VINE'S COMPLETE EXPOSITORY DICTIONARY OF OLD AND NEW TESTAMENT WORDS

WITH TOPICAL INDEX

W.E. VINE,

MERRILL F. UNGER, WILLIAM WHITE, JR.

THOMAS NELSON PUBLISHERS
Nashville • Atlanta • London • Vancouver

Published in Nashville, Tennessee, by Thomas Nelson, Inc. and distributed in Canada by Nelson/Word Canada.

Library of Congress Cataloging-in-Publication Data

Vine, W. E. (William Edwy), 1873–1949.
   [Complete expository dictionary with topical index]
   Vine's complete expository dictionary with topical index.
     p. cm.
   ISBN 0-7852-1160-8
   1. Bible—Dictionaries.   I. Title.
BS440.S746   1996
220.3—dc20

96-8956
CIP

Printed in the United States of America.

22 - 05 04

CONTENTS

Publisher's Preface (to the One-Volume Edition)

OLD TESTAMENT SECTION

NEW TESTAMENT SECTION
(following page 319)

PUBLISHER'S PREFACE

Vine's *Complete Expository Dictionary of Old and New Testament Words* combines in one volume W. E. Vine's *Expository Dictionary of New Testament Words* and *Nelson's Expository Dictionary of the Old Testament* by Merrill Unger and William White, Jr. The lasting popularity of these works has provided a convincing indication that serious students of the Bible would find this one-volume edition a useful and welcome addition to any reference library.

The publication of this volume provides a resource that will facilitate the study of biblical word meanings for those who may or may not have had formal training in Greek or Hebrew. At no other time has there been available a more complete language aid or study tool.

Vine's Complete Expository Dictionary of Old and New Testament Words allows the reader easy access to the alphabetized English equivalents of the Greek or Hebrew words from which they are translated. Throughout the text the most significant biblical words are illustrated by Scripture passages, comments, cross-references, ancient and modern meanings, precise etymologies, historical notes, and clearly defined technical information. Each original language is indexed, making this volume's format especially practical. Now, the addition of the exclusive Topical Index will make *Vine's* more useful than ever before. With the Index, you can confidently access all the Dictionary entries pertinent to specific New Testament ideas and teachings through convenient, time-saving Index entries.

It is a pleasure to offer a versatile reference work of this importance that will service the needs of beginning lay students and scholars alike.

Nelson's Expository Dictionary
of the
Old Testament

Edited by

Merrill F. Unger, Th.M., Th.D., Ph.D.
William White, Jr., Th.M., Ph.D.

CONTRIBUTORS

Gleason Archer

E. Clark Copeland

Leonard Coppes

Louis Goldberg

R. K. Harrison

Horace Hummel

George Kufeldt

Eugene H. Merrill

Walter Roehrs

Raymond Surburg

Willem van Gemeren

Donald Wold

FOREWORD

The *Expository Dictionary of the Old Testament* will be a useful tool in the hands of the student who has little or no formal training in the Hebrew language. It will open up the treasures of truth that often lie buried in the original language of the Old Testament, sometimes close to the surface and sometimes deeply imbedded far beneath the surface.

The student trained in Hebrew will find the *Expository Dictionary* to be a handy reference source. But the student without Hebrew training will experience a special thrill in being able to use this study tool in digging out truths from the Hebrew Bible not otherwise accessible to him.

It is, of course, possible to be a serious student of the Old Testament without having a knowledge of the Hebrew language. English translations and commentaries are of inestimable value and have their proper place. But a reference book that opens up the language in which the Scriptures were originally revealed and recorded, and which makes them available to readers unacquainted with the original tongue, has a value that at once becomes apparent.

As the language divinely chosen to record the prophecies of Christ, Hebrew possesses admirable qualities for the task assigned it. The language has a singularly rhythmic and musical quality. In poetic form, it especially has a noble dignity of style, combined with a vividness that makes it an effective vehicle for expression of sacred truth. The ideas behind its vocabulary give Hebrew a lively, picturesque nature.

Most Hebrew words are built upon verbal roots consisting of three consonants called *radicals.* There are approximately 1850 such roots in the Old Testament, from which various nouns and other parts of speech have been derived. Many of these roots represent theological, moral, and ceremonial concepts that have been obscured by the passage of time; recent archaeological and linguistic research is shedding new light on many of these concepts. Old Testament scholars find that biblical Hebrew can be compared with other Semitic languages such as Arabic, Assyrian, Ugaritic, Ethiopic, and Aramaic to discover the basic meaning of many heretofore obscure terms.

But it is not enough merely to have clarified the meaning of each root word. Each word can take on different shades of meaning as it is employed in various contexts, so one must study the various biblical occurrences of the word to arrive at an accurate understanding of its intended use.

This type of research has introduced students of Hebrew to a new world of understanding the Old Testament. But how can this material be made available to those who do not know Hebrew? That is the purpose of the present work.

Now the lay student can have before him or her the Hebrew root, or a Hebrew word based on that root, and can trace its development to its use in the passage before him. Moreover, he can acquire some appreciation of the richness and variety of the Hebrew vocabulary. For example, Hebrew synonyms often have pivotal doctrinal repercussions, as with the word *virgin* in Isaiah 7:14, compared with similar words meaning "young woman." In some cases, a play on words is virtually impossible to reflect in the English translation (e.g., Zeph. 2:4–7). Some Hebrew words can have quite different—sometimes exactly opposite—meanings in different contexts; thus the word *bārak* can mean "to bless" or "to curse," and *gā'al* can mean "to redeem" or "to pollute."

The lay student, of course, will suffer some disadvantage in not knowing Hebrew. Yet it is fair to say that an up-to-date expository dictionary that makes a happy selection of the more meaningful Hebrew words of the Old Testament will open up a treasure house of truth contained in the Hebrew Bible. It can offer a tremendous boon to the meaningful study of Scripture. It cannot fail to become an essential reference work for all serious students of the Bible.

MERRILL F. UNGER

INTRODUCTION

The writings of the New Testament are based in a large measure on God's revelation in the Old Testament. To understand the New Testament themes of Creation, Fall, and Restoration, it is necessary to read of their origin in the Old Testament.

The New Testament was written in a popular dialect of an Indo-European language, Greek. The Old Testament was written in the Semitic languages of Hebrew and Aramaic. For centuries, lay students of the Bible have found it very difficult to understand the structure of biblical Hebrew. Study guides to biblical Hebrew are designed for people who can read Hebrew—and many of them are written in German, which only compounds the difficulty.

This *Expository Dictionary* seeks to present about 500 significant terms of the Old Testament for lay readers who are not familiar with Hebrew. It describes the frequency, usage, and meaning of these terms as fully as possible. No source has been ignored in seeking to bring the latest Hebrew scholarship to the student who seeks it. It is hoped that this small reference book will enlighten Bible students to the riches of God's truth in the Old Testament.

A. The Place of Hebrew in History. Hebrew language and literature hold a unique place in the course of Western civilization. It emerged sometime after 1500 B.C. in the area of Palestine, along the eastern shore of the Mediterranean Sea. The Jewish people have used Hebrew continuously in one location or another to the present day. A modernized dialect of Hebrew (with spelling modifications) is the official language of the State of Israel.

When Alexander the Great came to power, he united the Greek city-states under the influence of Macedonia from about 330 B.C. to 323 B.C. Alexander and his generals virtually annihilated the social structures and languages of the ancient societies that their empire had absorbed. The Babylonians, Aramaeans, Persians, and Egyptians ceased to exist as distinct civilizations; only the Greek (Hellenistic) culture remained. Judaism was the only ancient religion and Hebrew the only ancient language that survived this onslaught.

The Hebrew Bible contains the continuous history of civilization from Creation to Roman times. It is the only record of God's dealings with humanity through His prophets, priests, and kings. In addition, it is the only ancient religious document that has survived completely intact.

Hebrew is related to Aramaic, Syriac, and such modern languages as Amharic and Arabic (both ancient and modern). It belongs to a group of languages known as the *Semitic* languages (so called because Scripture says that they were spoken by the descendants of Noah's son, Shem). The oldest known Semitic language is Akkadian, which was written in the "wedge-shaped" or *cuneiform* system of signs. The earliest Akkadian texts were written on clay tablets in about 2400 B.C. Babylonian and Assyrian are later dialects of Akkadian; both influenced the development of Hebrew. Because the Akkadian, Babylonian, and Assyrian languages were all used in Mesopotamia, they are classified as "East Semitic" languages.

The earliest evidence for the origins of "West Semitic" languages appears to be an inscription from the ancient city of Ebla. This was a little-known capital of a Semitic state in what is now Northern Syria. The tablets of Ebla are bilingual, written in both

Sumerian and Eblaite. The team of Italian archaeologists excavating Ebla have reported that these tablets contain a number of personal and place names mentioned in the Book of Genesis. Some of the tablets have been dated as early as 2400 B.C. Since Hebrew was also a West Semitic language, the publication of Ebla's texts may cast new light on many older Hebrew words and phrases.

The earliest complete series of pre-Hebrew texts comes from the ancient Canaanite city of Ugarit. Located on a cluster of hills in southern Lebanon, Ugarit has yielded texts that contain detailed information about the religion, poetry, and trade of the Canaanite people. The texts are dated between 1800 and 1200 B.C. These tablets contain many words and phrases that are almost identical to words found in the Hebrew Bible. The Ugaritic dialect illuminates the development of Old Hebrew (or Paleo-Hebrew). The poetic structure of the Ugaritic language is mirrored in many passages of the Old Testament, such as the "Song of Deborah" in Judges 5. The scribes of Ugarit wrote in a modified cuneiform script that was virtually alphabetic; this script prepared the way for using the simpler Phoenician writing system.

A number of texts from various parts of the Near East contain West Semitic words and phrases. The most important of these are the tablets from the ancient Egyptian city of Amarna. These tablets were written by the petty rulers of the Egyptian colonies of Syria-Palestine and by their overlord, the pharaoh. The tablets from the minor princes were written in Babylonian; but when the correspondent's scribe did not know the proper Babylonian word to express a certain idea, he substituted a Canaanite "gloss." These glosses tell us much about the words and spellings that were used in Palestine during the time when Paleo-Hebrew emerged as a distinct language.

The Hebrew language probably came into existence during the patriarchal period, about 2000 B.C. The language was reduced to writing in about 1250 B.C., and the earliest extant Hebrew inscription dates from about 1000 B.C. These early inscriptions were carved on stone; the oldest known Hebrew scrolls were found in the Qumran caves near the Dead Sea, and they date from the third century B.C. While some secular Hebrew texts have survived, the primary source for our knowledge of classical Hebrew is the Old Testament itself.

B. The Origin of the Hebrew Writing System. Greek tradition claims that Phoenicians invented the alphabet. Actually, this is only partially true, since the Phoenician writing system was not an alphabet as we know it today. It was a simplified *syllabary* system—in other words, its various symbols represent syllables rather than separate vocal components. The Hebrew writing system grew out of the Phoenician system.

The Hebrew writing system gradually changed over the centuries. From 1000 to 200 B.C., a rounded script (Old Phoenician style) was used. This script was last used for copying the biblical text and may be seen in the Dead Sea Scrolls. But after the Jews returned from their Babylonian Captivity, they began to use the square script of the Aramaic language, which was the official language of the Persian Empire. Jewish scribes adopted the Aramaic book hand, a more precise form of the script. When Jesus mentioned the "jot" and "tittle" of the Mosaic Law, He was referring to manuscripts in the square script. The book hand is used in all printed editions of the Hebrew Bible.

C. A Concise History of the Hebrew Bible. Undoubtedly the text of the Hebrew Bible was updated and revised several times in antiquity, and there was more than one textual tradition. Many archaic words in the Pentateuch suggest that Moses used early cuneiform documents in compiling his account of history. Scribes of the royal court under David and Solomon probably revised the text and updated obscure expressions. Apparently certain historical books, such as First and Second Kings and First and Second Chronicles, represent the official annals of the kingdom. These books represent the historical tradition of the priestly class.

The message of the prophets was probably written down sometime after the prophets delivered their message. There is a variety of writing styles among the prophetic books; and several, such as Amos and Hosea, seem to be closer to colloquial speech.

The text of the Old Testament was probably revised again during the time of King Josiah after the Book of Law was rediscovered (Second Kings 22–27; Second Chronicles 24–35). This would have taken place about 620 B.C. The next two centuries, which brought the Bablylonian Captivity, were the most momentous times in the history of Israel. When the Jews began to rebuild Jerusalem under Ezra and Nehemiah in 450 B.C., their common speech was the Aramaic language of the Persian court. This language became more popular among the Jews until it displaced Hebrew as the dominant language of Judaism in the Christian era. There is evidence that the Old Testament text was revised again at that time.

After the Greeks came to power under Alexander the Great, the preservation of Hebrew became a political issue; the conservative Jewish parties wanted to retain it. But the Jews of the *Diaspora*—those living outside of Palestine—depended upon versions of the biblical text in Aramaic (called the *Targums*) or Greek (called the *Septuagint*).

Both the Targums and Septuagint were translated from Hebrew manuscripts. There were substantial differences between these versions, and the Jewish rabbis went to great efforts to explain these differences.

After Jerusalem fell to the armies of the Roman general Titus, Jewish biblical scholars were scattered throughout the ancient world and the knowledge of Hebrew began to decline. From A.D. 200 to nearly A.D. 900, groups of scholars attempted to devise systems of vowel markings (later called *points*) to aid Jewish readers who no longer spoke Hebrew. The scholars who did this work are called *Masoretes,* and their markings are called the *Masora.* The Masoretic text that they produced represents the *consonants* that had been preserved from about 100 B.C. (as proven by the Dead Sea scrolls); but the *vowel markings* reflect the understanding of the Hebrew language in about A.D. 300. The Masoretic text dominated Old Testament studies in the Middle Ages, and it has served as the basis for virtually all printed versions of the Hebrew Bible.

Unfortunately, we have no complete text of the Hebrew Bible older than the tenth century A.D. The earliest complete segment of the Old Testament (the Prophets) is a copy dating from A.D. 895. While the Dead Sea scrolls yield entire books such as Isaiah, they do not contain a complete copy of the Old Testament text. Therefore, we must still depend upon the long tradition of Hebrew scholarship used in the printed editions of the Hebrew Bible.

The first complete printed edition of the Hebrew Bible was prepared by Felix Pratensis and published by Daniel Bomberg in Venice in 1516. A more extensive edition of the Hebrew Bible was edited by the Jewish-Christian scholar Jacob ben Chayyim in 1524. Some scholars continue to use the ben Chayyim text as the basic printed Hebrew Bible.

D. The Hebrew of the Old Testament. The Hebrew of the Old Testament does not have one neat and concise structure; the Old Testament was written over such a long span of time that we cannot expect to have one uniform linguistic tradition. In fact, the Hebrew of the three major sections of the Old Testament varies considerably. These three sections are known as the *Torah* (The Law), *Nebi'im* (The Prophets), and *Ketubim* (The Writings). In addition to the linguistic differences between the major sections, certain books of the Old Testament have their own peculiarities. For example, Job and Psalms have very ancient words and phrases similar to Ugaritic; Ruth preserves some archaic forms of Moabite speech; and First and Second Samuel reveal the rough, warlike nature of the colloquial idiom of the era of Solomon and David.

As Israel changed from being a confederation of tribes to a dynastic kingdom, the language changed from the speech of herdsmen and caravan traders to the literary language of a settled population. While the books of the New Testament reflect a Greek dialect as it was used over a span of about 75 years, the Old Testament draws upon various forms of the Hebrew language as it evolved over nearly 2,000 years. Therefore, certain texts—such as the early narrative of the Book of Exodus and the last of the Psalms—are virtually written in two different dialects and should be studied with this in mind.

E. Characteristics of the Hebrew Language. Because Hebrew is a Semitic language, its structure and function are quite different from Indo-European languages such as French, German, Spanish, and English. A number of Hebrew consonants cannot be transformed exactly into English letters. Therefore, our English transliterations of Hebrew words suggest that the language sounded very harsh and rough, but it probably was very melodious and beautiful.

Most Hebrew words are built upon a three-consonant root. The same root may appear in a noun, a verb, an adjective, and an adverb—all with the same basic meaning. For example, *keṯāb,* is a Hebrew noun meaning "book." A verbal form, *kāṯab,* means to "write." There is also the Hebrew noun *keṯōbeth,* which means "decoration" or "tattoo." Each of these words repeats the basic set of three consonants, giving them a similarity of sound that would seem awkward in English. It would seem ludicrous for an English writer to compose a sentence like, "The writer wrote the written writing of the writ." But this kind of repetition would be very common in biblical Hebrew. Many Old Testament texts, such as Genesis 49 and Numbers 23, use this type of repetition to play upon the meaning of words.

Hebrew also differs from English and other Indo-European languages in varying the form of a single part of speech. English has only one form of a particular noun or verb, while Hebrew may have two or more forms of the same basic part of speech. Scholars have studied these less common forms of Hebrew words for many centuries, and they have developed a vast literature about these words. Any study of the more important theological terms of the Old Testament must take these studies into consideration.

F. The Form of Words (Morphology). In principle, the basic Hebrew word consists of a three-consonant root and three vowels—two internal and one final (though the final vowel is often not pronounced). We might diagram the typical Hebrew word in this manner:

$$C_1 + V_1 + C_2 + V_2 + C_3 + V_3$$

Using the word *kātab* as an example, the diagram would look like this:

$$K + A + T + A + B + \underline{\quad}$$

The different forms of Hebrew words always keep the three consonants in the same relative positions, but they change the vowels inserted between the consonants. For example, *kōtēb* is the participle of *kātab,* while *kātôb* is the infinitive.

By extending the verbal forms of their words, Hebrew writers were able to develop very extensive and complex meanings. For example, they could do this by adding syllables at the beginning of the three-consonant root, like this:

Root = *KTB*
yi + *ketōb*—"let him write"
we + *kātab*—"and he will write"

Sometimes, a writer would double a consonant while keeping the three basic consonants in the same position. For example, he could take the root of KTB and make the word *wayyikᵉtōb,* meaning "and he caused to write."

The Hebrew writer could also add several different endings or *suffixes* to a basic verb to produce an entire clause. For example, using the verb *qātal* (meaning "to kill"), he could develop the word *qᵉtaltîhû* (meaning "I have killed him"). These examples emphasize the fact that Hebrew is a syllabic language. There are no unique consonantal combinations such as diphthongs (or glides) like *cl, gr, bl,* as in English.

G. Hebrew Word Order. The normal word order of a verbal sentence in a Hebrew narrative or prose passage is:

Verb—Object—Indirect Object or Pronoun—Subject

However, it is interesting to note that the Hebrew word order for a nominal sentence may parallel that of English:

Subject—Verb—Predicate Nominative/Adjective

Hebrew writers frequently departed from the verbal arrangement for the sake of emphasis. Yet a Hebrew sentence can seldom be translated into English word-for-word, because the result would be meaningless. Over the centuries, translators have developed standard ways to express these peculiar Semitic thought forms in Indo-European speech.

H. Foreign Words in Hebrew. The Old Testament uses foreign words in various ways, depending upon the context. Akkadian proper names often appear in the patriarchal narratives of Genesis. Here are some examples:

(Sumero-Akkadian) *Sumer* = Shinar (Hebrew)
(Akkadian) *Sharrukin* = *Nimrod* (Hebrew)

Several Egyptian terms appear in the narrative of Joseph, just as Bablylonian terms appear in the writings of Isaiah Jeremiah, and Persian words in the Book of Daniel.

None of these words have theological significance, however. There is little linguistic evidence that the religious concepts of Israel were borrowed from foreign sources.

The greatest inroad of a foreign idiom is the case of the Aramaic language, which appears in several isolated verses and some entire chapters of the Book of Daniel. As we have already noted, Aramaic became the primary religious language of the Jews living outside of Palestine after the Babylonian Captivity.

I. The Written Text of the Hebrew Bible. The Hebrew text of the Old Testament offers two immediate problems to the uninitiated reader. First is the fact that Hebrew is read from right to left, unlike Indo-European languages; each character of the text and its attendant symbols are read from top to bottom, as well as from right to left. Second is the fact that written Hebrew is a complicated system of syllable symbols, each of which has three components.

The first component is the sign for the consonant itself. Some of the less frequent consonantal signs stand for vowel sounds. (These letters are *aleph* [indicating the long *a* sound], *waw* [to indicate the long *u* sound], and *yod* [to indicate the "ee" sound—as in "see"].) The second component is the pattern of vowel points. The third component is the pattern of *cantellations,* which were added during the Middle Ages to aid cantors in singing the text. Some practice is required before a person is able to read the Hebrew text using all of the three components. The accompanying illustration shows the direction and sequence for reading the text. (Cantellations are omitted).

ENGLISH TRANSLITERATION: *'ashᵉrê hā'îsh 'ašher*

The specific vowel points and their sequence within the word indicate the weight or accentuation to be given to each syllable of the word. Different traditions within Judaism indicate different ways of pronouncing the same Hebrew word, and the vowel points of a particular manuscript will reflect the pronunciation used by the scribes who copied the manuscript. Many Slavic and Spanish speech patterns crept into the medieval Hebrew manuscripts, due to the Jews' association with Slavic and Spanish cultures during the Middle Ages. However, the use of Hebrew speech in modern Israel is tending to standardize the pronunciation of Hebrew.

The accompanying table indicates the transliterations accepted for Hebrew font by most biblical scholars today. It is the standard system, developed by the *Journal of Biblical Literature,* for use in writing and language instruction.

Consonants	Name	Transliteration
א	Alep	'
ב	Bet	b
ג	Gimel	g
ד	Dalet	d
ה	He	h
ו	Waw	w
ז	Zayin	z

	Name	Transliteration
ח	Ḥet	ḥ
ט	Ṭet	ṭ
י	Yod	y
כ, ך	Kap	k
ל	Lamed	l
מ, ם	Mem	m
נ, ן	Nun	n
ס	Samek	s
ע	Ayin	'
פ, ף	Pe	p
צ, ץ	Ṣade	ṣ
ק	Qop	q
ר	Reš	r
שׂ, שׁ	Śin, Šin	ś, š
ת	Taw	t

Vowels	Name	Transliteration
ֲ	pataḥ	ā
ֳ	qameṣ	a
ֱ	segol	e
ֵ	ṣere	ē
ִ	hireq	i
ֻ	qibbûṣ	u
ֲי	pataḥ yod	aw
ֱי	segol yod	ê
ֵי	ṣere yod	ê
ִי	hireq yod	î
וֹ	holem	ô
וּ	šûreq	û
ֲ	hatep-pataḥ	ŏ
ֳ	hatep-qameṣ	ă
ֱ	hatep-segol	ĕ

J. The Meaning of Hebrew Words. Christians have studied the Hebrew language with varying degrees of intensity as long as the church has existed. During the apostolic and early church age (A.D. 40–150), Christians had a great deal of interest in the Hebrew language. Eventually, they depended more heavily upon the Greek Septuagint for reading the Old Testament. In the early Middle Ages, Jerome had to employ Jewish scholars to help him in translating the official Latin Vulgate version of the Old Testament. There was little Christian interest in the Hebrew language in medieval times.

In the sixteenth century, a German Roman Catholic scholar named Johannes Reuchlin studied Hebrew with a Jewish rabbi and began to write introductory books in Latin about Hebrew for Christian students. He also compiled a small Hebrew-Latin dictionary. Reuchlin's work awakened an interest in Hebrew among Christian scholars that has continued to our own day. (The Jewish synagogues had passed on the meaning of the text for centuries, giving little attention to the mechanics of the Hebrew language itself. These traditional meanings are reflected in the King James Version, published after Reuchlin's studies.)

By comparing Akkadian, Ugaritic, Aramaic, and Hebrew languages, modern scholars have been able to understand the meaning of Hebrew words. Here are some of the keys that they have discovered:

1. Cognate Words. Foreign words that have sounds or constructions similar to Hebrew words are called *cognates.* Because words of different Semitic languages are based upon the same three-consonant root, cognates abound. In times past, these cognates gave rise to "folk etymology"—an unscholarly interpretation of words based upon folklore and tradition. Often these folk etymologies were used in interpreting the Old Testament. However, words that are *philological cognates* (form-related) are not necessarily *semantic cognates* (meaning-related). A good example is the Hebrew word *sar,* which means "prince." This same word is used in other Semitic languages, where it means "king."

For centuries, European students of Hebrew used Arabic philological cognates to decipher the meaning of obscure Hebrew words. This unreliable method is used by many of the older English dictionaries and lexicons.

2. Meaning from Context. It has often been said that the best commentary on Scripture is Scripture itself. Nowhere is this more true than in Hebrew word studies. The best method for determining the meaning of any Hebrew word is to study the context in which it appears. If it appears in many different contexts, then the meaning of the word can be found with greater accuracy. For the words that appear with very low frequency (four times or less), non-biblical Hebrew texts or other Semitic texts can help us locate the meaning of the word.

However, there is one caution: It is never wise to use one obscure word to try to determine the meaning of another obscure word. The most difficult words are those that occur only once in the Old Testament text; these are called *hapax legomena* (Greek, "read once"). Fortunately, all the Hebrew words of theological significance occur fairly frequently.

3. Poetic Parallelism. Fully one-third of the Old Testament is poetry. This amount of text is equal to the entire New Testament. English translators have tended to ignore the poetic structure of lengthy Old Testament passages, such as Isaiah 40–66 and the entire Book of Job; but the complexities of Hebrew poetry are vital to our understanding of the Old Testament. This can be seen by studying a modern English version of the Bible that prints poetic passages as such. Several verses from the Psalms in the RSV will illustrate the underlying structure of Hebrew poetry.

Note there is neither rhythm nor meter in Hebrew poetry, unlike most English poetry. Hebrew poetry repeats ideas or the relation of ideas in successive lines. Here is an example:

(I) O Magnify the Lord with me,
(II) And let us exalt His name together!

Notice that virtually every part of speech in Line I can be substituted for its equal in Line II. Scholars designate the individual words in Line I (or hemistych I) as "A" words and those in Line II (or hemistych II) as "B" words. Thus we see the pattern in these lines from Psalm 34:

Hemistych I: O magnify$_A$ the Lord$_A$ with me,$_A$
Hemistych II: Let us exalt$_B$ His name$_B$ together!$_B$

As one can readily see, the "A" words can be substituted for the "B" words without changing the meaning of the line, and the reverse is also true. This characteristic of Hebrew poetry is called *parallelism.* In scholarly studies of Hebrew poetry, paired words in a parallel structure are often marked with slanting parallel bars to show (a) which word usually occurs first—that is, the "A" word, (b) the fact that the two words form a parallel pair, and (c) which word is usually the second or "B." We can show this for the first verse of Psalm 34 in this manner:

O magnify / / exalt; the Lord / / His name; with me / / together.

This *Expository Dictionary* cites such pairs because they indicate important relationships in meaning. Many pairs are used over and over again, almost as synonyms. Thus the usage of Hebrew words in poetry becomes a very valuable tool for our understanding of their meaning. Most of the significant theological terms, including the names and titles of God, are found in such poetic pairs.

K. Theories of Translation. Theories of translation greatly affect our interpretation of our Hebrew words. We may describe the current dominant theories of translation as follows:

1. The Direct Equivalence Method. This method assumes that one will find only one English word to represent each Hebrew word that appears in the Old Testament text. Since some Hebrew words have no one-word equivalent in English, they are simply *transliterated* (turned into English letters). In this case, the reader must be taught what the transliterated term really meant. This method was used in the earliest translations of the New Testament, which attempted to bring the Latin equivalents of Greek words directly into English. This is how our early English versions adopted a large amount of Latin theological terminology, such as *justification, sanctification,* and *concupiscence.*

2. The Historico-Linguistic Method. This method attempts to find a limited number of English terms that will adequately express the meaning of a particular Hebrew term. A scholar using this method studies the historical record of how the word has been used and gives preference to its most frequent meaning in context. This method has been used in preparing the *Expository Dictionary.*

3. The Dynamic Equivalence Method. This method does not attempt to make any consistent use of an English word for a specific Hebrew word. Instead it endeavors to show the thrust or emphasis of a Hebrew word in each specific context. Thus it allows a very free, colloquial rendering of Old Testament passages. This enables lay readers to get the real kernel of meaning from a particular passage, but it makes Bible word study virtually impossible. For example, a comparison of the concordance for *The Living Bible* and the concordance for the RSV will show the difference in methods of translation. The RSV actually uses fewer different words than the KJV to translate the Hebrew Old Testament. *The Living Bible* uses many more specific words to reflect the subtle shades of meaning in the Hebrew text, thus making it impossible to trace how a particular Hebrew word has been used in different contexts.

This *Expository Dictionary* attempts to show the different methods of translation by indicating the different meanings of a Hebrew word given by various English versions.

L. How to Use This Book. When beginning a word study of a particular Hebrew term, you should obtain good editions of at least three English versions of the Old Testament. Always have a King James Version or a New King James Version, a more scholarly version such as the RSV or NASB, and a colloquial version such as the TEV. You should also have a good concordance to the KJV, NKJV or the RSV.

The *Expository Dictionary* gives wide ranges of meanings for most Hebrew words. They should not be substituted for each other without carefully reviewing the usage of the term in its different contexts. All Hebrew words have different meanings—sometimes even opposite meanings—so they should be studied in all of their occurrences, and not just one.

Strive for consistency in rendering a particular Hebrew word in different contexts. Seek the smallest number of equivalent English words. The contributors to this book have already done extensive research in the original languages and in modern scholarly literature. You can make the best use of their work by looking up the various usages of each word in order to get a balanced view.

Comparison and *frequency* are two fundamental factors in Bible word study. Write down the passages that you are comparing. Do not be afraid to look up all of the occurrences of a particular word. The time you spend will open up your Bible as it has never been opened before.

WILLIAM WHITE, JR.

A

ABOMINATION

A. Noun.

tô'ēbāh (תּוֹעֵבָה, 8441), "abomination; loathsome, detestable thing." Cognates of this word appear only in Phoenician and Targumic Aramaic. The word appears 117 times and in all periods.

First, *tô'ēbāh* defines something or someone as essentially unique in the sense of being "dangerous," "sinister," and "repulsive" to another individual. This meaning appears in Gen. 43:32 (the first occurrence): "... The Egyptians might not eat bread with the Hebrews; for that is an abomination unto the Egyptians." To the Egyptians, eating bread with foreigners was repulsive because of their cultural or social differences (cf. Gen. 46:34; Ps. 88:8). Another clear illustration of this essential clash of disposition appears in Prov. 29:27: "An unjust man is an abomination to the just: and he that is upright in the way is abomination to the wicked." When used with reference to God, this nuance of the word describes people, things, acts, relationships, and characteristics that are "detestable" to Him because they are contrary to His nature. Things related to death and idolatry are loathsome to God: "Thou shalt not eat any abominable thing" (Deut. 14:3). People with habits loathsome to God are themselves detestable to Him: "The woman shall not wear that which pertaineth unto a man, neither shall a man put on a woman's garment: for all that do so are abomination unto the Lord thy God" (Deut. 22:5). Directly opposed to *tô'ēbāh* are such reactions as "delight" and "loveth" (Prov. 15:8–9).

Second, *tô'ēbāh* is used in some contexts to describe pagan practices and objects: "The graven images of their gods shall ye burn with fire; thou shalt not desire the silver or gold that is on them, nor take it unto thee, lest thou be snared therein: for it is an abomination to the Lord thy God. Neither shalt thou bring an abomination into thine house ... " (Deut. 7:25–26). In other contexts, *tô'ēbāh* describes the repeated failures to observe divine regulations: "Because ye multiplied more than the nations that are round about you, and have not walked in my statutes, neither have kept my judgments, neither have done according to the judgments of the nations that are round about you; ... because of all thine abominations" (Ezek. 5:7, 9). *Tô'ēbāh* may represent the pagan cultic practices themselves, as in Deut. 12:31, or the people who perpetrate such practices: "For all that do these things are an abomination unto the Lord: and because of these abominations the Lord thy God doth drive them out from before thee" (Deut. 18:12). If Israelites are guilty of such idolatry, however, their fate will be worse than exile: death by stoning (Deut. 17:2–5).

Third, *tô'ēbāh* is used in the sphere of jurisprudence and of family or tribal relationships. Certain acts or characteristics are destructive of societal and familial harmony; both such things and the people who do them are described by *tô'ēbāh*: "These six things doth the Lord hate; yea, seven are an abomination unto him: ... a proud look, a lying tongue, and hands that shed innocent blood, a heart that deviseth wicked imaginations, ... and he that soweth discord among brethren" (Prov. 6:16–19). God says, "The scorner is an abomination to men" (Prov. 24:9) because he spreads his bitterness among God's people, disrupting unity and harmony.

B. Verb.

tā'ab (תָּעַב, 8581), "to abhor, treat as abhorrent, cause to be an abomination, act abominably." This verb occurs 21 times, and the first occurrence is in Deut. 7:26: "Neither shalt thou bring an abomination into thine house...."

TO ACCEPT

rāṣāh (רָצָה, 7521), "to be pleased, be pleased with, accept favorably, satisfy." This is a common term in both biblical and modern Hebrew. Found approximately 60 times in the text of the Old Testament, one of its first appearances is in

Gen. 33:10: "Thou wast pleased with me." In the RSV rendering of this verse, "favor" appears twice, the first time being a translation of *hēn*.

When *rāṣāh* expresses God's being pleased with someone, the English versions often translate it as "be delighted," which seems to reflect a sense of greater pleasure: " ... mine elect, in whom my soul delighteth" (Isa. 42:1); " ... thou hadst a favor unto them" (Ps. 44:3). This nuance is reflected also in Prov. 3:12, where *rāṣāh* is paralleled with *'āhab*, "to love": " ... for whom the Lord loveth he correcteth; even as a father the son in whom he delighteth."

On the other hand, when one must meet a certain requirement to merit *rāṣāh*, it seems more logical to translate it with "to please" or "to accept." For example: "Will the Lord be pleased with thousands of rams ...?" (Mic. 6:7); " ... burnt offerings and your meat offerings, I will not accept them ... " (Amos 5:22).

Rāṣāh can be used in the sense of "to pay for" or "to satisfy a debt," especially as it relates to land lying fallow in the sabbath years: "Then shall the land enjoy her sabbaths, as long as it lieth desolate, ... even then shall the land rest, and enjoy her sabbaths" (Lev. 26:34). Here the RSV, NASB, and NEB also translate *rāṣāh* as "enjoy." However, the context seems to require something like "the land shall repay (satisfy) its sabbaths." Similarly, the phrase, " ... her iniquity is pardoned" (Isa. 40:2), must mean "her iniquity is paid for" or "her punishment is accepted as satisfactory."

TO ADD

yāsap (יָסַף, 3254), "to add, continue, do again, increase, surpass." This verb occurs in the northwest Semitic dialects and Aramaic. It occurs in biblical Hebrew (around 210 times), post-biblical Hebrew, and in biblical Aramaic (once).

Basically, *yāsap* signifies increasing the number of something. It may also be used to indicate adding one thing to another, e.g., "And if a man eat of the holy thing unwittingly, then he shall put the fifth part thereof unto it, and shall give it unto the priest ... " (Lev. 22:14).

This verb may be used to signify the repetition of an act stipulated by another verb. For example, the dove that Noah sent out "returned not again" (Gen. 8:12). Usually the repeated action is indicated by an infinitive absolute, preceded by the preposition *lᵉ*—"And he did not have relations with her again." Literally, this reads "And he did not add again [*'ôd*] to knowing her [intimately]" (Gen. 38:26).

In some contexts *yāsap* means "to heighten," but with no suggestion of numerical increase.

God says, "The meek also shall increase [*yāsap*] their joy in the Lord ... " (Isa. 29:19). This same emphasis appears in Ps. 71:14: " ... and will yet praise thee more and more [*yāsap*]' or literally, "And I will add to all Thy praises." In such cases, more than an additional quantity of joy or praise is meant. The author is referring to a new quality of joy or praise—i.e., a heightening of them.

Another meaning of *yāsap* is "to surpass." The Queen of Sheba told Solomon, "Thy wisdom and prosperity exceedeth the fame which I heard," or literally, "You add [with respect to] wisdom and prosperity to the report which I heard" (1 Kings 10:7).

This verb may also be used in covenantal formulas, e.g., Ruth summoned God's curse upon herself by saying, "The Lord do so to me, and more also [*yāsap*], if ought but death part thee and me," or literally, "Thus may the Lord do to me, and thus may he add, if ... " (Ruth 1:17; cf. Lev. 26; Deut. 27–28).

ALL

A. Nouns.

kōl (כֹּל, 3605), "all; the whole." The noun *kōl*, derived from *kālal*, has cognates in Ugaritic, Akkadian, Phoenician, and Moabite. *Kōl* appears in biblical Hebrew about 5,404 times and in all periods. Biblical Aramaic attests it about 82 times.

The word can be used alone, meaning "the entirety," "whole," or "all," as in: "And thou shalt put all [*kōl*] in the hands of Aaron, and in the hands of his sons ... " (Exod. 29:24).

Kōl can signify everything in a given unit whose members have been selected from others of their kind: "That the sons of God saw the daughters of men that they were fair; and they took them wives of all which they chose" (Gen. 6:2).

kālîl (כָּלִיל, 3632), "whole offering." This word represents the "whole offering" from which the worshiper does not partake: "It is a statute for ever unto the Lord; it shall be wholly burnt" (Lev. 6:22).

B. Adjectives.

kōl (כֹּל, 3606), "all; whole; entirety; every; each." When *kōl* precedes a noun, it expresses a unit and signifies the whole: "These are the three sons of Noah: and of them was the whole earth overspread" (Gen. 9:19). *Kōl* may also signify the entirety of a noun that does not necessarily represent a unit: "All the people, both small and great" entered into the covenant (2 Kings 23:2). The use of the word in such instances tends to unify what is not otherwise a unit.

Kōl can precede a word that is only part of a larger unit or not part of a given unit at all. In this case, the prominent idea is that of "plurality," a heterogeneous unit: "And it came to pass from the time that he had made him overseer in his house, and over all that he had, that the Lord blessed the Egyptian's house for Joseph's sake; and the blessing of the Lord was upon all that he had in the house, and in the field" (Gen. 39:5).

Related to the preceding nuance is the use of *kōl* to express comprehensiveness. Not only does it indicate that the noun modified is a plurality, but also that the unit formed by the addition of *kōl* includes everything in the category indicated by the noun: "All the cities were ten with their suburbs for the families of the children of Kohath that remained" (Josh. 21:26). In Gen. 1:21 (its first occurrence), the word precedes a collective noun and may be translated "every": "And God created great whales, and every living creature that moveth, ... "

When used to refer to the individual members of a group, *kōl* means "every": "His hand will be against every man, and every man's hand against him" (Gen. 16:12). Another example: "Thy princes are rebellious, and companions of thieves: every one loveth gifts, and followeth after rewards" (Isa. 1:23). Related to this use is the meaning "none but."

In Deut. 19:15, *kōl* means "every kind of" or "any"; the word focuses on each and every member of a given unit: "One witness shall not rise up against a man for any iniquity, or for any sin, in any sin that he sinneth...." A related nuance appears in Gen. 24:10, but here the emphasis is upon "all sorts": "And the servant took ten camels of the camels of his master, and departed; for all [i.e., a variety of] the goods of his master were in his hand."

kālîl (כָּלִיל, 3632), "the entire; whole." In Num. 4:6, *kālîl* refers to the "cloth wholly of blue." In other words, it indicates "the entire" cloth.

C. Verb.

kālal (כָּלַל, 3634), "to perfect." This common Semitic root appears in biblical Hebrew only 3 times. Ezek. 27:11 is a good example: "... They have made thy beauty perfect [*kālal*]."

ALTAR

mizbēaḥ (מִזְבֵּחַ, 4196), "altar." This noun has cognates in Aramaic, Syriac, and Arabic. In each of these languages the consonantal root is *mdbh*. *Mizbēaḥ* occurs about 396 times in the Old Testament.

This word signifies a raised place where a sacrifice was made, as in Gen. 8:20 (its first biblical appearance): "And Noah builded an altar unto the Lord; and took of every clean beast, and of every clean fowl, and offered burnt offerings on the altar." In later references, this word may refer to a table upon which incense was burned: "And thou shalt make an altar to burn incense upon: of shittim wood shalt thou make it" (Exod. 30:1).

From the dawn of human history, offerings were made on a raised table of stone or ground (Gen. 4:3). At first, Israel's altars were to be made of earth—i.e., they were fashioned of material that was strictly the work of God's hands. If the Jews were to hew stone for altars in the wilderness, they would have been compelled to use war weapons to do the work. (Notice that in Exod. 20:25 the word for "tool" is *ḥereb*, "sword.")

At Sinai, God directed Israel to fashion altars of valuable woods and metals. This taught them that true worship required man's best and that it was to conform exactly to God's directives; God, not man, initiated and controlled worship. The altar that stood before the holy place (Exod. 27:1–8) and the altar of incense within the holy place (Exod. 30:1–10) had "horns." These horns had a vital function in some offerings (Lev. 4:30; 16:18). For example, the sacrificial animal may have been bound to these horns in order to allow its blood to drain away completely (Ps. 118:27).

Mizbēaḥ is also used of pagan altars: "But ye shall destroy their *altars,* break their images, and cut down their groves" (Exod. 34:13).

This noun is derived from the Hebrew verb *zābaḥ*, which literally means "to slaughter for food" or "to slaughter for sacrifice." *Zābaḥ* has cognates in Ugaritic and Arabic (*dbh*), Akkadian (*zibu*), and Phoenician (*zbh*). Another Old Testament noun derived from *zābaḥ* is *zebaḥ* (162 times), which usually refers to a sacrifice that establishes communion between God and those who eat the thing offered.

AMONG

A. Preposition.

qereb (קֶרֶב, 7130), "among." The first usage of this preposition is in Genesis: "Abram dwelled in the land of Canaan, and Lot dwelled in [among] the cities of the plain, and pitched his tent toward Sodom" (13:12). This word is used 222 times in the Old Testament; it is predominant in the Pentateuch (especially Deuteronomy) but is rare in the historical books (apart from the early books, Joshua and Judges). In the poetical books, *qereb* is used most often in the Book of Psalms. It occurs only once in Job and three times in Proverbs. It is fairly well represented in the prophetical books.

B. Noun.

qereb (קֶרֶב, 7130), "inward part; midst." As a noun, this word is related to the Akkadian root qarab, which means "midst." In Mishnaic and modern Hebrew, qereb generally means "midst" rather than "inward part" or "entrails."

One idiomatic usage of qereb denotes an inward part of the body that is the seat of laughter (Gen. 18:12) and of thoughts (Jer. 4:14). The Bible limits another idiomatic usage, meaning "inner parts," to animals: "Eat not of it raw, nor sodden at all with water, but roast with fire—his head with his legs, and with the purtenance thereof" (Exod. 12:9).

The noun approximates the prepositional use with the meaning of "midst" or "in." Something may be "in the midst of" a place: "Peradventure there be fifty righteous within [qereb] the city: wilt thou also destroy and not spare the place for the fifty righteous that are therein?" (Gen. 18:24). It may be in the midst of people: "Then Samuel took the horn of oil, and anointed him in the midst [qereb] of his brethren: and the Spirit of the Lord came upon David from that day forward" (1 Sam. 16:13).

God is said to be in the midst of the land (Exod. 8:22), the city of God (Ps. 46:4), and Israel (Num. 11:20). Even when He is close to His people, God is nevertheless holy: "Cry out and shout, thou inhabitant of Zion: for great is the Holy One of Israel in the midst [qereb] of thee" (Isa. 12:6; cf. Hos. 11:9).

The idiomatic use of qereb in Psalm 103:1—"Bless the Lord, O my soul: and all that is within me, bless his holy name"—is more difficult to discern because the noun is in the plural. It seems best to take "all that is within me" as a reference to the Psalmist's whole being, rather than to a distinct part of the body that is within him.

The Septuagint gives the following Greek translations of qereb: kardia, "heart [as seat of physical, spiritual, and mental life]" or "heart [figurative in the sense of being interior or central]"; koilia, "body cavity, belly"; and mesos, "middle" or "in the midst." The KJV gives these senses: "midst" and "inwards."

ANGEL

mal'āk (מַלְאָךְ, 4397), "messenger; angel." In Ugaritic, Arabic, and Ethiopic, the verb leʾak means "to send." Even though leʾak does not exist in the Hebrew Old Testament, it is possible to recognize its etymological relationship to mal'āk. In addition, the Old Testament uses the word "message" in Hag. 1:13; this word incorporates the meaning of the root leʾak, "to send." Another noun form of the root is melāʾkāh, "work," which appears 167 times. The name Malachi—literally, "my messenger"—is based on the noun mal'āk.

The noun mal'āk appears 213 times in the Hebrew Old Testament. Its frequency is especially great in the historical books, where it usually means "messenger": Judges (31 times), 2 Kings (20 times), 1 Samuel (19 times), and 2 Samuel (18 times). The prophetical works are very moderate in their usage of mal'āk, with the outstanding exception of the Book of Zechariah, where the angel of the Lord communicates God's message to Zechariah. For example: "Then I answered and said unto the angel that talked to me, 'What are these, my lord?' And the angel answered and said unto me, 'These are the four spirits [pl. of mal'āk] of the heavens, which go forth from standing before the Lord of all the earth'" (Zech. 6:4–5).

The word mal'āk denotes someone sent over a great distance by an individual (Gen. 32:3) or by a community (Num. 21:21), in order to communicate a message. Often several messengers are sent together: "And Ahaziah fell down through a lattice in his upper chamber that was in Samaria, and was sick: and he sent messengers [pl. of mal'āk] and said unto them, Go, inquire of Baal-zebub the god of Ekron whether I shall recover of this disease" (2 Kings 1:2). The introductory formula of the message borne by the mal'āk often contains the phrase "Thus says ...," or "This is what ... says," signifying the authority of the messenger in giving the message of his master: "Thus saith Jephthah, Israel took not away the land of Moab, nor the land of the children of Ammon" (Judg. 11:15).

As a representative of a king, the mal'āk might have performed the function of a diplomat. In 1 Kings 20:1ff., we read that Ben-hadad sent messengers with the terms of surrender: "He sent messengers to Ahab king of Israel into the city, and said unto him, Thus saith Ben-hadad ... " (1 Kings 20:2).

These passages confirm the important place of the mal'āk. Honor to the messenger signified honor to the sender, and the opposite was also true. David took personally the insult of Nabal (1 Sam. 25:14ff.); and when Hanun, king of Ammon, humiliated David's servants (2 Sam. 10:4ff.), David was quick to dispatch his forces against the Ammonites.

God also sent messengers. First, there are the prophetic messengers: "And the Lord God of their fathers sent to them by his messengers, rising up betimes, and sending; because he had compassion on his people, and on his dwelling place: But they mocked the messengers of God, and despised his words, and misused his prophets, until the wrath of the Lord arose against his people, till there was no remedy" (2 Chron. 36:15–16). Haggai called himself "the messenger of the Lord," *mal'āk Yahweh.*

There were also angelic messengers. The English word *angel* is etymologically related to the Greek word *angelos,* whose translation is similar to the Hebrew: "messenger" or "angel." The angel is a supernatural messenger of the Lord sent with a particular message. Two angels came to Lot at Sodom: "And there came two angels to Sodom at even; and Lot sat in the gate of Sodom: and Lot seeing them rose up to meet them; and he bowed himself with his face toward the ground ..." (Gen. 19:1). The angels were also commissioned to protect God's people: "For he shall give his angels charge over thee, to keep thee in all thy ways" (Ps. 91:11).

Third, and most significant, are the phrases *mal'āk Yahweh,* "the angel of the Lord," and *mal'āk 'ĕlōhîm,* "the angel of God." The phrase is always used in the singular. It denotes an angel who had mainly a saving and protective function: "For mine angel shall go before thee, and bring thee in unto the Amorites, and the Hittites, and the Perizzites, and the Canaanites, the Hivites, and the Jebusites: and I will cut them off" (Exod. 23:23). He might also bring about destruction: "And David lifted up his eyes, and saw the angel of the Lord stand between the earth and the heaven, having a drawn sword in his hand stretched out over Jerusalem. Then David and the elders of Israel, who were clothed in sackcloth, fell upon their faces" (1 Chron. 21:16).

The relation between the Lord and the "angel of the Lord" is often so close that it is difficult to separate the two (Gen. 16:7ff.; 21:17ff.; 22:11ff.; 31:11ff.; Exod. 3:2ff.; Judg. 6:11ff.; 13:21f.). This identification has led some interpreters to conclude that the "angel of the Lord" was the pre-incarnate Christ.

In the Septuagint the word *mal'āk* is usually translated by *angelos* and the phrase "angel of the Lord" by *angelos kuriou.* The English versions follow this twofold distinction by translating *mal'āk* as simply "angel" or "messenger" (KJV, RSV, NASB, NIV).

ANGER, BURNING

A. Verb.

hārāh (חָרָה, 2734), "to get angry, be angry." This verb appears in the Bible 92 times. In the basic stem, the word refers to the "burning of anger" as in Jonah 4:1. In the causative stem,

hārāh means "to become heated with work" or "with zeal for work" (Neh. 3:20).

B. Noun.

hārôn (חָרוֹן, 2740), "burning anger." The 41 occurrences of this word cover every period of the Bible. This word refers exclusively to divine anger as that which is "burning." *Ḥārôn* first appears in Exod. 32:12: "Turn from thy fierce wrath [*ḥārôn*], and repent of this evil against thy people."

TO ANOINT

A. Verb.

māšaḥ (מָשַׁח, 4886), "to anoint, smear, consecrate." A common word in both ancient and modern Hebrew, *māšaḥ* is also found in ancient Ugaritic. It occurs approximately 70 times in the Hebrew Old Testament.

The word is found for the first time in the Old Testament in Gen. 31:13: "... where thou anointedst the pillar, and ... vowedst a vow unto me ..." This use illustrates the idea of anointing something or someone as an act of consecration. The basic meaning of the word, however, is simply to "smear" something on an object. Usually oil is involved, but it could be other substances, such as paint or dye (cf. Jer. 22:14). The expression "anoint the shield" in Isa. 21:5 probably has more to do with lubrication than consecration in that context. When unleavened bread is "tempered with oil" in Exod. 29:2, it is basically equivalent to our act of buttering bread.

The Old Testament most commonly uses *māšaḥ* to indicate "anointing" in the sense of a special setting apart for an office or function. Thus, Elisha was "anointed" to be a prophet (1 Kings 19:16). More typically, kings were "anointed" for their office (1 Sam. 16:12; 1 Kings 1:39). Vessels used in the worship at the sacred shrine (both tabernacle and temple) were consecrated for use by "anointing" them (Exod. 29:36; 30:26; 40:9–10). In fact, the recipe for the formulation of this "holy anointing oil" is given in detail in Exod. 30:22–25.

B. Noun.

māšîaḥ (מָשִׁיחַ, 4899), "anointed one." A word that is important both to Old Testament and New Testament understandings is the noun *māšîaḥ,* which gives us the term *messiah.* As is true of the verb, *māšîaḥ* implies an anointing for a special office or function. Thus, David refused to harm Saul because Saul was "the Lord's anointed" (1 Sam. 24:6). The Psalms often express the messianic ideals attached to the Davidic line by using the phrase "the Lord's anointed" (Ps. 2:2; 18:50; 89:38, 51).

Interestingly enough, the only person named

"messiah" in the Old Testament was Cyrus, the pagan king of Persia, who was commissioned by God to restore Judah to her homeland after the Exile (Isa. 45:1). The anointing in this instance was more figurative than literal, since Cyrus was not aware that he was being set apart for such a divine purpose.

The New Testament title of *Christ* is derived from the Greek *Christos* which is exactly equivalent to the Hebrew *māšîaḥ*, for it is also rooted in the idea of "to smear with oil." So the term *Christ* emphasizes the special anointing of Jesus of Nazareth for His role as God's chosen one.

TO ANSWER

'ānāh (עָנָה, 6030), "to respond, answer, reply." This root occurs in most Semitic languages, although it bears many meanings. With the meaning that undergirds *'ānāh*, it appears in Ugaritic, Akkadian, Arabic, post-biblical Hebrew, and biblical Aramaic. It should be contrasted to *'ānāh*, meaning "oppress, subdue."

Biblical Hebrew attests the verb *'ānāh* about 320 times. One of the two meanings of *'ānāh* is "to respond," but not necessarily with a verbal response. For example, in Gen. 35:3 Jacob tells his household, "And let us arise, and go up to Bethel; and I will make there an altar unto God, who answered me in the day of my distress...." In Gen. 28:10ff., where this "answering" is recorded, it is quite clear that God initiated the encounter and that, although He spoke with Jacob, the emphasis is on the vision of the ladder and the relationship with God that it represented. This meaning is even clearer in Exod. 19:18, where we read that God reacted to the situation at Sinai with a sound (of thunder).

A nonverbal reaction is also indicated in Deut. 20:11. God tells Israel that before they besiege a city they should demand its surrender. Its inhabitants are to live as Israel's slaves "if it [the city] make thee answer of peace [literally, "responds peaceably"], and open unto thee...." In Job 30:20, Job says he cried out to God, who did not "respond" to him (i.e., did not pay any attention to him). In Isaiah 49:8 the Lord tells the Messiah, "In an acceptable time have I heard thee, and in a day of salvation have I helped thee...." Here responding ("hearing") is synonymously parallel to helping—i.e., it is an action (cf. Ps. 69:17; Isa. 41:17).

The second major meaning of *'ānāh* is "to respond with words," as when one engages in dialogue. In Gen. 18:27 (the first occurrence of *'ānāh*), we read: "Abraham answered and said" to the Lord, who had just spoken. In this formula, the two verbs represent one idea (i.e.,

they form an *hendiadys*). A simpler translation might be "respond," since God had asked no question and required no reply. On the other hand, when the sons of Heth "answer and say" (Gen. 23:5), they are responding verbally to the implied inquiry made by Abraham (v. 4). Therefore, they really do answer.

'Ānāh may mean "respond" in the special sense of verbally reacting to a truth discovered: "Then answered the five men that went to spy out the country of Laish, and said ..." (Judg. 18:14). Since no inquiry was addressed to them, this word implies that they gave a report; they responded to what they had discovered. In Deut. 21:7, the children of Israel are told how to respond to the rite of the heifer—viz., "They shall answer and say, Our hands have not shed this blood, neither have our eyes seen it."

'Ānāh can also be used in the legal sense of "testify": "Thou shalt not bear false witness against thy neighbor" (Exod. 20:16). Or we read in Exod. 23:2: "Thou shalt not follow a multitude to do evil...." In a similar sense, Jacob proposed that Laban give him all the spotted and speckled sheep of the flock, so that "my righteousness [will] answer [i.e., testify] for me in time to come, when it shall come [to make an investigation] for my hire before thy face ..." (Gen. 30:33).

TO ARISE

A. Verb.

qûm (קוּם, 6965), "to arise, stand up, come about." This word occurs in nearly every Semitic language, including biblical Hebrew and Aramaic. It occurs about 630 times in biblical Hebrew and 39 times in biblical Aramaic.

It may denote any movement to an erect position, such as getting up out of a bed (Gen. 19:33), or it can be used as the opposite of sitting or kneeling, as when Abraham "stood up from before his dead" (Gen. 23:3). It can also refer to the *result* of arising, as when Joseph saw his sheaf *arise* and remain erect (Gen. 37:7).

Qûm may be used by itself, with no direct object to refer to the origin of something, as when Isaiah says, "It shall not stand ..." (Isa. 7:7). Sometimes *qûm* is used in an intensive mood to signify empowering or strengthening: "Strengthen thou me according unto thy word" (Ps. 119:28). It is also used to denote the inevitable occurrence of something predicted or prearranged (Ezek. 13:6).

In a military context, *qûm* may mean "to engage in battle." In Ps. 18:38, for instance, God says, "I have wounded them that were not able to rise ..." (cf. 2 Sam. 23:10).

Qûm may also be used very much like *'āmad* to indicate the continuation of something—e.g., "Thy kingdom shall not continue" (1 Sam. 13:14). Sometimes it indicates validity, as when a woman's vow shall not "stand" (be valid) if her father forbids it (Num. 30:5). Also see Deut. 19:15, which states that a matter may be "confirmed" only by the testimony of two or more witnesses. In some passages, *qûm* means "immovable"; so Eli's eyes were "set" (1 Sam. 4:15).

Another special use of *qûm* is "rise up again," as when a childless widow complains to the elders, "My husband's brother refuseth to raise up unto his brother a name in Israel . . ." (Deut. 25:7). In other words, the brother refuses to continue that name or "raise it up again."

When used with another verb, *qûm* may suggest simply the beginning of an action. When Scripture says that "[Jacob] rose up, and passed over the [Euphrates] river" (Gen. 31:21), it does not mean that he literally stood up—merely that he began to cross the river.

Sometimes *qûm* is part of a compound verb and carries no special meaning of its own. This is especially true in commands. Thus Gen. 28:2 could simply be rendered, "Go to Padan-aram," rather than, "Arise, go . . ." (KJV). Other special meanings emerge when *qûm* is used with certain particles. With *'al*, "against," it often means "to fight against or attack": "A man riseth against his neighbor, and slayeth him . . ." (Deut. 22:26). This is its meaning in Gen. 4:8, the first biblical occurrence. With the particle *bᵉ* ("against"), *qûm* means "make a formal charge against": "One witness shall not rise up against a man . . ." (Deut. 19:15). With *lᵉ* ("for"), *qûm* means "to testify in behalf of": "Who will rise up for me against the evildoers?" (Ps. 94:16).The same construction can mean "to deed over," as when Ephron's field was deeded over (KJV, "made sure"—Gen. 23:17).

B. Noun.

māqôm (מָקוֹם, 4725), "place; height; stature; standing." The Old Testament contains three nouns related to *qûm*. The most important of these is *māqôm*, which occurs 401 times in the Old Testament. It refers to the place where something stands (1 Sam. 5:3), sits (1 Kings 10:19), dwells (2 Kings 8:21), or is (Gen. 1:9). It may also refer to a larger location, such as a country (Exod. 3:8) or to an undetermined "space between" (1 Sam. 26:13). A "place" is sometimes a task or office (Eccl. 10:4). This noun is used to signify a sanctuary—i.e., a "place" of worship (Gen. 22:3).

ARK

'ārôn (אָרוֹן, 727), "ark; coffin; chest; box." This word has cognates in Phoenician, Aramaic, Akkadian, and Arabic. It appears about 203 times in biblical Hebrew and in all periods.

In Gen. 50:26, this word represents a coffin or sarcophagus (as the same word does in Phoenician): "So Joseph died, being a hundred and ten years old: and they embalmed him, and he was put in a coffin in Egypt." This coffin was probably quite elaborate and similar to those found in ancient Egyptian tombs.

During the reign of Joash (or Jehoash), when the temple was repaired, money for the work was deposited in a "chest" with a hole in its lid. The high priest Jehoida prepared this chest and put it at the threshold to the temple (2 Kings 12:9).

In most occurrences, *'ārôn* refers to the "ark of the covenant." This piece of furniture functioned primarily as a container. As such the word is often modified by divine names or attributes. The divine name first modifies *'ārôn* in 1 Sam. 3:3: "And ere the lamp of God went out in the temple of the Lord, where the ark of God was, and Samuel was laid down to sleep. . . ." *'Ārôn* is first modified by God's covenant name, *Yahweh,* in Josh. 4:5. Judg. 20:27 is the first appearance of the "ark" as the ark of the covenant of *Elōhîm.* First Samuel 5:11 uses the phrase "the ark of the God [*'ĕlōhîm*] of Israel," and 1 Chron. 15:12 employs "the ark of the Lord [*Yahweh*] God [*'ĕlōhîm*] of Israel."

Sometimes divine attributes replace the divine name: "Arise, O Lord, into thy rest; thou, and the ark of thy strength" (Ps. 132:8). Another group of modifiers focuses on divine redemption (cf. Heb. 8:5). Thus *'ārôn* is often described as the "ark of the covenant" (Josh. 3:6) or "the ark of the covenant of the Lord" (Num. 10:33). As such, the ark contained the memorials of God's great redemptive acts—the tablets upon which were inscribed the Ten Commandments, an omer or two quarts of manna, and Aaron's rod. By Solomon's day, only the stone tablets remained in the ark (1 Kings 8:9). This chest was also called "the ark of the testimony" (Exod. 25:22), which indicates that the two tablets were evidence of divine redemption.

Exodus 25:10–22 tells us that this ark was made of acacia wood and measured 3 3/4 feet by 2 1/4 feet by 2 1/4 feet. It was gold-plated inside and outside, with a molding of gold. Each of its four feet had a golden ring at its top, through which passed unremovable golden carrying poles. The golden cover or mercy seat (place of propitiatory atonement) had the same dimensions as the top of the ark. Two golden cherubim sat on this cover facing each other, representing the heavenly majesty (Ezek. 1:10) that surrounds the living God.

In addition to containing memorials of divine redemption, the ark represented the presence of God. To be before it was to be in God's presence (Num. 10:35), although His presence was not limited to the ark (cf. 1 Sam. 4:3–11; 7:2, 6). The ark ceased to have this sacramental function when Israel began to regard it as a magical box with sacred power (a *palladium*).

God promised to meet Moses at the ark (Exod. 25:22). Thus, the ark functioned as a place where divine revelation was received (Lev. 1:1; 16:2; Num. 7:89). The ark served as an instrument through which God guided and defended Israel during the wilderness wandering (Num. 10:11). Finally, it was upon this ark that the highest of Israel's sacraments, the blood of atonement, was presented and received (Lev. 16:2ff.).

ARM

zᵉrôaʿ (זְרוֹעַ, 2220), "arm; power; strength; help." Cognates of *zᵉrôaʿ* occur both in Northwest and South Semitic languages. *Zᵉrôaʿ* is attested 92 times in biblical Hebrew and in all periods. The related word *'ezrôaʿ* appears twice (Job 31:22; Jer. 32:21). Biblical Aramaic attests *dra'* once and *'edrā* once.

Zᵉrôaʿ means "arm," a part of the body: "Blessed be he that enlargeth Gad: he dwelleth as a lion, and teareth the arm with the crown of the head" (Deut. 33:20). The word refers to arms in Gen. 49:24 (the first occurrence): "But his bow abode in strength, and the arms of his hands were made strong. . . . " The strength of his arms enabled him to draw the bow. In some passages, *zᵉrôaʿ* refers especially to the forearm: "It shall be as when the harvestman gathereth the corn, and reapeth the ears with his arm. . . . " (Isa. 17:5). Elsewhere, the word represents the shoulder: "And Jehu drew a bow with his full strength, and smote Jehoram between his arms . . . " (2 Kings 9:24).

Zᵉrôaʿ connotes the "seat of strength": "He teacheth my hands to war, so that a bow of steel is broken by mine arms" (Ps. 18:34). In Job 26:2, the poor are described as the arm that hath no strength.

God's strength is figured by anthropomorphisms (attributing to Him human bodily parts), such as His "stretched out arm" (Deut. 4:34) or His "strong arm" (Jer. 21:5). In Isa. 30:30, the word seems to represent lightning bolts: "And the Lord shall cause his glorious voice to be heard, and shall show the lighting down of his arm, with the indignation of his anger, and with the flame of a devouring fire, with scattering, and tempest, and hailstones" (cf. Job 40:9).

The arm is frequently a symbol of strength, both of man (1 Sam. 2:31) and of God (Ps. 71:18): "Now also when I am old and grayheaded, O God, forsake me not; until I have showed thy strength unto this generation, and thy power to every one that is to come." In Ezek. 22:6 *zᵉrôaʿ* may be translated "power": "Behold, the princes of Israel, every one were in thee to their power to shed blood." A third nuance is "help": "Assur also is joined with them: they have helped the children of Lot" (Ps. 83:8).

The word can represent political or military forces: "And the arms of the south shall not withstand, neither his chosen people, neither shall there be any strength to withstand" (Dan. 11:15; cf. Ezek. 17:9).

In Num. 6:19 *zᵉrôaʿ* is used of an animal's shoulder: "And the priest shall take the sodden shoulder of the ram . . . " (cf. Deut. 18:3).

ASHERAH

'ăšērāh (אֲשֵׁרָה, 842), "Asherah; Asherim (pl.)." This noun, which has an Ugaritic cognate, first appears in the Bible in passages anticipating the settlement in Palestine. The word's most frequent appearances, however, are usually in historical literature. Of its 40 appearances, 4 are in Israel's law code, 4 in Judges, 4 in prophetic books, and the rest are in 1 Kings and 2 Chronicles.

'Ăšērāh refers to a cultic object representing the presence of the Canaanite goddess Asherah. When the people of Israel entered Palestine, they were to have nothing to do with the idolatrous religions of its inhabitants. Rather, God said, "But ye shall destroy their altars, break their images, and cut down their groves ['ašērîm] . . . " (Exod. 34:13). This cult object was manufactured from wood (Judg. 6:26; 1 Kings 14:15) and it could be burned (Deut. 12:3). Some scholars conclude that it was a sacred pole set up near an altar to Baal. Since there was only one goddess with this name, the plural (*'ašērîm*) probably represents her several "poles."

'Ăšērāh signifies the name of the goddess herself: "Now therefore send, and gather to me all Israel unto mount Carmel, and the prophets of Baal four hundred and fifty, and the prophets of the groves ['ašērāh] four hundred, which eat at Jezebel's table" (1 Kings 18:19). The Canaanites believed that *'ašērāh* ruled the sea, was the mother of all the gods including Baal, and sometimes was his deadly enemy. Apparently,

the mythology of Canaan maintained that *'ašērāh* was the consort of Baal, who had displaced El as their highest god. Thus her sacred objects (poles) were immediately beside altars to Baal, and she was worshiped along with him.

TO ASK

A. Verb.

šā'al (שָׁאַל, 7592), "to ask, inquire, consult." This word is found in many Semitic languages, including ancient Akkadian and Ugaritic. It is found throughout the various periods of Hebrew and is used approximately 170 times in the Hebrew Bible. The first occurrence is found in Gen. 24:47, where the servant of Abraham asks Rebekah, "Whose daughter art thou?" It is commonly used for simple requests, as when Sisera asked for water from Jael (Judg. 5:25).

Since prayer often includes petition, *šā'al* is sometimes used in the sense of "praying for" something: "Pray for the peace of Jerusalem" (Ps. 122:6). In the idiomatic phrase, "to ask another of his welfare," it carries the sense of a greeting (cf. Exod. 18:7; Judg. 18:15; 1 Sam. 10:4). Frequently, it is used to indicate someone's asking for God's direction or counsel (Josh. 9:14; Isa. 30:2). In Ps. 109:10 it is used to indicate a begging: "Let his children be continually vagabonds, and beg."

B. Noun.

šeʼôl (שְׁאוֹל, 7585), "place of the dead." *Šā'al* seems to be the basis for an important noun in the Old Testament, *šeʼôl*. Found 65 times in the Hebrew Bible, *šeʼôl* refers to the netherworld or the underground cavern to which all buried dead go. Often incorrectly translated "hell" in the KJV, *šeʼôl* was not understood to be a place of punishment, but simply the ultimate resting place of all mankind (Gen. 37:35). Thus, it was thought to be the land of no return (Job 16:22; 17:14–16). It was a place to be dreaded, not only because it meant the end of physical life on earth, but also because there was no praise of God there (Ps. 6:5). Deliverance from it was a blessing (Ps. 30:3).

In some instances, it may be a symbol of distress or even plague; it is often used in parallel with "the Pit," another symbol of destruction. Much about *šeʼôl* was negative, so it is little wonder that the concept of hell developed from it in the intertestamental and New Testament literature. Yet it is also a place of reward for the righteous (Hos. 13:14; see p. 227).

Šeʼôl is translated variously in the English versions: "hell, pit, grave" (KJV); "netherworld" (NAB). Some versions simply give the transliteration, "Sheol" (RSV, JB, NASB).

ASSEMBLY

A. Noun.

qāhāl (קָהָל, 6951), "assembly; company." Cognates derived from this Hebrew noun appear in late Aramaic and Syriac. *Qāhāl* occurs 123 times and in all periods of biblical Hebrew.

In many contexts, the word means an assembly gathered to plan or execute war. One of the first of these is Gen. 49:6. In 1 Kings 12:3 (RSV), "all the assembly of Israel" asked Rehoboam to ease the tax burden imposed by Solomon. When Rehoboam refused, they withdrew from him and rejected their feudal (military) allegiance to him. For the application of *qāhāl* to an army, see Ezek. 17:17: "Neither shall Pharaoh with his mighty army and great company make for him in the war. . . ."

Quite often, *qāhāl* is used to denote a gathering to judge or deliberate. This emphasis first appears in Ezek. 23:45–47, where the "company" judges and executes judgment. In many passages, the word signifies an assembly representing a larger group: "David consulted with the commanders of thousands and of hundreds, with every leader. And David said to all the assembly of Israel . . ." (1 Chron. 13:1–2, RSV). Here, "the whole assembly" of Israel refers to the assembled leaders (cf. 2 Chron. 1:2). Thus, in Lev. 4:13 we find that the sin of the whole congregation of Israel can escape the notice of the "assembly" (the judges or elders who represent the congregation).

Sometimes *qāhāl* represents all the males of Israel who were eligible to bring sacrifices to the Lord: "He whose testicles are crushed or whose male member is cut off shall not enter the assembly of the Lord" (Deut. 23:1, RSV). The only eligible members of the assembly were men who were religiously bound together under the covenant, who were neither strangers (living in Israel temporarily) nor sojourners (permanent non-Hebrew residents) (Num. 15:15). In Num. 16:3 and 33, it is clear that the "assembly" was the worshiping, voting community (cf. 18:4).

Elsewhere, the word *qāhāl* is used to signify all the people of Israel. The whole congregation of the sons of Israel complained that Moses had brought them forth into the wilderness to kill the whole assembly with hunger (Exod. 16:3). The first occurrence of the word also bears the connotation of a large group: "And God Almighty bless thee, and make thee fruitful, and multiply thee, that thou mayest be a multitude [*qāhāl*] of people . . ." (Gen. 28:3).

B. Verb.

qāhal (קָהַל, 6950), "to gather." The verb *qāhal*, which occurs 39 times, is derived from the noun *qāhāl*. Like the noun, this verb appears in all periods of biblical Hebrew. It means "to gather" as a *qāhāl* for conflict or war, for religious purposes, and for judgment: "Then Solomon assembled the elders [*qāhal*] of Israel . . . " (1 Kings 8:1).

TO ATONE

A. Verb.

kāpar (כָּפַר, 3722), "to cover over, atone, propitiate, pacify." This root is found in the Hebrew language at all periods of its history, and perhaps is best known from the term *Yom Kippur,* "Day of Atonement." Its verbal forms occur approximately 100 times in the Hebrew Bible. *Kāpar* is first found in Gen. 6:14, where it is used in its primary sense of "to cover over." Here God gives Noah instructions concerning the ark, including, "Cover it inside and out with pitch" (RSV). (The KJV translates, "Pitch it within and without with pitch.")

Most uses of the word, however, involve the theological meaning of "covering over," often with the blood of a sacrifice, in order to atone for some sin. It is not clear whether this means that the "covering over" hides the sin from God's sight or implies that the sin is wiped away in this process.

As might be expected, this word occurs more frequently in the Book of Leviticus than in any other book, since Leviticus deals with the ritual sacrifices that were made to atone for sin. For example, Lev. 4:13–21 gives instructions for bringing a young bull to the tent of meeting for a sin offering. After the elders laid their hands on the bull (to transfer the people's sin to the bull), the bull was killed. The priest then brought some of the blood of the bull into the tent of meeting and sprinkled it seven times before the veil. Some of the blood was put on the horns of the altar and the rest of the blood was poured at the base of the altar of burnt offering. The fat of the bull was then burned on the altar. The bull itself was to be burned outside the camp. By means of this ritual, "the priest shall make an atonement [*kāpar*] for them, and it shall be forgiven them" (Lev. 4:20).

The term "atonement" is found at least 16 times in Lev. 16, the great chapter concerning the Day of Atonement. Before anything else, the high priest had to "make atonement" for himself and his house by offering a bull as a sin offering. After lots were cast upon the two goats, one was sent away into the wilderness as an atonement (v. 10), while the other was sacrificed and its blood sprinkled on the mercy seat as an atonement for the people (vv. 15–20). The Day of Atonement was celebrated only once a year. Only on this day could the high priest enter the holy of holies of the tabernacle or temple on behalf of the people of Israel and make atonement for them.

Sometimes atonement for sin was made apart from or without blood offerings. During his vision-call experience, Isaiah's lips were touched with a coal of fire taken from the altar by one of the seraphim. With that, he was told, "Thy sin is purged [*kāpar*]" (Isa. 6:7). The English versions translate the word variously as "purged" (KJV, JB); "forgiven" (RSV, NASB, TEV); and "wiped away" (NEB). In another passage, Scripture says that the guilt or iniquity of Israel would be "purged" (KJV, NEB) by the destruction of the implements of idolatrous worship (Isa. 27:9). In this case, the RSV renders *kāpar* as "expiated," while the NASB and TEV translate it as "forgiven."

B. Noun.

kappōret (כַּפֹּרֶת, 3727), "mercy seat; throne of mercy." This noun form of *kāpar* has been variously interpreted by the English versions as "mercy seat" (KJV, RSV); "cover" (NEB); "lid" (TEV); "throne of mercy" (JB); and "throne" (Knox). It refers to a slab of gold that rested on top of the ark of the covenant. Images of two cherubims stood on this slab, facing each other. This slab of gold represented the throne of God and symbolized His real presence in the worship shrine. On the Day of Atonement, the high priest sprinkled the blood of the sin offering on it, apparently symbolizing the blood's reception by God. Thus the *kappōret* was the central point at which Israel, through its high priest, could come into the presence of God.

This is further seen in the fact that the temple proper was distinguished from its porches and other accompanying structures by the name "place of the mercy seat (*kappōret*)" (1 Chron. 28:11). The Septuagint refers to the mercy seat as a "propitiary" (*hilasteirion*).

TO AVENGE

A. Verb.

nāqam (נָקַם, 5358), "to avenge, take vengeance, punish." This root and its derivatives occur 87 times in the Old Testament, most frequently in the Pentateuch, Isaiah, and Jeremiah; occasionally it occurs in the historical books and the Psalms. The root occurs also in Aramaic, Assyrian, Arabic, Ethiopic, and late Hebrew.

Lamech's sword song is a scornful challenge to his fellows and a blatant attack on the justice of God: " . . . for I have slain a man to my wounding, and a young man to my hurt. If Cain shall be avenged sevenfold, truly Lamech seventy and sevenfold" (Gen. 4:23–24).

The Lord reserves vengeance as the sphere of His own action: "To me belongeth vengeance, and recompense ... for he will avenge the blood of his servants, and will render vengeance to his adversaries" (Deut. 32:35, 43). The law therefore forbade personal vengeance: "Thou shalt not avenge, nor bear any grudge against the children of thy people, but thou shalt love thy neighbor as thyself: I am the Lord" (Lev. 19:18). Hence the Lord's people commit their case to Him, as David: "The Lord judge between me and thee [Saul], and the Lord avenge me of thee: but mine hand shall not be upon thee" (1 Sam. 24:12).

The Lord uses men to take vengeance, as He said to Moses: "Avenge the children of Israel of the Midianites.... And Moses spake unto the people, saying, Arm some of yourselves unto the war, and let them go against the Midianites, and avenge the Lord of Midian" (Num. 31:2–3). Vengeance for Israel is the Lord's vengeance.

The law stated, "And if a man smite his servant, or his maid, with a rod, and he die under his hand; he shall be surely punished" (Exod. 21:20). In Israel, this responsibility was given to the "avenger of blood" (Deut. 19:6). He was responsible to preserve the life and personal integrity of his nearest relative.

When a man was attacked because he was God's servant, he could rightly call for vengeance on his enemies, as Samson prayed for strength, " ... that I may be at once avenged of the Philistines for my two eyes" (Judg. 16:28).

In the covenant, God warned that His vengeance may fall on His own people: "And I will bring a sword upon you, that shall avenge the quarrel of my covenant ..." (Lev. 26:25). Isaiah thus says of Judah: "Therefore saith the Lord, the Lord of hosts ... Ah, I will ease me of mine adversaries, and avenge me of my enemies" (1:24).

B. Noun.

nāqām (נָקָם, 5359), "vengeance." The noun is first used in the Lord's promise to Cain: "Therefore whosoever slayeth Cain, vengeance shall be taken on him sevenfold" (Gen. 4:15).

In some instances a man may call for "vengeance" on his enemies, such as when another man has committed adultery with his wife: "For jealousy is the rage of a man: therefore he will not spare in the day of vengeance" (Prov. 6:34).

The prophets frequently speak of God's "vengeance" on His enemies: Isa. 59:17; Mic. 5:15; Nah. 1:2. It will come at a set time: "For it is the day of the Lord's vengeance, and the year of recompenses for the controversy of Zion" (Isa. 34:8).

Isaiah brings God's "vengeance" and redemption together in the promise of messianic salvation: "The Spirit of the Lord God is upon me; ... he hath sent me ... to proclaim the acceptable year of the Lord, and the day of vengeance of our God ..." (61:1–2). When Jesus announced that this was fulfilled in Himself, He stopped short of reading the last clause; but His sermon clearly anticipated that "vengeance" that would come on Israel for rejecting Him. Isaiah also said: "For the day of vengeance is in mine heart, and the year of my redeemed is come" (63:4).

TO AWAKE

'ûr (עוּר, 5782), "to awake, stir up, rouse oneself, rouse." This word is found in both ancient and modern Hebrew, as well as in ancient Ugaritic. It occurs approximately 80 times in the Hebrew Old Testament. Its first use in the Old Testament has the sense of "rousing" someone to action: "Awake, awake, Deborah" (Judg. 5:12). This same meaning is reflected in Ps. 7:6, where it is used in parallelism with "arise": "Arise, O Lord, in thine anger, ... awake for me to the judgment that thou hast commanded." The RSV translates this passage: " ... Awake, O my God; thou hast appointed a judgment." This probably is more in harmony with the total parallelism involved (arise/awake; Lord/God) than the KJ version. Also, the RSV's change from "for me" to "O my God" involves only a very slight change of one vowel in the word. (Remember that Hebrew vowels were not part of the alphabet. They were added after the consonantal text was written down.)

'Ûr commonly signifies awakening out of ordinary sleep (Zech. 4:1) or out of the sleep of death (Job 14:12). In Job 31:29, it expresses the idea of "being excited" or "stirred up": "If I ... lifted up myself when evil found him...." This verb is found several times in the Song of Solomon, for instance, in contrast with *sleep:* "I sleep, but my heart waketh ..." (5:2). It is found three times in an identical phrase: " ... that you stir not up, nor awake my love, till he please" (Song of Sol. 2:7; 3:5; 8:4).

B

BAAL, MASTER

ba'al (בַּעַל, 1167), "master; baal." In Akkadian, the noun *bēlu* ("lord") gave rise to the verb *bēlu* ("to rule"). In other northwest Semitic languages, the noun *ba'al* differs somewhat in meaning, as other words have taken over the meaning of "sir" or "lord." (Cf. Heb. *'ādôn.*) The Hebrew word *ba'al* seems to have been related to these homonyms.

The word *ba'al* occurs 84 times in the Hebrew Old Testament, 15 times with the meaning of "husband" and 50 times as a reference to a deity. The first occurrence of the noun *ba'al* is in Gen. 14:13: "And there came one that had escaped, and told Abram the Hebrew; for he dwelt in the plain of Mamre the Amorite, brother of Eshcol, and brother of Aner: and these were confederate with [literally, *"ba'al's* of a covenant with"] Abram."

The primary meaning of *ba'al* is "possessor." Isaiah's use of *ba'al* in parallel with *qānāh* clarifies this basic significance of *ba'al:* "The ox knoweth his owner [*qānāh*], and the ass his master's [*ba'al*] crib: but Israel does not know, my people doth not consider" (Isa. 1:3). Man may be the owner [*ba'al*] of an animal (Exod. 22:10), a house (Exod. 22:7), a cistern (Exod. 21:34), or even a wife (Exod. 21:3).

A secondary meaning, "husband," is clearly indicated by the phrase *ba'al ha-iššāh* (literally, "owner of the woman"). For example: "If men strive, and hurt a woman with child, so that her fruit depart from her, and yet no mischief follow: he shall be surely punished, according as the woman's husband [*ba'al ha-iššāh*] will lay upon him; and he shall pay as the judges determine" (Exod. 21:22). The meaning of *ba'al* is closely related to *îš* ("man"), as is seen in the usage of these two words in one verse: "When the wife of Uriah heard that Uriah her husband [*îš*] was dead, she mourned for her husband [*ba'al*]" (2 Sam. 11:26).

The word *ba'al* with another noun may signify a peculiar characteristic or quality: "And they said one to another, Behold, this dreamer cometh" (Gen. 37:19); the KJV offers a literal translation of the Hebrew—"master of dreams"—as an alternative.

Thirdly, the word *ba'al* may denote any deity other than the God of Israel. Baal was a common name given to the god of fertility in Canaan. In the Canaanite city of Ugarit, Baal was especially recognized as the god of fertility. The Old Testament records that Baal was "the god" of the Canaanites. The Israelites worshiped Baal during the time of the judges (Judg. 6:25–32) and of King Ahab. Elijah stood as the opponent of the Baal priests at Mount Carmel (1 Kings 18:21ff.). Many cities made Baal a local god and honored him with special acts of worship: Baal-peor (Num. 25:5), Baal-berith at Shechem (Judg. 8:33), Baal-zebub (2 Kings 1:2–16) at Ekron, Baal-zephon (Num. 33:7), and Baal-hermon (Judg. 3:3).

Among the prophets, Jeremiah and Hosea mention Baal most frequently. Hosea pictured Israel as turning to the baals and only returning to the Lord after a time of despair (Hos. 2:13, 17). He says that the name of *Ba'al* will no longer be used, not even with the meaning of "Lord" or "master," as the association was contaminated by the idolatrous practices: "And it shall be at that day, saith the Lord, that thou shalt call me Ishi; and shalt call me no more Ba-a-li [*ba'al*]. For I will take away the names of Ba-a-lim out of her mouth, and they shall no more be remembered by their name" (Hos. 2:16–17). In Hosea's and Jeremiah's time, the *ba'al* idols were still worshiped, as the peoples sacrificed, built high places, and made images of the *ba'alim* (plural).

In the Septuagint, the word *ba'al* is not uniformly translated: *kurios* ("lord, owner"); *aner* ("man, husband"); the simple transliteration; and *ba'al.* The KJV has these translations: "Baal, man, owner, husband, master."

BAND, ARMY

gᵉdûd (גְּדוּד, 1416), "band (of raiders); marauding band; raiding party; army; units (of an army); troops; bandits; raid." The 33 occurrences of this noun are distributed throughout every period of biblical Hebrew.

Basically, this word represents individuals or a band of individuals who raid and plunder an enemy. The units that perform such raids may be a group of outlaws ("bandits"), a special unit of any army, or an entire army. Ancient peoples frequently suffered raids from their neighbors. When the Amalekites "raided" Ziklag, looting and burning it while taking captive the wives and families of the men who followed David, he inquired of God, "Shall I pursue after this troop? shall I overtake them?" (1 Sam. 30:8). In this case, the "raiding band" consisted of the entire army of Amalek. This meaning of *gᵉdûd* occurs for the first time in Gen. 49:19: " ... A troop shall overcome him." Here the word is a collective noun referring to all the "band of raiders" to come. When Job described the glory of days gone by, he said he "dwelt as a king in the army [NASB, "troops"]" (Job 29:25). When David and his followers were called a *gᵉdûd,* they were being branded outlaws—men who lived by fighting and raiding (1 Kings 11:24).

In some passages, *gᵉdûd* signifies a smaller detachment of troops or a military unit or division: "And Saul's son had two men that were captains of bands" (2 Sam. 4:2). God sent against Jehoiakim "units" from the Babylonian army—"bands of the Chaldees, and bands of the Syrians, and bands of the Moabites, and bands of the children of Ammon . . . " (2 Kings 24:2).

The word can also represent individuals who are members of such raiding or military bands. The individuals in the household of Izrahiah, the descendant of Issachar, formed a military unit, "and with them by their generations, after the house of their fathers, were bands of soldiers for war, six and thirty thousand men . . ." (1 Chron. 7:4). Bildad asks the rhetorical question concerning God, "Is there any number [numbering] of his armies?" (Job 25:3).

The verb *gādad* means "to gather together against" (Ps. 94:21), "to make incisions into oneself" as a religious act (Deut. 14:1), "to roam about" (Jer. 30:23), or "to muster troops" (Mic. 5:1).

TO BE

hāyāh (הָיָה, 1961), "to become, occur, come to pass, be." This verb occurs only in Hebrew and Aramaic. The Old Testament attests *hāyāh* about 3,560 times, in both Hebrew and Aramaic.

Often this verb indicates more than simple existence or identity (this may be indicated by omitting the verb altogether). Rather, the verb makes a strong statement about the being or presence of a person or thing. Yet the simple meaning "become" or "come to pass" appears often in the English versions.

The verb can be used to emphasize the presence of a person (e.g., God's Spirit—Judg. 3:10), an emotion (e.g., fear—Gen. 9:2), or a state of being (e.g., evil—Amos 3:6). In such cases, the verb indicates that their presence (or absence) is noticeable—it makes a real difference to what is happening.

On the other hand, in some instances *hāyāh* does simply mean "happen, occur." Here the focus is on the simple occurrence of the events—as seen, for example, in the statement following the first day of creation: "And so it happened" (Gen. 1:7). In this sense, *hāyāh* is frequently translated "it came to pass."

The use of this verb with various particles colors its emphasis accordingly. In passages setting forth blessing or cursing, for example, this verb not only is used to specify the object of the action but also the dynamic forces behind and within the action. Gen. 12:2, for example, records that God told Abram: " . . . I will bless thee, and make thy name great; and thou shalt be [*hāyāh*] a blessing." Abram was already blessed, so God's pronouncement conferred upon him a future blessedness. The use of *hāyāh* in such passages declares the actual release of power, so that the accomplishment is assured— Abram will be blessed because God has ordained it.

In another set of passages, *hāyāh* constitutes intent rather than accomplishment. Hence, the blessing becomes a promise and the curse a threat (cf. Gen. 15:5).

Finally, in a still weaker use of *hāyāh,* the blessing or curse constitutes a wish or desire (cf. Ps. 129:6). Even here the verb is somewhat dynamic, since the statement recognizes God's presence, man's faithfulness (or rebellion), and God's intent to accomplish the result pronounced.

In miracle accounts, *hāyāh* often appears at the climax of the story to confirm the occurrence of the event itself. Lot's wife looked back and "became" a pillar of salt (Gen. 19:26); the use of *hāyāh* emphasizes that the event really occurred. This is also the force of the verb in Gen. 1:3, in which God said, "Let there *be* light." He accomplished His word so that there *was* light.

The prophets use *hāyāh* to project God's intervention in the future. By using this verb, they emphasize not so much the occurrence of predicted events and circumstances as the underlying divine force that will effect them (cf. Isa. 2:2).

Legal passages use *hāyāh* in describing God's relationship to His covenant people, to set forth what is desired and intended (cf. Exod. 12:16). When covenants were made between two partners, the formulas usually included *hāyāh* (Deut. 26:17–18; Jer. 7:23).

One of the most debated uses of *hāyāh* occurs in Exod. 3:14, where God tells Moses His name. He says: "I am [*hāyāh*] that I am [*hāyāh*]." Since the divine name *Jehovah* or *Yahweh* was well-known long before (cf. Gen. 4:1), this revelation seems to emphasize that the God who made the covenant was the God who kept the covenant. So Exod. 3:14 is more than a simple statement of identity: "I am that I am";

it is a declaration of divine control of all things (cf. Hos. 1:9).

TO BEAR

A. Verb.

yālad (יָלַד, 3205), "to bear, bring forth, beget, be delivered." This verb occurs in all Semitic languages and in nearly all verbal forms. The noteworthy exception is biblical Aramaic. However, the Aramaic verb is well attested outside the Bible. The verb *yālad* occurs about 490 times in the Bible.

Essentially, the word refers to the action of "giving birth" and its result, "bearing children." God cursed woman by multiplying her pain in "bringing forth" children (cf. Gen. 3:16, the first occurrence of *yālad*). The second meaning is exemplified by Gen. 4:18, which reports that Irad "begat" ("became the father of") Mehujael. This verb can also be used in reference to animals; in Gen. 30:39, the strong among Laban's flocks "birthed" striped, speckled, and spotted offspring.

One recurring theme in biblical history is typified by Abram and Sarah. They had no heirs, but God made them a promise and gave them a son (Gen. 16:1, 16). This demonstrates that God controls the opening of the womb (Gen. 20:17–18) and bestows children as an indication of His blessing. The prophets use the image of childbirth to illustrate the terror to overcome men in the day of the Lord (Isa. 13:8). Hosea uses the image of marriage and childbearing to describe God's relationship to Israel (1:3, 6, 8). One of the most hotly debated passages of Scripture, Isa. 7:14, uses this verb to predict the "birth" of Immanuel. Finally, the prophets sometimes mourn the day of their "birth" (Jer. 15:10).

Yālad describes the relationship between God and Israel at other places in the Bible as well. This relationship is especially relevant to the king who typifies the Messiah, the Son whom God "begot" (Ps. 2:7). God also says He "begot" the nation of Israel as a whole (Deut. 32:18). This statement is in noticeable contrast to Moses' disclaimer that he did not "birth" them (Num. 11:12) and, therefore, does not want to be responsible for them any longer.

The motif that God "gave birth" to Israel is picked up by Jeremiah. In Jer. 31:20, God states that His heart yearns for Ephraim His son (*yeled*). Ezekiel develops this motif in the form of an allegory, giving the names Aholah and Aholibah to Samaria and Jerusalem respectively, to those whom He "bore" (Ezek. 23:4, 37).

The Septuagint renders *yālad* with words connoting "giving birth" (*tinknein*) and "begetting" (*gennaō*).

B. Noun.

yeled (יֶלֶד, 3206), "boy; child." The noun *yeled* differs from *bēn* ("son"), which more exactly specifies the parental relationship. For example, the child that Naomi nursed was a "boy" (Ruth 4:16).

Yeled, which appears 89 times in the Bible, is rendered by several different Greek words. Other nouns built on the verb *yālad* include *yaldāh* ("girl"; 3 times), *yālîd* ("son" or "slave"; 3 times), *yillôd* ("newborn"; 5 times), *wālād* ("child"; once), *lēdâh* ("bringing forth" or "birth"; 4 times), *môledet* ("offspring, kindred, parentage"; 22 times), and *tôlēdôt* ("descendants, contemporaries, generation, genealogy, record of the family"; 39 times).

BEAST

beḥēmāh (בְּהֵמָה, 929), "beast; animal; domesticated animal; cattle; riding beast; wild beast." A cognate of this word appears in Arabic. Biblical Hebrew uses *beḥēmāh* about 185 times and in all periods of history.

In Exod. 9:25, this word clearly embraces even the larger "animals," all the animals in Egypt: "And the hail smote throughout all the land of Egypt all that was in the field, both man and beast.... " This meaning is especially clear in Gen. 6:7: "I will destroy man whom I have created from the face of the earth; both man, and beast, and the creeping thing, and the fowls of the air.... " In 1 Kings 4:33, this word seems to exclude birds, fish, and reptiles: "He [Solomon] spake also of beasts, and of fowl, and of creeping things, and of fishes."

The word *beḥēmāh* can be used of all the domesticated beasts or animals other than man: "And God said, Let the earth bring forth the living creature after his kind, cattle, and creeping thing, and [wild] beast of the earth after his kind ... " (Gen. 1:24, first occurrence). Psalm 8:7 uses *beḥēmāh* in synonymous parallelism with "oxen" and " sheep," as though it includes both: "All sheep and oxen, yea, and the beasts of the field." The word can, however, be used of cattle only: "Shall not their cattle and their substance and every beast of theirs [NASB, "animals"] be ours?" (Gen. 34:23).

In a rare use of the word, it signifies a "riding animal," such as a horse or mule: "And I arose in the night, I and some few men with me; neither told I any man what my God had put in my heart to do at Jerusalem: neither was there any beast with me, save the beast that I rode upon" (Neh. 2:12).

Infrequently, *beḥēmāh* represents any wild,

four-footed, undomesticated beast: "And thy carcase shall be meat unto all fowls of the air, and unto the beasts of the earth, and no man shall [frighten] them away" (Deut. 28:26).

BEHIND

A. Adverb.

'ahar (אַחַר, 310), "behind; after(wards)." A cognate of this word occurs in Ugaritic. 'Ahar appears about 713 times in biblical Hebrew and in all periods.

One adverbial use of 'ahar has a local-spatial emphasis that means "behind": "The singers went before, the players on instruments followed after ... " (Ps. 68:25). Another adverbial usage has a temporal emphasis that can mean "afterwards": "And I will fetch a morsel of bread, and comfort ye your hearts; after that ye shall pass on ... " (Gen. 18:5).

B. Preposition.

'ahar (אַחַר, 310), "behind; after." 'Ahar as a preposition can have a local-spatial significance, such as "behind": "And the man said, They are departed hence; for I heard them say, Let us go to Dothan" (Gen. 37:17). As such, it can mean "follow after": "And also the king that reigneth over you [will] continue following the Lord your God" (1 Sam. 12:14). 'Ahar can signify "after" with a temporal emphasis: "And Noah lived after the flood three hundred and fifty years" (Gen. 9:28, the first biblical occurrence of the word). This same emphasis may occur when 'ahar appears in the plural (cf. Gen. 19:6—local-spatial; Gen. 17:8—temporal).

C. Conjunction.

'ahar (אַחַר, 310), "after." 'Ahar may be a conjunction, "after," with a temporal emphasis: "And the days of Adam after he had begotten Seth were eight hundred years ... " (Gen. 5:4).

TO BELIEVE

A. Verb.

'aman (אָמַן, 539), "to be firm, endure, be faithful, be true, stand fast, trust, have belief, believe." Outside of Hebrew, this word appears in Aramaic (infrequently), Arabic, and Syriac. It appears in all periods of biblical Hebrew (about 96 times) and only in the causative and passive stems.

In the passive stem, 'aman has several emphases. First, it indicates that a subject is "lasting" or "enduring," which is its meaning in Deut. 28:59: "Then the Lord will make thy plagues wonderful, and the plagues of thy seed, even great plagues, and of long continuance, and sore sicknesses, and of long continuance." It also signifies the element of being "firm" or "trustworthy." In Isa. 22:23, 'aman refers to a "firm" place, a place into which a peg will be driven so that it will be immovable. The peg will remain firmly anchored, even though it is pushed so hard that it breaks off at the point of entry (Isa. 22:25). The Bible also speaks of "faithful" people who fulfill their obligations (cf. 1 Sam. 22:14; Prov. 25:13).

The nuance meaning "trustworthy" also occurs: "He that is of a faithful spirit concealeth the matter" (Prov. 11:13; cf. Isa. 8:2). An office-bearer may be conceived as an "entrusted one": "He removeth away the speech of the trusty [entrusted ones], and taketh away the understanding of the aged" (Job 12:20). In this passage, 'aman is synonymously parallel (therefore equivalent in meaning) to "elders" or "office-bearers." Thus, it should be rendered "entrusted ones" or "those who have been given a certain responsibility (trust)." Before receiving the trust, they are men "worthy of trust" or "trustworthy" (cf. 1 Sam. 2:35; Neh. 13:13).

In Gen. 42:20 (the first biblical appearance of this word in this stem), Joseph requests that his brothers bring Benjamin to him; "so shall your words be verified," or "be shown to be true" (cf. 1 Kings 8:26; Hos. 5:9). In Hos. 11:12, 'aman contrasts Judah's actions ("faithful") with those of Ephraim and Israel ("deceit"). So here 'aman represents both "truthfulness" and "faithfulness" (cf. Ps. 78:37; Jer. 15:18). The word may be rendered "true" in several passages (1 Kings 8:26; 2 Chron. 1:9; 6:17).

A different nuance of 'aman is seen in Deut. 7:9: " ... the faithful God, which keepeth covenant and mercy. ... " There is a good reason here to understand the word 'aman as referring to what God has done ("faithfulness"), rather than what He will do ("trustworthy"), because He has already proved Himself faithful by keeping the covenant. Therefore, the translation would become, " ... faithful God who has kept His covenant and faithfulness, those who love Him kept ... " (cf. Isa. 47:7).

In the causative stem, 'aman means "to stand fast," or "be fixed in one spot," which is demonstrated by Job 39:24: "He [a war horse] swalloweth the ground with fierceness and rage: neither believeth he that it is the sound of the trumpet."

Even more often, this stem connotes a psychological or mental certainty, as in Job 29:24: "If I laughed on them, they believed it not." Considering something to be trustworthy is an act of full trusting or believing. This is the emphasis in the first biblical occurrence of 'aman: "And [Abram] believed in the Lord; and he counted it to him for righteousness" (Gen. 15:6). The meaning here is that Abram was full of trust and confidence in God, and that he did not fear Him (v. 1). It was not primarily in God's words that he believed, but in God Himself. Nor does the text tell us that Abram believed God so as to accept what He said as "true" and "trustworthy" (cf. Gen. 45:26), but simply that he believed in God. In other words, Abram came to experience a personal relationship to God rather than an impersonal relationship with His promises. Thus, in Exod. 4:9 the meaning is, "if they do not believe in view of the two signs," rather than, "if they do not believe these two signs." The focus is on the act of believing, not on the trustworthiness of the signs. When God is the subject or object of the verb, the Septuagint almost always renders this stem of *'āman* with *pisteuō* ("to believe") and its composites. The only exception to this is Prov. 26:25.

A more precise sense of *'āman* does appear sometimes: "That they may believe that the Lord ... hath appeared unto thee" (Exod. 4:5; cf. 1 Kings 10:7).

In other instances, *'āman* has a cultic use, by which the worshiping community affirms its identity with what the worship leader says (1 Chron. 16:32). The "God of the *'āmēn*" (2 Chron. 20:20; Isa. 65:16) is the God who always accomplishes what He says; He is a "God who is faithful."

B. Nouns.

'ĕmûnāh (אֱמוּנָה, 530), "firmness; faithfulness; truth; honesty; official obligation." In Exod. 17:12 (the first biblical occurrence), the word means "to remain in one place": "And his [Moses'] hands were steady until the going down of the sun." Closely related to this use is that in Isa. 33:6: "And wisdom and knowledge shall be the stability of thy times...." In passages such as 1 Chron. 9:22, *'ĕmûnāh* appears to function as a technical term meaning "a fixed position" or "enduring office": "All these which were chosen to be porters in the gates were two hundred and twelve. These were reckoned by their genealogy in their villages, whom David and Samuel the seer did ordain in their set [i.e., established] office."

The most frequent sense of *'ĕmûnāh* is "faithfulness," as illustrated by 1 Sam. 26:23: "The Lord render to every man his righteousness and his faithfulness...." The Lord repays the one who demonstrates that he does what God demands.

Quite often, this word means "truthfulness," as when it is contrasted to false swearing, lying, and so on: "Run ye to and fro through the streets of Jerusalem, and see now, and know, and seek in the broad places thereof, if ye can find a man, if there be any that executeth judgment, that seeketh the truth [i.e., honesty]" (Jer. 5:1; cf. Jer. 5:2). Here *'ĕmûnāh* signifies the condition of being faithful to God's covenant, practicing truth, or doing righteousness. On the other hand, the word can represent the abstract idea of "truth": "This is a nation that obeyeth not the voice of the Lord their God, nor receiveth correction: truth [*'ĕmûnāh*] is perished, and is cut off from their mouth" (Jer. 7:28). These quotations demonstrate the two senses in which *'ĕmûnāh* means "true"—the personal sense, which identifies a subject as honest, trustworthy, faithful, truthful (Prov. 12:22); and the factual sense, which identifies a subject as being factually true (cf. Prov. 12:27), as opposed to that which is false.

The essential meaning of *'ĕmûnāh* is "established" or "lasting," "continuing," "certain." So God says, "And in mercy shall the throne be established: and he shall sit upon it in truth in the tabernacle of David, judging, and seeking judgment, and hasting righteousness" (cf. 2 Sam. 7:16; Isa. 16:5). Thus, the phrase frequently rendered "with lovingkindness and truth" should be rendered "with perpetual (faithful) lovingkindness" (cf. Josh. 2:14). He who sows righteousness earns a "true" or "lasting" reward (Prov. 11:18), a reward on which he can rely.

In other contexts, *'ĕmûnāh* embraces other aspects of the concept of truth: "[The Lord] hath remembered his mercy and his truth toward the house of Israel ..." (Ps. 98:3). Here the word does not describe the endurance of God but His "truthfulness"; that which He once said He has maintained. The emphasis here is on truth as a subjective quality, defined personally. In a similar sense, one can both practice (Gen. 47:29) and speak the "truth" (2 Sam. 7:28). In such cases, it is not a person's dependability (i.e., others can act on the basis of it) but his reliability (conformity to what is true) that is considered. The first emphasis is subjective and the second objective. It is not always possible to discern which emphasis is intended by a given passage.

'ĕmet (אֱמֶת, 571), "truth; right; faithful." This word appears 127 times in the Bible. The Septuagint translates it in 100 occurrences as "truth" (*aletheia*) or some form using this basic root. In Zech. 8:3, Jerusalem is called "a city of truth." Elsewhere, *'ĕmet* is rendered as the word "right" (*dikaios*): "Howbeit thou art just in all that is brought upon us; for thou hast done right, but we have done wickedly ..." (Neh. 9:33). Only infrequently (16 times) is *'ĕmet* translated "faithful" (*pistis*), as when Nehemiah

is described as "a faithful man, and feared God above many" (Neh. 7:2).

C. Adverb.

'āmēn (אָמֵן, 543), "truly; genuinely; amen; so be it." The term 'āmēn is used 30 times as an adverb. The Septuagint renders it as "truly" (*lethinos*) once; transliterates it as "amen" three times; and translates it as "so be it" (*genoitō*) the rest of the time. This Hebrew word usually appears as a response to a curse that has been pronounced upon someone, as the one accursed accepts the curse upon himself. By so doing, he binds himself to fulfill certain conditions or else be subject to the terms of the curse (cf. Deut. 29:15–26).

Although signifying a voluntary acceptance of the conditions of a covenant, the 'āmēn was sometimes pronounced with coercion. Even in these circumstances, the one who did not pronounce it received the punishment embodied in the curse. So the 'āmēn was an affirmation of a covenant, which is the significance of the word in Num. 5:22, its first biblical occurrence. Later generations or individuals might reaffirm the covenant by voicing their 'āmēn (Neh. 5:1–13; Jer. 18:6).

In 1 Kings 1:36, 'āmēn is noncovenantal. It functions as an assertion of a person's agreement with the intent of a speech just delivered: "And Benaiah the son of Jehoiada answered the king, and said, Amen: the Lord God of my lord the king say so too." However, the context shows that Benaiah meant to give more than just verbal assent; his 'āmēn committed him to carry out the wishes of King David. It was a statement whereby he obligated himself to do what David had indirectly requested of him (cf. Neh. 8:6).

BETWEEN

bên (בֵּין, 996), "between; in the midst of; among; within; in the interval of." A cognate of this word is found in Arabic, Aramaic, and Ethiopic. The approximately 375 biblical appearances of this word occur in every period of biblical Hebrew. Scholars believe that the pure form of this word is *bayin*, but this form never occurs in biblical Hebrew.

This word nearly always (except in 1 Sam. 17:4, 23) is a preposition meaning "in the interval of" or "between." The word may represent "the area between" in general: "And it shall be for a sign unto thee upon thine hand, and for a memorial between thine eyes . . . " (Exod. 13:9). Sometimes the word means "within," in the sense of a person's or a thing's "being in the area of": "The slothful man saith, There is a lion in the way; a lion is in the streets" (Prov.

26:13). In other places, *bên* means "among": "Shall the companions make a banquet of him [Leviathan]? Shall they part him among [give each a part] the merchants?" (Job 41:6). In Job 34:37, the word means "in the midst of," in the sense of "one among a group": "For he addeth rebellion unto his sin, he clappeth his hands among us. . . . "

The area separating two particular objects is indicated in several ways. First, by repeating *bên* before each object: "And God divided the light from the darkness" [literally, "between the light and between the darkness"] (Gen. 1:4); that is, He put an interval or space between them. In other places (more rarely), this concept is represented by putting *bên* before one object and the preposition *le* before the second object: "Let there be a firmament in the midst [*bên*] of the waters, and let it divide the waters from [*le*] the waters" (Gen. 1:6). In still other instances, this idea is represented by placing *bên* before the first object plus the phrase meaning "with reference to" before the second (Joel 2:17), or by *bên* before the first object and the phrase "with reference to the interval of" before the second (Isa. 59:2).

Bên is used in the sense of "distinguishing between" in many passages: "Let there be lights in the firmament of the heaven to divide the day from [*bên*] the night" (Gen. 1:14).

Sometimes *bên* signifies a metaphorical relationship. For example, "This is the token of the covenant which I make between [*bên*] me and you and every living creature . . . " (Gen. 9:12). The covenant is a contractual relationship. Similarly, the Bible speaks of an oath (Gen. 26:28) and of goodwill (Prov. 14:9) filling the metaphorical "space" between two parties.

This word is used to signify an "interval of days," or "a period of time": "Now that which was prepared for me was . . . once in ten days [literally, "at ten-day intervals"] store of all sorts of wine . . . " (Neh. 5:18).

In the dual form, *bên* represents "the space between two armies": "And there went out a champion [literally, "a man between the two armies"] out of the camp of the Philistines, named Goliath . . . " (1 Sam. 17:4). In ancient warfare, a battle or even an entire war could be decided by a contest between two champions.

TO BIND

'āsar (אָסַר, 631), "to bind, imprison, tie, gird, to harness." This word is a common Semitic term, found in both ancient Akkadian and Ugaritic, as well as throughout the history of the Hebrew language. The word occurs around 70 times in its verbal forms in the Hebrew Old

Testament. The first use of *'āsar* in the Hebrew text is in Gen. 39:20, which tells how Joseph was "imprisoned" after being wrongfully accused by Potiphar's wife.

The common word for "tying up" for security and safety, *'āsar* is often used to indicate the tying up of horses and donkeys (2 Kings 7:10). Similarly, oxen are "harnessed" to carts (1 Sam. 6:7, 10). Frequently, *'āsar* is used to describe the "binding" of prisoners with cords and various fetters (Gen. 42:24; Judg. 15:10, 12–13). Samson misled Delilah as she probed for the secret of his strength, telling her to "bind" him with bowstrings (Judg. 16:7) and new ropes (Judg. 16:11), none of which could hold him.

Used in an abstract sense, *'āsar* refers to those who are spiritually "bound" (Ps. 146:7; Isa. 49:9; 61:1) or a man who is emotionally "captivated" by a woman's hair (Song of Sol. 7:5). Strangely, the figurative use of the term in the sense of obligation or "binding" to a vow or an oath is found only in Num. 30, but it is used there a number of times (vv. 3, 5–6, 8–9, 11–12). This section also illustrates how such "binding" is variously rendered in the English versions: "bind" (RSV, KJV, NAB); "promises" (TEV); "puts himself under a binding obligation" (NEB, NASB); "takes a formal pledge under oath" (JB).

TO BLESS

A. Verb.

bārak (בָּרַךְ, 1288), "to kneel, bless, be blessed, curse." The root of this word is found in other Semitic languages which, like Hebrew, use it most frequently with a deity as subject. There are also parallels to this word in Egyptian.

Bārak occurs about 330 times in the Bible, first in Gen. 1:22: "And God blessed them, saying, Be fruitful and multiply, . . ." God's first word to man is introduced in the same way: "And God blessed them, and God said unto them, Be fruitful, and multiply . . ." (v. 28). Thus the whole creation is shown to depend upon God for its continued existence and function (cf. Ps. 104:27–30). *Bārak* is used again of man in Gen. 5:2, at the beginning of the history of believing men, and again after the Flood in Gen. 9:1: "And God blessed Noah and his sons. . . ." The central element of God's covenant with Abram is: "I will bless thee . . . and thou shalt be a blessing: And I will bless them that bless thee . . . and in thee shall all families of the earth be blessed" (Gen. 12:2–3). This "blessing" on the nations is repeated in Gen. 18:18; 22:18; and 28:14 (cf. Gen. 26:4; Jer. 4:2). In all of these instances, God's blessing goes out to the nations through Abraham or his seed. The Septuagint translates all of these occurrences of *bārak* in the passive, as do the KJV, NASB, and NIV. Paul quotes the Septuagint's rendering of Gen. 22:18 in Gal. 3:8.

The covenant promise called the nations to seek the "blessing" (cf. Isa. 2:2–4), but made it plain that the initiative in blessing rests with God, and that Abraham and his seed were the instruments of it. God, either directly or through His representatives, is the subject of this verb over 100 times. The Levitical benediction is based on this order: "On this wise ye shall bless the children of Israel . . . the Lord bless thee . . . and they shall put my name upon the children of Israel; and I will bless them" (Num. 6:23–27).

The passive form of *bārak* is used in pronouncing God's "blessing on men," as through Melchizedek: "Blessed be Abram of the most high God . . ." (Gen. 14:19). "Blessed be the Lord God of Shem . . ." (Gen. 9:26) is an expression of praise. "Blessed be the most high God, which hath delivered thine enemies into thy hand" (Gen. 14:20) is mingled praise and thanksgiving.

A common form of greeting was, "Blessed be thou of the Lord" (1 Sam. 15:13; cf. Ruth 2:4); "Saul went out to meet [Samuel], that he might salute him" (1 Sam. 13:10; "greet," NASB and NIV).

The simple form of the verb is used in 2 Chron. 6:13: "He . . . kneeled down . . . ." Six times the verb is used to denote profanity, as in Job 1:5: "It may be that my sons have sinned, and cursed God in their hearts."

B. Noun.

berākāh (בְּרָכָה, 1293), "blessing." The root form of this word is found in northwest and south Semitic languages. It is used in conjunction with the verb *bārak* ("to bless") 71 times in the Old Testament. The word appears most frequently in Genesis and Deuteronomy. The first occurrence is God's blessing of Abram: "I will make of thee a great nation, and I will bless thee, and make thy name great; and thou shalt be a blessing [*berākāh*]" (Gen. 12:2).

When expressed by men, a "blessing" was a wish or prayer for a blessing that is to come in the future: "And [God] give thee the blessing of Abraham, to thee, and to thy seed with thee; that thou mayest inherit the land wherein thou art a stranger, which God gave unto Abraham" (Gen. 28:4). This refers to a "blessing" that the patriarchs customarily extended upon their children before they died. Jacob's "blessings" on the tribes (Gen. 49) and Moses' "blessing"

(Deut. 33:1ff.) are other familiar examples of this.

Blessing was the opposite of a cursing (q^elā-lāh): "My father peradventure will feel me, and I shall seem to him as a deceiver; and I shall bring a curse upon me, and not a blessing" (Gen. 27:12). The blessing might also be presented more concretely in the form of a gift. For example, "Take, I pray thee, my blessing that is brought to thee; because God hath dealt graciously with me, and because I have enough. And he urged him, and he took it" (Gen. 33:11). When a "blessing" was directed to God, it was a word of praise and thanksgiving, as in: "Stand up and bless the Lord your God for ever and ever: and blessed be thy glorious name, which is exalted above all blessing and praise" (Neh. 9:5).

The Lord's "blessing" rests on those who are faithful to Him: "A blessing, if ye obey the commandments of the Lord your God, which I command you this day ..." (Deut. 11:27). His blessing brings righteousness (Ps. 24:5), life (Ps. 133:3), prosperity (2 Sam. 7:29), and salvation (Ps. 3:8). The "blessing" is portrayed as a rain or dew: "I will make them and the places round about my hill a blessing; and I will cause the shower to come down in his season; there shall be showers of blessing" (Ezek. 34:26; cf. Ps. 84:6). In the fellowship of the saints, the Lord commands His "blessing": "[It is] as the dew of Hermon, and as the dew that descended upon the mountains of Zion: for there the Lord commanded the blessing, even life for evermore" (Ps. 133:3).

In a few cases, the Lord made people to be a "blessing" to others. Abraham is a blessing to the nations (Gen. 12:2). His descendants are expected to become a blessing to the nations (Isa. 19:24; Zech. 8:13).

The Septuagint translates b^erākāh as eulogia ("praise; blessing"). The KJV has these translations: "blessing; present (gift)."

BLESSED

'ašrê (אַשְׁרֵי, 835), "blessed; happy." All but 4 of the 44 biblical occurrences of this noun are in poetical passages, with 26 occurrences in the Psalms and 8 in Proverbs.

Basically, this word connotes the state of "prosperity" or "happiness" that comes when a superior bestows his favor (blessing) on one. In most passages, the one bestowing favor is God Himself: "Happy art thou, O Israel: who is like unto thee, O people saved by the Lord" (Deut. 33:29). The state that the blessed one enjoys does not always appear to be "happy": "Behold, blessed [KJV, "happy"] is the man whom God correcteth: therefore despise not thou the chastening of the Almighty: for he maketh sore, and bindeth up ..." (Job 5:17–18). Eliphaz was not describing Job's condition as a happy one; it was "blessed," however, inasmuch as God was concerned about him. Because it was a blessed state and the outcome would be good, Job was expected to laugh at his adversity (Job 5:22).

God is not always the one who makes one "blessed." At least, the Queen of Sheba flatteringly told Solomon that this was the case (1 Kings 10:8).

One's status before God (being "blessed") is not always expressed in terms of the individual or social conditions that bring what moderns normally consider to be "happiness." So although it is appropriate to render 'ašrê as "blessed," the rendering of "happiness" does not always convey its emphasis to modern readers.

BLOOD

dām (דָּם, 1818) , "blood." This is a common Semitic word with cognates in all the Semitic languages. Biblical Hebrew attests it about 360 times and in all periods.

Dām is used to denote the "blood" of animals, birds, and men (never of fish). In Gen. 9:4, "blood" is synonymous with "life": "But flesh with the life thereof, which is the blood thereof, shall ye not eat." The high value of life as a gift of God led to the prohibition against eating "blood": "It shall be a perpetual statute for your generations throughout all your dwellings, that ye eat neither fat nor blood" (Lev. 3:17). Only infrequently does this word mean "blood-red," a color: "And they rose up early in the morning, and the sun shone upon the water, and the Moabites saw the water on the other side as red as blood" (2 Kings 3:22). In two passages, dām represents "wine": "He washed his garments in wine, and his clothes in the blood of grapes" (Gen. 49:11; cf. Deut. 32:14).

Dām bears several nuances. First, it can mean "blood shed by violence": "So ye shall not pollute the land wherein ye are: for blood it defileth the land: and the land cannot be cleansed of the blood that is shed therein ..." (Num. 35:33). Thus it can mean "death": "So will I send upon you famine and evil beasts, and they shall bereave thee; and pestilence and blood shall pass through thee; and I will bring the sword upon thee" (Ezek. 5:17).

Next, dām may connote an act by which a human life is taken, or blood is shed: "If there arise a matter too hard for thee in judgment, between blood and blood [one kind of homicide or another] ... " (Deut. 17:8). To "shed blood" is to commit murder: "Whoso sheddeth man's blood, by man shall his blood be shed ... " (Gen. 9:6). The second occurrence here means that the murderer shall suffer capital punishment. In other places, the phrase "to shed blood" refers to a non-ritualistic slaughter of an animal: "What man soever there be of the house of Israel, that killeth an ox, or lamb ... in the camp, or that killeth it out of the camp, and bringeth it not unto the door of the tabernacle of the congregation, to offer an offering unto the Lord before the tabernacle of the Lord; blood [guiltiness] shall be imputed unto that man" (Lev. 17:3–4).

In judicial language, "to stand against one's blood" means to stand before a court and against the accused as a plaintiff, witness, or judge: "Thou shalt not go up and down as a talebearer among thy people: neither shalt thou stand against the blood [i.e., act against the life] of thy neighbor ... " (Lev. 19:16). The phrase, "his blood be on his head," signifies that the guilt and punishment for a violent act shall be on the perpetrator: "For everyone that curseth his father or his mother shall be surely put to death: he hath cursed his father or his mother; his blood [guiltiness] shall be upon him" (Lev. 20:9). This phrase bears the added overtone that those who execute the punishment by killing the guilty party are not guilty of murder. So here "blood" means responsibility for one's dead: "And it shall be, that whosoever shall go out of the doors of thy house into the street, his blood shall be upon his head, and we will be guiltless: and whosoever shall be with thee in the house, his blood shall be on our head, if any hand be upon him" (Josh. 2:19).

Animal blood could take the place of a sinner's blood in atoning (covering) for sin: "For it is the blood that maketh an atonement for the soul" (Lev. 17:11). Adam's sin merited death and brought death on all his posterity (Rom. 5:12); so the offering of an animal in substitution not only typified the payment of that penalty, but it symbolized that the perfect offering would bring life for Adam and all others represented by the sacrifice (Heb. 10:4). The animal sacrifice prefigured and typologically represented the blood of Christ, who made the great and only effective substitutionary atonement, and whose offering was the only offering that gained life for those whom He represented. The shedding of His "blood" seals the covenant of life between God and man (Matt. 26:28).

TO BLOW

tāqaʻ (תָּקַע, 8628), "to strike, give a blast, clap, blow, drive." Found in both ancient and modern Hebrew, this word occurs in the Hebrew Old Testament nearly 70 times. In the verse where *tāqaʻ* first occurs, it is found twice: "Jacob had pitched [*tāqaʻ*] his tent in the mount: and Laban with his brethren pitched in the mount of Gilead" (Gen. 31:25). The meaning here is that of "striking" or "driving" a tent peg, thus "pitching" a tent. The same word is used of Jael's "driving" the peg into Sisera's temple (Judg. 4:21). The Bible also uses *tāqaʻ* to describe the strong west wind that "drove" the locusts into the Red Sea (Exod. 10:19).

Tāqaʻ expresses the idea of "giving a blast" on a trumpet. It is found seven times with this meaning in the story of the conquest of Jericho (Josh. 6:4, 8–9, 13, 16, 20).

To "strike" one's hands in praise or triumph (Ps. 47:1) or "shake hands" on an agreement (Prov. 6:1; 17:18; 22:26) are described by this verb. To "strike" the hands in an agreement was a surety or guarantor of the agreement.

BONE

ʻeṣem (עֶצֶם, 6106), "bone; body; substance; full; selfsame." Cognates of this word appear in Akkadian, Punic, Arabic, and Ethiopic. The word appears about 125 times in biblical Hebrew and in all periods.

This word commonly represents a human "bone." In Job 10:11, *ʻeṣem* is used to denote the bone as one of the constituent parts of the human body: "Thou hast clothed me with skin and flesh, and hast fenced me with bones and sinews." When Adam remarked of Eve that she was "bone of his bone," and flesh of his flesh, he was referring to her creation from one of his rib bones (Gen. 2:23--the first biblical appearance). *ʻEṣem* used with "flesh" can indicate a blood relationship: "And Laban said to [Jacob], Surely thou art my bone and my flesh" (Gen. 29:14).

Another nuance of this meaning appears in Job 2:5 where, used with "flesh," *ʻeṣem* represents one's "body": "But put forth thine hand now, and touch his bone and his flesh [his "body"]." A similar use appears in Jer. 20:9, where the word used by itself (and in the plural form) probably represents the prophet's entire "bodily frame": "Then I said, I will not make mention of him, nor speak any more in his name. But his word was in mine heart as a burning fire shut up in my bones. ... " Judg. 19:29 reports that a Levite cut his defiled and murdered concubine into twelve pieces "limb by limb" (according to her "bones" or bodily frame) and sent a part to each of the twelve tribes of Israel. In several passages, the plural form represents the "seat of vigor or sensation": "His bones are full of the sin of his youth ... " (Job 20:11; cf. 4:14).

In another nuance, 'eṣem is used for the "seat of pain and disease": "My bones are pierced in me in the night season: and my sinews take no rest" (Job 30:17).

The plural of 'eṣem sometimes signifies one's "whole being": "Have mercy upon me, O Lord; for I am weak: O Lord, heal me; for my bones are vexed" (Ps. 6:2). Here the word is synonymously parallel to "I."

This word is frequently used of the "bones of the dead": "And whosoever toucheth one that is slain with a sword in the open fields, or a dead body, or a bone of a man, or a grave, shall be unclean seven days" (Num. 19:16). Closely related to this nuance is the use of 'eṣem for "human remains," probably including a mummified corpse: "And Joseph took an oath of the children of Israel, saying, God will surely visit you, and ye shall carry up my bones from hence" (Gen. 50:25).

'Eṣem sometimes represents "animal bones." For example, the Passover lamb is to be eaten in a single house and "thou shalt not carry forth aught of the flesh abroad out of the house; neither shall ye break a bone thereof" (Exod. 12:46).

The word sometimes stands for the "substance of a thing": "And they saw the God of Israel: and there was under his feet as it were a paved work of a sapphire stone, and as it were the body of heaven in his clearness [as the bone of the sky]" (Exod. 24:10). In Job 21:23, the word means "full": "One dieth in his full strength. ... " At other points, 'eṣem means "same" or "selfsame": "In the selfsame day entered Noah, and Shem, and Ham and Japheth, the sons of Noah ... " (Gen. 7:13).

BOOK

sēper (סֵפֶר, 5612), "book; document; writing." *Sēper* seems to be a loanword from the Akkadian *sipru* ("written message," "document"). The word appears 187 times in the Hebrew Old Testament, and the first occurrence is in Gen. 5:1: "This is the book of the generations of Adam. When God created man, he made him in the likeness of God" (RSV). The word is rare in the Pentateuch except for Deuteronomy (11 times). The usage increases in the later historical books (Kings 60 times but Chronicles 24 times; cf. Esther 11 times and Nehemiah 9 times).

The most common translation of *sēper* is "book." A manuscript was written (Exod. 32:32; Deut. 17:18) and sealed (Isa. 29:11), to be read by the addressee (2 Kings 22:16). The sense of *sēper* is similar to "scroll" (*mᵉgillāh*): "Therefore go thou, and read in the roll [*sēper*] which thou hast written from my mouth, the words of the Lord in the ears of the people in the Lord's house upon the fasting day: and also thou shalt read them in the ears of all Judah that come out of their cities" (Jer. 36:6). *Sēper* is also closely related to "book" (*sipra*) (Ps. 56:8).

Many "books" are named in the Old Testament: the "book" of remembrance (Mal. 3:16), "book" of life (Ps. 69:28), "book" of Jasher (Josh. 10:13), "book" of the generations (Gen. 5:1), "book" of the Lord, "book" of the chronicles of the kings of Israel and of Judah, and the annotations on the "book" of the Kings (2 Chron. 24:27). Prophets wrote "books" in their lifetime. Nahum's prophecy begins with this introduction: "The burden of Nineveh. The book of the vision of Nahum the Elkoshite" (1:1).

Jeremiah had several "books" written in addition to his letters to the exiles. He wrote a "book" on the disasters that were to befall Jerusalem, but the "book" was torn up and burned in the fireplace of King Jehoiakim (Jer. 36). In this context, we learn about the nature of writing a "book." Jeremiah dictated to Baruch, who wrote with ink on the scroll (36:18). Baruch took the "book" to the Judeans who had come to the temple to fast. When the "book" had been confiscated and burned, Jeremiah wrote another scroll and had another "book" written with a strong condemnation of Jehoiakim and his family: "Then took Jeremiah another roll, and gave it to Baruch the scribe, the son of Neriah; who wrote therein from the mouth of Jeremiah all the words of the book which Jehoiakim king of Judah had burned in the fire: and there were added besides unto them many like words" (Jer. 36:32).

Ezekiel was commanded to eat a "book" (Ezek. 2:8–3:1) as a symbolic act of God's judgment on and restoration of Judah.

Sēper can also signify "letter." The prophet Jeremiah wrote a letter to the Babylonian exiles, instructing them to settle themselves, as they were to be in Babylon for 70 years: "Now these are the words of the letter (*sēper*) that Jeremiah the prophet sent from Jerusalem unto the residue of the elders which were carried away captives, and to the priests, and to the prophets, and to all the people whom Nebuchadnezzar had carried away captive from Jerusalem to Babylon ... " (Jer. 29:1).

The contents of the *sēper* varied. It might contain a written order, a commission, a request, or a decree, as in: "And [Mordecai] wrote in the king Ahasuerus' name, and sealed it [*sēper*] with the king's ring, and sent letters by posts on horseback, and riders on mules, camels, and young dromedaries" (Esth. 8:10). In divorcing his wife, a man gave her a legal document known as the *sēper* of divorce (Deut. 24:1). Here *sēper* meant a "certificate" or "legal document." Some other legal document might also be referred to as a *sēper*. As a "legal document," the *sēper* might be published or hidden for the appropriate time: "Thus saith the Lord of hosts, the God of Israel; Take these evidences [*sēper*], this evidence of the purchase, both which is sealed, and this evidence which is open; and put them in an earthen vessel, that they may continue many days" (Jer. 32:14).

The Septuagint gives the following translations: *biblion* ("scroll; document") and *gramma* ("letter; document; writing; book"). The KJV gives these senses: "book; letter; evidence."

BOOTY

šālāl (שָׁלָל, 7998), "booty; prey; spoil; plunder; gain." This word occurs 75 times and in all periods of biblical Hebrew.

Šālāl literally means "prey," which an animal tracks down, kills, and eats: "Benjamin shall raven as a wolf: in the morning he shall devour the prey [*šālāl*], and at night he shall divide the spoil" (Gen. 49:27--the first occurrence).

The word may mean "booty" or "spoil of war," which includes anything and everything a soldier or army captures from an enemy and carries off: "But the women, and the little ones, ... even all the spoil thereof, shalt thou take unto thyself ... " (Deut. 20:14). An entire nation can be "plunder" or a "spoil of war" (Jer. 50:10). To "save one's own life as booty" is to have one's life spared (cf. Jer. 21:9).

Šālāl is used in a few passages of "private plunder": "Woe unto them that ... turn aside the needy from judgment, and ... take away the right from the poor of my people, that widows may be their prey, and that they may rob the fatherless!" (Isa. 10:1-2).

This word may also represent "private gain": "The heart of her husband doth safely trust in her, so that he shall have no need of spoil" (Prov. 31:11).

BOSOM

hêq (חֵיק, 2436), "bosom; lap; base." Cognates of this word appear in Akkadian, late Aramaic, and Arabic. The word appears 38 times throughout biblical literature.

The word represents the "outer front of one's body" where beloved ones, infants, and animals are pressed closely: "Have I conceived all this people? have I begotten them, that thou shouldest say unto me, Carry them in thy bosom, as a nursing father beareth the sucking child ... " (Num. 11:12). In its first biblical appearance, *hêq* is used of a man's "bosom": "And Sarai said unto Abram, My wrong be upon thee: I have given my maid into thy bosom; and when she saw that she had conceived, I was despised in her eyes ... " (Gen. 16:5). The "husband of one's bosom" is a husband who is "held close to one's heart" or "cherished" (Deut. 28:56). This figurative inward sense appears again in Ps. 35:13: " ... My prayer returned into mine own bosom" (cf. Job 19:27). In 1 Kings 22:35, the word means the "inside" or "heart" of a war chariot.

Hêq represents a fold of one's garment above the belt where things are hidden: "And the Lord said furthermore unto him [Moses], Put now thine hand into thy bosom" (Exod. 4:6).

Various translations may render this word as "lap": "The lot is cast into the lap; but the whole disposing thereof is of the Lord" (Prov. 16:33). Yet "bosom" may be used, even where "lap" is clearly intended: "But the poor man had nothing, save one little ewe lamb, which he had bought and nourished up: and it grew up together with him, and with his children; it did eat of his own meat, and drank of his own cup, and lay in his bosom ... " (2 Sam. 12:3).

Finally, *hêq* means the "base of the altar," as described in Ezek. 43:13 (cf. Ezek. 43:17).

BOUNDARY

gᵉbûl (גְּבוּל, 1366), "boundary; limit; territory; closed area." This word has cognates in Phoenician and Arabic. It occurs about 240 times in biblical Hebrew and in all periods.

Gᵉbûl literally means "boundary" or "border." This meaning appears in Num. 20:23, where it signifies the border or boundary of the entire land of Edom. Sometimes such an imaginary line was marked by a physical barrier: " ... Arnon is the border of Moab, between Moab and the Amorites" (Num. 21:13). Sometimes *gᵉbûl* denoted ethnic boundaries, such as the borders of the tribes of Israel: "And unto the Reubenites and unto the Gadites I gave from Gilead even unto the river Arnon half the valley, and the border even unto the river Jabbok, which is the border of the children of Ammon ... " (Deut. 3:16). In Gen. 23:17, *gᵉbûl* represents the "border" of an individual's field or piece of ground: "And the field of Ephron, which was in Machpelah, which was before

Mamre, the field, and the cave which was therein, and all the trees that were in the field, that were in all the borders round about, were made sure." Fields were delineated by "boundary marks," whose removal was forbidden by law (Deut. 19:14; cf. Deut. 27:17).

Gᵉbûl can suggest the farthest extremity of a thing: "Thou hast set a bound that they may not pass over; that they turn not again to cover the earth" (Ps. 104:9).

This word sometimes represents the concrete object marking the border of a thing or area (cf. Ezek. 40:12). The "border" of Ezekiel's altar is signified by *gᵉbûl* (Ezek. 43:13) and Jerusalem's "surrounding wall" is represented by this word (Isa. 54:12).

Gᵉbûl represents the territory within certain boundaries: "And the border of the Canaanites was from Sidon, as thou comest to Gerar, unto Gaza; as thou goest, unto Sodom, and Gomorrah, and Admah, and Zeboim, even unto Lasha" (Gen. 10:19). In Exod. 34:24, Num. 21:22, 1 Chron. 21:12, and Ps. 105:31–32, *gᵉbûl* is paralleled to the "territory" surrounding and belonging to a city.

Gᵉbûlāh, the feminine form of *gᵉbûl,* occurs 9 times. *Gᵉbûlāh* means "boundary" in such passages as Isa. 10:13, and "territory" or "area" in other passages, such as Num. 34:2.

TO BOW, BEND

kāraʿ (כָּרַע, 3766), "to bow, bow down, bend the knee." This term is found in both ancient and modern Hebrew and in Ugaritic. It occurs in the Hebrew Old Testament approximately 35 times. *Kāraʿ* appears for the first time in the deathbed blessing of Jacob as he describes Judah: " . . . He stooped down, he couched as a lion" (Gen. 49:9).

The implication of *kāraʿ* seems to be the bending of one's legs or knees, since a noun meaning "leg" is derived from it. To "bow down" to drink was one of the tests for elimination from Gideon's army (Judg. 7:5–6). "Kneeling" was a common attitude for the worship of God (1 Kings 8:54; Ezra 9:5; Isa. 45:23; cf. Phil. 2:10).

"Bowing down" before Haman was required by the Persian king's command (Esth. 3:2–5). To "bow down upon" a woman was a euphemism for sexual intercourse (Job 31:10). A woman in process of giving birth was said to "bow down" (1 Sam. 4:19). Tottering or feeble knees are those that "bend" from weakness or old age (Job 4:4).

BREAD

lehem (לֶחֶם, 3899), "bread; meal; food; fruit." This word has cognates in Ugaritic, Syriac, Aramaic, Phoenician, and Arabic. *Lehem* occurs about 297 times and at every period of biblical Hebrew.

This noun refers to "bread," as distinguished from meat. The diet of the early Hebrews ordinarily consisted of bread, meat, and liquids: "And he humbled thee, and suffered thee to hunger, and fed thee with manna, which thou knewest not, neither did thy fathers know; that he might make thee know that man doth not live by bread only, but by every word that proceedeth out of the mouth of the Lord . . . " (Deut. 8:3). "Bread" was baked in loaves: "And it shall come to pass, that every one that is left in thine house shall come and crouch to him for a piece of silver and a morsel of bread . . . " (1 Sam. 2:36). Even when used by itself, *lehem* can signify a "loaf of bread": " . . . They will salute thee, and give thee two loaves of bread . . . " (1 Sam. 10:4). In this usage, the word is always preceded by a number. "Bread" was also baked in cakes (2 Sam. 6:19).

A "bit of bread" is a term for a modest meal. So Abraham said to his three guests, "Let a little water, I pray you, be fetched . . . and I will fetch a morsel of bread, and comfort ye your hearts . . . " (Gen. 18:4–5). In 1 Sam. 20:27, *lehem* represents an entire meal: " . . . Saul said unto Jonathan his son, Wherefore cometh not the son of Jesse to meat, neither yesterday, nor today?" Thus, "to make bread" may actually mean "to prepare a meal": "A feast is made for laughter, and wine maketh merry . . . " (Eccl. 10:19). The "staff of bread" is the "support of life": "And when I have broken the staff of your bread, ten women shall bake your bread in one oven, and they shall deliver you your bread again by weight: and ye shall eat, and not be satisfied" (Lev. 26:26). The Bible refers to the "bread of the face" or "the bread of the Presence," which was the bread constantly set before God in the holy place of the tabernacle or temple: "And thou shalt set upon the table showbread before me always" (Exod. 25:30).

In several passages, *lehem* represents the grain from which "bread" is made: "And the seven years of dearth began to come, according as Joseph had said: and the dearth was in all the lands; but in all the land of Egypt there was bread" (Gen. 41:54). The meaning "grain" is very clear in 2 Kings 18:32: "Until I come and take you away to a land like your own land, a land of corn and wine, a land of bread and vineyards. . . . "

Leḥem can represent food in general. In Gen. 3:19 (the first biblical occurrence), it signifies the entire diet: "In the sweat of thy face shalt thou eat bread...." This nuance may include meat, as it does in Judg. 13:15–16: "And Manoah said unto the angel of the Lord, I pray thee, let us detain thee, until we shall have made ready a kid for thee. And the angel of the Lord said unto Manoah, Though thou detain me, I will not eat of thy bread...." In 1 Sam. 14:24, 28, *leḥem* includes honey, and in Prov. 27:27 goat's milk. *Leḥem* may also represent "food" for animals: "He giveth to the beast his food, and to the young ravens which cry" (Ps. 147:9; cf. Prov. 6:8). Flesh and grain offered to God are called "the bread of God": "... For the offerings of the Lord made by fire, and the bread of their God, they do offer ..." (Lev. 21:6; cf. 22:13).

There are several special or figurative uses of *lehem.* The "bread" of wickedness is "food" gained by wickedness: "For [evil men] eat the bread of wickedness, and drink the wine of violence" (Prov. 4:17). Compare the "bread" or "food" gained by deceit (Prov. 20:17) and lies (23:3). Thus, in Prov. 31:27 the good wife "looketh well to the ways of her household, and eateth not the bread of idleness"—i.e., unearned food. The "bread of my portion" is the food that one earns (Prov. 30:8).

Figuratively, men are the "food" or prey for their enemies: "Only rebel not ye against the Lord, neither fear ye the people of the land; for they are bread for us ..." (Num. 14:9). The Psalmist in his grief says his tears are his "food" (Ps. 42:3). Evil deeds are likened to food: "[The evil man's] meat in his bowels is turned, it is the gall of asps within him" (Job 20:14). In Jer. 11:19, *lehem* represents "fruit from a tree" and is a figure of a man and his offspring: "... And I knew not that they had devised devices against me, saying, Let us destroy the tree with the fruit thereof, and let us cut him off from the land of the living, that his name may be no more remembered."

Maṣṣāh (מַצָּה, 4682), "unleavened bread." This noun occurs 54 times, all but 14 of them in the Pentateuch. The rest of the occurrences are in prose narratives or in Ezekiel's discussion of the new temple (Ezek. 45:21).

In the ancient Orient, household bread was prepared by adding fermented dough to the kneading trough and working it through the fresh dough. Hastily made bread omitted the fermented (leavened) dough: Lot "made them a feast, and did bake unleavened bread, and they did eat" (Gen. 19:3). In this case, the word represents bread hastily prepared for unexpected guests. The feasts of Israel often involved the use of unleavened bread, perhaps because of the relationship between fermentation, rotting, and death (Lev. 2:4ff.), or because unleavened bread reminded Jews of the hasty departure from Egypt and the rigors of the wilderness march.

BREADTH

rōhab (רֹחַב, 7341), "breadth; width; expanse." The noun *rōhab* appears 101 times and in all periods of biblical Hebrew.

First, the word refers to how broad a flat expanse is. In Gen. 13:17, we read: "Arise, walk through the land in the length of it and in the breadth of it; for I will give it unto thee." *Rōhab* itself sometimes represents the concept length, breadth, or the total territory: "... And the stretching out of his wings shall fill the breadth of thy land, O Immanuel" (Isa. 8:8). The same usage appears in Job 37:10, where the NASB renders the word "expanse." This idea is used figuratively in 1 Kings 4:29, describing the dimensions of Solomon's discernment: "And God gave Solomon wisdom and understanding exceeding much, and largeness [*rōhab*] of heart, even as the sand that is on the seashore."

Second, *rōhab* is used to indicate the "thickness" or "width" of an object. In its first biblical occurrence the word is used of Noah's ark: "The length of the ark shall be three hundred cubits, the breadth of it fifty cubits, and the height of it thirty cubits" (Gen. 6:15). In Ezek. 42:10, the word represents the "thickness" of a building's wall in which there were chambers (cf. Ezek. 41:9).

Rōhab is derived from the verb *rāhab,* as is the noun *rᵉhôb* or *rᵉhôb.*

Rᵉhôb (רְחוֹב, 7339) or *rᵉhōb* (רְחֹב, 7339), "town square." *Rᵉhôb* (or *rᵉhōb*) occurs 43 times in the Bible. Cognates of this noun appear in Ugaritic, Akkadian, and Aramaic. *Rᵉhôb* represents the "town square" immediately near the gate(s), as in Gen. 19:2 (the first occurrence). This "town square" often served for social functions such as assemblies, courts, and official proclamations.

TO BREAK

šābar (שָׁבַר, 7665), "to break, shatter, smash, crush." This word is frequently used in ancient Akkadian and Ugaritic, and is common throughout Hebrew. It is found almost 150 times in the Hebrew Bible. The first biblical occurrence of *šābar* is in Gen. 19:9, which tells how the men of Sodom threatened to "break" Lot's door to take his house guests.

The common word for "breaking" things,

šābar describes the breaking of earthen vessels (Judg. 7:20; Jer. 19:10), of bows (Hos. 1:5), of swords (Hos. 2:18), of bones (Exod. 12:46), and of yokes or bonds (Jer. 28:10, 12–13). Sometimes it is used figuratively to describe a "shattered" heart or emotion (Ps. 69:20; Ezek. 6:9). In its intensive sense, *šābar* connotes "shattering" something, such as the tablets of the Law (Exod. 32:19) or idol images (2 Kings 11:18), or the "shattering" of trees by hail (Exod. 9:25).

BREATH

hebel (הֶבֶל, 1892), "breath; vanity; idol." Cognates of this noun occur in Syriac, late Aramaic, and Arabic. All but 4 of its 72 occurrences are in poetry (37 in Ecclesiastes).

First, the word represents human "breath" as a transitory thing: "I loathe it; I would not live always: let me alone; for my days are vanity [literally, but a breath]" (Job 7:16).

Second, *hebel* means something meaningless and purposeless: "Vanity of vanities, saith the Preacher, vanity of vanities; all is vanity" (Eccl. 1:2).

Third, this word signifies an "idol," which is unsubstantial, worthless, and vain: "They have moved me to jealousy with that which is not God; they have provoked me to anger with their vanities ..." (Deut. 32:21--the first occurrence).

BROTHER

'āh (אָח, 251), "brother." This word has cognates in Ugaritic and most other Semitic languages. Biblical Hebrew attests the word about 629 times and at all periods.

In its basic meaning, *'āh* represents a "male sibling," a "brother." This is its meaning in the first biblical appearance: "And she again bare his brother Abel" (Gen. 4:2). This word represents a full brother or a half-brother: "And he said to him, Go, I pray thee, see whether it be well with thy brethren ..." (Gen. 37:14).

In another nuance, *'āh* can represent a "blood relative." Abram's nephew is termed his "brother": "And he brought back all the goods, and also brought again his brother Lot, and his goods, and the women also, and the people" (Gen. 14:16). This passage, however, might also reflect the covenantal use of the term whereby it connotes "ally" (cf. Gen. 13:8). In Gen. 9:25, *'āh* clearly signifies "relative": "Cursed be Canaan; a servant of servants shall he be unto his brethren." Laban called his cousin Jacob an *'āh*: "And Laban said unto Jacob, Because thou art my brother, shouldest thou therefore serve me for nought?" (Gen. 29:15). Just before this,

Jacob described himself as an *'āh* of Rachel's father (Gen. 29:12).

Tribes may be called *'āhîm*: "And [the tribe of] Judah said unto [the tribe of] Simeon his brother, Come up with me into my lot ..." (Judg. 1:3). The word *'āh* is used of a fellow tribesman: "With whomsoever thou findest thy gods, let him not live: before our brethren discern thou what is thine ..." (Gen. 31:32). Elsewhere it describes a fellow countryman: "And it came to pass in those days, when Moses was grown, that he went out unto his brethren, and looked on their burdens ..." (Exod. 2:11).

In several passages, the word *'āh* connotes "companion" or "colleague"—that is, a brother by choice. One example is found in 2 Kings 9:2: "And when thou comest thither, look out there Jehu the son of Jehoshaphat the son of Nimshi, and go in, and make him arise up from among his brethren, and carry him to an inner chamber" (cf. Isa. 41:6; Num. 8:26). Somewhat along this line is the covenantal use of the word as a synonym for "ally": "And Lot went out at the door unto them, and shut the door after him, and said, I pray you, brethren, do not so wickedly" (Gen. 19:6–7). Notice this same use in Num. 20:14 and 1 Kings 9:13.

'Āh can be a term of polite address, as it appears to be in Gen. 29:4: "And Jacob said unto them [shepherds, whose identity he did not know], My brethren, whence be ye?"

The word *'āh* sometimes represents someone or something that simply exists alongside a given person or thing: "And surely your blood of your lives will I require; at the hand of every beast will I require it, and at the hand of ... every man's brother will I require the life of man" (Gen. 9:5–6).

TO BUILD

A. Verb.
bānāh (בָּנָה, 1129), "to build, establish, construct, rebuild." This root appears in all the Semitic languages except Ethiopic and in all periods of Hebrew. In biblical Hebrew, it occurs about 375 times and in biblical Aramaic 23 times.

In its basic meaning, *bānāh* appears in Gen. 8:20, where Noah is said to have "constructed" an ark. In Gen. 4:17, *bānāh* means not only that Enoch built a city, but that he "founded" or "established" it. This verb can also mean "to manufacture," as in Ezek. 27:5: "They have made all thy ship boards of fir trees...." Somewhat in the same sense, we read that God "made" or "fashioned" Eve out of Adam's rib (Gen. 2:22--the first biblical occurrence). In like manner, Asa began with the cities of Geba and Mizpah and "fortified" them (1 Kings 15:22). In each case, the verb suggests adding to existing material to fashion a new object.

Bānāh can also refer to "rebuilding" something that is destroyed. Joshua cursed anyone who would rise up and rebuild Jericho, the city that God had utterly destroyed (Josh. 6:26).

Metaphorically or figuratively, the verb *bānāh* is used to mean "building one's house"—i.e., having children. Sarai said to Abram, "I pray thee, go in unto my maid; it may be that I may obtain children by her" (Gen. 16:2). It was the duty of the nearest male relative to conceive a child with the wife of a man who had died childless (Deut. 25:9); he thus helped "to build up the house" of his deceased relative. Used figuratively, "to build a house" may also mean "to found a dynasty" (2 Sam. 7:27).

B. Nouns.

bēn (בֵּן, 1121), "son." *bat* (בַּת, 1323), "daughter." These nouns are derived from the verb *bānāh*. They are actually different forms of the same noun, which occurs in nearly every Semitic language (except Ethiopic and Akkadian). Biblical occurrences number over 5,550 in the Hebrew and about 22 in Aramaic.

Basically, this noun represents one's immediate physical male or female offspring. For example, Adam "begat sons and daughters" (Gen. 5:4). The special emphasis here is on the physical tie binding a man to his offspring. The noun can also be used of an animal's offspring: "Binding his *foal* unto the vine, and his ass's *colt* unto the choice vine . . ." (Gen. 49:11). Sometimes the word *bēn*, which usually means "son," can mean "children" (both male and female). God told Eve that "in sorrow thou shalt bring forth children" (Gen. 3:16--the first occurrence of this noun). The words *bēn* and *bat* can signify "descendants" in general—daughters, sons, granddaughters, and grandsons. Laban complained to Jacob that he had not allowed him "to kiss my sons and my daughters" (Gen. 31:28; cf. v. 43).

The phrase, "my son," may be used by a superior to a subordinate as a term of familiar address. Joshua said to Achan, "My son, give, I pray thee, glory to the Lord God of Israel . . ." (Josh. 7:19). A special use of "my son" is a teacher's speaking to a disciple, referring to intellectual or spiritual sonship: "My son, if sinners entice thee, consent thou not" (Prov. 1:10). On the lips of the subordinate, "son" signifies conscious submission. Ben-hadad's servant Hazael took gifts to Elisha, saying, "Thy son Ben-hadad king of Syria hath sent me to thee" (2 Kings 8:9).

Bēn can also be used in an adoption formula:

"Thou art my Son; this day have I begotten thee" (Ps. 2:7). *Bēn* often is used in this sense of a king's relationship to God (i.e., he is God's adopted son). Sometimes the same word expresses Israel's relationship to God: "When Israel was a child, then I loved him, and called my son out of Egypt" (Hos. 11:1).

The Bible also refers to the heavenly court as the "sons of God" (Job 1:6). God called the elders of Israel the "sons [KJV, "children"] of the Most High" (Ps. 82:6). In Gen. 6:2, the phrase "sons of God" is variously understood as members of the heavenly court, the spiritual disciples of God (the sons of Seth), and the boastful among mankind.

Bēn may signify "young men" in general, regardless of any physical relationship to the speaker: "And [I] beheld among the simple ones, I discerned among the youths, a young man void of understanding" (Prov. 7:7). A city may be termed a "mother" and its inhabitants its "sons": "For he hath strengthened the bars of thy gates; he hath blessed thy children within thee" (Ps. 147:13).

Bēn is sometimes used to mean a single individual; thus Abraham ran to his flock and picked out a "son of a cow" (Gen. 18:7). The phrase "son of man" is used in this sense—God is asked to save the poor individuals, not the children of the poor (Ps. 72:4).

Bēn may also denote a member of a group. An example is a prophet who followed Elijah (1 Kings 20:35; cf. Amos 7:14).

This noun may also indicate someone worthy of a certain fate—e.g., "a stubborn and rebellious son" (Deut. 21:18).

Used figuratively, "son of" can mean "something belonging to"—e.g., "the arrow [literally, "the son of a bow"] cannot make him flee" (Job 41:28).

BULLOCK

pār (פַּר, 6499), "bullock." Cognates of this word appear in Ugaritic, Aramaic, Syriac, and Arabic. *Pār* appears about 132 times in the Bible and in every period, although most of its appearances are in prose contexts dealing with sacrifices to God.

Pār means "young bull," which is the significance in its first biblical appearance (Gen. 32:15), which tells us that among the gifts Jacob sent to placate Esau were "ten bulls." In Ps. 22:12, the word is used to describe "fierce, strong enemies": "Many bulls have compassed me: strong bulls of Bashan have beset me round." When God threatens the nations with judgment in Isa. 34:7, He describes their princes and warriors as "young bulls," which He will slaughter (cf. Jer. 50:27; Ezek. 39:18).

Pārāh is the feminine form of *pār,* and it is used disdainfully of women in Amos 4:1: "Hear this word, you cows [KJV, "kine"] of Bashan ..." (RSV). *Pārāh* occurs 25 times in the Old Testament, and its first appearance is in Gen. 32:15.

TO BURN

A. Verb.

śārap (שָׂרַף, 8313), "to burn." A common Semitic term, this word is found in ancient Akkadian and Ugaritic, as well as throughout the history of the Hebrew language. It occurs in its verb form nearly 120 times in the Hebrew Old Testament. *Śārap* is found first in Gen. 11:3 in the Tower of Babel story: "Go to, let us make brick, and burn them thoroughly."

Since burning is the main characteristic of fire, the term *śārap* is usually used to describe the destroying of objects of all kinds. Thus, the door of a city tower was "burned" (Judg. 9:52), as were various cities (Josh. 6:24; 1 Sam. 30:1), chariots (Josh. 11:6, 9), idols (Exod. 32:20; Deut. 9:21), and the scroll that Jeremiah had dictated to Baruch (Jer. 36:25, 27–28). The Moabites' "burning" of the bones of the king of Edom (Amos 2:1) was a terrible outrage to all ancient Semites. The "burning" of men's bodies on the sacred altar was a great act of desecration (1 Kings 13:2). Ezekiel "burned" a third of his hair as a symbol that part of the people of Judah would be destroyed (Ezek. 5:4).

Interestingly, *śārap* is never used for the "burning" of a sacrifice on the altar, although a few times it designates the disposal of refuse, unused sacrificial parts, and some diseased parts. The "burning" of a red heifer was for the purpose of producing ashes for purification (Lev. 19:5, 8).

B. Nouns.

śārap (שָׂרָף, 8314), "burning one; fiery being." In Num. 21:6, 8, the term *śārap* describes the serpents that attacked the Israelites in the wilderness. They are referred to as "fiery" serpents. A "fiery" flying serpent appears in Isa. 14:29, as well as in Isa. 30:6.

Śᵉrapîm (שְׂרָפִים, 8314), "burning, noble." *Śᵉrapîm* refers to the ministering beings in Isa. 6:2, 6, and may imply either a serpentine form (albeit with wings, human hands, and voices) or beings that have a "glowing" quality about them. One of the *śᵉrapîm* ministered to Isaiah by bringing a glowing coal from the altar.

TO BURN INCENSE

A. Verb.

qāṭar (קָטַר, 6999), "to burn incense, cause to rise up in smoke." The primary stem of this verb appears in Akkadian. Related forms appear in Ugaritic, Arabic, Phoenician, and post-biblical Hebrew. The use of this verb in biblical Hebrew is never in the primary stem, but only in the causative and intensive stems (and their passives).

The first biblical occurrence of *qāṭar* is in Exod. 29:13: "And thou shalt take all the fat that covereth the inwards, and caul that is above the liver, and the two kidneys, and the fat that is upon them, and *offer them up in smoke* on the altar." Technically this verb means "offering true offerings" every time it appears in the causative stem (cf. Hos. 4:13; 11:2), although it may refer only to the "burning of incense" (2 Chron. 13:11). Offerings are burned in order to change the thing offered into smoke (the ethereal essence of the offering), which would ascend to God as a pleasing or placating savor. The things sacrificed were mostly common foods, and in this way Israel offered up to God life itself, their labors, and the fruit of their labors.

Such offerings represent both the giving of the thing offered and a vicarious substitution of the offering for the offerer (cf. John 17:19; Eph. 5:2). Because of man's sinfulness (Gen. 8:21; Rom. 5:12), he was unable to initiate a relationship with God. Therefore, God Himself told man what was necessary in order to worship and serve Him. God specified that only the choicest of one's possessions could be offered, and the best of the offering belonged to Him (Lev. 4:10). Only His priests were to offer sacrifices (2 Kings 16:13). All offerings were to be made at the designated place; after the conquest, this was the central sanctuary (Lev. 17:6).

Some of Israel's kings tried to legitimatize their idolatrous offerings, although they were in open violation of God's directives. Thus the causative stem is used to describe, for example, Jeroboam's idolatrous worship: "So he offered upon the altar which he had made in Beth-el the fifteenth day of the eighth month, even in the month which he had devised of his own heart; and ordained a feast unto the children of Israel: and he offered upon the altar, and burnt incense" (1 Kings 12:33; cf. 2 Kings 16:13; 2 Chron. 28:4).

The intensive stem (occurring only after the Pentateuch) always represents "false worship." This form of *qāṭar* may represent the "total act of ritual" (2 Chron. 25:14). Such an act was usually a conscious act of idolatry, imitative of

Canaanite worship (Isa. 65:7). Such worship was blasphemous and shameful (Jer. 11:17). Those who performed this "incense-burning" were guilty of forgetting God (Jer. 19:4), while the practice itself held no hope for those who were involved in it (Jer. 11:12). Amos ironically told Israelites to come to Gilgal and Bethel (idolatrous altars) and "offer" a thank offering. This irony is even clearer in the Hebrew, for Amos uses *qāṭar* in the intensive stem.

B. Nouns.

qᵉṭōret (קְטֹרֶת, 7004), "incense." The first biblical occurrence of *qᵉṭōret* is in Exod. 25:6, and the word is used about 60 times in all. The word represents "perfume" in Prov. 27:9. *Qiṭṭēr* means "incense." This word appears once in the Old Testament, in Jer. 44:21. Another noun, *qᵉṭōrah*, also means "incense." This word's only appearance is in Deut. 33:10. *Qîṭôr* refers to "smoke; vapor." This word does not refer to the smoke of an offering, but to other kinds of smoke or vapor. The reference in Ps. 148:8 ("vapor") is one of its four biblical occurrences. *Muqṭār* means "the kindling of incense." The word is used only once, and that is in Mal. 1:11: " . . . And in every place incense shall be offered unto my name. . . . "

Miqṭeret means "censer; incense." The word occurs twice. *Miqṭeret* represents a "censer"—a utensil in which coals are carried—in 2 Chron. 26:19. The word refers to "incense" in Ezek. 8:11. *Mᵉqaṭṭērāh* refers to "incense altar." The word occurs once (2 Chron. 26:19). *Miqṭār* means a "place of sacrificial smoke; altar." The word appears once (Exod. 30:1).

TO BURY

A. Verb.

qābar (קָבַר, 6912), "to bury." This verb is found in most Semitic languages including Ugaritic, Akkadian, Arabic, Aramaic, Phoenician, and post-biblical Aramaic. Biblical Hebrew attests it about 130 times and in all periods.

This root is used almost exclusively of human beings. (The only exception is Jer. 22:19; see below.) This verb generally represents the act of placing a dead body into a grave or tomb. In its first biblical appearance, *qābar* bears this meaning. God told Abraham, "And thou shalt go to thy fathers in peace; thou shalt be buried in a good old age" (Gen. 15:15).

A proper burial was a sign of special kindness and divine blessing. As such, it was an obligation of the responsible survivors. Abraham bought the cave of Machpelah so that he might bury his dead. David thanked the men of Jabesh-gilead for their daring reclamation of the

bodies of Saul and Jonathan (1 Sam. 31:11–13), and for properly "burying" them. He said, "Blessed be ye of the Lord, that ye have showed this kindness unto your lord, even unto Saul, and have buried him" (2 Sam. 2:5). Later, David took the bones of Saul and Jonathan and buried them in their family tomb (2 Sam. 21:14); here the verb means both "bury" and "rebury." A proper burial was not only a kindness; it was a necessity. If the land were to be clean before God, all bodies had to be "buried" before nightfall: "His body shall not remain all night upon the tree, but thou shalt in any wise bury him that day; (for he that is hanged is accursed of God;) that thy land be not defiled, which the Lord thy God giveth thee for an inheritance" (Deut. 21:23). Thus, if a body was not buried, divine approval was withdrawn.

Not to be "buried" was a sign of divine disapproval, both on the surviving kinsmen and on the nation. Ahijah the prophet told Jeroboam's wife, "And all Israel shall mourn for him [Jeroboam's son], and bury him: for he only of Jeroboam shall come to the grave" (1 Kings 14:13). As for the rest of his family, they would be eaten by dogs and birds of prey (v. 11; cf. Jer. 8:2). Jeremiah prophesied that Jehoiakim would "be buried with the burial of an ass, drawn and cast forth beyond the gates of Jerusalem" (Jer. 22:19).

Bodies may be "buried" in caves (Gen. 25:9), sepulchers (Judg. 8:32), and graves (Gen. 50:5). In a few places, *qābar* is used elliptically of the entire act of dying. So in Job 27:15 we read: "Those that remain of him [his survivors] shall be buried in *death*: and his widows shall not weep."

B. Noun.

qeber (קֶבֶר, 6913), "grave; tomb; sepulcher." *Qeber* occurs 67 times, and in its first biblical appearance (Gen. 23:4) the word refers to a "tomb-grave" or "sepulcher." The word carries the meaning of "grave" in Jer. 5:16, and in Ps. 88:11, *qeber* is used of a "grave" that is the equivalent of the underworld. In Judg. 8:32, the word signifies a "family sepulcher." Jeremiah 26:23 uses the word for a "burial place," specifically an open pit.

TO BUY, ACQUIRE

qānāh (קָנָה, 7069), "to get, acquire, create, buy." A common Semitic word, *qānāh* is found in ancient and modern Hebrew and in ancient Akkadian and Ugaritic. It occurs in the text of the Hebrew Old Testament 84 times. The first occurrence of *qānāh* in the Old Testament is in Gen. 4:1: "I have gotten a man from the Lord." In this passage, *qānāh* expresses a basic meaning of God's "creating" or "bringing into being," so

Eve is really saying, "I have created a man-child with the help of the Lord." This meaning is confirmed in Gen. 14:19, 22 where both verses refer to God as "creator of heaven and earth" (KJV, NASB, "possessor"; RSV, "maker").

In Deut. 32:6, God is called the "father" who "created" Israel; a father begets or "creates," rather than "acquires" children. In the Wisdom version of the Creation story (Prov. 8:22–36), Wisdom herself states that "the Lord created me at the beginning of his work" (RSV, NEB, JB, TEV). "Possessed" (KJV, NASB) is surely not as appropriate in such a context.

When the Psalmist says to God, "Thou didst form my inward parts" (Ps. 139:13, RSV) he surely meant "create" (JB).

Qānāh is used several times to express God's redeeming activity in behalf of Israel, again reflecting "creativity" rather than "purchase." Exod. 15:16 is better translated, " . . . Thy people . . . whom thou hast created," rather than "thou hast purchased" (RSV). See also Ps. 74:2; 78:54.

The meaning "to buy" is expressed by *qānāh* frequently in contexts where one person makes a purchase agreement with another. The word is used to refer to "buying" a slave (Exod. 21:2) and land (Gen. 47:20).

C

CALAMITY

êd (אֵד, 343), "calamity; disaster." A possible cognate of this word appears in Arabic. Its 24 biblical appearances occur in every period of biblical Hebrew (12 in wisdom literature and only 1 in poetical literature, the Psalms).

This word signifies a "disaster" or "calamity" befalling a nation or individual. When used of a nation, it represents a "political or military event": "To me belongeth vengeance, and recompense; their foot shall slide in due time: for the day of their calamity is at hand, and the things that shall come upon them make haste" (Deut. 32:35—first occurrence). The prophets tend to use *êd* in the sense of national "disaster," while Wisdom writers use it for "personal tragedy."

TO CALL

A. Verb.

qārā' (קָרָא, 7121), "to call, call out, recite." This root occurs in Old Aramaic, Canaanite, and Ugaritic, and other Semitic languages (except Ethiopic). The word appears in all periods of biblical Hebrew.

Qārā' may signify the "specification of a name." Naming a thing is frequently an assertion of sovereignty over it, which is the case in the first use of *qārā':* "And God called the light Day, and the darkness he called Night" (Gen. 1:5). God's act of creating, "naming," and numbering includes the stars (Ps. 147:4) and all other things (Isa. 40:26). He allowed Adam to "name" the animals as a concrete demonstra-

tion of man's relative sovereignty over them (Gen. 2:19). Divine sovereignty and election are extended over all generations, for God "called" them all from the beginning (Isa. 41:4; cf. Amos 5:8). "Calling" or "naming" an individual may specify the individual's primary characteristic (Gen. 27:36); it may consist of a confession or evaluation (Isa. 58:13; 60:14); and it may recognize an eternal truth (Isa. 7:14).

This verb also is used to indicate "calling to a specific task." In Exod. 2:7, Moses' sister Miriam asked Pharaoh's daughter if she should go and "call" (summon) a nurse. Israel was "called" (elected) by God to be His people (Isa. 65:12), as were the Gentiles in the messianic age (Isa. 55:5).

To "call" on God's name is to summon His aid. This emphasis appears in Gen. 4:26, where men began to "call" on the name of the Lord. Such a "calling" on God's name occurs against the background of the Fall and the murder of Abel. The "calling" on God's name is clearly not the beginning of prayer, since communication between God and man existed since the Garden of Eden; nor is it an indication of the beginning of formal worship, since formal worship began at least as early as the offerings of Cain and Abel (Gen. 4:7ff.). The sense of "summoning" God to one's aid was surely in Abraham's mind when he "called upon" God's name (Gen. 12:8). "Calling" in this sense constitutes a prayer prompted by recognized need and directed to One who is able and willing to respond (Ps. 145:18; Isa. 55:6).

Basically, *qārā'* means "to call out loudly" in

order to get someone's attention so that contact can be initiated. So Job is told: "Call now, if there be any that will answer thee; and to which of the saints wilt thou turn?" (Job 5:11). Often this verb represents sustained communication, paralleling "to say" (*'āmar*), as in Gen. 3:9: "And the Lord God called unto Adam, and said unto him. . . . " *Qārā'* can also mean "to call out a warning," so that direct contact may be avoided: "And the leper in whom the plague is, his clothes shall be rent, and his head bare, and he shall put a covering upon his upper lip, and shall cry, Unclean, unclean" (Lev. 13:45).

Qārā' may mean "to shout" or "to call out loudly." Goliath "shouted" toward the ranks of Israel (1 Sam. 17:8) and challenged them to individual combat (duel). Sometimes ancient peoples settled battles through such combatants. Before battling an enemy, Israel was directed to offer them peace: "When thou comest nigh unto a city to fight against it, then proclaim peace unto it [call out to it in terms of peace]" (Deut. 20:10).

Qārā' may also mean "to proclaim" or "to announce," as when Israel proclaimed peace to the sons of Benjamin (Judg. 21:13). This sense first occurs in Gen. 41:43, where we are told that Joseph rode in the second chariot; "and they cried before him, Bow the knee." Haman recommended to King Ahasuerus that he adorn the one to be honored and "proclaim" ("announce") before him, "Thus shall it be done to the man whom the king delighteth to honor" (Esth. 6:9). This proclamation would tell everyone that the man so announced was honored by the king. The two emphases, "proclamation" and "announce," occur in Exod. 32:5: " . . . Aaron made proclamation, and said, Tomorrow is a feast to the Lord." This instance implies "summoning" an official assemblage of the people. In prophetic literature, *qārā'* is a technical term for "declaring" a prophetic message: "For the saying which he *cried* by the word of the Lord . . . shall surely come to pass" (1 Kings 13:32).

Another major emphasis of *qārā'* is "to summon." When Pharaoh discovered Abram's deceit concerning Sarai, he "summoned" ("called") Abram so that he might correct the situation (Gen. 12:18). Often the summons is in the form of a friendly invitation, as when Reuel (or Jethro) told his daughters to "invite him [Moses] to have something to eat" (Exod. 2:20, "that he may eat bread," KJV). The participial form of *qārā'* is used to denote "invited guests": "As soon as you enter the city you will find him before he goes up to the high place to eat . . . afterward *those who are invited* will eat" (1 Sam.

9:13, NASB). This verb is also used in judicial contexts, to mean being "summoned to court"; if a man is accused of not fulfilling his levirate responsibility, "then the elders of his city shall call him, and speak unto him . . . " (Deut. 25:8). *Qārā'* is used of "summoning" someone and/or "mustering" an army: "Why hast thou served us thus, that thou calledst us not, when thou wentest to fight with the Midianites?" (Judg. 8:1).

The meaning "to read" apparently arose from the meaning "to announce" and "to declare," inasmuch as reading was done out loud so that others could hear. This sense appears in Exod. 24:7. In several prophetic passages, the Septuagint translates *qārā'* "to read" rather than "to proclaim" (cf. Jer. 3:12; 7:2, 27; 19:2). *Qārā'* means "to read to oneself" only in a few passages.

At least once, the verb *qārā'* means "to dictate": "Then Baruch answered them, He [dictated] all these words unto me . . . and I wrote them with ink in the book" (Jer. 36:18).

B. Noun.

miqrā' (מִקְרָא, 4744), "public worship service; convocation." The word implies the product of an official summons to worship ("convocation"). In one of its 23 appearances, *miqrā'* refers to Sabbaths as "convocation days" (Lev. 23:2).

CAMP

mahăneh (מַנֶה, 4264), "camp; encampment; host." This noun derived from the verb *hānāh* occurs 214 times in the Bible, most frequently in the Pentateuch and in the historical books. The word is rare in the poetical and prophetic literature.

Those who travel were called "campers," or in most versions (KJV, RSV, NASB) a "company" or "group" (NIV), as in Gen. 32:8. Naaman stood before Elisha "with all his company" (2 Kings 5:15 NASB, NEB, "retinue"). Travelers, tradesmen, and soldiers spent much time on the road. They all set up "camp" for the night.

Jacob "encamped" by the Jabbok with his retinue (Gen. 32:10). The name *Mahanaim* (Gen. 32:2, "camps") owes its origin to Jacob's experience with the angels. He called the place *Mahanaim* in order to signify that it was God's "camp" (Gen. 32:2), as he had spent the night "in the camp" (Gen. 32:21) and wrestled with God (Gen. 32:24). Soldiers also established "camps" by the city to be conquered (Ezek. 4:2).

Usage of *mahăneh* varies according to context. First, it signifies a nation set over against another (Exod. 14:20). Second, the word refers to a division concerning the Israelites; each of the tribes had a special "encampment" in relation to the tent of meeting (Num. 1:52). Third, the word "camp" is used to describe the whole people of Israel: "And it came to pass on the third day in the morning, that there were thunders and lightnings, and a thick cloud upon the mount, and the voice of the trumpet exceeding loud; so that all the people that was in the *camp* trembled" (Exod. 19:16).

God was present in the "camp" of Israel: "For the Lord thy God walketh in the midst of thy camp, to deliver thee, and to give up thine enemies before thee; therefore shall thy camp be holy: that he see no unclean thing in thee, and turn away from thee" (Deut. 23:14). As a result, sin could not be tolerated within the camp, and the sinner might have to be stoned outside the camp (Num. 15:35).

The Septuagint translated *maḥăneh* by the Greek *parembole* ("camp; barracks; army") 193 times. Compare these Old Testament occurrences with the use of "camp" in Hebrews 13:11: "For the bodies of those beasts, whose blood is brought into the sanctuary by the high priest for sin, are burned without the camp."

In the English versions, the word is variously translated "camp; company; army" (KJV, RSV, NASB, NIV); "host" (KJV); "attendances; forces" (NIV).

CAN, MAY

yākōl (יָכֹל, 3201), "can, may, to be able, prevail, endure." This word is used about 200 times in the Old Testament, from the earliest to the latest writings. It is also found in Assyrian and Aramaic. As in English, the Hebrew word usually requires another verb to make the meaning complete.

Yākōl first occurs in Gen. 13:6: "And the land was not *able* to bear them, that they might dwell together...." God promised Abraham: "And I will make thy seed as the dust of the earth: so that if a man can number the dust of the earth, then shall thy seed also be numbered" (Gen. 13:16, NIV; cf. Gen. 15:5).

The most frequent use of this verb is in the sense of "can" or "to be able." The word may refer specifically to "physical ability," as in 1 Sam. 17:33: "You are not able to go against this Philistine to fight with him" (NASB). *Yākōl* may express "moral inability," as in Josh. 7:13: "... Thou canst not stand before thine enemies, until ye take away the accursed thing from among you." For a similar sense, see Jer. 6:10: "Behold, their ear is uncircumcised, and they cannot hearken...." In the negative sense, it may be used to express "prohibition": "Thou

mayest not eat within thy gates the tithe of thy corn..." (Deut. 12:17, NIV). Or the verb may indicate a "social barrier," as in Gen. 43:32: "... The Egyptians might not eat bread with the Hebrews; for that is an abomination unto the Egyptians" (KJV, RSV, NIV, NASB, "could not").

Yākōl is also used of God, as when Moses pleaded with God not to destroy Israel lest the nations say, "Because the Lord was not *able* to bring this people into the land..., therefore he hath slain them..." (Num. 14:16, NASB). The word may indicate a positive sense: "If it be so, our God whom we serve is *able* to deliver us..." (Dan. 3:17). The word *yākōl* appears when God limits His patience with the insincere: "When the Lord could no longer *endure* your wicked actions..., your land became an object of cursing..." (Jer. 44:22, NIV).

When *yākōl* is used without another verb, the sense is "to prevail" or "to overcome," as in the words of the angel to Jacob: "Your name will no longer be Jacob, but Israel, because you have struggled with God, and with men and have overcome" (Gen. 32:28, NIV, KJV, NASB, "prevailed"). With the word *yākōl*, God rebukes Israel's insincerity: "I cannot endure iniquity and the solemn assembly" (Isa. 1:13, NASB, NIV, "bear"). "... How long will it be ere they attain to innocency?" (Hos. 8:5, KJV, NASB, "will they be capable of").

There is no distinction in Hebrew between "can" and "may," since *yākōl* expresses both "ability" and "permission," or prohibition with the negative. Both God and man can act. There is no limit to God's ability apart from His own freely determined limits of patience with continued disobedience and insincerity (Isa. 59:1–2) and will (Dan. 3:17–18).

The Septuagint translates *yākōl* by several words, *dunamai* being by far the most common. *Dunamai* means "to be able, powerful." It is first used in the New Testament in Matt. 3:9: "... God is able of these stones to raise up children unto Abraham."

CANAAN; CANAANITE

kena'an (כְּנַעַן, 3667), "Canaan"; *kena'ănî* (כְּנַעֲנִי, 3669), "Canaanite; merchant." "Canaan" is used 9 times as the name of a person and 80 times as a place name. "Canaanite" occurs 72 times of the descendants of "Canaan," the inhabitants of the land of Canaan. Most occurrences of these words are in Genesis through Judges, but they are scattered throughout the Old Testament.

"Canaan" is first used of a person in Gen. 9:18: "... and Ham is the father of Canaan" (cf. Gen. 10:6). After a listing of the nations descended from "Canaan," Gen. 10:18–19 adds: "... and afterward were the families of the Canaanites spread abroad. And the border of the Canaanites was from Sidon, as thou comest to Gerar, unto Gaza; as thou goest, unto Sodom, and Gomorrah, ..." "Canaan" is the land west of the Jordan, as in Num. 33:51: "When ye are passed over Jordan into the land of Canaan" (cf. Josh. 22:9–11). At the call of God, Abram "... went forth to go into the land of Canaan; and into the land of Canaan they came.... And the Canaanite was then in the land" (Gen. 12:5–6). Later God promised Abram: "Unto thy seed have I given this land, ... [the land of] the Canaanites ..." (Gen. 15:18–20; cf. Exod. 3:8, 17; Josh. 3:10).

"Canaanite" is a general term for all the descendants of "Canaan": "When the Lord thy God shall bring thee into the land whither thou goest to possess it, and hath cast out many nations before thee ... the Canaanites ..." (Deut. 7:1). It is interchanged with Amorite in Gen. 15:16: "... for the iniquity of the Amorites is not yet full" (cf. Josh. 24:15, 18).

"Canaanite" is also used in the specific sense of one of the peoples of Canaan: "... and the Canaanites dwell by the sea, and by the coast of Jordan" (Num. 13:29; cf. Josh. 5:1; 2 Sam. 24:7). As these peoples were traders, "Canaanite" is a symbol for "merchant" in Prov. 31:24 and Job 41:6 and notably, in speaking of the sins of Israel, Hosea says, "He is a merchant, the balances of deceit are in his hand ..." (Hos. 7:12; cf. Zeph. 1:11).

Gen. 9:25–27 stamps a theological significance on "Canaan" from the beginning: "Cursed be Canaan; a servant of servants shall he be unto his brethren.... Blessed be the Lord God of Shem; and Canaan shall be his servant. And God shall enlarge Japheth ... and Canaan shall be his servant." Noah prophetically placed this curse on "Canaan" because his father had stared at Noah's nakedness and reported it grossly to his brothers. Ham's sin, deeply rooted in his youngest son, is observable in the Canaanites in the succeeding history. Leviticus 18 gives a long list of sexual perversions that were forbidden to Israel prefaced by the statement: "... and after the doings of the land of Canaan, whither I bring you, shall ye not do ..." (Lev. 18:3). The list is followed by a warning: "Defile not ye yourselves in any of these things: for in all these the nations are defiled which I cast out before you" (Lev. 18:24).

The command to destroy the "Canaanites" was very specific: "... thou shalt smite them, and utterly destroy them.... ye shall destroy

their altars, and break down their images.... For thou art a holy people unto the Lord thy God ..." (Deut. 7:2–6). But too often the house of David and Judah "built them high places, and images, and groves, on every high hill, and under every green tree. And there were also sodomites in the land: and they did according to all the abominations of the nations which the Lord cast out before the children of Israel" (1 Kings 14:23–24; cf. 2 Kings 16:3–4; 21:1–15). The nations were the "Canaanites"; thus "Canaanite" became synonymous with religious and moral perversions of every kind.

This fact is reflected in Zech. 14:21: "... and in that day there shall be no more the Canaanite in the house of the Lord of hosts." A "Canaanite" was not permitted to enter the tabernacle or temple; no longer would one of God's people who practiced the abominations of the "Canaanites" enter the house of the Lord.

This prophecy speaks of the last days and will be fulfilled in the New Jerusalem, according to Rev. 21:27: "And there shall in no wise enter into it any thing that defileth, neither whatsoever worketh abomination, or maketh a lie ..." (cf. Rev. 22:15).

These two words occur in Acts 7:11 and 13:19 in the New Testament.

TO CAST DOWN

šālak (שָׁלַךְ, 7993), "to throw, fling, cast, overthrow." This root seems to be used primarily in Hebrew, including modern Hebrew. *Šālak* is found 125 times in the Hebrew Bible. Its first use in the Old Testament is in Gen. 21:15, which says that Hagar "cast the child [Ishmael] under one of the shrubs."

The word is used to describe the "throwing" or "casting" of anything tangible: Moses "threw" a tree into water to sweeten it (Exod. 15:25); Aaron claimed he "threw" gold into the fire and a golden calf walked out (Exod. 32:24). Trees "shed" or "cast off" wilted blossoms (Job 15:33).

Šālak indicates "rejection" in Lam. 2:1: "How hath the Lord ... cast down from heaven unto the earth the beauty of Israel...." The word is used figuratively in Ps. 55:22: "Cast thy burden upon the Lord...."

CATTLE

'eleph (אֶלֶף, 504), "cattle; thousand; group." The first word, "cattle," signifies the domesticated animal or the herd animal. It has cognates in Aramaic, Akkadian, Ugaritic, and Phoenician. It appears only 8 times in the Bible, first in Deut. 7:13: "He will also bless the fruit of thy womb, and the fruit of thy land, thy corn,

and thy wine, and thine oil, the increase of thy kine [NASB, "herd"], and the flocks of thy sheep. . . ."

This noun is probably related to the verb *'ālap*, "to get familiar with, teach, instruct." This verb occurs 4 times, only in Job and Proverbs.

The related noun *'allûp* usually means "familiar; confident." It, too, occurs only in biblical poetry. In Ps. 144:14, *'allûp* signifies a tame domesticated animal: "That our oxen may be strong to labor; that there be no breaking in, nor going out. . . ."

The second word, "thousand," occurs about 490 times and in all periods of biblical Hebrew. It first appears in Gen. 20:16: "Behold, I have given thy brother a thousand pieces of silver. . . ."

The third word, "group," first occurs in Num. 1:16: "These were the renowned of the congregation, princes of the tribes of their fathers, heads of thousands [divisions] in Israel." It appears to be related to the word *'ellûp*, "leader of a large group," which is applied almost exclusively to non-Israelite tribal leaders (exceptions: Zech. 9:7; 12:5–6). *'Allûp* first occurs in Gen. 36:15: "These were [chiefs] of the sons of Esau. . . ."

TO CEASE

A. Verbs.
ḥādal (חָדַל, 2308), "to cease, come to an end, desist, forbear, lack." This word is found primarily in Hebrew, including modern Hebrew. In the Hebrew Old Testament, it is found fewer than 60 times. The first occurrence of *ḥādal* is in Gen. 11:8 where, after man's language was confused, "they left off building the city" (RSV).

The basic meaning of *ḥādal* is "coming to an end." Thus, Sarah's capacity for childbearing had long since "ceased" before an angel informed her that she was to have a son (Gen. 18:11). The Mosaic law made provision for the poor, since they would "never cease out of the land" (Deut. 15:11; Matt. 26:11). In Exod. 14:12, this verb is better translated "let us alone" for the literal "cease from us."

Šābat (שָׁבַת, 7673), "to rest, cease." This word occurs about 200 times throughout the Old Testament. The root also appears in Assyrian, Arabic, and Aramaic.

The verb first occurs in Gen. 2:2–3: "And on the seventh day God ended his work which he had made; and he *rested* on the seventh day from all his work which he had made. And God blessed the seventh day, and sanctified it: because that in it he had *rested* from all his work which God created and made."

The basic and most frequent meaning of

šābat is shown in Gen. 8:22: "While the earth remaineth, seedtime and harvest, and cold and heat, and summer and winter, and day and night shall not cease." This promise became a prophetic sign of God's faithfulness: "If those ordinances depart from before me, saith the Lord, then the seed of Israel also shall cease from being a nation before me for ever" (Jer. 31:36).

We find a variety of senses: " . . . Even the first day ye shall *put away* leaven out of your houses . . . " (Exod. 12:15). "Neither shalt thou suffer the salt of the covenant of thy God to *be lacking* from thy meat offering" (Lev. 2:13 NASB, KJV, NIV, "do not leave out"). Josiah "put down the idolatrous priests . . . " (2 Kings 23:5). "I will also eliminate harmful beasts from the land" (Lev. 26:6 NASB, KJV, "rid"; RSV, NIV, "remove").

B. Noun.
šabbāt (שַׁבָּת, 7676), "the sabbath." The verb *šābat* is the root of *šabbāt*: "Six days you are to do your work, but on the seventh day you shall cease from labor . . . " (Exod. 23:12, NASB, KJV, "rest"). In Exod. 31:15, the seventh day is called the "sabbath rest" (NASB, "a sabbath of complete rest").

A man's "rest" was to include his animals and servants (Exod. 23:12): even "in earing time and in harvest thou shalt rest" (Exod. 34:21). "It is a sign between me and the children of Israel for ever: for in six days the Lord made heaven and earth, and on the seventh day he rested, and was refreshed" (Exod. 31:17).

" . . . Then shall the land keep a sabbath unto the Lord" (Lev. 25:2). Six years' crops will be sown and harvested, but the seventh year "shall be a sabbath of rest unto the land, a sabbath for the Lord . . . " (Lev. 25:4). The feast of trumpets, the Day of Atonement, and the first and eighth days of the Feast of Tabernacles are also called "a sabbath observance" or "a sabbath of complete rest" (Lev. 23:24, 32, 39).

The "sabbath" was a "day of worship" (Lev. 23:3) as well as a "day of rest and refreshment" for man (Exod. 23:12). God "rested and was refreshed" (Exod. 31:17). The "sabbath" was the covenant sign of God's lordship over the creation. By observing the "sabbath," Israel confessed that they were God's redeemed people, subject to His lordship to obey the whole of His law. They were His stewards to show mercy with kindness and liberality to all (Exod. 23:12; Lev. 25).

By "resting," man witnessed his trust in God to give fruit to his labor; he entered into God's "rest." Thus "rest" and the "sabbath" were eschatological in perspective, looking to the accomplishment of God's ultimate purpose through the redemption of His people, to whom the "sabbath" was a covenant sign.

The prophets rebuked Israel for their neglect of the sabbath (Isa. 1:13; Jer. 17:21–27; Ezek. 20:12–24; Amos 8:5). They also proclaimed "sabbath" observance as a blessing in the messianic age and a sign of its fullness (Isa. 56:2–4; 58:13; 66:23; Ezek. 44:24; 45:17; 46:1, 3–4, 12). The length of the Babylonian Captivity was determined by the extent of Israel's abuse of the sabbatical year (2 Chron. 36:21; cf. Lev. 26:34–35).

CHARIOTRY

A. Nouns.

rekeb (רֶכֶב, 7393), "chariotry; chariot units; chariot horse; chariot; train; upper millstone." The noun *rekeb* appears 119 times and in all periods of biblical Hebrew.

The word is used collectively of an entire force of "military chariotry": "And he took six hundred chosen chariots, and all the [*chariotry*]" (Exod. 14:7, KJV, NASB, "chariots"). This use of *rekeb* might well be rendered "chariot-units" (the chariot, a driver, an offensive and a defensive man). The immediately preceding verse uses *rekeb* of a single "war-chariot" (or perhaps "chariot unit"). The following translation might better represent Exod. 14:6–7: "So he made his chariot ready and took his courtiers with him, and he took six hundred select chariot units, and all the chariotry of Egypt with defensive men."

In its first biblical appearance, *rekeb* means "chariotry": "And there went up with him both chariotry [KJV, "chariots"] and horsemen ..." (Gen. 50:9). In 2 Sam. 8:4, the word represents "chariot-horse": "... And David hamstrung [KJV, "houghed"] all the chariot horses.... " *Rekeb* also is used of the "chariot" itself: "... And the king was propped [KJV, "stayed"] up in his chariot against the Syrians ..." (1 Kings 22:35).

Next, *rekeb* refers to a "column" or "train of donkeys and camels": "And he saw a chariot with a couple of horsemen, a chariot of asses, and a chariot of camels ..." (Isa. 21:7).

Finally, *rekeb* sometimes signifies an "upper millstone": "No man shall take the nether or the upper millstone to pledge ..." (Deut. 24:6; cf. Judg. 9:53; 2 Sam. 11:21).

merkābāh (מֶרְכָּבָה, 4818), "war chariot." This word occurs 44 times. *Merkābāh* has cognates in Ugaritic, Syriac, and Akkadian. Like *rekeb*, it is derived from *rākab*. The word represents a "war-chariot" (Exod. 14:25), which may have been used as a "chariot of honor" (Gen.

41:43—the first occurrence). It may also be translated "traveling coach" or "cart" (2 Kings 5:21).

B. Verb.

rākab (רָכַב, 7392), "to ride upon, drive, mount (an animal)." This verb, which has cognates in Ugaritic and several other Semitic languages, occurs 78 times in the Old Testament. The first occurrence is in Gen. 24:61: "And Rebekah arose, and her damsels, and they rode upon the camels.... "

TO CHOOSE

A. Verb.

bāḥar (בָּחַר, 977), "to choose." This verb is found 170 times throughout the Old Testament. It is also found in Aramaic, Syriac, and Assyrian. The word has parallels in Egyptian, Akkadian, and Canaanite languages.

Bāḥar first occurs in the Bible in Gen. 6:2: "... They took them wives of all which they chose." It is often used with a man as the subject: "Lot chose [for himself] all the plain of Jordan ..." (Gen. 13:11). In more than half of the occurrences, God is the subject of *bāḥar*, as in Num. 16:5: "... The Lord will show who are his, and who is holy; ... even him whom he hath chosen will he cause to come near unto him."

Neh. 9:7–8 describes God's "choosing" (election) of persons as far back as Abram: "You are the Lord God, who chose Abram ... and you made a covenant with him" (NIV). *Bāḥar* is used 30 times in Deuteronomy, all but twice referring to God's "choice" of Israel or something in Israel's life. "Because he loved thy fathers, therefore he chose their seed after them ..." (Deut. 4:37). Being "chosen" by God brings people into an intimate relationship with Him: "... The children of the Lord your God: ... the Lord hath chosen thee to be a peculiar people unto himself, above all the nations that are upon the earth" (Deut. 14:1–2).

God's "choices" shaped the history of Israel; His "choice" led to their redemption from Egypt (Deut. 7:7–8), sent Moses and Aaron to work miracles in Egypt (Ps. 105:26–27), and gave them the Levites "to bless in the name of the Lord" (Deut. 21:5). He "chose" their inheritance (Ps. 47:4), including Jerusalem, where He dwelt among them (Deut. 12:5; 2 Chron. 6:5, 21). But "they have chosen their own ways, and ... I also will choose their delusions, and will bring their fears upon them ..." (Isa. 66:3–4). The covenant called men to respond to God's election: "... I have set before you life and death ...: therefore choose life ..." (Deut. 30:19; cf. Josh. 24:22).

The Greek Septuagint version translated *bāhar* chiefly by *eklegein*, and through this word the important theological concept of God's "choosing" came into the New Testament. The verb is used of God's or Christ's "choice" of men for service, as in Luke 6:13 ("of them he chose twelve ...") or of the objects of His grace: " ... He hath chosen us in him before the foundation of the world ..." (Eph. 1:4). John 15:16 expresses the central truth of election in both Testaments: "Ye have not chosen me, but I have chosen you, ... that ye should go and bring forth fruit, and that your fruit should remain...."

B. Noun.

bāhîr (בָּחִיר, 972), "chosen ones." Another noun, *bāhîr*, is used 13 times, always of the Lord's "chosen ones": "Saul, whom the Lord did choose" (2 Sam. 21:6); "ye children of Jacob, his chosen ones" (1 Chron. 16:13).

TO CIRCUMCISE

mûl (מוּל, 4135), "to circumcise, cut off." This verb occurs more than 30 times in the Old Testament. Its usage is continued in rabbinic and modern Hebrew. However, the verb "to cut off" is not found in other Semitic languages.

Most of the occurrences in the Old Testament take place in the Pentateuch (20 times) and Joshua (8 times). *Mûl* occurs most frequently in Genesis (17 times, 11 of them in Genesis 17 alone) and Joshua (8 times). *Mûl* occurs in 3 of the 7 verb patterns and in several rare patterns. It has no derivatives other than *mûlōt* in Exod. 4:26: "At that time she said, 'bridegroom of blood,' referring to circumcision" (NIV).

The physical act of circumcision was introduced by God as a sign of the Abrahamic covenant: "This is my covenant with you and your descendants after you ... Every male among you shall be circumcised. You are to undergo circumcision, and it will be the sign of the covenant between me and you" (Gen. 17:10–11, NIV). It was a permanent "cutting off" of the foreskin of the male organ, and as such was a reminder of the perpetuity of the covenantal relationship. Israel was enjoined to be faithful in "circumcising" all males; each male baby was to be "circumcised" on the eighth day (Gen. 17:12; Lev. 12:3). Not only were the physical descendants of Abraham "circumcised," but also those who were servants, slaves, and foreigners in the covenant community (Gen. 17:13–14).

The special act of circumcision was a sign of God's gracious promise. With the promise and covenantal relations, God expected that His people would joyously and willingly live up to His expectations, and thus demonstrate His rule on earth. To describe the "heart" attitude, several writers of Scripture use the verb "to circumcise." The "circumcision" of the flesh is a physical sign of commitment to God. Deuteronomy particularly is fond of the spiritual usage of the verb "to circumcise": "Circumcise your hearts, therefore, and do not be stiff-necked any longer" (Deut. 10:16, NIV; cf. 30:6). Jeremiah took over this usage: "Circumcise yourselves to the Lord, and take away the foreskins of your heart, ye men of Judah ..., because of the evil of your doings" (Jer. 4:4).

Few occurrences of the verb differ from the physical and the spiritual usage of "to circumcise." *Mûl* in the Book of Psalms has the meaning of "to cut off, destroy": "All the nations surrounded me, but in the name of the Lord I cut them off" (Ps. 118:10, NIV; cf. vv. 11–12).

The verb is translated as *peritemnō* in the Septuagint. The verb and the noun *peritomē* are used in both the physical and the spiritual sense. In addition to this, it also is a figure for baptism: "In him you were also circumcised, ... not with a circumcision alone by the hands of men but with the circumcision done by Christ, having been buried with him in baptism and raised with him through your faith in the power of God, who raised him from the dead" (Col. 2:11–12, NIV).

In the English versions, the verb is rendered "to circumcise," "to destroy" (KJV), as well as "to cut off" and "to wither" (RSV, NASB, NIV).

CITY

'îr (עִיר, 5892), "city; town; village; quarter [of a city]." Cognates of this word appear in Ugaritic, Phoenician, Sumerian, and old Arabic. This noun occurs about 1,092 times and in every period of biblical Hebrew.

The word suggests a "village." An unwalled village is represented by the Hebrew word *hāsēr*. *Qiryat*, a synonym of *'îr*, is an Aramaic loanword.

But *'îr* and its synonym do not necessarily suggest a walled city. This usage is seen in Deut. 3:5, where *'îr* may be a city standing in the open country (perhaps surrounded by dirt or stone ramparts for protection): "All these cities were fenced with high walls, gates, and bars; beside unwalled towns a great many." A comparison of Lev. 25:29 and Lev. 25:31 shows that *'îr* can be used as synonym of *hāsēr*: "And if a man sell a dwelling house in a walled city, then he may redeem it within a whole year after it is sold; ... but the houses of the villages [*hāsēr*] which have no wall round about them shall be counted as the fields of the country. . . . "

'*Îr* can signify not only a "village consisting of permanent houses" but also one in a permanent place, even though the dwellings are tents: "And Saul came to a *city* of Amalek, and laid wait in the valley" (1 Sam. 15:5).

In Gen. 4:17 (the first occurrence), the word '*îr* means a "permanent dwelling center" consisting of residences of stone and clay. As a rule, there are no political overtones to the word; '*îr* simply represents the "place where people dwell on a permanent basis." At some points, however, '*îr* represents a political entity (1 Sam. 15:5; 30:29).

This word can represent "those who live in a given town": "And when he came, lo, Eli sat upon a seat by the wayside watching: for his heart trembled for the ark of God. And when the man came into the city, and told it, *all the city* cried out" (1 Sam. 4:13).

'*Îr* can also signify only "a part of a city," such as a part that is surrounded by a wall: "Nevertheless David took the stronghold of Zion: the same is the *city* of David" (2 Sam. 5:7). Ancient cities (especially larger ones) were sometimes divided into sections (quarters) by walls, in order to make it more difficult to capture them. This suggests that, by the time of the statement just cited, '*îr* normally implied a "walled city."

TO BE CLEAN

A. Verb.

ṭāhēr (טָהֵר, 2891), "to be clean, pure." The root of this word appears over 200 times in various forms—as a verb, adjective, or noun.

Since the fall of Adam and Eve, none of their offspring is clean in the sight of the holy God: "Who can say, I have made my heart clean, I am pure from my sin?" (Prov. 20:9). Reminding Job that protestations of innocence are of no avail, Eliphaz asked: "Shall mortal man be more just than God? Shall a man be more pure than his Maker?" (Job 4:17).

There is hope, however, because God promised penitent Israel: "And I will cleanse them from all their iniquity, whereby they have sinned against me . . . " (Jer. 33:8). He said: " . . . I will save them out of all their dwelling places, wherein they have sinned, and will cleanse them: so they shall be my people, and I will be their God" (Ezek. 37:23).

The baleful effect of sin was recognized when a person contracted the dread disease of leprosy. After the priest diagnosed the disease, he could declare a person "clean" only after cleansing ceremonies had been performed: " . . . And he shall wash his clothes, also he shall wash his flesh in water, and he shall be clean" (Lev. 14:9).

God required that His people observe purification rites when they came into His presence for worship. On the Day of Atonement, for example, prescribed ceremonies were performed to "cleanse" the altar from "the uncleanness of the children of Israel" and to "hallow it" (Lev. 16:17–19; cf. Exod. 29:36ff.). The priests were to be purified before they performed their sacred tasks. Moses was directed to "take the Levites . . . and cleanse them" (Num. 8:6; cf. Lev. 8:5–13). After they had been held captive in the unclean land of Babylon, " . . . the priests and the Levites purified themselves, and purified the people, and the gates, and the wall [of the rebuilt city of Jerusalem]" (Neh. 12:30).

Cleansing might be achieved by physically removing the objects of defilement. During the reform of King Hezekiah, "the priests went into the inner part of the house of the Lord, to cleanse it, and brought out all the uncleanness that they found in the temple of the Lord . . . " (2 Chron. 29:16).

Some rites required blood as the purifying agent: "And he shall sprinkle of the blood upon it [the altar] with his finger seven times, and cleanse it, and hallow it from the uncleanness of the children of Israel" (Lev. 16:19). Sacrifices were offered to make atonement for a mother after childbirth: " . . . she shall bring . . . the one for the burnt offering, and the other for a sin offering: and the priest shall make an atonement for her, and she shall be clean" (Lev. 12:8).

B. Adjective.

ṭāhôr (טָהוֹר, 2889), "clean; pure." The word denotes the absence of impurity, filthiness, defilement, or imperfection. It is applied concretely to substances that are genuine or unadulterated, as well as describing an unstained condition of a spiritual or ceremonial nature.

Gold is a material frequently said to be free of baser ingredients. Thus the ark of the covenant, the incense altar, and the porch of the temple were "overlaid with pure gold" (Exod. 25:11; 37:11, 26; 2 Chron. 3:4). Some of the furnishings and utensils in the temple—such as the mercy seat, the lampstand, the dishes, pans, bowls, jars, snuffers, trays—were of "pure gold" (Exod. 37:6, 16–24). The high priest's vestment included "two chains of pure gold" and "a plate of pure gold" (Exod. 28:14, 22, 36).

God demands that His people have spiritual and moral purity, unsullied by sin. Anyone not clean of sin is subject to divine rejection and punishment. This contamination is never outgrown or overcome. Because sin pollutes one generation after another, Job asks: "Who can bring a clean thing out of an unclean?" (Job 14:4). All outward appearances to the contrary, it cannot be said that there is "one event . . . to the clean, and to the unclean" (Eccl. 9:2). Hope is available even to the chief of sinners, because any man can entreat the mercy of God and say: "Create in me a clean heart, O God; and renew a right spirit within me" (Ps. 51:10).

In sharp contrast with mankind's polluted nature and actions, "the words of the Lord are pure words . . ." (Ps. 12:6). The Lord is "of purer eyes than to behold evil" (Hab. 1:13).

"Clean" most frequently describes the purity maintained by avoiding contact with other human beings, abstaining from eating animals, and using things that are declared ceremonially clean. Conversely, cleansing results if ritual procedures symbolizing the removal of contamination are observed.

The people of the old covenant were told that "he that toucheth the dead body of any man shall be unclean seven days" (Num. 19:11). A priest was not to defile himself "for the dead among his people" except "for his kin, that is near unto him" (Lev. 21:1–2). This relaxation of the rule was even denied the high priest and a Nazarite during "all the days that he separateth himself unto the Lord" (Num. 6:6ff.).

Cleansing rituals emphasized the fact that the people were conceived and born in sin. Though conception and birth were not branded immoral (just as dying itself was not sinful), a woman who had borne a child remained unclean until she submitted to the proper purification rites (Lev. 12). Chapter 15 of Leviticus prescribes ceremonial cleansing for a woman having her menstrual flow, for a man having seminal emissions, and for "the woman also with whom man shall lie with seed of copulation" (Lev. 15:18).

To be ceremonially "clean," the Israelite also had to abstain from eating certain animals and even from touching them (Lev. 11; Deut. 14:3–21). After the Israelites settled in the Promised Land, some modifications were made in the regulations (Deut. 12:15, 22; 15:22).

Purification rites frequently involved the use of water. The person to be cleansed was required to wash himself and his clothes (Lev. 15:27). Water was sprinkled on the individual, on his tent, and on all its furnishings: "And a clean person shall take hyssop, and dip it in the water, and sprinkle it upon the tent, and upon all the vessels, and upon the persons that were there, and upon him that touched a bone, or the slain, or one dead, or a grave" (Num.

19:18). Sometimes the person being cleansed also had to change garments (Lev. 6:11).

However, the rites were not meritorious deeds, earning God's favor and forgiveness. Nor did the ceremonies serve their intended purpose if performed mechanically. Unless the rites expressed a person's contrite and sincere desire to be cleansed from the defilement of sin, they were an abomination to God and only aggravated a person's guilt. Anyone who appeared before Him in ritual and ceremony with "hands . . . full of blood" (Isa. 1:15) and did not plead for cleansing of his crimes was judged to be as wicked as the people of Sodom and Gomorrah. Zion's hope lay in this cleansing by means of an offering: "And they shall bring all your brethren for an offering unto the Lord out of all nations upon horses . . . as the children of Israel bring an offering in a clean vessel into the house of the Lord" (Isa. 66:20).

TO CLEAVE, CLING

dābaq (דָּבַק, 1692), "to cling, cleave, keep close." Used in modern Hebrew in the sense of "to stick to, adhere to," *dābaq* yields the noun form for "glue" and also the more abstract ideas of "loyalty, devotion." Occurring just over 60 times in the Hebrew Old Testament, this term is found very early in the text, in Gen. 2:24: "Therefore shall a man leave his father and his mother, and shall *cleave* unto his wife: and they shall be one flesh." This usage reflects the basic meaning of one object's (person's) being joined to another. In this sense, Eleazar's hand "cleaved" to the sword as he struck down the Philistines (2 Sam. 23:10). Jeremiah's linen waistcloth "clung" to his loins, symbolic of Israel's "clinging" to God (Jer. 13:11). In time of war and siege, the resulting thirst and famine caused the tongue "to cleave" to the roof of the mouth of those who had been so afflicted.

The literal statement, "My soul cleaveth unto the dust" (Ps. 119:25; RSV, "cleaves"), is better understood as one consults the other English versions: "I lie prone in the dust" (NEB); "Down in the dust I lie prostrate" (JB); "I lie prostrate in the dust" (NAB); "I lie defeated in the dust" (TEV).

The figurative use of *dābaq* in the sense of "loyalty" and "affection" is based on the physical closeness of the persons involved, such as a husband's closeness to his wife (Gen. 2:24), Shechem's affection for Dinah (Gen. 34:3), or Ruth's staying with Naomi (Ruth 1:14). "Cleaving" to God is equivalent to "loving" God (Deut. 30:20).

TO CLEAVE, SPLIT

bāqa‘ (בָּקַע, 1234), "to cleave, split, break open, break through." This word occurs in all the periods of the Hebrew language and is also found in ancient Ugaritic or Canaanite. It is the origin of the name of the famous Beqa Valley (which means "valley" or "cleft") in Lebanon.

In its verbal forms, *bāqa‘* is found some 50 times in the Hebrew Old Testament. The word is first used there in Gen. 7:11, which states that the "fountains of the great deep [were] broken up," resulting in the Flood. The everyday use of the verb is seen in references to "splitting" wood (Eccl. 10:9) and the ground "splitting" asunder (Num. 16:31). Serpents' eggs "split open" or "hatch out" their young (Isa. 59:5). City walls are "breached" or "broken into" in order to take them captive (Jer. 52:7). One of the horrors of war was the "ripping open" of pregnant women by the enemy (2 Kings 8:12; 15:16). Three times God is said "to split open" rocks or the ground in order to provide water for His people (Judg. 15:19; Ps. 74:15; Isa. 48:21).

In the figurative sense, it is said that the light of truth will "break forth as the morning" (Isa. 58:8). Using hyperbole or exaggeration, the historian who recorded the celebration for Solomon's coronation said that it was so loud "that the earth rent with the sound of them" (1 Kings 1:40). As here, the KJV often renders *bāqa‘* by "rent." In other contexts, it may be translated "burst; clave (cleave); tear; divide; break."

TO CLOTHE

lābaš (לָבַשׁ, 3847), "to put on (a garment), clothe, wear, be clothed." A common Semitic term, this word is found in ancient Akkadian and Ugaritic, in Aramaic, and throughout the history of the Hebrew language. The word occurs about 110 times in the text of the Hebrew Bible. *Lābaš* is found very early in the Old Testament, in Gen. 3:21: "Unto Adam also and to his wife did the Lord God make coats of skin, and *clothed* them." As always, God provided something much better for man than man could do for himself—in this instance, fig-leaf garments (Gen. 3:7).

Lābaš is regularly used for the "putting on" of ordinary clothing (Gen. 38:19; Exod. 29:30; 1 Sam. 28:8). The word also describes the "putting on" of armor (Jer. 46:4). Many times it is used in a figurative sense, as in Job 7:5: "My flesh is clothed [covered] with worms. . . ." Jerusalem is spoken of as "putting on" the Jews as they return after the Exile (Isa. 49:18). Often the figurative garment is an abstract quality: "For he put on righteousness as a breast-plate, . . . he put on garments of vengeance for clothing . . ." (Isa. 59:17). God is spoken of as being "clothed with honor and majesty" (Ps. 104:1). Job says, "I put on righteousness, and it clothed me . . ." (Job 29:14).

These abstract qualities are sometimes negative: "The prince shall be clothed [RSV, "wrapped"] with desolation" (Ezek. 7:27). "They that hate thee shall be clothed with shame" (Job 8:22). "Let mine adversaries be clothed with shame" (Ps. 109:29). A very important figurative use of *lābaš* is found in Judg. 6:34, where the stative form of the verb may be translated, "The spirit of the Lord clothed itself [was clothed] with Gideon." The idea seems to be that the Spirit of the Lord incarnated Himself in Gideon and thus empowered him from within. The English versions render it variously: "came upon" (KJV, NASB, JB); "took possession of" (NEB, RSV); "took control" (TEV); "wrapped round" (Knox).

CLOUD

‘ānān (עָנָן, 6051), "cloud; fog; storm cloud; smoke." Cognates of this word appear in Aramaic and Arabic. Its 87 appearances are scattered throughout the biblical material.

The word commonly means "cloud mass." *‘Ānān* is used especially of the "cloud mass" that evidenced the special presence of God: "And the Lord went before them by day in a pillar of a cloud, to lead them the way. . ."(Exod. 13:21). In Exod. 34:5, this presence is represented by *‘ānān* only: "And the Lord descended in the cloud, and stood with him [Moses] there, and proclaimed the name of the Lord."

When the ark of the covenant was brought into the holy place, "The cloud filled the house of the Lord, so that the priests could not stand to minister because of the cloud: for the glory of the Lord had filled the house of the Lord" (1 Kings 8:10–11). Thus the "cloud" evidenced the presence of God's glory. So the psalmist wrote that God was surrounded by "clouds and darkness" (Ps. 97:2); God appears as the controller and sovereign of nature. This description is somewhat parallel to the descriptions of Baal, the lord of the storm and god of nature set forth in Ugaritic mythology. The "cloud" is a sign and figure of "divine protection" (Isa. 4:5) and serves as a barrier hiding the fullness of divine holiness and glory, as well as barring sinful man's approach to God (Lam. 3:44). Man's relationship to God, therefore, is God-initiated and God-sustained, not humanly initiated or humanly sustained.

In its first biblical occurrence, *‘ānān* is used

in conjunction with God's sign that He would never again destroy the earth by a flood: "I do set my bow in the cloud, and it shall be for a token of a covenant between me and the earth" (Gen. 9:13). Elsewhere, the transitory quality of a cloud is used to symbolize the loyalty (Hos. 6:4) and existence of Israel (13:3). In Isa. 44:22, God says that after proper punishment He will wipe out, "as a thick cloud, thy transgressions, and, as a cloud, thy sins...."

'Ānān can mean "storm cloud" and is used to symbolize "an invading force": "Thou shalt ascend and come like a storm, thou shalt be like a cloud to cover the land, thou, and all thy bands, and many people with thee" (Ezek. 38:9; cf. Jer. 4:13). In Job 26:8, the storm cloud is said to be God's: "He bindeth up the waters in his thick clouds; and the cloud is not rent under them." In several passages, the thick storm cloud and the darkness accompanying it are symbols of "gloom" (Ezek. 30:18) and/or "divine judgment" (Ezek. 30:3).

'Ānān can represent the "smoke" arising from burning incense: "And he shall put the incense upon the fire before the Lord, that the cloud of the incense may cover the mercy seat that is upon the testimony, that he die not ..." (Lev. 16:13). This "cloud of smoke" may represent the covering between God's presence (above the mercy seat) and sinful man. If so, it probably also symbolizes the "divine glory." On the other hand, many scholars feel it represents the human prayers offered up to God.

TO COME

bô' (בּוֹא, 935), "to go in, enter, come, go." This root appears in most Semitic languages, but with varying meanings. For example, the meaning "come" appears in the Babylonian letters of Mari (1750–1697 B.C.). The corresponding Ugaritic word (1550–1200 B.C.) has the same significance as its Hebrew counterpart, while the Phoenician root (starting around 900 B.C.) means "come forth." *Bô'* occurs about 2,570 times in Old Testament Hebrew.

First, this verb connotes movement in space from one place toward another. The meaning "go in" or "enter" appears in Gen. 7:7, where it is said that Noah and his family "entered" the ark. In the causative stem, this verb can signify "cause to enter" or "bring into" (Gen. 6:19) or "bring unto" (its meaning in its first biblical occurrence, Gen. 2:19). In Gen. 10:19, the verb is used more absolutely in the phrase "as thou goest unto Sodom." Interestingly, this verb can also mean "to come" and "to return." Abram and his family "came" to the land of Canaan (Gen. 12:5), while in Deut. 28:6 God blessed the godly who "go forth" (to work in the morning) and "return" (home in the evening).

Sometimes *bô'* refers to the "going down" or "setting" of the sun (Gen. 15:12). It can connote dying, in the sense of "going to one's fathers" (Gen. 15:15). Another special use is the "going into one's wife" or "cohabitation" (Gen. 6:4). *Bô'* can also be used of movement in time. For example, the prophets speak of the "coming" day of judgment (1 Sam. 2:31). Finally, the verb can be used of the "coming" of an event such as the sign predicted by a false prophet (Deut. 13:2).

There are three senses in which God is said "to come." God "comes" through an angel (Judg. 6:11) or other incarnated being (cf. Gen. 18:14). He "appears" and speaks to men in dreams (Gen. 20:3) and in other actual manifestations (Exod. 20:20). For example, during the Exodus, God "appeared" in the cloud and fire that went before the people (Exod. 19:9).

Secondly, God promises to "come" to the faithful wherever and whenever they properly worship Him (Exod. 20:24). The Philistines felt that God had "come" into the Israelite camp when the ark of the covenant arrived (1 Sam. 4:7). This usage associated with formal worship may appear in Ps. 24:7, where the gates of Zion are said to open as the King of glory "enters" Jerusalem. Also, the Lord is "to return" ("come back") to the new temple described in Ezek. 43:2.

Finally, there is a group of prophetic pictures of divine "comings." This theme may have originated in the hymns sung of God's "coming" to aid His people in war (cf. Deut. 33:2). In the Psalms (e.g., 50:3) and prophets (e.g., Isa. 30:27), the Lord "comes" in judgment and blessing—a poetic figure of speech borrowed from ancient Near Eastern mythology (cf. Ezek. 1:4).

Bô' also is used to refer to the "coming" of the Messiah. In Zech. 9:9, the messianic king is pictured as "coming" on a foal of a donkey. Some of the passages pose especially difficult problems, such as Gen. 49:10, which prophesies that the scepter will remain in Judah "until Shiloh come." Another difficult passage is Ezek. 21:27: "until he come whose right it is." A very well-known prophecy using the verb *bô'* is that concerning the "coming" of the Son of Man (Dan. 7:13). Finally, there is the "coming" of the last day (Amos 8:2) and the Day of the Lord (Isa. 13:6).

The Septuagint translates this verb with many Greek words paralleling the connotations of the Hebrew verb, but especially with words meaning "to come," "to enter," and "to go."

TO COME NEAR, APPROACH

nāgaš (נָגַשׁ, 5066), "to approach, draw near, bring." Found primarily in biblical Hebrew, this word is also found in ancient Ugaritic. It occurs 125 times in the Hebrew text of the Old Testament. *Nāgaš* is used for the first time in the biblical text in Gen. 18:23, where Abraham is said to "draw near" to God to plead that Sodom be spared.

The word is often used to describe ordinary "contact" of one person with another (Gen. 27:22; 43:19). Sometimes *nāgaš* describes "contact" for the purpose of sexual intercourse (Exod. 19:15). More frequently, it is used to speak of the priests "coming into the presence of" God (Ezek. 44:13) or of the priests' "approach" to the altar (Exod. 30:20). Opposing armies are said "to draw near" to battle each other (Judg. 20:23; KJV, "go up"). Inanimate objects, such as the close-fitting scales of the crocodile, are said to be so "near" to each other that no air can come between them (Job 41:16). Sometimes the word is used to speak of "bringing" an offering to the altar (Mal. 1:7).

The English versions render *nāgaš* variously, according to context: "went near" (RSV); "moved closer" (TEV); "came close" (JB, NEB, NASB).

TO COME UP, ASCEND

A. Verb.

'ālāh (עָלָה, 5927), "to go up, ascend, offer up." This word occurs in all Semitic languages, including biblical Hebrew. The Old Testament attests it about 890 times.

Basically, *'ālāh* suggests movement from a lower to a higher place. That is the emphasis in Gen. 2:6 (the first occurrence of the word), which reports that Eden was watered by a mist or stream that "went up" over the ground. *'Ālāh* may also mean "to rise up" or "ascend." The king of Babylon said in his heart, "I will ascend into heaven" (Isa. 14:13). This word may mean "to take a journey," as in traveling from Egypt (Gen. 13:1) toward Palestine or other points northward. The verb may be used in a special sense meaning "to extend, reach"—for example, the border of Benjamin "went up ["extended, reached"] through the mountains westward" (Josh. 18:12).

The use of *'ālāh* to describe the journey from Egypt to Palestine is such a standard phrase that it often appears without the geographical reference points. Joseph told his brothers to "go up" to their father in peace (Gen. 44:17). Even the return from the Exile, which was a journey from north to south (Palestine), is described as

a "going up" (Ezra 2:1). Thus, the reference may be not so much to physically "going up," but to a figurative or spiritual "going up." This usage appears long before Ezra's time, when it is said that one "goes up" to the place where the sanctuary is located (cf. Deut. 17:8). The verb became a technical term for "making a pilgrimage" (Exod. 34:24) or "going up" before the Lord; in a secular context, compare Joseph's "going up" before Pharaoh (Gen. 46:31).

In instances where an enemy located himself in a superior position (frequently a higher place), one "goes up" to battle (Josh. 22:12). The verb can also refer merely to "going out" to make war against someone, even though there is no movement from a lower to a higher plane. So Israel "went up" to make war against the Moabites, who heard of the Israelites' approach while still dwelling in their cities (2 Kings 3:21). Even when *'ālāh* is used by itself, it can mean "to go to war"; the Lord told Phinehas, "Go up; for tomorrow I will deliver them into thine hand" (Judg. 20:28). On the other hand, if the enemy is recognized to be on a lower plane, one can "go down" (*yārad*) to fight (Judg. 1:9). The opposite of "going up" to war is not descending to battle, but "leaving off" (*'ālāh mē'al*), literally, "going up from against."

Another special use of *'ālāh* is "to overpower" (literally, "to go up from"). For example, the Pharaoh feared the Israelites lest in a war they join the enemy, fight against Egypt, and "overpower" the land (Exod. 1:10). "To go up" may also be used of "increasing in strength," as the lion that becomes strong from his prey: The lion "goes up from his prey" (Gen. 49:9; cf. Deut. 28:43).

Not only physical things can "go up." *'Ālāh* can be used also of the "increasing" of wrath (2 Sam. 11:20), the "ascent" of an outcry before God (Exod. 2:23), and the "continual" sound of battle (although "sound of" is omitted; cf. 1 Kings 22:35). The word can also be used passively to denote mixing two kinds of garments together, causing one "to lie upon" or "be placed upon" the other (Lev. 19:19). Sometimes "go up" means "placed," even when the direction is downward, as when placing a yoke upon an ox (Num. 19:2) or going to one's grave (Job 5:26). This may be an illustration of how Hebrew verbs can sometimes mean their opposite. The verb is also used of "recording" a census (1 Chron. 27:24).

The verb *'ālāh* is used in a causative stem to signify "presenting an offering" to God. In 63 cases, the word is associated with the presentation of the whole burnt offering (*'ōlāh*). *'Ālāh* is used of the general act of "presenting offerings" when the various offerings are mentioned in the same context (Lev. 14:20), or when the purpose of the offering is not specifically in mind (Isa. 57:6). Sometimes this verb means merely "to offer" (e.g., Num. 23:2).

B. Nouns.

elyôn (עֶלְיוֹן, 5945), "the upper; the highest." This word occurs 53 times. The use of *'elyôn* in Gen. 40:17 means "the upper" as opposed to "the lower." Where referring to or naming God, *'elyôn* means "the highest" (Gen. 14:18).

ma'ălāh (מַעֲלָה, 4699), "step; procession; pilgrimage." In some of its 47 biblical appearances, *ma'ălāh* signifies a "step" or "stair" (cf. Exod. 20:26). The word can also mean "procession" (Ps. 84:6).

TO COMMAND

ṣāwāh (צָוָה, 6680), "to command." This verb occurs only in biblical Hebrew (in all periods) and imperial Aramaic (starting from around 500 B.C.). Biblical occurrences number around 485.

Essentially, this verb refers to verbal communication by which a superior "orders" or "commands" a subordinate. The word implies the content of what was said. Pharaoh "ordered" ("commanded") his men concerning Abraham, and they escorted Abraham and his party out of Egypt (Gen. 12:20). This "order" defines an action relevant to a specific situation. *Ṣāwāh* can also connote "command" in the sense of the establishment of a rule by which a subordinate is to act in every recurring similar situation. In the Garden of Eden (the first appearance of this word in the Bible), God "commanded" ("set down the rule"): "Of every tree of the garden thou mayest freely eat: . . . " (Gen. 2:16). In this case, the word does not contain the content of the action but focuses on the action itself.

One of the recurring formulas in the Bible is "X did all that Y commanded him"—e.g., Ruth "did according to all that her mother-in-law bade her" (Ruth 3:6). This means that she carried out Naomi's "orders." A similar formula, "X did just as Y commanded," is first found in Num. 32:25, where the sons of Reuben and Gad say to Moses that they "will do as my lord commandeth." These formulas indicate the accomplishment of, or the intention to accomplish, the "orders" of a superior.

The verb *ṣāwāh* can be used of a commission or charge, such as the act of "commanding," "telling," or "sending" someone to do a particular task. In Gen. 32:4, Jacob "commissioned" his servants to deliver a particular message to his brother Esau. They acted as his emissaries.

Jacob commissioned (literally, "commanded") his sons to bury him in the cave of Machpelah (Gen. 49:30), and then he died. This "command" constituted a last will and testament— an obligation or duty. The verb again indicates, therefore, appointing someone to be one's emissary.

The most frequent subject of this verb is God. However, He is not to be questioned or "commanded" to explain the work of His hands (Isa. 45:11). He tells Israel that His "commands" are unique, requiring an inner commitment and not just external obedience, as the commands of men do (Gen. 29:13). His "ordering" is given to Moses from above the mercy seat (Exod. 25:22) and from His "commands" at Sinai (Lev. 7:38; cf. 17:1ff.). At other times when He "commands," the thing simply occurs; His word is active and powerful (Ps. 33:9). He also issues "orders" through and to the prophets (Jer. 27:4) who explain, apply, and speak His "commands" (Jer. 1:17).

COMMANDER

śar (שַׂר, 8269), "official; leader; commander; captain; chief; prince; ruler." This word, which has an Akkadian cognate, appears about 420 times in biblical Hebrew. The word is often applied to certain non-Israelite "officials or representatives of the king." This meaning appears in Gen. 12:15, its first biblical appearance: "The *princes* also of Pharaoh saw her [Sarah], and commended her before Pharaoh. . . . " In other contexts *śar* represents "men who clearly have responsibility over others"; they are "rulers or chieftains." *Śar* may mean simply a "leader" of a profession, a group, or a district, as Phichol was the "commander" of Abimelech's army (Gen. 21:22) and Potiphar was "an officer of Pharaoh's and captain of the [body]guard" (Gen. 37:36). In such usage, "chief" means "head official" (cf. Gen. 40:2). *Śarîm* (plural) were "honored men" (Isa. 23:8).

Śar is used of certain "notable men" within Israel. When Abner was killed by Joab, David said to his servants (palace officials), "Know ye not that there is a prince and a great man fallen this day in Israel?" (2 Sam. 3:38; cf. Num. 21:18). Joab, Abishai, and Ittai were "commanders" in David's army (cf. 2 Sam. 23:19). "Local leaders in Israel" are also called *śarîm*: "And the *princes* of Succoth said . . . " (Judg. 8:6).

In several passages, *śar* refers to the task of "ruling." Moses tried to break up a fight between two Hebrews and one of them asked him, "Who made thee a prince and a judge over us?" (Exod. 2:14). In such a context, *śar* means "leader," "ruler," and "judge": "Moreover thou shalt provide out of all the people able men, such as fear God, men of truth, hating covetousness; and place such over them, to be rulers of thousands, and rulers of hundreds, rulers of fifties, and rulers of tens ..." (Exod. 18:21). The "commander" of Israel's army was called a *śar* (1 Sam. 17:55).

In Judg. 9:30, *śar* represents a "ruler" of a city. Any government official might be called a *śar* (Neh. 3:14). "Religious officiants" who served in the temple of God were also called *śarîm* (Jer. 35:4).

The "leaders" or "chiefs" of the Levites (1 Chron. 15:16) or priests (Ezra 8:24) are *śarîm*. In 1 Chron. 24:5, the word appears to be a title: "Thus were they divided by lot, one sort with another; for the governors of the sanctuary [*śarîm qōdeš*], and governors of the house of God [*śarîm ha'ĕlōhîm*], were of the sons of Eleazar, and of the sons of Ithamar" (NASB, "officers of the sanctuary" and "officers of God").

In the Book of Daniel, *śar* is used of "superhuman beings" or "patron angels." Thus, Michael is the "prince" of Judah (Dan. 10:21; cf. Josh. 5:14). Daniel 8:25 speaks of a king who will arise and "stand up against the Prince of princes" (i.e., the Messiah).

COMMANDMENT

miṣwāh (מִצְוָה, 4687), "commandment." This noun occurs 181 times in the Old Testament. Its first occurrence is in Gen. 26:5, where *miṣwāh* is synonymous with *hōq* ("statute") and *tôrāh* ("law"): "Because that Abraham obeyed my voice, and kept my charge, my *commandments*, my statutes, and my laws."

In the Pentateuch, God is always the Giver of the *miṣwāh*: "All the commandments which I command thee this day shall ye observe to do, that ye may live, and multiply, and go in and possess the land which the Lord sware unto your fathers. And thou shalt remember all the way which the Lord thy God led thee these forty years in the wilderness, to humble thee, and to prove thee, to know what was in thine heart, whether thou wouldest keep his commandments, or no" (Deut. 8:1–2). The "commandment" may be a prescription ("thou shalt do ...") or a proscription ("thou shalt not do ..."). The commandments were given in the hearing of the Israelites (Exod. 15:26; Deut. 11:13), who were to "do" (Lev. 4:2ff.) and "keep" (Deut. 4:2; Ps. 78:7) them. Any failure to do so signified a covenantal breach (Num. 15:31), transgression (2 Chron. 24:20), and apostasy (1 Kings 18:18).

The plural of *miṣwāh* often denotes a "body of laws" given by divine revelation. They are God's "word": "Wherewithal shall a young man cleanse his way? By taking heed thereto according to thy word" (Ps. 119:9). They are also known as "the commandments of God."

Outside the Pentateuch, "commandments" are given by kings (1 Kings 2:43), fathers (Jer. 35:14), people (Isa. 29:13), and teachers of wisdom (Prov. 6:20; cf. 5:13). Only about ten percent of all occurrences in the Old Testament fit this category.

The Septuagint translations are: *entolē* ("commandment; order") and *prostagma* ("order; commandment; injunction").

COMPANION

A. Nouns.

rēaʿ (רֵעַ, 7453), "friend; companion." This noun is also represented in Akkadian, Ugaritic, and Aramaic. *Rēaʿ* appears 187 times in the Hebrew Old Testament, and it has an extensive range of meaning.

The basic meaning of *rēaʿ* is in the narrow usage of the word. A *rēaʿ* is a "personal friend" with whom one shares confidences and to whom one feels very close: "And the Lord spake unto Moses face to face, as a man speaketh unto his friend" (Exod. 33:11). The closeness of relationship is best expressed by those texts where the *rēaʿ* is like a brother or son, a part of the family: "For my brethren and companions' sakes ..." (Ps. 122:8; cf. Deut. 13:6). For this reason, when Zimri became king over Israel he killed not only all relatives of Baasha, but also his "friends" (1 Kings 16:11). In this sense, the word is a synonym of *'āh* ("brother") and of *qārôb* ("kin"): "... Go in and out from gate to gate throughout the camp, and slay every man his brother, and every man his *companion*, and every man his neighbor" (Exod. 32:27).

Similar to the above is the sense of "marriage partner": "His mouth is most sweet: yea, he is altogether lovely. This is my beloved, and this is my *friend*, O daughters of Jerusalem" (Song of Sol. 5:16). However, *rēaʿ* may also signify "illegitimate partners": "... If a man put away his wife, and she go from him, and become another man's, shall he return unto her again? shall not that land be greatly polluted? but thou has played the harlot with many lovers (*rēaʿ*); yet return again to me, saith the Lord" (Jer. 3:1). The prophet Hosea was commanded to take back his wife from her "friend" (lover), as she had played the adulteress long enough.

The wider usage of *rēaʿ* resembles the English word *neighbor*, the person with whom one associates regularly or casually without establishing close relations. One may borrow from his "neighbor" (Exod. 22:14), but not bear false witness (Exod. 20:16) nor covet his neighbor's possessions (Exod. 20:17–18). The laws regulate how one must not take advantage of one's "neighbors." The second greatest commandment, which Jesus reiterated—"Love thy neighbor as thyself" (Lev. 19:18)—receives reinforcement in the laws of the Pentateuch. The prophets charged Israel with breaking the commandment: They oppressed each other (Isa. 3:5) and desired their neighbors' wives (Jer. 5:8); they committed adultery with these women (Ezek. 18:6); they did not pay wages to the worker (Jer. 22:13); and they improperly took advantage of their "neighbors" (Ezek. 22:12). According to Proverbs, not loving one's neighbor is a sign of foolishness (Prov. 11:12).

The wider meaning comes to expression in the proverb of the rich man and his "friends": "Wealth maketh many friends; but the poor is separated from his neighbor" (Prov. 19:4). Here the "friend" is a person whose association is not long-lasting, whose friendship is superficial.

The Septuagint gives the following translations: *plesion* ("near; close by"), *philos* ("friend"). The KJV gives these senses: "neighbor; friend; fellow; companion."

Rē'eh also means "friend." This noun appears in 1 Kings 4:5: " . . . Zabud the son of Nathan was principal officer, and the king's *friend.* . . ." *Rē'āh* refers to a "female friend." See Judg. 11:37 for this usage: "And she said unto her father . . . let me alone two months, that I may go up and down upon the mountains, and bewail my virginity, I and my *fellows*" (cf. Judg. 11:38; Ps. 45:14). The noun *ra'yāh* means "beloved companion; bride." *Ra'yāh* occurs many times in the Song of Solomon: 1:9, 15; 2:2, 10, 13; 4:1, 7; 5:2; 6:4. *Re'ût* refers to a "fellow woman." This word is usually translated idiomatically in a reciprocal phrase of "one another," as in Zech. 11:9: "Then said I, I will not feed you: that that dieth, let it die; and that that is to be cut off, let it be cut off; and let the rest eat every one the flesh of *another.*"

B. Verb.

rā'āh (רָעָה, 7462), "to associate with." This word appears in Prov. 22:24: "Make no friendship with an angry man; and with a furious man thou shalt not go. . . ."

TO HAVE COMPASSION, BE MERCIFUL

A. Verb.

rāham (רָחַם, 7355), "to have compassion, be merciful, pity." The words from this root are found 125 times in all parts of the Old Testament. The root is also found in Assyrian, Ethiopic, and Aramaic.

The verb is translated "love" once: "I will love thee, O Lord. . . ." (Ps. 18:1). *Rāham* is also used in God's promise to declare His name to Moses: "I will make all my goodness pass before thee, and I will proclaim the name of the Lord before thee; and will be gracious to whom I will be gracious, and will *show mercy* on whom I will show mercy" (Exod. 33:19). So men pray: "Remember, O Lord, thy tender mercies and thy loving-kindnesses" (Ps. 25:6); and Isaiah prophesies messianic restoration: " . . . With great mercies will I gather thee. . . . But with everlasting kindness will I have mercy on thee, saith the Lord thy Redeemer" (Isa. 54:7–8). This is the heart of salvation by the suffering Servant-Messiah.

B. Nouns.

rehem (רֶחֶם, 7358), "bowels; womb; mercy." The first use of *rehem* is in its primary meaning of "womb": "The Lord had fast closed up all the wombs of the house of Abimelech" (Gen. 20:18). The word is personified in Judg. 5:30: "Have they not divided the prey; to every man a damsel or two . . . ?" In another figurative sense, the KJV reads in 1 Kings 3:26: "Her bowels yearned upon her son," which the NIV translates more idiomatically: "[She] was filled with compassion for her son." The greatest frequency is in this figurative sense of "tender love," such as a mother has for the child she has borne.

rahămîm (רַחֲמִים, 7356), "bowels; mercies; compassion." This noun, always used in the plural intensive, occurs in Gen. 43:14: "And God Almighty give you mercy [NASB, "compassion"]." In Gen. 43:30, it is used of Joseph's feelings toward Benjamin: "His bowels did yearn upon his brother." (NIV, "He was deeply moved at the sight of his brother.") *Rahămîm* is most often used of God, as by David in 2 Sam. 24:14: "Let us fall now into the hand of the Lord; for his mercies are great. . . ." We have the equivalent Aramaic word in Daniel's request to his friends: "That they would desire mercies of the God of heaven concerning this secret . . ." (Dan. 2:18).

The Greek version of the Old Testament *rāham* consists chiefly of three groups of words that come into the New Testament. *Eleos* is the most important, and it is used to translate several Hebrew words. Mary's song recalls the promise in Ps. 103:11, 17, where *eleos* translates both *rehem* and *hesed* as "mercy": "His mercy is on them that fear him from generation to generation" (Luke 1:50). *Rāham* is probably behind the often-heard plea: "Thou son of David, have mercy on us" (Matt. 9:27).

C. Adjective.

rahûm (רַחוּם, 7349), "compassionate; merciful." The adjective is used in that important proclamation of God's name to Moses: "The Lord, The Lord God, merciful and gracious ... " (Exod. 34:6, NASB, NIV, "compassionate").

TO COMPLETE

A. Verb.

šālam (שָׁלַם, 7999), "to finish, complete, repay, reward." The Hebrew root denotes perfection in the sense that a condition or action is "complete." This concept emerges when a concrete object is described. When sufficient building materials were at hand and workmen had enough time to apply them, "the wall [of Jerusalem] was finished" at the time of Nehemiah (Neh. 6:15). However, this Hebrew root is also found in words with so many nuances and applications that at times its original and basic intent is all but obscured. In the NASB, for example, *šālam* is represented with such words as: "fulfill, make up, restore, pay, repay, full, whole, wholly, entire, without harm, friendly, peaceably, to be at peace, make peace, safe, reward, retribution, restitution, recompense, vengeance, bribe, peace offering."

Perfection and completeness is primarily attributed to God. He is deficient in nothing; His attributes are not marred by any shortcomings; His power is not limited by weakness. God reminded Job of His uninhibited independence and absolute self-sufficiency: "Who hath prevented me, that I should repay him? Whatsoever is under the whole heaven is mine" (Job 41:11). And Job himself admitted: "And who shall repay him what he hath done?" (Job 21:31).

Without any deficiency or flaw in executing justice, God is likewise never lacking in mercy and power to bestow benevolences of every kind. Job is told by his friend: "If thou wert pure ... he would make the habitation of thy righteousness prosperous" (Job 8:6). He can make it happen that " ... to the righteous good shall be repaid" (Prov. 13:21). Cyrus says of the Lord: "He ... shall perform all my pleasure" (Isa. 44:28). The Lord will also " ... restore comforts unto him and to his mourners" who wept in the Babylonian exile (Isa. 57:18).

The God of perfect justice and goodness expects total devotion from His creatures. Job, suspected of not rendering the required obedience to his Maker, is therefore urged to "be at peace [with God]" (Job 22:21).

The concept of meeting one's obligation in full is basic in human relationships. Israel's social law required that the person causing injury or loss " ... shall surely make it good" (Exod. 22:14). "And he that killeth a beast shall make it good; beast for beast" (Lev. 24:18). In some instances, an offender " ... shall pay double unto his neighbor" (Exod. 22:9). David declared that the rich man who slaughtered the poor man's only lamb " ... shall restore the lamb fourfold ... " (2 Sam. 12:6). Debts were not to be left unpaid. After providing the widow with the amount needed, Elisha directed her: "Go sell the oil, and pay [*šālam*] thy debt ... " (2 Kings 4:7). "The wicked borroweth, and payeth not again ... " (Ps. 37:21). A robber who has mended his ways " ... give[s] again that he had robbed ... " (Ezek. 33:15).

National relationships were established on the basis of "complete" negotiations. Thus cities and peoples "made peace with Israel" after they agreed to Joshua's stipulations (Josh. 10:1). War between the two kingdoms ended when Jehoshaphat " ... made peace with the king of Israel" (1 Kings 22:44).

B. Adjective.

šālēm (שָׁלֵם, 8003), "perfect." God demanded total obedience from His people: "Let [their] heart therefore be perfect with the Lord our God, to walk in his statutes, and to keep his commandments ... " (1 Kings 8:61). Solomon failed to meet this requirement because " ... his heart was not perfect with the Lord his God" (1 Kings 11:4). Hezekiah, on the other hand, protested: " ... I have walked before thee in truth and with a perfect heart" (2 Kings 20:3).

In business transactions, the Israelites were required to " ... have a perfect and just weight, a perfect and just measure ... " (Deut. 25:15).

TO CONFESS

yādāh (יָדָה, 3034), "to confess, praise, give thanks." The root, translated "confess" or "confession" about twenty times in the KJV, is also frequently rendered "praise" or "give thanks." At first glance, the meanings may appear unrelated. But upon closer inspection, it becomes evident that each sense profoundly illumines and interprets the other.

Yādāh overlaps in meaning with a number of other Hebrew words implying "praise," such as *hālal* (whence *halleluyah*). Man is occasionally the object of *yādāh;* but far more commonly, God is the object.

The usual context seems to be public worship, where the worshipers affirm and renew their relationship with God. The subject is not primarily the isolated individual, but the congregation. Especially in the hymns and thanksgivings of the Psalter, it is evident that *yādāh* is a recital of, and thanksgiving for, Yahweh's mighty acts of salvation.

An affirmation or confession of God's undeserved kindness throws man's unworthiness into sharp relief. Hence, a confession of sin may be articulated in the same breath as a confession of faith or praise and thanksgiving. The confession is not a moralistic, autobiographical catalogue of sins—individual infractions of a legal code—but a confession of the underlying sinfulness that engulfs all mankind and separates us from the holy God. God is even to be praised for His judgments, by which He awakens repentance (e.g., Ps. 51:4). So one is not surprised to find praises in penitential contexts, and vice versa (1 Kings 8:33ff.; Neh. 9:2ff.; Dan. 9:4ff.). If praise inevitably entails confession of sin, the reverse is also true: The sure word of forgiveness elicits praise and thanksgiving on the confessor's part. This wells up almost automatically from the new being of the repentant person.

Often the direct object of *yādāh* is the "name" of Yahweh (e.g., Ps. 105:1; Isa. 12:4; 1 Chron. 16:8). In one sense, this idiom is simply synonymous with praising Yahweh. In another sense, however, it introduces the entire dimension evoked by the "name" in biblical usage. It reminds us that the holy God cannot be directly approached by fallen man, but only through His "name"— i.e., His Word and reputation, an anticipation of the incarnation. God reveals Himself only in His "name," especially in the sanctuary where He "causes His name to dwell" (a phrase especially frequent in Deuteronomy).

The vista of *yādāh* expands both vertically and horizontally—vertically to include all creation, and horizontally stretching forward to that day when praise and thanksgiving shall be eternal (e.g., Ps. 29; 95:10; 96:7–9; 103:19–22).

TO CONFRONT

qādam (קָדַם, 6923), "to meet, confront, go before, be before." This verb occurs 27 times and in every period of biblical Hebrew. Most often, this verb is used in a martial context. Such confrontations may be peaceful, as in the meeting of allies: "For thou [dost meet] him with the blessings of goodness ... " (Ps. 21:3). They may also be hostile: "The sorrows of hell compassed me about; the snares of death confronted (KJV, "prevented") me" (2 Sam. 22:6).

CONGREGATION

'ēdāh (עֵדָה, 5712), "congregation." This word may have etymologically signified a "company assembled together" for a certain purpose, similar to the Greek words *sunagoge* and *ekklesia,* from which our words "synagogue" and "church" are derived. In ordinary usage, *'ēdāh* refers to a "group of people." It occurs 149 times in the Old Testament, most frequently in the Book of Numbers. The first occurrence is in Exod. 12:3, where the word is a synonym for *qāhāl,* "assembly."

The most general meaning of *'ēdāh* is "group," whether of animals—such as a swarm of bees (Judg. 14:8), a herd of bulls (Ps. 68:30), and the flocking together of birds (Hos. 7:12)— or of people, such as the righteous (Ps. 1:5), the evildoers (Ps. 22:16), and the nations (Ps. 7:7).

The most frequent reference is to the "congregation of Israel" (9 times), "the congregation of the sons of Israel" (26 times), "the congregation" (24 times), or "all of the congregation" (30 times). Elders (Lev. 4:15), family heads (Num. 31:26), and princes (Num. 16:2; 31:13; 32:2) were placed in charge of the "congregation" in order to assist Moses in a just rule.

The Septuagint translation is *sunagoge* ("place of assembly"). The KJV has these translations: "congregation; company; assembly."

mô'ēd (מוֹעֵד, 4150), "appointed place of meeting; meeting." The noun *mô'ēd* appears in the Old Testament 223 times, of which 160 times are in the Pentateuch. The historical books are next in the frequency of usage (27 times).

The word *mô'ēd* keeps its basic meaning of "appointed," but varies as to what is agreed upon or appointed according to the context: the time, the place, or the meeting itself. The usage of the verb in Amos 3:3 is illuminating: "Can two walk together, except they be agreed?" Whether they have agreed on a time or a place of meeting, or on the meeting itself, is ambiguous.

The meaning of *mô'ēd* is fixed within the context of Israel's religion. First, the festivals came to be known as the "appointed times" or the set feasts. These festivals were clearly prescribed in the Pentateuch. The word refers to any "festival" or "pilgrimage festival," such as Passover (Lev. 23:15ff.), the feast of first fruits (Lev. 23:15ff.), the feast of tabernacles (Lev. 23:33ff.), or the Day of Atonement (Lev. 23:27). God condemned the people for observing the *mô'ēd* ritualistically: "Your new moons and your appointed feasts my soul hateth ... " (Isa. 1:14).

The word *mô'ēd* also signifies a "fixed place." This usage is not frequent: "For thou hast said in thine heart, I will ascend into heaven, I will exalt my throne above the stars of God: I will sit also upon the mount of the congregation [mô'ēd], in the sides of the north ..." (Isa. 14:13). "For I know that thou wilt bring me to death, and to *the house appointed* for all living" (Job 30:23).

In both meanings of mô'ēd—"fixed time" and "fixed place"—a common denominator is the "meeting" of two or more parties at a certain place and time—hence the usage of mô'ēd as "meeting." However, in view of the similarity in meaning between "appointed place" or "appointed time" and "meeting," translators have a real difficulty in giving a proper translation in each context. For instance, "He hath called an assembly [mô'ēd] against me" (Lam. 1:15) could be read: "He has called an appointed time against me" (NASB) or "He summoned an army against me" (NIV).

The phrase, "tabernacle of the congregation," is a translation of the Hebrew 'ōhel mô'ēd ("tent of meeting"). The phrase occurs 139 times— mainly in Exodus, Leviticus, and Numbers, rarely in Deuteronomy. It signifies that the Lord has an "appointed place" by which His presence is represented and through which Israel was assured that their God was with them. The fact that the tent was called the "tent of meeting" signifies that Israel's God was among His people and that He was to be approached at a certain time and place that were "fixed" (yā'ad) in the Pentateuch. In the KJV, this phrase is translated as "tabernacle of the congregation" (Exod. 28:43) because translators realized that the noun 'ēdāh ("congregation") is derived from the same root as mô'ēd. The translators of the Septuagint had a similar difficulty. They noticed the relation of mô'ēd to the root 'ûd ("to testify") and translated the phrase 'ōhel hamô'ēd as "tabernacle of the testimony." This phrase was picked up by the New Testament: "And after that I looked, and, behold, the temple of the tabernacle of the testimony in heaven was opened ..." (Rev. 15:5).

Of the three meanings, the appointed "time" is most basic. The phrase "tent of meeting" lays stress on the "place of meeting." The "meeting" itself is generally associated with "time" or "place."

The Septuagint has the following translations of mô'ēd: kairos ("time"), eorte ("feast; festival"). The English translators give these senses: "congregation" (KJV, RSV, NASB, NIV); "appointed time" (NASB); "appointed feast" (RSV, NASB); "set time" (RSV, NASB, NIV).

TO CONSUME

A. Verb.

kālāh (כָּלָה, 3615), "to cease, be finished, perish, be completed." This verb occurs in most Semitic languages and in all periods. In Hebrew, it occurs both in the Bible (about 210 times) and in post-biblical literature. The word does not appear in biblical Aramaic.

Basically, the word means "to cease or stop." Kālāh may refer to the "end" of a process or action, such as the cessation of God's creating the universe: "And on the seventh day God ended his work which he had made ..." (Gen. 2:2—the first occurrence of the word). The word can also refer to the "disappearance" of something: "And the water was *spent* in the bottle ..." (Gen. 21:15). Finally, kālāh can be used of "coming to an end" or "the process of ending": "The barrel of meal shall not waste" (1 Kings 17:14).

Kālāh can have the more positive connotation of "successfully completing" something. First Kings 6:38 says that the house of the Lord was "finished throughout all the parts thereof, and according to all [its plans]." In this same sense, the word of the Lord "is fulfilled": "Now in the first year of Cyrus king of Persia, that the word of the Lord by the mouth of Jeremiah might be fulfilled, the Lord stirred up the spirit of Cyrus king of Persia, that he made a proclamation ..." (Ezra 1:1).

Kālāh sometimes means "making a firm decision." David tells Jonathan that if Saul is very angry, "be sure that evil is determined by him" (1 Sam. 20:7).

Negatively, "to complete" something may mean "to make it vanish" or "go away." Kālāh is used in this sense in Deut. 32:23, when God says: "I will heap mischiefs upon them; I will spend mine arrows upon them." In other words, His arrows will "vanish" from His possession. This nuance is used especially of clouds: "As the cloud is consumed and vanisheth away ..." (Job 7:9). Another negative nuance is to "destroy" something or someone: "the famine shall consume the land" (Gen. 41:30). Along this same line is the use of kālāh in Isa. 1:28: " ... They that forsake the Lord shall be consumed"; here, however, the verb is a synonym for "dying" or "perishing." One's sight may also "vanish" and one may go blind: "But the eyes of the wicked shall fail, and they shall not escape ..." (Job 11:20). An altogether different emphasis appears when one's heart comes "to an end" or "stops within": "My soul longeth, yea, even fainteth for the courts of the Lord" (Ps. 84:2); the psalmist probably meant that his desire for God's presence was so intense that nothing else had any meaning for him—he "died" to be there.

B. Noun.

kālāh (כָּלָה, 3617), "consumption; complete annihilation." *Kālāh* appears 15 times; one occurrence is Neh. 9:31: "Nevertheless for thy great mercies' sake thou didst not utterly consume them, nor forsake them;...."

TO BE CONSUMED

A. Verb.

tāmam (תָּמַם, 8552), "to be complete, finished, perfect, spent, sound, used up, have integrity." Found in both ancient and modern Hebrew, this word also exists in ancient Ugaritic. *Tāmam* is found approximately 60 times in the Hebrew Old Testament in its verbal forms.

The basic meaning of this word is that of "being complete" or "finished," with nothing else expected or intended. When it was said that the temple was "finished" (1 Kings 6:22), this meant that the temple was "complete," with nothing else to add. Similarly, when the notation is made in Job 31:40, "The words of Job are ended [finished]," this indicates that the cycle of Job's speeches is "complete." *Tāmam* is sometimes used to express the fact that something is "completed" or "finished" with regard to its supply. Thus, money that is all spent is "finished" or "exhausted" (Gen. 47:15, 18). Jeremiah was given bread daily until "all the bread in the city [was] spent [exhausted]" (Jer. 37:21). When a people came "to a full end" (Num. 14:35, RSV), it meant that they were "consumed" or "completely destroyed." To "consume" the filthiness out of the people (Ezek. 22:15) meant "to destroy it" or "to make an end of it."

Tāmam sometimes expresses moral and ethical "soundness": "Then shall I be upright" (Ps. 19:13), says the psalmist, when God helps him to keep God's Law.

B. Adjective.

tām (תָּם, 8535), "perfect." When the adjectival form *tām* is used to describe Job (1:1), the meaning is not that he was really "perfect" in the ultimate sense, but rather that he was "blameless" (RSV) or "had integrity."

CONTINUALLY

A. Adverb.

tāmîd (תָּמִיד, 8548), "always; continually; regularly." This word comes from a root that means "to measure." The root is found in Assyrian, Aramaic, Arabic, and Phoenician. *Tāmîd* occurs 100 times in all parts of the Old Testament. It signifies what is to be done regularly or continuously without interruption.

Tāmîd is first used in Exod. 25:30: "And thou shalt set upon the table showbread before me

always" (KJV; NASB, "at all times"). Sometimes the continuity is explained by what follows, as in Isa. 21:8: "... My lord, I stand continually upon the watchtower in the daytime, and I am set in my ward whole nights."

Because of his covenant with Jonathan, David said to Mephibosheth: "... And you shall eat at my table regularly" (2 Sam. 9:7; cf. 2 Sam. 9:10, NASB; KJV, "continually"; RSV, "always").

Tāmîd occurs most frequently of the daily rituals in the tabernacle and temple: "Now this is that which thou shalt offer upon the altar; two lambs of the first year day by day continually" (Exod. 29:38). The variety in the English versions indicates that both ideas—regularity and continuousness—are present in the Hebrew word. In this passage, *tāmîd* indicates that these rituals were to be performed regularly and without interruption for the duration of the old covenant.

The word is also used of God. It describes His visible presence at the tabernacle: "So it was always: the cloud covered it by day, and the appearance of fire by night" (Num. 9:16). It describes His care for His people: "... let thy loving-kindness and thy truth continually preserve me" (Ps. 40:11); "And the Lord shall guide thee continually ..." (Isa. 58:11).

Tāmîd is also used of Jerusalem: "... thy walls are continually before me" (Isa. 49:16). The word describes man's response to God: "I have set the Lord always before me" (Ps. 16:8); "... his praise shall continually be in my mouth" (Ps. 34:1); "So I shall keep thy law continually, for ever and ever" (Ps. 119:44). In contrast, Israel is "a people that provoketh me to anger continually to my face" (Isa. 65:3). Finally, it is said of Zion eschatologically: "Therefore thy gates shall be open continually; they shall not be shut day nor night" (Isa. 60:11).

B. Adjective.

tāmîd (תָּמִיד, 8548), "continual." In Exod. 30:7–8, Aaron is commanded to burn incense morning and evening when he trims the lamps. He is told to offer "... a perpetual incense before the Lord throughout your generations" (KJV). The same Hebrew expression is used often of priestly functions (cf. Num. 28:6; Ezek. 46:15).

CONTINUITY

A. Noun.

tāmîd (תָּמִיד, 8548), "continuity." *Tāmîd* is often used as a noun. In Num. 4:7, the word is used with "bread," literally meaning "the bread of continuity" (NASB, "the continual bread") or the bread that is "always there." In other groups of passages, the word emphasizes "regular repetition": for example, Exod. 29:42 mentions, literally, "the burnt offering of continuity" (NASB, "continual burnt offering"), or the offering made every morning and evening. The "daily sacrifice" of Dan. 8:11 is also this continual burnt offering.

The nonreligious usage indicates that *tāmîd* describes "continuity in time," in the sense of a routine or habit. *Tāmîd* may also have the connotation of a routine that comes to an end when the job is completed: "And they shall sever out men of continual employment, passing through the land to bury with the passengers those that remain upon the face of the earth, to cleanse it: after the end of seven months shall they search" (Ezek. 39:14).

B. Adverb.

tāmîd (תָּמִיד, 8548), "continually; at all times; ever." A cognate of this word appears in Arabic. Biblical Hebrew attests it in all periods.

The word is used as an adverb meaning "continually." In its first occurrence, *tāmîd* represents "uninterrupted action": "And thou shalt set upon the table showbread before me always" (Exod. 25:30). In Jer. 6:7, we read: " . . . Before me continually is grief and wounds." In many passages, *tāmîd* bears the nuance of "regular repetition": "Now this is that which thou shalt offer upon the altar; two lambs of the first year day by day *continually.* The one lamb thou shalt offer in the morning; and the other lamb thou shalt offer at even . . . " (Exod. 29:38–39).

In poetic usage, *tāmîd* is found in the context of a fervent religious expression: "Mine eyes are ever toward the Lord; for he shall pluck my feet out of the net" (Ps. 25:15). It may express a firm belief in God's faithfulness: "Withhold not thou thy tender mercies from me, O Lord: let thy loving-kindness and thy truth continually preserve me" (Ps. 40:11).

COPPER

neḥōšet (נְחֹשֶׁת, 5178), "copper; bronze; bronze chains." Cognates of this word appear in Phoenician, Aramaic, Arabic, and Ethiopic. It is attested about 136 times in biblical Hebrew and in all periods.

Neḥōšet basically means "copper." This word refers to the metal ore: "A land wherein thou shalt eat bread without scarceness, thou shalt not lack any thing in it; a land whose stones are iron, and out of whose hills thou mayest dig [copper]" (Deut. 8:9). The word can also represent the refined ore: "And Zillah, she also bare Tubal-cain, an instructor of every artificer in copper [KJV, "brass"; NASB, "bronze"] and iron" (Gen. 4:22).

Inasmuch as it was a semiprecious metal, *neḥōšet* is sometimes listed as a spoil of war (2 Sam. 8:8). In such passages, it is difficult to know whether the reference is to copper or to copper mixed with tin (i.e., bronze). Certainly, "bronze" is intended in 1 Sam. 17:5, where *neḥōšet* refers to the material from which armor is made. Bronze is the material from which utensils (Lev. 6:21), altars (Exod. 38:30), and other objects were fashioned. This material could be polished (1 Kings 7:45) or shined (Ezra 8:27). This metal was less valuable than gold and more valuable than wood (Isa. 60:17).

Still another meaning of *neḥōšet* appears in Judg. 16:21: "But the Philistines took [Samson], and put out his eyes, and brought him down to Gaza, and bound him with fetters of [bronze]; and he did grind in the prison house." Usually, when the word has this meaning it appears in the dual form (in the singular form only in Lam. 3:7).

Deut. 28:23 uses *neḥōšet* to symbolize the cessation of life-giving rain and sunshine: "And thy heaven that is over thy head shall be [bronze], and the earth that is under thee shall be iron."

CORD

hebel (חֶבֶל, 2256), "cord; rope; tackle; measuring line; measurement; allotment; portion; region." Cognates of this word appear in Aramaic, Syriac, Ethiopic, Arabic, and Akkadian. The word appears about 50 times in the Old Testament.

Hebel primarily means "cord" or "rope." "Then she let them down by a rope through the window, for her house was built into the city wall" (Josh. 2:15, RSV). The word is used of "tent ropes" in Isa. 33:20: " . . . A tabernacle that shall not be taken down . . . neither shall any of the cords thereof be broken." A ship's "tackle" is the meaning of *hebel* in Isa. 33:23.

Used figuratively, *hebel* emphasizes "being bound." In 1 Kings 20:31, we read that the Syrians who fled into Aphek proposed to put sackcloth on their heads as a sign of repentance for attacking Israel, and to put "ropes" about their necks as a sign of submission to Israel's authority. Snares used "cords" or "ropes," forming a web or a noose into which the prey stepped and was caught. In this manner, the wicked would be caught by God (Job 18:10). In many passages, death is pictured as a hunter whose trap has been sprung and whose quarry is captured by the "cords" of the trap: "The cords of Sheol entangled me; the snares of death confronted me" (2 Sam. 22:6, RSV).

In other cases, the thing that "binds" is good: "I drew them with cords of a man, with bands of love ..." (Hos. 11:4). Eccl. 12:6 pictures human life as being held together by a silver "cord."

A "cord" could be used as a "measuring line": "And he smote Moab, and measured them with a line, casting them down to the ground; even with two lines measured he to put to death, and with one full line to keep alive" (2 Sam. 8:2). This meaning of *ḥebel* also occurs in Ps. 78:55: " ... And [He] divided them an inheritance by line." Compare Mic. 2:5: "Therefore thou shalt have none that shall cast a cord by lot in the congregation of the Lord." The act referred to by Micah appears in Ps. 16:6 as an image of one's life in general: "The lines are fallen unto me in pleasant places; yea, I have a goodly heritage."

Ḥebel also means "the thing measured or allotted": "For the Lord's portion is his people; Jacob is the lot of his inheritance" (Deut. 32:9). Here the use is clearly figurative, but in 1 Chron. 16:18 the "portion" of Israel's inheritance is a concrete "measured thing"; this nuance first appears in Josh. 17:5. In passages such as Deut. 3:4, the word is used of a "region" or "a measured area": " ... Threescore cities, all the region of Argob, the kingdom of Og in Bashan."

The word may refer to a group of people, describing them as that which is tied together— "a band": " ... Thou shalt meet a company of prophets coming down from the high place ..." (1 Sam. 10:5).

TO COUNSEL

A. Verb.

yā'aṣ (יָעַץ, 3289), "to advise, counsel, consult." Used throughout the history of the Hebrew language, this verb occurs in the Hebrew Old Testament approximately 80 times. *Yā'aṣ* is found first in Exod. 18:19, where Jethro says to his son-in-law Moses: "I will give thee counsel, and God shall be with thee." The word is found only one other time in the Hexateuch, and that is in Num. 24:14: "I will advise you" (NASB, RSV, "I will let you know"; JB, "let me warn you"; NEB, "I will warn you").

While *yā'aṣ* most often describes the "giving of good advice," the opposite is sometimes true. A tragic example was the case of King Ahaziah of Judah, whose mother "was his counselor to do wickedly" (2 Chron. 22:3). The idea of "decision" is expressed in Isa. 23:9: "The Lord of hosts hath purposed it" (RSV, NEB, NASB, "planned it"; JB, "decision").

B. Nouns.

yō'ēṣ (יָעֵץ, 3289), "counselor." Perhaps the most familiar use of this root is the noun form found in the messianic passage, Isa. 9:6. On the basis of the syntax involved, it is probably better to translate the familiar "Wonderful Counselor" (NASB, TEV) as "Wonder-Counsellor" (JB, NAB) or "Wonder of a Counsellor." The NEB renders it "in purpose wonderful." Another possibility is that of separating the terms: "Wonderful, Counselor" (KJV).

yā'aṣ (יָעַץ, 3289), "those who give counsel." *Yā'aṣ* is frequently used in its participial form, "those who give counsel," especially in connection with political and military leaders (2 Sam. 15:12; 1 Chron. 13:1).

COURT

ḥāṣēr (חָצֵר, 2691), "court; enclosure." This word is related to a common Semitic verb that has two meanings: "to be present," in the sense of living at a certain place (encampment, residence, court), and "to enclose, surround, press together." In the Hebrew Old Testament, *ḥāṣēr* appears about 190 times; its usage is well-distributed throughout, except for the minor prophets.

In some Hebrew dictionaries, the usage of *ḥāṣēr* as "settled abode," "settlement," or "village" is separated from the meaning "court." But most modern dictionaries identify only one root with two related meanings.

The first biblical occurrence of *ḥāṣēr* is in Gen. 25:16: "These are the sons of Ishmael, and these are their names, by their *towns*, and by their castles; twelve princes according to their nations." Here *ḥāṣēr* is related to the first meaning of the root; this occurs less frequently than the usage meaning "court." The *ḥāṣēr* ("settlement") was a place where people lived without an enclosure to protect them. The word is explained in Lev. 25:31: "But the houses of the villages which have no wall round about them shall be counted as the fields of the *country*: they may be redeemed, and they shall go out in the jubilee."

Ḥāṣēr signifies the "settlements" of semi-nomadic peoples: the Ishmaelites (Gen. 25:16), the Avim (Deut. 2:23), and Kedar (Isa. 42:11). *Ḥāṣēr* also denotes a "settlement" of people outside the city wall. The cities of Canaan were relatively small and could not contain the whole population. In times of peace, residents of the city might build homes and workshops for themselves outside the wall and establish a separate quarter. If the population grew, the king or governor often decided to enclose the new quarter by surrounding it with a wall and incorporating the section into the existing city, in order to protect the population from bandits and warriors. Jerusalem gradually extended its size westward; at the time of Hezekiah, it had grown into a large city. Huldah the prophetess lived in such a development, known in Hebrew as the *mišneh*: " . . . she dwelt in Jerusalem in the Second Quarter" (2 Kings 22:14, RSV).

The Book of Joshua includes Israel's victories in Canaan's major cities as well as the suburbs: "Ain, Remmon, and Ether, and Ashan; four cities and their villages . . ." (19:7; cf. 15:45, 47; 21:12).

The predominant usage of *ḥāṣēr* is "court," whether of a house, a palace, or the temple. Each house generally had a courtyard surrounded by a wall or else one adjoined several homes: "Nevertheless a lad saw them, and told Absalom: but they went both of them away quickly, and came to a man's house in Bahurim, which had a well in his court; whither they went down" (2 Sam. 17:18). Solomon's palace had several "courts"—an outer "court," an "enclosed space" around the palace, and a "court" around which the palace was built. Similarly, the temple had various courts. The psalmist expressed his joy in being in the "courts" of the temple, where the birds built their nests (Ps. 84:3); "For a day in thy courts is better than a thousand. I had rather be a doorkeeper in the house of my God, than to dwell in the tents of wickedness" (Ps. 84:10). God's people looked forward to the thronging together of all the people in God's "courts": " . . . In the courts of the Lord's house, in the midst of thee, O Jerusalem" (Ps. 116:19).

The Septuagint translations are: *aulē* ("courtyard; farm; house; outer court; palace"), *epaulis* ("farm; homestead; residence"), and *kōmē* ("village; small town"). The KJV gives these translations: "court; village; town."

COVENANT

bᵉrît (בְּרִית, 1285), "covenant; league; confederacy." This word is most probably derived from an Akkadian root meaning "to fetter"; it has parallels in Hittite, Egyptian, Assyrian, and Aramaic. *Bᵉrît* is used over 280 times and in all parts of the Old Testament. The first occurrence of the word is in Gen. 6:18: "But with thee [Noah] will I establish my covenant."

The KJV translates *bᵉrît* fifteen times as "league": " . . . Now therefore make ye a league with us" (Josh. 9:6). These are all cases of political agreement within Israel (2 Sam. 3:12–13, 21; 5:3) or between nations (1 Kings 15:19). Later versions may use "covenant," "treaty," or "compact," but not consistently. In Judg. 2:2, the KJV has: "And ye shall make no league with the inhabitants of this land. . . . " The command had been also given in Exod. 23:32; 34:12–16; and Deut. 7:2–6, where the KJV has "covenant."

The KJV translates *bᵉrît* as "covenant" 260 times. The word is used of "agreements between men," as Abraham and Abimelech (Gen. 21:32): "Thus they made a covenant at Beer-sheba. . . . " David and Jonathan made a "covenant" of mutual protection that would be binding on David's descendants forever (1 Sam. 18:3; 20:8, 16–18, 42). In these cases, there was "mutual agreement confirmed by oath in the name of the Lord." Sometimes there were also material pledges (Gen. 21:28–31).

Ahab defeated the Syrians: "So he made a covenant with [Ben-hadad], and sent him away" (1 Kings 20:34). The king of Babylon "took of the king's seed [Zedekiah], and made a covenant with him, and hath taken an oath of him . . ." (Ezek. 17:13, NIV, "treaty"). In such "covenants," the terms were imposed by the superior military power; they were not mutual agreements.

In Israel, the kingship was based on "covenant": " . . . David made a covenant [KJV, "league"] with them [the elders of Israel] in Hebron before the Lord . . ." (2 Sam. 5:3). The "covenant" was based on their knowledge that God had appointed him (2 Sam. 5:2); thus they became David's subjects (cf. 2 Kings 11:4, 17).

The great majority of occurrences of *bᵉrît* are of God's "covenants" with men, as in Gen. 6:18 above. The verbs used are important: "I will *establish* my covenant" (Gen. 6:18)—literally, "cause to stand" or "confirm." "I will *make* my covenant" (Gen. 17:2, RSV). "He *declared* to you his covenant" (Deut. 4:13). "My covenant which I *commanded* them . . ." (Josh. 7:11). "I have *remembered* my covenant. Wherefore . . . I will bring you out from under the burdens of the Egyptians" (Exod. 6:5–6). God will not reject Israel for their disobedience so as "to *destroy* them utterly, and to *break* my covenant with them . . ." (Lev. 26:44). "He will not . . . forget the covenant . . . which he *sware* unto them" (Deut. 4:31). The most common verb is "to cut [*kārat*] a covenant," which is always translated as in Gen. 15:18: "The Lord made a covenant with Abram." This use apparently comes from the ceremony described in Gen. 15:9–17 (cf. Jer. 34:18), in which God appeared as "a smoking furnace, and a burning lamp [flaming torch] that passed between those pieces" (Gen. 15:17). These verbs make it plain that God takes the sole initiative in covenant making and fulfillment.

"Covenant" is parallel or equivalent to the Hebrew words *dābār* ("word"), *ḥōq* ("statute"), *piqqûd* ("precepts"—Ps. 103:18, NASB), *'ēdāh* ("testimony"—Ps. 25:10), *tôrāh* ("law"—Ps. 78:10), and *ḥesed* ("lovingkindness"—Deut. 7:9, NASB). These words emphasize the authority and grace of God in making and keeping the "covenant," and the specific responsibility of man under the covenant. The words of the "covenant" were written in a book (Exod. 24:4, 7; Deut. 31:24–26) and on stone tablets (Exod. 34:28).

Men "enter into" (Deut. 29:12) or "join" (Jer. 50:5) God's "covenant." They are to obey (Gen. 12:4) and "observe carefully" all the commandments of the "covenant" (Deut. 4:6). But above all, the "covenant" calls Israel to "love the Lord thy God with all thine heart, and with all thy soul, and with all thy might" (Deut. 6:5). God's "covenant" is a relationship of love and loyalty between the Lord and His chosen people.

"… If ye will obey my voice indeed, and keep my covenant, then ye shall be a peculiar treasure unto me above all people … and ye shall be unto me a kingdom of priests, and a holy nation" (Exod. 19:5–6). "All the commandments … shall ye observe to do, that ye may live, and multiply, and go in and possess the land which the Lord sware unto your fathers" (Deut. 8:1). In the "covenant," man's response contributes to covenant fulfillment; yet man's action is not causative. God's grace always goes before and produces man's response.

Occasionally, Israel "made a covenant before the Lord, to walk after the Lord, and to keep his commandments …, to perform the words of this covenant that were written in this book" (2 Kings 23:3). This is like their original promise: "All that the Lord hath spoken we will do" (Exod. 19:8; 24:7). Israel did not propose terms or a basis of union with God. They responded to God's "covenant."

The wholly gracious and effective character of God's "covenant" is confirmed in the Septuagint by the choice of *diatheke* to translate *bᵉrit.* A *diatheke* is a will that distributes one's property after death according to the owner's wishes. It is completely unilateral. In the New Testament, *diatheke* occurs 33 times and is translated in the KJV 20 times as "covenant" and 13 times as "testament." In the RSV and the NASB, only "covenant" is used.

The use of "Old Testament" and "New Testament" as the names for the two sections of the Bible indicates that God's "covenant" is central to the entire book. The Bible relates God's "covenant" purpose, that man be joined to Him in loving service and know eternal fellowship with Him through the redemption that is in Jesus Christ.

TO CREATE

bārā' (בָּרָא, 1254), "to create, make." This verb is of profound theological significance, since it has only God as its subject. Only God can "create" in the sense implied by *bārā'.* The verb expresses creation out of nothing, an idea seen clearly in passages having to do with creation on a cosmic scale: "In the beginning God created the heaven and the earth" (Gen. 1:1; cf. Gen. 2:3; Isa. 40:26; 42:5). All other verbs for "creating" allow a much broader range of meaning; they have both divine and human subjects, and are used in contexts where bringing something or someone into existence is not the issue.

Bārā' is frequently found in parallel to these other verbs, such as *'āśāh*, "to make" (Isa. 41:20; 43:7; 45:7, 12; Amos 4:13), *yāṣar*, "to form" (Isa. 43:1, 7; 45:7; Amos 4:13), and *kûn*, "to establish." A verse that illustrates all of these words together is Isa. 45:18: "For thus saith the Lord that created [*bārā'*] the heavens; God himself that formed [*yāṣar*] the earth and made [*'āśāh*] it; he hath established [*kûn*] it, he created [*bārā'*] it not in vain, he formed [*yāṣar*] it to be inhabited: I am the Lord; and there is none else." The technical meaning of *bārā'* (to "create out of nothing") may not hold in these passages; perhaps the verb was popularized in these instances for the sake of providing a poetic synonym.

Objects of the verb include the heavens and earth (Gen. 1:1; Isa. 40:26; 42:5; 45:18; 65:17); man (Gen. 1:27; 5:2; 6:7; Deut. 4:32; Ps. 89:47; Isa. 43:7; 45:12); Israel (Isa. 43:1; Mal. 2:10); a new thing (Jer. 31:22); cloud and smoke (Isa. 4:5); north and south (Ps. 89:12); salvation and righteousness (Isa. 45:8); speech (Isa. 57:19); darkness (Isa. 45:7); wind (Amos 4:13); and a new heart (Ps. 51:10). A careful study of the passages where *bārā'* occurs shows that in the few nonpoetic uses (primarily in Genesis), the writer uses scientifically precise language to demonstrate that God brought the object or concept into being from previously nonexistent material.

Especially striking is the use of *bārā'* in Isaiah 40–65. Out of 49 occurrences of the verb in the Old Testament, 20 are in these chapters. Because Isaiah writes prophetically to the Jews in Exile, he speaks words of comfort based upon God's past benefits and blessings to His people. Isaiah especially wants to show that, since Yahweh is the Creator, He is able to deliver His people from captivity. The God of Israel has created all things: "I have made ['āśāh] the earth, and created [bārā'] man upon it: I, even my hands, have stretched out the heavens, and all their host have I commanded" (Isa. 45:12). The gods of Babylon are impotent nonentities (Isa. 44:12–20; 46:1–7), and so Israel can expect God to triumph by effecting a new creation (43:16–21; 65:17–25).

Though a precisely correct technical term to suggest cosmic, material creation from nothing, bārā' is a rich theological vehicle for communicating the sovereign power of God, who originates and regulates all things to His glory.

qānāh (קָנָה, 7069), "to get, acquire, earn." These basic meanings are dominant in the Old Testament, but certain poetic passages have long suggested that this verb means "create." In Gen. 14:19, Melchizedek blessed Abram and said: "Blessed be Abram by God Most High, maker [KJV, "possessor"] of heaven and earth" (RSV). Gen. 14:22 repeats this divine epithet. Deut. 32:6 makes this meaning certain in that qānāh is parallel to 'āśāh, "to make": "Is he not your father, who created (qānāh) you, who made ('āśāh) you and established (kûn) you?" (RSV). Ps. 78:54; 139:13; and Prov. 8:22–23 also suggest the idea of creation.

The cognate languages usually follow the Hebrew in the basic meaning of "to get, acquire." Ugaritic, however, attests the meaning "create." In fact, qny is the primary Ugaritic term to express creation. The close relationship of Hebrew and Ugaritic and the contextual meaning of qānāh as "create" in the Old Testament passages cited above argue for the use of qānāh as a synonym for "create" along with bārā', 'āśāh, and yāṣar.

'āśāh (עָשָׂה, 6213), "to create, do, make." This verb, which occurs over 2600 times in the Old Testament, is used as a synonym for "create" only about 60 times. There is nothing inherent in the word to indicate the nature of the creation involved; it is only when 'āśāh is parallel to bārā' that we can be sure that it implies creation.

Unfortunately, the word is not attested in cognate languages contemporary with the Old Testament, and its etymology is unclear. Because 'āśāh describes the most common of human (and divine) activities, it is ill-suited to communicate theological meaning—except where it is used with bārā' or other terms whose technical meanings are clearly established.

The most instructive occurrences of 'āśāh are in the early chapters of Genesis. Gen. 1:1 uses the verb bārā' to introduce the Creation account, and Gen. 1:7 speaks of its detailed execution: "And God made ['āśāh] the firma-

ment. . . ." Whether or not the firmament was made of existing material cannot be determined, since the passage uses only 'āśāh. But it is clear that the verb expresses creation, since it is used in that context and follows the technical word bārā'. The same can be said of other verses in Genesis: 1:16 (the lights of heaven); 1:25, 3:1 (the animals); 1:31; 2:2 (all his work); and 6:6 (man). In Gen. 1:26–27, however, 'āśāh must mean creation from nothing, since it is used as a synonym for bārā'. The text reads, "Let us make ['āśāh] man in our image, after our likeness. . . . So God created [bārā'] man in his own image. . . ." Similarly, Gen. 2:4 states: "These are the generations of the heavens and of the earth when they were created [bārā'], in the day that the Lord God made ['āśāh] the earth and the heavens." Finally, Gen. 5:1 equates the two as follows: "In the day that God created [bārā'] man, in the likeness of God made ['āśāh] he him." The unusual juxtaposition of bārā' and 'āśāh in Gen. 2:3 refers to the totality of creation, which God had "created" by "making."

It is unwarranted to overly refine the meaning of 'āśāh to suggest that it means creation from something, as opposed to creation from nothing. Only context can determine its special nuance. It can mean either, depending upon the situation.

TO CRY

ṣā'aq (צָעַק, 6817), "to cry, cry out, call." Found in both biblical and modern Hebrew, this word has the sense of "to shout, yell." The word is a close parallel to the very similar sounding word, zā'aq, also translated "to cry." The verb ṣā'aq is found about 55 times in the Hebrew Old Testament. The word occurs for the first time in Gen. 4:10: "The voice of thy brother's blood crieth unto me from the ground."

This word is often used in the sense of "crying out" for help. Sometimes it is man "crying out" to man: " . . . The people cried to Pharaoh for bread . . ." (Gen. 41:55). More often it is man "crying" to God for help: " . . . And the children of Israel cried out unto the Lord" (Exod. 14:10). The prophets always spoke sarcastically of those who worship idols: " . . . One shall cry unto him, yet can he not answer . . ." (Isa. 46:7). This word is frequently used to express "distress" or "need": " . . . He cried with a great and exceeding bitter cry . . ." (Gen. 27:34).

zā'aq (זָעַק, 2199), "to cry, cry out, call." This term is found throughout the history of the Hebrew language, including modern Hebrew.

The word occurs approximately 70 times in the Hebrew Old Testament. Its first occurrence is in the record of the suffering of the Israelite bondage in Egypt: "... And the children of Israel sighed by reason of the bondage, and they cried [for help] ... " (Exod. 2:23).

Zā'aq is perhaps most frequently used to indicate the "crying out" for aid in time of emergency, especially "crying out" for divine aid. God often heard this "cry" for help in the time of the judges, as Israel found itself in trouble because of its backsliding (Judg. 3:9, 15; 6:7; 10:10). The word is used also in appeals to pagan gods (Judg. 10:14; Jer. 11:12; Jonah 1:5). That *zā'aq* means more than a normal speaking volume is indicated in appeals to the king (2 Sam. 19:28).

The word may imply a "crying out" in distress (1 Sam. 4:13), a "cry" of horror (1 Sam. 5:10), or a "cry" of sorrow (2 Sam. 13:19). Used figuratively, it is said that "the stone shall cry out of the wall" (Hab. 2:11) of a house that is built by means of evil gain.

CUBIT

'ammāh (אַמָּה, 520), "cubit." This word has cognates in Akkadian, Ugaritic, and Aramaic. It appears about 245 times in biblical Hebrew and in all periods, but especially in Exod. 25–27; 37–38 (specifications of the tabernacle); 1 Kings 6–7 (the specifications of Solomon's temple and palace); and Ezek. 40–43 (the specifications of Ezekiel's temple).

In one passage, *'ammāh* means "pivot": "And the posts [literally, "sockets"] of the door moved at the voice of him that cried ... " (Isa. 6:4).

In almost every other occurrence, the word means "cubit," the primary unit of linear measurement in the Old Testament. Some scholars maintain that Israel's system of linear measurement was primarily based on the Egyptian system. In view of the history of Israel, this is a reasonable position. A "cubit" ordinarily was the distance from one's elbow to the tip of the middle finger. Since this distance varied from individual to individual, the "cubit" was a rather imprecise measurement. Yet the first appearance of *'ammāh* (Gen. 6:15) refers to the measurement of Noah's ark, which implies that the word must refer to a more precise length than the ordinary "cubit."

There was an official "cubit" in Egypt. In fact, there were both a shorter "cubit" (17.6 inches) and a longer "cubit" (20.65 inches). The Siloam inscription states that the Siloam tunnel was 1,200 "cubits" long. This divided by its measurement in feet (1,749) demonstrates that as late as Hezekiah's day (cf. 2 Chron. 32:4) the

"cubit" was about 17.5 inches or the shorter Egyptian cubit. Ezekiel probably used the Babylonian "cubit" in describing the temple. The Egyptian shorter cubit is only about three inches shorter than the longer cubit; on the other hand, the Babylonian shorter cubit was about four-fifths the length of the official royal "cubit," about a handbreadth shorter: "And behold a wall on the outside of the house round about, and in the man's hand a measuring reed of six cubits long by the cubit and a handbreadth ... " (Ezek. 40:5). In other words, it was the width of seven palms rather than six.

TO CURSE

A. Verbs.

qālal (קָלַל, 7043), "to be trifling, light, swift; to curse." This wide-ranging word is found in both ancient and modern Hebrew, in ancient Akkadian, and (according to some) in ancient Ugaritic. The word occurs about 82 times in the Hebrew Old Testament. As will be seen, its various nuances grow out of the basic idea of being "trifling" or "light," with somewhat negative connotations involved.

Qālal is found for the first time in Gen. 8:8: " ... To see if the waters had subsided ... " (RSV). Other English versions translate: "abated" (KJV, NASB); "dried up" (JB); "had lessened" (NEB); "had gone down" (TEV). All of these terms indicate a lessening of what had existed.

The idea of "to be swift" is expressed in the Hebrew comparative form. So, Saul and Jonathan "were swifter than eagles" (2 Sam. 1:23—literally, "more than eagles they were light"). A similar idea is expressed in 1 Sam. 18:23: "And David said, Seemeth it to you a light thing to a king's son-in-law ... ?"

Qālal frequently includes the idea of "cursing" or "making little or contemptible": "And he that curseth [belittles] his father, or his mother, shall surely be put to death" (Exod. 21:17). "To curse" had the meaning of an "oath" when related to one's gods: "And the Philistine cursed David by his gods" (1 Sam. 17:43). The negative aspect of "non-blessing" was expressed by the passive form: " ... The sinner being a hundred years old shall be accursed [by death]" (Isa. 65:20). Similar usage is reflected in: " ... Their portion is cursed in the earth ... " (Job 24:18).

The causative form of the verb sometimes expressed the idea of "lightening, lifting a weight": " ... Peradventure he will lighten his hand from off you ... " (1 Sam. 6:5); " ... so shall it be easier for thyself ... " (Exod. 18:22).

'ārar (אָרַר, 779), "to curse." This root is found

in South Arabic, Ethiopic, and Akkadian. The verb occurs 60 times in the Old Testament.

The first occurrence is in Gen. 3:14: "Thou [the serpent] art cursed above all cattle," and Gen. 3:17: "Cursed is the ground for thy [Adam's] sake." This form accounts for more than half of the occurrences. It is a pronouncement of judgment on those who break covenant, as: "Cursed is the man who ..." (twelve times in Deut. 27:15–26).

"Curse" is usually parallel with "bless." The two "curses" in Gen. 3 are in bold contrast to the two blessings ("And God blessed them ...") in Gen. 1. The covenant with Abraham includes: "I will bless them that bless thee, and curse [different root] him that curseth thee ..." (Gen. 12:3). Compare Jeremiah's "Cursed be the man that trusteth in man" and "Blessed is the man that trusteth in the Lord" (17:5, 7).

Pagans used the power of "cursing" to deal with their enemies, as when Balak sent for Balaam: "Come ..., curse me this people" (Num. 22:6). Israel had the ceremonial "water that causeth the curse" (Num. 5:18ff.).

God alone truly "curses." It is a revelation of His justice, in support of His claim to absolute obedience. Men may claim God's "curses" by committing their grievances to God and trusting in His righteous judgment (cf. Ps. 109:26–31).

The Septuagint translates 'ārar by epikatarasthai, its compounds and derivatives, by which it comes into the New Testament. "Curse" in the Old Testament is summed up in the statement: "Cursed be the man that obeyeth not the words of this covenant ..." (Jer. 11:3). The New Testament responds: "Christ hath redeemed us from the curse of the law, being made a curse for us: for it is written, Cursed is every one that hangeth on a tree ..." (Gal. 3:13).

B. Noun.

'ālāh (אָלָה, 423), "curse; oath." Cognates of this word appear in Phoenician and Arabic. The 36 Old Testament occurrences of this noun appear in every period of biblical literature.

In distinction from 'ārar ("to curse by laying an anathema on someone or something") and qālal ("to curse by abusing or by belittling"), 'ālāh basically refers to "the execution of a proper oath to legalize a covenant or agreement." As a noun, 'ālāh refers to the "oath" itself: "Then shalt thou be clear from this my oath, when thou comest to my kindred; and if they give not thee one, thou shalt be clear from my oath" (Gen. 24:41--the first occurrence). The "oath" was a "curse" on the head of the one who broke the agreement. This same sense appears in Lev. 5:1, referring to a general "curse" against anyone who would give false testimony in a court case.

So 'ālāh functions as a "curse" sanctioning a pledge or commission, and it can close an agreement or covenant. On the other hand, the word sometimes represents a "curse" against someone else, whether his identity is known or not.

D

DAY

yôm (יוֹם, 3117), "daylight; day; time; moment; year." This word also appears in Ugaritic, extrabiblical Hebrew or Canaanite (e.g., the Siloam inscription), Akkadian, Phoenician, and Arabic. It also appears in post-biblical Hebrew. Attested at every era of biblical Hebrew, yôm occurs about 2,304 times.

Yôm has several meanings. The word represents the period of "daylight" as contrasted with nighttime: "While the earth remaineth, seedtime and harvest, and cold and heat, and summer and winter, and day and night shall not cease" (Gen. 8:22). The word denotes a period of twenty-four hours: "And it came to pass, as she spake to Joseph day by day ..." (Gen. 39:10). Yôm can also signify a period of time of unspecified duration: "And God blessed the seventh day, and sanctified it: because that in it he had rested from all his work which God created and made" (Gen. 2:3). In this verse, "day" refers to the entire period of God's resting from creating this universe. This "day" began after He completed the creative acts of the seventh day and extends at least to the return of Christ. Compare Gen. 2:4: "These are the generations of the heavens and of the earth when they were created, in the day [beyôm] that the Lord God made the earth and the heavens...." Here "day" refers to the entire period envisioned in the first six days of creation. Another nuance appears in Gen. 2:17, where the word represents a "point of time" or "a moment": "But of the tree of the knowledge of good and evil, thou shalt not eat of it: for in the day [b*eyôm*] that thou eatest thereof thou shalt surely die." Finally, when used in the plural, the word may represent "year": "Thou shalt therefore keep this ordinance in his season from year to year [*yāmîm*]" (Exod. 13:10).

There are several other special nuances of *yôm* when it is used with various prepositions. First, when used with *ke* ("as," "like"), it can connote "first": "And Jacob said, Sell me this day [first] thy birthright" (Gen. 25:31). It may also mean "one day," or "about this day": "And it came to pass about this time, that Joseph went into the house to do his business . . ." (Gen. 39:11). On Joseph's lips, the phrase connotes "this present result" (literally, "as it is this day"): "But as for you, ye thought evil against me; but God meant it unto good, to bring to pass, as it is this day, to save much people alive" (Gen. 50:20). Adonijah used this same phrase to represent "today": "Let king Solomon swear unto me today that he will not slay his servant . . ." (1 Kings 1:51). Yet another nuance appears in 1 Sam. 9:13: "Now therefore get you up; for about this time ye shall find him." When used with the definite article *ha*, the noun may mean "today" (as it does in Gen. 4:14) or refer to some particular "day" (1 Sam. 1:4) and the "daytime" (Neh. 4:16).

The first biblical occurrence of *yôm* is found in Gen. 1:5: "And God called the light Day, and the darkness he called Night. And the evening and the morning were the first day." The second use introduces one of the most debated occurrences of the word, which is the duration of the days of creation. Perhaps the most frequently heard explanations are that these "days" are 24 hours long, indefinitely long (i.e., eras of time), or logical rather than temporal categories (i.e., they depict theological categories rather than periods of time).

The "day of the Lord" is used to denote both the end of the age (eschatologically) or some occurrence during the present age (non-eschatologically). It may be a day of either judgment or blessing, or both (cf. Isa. 2).

It is noteworthy that Hebrew people did not divide the period of daylight into regular hourly periods, whereas nighttime was divided into three watches (Exod. 14:24; Judg. 7:19). The beginning of a "day" is sometimes said to be dusk (Esth. 4:16) and sometimes dawn (Deut. 28:66–67).

TO DEAL OUT, DEAL WITH

gāmal (גָּמַל, 1580), "to deal out, deal with, wean, ripen." Found in both biblical and modern Hebrew, this word occurs 35 times in the Hebrew Old Testament. While the basic meaning of the word is "to deal out, with," the wide range of meaning can be seen in its first occurrence in the biblical text: "And the child grew, and was weaned . . ." (Gen. 21:8).

Gāmal is used most frequently in the sense of "to deal out to," such as in Prov. 31:12: "She will do him good and not evil. . . ." The word is used twice in 1 Sam. 24:17: " . . . Thou hast rewarded me good, whereas I have rewarded thee evil." The psalmist rejoices and sings to the Lord "because he hath dealt bountifully with me" (Ps. 13:6). This word can express ripening of grapes (Isa. 18:5) or bearing ripe almonds (Num. 17:8).

DEATH

māwet (מָוֶת, 4194), "death." This word appears 150 times in the Old Testament. The word *māwet* occurs frequently as an antonym of *hayyîm* ("life"): "I call heaven and earth to record this day against you, that I have set before you life and death, blessing and cursing: therefore choose life, that both thou and thy seed may live . . ." (Deut. 30:19). In the poetic language, *māwet* is used more often than in the historical books: Job–Proverbs (about 60 times), Joshua–Esther (about 40 times); but in the major prophets only about 25 times.

"Death" is the natural end of human life on this earth; it is an aspect of God's judgment on man: "But of the tree of the knowledge of good and evil, thou shalt not eat of it: for in the day that thou eatest thereof thou shalt surely die" (Gen. 2:17). Hence all men die: "If these men die the common death of all men . . . then the Lord hath not sent me" (Num. 16:29). The Old Testament uses "death" in phrases such as "the day of death" (Gen. 27:2) and "the year of death" (Isa. 6:1), or to mark an event as occurring before (Gen. 27:7, 10) or after (Gen. 26:18) someone's passing away.

"Death" may also come upon someone in a violent manner, as an execution of justice: "And if a man have committed a sin worthy of death and he be to be put to death, and thou hang him on a tree: his body shall not remain all night upon the tree . . ." (Deut. 21:22–23). Saul declared David to be a "son of death" because he intended to have David killed (1 Sam. 20:31; cf. Prov. 16:14). In one of his experiences, David composed a psalm expressing how close an encounter he had had with death: "When the waves of death compassed me, the floods of ungodly men made me afraid; the sorrows of hell compassed me about; the snares of death prevented me" (2 Sam. 22:5–6; cf. Ps. 18:5–6). Isaiah predicted the Suffering Servant was to die a violent death: "And he made his grave with the wicked, and with the rich in his death; because he had done no violence, neither was any deceit in his mouth" (Isa. 53:9).

Associated with the meaning of "death" is the meaning of "death by a plague." In a besieged city with unsanitary conditions, pestilence would quickly reduce the weakened population. Jeremiah alludes to this type of death as God's judgment on Egypt (43:11); note that "death" refers here to "death of famine and pestilence." Lamentations describes the situation of Jerusalem before its fall: " . . . Abroad the sword bereaveth, at home there is as death" (Lam. 1.20; cf. also Jer. 21:8–9).

Finally, the word *māwet* denotes the "realm of the dead" or *she'ōl*. This place of death has gates (Ps. 9:13; 107:18) and chambers (Prov. 7:27); the path of the wicked leads to this abode (Prov. 5:5).

Isaiah expected "death" to be ended when the Lord's full kingship would be established: "He will swallow up death in victory; and the Lord God will wipe away tears from off all faces; and the rebuke of his people shall he take away from off all the earth: for the Lord hath spoken it" (Isa. 25:8). Paul argued on the basis of Jesus' resurrection that this event had already taken place (1 Cor. 15:54), but John looked forward to the hope of the resurrection when God would wipe away our tears (Rev. 21:4).

Temûtāh means "death." One occurrence is in Ps. 79:11: "Let the sighing of the prisoner come before thee; according to the greatness of thy power preserve thou those that are appointed to die [literally, sons of death]" (cf. Ps. 102:20).

Māmôt refers to "death." *Māmôt* appears in Jer. 16:4: "They shall die of grievous deaths . . . " (cf. Ezek. 28:8).

DECEIT

šāw' (שָׁוְא, 7723), "deceit; deception; malice; falsity; vanity; emptiness." The 53 occurrences of *šāw'* are primarily in poetry.

The basic meaning of this word is "deceit" or "deception," "malice," and "falsehood." This meaning emerges when *šāw'* is used in a legal context: "Put not thine hand with the wicked to be an *unrighteous* witness" (Exod. 23:1). Used in cultic contexts, the word bears these same overtones but may be rendered variously. For example, in Ps. 31:6 the word may be

rendered "vain" (KJV, "lying"), in the sense of "deceitful" (cf. Ezek. 12:24). Eliphaz described the ungodly as those who trust in "emptiness" or "deception," though they gain nothing but emptiness as a reward for that trust (Job 15:31).

TO DELIVER

A. Verbs.

nātan (נָתַן, 5414), "to deliver, give, place, set up, lay, make, do." This verb occurs in the different Semitic languages in somewhat different forms. The form *nātan* occurs not only in Aramaic (including in the Bible) and in Hebrew (in all periods). The related forms *nadānu* (Akkadian) and *yātan* (Phoenician) are also attested. These verbs occur about 2,010 times in the Bible.

First, *nātan* represents the action by which something is set going or actuated. Achsah asked her father Caleb to "give" her a blessing, such as a tract of land with abundant water, as her dowry; she wanted him to "transfer" it from his possession to hers (Josh. 15:19). There is a technical use of this verb without an object: Moses instructs Israel to "give" generously to the man in desperate need (Deut. 15:10). In some instances, *nātan* can mean to "send forth," as in "sending forth" a fragrance (Song of Sol. 1:12). When used of a liquid, the word means to "send forth" in the sense of "spilling," for example, to spill blood (Deut. 21:8).

Nātan also has a technical meaning in the area of jurisprudence, meaning to hand something over to someone—for example, "to pay" (Gen. 23:9) or "to loan" (Deut. 15:10). A girl's parent or someone else in a responsible position may "give" her to a man to be his wife (Gen. 16:3), as well as presenting a bride price (Gen. 34:12) and dowry (1 Kings 9:16). The verb also is used of "giving" or "granting" a request (Gen. 15:2).

Sometimes, *nātan* can be used to signify "putting" ("placing") someone into custody (2 Sam. 14:7) or into prison (Jer. 37:4), or even of "destroying" something (Judg. 6:30). This same basic sense may be applied to "dedicating" ("handing over") something or someone to God, such as the first-born son (Exod. 22:29). Levites are those who have been "handed over" in this way (Num. 3:9). This word is used of "bringing reprisal" upon someone or of "giving" him what he deserves; in some cases, the stress is on the act of reprisal (1 Kings 8:32), or bringing his punishment on his head.

Nātan can be used of "giving" or "ascribing" something to someone, such as "giving" glory and praise to God (Josh. 7:19). Obviously, nothing is passed from men to God; nothing is added to God, since He is perfect. This means, therefore, that a worshiper recognizes and confesses what is already His.

Another major emphasis of *nātan* is the action of "giving" or "effecting" a result. For example, the land will "give" ("yield") its fruit (Deut. 25:19). In some passages, this verb means "to procure" ("to set up"), as when God "gave" ("procured, set up") favor for Joseph (Gen. 39:21). The word can be used of sexual activity, too, emphasizing the act of intercourse or "one's lying down" with an animal (Lev. 18:23).

God "placed" (literally, "gave") the heavenly lights into the expanse of the heavens (Gen. 1:17—the first occurrence of the verb). A garland is "placed" (literally, "given") upon one's head (Prov. 4:9). The children of Israel are commanded not to "set up" idols in their land.

A third meaning of *nātan* is seen in Gen. 17:5: " ... For a father of many nations have I made [literally, "given"] thee." There are several instances where the verb bears this significance.

Nātan has a number of special implications when used with bodily parts—for example, "to give" or "turn" a stubborn shoulder (Neh. 9:29). Similarly, compare expressions such as "turning [giving] one's face" (2 Chron. 29:6). To "turn [give] one's back" is to flee (Exod. 23:27). "Giving one's hand" may be no more than "putting it forth," as in the case of the unborn Zarah (Gen. 38:28). This word can also signify an act of friendship as when Jehonadab "gave his hand" (instead of a sword) to Jehu to help him into the chariot (2 Kings 10:15); an act of oathtaking, as when the priests "pledged" ("gave their hands") to put away their foreign wives (Ezra 10:19); and "making" or "renewing" a covenant, as when the leaders of Israel "pledged" themselves ("gave their hands") to follow Solomon (1 Chron. 29:24).

"To give something into someone's hand" is to "commit" it to his care. So after the Flood, God "gave" the earth into Noah's hand (Gen. 9:2). This phrase is used to express the "transfer of political power," such as the divine right to rule (2 Sam. 16:8). *Nātan* is used especially in a military and judicial sense, meaning "to give over one's power or control," or to grant victory to someone; so Moses said God would "give" the kings of Canaan into Israel's hands (Deut. 7:24). "To give one's heart" to something or someone is "to be concerned about it"; Pharaoh was not "concerned" about ("did not set his heart to") Moses' message from God (Exod. 7:23). "To put [give] something into one's heart" is to give one ability and concern to do

something; thus God "put" it in the heart of the Hebrew craftsmen to teach others (Exod. 36:2).

"To give one's face to" is to focus one's attention on something, as when Jehoshaphat was afraid of the alliance of the Transjordanian kings and "set [his face] to seek the Lord" (2 Chron. 20:3). This same phrase can merely mean "to be facing someone or something" (cf. Gen. 30:40). "To give one's face against" is a hostile action (Lev. 17:10). Used with *lipnê* (literally, "before the face of"), this verb may mean "to place an object before" or to "set it down before" (Exod. 30:6). It may also mean "to put before" (Deut. 11:26), "to smite" (cf. Deut. 2:33), or "to give as one's possession" (Deut. 1:8).

yāša' (יָשַׁע, 3467), "to deliver, help." Apart from Hebrew, this root occurs only in a Moabite inscription. The verb occurs over 200 times in the Bible. For example: "For thus saith the Lord God, the Holy One of Israel; In returning and rest shall ye be *saved;* in quietness and in confidence shall be your strength: and ye would not" (Isa. 30:15).

B. Nouns.

yešû'āh (יְשׁוּעָה, 3444), "deliverance." This noun appears 78 times in the Old Testament, predominantly in the Book of Psalms (45 times) and Isaiah (19 times). The first occurrence is in Jacob's last words: "I have waited for thy salvation, O Lord" (Gen. 49:18).

"Salvation" in the Old Testament is not understood as a salvation from sin, since the word denotes broadly anything from which "deliverance" must be sought: distress, war, servitude, or enemies. There are both human and divine deliverers, but the word *yešû'āh* rarely refers to human "deliverance." A couple of exceptions are when Jonathan brought respite to the Israelites from the Philistine pressure (1 Sam. 14:45), and when Joab and his men were to help one another in battle (2 Sam. 10:11). "Deliverance" is generally used with God as the subject. He is known as the salvation of His people: "But Jeshurun waxed fat, and kicked: thou art waxen fat, thou art grown thick, thou art covered with fatness; then he forsook God which made him, and lightly esteemed the Rock of his salvation" (Deut. 32:15; cf. Isa. 12:2). He worked many wonders in behalf of His people: "O sing unto the Lord a new song; for he hath done marvelous things: his right hand, and his holy arm, hath [worked salvation for him]" (Ps. 98:1).

Yešû'āh occurs either in the context of rejoicing (Ps. 9:14) or in the context of a prayer for "deliverance": "But I am poor and sorrowful: let thy salvation, O God, set me up on high" (Ps. 69:29).

Habakkuk portrays the Lord's riding on chariots of salvation (3:8) to deliver His people from their oppressors. The worst reproach that could be made against a person was that God did not come to his rescue: "Many there be which say of my soul, there is no help for him in God [literally, "he has no deliverance in God"]" (Ps. 3:2).

Many personal names contain a form of the root, such as *Joshua* ("the Lord is help"), *Isaiah* ("the Lord is help"), and *Jesus* (a Greek form of *yᵉšû'āh*).

yēša' (יֵשַׁע, 3468), "deliverance." This noun appears 36 times in the Old Testament. One appearance is in Ps. 50:23: "Whoso offereth praise glorifieth me: and to him that ordereth his conversation aright will I show the salvation of God."

tᵉšû'āh (תְּשׁוּעָה, 8668), "deliverance." *Tᵉšû'āh* occurs 34 times. One example is Isa. 45:17: "But Israel shall be saved in the Lord with an everlasting *salvation:* ye shall not be ashamed nor confounded world without end."

The Septuagint translations are: *soteria* and *soterion* ("salvation; preservation; deliverance") and *soter* ("savior; deliverer"). The KJV gives these translations: "salvation; deliverance; help."

TO DEPART

nāsa' (נָסַע, 5265), "to journey, depart, set out, march." Found throughout the development of the Hebrew language, this root is also found in ancient Akkadian. The word is used nearly 150 times in the Hebrew Bible. It occurs for the first time in Gen. 11:2, where *nāsa'* refers to the "migration" (RSV) of people to the area of Babylon. It is probably the most common term in the Old Testament referring to the movement of clans and tribes. Indeed, the word is used almost 90 times in the Book of Numbers alone, since this book records the "journeying" of the people of Israel from Sinai to Canaan.

This word has the basic meaning of "pulling up" tent pegs (Isa. 33:20) in preparation for "moving" one's tent and property to another place; thus it lends itself naturally to the general term of "traveling" or "journeying." Samson is said to have "pulled up" the city gate and posts (Judg. 16:3), as well as the pin on the weaver's loom (Judg. 16:14). *Nāsa'* is used to describe the "movement" of the angel of God and the pillar of cloud as they came between Israel and the pursuing Egyptians at the Sea of Reeds (Exod. 14:19). In Num. 11:31, the word refers to the "springing up" (NEB) of the wind that

brought the quail to feed the Israelites in the wilderness.

Nāsa' lends itself to a wide range of renderings, depending upon the context.

TO BE DESOLATE

šāmēm (שָׁמֵם, 8074), "to be desolate, astonished, appalled, devastated, ravaged." This verb is found in both biblical and modern Hebrew. It occurs approximately 90 times in the text of the Hebrew Old Testament. *Šāmēm* does not occur until Lev. 26:22: "Your high ways shall be desolate." Interestingly, the word occurs 25 times in the Book of Ezekiel alone, which may reflect either Ezekiel's times or (more likely) his personality.

Just how the meanings "be desolate," "be astonished," and "be appalled" are to be connected with each other is not clear. In some instances, the translator must make a subjective choice. For example, after being raped by her half-brother, Tamar is said to have remained in her brother Absalom's house, "desolate" (2 Sam. 13:20). However, she surely was "appalled" at what Amnon had done. Also, the traditional expression, "to be desolated," sometimes means much the same as "to be destroyed" (cf. Amos 7:9; Ezek. 6:4).

Šāmēm often expresses the idea of to "devastate" or "ravage": "I will destroy her vines" (Hos. 2:12). What one sees sometimes is so horrible that it "horrifies" or "appalls": "Mark me, and be astonished, and lay your hand upon your mouth [i.e., be speechless]" (Job 21:5).

TO DESPISE

mā'as (מָאַס, 3988), "to reject, refuse, despise." This verb is common in both biblical and modern Hebrew. It occurs about 75 times in the Hebrew Old Testament and is found for the first time in Lev. 26:15: " . . . If ye shall despise [RSV, "spurn"] my statutes. . . . "

God will not force man to do His will, so He sometimes must "reject" him: "Because thou hast rejected knowledge, I will also reject thee, that thou shalt be no priest to me . . ." (Hos. 4:6). Although God had chosen Saul to be king, Saul's response caused a change in God's attitude: "Because thou hast rejected the word of the Lord, he hath also rejected thee from being king" (1 Sam. 15:23).

As a creature of free choice, man may "reject" God: " . . . Ye have despised the Lord which is among you" (Num. 11:20). At the same time, man may "reject" evil (Isa. 7:15–16).

When the things that God requires are done with the wrong motives or attitudes, God "despises" such actions: "I hate, I despise your feast days ..." (Amos 5:21). Purity of heart and attitude are more important to God than perfection and beauty of ritual.

TO DESTROY

šāmad (שָׁמַד, 8045), "to destroy, annihilate, exterminate." This biblical word occurs also in modern Hebrew, with the root having the connotation of "religious persecution" or "forced conversion." *Šāmad* is found 90 times in the Hebrew Old Testament, the first time in Gen. 34:30: "I shall be destroyed."

This word always expresses complete "destruction" or "annihilation." While the word is often used to express literal "destruction" of people (Deut. 2:12; Judg. 21:16), *šāmad* frequently is part of an open threat or warning given to the people of Israel, promising "destruction" if they forsake God for idols (cf. Deut. 4:25–26). This word also expresses the complete "destruction" of the pagan high places (Hos. 10:8) of Baal and his images (2 Kings 10:28). When God wants to completely "destroy," He will sweep "with the [broom] of destruction" (Isa. 14:23).

šāḥat (שָׁחַת, 7843), "to corrupt, spoil, ruin, mar, destroy." Used primarily in biblical Hebrew, this word has cognate forms in a few other Semitic languages such as Aramaic and Ethiopic. It is used about 150 times in the Hebrew Bible and is found first in Gen. 6, where it is used 4 times in reference to the "corruption" that prompted God to bring the Flood upon the earth (Gen. 6:11–12, 17).

Anything that is good can be "corrupted" or "spoiled," such as Jeremiah's loincloth (Jer. 13:7), a vineyard (Jer. 12:10), cities (Gen. 13:10), and a temple (Lam. 2:6). *Šāḥat* has the meaning of "to waste" when used of words that are inappropriately spoken (Prov. 23:8). In its participial form, the word is used to describe a "ravening lion" (Jer. 2:30, RSV) and the "destroying angel" (1 Chron. 21:15). The word is used as a symbol for a trap in Jer. 5:26. *Šāḥat* is used frequently by the prophets in the sense of "to corrupt morally" (Isa. 1:4; Ezek. 23:11; Zeph. 3:7).

TO DEVISE

ḥāšab (חָשַׁב, 2803), "to think, account, reckon, devise, plan." This word is found throughout the historical development of Hebrew and Aramaic. Found at least 120 times in the Hebrew Bible, *ḥāšab* occurs in the text for the first time in Gen. 15:6, where it was said of Abraham: "He believed the Lord; and he reckoned

it to him as righteousness" (RSV). Here the term has the meaning of "to be imputed."

Frequently used in the ordinary sense of "thinking," or the normal thought processes (Isa. 10:7; 53:4; Mal. 3:16), *ḥāšab* also is used in the sense of "devising evil plans" (Gen. 50:20; Jer. 48:2). The word refers to craftsmen "inventing" instruments of music, artistic objects, and weapons of war (Exod. 31:4; 2 Chron. 26:15; Amos 6:5).

TO DIE

mût (מוּת, 4191), "to die, kill." This verb occurs in all Semitic languages (including biblical Aramaic) from the earliest times, and in Egyptian. The verb occurs about 850 times in biblical Hebrew and in all periods.

Essentially, *mût* means to "lose one's life." The word is used of physical "death," with reference to both man and beast. Gen. 5:5 records that Adam lived "nine hundred and thirty years: and he died." Jacob explains to Esau that, were his livestock to be driven too hard (fast), the young among them would "die" (Gen. 33:13). At one point, this verb is also used to refer to the stump of a plant (Job 14:8). Occasionally, *mût* is used figuratively of land (Gen. 47:19) or wisdom (Job 12:2). Then, too, there is the unique hyperbolic expression that Nabal's heart had "died" within him, indicating that he was overcome with great fear (1 Sam. 25:37).

In an intensive stem, this root is used of the last act inflicted upon one who is already near death. Thus Abimelech, his head having been cracked by a millstone, asked his armor-bearer to "kill" him (Judg. 9:54). In the usual causative stem, this verb can mean "to cause to die" or "to kill"; God is the one who "puts to death" and gives life (Deut. 32:39). Usually, both the subject and object of this usage are personal, although there are exceptions—as when the Philistines personified the ark of the covenant, urging its removal so it would not "kill" them (1 Sam. 5:11). Death in this sense may also be inflicted by animals (Exod. 21:29). This word describes "putting to death" in the broadest sense, including war and judicial sentences of execution (Josh. 10:26).

God is clearly the ultimate Ruler of life and death (cf. Deut. 32:39). This idea is especially clear in the Creation account, in which God tells man that he will surely die if he eats of the forbidden fruit (Gen. 2:17--the first occurrence of the verb). Apparently there was no death before this time. When the serpent questioned Eve, she associated disobedience with death (Gen. 3:3). The serpent repeated God's words, but negated them (Gen. 3:4). When Adam and

Eve ate of the fruit, both spiritual and physical death came upon Adam and Eve and their descendants (cf. Rom. 5:12). They experienced spiritual death immediately, resulting in their shame and their attempt to cover their nakedness (Gen. 3:7). Sin and/or the presence of spiritual death required a covering, but man's provision was inadequate; so God made a perfect covering in the form of a promised redeemer (Gen. 3:15) and a typological covering of animal skins (Gen. 3:21).

TO DISCERN

nākar (נָכַר, 5234), "to discern, regard, recognize, pay attention to, be acquainted with." This verb is found in both ancient and modern Hebrew. It occurs approximately 50 times in the Hebrew Old Testament. The first time *nākar* is used is in Gen. 27:23.

The basic meaning of the term is a "physical apprehension," whether through sight, touch, or hearing. Darkness sometimes makes "recognition" impossible (Ruth 3:14). People are often "recognized" by their voices (Judg. 18:3). *Nākar* sometimes has the meaning of "pay attention to," a special kind of "recognition": "Blessed be the man who took notice of you" (Ruth 2:19, RSV, KJV, "did take knowledge of"). This verb can mean "to be acquainted with," a kind of intellectual awareness: " . . . Neither shall his place know him any more" (Job 7:10; cf. Ps. 103:16). The sense of "to distinguish" is seen in Ezra 3:13: " . . . The people could not discern the noise of the shout of joy from the noise of the weeping of the people. . . ."

TO BE DISMAYED

ḥātat (חָתַת, 2865), "to be dismayed, shattered, broken, terrified." Used primarily in the Hebrew Old Testament, this verb has been identified in ancient Akkadian and Ugaritic texts by some scholars. The word is used approximately 50 times in the Hebrew Old Testament and occurs for the first time in Deut. 1:21 as Moses challenged Israel: "Do not fear or be dismayed" (RSV, NEB, "afraid"; KJV, JB, "discouraged"). As here, *ḥātat* is often used in parallelism with the Hebrew term for "fear" (cf. Deut. 31:8; Josh. 8:1; 1 Sam. 17:11). Similarly, *ḥātat* is frequently used in parallelism with "to be ashamed" (Isa. 20:5; Jer. 8:9).

An interesting figurative use of the word is found in Jer. 14:4, where the ground "is dismayed [KJV, "chapt"], for there was no rain." The meaning "to be shattered" is usually employed in a figurative sense, as with reference to the nations coming under God's judgment (Isa. 7:8; 30:31). The coming Messiah is to "shatter" or "break" the power of all His enemies (Isa. 9:4).

DISTRESS

A. Nouns.

ṣārāh (צָעָה, 6869), "distress; straits." The 70 appearances of *ṣārāh* occur in all periods of biblical literature, although most occurrences are in poetry (poetical, prophetical, and wisdom literature).

Ṣārāh means "straits" or "distress" in a psychological or spiritual sense, which is its meaning in Gen. 42:21 (the first occurrence): "We are verily guilty concerning our brother, in that we saw the anguish of his soul, when he besought us, and we would not hear. . . ."

ṣar (צַר, 6862), "distress." This word also occurs mostly in poetry. In Prov. 24:10, *ṣar* means "scarcity" or the "distress" caused by scarcity. The emphasis of the noun is sometimes on the feeling of "dismay" arising from a distressful situation (Job 7:11). In this usage the word *ṣar* represents a psychological or spiritual status. In Isa. 5:30, the word describes conditions that cause distress: " . . . If one look unto the land, behold darkness and *sorrow* . . . " (cf. Isa. 30:20). This nuance appears to be the most frequent use represented by *ṣar*.

B. Verb.

ṣārar (צָרַר, 6887), "to wrap, tie up, be narrow, be distressed, be in pangs of birth." This verb, which appears in the Old Testament 54 times, has cognates in Aramaic, Syriac, Akkadian, and Arabic. In Judg. 11:7, the word carries the meaning of "to be in distress."

C. Adjective.

ṣar (צַר, 6862), "narrow." *Ṣar* describes a space as "narrow" and easily blocked by a single person (Num. 22:26).

TO DIVIDE

A. Verb.

ḥālaq (חָלַק, 2505), "to divide, share, plunder, assign, distribute." Used throughout the history of Hebrew, this verb is probably reflected in the ancient Akkadian term for "field" i.e., that which is divided. The word is found approximately 60 times in the Hebrew Old Testament; it appears for the first time in Gen. 14:15, where it is said that Abram "divided his forces" (RSV) as he rescued his nephew Lot from the enemy. Apparently, Abram was "assigning" different responsibilities to his troops as part of his strategy. The sense of "dividing" or "allotting" is found in Deut. 4:19, where the sun, moon, and stars are said to have been "allotted" to all peoples by God. A similar use is seen in Deut. 29:26, where God is said not to have "allotted" false gods to His people.

Ḥālaq is used in the legal sense of "sharing" an inheritance in Prov. 17:2. The word is used three times in reference to "sharing" the spoils of war in 1 Sam. 30:24.

This verb describes the "division" of the people of Israel, as one half followed Tibni and the other half followed Omri (1 Kings 16:21). The word *ḥālaq* is also important in the description of the "dividing" of the land of Canaan among the various tribes and clans (Num. 26:52–55).

B. Noun.

ḥēleq (חֵלֶק, 2506), "portion; territory." The noun form of *ḥālaq* is used often in the biblical text. It has a variety of meanings, such as "booty" of war (Gen. 14:24), a "portion" of food (Lev. 6:17), a "tract" of land (Josh. 18:5), a spiritual "possession" or blessing (Ps. 73:26), and a chosen "pattern" or "life-style" (Ps. 50:18).

TO DIVINE, PRACTICE DIVINATION

qāsam (קָסַם, 7080), "to divine, practice divination." Cognates of this word appear in late Aramaic, Coptic, Syriac, Mandean, Ethiopic, Palmyran, and Arabic. This root appears 31 times in biblical Hebrew: 11 times as a verb, 9 times as a participle, and 11 times as a noun.

Divination was a pagan parallel to prophesying: "There shall not be found among you anyone who makes his son or daughter pass through the fire, one who uses divination.... For those nations, which you shall dispossess, listen to those who practice witchcraft and to diviners, but as for you the Lord your God has not allowed you to do so. The Lord your God will raise up for you a prophet like me from among you, from your countrymen; you shall listen to him" (Deut. 18:10, 14–15—first occurrence.)

Qāsam is a seeking after the will of the gods, in an effort to learn their future action or divine blessing on some proposed future action (Josh. 13:22). It seems probable that the diviners conversed with demons (1 Cor. 10:20).

The practice of divination might involve offering sacrifices to the deity on an altar (Num. 23:1ff.). It might also involve the use of a hole in the ground, through which the diviner spoke to the spirits of the dead (1 Sam. 28:8). At other times, a diviner might shake arrows, consult with household idols, or study the livers of dead animals (Ezek. 21:21).

Divination was one of man's attempts to know and control the world and the future, apart from the true God. It was the opposite of true prophecy, which essentially is submission to God's sovereignty (Deut. 18:14).

Perhaps the most perplexing uses of this word occur in Num. 22–23 and Prov. 16:10, where it seems to be an equivalent of prophecy. Balaam was well-known among the pagans as a diviner; at the same time, he recognized Yahweh as his God (Num. 22:18). He accepted money for his services and probably was not beyond adjusting the message to please his clients. This would explain why God, being angry, confronted him (Num. 22:22ff.), even though God had told him to accept the commission and go with his escort (22:20). It appears that Balaam was resolved to please his clients. Once that resolve was changed to submission, God sent him on his journey (22:35).

TO DO GOOD

A. Verb.

yāṭab (יָטַב, 3190), "to be good, do well, be glad, please, do good." This word is found in various Semitic languages, and is very common in Hebrew, both ancient and modern. *Yāṭab* is found approximately 100 times in biblical Hebrew. This verbal form is found first in the story of Cain and Abel, where it is used twice in one verse: "If you *do well*, will not your countenance be lifted up? And if you do not *do well*, sin is crouching at the door" (Gen. 4:7, NASB).

Among other nuances of the verb are "to deal well" (Exod. 1:20), "to play [a musical instrument] well" (1 Sam. 16:17), "to adorn, make beautiful" (2 Kings 9:30), and "to inquire diligently" (Deut. 17:4).

B. Adjective.

ṭôb (טוֹב, 2896), "good." This word occurs some 500 times in the Bible. Its first occurrence is in Gen. 1:4: "God saw that the light was good" (NASB). God appraises each day's creative work as being "good," climaxing it with a "very good" on the sixth day (Gen. 1:31).

As a positive term, the word is used to express many nuances of that which is "good," such as a "glad" heart (Judg. 18:20), "pleasing" words (Gen. 34:18), and a "cheerful" face (Prov. 15:13).

DOORWAY

A. Noun.

petaḥ (פֶּתַח, 6607), "doorway; opening; entrance; gate." This word appears 164 times in biblical Hebrew and in all periods.

Petaḥ basically represents the "opening through which one enters a building, tent, tower (fortress), or city." Abraham was sitting at the "doorway" of his tent in the heat of the day when his three heavenly visitors appeared (Gen.

18:1). Lot met the men of Sodom at the "doorway" of his home, having shut the door behind him (Gen. 19:6). Larger buildings had larger entryways, so in Gen. 43:19 *petah* may be rendered by the more general word, "entrance." In Gen. 38:14, *petah* may be translated "gateway": Tamar "sat in the gateway [KJV, "open place"]." Thus a *petah* was both a place to sit (a location) and an opening for entry (a passageway): " ... And the incense altar, and his staves, and the anointing oil, and the sweet incense, and the hanging for the *door* at the *entering in* of the tabernacle ... " (Exod. 35:15).

There are a few notable special uses of *petah*. The word normally refers to a part of the intended construction plans of a dwelling, housing, or building; but in Ezek. 8:8 it represents an "entrance" not included in the original design of the building: " ... When I had digged in the wall, behold a door." This is clearly not a doorway. This word may be used of a cave's "opening," as when Elijah heard the gentle blowing that signified the end of a violent natural phenomenon: " ... He wrapped his face in his mantle, and went out, and stood in the entering in of the cave" (1 Kings 19:13). In the plural form, *petah* sometimes represents the "city gates" themselves: "And her [Zion's] gates shall lament and mourn ... " (Isa. 3:26). This form of the word is used as a figure for one's lips; in Mic. 7:5, for example, the prophet mourns the low morality of his people and advises his hearers to trust no one, telling them to guard their lips (literally, the "openings" of their mouths).

In its first biblical occurrence, *petah* is used figuratively. The heart of men is depicted as a house or building with the Devil crouching at the "entrance," ready to subdue it utterly and destroy its occupant (Gen. 4:7).

B. Verb.

pātah (פָּתַח, 6605), "to open." This verb, which appears 132 times in the Old Testament, has attested cognates in Ugaritic, Akkadian, Arabic, and Ethiopic. The first occurrence is in Gen. 7:11.

Although the basic meaning of *pātah* is "to open," the word is extended to mean "to cause to flow," "to offer for sale," "to conquer," "to surrender," "to draw a sword," "to solve [a riddle]," "to free." In association with *min*, the word becomes "to deprive of."

DREAM

A. Noun.

halôm (חֲלוֹם, 2472), "dream." This noun appears about 65 times and in all periods of biblical Hebrew.

The word means "dream." It is used of the ordinary dreams of sleep: "Then thou scarest me with dreams, and terrifiest me through visions ... " (Job 7:14). The most significant use of this word, however, is with reference to prophetic "dreams" and/or "visions." Both true and false prophets claimed to communicate with God by these dreams and visions. Perhaps the classical passage using the word in this sense is Deut. 13:1ff.: "If there arise among you a prophet, or a dreamer of dreams, and giveth thee a sign or a wonder, and the sign or the wonder come to pass. ... " This sense, that a dream is a means of revelation, appears in the first biblical occurrence of *halôm* (or *halōm*): "But God came to Abimelech in a dream by night. . . " (Gen. 20:3).

B. Verb.

hālam (חָלַם, 2492), "to become healthy or strong; to dream." This verb, which appears 27 times in the Old Testament, has cognates in Ugaritic, Aramaic, Syriac, Coptic, Arabic, and Ethiopic. The meaning, "to become healthy," applies only to animals though "to dream" is used of human dreams. Gen. 28:12, the first occurrence, tells how Jacob "dreamed" that he beheld a ladder to heaven.

TO DRINK

šātāh (שָׁתָה, 8354), "to drink." This verb appears in nearly every Semitic language, although in biblical Aramaic it is not attested as a verb (the noun form *mishetteh* does appear). Biblical Hebrew attests *šātāh* at every period and about 215 times.

This verb primarily means "to drink" or "to consume a liquid," and is used of inanimate subjects, as well as of persons or animals. The verb *šāqāh*, which is closely related to *šātāh* in meaning, often appears both with animate and inanimate subjects. The first occurrence of *šātāh* reports that Noah "drank of the wine, and was drunken" (Gen. 9:21). Animals also "drink": "I will draw water for thy camels also, until they have done drinking" (Gen. 24:19). God says He does not "drink the blood of goats" (Ps. 50:13).

"To drink a cup" is a metaphor for consuming all that a cup may contain (Isa. 51:17). Not only liquids may be drunk, since *šātāh* is used figuratively of "drinking" iniquity: "How much more abominable and filthy is man, which drinketh iniquity like water?" (Job 15:16). Only infrequently is this verb used of inanimate subjects, as in Deut. 11:11: "But the land, whither ye go to possess it ... drinketh water of the rain of heaven. ... "

Šātāh may also be used of the initial act of "taking in" a liquid: "Is not this it in which my lord drinketh . . . ?" (Gen. 44:5). "To drink" from a cup does not necessarily involve consuming what is drunk. Therefore, this passage uses *šātāh* of "drinking in," and not of the entire process of consuming a liquid.

This word may be used of a communal activity: "And they went out into . . . the house of their god, and did eat and drink, and cursed Abimelech" (Judg. 9:27). The phrase "eat and drink" may mean "to eat a meal": "And they did eat and drink, he and the men that were with him, and tarried all night . . . " (Gen. 24:54). This verb sometimes means "to banquet" (which included many activities in addition to just eating and drinking), or "participating in a feast": " . . . Behold, they eat and drink before him, and say, God save king Adonijah" (1 Kings 1:25). In one case, *šātāh* by itself means "to participate in a feast": "So the king and Haman came to the banquet that Esther had prepared" (Esth. 5:5).

The phrase, "eating and drinking," may signify a religious meal—i.e., a communion meal with God. The seventy elders on Mt. Sinai "saw God, and did eat and drink" (Exod. 24:11). By this act, they were sacramentally united with God (cf. 1 Cor. 10:19). In contrast to this communion with the true God, the people at the foot of the mountain communed with a false god—they "sat down to eat and to drink, and rose up to play" (Exod. 32:6). When Moses stood before God, however, he ate nothing during the entire forty days and nights (Exod. 34:28). His communion was face-to-face rather than through a common meal.

Priests were commanded to practice a partial fast when they served before God—they were not to drink wine or strong drink (Lev. 10:9). They and all Israel were to eat no unclean thing. These conditions were stricter for Nazirites, who lived constantly before God. They were commanded not to eat any product of the vine (Num. 6:3; cf. Judg. 13:4; 1 Sam. 1:15). Thus, God laid claim to the ordinary and necessary processes of human living. In all that man does, he is obligated to recognize God's control of his existence. Man is to recognize that he eats and drinks only as he lives under God's rule; and the faithful are to acknowledge God in all their ways.

The phrase, "eating and drinking," may also signify life in general; "Judah and Israel were many, as the sand which is by the sea in multitude, eating and drinking, and making merry" (1 Kings 4:20; cf. Eccl. 2:24; 5:18; Jer. 22:15). In close conjunction with the verb "to be drunk (intoxicated)," *šātāh* means "to drink freely" or "to drink so much that one becomes drunk."

When Joseph hosted his brothers, they "drank, and were merry with him" (Gen. 43:34).

TO DRIVE OUT

nādaḥ (נָדַח, 5080), "to drive out, banish, thrust, move." This word is found primarily in biblical Hebrew, although in late Hebrew it is used in the sense of "to beguile." *Nādaḥ* occurs approximately 50 times in the Hebrew Old Testament, and its first use is in the passive form: "And lest thou . . . shouldest be driven to worship them. . . " (Deut. 4:19). The implication seems to be that an inner "drivenness" or "drawing away," as well as an external force, was involved in Israel's potential turning toward idolatry.

Nādaḥ expresses the idea of "being scattered" in exile, as in Jer. 40:12: "Even all the Jews returned out of all places whither they were driven. . . ." Job complained that any resource he once possessed no longer existed, for it "is . . . driven quite from me" (Job 6:13). Evil "shepherds" or leaders did not lead but rather "drove away" and scattered Israel (Jer. 23:2). The enemies of a good man plot against him "to thrust him down from his eminence" (Ps. 62:4, RSV).

DUST

'āpār (עָפָר, 6083), "dust; clods; plaster; ashes." Cognates of this word appear in Ugaritic, Akkadian, Aramaic, Syriac, and Arabic. It appears about 110 times in biblical Hebrew and in all periods.

This noun represents the "porous loose earth on the ground," or "dust." In its first biblical occurrence, *'āpār* appears to mean this porous loose earth: "And the Lord God formed man of the *dust* of the ground, and breathed into his nostrils the breath of life . . . " (Gen. 2:7). In Gen. 13:16, the word means the "fine particles of the soil": "And I will make thy [descendants] as the dust of the earth. . . ." In the plural, the noun can mean "dust masses" or "clods" of earth: " . . . While as yet he had not made the earth, nor the fields, nor the first clods [KJV, "highest part of the dust"; NASB, "dust"] of the world" (Prov. 8:26).

'Āpār can signify "dry crumbled mortar or plaster": "And he shall cause the house to be scraped within round about, and they shall pour out the dust that they scrape off without the city into an unclean place. . . " (Lev. 14:41). In Lev. 14:42, the word means "wet plaster": "And they shall take other stones, and put them in the place of those stones; and he shall take other mortar, and shall plaster the house." *'Āpār* represents "finely ground material" in Deut. 9:21:

"And I took your sin, the calf which ye had made, and burnt it with fire, and stamped it, and ground it very small, even until it was as small as dust: and I cast the dust thereof into the brook that descended out of the mount." *'Āpār* can represent the "ashes" of something that has been burned: "And the king commanded Hilkiah the high priest, and the priests of the second order, and the keepers of the door, to bring forth out of the temple of the Lord all the vessels that were made for Baal, and for the grove, and for all the host of heaven: and he burned them [outside] Jerusalem ... and carried the ashes of them unto Bethel" (2 Kings 23:4). In a similar use, the word represents the "ashes" of a burnt offering (Num. 19:17).

The "rubble" of a destroyed city sometimes is called "dust": "And Ben-hadad sent unto him, and said, The gods do so unto me, and more also, if the *dust* of Samaria shall suffice for handfuls for all the people that follow me" (1 Kings 20:10). In Gen. 3:14 the serpent was cursed with "dust" as his perpetual food (cf. Isa. 65:25; Mic. 7:17). Another nuance arising from the characteristics of dust appears in Job 28:6, where the word parallels "stones." Here the word seems to represent "the ground": "The stones of it are the place of sapphires: and it hath dust of gold."

'Āpār may be used as a symbol of a "large mass" or "superabundance" of something. This use, already cited (Gen. 13:16), appears again in its fulfillment in Num. 23:10: "Who can count the dust of Jacob, and the number of the fourth part of Israel?" "Complete destruction" is represented by *'āpār* in 2 Sam. 22:43: "Then did I beat them as small as the dust of the earth: I did stamp them as the mire of the street...." In Ps. 7:5, the word is used of "valuelessness" and "futility": "Let the enemy persecute my soul, and take it; yea, let him tread down my life upon the earth, and lay mine honor in the dust." To experience defeat is "to lick the dust" (Ps. 72:9), and to be restored from defeat is "to shake oneself from the dust" (Isa. 52:2). To throw "dust" ("dirt") at someone is a sign of shame and humiliation (2 Sam. 16:13), while mourning is expressed by various acts of self-abasement, which may include throwing "dust" or "dirt" on one's own head (Josh. 7:6). Abraham says he is but "dust and ashes," not really important (Gen. 18:27).

In Job 7:21 and similar passages, *'āpār* represents "the earth" of the grave: "For now shall I sleep in the dust; and thou shalt seek me in the morning, but I shall not be." This word is also used as a simile for a "widely scattered army": " ... For the king of Syria had destroyed

them, and had made them like the dust by threshing" (2 Kings 13:7).

TO DWELL

A. Verbs.

yāšab (יָשַׁב, 3427), "to dwell, sit, abide, inhabit, remain." The word occurs over 1,100 times throughout the Old Testament, and this root is widespread in other ancient Semitic languages.

Yāšab is first used in Gen. 4:16, in its most common connotation of "to dwell": "Cain went out ... and dwelt [NASB, "settled"; NIV, "lived"] in the land of Nod...." The word appears again in Gen. 18:1: "He [Abraham] *sat* in the tent door." In Gen. 22:5, *yāšab* is translated: "*Abide* ye here [NIV, "stay here"] with the ass; and I and the lad will go yonder and worship...." The word has the sense of "to remain": "Remain a widow at thy father's house ..." (Gen. 38:11), and it is used of God in a similar sense: "Thou, O Lord, remainest for ever; thy throne from generation to generation ..." (Lam. 5:19). The promise of restoration from captivity was: "And they shall build houses and inhabit them..." (Isa. 65:21).

Yāšab is sometimes combined with other words to form expressions in common usage. For example, "When he sitteth upon the throne of his kingdom" (Deut. 17:18; cf. 1 Kings 1:13, 17, 24) carries the meaning "begins to reign." "To sit in the gate" means "to hold court" or "to decide a case," as in Ruth 4:1–2 and 1 Kings 22:10. "Sit thou at my right hand" (Ps. 110:1) means to assume a ruling position as deputy. "There will I sit to judge all the heathen" (Joel 3:12) was a promise of eschatological judgment. "To sit in the dust" or "to sit on the ground" (Isa. 47:1) was a sign of humiliation and grief.

Yāšab is often used figuratively of God. The sentences, "I saw the Lord sitting on his throne" (1 Kings 22:19); "He that sitteth in the heavens shall laugh" (Ps. 2:4); and "God sitteth upon the throne of his holiness" (Ps. 47:8) all describe God as the exalted Ruler over the universe. The idea that God also "dwells" among men is expressed by this verb: "Shalt thou [David] build me a house for me to dwell in?" (2 Sam. 7:5; cf. Ps. 132:14). The usage of *yāšab* in such verses as 1 Sam. 4:4: " ... The Lord of hosts, which dwelleth between the cherubim," describes His presence at the ark of the covenant in the tabernacle and the temple.

The word is also used to describe man's being in God's presence: "One thing have I desired of the Lord, ... that I may dwell in the house of the Lord all the days of my life..." (Ps. 27:4;

cf. Ps. 23:6). "Thou shalt bring them in, and plant them in the mountain of thine inheritance, in the place, O Lord, which thou hast made for thee to dwell in. . . " (Exod. 15:17).

šākan (שָׁכַן, 7931), "to dwell, inhabit, settle down, abide." This word is common to many Semitic languages, including ancient Akkadian and Ugaritic, and it is found throughout all levels of Hebrew history. *Šākan* occurs nearly 130 times in Old Testament Hebrew.

Šākan is first used in the sense of "to dwell" in Gen. 9:27: " . . . And he shall dwell in the tents of Shem." Moses was commanded: "And let them make me a sanctuary, that I may dwell among them" (Exod. 25:8).

Šākan is a word from nomadic life, meaning "to live in a tent." Thus, Balaam "saw Israel abiding in his tents according to their tribes" (Num. 24:2). In that verse, *šākan* refers to temporary "camping," but it can also refer to being permanently "settled" (Ps. 102:28). God promised to give Israel security, "that they may dwell in a place of their own, and move no more . . . " (2 Sam. 7:10).

The Septuagint version of the Old Testament uses a great number of Greek words to translate *yāšab* and *šākan*. But one word, *katoikein*, is used by far more often than any other. This word also expresses in the New Testament the "dwelling" of the Holy Spirit in the church: "That Christ may dwell in your hearts by faith" (Eph. 3:17). The Greek word *skenein* ("to live in a tent") shares in this also, being the more direct translation of *šākan*. John 1:14 says of Jesus, "The Word was made flesh, and dwelt among us." The Book of Hebrews compares the tabernacle sacrifices of Israel in the wilderness with the sacrifice of Jesus at the true tabernacle: "Behold, the tabernacle of God is with men, and he will dwell [*skenein*] with them, and they shall be his people, and God himself shall be with them and be their God" (Rev. 21:3).

B. Noun.

miškān (מִשְׁכָּן, 4908), "dwelling place; tent." This word occurs nearly 140 times, and often refers to the wilderness "tabernacle" (Exod. 25:9). *Miškān* was also used later to refer to the "temple." This usage probably prepared the way for the familiar term *šᵉkînāh*, which was widely used in later Judaism to refer to the "presence" of God.

C. Participle.

yāšab (יָשַׁב, 3427), "remaining; inhabitant." This participle is sometimes used as a simple adjective: " . . . Jacob was a plain man, *dwelling* in tents" (Gen. 25:27). But the word is more often used as in Gen. 19:25: " . . . All the *inhabitants* of the cities."

E

EAR

A. Noun.

'ōzen (אֹזֶן, 241), "ear." The noun *'ōzen* is common to Semitic languages. It appears 187 times in the Old Testament, mainly to designate a part of the body. The first occurrence is in Gen. 20:8: "Abimelech rose early in the morning, and called all his servants, and told all these things in their ears: and the men were sore afraid."

The "ear" was the place for earrings (Gen. 35:4); thus it might be pierced as a token of perpetual servitude (Exod. 21:6).

Several verbs are found in relation to "ear": "to inform" (Ezek. 24:26), "to pay attention" (Ps. 10:17), "to listen" (Ps. 78:1), "to stop up" (Isa. 33:15), "to make deaf" (Isa. 6:10), and "to tingle" (1 Sam. 3:11).

Animals are also said to have "ears" (Prov. 26:17). God is idiomatically said to have "ears": "Hide not thy face from me in the day when I am in trouble; incline thine ear unto me; . . . when I call answer me speedily" (Ps. 102:2). In this particular passage, the NEB prefers a more idiomatic rendering: "Hide not thy face from me when I am in distress. Listen to my prayer and, when I call, answer me soon." Elsewhere, the KJV reads: "And Samuel heard all the words of the people, and he rehearsed them in the ears of the Lord" (1 Sam. 8:21); here the NIV renders "in the ears of" idiomatically as "before." The Lord "pierces" (i.e., opens up) ears (Ps. 40:6), implants ears (Ps. 94:9), and fashions ears (Prov. 20:12) in order to allow man to receive direction from his Creator. As the Creator, He also is able to hear and respond to the needs of His people (Ps. 94:9). The Lord reveals His words to the "ears" of his prophets: "Now the Lord had told Samuel in his ear a day before

Saul came, saying . . . " (1 Sam. 9:15). Since the Israelites had not responded to the prophetic message, they had made themselves spiritually deaf: "Hear now this, O foolish people, and without understanding; which have eyes, and see not; which have ears, and hear not" (Jer. 5:21). After the Exile, the people of God were to experience a spiritual awakening and new sensitivity to God's Word which, in the words of Isaiah, is to be compared to the opening of the "ears" (Isa. 50:5).

The KJV gives these renderings: "ear; audience; hearing."

EARTH

'ereṣ (אֶרֶץ, 776), "earth; land." This is one of the most common Hebrew nouns, occurring more than 2,500 times in the Old Testament. It expresses a world view contrary to ancient myths, as well as many modern theories seeking to explain the origin of the universe and the forces which sustain it.

'Ereṣ may be translated "earth," the temporal scene of human activity, experience, and history. The material world had a beginning when God "made the earth by His power," "formed it," and "spread it out" (Isa. 40:28; 42:5; 45:12, 18; Jer. 27:5; 51:15). Because He did so, it follows that "the earth is the Lord's" (Ps. 24:1; Deut. 10:1; Exod. 9:29; Neh. 9:6). No part of it is independent of Him, for "the very ends of the earth are His possession," including "the mountains," "the seas," "the dry land," "the depths of the earth" (Ps. 2:8; 95:4–5; Amos 4:13; Jonah 1:9).

God formed the earth to be inhabited (Isa. 45:18). Having "authority over the earth" by virture of being its Maker, He decreed to "let the earth sprout vegetation: of every kind" (Job 34:13; Gen. 1:11). It was never to stop its productivity, for "while the earth stands, seedtime and harvest, and cold and heat, and summer and winter, and day and night shall not cease" (Gen. 8:22). "The earth is full of God's riches" and mankind can "multiply and fill the earth and subdue it" (Ps. 104:24; Gen. 1:28; 9:1). Let no one think that the earth is an independent, self-contained mechanism, for "the Lord reigns" as He "sits on the vault of the earth" from where "He sends rain on the earth" (Ps. 97:1; Isa. 40:22; 1 Kings 17:14; Ps. 104:4).

As "the eyes of the Lord run to and fro throughout the earth," He sees that "there is not a just man on earth" (Eccl. 7:20). At an early stage, God endeavored to "blot out man . . . from the face of the earth" (Gen. 6:5–7). Though He relented and promised to "destroy never again all flesh on the earth," we can be

sure that "He is coming to judge the earth" (Gen. 7:16f.; Ps. 96:13). At that time, "the earth shall be completely laid waste" so that "the exalted people of the earth fade away" (Jer. 10:10; Joel 2:10; Isa. 33:3–6; Ps. 75:8). But He also provides a way of escape for all who heed His promise: "Turn to me and be saved, all the ends of the earth" (Isa. 45:22).

What the Creator formed "in the beginning" is also to have an end, for He will "create a new heaven and a new earth" (Isa. 65:17; 66:22).

The Hebrew word *'ereṣ* also occurs frequently in the phrase "heaven and earth" or "earth and heaven." In other words, the Scriptures teach that our terrestrial planet is a part of an all-embracing cosmological framework which we call the universe. Not the result of accident or innate forces, the unfathomed reaches of space and its uncounted components owe their origin to the Lord "who made heaven and earth" (Ps. 121:2; 124:8; 134:3).

Because God is "the possessor of heaven and earth," the whole universe is to reverberate in the praise of His glory, which is "above heaven and earth" (Gen. 14:19, 22; Ps. 148:13). "Shout, O heavens and rejoice, O earth": "let the heavens be glad and let the earth rejoice" (Ps. 49:13; 96:11). Such adoration is always appropriate, for "whatever the Lord pleases, He does in heaven and in earth, in the seas and in all deeps" (Ps. 135:6).

'Ereṣ does not only denote the entire terrestrial planet, but is also used of some of the earth's component parts. English words like *land, country, ground*, and *soil* transfer its meaning into our language. Quite frequently, it refers to an area occupied by a nation or tribe. So we read of "the land of Egypt," "the land of the Philistines," "the land of Israel," "the land of Benjamin," and so on (Gen. 47:13; Zech. 2:5; 2 Kings 5:2, 4; Judg. 21:21). Israel is said to live "in the land of the Lord" (Lev. 25:33f.; Hos. 9:13). When the people arrived at its border, Moses reminded them that it would be theirs only because the Lord drove out the other nations to "give you their land for an inheritance" (Deut. 4:38). Moses promised that God would make its soil productive, for "He will give rain for your land" so that it would be "a fruitful land," "a land flowing with milk and honey, a land of wheat and barley" (Deut. 11:13–15; 8:7–9; Jer. 2:7).

The Hebrew noun may also be translated "the ground" (Job 2:13; Amos 3:5; Gen. 24:52; Ezek. 43:14). When God executes judgment, "He brings down the wicked to the ground" (Ps. 147:6, NASB).

TO EAT

A. Verb.

'ākal (אָכַל, 398), "to eat, feed, consume, devour." This verb occurs in all Semitic languages (except Ethiopic) and in all periods, from the early Akkadian to the latest Hebrew. The word occurs about 810 times in Old Testament Hebrew and 9 times in Aramaic.

Essentially, this root refers to the "consumption of food by man or animals." In Gen. 3:6, we read that Eve took of the fruit of the tree of the knowledge of good and evil and "ate" it.

The function of eating is presented along with seeing, hearing, and smelling as one of the basic functions of living (Deut. 4:28). "Eating," as every other act of life, is under God's control; He stipulates what may or may not be eaten (Gen. 1:29). After the Flood, man was allowed to "eat" meat (Gen. 9:3). But under the Mosaic covenant, God stipulated that certain foods were not to be "eaten" (Lev. 11; Deut. 14), while others were permissible. This distinction is certainly not new, inasmuch as it is mentioned prior to the Flood (Gen. 7:2; cf. Gen. 6:19). A comparison of these two passages demonstrates how the Bible can speak in general terms, with the understanding that certain limitations are included. Hence, Noah was commanded to bring into the ark two of every kind (Gen. 6:19), while the Bible tells us that this meant two of every unclean and fourteen of every clean animal (Gen. 7:2). Thus, Gen. 9:3 implies that man could "eat" only the clean animals.

This verb is often used figuratively with overtones of destroying something or someone. So the sword, fire, and forest are said to "consume" men. The things "consumed" may include such various things as land (Gen. 3:17), fields (Isa. 1:7), offerings (Deut. 18:1), and a bride's purchase price (Gen. 31:15). 'Akal might also connote bearing the results of an action (Isa. 3:10). The word can refer not only to "eating" but to the entire concept "room and board" (2 Sam. 9:11, 13), the special act of "feasting" (Eccl. 10:16), or the entire activity of "earning a living" (Amos 7:12; cf. Gen. 3:19). In Dan. 3:8 and 6:24, "to eat one's pieces" is to charge someone maliciously. "To eat another's flesh," used figuratively, refers to tearing him to pieces or "killing him" (Ps. 27:2), although 'ākal may also be used literally, as when one "eats" human beings in times of serious famine (Lev. 26:29). Eccl. 4:5 uses the expression, "eat one's own flesh," for allowing oneself to waste away.

Abstinence from eating may indicate deep emotional upset, like that which overcame Hannah before the birth of Samuel (1 Sam. 1:7). It may also indicate the religious self-denial seen in fasting.

Unlike the pagan deities (Deut. 32:37–38), God "eats" no food (Ps. 50:13); although as a "consuming" fire (Deut. 4:24), He is ready to defend His own honor and glory. He "consumes" evil and the sinner. He will also "consume" the wicked like a lion (Hos. 13:8). There is one case in which God literally "consumed" food—when He appeared to Abraham in the form of three "strangers" (Gen. 18:8).

God provides many good things to eat, such as manna to the Israelites (Exod. 16:32) and all manner of food to those who delight in the Lord (Isa. 58:14), even the finest food (Ps. 81:16). He puts the Word of God into one's mouth; by "consuming" it, it is taken into one's very being (Ezek. 3:2).

B. Nouns.

'ōkel (אֹכֶל, 400), "food." This word occurs 44 times in the Old Testament. 'Okel appears twice in Gen. 41:35 with the sense of "food supply": "And let them gather all the food of those good years that come, and lay up corn under the hand of Pharaoh, and let them keep food in the cities." The word refers to the "food" of wild animals in Ps. 104:21: "The young lions roar after their prey, and seek their meat from God." 'Okel is used for "food" given by God in Ps. 145:15. The word may also be used for "food" as an offering, as in Mal. 1:12. A related noun, 'āklāh, also means "food." This noun has 18 occurrences in the Old Testament.

ELDER; AGED

zāqēn (זָקֵן, 2204, 2205), "old man; old woman; elder; old." Zāqēn occurs 174 times in the Hebrew Old Testament as a noun or as an adjective. The first occurrence is in Gen. 18:11: "Now Abraham and Sarah were old and well stricken in age; and it ceased to be with Sarah after the manner of women." In Gen. 19:4, the word "old" is used as an antonym of "young": "But before they lay down, the men of the city, even the men of Sodom, compassed the house round, both old and young [na'ar, "young man"], all the people from every quarter" (cf. Josh. 6:21). A similar usage of zāqēn and "young" appears in other Bible references: "But [Rehoboam] forsook the counsel of the old men, which they had given him, and consulted with the young men [yeled, "boy; child"] that were grown up with him . . . " (1 Kings 12:8). "Then shall the virgin rejoice in the dance, both young men [bāhûr] and old together: for I will turn their mourning into joy, and will comfort them, and make them rejoice from their sorrow" (Jer. 31:13). The "old man" is described as being advanced in days (Gen. 18:11), as being satisfied with life or full of years. A feminine form of *zāqēn* refers to an "old woman" (*zᵉqēnāh*).

The word *zāqēn* has a more specialized use with the sense of "elder" (more than 100 times). The "elder" was recognized by the people for his gifts of leadership, wisdom, and justice. He was set apart to administer justice, settle disputes, and guide the people of his charge. Elders are also known as officers (*šōtrîm*), heads of the tribes, and judges; notice the parallel usage: "Joshua called for all Israel, and for their *elders*, and for their heads, and for their judges, and for their officers, and said unto them; I am old and stricken in age . . . " (Josh. 23:2). The "elders" were consulted by the king, but the king could determine his own course of action (1 Kings 12:8). In a given city, the governing council was made up of the "elders," who were charged with the well-being of the town: "And Samuel did that which the Lord spake, and came to Bethlehem. And the elders of the town trembled at his coming, and said, Comest thou peaceably?" (1 Sam. 16:4). The elders met in session by the city gate (Ezek. 8:1). The place of meeting became known as the "seat" or "council" (KJV, "assembly") of the elders (Ps. 107:32).

The Septuagint gives the following translations: *presbutera* ("man of old; elder; presbyter"), *presbutes* ("old man; aged man"), *gerousia* ("council of elders"). The KJV gives various translations of *zāqēn:* "old; elder; old man; ancient." Note that the KJV distinguishes between "elder" and "ancient"; whenever the word *zāqēn* does not apply to age or to rule, the KJV uses the word "ancient."

Zāqān means "beard." The word *zāqān* refers to a "beard" in Ps. 133:2: "It is like the precious ointment upon the head, that ran down upon the beard, even Aaron's beard: that went down to the skirts of his garments. . . . " The association of "old age" with a "beard" can be made, but should not be stressed. The verb *zāqēn* ("to be old") comes from this noun.

ENCHANTER

'aššāp (אַשָּׁף, 825), "enchanter." Cognates of this word appear in Akkadian, Syriac, and biblical Aramaic (6 times). The noun appears only twice in biblical Hebrew, and only in the Book of Daniel.

The vocation of *ašipu* is known from earliest times in the Akkadian (Old Babylonian) society. It is not clear whether the *ašipu* was an assistant to a particular order of Babylonian priests (*mašmašu*) or an order parallel in func-

tion to the *mašmašu* order. In either case, the *ašipu* offered incantations to deliver a person from evil magical forces (demons). The sick often underwent actual surgery while the incantations were spoken.

In the Bible, *'aššāp* first occurs in Dan. 1:20: "And as for every matter of wisdom and understanding about which the king consulted them, he found them ten times better than all the magicians and enchanters (NASB, "conjurers") who were in his realm."

TO ENCOUNTER, BEFALL

qārā' (קָרָא, 7122), "to encounter, befall." *Qārā'* represents an intentional confrontation, whereby one person is immediately before another person. This might be a friendly confrontation, in which friend intentionally "meets" friend; so the kings of the valley came out to "meet" Abram upon his return from defeating the marauding army of Chedorlaomer (Gen. 14:17). A host may go forth to "meet" a prospective ally (Josh. 9:11; 2 Sam. 19:15). In cultic contexts, one "meets" God or "is met" by God (Exod. 5:3).

Qārā' may also be used of hostile "confrontation." In military contexts, the word often represents the "confrontation" of two forces to do battle (Josh. 8:5); so Israel is told: "Prepare to meet thy God, O Israel" (Amos 4:12). This verb infrequently may represent an "accidental meeting," so it is sometimes translated "befall" (Gen. 42:4).

END

A. Nouns.

'epes (אֶפֶס, 657), "end; not; nothing; only." The 42 occurrences of this word appear in every period of biblical literature. It has a cognate in Ugaritic. Basically, the noun indicates that a thing "comes to an end" and "is no more."

Some scholars suggest that this word is related to the Akkadian *apsu* (Gk. *abussos*), the chasm of fresh water at the edge of the earth (the earth was viewed as a flat surface with four corners and surrounded by fresh water). But this relationship is highly unlikely, since none of the biblical uses refers to an area beyond the edge of the earth. The idea of the "far reaches" of a thing is seen in passages such as Prov. 30:4: "Who hath gathered the wind in his fists? Who hath bound the waters in a garment? Who hath established all the ends [boundaries] of the earth?" (cf. Ps. 72:8). In other contexts, *'epes* means the "territory" of the nations other than Israel: " . . . With them he shall push the people together to the ends of the earth . . . " (Deut. 33:17). More often, this word represents the peoples who live outside the territory of Israel: "Ask of me, and I shall give thee the heathen for thine inheritance, and the [very ends] of the earth for thy possession" (Ps. 2:8). In Ps. 22:27, the phrase, "the ends of the world," is synonymously parallel to "all the [families] of the nations." Therefore, "the ends of the earth" in such contexts represents all the peoples of the earth besides Israel.

'Epes is used to express "non-existence" primarily in poetry, where it appears chiefly as a synonym of *'ayin* ("none, nothing"). In one instance, *'epes* is used expressing the "non-existence" of a person or thing and is translated "not" or "no": "Is there not yet any of the house of Saul, that I may show the kindness of God unto him?" (2 Sam. 9:3). In Isa. 45:6, the word means "none" or "no one": "That they may know from the rising of the sun, and from the west, that there is none beside me" (cf. v. 9).

In a few passages, *'epes* used as a particle of negation means "at an end" or "nothing": "And all her princes shall be nothing," or "unimportant" and "not exalted" to kingship (Isa. 34:12). The force of this word in Isa. 41:12 is on the "non-existence" of those so described: "... They that war against thee shall be as nothing, and as a thing of nought."

This word can also mean "nothing" in the sense of "powerlessness" and "worthlessness": "All nations before him are as nothing; and they are counted to him less than nothing, and [meaningless]" (Isa. 40:17).

In Num. 22:35, *'epes* means "nothing other than" or "only": "Go with the men: but only the word that I shall speak unto thee, that thou shall speak" (cf. Num. 23:13). In such passages, *'epes* (with the Hebrew particle *kî*) qualifies the preceding phrase. In 2 Sam. 12:14, a special nuance of the word is represented by the English "howbeit."

In Isa. 52:4, *'epes* preceded by the preposition *be* ("by; because of") means "without cause": "... And the Assyrian oppressed them without cause."

qēṣ (קֵץ, 7093), "end." A cognate of this word occurs in Ugaritic. Biblical Hebrew attests *qēṣ* about 66 times and in every period.

First, the word is used to denote the "end of a person" or "death": "And God said unto Noah, The end of all flesh is come before me ..." (Gen. 6:13). In Ps. 39:4, *qēṣ* speaks of the "farthest extremity of human life," in the sense of how short it is: "Lord, make me to know mine end, and the measure of my days, what it is; that I may know how frail I am."

Second, *qēṣ* means "end" as the state of "being annihilated": "He setteth an end to dark-

ness, and searcheth out all perfection ..." (Job 28:3).

Third, related to the previous meaning but quite distinct, is the connotation "farthest extremity of," such as the "end of a given period of time": "And after certain years [literally, "at the end of years"] he went down to Ahab to Samaria ..." (2 Chron. 18:2; cf. Gen. 4:3—the first biblical appearance).

A fourth nuance emphasizes a "designated goal," not simply the extremity but a conclusion toward which something proceeds: "For the vision is yet for an appointed time, but at the end it shall speak, and not lie ..." (Hab. 2:3).

In another emphasis, *qēṣ* represents the "boundary" or "limit" of something: "I have seen an end of all perfection" (Ps. 119:96).

In 2 Kings 19:23, the word (with the preposition *le*) means "farthest": "... And I will enter into the lodgings of his borders, and into the forest of his Carmel."

qāṣeh (קָצֶה, 7097), "end; border; extremity." The noun *qāṣeh* appears 92 times and in all periods of biblical Hebrew.

In Gen. 23:9, *qāṣeh* means "end" in the sense of "extremity": "That he may give me the cave of Machpelah, which he hath, which is in the end of his field. ..." The word means "[nearest] edge or border" in Exod. 13:20: "And they took their journey from Succoth, and encamped in the Etham, in the edge of the wilderness." At other points, the word clearly indicates the "farthest extremity": "If any of thine be driven out unto the outmost parts of heaven, from thence will the Lord thy God gather thee, and from thence will he fetch thee" (Deut. 30:4).

Second, *qāṣeh* can signify a "temporal end," such as the "end of a period of time"; that is the use in Gen. 8:3, the first biblical occurrence of the word: "... After the end of the hundred and fifty days the waters were abated."

One special use of *qāṣeh* occurs in Gen. 47:2, where the word is used with the preposition *min* ("from"): "And from among his brothers he took five men and presented them to Pharaoh" (RSV; cf. Ezek. 33:2). In Gen. 19:4, the same construction means "from every quarter (or "part") of a city": "... The men of the city, even the men of Sodom, compassed the house round, both old and young, all the people from every quarter." A similar usage occurs in Gen. 47:21, except that the phrase is repeated twice and is rendered "from one end of the borders of Egypt to the other." In Jer. 51:31, the phrase means "in every quarter" or "completely."

qāṣāh (קָצָה, 7098), "end; border; edge; extremity." The noun *qāṣāh* appears in the Bible 28 times and also appears in Phoenician. This word refers primarily to concrete objects. In a few instances, however, *qāṣāh* is used of abstract objects; one example is of God's way (Job 26:14): "These are but the *fringe* of his power; and how faint the whisper that we hear of him!" (NEB).

aḥărît (אַחֲרִית, 319), "hind-part; end; issue; outcome; posterity." Akkadian, Aramaic, and Ugaritic also attest this word. It occurs about 61 times in biblical Hebrew and in all periods; most of its occurrences are in poetry.

Used spatially, the word identifies the "remotest and most distant part of something": "If I take the wings of the morning, and dwell in the *uttermost* parts of the sea . . . " (Ps. 139:9).

The most frequent emphasis of the word is "end," "issue," or "outcome." This nuance is applied to time in a superlative or final sense: " . . . The eyes of the Lord thy God are always upon it, from the beginning of the year even unto the end of the year" (Deut. 11:12). A slight shift of meaning occurs in Dan. 8:23, where *aḥărît* is applied to time in a relative or comparative sense: "And in the latter time of their kingdom, when the transgressors are come to the full, a king of fierce countenance, and understanding dark sentences, shall stand up." Here the word refers to a "last period," but not necessarily the "end" of history. In a different nuance, the word can mean "latter" or "what comes afterward": "O that they were wise, that they understood this, that they would consider their latter end!" (Deut. 32:29). In some passages, *aḥărît* represents the "ultimate outcome" of a person's life. Num. 23:10 speaks thus of death: "Who can count the dust of Jacob, and the number of the fourth part of Israel? Let me die the death of the righteous, and let my last end be like his!"

In other passages, *aḥărît* refers to "all that comes afterwards." Passages such as Jer. 31:17 use the word of one's "descendants" or "posterity" (KJV, "children"). In view of the parallelism suggested in this passage, the first line should be translated "and there is hope for your posterity." In Amos 9:1, *aḥărît* is used of the "rest" (remainder) of one's fellows. Both conclusion and result are apparent in passages such as Isa. 41:22, where the word represents the "end" or "result" of a matter: "Let them bring them forth, and show us what shall happen: let them show the former things what they be, that we may consider them, and know the latter end of them; or declare us things for to come."

A third nuance of *aḥărît* indicates the "last" or the "least in importance": "Your mother shall be sore confounded; she that bare you shall be ashamed: behold, the hindermost of the na-

tions shall be a wilderness, a dry land, and a desert" (Jer. 50:12).

The fact that *aḥărît* used with "day" or "years" may signify either "a point at the end of time" or "a period of the end time" has created considerable debate on fourteen Old Testament passages. Some scholars view this use of the word as non-eschatological—that it merely means "in the day which follows" or "in the future." This seems to be its meaning in Gen. 49:1 (its first occurrence in the Bible): "Gather yourselves together, that I may tell you that which shall befall you in the last days." Here the word refers to the entire period to follow. On the other hand, Isa. 2:2 uses the word more absolutely of the "last period of time": "In the last days, . . . the mountain of the Lord's house shall be established [as the chief of the mountains] . . . ." Some scholars believe the phrase sometimes is used of the "very end of time": "Now I am come to make thee understand what shall befall thy people in the latter days: for yet the vision is for many days" (Dan. 10:14). This point, however, is much debated.

B. Adverb.

epes (אֶפֶס, 657), "howbeit; notwithstanding; however; without cause." This word's first occurrence is in Num. 13:28: "*Nevertheless* the people be strong that dwell in the land . . . ."

ENEMY

ōyēb (אֹיֵב, 341), "enemy." *Ōyēb* has an Ugaritic cognate. It appears about 282 times in biblical Hebrew and in all periods. In form, the word is an active infinitive (or more precisely, a verbal noun).

This word means "enemy," and is used in at least one reference to both individuals and nations: " . . . In blessing I will bless thee, and in multiplying I will multiply thy seed as the stars of the heaven, and as the sand which is upon the sea shore; and thy seed shall possess the gate of his enemies" (Gen. 22:17—the first occurrence). "Personal foes" may be represented by this word: "If thou meet thine enemy's ox or his ass going astray, thou shalt surely bring it back to him again" (Exod. 23:4). This idea includes "those who show hostility toward me": "But mine enemies are lively, and they are strong; and they that hate me wrongfully are multiplied" (Ps. 38:19).

One might be an "enemy" of God: " . . . The Lord will take vengeance on his adversaries, and he reserveth wrath for his enemies" (Nah. 1:2). God is the "enemy" of all who refuse to submit to His lordship: "But they rebelled, and vexed his holy Spirit: therefore he was turned to be their enemy . . . " (Isa. 63:10).

ṣar (צָר, 6862), "adversary; enemy; foe." This noun occurs 70 times in the Hebrew Old Testament, mainly in the Psalms (26 times) and Lamentations (9 times). The first use of the noun is in Gen. 14:20: "And blessed be the most high God, which hath delivered thine enemies into thy hand."

Ṣar is a general designation for "enemy." The "enemy" may be a nation (2 Sam. 24:13) or, more rarely, the "opponent" of an individual (cf. Gen. 14:20; Ps. 3:1). The Lord may also be the "enemy" of His sinful people as His judgment comes upon them (cf. Deut. 32:41–43). Hence, the Book of Lamentations describes God as an "adversary" of His people: "He hath bent his bow like an enemy [*'ōyēb*]: he stood with his right hand as an adversary [*ṣar*], and slew all that were pleasant to the eye in the tabernacle of the daughter of Zion: he poured out his fury like fire" (Lam. 2:4).

The word *ṣar* has several synonyms: *'ōyēb*, "enemy" (cf. Lam. 2:5); *śōnē'*, "hater" (Ps. 44:7); *rōdēp*, "persecutor" (Ps. 119:157); *'ārîṣ*, "tyrant; oppressor" (Job 6:23).

In the Septuagint, *ṣar* is generally translated by *echthros* ("enemy"). The KJV gives these translations: "enemy; adversary; foe."

EPHOD

'ēpôd (אֵפוֹד, 646), "ephod." This word, which appears in Assyrian and (perhaps) Ugaritic, occurs 49 times in the biblical Hebrew, 31 times in the legal prescriptions of Exodus—Leviticus and only once in biblical poetry (Hos. 3:4).

This word represents a close-fitting outer garment associated with worship. It was a kind of long vest, generally reaching to the thighs. The "ephod" of the high priest was fastened with a beautifully woven girdle (Exod. 28:27–28) and had shoulder straps set in onyx stones, on which were engraved the names of the twelve tribes. Over the chest of the high priest was the breastplate, also containing twelve stones engraved with the tribal names. Rings attached it to the "ephod." The Urim and Thummin were also linked to the breastplate.

Apparently, this "ephod" and attachments were prominently displayed in the sanctuary. David consulted the "ephod" to learn whether the people of Keilah would betray him to Saul (1 Sam. 23:9–12); no doubt the Urim and Thummim were used. The first biblical occurrence of the word refers to this high priestly ephod: "Onyx stones, and stones to be set in the ephod, and in the breastplate" (Exod. 25:7). So venerated was this "ephod" that replicas were sometimes made (Judg. 8:27; 17:1–5) and even worshiped. Lesser priests (1 Sam.

2:28) and priestly trainees wore less elaborate "ephods" made of linen whenever they appeared before the altar.

'Apuddāh means "ephod; covering." This word is a feminine form of *'ēpôd* (or *'ēpōd*). The word occurs 3 times, first in Exod. 28:8: "And the curious girdle of the ephod, which is upon it, shall be of ... gold, of blue, and purple, and scarlet, and fine twined linen."

TO ESCAPE

mālaṭ (מָלַט, 4422), "to escape, slip away, deliver, give birth." This word is found in both ancient and modern Hebrew. *Mālaṭ* occurs approximately 95 times in the Hebrew Old Testament. The word appears twice in the first verse in which it is found: "Flee for your life; ... flee to the hills, lest you be consumed" (Gen. 19:17, RSV). Sometimes *mālaṭ* is used in parallelism with *nûs*, "to flee" (1 Sam. 19:10), or with *bāraḥ*, "to flee" (1 Sam. 19:12).

The most common use of this word is to express the "escaping" from any kind of danger, such as an enemy (Isa. 20:6), a trap (2 Kings 10:24), or a temptress (Eccl. 7:26). When Josiah's reform called for burning the bones of false prophets, a special directive was issued to spare the bones of a true prophet buried at the same place: " ... So they let his bones alone ... " (2 Kings 23:18; literally, "they let his bones escape"). *Mālaṭ* is used once in the sense of "delivering a child" (Isa. 66:7).

EVENING

'ereb (עֶרֶב, 6153), "evening, night." The noun *'ereb* appears about 130 times and in all periods. This word represents the time of the day immediately preceding and following the setting of the sun. During this period, the dove returned to Noah's ark (Gen. 8:11). Since it was cool, women went to the wells for water in the "evening" (Gen. 24:11). It was at "evening" that David walked around on top of his roof to refresh himself and cool off, and observed Bathsheba taking a bath (2 Sam. 11:2). In its first biblical appearance, *'ereb* marks the "opening of a day": "And the evening and the morning were the first day" (Gen. 1:5). The phrase "between the evenings" means the period between sunset and darkness, "twilight" (Exod. 12:6; KJV, "in the evening").

Second, in a late poetical use, the word can mean "night": "When I lie down, I say, When shall I arise, and the *night* be gone? And I am full of tossings to and fro unto the dawning of the day" (Job 7:4).

EVER, EVERLASTING

'ôlām (עוֹלָם, 5769), "eternity; remotest time; perpetuity." This word has cognates in Ugaritic, Moabite, Phoenician, Aramaic, Arabic, and Akkadian. It appears about 440 times in biblical Hebrew and in all periods.

First, in a few passages the word means "eternity" in the sense of not being limited to the present. Thus, in Eccl. 3:11 we read that God had bound man to time and given him the capacity to live "above time" (i.e., to remember yesterday, plan for tomorrow, and consider abstract principles); yet He has not given him divine knowledge: "He hath made every thing beautiful in his time: also he hath set the world in their heart, so that no man can find out the work that God maketh from the beginning to the end."

Second, the word signifies "remotest time" or "remote time." In 1 Chron. 16:36, God is described as blessed "from everlasting to everlasting" (KJV, "for ever and ever"), or from the most distant past time to the most distant future time. In passages where God is viewed as the One Who existed before the creation was brought into existence, *'ôlām* (or *'ōlām*) may mean: (1) "at the very beginning": "Remember the former things [the beginning things at the very beginning] of old: for I am God, and there is none else..." (Isa. 46:9); or (2) "from eternity, from the pre-creation, till now": "Remember, O Lord, thy tender mercies and thy lovingkindnesses; for they have been ever of old [from eternity]" (Ps. 25:6). In other passages, the word means "from (in) olden times": "...Mighty men which were of old, men of renown" (Gen. 6:4). In Isa. 42:14, the word is used hyperbolically meaning "for a long time": "I have long time holden my peace; I have been still, and refrained myself...." This word may include all the time between the ancient beginning and the present: "The prophets that have been before me and before thee of old prophesied..." (Jer. 28:8). The word can mean "long ago" (from long ago): "For [long ago] I have broken thy yoke, and burst thy bands..." (Jer. 2:20). In Josh. 24:2, the word means "formerly; in ancient times." The word is used in Jer. 5:15, where it means "ancient": "Lo, I will bring a nation upon you from far, O house of Israel, saith the Lord: it is a mighty nation, it is an ancient nation...." When used with the negative, *'ôlām* (or *'ōlām*) can mean "never": "We are thine: thou never barest rule [literally, "not ruled from the most distant past"] over them..." (Isa. 63:19). Similar meanings emerge when the word is used without a preposition and in a genitive relationship to some other noun.

With the preposition *'ad*, the word can mean "into the indefinite future": "An Ammonite or Moabite shall not enter into the congregation of the Lord; even to their tenth generation shall they not enter into the congregation of the Lord for ever" (Deut. 23:3). The same construction can signify "as long as one lives": "I will not go up until the child be weaned, and then I will bring him, that he may appear before the Lord, and there abide *for ever*" (1 Sam. 1:22). This construction then sets forth an extension into the indefinite future, beginning from the time of the speaker.

In the largest number of its occurrences, *'ôlām* (or *'ōlām*) appears with the preposition *l*ᵉ. This construction is weaker and less dynamic in emphasis than the previous phrase, insofar as it envisions a "simple duration." This difference emerges in 1 Kings 2:33, where both phrases occur. *L*ᵉ*'ôlām* is applied to the curse set upon the dead Joab and his descendants. The other, more dynamic phrase (*'ad 'ôlām*), applied to David and his descendants, emphasizes the ever-continued, ever-acting presence of the blessing extended into the "indefinite future": "Their blood shall therefore return upon the head of Joab, and upon the head of his seed for ever [*l*ᵉ *'ôlām*]: but upon David, and upon his seed, and upon his house, and upon his throne, shall there be peace for ever [*'ad 'ôlām*] from the Lord." In Exod. 21:6 the phrase *l*ᵉ *'ôlām* means "as long as one lives": "...And his master shall bore his ear through with an awl; and he shall serve him for ever." This phrase emphasizes "continuity," "definiteness," and "unchangeability." This is its emphasis in Gen. 3:22, the first biblical occurrence of *'ôlām* (or *'ōlām*): "...And now, lest he put forth his hand, and take also of the tree of life, and eat, and live for ever...."

The same emphasis on "simple duration" pertains when *'ôlām* (or *'ōlām*) is used in passages such as Ps. 61:8, where it appears by itself: "So will I sing praise unto thy name for ever, that I may daily perform my vows." The parallelism demonstrates that *'ôlām* (or *'ōlām*) means "day by day," or "continually." In Gen. 9:16, the word (used absolutely) means the "most distant future": "And the bow shall be in the cloud; and I will look upon it, that I may remember the everlasting covenant between God and every living creature...." In other places, the word means "without beginning, without end, and ever-continuing": "Trust ye in the Lord for ever: for in the Lord Jehovah is everlasting strength" (Isa. 26:4).

The plural of this word is an intensive form.

TO BE EXALTED

A. Verb.

rûm (רוּם, 7311), "to be high, exalted." This root also appears in Ugaritic (with the radicals *r-m*), Phoenician, Aramaic (including biblical Aramaic, 4 times), Arabic, and Ethiopic. In extra-biblical Aramaic, it appears as *r'm.* The word occurs in all periods of biblical Hebrew and about 190 times. Closely related is the rather rare (4 times) *rmm*, "to rise, go away from."

Basically, *rûm* represents either the "state of being on a higher plane" or "movement in an upward direction." The former meaning appears in the first biblical occurrence of the word: "And the flood was forty days upon the earth; and the waters increased, and bare up the ark, and it was lifted [rose] up above the earth" (Gen. 7:17). Used of men, this verb may refer to their "physical stature"; for example, the spies sent into Canaan reported that "the people is greater and taller than we; the cities are great and walled up to heaven . . . " (Deut. 1:28).

The second emphasis, representing what is done to the subject or what it does to itself, appears in Ps. 12:8: "The wicked walk on every side, when the vilest men are exalted." The psalmist confesses that the Lord will "set me up upon a rock" so as to be out of all danger (Ps. 27:5). A stormy wind (Ps. 107:25) "lifts up" the waves of the sea. *Rûm* is used of the building of an edifice. Ezra confessed that God had renewed the people of Israel, allowing them "to set up the house of our God, and to repair the desolations thereof, and to give us a wall in Judah and Jerusalem" (Ezra 9:9; cf. Gen. 31:45). In Ezek. 31:4, this verb is used of "making a plant grow larger": "The waters made him [the cedar in Lebanon] great, the deep set him up on high. . . . " Since in Deut. 1:28 *gādal* ("larger") and *rûm* ("taller") are used in close connection, Ezek. 31:4 could be translated: "The waters made it grow bigger, the deep made it grow taller." Closely related to this nuance is the use of *rûm* to represent the process of child-rearing. God says through Isaiah: " . . . I have nourished [*gādal*] and brought up children, and they have rebelled against me" (Isa. 1:2).

Rûm sometimes means "to take up away from," as in Isa. 57:14: "Cast ye up, cast ye up, prepare the way, take up the stumbling block out of the way of my people." When used in reference to offerings, the word signifies the "removal of a certain portion" (Lev. 2:9). The presentation of the entire offering is also referred to as an "offering up" (Num. 15:19).

In extended applications, *rûm* has both negative and positive uses. Positively, this word can signify "to bring to a position of honor." So God says: "Behold, my servant shall deal prudently, he shall be exalted and extolled, and be very high" (Isa. 52:13). This same meaning occurs in 1 Sam. 2:7, where Hannah confessed: "The Lord maketh poor, and maketh rich: he bringeth low, and lifteth up." Used in a negative sense, *rûm* means "to be haughty": "And the afflicted people thou wilt save: but thine eyes are upon the haughty, that thou mayest bring them down" (2 Sam. 22:28).

Rûm is often used with other words in special senses. For example, to lift one's voice is "to cry aloud." Potiphar's wife reported that when Joseph attacked her, she "raised" her voice screaming. These two words (*rûm* and "voice") are used together to mean "with a loud voice" (Deut. 27:14).

The raising of the hand serves as a symbol of power and strength and signifies being "mighty" or "triumphant": "Were it not that I feared the wrath of the enemy, lest their adversaries should behave themselves strangely, and lest they should say, Our hand is high [literally, "is raised"] . . . " (Deut. 32:27). To raise one's hand against someone is to rebel against him. Thus, "Jeroboam . . . lifted up his hand against the king" (1 Kings 11:26).

The raising of one's horn suggests the picture of a wild ox standing in all its strength. This is a picture of "triumph" over one's enemies: "My heart rejoiceth in the Lord, mine horn is exalted in the Lord; my mouth is enlarged over mine enemies . . . " (1 Sam. 2:1). Moreover, horns symbolized the focus of one's power. Thus, when one's horn is "exalted," one's power is exalted. When one exalts another's horn, he gives him "strength": " . . . He [the Lord] shall give strength unto his king, and exalt the horn of his anointed" (1 Sam. 2:10).

Raising one's head may be a public gesture of "triumph and supremacy," as in Ps. 110:7, where it is said that after defeating all His enemies the Lord will "lift up the head." This nuance is sometimes used transitively, as when someone else lifts a person's head. Some scholars suggest that in such cases the verb signifies the action of a judge who has pronounced an accused person innocent by raising the accused's head. This phrase also came to signify "to mark with distinction," "to give honor to," or "to place in a position of strength": "But thou, O Lord, art a shield for me; my glory, and the lifter up of mine head" (Ps. 3:3).

To raise one's eyes or heart is to be "proud" and "arrogant": "Then thine heart be lifted up, and thou forget the Lord thy God, which brought thee forth out of the land of Egypt" (Deut. 8:14).

B. Nouns.

rûm (רוּם, 7312), "height; haughtiness." This word occurs 6 times, and it means "height" in Prov. 25:3. *Rûm* signifies "haughtiness" in Isa. 2:11.

mārôm (מָרוֹם, 4791), "higher plane; height; high social position." *Mārôm* appears about 54 times in biblical Hebrew. It also is attested in Ugaritic and Old South Arabic. In its first biblical occurrence (Judg. 5:18), *mārôm* means "a higher plane on the surface of the earth." Job 16:19 and Isa. 33:5 contain the word with the meaning of "the height" as the abode of God. Job 5:11 uses the word to refer to "a high social position." *Mārôm* can also signify "self-exaltation" (2 Kings 19:22; Ps. 73:8).

EXCEEDINGLY

A. Adverb.

meʿōd (מְאֹד, 3966), "exceedingly; very; greatly; highly." This word occurs about 300 times and in all periods of biblical Hebrew. A verb with a similar basic semantic range appears in Akkadian, Ugaritic, and Arabic.

Meʿōd functions adverbially, meaning "very." The more superlative emphasis appears in Gen. 7:18, where the word is applied to the "amount (quantity)" of a thing: "And the waters prevailed, and were increased greatly upon the earth. . . ." In Ps. 47:9, *meʿōd* is used of "magnifying" and "exaltation": " . . . For the shields of the earth belong unto God; he is greatly exalted." The doubling of the word is a means of emphasizing its basic meaning, which is "very much": "And the waters prevailed exceedingly (NASB, "more and more") upon the earth . . . " (Gen. 7:19).

B. Noun.

meʿōd (מְאֹד, 3966), "might." This word is used substantively in the sequence "heart . . . soul . . . might": "And thou shalt love the Lord thy God with all thine heart, and with all thy soul, and with all thy might" (Deut. 6:5).

EYE

ʿayin (עַיִן, 5869), "eye; well; surface; appearance; spring." *ʿAyin* has cognates in Ugaritic, Akkadian, Aramaic, and other Semitic languages. It occurs about 866 times and in all periods of biblical Hebrew (5 times in biblical Aramaic).

First, the word represents the bodily part, "eye." In Gen. 13:10, *ʿayin* is used of the "human eye": "And Lot lifted up his eyes, and beheld all the plain of Jordan. . . ." It is also used of the "eyes" of animals (Gen. 30:41), idols (Ps. 115:5), and God (Deut. 11:12—anthropomorphism). The expression "between the eyes" means "on the forehead": "And it shall be for a sign unto thee upon thine hand, and for a memorial between thine eyes, that the Lord's law may be in thy mouth . . . " (Exod. 13:9). "Eyes" are used as typical of one's "weakness" or "hurt": "And it came to pass, that when Isaac was old, and his eyes were dim, so that he could not see, he called Esau his eldest son, and said . . . " (Gen. 27:1). The "apple of the eye" is the central component, the iris: "Keep me as the apple of the eye" (Ps. 17:8). "Eyes" might be a special feature of "beauty": "Now he was ruddy, and withal [fair of eyes], and goodly to look to" (1 Sam. 16:12).

ʿAyin is often used in connection with expressions of "seeing": "And, behold, your eyes see, and the eyes of my brother Benjamin, that it is my mouth that speaketh unto you" (Gen. 45:12). The expression "to lift up one's eyes" is explained by a verb following it: one lifts up his eyes to do something—whatever the verb stipulates (cf. Gen. 13:10). "Lifting up one's eyes" may also be an act expressing "desire," "longing," "devotion": "And it came to pass after these things, that his master's wife [looked with desire at] Joseph . . . " (Gen. 39:7). The "eyes" may be used in gaining or seeking a judgment, in the sense of "seeing intellectually," "making an evaluation," or "seeking an evaluation or proof of faithfulness": "And thou saidst unto thy servants, Bring him down unto me, that I may set mine eyes upon him" (Gen. 44:21).

"Eyes" sometimes show mental qualities, such as regret: "Also regard not [literally, "do not let your eye look with regret upon"] your stuff; for the good of all the land of Egypt is yours" (Gen. 45:20).

"Eyes" are used figuratively of mental and spiritual abilities, acts and states. So the "opening of the eyes" in Gen. 3:5 (the first occurrence) means to become autonomous by setting standards of good and evil for oneself. In passages such as Prov. 4:25, "eye" represents a moral faculty: "Let thine eyes look right on, and let thine eyelids look straight before thee." Prov. 23:6 uses the word of a moral state (literally, "evil eye"): "Eat thou not the bread of [a selfish man], neither desire thou his dainty meats." An individual may serve as a guide, or one's "eyes": "And he said, Leave us not, I pray thee; forasmuch as thou knowest how we are to encamp in the wilderness, and thou mayest be to us instead of eyes" (Num. 10:31).

The phrase, "in the eye of," means "in one's view or opinion": "And he went in unto Hagar, and she conceived: and when she saw that she had conceived, her mistress was despised in her eyes" (Gen. 16:4).

Another phrase, "from the eyes of," may signify that a thing or matter is "hidden" from one's knowledge: "And a man lie with her carnally, and it be hid from the eyes of her husband, and [she be undetected]..." (Num. 5:13).

In Exod. 10:5, the word represents the "visible surface of the earth": "And they shall cover the face of the earth, that one cannot be able to see the earth...." Lev. 13:5 uses 'ayin to represent "one's appearance": "And the priest shall look on him the seventh day: and behold, if the plague in his sight be at a stay [NASB, "if in his eyes the infection has not changed"]...." A "gleam or sparkle" is described in the phrase, "to give its eyes," in passages such as Prov.

23:31: "Look not thou upon the wine when it is red, when it giveth his color [gives its eyes] in the cup...."

'Ayin also represents a "spring" (literally, an "eye of the water"): "And the angel of the Lord found her by a spring [KJV, "fountain"] of water in the wilderness, by the spring [KJV, "fountain"] on the way to Shur" (Gen. 16:7).

ma'yān (מַעְיָן, 4599), "spring." This word appears 23 times in the Old Testament. In Lev. 11:36, ma'yān means "spring": "Nevertheless a fountain or pit, wherein there is plenty of water, shall be clean: but that which toucheth their carcase shall be unclean." Another example is found in Gen. 7:11: "In the six hundredth year of Noah's life, in the second month, ... the same day were all the fountains of the great deep broken up, and the windows of heaven were opened."

F

FACE

pānîm (פָּנִים, 6440), "face." This noun appears in biblical Hebrew about 2,100 times and in all periods, except when it occurs with the names of persons and places, it always appears in the plural. It is also attested in Ugaritic, Akkadian, Phoenician, Moabite, and Ethiopic.

In its most basic meaning, this noun refers to the "face" of something. First, it refers to the "face" of a human being: "And Abram fell on his face: and God talked with him..." (Gen. 17:3). In a more specific application, the word represents the look on one's face, or one's "countenance": "And Cain was very [angry], and his countenance fell" (Gen. 4:5). To pay something to someone's "face" is to pay it to him personally (Deut. 7:10); in such contexts, the word connotes the person himself. Pānîm can also be used of the surface or visible side of a thing, as in Gen. 1:2: "The Spirit of God moved upon the face of the waters." In other contexts, the word represents the "front side" of something: "And thou shalt couple five curtains by themselves, and six curtains by themselves, and shalt double the sixth curtain in the forefront of the tabernacle" (Exod. 26:9). When applied to time, the word (preceded by the preposition lᵉ) means "formerly": "The Horim also dwelt in Seir [formerly]... (Deut. 2:12).

This noun is sometimes used anthropomorphically of God; the Bible speaks of God as though He had a "face": "... For therefore I have seen thy face, as though I had seen the face of God" (Gen. 33:10). The Bible clearly teaches that God is a spiritual being and ought not to be depicted by an image or any likeness whatever (Exod. 20:4). Therefore, there was no image or likeness of God in the innermost sanctuary—only the ark of the covenant was there, and God spoke from above it (Exod. 25:22). The word pānîm, then, is used to identify the bread that was kept in the holy place. The KJV translates it as "the showbread," while the NASB renders "the bread of the Presence" (Num. 4:7). This bread was always kept in the presence of God.

FAITHFULNESS

A. Noun.

'ĕmûnāh (אֱמוּנָה, 530), "faithfulness." This word occurs in Punic as emanethi ("certainty"). In the Hebrew Old Testament, the noun occurs 49 times, mainly in the Book of Psalms (22 times). The first occurrence of the word refers to Moses' hands: "But Moses' hands were heavy; and they took a stone, and put it under him, and he sat thereon; and Aaron and Hur stayed up his hands, the one on the one side, and the other on the other side; and his hands were *steady* until the going down of the sun" (Exod. 17:12).

The basic meaning of *'ĕmûnāh* is "certainty" and "faithfulness." Man may show himself "faithful" in his relations with his fellow men (1 Sam. 26:23). But generally, the Person to whom one is "faithful" is the Lord Himself: "And he charged them, saying, Thus shall ye do in the fear of the Lord, faithfully, and with a perfect heart" (2 Chron. 19:9). The Lord has manifested His "faithfulness" to His people: "He is the Rock, his work is perfect: for all his ways are judgment: a God of truth and without iniquity, just and right is he" (Deut. 32:4). All his works reveal his "faithfulness" (Ps. 33:4). His commandments are an expression of his "faithfulness" (Ps. 119:86); those who seek them are found on the road of "faithfulness": "I have chosen the way of *truth:* thy judgments have I laid before me" (Ps. 119:30). The Lord looks for those who seek to do His will with all their hearts. Their ways are established and His blessing rests on them: "A faithful man shall abound with blessings: but he that maketh haste to be rich shall not be innocent" (Prov. 28:20). The assurance of the abundance of life is in the expression quoted in the New Testament (Rom. 1:17; Gal. 3:11) from Hab. 2:4: "Behold, his soul which is lifted up is not upright in him: but the just shall live by his faith."

The word *'ĕmûnāh* is synonymous with *ṣedeq* ("righteousness"—cf. Isa. 11:5), with *hesed* ("lovingkindness"—cf. Ps. 98:3, NASB), and with *mišpāṭ* ("justice"—cf. Jer. 5:1).

The relationship between God and Israel is best described by the word *hesed* ("love"); but as a synonym, *'ĕmûnāh* fits very well. Hosea portrays God's relation to Israel as a marriage and states God's promise of "faithfulness" to Israel: "And I will betroth thee unto me for ever; yea, I will betroth thee unto me in righteousness, and in judgment, and in loving-kindness, and in mercies. I will even betroth thee unto me in *faithfulness:* and thou shalt [acknowledge] the Lord" (Hos. 2:19–20). In these verses, the words "righteousness," "judgment" ("justice"), "loving-kindness," "mercies," and "faithfulness" bear out the conclusion that the synonyms for *'ĕmûnāh* are covenantal terms expressive of God's "faithfulness" and "love." The assurance of the covenant and the promises is established by God's nature; He is "faithful."

Man's acts (Prov. 12:22) and speech (12:17) must reflect his favored status with God. As in the marriage relationship, "faithfulness" is not optional. For the relation to be established, the two parties are required to respond to each other in "faithfulness." Isaiah and Jeremiah condemn the people for not being "faithful" to God: "Run ye to and fro through the streets of Jerusalem, and see now, and know, and seek in the broad places thereof, if ye can find a man, if there be any that executeth judgment, that seeketh the *truth;* and I will pardon [this city]" (Jer. 5:1; cf. Isa. 59:4; Jer. 7:28; 9:3).

Faithfulness will be established in the messianic era (Isa. 11:5). The prophetic expectation was fulfilled in Jesus Christ, as his contemporaries witnessed in Him God's grace (cf. *hesed*) and truth (cf. *'ĕmûnāh*): "No man hath seen God at any time; the only begotten Son, which is in the bosom of the Father, he hath declared him" (John 1:18). It is significant that John puts these two terms side by side, even as they are found together in the Old Testament.

The Septuagint translations are: *aletheia* ("truthfulness; dependability; uprightness; truth; reality") and *pistos* ("trustworthy; faithfulness; reliability; rest; confidence; faith"). The KJV gives these translations: "faithfulness; truth; set office; faithfully; faithful. "

B. Verb.

'āman (אָמַן, 539), "to be certain, enduring; to trust, believe." This root is found in Akkadian, Ugaritic, and Phoenician. In the Old Testament, the word occurs fewer than 100 times.

Three words are derived from this verb: *'āmēn* ("amen"—30 times; e.g., Ps. 106:48), *'ĕmet* ("true"—127 times; e.g., Isa. 38:18), and *'ĕmûnāh* ("faithfulness").

FALSEHOOD

šeqer (שֶׁקֶר, 8267), "falsehood; lie." The presence of this root is limited to Hebrew and Old Aramaic. The word *šeqer* occurs 113 times in the Old Testament. It is rare in all but the poetic and prophetic books, and even in these books its usage is concentrated in Psalms (24 times), Proverbs (20 times), and Jeremiah (37 times). The first occurrence is in Exod. 5:9: "Let there more work be laid upon the men, that they may labor therein: and let them not regard vain words [lies]."

In about thirty-five passages, *šeqer* describes the nature of "deceptive speech": "to speak" (Isa. 59:3), "to teach" (Isa. 9:15), "to prophesy" (Jer. 14:14), and "to lie" (Mic. 2:11). It may also indicate a "deceptive character," as expressed in one's acts: "to deal treacherously" (2 Sam. 18:13) and "to deal falsely" (Hos. 7:1).

Thus *šeqer* defines a way of life that goes contrary to the law of God. The psalmist, desirous of following God, prayed: "Remove from me the way of lying: and grant me thy law graciously. I have chosen the way of truth: thy judgments have I laid before me" (Ps. 119:29–

30; cf. vv. 104, 118, 128). Here we see the opposites: "falsehood" and "faithfulness." As "faithfulness" is a relational term, "falsehood" denotes "one's inability to keep faith" with what one has said or to respond positively to the faithfulness of another being.

The Old Testament saint was instructed to avoid "deception" and the liar: "Keep thee far from a false matter; and the innocent and righteous slay thou not: for I will not justify the wicked" (Exod. 23:7; cf. Prov. 13:5).

The Septuagint has these translations: *adikos/adikia* ("unjust; unrighteous; wrongdoing; wickedness") and *pseudes* ("falsehood; lie"). The KJV gives these meanings: "lie; falsehood; false; falsely."

FAMILY

mišpāḥāh (מִשְׁפָּחָה, 4940), "family; clan." A form of this Hebrew word occurs in Ugaritic and Punic, also with the meaning of "family" or "clan." The word is found in the Dead Sea Scrolls, as well as in Mishnaic and modern Hebrew. *Mišpāḥāh* occurs 300 times in the Hebrew Old Testament. The word is first used in Gen. 8:19: "Every beast, every creeping thing, and every fowl, and whatsoever creepeth upon the earth, after their *kinds*, went forth out of the ark."

The word is related to the verbal root *šiphāh*, but the verbal form is absent from the Old Testament. Another noun form is *peḥah* ("maidservant"), as in Gen. 16:2: "And Sarai said unto Abram ... I pray thee, go in unto my maid...."

The noun *mišpāḥāh* is used predominantly in the Pentateuch (as many as 154 times in Numbers) and in the historical books, but rarely in the poetical literature (5 times) and the prophetical writings.

All members of a group who were related by blood and who still felt a sense of consanguinity belonged to the "clan" or "the extended family." Saul argued that since he belonged to the least of the "clans," he had no right to the kingship (1 Sam. 9:21). This meaning determined the extent of Rahab's family that was spared from Jericho: " ... And they brought out all her *kindred*, and left them without the camp of Israel" (Josh. 6:23). So the "clan" was an important division within the "tribe." The Book of Numbers gives a census of the leaders and the numbers of the tribes according to the "families" (Num. 1–4; 26). In capital cases, where revenge was desired, the entire clan might be taken: "And, behold, the whole family is risen against thine handmaid, and they said, Deliver him that smote his brother, that we may kill

him, for the life of his brother whom he slew; and we will destroy the heir also: and so they shall quench my coal which is left, and shall not leave to my husband neither name nor remainder upon the earth" (2 Sam. 14:7).

A further extension of the meaning "division" or "clan" is the idiomatic usage of "class" or "group," such as "the families" of the animals that left the ark (Gen. 8:19) or the "families" of the nations (Ps. 22:28; 96:7; cf. Gen. 10:5). Even God's promise to Abraham had reference to all the nations: "And I will bless them that bless thee, and curse him that curseth thee: and in thee shall all families of the earth be blessed" (Gen. 12:3).

The narrow meaning of *mišpāḥāh* is similar to our usage of "family" and similar to the meaning of the word in modern Hebrew. Abraham sent his servant to his relatives in Padan-aram to seek a wife for Isaac (Gen. 24:38). The law of redemption applied to the "close relatives in a family": "After that he is sold he may be redeemed again; one of his brethren may redeem him: Either his uncle, or his uncle's son, may redeem him, or any that is nigh of kin unto him of his family may redeem him; or if he be able, he may redeem himself" (Lev. 25:48–49).

In the Septuagint, several words are given as a translation: *demos* ("people; populace; crowd"), *phule* ("tribe; nation; people"), and *patria* ("family; clan"). The KJV translates *mišpāḥāh* with "family; kindred; kind." Most versions keep the translation "family"; but instead of "kindred" and "kind," some read "relative" (NASB) or "clan."

FAMINE

A. Noun.

rā'āb (רָעָב, 7458), "famine; hunger." This word appears about 101 times and in all periods of biblical Hebrew. *Rā'āb* means "hunger" as opposed to "thirst": "Therefore shalt thou serve thine enemies which the Lord shall send against thee, in hunger, and in thirst, and in nakedness, and in want of all things ... " (Deut. 28:48).

Another meaning of the word is "famine," or the lack of food in an entire geographical area: "And there was a famine in the land: and Abram went down into Egypt ... " (Gen. 12:10—the first occurrence). God used a "famine" as a means of judgment (Jer. 5:12), of warning (1 Kings 17:1), of correction (2 Sam. 21:1), or of punishment (Jer. 14:12), and the "famine" was always under divine control, being planned and used by Him. *Rā'āb* was also used to picture the "lack of God's word" (Amos 8:11; cf. Deut. 8:3).

B. Verb.

rā'ēb (רָעֵב, 7456), "to be hungry, suffer famine." This verb, which appears in the Old Testament 14 times, has cognates in Ugaritic (*rgb*), Arabic, and Ethiopic. The first biblical occurrence is in Gen. 41:55: "And when all the land of Egypt was famished. . . . "

C. Adjective.

rā'ēb (רָעֵב, 7456, 7457), "hungry." This word appears as an adjective 19 times. The first biblical occurrence is in 1 Sam. 2:5: " . . . And they that were hungry ceased: . . . "

FAR

rāḥaq (רָחַק, 7368), "far." A common Semitic term, this word was known in ancient Akkadian and Ugaritic long before the Hebrew of the Old Testament. *Rāḥaq* is a common word in modern Hebrew as well. The word is used about 55 times in the Hebrew Old Testament and it occurs for the first time in Gen. 21:16.

Rāḥaq is used to express "distance" of various types. It may be "distance" from a place (Deut. 12:21), as when Job felt that his friends kept themselves "aloof" from him (Job 30:10). Sometimes the word expresses "absence" altogether: " . . . The comforter that should relieve my soul is far from me . . . " (Lam. 1:16). "To be distant" was also "to abstain": "Keep thee far from a false matter" (Exod. 23:7).

Sometimes *rāḥaq* implies the idea of "exile": " . . . The Lord [removes] men far away" (Isa. 6:12). "To make the ends of the land distant" is "to extend the boundaries": " . . . thou hast increased the [borders of the land]" (Isa. 26:15).

FATHER

'āb (אָב, 1), "father; grandfather; forefather; ancestor." Cognates of this word occur in Ugaritic, Akkadian, Phoenician, and other Semitic languages. Biblical Hebrew attests it about 1,120 times and in all periods.

Basically, *'āb* relates to the familial relationship represented by the word "father." This is the word's significance in its first biblical appearance: "Therefore shall a man leave his father and his mother, and shall cleave unto his wife . . . " (Gen. 2:24). In poetical passages, the word is sometimes paralleled to *'ēm*, "mother": "I have said to corruption, Thou art my father: to the worm, Thou art my mother, and my sister" (Job 17:14). The word is also used in conjunction with "mother" to represent one's parents (Lev. 19:3). But unlike the word *'ēm*, *'āb* is never used of animals.

'Āb also means "grandfather" and/or "great-grandfather," as in Gen. 28:13: "I am the Lord God of Abraham thy [grand]father, and the God of Isaac. . . . " Such progenitors on one's mother's side were called "thy mother's father" (Gen. 28:2). This noun may be used of any one of the entire line of men from whom a given individual is descended: "But he [Elijah] himself went a day's journey into the wilderness, and came and sat down under a juniper tree: and he requested for himself that he might die; and said, It is enough; now, O Lord, take away my life; for I am not better than my fathers" (1 Kings 19:4). In such use, the word may refer to the first man, a "forefather," a clan (Jer. 35:6), a tribe (Josh. 19:47), a group with a special calling (1 Chron. 24:19), a dynasty (1 Kings 15:3), or a nation (Josh. 24:3). Thus, "father" does not necessarily mean the man who directly sired a given individual.

This noun sometimes describes the adoptive relationship, especially when it is used of the "founder of a class or station," such as a trade: "And Adah bare Jabal: he was the *father* of such as dwell in tents, and of such as have cattle" (Gen. 4:20).

'Āb can be a title of respect, usually applied to an older person, as when David said to Saul: "Moreover, my father, see, yea, see the skirt of thy robe in my hand . . . " (1 Sam. 24:11). The word is also applied to teachers: "And Elisha saw it, and he cried, My father, my father, the chariot of Israel, and the horsemen thereof . . . " (2 Kings 2:12). In 2 Kings 6:21, the word is applied to the prophet Elisha and in Judg. 17:10, to a priest; this word is also a title of respect when used of "one's husband": "Wilt thou not from this time cry unto me, My father, thou art the guide of my youth?" (Jer. 3:4). In Gen. 45:8, the noun is used of an "advisor": "So now it was not you that sent me hither, but God: and he hath made me a father [advisor] to Pharaoh, and lord of all his house, and a ruler throughout all the land of Egypt." In each case, the one described as "father" occupied a position or status and received the honor due to a "father."

In conjunction with *bayit* ("house"), the word *'āb* may mean "family": "In the tenth day of this month they shall take to them every man a lamb, according to the house of their fathers . . . " (Exod. 12:3). Sometimes the plural of the word used by itself can represent "family": " . . . These are the heads of the fathers [households] of the Levites according to their families" (Exod. 6:25).

God is described as the "father" of Israel (Deut. 32:6). He is the One who begot and protected them, the One they should revere and obey. Mal. 2:10 tells us that God is the "father" of all people. He is especially the "protector" or "father" of the fatherless: "A father of the fatherless, and a judge of the widows, is God in his holy habitation" (Ps. 68:5). As the "father" of a king, God especially aligns Himself to that man and his kingdom: "I will be his father, and he shall be my son. If he commit iniquity, I will chasten him with the rod of men, and with the stripes of the children of men" (2 Sam. 7:14). Not every king was a son of God—only those whom He adopted. In a special sense, the perfect King was God's adopted Son: "I will declare the decree: the Lord hath said unto me, Thou art my Son; this day have I begotten thee" (Ps. 2:7). The extent, power, and duration of His kingdom are guaranteed by the Father's sovereignty (cf. Ps. 2:8–9). On the other hand, one of the Messiah's enthronement names is "Eternal Father": " . . . And his name shall be called Wonderful, Counselor, The mighty God, The everlasting Father, The Prince of Peace" (Isa. 9:6).

FAVOR

A. Noun.

rāṣôn (רָצוֹן, 7522), "favor; goodwill; acceptance; will; desire; pleasure." The 56 occurrences of this word are scattered throughout Old Testament literature.

Rāṣôn represents a concrete reaction of the superior to an inferior. When used of God, *rāṣôn* may represent that which is shown in His blessings: "And for the precious things of the earth and fullness thereof, and for the *good will* of him that dwelt in the bush" (Deut. 33:16). Thus Isaiah speaks of the day, year, or time of divine "favor"—in other words, the day of the Lord when all the blessings of the covenant shall be heaped upon God's people (Isa. 49:8; 58:5; 61:2). In wisdom literature, this word is used in the sense of "what men can bestow": "He that diligently seeketh good procureth favor: but he that seeketh mischief, it shall come unto him" (Prov. 11:27). In Prov. 14:35, *rāṣôn* refers to what a king can or will do for someone he likes.

This word represents the position one enjoys before a superior who is favorably disposed toward him. This nuance is used only of God and frequently in a cultic context: " . . . And it [the plate engraved with "holy to the Lord"] shall be always upon his [the high priest's] forehead, that they may be accepted before the Lord" (Exod. 28:38). Being "accepted" means that God subjectively feels well disposed toward the petitioner.

Rāṣôn also signifies a voluntary or arbitrary decision. Ezra told the people of Israel to do the "will" of God, to repent and observe the law of Moses (Ezra 10:11). This law was dictated by God's own nature; His nature led Him to be concerned for the physical well-being of His people. Ultimately, His laws were highly personal; they were simply what God wanted His people to be and do. Thus the psalmist confessed his delight in doing God's "will," or His law (Ps. 40:8).

When a man does according to his own "will," he does "what he desires": "I saw the ram pushing westward, and northward, and southward; so that no beasts might stand before him, neither was there any that could deliver out of his hand; but he did according to his will, and became great" (Dan. 8:4). In Ps. 145:16, the word *rāṣôn* means "one's desire" or "what one wants" (cf. Esth. 1:8). This emphasis is found in Gen. 49:6 (the first occurrence): " . . . And in their self-will they [brought disaster upon themselves]."

B. Verb.

rāṣāh (רָצָה, 7521), "to be pleased with or favorable to, be delighted with, be pleased to, make friends with; be graciously received; make oneself favored." This verb, which occurs 50 times in the Old Testament, has cognates in Ugaritic, Aramaic, Syriac, and Arabic. Gen. 33:10 contains one appearance of this word: " . . . thou wast pleased with me."

TO FEAR

A. Verb.

yārē' (יָרֵא, 3372), "to be afraid, stand in awe, fear." This verb occurs in Ugaritic and Hebrew (both biblical and post-biblical). The Bible attests it approximately 330 times and in all periods.

Basically, this verb connotes the psychological reaction of "fear." *Yārē'* may indicate being afraid of something or someone. Jacob prayed: "Deliver me, I pray thee, from the hand of my brother, from the hand of Esau: for I fear him, lest he will come and smite me, and the mother with the children" (Gen. 32:11).

Used of a person in an exalted position, *yārē'* connotes "standing in awe." This is not simple fear, but reverence, whereby an individual recognizes the power and position of the individual revered and renders him proper respect. In this sense, the word may imply submission to a proper ethical relationship to God; the angel of the Lord told Abraham: " . . . I know that thou fearest God, seeing thou hast not withheld thy son, thine only son from me" (Gen. 22:12). The verb can be used absolutely to refer to the heavenly and holy attributes of something or someone. So Jacob said of Bethel: "How [awesome] is this place! this is none other but the house of God, and this is the gate of heaven" (Gen. 28:17). The people who were delivered from Egypt saw God's great power, "feared the Lord, and believed the Lord, and his servant Moses" (Exod. 14:31). There is more involved here than mere psychological fear. The people also showed proper "honor" ("reverence") for God and "stood in awe of" Him and of His servant, as their song demonstrates (Exod. 15). After experiencing the thunder, lightning flashes, sound of the trumpet, and smoking mountain, they were "afraid" and drew back; but Moses told them not to be afraid, "for God is come to prove you, and that his fear may be before your faces, that ye sin not" (Exod. 20:20). In this passage, the word represents "fear" or "dread" of the Lord. This sense is also found when God says, "fear not" (Gen. 15:1).

Yārē' can be used absolutely (with no direct object), meaning "to be afraid." Adam told God: "...I was afraid, because I was naked; and I hid myself" (Gen. 3:10—the first occurrence). One may be "afraid" to do something, as when Lot "feared to dwell in Zoar" (Gen. 19:30).

B. Nouns.

môrā' (מוֹרָא, 4172), "fear." The noun *môrā'*, which appears 12 times, is used exclusively of the fear of being before a superior kind of being. Usually it is used to describe the reaction evoked in men by God's mighty works of destruction and sovereignty (Deut. 4:24). Hence, the word represents a very strong "fear" or "terror." In the singular, this word emphasizes the divine acts themselves. *Môrā'* may suggest the reaction of animals to men (Gen. 9:2) and of the nations to conquering Israel (Deut. 11:25).

yir'āh (יִרְאָה, 3374), "fear; reverence." The noun *yir'āh* appears 45 times in the Old Testament. It may mean "fear" of men (Deut. 2:25), of things (Isa. 7:25), of situations (Jonah 1:10), and of God (Jonah 1:12); it may also mean "reverence" of God (Gen. 20:11).

FEAST

hag (חַג, 2282), "feast; festal sacrifice." Cognates of this noun appear in Aramaic, Syriac, and Arabic. Biblical Hebrew attests it about 62 times and in all periods, except in the wisdom literature.

This word refers especially to a "feast observed by a pilgrimage." That is its meaning in its first biblical occurrence, when Moses said to Pharaoh: "We will go with our young and with our old, with our sons and with our daughters, with our flocks and with our herds will we go; for we must hold a feast unto the Lord" (Exod.

10:9). *Hag* (or *hāg*) usually represents Israel's three annual "pilgrimage feasts," which were celebrated with processions and dances. These special feasts are distinguished from the sacred seasons ("festal assemblies"—Ezek. 45:17), the new moon festivals, and the Sabbaths (Hos. 2:11).

There are two unique uses of *hag*. First, Aaron proclaimed a "feast to the Lord" at the foot of Mt. Sinai. This "feast" involved no pilgrimage but was celebrated with burnt offerings, communal meals, singing, and dancing. The whole matter was displeasing to God (Exod. 32:5–7).

In two passages, *hag* represents the "victim sacrificed to God" (perhaps during one of the three annual sacrifices): "...Bind the [festal] sacrifice with cords, even unto the horns of the altar" (Ps. 118:27; cf. Exod. 23:18).

FIELD

śādeh (שָׂדֶה, 7704), "field; country; domain [of a town]." *Śādeh* has cognates in Akkadian, Phoenician, Ugaritic, and Arabic. It appears in biblical Hebrew about 320 times and in all periods.

This word often represents the "open field" where the animals roam wild. That is its meaning in its first biblical appearance: "And every plant of the field before it was in the earth, and every herb of the field before it grew: for the Lord God had not caused it to rain upon the earth..." (Gen. 2:5). Thus, "Esau was a cunning hunter, a man of the field; and Jacob was a plain man, dwelling in tents" (Gen. 25:27). A city in the "open field" was unfortified; David wisely asked Achish for such a city, showing that he did not intend to be hostile (1 Sam. 27:5). Dwelling in an unfortified city meant exposure to attack.

Śādeh represents the "fields surrounding a town" (Josh. 21:12; cf. Neh. 11:25). "Arable land," land that is either cultivated or to be cultivated, is also signified by *śādeh:* "If it be your mind that I should bury my dead out of my sight; hear me, and entreat for me to Ephron the son of Zohar, that he may give me the cave of Machpelah, which he hath, which is in the end of his field..." (Gen. 23:8–9). The entirety of one's cultivated or pasture land is called his "field": "And the king [David] said unto him [Mephibosheth], Why speakest thou any more of thy matters? I have said, Thou and Ziba divide the land [previously owned by Saul]" (2 Sam. 19:29).

Sometimes particular sections of land are identified by name: "And after this, Abraham buried Sarah his wife in the cave of the field of Machpelah before Mamre . . . " (Gen. 23:19).

śāday (שָׂדַי, 7704), "open field." *Śāday* occurs 12 times, only in poetical passages. Deut. 32:13 is the first biblical appearance: "He made him ride on the high places of the earth, that he might eat the increase of the fields; . . . "

TO FIGHT

A. Verb.

lāham (לָחַם, 3898), "to fight, do battle, engage in combat." This word is found in all periods of Hebrew, as well as in ancient Ugaritic. It occurs in the text of the Hebrew Bible more than 170 times. *Lāham* appears first in Exod. 1:10, where the Egyptian pharaoh expresses his fears that the Israelite slaves will multiply and join an enemy "to fight" against the Egyptians.

While the word is commonly used in the context of "armies engaged in pitched battle" against each other (Num. 21:23; Josh. 10:5; Judg. 11:5), it is also used to describe "single, hand-to-hand combat" (1 Sam. 17:32–33). Frequently, God "fights" the battle for Israel (Deut. 20:4). Instead of swords, words spoken by a lying tongue are often used "to fight" against God's servants (Ps. 109:2).

In folk etymology, *lāham* is often connected with *lehem*, the Hebrew term for "bread," on the contention that wars are fought for bread. There is, however, no good basis for such etymology.

B. Noun.

milhāmāh (מִלְחָמָה, 4421), "battle; war." This noun occurs more than 300 times in the Old Testament, indicating how large a part military experience and terminology played in the life of the ancient Israelites. Gen. 14:8 is an early occurrence of *milhāmāh:* "And there went out the king of Sodom, and the king of Gomorrah, . . . and they joined battle with them in the vale of Siddim."

TO FILL

A. Verb.

mālē' (מָלֵא, 4390), "to fill, fulfill, overflow, ordain, endow." This verb occurs in all Semitic languages (including biblical Aramaic) and in all periods. Biblical Hebrew attests it about 250 times.

Basically, *mālē'* means "to be full" in the sense of having something done to one. In 2 Kings 4:6, the word implies "to fill up": "And it came to pass, when the vessels were full, that she said. . . . " The verb is sometimes used figuratively as in Gen. 6:13, when God noted that "the earth is filled with violence."

Used transitively, this verb means the act or state of "filling something." In Gen. 1:22 (the first occurrence of the word), God told the sea creatures to "penetrate" the waters thoroughly but not exhaustively: "Be fruitful, and multiply, and fill the waters in the seas." *Mālē'* can also mean "to fill up" in an exhaustive sense: " . . . And the glory of the Lord filled the tabernacle" (Exod. 40:34). In this sense an appetite can be "filled up," "satiated," or "satisfied."

Mālē' is sometimes used in the sense "coming to an end" or "to be filled up," to the full extent of what is expected. For example, in 1 Kings 2:27 we read: "So Solomon thrust out Abiathar from being priest unto the Lord; that he might *fulfill* the word of the Lord, which he spake concerning the house of Eli in Shiloh." This constitutes a proof of the authority of the divine Word.

In a different but related nuance, the verb signifies "to confirm" someone's word. Nathan told Bathsheba: "Behold, while thou yet talkest there with the king, I also will come in after thee, and confirm thy words" (1 Kings 1:14). This verb is used to signify filling something to the full extent of what is necessary, in the sense of being "successfully completed": "When her days to be delivered were fulfilled . . . " (Gen. 25:24). This may also mean "to bring to an end"; so God tells Isaiah: "Speak ye comfortably to Jerusalem, and cry unto her, that her warfare is *accomplished* . . . " (Isa. 40:2).

Mālē' is used of "filling to overflowing"—not just filling up to the limits of something, but filling so as to go beyond its limits: "For Jordan overfloweth all his banks all the time of harvest" (Josh. 3:15).

A special nuance appears when the verb is used with "heart"; in such cases, it means "to presume." King Ahasuerus asked Esther: "Who is he, and where is he, that durst presume [literally, "fill his heart"] to do so?" (Esth. 7:5). To call out "fully" is to cry aloud, as in Jer. 4:5.

The word often has a special meaning in conjunction with "hand." *Mālē'* can connote "endow" ("fill one's hand"), as in Exod. 28:3: "And thou shalt speak unto all that are wisehearted, whom I have [endowed] with the spirit of wisdom. . . . " In Judg. 17:5, "to fill one's hand" is "to consecrate" someone to priestly service. A similar idea appears in Ezek. 43:26, where no literal hand is filled with anything, but the phrase is a technical term for "consecration": "Seven days shall they [make atonement for] the altar and purify it; and they shall consecrate themselves." This phrase is used not only of setting someone or something aside for special religious or cultic use, but of formally installing someone with the authority and responsibility to fulfill a cultic function (i.e., to be a priest). So God commands concerning Aaron and his sons: "And thou ... shalt anoint them, and consecrate them, and sanctify them, that they may minister unto me in the priest's office" (Exod. 28:41).

In military contexts, "to fill one's hand" is to prepare for battle. This phrase may be used of "becoming armed," as in Jer. 51:11: "Sharpen the arrows, fill the quivers." (KJV, "Make bright the arrows; gather the shields.") In a fuller sense, the phrase may signify the step immediately before shooting arrows: "And Jehu drew [literally, "filled his hand with"] a bow with his full strength ... " (2 Kings 9:24). It can also signify "being armed," or having weapons on one's person: "But the man that shall touch them must be [armed] with iron and the staff of a spear ... " (2 Sam. 23:7).

B. Adjective.

mālē' (מָלֵא, 4390), "full." The adjective *mālē'* appears 67 times. The basic meaning of the word is "full" or "full of" (Ruth 1:21; Deut. 6:11).

TO FIND

māṣā' (מָצָא, 4672), "to find, meet, get." This word is found in every branch of the Semitic languages (including biblical Aramaic) and in all periods. It is attested both in biblical (about 455 times) and post-biblical Hebrew.

Māṣā' refers to "finding" someone or something that is lost or misplaced, or "finding" where it is. The thing may be found as the result of a purposeful search, as when the Sodomites were temporarily blinded by Lot's visitors and were not able to "find" the door to his house (Gen. 19:11). In a very similar usage, the dove sent forth by Noah searched for a spot to land and was unable to "find" it (Gen. 8:9). On other occasions, the location of something or someone may be found without an intentional search, as when Cain said: "[Whoever] findeth me shall slay me" (Gen. 4:14).

Māṣā' may connote not only "finding" a subject in a location, but "finding something" in an abstract sense. This idea is demonstrated clearly by Gen. 6:8: "But Noah found grace in the eyes of the Lord." He found—"received"—something he did not seek. This sense also includes "finding" something one has sought in a spiritual or mental sense: "Mine hand had gotten much ... " (Job 31:25). Laban tells Jacob: " ... If I have found favor in thine eyes, [stay with me] ... " (Gen. 30:27). Laban is asking Jacob for a favor that he is seeking in an abstract sense.

Māṣā' can also mean "to discover." God told Abraham: "If I find in Sodom fifty righteous within the city, then I will spare all the place for their sakes" (Gen. 18:26). This same emphasis appears in the first biblical occurrence of the word: " ... But for Adam there was not found a help meet for him" (Gen. 2:20). As noted earlier, there can be a connotation of the unintentional here, as when the Israelites "found" a man gathering wood on the Sabbath (Num. 15:32). Another special nuance is "to find out," in the sense of "gaining knowledge about." For example, Joseph's brothers said: "God hath found out the iniquity of thy servants ... " (Gen. 44:16).

Māṣā' sometimes suggests "being under the power" of something, in a concrete sense. David told Abishai: " ... Take thou thy lord's servants, and pursue after him, lest he get him fenced cities, and escape us" (2 Sam. 20:6). The idea is that Sheba would "find," enter, and defend himself in fortified cities. So to "find" them could be to "take them over." This usage appears also in an abstract sense. Judah told Joseph: "For how shall I go up to my father, and the lad be not with me? lest peradventure I see the evil that shall come on my father" (Gen. 44:34). The word *māṣā'*, therefore, can mean not only to "find" something, but to "obtain" it as one's own: "Then Isaac sowed in that land, and received in the same year ... " (Gen. 26:12).

Infrequently, the word implies movement in a direction until one arrives at a destination; thus it is related to the Ugaritic root meaning "reach" or "arrive" (*mṣ'*). This sense is found in Job 11:7: "Canst thou by searching find out God?" (cf. 1 Sam. 23:17). In a somewhat different nuance, this meaning appears in Num. 11:22: "Shall the flocks and the herds be slain for them, to *suffice* them?"

FIRE

'ēš (אֵשׁ, 784), "fire." Cognates of this word occur in Ugaritic, Akkadian, Aramaic, and Ethiopic. The 378 occurrences of this word in biblical Hebrew are scattered throughout its periods.

In its first biblical appearance this word, *'ēš*, represents God's presence as "a torch of fire": "And it came to pass, that, when the sun went down, and it was dark, behold a smoking furnace, and a [flaming torch] ... " (Gen. 15:17). "Fire" was the instrument by which an offering was transformed into smoke, whose ascending heavenward symbolized God's reception of the offering (Lev. 9:24). God also consumed people with the "fire of judgment" (Num. 11:1; Ps.

89:46). Various things were to be burnt as a sign of total destruction and divine judgment (Exod. 32:20).

"Fire" often attended God's presence in theophanies (Exod. 3:2). Thus He is sometimes called a "consuming fire" (Exod. 24:17).

The noun *'iššeh*, meaning "an offering made by fire," is derived from *'ēš*.

FIRSTBORN

beˈkôr (בְּכוֹר, 1060), "firstborn." *Beˈkôr* appears about 122 times in biblical Hebrew and in all periods. The word represents the "firstborn" individual in a family (Gen. 25:13); the word can also represent the "firstborn" of a nation, collectively (Num. 3:46). The plural form of the word appears occasionally (Neh. 10:36); in this passage, the word is applied to animals. In other passages, the singular form of *beˈkôr* signifies a single "firstborn" animal (Lev. 27:26; KJV, "firstling") or collectively the "firstborn" of a herd (Exod. 11:5).

The "oldest" or "firstborn" son (Exod. 6:14) had special privileges within the family. He received the special family blessing, which meant spiritual and social leadership and a double portion of the father's possessions—or twice what all the other sons received (Deut. 21:17). He could lose this blessing through misdeeds (Gen. 35:22) or by selling it (Gen. 25:29–34). God claimed all Israel and all their possessions as His own. As a token of this claim, Israel was to give Him all its "firstborn" (Exod. 13:1–16). The animals were to be sacrificed, redeemed, or killed, while the male children were redeemed either by being replaced with Levites or by the payment of a redemption price (Num. 3:40ff.).

Israel was God's "firstborn"; it enjoyed a privileged position and blessings over all other nations (Exod. 4:22; Jer. 31:9).

The "first-born of death" is an idiom meaning a deadly disease (Job 18:13); the "first-born of the poor" is the poorest class of people (Isa. 14:30).

bikkûrîm (בִּכּוּרִים, 1061), "first fruits." This noun appears 16 times. The "first grain and fruit" harvested was to be offered to God (Num. 28:26) in recognition of God's ownership of the land and His sovereignty over nature. Bread of the "first fruits" was bread made of the first harvest grain, presented to God at Pentecost (Lev. 23:20). The "day of the first fruits" was Pentecost (Num. 28:26).

TO FLEE

bārah (בָּרַח, 1272), "to flee, pass through." Some scholars see this word, which is used throughout the history of the Hebrew language,

reflected in ancient Ugaritic as well. *Bārah* occurs about 60 times in the Hebrew Bible. The word first appears in Gen. 16:6, where it is said that Hagar "fled from her [Sarah's] face" as a result of Sarah's harsh treatment.

Men may "flee" from many things or situations. David "fled" from Naioth in Ramah in order to come to Jonathan (1 Sam. 20:1). Sometimes it is necessary to "flee" from weapons (Job 20:24). In describing flight from a person, the Hebrew idiom "from the presence of" (literally, "from the face of") is often used (Gen. 16:6, 8; 31:27; 35:1, 7).

In its figurative use, the word describes days "fleeing" away (Job 9:25) or frail man "fleeing" like a shadow (Job 14:2). A rather paradoxical use is found in Song of Sol. 8:14, in which "flee" must mean "come quickly": "Make haste [literally, "flee"], my beloved, and be thou like to a gazelle...."

nûs (נוּס, 5127), "to flee, escape, take flight, depart." This term is found primarily in biblical Hebrew, where it occurs some 160 times. *Nûs* occurs for the first time in Gen. 14:10, where it is used twice to describe the "fleeing" of the kings of Sodom and Gomorrah. *Nûs* is the common word for "fleeing" from an enemy or danger (Gen. 39:12; Num. 16:34; Josh. 10:6). The word is also used to describe "escape," as in Jer. 46:6 and Amos 9:1. In a figurative use, the word describes the "disappearance" of physical strength (Deut. 34:7), the "fleeing" of evening shadows (Song of Sol. 2:17), and the "fleeing away" of sorrow (Isa. 35:10).

FLESH

bāśār (בָּשָׂר, 1320), "flesh; meat; male sex organ." Cognates of this word appear in Ugaritic, Arabic, and Aramaic. Biblical Hebrew attests it about 270 times and in all periods.

The word means the "meaty part plus the skin" of men: "And the Lord God caused a deep sleep to fall upon Adam, and he slept: and he took one of his ribs, and closed up the flesh instead thereof" (Gen. 2:21—the first occurrence). This word can also be applied to the "meaty part" of animals (Deut. 14:8). Gen. 41:2 speaks of seven cows, sleek and "fat of flesh." In Num. 11:33, *bāśār* means the meat or "flesh" of the quail that Israel was still chewing. Thus the word means "flesh," whether living or dead.

Bāśār often means the "edible part" of animals. Eli's sons did not know God's law concerning the priests' portion, so "when any man offered sacrifice, the priest's [Eli's] servant came, while the flesh was [boiling], with a [three-pronged fork] in his hand" (1 Sam. 2:13). However, they insisted that "before they burnt the fat...., Give flesh to roast for the priest; for he will not have [boiled] flesh of thee, but raw" (literally, "living"—1 Sam. 2:15). *Bāśār*, then, represents edible animal "flesh" or "meat," whether cooked (Dan. 10:3) or uncooked. The word sometimes refers to "meat" that one is forbidden to eat (cf. Exod. 21:28).

This word may represent a part of the body. At some points, the body is viewed as consisting of two components, "flesh" and bones: "This is now bone of my bones, and flesh of my flesh: she shall be called Woman, because she was taken out of Man" (Gen. 2:23). That part of the "fleshly" element known as the foreskin was to be removed by circumcision (Gen. 17:11). In other passages, the elements of the body are the "flesh," the skin, and the bones (Lam. 3:4). Num. 19:5 mentions the "flesh," hide, blood, and refuse of a heifer. In Job 10:11, we read: "Thou hast clothed me with skin and flesh, and hast [knit] me with bones and sinews."

Flesh sometimes means "blood relative": "And Laban said to him [Jacob], Surely thou art my bone and my flesh" (Gen. 29:14). The phrase "your flesh" or "our flesh" standing alone may bear the same meaning: "Come, and let us sell him to the Ishmaelites, and let not our hand be upon him; for he is our brother and our flesh" (Gen. 37:27). The phrase *šᵉ'ēr bāśār* is rendered "blood relative" (Lev. 18:6; KJV, "near of kin").

About 50 times, "flesh" represents the "physical aspect" of man or animals as contrasted with the spirit, soul, or heart (the nonphysical aspect). In the case of men, this usage appears in Num. 16:22: "O God, the God of the spirits of all flesh, shall one man sin, and wilt thou be wroth with all the congregation?" In such passages, then, *bāśār* emphasizes the "visible and structural part" of man or animal.

In a few passages, the word appears to mean "skin," or the part of the body that is seen: "By reason of the voice of my groaning my bones cleave to my skin" (Ps. 102:5; 119:120). In passages such as Lev. 13:2, the ideas "flesh" and "skin" are clearly distinguished.

Bāśār sometimes represents the "male sex organ": "Speak unto the children of Israel, and say unto them, When any man hath a running issue out of his flesh [NASB, "body"], because of his issue he is unclean" (Lev. 15:2).

The term "all flesh" has several meanings. It means "all mankind" in Deut. 5:26: "For who is there of all flesh, that hath heard the voice of the living God...?" In another place, this phrase refers to "all living creatures within the cosmos," or all men and animals (Gen. 6:17).

FLOCK

ṣō'n (צֹאן, 6629), "flock; small cattle; sheep; goats." A similar word is found in Akkadian, Aramaic, and Syriac, and in the Tel Amarna tablets. In Hebrew, *ṣō'n* kept its meaning in all stages of the development of the language. The word occurs 273 times in the Hebrew Old Testament, with its first occurrence in Gen. 4:2. The word is not limited to any period of Hebrew history or to any type of literature. The Book of Genesis, with the narratives on the patriarchs in their pastoral setting, has the greatest frequency of usage (about 60 times).

The primary meaning of *ṣō'n* is "small cattle," to be distinguished from *bāqār* ("herd"). The word may refer to "sheep" only (1 Sam. 25:2) or to both "sheep and goats": "So shall my righteousness answer for me in time to come, when it shall come for my hire before thy face: every one that is not speckled and spotted among the goats, and brown among the sheep, that shall be counted stolen with me" (Gen. 30:33). The "flock" was an important economic factor in the ancient Near East. The animals were eaten (1 Sam. 14:32; cf. Ps. 44:11), shorn for their wool (Gen. 31:19), and milked (Deut. 32:14). They were also offered as a sacrifice, as when Abel sacrificed a firstling of his "flock" (Gen. 4:4).

In the metaphorical usage of *ṣō'n*, the imagery of a "multitude" may apply to people: "As the holy flock, as the flock of Jerusalem in her solemn feasts; so shall the waste cities be filled with flocks of men: and they shall know that I am the Lord" (Ezek. 36:38). God is viewed as the shepherd of His "flock," God's people: "Know ye that the Lord he is God: it is he that hath made us, and not we ourselves; we are his people, and the sheep of his pasture" (Ps. 100:3; cf. Ps. 23; 79:13; Mic. 7:14). In a period of oppression, the psalmist compared God's people to "sheep for the slaughter" (Ps. 44:22) and prayed for God's deliverance.

People without a leader were compared to a "flock" without a shepherd (1 Kings 22:17; cf. Zech. 10:2; 13:7). Jeremiah viewed the Judeans as having been guided astray by their shepherds, or leaders (Jer. 50:6). Similarly, Isaiah wrote: "All we like sheep have gone astray; we have turned every one to his own way; and the Lord hath laid on him the iniquity of us all" (Isa. 53:6).

The prophetic promise pertains to God's renewed blessing on the remnant of the "flock": "And I will gather the remnant of my flock out of all countries whither I have driven them, and will bring them again to their folds; and they shall be fruitful and increase" (Jer. 23:3). This would come to pass as the Messiah ("the Branch of David") will establish His rule over the people (vv. 5–6). This idea is also expressed by Ezekiel: "And I will set up one shepherd over them, and he shall feed them, even my servant David; he shall feed them, and he shall be their shepherd. And I the Lord will be their God, and my servant David a prince among them; I the Lord have spoken it" (Ezek. 34:23–24).

The Septuagint gives the following translations: *probaton* ("sheep") and *poimnion* ("flock"). The KJV gives these senses: "flocks; sheep; cattle."

FOLLOWING

'ahēr (אַחֵר, 312), "following; different; other." This word occurs about 166 times and in all periods of biblical Hebrew.

The first meaning of this word is temporal, and is seen in Gen. 17:21: "But my covenant will I establish with Isaac, which Sarah shall bear unto thee at this set time in the *next* year" (i.e., the year "following"). The first biblical occurrence of the word is in Gen. 4:25: "And Adam [had relations with] his wife again; and she bare a son, and called his name Seth: For God, said she, hath appointed me *another* seed instead of Abel. . . . "

This meaning of "different" or "another" also appears in Lev. 27:20: "And if he will not redeem the field, or if he have sold the field to another man, it shall not be redeemed any more." In Isa. 28:11, *'ahēr* defines tongue or language; hence it should be understood as "foreign": " For with stammering lips and *another* tongue will he speak to this people." Since this verse is quoted in 1 Cor. 14:21 as an Old Testament prophecy of tongues-speaking, *'ahēr* figures prominently in the debate on that subject.

Finally, *'ahēr* can mean "other." In this usage, the word distinguishes one thing from another without emphasizing any contrast. This is its meaning in Exod. 20:3: "Thou shalt have no other gods before me."

FOOL

'ĕwîl (אֱוִיל, 191), "fool." This word appears primarily in the wisdom literature. A person described by *'ĕwîl* generally lacks wisdom; indeed, wisdom is beyond his grasp (Prov. 24:7). In another nuance, "fool" is a morally undesirable individual who despises wisdom and discipline (Prov. 1:7; 15:5). He mocks guilt (Prov. 14:9), and is quarrelsome (Prov. 20:3) and li-

centious (Prov. 7:22). Trying to give him instruction is futile (Prov. 16:22).

FOOLISHNESS

'iwwelet (אִוֶּלֶת, 200), "foolishness; stupidity." This noun appears 25 times in the Old Testament. It can mean "foolishness" in the sense of violating God's law, or "sin" (Ps. 38:5). The word also describes the activities and life-style of the man who ignores the instructions of wisdom (Prov. 5:23). In another nuance, the noun means "thoughtless." Hence *'iwwelet* describes the way a young person is prone to act (Prov. 22:15) and the way any fool or stupid person chatters (Prov. 15:2).

nᵉbālāh (נְבָלָה, 5039), "foolishness; senselessness; impropriety; stupidity." This abstract noun appears 13 times in the Old Testament. Its use in 1 Sam. 25:25 signifies "disregarding God's will." *Nᵉbālāh* is most often used as a word for a serious sin (Gen. 34:7—the first occurrence).

FOOT

regel (רֶגֶל, 7272), "foot; leg." *Regel* is a word found in many Semitic languages, referring to a part of the body. In the Old Testament, the word is used a total of 245 times, with its first occurrence in Gen. 8:9.

Regel may refer to the "foot" of a human (Gen. 18:4), an animal (Ezek. 29:11), a bird (Gen. 8:9), or even a table (a rare usage; Exod. 25:26, KJV). The word's usage is also extended to signify the "leg": "And he had greaves of brass upon his legs, and a target of brass between his shoulders" (1 Sam. 17:6). *Regel* is used euphemistically for the genital area; thus urine is "water of the legs" (2 Kings 18:27) and pubic hair is "hair of the legs" (Isa. 7:20). The foot's low place gave rise to an idiom: "From the sole of the foot to the crown of the head" (cf. Deut. 28:35), signifying the "total extent of the body."

"Foot" may be a metaphor of "arrogance": "Let not the foot of pride come against me, and let not the hand of the wicked remove me" (Ps. 36:11). It is used to represent Israel: "Neither will I make the feet of Israel move any more out of the land which I gave their fathers; only if they will observe to do according to all that I have commanded them, and according to all the law that my servant Moses commanded them" (2 Kings 21:8).

In anthropomorphic expressions, God has "feet." Thus God revealed Himself with a pavement of sapphire as clear as the sky under His "feet" (Exod. 24:10). The authors of Scripture portray God as having darkness (Ps. 18:9) and clouds of dust beneath His "feet" (Nah. 1:3), and sending a plague out from His "feet" (Hab. 3:5). His "feet" are said to rest on the earth (Isa. 66:1); the temple is also the resting place of His "feet": "... And I will make the place of my feet glorious" (Isa. 60:13). Similarly, the seraphim had "feet," which they covered with a pair of wings as they stood in the presence of God (Isa. 6:2); the cherubim had "feet" that Ezekiel described (Ezek. 1:7).

The Septuagint gives the following translations: *pous* ("foot") and *skelos* ("leg").

TO FORGET

šākaḥ (שָׁכַח, 7911), "to forget." The common word meaning "to forget" appears in all periods of the Hebrew language; this term is also found in Aramaic. It occurs just over 100 times in the Hebrew Bible. *Šākaḥ* is found for the first time in the Old Testament in Gen. 27:45, when Rebekah urges Jacob to flee his home until Esau "forget that which thou hast done to him."

As the people worshiped strange gods, Jeremiah reminded Judah that "all thy lovers have forgotten thee; they seek thee not" (Jer. 30:14). But God does not "forget" His people: "Can a woman forget her suckling child, that she should not have compassion on the son of her womb? yea, they may forget, yet will I not forget thee" (Isa. 49:15). In spite of this, when destruction came, Judah complained: "Wherefore dost thou forget us for ever...?" (Lam. 5:20). Israel would often "forget" God's law (Hos. 4:6) and God's name (Jer. 23:27).

TO FORGIVE

sālaḥ (סָלַח, 5545), "to forgive." This verb appears 46 times in the Old Testament. The meaning "to forgive" is limited to biblical and rabbinic Hebrew; in Akkadian, the word means "to sprinkle," and in Aramaic and Syriac signifies "to pour out." The meaning of *sālaḥ* in Ugaritic is debatable.

The first biblical occurrence is in Moses' prayer of intercession on behalf of the Israelites: "... It is a stiffnecked people; and [forgive] our iniquity and our sin, and take us for thine inheritance" (Exod. 34:9). The basic meaning undergoes no change throughout the Old Testament. God is always the subject of "forgiveness." No other Old Testament verb means "to forgive," although several verbs include "forgiveness" in the range of meanings given a particular context (e.g., *nāsā'* and *'āwōn* in Exod. 32:32; *kāpar* in Ezek. 16:63).

The verb occurs throughout the Old Testament. Most occurrences of *sālaḥ* are in the sacrificial laws of Leviticus and Numbers. In the typology of the Old Testament, sacrifices fore-

shadowed the accomplished work of Jesus Christ, and the Old Testament believer was assured of "forgiveness" based on sacrifice: "And the priest shall make an atonement [for him in regard to his sin]" (Num. 15:25, 28), "And it shall be forgiven him" (Lev. 4:26; cf. vv. 20, 31, 35; 5:10, 13, 16, 18). The mediators of the atonement were the priests who offered the sacrifice. The sacrifice was ordained by God to promise ultimate "forgiveness" in God's sacrifice of His own Son. Moreover, sacrifice was appropriately connected to atonement, as there is no forgiveness without the shedding of blood (Lev. 4:20; cf. Heb. 9:22).

Out of His grace, God alone "forgives" sin. The Israelites experienced God's "forgiveness" in the wilderness and in the Promised Land. As long as the temple stood, sacrificial atonement continued and the Israelites were assured of God's "forgiveness." When the temple was destroyed and sacrifices ceased, God sent the prophetic word that He graciously would restore Israel out of exile and "forgive" its sins (Jer. 31:34).

The psalmist appealed to God's great name in his request for "forgiveness": "For thy name's sake, O Lord, pardon mine iniquity; for it is great" (Ps. 25:11). David praised God for the assurance of "forgiveness" of sins: "Bless the Lord, O my soul..., who forgiveth all thine iniquities..." (Ps. 103:2–3). The Old Testament saints, while involved in sacrificial rites, put their faith in God.

In the Septuagint, *sālaḥ* is most frequently translated by *hileos einai* ("to be gracious; be merciful"), *hilaskesthai* ("to propitiate, expiate") and *apievai* ("to forgive, pardon, leave, cancel"). The translation "to forgive" is found in most English versions (KJV, RSV, NASB, NIV), and at times also "to pardon" (KJV, RSV).

TO FORM

yāṣar (יָצַר, 3335), "to form, mold, fashion." A word common to Hebrew in all its periods, *yāṣar* is used in modern Hebrew in the sense of "to produce," or "to create." The word is found just over 60 times in the Hebrew Old Testament. The first occurrence in the Old Testament is in Gen. 2:7: "... God formed man of the dust of the ground," reflecting the basic meaning of "molding" something to a desired shape.

Yāṣar is a technical potter's word, and it is often used in connection with the potter at work (Isa. 29:16; Jer. 18:4, 6). The word is sometimes used as a general term of "craftsmanship or handiwork," whether molding, carving, or casting (Isa. 44:9–10, 12).

The word may be used to express the "forming" of plans in one's mind (Ps. 94:20; KJV, "frameth"). *Yāṣar* is frequently used to describe God's creative activity, whether literally or figuratively. Thus, God "formed" not only man (Gen. 2:7–8) but the animals (Gen. 2:19). God also "formed" the nation of Israel (Isa. 27:11; 45:9, 11); Israel was "formed" as God's special servant, even from the womb (Isa. 44:2, 24; 49:5). While yet in the womb, Jeremiah was "formed" to be a prophet (Jer. 1:5). God "formed" locusts as a special visual lesson for Amos (Amos 7:1); the great sea monster, Leviathan, was "formed" to play in the seas (Ps. 104:26).

The concreteness of ancient Hebrew thinking is vividly seen in a statement such as this: "I form the light, and create darkness ... " (Isa. 45:7). Similarly, the psalmist confessed to God: " ... Thou hast made summer and winter" (Ps. 74:17). God "formed" the spirit of man (Zech. 12:1), as well as the heart or mind of man (Ps. 33:15). *Yāṣar* is used to express God's "planning" or "preordaining" according to His divine purpose (Isa. 22:11; 46:11).

Almost one half of the uses of this word in the Old Testament are found in the Book of Isaiah, with God as the subject of most of them.

FORMER

ri'šôn (רִאשׁוֹן, 7223), "former; chief; first." This word comes from a common Semitic root that also yields *rō'š* ("head") and *rē'šît* ("beginning"). *Ri'šôn*, which appears 182 times (first in Gen. 8:13), is well represented throughout the entire Old Testament, with the exception of the poetic books and the minor prophets.

The basic meaning of *ri'šôn* is "first" in a series. The word is the antonym of *'aḥărôn* ("last"). On the one hand, *ri'šôn* may refer to the "first month" (Exod. 40:2), the "first day" (Exod. 12:15), the "former temple" (Ezra 3:12), or the "firstborn" (Gen. 25:25ff.).

On the other hand, the word may denote the "most prominent" in a series. Thus God is "the first" as well as "the last": "Who hath wrought and done it, calling the generations from the beginning? I the Lord, the first, and with the last; I am he" (Isa. 41:4). The most prominent people at a banquet sat in the "first place" (Esth. 1:14). The use of *ri'šôn* with "father" in "Thy first father hath sinned, and thy teachers have transgressed against me" (Isa. 43:27) expresses how Israel's beginnings started with sin and rebellion.

As a reference to time, *ri'šôn* signifies what has been—i.e., the "former." This usage appears in phrases meaning a "former position" (Gen. 40:13) and a "deceased husband" (Hos. 2:7).

The "prophets of the past" (Zech. 1:4) and "ancestors" (Lev. 26:45) are both best understood as expressions referring to the past. The prophetic phrase "former days" (unlike "latter days") expresses Israel's past sin and God's judgment on Israel: "Behold, the former things are come to pass, and new things do I declare: before they spring forth I tell you of them" (Isa. 42:9).

The Septuagint translations are: *proteros* ("earlier; former; superior"), *protos* ("first; earlier; earliest"), *emprosthen* ("ahead; in front"), *archē* ("beginning; first cause; ruler; rule"). The KJV gives these translations: "first; former; before; beginning."

TO FORSAKE

'āzab (עָזַב, 5800), "to leave, forsake, abandon, leave behind, be left over, let go." This word occurs in Akkadian and post-biblical Hebrew and Aramaic. Similar words appear in Arabic and Ethiopic. The word occurs in biblical Hebrew about 215 times and in all periods.

Basically *'āzab* means "to depart from something," or "to leave." This is the meaning of the word in its first biblical appearance: "[For this cause] shall a man leave his father and his mother, and shall cleave unto his wife ... " (Gen. 2:24). A special nuance of the word is "to leave in the lurch," or to leave someone who is depending upon one's services. So Moses said to Hobab the Midianite (Kenite): "Leave us not [in the lurch] I pray thee; forasmuch as thou knowest how we are to encamp in the wilderness, and thou mayest be to us instead of eyes" (Num. 10:31).

The word also carries the meaning "forsake," or "leave entirely." Such passages convey a note of finality or completeness. So Isaiah is to preach that " ... the land that thou abhorrest shall be forsaken of both her kings" (Isa. 7:16). In other places, the abandonment is complete but not necessarily permanent. God says that Israel is "as a woman forsaken and grieved in spirit.... For a small moment have I forsaken thee; but with great mercies will I gather thee" (Isa. 54:6–7). In Akkadian, this word carries a technical sense of "completely and permanently abandoned" or "divorced." Isaiah employs this sense in 62:4: "Thou shalt no more be termed Forsaken; ... but thou shalt be called [My delight is in her], and thy land [Married]. ... "

Another special use of the word is "to disregard advice": "But he forsook the counsel of the old men which they had given him ... " (1 Kings 12:8).

A second emphasis of *'āzab* is "to leave behind," meaning to allow something to remain while one leaves the scene. In Gen. 39:12, Joseph "left" his garment in the hand of Potiphar's wife and fled. The word may also refer to an intentional "turning over one's possessions to another's trust," or "leaving something in one's control." Potiphar "left all that he had in Joseph's hand" (Gen. 39:6).

In a somewhat different nuance, the word means to "let someone or something alone with a problem": "If thou see the ass of him that hateth thee lying under his burden, and wouldest forbear to help him . . ." (Exod. 23:5). Used figuratively, 'āzab means to "put distance between" in a spiritual or intellectual sense: "Cease from anger, and forsake wrath . . ." (Ps. 37:8).

The third emphasis of the word is "to be left over," or "to take most of something and leave the rest behind": "And thou shalt not glean thy vineyard, neither shalt thou gather every grape of thy vineyard; thou shalt leave them [over] for the poor and stranger: I am the Lord your God" (Lev. 19:10).

Finally, 'āzab can mean "to let go" or "allow to leave." The "stupid and senseless men" are those who make no provision for the future; they die leaving ("allowing it to go") their wealth to others (Ps. 49:10). A different nuance occurs in Ruth 2:16, where the verb means "to let something lie" on the ground. 'Azab can also mean "to give up": "He that covereth his sins shall not prosper: but whoso confesseth and forsaketh them [gives them up] shall have mercy" (Prov. 28:13), and the word can mean "to set free," as in 2 Chron. 28:14: "So the armed men left the captives and the spoil before the princes and all the congregation." 'Azab can signify "let go," or "make it leave." Concerning evil, Zophar remarks, " . . . [The wicked] forsake it not, but keep it still within his mouth" (Job 20:13).

'Azab can mean to "allow someone to do something," as in 2 Chron. 32:31, where "God left [Hezekiah], to try him, that he might know all that was in his heart"; God "let" Hezekiah do whatever he wanted. "Letting an activity go" may also signify its discontinuance: "I pray you, let us leave off this usury" (Neh. 5:10).

'Azab is sometimes used in a judicial technical sense of "being free," which is the opposite of being in bondage. The Lord will vindicate His people, and will have compassion on His servants "when he seeth that their power is gone, and there is none shut up, or left" (Deut. 32:36).

FRIEND

rēa' (רֵעַ, 7453), "friend; companion; fellow." This noun appears about 187 times in the Bible. The word refers to a "friend" in 2 Sam. 13:3: "But Amnon had a friend, whose name was Jonadab." The word may be used of a husband (Jer. 3:20) or a lover (Song of Sol. 5:16).

In another sense, *rēa'* may be used of any person with whom one has reciprocal relations: "And they said every one to his fellow, Come, and let us cast lots . . ." (Jonah 1:7). The word also appears in such phrases as "one another," found in Gen. 11:3: "And they said one to another . . ." (cf. Gen. 31:49).

Other related nouns that appear less frequently are *rē'eh*, which means "friend" about 5 times (e.g., 1 Kings 4:5); and *rē'āh*, which means "companion or attendant" (Judg. 11:38; Ps. 45:14).

FRUIT

A. Noun.

perî (פְּרִי, 6529), "fruit; reward; price; earnings; product; result." Cognates of this word appear in Ugaritic and Egyptian. *Perî* appears about 120 times in biblical Hebrew and in every period.

First, *perî* represents the mature edible product of a plant, which is its "fruit." This broad meaning is evident in Deut. 7:13: "He will also bless the fruit of thy womb, and the fruit of thy land, thy corn, and thy wine, and thine oil, the increase of thy kine and the flocks of thy sheep. . . ." In its first biblical appearance, the word is used to signify both "trees" and the "fruit" of trees: "And God said, Let the earth bring forth grass, the herb yielding seed, and the fruit tree yielding fruit after his kind . . ." (Gen. 1:11). In Ps. 107:34, the word is used as a modifier of land. The resulting term is "a fruitful land" in the sense of a "land of fruit."

Second, *perî* means "offspring," or the "fruit of a womb." In Deut. 7:13, the word represents "human offspring," but it can also be used of animal "offspring" (Gen. 1:22).

Third, the "product" or "result" of an action is, in poetry, sometimes called its "fruit": "A man shall say, Verily there is a reward for the righteous: verily he is a God that judgeth in the earth" (Ps. 58:11). Isa. 27:9 speaks of "the full price of the pardoning of his sin" (KJV, "all the fruit to take away his sin"), i.e., the result of God's purifying acts toward Israel. The wise woman buys and plants a field with her earnings or the "fruit of her hands" (Prov. 31:16). In other words, she is to be rewarded by receiving the "product" of her hands (Prov. 31:31). The righteous will be rewarded "according to his ways, according to the results of his deeds" (Jer. 17:10, NASB; cf. 21:14). In most passages similar to these, the NASB renders *pᵉrî* "fruit" (cf. Prov. 18:21).

B. Verb.

pārāh (פָּרָה, 6504), "to be fruitful, bear fruit." This verb appears 29 times in the Old Testament. Its first occurrence is in Gen. 1:22: "And God blessed them, saying, Be fruitful, and multiply, ... "

G

GARMENT

beged (בֶּגֶד, 899), "garment; covering; cloth; blanket; saddlecloth." This word appears in biblical Hebrew about 200 times and in all periods.

The word signifies any kind of "garment" or "covering," usually for human wear. *Beged* first appears in Gen. 24:53: "And the servant brought forth jewels of silver, and jewels of gold, and garments [KJV, "raiment"], and gave them to Rebekah. ... " Here the word represents "garments made of precious materials." The "garments" of widows, on the other hand, must have been quite common and valueless (Gen. 38:14). Certainly mourners' "garments" must have been very plain, if not torn (2 Sam. 14:2).

Beged sometimes refers to "outer garments." Thus in 2 Kings 7:15, the Syrian soldiers who fled from Jerusalem left behind their "clothes" and equipment; they left behind everything that would hinder their escape. Surely this did not include their essential "clothing." In Judg. 14:12, however, the word is distinguished from linen wrappings ("outer garments")—Samson promised the Philistines that if they would solve his riddle, he would give them "thirty linen wraps [KJV, "sheets"] and thirty change of garments" (cf. Judg. 17:10). The "holy garments" Moses was commanded to make for Aaron included everything he was to wear while officiating before the Lord: " ... A breastplate, and an ephod, and a robe, and an embroidered coat, a mitre, and a [sash]; and they shall make holy garments for Aaron ... " (Exod. 28:4).

In passages such as Num. 4:6, *beged* means "covering," in the sense of a large flat piece of cloth material to be laid over something: "And [they] shall put thereon the covering of badgers' skins, and shall spread over it a cloth wholly of blue. ... " When put over people, such clothes were probably "blankets": "Now king David was old and stricken in years; and they covered

him with blankets [KJV and NASB, "clothes"], but he gat no heat" (1 Kings 1:1). When put over beasts, such coverings were "saddlecloths" (Ezek. 27:20).

GATE

ša'ar (שַׁעַר, 8179), "gate." This word has cognates in Ugaritic, Arabic, Moabite, Aramaic, and Phoenician. Biblical Hebrew attests it about 370 times and in all periods.

Basically, this word represents a structure closing and enclosing a large opening through a wall, or a barrier through which people and things pass to an enclosed area. The "gate" of a city often was a fortified structure deeper than the wall. This is especially true of strong, well-fortified cities, as in the case of the first biblical appearance of the word: "And there came two angels to Sodom at even; and Lot sat in the gate of Sodom ... " (Gen. 19:1). Within major cities there were usually strongly fortified citadels with "gates" (Neh. 2:8). Certain "gates" were only the thickness of a curtain: "And for the gate of the court [of the tabernacle] shall be a hanging of twenty cubits ... " (Exod. 27:16). Later, the temple had large openings between its various courts: "Stand in the gate of the Lord's house, and proclaim there this word, and say, Hear the word of the Lord, all ye of Judah, that enter in at these gates to worship the Lord" (Jer. 7:2).

Exod. 32:26 speaks of an opening ("gate") in the barrier surrounding Israel's temporary camp at the foot of Sinai. Such camps often were enclosed with barriers of earth and/or rock. Ancient fortified cities had to find a source of water for periods of siege, and sometimes dams were built. Nah. 2:6 apparently refers to such a dam when it says: "The gates of the rivers shall be opened, and the palace shall be dissolved" (i.e., swept away). Both the underworld (Job

38:17) and heaven, the domain of God (Gen. 28:17), are pictured as cities with "gates."

The "gates" of ancient cities sometimes enclosed city squares or were immediately in front of squares (2 Chron. 32:6). The entry way (2 Chron. 23:15) could be secured with heavy doors that were attached to firmly embedded pillars and reinforced by bars (Judg. 16:3; cf. Ps. 147:13; Neh. 3:3). Palaces could be citadels with strongly fortified "gates" large enough to have rooms over them. During siege, such rooms housed warriors. It was such a room into which David climbed and wept over the death of his son Absalom (2 Sam. 18:33). "Gates" had rooms to house guards (Ezek. 40:7). The rooms bordering the "gates" could also be used to store siege supplies (Neh. 12:25).

The "gates" were the place where local courts convened: "And if the man like not to take his brother's wife, then let his brother's wife go up to the gate unto the elders, and say, My husband's brother refuseth . . . " (Deut. 25:7). The sentence sometimes was executed at the city "gates": "And I will fan them with a fan in the gates of the land; I will bereave them of children, I will destroy my people . . . " (Jer. 15:7). In this passage, all of the land of Israel is envisioned as a city at whose "gates" God gathers the offenders for trial, judgment, sentence, and punishment.

The phrase, "within the gates," means "within the area enclosed." Thus the sojourner who is "in your gates" is the foreigner who permanently lives in one of Israel's towns (Exod. 20:10). In passages such as Deut. 12:15, this phrase means "wherever you live": "Notwithstanding thou mayest kill and eat flesh in all thy gates. . . . "

TO GATHER

qābaṣ (קָבַץ, 6908), "to collect, gather, assemble." This verb also appears in Ugaritic, Arabic, Aramaic, and post-biblical Hebrew; a similar word (having the same radicals but a different meaning) occurs in Ethiopic. *Qābaṣ* appears in all periods of Hebrew and about 130 times in the Bible. The verb *'āsaph* is a near synonym to *qābaṣ*, differing from it only by having a more extensive range of meanings. *'Asap* duplicates, however, all the meanings of *qābaṣ*.

First, *qābaṣ* means "to gather" things together into a single location. The word may focus on the process of "gathering," as in Gen. 41:35 (the first occurrence): Joseph advised Pharaoh to appoint overseers to "gather all the food of those good years that come, and lay up corn under the hand of Pharaoh. . . . " The verb may also focus on the result of the process, as in Gen. 41:48: "And he gathered up all the food of the seven years, which were in the land of Egypt. . . . " Only in one passage does *qābaṣ* mean "to harvest" (Isa. 62:9): "But they that have gathered [harvested] it [grain] shall eat it, and praise the Lord; and they that have brought it [wine] together shall drink it in the courts of my holiness."

This verb is used metaphorically of things that can be "gathered" only in a figurative sense. So in Ps. 41:6, the enemy's "heart gathereth iniquity to itself" while visiting—i.e., the enemy considers how he can use everything he hears and sees against his host.

Qābaṣ is often used of "gathering" people or "assembling" them. This "gathering" is usually a response to a summons, but not always. In 1 Kings 11:24, David "gathered men unto him, and became captain over a [marauding] band." This action was not the result of a summons David issued, but resulted from reports that circulated about him. The entire story makes it quite clear that David was not seeking to set up a force rivaling Saul's. But when men came to him, he marshalled them.

Quite often this verb is used of "summoning" people to a central location. When Jacob blessed his sons, for example, he "summoned" them to him and then told them to gather around closer (Gen. 49:2). This same word is used of "summoning" the militia. All able-bodied men in Israel between the ages of 20 and 40 were members of the militia. In times of peace they were farmers and tradesmen; but when danger threatened, a leader would "assemble" them or "summon" them to a common location and organize them into an army (cf. Judg. 12:4). All Israel could be "summoned" or "gathered" for battle (as a militia); thus " . . . Saul gathered all Israel together, and they pitched in Gilboa" (1 Sam. 28:4). This military use may also signify "marshalling" a standing army in the sense of "setting them up" for battle. The men of Gibeon said: "All the kings of the Amorites that dwell in the mountains are gathered together against us" (Josh. 10:6). In 1 Kings 20:1, *qābaṣ* carries this sense in addition to overtones of "concentrating" an entire army against a particular point: "And Ben-hadad the king of Syria gathered all his host together: and there were thirty and two kings with him, and horses, and chariots: and he went up and besieged Samaria, and warred against it."

Ordered assemblies may include assemblies for covenant-making: "And Abner said unto David, I will arise and go, and will gather all Israel unto my lord the king, that they may make a league with thee . . . " (2 Sam. 3:21). In several instances, assemblies are "convened" for public worship activities: "Samuel said, Gather all Israel to Mizpeh. . . . And they gathered together to Mizpeh, and drew water, and poured it out before the Lord, and fasted on that day . . . " (1 Sam. 7:5–6; cf. Joel 2:16).

When *qābaṣ* appears in the intensive stem, God is often the subject. This usage connotes that something will result that would not result if things were left to themselves. The verb is used in this sense to refer to "divine judgment": "As they gathered silver, and brass . . . into the midst of the furnace, to blow the fire upon it, to melt it; so will I gather you in mine anger and in my fury (Ezek. 22:20). *Qābaṣ* is also applied to "divine deliverance": " . . . The Lord thy God will turn thy captivity, and have compassion upon thee, and will return and gather thee from all the nations, whither the Lord thy God hath scattered thee" (Deut. 30:3).

A special use of the verb *qābaṣ* appears in Joel 2:6, namely "to glow" or "glow with excitement" or "become pale [white]": "Before their face the people shall be much pained: all faces shall gather blackness."

'āsap (אָסַף, 622), "to gather, gather in, take away." This verb also occurs in Akkadian, Ugaritic, Phoenician, and Aramaic. It is attested at all periods of biblical literature, and it appears about 200 times.

Basically, *'āsap* refers to "bringing objects to a common point." This may mean to "gather" or "collect" something such as food. The first occurrence is when God told Noah to "gather" food to himself (Gen. 6:21). Eventually, the food was to go into the ark. This verb can also refer to "gathering" food at harvest time, or "harvesting": "And six years thou shalt sow thy land, and shalt gather in the fruits thereof" (Exod. 23:10). Second Kings 22:4 refers not to a process of going out and getting something together, but to standing still as someone brings money to one. Also notice Gen. 29:22: "And Laban gathered together all the men of the place, and made a feast"; this verse similarly focuses on the end product of gathering. But here the "gatherer" does not physically handle what is "gathered." He is simply the impetus or active cause for a congregating of all those men. God may "gather" a man to his fathers—i.e., cause him to die (2 Kings 22:20). Here the emphasis is on the end product, and God as the agent who "gathers."

'Āsap may represent not only the process of bringing things to a common location; the word may also represent "bringing" things to oneself. After the harvest is brought ("gathered") in from the threshing floor and wine vat, the Feast of Booths is to be celebrated (Deut. 16:13). In Deut. 22:2, a man is to "gather" into his home (bring home and care for) a lost animal whose owner cannot be found. In this manner, God "gathers" to Himself those abandoned by their family (Ps. 27:10). A special application of this nuance is to "receive hospitality": " . . . When he went in he sat him down in a street of the city: for there was no man that took them into his house to lodging" (Judg. 19:15). "To gather in" also may mean "to be consumed by"—God promises that His people "shall be no more consumed with hunger" (Ezek. 34:29). Finally, used in this way the verb can mean "to bring into," as when Jacob "gathered up his feet into the bed" (Gen. 49:33).

The third emphasis is the "withdrawal" or "removal" of something; the action is viewed from the perspective of one who loses something because someone has taken it ("gathered it in"). In Ps. 85:3, the "gathering" represents this sort of "withdrawal away from" the speaker. Thus, anger "disappears": "Thou hast taken away all thy wrath." Compare also Rachel's statement at the birth of Joseph: "God hath taken away my reproach" (Gen. 30:23). In this case, Sarah speaks of the "destruction" of her reproach. "To gather one's soul" is "to lose" one's life (Judg. 18:25). God can also be the agent who "gathers" or "takes away" a soul: "Gather not my soul with sinners . . . " (Ps. 26:9). In this sense, *'āsap* can mean "being cured" of a disease; "Would God my lord were with the prophet that is in Samaria! for he would recover him of his leprosy" (2 Kings 5:3).

GENERATION

dôr (דּוֹר, 1755), "generation." This noun belongs to a common Semitic root, which signifies "duration" in East Semitic and "generation" in West Semitic. The Akkadian words *daru* ("long duration") and *duru* ("circle") seem by form to be related to the root for the Hebrew word *dôr*.

In the Old Testament, the word *dôr* occurs about 166 times; as many as 74 of these are in the repetition "*dôr* plus *dôr*," meaning "alway." The first occurrence of the word is in Gen. 6:9: "These are the generations of Noah [the account of Noah]: Noah was a just man and perfect in his generations, and Noah walked with God."

First the concrete meaning of "generation" is the "period during which people live": "And the Lord said unto Noah, Come thou and all thy house into the ark; for thee have I seen righteous before me in this generation" (Gen. 7:1). A "generation" may be described as "stubborn" (Deut. 32:5—KJV, "perverse") or "righteous" (Ps. 14:5). Close to this meaning is the temporal element of *dôr:* A *dôr* is roughly the period of time from one's birth to one's maturity, which in the Old Testament corresponds to a period of about 40 years (Num. 14:33). Abraham received the promise that four "generations" of his descendants were to be in Egypt before the Promised Land would be inherited. Israel was warned to be faithful to the Lord, as the punishment for disobedience would extend to the fourth "generation" (Exod. 20:5); but the Lord's love extends to a thousand "generations" of those who love Him (Deut. 7:9).

The lasting element of God's covenantal faithfulness is variously expressed with the word *dôr:* "Thy faithfulness is unto all generations: thou hast established the earth, and it abideth" (Ps. 119:90).

The use of *dôr* in Isa. 51 teaches the twofold perspective of "generation," with reference to the future as well as to the past. Isaiah spoke about the Lord's lasting righteousness and said that His deliverance is everlasting (literally, "generation of generations"—v. 8); but in view of Israel's situation, Isaiah petitioned the Lord to manifest His loving strength on behalf of Israel as in the past (literally, "generations forever"—v. 9). Thus, depending on the context, *dôr* may refer to the past, the present, or the future.

The psalmist recognized the obligation of one "generation" to the "generations" to come: "One generation shall praise thy works to another, and shall declare thy mighty acts" (Ps. 145:4). Even the grey-haired man has the opportunity to instruct the youth (Ps. 71:17–18).

In the Septuagint, *dôr* is nearly always translated by *genea* ("generation"). The KJV translates it by "generation; age."

TO GIVE DRINK

šāqāh (שָׁקָה, 8248), "to give drink, irrigate, water." This verb is found in ancient Akkadian and Ugaritic, as well as in biblical and modern Hebrew. The word usually occurs in the causative sense, while its much more common counterpart, *šātāh*, is used primarily in the simple active form, "to drink." In its first occurrence in the biblical text, *šāqāh* expresses the idea of "to irrigate," or "to water": "But there went up a mist from the earth, and watered the whole face of the ground" (Gen. 2:6). In view of the Mesopotamian background of this passage, both linguistic and agricultural, the Hebrew word for "mist" probably is to be connected with the idea of an irrigation canal or system.

The dry climate of the Middle East makes *šāqāh* a most important word, since it expresses the act of "irrigating" or "watering" crops (Deut. 11:10). God "waters" the earth and causes plants to grow (Ps. 104:13–14). Figuratively, He "irrigates" His vineyard, Israel (Isa. 27:3).

A frequent use of *šāqāh* is to express the "giving of water to drink" to animals (Gen. 24:14, 46; 29:2–3, 7–8, 10). Men are given a variety of things to drink, such as water (Gen. 24:43), wine (Gen. 19:32; Amos 2:12), milk (Judg. 4:19), and vinegar (Ps. 69:21). In a symbol of divine judgment, God is said to give "poisoned water [KJV, "water of gall"] to drink" to Israel (Jer. 8:14; 9:15; 23:15). In this time of judgment and mourning, Israel was not to be given "the cup of consolation to drink" (Jer. 16:7).

A healthy person is one whose bones "are moistened" with marrow (Job 21:24; literally, whose bones "are watered" or "irrigated" with marrow).

GLORY

A. Noun.

tip'eret (תִּפְאֶרֶת, 8597), "glory; beauty; ornament; distinction; pride." This word appears about 51 times and in all periods of biblical Hebrew.

The word represents "beauty," in the sense of the characteristic enhancing one's appearance: "And thou shalt make holy garments for Aaron thy brother for glory and for beauty" (Exod. 28:2—the first occurrence). In Isa. 4:2, the word identifies the fruit of the earth as the "beauty" or "adornment" of the survivors of Israel.

Tip'eret (or *tip'arāh*) means "glory" in several instances. The word is used of one's rank. A crown of "glory" is a crown which, by its richness, indicates high rank—Wisdom will "[present you with] a crown of glory (NASB, "beauty")" (Prov. 4:9). "The hoary head is a crown of glory" (Prov. 16:31), a reward for righteous living. In Isa. 62:3, the phrase "crown of glory (NASB, "beauty")" is paralleled by "royal diadem." This word also modifies the greatness of a king (Esth. 1:4) and the greatness of the inhabitants of Jerusalem (Zech. 12:7). In each of these instances, this word emphasizes the rank of the persons or things so modified. The word is used of one's renown: " . . . And to make thee high above all nations which he hath made, in praise, and in name, and in honor [distinction]" (Deut. 26:19).

In another related nuance, *tip'eret* (or *tip'arāh*) is used of God, to emphasize His rank, renown, and inherent "beauty": "Thine, O Lord, is the greatness, and the power, and the glory, and the victory, and the majesty . . . " (1 Chron. 29:11).

This word represents the "honor" of a nation, in the sense of its position before God: "[He has] cast down from heaven unto the earth the beauty [honor or pride] of Israel . . . " (Lam. 2:1). This nuance is especially clear in passages such as Judg. 4:9: "I will surely go with thee: notwithstanding the journey that thou takest shall not be for thine honor [i.e., distinction]; for the Lord shall sell Sisera into the hand of a woman."

In Isa. 10:12, *tip'eret* (or *tip'arāh*) represents a raising of oneself to a high rank in one's own eyes: " . . . I will punish the fruit of the stout heart of the king of Assyria, and the glory of his high looks."

B. Verb.

pā'ar (פָּאַר, 6286), "to glorify." This verb occurs 13 times in biblical Hebrew. One appearance of this verb is in Isa. 60:9: " . . . And to the Holy One of Israel, because he hath gloried thee."

TO GO AWAY, LEAVE

A. Verb.

gālāh (גָּלָה, 1540), "to leave, depart, uncover, reveal." This verb occurs in Ugaritic, Phoenician, Arabic, imperial Aramaic, biblical Aramaic, and Ethiopic. Biblical Hebrew attests it in all periods and about 190 times. Some scholars divide this verb into two homonyms (two separate words spelled the same). If this division is accepted, *gālāh* (1) appears about 112 times and *gālāh* (2) about 75 times. Other scholars consider this one verb with an intransitive emphasis and a transitive emphasis. This seems more likely.

Intransitively, *gālāh* signifies "depart" or "leave." This meaning is seen clearly in 1 Sam. 4:21: "And she named the child Ichabod, saying, The glory is departed from Israel. . . . " Thus Isaiah 24:11 could be translated: "The gaiety of the earth departs." One special use of this sense of the verb is "to go into exile." The first biblical occurrence of *gālāh* carries this nuance: "And the children of Dan set up the graven image: and Jonathan . . . and his sons were priests to the tribe of Dan until the day of the *captivity* of the land" (Judg. 18:30), or until they lost control of the land and were forced to serve other gods.

The best-known Old Testament captivity was the one brought by God through the kings of Assyria and Babylon (1 Chron. 5:26; cf. Jer. 29:1).

Although *gālāh* is not used in this sense in the law of Moses, the idea is clearly present. If

Israel does not "observe to do all the words of this law that are written in this book, that thou mayest fear this glorious and fearful name, The Lord Thy God; . . . ye shall be plucked from off the land whither thou goest to possess it. And the Lord shall scatter thee among all people . . . " (Deut. 28:58, 63–64; cf. Lev. 26:27, 33). This verb can also be used of the "exile of individuals," such as David (2 Sam. 15:19).

This word may signify "making oneself naked." Noah "drank of the wine, and was drunken; and he was uncovered within his tent" (Gen. 9:21).

The transitive form occurs less frequently, but has a greater variety of meanings. "To uncover" another person may mean "to have sexual relations with" him or her: "None of you shall approach to any [blood relative of his] to uncover their nakedness: I am the Lord" (Lev. 18:6). Uncovering one's nakedness does not always, however, refer to sexual relations (cf. Exod. 20:26). Another phrase, "to uncover someone's skirts," means to have sexual relations with a person (Deut. 22:30).

In Isaiah 16:3, *gālāh* (2) (in the intensive stem) signifies "betray": " . . . Hide the outcasts [do not betray the fugitive]. . . . " This verb may also be used of "uncovering" (KJV, "discovering") things, of "laying them bare" so that they become visible: " . . . The foundations of the world were discovered at the rebuking of the Lord . . . " (2 Sam. 22:16). In a related sense Ezek. 23:18 speaks of "uncovering" harlotries, of "exposing" them constantly or leading a life of harlotry.

God's "uncovering" of Himself means that He "revealed" Himself (Gen. 35:7). "To uncover someone's ears" is to tell him something: "Now the day before Saul came, the Lord had revealed [literally, "had uncovered the ear"] to Samuel . . . " (1 Sam. 9:15, RSV). In this case, the verb means not simply "to tell," but "to tell someone something that was not known." Used in this sense, *gālāh* is applied to the "revealing" of secrets (Prov. 11:13) and of one's innermost feelings. Hence, Jer. 11:20 should be translated: "For unto thee have I revealed my case."

Thus *gālāh* can be used of "making something" openly known, or of "publicizing" it: "The copy of the writing for a commandment to be given in every province was published unto all people, that they should be ready against that day" (Esth. 3:14). Another nuance appears in Jer. 32:11, where *gālāh*, in connection with a deed of purchase, means "not sealed or closed up."

B. Noun.

gôlāh (גּוֹלָה, 1473), "exile; people exiled." This word makes 42 Old Testament appearances. Ezra 2:1 uses the word of "people returning from the exile." In other references, the word means "people in exile" (2 Kings 24:15). In 1 Chron. 5:22, *gôlāh* refers to the era of the "exile."

TO GO DOWN

yārad (יָרַד, 3381), "to descend, go down, come down." This verb occurs in most Semitic languages (including post-biblical Hebrew) and in all periods. In biblical Hebrew, the word appears about 380 times and in all periods.

Basically, this verb connotes "movement" from a higher to a lower location. In Gen. 28:12, Jacob saw a "ladder set up on the earth, and the top of it reached to heaven: and behold the angels of God ascending and descending on it." In such a use, the speaker or observer speaks from the point of destination, and the movement is "downward" toward him. Thus one may "go down" below or under the ground's surface (Gen. 24:16). The speaker may also speak as though he stands at the point of departure and the movement is away from him and "downward."

Interestingly, one may "go down" to a lower spot in order to reach a city's gates (Judg. 5:11) or to get to a city located on a lower level than the access road (1 Sam. 10:8)—usually one goes up to a city and "goes down" to leave a city (1 Sam. 9:27). The journey from Palestine to Egypt is referred to as "going down" (Gen. 12:10). This reference is not to a movement in space from a higher to a lower spot; it is a more technical use of the verb.

Yārad is used frequently of "dying." One "goes down" to his grave. Here the idea of spatial movement is present, but in the background. This "going down" is much more of a removal from the world of conscious existence: "For the grave cannot praise thee, death cannot celebrate thee: they that go down into the pit cannot hope for thy truth. The living, the living, he shall praise thee..." (Isa. 38:18–19). On the other hand, "going down to the dust" implies a return to the soil—i.e., a return of the body to the soil from which it came (Gen. 3:19). "All they that go down to the dust shall bow before him..." (Ps. 22:29). There is also the idea of the "descent" of the human soul into the realm of the dead. When Jacob mourned over Joseph, whom he thought to be dead, he said: "For I will go down into the grave unto my son mourning" (Gen. 37:35). Since one can "descend" into Sheol alive as a form of punishment (Num. 16:30), this phrase means more than the end of human life. This meaning is further established because Enoch was rewarded by being taken off the earth: "And Enoch walked with God: and he was not; for God took him" (Gen. 5:24); he was rewarded by not having "to descend" into Sheol.

Yārad may also be used of "coming down," when the emphasis is on "moving downward" toward the speaker: "And the Lord came down to see the city and the tower" of Babel (Gen. 11:5—the first biblical occurrence). This verb may also be used to express coming down from the top of a mountain, as Moses did when he "descended" from Sinai (Exod. 19:14). The word may be used of "dismounting" from a donkey: "And when Abigail saw David, she hasted, and lighted off the ass..." (1 Sam. 25:23). Abigail's entire body was not necessarily lower than before, so movement from a higher to a lower location is not indicated. However, she was no longer on the animal's back. So the verb here indicates "getting off" rather than getting down or descending. In a somewhat related nuance, one may "get out" of bed. Elijah told Ahaziah: "Thou shalt not come down from that bed on which thou art gone up..." (2 Kings 1:4). Again, the idea is not of descending *from* something. When one comes down from a bed, he stands up; he is higher than he was while yet in the bed. Therefore, the meaning here is "get out of" rather than "descend." This verb is used also to describe what a beard does—it "hangs down" (Ps. 133:2).

Yārad is used to indicate "coming away from" the altar: "And Aaron lifted up his hand toward the people, and blessed them, and came down from offering of the sin offering..." (Lev. 9:22). This special use is best seen as the opposite of "ascending to" the altar, which is not just a physical movement from a lower to a higher plane but a spiritual ascent to a higher realm of reality. For example, to "ascend" before a king is to go into the presence of someone who is on a higher social level. "To ascend" before God (represented by the altar) is to go before Someone on a higher spiritual plane. To stand before God is to stand in His presence, before His throne, on a higher spiritual plane. *Yārad* may thus be used of the humbled approach before God. God tells Moses that all the Egyptians shall "come down" to Him and bow themselves before Him (Exod. 11:8). Equally interesting is the occasional use of the verb to represent "descending" to a known sanctuary (cf. 2 Kings 2:2).

Figuratively, the verb has many uses. The "going down" of a city is its destruction (Deut.

20:20). When a day "descends," it comes to an end (Judg. 19:11). The "descent" of a shadow is its lengthening (2 Kings 20:11). Tears "flow down" the cheeks when one weeps bitterly (Jer. 13:17). *Yārad* is also used figuratively of a "descent in social position": "The stranger that is within thee shall get up above thee very high; and thou shalt come down very low" (Deut. 28:43).

At least once the word means "to go up." Jephthah's daughter said: "Let me alone two months, that I may go up and down upon the mountains, and bewail my virginity . . . " (Judg. 11:37).

TO GO OUT, GO FORTH

A. Verb.

yāṣa' (אָצָי, 3318), "to come forth, go out, proceed, go forth, bring out, come out." This verb occurs in all Semitic languages, including biblical Aramaic and Hebrew. It occurs in every period of Hebrew; the Old Testament attests the word about 1,070 times.

Basically, this word means "movement away" from some point, even as *bô'* ("come") means movement toward some point. *Yāṣa'* is the word used of "coming forth"—the observer is outside the point of departure but also speaks from the perspective of that departing point. For example, Gen. 2:10 (the first occurrence of the word) reports that a river "came forth" or "flowed out" from the garden of Eden.

In comparison to this continuing "going out," there is the one-time (punctiliar) "coming forth," as seen when all the animals "came out" of the ark (Gen. 9:10). Thus, Goliath the champion of the Philistines "went forward" from the camp to challenge the Israelites to a duel (1 Sam. 17:4). In the art of ancient warfare, a battle was sometimes decided on the basis of two duelers.

This verb may be used with "come" (*bô'*) as an expression for "constant activity." The raven Noah sent out "went forth to and fro" (literally, "in and out") until the water had abated (Gen. 8:7). Various aspects of a man's personality may "go forth," indicating that they "leave" him. When one's soul "departs" the body, the person dies (Gen. 35:18). When one's heart "departs," he loses all inner strength and confidence (Gen. 42:28).

Yāṣa' has a number of special uses. It can be used of "giving birth" (Exod. 21:22) or of "begetting" descendants (Gen. 17:6). The "going forth" of a year is its close, as in the harvest season (Exod. 23:16). Another special use of this verb has to do with "moving out" a camp for either a military campaign (1 Sam. 8:20) or

some other purpose (Deut. 23:10). "Going and coming" may also be used of "fighting" in wars. Toward the end of his life Moses said he was unable to "come and go" (Deut. 31:2; cf. Josh. 14:11). He probably meant that he could not engage in war (Deut. 31:3). On the other hand, this phrase can refer to the normal activities of life (1 Kings 3:7). *Yāṣa'* also has a cultic use, describing the "movement" of the priest in the tabernacle; bells were attached to the hem of the priest's robe so the people could follow his actions (Exod. 28:35).

When applied to God, the action of "going out" only infrequently refers to His "abandoning" a certain location. In Ezek. 10:18, the glory of the Lord "left" the "threshhold of the [temple], and stood over the cherubim," and eventually departed the temple altogether (Ezek. 10:19). Often this verb pictures the Lord as "going forth" to aid His people, especially in texts suggesting or depicting His appearances among men (theophanies; cf. Judg. 5:4). In Egypt, the Lord "went out" into the midst of the Egyptians to smite their first born (Exod. 11:4). The Lord's departure-point in such cases is variously represented as Seir (Judg. 5:4) and His heavenly dwelling place (Mic. 1:3), although it is often unexpressed.

The messenger of God also "goes forth" to accomplish specific tasks (Num. 22:32). God's providential work in history is described by Laban and Bethuel as "the thing proceedeth from the Lord" (Gen. 24:50). Also, "going out" from the Lord are His hand (Ruth 1:13), His Word (Isa. 55:11), His salvation (Isa. 51:5), His justice (Isa. 45:23), and His wisdom (Isa. 51:4).

Yāṣa' is not used of God's initial creative act, but only of His using what already exists to accomplish His purposes, such as His causing water to "come out" of the rock (Deut. 8:15). Because *yāṣa'* can mean "to bring forth," it is often used of "divine deliverance," as the One who "bringeth me forth from mine enemies" (2 Sam. 22:49) "into a large place" (2 Sam. 22:20). One of the most important formulas in the Old Testament uses the verb *yāṣa';* "the Lord [who] brought [Israel] out of [Egypt]"; He brought them from slavery into freedom (Exod. 13:3).

B. Nouns.

môṣā' (אָצוֹמ, 4161), "place of going forth; that which comes forth; going forth." The word occurs 23 times. *Môṣā'* is a word for "east" (cf. Ps. 19:6), where the sun rises ("goes forth"). The word also represents the "place of departure" or "exit" from the temple in Ezekiel's vision (Ezek. 42:11), and the "starting point" of a journey (Num. 33:2). *Môṣa'* may also refer to that which "comes forth," for example, an "utterance" (Num. 30:13), and the "going forth" of the morning and evening, the dawn and dusk (Ps. 65:8). Finally, the word can represent the "actual going forth" itself. So Hosea says that the Lord's "going forth" to redeem His people is as certain as the sunrise (6:3).

tôṣa'ôt (תּוֹצָאוֹת, 8444), "departure; place of departure." The word *tôṣa'ôt* can connote both the source or place of "departure" (Prov. 4:23) and the actual "departure" itself ("escape," Ps. 68:20). However, the word may also represent the extremity of a territory or its "border"—the place where one departs a given territory (Josh. 15:7).

GOAT-DEMONS

śā'îr (שָׂעִיר, 8163), "goat-demons; goat-idols." This word occurs 4 times in biblical Hebrew. In its first biblical appearance, the word represents "goat-demons" (some scholars translate it "goat-idols"): "And they shall no more offer their sacrifices unto devils [NASB, "goat demons"], after whom they have gone a whoring" (Lev. 17:7). This passage demonstrates that the word represents beings that were objects of pagan worship. Worship of these "demons" persisted long in the history of Israel, appearing under Jeroboam I (929–909 B.C.), who " . . . ordained him priests for the high places, and for the devils [RSV, "satyrs"], and for the calves which he had made" (2 Chron. 11:15). In this instance, *śā'îr* represents idols that Jeroboam had manufactured. Josiah's revival probably involved the breaking down of the high places of the goat-demons (2 Kings 23:8).

GOD

'ēl (אֵל, 410), "god." This term was the most common general designation of deity in the ancient Near East. While it frequently occurred alone, *'ēl* was also combined with other words to constitute a compound term for deity, or to identify the nature and functions of the "god" in some manner. Thus the expression "God, the God of Israel" (Gen. 33:20) identified the specific activities of Israel's God.

In the ancient world, knowledge of a person's name was believed to give one power over that person. A knowledge of the character and attributes of pagan "gods" was thought to enable the worshipers to manipulate or influence the deities in a more effective way than they could have if the deity's name remained unknown. To that extent, the vagueness of the term *'ēl* frustrated persons who hoped to obtain some sort of power over the deity, since the name gave little or no indication of the god's character.

This was particularly true for El, the chief Canaanite god. The ancient Semites stood in mortal dread of the superior powers exercised by the gods and attempted to propitiate them accordingly. They commonly associated deity with the manifestation and use of enormous power. Perhaps this is reflected in the curious Hebrew phrase, "the power [*'ēl*] of my hand" (Gen. 31:29, KJV; RSV, "It is in my power"; cf. Deut. 28:32). Some Hebrew phrases in the Psalms associated *'ēl* with impressive natural features, such as the cedar trees of Lebanon (Ps. 80:10) or mountains (Ps. 36:6). In these instances, *'ēl* conveys a clear impression of grandeur or majesty.

Names with *'ēl* as one of their components were common in the Near East in the second millennium B.C. The names Methusael (Gen. 4:18) and Ishmael (Gen. 16:11) come from a very early period. In the Mosaic period, *'ēl* was synonymous with the Lord who delivered the Israelites from bondage in Egypt and made them victorious in battle (Num. 24:8). This tradition of the Hebrew *'ēl* as a "God" who revealed Himself in power and entered into a covenant relationship with His people was prominent in both poetry (Ps. 7:11; 85:8) and prophecy (Isa. 43:12; 46:9). The name of *'ēl* was commonly used by the Israelites to denote supernatural provision or power. This was both normal and legitimate, since the covenant between "God" and Israel assured an obedient and holy people that the creative forces of the universe would sustain and protect at all times. Equally, if they became disobedient and apostate, these same forces would punish them severely.

'ĕlāh (אֱלָה, 426), "god." This Aramaic word is the equivalent of the Hebrew *'ĕlôah*. It is a general term for "God" in the Aramaic passages of the Old Testament, and it is a cognate form of the word *'allāh*, the designation of deity used by the Arabs. The word was used widely in the Book of Ezra, occurring no fewer than 43 times between Ezra 4:24 and 7:26. On each occasion, the reference is to the "God" of the Jewish people, whether the speaker or writer was himself Jewish or not. Thus the governor of the province "Beyond the River" (i.e., west of the river Euphrates) spoke to king Darius of the "house of the great God" (Ezra 5:8). So also Cyrus instructed Sheshbazzar, the governor, that the "house of God be builded" in Jerusalem (Ezra 5:15).

While the Persians were certainly not worshipers of the "God" of Israel, they accorded Him the dignity that befitted a "God of heaven" (Ezra 6:10). This was done partly through superstition; but the pluralistic nature of the newly-won Persian empire also required them to honor the gods of conquered peoples, in the interests of peace and social harmony. When Ezra himself used the word *'ĕlāh*, he frequently specified the God of the Jews. Thus he spoke of the "God of Israel" (5:1; 6:14), the "God of heaven" (5:12; 6:9) and "God of Jerusalem" (7:19); he also associated "God" with His house in Jerusalem (5:17; 6:3). In the decree of Artaxerxes, Ezra was described as "the priest, the scribe of the God of heaven" (7:12, 21). This designation would have sounded strange coming from a pagan Persian ruler, had it not been for the policy of religious toleration exercised by the Achaemenid regime. Elsewhere in Ezra, *'ĕlāh* is associated with the temple, both when it was about to be rebuilt (5:2, 13) and as a finished edifice, consecrated for divine worship (6:16).

In the only verse in the Book of Jeremiah that was written in Aramaic (10:11), the word *'ĕlāh* appears in plural form to describe "gods" that had not participated in the creation of the universe. Although such false "gods" were being worshiped by pagan nations (and perhaps worshiped by some of the Hebrews who were in exile in Babylonia), these deities would ultimately perish because they were not eternal in nature.

In the Book of Daniel, *'ĕlāh* was used both of heathen "gods" and the one true "God" of heaven. The Chaldean priests told Nebuchadnezzar: "And it is a rare thing that the king requireth, and there is none other that can show it before the king, except the gods, whose dwelling is not with flesh" (Dan. 2:11). The Chaldeans referred to such "gods" when reporting that Shadrach, Meshach, and Abed-nego refused to participate in idol worship on the plain of Dura (Dan. 3:12). The "gods" were enumerated by Daniel when he condemned Nebuchadnezzar's neglect of the worship of Israel's one true "God" (Dan. 5:23). In Dan. 3:25, the word refers to a divine being or messenger sent to protect the three Hebrews (Dan. 3:28). In Dan. 4:8–9, 18; and 5:11, the phrase "the spirit of the holy gods" appears (KJV, RSV, NEB, NIV). Elsewhere the references to *'ĕlāh* are to the living "God" whom Daniel worshiped.

'ĕlôah (אֱלוֹהַ, 433), "god." This Hebrew name for "God" corresponds to the Aramaic *'ĕlāh* and the Ugaritic *il* (or, if denoting a goddess, *ilt*). The origin of the term is unknown, and it is used rarely in Scripture as a designation of deity. Indeed, its distribution throughout the various books of the Bible is curiously uneven. *'Ĕlôah* occurs 40 times in the Book of Job between 3:4

and 40:2, while in the remainder of the Old Testament it is used no more than 15 times.

Certain scholars regard the word as being a singular version of the common plural form *'ĕlōhîm*, a plural of majesty. *'Ĕlôah* is commonly thought to be vocative in nature, meaning "O God." But it is not clear why a special form for the vocative in an address to God should be needed, since the plural *'ĕlōhîm* is frequently translated as a vocative when the worshiper is speaking directly to God, as in Ps. 79:1. There is an obvious general linguistic relationship between *'ĕlôah* and *'ĕlōhîm*, but determining its precise nature is difficult.

The word *'ĕlôah* is predominant in poetry rather than prose literature, and this is especially true of the Book of Job. Some scholars have suggested that the author of Job deliberately chose a description for godhead that avoided the historical associations found in a phrase such as "the God of Bethel" (Gen. 31:13) or "God of Israel" (Exod. 24:10). But even the Book of Job is by no means historically neutral, since places and peoples are mentioned in introducing the narrative (cf. Job 1:1, 15, 17). Perhaps the author considered *'ĕlôah* a suitable term for poetry and used it accordingly with consistency. This is also apparently the case in Ps. 18:31, where *'ĕlôah* is found instead of *'ēl*, as in the parallel passage of 2 Sam. 22:32. *'Ĕlôah* also appears as a term for God in Ps. 50:22; 139:19; and Prov. 30:5. Although *'ĕlôah* as a divine name is rarely used outside Job, its literary history extends from at least the second millennium B.C. (as in Deut. 32:15) to the fifth century B.C. (as in Neh. 9:17).

'ēl šadday (אֵל שַׁדַּי, 410, 7706), "God Almighty." This combination of *'ēl* with a qualifying term represents a religious tradition among the Israelites that was probably in existence by the third millennium B.C. A few centuries later, *šadday* appeared in Hebrew personal names such as Zurishaddai (Num. 1:6) and Ammishaddai (Num. 1:12). The earliest Old Testament appearance of the appellation as a title of deity ("God Almighty") is in Gen. 17:1, where "God" identifies Himself in this way to Abraham.

Unfortunately, the name is not explained in any manner; and even the directions "walk before me, and be thou perfect" throw no light on the meaning of *šadday*. Scholars have attempted to understand the word relating it to the Akkadian *šadū* ("mountain"), as though "God" had either revealed His mighty power in association with mountain phenomena such as volcanic eruptions, or that He was regarded strong and immutable, like the "everlasting hills" of the blessing of Jacob (Gen. 49:26). Certainly the associating of deity with mountains was an important part of Mesopotamian religion. The "gods" were believed to favor mountaintop dwellings, and the Sumerians constructed their staged temple-towers or ziggurats as artificial mountains for worship. It was customary to erect a small shrine on the uppermost stage of the ziggurat so that the patron deity could descend from heaven and inhabit the temple. The Hebrews began their own tradition of mountain revelation just after the Exodus, but by this time the name *'ēl šadday* had been replaced by the tetragrammaton of Yahweh (Exod. 3:15; 6:3).

'Ēl šadday served as the patriarchs' covenant name for "God," and continued as such until the time of Moses, when a further revelation took place (Exod. 6:3). The Abrahamic covenant was marked by a degree of closeness between "God" and the human participants that was distinctive in Hebrew history. "God Almighty" revealed Himself as a powerful deity who was able to perform whatever He asserted. But the degree of intimacy between *'ēl šadday* and the patriarchs at various stages shows that the covenant involved God's care and love for this growing family that He had chosen, protected, and prospered. He led the covenant family from place to place, being obviously present with them at all times. His covenant formulations show that He was not preoccupied with cultic rites or orgiastic celebrations. Instead, He demanded a degree of obedience that would enable Abraham and his descendants to walk in His presence, and live blameless moral and spiritual lives (Gen. 17:1). The true covenantal service of *'ēl šadday*, therefore, was not cultic or ritualistic, but moral and ethical in character.

In the early Mosaic era, the new redemptive name of "God" and the formulation of the Sinai covenant made *'ēl šadday* largely obsolete as a designation of deity. Subsequently, the name occurs about 35 times in the Old Testament, most of which are in the Book of Job. Occasionally, the name is used synonymously with the tetragrammaton of Yahweh (Ruth 1:21; Ps. 91:1–2), to emphasize the power and might of "God" in characteristic fashion.

'ēl 'ōlām (אֵל עוֹלָם, 410, 5769), "God of eternity; God the everlasting; God for ever." The word *'ōlām* has related forms in various ancient Near Eastern languages, all of which describe lengthy duration or distant time. The idea seems to be quantitative rather than metaphysical. Thus in Ugaritic literature, a person described as *'bd 'lm* was a "permanent slave," the term *'lm* (the same as the Hebrew *'ōlām*) expressing a

period of time that could not be measured other than as lengthy duration.

Only in rare poetic passages such as Ps. 90:2 are temporal categories regarded inadequate to describe the nature of God's existence as *'ēl 'ōlām*. In such an instance, the Creator is deemed to have been "from everlasting to everlasting"; but even this use of *'ōlām* expresses the idea of continued, measurable existence rather than a state of being independent of temporal considerations.

The name *'ēl 'ōlām* was associated predominantly with Beer-sheba (Gen. 21:25–34). The settlement of Beer-sheba was probably founded during the Early Bronze Age, and the Genesis narrative explains that the name means "well of the oath" (Gen. 21:31). But it could also mean "well of the seven"— i.e., the seven lambs that were set apart as witnesses of the oath.

Abraham planted a commemorative tree in Beer-sheba and invoked the name of the Lord as *'ēl 'ōlām*. The fact that Abraham subsequently stayed many days in the land of the Philistines seems to imply that he associated continuity and stability with *'ēl 'ōlām*, who was not touched by the vicissitudes of time. Although Beer-sheba may have been a place where the Canaanites worshiped originally, the area later became associated with the veneration of the God of Abraham.

At a subsequent period, Jacob journeyed to Beer-sheba and offered sacrifices to the God of Isaac his father. He did not offer sacrifices to *'ēl 'ōlām* by name, however; and although he saw a visionary manifestation of God, he received no revelation that this was the God Abraham had venerated at Beer-sheba. Indeed, God omitted any mention of Abraham, stating that He was the God of Jacob's father.

Gen. 21:33 is the only place in the Old Testament where the title *'ēl 'ōlām* occurs. Isa. 40:28 is the only other instance where *'ōlām* is used in conjunction with a noun meaning "God." *See also* LORD.

GOLD

zāhāb (זָהָב, 2091), "gold." This word has cognates in Arabic and Aramaic. It occurs about 385 times in biblical Hebrew and in every period.

Zāhāb can refer to "gold ore," or "gold in its raw state." This is its meaning in its first biblical appearance: "The name of the first is Pison: that is it which compasseth the whole land of Havilah, where there is gold" (Gen. 2:11). The word can also be used of "gold" which has already been refined: "But he knoweth the way that I take: when he hath tried me, I shall come forth as gold" (Job 23:10). "Gold" could be beaten (1 Kings 10:16) and purified (Exod. 25:11). One can also speak of the best "gold" (2 Chron. 3:5).

Zāhāb can be conceived of as an "object of wealth": "And Abram was very rich in cattle, in silver, and in gold" (Gen. 13:2). As such, the emphasis is on "gold" as a valuable or precious commodity. Consequently, the word is used in comparisons: "The gold and the crystal cannot equal it: and the exchange of it shall not be for jewels of fine gold" (Job 28:17).

"Gold" was often one of the spoils of war: "But all the silver, and gold, and vessels of brass and iron, are consecrated unto the Lord: they shall come into the treasury of the Lord" (Josh. 6:19).

"Gold" was bought and sold as an object of merchandise: "The merchants of Sheba and Raamah, they were thy merchants: they [paid for your wares] with chief of all spices, and with all precious stones, and gold" (Ezek. 27:22).

Zāhāb was used as a costly gift: "And Balaam answered and said unto the servants of Balak, If Balak would give me his house full of silver and gold, I [could not do anything] ... " (Num. 22:18).

This metal was used as a material to make jewelry and other valuable items: "And it came to pass, as the camels had done drinking, that the man took a golden earring of half a shekel weight, and two bracelets for her hands of ten shekels weight of gold ... " (Gen. 24:22). Solomon's temple was adorned with "gold" (1 Kings 6:20–28).

Gold was used as money, being exchanged in various weights and values (according to its weight): "And he made three hundred shields of beaten gold; three pound of gold went to one shield ... " (1 Kings 10:17; cf. 2 Sam. 12:30). "Gold" even existed in the form of "coins" (Ezra 2:69).

Zāhāb is used for the color "gold": "What be these two olive branches which through the two golden pipes empty the golden oil out of themselves?" (Zech. 4:12).

GOOD

A. Adjective.

ṭôb (טוֹב, 2896), "good; favorable; festive; pleasing; pleasant; well; better; right; best." This word appears in Akkadian, Aramaic, Arabic, Ugaritic, and Old South Arabic. Occurring in all periods of biblical Hebrew, it appears about 559 times.

This adjective denotes "good" in every sense of that word. For example, *ṭôb* is used in the sense "pleasant" or "delightful": "And he saw

that [a resting place] was good, and the land that it was pleasant; and bowed his shoulder to bear [burdens] ... " (Gen. 49:15). An extension of this sense appears in Gen. 40:16, where *ṭôb* means "favorable" or "in one's favor": "When the chief baker saw that the interpretation was good, he said unto Joseph. ... " In 1 Sam. 25:8, the emphasis is on the nuance "delightful" or "festal": " ... Let the young men find favor in thine eyes: for we come in a good day. ... " God is described as One who is "good," or One who gives "delight" and "pleasure": "But it is good for me to draw near to God: I have put my trust in the Lord God, that I may declare all thy works" (Ps. 73:28).

In 1 Sam. 29:6, this word describes human activities: " ... As the Lord liveth, thou hast been upright, and thy going out and thy coming in with me in the [army] is good in my sight. ... " *Ṭôb* can be applied to scenic beauty, as in 2 Kings 2:19: "Behold, I pray thee, the situation of this city is pleasant, as my lord seeth: but the water is naught, and the ground barren." Second Chron. 12:12 employs a related nuance when it applies the word to the conditions in Judah under King Rehoboam, after he humbled himself before God: " ... Things went well."

Ṭôb often qualifies a common object or activity. When the word is used in this sense, no ethical overtones are intended. In 1 Sam. 19:4, *ṭôb* describes the way Jonathan spoke about David: "And Jonathan spake good of David unto Saul his father, and said unto him, Let not the king sin against his servant, against David; because he hath not sinned against thee, and because his works have been [toward thee] very good." First Samuel 25:15 characterizes a people as "friendly" or "useful": "But the men were very good unto us, and we were not hurt, neither missed we any thing, as long as we were conversant with them, when we were in the fields. ... " Often this word bears an even stronger emphasis, as in 1 Kings 12:7, where the "good word" is not only friendly but eases the life of one's servants. God's "good word" promises life in the face of oppression and uncertainty: " ... There hath not failed one word of all his good promise, which he promised by the hand of Moses his servant" (1 Kings 8:56). *Ṭôb* often characterizes a statement as an important assertion for salvation and prosperity (real or imagined): "Is not this the word that we did tell thee in Egypt, saying, Let us alone, that we may serve the Egyptians? For it had been *better* for us to serve the Egyptians, than that we should die in the wilderness" (Exod. 14:12). God judged that man's circumstance without a wife or helpmeet was not "good" (Gen. 2:18). Elsewhere *ṭôb* is applied to an evaluation of one's well-being or of the well-being of a situation or thing: "And God saw the light, that it was good: and God divided the light from the darkness" (Gen. 1:4—the first occurrence).

Ṭôb is used to describe land and agriculture: "And I am come down to deliver them out of the [power] of the Egyptians, and to bring them up out of that land unto a good [fertile] land and a large, unto a land flowing with milk and honey . . ." (Exod. 3:8). This suggests its potential of supporting life (Deut. 11:17). Thus the expression "the good land" is a comment about not only its existing, but its potential, productivity. In such contexts the land is viewed as one aspect of the blessings of salvation promised by God; thus the Lord did not permit Moses to cross the Jordan and enter the land which His people were to inherit (Deut. 3:26–28). This aspect of the "good land" includes overtones of its fruitfulness and "pleasantness": "And he will take your fields, and your vineyards, and your oliveyards, even the best of them . . ." (1 Sam. 8:14).

Ṭôb is used to describe men or women. Sometimes it is used of an "elite corps" of people: "And he will take your menservants, and your maidservants, and your goodliest young men, and your asses . . ." (1 Sam. 8:16). In 2 Sam. 18:27, Ahimaaz is described as a "good" man because he comes with "good" military news. In 1 Sam. 15:28, the word has ethical overtones: "The Lord hath rent the kingdom of Israel from thee this day, and hath given it to a neighbor of thine, that is better than thou" (cf. 1 Kings 2:32). In other passages, *ṭôb* describes physical appearance: "And the damsel was very fair to look upon [literally, "good of appearance"] . . ." (Gen. 24:16). When applied to one's heart, the word describes "well-being" rather than ethical status. Therefore, the parallel idea is "joyous and happy": " . . . And they . . . went unto their tents joyful and glad of heart for all the goodness that the Lord had done for David . . ." (1 Kings 8:66). Dying "at a good old age" describes "advanced age," rather than moral accomplishment, but a time when due to divine blessings one is fulfilled and satisfied (Gen. 15:15).

Ṭôb indicates that a given word, act, or circumstance contributes positively to the condition of a situation. Often this judgment does not mean that the thing is actually "good," only that it is so evaluated: "When the chief baker saw that the interpretation was good . . ." (Gen. 40:16). The judgment may be ethical: "It is not

good that ye do: ought ye not to walk in the fear of our God because of the reproach of the heathen. . .?" (Neh. 5:9). The word may also represent "agreement" or "concurrence": "The thing proceedeth from the Lord: we cannot speak unto thee bad or good" (Gen. 24:50).

Ṭôb is often used in conjunction with the Hebrew word *rā'āh* ("bad; evil"). Sometimes this is intended as a contrast; but in other contexts it may mean "everything from good [friendly] to bad [unfriendly]," which is a way of saying "nothing at all." In other contexts, more contrast is suggested: "And what the land is that they dwell in, whether it be good or bad . . ." (Num. 13:19). In this case, the evaluation would determine whether the land could support the people well or not.

In Gen. 2:9, *ṭôb* contrasted with evil has moral overtones: " . . . the tree of life also in the midst of the garden, and the tree of knowledge of good and evil." The fruit of this tree, if consumed, would reveal the difference between moral evil and moral "good." This reference also suggests that, by eating this fruit, man attempted to determine for himself what "good" and evil are.

B. Verbs.

yāṭab (יָטַב, 3190), "to go well, be pleasing, be delighted, be happy." This verb appears 117 times in the Old Testament. The meaning of the word, as expressed in Neh. 2:6, is "pleased."

ṭôb (טוב, 2895), "to be joyful, glad, pleasant, lovely, appropriate, becoming, good, precious." *Ṭôb* has cognates in Akkadian and Arabic. The verb occurs 21 times in the Old Testament. Job 13:9 is one example of the word's meaning, "to be good": "Is it good that he should search you out?"

TO BE GRACIOUS, SHOW FAVOR

A. Verb.

ḥānan (חָנַן, 2603), "to be gracious, considerate; to show favor." This word is found in ancient Ugaritic with much the same meaning as in biblical Hebrew. But in modern Hebrew *ḥānan* seems to stress the stronger meaning of "to pardon or to show mercy." The word occurs around 80 times in the Hebrew Old Testament, the first time in Gen. 33:5: "The children which God hath graciously given thy servant." Generally, this word implies the extending of "favor," often when it is neither expected nor deserved. *Ḥānan* may express "generosity," a gift from the heart (Ps. 37:21). God especially is the source of undeserved "favor" (Gen. 33:11), and He is asked repeatedly for such "gracious" acts as only He can do (Num. 6:25; Gen. 43:29). The psalmist prays: "... Grant me thy law graciously" (Ps. 119:29).

God's "favor" is especially seen in His deliverance from one's enemies or surrounding evils (Ps. 77:9; Amos 5:15). However, God extends His "graciousness" in His own sovereign way and will, to whomever He chooses (Exod. 33:19).

In many ways, *ḥānan* combines the meaning of the Greek *haris* (with the general classical Greek sense of "charm" or "graciousness") and the New Testament sense of "undeserved favor" or "mercy."

B. Noun.

ḥēn (חֵן, 2580), "favor; grace." The root with the meaning "to favor someone" is a common Semitic term. In Akkadian, the verb *enēnu* ("to have compassion") is related to *hinnu* ("favor"), which occurs only as a proper noun. The Hebrew noun *ḥēn* occurs 69 times, mainly in the Pentateuch and in the historical books through Samuel. The word's frequency increases in the poetic books, but it is rare in the prophetic books. The first occurrence is in Gen. 6:8: "But Noah found grace in the eyes of the Lord."

The basic meaning of *ḥēn* is "favor." Whatever is "pleasant and agreeable" can be described by this word. When a woman is said to have *ḥēn*, she is a "gracious" woman (Prov. 11:16); or the word may have the negative association of being "beautiful without sense" (Prov. 31:30). A person's speech may be characterized by "graciousness": "He that loveth pureness of heart, for the grace of his lips the king shall be his friend" (Prov. 22:11; cf. Ps. 45:2).

Ḥēn also denotes the response to whatever is "agreeable." The verbs used with "favor" are: "give favor" (Gen. 39:21), "obtain favor" (Exod. 3:21), and "find favor" (Gen. 6:8, RSV). The idioms are equivalent to the English verbs "to like" or "to love": "[She] said to him, Why have I found favor in your eyes, that you should take notice of me, when I am a foreigner?" (Ruth 2:10, RSV).

The Septuagint translations are: *charis* ("grace; favor; graciousness; attractiveness") and *eleos* ("mercy; compassion; pity").

C. Adjective.

ḥannûn (חַנּוּן, 2587), "gracious." One of the word's 13 occurrences is in Exod. 34:6: "And the Lord passed by before him [Moses], and proclaimed, The Lord, The Lord God, merciful and gracious, long-suffering, and abundant in goodness and truth...."

TO BE GREAT, HEAVY

A. Verbs.

kābēd (כָּבֵד, 3515), "to be heavy, weighty, burdensome, dull, honored, glorious." This word is a common Semitic term, one that is found frequently in ancient Akkadian and Ugaritic, as well as in Hebrew of all periods. *Kābēd* occurs more than 150 times in the Hebrew Bible. The verb's first occurrence is in Gen. 13:2 in the sense of "being rich": "And Abram was very rich...." This usage vividly illustrates the basic implications of the word. Whenever *kābēd* is used, it reflects the idea of "weightiness," or that which is added to something else. Thus, to be "very rich" means that Abram was heavily "weighted down" with wealth. This idea also explains how the word can be used to indicate the state of "being honored" or "glorious," for honor and glory are additional qualities that are added to a person or thing.

"To be heavy" includes negative as well as positive aspects. Thus, calamity is "heavier than the sand of the sea" (Job 6:3), and the hand of God is "very heavy" in punishing the Philistines (1 Sam. 5:11). Bondage and heavy work are "heavy" on the people (Exod. 5:9; Neh. 5:18). Eyes (Gen. 48:10) and ears (Isa. 59:1) that have become insensitive, or "dull," have had debilitating conditions added to them, whether through age or other causes. The heart of a man may become excessively "weighted" with stubbornness and thus become "hardened" (Exod. 9:7).

"To honor" or "glorify" anything is to add something which it does not have in itself, or that which others can give. Children are commanded to "honor" their parents (Exod. 20:12; Deut. 5:16); Balak promised "honor" to Balaam (Num. 22:17); Jerusalem (Lam. 1:8) and the Sabbath (Isa. 58:13) are "honored" or "made glorious." Above all, "honor" and "glory" are due to God, as repeatedly commanded in the biblical text: "Honor the Lord with thy substance" (Prov. 3:9); "Let the Lord be glorified" (Isa. 66:5); "Glorify ye the Lord" (Isa. 24:15).

Kābēd is also the Hebrew word for "liver," apparently reflecting the sense that the liver is the heaviest of the organs of the body.

rābab (רָבַב, 7231), "to be numerous, great, large, powerful." This verb, which occurs 24 times in biblical Hebrew, appears in most other Semitic languages as well. The first occurrence means "to be (or become) numerous" (Gen. 6:1). *Rābab* can also mean "to be great" in size, prestige, or power (cf. Gen. 18:20; Job 33:12; Ps. 49:16). With a subject indicating time, this verb implies "lengthening" (Gen. 38:12), and with special subjects the word may imply "extension of space" (Deut. 14:24).

B. Nouns.

rōb (רֹב, 7230), "multitude; abundance." This noun occurs about 150 times in biblical Hebrew. The word basically means "multitude" or "abundance"; it has numerical implications apparent in its first biblical appearance: "I will multiply thy seed exceedingly, that it shall not be numbered for multitude" (Gen. 16:10).

When applied to time or distance, *rōb* indicates a "large amount" or "long": "And these bottles of wine, which we filled, were new; and, behold, they be rent: and these our garments and our shoes are become old by reason of the very long journey" (Josh. 9:13). In several passages, the word is applied to abstract ideas or qualities. In such cases, *rōb* means "great" or "greatness": " . . . This that is glorious in his apparel, traveling in the greatness of his strength" (Isa. 63:1).

The preposition *le* when prefixed to the noun *rōb* sometimes forms an adverbial phrase meaning "abundantly": "For it was little which thou hadst before I came, and it is now increased unto a multitude . . ." (Gen. 30:30). The same phrase bears a different sense in 1 Kings 10:10, where it seems to be almost a substantive: "There came no more such abundance of spices as these which the queen of Sheba gave to king Solomon." The phrase literally appears to mean "great" with respect to "multitude." This phrase is applied to Uzziah's building activities: " . . . And on the wall of Ophel he built much" (2 Chron. 27:3), where it means "much." This phrase is extended by the addition of *'ad*. Thus we have *'ad lerōb*, meaning "exceeding much": "Since the people began to bring the offerings into the house of the Lord, we have had enough to eat, and have left plenty [literally, "the remainder is exceeding much"] . . ." (2 Chron. 31:10).

rab (רַב, 7227), "chief." This word is a transliteration of the Akkadian *rab*, an indication of "military rank" similar to our word *general*. The first appearance: "And it came to pass, that at midnight [literally, "the middle of the *officers* of his house]. . . ." One should especially note the titles in Jeremiah: "And all the princes [officials] of the king of Babylon came in, and sat in the middle gate, even Nergal-shar-ezer, Samgar-nebo, Sarsechim, Rab-saris, Nergal-sharezer, Rab-mag, with all the residue of the princes of the king of Babylon" (39:3). Verses 9, 10, 11, and 13 of Jeremiah 39 mention Nebuzaradan as the "captain" of the bodyguard.

C. Adjective.

rab (רַב, 7227), "many; great; large; prestigious; powerful." This adjective has a cognate in biblical Aramaic. The Hebrew word appears about 474 times in the Old Testament and in all periods.

First, this word represents plurality in number or amount, whether applied to people or to things. *Rab* is applied to people in Gen. 26:14: "For he [Isaac] had possession of flocks, and possession of herds, and great store of servants. . . ." In Gen. 13:6, the word is applied to things: "And the land was not able to bear them, that they might dwell together: for their substance was great, so that they could not dwell together." This word is sometimes used of "large groups of people" (Exod. 5:5). This basic idea of "numerical multiplicity" is also applied to amounts of liquids or masses of non-liquids: "And Moses lifted up his hand, and with his rod he smote the rock twice: and the water came out abundantly . . ." (Num. 20:11); a "great" amount of water came forth. Rebekah told Abraham's servant that her father had "straw and provender enough, and room to lodge in" (Gen. 24:25).

The phrase "many waters" is a fixed phrase meaning the "sea": " . . . Thou whom the merchants of Zidon, that pass over the sea, have replenished. And by great waters the seed of Sihor, the harvest of the river, is her revenue . . ." (Isa. 23:2–3). "And the channels of the sea appeared, the foundations of the world were discovered, at the rebuking of the Lord, at the blast of the breath of his nostrils. He sent from above, he took me; he drew me out of many waters . . ." (2 Sam. 22:16–17). This imagery is used in several Old Testament poetical passages; it would be wrong to conclude that this view of the world was true or actual. On the other hand, Gen. 7:11 uses a related phrase as a figure of the "sources of all water": " . . . The same day were all the fountains of the great deep broken up. . . ."

Used in conjunction with "days" or "years," *rab* means "long," and the resulting phrase means "a long time": "And Abraham sojourned in the Philistines' land many days" (Gen. 21:34).

The word can be used metaphorically, describing an abstract concept: "And God saw that the wickedness of man was great in the earth, and that every imagination of the thoughts of his heart was only evil continually" (Gen. 6:5—the first biblical occurrence). This use of *rab* does not describe the relative *value* of the thing modified, but its numerical recurrence. The statement implies, however, that man's constant sinning was more reprehensible than the more occasional sinning previously committed.

When *rab* is applied to land areas, it means "large" (1 Sam. 26:13). This usage is related to the usual meaning of the Semitic cognates, which represent "size" rather than numerical multiplicity (also cf. *gādal*): "And the Lord delivered them into the hand of Israel, who smote them, and chased them unto great Zidon ... " (Josh. 11:8). When God is called the "great King" (Ps. 48:2), the adjective refers to His superior power and sovereignty over all kings (vv. 4ff.). This meaning emerges in Job 32:9: "The great may not be wise, nor may elders understand justice" (cf. Job 35:9). Uses such as these in Job emphasize "greatness in prestige," whereas passages such as 2 Chron. 14:11 emphasize "strength and might": "Lord, there is none like thee to help [in battle], between the mighty and the weak" (RSV).

TO BE GUILTLESS

A. Verb.

nāqāh (נָקָה, 5352), "to be pure, innocent." Only in Hebrew does this verb mean being "innocent." In Aramaic and Arabic it occurs with the meaning of being "clean." The verb is found 44 times in the Old Testament.

Isaiah described the future of Jerusalem as an empty ("cleaned out") city: "The gates of Zion will lament and mourn; *destitute*, she will sit on the ground" (Isa. 3:26, NIV). On the more positive side, a land may also be "cleansed" of robbers: " ... Every thief will be banished [KJV, "cut off"] and everyone who swears falsely will be banished" (Zech. 5:3, NIV).

The verb is more often used to mean being "free" (with the preposition *min*). The first occurrence in the Old Testament is in Gen. 24:8, and is illustrative of this usage. Abraham ordered his servant to find a wife for Isaac. The servant pledged that he would fulfill his commission; however, if he did not succeed—that is, in case the woman was unwilling to make the long journey with him—Abraham would free him: " ... Then thou shalt be clear from this my oath. ... " The freedom may be from an oath (cf. Gen. 24:8, 41), from wrongdoing (Num. 5:31), or from punishment (Exod. 21:19; Num. 5:28). The translations vary in these contexts.

The verb *nāqāh* also appears with the legal connotation of "innocence." First, a person may be declared "innocent," or "acquitted." David prayed: "Keep your servant also from willful sins. ... Then will I be blameless, innocent of great transgression" (Ps. 19:13, NIV). On the other hand, the sinner is not "acquitted" by God: "I still dread all my sufferings, for I know you will not hold me innocent" (Job 9:28, NIV). The punishment of the person who is not "acquitted" is also expressed by a negation of the verb *nāqāh:* "The Lord will not hold anyone guiltless who misuses his name" (Exod. 20:7, NIV; "The Lord will not leave unpunished," NEB). "I will discipline you but only with justice; I will not let you go entirely unpunished" (Jer. 30:11, NIV). The fate of the wicked is the judgment of God: " ... the wicked shall not be *unpunished:* but the seed of the righteous shall be delivered [*mālat*]" (Prov. 11:21).

The verb is translated in the Septuagint generally as *athos* ("to be innocent, guiltless"). However, the range of the meaning of the Hebrew word is wider. It extends from "to be emptied [cleaned out]" to the legal jargon of "acquittal." In English versions, there is no uniformity of translation: "to be innocent, unpunished, acquitted, cleansed, held innocent" (KJV, RSV, NIV); "to be guiltless, free, cut off" (RSV); "to be deserted, purged" (NASB); "to be released, banished" (NIV).

B. Adjective.

nāqî (נָקִי, 5355), "innocent." This adjective appears 43 times in the Old Testament. One occurrence is in Ps. 15:5, which says of the righteous man, " ... Nor does he take a bribe against the innocent" (NASB).

H

HALF

A. Noun.

ḥăṣî (חֲצִי, 2677), "half; halfway; middle." This word appears about 123 times and in all periods of biblical Hebrew.

First, the word is used to indicate "half" of anything. This meaning first occurs in Exod. 24:6: "And Moses took half of the blood, and put it in basins; and half of the blood he sprinkled on the altar."

Second, *ḥăṣî* can mean "middle," as it does

in its first biblical appearance: "And it came to pass, that at midnight [literally, "the middle of the night"] the Lord smote all the first-born in the land of Egypt . . . " (Exod. 12:29). In Exod. 27:5, the word means "halfway": "And thou shalt put it under the compass of the altar beneath, that the net may be even to the midst [i.e., up to the middle] of the altar."

B. Verb.

ḥāṣāh (חָצָה, 2673), "to divide, reach unto." This verb appears about 15 times in biblical Hebrew and has cognates in Phoenician, Moabite, and Arabic. The word most commonly means "to divide," as in Exod. 21:35: " . . . Then they shall sell the live ox, and divide the money of it. . . . "

HAND

yād (יָד, 3027), "hand; side; border; alongside; hand-measure; portion; arm (rest); monument; manhood (male sex organ); power; rule." This word has cognates in most of the other Semitic languages. Biblical Hebrew attests it about 1,618 times and in every period.

The primary sense of this word is "hand": "And the Lord God said, Behold, the man is become as one of us, to know good and evil: and now, lest he put forth his hand, and take also of the tree of life . . . " (Gen. 3:22—the first biblical occurrence). Sometimes the word is used in conjunction with an object that can be grasped by the "hand": "And if he smite him with throwing a stone [literally, "hand stone"] . . . " (Num. 35:17). In a similar usage, the word means "human": " . . . He shall also stand up against the Prince of princes; but he shall be broken without hand [i.e., human agency]" (Dan. 8:25; cf. Job 34:20).

In Isa. 49:2, "hand" is used of God; God tells Moses that He will put His "hand" over the mouth of the cave and protect him. This is a figure of speech, an anthropomorphism, by which God promises His protection. God's "hand" is another term for God's "power" (cf. Jer. 16:21). The phrase "between your hands" may mean "upon your chest": "And one shall say unto him, What are these wounds in thine hands [upon your chest]?" (Zech. 13:6).

Yād is employed in several other noteworthy phrases. The "lifting of the hand" may be involved in "taking an oath" (Gen. 14:22). "Shaking" [literally, "giving one's hand"] is another oath-taking gesture (cf. Prov. 11:21). For "one's hands to be on another" (Gen. 37:27) or "laid upon another" (Exod. 7:4) is to do harm to someone. "Placing one's hands with" signifies "making common cause with someone" (Exod. 23:1). If one's hand does not "reach"

something, he is "unable to pay" for it (Lev. 5:7, RSV). When one's countryman is "unable to stretch out his hand to you," he is not able to support himself (Lev. 25:35).

"Putting one's hand on one's mouth" is a gesture of silence (Prov. 30:32). "Placing one's hands under someone" means submitting to him (1 Chron. 29:24). "Giving something into one's hand" is entrusting it to him (Gen. 42:37).

A second major group of passages uses *yād* to represent the location and uses of the hand. First, the word can mean "side," where the hand is located: "And Absalom rose up early, and stood *beside* the way of the gate . . . " (2 Sam. 15:2). In 2 Chron. 21:16, the word means "border": "Moreover the Lord stirred up against Jehoram the spirit of the Philistines, and of the Arabians, that were near [literally, "by the hand of"] the Ethiopians." A similar use in Exod. 25 applies this word to the "banks" of the Nile River: "And the daughter of Pharaoh came down to wash herself at the river; and her maidens walked *along by* the [Nile]. . . . " In this sense, *yād* can represent "length and breadth." In Gen. 34:21 we read that the land was (literally) "broad of hands": "These men are peaceable with us; therefore let them dwell in the land, and trade therein; for the land, behold, it is large enough for them. . . . "

Second, since the hand can receive only a part or fraction of something, the word can signify a "part" or "fraction": "And he took and sent [portions] unto them from before him: but Benjamin's [portion] was five times so much as any of theirs" (Gen. 43:34).

Third, *yād* comes to mean that which upholds something, a "support" (1 Kings 7:35ff.) or an "arm rest" (1 Kings 10:19).

Fourth, since a hand may be held up as a "sign," *yād* can signify a "monument" or "stele": " . . . Saul came to Carmel, and, behold, he set him up a place [monument], and is gone about, and passed on, and gone down to Gilgal" (1 Sam. 15:12).

Fifth, *yād* sometimes represents the "male sex organ": " . . . And art gone up; thou hast enlarged thy bed, and made thee a covenant with them; thou lovedst their bed where thou sawest it [you have looked on their *manhood*]" (Isa. 57:8; cf. v. 10; 6:2; 7:20).

In several passages, *yād* is used in the sense of "power" or "rule": "And David smote Hadarezer king of Zobah unto Hamath, as he went to stablish his dominion by the river Euphrates" (1 Chron. 18:3). "To be delivered into one's hands" means to be "given into one's power": "God hath delivered him into mine hand; for he is shut in, by entering into a town that hath gates and bars" (1 Sam. 23:7; cf. Prov. 18:21).

"To fill someone's hand" may be a technical term for "installing him" in office: "And thou shalt put them upon Aaron thy brother, and his sons with him; and shalt anoint them, and consecrate them [literally, "fill their hands"], and sanctify them, that they may minister unto me in the priest's office" (Exod. 28:41).

Yād is frequently joined to the preposition *b*ᵉ and other prepositions as an extension; there is no change in meaning, only a longer form: "For what have I done? or what evil is in mine hand?" (1 Sam. 26:18).

TO HASTEN, MAKE HASTE

māhar (מָהַר, 4116), "to hasten, make haste." This verb and various derivatives are common to both ancient and modern Hebrew. *Māhar* occurs approximately 70 times in the Hebrew Bible; it appears twice in the first verse in which it is found: "And Abraham *hastened* into the tent unto Sarah, and said, *Make ready quickly* three measures of fine meal . . ." (Gen. 18:6). *Māhar* often has an adverbial use when it appears with another verb, such as in Gen. 18:7: ". . . hasted to dress it" (or "quickly prepared it").

TO HATE

A. Verb.

śānē' (שָׂנֵא, 8130), "to hate, set against." This verb appears in Ugaritic, Moabite, Aramaic, and Arabic. It appears in all periods of Hebrew and about 145 times in the Bible.

Śānē' represents an emotion ranging from intense "hatred" to the much weaker "set against" and is used of persons and things (including ideas, words, inanimate objects).

The strong sense of the word typifies the emotion of jealousy; and therefore, *śānē'* is the feeling Joseph's brothers experienced because their father preferred him (Gen. 37:4; cf. v. 11). This "hatred" increased when Joseph reported his dreams (Gen. 37:8). Obviously, the word covers emotion ranging from "bitter disdain" to outright "hatred," for in Gen. 37:18ff. the brothers plotted Joseph's death and achieved his removal.

This emphasis can be further heightened by a double use of the root. Delilah's father told Samson: "I verily thought that thou hadst utterly hated her [literally, "hating, you hated her"] . . ." (Judg. 15:2).

One special use of *śānē'* is ingressive, indicating the initiation of the emotion. So "Amnon hated [literally, "began to hate"] her exceedingly; so that the hatred wherewith he hated

["began to hate"] her was greater than the love wherewith he had loved her" (2 Sam. 13:15). This emphasis appears again in Jer. 12:8: "Mine heritage is unto me as a lion in the forest; it crieth out against me: therefore have I [come to hate] it" (also cf. Hos. 9:15).

In a weaker sense, *śānē'* signifies "being set against" something. Jethro advised Moses to select men who hated ["were set against"] covetousness to be secondary judges over Israel (Exod. 18:21). A very frequent but special use of the verb means "to be unloved." For example, *śānē'* may indicate that someone is "untrustworthy," therefore an enemy to be ejected from one's territory. This sense is found in an early biblical occurrence, in which Isaac said to Abimelech and his army: "Wherefore come ye to me, seeing ye hate me, and have sent me away from you?" (Gen. 26:27). The word may mean "unloved" in the sense of deteriorating marital relations: "And the damsel's father shall say unto the elders, I gave my daughter unto this man to wife, and he hateth [i.e., turned against] her" (Deut. 22:16). This nuance is especially clear in Ezek. 23:28, where the verb is in synonymous parallelism to "alienated": "Behold, I will deliver thee into the hand of them whom thou hatest, into the hand of them from whom thy mind is alienated." In the case of two wives in a family, in which one was preferred over the other, it may be said that one was loved and the other "hated" (Deut. 21:15). This emphasis is found in Gen. 29:31: "And when the Lord saw that Leah was hated, he opened her womb; but Rachel was barren." The word, used as a passive participle, represents a spurned woman: ". . . An odious [unloved] woman when she is married . . ." (Prov. 30:23).

B. Noun.

śin'āh (שִׂנְאָה, 8135), "hatred." This noun occurs 17 times in the Old Testament. Num. 35:20 is one occurrence: "And if he stabbed him from hatred, or hurled at him, lying in wait . . ." (RSV).

HEAD

A. Nouns.

rō'š (רֹאשׁ, 7218), "head; top; first; sum." Cognates of *rō'š* appear in Ugaritic, Akkadian, Phoenician, biblical Aramaic, Arabic, and Ethiopic. *Rō'š* and its alternate form *rē'š* appear about 596 times in biblical Hebrew.

This word often represents a "head," a bodily part (Gen. 40:20). *Rō'š* is also used of a decapitated "head" (2 Sam. 4:8), an animal "head" (Gen. 3:15), and a statue "head" (Dan. 2:32). In Dan. 7:9, where God is pictured in human form, His "head" is crowned with hair like pure wool (i.e., white).

To "lift up one's own head" may be a sign of declaring one's innocence: "If I be wicked, woe unto me; and if I be righteous, yet will I not lift up my head. I am full of confusion; therefore see thou mine affliction" (Job 10:15). This same figure of speech may indicate an intention to begin a war, the most violent form of self-assertion: "For, lo, thine enemies make a tumult: and they that hate thee have lifted up the head" (Ps. 83:2). With a negation, this phrase may symbolize submission to another power: "Thus was Midian subdued before the children of Israel, so that they lifted up their heads no more" (Judg. 8:28). Used transitively (i.e., to lift up someone else's "head"), this word may connote restoring someone to a previous position: "Yet within three days shall Pharaoh lift up thine head, and restore thee unto thy place..." (Gen. 40:13). It can also denote the release of someone from prison: "... Evil-merodach king of Babylon in the year that he began to reign did lift up the head of Jehoiachin king of Judah out of prison" (2 Kings 25:27).

With the verb *rûm* ("to raise"), *rō'š* can signify the victory and power of an enthroned king—God will "lift up [His] head," or exert His rule (Ps. 110:7). When God lifts up (*rûm*) one's "head," He fills one with hope and confidence: "But thou, O Lord, art a shield for me; my glory, and the lifter up of mine head" (Ps. 3:3).

There are many secondary nuances of *rō'š*. First, the word can represent the "hair on one's head": "And on the seventh day, he shall shave all his hair off his *head;* he shall shave off his beard and his eyebrows, all his hair" (Lev. 14:9, RSV).

The word can connote unity, representing every individual in a given group: "Have they not sped? have they not divided the prey; to every man a damsel or two..." (Judg. 5:30). This word may be used numerically, meaning the total number of persons or individuals in a group: "Take ye the sum of all the congregation of the children of Israel, after their families, by the house of their fathers, with the number of their names, every male by their polls" (Num. 1:2).

Rō'š can also emphasize the individual: "And there was a great famine in Samaria: and, behold, they besieged it, until an ass's head [i.e., an individual donkey] was sold for fourscore pieces of silver..." (2 Kings 6:25). It is upon the "head" (upon the person himself) that curses and blessings fall: "The blessings of thy father have prevailed above the blessings of my progenitors...: they shall be on the head of Joseph..." (Gen. 49:26).

Rō'š sometimes means "leader," whether appointed, elected, or self-appointed. The word can be used of the tribal fathers, who are the leaders of a group of people: "And Moses chose able men out of all Israel, and made them heads over the people..." (Exod. 18:25). Military leaders are also called "heads": "These be the names of the mighty men whom David had: The Tachmonite that sat in the seat, chief among the captains..." (2 Sam. 23:8). In Num. 1:16, the princes are called "heads" (cf. Judg. 10:18). This word is used of those who represent or lead the people in worship (2 Kings 25:18—the chief priest).

When used of things, *rō'š* means "point" or "beginning." With a local emphasis, the word refers to the "top" or summit of a mountain or hill: "... Tomorrow I will stand on the top of the hill with the rod of God in mine hand" (Exod. 17:9). Elsewhere the word represents the topmost end of a natural or constructed object: "Go to, let us build us a city and a tower, whose top may reach unto heaven..." (Gen. 11:4).

In Gen. 47:31, the word denotes the "head" of a bed, or where one lays his "head." In 1 Kings 8:8, *rō'š* refers to the ends of poles. The word may be used of the place where a journey begins: "Thou hast built thy high place at every head of the way..." (Ezek. 16:25); cf. Dan. 7:1: "the sum of the matters...." This sense of the place of beginning appears in Gen. 2:10 (the first occurrence): "And a river went out of Eden to water the garden; and from thence it was parted, and became [the source of four rivers]." This nuance identifies a thing as being placed spatially in front of a group; it stands in front or at the "head" (Deut. 20:9; cf. 1 Kings 21:9). The "head" of the stars is a star located at the zenith of the sky (Job 22:12). The "head" cornerstone occupies a place of primary importance. It is the stone by which all the other stones are measured; it is the chief cornerstone (Ps. 118:22).

This word may have a temporal significance, meaning "beginning" or "first." The second sense is seen in Exod. 12:2: "This month shall be unto you the beginning of months...." In 1 Chron. 16:7 the word describes the "first" in a whole series of acts: "Then on that day David delivered first this psalm to thank the Lord into the hand of Asaph and his brethren."

Rō'š may also have an estimative connotation: "Take thou also unto thee [the finest of] spices..." (Exod. 30:23).

rē'šît (רֵאשִׁית, 7225), "beginning; first; choicest." The abstract word *rē'šît* corresponds to the temporal and estimative sense of *rō'š*. *Rē'šît* connotes the "beginning" of a fixed period of time: "... The eyes of the Lord thy God are always upon it, from the beginning of the year even unto the end of the year" (Deut. 11:12). The "beginning" of one's period of life is intended in Job 42:12: "So the Lord blessed the latter end of Job more than his beginning...." This word can represent a point of departure, as it does in Gen. 1:1 (the first occurrence): "In the beginning God created the heaven and the earth." Estimatively, this word can mean the "first" or "choicest": "The first of the first fruits of thy land thou shalt bring into the house of the Lord thy God" (Exod. 23:19). This nuance of *rē'šît* may appear in the comparative sense, meaning "choicest" or "best." Dan. 11:41 exhibits the nuance of "some": "... But these shall escape out of his hand, even Edom, and Moab, and the chief [NASB, "foremost"] of the children of Ammon" (Dan. 11:41).

Used substantively, the word can mean "first fruits": "As for the oblation of the first fruits, ye shall offer them unto the Lord: but they shall not be burnt on the altar for a sweet savor" (Lev. 2:12). "... The first fruits of them which they shall offer unto the Lord, them have I given thee" (Num. 18:12). Sometimes this word represents the "first part" of an offering: "Ye shall offer up a cake of the first of your dough for a heave offering..." (Num. 15:20).

B. Adjective.

ri'šôn (רִאשׁוֹן, 7223), "first; foremost; preceding; former." This word occurs about 182 times in biblical Hebrew. It denotes the "first" in a temporal sequence: "And it came to pass in the six hundredth and first year, in the first month, the first day of the month..." (Gen. 8:13). In Ezra 9:2, *ri'šôn* is used both of precedence in time and of leadership: "... The holy seed have mingled themselves with the people of those lands: yea, the hand of the princes and rulers hath been chief in this trespass."

A second meaning of this adjective is "preceding" or "former": "... Unto the place of the altar, which he had made there at the first..." (Gen. 13:4). Gen. 33:2 uses this word locally: "And he put the handmaids and their children foremost, and Leah and her children after, and Rachel and Joseph hindermost." The "former ones" are "ancestors": "But I will for their sakes remember the covenant of their ancestors, whom I brought forth out of the land of Egypt in the sight of the heathen..." (Lev. 26:45). But in most cases, this adjective has a temporal emphasis.

TO HEAL

rāpā' (רָפָא, 7495), "to heal." This word is common to both ancient and modern Hebrew. It occurs approximately 65 times in the Hebrew Old Testament, appearing first in Gen. 20:17: "... God healed Abimelech."

"To heal" may be described as "restoring to normal," an act which God typically performs. Thus, appeals to God for healing are common: "... O Lord, heal me; for my bones are vexed" (Ps. 6:2); "Heal me, O Lord, and I shall be healed..." (Jer. 17:14). Not only are human diseases "healed," but bad water is restored to normal or "healed" (2 Kings 2:22); salt water is "healed" or made fresh (Ezek. 47:8); even pottery is "healed" or restored (Jer. 19:11).

A large number of the uses of *rāpā'* express the "healing" of the nation—such "healing" not only involves God's grace and forgiveness, but also the nation's repentance. Divine discipline leads to repentance and "healing": "Come, and let us return unto the Lord: for he hath torn, and he will heal us..." (Hos. 6:1). God promises: "For I will restore health unto thee, and I will heal thee of thy wounds, saith the Lord..." (Jer. 30:17). Even foreign cities and powers can know God's "healing" if they repent (Jer. 51:8–9).

False prophets are condemned because they deal only with the symptoms and not with the deep spiritual hurts of the people: "They have healed also the hurt of the daughter of my people slightly, saying, Peace, peace; when there is no peace" (Jer. 6:14; also 8:11).

TO HEAR

A. Verb.

šāma' (שָׁמַע, 8085), "to hear, hearken, listen, obey, publish." This word occurs throughout the Semitic languages including biblical Hebrew and Aramaic. *Šāma'* occurs in all historical layers of Hebrew, and about 1,160 times in the Bible. The word is attested 9 times in biblical Aramaic.

Basically, this verb means to "hear" something with one's ears, but there are several other nuances. In Gen. 37:17, a man told Joseph that he "heard" Joseph's brothers say, "Let us go to Dothan"; in other words, he unintentionally "overheard" them say it. *Šāma'* can also be used of "eavesdropping, or intentionally listening in on a conversation; so Sarah "overheard" what the three men said to Abram (Gen. 18:10).

Joseph asked his brothers to "listen" as he recounted what he had dreamed (Gen. 37:6). In 1 Chron. 28:2, David told his audience to "listen" as he spoke; they were to give him their undivided attention.

To "hear" something may imply to "have knowledge," as when Abimelech told Abraham that he did not know about the controversy over the wills because no one had told him and neither had he "heard" it (Gen. 21:26). *Šāma'* may also imply to "gain knowledge" or to "get knowledge": " . . . The Chaldeans that besieged Jerusalem heard [the report] . . . " (Jer. 37:5).

Again, the word may mean to "come into knowledge about." Moses told the unclean men to wait while he "listened" to what the Lord would command regarding them (Num. 9:8). His intent clearly was more than just to "hear" something; he intended to "gain some knowledge" from the Lord.

The verb can represent the mere "hearing" of something, as when Adam and Eve "heard" the sound of God walking in the garden (Gen. 3:8—first biblical occurrence). To "make someone hear" something (without any specification of what was heard) suggests "summoning" the person (1 Kings 15:22).

"Hearing" can be both intellectual and spiritual. Spiritually, one may "hear" God's Word (Num. 24:4), or "learn" it from God. Conversely, God told Abraham that He had "heard" his prayer and would act accordingly (Gen. 17:20). In this context, to "hear" means not only to hear what is said, but to agree with its intention or petition (cf. Gen. 16:11). In the case of hearing and hearkening to a higher authority, *šāma'* can mean to "obey." In Abraham's seed, all nations would be blessed because he "heard" (obeyed) God's voice (Gen. 22:18).

Another nuance of intellectual "hearing" appears in Gen. 11:7, in which we are told that God planned to confuse human language, "that they may not understand one another's speech."

To have a "hearing heart" is to have "discernment" or "understanding" (1 Kings 3:9). Certainly when Moses told Israel's judges to "hear" cases, he meant more than listening with one's ear. He meant for them to examine the merits of a case, so as to render a just decision (Deut. 1:16).

B. Nouns.

šôma' (שׁוֹמַע, 8089), means "things heard by accident; hearsay." This word appears infrequently in the Old Testament, as in Josh. 6:27: "So the Lord was with Joshua; and his *fame* was noised throughout all the country."

šēma' (שֵׁמַע, 8088), "something heard by design; report." The Old Testament attests this word 17 times. Gen 29:13 contains one occurrence: "And it came to pass, when Laban heard the tidings [*šēma'*] of Jacob his sister's son. . . . "

šᵉmû'āh (שְׁמוּעָה, 8052), "revelation; something heard." This word appears 27 times. One appearance is in Isa. 28:9: "Whom shall he teach knowledge? and whom shall he make to understand doctrine [*šᵉmû'āh*]?"

HEART

A. Noun.

lēb (לֵב, 3820), "heart; mind; midst." *Lēb* and its synonym *lēbāb* appear 860 times in the Old Testament. The law, prophets, and Psalms often speak of the "heart." The root occurs also in Akkadian, Assyrian, Egyptian, Ugaritic, Aramaic, Arabic, and post-biblical Hebrew. The corresponding Aramaic nouns occur seven times in the Book of Daniel.

"Heart" is used first of man in Gen. 6:5: "And God saw that the wickedness of man was great in the earth, and that every imagination of the thoughts of his heart was only evil continually." In Gen. 6:6 *lēb* is used of God: "And it repented the Lord that he had made man on the earth, and it grieved him at his heart."

"Heart" may refer to the organ of the body: "And Aaron shall bear the names of the children of Israel in the breastplate of judgment upon his heart, when he goeth in unto the holy place . . . " (Exod. 28:29); " . . . [Joab] took three darts in his hand, and thrust them through the heart of Absalom . . . " (2 Sam. 18:14); "My heart panteth . . . " (Ps. 38:10).

Lēb may also refer to the inner part or middle of a thing: " . . . and the depths were congealed in the heart of the sea" (Exod. 15:8); " . . . and the mountain burned with fire in the midst [RSV, "to the heart"] of heaven . . . " (Deut. 4:11, KJV); "Yea, thou shalt be as he that lieth down in the midst of the sea . . . " (Prov. 23:34).

Lēbāb can be used of the inner man, contrasted to the outer man, as in Deut. 30:14: "But the word is very nigh unto thee, in thy mouth, and in thy heart, that thou mayest do it" (cf. Joel 2:13); " . . . man looketh on the outward appearance, but the Lord looketh on the heart" (1 Sam. 16:7). *Lēbāb* is often compounded with "soul" for emphasis, as in 2 Chron. 15:12; "And they entered into a covenant to seek the Lord God of their fathers with all their heart and with all their soul" (cf. 2 Chron. 15:15). *Nepeš* ("soul; life; self") is translated "heart" fifteen times in the KJV. Each time, it connotes the "inner man": "For as he thinketh in his heart [*nepeš*], so is he" (Prov. 23:7).

Lēb can be used of the man himself or his personality: "Then Abraham fell upon his face and laughed, and said in his heart, ... " (Gen. 17:17); " ... my heart had great experience ... " (Eccl. 1:16). *Lēb* is also used of God in this sense: "And I will give you pastors according to mine heart" (Jer. 3:15).

The seat of desire, inclination, or will can be indicated by "heart": "Pharaoh's heart is hardened ... " (Exod. 7:14); " ... whosoever is of a willing heart, let him bring it ... " (Exod. 35:5; cf. vv. 21, 29); "I will praise thee, O Lord my God, with all my heart ... " (Ps. 86:12). *Lēb* is also used of God in this sense: " ... and I will plant them in this land assuredly with my whole heart and with my whole soul" (Jer. 32:41). Two people are said to be in agreement when their "hearts" are right with each other: "Is thine heart right, as my heart is with thy heart?" (2 Kings 10:15). In 2 Chron. 24:4, " ... Joash was minded to repair the house of the Lord" (Heb. "had in his heart").

The "heart" is regarded as the seat of emotions: "And thou shalt love the Lord thy God with all thine heart, ... " (Deut. 6:5); " ... and when he [Aaron] seeth thee, he will be glad in his heart" (Exod. 4:14; cf. 1 Sam. 2:1). So there are "merry" hearts (Judg. 16:25), "fearful" hearts (Isa. 35:4), and hearts that "trembled" (1 Sam. 4:13).

The "heart" could be regarded as the seat of knowledge and wisdom and as a synonym of "mind." This meaning often occurs when "heart" appears with the verb "to know": "Thus you are to know in your heart ... " (Deut. 8:5, NASB); and "Yet the Lord hath not given you a heart to perceive [know] ... " (Deut. 29:4, KJV; RSV, "mind"). Solomon prayed, "Give therefore thy servant an understanding heart to judge thy people, that I may discern between good and bad ... " (1 Kings 3:9; cf. 4:29). Memory is the activity of the "heart," as in Job 22:22: " ... lay up his [God's] words in thine heart."

The "heart" may be the seat of conscience and moral character. How does one respond to the revelation of God and of the world around him? Job answers: " ... my heart shall not reproach me as long as I live" (27:6). On the contrary, "David's heart smote him ... " (2 Sam. 24:10). The "heart" is the fountain of man's deeds: " ... in the integrity of my heart and innocency of my hands I have done this" (Gen. 20:5; cf. v. 6). David walked "in uprightness of heart" (1 Kings 3:6) and Hezekiah "with a perfect heart" (Isa. 38:3) before God. Only the man with "clean hands, and a pure heart" (Ps. 24:4) can stand in God's presence.

Lēb may refer to the seat of rebellion and pride. God said: " ... for the imagination of man's heart is evil from his youth" (Gen. 8:21).

Tyre is like all men: "Because thine heart is lifted up, and thou hast said, I am a God" (Ezek. 28:2). They all become like Judah, whose "sin ... is graven upon the table of their heart" (Jer. 17:1).

God controls the "heart." Because of his natural "heart," man's only hope is in the promise of God: "A new heart also will I give you, ... and I will take away the stony heart out of your flesh, and I will give you a heart of flesh" (Ezek. 36:26). So the sinner prays: "Create in me a clean heart, O God" (Ps. 51:10); and " ... unite my heart [give me an undivided heart] to fear thy name" (Ps. 86:11). Also, as David says, "I know also, my God, that thou triest the heart, and hast pleasure in uprightness" (1 Chron. 29:17). Hence God's people seek His approval: " ... try my reins and my heart" (Ps. 26:2).

The "heart" stands for the inner being of man, the man himself. As such, it is the fountain of all he does (Prov. 4:4). All his thoughts, desires, words, and actions flow from deep within him. Yet a man cannot understand his own "heart" (Jer. 17:9). As a man goes on in his own way, his "heart" becomes harder and harder. But God will circumcise (cut away the uncleanness of) the "heart" of His people, so that they will love and obey Him with their whole being (Deut. 30:6).

B. Adverb.

lēb (לֵב, 3820), "tenderly; friendly; comfortably." *Lēb* is used as an adverb in Gen. 34:3: "And his soul clave unto Dinah ... and he loved the damsel, and spake kindly unto the damsel." In Ruth 4:13, the word means "friendly": " ... thou hast spoken friendly unto thine handmaid. ... " The word means "comfortably" in 2 Chron. 30:22 and in Isa. 40:2.

HEAVENS

šāmayim (שָׁמַיִם, 8064), "heavens; heaven; sky." This general Semitic word appears in languages such as Ugaritic, Akkadian, Aramaic, and Arabic. It occurs 420 times and in all periods of biblical Hebrew.

First, *šāmayim* is the usual Hebrew word for the "sky" and the "realm of the sky." This realm is where birds fly. God forbids Israel to make any "likeness of any winged fowl that flieth in the air" (Deut. 4:17). When Absalom's hair caught in the branches of a tree, he hung suspended between the "heaven" and the earth (2 Sam. 18:9). This area, high above the ground but below the stars and heavenly bodies, is often the locus of visions: "And David lifted up his eyes, and saw the angel of the Lord stand between the earth and the heaven, having a drawn sword in his hand stretched out over Jerusalem" (1 Chron. 21:16).

Second, this word represents an area farther removed from the earth's surface. From this area come such things as frost (Job 38:29), snow (Isa. 55:10), fire (Gen. 19:24), dust (Deut. 28:24), hail (Josh. 10:11), and rain: "The fountains also of the deep and the windows of heaven were stopped, and the rain from heaven was restrained" (Gen. 8:2). This realm is God's storehouse; God is the dispenser of the stores and Lord of the realm (Deut. 28:12). This meaning of *šāmayim* occurs in Gen. 1:7–8: "And God made the firmament, and divided the waters which were under the firmament from the waters which were above the firmament: and it was so. And God called the firmament Heaven."

Third, *šāmayim* also represents the realm in which the sun, moon, and stars are located: "And God said, Let there be lights in the firmament of the heaven to divide the day from the night . . ." (Gen. 1:14). This imagery is often repeated in the Creation account and in poetical passages. Thus the "heavens" can be stretched out like a curtain (Ps. 104:2) or rolled up as a scroll (Isa. 34:4).

Fourth, the phrase "heaven and earth" may denote the entire creation. This use of the word appears in Gen. 1:1: "In the beginning God created the heaven and the earth."

Fifth, "heaven" is the dwelling place of God: "He that sitteth in the heavens shall laugh: the Lord shall have them in derision" (Ps. 2:4; cf. Deut. 4:39). Again, note Deut. 26:15: "Look down from thy holy habitation, from heaven, and bless thy people Israel. . . ." Another expression representing the dwelling place of God is "the highest heaven [literally, the heaven of heavens]." This does not indicate height, but an absolute—i.e., God's abode is a unique realm not to be identified with the physical creation: "Behold the heaven and the heaven of heavens is the Lord's thy God, the earth also, with all that therein is" (Deut. 10:14).

TO HELP

'āzar (עָזַר, 5826), "to help, assist, aid." This word and its derivatives are common in both ancient and modern Hebrew. The verb occurs about 80 times in the biblical text. *'Āzar* is first found in the Old Testament in Jacob's deathbed blessing of Joseph: " . . . The God of thy father, who shall help thee . . ." (Gen. 49:25).

Help or aid comes from a variety of sources: Thirty-two kings "helped" Ben-hadad (1 Kings 20:6); one city "helps" another (Josh. 10:33); even false gods are believed to be of "help"

(2 Chron. 28:23). Of course, the greatest source of help is God Himself; He is "the helper of the fatherless" (Ps. 10:14). God promises: "I will help thee" (Isa. 41:10); "and the Lord shall help them, and deliver them . . ." (Ps. 37:40).

HERD

bāqār (בָּקָר, 1241), "herd; cattle." This noun has cognates in Arabic and Aramaic. It appears about 180 times in biblical Hebrew and in all periods.

One meaning of the word is "cattle." Such beasts were slaughtered for food, and their hides were presented as offerings to God (Num. 15:8). This meaning of *bāqār* is in Gen. 12:16 (the first biblical occurrence): "And he [Pharaoh] entreated Abram well for her [Sarah's] sake: and he had sheep, and oxen, and he asses. . . ." These were grazing beasts (1 Chron. 27:29) and were eaten (1 Kings 4:23). These animals pulled carts (2 Sam. 6:6) and plows (Job 1:14), and carried burdens on their backs (1 Chron. 12:40).

Bāqār often refers to a group of cattle or "herd" (both sexes), as it does in Gen. 13:5: "And Lot also, which went with Abram, had flocks, and herds [in the Hebrew, this word appears in a singular form] and tents." The word can represent a "small group of cattle" (not a herd; cf. Gen. 47:17; Exod. 22:1) or even a pair of oxen (Num. 7:17). A single ox is indicated either by some other Hebrew word or called an offspring of oxen (Gen. 18:7).

Bāqār also refers to statues of oxen: "It [the altar of burnt offerings] stood upon twelve oxen, three looking toward the north, and three looking toward the west, and three looking toward the south, and three looking toward the east . . ." (1 Kings 7:25).

Some scholars believe this noun is related to the verb *bāqār* ("to seek out") and to the noun *bōqer* ("morning").

HERO

A. Nouns.

gibbôr (גִּבּוֹר, 1368), "hero." This word appears 159 times in the Old Testament. The first occurrence of *gibbôr* is in Gen. 6:4: "There were giants in the earth in those days; and also after that, when the sons of God came in unto the daughters of men, and they bare children to them, the same became *mighty men* which were of old, men of renown."

In the context of battle, the word is better understood to refer to the category of warriors. The *gibbôr* is the proven warrior; especially is this true when *gibbôr* is used in combination with *ḥayil* ("strength"). The KJV gives a literal translation, "mighty men [*gibbôr*] of valor [*hayil*]," whereas the NIV renders the phrase idiomatically, "fighting men" (cf. Josh. 1:14). David, who had proven himself as a warrior, attracted "heroes" to his band while he was being pursued by Saul (2 Sam. 23). When David was enthroned as king, these men became a part of the elite military corps. The phrase *gibbôr hayil* may also refer to a man of a high social class, the landed man who had military responsibilities. Saul came from such a family (1 Sam. 9:1); so also Jeroboam (1 Kings 11:28).

The king symbolized the strength of his kingdom. He had to lead his troops in battle, and as commander he was expected to be a "hero." Early in David's life, he was recognized as a "hero" (1 Sam. 18:7). The king is described as a "hero": "Gird thy sword upon thy thigh, O most *Mighty*, with thy glory and thy majesty" (Ps. 45:3). The messianic expectation included the hope that the Messiah would be "mighty": "For unto us a child is born, unto us a son is given: and the government shall be upon his shoulder; and his name shall be called Wonderful, Counselor, The *mighty* God, The everlasting Father, The Prince of Peace" (Isa. 9:6).

Israel's God was a mighty God (Isa. 10:21). He had the power to deliver: "The Lord thy God in the midst of thee is mighty; he will save, he will rejoice over thee with joy; he will rest in his love, he will joy over thee with singing" (Zeph. 3:17). Jeremiah's moving confession (32:17ff.) bears out the might of God in creation (v. 17) and in redemption (vv. 18ff.). The answer to the emphatic question, "Who is this King of glory?" in Psalm 24 is: "The Lord strong and mighty, the Lord mighty in battle" (v. 8).

The Septuagint gives the following translations: *dunatos* ("powerful; strong; mighty; able ruler") and *ischuros* ("strong; mighty; powerful"). The KJV gives these senses: "mighty men; mighty one; strong; violent."

geber (גֶּבֶר, 181), "man." This word occurs 66 times in the Old Testament, once in 1 Chron. 23:3: "Now the Levites were numbered from the age of thirty years and upward: and their number by their polls, man by man, was thirty and eight thousand."

B. Verb.
gābar (גָּבַר, 1396), "to be strong." The root meaning "to be strong" appears in all Semitic languages as a verb or a noun, but the verb occurs only 25 times in the Old Testament. Job 21:7 contains an occurrence of *gābar*: "Wherefore do the wicked live, become old, yea, are mighty in power?"

C. Adjective.
gibbôr (גִּבּוֹר, 1368), "strong." *Gibbôr* may be translated by the adjective "strong" in the following contexts: a "strong" man (1 Sam. 14:52), a "strong" lion (Prov. 30:30), a mighty hunter (Gen. 10:9), and the mighty ones (Gen. 6:1–4).

TO HIDE

sātar (סָתַר, 5641), "to conceal, hide, shelter." This verb and various derivatives are found in modern Hebrew as well as in biblical Hebrew. *Sātar* occurs approximately 80 times in the Old Testament. The word is found for the first time in Gen. 4:14 as Cain discovers that because of his sin, he will be "hidden" from the presence of God, which implies a separation.

In the so-called Mizpah Benediction (which is really a warning), *sātar* again has the sense of "separation": "The Lord watch between me and thee, when we are absent one from another" (Gen. 31:49). To "hide oneself" is to take refuge: "Doth not David hide himself with us . . . ?" (1 Sam. 23:19). Similarly, to "hide" someone is to "shelter" him from his enemy: " . . . The Lord hid them" (Jer. 36:26).

To pray, "Hide thy face from my sins" (Ps. 51:9), is to ask God to ignore them. But when the prophet says, "And I will wait upon the Lord, that hideth his face from the house of Jacob . . . " (Isa. 8:17), he means that God's favor has been withdrawn. Similarly, Judah's sins have "hidden" God's face from her (Isa. 59:2).

HIGH

A. Adjective.
gābōah (גָּבֹהַּ, 1364), "high; exalted." This adjective occurs about 24 times. The root seen in this adjective, in the verb *gābah* and in the noun *gōbah*, occurs in every period of biblical Hebrew.

This word means "high, lofty, tall in dimension": "And the waters [of the flood] prevailed exceedingly upon the earth; and all the high hills, that were under the whole heaven, were covered" (Gen. 7:19—the first occurrence). When used of a man, *gābōah* means "tall": Saul was "higher than any of the people" (1 Sam. 9:2; cf. 16:7). In Dan. 8:2, *gābōah* describes the length of a ram's horns: " . . . And the two horns were high; but one was higher than the other, and the higher came up last."

The word means "high or exalted in station": "Thus saith the Lord God; Remove the diadem, and take off the crown: this shall not be the same: exalt him that is low, and abase him that is high" (Ezek. 21:26). In Eccl. 5:8, this connotation of "one of high rank" may be expressed in the translation "official" (RSV).

Gābōah may be used of a psychological state, such as "haughtiness": "Talk no more so exceeding proudly [this double appearance of the word emphasizes it]; let not arrogancy come out of your mouth . . . " (1 Sam. 2:3).

'elyôn (עֶלְיוֹן, 5945), "high; top; uppermost; highest; upper; height." The 53 occurrences of this word are scattered throughout biblical literature.

This word indicates the "uppermost" (as opposed to the lower): " . . . I had three white baskets on my head: And in the uppermost basket there was of all manner of bakemeats . . . " (Gen. 40:16–17). In Ezek. 42:5, *'elyôn* describes the "uppermost" of three stories: "Now the upper chambers were shorter: for the galleries were higher than these, than the lower, and than the middlemost of the building." A figurative use of the word appears in 2 Chron. 7:21, where it modifies the dynasty (house) of Solomon. The messianic Davidic king will be God's firstborn, "higher than the kings of the earth" (Ps. 89:27).

In many passages, *'elyôn* means "upper," in the sense of the top or higher of two things: " . . . the border of their inheritance on the east side was Ataroth-addar, unto Beth-horon the upper" (Josh. 16:5; cf. 2 Chron. 8:5).

This word is frequently used in a name (*el 'elyôn*) of God; it describes Him as the Most High, the "highest" and only Supreme Being. The emphasis here is on divine supremacy rather than divine exclusiveness: "And Melchizedek king of Salem brought forth bread and wine: and he was the priest of the most *high God*" [*el 'elyôn*] (Gen. 14:18—the first occurrence). This name for a god also appears in extra-biblical Palestinian documents.

Also the figurative use of *'elyôn* to describe the "house" or dynasty of Israel takes an unusual turn in 1 Kings 9:8, where the kingdom is said to be the "height" of astonishment: "And at this house, which [will be a heap of ruins], every one that passeth by it shall be astonished, and shall hiss; and they shall say, Why hath the Lord done thus unto this land, and to this house?"

B. Verb.

gābāh (גָּבַה, 1362), "to be high, exalted, lofty." This verb, which occurs 38 times in the Bible, has cognates in Akkadian, Aramaic, and Arabic. Its meanings parallel those of the adjective. It may mean "to be high, lofty." In this sense, it is used of trees (Ezek. 19:11), the heavens (Job 35:5), and a man (1 Sam. 10:23). It may mean "to be exalted" in dignity and honor

(Job 36:7). Or it may simply mean "to be lofty," used in the positive sense of "being encouraged" (2 Chron. 17:6) or in the negative sense of "being haughty or proud" (2 Chron. 26:16).

C. Noun.

gōbah (גֹּבַה, 1363), "height; exaltation; grandeur; haughtiness; pride." This noun, which occurs 17 times in biblical Hebrew, refers to the "height" of things (2 Chron. 3:4) and of men (1 Sam. 17:4). It may also refer to "exaltation" or "grandeur" (Job 40:10), and to "haughtiness" or "pride" (2 Chron. 32:26).

HIGH PLACE

bāmāh (בָּמָה, 1116), "high place." This noun occurs in other Semitic languages, meaning the "back" of an animal or of a man (Ugaritic), the incline or "back" of a mountain (Akkadian), and the "block" (of stone) or grave of a saint (Arabic). *Bāmāh* is used about 100 times in biblical Hebrew, and the first occurrence is in Lev. 26:30: "And I will destroy your high places, and cut down your images, and cast your carcases upon the carcases of your idols, and my soul shall abhor you." Most of the uses are in the Books of Kings and Chronicles, with the sense of "cultic high place." The word is rarely used in the Pentateuch or in the poetic or prophetic literature.

Bāmāh with the sense of "back" is still to be found in the Hebrew Old Testament: "So your enemies shall cringe before you, and you shall tread upon their high places" (Deut. 33:29, NASB). Compare this with the NEB "Your enemies come crying to you, and you shall trample their bodies [*bāmāh*] underfoot."

The Bible's metaphorical use of the "backs" of the clouds and the waves of the sea gives problems to translators: "I will ascend above the heights [*bāmāh*] of the clouds; I will be like the most High" (Isa. 14:14), and "[He] alone spreadeth out the heavens, and treadeth upon the waves [literally, "high places"] of the sea" (Job 9:8). A similar problem is found in Ps. 18:33 (cf. 2 Sam. 22:34; Hab. 3:19): "He maketh my feet like hinds' feet, and setteth me upon my high places." In these passages, *bāmāh* must be understood idiomatically, meaning "authority."

The word is used metaphorically to portray the Lord as providing for His people: "He made him ride on the high places of the earth, that he might eat the increase of the fields; and he made him to suck honey out of the rock, and oil out of the flinty rock" (Deut. 32:13; cf. Isa. 58:14). The idiom, "to ride upon the high places of the earth," is a Hebraic way of expressing God's protection of His people. It expresses the exalted nature of Israel, whose God is the Lord.

Not every literal *bāmāh* was a cultic high place; the word may simply refer to a geographical unit; cf. "Therefore shall Zion for your sake be plowed as a field, and Jerusalem shall become heaps, and the mountain of the [temple] as the high places of the forest" (cf. Amos 4:13; Mic. 3:12). The Canaanites served their gods on these hills, where pagan priests presented the sacrifices to the gods: Israel imitated this practice (1 Kings 3:2), even when they sacrificed to the Lord. The surrounding nations had high places dedicated to Chemosh (1 Kings 11:7), Baal (Jer. 19:5), and other deities. On the "high place," a temple was built and dedicated to a god: "[Jeroboam] made a house of high places, and made priests of the lowest of the people, which were not of the sons of Levi" (1 Kings 12:31). Cultic symbols were added as decoration; thus, the sacred pillars (*'ašērāh*) and sacred trees or poles (*maṣṣēbāh*) were associated with a temple: "For they also built them high places, and [sacred stones], and groves, on every high hill [*gib'āh*], and under every green tree" (1 Kings 14:23; cf. 2 Kings 16:4).

Before the temple was built, Solomon worshiped the Lord at the great *bāmāh* of Gideon (1 Kings 3:4). This was permissible until the temple was constructed; however, history demonstrates that Israel soon adopted these "high places" for pagan customs. The *bāmāh* was found in the cities of Samaria (2 Kings 23:19), in the cities of Judah (2 Chron. 21:11), and even in Jerusalem (2 Kings 23:13). The *bāmāh* was a place of cult prostitution: "[They] pant after the dust of the earth on the head of the poor, and turn aside the way of the meek: and a man and his father will go in unto the same maid, to profane my holy name: And they lay themselves down upon clothes laid to pledge by every altar, and they drink the wine of the condemned in the house of their god" (Amos 2:7–8).

The Septuagint gives the following translations: *hupselos* ("high; lofty; elevated"), *bama* (a transliteration of the Hebrew), *bomos* ("altar"), *stele* ("pillar") and *hupsos* ("height; high place").

HOLY

A. Adjective.
qādôš (קָדוֹשׁ, 6918), "holy." The Semitic languages have two separate original forms of the root. The one signifies "pure" and "devoted," as in Akkadian *qadistu* and in Hebrew *qādēš*, "holy." The word describes something or someone. The other signifies "holiness" as a situation

or as an abstract, as in Arabic *al-qaddus* "the most holy or most pure." In Hebrew the verb *qādaš* and the word *qādēš* combine both elements: the descriptive and the static. The traditional understanding of "separated" is only a derived meaning, and not the primary.

Qādôš is prominent in the Pentateuch, poetic and prophetic writings, and rare in the historical books. The first of its 116 occurrences is in Exod. 19:16: "And ye shall be unto me a kingdom of priests, and a holy nation. These are the words which thou shalt speak unto the children of Israel."

In the Old Testament *qādôš* has a strongly religious connotation. In one sense the word describes an object or place or day to be "holy" with the meaning of "devoted" or "dedicated" to a particular purpose: "And the priest shall take holy water in an earthen vessel . . ." (Num. 5:17). Particularly the sabbath day is "devoted" as a day of rest: "If thou turn away thy foot from the sabbath, from doing thy pleasure on my holy day; and call the sabbath a delight, the holy of the Lord, honorable; and shalt honor him, not doing thine own ways, nor finding thine own pleasure, nor speaking thine own words: Then shalt thou delight thyself in the Lord . . ." (Isa. 58:13–14). The prescription is based on Gen. 2:3 where the Lord "sanctified," or "dedicated," the sabbath.

God has dedicated Israel as His people. They are "holy" by their relationship to the "holy" God. All of the people are in a sense "holy," as members of the covenant community, irrespective of their faith and obedience: "And they gathered themselves together against Moses and against Aaron, and said unto them, Ye take too much upon you, seeing all the congregation are holy, every one of them, and the Lord is among them: wherefore then lift ye up yourselves above the congregation of the Lord?" (Num. 16:3). God's intent was to use this "holy" nation as a "holy," royal priesthood amongst the nations (Exod. 19:6). Based on the intimate nature of the relationship, God expected His people to live up to His "holy" expectations and, thus, to demonstrate that they were a "holy nation": "And ye shall be holy unto me: for I the Lord am holy, and have severed you from other people, that ye should be mine" (Lev. 20:26).

The priests were chosen to officiate at the Holy Place of the tabernacle/temple. Because of their function as intermediaries between God and Israel and because of their proximity to the temple, they were dedicated by God to the office of priest: "They shall be holy unto their God, and not profane the name of their God: for the offerings of the Lord made by fire, and the bread of their God, they do offer: therefore they shall be holy. They shall not take a wife that is a whore, or profane; neither shall they take a woman put away from her husband: for he is holy unto his God. Thou shalt sanctify him therefore; for he offereth the bread of thy God: he shall be holy unto thee: for I the Lord, which sanctify you, am holy" (Lev. 21:6–8). Aaron as the high priest was "the holy one of the Lord" (Ps. 106:16, NASB).

The Old Testament clearly and emphatically teaches that God is "holy." He is "the Holy One of Israel" (Isa. 1:4), the "holy God" (Isa. 5:16), and "the Holy One" (Isa. 40:25). His name is "Holy": "For thus saith the high and lofty One that inhabiteth eternity, whose name is Holy; I dwell in the high and holy place, with him also that is of a contrite and humble spirit, to revive the spirit of the humble, and to revive the heart of the contrite ones" (Isa. 57:15). The negative statement, "There is none holy as the Lord: for there is none besides thee: neither is there any rock like our God" (1 Sam. 2:2), explains that He is most "holy" and that no one is as "holy" as He is. Also the angels in the heavenly entourage are "holy": "And the valley of my mountains shall be stopped up, for the valley of the mountains shall touch the side of it; and you shall flee as you fled from the earthquake in the days of Uzziah king of Judah. Then the Lord your God will come, and all the holy ones [KJV, "saints"] with him" (Zech. 14:5, RSV). The seraphim proclaimed to each other the holiness of God: "And one cried unto another, and said, Holy, holy, holy, is the Lord of hosts: the whole earth is full of his glory" (Isa. 6:3).

In the Septuagint the word *hagios* ("holy") stands for the Hebrew *qādôsh*.

B. Verb.

qādēš (קָדֵשׁ, 6942) or *qādaš* (קָדַשׁ, 6942), "to be holy; to sanctify." This verb, which occurs 175 times, can mean "to be holy" (Exod. 29:37; Lev. 6:18) or "to sanctify": "Hear me, ye Levites, sanctify now yourselves, and sanctify the house of the Lord God of your fathers, and carry forth the filthiness out of the holy place" (2 Chron. 29:5).

C. Nouns.

qōdeš (קֹדֶשׁ, 6944), "holiness; holy thing; sanctuary." This noun occurs 469 times with the meanings: "holiness" (Exod. 15:11); "holy thing" (Num. 4:15); and "sanctuary" (Exod. 36:4).

Another noun, *qādēš*, means "temple-prostitute" or "sodomite": "There shall be no whore of the daughters of Israel, nor a sodomite of the sons of Israel" (Deut. 23:17). The noun is found 11 times.

TO HONOR

A. Verbs.

kābēd (כָּבֵד, 3513), "to honor." This verb occurs about 114 times and in all periods of biblical Hebrew. Its cognates appear in the same languages as those of the noun *kābôd*. One occurrence of *kābēd* is in Deut. 5:16: "Honor thy father and thy mother, as the Lord thy God hath commanded thee. . . ."

hādar (הָדַר, 1921), "to honor, prefer, exalt oneself, behave arrogantly." This verb, which appears 8 times in biblical Hebrew, has cognates only in Aramaic although some scholars suggest cognates in Egyptian and Syriac.

The word means "to honor" or "to prefer" in Exod. 23:3: "Neither shalt thou countenance a poor man in his cause." In Prov. 25:6 *hādar* means "to exalt oneself" or "to behave arrogantly."

B. Nouns.

kābôd (כָּבוֹד, 3519), "honor; glory; great quantity; multitude; wealth; reputation [majesty]; splendor." Cognates of this word appear in Ugaritic, Phoenician, Arabic, Ethiopic, and Akkadian. It appears about 200 times in biblical Hebrew and in all periods.

Kābôd refers to the great physical weight or "quantity" of a thing. In Nah. 2:9 one should read: "For there is no limit to the treasure—a great quantity of every kind of desirable object." Isa. 22:24 likens Eliakim to a peg firmly anchored in a wall upon which is hung "all the [weighty things] of his father's house." This meaning is required in Hos. 9:11, where *kābôd* represents a great crowd of people or "multitude": "As for Ephraim, their [multitude] shall fly away. . . ." The word does not mean simply "heavy," but a heavy or imposing quantity of things.

Kābôd often refers to both "wealth" and significant and positive "reputation" (in a concrete sense). Laban's sons complained that "Jacob hath taken away all that was our father's; and of that which was our father's hath he gotten all this [wealth]" (Gen. 31:1—the first biblical occurrence). The second emphasis appears in Gen. 45:13, where Joseph told his brothers to report to his "father . . . all my [majesty] in Egypt." Here this word includes a report of his position and the assurance that if the family came to Egypt, Joseph would be able to provide for them. Trees, forests, and wooded hills have an imposing quality, a richness or "splendor." God will punish the king of Assyria by destroying most of the trees in his forests, "and shall consume the glory of his forest, . . . and the rest of the trees of his forest shall be few, that a child may write them" (Isa. 10:18–19). In Ps. 85:9 the idea of richness or abundance predominates: "Surely his salvation is nigh them that fear him; that glory [or abundance] may dwell in our land." This idea is repeated in Ps. 85:12: "Yea, the Lord shall give that which is good; and our land shall yield her increase."

Kābôd can also have an abstract emphasis of "glory," imposing presence or position. Phinehas' wife named their son Ichabod, "saying, The glory is departed from Israel: because the ark of God was taken, and because of her father-in-law and her husband" (they, the high priests, had died; 1 Sam. 4:21). In Isa. 17:3 *kābôd* represents the more concrete idea of a fullness of things including fortified cities, sovereignty (self-rule), and people. Among such qualities is "honor," or respect and position. In Isa. 5:13 this idea of "honor" is represented by *kābôd:* "...And their [my people's] honorable men are famished, and their multitude dried up with thirst." Thus the word *kābôd* and its parallel (the multitude) represent all the people of Israel: the upper classes and the common people. In many passages the word represents a future rather than a present reality: "In that day shall the branch of the Lord be beautiful and glorious..." (Isa. 4:2).

When used in the sense of "honor" or "importance" (cf. Gen. 45:13) there are two nuances of the word. First, *kābôd* can emphasize the position of an individual within the sphere in which he lives (Prov. 11:16). This "honor" can be lost through wrong actions or attitudes (Prov. 26:1, 8) and evidenced in proper actions (Prov. 20:3; 25:2). This emphasis then is on a relationship between personalities. Second, there is a suggestion of nobility in many uses of the word, such as "honor" that belongs to a royal family (1 Kings 3:13). Thus, *kābôd* can be used of the social distinction and position of respect enjoyed by nobility.

When applied to God, the word represents a quality corresponding to Him and by which He is recognized. Joshua commanded Achan to give glory to God, to recognize His importance, worth, and significance (Josh. 7:19). In this and similar instances "giving honor" refers to doing something; what Achan was to do was to tell the truth. In other passages giving honor to God is a cultic recognition and confession of God as God (Ps. 29:1). Some have suggested that such passages celebrate the sovereignty of God over nature wherein the celebrant sees His "glory" and confesses it in worship. In other places the word is said to point to God's sovereignty over history and specifically to a future manifestation of that "glory" (Isa. 40:5). Still other passages relate the manifestation of divine "glory" to past demonstrations of His sovereignty over history and peoples (Exod. 16:7; 24:16).

hādār (הָדָר, 1926), "honor; splendor." Cognates of this word appear only in Aramaic. Its 31 appearances in the Bible are exclusively in poetic passages and in all periods.

First, *hādār* refers to "splendor" in nature: "And ye shall take you on the first day the boughs of goodly trees [literally, trees of splendor or beauty]..." (Lev. 23:40—the first occurrence).

Second, this word is a counterpart to Hebrew words for "glory" and "dignity." Thus *hādār* means not so much overwhelming beauty as a combination of physical attractiveness and social position. The Messiah is said to have "no form nor [majesty]; and when we shall see him, there is no beauty that we should desire him" (Isa. 53:2). Mankind is crowned with "glory and honor" in the sense of superior desirability (for God) and rank (Ps. 8:5). In Prov. 20:29 *hādār* focuses on the same idea—an aged man's mark of rank and privilege is his gray hair. This reflects the theme present throughout the Bible that long life is a mark of divine blessing and results (often) when one is faithful to God, whereas premature death is a result of divine judgment. The ideas of glorious brilliance, preeminence, and lordship are included in *hādār* when it is applied to God: "Glory and honor are in his presence; strength and gladness are in his place" (1 Chron. 16:27). Not only are these characteristics of His sanctuary (Ps. 96:6) but He is clothed with them (Ps. 104:1). This use of *hādār* is rooted in the ancient concept of a king or of a royal city. God gave David all good things: a crown of gold on his head, long life, and glory or "splendor" and majesty (Ps. 21:3–5). In the case of earthly kings their beauty or brilliance usually arises from their surroundings. So God says of Tyre: "They of Persia and of Lud and of Phut were in thine army, thy men of war: they hanged the shield and helmet in thee; they set forth thy comeliness [honor]. The men of Arvad with thine army were upon thy walls round about, and the Gammadim were in thy towers: they hanged their shields upon thy walls round about; they have made thy beauty perfect" (Ezek. 27:10–11). God, however, manifests the characteristic of "honor or splendor" in Himself.

The noun *hădārāh* means "majesty; splendor; exaltation; adornment." This noun appears 5 times in the Bible. The word implies "majesty or exaltation" in Prov. 14:28: "In a multitude of people is the glory of a King, but without people a prince is ruined" (RSV). *Hădārāh* refers to "adornment" in Ps. 29:2.

C. Adjective.

kābēd (כָּבֵד, 3515), "heavy; numerous; severe; rich." The adjective *kābēd* occurs about 40 times. Basically this adjective connotes "heavy." In Exod. 17:12 the word is used of physical weight: "But Moses' hands were heavy; and they took a stone, and put it under him, and he sat thereon; and Aaron and Hur stayed up his hands...." This adjective bears the connotation of heaviness as an enduring, ever-present quality, a lasting thing. Used in a negative but extended sense, the word depicts sin as a yoke ever pressing down upon one: "For mine iniquities are gone over mine head: as a heavy burden they are too heavy for me" (Ps. 38:4). A task can be described as "heavy" (Exod. 18:18). Moses argued his inability to lead God's people out of Egypt because he was "slow of speech, and of a slow tongue"; his speech or tongue was not smooth-flowing but halting (heavy; Exod. 4:10). This use of *kābēd* appears with an explanation in Ezek. 3:6, where God is describing the people to whom Ezekiel is to minister: "... not to many people of a strange speech and of a hard language, whose words thou canst not understand." Another nuance of this word appears in Exod. 7:14, where it is applied to Pharaoh's heart: "Pharaoh's heart is hardened, he refuseth to let the people go." In all such contexts *kābēd* depicts a burden which weighs down one's body (or some part of it) so that one is either disabled or unable to function successfully.

A second series of passages uses this word of something that falls upon or overcomes one. So God sent upon Egypt a "heavy" hail (Exod. 9:18), a "great" swarm of insects (8:24), "numerous" locusts, and a "severe" pestilence (9:3). The first appearance of the word belongs to this category: "... The famine was [severe] in the land" of Egypt (Gen. 12:10).

Used with a positive connotation, *kābēd* can describe the amount of "riches" one has: "And Abram was very rich in cattle, in silver, and in gold" (Gen. 13:2). In Gen. 50:9 the word is used to modify a group of people, "a very great company." The next verse uses *kābēd* in the sense of "imposing" or "ponderous": "... They mourned with a great and very sore lamentation...."

This adjective is never used of God.

HORSE

sûs (סוּס, 5483), "horse." Cognates of this word appear in Ugaritic, Akkadian, Egyptian, and Syriac. It appears in biblical Hebrew about 138 times and in all periods.

The first biblical appearance of *sûs* is in Gen. 47:17: "And they brought their cattle unto Joseph: and Joseph gave them bread in exchange for horses, and for the flocks, and for the cattle of the herds, and for the asses...." In the second quarter of the second millennium the chariot became a major military weapon and "horses" a very desirable commodity. This was the time of Joseph. It was not until the end of the second millennium that a rudimentary cavalry appeared on the battlefield. In the period of the eighth-century prophets and following, "horses" became a sign of luxury and apostasy (Isa. 2:7; Amos 4:10) inasmuch as Israel's hope for freedom and security was to be the Lord: "But he [the king] shall not multiply horses to himself, nor cause the people to return to Egypt, to ... multiply horses ..." (Deut. 17:16).

The "horses" of God are the storm clouds with which he treads upon the sea (Hab. 3:15).

HOST

A. Noun.

șābā' (צָבָא, 6633), "host; military service; war; army; service; labor; forced labor; conflict." This word has cognates in either a verbal or noun form in Akkadian, Ugaritic, Arabic, and Ethiopic. The noun form occurs 486 times in biblical Hebrew and in all periods of the language.

This word involves several interrelated ideas: a group; impetus; difficulty; and force. These ideas undergird the general concept of "service" which one does for or under a superior rather than for himself. *Șābā'* is usually applied to "military service" but is sometimes used of "work" in general (under or for a superior). In Num. 1:2-3 the word means "military service": "Take ye the sum of all the congregation of the children of Israel ... from twenty years old and upward, all that are able to go forth to war in Israel...." The idea is more concrete in Josh. 22:12, where the word represents serving in a military campaign: "And when the children of Israel heard of it, the whole congregation of the children of Israel gathered themselves together at Shiloh, to go to war against them." Num. 31:14 uses *șābā'* of the actual battling itself: "And Moses was wroth with the officers of the [army], ... which came from the battle."

The word can also represent an "army host": "And Eleazer the priest said unto the men of war which went to the battle ..." (Num. 31:21). Even clearer is Num. 31:48: "And the officers which were over thousands of the host, the captains of thousands, and captains of hundreds, came near unto Moses."This meaning first appears in Gen. 21:22, which mentions Phichol, the captain of Abimelech's "army." At several points this is the meaning of the feminine plural: "And it shall be, when the officers have made an end of speaking unto the people, that they shall make captains of the armies to lead the people" (Deut. 20:9). In Num. 1, 2, and 10, where *ṣābā'* occurs with regard to a census of Israel, it is suggested that this was a military census by which God organized His "army" to march through the wilderness. Some scholars have noted that the plan of the march, or the positioning of the tribes, recalls the way ancient armies were positioned during military campaigns. On the other hand, groupings of people might be indicated regardless of military implications, as seems to be the case in passages such as Exod. 6:26: "These are that Aaron and Moses, to whom the Lord said, Bring out the children of Israel from the land of Egypt according to their armies."

That *ṣābā'* can refer to a "nonmilitary host" is especially clear in Ps. 68:11: "The Lord gave the word: great was the company of those that published it." The phrase "hosts of heaven" signifies the stars as visual indications of the gods of the heathen: "And them that worship the host of heaven upon the housetops; and them that worship and that swear by the Lord, and that swear by Malcham..." (Zeph. 1:5). This meaning first appears in Deut. 4:19. Sometimes this phrase refers to the "host of heaven," or the angels: "And [Micaiah] said, Hear thou therefore the word of the Lord: I saw the Lord sitting on his throne, and all the host of heaven [the angels] standing by him on his right hand and on his left" (1 Kings 22:19). God Himself is the commander of this "host" (Dan. 8:10–11). In Josh. 6:14 the commander of the "host" of God confronted Joshua. This heavenly "host" not only worships God but serves to do all His will: "Bless ye the Lord, all ye his hosts; ye ministers of his, that do his pleasure" (Ps. 103:21).

Another meaning of the phrase "the host(s) of heaven" is simply "the numberless stars": "As the host of heaven cannot be numbered, neither the sand of the sea measured: so will I multiply the seed of David my servant, and the Levites that minister unto me" (Jer. 33:22). This phrase can include all the heavenly bodies, as it does in Ps. 33:6: "By the word of the Lord were the heavens made; and all the host of them by the breath of his mouth." In Gen. 2:1 *ṣābā'* includes the heavens, the earth, and everything in the creation: "Thus the heavens and the earth were finished, and all the host of them."

The meaning "nonmilitary service in behalf of a superior" emerges in Num. 4:2–3: "Take the sum of the sons of Kohath... from thirty years old and upward even until fifty years old, all that enter [the service], to do the work in the tabernacle of the congregation." In Job 7:1 the word represents the burdensome everyday "toil" of mankind: "Is there not an appointed time to man upon earth? Are not his days also like the days of a hireling?" In Job 14:14 *ṣābā'* seems to represent "forced labor." In Dan. 10:1 the word is used for "conflict": "In the third year of Cyrus king of Persia a word was revealed to Daniel, who was named Belteshazzar. And the word was true, and it was a great conflict" [RSV; KJV, "time appointed"].

B. Verb.

ṣābā' (צָבָא, 6633), "to wage war, to muster an army, to serve in worship." This verb appears 14 times in biblical Hebrew. *Ṣābā'* means "to wage war" in Num. 31:7: "And they warred against the Midianites, as the Lord commanded Moses...." The word is used in 2 Kings 25:19 to refer to "mustering an army." Another sense of *ṣābā'* appears in Num. 4:23 with the meaning of "serving in worship": "...all that enter in to perform the service, to do the work in the tabernacle of the congregation."

HOUSE

bayit (בַּיִת, 1004), "house or building; home; household; land." The noun has cognates in most other Semitic languages including biblical Aramaic. *Bayit* appears about 2,048 times in biblical Hebrew (44 times in Aramaic) and in all periods.

First, this noun denotes a fixed, established structure made from some kind of material. As a "permanent dwelling place" it is usually distinguished from a tent (2 Sam. 16:21, cf. v. 22). This word can even be applied to a one-room dwelling: "And he [Lot] said [to the two angels], Behold now, my lords, turn in, I pray you, into your servant's house..." (Gen. 19:2). *Bayit* is also distinguished from temporary booths or huts: "And Jacob journeyed to Succoth, and built him a house, and made booths for his cattle..." (Gen. 33:17). In Ps. 132:3 the word means "dwelling-living-place" and is used in direct conjunction with "tent" (literally, "tent of my house"): "Surely I will not come into the tabernacle of my house, nor go up into my bed." A similar usage appears in 1 Chron. 9:23 (literally, "the tent house"): "So they and their children had the oversight of the gates of the house of the Lord, namely, the house of the tabernacle, by wards."

Second, in many passages (especially when

the word is joined to the word God) *bayit* represents a place of worship or "sanctuary": "The first of the first fruits of thy land thou shalt bring into the house of the Lord thy God" (Exod. 23:19). Elsewhere this noun signifies God's temple in Jerusalem: "And against the wall of the house he built chambers round about, against the walls of the house round about, both of the temple and of the oracle ..." (1 Kings 6:5). Sometimes the word has this meaning although it is not further defined (cf. Ezek. 41:7).

Third, *bayit* can signify rooms and/or wings of a house: "And let the king appoint officers in all the provinces of his kingdom, that they may gather together all the fair young virgins unto Shushan the palace, to the [harem] (literally, to the house of the women; Esth. 2:3). ... " In this connection *bayit* can also represent the inside of a building or some other structure as opposed to the outside: "Make thee an ark of gopher wood; rooms shalt thou make in the ark, and shalt pitch it within and without with pitch" (Gen. 6:14—the first biblical occurrence).

Fourth, *bayit* sometimes refers to the place where something or someone dwells or rests. So the underworld (Sheol) is termed a "home": "If I wait, the grave is mine house: I have made my bed in the darkness" (Job 17:13). An "eternal home" is one's grave: " ... Man goeth to his long home, and the mourners go about the streets" (Eccl. 12:5). "House" can also mean "place" when used with "grave," as in Neh. 2:3: "Let the king live for ever: why should not my countenance be sad, when the city, the place of my fathers' sepulchres. ... " *Bayit* means a receptacle (NASB, "box") in Isa. 3:20. In 1 Kings 18:32 the "house of two seeds" is a container for seed: "And with the stones he built an altar in the name of the Lord: and he made a trench about the altar, as great as would contain [literally, "a house of"] two measures of seed." Houses for bars are supports: "And thou shalt overlay the boards with gold, and make their rings of gold for places [literally, "houses"] for the bars" (Exod. 26:29). Similarly, see "the places [house] of the two paths," a crossing of two paths, in Prov. 8:2. The steppe is termed the "house of beasts": " ... whose house I have made the wilderness, and the barren land his dwellings [house of beasts]" (Job 39:6).

Fifth, *bayit* is often used of those who live in a house, i.e., a "household": "Come thou and all thy house into the ark ... " (Gen. 7:1). In passages such as Josh. 7:14 this word means "family": " ... And it shall be, that the tribe which the Lord taketh shall come according to the families thereof; and the family which the

Lord shall take shall come by households [literally, by house or by those who live in a single dwelling]. ... " In a similar nuance this noun means "descendants": "And there went a man of the house of Levi, and took to wife a daughter of Levi" (Exod. 2:1). This word can be used of one's extended family and even of everyone who lives in a given area: "And the men of Judah came, and there they anointed David king over the house of Judah" (2 Sam. 2:4). Gen. 50:4, however, uses *bayit* in the sense of "a royal court" or all the people in a king's court: "And when the days of his mourning were past, Joseph spake unto the house of Pharaoh. ... " The ideas "royal court" and "descendant" are joined in 1 Sam. 20:16: "So Jonathan made a covenant with the house of David. ... "

In a few passages *bayit* means "territory" or "country": "Set the trumpet to thy mouth. He shall come as an eagle against the house of the Lord ... " (Hos. 8:1; 9:15; Jer. 12:7; Zech. 9:8).

TO HUMBLE (SELF)

A. Verbs.

kāna' (כָּנַע, 3665), "to be humble, to humble, subdue." This biblical Hebrew word is also found in modern Hebrew. The word can mean "to humble, to subdue," and it can have a passive or reflexive use, "to be humble" or "to humble oneself." While *kāna'* occurs some 35 times in the Hebrew Old Testament, the word is not found until Deut. 9:3: " ... The Lord thy God ... shall destroy them, and he shall bring them down. ... " *Kāna'* is frequently used in this sense of "subduing, humbling," enemies (2 Sam. 8:1; 1 Chron. 17:10; Ps. 81:14). "To humble oneself" before God in repentance is a common theme and need in the life of ancient Israel (Lev. 26:41; 2 Chron. 7:14; 12:6–7, 12).

šāpēl (שָׁפֵל, 8213), "to be low, become low; sink down; be humiliated; be abased." This root appears in most Semitic languages (except Ethiopic) with the basic meaning "to be low" and "to become low." *Šāpēl* occurs about twenty-five times in the Old Testament. It is a poetic term.

The verb, as can be expected in poetic usage, is generally used in a figurative sense. *Šāpēl* rarely denotes a literal lowness. Even in passages where the meaning may be taken literally, the prophet communicates a spiritual truth: " ... The high [trees] of stature shall be hewn down, and the haughty shall be humbled" (Isa. 10:33), or "Every valley shall be exalted, and every mountain and hill shall be made low ... " (Isa. 40:4). Isaiah particularly presented Judah's sin as one of rebellion, self-exaltation, and pride (2:17; 3:16–17). In the second chapter he repeated God's indictment on human pride. When the Lord comes in judgment, He will not tolerate pride: " ... The Lord alone shall be exalted in that day" (Isa. 2:11); then "the Lord of hosts shall be upon every one that is proud and lofty, and upon every one that is lifted up; and he shall be brought low" (Isa. 2:12). Isaiah applied to Judah the principle found in Proverbs: "A man's pride shall bring him low: but honor shall uphold the humble in spirit" (Prov. 29:23).

Pride and self-exaltation have no place in the life of the godly, as the Lord "brings low" a person, a city, and a nation: "The Lord maketh poor, and maketh rich: he bringeth low, and lifteth up" (1 Sam. 2:7).

The prophets called the people to repent and to demonstrate their return to God by lowliness. Their call was generally unheeded. Ultimately the Exile came, and the people were humbled by the Babylonians. Nevertheless, the promise came that, regardless of the obstacles, God would initiate the redemption of His people. Isaiah expressed the greatness of the redemption in this way: "Prepare ye the way of the Lord. ... Every valley shall be exalted, and every mountain and hill shall be made low. ... And the glory of the Lord shall be revealed. ... " (Isa. 40:3–5).

In the Septuagint *šāpēl* is represented by *tapeinō* ("to level, be humble, humiliate"). It is translated in English versions as "to be low" (KJV, RSV, NASB, NIV); "to bring low" (KJV, RSV); "to bring down" (NASB, NIV); "to be humble" (KJV, RSV, NASB, NIV).

B. Nouns.

Some nouns related to this verb occur infrequently. *Šēpel* refers to a "low condition, low estate." This word appears twice (Ps. 136:23; Eccl. 10:6). The noun *šiplāh* means a "humiliated state." This noun occurs once: "When it shall hail, coming down on the forest; and the city shall be low in a low place" (Isa. 32:19); the city is leveled completely. *Šᵉpēlah* means "lowland." This word is used most often as a technical designation for the low-lying hills of the Judean hill country (cf. Deut. 1:7; Josh. 9:1). *Šiplût* refers to a "sinking." This noun's single appearance is in Eccl. 10:18: "By much slothfulness the building decayeth; and through idleness [*šiplût*] of the hands the house droppeth through." The word implies a negligence or "sinking" of the hands.

C. Adjective.

šāpāl (שָׁפָל, 8217), means "low; humble." This word means "low" in Ezek. 17:24: "And all the trees of the field shall know that I the Lord have brought down the high tree, have exalted the low tree.... " In Isa. 57:15 *šāpāl* refers to "humble": " ... I dwell in the high and holy place, with him also that is of a contrite and humble spirit, to revive the spirit of the humble, and to revive the heart of the contrite ones."

TO BE HUMBLED, AFFLICTED

A. Verb.

'ānāh (עָנָה, 6031), "to be afflicted, be bowed down, be humbled, be meek." This word, common to both ancient and modern Hebrew, is the source of several important words in the history and experience of Judaism: "humble, meek, poor, and affliction." *'Anāh* occurs approximately 80 times in the Hebrew Old Testament. It is found for the first time in Gen. 15:13: " ... they shall afflict them four hundred years."

'Anāh often expresses harsh and painful treatment. Sarai "dealt hardly" with Hagar (Gen. 16:6). When Joseph was sold as a slave, his feet were hurt with fetters (Ps. 105:18). Frequently the verb expresses the idea that God sends affliction for disciplinary purposes: " ... the Lord thy God led thee these forty years in the wilderness, to humble thee, and to prove thee, to know what was in thine heart ... " (Deut. 8:2; see also 1 Kings 11:39; Ps. 90:15). To take a woman sexually by force may be "to humble" her (Gen. 34:2, KJV, RSV), but the word is more appropriately translated "dishonor" (JB, NEB).

In the Day of Atonement observance, "to humble oneself" is probably connected with the requirement for fasting on that day (Lev. 23:28–29).

B. Noun.

'ānî (עָנִי, 6041), "poor; humble; meek." Especially in later Israelite history, just before the Exile and following, this noun came to have a special connection with those faithful ones who were being abused, taken advantage of, by the rich (Isa. 29:19; 32:7; Amos 2:7). The prophet Zephaniah's reference to them as the "meek of the earth" (Zeph. 2:3) set the stage for Jesus' concern and ministry to the "poor" and the "meek" (Matt. 5:3, 5; Luke 4:18; cf. Isa. 61:1). By New Testament times, "the poor of the land" were more commonly known as *'am ha'āreṣ*, "the people of the land."

I

IDOL

tᵉrāpîm (תְּרָפִים, 8655), "idol; household idol; cultic mask; divine symbol." This word is a loanword from Hittite-Hurrian (*tarpiš*) which in West Semitic assumes the basic form *tarpi*. Its basic meaning is "spirit" or "demon." Biblical Hebrew attests this word 15 times.

Tᵉrāpîm first appears in Gen. 31:19: "And Laban went to shear his sheep: and Rachel had stolen the [household gods] that were her father's." Hurrian law of this period recognized "household idols" as deeds to the family's succession and goods. This makes these *tᵉrāpîm* (possibly a plural of majesty as is *'elōhîm* when used of false gods; cf. 1 Kings 11:5, 33) extremely important to Laban in every way.

In 1 Sam. 19:13 we read that "Michal took the *tᵉrāpîm* [here a plural of "majesty"] and laid it on the bed, and put a quilt of goat's hair at its head, and covered it with blankets" (author's translation). In view of 1 Sam. 19:11, where it is said that they were in David's private quarters, supposing that this *tᵉrāpîm* was a "household idol" is difficult, although not impossible. Some scholars suggest that this was a "cultic" mask used in worshiping God.

Either of the former suggestions is the possible meaning of the word in the Micah incident recorded in Judg. 17–18. Notice in Judg. 17:5: "... Micah had a house of gods, and made an ephod, and *tᵉrāpîm*, and consecrated one of his sons, who became his priest." In Judg. 18:14 *tᵉrāpîm* appears to be distinguished from idols: "... there is in these houses an ephod, and *tᵉrāpîm*, and a graven image, and a molten image?" The verses that follow suggest that the graven image and the molten image may have been the same thing: Judg. 18:17 uses all four words in describing what the Danites stole; Judg. 18:20 omits "molten image" from the list; and Judg. 18:31 reports that only the graven image was set up for worship. We know that the ephod was a special priestly garment. Could it be that *tᵉrāpîm* was a "cultic mask" or some other symbol of the divine presence?

Thus *tᵉrāpîm* may signify an "idol," a "cultic mask," or perhaps a "symbol of the divine presence." In any case the item is associated with pagan worship and perhaps with worship of God.

'ĕlîl (אֱלִיל, 457), "idol; gods; nought; vain." The 20 occurrences of this noun are primarily in Israel's legal code and the prophetic writings (especially Isaiah). Cognates of this word appear in Akkadian, Syriac, and Arabic.

This disdainful word signifies an "idol" or "false god." *'Ĕlîl* first appears in Lev. 19:4: "Turn ye not unto idols, nor make to yourselves molten gods. ... " In Lev. 26:1 the *'ĕlîlîm* are what Israel is forbidden to make: "Ye shall make you no idols. ... " The irony of this is biting not only with respect to the usual meaning of this word but also in view of its similarity to the usual word for God (*'ĕlōhîm;* cf. Ps. 96:5): "For all the gods [*'ĕlōhîm*] of the people are idols [*'ĕlîlîm*] ... " (1 Chron. 16:26).

Second, this word can mean "nought" or "vain." 1 Chron. 16:26 might well be rendered: "For all the gods of the people are nought." This nuance appears clearly in Job 13:4: "But ye are forgers of lies; ye are all physicians of no value [physicians of vanity]." Jeremiah told Israel that their prophets were "prophesy [ing] unto you a false vision and divination, and a thing of nought ... "(14:14).

gillûlîm (גִּלּוּלִים, 1544), "idols." Of the 48 occurrences of this word, all but 9 appear in Ezekiel. This word for "idols" is a disdainful word and may originally have meant "dung pellets": "And I will destroy your high places, and cut down your images, and cast your carcases upon the carcases of your idols, and my soul shall abhor you" (Lev. 26:30).

This word and others for "idol" exhibit the horror and scorn that biblical writers felt toward them. In passages such as Isa. 66:3 the word for "idol," *'āwen*, means "uncanny or wickedness." Jer. 50:38 evidences the word *'ēmîm*, which means "fright or horror." The word *'ĕlîl* appears for "idol" in Lev. 19:4; it means "nothingness or feeble." 1 Kings 15:13 uses the Hebrew word, *mipleset*, meaning a "horrible thing, a cause of trembling." A root signifying to make an image or to shape something, *'ṣb* (a homonym of the root meaning "sorrow and grief") is used in several passages (cf. 1 Sam. 31:9).

TO INHERIT

A. Verb.

nāhal (נָחַל, 5157), "to inherit, get possession of, take as a possession." This term is found in both ancient and modern Hebrew, as well as in ancient Ugaritic. It is found around 60 times in the Hebrew Old Testament. The first time *nāhal* is used in the Old Testament text is in Exod. 23:30: "inherit the land." The RSV "possess" translates more appropriately here, since the land of Canaan was not literally an inheritance in the usual sense of the word, but a possession, that which was due her, through God's direct intervention. In fact, in most cases of the use of *nāḥal* in the Old Testament, the word has the basic sense of "to possess" rather than "to inherit" by means of a last will and testament. One of the few instances of "to inherit" by last will and testament is in Deut. 21:16: " . . . when he maketh his sons to inherit that which he hath. . . ." This clause is more literally translated "in the day he causes his sons to inherit that which is his."

When Moses prayed: " . . . O Lord, . . . take us for thine inheritance" (Exod. 34:9), he did not mean that God should "inherit" through a will, but that He should "take possession of" Israel. The meaning "to get as a possession" is seen in its figurative use. Thus, "the wise shall inherit [possess as their due] glory" (Prov. 3:35); "the upright shall have good things in possession" (Prov. 28:10); "our fathers have inherited lies" (Jer. 16:19); "he that troubleth his own house shall inherit the wind" (Prov. 11:29).

B. Noun.

nahălāh (נַחֲלָה, 5159), "possession; property; inheritance." This noun is used frequently (220 times), but mainly in the Pentateuch and Joshua. It is rare in the historical books. The first occurrence of the word is in Gen. 31:14: "And Rachel and Leah answered and said unto him, Is there yet any portion or inheritance for us in our father's house?"

The basic translation of *nahălāh* is "inheritance": "And Naboth said to Ahab, The Lord forbid it me, that I should give the inheritance of my fathers unto thee" (1 Kings 21:3). The word more appropriately refers to a "possession" to which one has received the legal claim. The usage of *nahălāh* in the Pentateuch and Joshua indicates that the word often denotes that "possession" which all of Israel or a tribe or a clan received as their share in the Promised Land. The share was determined by lot (Num. 26:56) shortly before Moses' death, and it fell upon Joshua to execute the division of the "possession": "So Joshua took the whole land, according to all that the Lord said unto Moses; and Joshua gave it for an inheritance unto Israel according to their divisions by their tribes" (Josh. 11:23). After the Conquest the term "inheritance" is no longer used to refer to newly gained territory by warfare. Once "possession" had been taken of the land, the legal process came into operation by which the hereditary property was supposed to stay within the family. For this reason Naboth could not give his rights over to Ahab (1 Kings 21:3–4). One could redeem the property, whenever it had come into other hands, as did Boaz, in order to maintain the name of the deceased: "Moreover Ruth the Moabitess, the wife of Mahlon, have I purchased to be my wife, to raise up the name of the dead upon his inheritance, that the name of the dead be not cut off from among his brethren, and from the gate of his place" (Ruth 4:10).

Metaphorically, Israel is said to be God's "possession": "But the Lord hath taken you, and brought you forth out of the iron furnace, even out of Egypt, to be unto him a people of inheritance, as ye are this day" (Deut. 4:20). Within the special covenantal status Israel experienced the blessing that its children were a special gift from the Lord (Ps. 127:3). However, the Lord abandoned Israel as His "possession" to the nations (cf. Isa. 47:6), and permitted a remnant of the "possession" to return: "Who is a God like unto thee, that pardoneth iniquity, and passeth by the transgression of the remnant of his heritage? he retaineth not his anger for ever, because he delighteth in mercy" (Mic. 7:18).

On the other hand, it can even be said that the Lord is the "possession" of His people. The priests and the Levites, whose earthly "possessions" were limited, were assured that their "possession" is the Lord: "Wherefore Levi hath no part nor inheritance with his brethren; the Lord is his inheritance, according as the Lord thy God promised him" (Deut. 10:9; cf. 12:22; Num. 18:23).

The Septuagint gives the following translations: *kleronomia* ("inheritance; possession; property"), and *kleros* ("lot; position; share"). The KJV gives these senses: "inheritance, heritage."

INIQUITY

A. Verb.

'āwāh (עָוָה, 5753), "to do iniquity." This verb appears in the Bible 17 times. In Arabic this verb appears with the meaning "to bend" or "to deviate from the way." *'Āwāh* is often used as a synonym of *ḥāṭā'*, "to sin," as in Ps. 106:6: "We have sinned [*ḥāṭā'*] with our fathers, we have committed iniquity [*'āwāh*], we have done wickedly [*rāša'*]."

B. Nouns.

'āwōn (עָוֹן, 5771), "iniquity; guilt; punishment." This noun, which appears 231 times in the Old Testament, is limited to Hebrew and biblical Aramaic. The prophetic and poetic books employ *'āwōn* with frequency. The Pentateuch as a whole employs the word about 50

times. In addition to these, the historical books infrequently use *'āwōn*. The first use of *'āwōn* comes from Cain's lips, where the word takes the special meaning of "punishment": "And Cain said unto the Lord, My punishment is greater than I can bear" (Gen. 4:13).

The most basic meaning of *'āwōn* is "iniquity." The word signifies an offense, intentional or not, against God's law. This meaning is also most basic to the word *ḥaṭṭā't*, "sin," in the Old Testament, and for this reason the words *ḥaṭṭā't* and *'āwōn* are virtually synonymous; "Lo, this [the live coal] hath touched thy [Isaiah's] lips; and thine iniquity [*'āwōn*] is taken away, and thy sin [*ḥaṭṭā't*] purged" (Isa. 6:7).

"Iniquity" as an offense to God's holiness is punishable. The individual is warned that the Lord punishes man's transgression: "But every one shall die for his own iniquity: every man that eateth the sour grape, his teeth shall be set on edge" (Jer. 31:30). There is also a collective sense in that the one is responsible for the many: "Thou shalt not bow down thyself to them, nor serve them: for I the Lord thy God am a jealous God, visiting the iniquity of the fathers upon the children unto the third and fourth generation of them that hate me" (Exod. 20:5). No generation, however, was to think that it bore God's judgment for the "iniquity" of another generation: "Yet say ye, Why? doth not the son bear the iniquity of the father? When the son hath done that which is lawful and right, and hath kept all my statutes, and hath done them, he shall surely live. The soul that sinneth, it shall die. The son shall not bear the iniquity of the father, neither shall the father bear the iniquity of the son: the righteousness of the righteous shall be upon him, and the wickedness of the wicked shall be upon him" (Ezek. 18:19–20).

Israel went into captivity for the sin of their fathers and for their own sins: "And the heathen shall know that the house of Israel went into captivity for their iniquity; because they trespassed against me, therefore hid I my face from them, and gave them into the hand of their enemies: so fell they all by the sword" (Ezek. 39:23).

Serious as "iniquity" is in the covenantal relationship between the Lord and His people, the people are reminded that He is a living God who willingly forgives "iniquity": "Keeping mercy for thousands, forgiving iniquity and transgression and sin, and that will by no means clear the guilty; visiting the iniquity of the fathers upon the children, and upon the children's children, unto the third and to the fourth generation" (Exod. 34:7). God expects confession

of sin: "I acknowledged my sin unto thee, and mine iniquity have I not hid. I said, I will confess my transgressions unto the Lord; and thou forgavest the iniquity of my sin" (Ps. 32:5), and a trusting, believing heart which expresses the humble prayer: "Wash me thoroughly from mine iniquity, and cleanse me from my sin" (Ps. 51:2).

Isaiah 53 teaches that God put upon Jesus Christ our "iniquities" (v. 6), that He having been bruised for our "iniquities" (v. 5) might justify those who believe on Him: "He shall see of the travail of his soul, and shall be satisfied: by his knowledge shall my righteous servant justify many; for he shall bear their iniquities" (Isa. 53:11).

The usage of *'āwōn* includes the whole area of sin, judgment, and "punishment" for sin. The Old Testament teaches that God's forgiveness of "iniquity" extends to the actual sin, the guilt of sin, God's judgment upon that sin, and God's punishment of the sin. "Blessed is the man unto whom the Lord imputeth not iniquity, and in whose spirit there is no guile" (Ps. 32:2).

In the Septuagint the word has the following renderings: *adikia* ("wrongdoing; unrighteousness; wickedness"); *hamartia* ("sin; error"); and *anomia* ("lawlessness"). In the English versions the translation "iniquity" is fairly uniform. The RSV and NIV give at a few places the more specialized rendering "guilt" or the more general translation "sin."

'āwen (אָוֶן, 205), "iniquity; misfortune." This noun is derived from a root meaning "to be strong," found only in the Northwest Semitic languages. The word occurs about 80 times and almost exclusively in poetic-prophetic language. The usage is particularly frequent in the poetical books. Isaiah's use stands out among the prophets. The first occurrence is in Num. 23:21: "He hath not beheld iniquity in Jacob, neither hath he seen perverseness in Israel: the Lord his God is with him, and the shout of a king is among them."

The meaning of "misfortune" comes to expression in the devices of the wicked against the righteous. The psalmist expected "misfortune" to come upon him: "And if he come to see me, he speaketh vanity: his heart gathereth iniquity to itself; when he goeth abroad, he telleth it" (Ps. 41:6). *'Āwen* in this sense is synonymous with *'ēd*, "disaster" (Job 18:12). In a real sense *'āwen* is part of human existence, and as such the word is identical with *'āmāl*, "toil," as in Ps. 90:10: "The days of our years are threescore years and ten; and if by reason of strength they be fourscore years, yet is their strength labor and sorrow; for it is soon cut off, and we fly away."

'Āwen in a deeper sense characterizes the way of life of those who are without God: "For the vile person will speak villany, and his heart will work iniquity, to practice hypocrisy, and to utter error against the Lord, to make empty the soul of the hungry, and he will cause the drink of the thirsty to fail" (Isa. 32:6). The being of man is corrupted by "iniquity." Though all of mankind is subject to 'āwen ("toil"), there are those who delight in causing difficulties and "misfortunes" for others by scheming, lying, and acting deceptively. The psalmist puts internalized wickedness this way: "Behold, he travaileth with iniquity, and hath conceived mischief, and brought forth falsehood" (Ps. 7:14; cf. Job 15:35).

Those who are involved in the ways of darkness are the "workers of iniquity," the doers of evil or the creators of "misfortune" and disaster. Synonyms for 'āwen with this sense are ra', "evil," and rāšā', "wicked," opposed to "righteousness" and "justice." They seek the downfall of the just (Ps. 141:9). Between Ps. 5:5 and 141:9 there are as many as 16 references to the workers of evil (cf. "The foolish shall not stand in thy sight: thou hatest all workers of iniquity"—Ps. 5:5). In the context of Ps. 5, the evil spoken of is falsehood, bloodshed, and deceit (v. 6). The qualitative aspect of the word comes to the best expression in the verbs with 'āwen. The wicked work, speak, beget, think, devise, gather, reap, and plow 'āwen, and it is revealed ("comes forth") by the misfortune that comes upon the righteous. Ultimately when Israel's religious festivals (Isa. 1:13) and legislation (Isa. 10:1) were affected by their apostate way of life, they had reduced themselves to the Gentile practices and way of life. The prophetic hope lay in the period after the purification of Israel, when the messianic king would introduce a period of justice and righteousness (Isa. 32) and the evil men would be shown up for their folly and ungodliness.

The Septuagint has several translations: *anomia* ("lawlessness"); *kopos* ("work; labor; toil"); *mataios* ("empty; fruitless; useless; powerless"); *poneria* ("wickedness; maliciousness; sinfulness"); and *adikia* ("unrighteousness; wickedness; injustice"). The KJV has these translations: "iniquity; vanity; wickedness."

INSTRUCTION

A. Noun.

mûsār (מוּסָר, 4148), "instruction; chastisement; warning." This noun occurs 50 times, mainly in Proverbs. The first occurrence is in

Deut. 11:2: "... I speak not with your children which have not known, and which have not seen the chastisement of the Lord your God, his greatness, his mighty hand, and his stretched out arm."

One of the major purposes of the wisdom literature was to teach wisdom and *mûsār* (Prov. 1:2). *Mûsār* is discipline, but more. As "discipline" it teaches how to live correctly in the fear of the Lord, so that the wise man learns his lesson before temptation and testing: "Then I saw, and considered it well: I looked upon it, and received instruction" (Prov. 24:32). This "discipline" is training for life; hence, paying attention to *mûsār* is important. Many verbs bear out the need for a correct response: "hear, obey, love, receive, obtain, take hold of, guard, keep." Moreover, the rejection is borne out by many verbs connected with *mûsār:* "reject, hate, ignore, not love, despise, forsake." When *mûsār* as "instruction" has been given, but was not observed, the *mûsār* as "chastisement" or "discipline" may be the next step: "Foolishness is bound in the heart of a child; but the rod of correction shall drive it far from him" (Prov. 22:15).

Careful attention to "instruction" brings honor (Prov. 1:9), life (Prov. 4:13), and wisdom (Prov. 8:33), and above all it pleases God: "For whoso findeth me findeth life, and shall obtain favor of the Lord" (Prov. 8:35). The lack of observance of "instruction" brings its own results: death (Prov. 5:23), poverty, and shame (Prov. 13:18), and is ultimately a sign that one has no regard for one's own life (Prov. 15:32).

The receptivity for "instruction" from one's parents, teacher, the wise, or the king is directly corollary to one's subjugation to God's discipline. The prophets charged Israel with not receiving God's discipline: "O Lord, are not thine eyes upon the truth? thou hast stricken them, but they have not grieved; thou hast consumed them, but they have refused to receive correction: they have made their faces harder than a rock; they have refused to return" (Jer. 5:3). Jeremiah asked the men of Judah and the inhabitants in the besieged Jerusalem to pay attention to what was happening around them, that they still might subject themselves to "instruction" (35:13). Isaiah predicted that God's chastisement on man was carried by the Suffering Servant, bringing peace to those who believe in Him: "But he was wounded for our transgressions, he was bruised for our iniquities: the chastisement of our peace was upon him; and with his stripes we are healed" (53:5).

The Septuagint has the translation of *paideia* ("upbringing; training; instruction"). The Greek word is the basis for our English word *peda-gogy*, "training of a child." The KJV has the translations: "instruction; correction; chastisement; chastening."

B. Verb.

yāsar (יָסַר, 3256), "to discipline." This verb occurs in Hebrew and Ugaritic with the sense of "to discipline." Outside of these languages the root is not represented. The verb appears 42 times in the Old Testament; cf. Prov. 19:18: "Chasten thy son while there is hope, and let not thy soul spare for his crying."

J

TO BE JEALOUS, ZEALOUS

A. Verb.

qānā' (קָנָא, 7065), "to be jealous; to be zealous." This verb, derived from the noun *qin'āh*, occurs 34 times in the Old Testament. The root appears in several Semitic languages with the meaning "to be zealous" (Aramaic and Ethiopic). In Ugaritic and Arabic the root occurs, but it is questionable if the root is related to the meaning "to be zealous"; the meaning in Ugaritic text is uncertain, and the meaning in Arabic, "became intensely red," is not to be explained etymologically. The verb *qānā'* appears in rabbinic Hebrew.

At the interhuman level *qānā'* has a strongly competitive sense. In its most positive sense the word means "to be filled with righteous zeal or jealousy." The law provides that a husband who suspects his wife of adultery can bring her to a priest, who will administer a test of adultery. Whether his accusation turns out to be grounded or not, the suspicious man has a legitimate means of ascertaining the truth. In his case a spirit of jealousy has come over him, as he "is jealous" of his wife (Num. 5:30). However, even in this context (Num. 5:12–31), the jealousy has arisen out of a spirit of rivalry which cannot be tolerated in a marriage relationship. The jealousy must be cleared by a means ordained by the law and administered by the priests. *Qānā'*, then, in its most basic sense is the act of advancing one's rights to the exclusion of the rights of others: " . . . Ephraim shall not envy Judah, and Judah shall not vex Ephraim" (Isa. 11:13). Saul sought to murder the Gibeonite enclave "in his zeal to the children of Israel and Judah" (2 Sam. 21:2). Next, the word signifies the attitude of envy toward an opponent. Rachel in her barren state "envied her sister" (Gen. 30:1) and in the state of envy approached Jacob: "Give me children, or else I die." The Philistines envied Isaac because of the multitude of his flocks and herds (Gen. 26:14).

The Bible contains a strong warning against being envious of sinners, who might prosper and be powerful today, but will be no more tomorrow: "Do not envy a violent man or choose any of his ways" (Prov. 3:31, NIV; cf. Ps. 37:1).

In man's relation to God, the act of zeal is more positively viewed as the act of the advancement of God and His glory over against substitutes. The tribe of Levi received the right to service because "he was zealous for his God" (Num. 25:13). Elijah viewed himself as the only faithful servant left in Israel: "I have been very jealous for the Lord God of hosts: for the children of Israel have forsaken thy covenant . . . And I, even I only, am left . . . " (1 Kings 19:10). However, the sense of *qānā'* is "to make jealous," that is, "to provoke to anger": "They provoked him to jealousy with strange gods, with abominations provoked they him to anger" (Deut. 32:16).

God is not tainted with the negative connotation of the verb. His holiness does not tolerate competitors or those who sin against Him. In no single passage in the whole Old Testament is God described as envious. Even in those texts where the adjective "jealous" is used, it might be more appropriate to understand it as "zealous." When God is the subject of the verb *qānā'*, the meaning is "be zealous," and the preposition *le* ("to, for") is used before the object: His holy name (Ezek. 39:25); His land (Joel 2:18); and His inheritance (Zech. 1:14). Cf. Zech. 8:2: "This is what the Lord Almighty says: I am very jealous for Zion; I am burning with jealousy for her" (NIV), where we must interpret "jealous[y]" as "zealous" and "zeal."

In the Septuagint the word *zelos* ("zeal; ardor; jealousy") brings out the Hebrew usage. In the English versions similar translations are given: "to be jealous" or "to be zealous" (KJV, RSV, NASB, NIV) and "to be envious" (KJV and NIV).

B. Noun.

qin'āh (קִנְאָל, 7068), "ardor; zeal; jealousy." This noun occurs 43 times in biblical Hebrew. One occurrence is in Deut. 29:20: "The Lord will not spare him, but then the anger of the Lord and his jealousy shall smoke against that man...."

C. Adjectives.

qannā' (קַנָּא, 7067), "jealous." This adjective occurs 6 times in the Old Testament. The word refers directly to the attributes of God's justice and holiness, as He is the sole object of human worship and does not tolerate man's sin. One appearance is in Exod. 20:5: "... For I the Lord thy God am a jealous God, visiting the iniquity of the fathers upon the children unto the third and fourth generation of them that hate me."

The adjective qannô' also means "jealous." This word appears only twice, with implications similar to qannā'. Josh. 24:19 is one example: "And Joshua said unto the people, Ye cannot serve the Lord: for he is a holy God; he is a jealous God; he will not forgive your transgressions nor your sins." Nah. 1:2 contains the other occurrence of qannô'.

TO JUDGE

A. Verb.

šāpaṭ (שָׁפַט, 8199), "to judge, deliver, rule." This verb also occurs in Ugaritic, Phoenician, Arabic, Akkadian, and post-biblical Hebrew. Biblical Hebrew attests šāpaṭ around 125 times and in all periods.

In many contexts this root has a judicial sense. Šāpaṭ refers to the activity of a third party who sits over two parties at odds with one another. This third party hears their cases against one another and decides where the right is and what to do about it (he functions as both judge and jury). So Sarai said to Abram: "My wrong [outrage done me] be upon thee [in your lap]: I have given my maid into thy bosom; and when she saw that she had conceived, I was despised in her eyes: the Lord judge between me and thee" (Gen. 16:5—the first occurrence of the word). Sarai had given Hagar to Abram in her stead. This act was in keeping with ancient Nuzu law, which Abram apparently knew and followed. The legal rights to the child would be Sarai's. This would mean that Hagar "did all the work" and received none of the privileges. Consequently she made things miserable for Sarai. As the tribal and family head Abram's responsibility was to keep things in

order. This he did not do. Thus Sarai declares that she is innocent of wrongdoing; she has done nothing to earn Hagar's mistreatment, and Abram is at fault in not getting the household in order. Her appeal is: since Abram has not done his duty (normally he would be the judge of tribal matters), "the Lord decide" between us, that is, in a judicial sense, as to who is in the right. Abram granted the legitimacy of her case and handed Hagar over to her to be brought into line (Gen. 16:6).

Šāpaṭ also speaks of the accomplishing of a sentence. Both this concept and those of hearing the case and rendering a decision are seen in Gen. 18:25, where Abraham speaks of "the Judge [literally, "One who judges"] of all the earth." In 1 Sam. 3:13 the emphasis is solely on "delivering" the sentence: "For I have told him that I will judge his house for ever for the iniquity which he knoweth...."

In some cases "judging" really means delivering from injustice or oppression. David says to Saul: "The Lord therefore be judge and judge between me and thee, and see, and plead my cause, and deliver me out of thine hand" (1 Sam. 24:15). This sense (in addition to the judicial sense), "to deliver," is to be understood when one speaks of the judges of Israel (Judg. 2:16): "Nevertheless the Lord raised up judges, which delivered them out of the hand of those that [plundered] them."

Šāpaṭ can be used not only of an act of deliverance, but of a process whereby order and law are maintained within a group. This idea also is included in the concept of the judges of Israel: "And Deborah, a prophetess, the wife of Lapidoth, she judged Israel at that time" (Judg. 4:4). This activity was judicial and constituted a kind of ruling over Israel. Certainly ruling is in mind in Num. 25:5: "And Moses said unto the judges of Israel, 'Slay ye every one his men that were joined unto Baal-Peor'" (1 Sam. 8:1).

The military deliverer was the head over a volunteer army summoned when danger threatened (militia). In the time of Samuel this procedure proved inadequate for Israel. They wanted a leader who would organize and lead a standing army. They asked Samuel, therefore, for a king such as the other nations had, one who was apt and trained in warfare, and whose successor (son) would be carefully trained, too. There would be more continuity in leadership as a result. Included in this idea of a king who would "judge" them like the other nations was the idea of a ruler; in order to sustain a permanent army and its training, the people had to be organized for taxation and conscription. This is what is in view in 1 Sam. 8:6–18 as Samuel explains.

B. Nouns.

mišpāṭ (מִשְׁפָּט, 4941), "judgment; rights." This noun, which appears around 420 times, also appears in Ugaritic.

This word has two main senses; the first deals with the act of sitting as a judge, hearing a case, and rendering a proper verdict. Eccl. 12:14 is one such occurrence: "For God shall bring every work into judgment, with every secret thing, whether it be good, or whether it be evil."

Mišpāṭ can also refer to the "rights" belong-

ing to someone (Exod. 23:6). This second sense carries several nuances: the sphere in which things are in proper relationship to one's claims (Gen. 18:19—the first occurrence); a judicial verdict (Deut. 17:9); the statement of the case for the accused (Num. 27:5); and an established ordinance (Exod. 21:1).

The noun *šĕpāṭîm* refers to "acts of judgment." One of the 16 occurrences is in Num. 33:4: "For the Egyptians buried all their firstborn, which the Lord had smitten among them: upon their gods also the Lord executed judgments."

K

TO KEEP, OVERSEE

A. Verb.

nāṣaḥ (נָצַח, 5329), "to keep, oversee, have charge over." The word appears as "to set forward" in the sense of "to oversee or to lead" in 1 Chron. 23:4, 2 Chron. 34:12, Ezra 3:8, and Ezra 3:9: "Then stood Jeshua with his sons and his brethren, Kadmiel and his sons, the sons of Judah, together, to set forward the workmen in the house of God...." The word appears as "to oversee" in 2 Chron. 2:2: "And Solomon told out threescore and ten thousand men to bear burdens... and three thousand and six hundred to oversee them."

B. Participle.

nāṣṣēaḥ (נָצֵח, 5329), "overseer; director." Used throughout the history of the Hebrew language, this root is used in the noun sense in modern Hebrew to mean "eternity, perpetuity." While this word is used approximately 65 times in the Hebrew Old Testament, almost all of them (except for 5 or 6) are participles, used as verbal-nouns. The participial form has the meaning of "overseer, director," reflecting the idea that one who is pre-eminent or conspicuous is an "overseer." Thus, *nāṣṣēaḥ* is found in the Book of Psalms a total of 55 times in the titles of various psalms (Ps. 5, 6, 9, et al.) with the meaning, "To the choirmaster" (JB, RSV). Other versions render it "choir director" (NASB); "chief musician" (KJV); and "leader" (NAB). The significance of this title is not clear. Of the 55 psalms involved, 39 are connected with the name of David, 9 with Korah, and 5 with Asaph, leaving only two anonymous psalms.

The Hebrew preposition meaning "to" or "for" which is used with this participle could mean assignment to the person named, or perhaps more reasonably, an indication of a collection of psalms known by the person's name. This title is found also at the end of Hab. 3, showing that this psalm was part of a director's collection.

The word refers to "overseers" in 2 Chron. 2:18: "... and three thousand and six hundred overseers to set the people a work."

C. Adjective.

Nāṣaḥ is used only in Jer. 8:5 in the sense of "enduring": "Why then is this people of Jerusalem slidden back by a perpetual backsliding?"

TO KEEP, WATCH, GUARD

A. Verb.

nāṣar (נָצַר, 5341), "to watch, to guard, to keep." Common to both ancient and modern Hebrew, this verb is found also in ancient Ugaritic. It occurs some 60 times in the Hebrew Old Testament. *Nāṣar* is found for the first time in the biblical text in Exod. 34:7, where it has the sense of "keeping with faithfulness." This meaning is usually found when man is the subject: "keeping" the covenant (Deut. 33:9); "keeping" the law (Ps. 105:45 and 10 times in Ps. 119); "keeping" the rules of parents (Prov. 6:20).

Nāṣar is frequently used to express the idea of "guarding" something, such as a vineyard (Isa. 27:3) or a fortification (Nah. 2:1). "To watch" one's speech is a frequent concern, so advice is given "to watch" one's mouth (Prov. 13:3), the tongue (Ps. 34:13), and the lips (Ps.

141:3). Many references are made to God as the one who "preserves" His people from dangers of all kinds (Deut. 32:10; Ps. 31:23). Generally, *nāṣar* is a close synonym to the much more common verb, *šāmar*, "to keep, tend."

Sometimes "to keep" has the meaning of "to besiege," as in Isa. 1:8, " ... as a besieged city."

šāmar (שָׁמַר, 8104), "to keep, tend, watch over, retain." This verb occurs in most Semitic languages (biblical Aramaic attests only a noun formed from this verb). Biblical Hebrew attests it about 470 times and in every period.

Šāmar means "to keep" in the sense of "tending" and taking care of. So God put Adam "into the garden of Eden to dress it and to keep it" (Gen. 2:15—the first occurrence). In 2 Kings 22:14 Harhas is called "keeper of the wardrobe" (the priest's garments). Satan was directed "to keep," or "to tend" (so as not to allow it to be destroyed) Job's life: "Behold, he is in thine hand; but save his life" (Job 2:6). In this same sense God is described as the keeper of Israel (Ps. 121:4).

The word also means "to keep" in the sense of "watching over" or giving attention to. David, ironically chiding Abner for not protecting Saul, says: "Art not thou a valiant man? and who is like to thee in Israel? wherefore then hast thou not kept thy lord the king?" (1 Sam. 26:15). In extended application this emphasis comes to mean "to watch, observe": "And it came to pass, as she continued praying before the Lord, that Eli [was watching] her mouth" (1 Sam. 1:12). Another extended use of the verb related to this emphasis appears in covenantal contexts. In such cases "keep" means "to watch over" in the sense of seeing that one observes the covenant, keeping one to a covenant. God says of Abraham: "For I know him, that he will command his children and his household after him, and they shall keep the way of the Lord, to do justice and judgment ... " (Gen. 18:19). As God had said earlier, "Thou shalt keep my covenant therefore, thou, and thy seed after thee in their generations" (Gen. 17:9). When used in close connection with another verb, *šāmar* can signify carefully or watchfully doing that action: "And he answered and said, Must I not take heed to speak that which the Lord hath put in my mouth?" (Num. 23:12). Not only does *šāmar* signify watching, but it signifies doing it *as a watchman* in the sense of fulfilling a responsibility: "And the spies saw a man come forth out of the city ... " (Judg. 1:24).

In a third group of passages this verb means "to keep" in the sense of saving or "retaining." When Jacob told his family about his dream,

"his brethren envied him; but his father observed the saying" (Gen. 37:11); he "retained" it mentally. Joseph tells Pharaoh to appoint overseers to gather food: "And let them ... lay up corn under the hand of Pharaoh, and let them keep food in the cities" (Gen. 41:35); let them not give it out but see that it is "retained" in storage.

In three passages *šāmar* seems to have the same meaning as the Akkadian root, "to revere." So the psalmist says: "I have hated them that regard [revere] lying vanities: but I trust in the Lord" (Ps. 31:6).

B. Nouns.

mišmār (מִשְׁמָר, 4929), "guard; guardpost." In the first of its 22 occurrences *mišmār* means "guard": "And he put them in ward [*mišmār*] in the house of the captain of the guard, into the prison ... " (Gen. 40:3). The word implies "guardpost" in Neh. 7:3. The word also refers to men on "guard" (Neh. 4:23) and to groups of attendants (Neh. 12:24).

mišmeret (מִשְׁמֶרֶת, 4931), "those who guard; obligation." This noun appears 78 times. The word refers to "those who guard" in 2 Kings 11:5: " ... A third part of you that enter in on the sabbath shall even be keepers of the watch of the king's house." In Gen. 26:5 the word refers to an "obligation": "Because that Abraham obeyed my voice, and kept my *charge,* my commandments, my statutes, and my laws."

Some other nouns are related to the verb *šāmar*. *Sᵉmarîm* refers to "dregs of wine, lees." One of the 4 appearances of this word is in Isa. 25:6: " ... shall the Lord of hosts make unto all people a feast of fat things, a feast of wines on the lees, of fat things full of marrow, of wines on the lees well refined." The noun *šāmrāh* means "guard, watch." The single appearance of this word is in Ps. 141:3. *Šimmurîm* means a "night vigil." In Exod. 12:42 this word carries the meaning of "night vigil" in the sense of "night of watching": "It is a night to be much observed unto the Lord for bringing them out from the land of Egypt: this is that night of the Lord to be observed of all the children of Israel in their generations." This noun occurs twice in this entry and in no other verse. *'Ašmûrāh* (or *'ašmōret*) refers to "watch." This noun occurs 7 times and in Exod. 14:24 refers to "morning watch": " ... that in the morning watch the Lord looked unto the host of the Egyptians. ... "

TO KILL

šāḥaṭ (שָׁחַט, 7819), "to slaughter, kill." This word is common to both ancient and modern Hebrew, as well as ancient Ugaritic. The idea that the ancient Akkadian term *šahaṣu* ("to flay") may be related appears to have some support in the special use of *šāhat* in 1 Kings 10:16–17: "beaten gold" (see also 2 Chron. 9:15–16). *Šāhat* occurs in the Hebrew Bible approximately 80 times. It first appears in Gen. 22:10: "And Abraham ... took the knife to slay his son." Expressing "slaying" for sacrifice is the most frequent use of *šāhat* (51 times); and as might be expected, the word is found some 30 times in the Book of Leviticus alone.

Šāhat sometimes implies the "slaughtering" of animals for food (1 Sam. 14:32, 34; Isa. 22:13). The word is used of the "killing" of people a number of times (Judg. 12:6; 1 Kings 18:40; 2 Kings 10:7, 14). Sometimes God is said "to slay" people (Num. 14:16). Backslidden Judah went so far as "to slaughter" children as sacrifices to false gods (Ezek. 16:21; 23:39; Isa. 57:5).

hārag (הָרַג, 2026), "to kill, slay, destroy." This term is commonly used in modern Hebrew in its verb and noun forms to express the idea of "killing, slaughter." The fact that it is found in the Old Testament some 170 times reflects how commonly this verb was used to indicate the taking of life, whether animal or human. *Hārag* is found for the first time in the Old Testament in the Cain and Abel story (Gen. 4:8; also vv. 14–15).

Rarely suggesting premeditated killing or murder, this term generally is used for the "killing" of animals, including sacrificially, and for ruthless personal violence of man against man. *Hārag* is not the term used in the sixth commandment (Exod. 20:13; Deut. 5:17). The word there is *rāṣah*, and since it implies premeditated killing, the commandment is better translated: "Do not murder," as most modern versions have it.

The word *hārag* often means wholesale slaughter, both in battle and after battle (Num. 31:7–8; Josh. 8:24; 2 Sam. 10:18). The word is only infrequently used of men's killing at the command of God. In such instances, the causative form of the common Hebrew verb for "to die" is commonly found. In general, *hārag* refers to violent "killing" and destruction, sometimes even referring to the "killing" of vines by hail (Ps. 78:47).

rāṣah (רָצַח, 7523), "to kill, murder, slay." This verb occurs more than 40 times in the Old Testament, and its concentration is in the Pentateuch. *Rāṣah* is rare in rabbinic Hebrew, and its usage has been increased in modern Hebrew with the exclusive meaning of "to murder." Apart from Hebrew, the verb appears in Arabic with the meaning of "to bruise, to crush."

Rāṣah occurs primarily in the legal material of the Old Testament. This is not a surprise, as God's law included regulations on life and provisions for dealing with the murderer. The Decalogue gives the general principle in a simple statement, which contains the first occurrence of the verb: "Thou shalt not kill [murder]" (Exod. 20:13). Another provision pertains to the penalty: "Whoso killeth any person, the murderer shall be put to death by the mouth of witnesses ..." (Num. 35:30). However, before a person is put to death, he is assured of a trial.

The Old Testament recognizes the distinction between premeditated murder and unintentional killing. In order to assure the rights of the manslayer, who unintentionally killed someone, the law provided for three cities of refuge (Num. 35; Deut. 19; Josh. 20; 21) on either side of the Jordan, to which a manslayer might flee and seek asylum: " ... that the slayer may flee thither, which killeth any person at unawares" (Num. 35:11). The provision gave the manslayer access to the court system, for he might be "killed" by the blood avenger if he stayed within his own community (Num. 35:21). He is to be tried (Num. 35:12), and if he is found to be guilty of unintentional manslaughter, he is required to stay in the city of refuge until the death of the high priest (Num. 35:28). The severity of the act of murder is stressed in the requirement of exile even in the case of unintentional murder. The man guilty of manslaughter is to be turned over to the avenger of blood, who keeps the right of killing the manslayer if the manslayer goes outside the territory of the city of refuge before the death of the high priest. On the other hand, if the manslayer is chargeable with premeditated murder (examples of which are given in Num. 35:16–21), the blood avenger may execute the murderer without a trial. In this way the Old Testament underscores the principles of the sanctity of life and of retribution; only in the cities of refuge is the principle of retribution suspended.

The prophets use *rāṣah* to describe the effect of injustice and lawlessness in Israel: " ... because there is no truth, nor mercy, nor knowledge of God in the land. By swearing, and lying, and killing, and stealing, and committing adultery ..." (Hos. 4:1–2; cf. Isa. 1:21; Jer. 7:9). The psalmist, too, metaphorically expresses the deprivation of the rights of helpless murder victims: "They slay the widow and the stranger, and murder the fatherless" (Ps. 94:6).

The Septuagint gives the following translation: *phoneuein* ("murder; kill; put to death"). The KJV gives these senses: "kill; murder; be put to death; be slain."

KINGDOM

malkût (מַלְכוּת, 4438), "kingdom; reign; rule." The word *malkût* occurs 91 times in the Hebrew Old Testament and apparently belongs to late biblical Hebrew. The first occurrence is in Num. 24:7: "He shall pour the water out of his buckets, and his seed shall be in many waters, and his king shall be higher than Agag, and his kingdom shall be exalted."

The word *malkût* denotes: (1) the territory of the kingdom: "When he showed the riches of his glorious kingdom and the honor of his excellent majesty many days, even a hundred and fourscore days" (Esth. 1:4); (2) the accession to the throne: "For if thou altogether holdest thy peace at this time, then shall there enlargement and deliverance arise to the Jews from another place; but thou and thy father's house shall be destroyed: and who knoweth whether thou art come to the kingdom for such a time as this?" (Esth. 4:14); (3) the year of rule: "So Esther was taken unto king Ahasuerus into his house royal in the tenth month, which is the month Tebeth, in the seventh year of his reign" (Esth. 2:16); and (4) anything "royal" or "kingly": throne (Esth. 1:2), wine (Esth. 1:7), crown (Esth. 1:11), word (Esth. 1:19), garment (Esth. 6:8), palace (Esth. 1:9), scepter (Ps. 45:6), and glory (Ps. 145:11–12).

The Septuagint translations of *malkût* are: *basileia* ("kingship; kingdom; royal power") and *basileus* ("king").

mamlākāh (מַמְלָכָה, 4467), "kingdom; sovereignty; dominion; reign." The word appears about 115 times throughout the Old Testament. *Mamlākāh* occurs first in Gen. 10:10: "And the beginning of his kingdom was Babel, and Erech, and Accad, and Calneh, in the land of Shinar" in the sense of the "realm" of the kingdom.

The basic meaning of *mamlākāh* is the area and people that constitute a "kingdom." The word refers to non-Israelite nations who are ruled by a *melek*, "king": "And it shall come to pass after the end of seventy years, that the Lord will visit Tyre, and she shall turn to her hire, and shall commit fornication with all the kingdoms of the world upon the face of the earth" (Isa. 23:17). *Mamlākāh* is a synonym for *'am*, "people," and *gôy*, "nation": " . . . they went from one nation to another, from one kingdom to another people" (Ps. 105:13). *Mamlākāh* also denotes Israel as God's "kingdom": "And ye shall be unto me a kingdom of priests, and a holy nation" (Exod. 19:6). The Davidic king was the theocratic agent by whom God ruled over and blessed His people: "And thine house and thy kingdom shall be established for ever

before thee: thy throne shall be established for ever" (2 Sam. 7:16). Nevertheless, the one *mamlākāh* after Solomon was divided into two kingdoms which Ezekiel predicted would be reunited: " And I will make them one nation in the land upon the mountains of Israel; and one king shall be king to them all: and they shall be no more two nations, neither shall they be divided into two kingdoms . . . " (Ezek. 37:22).

Close to the basic meaning is the usage of *mamlākāh* to denote "king," as the king was considered to be the embodiment of the "kingdom." He was viewed as a symbol of the kingdom proper: "Thus saith the Lord God of Israel, I brought up Israel out of Egypt, and delivered you out of the hand of the Egyptians, and out of the hand of all kingdoms, and of them that oppressed you" (1 Sam. 10:18; in Hebrew the noun "kingdoms" is feminine and the verb "oppress" has a masculine form, signifying that we must understand "kingdoms" as "kings").

The function and place of the king is important in the development of the concept "kingdom." "Kingdom" may signify the head of the kingdom. The word further has the meaning of the royal "rule," the royal "sovereignty," and the "dominion." The royal "sovereignty" was taken from Saul because of his disobedience (1 Sam. 28:17). "Royal sovereignty" is also the sense in Jer. 27:1: "In the beginning of the reign of Jehoiakim. . . . " The Old Testament further defines as expressions of the royal "rule" all things associated with the king: (1) the throne: "And it shall be, when he sitteth upon the throne of his kingdom, that he shall write him a copy of this law in a book out of that which is before the priests the Levites" (Deut. 17:18); (2) the pagan sanctuary supported by the throne: "But prophesy not again any more at Beth-el: for it is the king's chapel, and it is the king's court" (Amos 7:13); and (3) a royal city: "And David said unto Achish, If I have now found grace in thine eyes, let them give me a place in some town in the country, that I may dwell there: for why should thy servant dwell in the royal city with thee?" (1 Sam. 27:5).

All human rule is under God's control. Consequently the Old Testament fully recognizes the kingship of God. The Lord ruled as king over His people Israel (1 Chron. 29:11). He graciously ruled over His people through David and his followers until the Exile (2 Chron. 13:5).

In the New Testament usage all the above meanings are to be associated with the Greek word *basileia* ("kingdom"). This is the major translation of *mamlākāh* in the Septuagint, and as such it is small wonder that the New Testament authors used this word to refer to God's "kingdom": the realm, the king, the sovereignty, and the relationship to God Himself.

melek (מֶלֶךְ, 4428), "king." This word occurs about 2,513 times in the Old Testament. It is found several times in Gen. 14:1: "And it came to pass in the days of Amraphel king of Shinar, Arioch king of Ellasar, Chedorlaomer king of Elam, and Tidal king of nations."

TO KNOW

A. Verb.

nākar (נָכַר, 5234), "to know, regard, recognize, pay attention to, be acquainted with." This verb, which is found in both ancient and modern Hebrew, occurs approximately 50 times in the Hebrew Old Testament. The first time is in Gen. 27:23: "...he did not recognize him" (RSV).

The basic meaning of the term is a physical apprehension, whether through sight, touch, or hearing. Darkness sometimes makes recognition impossible (Ruth 3:14). People are often "recognized" by their voices (Judg. 18:3). *Nākar* sometimes has the meaning "pay attention to," a special kind of recognition: "Blessed be the man who took notice of [KJV, "took knowledge of"] you" (Ruth 2:19, RSV).

This verb can mean "to be acquainted with," a kind of intellectual awareness: "...neither shall his place know him any more" (Job 7:10; cf. Ps. 103:16).

The sense of "to distinguish" is seen in Ezra 3:13: "... The people could not discern the noise of the shout of joy from the noise of the weeping of the people...."

yāda' (יָדַע, 3045), "to know." This verb occurs in Ugaritic, Akkadian, Phoenician, Arabic (infrequently), biblical Aramaic, and in Hebrew in all periods. This verb occurs about 1,040 times (995 in Hebrew and 47 in Aramaic) in the Bible.

Essentially *yāda'* means: (1) to know by observing and reflecting (thinking), and (2) to know by experiencing. The first sense appears in Gen. 8:11, where Noah "knew" the waters had abated as a result of seeing the freshly picked olive leaf in the dove's mouth; he "knew" it after observing and thinking about what he had seen. He did not actually see or experience the abatement himself.

In contrast to this knowing through reflection is the knowing which comes through experience with the senses, by investigation and proving, by reflection and consideration (firsthand knowing). Consequently *yāda'* is used in synonymous parallelism with "hear" (Exod. 3:7), "see" (Gen. 18:21), and "perceive, see" (Job 28:7).

Joseph told his brothers that were they to leave one of their number with him in Egypt then he would "know," by experience, that they were honest men (Gen. 42:33). In the Garden of Eden, Adam and Eve were forbidden to eat of the tree whose fruit if eaten would give them the experience of evil and, therefore, the knowledge of both good and evil. Somewhat characteristically the heart plays an important role in knowing. Because they experienced the sustaining presence of God during the wilderness wandering, the Israelites "knew" in their hearts that God was disciplining or caring for them as a father cares for a son (Deut. 8:5). Such knowing can be hindered by a wrongly disposed heart (Ps. 95:10).

Thirdly, this verb can represent that kind of knowing which one learns and can give back. So Cain said that he did not "know" he was Abel's keeper (Gen. 4:9), and Abram told Sarai that he "knew" she was a beautiful woman (Gen. 12:11). One can also "know" by being told—in Lev. 5:1 a witness either sees or otherwise "knows" (by being told) pertinent information. In this sense "know" is paralleled by "acknowledge" (Deut. 33:9) and "learn" (Deut. 31:12–13). Thus, little children not yet able to speak do not "know" good and evil (Deut. 1:39); they have not learned it so as to tell another what it is. In other words, their knowledge is not such that they can distinguish between good and evil.

In addition to the essentially cognitive knowing already presented, this verb has a purely experiential side. The "knower" has actual involvement with or in the object of the knowing. So Potiphar was unconcerned about (literally, "did not know about") what was in his house (Gen. 39:6)—he had no actual contact with it. In Gen. 4:1 Adam's knowing Eve also refers to direct contact with her—in a sexual relationship. In Gen. 18:19 God says He "knows" Abraham; He cared for him in the sense that He chose him from among other men and saw to it that certain things happened to him. The emphasis is on the fact that God "knew" him intimately and personally. In fact, it is parallel in concept to "sanctified" (cf. Jer. 1:5). A similar use of this word relates to God's relationship to Israel as a chosen or elect nation (Amos 3:2).

Yāda' in the intensive and causative stems is used to express a particular concept of revelation. God did not make Himself known by His name Jehovah to Abraham, Isaac, and Jacob. He did reveal that name to them, that He was the God of the covenant. Nevertheless, the covenant was not fulfilled (they did not possess the Promised Land) until the time of Moses. The statement in Exod. 6:3 implies that now God was going to make Himself known "by His name"; He was going to lead them to possess the land. God makes Himself known through revelatory acts such as bringing judgment on the wicked (Ps. 9:16) and deliverance to His people (Isa. 66:14). He also reveals Himself through the spoken word—for example, by the commands given through Moses (Ezek. 20:11), by promises like those given to David (2 Sam. 7:21). Thus, God reveals Himself in law and promise.

"To know" God is to have an intimate experiential knowledge of Him. So Pharaoh denies that he knows Jehovah (Exod. 5:2) or that he recognizes His authority over him. Positively "to know" God is paralleled to fear Him (1 Kings 8:43), to serve (1 Chron. 28:9), and to trust (Isa. 43:10).

B. Noun.

da'at (דַּעַת, 1847), "knowledge." Several nouns are formed from *yāda'*, and the most frequently occurring is *da'at*, which appears 90 times in the Old Testament. One appearance is in Gen. 2:9: " . . . and the tree of knowledge of good and evil." The word also appears in Exod. 31:3.

C. Particle.

maddûa' (מַדּוּעַ, 4069), "why." This word, which occurs 72 times, is related to the verb *yāda'*. The word is found in Exod. 1:18: " . . . Why have ye done this thing, and have saved the men children alive?"

L

LABOR

A. Noun.

'āmāl (עָמָל, 5999), "labor; toil; anguish; troublesome work; trouble; misery." Cognates of this noun and the verb from which it is derived occur in Aramaic, Arabic, and Akkadian. The 55 occurrences of the noun are mostly in later poetic and prophetic literature (Gen. 41:51; Deut. 26:7; Judg. 10:16).

First, the word means "labor" in the sense of toil: " . . . The Lord heard our voice, and looked on our affliction, and our labor, and our oppression" (Deut. 26:7). In Isa. 53:11 *'āmāl* is used of the toilsome "labor" of the Messiah's soul: "He shall see of the travail of his soul. . . . "

Second, something gained by toil or labor is *'āmāl*: "[He] gave them the lands of the heathen: and they inherited the labor of the people [i.e., of the land of Palestine]" (Ps. 105:44).

Third, *'āmāl* means "troublesome work"; the emphasis is on the difficulty involved in a task or work as troublesome and burdensome: "What profit hath a man of all his labor [troublesome labor] which he taketh under the sun?" (Eccl. 1:3). All 17 appearances of the word in Ecclesiastes bear this meaning.

Fourth, sometimes the emphasis shifts to the area of trouble so that an enterprise or situation is exclusively troublesome or unfortunate: " . . . For God, said he, hath made me forget all my toil, and all my father's house" (Gen. 41:51—the first occurrence). In Judg. 10:16 we read that God "was grieved for the misery of Israel."

Fifth, *'āmāl* can have an ethical connotation and is used as a word for sin. The wicked man "travaileth with iniquity, and hath conceived mischief, and brought forth falsehood" (Ps. 7:14; cf. Job 4:8).

Another noun *'āmēl* means "laborer, sufferer." This word appears infrequently in biblical Hebrew. In Prov. 16:26 the word refers to "laborer": "He that laboreth, laboreth for himself; for his mouth craveth it of him." In Job 3:20 *'āmēl* refers to a "sufferer": "Wherefore is light given to him that is in misery. . . . "

B. Verbs.

'āmal (עָמַל, 5998), "to labor." This verb occurs 11 times in biblical Hebrew and only in poetry. *'Āmal* appears several times in Ecclesiastes (2:11, 19, 21; 5:16). The verb is also found in Ps. 127:1: "Except the Lord build the house, they labor in vain that build it. . . . "

'Āmēl means "toiling." This verb occurs only in a few instances in Ecclesiastes. One occurrence is in Eccl. 3:9: "What profit hath he that worketh in that wherein he laboreth?"

LAMB (MALE)

kebeś (כֶּבֶשׂ, 3532), "lamb (male); kid." The Akkadian cognate of this noun means "lamb," whereas the Arabic cognate signifies "a young ram." The word occurs 107 times in the Hebrew Old Testament, and especially in the Pentateuch.

The *kebeś* is a "young lamb" which is nearly always used for sacrificial purposes. The first usage in Exodus pertains to the Passover: "Your lamb shall be without blemish, a male of the first year: ye shall take it out from the sheep, or from the goats" (Exod. 12:5). The word *gᵉdî*, "kid," is a synonym for *kebeś*: "The wolf also shall dwell with the lamb [*kebeś*], and the leopard shall lie down with the kid [*gᵉdî*]; and the calf and the young lion and the fatling together; and a little child shall lead them" (Isa. 11:6). The traditional translation "lamb" leaves the gender uncertain. In Hebrew the word *kebeś* is masculine, whereas the *kibśah*, "young ewe lamb," is feminine; cf. "And Abraham set seven ewe lambs of the flock by themselves" (Gen. 21:28).

The Septuagint gives the following translations: *amnos* ("lamb"); *probaton* ("sheep"); and *arnos* ("lamb"). The KJV gives these senses: "lamb; sheep."

LAND

'ădāmāh (אֲדָמָה, 127), "ground; land; earth." This noun also occurs in Arabic. Hebrew occurrences number about 224 and cover every period of biblical Hebrew.

Initially this noun represents arable "ground" (probably red in color). As such it supports water and plants: "But there went up a mist from the earth, and watered the whole face of the ground" (Gen. 2:6). This meaning is in Gen. 1:25, where it first appears: " ... every thing that creepeth upon the earth. ... " The word is contrasted to unproductive soil, or "waste land," and the generic word for the surface of the planet "earth," which may represent either or both of the preceding words. The body of the first man, Adam, was formed exclusively from the *'ădāmāh* (cf. Gen. 2:9): "And the Lord God formed man [*'ādām*] of the dust of the ground [*'ădāmāh*] ... " (Gen. 2:7).

'Ădāmāh may be used specifically to describe what has been and will be cultivated by a given group of people, or what they possess to this end: "Look down from thy holy habitation, from heaven, and bless thy people Israel, and the land which thou hast given us, as thou swarest unto our fathers, a land that floweth with milk and honey" (Deut. 26:15). A further variation of this nuance refers to the actual soil itself: "Shall there not then, I pray thee, be given to thy servant two mules' burden of earth [with which to build an altar to the true God]?" (2 Kings 5:17).

In Exod. 3:5 *'ădāmāh* is used more in the sense "ground," what is below one's feet irrespective of its cultivable properties: " ... Put off thy shoes from off thy feet, for the place whereon thou standest is holy *ground*."

The nuance "property" or "possession" comes more clearly to the fore in passages such as Zech. 2:12: "And the Lord shall inherit Judah his portion in the holy land ... " (cf. Ps. 49:11). Although *'ădāmāh* is never used politically, its use as "landed property" or "home country" sometimes approaches that sense (cf. Isa. 14:2; 19:17; and especially Ezek. 7:2). Isa. 15:9: " ... For I will bring more upon Dimon, lions upon him that escapeth of Moab, and upon the remnant of the land," further illustrates this usage.

Throughout the Old Testament there is a relationship between *'ădām*, "man," and the *'ădāmāh*. The two words have an etymological affinity inasmuch as they both appear to be derived from the verb *'ādōm*, "to be red." If Adam were to remain obedient to God, the "ground" would give forth its fruit. Hence, the "ground" was God's possession and under His command (Gen. 2:6). He made it respond to His servant. The entry of sin disrupted the harmony between man and the "ground," and the "ground" no longer responded to man's care. His life moved in and toward death rather than upward and toward life. Increased human rebellion caused decreased fruitfulness of the "ground" (Gen. 4:12, 14; cf. 8:21). In Abraham the promised redemption (Gen. 3:15) took the form of the restoration of a proper relation between God and man and between man and the "ground" (Gen. 28:14–15). Under Moses the fruitfulness of the "ground" depended on the obedience of God's people (cf. Deut. 11:17).

'ereṣ (אֶרֶץ, 776), "land (the whole earth); dry land; ground; land (political); underworld." This word has cognates in Ugaritic, Phoenician-Punic, Moabite, Akkadian, Aramaic (here the radicals are *'rq* or *'r'*), and Arabic (*'rd*). *'Ereṣ* occurs in biblical Hebrew about 2,504 times (22 times in biblical Aramaic) and in all periods.

The word often represents the whole surface of this planet and, together with the word "heavens," describes the entire physical creation and everything in it. This meaning is in its first biblical occurrence: "In the beginning God created the heaven and the earth" (Gen. 1:1).

'Ereṣ sometimes means "land" as contrasted to sea or water. This use, for example, is in Exod. 20:11: "For in six days the Lord made heaven and earth, the sea, and all that in them is, and rested the seventh day. ... " This more narrow meaning first appears in Gen. 1:10,

where God called the dry ground "land." Here "land" includes desert and arable land, valleys and mountains—everything that we know today as continents and islands.

'Ereṣ refers to the physical "ground" under the feet of men and animals. Upon the "ground" creep all creeping things: "Let us make man in our image, after our likeness: and let them have dominion . . . over every creeping thing that creepeth upon the earth" (Gen. 1:26). Dust lies upon the *'ereṣ* (Exod. 8:16), and rain and dew fall on it (Gen. 2:5).

'Ereṣ may be used geographically, i.e., to identify a territory: "And Haran died before his father Terah in the land of his nativity" (Gen. 11:28).

'Ereṣ sometimes bears a political connotation and represents both a given political territory and the people who live there: "And there was no bread in all the land; for the famine was very sore, so that the land of Egypt and all the land of Canaan fainted by reason of the famine" (Gen. 47:13). Not only the "land" languished, but (and especially) the people suffered.

Next, in several passages this noun has both geographical and political overtones and identifies the possession or inheritance of a tribe. This emphasis is in Num. 32:1: "Now the children of Reuben and the children of Gad had a very great multitude of cattle: and when they saw the land of Jazer, and the land of Gilead, that, behold, the place was a place for cattle. . . ."

In a seldom used, but interesting, nuance *'ereṣ* represents the "underworld": "But those that seek my soul, to destroy it, shall go into the lower parts of the earth" (Ps. 63:9). Sometimes even used by itself (absolutely) this noun represents the "underworld": "I went down to the bottoms of the mountains; the earth with her bars was about me for ever . . ." (Jonah 2:6). The Akkadian cognates sometimes bear this same meaning. Other Old Testament passages where some scholars find this meaning are Exod. 15:12; Ps. 71:20; and Jer. 17:13.

LAST

A. Adjective.

'aḥărôn (אַחֲרוֹן, 314), "at the back; western; later; last; future." This word occurs about 51 times in biblical Hebrew.

'Aḥărôn has a local-spatial meaning. Basically, it means "at the back": "And he put the handmaids and their children foremost, and Leah and her children after, and Rachel and Joseph hindermost" (Gen. 33:2—the first biblical appearance). When applied elsewhere, the word means "western": "Every place whereon

the soles of your feet shall tread shall be yours: from the wilderness and Lebanon, from the river, the river Euphrates, even unto the uttermost [western] sea shall your coast be" (Deut. 11:24).

Used temporally, *'aḥărôn* has several nuances. First, it means "last" as contrasted to the first of two things: "And it shall come to pass, if they will not believe thee, neither hearken to the voice of the first sign, that they will believe the voice of the latter sign" (Exod. 4:8). Second, it can represent the "last" in a series of things or people: "Ye are my brethren, ye are my bones and my flesh: wherefore then are ye the last to bring back the king?" (2 Sam. 19:12). The word also connotes "later on" and/or "afterwards": "But thou shalt surely kill him; thine hand shall be first upon him to put him to death, and afterwards the hand of all the people" (Deut. 13:9). Next the emphasis can be on the finality or concluding characteristic of a given thing: "Now these be the last words of David" (2 Sam. 23:1).

'Aḥărôn connotes "future," or something that is yet to come: " . . . So that the generation to come of your children that shall rise up after you, and the stranger that shall come from a far land, shall say, when they see the plagues of that land . . ." (Deut. 29:22).

The combination of "first" and "last" is an idiom of completeness: "Now the rest of the acts of Solomon, first and last, are they not written in the book of Nathan the prophet, and in the prophecy of Ahijah the Shilonite, and in the visions of Iddo the seer against Jeroboam the son of Nebat?" (2 Chron. 9:29). Likewise the phrase expresses the sufficiency of the Lord, since He is said to include within Himself the "first" as well as the "last": "Thus saith the Lord the King of Israel, and his Redeemer the Lord of hosts; I am the first, and I am the last; and beside me there is no God" (Isa. 44:6; cf. 48:12). These verses affirm that there is no other God, because all exists in Him.

B. Verb.

'āhar (אָחַר, 309), "to tarry, remain behind, delay." Other words derived from this verb are: "other," "after (wards)," "backwards." *'Āhar* appears in Exod. 22:29 with the meaning "delay": "Thou shalt not delay to offer the first of thy ripe fruits, and of thy liquors: the firstborn of thy sons shalt thou give unto me."

LAW

A. Noun.

tôrāh (תּוֹרָה, 8451), "law; direction; instruction." This noun occurs 220 times in the Hebrew Old Testament.

In the wisdom literature, where the noun does not appear with a definite article, *tôrāh* signifies primarily "direction, teaching, instruction": "The law of the wise is a fountain of life, to depart from the snares of death" (Prov. 13:14), and "Receive, I pray thee, the law from his mouth, and lay up his words in thine heart" (Job 22:22). The "instruction" of the sages of Israel, who were charged with the education of the young, was intended to cultivate in the young a fear of the Lord so that they might live in accordance with God's expectations. The sage was a father to his pupils: "Whoso keepeth the law is a wise son: but he that is a companion of riotous men shameth his father" (Prov. 28:7; cf. 3:1; 4:2; 7:2). The natural father might also instruct his son in wise living, even as a God-fearing woman was an example of kind "instruction": "She openeth her mouth with wisdom; and in her tongue is the law of kindness" (Prov. 31:26).

The "instruction" given by God to Moses and the Israelites became known as "the law" or "the direction" (*hā-tôrāh*), and quite frequently as "the Law of the Lord": "Blessed are the undefiled in the way, who walk in the law of the Lord" (Ps. 119:1), or "the Law of God": "Also day by day, from the first day unto the last day, [Ezra] read in the book of the law of God" (Neh. 8:18), and also as "the Law of [given through] Moses": "Remember ye the law of Moses my servant, which I commanded unto him in Horeb for all Israel . . . " (Mal. 4:4). The word can refer to the whole of the "law": "For he established a testimony in Jacob, and appointed a law in Israel, which he commanded our fathers, that they should make them known to their children" (Ps. 78:5), or to particulars: "And this is the law which Moses set before the children of Israel . . . " (Deut. 4:44).

God had communicated the "law" that Israel might observe and live: "And what nation is there so great, that hath statutes and judgments so righteous as all this law, which I set before you this day?" (Deut. 4:8). The king was instructed to have a copy of the "law" prepared for him at his coronation (Deut. 17:18). The priests were charged with the study and teaching of, as well as the jurisprudence based upon, the "law" (Jer. 18:18). Because of rampant apostasy the last days of Judah were times when there were no teaching priests (2 Chron. 15:3); in fact, in Josiah's days the "law" (whether the whole Torah, or a book or a part) was recovered: "And Hilkiah . . . said to Shaphan the scribe, I have found the book of the law in the house of the Lord" (2 Chron. 34:15).

The prophets called Israel to repent by returning to the *tôrāh* ("instruction") of God (Isa. 1:10). Jeremiah prophesied concerning God's new dealing with His people in terms of the New Covenant, in which God's law is to be internalized, God's people would willingly obey Him: "But this shall be the covenant that I will make with the house of Israel; After those days, saith the Lord, I will put my law in their inward parts, and write it in their hearts; and will be their God, and they shall be my people" (Jer. 31:33). The last prophet of the Old Testament reminded the priests of their obligations (Mal. 2) and challenged God's people to remember the "law" of Moses in preparation for the coming Messiah (Mal. 4:4).

The Septuagint gives the following translations: *nomos* ("law; rule"); *nomimos* ("conformable to law; lawful"); *entole* ("command-[ment]; order"); and *prostagma* ("order; commandment; injunction").

B. Verb.

yārāh (יָרָה, 3384), "to throw, cast, direct, teach, instruct." The noun *tôrāh* is derived from this root. The meaning "to cast" appears in Gen. 31:51: "And Laban said to Jacob, Behold this heap, and behold this pillar, which I have cast betwixt me and thee." *Yārāh* means "to teach" in 1 Sam. 12:23: " . . . but I will teach you the good and the right way."

TO BE LEFT, REMAIN

A. Verb.

yātar (יָתַר, 3498), "to be left; remain over; excel; show excess." This word is found in various Semitic languages, ranging from ancient Akkadian to modern Hebrew. In its verb forms, the word is found just over 100 times in the Hebrew Bible. *Yātar* occurs for the first time in the biblical text in Gen. 30:36, where it is stated that "Jacob fed the rest of Laban's flocks." This statement reflects the word's frequent use to show separation from a primary group. Thus, Jacob "was left alone" (Gen. 32:24) when his family and flocks went on beyond the brook Jabbok.

Sometimes the word indicates survivors, as in 2 Sam. 9:1: "Is there yet any that is left of the house of Saul . . . ?" The remnant idea is reflected in Ezek. 6:8: "Yet will I leave a remnant, that ye may have some that shall escape the sword. . . . "

B. Noun.

yeter (יֶתֶר, 3499), "remainder; excess." This noun occurs nearly 100 times. As "remainder, excess," it is used especially in the sense of a lesser number or quality as compared to something of primary importance. So, *yeter* is used to refer to "the rest of the vessels" left in Jerusalem by Nebuchadnezzar (Jer. 27:19–20, RSV), and the men who were left after Joab had assigned his picked men in the battle lines (2 Sam. 10:10). Occasionally *yeter* is used to indicate "excess" in a negative way, so the literal "lip of excess" has the meaning of "false speech" (Prov. 17:7, RSV).

A few times this noun implies "superiority" or "pre-eminence," as in Gen. 49:3, where Jacob describes his son Reuben as being "pre-eminent in pride and pre-eminent in power" (RSV). The name of Jethro, Moses' father-in-law, is derived from this word.

TO LIE

A. Verb.

šākab (שָׁכַב, 7901), "to lie down, lie, have sexual intercourse with." This word also occurs in Ugaritic, Akkadian, Ethiopic, post-biblical Aramaic, and post-biblical Hebrew. Biblical Hebrew attests it about 160 times and in all periods.

Basically this verb signifies a person's lying down—though in Job 30:17 and Eccl. 2:23 it refers to something other than a human being. *Šākab* is used of the state of reclining as opposed to sitting: "And every thing that she lieth upon in her [menstruation] shall be unclean: every thing also that she sitteth upon . . . " (Lev. 15:20). This general sense appears in several nuances. First, there is the meaning "to lie down to rest." Elisha "came thither, and he turned into the chamber [which the Shunammite had prepared for his use], and lay there" (2 Kings 4:11). Job remarks that his gnawing pains "take no rest" (Job 30:17; cf. Eccl. 2:23).

Šākab can also be used of lying down on a bed, for example, when one is sick. Jonadab told Amnon: "Lay thee down on thy bed, and make thyself [pretend to be] sick . . . " (2 Sam. 13:5). The word can be used as an equivalent of the phrase "to go to bed": "But before they [Lot's visitors] lay down, the men of the city, even the men of Sodom, compassed the house round . . . " (Gen. 19:4—the first occurrence of the verb). *Šākab* also signifies "lying down asleep." The Lord told Jacob: " . . . The land whereon thou liest, to thee will I give it, and to thy seed" (Gen. 28:13).

In Exod. 22:26–27 the verb denotes the act of sleeping more than the lying down: "If thou at all take thy neighbor's raiment to pledge, thou shalt deliver it unto him by that the sun goeth down . . . [In what else] shall he sleep?" *Šākab* can also be used to mean "lodge" and thus refers to sleeping and eating. Israel's spies lodged with Rahab: "And they went, and came

into a harlot's house, named Rahab, and lodged there" (Josh. 2:1; cf. 2 Kings 4:11).

This verb can mean "to lie down" in a figurative sense of to be humbled or to be robbed of power. The trees of Lebanon are personified and say concerning the king of Babylon: "Since thou art laid down, no feller [tree cutter] is come up against us" (Isa. 14:8).

Used reflexively, *šākab* means "to humble oneself, to submit oneself": "We lie down in our shame . . . " (Jer. 3:25).

Another special nuance is "to put something on its side": "Who can number the clouds in wisdom? Or who can [tip] the bottles of heaven, when the dust groweth into hardness, and the clods cleave fast together?" (Job 38:37–38).

A second emphasis of *šākab* is "to die," to lie down in death. Jacob instructed his sons as follows: "But I will lie with my fathers, and thou shalt carry me out of Egypt, and bury me in their burying place" (Gen. 47:30). This phrase ("lie down with one's fathers") does not necessarily refer to being buried or to dying an honorable death (cf. 1 Kings 22:40) but is a synonym for a human's dying. (It is never used of animals or inanimate things.) The idea is that when one dies he no longer stands upright. Therefore, to "lie with one's fathers" parallels the concept of "lying down" in death. *Šākab*, as 1 Kings 22:40 suggests, can refer to the state of being dead ("so Ahab slept with his fathers"), since v. 37 already reports that he had died and was buried in Samaria. The verb used by itself may mean "to die," or "to lie dead"; cf. "At her feet he bowed, he fell, he lay [dead]: at her feet he bowed, he fell: where he bowed, there he fell down dead" (Judg. 5:27).

A third major use of *šākab* is "to have sexual relations with." The first occurrence of this use is in Gen. 19:32, where Lot's daughters say: "Come, let us make our father drink wine, and we will lie with him, that we may preserve seed of our father." Even when a physical "lying down" is not necessarily in view, the word is used of having sexual relations: "Whosoever lieth with a beast shall surely be put to death" (Exod. 22:19). The word is also used of homosexual activities (Lev. 18:22).

B. Nouns.

miškāb (מִשְׁכָּב, 4904), "place to lie; couch; bed; act of lying." This noun appears 46 times in the Old Testament. In Gen. 49:4 *miškāb* is used to mean a "place to lie" or "bed": " . . . because thou wentest up to thy father's bed. . . . " The word refers to the "act of lying" in Num. 31:17: " . . . kill every woman that hath known man by lying with him."

Šᵉkābāh means "layer of dew." In one of its

9 appearances, *s͞ekābāh* refers to a "layer of dew": " . . . and in the morning the dew lay round about the host" (Exod. 16:13).

S͞ekōbet refers to "copulation." This noun occurs rarely (4 times), as in Lev. 18:20: "Moreover thou shalt not lie carnally with thy neighbor's wife, to defile thyself with her."

TO LIGHT

A. Verb.

'ôr (אוֹר, 216), "to become light, become lighted up (of daybreak), give light, cause light to shine." This verb is found also in Akkadian and Canaanite. The Akkadian word *urru* means "light," but generally "day."

'Ôr means "to become light" in Gen. 44:3: "As soon as the morning was light, the men were sent away, they and their asses." The word means "to give light" in Num. 8:2: " . . . the seven lamps shall give light over against the candlestick."

B. Nouns.

'ôr (אוֹר, 216), "light." This noun appears about 120 times and is clearly a poetic term.

The first occurrence of *'ôr* is in the Creation account: "And God said, Let there be light: and there was light" (Gen. 1:3). Here "light" is the opposite of "darkness." The opposition of "light" and "darkness" is not a unique phenomenon. It occurs frequently as a literary device: "Woe unto them that call evil good, and good evil; that put darkness for light, and light for darkness; that put bitter for sweet, and sweet for bitter!" (Isa. 5:20); and "In that day they shall roar against them like the roaring of the sea: and if one look unto the land, behold darkness and sorrow, and the light is darkened in the heavens thereof" (Isa. 5:30). In Hebrew various antonyms of *'ôr* are used in parallel constructions: "The people that walked in darkness have seen a great light: they that dwell in the land of the shadow of death, upon them hath the light shined" (Isa. 9:2).

The basic meaning of *'ôr* is "daylight" (cf. Gen. 1:3). In the Hebrew mind the "day" began at the rising of the sun: "And he shall be as the light of the morning, when the sun riseth, even a morning without clouds; as the tender grass springeth out of the earth by clear shining after rain" (2 Sam. 23:4). The "light" given by the heavenly bodies was also known as *'ôr:* "Moreover the light of the moon shall be as the light of the sun, and the light of the sun shall be sevenfold, as the light of seven days, in the day that the Lord bindeth up the breach of his people, and healeth the stroke of their wound" (Isa. 30:26).

In the metaphorical use *'ôr* signifies life over against death: "For thou hast delivered my soul from death: wilt not thou deliver my feet from falling, that I may walk before God in the light of the living?" (Ps. 56:13). To walk in the "light" of the face of a superior (Prov. 16:15), or of God (Ps. 89:15), is an expression of a joyful, blessed life in which the quality of life is enhanced. The believer is assured of God's "light," even in a period of difficulty; cf. "Rejoice not against me, O mine enemy: when I fall, I shall arise; when I sit in darkness, the Lord shall be a light unto me" (Mic. 7:8; cf. Ps. 23:4).

In the Septuagint *'ôr* has many translations, of which *phos* ("light") is most frequent.

The noun *'ûr* means "shine; light-giving." This word occurs infrequently, once in Isa. 50:11: "Behold, all ye that kindle a fire, that compass yourselves about with sparks: walk in the light [*'ûr*] of your fire, and in the sparks that ye have kindled."

'Ôrāh refers to "light." This noun means "light" in Ps. 139:12: "Yea, the darkness hideth not from thee; but the night shineth as the day: the darkness and the light are both alike to thee."

Mā'ôr also means "light." This noun appears about 20 times. *Mā'ôr* occurs more than once in Gen. 1:16: "And God made two great lights; the greater light to rule the day, and the lesser light to rule the night: he made the stars also."

LIKENESS

A. Verb.

dāmāh (דָּמָה, 1819), "to be like, resemble, be or act like, liken or compare, devise, balance or ponder." This verb appears in biblical Hebrew about 28 times. Cognates of this word appear in biblical Aramaic, Akkadian, and Arabic. *Dāmāh* means "to be like" in Ps. 102:6: "I am like a pelican of the wilderness: I am like an owl of the desert."

B. Noun.

d͞emût (דְּמוּת, 1823), "likeness; shape; figure; form; pattern." All but 5 of the 25 appearances of this word are in poetical or prophetical books of the Bible.

First, the word means "pattern," in the sense of the specifications from which an actual item is made: "Now King Ahaz went to Damascus . . . and saw the altar which was at Damascus; and King Ahaz sent to Urijah the priest the pattern of the altar and its model, according to all its workmanship" (2 Kings 16:10, NASB).

Second, *d͞emût* means "shape" or "form," the thing(s) made after a given pattern. In 2 Chron. 4:3 the word represents the "shape" of a bronze statue: "And under it was the similitude of oxen, which did compass it round about: ten in a cubit, compassing the sea round about." In such passages *dᵉmût* means more than just "shape" in general; it indicates the "shape" in particular. In Ezek. 1:10, for example, the word represents the "form" or "likeness" of the faces of the living creatures Ezekiel describes. In Ezek. 1:26 the word refers to what something seemed to be rather than what it was: "And above the firmament that was over their heads was the likeness of a throne. . . . "

Third, *dᵉmût* signifies the original after which a thing is patterned: "To whom then will ye liken God? or what likeness will ye compare unto him?" (Isa. 40:18). This significance is in its first biblical appearance: "And God said, Let us make man in our image, after our likeness . . . " (Gen. 1:26).

Fourth, in Ps. 58:4 the word appears to function merely to extend the form but not the meaning of the preposition *kᵉ*: "Their poison is like the poison of a serpent. . . . "

LION

'ărî (אֲרִי, 738), "lion." This apparently Aramaic loan word finds a cognate only in Aramaic. Occurring in all periods of biblical Hebrew, it is attested 83 times.

The word represents a "full-grown lion." This word should be compared to: (1) *gûr* (Gen. 49:9), a suckling lion; (2) *šaḥal* (Hos. 5:14), a young lion which no longer is a suckling; and (3) *kᵉpîr* (Judg. 14:5), a young lion which no longer is a suckling and which hunts for its food independently.

The "lion" was a much-feared beast (Amos 3:12) found mostly in the Trans-jordan (Jer. 49:19) and in the mountainous areas (Song of Sol. 4:8). The various characteristics of the "lion" make it a frequent figure of strength and power (Judg. 14:18), of plundering (Gen. 49:9), and of malicious scheming (Ps. 10:9).

LIP

śāpāh (שָׂפָה, 8193), "lip; edge." This Hebrew word is related to cognate languages where a similar word signifies "lip" or "edge" (cf. Akkadian *saptu*). *Śāpāh* has undergone little change in the history of the Hebrew language. It occurs about 175 times in the Old Testament, mainly in the poetic literature. The word is most frequent in the prophetical books, except for Isaiah (13 times) and Ezekiel (7 times).

"Lip" is first a part of the body. Isaiah's "lips" were ritually cleansed by the burning coal (Isa. 6:7). The compression of the "lips" was an indication of evil thoughts or motivation: "He shutteth his eyes to devise froward things: mov-

ing his lips he bringeth evil to pass" (Prov. 16:30).

The use of "lip" as an organ of speech is more frequent. With the lips, or human speech, one may flatter (Ps. 12:3), lie (Ps. 31:18), speak mischief (Ps. 140:9), and speak perversity (Prov. 4:24). On the other hand, the "lip" (speech) of the people of God is described as not sinful (Job 2:10), rejoicing (Job 8:21), prayerful (Ps. 17:1), God's word (Ps. 119:13), truthful (Prov. 12:19), wise (Prov. 14:7; 15:7), righteous (Prov. 16:13), and excellent (Prov. 17:7). In all these examples "the lip" signifies a manner of speech; cf. "Excellent speech becometh not a fool: much less do lying lips a prince" (Prov. 17:7).

The use of *śāpāh* is similar to that of *lāšôn*, "tongue," in that both words denote speech and also human language. *Śāpāh* with the meaning of human language occurs in the phrase "the language of Canaan" (Isa. 19:18). Isaiah described foreign language as "deeper speech than thou canst perceive" (literally, "depths of lip"; 33:19).

The metaphorical use of *śāpāh* ("edge") appears mainly in the narrative literature. The word denotes the shore of a sea (Gen. 22:17) or of a river (Gen. 41:3), or the edge of material (Exod. 26:4), or the brim of a vessel (1 Kings 7:23).

The Septuagint translation is *cheilos* ("lip; shore; bank"); and the KJV has these translations: "lip; bank; brim; edge; language; shore; and speech."

TO LIVE

A. Verb.

hāyāh (חָיָה, 2421), "to live." This verb, which has cognates in most other Semitic languages (except Akkadian), occurs 284 times in biblical Hebrew and in all periods. In the ground stem this verb connotes "having life": "And Adam lived a hundred and thirty years . . . " (Gen. 5:3). A similar meaning appears in Num. 14:38 and Josh. 9:21.

The intensive form of *hāyāh* means "to preserve alive": " . . . Two of every sort shalt thou bring into the ark, to keep them alive with thee . . . " (Gen. 6:19). This word may also mean "to bring to life" or "to cause to live": " . . . I dwell . . . with him also that is of a contrite and humble spirit, to revive the spirit of the humble, and to revive the heart of the contrite ones" (Isa. 57:15).

"To live" is more than physical existence. According to Deut. 8:3, "man doth not live by bread only, but by every word that proceedeth out of the mouth of the Lord doth man live." Moses said to Israel: " . . . Love the Lord thy

God ... that thou mayest live and multiply" (Deut. 30:16).

B. Noun.

hay (חַי, 2416), "living thing; life." The use of this word occurs only in the oath formula "as X lives," literally, "by the life of X": "And he said, They were my brethren, even the sons of my mother: as the Lord liveth, if ye had saved them alive, I would not slay you" (Judg. 8:19). This formula summons the power of a superior to sanction the statement asserted. In Judg. 8:19 God is the witness to Gideon's pledge to kill his enemies and this statement that they brought the penalty on themselves. A similar use appears in Gen. 42:15 except that the power summoned is Pharaoh's: "Hereby ye shall be proved: By the life of Pharaoh ye shall not go forth hence, except your youngest brother come hither." In 1 Sam. 1:26 Hannah employs a similar phrase summoning Eli himself to attest the truthfulness of her statement: "And she said, Oh my lord, as thy soul liveth, my lord, I am the woman that stood by thee here, praying unto the Lord." Only God swears by His own power: "And the Lord said, I have pardoned according to thy word: But as truly as I live, all the earth shall be filled with the glory of the Lord" (Num. 14:20–21).

The feminine form of the word, *hayyāh*, means "living being" and is especially used of animals. When so used, it usually distinguishes wild and undomesticated from domesticated animals; the word connotes that the animals described are untamed: "And God remembered Noah, and every living thing, and all the cattle that was with him in the ark ... " (Gen. 8:1). Job 37:8 uses *hayyāh* of rapacious beasts: "Then the beasts go into dens, and remain in their places." This same word may also connote "evil beast": "Come now therefore, and let us slay him, and cast him into some pit, and we will say, Some evil beast hath devoured him ... " (Gen. 37:20). In another nuance the word describes land animals as distinct from birds and fish: "Be fruitful, and multiply, and replenish the earth, and subdue it: and have dominion over the fish of the sea, and over the fowl of the air, and over every living thing that moveth upon the earth" (Gen. 1:28).

Infrequently *hayyāh* represents a domesticated animal: "And the cities shall they have to dwell in; and the suburbs of them shall be for their cattle, and for their goods, and for all their beasts" (Num. 35:3). Sometimes this word is used of "living beings" in general: "Also out of the midst thereof came the likeness of four living creatures" (Ezek. 1:5). In such passages the word is synonymous with the Hebrew word *nepeš*.

The plural of the noun *hay, hayyîm*, is a general word for the state of living as opposed to that of death. This meaning is in Deut. 30:15: "See, I have set before thee this day life and good, and death and evil." Notice also Gen. 27:46: "And Rebekah said to Isaac, I am weary of my life because of the daughters of Heth.... " In a second nuance the plural signifies "lifetime," or the days of one's life: " ... And dust shalt thou eat all the days of thy life" (Gen. 3:14). The phrase "the years of one's life" represents the same idea: "And Sarah was a hundred and seven and twenty years old: these were the years of the life of Sarah" (Gen. 23:1). The "breath of life" in Gen. 2:7 is the breath that brings "life": "And the Lord God formed man of the dust of the ground, and breathed into his nostrils the breath of life; and man became a living soul" (cf. Gen. 6:17).

The "tree of life" is the tree which gives one eternal, everlasting "life." Therefore, it is the tree whose fruit brings "life": "And out of the ground made the Lord God to grow every tree that is pleasant to the sight, and good for food; the tree of life also in the midst of the garden ... " (Gen. 2:9). In another nuance this word suggests a special quality of "life," life as a special gift from God (a gift of salvation): "I call heaven and earth to record this day against you, that I have set before you life and death, blessing and cursing: therefore choose life, that both thou and thy seed may live" (Deut. 30:19). The plural of the word can represent "persons who are alive," or living persons: "And he stood between the dead and the living; and the plague was stayed" (Num. 16:48).

C. Adjective.

hay (חַי, 2416), "alive; living." This word has cognates in Ugaritic, Canaanite, Phoenician, Punic, and Aramaic. It occurs about 481 times in biblical Hebrew and in all periods.

The word *hay* is used both as an adjective and as a noun. Used adjectivally it modifies men, animals, and God, but never plants. In Gen. 2:7 the word used with the noun *nepeš* ("soul, person, being") means a "living" person: "And the Lord God formed man of the dust of the ground, and breathed into his nostrils the breath of life; and man became a living soul." The same two words are used in Gen. 1:21 but with a slightly different meaning: "And God created ... every living creature that moveth, which the waters brought forth abundantly, after their kind.... " Here a living *nepeš* ("creature") is an animal. Deut. 5:26 refers to God as the "living" God, distinguishing Him from the lifeless gods/idols of the heathen.

In a related nuance *hay* describes flesh (animal meat or human flesh) under the skin, or "raw flesh." In Lev. 13:10 one reads that leprosy involved seeing quick (alive), raw (*hay*) flesh: "And the priest shall see him: and, behold, if the rising be white in the skin, and it have turned the hair white, and there be quick raw flesh in the rising...." The same words (*bāśar hay*) are applied to dead, raw (skinned) animal flesh: "Give flesh to roast for the priest; for he will not have [boiled] flesh of thee, but raw" (1 Sam. 2:15).

Applied to liquids, *hay* means "running"; it is used metaphorically describing something that moves: "And Isaac's servants digged in the valley, and found there a well of springing water" (Gen. 26:19). In Jer. 2:13 the NASB translates "living" waters, or waters that give life (cf. Jer. 17:13; Zech. 14:8). The Song of Solomon uses the word in a figure of speech describing one's wife; she is "a well of living waters" (4:15). The emphasis is not on the fact that the water flows but on its freshness; it is not stagnant, and therefore is refreshing and pleasant when consumed.

LOAD

maśśā' (מַשָּׂא, 4853), "load; burden; tribute; delight." The 43 occurrences of this word are scattered throughout the periods of biblical Hebrew.

The word means that which is borne by a man, an ass, a mule, or a camel: "If thou see the ass of him that hateth thee lying under his burden, and wouldest forbear to help him ..." (Exod. 23:5—the first occurrence). A "load" may be hung on a peg (Isa. 22:25). This word is used figuratively of spiritual "loads" one is carrying: "For mine iniquities are gone over mine head: as a heavy burden they are too heavy for me" (Ps. 38:4).

Maśśā' means "burden" in the sense of something burdensome, a hardship. Moses asked God: "... Wherefore have I not found favor in thy sight, that thou layest the burden of all this people upon me?" (Num. 11:11).

Once the word represents that which is borne to a lord, a "tribute": "Also some of the Philistines brought Jehoshaphat presents, and tribute silver ..." (2 Chron. 17:11).

In Ezek. 24:25 *maśśā'* bears a unique meaning: "Will it not be on the day when I take from them their stronghold, the joy of their pride, the desire of their eyes, and their heart's delight [or, the longing of their soul], their sons and their daughters ..." (NASB).

maśśā' (מַשָּׂא, 4853), "utterance; oracle."

This noun, closely related to the above noun, is used 21 times. *Maśśā'* means "utterance" or "oracle": "For remember, when you and I rode side by side behind Ahab his father, how the Lord uttered this oracle against him" (2 Kings 9:25, RSV). In Jer. 23:33–38 the word appears to connote both a burden and an oracle.

TO LOOK

nābaṭ (נָבַט, 5027), "to look, regard, behold." This verb is found in both ancient and modern Hebrew. It occurs approximately 70 times in the Old Testament. The first use of this term is in Gen. 15:5, where it is used in the sense of "take a good look," as God commands Abraham: "Look now toward heaven, and [number] the stars...."

While *nābaṭ* is commonly used of physical "looking" (Exod. 3:6), the word is frequently used in a figurative sense to mean a spiritual and inner apprehension. Thus, Samuel is told by God: "Look not on his countenance ..." (1 Sam. 16:7) as he searched for a king among Jesse's sons. The sense of "consider" (with insight) is expressed in Isa. 51:1–2: "... Look unto the rock whence ye are hewn.... Look unto Abraham your father...." "Pay attention to" seems to be the meaning in Isa. 5:12: "... they regard not the work of the Lord...."

LOOSE CONDUCT

A. Noun.

zimmāh (זִמָּה, 2154), "loose conduct; lewdness." The 28 occurrences of this noun are all in legal and poetical books of the Bible, except for a single occurrence in Judges.

This noun signifies "loose or infamous conduct" and is used most often with regard to illicit sexual conduct: "Thou shalt not uncover the nakedness of a woman and her daughter, ... or her daughter's daughter, to uncover her nakedness; for they are her near kinswomen: it is wickedness" (Lev. 18:17—the first occurrence). Rejection of God's law or spiritual adultery may be represented by *zimmāh* (Ps. 119:150; cf. Ezek. 16:12–28). A plan or scheme identified by the word is, therefore, a "harlotrous" plan (Ps. 26:10).

mᵉzimmāh (מְזִמָּה, 4209), "purpose; evil device; evil thoughts; discretion." This noun occurs 19 times. The word means "purpose" in Job 42:2: "I know that thou canst do all things, and that no purpose of time can be thwarted" (RSV). *Mᵉzimmāh* refers to "evil device" in Jer. 11:15: "What hath my beloved to do in mine house, seeing she hath wrought lewdness with many...." In Job 21:27 the word is used to mean "evil thoughts," and in Prov. 1:4 the word is used for "discretion."

B. Verb.

zāmam (זָמַם, 2161), "to ponder, to cogitate." The noun mᵉzimmāh is derived from this verb that occurs 13 times. In Zech. 8:14–15 the word appears to carry the sense of "to ponder": "For thus saith the Lord of hosts; As I thought to punish you, when your fathers provoked me to wrath . . . and I repented not: So again have I thought in these days to do well unto Jerusalem and to the house of Judah: fear ye not."

LORD

'ādôn (אָדוֹן, 113), or 'ădōnāy (אֲדֹנָי, 113), "lord; master; Lord." Cognates of this word appear in Ugaritic and Phoenician. The form 'ādôn appears 334 times, while the form 'ădōnāy (used exclusively as a divine name) appears 439 times.

Basically, 'ādôn means "lord" or "master." It is distinguished from the Hebrew word ba'al, which signifies "possessor" or "owner." 'Adôn basically describes the one who occupies the position of a "master" or "lord" over a slave or servant: "And the servant put his hand under the thigh of Abraham his master . . . " (Gen. 24:9). It is used of kings and their most powerful aides. Joseph told his brothers: "So now it was not you that sent me hither, but God: and he hath made me a father [i.e., an adviser] to Pharaoh, and lord of all his house, and a ruler throughout all the land of Egypt" (Gen. 45:8; cf. 42:30). Only once is this word used in the sense of "owner" or "possessor" (1 Kings 16:24).

'Adôn is often used as a term of polite address. In some cases, the one so named really occupies a position of authority. In Gen. 18:12 (the first occurrence) Sarah called Abraham her "lord." On the other hand, this may be a purely honorary title by which the speaker intends to indicate his submission to the one so addressed. Jacob instructed his slaves to speak to "my lord Esau" (Gen. 32:18); i.e., Jacob called his brother Esau "lord." In places where the speaker is addressing someone calling him "lord," the word virtually means "you."

When applied to God, 'ādôn is used in several senses. It signifies His position as the one who has authority (like a master) over His people to reward the obedient and punish the disobedient: "Ephraim provoked him to anger most bitterly: therefore shall he leave his blood upon him, and his reproach shall his Lord return unto him" (Hos. 12:14). In such contexts God is conceived as a Being who is sovereign ruler and almighty master. The word is often a title of respect, a term of direct address usually assuming a specific concrete lord-vassal or master-servant relationship (Ps. 8:1). In some cases the word appears to be a title suggesting God's relationship to and position over Israel: "Three times in the year all thy males shall appear before the Lord God" (Exod. 23:17). In such contexts 'ādôn is a formal divine name and should probably be transliterated if the proper emphasis is to be retained. In the form 'ădōnāy the word means "Lord" par excellence or "Lord over all," even as it sometimes does in the form 'ādôn (cf. Deut. 10:17, where God is called the "God of gods, and Lord of lords"; Josh. 3:11, where He is called the "Lord of all the earth").

The word 'ădōnāy appears in Gen. 15:2: "And Abram said, Lord God, what wilt thou give me, seeing I go childless, ..." This word frequently appears in Psalms (Ps. 68:17; 86:3) and Isaiah (Isa. 29:13; 40:10).

yᵉhwāh (יְהוָה, 3068), "Lord." The Tetragrammaton YHWH appears without its own vowels, and its exact pronunciation is debated (Jehovah, Yehovah, Jahweh, Yahweh). The Hebrew text does insert the vowels for 'ădōnāy, and Jewish students and scholars read 'ădōnāy whenever they see the Tetragrammaton. This use of the word occurs 6,828 times. The word appears in every period of biblical Hebrew.

The divine name YHWH appears only in the Bible. Its precise meaning is much debated. God chose it as His personal name by which He related specifically to His chosen or covenant people. Its first appearance in the biblical record is Gen. 2:4: "These are the generations of the heavens and of the earth when they were created, in the day that the Lord God made the earth and the heavens." Apparently Adam knew Him by this personal or covenantal name from the beginning, since Seth both called his son Enosh (i.e., man as a weak and dependent creature) and began (along with all other pious persons) to call upon (formally worship) the name of YHWH, "the Lord" (Gen. 4:26). The covenant found a fuller expression and application when God revealed Himself to Abraham (Gen. 12:8), promising redemption in the form of national existence. This promise became reality through Moses, to whom God explained that He was not only the "God who exists" but the "God who effects His will": "Thus shalt thou say unto the children of Israel, The Lord [YHWH] God of your fathers, the God of Abraham, the God of Isaac, and the God of Jacob, hath sent me unto you: this is my name for ever, and this is my memorial unto all generations. Go, and gather the elders of Israel together, and say unto them, The Lord [YHWH] God of your fathers, the God of Abraham, of Isaac, and of Jacob, appeared unto me, saying, I have surely visited you, and seen that which is done to you in Egypt: And I have said, I will bring you up out of the affliction of Egypt unto the land of the Canaanites. . ." (Exod. 3:15–17). So God explained the meaning of "I am who I am" (Exod. 3:14). He spoke to the fathers as YHWH, but the promised deliverance and, therefore, the fuller significance or experienced meaning of His name were unknown to them (Exod. 6:2–8).

LOT

gôrāl (גּוֹרָל, 1486), "lot." This word is attested 77 times and in all periods of the language (if a traditional view of the formation of the canon is accepted).

Gôrāl represents the "lot" which was cast to discover the will of God in a given situation: "And Aaron shall cast lots upon the two goats; one lot for the Lord, and the other lot for the scapegoat" (Lev. 16:8—the first occurrence). Exactly what casting the "lot" involved is not known.

Since the land of Palestine was allocated among the tribes by the casting of the "lot," these allotments came to be known as their lots: "This then was the lot of the tribe of the children of Judah by their families; even to the border of Edom. . ." (Josh. 15:1).

In an extended use the word *gôrāl* represents the idea "fate" or "destiny": "And behold at eveningtide trouble; and before the morning he is not. This is the portion of them that spoil us, and the lot of them that rob us" (Isa. 17:14). Since God is viewed as controlling all things absolutely, the result of the casting of the "lot" is divinely controlled: "The lot is cast into the lap; but the whole disposing thereof is of the Lord" (Prov. 16:33). Thus, providence (divine control of history) is frequently figured as one's "lot."

TO LOVE

A. Verb.

'āhab (אָהַב, 157) or *'āhēb* (אָהֵב, 157), "to love; like." This verb occurs in Moabite and Ugaritic. It appears in all periods of Hebrew and around 250 times in the Bible.

Basically this verb is equivalent to the English "to love" in the sense of having a strong emotional attachment to and desire either to possess or to be in the presence of the object. First, the word refers to the love a man has for a woman and a woman for a man. Such love is rooted in sexual desire, although as a rule it is desire within the bounds of lawful relationships: "And

Isaac brought her into his mother Sarah's tent, and took Rebekah, and she became his wife; and he loved her. . ." (Gen. 24:67). This word may refer to an erotic but legal love outside marriage. Such an emotion may be a desire to marry and care for the object of that love, as in the case of Shechem's love for Dinah (Gen. 34:3). In a very few instances *'āhab* (or *'āhēb*) may signify no more than pure lust—an inordinate desire to have sexual relations with its object (cf. 2 Sam. 13:1). Marriage may be consummated without the presence of love for one's marriage partner (Gen. 29:30).

'Āhab (or *'āhēb*) seldom refers to making love (usually this is represented by *yāda'*, "to know," or by *šākab*, "to lie with"). The word does seem to have this added meaning, however, in 1 Kings 11:1: "But King Solomon loved many strange women, together with the daughter of Pharaoh . . ." (cf. Jer. 2:25). Hosea appears to use this nuance when he writes that God told him to "go yet, love a woman beloved of her friend, yet an adulteress. . ." (3:1). This is the predominant meaning of the verb when it appears in the causative stem (as a participle). In every instance except one (Zech. 13:6) *'āhab* (or *'āhēb*) signifies those with whom one has made or intends to make love: "Go up to Lebanon, and cry; and lift up thy voice in Bashan, and cry from the passages: for all thy lovers are destroyed" (Jer. 22:20; cf. Ezek. 16:33).

'Āhab (or *'āhēb*) is also used of the love between parents and their children. In its first biblical appearance, the word represents Abraham's special attachment to his son Isaac: "And he said, Take now thy son, thine only son Isaac, whom thou lovest. . ." (Gen. 22:2). *'Āhab* (or *'āhēb*) may refer to the family love experienced by a daughter-in-law toward her mother-in-law (Ruth 4:15). This kind of love is also represented by the word *rāḥam*.

'Āhab (or *'āhēb*) sometimes depicts a special strong attachment a servant may have toward a master under whose dominance he wishes to remain: "And if the servant shall plainly say, I love my master, my wife, and my children; I will not go out free. . ." (Exod. 21:5). Perhaps there is an overtone here of family love; he "loves" his master as a son "loves" his father (cf. Deut. 15:16). This emphasis may be in 1 Sam. 16:21, where we read that Saul "loved [David] greatly." Israel came "to love" and deeply admire David so that they watched his every move with admiration (1 Sam. 18:16).

A special use of this word relates to an especially close attachment of friends: " . . . The soul of Jonathan was knit with the soul of David, and Jonathan loved him as his own soul"

(1 Sam. 18:1). In Lev. 19:18: "... Thou shalt love thy neighbor as thyself..." (cf. Lev. 19:34; Deut. 10:19) '*āhab* (or '*āhēb*) signifies this brotherly or friendly kind of love. The word suggests, furthermore, that one seek to relate to his brother and all men according to what is specified in the law structure God gave to Israel. This was to be the normal state of affairs between men.

This verb is used politically to describe the loyalty of a vassal or a subordinate to his lord—so Hiram of Tyre "loved" David in the sense that he was completely loyal (1 Kings 5:1).

The strong emotional attachment and desire suggested by '*āhab* (or '*āhēb*) may also be fixed on objects, circumstances, actions, and relationships.

B. Noun.

'*ahăbāh* (אַהֲבָה, 160), "love." This word appears about 55 times, and it represents several kinds of "love." The first biblical occurrence of '*ahăbāh* is in Gen. 29:20; there the word deals with the "love" between man and wife as a general concept. In Hos. 3:1 the word is used of "love" as a sexual activity. '*Ahăbāh* means "love" between friends in 1 Sam. 18:3: "Then Jonathan and David made a covenant because he loved him as his own soul." The word refers to Solomon's "love" in 1 Kings 11:2 and to God's "love" in Deut. 7:8.

C. Participle.

'*āhab* (אָהַב, 157), "friend." This word used as a participle may mean "friend": "... The rich hath many friends" (Prov. 14:20).

LOVING-KINDNESS

A. Noun.

ḥesed (חֶסֶד, 2617), "loving-kindness; steadfast love; grace; mercy; faithfulness; goodness; devotion." This word is used 240 times in the Old Testament, and is especially frequent in the Psalter. The term is one of the most important in the vocabulary of Old Testament theology and ethics.

The Septuagint nearly always renders *ḥesed* with *eleos* ("mercy"), and that usage is reflected in the New Testament. Modern translations, in contrast, generally prefer renditions close to the word "grace." KJV usually has "mercy," although "loving-kindness" (following Coverdale), "favor," and other translations also occur. RSV generally prefers "steadfast love." NIV often offers simply "love."

In general, one may identify three basic meanings of the word, which always interact: "strength," "steadfastness," and "love." Any understanding of the word that fails to suggest all three inevitably loses some of its richness.

"Love" by itself easily becomes sentimentalized or universalized apart from the covenant. Yet "strength" or "steadfastness" suggests only the fulfillment of a legal or other obligation.

The word refers primarily to mutual and reciprocal rights and obligations between the parties of a relationship (especially Yahweh and Israel). But *ḥesed* is not only a matter of obligation; it is also of generosity. It is not only a matter of loyalty, but also of mercy. The weaker party seeks the protection and blessing of the patron and protector, but he may not lay absolute claim to it. The stronger party remains committed to his promise, but retains his freedom, especially with regard to the manner in which he will implement those promises. *Ḥesed* implies personal involvement and commitment in a relationship beyond the rule of law.

Marital love is often related to *ḥesed*. Marriage certainly is a legal matter, and there are legal sanctions for infractions. Yet the relationship, if sound, far transcends mere legalities. The prophet Hosea applies the analogy to Yahweh's *ḥesed* to Israel within the covenant (e.g., 2:21). Hence, "devotion" is sometimes the single English word best capable of capturing the nuance of the original. The RSV attempts to bring this out by its translation, "steadfast love." Hebrew writers often underscored the element of steadfastness (or strength) by pairing *ḥesed* with '*ĕmet* ("truth, reliability") and '*ĕmûnāh* ("faithfulness").

Biblical usage frequently speaks of someone "doing," "showing," or "keeping" *ḥesed*. The concrete content of the word is especially evident when it is used in the plural. God's "mercies," "kindnesses," or "faithfulnesses" are His specific, concrete acts of redemption in fulfillment of His promise. An example appears in Isa. 55:3: "... And I will make an everlasting covenant with you, even the sure mercies of David."

Ḥesed has both God and man as its subject. When man is the subject of *ḥesed*, the word usually describes the person's kindness or loyalty to another; cf. 2 Sam. 9:7: "And David said ... I will surely show thee [Mephibosheth] kindness for Jonathan thy father's sake...." Only rarely is the term applied explicitly to man's affection or fidelity toward God; the clearest example is probably Jer. 2:2: "Go and cry in the ears of Jerusalem, saying, thus saith the Lord; I remember thee, the kindness of thy youth, the love of thine espousals, when thou wentest after me in the wilderness...."

Man exercises *ḥesed* toward various units within the community—toward family and relatives, but also to friends, guests, masters, and servants. *Hesed* toward the lowly and needy is often specified. The Bible prominently uses the term *hesed* to summarize and characterize a life of sanctification within, and in response to, the covenant. Thus, Hos. 6:6 states that God desires "mercy [RSV, "steadfast love"] and not sacrifice" (i.e., faithful living in addition to worship). Similarly, Mic. 6:8 features *hesed* in the prophets' summary of biblical ethics: " . . . and what doth the Lord require of thee, but . . . to love *mercy*. . .?"

Behind all these uses with man as subject, however, stand the repeated references to God's *hesed*. It is one of His most central characteristics. God's loving-kindness is offered to His people, who need redemption from sin, enemies, and troubles. A recurrent refrain describing God's nature is "abounding/plenteous in *hesed*" (Exod. 34:6; Neh. 9:17; Ps. 103:8; Jonah 4:2). The entire history of Yahweh's covenantal relationship with Israel can be summarized in terms of *hesed*. It is the one permanent element in the flux of covenantal history. Even the Creation is the result of God's *hesed* (Ps. 136:5–9). His love lasts for a "thousand generations" (Deut. 7:9; cf. Deut. 5:10 and Exod. 20:6), indeed "forever" (especially in the refrains of certain psalms, such as Ps. 136).

Words used in synonymous parallelism with *hesed* help to define and explain it. The word most commonly associated with *hesed* is *'ĕmet* ("fidelity; reliability"): " . . . Let thy loving-kindness [*hesed*] and thy truth [*'ĕmet*] continually preserve me." *'Ĕmûnāh* with a similar meaning is also common: "He hath remembered his mercy [*hesed*] and his truth [*'ĕmûnāh*] toward the house of Israel. . . . " This emphasis is especially appropriate when God is the subject, because His *hesed* is stronger and more enduring than man's. Etymological investigation suggests that *hesed's* primitive significance may have been "strength" or "permanence." If so, a puzzling use of *hesed* in Isa. 40:6 would be explained: "All flesh is grass, and all the goodliness thereof is as the flower of the field."

The association of *hesed* with "covenant" keeps it from being misunderstood as mere providence or love for all creatures; it applies primarily to God's particular love for His chosen and covenanted people. "Covenant" also stresses the reciprocity of the relationship; but since God's *hesed* is ultimately beyond the covenant, it will not ultimately be abandoned, even when the human partner is unfaithful and must be disciplined (Isa. 54:8, 10). Since its final triumph and implementation is eschatological, *hesed* can imply the goal and end of all salvation-history (Ps. 85:7, 10; 130:7; Mic. 7:20).

The proper noun *Hasdiah* (1 Chron. 3:20) is related to *hesed*. The name of Zerubbabel's son means "Yahweh is faithful/gracious," a fitting summary of the prophet's message.

B. Adjective.

hāsîd (חָסִיד, 2623), "pious; devout; faithful; godly." The adjective *hāsîd*, derived from *hesed*, is often used to describe the faithful Israelite. God's *hesed* provides the pattern, model, and strength by which the life of the *hāsîd* is to be directed. One reference to the "godly" man appears in Ps. 12:1: "Help, Lord; for the godly man ceaseth; for the faithful fail from among the children of men." Usually a suffix or possessive pronoun referring to God is attached to the word, indicating His special attachment to those who pattern their lives after His: "O love the Lord, all ye his saints [literally, "His pious ones"; NASB, "His godly ones"]: for the Lord preserveth the faithful, and plentifully rewardeth the proud doer" (Ps. 31:23).

Following the Greek *hosios* and Latin *sanctus*, the KJV often renders the word "saint"—which must be understood in the sense of sanctification [dependent upon grace], not moralistically [of native goodness].

M

TO MAGNIFY

A. Verb.

gādal (גָּדַל, 1431), "to become strong, grow up, be great or wealthy, evidence oneself as great (magnified), be powerful, significant, or valuable." This verb occurs elsewhere only in Ugaritic and Arabic; it is not attested in biblical Aramaic or post-biblical Hebrew. In other Semitic languages the meaning of the word is generally represented by roots with the radicals *rbh*, and such a root exists in biblical Hebrew as a synonym of *gādal*. These two synonyms differ, however, inasmuch as *gādal* does not refer to numerical increase (except perhaps in Gen. 48:19). The Bible attests *gādal* about 120 times and in every period.

This verb can signify the increasing of size and age as with the maturing process of human life: "And the child grew, and was weaned ... " (Gen. 21:8). The word also depicts the "growing up" of animals (2 Sam. 12:3) and plants (Isa. 44:14) and the maturing of animal horns (Dan. 8:9) and other growing things. In the intensive stem *gādal* indicates that this rearing has occurred: " ... I have nourished and brought up children ... " (Isa. 1:2). This stem may also imply permission: " ... [He] shall let the locks of the hair of his head grow" (Num. 6:5).

Gādal can represent the status of "being great or wealthy." Abraham's servant reported: "And the Lord hath blessed my master greatly; and he is become great ... " (Gen. 24:35)—here the word represents the conclusion of a process. In the intensive stem the verb sets forth a fact, as when God said: "And I will make of thee a great nation, and I will bless thee, and make thy name great ... " (Gen. 12:2—the first biblical occurrence of the verb).

This word is sometimes used with the meaning "to be great, to evidence oneself as great": "And now, I beseech thee, let the power of my Lord be great, according as thou hast spoken ... " (Num. 14:17). Moses is praying that God will demonstrate that He is truly great, even as He has said, and do so not by destroying His people. Such an act (destroying Israel) would make onlookers conclude that God was not able to accomplish what He had promised. If, however, He would bring Israel into Palestine, this would exhibit His greatness before the nations. This same sense appears in 2 Sam. 7:22, except with the added overtone of "magnified," "praised as great": "Wherefore thou art great, O Lord God: for there is none like thee, neither is there any God besides thee, according to all that we have heard with our ears."

Another emphasis of *gādal* is "to be great, powerful, important, or valuable." This nuance arises when the word is applied to kings. Pharaoh said to Joseph: "Thou shalt be over my house, and according unto thy word shall all my people be ruled: only in the throne will I be greater [more powerful and honored] than thou" (Gen. 41:40). The Messiah "shall stand and feed in the strength of the Lord, in the majesty of the name of the Lord his God; and they shall abide: for now shall he be great unto the ends of the earth" (Mic. 5:4); He will be powerful to the ends of the earth. The nuance "to be valuable" appears in 1 Sam. 26:24 when

David said to Saul: "And, behold, as thy life was much set by this day in mine eyes, so let my life be much set by in the eyes of the Lord, and let him deliver me out of all tribulation." In this statement the second use of the verb is in the intensive stem. Perhaps the force of this could be expressed if one were to translate: "So may my life be very highly valued ... "

In the reflexive stem *gādal* may signify "to magnify oneself." God says: "Thus will I magnify myself, and sanctify myself; and I will be known in the eyes of many nations ... " (Ezek. 38:23). The context shows that He will bring judgment. In this way He "magnifies Himself," or shows Himself to be great and powerful. On the other hand, a false statement of greatness and power is an empty boast. So *gādal* can mean "to boast": "Shall the axe boast itself against him that heweth therewith? or shall the saw magnify itself against him that shaketh it?" (Isa. 10:15). In the causative stem the verb may signify "to assume great airs": "If indeed ye will magnify yourselves against me, and plead against me my reproach ... " (Job 19:5). A nuance appears in Job 7:17, where *gādal* is in the intensive stem, suggesting an estimation of greatness: "What is man, that thou shouldest magnify him? and that thou shouldest set thine heart upon him?" (Ps. 8:4). When man is so insignificant, why then does God esteem him so important?

B. Nouns.

gᵉdûllāh (גְּדוּלָּה, 1420), "greatness; great dignity; great things." This noun occurs 12 times. It means "greatness" in Ps. 71:21: "Thou shalt increase my greatness, and comfort me on every side." *Gᵉdûllāh* may refer also to "great dignity" (Esth. 6:3) and to "great things" (2 Sam. 7:21).

gōdel (גֹּדֶל, 1433), "greatness." This noun appears 13 times. *Gōdel* means "greatness" in terms of size (Ezek. 31:7), of divine power (Ps. 79:11), of divine dignity (Deut. 32:3), of divine majesty (Deut. 3:24), of divine mercy (Num. 14:19), or of the false greatness of one's heart (insolence; Isa. 9:9).

migdāl (מִגְדָּל, 4026), "strong place; wooden podium." This noun, which occurs 49 times, usually refers to a tower or a "strong place" (Gen. 11:4–5), but it also occurs once to refer to a "wooden podium": "And Ezra the scribe stood upon a pulpit of wood ... " (Neh. 8:4).

C. Adjectives.

gādôl (גָּדוֹל, 1419), "great." The adjective *gādôl* is the most frequently appearing word related to the verb *gādal* (about 525 times). *Gādôl* is used of extended dimension (Gen. 1:21), of number (Gen. 12:2), of power (Deut. 4:37), of punishment (Gen. 4:13), and of value or importance (Gen. 39:9).

The verb *gādal* and the related adjective *gādôl* may each be used to make distinctive statements. In Hebrew one may say "he is great" both by using the verb alone and by using the pronoun and the adjective *gādôl*. The first sets forth a standing and existing condition—so Mal. 1:5 could be rendered: "The Lord is magnified beyond the borders of Israel." The second construction announces newly experienced information to the recipient, as in Isa. 12:6: "... Great is the Holy One of Israel in the midst of thee." This information was known previously, but recent divine acts have made it to be experienced anew. The emphasis is on the freshness of the experience.

Another adjective *gādēl* means "becoming great; growing up." This verbal adjective occurs 4 times, once in Gen. 26:13: "And the man waxed great, and went forward, and grew until he became very great."

MAIDEN, VIRGIN

bᵉtûlāh (בְּתוּלָה, 1330), "maiden, virgin." Cognates of this word appear in Ugaritic and Akkadian. Its 50 biblical occurrences are distributed throughout every period of Old Testament literature.

This word can mean "virgin," as is clear in Deut. 22:17, where if a man has charged that "I found not thy daughter a maid," the father is to say, "And yet these are the tokens of my daughter's virginity [*bᵉtûlîm*]. The text continues: "And they shall spread the cloth before the elders of the city." The husband was to be chastised and fined (which was given to the girl's father), "because he hath brought up an evil name upon a virgin of Israel" (Deut. 22:19). If she was found not to be a "virgin," she was to be stoned to death "because she hath wrought folly in Israel, to play the whore in her father's house" (Deut. 22:21).

In several passages this word merely means a grown-up girl or a "maiden"; it identifies her age and marital status. The prophets who denounce Israel for playing the harlot also called her the *bᵉtûlāh* of Yahweh, or the *bᵉtûlāh* (daughter) of Israel (Jer. 31:4, 21). The other nations are also called *bᵉtûlôth:* Isa. 23:12—Zidon; Isa. 47:1—Babylon; Jer. 46:11—Egypt. These nations are hardly being commended for their purity! In Ugaritic literature the word is used frequently of the goddess Anat, the sister of Baal and hardly a virgin. What was true of her and figuratively of these nations (including Israel) was that she was a vigorous young woman at the height of her powers and not married. Thus *bᵉtûlāh* is often used in parallelism with the Hebrew *bāḥûr*, which signifies a young man, regardless of his virginity, who is at the height of his powers (Deut. 32:25). In such contexts virility and not virginity is in view. Because of this ambiguity Moses described Rebekah as a young girl (*na'ărāh*) who was "very fair to look upon, a virgin [*bᵉtûlāh*], neither had any man known her" (Gen. 24:16—the first occurrence of the word).

Both the masculine and feminine forms appear in Isa. 23:4: "... I travail not, nor bring forth children, neither do I nourish up young men (*bᵉtûlîm*), nor bring up virgins (*bᵉtûlôt*). A similar occurrence is found in Lam. 1:18: "... Behold my sorrow: my *virgins* and my *young* men are gone into captivity" (cf. Lam. 2:21; Zech. 9:17).

The standard edition of William Gesenius' lexicon by Brown, Driver, and Briggs (BDB) observes that the Assyrian word *batultu* (masc. *batulu*) is a cognate of *bᵉtûlāh*. This Assyrian word means "maiden" or "young man."

Most scholars agree that *bᵉtûlāh* and *batultu* are phonetically related; yet they disagree as to whether they are true cognates. Various Old Testament contexts indicate that *bᵉtûlāh* should be translated "maiden" more often than "virgin." If this is true, the BDB etymology is probably correct.

TO MAKE (CUT) A COVENANT

A. Verb.

kārat (כָּרַת, 3772), "to cut off, cut down, fell, cut or make (a covenant or agreement)." This verb also occurs in Akkadian, Moabite, and post-biblical Hebrew. In biblical Hebrew it is attested about 290 times and in all periods.

Basically *kārat* means "to sever" something from something else by cutting it with a blade. The nuance depends upon the thing being cut off. In the case of a branch, one "cuts it down" (Num. 13:23), and one "[swings] the axe to cut down the tree" (Deut. 19:5). The word is also used of "chopping down" wooden idols (Exod. 34:13). *Kārat* can signify "chopping off" a man's head and feet (1 Sam. 5:4). In Jer. 34:18 this verb means "to cut into two pieces." "Cut off" may also imply cutting off in the sense of circumcision. In Exod. 4:25 Zipporah took a flint knife and "cut off" her son's foreskin. In a related but different usage this word appears in Num. 11:33, where it means "to chew" meat.

"To cut off" can mean "to exterminate or destroy." God told Noah that "all flesh [shall never again] be cut off ... by the waters of a flood ..." (Gen. 9:11—the first occurrence of the word). *Kārat* can be used of spiritual and social extermination. A person "cut off" in this manner is not necessarily killed but may be driven out of the family and removed from the blessings of the covenant. God told Abraham that "the uncircumcised man child whose flesh of his foreskin is not circumcised, that soul shall be cut off from his people; he hath broken my covenant" (Gen. 17:14).

One of the best known uses of this verb is "to make" a covenant. The process by which God made a covenant with Abraham is called "cutting": "In the same day the Lord made a covenant with Abram . . ." (Gen. 15:18). The word "covenant" appears nine times before this in Genesis, but it is not connected with kārat. A synonym to this verb appears in this immediate context (Gen. 15:10) and is directly related to the process of making the covenant. Furthermore, hereafter in Genesis and throughout the Bible kārat is frequently associated with making a covenant. This verb, therefore, constitutes a rather technical term for making a covenant. In Genesis it often alludes to an act by which animals were cut in two and the party taking the oath passed between the pieces. This act was not created by God especially to deal with Abraham but was a well-known practice at that time among many men.

Later, "cutting" a covenant did not necessarily include this act but seems to be an allusion to the Abrahamic covenantal process (cf. Jer. 34:18). In such a covenant the one passing through the pieces pledged his faithfulness to the covenant. If that faithfulness was broken, he called death upon himself, or the same fate which befell the animals. In some cases it is quite clear that no literal cutting took place and that kārat is used in a technical sense of "making an agreement in writing" (Neh. 9:38).

B. Nouns.

kerîtût (כְּרִיתֻת, 3748), refers to a "bill of divorcement." This word implies the cutting off of a marriage by means of a "bill of divorcement": "When a man hath taken a wife, and married her, and it come to pass that she find no favor in his eyes, because he hath found some uncleanness in her: then let him write her a bill of divorcement, and give it in her hand, and send her out of his house" (Deut. 24:1). Kerîtût appears 4 times.

Kerutôt means "beams." This noun, which occurs only 3 times, refers to "beams" in the sense of things "cut off" in 1 Kings 6:36: "And he built the inner court with three rows of hewed stone, and a row of cedar beams."

TO MAKE HASTE, HASTEN

māhar (מָהַר, 4116), "to hasten; make haste." This verb, along with various derivatives, is common to both ancient and modern Hebrew.

It occurs approximately 70 times in the Hebrew Bible. Māhar occurs twice in the first verse in which it is found: "And Abraham hastened into the tent unto Sarah, and said, Make ready quickly three measures of fine meal . . . " (Gen. 18:6).

Māhar often has an adverbial use when it is used with another verb, such as in Gen. 18:7: " . . . hasted to prepare it" (or, "quickly prepared it"). Anyone who yields to seduction is likened by the wise man to a bird that rushes into a snare (Prov. 7:23).

MALE

A. Noun.

zākār (זָכָר, 2145), "male." Cognates of this word appear in Akkadian, Aramaic, and Arabic. It occurs 82 times and usually in early prose (Genesis through Deuteronomy), only 5 times in the biblical prophets, and never in biblical wisdom or poetical literature.

Zākār emphasizes "maleness" as over against "femaleness"; this word focuses on the sex of the one so named. Thus, "God created man in his own image, in the image of God created he him; male and female created he them" (Gen. 1:27). The word can be used not only of an "adult male" but also of a "male child" (Lev. 12:7). Zākār is used collectively in many passages—in singular form, with a plural reference (Judg. 21:11).

In some contexts the word represents a "male animal": "And of every living thing of all flesh, two of every sort shalt thou bring into the ark, to keep them alive with thee; they shall be male and female" (Gen. 6:19).

B. Adjective.

zākār (זָכָר, 2145), "male." Sometimes zākār is used as an adjective: "Number all the firstborn of the males of the children of Israel from a month old and upward . . ." (Num. 3:40). The word appears in Jer. 20:15: "A man child is born unto thee; making him very glad."

MAN

A. Nouns.

'ādām (אָדָם, 120), "man; mankind; people; someone (indefinite); Adam (the first man)." This noun appears in Ugaritic, Phoenician, and Punic. A word with the same radicals occurs in old South Arabic meaning "serf." In late Arabic the same radicals mean not only "mankind" but "all creation." Akkadian admu signifies "child." The Hebrew word appears about 562 times and in all periods of biblical Hebrew.

This noun is related to the verb 'ādōm, "to be red," and therefore probably relates to the original ruddiness of human skin. The noun connotes "man" as the creature created in God's image, the crown of all creation. In its first appearance *'ādām* is used for mankind, or generic man: "And God said, Let us make man in our image, after our likeness ... " (Gen. 1:26). In Gen. 2:7 the word refers to the first "man," Adam: "And the Lord God formed man of the dust of the ground, and breathed into his nostrils the breath of life; and man became a living soul."

Throughout Gen. 2:5–5:5 there is a constant shifting and interrelationship between the generic and the individual uses. "Man" is distinguished from the rest of the creation insofar as he was created by a special and immediate act of God: he alone was created in the image of God (Gen. 1:27). He consisted of two elements, the material and the nonmaterial (Gen. 2:7). From the outset he occupied an exalted position over the rest of the earthly creation and was promised an even higher position (eternal life) if he obeyed God: "And God blessed them, and God said unto them, Be fruitful, and multiply, and replenish the earth, and subdue it: and have dominion over the fish of the sea, and over the fowl of the air, and over every living thing that moveth upon the earth" (Gen. 1:28; cf. 2:16–17). In Gen. 1 "man" is depicted as the goal and crown of creation, while in Gen. 2 the world is shown to have been created as the scene of human activity. "Man" was in God's image with reference to his soul and/or spirit. (He is essentially spiritual; he has an invisible and immortal aspect which is simple or indivisible.) Other elements of this image are his mind and will, intellectual and moral integrity (he was created with true knowledge, righteousness, and holiness), his body (this was seen as a fit organ to share immortality with man's soul and the means by which dominion over the creation was exercised), and dominion over the rest of the creation.

The Fall greatly affected the nature of "man," but he did not cease to be in God's image (Gen. 9:6). Fallen "man" occupies a new and lower position before God: "And God saw that the wickedness of man was great in the earth, and that every imagination of the thoughts of his heart was only evil continually" (Gen. 6:5; cf. 8:21). No longer does "man" have perfect communion with the Creator; he is now under the curse of sin and death. Original knowledge, righteousness, and holiness are destroyed. Restoration to his proper place in the creation and relationship to the Creator comes only through spiritual union with the Christ, the second Adam (Rom. 5:12–21). In some later passages of Scripture *'ādām* is difficult to distinguish from

'îš—man as the counterpart of woman and/or as distinguished in his maleness.

Sometimes *'ādām* identifies a limited and particular "group of men": "Behold, waters rise up out of the north, and shall be an overflowing flood, and shall overflow the land [of the Philistines], and all that is therein; the city, and them that dwell therein: then the men [used in the singular] shall cry, and all the inhabitants of the land shall howl" (Jer. 47:2). When used of a particular group of individual "men," the noun appears in the phrase "sons of men": "And the Lord came down to see the city and the tower, which the children of men builded" (Gen. 11:5). The phrase "son of man" usually connotes a particular individual: "God is not a man [*'îš*], that he should lie; neither the son of man, that he should repent ... " (Num. 23:19; cf. Ezek. 2:1). The one notable exception is the use of this term in Dan. 7:13–14: "I saw in the night visions, and, behold, one like the Son of man [*'ĕnôš*] came with the clouds of heaven.... His dominion is an everlasting dominion, which shall not pass away ... " Here the phrase represents a divine being.

'Ādām is also used in reference to any given man, or to anyone male or female: "When a man [anyone] shall have in the skin of his flesh a rising, a scab, or bright spot, and it be in the skin of his flesh like the plague of leprosy; then he shall be brought unto Aaron ... " (Lev. 13:2).

The noun *'ōdem* means "ruby." This word occurs 3 times and in Hebrew only. It refers to the red stone, the "ruby" in Exod. 28:17: " ... the first row shall be a sardius [*'ōdem*], a topaz, and a carbuncle .... "

geber (גֶּבֶר, 1397), "man." This word occurs 60 times in the Hebrew Old Testament, and its frequency of usage is higher (32 times, nearly half of all the occurrences) in the poetical books. The word occurs first in Exod. 10:11: "Not so: go now ye that are *men*, and serve the Lord; for that ye did desire."

The root meaning "to be strong" is no longer obvious in the usage of *geber*, since it is a synonym of *'îš*: "Thus saith the Lord, Write ye this man [*'îš*] childless, a man [*geber*] that shall not prosper in his days: for no man of his seed shall prosper, sitting upon the throne of David ... " (Jer. 22:30). Other synonyms are *zākār*, "male" (Jer. 30:6); *'ĕnôš*, "man" (Job 4:17); and *'ādām*, "man" (Job 14:10). A *geber* denotes a "male," as an antonym of a "woman"; cf. "The woman [*'iššāh*] shall not wear that which pertaineth unto a man, neither shall a man [*geber*] put on a woman's [*'iššāh*] garment:

for all that do so are abomination unto the Lord thy God" (Deut. 22:5).

In standardized expressions of curse and blessing *geber* also functions as a synonym for *'îš*, "man." The expression may begin with "Cursed be the man" (*geber;* Jer. 17:5) or "Blessed is the man" (*geber;* Ps. 34:8), but these same expressions also occur with *'îš* (Ps. 1:1; Deut. 27:15).

The Septuagint gives the following translations: *aner* ("man"); *anthropos* ("human being; man"); and *dunatos* ("powerful or strong ones").

'îš (אִישׁ, 376), "man; husband; mate; human being; human; somebody; each; every." Cognates of this word appear in Phoenician, Punic, old Aramaic, and old South Arabic. This noun occurs about 2,183 times and in all periods of biblical Hebrew. The plural of this noun is usually *'ănāšîm*, but 3 times it is *'îšîm* (Ps. 53:3).

Basically, this word signifies "man" in correspondence to woman; a "man" is a person who is distinguished by maleness. This emphasis is in Gen. 2:24 (the first biblical occurrence): "Therefore shall a man leave his father and his mother, and shall cleave unto his wife...." Sometimes the phrase "man and woman" signifies anyone whatsoever, including children: "If an ox gore a man or a woman, that they die: then the ox shall be surely stoned..." (Exod. 21:28). This phrase can also connote an inclusive group, including children: "And they utterly destroyed all that was in the city, both man and woman, young and old, and ox, and sheep, and ass, with the edge of the sword" (Josh. 6:21). This idea is sometimes more explicitly expressed by the word series "men, women, and children": "Gather the people together, men, and women, and children, and thy stranger that is within thy gates..." (Deut. 31:12).

'îš is often used in marriage contexts (cf. Gen. 2:24) meaning "husband" or "mate": "Take ye wives, and beget sons and daughters; and take wives for your sons, and give your daughters to husbands, that they may bear sons and daughters..." (Jer. 29:6). A virgin is described as a lass who has not known a "man" ("husband"): "...And she went with her companions, and bewailed her virginity upon the mountains. And it came to pass at the end of two months, that she returned unto her father, who did with her according to his vow which he had vowed: and she knew no man" (Judg. 11:38–39). The sense "mate" appears in Gen. 7:2, where the word represents male animals: "Of every clean beast thou shalt take to thee by sevens, the male and his female...."

One special nuance of *'îš* appears in passages such as Gen. 3:6, where it means "husband," or one responsible for a wife or woman and revered by her: "[And she] gave also unto her husband with her: and he did eat." This emphasis is in Hos. 2:16 where it is applied to God (cf. the Hebrew word *ba'al*).

Sometimes this word connotes that the one so identified is a "man" *par excellence.* As such he is strong, influential, and knowledgeable in battle: "Be strong, and quit yourselves like men, O ye Philistines, that ye be not servants unto the Hebrews..." (1 Sam. 4:9).

In a few places *'îš* is used as a synonym of "father": "We are all sons of one man..." (Gen. 42:11, RSV). In other passages the word is applied to a son (cf. Gen. 2:24).

In the plural the word can be applied to groups of men who serve or obey a superior. Pharaoh's men escorted Abraham: "And Pharaoh commanded his men concerning him: and they sent him away..." (Gen. 12:20). In a similar but more general sense, the word may identify people who belong to someone or something: "For all these abominations have the men of the land done, which were before you, and the land is defiled" (Lev. 18:27).

Infrequently (and in later historical literature) this word is used as a collective noun referring to an entire group: "And his servant said,... Should I set this before a hundred men?" (2 Kings 4:43).

Many passages use *'îš* in the more general or generic sense of "man" (*'ādām*), a human being: "He that smiteth a man, so that he die, shall be surely put to death" (Exod. 21:12). Even if one strikes a woman or child and he or she dies, the attacker should be put to death. Again, notice Deut. 27:15: "Cursed be the man that maketh any graven or molten image...." This is the sense of the word when it is contrasted with animals: "But against any of the children of Israel shall not a dog move his tongue, against man or beast..." (Exod. 11:7). The same nuance appears when man over against God is in view: "God is not a man, that he should lie..." (Num. 23:19).

Sometimes *'îš* is indefinite, meaning "somebody" or "someone" ("they"): "And I will make thy seed as the dust of the earth: so that if a man can number the dust of the earth, then shall thy seed also be numbered" (Gen. 13:16). In other passages the word suggests the meaning "each" (Gen. 40:5). Closely related to the previous nuance is the connotation "every" (Jer. 23:35).

The word *'îšôn* means "little man." This diminutive form of the noun, which appears 3 times, has a cognate in Arabic. Although it literally means "little man," it signifies the pupil of the eye and is so translated (cf. Deut. 32:10, NASB; RSV and KJV, "apple of his eye").

'ĕnôš (אֱנוֹשׁ, 582), "man." This common Semitic word is the usual word for "man" (generic) in biblical Aramaic (This meaning is served by Hebrew 'ādām). It occurs 25 times in biblical Aramaic and 42 times in biblical Hebrew. Hebrew uses 'ĕnôš exclusively in poetical passages. The only apparent exception is 2 Chron. 14:11, but this is a prayer and, therefore, uses poetical words.

'Ĕnôš never appears with the definite article and at all times except once (Ps. 144:3) sets forth a collective idea, "man." In most cases where the word occurs in Job and the Psalms it suggests the frailty, vulnerability, and finitude of "man" as contrasted to God: "As for man, his days are as grass: as a flower of the field, so he flourisheth" (Ps. 103:15). As such "man" cannot be righteous or holy before God: "Shall mortal man be more just than God? Shall a man be more pure than his Maker?" (Job 4:17). In the Psalms this word is used to indicate the enemy: "Arise, O Lord; let not man prevail: let the heathen be judged in thy sight" (Ps. 9:19). Here the parallelism shows that 'ĕnôš is synonymous with "nations," or the enemy. They are, therefore, presented as weak, vulnerable, and finite: "Put them in fear, O Lord: that the nations may know themselves to be but men" (Ps. 9:20).

'Ĕnôš may connote "men" as weak but not necessarily morally weak: "Blessed is the man that doeth this, and the son of man that layeth hold of it" (Isa. 56:2). In this passage the 'ĕnôš is blessed because he has been morally strong.

In a few places the word bears no moral overtones and represents "man" in a sense parallel to Hebrew 'ādām. He is finite as contrasted to the infinite God: "I said, I would scatter them into corners, I would make the remembrance of them to cease from among men" (Deut. 32:26—the first biblical occurrence).

bāḥûr (בָּחוּר, 970), "young man." The 44 occurrences of this word are scattered throughout every period of biblical Hebrew.

This word signifies the fully developed, vigorous, unmarried man. In its first occurrence bāḥûr is contrasted to bᵉtûlāh, "maiden": "The sword without, and terror within, shall destroy both the young man and the virgin, the suckling also with the man of gray hairs" (Deut. 32:25). The strength of the "young man" is contrasted with the gray hair (crown of honor) of old men (Prov. 20:29).

The period during which a "young man" is in his prime (could this be the period during which he is eligible for the draft—i.e., age 20–50?) is represented by the two nouns, bᵉḥûrîm and bᵉḥûrôt, both of which occur only once. Bᵉḥûrîm is found in Num. 11:28.

B. Verb.

bāḥar (בָּחַר, 977), "to examine, choose, select, choose out, elect, prefer." This verb, which occurs 146 times in biblical Hebrew, has cognates in late Aramaic and Coptic. The poetic noun bāḥîr, "chosen or elect one(s)," is also derived from this verb. Not all scholars agree that these words are related to the noun bāḥûr. They would relate it to the first sense of bhr, whose cognate in Akkadian has to do with fighting men. The word means "choose or select" in Gen. 6:2: ". . . and they took them wives of all which they chose."

TO BE MARVELOUS

A. Verb.

pālā' (פָּלָא, 6381), "to be marvelous, be extraordinary, be beyond one's power to do, do wonderful acts." As can be seen from the suggested meanings, this verb is not easy to define. As a denominative verb, it is based on the noun for "wonder, marvel," so it expresses the idea of doing or making a wondrous thing. Found in both biblical and modern Hebrew, pālā' occurs some 70 times in the Hebrew Old Testament. The verb is found for the first time in Gen. 18:14: "Is any thing too hard for the Lord?"

Pālā' is used primarily with God as its subject, expressing actions that are beyond the bounds of human powers or expectations. This idea is well expressed by the psalmist: "This is the Lord's doing; it is marvelous in our eyes" (Ps. 118:23). Deliverance from Egypt was the result of God's wondrous acts: "And I will stretch out my hand, and smite Egypt with all my wonders which I will do in [it] . . ." (Exod. 3:20). Praise is constantly due God for all His wonderful deeds (Ps. 9:1). At the same time, God does not require anything of His people that is too hard for them (Deut. 30:11). Although something may appear impossible to man, it still is within God's power: "If it be marvelous in the eyes of the remnant of this people in these days, should it also be marvelous in mine eyes? saith the Lord of hosts" (Zech. 8:6).

B. Noun.

pele' (פֶּלֶא, 6382), "wonder; marvel." This noun frequently expresses the "wonder," the extraordinary aspects, of God's dealings with His people (Exod. 15:11; Ps. 77:11; Isa. 29:14). The messianic title, "marvel of a counselor" (Isa. 9:6; KJV, RSV, "wonderful counselor"), points toward God's Anointed continuing the marvelous acts of God.

TO MEASURE

A. Verb.

mādad (מָדַד, 4058), "to measure, measure off, extend." Found in both ancient and modern Hebrew, in modern usage this word has the nuance of "to survey." The word has cognates in Akkadian, Phoenician, and Arabic. It occurs 53 times in the text of the Hebrew Old Testament. The basic meaning of the verb is illustrated in its first occurrence in the Old Testament: "... they did mete it with an omer..." (Exod. 16:18). *Mādad* is used not only of "measuring" volume but also of "measuring" distance (Deut. 21:2) and length (Num. 35:5).

A rather gruesome use is found in 2 Sam. 8:2, where, after defeating the Moabites, David "measured them with a line, casting them down to the ground; even with two lines measured he to put to death, and with one full line to keep alive."

The greatness of the creator God is expressed in the question, "Who hath measured the waters in the hollow of his hand...?" (Isa. 40:12). Also, God "stood, and measured [NASB, "surveyed"] the earth" (Hab. 3:6).

Mādad can express the idea of extending, stretching: "And he stretched himself upon the child three times..." (1 Kings 17:21).

B. Noun.

middāh (מִדָּה, 4060), "measure; measurement; extent; size; stature; section; area." Of the 53 times this noun appears, 25 appearances are in Ezekiel. The rest of the word's occurrences are scattered throughout every period of biblical Hebrew.

This noun refers to the act of "measurement": "You shall do no wrong in judgment, in measures of length or weight or quantity" (Lev. 19:35, RSV). In Ezek. 41:17 this word is used of length "measurement," and in Job 28:25 of liquid "measurement."

Second, *middāh* means the thing measured, or the "size." Exod. 26:2 (the first occurrence) specifies: "... Every one of the curtains shall have one measure [the same size]." The word can also refer to the duration of one's life: "Lord, make me to know [realize] mine end, and the measure of my days [how short my life really is]..." (Ps. 39:4). A "man of measure" is one of great "stature or size": "And he [Benaiah] slew an Egyptian, a man of great stature, five cubits [about 7½ feet] high ..." (1 Chron. 11:23).

Third, *middāh* sometimes represents a "measured portion" of a thing: "Malchijah the son of Harim, and Hashub the son of Pahath-moab, repaired the other piece, and the tower of the furnaces" (Neh. 3:11). In Ezek. 45:3 the word appears to represent a "measured area."

TO MEDITATE

hāgāh (הָגָה, 1897), "to meditate, moan, growl, utter, speak." This word is common to both ancient and modern Hebrew. Found only 25 times in the Hebrew Old Testament, it seems to be an onomatopoetic term, reflecting the sighing and low sounds one may make while musing, at least as the ancients practiced it. This meaning is seen in its first occurrence in the text: "This book of the law shall not depart out of thy mouth; but thou shalt meditate therein day and night..." (Josh. 1:8). Perhaps the most famous reference "to meditating" on the law day and night is Ps. 1:2.

Hāgāh also expresses the "growl" of lions (Isa. 31:4) and the "mourning" of doves (Isa. 38:14). When the word is used in the sense of "to mourn," it apparently emphasizes the sorrowful sounds of mourning, as seen in this parallelism: "Therefore will I howl for Moab, and I will cry out for all Moab; mine heart shall mourn for the men of Kir-heres" (Jer. 48:31). The idea that mental exercise, planning, often is accompanied by low talking seems to be reflected by Prov. 24:1–2: "Be not thou envious against evil men,... for their heart studieth destruction, and their lips talk of mischief."

MESSIAH

A. Nouns.

māšîaḥ (מָשִׁיחַ, 4899), "anointed one; Messiah." Of the 39 occurrences of *māšîaḥ*, none occurs in the wisdom literature. They are scattered throughout the rest of biblical literary types and periods.

First, *māšîaḥ* refers to one who is anointed with oil, symbolizing the reception of the Holy Spirit, enabling him to do an assigned task. Kings (1 Sam. 24:6), high priests, and some prophets (1 Kings 19:16) were so anointed: "If the priest that is anointed do sin according to the sin of the people..." (Lev. 4:3—the first biblical appearance). In the case of Cyrus, he was anointed with God's Spirit only and commissioned an "anointed deliverer" of Israel (Isa. 45:1). The patriarchs, too, are called "anointed ones": "Touch not mine anointed, and do my prophets no harm" (Ps. 105:15).

Second, the word is sometimes transliterated "Messiah." After the promise to David (2 Sam. 7:13) *māšîaḥ* refers immediately to the Davidic dynasty, but ultimately it points to the "Messiah," Jesus the Christ: "The kings of the earth [take their stand], and the rulers take counsel together, against the Lord, and against his Anointed . . . " (Ps. 2:2). In Dan. 9:25 the word is transliterated: "Know therefore and understand, that from the going forth of the commandment to restore and to build Jerusalem unto the Messiah the Prince. . . . " The New Testament also attests the word in this latter meaning (John 1:41). Most frequently in the New Testament the word is translated ("Christ") rather than transliterated ("Messiah"). *See also* ANOINT.

mišḥāh (מִשְׁחָה, 4888), "anointment." This noun occurs 21 times and only in Exodus, Leviticus, and Numbers. It always follows the Hebrew word for oil. The first occurrence is Exod. 25:6: "Oil for the light, spices for anointing oil, and for sweet incense."

B. Verb.

māšah (מָשַׁח, 4886), "to smear with oil or paint, anoint." This verb, which appears 69 times in biblical Hebrew, has cognates in Ugaritic, Akkadian, Aramaic, and Arabic. The objects of this verb are people, sacrificial victims, and objects of worship. Aaron and his sons are the objects of this verb in Exod. 30:30: "And thou shalt anoint Aaron and his sons, and consecrate them, that they may minister unto me in the priest's office."

MIDST

tāwek (תָּוֶךְ, 8432), "midst; middle." This word, which also appears in Ugaritic, occurs about 418 times in biblical Hebrew and in all periods.

Tāwek indicates the part of a space, place, number of people, things, or line which is not on the end or outside edge. This emphasis is in Gen. 9:21: "And he [Noah] drank of the wine, and was drunken; and he was uncovered within [literally, "in the midst of"] his tent. In many contexts the word means "among," not necessarily in the middle: " . . . And he [Pharaoh] lifted up the head of the chief butler and the chief baker among [literally, "in the midst of"] his servants" (Gen. 40:20). Exod. 14:29 uses *tāwek* as an extension of the word "through": "But the children of Israel walked upon dry land in the midst of the sea. . . . " The idea "within" can be emphasized with the addition of words like *me'îm*, "belly, inwards," or *lēb*, "heart": " . . . My heart is like wax; it is melted in the midst of my bowels" (Ps. 22:14). This word also sometimes means simply "in" in the sense of "mixed into something": "And they did beat the gold into thin plates, and cut it into wires, to work it in the blue . . . " (Exod. 39:3).

Tāwek can mean "middle" when applied to an object or person between two others: "And they made bells of pure gold, and put the bells between the pomegranates upon the hem of the robe . . . " (Exod. 39:25). The same sense but a different translation is required in Judg. 15:4: "And Samson went and caught three hundred foxes, and took firebrands, and turned tail to tail, and put a firebrand in the midst between two tails." This appears to be the meaning of the word in its first biblical occurrence: "And God said, Let there be a firmament in the midst of the waters, and let it divide the waters from the waters" (Gen. 1:6). In Num. 35:5 the word means "in the center": "And ye shall measure from without the city on the east side two thousand cubits, and on the south side two thousand cubits, and on the west side two thousand cubits, and on the north side two thousand cubits; and the city shall be in the midst. . . . " In other passages this word signifies the hypothetical center line dividing something into two equal parts: "And he [Abraham] took unto him all these, and divided them in the midst, and laid each piece one against another . . . " (Gen. 15:10; cf. Ezek. 15:4).

In a few instances *tāwek* is used substantively, meaning "the middle or the center part of a thing": "Sihon king of the Amorites . . . ruled from Aroer, which is upon the bank of the river Arnon, and from the middle of the river . . . " (Josh. 12:2).

The word occurs only 7 times without a preceding preposition.

MIGHT

gᵉbûrāh (גְּבוּרָה, 1369), "might." This noun is found 61 times in the Hebrew Old Testament, predominantly in poetic books and in Isaiah and Jeremiah. The first occurrence is in Exod. 32:18: "And he said, It is not the voice of them that shout for *mastery*, neither is it the voice of them that cry for being overcome: but the noise of them that sing do I hear."

The primary meaning of *gᵉbûrāh* is "power" or "strength." Certain animals are known for their "strength," such as horses (Ps. 147:10) and crocodiles (Job 41:4). Man also demonstrates "might" in heroic acts (Judg. 8:21) and in war (Isa. 3:25). David's powerful regime is expressed as a "kingship of *gᵉbûrāh*" (1 Chron. 29:30; KJV, "his reign and his might"). Since both physical strength and wisdom were necessary for leadership, these two qualities are joined together: "Counsel is mine, and sound wisdom: I am understanding; I have strength" (Prov. 8:14). Also Micah, being filled with the Holy Spirit, said: "But truly I am full of power by the spirit of the Lord, and of judgment, and of might, to declare unto Jacob his transgression, and to Israel his sin" (Mic. 3:8). In messianic expectations the prophets projected the Messiah's special role as a demonstration of "might" and counsel: "And the spirit of the Lord shall rest upon him, the spirit of wisdom and understanding, the spirit of counsel and might, the spirit of knowledge and of the fear of the Lord" (Isa. 11:2).

The Psalms ascribe "might" to God. These characterizations are found either in the context of "praise": " . . . which by his strength setteth fast the mountains; being girded with power" (Ps. 65:6), or in the context of prayer: "Save me, O God, by thy name, and judge me by thy strength" (Ps. 54:1). The Lord's "might" is a manifestation of His wisdom: "With him is wisdom and strength, he hath counsel and understanding" (Job 12:13). In the plural g^ebûrāh denotes God's mighty deeds of the past: "O Lord God, thou hast begun to show thy servant thy greatness, and thy mighty hand: for what God is there in heaven or in earth, that can do according to thy works, and according to thy might?" (Deut. 3:24).

The Septuagint gives the following translations: *dunasteis* ("ruler, sovereign; court official"); *ischus* ("strength; power; might"); and *dunamis* ("power; strength; might; ability; capability"). The KJV gives these senses: "might; strength; power; mighty acts."

TO MINISTER, SERVE

A. Verb.

šārat (שָׁרַת, 8334), "to minister, serve, officiate." This word is a common term in Hebrew usage, ancient and modern, in various verbal and noun forms. It occurs in ancient Phoenician, and some see it in ancient Ugaritic as well. *Šārat* is found just under 100 times in the Hebrew Old Testament. The first time it is used in the Hebrew Bible is in the story of Joseph as he becomes the slave of Potiphar: "And Joseph found grace in his sight, and he served [RSV, "attended"] him. . ." (Gen. 39:4).

As a term for serving or ministering, *šārat* is to be distinguished from the term for more menial serving, *'ābad*, from which the word meaning "slave" or "servant" is derived. *Šārat* is characteristically used of "serving" done by royal household workers (2 Sam. 13:17; 1 Kings 10:5). In the manner of the modern "public servant" idea, the word is used in reference to court officials and royal servants (1 Chron. 27:1; 28:1; Esth. 1:10).

Elisha "ministered" to Elijah (1 Kings 19:21).

Foreign kings are "to minister" to God's people (Isa. 60:10).

This term is used most frequently as the special term for service in worship. The Levitical priests "stand before the Lord to minister unto him" (Deut. 10:8). They also are "to stand before the congregation to minister unto them" (Num. 16:9). In the post-exilic temple, the Levites who had earlier "ministered" in idolatry will not be allowed "to serve" as priests but rather as maintenance workers in the temple (Ezek. 44:11–14).

B. Noun.

šārat (שָׁרַת, 8334), "minister; servant." The noun form of the verb appears several times meaning "minister" or "servant." As Moses' right-hand man Joshua is referred to as "minister" (KJV), "servant" (RSV, JB, NASB), "assistant" (NEB), or "aide" (NAB) in Exod. 24:13. Angels are God's "ministers . . . that do his pleasure" (Ps. 103:21; cf. Ps. 104:4).

MORNING

A. Noun.

bōqer (בֹּקֶר, 1242), "morning." This word occurs about 214 times and in every period of biblical Hebrew.

This word means "morning," though not the period of time before noon. Rather it indicates the point of time at which night is changing to day or that time at the end of night: "And Moses stretched forth his rod over the land of Egypt, and the Lord brought an east wind upon the land all that day, and all that night; and when it was morning, the east wind brought the locusts" (Exod. 10:13).

Bōqer can represent the time just before the rising of the sun. In Judg. 19:25 we read that the men of Gibeah raped and abused the Levite's concubine "all the night until the morning: and when the day began to spring, they let her go" (cf. Ruth 3:13). In the ancient Near East the night was divided into three watches. The last period of the night was called the morning watch (Exod. 14:24). It lasted from 2:00 A.M. until sunrise, and in such a context the word indicates this period of time.

Bōqer can mean "daybreak" or "dawn." In Exod. 14:27 it is reported that the water of the Red Sea "returned to his [normal state] when the morning appeared [literally, "at the turning of the morning"]." *Bōqer* is used as a synonym of "dawn" in Job 38:12: "Hast thou commanded the morning since thy days; and caused the dayspring to know his place . . . ?"

Sometimes *bōqer* appears to mean "early morning," or shortly after daybreak: "And Joseph came in unto them in the morning, and looked upon them and, behold, they were sad" (Gen. 40:6). Thus, Moses "rose up early in the morning" and went up to Mount Sinai; he arose before daybreak so he could appear before God in the "morning" as God had commanded (Exod. 34:2, 4). In the "morning" Jacob saw that his bride was Leah rather than Rachel (Gen. 29:25; cf. 1 Sam. 29:10).

As the opposite of night the word represents the entire period of daylight. The psalmist prays that it is good "to show forth thy loving-kindness in the morning, and thy faithfulness every night" (Ps. 92:2), in other words, to always be praising God (cf. Amos 5:8).

In Ps. 65:8 *bōqer* represents a place, specifically, the place where the sun rises: "They also that dwell in the uttermost parts are afraid at thy tokens: thou makest the outgoings of the morning and evening to rejoice."

At least once the word appears to represent the resurrection: "Like sheep they [the ungodly] are laid in the grave; death shall feed on them; and the upright shall have dominion over them in the morning . . ." (Ps. 49:14).

Bōqer can mean "morrow" or "next day." This meaning first appears in Exod. 12:10, where God tells Israel not to leave any of the Passover "until the morning; and that which remaineth of it until the morning ye shall burn with fire" (cf. Lev. 22:30).

B. Verb.

bāqar (בָּקַר, 1239), "to attend, bestow care on, seek with pleasure." Although this verb is found only 7 times in biblical Hebrew, it occurs in early, middle, and late periods and in both prose and poetry. The word has cognates in Arabic and Nabataean. Some scholars relate to this verb the noun *bāqār*, "herd, cattle, ox."

In Lev. 13:36 *bāqar* means "to attend to": " . . . If the scall be spread in the skin, the priest shall not seek for yellow hair. . . . " The word implies "to seek with pleasure or delight" in Ps. 27:4: " . . . to behold the beauty of the Lord, and *to inquire* in his temple."

MOTHER

ēm (אֵם, 517), "mother; grandmother; stepmother." Cognates of this word appear in nearly all Semitic languages including Ugaritic and Aramaic. Biblical Hebrew attests it 220 times and in all periods.

The basic meaning of the word has to do with the physical relationship of the individual called "mother." This emphasis of the word is in Gen. 2:24 (the first biblical appearance): "Therefore shall a man leave his father and his mother, and shall cleave unto his wife. . . . " *Ēm* sometimes represents an animal "mother":

"Likewise shalt thou do with thine oxen, and with thy sheep: seven days it shall be with its [mother]; on the eighth day thou shalt give it me" (Exod. 22:30). The phrase "father and mother" is the biblical phrase for parents: "And he brought up Hadassah, that is, Esther, his uncle's daughter: for she had neither father nor mother [living]" (Esth. 2:7). The "son of one's mother" is his brother (Gen. 43:29), just as the "daughter of one's mother" is his sister (Gen. 20:12). These phrases usually emphasize that the persons so represented are whole brothers or sisters, whereas the Hebrew words *'āh*, ("brother") and *'āhôt*, ("sister") meaning both whole and half siblings, leave the issue unclear. On the other hand, in Gen. 27:29 this phrase appears to mean peoples more distantly related: "Let people serve thee, and nations bow down to thee: be lord over thy brethren, and let thy mother's sons bow down to thee: cursed be every one that curseth thee, and blessed be he that blesseth thee."

Ēm can represent blood relatives further removed than one's mother. In 1 Kings 15:10 the word means "grandmother": "And forty and one years reigned he in Jerusalem. And his [grand]mother's name was Maachah, the daughter of Abishalom." This word can also mean "stepmother." When Joseph told his dream to his family, "his father rebuked him, and said unto him, What is this dream that thou hast dreamed? Shall I and thy [step]mother and thy brethren indeed come to bow down ourselves to thee to the earth?" (Gen. 37:10; cf. 35:16ff., where we read that Rachel died). The word can signify a mother-in-law, or the mother of one's wife: "And if a man take a wife and her mother, it is wickedness . . . " (Lev. 20:14). The woman through whom a nation originated is called its "mother"; she is the first or tribal "mother," an ancestress: "Thus saith the Lord God unto Jerusalem; Thy birth and thy nativity is of the land of Canaan; thy father was an Amorite, and thy mother a Hittite" (Ezek. 16:3). Even further removed physically is Eve, "the mother of all living" (Gen. 3:20).

Ēm can represent all one's female forebears: "Let the iniquity of his fathers be remembered with the Lord; and let not the sin of his mother be blotted out" (Ps. 109:14).

A group of people, a people, or a city may be personified and called a "mother." Hosea calls the priests (probably) the "mother" of Israel: " . . . And the prophet also shall fall with thee in the night, and I will destroy thy mother" (Hos. 4:5). The people of Israel, the northern kingdom, are the "mother" of Judah: "Where is the bill of your mother's divorcement, whom

I have put away? or which of my creditors is it to whom I have sold you? Behold, for your iniquities have ye sold yourselves, and for your transgressions is your mother put away" (Isa. 50:1; cf. Hos. 2:4, 7).

An important city may be called a "mother" of its citizens: " . . . Thou seekest to destroy a city and a mother in Israel. . ." (2 Sam. 20:19).

The title "mother in Israel" was a title of respect in Deborah's day (Judg. 5:7).

"The mother of a way" is the starting point for roads: "For the king of Babylon stood at the parting of the way, at the head of the two ways, to use divination . . . " (Ezek. 21:21).

MOUNTAIN RANGE

har (הַר, 2022), "mountain range; mountainous region; mount." This word also appears in Ugaritic, Phoenician, and Punic. Biblical Hebrew attests it about 558 times and in all periods.

In its first biblical appearance *har* refers to the "mountain range" upon which Noah's ark came to rest (Gen. 8:4). In the singular form the word can mean a "mountain range" or the "mountains" of a given area: " . . . And [he] set his face toward the mount [NASB, "hill country"] Gilead" (Gen. 31:21). Jacob was fleeing from Laban toward the "mountains" where he thought to find protection. A further extension of this meaning applies this word to an area which is primarily mountainous; the word focuses on the territory in general rather than on the mountains in particular: "And they gave them the city of Arba the father of Anak, which city is Hebron, in the hill country of Judah, with the suburbs thereof round about it" (Josh. 21:11).

The word can be used of particular "mountains": " . . . And he led the flock to the backside of the desert, and came to the mountain of God, even to Horeb" (Exod. 3:1). In this particular instance "the mountain of God" refers to Horeb. Elsewhere it is Jerusalem: "Why leap ye, ye high hills? This is the hill which God desireth to dwell in; yea, the Lord will dwell in it for ever" (Ps. 68:16).

Har signifies inhabitable sites situated on hills and/or mountainsides: "And at that time came Joshua, and cut off the Anakim from the mountains, from Hebron, from Debir, from Anab, and from all the mountains of Judah, and from all the mountains of Israel: Joshua destroyed them utterly with their cities" (Josh. 11:21). In this regard, compare Deut. 2:37: "Only unto the land of the children of Ammon thou camest not, nor unto any place of the river Jabbok, nor unto the cities in the mountains, nor unto what-

soever the Lord our God forbade us." A comparison of Judg. 1:35 and Josh. 19:41 shows that Mount Heres is the same as the city of Heres.

In the poetical literature of the Old Testament, the view of the world held by men of that era finds its reflection. One can speak of the foundations of the mountains as rooted in the underworld (Deut. 32:22), serving to support the earth as the "bars" of the earth (Jonah 2:6). Mountain peaks may be said to reach into the heavens where God dwells (Isa. 24:21; in Gen. 11:4, the men who built the tower at Babel erroneously thought they were going to reach God's dwelling place). Although it would be wrong to conclude that God is setting forth this understanding of creation, yet He used it in explaining His word to men just as He used other contemporaneous ideas. Since "mountains" were associated with deity (Isa. 14:13), God chose to make great revelations on "mountains," concretely impressing the recipients with the solemnity and authority of the message (Deut. 27; Josh. 8:30–35). At the same time such locations provided for better audibility and visibility (Judg. 9:7; 2 Chron. 13:4). "Mountains" often serve as a symbol of strength (Zech. 4:7) inasmuch as they carried mythological significance since many people thought of them as sacred areas (Jer. 3:22–23), and they were the locations of strong fortresses (Josh. 10:6). Even the "mountains" tremble before the Lord; He is mightier than they are (Job 14:18).

TO MOURN

'ābal (אָבַל, 56), "to mourn, lament." This word is common to both ancient and modern Hebrew. Found in the Hebrew Old Testament 39 times, *'ābal* is used in the simple, active verbal form primarily in poetry, and usually in a figurative sense. When it is used of mourning for the dead in a literal sense, the word is found in prose sections and in the reflexive form, indicating action back on the subject. It first occurs in Gen. 37:34: "And Jacob . . . mourned for his son many days."

When used in the figurative sense, *'ābal* expresses "mourning" by gates (Isa. 3:26), by the land (Isa. 24:4), and by pastures (Amos 1:2). In addition to mourning for the dead, "mourning" may be over Jerusalem (Isa. 66:10), over sin (Ezra 10:6), or over God's judgment (Exod. 33:4). One may pretend to be a mourner (2 Sam. 14:2) simply by putting on mourning clothes.

MOUTH

peh (פֶּה, 6310), "mouth; edge; opening; entrance; collar; utterance; order; command; evidence." This word has cognates in Ugaritic, Akkadian, Arabic, Aramaic, and Amorite. It appears about 500 times and in every period of biblical Hebrew.

First, the word means "mouth." It is often used of a human "mouth": "And he shall be thy spokesman unto the people: and he shall be, even he shall be to thee instead of a mouth . . ." (Exod. 4:16). In passages such as Num. 22:28 this word represents an animal's "mouth": "And the Lord opened the mouth of the ass, and she said unto Balaam. . . ." When used of a bird's "mouth" it refers to its beak: "And the dove came in to him in the evening; and, lo, in her mouth was an olive leaf plucked off . . ." (Gen. 8:11). This word may be used figuratively of "the mouth of the ground," referring to the fact that liquid went into the ground—the ground drank it: "And now art thou cursed from the earth, which hath opened her mouth to receive thy brother's blood from thy hand" (Gen. 4:11—the first biblical occurrence). A similar use appears in Ps. 141:7: "Our bones are scattered at the grave's mouth. . . ." In this case Sheol is perhaps conceived as a pit and then personified with its "mouth" consuming men once they die.

Second, this word can be used in an impersonal, nonpersonified sense of an "opening": "And he looked, and behold a well in the field, and, lo, there were three flocks of sheep lying by it; for out of that well they watered the flocks: and a great stone was upon the well's mouth" (Gen. 29:2). In Isa. 19:7 this word represents the "edge" of a river: "The paper reeds by the brooks, by the mouth of the brooks, and every thing sown by the brooks, shall wither, be driven away. . . ." Gen. 42:27 uses *peh* to refer to an orifice, or the area within the edges of a sack's opening: " . . . He espied his money; for, behold, it was in his sack's mouth." A similar use appears in Josh. 10:18, where the word is used of a cave "entrance" or "opening." *Peh* can mean not only an opening which is closed in on all sides but a city gate, an opening opened at the top: " . . . at the gates, at the entry of the city, at the coming in at the doors" (Prov. 8:3). Exod. 28:32 uses this word to mean an "opening" in a tunic around which a collar would be woven: "And there shall be a hole in the top of it, in the midst thereof: it shall have a binding of woven work round about the hole of it, as it were the hole of a habergeon, that it be not rent." Job 30:18 uses the word of

the "collar" itself: "By the great force of my disease is my garment changed: it bindeth me about as the collar of my coat" (cf. Ps. 133:2).

In several passages *peh* represents the edge of a sword, perhaps in the sense of the part that consumes and/or bites: "And they slew Hamor and Shechem his son with the edge of the sword . . ." (Gen. 34:26).

Several noteworthy idioms employ *peh*. In Josh. 9:2 "with one mouth" means "with one accord": " . . . That they gathered themselves together, to fight with Joshua and with Israel, with one accord." In Num. 12:8 God described His unique communication as "mouth to mouth" or person to person. A similar construction appears in Jer. 32:4 (cf. 34:3, which has the same force): "And Zedekiah king of Judah shall not escape out of the hand of the Chaldeans, hut shall surely be delivered into the hand of the king of Babylon, and shall speak with him mouth to mouth, and his eyes shall behold his eyes." The phrase "from mouth to mouth" or "mouth to mouth" can mean "from end to end": "And they came into the house of Baal; and the house of Baal was full from one end to another" (2 Kings 10:21). "With open mouth" is a phrase which emphasizes greedy consumption: "The Syrians before, and the Philistines behind; and they shall devour Israel with open mouth" (Isa. 9:12). Placing one's hands on one's mouth is a gesture of silence (Job 29:9). "To ask someone's mouth" is to ask him personally: "We will call the damsel, and inquire at her mouth [NASB, "consult her wishes"]" (Gen. 24:57).

This word can also stand for "utterance" or "order": "Thou shalt be over my house, and according unto thy word shall all my people be ruled . . ." (Gen. 41:40). "The mouth of two witnesses" means their testimony: "Whoso killeth any person, the murderer shall be put to death by the mouth of witnesses. . ." (Num. 35:30). In Jer. 36:4 "from the mouth of Jeremiah" means "by dictation": " . . . And Baruch wrote from the mouth of Jeremiah all words of the Lord . . . upon a [scroll]."

Peh used with various prepositions has special meanings. (1) Used with *kᵉ*, it means "according to." In Lev. 25:52 this construction has the special nuance "in proportion to": "And if there remain but few years unto the year of jubilee, then he shall count with him, and according unto [in proportion to] his years shall he give him again the price of his redemption." The meaning "according to" appears in passages such as Num. 7:5: "Take it of them, that they may be to do the service of the tabernacle of the congregation; and thou shalt give them unto the Levites, to every man according to his service." The phrase means "as much as" in Exod. 16:21. A different nuance appears in Job 33:6: "Behold, I am according to thy wish in God's stead...." (2) When the word is preceded by *lᵉ*, its meanings are quite similar to those just discussed. In Lev. 25:51 it means "in proportion to." Jer. 29:10 uses the word in the sense "according to": "After seventy years be accomplished at Babylon," which can be read literally, "according to the fullness of the seventy years of Babylon." (3) With *'al* the word also means "according to" or "in proportion to" (cf. Lev. 27:18).

The phrase *pî šᵉnayim* (literally, "two mouths") has two different meanings. In Deut. 21:17 it means "double portion" (two parts): "But he shall acknowledge the son of the hated for the first-born, by giving him a double portion of all that he hath...." This same phrase, however, also means "two thirds": "And it shall come to pass, that in all the land, saith the Lord, two parts therein shall be cut off and die; but the third shall be left therein" (Zech. 13:8).

TO MULTIPLY, INCREASE

A. Verb.

rābāh (רָבָה, 7235), "to multiply, become numerous, become great." This verb also occurs in Akkadian, Arabic, Amorite, and biblical Aramaic. Biblical Hebrew attests it about 220 times and in all periods. This word should be compared to *gādal* and *rābab*.

Basically this word connotes numerical increase. It can refer to the process of increasing numerically: God told the sea and air creatures to "be fruitful, and multiply" (Gen. 1:22—the first occurrence). In Gen. 38:12 the word refers to the end result in the sense that a great many of something existed: "And in process of time the daughter of Shuah Judah's wife died [literally, "and the days became multiplied"]...." When used with "days," the word may also signify "long life": "... I shall multiply my days as the sand" (Job 29:18: cf. Prov. 4:10). *Rābāh* sometimes refers to increasing in wealth, although in such cases the material is clearly specified (cf. Deut. 8:13: "... and thy silver and thy gold is multiplied").

This verb can be used of being quantitatively large. In Gen. 7:17 the waters are said to have "increased, and bare up the ark, and it was lifted up above the earth." So here the verb means "to increase in quantity." A similar use occurs in Gen. 15:1, where God tells Abram: "I am... thy exceeding great reward." The first instance speaks of the process of increasing and

the latter of the end product (something that is larger).

In a special nuance this verb signifies the process of growing up: "Their young ones are in good liking, they grow up [in the open field]" (Job 39:4). *Rābāh* can also be used of the end product: "I have caused thee to multiply as the bud of the field, and thou hast increased and waxen great, and thou art come to excellent ornaments: thy breasts are fashioned, and thine hair is grown..." (Ezek. 16:7). A somewhat different nuance occurs in Ezek. 19:2, where the verb speaks of a parent's care for an offspring: "... She nourished her whelps."

Rābāh is sometimes used with another verb to signify its increase in occurrence or frequency. In some passages it signifies that a process is continuing: "The people bring much more than enough for the service of the work..." (Exod. 36:5), literally, "the people continue to bring." It can also signify a great number of times with the sense of "repeatedly." The sinner is urged to return to God, "for he will abundantly pardon" (Isa. 55:7). This sense appears clearly in Amos 4:4: "Come to Beth-el, and transgress; at Gilgal multiply transgression...."

B. Nouns.

'arbeh (אַרְבֶּה, 697), "locust." This noun, which occurs 24 times, refers to a kind of swarming "locust": "Stretch out thine hand over the land of Egypt for the locusts, that they may come up upon the land of Egypt, and eat every herb of the land..." (Exod. 10:12).

Several other nouns related to this verb appear infrequently. *Marbeh*, which appears once, means "abundance" (Isa. 33:23). *Marbît*, which is found 5 times, refers to a "greater number" (1 Sam. 2:33) or the "greater half" (2 Chron. 9:6). *Tarbût* has a single appearance to mean "increase" (Num. 32:14). *Tarbît*, which occurs 6 times, can mean "interest, increment, usury" (Lev. 25:36).

MULTITUDE

A. Noun.

hāmôn (הָמוֹן, 1995), "multitude; lively commotion; agitation; tumult; uproar; commotion; turmoil; noise; crowd; abundance." This noun appears 85 times in biblical Hebrew and in all periods.

The word represents a "lively commotion or agitation": "Look down from heaven, and behold from the habitation of thy holiness and of thy glory: where is thy zeal and thy strength, the sounding of thy bowels and of thy mercies toward me?" (Isa. 63:15).

Hāmôn represents the stirring or agitation of

a crowd of people: "When Joab sent the king's servant, and me thy servant, I saw a great tumult, but I knew not what it was" (2 Sam. 18:29). In Isa. 17:12 the word is synonymously parallel to *šā'ôn*, "rumbling": "Woe to the multitude of many people, which make a noise like the noise of the seas; and to the rushing of nations, that make a rushing like the rushing of mighty waters!"

Sometimes *hāmôn* represents the noise raised by an agitated crowd of people (a "tumult"): "And when Eli heard the noise of the crying, he said, What meaneth the noise of this tumult [raised by the report that the battle was lost]?" (1 Sam. 4:14). In Isa. 13:4 the word represents the mighty sound of a gathering army rather than the confused outcry of a mourning city: "The noise of a multitude in the mountains, like as of a great people; a tumultuous noise of the kingdoms of nations gathered together: the Lord of hosts mustereth the host of the battle." A young lion eating his prey is not disturbed by the noise of a band of shepherds trying to scare him off (Isa. 31:4). There are exceptions to the rule that the word represents the sound of a large number of people. In 1 Kings 18:41 *hāmôn* signifies the roar of a heavy downpour of rain (cf. Jer. 10:13), and in Jer. 47:3 it represents the tumult of chariots.

Hāmôn sometimes means a "multitude or crowd" from which a tumult may arise. Frequently the word represents a large army: "And I will draw unto thee, to the river Kishon, Sisera, the captain of Jabin's army, with his chariots and his multitude [NASB, "many troops"]..." (Judg. 4:7; cf. 1 Sam. 14:16). Elsewhere *hāmôn* represents a whole people: "And he dealt among all the people, even among the whole multitude of Israel..." (2 Sam. 6:19). Finally, any great throng, or a great number of people (Gen. 17:4—the first occurrence) may be represented by this word.

A great number of things can be indicated by *hāmôn*: "O Lord our God, all this store that we have prepared to build thee a house for thine holy name..." (1 Chron. 29:16).

Abundance of possessions or wealth is indicated by *hāmôn*, as in: "A little that a righteous man hath is better than the riches of many wicked" (Ps. 37:16; cf. Eccl. 5:10—parallel to "silver" [money]; Isa. 60:5).

Finally, *hāmôn* refers to a group of people organized around a king, specifically, his courtiers: "Son of man, speak unto Pharaoh king of Egypt, and to his multitude [his train or royal retinue]; Whom art thou like in thy greatness?" (Ezek. 31:2). Thus in Ps. 42:4 the word can represent a festival procession, a kind of train.

B. Verb.

hāmāh (הָמָה, 1993), "to make a noise, be tumultuous, roar, groan, bark, sound, moan." This verb, which occurs 33 times in biblical Hebrew, has cognates in Aramaic and Arabic. Psalm 83:2 contains one appearance: "For, lo, thine enemies make a tumult: and they that hate thee have lifted up the head."

N

NAKEDNESS

A. Nouns.

'erwāh (עֶרְוָה, 6172), "nakedness; indecent thing." Thirty-two of the 53 occurrences of this noun are in the social laws of Lev. 18, 20. The rest of its appearances are scattered throughout the various periods of Old Testament literature with the notable exception of poetical literature.

This word represents male or female sexual organs. In its first biblical appearance *'erwāh* implies shameful exposure: "And Ham, the father of Canaan, saw the nakedness of his father.... And Shem and Japheth took a garment, and laid it upon both their shoulders, and went backward, and covered the nakedness of their father; and their faces were backward, and they saw not their father's nakedness" (Gen. 9:22–23). This word is often used of female nakedness (the uncovered sex organs) and is symbolical of shame. In Lam. 1:8 plundered, devastated Jerusalem is pictured as a woman whose nakedness is exposed. To uncover one's nakedness is a frequent euphemism for cohabitation: "None of you shall approach to any that is near of kin to him, to uncover their nakedness: I am the Lord" (Lev. 18:6).

The phrase "indecent thing" represents any uncleanness in a military camp or any violation of the laws of sexual abstinence—nocturnal emission not properly cleansed, sexual cohabitation and other laws of purity (for example, excrement buried in the camp): "For the Lord thy God walketh in the midst of thy camp, to deliver thee, and to give up thine enemies before thee; therefore shall thy camp be holy: that he see no unclean thing [literally, "a matter of an indecent thing"] in thee, and turn away from thee" (Deut. 23:14). In Deut. 24:1 *'erwāh* appears to bear this emphasis on any violation of the laws of purity—if a groom is dissatisfied with his bride "because he hath found some *uncleanness* in her," he may divorce her. Obviously this evidence is not of previous cohabitation, since such a sin merits death (Deut. 22:13ff.).

The "undefended parts" or "nakedness" of a land is represented by *'erwāh* in Gen. 42:9: "Ye are spies; to see the nakedness of the land ye are come."

Other nouns related to this word appear less often. *Ma'ar*, which refers to "sexual nakedness," appears in a figurative sense in Nah. 3:5. *'Êrōm* appears as a noun abstract in several instances. This word represents the more general idea of being without clothes, with no necessary suggestion of shamefulness; it means the "state of being unclothed." In Ezek. 16:7, 39 the word *'êrōm* appears as "naked," but it can literally be translated as "nakedness" or one being in his "nakedness."

Two nouns, *ta'ar* and *môrāh*, have a different significance. *Ta'ar*, which occurs 13 times, means "razor" (Num. 6:5) or a "knife" to sharpen scribal pens (Jer. 36:23). The word's meaning of a "sword sheath" (1 Sam. 17:51) has a cognate in Ugaritic. *Môrāh* also means "razor" (1 Sam. 1:11).

B. Adjectives.

'ārôm (עָרוֹם, 6174), or *'ārōm* (עָרֹם, 6174), "naked." This word occurs 16 times. The first occurrence is in Gen. 2:25: "And they were both naked, the man and his wife, and were not ashamed."

Another adjective, found 6 times in biblical poetry, is *'eryāh*. It appears to be a variant spelling of *'erwāh*. One appearance is in Ezek. 16:22: " . . . When thou wast naked and bare. . . . "

C. Verb.

'ārāh (עָרָה, 6168), "to pour out, make bare, destroy, spread oneself out." This verb, which appears 14 times in biblical Hebrew, has cognates in Akkadian, Phoenician, Egyptian, and Syriac. The word means "to pour out" in Isa. 32:15: " Until the spirit be poured upon us from on high. . . . " The verb implies "to make bare" in Lev. 20:19. *'Ārāh* is used in the sense of "to destroy" in Isa. 3:17: "Therefore the Lord will smite with a scab the crown of the head of the

daughters of Zion, and the Lord will discover their secret parts." In Ps. 37:35 the word means "to spread oneself out."

NAME

šēm (שֵׁם, 8034), "name; reputation; memory; renown." Cognates of this word appear in Akkadian, Ugaritic, Phoenician, Aramaic, and Arabic. This word appears about 864 times and in all periods of biblical Hebrew.

It is not always true that an individual's "name" reveals his essence. Names using foreign loan words and ancient words were probably often not understood. Of course, names such as "dog" (Caleb) and "bee" (Deborah) were not indicative of the persons who bore them. Perhaps some names indicated a single decisive characteristic of their bearer. In other cases, a "name" recalls an event or mood which the parent(s) experienced at or shortly before the child's birth and/or naming. Other names make a statement about an individual. This sense of a name as an identification appears in Gen. 2:19 (an early occurrence of this word): " . . . And whatsoever Adam called every living creature, that was the name thereof." On the other hand, the names by which God revealed Himself (*'Ădōnāy, 'El, 'Ĕlōhîm*) do reflect something of His person and work.

Šēm can be a synonym for "reputation" or "fame": "Go to, let us build us a city and a tower, whose top may reach unto heaven; and let us make us a name; lest we be scattered abroad upon the face of the whole earth" (Gen. 11:4). To "give a name for one" is to make him famous: "And what one nation in the earth is like thy people, even like Israel, whom God went to redeem for a people to himself, and to make a name, and to do for you great things and terrible, for thy land . . . " (2 Sam. 7:23). If a name goes forth for one, his "reputation" of fame is made known: "And thy renown went forth among the heathen for thy beauty . . . " (Ezek. 16:14). Fame may include power: "And he lifted up his spear against three hundred, and slew them, and had the name among three" (2 Sam. 23:18). This sense, "men of reputation," appears in Gen. 6:4: " . . . mighty men which were of old, men of renown."

This word is sometimes a synonym for "memory" or "reputation" (that which remains): " . . . And so they shall quench my coal which is left, and shall not leave to my husband neither name nor remainder upon the earth" (2 Sam. 14:7). In this respect "name" may include property, or an inheritance: "Why should the name of our father be done away from among his family, because he hath no son?

Give unto us therefore a possession among the brethren of our father" (Num. 27:4).

Šēm can connote "renown" and "continuance" (in those remaining after one): "And they rose up before Moses, with certain of the children of Israel, two hundred and fifty princes of the assembly, famous in the congregation, men of renown" (Num. 16:2). This significance is in the phrase "to raise up his name after him": "What day thou buyest the field of the hand of Naomi, thou must buy it also of Ruth the Moabitess, the wife of the dead, to raise up the name of the dead upon his inheritance" (cf. Deut. 9:14; 25:6; Ruth 4:5).

NATION

gôy (גּוֹי, 1471), "nation; people; heathen." Outside the Bible, this noun appears only in the Mari texts (Akkadian) and perhaps in Phoenician-Punic. This word occurs about 56 times and in all periods of biblical Hebrew.

Gôy refers to a "people or nation," usually with overtones of territorial or governmental unity/identity. This emphasis is in the promise formulas where God promised to make someone a great, powerful, numerous "nation" (Gen. 12:2). Certainly these adjectives described the future characteristics of the individual's descendants as compared to other peoples (cf. Num. 14:12). So *gôy* represents a group of individuals who are considered as a unit with respect to origin, language, land, jurisprudence, and government. This emphasis is in Gen. 10:5 (the first occurrence): "By these were the isles of the Gentiles divided in their lands; every one after his tongue, after their families, in their nations." Deut. 4:6 deals not with political and national identity but with religious unity, its wisdom, insight, righteous jurisprudence, and especially its nearness to God: "Keep therefore and do them; for this is your wisdom and your understanding in the sight of the nations, which shall hear all these statutes, and say, Surely this great nation is a wise and understanding people." Certainly all this is viewed as the result of divine election (Deut. 4:32ff.). Israel's greatness is due to the greatness of her God and the great acts He has accomplished in and for her.

The word *'am*, "people, nation," suggests subjective personal interrelationships based on common familial ancestry and/or a covenantal union, while *gôy* suggests a political entity with a land of its own: "Now therefore, I pray thee, if I have found grace in thy sight, show me thy way, that I may know thee, that I may find grace in thy sight: and consider that this nation is thy people" (Exod. 33:13). *Gôy* may be used of a people, however, apart from its territorial

identity: "And ye shall be unto me a kingdom of priests, and a holy nation" (Exod. 19:6).

Gôy is sometimes almost a derogatory name for non-Israelite groups, or the "heathen": "And I will scatter you among the heathen, and will draw out a sword ..." (Lev. 26:33). This negative connotation is not always present, however, when the word is used of the heathen: "For from the top of the rocks I see him, and from the hills I behold him: lo, the people shall dwell alone, and shall not be reckoned among the nations" (Num. 23:9). Certainly in contexts dealing with worship the *gôyim* are the non-Israelites: "They feared the Lord, and served their own gods, after the manner of the nations whom they carried away from thence" (2 Kings 17:33). In passages such as Deut. 4:38 *gôyim* specifically describes the early inhabitants of Canaan prior to the Israelite conquest. Israel was to keep herself apart from and distinct from the "heathen" (Deut. 7:1) and was an example of true godliness before them (Deut. 4:6). On the other hand, as a blessing to all the nations (Gen. 12:2) and as a holy "nation" and kingdom of priests (Exod. 19:6), Israel was to be the means by which salvation was declared to the nations (heathen) and they came to recognize God's sovereignty (Isa. 60). So the Messiah is the light of the nations (Isa. 49:6).

NEEDY (PERSON)

A. Noun.

'ebyôn (אֶבְיוֹן, 34), "needy (person)." This word also occurs in Ugaritic and Ethiopic. Biblical Hebrew attests it about 60 times (33 times in the Psalms alone) and in all periods.

This noun refers, first, to someone who is poor in a material sense. Such a one may have lost the land of his inheritance: "But the seventh year thou shalt let it rest and lie still; that the poor of thy people may eat: and what they leave the beasts of the field shall eat" (Exod. 23:11). He has come into difficult financial straits (Job 30:25) and perhaps lacks clothing (Job 31:19) or food (Ps. 132:15).

Secondly, *'ebyôn* may refer to the lack of social standing which causes a need for protection. The first biblical occurrence bears this emphasis. God guarantees protection for such a one: "Thou shalt not wrest the judgment of thy poor in his cause" (Exod. 23:6). The godly man defends the needy and defenseless: "I was a father to the poor: and the cause which I knew not I searched out" (Job 29:16; cf. Prov. 31:9; Rom. 3:14–15). Divine provisions are encased in the Mosaic stipulations such as the seventh-year reversion of ancestral hereditary lands (Exod. 23:11), cancellation of loans (Deut.

15:4), and special extension of loans (Deut. 15:7, 9, 11).

Thirdly, this noun sometimes describes one's spiritual condition before God: "Thus saith the Lord; For three transgressions of Israel, and for four, I will not turn away the punishment thereof; because they sold the righteous for silver, and the poor for a pair of shoes" (Amos 2:6). In this verse 'ebyôn is in synonymous parallelism to "righteous," which means that it describes a moral quality.

B. Verb.

'ābāh (אָבָה, 14), "to accede, accept, consent." This verb, which occurs about 52 times and in all periods of biblical Hebrew, is sometimes associated with the noun 'ebyôn, "needy (person)." The same radicals appear in Akkadian ("to wish"), Arabic ("to refuse"), Aramaic ("to want"), and Egyptian ("to desire"). This verb means "to consent to" in Deut. 13:8: "Thou shalt not consent unto him, nor hearken unto him. . . ."

NEW; NEW MOON

A. Verb.

hādaš (חָדַשׁ, 2318), "to renew." This verb occurs in post-Mosaic literature (with the exception of Job 10:17). The root is found in all the Semitic languages with the same sense; usually the radicals are h-d-th. The first appearance of hādaš in the Bible is in 1 Sam. 11:14: "Then said Samuel to the people, Come, and let us go to Gilgal, and renew the kingdom there."

B. Noun.

hōdeš (חֹדֶשׁ, 2320), "new moon; month." This noun occurs about 283 times in biblical Hebrew and in all periods.

The word refers to the day on which the crescent reappears: "So David hid himself in the field: and when the new moon was come, the king sat him down to eat meat" (1 Sam. 20:24). Isa. 1:14 uses this word of the feast which occurred on that day: "Your new moons [festivals] and your appointed feasts my soul hateth . . ." (cf. Num. 28:14; 29:6).

Hōdeš can refer to a "month," or the period from one new moon to another. The sense of a measure of time during which something happens occurs in Gen. 38:24: "And it came to pass about three months after, that it was told Judah. . . ." In a related nuance the word refers not so much to a measure of time as to a period of time, or a calendar month. These "months" are sometimes named (Exod. 13:4) and sometimes numbered (Gen. 7:11).

C. Adjective.

hādāš (חָדָשׁ, 2319), "new; renewed." This adjective appears 53 times in biblical Hebrew.

Hādāš means "new" both in the sense of recent or fresh (as the opposite of old) and in the sense of something not previously existing. The first nuance appears in Lev. 23:16: "Even unto the morrow after the seventh sabbath shall ye number fifty days; and ye shall offer a new meat offering unto the Lord." The first biblical occurrence of hādāš (Exod. 1:8) demonstrates the second meaning: "Now there arose up a new king over Egypt, which knew not Joseph." This second nuance occurs in Isaiah's discussion of the future salvation. For example, in Isa. 42:10 a new saving act of God will bring forth a new song of praise to Him: "Sing unto the Lord a new song, and his praise from the end of the earth. . . . " The Psalter uses the phrase "a new song" in this sense; a new saving act of God has occurred and a song responding to that act celebrates it. The "new" is often contrasted to the former: "Behold, the former things are come to pass, and new things do I declare: before they spring forth I tell you of them" (Isa. 42:9). Jer. 31:31–34 employs this same nuance speaking of the new covenant (cf. Ezek. 11:19; 18:31).

A unique meaning appears in Lam. 3:23, where hādāš appears to mean "renewed"; just as God's creation is renewed and refreshed, so is His compassion and loving-kindness: "They are new every morning: great is thy faithfulness." This nuance is more closely related to the verb from which this word is derived.

NIGHT

laylāh (לַיְלָה, 3915), "night." Cognates of this noun appear in Ugaritic, Moabite, Akkadian, Aramaic, Syrian, Arabic, and Ethiopic. The word appears about 227 times in biblical Hebrew and in all periods.

Laylāh means "night," the period of time during which it is dark: "And God called the light Day, and the darkness he called Night" (Gen. 1:5—the first biblical appearance). In Exod. 13:21 and similar passages the word means "by night," or "during the night": "And the Lord went before them by day in a pillar of cloud . . . and by night in a pillar of fire, to give them light; to go by day and night." This word is used figuratively of protection: "Take counsel, execute judgment; make thy shadow as the night in the midst of the noonday; hide the outcasts; [betray] not him that wandereth" (Isa. 16:3). Laylāh also figures deep calamity without the comforting presence and guidance of God, and/or other kinds of distress: "Where is God my maker, who giveth songs in the night . . . ?" (Job 35:10).

During Old Testament times the "night" was

divided into three watches: (1) from sunset to 10 P.M. (Lam. 2:19), (2) from 10 P.M. to 2 A.M. (Judg. 7:19), and (3) from 2 A.M. to sunrise (Exod. 14:24).

NO

'ayin (אַיִן, 369), "no; not; nothing; or else, nor." Cognates of this word appear in Akkadian, Ugaritic, and Phoenician (Punic). The word appears 789 times in biblical Hebrew and in all periods.

'Ayin may be used absolutely, with no suffixes and not in a construct chain. When so used the word signifies nonexistence. This is its use and significance in Gen. 2:5 (the first occurrence): "... And there was not a man to till the ground." Preceded by the particle *'im*, the word may mean "not": "Is the Lord among us, or not?" (Exod. 17:7). In Gen. 30:1 this construction means "or else." In other contexts the word means "nothing": "... Mine age is as nothing before thee ..." (Ps. 39:5).

In the construct state *'ayin* has the same basic meaning. In one special nuance the word is virtually a predicate meaning "there is not" or "we do not have" (Num. 14:42; cf. Gen. 31:50). In several contexts the word might be translated "without": "Without counsel purposes are disappointed ..." (Prov. 15:22). Preceded by the preposition *min*, *'ayin* can mean "because" (Jer. 7:32). Elsewhere the word expresses simple negation: "They have ears, but they hear not; neither is there any breath in their mouths" (Ps. 135:17).

With a suffixed pronoun *'ayin* negates the existence of the one or thing so represented; with the suffixed pronoun "he," the word means "he was no longer": "And Enoch walked with God: and he was [no longer]; for God took him" (Gen. 5:24).

This word should be distinguished from another *'ayin* meaning "whence," or "from where."

NOBLE

A. Nouns.

'addîr (אַדִּיר, 117), "noble; principal; stately one." As a noun, *'addîr* is paralleled to "mighty" in Judg. 5:13: "Then he made him that remaineth have dominion over the nobles among the people: the Lord made me have dominion over the mighty." The word also occurs in Jer. 14:3 and Jer. 30:21. In 2 Chron. 23:20 *'addîr* is paralleled to "captains and governors." The word is applied to the Messiah; the Messiah is none other than God Himself: "But there the glorious Lord will be unto us a place of broad rivers ..." (Isa. 33:21).

Two less frequently occurring nouns are *'adderet* and *'eder*. *'Adderet* may mean "luxurious outer garment, mantle, cloak." This word appears in Gen. 25:25 to mean "mantle." *'Eder* may refer to a "luxurious outer garment" (Mic. 2:8).

B. Adjectives.

'addîr (אַדִּיר, 117), "mighty; majestic." The word *'addîr* (adjective or noun) occurs about 26 times in biblical Hebrew and mostly in poetical passages (of all periods). Ugaritic and Phoenician attest cognates of the word.

In its first appearance the adjective *'addîr* describes God's superior (majestic) holiness which was demonstrated by His delivering Israel from Egyptian bondage: "Who is like unto thee, O Lord, among the gods? Who is like thee, glorious in holiness, fearful in praises, doing wonders?" (Exod. 15:11). The idea of superior power is also suggested here (cf. Exod. 15:6; 1 Sam. 4:8). It is God's eternal and sovereign might which overcame His enemies: "and [he] slew famous kings" (Ps. 136:18)—He was/is mightier than mighty kings. Hence, His name (His person) is lauded as sovereign in power and majesty: "O Lord, our Lord, how majestic is thy name in all the earth" (Ps. 8:1 NASB). The word, therefore, has two implications: might and splendor. Only God is Lord (exercises *'addîr*) over the oceans (Ps. 93:4) and the mountains (Ps. 76:4).

God also exalts other things; He makes them majestic. Israel's exaltation is described in the figure of a cedar (Ezek. 17:23).

Two other adjectives are related to this word. *'Adderet* used as an adjective and a noun appears 12 times. In Ezek. 17:8 the word implies "noble or majestic": "It was planted in a good soil by great waters ... that it might be a goodly [*'adderet*] vine." *'Eder* occurs once as an adjective (Zech. 11:13); there it modifies the value of an amount of money.

C. Verb.

'ādar (אָדַר, 142), "to be majestic." This verb occurs only twice and in a poetical usage. The word appears in Isa. 42:21: "The Lord is well pleased for his righteousness' sake; he will magnify the law, and make it honorable [*'ādar*]." The word also appears in Exod. 15:11.

NOSE

A. Noun.

'ap (אַף, 639), "nose; nostrils; face; wrath; anger." This general Semitic word has cognates in Akkadian, Ugaritic, Phoenician, Aramaic, and Arabic. This word appears in every period of biblical Hebrew and about 277 times.

The fundamental meaning of the word is

"nose," as a literal part of the body. *'Ap* bears this meaning in the singular, while the dual refers to the "nostrils" through which air passes in and out: "And the Lord God formed man of the dust of the ground, and breathed into his nostrils the breath of life" (Gen. 2:7—the first biblical occurrence).

In other contexts *'ap* in the dual represents the "entire face." God cursed Adam saying: "In the sweat of thy face shalt thou eat bread, till thou return unto the ground . . ." (Gen. 3:19). This emphasis appears often with the phrase "to bow one's face to the ground": " . . . And Joseph's brethren came, and bowed down themselves before him with their faces to the earth" (Gen. 42:6).

The words "length of face or nostrils" constitute an idiom meaning "longsuffering" or "slow to anger." It is used both of God and of man: "The Lord, The Lord God, merciful and gracious, long-suffering, and abundant in goodness and truth" (Exod. 34:6). The contrasting idiom, meaning "quick to anger," might literally mean "short of face/nostrils." It implies a changeable countenance, a capricious disposition. Prov. 14:17 uses this idiom with a little stronger emphasis: "He that is soon angry dealeth foolishly: and a man of wicked devices is hated." The accuracy of this translation is supported by the parallelism of the phrase and "a man of evil devices." Clearly *'ap* must mean something evil in God's sight.

Finally, the dual form can mean "wrath" (only in 4 passages): "Surely the churning of milk bringeth forth butter, and the wringing of the nose bringeth forth blood: so the forcing of wrath bringeth forth strife" (Prov. 30:33; cf. Exod. 15:8).

The singular form means "nose" about 25 times. In Num. 11:19–20 the word represents a human nose: "You [Israel] shall . . . eat [the meat God will supply] . . . a whole month, until it comes out of your nostrils and becomes loathsome to you" (NASB). Isa. 2:22 makes it clear that the word represents the place where the breath is: "Stop regarding man, whose breath of life is in his nostrils" (NASB). Perhaps the NASB translation in such passages is acceptable. The first passage, however, refers to the two holes or nostrils, while the second passage appears to refer to the entire frontal part of the nasal passages (where one is aware of breath being present). This word may be used of the structure protruding from one's face: " . . . They shall take away thy nose and thine ears; and thy remnant shall fall by the sword . . ." (Ezek. 23:25; cf. Song of Sol. 7:4). *'Ap* is applied also to the "nose" of animals. In Job 40:24, God speaks of

a large water animal: "He taketh it with his eyes: his nose pierceth through snares."

The word can be used anthropomorphically of God. Certainly passages such as Deut. 4:15–19 make it clear that God is a Spirit (John 4:24) and has not a body like men. Yet, speaking figuratively, it may be said: "They shall teach Jacob thy judgments, and Israel thy law: they shall put incense before thee [literally, "in thy nostrils"], and whole burnt sacrifice upon thine altar" (Deut. 33:10; cf. Ps. 18:8, 15). The idiom "high of nose" means "haughty" (cf. the English idiom "to have one's nose in the air"): "The wicked, through the pride of his countenance, will not seek after God . . ." (Ps. 10:4).

The singular form often means "anger" or "wrath." This meaning first appears in Gen. 30:2: "And Jacob's anger was kindled against Rachel. . . ." This meaning is applied to God as a figure of speech (anthropopathism) whereby He is attributed human emotions. Since God is infinite, eternal, and unchangeable and since anger is an emotion representing a change in one's reaction (cf. Num. 25:4), God does not really become angry, He only appears to do so in the eyes of men (cf. Prov. 29:8). The Spirit of God can seize a man and move him to a holy "anger" (Judg. 14:19; 1 Sam. 11:6).

B. Verb.

'ānap (אָנַף, 599), "to be angry." This verb, which has cognates in most of the Semitic languages, occurs 39 times in biblical Hebrew and in all periods. The verb appears in Isa. 12:1: "O Lord, I will praise thee: though thou wast angry with me. . . . "

FOR NOTHING

ḥinnām (חִנָּם, 2600), "for nothing; for no purpose; useless; without a cause; for no reason." The 32 appearances of this word are scattered throughout every period of biblical Hebrew.

This substantive is used chiefly as an adverb. *Ḥinnām* means "for nought": "And Laban said unto Jacob, Because thou art my brother, shouldest thou therefore serve me for nought? tell me, what shall thy wages be?" (Gen. 29:15—the first occurrence). The word means "in vain," or "for no purpose": "Surely in vain the net is spread in the sight of any bird" (Prov. 1:17). Finally, *ḥinnām* means "for no cause": " . . . Wherefore then wilt thou sin against innocent blood, to slay David without a cause?" (1 Sam. 19:5).

The verb *ḥānan* and the noun *ḥēn* are related to this word.

TO NUMBER, COUNT

A. Verb.

sāpar (סָפַר, 5608), "to number, count, proclaim, declare." The relationship of this verb to similar verbs in other languages is greatly debated, but it does occur in Ugaritic, Ethiopic, and Old South Arabic. Attested in all periods of biblical Hebrew, it appears about 110 times.

In the basic verbal form this verb signifies "to number or count." This meaning is in its first biblical appearance, Gen. 15:5: "Look now toward heaven, and tell the stars, if thou be able to number them. . . . " Here the counting is a process which has no completion in view. In Lev. 15:13 the emphasis is on a completed task: "And when [the man with the discharge becomes cleansed]; then he shall number to himself seven days for his cleansing, and wash his clothes, and bathe his flesh. . . . " Another nuance of this usage is "to count up" or "to take a census": "And David's heart smote him after that he had numbered the people" (2 Sam. 24:10). The verb is also used of assigning persons to particular jobs: "And Solomon told out threescore and ten thousand men to bear burdens . . . " (2 Chron. 2:2). Another special use appears in Ezra 1:8, where *sāpar* means "to count out according to a list" as the recipient listens: "Even those [the temple furnishings] did Cyrus king of Persia bring forth by the hand of Mithredath the treasurer, and numbered them unto Sheshbazzar, the prince of Judah." In Ps. 56:8 the word signifies "taking account of," or being aware and concerned about each detail of: "Thou tellest my wanderings. . . . " This verb can also mean "to measure," in the sense of what one does with grain: "And Joseph gathered corn as the sand of the sea, very much, until he left numbering; for it was without number" (Gen. 41:49). Finally, the verb *sāpar* can represent recording something in writing, or enumerating. So, "the Lord shall count, when he writeth up the people, that this man was born there" (Ps. 87:6).

In about 90 instances this verb appears in an intensive form. For the most part the verb in this form means "to recount," to orally list in detail. The one exception to this significance is Job 38:37: "Who can number the clouds in wisdom? Or who can stay the bottles of heaven . . . ?" In every other instance the verb signifies a vocal statement (listing or enumeration) of a series of given facts. In Gen. 24:66 Eliezer, Abraham's servant, "told Isaac all things that he had done"; he gave him a summarized but complete account of his activities. Thus Isaac knew who Rebekah was, and why she was there, so he took her to be his wife. In a similar but somewhat different sense Jacob "told Laban" who he was, that he was from the same family (Gen. 29:13). In this case the word represents something other than a report; it represents an account of Jacob's genealogy and perhaps of the events of his parents' lives. This emphasis on accurate recounting is especially prominent in Num. 13:27, where the spies report back to Moses concerning what they saw in Palestine. Even more emphatic is Exod. 24:3, where one word represents a detailed repetition of what Moses heard from God: "And Moses came and told the people all the words of the Lord, and all the judgments. . . . " Again, in Isa. 43:26 a detailed and accurate recounting is clearly in view. In this case the prophet has in mind the presentation of a law case: "Put me in remembrance: let us plead together: declare thou, that thou mayest be justified." Because of the predominant meaning presented above, Ps. 40:5 could be translated: "If I would declare and speak of them, they would be too numerous to recount" (instead of "to count").

In at least one case the verb in the intensive stem means "to exhibit," "to recount or list in detail by being a living example." This meaning first appears in Exod. 9:16, where God tells Moses to say to Pharaoh: "And in very deed for this cause have I raised thee up, for to show in thee my power; and that my name may be declared throughout all the earth."

B. Nouns.

mispār (מִסְפָּר, 4557), "measure; (a certain) number; account." This noun occurs about 132 times. *Mispār* can mean "measure" (quantity) as in Gen. 41:49. In Gen. 34:30, the first biblical occurrence, the word refers to "a certain number" in the sense of the sum total of individuals that are counted: " . . . and I being few in number, they shall gather themselves together against me, and slay me. . . . " The word means "account" (what is set forth in a detailed report) in Judg. 7:15.

sēper (סֵפֶר, 5612), "book; tablet." This noun occurs in Akkadian, Phoenician, and Aramaic (including biblical Aramaic), and in all periods of biblical Hebrew. It occurs 187 times in the Old Testament. Basically this word represents something one writes upon. So in Exod. 17:14 "the Lord said unto Moses, Write this for a memorial in a book." In Isa. 30:8 *sēper* represents a tablet. In Gen. 5:1 (the first biblical occurrence of this word) it signifies something that has been written upon, or a written record: "This is the book of the generations of Adam." Such a written document may be a summary of God's law (Exod. 24:7). During the monarchy *sēper* came to represent a letter (2 Sam. 11:14). Even later it means a king's written decree sent throughout his empire (Esth. 1:22). Usually the word means "book" (Exod. 32:32)—a complete record of whatever one wants to preserve accurately. Often this word can signify the way a people writes, the written language or script (Isa. 29:11).

sōpēr (סֹפֵר, 5608), "scribe." *Sōpēr*, which occurs about 50 times in biblical Hebrew, appears also in Akkadian, Ugaritic, and Aramaic. In the early monarchy the chief "scribe" was the highest court official next to the king (2 Sam. 8:17). His job was to receive and evaluate all royal correspondence—to answer the unimportant and give the rest to the proper officer or to the king himself. He also wrote and/or composed royal communications to those within the kingdom. There was probably an entire corps of lesser scribes under his direction. As a highly trusted official he was sometimes involved in counting and managing great influxes of royal revenue (2 Kings 12:10) and in certain diplomatic jobs (2 Kings 19:2). Later *sōpēr* represented the Jewish official in the Persian court who was responsible for Jewish belongings (Ezra 7:11). In the post-exilic community this word came to mean someone who was learned in the Old Testament Scripture and especially the Mosaic Law (the Pentateuch; Ezra 7:6). The word first occurs in Judg. 5:14, where its meaning is debated. The NASB translates it "office"; some scholars translate it "scribe" (KJV, "they that handle the pen of the writer").

Some other nouns are related to the verb *sāpar*. Three of them occur only once: *sᵉpār*, "numbering or census" (2 Chron. 2:17); *siprāh*, "book" (Ps. 56:8); *sᵉpōrāh*, "number or sum" (Ps. 71:15).

TO NUMBER, VISIT, PUNISH

A. Verb.

pāqad (פָּקַד, 6485), "to number, visit, be concerned with, look after, make a search for, punish." This very ancient Semitic word is found in both Akkadian and Ugaritic long before it appears in Hebrew. It is used over 285 times in the Old Testament. The first occurrence is in Gen. 21:1 ("The Lord visited Sarah") in the special sense of "to intervene on behalf of," so as to demonstrate the divine intervention in the normal course of events to bring about or fulfill a divine intent. Often this intervention is by miraculous means.

The verb is used in an expression which is unique to Hebrew and which shows great intensity of meaning. Such an occurrence appears in Exod. 3:16ff., in which it is used twice in two different grammatical forms to portray the intensity of the action; the text reads (literally): "Looking after, I have looked after" (KJV, "I have surely visited"). The usage refers to God's intervention in His saving the children of Israel from their bondage in Egypt. The same verb in a similar expression can also be used for divine intervention for punishment: "Shall I not visit them for these things?" (Jer. 9:9), which means literally: "Shall I not punish them for these things?"

Hebrew usage also allows a use which applies to the speaker in a nearly passive sense. This is termed the reflexive, since it turns back upon the speaker. *Pāqad* is used in such a sense meaning "be missed, be lacking," as in 1 Sam. 25:7: ". . . Neither was there aught missing. . . ."

However, the most common usage of the verb in the whole of the Old Testament is in the sense of "drawing up, mustering, or numbering," as of troops for marching or battle (Exod. 30:12 and very frequently in Numbers; less so in 1 and 2 Samuel). Recent English versions have tended to use the meaning "take a census," but this equivalent seems to encompass only part of the actual meaning. The verb is used in this sense fully 100 times in the historical books.

The term has such a wide application of meanings on the whole that the Greek Septuagint and the Latin Vulgate versions use a number of terms to translate the single Hebrew word. The usage in the English versions also varies: "number, visit, punish" (KJV, RSV); "take a census, take note of, visit, punish" (NASB); "did as promised, to see, visit, punish," and other variations (LB); "blessed, seen, to take a census" (TEV); "take note of, to witness, visit, punish" (NAB); "take a census, be gracious, punish," and other variations (NIV).

B. Noun.

pāqîd (פָּקִיד, 6496), "one who looks after." This noun, derived from *pāqad* in the sense "to number, muster, draw up (troops)," possibly means "one who draws up troops," hence "officer" (2 Chron. 24:11). Another example of this meaning occurs in Jer. 20:1: "Now Pashur the son of Immer the priest, who was also chief governor in the house of the Lord. . . ."

O

TO OFFER

A. Verb.

qārab (קָרַב, 7126), "to offer, come near, approach." This word appears in nearly all branches of the Semitic languages from the earliest times and at all periods. Hebrew also attests the verb at all periods and about 295 times. (It appears 9 times in biblical Aramaic.)

In general *qārab* signifies "approach or coming near someone or something" apart from any sense of intimacy. In Gen. 12:11 (the first biblical occurrence) the word is used of spatial proximity, of being spatially close to something: "And it came to pass, when he was come near to enter into Egypt, that he said unto Sarai his wife...." Usually the word represents being so close to something (or someone) that the subject can see (Exod. 32:19), speak to (Num. 9:6), or even touch (Exod. 36:2) the object or person in question.

This verb also is used of temporal nearness, in the sense that something is about to occur. *Qārab* can be used of the imminence of joyous occasions, such as religious feasts: "Beware that there be not a thought in thy wicked heart, saying, The seventh year, the year of release, is at hand..." (Deut. 15:9). The word is also used of the imminence of foreboding events: "...Esau said in his heart, The days of mourning for my father are at hand [literally, "my father will soon die"]..." (Gen. 27:41).

Qārab is used in a number of technical senses. In all these instances personal involvement is suggested; the idea is not simply being close to something (someone) but being actively and personally involved with it (him). In military contexts the word signifies armed conflict. In Deut. 2:37 the Lord commended Israel because "unto the land of the children of Ammon thou camest not." Yet in Deut. 2:19 He allowed them to "come nigh" that land: "And when thou comest nigh over against the children of Ammon, distress them not, nor meddle with them...." The later passage (Deut. 2:37) uses the word technically, to close in battle. Therefore, Israel did not come close to the land of Ammon; they did not close in battle with them (cf. Josh. 8:5). In some passages this martial coloring is not immediately obvious to the casual reader but is nonetheless present: "When the wicked... came upon me to eat up my flesh..." (Ps. 27:2). Ps. 27:3 ("though a host should encamp against me") substantiates that

this use of the verb is "to close in battle" (cf. Ps. 91:10; 119:150).

Qārab is used technically of having sexual relations. In Gen. 20:4 before Abimelech states his innocence with regard to Sarah we read he "had not come near her" (cf. Deut. 22:14; Isa. 8:3).

In another technical use the word represents every step one performs in presenting his offering and worship to God. This idea first appears in Exod. 3:5 where God tells Moses not to "draw near" before removing his sandals. Later Israel's meeting with God's representative was a drawing near to God (Exod. 16:9). At Sinai they drew near to receive God's law (Deut. 5:23, 27). In the causative stem the verb often represents the sacrificial presentation of offerings (Lev. 1:14) through the priests (Lev. 1:5) to the Lord (Lev. 1:13).

Israel also came near the Lord's representative in serious legal cases so that God the great King and Judge could render a decision (Josh. 7:14). In the eschaton all peoples are to gather before God; they are "to come near" Him to hear and receive His judgment (Isa. 41:1; 48:16).

B. Nouns.

qorbān (קָרְבָּן, 7133), "offering; oblation." This noun occurs about 80 times in biblical Hebrew. The word is also found in Ethiopic and old South Arabic. The first occurrence of the word is used of an "offering" presented as a sacrifice: "If any man of you bring an offering unto the Lord, ye shall bring your offering of the cattle, even of the herd, and of the flock" (Lev. 1:2).

Some other related nouns appear less frequently: *qārôb*, "neighbor" (Exod. 32:27); *qir-bāh* occurs twice with the meaning of drawing near to worship God and offer sacrifice (Ps. 73:28; Isa. 58:2); *qurbān*, which appears twice, means "supply, offering" (Neh. 10:35; 13:31)—it appears to be a late pronunciation of *qorbān*. The word *q^erāb*, which appears 8 times, is an Aramaic loan word; it means "war, battle," or the actual engaging in battle (Ps. 55:18).

C. Adjectives.

qārôb (קָרוֹב, 7138), "near." This word occurs about 77 times. *Qārôb* can represent nearness in space (Gen. 19:20—the first biblical occurrence) and an epistemological nearness (Deut. 30:14). The adjective also appears in Ezek. 6:12: "He that is far off shall die of the pestilence; and he that is near shall fall by the sword. . . . "

The adjective *qārēb* parallels *qārôb* in meaning. *Qārēb*, which occurs 11 times, means "near"; it represents intimate proximity (usually in a cultic context referring to cultic activity). One appearance is in Ezek. 45:4: "The holy portion of the land shall be for the priests the ministers of the sanctuary, which shall come near to minister unto the Lord. . . ."

OFFERING

minḥāh (מִנְחָה, 4503), "meat [cereal] offering; offering; tribute; present; gift; sacrifice; oblation." The KJV characteristically translates the word as "meat offering," using it some 40 times in this way in both Leviticus and Numbers alone. The word "meat" in this KJV use really means "food"; the RSV's rendering, "cereal offering," generally is much more accurate. *Minḥāh* is found some 200 times in the Old Testament.

Minḥāh is found in all periods of Hebrew, although in modern Hebrew, while it is commonly used in the sense of "gift," it also is used to refer to "afternoon prayers." This latter use is an obvious echo of the Old Testament liturgy connected with sacrifices. It appears in other Semitic languages such as Arabic and Phoenician, and seems to be used in ancient Ugaritic in the sense of "tribute/gift." *Minḥāh* occurs for the first time in the Old Testament in Gen. 4:3: " . . . Cain brought of the fruit of the ground an offering unto the Lord." This use reflects the most common connotation of *minḥāh* as a "vegetable or cereal offering."

Minḥāh is used many times in the Old Testament to designate a "gift" or "present" which is given by one person to another. For example, when Jacob was on his way back home after twenty years, his long-standing guilt and fear of Esau prompted him to send a rather large "present" (bribe) of goats, camels, and other animals (Gen. 32:13–15). Similarly, Jacob directed his sons to "carry down the man a present" (Gen. 43:11) to appease the Egyptian ruler that later turned out to be his lost son Joseph. Those who came to hear Solomon's great wisdom all brought to him an appropriate "present" (1 Kings 10:25), doing so on a yearly basis.

Frequently *minḥāh* is used in the sense of "tribute" paid to a king or overlord. The delivering of the "tribute" of the people of Israel to the king of Moab by their judge-deliverer became the occasion for the deliverance of Israel from Moabite control as Ehud assassinated Eglon by a rather sly maneuver (Judg. 3:15–23). Years later when David conquered the Moabites, they "became servants to David and brought gifts [tribute]" (2 Sam. 8:2). Hosea proclaimed to Israel that its pagan bull-god would "be carried unto Assyria for a present [tribute]" (Hos. 10:6). Other passages where *minḥāh* has the meaning of "tribute" are: Ps. 72:10; 1 Kings 4:21; 2 Kings 17:3–4.

Minḥāh is often used to refer to any "offering" or "gift" made to God, whether it was a "vegetable offering" or a "blood sacrifice." The story of Cain and Abel vividly illustrates this general usage: " . . . Cain brought of the fruit of the ground an offering unto the Lord. And Abel, he also brought of the firstlings of his flock and of the fat thereof. And the Lord had respect unto Abel and to his offering: But unto Cain and to his offering he had not respect" (Gen. 4:3–5). The animal sacrifices which were misappropriated by the wicked sons of Eli were simply designated as "the offering of the Lord" (1 Sam. 2:17). In each case "offering" is the translation of *minḥāh*.

A common use of *minḥāh*, especially in later Old Testament texts, is to designate "meat [grain/cereal] offerings." Sometimes it referred to the "meat [cereal] offering" of first fruits, "green ears of corn, dried by the fire. . . . " (Lev. 2:14). Such offerings included oil and frankincense which were burned with the grain. Similarly, the "meat [grain] offering" could be in the form of finely ground flour upon which oil and frankincense had been poured also. Sometimes the oil was mixed with the "meat [cereal] offering" (Lev. 14:10, 21; 23:13; Num. 7:13), again in the form of fine flour. The priest would take a handful of this fine flour, burn it as a memorial portion, and the remainder would belong to the priest (Lev. 2:9–10). The "meat [cereal] offering" frequently was in the form of fine flour which was mixed with oil and then formed into cakes and baked, either in a pan or on a griddle (Lev. 2:4–5). Other descriptions of this type of baked "meat [cereal] offering" are found in Num. 6:15 and Lev. 7:9. These baked "meat [cereal] offerings" were always to be made without leaven, but were to be mixed with salt and oil (Lev. 2:11, 13).

The *minḥāh* was prescribed as a "meat offering" of flour kneaded with oil to be given along with the whole burnt offering. A libation of wine was to be given as well. This particular rule applied especially to the Feast of Weeks or Pentecost (Lev. 23:18), to the daily "continual offering" (Exod. 29:38–42), and to all the whole burnt offerings or general sacrifices (Num. 15:1–16). The "meat [cereal] offering" was to be burned, while the wine seems to have been poured out at the foot of the altar like blood of the sacrificial animal.

The regular daily morning and evening sacrifices included the *minḥāh* and were specifically referred to as "meat [cereal] offering of the morning" (Exod. 29:41; cf. Num. 28:8) and as "the evening meat [cereal] offering" (2 Kings 16:15; cf. Ezra 9:4–5 and Ps. 141:2, "evening sacrifice").

Minḥāh provides an interesting symbolism for the prophet when he refers to the restoration of the Jews: "And they shall bring all your brethren for an offering unto the Lord out of all nations upon horses, and in chariots . . . to my holy mountain Jerusalem, saith the Lord, as the children of Israel bring an offering in a clean vessel into the house of the Lord" (Isa. 66:20). In his vision of the universal worship of God, even in Gentile lands, Malachi saw the *minḥāh* given as "a pure offering" to God by believers everywhere (Mal. 1:11).

tᵉrûmāh (תְּרוּמָה, 8641), "heave offering; offering; oblation." This word is found in the literature of ancient Ugarit in the term, "bread of offering," as well as in all periods of Hebrew. In modern Hebrew it is often used in the sense of "contribution," quite like the use found in Ezek. 45:13, 16, where it refers to a contribution to be given to the prince. *Tᵉrûmāh* is found approximately 70 times in the Old Testament, being used for the first time in the Old Testament text in Exod. 25:2: "Speak unto the children of Israel, that they bring me an offering: of every man that giveth it willingly with the heart ye shall take my offering."

In more than a third of its occurrences in the text, the KJV translates *tᵉrûmāh* as "heave offering," all of these instances being found in Exodus, Leviticus, Numbers (where the majority are found), and Deuteronomy. This translation apparently is derived from the fact that the word is based on the common Semitic root, "to be high, exalted." The inference seems to be that such "offerings" were raised high by the priest in some sort of motion as it was placed on the altar. This is clearly illustrated in Num. 15:20: "Ye shall offer up a cake of the first of your dough for a heave offering: as ye do the heave offering of the threshing floor, so shall ye heave it." From texts like this, it appears that *tᵉrûmāh* was used in the early period to refer to "contributions" or "gifts" which consisted of the produce of the ground, reflecting the agricultural character of early Israel. See Deut. 12:6, 11, 17 for other examples.

Tᵉrûmāh often is used to designate those gifts or contributions to God, but which were set apart specifically for the priests: "And every offering of all the holy things of the children of Israel, which they bring unto the priest, shall be

his" (Num. 5:9). Such "offerings" were to go to the priests because of a special covenant God had made: "All the holy offerings which the people of Israel present to the Lord I give to you [Aaron], and to your sons and daughters with you, as a perpetual due; it is a covenant of salt for ever before the Lord for you and for your offspring with you" (Num. 18:19, RSV). Such offerings, or contributions, sometimes were of grain or grain products: "Besides the cakes, he shall offer for his offering leavened bread with the sacrifice of thanksgiving of his peace offerings. And of it he shall offer one out of the whole oblation for a heave offering unto the Lord, and it shall be the priest's that sprinkleth the blood of the peace offerings" (Lev. 7:13–14). Part of the animal sacrifices was also designated as a *tᵉrûmāh* for the priests: "And the right shoulder shall ye give unto the priest for a heave offering of the sacrifices of your peace offerings" (Lev. 7:32; cf. Lev. 10:14–15; Num. 6:20). Such contributions to the priests obviously were given to provide the needed foodstuffs for the priests and their families since their tribe, Levi, was given no land on which to raise their own food.

While all the priests had to be from the tribe of Levi, inheriting their office through their fathers, not all Levites could function as priests. For one thing, there were too many of them. Also, some were needed to work in the tabernacle, and later the temple, as maintenance and cleanup people, something that is readily understandable when one thinks of all that was involved in the sacrificial system. The Levites actually lived in various parts of Israel, and they were the welfare responsibility of the Israelites among whom they lived. They, like the widow, the orphan, and the resident alien, were to be given the tithe of all farm produce every third year (Deut. 14:28–29). The Levites, then, were to tithe the tithe they received, giving their own tithe from what they received from the people to the Lord. Part of that tithe was to be a *tᵉrûmāh* or "heave offering" to the priests, the descendants of Aaron (see Num. 18:25–32).

In order to provide for the materials necessary for the construction of the wilderness tabernacle, Moses was instructed to receive an "offering" or *tᵉrûmāh*. The "offering" was to consist of all kinds of precious metals and stones, as well as the usual building materials such as wood and skins (Exod. 25:3–9). When Moses announced this to the people of Israel, he said: "Take ye from among you an offering unto the Lord; whosoever is of a willing heart, let him bring it, an offering of the Lord . . ." (Exod. 35:5), following this with a list of the needed materials (Exod. 35:6–8). The implication here is twofold: the *t*ᵉ*rûmāh* is really the Lord's, and it is best given freely, willingly, from a generous heart. In the Second Temple Period, following the Exile, the silver and gold and the vessels for the temple are called "the offering for the house of our God" (Ezra 8:25), also signifying a contribution.

The *t*ᵉ*rûmāh* sometimes was an "offering" which had the meaning of a tax, an obligatory assessment which was made against every Israelite male who was twenty years old or older, to be paid for the support of the tabernacle and, later, the temple (Exod. 30:11–16). This tax was levied on all males without any allowance for their financial situation: "The rich shall not give more, and the poor shall not give less than half a shekel, when they give an offering unto the Lord, to make an atonement for your souls" (Exod. 30:15). This tax actually had its basis in the census or count of the male population, the tax then being required as a ransom or atonement from the wrath of God because such a census was taken (2 Sam. 24:1). The practical aspect of it was that it provided needed financial support for the sanctuary. Another example of *t*ᵉ*rûmāh* in the sense of taxes may be seen in Prov. 29:4: "The king by judgment establisheth the land; but he that receiveth gifts overthroweth it." Solomon's heavy taxation which led to the split of the kingdom may be a case in point (1 Kings 12).

A very different use of *t*ᵉ*rûmāh* is found in Ezek. 45:1; 48:9, 20–21, where it refers to an "oblation" which was that portion of land on which the post-exilic temple was to be built, as well as accommodations for the priests and Levites. This tract of land is referred to as "the holy oblation" (Ezek. 48:20; RSV, "holy portion"), since it belongs to God just as much as the *t*ᵉ*rûmāh* which was given to Him as a sacrifice.

qorbān (קָרְבָּן, 7133), "offering; oblation; sacrifice." *Qorbān* is found in various Semitic languages and is derived from the verb "to come/bring near." It is found in ancient Akkadian in the sense of "a present," while a form of the verb is found in Ugaritic to refer to the offering of a sacrifice. Found throughout the history of Hebrew, in late or modern Hebrew it is used in the sense of "offering" and "consecration." In the Septuagint, it is often rendered as "gift."

While the root, "to come/bring near," is found literally hundreds of times in the Old Testament, the derived noun *qorbān* occurs only about 80 times. All but two of the occurrences in the Old Testament are found in the books of Numbers and Leviticus. The two exceptions are

in Ezekiel (20:28; 40:43), a book which has a great concern for ritual. The word occurs for the first time in Lev. 1:2.

Qorbān may be translated as "that which one brings near to God or the altar." It is not surprising, then, that the word is used as a general term for all sacrifices, whether animal or vegetable. The very first reference to "sacrifice" in Leviticus is to the *qorbān* as a burnt "offering": "If any man of you bring an offering unto the Lord, ye shall bring your offering of the cattle, even of the herd, and of the flock. If his offering be a burnt sacrifice . . . " (Lev. 1:2–3; cf. Lev. 1:10; 3:2, 6; 4:23). The first reference to *qorbān* as a "meat [cereal] offering" is in Lev. 2:1: "And when any will offer a meat offering unto the Lord, his offering shall be of fine flour. . . . "

What is perhaps the best concentration of examples of the use of *qorbān* is Numbers 7. In this one chapter, the word is used some 28 times, referring to all kinds of animal and meat [cereal] offerings, but with special attention to the various silver and gold vessels which were offered to the sanctuary. For example, Eliab's "offering was one silver charger, the weight whereof was a hundred and thirty shekels, one silver bowl of seventy shekels, . . . both of them full of fine flour mingled with oil for a meat offering; One golden spoon of ten shekels, full of incense; One young bullock, one ram, one lamb of the first year, for a burnt offering" (Num. 7:25–27).

In the two uses found in Ezekiel, both are in the general sense of "offering." In Ezek. 20:28 the word refers to the pagan "provocation of their offering" which apostate Israel gave to other gods, while in Ezek. 40:43, *qorbān* refers to regular animal sacrifices.

qurbān (קֻרְבָּן, 7133), "wood offering." *Qurbān* is closely related to *qārbān*, and it is found in Neh. 10:34; 13:31. Here it refers to the "wood offering" which was to be provided for the burning of the sacrifices in the Second Temple. Lots were to be cast among the people, priests, and Levites to determine who would bring in the "wood offering" or fuel at the scheduled times throughout the year.

ʿōlāh (עוֹלָה, 5930), "whole burnt offering." This word has cognates in late and biblical Aramaic. It occurs about 280 times in biblical Hebrew and at all periods.

In its first biblical occurrence *ʿōlāh* identifies a kind of "offering" presented to God: "And Noah builded an altar unto the Lord; and took of every clean beast, and of every clean fowl, and offered burnt offerings on the altar" (Gen. 8:20). Its second nuance appears in Lev. 1:4, where it represents the "thing being offered":

"And he shall put his hand upon the head of the burnt offering; and it shall be accepted for him to make atonement for him."

This kind of "offering" could be made with a bull (Lev. 1:3–5), a sheep, a goat (Lev. 1:10), or a bird (Lev. 1:14). The offerer laid his hands on the sacrificial victim, symbolically transferring his sin and guilt to it. After he slew the animal (on the north side of the altar), the priest took its blood, which was presented before the Lord prior to being sprinkled around the altar. A bird was simply given to the priest, but he wrung its neck and allowed its blood to drain beside the altar (Lev. 1:15). This sacrifice effected an atonement, a covering for sin necessary before the essence of the sacrifice could be presented to God. Next, the "offering" was divided into sections. They were carefully purified (except those parts which could not be purified) and arranged on the altar (Lev. 1:6–9, 12–13). The entire sacrifice was then consumed by the fire and its essence sent up to God as a placating (pleasing) odor. The animal skin was given to the priest as his portion (Lev. 7:8).

The word *ōlāh* was listed first in Old Testament administrative prescriptions and descriptions as the most frequent offering. Every day required the presentation of a male lamb morning and evening—the continual "whole burnt offering" (Exod. 29:38–42). Each month was consecrated by a "whole burnt offering," of two young bulls, one ram, and seven male lambs (Num. 28:11–14). The same sacrifice was mandated, for each day of the Passover-Unleavened Bread feast (Num. 28:19–24), and the Feast of Weeks (Num. 28:26–29). Other stated feasts required "burnt offerings" as well. The various purification rites mandated both "burnt" and sin "offerings."

The central significance of *ōlāh* as the "whole burnt offering" was the total surrender of the heart and life of the offerer to God. Sin offerings could accompany them when the offerer was especially concerned with a covering or expiation for sin (2 Chron. 29:27). When peace offerings accompanied "burnt offerings," the offerer's concern focused on fellowship with God (2 Chron. 29:31–35). Before the Mosaic legislation, it appears, the "whole burnt offering" served the full range of meanings expressed in all the various Mosaic sacrifices.

'iššeh (אִשֶּׁה, 801), "fire offering." Sixty-two of the 64 appearances of this word occur in the sacramental prescriptions of Exodus-Deuteronomy. The other two occurrences (Josh. 13:14; 1 Sam. 2:28) bear the same meaning and sacramental context.

All legitimate sacrifices had to be presented before God at His altar, and all of them involved burning to some degree. Thus they may all be called fire offerings. The word *'iššeh* first occurs in Exod. 29:18: "And thou shalt burn the whole ram upon the altar: it is a burnt offering unto the Lord: it is a sweet savor, an offering made by fire unto the Lord."

'āšām (אָשָׁם, 817), "guilt offering; offense; guilt; gift of restitution; gift of atonement." The noun *'āšām* occurs 46 times in biblical Hebrew; 33 of its occurrences are in the Pentateuch.

The most frequent meaning of the word is "guilt offering": "And he shall bring his trespass [guilt] offering unto the Lord for his sin which he hath sinned . . ." (Lev. 5:6). This specialized kind of sin offering (Lev. 5:7) was to be offered when someone had been denied what was due to him. The valued amount defrauded was to be repaid plus 20 percent (Lev. 5:16; 6:5). Ritual infractions and periods of leprosy and defilement took from God a commodity or service rightfully belonging to Him and required repayment plus restitution. Every violation of property rights required paying full reparation and the restitution price (20 percent) to the one violated as well as presenting the guilt offering to God as the Lord of all (i.e., as a feudal lord over all). If the offended party was dead, reparation and restitution were made to God (i.e., given to the priests; Num. 5:5–10). Usually the "guilt offering" consisted of a ram (Lev. 5:15) or a male lamb. The offerer presented the victim, laying his hands on it. The priest sprinkled its blood around the altar, burned the choice parts on the altar, and received the rest as food (Lev. 7:2–7). When a cleansed leper made this offering, blood from the sacrifice was applied to the man's right ear, right thumb, and right big toe (Lev. 14:14).

In some passages, *'āšām* is used of an offense against God and the guilt incurred by it: "And Abimelech said, What is this thou hast done unto us? One of the people might lightly have lain with thy wife, and thou shouldest have brought guiltiness upon us" (Gen. 26:10—the first occurrence). There is an added sense here that the party offended would punish the perpetrator of the crime.

In two verses (Num. 5:7–8), *'āšām* represents the repayment made to one who has been wronged: "Then they shall confess their sin which they have done: and he shall recompense his trespass with the principal thereof, and add unto it the fifth part thereof, and give it unto him against whom he hath trespassed." In the Hebrew the word is the value of the initial thing taken from the injured party, which value is to be returned to him, i.e., the reparation or restitution itself. This basic idea is extended so that the word comes to mean a gift made to God to remove guilt (1 Sam. 6:3), or atone for sin (Isa. 53:10) other than the specified offerings to be presented at the altar.

(OLIVE) OIL

A. Nouns.

šemen (שֶׁמֶן, 8081), "(olive) oil; olive; perfume; olivewood." Cognates of this word appear in Ugaritic, Akkadian, Phoenician, Syriac, Arabic, and Aramaic. This word appears about 190 times and in all periods of biblical Hebrew.

Šemen means olive "oil": "And Jacob rose up early in the morning, and took the stone that he had put for his pillows, and set it up for a pillar, and poured oil upon the top of it" (Gen. 28:18). Olive "oil" was also used to anoint a future office bearer (Exod. 25:6; 2 Kings 9:6); one's head as a sign of mourning (2 Sam. 14:2); one's head as a sign of rejoicing (Ps. 23:5); and one's ear lobe, thumb, and toe as a ritual cleansing (Lev. 14:17). *Šemen* is used as a preservative on shield-leather (2 Sam. 1:21) and in baking (Exod. 29:2) and as a medication (Ezek. 16:9). This "oil" is burned for light (Exod. 25:6). Its many uses made olive oil a valuable trade item (Ezek. 27:17).

In many contexts *šemen* perhaps means the "olive" itself: " ... But ye, gather ye wine, and summer fruits, and oil, and put them in your vessels ... " (Jer. 40:10).

Once the word appears to mean lavish dishes, or dishes mixed with much oil: "And in this mountain shall the Lord of hosts make unto all people a feast of fat things [NASB, "lavish banquet"]" (Isa. 25:6).

Šemen is "a kind of perfume," or olive oil mixed with certain odors to make a perfume, in passages such as Song of Sol. 1:3: "Because of the savor of thy good ointments [NASB, "oils"] thy name is as ointment poured forth. ... "

Šemen sometimes modifies "wood": "In the inner sanctuary he made two cherubim of olivewood, each ten cubits high" (1 Kings 6:23, RSV).

A related noun *mišmān* appears 4 times. It means "stout or vigorous ones" (Isa. 10:16) and "fertile spots" (Dan. 11:24).

B. Verb.

The verb *šāman*, which appears 5 times, has cognates in Aramaic, Syriac, and Arabic. The word means "to grow or be fat" (Neh. 9:25; Jer. 5:28).

C. Adjective.

The adjective *šāmēn*, which occurs 10 times, in Ugaritic cognates means: "fat" (Ezek. 34:16); "rich" in the sense of fattening (Gen. 49:20—the first occurrence); "fertile" (Num. 13:20); "robust or muscular" (Judg. 3:29); and "large" (Hab. 1:16).

TO OVERLAY, SPY

A. Verb.

ṣāpāh (צָפָה, 6822), "to overlay, spy, keep watch." This word is found in both biblical and modern Hebrew, and some scholars suggest that it exists in Ugaritic. *Ṣāpāh* is found in the text of the Hebrew Bible about 37 times. It occurs for the first time in the Old Testament in the so-called Mizpah Benediction: "The Lord watch between me and thee ... " (Gen. 31:49). The meaning in this context is "to watch" with a purpose, that of seeing that the covenant between Laban and Jacob was kept. Thus, the statement by Laban is more of a threat than a benediction. Similarly, when God's "eyes behold the nations" (Ps. 66:7), it is much more than a casual look. Perhaps in most uses, the connotation of "to spy" would be the most accurate.

B. Participle.

The participial form of *ṣāpāh* is often used as a noun, *ṣōpeh*, meaning "watchman," or one whose task it is "to keep close watch" (2 Sam. 13:34).

TO OVERTAKE

nāśag (נָשַׂג, 5381), "to reach, overtake, attain." This verb is found in both ancient and modern Hebrew. It is used in the text of the Hebrew Old Testament approximately 50 times, the first time being Gen. 31:25: "Then Laban overtook Jacob." Often it is used in connection with the verb, "to pursue, follow," as in Gen. 44:4: " ... follow after the men; and when thou dost overtake them. ... " *Nāśag* is sometimes used in the figurative sense to describe "being overtaken" by something undesirable or unwanted, such as war (Hos. 10:9), the sword (Jer. 42:16), or curses (Deut. 28:15, 45). Fortunately, blessings may "overtake" those who are obedient (Deut. 28:2). *Nāśag* may mean "to attain to" something, "to come into contact" with it: "The sword of him that layeth at him [Leviathan] ... " (Job 41:26). Used figuratively, "The ransomed of the Lord ... shall obtain joy and gladness ... " (Isa. 35:10). Jacob complained: " ... the days of the years of my pilgrimage ... have not attained unto the days of the years of the life of my fathers ... " (Gen. 47:9).

P

PALM (OF HAND)

A. Noun.

kap (כַּף, 3709), "palm (of hand)." Cognates of this noun are attested in Akkadian, Ugaritic, Aramaic, Arabic, Ethiopic, and Egyptian. It appears about 193 times in biblical Hebrew and at all periods.

Basically, *kap* represents the "palm," the hollow part of the hand as distinguished from its fingers, thumbs, and back. Thus we read that part of the ritual for cleansing a leper is that a "priest shall take some of the log of oil, and pour it into the palm of his own left hand" (Lev. 14:15).

The word represents the entire inside of the hand when it is cupped, or the "hollow of the hand." God told Moses: "... While my glory passeth by, that I will put thee in a clift of the rock, and will cover thee with my hand while I pass by" (Exod. 33:22; cf. Ps. 139:5).

This word means fist, specifically the inside of a fist. The woman of Zarephath told Elijah: "... I have not a cake, but a handful of meal in a barrel, and a little oil in a cruse ... " (1 Kings 17:12). This was, indeed, a very small amount of flour—enough for only one little biscuit.

Kap also refers to the flat of the hand, including the fingers and the thumb. These are what one claps together in joy and applause: "And he brought forth the king's son, and put the crown upon him, and gave him the testimony; and they made him king, and anointed him; and they clapped their hands, and said, God save the king" (2 Kings 11:12). Clapping the hands may also be an expression of scorn and contempt (Num. 24:10). The flat of the hands may be raised heavenward in prayer to symbolize one's longing to receive. Moses told Pharaoh: "As soon as I am gone out of the city, I will spread abroad my hands unto the Lord ... " (Exod. 9:29).

This word can suggest the inside part of a hand grasp as distinguished from the hand as a whole: "And the Lord said unto Moses, Put forth thine hand, and take it by the tail. And he put forth his hand, and caught it, and it became a rod in his hand" (Exod. 4:4). A mutual hand grasp may signify entrance into a pledge (Prov. 6:1). To take one's life (*nepeš*) into one's own hands is to put oneself into danger (Judg. 12:3).

In many passages *kap* is synonymous with the entire hand. Jacob tells Laban that "God

hath seen ... the labor of my hands ... " (Gen. 31:42). Perhaps the same nuance occurs in passages such as Gen. 20:5: "... In the integrity of my heart and innocency of my hands have I done this."

The word may be used symbolically and figuratively meaning "power." Gideon complained to the Angel of the Lord that "now the Lord hath forsaken us, and delivered us into the hands [the power] of the Midianites" (Judg. 6:13). Israel was not literally in the Midianites' hands but was dominated by them and under their control.

Once the word represents animal paws: "And whatsoever goeth upon his paws, among all manner of beasts that go on all four, those are unclean unto you ... " (Lev. 11:27).

In many passages *kap* signifies the sole of the foot, the hollow part. This meaning appears in Gen. 8:9 (first biblical appearance): "But the dove found no rest for the sole of her foot ... " (cf. Josh. 3:13 where the word is used of the sole of a human foot).

Various hollow, bending, or beaten objects are represented by *kap*. First, it is used of a thigh joint: "And when he [the Angel of the Lord] saw that he prevailed not against him [Jacob], he touched the hollow of his thigh; and the hollow of Jacob's thigh was out of joint, as he wrestled with him" (Gen. 32:25). Second, a certain shaped pan or vessel is called a *kap:* "And thou shalt make the dishes thereof, and spoons thereof, and covers thereof, and bowls thereof, to cover withal: of pure gold shalt thou make them" (Exod. 25:29). Third, the word is used of the hollow of a sling: "... And the souls of thine enemies, them shall he sling out, as out of the middle of a sling" (1 Sam. 25:29). Next, the huge hand-shaped branches of palm trees are represented by the word: "And ye shall take you on the first day the boughs of goodly trees, branches of palm trees, and the boughs of thick trees ... " (Lev. 23:40). Finally, in Song of Sol. 5:5 this word represents the bent piece of metal or wood which forms a door handle.

B. Verb.

kāpap (כָּפַף, 3721), "to bend, bow down." This word appears 5 times in biblical poetry and has cognates in Akkadian and Arabic. The verb occurs in Isa. 58:5: "... is it to bow down his head as a bulrush, and to spread sackcloth and ashes under him?"

PART

A. Particle.

bad (בַּד, 905), "part; portion; limbs; piece of cloth; pole; shoot; alone; by themselves; only; apart from; besides; aside from." This word occurs about 219 times and in all periods of biblical Hebrew.

First, *bad* means a "part or portion" of something. In Exod. 30:34 it refers to the portion or amount of spices mixed together to make incense for the worship of God. In Job 18:13 the word represents the members or parts of the wicked (cf. Job 41:12—"limbs" of a crocodile).

Second, the word means a piece of cloth: "And thou shalt make them linen breeches to cover their nakedness..." (Exod. 28:42—first occurrence of this nuance). This word is always used of a priestly garment or at least of a garment worn by one who appears before God or His altar.

Third, *bad* can mean a long piece of wood or woody material. The ark, altars, and table of the Bread of the Presence were carried by staves passed through rings attached to these articles: "And thou shalt put the staves into the rings by the sides of the ark, that the ark may be borne with them" (Exod. 25:14—first occurrence of this nuance). In Ezek. 19:14 *bad* is used of the "shoots" or limbs of a vine; "And fire is gone out of a rod of her branches..." (cf. Ezek. 17:6). The gates of a city are *badîm* (Job 17:16).

Fourth, in most of its appearances (152 times) this word is preceded by the preposition *lᵉ*. This use means "alone" (89 times): "And the Lord God said, It is not good that the man should be alone; I will make him a help meet for him" (Gen. 2:18—first occurrence of the word). In a second nuance the phrase identifies a unit by itself, a single unit: "And thou shalt couple five curtains by themselves, and six curtains by themselves..." (Exod. 26:9). Twice the word is used as an adverb of limitation meaning "only": "Lo, this only have I found, that God hath made man upright; but they have sought out many inventions" (Eccl. 7:29). When followed by the preposition *min* (or *ʿal*) the word functions as an adverb meaning "apart from" or "besides": "And the children of Israel journeyed from Rameses to Succoth, about six hundred thousand on foot that were men, beside children" (Exod. 12:37). In Num. 29:39 the translation "besides" is appropriate: "These things ye shall do unto the Lord in your set feasts, beside your vows, and your freewill offerings...." In 33 passages the word is preceded by the preposition *min* but still means "besides."

B. Verb.

bādad (בָּדַד, 909), "to be isolated, be alone." This verb has an Arabic cognate. One of its 3 appearances is in Ps. 102:7: "I watch, and am as a sparrow alone upon the housetop."

TO PASS ON, PASS AWAY

ḥālap (חָלַף, 2498), "to pass on, pass away, change, overstep, transgress." Common to both biblical and modern Hebrew, this term appears approximately 30 times in the Hebrew Old Testament. When used in the simple active form, *ḥālap* occurs only in poetry (except for 1 Sam. 10:3), and it has the meaning of "to pass on, through." The word is typically used in narrative or prose with the meaning of "to change." With this meaning *ḥālap* first occurs in the Old Testament in Gen. 31:7: "... Your father hath deceived me, and changed my wages ten times..." (cf. Gen. 31:41). *Ḥālap* expresses the "sweeping on" of a flood (Isa. 8:8), of a whirlwind (Isa. 21:1), and of God Himself (Job 9:11). The word has the meaning of "to pass away or to vanish," with reference to days (Job 9:26), the rain (Song of Sol. 2:11), and idols (Isa. 2:18). Not only wages, but garments are "changed" (Gen. 35:2; Ps. 102:26). "To change" is "to renew" strength (Isa. 40:31; 41:1); a tree appears "to be renewed" when it sprouts again (Job 14:7).

TO PASS OVER

A. Verb.

ʿābar (עָבַר, 5674), "to pass away, pass over." This verb occurs in all Semitic languages and at all periods of those languages, including biblical Hebrew and Aramaic. The Bible attests about 550 uses of this verb in Hebrew.

The verb refers primarily to spatial movement, to "moving over, through, or away from." This basic meaning can be used of "going over or through" a particular location to get to the other side, as when Jacob "crossed over" the Euphrates to escape Laban (Gen. 31:21). Another specific use of this general meaning is to pass through something; Ps. 8:8 speaks of whatever "passes through" the sea as being under Adam's control. *ʿĀbar* can also merely mean "to go as far as"—Amos tells his audience not to "cross over" to Beer-sheba (Amos 5:5). "To go as far as" an individual is to overtake him (2 Sam. 18:23). Abram "passed through" Canaan as far as Mamre; he did not go out of the land (cf. Gen. 12:6). The word can also be used of "passing by" something; Abraham begged the three men not "to pass by" him but to stop and refresh themselves (Gen. 18:3). *'Abar* is sometimes used of "passing over" a law, order, or covenant as if it were not binding. When the people decided to enter Palestine against the command of God, Moses said, "Wherefore now do ye transgress the commandment of the Lord?" (Num. 14:41).

This verb first occurs in Gen. 8:1 where it means "pass over on top of." God caused the wind "to pass over" the flood waters and to carry them away.

The word can also mean "to pass away," to cease to be, as in Gen. 50:4 where the days of mourning over Jacob "were past."

A number of technical phrases where this root has a regular and specialized meaning appear. For example, one who "passes over" the sea is a seafarer or sailor (Isa. 23:2—a similar technical usage appears in Akkadian). *'Abar* is used in business affairs with silver or money in the sense of reckoning money according to the "going" (passing) rate (Gen. 23:16ff.). In Song of Sol. 5:5 (RSV) the verb is used to mean "flow" as what a liquid does ("flowing" or "liquid" myrrh). The phrase "pass over to be numbered" is a phrase meaning to move from one status to another (to move into the ranks of the militia) in Exod. 30:13–14.

The intensive stem of *'ābar* is used in two special senses: of "overlaying" with precious metals (1 Kings 6:21) and of the ox's act of making a cow pregnant (Job 21:10). The verb also has special meanings in the causative stem: "to devote" the firstborn to the Lord (Exod. 13:12); "to offer" a child by burning him in fire (Deut. 18:10); "to make" a sound "come forth" (Lev. 25:9); "to sovereignly transfer" a kingdom or cause it to pass over to another's leadership (2 Sam. 3:10); "to put away or cause to cease" (1 Kings 15:12); and "to turn" something "away" (Ps. 119:37).

B. Nouns.

'ibrî (עִבְרִי, 5680), "Hebrew." The origin and meaning of this word, which appears 34 times, is much debated. The word is an early generic term for a variety of Semitic peoples and is somewhat akin to our word *barbarian*. So Abram is identified as a "Hebrew" (Gen. 14:13). This ethnic term indicates family origin whereas the term "sons of Israel" is a political and religious term. Unquestionably in the ancient Near East "Hebrew" was applied to a far larger group than the Israelites. The word occurs in Ugaritic, Egyptian, and Babylonian writings describing a diverse mixture of nomadic wanderers or at least those who appear to have at one time been nomadic. Sometimes the word

seems to be a term of derision. Such usage recalls 1 Sam. 29:3, where the Philistine leaders asked Achish, "What do these Hebrews here?" There is considerable debate about identifying Hebrew with the well-known Habiru (Semitic warlords) who occupied Egypt in the first half of the second millennium B.C.

Several other nouns are derived from the verb *'ābar*. *'Eber*, which occurs 89 times, refers to the "side" (1 Sam. 14:1) or "edge" (Exod. 28:26) of something. When speaking of rivers or seas, *'ēber* means the "edge or side opposite the speaker" or "the other side" (Josh. 2:10). *Ma'bārāh*, which appears 8 times, means "ford" (Josh. 2:7) and "ravine" or "passage" (1 Sam. 14:4). *Ma'ăbār* appears 3 times to mean: "sweep" (of a staff, Isa. 30:32); "ford" (Gen. 32:22); and "ravine" or "passage" (1 Sam. 13:23). *'Ăbārāh*, which occurs twice, means "crossing or ford" (2 Sam. 19:18, RSV).

PEACE

A. Nouns.

šālôm (שָׁלוֹם, 7965), "peace; completeness; welfare; health." The root is a common Semitic root with the meaning "peace" in Akkadian, Ugaritic, Phoenician, Aramaic, Syriac, Arabic, and Ethiopic.

Šālôm is a very important term in the Old Testament and has maintained its place in Mishnaic, rabbinic, and modern Hebrew. In Israel today, people greet the newcomer and each other with the words *māh šlomka*, ("what is your peace," "how are you doing,") and they ask about the "peace" ("well-being") of one's family.

The use of *šālôm* is frequent (237 times) and varied in its semantic range. The first two occurrences in Genesis already indicate the changes in meaning: "And thou shalt go to thy fathers in peace [*šālôm* in the sense of "in tranquility," "at ease," "unconcerned"]; thou shalt be buried in a good old age" (Gen. 15:15); and "that thou wilt do us no hurt, as we have not touched thee, and as we have done unto thee nothing but good, and have sent thee away in peace [*šālôm* with the meaning of "unharmed" and "unhurt"] . . . " (Gen. 26:29). Yet, both uses are essentially the same, as they express the root meaning of "to be whole." The phrase *îš šlômî* ("friend of my peace") in Ps. 41:9, "Yea, mine own familiar friend [literally, "friend of my peace"], in whom I trusted, which did eat of my bread, hath lifted up his heel against me" (cf. Jer. 20:10), signifies a state in which one can feel at ease, comfortable with someone. The relationship is one of harmony and wholeness, which is the opposite of the state of strife and war: "I am for peace: but when I speak, they are for war" (Ps. 120:7). *Šālôm* as a harmonious state of the soul and mind encourages the development of the faculties and powers. The state of being at ease is experienced both externally and internally. In Hebrew it finds expression in the phrase *bešālôm* ("in peace"): "I will both lay me down in peace [*bešālôm*], and sleep: for thou, Lord, only makest me dwell in safety" (Ps. 4:8).

Closely associated to the above is the meaning "welfare," specifically personal "welfare" or "health." This meaning is found in questions: "And Joab said to Amasa, Art thou in health, my brother? And Joab took Amasa by the beard with the right hand to kiss him" (2 Sam. 20:9), or in the prepositional phrase *lešālôm* with the verb "to ask": "And he asked them of their welfare, and said, Is your father well, the old man of whom ye spake? Is he yet alive?" (Gen. 43:27).

Šālôm also signifies "peace," indicative of a prosperous relationship between two or more parties. *Šālôm* in this sense finds expression in speech: "Their tongue is as an arrow shot out; it speaketh deceit: one speaketh peaceably [literally, "in peace"] to his neighbor with his mouth, but in heart he layeth his wait" (Jer. 9:8); in diplomacy: "Howbeit Sisera fled away on his feet to the tent of Jael the wife of Heber the Kenite: for there was peace between Jabin the king of Hazor and the house of Heber the Kenite" (Judg. 4:17); and in warfare: " . . . If it make thee answer of peace, and open unto thee, then it shall be, that all the people that is found therein shall be tributaries unto thee, and they shall serve thee" (Deut. 20:11).

Isaiah prophesied concerning the "prince of peace" (Isa. 9:6), whose kingdom was to introduce a government of "peace" (Isa. 9:7). Ezekiel spoke about the new covenant as one of "peace": "Moreover I will make a covenant of peace with them; it shall be an everlasting covenant with them: and I will place them, and multiply them, and will set my sanctuary in the midst of them for evermore" (Ezek. 37:26). Psalm 122 is one of those great psalms in celebration of and in prayer for the "peace of Jerusalem": "Pray for the peace of Jerusalem: they shall prosper that love thee" (Ps. 122:6). In benedictions God's peace was granted to His people: " . . . Peace shall be upon Israel" (Ps. 125:5).

The Septuagint gives the following translations: *eirene* ("peace; welfare; health"); *eirenikos* ("peaceable; peaceful"); *soteria* ("deliverance;

preservation; salvation"); and *hugiainein* ("be in good health; sound").

Another related noun is *šelem*, which occurs 87 times, and means "peace offering": "And he sent young men of the children of Israel, which offered burnt offerings, and sacrificed peace offerings of oxen unto the Lord" (Exod. 24:5).

B. Verbs.

šālēm (שָׁלֵם, 7999), "to be complete, be sound." This verb occurs 103 times. The word signifies "to be complete" in 1 Kings 9:25: "So he finished the house."

Another verb, *šālam*, means "to make peace": "When a man's ways please the Lord, he maketh even his enemies to be at peace with him" (Prov. 16:7).

C. Adjective.

šālēm (שָׁלֵם, 8003), "complete; perfect." This word is found in Gen. 15:16 with the meaning of not quite "complete": "But in the fourth generation they shall come hither again: for the iniquity of the Amorites is not yet full." The word means "perfect" in Deut. 25:15.

PEOPLE

'am (עַם, 5971), "people; relative." This common Semitic word has cognates in Akkadian, Amorite, Phoenician, Ugaritic, Punic, Moabite, Aramaic, and Arabic. This word occurs about 1,868 times and at all periods of biblical Hebrew.

The word bears subjective and personal overtones. First, *'am* represents a familial relationship. In Ruth 3:11 the word means "male kinsmen" with special emphasis on the paternal relationship: "And now, my daughter, fear not; I will do to thee all that thou requirest: for all the city of my people doth know that thou art a virtuous woman." Here the word is a collective noun insofar as it occurs in the singular; indeed, it is almost an abstract noun. In the plural the word refers to all the individuals who are related to a person through his father: "But he shall not defile himself, being a chief man among his people, to profane himself" (Lev. 21:4). This emphasis of the word is related to the meaning of its cognates in Ugaritic (clan), Arabic (uncle on one's father's side), and Nabataean (uncle on one's father's side). The word is quite often combined with divine names and titles in people's names (theophoric names) where God is set forth as the God of a particular tribe, clan, or family—for example, Jekameam (God has raised up a clan or family, 1 Chron. 23:19) and Jokneam (God has created a clan or family, Josh. 12:22).

Second, *'am* may signify those relatives (including women and children) who are grouped together locally whether or not they permanently inhabit a given location: "Then Jacob was greatly afraid and distressed: and he divided the people that was with him, and the flocks, and herds, and the camels, into two bands" (Gen. 32:7).

Third, this word may refer to the whole of a nation formed and united primarily by their descent from a common ancestor. Such a group has strong blood ties and social interrelationships and interactions. Often they live and work together in a society in a common location. This is the significance of the word in its first biblical appearance: "And the Lord said, Behold, the people is one, and they have all one language..." (Gen. 11:6). Hence, in this usage 'am refers not simply to male relatives but to men, women, and children.

'Am may also include those who enter by religious adoption and marriage. The people of Israel initially were the descendants of Jacob (Israel) and their families: "And he said unto his people [Egyptians], Behold, the people of the children of Israel are more and mightier than we" (Exod. 1:9). Later the basic unity in a common covenant relationship with God becomes the unifying factor underlying 'am. When they left Egypt, the people of Israel were joined by many others: "And a mixed multitude went up also with them; and flocks, and herds, even very much cattle" (Exod. 12:38). Such individuals and their families were taken into Israel before they observed the Passover: "And when a stranger shall sojourn with thee, and will keep the passover to the Lord, let all his males be circumcised, and then let him come near and keep it; and he shall be as one that is born in the land..." (Exod. 12:48). There is another mention of this group (perhaps) in Num. 11:4: "And the mixed multitude that was among them fell a lusting: and the children of Israel also wept again, and said...."

After that, however, we read of them no more. By the time of the conquest we read only of the "people" ('am) of Israel entering the land of Canaan and inheriting it (Judg. 5:11). Passages such as Deut. 32:9 clearly focus on this covenantal relationship as the basis of unity: "For the Lord's portion is his people; Jacob is the lot of his inheritance." This sense certainly emerges in the concept "to be cut off from one's people": "And the uncircumcised man child whose flesh of his foreskin is not circumcised, that soul shall be cut off from his people; he hath broken my covenant" (Gen. 17:14).

'Am can mean all those physical ancestors who lived previously and are now dead. So Abraham was gathered to his people: "Then Abraham gave up the ghost, and died in a good old age, an old man, and full of years; and was gathered to his people" (Gen. 25:8). There might be covenantal overtones here in the sense that Abraham was gathered to all those who were true believers. Jesus argued that such texts taught the reality of life after death (Matt. 22:32).

'Am can represent the individuals who together form a familial (and covenantal) group within a larger group: "Zebulun and Naphtali were a people that jeoparded their lives unto the death in the high places of the field [on the battlefield]" (Judg. 5:18). Some scholars have suggested that the reference here is to a fighting unit with the idea of blood relationship in the background. One must never forget, however, that among nomadic and semi-nomadic tribes there is no distinction between the concepts "militia" and "kinsmen": "And the Lord said unto Joshua, Fear not, neither be thou dismayed: take all the people of war with thee, and arise..." (Josh. 8:1). Compare Josh. 8:5 where 'am by itself means fighting unit: "And I, and all the people that are with me, will approach unto the city..." (cf. Gen. 32:7).

'Am may signify the inhabitants of a city regardless of their familial or covenantal relationship; it is a territorial or political term: "And Boaz said unto the elders, and unto all the people, Ye are witnesses..." (Ruth 4:9).

This noun can be used of those who are privileged. In the phrase "people of the land" 'am may signify those who have feudal rights, or those who may own land and are especially protected under the law: "And Abraham stood up, and bowed himself to the people of the land, even to the children of Heth" (Gen. 23:7). This sense of a full citizen appears when the phrase is used of Israel, too (cf. 2 Kings 11:14ff.). In some contexts this phrase excludes those of high office such as the king, his ministers, and priests; "For, behold, I have made thee this day a defenced city, and an iron pillar, and brazen walls against the whole land, against the kings of Judah, against the princes thereof, against the priests thereof, and against the people of the land" (Jer. 1:18). In Lev. 4:27 this same phrase signifies the entire worshiping community of Israel: "And if any one of the common people [people of the land] sin through ignorance...." The sense of privileged people with a proper relationship to and unique knowledge of God appears in Job 12:2: "No doubt but ye are the people, and wisdom shall die with you." Could it be that in Isa. 42:5 all mankind are conceived to be the privileged recipients of divine revelation and blessing:

"Thus saith God the Lord, he that created the heavens, and stretched them out; he that spread forth the earth, and that which cometh out of it; he that giveth breath unto the people upon it, and spirit to them that walk therein."

Finally, sometimes 'am used of an entire nation has political and territorial overtones. As such it may be paralleled to the Hebrew word with such overtones (gôy): "For thou art a holy people unto the Lord thy God, and the Lord hath chosen thee to be a peculiar people unto himself, above all the nations that are upon the earth" (Deut. 14:2; cf. Exod. 19:5–6).

PERADVENTURE

'ûlay (אוּלַי, 194), "peradventure; perhaps; suppose; if; less." The 43 occurrences of this word appear in every period of biblical Hebrew.

This word meaning "peradventure or perhaps" usually expresses a hope: "Behold now, the Lord hath restrained me from bearing: I pray thee, go in unto my maid; it may be that I may obtain children by her" (Gen. 16:2—the first occurrence). Elsewhere 'ûlay expresses fear or doubt: "Peradventure the woman will not be willing to follow me unto this land; must I needs bring thy son again unto the land from whence thou camest?" (Gen. 24:5).

If followed by another clause the word almost functions to introduce a protasis: "Peradventure there be fifty righteous within the city: wilt thou also destroy..." (Gen. 18:24).

In Num. 22:33 the word has a different force: "And the ass saw me, and turned from me these three times: unless she had turned from me, surely now also I had slain thee, and saved her alive."

PERFECT

A. Adjectives.

tāmîm (תָּמִים, 8549), "perfect; blameless; sincerity; entire; whole; complete; full." The 91 occurrences of this word are scattered throughout biblical literature with 51 of them in passages dealing with cultic offerings.

Tāmîm means "complete," in the sense of the entire or whole thing: "And he shall offer of the sacrifice of the peace offering an offering made by fire unto the Lord; the fat thereof, and the whole rump, it shall he take off hard by the backbone..." (Lev. 3:9). The sun stood still for the "whole" day while Joshua fought the Gibeonites (Josh. 10:13). In Lev. 23:15 God commands that there be seven "complete" sabbaths after the first fruit feast plus fifty days and then that the new grain offering be presented. A house within a walled city must be purchased back within a "full" year if it is to remain the permanent property of the seller (Lev. 25:30).

This word may mean "intact," or not cut up into pieces: "Behold, when it was whole, it [a piece of wood] was meet for no work..." (Ezek. 15:5).

Tāmîm may mean incontestable or free from objection. In Deut. 32:4 the word modifies God's work: "His work is perfect." The people of God are to avoid the idolatrous practices of the Canaanites. They are to "be perfect with the Lord thy God" (Deut. 18:13). Used in such contexts the word means the one so described externally meets all the requirements of God's law (cf. Ps. 18:23). This word modifies the victim to be offered to God (51 times). It means that the victim has no blemish (Lev. 22:18–21) as "blemish" is defined by God: "Ye shall offer at your own will a male without blemish, of the beeves, of the sheep, or of the goats" (Lev. 22:19).

In several contexts the word has a wider background. When one is described by it, there is nothing in his outward activities or internal disposition that is odious to God; "... Noah was a just man and perfect in his generations, and Noah walked with God" (Gen. 6:9). This word describes his entire relationship to God. In Judg. 9:16, where tāmîm describes a relationship between men it is clear that more than mere external activity is meant: "Now therefore, if ye have done truly and sincerely [literally, "in a sincere manner"], in that ye have made Abimelech king...." This extended connotation of this nuance is also evidenced when one compares Gen. 17:1 with Rom. 4 where Paul argues that Abraham fulfilled God's condition but that he did so only through faith.

Another adjective, tām, appears 15 times. With a cognate in Ugaritic the word means "complete or perfect" (Song of Sol. 5:2, RSV), "sound or wholesome" (Gen. 25:27), and "complete, morally innocent, having integrity" (Job 1:8).

B. Noun.

tōm (תֹּם, 8537), "completeness." This noun, which occurs 25 times, signifies "completeness" in the following senses: fullness (Job 21:23), innocency or simplicity (2 Sam. 15:11), integrity (Gen. 20:5).

C. Verb.

tāmam (תָּמַם, 8552), "to be complete, be finished, be consumed, be without blame." This verb, which appears 64 times, has cognates in Aramaic, Syriac, and Arabic. The word means "to be finished or completed" in Gen. 47:18: "When that year was ended, they came unto him...."

TO PERISH

A. Verb.

'ābad (אָבַד, 6), "to perish, die, be lost, go astray, go to ruin, succumb, be carried off, fail." The word occurs in all the branches of the Semitic languages including biblical Aramaic. Biblical Hebrew attests this verb at every time period and about 120 times.

Basically 'ābad represents the disappearance of someone or something. In its strongest sense the word means "to die or to cease to exist." The Lord warned Israel that disobedience and godlessness would be punished by their removal from the Promised Land and death in a foreign land: "And ye shall perish among the heathen, and the land of your enemies shall eat you up" (Lev. 26:38). This sense may be further heightened by the use of the intensive stem so that the verb comes to mean "utterly destroy." The stem also changes the force of the verb from intransitive to transitive. So God told Israel "to utterly destroy" ("bring to non-existence") the false gods of Canaan: " ... [Utterly] destroy all their pictures and [utterly] destroy all their molten images ... " (Num. 33:52). The force of this command was further heightened when He said: "Ye shall utterly destroy all the places, wherein the nations which ye shall possess served their gods ... and destroy the names of them out of that place" (Deut. 12:2–3). This intensified sense is used of the destruction of peoples (armies), too; as for Pharaoh's army, "the Lord hath destroyed them unto this day" (Deut. 11:4).

A somewhat different emphasis of 'ābad is "to go to ruin" or "to be ruined." After the second plague Pharaoh's counsellors told him to grant Israel's request to leave because the nation was in ruins: " ... knowest thou not yet that Egypt is destroyed [ruined]?" (Exod. 10:7—the first biblical occurrence). In a similar sense Moab is said "to be ruined" or laid waste: "Woe to thee, Moab! Thou art undone [NASB, "ruined"], O people of Chemosh ... We have shot at them; Heshbon is perished even unto Dibon, and we have laid them waste even unto Nophah ... " (Num. 21:29–30).

Closely related to the immediately preceding emphasis is that of "to succumb." This use of 'ābad focuses on the process rather than the conclusion. The sons of Israel spoke to Moses about the disastrous effects of everyone drawing near to God. They needed some mediators (priests) who could focus on keeping ritualistically prepared so they would not die when they approached God. They used the verb, therefore, in the sense of the nation gradually perishing, or "succumbing" to death: "Behold, we die, we perish, we all perish. Whosoever cometh any thing near unto the tabernacle of the Lord shall die: shall we be consumed with dying?" (Num. 17:12–13). God responds by establishing the priesthood so "that there be no wrath any more upon the children of Israel" (Num. 18:5).

'Ābad can also speak of being carried off to death or destruction by some means. The leaders of the rebellion against the Aaronic priesthood (Korah, Dathan, and Abiram) and their families were swallowed up by the ground: " ... and the earth closed upon them: and they perished from among the congregation" (Num. 16:33). This same nuance appears when God says the people will "perish" from off the land if they do not keep the covenant: " ... Ye shall soon utterly perish from off the land whereunto ye go over Jordan to possess it; ye shall not prolong your days upon it, but shall utterly be destroyed" (Deut. 4:26). As a nation they will be destroyed as far as the land is concerned.

The verb may mean to disappear but not be destroyed, in other words "to be lost." God instructs Israel concerning lost possessions: "In like manner shalt thou do with his ass; and so shalt thou do with his raiment; and with all lost things of thy brother's, which he hath lost, and thou hast found, shalt thou do likewise: thou mayest not hide thyself" (Deut. 22:3). Israel is called "lost sheep" whose "shepherds have caused them to go astray" (Jer. 50:6).

Another nuance of the verb is "to go astray" in the sense of wandering. At the dedication of the first fruits Israel is to recognize God's rights to the land, that He is the landowner and they are the temporary tenants, by confessing "a Syrian ready to perish was my father" (Deut. 26:5; NASB, "my father was a wandering Aramean").

Finally, 'ābad can be applied to human qualities which are lessening or have lessened: "For they are a nation void of counsel, neither is there any understanding in them" (Deut. 32:28). The word can also be used of the failure of human wisdom as in Ps. 146:4: as for men "his breath goeth forth, he returneth to his earth; in that very day his thoughts perish."

B. Nouns.

There are four nouns related to the verb. 'Ăbēdāh, which is found 4 times, refers to a "thing which has been lost" (Exod. 22:9). The noun 'ăbaddôn occurs 6 times and means "the place of destruction" (Job 26:6). 'Abdān occurs once with the meaning "destruction" (Esth. 9:5). A variant spelling 'ābdān also occurs twice with the meaning "destruction" (Esth. 8:6; 9:5).

PESTILENCE

deber (דֶּבֶר, 1698), "pestilence." The meaning of the cognate word varies in other Semitic languages from the Hebrew. In Ugaritic, *dbr* probably signifies "death." The Arabic word *dabrat* means "misfortune," similar to the Akkadian *dibiru*, "misfortune." The word occurs fewer than 60 times in the Old Testament, and mainly in the prophets Jeremiah and Ezekiel.

The meaning of *deber* is best denoted by the English word "pestilence" or "plague." A country might be quickly reduced in population by the "plague" (cf. 2 Sam. 24:13ff.). The nature of the "plague" (bubonic or other) is often difficult to determine from the contexts, as the details of medical interest are not given or are scanty. In the prophetical writings, the "plague" occurs with other disasters: famine, flood, and the sword: "When they fast, I will not hear their cry; and when they offer burnt offering and an oblation, I will not accept them: but I will consume them by the sword, and by the famine, and by the pestilence" (Jer. 14:12).

The Septuagint gives the following translation: *thanatos* ("death").

PILLAR

'ayil (אַיִל, 352), "pillar." This word appears 22 times and only once outside Ezek. 40–41: "And for the entering of the oracle he made doors of olive tree: the lintel [pillar] and side posts were a fifth part of the wall" (1 Kings 6:31).

maṣṣēbāh (מַצֵּבָה, 4676), "pillar; monument; sacred stone." This word is derived from the verb *nāṣab*, and it is found about 35 times.

This word refers to a "pillar" as a personal memorial in 2 Sam. 18:18: "Now Absalom in his lifetime had taken and reared up for himself a pillar... and he called the pillar after his own name: and it is called unto this day, Absalom's place." In Gen. 28:18 the "monument" is a memorial of the Lord's appearance. *Maṣṣēbāh* is used in connection with the altar built by Moses in Exod. 24:4, and it refers to "sacred stones or pillars."

PIOUS

ḥāsîd (חָסִיד, 2623), "one who is pious, godly." Psalms contains 25 of the 32 appearances of this word.

Basically, *ḥāsîd* means one who practices *hesed* ("loving-kindness"), so it is to be translated the "pious" or "godly one." The word's first biblical occurrence is in Deut. 33:8 where it represents a human being: "Give to Levi thy Thummim, and thy Urim to thy godly one" (RSV). The word appears in Ps. 32:6: "For this shall every one that is godly pray unto thee in a time when thou mayest be found...." The word is applied to God in Ps. 145:17: "The Lord is righteous in all his ways, and holy in all his works."

This noun is derived from the noun *hesed.*

PIT

be'ēr (בְּאֵר, 875), "pit; well." Cognates of this noun appear in Ugaritic, Akkadian, Arabic, Phoenician, Aramaic, and Ethiopic. This word appears 37 times in the Bible with no occurrences in the Old Testament prophetic books.

Be'ēr means a "well" in which there may be water. (By itself the word does not always infer the presence of water.) The word refers to the "pit" itself whether dug or natural: "And Abraham reproved Abimelech because of a well of water, which Abimelech's servants had violently taken away" (Gen. 21:25). Such a "well" may have a narrow enough mouth that it can be blocked with a stone which a single strong man could move (Gen. 29:2, 10). In the desert country of the ancient Near East a "well" was an important place and its water the source of deep satisfaction for the thirsty. This concept pictures the role of a wife for a faithful husband (Prov. 5:15).

A "pit" may contain something other than water. In its first biblical appearance *be'ēr* is used of tar pits: "And the vale of Siddim was full of slimepits..." (Gen. 14:10). A "pit" may contain nothing as does the "pit" which becomes one's grave (Ps. 55:23, "pit of the grave"). In some passages the word was to represent more than a depository for the body but a place where one exists after death (Ps. 69:15). Since Babylonian mythology knows of such a place with gates that shut over the deceased, it is not at all unreasonable to see such a place alluded to (minus the erroneous ideas of the pagans) in the Bible.

TO PLANT

nāṭa' (נָטַע, 5193), "to plant." Common in both ancient and modern Hebrew, this word is also found in ancient Ugaritic. It occurs approximately 60 times in the Hebrew Old Testament. The word is used for the first time in the text in Gen. 2:8: "And the Lord God planted a garden eastward in Eden...." The regular word for planting trees and vineyards, *nāṭa'* is used figuratively of planting people: "Yet I had planted thee [Judah] a noble vine..." (Jer. 2:21). This use is a close parallel to the famous "Song of the Vineyard" (Isa. 5:1–10) where Israel and Judah are called God's "pleasant planting" (Isa.

5:7, RSV). *Nāṭaʿ* is used in Isa. 17:10 in an unusual description of idolatry: " . . . Therefore shalt thou plant pleasant plants, and shalt set it with strange slips." The NEB (much like the JB) translates more specifically: "Plant them, if you will, your gardens in honor of Adonis" (Adonis was the god of vegetation). "To plant" sometimes has the meaning of "to establish." Thus, God promises in the latter days, "I will plant them upon their land" (Amos 9:15).

TO PLEAD

A. Verb.

rîb (רִיב, 7378), "to plead, strive, conduct a legal case, make a charge." Found in both biblical and modern Hebrew, this term occurs as a verb some 70 times. It appears in the text for the first time in Gen. 26:20: "And the herdmen of Gerar did strive with Isaac's herdmen. . . ." Such "striving" with words is found frequently in the biblical text (Gen. 31:36; Exod. 17:2). Sometimes contentious words lead to bodily struggle and injury: "And if men strive together, and one smite another . . . " (Exod. 21:18). The prophets use *rîb* frequently to indicate that God has an indictment, a legal case, against Israel: "The Lord standeth up to plead, and standeth to judge the people" (Isa. 3:13). In one of his visions, Amos noted: " . . . the Lord God called to contend by fire . . . " (Amos 7:4, KJV; RSV, "calling for a judgment"). Micah 6 is a classic example of such a legal case against Judah, calling on the people "to plead" their case (6:1) and progressively showing how only God has a valid case (6:8).

B. Noun.

rîb (רִיב, 7379), "strife; dispute." This word appears as a noun 60 times. The word appears twice in Mic. 6:2: "Hear ye, O mountains, the Lord's controversy, and ye strong foundations of the earth: for the Lord hath a controversy with his people, and he will plead with Israel."

PLEASURE

A. Noun.

ḥēpeṣ (חֵפֶץ, 2656), "pleasure; delight; desire; request; affair; thing." None of the 39 occurrences of this word appear before First Samuel. All its occurrences are scattered through the rest of biblical literature.

This word often means "pleasure" or "delight": "Hath the Lord as great delight in burnt offerings and sacrifices, as in obeying the voice of the Lord?" (1 Sam. 15:22—the first occurrence). Thus "the preacher [writer of Ecclesiastes] sought to find out acceptable [*ḥēpeṣ*] words: and that which was written was upright, even words of truth" (Eccl. 12:10), words that

were both true and aesthetically pleasing. A good wife works with "hands of delight," or hands which delight in her work because of her love for her family; "she seeketh wool, and flax, and worketh willingly [in delight] with her hands" (Prov. 31:13).

Ḥēpeṣ can mean not simply what one takes pleasure in or what gives someone delight but one's wish or desire: "Although my house be not so with God; yet he hath made with me an everlasting covenant, ordered in all things, and sure: for this is all my salvation, and all my desire, although he make it not to grow" (2 Sam. 23:5). "To do one's desire" is to grant a request (1 Kings 5:8). "Stones of desire" are precious stones (Isa. 54:12).

Third, *ḥēpeṣ* sometimes represents one's affairs as that in which one takes delight: " . . . There is . . . a time to every purpose [literally, delight] under the heaven" (Eccl. 3:1). In Isa. 58:13 the first occurrence of this word means "pleasure" or "delight," while the last occurrence indicates an affair or matter in which one delights: "If thou turn away thy foot from the sabbath, from doing thy pleasure on my holy day; and call the sabbath a delight, the holy of the Lord, honorable; and shalt honor him, not doing thine own ways, nor finding thine own pleasure, nor speaking thine own words."

Finally, in one passage this word means "affair" in the sense of a "thing" or "situation": "If thou seest the oppression of the poor, and violent perverting of judgment and justice in a province, marvel not at the matter [NASB, "sight"] . . . ". (Eccl. 5:8).

B. Verb.

ḥāpēṣ (חָפֵץ, 2654), "to take pleasure in, take care of, desire, delight in, have delight in." This verb, which occurs 72 times in biblical Hebrew, has cognates in Arabic, Phoenician, Syriac, and Arabic. *Ḥāpēṣ* means "to delight in" in 2 Sam. 15:26: "But if he thus say, I have no delight in thee; behold, here am I, let him do to me as seemeth good unto him."

C. Adjective.

ḥāpēṣ (חָפֵץ, 2655), "delighting in, having pleasure in." This adjective appears 12 times in biblical Hebrew. The word is found in Ps. 35:27: "Let the Lord be magnified, which hath pleasure in the prosperity of his servant."

TO PLOW

A. Verb.

ḥāraš (חָרַשׁ, 2790), "to plow, engrave, work in metals." This word occurs in ancient Ugaritic, as well as in modern Hebrew where it has the primary sense of "to plow." It is found approximately 50 times in the Hebrew Old Testament. A fitting word for the agricultural nature of Israelite culture, *hāraš* is frequently used of "plowing" a field, usually with animals such as oxen (1 Kings 19:19). The imagery of cutting up or tearing up a field with a plow easily lent itself to the figurative use of the word to mean mistreatment by others: "The plowers plowed upon my back: they made long their furrows" (Ps. 129:3). The word is used to express the plotting of evil against a friend in Prov. 3:29: "Devise not evil against thy neighbor, seeing he dwelleth securely by thee [literally, "do not plow evil"]."

The use of *hāraš* in the sense of "working or engraving" metals is not used in the Old Testament as much as it might have been if Israel had been as given to such craftsmanship as her neighbors, or perhaps because of the commandment against images (Exod. 20:4). The word is used in 1 Kings 7:14: " . . . His father was a man of Tyre, a worker in brass [literally, "a man who works in brass"]. . . ." The first occurrence of *hāraš* is in Gen. 4:22 where it is used of the "artificer in brass and iron." The figurative use of "engraving" is vividly seen in the expression describing the extent of Israel's sin: "The sin of Judah is written with a pen of iron, and with the point of a diamond: it is graven upon the table of their heart . . ." (Jer. 17:1).

An updating or correction of the KJV is called for in 1 Sam. 8:12 where *hāraš* is translated by the old English term, "to ear the ground"!

B. Noun.

hārāš (חָרָשׁ, 2796), "engraver; artificer." The prophets denounced the craftsmanship of these workers in metals when they made images (Isa. 40:20; Hos. 8:6). A more positive approach to the word is conveyed in 1 Chron. 29:5: "The gold for things of gold . . . and for all manner of work to be made by the hands of artificers. And who then is willing to consecrate his service this day unto the Lord?"

TO POLLUTE

hālal (חָלַל, 2490), "to pollute, defile, profane, begin." This word is used more than 225 times in the Old Testament. As a verb, *hālal* is used in what seem to be two quite different ways. In one sense, the word means "to pollute" or "to profane." In the second usage the word has the sense of "to begin."

The most frequent use of this Hebrew root is in the sense of "to pollute, defile." This may be a ritual defilement, such as that resulting from contact with a dead body (Lev. 21:4), or the ceremonial profaning of the sacred altar by the use of tools in order to shape the stones (Exod.

20:25). Holy places may be profaned (Ezek. 7:24); the name of God (Ezek. 20:9) and even God Himself (Ezek. 22:26) may be profaned. The word is often used to describe the defilement which results from illicit sexual acts, such as harlotry (Lev. 21:9) or violation of one's father's bed (Gen. 49:4—the first occurrence).

In more than 50 instances, this root is used in the sense of "to begin." Perhaps the most important of such uses is found in Gen. 4:26. There it is stated that after the birth of Seth, who was born to Adam and Eve after the murder of Abel by Cain, "men began to call upon the name of the Lord" (RSV). The Septuagint translates it something like this: "he hoped [trusted] to call on the name of the Lord God." The Jerusalem Bible says: "This man was the first to invoke the name of Yahweh." One must ask whether the writer meant to say that it was not until the birth of Enosh, the son of Seth, that people "began" to call on the name of the Lord altogether, or whether he meant that this was the first time the name Yahweh was used. In view of the accounts in Gen. 1–3, neither of these seems likely. Perhaps the writer is simply saying that in contrast to the apparent non-God-fearing attitude expressed by Cain, the generation beginning with Seth and his son Enosh was known for its God-fearing way of life. Perhaps, in view of the passive intensive verb form used here, the meaning is something like this: "Then it was begun again to call on the name of the Lord."

POOR (PERSON), WEAK (PERSON)

A. Nouns.

ʿānî (עָנִי, 6041), "poor; weak; afflicted; humble." This word, which also appears in early Aramaic and post-biblical Hebrew, occurs in biblical Hebrew about 76 times and in all periods.

This noun is frequently used in synonymous parallelism with *ʾebyôn* ("needy") and/or *dal* ("poor"). It differs from both in emphasizing some kind of disability or distress. A hired servant as one who is in a lower (oppressive) social and material condition is described both as an *ʾebyôn* and *ʿānî*: "Thou shalt not oppress a hired servant that is poor and needy, whether he be of thy brethren, or of thy strangers that are in thy land within thy gates: At his day thou shalt give him his hire, neither shall the sun go down upon it; for he is poor, and setteth his heart upon it: lest he cry against thee unto the Lord, and it be sin unto thee" (Deut. 24:14–15). If wrongly oppressed, he can call on God for defense. Financially, the *'ānî* lives from day to day and is socially defenseless, being subject to oppression. In its first biblical occurrence the *'ānî* is guaranteed (if men obey God's law) his outer garment for warmth at night even though that garment might be held as collateral during the day: "If thou lend money to any of my people that is poor by thee, thou shall not be to him as a usurer, neither shalt thou lay upon him usury" (Exod. 22:25). The godly protect and deliver the "afflicted" (Isa. 10:2; Ezek. 18:17), while the ungodly take advantage of them, increasing their oppressed condition (Isa. 58:7). The king is especially charged to protect the *'ānî*: "Open thy mouth, judge righteously, and plead the cause of the poor and needy" (Prov. 31:9).

'Ānî can refer to one who is physically oppressed: "Therefore hear now this, thou afflicted, and drunken, but not with wine" (Isa. 51:21).

Physical oppression is sometimes related to spiritual oppression as in Ps. 22:24: "For he hath not despised nor abhorred the affliction of the afflicted; neither hath he hid his face from him...." Outward affliction frequently leads to inner spiritual affliction and results in an outcry to God: "Turn thee unto me, and have mercy upon me; for I am desolate and afflicted" (Ps. 25:16). Even apart from outward affliction, the pious are frequently described as the "afflicted" or "poor" for whom God provides: "Thy congregation hath dwelt therein: thou, O God, hast prepared of thy goodness for the poor" (Ps. 68:10). In such cases spiritual poverty and want are clearly in view.

Sometimes the word means "humble" or "lowly," as it does in Zech. 9:9, where it describes the Messiah: "Behold, thy King cometh unto thee: he is just, and having salvation; lowly, and riding upon an ass..." (cf. Ps. 18:27; Prov. 3:34; Isa. 66:2).

Related to *'ānî* is the noun *'onî*, "affliction." It appears about 36 times and in all periods of biblical Hebrew. *'Onî* represents the state of pain and/or punishment resulting from affliction. In Deut. 16:3 the shewbread is termed the bread of "affliction" because it is a physical reminder of sin, the cause of "affliction" (Ps. 25:18), the hardship involved in sin (especially the Egyptian bondage), and divine deliverance from sin (Ps. 119:50).

'Ānî is also related to the word *'ānāwāh*, "humility, gentleness." This word occurs only 5 times, setting forth the two characteristics gained from affliction. Applied to God, it represents His submission to His own nature (Ps. 45:4).

dal (דַּל, 1800), "one who is low, poor, reduced, helpless, weak." This noun also appears in Ugaritic. It occurs in biblical Hebrew about 47 times and in all periods.

Dal is related to, but differs from, *'ānî* (which suggests affliction of some kind), *'ebyôn* (which emphasizes need), and *rāš* (which suggests destitution). The *dallîm* constituted the middle class of Israel—those who were physically deprived (in the ancient world the majority of people were poor). For example, the *dallîm* may be viewed as the opposite of the rich (Exod. 30:15; cf. Ruth 3:10; Prov. 10:15).

In addition, the word may connote social poverty or lowliness. As such, *dal* describes those who are the counterparts of the great: "Ye shall do no unrighteousness in judgment: thou shalt not respect the person of the poor, nor honor the person of the mighty: but in righteousness shalt thou judge thy neighbor" (Lev. 19:15; cf. Amos 2:7).

When Gideon challenged the Lord's summoning him to deliver Israel, he emphasized that his clan was too weak to do the job: "And he said unto him, Oh my Lord, wherewith shall I save Israel? behold, my family is poor in Manasseh..." (Judg. 6:15; cf. 2 Sam. 3:1). God commands that society protect the poor, the lowly, and the weak: "Thou shalt not follow a multitude to do evil; neither shalt thou speak in a cause to decline after many to wrest judgment: neither shalt thou countenance a poor man in his cause" (Exod. 23:2–3; cf. Lev. 14:21; Isa. 10:2). He also warns that if men fail to provide justice, He will do so (Isa. 11:4).

A fourth emphasis appears in Gen. 41:19 (the first biblical appearance of the word), where *dal* is contrasted to "healthy" or "fat": "And behold, seven other kine came up after them, poor and very ill-favored and leanfleshed...." Thus, *dal* indicates a physical condition and appearance of sickliness. It is used in this sense to describe Amnon's appearance as he longed for Tamar (2 Sam. 13:4).

Dal is used (very infrequently) of spiritual poverty (in such cases it is sometimes paralleled to *'ebyôn*): "Therefore I said, Surely these are poor; they are foolish: for they know not the way of the Lord, nor the judgment of their God" (Jer. 5:4). Some scholars argue that here the word means "ignorance," and as the context shows, this is ignorance in the knowledge of God's word.

Another noun, *dallāh*, is related to *dal*. *Dallāh*, which appears about 8 times, means "poverty; dishevelled hair." The word appears in 2 Kings 24:14: "...none remained, save the poorest sort of the people of the land," where *dallāh* emphasizes the social lowliness and "poverty" of those people whom it describes. In Song of Sol. 7:5 the word refers to "dishevelled hair" in the sense of something that hangs down.

B. Verbs.

dālal (דָּלַל, 1809), "to be low, hang down." This verb appears only 8 times in the Bible and always in poetical passages. It has cognates or near cognates in Arabic, Ethiopic, Akkadian, and extra-biblical Hebrew. The word appears in Ps. 79:8: "O remember not against us former iniquities: let thy tender mercies speedily prevent us; for we are brought very low."

'ānāh (עָנָה, 6031), "to afflict, oppress, humble." This verb, which also appears in Arabic, occurs about 74 times in biblical Hebrew and in every period. The first occurrence is in Gen. 15:13: "Know of a surety that thy seed shall be a stranger in a land that is not theirs, and shall serve them; and they shall afflict them four hundred years."

C. Adjective.

'ānāw (עָנָו, 6035), "humble; poor; meek." This adjective, which appears about 21 times in biblical Hebrew, is closely related to *'ānî* and derived from the same verb. Sometimes this word is synonymous with *'ānî*. Perhaps this is due to the well-known *waw-yodh* interchange. *'Ānāw* appears almost exclusively in poetical passages and describes the intended outcome of affliction from God, namely "humility." In its first appearance the word depicts the objective condition as well as the subjective stance of Moses. He was entirely dependent on God and saw that he was: "Now the man Moses was very meek, above all the men which were upon the face of the earth" (Num. 12:3).

TO POSSESS

A. Verb.

yāraš (יָרַשׁ, 3423), "to inherit, subdue, take possession, dispossess, impoverish." This word is attested in all Semitic languages except Akkadian, Phoenician, and biblical Aramaic. The word appears in all periods of Hebrew; the Bible attests it about 260 times.

Basically *yāraš* means "to inherit." The verb can connote the state of being designated as an heir. Abram said to God: "Behold, to me thou hast given no [offspring]: and, lo, one born in my house is mine heir [literally, "is the one who is inheriting me"]" (Gen. 15:3—the first biblical occurrence of the word). Whatever Abram had to be passed on to his legal descendants was destined to be given to his servant. Hence his servant was his legally designated heir.

This root can also represent the status of having something as one's permanent possession, as a possession which may be passed on to one's legal descendants. God told Abram: "I am the Lord that brought thee out of Ur of the Chaldees, to give thee this land to inherit it" (Gen. 15:7). *Yāraš* can mean "to take over as a permanent possession": "And if his father have no brethren, then ye shall give his inheritance unto his kinsman that is next to him of his family, and he shall possess it . . ." (Num. 27:11). The verb sometimes means to take something over (in the case of the Promised Land) by conquest as a permanent possession: "The Lord shall make the pestilence cleave unto thee, until he have consumed thee from off the land, whither thou goest to possess it" (Deut. 28:21).

When people are the object, *yāraš* sometimes means "to dispossess" in the sense of taking away their inheritable goods and putting them in such a social position that they cannot hold possessions or inherit permanent possessions: "The Horim also dwelt in Seir beforetime; but the children of Esau succeeded them, when they had destroyed them from before them, and dwelt in their stead . . . " (Deut. 2:12). To cause someone to be dispossessed is "to impoverish" him: "The Lord maketh poor, and maketh rich . . . " (1 Sam. 2:7), the Lord makes one to be without permanent inheritable possessions.

B. Nouns.

Several nouns related to *yāraš* occur infrequently in biblical Hebrew. *Yerēšāh*, which appears twice, means "something given as a permanent possession; to be taken over by conquest" (Num. 24:18). *Yeruššāh* occurs 14 times; it means "to have as a possession" (Deut. 2:5), "to be designated as a possession, to receive as a possession" (Deut. 2:9). The noun *môrāš* means "a place one has as a permanent possession" in its 2 appearances (Isa. 14:23; Obad. 17). *Môrāšāh*, which occurs 9 times, can refer to "a place one has as a permanent possession" (Exod. 6:8), "a thing one has as a permanent possession" (Deut. 33:4), and "people to be dispossessed" (Ezek. 25:4).

Some scholars associate *rešet*, "net," with *yāraš*. Hence, a "net" is conceived as a thing which receives and holds (possesses) something or someone (Job 18:8). Others suggest that *rešet* can also mean "pit" (cf. Ps. 9:15; 35:7–8).

POSSESSION

segullāh (סְגֻלָּה, 5459), "possession." Cognates of this word appear in late Aramaic and Akkadian. This word occurs only 8 times.

Segullāh signifies "property" in the special sense of a private possession one personally acquired and carefully preserves. Six times this word is used of Israel as God's personally acquired (elected, delivered from Egyptian bondage, and formed into what He wanted them to be), carefully preserved, and privately possessed people: "Now therefore, if ye will obey my voice indeed, and keep my covenant, then ye shall be a peculiar treasure [NASB, "possession"] unto me above all people: for all the earth is mine" (Exod. 19:5—first occurrence).

TO POUR, FLOW

yāṣaq (יָצַק, 3332), "to pour, pour out, cast, flow." Commonly used throughout the history of the Hebrew language, this word occurs in ancient Ugaritic with the same nuances as in the Old Testament. *Yāṣaq* occurs in the Hebrew Bible just over 50 times. The word is used first in Gen. 28:18, where it is said that after Jacob had slept at Bethel with his head resting on a stone, he "poured oil upon the top of it." He again "poured" oil on a stone pillar at Bethel while on his return trip home twenty years later (Gen. 35:14). The idea expressed in these two instances and others (Lev. 8:12; 21:10) is that of anointing with oil; it is not the ordinary term for "to anoint." (The regular term for "to anoint" is *māšah*, which gives us the word "messiah.")

Many things may "be poured out," such as oil in sacrifice (Lev. 2:1), water for washing purposes (2 Kings 3:11), and pottage for eating (2 Kings 4:41). This verb is used to express the idea of "pouring out" or "casting" molten metals (Exod. 25:12; 26:37; 1 Kings 7:46). The idea of "pouring upon or infusing" someone is found in Ps. 41:8: "A wicked thing is poured out upon him" (NASB). The context seems to imply the infusion of a sickness, as interpreted by the JB: "This sickness is fatal that has overtaken him."

šāpak (שָׁפַךְ, 8210), "to pour out, pour, shed." A common Semitic word, this verb is found in both ancient Akkadian and Ugaritic, as well as throughout Hebrew. *Šāpak* occurs just over 100 times in the text of the Hebrew Bible. In its first use in the Old Testament, the word is part of the general principle concerning the taking of human life: "Whoso sheddeth man's blood, by man shall his blood be shed . . ." (Gen. 9:6). While it is frequently used in this sense of "shedding" or "pouring out" blood, the word is commonly used of the "pouring out" of the contents of a vessel, such as water (Exod. 4:9; 1 Sam. 7:6), plaster or dust (Lev. 14:41), and drink offerings to false gods (Isa. 57:6).

In its figurative use, *šāpak* indicates the "pouring out" of God's wrath (Hos. 5:10), of contempt (Job 12:21), of wickedness (Jer.

14:16), and of the Spirit of God (Ezek. 39:29). The psalmist describes his helpless condition in this picturesque phrase: "I am poured out like water" (Ps. 22:14, KJV; NEB, "My strength drains away like water"; JB, "I am like water draining away").

POWER

kōah (כֹּח, 3581), "strength; power; force; ability." This Hebrew word is used in biblical, rabbinic, and modern Hebrew with little change in meaning. The root is uncertain in Hebrew, but the verb is found in Arabic (*wakaha*, "batter down," and *kwḥ*, "defeat"). *Kōah*, which occurs 124 times, is a poetic word as it is used most frequently in the poetic and prophetical literature.

The basic meaning of *kōah* is an ability to do something. Samson's "strength" lay in his hair (Judg. 16:5), and we must keep in mind that his "strength" had been demonstrated against the Philistines. Nations and kings exert their "powers" (Josh. 17:17; Dan. 8:24). It is even possible to say that a field has *kōah*, as it does or does not have vital "powers" to produce and harvest: "When thou tillest the ground, it shall not henceforth yield unto thee her strength [i.e., crops] . . ." (Gen. 4:12—the first occurrence). In the Old Testament it is recognized that by eating one gains "strength" (1 Sam. 28:22), whereas one loses one's "abilities" in fasting (1 Sam. 28:20); "And he arose, and did eat and drink, and went in the strength of that meat forty days and forty nights unto Horeb the mount of God" (1 Kings 19:8).

The above definition of *kōah* fits well in the description of Daniel and his friends: "Children in whom was no blemish, but well-favored, and skillful in all wisdom, and cunning in knowledge, and understanding science, and such as had ability [*kōah*] in them to stand in the king's palace, and whom they might teach the learning and the tongue of the Chaldeans" (Dan. 1:4). The "ability" is here not physical but mental. They were talented in having the intellectual acumen of learning the skills of the Babylonians and thus training for being counselors to the king. The internal fortitude was best demonstrated by the difficulties and frustrations of life. A strong man withstood hard times. The proverb bears out this important teaching: "If thou faint in the day of adversity, thy strength is small" (Prov. 24:10).

A special sense of *kōah* is the meaning "property." The results of native "abilities," the development of special gifts, and the manifestation of one's "strength" led often to prosperity and riches. Those who returned from the Exile gave willingly out of their riches (*kōaḥ*) to the building fund of the temple (Ezra 2:69). A proverb warns against adultery, because one's "strength," or one's wealth, may be taken by others: "Lest strangers be filled with thy wealth [*kōaḥ*]; and thy labors be in the house of a stranger" (Prov. 5:10).

In the Old Testament, God had demonstrated His "strength" to Israel. The language of God's "strength" is highly metaphorical. God's right hand gloriously manifests His "power" (Exod. 15:6). His voice is loud: "The voice of the Lord is powerful; the voice of the Lord is full of majesty" (Ps. 29:4). In His "power," He delivered Israel from Egypt (Exod. 32:11) and brought them through the Red Sea (Exod. 15:6; cf. Num. 14:13). Even as He advances the rights of the poor and needy (Isa. 50:2), He brought the Israelites as a needy people into the Promised Land with His "power": "He hath showed his people the power of his works, that he may give them the heritage of the heathen" (Ps. 111:6). He delights in helping His people; however, the Lord does not tolerate self-sufficiency on man's part. Isaiah rebuked the king of Assyria for his arrogance in claiming to have been successful in his conquests (10:12–14), and he remarked that the axe (Assyria) should not boast over the one who chops (God) with it (v. 15). Likewise God had warned His people against pride in taking the land of Canaan: "And thou say in thine heart, My power [*kōaḥ*] and the might of mine hand hath gotten me this wealth. But thou shalt remember the Lord thy God: for it is he that giveth thee power [*kōaḥ*] to get wealth, that he may establish his covenant which he sware unto thy fathers, as it is this day" (Deut. 8:17–18). The believer must learn to depend upon God and trust in Him: "This is the word of the Lord unto Zerubbabel, saying, Not by might, nor by power, but by my spirit, saith the Lord of hosts" (Zech. 4:6).

The Septuagint gives the following translations: *ischus* ("strength; power; might") and *dunamis* ("power; might; strength; force; ability; capability").

TO PRAISE

A. Verbs.

hālal (הָלַל, 1984), "to praise, celebrate, glory, sing (praise), boast." The meaning "to praise" is actually the meaning of the intensive form of the Hebrew verb *hālal*, which in its simple active form means "to boast." In this latter sense *hālal* is found in its cognate forms in ancient Akkadian, of which Babylonian and Assyrian are dialects. The word is found in Ugaritic in the sense of "shouting," and perhaps "jubila-

tion." Found more than 160 times in the Old Testament, *hālal* is used for the first time in Gen. 12:15, where it is noted that because of Sarah's great beauty, the princes of Pharaoh "praised" (KJV, "commended") her to Pharaoh.

While *hālal* is often used simply to indicate "praise" of people, including the king (2 Chron. 23:12) or the beauty of Absalom (2 Sam. 14:25), the word is usually used in reference to the "praise" of God. Indeed, not only all living things but all created things, including the sun and moon, are called upon "to praise" God (Ps. 148:2–5, 13; 150:1). Typically, such "praise" is called for and expressed in the sanctuary, especially in times of special festivals (Isa. 62:9).

The Hebrew name for the Book of Psalms is simply the equivalent for the word "praises" and is a bit more appropriate than "Psalms," which comes from the Greek and has to do with the accompaniment of singing with a stringed instrument of some sort. It is little wonder that the Book of Psalms contains more than half the occurrences of *hālal* in its various forms. Psalms 113–118 are traditionally referred to as the "Hallel Psalms," because they have to do with praise to God for deliverance from Egyptian bondage under Moses. Because of this, they are an important part of the traditional Passover service. There is no reason to doubt that these were the hymns sung by Jesus and His disciples on Maundy Thursday when He instituted the Lord's Supper (Matt. 26:30).

The word *hālal* is the source of "Hallelujah," a Hebrew expression of "praise" to God which has been taken over into virtually every language of mankind. The Hebrew "Hallelujah" is generally translated "Praise the Lord!" The Hebrew term is more technically translated "Let us praise Yah," the term "Yah" being a shortened form of "Yahweh," the unique Israelite name for God. The term "Yah" is found in the KJV rendering of Ps. 68:4, reflecting the Hebrew text; however, the Jerusalem Bible (JB) translates it with "Yahweh." Most versions follow the traditional translation "Lord," a practice begun in Judaism before New Testament times when the Hebrew term for "Lord" was substituted for "Yahweh," although it probably means something like "He who causes to be." The Greek approximation of "Hallelujah" is found 4 times in the New Testament in the form "Alleluia" (Rev. 19:1, 3–4, 6). Christian hymnody certainly would be greatly impoverished if the term "Hallelujah" were suddenly removed from our language of praise.

yādāh (יָדָה, 3034), "to give thanks, laud, praise." A common Hebrew word in all its periods, this verb is an important word in the language of worship. *Yādāh* is found nearly 120 times in the Hebrew Bible, the first time being in the story of the birth of Judah, Jacob's son who was born to Leah: "And she conceived again and bore a son, and said, This time I will praise the Lord; therefore she called his name Judah" (Gen. 29:35, RSV).

As is to be expected, this word is found most frequently in the Book of Psalms (some 70 times). As an expression of thanks or praise, it is a natural part of ritual or public worship as well as personal praise to God (Ps. 30:9, 12; 35:18). Thanks often are directed to the name of the Lord (Ps. 106:47; 122:4).

The variation in translation may be seen in 1 Kings 8:33: "confess" thy name (KJV, NEB, NASB); "acknowledge" (RSV); "praise" (JB, NAB).

B. Nouns.

tᵉhillāh (תְּהִלָּה, 8416), "glory; praise; song of praise; praiseworthy deeds." *Tᵉhillāh* occurs 57 times and in all periods of biblical Hebrew.

First, this word denotes a quality or attribute of some person or thing, "glory or praiseworthiness": "He is thy praise, and he is thy God, that hath done for thee these great and terrible things, which thine eyes have seen" (Deut. 10:21). Israel is God's "glory" when she exists in a divinely exalted and blessed state: "And give him no rest, till he establish, and till he make Jerusalem a praise in the earth" (Isa. 62:7; cf. Jer. 13:11).

Second, in some cases *tᵉhillāh* represents the words or song by which God is publicly lauded, or by which His "glory" is publicly declared: "My praise [the Messiah is speaking here] shall be of thee in the great congregation. . ." (Ps. 22:25). Ps. 22:22 is even clearer: "I will declare thy name unto my brethren: in the midst of the congregation will I praise thee."

In a third nuance *tᵉhillāh* is a technical-musical term for a song (*šīr*) which exalts or praises God: "David's psalm of praise" (heading for Ps. 145; v. 1 in the Hebrew). Perhaps Neh. 11:17 refers to a choirmaster or one who conducts such singing of "praises": "And Mattaniah . . . , the son of Asaph, was the principal to begin the thanksgiving in prayer [who at the beginning was the leader of praise at prayer]. . . ."

Finally, *tᵉhillāh* may represent deeds which are worthy of "praise," or deeds for which the doer deserves "praise and glory." This meaning is in the word's first biblical appearance: "Who is like unto thee, O Lord, among the gods? Who is like thee, glorious in holiness, fearful in praises [in praiseworthy deeds], doing wonders [miracles]?" (Exod. 15:11).

Two other related nouns are *mahălāl* and *hillûlîm*. *Mahălāl* occurs once (Prov. 27:21) and

denotes the degree of "praise" or its lack. *Hillûlîm*, which occurs twice, means "festal jubilation" in the fourth year at harvest time (Lev. 19:24, RSV; Judg. 9:27, NASB).

tôdāh (תּוֹדָה, 8426), "thanksgiving." This important noun form, found some 30 times in the Old Testament, is used there in the sense of "thanksgiving." The word is preserved in modern Hebrew as the regular word for "thanks." In the Hebrew text *tôdāh* is used to indicate "thanksgiving" in songs of worship (Ps. 26:7; 42:4). Sometimes the word is used to refer to the thanksgiving choir or procession (Neh. 12:31, 38). One of the peace offerings, or "sacrings," was designated the thanksgiving offering (Lev. 7:12).

TO PRAY

A. Verb.

pālal (פָּלַל, 6419), "to pray, intervene, mediate, judge." Found in both biblical and modern Hebrew, this word occurs 84 times in the Hebrew Old Testament. The word is used 4 times in the intensive verbal form; the remaining 80 times are found in the reflexive or reciprocal form, in which the action generally points back to the subject. In the intensive form *pālal* expresses the idea of "to mediate, to come between two parties," always between human beings. Thus, "if a man sins against a man, God will mediate for him. . ." (1 Sam. 2:25, RSV). "To mediate" requires "making a judgment," as in Ezek. 16:52: "Thou also, which hast judged thy sisters. . . . " In the remaining 2 references in which the intensive form is used, *pālal* expresses "making a judgment" in Gen. 48:11 and "coming between" in Ps. 106:30.

The first occurrence of *pālal* in the Old Testament is in Gen. 20:7, where the reflexive or reciprocal form of the verb expresses the idea of "interceding for, prayer in behalf of": " . . . He shall pray for thee. . . . " Such intercessory praying is frequent in the Old Testament: Moses "prays" for the people's deliverance from the fiery serpents (Num. 21:7); he "prays" for Aaron (Deut. 9:20); and Samuel "intercedes" continually for Israel (1 Sam. 12:23). Prayer is directed not only toward Yahweh but toward pagan idols as well (Isa. 44:17). Sometimes prayer is made to Yahweh that He would act against an enemy: "That which thou hast prayed to me against Sennacherib king of Assyria I have heard" (2 Kings 19:20).

Just why this verb form is used to express the act of praying is not completely clear. Since this verb form points back to the subject, in a reflexive sense, perhaps it emphasizes the part which the person praying has in his prayers. Also, since the verb form can have a reciprocal meaning between subject and object, it may emphasize the fact that prayer is basically communication, which always has to be two-way in order to be real.

B. Noun.

tᵉpillāh (תְּפִלָּה, 8605), "prayer." This word, which appears 77 times in biblical Hebrew, is the most general Hebrew word for "prayer." It first appears in 1 Kings 8:28: "Yet have thou respect unto the prayer of thy servant, and to his supplication. . . ." In the eschaton God's house will be a house of "prayer" for all peoples (Isa. 56:7); it will be to this house that all nations will come to worship God. The word can mean both a non-liturgical, non-poetical "prayer" and a liturgical, poetical "prayer." In the latter special meaning *tᵉpillāh* is used as a psalm title in 5 psalms and as the title of Habakkuk's prayer (Hab. 3:1). In these uses *tᵉpillāh* means a prayer set to music and sung in the formal worship service. In Ps. 72:20 the word describes all the psalms or "prayers" of Psalms 1–72, only one of which is specifically called a "prayer" (17:1).

PRECIOUS

A. Adjective.

yāqār (יָקָר, 3368), "precious; rare; excellent; weighty; noble." Although none of the 35 biblical appearances of this word occurs before First Samuel, they are scattered throughout the rest of the Bible.

First, *yāqār* means "precious" in the sense of being rare and valuable: "And he took their king's crown from off his head, the weight whereof was a talent of gold with the precious stones: and it was set on David's head" (2 Sam. 12:30). The emphasis is on the nuance "rare" in 1 Sam. 3:1: "And the word of the Lord was precious in those days; there was no open vision."

Second, the word can focus on the value of a thing: "How excellent is thy loving-kindness, O God!" (Ps. 36:7).

Third, this word means "weighty" or "noble": "A little foolishness is weightier than wisdom and honor" (Eccl. 10:1, NASB); like dead flies which make perfume stink, so a little foolishness spoils wisdom and honor—it is worth more in a negative sense (cf. Lam. 4:2).

B. Verb.

yāqar (יָקַר, 3365), "to be difficult, be valued from, be valued or honored, be precious." This verb, which occurs 11 times in biblical Hebrew, has cognates in Ugaritic, Arabic, and Akkadian. The word means "to be precious" in 1 Sam. 26:21: "Then said Saul, I have sinned: return,

my son David: for I will no more do thee harm, because my soul was precious in thine eyes this day. . . ."

C. Noun.

yᵉqār (יְקָר, 3366), "precious thing; value; price; splendor; honor." This noun, which appears 16 times in biblical Hebrew, is Aramaic in form. The word signifies "value or price" (Zech. 11:13), "splendor" (Esth. 1:4), and "honor" (Esth. 8:16). In Jer. 20:5 the word refers to "precious things": "Moreover I will deliver all the strength of this city, and all the labors thereof, and all the precious things thereof. . . ."

TO PREPARE

A. Verb.

kûn (כּוּן, 3559), "to be established, be readied, be prepared, be certain, be admissible." This verb occurs in nearly every Semitic language (not in biblical Aramaic). *Kûn* appears in the Bible about 220 times and in all periods of Hebrew.

This root used concretely connotes being firmly established, being firmly anchored and being firm. The first meaning is applied to a roof which is "firmly established" on pillars. So Samson said to the lad who was leading him: "Suffer me that I may feel the pillars whereupon the house standeth, that I may lean upon them" (Judg. 16:26). In a similar sense the inhabited earth "is firmly established or anchored"; it is immovable: " . . . The world also is stablished, that it cannot be moved" (Ps. 93:1). In Ps. 75:3 the image shifts to the earth "firmly established" upon pillars. In Ps. 65:6 the divine establishing of the mountains is synonymous with divine creating. The verb also means "to be firm": "And you grew up and became tall and arrived at [the age for fine ornaments]; your breasts were formed, and your hair had grown" (Ezek. 16:7, RSV).

Used abstractly, *kûn* can refer to a concept as "established," or "fixed" so as to be unchanging and unchangeable: "And for that the dream was doubled unto Pharaoh twice; it is because the thing is established by God, and God will shortly bring it to pass" (Gen. 41:32—the first occurrence of the word). In somewhat the same sense one can speak of the light of day "being firmly established," or having fully arrived: "But the path of the just is as the shining light, that shineth more and more unto the perfect day" (Prov. 4:18). *Kûn* can be used of the "establishing" of one's descendants, of seeing them prosperous (Job 21:8).

Something can be "fixed" in the sense of "being prepared or completed": "Now all the work of Solomon was prepared unto the day of the foundation of the house of the Lord. . ." (2 Chron. 8:16).

An "established" thing can be something that is enduring. In 1 Sam. 20:31 Saul tells Jonathan: "For as long as the son of Jesse liveth upon the ground, thou shalt not be established, nor thy kingdom." Truthful lips (what they say) "shall be established," or will endure forever (Prov. 12:19). One's plans "will endure" (be established) if he commits his works to the Lord (Prov. 16:3).

Kûn can also mean "to be established" in the sense of "being ready." So Josiah told the people "to prepare" themselves for the Passover (2 Chron. 35:4). This same sense appears in Exod. 19:11: "And be ready against the third day: for the third day the Lord will come down in the sight of all the people upon mount Sinai." A somewhat different nuance appears in Job 18:12; Bildad says that wherever godlessness breaks out, there is judgment: " . . . Destruction shall be ready at his side." That is, calamity is "fixed or prepared" so that it exists potentially even before godlessness breaks out.

Something "fixed" or "established" can "be certain": "Then shalt thou inquire, and make search, and ask diligently; and, behold, if it be truth, and the thing certain. . ." (Deut. 13:14). In a somewhat different nuance the thing can be trustworthy or true. The psalmist says of the wicked that "there is no faithfulness in their mouth" (Ps. 5:9). A further development of this emphasis is that a matter "may be admissible"—so Moses said to Pharaoh: "It is not meet so to do; for we shall sacrifice the abomination of the Egyptians to the Lord our God. . ." (Exod. 8:26).

When one "fixes" an arrow on the bow, he takes aim or "prepares" to shoot his bow (cf. Ps. 7:12).

B. Nouns.

mᵉkônāh (מְכוֹנָה, 4350), "proper place; base." This noun occurs 25 times; it means "proper place" in Ezra 3:3: "And they set the altar upon his bases. . . ." The word refers to "bases" in 1 Kings 7:27.

Two other nouns are related to the verb *kûn. Mākôn*, which appears 17 times, means "an established place or site" (Exod. 15:17). *Tᵉkûnāh*, which makes 3 appearances, means "fixed place" as in Job 23:3 or "fixed matter" as in Ezek. 43:11: " . . . Show them the form of the house, and the fashion [*tᵉkûnāh*] thereof. . . ."

C. Adjective.

kēn (כֵּן, 3651), "right; veritable; honest." This adjective occurs 24 times in biblical Hebrew. The word implies "honest or righteous" in Gen.

42:11: "We are all one man's sons; we are true men, thy servants are no spies." The word means not "right" in 2 Kings 17:9.

PRIDE

A. Verb.

gā'āh (גָּאָה, 1342), "to be proud, be exalted." This verb appears 7 times in biblical Hebrew. The word appears in Exod. 15:1 in the sense of "to be exalted": "I will sing to the Lord, for He is highly exalted [KJV, "he hath triumphed"]; The horse and its rider He has hurled into the sea" (NASB).

B. Nouns.

gā'ôn (גָּאוֹן, 1347), "pride." This root occurs only in northwest Semitic languages, as in Ugaritic: *gan*, "pride." This noun is a poetic word, which is found only in poetic books, the prophets (12 times in Isaiah), Moses' song (Exod. 15:7), and Leviticus (26:19). In rabbinic Hebrew, *gā'ôn* signifies a man of great learning. A *gā'ôn* was the head of the rabbinic academies of Susa and Pumpedita in Babylonia. Saadiah Gaon was one of the most outstanding.

In a positive sense *gā'ôn*, like the verb, signifies "excellence" or "majesty." God's "majesty" was expressed in Israel's deliverance through the Red Sea (Exod. 15:7). Israel as the redeemed people, then, is considered to be an expression of God's "majesty": "He shall choose our inheritance for us, the excellency of Jacob whom he loved" (Ps. 47:4). The meaning of *gā'ôn* is here close to that of *kābôd*, "glory."

Related to "majesty" is the word *gā'ôn* attributed to nature as something mighty, luxuriant, rich, and thick. The poets use the word to refer to the proud waves (Job 38:11) or the thick shrubbery by the Jordan; cf. "If thou hast run with the footmen, and they have wearied thee, then how canst thou contend with horses? and if in the land of peace, wherein thou trustedst, they wearied thee, then how wilt thou do in the swelling [literally, "majesty"] of Jordan?" (Jer. 12:5; cf. 49:19; 50:44).

The majority of the uses of *gā'ôn* are negative in that they connote human "pride" as an antonym for humility (Prov. 16:18). Proverbs puts *gā'ôn* together with arrogance, evil behavior, and perverse speech. In her independence from the Lord, Israel as a majestic nation, having been set apart by a majestic God, had turned aside and claimed its excellence as a prerogative earned by herself. The new attitude of insolence was not tolerated by God: "The Lord God hath sworn by himself, saith the Lord the God of hosts, I abhor the excellency of Jacob, and hate his palaces: therefore will I deliver up the city with all that is therein" (Amos 6:8).

The Septuagint translations are: *hubris* ("insolence; arrogance") and *huperephania* ("arrogance; haughtiness; pride").

Some other nouns are related to *gā'ôn. Gē'āh* occurs once to mean "pride" (Prov. 8:13). The noun *ga'ăwāh*, which is found 19 times, also means "pride": "And all the people shall know, even Ephraim and the inhabitant of Samaria, that say in the pride and stoutness of heart. . ." (Isa. 9:9). *Gē'ût* appears 8 times and refers to "majesty": "Let favor be showed to the wicked, yet will he not learn righteousness: in the land of uprightness will he deal unjustly, and will not behold the majesty of the Lord" (Isa. 26:10).

C. Adjectives.

The adjective *gē'*, which is thought to be a scribal error for *gē'eh*, appears only once as "proud" (Isa. 16:6). *Gē'eh* also means "proud" in its 8 occurrences, once in Isa. 2:12: "For the day of the Lord of hosts shall be upon every one that is proud and lofty. . . ."

Ga'ăyôn, which means "pride," appears once in biblical Hebrew (Ps. 123:4).

PRIEST; PRIESTHOOD

A. Noun.

kōhēn (כֹּהֵן, 3548), "priest." This word is found 741 times in the Old Testament. More than one-third of the references to the "priests" are found in the Pentateuch. Leviticus, which has about 185 references, is called the "manual of the priests."

The term *kōhēn* was used to refer not only to the Hebrew priesthood but to Egyptian "priests" (Gen. 41:50; 46:20; 47:26), the Philistine "priests" (1 Sam. 6:2), the "priests" of Dagon (1 Sam. 5:5), "priests" of Baal (2 Kings 10:19), "priests" of Chemosh (Jer. 48:7), and "priests" of the Baalim and Asherim (2 Chron. 34:5).

Joseph married the daughter of the "priest" of On (Gen. 41:45), and she bore him two sons, Ephraim and Manasseh (Gen. 46:20). Joseph did not purchase the land of the "priests" of Egypt, because the Egyptian "priests" received regular allotments from Pharaoh (Gen. 47:22).

A "priest" is an authorized minister of deity who officiates at the altar and in other cultic rites. A "priest" performs sacrificial, ritualistic, and mediatorial duties; he represents the people before God. By contrast, a "prophet" is an intermediary between God and the people.

The Jewish priestly office was established by the Lord in the days of Moses. But prior to the institution of the high priesthood and the priestly office, we read of the priesthood of Melchizedek (Gen. 14:18) and of Midianite "priests" (Exod. 2:16; 3:1; 18:1). In Exod. 19:24, other "priests" are mentioned: these may have been either Midianite "priests" or "priests" in Israel prior to the official establishment of the Levitical priesthood. No doubt priestly functions were performed in pre-Mosaic times by the head of the family, such as Noah, Abraham, and Job. After the Flood, for example, Noah built an altar to the Lord (Gen. 8:20–21). At Bethel, Mamre, and Moriah, Abraham built altars. In Gen. 22:12–13, we read that Abraham was willing to offer his son as a sacrifice. Job offered up sacrifices for his sinning children (Job 1:5).

The priesthood constituted one of the central characteristics of Old Testament religion. A passage showing the importance of the priesthood is Num. 16:5–7: "And he spake unto Korah and unto all his company, saying, Even tomorrow the Lord will show who are his, and who is holy; and will cause him to come near unto him: even him whom he hath chosen will he cause to come near unto him. This do; Take you censers, Korah, and all his company; And put fire therein, and put incense in them before the Lord . . . the man whom the Lord doth choose, he shall be holy. . . ."

God established Moses, Aaron, and Aaron's sons Nadab, Abihu, Eleazar, and Ithamar as "priests" in Israel (Exod. 28:1, 41; 29:9, 29–30). Because Nadab and Abihu were killed when they "offered strange fire before the Lord," the priesthood was limited to the lines of Eleazar and Ithamar (Lev. 10:1–2; Num. 3:4; 1 Chron. 24:2).

However, not all individuals born in the family of Aaron could serve as "priest." Certain physical deformities excluded a man from that perfection of holiness which a "priest" should manifest before Yahweh (Lev. 21:17–23). A "priest" who was ceremonially unclean was not permitted to perform his priestly duties. Lev. 21:1–15 gives a list of ceremonial prohibitions that forbade a "priest" from carrying out his duties.

Exod. 29:1–37 and Lev. 8 describe the seven-day consecration ceremony of Aaron and his sons. Both the high priest (*kōhēn haggadōl*) and his sons were washed with water (Exod. 29:4). Then Aaron the high priest dressed in holy garments with a breastplate over his heart, and there was placed on his head a holy crown—the mitre or turban (Exod. 29:5–6). After that, Aaron was anointed with oil on his head (Exod. 29:7; cf. Ps. 133:2). Finally, the blood of a sacrificial offering was applied to Aaron and his sons (Exod. 29:20–21). The consecrating bloodmark was placed upon the tip of the right ear, on the thumb of the right hand, and on the great toe of the right foot.

The duties of the priesthood were very clearly defined by the Mosaic law. These duties were assumed on the eighth day of the service of consecration (Lev. 9:1). The Lord told Aaron: "Therefore thou and thy sons with thee shall keep your priest's office for every thing of the altar, and within the veil; and ye shall serve . . ." (Num. 18:7).

The "priests" were to act as teachers of the Law (Lev. 10:10–11; Deut. 33:10; 2 Chron. 5:3; 17:7–9; Ezek. 44:23; Mal. 2:6–9), a duty they did not always carry out (Mic. 3:11; Mal. 2:8). In certain areas of health and jurisprudence, "priests" served as limited revelators of God's will. For example, it was the duty of the "priest" to discern the existence of leprosy and to perform the rites of cleansing (Lev. 13–14). Priests determined punishments for murder and other civil matters (Deut. 21:5; 2 Chron. 19:8–11).

B. Verb.

kāhan (כָּהַן, 3547), "to act as a priest." This verb, which appears 23 times in biblical Hebrew, is derived from the noun *kōhēn*. The verb appears only in the intensive stem. One occurrence is in Exod. 28:1: "And take thou unto thee Aaron thy brother, and his sons with him, from among the children of Israel, that he may minister unto me in the priest's office. . . ."

PRINCE

A. Nouns.

nāśî' (נְשִׂיא, 5387), "prince; chief; leader." This noun appears 129 times in biblical Hebrew. An early occurrence of *nāśî'* is in Gen. 23:6: "Hear us, my lord: thou art a mighty prince among us. . . ." The books of Numbers and Ezekiel use the word most frequently. Elsewhere it rarely occurs.

Though the origin and meaning of *nāśî'* are controversial, it is clearly associated with leadership, both Israelite and non-Israelite. M. Noth proposed the idea that the *nāśî'* was originally a tribal representative or a "deputy, chief." Ishmael was promised to give rise to twelve "princes" (Gen. 17:20; cf. 25:16); the Midianites had "princes" (Num. 25:18), as well as the Amorites (Josh. 13:21), the peoples of the sea (Ezek. 26:16), Kedar (Ezek. 27:21), Egypt (Ezek. 30:13), and Edom (Ezek. 32:29). Also Israel had her "princes" ("rulers"): " . . . On the sixth day they gathered twice as much bread, two omers for one man: and all the rulers of the congregation came and told Moses" (Exod. 16:22). The "princes" ("leaders") of Israel did not only participate in the civil leadership; they were also regarded as pillars in Israelite religious

life, the upholders of the covenantal way of life: "And Moses called unto them; and Aaron and all the rulers of the congregation returned unto him: and Moses talked with them" (Exod. 34:31; cf. Josh. 22:30). Hence, Israel was to obey her "leaders": "Thou shalt not revile the gods, nor curse the ruler of thy people" (Exod. 22:28).

The Septuagint translation is *arxon* ("ruler; lord; prince; authority; official"), and the KJV has these translations: "prince; captain; chief; ruler."

Another noun, *neśî'îm*, is related to *nāśî'*. The word, which is found 4 times, means "clouds": "Whoso boasteth himself of a false gift is like clouds and wind without rain" (Prov. 25:14; cf. Ps. 135:7; Jer. 10:13; 51:16).

B. Verb.

nāśā' (נָשָׂא, 5375), "to lift up, carry." This verb appears 654 times in the Old Testament; once in Gen. 44:1: "Fill the men's sacks with food, as much as they can carry. . . ."

PROPERTY

A. Noun.

'ăhuzzāh (אֲחֻזָּה, 272), "property; possession." This word appears 66 times, with most of its appearances being in Genesis-Joshua and Ezekiel.

Essentially *'ăhuzzāh* is a legal term usually used of land, especially family holdings to be passed down to one's heirs. In Gen. 17:13 (an early occurrence of the word) Abram is promised the territory of Palestine as a familial or tribal possession until the indiscriminate future. In Gen. 23:20 (cf. vv. 4, 9) the word bears a similar meaning. The difference appears to be that here no feudal responsibilities were attached to this "possession." However, the rather small lot belonged to Abraham and his descendants as a burial site: "And the field, and the cave that is therein, were made sure unto Abraham for a possession of a burying place by the sons of Heth" (Gen. 23:20).

In Lev. 25:45–46 non-Israelites could also be inheritable property, but a fellow Israelite could not. The "inheritable property" of the Levites was not fields but the Lord Himself (Ezek. 44:28).

B. Verb.

'āhaz (אָחַז, 270), "to seize, grasp, hold fast, bolt (a door)." This verb, which occurs 64 times in biblical Hebrew, occurs also in most other Semitic languages. The verb appears in Gen. 25:26: " . . . And his hand took hold on Esau's heel. . . ." The meaning of "to bolt" (a door) appears in Neh. 7:3: " . . . Let them shut and

bolt [KJV, "bar"] the doors" (NASB). In 2 Chron. 9:18, *'āhaz* means "fastened."

TO PROPHESY

A. Verb.

nābā' (נָבָא, 5012), "to prophesy." This word appears in all periods of the Hebrew language. It seems to be related to the ancient Akkadian word *nabû*, which in its passive form means "to be called." The word is found in the biblical Hebrew text about 115 times. Its first appearance is in 1 Sam. 10:6, where Saul is told by Samuel that when he meets a certain band of ecstatic prophets, he too will "prophesy with them, and . . . be turned into another man." This incident points up the fact that there is a certain amount of ambiguity in the biblical use of both the verb and the noun forms, just as there is in the English "to prophesy" and "prophet." Thus, there is a wide range of meanings reflected in the term in the Old Testament.

Most frequently *nābā'* is used to describe the function of the true prophet as he speaks God's message to the people, under the influence of the divine spirit (1 Kings 22:8; Jer. 29:27; Ezek. 37:10). "To prophesy" was a task that the prophet could not avoid: "The Lord God hath spoken, who can but prophesy?" (Amos 3:8; cf. Jer. 20:7, where Jeremiah says that he was both attracted to and forced into being a prophet). While the formula "The word of the Lord came [to the prophet]" is used literally hundreds of times in the Old Testament, there is no real indication as to the manner in which it came— whether it came through the thought-processes, through a vision, or in some other way. Sometimes, especially in the earlier prophets, it seems that some kind of ecstatic experience may have been involved, as in 1 Sam. 10:6, 11; 19:20. Music is sometimes spoken of as a means of prophesying, as in 1 Chron. 25:1–3.

The false prophets, although not empowered by the divine spirit, are spoken of as prophesying also: " . . . I have not spoken to them, yet they prophesied" (Jer. 23:21). The false prophet is roundly condemned because he speaks a nonauthentic word: " . . . Prophesy against the prophets of Israel that prophesy, and say thou unto them that prophesy out of their own hearts, Hear ye the word of the Lord; . . . Woe unto the foolish prophets, that follow their own spirit, and have seen nothing!" (Ezek. 13:2–3). The false prophet especially is subject to frenzied states of mind which give rise to his prophesying, although the content of such activity is not clearly spelled out (1 Kings 22:10). The point is that in the biblical context "to prophesy" can refer to anything from the frenzied ecstaticism of a false prophet to the cold sober proclamation of God's judgment by an Amos or an Isaiah.

"To prophesy" is much more than the prediction of future events. Indeed, the first concern of the prophet is to speak God's word to the people of his own time, calling them to covenant faithfulness. The prophet's message is conditional, dependent upon the response of the people. Thus, by their response to this word, the people determine in large part what the future holds, as is well illustrated by the response of the Ninevites to Jonah's preaching. Of course, prediction does enter the picture at times, such as in Nahum's prediction of the fall of Nineveh (Nah. 2:13) and in the various messianic passages (Isa. 9:1–6; 11:1–9; 52:13–53:12).

B. Noun.

nābî' (נָבִיא, 5030), "prophet." The word has a possible cognate in Akkadian. It occurs about 309 times in biblical Hebrew and in all periods.

Nābî' represents "prophet," whether a true or false prophet (cf. Deut. 13:1–5). True prophets were mouthpieces of the true God. In 1 Chron. 29:29 three words are used for "prophet": "Now the acts of David the king, first and last, behold, they are written in the Book of Samuel the Seer [*rō'eh*] and in the Book of Nathan the Prophet [*nābî'*], and in the Book of Gad the Seer [*hōzēh*]." The words translated "seer" emphasize the means by which the "prophet" communicated with God but do not identify the men as anything different from prophets (cf. 1 Sam. 9:9). The first occurrence of *nābî'* does not help to clearly define it either: "Now therefore restore the man [Abraham] his wife; for he is a prophet, and he shall pray for thee, and thou shalt live . . . " (Gen. 20:7).

The second occurrence of *nābî'* establishes its meaning: "And the Lord said unto Moses, See, I have made thee a god to Pharaoh: and Aaron thy brother shall be thy prophet" (Exod. 7:1). The background of this statement is Exod. 4:10–16, where Moses argued his inability to speak clearly. Hence, he could not go before Pharaoh as God's spokesman. God promised to appoint Aaron (Moses' brother) to be the speaker: "And he shall be thy spokesman unto the people: and he shall be, even he shall be to thee instead of a mouth, and thou shalt be to him instead of God" (Exod. 4:16). Exod. 7:1 expresses the same idea in different words. It is clear that the word "prophet" is equal to one who speaks for another, or his mouth.

This basic meaning of *nābî'* is supported by other passages. In the classical passage Deut. 18:14–22, God promised to raise up another "prophet" like Moses who would be God's spokesman (v. 18). They were held responsible for what he told them and were admonished to obey him (Deut. 18:19). However, if what the "prophet" said proved to be wrong, he was to be killed (Deut. 18:20). Immediately, this constitutes a promise and definition of the long succession of Israel's prophets. Ultimately, it is a promise of the Great Prophet, Jesus Christ (cf. Acts 3:22–23). The "prophet" or dreamer of dreams might perform miracles to demonstrate that he was God's man, but the people were to look to the message rather than the miracle before they heeded his message (Deut. 13:1–5).

In the plural *nābî'* is used of some who do not function as God's mouthpieces. In the time of Samuel there were men who followed him. They went about praising God (frequently with song) and trying to stir the people to return to God (1 Sam. 10:5, 10; 19:20). Followers of Elijah and Elisha formed into groups to assist and/or to learn from these masters. They were called sons of the prophets (1 Kings 20:35). Used in this sense, the word *nābî'* means a companion and/or follower of a prophet.

The word is also used of "heathen prophets": "Now therefore send, and gather to me all Israel unto mount Carmel, and the prophets of Baal four hundred and fifty, and the prophets of the groves four hundred, which eat at Jezebel's table" (1 Kings 18:19).

This word has a feminine form, "prophetess" (*nᵉbî'āh*), which appears 6 times. In Exod. 15:20 Miriam is called a "prophetess." Isaiah's wife, too, is called a "prophetess" (Isa. 8:3). This usage may be related to the meaning "a companion and/or follower of a prophet."

TO PROSPER

sālēaḥ (צָלֵחַ, 6743), "to succeed, prosper." This word is found in both ancient and modern Hebrew. Occurring some 65 times in the text of the Hebrew Old Testament, the word is first found in Gen. 24:21: " ... whether the Lord had made his journey prosperous [literally, "to prosper"] or not." This word generally expresses the idea of a successful venture, as contrasted with failure. The source of such success is God: " ... as long as he sought the Lord, God made him to prosper" (2 Chron. 26:5). In spite of that, the circumstances of life often raise the question, "Wherefore doth the way of the wicked prosper?" (Jer. 12:1).

Sālēaḥ is sometimes used in such a way as to indicate "victory": "In your majesty ride forth victoriously" (Ps. 45:4, RSV; the KJV rendering, "ride prosperously," is not nearly so appropriate).

TO PROVOKE (ANGER)

kā'as (כָּעַס, 3707), "to provoke, vex, make angry." This word is common throughout the history of Hebrew and is used in modern Hebrew in the sense of "to be angry, to rage." It occurs some 55 times in the Hebrew Old Testament.

A word that is characteristic of the Book of Deuteronomy, it seems fitting that *kā'as* is found for the first time in the Old Testament in that book: " ... To provoke him to anger" (Deut. 4:25). The word is characteristic also of the books of Jeremiah and Kings. A review of the uses of this verb shows that around 80 percent of them involve Yahweh's "being provoked to anger" by Israel's sin, especially its worship of other gods. One such example is in 2 Kings 23:19: "And all the houses also of the high places that were in the cities of Samaria, which the kings of Israel had made to provoke the Lord to anger, Josiah took away...."

TO PURSUE

rādap (רָדַף, 7291), "to pursue, follow after, pass away, persecute." This verb also appears in Coptic, Syriac, Mandaean, Arabic, and post-biblical Aramaic. It appears in the Bible about 135 times and in all periods.

The basic meaning of this verb is "to pursue after" an enemy with the intent of overtaking and defeating him. In most of its occurrences *rādap* is a military term. It first occurs in Gen. 14:14, where it is reported that Abram mustered his men (318 men) and "pursued them [men who took his brother] unto Dan." A nuance of this verb is "to pursue" a defeated enemy with the intent of killing him: "And he divided himself against them, he and his servants, by night, and smote them, and pursued them unto Hobah, which is on the left hand of Damascus" (Gen. 14:15). The one pursued is not always a hostile force—so Laban "took his brethren [army] with him, and pursued after him [Jacob] seven days' journey; and they overtook him in the mount Gilead" (Gen. 31:23). At times *rādap* signifies pursuing without having a specific location or direction in mind, as in hunting for someone. This meaning is in 1 Sam. 26:20—David asked Saul why he was exerting so much effort on such an unimportant task (namely, pursuing him), "as when one doth hunt a partridge in the mountains." The word occurs in Josh. 2:5, where Rahab tells the soldiers of Jericho: " ... Whither the men [Israelite spies] went I wot not: pursue after them quickly;

for ye shall overtake them." This verse embodies the meaning first mentioned, but by Josh. 2:22 the emphasis has shifted to hunting, not intentional pursuit after an enemy whose location is known but a searching for an enemy in order to kill him: "And they went, and came unto the mountain, and abode there three days, until the pursuers were returned: and the pursuers sought them throughout all the way, but found them not."

In another nuance *rādap* can signify "to put to flight" or "to confront and cause to flee." Moses reminded the Israelites that "the Amorites . . . came out against you, and chased you, as bees do, and destroyed you in Seir, even unto Hormah" (Deut. 1:44). Bees do not pursue their victims, but they certainly do put them to flight, or cause them to flee. In Josh. 23:10 Israel is reminded: "One man of you shall chase a thousand: for the Lord your God he it is that fighteth for you, as he hath promised you" (cf. Lev. 26:8).

Used in another sense, *rādap* signifies the successful accomplishment of a pursuit; the pursuer overtakes the pursued but does not utterly destroy him (in the case of an army) and, therefore, continues the pursuit until the enemy is utterly destroyed. So Israel is warned of the penalty of disobedience to God: "The Lord shall smite thee with a consumption, and with a fever . . .; and they shall pursue thee until thou perish" (Deut. 28:22; cf. v. 45). This is the emphasis when God admonishes Israel: "That which is altogether just shalt thou follow, that thou mayest live, and inherit the land . . . "

(Deut. 16:20); Israel is "to pursue" justice and only justice, as a goal always achieved but never perfected. They are to always have justice in their midst, and always "to pursue" it. This same sense appears in other figurative uses of the word: "Surely goodness and mercy shall follow me all the days of my life . . . " (Ps. 23:6; cf. Isa. 1:23; 5:11; Hos.6:3).

In a related meaning *rādap* can signify "follow after." This is not with any intention to do harm to the one pursued but merely "to overtake" him. So Gehazi "pursued" (followed after) Naaman, overtook him, and asked him for a talent of silver and two changes of clothes (2 Kings 5:21–22). The word also means "to follow after" in the sense of "practicing," or following a leader: "They also that render evil for good are mine adversaries; because I follow the thing that good is" (Ps. 38:20; cf. 119:150; Prov. 21:21).

The third meaning of *rādap*, "to persecute," represents the constant infliction of pain or trouble upon one's enemies. This meaning is seen in Deut. 30:7: "And the Lord thy God will put all these curses upon thine enemies, and on them that hate thee, which persecuted thee" (cf. Job 19:22, 28).

A special use of *rādap* appears in Eccl. 3:15: " . . . God requireth [holds men accountable for] that which is past." Men should serve God (literally, "fear him") because God controls all things. Men should be on His side, since He is totally sovereign. The intensive stem sometimes means to pursue relentlessly and passionately as a harlot "pursues" her lovers (Prov. 11:19).

R

RAM

'ayil (אַיִל, 352), "ram." This word, which has cognates in Ugaritic, Egyptian, and Coptic, occurs in biblical Hebrew about 164 times and in all periods.

'Ayil represents a male sheep or "ram." The word first appears in Gen. 15:9, where God told Abram: "Take me a heifer of three years old, and a she goat of three years old, and a ram of three years old, and a turtledove, and a young pigeon." These animals were often used in sacrificing (cf. Gen. 22:13). They were eaten (Gen. 31:38), and the wool used to make clothing (cf.

2 Kings 3:4). Consequently, as highly valuable animals, such "rams" were selected by Jacob to be part of a peace present sent to Esau (Gen. 32:14).

Many passages use *'ayil* as a figure of despots or mighty men: "Then the dukes of Edom shall be amazed; the mighty men of Moab, trembling shall take hold upon them . . . " (Exod. 15:15). The king of Babylon deported Judah's kings, princes, and the "mighty of the land" (Ezek. 17:13). In the first instance the word represents chiefs in the sense of head political figures, whereas in the second use it appears to signify lesser figures. An even more powerful figure is in view in Ezek. 31:11, where *'ayil* represents a central, powerful, earthly figure who will ruthlessly destroy Assyria: "I have therefore delivered him into the hand of the mighty one of the heathen; he shall surely deal with him: I have driven him out for his wickedness."

yôbēl (יוֹבֵל, 3104), "ram; ram's horn; jubilee year." Cognates of this word appear in late Aramaic, Phoenician, and Arabic. The 27 biblical appearances of the noun all occur before the Book of Judges.

First, this word means "ram's horn": "When the ram's horn [KJV, "trumpet"] sounds a long blast, they shall come up to the mountain" (Exod. 19:13—the first occurrence). In Josh. 6:5 the word is preceded by the Hebrew word for "horn," which is modified by *yôbēl*, "horn of a ram."

Second, this word signifies "jubilee year." The law concerning this institution is recorded in Lev. 25:8–15; 27:16–25. In the fiftieth year on the Day of Atonement jubilee was to be declared. All land was to return to the individual or family to whom it had originally belonged by inheritance, even if he (or she) were in bondservice. When land was valued in anticipation of selling it or devoting it to God, it was to be valued in terms of anticipated productivity prior to the year of jubilee. Between jubilees land might be redeemed for its productivity value. City property, however, must be redeemed within a year of its sale or loss. Levitical property was not subject to these rules. Israelites who fell into bondage were to be released in the jubilee year, or redeemed in the interim period.

TO REBEL

A. Verb.

mārāh (מָרָה, 4784), "to rebel, be contentious." The meaning of "being rebellious" is limited to the Hebrew language, as the meaning of this verb in other Semitic languages differs: "to make angry" (Aramaic), "to contend with" (Syriac), and "to dispute with" (Arabic). *Mārāh* occurs some 50 times in the Old Testament, and its usage is scattered throughout the Old Testament (historical, prophetic, poetic, and legal literature). Some personal names are partly composed of the verb: *Meraiah* ("stubborn headed"; Neh. 12:12) and *Miriam* ("stubborn headed," if actually derived from the verb).

Mārāh signifies an opposition to someone motivated by pride: "If a man have a stubborn [*sārar*] and rebellious [*mārāh*] son, which will not obey the voice of his father..." (Deut. 21:18). The sense comes out more clearly in Isa. 3:8 (NASB): "For Jerusalem has stumbled, and Judah has fallen, Because their speech and their actions are against the Lord, To rebel against His glorious presence."

More particularly, the word generally connotes a rebellious attitude against God. Several prepositions are used to indicate the object of rebellion (*'im, ēt*, generally translated as "against"): "... Ye have been rebellious against [*'im*] the Lord" (Deut. 9:7); "... She hath been rebellious against [*ēt*] me..." (Jer. 4:17).

The primary meaning of *mārāh* is "to disobey." Several passages attest to this: "... Forasmuch as thou hast disobeyed the mouth of the Lord, and hast not kept the commandment which the Lord thy God commanded thee" (1 Kings 13:21); cf. 1 Kings 13:26: "It is the man of God, who was disobedient unto the word of the Lord...."

The Old Testament sometimes specifically states that someone "rebelled" against the Lord; at other times it may refer to a rebelling against the word of the Lord (Ps. 105:28; 107:11), or against the mouth of God (KJV, "word"; NIV, "command"; cf. Num. 20:24; Deut. 1:26, 43; 9:23; 1 Sam. 12:14–15). The intent of the Hebrew is to signify the act of defying the command of God: "The Lord is righteous; for I have rebelled against his commandment..." (Lam. 1:18).

The verb *mārāh* is at times strengthened by a form of the verb *sārar* ("to be stubborn"): "[They] might not be as their fathers, a stubborn [*sārar*] and rebellious [*mārāh*] generation; a generation that set not their heart aright..." (Ps. 78:8; cf. Deut. 21:18, 20; Jer. 5:23).

An individual (Deut. 21:18, 20), a nation (Num. 20:24), and a city (Zeph. 3:1) may be described as "being rebellious." Zephaniah gave a vivid image of the nature of the rebellious spirit: "Woe to her that is rebellious and defiled, the oppressing city! She listens to no voice, she accepts no correction. She does not trust in the Lord, she does not draw near to her God" (Zeph. 3:1–2, RSV).

The Septuagint translates *mārāh* by *parepikraino* ("make bitter; make angry; provoke; be rebellious") and by *atheteo* ("to reject; not to recognize"). The English versions give the meanings "rebel; provoke" (KJV, RSV, NIV).

B. Nouns.

merî (מְרִי, 4805), "rebellion." This word occurs infrequently: "For I know thy rebellion, and thy stiff neck..." (Deut. 31:27; cf. Prov. 17:11).

The noun *merātayim* means "double rebellion." This reference to Babylon (Jer. 50:21) is generally not translated (KJV, RSV, and NIV, "Merathaim").

C. Adjective.

mᵉrî (מְרִי, 4805), "rebellious." This word occurs 23 times, mainly in Ezekiel. The word modifies "house" (referring to Israel) in Ezek. 2:8: "... Be not thou rebellious like that rebellious house...."

TO RECKON

A. Verb.

yāḥaś (יָחַשׂ, 3187), "to reckon (according to race or family)." In Aramaic, *yāḥaś* appears in the Targumim for the Hebrew *mišpāḥāh* ("family") and *tôlēdôt* ("genealogy or generations"). This word occurs about 20 times in the Old Testament.

In 1 Chron. 5:17 *yāḥaś* means "reckoned by genealogies": "All these were reckoned by genealogies in the days of Jothan King of Judah..." (cf. 1 Chron. 7:5). A similar use is found in Ezra 2:62: "These sought their register among those that were reckoned by genealogy, but they were not found..." (NASB, "searched among their ancestral registration").

The Septuagint renders *yāḥaś* variously: *ogdoēkonta* ("genealogy... to be reckoned"); *arithmos* ("member of them; father their genealogy"); *paratoxin* ("member throughout the genealogy"); *sunodias* ("reckoned by genealogy").

B. Noun.

yahaś (יַחַשׂ, 3188), "genealogy." This word appears in the infinitive form as a noun to indicate a register or table of genealogy: "And the number throughout the genealogy of them that were apt to the war, and to battle was twenty and six thousand men" (1 Chron. 7:40; cf. 2 Chron. 31:18). Another rendering concerning the acts of Rehoboam, recorded in the histories of Shemaiah (2 Chron. 12:15), meant that the particulars were related in a genealogical table.

TO RECOMPENSE, REWARD

šālam (שָׁלַם, 7999), "to recompense, reward, be whole, be complete, sound." A common Semitic term, this verb is found in ancient Akkadian and Ugaritic and in all periods of Hebrew. The root is familiar to most people in the word *šālôm*, which is the common Jewish greeting. The verb *šālam* occurs just over 100 times in the Hebrew Bible.

In its first occurrence in the Old Testament, the word has the sense of "repaying" or "restoring": "Why have you returned evil for good?" (Gen. 44:4, RSV). Sometimes it means "to complete or finish"—for example, completing the temple (1 Kings 9:25). In Lev. 24:18, *šālam* describes compensation for injury: "And he that killeth a beast shall make it good [life for life]."

Perhaps it should be noted that the Arabic terms *Muslim* and *Islam* are derived from the Arabic cognate to *šālam* and imply "submission to Allah."

TO REDEEM

A. Verbs.

gā'al (גָּאַל, 1350), "to redeem, deliver, avenge, act as a kinsman." This word group is used 90 times, chiefly in the Pentateuch, Psalms, Isaiah, and Ruth. The root appears to be almost exclusively Hebrew, the only cognate being an Amorite proper name.

The first occurrence of *gā'al* is in Gen. 48:16: "The angel which redeemed me [Jacob] from all evil..." (KJV), means as in the NIV, "delivered me from all harm." Its basic use had to do with the deliverance of persons or property that had been sold for debt, as in Lev. 25:25: "If thy brother be waxen poor, and hath sold away some of his possession, and if any of his kin come to redeem it, then shall he redeem that which his brother sold." If he prospers, the man himself may "redeem" it (Lev. 25:26). A poor man may sell himself to a fellow Israelite (Lev. 25:39) or to an alien living in Israel (Lev. 25:47). The responsibility "to redeem" belonged to the nearest relative—brother, uncle, uncle's son, or a blood relative from his family (Lev. 25:25, 48–49). The person (kinsman) who "redeemed" the one in financial difficulties was known as a kinsman-redeemer, as the NIV translates the word in Ruth 2:20. In Deut. 19:6 the redeemer is called the "avenger of blood" whose duty it was to execute the murderer of his relative. The verb occurs in this sense 12 times and is translated "revenger" in KJV (Num. 35:19, 21, 24, 27) or "avenger" (Num. 35:12; always so in NASB and NIV).

The Book of Ruth is a beautiful account of the kinsman-redeemer. His responsibility is summed up in Ruth 4:5: "What day thou buyest the field of the hand of Naomi, thou must buy it also of Ruth the Moabitess, the wife of the dead, to raise up the name of the dead upon his inheritance." Thus the kinsman-redeemer was responsible for preserving the integrity, life, property, and family name of his close relative or for executing justice upon his murderer.

The greater usage of this word group is of God who promised: "... I am the Lord... I will redeem you with a stretched out arm and with great judgments" (Exod. 6:6; cf. Ps. 77:15). Israel confessed: "Thou in thy mercy hast led forth the people which thou hast *redeemed*..." (Exod. 15:13). "And they remembered that God was their rock, and the high God their redeemer" (Ps. 78:35).

The Book of Isaiah evidences the word "Redeemer" used of God 13 times, all in chapters 41–63, and *gā'al* is used 9 times of God, first in 43:1: "Fear not; for I have redeemed thee, I have called thee by thy name; thou art mine." *Gā'al* is used of deliverance from Egypt (51:10; 63:9) and from captivity in Babylon (48:20; 52:3, 9; 62:12). Israel's "Redeemer" is "the Holy One of Israel" (41:14), "the creator of Israel, your King" (43:14–15), "the Lord of hosts" (44:6), and "the mighty One of Jacob" (49:26). Those who share His salvation are "the redeemed" (35:9).

The Book of Psalms often places spiritual redemption in parallel with physical redemption. For example: "Draw nigh unto my soul, and redeem it: // deliver me because of mine enemies" (Ps. 69:18). "Bless the Lord, O my soul, and forget not all his benefits: . . . who redeemeth thy life from destruction; who crowneth thee with loving-kindness and tender mercies" (Ps. 103:2, 4).

pādāh (פָּדָה, 6299), "to redeem, ransom." Originally, the usage of this word overlapped with that of *kāpar;* both meant "to ransom." In theological usage, however, each root tended to develop in different directions, so that they can often be considered synonymous only in a very broad sense.

Pādāh indicates that some intervening or substitutionary action effects a release from an undesirable condition. In more secular contexts, it implies a payment of some sort. But 1 Sam. 14:45 indicates that money is not intrinsic in the word; Saul is determined to execute Jonathan for his involuntary transgression, but " . . . the people rescued Jonathan, that he died not." Slavery appears as a condition from which one may be "ransomed" (Exod. 21:8; Lev. 19:20).

The word is connected with the laws of the firstborn. As a reminder of slaying all the Egyptian firstborn but sparing the Israelites, God retained an eternal claim on the life of all Israelite firstborn males, both of men and of cattle. The latter were often sacrificed, "but all the firstborn of my children I redeem" (Exod. 13:15). God accepted the separation of the tribe of Levi for liturgical service in lieu of all Israelite firstborn (Num. 3:40ff.). However, the Israelite males still had to be "redeemed" (*pādāh*) from this service by payment of specified "redemption money" (Num. 3:44–51).

When God is the subject of *pādāh*, the word emphasizes His complete, sovereign freedom to liberate human beings. Sometimes God is said to "redeem" individuals (Abraham, Isa. 29:22; David, 1 Kings 1:29; and often in the Psalter,

e.g., 26:11; 21:5; 71:23); but usually Israel, the elect people, is the beneficiary. Sometimes the redemption or deliverance is proclaimed absolutely (2 Sam. 7:23; Ps. 44:26; Hos. 7:13); but the subject is said to be "ransomed" from a specific oppression. At other times, the reference is less explicit—e.g., from "troubles" (Ps. 25:22) and from "wicked" men (Jer. 15:21). Only once is *pādāh* used to describe liberation from sin or iniquity: "And he shall redeem Israel from all his iniquity" (Ps. 130:8).

kāpar (כָּפַר, 3722), "to ransom, atone, expiate, propitiate." *Kāpar* has an initial secular and non-theological range quite parallel to *pādāh*. In addition, however, *kāpar* became a technical term in Israel's sacrificial rituals. On its most basic level of meaning, *kāpar* denotes a material transaction or "ransom."

Sometimes man is the subject of *kāpar*. In 2 Sam. 21:3, David asks the Gibeonites, " . . . And wherewith shall I make the atonement, that ye may bless the inheritance of the Lord?" He receives in answer the advice to hang seven of Saul's sons in compensation. In Exod. 32:30, Moses ascends the mountain yet a third time in an effort to "make an atonement" for the people's sin (apparently merely by intercession, although this is not explicitly stated). Isa. 27:9 speaks of "purging" Israel's guilt by banishing idolatrous objects. In Num. 25:13, Phinehas is said to have "made an atonement for the children of Israel" by spearing a couple during orgiastic worship of Baal.

God is often the subject of *kāpar* in this general sense, too. In 2 Chron. 30:18, Hezekiah prays for God to "pardon" those who were not ritually prepared for the Passover. At the conclusion of the Song of Moses, Yahweh is praised because He "will atone for His land and His people" (Deut. 32:43, NASB). Similar general uses of the word appear in Ps. 65:3; 78:38; and Dan. 9:24. Jeremiah once uses *kāpar* to pray bitterly that Yahweh not "forgive" the iniquity of those plotting to slay him (Jer. 18:23), and in Ps. 79:9 the word means "to purge" sin.

Most often *kāpar* is used in connection with specific rites, and the immediate subject is a priest. All types of ritual sacrifice are explained in terms of *kāpar*. We find the priests' smearing of blood on the altar during the "sin offering" (*haṭṭā't*) described as "atonement" (Exod. 29:36–37; Lev. 4:20, 31; 10:17; Num. 28:22; 29:5; Neh. 10:33). The use of blood is not quite so prominent in sacrifices, but the relation to "atonement" still holds. It is clearly true of the "guilt offering" (Lev. 5:16, 18; 6:7; 7:7; 14:21; 19:22; Num. 5:8). The principle holds even when the poor cannot afford an animal or birds, and they sacrifice only a little flour—i.e., where obviously no blood is involved (Lev. 5:11–13). Making "atonement" (*kāpar*) is also part of the purpose of the "burnt offering" (Lev. 1:4; Num. 15:25). The only major type of sacrifice not classified an "atonement" in Leviticus is the "cereal offering" (*minḥāh*) of chapter 2; but Ezek. 45:15, 17 does include it under that heading. First Chron. 6:49 applies the concept to the priestly ministry in general. The connection of all of the rituals with *kāpar* peaks in the complex ceremony of the annual Day of Atonement (*Yom Kippur*), as described in detail in Lev. 16.

Most English versions prefer to render *kāpar* with the more neutral term "atone" or even "ransom." But various translations often have "expiate" or "propitiate" as well. The terms are partly synonymous. In any sacrifice, the action is directed both toward God (*propitiation*) and toward the offense (*expiation*). "Expiate," "atone," and even "forgive" (if related to sacrifice) all have God as their primary subject, while "propitiation" addresses God as object.

All the sacrifices in the world would not satisfy God's righteousness (e.g., Mic. 6:7; Ps. 50:7–15). Hence God alone can provide an atonement or expiation for sin, by which His wrath is assuaged. The righteous God is neither implacable nor capricious, but provides Himself the "ransom" or substitute sacrifice that would satisfy Him. The priest at the altar represents God Himself, bringing the requisite offering before God; sacrifice is not essentially man's action, but God's own act of pardoning mercy.

B. Noun.

geʾullāh (גְּאֻלָּה, 1353), "(right of) redemption." This word is used in regard to deliverance of persons or property that had been sold for debt. The law required that the "right of redemption" of land and of persons be protected (Lev. 25:24, 48). The redemption price was determined by the number of years remaining until the release of debts in the year of jubilee (Lev. 25:27–28). The word *geʾullāh* also occurs in Jer. 32:7: "Behold, Hanameel the son of Shallum thine uncle shall come unto thee, saying, Buy thee my field that is in Anathoth: for the right of redemption is thine to buy it."

The noun related to *pādāh* is *peḏût*. It occurs about 5 times and means "ransom or redemption": "He sent redemption unto his people: he hath commanded his covenant for ever ..." (Ps. 111:9).

TO REIGN

mālak (מֶלֶךְ, 4427), "to reign, be king (or queen)." This root appears in most Semitic languages, although it means "advice" and "coun-sel" in Akkadian (and biblical Aramaic) and "own" exclusively in Ethiopic (and old South Arabic). In the Northwest Semitic dialects the root has a common meaning. The verbal form occurs in every period of Hebrew and about 350 times in the Bible.

Basically the word means to fill the functions of ruler over someone. To hold such a position was to function as the commander-in-chief of the army, the chief executive of the group, and to be an important, if not central, religious figure. The king was the head of his people and, therefore, in battle were the king to be killed, his army would disperse until a new king could be chosen. The first appearance of *mālak* is in Gen. 36:31: "And these are the kings that reigned in the land of Edom, before there reigned any king over the children of Israel." The king "reigned" as the earthly representative of the god (or God) who was recognized as the real king. Thus, he was considered to be god's (God's) son. This same idea recurs in Israel (Ps. 2:6). In Israel, too, God was the King: "The Lord shall reign for ever and ever" (Exod. 15:18). That the word can also be used of what a queen does when she "reigns" proves that it refers to the function of anyone in the office of king: "And he was with her hid in the house of the Lord six years. And Athaliah did reign over the land" (2 Kings 11:3).

Mālak can also be used of the idea "to become king"—someone was made, or made himself, a king: "And Bela died, and Jobab the son of Zerah of Bozrah reigned in his stead" (Gen. 36:33). This verb can be used of the assumption of a kingly reign, or of "beginning to reign": "Saul reigned one year; and when he had reigned two years over Israel ... " (1 Sam. 13:1; cf. Prov. 30:22). Finally, the verb is used of receiving the title of queen (or king) whether or not one receives any political or military power. So it was said: "And let the maiden which pleaseth the king be queen instead of Vashti" (Esth. 2:4).

TO REJOICE

A. Verb.

śāmaḥ (שָׂמַח, 8055), "to rejoice, be joyful." This verb also occurs in Ugaritic (where its radicals are *śh-m-h*) and perhaps in Aramaic-Syriac. It appears in all periods of Hebrew and about 155 times in the Bible.

Śāmaḥ usually refers to a spontaneous emotion or extreme happiness which is expressed in some visible and/or external manner. It does not normally represent an abiding state of well-being or feeling. This emotion arises at festivals, circumcision feasts, wedding feasts, harvest feasts, the overthrow of one's enemies, and other such events. The men of Jabesh broke out joyously when they were told that they would be delivered from the Philistines (1 Sam. 11:9).

The emotion expressed in the verb *śāmaḥ* usually finds a visible expression. In Jer. 50:11 the Babylonians are denounced as being glad and "jubilant" over the pillage of Israel. Their emotion is expressed externally by their skipping about like a threshing heifer and neighing like stallions. The emotion represented in the verb (and concretized in the noun *śimḥāh*) is sometimes accompanied by dancing, singing, and playing musical instruments. This was the sense when David was heralded by the women of Jerusalem as he returned victorious over the Philistines (1 Sam. 18:6). This emotion is usually described as the product of some external situation, circumstance, or experience, such as found in the first biblical appearance of *śāmaḥ*: God told Moses that Aaron was coming to meet him and "when he seeth thee, he will be glad in his heart" (Exod. 4:14). This passage speaks of inner feeling which is visibly expressed. When Aaron saw Moses, he was overcome with joy and kissed him (v. 27).

Therefore, the verb *śāmaḥ* suggests three elements: (1) a spontaneous, unsustained feeling of jubilance, (2) a feeling so strong that it finds expression in some external act, and (3) a feeling prompted by some external and unsustained stimulus.

This verb is used intransitively signifying that the action is focused on the subject (cf. 1 Sam. 11:9). God is sometimes the subject, the one who "rejoices and is jubilant": "The glory of the Lord shall endure for ever: the Lord shall rejoice in his works" (Ps. 104:31). The godly are to "be glad in the Lord, and rejoice ... and shout for joy ... " (Ps. 32:11). *Śāmaḥ* can also mean "to be joyful or glad." In the place the Lord chooses, Israel is "to be joyful" in all in which the Lord blesses them (Deut. 12:7). Used thus the verb describes a state into which one places himself under given circumstances. It has a further and technical sense describing all that one does in making a feast before God: "And ye shall take you on the first day the boughs of goodly trees, branches of palm trees, and the boughs of thick trees, and willows of the brook; and ye shall rejoice before the Lord your God seven days" (Lev. 23:40).

In a few cases the verb describes an ongoing state. In 1 Kings 4:20 the reign of Solomon is summarized as follows: "Judah and Israel were many, as the sand which is by the sea in multitude, eating and drinking, and making merry."

B. Noun.

śimḥāh (שִׂמְחָה, 8057), "joy." This noun, which also occurs in Ugaritic, is found 94 times in biblical Hebrew. *Śimḥāh* is both a technical term for the external expression of "joy" (Gen. 31:27—the first biblical occurrence; cf. 1 Sam. 18:6; Jer. 50:11) and (usually) a representation of the abstract feeling or concept "joy" (Deut. 28:47). In another technical use this noun signifies the entire activity of making a feast before God: "And all the people went their way to eat, and to drink, and to send portions, and to make great mirth [literally, "to make a great rejoicing"] ... " (Neh. 8:12).

The noun catches the concrete coloring of the verb, as in Isa. 55:12: "For ye shall go out with joy ...: the mountains and the hills shall break forth before you into singing, and all the trees of the field shall clap their hands."

C. Adjective.

śāmēaḥ (שָׂמֵחַ, 8056), "joyful; glad." This adjective occurs 21 times in the Old Testament. The first biblical occurrence is in Deut. 16:15: "Seven days shalt thou keep a solemn feast unto the Lord thy God in the place which the Lord shall choose: because the Lord thy God shall bless thee ... therefore thou shalt surely rejoice."

TO REMAIN

lûn (לוּן, 3885), "to remain, lodge, spend the night, abide." Found also in ancient Ugaritic, this word continues in use from biblical Hebrew until now. The modern Hebrew term for "hotel" is derived from this term. *Lûn* is used approximately 60 times in the Hebrew Old Testament. Its first occurrence is in Gen. 19:2, where it is used twice: "Behold now, my lords, turn in, I pray you, into your servant's house, and tarry all night. ... And they said, Nay; but we will abide in the street all night."

While it is usually used concerning human beings spending the night, *lûn* is sometimes used of animals, such as the wild ox (Job 39:9, NASB; KJV, "unicorn"), the pelican and the hedgehog (Zeph. 2:14, NASB; KJV, "the cormorant and the bittern"). The word does not necessarily mean sleeping through the night, but may be used to indicate being located in one place for the night: "Thou shalt not ... [let] the fat of my sacrifice remain until the morning [literally, "pass the night until morning"] (Exod. 23:18). In a similar way, the figurative use of the word often has the connotation of "abiding, remaining": " ... Mine error remaineth [NASB, "lodges"] with myself" (Job 19:4); " ... Righteousness lodged in it ... " (Isa. 1:21); "His soul shall dwell at ease . . ." (Ps. 25:13); " . . . [He] shall abide satisfied . . ." (Prov. 19:23).

REMAINDER; REMNANT

A. Nouns.

yeter (יֶתֶר, 3499), "remainder; remnant." *Yeter* appears 94 times in the Hebrew Old Testament. The word occurs mainly (about 45 times) in the historical books in the stereotype phrase "the rest of the acts," as in "And the rest of the acts of Solomon [the events of Solomon's reign], and all that he did, and his wisdom, are they not written in the Book of the Acts of Solomon?" (1 Kings 11:41). In these verses, *yeter* is used to refer to those events which have not been included in the works of the biblical historiographers.

The more general meaning of *yeter* is "whatever remains": the prey (Num. 31:32); the giants (Deut. 3:11); the kingdom (Josh. 13:27); and the people (Judg. 7:6). A good illustration is found in Joel's teaching on the locusts: "That which the palmerworm hath left hath the locust eaten; and that which the locust hath left hath the cankerworm eaten; and that which the cankerworm hath left hath the caterpillar eaten" (Joel 1:4).

The prophets used *šᵉʾērît* as a technical term for "the remnant of Israel." They predicted that after the Exile a "remnant" of God-fearing people would return to the land (cf. Hag. 2:2–3). Few prophets (Micah; Zeph. 2:9) employ *yeter* for this purpose: "Therefore will he give them up, until the time that she which travaileth hath brought forth: then the remnant [*yeter*] of his brethren shall return unto the children of Israel" (Mic. 5:3).

The Septuagint translations are: *loipos* ("remaining; rest; remainder") and *kataloipos* ("what is left; remaining").

Several other nouns which appear infrequently are related to *yeter*. *Yôtēr* ("advantage; excess; over,") can be found in Eccl. 6:8: "For what advantage does the wise man have over the fool?" (NASB). *Yitrāh* means "abundance" or "riches" and occurs only in Jer. 48:36. *Yitrôn* can refer to "advantage, gain, profit," and this word appears only in Ecclesiastes (cf. Eccl. 1:3; 2:11). *Yôteret*, "appendage of the liver," occurs about 10 times (cf. Exod. 29:13, 22; Lev. 3:4, 10, 15). *Môtār*, which means "abundance, superiority, profit," is found in Prov. 14:23. *See also* REMNANT.

B. Verb.

yātar (יָתַר, 3498), "to be superfluous." This verb is related to other Semitic languages, where the root *yātar/watar* signifies the state of abundance (Ugaritic, Phoenician, Arabic). In Hebrew many forms are derived from the verb *yātar*. The word occurs about 107 times, once in Dan. 10:13: "But the prince of the kingdom of Persia withstood me one and twenty days: but, lo, Michael, one of the chief princes, came to help me; and I remained there with the kings of Persia."

TO REMEMBER

A. Verb.

zākar (זָכַר, 2142), "to remember, think of, mention." This root is found in Assyrian, Aramaic, Arabic, and Ethiopic. The group of words (the verb and the three nouns derived from it) is found throughout the Old Testament. The first occurrence of *zākar* is in Gen. 8:1 with God as the subject: "God remembered Noah . . . : and God made a wind to pass over the earth, and the waters assuaged." In Gen. 9:15 God said to Noah: "And I will remember my covenant . . . ; and the waters shall no more become a flood to destroy all flesh." As in these two cases (cf. Gen. 6:18), "remember" is used of God in respect to His covenant promises and is followed by an action to fulfill His covenant. God delivered Lot from Sodom because of His covenant with Abraham to bless all the nations through him (Gen. 18:17–33): "God remembered Abraham, and brought Lot out of the catastrophe . . ." (Gen. 19:29, NIV). This marks the history of Israel at every major point: "And I have also heard the groaning of the children of Israel, . . . and I have remembered my covenant. . . . and I will bring you out from under the burdens of the Egyptians . . ." (Exod. 6:5–6). The promise "to remember" was repeated in the covenant at Sinai (Lev. 26:40–45), God's remembrance was sung in the Psalms (98:3; 105:8, 42; 106:45), and the promise was repeated by the prophets in regard to restoration from captivity (Ezek. 16:60). The new covenant promise is: " . . . I will forgive their iniquity, and I will remember their sin no more" (Jer. 31:34).

Because of this God's people pray, as Moses: "Turn from thy fierce wrath. . . . Remember Abraham, Isaac, and Israel, thy servants, to whom thou swarest . . ." (Exod. 32:12–13); or Nehemiah: "Remember . . . the word that thou commandedst thy servant Moses . . ." (Neh. 1:8, quoting Lev. 26:33); or the psalmist: "Remember not the sins of my youth, nor my transgressions: according to thy mercy remember thou me . . ." (Ps. 25:7); or Jeremiah: " . . . Remember, break not thy covenant with us" (Jer. 14:21).

Men also "remember." Joseph said to Pharaoh's butler: "But think on me . . . , and make mention of me unto Pharaoh ... " (Gen. 40:14; NIV, "remember ... and mention"). Again, "to remember" means more than "to recall"; it means "to retain in thought" so as to tell someone who can take action (cf. Ps. 20:7). *Zākar* may have more specific connotations in certain circumstances: "Hear ye this, O house of Jacob, ... which swear by the name of the Lord, ... and make mention of the God of Israel. . ." (Isa. 48:1). The NASB and the NIV translate the last clause "and invoke the God of Israel"; and the RSV has "confess." All point to the mention of God's name in worship. David appointed "Levites as ministers before the ark of the Lord, to invoke ... the Lord ... " (1 Chron. 16:4, RSV; NASB, "to celebrate"; NIV, "to make petition").

The covenant commanded Israel to "remember this day, in which ye came out from Egypt ... " (Exod. 13:3); to "remember the sabbath day ... " (Exod. 20:8); to "remember that thou wast a servant in the land of Egypt, and that the Lord thy God brought thee out thence through a mighty hand ... " (Deut. 5:15 and often); and to "remember his marvelous works ... " (Ps. 105:5; cf. 1 Chron. 16:15). But "the children of Israel remembered not the Lord their God, who had delivered them out of the hands of all their enemies ... " (Judg. 8:34; cf. Ps. 78:42).

B. Nouns.

zēker (זֵכֶר, 2143) or *zeker* (זֶכֶר, 2143), "remembrance; memorial." Of His covenant name, YHWH ("Lord"), God said: " ... This is my memorial unto all generations" (Exod. 3:15; cf. Ps. 30:4; 135:13). The name would recall His acts of covenant fulfillment. Moses was told to write an account of the war with Amalek "for a memorial [*zikkārôn*] in a book, and rehearse it in the ears of Joshua: for I will utterly put out the remembrance [*zeker* or *zēker*] of Amalek from under heaven" (Exod. 17:14).

The noun *zikkārôn* has similar meanings. God gave the bronze plates covering the altar (Num. 16:40) and the heap of stones at the Jordan (Josh. 4:7, 20–24) as perpetual "memorials" for the sons of Israel. The names of the twelve tribes of Israel were engraved on two stones that were attached to the ephod as "stones of memorial unto the children of Israel: and Aaron shall bear their names before the Lord ... " (Exod. 28:12; cf. v. 29). When Israel went into battle, and when they offered sacrifice, they were to blow trumpets "that they may be to you for a memorial before your God" (Num. 10:9–10).

The noun *'azkārāh* means "memorial offering," and it occurs primarily in Leviticus.

"Memorials" were directed toward God. A "memorial" portion of each meal offering was burnt on the altar (Lev. 2:2, 9, 16), in other words a small portion in place of the whole amount.

The Septuagint translates these words by several derivatives from one root, *mimneskō*, by which the idea comes into the New Testament. Zechariah praised the Lord God that He had "raised up a horn of salvation for us in the house of his servant David ... and to remember his holy covenant ... " (Luke 1:69–73). Our need for a reminder is met in "This do in remembrance of me" (1 Cor. 11:24–25).

REMNANT

A. Nouns.

šᵉ'ērît (שְׁאֵרִית, 7611), "rest; remnant; residue." The idea of the "remnant" plays a prominent part in the divine economy of salvation throughout the Old Testament. The "remnant" concept is applied especially to the Israelites who survived such calamities as war, pestilence, and famine—people whom the Lord in His mercy spared to be His chosen people: "For out of Jerusalem shall go forth a remnant, and they that escape out of mount Zion: the zeal of the Lord of hosts shall do this" (2 Kings 19:31; cf. Ezra 9:14).

The Israelites repeatedly suffered major catastrophes that brought them to the brink of extinction. So they often prayed as in Jer. 42:2: "Let, we beseech thee, our supplication be accepted before thee, and pray for us unto the Lord thy God, even for all this remnant; (for we are left but a few of many, as thine eyes do behold us:)."

Isaiah used the word *šᵉ'ērît* 5 times to denote those who would be left after the Assyrian invasions: "For out of Jerusalem shall go forth a remnant, and they that escape out of mount Zion: the zeal of the Lord of hosts shall do this" (Isa. 37:32).

Micah also announced the regathering of the Jewish people after the Exile. Thus Micah prophesied: "I will surely assemble them together, O Jacob, all of thee; I will surely gather the remnant of Israel ... " (2:12). In Mic. 4:7 he predicted: "And I will make her that halted a remnant and her that was cast far off a strong nation: and the Lord shall reign over them in mount Zion from henceforth, even for ever." In 5:7–8 and 7:18, Micah announces a similar idea.

Jeremiah discussed the plight of the Jews who fled to Egypt after Jerusalem's capture by Nebuchadnezzar: "Likewise when all the Jews that were in Moab, and among the Ammonites, and in Edom, and that were in all the countries, heard that the King of Babylon had left a remnant of Judah.... Then Johanan the son of Kareah spake to Gedaliah in Mizpah secretly, saying, Let me go, I pray thee, and I will slay Ishmael ... wherefore should he slay thee, that all the Jews which are gathered unto thee should be scattered, and the remnant in Judah perish?" (Jer. 40:11, 15).

Zephaniah, a seventh-century prophet, identified the "remnant" with the poor and humble (2:3, 7; 3:12–13). Zechariah announced that a "remnant" would be present at the time of the coming of the Messiah's kingdom (12:10–13:1; 13:8–9).

šᵉ'ār (שְׁאָר, 7605), "rest; remnant; residue." Isaiah describes the "remnant" of Israel: "And it shall come to pass in that day, that the remnant of Israel, and such as are escaped of the house of Jacob, shall no more again stay upon him that smote them; but shall stay upon the Lord, the Holy One of Israel, in truth" (Isa. 10:20).

Notice that a twofold theme emerges from most prophetic passages concerning the "remnant": (1) A "remnant" will survive when the people are subjected to punishment, and (2) the fact that a "remnant" does survive and does remain contains a note of hope for the future. Isa. 10:21 announces: "The remnant shall return, even the remnant of Jacob, unto the mighty God." In Isa. 11:11, the prophet proclaims: "And it shall come to pass in that day, that the Lord shall set his hand again the second time to recover the remnant of his people, which shall be left from Assyria, and from Egypt, and from Pathros, and from Cush, and from Elam, and from Shinar, and from Hamath, and from the islands of the sea." *See also* REMAINDER.

B. Verb.

šā'ar (שָׁאַר, 7604), "to remain, be left over." This verb and its noun derivatives occur about 220 times in the Old Testament.

Noah and his family were a "remnant" delivered by the Flood: "...And Noah only remained alive, and they that were with him in the ark" (Gen. 7:23). In the days of Elijah, when God's chosen people in the northern kingdom had fallen into apostasy, the Lord announced: "Yet I have left me seven thousand in Israel, all the knees which have not bowed unto Baal..." (1 Kings 19:18).

In the pre-exilic period, this remnant idea is stressed by Isaiah. Isaiah tells of the judgment on the earth from which a remnant will "remain": "Therefore hath the curse devoured the earth, and they that dwell therein are desolate: therefore the inhabitants of the earth are burned, and few men left" (Isa. 24:6). Isa. 4:3 refers to a "remnant" which shares holiness: "And it shall come to pass, that he that is left [šā'ar], and he that remaineth in Jerusalem, shall be called holy...."

In the writing prophets, the idea of the "remnant" acquired a growing significance. Yet the idea may be found as early as the Pentateuch. The idea of "those being left" or "having escaped," especially a portion of the Israelite people, may be traced back to Deut. 4:27: "And the Lord shall scatter you among the nations, and ye shall be left few in number among the heathen, whither the Lord shall lead you" (cf. Deut. 28:62). In these passages, Moses warns that if Israel failed to live up to the stipulations of the Mosaic covenant, the Lord would scatter them among the nations, and then He would regather a "remnant."

In Neh. 1:2–3, the condition of the "remnant" of Israel is described: "...And I asked them concerning the Jews that had escaped, which were left of the captivity, and concerning Jerusalem. And they said unto me, the remnant that are left of the captivity there in the province are in great affliction and reproach...."

TO REMOVE, DEPART

A. Verb.

nāśā' (נָשָׂא, 5375), "to remove, depart, carry away." This verb occurs in all Semitic languages including biblical Aramaic and in all periods of Hebrew. The Bible attests this Hebrew word about 650 times.

The meaning "to lift up" or "to bear" is seen, for example, in Gen. 7:17 (the first occurrence of this word), where it is reported that the waters "lifted up" the ark. A special use of this emphasis occurs in Job 6:2, where Job prays that his trouble be laid ("lifted up") in the balances because he believes his trouble far outweighs his sin. Then there is the sense "to bear up" or "to support," as a loaded donkey "bears up" his load (Gen. 45:23). Then, too, nāśā' can be used of bearing something away—David and his men "took away" the abandoned Philistine idols; they lifted them up, bore them, and carried them away (2 Sam. 5:21, RSV). This same nuance is applied to marriage, or taking a wife (Ruth 1:4). The same expression means to steal (or plunder) a wife (Judg. 21:23). The phrase "lift up ... heads" sometimes means "to take a census" (KJV, "to number")—the Lord told Moses to "lift up" the heads of the sons of Israel (Exod. 30:12). This latest phrase may well be an evidence of direct influence from the Akkadian language.

Often *nāśā'* is used as a part of a gesture—for example, "to lift up" one's hand. This gesture can be hostile (2 Sam. 20:21), a part of taking an oath (Exod. 6:8), something done while praying (Ps. 28:9) and signaling (Isa. 49:22). "To lift up the head" can mean to be or declare independence in power and control (Judg. 8:28). The same phrase can be used of being free (2 Kings 25:27; cf. Gen. 40:13), while losing one's head can mean dying (cf. Gen. 40:19). To "lift one's face" means to be able to look someone straight in the eye, to have a clear conscience toward someone or with reference to something (2 Sam. 2:22), or to anticipate that things will go well (Job 22:26). God says He will "accept" Lot's request; He reassures Lot that things will go the way he wants them to (Gen. 19:21). This phrase can mean "to be well disposed toward" or "to respect" (2 Kings 3:14), and "to be biased in favor of" (Job 13:8). God's "raising His face on one" means that He will show one His favor (Num. 6:26). To raise one's eyes is to see (Gen. 13:10) and to lust for someone (Gen. 39:7).

Nāśā' can also be used with words for sounds and verbal communication. "To lift" one's voice often means to wail (Gen. 21:16). It can also mean to call out loudly (Judg. 9:7), to speak (a proverb; Num. 23:7), to declare (an oracle; 2 Kings 9:25), to slander (Ps. 15:3), to carry (a false rumor; Exod. 23:1), and to speak a name (Exod. 20:7).

This verb can be used with "soul," in the sense "to lift up" one's soul. This means "to hand oneself over to" or "to be dependent on" something—the poor man "lifts up his soul" to his wages (Deut. 24:15).

Sometimes *nāśā'* means "to support"—Gen. 13:6 says the land could not support, or provide enough sustenance for, Abraham's and Lot's parties.

The Bible speaks of bearing sin and iniquity in Exod. 28:38, where it is said that Aaron "may bear the iniquity of the holy things"; the sin of the holy things will be on Aaron, who is "holy to the Lord" (v. 36). In Gen. 18:24 Abraham pleads with God to spare Sodom and Gomorrah and to bear away the sin of the place.

B. Nouns.

nāśî' (נָשִׂיא, 5387), "(elected) chief." This noun appears 130 times, and it refers to one lifted up publicly: " ... Twelve princes shall he beget, and I will make him a great nation" (Gen. 17:20; cf. Num. 1:44).

Several other related nouns occur less frequently. *Maśśā'* appears 45 times as "load" or "bearing" (Num. 11:11) and 21 times as "utter-ance" (2 Kings 9:25). *Maś'ēt*, which occurs 16 times, refers to the "action of lifting up" (cf. Ps. 141:2) and to "something lifted up" (Gen. 43:34). *Śe'ēt* occurs 14 times, with 2 senses: (1) a "lifting up," such as an "uprising" (Job 41:25), and "dignity" (Gen. 49:3); and (2) something that is "lifted up," such as a swelling or blotch (Lev. 13:2). *Neśî'îm* occurs 4 times with the meaning "damp, fog, hovering clouds" (Jer. 10:13). Both *maśśā'āh* (Isa. 30:27) and *śî'* (Job 20:6) occur only once.

TO REND, TEAR

qāra' (קָרַע, 7167), "to rend, tear, tear away." This word is common to both ancient and modern Hebrew. Used some 63 times in the Hebrew Old Testament, it is found for the first time in Gen. 37:29: " ... He rent his clothes." In the expression, "to tear one's clothes," *qāra'* is used 39 times. Usually such "rending" of clothes is an expression of grief (Gen. 37:34; 44:13; 2 Sam. 13:19).

Sometimes the word is used in a symbolic act, such as Ahijah's "tearing" a new garment into twelve pieces and sending them to the twelve tribes as a symbol of coming division (1 Kings 11:30). Samuel used *qāra'* figuratively when he said to Saul: "The Lord hath rent the kingdom of Israel from thee this day ... " (1 Sam. 15:28). Wild animals "rend" or "tear" their prey (Hos. 13:8).

TO REPENT

nāham (נָחַם, 5162), "to repent, comfort." *Nāham* apparently means "to repent" about 40 times and "to comfort" about 65 times in the Old Testament. Scholars assert several views in trying to ascertain the meaning of *nāham* by connecting the word to a change of the heart or disposition, a change of mind, a change of purpose, or an emphasis upon the change of one's conduct.

Most uses of the term in the Old Testament are connected with God's repentance: " ... It repented the Lord that he had made man. . ." (Gen. 6:6); "And the Lord repented [NASB, "changed his mind"] of the evil which he thought to do unto his people" (Exod. 32:14, KJV). Sometimes the Lord "repented" of the discipline He had planned to carry out concerning His people: "If that nation, against whom I have pronounced, turn from their evil, I will repent of the evil that I thought to do unto them" (Jer. 18:8); "If it do evil in my sight, that it obey not my voice, then I will repent of the good. . ." (Jer. 18:10); "And rend your heart, and not your garments, and turn unto the Lord your God: for he is gracious and merciful, slow to anger ... and repenteth him of evil" (Joel 2:13). In other instances, the Lord changed His mind; obviously, He changed when man changed to make the right choices, but He could not change His attitude toward evil when man continued on the wrong course. As God changed His actions, He always remained faithful to His own righteousness.

In some situations, God was weary of "repenting" (Jer. 15:6), suggesting that there might be a point beyond which He had no choice but to implement His discipline. An instance of this action was in Samuel's word to Saul, that God took the kingdom from Israel's first king and intended to give it to another; Samuel declared, "And also the Strength of Israel will not lie nor repent; for he is not a man, that he should repent" (NASB, "change His mind"; 1 Sam. 15:29).

God usually changed His mind and "repented" of His actions because of man's intercession and repentance of his evil deeds. Moses pleaded with God as the intercessor for Israel: "Turn from thy fierce wrath, and repent of this evil against thy people" (Exod. 32:12). The Lord did that when He " ... repented [changed His mind] of the evil which he thought to do unto his people" (Exod. 32:14). As God's prophet preached to Nineveh, " ... God saw their works, that they turned from their evil way; and God repented of the evil, that he had said that he would do unto them ... " (Jonah 3:10). In such instances, God "repented," or changed His mind, to bring about a change of plan. Again, however, God remained faithful to His absolutes of righteousness in His relation to and with man.

Other passages refer to a change (or lack of it) in man's attitude. When man did not "repent" of his wickedness, he chose rebellion (Jer. 8:6). In the eschatological sense, when Ephraim (as a representative of the northern branch of Israel) will "repent" (Jer. 31:19), God then will have mercy (Jer. 31:20).

Man also expressed repentance to other men. Benjamin suffered greatly from the crime of immorality (Judg. 19-20): "And the children of Israel [eleven tribes] repented them from Benjamin their brother, and said, There is one tribe cut off from Israel this day" (Judg. 21:6; cf. v. 15).

Nāham may also mean "to comfort." The refugees in Babylon would be "comforted" when survivors arrived from Jerusalem (Ezek. 14:23); the connection between "comfort" and "repent" here resulted from the calamity God brought upon Jerusalem as a testimony to the truth of His Word. David "comforted" Bath-

sheba after the death of her child born in sin (2 Sam. 12:24); this probably indicates his repentance of what had happened in their indiscretion.

On the other hand, the word was used in the human sense of "comfort." Job asked his three companions, "How then comfort ye me in vain, seeing in your answers there remaineth falsehood?" (Job 21:34; he meant that their attitude seemed cruel and unfeeling). The psalmist looked to God for "comfort": "Thou shalt increase my greatness, and comfort me on every side" (Ps. 71:21). In an eschatological sense, God indicated that He would "comfort" Jerusalem with the restoration of Israel, as a mother comforts her offspring (Isa. 66:13).

REPROACH

A. Noun.

herpāh (חֶרְפָּה, 2781), "reproach." This noun occurs in the Old Testament and in rabbinic Hebrew. Its use in modern Hebrew has been taken over by other nouns. *Herpāh* occurs 70 times in the Hebrew Old Testament. It is rare in the Pentateuch and in the historical books. The noun appears most frequently in the Book of Psalms, in the major prophets, and in Daniel. The first occurrence is in Gen. 30:23: "And she conceived, and bare a son; and said, God hath taken away my reproach."

"Reproach" has a twofold usage. On the one hand, the word denotes the state in which one finds himself. The unmarried woman (Isa. 4:1) or the woman without children (Gen. 30:23) carried a sense of disgrace in a society where marriage and fertility were highly spoken of. The destruction of Jerusalem and the Exile brought Judah to the state of "reproach": "O Lord, according to all thy righteousness, I beseech thee, let thine anger and thy fury be turned away from thy city Jerusalem, thy holy mountain: because for our sins, and for the iniquities of our fathers, Jerusalem and thy people are become a reproach to all that are about us" (Dan. 9:16). On the other hand, the disgrace found in a person or a nation became the occasion for taunting the oppressed. The disgraced received abuse by the words spoken against them and by the rumors which were spread about them.

Whatever the occasion of the disgrace was, whether defeat in battle, exile, or enmity, the psalmist prayed for deliverance from the "reproach": "Remove from me reproach and contempt; for I have kept thy testimonies" (Ps. 119:22—see context; cf. Ps. 109:25). The verbal abuse that could be heaped upon the unfortunate is best evidenced by the synonyms found with *herpāh* in Jer. 24:9: "And I will deliver them to be removed into all the kingdoms of the earth for their hurt, to be a reproach and a proverb, a taunt and a curse, in all places whither I shall drive them." Several prophets predicted that Israel's judgment was partly to be experienced by the humiliating "reproach" of the nations: "And I will persecute them with the sword, with the famine, and with the pestilence, and will deliver them to be removed to all the kingdoms of the earth, to be a curse, and an astonishment, and a hissing, and a reproach, among all the nations whither I have driven them" (Jer. 29:18; cf. Ezek. 5:14). However, the Lord graciously promised to remove the "reproach" at the accomplishment of His purpose: "He will swallow up death in victory; and the Lord God will wipe away tears from off all faces; and the rebuke of his people shall he take away from off all the earth . . . " (Isa. 25:8).

The Septuagint translations are: *oneidismos* ("reproach; reviling; disgrace; insult") and *oneidos* ("disgrace; reproach; insult"). The KJV gives these translations: "reproach; shame; rebuke."

B. Verb.

hārap (חָרַף, 2778), "to say sharp things, reproach." The root with the meaning "to be sharp" is found in Northwest and South Semitic languages. In Hebrew the verb refers to a manner of speech, i.e., to reproach someone. The word appears about 50 times in the Old Testament, once in Ps. 42:10: "As with a sword in my bones, mine enemies reproach me; while they say daily unto me, Where is thy God?"

TO REPROVE

yākah (יָכַח, 3198), "to decide, prove, convince, judge." As in biblical Hebrew, this verb is found in modern Hebrew primarily in the causative forms. It occurs some 60 times in the text of the Hebrew Bible. The first occurrence of the word is in Gen. 20:16, where the KJV translates: " . . . She was reproved." The context indicates, however, that Abraham, Sarah's husband, deserved being "reproved" in our modern meaning of the word, but that Sarah actually was "cleared" (NASB).

It is evident in most of the uses of *yākah* that there is a value judgment involved, as in Ps. 50:21: " . . . I will reprove thee, and [lay the charge before thee]." Negative judgments may lead to reproof, especially by God (Job 5:17). Such divine reproof may be physical: " . . . I will chasten him with the rod of men . . . " (2 Sam. 7:14). But it is the conviction of the wise man that "the Lord reproves him whom he loves" (Prov. 3:12, RSV).

TO REST, REMAIN

nûah (נוּחַ, 5117), "to rest, remain, be quiet." This word is common to ancient and modern Hebrew, as well as ancient Akkadian and Ugaritic. It occurs in the text of the Old Testament approximately 65 times; the first occurrence is in Gen. 8:4: "And the ark [came to rest] . . . upon the mountains of Ararat." This illustrates the frequent use of this word to show a physical settling down of something at some particular place. Other examples are birds (2 Sam. 21:10), insects (Exod. 10:14), and soles of feet in the waters of the Jordan (Josh. 3:13).

"To rest" sometimes indicates a complete envelopment and thus permeation, as in the spirit of Elijah "resting" on Elisha (2 Kings 2:15), the hand of God "resting" on the mountain (Isa. 25:10), and when Wisdom "resteth in the heart of him that hath understanding" (Prov. 14:33). Frequently *nûah* means "to be quiet" or "to rest" after hard work (Exod. 20:11), from onslaught of one's enemies (Esth. 9:16), from trouble (Job 3:26), and in death (Job 3:17). The word may mean "to set one's mind at rest," as when a child receives the discipline of his parent (Prov. 29:17). Sometimes *nûah* means "to leave at rest" or "to allow to remain." Thus, God "allowed" the pagan nations "to remain" in Canaan during Joshua's lifetime (Judg. 2:23). God threatened to abandon the Israelites in the wilderness (Num. 32:15).

It should be noted that while *nûah* is used sometimes as a synonym for *šābat*, "to cease, to rest" (Exod. 20:11), *šābat* really is basically "to cease" from work which may imply rest, but not necessarily so. The writer of Gen. 2:3 is not stressing rest from work but rather God's ceasing from His creative work since it was complete.

TO RETURN

A. Verb.

šûb (שׁוּב, 7725), "to return or go back, bring back." This verb occurs in several Semitic languages (not in Phoenician-Punic and Ethiopic) including Ugaritic (1550–1200 B.C.) and in all periods of Hebrew. It occurs about 1,060 times in biblical Hebrew and about 8 times in biblical Aramaic (in the form *tûb*).

The basic meaning of the verb is movement back to the point of departure (unless there is evidence to the contrary). In the first occurrence of this verb God told Adam that he and Eve would "eat bread, till thou return unto the ground; for out of it wast thou taken: for dust thou art, and unto dust shalt thou return" (Gen. 3:19).

Used in this emphasis, *šûb* can be applied specifically of returning along a path already traversed: "So Esau returned that day on his way unto Seir" (Gen. 33:16). The word can mean "turn away from," as in Ps. 9:3: "When mine enemies are turned back . . . ," or "reverse a direction," as in 2 Kings 20:10: " . . . Let the shadow return backward ten degrees." It can mean the opposite of going out, as when the raven Noah sent forth was constantly going "to and fro" (Gen. 8:7)—this phrase, however, may also mean merely constant movement; the raven went about constantly "here and there" (cf. NASB). In Gen. 8:3 the word is used of the receding of the flood water; the water went (*hālak*) down (*šûb*, "returned") steadily.

The verb can also mean "to follow after": "Behold, thy sister-in-law is gone back unto her people, and unto her gods: return thou after thy sister-in-law" (Ruth 1:15).

Šûb can imply the cessation of something. In this sense, the word can imply "to go away or disappear": "And tarry with him a few days, until thy brother's fury turn away" (Gen. 27:44). It can refer to the initiation of the cessation of something. In some cases violence is the means of bringing something to cease: "How then wilt thou turn away the face of one captain of the least of my master's servants . . . " (2 Kings 18:24). In Isa. 47:10 the verb implies both turning away and destroying: "Thy wisdom and thy knowledge, it hath perverted thee. . . . "

In the case of spiritually returning (metaphorically) to the Lord, *šûb* can mean "turning away from" following Him (Num. 14:43), "turning from" pursuing evil (1 Kings 8:35), and "to return" to Him and obey Him (Deut. 30:2). The verb can also be used in close relation to another verb to indicate the repetition of an action presented by the other verb: " . . . I will again feed and keep thy flock" (Gen. 30:31).

B. Nouns.

mešûbāh (מְשׁוּבָה, 4878), "backturning; apostasy." This noun occurs 12 times, and it refers to "backsliding" in Hos. 14:4: "I will heal their backsliding, I will love them freely: for mine anger is turned away from him."

Other nouns related to the verb *šûb* occur less frequently. *Tešûbāh* is found 8 times, and it may mean "return" or "beginning" (1 Sam. 7:17) and "answer" (Job 21:34). *Šûbāh* occurs once to mean "coming back" or "turning back" (Isa. 30:15).

TO RIDE

rākab (רָכַב, 7392), "to ride, cause to ride." Already found in ancient Akkadian and Uga-

ritic, this word is also common to both ancient and modern Hebrew. It occurs approximately 70 times in the text of the Hebrew Bible and is found for the first time in Gen. 24:61: "And Rebekah arose, and her damsels, and they rode upon the camels. . . . " In addition to camels, the biblical account records the riding of mules (2 Sam. 13:29), asses (1 Sam. 25:42), horses (Zech. 1:8), and chariots (2 Kings 9:16). "To ride" upon horses is symbolic of an alliance with Assyria (Hos. 14:3).

Isaiah's statement that "the Lord rideth upon a swift cloud" (Isa. 19:1) is an interesting parallel to the Ugaritic text's reference to the god Baal as "a rider on the clouds." This is not to equate Baal with God, but simply to note the similar imagery which is used, and the apparent influence of one literature on another.

RIGHT HAND

yāmîn (יָמִין, 3225), "right hand." This word has cognates attested in Ugaritic, Arabic, Syriac, Aramaic, and Ethiopic. It appears about 137 times and in all periods of biblical Hebrew.

First, the word represents the bodily part called the "right hand": "And Joseph took them both, Ephraim in his right hand toward Israel's left hand, and Manasseh in his left hand toward Israel's right hand . . . " (Gen. 48:13). Ehud was "bound as to his right hand"; he was left-handed: "But when the children of Israel cried unto the Lord, the Lord raised them up a deliverer, Ehud the son of Gera, a Benjamite, a man lefthanded . . . " (Judg. 3:15). *Yāmîn* may be used in a figurative sense. God's taking one's "right hand" means that He strengthens him: "For I the Lord thy God will hold thy right hand, saying unto thee, Fear not: I will help thee" (Isa. 41:13). The Bible speaks anthropomorphically, attributing to God human parts and, in particular, a "right hand" (Exod. 15:6). The Bible teaches that God is a spirit and has no body or bodily parts (cf. Exod. 20:4; Deut. 4:15-19). This figure is used of God's effecting His will among men and of His working in their behalf (showing His favor): "And I said, This is my infirmity: but I will remember the years of the right hand of the Most High" (Ps. 77:10).

Second, *yāmîn* represents the direction, to the "right." In this use the word can specify the location of someone or something: "But the children of Israel walked upon dry land in the midst of the sea; and the waters were a wall unto them on their right hand, and on their left" (Exod. 14:29). In other contexts *yāmîn* signifies "direction toward": "Is not the whole land before thee? Separate thyself, I pray thee, from me: if thou wilt take the left hand, then I will go to the right; or if thou depart to the right hand, then I will go to the left" (Gen. 13:9— the first biblical appearance).

Third, *yāmîn* can be used of bodily parts other than the right hand. In Judg. 3:16 the word is used of one's thigh (literally, "thigh of the right hand"): "But Ehud made him a dagger which had two edges, of a cubit length; and he did gird it under his raiment upon his right thigh." The word is used in 1 Sam. 11:2 in conjunction with one's eye and in Exod. 29:22 with a thigh.

Fourth, this word is used to mean "south," since the south is on one's "right" when he faces eastward: "Then came up the Ziphites to Saul to Gibeah, saying, Doth not David hide himself with us in strongholds in the wood, in the hill of Hachilah, which is on the south of Jeshimon?" (1 Sam. 23:19).

Yᵉmānî (יְמָנִי, 3233), "right hand; on the right side; the right side (of one's body); southern." This noun appears 25 times in the Old Testament. *Yᵉmānî* means "right hand" in Exod. 29:20, the first biblical occurrence. In 1 Kings 7:21 the word refers to the "right side" in regard to a location. *Yᵉmānî* appears in Ezek. 4:6 with the meaning of the "right side" of the body. The word implies "southern" in 1 Kings 6:8: "The door for the middle chamber was in the right side [southern side] of the house. . . ."

tēmān (תֵּמָן, 8486), "south; southern quarter; southwards." This noun makes 22 biblical appearances. In its first biblical occurrence (Exod. 26:18), the word refers to the direction "southward." *Tēmān* can mean "south" or "southern quarter" as in Josh. 15:1.

TO BE RIGHTEOUS

A. Verb.

ṣādaq (צָדַק, 6663), "to be righteous, be in the right, be justified, be just." This verb, which occurs fewer than 40 times in biblical Hebrew, is derived from the noun *ṣedeq*. Nowhere is the issue of righteousness more appropriate than in the problem of the suffering of the righteous presented to us in Job, where the verb occurs 17 times. Apart from the Book of Job the frequency of *ṣādaq* in the various books is small. The first occurrence of the verb is in Gen. 38:26, where Judah admits that Tamar was just in her demands: "She hath been more righteous than I; because that I gave her not to Shelah my son."

The basic meaning of *ṣādaq* is "to be righteous." It is a legal term which involves the whole process of justice. God "is righteous" in all of His relations, and in comparison with Him man is not righteous: "Shall mortal man be more just [righteous] than God?" (Job 4:17). In a derived sense, the case presented may be characterized as a just cause in that all facts indicate that the person is to be cleared of all charges. Isaiah called upon the nations to produce witnesses who might testify that their case was right: "Let them bring forth their witnesses, that they may be justified: or let them hear, and say, It is truth" (43:9). Job was concerned about his case and defended it before his friends: " . . . Though I were righteous, yet would I not answer, but I would make supplication to my judge" (9:15). *Ṣādaq* may also be used to signify the outcome of the verdict, when a man is pronounced "just" and is judicially cleared of all charges. Job believed that the Lord would ultimately vindicate him against his opponents (Job 13:18).

In its causative pattern, the meaning of the verb brings out more clearly the sense of a judicial pronouncement of innocence: "If there be a controversy between men, and they come unto judgment, that the judges may judge them; then they shall justify [*ṣādaq*] the righteous [*ṣaddîq*], and condemn the wicked" (Deut. 25:1). The Israelites were charged with upholding righteousness in all areas of life. When the court system failed because of corruption, the wicked were falsely "justified" and the poor were robbed of justice because of trumped-up charges. Absalom, thus, gained a large following by promising justice to the landowner (2 Sam. 15:4). God, however, assured Israel that justice would be done in the end: "Thou shalt not wrest the judgment of thy poor in his cause. Keep thee far from a false matter; and the innocent and righteous slay thou not: for I will not justify the wicked" (Exod. 23:6–7). The righteous person followed God's example. The psalmist exhorts his people to change their judicial system: "Defend the poor and fatherless: do justice to the afflicted and needy" (Ps. 82:3).

Job's ultimate hope was in God's declaration of justification. The Old Testament is in agreement with this hope. When injustice prevails, God is the One who "justifies."

The Septuagint translates the verb by *dikaiaō* ("to do justice, justly, to vindicate"). In the English versions a frequent translation is "to justify" (KJV, RSV, NASB, NIV); modern versions also give the additional translations "to be vindicated" (RSV, NASB, NIV) and "to acquit" (RSV, NIV).

B. Nouns.

ṣedeq (צֶדֶק, 6664); *ṣᵉdāqāh* (צְדָקָה, 6666), "righteousness." These nouns come from a Semitic root which occurs in Hebrew, Phoenician, and Aramaic with a juristic sense. In Phoenician and Old Aramaic it carries the sense of "loyalty" demonstrated by a king or priest as a servant of his own god. In these languages a form of the root is combined with other words or names, particularly with the name of a deity, in royal names. In the Old Testament we meet the name Melchizedek ("king of righteousness"). A more limited meaning of the root is found in Arabic (a South Semitic language): "truthfulness" (of propositions). In rabbinic Hebrew the noun ṣedāqāh signifies "alms" or "demonstrations of mercy."

The word ṣedāqāh, which occurs 157 times, is found throughout the Old Testament (except for Exodus, Leviticus, 2 Kings, Ecclesiastes, Lamentations, Habbakuk, and Zephaniah). Ṣedeq, which occurs 119 times, is found mainly in poetic literature. The first usage of ṣedeq is: "Ye shall do no unrighteousness in judgment: thou shalt not respect the person of the poor, nor honor the person of the mighty: but in righteousness shalt thou judge thy neighbor" (Lev. 19:15); and of ṣedāqāh is: "[Abram] believed in the Lord; and he counted it to him for righteousness" (Gen. 15:6).

Translators have found it difficult to translate these two words. The older translations base their understanding on the Septuagint with the translation dikaiosune ("righteousness") and on the Vulgate iustitia ("justice"). In these translations the legal relationship of humans is transferred to God in an absolute sense as the Lawgiver and with the perfections of justice and "righteousness."

Exegetes have spilled much ink in an attempt to understand contextually the words ṣedeq and ṣedāqāh. The conclusions of the researchers indicate a twofold significance. On the one hand, the relationships among people and of a man to his God can be described as ṣedeq, supposing the parties are faithful to each other's expectations. It is a relational word. In Jacob's proposal to Laban, Jacob used the word ṣedāqāh to indicate the relationship. The KJV gives the following translation of ṣedāqāh: "So shall my righteousness answer for me in time to come, when it shall come for my hire before thy face . . ." (Gen. 30:33). The NASB gives the word "righteousness" in a marginal note, but prefers the word "honesty" in the text itself. The NEB reads "fair offer" instead. Finally, the NIV has: "And my honesty [ṣedāqāh] will testify for me in the future, whenever you check on the wages you have paid me." On the other hand, "righteousness" as an abstract or as the legal status of a relationship is also present in the Old Testament. The locus classicus is Gen. 15:6:

" . . . And he [the Lord] counted it to him [Abraham] for righteousness."

Regrettably, in a discussion of the dynamic versus the static sense of the word, one or the other wins out, though both elements are present. The books of Psalms and of the prophets particularly use the sense of "righteousness" as a state; cf. "Hearken to me, ye that follow after righteousness, ye that seek the Lord: look unto the rock whence ye are hewn, and to the hole of the pit whence ye are digged" (Isa. 51:1); and "My righteousness is near; my salvation is gone forth, and mine arms shall judge the people; the isles shall wait upon me, and on mine arm shall they trust" (Isa. 51:5). The NEB exhibits this tension between dynamic and static in the translation of ṣedeq: "My victory [instead of righteousness] is near, my deliverance has gone forth and my arm shall rule the nations; for me coasts and islands shall wait and they shall look to me for protection" (Isa. 51:5). Thus, in the discussion of the two nouns below, the meanings lie between the dynamic and the static.

Ṣedeq and ṣedāqāh are legal terms signifying justice in conformity with the legal corpus (the Law; Deut. 16:20), the judicial process (Jer. 22:3), the justice of the king as judge (1 Kings 10:9; Ps. 119:121; Prov. 8:15), and also the source of justice, God Himself: "Judge me, O Lord my God, according to thy righteousness; and let them not rejoice over me. . . . And my tongue shall speak of thy righteousness and of thy praise all the day long" (Ps. 35:24, 28).

The word "righteousness" also embodies all that God expects of His people. The verbs associated with "righteousness" indicate the practicality of this concept. One judges, deals, sacrifices, and speaks righteously; and one learns, teaches, and pursues after righteousness. Based upon a special relationship with God, the Old Testament saint asked God to deal righteously with him: "Give the king thy judgments, O God, and thy righteousness unto the king's son" (Ps. 72:1).

The Septuagint gives the following translations: dikaios ("those who are upright, just, righteous, conforming to God's laws"); dikalosunē ("righteousness; uprightness"); and eleemosunē ("land deed; alms; charitable giving"). The KJV gives the senses "righteousness; justice."

C. Adjective.

ṣaddîq (צַדִּיק, 6662), "righteous; just." This adjectival form occurs 206 times in biblical Hebrew. In Old Aramaic the adjective signifies "loyalty" of a king or high priest to his personal god, often represented by a gift to the god. Similarly in Phoenician, the noun and adjective apply to the loyal relationship of the king before the gods. The word is used of God in Exod. 9:27: "I have sinned this time: the Lord is righteous, and I and my people are wicked." *Ṣaddîq* is used of a nation in Gen. 20:4: "...And he said, Lord, wilt thou slay also a righteous nation?"

TO RISE UP EARLY

šākam (שָׁכַם, 7925), "to rise early, start early." Found in both biblical and modern Hebrew, this verb occurs some 65 times in the Hebrew Old Testament. It is found for the first time in Gen. 19:2: "...And ye shall rise up early, and go on your ways." As in this instance, many of the instances of the use of *šākam* are in connection with traveling. Thus, it may be used with verbs of going (as above) or encamping (Judg. 7:1). The word is used some 30 times in reference to rising early in the morning, as in 1 Sam. 29:10, in which this phrase appears twice: "Wherefore now rise up early in the morning with thy master's servants that are come with thee: and as soon as ye be up early in the morning, and have light, depart."

A number of times in the Book of Jeremiah, "rising up early" is used with "speaking" (7:13; 25:3; 35:14), "sending" (7:25; 25:4; 29:19; 35:15; 44:4), "protesting" (11:7), or "teaching" (32:33). Ps. 127:2 gives some interesting advice while using this word: "It is vain for you to rise up early, to sit up late, to eat the bread of sorrows: for so he giveth his beloved sleep."

RIVER; WADI

A. Nouns.

nahal (נַחַל, 5158), "wadi (or wady); torrent-valley; torrent; river; shaft." This root also occurs in Akkadian, post-biblical Hebrew, and Syriac. In Arabic these same radicals mean "palm tree." *Nahal* occurs about 139 times in biblical Hebrew and in all periods.

This noun represents a dry valley in which water runs during the rainy season: "And Isaac departed thence, and pitched his tent in the valley of Gerar, and dwelt there" (Gen. 26:17—the first biblical appearance). The word can signify the "wady" when it is full of rushing water. Indeed, it appears to describe the rushing water itself: "And he took them, and sent them over the brook..." (Gen. 32:23). Sometimes *nahal* means a permanent stream or "river": "These shall ye eat of all that are in the waters: whatsoever hath fins and scales in the waters, in the seas, and in the rivers, them shall ye eat" (Lev. 11:9). Finally, the word represents a miner's shaft (only once in the Scripture): "They

open shafts in a valley away from where men live" (Job 28:4, RSV).

The Pentateuch consistently distinguishes between extra-Egyptian waterways (calling them *nahal*, 13 times, and *nāhār*, 13 times) and inter-Egyptian waterways (calling them *yᵉ'ôr*). This distinction demonstrates the kind of firsthand knowledge and historical concern expected from a mature eyewitness.

Nahal is used figuratively of many things that emerge and disappear suddenly or that have extreme onrushing power such as the pride of nations (Isa. 66:12), the strength of the invader (Jer. 47:2), and the power of the foe (Ps. 18:4). Torrents of oil do not please God if the offerer's heart is wrongly disposed (Mic. 6:7). God overfloods the godly with torrents of His good pleasure (Ps. 36:8). The eschaton is typified by streams, or torrents, in the desert (Ezek. 47:5–19; cf. Exod. 17:3ff.).

nāhār (נָהָר, 5104), "river; stream; canal; current." Cognates of this word are attested in Ugaritic, Akkadian, Aramaic, and Arabic. The word appears about 120 times in biblical Hebrew and in all periods.

First, this word usually refers to permanent natural watercourses. In its first biblical appearance *nāhār* represents the primeval "rivers" of Eden: "And a river went out of Eden to water the garden; and from thence it was parted, and became into four heads" (Gen. 2:10).

In some passages *nāhār* may represent a "canal(s)": "Say unto Aaron, Take thy rod, and stretch out thine hand upon the waters of Egypt, upon their streams [the branches of the Nile], upon their rivers [canals], and upon their ponds..." (Exod. 7:19; cf. Ezek. 1:1).

Third, this word is used of "ocean currents": "For thou hadst cast me into the deep, in the midst of the seas; and the floods compassed me about: all thy billows and thy waves passed over me" (Jonah 2:3).

Fourth, *nāhār* is used of underground streams: "For he hath founded it [the earth] upon the seas, and established it upon the floods" (Ps. 24:2). This passage appears to be a literary allusion to the pagan concept of the creation and structure of the world—the next verse is "Who shall ascend into the hill of the Lord?" (Ps. 24:3).

This word plays a prominent role in the figure of divine blessing set forth in Ps. 46:4: "There is a river, the streams whereof shall make glad the city of God...." This may be an allusion to the primeval "river" in Eden whose water gave life to the garden. In Isa. 33:21 the same Jerusalem is depicted as having "rivers" of blessing: "...A place of broad rivers and streams; wherein shall go no galley with oars, neither shall gallant ship pass thereby" (cf. Isa. 48:18). In other passages a "river" is a figure of trouble and difficulty: "When thou passest through the waters, I will be with thee; and through the rivers, they shall not overflow thee..." (Isa. 43:2). This is in marked contrast to the use of the same idea in Isa. 66:12, where an "overflowing stream" depicts respectively the onrush of God's glory and divine peace.

B. Verb.

nāhar (נָהַר, 5102), "to flow." This verb, derived from the noun *nāhār*, occurs 3 times in biblical Hebrew. The first occurrence is in Isa. 2:2: "And it shall come to pass in the last days, that the mountain of the Lord's house shall be established in the top of the mountains, and shall be exalted above the hills; and all nations shall flow unto it."

ROCK

sûr (צוּר, 6697), "rock; rocky wall; cliff; rocky hill; mountain; rocky surface; boulder." Cognates of this word appear in Amorite, Phoenician, Ugaritic, and Aramaic. Other than in names of places and persons, the word appears 70 times in biblical Hebrew and in all periods.

First, *sûr* means "rocky wall" or "cliff." This is probably what Moses struck in Exod. 17:6: "Behold, I will stand before thee there upon the rock in Horeb; and thou shalt smite the rock, and there shall come water out of it...." Thus God hid Moses in a cleft of the "rocky cliff" (Exod. 33:21–22).

Second, the word frequently means "rocky hill" or "mountains." This emphasis clearly emerges in Isa. 2:10, 19: "Enter into the rock, and hide thee in the dust.... And [men] shall go into the holes of the rocks, and into the caves of the earth...." Thus "rock" is an abbreviation for "caves of the rocks." A lookout sees someone "from the top of the rocks [hills]..., from the hills" (Num. 23:9). The "rock" (mountains or hills) flowing with honey and oil figures the abundant overflowing blessing of God (Deut. 32:13). The "rock" (or mountain) serves as a figure of security (Ps. 61:2), firmness (Job 14:18), and something that endures (Job 19:24).

Third, *sûr* can mean "rocky ground" or perhaps a large flat "rock": "And Rizpah the daughter of Aiah took sackcloth, and spread it for her upon the rock..." (2 Sam. 21:10; cf. Prov. 30:19).

Fourth, in some passages the word means "boulder," in the sense of a rock large enough to serve as an altar: "...There rose up fire out of the rock, and consumed the flesh and the unleavened cakes..." (Judg. 6:21).

"Rock" is frequently used to picture God's support and defense of His people (Deut. 32:15). In some cases this noun is an epithet, or meaningful name, of God (Deut. 32:4), or of heathen gods: "For their rock [god] is not as our Rock [God]..." (Deut. 32:31).

Finally, Abraham is the source (rock) from which Israel was hewn (Isa. 51:1).

TO RULE

māšal (מָשַׁל, 4910), "to rule, reign, have dominion." This term is common in both ancient and modern Hebrew. It is found approximately 100 times in the text of the Hebrew Old Testament. The word is used for the first time in the Old Testament in Gen. 1:18, where the sun, moon, and stars are designated "to rule over the day and over the night...."

Māšal is used most frequently in the text to express the "ruling or dominion" of one person over another (Gen. 3:16; 24:2). Cain is advised "to rule over" or "master" sin (Gen. 4:7). Joseph's brothers respond to his dreams with the angry question: "Shalt thou indeed reign over us?" (Gen. 37:8; the Hebrew verb here is literally "ruling will you rule," the repetition of the same root giving the needed emphasis).

As Creator and Sovereign over His world, God "ruleth by his power for ever" (Ps. 66:7). When God allowed Israel to have a king, it was with the condition that God was still the ultimate King and that first loyalty belonged to Him (Deut. 17:14–20). This theocratic ideal is perhaps best expressed by Gideon: "I will not rule over you, neither shall my son rule over you: the Lord shall rule over you" (Judg. 8:23). With the possible exception of David, no king of Israel fully lived up to the theocratic ideal, and David himself had some problems with it.

TO RUN

A. Verb.

rûs (רוּץ, 7323), "to hasten, run." This verb also appears in Ethiopic, Aramaic (where it is spelled *rᵉhas*), and Akkadian (where it means "hasten to one's aid"). It appears about 80 times in the Bible and in all periods of the language.

In some contexts *rûs* signifies moving very quickly or "hastening" rather than running. This appears to be the emphasis in its first occurrence, where we are told that "when [Abraham] saw them [the three men], he ran to meet them from the tent door..." (Gen. 18:2). Abraham did not run to meet the three men but instead moved very quickly to meet them. So, also, Abraham probably did not run but "hastened" to his herd to choose the animal for the meal (cf. Gen. 18:7). This meaning is confirmed by Isa. 59:7, where the verb is in synonymous parallelism with *māhar* ("to hasten"): "Their [the wicked's] feet run to evil, and they make haste to shed innocent blood...." The sense "hasten" or "move quickly" also appears in Gen. 41:14, where we are told that "Pharaoh sent and called Joseph, and they brought him hastily out of the dungeon...." It appears again in the sense "quickly" in Ps. 68:31: "...Let Ethiopia hasten to stretch out her hands to God" (RSV).

Usually this word means "to run." This significance is quite clear in Josh. 8:19, where it is reported that the Israelites in ambush (against Ai) "arose quickly out of their place, and they ran as soon as he [Joshua] had stretched out his hand: and they entered into the city, and took it...." This is a military picture. It describes the height of battle when a troop rushes/runs headlong into the enemy or their camp. Samuel told Israel that God would give them a king after their own hearts (one that met their standards) but that he would make their sons "run" before his chariots, or "run" headlong into battle (1 Sam. 8:11). It was not having a king that was evil, for God had provided for a king in the Mosaic law (cf. Deut. 17:14ff.). The people sinned because they wanted a king who would be like the kings over other peoples. He would be primarily a military leader. Therefore, God responded that He would give them the kind of king they wanted but that their battles would be won at the cost of their sons' lives. David, the man after God's own heart (the man of God's choosing), was an imperfect king, but when he repented and obeyed God, battles were won without the loss of Israelite lives. This military sense of charging into battle appears metaphorically, describing the lifestyle of the wicked—they "rush" headlong at God (Job 15:26). This emphasis also explains the rather difficult passage 2 Sam. 22:30: "For by thee I have run through a troop...," which means to charge at the enemy (cf. NASB, "margin").

Rûṣ is also used of "running away from" something or someone. In the battle against Midian when Gideon and his band routed the unsuspecting enemy, "all the host [Midianites] ran, and cried, and fled" (Judg. 7:21). But as with the previous emphasis, so this nuance of "to run away from" may be used in non-military contexts. In 1 Sam. 20:36 the verb signifies running away from someone in search of something, in the sense of not fleeing but pursuing. Jonathan told his aide: "Run, find out now the arrows which I shoot."

Rûṣ can signify "running" into somewhere not only in a hostile sense but in order to be united with or hidden by it. For example, the sage confesses that "the name of the Lord is a strong tower: the righteous runneth into it, and is safe" (Prov. 18:10). The goal of "running" may be unspecified while the direction or path is emphasized. So used, *rûṣ* means to pursue a particular course of action: "I will run the way of thy commandments..." (Ps. 119:32).

The word is used in several technical senses. Kings and pretenders to the throne demonstrate their exalted position by having runners precede their chariots (2 Sam. 15:1). Perhaps this was in direct response to Samuel's description in 1 Sam. 8:11. Runners also served as official messengers; so Ahimaaz son of Zadok said: "Let me now run, and bear the king [David] tidings, how that the Lord hath avenged him of his enemies [Absalom]" (2 Sam. 18:19).

There are a few additional special nuances of *rûṣ*. In Song of Sol. 1:4 the word has something to do with love-making, so the translation "let us run together" (NASB) is probably misleading. Perhaps one might translate: "Draw me after you and let us hasten [to make love]; the king has brought me into his bed chambers." In Hag. 1:9 the word means "to busy oneself": "Because of mine house that is waste, and ye run every man unto his own house." Finally, Hab. 2:2 uses this verb to mean "to read quickly," or fluently: "Write the vision, and make it plain upon tables, that he may run that readeth it."

B. Noun.

mērûṣ means "running; course." This noun, which occurs only 4 times in biblical Hebrew, represents both the mode of running (2 Sam. 18:27) and the course one runs (Jer. 23:10).

S

SACRIFICE

zebaḥ (זֶבַח, 2077), "sacrifice." This root with the meaning "to sacrifice" is represented in other Semitic languages: Akkadian, Ugaritic, Phoenician, Aramaic, and Arabic. *Zebaḥ* continued to be used in Mishnaic Hebrew, and its use is greatly reduced in modern Hebrew, since there is no temple. The word is used 162 times in the Hebrew Old Testament and in all periods. The first occurrence is in Gen. 31:54: "Then Jacob offered sacrifice upon the mount, and called his brethren to eat bread: and they did eat bread, and tarried all night in the mount."

The basic meaning of *zebaḥ* is "sacrifice." When a "sacrifice" had been slaughtered by the priest, he then offered it to God. The purpose was not just to create communion between God and man; rather, the "sacrifice" represented the principle that, without the shedding of blood, there is no forgiveness of sins (Lev. 17:11; cf. Heb. 9:22). In the act of "sacrifice" the faithful Israelite submitted himself to the priest, who, in keeping with the various detailed regulations (see Leviticus), offered the "sacrifice" in accordance with God's expectations. The "sacrifices" are the Passover "sacrifice" (Exod. 12:27), "sacrifice" of the peace offering (Lev. 3:1ff.), "sacrifice" of thanksgiving (Lev. 7:12), and "sacrifice" of the priest's offering (*qārbān;* Lev. 7:16). The *zebaḥ* was not like the burnt offering (*'ōlāh*), which was completely burnt on the altar; and it was unlike the sin offering (*ḥaṭṭā't*), where the meat was given to the priest, for most of the meat of the *zebaḥ* was returned to the person who made the "sacrifice." The fat was burned on the altar (Lev. 3:4–5), and the blood was poured out around the altar (3:2). The person who made the *zebaḥ* had to share the meat with the officiating priest (Exod. 29:28; Lev. 7:31–35; Deut. 18:3).

In view of the fact that the people shared in the eating of the *zebaḥ*, the "sacrifice" became a communal meal in which the Lord hosted His people. Zephaniah's message of judgment is based on this conception of "sacrifice": "Hold thy peace at the presence of the Lord God: for the day of the Lord is at hand: for the Lord hath prepared a sacrifice, he hath bid his guests" (Zeph. 1:7). The Israelite came to the temple with the animal to be sacrificed. It was butchered, boiled, and eaten in the area of the sanctuary (1 Sam. 2:13). Apart from the sanctuaries, the Israelites also celebrated God's goodness together in their native villages. The story of Samuel gives several good illustrations of this custom (cf. 1 Sam. 9:13; 16:2–3).

The prophets looked with condemnation on apostate Israel's "sacrifices": "To what purpose is the multitude of your sacrifices unto me? saith the Lord: I am full of the burnt offerings of rams, and the fat of fed beasts; and I delight not in the blood of bullocks, or of lambs, or of he goats" (Isa. 1:11). Hosea spoke about the necessity of Israel's love for God: "For I desired mercy, and not sacrifice; and the knowledge of God more than burnt offerings" (Hos. 6:6). Samuel the prophet rebuked Saul with the familiar words: "Hath the Lord as great delight in burnt offerings and sacrifices, as in obeying the voice of the Lord? Behold, to obey is better than sacrifice, and to hearken than the fat of rams" (1 Sam. 15:22). David knew the proper response to God when he had sinned: "For thou desirest not sacrifice; else would I give it: thou delightest not in burnt offering. The sacrifices of God are a broken spirit: a broken and a contrite heart, O God, thou wilt not despise" (Ps. 51:16–17).

The Septuagint gives the following translation: *thusia* ("sacrifice; offering"). The KJV gives these senses: "sacrifice; offering."

TO SANCTIFY

A. Verb.

qādaš (קָדַשׁ, 6942), "to sanctify, be holy." This verb also appears in Phoenician, biblical Aramaic, and Ethiopic. In Ugaritic *q-d-š* signifies "sanctuary," and in Old Babylonian *qadāšu* means "shine." *Qādaš* appears about 170 times in biblical Hebrew and in all periods of the language.

In the primary stem the verb signifies an act whereby, or a state wherein, people or things are set aside for use in the worship of God: they are consecrated or "made sacred." By this act and in this state the thing or person consecrated is to be withheld from workaday use (or profane use) and to be treated with special care as a possession of God. The first use of *qādaš* in this stem focuses on the act: "And thou shalt take of the blood that is upon the altar, and of the anointing oil, and sprinkle it upon Aaron, and upon his garments, and upon his sons, and upon the garments of his sons with him: and he shall be hallowed, and his garments, and his sons, and his sons' garments with him" (Exod. 29:21). There are also overtones of ethical-moral (spiritual) holiness here since the atoning blood was applied to the people involved. The state appears to be emphasized when the word is used in Exod. 29:37: "Seven days thou shalt make an atonement for the altar, and sanctify it; and it shall be an altar most holy: whatsoever toucheth the altar shall be holy." Thus, whatever touches the altar enters into a new state. Now it belongs to God to be used solely by Him in the way He sees fit. In some cases this means destruction (2 Sam. 6:6ff.), while in others it means such things are to be used only by those who are ritualistically pure (Num. 4:15; 1 Sam. 21:6). It might mean that such things are to be used in the sanctuary itself (Num. 16:37ff.).

In some passages qādaš seems to mean the opposite of "holy," defiled so as not to be usable to Israel (God's consecrated people): "Thou shalt not sow thy vineyard with [two kinds of] seeds: lest the fruit of thy seed which thou hast sown, and the fruit of thy vineyard, be defiled" (Deut. 22:9; cf. Ezek. 44:19; 46:20, etc.).

In the passive stem the verb means "to prove oneself holy." So Moses wrote: "This is the water of Meribah; because the children of Israel strove with the Lord, and he was sanctified in them" (Num. 20:13). This proving refers not to an act of judgment against sin (an ethical-moral holiness) but a miraculous act of deliverance. Some scholars see an emphasis here on divine power, arguing that at this stage of their history Israel's concept of holiness was similar to that of the pagans, namely, that "holy" signified the presence of extraordinary power. A similar use of the word occurs in the prophet's promise of the future restoration of Israel: "When I . . . am sanctified in them in the sight of many nations . . ." (Ezek. 39:27).

Another emphasis of this stem appears in Lev. 10:3 (its first biblical appearance), "to be treated as holy": " . . . I will be sanctified in them that come nigh me [approach me in formal worship], and before all the people I will be glorified." Again, the emphasis appears to be on divine power; God will have people obey Him and view Him as a powerful (holy) God. There is an ethical-moral overtone here, too, for God desires His people to obey Him, to hate sin and love righteousness (cf. Isa. 5:16). It is love not fear that lies at the root of Israel's relationship to their God (Deut. 6:3, 5ff.).

Finally, this stem may be used as a true passive of the primary stem in the sense of "to be consecrated or set aside for God's use": "And there [the tent of meeting] I will meet with the children of Israel, and the tabernacle shall be sanctified by my glory" (Exod. 29:43).

Qādaš has several emphases in the intensive stem. First, it can mean "to declare something holy" or to declare it to be used exclusively for celebrating God's glory. In Gen. 2:3 (the first biblical occurrence of the word) "God blessed the seventh day, and sanctified it: because that in it he had rested from all his work which God created and made." A related meaning of the word appears in the Ten Commandments: "Remember the sabbath day, to keep it holy" (Exod. 20:8). Israel is to remember the Sabbath by keeping it holy, by celebrating God's person or worshiping Him in the way He specifies. In a still different nuance, "to sanctify" a holy day means to proclaim it, to bind oneself and one's fellows to keep it holy when it comes. This sense can be applied to pagan holy days: "Proclaim a solemn assembly for Baal. And they proclaimed it" (2 Kings 10:20). In Joel 1:14 the verb is applied to Israel's holy days: "Sanctify ye a fast, call a solemn assembly. . . ." Thus, the word comes to mean "to declare" and "to make proper preparations for." In this sense it is sometimes applied to warfare: "Prepare ye war against her; arise, and let us go up at noon" (Jer. 6:4; cf. Mic. 3:5). Even pagans declare holy war: "Set ye up a standard in the land, blow the trumpet among the nations, prepare the nations against her, call together against her the kingdoms of Ararat, Minni . . ." (Jer. 51:27).

This stem may also be used of putting something or someone into a state reserved exclusively for God's use: "Sanctify unto me all the first-born, whatsoever openeth the womb among the children of Israel, both of man and of beast: it is mine" (Exod. 13:2). The first-born of every beast is to be offered up to God by being given to the temple or killed (Exod. 13:12–13). The first son may be redeemed (bought back from the Lord; Num. 18:15–16) or given to the temple (1 Sam. 1:24).

Qādaš may also be used in the sense of making something or someone cultically pure and meeting all God's requirements for purity in persons or things used in the formal worship of Him. This act appears in Exod. 19:10, where God told Moses to "go unto the people, and sanctify them today and tomorrow, and let them wash their clothes." Thus consecrated, the people could come into God's presence. In a related sense, the verb means "to set someone aside for divine service." Although the primary emphasis here is ritualistic, there are ethical-moral overtones. Thus, God directed Moses to have the artisans make special clothing for Aaron: " . . . And they shall make holy garments for Aaron thy brother, . . . that he may minister unto me in the priest's office" (Exod.

28:4). When the consecration occurred, Aaron and his sons were sprinkled with the blood of the atonement. Such an offering necessitated their confessing their sin and submitting to a substitutionary (albeit typological) sacrifice. Used in this sense the word describes the necessary step preceding ordination to the priestly office.

Qādaš is also applied to the consecration of things by placing them into a state of ritualistic or cultic purity and dedicating them solely to God's use (cultic use; cf. Exod. 29:36; Lev. 16:19). In some cases consecrating something to God requires no act upon the object, but leaving it entirely alone. Moses acknowledges to God that "the people cannot come up to mount Sinai: for thou chargedst us, saying, Set bounds about the mount, and sanctify it" (Exod. 19:23). In Isa. 29:23–24 the verb means "to recognize God as holy," as the only real source of truth, and to live according to His laws: "But when he [the house of Jacob] seeth his children, the work of mine hands, in the midst of him, they shall sanctify my name, and sanctify the Holy One of Jacob, and shall fear the God of Israel. They also that erred in spirit shall come to understanding, and they that murmured shall learn doctrine." In Ezek. 36:23 *qādaš* means "to prove oneself to be holy, or to demonstrate and vindicate one's holiness."

In the causative stem the word means "to give for God's use": "And it shall be upon Aaron's forehead, that Aaron may bear the iniquity of the holy things, which the children of Israel shall hallow..." (Exod. 28:38). The act whereby someone gives things to God is also described by the word *qādaš*. The priests performed the actual consecration ceremony while an individual decided that something he owned was to be given to God: "... King David did dedicate [these vessels] unto the Lord..." (2 Sam. 8:11). In Lev. 27:14ff. several objects are listed which may be given to God as a gift and which may be redeemed by substitutionary payments. In Num. 8:17 God identified "sanctifying" the first-born and killing them. Thus, they were removed from profane use and taken over completely by God: "... On the day that I smote every first-born in the land of Egypt I sanctified them for myself."

God's consecrating something or someone may also mean that He accepts that person or thing as in His service: "... I have hallowed this house, which thou hast built, to put my name there for ever; and mine eyes and mine heart shall be there perpetually" (1 Kings 9:3). In a more emphatic nuance the word is a correlative of election, signifying God's appointing

someone to His service: "... Before thou camest forth out of the womb I sanctified thee, and I ordained thee a prophet unto the nations" (Jer. 1:5; cf. 12:3). This verb also means "to prepare to approach God": "... For the Lord hath prepared a sacrifice, he hath bid his guests" (Zeph. 1:7). Here, since the word is synonymously parallel to the concept "prepare," or "make ready," it, too, refers to making ready. In Num. 20:12 the stem presents the word in the meaning "trust as holy"; Moses did not follow God's orders recognizing His demand for perfect obedience (cf. Isa. 8:13).

B. Nouns.

qōdeš (קֹדֶשׁ, 6944), "holy thing." This noun, which occurs about 470 times in biblical Hebrew, also appears in Ugaritic. Appearing in all periods of biblical Hebrew, it reflects several of the verbal meanings just presented. First, *qōdeš* is used of things or people belonging to God. All Israel is holy (Exod. 30:31), separated to God's service, and therefore should keep itself separated to that service by observing the distinction between things holy (allowed by God) and things unclean (Lev. 10:10).

The word also describes things set aside for exclusive use by God's people (Isa. 35:8). It is used of a more narrow sense of "sacred," or something set aside for use in the temple (cultic use). So the word describes the priestly (sacred) garments (Exod. 28:2). It can be used of sacred things given to the Lord (to be used in the sanctuary and/or by the priests and Levites; Exod. 28:38) and sacred things to be used only by the priests and/or Levites (Exod. 29:32–33). In some cases such dedicated (sacred) gifts may be given to others—at the Lord's direction (Deut. 26:13). In a similar sense *qōdeš* describes sacred things appointed for sacrifice and ritualistic-cultic worship (Exod. 30:25; Lev. 27:10). Israel is to set aside certain sacred days (Sabbaths) exclusively for divine service—for rest from labor (Exod. 20:10), rest in the Lord (Deut. 5:14), and holy convocation (Exod. 12:16).

Qōdeš can also be used of what God makes a person, place, or thing to be. He designates a place to be His (Exod. 3:5—the first biblical appearance of the word), that is, separate and unique. Even more, God designates His sanctuary a holy place (Exod. 36:1). The outer part of the sanctuary is *the* holy place, the inner part the holy of holies (Exod. 26:33), and the altar a most holy place. This means that to varying degrees these places are identified with the holy God (2 Sam. 6:10–11), the God who is separate from and hates all that is death and/or associated with death and idolatry (Ezek. 39:25). This word is also used (infrequently) to describe God's majestic holiness, in that He is without equal and without imperfection (Exod. 15:11). In at least one place the emphasis is on God's holiness as power (Jer. 23:9).

The noun *miqdāš*, which occurs in biblical Hebrew about 74 times, appears in Aramaic and post-biblical Hebrew. The word represents a "sacred place" or "sanctuary," a place set aside by men upon God's direction and acceptance as the place where He meets them and they worship Him (Exod. 15:17—the first biblical occurrence of the word).

The noun *qādēš*, which occurs about 11 times in biblical Hebrew, indicates a "cult prostitute," whether female (Gen. 38:21—the first biblical appearance) or male. Male cultic prostitutes were homosexuals (1 Kings 22:46). This noun appears in the Pentateuch, all periods of historical writings, and Hosea and Job.

C. Adjective.

qādôš (קָדוֹשׁ, 6918), "holy." The adjective *qādôš* occurs about 116 times in biblical Hebrew and in all periods. This adjective is more focused in emphasis than the noun *qōdeš*. *Qādôš* can refer (infrequently) to cultic holiness, or ritualistic ceremonial holiness (Num. 5:17). Its most frequent use, however, represents God's majestic (1 Sam. 2:2), moral (Lev. 11:44), and dynamistic holiness (holiness as power; 1 Sam. 6:20). The word is also used of what God claims for Himself, what is consecrated to His service (Exod. 29:31). When applied to people, the word may mean "set apart for God" (Ps. 16:3), ritualistically separated to Him (Exod. 19:6—the first biblical occurrence of the word), and thoroughly purified and perfected by Him from all moral evil (Isa. 4:3). Infrequently *qādôš* is used of non-human beings, separate from this world and endued with great power (Job 5:1; Dan. 8:13).

SATAN

śāṭān (שָׂטָן, 7854), "adversary; Satan." This word appears 24 times in the Old Testament. Most uses of the term relate to the cosmic struggle in the unseen world between God and the opposing forces of darkness.

In Ps. 38:20, David cried out because he was the target of attack by his "adversaries." Possibly David suffered because of mistakes he made; and within the permissive will of God, He used David's enemies to discipline His servant.

In another psalm of distress by an individual, a godly man expressed his deep faith in the Lord. The writer prayed concerning those who were "adversaries" to his soul: "Let them be confounded and consumed that are adversaries to my soul; let them be covered with reproach and dishonor that seek my hurt" (Ps. 71:13). He expressed the reality of the powers of darkness against an individual who sought to live for God.

Imprecatory psalms call for judgment upon one's enemies, reflecting the battle in the unseen world between darkness and light. David's enemies became his "adversaries," but he continued to pray for them (Ps. 109:4). Because those enemies repaid him evil for good and hatred for his love, the king prayed: "Set thou a wicked man over him: and let Satan stand at his right hand" (Ps. 109:6). When they spoke evil against his soul, David called for the Lord's reward against his "adversaries" (Ps. 109:20), and finally, because David's accusers had intended him so much harm, he asked that his accusers be clothed with shame and dishonor (Ps. 109:29). In all of these passages, God worked indirectly by permitting individuals to act as "adversaries" of His people.

In another instance, David was merciful with members of Saul's family who cursed him and wished him harm when he fled from Absalom (2 Sam. 16:5ff.). David restrained his army commanders from killing Saul's family who had repented of their misdeeds. The king did not want his officers to be his "adversaries" on the day of victory and joy (2 Sam. 19:22).

God can also be the "adversary." When Balaam went to curse the sons of Israel, God warned him not to do so. When the prophet persisted, God disciplined him: "And God's anger was kindled because he went: and the angel of the Lord stood in the way for an adversary against him" (Num. 22:22). God stood as an "adversary" because no curse could undo the covenants and agreements already made with Israel.

God took up a controversy with Solomon. When Solomon added more and more pagan wives to his harem, God was greatly displeased (Deut. 17:17). But when the king built pagan shrines for his wives, God raised up "adversaries" against him (1 Kings 11:14), a direct action which caused the Edomites and Syrians to revolt against Israel.

Another special instance of intervention was the occasion when " . . . Satan [literally, "an adversary"] stood up against Israel, and provoked David to number Israel" (1 Chron. 21:1). (No definite article is here in Hebrew and, therefore, "an adversary" is in mind.) In a parallel passage the Lord moved David to number Israel and Judah (2 Sam. 24:1). Even as the Lord stirred up an "adversary" against Solomon, so here

God took a direct action to test David to help him learn a vital lesson. God tests believers to help them make the right choices and not depend upon their own human strength.

In the Book of Job, the word *Satan* always has the definite article preceding it (Job 1:6–12; 2:1–7), so the term emphasizes Satan's role as "the adversary." God permitted Satan to test Job's faith, and the adversary inflicted the patriarch with many evils and sorrows. Satan was not all-powerful because he indicated that he could not get beyond God's protection of Job (Job 1:10). He penetrated the "hedge" only with God's permission and only for specific instances that would demonstrate God's righteousness. Job became the battleground between the forces of darkness and light. He learned that Satan could be defeated by making the right choices and that God can be glorified in every circumstance.

Zechariah recorded a vision of " . . . Joshua the high priest standing before the angel of the Lord, and Satan standing at his right hand to resist him" (literally, "be his adversary"; Zech. 3:1). The Lord rebuked "the adversary" (Zech. 3:2). Satan was once again in conflict with God's purposes and the angels of God, but "the adversary" was not all-powerful and was subject to rebuke by God Himself.

A general usage of *śātān* ("adversary") appears in 1 Kings 5:4: "But now the Lord my God hath given me rest on every side, so that there is neither adversary or evil occurrent." In another instance, David went over to the side of the Philistines; in attempting to fight with them against Israel, some of the Philistine leaders doubted David's sincerity and felt that he would be "an adversary" in any battle between the two armies (1 Sam. 29:4).

In the Septuagint, the word is *diabolos.*

TO BE SATISFIED

śāba' (שָׂבַע, 7646), "to be satisfied, sated, surfeited." This word is found in Akkadian and Ugaritic, as well as in all periods of Hebrew. It occurs some 96 times in the Hebrew Old Testament. In its first occurrence in the Old Testament text, *śāba'* expresses the idea of "being filled, sated": " . . . When the Lord shall give you in the evening flesh to eat, and in the morning bread to the full . . . " (Exod. 16:8). As here, the word is frequently used in parallelism with "to eat," or "to graze" when used with cattle or sheep (Jer. 50:19). The earth too "can be sated, have its fill," of rain (Job 38:27).

In a notoriously difficult verse (Hab. 2:5), wine seems to be referred to as never "being satisfied, never having enough." Instead of "wine," the Habakkuk Dead Sea Scroll reads "wealth," which seems more appropriate in the context which points to Assyria as the concern of Habakkuk's complaint.

Śāba' sometimes expresses "being surfeited with," as in Prov. 25:16: "Hast thou found honey? Eat so much as is sufficient for thee, lest thou be filled therewith, and vomit it." God too can "become surfeited," especially when men offer sacrifices with the wrong motives: " . . . I am full of the burnt offerings of rams . . . " (Isa. 1:11). The wise man noted that the lazy man "that followeth after vain persons shall have poverty enough [be surfeited with poverty]" (Prov. 28:19; to translate "will have plenty of poverty," as does the RSV, is not quite strong enough).

Śāba' often expresses God's "satisfying, supplying," man with his material needs: " . . . Who satisfieth thy mouth with good things; so that thy youth is renewed like the eagle's" (Ps. 103:5). But even when God "fed them to the full," Israel was not satisfied and went after strange gods (Jer. 5:7). Used in parallelism with "to enrich" in Ezek. 27:33, *śāba'* implies something of enriching as well: " . . . Thou filledst many people; . . . thou didst enrich the kings of the earth. . . . "

TO SAVE

A. Verb.

yāša' (יָשַׁע, 3467), "to help, deliver, save." Outside Hebrew this word is attested only in Moabite. It appears in all periods of Hebrew (including post-biblical Hebrew) and in biblical Hebrew about 205 times. The verb occurs only in the causative and passive stems.

Essentially the word means "to remove or seek to remove someone from a burden, oppression, or danger." In Exod. 2:17 (the first appearance of this verb) *yāša'* signifies to remove someone from a burden or job: " . . . Moses stood up and helped them, and watered their flock." The word is frequently used of removing or seeking to remove someone from the danger of defeat: "And the men of Gibeon sent unto Joshua . . . saying, slack not thy hand from thy servants; come up to us quickly, and save us, and help us . . . " (Josh. 10:6). This is a request to preserve them from possible death. The real danger is not yet upon them but soon will be. The Gibeonites see in Israel their only help.

Yāša' is used in other situations as when Jephthah tells the Ephraimites that they had been summoned to the war at a crucial time but did not respond and "delivered me not out of their [children of Ammon] hands" (Judg. 12:2). Here the emphasis is "set free," or "liberate," in other words, to remove someone from a condition already upon him. Militarily the word can also be used of "helping," emphasizing the union of forces so as to forge a single and stronger fighting unit. This is no last-ditch stand for the unit being helped. So Joab told Abishai: "If the Syrians be too strong for me, then thou shalt help me ... " (2 Sam. 10:11). Also, compare: "So the Syrians feared to help [to serve as an ally of] the children of Ammon any more" (2 Sam. 10:19).

In the realm of justice and civil law *yāša'* represents an obligation on the part of anyone who hears an outcry of one being mistreated: "For he [the rapist] found her [the one he was about to rape] in the field, and the betrothed damsel cried, and there was none to save her" (Deut. 22:27; cf. 28:29). Therefore, one may appeal especially to the king as the one obligated to help maintain one's rights: "And when the woman of Tekoah spake to the king, she fell on her face to the ground, and did obeisance, and said, Help, O king" (2 Sam. 14:4; cf. 2 Kings 6:26). The king also "delivered" his people from subjection to their enemies (1 Sam. 10:27; Hos. 13:10). Jeremiah says of the messianic king: "In his days Judah shall be saved, and Israel shall dwell safely ... " (23:6). Here *yāša'* is paralleled by "dwell safely," a phrase which identifies the meaning of *yāša'* as "to be preserved from danger." Ultimately, God is the Great King who "goeth with you, to fight for you against your enemies, to save you [deliver you from danger]" (Deut. 20:4), and the Judge of all Israel.

The word appears in many prayer petitions: "Arise, O Lord; save me, O my God ... " (Ps. 3:7). This is a combination, therefore, of military emphasis (a prayer for deliverance from some enemy by forceful interference) and judicial emphasis (a prayer for that which is the petitioner's due and the obligation of the one petitioned—in God's case the obligation is self-imposed through the establishment of the covenantal relationship; cf. Ps. 20:9). In other instances the judicial obligation is in view: "He [the Lord's anointed king] shall judge the poor of the people, he shall save the children of the needy, and shall break in pieces the oppressor" (Ps. 72:4). In this passage the word in synonymous parallelism to *yāša'* is *šāpaṭ*, "to see that legal justice is executed." Very often the psalmist has in view the spiritual aspect of God's eternal covenant. This is clear in passages such as Ps. 86, where David confesses that, although the ruler of Israel, he is humbled (godly), and that, although enjoying kingly wealth, he is needy (trusting in God). On the basis of these spiritual conditions he prays for God's covenantal response: "Preserve my soul; for I am holy: O thou my God, save thy servant that trusteth in thee" (Ps. 86:2). The blessings sought here are both eternal (Ps. 86:11–13) and temporal (Ps. 86:14–17).

B. Nouns.

yᵉšû'āh (יְשׁוּעָה, 3444), "salvation." This word appears about 78 times and refers primarily to God's acts of help which have already occurred and been experienced. In Gen. 49:18 (the first biblical occurrence), the word includes the idea of "salvation" through divinely appointed means and from inequity. In 1 Sam. 14:45 *yᵉšû'āh* is used of a human act: "And the people said unto Saul, Shall Jonathan die, who hath wrought this great salvation in Israel?" The word is used infrequently of deliverance and/or help effected by things (Isa. 12:3).

The noun *tᵉšû'āh* also means "salvation." It occurs about 34 times. The word is frequently joined with responses of thanksgiving and rejoicing (Judg. 15:18—the first occurrence; 1 Sam. 11:13). *Tᵉšû'āh*, therefore, is sometimes rendered "deliverance" (Judg. 15:18), "victory" (2 Sam. 19:2), as well as "salvation" (Isa. 45:17). The idea of "salvation" is that of preservation from threatened, impending, and perhaps deserved danger and suffering. *Tᵉšû'āh* is used in a few instances of a human act: "Where no counsel is, the people fall: but in the multitude of counselors there is safety" (Prov. 11:14).

The noun *yēša'*, which occurs 36 times, signifies that which God will do in man's behalf (2 Sam. 22:3), or that which has been done by Him for man (2 Sam. 22:36). In two instances this word means simply the general absence of oppression and need (Job 5:4, 11). The word may be translated as "salvation" or "safety."

The noun *môšā'ōt* occurs only once to mean "saving acts" (Ps. 68:20).

SAVOR

A. Noun.

rêaḥ (רֵיחַ, 7381), "savor; smell; fragrance; aroma." Of the 61 appearances of this word, 43 refer specifically to sacrifices made to God and appear in Genesis-Numbers and Ezekiel.

This word refers to the "scent or smell" of a person or thing: "And he [Jacob] came near, ... and he [Isaac] smelled the smell of his raiment ... " (Gen. 27:27). In Song of Sol. 1:12 *rêaḥ* signifies the "fragrance" of perfume and in Song of Sol. 2:3 the "fragrance" of a flower. This word is used of a bad "smell" in Exod. 5:21: " ... Because ye have made our savor to be abhorred [have made us odious] in the eyes of Pharaoh. ... "

Most frequently *rêah* is used of the "odor" of a sacrifice being offered up to God. The sacrifice, or the essence of the thing it represents, ascends to God as a placating "odor": "And the Lord smelled a sweet [NASB, "soothing"] savor..." (Gen. 8:21—the first occurrence of the word).

B. Verb.

rûah (רוּחַ, 7306), "to perceive, enjoy, smell." Gen. 8:21 is the first occurrence: "And the Lord smelled a sweet savor...." The word appears about 14 times.

TO SAY, SPEAK, ANSWER

A. Verb.

'āmar (אָמַר, 559), "to say, speak, tell, command, answer." This verb occurs in all Semitic languages and in all periods of those languages although it has the meaning "to say, speak" only in the so-called Northwest Semitic dialects (except in Ugaritic) and in Aramaic. Elsewhere the word means "to say" or "to see." This verb is used about 5,280 times in Old Testament Hebrew.

'Āmar refers to the simple act of communicating with the spoken word. Usually the word is used of direct speech ("say"), although it may be used of indirect speech as well ("speak").

The usual subject of this verb is some self-conscious personality—man (Gen. 2:23) or God (Gen. 1:3—the first occurrence of the word). Infrequently animals (Gen. 3:1) or, in figures of speech such as personification, inanimate objects "say" something (Judg. 9:8ff.). This verb bears many connotations and in some passages is better translated accordingly. The KJV renders this verb "answer" 98 times ("say as a response"), while the NASB translates such passages "said." In Gen. 9:8 we read: "God spoke to Noah" (NASB); the specific content of the communication is not immediately detailed. In Gen. 22:2 Abraham is to offer Isaac on the "mountain of which" God "tells [says to] him" (NASB). Moses requests Pharaoh to let Israel go and sacrifice to God as He "commands" them (Exod. 8:27); the force of God's speaking is more than merely making a statement: It is authoritative.

In addition to these frequently occurring connotations, *'āmar* is rendered with many words representing various aspects of spoken communication, such as "appoint" or "assign" (1 Kings 11:18), "mention" or "name" (Gen. 43:27), "call" (Isa. 5:20), and "promise" (2 Kings 8:19). Although not always so translated, this word can imply the act of thinking within oneself (Gen. 44:28) and the intention to do something (Exod. 2:14).

When used of divine speaking, this verb may refer to simple communication (Gen. 1:26). Often, however, there is a much fuller sense where God's saying effects the thing spoken (cf. Gen. 1). The phrase "thus says the Lord," so frequent in the prophets, has been analyzed as a message-formula. Ancient Near Eastern letters from, for example, Mari (1750–1697 B.C.) and Amarna (1400–1360 B.C.) contain a similar formula. One might compare our letters which open with "Dear sir." Divine messages are often concluded with the words "says the Lord." The Bible recognizes that behind the divine speaking is divine authority and power.

The Septuagint renders this verb by over 40 different Greek words and most often by *legō* ("to say") and *eipen* ("he said").

B. Nouns.

'ēmer (אֵמֶר, 561), "word; speech." This noun appears 48 times. *'Ēmer* refers to "words" in Prov. 2:1: "My son, if thou wilt receive my words, and hide my commandments with thee."

Several other nouns are related to the verb *'āmar*. *'Imrāh* also means "word, speech," and it occurs 37 times. One occurrence of *'imrāh* is in 2 Sam. 22:31 (cf. Ps. 18:30). The noun *'ōmer* is found 6 times and means "word, speech, promise" (Ps. 68:11; Hab. 3:9). *Ma'amār* and *mē'mar* mean "word, command." *Ma'amār* occurs 3 times (Esth. 1:15; 2:22; 9:32), and *mē'mar* occurs twice (Ezra 6:9; Dan. 4:17).

TO SAY, UTTER, AFFIRM

A. Verb.

ne'um (נְאֻם, 5002), "to say, utter an affirmation, speak." The word is a verbal form of the verb *nā'am*, which occurs only once in the entire Old Testament: "Behold, I am against the prophets, saith [*ne'um*] the Lord, that use their tongues, and say [*nā'am*], He saith [*ne'um*]" (Jer. 23:31). The word *ne'um* appears as many as 361 times and, because of the frequency in the prophetical books, it is characteristic of prophetic speech.

Ne'um is an indicator which generally appears at the end of the quotation: "What mean ye that ye beat my people to pieces, and grind the faces of the poor? saith [*ne'um*] the Lord God of hosts" (Isa. 3:15). The word may also be found in the middle of an argument: "And I raised up of your sons for prophets, and of your young men for Nazarites. Is it not even thus, O ye children of Israel? saith [*ne'um*] the Lord. But ye gave the Nazarites wine to drink; and commanded the prophets, saying, Prophesy not" (Amos 2:11–12).

B. Noun.

n^e'um (נְאֻם, 5002), "utterance; saying." The use of *n^e'um* is rare at the beginning of a statement: "The Lord said unto my Lord [literally, "a statement of Jehovah to my Lord"] , Sit thou at my right hand, until I make thine enemies thy footstool" (Ps. 110:1).

With one exception (Prov. 30:1) in the sayings of Agur, the usage throughout the Old Testament is virtually limited to a word from God. In Numbers the utterances of Balaam are introduced with the formula "and he uttered his oracle": "The *oracle* of Balaam the son of Beor, the *oracle* of the man whose eye is opened" (Num. 24:3, RSV; cf. v. 15). David's concluding words begin with these words: "Now these are the last words of David: The *oracle* of David, the son of Jesse, the *oracle* of the man who was raised on high, the anointed of the God of Jacob, the sweet psalmist of Israel" (2 Sam. 23:1, RSV). Apart from these instances there are a few more examples, but as a rule *n^e'um* is a prophetic term, which even beyond the prophetical literature is associated with a word from God.

The Septuagint gives the following translation(s): *legein* ("utterance in words") and *hode* (used with reference to what follows, e.g., "this is what . . . says").

TO SCATTER

pûṣ (פּוּץ, 6327), "to scatter, disperse, be scattered." This term is found in both ancient and modern Hebrew. Occurring some 65 times in the Hebrew Old Testament, the word is found for the first time in Gen. 10:18: " . . . The families of the Canaanites spread abroad." The word is used 3 times in the story of the tower of Babel (Gen. 11:4, 8–9), apparently to emphasize how men and their languages "were spread" throughout the world.

Pûṣ, in the sense of "scattering," often has an almost violent connotation to it. Thus, when Saul defeated the Ammonites, "they which remained were scattered, so that two of them were not left together" (1 Sam. 11:11). Such "scattering" of forces seems to have been a common thing after defeats in battle (1 Kings 22:17; 2 Kings 25:5). Many references are made to Israel as a people and nation "being scattered" among the nations, especially in the imagery of a scattered flock of sheep (Ezek. 34:5–6; Zech. 13:7). Ezekiel also promises the gathering together of this scattered flock: " . . . I will even gather you from the people, . . . where ye have been scattered . . . " (Ezek. 11:17; 20:34, 41).

In a figurative sense, this word is used to refer to lightning as arrows which God "scatters" (2 Sam. 22:15). According to Job, "the clouds scatter his lightning" (Job 37:11, RSV). No harvest is possible unless first the seeds "are scattered" in rows (Isa. 28:25).

SEA

yām (יָם, 3220), "sea; ocean." This word has cognates in Aramaic, Akkadian, Ugaritic, Phoenician, and Ethiopic. It occurs about 390 times and in all periods of biblical Hebrew.

This word refers to the body of water as distinct from the land bodies (continents and islands) and the sky (heavens): "For in six days the Lord made heaven and earth, the sea and all that in them is . . . " (Exod. 20:11). Used in this sense *yām* means "ocean." This is its meaning in Gen. 1:10, its first biblical appearance; unlike the use in the singular, where the word is a collective noun, it appears here in the plural: "And God called the dry land Earth; and the gathering together of the waters called he Seas. . . . "

Yām may be used of "seas," whether they are salty or fresh. The Great Sea is the Mediterranean: "From the wilderness and this Lebanon even unto the great river, the river Euphrates, all the land of the Hittites, and unto the Great Sea toward the going down of the sun, shall be your coast" (Josh. 1:4). This sea is also called the sea of the Philistines (Exod. 23:31) and the hinter or western sea (Deut. 11:24; KJV, "uttermost sea"). The Dead Sea is called the Salt Sea (Gen. 14:3), the Arabah (Deut. 3:17; KJV, "plain"), and the east sea (Ezek. 47:18). Thus, *yām* can be used of an inland salty "sea." It can also be used of a fresh water "sea" such as the Sea of Galilee: " . . . And the border shall descend, and shall reach unto the side of the Sea of Chinnereth eastward" (Num. 34:11).

The word is sometimes used of the direction west or westward, in the sense of toward the (Great) Sea: "Lift up now thine eyes, and look from the place where thou art northward, and southward, and eastward, and westward" (Gen. 13:14). In Gen. 12:8 *yām* means "on the west side": "And he removed from thence unto a mountain on the east of Beth-el, and pitched his tent, having Beth-el on the west, and Hai on the east. . . . " This word can also refer to a side of something and not just a direction, but it is the side that faces westward: "He turned about to the west side . . . " (Ezek. 42:19). Exod. 10:19 uses *yām* as an adjective modifying "wind": "And the Lord turned a mighty strong west wind, which took away the locusts. . . . "

Yām is used of the great basin immediately in front of the Holy Place: "And the pillars of brass that were in the house of the Lord, and the bases, and the brazen sea that was in the house of the Lord, did the Chaldees break in pieces, and carried the brass of them to Babylon" (2 Kings 25:13). This is also called the "sea" of cast metal (1 Kings 7:23; KJV, "molten sea") or simply the "sea" (Jer. 27:19).

Yām is used of mighty rivers such as the Nile: "And the waters shall fail from the sea, and the river shall be wasted and dried up" (Isa. 19:5). This statement occurs in the middle of a prophecy against Egypt. Therefore, "the river" is the Nile. But since the term "river" is in synonymous parallelism to "the sea," this latter term also refers to the Nile. Ezek. 32:2 uses *yām* of the branches of the Nile: " ... And thou art as a whale in the seas: and thou camest forth with thy rivers, and troubledst the waters with thy feet, and fouledst their rivers." This word can also be used of the Euphrates River (Jer. 51:36).

In some instances the word *yām* may represent the Canaanite god Yamm, "which alone spreadeth out the heavens, and treadeth upon the waves of the sea" (Job 9:8). If understood as a statement about Yamm, this passage would read: "and tramples upon the back of Yamm." The parallelism between "heavens" and "seas," however, would lead us to conclude that the reference here is to the literal "sea." Ps. 89:9–10 is a more likely place to see a mention of Yamm, for there the word is identified as one of God's enemies in immediate proximity to the goddess Rahab: "Thou rulest the raging of the sea [Yamm]: when the waves thereof arise, thou stillest them. Thou hast broken Rahab in pieces, as one that is slain; thou hast scattered thine enemies with thy strong arm." Especially note Job 7:12: "Am I a sea [Yamm], or a whale, that thou settest a watch over me?" (cf. Job 26:12; Ps. 74:13).

SECRET

sôd (סוֹד, 5475), "secret or confidential plan(s); secret or confidential talk; secret; council; gathering; circle." This noun occurs 21 times in biblical Hebrew.

Sôd means, first, "confidential talk": "Hide me from the secret counsel of the wicked ... " (Ps. 64:2). In Prov. 15:22 the word refers to plans which one makes on one's own and before they are shared by others: "Without counsel [self-made] purposes are disappointed: but in the multitude of counselors they [succeed]." Sometimes the word signifies simply a talk about something that should be kept confidential: "Debate thy cause with thy neighbor himself; and discover not a secret to another" (Prov. 25:9).

Second, the word represents a group of intimates with whom one shares confidential matters: "O my soul, come not thou into their [Simeon's and Levi's] secret; unto their assembly, mine honor, be not thou united ... " (Gen. 49:6—the first occurrence of the word). Jer. 6:11 speaks of the "assembly [informal but still sharing confidential matters] of young men together." To "have sweet counsel" is to be in a group where everyone both shares and rejoices in what is being discussed and/or done (Ps. 55:14).

SECURITY

A. Nouns.

mibṭāḥ (מִבְטָח, 4009), "the act of confiding; the object of confidence; the state of confidence or security." This word occurs 15 times. The word refers to "the act of confiding" in Prov. 21:22: "A wise man scaleth the city of the mighty, and casteth down the strength of the confidence thereof." *Mibṭāḥ* means the "object of confidence" in Job 8:14 and the "state of confidence or security" in Prov. 14:26.

Beṭaḥ is a noun meaning "security, trust." One occurrence is in Isa. 32:17: " ... And the effect of righteousness quietness and assurance [*beṭaḥ*] for ever."

B. Verb.

bāṭaḥ (בָּטַח, 982), "to be reliant, trust, be unsuspecting." This verb, which occurs 118 times in biblical Hebrew, has a possible Arabic cognate and a cognate in late Aramaic. The word means "to trust" in Deut. 28:52: "And he shall besiege thee in all thy gates, until thy high and fenced walls come down, wherein thou trustedst, throughout all thy land. ... "

C. Adjective.

beṭaḥ (בֶּטַח, 982), "secure." In two passages this word is used as an adjective suggesting trust and security: "And Gideon went up ... and smote the host: for the host was secure [unsuspecting]" (Judg. 8:11; cf. Isa. 32:17).

D. Adverb.

beṭaḥ (בֶּטַח, 983), "securely." The occurrences of this word appear in all periods of biblical Hebrew.

In its first occurrence *beṭaḥ* emphasizes the status of a city which was certain of not being attacked: " ... Two of the sons ... took each man his sword, and came upon the city boldly, and slew all the males" (Gen. 34:25). Thus the city was unsuspecting regarding the impending attack. In passages such as Prov. 10:9 (cf. Prov. 1:33) *beṭaḥ* emphasizes a confidence and the absence of impending doom: "He that walketh uprightly walketh surely: but he that perverteth his ways shall be known [faces certain judgment]." Israel dwells in security apart from any possible doom or danger because God keeps her completely safe (Deut. 33:12, 28; cf. 12:10). This condition is contingent on their faithfulness to God (Lev. 25:18–19). In the eschaton, however, such absence of danger is guaranteed by the Messiah's presence (Jer. 23:5–6).

TO SEE, PERCEIVE

A. Verb.

rā'āh (רָאָה, 7200), "to see, observe, perceive, get acquainted with, gain understanding, examine, look after (see to), choose, discover." This verb occurs only in Moabite and all periods of Hebrew. It appears in the Bible about 1,300 times.

Basically *rā'āh* connotes seeing with one's eyes: Isaac's "eyes were dim, so that he could not see" (Gen. 27:1). This is its meaning in Gen. 1:4, its first biblical appearance. The word can be used in the sense of seeing only what is obvious: "... For the Lord seeth not as man seeth..." (1 Sam. 16:7). This verb can also mean "to observe": "... And there were upon the roof about three thousand men and women, that beheld while Samson made sport" (Judg. 16:27). The second primary meaning is "to perceive," or to be consciously aware of—so idols "neither see, nor hear" (Deut. 4:28). Third, *rā'āh* can represent perception in the sense of hearing something—God brought the animals before Adam "to see what he would call them" (Gen. 2:19). In Isa. 44:16 the verb means "to enjoy": "... I am warm, I have seen the fire." It can also mean "to realize" or "to get acquainted with": "When I applied mine heart to know wisdom, and to see the business that is done upon the earth..." (Eccl. 8:16). The rebellious men of Jerusalem tell God they will not "see sword nor famine"; they will not experience it (Jer. 5:12).

This verb has several further extended meanings. For example, *rā'āh* can refer to "perceiving or ascertaining" something apart from seeing it with one's eyes, as when Hagar saw that she had conceived (Gen. 16:4). It can represent mentally recognizing that something is true: "We saw certainly that the Lord was with thee..." (Gen. 26:28). Seeing and hearing together can mean "to gain understanding": "... Kings shall shut their mouths at him: for that which had not been told them shall they see; and that which they had not heard shall they consider" (Isa. 52:15). In Mal. 3:18 the verb means "to distinguish": "Then shall ye return, and discern between the righteous and

the wicked...." The word can mean to consider the fact that Israel is God's people (Exod. 33:13).

In addition to these uses of *rā'āh* referring to intellectual seeing, there is seeing used in the sense of living. "To see the light" is to live life (Job 3:16; cf. 33:28). It can mean "experience" in the sense of what one is aware of as he lives: "Even as I have seen, they that plow iniquity... reap the same" (Job 4:8). In 2 Kings 25:19 the verb is used in the unique sense of "having trusted concourse with" when it speaks of the five advisors of the king.

A fourth idea of seeing is "to examine": "And the Lord came down to see the city and the tower..." (Gen. 11:5). This examining can have to do with more than looking something over; it can refer to looking after or supervising something (Gen. 39:23). Used in this sense *rā'āh* can imply looking upon with joy or pain. Hagar asked that she not be allowed to look on the death of Ishmael (Gen. 21:16). This verb may be used of attending to or visiting—so Jonadab said to Amnon: "... When thy father cometh to see thee, say unto him..." (2 Sam. 13:5). When Joseph advised Pharaoh "to look out a man discreet and wise," he was telling him to choose or select such a man (Gen. 41:33). "To examine" may also be "to observe" someone in order to imitate what he does (Judg. 7:17), or "to discover" something (find it out; Judg. 16:5).

B. Nouns.

rō'eh (רֹאֶה, 7203), "seer; vision." *Rō'eh*, which occurs 11 times, refers to a "prophet" (emphasizing the means by which revelation was received; 1 Sam. 9:9) and to "vision" (Isa. 28:7).

Several other nouns are related to the verb *rā'āh. R*ᵉ*'î* appears once to mean "looking-glass" (Job 37:18). *Rō'î*, which occurs 4 times, means "looking, appearance" (1 Sam. 16:12, NASB). *R*ᵉ*'ût* occurs once, and it means "look" (Eccl. 5:11). *Mar'āh* means "visionary appearance" or "(prophetic) vision" (Gen. 46:2) and "looking glasses" (Exod. 38:8); this word appears 12 times. Of its 15 occurrences the noun *tō'ar* means "form, shape" in 1 Sam. 28:14 and "stately appearance" in 1 Sam. 25:3. *Mar'eh* occurs 103 times; this word and *tō'ar* are descriptive of blessing in Gen. 39:6: "Now Joseph was handsome in form [*tō'ar*] and appearance [*mar'eh*]" (NASB). *Mar'eh* refers more to external "appearance" (Gen. 2:9), and the word can also connote "sight" as in a range of vision (Lev. 13:3) and "sight" in the sense of a supernatural "sight" or manifestation (Exod. 3:3).

TO SEEK

A. Verbs.

bāqaš (בָּקַשׁ, 1245), "to seek, search, consult." This verb occurs only in Ugaritic, Phoenician, and Hebrew (both biblical and post-biblical). It appears in the Bible about 220 times and in all periods.

Basically *bāqaš* means "to seek" to find something that is lost or missing, or, at least, whose location is unknown. In Gen. 37:15 a man asks Joseph: "What seekest thou?" A special nuance of this sense is "to seek out of a group; to choose, select" something or someone yet undesignated, as in 1 Sam. 13:14: " ... The Lord hath sought him a man after his own heart...." To seek one's face is "to seek" to come before him, or to have a favorable audience with him; all the world "was seeking" the presence of Solomon (1 Kings 10:24). In a similar sense one may "seek" God's face by standing before Him in the temple praying (2 Sam. 21:1).

The sense "seek to secure" emphasizes the pursuit of a wish or the accomplishing of a plan. Moses asked the Levites who rebelled against the unique position of Aaron and his sons: " ... Seek ye the priesthood also?" (Num. 16:10). This usage may have an emotional coloring, such as, "to aim at, devote oneself to, and be concerned about." So God asks the sons of men (mankind): " ... How long will ye turn my glory into shame? How long will ye love vanity, and seek after [sin]?" (Ps. 4:2). Cultically one may "seek" to secure God's favor or help: "And Judah gathered themselves together, to ask help of the Lord ... " (2 Chron. 20:4). In such usages the intellectual element usually is in the background; there is no seeking after information. An exception to this is Judg. 6:29: "And when they inquired [*dāraš*] and asked [*bāqaš*], they said, Gideon the son of Joash hath done this thing." Infrequently this verb is used of seeking information from God (Exod. 33:7). In a similar sense one may "seek" God's face (2 Sam. 21:1). Here *bāqaš* is clearly used of searching for information (a cognitive pursuit). Also, compare the pursuit of wisdom (Prov. 2:4).

This sense of "seeking to secure" may also be used of seeking one's life (*nepeš*). God told Moses to "go, return into Egypt: for all the men are dead which sought thy life" (Exod. 4:19). *Bāqaš* may be used with this same nuance but without *nepeš*—so Pharaoh "sought to slay Moses" (Exod. 2:15). Only twice is this nuance applied to seeking to procure one's good as in Ps. 122:9: "Because of the house of the Lord our God I will seek thy good" (usually *dāraš* is used of seeking one's good).

About 20 times *bāqaš* means to hold someone responsible for something because the speaker has a (real or supposed) legal right to it. In Gen. 31:39 (the first biblical occurrence of the verb) Jacob points out to Laban that regarding animals lost to wild beasts, "of my hand didst thou require it."

Only infrequently is *bāqaš* used of seeking out a place, or as a verb of movement toward a place. So Joseph "sought [a place] to weep; and he entered into his chamber, and wept there" (Gen. 43:30).

Theologically, this verb can be used not only "to seek" a location before the Lord (to stand before Him in the temple and seek to secure His blessing), but it may also be used of a state of mind: "But if from thence thou shalt seek the Lord thy God, thou shalt find him, if thou seek him [*dāraš*] with all thy heart and with all thy soul" (Deut. 4:29). In instances such as this where the verb is used in synonymous parallelism with *dāraš*, the two verbs have the same meaning.

dāraš (דָּרַשׁ, 1875), "to seek, inquire, consult, ask, require, frequent." This word is a common Semitic word, being found in Ugaritic and Syriac as well as in Hebrew in its various periods. It is commonly used in modern Hebrew in its verbal form for "to interpret, expound" and then in its derived noun forms for "sermon, preacher." Occurring more than 160 times in the Old Testament, *dāraš* is first used in Gen. 9:5: "And surely your blood of your lives will I require...." It often has the idea of avenging an offense against God or the shedding of blood (see Ezek. 33:6).

One of the most frequent uses of this word is in the expression "to inquire of God," which sometimes indicates a private seeking of God in prayer for direction (Gen. 25:22), and often it refers to the contacting of a prophet who would be the instrument of God's revelation (1 Sam. 9:9; 1 Kings 22:8). At other times this expression is found in connection with the use of the Urim and Thummim by the high priest as he sought to discover the will of God by the throwing of these sacred stones (Num. 27:21). Just what was involved is not clear, but it may be presumed that only yes-or-no questions could be answered by the manner in which these stones fell. Pagan people and sometimes even apostate Israelites "inquired of" heathen gods. Thus, Ahaziah instructed messengers: "Go, inquire of Baal-zebub the god of Ekron whether I shall recover of this disease" (2 Kings 1:2). In gross violation of the Mosaic law (Deut. 18:10–

11), Saul went to the witch of Endor "to inquire of" her, which in this instance meant that she was to call up the spirit of the dead prophet Samuel (1 Sam. 28:3ff.). Saul went to the witch of Endor as a last resort, saying, "Seek out for me a woman who is a medium, that I may go to her and *inquire* of her" (1 Sam. 28:7, RSV).

This word is often used to describe the "seeking of" the Lord in the sense of entering into covenantal relationship with Him. The prophets often used *dāraš* as they called on the people to make an about-face in living and instead "seek ye the Lord while he may be found . . . " (Isa. 55:6).

B. Noun.

Midraš can mean "study; commentary; story." This noun occurs a few times in late biblical Hebrew (2 Chron. 13:22); it is commonly used in post-biblical Judaism to refer to the various traditional commentaries by the Jewish sages. One occurrence of the word is in 2 Chron. 24:27: "Now concerning his sons, and the greatness of the burdens laid upon him . . . they are written in the story [commentary] of the Book of the Kings."

TO SELL

mākar (מָכַר, 4376), "to sell." Common in both ancient and modern Hebrew, this word is also found in ancient Akkadian and Ugaritic. It occurs approximately 70 times in the text of the Hebrew Old Testament and is found for the first time in the Old Testament in Gen. 25:31: "And Jacob said, Sell me this day thy birthright."

Anything tangible may be "sold," such as land (Gen. 47:20), houses (Lev. 25:29), animals (Exod. 21:35), and human beings as slaves (Gen. 37:27–28). Daughters were usually "sold" for an agreed bride price (Exod. 21:7).

Mākar is often used in the figurative sense to express various actions. Nineveh is accused of "selling" or "betraying" other nations (Nah. 3:4). Frequently it is said that God "sold" Israel into the power of her enemies, meaning that He gave them over entirely into their hands (Judg. 2:14). Similarly, it was said that "the Lord shall sell Sisera into the hand of a woman" (Judg. 4:9). "To be sold" sometimes means to be given over to death (Esth. 7:4).

TO SEND

A. Verb.

šālah (שָׁלַח, 7971), "to send, stretch forth, get rid of." This verb occurs in the Northwest Semitic languages (Hebrew, Phoenician, and Aramaic). It occurs in all periods of Hebrew and in the Bible about 850 times. Biblical Aramaic uses this word 14 times.

Basically this verb means "to send," in the sense of (1) to initiate and to see that such movement occurs or (2) to successfully conclude such an action. In Gen. 32:18 the second emphasis is in view—these animals are "a present sent unto my lord Esau." In Gen. 38:20 the first idea is in view: When "Judah sent the kid by the hand of his friend. . ., he found her not"; it never reached its goal. In 1 Sam. 15:20 Saul told Samuel about the "way which the lord sent" him; here, too, the emphasis is on the initiation of the action.

The most frequent use of *šālah* suggests the sending of someone or something as a messenger to a particular place: " . . . He shall send his angel before thee, and thou shalt take a wife unto my son from thence" (Gen. 24:7); God's angel (messenger) will be sent to Nahor to prepare things for the successful accomplishment of the servant's task. One may also "send a word" by the hand of a messenger (fool); one may send a message (Prov. 26:6), send a letter (2 Sam. 11:14), and send instructions (Gen. 20:2).

Šālah can refer to shooting arrows by sending them to hit a particular target: "And he sent out arrows, and scattered them . . . " (2 Sam. 22:15). In Exod. 9:14 God "sends" His plague into the midst of the Egyptians; He "sends" them forth and turns them loose among them. Other special meanings of this verb include letting something go freely or without control: "Thou givest thy mouth to evil . . . " (Ps. 50:19).

Quite often this verb means "to stretch out." God was concerned lest after the Fall Adam "put forth his hand, and take also of the tree of life" (Gen. 3:22). One may stretch forth a staff (1 Sam. 14:27) or a sickle (Joel 3:13).

For the most part the intensive stems merely intensify the meanings already set forth, but the meaning "to send away" is especially frequent: " . . . Abner was no longer with David in Hebron, for David had sent him away . . . " (2 Sam. 3:22, NIV). That is, David "let him go" (v. 24, NIV). God sent man out of the garden of Eden; He made man leave (Gen. 3:23—the first occurrence of the verb). Noah sent forth a raven (Gen. 8:7). *Šālah* can also mean to give someone a send off, or "to send" someone on his way in a friendly manner: " . . . And Abraham went with them to bring them on the way [send them off]" (Gen. 18:16). In Deut. 22:19 the word is used of divorcing a wife, or sending her away.

This verb can signify "to get rid of" something: "They bow themselves, they bring forth their young ones, they cast out their [labor pains]" (Job 39:3). It can also be used of setting a bondservant free: "And when thou sendest him out free from thee, thou shalt not let him go away empty" (Deut. 15:13). In a less technical sense *šalaḥ* can mean to release someone held by force. The angel with whom Jacob wrestled said: "Let me go, for the day breaketh" (Gen. 32:26). Yet another nuance is "to hand someone over," as in Ps. 81:12: "So I gave them up unto their own hearts' lust. . . ." *Šalaḥ* can also mean to set something afire, as in "set the city on fire" (Judg. 1:8).

In the passive sense the verb has some additional special meanings; in Prov. 29:15 it means "to be left to oneself": " . . . But a child left to himself [who gets his own way] bringeth his mother to shame."

B. Nouns.
Mišlaḥ means "outstretching; undertaking." This noun occurs 7 times. The word refers to an "undertaking" in Deut. 28:8: "The Lord shall command the blessing upon thee in thy storehouses, and in all that thou settest thine hand unto; and he shall bless thee. . . ." The phrase "that thou settest" embodies the meaning of *mišlaḥ* here (cf. Deut. 28:20).

Other nouns are related to *šalaḥ*. *Šillûḥîm* occurs 3 times and means "presents" in the sense of something sent out to or with someone (1 Kings 9:16). *Mišlôaḥ* is found 3 times and refers to "the act of sending" (Esth. 9:19, 22) or "the place hands reach when stretched forth" (Isa. 11:14, RSV). *Šelaḥ* means " something sent forth as a missile," and it can refer to a sword or a weapon. *Šelaḥ* occurs 8 times (2 Chron. 32:5; Job 33:18; Neh. 4:17). The proper noun *shiloāh* appears in Isa. 8:6 and refers to a channel through which water is sent forth.

TO SEPARATE

A. Verbs.
pārad (פָּרַד, 6504), "to divide, separate." This word and its derivatives are common to both ancient and modern Hebrew. It is found in the text of the Hebrew Old Testament only about 25 times. *Pārad* occurs for the first time in the text in Gen. 2:10: "And a river went out of Eden . . . and from thence it was parted, and became into four heads." The meaning here must be "dividing into four branches."

This word often expresses separation of people from each other, sometimes with hostility: "Separate thyself . . . from me . . . " (Gen. 13:9). A reciprocal separation seems to be implied in the birth of Jacob and Esau: "Two nations are in thy womb, and two manner of people shall be separated from thy bowels . . . " (Gen. 25:23). Sometimes economic status brings about separation: " . . . The poor is separated

from his neighbor" (Prov. 19:4). Generally speaking, *pārad* has more negative than positive connotations.

nāzar (נָזַר, 5144), "to separate, be separated." This verb occurs about 10 times in the Old Testament. The root *nāzar* is a common Semitic verb. In Akkadian, *nazāru* meant "to curse," but in West Semitic it connoted "to dedicate." Students of Semitic languages often relate Hebrew *nāzar* to *nadhar* ("to vow").

"To separate" and "to consecrate" are not distinguished from one another in the early Old Testament books. For example, the earliest use of *nāzar* in the Pentateuch is in Lev. 15:31: "Thus shall ye *separate* the children of Israel from their uncleanness; that they die not in their uncleanness, when they defile my tabernacle that is among them." Here Moses uses the word in a cultic sense, meaning a kind of "consecration." A comparison of various twentieth-century translations will show that *nāzar* in Lev. 22:2 is sometimes rendered "to separate," and sometimes "to dedicate." The NIV translates this verse: "Tell Aaron and his sons to treat with respect the sacred offerings the Israelites *consecrated* to me, so that they will not profane my holy name. I am the Lord."

In the days of the prophet Zechariah, Jews asked the Lord whether certain fasts which they had voluntarily adopted were to be continued and observed. "When they had sent unto the house of God Sherezer and Regemmelech, and their men, to pray before the Lord, And to speak unto the priests which were in the house of the Lord of hosts, and to the prophets, saying, Should I weep in the fifth month, separating myself [NASB, "abstain"], as I have done these so many years?" (Zech. 7:2–3). The Lord's response stated that it was no longer necessary and therefore needed not to be continued.

In prophetic literature, the verb *nāzar* indicates Israel's deliberate separation from Jehovah to dedication of foreign gods or idols. In Hos. 9:10, the various versions differ in their rendering of *nāzar:* "I found Israel like grapes in the wilderness; I saw your fathers as the firstripe in the fig tree at her first time: but they went to Baal-peor, and separated [NASB, "devoted"; NEB, RSV, "consecrated"] themselves unto that shame; and their abominations were according as they loved." The prophet Ezekiel employed *nāzar:* "For every one of the house of Israel, or of the stranger that sojourneth in Israel, which separateth himself from me, and setteth up his idols in his heart, and putteth the stumbling block of his iniquity before his face, and cometh to a prophet to inquire of him concerning me; I the Lord will answer him by myself" (Ezek. 14:7).

B. Noun.

nāzîr (נָזִיר, 5139), "one who is separated; Nazarite." There are 16 occurrences of the word in the Old Testament. The earliest use of *nāzîr* is found in Gen. 49:26: "The blessings of thy father ... shall be on the head of Joseph ... that was *separate* from his brethren" (cf. Deut. 33:16). Some modern-speech translators have translated *nāzîr* in these two verses as "prince" (NIV, NEB, NAB). The KJV and RSV render the phrase "separate from his brethren." This interpretation might be justified by assuming that Joseph was separated from his brethren to become the savior of his father, his brethren, and their families.

Most frequently in Old Testament usage, *nāzîr* is an appellation for one who vowed to refrain from certain things for a period of time: "And this is the law of the Nazarite, when the days of his separation are fulfilled: he shall be brought unto the door of the tabernacle of the congregation" (Num. 6:13).

According to Num. 6, a lay person of either sex could take a special vow of consecration to God's service for a certain period of time. A "Nazarite" usually made a vow voluntarily; however, in the case of Samson (Judg. 13:5, 7) his parents dedicated him for life. Whether or not this idea of separation to God was distinctive alone to Israel has been debated. Num. 6:1–23 laid down regulatory laws pertaining to Nazaritism. There were two kinds of "Nazarites": the temporary and the perpetual. The first class was much more common than the latter kind. From the Bible we have knowledge only of Samson, Samuel, and John the Baptist as persons who were lifelong "Nazarites."

According to the Mishna, the normal time for keeping a Nazarite vow was thirty days; but sometimes a double vow was taken, lasting sixty days. In fact, a vow was sometimes undertaken for a hundred days.

During the time of his vow, a "Nazarite" was required to abstain from wine and every kind of intoxicating drink. He was also forbidden to cut the hair of his head or to approach a dead body, even that of his nearest relative. If a "Nazarite" accidently defiled himself, he had to undergo certain rites of purification and then had to begin the full period of consecration over again. The "Nazarite" was "holy unto the Lord," and he wore upon his head a diadem of his consecration.

There is but one reference in the prophetic literature to "Nazarites": The prophet Amos complained that the Lord had given the Israel-ites, Nazarites and prophets as spiritual leaders, but that the people "gave the Nazarites wine to drink; and commanded the prophets, saying, Prophesy not" (Amos 2:11–12).

The New Testament occasionally refers to what appear to have been Nazarite vows. For example, Acts 18:18 says that Paul sailed with Priscilla and Aquila, "having shorn his head ... for he had a vow" (cf. Acts 21:23–24).

TO SERVE

A. Verbs.

šārat (שָׁרַת, 8334), "to serve, minister." This word occurs less than 100 times in the Old Testament. In the vast majority of instances, *šārat* appears in the form of an infinitive or participle. When the participle is translated as a verbal noun, such as "servant" or "minister," it loses the connotation of duration or repetition. Another grammatical feature of *šārat* is its usage exclusively in the intensive form.

The reader of a modern English version can no longer be aware of the distinctive meaning of *šārat* because it and its synonym, *'ābad* (or *'ebed*), are both rendered "serve" or "servant."

Šārat often denotes "service" rendered in connection with Israel's worship; about 60 of its 97 occurrences have this meaning. When Samuel was still a boy, he " ... did minister unto the Lord before Eli the priest" (1 Sam. 2:11), and the Lord called to him while he " ... ministered unto the Lord before Eli" (1 Sam. 3:1). This kind of "service" was to honor only the Lord, for Israel was not to be "as the heathen, as the families of the countries; to serve wood and stone" (Ezek. 20:32). In the temple of Ezekiel's vision, those Levites who had " ... ministered unto them [the people] before their idols ... " were forbidden by the Lord to serve as priests (Ezek. 44:12). Furthermore, " ... the Lord separated the tribe of Levi ... to minister unto him, and to bless in his name ... " (Deut. 10:8). From the tribe of Levi, Moses was to anoint Aaron and his sons and consecrate them, that they may "minister" as priests (Exod. 29:30). Those not of the family of Aaron, though chosen "to minister unto him forever," acted as assistants to the priests, performing such physical tasks as keeping the gates, slaughtering the burnt offering, caring for the altars and the utensils of the sanctuary (1 Chron. 15:2; Ezek. 44:11). But Isaiah foresees the time when " ... the sons of strangers ... shall minister unto thee" (Isa. 60:10).

In a number of situations, the word is used to denote "service" rendered to a fellow human being. Though the person "served" usually is of a higher rank or station in life, this word never describes a slave's servitude to his master. Moses was instructed: "Bring the tribe of Levi near, and present them before Aaron, the priest, that they may minister [NASB, "serve"] unto him" (Num. 3:6; cf. 8:26). Elisha "ministered" to Elijah (1 Kings 19:21). Abishag is said to have "ministered" unto David (1 Kings 1:15). Various kinds of officials "ministered" to David (1 Chron. 28:1). David's son Amnon had a "servant that ministered unto him" (2 Sam. 13:17). There were seven eunuchs that "served in the presence of Ahasuerus the king . . ." (Esth. 1:10). He also had "servants that ministered unto him . . ." (Esth. 2:2).

'*ābad* (עָבַד, 5647), "to serve, cultivate, enslave, work." This root is used widely in Semitic and Canaanite languages. This verb appears about 290 times in all parts of the Old Testament.

The verb is first used in Gen. 2:5: " . . . And there was not a man to till the ground." God gave to man the task "to dress [the ground]" (Gen. 2:15; 3:23; cf. 1:28, NASB). In Gen. 14:4 "they served Chedorlaomer . . ." means that they were his vassals. God told Abraham that his descendants would "serve" the people of a strange land 400 years (Gen. 15:13), meaning, as in the NIV, "to be enslaved by."

'*Ābad* is often used toward God: " . . . Ye shall serve God upon this mountain" (Exod. 3:12), meaning "to worship" as in the NASB and the NIV. The word is frequently used with another verb: "Thou shalt fear the Lord thy God, and serve him . . ." (Deut. 6:13), or " . . . hearken diligently unto my commandments which I command you this day, to love the Lord your God, and to serve him . . ." (Deut. 11:13). All nations are commanded: "Serve the Lord with gladness . . ." (Ps. 100:2). In the reign of Messiah, "all nations shall serve him" (Ps. 72:11). The verb and the noun may be used together as in Num. 8:11: "And Aaron shall offer the Levites before the Lord . . . that they may execute the service of the Lord."

B. Nouns.

'*ăbôdāh* (עֲבוֹדָה, 5656), "work; labors; service." This noun appears 145 times in the Hebrew Old Testament, and the occurrences are concentrated in Numbers and Chronicles. '*Ăbôdāh* is first used in Gen. 29:27: " . . . We will give thee this also for the service which thou shalt serve with me. . . ."

The more general meaning of '*ăbôdāh* is close to our English word for "work." "Labor" in the field (1 Chron. 27:26), daily "work" from morning till evening (Ps. 104:23), and "work" in the linen industry (1 Chron. 4:21) indicate a use with which we are familiar. To this, it must

be added that '*ăbôdāh* may also be "hard labor," such as that of a slave (Lev. 25:39) or of Israel while in Egypt: "Go ye, get you straw where ye can find it: yet not aught of your work shall be diminished" (Exod. 5:11).

The more limited meaning of the word is "service." Israel was in the "service" of the Lord: "But that it may be a witness between us, and you, and our generations after us, that we might do the *service* of the Lord before him with our burnt offerings, and with our sacrifices, and with our peace offerings; that your children may not say to our children in time to come, Ye have no part in the Lord" (Josh. 22:27). Whenever God's people were not fully dependent on Him, they had to choose to serve the Lord God or human kings with their requirements of forced "labor" and tribute: "Nevertheless they shall be his servants; that they may know my service, and the service of the kingdoms of the countries" (2 Chron. 12:8).

Further specialization of the usage is in association with the tabernacle and the temple. The priests were chosen for the "service" of the Lord: "And they shall keep his charge, and the charge of the whole congregation before the tabernacle of the congregation, to do the service of the tabernacle" (Num. 3:7). The Levites also had many important functions in and around the temple; they sang, played musical instruments, and were secretaries, scribes, and doorkeepers (2 Chron. 34:13; cf. 8:14). Thus anything, people and objects (1 Chron. 28:13), associated with the temple was considered to be in the "service" of the Lord. Our understanding of "worship," with all its components, comes close to the Hebrew meaning of '*ăbôdāh* as "service"; cf. "So all the service of the Lord was prepared the same day, to keep the passover, and to offer burnt offerings upon the altar of the Lord, according to the commandment of King Josiah" (2 Chron. 35:16).

The Septuagint translations are: *leitourgia* ("service"); *doulia* ("slavery"); *ergon* ("work; deed; occupation"); and *ergasia* ("pursuit; practice; working; profit; gain"). The KJV gives these senses: "service; bondage; work."

'*ebed* (עֶבֶד, 5650), "servant." This noun appears over 750 times in the Old Testament. '*Ebed* first appears in Gen. 9:25: " . . . A servant of servants shall he [Canaan] be unto his brethren," meaning "the lowest of slaves" (NIV). A "servant" may be bought with money (Exod. 12:44) or hired (1 Kings 5:6). The often repeated statement of God's redemption of Israel is: "I brought you out of the house of slaves" (Exod. 13:3, Heb. 2:15; KJV, RSV, "bondage"; NASB, NIV, "slavery"). '*Ebed* was used as a mark of humility and courtesy, as in Gen. 18:3: "... Pass not away, I pray thee, from thy servant" (cf. Gen. 42:10). Moses addressed God: "O my Lord, I am not eloquent, neither heretofore, nor since thou hast spoken unto thy servant ..." (Exod. 4:10). It is the mark of those called by God, as in Exod. 14:31: "...[They] believed the Lord, and his servant Moses." God claimed: "For unto me the children of Israel are servants ..." (Lev. 25:55; cf. Isa. 49:3). "And the Lord spake by his servants the prophets ..." (2 Kings 21:10). The psalmist said: "I am thy servant" (116:16), indicating the appropriateness of the title to all believers.

Of prime significance is the use of "my servant" for the Messiah in Isaiah (42:1–7; 49:1–7; 50:4–10; 52:13–53:12). Israel was a blind and deaf "servant" (Isa. 42:18–22). So the Lord called "my righteous servant" (Isa. 53:11; cf. 42:6) "[to bear] the sin of many" (Isa. 53:12), "that thou mayest be my salvation unto the end of the earth" (Isa. 49:6).

The "servant" was not a free man. He was subject to the will and command of his master. But one might willingly and lovingly submit to his master (Exod. 21:5), remaining in his service when he was not obliged to do so. Hence it is a very fitting description of the relationship of man to God.

The Septuagint translates *'ābad* and its nouns by 7 different Greek roots that give more specific meanings to the term. Through these the basic uses of *'ābad* come into the New Testament. Notable is Jesus' fulfillment of the Servant of the Lord in Isaiah: "That signs and wonders may be done by the name of thy holy child Jesus" (Acts 4:30; RSV, NASB, NIV, "servant Jesus"); and another important use is Paul's personal use of "a servant of Jesus Christ" (Rom 1:1; KJV, RSV, NIV; but more precisely, "bond servant" in NASB).

C. Participle.

šārat (שָׁרַת, 8334), "servant; minister." This word is most regularly translated "minister"; Josh. 1:1 is one example: "Now after the death of Moses the servant [*'ebed*] of the Lord it came to pass, that the Lord spake unto Joshua, the son of Nun, Moses' minister [*šārat*]...." Ezek. 46:24 refers to a place in the temple complex which is reserved for "... the ministers of the house...."

The privilege of serving the Lord is not restricted to human beings: "Bless ye the Lord, all ye his hosts [angels]; ye ministers of his, that do his pleasure" (Ps. 103:21). Fire and wind, conceived poetically as persons, are also God's "ministers" (Ps. 104:3–4).

Joshua was the "minister" of Moses (Exod.

24:13), and Elisha had a "servitor" (2 Kings 4:43; NASB, "attendant").

TO SET, PLACE

šît (שִׁית, 7896), "to put, place, set, station, fix." In addition to biblical Hebrew, this verb is found frequently in ancient Ugaritic. It occurs more than 80 times in the Hebrew Old Testament, for the first time in Gen. 3:15: "And I will put enmity between thee and the woman...."

Generally speaking, this word is a term of physical action, typically expressing movement from one place to another. Often it expresses "putting" hands on someone or something: "... Joseph shall put his hand upon thine eyes [close your eyes]" (Gen. 46:4). One may "put on" ornaments (Exod. 33:4); Naomi laid her "grandchild" Obed in her bosom (Ruth 4:16); a fine may be "laid" on someone for injury (Exod. 21:22). Sheep may be "set" or stationed, at a particular place (Gen. 30:40).

"To set" one's heart to something is to give heed to, to pay attention (Exod. 7:23; RSV, "he did not lay even this to heart"). To set one's heart may also be to reflect: "Then I saw, and considered it [set my heart to it]..." (Prov. 24:32). "To set" boundaries is "to set," or "fix," limits: "And I will set thy bounds from the Red Sea even unto the sea of the Philistines..." (Exod. 23:31). When Job cries: "Oh... that thou wouldest appoint me a set time, and remember me!" (Job 14:13), he wants limits "set" for him.

Šît is sometimes used to express the making of something: "... I will make him prince..." (1 Kings 11:34); "And I will lay it waste..." (Isa. 5:6); "... I will make thee a wilderness..." (Jer. 22:6).

TO SET IN ORDER

'ārak (עָרַךְ, 6186), "to arrange, set in order, compare." While it occurs some 75 times in the Hebrew Old Testament, this root is also found in modern Hebrew, being connected with "editing" and "dictionary." The word is first found in the Old Testament in Gen. 14:8: "... They joined battle [literally, "they arranged," referring to opposing battle lines]...." It is used in this way many times in the record of the battles of Israel.

A common word in everyday life, *'ārak* often refers to "arranging" a table (Isa. 21:5; Ezek. 23:41). The word is used several times in the Book of Job with reference to "arranging" or "setting" words "in order," as in an argument or rebuttal (Job 32:14; 33:5; 37:19). In Job 13:18, Job declares: "Behold now, I have ordered my cause [literally, "I have set my judgment in order"]...." "To arrange in order" makes it possible "to compare" one thing with another. So, to show the superiority of God over the idols, the prophet asks: "To whom then will ye liken God? or what likeness will ye compare unto him?" (Isa. 40:18).

TO SET ON, SET UP

A. Verb.

sîm (שִׂים, 7760), "to put, place, set, fix." This word also appears in Akkadian (as *shamu*), Aramaic (including biblical Aramaic), Arabic, and Ethiopic. It appears about 580 times in biblical Hebrew, in all periods, and almost exclusively in the primary stem.

In its first biblical appearance *sîm* means "to put or place someone somewhere": "And the Lord God planted a garden eastward in Eden; and there he put the man whom he had formed" (Gen. 2:8). In Exod. 40:8 the verb means "to set up," in the sense of "to place or put something so that it is perpendicular or vertical": "And thou shalt set up the court round about, and hang up the hanging at the court gate." Other things are "set up" in a figurative sense, like a wall. So Micah speaks of "setting up" a siege, a wall, around a city: "... He hath laid siege against us ..." (Mic. 5:1; cf. 1 Kings 20:12). This image is also used figuratively of a human wall in one's path: "I remember that which Amalek did to Israel, how he laid wait for him in the way, when he came up from Egypt" (1 Sam. 15:2).

Sîm is used sometimes in the sense "to set over, impose on" (negatively): "Therefore they did set [imposed] over them taskmasters to afflict them with their burdens" (Exod. 1:11). A more positive use of the word in the sense "to appoint" (where the appointment is pleasing to the wards) appears in 1 Sam. 8:5—the elders of Israel asked the aged Samuel: "... Now make us a king to judge us like all the nations." In such usages one in authority determines or is asked to determine something. This is the focus of the word in Num. 24:23, where Balaam said: "Alas, who shall live when God doeth this!"

This verb means "to make," as it does in Zeph. 3:19: "... And I will get them praise and fame [make their shame into praise and fame] in every land where they have been put to shame."

In some passages *sîm* is used in the figurative sense of setting something or putting it before one's mind: "... They have not set God before them" (Ps. 54:3). The same phrase is used in a literal sense in Ezek. 14:4 (cf. NIV).

Sîm also means "to put down" in the sense of literally setting something on the ground, on a chair, or a flat surface: "... Abraham built an altar there, and laid the wood in order, and bound Isaac his son, and laid him on the altar upon the wood" (Gen. 22:9). In a related sense one "puts down" a distance or space between himself and someone else: "And he set three days' journey betwixt himself and Jacob ..." (Gen. 30:36). In Job 4:18 the word means to charge someone with an error, or "to put it down" against or to him. Closely related to this legal use of *sîm* is 1 Sam. 22:15, where it means "to impute" (lay to one's charge), and Deut. 22:8, where it means "to bring guilt upon oneself." Other passages use this verb of putting clothing on, in the sense of setting it down upon one's body (Ruth 3:3). So, too, one may obligate someone with a task: one may impose it upon him (Exod. 5:8).

When used with "hand," *sîm* may signify putting (Exod. 4:21) or taking something (Judg. 4:21) into one's grasp. Closely related is the phrase "putting hands on," or "arresting" (2 Kings 11:16).

This verb may be used in the sense of "giving for" (in behalf of). So Job says: "Lay down now, put me in a surety with thee ...," or give a pledge for me (Job 17:3). In a related sense the Servant of the Lord would "make his soul an offering for sin" (Isa. 53:10).

In Dan. 1:7 *sîm* signifies "to assign something to, or give to"; the commander of the officials assigned new names to them. In Job 5:8 this giving constitutes handing over one's cause to another, while in Exod. 21:1 it represents fully stating God's word in the presence of His people so as to make it possible for them to receive it fully.

To place or put something on one's heart means to consider it (Isa. 47:7) or to pay heed to it (1 Sam. 21:12).

The meaning "to fix," as to fix something in a particular place, appears in Gen. 24:47: "... And I put the earring upon her face, and the bracelets upon her hands." So, too, in Deut. 14:1 God commands Israel not "to fix" a bald spot on their foreheads for the sake of the dead. Other things may be so "fixed," such as plants (Isa. 28:25) and ashes (Lev. 6:10).

The word means "to make" in Exod. 4:11: "Who hath made man's mouth? or who maketh the dumb, or deaf ...?" The first nuance here signifies the creation of the thing (fixing its nature) and the second its disposition (fixing its use; cf. Gen. 13:16). Closely related is the use of the verb to represent "to state, to appoint, or to assign"; in Exod. 21:13, God will appoint a place for the manslayer to flee. In an extended sense *śîm* signifies "to assign to continue," or "to preserve": "And God sent me before you to preserve you a posterity in the earth, and to save your lives by a great deliverance" (Gen. 45:7). Thus, to set a remnant is to keep it alive. Therefore, *śîm* means "to preserve." To set glory and praise to the Lord is to establish it by stating it (Josh. 7:19). God's establishing the plagues on Pharaoh is also an appointing (Exod. 8:12).

B. Noun.

Tᵉśûmet, means "something laid down; a deposit or joint property." This noun occurs only once in biblical Hebrew: "If a soul sin, and commit a trespass against the Lord, and lie unto his neighbor in that which was delivered him to keep, or in fellowship [*tᵉśûmet*] . . . " (Lev. 6:2).

SHAME

A. Verb.

bôš (בּוּשׁ, 954), "to be ashamed, feel ashamed." This verb, which occurs 129 times in biblical Hebrew, has cognates in Ugaritic, Akkadian, and Arabic. The word has overtones of being or feeling worthless. *Bôš* means "to be ashamed" in Isa. 1:29: "For they shall be ashamed of the oaks which ye have desired, and ye shall be confounded for the gardens that ye have chosen."

B. Noun.

bōšet (בֹּשֶׁת, 1322), "shame; shameful thing." The 30 appearances of this noun are mostly in poetic materials—only 5 appearances are in historical literature.

This word means a "shameful thing" as a substitute for the name Baal: "For shame hath devoured the labor of our fathers from our youth . . . " (Jer. 3:24; cf. Jer. 11:13; Hos. 9:10). This substitution also occurs in proper names: Ish-bosheth (2 Sam. 2:8), the "man of shame," was originally Esh-baal (cf. 1 Chron. 8:33), the "man of Baal."

This word represents both "shame and worthlessness": "Thou son of the perverse rebellious woman, do not I know that thou hast chosen the son of Jesse . . . unto the confusion of thy mother's nakedness" (1 Sam. 20:30). The "shame of one's face" (2 Chron. 32:21) may well mean being red-faced or embarrassed.

SHEOL

šᵉ'ôl (שְׁאוֹל, 7585), "Sheol." The 65 occurrences of this word are distributed throughout every period of biblical Hebrew.

First, the word means the state of death: "For in death there is no remembrance of thee: in the *grave* who shall give thee thanks?" (Ps. 6:5; cf. 18:5). It is the final resting place of all men: "They spend their days in wealth, and in a moment go down to the *grave*(Job 21:13). Hannah confessed that it was the omnipotent God who brings men to *šᵉ'ôl* (death) or kills them (1 Sam. 2:6). "Sheol" is parallel to Hebrew words for "pit" or "hell" (Job 26:6), "corruption" or "decay" (Ps. 16:10), and "destruction" (Prov. 15:11).

Second, "Sheol" is used of a place of conscious existence after death. In the first biblical appearance of the word Jacob said that he would "go down into the *grave* unto my son mourning" (Gen. 37:35). All men go to "Sheol"—a place and state of consciousness after death (Ps. 16:10). The wicked receive punishment there (Num. 16:30; Deut. 32:22; Ps. 9:17). They are put to shame and silenced in "Sheol" (Ps. 31:17). Jesus alluded to Isaiah's use of *šᵉ'ôl* (14:13–15) in pronouncing judgment on Capernaum (Matt. 11:23), translating "Sheol" as "Hades" or "Hell," meaning the place of conscious existence and judgment. It is an undesirable place for the wicked (Job 24:19) and a refuge for the righteous (Job 14:13). Thus "Sheol" is also a place of reward for the righteous (Hos. 13:14; cf. 1 Cor. 15:55). Jesus' teaching in Luke 16:19–31 seems to reflect accurately the Old Testament concept of *šᵉ'ôl;* it is a place of conscious existence after death, one side of which is occupied by the suffering, unrighteous dead separated by a great chasm from the other side peopled by the righteous dead enjoying their reward.

TO SHEPHERD

A. Verb.

rā'āh (רָעָה, 7462), "to pasture, shepherd." This common Semitic root appears in Akkadian, Phoenician, Ugaritic, Aramaic, and Arabic. It is attested in all periods of Hebrew and about 170 times in the Bible. (The word should be distinguished from the verb "to have dealings with or associate with.")

Rā'āh represents what a shepherd allows domestic animals to do when they feed on grasses in the fields. In its first appearance Jacob tells the shepherds: "Lo, it is yet high day, neither is it time that the cattle should be gathered together: water ye the sheep, and go and feed them" (Gen. 29:7). *Rā'āh* can also represent the entire job of a shepherd. So "Joseph, being seventeen years old, was feeding the flock with his brethren; and [he was still a youth]" (Gen. 37:2). Used metaphorically this verb represents a leader's or a ruler's relationship to his people. At Hebron the people said to David: "Also in time past, when Saul was king over us, thou wast he that leddest out and broughtest in Israel: and the Lord said to thee, Thou shalt feed my people Israel, and thou shalt be a captain over Israel" (2 Sam. 5:2). The verb is used figuratively in the sense "to provide with nourishment" or "to enliven": "The lips of the righteous feed many: but fools die for want of wisdom" (Prov. 10:21).

Rā'āh is used intransitively describing what cattle do when they feed on the grass of the field. So Pharaoh dreamed that "there came up out of the river seven well-favored kine and fatfleshed; and they fed in a meadow" (Gen. 41:2). This usage is applied metaphorically to men in Isa. 14:30: "And [those who are most helpless] shall feed, and the needy shall lie down in safety...." This word is used to describe destruction: "Also the children of Noph and Tahapanes have broken [literally, "consumed as a domestic animal utterly bares a pasture"] the crown of thy head" (Jer. 2:16).

B. Nouns.

rō'ēh (רֹעֶה, 7462), "shepherd." This noun occurs about 62 times in the Old Testament. It is applied to God, the Great Shepherd, who pastures or feeds His sheep (Ps. 23:1–4; cf. John 10:11). This concept of God, the Great Shepherd, is very old, having first appeared in the Bible on Jacob's lips in Gen. 49:24: "... From thence is the shepherd, the stone of Israel."

When applied to human kings, *rō'ēh* recalls its usage among non-Israelites. There it depicts the king as the head of the cultus (official public worship) and the mediator between the god(s) and men. It also suggests that he is the center of national unity, the supreme protector and leader of the nation, the bestower of every earthly blessing, and the dispenser of justice. Interestingly, no biblical king claimed the title *rō'ēh* for himself (cf. 2 Sam. 5:2). In later times leaders other than the kings were also called "shepherds" (cf. Isa. 44:28; Ezek. 34:2).

Other nouns derived from the verb *rā'āh* occur infrequently. *Mir'eh*, which occurs 12 times, means "pasture or pasturage" in the sense of where animals graze, and/or what they graze on (Gen. 47:4). *Mar'ît* appears 10 times and refers to a "pasture" (Ps. 74:1). *R'î* is found once and means "pasture" (1 Kings 4:23).

TO SHUT

sāgar (סָגַר, 5462), "to shut, close, shut up or imprison." Found in ancient Ugaritic, this verb is common also in ancient and modern Hebrew. It is found some 80 times in the text of the Hebrew Old Testament. *Sāgar* is used for the first time in the Old Testament in the story of the creation of the woman from the rib of the man: "And the Lord God ... closed up the flesh instead thereof" (Gen. 2:21).

The obvious use of this verb is to express the "shutting" of doors and gates, and it is used in this way many times in the text (Gen. 19:10; Josh. 2:7). More specialized uses are: fat closing over the blade of a sword (Judg. 3:22) and closing up a breach in city walls (1 Kings 11:27).

Figuratively, men may "close their hearts to pity" (Ps. 17:10, RSV; KJV, "They are inclosed in their own fat," with "fat" symbolizing an unresponsive heart). In the books of Samuel, *sāgar* is used in the special sense of "to deliver up," implying that all avenues of escape "are closed": "This day will the Lord deliver thee into mine hand ..." (1 Sam. 17:46; cf. 1 Sam. 24:18; 26:8; 2 Sam. 18:28).

In Lev. 13–14, in which the priest functions as a medical inspector of contagious diseases, *sāgar* is used a number of times in the sense of "to isolate, to shut up" a sick person away from other people (*see* Lev. 13:5, 11, 21, 26). The more extreme sense of "to imprison" is found in Job 11:10: "If he cut off, and shut up, or gather together, then who can hinder him?"

TO BE SICK

A. Verb.

hālāh (חָלָה, 2470), "to be sick, weak." This verb is common in all periods of the Hebrew language and occurs approximately 60 times in the Hebrew Bible. It is found in the text for the first time near the end of the Book of Genesis when Joseph is told: "Behold, thy father is sick ..." (Gen. 48:1).

A survey of the uses of *hālāh* shows that there was a certain lack of precision in many of its uses, and that the context would be the deciding factor in its meaning. When Samson told Delilah that if he were tied up with bowstrings he would "be weak, and be as another man" (Judg. 16:7), the verb obviously did not mean "become sick," unless being sick implied being less than normal for Samson. When Joram is described as being sick because of wounds suffered in battle (2 Kings 8:29, RSV), perhaps it would be better to say that he was weak. Sacrificial animals that are described as being lame or "sick" (Mal. 1:8) are actually imperfect or not acceptable for sacrifice.

This word is sometimes used in the figurative sense of overexerting oneself, thus becoming "weak." This is seen in the various renderings of Jer. 12:13: "They have put themselves to pain ..." (KJV); "they have tired themselves out ..." (RSV); "they have worn themselves out" (JB); "they sift but get no grain" (NEB). The versions are divided in the translation of Song of Sol. 2:5, which the KJV, RSV, and JB translate "sick of/with love," while the NEB and NAB make it "faint with love." The NASB renders it "lovesick," but the TEV is probably closest to the meaning when it says "weak with passion."

B. Noun.

hŏlî (חֲלִי, 2483), "sickness." This noun occurs about 23 times. The use of this word in the description of the Suffering Servant in Isa. 53:3–4 has resulted in various translations. The RSV, KJV, and NASB render it "grief." It is "sufferings" in the NEB, JB, TEV and "infirmity" in the NAB.

The meaning of "sickness" occurs in Deut. 7:15: "And the Lord will take away from thee all *sickness*, and will put none of the evil diseases [*madweh*] of Egypt...." *Hŏlî* is used metaphorically as a distress of the land in Hos. 5:13.

SIGN

'ôt (אוֹת, 226), "sign; mark." Cognates of this word appear in Aramaic and Arabic. It occurs 78 times in biblical Hebrew and in all periods of the language.

This word represents something by which a person or group is characteristically marked. This is its emphasis in Gen. 4:15: "And the Lord set a mark [NASB, "sign"] upon Cain, lest any finding him should kill him." In Exod. 8:23 God promises to "put a division between my people and thy people: tomorrow shall this sign be" (cf. Exod. 12:13). Num. 2:2 uses *'ôt* to represent a military banner, while Job 21:29 uses the word of the identifying banners of nomadic tribes. Rahab asked her Israelite guests for a trustworthy "mark" (NASB, "pledge of truth"), which they stipulated to be the scarlet cord by which she lowered them out of her window and outside Jericho's walls (Josh. 2:12, 18).

The word means "sign" as a reminder of one's duty. This usage first appears in Gen. 9:12: "This [the rainbow] is the token of the covenant which I make between me and you and every living creature..." (cf. vv. 4–15).

A reminding token is represented by *'ôt:* "And it [the observance of the Feast of Unleavened Bread] shall be for a sign unto thee upon thine hand, and for a memorial between thine eyes, that the Lord's law may be in thy mouth..." (Exod. 13:9).

A "sign" eventually showing the truth of a statement is indicated by *'ôt:* "Certainly I will be with thee; and this shall be a token unto thee, that I have sent thee: When thou hast brought forth the people out of Egypt, ye shall serve God upon this mountain" (Exod. 3:12).

In passages such as Exod. 4:8 *'ôt* represents a miraculous "sign": "And it shall come to pass, if they will not believe thee, neither hearken to the voice of the first sign, that they will believe the voice of the latter sign." "Signs" are attestations of the validity of a prophetic message, but they are not the highest or final test of a prophet; he must speak in conformity to past revelation (cf. Deut. 13:1–5).

Several passages use *'ôt* of omens and/or indications of future events: "But if they say thus, Come up unto us; then we will go up: for the Lord hath delivered them into our hand: and this shall be a sign unto us" (1 Sam. 14:10).

An *'ôt* can be a "warning sign": "The censers of these sinners against their own souls, let them make them broad plates for a covering of the altar: for they offered them before the Lord, therefore they are hallowed: and they shall be a sign unto the children of Israel" (Num. 16:38).

The first occurrence of *'ôt* is in Gen. 1:14. Here it refers to the stars, indicators of the time of day and seasons.

SILVER

A. Noun.

kesep (כֶּסֶף, 3701), "silver; money; price; property." This word has cognates in Akkadian, Ugaritic, Phoenician, and Aramaic. It occurs about 402 times in biblical Hebrew and in all periods.

This word represents the "metal ore silver": "Take away the dross from the silver, and there shall come forth a vessel for the finer" (Prov. 25:4; cf. Job 28:1).

Kesep may signify the "metal silver," or what has been refined from silver ore: "And the servant brought forth jewels of silver, and jewels of gold..." (Gen. 24:53). As a precious metal "silver" was not as valuable as gold— probably because it is not so rare: "And all king Solomon's drinking vessels were of gold, and all the vessels of the house of the forest of Lebanon were of pure gold; none were of silver: it was nothing accounted of in the days of Solomon" (1 Kings 10:21).

"Silver" was often a form of wealth. This is the meaning of *kesep* in Gen. 13:2 (the first biblical occurrence): "And Abram was very rich in cattle, in silver, and in gold." Silver pieces (not coins) were used as money: "Then Joseph commanded to fill their sacks with corn, and to restore every man's money into his sack..." (Gen. 42:25). Frequently the word absolutely (by itself) and in the singular form means "pieces of silver": "Behold, I have given thy brother a thousand pieces of silver..." (Gen. 20:16). In Lev. 25:50 the word is used in the general sense of "money, value, price": "And he shall reckon with him that bought him from the year that he was sold to him unto the year of jubilee: and the price of his sale shall be according unto the number of years. . . . "

Since it was a form of wealth, "silver" often was one of the spoils of war: "The kings came, they fought; . . . they got no spoils of silver" (Judg. 5:19, RSV).

This word may be used in the sense of "valuable property": "Notwithstanding, if he [the slave who has been beaten] continue a day or two, he shall not be punished: for he is his money" (Exod. 21:21).

Kesep sometimes represents the color "silver": "Though ye have lain among the pots, yet shall ye be as the wings of a dove covered with silver, and her feathers with yellow gold" (Ps. 68:13).

B. Verb.

Kāsap means "to long for." Some scholars derive *kesep* from this verb which occurs 5 times in the biblical text. *Kāsap* means "to long for" in the sense of "to be pale by reason of longing": "And now, though thou wouldest needs be gone, because thou sore longedst after thy father's house, yet wherefore hast thou stolen my gods?" (Gen. 31:30).

SIN

A. Nouns.

'āwen (אָוֶן, 205), "iniquity; vanity; sorrow." Some scholars believe that this term has cognates in the Arabic words *'āna*, ("to be fatigued, tired") and *'aynun* ("weakness; sorrow; trouble"), or with the Hebrew word *'ayin* ("nothingness"). This relationship would imply that *'āwen* means the absence of all that has true worth; hence, it would denote "moral worthlessness," as in the actions of wrongdoing, evil devising, or false speaking.

Other scholars believe that the term implies a "painful burden or difficulty"—i.e., that sin is a toilsome, exhausting load of "trouble and sorrow," which the offender causes for himself or others. This meaning is indicated in Ps. 90:10: "The days of our years are three score years and ten; and if by reason of strength they be fourscore years, yet is their strength labor and *sorrow* [RSV, "trouble"]. . . . " A similar meaning appears in Prov. 22:8: "He that soweth iniquity shall reap vanity [*'āwen*]: and the rod of his anger shall fail."

'Āwen may be a general term for a crime or offense, as in Micah 2:1: "Woe to them that devise iniquity . . . " (cf. Isa. 1:13). In some passages, the word refers to falsehood or deception: "The words of his mouth are *iniquity* and deceit: he hath left off to be wise, and to do good" (Ps. 36:3). "For the idols have spoken *vanity* [NASB,

"iniquity"] . . . " (Zech. 10:2). Isa. 41:29 portrays idols deceiving their worshipers: "Behold, they are all *vanity;* their works are nothing: Their molten images are wind and confusion."

'āšām (אָשָׁם, 817), "sin; guilt; guilt offering; trespass; trespass offering." Cognates appear in Arabic as *'ithmun* ("sin; offense; misdeed; crime"), *'athima* ("to sin, err, slip"), and *'āthimun* ("sinful; criminal; evil; wicked"); but the Arabic usage does not include the idea of restitution. In the Ugaritic texts of Ras Shamra, the word *atm* occurs in similar passages. Scholars believe this Ugaritic word may mean "offense" or "guilt offering," but this cannot be ascertained.

'Āšām implies the condition of "guilt" incurred through some wrongdoing, as in Gen. 26:10: "And Abimelech said, . . . one of the people might lightly have lain with thy wife, and thou shouldest have brought guiltiness upon us." The word may also refer to the offense itself which entails the guilt: "For Israel hath not been forsaken . . . though their land was filled with sin against the Holy One of Israel" (Jer. 51:5). A similar meaning of the word appears in Ps. 68:21: "But God shall wound the head of his enemies and the hairy scalp of such a one as goeth on still in his trespasses [RSV, "guilty ways"; NASB, "guilty deeds"]."

Most occurrences of *'āšām* refer to the compensation given to satisfy someone who has been injured, or to the "trespass offering" or "guilt offering" presented on the altar by the repentant offender after paying a compensation of six-fifths of the damage inflicted (Num. 5:7–8). The "trespass offering" was the blood sacrifice of a ram: "And he shall bring a ram without blemish out of the flock, with thy estimation, for a trespass offering, unto the priest: and the priest shall make an atonement for him concerning his ignorance wherein he erred and wist it not, and it shall be forgiven him" (Lev. 5:18; cf. Lev. 7:5, 7; 14:12–13). The most significant theological statement containing *'āšām* is in Isa. 53:10, which says that the servant of Yahweh was appointed as an *'āšām* for sinful mankind. This suggests that His death furnished a 120–percent compensation for the broken law of God.

'āmāl (עָמָל, 5999), "evil; trouble; misfortune; mischief; grievance; wickedness; labor." This noun is related to the Hebrew verb *'āmal* ("to labor, toil"). The Arabic cognate *'amila* means "to get tired from hard work." The Aramaic *'amal* means "make" or "do," with no necessary connotation of burdensome labor. The Phoenician Canaanite usage of this term was closer to

the Arabic; the Book of Ecclesiastes (which shows considerable Phoenician influence) clearly represents this use: "Yea, I hated all my *labor* which I had taken under the sun . . ." (Eccl. 2:18). "And also that every man should eat and drink, and enjoy the good of all his *labor* . . ." (Eccl. 3:13). A related example appears in Ps. 107:12: "Therefore he brought down their heart with *labor;* they fell down and there was none to help."

In general, *'āmāl* refers either to the trouble and suffering which sin causes the sinner or to the trouble that he inflicts upon others. Jer. 20:18 depicts self-inflicted sorrow: "Wherefore came I forth out of the womb to see labor [*'āmāl*] and sorrow [*yāgôn*], that my days should be consumed with shame?" Another instance is found in Deut. 26:7: "And when we cried unto the Lord God of our fathers, the Lord heard our voice, and looked on our affliction [*'onî*], and our labor [*'āmāl*], and our oppression [*laḥaṣ*]."

Job 4:8 illustrates the sense of trouble as mischief inflicted on others: " . . . They that plow iniquity [*'āwen*], and sow wickedness [*'āmāl*] reap the same." The word appears in Ps. 140:9: "As for the head of those that compass me about, let the mischief of their own lips cover them." Hab. 1:3 also refers to the trouble inflicted on others: "Why dost thou show me iniquity [*'āwen*], and cause me to behold grievance [*'āmāl*]? For spoiling and violence are before me; and there are that raise up strife and contention."

'āwōn (עָוֹן, 5771), "iniquity." This word is derived from the root *'āwāh,* which means "to be bent, bowed down, twisted, perverted" or "to twist, pervert." The Arabic cognate *'awā* means "to twist, bend down"; some scholars regard the Arabic term *gharā* ("to err from the way") as the true cognate, but there is less justification for this interpretation.

'Āwōn portrays sin as a perversion of life (a twisting out of the right way), a perversion of truth (a twisting into error), or a perversion of intent (a bending of rectitude into willful disobedience). The word "iniquity" is the best single-word equivalent, although the Latin root *iniquitas* really means "injustice; unfairness; hostile; adverse."

'Āwōn occurs frequently throughout the Old Testament in parallelism with other words related to sin, such as *ḥaṭṭā't* ("sin") and *peša'* ("transgression"). Some examples are 1 Sam. 20:1: "And David . . . said before Jonathan, what have I done? what is mine iniquity [*'āwōn*]? and what is my sin [*ḥaṭṭā't*] before thy father, that he seeketh my life?" (cf. Isa. 43:24; Jer. 5:25). Also note Job 14:17: "My transgres-

sion [*peša'*] is sealed up in a bag, and thou sewest up mine iniquity [*'āwōn*]" (cf. Ps. 107:17; Isa. 50:1).

The penitent wrongdoer recognized his "iniquity" in Isa. 59:12: "For our transgressions are multiplied before thee, and our sins testify against us: for our transgressions are with us; and as for our iniquities, we know them" (cf. 1 Sam. 3:13). "Iniquity" is something to be confessed: "And Aaron shall lay both his hands upon the head of the live goat, and confess over him all the iniquities of the children of Israel . . ." (Lev. 16:21). "And the seed of Israel . . . confessed their sins, and the iniquities of their fathers" (Neh. 9:2; cf. Ps. 38:18).

The grace of God may remove or forgive "iniquity": "And unto him he said, Behold, I have caused thine iniquity to pass from thee . . ." (Zech. 3:4; cf. 2 Sam. 24:10). His atonement may cover over "iniquity": "By mercy and truth iniquity is purged; and by the fear of the Lord men depart from evil" (Prov. 16:6; cf. Ps. 78:38).

'Āwōn may refer to "the guilt of iniquity," as in Ezek. 36:31: "Then shall ye remember your own evil ways . . . and shall loathe yourselves in your own sight for your iniquities and for your abominations" (cf. Ezek. 9:9). The word may also refer to "punishment for iniquity": "And Saul sware to her by the Lord, saying, As the Lord liveth, there shall no punishment happen to thee for this thing" (1 Sam. 28:10). In Exod. 28:38, *'āwōn* is used as the object of *nāśā'* ("to bear, carry away, forgive"), to suggest bearing the punishment for the "iniquity" of others. In Isa. 53:11, we are told that the servant of Yahweh bears the consequences of the "iniquities" of sinful mankind, including Israel.

rāšā' (רָשָׁע, 7563), "wicked; criminal; guilty." Some scholars relate this word to the Arabic *raš'a* ("to be loose, out of joint"), although that term is not actively used in literary Arabic. The Aramaic cognate *ršša'* means "to be wicked" and the Syriac *apel* ("to do wickedly").

Rāšā' generally connotes a turbulence and restlessness (cf. Isa. 57:21) or something disjointed or ill-regulated. Thus Robert B. Girdlestone suggests that it refers to the tossing and confusion in which the wicked live, and to the perpetual agitation they cause to others.

In some instances, *rāšā'* carries the sense of being "guilty of crime": "Thou shalt not raise a false report: put not thine hand with the wicked to be an unrighteous witness" (Exod. 23:1); "Take away the wicked from before the king, and his throne shall be established in righteousness" (Prov. 25:5). "An ungodly witness scorneth judgment: and the mouth of the *wicked* [plural form] devoureth iniquity" (Prov. 19:28; cf. Prov. 20:26).

Justifying the "wicked" is classed as a heinous crime: "He that justifieth the wicked, and he that condemneth the just, even they both are abomination to the Lord" (Prov. 17:15; cf. Exod. 23:7).

The *rāšā'* is guilty of hostility to God and His people: "Arise, O Lord, disappoint him, cast him down: deliver my soul from the wicked, which is thy sword" (Ps. 17:13); "Oh let the wickedness of the *wicked* [plural form] come to an end; but establish the just . . . " (Ps. 7:9). The word is applied to the people of Babylon in Isa. 13:11 and to the Chaldeans in Hab. 1:13.

ḥaṭṭā't (חַטָּאת, 2403), "sin; sin-guilt; sin-purification; sin offering." The noun *ḥaṭṭā't* appears about 293 times and in all periods of biblical literature.

The basic nuance of this word is "sin" conceived as missing the road or mark (155 times). *Ḥaṭṭā't* can refer to an offense against a man: "And Jacob was wroth, and chode with Laban: and Jacob answered and said to Laban, What is my trespass [*pešaʻ*]? what is my sin, that thou hast so hotly pursued after me?" (Gen. 31:36). It is such passages which prove that *ḥaṭṭā't* is not simply a general word for "sin"; since Jacob used two different words, he probably intended two different nuances. In addition, a full word study shows basic differences between *ḥaṭṭā't* and other words rendered "sin."

For the most part this word represents a sin against God (Lev. 4:14). Men are to return from "sin," which is a path, a life-style, or act deviating from that which God has marked out (1 Kings 8:35). They should depart from "sin" (2 Kings 10:31), be concerned about it (Ps. 38:18), and confess it (Num. 5:7). The noun first appears in Gen. 4:7, where Cain is warned that "sin lieth at the door." This citation may introduce a second nuance of the word—"sin" in general. Certainly such an emphasis appears in Ps. 25:7, where the noun represents rebellious sin (usually indicated by *pāšaʻ*): "Remember not the sins of my youth, nor my transgressions. . . . "

In a few passages the term connotes the guilt or condition of sin: " . . . The cry of Sodom and Gomorrah is great, and . . . their sin is very grievous" (Gen. 18:20).

The word means "purification from sin" in two passages: "And thus shalt thou do unto them, to cleanse them: Sprinkle water of purifying upon them . . . " (Num. 8:7; cf. 19:9).

Ḥaṭṭā't means "sin offering" (135 times). The law of the "sin offering" is recorded in Lev. 4–5:13; 6:24–30. This was an offering for some specific "sin" committed unwittingly, without intending to do it and perhaps even without knowing it at the time (Lev. 4:2; 5:15).

Also derived from the verb *ḥātā'* is the noun *ḥēt'*, which occurs 33 times in biblical Hebrew. This word means "sin" in the sense of missing the mark or the path. This may be sin against either a man (Gen. 41:9—the first occurrence of the word) or God (Deut. 9:18). Second, it connotes the "guilt" of such an act (Num. 27:3). The psalmist confessed that his mother was in the condition of sin and guilt (cf. Rom. 5:12) when he was conceived (Ps. 51:5). Finally, several passages use this word for the idea of "punishment for sin" (Lev. 20:20).

The noun *ḥaṭṭā't*, with the form reserved for those who are typified with the characteristic represented by the root, is used both as an adjective (emphatic) and as a noun. The word occurs 19 times. Men are described as "sinners" (1 Sam. 15:18) and as those who are liable to the penalty of an offense (1 Kings 1:21). The first occurrence of the word is in Gen. 13:13: "But the men of Sodom were wicked and sinners before the Lord exceedingly."

B. Adjectives.

rāšā' (רָשָׁע, 7563), "wicked; guilty." In the typical example of Deut. 25:2, this word refers to a person "guilty of a crime": "And it shall be, if the wicked man be worthy to be beaten, that the judge shall cause him . . . to be beaten. . . . " A similar reference appears in Jer. 5:26: "For among my people are found *wicked* [plural form] men: they lay wait, as he that setteth snares; they set a trap, they catch men." *Rāšā'* is used specifically of murderers in 2 Sam. 4:11: "How much more, when wicked men have slain a righteous person in his own house upon his bed? . . . " The expression "guilty of death" (*rāšā' lāmût*) occurs in Num. 35:31 and is applied to a murderer.

Pharaoh and his people are portrayed as "wicked" people guilty of hostility to God and His people (Exod. 9:27).

ra' (רַע, 7451), "bad; evil; wicked; sore." The root of this term is disputed. Some scholars believe that the Akkadian term *raggu* ("evil; bad") may be a cognate. Some scholars derive *ra'* from the Hebrew word *rā'a'* ("to break, smash, crush"), which is a cognate of the Hebrew *rāṣaṣ* ("to smash, break to pieces"); *rāṣaṣ* in turn is related to the Arabic *radda* ("to crush, bruise"). If this derivation were correct, it would imply that *ra'* connotes sin in the sense of destructive hurtfulness; but this connotation is not appropriate in some contexts in which *ra'* is found.

Ra' refers to that which is "bad" or "evil," in

a wide variety of applications. A greater number of the word's occurrences signify something morally evil or hurtful, often referring to man or men: "Then answered all the wicked men and men of Belial, of those that went with David . . . " (1 Sam. 30:22). "And Esther said, the adversary and enemy is the wicked Haman" (Esth. 7:6). "There they cry, but none giveth answer, because of the pride of evil men" (Job 35:12; cf. Ps. 10:15). *Ra'* is also used to denote evil words (Prov. 15:26), evil thoughts (Gen. 6:5), or evil actions (Deut. 17:5, Neh. 13:17). Ezek. 6:11 depicts grim consequences for Israel as a result of its actions: "Thus saith the Lord God; smite with thine hand, and stamp with thy foot, and say, Alas for all the evil abominations of the house of Israel! For they shall fall by the sword, by the famine, and by the pestilence."

Ra' may mean "bad" or unpleasant in the sense of giving pain or causing unhappiness: "And Jacob said unto Pharaoh, . . . Few and evil have the days of the years of my life been . . . " (Gen. 47:9). "And when the people heard these evil tidings, they mourned . . . " (Exod. 33:4; cf. Gen. 37:2). "Correction is grievous [*ra'*] unto him that forsaketh the way: and he that hateth reproof shall die" (Prov. 15:10).

Ra' may also connote a fierceness or wildness: "He cast upon them the fierceness of his anger, wrath, and indignation, and trouble, by sending evil [*ra'*] angels among them" (Ps. 78:49). "Some evil beast hath devoured him . . . " (Gen. 37:20; cf. Gen. 37:33; Lev. 26:6).

In less frequent uses, *ra'* implies severity: "For thus saith the Lord God; How much more when I send my four sore [*ra'*] judgments upon Israel . . . " (Ezek. 14:21; cf. Deut. 6:22); unpleasantness: "And the Lord will take away from thee all sickness, and will put more of the evil diseases of Egypt . . . upon thee . . . " (Deut. 7:15; cf. Deut. 28:59); deadliness: "When I shall send upon them the evil arrows of famine, which shall be for their destruction . . . " (Ezek. 5:16; cf. "hurtful sword," Ps. 144:10); or sadness: "Wherefore the king said unto me, why is thy countenance sad . . . " (Neh. 2:2).

The word may also refer to something of poor or inferior quality, such as "bad" land (Num. 13:19), "naughty" figs (Jer. 24:2), "ill-favored" cattle (Gen. 41:3, 19), or a "bad" sacrificial animal (Lev. 27:10, 12, 14).

In Isa. 45:7 Yahweh describes His actions by saying, " . . . I make peace, and create evil [*ra'*] . . . "; moral "evil" is not intended in this context, but rather the antithesis of *šālôm*

("peace; welfare; well-being"). The whole verse affirms that as absolute Sovereign, the Lord creates a universe governed by a moral order. Calamity and misfortune will surely ensue from the wickedness of ungodly men.

C. Verbs.
'ābar (עָבַר, 5674), "to transgress, cross over, pass over." This word occurs as a verb only when it refers to sin. *'Ābar* often carries the sense of "transgressing" a covenant or commandment—i.e., the offender "passes beyond" the limits set by God's law and falls into transgression and guilt. This meaning appears in Num. 14:41: "And Moses said, wherefore now do ye transgress the commandment of the Lord? but it shall not prosper." Another example is in Judg. 2:20: "And the anger of the Lord was hot against Israel; and he said, Because that this people hath transgressed my covenant which I commanded their fathers, and have not hearkened unto my voice" (cf. 1 Sam. 15:24; Hos. 8:1).

Most frequently, *'ābar* illustrates the motion of "crossing over" or "passing over." (The Latin *transgredior*, from which we get our English word *transgress*, has the similar meaning of "go beyond" or "cross over.") This word refers to crossing a stream or boundage ("pass through," Num. 21:22), invading a country ("passed over," Judg. 11:32), crossing a boundary against a hostile army ("go over," 1 Sam. 14:4), marching over ("go over," Isa. 51:23), overflowing the banks of a river or other natural barriers ("pass through," Isa. 23:10), passing a razor over one's head ("come upon," Num. 6:5), and the passing of time ("went over," 1 Chron. 29:30).

hātā' (חָטָא, 2398), "to miss, sin, be guilty, forfeit, purify." This verb occurs 238 times and in all parts of the Old Testament. It is found also in Assyrian, Aramaic, Ethiopic, Sabean, and Arabic.

The basic meaning of this verb is illustrated in Judg. 20:16: There were 700 left-handed Benjamite soldiers who "could sling stones at a hair breadth, and not *miss*." The meaning is extended in Prov. 19:2: "He who makes haste with his feet *misses* the way" (RSV, NIV, KJV, NASB, "sinneth"). The intensive form is used in Gen. 31:39: "That which was torn of beasts I brought not unto thee; I bare the *loss* of it. . . . "

From this basic meaning comes the word's chief usage to indicate moral failure toward both God and men, and certain results of such wrongs. The first occurrence of the verb is in Gen. 20:6, God's word to Abimelech after he had taken Sarah: "Yes, I know that in the integrity of your heart you have done this, and also

I have kept you from sinning against Me" (NASB; cf. Gen. 39:9).

Sin against God is defined in Josh. 7:11: "Israel hath sinned, and they have also transgressed my covenant which I commanded them. . . ." Also note Lev. 4:27: "And if any one of the common people sin through ignorance, while he doeth somewhat against any of the commandments of the Lord concerning things which ought not to be done, and be guilty." The verb may also refer to the result of wrongdoing, as in Gen. 43:9: " . . . Then let me bear the blame for ever." Deut. 24:1–4, after forbidding adulterous marriage practices, concludes: " . . . For that is abomination before the Lord: and thou shalt not cause the land to sin . . ." (KJV); the RSV renders this passage: "You shall not bring guilt upon the land." Similarly, those who pervert justice are described as "those who by a word make a man out to be guilty" (Isa. 29:21, NIV). This leads to the meaning in Lev. 9:15: "And he . . . took the goat . . . and slew it, and offered it for sin. . . ." The effect of the offerings for sin is described in Ps. 51:7: "Purge me with hyssop, and I shall be clean . . ." (cf. Num. 19:1–13). Another effect is seen in the word of the prophet to evil Babylon: "You have forfeited your life" (Hab. 2:10, RSV, NIV; KJV, NASB, " sinned against").

The word is used concerning acts committed against men, as in Gen. 42:22: "Spake I not unto you, saying, Do not sin against the child . . .?" and 1 Sam. 19:4: "Do not let the king sin against his servant David, since he has not sinned against you . . . " (NASB; NIV, "wrong, wronged").

The Septuagint translates the group of words with the verb *hamartanō* and derived nouns 540 times. They occur 265 times in the New Testament. The fact that all "have sinned" continues to be emphasized in the New Testament (Rom. 3:10–18, 23; cf. 1 Kings 8:46; Ps. 14:1–3; Eccl. 7:20). The New Testament development is that Christ, "having made one sacrifice for sins for all time sat down at the right hand of God. . . . For by one offering he has perfected for all time those who are being sanctified" (Heb. 10:12–14, NASB).

TO SING

A. Verbs.

rānan (רָנַן, 7442), "to sing, shout, cry out." Found in both ancient and modern Hebrew, this word is used in modern Hebrew in the sense of "to chant, sing." It occurs approximately 50 times in the Hebrew Old Testament, with about half of these uses being in the Book of Psalms, where there is special emphasis on "singing"

and "shouting" praises to God. *Rānan* is found for the first time in Lev. 9:24 at the conclusion of the consecration of Aaron and his sons to the priesthood. When the fire fell and consumed the sacrifice, the people "shouted, and fell on their faces."

Rānan is often used to express joy, exultation, which seems to demand loud singing, especially when it is praise to God: "Cry out and shout, thou inhabitant of Zion: for great is the Holy One of Israel in the midst of thee" (Isa. 12:6). When Wisdom calls, she cries aloud to all who will hear (Prov. 8:3). To shout for joy (Ps. 32:11) is to let joy ring out!

šîr (שִׁיר, 7891), "to sing." This word appears frequently in ancient and modern Hebrew, as well as in ancient Ugaritic. While it occurs almost 90 times in the Hebrew Old Testament, it is not used until Exod. 15:1: "Then sang Moses and the children of Israel this song unto the Lord. . . . " One might wonder if it took the miracle of the Exodus from Egypt to give the Israelites something "to sing" about!

Over one quarter of the instances of *šîr* are found in the Book of Psalms, often in the imperative form, calling the people to express their praise to God in singing. One such example is found in Ps. 96:1: "O sing unto the Lord a new song: sing unto the Lord, all the earth." Frequently *šîr* is found in parallelism with *zāmar*, "to sing" (Ps. 68:4, 32).

B. Participle.

šîr (שִׁיר, 7891), "singers." In the Books of Chronicles, *šîr* is used in the participial form some 33 times to designate the Levitical "singers" (1 Chron. 15:16). "Female singers" are referred to occasionally (2 Sam. 19:35; 2 Chron. 35:25; Eccl. 2:8).

C. Noun.

šîr (שִׁיר, 7892), "song." This noun is found about 30 times in the titles of various psalms as well as elsewhere in the Old Testament. *Šîr* is used of a joyous "song" in Gen. 31:27: " . . . And didst not tell me, that I might have sent thee away with mirth, and with songs, with tabret, and with harp?" In Judg. 5:12 the word refers to a triumphal "song," and in Neh. 12:46 the word is used of a religious "song" for worship.

The book that is commonly designated "The Song of Solomon" actually has the title "The Song of Songs" in Hebrew. While this love "song" continues to create questions in the minds of many regarding its inclusion in the biblical canon, it must have had some special meaning to have earned the title it has. Rather than rationalize its place in the canon by stating that it is an allegory of the love between God and Israel, and then Christ and the church, perhaps one should simply recognize that it is a love "song," pure and simple, and that love has its rightful place in the divine plan for mature men and women.

SISTER

'āhôt (אָחוֹת, 269), "sister." Like the words for "brother" and "father," this noun is common to many Semitic languages. Whereas "brother" appears 629 times, "sister" occurs only 114 times. The usage is rare in the poetic literature with the exception of the Song of Solomon (7 times). The first occurrence is in Gen. 4:22: "And Zillah, she also bare Tubal-cain, an instructor of every artificer in brass and iron: and the sister of Tubal-cain was Naamah."

The translation of "sister" for *'āhôt* is only the beginning. In Hebrew custom the word was a term employed to refer to the daughter of one's father and mother (Gen. 4:22) or one's half-sister (Gen. 20:12). It may also refer to one's aunt on the father's side (Lev. 18:12; 20:19) or on the mother's side (Lev. 18:13; 20:19).

The use of *'āhôt* more generally denotes female relatives: "And they blessed Rebekah, and said unto her, Thou art our sister, be thou the mother of thousands of millions, and let thy seed possess the gate of those which hate them" (Gen. 24:60). This meaning lies behind the metaphorical use, where two divisions of a nation (Judah and Israel; Jer. 3:7) and two cities (Sodom and Samaria; Ezek. 16:46) are portrayed as sisters—Hebrew names of geographical entities are feminine.

The more specialized meaning "beloved" is found only in Song of Sol. 4:9: "Thou hast ravished my heart, my sister [or beloved], my spouse; thou hast ravished my heart with one of thine eyes, with one chain of thy neck." Here *'āhôt* is used as a term of endearment rather than a term for a blood relative.

The Septuagint translates the word *adelphe* ("sister").

TO SLAUGHTER

A. Verb.

zābah (זָבַח, 2076), "to slaughter, sacrifice." This word is a common Semitic term for sacrifice in general, although there are a number of other terms used in the Old Testament for specific sacrificial rituals. There is no question that this is one of the most important terms in the Old Testament; *zābah* is found more than 130 times in its verbal forms and its noun forms occur over 500 times. The first time the verb occurs is in Gen. 31:54, where "Jacob offered

sacrifice upon the mount." In Exod. 20:24 the word is used in relation to the kinds of sacrifices to be made.

While there were grain and incense offerings prescribed as part of the Mosaic laws dealing with sacrifice (see Lev. 2), the primary kind of sacrifice was the blood offering which required the slaughter of an animal (cf. Deut. 17:1; 1 Chron. 15:26). This blood was poured around the altar, for the blood contained the life, as stated in Lev. 17:11: "For the life of the flesh is in the blood; and I have given it for you upon the altar to make atonement for your souls; for it is the blood that makes atonement, by reason of the life" (RSV). Since the blood was the vehicle of life, it belonged to God alone. Because the blood is the life, and because it is given to God in the process of pouring it about the altar, it becomes the means of expiating sin, as an offering for sin and not because it becomes a substitute for the sinner.

Zābah is also used as a term for "slaughter for eating." This usage is closely linked with "slaughter for sacrifice" since all eating of flesh was sacrificial among ancient Hebrews. The word carries this meaning in 1 Kings 19:21: "And he returned back from him, and took a yoke of oxen, and slew them, and boiled their flesh . . . and gave unto the people, and they did eat."

B. Nouns.

zebah (זֶבַח, 2077), "sacrifice." This noun occurs more than 160 times in biblical Hebrew. The "sacrifice" which was part of a covenant ritual involved the sprinkling of the blood on the people and upon the altar, which presumably symbolized God as the covenant partner (see Exod. 24:6–8). Another special "sacrifice" was "the sacrifice of the feast of the passover" (Exod. 34:25). In this case the sacrificial lamb provided the main food for the passover meal, and its blood was sprinkled on the doorposts of the Israelite homes as a sign to the death angel.

The "sacrifice" of animals was in no way unique to Israelite religion, for sacrificial rituals generally are part of all ancient religious cults. Indeed, the mechanics of the ritual were quite similar, especially between Israelite and Canaanite religions. However, the differences are very clear in the meanings which the rituals had as they were performed either to capricious Canaanite gods or for the one true God who kept His covenant with Israel.

The noun *zebah* is used of "sacrifices" to the one true God in Gen. 46:1: "And Israel took his journey with all that he had . . . and offered sacrifices unto the God of his father Isaac" (cf. Exod. 10:25; Neh. 12:43). The noun refers to "sacrifices" to other deities in Exod. 34:15: "Lest thou make a covenant with the inhabitants of the land, and they go a whoring after their gods, and do sacrifice unto their gods, and one call thee, and thou eat of his sacrifice" (cf. Num. 25:2; 2 Kings 10:19).

The idea of "sacrifice" certainly is taken over into the New Testament, for Christ became "the Lamb of God, who takes away the sin of the world" (John 1:29, RSV). The writer of Hebrews makes much of the fact that with the "sacrifice" of Christ, no more sacrifices are necessary (Heb. 9).

mizbēaḥ (מִזְבֵּחַ, 4196), "altar." This word is used more than 400 times in the Old Testament. This frequent use is obviously another direct evidence of the centrality of the sacrificial system in Israel. The first appearance of *mizbēaḥ* is in Gen. 8:20, where Noah built an "altar" after the Flood.

Countless "altars" are referred to as the story of Israel progresses on the pages of the Old Testament: that of Noah (Gen. 8:20); of Abram at Sichem (Gen. 12:7), at Beth-el (Gen. 12:8), and at Moriah (Gen. 22:9); of Isaac at Beersheba (Gen. 26:25); of Jacob at Shechem (Gen. 33:20); of Moses at Horeb (Exod. 24:4); of Samuel at Ramah (1 Sam. 7:17); of the temple in Jerusalem (1 Kings 6:20; 8:64); and of the two "altars" planned by Ezekiel for the restored temple (Ezek. 41:22; 43:13–17).

SMALL

A. Adjectives.

qātān (קָטָן, 6996), "small; youngest"; *qāṭōn* (קָטֹן, 6994), "small; young; insignificant." These adjectives are synonymous. Both occur in all periods of biblical Hebrew—*qātān*, 47 times; *qāṭōn*, 56 times.

Qāṭōn in its first appearance means "small and insignificant": "And God made two great lights; the greater light to rule the day, and the lesser light to rule the night . . ." (Gen. 1:16). The first appearance of *qātān* bears the sense "youngest": "And Noah awoke from his wine, and knew what his younger son had done unto him" (Gen. 9:24).

In their first nuance, "small," the words are often contrasted to *gādôl*, "great": "And all the vessels of the house of God, great and small, and the treasures of the house of the Lord . . ." (2 Chron. 36:18). Other uses of the words to mean "small" include their application to the size of a set of weights (Deut. 25:13), to the size of the smallest finger of one's hand (1 Kings 12:10), and to the degree of seriousness of a given sin (Num. 22:18).

In the sense "young" these words refer to the relative age of an individual: "And the Syrians had gone out by companies, and had brought away captive out of the land of Israel a little maid . . ." (2 Kings 5:2). Notice 2 Kings 5:14: "Then went he down, and dipped himself seven times in Jordan, according to the saying of the man of God: and his flesh came again like unto the flesh of a little child. . . ." In a related use the word is comparative, contrasting the age of a given individual with that of his sibling(s): "Hereby ye shall be proved: By the life of Pharaoh ye shall not go forth hence, except your youngest brother come hither" (Gen. 42:15).

Finally, these adjectives can represent the idea "insignificant," or small in importance or strength: "Ye shall not respect persons in judgment; but ye shall hear the small as well as the great . . ." (Deut. 1:17). In a related nuance *qāṭōn* signifies "low in social standing": "When thou wast little in thine own sight, wast thou not made the head of the tribes of Israel . . . ?" (I Sam. 15:17). In Exod. 18:22 the word suggests triviality: "And let them judge the people at all seasons: and it shall be, that every great matter they shall bring unto thee, but every small matter they shall judge. . . ."

B. Verb.

Qāṭōn means "to be small, insignificant." This verb occurs 4 times in biblical Hebrew and emphasizes smallness in quality or quantity. The word refers to "being insignificant" in Gen. 32:10: "I am not worthy of the least of all the mercies, and of all the truth, which thou hast showed unto thy servant . . ." (cf. 2 Sam. 7:19, NASB). In Amos 8:5, *qāṭōn* refers to "making small."

TO SOJOURN, DWELL

A. Verb.

gûr (גּוּר, 1481), "to dwell as a client, sojourn." This verb occurs only in Northwest Semitic and outside Hebrew only as a noun. In biblical Hebrew the verb *gûr* occurs 84 times and in every period of the language. This sense of *gûr* should be distinguished from one that means "to be afraid of" (Num. 22:3).

This verb means "to dwell in a land as a client." The first occurrence of the word is in Gen. 12:10, where it is reported that Abram journeyed to Egypt and dwelt there as a client. In Gen. 21:23, Abraham makes a covenant with Abimelech, saying, " . . . According to the kindness that I have done unto thee, thou shalt do unto me, and to the land wherein thou hast sojourned."

B. Nouns.

gēr (רֵג, 1616), "client; stranger." *Gēr* occurs about 92 times and in every period of biblical Hebrew.

A "client" was not simply a foreigner (*nākrî*) or a stranger (*zār*). He was a permanent resident, once a citizen of another land, who had moved into his new residence. Frequently he left his homeland under some distress, as when Moses fled to Midian (Exod. 2:22). Whether the reason for his journey was to escape some difficulty or merely to seek a new place to dwell, he was one who sought acceptance and refuge. Consequently he might also call himself a *tôšāb*, a settler. Neither the settler nor the "client" could possess land. In the land of Canaan the possession of land was limited to members or descendants of the original tribal members. Only they were full citizens who enjoyed all the rights of citizenry, which meant sharing fully in the inheritance of the gods and forefathers—the feudal privileges and responsibilities (cf. Ezek. 47:22).

In Israel a *gēr*, like a priest, could possess no land and enjoyed the special privileges of the third tithe. Every third year the tithe of the harvest was to be deposited at the city gate with the elders and distributed among "the Levite, (because he hath no part nor inheritance with thee,) and the stranger, and the fatherless, and the widow, which are within thy gates ..." (Deut. 14:29). In the eschaton such "clients" were to be treated as full citizens: "And it shall come to pass, that ye shall divide it [the land] by lot for an inheritance unto you, and to the strangers that sojourn among you, which shall beget children among you: and they shall be unto you as born in the country among the children of Israel; they shall have inheritance with you among the tribes of Israel" (Ezek. 47:22). Under the Mosaic law aliens were not slaves but were usually in the service of some Israelite whose protection they enjoyed (Deut. 24:14). This, however, was not always the case. Sometimes a "client" was rich and an Israelite would be in his service (Lev. 25:47).

The *gēr* was to be treated (except for feudal privileges and responsibilities) as an Israelite, being responsible to and protected by the law: "Hear the causes between your brethren, and judge righteously between every man and his brother, and the stranger that is with him" (Deut. 1:16); "ye shall therefore keep my statutes and my judgments, and shall not commit any of these abominations; neither any of your own nation, nor any stranger that sojourneth among you" (Lev. 18:26); "ye shall have one manner of law, as well for the stranger, as for one of your own country: for I am the Lord your God" (Lev. 24:22). The *gēr* also enjoyed the Sabbath rest (Lev. 25:6) and divine protection (Deut. 10:18). God commanded Israel to love the "client" as himself (Lev. 19:34).

The *gēr* could also be circumcised (Exod. 12:48) and enjoy all the privileges of the true religion: the Passover (Exod. 12:48–49), the Atonement feast (Lev. 16:29), presenting offerings (Lev. 17:8), and all the feasts (Deut. 16:11). He was also obligated to keep the purity laws (Lev. 17:15).

Israel is told that God is the true owner of all the land and its people are but "clients" owing Him feudal obedience (Lev. 19:34; Deut. 10:19). They are admonished to treat the client with justice, righteousness, and love because like Abraham (Gen. 23:4) they were "clients" in Egypt (Exod. 22:21). In legal cases the "client" could appeal directly to God the great feudal Lord (Lev. 24:22).

Two other nouns related to *gûr* are *mᵉgûrîm* and *gērût*. *Mᵉgûrîm* occurs 11 times and refers to the "status or condition of being a client" (Gen. 17:8) and to a "dwelling where one is a client" (Job 18:19). *Gērût* appears once to refer to a "place where clients dwell" (Jer. 41:17). Some scholars think this word is a proper name, a part of a place name.

SOUL; SELF; LIFE

A. Noun.

nepeš (שֶׁפֶנ, 5315), "soul; self; life; person; heart." This is a very common term in both ancient and modern Semitic languages. It occurs over 780 times in the Old Testament and is evenly distributed in all periods of the text with a particularly high frequency in poetic passages.

The basic meaning is apparently related to the rare verbal form, *nāpaš*. The noun refers to the essence of life, the act of breathing, taking breath. However, from that concrete concept, a number of more abstract meanings were developed. In its primary sense the noun appears in its first occurrence in Gen. 1:20: "the moving creature that hath life," and in its second occurrence in Gen. 2:7: "living soul."

However, in over 400 later occurrences it is translated "soul." While this serves to make sense in most passages, it is an unfortunate mistranslation of the term. The real difficulty of the term is seen in the inability of almost all English translations to find a consistent equivalent or even a small group of high-frequency equivalents for the term. The KJV alone uses over 28 different English terms for this one Hebrew word. The problem with the English term "soul" is that no actual equivalent of the term or the idea behind it is represented in the Hebrew language. The Hebrew system of thought does not include the combination or opposition of the terms "body" and "soul," which are really Greek and Latin in origin. The Hebrew contrasts two other concepts which are not found in the Greek and Latin tradition: "the inner self" and "the outer appearance" or, as viewed in a different context, "what one is to oneself" as opposed to "what one appears to be to one's observers." The inner person is *nepeš*, while the outer person, or reputation, is *šēm*, most commonly translated "name." In narrative or historical passages of the Old Testament, *nepeš* can be translated as "life" or "self," as in Lev. 17:11: "For the life of the flesh is in the blood: and I have given it to you upon the altar to make an atonement for [yourselves]. . . ." Needless to say, the reading "soul" is meaningless in such a text.

But the situation in the numerous parallel poetic passages in which the term appears is much more difficult. The Greek Septuagint and the Latin Vulgate both simply use the Greek and Latin equivalent "soul," especially in the Psalms. The first occurrence is in Ps. 3:2: "Many are saying of my soul, // There is no deliverance for him in God" (NASB). The next occurrence is in Ps. 6:3: "And my soul is greatly dismayed; // But Thou, O Lord—how long?" (NASB). In both passages the parallel contrast is between *nepeš* and some aspect of the self, expressed as "him" in Ps. 3:2 and not expressed but understood in Ps. 6:3. There is no distinction as to whether it appears as an "A" or "B" word in the parallelism. However, since Hebrew rejects repeating the same noun in both halves of a poetic line, *nepeš* is often used as the parallel for the speaker, primary personal subject, and even for God, as in Ps. 11:5: "The Lord trieth the righteous: but the wicked // and him that loveth violence [he himself] hateth." Such passages are frequent, and a proper understanding of the word enlightens many well-known passages, such as Ps. 119:109: "My life is continually in my hand, // Yet I do not forget Thy law" (NASB).

The versions vary widely in their readings of *nepeš*, with the more contemporary versions casting widely for meanings.

B. Verb.

Nāpaš means "to breathe; respire; be refreshed." This verb, which is apparently related to the noun *nepeš*, appears 3 times in the Old Testament (Exod. 23:12; 31:17). The other appearance is in 2 Sam. 16:14: "And the king, and all the people that were with him, came weary, and refreshed themselves there."

TO SOW

A. Verb.

zāra' (זָרַע, 2232), "to sow, scatter seed, make pregnant." Common throughout the history of the Hebrew language, this root is found in various Semitic languages, including ancient Akkadian. The verb is found approximately 60 times in the Hebrew Old Testament. It occurs first in Gen. 1:29 in the summary of the blessings of creation which God has given to mankind: " . . . In the which is the fruit of a tree yielding seed. . . ."

In an agricultural society such as ancient Israel, *zāra'* would be most important and very commonly used, especially to describe the annual sowing of crops (Judg. 6:3; Gen. 26:12). Used in the figurative sense, it is said that Yahweh "will sow" Israel in the land (Hos. 2:23); in the latter days, Yahweh promises: " . . . I will sow the house of Israel and the house of Judah with the seed of man, and with the seed of beast" (Jer. 31:27). Of great continuing comfort are the words, "They that sow in tears shall reap in joy" (Ps. 126:5). The universal law of the harvest, sowing and reaping, applies to all areas of life and experience.

A good example of the need for free translation of the inherent meaning rather than a strictly literal rendering involves *zāra'*, in both its verb and noun forms. This is found in Num. 5, which describes the law of trial by ordeal in the case of a wife accused of infidelity. If she was found innocent, it was declared: " . . . She shall be free, and shall conceive [*zāra'*] seed [*zera'*]" (Num. 5:28). This phrase is literally: "She shall be acquitted and shall be seeded seed," or "She shall be made pregnant with seed."

An Old Testament name, Jezreel, has been connected with this root. Jezreel ("God sows") refers both to a city and valley near Mt. Gilboa (Josh. 17:16; 2 Sam. 2:9) and to the symbolically named son of Hosea (Hos. 1:4).

B. Noun.

zera' (זֶרַע, 2233), "seed; sowing; seedtime; harvest; offspring; descendant(s); posterity." This word occurs about 228 times in biblical Hebrew and in all periods. It has cognates in Aramaic, Phoenician, Arabic, Ethiopic, and Akkadian.

Zera' refers to the process of scattering seed, or "sowing." This is the emphasis in Gen. 47:24: "And it shall come to pass in the increase, that ye shall give the fifth part unto Pharaoh, and four parts shall be your own, for seed of the field, and for your food . . . ." Num. 20:5 should be rendered: "It [the wilderness] is not a place of sowing [NASB, "grain"] or figs or vines or pomegranates, nor is there water to drink." Ezek. 17:5 should be rendered: "He also took some of the seed of the land and planted it in a field [suitable for] sowing" (NASB, "in a fertile field"). A closely related emphasis occurs in passages such as Gen. 8:22, where the word represents "sowing" as a regularly recurring activity: "While the earth remaineth, seedtime and harvest, and cold and heat . . . shall not cease."

Zera' frequently means "seed." There are several nuances under this emphasis, the first being what is sown to raise crops for food. The Egyptians told Joseph: "Buy us and our land for bread, and we and our land will be servants unto Pharaoh: and give us seed, that we may live, and not die, that the land be not desolate" (Gen. 47:19). The word represents the product of a plant: "Let the earth bring forth grass, the herb yielding seed [food], and the fruit tree yielding fruit after his kind, whose seed is in itself . . . " (Gen. 1:11—the first biblical appearance). In this and other contexts zera' specifically refers to "grain seed," or "edible seed" (cf. Lev. 27:30). This may be the meaning of the word in 1 Sam. 8:15: "And he will take the tenth of your seed, and of your vineyards . . . ." However, it is possible that here the word refers to arable land, as does its Akkadian cognate. In other contexts the word represents an entire "crop or harvest": "For the seed [harvest] shall be prosperous; the vine shall give her fruit, and the ground shall give her increase, and the heavens shall give their dew . . . " (Zech. 8:12). In Isa. 23:3 zera' and the usual Hebrew word for "harvest" (qāṣîr) are in synonymous parallelism.

Zera' sometimes means "semen," or a man's "seed": "And if any man's seed of copulation go out from him [if he has a seminal emission] . . . " (Lev. 15:16). A beast's "semen" can also be indicated by this word (Jer. 31:27). Zera' often means "offspring." Only rarely is this nuance applied to animals: "And I will put enmity between thee [the devil] and the woman [Eve], and between thy seed and her seed . . . " (Gen. 3:15). This verse uses the word in several senses. The first appearance means both the descendants of the snake and those of the spiritual being who used the snake (evil men). The second appearance of the word refers to all the descendants of the woman and ultimately to a particular descendant (Christ). In Gen. 4:25 zera' appears not as a collective noun but refers to a particular and immediate "offspring"; upon the birth of Seth, Eve said: "God . . . hath ap-

pointed me another seed [offspring] . . . ." Gen. 46:6 uses the word (in the singular) of one's entire family including children and grandchildren (cf. Gen. 17:12). One's larger family, including all immediate relatives, is included in the word in passages such as 1 Kings 11:14. The word is used of an entire nation of people in Esth. 10:3.

Zera' is used of groups and individuals marked by a common moral quality. This usage was already seen in Gen. 3:15. Isa. 65:23 mentions the "seed" of the blessed of God. The Messiah or Suffering Servant will see His "offspring," or those who believe in and follow Him (Isa. 53:10). We also read about the followers of the righteous (Prov. 11:21), the faithful "seed" (Jer. 2:21), and godly "offspring." In each case this word represents those who are united by being typified by the modifier of zera'. Several other passages exhibit the same nuance except that zera' is modified by an undesirable quality.

TO SPEAK

A. Verb.

dābar (דָּבַר, 1696), "to speak, say." This verb occurs in all periods of Hebrew, in Phoenician (starting from around 900 B.C.), and in imperial Aramaic (starting from about 500 B.C.). In Old Testament Hebrew it occurs about 1,125 times.

This verb focuses not only on the content of spoken verbal communication but also and especially on the time and circumstances of what is said. Unlike 'āmar, "to say," dābar often appears without any specification of what was communicated. Those who "speak" are primarily persons (God or men) or organs of speech. In Gen. 8:15 (the first occurrence of this verb) God "spoke" to Noah, while in Gen. 18:5 one of the three men "spoke" to Abraham. Exceptions to this generalization occur, for example, in Job 32:7, where Elihu personifies "days" (a person's age) as that which has the right "to speak" first. In 2 Sam. 23:2 David says that the Spirit of the Lord "spoke" to him; contrary to many (especially liberal) scholars, this is probably a reference to the Holy Spirit (cf. NASB).

Among the special meanings of this verb are "to say" (Dan. 9:21), "to command" (2 Kings 1:9), "to promise" (Deut. 6:3), "to commission" (Exod. 1:17), "to announce" (Jer. 36:31), "to order or command" (Deut. 1:14), and "to utter a song" (Judg. 5:12). Such secondary meanings are, however, quite infrequent.

B. Nouns.

dābār (דָּבָר, 1697), "word; matter; something." This noun occurs 1,440 times.

The noun dābār refers, first, to what is said,

to the actual "word" itself; whereas *'emer* is essentially oral communication (the act of speaking). Before the dispersion from the tower of Babel all men spoke the same "words" or language (Gen. 11:1). This noun can also be used of the content of speaking. When God "did according to the word of Moses" (Exod. 8:13), He granted his request. The noun can connote "matter" or "affair," as in Gen. 12:17, where it is reported that God struck Pharaoh's household with plagues because of the "matter of Sarah" (KJV, "because of Sarai"). A rather specialized occurrence of this sense appears in references to records of the "events of a period" (cf. 1 Kings 14:19) or the activities of a particular person (1 Kings 11:41; cf. Gen. 15:1). *Dābār* can be used as a more general term in the sense of "something"—so in Gen. 24:66 the "everything" (KJV, "all things") is literally "all of something(s)"; it is an indefinite generalized concept rather than a reference to everything in particular. This noun also appears to have had almost a technical status in Israel's law procedures. Anyone who had a "matter" before Moses had a law case (Exod. 18:16).

As a biblical phrase "the word of the Lord" is quite important; it occurs about 242 times. Against the background just presented it is important to note that "word" here may focus on the content (meaning) of what was said, but it also carries overtones of the actual "words" themselves. It was the "word of the Lord" that came to Abram in a vision after his victory over the kings who had captured Lot (Gen. 15:1). In most cases this is a technical phrase referring expressly to prophetic revelation (about 225 times). It has been suggested that this phrase has judicial overtones although there are only 7 passages where this is certain (cf. Num. 15:31). This noun is used twice of God's "affairs" in the sense of the care of the temple (1 Chron. 26:32).

The "word" of God indicates God's thoughts and will. This should be contrasted with His name, which indicates His person and presence. Therefore, God's "word" is called "holy" only once (cf. Ps. 105:42), while His name is frequently called "holy."

There is much discussion regarding the "word" as a hypostatization of divine reality and attributes as seen, for example, in John 1:1: "In the beginning was the Word." This theme is rooted in such Old Testament passages as Isa. 9:8: "The Lord sent a word into Jacob..." (cf. 55:10–11; Ps. 107:20; 147:15). Some scholars argue that this is no more than the poetical device of personification and does not foreshadow John's usage. Their evidence is that human attributes are frequently separated from

a man and objectivized as if they had a separate existence (cf. Ps. 85:11–12).

The Septuagint translates the noun *dābār* with two words respectively carrying overtones of the (1) content and (2) form of speaking: (1) *logos* and (2) *rēma*.

Several other nouns related to the verb *dābar* occur infrequently. *Dibrāh*, which occurs 5 times, means "cause, manner" (Job 5:8). *Dabberet* means "word" once (Deut. 33:3). *Dᵉbôrāh* appears 5 times and refers to "honey bee" (Deut. 1:44; Ps. 118:12). *Midbār* refers to "speaking" once (Song of Sol. 4:3).

SPIRIT; BREATH

rûah (רוּחַ, 7307), "breath; air; strength; wind; breeze; spirit; courage; temper; Spirit." This noun has cognates in Ugaritic, Aramaic, and Arabic. The word occurs about 378 times and in all periods of biblical Hebrew.

First, this word means "breath," air for breathing, air that is being breathed. This meaning is especially evident in Jer. 14:6: "And the wild asses did stand in the high places, they snuffed up the wind like dragons...." When one's "breath" returns, he is revived: "... When he [Samson] had drunk [the water], his spirit [literally, "breath"] came again, and he revived..." (Judg. 15:19). Astonishment may take away one's "breath": "And when the queen of Sheba had seen all Solomon's wisdom, and the house that he had built, And the meat of his table,... there was no more spirit in her [she was overwhelmed and breathless]" (1 Kings 10:4–5). *Rûah* may also represent speaking, or the breath of one's mouth: "By the word of the Lord were the heavens made; and all the host of them by the breath of his mouth"(Ps. 33:6; cf. Exod. 15:8; Job 4:9; 19:17).

Second, this word can be used with emphasis on the invisible, intangible, fleeting quality of "air": "O remember that my life is wind: mine eyes shall no more see good" (Job 7:7). There may be a suggestion of purposelessness, uselessness, or even vanity (emptiness) when *rûah* is used with this significance: "And the prophets shall become wind, and the word is not in them..." (Jer. 5:13). "Windy words" are really "empty words" (Job 16:3), just as "windy knowledge" is "empty knowledge" (Job 15:2; cf. Eccl. 1:14, 17—"meaningless striving"). In Prov. 11:29 *rûah* means "nothing": "He that troubleth his own house shall inherit the wind...." This nuance is especially prominent in Eccl. 5:15–16: "And he came forth of his mother's womb, naked shall he return to go as he came, and shall take nothing of his labor, which he may carry away in his hand. And this also is a sore evil, that in all points as he came, so shall he go: and what profit hath he that hath labored for the wind?"

Third, *rûaḥ* can mean "wind." In Gen. 3:8 it seems to mean the gentle, refreshing evening breeze so well known in the Near East: "And they heard the voice of the Lord God walking in the garden in the cool [literally, "breeze"] of the day...." It can mean a strong, constant wind: "... And the Lord brought an east wind upon the land all that day, and all that night..." (Exod. 10:13). It can also signify an extremely strong wind: "And the Lord turned a mighty strong west wind..." (Exod. 10:19). In Jer. 4:11 the word appears to represent a gale or tornado (cf. Hos. 8:7). God is the Creator (Amos 4:13) and sovereign Controller of the winds (Gen. 8:1; Num. 11:31; Jer. 10:13).

Fourth, the wind represents direction. In Jer. 49:36 the four winds represent the four ends of the earth, which in turn represent every quarter: "And upon Elam will I bring the four winds [peoples from every quarter of the earth] from the four quarters of heaven, and will scatter them toward all those winds; and there shall be no nation whither the outcasts of Elam shall not come." Akkadian attests the same phrase with the same meaning, and this phrase begins to appear in Hebrew at a time when contact with Akkadian-speaking peoples was frequent.

Fifth, *rûaḥ* frequently represents the element of life in a man, his natural "spirit": "And all flesh died that moved upon the earth, ... All in whose nostrils was the breath of life..." (Gen. 7:21–22). In these verses the animals have a "spirit" (cf. Ps. 104:29). On the other hand, in Prov. 16:2 the word appears to mean more than just the element of life; it seems to mean "soul": "All the ways of a man are clean in his own eyes; but the Lord weigheth the spirits [NASB, "motives"]." Thus, Isaiah can put *nepeš*, "soul," and *rûaḥ* in synonymous parallelism: "With my soul have I desired thee in the night; yea, with my spirit within me will I seek thee early..." (26:9). It is the "spirit" of a man that returns to God (Eccl. 12:7).

Sixth, *rûaḥ* is often used of a man's mind-set, disposition, or "temper": "Blessed is the man unto whom the Lord imputeth not iniquity, and in whose spirit there is no guile" (Ps. 32:2). In Ezek. 13:3 the word is used of one's mind or thinking: "Woe unto the foolish prophets, that follow their own spirits, and have seen nothing" (cf. Prov. 29:11). *Rûaḥ* can represent particular dispositions, as it does in Josh. 2:11: "And as soon as we had heard these things, our hearts did melt, neither did there remain any more courage in any man, because of you..." (cf.

Josh. 5:1; Job 15:13). Another disposition represented by this word is "temper": "If the spirit [temper] of the ruler rise up against thee, leave not thy place..." (Eccl. 10:4). David prayed that God would "restore unto me the joy of thy salvation; and uphold me with thy free Spirit" (Ps. 51:12). In this verse "joy of salvation" and "free Spirit" are parallel and, therefore, synonymous terms. Therefore, " spirit" refers to one's inner disposition, just as "joy" refers to an inner emotion.

Seventh, the Bible often speaks of God's "Spirit," the third person of the Trinity. This is the use of the word in its first biblical occurrence: "And the earth was without form, and void; and darkness was upon the face of the deep. And the Spirit of God moved upon the face of the waters" (Gen. 1:2). Isa. 63:10–11 and Ps. 51:12 specifically speak of the "holy or free Spirit."

Eighth, the non-material beings (angels) in heaven are sometimes called "spirits": "And there came forth a spirit, and stood before the Lord, and said, I will persuade him" (1 Kings 22:21; cf. 1 Sam. 16:14).

Ninth, the "spirit" may also be used of that which enables a man to do a particular job or that which represents the essence of a quality of man: "And Joshua the son of Nun was full of the spirit of wisdom; for Moses had laid his hands upon him..." (Deut. 34:9). Elisha asked Elijah for a double portion of his "spirit" (2 Kings 2:9) and received it.

SPIRIT (OF THE DEAD), NECROMANCER

'ôb (אוֹב, 178), "spirit (of the dead); necromancer; pit." This word has cognates in Sumerian, Akkadian, and Ugaritic, where the meanings "pit" and "spirit of one who has died" occur. In its earliest appearances (Sumerian), *'ôb* refers to a pit out of which a departed spirit may be summoned. Later Assyrian texts use this word to denote simply a pit in the ground. Akkadian texts describe a deity that is the personification of the pit, to whom a particular exorcism ritual was addressed. Biblical Hebrew attests this word 16 times.

The word usually represents the troubled spirit (or spirits) of the dead. This meaning appears unquestionably in Isa. 29:4: "... Thy voice shall be, as of one that hath a familiar spirit, out of the ground, and thy speech shall whisper out of the dust."

Its second meaning, "necromancer," refers to a professional who claims to summon forth such spirits when requested (or hired) to do so:

"Regard not them that have familiar spirits, neither seek after wizards" (Lev. 19:31—first occurrence). These mediums summoned their "guides" from a hole in the ground. Saul asked the medium (witch) of Endor, "Divine for me from the hole ['ôb] (1 Sam. 28:8, author's translation).

God forbade Israel to seek information by this means, which was so common among the pagans (Lev. 19:31; Deut. 18:11). Perhaps the pagan belief in manipulating one's basic relationship to a god (or gods) explains the relative silence of the Old Testament regarding life after death. Yet God's people believed in life after death, from early times (e.g., Gen. 37:35; Isa. 14:15ff.).

Necromancy was so contrary to God's commands that its practitioners were under the death penalty (Deut. 13). Necromancers' unusual experiences do not prove that they truly had power to summon the dead. For example, the medium of Endor could not snatch Samuel out of God's hands against His wishes. But in this particular incident, it seems that God rebuked Saul's apostasy, either through a revived Samuel or through a vision of Samuel. Mediums do not have power to summon the spirits of the dead, since this is reprehensible to God and contrary to His will.

SPLENDOR

hôd (הוד, 1935), "splendor; majesty; authority." A possible cognate of this word appears in Arabic. All but 4 of its 24 biblical appearances occur in poetry.

The basic significance of "splendor and majesty" with overtones of superior power and position is attested in the application of this word to kings: "Therefore thus saith the Lord concerning Jehoiakim the son of Josiah king of Judah; They shall not lament for him, saying, Ah my brother! or, Ah sister! they shall not lament for him, saying, Ah lord! or, Ah his glory!" (Jer. 22:18). This concept is equally prominent when the word is used of God: "Fair weather cometh out of the north: with God is terrible majesty" (Job 37:22).

In many cases *hôd* focuses on "dignity and splendor" with overtones of superior power and position but not to the degree seen in oriental kings: "And thou shalt put some of thine honor upon him, that all the congregation of the children of Israel may be obedient" (Num. 27:20— the first occurrence of the word). When used of the olive tree (Hos. 14:6), *hôd* focuses on its "splendor and dignity" as the most desired and desirable of the trees (cf. Judg. 9:9–15). The proud carriage of a war horse and seeming bravery in the face of battle lead God to say, "The glory of his nostrils is terrible" (Job 39:20). In every use of the word the one so described evokes a sense of amazement and satisfaction in the mind of the beholder.

TO SPREAD OUT

pāraś (פרש, 6566), "to spread out, scatter, display." Found in both ancient and modern Hebrew, this word occurs approximately 65 times in the Hebrew Old Testament. It is found for the first time in Exod. 9:29: "... I will spread abroad my hands unto the Lord...." Such stretching of the hands probably reflected the characteristic posture of prayer in the Bible (cf. Ps. 143:6; Isa. 1:15).

Pāraś sometimes expresses the "spreading out" of a garment to its widest extent (Judg. 8:25). It is commonly used of wings' "being spread," opened fully (Deut. 32:11; 1 Kings 6:27). "To spread out" a net is to set a snare or trap (Hos. 7:12). Sometimes "to spread out" is "to display": "... A fool layeth open his folly" (Prov. 13:16). "To spread" may mean "to cover over" and thus to hide from vision: "And the woman took and spread a covering over the well's mouth, and spread ground corn thereon; and the thing was not known" (2 Sam. 17:19). In some instances, "to spread" may have a more violent meaning of "to scatter": "... They that remain shall be scattered toward all winds..." (Ezek. 17:21).

TO SPRINKLE

zāraq (זרק, 2236), "to throw; sprinkle; strew; toss; scatter abundantly." This word is found in both ancient and modern Hebrew and is used in ancient Akkadian in the sense of "to spray." Used 35 times in the text of the Hebrew Old Testament, in 26 of those times it expresses the "throwing" or "sprinkling" of blood against the sacrificial altar or on the people. Thus, it appears very often in Leviticus (1:5, 11; 3:2, 8, 13 et al.).

Ezekiel's version of "the New Covenant" includes the "sprinkling" of the water of purification (Ezek. 36:25). In the first use of *zāraq* in the Old Testament, it describes the "throwing" of handful of dust into the air which would settle down on the Egyptians and cause boils (Exod. 9:8, 10). In his reform, Josiah ground up the Canaanite idol images and "scattered, strewed," the dust over the graves of idolworshipers (2 Chron. 34:4). In Ezekiel's vision of the departure of God's glory from the temple, the man in linen takes burning coals and "scatters" them over Jerusalem (Ezek. 10:2).

TO STAND

A. Verbs.

nāṣab (נָצַב, 5324), "to stand, station, set up, erect." Found in both ancient and modern Hebrew, this word goes back at least to ancient Ugaritic. It is found approximately 75 times in the Hebrew Bible. Its first occurrence in the Old Testament is in Gen. 18:2: "... Three men stood by him ...."

There are various ways of standing. One may "stand" for a definite purpose at a particular spot: "... Wait for him by the river's brink ..." (Exod. 7:15, RSV; literally, "stand by the river's bank"). One often stands upright: "... And stood every man at his tent door ..." (Exod. 33:8); "... my sheaf arose, and also stood upright ..." (Gen. 37:7). One who is "stationed" in a position is usually over someone else: "And Azariah the son of Nathan was over the officers [literally, "those standing over"] ..." (1 Kings 4:5). "To stand" something may be "to erect" something: "And Jacob set up a pillar ..." (Gen. 35:14). The waters of the Sea of Reeds were said to "stand as a heap" (Ps. 78:13). To fix a boundary is "to establish or erect" a boundary marker (Deut. 32:8).

'āmad (עָמַד, 5975), "to take one's stand; stand here or be there; stand still." Outside biblical Hebrew, where it occurs about 520 times and in all periods, this verb is attested only in Akkadian ("to stand, lean on"). A word spelled the same way appears in Arabic, but it means "to strive after."

The basic meaning of this verb is "to stand upright." This is its meaning in Gen. 18:8, its first biblical occurrence. It is what a soldier does while on watch (2 Sam. 18:30). From this basic meaning comes the meaning "to be established, immovable, and standing upright" on a single spot; the soles of the priests' feet "rested" (stood still, unmoving) in the waters of the Jordan (Josh. 3:13). Also, the sun and the moon "stood still" at Joshua's command (Josh. 10:13). Idols "stand upright" in one spot, never moving. The suggestion here is that they never do anything that is expected of living things (Isa. 46:7). *'Āmad* may be used of the existence of a particular experience. In 2 Sam. 21:18 there "was" (*hāyah*) war again, while in 1 Chron. 20:4 war "existed" or "arose" (*'āmad*) again. Cultically (with reference to the formal worship activities) this verb is used of approaching the altar to make a sacrifice. It describes the last stage of this approaching, "to stand finally and officially" before the altar (before God; cf. Deut. 4:11). Such standing is not just a standing still

doing nothing but includes all that one does in ministering before God (Num. 16:9).

In other contexts *'āmad* is used as the opposite of verbs indicating various kinds of movement. The psalmist praises the man who does not walk (behave according to) in the counsel of the ungodly or "stand" (serve) in the path of the sinful (Ps. 1:1). Laban told Abraham not "to stand" (remain stationary, not entering) outside his dwelling but to come in (Gen. 24:31). The verb can suggest "immovable," or not being able to be moved. So the "house of the righteous shall stand" (Prov. 12:7). Yet another nuance appears in Ps. 102:26, which teaches the indestructibility and/or eternity of God—the creation perishes but He "shalt endure [will ever stand]." This is not the changelessness of doing nothing or standing physically upright, but the changelessness of ever-existing being, a quality that only God has in Himself. All other existing depends upon Him; the creation and all creatures are perishable. In a more limited sense the man who does not die as the result of a blow "stands," or remains alive (Exod. 21:21). In a military context "to stand" refers to gaining a victory: "Behold, two kings stood not before him: how then shall we stand?" (2 Kings 10:4; cf. Judg. 2:14).

'Āmad can be used of the ever unchanged content and/or existence of a document (Jer. 32:14), a city (1 Kings 15:4), a people (Isa. 66:22), and a divine worship (Ps. 19:9).

Certain prepositions sometimes give this verb special meanings. Jeroboam "ordained" (made to stand, to minister) priests in Bethel (1 Kings 12:32). With "to" the verb can signify being in a certain place to accomplish a predesignated task—so Moses said that certain tribes should "stand upon mount Gerizim to bless the people" (Deut. 27:12). With this same preposition this verb can be used judicially of (1) the act of being in court, or standing before a judge (1 Kings 3:16), and (2) the position (whether literal or figurative) assumed by a judge when pronouncing the sentence (Ezek. 44:24) or delivering judgment (Isa. 3:13; cf. Exod. 17:6). With the preposition "before" *'āmad* is used to describe the service of a servant before a master—so Joshua "stood" before Moses (Deut. 1:38). This is not inactivity but activity.

In Neh. 8:5 the verb means "to stand up or rise up"; when Ezra opened the book, all the people "stood up" (cf. Dan. 12:13).

The Septuagint renders *'āmad* usually with a verb meaning "to stand" and, where the contexts show it refers to temporal standing, with verbs meaning "to abide or remain."

B. Nouns.

'ammûd (עַמּוּד, 5982), "pillar; standing place." The noun 'ammûd occurs 111 times and usually signifies something that stands upright like a "pillar" (Exod. 26:32; Judg. 16:25). It may occasionally refer to a "standing place" (2 Kings 11:14).

Several other nouns are derived from the verb 'āmad. 'Ōmed occurs 9 times and refers to "standing places" (2 Chron. 30:16). 'Emdāh means "standing ground" once (Mic. 1:11). Ma'ămād, which occurs 5 times, refers to "service" in 2 Chron. 9:4 and to "office or function" (in someone's service) in 1 Chron. 23:28. Mā'omād occurs once to mean "standing place" or "foothold" (Ps. 69:2).

STATUE

ṣelem (צֶלֶם, 6754), "statue; image; copy." Cognates of this word appear in Ugaritic and Phoenician (perhaps), Akkadian, Aramaic, and Arabic. Old Testament Hebrew attests it 17 times.

This word means "statue": "And all the people of the land went into the house of Baal, and brake it down; his altars and his images brake they in pieces thoroughly..." (2 Kings 11:18; cf. Num. 33:52).

This word signifies an "image or copy" of something in the sense of a replica: "Wherefore ye shall make images of your emerods, and images of your mice that mar the land; and ye shall give glory unto the God of Israel..." (1 Sam. 6:5). In Ezek. 23:14 ṣelem represents a wall painting of some Chaldeans.

The word also means "image" in the sense of essential nature. So Adam "begat a son in his own likeness, after his image; and called his name Seth" (Gen. 5:3). Human nature in its internal and external characteristics is what is meant here rather than an exact duplicate. So, too, God made man in His own "image," reflecting some of His own perfections: perfect in knowledge, righteousness, and holiness, and with dominion over the creatures (Gen. 1:26). Being created in God's "image" meant being created male and female, in a loving unity of more than one person (Gen. 1:27). It is noteworthy that in Gen. 1:26 (the first occurrence of the word) the "image" of God is represented by two Hebrew words (ṣelem and dᵉmût); by ṣelem alone in Gen. 1:27 and 9:6; and by dᵉmût alone in Gen. 5:1. This plus the fact that in other contexts the words are used exactly the same leads to the conclusion that the use of both in passages such as Gen. 1:26 is for literary effect.

In Ps. 39:6 ṣelem means "shadow" of a thing which represents the original very imprecisely, or it means merely a phantom (ghost?), a thing which represents the original more closely but lacks its essential characteristic (reality): "Surely every man walketh in a vain show [ṣelem]; surely they are disquieted in vain: he heapeth up riches, and knoweth not who shall gather them" (cf. Ps. 73:20—the word represents a "dream image").

STATUTE, ORDINANCE

A. Nouns.

ḥōq (חֹק, 2706), "statute; prescription; rule; law; regulation." This noun is derived from the verb ḥāqaq, "to cut in, determine, decree." Ḥōq occurs 127 times in biblical Hebrew.

The first usage of ḥōq is in Gen. 47:22: "Only the land of the priests bought he not; for the priests had a portion [ḥōq] assigned them of Pharaoh...." This word is frequent in Deuteronomy and Psalms and rare in the historical books and in the prophets.

The meaning of ḥōq in the first occurrence (Gen. 47:22) differs from the basic meaning of "statute." It has the sense of something allotted or apportioned. A proverb speaks about "the food that is my portion" (Prov. 30:8, NASB; KJV, "food convenient for me"; literally, "food of my prescription or portion"). Job recognized in his suffering that God does what is appointed for him: "For he performeth the thing that is appointed for me [literally, "he will perform my Law"]..." (23:14). The "portion" may be something that is due to a person as an allowance or payment. The Egyptian priests received their income from Pharaoh (Gen. 47:22), even as God permitted a part of the sacrifice to be enjoyed by the priests: "And it shall be Aaron's and his sons' [as their portion] for ever from the children of Israel: for it is a heave offering..." (Exod. 29:28).

The word ḥōq also signifies "law," or "statute." In a general sense it refers to the "laws" of nature like rain: "When he made a decree for the rain, and a way for the lightning of the thunder" (Job 28:26; cf. Jer. 5:22); and the celestial bodies: "He hath also stablished them for ever and ever: he hath made a decree which shall not pass" (Ps. 148:6 cf.). "Thus saith the Lord, which giveth the sun for a light by day, and the ordinances of the moon and of the stars for a light by night, which divideth the sea when the waves thereof roar; The Lord of hosts is his name: If those ordinances depart from before me, saith the Lord, then the seed of Israel also shall cease from being a nation before me for ever" (Jer. 31:35–36). Moreover, the word ḥōq denotes a "law" promulgated in a country:

"And Joseph made it a law over the land of Egypt unto this day, that Pharaoh should have the fifth part; except the land of the priests only, which became not Pharaoh's" (Gen. 47:26).

Finally, and most important, the "law" given by God is also referred to as a *ḥōq:* "When they have a matter, they come unto me; and I judge between one and another, and I do make them know the statutes [*ḥōq*] of God, and his laws [*tôrāh*]" (Exod. 18:16). The word's synonyms are *miṣwāh*, "commandment"; *mišpāṭ*, "judgment"; *bᵉrît*, "covenant"; *tôrāh*, "law"; and *ʿēdût*, "testimony." It is not easy to distinguish between these synonyms, as they are often found in conjunction with each other: "Ye shall diligently keep the commandments [*miṣwāh*] of the Lord your God, and his testimonies [*ʿēdāh*], and his statutes [*ḥōq*], which he hath commanded thee" (Deut. 6:17).

ḥuqqāh (חֻקָּה, 2708), "statute; regulation; prescription; term." This noun occurs about 104 times.

Ḥuqqāh is found for the first time in God's words of commendation about Abraham to Isaac: "Because that Abraham obeyed my voice, and kept my charge, my commandments [*miṣwāh*], my statutes [*ḥuqqāh*], and my laws [*tôrāh*]" (Gen. 26:5), together with its synonyms *mišmeret, miṣwāh*, and *tôrāh.* The primary use of *ḥuqqāh* is in the Pentateuch, especially in Leviticus and Numbers. It is extremely rare in the poetical books and in the prophetic writings (except for Jeremiah and Ezekiel).

The meaning of "fixed" is similar to the usage of *ḥōq*, in the sense of the laws of nature: "Thus saith the Lord; If my covenant be not with day and night, and if I have not appointed the ordinances of heaven and earth" (Jer. 33:25; cf. Job 38:33). Even as the Israelites had a period of rainfall from October to April, there was a fixed period of harvest (from April to June): "Neither say they in their heart, Let us now fear the Lord our God, that giveth rain, both the former and the latter, in his season: he reserveth unto us the appointed weeks of the harvest" (Jer. 5:24). In addition to regularity of nature, the word *ḥuqqāh* signifies regular payment to the priests: "Which the Lord commanded to be given them of the children of Israel, in the day that he anointed them, by a statute for ever throughout their generations" (Lev. 7:36).

In non-religious usage, the word *ḥuqqāh* refers to the customs of the nations: "After the doings of the land of Egypt, wherein ye dwelt, shall ye not do: and after the doings of the land of Canaan, whither I bring you, shall ye not do: neither shall ye walk in their ordinances" (Lev. 18:3; cf. 20:23). The reason for the requirement to abstain from the pagan practices is that they were considered to be degenerate (Lev. 18:30).

The most significant usage of *ḥuqqāh* is God's "law." It is more specific in meaning than *ḥōq*. Whereas *ḥōq* is a general word for "law," *ḥuqqāh* denotes the "law" of a particular festival or ritual. There is the "law" of the Passover (Exod. 12:14), Unleavened Bread (Exod. 12:17), Feast of Tabernacles (Lev. 23:41), the Day of Atonement (Lev. 16:29ff.), the priesthood (Exod. 29:9), and the blood and fat (Lev. 3:17).

The word *ḥuqqāh* has many synonyms. At times it forms a part of a series of three: "Beware that thou forget not the Lord thy God, in not keeping his commandments [*miṣwāh*], and his judgments [*mišpāṭ*], and his statutes [*ḥuqqāh*], which I command thee this day" (Deut. 8:11), and at other times of a series of four: "Therefore thou shalt love the Lord thy God, and keep his charge [*mišmeret*], and his statutes [*ḥuqqāh*] and his judgments [*mišpāṭ*], and his commandments [*miṣwāh*], always" (Deut. 11:1; cf. Gen. 26:5 with *tôrāh* instead of *mišpāṭ*).

The "statutes" of people are to be understood as the practices contrary to God's expectations: "For the statutes of Omri are kept, and all the works of the house of Ahab, and ye walk in their counsels; that I should make thee a desolation, and the inhabitants thereof a hissing: therefore ye shall bear the reproach of my people" (Mic. 6:16). The prophet Ezekiel condemned Judah for rejecting God's holy "statutes": "And she hath changed my judgments into wickedness more than the nations, and my statutes [*ḥuqqāh*] more than the countries that are round about her: for they have refused my judgments and my statutes [*ḥuqqāh*], they have not walked in them" (Ezek. 5:6). He also challenged God's people to repent and return to God's "statutes" that they might live: "If the wicked restore the pledge, give again that he had robbed, walk in the statutes of life, without committing iniquity; he shall surely live, he shall not die" (Ezek. 33:15).

The Septuagint gives the following translations of both *ḥōq* and *ḥuqqāh: prostagma* ("order; command; injunction"); *dikaioma* ("regulation; requirement; commandment"); and *nomimos* ("lawful; conformable to law"). A translation of *ḥōq* is *diatheke* ("last will; testament; covenant"). A translation of *ḥuqqāh* is *nomos* ("law").

B. Verb.

ḥāqaq (חָקַק, 2710), "to cut in, determine, decree." This root is found in Semitic languages with the above meaning or with the sense "to be true" (Arabic), "to be just" (Akkadian). This verb occurs less than 20 times in the Old Testament.

Hāqaq is used in Isa. 22:16 with the meaning "to cut in": ". . . That graveth a habitation for himself in a rock." In Isa. 10:1 the verb is used of "enacting a decree": "Woe unto them that decree unrighteous decrees, and that write grievousness which they have prescribed."

STEP

A. Noun.

pa'am (פַּעַם, 6471), "step; foot; hoofbeats; pedestal; stroke; anvil." This noun's attested cognates appear in Ugaritic (*pʿn*) and Phoenician. Biblical occurrences of this word number about 117 and appear in every period of the language.

The nuances of this word are related to the basic meaning "a human foot." The psalmist uses this meaning in Ps. 58:10: "The righteous shall rejoice when he seeth the vengeance: he shall wash his feet in the blood of the wicked." In Exod. 25:12 the word is applied to the "pedestals or feet" of the ark of the covenant: "And thou shalt cast four rings of gold for it, and put them in the four [feet] thereof; and two rings shall be in the one side of it, and two rings in the other side of it." Elsewhere the word signifies the "steps" one takes, or "footsteps": "Hold up my goings in thy paths, that my footsteps slip not" (Ps. 17:5). Judg. 5:28 applies the word to the "steps" of a galloping horse, or its hoofbeats. This focus on the falling of a foot once is extended to the "stroke" of a spear: "Then said Abishai to David, . . . let me pin him to the earth with one stroke of the spear . . ." (1 Sam. 26:8, RSV). Finally, *pa'am* represents a foot-shaped object, an "anvil" (Isa. 41:7).

B. Adverb.

pa'am (פַּעַם, 6471), "once; now; anymore." This word functions as an adverb with the focus on an occurrence or time. In Exod. 10:17 the word bears this emphasis: "Now therefore forgive, I pray thee, my sin *only this once*, and entreat the Lord your God. . . . " The first biblical appearance of the word focuses on the finality, the absoluteness, of an event: "This is now bone of my bones . . ." (Gen. 2:23). The thrust of this meaning appears clearly in the translation of Gen. 18:32—Abraham said to God: "Oh, let not the Lord be angry, and I will speak yet but this once [only one more time]. . . . "

STONE

'eben (אֶבֶן, 68), "stone." A comparison of Semitic languages shows that *'eben* was the common word for "stone" among the ancients. Exact philological and semantic cognates are found in Akkadian, Ugaritic, Phoenician, Aramaic, Old South Arabic, and several Ethiopic dialects. The Greek Old Testament usually has *lithos* (λίθος) for *'eben*. Used almost exclusively for movable stone(s), *'eben* is to be distinguished from *sela'*, "rock," and *ṣûr*, "cliff."

The noun *'eben* occurs in the Old Testament 260 times, with almost equal frequency in the singular (and collective) as in the plural. It appears more frequently in prose than in poetry.

Palestine was (and is) famous for its ubiquitous "stone." So much was "stone" a part of the ancient writer's consciousness that it served the literary interests of simile (Exod. 15:5), metaphor (Ezek. 11:19), and hyperbole (1 Kings 10:27; 2 Chron. 1:15; 9:27). That building with "stone" was the rule rather than the exception in Palestine is suggested by the biblical writer's allusion to the Mesopotamian custom of using clay bricks (Gen. 11:3). Yet it seems that Israelite craftsmen at the time of David lagged behind somewhat in the art of stonework, for stonemasons from Tyre were employed in constructing the royal residence (2 Sam. 5:11).

Beyond their use as a construction material, "stones" served as covers for wells (Gen. 29:3ff.), storage containers (Exod. 7:19), weights (Deut. 25:13; Prov. 11:1), and slingstones (1 Sam. 17:49). Plumblines were suspended stones (Isa. 34:11); pavement was sometimes made of "stone" (2 Kings 16:17); and the Bible speaks of hailstones (Josh. 10:11; Ezek. 13:11ff.). The Israelite custom of cave burials presumes stone tombs (Isa. 14:19); on 3 occasions when bodies were not interred, they were heaped with "stones" (Josh. 7:26; 8:29; 2 Sam. 18:17).

Pentateuchal laws relating to purity-impurity concepts stipulated that certain crimes were punishable by stoning. The standard formula employed either the verb *rāgam* or *sāqal* followed by a preposition and the noun *'eben*. Included under this penalty were the crimes of blasphemy (Lev. 24:23; Num. 15:35–36), Molech worship (Lev. 20:2), idolatry (Deut. 13:10), and prostitution (Deut. 22:21, 24). Originally, stoning was a means of merely expelling the lawbreaker from the community; however, in ancient Israel it was a means of capital punishment whereby the community could rid itself of the impure offender without coming into direct contact with him.

As for the cult, the carved "stone" figurines commonly worshiped throughout the ancient Near East were strictly forbidden to Israel (Lev. 26:1). To carve "stone" which was to be used in the cult was to profane it (Exod. 20:25). Altars and memorials especially common to the patriarchal age and the period of the Conquest were all made of unhewn "stones" (Gen. 28:18ff.; 31:45; Josh. 4:5; 24:26–27). Of the cult objects in Israel's wilderness shrine, only the tablets of the Decalogue were made of "stone" (Exod. 24:12; 34:1, 4; Deut. 4:13; Ezek. 40:42—the stone tables of Ezekiel's temple served only utilitarian purposes).

Precious "stones" such as onyx (Gen. 2:12) and sapphire (Ezek. 1:26) are mentioned frequently in the Bible, especially with regard to the high priest's ephod and breastplate (Exod. 39:6ff.). The expensiveness of the high priest's garments corresponded to the special workmanship of the most holy place where Aaron served.

In certain texts, 'eben has been given theological interpretations. God is called the "stone of Israel" in Gen. 49:24. And several occurrences of 'eben in the Old Testament have been viewed as messianic, as evidenced by the Greek Old Testament, rabbinic writings, and the New Testament; among them: Gen. 28:18; Ps. 118:22; Isa. 8:14; 28:16; Dan. 2:34; Zech. 4:7.

STREET

A. Noun.

hûṣ (חוּץ, 2351), "street." This word, of uncertain origin, appears in biblical, mishnaic, and modern Hebrew. In the Old Testament the total number of occurrences of the noun and adverb is about 160.

A particular use of hûṣ denotes the place outside the houses in a city, or the "street." The "street" was the place for setting up bazaars: "The cities, which my father took from thy father, I will restore; and thou shalt make streets for thee in Damascus, as my father made in Samaria" (1 Kings 20:34). Craftsmen plied their trade on certain "streets" named after the guild—for example, the Bakers' Street: "Then Zedekiah the king commanded that they should commit Jeremiah into the court of the prison, and that they should give him daily a piece of bread out of the bakers' street, until all the bread in the city were spent" (Jer. 37:21). The absence of justice in the marketplace was an indication of the wickedness of the whole population of Jerusalem. Jeremiah was called to check in the "streets" to find an honest man: "Run ye to and fro through the streets of Jerusalem, and see now, and know, and seek in the broad places thereof, if ye can find a man, if there be any that executeth judgment, that seeketh the truth; and I will pardon it" (5:1).

Other descriptions of the "streets" are given by the prophets. Several mention that the "streets" were muddy: " . . . And to tread them down like the mire of the streets" (Isa. 10:6; cf. Mic. 7:10; Zech. 10:5). Others make reference to the blood (Ezek. 28:23), the famished (Lam. 2:19), and the dead (Nah. 3:10) which filled the "streets" in times of war.

The area outside a city was also known as the hûṣ. In this case it is better translated as "open country" or "field"; cf. "That our garners may be full, affording all manner of store; that sheep may bring forth thousands and ten thousands in our streets" (Ps. 144:13, KJV; RSV, "fields"; cf. Job 5:10; Prov. 8:26).

B. Adverb.

hûṣ (חוּץ, 2351), "outside." The first occurrence of this word is in Gen. 6:14: "Make thee an ark of gopher wood; rooms shalt thou make in the ark, and shalt pitch it within and without [hûṣ] with pitch."

By hûṣ the general idea of "the outside" is intimated. It is sometimes indeterminate where "outside" is, especially when connected with a verb: "You shall also have a place outside the camp; he may not reenter the camp" (Deut. 23:12, NASB). The area could be "outside" a house, tent, city, or camp—hence the adverbial usage of "outside." The word is also connected with a preposition with the sense of "in, to, on, toward the outside": "If he rise again, and walk abroad upon his staff, then shall he that smote him be quit: only he shall pay for the loss of his time, and shall cause him to be thoroughly healed" (Exod. 21:19).

STRENGTH

hayil (חַיִל, 2458), "strength; power; wealth; property; capable; valiant; army; troops; influential; upper-class people (courtiers)." The cognates of this word have been found in Aramaic, Akkadian, Syriac, Arabic, and Ethiopic. Biblical Hebrew attests it about 245 times and in all periods.

First, this word signifies a faculty or "power," the ability to effect or produce something. The word is used of physical "strength" in the sense of power that can be exerted: "If the iron be blunt, and he do not whet the edge, then must he put to more strength . . . " (Eccl. 10:10). Quite often this word appears in a military context. Here it is the physical strength, power, and ability to perform in battle that is in view. This idea is used of men in 1 Sam. 2:4: "The bows of the mighty men are broken, and they that stumbled are girded with strength" (cf. Ps. 18:32, 39). Ps. 33:17 applies the word to a war horse. An interesting use of hayil appears in Num. 24:17–18, where Balaam prophesied the destruction of Moab and Edom at the hands of Israel: "And Edom shall be a possession, Seir also shall be a possession for his enemies; and

Israel shall do valiantly" (v. 18). The idea here is dynamic; something is happening. One might also render this phrase: "Israel performs mightily." This translation of the word is somewhat inexact; a noun is translated as an adverb.

Second, *hayil* means "wealth, property." This nuance of the word focuses on that which demonstrates one's ability, his wealth or goods; Levi, Simeon, and their cohorts attacked the Shechemites: "And all their wealth, and all their little ones, and their wives took they captive, and spoiled even all that was in the house" (Gen. 34:29—the first biblical occurrence of the word). In Num. 31:9 *hayil* includes all the possessions of the Midianites except the women, children, cattle, and flocks. Thus it seems to be a little narrower in meaning. When this nuance is used with the Hebrew word "to do or make," the resulting phrase means "to become wealthy or make wealth" (cf. Deut. 8:18; Ruth 4:11). This is in marked contrast to the emphasis of the same construction in Num. 24:18. Joel 2:22 uses *hayil* in the sense of "wealth" or products of the ability of a tree to produce fruit.

Third, several passages use the word in the sense of "able." In Gen. 47:6 the ability to do a job well is in view. Pharaoh told Joseph: "The land of Egypt is before thee; in the best of the land make thy father and brethren to dwell; in the land of Goshen let them dwell: and if thou knowest any men of activity [capable men] among them, then make them rulers over my cattle." This word can also represent the domestic skills of a woman—Ruth is described as a woman of ability and, therefore, either potentially or actually a good wife (Ruth 3:11; Prov. 12:4). When applied to men, *hayil* sometimes focuses on their ability to conduct themselves well in battle as well as being loyal to their commanders (1 Sam. 14:52; 1 Kings 1:42). When used in such contexts, the word may be translated "valiant": "And there was sore war against the Philistines all the days of Saul: and when Saul saw any strong man, or any valiant man, he took him unto him" (1 Sam. 14:52; cf. Num. 24:18; 1 Sam. 14:48).

Fourth, this word sometimes means "army"; "And I will harden Pharaoh's heart, that he shall follow after them; and I will be honored upon Pharaoh, and upon all his host [army]..." (Exod. 14:4). The word can also refer to the army as troops in the sense of a combination of a lot of individuals. Under such an idea the word can represent the members of an army distributed to perform certain functions. Jehoshaphat "placed forces in all the fenced cities of Judah, and set garrisons in the land of Judah..." (2 Chron. 17:2). This is also the emphasis in 1 Kings 15:20: "Ben-hadad ... sent the captains of the hosts which he had [NASB, "commanders of his armies"] against the cities of Israel...."

Fifth, *hayil* sometimes represents the "upper class," who, as in all feudal systems, were at once soldiers, wealthy, and influential; Sanballat "spake before his brethren and the army of Samaria," i.e., in the royal court (NASB, "wealthy men"; Neh. 4:2). The Queen of Sheba was accompanied by a large escort of upper-class people from her homeland: "And she came to Jerusalem with a very great train..." (1 Kings 10:2).

TO STRETCH OUT

A. Verb.

nātāh (נָטָה, 5186), "to stretch forth, spread out, stretch down, turn aside." This verb also occurs in Arabic, late Aramaic, and post-biblical Hebrew. The Bible attests it in all periods and about 215 times.

Nātāh connotes "extending something outward and toward" something or someone. So God told Moses: "...I will redeem you with a stretched out arm, and with great judgments" (Exod. 6:6). This is a figure of God's active, sovereign, and mighty involvement in the affairs of men. So this phrase means "to stretch out" something until it reaches a goal. The verb can also mean "to stretch out toward" but not to touch or reach anything. God told Moses to tell Aaron to take his staff in hand (cf. Exod. 9:23) and "stretch it out." This act was to be done as a sign. The pointed staff was a visible sign that God's power was directly related to God's messengers: "...Take thy rod, and stretch out thine hand upon the waters of Egypt, upon their streams, upon their rivers, and upon their ponds...," over all the water in Egypt (Exod. 7:19). God "stretched out" (offered) 3 things to David (1 Chron. 21:10); this is a related sense with the absence of anything physical being "stretched out."

This verb may connote "stretch out" but not toward anything. When a shadow "stretches out," it lengthens. Hezekiah remarked: "It is a light thing for the shadow to go down ten degrees..." (2 Kings 20:10), to grow longer. *Nātāh* may be used in this sense without an object and referring to a day. The Levite was asked to "comfort thine heart, I pray thee. And they tarried until afternoon [literally, the "stretching" (of the day, or of the shadows)]..." (Judg. 19:8). "To stretch out" one's limbs full length is to recline: "And they lay themselves down upon clothes laid to pledge by every altar..." (Amos 2:8). This is a figure of temple prostitution. This verb may also mean "to extend" in every direction. It represents what one does in pitching a tent by unrolling the canvas (or skins sewn together) and "stretching it out." The end product is that the canvas is properly "spread out." Abram "pitched his tent, having Beth-el on the west, and Hai on the east ..." (Gen. 12:8—the first appearance of the word). This act and its result is used as a figure of God's creating the heavens: "... Which alone spreadeth out the heavens ..." (Job 9:8).

This verb also implies "stretching down toward" so as to reach something. Earlier in the Bible Rebekah was asked to "let down thy pitcher, ... that I may drink" (Gen. 24:14); she was asked to "stretch it down" into the water. This is the nuance when God is said to have "inclined [stretched down] unto me, and heard my cry" (Ps. 40:1). Issachar is described as a donkey which "bowed his shoulder to bear [burdens]" (Gen. 49:15). In somewhat the same sense the heavens are bowed; the heavens are made to come closer to the earth. This is a figure of the presence of thick clouds: "He bowed the heavens also, and came down: and darkness was under his feet" (Ps. 18:9). The somewhat new element here is that the heavens do not touch the speaker but only "stretch downward" toward him.

This verb may mean "to turn aside" in the sense of "to visit": "... Judah went down from his brethren, and turned in to [visited] a certain Adullamite ..." (Gen. 38:1). Another special nuance appears in Num. 22:23, where it means "to go off the way": "And the ass saw the angel of the Lord standing in the way ..., and the ass turned aside out of the way...." Applied to human relationships, this may connote seduction: "With her much fair speech she caused him to yield ..." (Prov. 7:21).

B. Nouns.

maṭṭeh (מַטֶּה, 4294), "rod; staff; tribe." This noun occurs about 250 times. In Gen. 38:18 the word refers to a shepherd's "staff": "And he said, What pledge shall I give thee? And she said, Thy signet, and thy bracelets, and thy staff that is in thine hand." The word is used to refer to a number of kinds of "rods": A "rod" which symbolizes spiritual power, such as Moses' rod (Exod. 4:2), Aaron's rod (Exod. 7:9), and the sorcerers' rods (Exod. 7:12), and rods symbolizing authority (Num. 17:7). This noun is often used elliptically instead of "the rod of the tribe of"; the word signifies "tribe" (cf. Exod. 31:2). *Maṭṭeh* is also used in the phrase "the staff of bread," of staves around which loaves are suspended to keep them from mice (Lev. 26:26).

Some other nouns are related to the verb *nāṭāh*. *Mûṭṭôt* occurs once (Isa. 8:8) and refers to the "stretching out" of wings. *Miṭṭāh* occurs about 29 times and means something which is stretched out. *Miṭṭāh* is used of a couch (Song of Sol. 3:7) and of a metal framework (Esth. 1:6). *Miṭṭāh* may also refer to a room, a bedchamber (2 Kings 11:2).

C. Adverb.

maṭṭāh (מַטָּה, 4295), "downwards; beneath." This word occurs about 17 times. It means "beneath" (Deut. 28:13), "downward" (2 Kings 19:30), and "underneath" (Exod. 28:27).

STRIFE

A. Verb.

rîb (רִיב, 7378), "to strive, contend." This verb occurs 65 times and in all periods of biblical Hebrew.

In Exod. 21:18 *rîb* is used in connection with a physical struggle: "And if men strive together, and one smite another with a stone, or with his fist, and he die not...." *Rîb* appears in Judg. 6:32 with the meaning of "to contend against" through words.

B. Nouns.

rîb (רִיב, 7379), "strife; quarrel; dispute; case; contentions; cause." This noun has a cognate only in Aramaic. Its 60 occurrences appear in all periods of biblical Hebrew.

The noun *rîb* is used of conflicts outside the realm of law cases and courts. This conflict between individuals may break out into a quarrel, as in Prov. 17:14: "The beginning of strife is as when one letteth out water: therefore leave off contention, before it be meddled with." In Gen. 13:7–8 (the first occurrence of *rîb*) the word is used of "contention" prior to open fighting between two groups: "And there was a strife between the herdmen of Abram's cattle and the herdmen of Lot's cattle...." In such a case the one with the "strife" is clearly the guilty party.

Rîb sometimes represents a "dispute" between two parties. This "dispute" is set in the context of a mutual law structure binding both parties and a court which is empowered to decide and execute justice. This may involve "contention" between two unequal parties (an individual and a group), as when all Israel quarreled with Moses, asserting that he had not kept his end of the bargain by adequately providing for them. Moses appealed to the Judge, who vindicated him by sending water from a rock (cliff?) smitten by Moses: "And he called the name of the place Massah, and Meribah, because of the chiding [quarrel] of the children of Israel ..." (Exod. 17:7). God decided who was the guilty party, Moses or Israel. The "contention" may be between two individuals as in Deut. 25:1, where the two disputants go to court (having a "case or dispute" does not mean one is a wrongdoer): "If there be a controversy between men, and they come unto judgment, that the judges may judge them; then they shall justify the righteous, and condemn the wicked." So in Isa. 1:23 the unjust judge accepts a bribe and does not allow the widow's just "cause" (NASB, "widow's plea") to come before him. Prov. 25:8–9 admonishes the wise to "debate thy cause with thy neighbor" when that neighbor has "put thee to shame."

Rîb may represent what goes on in an actual court situation. It is used of the entire process of adjudication: "Neither shalt thou [be partial to] a poor man in his cause" (Exod. 23:3; cf. Deut. 19:17). It is also used of the various parts of a lawsuit. In Job 29:16, Job defends his righteousness by asserting that he became an advocate for the defenseless: "I was a father to the poor: and the cause which I knew not I searched out." Here, then, the word means the false charge brought against a defendant. Earlier in the Book of Job (13:6), *rîb* represents the argument for the defense: "Hear now my reasoning, and hearken to the pleadings of my lips." Elsewhere the word represents the argument for the prosecution: "Give heed to me, O Lord, and hearken to the voice of them that contend with me [literally, "the men presenting the case for the prosecution"]" (Jer. 18:19). Finally, in Isa. 34:8 *rîb* signifies a "case" already argued and won and awaiting justice: "For it is the day of the Lord's vengeance, and the year of recompenses for the controversy of Zion."

Two other related nouns occur rarely. *Merîbāh* occurs twice, and it means "strife." The word refers to an extra-legal (Gen. 13:8) and to a legal confrontation (Num. 27:14). *Yārîb* appears 3 times to mean "disputant; opponent; adversary" (Ps. 35:1; Isa. 49:25; Jer. 18:19).

TO BE STRONG

A. Verb.

ḥāzaq (חָזַק, 2388), "to be strong, strengthen, harden, take hold of." This verb is found 290 times in the Old Testament. The root also exists in Aramaic and Arabic.

The word first occurs in Gen. 41:56: "... And the famine waxed sore in the land of Egypt" (NASB, NIV, "was severe"). The strong form of the verb is used in Exod. 4:21: "... I will harden his [Pharaoh's] heart...." This statement is found 8 times. Four times we read: "Pharaoh's heart was hard" (Exod. 7:13, 22; 8:19; 9:35, NIV; KJV, RSV, NASB, "was hard-

ened"). In Exod. 9:34 Pharaoh's responsibility is made clear by the statement "he sinned yet more, and hardened his heart...."

In the sense of personal strength *ḥāzaq* is first used in Deut. 11:8 in the context of the covenant: "Therefore shall ye keep all the commandments which I command you this day, that ye may be strong, and go in and possess the land...." Moses was commanded to "charge Joshua, and encourage him" (Deut. 3:28). The covenant promise accompanies the injunction to "be strong and of a good courage": "... For the Lord thy God, he it is that doth go with thee; he will not fail thee, nor forsake thee" (Deut. 31:6). The same encouragement was given to the returned captives as they renewed the work of rebuilding the temple (Zech. 8:9, 13; cf. Hag. 2:4).

If in the above examples there is moral strength combined with physical, the latter is the sense of Judg. 1:28: "And it came to pass, when Israel was strong, that they put the Canaanites to [forced labor]...." Israel sinned and the Lord "strengthened Eglon the king of Moab against Israel" (Judg. 3:12). The word is used in reference to a building: "... The priests had not repaired the breaches of the house" (2 Kings 12:6), or to a city: "Moreover Uzziah built towers in Jerusalem ... and fortified them" (2 Chron. 26:9). In battle *ḥāzaq* means: "So David prevailed over the Philistine ..." (1 Sam. 17:50).

As the prophet said, "For the eyes of the Lord run to and fro throughout the whole earth, to show himself strong in the behalf of them [NASB, "to strongly support them"] whose heart is perfect toward him" (2 Chron. 16:9). To His Servant, the Messiah, God said: "I ... will hold thine hand ..." (Isa. 42:6); and to Cyrus He said: "... Whose right hand I have holden ..." (Isa. 45:1).

Other noteworthy uses of the word are: "... Thou shalt relieve him [a poor Israelite]..." (Lev. 25:35); and "... [Saul] laid hold upon the skirt of his mantle, and it rent" (1 Sam. 15:27).

In summary, this word group describes the physical and moral strength of man and society. God communicates strength to men, even to the enemies of His people as chastisement for His own. Men may turn their strength into stubbornness against God.

B. Adjective.

ḥāzāq (חָזָק, 2389), "strong; mighty; heavy; severe; firm; hard." This adjective occurs about 56 times and in all periods of biblical Hebrew.

First, the word means "firm" or "hard" in the sense that something is impenetrable. In

Ezek. 3:8–9 the prophet's face is compared to rock; God has made him determined to his task just as Israel is determined not to listen to him: "Behold, I have made thy face [hard] against their faces, and thy forehead [hard] against their foreheads. As an adamant harder than flint have I made thy forehead. . . . " Job 37:18 uses *ḥāzāq* of molten solidified metal.

Second, this word means "strong." In its basic meaning it refers to physical strength. God's hand (an anthropomorphism; cf. Deut. 4:15, 19) as a symbol of His effecting His will among men is "strong": "And I am sure that the king of Egypt will not let you go, no, not by a mighty hand" (Exod. 3:19—the first biblical occurrence). This word modifies a noun, specifying that it is the opposite of weak, or unable to effect anything (Num. 13:18). Isaiah speaks of God's "sore and great and strong sword" (27:1). When Ezekiel wrote of "fat and strong" animals, he probably meant that they were well fed and healthy (34:16).

Third, *ḥāzāq* means "heavy." When applied to a battle or war, it describes the event(s) as severe (1 Sam. 14:52). The word is also used to indicate a severe sickness (1 Kings 17:17) and famine (1 Kings 18:2).

TO STUMBLE, BE WEAK

kāšal (בָּשַׁל, 3782), "to stumble, stagger, totter, be thrown down." As in biblical Hebrew, this word is used in modern Hebrew in the sense of "to stumble, fail." It occurs in the text of the Hebrew Old Testament approximately 60 times, the first time being in Lev. 26:37: "And they shall fall one upon another. . . . " This use illustrates the basic idea that one "stumbles" because of something or over something. Heavy physical burdens cause one "to stagger": " . . . The children fell under the [loads of] wood" (Lam. 5:13).

This word is often used figuratively to describe the consequences of divine judgment on sin: "Behold, I will lay stumbling blocks before this people, and the fathers and the sons together shall fall upon them . . . " (Jer. 6:21). Babylon, too, will know God's judgment: "And the most proud shall stumble and fall . . . " (Jer. 50:32). When the psalmist says: "My knees totter from my fasting" (Ps. 109:24, NAB), he means: "My knees are weak" (as translated by KJV, NASB, RSV, JB, NEB, TEV).

STUPID FELLOW

kᵉsîl (כְּסִיל, 3684), "stupid fellow; dull person; fool." This word occurs in the Old Testament 70 times. All of its occurrences are in wisdom literature except 3 in the Psalms.

The *kᵉsîl* is "insolent" in religion and "stupid or dull" in wise living (living out a religion he professes). In Ps. 92:6 the first emphasis is especially prominent: "A brutish man knoweth not; neither doth a fool understand this." The psalmist is describing an enemy of God who knew God and His word but, seeing the wicked flourishing, reasoned that they have the right life-style (Ps. 92:7). They have knowledge of God but do not properly evaluate or understand what they know. The second emphasis is especially prominent in wisdom contexts: "How long, ye simple ones, will ye love simplicity? and the scorners delight in their scorning, and fools hate knowledge?" (Prov. 1:22). In such contexts the person so described rejects the claims and teachings of wisdom. However, in the Bible wisdom is the practical outworking of one's religion. Therefore, even in these contexts there is a clear connotation of insolence in religion.

Kesel means "stupidity; imperturbability; confidence." This noun occurs 6 times. It means "stupidity" in Eccl. 7:25 and "confidence" in Prov. 3:26. The meaning of "confidence" also appears in Job 31:24: "If I have made gold my hope. . . . "

SUBURBS

A. Noun.

migrāš (מִגְרָשׁ, 4054), "suburbs; pasture land; open land." This noun occurs about 100 times, mainly in Joshua and First Chronicles. It denotes the untilled ground outside a city or the "pasture land" belonging to the cities: "For the children of Joseph were two tribes, Manasseh and Ephraim: therefore they gave no part unto the Levites in the land, save cities to dwell in, with their suburbs for their cattle and for their substance" (Josh. 14:4).

Ezekiel describes a strip of land for the Levites around the city. Part of the land was to be used for houses and part to be left: "And the five thousand, that are left in the breadth over against the five and twenty thousand, shall be a profane place for the city, for dwelling, and for suburbs: and the city shall be in the midst thereof" (Ezek. 48:15).

The Septuagint translates the word *perisporia* ("suburb").

B. Verb.

gāraš (גָּרַשׁ, 1644), "to drive out, cast out." This verb occurs about 45 times. An early occurrence in the Old Testament is in Exod. 34:11: " . . . Behold, I drive out before thee the Amorite, and the Canaanite. . . . " The word may be used of a divorced woman as in Lev.

21:7—a woman that is "put away from her husband."

SUFFICIENCY

day (דַי, 1767), "sufficiency; the required; enough." Cognates of this word appear in late Aramaic, Syriac, and Phoenician. Its 42 biblical occurrences appear in all periods of biblical Hebrew.

The word is translated variously according to the needs of a given passage. The meaning "sufficiency" is clearly manifested in Exod. 36:7: "For the stuff they had was sufficient for all the work to make it, and too much." A different translation is warranted in Jer. 49:9: "If thieves [come] by night, they will destroy till they have enough" (cf. Obad. 5). In Prov. 25:16 the word means only what one's digestive system can handle: "Hast thou found honey? Eat so much as is sufficient for thee, lest thou be filled therewith, and vomit it." Other passages use this word of money (Deut. 15:8). In Jer. 51:58 *day* preceded by the preposition *be* means "only for": " ... The people shall labor in vain [only for nothing], and the folk in the fire [only for fire], and they shall be weary." The phrase "as long as there is need" signifies until there is no more required (Mal. 3:10, NEB; KJV, "that there shall not be room enough to receive it"). The word first appears in Exod. 36:5 and is preceded by the preposition *min:* "The people bring much more than enough for the service of the work, which the Lord commanded to make."

There are many special uses of *day* where the basic meaning is in the background and the context dictates a different nuance. In Job 39:25 the word preceded by the preposition *be* may be rendered "as often as": "As often as the trumpet sounds he says, Aha!" (NASB). When preceded by the preposition *ke*, "as," the word usually means "according to": " ... The judge shall cause him to lie down, and to be beaten before his face, according to his fault, by a certain number" (Deut. 25:2). Preceded by *min*, "from," the word sometimes means "regarding the need." This illuminates passages such as 1 Sam. 7:16: "And he [Samuel] went from year to year [according to the need of each year; NASB, "annually"] in circuit to Beth-el ... " (cf. Isa. 66:23). In other places this phrase (*day* preceded by *min*) signifies "as often as": "Then the princes of the Philistines went forth: and it came to pass, after [NASB, "as often as"] they went forth, that David behaved himself more wisely than all the servants of Saul ... " (1 Sam. 18:30).

SUN

šemeš (שֶׁמֶשׁ, 8121), "sun; Shamshu (?); sun-shield; battlement." Cognates of this word occur in Ugaritic (*š-p-š*), Akkadian, Aramaic, Phoenician, and Arabic. It appears 134 times in biblical Hebrew and in all periods.

This word means "sun": "And when the sun was going down, a deep sleep fell upon Abram ... " (Gen. 15:12—the first occurrence of the word). The "wings of the sun" are probably its rays (Mal. 4:2). The "sun" and especially its regularity supported by divine sovereignty (Gen. 8:22) figures the security of God's allies: "So let all thine enemies perish, O Lord: but let them that love him be as the sun when he goeth forth in his might" (Judg. 5:31). God can also make the "sun" stand still when He wishes (Josh. 10:12–13) or darken as an indication of His judgment upon His enemies and salvation for His people (Joel 2:31–32). The "sun" and all the heavenly bodies were created by God (Gen. 1:16) and are summoned to praise Him (Ps. 148:3). The Canaanites and other people worshiped the "sun" as a god, and this paganism appeared among Israelites in times of spiritual decline (Deut. 4:19). In 2 Kings 23:5 perhaps one could translate: "Those who burned incense to Shamshu" (cf. v. 11). Perhaps passages like Ps. 148:3 are allusions to the sun god (although this is questionable).

Šemeš is used in phrases indicating direction. The east is "the rising of the sun": "And they journeyed from Oboth, ... toward the sunrising" (Num. 21:11). The west is "the setting of the sun": "Are they not on the other side of Jordan, by the way where the sun goeth down ... ?" (Deut. 11:30).

In Ps. 84:11 the word represents a sun-shaped shield: "For the Lord God is a sun and shield. ... "

Šemeš may be a structural term: "And I will make thy windows [NASB, "battlements"] of agates, and thy gates of carbuncles ... " (Isa. 54:12).

There are a few noteworthy phrases related to *šemeš*. To be "before the sun" or "before the eyes of the sun" is to be openly exposed: "Take all the heads of the people, and hang them up before the Lord against the sun [NASB, "in broad daylight"]. . ." (Num. 25:4). To "see the sun" is "to live": " ... Like the untimely birth of a woman, that they may not see the sun" (Ps. 58:8). Something "under the sun" is life lived on the earth apart from God in contrast to life lived on earth with a proper relationship with God (Eccl. 1:3).

TO SWALLOW

bāla' (בָּלַע, 1104), "to swallow, engulf." Commonly used throughout the history of the Hebrew language, this word is also found in ancient Akkadian, as well as several other Semitic languages. It occurs about 50 times in the Hebrew Old Testament. *Bāla'* is first used in Gen. 41:7 in Pharaoh's dream of seven lean ears of grain "swallowing up" the seven plump ears.

While it is used of the normal physical swallowing of something quite frequently, such as Jonah's "being swallowed" by the great fish (Jonah 1:17), the word is used more often in the figurative sense, often implying destruction. Thus, the violent "overwhelm" the innocent (Prov. 1:11–12); an enemy "swallows" those he conquers "like a dragon" (Jer. 51:34); and the false prophet and priest "are swallowed up of wine" (Isa. 28:7; RSV, "confused with").

TO SWEAR

šāba' (שָׁבַע, 7650), "to swear; take an oath." This is a common word throughout the history of the Hebrew language. The fact that it occurs more than 180 times in the Hebrew Bible attests to its importance there also. *Šāba'* occurs for the first time in the Hebrew Bible in Gen. 21:23–24, where Abimelech requests Abraham to " . . . swear unto me here by God that thou wilt not deal falsely with me, nor with my son. . . . And Abraham said, I will swear."

Often "to swear or to take an oath" is to strongly affirm a promise. Thus, Joshua instructs the spies concerning Rahab of Jericho: "Go into the harlot's house, and bring out thence the woman, and all that she hath, as ye sware unto her" (Josh. 6:22). David and Jonathan strongly affirmed their love for each other with an oath (1 Sam. 20:17). Allegiance to God is pledged by an oath (Isa. 19:18). Zephaniah condemns the idolatrous priests "that worship and that swear by the Lord, and that swear by Malcham [the Ammonite god]" (Zeph. 1:5). In making and upholding His promises to men, God often "swears" by Himself. To Abraham after his test involving His command to sacrifice his son Isaac, God said: "By myself have I sworn, saith the Lord, for because thou hast done this thing, and hast not withheld thy son, thine only son: That in blessing I will bless thee . . . " (Gen. 22:16–17; cf. Isa. 45:23; Jer. 22:5). God also "swears" by His holiness (Amos 4:2).

The root for "to swear" and the root for "seven" are the same in Hebrew, and since the number seven is the "perfect number," some have conjectured that "to swear" is to somehow "seven oneself," thus to bind oneself with seven things. Perhaps this is paralleled by the use of "seven" in Samson's allowing himself to be bound by seven fresh bowstrings (Judg. 16:7) and weaving the seven locks of his head (Judg. 16:13). The relationship between "to swear" and "seven" is inconclusive.

SWORD

A. Noun.

hereb (חֶרֶב, 2719), "sword; dagger; flint knife; chisel." This noun has cognates in several other Semitic languages including Ugaritic, Aramaic, Syriac, Akkadian, and Arabic. The word occurs about 410 times and in all periods of biblical Hebrew.

Usually *hereb* represents an implement that can be or is being used in war, such as a "sword." The exact shape of that implement, however, is not specified by this word. Present-day archaeology has unearthed various sickle swords and daggers from the earliest periods. Sickle swords are so named because they are shaped somewhat like a sickle with the outer edge of the arc being the cutting edge. These were long one-edged "swords." This is what *hereb* refers to when one reads of someone's being slain with the edge of the "sword": "And they slew Hamor and Shechem his son with the edge of the sword, and took Dinah out of Shechem's house . . . " (Gen. 34:26). The first biblical occurrence of the word (Gen. 3:24) probably also represents such an implement: " . . . And he placed at the east of the garden of Eden cherubim, and a flaming sword which turned every way. . . . "

The precise meaning of *hereb* is confused, however, by its application to what we know as a "dagger," a short two-edged sword: "But Ehud made him a dagger which had two edges, of a cubit [eighteen to twenty-four inches] length . . . " (Judg. 3:16).

The sickle sword was probably the implement used up to and during the conquest of Palestine. About the same time the Sea Peoples (among whom were the Philistines) were invading the ancient Near East. They brought with them a new weapon—the long two-edged "sword." The first clear mention of such a "sword" in the biblical record appears in 1 Sam. 17:51: "Therefore David ran, and stood upon the Philistine [Goliath], and took his sword, and drew it out of the sheath thereof, and slew him. . . . " Perhaps Saul also used the highly superior Philistine armor and "sword" (1 Sam. 17:39), but this is not clear. It is also possible that the angel who confronted Balaam with a drawn "sword" wielded a long two-edged "sword" (Num. 22:23). Certainly this would have made him (humanly speaking) a much more formidable sight. By the time of David, with his expertise and concern for warfare, the large two-edged "sword" was much more prominent if not the primary kind of "sword" used by Israel's heavy infantry.

This two-edged "sword" can be compared to a tongue: "... Even the sons of men, whose teeth are spears and arrows, and their tongue a sharp sword" (Ps. 57:4). This usage tells us not only about the shape of the "sword" but that such a tongue is a violent, merciless, attacking weapon. In Gen. 27:40 "sword" is symbolic of violence: "And by thy sword shalt thou live...." Prov. 5:4 uses *ḥereb* (of a long two-edged "sword") to depict the grievous result of dealing with an adulteress; it is certain death: "But her end is bitter as wormwood, sharp as a two-edged sword."

The "sword" is frequently depicted as an agent of God. It is not only used to safeguard the garden of Eden, but figures the judgment of God executed upon His enemies: "For my sword shall be bathed in heaven: behold, it shall come down upon Idumea ..." (Isa. 34:5; cf. Deut. 28:22).

Ḥereb may be used of various other cutting implements. In Josh. 5:2 it means "knife": "Make thee sharp knives, and circumcise again the children of Israel the second time." Ezek. 5:1 uses *ḥereb* of a barber's "razor": "And thou, son of man, take thee a sharp knife, take thee a barber's razor, and cause it to pass upon thine head and upon thy beard...." The exact size and shape of this tool cannot be determined, but it is clear that it was used as a razor.

This word can also be used of tools ("chisels") for hewing stone: "And if thou wilt make me an altar of stone, thou shalt not build it of hewn stone: for if thou lift up thy tool upon it, thou hast polluted it" (Exod. 20:25). The fact that a "sword," an implement of death, would be used to cut the stone for an altar, the instrument of life, explains why this action would profane the altar.

B. Verb.

Ḥārab means "to smite down, slaughter." This verb, which appears 3 times in biblical Hebrew, has cognates in Arabic. The word appears in 2 Kings 3:23: "This is blood: the kings are surely slain...."

T

TABERNACLE

A. Noun.

miškān (מִשְׁכָּן, 4908), "dwelling place; tabernacle; shrine." This word appears 139 times and refers in its first occurrence to the "tabernacle": "According to all that I show thee, after the pattern of the tabernacle, and the pattern of all the instruments thereof, even so shall ye make it" (Exod. 25:9). *Miškān* is found primarily in Exodus and Numbers, and it always designates the sanctuary. With this meaning it is a synonym for the phrase "tent of meeting." In total, 100 out of the 139 uses of *miškān* throughout the Old Testament signify the tabernacle as "dwelling place." God dwelt amidst His people in the wilderness, and His presence was symbolically manifest in the tent of meeting. The word *miškān* places the emphasis on the representative presence of God: "And I will set my tabernacle among you: and my soul shall not abhor you. And I will walk among you, and will be your God, and ye shall be my people. I am the Lord your God, which brought you forth out of the land of Egypt, that ye should not be their bondmen; and I have broken the bands of your yoke, and made you go upright" (Lev. 26:11–13). Hence, sin among the Israelites defiled God's "dwelling-place" (Lev. 15:31; cf. Num. 19:13).

Whereas the "tabernacle" was mobile, the temple was built for the particular purpose of religious worship: "... I have not dwelt in any house since the time that I brought up the children of Israel out of Egypt, even to this day, but have walked in a tent and in a tabernacle" (2 Sam. 7:6). Solomon built it and the finished structure was known as "the house," the temple, instead of the dwelling place (*miškān*). In later literature *miškān* is a poetic synonym for "temple": "I will not give sleep ... until I find out a place for the Lord, a *habitation* for the mighty God of Jacob" (Ps. 132:4–5). The meaning of *miškān* was also extended to include the whole area surrounding the temple, as much as the city Jerusalem: "There is a river, the streams whereof shall make glad the city of God, the holy place of the tabernacles of the Most High" (Ps. 46:4), "the Lord loveth the gates of Zion more than all the dwellings of Jacob" (Ps. 87:2).

The defilement of the city and the temple area was sufficient reason for God to leave the temple (Ezek. 10) and to permit the destruction of His "dwelling place" by the brutish Babylonians: "They have cast fire into thy sanctuary, they have defiled by casting down the dwelling place of thy name to the ground" (Ps. 74:7). In the Lord's providence He had planned to restore His people and the temple so as to assure them of His continued presence: "My tabernacle also shall be with them: yea, I will be their God, and they shall be my people. And the heathen shall know that I the Lord do sanctify Israel, when my sanctuary shall be in the midst of them for evermore" (Ezek. 37:27–28). John comments that Jesus Christ was God's "tabernacle": "And the Word was made flesh, and dwelt among us, (and we beheld his glory, the glory as of the only begotten of the Father,) full of grace and truth" (John 1:14), and Jesus later referred to Himself as the temple: "But He spake of the temple of his body" (John 2:21).

In non-religious use *miškān* is "the dwelling place" of an individual (Num. 16:24), of Israel (Num. 24:5), and of strangers (Hab. 1:6).

The usual translation of *miškān* in the Septuagint is *skene* ("dwelling; booth"), which is also the translation for *'ōhel*, "tent." It has been suggested that the similarity in sound of the Hebrew *šākan* and the Greek *skene* influenced the translation. Another translation is *skenoma* ("tent; dwelling; lodging"). The translations in the KJV are: "tabernacle; dwelling place; dwelling; habitation."

B. Verb.

šākan (שָׁכַן, 7934), "to dwell, inhabit." This verb, which occurs about 129 times in biblical Hebrew, is found also in other Semitic languages. In Akkadian *šakānu*, "to lay, to set up, to be situated," has many forms, such as the noun *maskana*, "dwelling place." One occurrence of the verb is in Ps. 37:27: "Depart from evil, and do good; and dwell for evermore."

TO TAKE, HANDLE

tāpaś (תָּפַשׂ, 8610), "to catch, seize, lay hold of, grasp, play." This verb is found in both biblical and modern Hebrew. It occurs approximately 60 times in the Hebrew Old Testament. The word is found for the first time in Gen. 4:21, where it expresses the idea of grasping something in one's hand in order to use it: "... He was the father of all such as handle the

harp and organ." Other things that are "seized" with the hand, or "handled," are: swords (Ezek. 21:11), shields (Jer. 46:9), bows (Amos 2:15), and sickles (Jer. 50:16). The expert in *tôrāh*, "law," is one who "handles" the law, but he sometimes mishandles it also: "... They that handle the law knew me not ... " (Jer. 2:8).

"To seize" someone may be to arrest him: "... Irijah took [NASB, "arrested"] Jeremiah, and brought him to the princes" (Jer. 37:14). Frequently, *tāpaś* is used in the sense of "to capture": "And the king of Ai they took alive, and brought him to Joshua" (Josh. 8:23). "To lay hold of," or "seize," hearts is to terrorize: "That I may take the house of Israel in their own heart, because they are all estranged from me through their idols" (Ezek. 14:5).

'āḥaz (אָחַז, 270), "to seize, grasp, take hold, take possession." Found in various Semitic languages, including ancient Akkadian, this word is a common one throughout the stages of the Hebrew language. It occurs almost 70 times in the Hebrew Old Testament. It is used for the first time in the Old Testament in the passive sense with reference to the ram "caught in a thicket by his horns" (Gen. 22:13) and thus became a substitute for Isaac.

While *'āḥaz* is a common term for taking hold of things physically, such as Jacob's "taking hold" of Esau's heel (Gen. 25:26), *'āḥaz* is frequently used in a metaphorical or figurative sense. In His wrath, God "seized" Job by the neck (Job 16:12). On the other hand, the psalmist testifies that in His grace, God "holds" his right hand (Ps. 73:23). Pain and trembling "seize" the enemies of Israel (Exod. 15:14–15). Horror "seizes" the people of the east (Job 18:20).

This word gives us the name of Ahaz, king of Judah (2 Kings 16).

TO TAKE AWAY

A. Verbs.

lāqaḥ (לָקַח, 3947), "to take, receive, take away." This word occurs in all Semitic languages and in all periods of Hebrew. It occurs about 965 times in the Old Testament.

Primarily this word means "to take, grasp, take hold of," as when Noah reached out and "took hold of" the dove to bring it back into the ark (Gen. 8:9). A secondary meaning is "to take away, remove, take to oneself," as when the invading kings "took away" and "took to themselves" all the movable goods of the cities of the plain (Gen. 14:11). Sometimes this verb implies "to receive something from someone." So Abraham asks Ephron the Hittite to "receive from" his hand payment for the field which contained the sepulchre (Gen. 23:13). With the particle "for" *lāqaḥ* means "to take someone or something," as when Joseph's brothers remarked that they were afraid he was scheming "to take" them to be slaves, mentioned in Gen. 43:18. Another secondary use of this word is "to transfer" a thing, concept, or emotion, such as "take vengeance" (Isa. 47:3), "receive reproach" (Ezek. 36:30), and "receive a [whisper]" (Job 4:12). In other passages this verb is virtually a helping verb serving to prepare for an action stipulated in a subsequent verb; God "took" Adam and put him into the garden of Eden (Gen. 2:15—the first occurrence of the verb). Finally, this word can be used elliptically, suggesting the phrase "take and bring," but only "taken" is written. Noah is told to "take" (and bring) clean animals by sevens into the ark (Gen. 7:2).

This verb is used of God in several connections. Sometimes God is pictured as having bodily parts (anthropomorphically). This is the implication of Gen. 2:15, where the Lord "took" Adam and put him into Eden. God's taking sometimes connotes election, as when He "took" Abraham from his father's house (Gen. 24:7). He also "takes" in the sense of taking to Himself or accepting. Thus, He "accepts" offerings (Judg. 13:23) and prayers (Ps. 6:9). God "takes away" in judgment David's wives (2 Sam. 12:11) and the kingdom (1 Kings 11:34).

Of special interest is the use of the verb in the absolute sense: God "took away" Enoch so that he was not found on earth (Gen. 5:24). This meaning of receiving one into heaven to Himself seems to be the force of Ps. 73:24 and perhaps of Ps. 49:15.

lākad (לָכַד, 3920), "to capture; seize; take captive." This term is found in both ancient and modern Hebrew. It occurs about 120 times in biblical Hebrew and is found for the first time in the text in Num. 21:32, where the Israelites are said to have taken the villages of the Amorites.

The act of "capturing, seizing" is usually connected with fighting wars or battles, so a variety of objects may be taken. Cities are often "captured" in war (Josh. 8:21; 10:1; Judg. 1:8, 12). Land or territory also is taken as booty of war (Josh. 10:42; Dan. 11:18). Strategic geographic areas such as watercourses "are captured" (Judg. 3:28). Sometimes kings and princes "are seized" in battle (Judg. 7:25; 8:12, 14), as well as fighting men and horses (2 Sam. 8:4). Saul is spoken of as actually taking the kingdom, apparently by force of arms (1 Sam. 14:47). In establishing the source of Israel's defeat by Ai,

lots were used "to take or separate" the guilty party, Achan and his family (Josh. 7:14).

Occasionally *lākad* is used in the figurative sense, especially in terms of men "being caught" in the trap of divine judgment (Ps. 9:15; Isa. 8:15; 24:18).

B. Nouns.

leqaḥ (לֶקַח, 3948), "teaching; instruction; persuasiveness; understanding." The word is used in the sense of something taken in. This noun occurs 9 times in the Old Testament, several times in Proverbs. One occurrence is in Prov. 1:5: "A wise man will hear, and will increase learning. . . ." The word refers to "persuasiveness" in Prov. 7:21.

Several other nouns are related to *lāqaḥ*. *Malqôaḥ* refers to "things taken in warfare," and it appears 7 times (Num. 31:32). *Malqôaḥ* also means "jaws" once (Ps. 22:15). *Melqāhayim* refers to "snuffers" (Exod. 37:23), and it is found 6 times. *Miqqāḥ* occurs once to mean "taking" (2 Chron. 19:7). *Maqqāḥôt* means "wares" once (Neh. 10:31).

TO TEACH

A. Verbs.

lāmad (לָמַד, 3925), "to teach, learn, cause to learn." This common Semitic term is found throughout the history of the Hebrew language and in ancient Akkadian and Ugaritic. *Lāmad* is found approximately 85 times in the text of the Hebrew Old Testament. In its simple, active form, this verb has the meaning "to learn," but it is also found in a form giving the causative sense, "to teach." This word is first used in the Hebrew Old Testament in Deut. 4:1: ". . . Hearken, O Israel, unto the statutes and unto the judgments, which I teach you. . . ."

In Deut. 5:1 *lāmad* is used of learning God's laws: "Hear, O Israel, the statutes and judgments which I speak in your ears this day, that ye may learn them, and keep, and do them." A similar meaning occurs in Ps. 119:7. The word may be used of learning other things: works of the heathen (Ps. 106:35); wisdom (Prov. 30:3); and war (Mic. 4:3).

About half the occurrences of *lāmad* are found in the books of Deuteronomy and Psalms, underlining the teaching emphasis found in these books. Judaism's traditional emphasis on teaching and thus preserving its faith clearly has its basis in the stress on teaching the faith found in the Old Testament, specifically Deut. 6:4–9. Following the Shema', the "watchword of Judaism" that declares that Yahweh is One (Deut. 6:4), is the "first great commandment" (Deut. 6:5; Mark 12:28–29). When Moses delivered the Law to his people, he said,

" ... The Lord commanded me at that time to teach you statutes and judgments ... " (Deut. 4:14).

The later Jewish term *talmud*, "instruction," is derived from this verb.

yārāh (יָרָה, 3384),"to throw, teach, shoot, point out." Found in all periods of the Hebrew language, this root is also found in ancient Ugaritic with the sense of "to shoot"; modern Hebrew uses the word to express the firing of a gun. *Yārāh* occurs approximately 80 times in the Hebrew Old Testament.

The first use of this verb in the Old Testament is in Gen. 31:51: " ... Behold this pillar, which I have cast betwixt me and thee." This basic meaning, "to throw or cast," is expressed in "casting" lots (Josh. 18:6) and by Pharaoh's army "being cast" into the sea (Exod. 15:4).

The idea of "to throw" is easily extended to mean the shooting of arrows (1 Sam. 20:36–37). "To throw" seems to be further extended to mean "to point," by which fingers are thrown in a certain direction (Gen. 46:28; Prov. 6:13).

From this meaning it is only a short step to the concept of teaching as the "pointing out" of fact and truth. Thus, Bezaleel was inspired by God "to teach" others his craftsmanship (Exod. 35:34); the false prophets "teach" lies (Isa. 9:15); and the father "taught" his son (Prov. 4:4). It was the responsibility of the priests to interpret and "to teach" those things that had to do with ceremonial requirements and God's judgments: "They shall teach Jacob thy judgments, and Israel thy law ... " (Deut. 33:10; cf. Deut. 17:10–11). Interestingly, priests at a later time were said "to teach" for hire, presumably "to teach" what was wanted rather than true interpretation of God's word (Mic. 3:11).

B. Noun.
tôrāh (תּוֹרָה, 8451), "direction; instruction; guideline." From *yārāh* is derived *tôrāh*, one of the most important words in the Old Testament. Seen against the background of the verb *yārāh*, it becomes clear that *tôrāh* is much more than law or a set of rules. *Tôrāh* is not restriction or hindrance, but instead the means whereby one can reach a goal or ideal. In the truest sense, *tôrāh* was given to Israel to enable her to truly become and remain God's special people. One might say that in keeping *tôrāh*, Israel was kept. Unfortunately, Israel fell into the trap of keeping *tôrāh* as something imposed, and for itself, rather than as a means of becoming what God intended for her. The means became the end. Instead of seeing *tôrāh* as a guideline, it became an external body of rules, and thus a weight rather than a freeing and guiding power. This burden, plus the legalism of Roman law, forms the background of the New Testament tradition of law, especially as Paul struggles with it in his Letter to the church at Rome.

C. Adjective.
Limmûd means "taught." This adjective forms an exact equivalent to the New Testament idea of "disciple, one who is taught." This is well expressed in Isa. 8:16: " ... Seal the law among my disciples." The word also occurs in Isa. 54:13: "And all thy children shall be taught of the Lord. ... "

TO TELL

A. Verb.
nāgad (נָגַד, 5046), "to tell, explain, inform." An exact equivalent to this verb is not known outside biblical Hebrew except in late Aramaic. The verb occurs around 335 times and in all periods of biblical Hebrew.

The first emphasis of the word is "to tell." This especially means that A (frequently a messenger or some other person who has witnessed something) "tells" B (the one to whom the report is made) C (the report). In such instances B (the one told) is spatially separated from the original source of the information. So, in Gen. 9:22, Ham (A) saw his father naked and went outside the tent and "told" his brothers (B) what he had seen (C).

In another group of passages *nāgad* represents the reporting of a messenger about a matter of life-or-death importance for the recipient. So a fugitive "came ... and told Abram" that Lot had been captured and led away captive (Gen. 14:13). A note of this emotionally charged situation is seen in Jacob's message to Esau: " ... I have sent to tell my lord, that I may find grace in thy sight" (Gen. 32:5). Although not a report from a messenger from afar, Gen. 12:18 uses the verb of a report that is of crucial importance to the one addressed. Pharaoh asked Abram: "Why didst thou not tell me that she was thy wife?" Gen. 12:17 reports that because Pharaoh had taken Sarai into his harem to become his wife, God had smitten his household with great plagues.

Finally, *nāgad* means "to explain or reveal" something one does not otherwise know. In Gen. 3:11 (the first biblical occurrence of the word) God asked Adam: "Who told thee that thou wast naked?" This was information immediately before them but not previously grasped by them. This usage appears in Gen. 41:24, where Pharaoh said of his dream: " ... I told this unto the magicians; but there was none that could declare it to me." Similarly, David made certain there were no survivors from the Philistine cities he looted so no one would "tell" it to Achish (1 Sam. 27:11). This word some-times has a more forceful significance—God told the prophet to "show my people their transgression" (Isa. 58:1).

B. Noun.

nāgîd (נָגִיד, 5057), "chief leader." This noun occurs 44 times in biblical Hebrew. In 1 Sam. 9:16 the word is used as a "chief leader" that is equivalent to a king: "Tomorrow about this time I will send thee a man out of the land of Benjamin, and thou shalt anoint him to be captain over my people Israel. . . . " *Nāgîd* ap-pears in 1 Chron. 9:11 to refer to a "chief leader" (ruler) of a smaller region. The word may also be used of a head of a family (1 Chron. 9:20).

C. Preposition.

neged (נֶגֶד, 5048), "before; in the presence of; in the sight of; in front of; in one's estimation; straight ahead." This word occurs 156 times in biblical Hebrew as a preposition and an adverb. Basically the word indicates that its object is immediately "before" something or someone. It is used in Gen. 2:18, where God said He would make Adam "a help meet for him," or some-one to correspond to him, just as the males and females of the animals corresponded to (matched) one another. To be immediately "be-fore" the sun is to be fully in the sunlight (Num. 25:4). In Exod. 10:10 Pharaoh told Moses that evil was immediately "before" his face, or was in his mind. *Neged* signifies "in front of" (Exod. 19:2), "before" in the sense of "in one's estima-tion" (Isa. 40:17), and "straight ahead (before)" (Josh. 6:5). In combination with other particles *neged* means "contrary to" (Num. 22:32).

D. Adverb.

neged (נֶגֶד, 5048), "opposite; over against." This meaning of *neged* appears in Gen. 21:16: "And she went, and sat her down over against him a good way off. . . . "

TEMPLE

hêkāl (הֵיכָל, 1964), "palace; temple." This word is indirectly derived from the Sumerian *é-gal*, "large house, palace," and more directly from the Akkadian *ēkallu*, "large house." The influence of the Akkadian *ēkallu* spread to the Northwest Semitic languages. In post-biblical Hebrew the meaning became limited to "tem-ple." The *Hekhal Shlomo* ("Temple of Solomon") in modern Jerusalem signifies the building of Israel's chief rabbinate, in absence of the tem-ple. The word occurs 78 times from First Sam-uel to Malachi, most frequently in Ezekiel. The first usage pertains to the tabernacle at Shiloh (1 Sam. 1:9).

The word "palace" in English versions may

have one of three Hebrew words behind it: *hêkāl, bayit,* or *'armôn*. The Sumero-Akkadian meaning "palace" for *hêkāl* is still to be found in biblical Hebrew. The *hêkāl* with its 15 usages as "palace" refers to the palaces of Ahab (1 Kings 21:1), of the king of Babylon (2 Kings 20:18), and of Nineveh (Nah. 2:6). The "pal-ace" was luxuriously decorated and the resi-dents enjoyed the fulfillment of their pleasures; cf.: "And the wild beasts of the islands shall cry in their desolate houses, and dragons in their pleasant palaces: and her time is near to come, and her days shall not be prolonged" (Isa. 13:22). The psalmist compared beautiful girls to fine pillars in an ornate "palace": " . . . That our sons may be as plants grown up in their youth; that our daughters may be as corner stones, polished after the similitude of a palace" (Ps. 144:12). Amos prophesied that the "songs of the palace" (KJV, "temple") were to turn to wailing at the destruction of the northern king-dom (Amos 8:3, NASB).

Hêkāl with the meaning "temple" is gener-ally clarified in the context by two markers that follow. The first marker is the addition "of the Lord": "And when the builders laid the foun-dation of the temple of the Lord, they set the priests in their apparel with trumpets, and the Levites the sons of Asaph with cymbals, to praise the Lord, after the ordinance of David king of Israel" (Ezra 3:10). The second marker is a form of the word *qōdeš*, "holy": "O God, the heathen are come into thine inheritance; thy holy temple have they defiled; they have laid Jerusalem on heaps" (Ps. 79:1). Sometimes the definite article suffices to identify the "temple in Jerusalem": "In the year that King Uzziah died I saw also the Lord sitting upon a throne, high and lifted up, and his train filled the temple" (Isa. 6:1), especially in a section dealing with the "temple" (Ezek. 41).

The Old Testament also speaks about the heavenly *hêkāl*, the *hêkāl* of God. It is difficult to decide on a translation, whether "palace" or "temple." Most versions opt in favor of the "temple" idea: "Hear, all ye people; hearken, O earth, and all that therein is: and let the Lord God be witness against you, the Lord from his holy temple" (Mic. 1:2; cf. Ps. 5:7; 11:4; Hab. 2:20). "In my distress I called upon the Lord, and cried to my God: and he did hear my voice out of his temple, and my cry did enter into his ears" (2 Sam. 22:7). However, since Scripture portrays the presence of the royal judgment throne in heaven, it is not altogether impossible that the original authors had a royal "palace" in mind. The imagery of the throne, the "pal-ace," and judgment seems to lie behind Ps.

11:4–5. "The Lord is in his holy temple, the Lord's throne is in heaven: his eyes behold, his eyelids try, the children of men. The Lord trieth the righteous: but the wicked and him that loveth violence his soul hateth."

The Septuagint has the words *naos* ("temple") and *oikos* ("house; palace; dwelling; household").

TENT

'ōhel (אֹהֶל, 168), "tent; home; dwelling; habitation." Cognates of this word appear in Ugaritic, Phoenician, and Arabic. It appears about 343 times in biblical Hebrew and in all periods.

First, this word refers to the mobile structure called a "tent." This is its meaning in Gen. 4:20: "And Adah bare Jabal: he was the father of such as dwell in tents, and of such as have cattle." These are what nomadic Bedouins normally live in. "Tents" can also be used as housing for animals: "They smote also the tents of cattle [NASB, "those who owned"], and carried away sheep and camels in abundance . . ." (2 Chron. 14:15). Soldiers lived in "tents" during military campaigns (1 Sam. 17:54). A "tent" was pitched on top of a house so everyone could see that Absalom went in to his father's concubines (2 Sam. 16:22). This constituted an open rejection of David's dominion and a declaration that he (Absalom) was claiming the throne.

Second, the word is a synonym for "home, dwelling," and "habitation." This emphasis is especially evident in Judg. 19:9: " . . . Behold, the day groweth to an end, lodge here, that thine heart may be merry; and tomorrow get you early on your way, that thou mayest go home." This meaning appears in the phrase "to your tents": "We have no part in David, neither have we inheritance in the son of Jesse: every man to his tents, O Israel" (2 Sam. 20:1). The "tabernacle" ("tent") of David, therefore, is his dwelling place or palace (Isa. 16:5). Similarly, the "tabernacle" ("tent") of the daughter of Zion is Israel's capital, or what Israel inhabits—Jerusalem (Lam. 2:4).

Third, *'ōhel* may represent those who dwell in the dwellings of a given area or who form a unit of people. Thus the "tents" of Judah are her inhabitants: "The Lord also shall save the tents of Judah first, that the glory of the house of David and the glory of the inhabitants of Jerusalem do not magnify themselves against Judah" (Zech. 12:7; cf. Ps. 83:6).

Bedouin "tents" today (as in the past) are constructed of strong black cloth of woven goat's hair. They are shaped variously. The women pitch them by stretching the cloth over poles and tying it down with cords of goat's hair or hemp. Wooden mallets are used to drive the tent pegs into the ground (Judg. 4:21). Sometimes the structure is divided in order to separate families or to separate animals from people (2 Chron. 14:15). The back of the "tent" is closed and the front open. The door is made by turning back the fold where the two ends of the cloth meet (Gen. 18:1). The "tent" and all its contents are transported on the back of a single pack animal. Richer people cover the floor with mats of various materials. A chief or sheikh may have several "tents"—one for himself and his guest(s), another for his wives and other females in his immediate family, and still another for the animals (Gen. 31:33).

Before the construction of the tabernacle Moses pitched a "tent" outside the camp (Exod. 33:7). There he met with God. The "tent" outside the camp persisted as a living institution for only a short period after the construction of the tabernacle and before the departure from Sinai (Num. 11:16ff.; 12:4ff.). Eventually the ark of the covenant was moved into the tabernacle (Exod. 40:21) where the Lord met with Moses and spoke to Israel (Exod. 29:42). This structure is called the tent of meeting inasmuch as it contained the ark of the covenant and the tables of testimony (Num. 9:15). As the tent of meeting it was the place where God met with His people through Moses (or the high priest) and revealed His will to them (1 Sam. 2:22).

TO TEST

A. Verb.

sārap (צָרַף, 6884), "to refine, try, smelt, test." This root with the basic meaning of smelting and refining is found outside the Old Testament in Akkadian, Phoenician, and Syriac. In Arabic an adjective derived from the verb means "pure, unmixed," describing the quality of wine. *Sārap* has maintained the meaning "to refine" in rabbinic and modern Hebrew, but lost the primary significance of "to smelt" in modern Hebrew.

The verb occurs fewer than 35 times in the Old Testament, mainly in the prophets and in the Book of Psalms. The first occurrence is in the story of Gideon, where 10,000 are "being tested" and only 300 are chosen to fight with Gideon against the Midianites: "And the Lord said unto Gideon, The people are yet too many; bring them down unto the water, and I will try them for thee there . . . " (Judg. 7:4). The meaning in this context is "to test," to find out who is qualified for battle. The only other occurrence of the verb in Judges is equivalent to a noun in English: "smith," in this context a silversmith (17:4).

Jeremiah describes the process of smelting and refining: "The bellows [blow fiercely], the lead is consumed of the fire; the founder melteth in vain: for the wicked are not plucked away" (Jer. 6:29), and the failure of refining the silver leads to rejection (Jer. 6:30). The process (smelting) and the result (refining) are often considered together. It is difficult to separate them in biblical usage. Hence, the work of the smith involves smelting, refining, and particularly the use of the refined metals in making the final product: "The workman melteth a graven image, and the goldsmith spreadeth it over with gold, and casteth silver chains" (Isa. 40:19). He used a hammer and anvil in making fine layers of gold used in plating the form (Isa. 41:7).

Ṣārap is also used metaphorically with the sense "to refine by means of suffering." The psalmist describes the experience of Israel in this way: "For thou, O God, hast proved us: thou hast tried us, as silver is tried. Thou ... laidst affliction upon our loins.... We went through fire and through water: but thou broughtest us out into a wealthy place" (Ps. 66:10–12). God's judgment is also described as a process of refining: "And I will ... purely purge away thy dross, and take away all thy tin" (Isa. 1:25). Those who were thus purified are those who call on the name of the Lord and receive the gracious benefits of the covenant (Zech. 13:9). The coming of the messenger of the covenant (Jesus Christ) is compared to the work of a smith: "But who may abide the day of his coming? and who shall stand when he appeareth? for he is like a refiner's fire.... And he shall sit as a refiner and purifier of silver: and he shall purify the sons of Levi, and purge them as gold and silver ... " (Mal. 3:2–3). The believer can take comfort in the Word of God which alone on earth is tried and purified and by which we can be purified: "Thy promise is well tried, and thy servant loves it" (Ps. 119:140, RSV; cf. Ps. 18:30; Prov. 30:5).

Ṣārap has the following translations in the Septuagint: *purao* ("to burn; to make red hot") and *chruso-o* ("to gild; to overlay with gold"). The KJV gives the following translations: "to refine; try; melt; founder; goldsmith." In the RSV, NASB, and NIV the verb "to test" is given instead of "to try."

B. Nouns.
Two nouns derived from the verb *ṣārap* occur rarely. *Ṣōrpî* occurs once to mean "goldsmith" (Neh. 3:31). *Maṣrēp* occurs twice and refers to a "crucible": "The fining pot is for silver, and the furnace is for gold: but the Lord trieth the hearts" (Prov. 17:3; cf. Prov. 27:21).

TESTIMONY

ʿēdût (עֵדוּת, 5715), "testimony; ordinance." The 83 occurrences of this word are scattered throughout all types of biblical literature and all periods (although not before the giving of the law at Mount Sinai).

This word refers to the Ten Commandments as a solemn divine charge or duty. In particular, it represents those commandments as written on the tablets and existing as a reminder and "testimony" of Israel's relationship and responsibility to God: "And he gave unto Moses, when he had made an end of communing with him upon Mount Sinai, two tables of testimony, tables of stone, written with the finger of God" (Exod. 31:18). Elsewhere these tablets are called simply "the testimony" (Exod. 25:16). Since they were kept in the ark, it became known as the "ark of the testimony" (Exod. 25:22) or simply "the testimony": "As the Lord commanded Moses, so Aaron laid it up before the Testimony, to be kept" (Exod. 16:34—the first biblical occurrence of the word). The tabernacle as the housing for the ark containing these tablets was sometimes called the "tabernacle of testimony" (Exod. 38:21) or the "tent of the testimony" (Num. 9:15).

The word sometimes refers to the entire law of God: "The law of the Lord is perfect, converting the soul: the testimony of the Lord is sure, making wise the simple" (Ps. 19:7). Here *ʿēdût* is synonymously parallel to "law," making it a synonym to that larger concept. Special or particular laws are sometimes called "testimonies": "And keep the charge of the Lord thy God, to walk in his ways, to keep his statutes, and his commandments, and his judgments, and his testimonies ... " (1 Kings 2:3). In Ps. 122:4 the annual pilgrimage feasts are called "the testimony of Israel."

THERE IS

yēš (יֵשׁ, 3426), "there is; substance; he/she/it is/are." Cognates of this word are attested in Ugaritic, Aramaic, Akkadian, Amorite, and Arabic. It appears about 137 times and in all periods of biblical Hebrew.

This particle is used substantively only in Prov. 8:21: " ... That I may cause those that love me to inherit substance; and I will fill their treasures."

In all other appearances the word asserts existence with emphasis. Sometimes *yēš* appears with a predicate following, as it does in Gen. 28:16: "And Jacob awaked out of his sleep, and he said, Surely the Lord is in this place; and I knew it not." In a few passages the word is used as a response to an inquiry: "Is the seer here? And they [the young maidens] answered them, and said, He is; behold, he is before you ... " (1 Sam. 9:11–12). Used absolutely the word can mean "there is/are/was/were," as it does in Gen. 18:24 (the first biblical appearance): "Peradventure there be fifty righteous within the city ... ?" In many contexts *yēš* used in framing questions or protestations suggests doubt that the matter queried exists or is to be found: "As the Lord thy God liveth, there is no nation or kingdom, whither my lord hath not sent to seek thee: and when they said, He is not there; he took an oath of the kingdom and nation, that they found thee not" (1 Kings 18:10). This is especially clear in Jer. 5:1, where God commands the prophet to go and seek "if ye can find a man, if there be any that executeth judgment, that seeketh the truth. ... "

There are several other special uses of *yēš*. Used with the particle *'im* and a participle, it emphasizes abiding intention: "And I came this day unto the well, and said, O Lord God of my master Abraham, if now thou do prosper my way which I go [literally, if there surely is a prospering of my way; or if it surely is that you intend to prosper] ... " (Gen. 24:42). Possession is sometimes indicated by *yēš* plus the preposition *le*: "And Esau said, I have enough, my brother ... " (Gen. 33:9). Used with the infinitive and the preposition *le*, *yēš* signifies possibility—Elisha told the Shunammite woman: " ... Behold, thou hast been careful for us with all this care; what is to be done for thee? *wouldest* thou be spoken for to the king, or to the captain of the host [is it possible that you want me to speak a word in your behalf to]?" (2 Kings 4:13).

TO THINK, DEVISE

A. Verb.

hāšab (חָשַׁב, 2803), "to think, devise, purpose, esteem, count, imagine, impute." This word appears 123 times in the Old Testament, and it implies any mental process involved in planning or conceiving.

Hāšab can be translated as "devise" in association with the sense of "to think and reckon." A gifted person of God "devises" excellent works in gold and other choice objects (Exod. 35:35). The word may deal with evil, as when Haman "devised" an evil plot against the Jewish people (Esth. 8:3). David issued his prayer against those who "devise" evil toward him as a servant of the Lord (Ps. 35:4), and the scoundrel "devises" perverse things in Prov. 16:30. Other verses indicating an immoral intent behind the action of "devising" are Jer. 18:11; 18:18; Ezek. 11:2.

The word may mean "think." Some "thought" to do away with David by sending him against the Philistines (1 Sam. 18:25); Judah "thought" Tamar to be a harlot (Gen. 38:15); and Eli "thought" Hannah was drunk (1 Sam. 1:13). God repented of the evil concerning the judgment he "thought" to bring upon Israel (Jer. 18:8). Those who fear the Lord may also "think" upon His name (Mal. 3:16).

Hāšab may be rendered "to purpose" or "esteem." God asked Job if he could tame the Leviathan, who " ... esteemeth him as straw, and brass as rotten wood" (Job 41:27). A classic usage of "esteem" appears in Isa. 53:3–4: "He [the Messiah] is despised and rejected of men; a man of sorrows, and acquainted with grief; and we hid as it were our faces from him; he was despised, and we esteemed him not. Surely he hath borne our griefs. ... Yet we did esteem him stricken, smitten of God, and afflicted." Some uses of "to purpose" have a malevolent intent. David's enemies have "purpose" to overthrow him (Ps. 140:4). God repented of the evil He "purposed" to do concerning Israel (Jer. 26:3), and perhaps the people will repent when they hear the evil God has "purposed" against the nation (Jer. 36:3). On the other hand, God "purposes" evil against the land of the Chaldeans in His judgment after using them for the purification of His people, Israel (Jer. 50:45).

Translated as "count," the word is used in a number of ways. It had a commercial connotation, as when land was being redeemed and the price was established, based on the value of crops until the next year of Jubilee: "Then let him count the years of the sale thereof, and restore the overplus ... " (Lev. 25:27). The same idea concerns the provisions for the Levites when Israel offered their gifts to the Lord (Num. 18:30). "Count" may imply "to be thought or reckoned." Bildad declared to Job, "Wherefore are we counted as beasts, and reputed vile in your sight?" (Job 18:3). Those who seek to live for the Lord are "counted" as sheep for the slaughter (Ps. 44:22). The foolish person, when he holds his peace, is "counted" as wise (Prov. 17:28). A theological emphasis exists in God's reward of Abraham, when the patriarch believed God and His word: "And he believed in the Lord; and he counted it to him for righteousness" (Gen. 15:6).

Most uses of *hāšab* translated as "imagine" bear an evil connotation. Job chided his friends: "Do ye imagine to reprove words, and the speeches of one that is desperate ... " (Job

6:26); David's enemies "imagined" a mischievous device (Ps. 21:11); and Nahum complained of those who "imagine" evil against the Lord (Nah. 1:11).

Other unique translations of *hāšab* occur. In order to approach God, Asaph had to remember and "consider" the days of old (Ps. 77:5). God had a controversy with Nebuchadnezzar, king of Babylon, because he "conceived" a plan against Him and His people (Jer. 49:30). The prophet Amos cites people who "invent" instruments of music and enjoy it (Amos 6:5). Huram of Tyre sent a man to help Solomon in the building of the temple, who knew how to "find out" all the works of art—i.e., he could work in various metals and fabrics to design a work of beauty (2 Chron. 2:14). Joseph had to remind his brethren that he did not seek to do them harm because they had sold him into slavery, since God "meant" it for the good of the preservation of Jacob's sons (Gen. 50:20).

Infrequently, *hāšab* is translated as "impute": "And if any of the flesh of the sacrifice of his peace offerings be eaten at all on the third day, it shall not be accepted, neither shall it be imputed unto him that offereth it; it shall be an abomination" (Lev. 7:18). When an Israelite killed a sacrifice in any place except an appointed altar, the blood was "imputed" to that man; the substitute sacrifice would not atone for the offerer at all, and the offerer would bear his own guilt (Lev. 17:4). David could praise God for forgiveness because the Lord will not "impute" iniquity after he had confessed his sin (Ps. 32:2).

B. Adjective.

hāšab (חָשֵׁב, 2803), "cunning." This word is applied to those who performed "cunning" work with parts of the tabernacle: "And with him was Aholiab, son of Ahisamach, ... an engraver, and a cunning workman ... " (Exod. 38:23). This meaning of *hāšab* as "cunning" appears 11 times in Exodus. But this skill was more than human invention—it indicated how the Spirit of God imparts wisdom, understanding, and knowledge (cf. Exod. 36:8; 39:3).

THRONE

kissē' (בִּסֵּא, 3678), "throne; seat." This word, with the basic meaning "seat of honor," occurs in many Semitic languages (Ugaritic, Phoenician, Aramaic, Syriac, Arabic) and in ancient Egyptian.

Kissē' occurs 130 times in the Hebrew Old Testament and, as is to be expected, the frequency is greater in the historical books and the prophetical works. It is rare in the Pentateuch. The first usage of *kissē'* is in Gen. 41:40: "Thou

shalt be over my house, and according unto thy word shall all my people be ruled: only in the throne will I be greater than thou." In modern Hebrew the word mainly denotes a "chair," and "throne" is further described as a "royal chair."

In the Old Testament the basic meaning of *kissē'* is "seat" or "chair." Visitors were seated on a chair (1 Kings 2:19), as well as guests (2 Kings 4:10) and older men (1 Sam. 1:9). When the king or elders assembled to administer justice, they sat on the throne of justice (Prov. 20:8; cf. Ps. 9:4). In these contexts *kissē'* is associated with honor. However, in the case of the prostitute (Prov. 9:14) and soldiers who set up their chairs (Jer. 1:15—*kissē'* may mean "throne" here; cf. KJV, NASB, NIV), *kissē'* signifies a place and nothing more.

The more frequent sense of *kissē'* is "throne" or "seat of honor," also known as the "royal seat": "And it shall be, when he sitteth upon the throne of his kingdom, that he shall write him a copy of this law in a book out of that which is before the priests the Levites" (Deut. 17:18; cf. 1 Kings 1:46). Since the Davidic dynasty received the blessing of God, the Old Testament has a number of references to "the throne of David" (2 Sam. 3:10; Jer. 22:2, 30; 36:30): "Of the increase of his government and peace there shall be no end, upon the throne of David, and upon his kingdom, to order it, and to establish it with judgment and with justice from henceforth even for ever" (Isa. 9:7). The "throne of Israel" is a synonymous phrase for "throne of David" (1 Kings 2:4; cf. 8:20, 25; 9:5; 10:9; 2 Kings 10:30; 15:12, etc.).

The physical appearance of the "throne" manifested the glory of the king. Solomon's "throne" was an artistic product with ivory inlays, the wood covered with a layer of fine gold (1 Kings 10:18).

The word *kissē'* was also used to represent "kingship" and the succession to the throne. David had sworn that Solomon would sit on his "throne" (1 Kings 1:13; cf. 2 Kings 10:3).

Above all human kingship and "thrones" was the God of Israel: "God reigneth over the heathen: God sitteth upon the throne of his holiness" (Ps. 47:8). The Israelites viewed God as the ruler who was seated on a "throne." Micaiah said in the presence of Ahab and Jehoshaphat: "Hear thou therefore the word of the Lord: I saw the Lord sitting on his throne, and all the host of heaven standing by him on his right hand and on his left" (1 Kings 22:19). Isaiah received a vision of God's glory revealed in the temple (Isa. 6:1). The presence of the Lord in Jerusalem also gave rise to the conception that Jerusalem was the throne of God (Jer. 3:17).

The Septuagint translation is *thronos* ("throne; dominion; sovereignty").

TIME

A. Noun.

'ēt (עֵת, 6256), "time; period of time; appointed time; proper time; season." This word also appears in Phoenician, post-biblical Hebrew, Arabic (where the same radicals constitute a verb signifying "to appear"), and Akkadian (where these radicals form an adverb signifying "at the time when"). *'Ēt* appears about 290 times in the Bible and in all periods.

Basically this noun connotes "time" conceived as an opportunity or season. First, the word signifies an appointed, fixed, and set time or period. This is what astrologers claimed to discern: "Then the king said to the wise men, which knew the times ..." (Esth. 1:13). God alone, however, knows and reveals such "appointed times": " ... In the time of their visitation they shall be cast down, saith the Lord" (Jer. 8:12).

This noun also is used of the concept "proper or appropriate time." This nuance is applied to the "time" God has appointed for one to die: "Be not over much wicked, neither be thou foolish: why shouldest thou die before thy time?" (Eccl. 7:17). It is used of the "appropriate or suitable time" for a given activity in life: "He hath made every thing beautiful in his time ..." (Eccl. 3:11; cf. Ps. 104:27). Finally, the "appropriate time" for divine judgment is represented by *'ēt:* "It is time for thee, Lord, to work: for they have made void thy law" (Ps. 119:126).

A third use connotes "season," or a regular fixed period of time such as springtime: "And he said, I will certainly return unto thee according to the time of life; and, lo, Sarah thy wife shall have a son" (Gen. 18:10). Similarly, the word is used of the rainy "season" (Ezra 10:13), the harvest "time" (Jer. 50:16), the migratory "period" (Jer. 8:7), and the mating "season" (Gen. 31:10).

This noun also is applied to differing "extensions of time." In its first biblical appearance, for example, *'ēt* represents the "time" (period of the day) when the sun is setting: "And the dove came in to him in the evening [literally, time of the evening] ..." (Gen. 8:11). The word is used of special occasions such as the birth of a child (Mic. 5:3) and of periods during which certain conditions persist (Exod. 18:22; Dan. 12:11).

B. Verb.

'Ānāh means "to be exercised." The noun *'ēt* may be derived from this verb which occurs only 3 times in Hebrew poetry (cf. Eccl. 1:13). It may be related to an Arabic root meaning "to be disquieted or disturbed about something," an Ethiopic root and old South Arabic root meaning "to be concerned about." In later Hebrew this root means "to worry."

TOGETHER

A. Adverbs.

yaḥad (יַחַד, 3162), "together; alike; all at once; all together." *Yaḥad* appears about 46 times and in all periods of biblical Hebrew.

Used as an adverb, the word emphasizes a plurality in unity. In some contexts the connotation is on community in action. Goliath challenged the Israelites, saying: "I defy the armies of Israel this day; give me a man, that we may fight together" (1 Sam. 17:10). Sometimes the emphasis is on commonality of place: " ... And it came to pass, that they which remained were scattered, so that two of them were not left together" (1 Sam. 11:11). The word can be used of being in the same place at the same time: "And he delivered them into the hands of the Gibeonites, and they hanged them in the hill before the Lord: and they fell all seven together ..." (2 Sam. 21:9). In other passages *yaḥad* means "at the same time": "O that my grief were thoroughly weighed, and my calamity laid in the balances together!" (Job 6:2).

In many poetic contexts *yaḥad* is a near synonym of *kullām*, "altogether." *Yaḥad*, however, is more emphatic, meaning "all at once, all together." In Deut. 33:5 (the first biblical occurrence) the word is used emphatically, meaning "all together," or "all of them together": "And he was king in Jeshurun, when the heads of the people and the tribes of Israel were gathered together." Cf.: "Surely men of low degree are vanity, and men of high degree are a lie: to be laid in the balance, they are altogether lighter than vanity" (Ps. 62:9). In such contexts *yaḥad* emphasizes the totality of a given group (cf. Ps. 33:15).

Yaḥad also sometimes emphasizes that things are "alike" or that the same thing will happen to all of them: "The fool and the stupid alike must perish" (Ps. 49:10, RSV).

yaḥdāw, (יַחְדָּו, 3162), "all alike; equally; all at once; all together." The second adverbial form, *yaḥdāw* appears about 92 times. It, too, speaks of community in action (Deut. 25:11), in place (Gen. 13:6—the first biblical appearance of this form), and in time (Ps. 4:8). In other places it, too, is synonymous with *kullām*, "altogether." In Isa. 10:8 *yahdāw* means "all alike," or "equally": "Are not my princes altogether kings?" In Exod. 19:8 this word implies "all at once" as well as "all together": "And all the people answered together, and said...." The sense "alike" appears in Deut. 12:22: "Even as the roebuck and the hart is eaten, so thou shalt eat them: the unclean and the clean shall eat of them alike."

B. Verb.

Yāḥad means "to be united, meet." This verb appears in the Bible 4 times and has cognates in Aramaic, Ugaritic, Arabic, Ethiopic, and Akkadian. One occurrence is in Gen. 49:6: "O my soul, come not thou into their secret; unto their assembly, mine honor, be not thou united...."

C. Nouns.

yāḥîd (דְּחִיד, 3173), "very self, only; solitary; lonely." This word appears 12 times as a noun or as an adjective. *Yāḥîd* has cognates in Ugaritic, Aramaic, and Syriac. The word can be used meaning "self, my soul": "Deliver my soul from the sword, my life [NASB, "only life"; KJV, "darling"] from the power of the dog" (Ps. 22:20, RSV; cf. Ps. 35:17).

Sometimes this word means "only": "Take now thy son, thine only son Isaac, whom thou lovest..." (Gen. 22:2—the first biblical occurrence of the word). In two passages this word means "solitary" or "lonely": "Turn thee unto me, and have mercy upon me; for I am desolate [RSV, "lonely"] and afflicted" (Ps. 25:16; cf. Ps. 68:6).

The noun *yāḥad* occurs only once to mean "unitedness." David said to the Benjaminites: "If ye be come peaceably unto me to help me, mine heart shall be knit unto you [I am ready to become one (or united) with you]..." (1 Chron. 12:17). This usage of the word as a substantive is unusual.

TOMORROW

A. Noun.

māhār (מְחָר, 4279), "tomorrow." This word has cognates in late Aramaic, Egyptian, Syriac, Phoenician, and Akkadian (here it appears with the word for "day"). *Māhār* appears as a noun or an adverb about 52 times in biblical Hebrew and in all periods of the language.

The word means the day following the present day: "...Tomorrow is the rest of the holy sabbath unto the Lord: bake that which ye will bake today..." (Exod. 16:23). *Māhār* also occurs as a noun in Prov. 27:1: "Boast not thyself of tomorrow; for thou knowest not what a day may bring forth."

B. Adverbs.

māhār (מְחָר, 4279), "tomorrow." The basic meaning of this word is clearly set forth in Exod. 19:10: "And the Lord said unto Moses, Go unto the people, and sanctify them today and tomorrow, and let them wash their clothes." In a few passages the Akkadian idiom is closely paralleled—the phrase *yôm māhār* is used: "So shall my righteousness answer for me in time to come [later]..." (Gen. 30:33). In most passages *māhār* by itself (used absolutely) means "tomorrow": "Behold, I go out from thee, and I will entreat the Lord that the swarms of flies may depart from Pharaoh, from his servants, and from his people, tomorrow..." (Exod. 8:29). Interestingly, in Exod. 8:10 the phrase *leāhār* (which appears 5 times in the Bible) is used: "And he said, Tomorrow." Used with the preposition *ke*, the word means "tomorrow about this time": "Behold, tomorrow about this time I will cause it to rain a very grievous hail..." (Exod. 9:18).

māhŏrāt (מֶחֱרָת, 4283) "the next day." Closely related to the noun *māhār* is this adverb, which occurs about 32 times and in all periods of biblical Hebrew. About 28 times *māhŏrāt* is joined to the preposition *min* to mean "on the next day." This is its form and meaning in its first biblical appearance: "And it came to pass on the morrow..." (Gen. 19:34). In 3 passages this adverb is preceded by the preposition *le*, but the meaning is the same: "And David smote them from the twilight even unto the evening of the next day..." (1 Sam. 30:17). In Num. 11:32 *māhŏrāt* appears after *yôm*, "day," and is preceded by the definite article: "And the people stood up all that day, and all that night, and all the next day, and they gathered the quails...." First Chron. 29:21 displays yet another construction, with the same meaning: "...On the morrow after that day...."

C. Verb.

'Āhar means "to be behind, tarry, defer." This verb, which occurs rarely in biblical Hebrew, is usually considered the root of *māhār*, "tomorrow." This verb appears in Prov. 23:30: "They that tarry long at the wine; they that go to seek mixed wine." The meaning of "to tarry" also occurs in Judg. 5:28: "Why tarry the wheels of his chariots?"

TONGUE

lāšôn (לָשׁוֹן, 3956), "tongue; language; speech." This word is thought to have the root meaning "to lick," but this is a conjecture. The noun occurs in Ugaritic, Akkadian (*Lišānu*), Phoenician, and Arabic. In the Hebrew Old Testament it appears 115 times, mainly in the poetic and, to a lesser extent, in the prophetical books. The first occurrence is in Gen. 10:5: "By these were the isles of the Gentiles divided in their lands; every one after his tongue, after their families, in their nations."

The basic meaning of *lāšôn* is "tongue," which as an organ of the body refers to humans (Lam. 4:4) and animals (Exod. 11:7; Job 41:1) The extended meaning of the word as an organ of speech occurs more frequently. A person may be "heavy" or "slow" of tongue or have a stammering "tongue" (Exod. 4:10); or he may be fluent and clear: "The heart also of the rash shall understand knowledge, and the tongue of the stammerers shall be ready to speak plainly" (Isa. 32:4). And see the description of the "tongue" in Ps. 45:1: "My heart is inditing a good matter: I speak of the things which I have made touching the King: my tongue is the pen of a ready writer." The word is often better translated as "speech," because of the negative and positive associations of *lāšôn*. Especially in the wisdom literature the manner of one's "speech" is considered to be the external expression of the character of the speaker. The fool's "speech" is unreliable (Ps. 5:9), deceitful (Ps. 109:2; 120:2–3; Prov. 6:17), boastful (Ps. 140:11), flattering (Prov. 26:28), slanderous (Ps. 15:3), and subversive (Prov. 10:31). The "tongue" of the righteous man heals (Prov. 15:4). While the "tongue" may be as sharp as a sword (Ps. 57:4), it is a means of giving life to the righteous and death to the wicked: "Death and life are in the power of the tongue: and they that love it shall eat the fruit thereof" (Prov. 18:21; cf. 21:23; 25:15). The biblical authors speak of divine inspiration as the Lord's enabling them to speak: "The Spirit of the Lord spake by me, and his word was in my tongue" (2 Sam. 23:2; cf. Prov. 16:1). "Tongue" with the meaning "speech" has as a synonym *peh*, "mouth" (Ps. 66:17), and more rarely *śāpāh*, "lip" (Job 27:4).

A further extension of meaning is "language." In Hebrew both *śāpāh* and *lāšôn* denote a foreign "language": "For with stammering lips and another tongue will he speak to this people" (Isa. 28:11). The foreigners to the "language" are well described in these words: "Thou shalt not see a fierce people, a people of a deeper speech than thou canst perceive; of a stammering tongue, that thou canst not understand" (Isa. 33:19).

Lāšôn also refers to objects that are shaped in the form of a tongue. Most important is the "tongue of fire," which even takes the character of "eating" or "devouring": "Therefore as the [tongues of fire] devoureth the stubble, and the

flame consumeth the chaff . . . " (Isa. 5:24). The association in Isaiah of God's appearance in judgment with smoke and fire gave rise to a fine literary description of the Lord's anger: "Behold, the name of the Lord cometh from far, burning with his anger, and the burden thereof is heavy: his lips are full of indignation, and his tongue as a devouring fire" (Isa. 30:27). Notice the words "lips" and "tongue" here with the meaning of "flames of fire," even though the language evokes the representation of a tongue (as an organ of the body) together with a tongue (of fire). Also a bar of gold (Josh. 7:21) and a bay of the sea (Isa. 11:15) shaped in the form of a tongue were called *lāšôn*.

The Septuagint translation is *glossa* ("tongue; language").

TO TOUCH

A. Verb.

nāga‘ (נָגַע, 5060), "to touch, strike, reach, smite." Common throughout the history of the Hebrew language, this word is also found in Aramaic. It is used some 150 times in the Hebrew Old Testament. *Nāga‘* first occurs in Gen. 3:3 in the Garden of Eden story, where the woman reminds the serpent that God had said: "Ye shall not eat of [the fruit of the tree which is in the midst of the garden], neither shall ye touch it. . . ." This illustrates the common meaning of physical touch involving various kinds of objects: Jacob's thigh was "touched" by the man at Jabbok (Gen. 32:25, 32); the Israelites were commanded not "to touch" Mount Horeb under pain of death (Exod. 19:12); and unclean things were not "to be touched" (Lev. 5:2–3).

Sometimes *nāga‘* is used figuratively in the sense of emotional involvement: "And Saul also went home to Gibeah; and there went with him a band of men, whose hearts God had touched" (1 Sam. 10:26; NEB, "had moved"). The word is used to refer to sexual contact with another person, such as in Gen. 20:6, where God tells Abimelech that He did not allow him "to touch" Sarah, Abraham's wife (cf. Prov. 6:29). To refer to the touch of God's hand means that divine chastisement has been received: " . . . Have pity upon me, O ye my friends; for the hand of God hath touched me" (Job 19:21).

The word is commonly used also to describe "being stricken" with a disease: King Uzziah "was smitten" with leprosy (2 Chron. 26:20).

B. Noun.

nega‘ (נֶגַע, 5061), "plague: stroke; wound." This noun formed from *nāga‘* occurs about 76 times in the Old Testament. The word refers to a "plague" most frequently (Gen. 12:17; Exod.

11:1). *Nega'* can also mean "stroke" (Deut. 17:8; 21:5) or "wound" (Prov. 6:33). Each meaning carries with it the sense of a person "being stricken or smitten in some way."

TOWER

migdāl (מִגְדָּל, 4026), "tower; small fortress; watchtower; podium." Cognates of this word appear in Ugaritic, Aramaic, Syriac, and Akkadian. The word occurs about 50 times in biblical Hebrew.

Migdāl means "tower." This is its use in Gen. 11:4 (the first occurrence of the word): "And they said, Go to, let us build us a city and a tower, whose top may reach unto heaven. . . ."

The word often refers to a "small fortress": "And he went up thence to Penuel, and spake unto them likewise: and the men of Penuel answered him as the men of Succoth had answered him. And he spake also unto the men of Penuel, saying, When I come again in peace, I will break down this tower" (Judg. 8:8–9).

Migdāl sometimes means "watchtower," one of the specially fortified towers safeguarding the gates of a city and spaced along city walls: "Moreover Uzziah built towers in Jerusalem at the corner gate, and at the valley gate, and at the [corner buttress], and fortified them" (2 Chron. 26:9).

In Neh. 8:4 the word is used of a wooden "podium": "And Ezra the scribe stood upon a pulpit of wood, which they had made for the purpose. . . ."

TO TRANSGRESS

A. Verb.

pāša' (פָּשַׁע, 6586), "to transgress, rebel." Apart from biblical Hebrew, this verb occurs in post-biblical Hebrew, in Palestinian Aramaic, and in Syriac, where it has the significance of "to be terrified" or "to be tepid, to be insipid." It does not appear in any other Semitic languages. The verb occurs 41 times in the Old Testament. It is not found in the Pentateuch. The first occurrence is in Solomon's prayer at the occasion of the dedication of the temple: "And forgive Thy people who have sinned against Thee and all their transgressions which they have transgressed against Thee . . ." (1 Kings 8:50, NASB).

The basic sense of *pāša'* is "to rebel." There are two stages of rebellion. First, the whole process of rebellion has independence in view: "Then Moab rebelled against Israel after the death of Ahab" (2 Kings 1:1). Second, the final result of the rebellion is the state of independence: "In his days Edom revolted from under the hand of Judah, and made a king over themselves" (2 Kings 8:20, NASB). A more radical meaning is the state of rebellion in which there is no end of the rebellion in view. The process is no longer goal-oriented. The state thus described refers to a *status quo*: "So Israel rebelled against the house of David unto this day" (1 Kings 12:19). The prepositions used (*be*, "against," and more rarely *mittahat yād*, "from under the hand") indicate the object of revolt. The usage of *mittahat yād* with *pāša'* fits into the category of rebellion with no goal in view (2 Chron. 21:8, 10). It is best translated as an absolute, radical act ("to break away from").

Thus far, the usage has a king or a nation as the object of the revolt. Translations generally give the rendering "transgress" for *pāša'* when the act is committed against the Lord: "Woe unto them! for they have fled from me: destruction unto them! because they have transgressed against me . . ." (Hos. 7:13). This meaning also appears in Isa. 66:24: "And they shall go forth, and look upon the carcases of the men that have transgressed against me. . . ." The preposition *be*, "against," before the name of God occurs about 10 times. In each case the act is an expression of an apostate way of life: "In transgressing and lying against the Lord, and departing away from our God, speaking oppression and revolt, conceiving and uttering from the heart words of falsehood" (Isa. 59:13).

The Septuagint translators are not consistent in the translation of *pāša'*. The most common translations are: *asebeo* ("to act unpiously"); *aphistemi* ("to go away, withdraw"); *anomos* ("lawless"); and *hamartia* ("sin"). The KJV gives these senses: "transgress; revolt; rebel."

B. Noun.

peša' (פֶּשַׁע, 6588), "transgression; guilt; punishment; offering." A cognate of this word appears in Ugaritic. *Peša'* appears 93 times and in all periods of biblical Hebrew.

Basically, this noun signifies willful deviation from, and therefore rebellion against, the path of godly living. This emphasis is especially prominent in Amos 2:4: "For three transgressions of Judah, and for four, I will not turn away the punishment thereof; because they have despised the law of the Lord, and have not kept his commandments, and their lies caused them to err, after the which their fathers have walked." Such a willful rebellion from a prescribed or agreed-upon path may be perpetrated against another man: " . . . Jacob answered and said to Laban, What is my trespass? what is my sin, that thou hast so hotly pursued after me?" (Gen. 31:36—the first occurrence of the word). Jacob is asking what he has done by way of violating or not keeping his responsibility (contract) with Laban. A nation can sin in this sense against another nation: "For three transgressions of Damascus, and for four . . . because they have threshed Gilead with threshing instruments of iron" (Amos 1:3). Usually, however, *peša'* has immediate reference to one's relationship to God.

This word sometimes represents the guilt of such a transgression: "I am clean, without [guilt of] transgression, I am innocent; neither is there iniquity in me" (Job 33:9).

Peša' can signify the punishment for transgression: "And a host was given him against the daily sacrifice by reason of transgression . . ." (Dan. 8:12); "How long shall be the vision concerning the daily sacrifice, and [punishment for] the transgression of desolation, to give both the sanctuary and the host to be trodden under foot?" (Dan. 8:13).

Finally, in Mic. 6:7 *peša'* signifies an offering for "transgression": "Shall I give my first-born for my transgression [NASB, "for my rebellious acts"] . . . ?"

TREE

ēṣ (עֵץ, 6086), "tree; wood; timber; stick; stalk." This word has cognates in Ugaritic, Akkadian, Phoenician, Aramaic ('ē'), and Arabic. It occurs about 325 times in biblical Hebrew and in all periods.

In its first biblical appearance *ēṣ* is used as a collective noun representing all trees bearing fruit (Gen. 1:11). In Exod. 9:25 the word means "tree" indiscriminately: " . . . And the hail smote every herb of the field, and brake every tree of the field." God forbids Israel to destroy the orchards around besieged cities: "When thou shalt besiege a city a long time, in making war against it to take it, thou shalt not destroy the trees . . . : for thou mayest eat of them [literally, " . . . its tree or orchard . . . for you may eat from it . . ."] . . . " (Deut. 20:19).

This word may signify a single "tree," as it does in Gen. 2:9: " . . . The tree of life also in the midst of the garden, and the tree of knowledge of good and evil."

This word may be used of the genus "tree." So Isa. 41:19 lists the olive "tree" and the box "tree" in the midst of a long list of various species of trees.

Ēṣ can mean "wood." Thus, Deut. 16:21 should read: "You shall not plant for yourself an Asherah of any kind of wood" (NASB, "any kind of tree"). This word can represent "wood" as a material from which things are constructed, as a raw material to be carved: " . . . And in carving of timber, to work in all manner of workmanship" (Exod. 31:5). Large unpro-

cessed pieces of "wood or timber" are also signified by *ēṣ*: "Go up to the mountain, and bring wood [timber], and build the house . . ." (Hag. 1:8). The end product of wood already processed and fashioned into something may be indicated by *ēṣ*: "And upon whatsoever any of them, when they are dead, doth fall, it shall be unclean; whether it be any vessel of wood . . ." (Lev. 11:32). This word means "stick" or "piece of wood" in Ezek. 37:16: " . . . Thou son of man, take thee one stick, and write upon it. . . . " This may also refer to a "pole" or "gallows": " . . . Within three days shall Pharaoh lift up thy head from off thee, and shall hang thee on a tree [gallows or pole] . . . " (Gen. 40:19). *Ēṣ* once means "stalk": "But she had brought them up to the roof of the house, and hid them with the stalks of flax, which she had laid in order upon the roof" (Josh. 2:6).

'ayil (אַיִל, 352), "large, mighty tree." This word occurs 4 times and only in poetical passages. This does not mean a particular genus or species of tree but merely a large, mighty tree: "For they shall be ashamed of the [mighty trees] [KJV, RSV, NASB, "oaks"] which ye have desired . . . " (Isa. 1:29—the first biblical occurrence).

ēlôn (אֵלוֹן, 436), "large tree." This noun is probably related to *'ayil*, "large tree." *Ēlôn* occurs 10 times and only in relation to places of worship. It may well be that these were all ancient cultic sites. The word does not represent a particular genus or species of tree but, like the noun to which it is related, simply a "big tree": "Gaal spoke again and said, Look, men are coming down from the center of the land, and one company is coming from the direction of the Diviners' oak [KJV, "Meonenim"; NASB, "oak"]" (Judg. 9:37, RSV). Judg. 9:6 speaks of the "tree of the pillar" (KJV, "plain of the pillar") in Shechem where the men of Shechem and Beth-millo made Abimelech king.

TO TRESPASS

A. Verb.

mā'al (מָעַל, 4603), "to trespass, act unfaithfully." This verb is not very common in Hebrew, biblical or rabbinic. It occurs 35 times in the Hebrew Old Testament, particularly in late Hebrew. Translations may give a separate translation of the verb and the noun *ma'al*, but most combine them into one phrase in which the verb takes the meaning of "to act" or "to commit"—e.g., Josh. 7:1: "But the children of Israel committed [*mā'al*] a trespass [*ma'al*] in the accursed thing . . . " (KJV); "But the Israelites acted unfaithfully" (NIV). Some versions give the sense more freely: "But the people of Israel broke faith" (RSV); "But the Israelites defied the ban" (NEB).

The first occurrence of the verb (together with the noun) is found in Lev. 5:15: "If a soul commit a trespass, and sin through ignorance...." The sense of the verb is similar to the verb "to sin." In fact, in the next chapter the verb for "to sin" and *mā'al* are used together: "If a soul sin, and commit a trespass against the Lord, and lie unto his neighbor..." (Lev. 6:2). The combining of these two usages in Leviticus is significant. First, it shows that the verb may be a synonym for "to sin." *Mā'al* has basically this meaning in Lev. 5:15, since the sin is here out of ignorance instead of a deliberate act of treachery. Second, the meaning of *mā'al* is further expressed by a verb indicating the intent of being unfaithful to one's neighbor for personal profit ("commit a trespass against the Lord, and lie unto his neighbor...").

The offense is against God, even when one acts unfaithfully against one's neighbor. In 2 Chron. 29:6 we read: "For our fathers have trespassed, and done that which was evil in the eyes of the Lord our God, and have forsaken him..."; and Daniel prayed: "... Because of their trespass that they have trespassed against thee" (Dan. 9:7; cf. NIV, "... because of our unfaithfulness to you").

In view of the additional significance of "treachery," many versions translate the verb "to act unfaithfully" or "to act treacherously" instead of "to transgress" or "to commit a trespass." Both the verb and the noun have strongly negative overtones, which the translator must convey in English. When God spoke to Ezekiel: "Son of man, when the land sinneth against me by trespassing grievously, then will I stretch out mine hand upon it, and... cut off man and beast from it" (Ezek. 14:13), He communicated also His displeasure with Israel's rebellious, treacherous attitude. This is communicated in other versions: "Son of man, if a country sins against me by being unfaithful..." (NIV); "Son of man, if a country sins against Me by committing unfaithfulness..." (NASB).

The verb *mā'al* generally expresses man's unfaithfulness to God (Lev. 26:40; Deut. 32:51; 2 Chron. 12:2; Ezra 10:2; Ezek. 14:13). The word further signifies man's unfaithfulness to his fellow man; particularly it is illustrative of unfaithfulness in marriage: "If any man's wife go aside, and commit a trespass against him, And a man lie with her carnally..." (Num. 5:12–13). In this sense also must Lev. 6:2 be understood: "If anyone sins and is unfaithful to the Lord by deceiving his neighbor about something entrusted to him..." (NIV).

In the Septuagint we find these translations: *athetein* ("to nullify; reject; commit an offense"); *asunthetein* ("to be faithless"); and *aphistaveiv* ("to mislead; withdraw"). Modern versions set forth more explicitly the overt nature of the sin than the KJV ("trespass; transgress"): RSV, NASB, NIV, "act or be unfaithful"; RSV, NASB, "to break faith."

B. Noun.

ma'al (מַעַל, 4604), "trespass; unfaithful, treacherous act." This noun is used 29 times in biblical Hebrew. In addition to the primary sense of "trespass," given in KJV, there may be an indication of the motivation through which the sin was committed. Most of the usages support the idea of "faithlessness, treachery." It is an act committed by a person who knows better but who, for selfish motives, acts in bad faith. The story of Achan bears out the attitude of treachery (Josh. 7:1). Joshua challenged Israel not to follow the example of Achan: "Did not Achan the son of Zerah commit [*mā'al*] a trespass [*ma'al*] in the accursed thing, and wrath fell on all the congregation of Israel?" (Josh. 22:20).

In 2 Chron. 29:19 the "faithlessness" was committed against God: "Moreover all the vessels which king Ahaz in his reign did cast away in his transgression...." *Ma'al* also appears in Ezra 9:2: "... Yea, the hand of the princes and rulers hath been chief in this trespass."

TRIBE

A. Nouns.

maṭṭeh (מַטֶּה, 4294), "staff; rod; shaft; branch; tribe." This noun is a distinctively Hebrew word. It occurs 251 times; the first usage is in Gen. 38:18: "And he said, What pledge shall I give thee? And she said, Thy signet, and thy bracelets, and thy staff that is in thine hand." The word appears most frequently in Numbers and Joshua, generally with the meaning "tribe" in these books.

The basic meaning of *maṭṭeh* is "staff." The use of the "staff" was in shepherding. Judah was a shepherd and gave his "staff" to his daughter-in-law, Tamar, as a pledge of sending her a kid of the flock (Gen. 38:17–18). Moses was a shepherd when he saw the vision of the burning bush and when the Lord turned his "staff" into a snake as a sign of His presence and power with Moses' mission (Exod. 4:2ff.). His "staff" figured prominently throughout the wilderness journeys and was known as "the staff of God" because of the miraculous power connected with it: "And Moses said unto Joshua, Choose us out men, and go out, fight with Amalek: tomorrow I will stand on the top of the hill with the rod of God in mine hand" (Exod. 17:9). The "staff" was also a token of authority. The Egyptian magicians had "staffs" as symbols of their authority over the magical realm by which they duplicated several miracles (Exod. 7:12). Aaron had a "rod," which alone sprouted and put forth buds, whereas eleven rods "from all their leaders according to their father's household" (Num. 17:2, NASB) did not put forth buds.

The "staff" further signifies authority or power over another nation: "For thou hast broken the yoke of his burden, and the staff of his shoulder, the rod of his oppressor, as in the day of Midian" (Isa. 9:4). God gave to Assyria His "staff"; they received His authority, divine permission, to wield the sword, to plunder, and to destroy: "O Assyrian, the rod of mine anger, and the staff in their hand is mine indignation. I will send him against a hypocritical nation, and against the people of my wrath will I give him a charge, to take the spoil, and to take the prey, and to tread them down like the mire of the streets" (Isa. 10:5–6). The psalmist, in his expectation that the messianic rule included God's authority and judgment over the Gentiles, views the messianic rule as a strong "staff": "The Lord shall send the rod of thy strength out of Zion: rule thou in the midst of thine enemies" (Ps. 110:2). Similarly, the prophet Ezekiel said, "Fire is gone out of a *rod* of her branches, which hath devoured her fruit, so that she hath no strong *rod* to be a scepter to rule" (Ezek. 19:14). The figurative usage of *maṭṭeh* occurs in the idiom *maṭṭeh-leḥem*, "staff of bread." This poetic idiom refers to the food supply, and it is found mainly in Ezekiel: "Moreover he said unto me, Son of man, behold, I will break the staff of bread in Jerusalem: and they shall eat [rationed food in anxiety and drink rationed water in despair]" (Ezek. 4:16; cf. 14:13).

A derived sense of *maṭṭeh* is "tribe," which is used as many as 183 times. The "tribes" of Israel are each designated as *maṭṭeh:* "And these are the countries which the children of Israel inherited in the land of Canaan, which Eleazar the priest, and Joshua the son of Nun, and the heads of the fathers of the tribes of the children of Israel, distributed for inheritance to them" (Josh. 14:1). It is possible that the *maṭṭeh* ("staff"), as a symbol of authority, first applied to the tribal leader and thereafter by extension to the whole "tribe."

The several meanings of *maṭṭeh* are reflected in the Septuagint: *phule* ("tribe; nation; people") and *rabdos* ("rod; staff; scepter").

šēbeṭ (שֵׁבֶט, 7626), "tribe; rod." In modern Hebrew this word mainly denotes "tribe" as a technical term. In Akkadian the related verb *šabaṭu* signifies "to smite," and the noun *šabbiṭu* means "rod" or "scepter." A synonym of the Hebrew *šēbeṭ* is *maṭṭeh*, also "rod" or "tribe," and what is applicable to *maṭṭeh* is also relevant to *šēbeṭ*.

The "rod" as a tool is used by the shepherd (Lev. 27:32) and the teacher (2 Sam. 7:14). It is a symbol of authority in the hands of a ruler, whether it is the scepter (Amos 1:5, 8) or an instrument of warfare and oppression: "Thou shalt break them with a rod of iron; thou shalt dash them in pieces like a potter's vessel" (Ps. 2:9; cf. Zech. 10:11). The symbolic element comes to expression in a description of the messianic rule: "But with righteousness shall he judge the poor, and reprove with equity for the meek of the earth: and he shall smite the earth with the rod of his mouth . . ." (Isa. 11:4).

The word *šēbeṭ* is most frequently used (143 times) to denote a "tribe," a division in a nation. It is the preferred term for the twelve "tribes" of Israel (Gen. 49:16; Exod. 28:21). Jeremiah referred to all of Israel as the "tribe": "The portion of Jacob is not like them; for he is the former of all things: and Israel is the rod of his inheritance: the Lord of hosts is his name" (51:19).

The Septuagint translations are: *phule* ("tribe; nation; people"); *rabdos* ("rod; staff"); and *skeptron* ("scepter; tribe").

B. Verb.

nāṭāh (נָטָה, 5186), "to stretch out, spread out, extend." This root occurs in biblical, mishnaic, and modern Hebrew and in Arabic with the same meaning. One occurrence of *nāṭāh* is in Exod. 9:22: "Stretch forth thine hand toward heaven. . . ."

TO TURN

A. Verbs.

hāpak (הָפַךְ, 2015), "to turn, overturn, change, transform, turn back." A common word throughout the various periods of Hebrew, this term occurs in other Semitic languages, including ancient Akkadian. It is found almost 100 times in biblical Hebrew. Used for the first time in the biblical text in Gen. 3:24, the Hebrew verb form there indicates reflexive action: ". . . A flaming sword which turned every way [NAB, "revolving"; NEB, "whirling"] . . ."

In its simplest meaning, *hāpak* expresses the turning from one side to another, such as "turning" one's back (Josh. 7:8), or "as a man wipeth a dish, wiping it, and turning it upside down" (2 Kings 21:13). Similarly, Hosea refers to Israel as being "a cake not turned" (Hos. 7:8). The meaning of "transformation" or "change" is vividly illustrated in the story of Saul's encounter with the Spirit of God. Samuel promised that Saul would "be changed into another man" (1 Sam. 10:6, JB), and when the Spirit came on him, "God changed his heart" (1 Sam. 10:9, JB). Other examples of change are the "changing" of Pharaoh's mind (Exod. 14:5; literally, "the heart of Pharaoh... was turned"); the "turning" of Aaron's rod into a serpent (Exod. 7:15); dancing "turned" to mourning (Lam. 5:14); water "turned" into blood (Exod. 7:17); and the sun "turned" to darkness and the moon to blood (Joel 2:31). Ps. 41:3 presents a difficult translation problem in its use of *hāpak*. Literally, it reads: "All his bed you [Yahweh] change in his sickness." In view of the poetic parallelism involved, restoration of health must be meant. Thus, the RSV translates: "In his sickness thou healest all his infirmities." Perhaps only a refreshing of the bed is meant, so the NEB translates: "He turns his bed when he is ill."

The KJV rendering of Isa. 60:5 sounds strange to our modern ears: "The abundance of the sea shall be converted unto thee...." A slight improvement is given by the RSV, which reads: "The abundance of the sea shall be turned to you." The meaning is best captured by the JB: "The riches of the sea shall be lavished upon you."

sābab (סָבַב, 5437), "to turn, go around, turn around (change direction)." This verb occurs only in Hebrew (including post-biblical Hebrew) and Ugaritic. Nouns using these radicals appear in Arabic and Akkadian. Biblical Hebrew attests the word in all periods and about 160 times.

Basically this verb represents a circular movement—"to take a turning." First, it refers to such movement in general. The first occurrence of *sābab* having this emphasis is in Gen. 42:24, where Joseph "turned himself about" from his brothers and wept. Here the verb does not tell the precise direction of his departure, only that he left their presence. Similarly, when Samuel was told that Saul went to Carmel and "is gone about, and passed on, and gone down to Gilgal" (1 Sam. 15:12), we are not told that he reversed direction in order to get from his origin to Carmel and Gilgal. God led Israel out of the way (by an out-of-the-way route) when He took them into the Promised Land. He wanted to avoid having them face war with the Philistines, an event that was unavoidable if they proceeded directly north from Egypt to Palestine. Therefore, He led them through the wilderness—a back route into the land: "But God led the people about, through the way of the wil-

derness of the Red Sea..." (Exod. 13:18). Perhaps one of the passages where this meaning is clearest is Prov. 26:14, which speaks of the "turning" of a door on its hinges. An extension of this meaning occurs in 1 Sam. 5:8-9, "to remove, to take away": "And they answered, Let the ark of the God of Israel be carried about [taken away] unto Gath. And they carried the ark of the God of Israel about thither" (cf. 2 Kings 16:18).

A second emphasis of *sābab* is "to go around," in the sense of to proceed or be arranged in a circle. Joseph tells his family: "... Lo, my sheaf arose, and also stood upright; and, behold, your sheaves stood round about, and made obeisance to my sheaf" (Gen. 37:7). They moved so as to surround his sheaf. This is the action pictured when Israel besieged Jericho, except with the further nuance of encircling in a processional and religious march: "And ye shall compass the city, all ye men of war, and go round about the city once" (Josh. 6:3). "To travel" and "to return" are used together to represent traveling a circuit. It is said of Samuel that he used to go annually "in circuit" (1 Sam. 7:16). Another variation of this emphasis is "to go around" a territory in order to avoid crossing through it: "And they journeyed from mount Hor by the way of the Red Sea, to compass [go around] the land of Edom: and the soul of the people was much discouraged because of the way" (Num. 21:4).

Sābab is also used of the completion of this movement, the state of literally or figuratively surrounding something or someone. The very first biblical occurrence of the word carries this force (according to many scholars): "The name of the first is Pison: that is it which compasseth [flows around] the whole land of Havilah..." (Gen. 2:11). Judg. 16:2, where the Gazites "compassed [Samson] in, and laid wait for him all night in the gate of the city," represents another occurrence of this nuance. When David spoke of the cords (as a trap) of Sheol "surrounding" him (2 Sam. 22:6), he meant that they actually touched him and held him fast. *Sābab* can be used of sitting down around a table. So Samuel told Jesse to fetch David, "for we will not sit down till he come hither" (1 Sam. 16:11).

A third use of this verb is "to change direction." This can be a change of direction *toward:* "Neither shall the inheritance remove from one tribe to another tribe..." (Num. 36:9); the usual direction of passing on an inheritance is down family lines, and God's commandment that the daughters of Zelophehad marry within their father's families would make certain that this movement of things not be interrupted. This emphasis appears more clearly in 1 Sam. 18:11: "And David [escaped] out of his presence twice"; it is certain that David is putting as much space between himself and Saul as possible. He is "running away or turning away" (cf. 1 Sam. 22:17). *Sābab* may also refer to a change of direction, as in Num. 34:4: "And your border shall turn. . . ."

There are three special nuances under this emphasis. First, the verb may mean "to roam through" as a scout looking for water: ". . . And they fetched a compass [made a circuit] of seven days' journey: and there was no water for the host, and for the cattle that followed them" (2 Kings 3:9). Some scholars suggest that this is the idea expressed in Gen. 2:11—that the Pison meandered through Havilah rather than flowed around it. Second, *sabab* may be used of "turning something over" to someone. So Adonijah said of Solomon: ". . . The kingdom was mine, . . . howbeit the kingdom is turned about, and is become my brother's . . ." (1 Kings 2:15). Third, *sabab* may be used of "changing or turning one thing into another": "And the land shall be turned as a plain from Geba to Rimmon south of Jerusalem . . ." (Zech. 14:10).

B. Nouns.

sābîb (סָבִיב, 5439), "area round about; circuit." This word appears about 336 times in biblical Hebrew. The word can be used as a noun, but it usually occurs as an adverb or preposition. In 1 Chron. 11:8 *sābîb* refers to the "parts round about": "And he built the city round about, even from Millo round about. . . ." The word may also be used for "circuits": ". . . And the wind returneth again according to his circuits" (Eccl. 1:6). The first biblical appearance of the word is in Gen. 23:17, and it refers to "within the circuit of."

Other nouns are related to the verb *sābab*. *Sibbāh* and *nᵉsibbāh* both refer to "turn of affairs"; *sibbāh* is found in 1 Kings 12:15 and *nᵉsibbāh* in 2 Chron. 10:15. *Mûsab* occurs once with the meaning of "circular passage": ". . . For the winding about of the house went still upward round about the house . . ." (Ezek. 41:7). *Mēsab* occurs 4 times, and it refers to "that which surrounds or is round." *Mēsab* refers to a "round table" (Song of Sol. 1:12) and to "places round about" Jerusalem (2 Kings 23:5).

TO TURN TOWARDS, TURN BACK

A. Verb.

pānāh (פָּנָה, 6437), "to turn towards, turn back, turn around, attach to, pass away, make clear." This verb also appears in Syriac and post-biblical Hebrew and post-biblical Aramaic. Related verbs which have the same radicals with a somewhat different meaning occur in Arabic and Ethiopic. The Bible attests *pānāh* about 155 times and in all periods.

Most occurrences of this verb carry the sense "to turn in another direction"; this is a verb of either physical or mental motion. Used of physical motion, the word signifies turning so as to move in another direction: "Ye have compassed this mountain long enough: turn you northward" (Deut. 2:3). *Pānāh* can also mean to turn so as to face or look at something or someone: "And it came to pass, as Aaron spake unto the whole congregation of the children of Israel, that they looked toward the wilderness . . ." (Exod. 16:10). "Turning toward" something may also signify looking at, or seeing it: "Remember thy servants, Abraham, Isaac, and Jacob; look not unto [do not see] the stubbornness of this people, nor to their wickedness, nor to their sin" (Deut. 9:27). A further extension in meaning is seen in Hag. 1:9, where *pānāh* means "to look for," or to expect: "Ye looked for much, and, lo, it came to little. . . ."

Another focus of meaning is "to turn back" so as to see. This is found in Josh. 8:20: "When the men of Ai turned back and looked, behold . . ." (NASB). In other passages the verb means "to turn around," in the sense of to look in every direction. So Moses "looked this way and that way, and when he saw there was no man, he slew the Egyptian, and hid him in the sand" (Exod. 2:12).

In the sense of "to turn around" *pānāh* is used of changing one's direction so as to leave the scene. So "the men turned their faces from thence, and went toward Sodom . . ." (Gen. 18:22—the first biblical occurrence of the verb).

Used of intellectual and spiritual turning, this verb signifies attaching oneself to something. God commanded Israel: "Turn ye not unto idols, nor make to yourselves molten gods . . ." (Lev. 19:4); they should not shift their attention to and attach themselves to idols. In an even stronger use this verb represents dependence on someone: ". . . Which bringeth their iniquity to remembrance, when they shall look after [depend on] them . . ." (Ezek. 29:16). "To turn towards" sometimes means to pay attention to someone. Job tells his friends: "Now . . . look upon me; for it is evident unto you if I lie" (Job 6:28).

In a still different emphasis the word connotes the "passing away" of something, such as the turning away of a day: "And Isaac went out to meditate in the field at the eventide ... "—he went out "at the turning of the evening" (Gen. 24:63). Similarly the Bible speaks of the dawn as the "turning of the morning" (Exod. 14:27). The "turning of the day" is the end of the day (Jer. 6:4).

Used in a military context, *pānāh* can signify giving up fighting or fleeing before one's enemies. Because of Achan's sin the Lord was not with Israel at the battle of Ai: "Therefore the children of Israel could not stand before their enemies, but turned their backs before their enemies, because they were accursed ... " (Josh. 7:12).

In the intensive stem the verb means "to remove," to take away: "The Lord hath taken away thy judgments, he hath cast out thine enemy ... " (Zeph. 3:15). "To clear a house" (to set things in order) is often the means by which conditions are prepared for guests: "Come in, thou blessed of the Lord; wherefore standest thou without? for I have prepared the house ... " (Gen. 24:31). Another nuance is "to prepare" a road for a victory march; Isaiah says: "Prepare ye the way of the Lord, make straight in the desert a highway for our God" (Isa. 40:3; cf. Matt. 3:3).

B. Nouns.
pinnāh (פִּנָּה, 6438), "corner." This noun occurs 30 times in the Old Testament. The word refers to "corners" in Exod. 27:2: "And thou shalt make the horns of it upon the four corners thereof.... " In 2 Kings 14:13 the word refers to a corner-tower, and in Judg. 20:2 *pinnāh* is used figuratively of a "chief" as the "corner" or defense of the people.

The noun *pānîm* is also related to the verb *pānāh*. It occurs 2,100 times to refer to the "face" of something. An early occurrence of the word is in Gen. 17:3.

C. Adjective.
penîmî (פְּנִימִי, 6442), "inner." This adjective occurs about 33 times, and it refers to a part of a building, usually a temple. One occurrence is in 1 Kings 6:27: "And he set the cherubim within the inner house.... "

D. Adverb.
penîmāh (פְּנִימָה, 6441), "within." This word occurs about 12 times. One appearance is in 1 Kings 6:18: "And the cedar of the house within was carved with knobs and open flowers.... " Here the word refers to the inside of the house.

U

TO BE UNCLEAN
A. Verb.
ṭāmē' (טָמֵא, 2930), "to be unclean." This root is limited to Hebrew, Aramaic, and Arabic. The verb occurs 160 times in biblical Hebrew and mainly in Leviticus, as in Lev. 11:26: "The carcases of every beast which divideth the hoof, and is not clovenfooted, nor cheweth the cud, are unclean unto you: every one that toucheth them shall be unclean." *Ṭāmē'* is the opposite of *ṭāhēr*, "to be pure."

B. Noun.
ṭum'āh (טֻמְאָה, 2932), "uncleanness." This noun is derived from *ṭāmē'*. *Ṭum'āh* occurs 37 times in biblical Hebrew. The word occurs in Num. 5:19: "And the priest shall charge her by an oath, and say unto the woman, If no man have lain with thee, and if thou hast not gone aside to uncleanliness with another instead of thine husband, be thou free from this bitter water that causeth the curse." Here the word refers to sexual "uncleanness." *Ṭum'āh* occurs twice in Lev. 16:16 and refers to ethical and religious "uncleanness."

C. Adjective.
ṭāmē' (טָמֵא, 2931), "unclean." This adjective occurs 89 times in the Old Testament. The frequency of the word is high in Leviticus. Its first occurrence is also in Leviticus: "Or if a soul touch any unclean thing, whether it be a carcase of an unclean beast, or a carcase of unclean cattle, or the carcase of unclean creeping things, and if it be hidden from him; he also shall be unclean, and guilty" (5:2).

The usage of *ṭāmē'* in the Old Testament resembles that of *ṭāhôr*, "pure." First, uncleanness is a state of being. The leper was compelled to announce his uncleanness wherever he went (Lev. 13:45); however, even here there is a religious overtone, in that his uncleanness was ritual. Hence, it is more appropriate to recognize that the second usage is most basic. *Ṭāmē'* in the religio-cultic sense is a technical term denoting a state of being ceremonially unfit. Animals, carcases, unclean people, and objects conveyed the impurity to those who touched them: "And whatsoever the unclean person toucheth shall be unclean; and the soul that toucheth it shall lie unclean until even" (Num. 19:22). The impurity could also be brought about by a seminal issue (Lev. 15:2) or a menstrual period (Lev. 15:25), and whatever the unclean touched was also rendered "unclean."

The Septuagint translations are: *akathartos* ("impure; unclean") and *miaino* ("stain; defile"). The KJV gives these translations: "unclean; defiled; polluted."

TO UNDERSTAND

A. Verbs.

śakal (שָׂכַל, 7919), "to be prudent, act wisely, give attention to, ponder, prosper." This word, which is common to both ancient and modern Hebrew, is found approximately 75 times in the text of the Hebrew Bible. Its first use in the text, in Gen. 3:6, contributes to an interesting paradox, for while the forbidden fruit was "to be desired to make one wise," it was a very unwise thing to take it!

The basic meaning of *śakal* seems to be "to look at, to give attention to," as illustrated in this parallelism: "That they may see, and know, and consider, and understand ..." (Isa. 41:20). From this develops the connotation of insight, intellectual comprehension: "Let not the wise man glory in his wisdom ... But let him that glorieth glory in this, that he understandeth and knoweth me ... " (Jer. 9:23–24). As here, it is frequently used along with and in parallelism to the Hebrew *yāda'*, "to know" (primarily experientially). As is true of *ḥakam*, "to be wise," *śakal* never concerns abstract prudence, but acting prudently: "Therefore the prudent shall keep silence ... " (Amos 5:13); " ... He hath left off to be wise ... " (Ps. 36:3).

bîn (בִּין, 995), "to understand, be able, deal wisely, consider, pay attention to, regard, notice, discern, perceive, inquire." This verb, which occurs 126 times in biblical Hebrew, has cognates in Ugaritic, Arabic, Ethiopic, late Aramaic, and Syriac. *Bîn* appears in all periods of biblical Hebrew.

Bîn appears in Jer. 9:12 with the meaning "to understand": "Who is the wise man, that may understand this?" In Job 6:30 the word means "to discern," and in Deut. 32:7 it means "to consider."

B. Nouns.

bînāh (בִּינָה, 998), "understanding." *Bînāh* appears 37 times and in all periods of biblical

Hebrew even though it belongs primarily to the sphere of wisdom and wisdom literature.

This noun represents the "act of understanding": "And in all matters of wisdom and understanding, that the king inquired of them, he found them ten times better than all the magicians ... " (Dan. 1:20).

Elsewhere *bînāh* signifies the faculty "understanding": " ... The spirit of my understanding causeth me to answer" (Job 20:3).

In other passages the object of knowledge, in the sense of what one desires to know, is indicated by *bînāh*: "Keep therefore and do them [God's laws]: for this is your wisdom and your understanding in the sight of the nations, which shall hear all these statutes ... " (Deut. 4:6; cf. 1 Chron. 22:12). God's law, therefore, is wisdom and "understanding"—what one should know.

This word is sometimes personified: "Yea, if thou criest after knowledge, and liftest up thy voice for understanding; if thou seekest her as silver, and searchest for her as for hid treasures ... " (Prov. 2:3–4).

tᵉbûnāh (תְּבוּנָה, 8394), "understanding." This word, which occurs 42 times, is also a wisdom term. Like *bînāh*, it represents the act (Job 26:12), faculty (Exod. 31:3), object (Prov. 2:3), and personification of wisdom (Prov. 8:1).

maśkîl (מַשְׂכִּיל, 4905), "didactic psalm(?)." This noun form, derived from *śakal*, is found in the title of 13 psalms and also in Ps. 47:7. Scholars are not agreed on the significance of this term, but on the basis of the general meaning of *śakal*, such psalms must have been considered didactic or teaching psalms.

UPRIGHT

A. Adjective.

yāšar (יָשָׁר, 3477), "upright; right; righteous; just." This adjective occurs first in Exodus in the idiom "right in his eyes": "[He] said, If thou wilt diligently hearken to the voice of the Lord thy God, and wilt do that which is right in his sight, and wilt give ear to his commandments, and keep all his statutes, I will put none of these diseases upon thee, which I have brought upon the Egyptians: for I am the Lord that healeth thee" (Exod. 15:26). Its usage is infrequent in the Pentateuch and in the prophetical writings. Predominantly a poetic term, *yāšar* also occurs idiomatically ("to do what is right") in the historical books; cf. 1 Kings 15:5: "Because David did that which was right in the eyes of the Lord, and turned not aside from any thing that he commanded him all the days of his life, save only in the matter of Uriah the Hittite."

The basic meaning is the root meaning "to

be straight" in the sense of "to be level." The legs of the creatures in Ezekiel's vision were straight (Ezek. 1:7). The Israelites designated an easy road for traveling as a "level road." It had few inclines and declines compared to the mountain roads (cf. Jer. 31:9: "They shall come with weeping, and with supplications will I lead them: I will cause them to walk by the rivers of water in a straight way, wherein they shall not stumble: for I am a father to Israel, and Ephraim is my firstborn").

Yāšār with the meaning "right" pertains to things and to abstracts. Samuel promised himself to instruct God's people in "the good and the right way" (1 Sam. 12:23). Nehemiah thanked God for having given just ordinances: "Thou camest down also upon mount Sinai, and spakest with them from heaven, and gavest them right judgments, and true laws, good statutes and commandments" (Neh. 9:13). Based on His revelation God expected His people to please Him in being obedient to Him: "And thou shalt do that which is right and good in the sight of the Lord: that it may be well with thee, and that thou mayest go in and possess the good land which the Lord sware unto thy fathers" (Deut. 6:18).

When *yāšār* pertains to people, it is best translated "just" or "upright." God is the standard of uprightness for His people: "Good and upright is the Lord: therefore will he teach sinners in the way" (Ps. 25:8). His word (Ps. 33:4), judgments (Ps. 19:9), and ways (Hos. 14:9) reveal His uprightness and are a blessing to His people. The believer follows Him in being "upright" in heart: "Be glad in the Lord, and rejoice, ye righteous; and shout for joy, all ye that are upright in heart" (Ps. 32:11; cf. 7:10; 11:2). In their daily walk they manifest that they are walking on the narrow road: "The wicked have drawn out the sword, and have bent their bow, to cast down the poor and needy, and to slay

such as be of upright conversation" (Ps. 37:14). The "just" are promised God's blessing upon their lives (Prov. 11:10–11).

Finally, *yāšār* is also the abstract "rightness," especially when the Hebrew word has the definite article (*hayyāšār*, "the right"): "Hear this, I pray you, ye heads of the house of Jacob, and princes of the house of Israel, that abhor judgment, and pervert all equity [all that is right]" (Mic. 3:9).

The Septuagint translations are: *arestos* ("pleasing"); *dikaios* ("upright; just; righteous"); *euthes* ("upright"); and *euthus* ("straight").

B. Verb.

yāšar (יָשַׁר, 3474), "to be straight, be smooth, be right." This verb, which occurs rarely, has many derivatives in the Bible.

In Akkadian the verb *išaru* signifies "to be straight, bring in order," and the noun *mišarum* denotes justice and an upright way of life. The Hebrew word has many related words in other Semitic languages (Phoenician, Ugaritic) and even in Egyptian.

One occurrence of the verb is in 1 Chron. 13:4: "And all the congregation said that they would do so: for the thing was right in the eyes of all the people." In this usage *yāšar* has the sense of being pleasing or agreeable. In Hab. 2:4 the word implies an ethical uprightness.

C. Nouns.

yošer (יֹשֶׁר, 3476), "straightness." This noun occurs about 15 times. One occurrence is in Prov. 2:13: "Who leave the paths of uprightness, to walk in the ways of darkness."

Other nouns occur less frequently. *Yišrāh* means "uprightness" and occurs once (1 Kings 3:6). The noun *yᵉšurûn* is an honorific title for Israel (Deut. 32:15; 33:5). *Mîšôr* means "level place, uprightness." In 1 Kings 20:23 *mîšôr* refers to "level country"; in Isa. 11:4 the word refers to "uprightness": " . . . And reprove with equity for the meek of the earth. . . . "

V

VESSEL

kᵉlî (כְּלִי, 3627), "vessel; receptacle; stuff; clothing; utensil; tool; instrument; ornament or jewelry; armor or weapon; male sex organ." A cognate to this word appears in Akkadian. *Kᵉlî* appears in biblical Hebrew about 320 times and in all periods.

This word is used of "receptacles" of various kinds used for storing and transporting. Thus, Jacob said to Laban: "Whereas thou hast searched through all my stuff [literally, receptacles], what hast thou found of all thy household stuff [literally, from all the receptacles of thy house]?" (Gen. 31:37). Such "receptacles" may be made of wood (Lev. 11:32) or potsherd or clay (Lev. 6:28). They may be used to hold documents (Jer. 32:14), wine, oil, fruits (Jer. 40:10), food (Ezek. 4:9), beverage (Ruth 2:9), or bread (1 Sam. 9:7). Even a shepherd's bag is a *keli* (1 Sam. 17:40). In 1 Sam. 17:22 the word is used of baggage, or "receptacles" (his shepherd's bag?) and what is in them: "And David left his carriage in the hand of the [baggage keeper]...." The sailors on the ship in which Jonah sailed "cast forth the wares [cargo]... into the sea, to lighten it of them" (Jon. 1:5).

Ships are called "receptacles," presumably because they can hold people: "That sendeth ambassadors by the sea, even in vessels of bulrushes upon the waters..." (Isa. 18:2).

Keli can mean "clothing": "The woman shall not wear that which pertaineth unto a man, neither shall a man put on a woman's garment: for all that do so are abomination unto the Lord thy God" (Deut. 22:5).

The word may be used of various "vessels and utensils": "And the four tables were of hewn stone for the burnt offering...: whereupon also they laid the instruments wherewith they slew the burnt offering and the sacrifice" (Ezek. 40:42). In Gen. 45:20 this word refers to movable but large possessions: Pharaoh told Joseph to tell his brothers to take wagons and bring their family to Egypt, and "regard not your stuff; for the good of all the land of Egypt is yours." Thus in Exod. 27:19 the word represents all the furniture and utensils of the tabernacle (cf. Num. 3:8). Samuel warned Israel that the king on whom they insisted would organize them into levees (work crews) "to [plow] his ground, and to reap his harvest, and to make his instruments of war, and instruments of his chariots" (1 Sam. 8:12). More narrowly, *keli* may be used of oxen harnesses: "... Behold, here be oxen for burnt sacrifice, and threshing instruments and other instruments of the oxen for wood" (2 Sam. 24:22).

This word may be used of various "implements or tools": "Simeon and Levi are brethren; instruments of cruelty are in their habitations" (Gen. 49:5). In Jer. 22:7 the word represents "tools" with which trees may be cut down: "And I will prepare destroyers against thee, every one with his weapons: and they shall cut down thy choice cedars, and cast them into the fire." Isaac told Esau to take his gear, his quiver, and his bow, "and go out to the field, and take me some venison" (Gen. 27:3).

Weapons for war are called "implements": "And they [the Israelites] went after them unto Jordan: and, lo, all the way was full of garments and vessels, which the Syrians had cast away in

their haste" (2 Kings 7:15). A bearer of implements is an armor-bearer (Judg. 9:54). A house of arms or an armory is referred to in 2 Kings 20:13.

In Amos 6:5 and such passages (2 Chron. 5:13; 7:6; 23:13; cf. Ps. 71:22) "musical instruments" are called *kelim*: "That chant to the sound of the viol, and invent to themselves instruments of music...."

Keli stands for various kinds of "precious ornaments": "And the servant brought forth jewels of silver, and jewels of gold, and raiment, and gave them to Rebekah..." (Gen. 24:53—the first biblical appearance of the word). Such "precious ornaments" adorned the typical bride: "I will greatly rejoice in the Lord, my soul shall be joyful in my God; for he hath clothed me with the garments of salvation, he hath covered me with the robe of righteousness, as a bridegroom decketh himself with ornaments, and as a bride adorneth herself with her jewels" (Isa. 61:10).

In 1 Sam. 21:5 *keli* may refer to the "male sex organ." This certainly makes more sense than if the word is rendered "vessels," since the matter under discussion is the ritualistic purity of David's men: "Of a truth women have been kept from us about these three days, since I came out, and the vessels [sex organs] of the young men are holy...."

VINEYARD

kerem (כֶּרֶם, 3754), "vineyard." This Hebrew word is related to other Semitic languages (Akkadian, *karmu*; Arabic, *karm*). The word is evenly distributed throughout the Old Testament and is used 92 times. The first occurrence is in Gen. 9:20.

Isaiah gives a vivid description of the work involved in the preparation, planting, and cultivation of a "vineyard" (Isa. 5:1–7). The "vineyard" was located on the slopes of a hill (Isa. 5:1). The soil was cleared of stones before the tender vines were planted (Isa. 5:2). A watchtower provided visibility over the "vineyard" (Isa. 5:2), and a winevat and place for crushing the grapes were hewn out of the rock (Isa. 5:2). When all the preparations were finished, the "vineyard" was ready and in a few years it was expected to produce crops. In the meantime the *kerem* required regular pruning (Lev. 25:3–4). The time between planting and the first crop was of sufficient import as to free the owner from military duty: "And what man is he that hath planted a vineyard, and hath not yet eaten of it?" (Deut. 20:6).

The harvest time was a period of hard work and great rejoicing. The enjoyment of the "vineyard" was a blessing of God: "And they shall build houses, and inhabit them; and they shall plant vineyards, and eat the fruit of them" (Isa. 65:21). The failure of the "vineyard" to produce or the transfer of ownership of one's "vineyard" was viewed as God's judgment: "Forasmuch therefore as your treading is upon the poor, and ye take from him burdens of wheat: ye have built houses of hewn stone, but ye shall not dwell in them; ye have planted pleasant vineyards, but ye shall not drink wine of them" (Amos 5:11; cf. Deut. 28:30).

The words "vineyard" and "olive grove" (zayit) are often found together in the biblical text. These furnished the two major permanent agricultural activities in ancient Israel, as both required much work and time before the crops came in. God promised that the ownership of the "vineyards" and orchards of the Canaanites was to go to His people as a blessing from Him (Deut. 6:11–12). God's judgment to Israel extended to the "vineyards." The rejoicing in the "vineyard" would cease (Isa. 16:10) and the carefully cultivated "vineyard" would be turned into a thicket with thorns and briers (cf. Isa. 32:12–13). The "vineyard" would be reduced to a hiding place of wild animals and a grazing place for goats and wild donkeys (Isa. 32:14). The postexilic hope lay in God's blessings on the agricultural activity of His people: "And I will bring again the captivity of my people of Israel, and they shall build the waste cities, and inhabit them; and they shall plant vineyards, and drink the wine thereof; they shall also make gardens, and eat the fruit of them" (Amos 9:14).

The "vineyards" were located mainly in the hill country and in the low-lying hill country. The Bible mentions the "vineyard" at Timnath (Judg. 14:5), Jezreel (1 Kings 21:1), the hill country of Samaria (Jer. 31:5), and even at En-gedi (Song of Sol. 1:14).

The metaphorical use of kerem allows the prophet Isaiah to draw an analogy between the "vineyard" and Israel: "For the vineyard of the Lord of hosts is the house of Israel . . ." (Isa. 5:7). It has also been suggested that the "vineyard" in the Song of Solomon is better understood metaphorically as "person": "Look not upon me, because I am black, because the sun hath looked upon me: my mother's children were angry with me; they made me the keeper of the vineyards; but mine own vineyard have I not kept" (Song of Sol. 1:6).

VIOLENCE

A. Noun.

hāmās (חָמָס, 2555), "violence; wrong; maliciousness." This word appears about 60 times and in all periods of biblical Hebrew.

Basically hāmās connotes the disruption of the divinely established order of things. It has a wide range of nuances within this legal sphere. The expression "a witness in the case of violent wrongdoing" means someone who bears witness in a case having to do with such an offense (cf. Deut. 19:16). In this context the truthfulness of the witness is not established except upon further investigation (Deut. 19:18). Once he was established as a false witness, the penalty for the crime concerning which he bore false witness was to be executed against the lair (cf. Deut. 19:19). In Exod. 23:1 Israel is admonished: " . . . Put not thine hand with the wicked to be an unrighteous witness," i.e., a witness who in accusing someone of a violent crime intends to see the accused punished severely.

Hāmās perhaps connotes a "violent wrongdoing" which has not been righted, the guilt of which lies on an entire area (its inhabitants) disrupting their relationship with God and thereby interfering with His blessings.

It is this latter sense which appears in the phrase "the earth was full of violent wrongdoing": "The earth also was corrupt before God, and the earth was filled with violence" (Gen. 6:11—the first occurrence of the word). Thus, in Gen. 16:5 Sarai summons God to judge between Abram and herself because he has not acted properly toward her keeping Hagar in submission: "My wrong [done me] be upon thee: I have given my maid into thy bosom; and when she saw that she had conceived, I was despised in her eyes: the Lord judge between me and thee." Abram as God's judge (in God's stead) accepts the correctness of her case and commits Hagar to Sarai's care to be dealt with properly.

B. Verb.

Hāmas means "to treat violently." This verb, which occurs 7 times in biblical Hebrew, has cognates in Aramaic, Akkadian, and Arabic. This verb appears in Jer. 22:3 with the meaning of "to do no violence": " . . . And do no wrong, do no violence to the stranger, the fatherless, nor the widow, neither shed innocent blood in this place."

VIRGIN

'almāh (עַלְמָה, 5959), "virgin; maiden." This noun has an Ugaritic cognate, although the masculine form also appears in Aramaic, Syriac, and Arabic. The feminine form of the root appears 9 times; the only 2 appearances of the masculine form ('elem) are in First Samuel. This suggests that this word was used rarely, perhaps because other words bore a similar meaning.

That *'almāh* can mean "virgin" is quite clear in Song of Sol. 6:8: "There are threescore queens, and fourscore concubines, and virgins [NASB, "maidens"] without number." Thus all the women in the court are described. The word *'almāh* represents those who are eligible for marriage but are neither wives (queens) nor concubines. These "virgins" all loved the king and longed to be chosen to be with him (to be his bride), even as did the Shulamite who became his bride (1:3–4). In Gen. 24:43 the word describes Rebekah, of whom it is said in Gen. 24:16 that she was a "maiden" with whom no man had had relations. Solomon wrote that the process of wooing a woman was mysterious to him (Prov. 30:19). Certainly in that day a man ordinarily wooed one whom he considered to be a "virgin." There are several contexts, therefore, in which a young girl's virginity is expressly in view.

Thus *'almāh* appears to be used more of the concept "virgin" than that of "maiden," yet always of a woman who had not borne a child. This makes it the ideal word to be used in Isa. 7:14, since the word *b^etûlāh* emphasizes virility more than virginity (although it is used with both emphases, too). The reader of Isa. 7:14 in the days preceding the birth of Jesus would read that a "virgin who is a maiden" would conceive a child. This was a possible, but irregular, use of the word since the word can refer merely to the unmarried status of the one so described. The child immediately in view was the son of the prophet and his wife (cf. Isa. 8:3) who served as a sign to Ahaz that his enemies would be defeated by God. On the other hand, the reader of that day must have been extremely uncomfortable with this use of the word, since its primary connotation is "virgin" rather than "maiden." Thus the clear translation of the Greek in Matt. 1:23 whereby this word is rendered "virgin" satisfies its fullest implication. Therefore, there was no embarrassment to Isaiah when his wife conceived a son by him, since the word *'almāh* allowed for this. Neither is there any embarrassment in Matthew's understanding of the word.

VISION

A. Nouns.

ḥāzôn (חָזוֹן, 2377), "vision." None of the 34 appearances of this word appear before First Samuel, and most of them are in the prophetic books.

Ḥāzôn almost always signifies a means of divine revelation. First, it refers to the means itself, to a prophetic "vision" by which divine messages are communicated: "The days are prolonged, and every vision faileth" (Ezek. 12:22). Second, this word represents the message received by prophetic "vision": "Where there is no vision, the people perish: but he that keepeth the law, happy is he" (Prov. 29:18). Finally, *ḥāzôn* can represent the entirety of a prophetic or prophet's message as it is written down: "The vision of Isaiah the son of Amoz . . ." (Isa. 1:1). Thus the word inseparably related to the content of a divine communication focuses on the means by which that message is received: "And the word of the Lord was precious in those days; there was no open vision" (1 Sam. 3:1—the first occurrence of the word). In Isa. 29:7 this word signifies a non-prophetic dream.

ḥizzāyôn (חִזָּיוֹן, 2384), "vision." This noun, which occurs 9 times, refers to a prophetic "vision" in Joel 2:28: "And it shall come to pass afterward, that I will pour out my spirit upon all flesh; and your sons and your daughters shall prophesy, your old men shall dream dreams, your young men shall see visions." *Ḥizzāyôn* refers to divine communication in 2 Sam. 7:17 (the first biblical occurrence) and to an ordinary dream in Job 4:13.

B. Verb.

ḥāzāh (חָזָה, 2372), "to see, behold, select for oneself." This verb appears 54 times and in every period of biblical Hebrew. Cognates of this word appear in Ugaritic, Aramaic, and Arabic. It means "to see or behold" in general (Prov. 22:29), "to see" in a prophetic vision (Num. 24:4), and "to select for oneself" (Exod. 18:21—the first occurrence of the word).

In Lam. 2:14 the word means "to see" in relation to prophets' vision: "Thy prophets have seen vain and foolish things for thee: and they have not discovered thine iniquity. . . ."

VOICE

qôl (קוֹל, 6963), "voice; sound; noise." This word also appears in Ugaritic ("sound"), Akkadian ("call"), Arabic ("say"), and in Phoenician, Ethiopic, and old South Arabic ("voice"). *Qôl* appears about 506 times in the Bible and in all periods.

In its first meaning the word denotes a "sound" produced by vocal cords. This includes the human "voice": "And there was no day like that before it or after it, that the Lord hearkened unto the voice of a man: for the Lord fought for Israel" (Josh. 10:14). The word also includes vocal "sounds" produced by animals: "And Samuel said, What meaneth then this bleating [literally, sound] of the sheep in mine ears, and the lowing [literally, sound] of the oxen which I hear?" (1 Sam. 15:14). In this regard *qôl* is used of the "voice" of personified inanimate objects or things: "And he said, What hast thou done? the voice of thy brother's blood crieth unto me from the ground" (Gen. 4:10).

The second meaning, "sound" or "noise," appears especially in poetical passages and covers a great variety of "noises and sounds," such as the "noise or sound" of battle: "And when Joshua heard the noise of the people as they shouted, he said unto Moses, There is a noise of war in the camp" (Exod. 32:17). It can be used of the "sound" of words (Deut. 1:34), water (Ezek. 1:24), weeping (Isa. 65:19), and thunder (Exod. 9:23).

The word can also represent the thing that is spoken: "And unto Adam he said, Because thou hast hearkened unto the voice of thy wife, and hast eaten of the tree of which I commanded thee . . . " (Gen. 3:17). In an extended nuance *qôl* signifies the thing said, even though it is written down: "Then he wrote a letter the second time to them, saying, If ye be mine, and if ye will hearken unto my voice . . . " (2 Kings 10:6).

There are several special phrases related to *qôl*. "To lift up one's *voice* and weep" signifies many things including crying out for help (Gen. 39:14), mourning for present or anticipated tragedy (Gen. 21:16), and the "sound" of disaster (Num. 16:34) or joy (Gen. 29:11).

"To hearken to one's voice" means such things as taking note of something and believing it (Gen. 4:23), following another's suggestions (Gen. 3:17), complying with another's request (Gen. 21:12), obeying another's command (Gen. 22:18), and answering a prayer (2 Sam. 22:7).

Theologically the word is crucial in contexts relating to prophecy. The prophet's "voice" is God's "voice" (Exod. 3:18; cf. 7:1; Deut. 18:18–19). God's "voice" is sometimes the roar of thunder (Exod. 9:23, 29) or a "still small voice" (1 Kings 19:12). Thunder demonstrated God's tremendous power and evoked fear and submission. In covenantal contexts God stipulates that His "voice," heard in both the roar of thunder and the prophetic message, is authoritative and when obeyed brings reward (Exod. 19:5; 1 Sam. 12:14–18). The blast ("sound") of a trumpet is used to signify divine power (Josh. 6:5) and presence (2 Sam. 6:15).

Interestingly the first biblical appearance of *qôl* (Gen. 3:8) is a highly debated passage. Exactly what did Adam and Eve hear in the garden? Was it the sound of God walking (cf. 1 Kings 14:6)?

VOW

A. Verb.

nādar (נָדַר, 5087), "to vow." This verb occurs in Semitic languages (Ugaritic, Phoenician, and Aramaic). In Phoenician-Punic inscriptions the verb and also the noun derived from it frequently denote human sacrifices and in a more general sense signify a gift. In the Old Testament *nādar* occurs 31 times.

The distribution of the verb is over the entire Old Testament (narrative, legal, poetic, but more rarely in the prophetic books). Beyond the Old Testament the verb occurs in the Dead Sea Scrolls, rabbinic Hebrew, medieval and modern Hebrew. However, its usage declined from post-Exilic times onward.

Both men and women could "vow" a vow. Numbers 30 deals with the law concerning vows; cf. Num. 30:2: "If a man vow a vow unto the Lord, or swear an oath to bind his soul with a bond . . . "; and Num. 30:3: "If a woman also vow a vow unto the Lord, and bind herself by a bond. . . . "

The Septuagint has *euchomai* ("to wish").

B. Noun.

neder (נֶדֶר, 5088), "vow; votive offering." This noun occurs 60 times in biblical Hebrew and is often used in conjunction with the verb (19 times): " . . . Any of thy vows which thou vowest . . . " (Deut. 12:17). Modern versions compress the noun and verb into one idiom: "Or whatever you have vowed to give" (NIV), or give a technical usage to the noun: "Or any of your votive offerings which you vow" (RSV).

The vow has two basic forms, the unconditional and the conditional. The unconditional is an "oath" where someone binds himself without expecting anything in return: "I will pay my vows unto the Lord now in the presence of all his people" (Ps. 116:14). The obligation is binding upon the person who has made a "vow." The word spoken has the force of an oath which generally could not be broken: "If a man vow a vow unto the Lord, or swear an oath to bind his soul with a bond; he shall not break his word, he shall do [everything he said] " (Num. 30:2). The conditional "vow" generally had a preceding clause before the oath giving the conditions which had to come to pass before the "vow" became valid: "And Jacob vowed a vow, saying, If God will be with me, and will [watch over me] . . . , so that I come again to my father's house in peace; then shall the Lord be my God . . . and of all that thou shalt give me I will surely give the tenth unto thee" (Gen. 28:20–22).

"Vows" usually occurred in serious situations. Jacob needed the assurance of God's presence before setting out for Padan-aram (Gen. 28:20–22); Jephthah made a rash "vow" before battle (Judg. 11:30; cf. Num. 21:1–3); Hannah greatly desired a child (1 Sam. 1:11), when she made a "vow." Though conditional "vows" were often made out of desperation, there is no question of the binding force of the "vow." Ecclesiastes amplifies the Old Testament teaching on "vowing": "When thou vowest a vow unto God, defer not to pay it. . . . Better is it that thou shouldest not vow, than that thou shouldest vow and not pay. . . . Neither say thou before the angel, that it was an error" (5:4–6). First, a "vow" is always made to God. Even non-Israelites made "vows" to Him (Jonah 1:16). Second, a "vow" is made voluntarily. It is never associated with a life of piety or given the status of religious requirement in the Old Testament. Third, a "vow" once made must be kept. One cannot annul the "vow." However, the Old Testament allows for "redeeming" the "vow"; by payment of an equal amount in silver, a person, a field, or a house dedicated by "vow" to the Lord could be redeemed (Lev. 27:1–25).

This practice, however, declined in Jesus' time, and therefore the Talmud frowns upon the practice of "vowing" and refers to those who vow as "sinners."

Neder signifies a kind of offering: "And thither ye shall bring your burnt offerings, and your sacrifices, and your tithes, and [contributions] of your hand, and your vows, and your freewill offerings . . ." (Deut. 12:6). In particular the word represents a kind of peace or "votive offering" (Ezra 7:16). It also is a kind of thank offering: "Behold upon the mountains the feet of him that bringeth good tidings, that publisheth peace! . . . Perform thy vows . . ." (Nah. 1:15). Here even Gentiles expressed their thanks to God presumably with a gift promised upon condition of deliverance (cf. Num. 21:1–3). Such offerings may also be expressions of zeal for God (Ps. 22:25). One can give to God anything not abominable to Him (Lev. 27:9ff.; Deut. 23:18), including one's services (Lev. 27:2). Pagans were thought to feed and/or tend their gods, while God denied that "vows" paid to Him were to be so conceived (Ps. 50:9–13). In paganism the god rewarded the devotee because of and in proportion to his offering. It was a contractual relationship whereby the god was obligated to pay a debt thus incurred. In Israel no such contractual relationship was in view.

The Israelites' unique and concrete demonstrations of love for God show that under Moses love (Deut. 6:4) was more than pure legalism; it was spiritual devotion. God's Messiah was pledged to offer Himself as a sacrifice for sin (Ps. 22:25; cf. Lev. 27:2ff.). This was the only sacrifice absolutely and unconditionally acceptable to God. Every man is obliged to pay the "vow" before God: "Praise waiteth for thee, O God in Zion: and unto thee shall the vow be performed. . . . Unto thee shall all flesh come" (Ps. 65:1–2).

The Septuagint has *euche* ("prayer; oath; vow").

W

TO WALK

A. Verb.

hālak (הָלַךְ, 1980), "to go, walk, behave." This verb appears in most Semitic languages (although it has a different meaning in Arabic). It is attested in all periods of Hebrew. Old Testament Hebrew attests it about 1,550 times, while the Aramaic uses it a few times.

Essentially, this root refers to movement without any suggestion of direction in the sense of going, whether of man (Gen. 9:23), beasts (Gen. 3:14), or inanimate objects (Gen. 2:14— the first occurrence of the word). In cases other than men (where it means "to walk") *hālak* may be translated "to go." It is used sometimes with a special emphasis on the end or goal of the action in mind; men are but flesh, "a wind that passeth [goes] away, and cometh not again" (Ps. 78:39). Applied to human existence the word suggests "going to one's death," as in Gen. 15:2, when Abraham says: "O Lord God, what wilt thou give me, since I am [going to my death] childless . . . ?" (NASB). This verb can also be used of one's behavior, or the way one "walks in life." So he who "walks" uprightly shall be blessed of God (Isa. 33:15). This does not refer to walking upright on one's feet but to living a righteous life.

This root is used in various other special ways. It may be used to emphasize that a certain thing occurred; Jacob went and got the kid his mother requested, in other words, he actually did the action (Gen. 27:14). In Gen. 8:3 the waters of the flood steadily receded from the surface of the earth. Sometimes this verb implies movement away from, as in Gen. 18:33, when the Lord "departed" from Abraham.

God is said to "walk" or "go" in three senses. First, there are certain cases where He assumed some kind of physical form. For example, Adam and Eve heard the sound of God "walking" to and fro in the garden of Eden (Gen. 3:8). He "walks" on the clouds (Ps. 104:3) or in the heavens (Job 22:14); these are probably anthropomorphisms (God is spoken of as if He had bodily parts). Even more often God is said to accompany His people (Exod. 33:14), to go to redeem (deliver) them from Egypt (2 Sam. 7:23), and to come to save them (Ps. 80:2). The idea of God's "going" ("walking") before His people in the pillars of fire and cloud (Exod. 13:21) leads to the idea that His people must "walk" behind Him (Deut. 13:5). Quite often the people are said to have "walked" or to be warned against "walking behind" foreign gods (Deut. 4:3). Thus, the rather concrete idea of following God through the wilderness moves to "walking behind" Him spiritually. Some scholars suggest that "walking behind" pagan gods (or even the true God) arose from the pagan worship where the god was carried before the people as they entered the sanctuary. Men may also "walk . . . after the imagination of their evil heart," or act stubbornly (Jer. 3:17). The pious followed or practiced God's commands; they "walked" in righteousness (Isa. 33:15), in humility (Mic. 6:8), and in integrity (Ps. 15:2). They also "walk with God" (Gen. 5:22), and they live in His presence, and "walk before" Him (Gen. 17:1), in the sense of living responsibly before Him.

B. Nouns.

hălîkāh (חֲלִיכָה, 1979), "course; doings; traveling company; caravan; procession." This noun occurs 6 times in the Old Testament.

This word conveys several nuances. In Nah. 2:5 *hălîkāh* refers to a "course": "He shall recount his worthies: they shall stumble in their walk. . . ." The word means "doings" in Prov. 31:27. It may also mean "traveling-company" or "caravan" as in Job 6:19 or a "procession" as in Ps. 68:24.

Several other related nouns occur infrequently. *Mahălāk*, which appears 5 times, means "passage" (Ezek. 42:4) and "journey" (Neh. 2:6). *Hēlek* occurs twice and means a

"visitor" (2 Sam. 12:4). *Hālîk* appears once with the meaning "steps" (Job 29:6). *Tahălukōt* occurs once to mean "procession," specifically a thanksgiving procession (Neh. 12:31).

WALL

hômāh (חוֹמָה, 2346), "wall." This word is found in several Semitic languages and even in Egyptian. In Phoenician, it has the more restricted significance of "fortifications." It is thought that the root meaning is "to protect," as in the Arabic *chama*, "to protect."

Hômāh occurs about 120 times in the Hebrew Bible. Its first occurrence is in Exod. 14:22: "And the children of Israel went into the midst of the sea upon the dry ground: and the waters were a wall unto them on their right hand, and on their left." It is rare in the Pentateuch, in the historical books, and in the poetical books. The most frequent use is in Nehemiah, where Nehemiah is in charge of the rebuilding of the "wall" of Jerusalem.

The primary meaning of *hômāh* is a "wall" around a city, since in ancient Israel people had to protect themselves by constructing such a well-fortified "wall" (cf. Lev. 25:29–30). Stones were used in the construction of the "wall": "Now Tobiah the Ammonite was by him, and he said, Even that which they build, if a fox go up, he shall even break down their stone wall" (Neh. 4:3). The "wall" was also strengthened by thickness and other devices. From Solomonic times double walls (casemate) served a strategic purpose in that they were easy to construct and could be filled in with rocks and dirt in the case of a siege. There was also another possibility during a siege: "And the city was broken up, and all the men of war fled by night by the way of the gate between two walls, which is by the king's garden: (now the Chaldees were against the city round about:) . . . " (2 Kings 25:4).

In the case of war the enemy besieged a city and made efforts to breach the "wall" with a battering ram. The goal was to force a breach wide enough for the troops to enter into the city; "And Jehoash king of Israel took Amaziah king of Judah, the son of Jehoash the son of Ahaziah, at Beth-shemesh, and came to Jerusalem, and brake down the wall of Jerusalem from the gate of Ephraim unto the corner gate, four hundred cubits [about six hundred feet]" (2 Kings 14:13). At the time of Nebuchadnezzar's invasion and victory over Jerusalem, he had the "walls" of the city demolished: "And they burnt the house of God, and brake down the wall of Jerusalem, and burnt all the palaces thereof with fire, and destroyed all the goodly vessels thereof" (2 Chron. 36:19). For this reason Nehemiah had to help his unsuccessful compatriots to rebuild the "wall" about 135 years later: "Then said I unto them, Ye see the distress that we are in, how Jerusalem lieth waste, and the gates thereof are burned with fire: come, and let us build up the wall of Jerusalem, that we be no more a reproach" (Neh. 2:17).

Hômāh also referred to any "wall," whether around buildings or parts of the city such as the temple precincts: "And behold a wall on the outside of the house round about, and in the man's hand a measuring reed of six cubits long by the cubit and a handbreadth: so he measured the breadth of the building, one reed; and the height, one reed" (Ezek. 40:5).

The Septuagint gives the following translation: *teichos* ("wall").

WAR

A. Noun.

milhāmāh (מִלְחָמָה, 4421), "war; battle; skirmish; combat." This word has a cognate only in Ugaritic. Biblical Hebrew attests it 315 times and in all periods.

This word means "war," the over-all confrontation of two forces (Gen. 14:2). It can refer to the engagement in hostilities considered as a whole, the "battle": " . . . And they joined battle with them in the vale of Siddim" (Gen. 14:8). This word is used not only of what is intended but of the hand-to-hand fighting which takes place: "And when Joshua heard the noise of the people as they shouted, he said unto Moses, There is a noise of war in the camp" (Exod. 32:17). *Milhāmāh* sometimes represents the art of soldiering, or "combat": "The Lord is a man of war . . . " (Exod. 15:3).

There are several principles which were supposed to govern "war" in the Old Testament. Unjust violence was prohibited, but "war" as a part of ancient life was led (Judg. 4:13) and used by God (Num. 21:14). If it was preceded by sacrifices recognizing His leadership and sovereignty (1 Sam. 7:9) and if He was consulted and obeyed (Judg. 20:23), Israel was promised divine protection (Deut. 20:1–4). Not one life would be lost (Josh. 10:11). God's presence in "battle" was symbolized by the ark of the covenant (1 Sam. 4:3–11). His presence necessitated spiritual and ritualistic cleanliness (Deut. 23:9–14). Before and during "battle," trumpets were blown placing the cause before God in anticipation of the victory and gratitude for it (Num. 10:9–10), as well as to relay the orders of the commanders. A war cry accompanied the initiation of "battle" (Josh. 6:5). At the

beginning Israel's army consisted of every man over twenty and under fifty (Num. 1:2–3). Sometimes only certain segments of this potential citizens' army were summoned (Num. 31:3–6). There were several circumstances which could exempt one from "war" (Num. 1:48–49; Deut. 20:5–8). Under David and Solomon there grew a professional army. It was especially prominent under Solomon, whose army was renowned for its chariotry. Cities outside Palestine were to be offered terms of surrender before being attacked. Compliance meant subjugation to slavery (Deut. 20:10–11). Cities and peoples within the Promised Land were to be utterly wiped out. They were under the ban (Deut. 2:34; 3:6; 20:16–18). This made these battles uniquely holy battles (a holy war) where everything was especially devoted and sacrificed to God. Israel's kings were admonished to trust in God as their strength rather than in a great many horses and chariots (Deut. 17:16). Her armies were forbidden to cut down fruit trees in order to build siege equipment (Deut. 20:19–20). Soldiers were paid by keeping booty won in "battle" (Num. 31:21–31). The entire army divided the spoil—even those in the rear guard (Num. 31:26–47; Judg. 5:30). God, too, was appointed a share (Num. 31:28–30).

B. Verb.

lāham (לָחַם, 3898), "to engage in battle, fight, wage war." This verb occurs 171 times in biblical Hebrew. The first appearance is in Exod. 1:10: "Come on, let us deal wisely with them; lest they multiply, and it come to pass, that, when there falleth out any war, they join also unto our enemies, and fight against us, and so get them up out of the land."

TO WASH

rāhas (רָחַץ, 7364), "to wash, bathe." This word is common to both ancient and modern Hebrew and is found in ancient Ugaritic as well. It is used some 72 times in the text of the Hebrew Old Testament. The first occurrence of the word in the text illustrates one of its most common uses: "Let a little water . . . be fetched, and wash your feet . . . " (Gen. 18:4).

When the word is used figuratively to express vengeance, the imagery is a bit more gruesome: " . . . He shall wash his feet in the blood of the wicked" (Ps. 58:10). Pilate's action in Matt. 27:24 is reminiscent of the psalmist's statement "I will wash mine hands in innocency" (Ps. 26:6). The parts of a sacrificial animal usually "were washed" before they were burned on the altar (Exod. 29:17). *Rāhas* is frequently used in the sense of "bathing" or "washing" oneself

(Exod. 2:5; 2 Sam. 11:2). Beautiful eyes are figuratively described as "washed with milk" (Song of Sol. 5:12).

kābas (כָּבַס, 3526), "to wash." A common term throughout the history of Hebrew for the "washing" of clothes, this word is found also in ancient Ugaritic and Akkadian, reflecting the treading aspect. *Kābas* occurs in the Hebrew Old Testament 51 times. It is found for the first time in the Old Testament in Gen. 49:11 as part of Jacob's blessing on Judah: " . . . He washed his garments in wine. . . . "

The word is used in the Old Testament primarily in the sense of "washing" clothes, both for ordinary cleansing (2 Sam. 19:24) and for ritual cleansing (Exod. 19:10, 14; Lev. 11:25). It is often used in parallelism with the expression "to wash oneself," as in Lev. 14:8–9. *Kābas* is used in the sense of "washing" or "bathing" oneself only in the figurative sense and in poetic usage, as in Jer. 4:14: "O Jerusalem, wash thine heart from wickedness, that thou mayest be saved."

WATCH

A. Nouns.

mišmeret (מִשְׁמֶרֶת, 4931); *mišmār* (מִשְׁמָר, 4929), "watch; guard; post; confinement; prison; custody; division." The first or feminine form of this word appears 78 times, while the masculine form is attested 22 times. These forms are scattered through biblical literature.

The noun *mišmār* means a "military watch" over a city: "Nevertheless we made our prayer unto our God, and set a watch against them day and night because of them [our enemies]" (Neh. 4:9). This word represents the place where a guard or watchman fulfills his task: " . . . And appoint watches of the inhabitants of Jerusalem, every one in his watch, and every one to be over against his house" (Neh. 7:3). Someone who guards something keeps "watch" over it: "Mattaniah, and Bakbukiah, . . . were porters keeping the ward at the thresholds of the gates" (Neh. 12:25). In Job 7:12 *mišmār* means "watch" or "guard" in general (over a potentially dangerous criminal): "Am I a sea, or a whale, that thou settest a watch over me?"

Mišmār can also represent a "place of confinement," such as a jail: "And he put them in ward in the house of the captain of the guard, into the prison, the place where Joseph was bound" (Gen. 40:3—the first occurrence of the word). Joseph put his brothers "into ward three days" (Gen. 42:17) and thereafter allowed 9 of them to return to Palestine to get Benjamin (an act supposedly proving they were not spies) while 1 of them remained in the Egyptian "prison" (Gen. 42:19). Under Mosaic law there were to be no prisons where people were held for extended periods after being convicted of a crime. Instead, those charged were held for a very short time (sometimes) immediately preceding trial until the trial could be arranged (Lev. 24:12). After the trial the guilty party was killed, punished, fined, or indentured until he worked out his fine.

Mišmār sometimes represents a group of attendants, especially in the temple. In this nuance the word may represent the temple guard-units: "To Shuppim and Hosah the lot came forth westward, with the gate Shallecheth, by the causeway of the going up, ward against ward" (1 Chron. 26:16). However, in Neh. 12:24 the service rendered is the Levitical service in general, therefore, "division corresponding to division." All these Levitical "divisions" constituted the full services of the temple (Neh. 13:14).

The noun *mišmeret* appears with the same meanings as those just set forth. It can mean a "military watchman or guard" (cf. Neh. 7:3). In Isa. 21:8 the word signifies the place where one keeps watch: " . . . I am set in my *wards* whole nights. . . . " The phrase "to keep watch," in the sense of to fulfill the function of a watchman or guard, appears with *mišmeret* in 2 Kings 11:5: "A third part of you that enter in on the sabbath shall even be keepers of the watch of the king's house." *Mišmeret* represents a place of confinement in 2 Sam. 20:3: David put 10 of his concubines who had been defiled by Absalom into a house of confinement (NASB, "under guard").

Mišmeret often is used to represent a more abstract idea than *mišmār*, whereas *mišmār* means the units of Levites who served the Lord (perhaps with the exception of Neh. 13:30, where *mišmeret* may mean "service-unit"). *Mišmeret* refers to the priestly or Levitical service itself: "Therefore shall ye abide at the door of the tabernacle of the congregation day and night seven days, and keep the charge of the Lord . . . " (Lev. 8:35). Num. 3:25 speaks of the duties of the Levites in the tent of meeting. The Levites were to "keep the charge of the tabernacle of testimony" (Num. 1:53). The word, therefore, suggests both regularly prescribed act and obligation. The latter idea alone appears in Num. 8:26, where God allows Levites over 50 to serve in extraordinary circumstances, to keep an obligation.

This word often refers to divine obligation or service in general, a non-cultic obligation: "Because that Abraham obeyed my voice, and kept my charge, my commandments, my statutes, and my laws" (Gen. 26:5—the first occurrence of *mišmeret;* cf. Deut. 11:1).

B. Verb.

šāmar (שָׁמַר, 8104), "to keep, watch." This verb occurs 468 times in the Old Testament. The word means "to watch" in Job 14:16: "For now thou numberest my steps: dost thou not watch over my sin?"

WATER

mayim (מַיִם, 4325), "water; flood." This word has cognates in Ugaritic and old South Arabic. It occurs about 580 times and in every period of biblical Hebrew.

First, "water" is one of the original basic substances. This is its significance in Gen. 1:2 (the first occurrence of the word): "And the Spirit of God moved upon the face of the waters." In Gen. 1:7 God separated the "waters" above and the "waters" below (cf. Exod. 20:4) the expanse of the heavens.

Second, the word represents that which is in a well, "water" to be drunk (Gen. 21:19). "Living water" is "water" that flows: "And Isaac's servants digged in the valley, and found there a well of springing [living] water..." (Gen. 26:19). "Water" of oppression or affliction is so designated because it is drunk in prison: "Put this fellow in the prison, and feed him with bread of affliction and with water of affliction, until I come in peace" (1 Kings 22:27). Job 9:30 speaks of slush or snow water: "If I wash myself with snow water, and make my hands never so clean...."

Third, *mayim* can represent liquid in general: "...For the Lord our God hath put us to silence, and given us water of gall to drink, because we have sinned against the Lord" (Jer. 8:14). The phrase, *me raglayim* ("water of one's feet") is urine: "Hath my master sent me to thy master, and to thee, to speak these words? hath he not sent me to the men which sit on the wall, that they may eat their own dung, and drink their own piss [water of their feet] with you?" (2 Kings 18:27; cf. Isa. 25:10).

Fourth, in Israel's cultus "water" was poured or sprinkled (no one was ever immersed into water), symbolizing purification. So Aaron and his sons were to be washed with "water" as a part of the rite consecrating them to the priesthood: "And Aaron and his sons thou shalt bring unto the door of the tabernacle of the congregation, and shalt wash them with water" (Exod. 29:4). Parts of the sacrificial animal were to be ritually cleansed with "water" during the sacrifice: "But his inwards and his legs shall he wash in water..." (Lev. 1:9). Israel's rites sometimes include consecrated "water": "And the priest shall take holy water in an earthen vessel; and of the dust that is in the floor of the tabernacle the priest shall take, and put it into the water" (Num. 5:17). "Bitter water" was used in Israel's rituals, too: "And the priest shall set the woman before the Lord, and uncover the woman's head, and put the offering of memorial in her hands, which is the jealousy offering: and the priest shall have in his hand the bitter water that causeth the curse" (Num. 5:18). It was "water" which when drunk brought a curse and caused bitterness (Num. 5:24).

Fifth, in proper names this word is used of springs, streams, or seas and/or the area in the immediate vicinity of such bodies of water: "Say unto Aaron, Take thy rod, and stretch out thine hand upon the waters of Egypt, upon their streams, upon their rivers, and upon their ponds, and upon all their pools of water, that they may become blood..." (Exod. 7:19).

Sixth, this word is used figuratively in many senses. *Mayim* symbolizes danger or distress: "He sent from above, he took me; he drew me out of many waters" (2 Sam. 22:17). Outbursting force is represented by *mayim* in 2 Sam. 5:20: "The Lord hath broken forth upon mine enemies before me, as the [break-through] of waters." "Mighty waters" describes the onrush of the godless nations against God: "The nations shall rush like the rushing of many waters..." (Isa. 17:13). Thus the word is used to picture something impetuous, violent, and overwhelming: "Terrors take hold on him as waters, a tempest stealeth him away in the night" (Job 27:20). In other passages "water" is used to represent timidity: "...Wherefore the hearts of the people melted, and became as water" (Josh. 7:5). Related to this nuance is the connotation "transitory": "...Because thou shalt forget thy misery, and remember it as waters that pass away" (Job 11:16). In Isa. 32:2 "water" represents that which is refreshing: "And a man shall be as a hiding place from the wind, and a covert from the tempest; as rivers of water in a dry place, as the shadow of a great rock in a weary land." Rest and peace are figured by waters of rest, or quiet waters: "...He leadeth me beside the still waters" (Ps. 23:2). Similar ideas are involved when one's wife's charms are termed "water of life" or "water which enlivens": "Drink waters out of thine own cistern, and running waters out of thine own well" (Prov. 5:15). Outpoured "water" represents bloodshed (Deut. 12:16), wrath (Hos. 5:10), justice (Amos 5:24; KJV, "judgment"), and strong feelings (Job 3:24).

tehôm (תְּהוֹם, 8415), "deep water; ocean; water table; waters; flood of waters." Cognates of this word appear in Ugaritic, Akkadian (as early as Ebla, around 2400–2250 B.C.), and Arabic. The 36 occurrences of this word appear almost exclusively in poetical passages but in all historical periods.

The word represents the "deep water" whose surface freezes when cold: "The waters are hid as with a stone, and the face of the deep is frozen" (Job 38:30). In Ps. 135:6 t°hôm is used of the "ocean" in contrast to the seas: "Whatsoever the Lord pleased, that did he in heaven, and in earth, in the seas, and all deep places [in the entire ocean]" (cf. Ps. 148:7 et al.).

The word has special reference to the deep floods or sources of water. Sailors in the midst of a violent storm "mount up to the heaven, they go down again to the depths" (Ps. 107:26). This is hyperbolic or exaggerated poetical talk, but it presents the "depths" as the opposite of the heavens or skies. This emphasis is especially prominent in the Song of Moses, where the word represents the ever-existing (but not eternal), ever-threatening, and perilous "deep," not simply an element of nature but a dangerous element: "The depths have covered them: they sank into the bottom as a stone" (Exod. 15:5). On the other hand, in such contexts t°hôm may mean no more than "deep water" into which heavy objects quickly sink.

T°hôm can represent an inexhaustible source of water or, by way of poetic comparison, of blessing: " . . . With blessings of heaven above, blessings of the deep that lieth under . . . " (Gen. 49:25). In such contexts the word represents the "water table" always available below the surface of the earth—what was tapped by digging wells, out of which flowed springs, and what was one with the waters beneath the surface of oceans, lakes, seas, and rivers. This was what God opened together with the waters above the expanse (Gen. 7:11; cf. 1:7) and what later was closed to cause and terminate the great Flood (Gen. 8:2; cf. Ps. 33:6; 104:6; Ezek. 26:19). In such contexts the word represents a "flood of waters" (Ps. 33:6).

In Gen. 1:2 (the first occurrence of the word) t°hôm is used of "all waters" which initially covered the surface of the entire earth: " . . . And darkness was upon the face of the *deep*" (cf. Prov. 3:20; 8:24, 27–28).

WAY

A. Nouns.

derek (דֶּרֶךְ, 1870), "way (path, road, highway); distance; journey; manner, conduct; condition; destiny." This noun has cognates in Akkadian, Ugaritic (where it sometimes means "power" or "rule"), Phoenician, Punic, Arabic,

and Aramaic. It occurs about 706 times in biblical Hebrew and in all periods.

First, this word refers to a path, a road, or a highway. In Gen. 3:24 (the first occurrence of the word) it means "path" or "route": " . . . And he placed at the east of the garden of Eden cherubim, and a flaming sword which turned every [direction], to [guard] the way of the tree of life." Sometimes, as in Gen. 16:7, the word represents a pathway, road, or route: "And the angel of the Lord found her by a fountain of water in the wilderness, by the fountain in the way to Shur." The actual road itself is represented in Gen. 38:21: "Where is the [temple prostitute], that was openly by the wayside?" (In Num. 20:17 the word means "highway," a well-known and well-traveled road: " . . . We will go by the king's highway, we will not turn to the right hand nor to the left, until we have passed thy borders."

Second, this noun represents a "distance" (how far or how long) between two points: "And he set three days' journey [a distance of three days] betwixt himself and Jacob . . . " (Gen. 30:36).

In other passages *derek* refers to the action or process of "taking a journey": "And to his father he sent after this manner; ten asses laden with the good things of Egypt, and ten she asses laden with corn and bread and meat for his father by the way [on the journey]" (Gen. 45:23). In an extended nuance *derek* means "undertaking": "If thou turn away thy foot from the sabbath, from doing thy pleasure on my holy day; and call the sabbath a delight, the holy of the Lord, honorable; and shalt honor him, not doing thine own ways, nor finding thine own pleasure . . . " (Isa. 58:13). Cf. Gen. 24:21: "And the man wondering at her held his peace, to wit whether the Lord had made his journey prosperous or not" (cf. Deut. 28:29).

In another emphasis this word connotes how and what one does, a "manner, custom, behavior, mode of life": "Our father is old, and there is not a man in the earth to come in unto us after the manner of all the earth" (Gen. 19:31). In 1 Kings 2:4 *derek* is applied to an activity that controls one, one's life-style: "If thy children take heed to their way, to walk before me in truth with all their heart and with all their soul, there shall not fail thee . . . a man on the throne of Israel." In 1 Kings 16:26 *derek* is used of Jeroboam's attitude: "For he walked in all the way of Jeroboam the son of Nebat, and in his sin wherewith he made Israel to sin. . . . " Deeds, or specific acts, may be connoted by this noun: "Lo, these are parts of his ways; but how little a portion is heard of him? But the thunder of his power who can understand?" (Job 26:14).

Derek refers to a "condition" in the sense of what has happened to someone. This is clear by the parallelism of Isa. 40:27: "Why sayest thou, O Jacob, and speakest, O Israel, My way is hid from the Lord, and [the justice due to me is passed away] from my God?" In one passage *derek* signifies the overall course and fixed path of one's life, or his "destiny": "O Lord, I know that the way of man is not in himself: it is not in man that walketh to direct his steps" (Jer. 10:23).

Finally, this word sometimes seems to bear the meaning of its Ugaritic cognate, "power" or "rulership": "Only acknowledge thine iniquity, that thou hast transgressed against the Lord thy God, and hast scattered thy ways [NASB, "favors"] to the strangers under every green tree . . . " (Jer. 3:13; cf. Job 26:14; 36:23; 40:19; Ps. 67:2; 110:7; 119:37; 138:5; Prov. 8:22; 19:16; 31:3; Hos. 10:13; Amos 8:14). Some scholars, however, contest this explanation of these passages.

'ōraḥ (אֹרַח, 734), "way; path; course; conduct; manner." Cognates of this word appear in Akkadian, Arabic, and Aramaic. Its 57 occurrences in biblical Hebrew are all in poetry except Gen. 18:11.

In meaning this word parallels Hebrew *derek*, which it often synonymously parallels. First, *'ōraḥ* means "path" or "way" conceived as a marked-out, well-traveled course: "Dan shall be a serpent by the way, an adder in the path, that biteth the horse heels . . . " (Gen. 49:17). In Judg. 5:6 the word means "highway": "In the days of Shamgar . . . the highways were unoccupied, and the travelers walked through byways." When the sun is likened to a "strong man" who rejoices "to run a race" (Ps. 19:5), *'ōraḥ* represents a race course rather than a highway or a primitive, snake-laden path. The man who makes his path straight goes directly on his journey, not turning aside for the beckoning harlot (Prov. 9:15). So here the word represents the "course" one follows between his departure and arrival conceived in terms of small units, almost step by step. In Ps. 8:8 the word represents the ocean currents: " . . . The fowl of the air and the fish of the sea, and whatsoever passeth through the paths of the seas."

'Ōraḥ signifies the ground itself as the path upon which one treads: "He pursued them, and passed safely; even by the way that he had not gone with his feet" (Isa. 41:3).

In Job 30:12 the word seems to represent an obstruction or dam: " . . . They push away my feet, and they raise up against me the ways of their destruction."

The word can refer to a recurring life event typical of an individual or a group. In its first biblical occurrence (Gen. 18:11) it is used of "the manner of women" (menstruation). Job 16:22 mentions the "way whence I shall not return," or death, while other passages speak of life actions (Job 34:11; literally, "conduct") or life-style (Prov. 15:10: "Correction is grievous unto him that forsaketh the way . . . "—prescribed life-style; Prov. 5:6: "Lest thou shouldest ponder the path [which is typified by] life . . . "). Thus, *'ōraḥ* sometimes figures a proper course of action or proceeding within a given realm— "the path of judgment" (Isa. 40:14).

The noun *'ōrḥāh*, which occurs 3 times, represents a "wandering company" or a "caravan" (Gen. 37:25).

B. Verb.

'Āraḥ means "to go, wander." This word, which occurs 6 times in biblical Hebrew, has cognates in Phoenician, Ethiopic, Aramaic, and Syriac. One example of this verb's usage is found in Job 34:7–8: "What man is like Job . . . which goeth in company with the workers of iniquity, and walketh with wicked men."

WEAKER ONE, LITTLE ONE

tap (טַף, 2945), "weaker one; child; little one." Cognates of this noun appear in Arabic and Ethiopic. All but 4 of the 42 occurrences of this word are in prose literature and mostly in early (pre-monarchy) prose narrative.

Basically this word signifies those members of a nomadic tribe who are not able to march or who can only march to a limited extent. The word implies the "weaker ones." Thus we read of the men and the *ṭāpîm*, or the men and those who were unable to move quickly over long stretches: "And Judah said unto Israel, his father, Send the lad with me, and we will arise and go; that we may live, and not die, both we, and thou, and also our little ones" (Gen. 43:8). This nuance is clearer in Gen. 50:7–8: "And Joseph went up to bury his father; and with him went up all the servants of Pharaoh, the elders of his house, and all the elders of the land of Egypt, and all the house of Joseph, and his brethren, and his father's house: only their little ones, and their flocks, and their herds, they left in the land of Goshen." They left the women and the aged to take care of the beasts and babies. These verses certainly make it clear that only men went along.

In several passages *tap* represents only the children and old ones: "And all their wealth, and all their little ones, and their wives took they captive, and spoiled even all that was in the house" (Gen. 34:29, first occurrence). All the able-bodied men of Shechem were killed (Gen. 34:26).

Sometimes the word means "children": "But all the women children [NASB, "girls"], that have not known a man by lying with him, keep alive for yourselves" (Num. 31:18; cf. v. 17).

WEALTH

hôn (הוֹן, 1952), "wealth; substance; riches; possessions; enough." The 26 occurrences of this word are almost wholly in wisdom literature, with 17 of them in the Book of Proverbs. This word appears only in the singular form.

Hôn usually refers to movable goods considered as "wealth": "But if he [the thief] be found, he shall restore seven-fold; he shall give all the substance of his house" (Prov. 6:31; cf. Ezek. 27:12). "Wealth" can be good and a sign of blessing: "Wealth and riches shall be in his [the righteous man's] house: and his righteousness endureth for ever" (Ps. 112:3). The creation is God's wealth: "I have rejoiced in the way of thy testimonies, as much as in all riches" (Ps. 119:14). In the Proverbs "wealth" is usually an indication of ungodliness: "The rich man's wealth is his strong city: the destruction of the poor is their poverty" (Prov. 10:15).

This word can also represent any kind of concrete "wealth": " . . . If a man would give all the substance of his house for love, it would utterly be contemned" (Song of Sol. 8:7). This is the significance of the word in its first occurrence: "Thou sellest thy people for nought and dost not increase thy wealth by their price" (Ps. 44:12). "Wealth" in general is meant in Prov. 12:27: "The slothful man roasteth not that which he took in hunting: but the substance of a diligent man is precious."

Finally, *hôn* means "enough" (only in Prov. 30:15–16): "The horseleech hath two daughters, crying, Give, Give. There are three things that are never satisfied, yea, four things say not, It is enough: the grave; and the barren womb; the earth that is not filled with water; and the fire that saith not, It is enough."

WEEK

šābûaʿ (שָׁבוּעַ, 7620), "week." This noun appears about 20 times in biblical Hebrew. In Gen. 29:27 it refers to an entire "week" of feasting. Exod. 34:22 speaks of a special feast in Israel's religious calendar: "And thou shalt observe the feast of weeks, of the first fruits of wheat harvest, and the feast of ingathering at the year's end." In Lev. 12:5 the word appears with the dual suffix and signifies a period of

two weeks: "But if she bear a maid child, then she shall be unclean two weeks. . . . "

TO GO A WHORING, BE A HARLOT

zānāh (זָנָה, 2181), "to go a whoring, commit fornication, be a harlot, serve other gods." This is the regular term denoting prostitution throughout the history of Hebrew, with special nuances coming out of the religious experience of ancient Israel. The word occurs approximately 90 times in the Hebrew Old Testament. It is used for the first time in the text at the conclusion of the story of the rape of Dinah by Shechem, as her brothers excuse their revenge by asking: "Should he deal with our sister as with a harlot?" (Gen. 34:31).

While the term means "to commit fornication," whether by male or by female, it is to be noted that it is almost never used to describe sexual misconduct on the part of a male in the Old Testament. Part of the reason lies in the differing attitude in ancient Israel concerning sexual activity by men and women. The main reason, however, is the fact that this term is used most frequently to describe "spiritual prostitution" in which Israel turned from God to strange gods. Deut. 31:16 illustrates this meaning: "And the Lord said unto Moses, Behold, thou shalt sleep with thy fathers; and this people will rise up, and go a whoring after the gods of the strangers of the land, whither they go to be among them, and will forsake me, and break my covenant which I have made with them."

Zānāh became, then, the common term for spiritual backsliding. The act of harloting after strange gods was more than changing gods, however. This was especially true when Israel went after the Canaanite gods, for the worship of these pagan deities involved actual prostitution with cult prostitutes connected with the Canaanite shrines. In the Old Testament sometimes the use of the phrase "go a whoring after" gods implies an individual's involvement with cult prostitutes. An example might be in Exod. 34:15–16: "Lest thou make a covenant with the inhabitants of the land, and they go a whoring after their gods, and do sacrifice unto their gods. . . . And thou take of their daughters unto thy sons, and their daughters go a whoring after their gods, and make thy sons go a whoring after their gods."

The religious theory behind such activity at the Canaanite shrine was that such sexual activity with cult prostitutes, both male and female, who represented the gods and goddesses of the Canaanite fertility cult, would stimulate fertility in their crops and flocks. Such cult prostitutes were not designated as prostitutes but rather "holy ones" or "set-apart ones," since the Semitic term for "holy" means, first of all, to be set apart for a special use. This is illustrated in Deut. 23:17: "There shall be no cult prostitute [set-apart one] of the daughters of Israel, neither shall there be a cult prostitute of the sons of Israel" (RSV; KJV, "whore of the daughters of Israel" and "sodomite of the sons of Israel"). This theme of religious harlotry looms large in the prophets who denounce this backsliding in no uncertain terms. Ezekiel minces no words as he openly calls both Judah and Israel "harlots" and vividly describes their backsliding in sexual terms (Ezek. 16:6–63; 23).

The Book of Hosea, in which Hosea's wife Gomer became unfaithful and most likely was involved in such cult prostitution, again illustrates not only Hosea's heartbreak but also God's own heartbreak because of the unfaithfulness of his wife, Israel. Israel's unfaithfulness appears in Hos. 9:1: "Rejoice not, O Israel, for joy, as other people: for thou hast gone a whoring from thy God, thou hast loved a reward upon every cornfloor."

WICKED

A. Nouns.

rāšā' (רָשָׁע, 7563), "wicked; ungodly; guilty." *Rāšā'* occurs only in Hebrew and late Aramaic. The word occurs about 260 times as a noun or an adjective and especially in the poetic literature of the Old Testament. It is rare in the Pentateuch and in the historical books. Its frequency increases in the prophetical books.

The narrow meaning of *rāšā'* lies in the concept of "wrongdoing" or "being in the wrong." It is a legal term. The person who has sinned against the law is guilty: "They that forsake the law praise the wicked: but such as keep the law contend with them" (Prov. 28:4). When in Israel's history justice did not prevail, the "guilty" were acquitted: " ... When the wicked beareth rule, the people mourn" (Prov. 29:2; cf. 2 Chron. 6:23).

Rāšā' also denotes the category of people who have done wrong, are still living in sin, and are intent on continuing with wrongdoing. This is the more general meaning of the word. The first psalm exhorts the godly not to imitate the deeds and behavior of the ungodly, wicked people. The "wicked" does not seek God (Ps. 10:4); he challenges God (Ps. 10:13). In his way of life the "wicked" loves violence (Ps. 11:5), oppresses the righteous (Ps. 17:9), does not repay his debts (Ps. 37:21), and lays a snare to trap the righteous (Ps. 119:110). Ps. 37 gives a vivid

description of the acts of the "wicked" and also of God's judgment upon them. Facing the terrible force of the "wicked," the righteous prayed for God's deliverance and for His judgment upon them. This theme of judgment has already been anticipated in Ps. 1:6: "For the Lord knoweth the way of the righteous: but the way of the ungodly shall perish." The expectation of the righteous includes God's judgment on the "wicked" in this life that they might be ashamed (Ps. 31:17), be overcome by sorrows (Ps. 32:10), fall by their devices (Ps. 141:10), and die a premature death (Prov. 10:27), and that their remembrance will be no more (Prov. 10:7). It is expected that at the time of their death there will be great shouting: "When it goeth well with the righteous, the city rejoiceth: when the wicked perish, there is shouting" (Prov. 11:10).

The judgment upon the "wicked" is particularly strong in Proverbs, where the authors contrast the advantages of wisdom and righteousness and the disadvantages of the "wicked" (cf. 2:22: "But the wicked shall be cut off from the earth, and the transgressors shall be rooted out of it"). In Job another theme finds expression: why are the "wicked" not cut off? "Wherefore do the wicked live, become old, yea, are mighty in power?" (21:7). There is no clear answer to this question in the Old Testament. Malachi predicts a new age in which the distinction of the righteous and the "wicked" will be clear and where the righteous will triumph: "Then shall ye return, and discern between the righteous and the wicked, between him that serveth God and him that serveth him not" (Mal. 3:18).

The Septuagint has three translations of *rāšā'*: *asebes* ("godless; impious"); *hamartolos* ("sinner; sinful"), and *anomos* ("lawless").

Two other related nouns occur in the Old Testament. *Rēša'*, which is found about 30 times, usually means "wickedness": "Remember thy servants, Abraham, Isaac, and Jacob; look not unto the stubborness of this people, nor to their wickedness, nor to their sin" (Deut. 9:27). *Riš'āh*, which appears about 15 times, refers to "wickedness" or "guilt": "For my righteousness the Lord hath brought me in to possess this land: but for the wickedness of these nations the Lord doth drive them out from before thee" (Deut. 9:4).

B. Adjective.

rāšā' (רָשָׁע, 7563), "wicked; guilty." This word may also be used as an adjective. In some cases a person is so guilty that he deserves death: " ... If the wicked man be worthy to be beaten, that the judge shall cause him to lie down, and to be beaten before his face . . . by a certain number" (Deut. 25:2). The characteristics of a "wicked" person qualify him as a godless, impious man: "How much more, when wicked men have slain a righteous person in his own house upon his bed? shall I not therefore now require his blood of your hand, and take you away from the earth?" (2 Sam. 4:11; cf. Ezek. 3:18–19).

C. Verb.

rāša' (רָשַׁע, 7561), "to be wicked, act wickedly." This verb is derived from the noun *rāšā'*. There is a similar root in Ethiopic and Arabic, with the respective meanings "to forget" and "to be loose." This verb appears in 2 Chron. 6:37: "Yet if they bethink themselves in the land whither they are carried captive, and turn and pray unto thee in the land of their captivity, saying, We have sinned, we have done amiss, and have dealt wickedly."

WICKEDNESS

beliya'al (בְּלִיַּעַל, 1100), "wickedness; wicked; destruction." The 27 occurrences of this noun are scattered throughout the periods of biblical Hebrew.

The basic meaning of this word appears in a passage such as Judg. 20:13, where the sons of *beliya'al* are perpetrators of wickedness (they raped and murdered a man's concubine): "Now therefore deliver us the men, the children of Belial [NASB, "worthless fellows"] which are in Gibeah, that we may put them to death, and put away evil from Israel." In its first appearance the word represents men who lead others into idolatry: "Certain men, the children of Belial, are gone out from among you, and have [seduced] the inhabitants of their city . . . " (Deut. 13:13). In Deut. 15:9 the word modifies Hebrew *dābār*, "word" or "matter." Israel is warned to avoid "wicked" words (thoughts) in their hearts. *Beliya'al* is a synonym for *rāšā'* ("wicked rebellious one") in Job 34:18. In Nah. 1:11 the wicked counselor plots evil against God. The psalmist uses *beliya'al* as a synonym of death: "The cords of death encompassed me, and the torrents of ungodliness [KJV, "floods of ungodly men"] terrified me" (Ps. 18:4, NASB).

WIDOW

'almānāh (אַלְמָנָה, 490), "widow." Cognates of this word appear in Aramaic, Arabic, Akkadian, Phoenician, and Ugaritic. Biblical Hebrew attests it 55 times and in all periods.

The word represents a woman who, because of the death of her husband, has lost her social and economic position. The gravity of her situation was increased if she had no children. In such a circumstance she returned to her father's home and was subjected to the Levirate rule whereby a close male relative surviving her husband was to produce a child through her in her husband's behalf: "Then said Judah to Tamar his daughter-in-law, Remain a widow at thy father's house, till Shelah my son be grown . . . " (Gen. 38:11—the first occurrence of the word). These words constitute a promise to Tamar that the disgrace of being without both husband and child would be removed when Shelah was old enough to marry. Even if children had been born before her husband's death, a widow's lot was not a happy one (2 Sam. 14:5). Israel was admonished to treat "widows" and other socially disadvantaged people with justice, God Himself standing as their protector (Exod. 22:21–24).

Wives whose husbands shut them away from themselves are sometimes called "widows": "And David came to his house at Jerusalem; and the king took the ten women his concubines, whom he had left to keep the house, and put them in ward, and fed them, but went not in unto them. So they were shut up unto the day of their death, living in widowhood" (2 Sam. 20:3).

Destroyed, plundered Jerusalem is called a "widow" (Lam. 1:1).

TO WILL, BE WILLING

'ābāh (אָבָה, 14), "to will, be willing, consent." Common throughout the history of the Hebrew language, this word occurs in the Hebrew Bible just over 50 times. It is found for the first time in Gen. 24:5, where Abraham's servant who is about to be sent to find a wife for Isaac says: "Peradventure the woman will not be willing to follow me unto this land . . . ?"

It is to be noted that in all but 2 instances of its use in the Old Testament (Job 39:9; Isa. 1:19), the word is used with a negation, to indicate lack of willingness or consent. Even in these two positive uses, there seems to be a negative aspect or expectation implied. Job asks: "Will the unicorn be willing to serve thee . . . ?" (Job 39:9); and Isaiah seems almost hopeless as he says to Judah: "If ye be willing and obedient, ye shall eat the good of the land" (Isa. 1:19).

WINE

yayin (יַיִן, 3196), "wine." Cognates of this word appear in Akkadian, Ugaritic, Aramaic, Arabic, and Ethiopic. It appears about 141 times and in all periods of biblical Hebrew.

This is the usual Hebrew word for fermented grape. It is usually rendered "wine." Such "wine" was commonly drunk for refreshment: "And Melchizedek king of Salem brought forth bread and wine..." (Gen. 14:18; cf. 27:25). Passages such as Ezek. 27:18 inform us that "wine" was an article of commerce: "Damascus was thy merchant in the multitude of the wares of thy making, for the multitude of all riches; in the wine of Helbon, and white wool." Strongholds were supplied with "wine" in case of siege (2 Chron. 11:11). Proverbs recommends that kings avoid "wine" and strong drink but that it be given to those troubled with problems that they might drink and forget their problems (Prov. 31:4–7). "Wine" was used to make merry, to make one feel good without being intoxicated (2 Sam. 13:28).

Second, "wine" was used in rejoicing before the Lord. Once a year all Israel is to gather in Jerusalem. The money realized from the sale of a tithe of all their harvest was to be spent "for whatsoever thy soul lusteth after, for oxen, or for sheep, or for wine, or for strong drink, or for whatsoever thy soul desireth: and thou shalt eat there before the Lord thy God, and thou shalt rejoice..." (Deut. 14:26). "Wine" was offered to God at His command as part of the prescribed ritual (Exod. 29:40). Thus it was part of the temple supplies available for purchase by pilgrims so that they could offer it to God (1 Chron. 9:29). Pagans used "wine" in their worship, but "their wine is the poison of dragons, and the cruel venom of asps" (Deut. 32:33).

Yayin clearly represents an intoxicating beverage. This is evident in its first biblical appearance: "And Noah began to be a husbandman, and he planted a vineyard: and he drank of the wine, and was drunken..." (Gen. 9:20–21). The word is used as a synonym of *tîrôš*, "new wine," in Hos. 4:11, where it is evident that both can be intoxicating. *Tîrôš* is distinguished from *yayin* by referring only to new wine not fully fermented; *yayin* includes "wine" at any stage. In Gen. 27:28 (the first biblical occurrence of the word) Jacob's blessing includes the divine bestowal of an abundance of new wine. In 1 Sam. 1:15 *yayin* parallels *šēkār*, "strong drink." *Šēkār* in early times included wine (Num. 28:7) but meant strong drink made from any fruit or grain (Num. 6:3). People in special states of holiness were forbidden to drink "wine," such as the Nazarites (Num. 6:3), Samson's mother (Judg. 13:4), and priests approaching God (Lev. 10:9).

In Gen. 9:24 *yayin* means drunkenness: "And Noah awoke from his wine...."

WING

kānāp (כָּנָף, 3671), "wing." The Hebrew word is represented in Semitic languages (Ugaritic, Akkadian, Aramaic, Syriac, and Arabic) and in Egyptian. *Kānāp* has maintained its meaning in rabbinic and modern Hebrew.

In the Old Testament *kānāp* occurs first in the Creation account: "And God created great whales, and every living creature that moveth, which the waters brought forth abundantly, after their kind, and every winged fowl after his kind: and God saw that it was good" (Gen. 1:21; cf. Ps. 78:27). In the biblical usage the idiom "every bird wing" denotes the class of birds; cf. "They, and every beast after his kind, and all the cattle after their kind, and every creeping thing that creepeth upon the earth after his kind, and every fowl after his kind, every bird of every sort" (Gen. 7:14). This phrase is translated in the KJV, "any winged fowl" (Deut. 4:17; cf. NASB, "any winged bird that flies in the sky").

The word "wing" appears 109 times in the Hebrew Old Testament, with particular concentration in the description of the 2 cherubim of wood in Solomon's temple and in Ezekiel's vision of the "creatures," or cherubim. Elsewhere the Bible speaks of "wings" of the cherubim (Exod. 25:20; 37:9) and of the seraphim (Isa. 6:2).

As an extension of the usage "wing," *kānāp* signifies "extremity." The seam or lower part of a garment was known as the *kānāp*. In the "fold" (*kānāp*; KJV, "skirt") of the garment one could carry things (Hag. 2:12). Saul tore the edge (*kānāp*; KJV, "skirt") of Samuel's robe (1 Sam. 15:27). The extremity of a land on the world was also known by the word *kānāp* and is translated by "corner" in English: "And he shall set up an ensign for the nations, and shall assemble the outcasts of Israel, and gather together the dispersed of Judah from the four corners of the earth" (Isa. 11:12; cf. Job 37:3; 38:13; Ezek. 7:2).

In the metaphorical use God is said to protect His people as a bird protects her young with her "wings" (Deut. 32:11). The psalmist expressed God's care and protection as a "shadow" of the "wings" (Ps. 17:8; cf. 36:7; 57:1; 61:4; 63:7; 91:45). In keeping with this usage Malachi looked forward to a new age, when "the Sun of righteousness [will] arise with healing in his wings; and ye shall go forth, and grow up as calves of the stall" (4:2).

When the nations are compared to birds, the association is that of terror and conquest. This is best expressed in Ezekiel's parable of the two eagles and the vine: "And say, Thus saith the Lord God; A great eagle with great wings, longwinged, full of feathers, which had divers colors, came unto Lebanon, and took the highest branch of the cedar: he cropped off the top of his young twigs, and carried it into a land of traffic; he set it in a city of merchants" (Ezek. 17:3–4). The believer is enjoined to seek refuge with God when adversity strikes him or adversaries surround him: "He shall cover thee with his feathers, and under his wings shall thou trust: his truth shall be thy shield and buckler" (Ps. 91:4).

The Septuagint gives the following translations: *pteruks* ("wing; pinion"); *pterugion* ("end; edge"); and *pteroros* ("feathered; winged") The KJV gives these senses: "wing; skirt; border; corner."

WISE, SKILLED

A. Adjective.

ḥākām (חָכָם, 2450), "wise; skillful; practical." This word plus the noun *ḥakᵉmāh* and the verb "to be wise" signify an important element of the Old Testament religious point of view. Religious experience was not a routine, a ritual, or faith experience. It was viewed as a mastery of the art of living in accordance with God's expectations. In their definition, the words "mastery" and "art" signify that wisdom was a process of attainment and not an accomplishment. The secular usage bears out the importance of these observations.

Ḥākām appears 132 times in the Hebrew Old Testament. It occurs most frequently in Job, Proverbs, and Ecclesiastes, for which reason these books are known as "wisdom literature". The first occurrence of *ḥākām* is in Gen. 41:8: "And it came to pass in the morning that his spirit was troubled; and he sent and called for all the magicians of Egypt, and all the wise men thereof: and Pharaoh told them his dream; but there was none that could interpret them unto Pharaoh."

The *ḥākām* in secular usage signified a man who was a "skillful" craftsman. The manufacturers of the objects belonging to the tabernacle were known to be wise, or experienced in their crafts (Exod. 36:4). Even the man who was skillful in making idols was recognized as a craftsman (Isa. 40:20; cf. Jer. 10:9). The reason for this is to be found in the man's skill, craftsmanship, and not in the object which was being manufactured. Those who were experienced in life were known as "wise," but their wisdom is not to be confused with the religious usage. Cleverness and shrewdness characterized this type of wisdom. Amnon consulted Jonadab,

who was known as a shrewd man (2 Sam. 13:3), and followed his plan of seducing his sister Tamar. Joab hired a "wise" woman to make David change his mind about Absalom (2 Sam. 14:2).

Based on the characterization of wisdom as a skill, a class of counselors known as "wise men" arose. They were to be found in Egypt (Gen. 41:8), in Babylon (Jer. 50:35), in Tyre (Ezek. 27:9), in Edom (Obad. 8), and in Israel. In pagan cultures the "wise" man practiced magic and divination: "Then Pharaoh also called the wise men and the sorcerers: now the magicians of Egypt, they also did in like manner with their enchantments" (Exod. 7:11); and "... that frustrateth the tokens of the liars, and maketh diviners mad; that turneth wise men backward, and maketh their knowledge foolish" (Isa. 44:25).

The religious sense of *ḥākām* excludes delusion, craftiness, shrewdness, and magic. God is the source of wisdom, as He is "wise": "Yet he also is wise, and will bring evil, and will not call back his words: but will arise against the house of the evildoers, and against the help of them that work iniquity" (Isa. 31:2). The man or woman who, fearing God, lives in accordance with what God expects and what is expected of him in a God-fearing society is viewed as an integrated person. He is "wise" in that his manner of life projects the fear of God and the blessing of God rests upon him. Even as the craftsman is said to be skillful in his trade, the Old Testament *ḥākām* was learning and applying wisdom to every situation in life, and the degree in which he succeeded was a barometer of his progress on the road of wisdom.

The opposite of the *ḥākām* is the "fool" or wicked person, who stubbornly refuses counsel and depends on his own understanding: "For the turning away of the simple shall slay them, and the prosperity of fools shall destroy them" (Prov. 1:32; cf. Deut. 32:5–6; Prov. 3:35).

B. Noun.

ḥokmāh (חָכְמָה, 2451), "wisdom; experience; shrewdness." This word appears 141 times in the Old Testament. Like *ḥākām*, most occurrences of this word are in Job, Proverbs, and Ecclesiastes.

The *ḥākām* seeks after *ḥokmāh,* "wisdom." Like *ḥākām*, the word *ḥokmāh* can refer to technical skills or special abilities in fashioning something. The first occurrence of *ḥokmāh* is in Exod. 28:3: "And thou shalt speak unto all that are wisehearted, whom I have filled with the spirit of wisdom, that they may make Aaron's garments to consecrate him, that he may minister unto me in the priest's office." This first occurrence of the word in the Hebrew Bible bears this out as well as the description of the workers on the tabernacle. The artisan was considered to be endowed with special abilities given to him by God: "And he hath filled him with the spirit of God, in wisdom, in understanding, and in knowledge, and in all manner of workmanship" (Exod. 35:31).

Hokmāh is the knowledge and the ability to make the right choices at the opportune time. The consistency of making the right choice is an indication of maturity and development. The prerequisite for "wisdom" is the fear of the Lord: "The fear of the Lord is the beginning of knowledge: but fools despise wisdom and instruction" (Prov 1:7). "Wisdom" is viewed as crying out for disciples who will do everything to pursue her (Prov. 1:20). The person who seeks *hokmāh* diligently will receive understanding: "For the Lord giveth wisdom: out of his mouth cometh knowledge and understanding" (Prov. 2:6); he will benefit in his life by walking with God: "That thou mayest walk in the way of good men, and keep the paths of the righteous" (Prov. 2:20). The advantages of "wisdom" are many: "For length of days, and long life, and peace, shall they add to thee. Let not mercy and truth forsake thee: bind them about thy neck; write them upon the table of thine heart: so shalt thou find favor and good understanding in the sight of God and man" (Prov. 3:2–4). The prerequisite is a desire to follow and imitate God as He has revealed Himself in Jesus Christ, without self-reliance and especially *not* in a spirit of pride: "A wise man will hear, and will increase learning; and a man of understanding shall attain unto wise counsels: to understand a proverb, and the interpretation; the words of the wise, and their dark sayings. The fear of the Lord is the beginning of knowledge: but fools despise wisdom and instruction" (Prov. 1:5–7). The fruits of *hokmāh* are many, and the Book of Proverbs describes the characters of the *hākām* and *hokmāh*. In New Testament terms the fruits of "wisdom" are the same as the fruits of the Holy Spirit; cf. "But the fruit of the Spirit is love, joy, peace, long-suffering, gentleness, goodness, faith, meekness, temperance: against such there is no law" (Gal. 5:22–23); "But the wisdom that is from above is first pure, then peaceable, gentle, and easy to be entreated, full of mercy and good fruits, without partiality, and without hypocrisy. And the fruit of righteousness is sown in peace of them that make peace" (James 3:17–18).

The importance of "wisdom" explains why books were written about it. Songs were composed in celebration of "wisdom" (Job 28).

Even "wisdom" is personified in Proverbs. *Hokmāh* as a person stands for that divine perfection of "wisdom" which is manifest in God's creative acts. As a divine perfection it is visible in God's creative acts: "Doth not wisdom cry: and understanding put forth her voice? . . . I wisdom dwell with prudence, and find out knowledge of witty inventions. . . . The Lord possessed me in the beginning of his way, before his works of old. . . . Then I was by him, as one brought up with him: and I was daily his delight, rejoicing always before him. . . . Now therefore hearken unto me, O ye children: for blessed are they that keep my ways" (Prov. 8:1, 12, 22, 30, 32).

The Septuagint translations are: *sophos* ("clever; skillful; experienced; wise; learned"); *phronimos* ("sensible; thoughtful; prudent; wise"); and *sunetos* ("intelligent; sagacious; wise"). The kjv gives these translations: "wise; wise man; cunning."

C. Verb.

hākam (חָכַם, 2449), "to be wise, act wisely, make wise, show oneself wise." This root, which occurs 20 times in the Old Testament, appears in other Semitic languages, such as in the Akkadian word *hakamu.* The word means "to be wise" in Prov. 23:15: "My son, if thine heart be wise, my heart shall rejoice, even mine." In Ps. 119:98 *hākam* means "to make wise": "Thou through thy commandments hast made me wiser than mine enemies: for they are ever with me."

TO WITHER

yābēš (יָבֵשׁ, 3001), "to be dry, be dried up, be withered." This term is found throughout the development of the Hebrew language and a few other Semitic languages. It is found approximately 70 times in the Hebrew Old Testament. In its verbal form *yābēš* is found for the first time in Gen. 8:7, when after the Flood, "the waters were dried up from the earth." However, the noun derivative, *yabbāšāh*, which means "dry ground," already occurs in Gen. 1:9.

Physical "drying up" can involve bread (Josh. 9:5), the ground in time of drought (Jer. 23:10; Amos 4:7), brooks and streams (1 Kings 17:7), and crops (Isa. 42:15). The shortness of man's life is compared to the "drying up" of grass (Ps. 90:6; 102:11; Isa. 40:7). Because of affliction, the heart too "withers" like the grass (Ps. 102:4). In his parable of the vine, Ezekiel likens God's judgment on Judah to the "withering" of a vine that is pulled up (Ezek. 17:9–10). Because of his disobedience, Jeroboam's hand "is dried up" as judgment from God (1 Kings 13:4). Psychosomatic awareness is clearly demonstrated in Prov. 17:22: "...A broken spirit drieth the bones."

WITNESS

A. Noun.

ēd (עֵד, 5707), "witness." The 69 occurrences of this word are scattered throughout the various biblical literary genres and periods although it does not appear in historical literature outside the Pentateuch.

This word has to do with the legal or judicial sphere. First, in the area of civil affairs the word can mean someone who is present at a legal transaction and can confirm it if necessary. Such people worked as notaries, e.g., for an oral transfer of property: "Now this was the manner in former time in Israel concerning redeeming and concerning changing, for to confirm all things .... And Boaz said unto the elders, and unto all the people, Ye are witnesses this day, that I have bought all that was Elimelech's, and all that was Chilion's and Mahlon's, of the hand of Naomi" (Ruth 4:7, 9). At a later time the "witnesses" not only acted to attest the transaction and to confirm it orally, but they signed a document or deed of purchase. Thus "witness" takes on the new nuance of those able and willing to affirm the truth of a transaction by affixing their signatures: "And I gave the evidence of the purchase unto Baruch the son of Neriah ... in the sight of Hanameel mine uncle's son, and in the presence of the witnesses that subscribed the book of the purchase ... " (Jer. 32:12). An object or animal(s) can signify the truthfulness of an act or agreement. Its very existence or the acceptance of it by both parties (in the case of the animals given to Abimelech in Gen. 21:30) bears witness: "Now therefore come thou, let us make a covenant, I and thou; and let it be for a witness between me and thee [let it attest to our mutual relationship]" (Gen. 31:44—the first biblical occurrence of the word). Jacob then set up a stone pillar or heap as a further "witness" (Gen. 31:48) calling upon God to effect judgment if the covenant were broken.

In Mosaic criminal law the accused has the right to be faced by his/her accuser and to give evidence of his/her innocence. In the case of a newly married woman charged by her own husband, his testimony is sufficient to prove her guilty of adultery unless her parents have clear evidence proving her virginity before her marriage (Deut. 22:14ff.). Usually the accused is faced with someone who either saw or heard of his guilt: "And if a soul sin, and hear the voice of swearing, and is a witness, whether he hath seen or known of it..." (Lev. 5:1). Heavy penalties fell on anyone who lied to a court. The ninth commandment may well have immediate reference to such a concrete court situation (Exod. 20:16). If so, it serves to sanction proper judicial procedure, to safeguard individuals from secret accusation and condemnation and giving them the right and privilege of self-defense. In the exchange between Jacob and Laban mentioned above, Jacob also cites God as a "witness" (Gen. 31:50) between them, the one who will see violations; God, however, is also the Judge. Although human courts are (as a rule) to keep judge and "witness" separate, the "witnesses" do participate in executing the penalty upon the guilty party (Deut. 17:7), even as God does.

B. Verb.

'ûd (עוּד, 5749), "to take as witness, bear witness, repeat, admonish, warn, assure protection, relieve." This verb, which occurs 42 times in biblical Hebrew, has cognates in Ugaritic (perhaps), Arabic, Aramaic, Syriac, Phoenician, and Ethiopic.

In 1 Kings 21:10 *'ûd* means "to bear witness": "And set two men, sons of Belial, before him, to bear witness against him. . . ." The word means "to warn" in Jer. 6:10: "To whom shall I speak, and give warning, that they may hear?"

WOMAN

'iššāh (אִשָּׁה, 802), "woman; wife; betrothed one; bride; each." This word has cognates in Akkadian, Ugaritic, Aramaic, Arabic, and Ethiopic. It appears about 781 times in biblical Hebrew and in all periods of the language.

This noun connotes one who is a female human being regardless of her age or virginity. Therefore, it appears in correlation to "man" (*'îš*): "... She shall be called Woman, because she was taken out of Man" (Gen. 2:23). This is its meaning in its first biblical usage: "And the rib, which the Lord God had taken from man [*'ādām*], made he a woman, and brought her unto the man" (Gen. 2:22). The stress here is on identification of womanhood rather than a family role.

The stress on the family role of a "wife" appears in passages such as Gen. 8:16: "Go forth of the ark, thou, and thy wife, and thy sons, and thy sons' wives with thee."

In one special nuance the word connotes "wife" in the sense of a woman who is under a man's authority and protection; the emphasis is on the family relationship considered as a legal and social entity: "And Abram took Sarai his wife and Lot his brother's son, and all their substance that they had gathered . . . " (Gen. 12:5).

In Lam. 2:20 'iššāh is a synonym for "mother": "Shall the women eat their [offspring, the little ones who were born healthy]?" In Gen. 29:21 (cf. Deut. 22:24) it appears to connote "bride" or "betrothed one": "And Jacob said unto Laban, Give me my wife, for my days are fulfilled, that I may go in unto her." Eccl. 7:26 uses the word generically of "woman" conceived in general, or womanhood: "And I find more bitter than death the woman, whose heart is snares and nets . . . " (cf. Gen. 31:35).

This word is used only infrequently of animals: "Of every clean beast thou shalt take to thee by sevens, the male and his female: and of beasts that are not clean by two, the male and his female" (Gen. 7:2).

This word can also be used figuratively describing foreign warriors and/or heroes as "women," in other words as weak, unmanly, and cowardly: "In that day shall Egypt be like unto women: and it shall be afraid and fear because of the shaking of the hand of the Lord of hosts. . . " (Isa. 19:16).

In a few passages 'iššāh means "each" or "every": "But every woman shall borrow of her neighbor, and of her that sojourneth in her house. . . " (Exod. 3:22; cf. Amos 4:3). A special use of this nuance occurs in passages such as Jer. 9:20, where in conjunction with rᵉ'ût ("neighbor") it means "one" (female): "Yet hear the word of the Lord, O ye women, and let your ear receive the word of his mouth, and teach your daughters wailing, and every one her neighbor lamentation."

WONDER

môpēt (מוֹפֵת, 4159), "wonder; sign; portent." The 36 appearances of this word are in all periods of biblical literature except wisdom literature. Poetical literature manifests it only 5 times and only in the Psalter.

First, this word signifies a divine act or a special display of divine power: "When thou goest to return into Egypt, see that thou do all those wonders before Pharaoh, which I have put in thine hand . . . " (Exod. 4:21—the first biblical occurrence of the word). Acts effecting the divine curses are called "wonders." Thus the word does not necessarily refer to a miraculous act, if "miracle" means something outside the realm of ordinary providence.

Second, the word can represent a "sign" from God or a token of a future event: "This is the sign which the Lord hath spoken: Behold, the altar shall be rent, and the ashes that are upon

it shall be poured out" (1 Kings 13:3). This sense sometimes has the nuance "symbol": "Now listen, Joshua the high priest, you and your friends who are sitting in front of you—indeed they are men who are a symbol . . . " (Zech. 3:8, NASB; cf. Ps. 71:7).

TO WORK

A. Verbs.

pā'al (פָּעַל, 6466), "to do, work." Common to both ancient and modern Hebrew, this word is used in modern Hebrew in the sense of "to work, to act, to function." Found only 57 times in the Hebrew Old Testament, it is used primarily as a poetic synonym for the much more common verb 'āśāh, "to do, to make." Thus, almost half the occurrences of this verb are in the Book of Psalms. *Pā'al* is used for the first time in the Old Testament in the Song of Moses: " . . . The place, O Lord, which thou hast made for thee to dwell in. . ." (Exod. 15:17). There is no distinction in the use of this verb, whether God or man is its subject. In Ps. 15:2 man is the subject: "He that walketh uprightly and worketh righteousness, and speaketh the truth in his heart."

'āśāh (עָשָׂה, 6213), "to make, do, create." This root also occurs in Moabite and Phoenician (only in a proper name). It occurs in early extra-biblical Hebrew, Hebrew, and about 2,625 times in the Bible (in all periods). It should be distinguished from the second sense of 'āśāh, "to squeeze."

In its primary sense this verb represents the production of various objects. This includes making images and idols: "Thou shalt not make unto thee any graven image . . . " (Exod. 20:4). The verb can mean to make something into something: "And the residue thereof he maketh a god, even his graven image . . . " (Isa. 44:17). In an extended use this verb means to prepare a meal, a banquet, or even an offering: "And he [Abraham] took butter, and milk, and the calf which he had dressed, and set it before them [his three guests] . . . " (Gen. 18:8).

In Gen. 12:5 'āśāh means "to acquire" (as it often does): "And Abram took Sarai his wife, and Lot his brother's son, and all their substance that they had gathered, and the souls that they had gotten in Haran. . . . " The "souls that they had gotten" probably were slaves.

Used in association with "Sabbath" or the name of other holy days, this word signifies "keeping" or "celebrating": "All the congregation of Israel shall keep it [the Passover]" (Exod. 12:47). In a related sense the word means "to spend" a day: "For who knoweth what is good for man in this life, all the days of his vain life which he spendeth as a shadow?" (Eccl. 6:12).

Depending upon its object, *'āśāh* has several other nuances within the general concept of producing some product. For example, with the object "book" the verb means "to write": "... Of making many books there is no end..." (Eccl. 12:12). The Bible also uses this word of the process of war: "These made war with Bera king of Sodom..." (Gen. 14:2). Sometimes the word represents an action: "And Joshua made peace with them, and made a league with them..." (Josh. 9:15). "To make a mourning" is to observe it: "... And he [Joseph] made a mourning for his father seven days" (Gen. 50:10). With "name" the verb means "to gain prominence and fame": "Go to, let us build us a city and a tower, whose top may reach unto heaven; and let us make us a name..." (Gen. 11:4). With the word "workmanship" the word signifies "to work": "And I have filled him with the spirit of God..., and in all manner of workmanship,... to work in gold, and in silver, and in brass" (Exod. 31:3–4).

'Āśāh may represent the relationship of an individual to another in his action or behavior, in the sense of what one does. So Pharaoh asks Abram: "What is this that thou hast done unto me?" (Gen. 12:18). Israel pledged: "All that the Lord hath said will we do, and be obedient" (Exod. 24:7). With the particle *le* the verb signifies inflicting upon another some act or behavior: "Then Abimelech called Abraham, and said unto him, What hast thou done unto us?" (Gen. 20:9). With the particle *'im* the word may mean "to show," or "to practice" something toward someone. The emphasis here is on an ongoing mutual relationship between two parties obligating them to a reciprocal act: "O Lord God of my master Abraham, I pray thee, send me good speed this day, and show kindness unto my master Abraham" (Gen. 24:12). In Gen. 26:29 *'āśāh* appears twice in the sense "to practice toward": "That thou wilt do us no harm, as we have not touched thee, and as we have done unto thee nothing but good...."

Used absolutely this verb sometimes means "to take action": "Let Pharaoh do this, and let him appoint officers over the land..." (Gen. 41:34). In the Hebrew *'āśāh* has no object in this passage—it is used absolutely. Used in this manner it may also signify "to be active": "She seeketh wool, and flax, and worketh willingly with her hands" (Prov. 31:13). In 1 Chron. 28:10 the verb (used absolutely) means "to go to work," to go about doing a task: "Take heed now; for the Lord hath chosen thee to build a house for the sanctuary: be strong, and do it."

This verb used of plants signifies "bringing forth." In Gen. 1:11 it means "to bear" fruit: "... And the fruit tree [bearing] fruit after his kind...." In another nuance this verb represents what a plant does in producing grain: "... It hath no stalk: the bud shall yield no meal..." (Hos. 8:7). The word signifies the production of branches, too: "It was planted in a good soil by great waters, that it might bring forth branches, and that it might bear fruit, that it might be a goodly vine" (Ezek. 17:8).

'Āśāh is used theologically of man's response to divine commands. God commanded Noah: "Make thee an ark of gopher wood..." (Gen. 6:14). Similarly Israel was commanded "to construct" a sanctuary for God (Exod. 25:8). The manipulation of the blood of the sacrifice is what the priest is to do (Lev. 4:20). The entire cultic activity is described by *'āśāh:* "As he hath done this day, so the Lord hath commanded to do..." (Lev. 8:34). Thus in his acts a man demonstrates his inward commitment and, therefore, his relationship to God (Deut. 4:13). Doing God's commands brings life upon a man (Lev. 18:5).

This verb is also applied specifically to all aspects of divine acts and actions. In the general sense of His actions toward His people Israel, the word first occurs in Gen. 12:2, where God promises "to make" Abram a great nation. *'Āśāh* is also the most general Old Testament expression for divine creating. Every aspect of this activity is described by this word: "For in six days the Lord made heaven and earth..." (Exod. 20:11). This is its meaning in its first biblical occurrence: "And God made the firmament, and divided the waters which were under the firmament from the waters which were above the firmament..." (Gen. 1:7). This word is used of God's acts effecting the entire created world and individual men (Exod. 20:6). God's acts and words perfectly correspond, so that what He says He does, and what He does is what He has said (Gen. 21:1; Ps. 115:3).

B. Noun.

ma'āśeh (מַעֲשֶׂה, 4639), "work; deed; labor; behavior." This noun is used 235 times in biblical Hebrew. Lamech, Noah's father, in expressing his hope for a new world, used the noun for the first time in the Old Testament: "And he called his name Noah, saying, This same shall comfort us concerning our work and toil of our hands, because of the ground which the Lord hath cursed" (Gen. 5:29). The word is scattered throughout the Old Testament and all types of literature.

The basic meaning of *ma'ăśeh* is "work." Lamech used the word to signify agricultural labor (Gen. 5:29). The Israelites were commanded to celebrate the Festival of the Firstfruits, as it signified the blessing of God upon their "labors" (Exod. 23:16). It is not to be limited to this. As the word is the most general word for "work," it may be used to refer to the "work" of a skillful craftsman (Exod. 26:1), a weaver (26:36), a jeweler (28:11), and a perfumer (30:25). The finished product of the worker is also known as *ma'ăśeh*: "And in the uppermost basket there was of all manner of bakemeats [literally, "work of a baker"] for Pharaoh. . . . " (Gen. 40:17); "And Moses and Eleazar the priest took the gold of them, even all wrought jewels" [literally, "articles of work"] (Num. 31:51). The artisan plied his craft during the work week, known in Hebrew as "the days of work," and rested on the Sabbath: "Thus saith the Lord God; The gate of the inner court that looketh toward the east shall be shut the six working days; but on the sabbath it shall be opened, and in the day of the new moon it shall be opened" (Ezek. 46:1; cf. Exod. 23:12).

The phrase "work of one's hands" signifies the worthlessness of the idols fashioned by human hands: "Asshur shall not save us; we will not ride upon horses: neither will we say any more to the work of our hands, Ye are our gods: for in thee the fatherless findeth mercy" (Hos. 14:3). However, the prayer of the psalmist includes the request that the "works" of God's people might be established: "And let the beauty of the Lord our God be upon us: and establish thou the work of our hands upon us; yea, the work of our hands establish thou it" (Ps. 90:17). Since the righteous work out God's work and are a cause of God's rejoicing, "the glory of the Lord shall endure for ever: the Lord shall rejoice in his works" (Ps. 104:31).

In addition to "work," *ma'ăśeh* also denotes "deed," "practice," or "behavior." Joseph asked his brothers, accused of having taken his cup of divination: "What deed is this that ye have done? wot ye not that such a man as I can certainly divine?" (Gen. 44:15). The Israelites were strongly commanded not to imitate the grossly immoral behavior of the Canaanites and the surrounding nations: "After the doings of the land of Egypt, wherein ye dwelt, shall ye not do: and after the doings of the land of Canaan, whither I bring you, shall ye not do: neither shall ye walk in their ordinances" (Lev. 18:3; cf. Exod. 23:24). However, the Israelites did not listen to the warning, and they "were mingled among the heathen, and learned their works. . . . Thus were they defiled with their

own works, and went a whoring with their own inventions" (Ps. 106:35, 39).

Thus far, we have dealt with *ma'ăśeh* from man's perspective. The word may have a positive connotation ("work, deed") as well as a negative ("corrupt practice"). The Old Testament also calls us to celebrate the "work" of God. The psalmist was overwhelmed with the majesty of the Lord, as he looked at God's "work" of creation: "When I consider thy heavens, the work of thy fingers, the moon and the stars, which thou hast ordained" (Ps. 8:3; cf. 19:1; 102:25). The God of Israel demonstrated His love by His mighty acts of deliverance on behalf of Israel: "And Israel served the Lord all the days of Joshua, and all the days of the elders that [out] lived Joshua, and which had known all the works of the Lord, that he had done for Israel" (Josh. 24:31; cf. versions).

All of God's "works" are characterized by faithfulness to His promises and covenant: "For the word of the Lord is right; and all his works are done in truth" (Ps. 33:4).

Ma'ăśeh is translated in the Greek as *ergon* ("deed; action; manifestation") and *poiema* ("what is made; work; creation"). English translations are "work" (KJV, RSV, NASB, NIV), "doing" (KJV and RSV), "practice" (NASB, NIV).

TO WORSHIP

šāhāh (שָׁחָה, 7812), "to worship, prostrate oneself, bow down." This word is found in modern Hebrew in the sense of "to bow or stoop," but not in the general sense of "to worship." The fact that it is found more than 170 times in the Hebrew Bible shows something of its cultural significance. It is found for the first time in Gen. 18:2, where Abraham "bowed himself toward the ground" before the 3 messengers who announced that Sarah would have a son.

The act of bowing down in homage is generally done before a superior or a ruler. Thus, David "bowed" himself before Saul (1 Sam. 24:8). Sometimes it is a social or economic superior to whom one bows, as when Ruth "bowed" to the ground before Boaz (Ruth 2:10). In a dream, Joseph saw the sheaves of his brothers "bowing down" before his sheaf (Gen. 37:5, 9–10). *Šāhāh* is used as the common term for coming before God in worship, as in 1 Sam. 15:25 and Jer. 7:2. Sometimes it is in conjunction with another Hebrew verb for bowing down physically, followed by "worship," as in Exod. 34:8: "And Moses made haste, and bowed his head toward the earth, and worshiped." Other gods and idols are also the object of such worship by one's prostrating oneself before them (Isa. 2:20; 44:15, 17).

WRATH

A. Noun.

hēmāh (חֵמָה, 2534), "wrath; heat; rage; anger." This noun occurs in Semitic languages with the meanings "heat, wrath, poison, venom." The noun, as well as the verb *yāham*, denotes a strong emotional state. The noun is used 120 times, predominantly in the poetic and prophetic literature, especially Ezekiel.

The first usage of *hēmāh* takes place in the story of Esau and Jacob. Jacob is advised to go to Haran with the hope that Esau's "anger" will dissipate: "And tarry with him a few days, until thy brother's fury turn away" (Gen. 27:44).

The word indicates a state of anger. Most of the usage involves God's "anger." His "wrath" is expressed against Israel's sin in the wilderness: "For I was afraid of the anger and hot displeasure, wherewith the Lord was wroth against you to destroy you" (Deut. 9:19). The psalmist prayed for God's mercy in the hour of God's "anger": "O Lord, rebuke me not in thine anger, neither chasten me in thy hot displeasure" (Ps. 6:1). God's "anger" against Israel was ultimately expressed in the exile of the Judeans to Babylon: "The Lord hath accomplished his fury; he hath poured out his fierce anger, and hath kindled a fire in Zion, and it hath devoured the foundations thereof" (Lam. 4:11).

The metaphor "cup" denotes the judgment of God upon His people. His "wrath" is poured out: "Therefore he hath poured upon him the fury of his anger, and the strength of battle: and it hath set him on fire round about, yet he knew not; and it burned him, yet he laid it not to heart" (Isa. 42:25); and the "cup of wrath" is drunk: "Awake, awake, stand up, O Jerusalem, which hast drunk at the hand of the Lord the cup of his fury; thou hast drunken the dregs of the cup of trembling ... " (Isa. 51:17).

Thus, God as the Almighty Potentate is angered by the sins and the pride of His people, as they are an insult to His holiness. In a derived sense, the rulers on earth are also described as those who are angered, but their "anger" is aroused from circumstances over which they have no control. Naaman was angry with Elisha's advice (2 Kings 5:11–12); Ahasuerus became enraged with Vashti's refusal to display her beauty before the men (Esth. 1:12).

Hēmāh also denotes man's reaction to everyday circumstances. Man's "rage" is a dangerous expression of his emotional state, as it inflames everybody who comes close to the person in rage. "Wrath" may arise for many reasons.

Proverbs speaks strongly against *hēmāh*, as jealousy (6:34); cf. "Wrath is cruel, and anger is outrageous; but who is able to stand before envy?" (Prov. 27:4; cf. Ezek. 16:38). The man in rage may be culpable of crime and be condemned: "Be ye afraid of the sword: for wrath bringeth the punishments of the sword, that ye may know there is a judgment" (Job 19:29). The wise response to "rage" is a soft answer: "A soft answer turneth away wrath: but grievous words stir up anger" (Prov. 15:1).

Hēmāh is associated with *qin'āh*, "jealousy," and also with *nāqām*, "vengeance," as the angered person intends to save his name or avenge himself on the person who provoked him. In God's dealing with Israel He was jealous of His Holy name, for which reason He had to deal justly with idolatrous Israel by avenging Himself: "That it might cause fury to come up to take vengeance; I have set her blood upon the top of a rock, that it should not be covered" (Ezek. 24:8); but He also avenges His people against their enemies: "God is jealous, and the Lord revengeth; the Lord revengeth, and is furious; the Lord will take vengeance on his adversaries, and he reserveth wrath for his enemies" (Nah. 1:2). Other synonyms of *hēmāh* are *'ap*, "anger," and *qesep*, "wrath," as in Deut. 29:27 and Jer. 21:5.

There are two special meanings of *hēmāh*. One is "heat," as in "the Spirit lifted me up, and took me away, and I went in bitterness, in the heat of my spirit; but the hand of the Lord was strong upon me" (Ezek. 3:14). The other is "poison," or "venom," as in Deut. 32:33: "Their wine is the poison of dragons, and the cruel venom of asps."

The Septuagint gives the following translations: *orge* ("anger; indignation; wrath") and *thumos* ("passion; anger; wrath; rage"). The KJV gives these senses: "fury; wrath; poison."

B. Verb.

yāham (יָחַם, 3179), "to be fiery, be hot." This verb, which occurs only 10 times in biblical Hebrew, is the root of the noun *hēmāh*.

In Deut. 19:6 *yāham* means "to be hot": "Lest the avenger of the blood pursue the slayer, while his heart is hot, and overtake him. . . . "

TO WRITE

A. Verb.

kātab (כָּתַב, 3789), "to write, inscribe, describe, take dictation, engrave." This verb appears in most Semitic languages (not in Akkadian or Ugaritic). Biblical Hebrew attests around 203 occurrences (in all periods) and biblical Aramaic 7 occurrences.

Basically, this verb represents writing down a

message. The judgment (ban) of God against the Amalekites was to be recorded in the book (scroll): "And the Lord said unto Moses, Write this for a memorial in a book, and rehearse it in the ears of Joshua: for I will utterly put out the remembrance of Amalek from under heaven" (Exod. 17:14—the first biblical occurrence of the word).

One may "write" upon a stone or "write" a message upon it. Moses told Israel that after crossing the Jordan "thou shalt set thee up great stones, and plaster them with plaster: and thou shalt write upon them all the words of this law . . ." (Deut. 27:2–3).

This use of the word implies something more than keeping a record of something so that it will be remembered. This is obvious in the first passage because the memory of Amalek is "to be recorded" and also blotted out. In such passages "to be recorded," therefore, refers to the unchangeableness and binding nature of the Word of God. God has said it, it is fixed, and it will occur. An extended implication in the case of divine commands is that man must obey what God "has recorded" (Deut. 27:2–3). Thus, such uses of the word describe a fixed body of authoritative instruction, or a canon. These 2 passages also show that the word does not tell us anything specific about how the message was composed. In the first instance Moses seems not to have merely "recorded" as a secretary but "to have written" creatively what he heard and saw. Certainly in Exod. 32:32 the word is used of creative writing by the author; God was not receiving dictation from anyone when He "inscribed" the Ten Commandments. In Deut. 27:2–3 the writers must reproduce exactly what was previously given (as mere secretaries).

Sometimes kātab appears to mean "to inscribe" and "to cover with inscription." The 2 tablets of the testimony which were given to Moses by God were "tables of stone, written [fully inscribed] with the finger of God" (Exod. 31:18). The verb means not only to write in a book but "to write a book," not just to record something in a few lines on a scroll but to complete the writing. Moses prays: "Yet now, if thou wilt forgive their sin—; and if not, blot me, I pray thee, out of thy book which thou hast written" (Exod. 32:32). Here "book" probably refers to a scroll rather than a book in the present-day sense.

Among the special uses of kātab is the meaning "to record a survey." At Shiloh, Joshua told Israel to choose three men from each tribe "and they shall arise, and go through the land, and describe it . . ." (Josh. 18:4).

A second extended nuance of kātab is "to receive dictation": "And Baruch wrote from the mouth of Jeremiah . . ." (Jer. 36:4). The word can also be used of signing one's signature: "And because of all this we make [are cutting] a sure covenant, and write it; and our princes, Levites, and priests, seal unto it" (Neh. 9:38). Thus they "cut," or completed, the agreement by having the representatives sign it. The cutting was the signing.

B. Nouns.

kᵉtāb (כְּתָב, 3791), "something written; register; scripture." This noun occurs 17 times in the Old Testament.

In 1 Chron. 28:19 kᵉtāb is used to mean "something written," such as an edict: "All this, said David, the Lord made me understand in writing by his hand upon me, even all the works of this pattern." The word also refers to a "register" (Ezra 2:62) and to "scripture" (Dan. 10:21).

Two other related nouns are kᵉtōbet and miktāb. Kᵉtōbet occurs once to mean something inscribed, specifically a "tatooing" (Lev. 19:28). Miktāb appears about 9 times and means "something written, a writing" (Exod. 32:16; Isa. 38:9).

TO BE WROTH, ANGRY

A. Verb.

qāṣap (קָצַף, 7107), "to be wroth, angry." This verb appears 34 times and is found mainly in the Pentateuch and in the prophets, and a few times in the historical books and the poetic literature. The word is used in rabbinic Hebrew, but its use in modern Hebrew has been displaced by other verbs. It is an ancient Canaanite word; as a gloss it appeared in the Amarna Tablets with the meaning "to become worried," or according to others, "to be embittered." The relation with the Arabic cognate qasafa is doubtful.

The general meaning of qāṣap is a strong emotional outburst of anger, especially when man is the subject of the reaction. The first usage of the word brings this out: "And Pharaoh was wroth against two of his officers . . . and he put them in [custody] . . ." (Gen. 40:2–3; cf. 41:10). Moses became bitterly angry with the disobedient Israelites (Exod. 16:20). The leaders of the Philistines "were wroth" with Achish (1 Sam. 29:4), and Naaman was strongly irritated by Elisha's lack of a sense of protocol (2 Kings 5:11). Elisha expressed his anger with Joash, king of Israel (2 Kings 13:19). King Ahasuerus deposed Vashti in his anger (Esth. 1:12). In these examples an exalted person (generally a king) demonstrated his royal anger in radical measures against his subjects. He was in a position "to be angered" by the response of his subjects. It is rarer for a person "to become angry" with an equal. It is even rarer for a subject "to be angry" with his superior: "... Two of the king's chamberlains ... were wroth, and sought to lay hand on the king Ahasuerus" (Esth. 2:21).

The noun derived from qāṣap particularly refers to God's anger. The verb qāṣap is used 11 times to describe man's anger and 18 times to refer to God's anger. This fact, coupled with the observation that the verb generally is an expression of a superior against a subject, explains why the biblical text more frequently uses qāṣap to describe God's anger. The object of the anger is often indicated by the preposition 'al ("against"). "For I was afraid of the anger ['ap] and hot displeasure [ḥēmāh], wherewith the Lord was wroth [qāṣap] against ['al] you to destroy you" (Deut. 9:19). The Lord's anger expresses itself against disobedience (Lev. 10:6) and sin (Eccl. 5:5ff.). However, people themselves can be the cause for God's anger (Ps. 106:32). In the wilderness the Israelites provoked God to wrath by their disobedience and lack of faith: "Remember, and forget not, how thou provokedst the Lord thy God to wrath in the wilderness: from the day that thou didst depart out of the land of Egypt, until ye came unto this place, ye have been rebellious against the Lord" (Deut. 9:7; cf. vv. 8, 22). Moses spoke about God's wrath against Israel's disobedience which would in time be the occasion for the Exile (Deut. 29:27), and the prophets amplify Moses' warning of God's coming "wrath" (Jer. 21:5). After the Exile, God had compassion on Israel and turned His anger against Israel's enemies (Isa. 34:2).

In the Greek version we find the following translations: orgizomai ("to be angry") and lupew ("to grieve, to pain, to be sad").

B. Noun.

qeṣep (קֶצֶף, 7110), "wrath." This noun occurs 28 times in biblical Hebrew and generally with reference to God. One occurrence of God's "wrath" is in 2 Chron. 29:8: "Wherefore the wrath of the Lord was upon Judah and Jerusalem. . . ." An example of man's "wrath" appears in Esth. 1:18: "Likewise shall the ladies of Persia and Media say this day unto all the king's princes, which have heard of the deed of the queen. Thus shall there arise too much contempt and wrath" (cf. Eccl. 5:17).

Y

YEAR

šānāh (שָׁנָה, 8141), "year." This word has cognates in Ugaritic, Akkadian, Arabic, Aramaic, and Phoenician. Biblical Hebrew attests it about 877 times and in every period.

This Hebrew word signifies "year": "And God said, Let there be lights in the firmament of the heaven to divide the day from the night; and let them be for signs, and for seasons, and for days, and years" (Gen. 1:14—the first biblical occurrence of the word). There are several ways of determining what a "year" is. First, the "year" may be based on the relationship between the seasons and the sun, the solar year or agricultural year. Second, it can be based on a correlation of the seasons and the moon (lunar year). Third, the "year" may be decided on the basis of the correlation between the movement of the earth and the stars (stellar year). At many points the people of the Old Testament period set the seasons according to climatic or agricultural events; the year ended with the grape and fruit harvest in the month Elul: "[Thou shalt keep] the feast of harvest, the first fruits of thy labors, which thou hast sown in the field: and the feast of ingathering, which is in the end of the year, when thou hast gathered in thy labors out of the field" (Exod. 23:16).

The Gezer calendar shows that by the time it was written (about the tenth century B.C.) some in Palestine were using the lunar calendar, since it exhibits an attempt to correlate the agricultural and lunar systems. The lunar calendar began in the spring (the month Nisan, March-April) and had twelve lunations, or periods between new moons. It was necessary periodically to add a thirteenth month in order to synchronize the lunar calendar and the number of days in a solar year. The lunar calendar also seems to have underlain Israel's religious system with a special rite to celebrate the first day of each lunar month (Num. 28:11–15). The major feasts, however, seem to be based on the agricultural cycle, and the date on which they were celebrated varied from year to year according to work in the fields (e.g., Deut. 16:9–12). This solar-agricultural year beginning in the spring is similar to (if not derived from) the Babylonian calendar—the names of the months are Babylonian derivatives. These 2 systems, therefore, appear side by side at least from the time of Moses. An exact picture of the Old Testament "year" is difficult, if not impossible, to obtain.

YOUTH

na'ar (נַעַר, 5288), "youth; lad; young man." This word is found in Ugaritic, and it seems that the Egyptian word *na-arma* ("armed retainers") is also related to the West Semitic usage. The root with the meaning of "youth" occurs only as a noun and occurs in Hebrew in the feminine (*na'ărāh*, "young girl") as well as the masculine form (e.g., Gen. 24:14).

Na'ar occurs 235 times in the Hebrew Old Testament. Its use is predominant in the Pentateuch and in the historical books. The first occurrence is in Gen. 14:23–24: "... I will not take any thing... save only that which the young men have eaten, and the portion of the men which went with me, Aner, Eshcol, and Mamre; let them take their portion."

The basic meaning of *na'ar* is "youth," over against an older man. At times it may signify a very young child: "For before the child shall know to refuse the evil, and choose the good, the land that thou abhorrest shall be forsaken of both her kings" (Isa. 7:16). Generally *na'ar* denotes a "young man" who is of marriageable age but is still a bachelor. We must keep in mind the opposition of youth and old age, so that we can better understand that Jeremiah, while claiming to be only a "youth," was not necessarily a youngster. In truth, he argued that he did not have the experience of the older men, when he said: "Ah, Lord God! behold, I cannot speak: for I am a child" (Jer. 1:6).

Absalom was considered a *na'ar*, even though he was old enough to lead the troups in rebellion against David: "And the king commanded Joab and Abishai and Ittai, saying, Deal gently for my sake with the young man, even with Absalom" (2 Sam. 18:5).

A derived meaning of *na'ar* is "servant." Jonathan used a "servant" as armorbearer: "Now it came to pass upon a day, that Jonathan the son of Saul said unto the young man that bare his armor, Come, and let us go over to the Philistines' garrison, that is on the other side" (1 Sam. 14:1). The *na'ar* ("servant") addressed his employer as "master": "And when they were by Jebus, the day was far spent; and the servant said unto his master, Come, I pray thee, and let us turn into this city of the Jebusites, and lodge in it" (Judg. 19:11). Kings and officials had "servants" who were referred to by the title *na'ar*. In this context the word is better translated as "attendant," as in the case of the attendants of King Ahasuerus, who gave counsel to the king: "Then said the king's servants [NASB, "attendants"] that ministered unto him, Let there be fair young virgins sought for the king" (Esth. 2:2). When a *na'ar* is commissioned to carry messages, he is a "messenger." Thus, we see that the meaning of the word *na'ar* as "servant" does not denote a "slave" or a performer of low duties. He carried important documents, was trained in the art of warfare, and even gave counsel to the king.

Another noun *nō'ar* means "youth." This noun appears only 4 times in the Bible, once in Ps. 88:15: "I am afflicted and ready to die from my youth up: while I suffer thy terrors I am distracted" (cf. Job 36:14).

The Septuagint gives the following translation(s): *paidarion* ("little boy; boy; child; young slave"); *neos* ("novice"); *neaniskos* ("youth; young man; servant"); *paidion* ("infant; child"); *pais* ("child"); and *neanias* ("youth; young man").

ENGLISH WORD INDEX

A

abandon, to, 87-88
abased, to be, 118-119
abhor, to, 1
abhorrent, to treat as, 1
abide, to, 64-65, 197-198
ability, 183-184
able, to be, 31, 273
abominably, to act, 1
abomination, 1
abomination, to cause to be an, 1
abundance, 102, 156
accede, to, 160
accept, to, 160
accept favorably, to, 1
acceptance, 79
accident, things heard by, 108
account, 163
account, to, 59
acquainted with, to be (get), 60, 130, 219
acquire, to, 28-29, 52
Adam (the first man), 146-147
add, to, 2
admissible, to be, 186-187
admonish, to, 292
adversary, 71, 213-214
advise, to, 49
affair, 179
affirmation, to utter an, 216-217
afflict, to, 182
afflicted, to be, 119, 180-182
afraid, to be, 79-80
after, 15
afterwards, 15
again, to do, 2
agitation, 156-157
aid, to, 110
air, 240-241
alike, 263-264
alive, 138-139
all, 2-3
all at once, 263-264
allotment, 48-49
all together, 263-264
alone, 172
alone, to be, 172
alongside, 104
altar, 3, 28
always, 47
amen, 17
among, 3-4, 17
ancestor, 78-79
angel, 4-5
anger, 161-162, 296
anger, burning, 5
angry, to be (get), 5, 162, 297-298
angry, to make, 191

anguish, 131
animal, domesticated, 14-15
annihilate, to, 59
annihilation, complete, 47
anoint, to, 5, 151
anointed one, 5-6, 150-151
anointment, 151
answer, to, 6, 216
anvil, 246
anymore, 246
apart from, 172
apostasy, 203
appalled, to be, 58
appearance, 74-75
appointed time, 263
approach, to, 40, 165
appropriate, to be, 100
ardor, 125
area, 150
area, closed, 22-23
area round about, 271-272
arise, to, 6-7
ark, 7-8
arm, 8
armor, 274-275
arm(rest), 104
army, to muster an, 12-13, 116-117, 247-248
aroma, 215-216
around, to go, 269-271
arrange, to, 225-226
arrogantly, to behave, 114
artificer, 179-180
ascend, to, 40
ashamed, to be, 227
ashamed, to feel, 227
asherah, 8-9
asherim, 8-9
ashes, 63-64
aside from, 172
ask, to, 9, 220
assemble, to, 90-91
assembly, 9
assign, to, 60
assist, to, 110
associate with, to, 43
astonished, to be, 58
astray, to go, 171
at all times, 48
atone, to, 10, 194-196
atonement, gift of, 166-170
attach to, 271-272
attain, to, 170
attend, to, 153
attention, to give (pay), 60, 130-131, 273
authority, 242
avenge, to, 10-11, 194-196
awake, to, 11

away, to take, 255-256
awe, to stand in, 79-80

B

baal, 12
back, at the, 133
backturning, 203-204
balance, to, 136
band, marauding, 12-13
bandits, 12
band (of raiders), 12-13
banish, to, 63
bare, to make, 158
bark, to, 157
base, 22, 186-187
bathe, to, 281-282
battle, 81, 281
battle, to do, 81
battle, to engage in, 281
battlement, 252
be, to, 13-14
beams, 146
bear, to, 14
bear fruit, to, 89
beast, riding, wild, 14-15
beauty, 92-93
become, to, 13
becoming, to be, 100
bed, 135
befall, to, 68
before, 258
before, to be, to go, 45
beget, to, 14
begin, to, 180
beginning, 106-107
behave, to, 279-280
behavior, 293-295
behind, 15, to be, 264, to remain, 133
behold, to, 139, 277
belief, to have, 15
believe, to, 15-16, 76
bend, to, 171
bend the knee, to, 23
beneath, 248
besides, 171
best, 99-100
bestow care on, to, 153
betrothed one, 292-293
better, 99-100
between, 17
beyond one's power, to be, 149
bind, to, 17-18
birth, to be in pangs of, 60
birth, to give, 71
blame, to be without, 176
blameless, 176

blanket, 89
blast, to give a, 20
bless, to, 18-19
blessed, 19
blessed, to be, 18
blessing, 18-19
blood, 19-20
blow, to, 20
boast, to, 184-185
body, 20-21
bolt a door, to, 189-190
bone, 20-21
book, 21-22, 163-164
booty, 22
border, 60-70, 104
bosom, 22
boulder, 208
boundary, 22-23
bow, to, 23
bow down, to, 23, 171, 295-296
bowed down, to be, 119
bowels, 43
box, 7-8
boy, 14
branch, 267-268
bread, 23-24
breadth, 24
break, to, 24-25, break open, 38,
      break through, 38
breath, 25, 240
breathe, to, 237-238
breeze, 240
bride, 292-293
bring, to 40, bring back 203-204,
      bring forth 14, bring out, 95
broken, to be, 60
bronze, 48
bronze chains, 48
brother, 25
build, to, 25-26
building, house or, 117-118
bullock, 26-27
burden, 139
burdensome, to be, 101
burn, to, 27
burning, 27
burning one, 27
bury, to, 28
buy, to, 28-29

C

calamity, 29
call, to, 29-30
call out, to, 52-53
camp, 30-31
can, 31
Canaan, 31-32
Canaanite, 31-32
capable, 247-248
captain, 41-42
captive, to take, 255
capture, to, 255

caravan, 280
carried off, to be, 177
carry, to, 189, carry away, 200-
      210
case, 248
cast, to, 32, 134, 183, cast out,
      251-252
catch, to, 255
cattle, 14, 32-33, 110, small, 84-
      85
cause, 249-250
cease, to, 33, 46
celebrate, to, 184-185
censer, 28
cereal offering, 165-166
certain, to be, 76, 186-187
change, to, 172, 269-270
charge, to make a, 179
charge over, to have, 126
chariot, 34
chariotry, 34
chastisement, 123-124
chest, 7
chief, 41-42, 87, 102, 189
chief (elected), 201
chief leader, 258
child, 14, 285-286
chisel, 253-254
choicest, 106-107
choose, to, 56-57, 149, choose
      out, 149
chosen ones, 35, 219
circle, 218-219
circuit, 269-270
circumcise, to, 35
city, 35-36
clan, 77
clap, to, 20
clean, 36-37
clean, to be, 36
clear, to make, 269-270
cleave, to, 37-38
client, 236-237
cliff, 208
cling, to, 37
clods, 63-64
close, to, 228
close, to keep, 37
closed area, 22-23
cloth, 89, piece of, 172
clothe, to, 38
clothed, to be, 38
clothing, 274
cloud, 38-39
coffin, 7-8
cogitate, to, 140
collar, 155-156
collect, to, 90-91
combat, 281, to engage in, 81
come, to, 39
come down, to, 94-95
come forth, to, 95
come near, to, 40

come out, to, 95
comes forth, that which, 95-96
come up, to, 40-41
comfort, to, 201-202
command, 155-156
command, to, 41, 216
commander, 41-42
commandment, 42
commotion, 156-157
commotion, lively, 156-157
companion, 42-43, 88
company, 9
compare, 225-226
compare, to, 136
compassion, to have, 43-44
compassionate, 44
complete, 174, 176
complete, to, 44
complete, to be, 46, 174, 176, 194
completed to be, 46
completeness, 174, 176
condition, 284-285
condition, low, 119
conduct, 284-285, loose, 139-140
conduct a legal case, to, 179
conceal, to, 111
concerned with, to be, 164
confederacy, 50-51
confess, to, 44-45
confidence, 218-219
confidential plan(s), 218
confidential talk, 218
confiding, the act of, 218-219
confinement, 282-283
conflict, 116-117
confront, to, 45
congregation, 45-46
consecrate, to, 5-6
consent, to, 160, 288
consider, to, 273
considerate, to be, 100-101
construct, to, 25-26
consult, to, 9, 49, 220-221
consume, to, 67
consumed, to be, 177
consumption, 47
contend, to, 249-250
contentions, 249-250
contentious, to be, 193
continual, 47
continually, 47-48
continue, to, 2
continuity, 47-48
convince, to, 203
convocation, 30
copper, 48
copy, 244
cord, 48-49
corner, 271-272
corrupt, to, 59
couch, 135
courage, 240-241
course, 279-280, 285
court, 49-50

expiate, to, 195-196
explain, to, 257
extend, to, 150
extent, 150
exterminate, to, 59
extraordinary, to be, 149
extremity, 69-70
eye, 74-75

F

face, 75, 161-162
fail, to, 177
faithful, 143
faithful, to be, 15-16
faithfulness, 15-16, 75-76, 142
falsehood, 76-77
falsity, 56
family, 77
famine, 77
famine, to suffer, 78
far, 78
fashion, to, 86-87
fast, to stand, 15
father, 78-79
favor, 79, 101
favorable, 99-100
favorable, to be, 79
favored, to make oneself, 79
fear, 79-80
fear, to, 79-80
feast, 80
feed, to, 67
fell, to, 145-146
fellow, 88
festal sacrifice, 80
festive, 99-100
field, 80-81, open, 81
fiery, to be, 296
fiery being, 27
fight, to, 81, 281
figure, 136-137
fill, to, 81-82
find, to, 82
finish, to, 44
finished, to be, 46, 176
fire, 82-83
fire offering, 169
firm, 250-251
firm, to be, 15-16
firmness, 16
first, 87, 105-107
firstborn, 83
first fruits, 83
fix, to, 225
flee, to, 83
flesh, 83-84
flight, to take, 83
fling, to, 32
flock, 84-85
flood, 283-284
flow, to, 183
foe, 71

fog, 38-39
follow after, to, 191-192
following, 85
food, 23-24, 67
fool, 85, 251
foolishness, 85
foot, 85-86, 246
forbear, to, 33
force, 183-184
forced labor, 116-117
forefather, 78-79
foremost, 107
forfeit, to, 233-234
forget, to, 86
forgive, to, 86
form, 136-137
form, to, 86-87
former, 87, 107
fornication, to commit, 286-287
forsake, to, 87-88
fortress, small, 266
fragrance, 215-216
frequent, to, 220-221
friend, 42-43, 88, 142
friendly, 109
friends with, to make, 79
front of, in, 258
fruit, 23-24, 88-89
fruit, to bear, 89
fulfill, 81-82
full, 20-21, 82, 176
future, 133

G

gain, 22
garment, 89
gate, 61-62, 89-90
gather, to, 10, 90-91
gather in, to, 91
gathering, 218
genealogy, 194
generation, 91-92
genuinely, 17
get, to, 28-29, 52, 82
gift, 166-170
gird, to, 17-18
give, to, 56-57
glad, 197
glad, to be, 61, 100
glorify, to, 93
glorious, to be, 101-102
glory, 92-93, 114-115, 184
glory, to, 184-185
go, to, 39, 279-280
goat-demons, 96
goat-idols, 96
goats, 84-85
go back, to, 203-204
go down, to, 94-95
go forth, to, 95-96
god (God), 96-98
God Almighty, 97-98

God for Ever, 98
God of Eternity, 98
God the Everlasting, 98
godly, 143, 178
gods, 120
gods, to serve other, 286-287
going forth, 95-96
going forth, place of, 95-96
gold, 98-99
good, 61, 100-101
good, to be, 61, 100
good, to do, 61
goodness, 142-143
goodwill, 79
go out, to, 95-96
grace, 101, 142-143
gracious, 101
gracious, to be, 100-101
graciously received, to be, 79
grandeur, 112
grandfather, 78-79
grandmother, 153-154
grasp, to, 189-190, 255
grave, 28
great, 102-103, 144-145
great, to be, 101-102, 143-144
great, to become, 156
great dignity, 144
greatly, 74
great (magnified), to evidence
    oneself as, 143-144
greatness, 144
great things, 144
grievance, 230-231
groan, to, 157
ground, 132-133
group, 32-33
growl, to, 150
grow up, to, 143-144
guard, 127, 282-283
guard, to, 126-127
guardpost, 127
guideline, 257
guilt, 121-122, 169, 230-234,
    266-267
guilt offering, 169, 230
guilty, 231-232, 287-288
guilty, to be, 231-232

H

habitation, 259
half, 103-104
halfway, 103-104
hand, 104-105
hand, palm of, 171
hand-measure, 104-105
hang down, to, 192
happy, 19
happy, to be, 100
hard, 250-251
harden, to, 250
harlot, to be a, 286-287

harness, to, 17-18
harvest, 238-239
haste, to make, 105, 146
hasten, to, 105, 146, 208-209
hate, to, 105
hatred, 105
haughtiness, 74, 112
head, 105-107
heal, to, 107
health, 173-174
healthy, to become, 62
hear, to, 107-108
heard, something, 108
hearken, to, 107-108
hearsay, 108
heart, 108-109, 237-238
heat, 296
heathen, 159
heaven, 109-110
heavens, 109-110
heave offering, 167-168
heavy, 116, 250-251
heavy, to be, 101-102
Hebrew, 173
height, 7, 74, 112
he is, 260-261
help, 8
help, to, 110, 214-215
helpless, one who is, 181-182
herd, 110
hero, 110-111
hide, to, 111
high, 111-112
high, to be, 73-74, 112
higher plane, 74
highest, 112
highest, the, 41
highly, 74
high place, 112-113
highway, 284-285
hill, rocky, 208
hind-part, 70
hold, to take, 255
hold fast, to, 189-190
hold of, to lay, 255
holiness, 114
holy, 113-114, 213
holy, to be, 114, 210-212
holy thing, 114, 212
home, 117-118, 259
honest, 187
honesty, 16-17
honor, 114-115, 186
honor, to, 114-116
honored, to be, 101-102, 186
hoofbeats, 246
horse, 116, chariot, 34
host, 20-31, 116-117
hot, to be, 296
house, 117-118
household, 117-118
household idol, 120
howbeit, 70
however, 70

human, 148-149
human being, 148-149
humble, 119, 180-181
humble, to, 118-119
humble, to be, 118-119
humbled, to be, 119
humiliated, to be, 119
hunger, 77
hungry, 78
hungry, to be, 78
husband, 148-149

I

idol, 25, 120
idol, household, 120
idols, 120
if, 176
image, 244
imagine, to, 261-262
impoverish, to, 182
imprison, to, 17-18, 228
impropriety, 85
impute, to, 261-262
in, to go, 39
incense, 28
incense, to burn, 27-28
incense altar, 28
increase, to, 2
indecent thing, 157-158
influential, 247-248
inform, to, 257-258
inhabit, to, 64-65, 255
inhabitant, 65
inherit, to, 120-121, 182
inheritance, 121
iniquity, 121-122, 230-232
iniquity, to do, 121
inner, 272
innocent, 103
innocent, to be, 103
inquire, to, 9, 220-221
inscribe, to, 296-297
insignificant, to be, 236
instruct, to, 134
instruction, 123-124, 133-134,
    256
instrument, 274-275
integrity, to have, 47
interval of, in the, 17
intervene, to, 185-186
inward part, 4
irrigate, to, 92
isolated, to be, 172
issue, 70
it is, 260-261

J

jealous, 125
jealous, to be, 124-125
jealousy, 125

jewelry, 274-275
journey, 284-285
journey, to, 58
joy, 197
joyful, 197
joyful, to be, 100, 196-197
judge, to, 125-126, 185-186, 203
judgment, 126
just, 206-207
just, to be, 205
justified, to be, 205

K

keep, to, 126, 283
kid, 131-132
kill, to, 59-60, 127-128
king, 130
king, to be, 196
kingdom, 129-130
kinsman, to act as a, 194-195
knee, to bend the, 23
kneel, to, 18
knife, flint, 253-254
know, to, 130-131
knowledge, 131

L

labor, 116-117, 131, 294-295
labor, forced, 116-117
labor, to, 131
labors, 224
lack, to, 33
lad, 299
lamb (male), 131-132
lament, to, 154
land, 66, 117-118, 132-133
land (political), 133
land (the whole earth), 132-133
land, dry, 132-133
land, open, 251
land, pasture, 251
language, 264-265
lap, 22
large, 102-103
large, to be, 101-102
large tree, 267
last, 133
later, 133
laud, to, 184-185
law, 133-134, 244-245
lay hold of, to, 255
lay, to, 56-57
leader, 41-42, 189
league, 50-51
learn, to, 256-257
learn, to cause to, 256-257
leave, to, 87-88, 93
leave behind, to, 87-88
left, to be, 134
left over, to be, 87-88, 200

quarrel, 249-250
quarter (of a city), 35-36
queen, to be, 196
quiet, to be, 203

R

rage, 296
raid, 12-13
raiding party, 12-13
ram, young, 131-132, 192-193
ransom, to, 194-195
rare, 186
ravaged, to be, 58
reach, to, 265
reach unto, to, 104
readied, to be, 186-187
reason, for no, 162
rebel, to, 193-194
rebellion, 193
rebellious, 193
rebuild, to, 25-26
receive, to, 255-256
received, to be graciously, 79
receptacle, 274
recite, to, 29-30
reckon, to, 59, 194
recognize, to, 60, 130-131
recompense, to, 194
recount, to, 163
redeem, to, 194-196
redemption, (right of), 196
reduced, one who is, 180-182
refine, to, 259-260
refreshed, to be, 238
refuse, to, 58-59
regard, to, 60, 130-131, 139
region, 48-49
register, 296
regularly, 47
regulation, 244-246
reign, 129, 196
reign, to, 196
reject, to, 58-59
rejoice, to, 196-197
relative, 174-176
reliant, to be, 218-219
relieve, to, 292
remain, to, 64-65, 197-199, 202
remainder, 134-135, 198
remaining, 65
remain over, to, 134
remember, to, 198
remembrance, 199
remnant, 199-200
remotest time, 72
remove, to, 200-201
rend, to, 201
renew, to, 160
renewed, 160
renown, 158-159
repay, to, 44
repeat, to, 292

repent, to, 201-202
reply, to, 6
report, 108
reproach, 202-203
reputation, 114-116, 158-159
request, 179
require, to, 220-221
required, the, 252
resemble, to, 136
residue, 199-200
respire, to, 237-238
respond, to, 6
rest, 199-200
rest, to, 203
restitution, gift of, 166-170
result, 88-89
retain, to, 127
return, to, 203
reveal, to, 93
revelation, 108
reverence, 80
reward, 88-89
reward, to, 44
rich, 116
riches, 286
ride, to, 204
ride, to cause to, 204
ride upon, to, 34
riding beast, 14-15
rid of, to get, 221
right, 99-100, 187, 273-274
right, to be, 273-274
right, to be in the, 205
righteous, 205-206
righteous, to be, 205-206
righteousness, 205-206, 273-274
right hand, 204
rights, 126
right side, on the, 205
ripen, to, 55
rise early, to, 207
river, 207-208
road, 284
roar, to, 157
rock, 208
rocky hill, 208
rocky surface, 208
rocky wall, 208
rod, 248-249, 268-269
rope, 48-49
round about, 271
rouse, to, 11
rouse oneself, to, 11
ruin, to, 59
ruin, to go to, 177
rule, 104-105, 129-130, 208
rule, to, 125-126, 244-245
ruler, 41-42
running, 209
run, to, 208-209

S

sabbath, the, 33-34

sacrifice, 210
sacrifice, to, 235
sacrificial smoke, place of, 28
saddlecloth, 89
salvation, 214
sanctify, to, 114, 210-213
sanctuary, 114
Satan, 213-214
sated, to be, 214
satisfied, to be, 214
satisfy, to, 1-2
save, to, 214
savor, 215-216
say, to, 216, 239
saying, 217
say sharp things, to, 202-203
scatter, to, 217, 242
scatter abundantly, to, 242
scattered, to be, 217
scatter seed, to, 238
scribe, 164
scripture, 296-297
sea, 217
search, to, 164, 220
season, 263
seat, 262
secret, 218
secret plans, 218
secret talk, 218
section, 150
secure, 218
securely, 218
security, the state of, 218
see, to, 219, 277
seed, 217
seed, to scatter, 217
seedtime, 220
seek, to, 220
seek with pleasure, to, 153
seer, 277
seize, to, 189, 255
select, to, 149, 219
self, 237-238
selfsame, 21
sell, to, 221
send, to, 221
send away, to, 221
senselessness, 85
separate, to, 222-223
separated, one who is, 223
separated, to be, 222-223
sepulcher, 28
servant, 152, 223
serve, to, 152, 223
serve other gods, to, 286-287
service, 116-117, 224
service, military, 116-117
set, to, 225-227
set against, to, 105
set in order, to, 225
set out, to, 58, 225
settle down, to, 65
set up, to, 56-57, 225
severe, 116

HEBREW WORD INDEX

This index lists the transliterated Hebrew words which are found in *Nelson's Expository Dictionary of Old Testament Words*. Immediately following each Hebrew word are two numbers set in brackets and set off from one another by a semicolon. The first is the reference number assigned to that word in the Hebrew and Chaldee Dictionary of *Strong's Exhaustive Concordance of the Bible*. By using a word's reference number, the student can then use *Strong's Concordance* to find every biblical reference where the indexed word may be found. The second number refers to the page in the *Hebrew and English Lexicon of the Old Testament* by Brown, Driver, and Briggs (BDB) where the word is listed. The lower case letter adjoining the BDB number refers to the quarter of the page on which the indexed word is found. Thus, *a* refers to the upper left, *b* the lower left, *c* the upper right, and *d* the lower right. The student can use the BDB number to discover the various forms and meanings the word takes in the Old Testament.

The page or pages on which an indexed word is found in *Nelson's Expository Dictionary of Old Testament Words* are listed immediately following the bracketed reference and BDB numbers.

A

'āb [1; 3a] 78, 79

'ābad [5647; 712b] 152, 177, 223, 224

'ăbaddôn [11; 2b] 177

'ābāh [14; 2c] 160, 288

'ābal [56; 5b] 154

'ābar [5674; 716d] 172, 173, 233

'ăbārāh [5679; 720b] 173

'ăbēdāh [9; 2b] 177

'abdān [13; 2b] 177

'ăbôdāh [5656; 715a] 224

'ad [5703, 5705; 723c, 1105b] 2, 72, 102

'ādām [120; 9a] 132, 146, 147, 148, 149, 292

'ădāmāh [127; 9c] 132

'ādār [142; 12a] 161

'adderet [155; 12b] 161

'addîr [117; 12b] 161

'ādōm [119; 10a] 132, 146, 147

'ādôn [113; 10d] 12, 140

'ădōnāy [136; 10d] 140, 158

'āh [251; 26b] 25, 42, 153, 154

'āhab [157; 13b] 141, 142

'ahăbāh [160; 13b] 142

'āhar [309, 310; 29b, 29d] 15, 133, 264

'ahărît [319, 320; 31a, 1079d] 70

'ahărôn [314; 30d] 87, 133

'āhaz [270; 28a] 189, 190, 255

'āhēb [157; 12d] 141, 142

'aher [312; 29c] 85

'āhîm [251; 26b] 25

'āhôt [269; 27d] 153, 235

'ăhuzzāh [272; 28c] 189

'ākal [398; 37a] 67

'āklāh [402; 38b] 67

'ālāh [423; 46d] 54

'ālāh [5927; 748a] 40

'allāh [427; 47c] 96

'allûp [441; 48d] 33

'almāh [5959; 761c] 276, 277

'almānāh [490; 48b] 288

'am [5971; 766b] 129, 159, 174, 175, 176

'āmad [5975; 763c] 7, 243

'āmāl [5999; 765d] 122, 123, 131, 231

'āman [539; 1081a] 15, 16, 76

'āmar [559; 55c] 30, 216, 239

'āmēl [6001; 766a] 131

'āmēn [543; 53b] 76

'ammāh [520; 52a] 53

'ammûd [5982; 765a] 244

'ānāh [6030, 6031; 772c, 775d, 776a] 6, 119, 182

'ānān [6051; 777d] 38, 39

'ānap [599, 60a] 162

'ānāšîm [376; 35d] 148

'ānāw [6035; 776c] 182

'ănāwāh [6038; 776c] 181

'ănî [6041; 776d] 119, 180, 181

'ap [639; 60a] 161, 162, 296

'āpār [6083; 779c] 63, 64

'apuddāh [642; 65d] 71

'ārāh [732; 72d] 285

'ārāh [6168; 788c] 158

'ārak [6186; 789b] 225, 226

'ārar [779; 76c] 53, 54

'arbeh [697; 916a] 156

'ărî [738; 71c] 137

'ărîṣ [6184; 792a] 71

'armôn [759; 74d] 258

'ărōm [6174; 735d] 158

'ārôn [727; 75b] 7

'āśāh [6213; 796b] 51, 52, 293, 294

'āšām [817; 79d] 169, 170, 230

'āsap [622; 62a] 90, 91

'ašērāh [842; 81b] 8, 113

'ašērîm [842; 81b] 8

'ašmōret [821; 1038a] 127

'ašmûrāh [821; 1038a] 127

'ašrê [835; 80d] 19

'aššāp [825; 80b] 68

'āwāh [5753; 730c, 731c] 121, 231

'āwen [205; 19d] 120, 122, 123, 230

'āwōn [5771; 730d] 86, 121, 122, 231

'ayil [352; 17d, 18a,b] 178, 192, 193, 267

'ayin [369; 34a] 69, 230

'ayin [5869; 744a] 74, 75, 161

'āzab [5800; 736d] 87, 88

'āzar [5826; 740b] 110

'azkārāh [234; 272b] 199

B

ba'al [1167; 127b] 12, 140, 148

bad [905, 906; 94c, 94b] 172

bādad [909; 94d] 172

bāhar [977; 103d] 34, 35, 149

bāhîr [972; 104c] 35, 149

bāhûr [970; 104c] 67, 145, 149

bāla' [1104; 108c] 253

bāmāh [1116; 119a] 112, 113

bānāh [1129; 124a] 25, 26

bāqa' [1234; 131d] 38

bāqar [1239; 133a] 153

bāqar [1241; 133a] 84, 110

bāqaš [1245; 134c] 220
bārā' [1254; 135d] 51, 52
bārah [1272; 137d] 71, 83
bārak [1288; 138c] 18
bāśār [1320; 142b] 83, 84, 139
bātah [982; 105a] 218
bat [1323; 123a] 26
bayit [1004; 108c] 78, 117, 118, 258
be'ēr [875; 91c] 178
beged [899; 93d] 89
behemāh [929; 96d] 14
behûrôt [979; 104c] 149
bekôr [1060; 114a] 83
beliya'al [1100; 116a] 288
bēn [1121; 119d] 14, 26
bên [996; 1084b] 17
berākāh [1295; 140a] 18, 19
berît [1285; 136b] 50, 51, 245
beṭah [983; 105b] 218
betûlîm [1331; 144a] 145
betûlôth [1330; 143d] 145
bikkûrîm [1061; 114c] 83
bîn [995; 106c] 273
bînāh [998; 1084b] 273
bô' [935; 97c] 39, 95
bōqer [1242; 133c] 110, 152, 153
bôš [954; 101d] 227
bōšet [1322; 102a] 227

D

da'at [1847; 395c] 131
dābaq [1692; 179c] 37
dābar [1696; 180b] 239
dābār [1697; 182a] 50, 239, 288
dabberet [1703; 184c] 240
dal [1800; 195d] 181, 182
dālal [1809; 195c] 182
dallāh [1803; 195d] 182
dallîm [1800; 195d] 181
dām [1818; 196b] 19, 20
dāmāh [1819; 197d] 136
dāraš [1875; 205a] 220, 221
day [1767; 191b] 252
deber [1698; 184a] 178
debôrāh [1682; 184b] 240
demût [1823; 198b] 136, 137, 244
derek [1870; 202c] 284, 285
dibrāh [1700; 184a] 240
dōr [1755; 189c] 91, 92

E

'ebed [5650; 713d] 224, 225
'eben [68; 6b] 246, 247
'ēber [5676; 719b] 173
'ebyôn [34, 2d] 159, 160, 181
'ēd [5707; 729c] 292
'ēd [343; 15c] 29, 122
'ēdāh [5713; 730a] 51, 245
'ēdāh [5712; 417a] 45, 46

'eder [145; 12a] 161
'ēdût [5715; 730b] 245, 260
'ēl [410; 41d] 96, 97, 98, 158
'ēlāh [426; 1080c] 96, 97
'elem [5958; 761c] 276, 277
'elep [504; 48c] 32, 33
'elyôn [5945; 751b] 41, 112
'ĕlîl [457; 47b] 120
'ĕlôah [433; 43a] 97
'ĕlōhîm [430; 43b] 5, 7, 97, 120, 158
'ēlôn [436; 18d] 267
'ēm [517; 51c] 78, 153, 154
'emdāh [5979; 765a] 244
'ēmer [561; 56d] 216, 240
'ĕmet [571; 54a] 16, 76, 142, 143
'ēmîm [367; 33d] 120
'ĕmûnāh [530; 53c] 16, 75, 76, 142, 143
'ĕnôš [582; 60d] 147, 148, 149
'epes [657; 67a] 68, 69, 70
'ēpôd [646; 65b] 71
'ereb [6153; 787d] 71
'ereṣ [776; 75d] 66, 132, 133
'erwāh [6172; 788d] 157, 158
'eryāh [6181; 789a] 158
'ērōm [5903; 735d] 158
'ēš [784; 77b] 82, 83
'ēs [6086; 781c] 267
'eṣem [6106; 782c] 20, 21
'ēt [6256; 773b] 263
'ĕwîl [191; 17b] 85
'ezrôa' [248; 284b]8

G

gā'āh [1342; 144b] 187
gā'al [1350; 146b] 194, 195
ga'ăwāh [1346; 144d] 188
ga'ăyôn [1349; 145b] 188
gābāh [1362; 147a] 111, 112
gābar [1396; 149c] 111
gābōah [1364; 147a] 111
gādad [1413; 151a] 13
gādal [1431; 152a] 73, 103, 143, 144, 156
gādēl [1432; 152d] 145
gādôl [1419; 152d] 144, 236
gālāh [1540; 162d] 93
gāmal [1580; 168a] 55
gā'ôn [1347; 144d] 187, 188
gāraš [1644; 176c] 251, 252
gē' [1341; 144b] 188
gē'āh [1344; 144d] 188
geber [1397; 149d] 111, 147, 148
gebûl [1366; 147d] 22, 23
gebûlāh [1367; 148b] 23
gebûrāh [1369; 150b] 151, 152
gedî [1423; 152a] 132
gedûd [1416; 151b] 12, 13
gedùllāh [1420; 153c] 144
gē'eh [1343; 144b] 188
gēr [1616; 158a] 237

gērût [1628; 158c] 237
ge'ullāh [1353; 145d] 196
gē'ût [1348; 145a] 188
gibbôr [1368; 150a] 110, 111
gib'āh [1389; 148d] 113
gillûlîm [1544; 165c] 120
gōbah [1363; 147b] 111, 112
gōdel [1433; 152d] 144
gôlāh [1473; 163c] 94
gôrāl [1486; 174a] 141
gôy [1471; 156c] 159, 176
gôyim [1471; 156c] 159
gûr [1481, 1482; 157c, 158d] 137, 236, 237

H

hādal [2308; 292d] 33
hādar [1921; 213d] 114
hādār [1926; 214a] 115
hădārah [1927; 214c] 115, 116
hādaš [2318; 293d] 160
hādāš [2319; 294a] 160
hag [2282; 290d] 80
hāgāh [1897; 211c] 150
hākam [2449; 314b] 273, 291
hākām [2450; 314c] 290, 291
hālāh [2470; 318c] 228, 229
hālak [1980; 229d] 204, 279, 280
hālal [1984; 237d] 184
hālal [2490; 320a] 180
hālam [2492; 321b] 62
hālap [2498; 322a] 172
hālaq [2505; 323c] 60, 61
hālîk [1978; 237b] 280
halîkāh [1979; 237b] 280
halleluyah [1984; 238b] 44
halôm [2472; 321c] 62
halōm [2492; 321b] 62
hāmāh [1993; 242a] 157
hāmas [2554; 329b] 276
hāmās [2555; 329b, 329c] 276
hāmôn [1995; 242b] 156, 157
hānāh [2583; 333b] 30
hānan [2603; 1093b] 100, 101, 162
hannûn [2587; 337a] 101
hāpak [2015; 245b] 269, 270
hāpēs [2654, 2655; 342c, 343a] 179
hāqaq [2710; 349a] 245, 246
har [2022; 249a] 154
hārab [2717; 352b] 254
hārag [2026; 246d] 128
hārāh [2734; 354a] 5
hārap [2778; 357c] 203
hāraš [2790; 361a] 179, 180
hārāš [2796; 360d] 180
hārôn [2740; 354c] 5
hāšab [2803; 362d] 59, 261, 262
hāsîd [2623; 339c] 143, 178
hāṭā' [2398; 306c] 121, 232, 233
hātat [2865; 369a] 60

mᵉkônāh [4350; 467d] 187
mᵉl'kāh [4399; 521d] 4
melek [4428; 572d] 130
melqāhayim [4457; 544c] 256
mē'mar [3983; 1081b] 216
mᵉ'ôd [3966; 547b] 74
mᵉqaṭṭērāh [4729; 883b] 28
merkābāh [4818; 939d] 34
mᵉrî [4805; 598b] 193, 194
mᵉrîbāh [4808; 937b] 250
mērûṣ [4793; 930c] 209
mēsab [4524; 687b] 271
mᵉšûbāh [4878; 1000b] 204
mᵉzimmāh [4209; 273c] 139, 140
mibṭāh [4009; 105c] 218
middāh [4060; 551c] 150
midbār [4057; 184c] 240
midraš [4097; 205d] 221
migdāl [4026; 153d] 144, 266
migrāš [4054; 177b] 251
miktāb [4385; 508b] 297
milḥāmāh [4421; 536a] 81, 281
min [4480; 577d] 69, 103, 161, 172
minhāh [4503; 585a] 166, 167, 196
mipleṣet [4656; 814a] 120
miqdāš [4720; 874a] 213
miqqāh [4727; 899d] 256
miqrā' [4744; 896d] 30
miqṭār [4729; 883b] 28
miqṭeret [4730; 883b] 28
mir'eh [4829; 945c] 228
mišḥāh [4888; 603b] 151
miškāb [4904; 1012d] 135
miškān [4908; 1015c] 64, 254, 255
mišlah [4916; 1020a] 222
mišlôah [4916; 1020a] 222
mišmān [4924; 1032d] 170
mišmār [4929; 1038b] 127, 282, 283
mišmeret [4931; 1038b] 127, 245, 282, 283
mišneh [4932; 1041c] 50
mîšôr [4334; 449d] 274
mišpāhāh [4940; 1046c] 77, 194
mispār [4557; 708d] 163
mišpāṭ [4941; 1048b] 76, 126, 245
miṣwāh [4687; 846b] 42, 245
miṭṭāh [4296; 641d] 249
mizbēah [4196; 258a] 3, 236
mô'ēd [4150; 417b] 45, 46
môledet [4138; 409d] 14
môpēt [4159; 68d] 293
môrā' [4172; 432b] 80
môrāh [4177; 559a] 158
môrāš [4180; 440c] 182
môrāšāh [4181; 440c] 182
môṣā' [4161; 425d] 95
môšā'ôt [4190; 448a] 215
môtār [4195; 452d] 198
mûl [4135; 557d] 35

mûsab [4141; 687c] 271
mûsār [4148; 416b] 123, 124
mût [4191; 559b] 59, 60
muṭṭôt [4298; 642a] 249

N

nā'am [5001; 610c] 216
na'ar [5288; 654c] 67, 299
na'ārāh [5291; 655a] 145, 299
nābā' [5012; 612a] 190
nābaṭ [5027; 613c] 139
nābî' [5030; 611c] 190, 191
nahal [5159; 635a] 121
nahal [5157; 635c] 120, 121
nahălāh [5159; 635a] 121
nāham [5162; 636d] 201, 202
nādah [5080; 623a] 63
nādar [5087; 623d] 278
nāga' [5060; 619a] 265
nāgad [5046; 616c] 257, 258
nāgash [5066; 620c] 40
nāgîd [5057; 617d] 258
nāhār [5104; 625c] 207
nāhar [5102; 625c] 208
nākar [5234; 647d] 60, 130
nākrî [5237; 648d] 237
nāpaš [5314; 661c] 237, 238
nāqāh [5352; 667a] 103
nāqam [5358; 667d] 10, 11
nāqām [5359; 668b] 11, 296
nāqî [5355; 667c] 103
nāsa' [5265; 652a] 58, 86
nāśā' [5375; 669d] 189, 200, 201
nāṣab [5324; 662a] 178, 243
nāśag [5381; 969c] 170
nāṣah [5329; 663d] 126
nāṣar [5341; 665c] 126
nāśî' [5387; 672b] 189, 201
nāta' [5193; 642b] 178, 179
nātāh [5186; 639d] 248, 249, 269
nātan [5414; 678a] 56, 57
nāzar [5144; 634c] 222, 223
nāzîr [5139; 634c] 223
nᵉbālāh [5039; 615a] 85
nᵉbî'āh [5031; 612c] 191
neder [5088; 623d] 278, 279
nega' [5061; 619c] 265, 266
neged [5048; 617a] 258
nᵉhōšet [5178; 638d] 48
nepeš [5315; 659b] 108, 138, 139, 171, 220
nᵉsibbāh [5252; 687c] 271
nᵉśî'îm [5387; 672b] 189, 201
nᵉ'um [5002; 610b] 216, 217
nō'ar [5290; 655a] 299
nûah [5117; 628a] 203
nûs [5127; 630c] 71, 83

O

'ôb [178; 15b] 241, 242

'ôd [5749; 728c] 2, 72, 102
'ôdem [124; 10b] 147
'ôhel [168; 13d] 46, 255, 259
'ôkel [400; 38a] 67
'ôlāh [5930; 750b] 40, 168, 169, 210
'ôlām [5769; 761d] 72, 98
'ômed [5977; 765a] 244
'ômer [562; 56d] 216
'onî [6040; 777a] 181, 231
'ôr [216; 21c] 136
'ôrah [734; 73a] 285
'ôrāh [219; 21d] 136
'ôrhāh [736; 73c] 285
'ôt [226; 16d] 229
'ôyēb [341; 33b] 70, 71
'ôzen [241; 23d] 65

P

pā'al [6466; 821b] 293
pa'am [6471; 821d] 246
pā'ar [6286; 802b] 93
pādāh [6299; 804a] 195
pālā' [6381; 810c] 149
pālal [6419; 813a] 185, 186
pānāh [6437; 815a] 271, 272
pānîm [6440; 815d] 75, 272
pāqad [6485; 823b] 164
pāqîd [6496; 824b] 164
pār [6499; 830d] 26
pārad [6504; 825b] 222
pārāh [6509, 6510; 826a, 831a] 27, 89
pāraš [6566; 831a] 242
pāša' [6586; 833b] 232, 266
pātah [6605; 834d] 62
pᵉdût [6304; 804b] 196
peh [6310; 804d] 155, 156, 265
pele' [6382; 810b] 149, 150
pᵉnîmāh [6441; 819b] 272
pᵉnîmî [6442; 819b] 272
pᵉrî [6529; 826b] 88, 89
peša' [6588; 833b] 231, 266, 267
petah [6607; 835d] 61, 62
pinnāh [6438; 819c] 272
piqqûd [6490; 824b] 51
pûṣ [6327; 806d] 217

Q

qābar [6912; 868b] 28
qābaṣ [6908; 867c] 90, 91
qādam [6923; 869d] 45
qādaš [6942; 872d] 113, 210, 211, 212
qādēš [6942, 6945; 872d, 873c] 114, 212, 213
qādôš [6918; 872c] 113, 213
qāhal [6950; 874d] 10
qāhāl [6951; 874c] 9, 10, 45
qālal [7043; 886b] 53, 54

zār [2114; 266b] 237
zāra' [2232; 281b] 238
zāraq [2236; 284c] 242
zayit [2132; 268b] 276

zebaḥ [2077; 257b] 3, 210, 235, 236
zeker [2143; 271b] 199
*z*e*qēnāh* [2205; 279a] 68

zera' [2233; 282a] 238, 239
*z*e*rôa'* [2220; 283d] 8
zikkārôn [2146; 272a] 199
zimmāh [2154; 273b] 140

An Expository Dictionary
of
New Testament Words

with their Precise Meanings
for English Readers

by
W. E. Vine, M.A.

PUBLISHER'S PREFACE

This new edition of W. E. Vine's *An Expository Dictionary of New Testament Words* includes many new features and provides the Bible student with a number of significant additional benefits. The new typesetting has allowed for numerous factual and typographical errors to be corrected, for British spellings to be changed to their more familiar American counterparts, and for a new two-column format that is easier to use than the previous edition. Additionally, the numbering system found in the Greek lexicon of *The New Strong's Exhaustive Concordance of the Bible* (1984) is included immediately following the Greek word in each entry, as well as in the Index. The reader is encouraged to read the following instructions to gain the fullest benefit of this added feature.

1. Words not listed in *Strong's* Greek lexicon but which are simple compounds of other words that are listed are indicated by a combination of numbers (for instance, *diachleuazo,* 1223 and 5512).

2. Phrases of two or more words (for instance, *men oun, ei me*) are not numbered in the main text of *Vine's* unless there is a separate entry for them in *Strong's.*

3. Irregular verbs that are listed separately in *Vine's,* but not in *Strong's,* are indicated as a tense of the verb (for instance, *eipon,* aorist of 3004).

4. Intensives, diminuitives, comparatives, or similar forms of other words not listed in *Strong's* are indicated with a single asterisk (for instance, *eleeinoteros,* from *eleeinos* is 1652*).

5. Differing gender, number, or verb forms (for instance, infinitive or participle) of other words not listed in *Strong's* are indicated with a double asterisk (for instance, *opsia,* from *opsion,* is 3798**).

6. Variant spellings of forms of other words not listed in *Strong's* are indicated with a "v" following the number (for instance, *ektromos,* a variant of *entromos,* is 1790v).

7. Derivatives or roots of other words not listed in *Strong's* are indicated with a "d" following the number (for instance, *genema,* a derivative of *ginomai,* is 1096d).

8. Words not listed in *Strong's* are indicated with an "a" following the number of the word that would precede them alphabetically if they were included in *Strong's.*

Character	Name	Transliteration
α	alpha	a
β	beta	b
γ	gamma	g
δ	delta	d
ε	epsilon	e
ζ	zeta	z
η	eta	ē
θ	theta	th
ι	iota	i
κ	kappa	k
λ	lambda	l
μ	mu	m

ν	nu	n
ξ	xi	x
o	omicron	o
π	pi	p
ρ	rho	r
σ, s	sigma	s
τ	tau	t
υ	upsilon	u or y
ϕ	phi	ph
χ	chi	ch
ψ	psi	ps
ω	omega	ō
'	rough breathing mark	h

In the Index we have included two numbers following each entry word, set with brackets. The first number is the *Strong's* reference; the second refers to the page number in *A Greek-English Lexicon of the New Testament and Other Early Christian Literature* by Bauer, Arndt, and Gingrich, Second Edition (Chicago: 1979). In this way the beginning student can best be directed to the place where the various forms and meanings a word takes in the New Testament are explained and illustrated.

We are pleased to add this new and corrected edition of *Vine's* to our list. We therefore send it forth with the same intention Professor Vine expressed in 1939, that it might benefit those who study and teach the Bible "in their knowledge of God and His Word and in helping to equip them in their use and ministry of the Holy Scriptures."

The Publishers

FOREWORD

Anyone who makes a serious and substantial contribution to the understanding of the New Testament renders a public service, for if religion is the foundation of morality, by the knowledge of God is the welfare of the people. As a book the New Testament stands alone and supreme, simple in its profoundness, and profound in its simplicity. It is the record, in twenty-seven Writings, of the origin, nature, and progress of Christianity, and in the quality of its influence it has done more for the world than all other books together.

We are more than fortunate to have this Book in a Version made immortal by William Tyndale, and we are grateful to have it also in the Revised Versions of 1611, and 1881–1885. But the fact remains that they who are entirely dependent upon a Version must miss very much of the glory and richness of these Writings. Provided there is spiritual appreciation, he who can read the New Testament in the language in which it was written stands to get the most out of it. But, of course, all cannot do this, although the accomplishment is by no means the preserve of the linguistic scholar. Yet the average reader is not wholly cut off from the treasures which lie in the Greek of the New Testament, for these have been put within our reach by means of Grammars and Lexicons, the special purpose of which has been to aid the English reader. So far as my acquaintance with these works goes, I do not hesitate to say that this Expository Dictionary more completely fulfills this design than any other such effort, in that it is at once a concordance, a dictionary, and a commentary, produced in the light of the best available scholarship.

Without encumbering this work with philological technicalities and extra-biblical references, Mr. Vine puts at the disposal of the English reader the labors of a lifetime bestowed devoutly upon the New Testament.

To several of the features of this Dictionary I would like to call attention.

First, it shows how rich is the language of the New Testament in words which present shades of the meaning of some common idea.

A good illustration of this is found on pages 108–110, under *Come,* and its related thoughts [e.g., *Appear,* pp. 31–32]. Here, including the compounds, upwards of fifty words are employed to express one general thought, and the employment of any one of these, in any given passage, has precise historical or spiritual significance. If this root idea is followed out, for example, in its bearing on Christ's Second Advent, it is profoundly important to apprehend the significance respectively of *erchomai, heko, phaino, epiphaino, parousia, apokalupsis,* and *epiphaneia.*

Second, this Dictionary indicates the doctrinal bearing which the use of chosen words has. A case in point will be found on page 29, under *Another.* The use of *allos* and *heteros* in the New Testament should be carefully examined, for *another numerically* must not be confounded with *another generically.* Mr. Vine points this out in John 14:16. When Christ said, "I will make request of the Father, and He shall give you another Helper (*allon Parakleton*)," He made a tremendous claim both for Himself and for the Spirit, for *allos* here implies the personality of the Spirit, and the equality of both Jesus and the Spirit with the Father. See also Mr. Vine's reference to the use of these words in Galatians 1:6 and 7. For an illustration of how one word can have a variety of meanings see pages 146–147 under *Day.* Unless such expressions as "man's day," "day of the Lord," and "day of Christ," are distinguished, one cannot understand the dispensational teaching of the New Testament. In this connection, the RV must be followed in 2 Thess. 2:2.

Third, this Dictionary shows how very many New Testament words are compounds, and how important are prepositional prefixes.

I think it was Bishop Westcott who said that New Testament doctrine is largely based on its prepositions; in any case the importance of them can scarcely be exaggerated. These added to a word either emphasize or extend its meaning, and many such words have become Anglicized. For illustration take the three words *anabolism, katabolism,* and *metabolism.* These words are used in relation to biology and physiology. The root word in each is *ballo,* "to cast, or throw," and each has a prepositional prefix; in the first, *ana,* "up"; in the second, *kata,* "down"; and in the third, *meta,* "with." *Metabolism* tells of the chemical changes in living cells, by which the energy is provided for the vital processes and activities, and new material is assimilated to repair the waste; by a proper *metabolism* or *throwing-together* of the substances of the body, health is promoted. This building up of the nutritive substances into the more complex living protoplasm is *anabolism,* or *throwing-up;* and the want of this results in *katabolism,* or *throwing-down* of protoplasm. Now, two of the three words occur in the New Testament. For *metaballo* see pp. 95–96; and for *kataballo,* p. 91, in both cases all the references are given (see Preface, p. xii, par. 4).

For the possible range of prefixes to one word, see pages 108–109; *Come,* with *eis,* and *ek,* and *epi,* and *dia,* and *kata,* and *para,* and *pros,* and *sun;* and two of the eleven compounds are double. No. 4 with *epi* and *ana;* and No. 8 with *para* and *eis.* These illustrations are sufficient to show the scope and simplicity of this work and consequently its immense usefulness to the English reader.

Fourth, this Dictionary is compiled in the light of the new knowledge which has come to us by the discovery of the papyri. During the last fifty years this light has been brought to bear upon the New Testament with precious and priceless results. In olden days in Egypt it was a custom not to burn waste paper, but to dump it outside the town, and the sands of the desert swept over it, and buried it, and for centuries a vast mass of such rubbish has lain there. However, in 1896–1897 Dr. Grenfell and Dr. Hunt began digging at Oxyrhynchus and discovered a number of papyri, among which was a crumpled leaf, written on both sides in uncial characters, which proved to be a collection of Sayings attributed to Jesus, Logia which Dr. J. Hope Moulton believed to be genuine. These and very many other papyri were classified and edited and one day when Dr. Deissmann was casually looking at a volume of these in the University Library at Heidelberg, he was impressed by the likeness of the language to that with which he was familiar in his study of the Greek New Testament. By further study the great discovery was made that New Testament Greek is not the Attic of the Classics, nor is it "a language of the Holy Ghost" as one scholar called it, but it is the ordinary vernacular Greek of that period, the language of everyday life, as it was spoken and written by the ordinary men and women of the day, tradesmen, soldiers, schoolboys, lovers, clerks, and so on, that is, the *koine,* or "Common" Greek of the great Graeco-Roman world.

In illustration of this, look at Col. 2:14, which has several words which are found in the papyri; and take one of these, *Cheirographon,* "handwriting." This means a memorandum of debt, "a writing by hand" used in public and private contracts, and it is a technical word in the Greek papyri. A large number of ancient notes of hand have been published and of these Dr. Deissmann says, "a stereotyped formula in these documents is the promise to pay back the borrowed money, 'I will repay'; and they all are in the debtor's own hand, or, if he could not write, in the handwriting of another acting for him, with the express remark, 'I have written for him.'" In such a note-of-hand, belonging to the first century and with reference to a hundred silver drachmae, one named Papus wrote on behalf of two people who could not write, "which we will also repay, with any other that we owe, I Papus wrote for him who is not able to write."

Now, this expression occurs in the New Testament twice, in the parable of "The Lord and his Servants," "have patience with me, and I will pay thee all," and in Paul's note to Philemon concerning Onesimus, "if he hath wronged thee, or oweth thee ought, put that on mine account. I Paul have written it with mine own hand, I will repay it."

In the famous Florentine papyrus of A.D. 85, the governor of Egypt gives this order in the course of a trial,—"Let the hand-writing" of Col. 2:14. Many such illustrations might be given, from which we see that the papyri have a distinct expository value.

In Lexicons previous to this discovery are to be found lists of what are called *hapax legomena,* words which occur once only, and many of which, it was supposed, were created by the Holy Spirit for the conveyance of Christian truth, but now all or nearly all such words have been found in the papyri. The Holy Spirit did not create a special language for Christianity, but used the colloquial tongue of the time; He employed the cosmopolitan Greek. This fact has radically affected our approach to the New Testament, and although, in view of the magnitude of this Dictionary, it has been impossible to do more than make a reference here and there to this learning, yet the whole is produced in the light of it, and so represents present day scholarship.

I might have made reference also to etymological, cross-reference, and other values in this work, but perhaps enough has been said to indicate its scope and usefulness. Mr. Vine has done a great service to the non-academic reader of the New Testament, and those also who are most familiar with the original tongue may learn much from these pages.

W. Graham Scroggie, D.D.
(Edin.)

FOREWORD
TO NEW ONE-VOLUME EDITION

Nearly twelve years have gone by since the first edition of this *Expository Dictionary* was completed. During these years the work has had ample opportunity to prove its worth as a handbook for serious students of the English Bible. And the high hopes with which the enterprise was launched have been justified not only by the warm welcome each volume of the first edition received as it appeared but also by the increasing sense of indebtness which Bible students all over the world have felt as they have come to know its value by daily use. Mr. Vine himself has passed from our midst in the meantime, but his biblical ministry survives in a wide range of published works, at the head of which stands his *Expository Dictionary.* It is a welcome token of its continued usefulness that the publishers have now decided to reissue it in a one-volume edition.

There is no work just like this. The English reader with little or no Greek has, of course, the standard concordances, notably Wigram's *Englishman's Greek Concordance;* the student of Greek has his Grimm-Thayer, Moulton-Milligan, and Bauer. These works provide the lexical skeleton; Mr. Vine's work clothes that skeleton with the flesh and sinews of living exposition, and makes available for the ordinary reader the expert knowledge contained in the more advanced works. In fact, this *Expository Dictionary* comes as near as possible to doing for the non-specialist what is being done for the specialist by Kittel's encyclopaedic *Theological Dictionary of the New Testament.*

A work of this kind, of course, cannot be expected to record every occurrence of each word in the New Testament. But all important and significant occurrences are mentioned, and many of the entries in fact are exhaustive, especially those dealing with words which do not occur very often. By the helpful system of cross-references the reader can see at a glance not only which Greek words are represented by one English word, but also which other English words, if any, are used to translate each Greek word. It is a further advantage that both KJV and RV renderings are listed.

Mr. Vine's Greek scholarship was wide, accurate, and up-to-date, and withal unobtrusive. Casual readers will hardly realize the wealth of ripe learning, the years of hard work, of which they may reap the fruit in this work. To his thorough mastery of the classical idiom the author added a close acquaintance with the Hellenistic vernacular and used his knowledge of both to illustrate the meaning of New Testament words. And bearing in mind the New Testament writers' familiarity with the Septuagint and its influence on their language, he has enhanced the value of his work by giving select references to Septuagint usages.

There are few human pursuits more fascinating than the study of words. As vehicles for conveying the thoughts, feelings, and desires of men, they have an abiding interest; how supremely interesting, then, should be the study of those "healthful words" in which the revelation of God Himself has been conveyed!

Yet words, divorced from their meanings, are but empty sounds; instead of being a vehicle of thought, they become a substitute for it. "Words," said Thomas Hobbes, "are wise men's counters; they do but reckon by them: but they are the money of fools." We must know what values to attach to them if we are to profit by them.

Words are not static things. They change their meanings with the passage of time. Many words used in the KJV no longer possess in current English the meanings they had in 1611. We do not now use "prevent" in the sense of "precede," or "carriage" in the sense of "baggage." These changes of meaning may be inferred from the context, but there are other changes which might not be so readily noticed. An important example is the word "atonement," one of the great technical terms of theology. When this word retained its etymological sense of "at-one-ment," it was an appropriate rendering for Gk. *katallage,* and is so used in the KJV of Rom. 5:11. But "atonement" has long since ceased to be an English equivalent of "reconciliation," and its continued use leads to confusion of thought on a theme of the utmost importance. A study of the articles on PROPITIATE, RANSOM, and RECONCILE in this work will greatly clarify the reader's understanding of the biblical presentation of what is commonly called "the doctrine of the atonement."

Not only in recent English, but in ancient Greek as well, we find words changing their meanings. Biblical exegetes of an earlier day were at a disadvantage in having to read New Testament words in the light of their classical usage of four or five centuries earlier. But they recognized certain marked differences between classical and New Testament Greek, and knowing no other Greek quite like that of the New Testament, they concluded that it must be a specially devised "language of the Holy Ghost." During the last seventy or eighty years, however, many documents have been found in the Near East written in this same Greek, from which we have learned the very salutary lesson that the "language of the Holy Ghost" is nothing other than the language of the common people. (One example of a change in the meaning of a Greek word between classical and New Testament times is pointed out in a note at the end of the entry on PUNISHMENT.)

There can be no true biblical theology unless it is based on sound biblical exegesis, and there can be no sound biblical exegesis unless a firm textual and grammatical foundation has been laid for it. Such a foundation is laid in this *Expository Dictionary,* but it provides much more than a foundation. The work is full of careful exegesis, and the student or teacher who makes it his constant companion in the study of Scripture will find that he can afford to dispense with a large number of lesser aids. In fact, it is so valuable a handbook to the study of the New Testament that many of us who have learned to use it regularly wonder how we ever got on without it. It has established a well-deserved reputation for itself and really needs no special commendation such as this, but it is a pleasure to commend it afresh and to wish it a long term of service in its new format.

F. F. BRUCE,
Head of the Department of Biblical
History of Literature in the
University of Sheffield.

September, 1952

PREFACE

To ascertain the exact meaning of the words and phraseology of the originals of the Holy Scriptures is of great importance, particularly those which have a variety of meanings in English. The research work of the past fifty years, with the discovery of a large number of inscriptions and documents, and especially of the non-literary writings in the tombs and dust heaps of Egypt, has yielded much light upon the use and meaning of the language of the originals. The importance of the Egyptian papyri writings, etc., lies in the fact that they were written during the period in which the writers of the New Testament lived. Proof has thus been provided that the language of the New Testament was not a debased form of literary Greek corrupted by Hebrew idioms, but that in the main it was the vernacular, the speech of the everyday life of the people in the countries which came under Greek influence through the conquests of Alexander the Great. As the result of those conquests, the ancient Greek dialects became merged into one common speech, the *Koine* or "common" Greek. In one form this language became the literary *Koine,* or Hellenistic, of such writers as Josephus. In its spoken form it was the everyday speech of millions of people throughout the Graeco-Roman world, and in the providence of God it was under these conditions and in this world-language that the New Testament was written.

The fruit of these researchers has been provided in such volumes as the *Vocabulary of the Greek Testament,* by J. H. Moulton and G. Milligan, the *Grammar of the New Testament Greek* by the former and the book entitled *New Testament Documents* by the latter, *Bible Studies* by G. A. Deissmann, *Light from the Ancient East* by A. Deissmann, and similarly well-known works by W. M. Ramsay. References will be found to some of these in the following pages.

The present volumes are produced especially for the help of those who do not study Greek, though it is hoped that those who are familiar with the original will find them useful.

The work is of an expository character, comments being given on various passages referred to under the different headings. The doctrines of Scripture are dealt with at some length, and notes are provided on matters historical, technical, and etymological.

In cases where an English word translates a variety of Greek words the latter are given in English form. Where there are no such variations, each word is dealt with according to its occurrences and usage in the New Testament, reference being made to the differences between the Authorized and Revised Versions.

The method of the *Dictionary* provides an exhaustive presentation of synonymous words. Where a word in the original has a variety of English renderings, a list is given of these at the close of the note on each word. The list provides in this way a comprehensive study of the use of any given word in the original. In cases where a list has already been given, only the first of these meanings is usually mentioned. There is thus a twofold presentation, firstly, of the different Greek words for one English word, secondly, of the different English meanings attached to a single Greek word.

The subject-matter is also analyzed under the various parts of speech. To take an example, DILIGENCE, DILIGENT, DILIGENTLY, are associated in one heading, and the forms in the original are divided respectively under the sections, Nouns, Verbs, Adjectives, Adverbs. The parts of speech are not given in the same order in every case.

The order is largely dependent upon the greater prominence which a word receives in the original. Other considerations have made a variety in this respect advisable.

In many cases the student is referred to the occurrences in the Septuagint Version, especially where that Version presents a comparatively small number of occurrences or contains only one instance of the use. Reference to the Apocryphal books of the Old Testament is omitted.

The sign (¶) at the close of the treatment of a word indicates that all its occurrences in the original are mentioned. The *Dictionary* thus partakes to a considerable extent of the nature of a concordance.

In many instances all the occurrences and usages of a word are analyzed in a list, showing the different meanings as indicated by the context in each passage of the New Testament.

Considerable use has been made of the two commentaries, written jointly by Mr. C. F. Hogg of London and the present writer, upon the Epistle to the Galatians and the two Epistles to the Thessalonians. I have also made use of Hastings' *Dictionary of the Bible,* Abbott-Smith's *Manual Greek Lexicon of the New Testament,* the larger works by Cremer and by Thayer's Grimm, and of A. T. Robertson's *Grammar of the Greek New Testament in the Light of Historical Research;* also of such works as Trench's *New Testament Synonyms.*

A criticism may be raised in regard to a work like this that it would provide students who know little or nothing of the original with an opportunity of airing some knowledge of Greek. Even supposing that such a criticism were valid, the general advantage of the method adopted should outweigh the danger of such proclivities.

I wish to express my great indebtedness to, and appreciation of, the kind assistance of the Rev. H. E. Guillebaud, M.A., of Cambridge, and T. W. Rhodes, Esqre., M.A., recently of Madrid, who have made copious and useful suggestions and emendations, and have cooperated in going through the proofs.

It is with a sense of deep gratitude that I express my indebtedness to a friend Mr. F. F. Bruce, for his wholehearted assistance in going through the typescript and making corrections and valuable suggestions previous to its being printed, and in proofreading subsequently, whose efficiency, as a classical scholar, and whose knowledge of the originals, have enhanced the value of the work.

I trust that notwithstanding imperfections and limitations of treatment the work may afford assistance to Bible students in enabling them to increase in their knowledge of God and His Word and in helping to equip them in their use and ministry of the Holy Scriptures.

W. E. VINE

Bath,
February, 1939

A

Notes: In the following pages † indicates that the word referred to (preposition, conjunction, or particle) is not dealt with in this volume.

¶ indicates that all the NT occurrences of the Greek word under consideration are mentioned under the heading or sub-heading.

ABASE

tapeinoō (ταπεινόω, 5013) signifies "to make low, bring low," (*a*) of bringing to the ground, making level, reducing to a plain, as in Luke 3:5; (*b*) metaphorically in the active voice, to bring to a humble condition, "to abase," 2 Cor. 11:7, and in the passive, "to be abased," Phil. 4:12; in Matt. 23:12; Luke 14:11; 18:14, the KJV has "shall be abased," the RV "shall be humbled." It is translated "humble yourselves" in the middle voice sense in Jas. 4:10; 1 Pet. 5:6; "humble," in Matt. 18:4; 2 Cor. 12:21 and Phil. 2:8. See HUMBLE, LOW.¶ Cf., *tapeinos*, "lowly," *tapeinōsis*, "humiliation," and *tapeino-phrosunē*, "humility."

ABBA

abba (ἀββᾶ, 5) is an Aramaic word, found in Mark 14:36; Rom. 8:15 and Gal. 4:6. In the Gemara (a Rabbinical commentary on the Mishna, the traditional teaching of the Jews) it is stated that slaves were forbidden to address the head of the family by this title. It approximates to a personal name, in contrast to "Father," with which it is always joined in the NT. This is probably due to the fact that, *abba* having practically become a proper name, Greek-speaking Jews added the Greek word *patēr*, "father," from the language they used. *Abba* is the word framed by the lips of infants, and betokens unreasoning trust; "father" expresses an intelligent apprehension of the relationship. The two together express the love and intelligent confidence of the child.

ABHOR

1. *apostugeō* (ἀποστυγέω, 655) denotes "to shudder" (*apo*, "from," here used intensively, *stugeō*, "to hate") hence, "to abhor," Rom. 12:9. ¶

2. *bdelussō* (βδελύσσω, 948), "to render foul" (from *bdeō*, "to stink"), "to cause to be abhorred" (in the Sept. in Exod. 5:21; Lev. 11:43; 20:25, etc.), is used in the middle voice, signifying "to turn oneself away from" (as if from a stench); hence, "to detest," Rom. 2:22. In Rev. 21:8 it denotes "to be abominable." See ABOMINABLE.¶

ABIDE, ABODE

A. Verbs.

1. *menō* (μένω, 3306), used (*a*) of place, e.g., Matt. 10:11, metaphorically 1 John 2:19, is said of God, 1 John 4:15; Christ, John 6:56; 15:4, etc.; the Holy Spirit, John 1:32–33; 14:17; believers, John 6:56; 15:4; 1 John 4:15, etc.; the Word of God, 1 John 2:14; the truth, 2 John 2, etc.; (*b*) of time; it is said of believers, John 21:22–23; Phil. 1:25; 1 John 2:17; Christ, John 12:34; Heb. 7:24; the Word of God, 1 Pet. 1:23; sin, John 9:41; cities, Matt. 11:23; Heb. 13:14; bonds and afflictions, Acts 20:23; (*c*) of qualities; faith, hope, love, 1 Cor. 13:13; Christ's love, John 15:10; afflictions, Acts 20:23; brotherly love, Heb. 13:1; the love of God, 1 John 3:17; the truth, 2 John 2.

The RV usually translates it by "abide," but "continue" in 1 Tim. 2:15; in the following, the RV substitutes "to abide" for the KJV, "to continue," John 2:12; 8:31; 15:9; 2 Tim. 3:14; Heb. 7:24; 13:14; 1 John 2:24. Cf. the noun *monē*, below. See CONTINUE, DWELL, ENDURE, REMAIN, STAND, TARRY.

2. *epimenō* (ἐπιμένω, 1961), "to abide in, continue in, tarry," is a strengthened form of *menō* (*epi*, "intensive"), sometimes indicating perseverance in continuing, whether in evil,

Rom. 6:1; 11:23, or good, Rom. 11:22; 1 Tim. 4:16. See CONTINUE, TARRY.

3. *katamenō* (καταμένω, 2650), *kata*, "down" (intensive), and No. 1, is used in Acts 1:13. The word may signify "constant residence," but more probably indicates "frequent resort." In 1 Cor. 16:6, it denotes "to wait."¶

4. *paramenō* (παραμένω, 3887), "to remain beside" (*para*, "beside"), "to continue near," came to signify simply "to continue," e.g., negatively, of the Levitical priests, Heb. 7:23. In Phil. 1:25, the apostle uses both the simple verb *menō* and the compound *paramenō* (some mss. have *sumparamenō*), to express his confidence that he will "abide," and "continue to abide," with the saints. In 1 Cor. 16:6 some mss. have this word. In Jas. 1:25, of steadfast continuance in the law of liberty. See CONTINUE.¶

5. *hupomenō* (ὑπομένω, 5278), lit., "to abide under" (*hupo*, "under"), signifies "to remain in a place instead of leaving it, to stay behind," e.g., Luke 2:43; Acts 17:14; or "to persevere," Matt. 10:22; 24:13; Mark 13:13; in each of which latter it is used with the phrase "unto the end"; or "to endure bravely and trustfully," e.g., Heb. 12:2–3, 7, suggesting endurance under what would be burdensome. See also Jas. 1:12; 5:11; 1 Pet. 2:20. Cf., *makrothumeō*, "to be longsuffering." See ENDURE, SUFFER, TAKE, *Notes* (12), TARRY.

6. *prosmenō* (προσμένω, 4357), "to abide still longer, continue with" (*pros*, "with") is used (*a*) of place, Matt. 15:32; Mark 8:2; Acts 18:18; 1 Tim. 1:3; (*b*) metaphorically, "of cleaving unto a person," Acts 11:23, indicating persistent loyalty; of continuing in a thing, Acts 13:43; 1 Tim. 5:5. See CLEAVE, CONTINUE, TARRY.¶ In the Sept., Judg. 3:25.¶

7. *diatribō* (διατρίβω, 1304), lit., "to wear through by rubbing, to wear away" (*dia*, "through," *tribō*, "to rub"), when used of time, "to spend or pass time, to stay," is found twice in John's gospel, 3:22 and 11:54, RV "tarried," instead of "continued"; elsewhere only in the Acts, eight times, 12:19; 14:3, 28; 15:35; 16:12; 20:6; 25:6, 14. See CONTINUE, TARRY.¶

8. *anastrephō* (ἀναστρέφω, 390), used once in the sense of "abiding," Matt. 17:22, frequently denotes "to behave oneself, to live a certain manner of life"; here the most reliable mss. have *sustrephomai*, "to travel about." See BEHAVE, CONVERSATION, LIVE, OVERTHROW, PASS, RETURN.

9. *aulizomai* (αὐλίζομαι, 835), "to lodge," originally "to lodge in the *aulē*, or courtyard," is said of shepherds and flocks; hence, to pass the night in the open air, as did the Lord, Luke

21:37; "to lodge in a house," as of His visit to Bethany, Matt. 21:17.¶

10. *agrauleō* (ἀγραυλέω, 63), "to lodge in a fold in a field" (*agros*, "a field," *aulē*, "a fold"), is used in Luke 2:8.¶ See LODGE.

11. *histēmi* (ἵστημι, 2476), "to stand, to make to stand," is rendered "abode" in John 8:44, KJV; "continue," in Acts 26:22. In these places the RV corrects to "stood" and "stand." This word is suggestive of fidelity and stability. It is rendered "lay... to the charge" in Acts 7:60. See APPOINT, CHARGE, ESTABLISH, HOLDEN, PRESENT, SET, STANCH, STAND.

12. *poieō* (ποιέω, 4160), "to do, make," is used of spending a time or tarrying, in a place, Acts 15:33; 20:3; in 2 Cor. 11:25 it is rendered "I have been (a night and a day)"; a preferable translation is "I have spent," as in Jas. 4:13, "spend a year" (RV). So in Matt. 20:12. Cf., the English idiom "did one hour"; in Rev. 13:5 "continue" is perhaps the best rendering. See DO.

B. Noun.

monē (μονή, 3438), "an abode" (akin to No. 1), is found in John 14:2, "mansions" (RV marg., "abiding places"), and 14:23, "abode."¶

ABILITY, ABLE

A. Nouns.

1. *dunamis* (δύναμις, 1411) is (*a*) "power, ability," physical or moral, as residing in a person or thing; (*b*) "power in action," as, e.g., when put forth in performing miracles. It occurs 118 times in the NT. It is sometimes used of the miracle or sign itself, the effect being put for the cause, e.g., Mark 6:5, frequently in the Gospels and Acts. In 1 Cor. 14:11 it is rendered "meaning"; "force" would be more accurate. Cf., the corresponding verbs, B, 1, 2, 3 and the adjective C. 1, below. See ABUNDANCE, DEED, MIGHT, POWER, STRENGTH, VIOLENCE, VIRTUE, WORK.

2. *ischus* (ἰσχύς, 2479), connected with *ischō* and *echō*, "to have, to hold" (from the root *ech*—, signifying "holding"), denotes "ability, force, strength"; "ability" in 1 Pet. 4:11, KJV (RV, "strength"). In Eph. 1:19 and 6:10, it is said of the strength of God bestowed upon believers, the phrase "the power of His might" indicating strength afforded by power. In 2 Thess. 1:9, "the glory of His might" signifies the visible expression of the inherent personal power of the Lord Jesus. It is said of angels in 2 Pet. 2:11 (cf., Rev. 18:2, KJV, "mightily"). It is ascribed to God in Rev. 5:12 and 7:12. In Mark 12:30, 33, and Luke 10:27 it describes the full extent of the power wherewith we are to love God. See MIGHT, POWER, STRENGTH.¶

B. Verbs.

1. *dunamai* (δύναμαι, 1410), "to be able, to have power," whether by virtue of one's own ability and resources, e.g., Rom. 15:14; or through a state of mind, or through favorable circumstances, e.g., 1 Thess. 2:6; or by permission of law or custom, e.g., Acts 24:8, 11; or simply "to be able, powerful," Matt. 3:9; 2 Tim. 3:15, etc. See CAN, MAY, POSSIBLE, POWER.

2. *dunamoō* (δυναμόω, 1412), "to make strong, confirm," occurs in Col. 1:11 (some authorities have the 1st aorist or momentary tense, in Heb. 11:34 also). Cf. *endunamoō*, "to enable, strengthen."¶

3. *dunateō* (δυνατέω, 1414) signifies "to be mighty, to show oneself powerful," Rom. 4:14; 2 Cor. 9:8; 13:3. See A, No. 1.¶

4. *ischuō* (ἰσχύω, 2480), akin to A, No. 2, "to be strong, to prevail," indicates a more forceful strength or ability than *dunamai*, e.g., Jas. 5:16, where it is rendered "availeth much" (i.e., "prevails greatly"). See AVAIL, CAN, DO, MAY, PREVAIL, STRENGTH, WORK.

Note: Still stronger forms are *exischuō*, "to be thoroughly strong," Eph. 3:18, "may be strong" (not simply "may be able," KJV).¶; *katischuō*, Matt. 16:18, and Luke 23:23, in the former, of the powerlessness of the gates of Hades to prevail against the Church; in the latter, of the power of a fierce mob to prevail over a weak ruler (see *Notes on Galatians,* by Hogg and Vine, p. 251); also Luke 21:36. The prefixed prepositions are intensive in each case.¶

5. *echō* (ἔχω, 2192), "to have," is translated "your ability" in 2 Cor. 8:11, and "ye may be able" in 2 Pet. 1:15, and is equivalent to the phrase "to have the means of." See CAN, HAVE.

6. *euporeō* (εὐπορέω, 2141), lit., "to journey well" (*eu*, "well," *poreō*, "to journey"), hence, "to prosper," is translated "according to (his) ability," in Acts 11:29.¶

Note: Hikanoō, corresponding to the adjective *hikanos* (see below) signifies "to make competent, qualify, make sufficient"; in 2 Cor. 3:6, KJV, "hath made (us) able"; RV, "hath made us sufficient"; in Col. 1:12, "hath made (us) meet." See ENOUGH, SUFFICIENT.¶

C. Adjectives.

1. *dunatos* (δυνατός, 1415), corresponding to A, No. 1, signifies "powerful." See, e.g., Rom. 4:21; 9:22; 11:23; 12:18; 15:1; 1 Cor. 1:26; 2 Cor. 9:8. See MIGHTY, POSSIBLE, POWER, STRONG.

2. *hikanos* (ἱκανός, 2425), translated "able," is to be distinguished from *dunatos*. While *dunatos* means "possessing power," *hikanos*, primarily, "reaching to," has accordingly the meaning "sufficient." When said of things it

signifies "enough," e.g., Luke 22:38; when said of persons, it means "competent," "worthy," e.g., 2 Cor. 2:6, 16; 3:5; 2 Tim. 2:2. See CONTENT, ENOUGH, GOOD, GREAT, LARGE, LONG, MANY, MEET, MUCH, SECURITY, SUFFICIENT, WORTHY.

Note: Ischuros denotes "strong, mighty"; in an active sense, "mighty," in having inherent and moral power, e.g., Matt. 12:29; 1 Cor. 4:10; Heb.6:18.

ABOARD

epibainō (ἐπιβαίνω, 1910), "to go upon" (*epi*, "upon," *bainō*, "to go"), is once translated "we went aboard," Acts 21:2, the single verb being short for "going aboard ship." In v. 6 it is rendered "we went on board"; in 27:2 "embarking"; in Matt. 21:5, "riding upon." See COME, No. 16.

ABOLISH

katargeō (καταργέω, 2673), lit., "to reduce to inactivity" (*kata*, "down," *argos*, "inactive"), is translated "abolish" in Eph. 2:15 and 2 Tim. 1:10, in the RV only in 1 Cor. 15:24, 26. It is rendered "is abolished" in the KJV of 2 Cor. 3:13; the RV corrects to "was passing away" (marg., "was being done away"). In this and similar words not loss of being is implied, but loss of well being.

The barren tree was cumbering the ground, making it useless for the purpose of its existence, Luke 13:7; the unbelief of the Jews could not "make of none effect" the faithfulness of God, Rom. 3:3; the preaching of the gospel could not "make of none effect" the moral enactments of the Law, 3:31; the Law could not make the promise of "none effect," 4:14; Gal. 3:17; the effect of the identification of the believer with Christ in His death is to render inactive his body in regard to sin, Rom. 6:6; the death of a woman's first husband discharges her from the law of the husband, that is, it makes void her status as his wife in the eyes of the law, 7:2; in that sense the believer has been discharged from the Law, 7:6; God has chosen things that are not "to bring to nought things that are," i.e., to render them useless for practical purposes, 1 Cor. 1:28; the princes of this world are "brought to nought," i.e., their wisdom becomes ineffective, 2:6; the use for which the human stomach exists ceases with man's death, 6:13; knowledge, prophesyings, and that which was in part were to be "done away," 1 Cor. 13:8, 10, i.e., they were to be rendered of no effect after their temporary use was fulfilled; when the apostle became a man he did away with the ways of a child, v. 11; God is going to abolish all rule and authority and power, i.e., He is going to render them inactive, 1 Cor. 15:24; the last enemy that shall be abolished, or reduced to inactivity, is death, v. 26; the glory shining in the face of Moses, "was passing away," 2 Cor. 3:7, the transitoriness of its character being of a special significance; so in vv. 11, 13; the veil upon the heart of Israel is "done away" in Christ, v. 14; those who seek justification by the Law are "severed" from Christ, they are rendered inactive in relation to Him, Gal. 5:4; the essential effect of the preaching of the Cross would become inoperative by the preaching of circumcision, 5:11; by the death of Christ the barrier between Jew and Gentile is rendered inoperative as such, Eph. 2:15; the Man of Sin is to be reduced to inactivity by the manifestation of the Lord's *Parousia* with His people, 2 Thess. 2:8; Christ has rendered death inactive for the believer, 2 Tim. 1:10, death becoming the means of a more glorious life, with Christ; the Devil is to be reduced to inactivity through the death of Christ, Heb. 2:14. See CEASE, CUMBER, DESTROY, DO, *Note* (7), OF NONE EFFECT, NOUGHT, PUT, No. 19, VOID.¶

ABOMINABLE, ABOMINATION

A. Adjectives.

1. *athemitos* (ἀθέμιτος, 111) occurs in Acts 10:28, "unlawful," and 1 Pet. 4:3, "abominable" (*a*, negative, *themitos*, an adjective from *themis*, "law"), hence, "unlawful." See UNLAWFUL.¶

2. *bdeluktos* (βδελυκτός, 947), Titus 1:16, is said of deceivers who profess to know God, but deny Him by their works.¶

B. Verb.

bdelussō (βδελύσσω, 948): see ABHOR, No. 2.

C. Noun.

bdelugma (βδέλυγμα, 946), akin to A, No. 2 and B, denotes an "object of disgust, an abomination." This is said of the image to be set up by Antichrist, Matt. 24:15; Mark 13:14; of that which is highly esteemed amongst men, in contrast to its real character in the sight of God, Luke 16:15. The constant association with idolatry suggests that what is highly esteemed among men constitutes an idol in the human heart. In Rev. 21:27, entrance is forbidden into the Holy City on the part of the unclean, or one who "maketh an abomination and a lie." It is also used of the contents of the golden cup in the hand of the evil woman described in Rev. 17:4, and of the name ascribed to her in the following verse.¶

For ABOUND see ABUNDANCE

ABOUT

A. Adverbs, etc.

Besides prepositions, the following signify "about":—

1. *kuklothen* (κυκλόθεν, 2943), "round about, or all round" (from *kuklos*, "a circle, cycle"), is found in the Apocalypse only, 4:3–4, 8.¶

2. *kuklō* (κύκλῳ, 2945), the dative case of *kuklos* (see above), means "round about," lit., "in a circle." It is used in the same way as No. 1, Mark 3:34; 6:6, 36; Luke 9:12; Rom. 15:19; Rev. 4:6; 5:11; 7:11.¶

3. *pou* (ποῦ, 4225), an indefinite particle, signifying "somewhere, somewhere about, nearly," has a limiting force, with numerals, e.g., Rom. 4:19. In referring to a passage in the OT, it is translated "somewhere," in the RV of Heb. 2:6 and 4:4 (KJV, "in a certain place"); by not mentioning the actual passage referred to, the writer acknowledged the familiar acquaintance of his readers with the OT. See PLACE.

4. *hōs* (ὡς, 5613) usually means "as." Used with numerals it signifies "about," e.g., Mark 5:13; 8:9; John 1:40; 6:19; 11:18; Acts 1:15; Rev. 8:1.

5. *hōsei* (ὡσεί, 5616), "as if," before numerals, denotes "about, nearly, something like," with perhaps an indication of greater indefiniteness than No. 4, e.g., Matt. 14:21; Luke 3:23; 9:14, 28; Acts 2:41; with a measure of space, Luke 22:41, "about a stone's cast." See LIKE.

B. Verb.

mellō (μέλλω, 3195) signifies (*a*) "of intention, to be about to do something," e.g., Acts 3:3; 18:14; 20:3; Heb. 8:5; (*b*) "of certainty, compulsion or necessity, to be certain to act," e.g., John 6:71. See ALMOST, BEGIN, COME, INTEND, MEAN, MIND, POINT OF (at), READY, SHALL, SHOULD, TARRY.

Note: *Zēteō*, "to seek," is translated "were about" in the KJV of Acts 27:30; RV, correctly, "were seeking to."

ABOVE

The following adverbs have this meaning (prepositions are omitted here):—

1. *anō* (ἄνω, 507) denotes "above, in a higher place," Acts 2:19 (the opposite to *katō*, "below"). With the article it means "that which is above," Gal. 4:26; Phil. 3:14, "the high calling" (RV marg., "upward"); with the plural article, "the things above," John 8:23, lit., "from the things above"; Col. 3:1–2. With *heōs*, "as far as," it is translated "up to the brim," in John 2:7. It has the meaning "upwards" in John 11:41 and Heb. 12:15. See BRIM, HIGH, UP.¶

2. *anōteron* (ἀνώτερον, 511), the comparative degree of No. 1, is the neuter of the adjective *anōteros*. It is used (*a*) of motion to a higher place, "higher," Luke 14:10; (*b*) of location in a higher place, i.e., in the preceding part of a passage, "above" Heb. 10:8. See HIGHER.¶

3. *epanō* (ἐπάνω, 1883), *epi*, "over," *anō*, "above," is used frequently as a preposition with a noun; adverbially, of number, e.g., Mark 14:5, RV; 1 Cor. 15:6.

Note: In Acts 4:22, KJV, the adjective *pleion*, "more," is translated "above," the RV corrects to "more than (forty years)."

4. *anōthen* (ἄνωθεν, 509), "from above," is used of place, (*a*) with the meaning "from the top," Matt. 27:51; Mark 15:38, of the temple veil; in John 19:23, of the garment of Christ, lit., "from the upper parts" (plural); (*b*) of things which come from heaven, or from God in Heaven, John 3:31; 19:11; Jas. 1:17; 3:15, 17. It is also used in the sense of "again." See AGAIN.

For **ABROAD,** see the verbs with which it is used, **DISPERSE, NOISE, SCATTER, SHEED, SPREAD**

ABSENCE, ABSENT

A. Noun.

apousia (ἀπουσία, 666), lit., "a being away from," is used in Phil. 2:12, of the apostle's absence from Philippi, in contrast to his parousia, his presence with the saints there "parousia" does not signify merely "a coming," it includes or suggests "the presence" which follows the arrival.¶

B. Verbs.

1. *apeimi* (ἄπειμι, 548), "to be absent" (*apo*, "from," *eimi*, "to be"), is found in 1 Cor. 5:3; 2 Cor. 10:1, 11; 13:2, 10; Phil. 1:27; Col. 2:5. See GO.¶

2. *ekdēmeō* (ἐκδημέω, 1553), lit., "to be away from people" (*ek*, "from," or "out of," *dēmos*, "people"), came to mean either (*a*) "to go abroad, depart"; the apostle Paul uses it to speak of departing from the body as the earthly abode of the spirit, 2 Cor. 5:8; or (*b*) "to be away"; in the same passage, of being here in the body and absent from the Lord (v. 6), or being absent from the body and present with the Lord (v. 8). Its other occurrence is in v. 9.¶

C. Preposition.

ater (ἄτερ, 817) means "without," Luke 22:35, "without purse"; in v. 6, "in the absence (of the multitude)," marg., "without tumult." See WITHOUT.¶

ABSTAIN, ABSTINENCE

apechō (ἀπέχω, 568), "to hold oneself from" (*apo*, "from," *echomai*, the middle voice of *echō*, "to have," i.e., to keep oneself from), in the NT, invariably refers to evil practices, moral and ceremonial, Acts 15:20, 29; 1 Thess. 4:3; 5:22; 1 Tim. 4:3; 1 Pet. 2:11; so in the Sept. in Job 1:1; 2:3. See ENOUGH, RECEIVE.¶

Note: The noun "abstinence" in Acts 27:21, KJV, translates *asitia*, "without food," RV (*a*, negative, *sitos*, "food"). Cf. *asitos*, "fasting," v. 33.¶

ABUNDANCE, ABUNDANT, ABUNDANTLY, ABOUND

A. Nouns.

1. *hadrotēs* (ἁδρότης, 100), which, in 2 Cor. 8:20, in reference to the gifts from the church at Corinth for poor saints in Judea, the RV renders "bounty" (KJV, "abundance"), is derived from *hadros*, "thick, fat, full-grown, rich" (in the Sept. it is used chiefly of rich and great men, e.g., Jer. 5:5). In regard, therefore, to the offering in 2 Cor. 8:20 the thought is that of bountiful giving, a fat offering, not mere "abundance".¶

2. *perisseia* (περισσεία, 4050), "an exceeding measure, something above the ordinary," is used four times; Rom. 5:17, "of abundance of grace"; 2 Cor. 8:2, "of abundance of joy"; 2 Cor. 10:15, of the extension of the apostle's sphere of service through the practical fellowship of the saints at Corinth; in Jas. 1:21 it is rendered, metaphorically, "overflowing," KJV "superfluity," with reference to wickedness. Some would render it "residuum," or "what remains." See No. 3.¶

3. *perisseuma* (περίσσευμα, 4051) denotes "abundance" in a slightly more concrete form, 2 Cor. 8:13–14, where it stands for the gifts in kind supplied by the saints. In Matt. 12:34 and Luke 6:45 it is used of the "abundance" of the heart; in Mark 8:8, of the broken pieces left after feeding the multitude "that remained over"(KJV "that was left"). See REMAIN.¶ In the Sept., Eccl. 2:15.¶

4. *huperbolē* (ὑπερβολή, 5236), lit., "a throwing beyond" (*huper*, "over," *ballō*, "to throw"), denotes "excellence, exceeding greatness," of the power of God in His servants, 2 Cor. 4:7; of the revelations given to Paul, 12:7; with the preposition *kata*, the phrase signifies "exceeding," Rom. 7:13; "still more excellent," 1 Cor. 12:31; "exceedingly," 2 Cor. 1:8; "beyond measure," Gal. 1:13; and, in a more extended phrase, "more and more exceedingly," 2 Cor. 4:17. See EXCELLENCY, EXCELLENT, MEASURE.¶

B. Verbs.

1. *perisseuō* (περισσεύω, 4052), akin to A, Nos. 2 and 3, is used intransitively (*a*) "of exceeding a certain number, or measure, to be over, to remain," of the fragments after feeding the multitude (cf. *perisseuma*), Luke 9:17; John 6:12–13; "to exist in abundance"; as of wealth, Luke 12:15; 21:4; of food, 15:17. In this sense it is used also of consolation, 2 Cor. 1:5; of the effect of a gift sent to meet the need of saints, 2 Cor. 9:12; of rejoicing, Phil. 1:26; of what comes or falls to the lot of a person in large measure, as of the grace of God and the gift by the grace of Christ, Rom. 5:15; of the sufferings of Christ, 2 Cor. 1:5. In Mark 12:44 and Luke 21:4, the RV has "superfluity."

(*b*) "to redound to, or to turn out abundantly for something," as of the liberal effects of poverty, 2 Cor. 8:2; in Rom. 3:7, argumentatively, of the effects of the truth of God, as to whether God's truthfulness becomes more conspicuous and His glory is increased through man's untruthfulness; of numerical increase, Acts 16:5.

(*c*) "to be abundantly furnished, to abound in a thing," as of material benefits, Luke 12:15; Phil. 4:18 of spiritual gifts; 1 Cor. 14:12, or "to be pre-eminent, to excel, to be morally better off," as regards partaking of certain meats; 1 Cor. 8:8, "are we the better"; "to abound" in hope, Rom. 15:13; the work of the Lord, 1 Cor. 15:58; faith and grace, 2 Cor. 8:7; thanksgiving, Col. 2:7; walking so as to please God, Phil. 1:9; 1 Thess. 4:1, 10; of righteousness, Matt. 5:20; of the Gospel, as the ministration of righteousness, 2 Cor. 3:9, "exceed."

It is used transitively, in the sense of "to make to abound," e.g., to provide a person richly so that he has "abundance," as of spiritual truth, Matt. 13:12; the right use of what God has entrusted to us, 25:29; the power of God in conferring grace, 2 Cor. 9:8; Eph. 1:8; to "make abundant" or to cause to excel, as of the effect of grace in regard to thanksgiving, 2 Cor. 4:15; His power to make us "to abound" in love, 1 Thess. 3:12. See BETTER, ENOUGH, EXCEED, EXCEL, INCREASE, REDOUND, REMAIN.¶

2. *huperperisseuō* (ὑπερπερισσεύω, 5248), a strengthened form of No. 1, signifies "to abound exceedingly," Rom. 5:20, of the operation of grace; 2 Cor. 7:4, in the middle voice, of the apostle's joy in the saints. See JOYFUL.¶

3. *pleonazō* (πλεονάζω, 4121), from *pleion*, or *pleon*, "more" (greater in quantity), akin to *pleō*, "to fill," signifies, (*a*) intransitively, "to superabound," of a trespass or sin, Rom. 5:20; of grace, Rom. 6:1; 2 Cor. 4:15; of spiritual fruit, Phil. 4:17; of love, 2 Thess. 1:3; of various fruits, 2 Pet. 1:8; of the gathering of the manna,

2 Cor. 8:15, "had . . . over"; (*b*) transitively, "to make to increase," 1 Thess. 3:12. See INCREASE, OVER. ¶

4. *huperpleonazō* (ὑπερπλεονάζω, 5250), a strengthened form of No. 3, signifying "to abound exceedingly," is used in 1 Tim. 1:14, of the grace of God.¶

5. *plēthunō* (πληθύνω, 4129), a lengthened form of *plēthō*, "to fill," akin to No. 3, and to *plēthos*, "a multitude," signifies "to increase, to multiply," and, in the passive voice, "to be multiplied," e.g., of iniquity, Matt. 24:12, RV. See MULTIPLY.

Note: *Huperballō*, akin to A, No. 4, "to exceed, excel," is translated "passeth" in Eph. 3:19. See also 2 Cor. 3:10 (RV, "surpasseth"; KJV, "excelleth"); 9:14, "exceeding"; Eph. 1:19; 2:7. See EXCEED, EXCEL.¶

C. Adjectives.

1. *perissos* (περισσός, 4053), akin to B, No. 1, "abundant," is translated "advantage" in Rom. 3:1, "superfluous" in 2 Cor. 9:1. See ADVANTAGE, MORE, B, No. 2, SUPERFLUOUS.

2. *perissoteros* (περισσότερος, 4055), the comparative degree of No. 1, is translated as follows: in Matt. 11:9, and Luke 7:26, RV, "much more" (KJV, "more"); in Mark 12:40, "greater"; in Luke 12:4, 48, "more"; in 1 Cor. 12:23–24, "more abundant"; in 2 Cor. 2:7, "overmuch"; in 2 Cor. 10:8, RV, "abundantly"; KJV, "more." See GREATER, MORE, OVERMUCH.

D. Adverbs.

1. *perissōs* (περισσῶς, 4057), corresponding to Adjective No. 1 above, is found in Matt. 27:23, RV, "exceedingly," KJV, "the more"; Mark 10:26, RV, "exceedingly," KJV, "out of measure"; 15:14; Acts 26:11, "exceedingly." See EXCEEDINGLY, B, No. 4, MEASURE, B, No. 2, MORE.¶

2. *perissoteros* (περισσοτέρως, 4056), the adverbial form of No. 2, above, means "more abundantly"; in Heb. 2:1, lit., "we ought to give heed more abundantly." It is most frequent in 2 Cor. In 11:23, see the RV. See EARNEST, EXCEEDINGLY, RATHER.

3. *huperperissōs* (ὑπερπερισσῶς, 5249), a strengthened form of No. 1, signifies "exceeding abundantly," Mark 7:37.¶

4. *huperekperissou* (ὑπερεκπερισσοῦ, 5228, 1537, and 4053), a still further strengthened form, is translated "exceeding abundantly" in Eph. 3:20; "exceedingly" in 1 Thess. 3:10; 5:13. See EXCEEDINGLY.¶

Note: *Huperballontōs*, akin to A, No. 4, denotes "above measure," 2 Cor. 11:23.¶

5. *plousiōs* (πλουσίως, 4146), connected with *ploutos*, "riches," is rendered "abundantly," Titus 3:6 and 2 Pet. 1:11; "richly," Col. 3:16

and 1 Tim. 6:17. It is used of (*a*) the gift of the Holy Spirit; (*b*) entrance into the coming kingdom; (*c*) the indwelling of the Word of Christ; (*d*) material benefits. See RICHLY.¶

Notes: (1) *Dunamis*, "power," is translated "abundance" in the KJV of Rev. 18:3 (RV and KJV marg., "power").

(2) *Polus*, "much, many," is rendered "abundant" in 1 Pet. 1:3, KJV (marg., "much"), RV, "great."

(3) For the verbs *plouteō* and *ploutizō*, see RICH and ENRICH.

(4) For *ploutos*, "wealth, riches," and *plousios*, "rich," see RICH.

ABUSE, ABUSERS

A. Verb.

katachraomai (καταχράομαι, 2710), lit., "to use overmuch" (*kata*, "down," intensive, *chraomai*, "to use"), is found in 1 Cor. 7:31, with reference to the believer's use of the world (marg., "use to the full"), and 1 Cor. 9:18, KJV, "abuse," RV, "use to the full." See USE.¶

B. Noun.

For the noun *arsenokoitēs*, see 1 Cor. 6:9, and 1 Tim. 1:10.¶

For ABYSS see BOTTOM

ACCEPT, ACCEPTED, ACCEPTABLE

A. Verbs.

1. *dechomai* (δέχομαι, 1209) signifies "to accept," by a deliberate and ready reception of what is offered (cf. No. 4), e.g., 1 Thess. 2:13, RV, "accepted"; 2 Cor. 8:17; 11:4. See RECEIVE, TAKE.

2. *apodechomai* (ἀποδέχομαι, 588), consisting of *apo*, "from," intensive, and No. 1, expresses *dechomai* more strongly, signifying "to receive heartily, to welcome," Luke 8:40 (RV, "welcomed," KJV, "gladly received"); Acts 2:41; 18:27; 24:3; 28:30. See RECEIVE, WELCOME.

3. *prosdechomai* (προσδέχομαι, 4327), *pros*, "to," and No. 1, "to accept favorably, or receive to oneself," is used of things future, in the sense of expecting; with the meaning of "accepting," it is used negatively in Heb. 11:35, "not accepting their deliverance"; of receiving, e.g., Luke 15:2; Rom. 16:2; Phil. 2:29. See ALLOW, LOOK (for), RECEIVE, TAKE, WAIT.

4. *lambanō* (λαμβάνω, 2983), almost synonymous with *dechomai*, is distinct from it, in that it sometimes means "to receive as merely a self-prompted action," without necessarily signifying a favorable reception, Gal. 2:6. See AT-

TAIN, CALL, CATCH, HAVE, HOLD, OBTAIN, RECEIVE, TAKE.

Note: The verb *charitoō*, "to make acceptable," is translated "made accepted," in Eph. 1:6, KJV; RV, "freely bestowed."

B. Adjectives.

The following adjectives are translated "acceptable," or in some cases "accepted." The RV more frequently adopts the former rendering.

1. *dektos* (δεκτός, 1184), akin to No. 1, denotes "a person or thing who has been regarded favorably," Luke 4:19, 24; Acts 10:35; 2 Cor. 6:2 (in this verse No. 3 is used in the second place); Phil. 4:18.¶

2. *apodektos* (ἀπόδεκτός, 587), a strengthened form of No. 1 (*apo*, "from," used intensively), signifies "acceptable," in the sense of what is pleasing and welcome, 1 Tim. 2:3; 5:4.¶

3. *euprosdektos* (εὐπρόσδεκτος, 2144), a still stronger form of No. 1, signifies a "very favorable acceptance" (*eu*, "well," *pros*, "towards," No. 1), Rom. 15:16, 31; 2 Cor. 6:2; 8:12; 1 Pet. 2:5.¶

4. *euarestos* (εὐάρεστος, 2101), *eu*, "well," *arestos*, "pleasing," is rendered "acceptable," in the KJV of Rom. 12:1–2; 14:18; in 2 Cor. 5:9, "accepted"; Eph. 5:10. The RV usually has "well-pleasing"; so KJV and RV in Phil. 4:18; Col. 3:20; in Titus 2:9, "please well," KJV; Heb. 13:21. See PLEASING.¶

C. Adverb.

euarestōs (εὐαρέστως, 2102), corresponding to B, No. 4, is used in Heb. 12:28, "so as to please." See PLEASE.¶

D. Nouns.

1. *apodochē* (ἀποδοχή, 594), akin to B, No. 2, signifies "worthy to be received with approbation, acceptation," 1 Tim. 1:15; 4:9. The phrase in 1:15 is found in a writing in the 1st century expressing appreciation of a gift from a princess.¶

2. *charis* (χάρις, 5485), "grace," indicating favor on the part of the giver, "thanks" on the part of the receiver, is rendered "acceptable" in 1 Pet. 2:19–20. See margin. See BENEFIT, FAVOR, GRACE, LIBERALITY, PLEASURE, THANK.

ACCESS

prosagōgē (προσαγωγή, 4318), lit., "a leading or bringing into the presence of" (*pros*, "to," *agō*, "to lead"), denotes "access," with which is associated the thought of freedom to enter through the assistance or favor of another. It is used three times, (*a*) Rom. 5:2, of the "access" which we have by faith, through our Lord Jesus Christ, into grace; (*b*) Eph. 2:18, of our "access" in one Spirit through Christ, unto the Father; (*c*) Eph. 3:12, of the same "access," there said to be "in Christ," and which we have "in confidence through our faith in Him." This "access" involves the acceptance which we have in Christ with God, and the privilege of His favor towards us. Some advocate the meaning "introduction."¶

ACCOMPANY

A. Verbs.

1. *sunepomai* (συνέπομαι, 4902), lit., "to follow with" (*sun*, "with," *hepomai*, "to follow"), came to mean simply "to accompany," Acts 20:4.¶

2. *sunerchomai* (συνέρχομαι, 4905), chiefly used of "assembling together," signifies "to accompany," in Luke 23:55; John 11:33; Acts 9:39; 10:45; 11:12; 15:38; 21:16. In Acts 1:21 it is said of men who had "companied with" the apostles all the time the Lord Jesus was with them. See ASSEMBLE, COME, COMPANY, GO, RESORT.

3. *echō* (ἔχω, 2192), "to have," is rendered "accompany," in Heb. 6:9, "things that accompany salvation." The margin gives perhaps the better sense, "things that are near to salvation."

4. *propempō* (προπέμπω, 4311), translated "accompanied," in Acts 20:38, KJV, lit. means "to send forward"; hence, of assisting a person on a journey either (*a*) in the sense of fitting him out with the requisites for it, or (*b*) actually "accompanying" him for part of the way. The former seems to be indicated in Rom. 15:24 and 1 Cor. 16:6, and v. 11, where the RV has "set him forward." So in 2 Cor. 1:16 and Titus 3:13, and of John's exhortation to Gaius concerning traveling evangelists, "whom thou wilt do well to set forward on their journey worthily of God," 3 John 6, RV. While personal "accompaniment" is not excluded, practical assistance seems to be generally in view, as indicated by Paul's word to Titus to set forward Zenas and Apollos on their journey and to see "that nothing be wanting unto them." In regard to the parting of Paul from the elders of Ephesus at Miletus, personal "accompaniment" is especially in view, perhaps not without the suggestion of assistance, Acts 20:38, RV "brought him on his way"; "accompaniment" is also indicated in 21:5; "they all with wives and children brought us on our way, till we were out of the city." In Acts 15:3, both ideas perhaps are suggested. See BRING, CONDUCT.¶

ACCOMPLISH, ACCOMPLISHMENT

A. Verbs.

1. *exartizō* (ἐξαρτίζω, 1822), "to fit out," (from *ek*, "out," and a verb derived from *artos*,

"a joint"), means "to furnish completely," 2 Tim. 3:17, or "to accomplish," Acts 21:5, there said of a number of days, as if to render the days complete by what was appointed for them. See FURNISH.¶ In the Sept., Exod. 28:7.¶

2. *plēroō* (πληρόω, 4137), "to fulfill, to complete, carry out to the full" (as well as to fill), is translated "perfect" in Rev. 3:2, KJV; RV, "I have found no works of thine fulfilled before My God"; "accomplish" in Luke 9:31. See COMPLETE, END, EXPIRE, FILL, FULFILL, FULL, PREACH.

Note: Its strengthened form, *ekplēroō*, "to fulfill," lit., "fill out," is used in Acts 13:33, of the fulfillment of a divine promise of the resurrection of Christ.

3. *teleō* (τελέω, 5055), "to finish, to bring to an end" (*telos*, "an end"), frequently signifies, not merely to terminate a thing, but to carry out a thing to the full. It is used especially in the Apocalypse, where it occurs eight times, and is rendered "finish" in 10:7; 11:7, and in the RV of 15:1, which rightly translates it "(in them) is finished (the wrath of God)." So in v. 8; in 17:17, RV, "accomplish," and "finish" in 20:3, 5, 7; in Luke 2:39, RV, "accomplish," for KJV, "performed." See END, EXPIRE, FILL, FINISH, FULFILL, GO, No. 5, PAY, PERFORM.

4. *epiteleō* (ἐπιτελέω, 2005), *epi*, "up," intensive, and No. 3, is a strengthened form of that verb, in the sense of "accomplishing." The fuller meaning is "to accomplish perfectly"; in Rom. 15:28, RV, "accomplish"; "perfecting" in 2 Cor. 7:1; "complete" in 8:6 and 11; "completion" in the latter part of this 11th verse, which is better than "performance"; "perfected" in Gal. 3:3; "perfect" in Phil. 1:6. In Heb. 8:5 the margin rightly has "complete" instead of "make," with regard to the tabernacle. In Heb. 9:6 it is translated "accomplish" and in 1 Pet. 5:9. See COMPLETE, DO, FINISH, MAKE, PERFECT, PERFORM.¶

5. *teleioō* (τελειόω, 5048), though distinct grammatically from *teleō*, has much the same meaning. The main distinction is that *teleō* more frequently signifies "to fulfill," *teleioō*, more frequently, "to make perfect," one of the chief features of the Epistle to the Hebrews, where it occurs nine times. It is rendered "accomplish" in the RV of John 4:34; 5:36; 17:4, and Acts 20:24. See CONSECRATE, FINISH, FULFILL, PERFECT.

6. *plēthō* (πλήθω, 4130), "to fulfill," is translated "accomplished" in the KJV of Luke 1:23; 2:6, 21–22 (RV, "fulfilled"). See FILL, No. 5, FURNISH, *Note.*

B. Noun.

ekplērōsis (ἐκπλήρωσις, 1604), see A, No. 2, *Note,* means "an entire fulfillment" (*ek,* "out," *plērosis,* "a filling"), Acts 21:26, of the "fulfillment" of days of purification.¶

ACCORD

A. Adverb.

homothumadon (ὁμοθυμαδόν, 3661), "of one accord" (from *homos,* "same," *thumos,* "mind"), occurs eleven times, ten in the Acts, 1:14; 2:46; 4:24; 5:12; 7:57; 8:6; 12:20; 15:25; 18:12; 19:29, and the other in Rom. 15:6, where, for KJV, "with one mind," the RV has "with one accord," as throughout the Acts. See MIND.¶

Note: In Acts 2:1, the adverb *homou,* "together," is so rendered in the RV, for KJV, "of one accord."

B. Adjectives.

"Of one's own accord."

1. *authairetos* (αὐθαίρετος, 830), from *autos,* "self," and *haireomai,* "to choose, self-chosen, voluntary, of one's own accord," occurs in 2 Cor. 8:3 and 17, of the churches of Macedonia as to their gifts for the poor saints in Judea, and of Titus in his willingness to go and exhort the church in Corinth concerning the matter. In 8:3 the RV translates it "(gave) of their own accord," consistently with the rendering in v. 17. See WILLING.¶

2. *automatos* (αὐτόματος, 844), from *autos,* "self," and a root *ma*—, signifying "desire," denotes of oneself, moved by one's own impulse. It occurs in Mark 4:28, of the power of the earth to produce plants and fruits of itself; Acts 12:10, of the door which opened of its own accord. See SELF.¶ In the Sept., Lev. 25:5, "spontaneous produce"; v. 11, "produce that comes of itself"; Josh. 6:5; 2 Kings 19:29,"(that which groweth) of itself"; Job 24:24, of an ear of corn "(falling off) of itself (from the stalk)."¶

3. *sumpsuchos* (σύμψυχο, 4861), lit., "fellow-souled or minded" (*sun,* "with," *psuchē,* "the soul"), occurs in Phil. 2:2, "of one accord."¶

ACCORDING AS

1. *kathoti* (καθότι, 2530), from *kata,* "according to," and *hoti,* "that," lit., "because that," Luke 1:7; 19:9; Acts 2:24, is translated "according as" in Acts 2:45, RV (KJV, "as") and in 4:35; "inasmuch as," 17:31.¶

2. *kathōs* (καθώς, 2531), from *kata,* "according to," and *hōs,* "as," signifies "according as" or "even as," e.g., 1 Cor. 1:31; 2 Cor. 9:7.

3. *hōs* (ὡς, 5613) is sometimes rendered "according as," e.g., Rev. 22:12; in 2 Pet. 1:3, the RV has "seeing that," for the KJV "according as."

4. *katho* (καθό, 2526) : see INASMUCH AS.

For **ACCORDING TO** see *Note* †, p. 1

ACCOUNT (-ED) (Verbs and Noun)

A. Verbs.

1. *dokeō* (δοκέω, 1380), primarily, "to be of opinion, think, suppose," also signifies "to seem, be accounted, reputed," translated "accounted" in Mark 10:42; Luke 22:24. It is not used ironically here, nor in Gal. 2:2, 6, 9, "those who were of repute." See REPUTE, SEEM, SUPPOSE, THINK.

2. *ellogeō* (or-*aō*) (ἐλλογέω, 1677), "to put to a person's account," Philem. 18, is used of sin in Rom. 5:13, "reckon" (KJV, "impute"). See IMPUTE, No. 2.¶

3. *hēgeomai* (ἡγέομαι, 2233) primarily signifies "to lead"; then, "to consider"; it is translated "accounting" in Heb. 11:26, RV (KJV, "esteeming"); 2 Pet. 3:15, "account." See CHIEF, COUNT, ESTEEM, GOVERNOR, JUDGE, RULE, SUPPOSE, THINK.

4. *logizomai* (λογίζομαι, 3049) primarily signifies "to reckon," whether by calculation or imputation, e.g., Gal. 3:6 (RV, "reckoned"); then, to deliberate, and so to suppose, "account," Rom. 8:36; 14:14 (KJV, "esteemeth"); John 11:50; 1 Cor. 4:1; Heb. 11:19; (KJV, "consider"); Acts 19:27 ("made of no account"; KJV, "despised"); 1 Pet. 5:12 (KJV, "suppose"). It is used of love in 1 Cor. 13:5, as not taking "account" of evil, RV (KJV, "thinketh"). In 2 Cor. 3:5 the apostle uses it in repudiation of the idea that he and fellow-servants of God are so self-sufficient as to "account anything" (RV) as from themselves (KJV, "think"), i.e., as to attribute anything to themselves. Cf. 12:6. In 2 Tim. 4:16 it is used of laying to a person's "account" (RV) as a charge against him (KJV, "charge").

Note: In Phil. 4:8 it signifies "to think upon a matter by way of taking account of its character" (RV marg.). See CONCLUDE, COUNT, CHARGE, ESTEEM, IMPUTE, NUMBER, REASON, RECKON, SUPPOSE, THINK.

5. *kataxioō* (καταξιόω, 2661) denotes "to account worthy" (*kata,* "intensive," *axios,* "worthy"), "to judge worthy," Luke 20:35; some mss. have it in 21:36 (so the KJV); the most authentic mss. have the verb *katischuō,* "to prevail"; Acts 5:41, "were counted worthy"; so 2 Thess. 1:5.¶

6. *exoutheneō* (ἐξουθενέω, 1848), "to make of no account," frequently signifies "to despise." In 1 Cor. 6:4, it is used, not in a contemptuous sense, but of gentile judges, before whom the

saints are not to go to law with one another, such magistrates having no place, and therefore being "of no account" (RV), in the church. The apostle is not speaking of any believers as "least esteemed" (KJV). In 2 Cor. 10:10, for KJV, "contemptible," the RV suitably has "of no account." See DESPISE.

B. Noun.

logos (λόγος, 3056), "a word or saying," also means "an account which one gives by word of mouth" (cf. No. 4), Matt. 12:36; Matt. 18:23, RV, "reckoning"; 16:2; Acts 19:40; 20:24 (KJV, "count"); Rom. 14:12; Phil. 4:17; Heb. 13:17; 1 Pet. 4:5. See CAUSE, COMMUNICATION, DO, DOCTRINE, FAME, INTENT, MATTER, MOUTH, PREACHING, QUESTION, REASON, RECKONING, RUMOR, SAYING, SHEW, SPEECH, TALK, THING, TIDINGS, TREATISE, UTTERANCE, WORD, WORK.

ACCURATELY

akribōs (ἀκριβῶς, 199) is correctly translated in the RV of Luke 1:3, "having traced the course of all things accurately" (KJV, "having had perfect understanding"). It is used in Matt. 2:8, of Herod's command to the wise men as to searching for the young Child (RV, "carefully"; KJV, "diligently"); in Acts 18:25, of Apollos' teaching of "the things concerning Jesus" (RV, "carefully"; KJV, "diligently"); in Eph. 5:15, of the way in which believers are to walk (RV, "carefully"; KJV, "circumspectly"); in 1 Thess. 5:2, of the knowledge gained by the saints through the apostle's teaching concerning the Day of the Lord (RV and KJV, "perfectly"). The word expresses that "accuracy" which is the outcome of carefulness. It is connected with *akros*, "pointed."

This word and its other grammatical forms, *akribeia, akribēs, akribesteron* and *akriboō*, are used especially by Luke, who employs them eight times out of the thirteen in the NT; Matthew uses them three times, Paul twice. See CAREFUL, DILIGENT, EXACTLY, PERFECT.¶

For **ACCURSED** see **CURSE**, A, No. 3

ACCUSATION, ACCUSE

A. Nouns.

1. *aitia* (αἰτία, 156) probably has the primary meaning of "a cause, especially an occasion of something evil, hence a charge, an accusation." It is used in a forensic sense, of (*a*) an accusation, Acts 25:18 (RV, "charge"), 27; (*b*) a crime, Matt. 27:37; Mark 15:26; John 18:38; 19:4, 6; Acts 13:28; 23:28; 28:18. See CASE, CAUSE, CHARGE, CRIME, FAULT.

2. *aitiōma* (αἰτίωμα, 157), "an accusation," expressing No. 1 more concretely, is found in Acts 25:7, RV, "charges," for KJV, "complaints." See COMPLAINT.¶

3. *enklēma* (ἔγκλημα, 1462) is "an accusation made in public," but not necessarily before a tribunal. That is the case in Acts 23:29, "laid to his charge." In 25:16 it signifies a matter of complaint; hence, the RV has "the matter laid against him" (KJV, "crime"). See CHARGE, CRIME.¶

4. *katēgoria* (κατηγορία, 2724), "an accusation," is found in John 18:29; 1 Tim. 5:19 and Titus 1:6, lit., "not under accusation." This and the verb *katēgoreō*, "to accuse," and the noun *katēgoros*, "an accuser" (see below), all have chiefly to do with judicial procedure, as distinct from *diaballō*, "to slander." It is derived from *agora*, "a place of public speaking," prefixed by *kata*, "against"; hence, it signifies a speaking against a person before a public tribunal. It is the opposite to *apologia*, "a defense."¶

Note: Krisis, which has been translated "accusation," in the KJV of 2 Pet. 2:11 and Jude 9 (RV, "judgement"), does not come under this category. It signifies "a judgment, a decision given concerning anything."

B. Verbs.

1. *diaballō* (διαβάλλω, 1225), used in Luke 16:1, in the passive voice, lit. signifies "to hurl across" (*dia*, "through," *ballō*, "to throw"), and suggests a verbal assault. It stresses the act rather than the author, as in the case of *aitia* and *katēgoria. Diabolos* is connected.¶

2. *enkaleō* (ἐγκαλέω, 1458), — see A, No. 3, "to bring a charge against, or to come forward as an accuser against," lit. denotes "to call in" (*en*, "in," *kaleō*, "to call"), i.e., "to call (something) in or against (someone)"; hence, "to call to account, to accuse," Acts 19:38, RV (KJV, "implead"); in v. 40, "accused" (KJV, "call in question"). It is used in four other places in the Acts, 23:28–29; 26:2, 7, and elsewhere in Rom. 8:33, "shall lay to the charge." See CALL, IMPLEAD.¶

3. *epēreazō* (ἐπηρεάζω, 1908), besides its more ordinary meaning, "to insult, treat abusively, despitefully," Luke 6:28, has the forensic significance "to accuse falsely," and is used with this meaning in 1 Pet. 3:16, RV, "revile." See DESPITEFULLY, REVILE.¶

4. *katēgoreō* (κατηγορέω, 2723), "to speak against, accuse" (cf. A, No. 4), is used (*a*) in a general way, "to accuse," e.g., Luke 6:7, RV, "how to accuse"; Rom. 2:15; Rev. 12:10; (*b*) before a judge, e.g., Matt. 12:10; Mark 15:4 (RV, "witness against"); Acts 22:30; 25:16. In

Acts 24:19, RV renders it "make accusation," for the KJV, "object." See OBJECT, WITNESS.

5. *sukophanteō* (συκοφαντέω, 4811), (Eng., "sycophant") means (a) "to accuse wrongfully"; Luke 3:14 (KJV and RV, margin); RV, "exact wrongfully"; (b) "to exact money wrongfully, to take anything by false accusation," Luke 19:8, and the RV text of 3:14. It is more frequently found in the Sept.; see Gen. 43:18, "to inform against"; Lev. 19:11, "neither shall each falsely accuse his neighbor"; Job 35:9, "they that are oppressed by false accusation"; Ps. 119:122, "let not the proud accuse me falsely"; Prov. 14:31 and 22:16, "he that oppresses the needy by false accusation."

The word is derived from *sukon*, "a fig," and *phainō*, "to show." At Athens a man whose business it was to give information against anyone who might be detected exporting figs out of the province, is said to have been called a *sukophantēs* (see Note (2) below). Probably, however, the word was used to denote one who brings figs to light by shaking the tree, and then in a metaphorical sense one who makes rich men yield up their fruit by "false accusation." Hence in general parlance it was used to designate "a malignant informer," one who accused from love of gain. See EXACT.¶

Note: Proaitiaomai denotes "to bring a previous charge against", Rom. 3:9, RV. See CHARGE.¶

ACCUSER

1. *diabolos* (διάβολος, 1228), "an accuser" (cf. ACCUSE, B, No. 1), is used 34 times as a title of Satan, the Devil (the English word is derived from the Greek); once of Judas, John 6:70, who, in his opposition to God, acted the part of the Devil. Apart from John 6:70, men are never spoken of as devils. It is always to be distinguished from *daimōn*, "a demon." It is found three times, 1 Tim. 3:11; 2 Tim. 3:3; Titus 2:3, of false accusers, slanderers.

2. *katēgoros* (κατήγορος, 2725), "an accuser," is used in John 8:10; Acts 23:30, 35; 24:8; 25:16, 18. In Rev. 12:10, it is used of Satan.¶ In the Sept., Prov. 18:17.¶

Notes: (1) *Sukophantia*, "a false accusation or oppression," is used in Eccl. 5:7; 7:8; Ps. 119:134 and Amos 2:8 (not in the NT). See No. 5, above.

(2) *Sukophantēs*, "a false accuser, or oppressor," occurs in Ps. 72:4; Prov. 28:16 (not in the NT).

ACKNOWLEDGE (-MENT)

A. Verb.

epiginōskō (ἐπιγινώσκω, 1921) signifies (a) "to know thoroughly" (*epi*, "intensive," *ginōskō*, "to know"); (b) "to recognize a thing to be what it really is, to acknowledge," 1 Cor. 14:37 (RV, "take knowledge of"); 16:18; 2 Cor. 1:13–14. See KNOW, KNOWLEDGE, PERCEIVE.

Note: In 1 John 2:23, "acknowledgeth" translates the verb *homologeō*, "to confess," RV, "confesseth."

B. Noun.

epignōsis (ἐπίγνωσις, 1922), akin to A, "full, or thorough knowledge, discernment, recognition," is translated "acknowledging" in the KJV of 2 Tim. 2:25; Titus 1:1 and Philem. 6 (in all three, RV, "knowledge," properly, "thorough knowledge"). In Col. 2:2, KJV, "acknowledgement," RV, "that they may know" (i.e., "unto the full knowledge"). See KNOWLEDGE.

ACQUAINTANCE

1. *gnōstos* (γνωστός, 1110), from *ginōskō*, "to know," signifies "known, or knowable"; hence, "one's acquaintance"; it is used in this sense, in the plural, in Luke 2:44 and 23:49. See KNOWN, NOTABLE.

2. *idios* (ἴδιος, 2398), "one's own," is translated "acquaintance" in the KJV of Acts 24:23, "friends" (RV). See COMPANY.

For **ACROSS** (Acts 27:5, RV), see *Note* †, p. 1

ACT

1. *epautophōrō* (ἐπαυτοφώρω, 1888) primarily signifies "caught in the act of theft" (*epi*, "upon," intensive, *autos*, "self," *phōr*, "a thief"); then, "caught in the act" of any other crime, John 8:4. In some texts the preposition *epi* is detached from the remainder of the adjective, and appears as *ep' autophōrō*.¶

2. *dikaiōma* (δικαίωμα, 1345) signifies "an act of righteousness, a concrete expression of righteousness," as in the RV of Rom. 5:18, in reference to the death of Christ; the KJV wrongly renders it "the righteousness of One." The contrast is between the one trespass by Adam and the one act of Christ in His atoning Death. In Rev. 15:4 and 19:8, the word is used in the plural to signify, as in the RV, "righteous acts," respectively, of God, and of the saints. See JUDGMENT, JUSTIFICATION, ORDINANCE, RIGHTEOUSNESS.

3. *prassō* (πράσσω, 4238), "to do, to practice," is translated "act" in the RV of Acts 17:7

(KJV, "do"). See COMMIT, DO, EXACT, KEEP, RE-QUIRE, USE.

ACTIVE

energēs (ἐνεργής, 1756), lit., "in work" (cf. Eng., "energetic"), is used (*a*) of the Word of God, Heb. 4:12 (RV, "active," KJV, "powerful"); (*b*) of a door for the Gospel, 1 Cor. 16:9, "effectual"; (*c*) of faith, Philem. 6, "effectual." See EFFECTUAL, POWERFUL. Cf. the synonymous words *dunatos* and *ischuros* (see ABLE).¶

ACTUALLY

holōs (ὅλως, 3654), from *holos*, "all, whole," is translated "actually" in 1 Cor. 5:1, RV ("it is actually reported"); the KJV "commonly" does not convey the meaning. In 6:7 it is translated "altogether" (KJV, "utterly"); in 15:29, "at all," as in Matt. 5:34. See ALL, ALTOGETHER.¶

ADD

1. *epitithēmi* (ἐπιτίθημι, 2007), lit., "to put upon" (*epi*, "upon," *tithēmi*, "to put"), has a secondary and somewhat infrequent meaning, "to add to," and is found in this sense in Mark 3:16–17, lit., "He added the name Peter to Simon," "He added to them the name Boanerges," and Rev. 22:18, where the word is set in contrast to "take away from" (v. 19). See LADE, LAY, PUT, SET.

2. *prostithēmi* (προστίθημι, 4369), "to put to" (*pros*, "to," *tithēmi*, "to put"), "to add, or to place beside" (the primary meaning), in Luke 17:5 is translated "increase," in the request "increase our faith"; in Luke 20:11–12, "he sent yet" (KJV, "again he sent"), lit., "he added and sent," as in 19:11, "He added and spake." In Acts 12:3, RV, "proceeded," KJV, "proceeded further" (of repeating or continuing the action mentioned by the following verb); in Acts 13:36,"was laid unto"; in Heb. 12:19, "more ... be spoken," (lit., "that no word should be added"). In Gal. 3:19, "What then is the law? It was "added" because of transgressions, there is no contradiction of what is said in v. 15, where the word is *epidiatasso* (see No. 4), for there the latter word conveys the idea of supplementing an agreement already made; here in v. 19 the meaning is not that something had been 'added' to the promise with a view to complete it, which the apostle denies, but that something had been given "in addition" to the promise, as in Rom. 5:20, "The law came in beside." See GIVE, INCREASE, LAY, PROCEED, SPEAK.

3. *prosanatithēmi* (προσανατίθημι, 4323), lit., "to lay upon in addition," came to be used in the sense of putting oneself before another, for the purpose of consulting him; hence simply "to consult, to take one into counsel, to confer." With this meaning it is used only in Gal. 1:16. In Gal. 2:2, a shorter form, *anatithēmi*, is used, which means "to lay before" (KJV, "communicated unto"). This less intensive word may have been purposely used there by the apostle to suggest that he described to his fellow apostles the character of his teaching, not to obtain their approval or their advice concerning it, but simply that they might have the facts of the case before them on which they were shortly to adjudicate.

It was also used to signify "to communicate, to impart." With this meaning it is used only in Gal. 2:6, in the middle voice, the suggestion being to "add" from one's store of things. In regard to his visit to Jerusalem the apostle says "those who were of repute imparted nothing to me" (KJV, "in conference added"), that is to say, they neither modified his teaching nor "added" to his authority. See CONFER.¶

4. *epidiatassō* (ἐπιδιατάσσω, 1928), lit., "to arrange in addition" (*epi*, "upon," *dia*, "through," *tassō*, "to arrange"), is used in Gal. 3:15 ("addeth," or rather, "ordains something in addition"). If no one does such a thing in the matter of a human covenant, how much more is a covenant made by God inviolable! The Judaizers by their "addition" violated this principle, and, by proclaiming the divine authority for what they did, they virtually charged God with a breach of promise. He gave the Law, indeed, but neither in place of the promise nor to supplement it.¶

5. *pareispherō* (παρεισφέρω, 3923), "to bring in besides" (*para*, "besides," *eis*, "in," *pherō*, "to bring"), means "to add," 2 Pet. 1:5, "adding on your part" (RV); the words "on your part" represent the intensive force of the verb; the KJV, "giving" does not provide an adequate meaning.¶

6. *epichorēgeō* (ἐπιχορηγέω, 2023) is translated "add" in the KJV of 2 Pet. 1:5. Its meaning is "to supply, to minister" (*epi*, "to," *chorēgeō*, "to minister"); RV, "supply." See MINISTER.

7. *didōmi* (δίδωμι, 1325), "to give," is translated "add," in Rev. 8:3, RV, for KJV, "offer" (marg., "add"). See GIVE.

Note: In Phil. 1:17, RV, *egeirō*, "to raise," is translated "add" in the KJV (RV, "raise up"). See BRING, A, No. 6.

For **ADDICTED** (KJV, of 1 Cor. 16:15) see SET, No. 10

ADJURE

1. *horkizo* (ὁρκίζω, 3726), "to cause to swear, to lay under the obligation of an oath" (*horkos*, Mark 5:7; Acts 19:13), is connected with the Heb. word for a thigh, cf. Gen. 24:2, 9; 47:29. Some mss. have this word in 1 Thess. 5:27. The most authentic have No. 3 (below). See CHARGE.¶

2. *exorkizō* (ἐξορκίζω, 1844), an intensive form of No. 1, signifies "to appeal by an oath, to adjure," Matt. 26:63.¶ In the Sept., Gen. 24:3; Judg. 17:2; 1 Kings 22:16.¶

3. *enorkizō* (ἐνορκίζω, 1722 and 3726), "to put under (or bind by) an oath," is translated "adjure" in the RV of 1 Thess. 5:27 (KJV, "charge").¶ In the Sept., Neh. 13:25.¶

Note: The synonymous verb *omnumi* signifies "to make an oath, to declare or promise with an oath." See, e.g., Mark 6:23, in contrast to 5:7 (*horkizō*). See OATH and SWEAR.

For the KJV **ADMINISTER** and **ADMINISTRATION** see **MINISTER** and **MINISTRATION, SERVE,** and **SERVICE**

For the KJV **ADMIRATION** and **ADMIRE** see **WONDER** and **MARVEL**

ADMONITION, ADMONISH

A. Noun.

nouthesia (νουθεσία, 3559), lit., "a putting in mind" (*nous*, "mind," *tithēmi*, "to put"), is used in 1 Cor. 10:11, of the purpose of the Scriptures; in Eph. 6:4, of that which is ministered by the Lord; and in Titus 3:10, of that which is to be administered for the correction of one who creates trouble in the church. *Nouthesia* is "the training by word," whether of encouragement, or, if necessary, by reproof or remonstrance. In contrast to this, the synonymous word *paideia* stresses training by act, though both words are used in each respect.¶

B. Verbs.

1. *noutheteō* (νουθετέω, 3560), cf. the noun above, means "to put in mind, admonish," Acts 20:31 (KJV, "warn"); Rom. 15:14; 1 Cor. 4:14 (KJV, "warn"); Col. 1:28 (KJV, "warning"); Col. 3:16; 1 Thess. 5:12, 14 (KJV, "warn"); 2 Thess. 3:15.

It is used, (*a*) of instruction, (*b*) of warning. It is thus distinguished from *paideuō*, "to correct by discipline, to train by act," Heb. 12:6; cf. Eph. 6:4.

"The difference between 'admonish' and 'teach' seems to be that, whereas the former has mainly in view the things that are wrong and call for warning, the latter has to do chiefly with the impartation of positive truth, cf. Col. 3:16; they were to let the Word of Christ dwell richly in them, so that they might be able (1) to teach and 'admonish' one another, and (2) to abound in the praises of God.

"Admonition differs from remonstrance, in that the former is warning based on instruction; the latter may be little more than expostulation. For example, though Eli remonstrated with his sons, 1 Sam. 2:24, he failed to admonish them, 3:13, LXX. Pastors and teachers in the churches are thus themselves admonished, i.e., instructed and warned, by the Scriptures, 1 Cor. 10:11, so to minister the Word of God to the saints, that, naming the Name of the Lord, they shall depart from unrighteousness, 2 Tim. 2:19."* See WARN.¶

2. *paraineō* (παραινέω, 3867), "to admonish by way of exhorting or advising," is found in Acts 27:9 ("Paul admonished them") and v. 22 ("and now I exhort you"). See EXHORT.¶

3. *chrēmatizō* (χρηματίζω, 5537), primarily, "to transact business," then, "to give advice to enquirers" (especially of official pronouncements of magistrates), or "a response to those consulting an oracle," came to signify the giving of a divine "admonition" or instruction or warning, in a general way; "admonished" in Heb. 8:5, KJV (RV, "warned"). Elsewhere it is translated by the verb "to warn."

The word is derived from *chrēma*, "an affair, business." Names were given to men from the nature of their business (see the same word in Acts 11:26; Rom. 7:3); hence, the idea of dealing with a person and receiving instruction. In the case of oracular responses, the word is derived from *chrēsmos*, "an oracle." See CALL, REVEAL, SPEAK, WARN.

ADO

thorubeō (θορυβέω, 2350), "to make an uproar, to throw into confusion, or to wail tumultuously," is rendered "make . . . ado," in Mark 5:39; elsewhere in Matt. 9:23; Acts 17:5; 20:10. See NOISE, TROUBLE, UPROAR. ¶

Note: For the corresponding noun, *thorubos*, see TUMULT, UPROAR.

ADOPTION

huiothesia (υἱοθεσία, 5206), from *huios*, "a son," and *thesis*, "a placing," akin to *tithēmi*, "to place," signifies the place and condition of a son given to one to whom it does not naturally

---

* From *Notes on Thessalonians*, by Hogg and Vine, pp. 179–180.

belong. The word is used by the apostle Paul only.

In Rom. 8:15, believers are said to have received "the Spirit of adoption," that is, the Holy Spirit who, given as the Firstfruits of all that is to be theirs, produces in them the realization of sonship and the attitude belonging to sons. In Gal. 4:5 they are said to receive "the adoption of sons," i.e., sonship bestowed in distinction from a relationship consequent merely upon birth; here two contrasts are presented, (1) between the sonship of the believer and the unoriginated sonship of Christ, (2) between the freedom enjoyed by the believer and bondage, whether of Gentile natural condition, or of Israel under the Law. In Eph. 1:5 they are said to have been foreordained unto "adoption as sons" through Jesus Christ, RV; the KJV, "adoption of children" is a mistranslation and misleading. God does not "adopt" believers as children; they are begotten as such by His Holy Spirit through faith. "Adoption" is a term involving the dignity of the relationship of believers as sons; it is not a putting into the family by spiritual birth, but a putting into the position of sons. In Rom. 8:23 the "adoption" of the believer is set forth as still future, as it there includes the redemption of the body, when the living will be changed and those who have fallen asleep will be raised. In Rom. 9:4 "adoption" is spoken of as belonging to Israel, in accordance with the statement in Exod. 4:12, "Israel is My Son." Cf. Hos. 11:1. Israel was brought into a special relation with God, a collective relationship, not enjoyed by other nations, Deut. 14:1; Jer. 31:9, etc.¶

ADORN, ADORNING

A. Verb.

kosmeō (κοσμέω, 2885), primarily "to arrange, to put in order" (Eng., "cosmetic"), is used of furnishing a room, Matt. 12:44; Luke 11:25, and of trimming lamps, Matt. 25:7. Hence, "to adorn, to ornament," as of garnishing tombs, Matt. 23:29; buildings, Luke 21:5; Rev. 21:19; one's person, 1 Tim. 2:9; 1 Pet. 3:5; Rev. 21:2; metaphorically, of "adorning a doctrine," Titus 2:10. See GARNISH, TRIM.¶

B. Noun.

kosmos (κόσμος, 2889), "a harmonious arrangement or order," then, "adornment, decoration," came to denote "the world, or the universe, as that which is divinely arranged." The meaning "adorning" is found in 1 Pet. 3:3. Elsewhere it signifies "the world." Cf. kosmios, decent, modest, 1 Tim. 2:9; 3:2. See WORLD.

ADULTERER (-ESS), ADULTEROUS, ADULTERY

A. Nouns.

1. moichos (μοιχός, 3432) denotes one "who has unlawful intercourse with the spouse of another," Luke 18:11; 1 Cor. 6:9; Heb. 13:4. As to Jas. 4:4, see below.¶

2. moichalis (μοιχαλίς, 3428), "an adulteress," is used (a) in the natural sense, 2 Pet. 2:14; Rom. 7:3; (b) in the spiritual sense, Jas. 4:4; here the RV rightly omits the word "adulterers." It was added by a copyist. As in Israel the breach of their relationship with God through their idolatry, was described as "adultery" or "harlotry" (e.g., Ezek. 16:15, etc.; 23:43), so believers who cultivate friendship with the world, thus breaking their spiritual union with Christ, are spiritual "adulteresses," having been spiritually united to Him as wife to husband, Rom. 7:4. It is used adjectively to describe the Jewish people in transferring their affections from God, Matt. 12:39; 16:4; Mark 8:38. In 2 Pet. 2:14, the lit. translation is "full of an adulteress" (RV, marg.).¶

3. moicheia (μοιχεία, 3430), "adultery," is found in Matt. 15:19; Mark 7:21; John 8:3 (KJV only).¶

B. Verbs.

1. moichaō (μοιχάω, 3429), used in the middle voice in the NT, is said of men in Matt. 5:32; 19:9; Mark 10:11; of women in Mark 10:12.¶

2. moicheuō (μοιχεύω, 3431) is used in Matt. 5:27–28, 32 (in v. 32 some texts have No. 1); 19:18; Mark 10:19; Luke 16:18; 18:20; John 8:4; Rom. 2:22; 13:9; Jas. 2:11; in Rev. 2:22, metaphorically, of those who are by a Jezebel's solicitations drawn away to idolatry. ¶

ADVANCE

prokoptō (προκόπτω, 4298), lit., "to strike forward, cut forward a way," i.e., to make progress, is translated "advanced" in Luke 2:52, RV, of the Lord Jesus (KJV, "increased"); in Gal. 1:14 "advanced," of Paul's former progress in the Jews' religion (KJV, "profited"); in Rom. 13:12, "is far spent," of the "advanced" state of the "night" of the world's spiritual darkness; in 2 Tim. 2:16, "will proceed further," of profane babblings; in 3:9, "shall proceed no further," of the limit divinely to be put to the doings of evil men; in v. 13, of the progress of evil men and impostors, "shall wax," lit., "shall advance to the worse." See INCREASE, PROCEED, PROFIT, SPENT, WAX. ¶

Note: The corresponding noun prokopē is found in Phil. 1:12 and 25, "progress" (KJV, "furtherance"); 1 Tim. 4:15, "progress" (KJV, "profiting," an inadequate meaning).¶

ADVANTAGE

A. Nouns.

1. *perissos* (περισσός, 4053), primarily, "what is above and over, superadded," hence came to denote "what is superior and advantageous," Rom. 3:1, in a comparison between Jew and Gentile; only here with this meaning. See ABUNDANT, C, No. 1.

2. *ophelos* (ὄφελος, 3786), akin to *ophellō*, "to increase," comes from a root signifying "to increase"; hence, "advantage, profit"; it is rendered as a verb in its three occurrences, 1 Cor. 15:32 (KJV, "advantageth"; RV, "doth it profit"); Jas. 2:14, 16, lit., "What (is) the profit?" See PROFIT.¶ In the Sept., Job 15:3.¶

3. *ōpheleia* (ὠφέλεια, 5622), an alternative form to No. 2, akin to C, No. 1, is found in Rom. 3:1, "profit," and Jude 16, "advantage." (i.e., they shew respect of persons for the sake of what they may gain from them). See PROFIT.¶

Note: Ōphelimos, "profitable," is used only in the Pastoral Epistles, 1 Tim. 4:8; 2 Tim. 3:16; Titus 3:8. See PROFIT.¶

B. Verbs.

1. *ōpheleō* (ὠφελέω, 5623) signifies "to be useful, do good, profit," Rom. 2:25; with a negative, "to be of no use, to effect nothing," Matt. 27:24; John 6:63, "profiteth"; 12:19, "prevail"; in Luke 9:25, KJV, "(what is a man) advantaged ?" RV, "profited." See BETTERED (to be), PREVAIL, PROFIT.

2. *pleonekteō* (πλεονεκτέω, 4122), lit., "to seek to get more" (*pleon*, "more," *echō*, "to have"); hence, "to get an advantage of, to take advantage of." In 2 Cor. 7:2 the KJV has "defrauded," the RV, "took advantage of"; in 1 Thess. 4:6, KJV, "defraud," RV, "wrong." In the other three places the RV consistently translates it by the verb "to take advantage of," 2 Cor. 2:11, of Satan's effort to gain an "advantage" over the church, through their neglect to restore the backslider; in 2 Cor. 12:17–18, KJV, "make a gain of." See DEFRAUD, GAIN, WRONG.¶

Note: Cf. pleonektēs, "a covetous person," *pleonexia*, "covetousness."

ADVENTURE

didōmi (δίδωμι, 1325), "to give," is once used of giving oneself to go into a place, "to adventure" into, Acts 19:31, of Paul's thought of going into the midst of the mob in the theater at Ephesus. See BESTOW, COMMIT, DELIVER, GIVE.

ADVERSARY

A. Noun.

antidikos (ἀντίδικος, 476), firstly, "an opponent in a lawsuit," Matt. 5:25 (twice); Luke 12:58; 18:3, is also used to denote "an adversary or an enemy," without reference to legal affairs, and this is perhaps its meaning in 1 Pet. 5:8, where it is used of the Devil. Some would regard the word as there used in a legal sense, since the Devil accuses men before God.¶

B. Verb.

antikeimai (ἀντικείμαι, 480) is, lit., "to lie opposite to, to be set over against." In addition to its legal sense it signifies "to withstand"; the present participle of the verb with the article, which is equivalent to a noun, signifies "an adversary," e.g., Luke 13:17; 21:15; 1 Cor. 16:9; Phil. 1:28; 1 Tim. 5:14. This construction is used of the Man of Sin, in 2 Thess. 2:4, and is translated "He that opposeth," where, adopting the noun form, we might render by "the opponent and self-exalter against. . . ." In Gal. 5:17 it is used of the antagonism between the Holy Spirit and the flesh in the believer; in 1 Tim. 1:10, of anything, in addition to persons, that is opposed to the doctrine of Christ. In these two places the word is rendered "contrary to."¶ In the Sept. it is used of Satan, Zech. 3:1, and of men, Job 13:24; Isa. 66:6. See CONTRARY, OPPOSE.¶

C. Adjective.

hupenantios (ὑπεναντίος, 5227), "contrary, opposed," is a strengthened form of *enantios* (*en*, "in," and *antios*, "set against"). The intensive force is due to the preposition *hupo*. It is translated "contrary to," in Col. 2:14, of ordinances; in Heb. 10:27, "adversaries." In each place a more violent form of opposition is suggested than in the case of *enantios*. See CONTRARY.¶

For **ADVERSITY**, in Heb. 13:3, where the verb *kakoucheomai* is translated in the KJV, "suffer adversity," see SUFFER, (*b*), No. 6.

ADVICE, ADVISE

1. *gnōmē* (γνώμη, 1106), connected with *ginōskō*, "to know, perceive," firstly means "the faculty or knowledge, reason"; then, "that which is thought or known, one's mind." Under this heading there are various meanings: (1) a view, judgment, opinion, 1 Cor. 1:10; Philem. 14; Rev. 17:13, 17; (2) an opinion as to what ought to be done, either (*a*) by oneself, and so a resolve, or purpose, Acts 20:3; or (*b*) by others, and so, judgment, advice, 1 Cor. 7:25,

40; 2 Cor. 8:10. See AGREE, JUDGMENT, MIND, PURPOSE, WILL.¶

2. *boulē* (βουλή, 1012), from a root meaning "a will," hence "a counsel, a piece of advice," is to be distinguished from *gnōmē; boulē* is the result of determination, *gnōmē* is the result of knowledge. *Boulē* is everywhere rendered by "counsel" in the RV except in Acts 27:12, "advised," lit., "gave counsel." In Acts 13:36 the KJV wrongly has "by the will of God fell on sleep"; the RV, "after he had served the counsel of God, fell on sleep." The word is used of the counsel of God, in Luke 7:30; Acts 2:23; 4:28; 13:36; 20:27; Eph. 1:11; Heb. 6:17; in other passages, of the counsel of men, Luke 23:51; Acts 27:12, 42; 1 Cor. 4:5. See COUNSEL, WILL.¶

For ADVOCATE see COMFORTER

AFAR

1. *makran* (μακράν, 3112), from *makros*, "far," Matt. 8:20 (KJV, "a good way"; RV, "afar"), "a long way off," is used with *eis*, "unto," in Acts 2:39, "afar off." With the article, in Eph. 2:13, 17, it signifies "the (ones) far off." See FAR and WAY.

2. *makrothen* (μακρόθεν, 3113), also from *makros*, signifies "afar off, from far," Matt. 26:58; 27:55, etc. It is used with *apo*, "from," in Mark 5:6; 14:54; 15:40, etc.; outside the Synoptists, three times, Rev. 18:10, 15, 17.

3. *porrōthen* (πόρρωθεν, 4207), "afar off," from *porrō*, "at a distance, a great way off," is found in Luke 17:12 and Heb. 11:13.¶

Note: In 2 Pet. 1:9, *muōpazō*, "to be short-sighted," is translated "cannot see afar off" (KJV); RV, "seeing only what is near."

AFFAIR (-S)

pragmatia, or *pragmateia* (πραγματία, 4230), from *pragma*, "a deed," denotes "a business, occupation, the prosecution of any affair"; in the plural, "pursuits, affairs (of life)," 2 Tim. 2:4.¶

Notes: (1) *Ta kata*, lit., "the (things), with, or respecting a (person)," is translated "affairs" in Eph. 6:21 and Col. 4:7, RV.

(2) *Ta peri*, lit., "the (things) concerning (a person)," is translated "affairs" in the KJV of Eph. 6:22 and Phil. 1:27 (RV, "state," in each place).

AFFECT

kakoō (κακόω, 2559), from *kakos*, "evil, to treat badly, to hurt," also means "to make evil affected, to embitter," Acts 14:2. See EVIL, HARM, HURT.

Note: Zēloō, akin to *zeō*, "to boil" (Eng.,

"zeal"), means (*a*) "to be jealous," Acts 7:9; 17:5; "to envy," 1 Cor. 13:4; "to covet," Jas. 4:2; in a good sense ("jealous over"), in 2 Cor. 11:2; (*b*) "to desire earnestly," 1 Cor. 12:31; 14:1, 39; "to take a warm interest in, to seek zealously," Gal. 4:17–18, KJV, "zealously affect," "to be zealously affected." The RV corrects this to "zealously seek," etc. See COVET, DESIRE, ENVY, JEALOUS, ZEALOUS.¶

AFFECTION (-S), AFFECTED

A. Nouns.

1. *pathos* (πάθος, 3806), from *paschō*, "to suffer," primarily denotes whatever one suffers or experiences in any way; hence, "an affection of the mind, a passionate desire." Used by the Greeks of either good or bad desires, it is always used in the NT of the latter, Rom. 1:26 (KJV, "affections," RV, "passions"); Col. 3:5 (KJV, "inordinate affection," RV, "passion"); 1 Thess. 4:5 (KJV, "lust," RV, "passion"). See LUST.¶

2. *splanchna* (σπλάγχνα, 4698), lit., "the bowels," which were regarded by the Greeks as the seat of the more violent passions, by the Hebrews as the seat of the tender "affections"; hence the word denotes "tender mercies" and is rendered "affections" in 2 Cor. 6:12 (KJV, "bowels"); "inward affection," 2 Cor. 7:15. See BOWELS, COMPASSION, HEART, MERCY. Cf. *epithumia*, "desire."

3. *pathēma* (πάθημα, 3804), akin to No. 1, translated "affections" in Gal. 5:24, KJV, is corrected to "passions" in the RV. See AFFLICTION, B, No. 3.

B. Adjectives.

1. *astorgos* (ἄστοργος, 794) signifies "without natural affection" (*a*, negative, and *storgē*, "love of kindred," especially of parents for children and children for parents; a fanciful etymology associates with this the "stork"), Rom. 1:31; 2 Tim. 3:3.¶

2. *philostorgos* (φιλόστοργος, 5387), "tenderly loving" (from *philos*, "friendly," *storgē*, see No. 1), is used in Rom. 12:10, RV, "tenderly affectioned" (KJV, "kindly affectioned").¶

Notes: (1) *Phroneō*, "to think, to set the mind on," implying moral interest and reflection, is translated "set your affection on" in Col. 3:2, KJV (RV, "set your mind on"). See CAREFUL, MIND, REGARD, SAVOR, THINK, UNDERSTAND.

(2) For *homeiromai* (or *himeiromai*), "to be affectionately desirous of," 1 Thess. 2:8, see DESIRE.¶

AFFIRM

1. *diabebaioomai* (διαβεβαιόομαι, 1226), *dia*, "intensive," and *bebaioō*, "to confirm, make sure," denotes "to assert strongly," "affirm con-

fidently," 1 Tim. 1:7; Titus 3:8 (KJV, "affirm constantly").¶

2. *diischurizomai* (διϊσχυρίζομαι, 1340), as in No. 1, and *ischurizosai*, "to corroborate" (*ischuros* "strong"; see ABILITY, A, No. 2 and C, No. 2, *Note*), primarily signifies "to lean upon," hence, "to affirm stoutly, assert vehemently," Luke 22:59; Acts 12:15.¶

3. *phaskō* (φάσκω, 5335), a frequentative form of the verb *phēmi* (No. 4), denotes "to allege, to affirm by way of alleging or professing," Acts 24:9 (RV, "affirming," KJV, "saying"); 25:19; Rom. 1:22, "professing." Some mss. have it in Rev. 2:2, instead of the verb *legō*, "to say." See PROFESS, SAY.¶

4. *phēmi* (φημί, 5346), "to say" (primarily by way of enlightening, explaining), is rendered "affirm" in Rom. 3:8. See SAY.

AFFLICT (-ED), AFFLICTION

A. Verbs.

1. *kakoō* (κακόω, 2559) is translated "afflict," in Acts 12:1, RV (KJV, "vex"). See AFFECT.

2. *kakoucheō* (κακουχέω, 2558), from *kakos*, "evil," and *echō*, "to have," signifies, in the passive voice, "to suffer ill, to be maltreated, tormented," Heb. 11:37 (KJV, "tormented," RV, "afflicted"); 13:3, KJV, "suffer adversity," RV, "evil entreated." See ENTREAT, TORMENT.¶ In the Sept., 1 Kings, 2:26; 11:39.¶

Note: Sunakoucheō (*sun*, "with," and No. 1), "to be evil entreated with," is used in Heb. 11:25.¶

3. *kakopatheō* (κακοπαθέω, 2553), from *kakos*, "evil," *pathos*, "suffering," signifies "to suffer hardship." So the RV in 2 Tim. 2:9; and 4:5; in Jas. 5:13, "suffer" (KJV, "afflicted "). See ENDURE, SUFFER.¶

Note: For *sunkakopatheō*, 2 Tim. 1:8, see HARDSHIP.

4. *thlibō* (θλίβω, 2346), "to suffer affliction, to be troubled," has reference to sufferings due to the pressure of circumstances, or the antagonism of persons, 1 Thess. 3:4; 2 Thess. 1:6–7; "straitened," in Matt. 7:14 (RV); "throng," Mark 3:9; "afflicted," 2 Cor. 1:6; 7:5 (RV); 1 Tim. 5:10; Heb. 11:37; "pressed," 2 Cor. 4:8. Both the verb and the noun (see B, No. 4), when used of the present experience of believers, refer almost invariably to that which comes upon them from without. See NARROW, PRESS, STRAITENED, THRONG, TRIBULATION, TROUBLE. ¶

5. *talaipōreō* (ταλαιπωρέω, 5003), "to be afflicted," is used in Jas. 4:9, in the middle voice ("afflict yourselves"). It is derived from *tlaō*, "to bear, undergo," and *pōros*, "a hard substance, a callus," which metaphorically came to signify that which is miserable.¶

Note: Talaipōria (akin to No. 5) denotes "misery, hardship," Rom. 3:16; Jas. 5:1.¶ The corresponding adjective is *talaipōros*, "wretched," Rom. 7:24; Rev. 3:17.¶

B. Nouns.

1. *kakopatheia* (κακοπάθεια, 2552), from *kakos*, "evil," and *paschō*, "to suffer" is rendered "suffering" in Jas. 5:10, RV (KJV, "suffering affliction").¶ In Sept., Mal. 1:13.¶

2. *kakōsis* (κάκωσις, 2561), "affliction, ill treatment," is used in Acts 7:34.¶

3. *pathēma* (πάθημα, 3804), from *pathos*, "suffering," signifies "affliction." The word is frequent in Paul's epistles and is found three times in Hebrews, four in 1 Peter; it is used (*a*) of "afflictions," Rom. 8:18, etc.; of Christ's "sufferings," 1 Pet. 1:11; 5:1; Heb. 2:9; of those as shared by believers, 2 Cor. 1:5; Phil. 3:10; 1 Pet. 4:13; 5:1; (*b*) of "an evil emotion, passion," Rom. 7:5; Gal. 5:24. The connection between the two meanings is that the emotions, whether good or evil, were regarded as consequent upon external influences exerted on the mind (cf. the two meanings of the English "passion"). It is more concrete than No. 1, and expresses in sense (*b*) the uncontrolled nature of evil desires, in contrast to *epithumia*, the general and comprehensive term, lit., "what you set your heart upon" (Trench, *Syn.* § lxxxvii). Its concrete character is seen in Heb. 2:9. See AFFECTION, MOTION, PASSION, SUFFERING.

Note: The corresponding verbal form *pathētos*, used in Acts 26:23 or the sufferings of Christ, signifies "destined to suffer."¶

4. *thlipsis* (θλίψις, 2347) primarily means "a pressing, pressure" (see A, No. 4), anything which burdens the spirit. In two passages in Paul's Epistles it is used of future retribution, in the way of "affliction," Rom. 2:9; 2 Thess. 1:6. In Matt. 24:9, the KJV renders it as a verb, "to be afflicted," (RV, "unto tribulation"). It is coupled with *stenochōria*, "anguish," in Rom. 2:9; 8:35; with *anankē*, "distress," 1 Thess. 3:7; with *diōgmos*, "persecution," Matt. 13:21; Mark 4:17; 2 Thess. 1:4. It is used of the calamities of war, Matt. 24:21, 29; Mark 13:19, 24; of want, 2 Cor. 8:13, lit., "distress for you"; Phil. 4:14 (cf. 1:16); Jas. 1:27; of the distress of woman in childbirth, John 16:21; of persecution, Acts 11:19; 14:22; 20:23; 1 Thess. 3:3, 7; Heb. 10:33; Rev. 2:10; 7:14; of the "afflictions" of Christ, from which (His vicarious sufferings apart) his followers must not shrink, whether sufferings of body or mind, Col. 1:24; of sufferings in general, 1 Cor. 7:28; 1 Thess. 1:6, etc. See ANGUISH, BURDENED, DISTRESS, PERSECUTION, TRIBULATION, TROUBLE.

AFFRIGHTED

A. Adjective.

emphobos (ἔμφοβος, 1719), lit., "in fear" (*en*, "in," *phobos*, "fear"), means "affrighted," Luke 24:5, RV (KJV, "afraid"); 24:37; Acts 10:4, RV (KJV, "afraid"); Rev. 11:13. The RV omits it in Acts 22:9. See TREMBLE.

B. Verbs.

1. *pturō* (πτύρω, 4426), "to frighten, scare," is used in the passive voice in Phil. 1:28, "be affrighted," RV, "be terrified," KJV. See TERRIFY.¶

2. *ekthambeō* (ἐκθαμβέω, 1568), "to throw into terror," is used in the passive sense, "to be amazed, affrighted," Mark 16:5-6, KJV (RV, "amazed"); Mark 9:15, "were greatly amazed"; 14:33, "to be greatly amazed" (RV), "to be sore amazed" (KJV). See AMAZE, B, No. 4.¶

For AFOOT see FOOT, B, No. 2

AFORE, AFOREHAND

The Greek words with these meanings consist of prefixes to verbs, signifying "to come, prepare, promise, write afore," etc. See these words.

AFOREPROMISED

proepangellomai (προεπαγγέλλομαι, 4279), "to promise before" (*pro*, "before", *epangellomai*, "to promise"), is translated by the one word "aforepromised," in the RV of 2 Cor. 9:5; in Rom. 1:2, "promised afore."¶

AFORETIME

1. *pote* (ποτέ, 4218) signifies "once, at some time," John 9:13 (cf. *proteron*, in v. 8); Eph. 2:2, 11; Col. 3:7; Titus 3:3; Philem. 11; 1 Pet. 3:5, 20. In all these the RV translates it "aforetime." The KJV varies it with "in time past," "some time," "sometimes," "in the old time."

2. *proteron* (πρότερον, 4386), the comparative of *pro*, "before, aforetime," as being definitely antecedent to something else, is more emphatic than *pote* in this respect. See, e.g., John 6:62; 7:50; 9:8; 2 Cor. 1:13; Gal. 4:13; 1 Tim. 1:13; Heb. 4:6; 7:27; 10:32; 1 Pet. 1:14. See BEFORE, FIRST, FORMER.¶

For AFRAID see AFFRIGHTED, A, FEAR, A, No. 2, B, No. 3, D, SORE

For AFRESH see CROSS, CRUCIFY, B

AFTER, AFTERWARD (-S)

The following are adverbs only. For prepositions and conjunctions see Note † p. 1.

1. *ekeithen* (ἐκεῖθεν, 1564), "thence," is once used to signify "afterwards," in the sense of "then, from that time," Acts 13:21. See THENCE.

2. *hexēs* (ἑξῆς, 1836) denotes "after" with the significance of a succession of events, an event following next in order after another, Luke 7:11; 9:37; Acts 21:1; 25:17; 27:18.¶

3. *kathexēs* (καθεξῆς, 2517), a strengthened form of No. 2, denotes "afterward," or "in order" (*kata*, "according to," and No. 2), Luke 1:3; 8:1; Acts 3:24; 11:4; 18:23.¶

4. *metepeita* (μετέπειτα, 3347), "afterwards," without necessarily indicating an order of events, as in Nos. 1 and 2, is found in Heb. 12:17.¶

5. *husteron* (ὕστερον, 5305), "afterwards," with the suggestion of at length, is found in Matt. 4:2; 21:29, 32, 37 (KJV, "last of all"); 22:27; 25:11; 26:60 (KJV, "at the last"); Mark 16:14; Luke 4:2; 20:32 (KJV, "last"); John 13:36; Heb. 12:11. See LAST.¶

Note: Eita and *epeita*, "then, afterwards," or "thereupon," are translated "afterward" or "afterwards" in the KJV of Mark 4:17 (*eita*) and Gal. 1:21; 1 Cor. 15:23, 46 (*epeita*); always "then" in the RV. See THEN.

AGAIN

1. *dis* (δίς, 1364), the ordinary numeral adverb signifying twice, is rendered "again" in Phil. 4:16, "ye sent once and again unto my need," and in 1 Thess. 2:18, where Paul states that he would have come to the Thessalonians "once and again," that is, twice at least he had attempted to do so. See TWICE.

2. *palin* (πάλιν, 3825), the regular word for "again," is used chiefly in two senses, (*a*) with reference to repeated action; (*b*) rhetorically, in the sense of "moreover" or "further," indicating a statement to be added in the course of an argument, e.g., Matt. 5:33; or with the meaning "on the other hand, in turn," Luke 6:43; 1 Cor. 12:21; 2 Cor. 10:7; 1 John 2:8. In the first chapter of Hebrews, v. 5, *palin* simply introduces an additional quotation; in v. 6 this is not so. There the RV rightly puts the word "again" in connection with "He bringeth in the firstborn into the world," "When He again bringeth, etc." That is to say, *palin* is here set in contrast to the time when God *first* brought His Son into the world. This statement, then, refers to the future second advent of Christ. The word is used far more frequently in the Gospel of John than in any other book in the New Testament.

Note: Other words are rendered "again" in the KJV, which the RV corrects, namely, *deuteros* and *anōthen*. *Deuteros* signifies "a second time," John 9:24; Acts 11:9. *Anōthen* signifies "from above, or anew." See the RV of John 3:3, 7, and the KJV and RV of v. 31. Nicodemus was not puzzled about birth from heaven; what perplexed him was that a person must be born a second time. This the context makes clear. This is really the meaning in Gal. 4:9, where it is associated with *palin*, "over again." The idea is "anew," for, though the bondage would be the same in essence and effect, it would be new in not being in bondage to idols but to the Law. See also Matt. 27:51; Mark 15:38; John 19:23, "from the top." *Anōthen* may mean "from the first," in Luke 1:3 and Acts 26:5. For the meaning "from above," see Jas. 1:17; 3:15, 17.¶

For **AGAINST** see *Note* †, p. 1

AGE

A. Nouns.

1. *aiōn* (αἰών, 165), "an age, era" (to be connected with *aei*, "ever," rather than with *aō*, "to breathe"), signifies a period of indefinite duration, or time viewed in relation to what takes place in the period.

The force attaching to the word is not so much that of the actual length of a period, but that of a period marked by spiritual or moral characteristics. This is illustrated in the use of the adjective [see Note (1) below] in the phrase "life eternal," in John 17:3, in respect of the increasing knowledge of God.

The phrases containing this word should not be rendered literally, but consistently with its sense of indefinite duration. Thus *eis ton aiōna* does not mean "unto the age" but "for ever" (see, e.g., Heb. 5:6). The Greeks contrasted that which came to an end with that which was expressed by this phrase, which shows that they conceived of it as expressing interminable duration.

The word occurs most frequently in the Gospel of John, the Hebrews and Revelation. It is sometimes wrongly rendered "world." See COURSE, ETERNAL, WORLD. It is a characteristic word of John's gospel.

Notes: (1) *Aiōnios*, the adjective corresponding, denoting "eternal," is set in contrast with *proskairos*, lit., "for a season," 2 Cor. 4:18. It is used of that which in nature is endless, as, e.g., of God, Rom. 16:26, His power, 1 Tim. 6:16, His glory, 1 Pet. 5:10, the Holy Spirit, Heb. 9:14, redemption, Heb. 9:12, salvation, 5:9, life in Christ, John 3:16, the resurrection body, 2 Cor. 5:1, the future rule of Christ, 2 Pet. 1:11, which is declared to be without end, Luke 1:33, of sin that never has forgiveness, Mark 3:29, the judgment of God, Heb. 6:2, and of fire, one of

its instruments, Matt. 18:8; 25:41; Jude 7. See ETERNAL, EVERLASTING.

(2) In Rev. 15:3, the RV has "King of the ages," according to the texts which have *aiōnōn*, the KJV has "of saints" (*hagiōn*, in inferior mss.). There is good ms. evidence for *ethnōn*, "nations," (KJV, marg.), probably a quotation from Jer. 10:7.

2. *genea* (γενεά, 1074), connected with *ginomai*, "to become," primarily signifies "a begetting, or birth"; hence, that which has been begotten, a family; or successive members of a genealogy, Matt. 1:17, or of a race of people, possessed of similar characteristics, pursuits, etc., (of a bad character) Matt. 17:17; Mark 9:19; Luke 9:41; 16:8; Acts 2:40; or of the whole multitude of men living at the same time, Matt. 24:34; Mark 13:30; Luke 1:48; 21:32; Phil. 2:15, and especially of those of the Jewish race living at the same period, Matt. 11:16, etc. Transferred from people to the time in which they lived, the word came to mean "an age," i.e., a period ordinarily occupied by each successive generation, say, of thirty or forty years, Acts 14:16; 15:21; Eph. 3:5; Col. 1:26; see also, e.g., Gen. 15:16. In Eph. 3:21 *genea* is combined with *aiōn* in a remarkable phrase in a doxology: "Unto Him be the glory in the church and in Christ Jesus, unto all generations for ever and ever (wrongly in KJV 'all ages, world without end')." The word *genea* is to be distinguished from *aiōn*, as not denoting a period of unlimited duration. See GENERATION, NATION, TIME.

3. *hēlikia* (ἡλικία, 2244), primarily "an age," as a certain length of life, came to mean (*a*) "a particular time of life," as when a person is said to be "of age," John 9:21, 23, or beyond a certain stage of life, Heb. 11:11; (*b*) elsewhere only "of stature," e.g., Matt. 6:27; Luke 2:52; 12:25; 19:3; Eph. 4:13. Some regard Matt. 6:27 and Luke 12:25 as coming under (*a*). It is to be distinguished from *aiōn* and *genea*, since it has to do simply with matters relating to an individual, either his time of life or his height. See STATURE.¶

4. *hēmera* (ἡμέρα, 2250), "a day," is rendered "age" in Luke 2:36, "of a great age" (lit., "advanced in many days"). In Luke 3:23 there is no word in the original corresponding to age. The phrase is simply "about thirty years." See DAY, JUDGMENT, TIME, YEAR.

B. Adjectives.

1. *huperakmos* (ὑπέρακμος, 5230) in 1 Cor. 7:36 is rendered "past the flower of her age"; more lit., "beyond the bloom or flower (*acme*) of life."¶

2. *teleios* (τέλειος, 5046), "complete, per-

fect," from *telos*, "an end," is translated "of full age" in Heb. 5:14, KJV (RV, "fullgrown man").

Note: In Mark 5:42, RV, "old," KJV, "of the age of," is, lit., "of twelve years." For "of great age," Luke 2:36, see STRICKEN. For "of mine own age," Gal. 1:14, RV, see EQUAL, B, No. 2.

AGED

A. Nouns.

1. *presbutēs* (πρεσβύτης, 4246), "an elderly man," is a longer form of *presbus*, the comparative degree of which is *presbuteros*, "a senior, elder," both of which, as also the verb *presbeuō*, "to be elder, to be an ambassador," are derived from *proeisbainō*, "to be far advanced." The noun is found in Luke 1:18, "an old man"; Titus 2:2, "aged men," and Philem. 9, where the RV marg., "Paul an ambassador," is to be accepted, the original almost certainly being *presbeutēs* (not *presbutēs*), "an ambassador." So he describes himself in Eph. 6:20. As Lightfoot points out, he is hardly likely to have made his age a ground of appeal to Philemon, who, if he was the father of Archippus, cannot have been much younger than Paul himself. See OLD.

2. *presbutis* (πρεσβῦτις, 4247), the feminine of No. 1, "an aged woman," is found in Titus 2:3.¶

B. Verb.

gēraskō (γηράσκω, 1095), from *gēras*, "old age," signifies "to grow old," John 21:18 ("when thou shalt be old") and Heb. 8:13 (RV, "that which ... waxeth aged," KJV, "old"). See OLD.¶

For **AGO** see **LONG**, A, No. 5, and in combination with other words

AGONY

agōnia (ἀγωνία, 74), Eng., "agony," was used among the Greeks as an alternative to *agōn*, "a place of assembly"; then for the contests or games which took place there, and then to denote intense emotion. It was more frequently used eventually in this last respect, to denote severe emotional strain and anguish. So in Luke 22:44, of the Lord's "agony" in Gethsemane.¶

AGREE, AGREEMENT

A. Verbs.

1. *sumphōneō* (συμφωνέω, 4856), lit., "to sound together" (*sun*, "together," *phōnē*, "a sound"), i.e., "to be in accord, primarily of musical instruments," is used in the NT of the "agreement" (*a*) of persons concerning a matter, Matt. 18:19; 20:2, 13; Acts 5:9; (*b*) of the writ-

ers of Scripture, Acts 15:15; (*c*) of things that are said to be congruous in their nature, Luke 5:36.¶

Note: Cf. *sumphōnēsis*, "concord," 2 Cor. 6:15,¶, and *sumphōnia*, "music," Luke 15:25.¶

2. *suntithēmi* (συντίθημι, 4934), lit., "to put together" (*sun*, "with," *tithēmi*, "to put"), in the middle voice, means "to make an agreement, or to assent to"; translated "covenanted" in Luke 22:5; "agreed" in John 9:22, and Acts 23:20;"assented" in Acts 24:9.¶

Note: For the synonym *sunkatatithēmi*, a strengthened form of No. 2, see CONSENT, No. 4.

3. *eunoeō* (εὐνοέω, 2132), lit., "to be well-minded, well-disposed" (*eu*, "well," *nous*, "the mind"), is found in Matt. 5:25, "agree with."¶

4. *peithō* (πείθω, 3982), "to persuade," is rendered "agreed" in Acts 5:40, where the meaning is "they yielded to him." See ASSURE, BELIEVE, CONFIDENT, FRIEND, OBEY, PERSUADE, TRUST, YIELD.

B. Nouns.

1. *gnōmē* (γνώμη, 1106), "mind, will," is used with *poieō*, "to make," in the sense of "to agree," Rev. 17:17 (twice), lit., "to do His mind, and to make one mind"; RV, "to come to one mind," KJV, "to agree." See ADVICE, JUDGMENT, MIND, PURPOSE, WILL.

2. *sunkatathesis* (συνκατάθεσις, 4783), akin to A, No. 3, occurs in 2 Cor. 6:16. ¶

C. Adjectives.

1. *asumphōnos* (ἀσύμφωνος, 800), "inharmonious" (*a*, negative, *sumphōnos*, "harmonious"), is used in Acts 28:25, "they agreed not."¶

2. *isos* (ἴσος, 2470), "equal," is used with the verb to be, signifying "to agree," Mark 14:56, 59, lit., "their thought was not equal one with the other." See EQUAL, LIKE, MUCH.

Note: Sumphōnos, "harmonious, agreeing," is used only with the preposition *ek* in the phrase *ek sumphōnou*, "by consent," lit., "out of agreement," 1 Cor. 7:5. In Mark 14:70 some texts have the verb *homoiazō*, "agreeth," KJV.

For **AGROUND** see **RUN**, No. 11

AH!

1. *oua* (οὐά, 3758), an interjection of derision and insult, is translated "Ha!" in Mark 15:29, RV.¶

2. *ea* (ἔα, 1436), an interjection of surprise, fear and anger, was the ejaculation of the man with the spirit of an unclean demon, Luke 4:34, RV; the KJV renders it "Let us alone" (see RV, marg.).¶

AIM

philotimeomai (φιλοτιμέομαι, 5389), lit., "to be fond of honor" (*phileō*, "to love," *timē*, "honor"), and so, actuated by this motive, "to strive to bring something to pass"; hence, "to be ambitious, to make it one's aim," Rom. 15:20, of Paul's "aim" in gospel pioneering, RV (KJV, "strive"); 2 Cor. 5:9, of the "aim" of believers "to be well-pleasing" unto the Lord, RV (KJV, "labor"); in 1 Thess. 4:11, of the "aim" of believers to be quiet, do their own business and work with their own hands; both versions translate it "study." Some would render it, "strive restlessly"; perhaps "strive earnestly" is nearer the mark, but "make it one's aim" is a good translation in all three places. See LABOR, STRIVE, STUDY.¶

AIR

1. *aēr* (ἀήρ, 109), Eng., "air," signifies "the atmosphere," certainly in five of the seven occurrences, Acts 22:23; 1 Cor. 9:26; 14:9; Rev. 9:2; 16:17, and almost certainly in the other two, Eph. 2:2 and 1 Thess. 4:17.¶

2. *ouranos* (οὐρανός, 3772) denotes "the heaven." The RV always renders it "heaven." The KJV translates it "air" in Matt. 8:20. In the phrase "the fowls (or birds) of the heaven" the KJV always has "air"; "sky" in Matt. 16:2-3; Luke 12:56; in all other instances "heaven." The word is probably derived from a root meaning to cover or encompass. See HEAVEN, SKY.

For ALABASTER see CRUSE

For ALAS! see WOE

ALBEIT

hina (ἵνα, 2443), a conjunction, meaning "that," and so rendered in Philem. 19, RV, for KJV, "albeit."

ALIEN

allotrios (ἀλλότριος, 245), primarily, "belonging to another" (the opposite to *idios*, "one's own"), came to mean "foreign, strange, not of one's own family, alien, an enemy"; "aliens" in Heb. 11:34, elsewhere "strange," etc. See MAN'S, *Note* (1), STRANGE, STRANGER.

ALIENATE

apallotrioō (ἀπαλλοτριόω, 526) consists of *apo*, "from," and the above; it signifies "to be rendered an alien, to be alienated." In Eph. 2:12 the RV corrects to the verbal form "alienated," for the noun "aliens"; elsewhere in Eph. 4:18 and Col. 1:21; the condition of the unbeliever is presented in a threefold state of "alienation," (*a*) from the commonwealth of Israel, (*b*) from the life of God, (*c*) from God Himself.¶ The word is used of Israelites in the Sept. of Ezek. 14:5 ("estranged") and of the wicked in general, Ps. 58:3.

ALIKE

Note: In Rom. 14:5, this word is in italics. This addition is not needed in the translation.

For ALIVE see LIFE, C, LIVE, No. 6

ALL

A. Adjectives.

1. *pas* (πᾶς, 3956) radically means "all." Used without the article it means "every," every kind or variety. So the RV marg. in Eph. 2:21, "every building," and the text in 3:15, "every family," and the RV marg. of Acts 2:36, "every house"; or it may signify "the highest degree," the maximum of what is referred to, as, "with all boldness" Acts 4:29. Before proper names of countries, cities and nations, and before collective terms, like "Israel," it signifies either "all" or "the whole," e.g., Matt. 2:3; Acts 2:36. Used with the article, it means the whole of one object. In the plural it signifies "the totality of the persons or things referred to." Used without a noun it virtually becomes a pronoun, meaning "everyone" or "anyone." In the plural with a noun it means "all." The neuter singular denotes "everything" or "anything whatsoever." One form of the neuter plural (*panta*) signifies "wholly, together, in all ways, in all things," Acts 20:35; 1 Cor. 9:25. The neuter plural without the article signifies "all things severally," e.g., John 1:3; 1 Cor. 2:10; preceded by the article it denotes "all things," as constituting a whole, e.g., Rom. 11:36; 1 Cor. 8:6; Eph. 3:9. See EVERY, *Note* (1), WHOLE.

2. *hapas* (ἅπας, 537), a strengthened form of *pas*, signifies "quite all, the whole," and, in the plural, "all, all things." Preceded by an article and followed by a noun it means "the whole of." In 1 Tim. 1:16 the significance is "the whole of His longsuffering," or "the fulness of His longsuffering." See EVERY, WHOLE.

3. *holos* (ὅλος, 3650), "the whole, all," is most frequently used with the article followed by a noun, e.g., Matt. 4:23. It is used with the article alone, in John 7:23, "every whit"; Acts 11:26; 21:31; 28:30; Titus 1:11; Luke 5:5, in the best texts. See ALTOGETHER.

Note: The adjective *holoklēros*, lit., "whole-lot, entire," stresses the separate parts which constitute the whole, no part being incomplete. See ENTIRE.

B. Adverbs.

1. *holōs* (ὅλως, 3654) signifies "at all," Matt. 5:34; 1 Cor. 15:29; "actually," 1 Cor. 5:1, RV (KJV, wrongly, "commonly"); "altogether," 1 Cor. 6:7 (KJV, "utterly").¶

Notes: (1) *Holotelēs*, from A, No. 3, and *telos*, "complete," signifies "wholly, through and through," 1 Thess. 5:23, lit., "whole complete"; there, not an increasing degree of sanctification is intended, but the sanctification of the believer in every part of his being.¶

(2) The synonym *katholou*, a strengthened form of *holou* signifies "at all," Acts 4:18.¶

2. *pantōs* (πάντως, 3843), when used without a negative, signifies "wholly, entirely, by all means," Acts 18:21 (KJV); 1 Cor. 9:22; "altogether," 1 Cor. 9:10; "no doubt, doubtless," Luke 4:23, RV (KJV, "surely"); Acts 28:4. In 21:22 it is translated "certainly," RV, for KJV, "needs" (lit., "by all means"). With a negative it signifies "in no wise," Rom. 3:9; 1 Cor. 5:10; 16:12 ("at all"). See ALTOGETHER, DOUBT (NO), MEANS, SURELY, WISE.¶

C. Pronoun.

hosa (ὅσα, 3745), the neuter plural of *hosos*, "as much as," chiefly used in the plural, is sometimes rendered "all that," e.g., Acts 4:23; 14:27. It really means "whatsoever things." See Luke 9:10, RV, "what things."

ALLEGE

paratithēmi (παρατίθημι, 3908), "to place beside or to set before" (*para*, "beside," *tithēmi*, "to put"), while often used in its literal sense of material things, as well as in its more common significance, "to commit, entrust," twice means "to set before one in teaching," as in putting forth a parable, Matt. 13:24, 31, RV. Once it is used of setting subjects before one's hearers by way of argument and proof, of Paul, in "opening and alleging" facts concerning Christ, Acts 17:3. See COMMEND, COMMIT, PUT, SET.

Note: Legō is rendered "put forth" in the KJV of Luke 14:7; but *legō* signifies "to speak"; hence, the RV, "spake." The KJV seems to be an imitation of *paratithēmi* in Matt. 13:24, 31. See SAY.

ALLEGORY

allēgoreō (ἀλληγορέω, 238), translated in Gal. 4:24 "contain an allegory" (KJV, "are an allegory"), formed from *allos*, "other," and *agoreuō*, "to speak in a place of assembly" (*agora*, "the market-place"), came to signify "to speak," not according to the primary sense of the word, but so that the facts stated are applied to illustrate principles. The "allegorical" meaning does not do away with the literal meaning of the narrative. There may be more than one "allegorical" meaning though, of course, only one literal meaning. Scripture histories represent or embody spiritual principles, and these are ascertained, not by the play of the imagination, but by the rightful application of the doctrines of Scripture.¶

For **ALLELUIA** (which has been robbed of its initial aspirate) see **HALLELUJAH**

For **ALLOTTED** see **CHARGE,** A (*b*), No.4

ALLOW

1. *dokimazō* (δοκιμάζω, 1381), "to prove with a view to approving," is twice translated by the verb "to allow" in the KJV; the RV corrects to "approveth" in Rom. 14:22, and "have been approved," 1 Thess. 2:4, of being qualified to be entrusted with the gospel; in Rom. 1:28, with the negative, the RV has "refused," for KJV, "did not like." See APPROVE.

2. *ginōskō* (γινώσκω, 1097), "to know," is rendered "allow" in Rom. 7:15 (KJV); the RV has "that which I do I know not"; i.e., "I do not recognize, as a thing for which I am responsible." See AWARE, CAN, FEEL, KNOW, PERCEIVE, RESOLVE, SPEAK, SURE, UNDERSTAND.

3. *suneudokeō* (συνευδοκέω, 4909), "to consent or fully approve" (*sun*, "with," *eu*, "well," *dokeō*, "to think"), is translated "allow" in Luke 11:48; "was consenting" in Acts 8:1; 22:20. See CONSENT.

4. *prosdechomai* (προσδέχομαι, 4327), mistranslated "allow" in Acts 24:15, KJV, means "to wait for," in contrast to rejection, there said of entertaining a hope; hence the RV, "look for." See ACCEPT, A, No. 3.

For **ALLURE** see **BEGUILE,** No. 4, **ENTICE**

ALMIGHTY

pantokratōr (παντοκράτωρ, 3841), "almighty, or ruler of all" (*pas*, "all," *krateō*, "to hold, or to have strength"), is used of God only, and is found, in the Epistles, only in 2 Cor. 6:18, where the title is suggestive in connection with the context; elsewhere only in the Apocalypse, nine times. In one place, 19:6, the KJV has "omnipotent"; RV, "(the Lord our God,) the Almighty."¶ The word is introduced in the Sept. as a translation of "Lord (or God) of hosts," e.g., Jer. 5:14 and Amos 4:13.

ALMOST

A. Adverb.
schedon (σχεδόν, 4975) is used either (*a*) of locality, Acts 19:26, or (*b*) of degree, Acts 13:44; Heb. 9:22.¶

B. Verb.
mellō (μέλλω, 3195), "to be about to do anything, or to delay," is used in connection with a following verb in the sense of "almost," in Acts 21:27, lit., "And when the seven days were about to be completed." In Acts 26:28 the KJV, "Almost thou persuadest me to be a Christian" obscures the sense; the RV rightly has "with but little persuasion"; lit., "in a little." See ABOUT, B.

ALMS, ALMSDEEDS

eleēmosunē (ἐλεημοσύνη, 1654), connected with *eleēmōn*, "merciful," signifies (*a*) "mercy, pity, particularly in giving alms," Matt. 6:1 (see below), 2–4; Acts 10:2; 24:17; (*b*) the benefaction itself, the "alms" (the effect for the cause), Luke 11:41; 12:33; Acts 3:2–3, 10; 9:36, "almsdeeds"; 10:2, 4, 31.¶

Note: In Matt. 6:1, the RV, translating *dikaiosunē*, according to the most authentic texts, has "righteousness," for KJV, "alms."

ALOES

aloē (ἀλόη, 250), "an aromatic tree," the soft, bitter wood of which was used by Orientals for the purposes of fumigation and embalming, John 19:39 (see also Num. 24:6; Ps. 45:8; Prov. 7:17).¶ In the Sept., Song of Sol. 4:14.¶

ALONE (LET ALONE)

A. Adjective.
monos (μόνος, 3441) denotes "single, alone, solitary," Matt. 4:4, etc. See ONLY, SELF.

B. Adverbs.
1. *monon* (μόνον, 3441), the neuter of A, meaning "only, exclusively," e.g., Rom. 4:23; Acts 19:26, is translated "alone" in the KJV of John 17:20; RV, "only." See ONLY.

2. *kata monas* (κατὰ μόνας, 2651) signifies "apart, in private, alone," Mark 4:10; Luke 9:18. Some texts have the phrase as one word.¶

C. Verb.
aphiēmi (ἀφίημι, 863) signifies "to send away, set free"; also "to let alone," Matt. 15:14; Mark 14:6; Luke 13:8; John 11:48; 12:7 (RV, "suffer her"); in Acts 5:38 some texts have *easate* from *eaō*, "to permit." See CRY, FORGIVE, FORSAKE, LAY, *Note* (2), LEAVE, LET, OMIT, PUT, No. 16, *Note*, REMIT, SEND, SUFFER, YIELD.

Notes: (1) The phrase *kath' heautēn* means "by (or in) itself," Jas. 2:17, RV, for KJV, "being alone" (see KJV, marg.).

(2) The phrase *kat' idian*, Mark 4:34, signifies "in private," "privately," RV (KJV, "when they were alone").

(3) For "let us alone" see AH !

For ALONG see the RV of Acts 17:23 and 27:13

For ALOUD see CRY, B, No. 2

ALREADY

ēdē (ἤδη, 2235) is always used of time in the NT and means "now, at (or by) this time," sometimes in the sense of "already," i.e., without mentioning or insisting upon anything further, e.g., 1 Tim. 5:15. In 1 Cor. 4:8 and 1 John 2:8, the RV corrects the KJV "now," and, in 2 Tim. 4:6, the KJV, "now ready to be," by the rendering "already."

See also John 9:27 (KJV, "already," RV, "even now") and 1 Cor. 6:7 (KJV, "now," RV, "already").

Notes: (1) *Phthanō*, "to anticipate, be beforehand with," signifies "to attain already," in Phil. 3:16. See ATTAIN, COME, PRECEDE.

(2) *Proamartanō*, "to sin before, or heretofore," is translated "have sinned already" in 2 Cor. 12:21, KJV; both versions have "heretofore" in 13:2.

ALSO

1. *kai* (καί, 2532) has three chief meanings, "and," "also," "even." When *kai* means "also" it precedes the word which it stresses. In English the order should be reversed. In John 9:40, e.g., the RV rightly has "are we also blind?" instead of "are we blind also?" In Acts 2:26 the RV has "moreover My flesh also," instead of "moreover also ... " See EVEN.

2. *eti* (ἔτι, 2089), "yet" or "further," is used (*a*) of time, (*b*) of degree, and in this sense is once translated "also," Luke 14:26, "his own life also." Here the meaning probably is "and, further, even his own life" (the force of the *kai* being "even"). No other particles mean "also." See EVEN, FURTHER, LONGER, MORE, MOREOVER, STILL, THENCEFORTH, YET.

Note: The particle *te* means "both" or "and."

ALTAR

1. *thusiastērion* (θυσιαστήριον, 2379), probably the neuter of the adjective *thusiastērios*, is derived from *thusiazō*, "to sacrifice." Accordingly it denotes an "altar" for the sacrifice of victims, though it was also used for the "altar"

of incense, e.g., Luke 1:11. In the NT this word is reserved for the "altar" of the true God, Matt. 5:23–24; 23:18–20, 35; Luke 11:51; 1 Cor. 9:13; 10:18, in contrast to *bōmos*, No. 2, below. In the Sept. *thusiastērion* is mostly, but not entirely, used for the divinely appointed altar; it is used for idol "altars," e.g., in Judg. 2:2; 6:25; 2 Kings 16:10.

2. *bōmos* (βωμός, 1041), properly, "an elevated place," always denotes either a pagan "altar" or an "altar" reared without divine appointment. In the NT the only place where this is found is Acts 17:23, as this is the only mention of such. Three times in the Sept., but only in the Apocrypha, *bōmos* is used for the divine altar. In Josh. 22 the Sept. translators have carefully observed the distinction, using *bōmos* for the altar which the two and a half tribes erected, vv. 10–11, 16, 19, 23, 26, 34, no divine injunction being given for this; in vv. 19, 28–29, where the altar ordained of God is mentioned, *thusiastērion* is used.¶

For ALTERED see OTHER, No. 2

For ALTHOUGH see *Note* †, p. 1

ALTOGETHER

A. Adjective.

holos (ὅλος, 3650), "whole," is rendered "altogether" in John 9:34. It is sometimes subjoined to an adjective or a verb, as in this case, to show that the idea conveyed by the adjective or verb belongs to the whole person or thing referred to. So here, lit., "thou wast altogether (i.e., completely) born in sins." Cf. Matt. 13:33, RV; Luke 11:36; 13:21; John 13:10, RV (rendered "every whit"). See ALL, and EVERY WHIT.

B. Adverbs.

1. *pantōs* (πάντως, 3843), from *pas*, "all," is translated in various ways. The rendering "altogether" is found only in 1 Cor. 5:10 (where the RV margin gives the alternative meaning, "not at all" (meaning the fornicators of this world) and 9:10 (marg., "doubtless"). The other renderings are, in Luke 4:23, "doubtless" (KJV, "surely"); in Acts 18:21, "by all means," (KJV, "only"); so in 1 Cor. 9:22, both RV and KJV; in Acts 21:22, "certainly" (KJV, "needs," which does not give an accurate meaning); in Acts 28:4, "no doubt"; in Rom. 3:9, "in no wise" (lit., "not at all"), so in 1 Cor. 16:12. In Acts 26:29 the KJV has given a misleading rendering in the phrase "both almost and altogether"; there is no Greek word here which means "altogether"; the RV corrects to "whether with little or with much." See ALL.¶

2. *holōs* (ὅλως, 3654) denotes "altogether or

actually, or assuredly." See ACTUALLY, and ALL, B, No. 1.

ALWAY, ALWAYS

1. *aei* (ἀεί, 104) has two meanings: (*a*) "perpetually, incessantly," Acts 7:51; 2 Cor. 4:11; 6:10; Titus 1:12; Heb. 3:10; (*b*) "invariably, at any and every time," of successive occurrences, when some thing is to be repeated, according to the circumstances, 1 Pet. 3:15; 2 Pet. 1:12. See EVER.¶

2. *hekastote* (ἑκάστοτε, 1539), from *hekastos*, "each," is used in 2 Pet. 1:15, RV, "at every time" (KJV, "always"). See TIME.¶

3. *diapantos* (διαπαντός, 1275) is, lit., "through all," i.e., through all time, (*dia*, "through," *pas*, "all"). In the best texts the words are separated. The phrase, which is used of the time throughout which a thing is done, is sometimes rendered "continually," sometimes "always"; "always" or "alway" in Mark 5:5; Acts 10:2; 24:16; Rom. 11:10; "continually" in Luke 24:53; Heb. 9:6; 13:15, the idea being that of a continuous practice carried on without being abandoned. See CONTINUALLY.¶

4 and 5. *pantē* (πάντη, 3839) and *pantote* (πάντοτε, 3842) are derived from *pas*, "all." The former is found in Acts 24:3.¶ The latter is the usual word for "always." See EVER, EVERMORE.

Note: Two phrases, rendered "always" or "alway" in the KJV, are *en panti kairō* (lit., "in every season"), Luke 21:36, RV, "at every season," Eph. 6:18, RV, "at all seasons," and *pasas tas hēmeras*, (lit., "all the days"), Matt. 28:20, KJV and RV, "alway."

AMAZE, AMAZEMENT

A. Nouns.

1. *ekstasis* (ἔκστασις, 1611) is, lit., "a standing out" (*ek*, "out of," *stasis*, "a standing"). Eng. "ecstasy" is a transliteration. It is translated "amazement" in Acts 3:10. It was said of any displacement, and especially, with reference to the mind, of that alteration of the normal condition by which the person is thrown into a state of surprise or fear, or both; or again, in which a person is so transported out of his natural state that he falls into a trance, Acts 10:10; 11:5; 22:17. As to the other meaning, the RV has "amazement" in Mark 5:42 and Luke 5:26, but "astonishment" in Mark 16:8. See TRANCE.¶

2. *thambos* (θάμβος, 2285), "amazement, wonder," is probably connected with a root signifying "to render immovable"; it is frequently associated with terror as well as astonishment, as with the verb (No. 3, below) in Acts

9:6. It occurs in Luke 4:36; 5:9; Acts 3:10. See WONDER.¶

Note: Ptoēsis signifies "terror," not "amazement," 1 Pet. 3:6, RV.¶

B. Verbs.

1. existēmi (ἐξίστημι, 1839), akin to A, No. 1, lit. means "to stand out from." Like the noun, this is used with two distinct meanings : (a) in the sense of amazement, the word should be invariably rendered "amazed," as in the RV, e.g., in the case of Simon Magus (for KJV, "bewitched"), Acts 8:9 and 11. It is used, in the passive voice, of Simon himself in the 13th v., RV, "he was amazed," for KJV, "wondered." "Amaze" is preferable to "astonish" throughout; (b) in Mark 3:21 and 2 Cor. 5:13 it is used with its other meaning of being beside oneself. See BESIDE ONESELF (to be), BEWITCH, WONDER.

2. ekplēssō (ἐκπλήσσω, 1605), from ek, "out of," plēssō, "to strike," lit., "to strike out," signifies "to be exceedingly struck in mind, to be astonished" (ek, intensive). The English "astonish" should be used for this verb, and "amaze" for existēmi, as in the RV; see Matt. 19:25; Luke 2:48; 9:43.

3. thambeō (θαμβέω, 2284), akin to A, No. 2, is used in Mark 1:27; 10:24, 32 (and Acts 9:6, KJV). The RV has "amazed" in each place; KJV, "astonished," in Mark 10:24.¶

4. ekthambeō (ἐκθαμβέω, 1568), an intensive form of No. 3, is found in Mark's gospel only; in 9:15, "were greatly amazed"; in 14:33, KJV, "were sore amazed"; in 16:5, RV, "were amazed," KJV, "were affrighted"; in v. 6, RV, "be not amazed," KJV, "be not affrighted." See AFFRIGHTED.¶

C. Adjective.

ekthambos (ἔκθαμβος, 1569), a strengthened form of A, No. 2, is found in Acts 3:11. The intensive force of the word is brought out by the rendering "greatly wondering. See WONDER.¶

AMBASSADOR, AMBASSAGE

A. Verb.

presbeuō (πρεσβεύω, 4243) denotes (a) "to be elder or eldest, prior in birth or age"; (b) "to be an ambassador," 2 Cor. 5:20, and Eph. 6:20; for Philem. 9 see under AGED. There is a suggestion that to be an "ambassador" for Christ involves the experience suggested by the word "elder." Elder men were chosen as "ambassadors."

B. Noun.

presbeia (πρεσβεία, 4242), primarily, "age, eldership, rank," hence, "an embassy or ambassage," is used in Luke 14:32; in 19:14, RV, "ambassage," for KJV, "message."¶

AMEN

amēn (ἀμήν, 281) is transliterated from Hebrew into both Greek and English. "Its meanings may be seen in such passages as Deut. 7:9, 'the faithful (the Amen) God,' Isa. 49:7, 'Jehovah that is faithful.' 65:16, 'the God of truth,' marg., 'the God of Amen.' And if God is faithful His testimonies and precepts are "sure (amen)," Ps. 19:7; 111:7, as are also His warnings, Hos. 5:9, and promises, Isa. 33:16; 55:3. 'Amen' is used of men also, e.g., Prov. 25:13.

"There are cases where the people used it to express their assent to a law and their willingness to submit to the penalty attached to the breach of it, Deut. 27:15, cf. Neh. 5:13. It is also used to express acquiescence in another's prayer, 1 Kings 1:36, where it is defined as "(let) God say so too," or in another's thanksgiving, 1 Chron. 16:36, whether by an individual, Jer. 11:5, or by the congregation, Ps. 106:48.

"Thus 'Amen' said by God 'it is and shall be so,' and by men, 'so let it be.' "

"Once in the NT 'Amen' is a title of Christ, Rev. 3:14, because through Him the purposes of God are established, 2 Cor. 1:20.

"The early Christian churches followed the example of Israel in associating themselves audibly with the prayers and thanksgivings offered on their behalf, 1 Cor. 14:16, where the article 'the' points to a common practice. Moreover this custom conforms to the pattern of things in the Heavens, see Rev. 5:14, etc.

"The individual also said 'Amen' to express his 'let it be so' in response to the Divine 'thus it shall be,' Rev. 22:20. Frequently the speaker adds 'Amen' to his own prayers and doxologies, as is the case at Eph. 3:21, e.g.

"The Lord Jesus often used 'Amen,' translated 'verily,' to introduce new revelations of the mind of God. In John's Gospel it is always repeated, 'Amen, Amen,' but not elsewhere. Luke does not use it at all, but where Matthew, 16:28, and Mark, 9:1, have 'Amen,' Luke has 'of a truth'; thus by varying the translation of what the Lord said, Luke throws light on His meaning."* See VERILY.

AMEND

echō (2192) kompsoteron (2866), lit., "to have more finely," i.e., "to be better," is used in John 4:52, "to amend." The latter word in the phrase is the comparative of kompsos, "elegant, nice, fine." Cf. Eng., "he's doing nicely."¶

---

* From Notes on Galatians, by Hogg and Vine, pp. 26, 27.

AMETHYST

amethustos (ἀμέθυστος, 271), primarily meaning "not drunken" (*a*, negative, and *methu*, "wine"), became used as a noun, being regarded as possessing a remedial virtue against drunkenness. Pliny, however, says that the reason for its name lay in the fact that in color it nearly approached that of wine, but did not actually do so, Rev. 21:20.¶

For AMIDST see MIDST

AMISS

A. Adjective.

atopos (ἄτοπος, 824), lit., "out of place" (*a*, negative, *topos*, "a place"), denotes unbecoming, not befitting. It is used four times in the NT, and is rendered "amiss" three times in the RV; in the malefactor's testimony of Christ, Luke 23:41; in Festus' words concerning Paul, Acts 25:5, "if there is anything amiss in the man" (KJV, "wickedness"); in Acts 28:6, of the expected effect of the viper's attack upon Paul (KJV, "harm"); in 2 Thess. 3:2, of men capable of outrageous conduct, "unreasonable." See HARM, UNREASONABLE.

B. Adverb.

kakōs (κακῶς, 2560), akin to *kakos*, "evil," is translated "amiss" in Jas. 4:3; elsewhere in various ways. See EVIL, GRIEVOUS, MISERABLE, SORE.

For AMONG see Note †, p. 1

For ANATHEMA see CURSE

ANCHOR

ankura (ἄγκυρα, 45), (Eng., "anchor"), was so called because of its curved form (*ankos*, "a curve"), Acts 27:29–30, 40; Heb. 6:19. In Acts 27:13 the verb *airō*, "to lift," signifies "to lift anchor" (the noun being understood), RV, "they weighed anchor" (KJV, "loosing thence").¶

ANEW

anōthen (ἄνωθεν, 509), lit., "from above," in the phrase rendered "anew" in the RV (KJV, "again") of John 3:3, 7. See AGAIN.

Note: In Phil. 3:21 "fashion anew" translates the verb *metaschēmatizō*, which signifies "to change the form of".

ANGEL

angelos (ἄγγελος, 32), "a messenger" (from *angellō*, "to deliver a message"), sent whether by God or by man or by Satan, "is also used of a guardian or representative in Rev. 1:20, cf. Matt. 18:10; Acts 12:15 (where it is better understood as 'ghost'), but most frequently of an order of created beings, superior to man, Heb. 2:7; Ps. 8:5, belonging to Heaven, Matt. 24:36; Mark 12:25, and to God, Luke 12:8, and engaged in His service, Ps. 103:20. "Angels" are spirits, Heb. 1:14, i.e., they have not material bodies as men have; they are either human in form, or can assume the human form when necessary, cf. Luke 24:4, with v. 23, Acts 10:3 with v. 30.

"They are called 'holy' in Mark 8:38, and 'elect,' 1 Tim. 5:21, in contrast with some of their original number, Matt. 25:41, who 'sinned,' 2 Pet. 2:4, 'left their proper habitation,' Jude 6, *oikētērion*, a word which occurs again, in the NT, only in 2 Cor. 5:2. Angels are always spoken of in the masculine gender, the feminine form of the word does not occur."*

Note: Isangelos, "equal to the angels," occurs in Luke 20:36.¶

ANGER, ANGRY (to be)

A. Noun.

orgē (ὀργή, 3709), originally any "natural impulse, or desire, or disposition," came to signify "anger," as the strongest of all passions. It is used of the wrath of man, Eph. 4:31; Col. 3:8; 1 Tim. 2:8; Jas. 1:19–20; the displeasure of human governments, Rom. 13:4–5; the sufferings of the Jews at the hands of the Gentiles, Luke 21:23; the terrors of the Law, Rom. 4:15; "the anger" of the Lord Jesus, Mark 3:5; God's "anger" with Israel in the wilderness, in a quotation from the OT, Heb. 3:11; 4:3; God's present "anger" with the Jews nationally, Rom. 9:22; 1 Thess. 2:16; His present "anger" with those who disobey the Lord Jesus in His gospel, John 3:36; God's purposes in judgment, Matt. 3:7; Luke 3:7; Rom. 1:18; 2:5, 8; 3:5; 5:9; 12:19; Eph. 2:3; 5:6; Col. 3:6; 1 Thess. 1:10; 5:9. See INDIGNATION, VENGEANCE, WRATH.¶

Notes: (1) *Thumos*, "wrath" (not translated "anger"), is to be distinguished from *orgē*, in this respect, that *thumos* indicates a more agitated condition of the feelings, an outburst of wrath from inward indignation, while *orgē* suggests a more settled or abiding condition of mind, frequently with a view to taking revenge. *Orgē* is less sudden in its rise than *thumos*, but more lasting in its nature. *Thumos* expresses more the inward feeling, *orgē* the more active emotion. *Thumos* may issue in revenge, though it does not necessarily include it. It is character-

* From *Notes on Thessalonians*, by Hogg and Vine, p. 229.

istic that it quickly blazes up and quickly subsides, though that is not necessarily implied in each case.

(2) *Parorgismos*, a strengthened form of *orgē*, and used in Eph. 4:26, RV margin, "provocation," points especially to that which provokes the wrath, and suggests a less continued state than No. (1). "The first keenness of the sense of provocation must not be cherished, though righteous resentment may remain" (Westcott). The preceding verb, *orgizō*, in this verse implies a just occasion for the feeling. This is confirmed by the fact that it is a quotation from Ps. 4:4 (Sept.), where the Hebrew word signifies to quiver with strong emotion.

Thumos is found eighteen times in the NT, ten of which are in the Apocalypse, in seven of which the reference is to the wrath of God; so in Rom. 2:8, RV, "wrath (*thumos*) and indignation" (*orgē*); the order in the KJV is inaccurate. Everywhere else the word *thumos* is used in a bad sense. In Gal. 5:20, it follows the word "jealousies," which when smoldering in the heart break out in wrath. *Thumos* and *orgē* are coupled in two places in the Apocalypse, 16:19, "the fierceness (*thumos*) of His wrath" (*orgē*); and 19:15, "the fierceness of the wrath of Almighty God." See WROTH (be).

(3) *Aganaktēsis* originally signified "physical pain or irritation" (probably from *agan*, "very much," and *achomai*, "to grieve"), hence, "annoyance, vexation," and is used in 2 Cor. 7:11, "indignation."¶

B. Verbs.

1. *orgizō* (ὀργίζω, 3710), "to provoke, to arouse to anger," is used in the middle voice in the eight places where it is found, and signifies "to be angry, wroth." It is said of individuals, in Matt. 5:22; 18:34; 22:7; Luke 14:21; 15:28, and Eph. 4:26 (where a possible meaning is "be ye angry with yourselves"); of nations, Rev. 11:18; of Satan as the Dragon, 12:17. See WRATH.¶

2. *parorgizō* (παροργίζω, 3949) is "to arouse to wrath, provoke" (*para*, used intensively, and No. 1); Rom. 10:19, "will I anger"; Eph. 6:4, "provoke to wrath." See PROVOKE.¶

3. *cholaō* (χολάω, 5520), connected with *cholē*, "gall, bile," which became used metaphorically to signify bitter anger, means "to be enraged," John 7:23, "wroth," RV, in the Lord's remonstrance with the Jews on account of their indignation at His having made a man whole on the Sabbath Day.¶

Notes: (1) *Thumomacheō* (from *thumos*, "wrath," *machomai*, "to fight") originally denoted to fight with great animosity, and hence came to mean "to be very angry, to be exasper-ated," Acts 12:20, of the anger of Herod, "was highly displeased."¶

(2) *Thumoō*, the corresponding verb, signifies "to provoke to anger," but in the passive voice "to be wroth," as in Matt. 2:16, of the wrath of Herod, "was exceeding wroth."¶

(3) *Aganakteō*, see A, *Note* (3), is rendered in various ways in the seven places where it is used; "moved with indignation," Matt. 20:24 and 21:15, RV (KJV, "sore displeased"); "had indignation," Matt. 26:8; Mark 14:4. In Mark 10:14 the RV has "was moved with indignation" (KJV, "was much displeased"), said of the Lord Jesus. The same renderings are given in v. 41. In Luke 13:14 (KJV, "with indignation"), the RV rightly puts "being moved with indignation." These words more particularly point to the cause of the vexation. See DISPLEASE, INDIGNATION.¶

(4) In Col. 3:21, *erethizō* signifies "to provoke." The RV correctly omits "to anger."

C. Adjective.

orgilos (ὀργίλος, 3711), "angry, prone to anger, irascible" (see B, Nos. 1, 2), is rendered "soon angry" in Titus 1:7.¶

ANGUISH

A. Nouns.

1. *thlipsis* (θλῖψις, 2347): see AFFLICTION (No. 4).

2. *stenochōria* (στενοχωρία, 4730), lit., "narrowness of place" (*stenos*, "narrow," *chōra*, "a place"), metaphorically came to mean the "distress arising from that condition, anguish." It is used in the plural, of various forms of distress, 2 Cor. 6:4 and 12:10, and of "anguish" or distress in general, Rom. 2:9; 8:35, RV, "anguish" for KJV, "distress." The opposite state, of being in a large place, and so metaphorically in a state of joy, is represented by the word *platusmos* in certain Psalms as, e.g., Ps. 118:5; see also 2 Sam. 22:20. See DISTRESS.¶

3. *sunochē* (συνοχή, 4928), lit., "a holding together, or compressing" (*sun*, "together," *echō*, "to hold"), was used of the narrowing of a way. It is found only in its metaphorical sense, of "straits, distress, anguish," Luke 21:25, "distress of nations," and 2 Cor. 2:4, "anguish of heart." See DISTRESS.¶

Note: Anankē is associated with *thlipsis*, and signifies a condition of necessity arising from some form of compulsion. It is therefore used not only of necessity but of distress, Luke 21:23; 1 Thess. 3:7, and in the plural in 2 Cor. 6:4; 12:10.

B. Verbs.

1. *stenochōreō* (στενοχωρέω, 4729), akin to A, No. 2, lit., "to crowd into a narrow space,"

or, in the passive voice "to be pressed for room," hence, metaphorically, "to be straitened," 2 Cor. 4:8 and 6:12 (twice), is found in its literal sense in two places in the Sept., in Josh. 17:15 and Isa. 49:19, and in two places in its metaphorical sense, in Judg. 16:16, where Delilah is said to have pressed Samson sore with her words continually, and to have "straitened him," and in Isa. 28:20. See DISTRESS, STRAITENED.¶

2. *sunechō* (συνέχω, 4912), akin to A, No. 3, lit., "to hold together," is used physically of being held, or thronged, Luke 8:45; 19:43; 22:63; of being taken with a malady, Matt. 4:24; Luke 4:38; Acts 28:8; with fear, Luke 8:37; of being straitened or pressed in spirit, with desire, Luke 12:50; Acts 18:5; Phil. 1:23; with the love of Christ, 2 Cor. 5:14. In one place it is used of the stopping of their ears by those who killed Stephen. See CONSTRAIN, HOLD, KEEP, PRESS, SICK (lie), STOP, STRAIT (be in a), STRAITENED, TAKE, THRONG.

3. *odunaō* (ὀδυνάω, 3600), in the middle and passive voices, signifies "to suffer pain, be in anguish, be greatly distressed" (akin to *odunē*, "pain, distress"); it is rendered "sorrowing" in Luke 2:48; in 16:24–25, RV, "in anguish," for KJV, "tormented"; in Acts 20:38, "sorrowing." See SORROW, TORMENT.¶

For **ANIMALS** (2 Pet. 2:12, RV), see **NATURAL**

ANISE

anēthon (ἄνηθον, 432), "dill, anise," was used for food and for pickling, Matt. 23:23.¶

ANKLE-BONES

sphuron (σφυρόν, 4974) or *sphudron* (σφυδρόν, 4974a) denotes the "ankle, or ankle-bone" (from *sphura*, "a hammer," owing to a resemblance in the shape), Acts 3:7.¶

ANNOUNCE

anangellō (ἀναγγέλλω, 312), "to declare, announce" (*ana*, "up," *angellō*, "to report"), is used especially of heavenly messages, and is translated "announced" in the RV of 1 Pet. 1:12, for KJV, "reported," and in 1 John 1:5, RV, "announce," for KJV, "declare." See DECLARE, REHEARSE, REPORT, SHOW, SPEAK, TELL.

ANOINT, ANOINTING

A. Verbs.

1. *aleiphō* (ἀλείφω, 218) is a general term used for "an anointing" of any kind, whether of physical refreshment after washing, e.g., in the Sept. of Ruth 3:3; 2 Sam. 12:20; Dan. 10:3;

Micah 6:15; in the NT, Matt. 6:17; Luke 7:38, 46; John 11:2; 12:3; or of the sick, Mark 6:13; Jas. 5:14; or a dead body, Mark 16:1. The material used was either oil, or ointment, as in Luke 7:38, 46.¶ In the Sept. it is also used of "anointing" a pillar, Gen. 31:13, or captives, 2 Chron. 28:15, or of daubing a wall with mortar, Ezek. 13:10–12, 14–15; and, in the sacred sense, of "anointing" priests, in Exod. 40:15 (twice), and Num. 3:3.

2. *chriō* (χρίω, 5548) is more limited in its use than No. 1; it is confined to "sacred and symbolical anointings"; of Christ as the "Anointed" of God, Luke 4:18; Acts 4:27; 10:38, and Heb. 1:9, where it is used metaphorically in connection with "the oil of gladness." The title Christ signifies "The Anointed One," The word (*Christos*) is rendered "(His) Anointed" in Acts 4:26, RV. Once it is said of believers, 2 Cor. 1:21. *Chriō* is very frequent in the Sept., and is used of kings, 1 Sam. 10:1, and priests, Ex. 28:41, and prophets, 1 Kings 19:16. Among the Greeks it was used in other senses than the ceremonial, but in the Scriptures it is not found in connection with secular matters.¶

Note: The distinction referred to by Trench (*Syn.* § xxxviii), that *aleiphō* is the mundane and profane, *chriō*, the sacred and religious word, is not borne out by evidence. In a papyrus document *chrisis* is used of "a lotion for a sick horse" (Moulton and Milligan, *Vocab. of Greek Test*).

3. *enchriō* (ἐγχρίω, 1472), primarily, "to rub in," hence, "to besmear, to anoint," is used metaphorically in the command to the church in Laodicea to "anoint" their eyes with eyesalve, Rev. 3:18.¶ In the Sept., Jer. 4:30, it is used of the "anointing" of the eyes with a view to beautifying them.

4. *epichriō* (ἐπιχρίω, 2025), primarily, "to rub on" (*epi*, "upon"), is used of the blind man whose eyes Christ "anointed," and indicates the manner in which the "anointing" was done, John 9:6, 11.¶

5. *murizō* (μυρίζω, 3462) is used of "anointing" the body for burial, in Mark 14:8.¶

B. Noun.

chrisma (χρίσμα, 5545), the corresponding noun to No. 2, above, signifies "an unguent, or an anointing." It was prepared from oil and aromatic herbs. It is used only metaphorically in the NT; by metonymy, of the Holy Spirit, 1 John 2:20, 27, twice. The RV translates it "anointing" in all three places, instead of the KJV "unction" and "anointing."

That believers have "an anointing from the Holy One" indicates that this anointing renders them holy, separating them to God. The passage teaches that the gift of the Holy Spirit is the all-efficient means of enabling believers to possess a knowledge of the truth. In the Sept., it is used of the oil for "anointing" the high priest, e.g., Exod. 29:7, lit., "Thou shalt take of the oil of the anointing." In Exod. 30:25, etc., it is spoken of as "a holy anointing oil." In Dan. 9:26 *chrisma* stands for the "anointed" one, "Christ," the noun standing by metonymy for the person Himself, as for the Holy Spirit in 1 John 2. See UNCTION.¶

Notes: (1) *Aleimma*, akin to A, No. 1 (not in the NT), occurs three times in the Sept., Exod. 30:31, of the "anointing" of the priests; Isa. 61:3, metaphorically, of the oil of joy; Dan. 10:3, of physical refreshment.

(2) *Muron*, a word akin to A, No. 5, denotes "ointment." The distinction between this and *elaion*, "oil," is observable in Christ's reproof of the Pharisee who, while desiring Him to eat with him, failed in the ordinary marks of courtesy; "My head with oil (*elaion*) thou didst not anoint, but she hath anointed My feet with ointment" (*muron*), Luke 7:46.

ANON

Note: This is the KJV rendering of *euthus*, in Matt. 13:20 and Mark 1:30, RV, "straightway."

ANOTHER

allos (ἄλλος, 243) and *heteros* (ἕτερος, 2087) have a difference in meaning, which despite a tendency to be lost, is to be observed in numerous passages. *Allos* expresses a numerical difference and denotes "another of the same sort"; *heteros* expresses a qualitative difference and denotes "another of a different sort." Christ promised to send "another Comforter" (*allos*, "another like Himself," not *heteros*), John 14:16. Paul says "I see a different (KJV, "another") law," *heteros*, a law different from that of the spirit of life (not *allos*, "a law of the same sort"), Rom. 7:23. After Joseph's death "another king arose," *heteros*, one of quite a different character, Acts 7:18. Paul speaks of "a different gospel (*heteros*), which is not another" (*allos*, another like the one he preached), Gal. 1:6–7. See *heteros* (not *allos*) in Matt. 11:3, and Acts 27:1; in Luke 23:32 *heteroi* is used of the two malefactors crucified with Christ. The two words are only apparently interchanged in 1 Cor. 1:16 and 6:1; 12:8–10; 14:17 and 19, e.g., the difference being present, though not so readily discernible.

They are not interchangeable in 1 Cor. 15:39–41; here *heteros* is used to distinguish the heavenly glory from the earthly, for these differ in genus, and *allos* to distinguish the flesh of men, birds, and fishes, which in each case is flesh differing not in genus but in species. *Allos* is used again to distinguish between the glories of the heavenly bodies, for these also differ not in kind but in degree only. For *allos*, see MORE, OTHER, etc. For *heteros*, see OTHER, STRANGE.

Note: The distinction comes out in the compounds of *heteros*, viz., *heteroglōssos*, "strange tongues," 1 Cor. 14:21; ¶; *heterodidaskaleō*, "to teach a different doctrine," 1 Tim. 1:3; 6:3; ¶; *heterozugō*, "to be unequally yoked" (i.e., with those of a different character), 2 Cor. 6:14.¶

ANSWER

A. Nouns.

1. *apokrisis* (ἀπόκρισις, 612), lit., "a separation or distinction," is the regular word for "answer," Luke 2:47; 20:26; John 1:22 and 19:9.¶

2. *apokrima* (ἀπόκριμα, 610), akin to No. 1, denotes a judicial "sentence," 2 Cor. 1:9, KJV, and RV, margin, or an "answer" (RV, text), an answer of God to the apostle's appeal, giving him strong confidence. In an ancient inscription it is used of an official decision. In a papyrus document it is used of a reply to a deputation. See SENTENCE.¶

3. *chrēmatismos* (χρηματισμός, 5538), "a divine response, an oracle," is used in Rom. 11:4, of the answer given by God to Elijah's complaint against Israel.¶ See the verb under CALL.

4. *apologia* (ἀπολογία, 627), a "verbal defense, a speech in defense," is sometimes translated "answer," in the KJV, Acts 25:16; 1 Cor. 9:3; 2 Tim. 4:16, all which the RV corrects to "defense." See Acts 22:1; Phil. 1:7, 16; 2 Cor. 7:11, "clearing." Once it signifies an "answer," 1 Pet. 3:15. Cf. B, No. 4. See CLEARING, DEFENSE.¶

Note: Eperōtēma, 1 Pet. 3:21, is not, as in the KJV, an "answer." It was used by the Greeks in a legal sense, as a" demand or appeal." Baptism is therefore the ground of an "appeal" by a good conscience against wrong doing.¶

B. Verbs.

1. *apokrinomai* (ἀποκρίνομαι, 611), akin to A, No. 1, above, signifies either "to give an answer to a question" (its more frequent use) or "to begin to speak," but always where something has preceded, either statement or act to which the remarks refer, e.g., Matt. 11:25; Luke 14:3; John 2:18. The RV translates by "answered," e.g., Matt. 28:5; Mark 12:35; Luke 3:16, where some have suggested "began to say" or "uttered solemnly," whereas the speaker is replying to the unuttered thought or feeling of those addressed by him.

2. *antapokrinomai* (ἀνταποκρίνομαι, 470), *anti*, "against," and No. 1, a strengthened form, "to answer by contradiction, to reply against," is found in Luke 14:6 and Rom. 9:20.¶

3. *hupolambanō* (ὑπολαμβάνω, 5274) signifies (*a*) "to take or bear up from beneath," Acts 1:9; (*b*) "to receive," 3 John 8; (*c*) "to suppose," Luke 7:43; Acts 2:15; (*d*) "to catch up (in speech), to answer," Luke 10:30; in sense (*d*) it indicates that a person follows what another has said, either by controverting or supplementing it. See RECEIVE, SUPPOSE.¶

4. *apologeomai* (ἀπολογέομαι, 626), cf. A, No. 4, lit., "to talk oneself off from" (*apo*, "from," *legō*, "to speak"), "to answer by way of making a defense for oneself" (besides its meaning "to excuse," Rom. 2:15; 2 Cor. 12:19), is translated "answer" in Luke 12:11; 21:14; in Acts 19:33, KJV and RV both have "made defense"; in Acts 24:10; 25:8; 26:1–2, the RV has the verb to make a defense, for the KJV, "to answer," and in 26:24 for the KJV, "spake for himself." See DEFENSE, EXCUSE, SPEAK.¶

5. *antilegō* (ἀντιλέγω, 483), "to speak against," is rendered "answering again" in the KJV of Titus 2:9 (RV, "gainsaying"). See CONTRADICT, DENY, GAINSAY, SPEAK.

6. *sustoicheō* (συστοιχέω, 4960), lit., "to be in the same line or row with" (*sun*, "with," *stoichos*, "a row"), is translated "answereth to" in Gal. 4:25.¶

Note: Cf. *stoicheō*, "to walk" (in line), 5:25; 6:16. For *hupakouō*, rendered to answer in Acts 12:13, RV, see HEARKEN, No. 1, *Note.*

ANTICHRIST

antichristos (ἀντίχριστος, 500) can mean either "against Christ" or "instead of Christ," or perhaps, combining the two, "one who, assuming the guise of Christ, opposes Christ" (Westcott). The word is found only in John's epistles, (*a*) of the many "antichrists" who are forerunners of the "Antichrist" himself, 1 John 2:18, 22; 2 John 7; (*b*) of the evil power which already operates anticipatively of the "Antichrist," 1 John 4:3.¶

What the apostle says of him so closely resembles what he says of the first beast in Rev. 13, and what the apostle Paul says of the Man of Sin in 2 Thess. 2, that the same person seems to be in view in all these passages, rather than the second beast in Rev. 13, the false prophet; for the latter supports the former in all his Antichristian assumptions.

Note: The term *pseudochristos*, "a false Christ," is to be distinguished from the above; it is found in Matt. 24:24 and Mark 13:22. The false Christ does not deny the existence of

Christ, he trades upon the expectation of His appearance, affirming that he is the Christ. The Antichrist denies the existence of the true God (Trench, *Syn.* § xxx).¶

For ANXIETY and ANXIOUS see CARE, A, No. 1, B, No. 1

For ANY see *Note* †, p. 1

ANYTHING

Note: See the RV of Mark 15:5; John 16:23; 1 Tim. 6:7; in Luke 24:41, the RV suitably has "anything to eat," for, KJV, "any meat."

APART

1. *chōris* (χωρίς, 5565) is used both as an adverb and as a preposition. As an adverb it signifies "separately, by itself," John 20:7, of the napkin which had been around the Lord's head in the tomb; as a preposition (its more frequent use), "apart from, without, separate from." It is rendered "apart from" in the RV of John 15:5; Rom. 3:21, 28; 4:6; 2 Cor. 12:3; Heb. 9:22, 28; 11:40; Jas. 2:18, 20, 26. See BESIDE, WITHOUT.

Note: The opposite of *chōris* is *sun*, "with." A synonymous preposition, *aneu*, denotes "without," Matt. 10:29; 1 Pet. 3:1 and 4:9.¶

2. *kat' idian* (κατ᾽ ἰδίαν), lit., "according to one's own," i.e., privately, alone, is translated "apart" in Matt. 14:13, 23; 17:1, 19; 20:17; Mark 6:31–32 (KJV, "privately"); 9:2.

3. *kata monas* (κατὰ μόνας, 2651): see ALONE.

APIECE

ana (ἀνά, 303), used with numerals or measures of quantity with a distributive force, is translated "apiece" in Luke 9:3, "two coats apiece," KJV; in John 2:6, "two or three firkins apiece." In Matt. 20:9–10, "every man a penny," is a free rendering for "a penny apiece"; in Luke 9:14, the RV adds "each" to translate the *ana;* in 10:1, *ana duo* is "two by two." See Rev. 4:8, "each." See EACH, EVERY.

APOSTLE, APOSTLESHIP

1. *apostolos* (ἀπόστολος, 652) is, lit., "one sent forth" (*apo*, "from," *stellō*, "to send"). "The word is used of the Lord Jesus to describe His relation to God, Heb. 3:1; see John 17:3. The twelve disciples chosen by the Lord for special training were so called, Luke 6:13; 9:10. Paul, though he had seen the Lord Jesus, 1 Cor. 9:1; 15:8, had not 'companied with' the Twelve 'all the time' of His earthly ministry, and hence was not eligible for a place among them, according

to Peter's description of the necessary qualifications, Acts 1:22. Paul was commissioned directly, by the Lord Himself, after His Ascension, to carry the gospel to the Gentiles.

"The word has also a wider reference. In Acts 14:4, 14, it is used of Barnabas as well as of Paul; in Rom. 16:7 of Andronicus and Junias. In 2 Cor. 8:23 (RV, margin) two unnamed brethren are called 'apostles of the churches'; in Phil. 2:25 (RV, margin) Epaphroditus is referred to as 'your apostle.' It is used in 1 Thess. 2:6 of Paul, Silas and Timothy, to define their relation to Christ."*

2. *apostolē* (ἀποστολή, 651), "a sending, a mission," signifies an apostleship, Acts 1:25; Rom. 1:5; 1 Cor. 9:2; Gal. 2:8.¶

Note: Pseudapostoloi, "false apostles," occurs in 2 Cor. 11:13.¶

APPAREL, APPARELLED

1. *esthēs* (ἐσθής, 2066) and *esthēsis* (ἔσηνσις, 2067), connected with *hennumi*, "to clothe" means "clothing, raiment," usually suggesting the ornate, the goodly. The former is found in Luke 23:11, RV, "apparel" (KJV, "robe"); 24:4 (KJV, "garments"); Acts 10:30 (KJV, "clothing"); 12:21; Jas. 2:2 (RV, "clothing," twice; KJV, "apparel" and "raiment"); 2:3 ("clothing"). *Esthēsis* is used in Acts 1:10, "apparel." See CLOTHING.¶

2. *himation* (ἱμάτιον, 2440), a diminutive of *heima*, "a robe," was used especially of an outer cloak or mantle, and in general of raiment, "apparel" in 1 Pet. 3:3. The word is not in the original in the next verse, but is supplied in English to complete the sentence. See CLOTHING No. 2, GARMENT, RAIMENT, ROBE.

3. *himatismos* (ἱματισμός, 2441), a collective word, is translated "apparelled" in Luke 7:25, and preceded by *en*, "in," lit., "in apparel." See CLOTHING, No. 4, RAIMENT, VESTURE.

4. *katastolē* (καταστολή, 2689), connected with *katastellō*, "to send or let down, to lower" (*kata*, "down," *stellō*, "to send"), was primarily a garment let down; hence, "dress, attire," in general (cf. *stolē*, a loose outer garment worn by kings and persons of rank,—Eng., "stole"); 1 Tim. 2:9, "apparel." See CLOTHING.¶

APPARITION

phantasma (φάντασμα, 5326), "a phantasm or phantom" (from *phainō*, "to appear"), is translated "apparition" in the RV of Matt. 14:26 and Mark 6:49 (KJV, "spirit").¶ In the Sept., Job 20:8; Isa. 28:7.¶

* From *Notes on Thessalonians*, by Hogg and Vine, pp. 59–60.

APPEAL

epikaleō (ἐπικαλέω, 1941), "to call upon," has the meaning "appeal" in the middle voice, which carries with it the suggestion of a special interest on the part of the doer of an action in that in which he is engaged. Stephen died "calling upon the Lord," Acts 7:59. In the more strictly legal sense the word is used only of Paul's "appeal" to Caesar, Acts 25:11–12, 21, 25; 26:32; 28:19. See CALL (upon), SURNAME. See also *eperotēma*, under ANSWER.

APPEAR, APPEARING

A. Verbs.

1. *phainō* (φαίνω, 5316) signifies, in the active voice, "to shine"; in the passive, "to be brought forth into light, to become evident, to appear." In Rom. 7:13, concerning sin, the RV has "might be shewn to be," for KJV, "appear."

It is used of the "appearance" of Christ to the disciples, Mark 16:9; of His future "appearing" in glory as the Son of Man, spoken of as a sign to the world, Matt. 24:30; there the genitive is subjective, the sign being the "appearing" of Christ Himself; of Christ as the light, John 1:5; of John the Baptist, 5:35; of the "appearing" of an angel of the Lord, either visibly, Matt. 1:20, or in a dream, 2:13; of a star, 2:7; of men who make an outward show, Matt. 6:5; 6:18 (see the RV); 23:27–28; 2 Cor. 13:7; of tares, Matt. 13:26; of a vapor, Jas. 4:14; of things physical in general, Heb. 11:3; used impersonally in Matt. 9:33, "it was never so seen"; also of what appears to the mind, and so in the sense of to think, Mark 14:64, or to seem, Luke 24:11 (RV, "appeared"). See SEE, SEEM, SHINE, THINK.

2. *epiphainō* (ἐπιφαίνω, 2014), a strengthened form of No. 1 but differing in meaning, *epi* signifying "upon," is used in the active voice with the meaning "to give light," Luke 1:79; in the passive voice, "to appear, become visible." It is said of heavenly bodies, e.g., the stars, Acts 27:20 (RV, "shone"); metaphorically, of things spiritual, the grace of God, Titus 2:11; the kindness and the love of God, 3:4. See LIGHT.¶ Cf. *epiphaneia*, B, No. 2.

3. *anaphainō* (ἀναφαίνω, 398), *ana*, "forth, or up," perhaps originally a nautical term, "to come up into view," hence, in general, "to appear suddenly," is used in the passive voice, in Luke 19:11, of the Kingdom of God; active voice, in Acts 21:3, "to come in sight of," RV; "having sighted" would be a suitable rendering (KJV, "having discovered").¶

4. *phaneroō* (φανερόω, 5319), akin to No. 1, signifies, in the active voice, "to manifest"; in the passive voice, "to be manifested"; so, regu-

larly, in the RV, instead of "to appear." See 2 Cor. 7:12; Col. 3:4; Heb. 9:26; 1 Pet 5:4; 1 John 2:28; 3:2; Rev. 3:18. To be manifested, in the Scriptural sense of the word, is more than to "appear." A person may "appear" in a false guise or without a disclosure of what he truly is; to be manifested is to be revealed in one's true character; this is especially the meaning of *phaneroō*, see, e.g., John 3:21; 1 Cor. 4:5; 2 Cor. 5:10–11; Eph. 5:13.

5. *emphanizō* (ἐμφανίζω, 1718), from *en*, "in," intensive, and *phainō*, "to shine," is used, either of "physical manifestation," Matt. 27:53; Heb. 9:24; cf. John 14:22, or, metaphorically, of "the manifestation of Christ" by the Holy Spirit in the spiritual experience of believers who abide in His love, John 14:21. It has another, secondary meaning, "to make known, signify, inform." This is confined to the Acts, where it is used five times, 23:15, 22; 24:1; 25:2, 15. There is perhaps a combination of the two meanings in Heb. 11:14, i.e., to declare by oral testimony and to "manifest" by the witness of the life. See INFORM, MANIFEST, SHEW, SIGNIFY.¶

6. *optomai* (ὄπτομαι, 3700), "to see" (from *ōps*, "the eye"; cf. Eng. "optical," etc.), in the passive sense, "to be seen, to appear," is used (a) objectively, with reference to the person or thing seen, e.g., 1 Cor. 15:5–8, RV "appeared," for KJV, "was seen"; (b) subjectively, with reference to an inward impression or a spiritual experience, John 3:36, or a mental occupation, Acts 18:15, "look to it"; cf. Matt. 27:4, 24, "see (thou) to it," "see (ye) to it," throwing responsibility on others. *Optomai* is to be found in dictionaries under the word *horaō*, "to see"; it supplies some forms that are lacking in that verb.

These last three words, *emphanizō*, *phaneroō* and *optomai* are used with reference to the "appearances" of Christ in the closing verses of Heb. 9; *emphanizō* in v. 24, of His presence before the face of God for us; *phaneroō* in v. 26, of His past manifestation for "the sacrifice of Himself"; *optomai* in v. 28, of His future "appearance" for His saints.

7. *optanō* (ὀπτάνω, 3700), in the middle voice signifies "to allow oneself to be seen." It is rendered "appearing" in Acts 1:3, RV, for KJV, "being seen," of the Lord's "appearances" after His resurrection; the middle voice expresses the personal interest the Lord took in this.¶

Note: In Acts 22:30 *sunerchomai* (in its aorist form), "to come together," is translated "appear," KJV; RV, "come together."

B. Nouns.

1. *apokalupsis* (ἀποκάλυψις, 602), lit., "an uncovering, unveiling" (*apo*, "from," *kaluptō*,

"to hide, cover"), denotes "a revelation, or appearing" (Eng., apocalypse). It is translated "the appearing" in 1 Pet. 1:7, KJV (RV, "revelation"). See COMING, MANIFESTATION, REVELATION.

2. *epiphaneia* (ἐπιφάνεια, 2015), "epiphany," lit., "a shining forth," was used of the "appearance" of a god to men, and of an enemy to an army in the field, etc. In the NT it occurs of (a) the advent of the Savior when the Word became flesh, 2 Tim. 1:10; (b) the coming of the Lord Jesus into the air to the meeting with His saints, 1 Tim. 6:14; 2 Tim. 4:1, 8; (c) the shining forth of the glory of the Lord Jesus "as the lightning cometh forth from the east, and is seen even unto the west," Matt. 24:27, immediately consequent on the unveiling, *apokalupsis*, of His *Parousia* in the air with His saints, 2 Thess. 2:8; Titus 2:13.¶*

Notes: (1) *Phanerōsis*, akin to A, No. 4, "a manifestation," is used in 1 Cor. 12:7 and 2 Cor. 4:2.¶

(2) For *phaneros*, wrongly translated "may appear," in 1 Tim. 4:15, KJV (RV, "may be manifest," not mere appearance), see MANIFEST.

(3) *Emphanēs*, akin to A, No. 5, "manifest," is used in Acts 10:40 and Rom. 10:20. See MANIFEST, OPENLY.¶

(4) For *adēlos*, "which appear not," Luke 11:44, see UNCERTAIN.

APPEARANCE

A. Nouns.

1. *eidos* (εἶδος, 1491), properly "that which strikes the eye, that which is exposed to view," signifies the "external appearance, form, or shape," and in this sense is used of the Holy Spirit in taking bodily form, as a dove, Luke 3:22; of Christ, 9:29, "the fashion of His countenance." Christ used it, negatively, of God the Father, when He said "Ye have neither heard His voice at any time, nor seen His form," John 5:37. Thus it is used with reference to each person of the Trinity. Probably the same meaning attaches to the word in the apostle's statement, "We walk by faith, not by sight (*eidos*)," 2 Cor. 5:7, where *eidos* can scarcely mean the act of beholding, but the visible "appearance" of things which are set in contrast to that which directs faith. The believer is guided, then, not only by what he beholds but by what he knows to be true though it is invisible.

It has a somewhat different significance in 1 Thess. 5:22, in the exhortation, "Abstain from every form of evil," i.e., every sort or kind of evil (not "appearance," KJV). This meaning was common in the papyri, the Greek writings of the closing centuries, B.C., and the New Testament era. See FASHION, SHAPE, SIGHT.¶ Cf. No. 4.

2. *prosōpon* (πρόσωπον, 4383), pros, "towards," *ōps*, "an eye," lit., "the part round the eye, the face," in a secondary sense "the look, the countenance," as being the index of the inward thoughts and feelings (cf. 1 Pet. 3:12, there used of the face of the Lord), came to signify the presentation of the whole person (translated "person," e.g., in Matt. 22:16). Cf. the expression in OT passages, as Gen. 19:21 (KJV marg., "thy face"), where it is said by God of Lot, and 33:10, where it is said by Jacob of Esau; see also Deut. 10:17 ("persons"), Lev. 19:15 ("person"). It also signifies the presence of a person, Acts 3:13; 1 Thess. 2:17; or the presence of a company, Acts 5:41. In this sense it is sometimes rendered "appearance," 2 Cor. 5:12. In 2 Cor. 10:7, KJV, "appearance," the RV corrects to "face." See COUNTENANCE, FACE, FASHION, PERSON, PRESENCE.

3. *opsis* (ὄψις, 3799), from *ōps*, "the eye," connected with *horaō*, "to see" (cf. No. 2), primarily denotes "seeing, sight"; hence, "the face, the countenance," John 11:44 ("face"); Rev. 1:16 ("countenance"); the outward "appearance," the look, John 7:24, only here, of the outward aspect of a person. See COUNTENANCE, FACE.

4. *eidea* (εἰδέα, 5324), "an aspect, appearance," is used in Matt. 28:3, RV, "appearance"; KJV, "countenance." ¶

B. Verb.

phantazō (φαντάζω, 5324), "to make visible," is used in its participial form (middle voice), with the neuter article, as equivalent to a noun, and is translated "appearance," RV, for KJV, "sight," Heb. 12:21.¶

APPEASE

katastellō (καταστέλλω, 2687), "to quiet" (lit., "to send down," *kata*, "down," *stellō*, "to send"), in the passive voice, "to be quiet, or to be quieted," is used in Acts 19:35 and 36, in the former verse in the active voice, KJV, "appeased"; RV, "quieted"; in the latter, the passive, "to be quiet" (lit., 'to be quieted'). See QUIET.¶

APPOINT, APPOINTED

1. *histēmi* (ἵστημι, 2476), "to make to stand," means "to appoint," in Acts 17:31, of the day in which God will judge the world by Christ. In Acts 1:23, with reference to Joseph and Barnabas, the RV has "put forward"; for these were not both "appointed" in the accepted sense of the term, but simply singled out, in

order that it might be made known which of them the Lord had chosen. See ABIDE, No. 10.

2. *kathistēmi* (καθίστημι, 2525), a strengthened form of No. 1, usually signifies "to appoint a person to a position." In this sense the verb is often translated "to make" or "to set," in appointing a person to a place of authority, e.g., a servant over a household, Matt. 24:45, 47; 25:21, 23; Luke 12:42, 44; a judge, Luke 12:14; Acts 7:27, 35; a governor, Acts 7:10; man by God over the work of His hands, Heb. 2:7. It is rendered "appoint," with reference to the so-called seven deacons in Acts 6:3. The RV translates it by "appoint" in Titus 1:5, instead of "ordain," of the elders whom Titus was to "appoint" in every city in Crete. Not a formal ecclesiastical ordination is in view, but the "appointment," for the recognition of the churches, of those who had already been raised up and qualified by the Holy Spirit, and had given evidence of this in their life and service (see No. 11). It is used of the priests of old, Heb. 5:1; 7:28; 8:3 (RV, "appointed"). See CONDUCT, MAKE, ORDAIN, SET.

3. *tithēmi* (τίθημι, 5087), "to put," is used of "appointment" to any form of service. Christ used it of His followers, John 15:16 (RV, "appointed" for KJV, "ordained"). "I set you" would be more in keeping with the metaphor of grafting. The verb is used by Paul of his service in the ministry of the gospel, 1 Tim. 1:12 (RV, "appointing" for "putting"); 2:7 (RV, "appointed" for "ordained"); and 2 Tim. 1:11 (RV, "appointing" for "putting"); of the overseers, or bishops, in the local church at Ephesus, as those "appointed" by the Holy Ghost, to tend the church of God, Acts 20:28 ("hath made"); of the Son of God, as appointed Heir of all things, Heb. 1:2. It is also used of "appointment" to punishment, as of the unfaithful servant, Matt. 24:51; Luke 12:46; of unbelieving Israel, 1 Pet. 2:8. Cf. 2 Pet. 2:6. See BOW, COMMIT, CONCEIVE, LAY, MAKE, ORDAIN, PURPOSE, PUT, SET, SINK.

Note: Akin to *tithēmi* is the latter part of the noun *prothesmia*, Gal. 4:2, of a term or period "appointed."¶

4. *diatithēmi* (διατίθημι, 1303), a strengthened form of No. 3 (*dia*, "through," intensive), is used in the middle voice only. The Lord used it of His disciples with reference to the kingdom which is to be theirs hereafter, and of Himself in the same respect, as that which has been "appointed" for Him by His Father, Luke 22:29. For its use in connection with a covenant, see MAKE and TESTATOR.

5. *tassō* (τάσσω, 5021), "to place in order, arrange," signifies "to appoint," e.g., of the place where Christ had "appointed" a meeting with

His disciples after His resurrection, Matt. 28:16; of positions of military and civil authority over others, whether "appointed" by men, Luke 7:8, or by God, Rom. 13:1, "ordained." It is said of those who, having believed the gospel, "were ordained to eternal life," Acts 13:48. The house of Stephanas at Corinth had "set themselves" to the ministry of the saints (KJV, "addicted"), 1 Cor. 16:15. Other instances of the arranging of special details occur in Acts 15:2; 22:10; 28:23. See DETERMINE, ORDAIN, SET.¶

6. *diatassō* (διατάσσω, 1299), a strengthened form of No. 5 (*dia*, "through," intensive), frequently denotes "to arrange, appoint, prescribe," e.g., of what was "appointed" for tax collectors to collect, Luke 3:13; of the tabernacle, as "appointed" by God for Moses to make, Acts 7:44; of the arrangements "appointed" by Paul with regard to himself and his travelling companions, Acts 20:13; of what the apostle "ordained" in all the churches in regard to marital conditions, 1 Cor. 7:17; of what the Lord "ordained" in regard to the support of those who proclaimed the gospel, 1 Cor. 9:14; of the Law as divinely "ordained," or administered, through angels, by Moses, Gal. 3:19.

In Titus 1:5, KJV, "had appointed thee," the sense is rather that of commanding, RV, "gave thee charge." See COMMAND, No. 1, ORDAIN, ORDER.

7. *suntassō* (συντάσσω, 4929), *sun*, "with," and No. 5, lit., "to arrange together with", hence "to appoint, prescribe," is used twice, in Matt. 26:19 of what the Lord "appointed" for His disciples, and in 27:10, in a quotation concerning the price of the potter's field.¶

8. *protassō* (προτάσσω, 4384), *pro*, "before," and No. 5, "to appoint before," is used in Acts 17:26 (RV, "appointed"), of the seasons arranged by God for nations, and the bounds of their habitation.¶

9. *keimai* (κεῖμαι, 2749), "to lie," is used in 1 Thess. 3:3 of the "appointment" of affliction for faithful believers. It is rendered "set" in Luke 2:34 and Phil. 1:16, RV, where the sense is the same. The verb is a perfect tense, used for the perfect passive of *tithēmi*, "to place," "I have been placed," i.e., "I lie." See LAY, LIE, MADE (be), SET.

10. *apokeimai* (ἀπόκειμαι, 606), *apo*, "from," and No. 9, signifies "to be laid, reserved," Luke 19:20; Col. 1:5; 2 Tim. 4:8; "appointed," in Heb. 9:27, where it is said of death and the judgment following (RV, marg., "laid up"). See LAY.¶

11. *cheirotoneō* (χειροτονέω, 5500), primarily used of voting in the Athenian legislative assembly and meaning "to stretch forth the

hands" (*cheir*, "the hand," *teinō*, "to stretch"), is not to be taken in its literal sense; it could not be so taken in its compound *procheirotoneō*, "to choose before," since it is said of God, Acts 10:41. *Cheirotoneō* is said of "the appointment" of elders by apostolic missionaries in the various churches which they revisited, Acts 14:23, RV, "had appointed," i.e., by the recognition of those who had been manifesting themselves as gifted of God to discharge the functions of elders (see No. 2). It is also said of those who were "appointed" (not by voting, but with general approbation) by the churches in Greece to accompany the apostle in conveying their gifts to the poor saints in Judea, 2 Cor. 8:19. See CHOOSE, ORDAIN.¶

12. *procheirizō* (προχειρίζω, 4400), from *procheiros*, "at hand," signifies (*a*) "to deliver up, appoint," Acts 3:20 (RV, "appointed"); (*b*) in the middle voice, "to take into one's hand, to determine, appoint beforehand," translated "appointed" in Acts 22:14, RV (for KJV, "hath chosen"), and "to appoint" in 26:16 (for KJV, "to make").¶

13. *horizō* (ὁρίζω, 3724) (Eng., "horizon"), lit., "to mark by a limit," hence, "to determine, ordain," is used of Christ as ordained of God to be a judge of the living and the dead, Acts 17:31; of His being "marked out" as the Son of God, Rom. 1:4; of divinely appointed seasons, Acts 17:26, "having determined." See DEFINE.

14. *anadeiknumi* (ἀναδείκνυμι, 322), lit., "to show up, to show clearly," also signifies "to appoint to a position or a service"; it is used in this sense of the 70 disciples, Luke 10:1; for the meaning "show," see Acts 1:24.¶

15. *poieō* (ποιέω, 4160), "to do, to make," is rendered "appointed" in Heb. 3:2, of Christ. For Mark 3:14, RV, see ORDAIN, *Note* (2).

Note: Epithanatios, "appointed to death," doomed to it by condemnation, 1 Cor. 4:9, KJV, is corrected to "doomed to death" in the RV (*epi*, "for," *thanatos*, "death").

For APPORTIONED (RV in 2 Cor. 10:13) see DISTRIBUTE

APPREHEND

1. *katalambanō* (καταλαμβάνω, 2638) properly signifies "to lay hold of"; then, "to lay hold of so as to possess as one's own, to appropriate." Hence it has the same twofold meaning as the Eng. "to apprehend"; (*a*), "to seize upon, take possession of," (1) with a beneficial effect, as of "laying hold" of the righteousness which is of faith, Rom. 9:30 (not there a matter of attainment, as in the Eng. versions, but of ap-

propriation); of the obtaining of a prize, 1 Cor. 9:24 (RV, "attain"); of the apostle's desire "to apprehend," or "lay hold of," that for which he was apprehended by Christ, Phil. 3:12–13; (2) with a detrimental effect, e.g., of demon power, Mark 9:18; of human action in seizing upon a person, John 8:3–4; metaphorically, with the added idea of overtaking, of spiritual darkness in coming upon people, John 12:35; of the Day of the Lord, in suddenly coming upon unbelievers as a thief, 1 Thess. 5:4; (b), "to lay hold of" with the mind, to understand, perceive, e.g., metaphorically, of darkness with regard to light, John 1:5, though possibly here the sense is that of (a) as in 12:35; of mental perception, Acts 4:13; 10:34; 25:25; Eph. 3:18. See ATTAIN, No. 2, COME, *Note* (8), FIND, OBTAIN, OVERTAKE, PERCEIVE, TAKE.¶

Note: Cf. *epilambanō*, "to take hold of," always in the middle voice in the NT. See HOLD.

2. *piazō* (πιάζω, 4084), "to lay hold of," with the suggestion of firm pressure or force, is used in the Gospels only in John, six times of efforts to seize Christ and is always rendered "take" in the RV, 7:30, 32, 44; 8:20; 10:39; 11:57. The KJV has "laid hands on" in 8:20. In Acts 12:4 and 2 Cor. 11:32 (KJV), it is translated respectively "apprehended" and "apprehend" (RV, "had taken," and "take"). In Rev. 19:20 it is used of the seizure of the Beast and the False Prophet. In John 21:3, 10 it is used of catching fish. Elsewhere in Acts 3:7. See CATCH, LAY HANDS ON, TAKE.¶ In the Sept., Song of Sol. 2:15.¶

APPROACH

A. Verb.

engizō (ἐγγίζω, 1448), "to draw near, to approach," from *engus*, "near," is used (a) of place and position, literally and physically, Matt. 21:1; Mark 11:1; Luke 12:33; 15:25; figuratively, of drawing near to God, Matt. 15:8; Heb. 7:19; Jas. 4:8; (b) of time, with reference to things that are imminent, as the kingdom of heaven, Matt. 3:2; 4:17; 10:7; the kingdom of God, Mark 1:15; Luke 10:9, 11; the time of fruit, Matt. 21:34; the desolation of Jerusalem, Luke 21:8; redemption, 21:28; the fulfillment of a promise, Acts 7:17; the Day of Christ in contrast to the present night of the world's spiritual darkness, Rom. 13:12; Heb. 10:25; the coming of the Lord, Jas. 5:8; the end of all things, 1 Pet. 4:7. It is also said of one who was drawing near to death, Phil. 2:30. See COME, *Note* (16), DRAW, B, No. 1, HAND (at), NIGH.

B. Adjective.

aprositos (ἀπρόσιτος, 676), "unapproachable, inaccessible" (a), negative, and an adjective formed from *proseimi*, "to go to"), is used, in 1 Tim. 6:16, of the light in which God dwells (KJV, "which no man can approach unto"; RV, "unapproachable").¶

APPROVE, APPROVED

A. Verbs.

1. *dokimazō* (δοκιμάζω, 1381), primarily, of metals (e.g., the Sept. of Prov. 8:10; 17:3), signifies "to prove," e.g., 1 John 4:1, more frequently to prove with a view to approval, e.g., Rom. 1:28, KJV, "they did not like to retain God in their knowledge"; RV, "they refused"; marg., "did not approve," the true meaning. Their refusal was not the outcome of ignorance; they had the power to make a deliberate choice; they willfully disapproved of having God in their knowledge.

In the next chapter, the apostle speaks of the Jew as "approving things that are excellent," 2:18. The Jew knew God's will, and mentally "approved" of the things in which God had instructed him out of the Law.

In Rom. 14:22, he is said to be happy who "judgeth not himself in that which he approveth"; that is to say, in that which he "approves" of after having put the matter to the test. The KJV "alloweth" has not now this meaning.

As to the gifts from the church at Corinth for poor saints in Judea, those who were "approved" by the church to travel with the offering would be men whose trustworthiness and stability had been proved, 1 Cor. 16:3 (the RV margin seems right, "whomsoever ye shall approve, them will I send with letters"); cf. 2 Cor. 8:22.

In Phil. 1:10 the apostle prays that the saints may "approve the things that are excellent" or "things that differ," i.e., "approve" after distinguishing and discerning.

In 1 Thess. 2:4, the apostle and his fellow-missionaries were "approved of God to be entrusted with the Gospel" (not "allowed," KJV). Not permission to preach, but divine "approval" after divine testing is intended. See ALLOW, DISCERN, EXAMINE, LIKE, PROVE, REFUSE, TRY.

Note: Cf. *dokimē*, "proof, experience"; see also B.

2. *sunistēmi* (συνίστημι, 4921), lit., "to set together" (*sun*, "with," *histēmi*, "to stand"), hence signifies "to set one person or thing with another by way of presenting and commending." This meaning is confined to Romans and 2 Corinthians. The saints at Corinth had "approved themselves in everything to be pure," in the matter referred to, 2 Cor. 7:11. The word often denotes "to commend," so as to meet with

approval, Rom. 3:5; 5:8; 16:1; 2 Cor. 4:2; 6:4 (RV); 10:18; 12:11, etc. See COMMEND, COMPACTED, CONSIST (No. 2), STAND.

3. *apodeiknumi* (ἀποδείκνυμι, 584), lit., "to point out, to exhibit" (*apo*, "forth," *deiknumi*, "to show"), is used once in the sense of proving by demonstration, and so bringing about an "approval." The Lord Jesus was "a Man approved of God by mighty works and wonders and signs," Acts 2:22. See PROVE, SET, No. 17, SHEW.

B. Adjective.

dokimos (δόκιμος, 1384), akin to *dechomai*, "to receive," always signifies "approved"; so the RV everywhere, e.g., in Jas. 1:12 for KJV, "when he is tried." The word is used of coins and metals in the Sept.; in Gen. 23:16, "four hundred didrachms of silver approved with merchants"; in Zech. 11:13, in regard to the 30 pieces of silver, "Cast them into a furnace and I will see if it is good (approved) metal."

APRON

simikinthion (σιμικίνθιον, 4612), "a thing girded round half the body" (Latin, *semicinctium*), was a narrow apron, or linen covering, worn by workmen and servants, Acts 19:12.¶

For APT see TEACH, B

ARCHANGEL

archangelos (ἀρχάγγελος, 743) "is not found in the OT, and in the NT only in 1 Thess. 4:16 and Jude 9, where it is used of Michael, who in Daniel is called 'one of the chief princes,' and 'the great prince' (Sept., 'the great angel'), 10:13, 21; 12:1. Cf. also Rev. 12:7.... Whether there are other beings of this exalted rank in the heavenly hosts, Scripture does not say, though the description 'one of the chief princes' suggests that this may be the case; cf. also Rom. 8:38; Eph. 1:21; Col. 1:16, where the word translated 'principalities' is *archē*, the prefix in archangel."* In 1 Thess. 4:16 the meaning seems to be that the voice of the Lord Jesus will be of the character of an "archangelic" shout. ¶

For ARIGHT (RV of 2 Tim. 2:15) see HANDLE, No. 5

ARISE, AROSE, AROUSE, RAISE, RISE, ROUSE

1. *anistēmi* (ἀνίστημι, 450), "to stand up or to make to stand up," according as its use is

intransitive or transitive (*ana*, "up," *histēmi*, "to stand"), is used (*a*) of a physical change of position, e.g., of "rising" from sleep, Mark 1:35; from a meeting in a synagogue, Luke 4:29; of the illegal "rising" of the high priest in the tribunal in Matt. 26:62; of an invalid "rising" from his couch, Luke 5:25; the "rising" up of a disciple from his vocation to follow Christ, Luke 5:28; cf. John 11:31; "rising" up from prayer, Luke 22:45; of a whole company, Acts 26:30; 1 Cor. 10:7; (*b*) metaphorically, of "rising" up antagonistically against persons, e.g. of officials against people, Acts 5:17; of a seditious leader, 5:36; of the "rising" up of Satan, Mark 3:26; of false teachers, Acts 20:30; (*c*) of "rising" to a position of preeminence or power; e.g., of Christ as a prophet, Acts 3:22; 7:37; as God's servant in the midst of the nation of Israel, Acts 3:26; as the Son of God in the midst of the nation, 13:33 (not here of resurrection, but with reference to the Incarnation: the KJV "again" has nothing corresponding to it in the original, it was added as a misinterpretation: the mention of His resurrection is in the next verse, in which it is stressed by way of contrast and by the addition, "from the dead"); as a priest, Heb. 7:11, 15; as king over the nations, Rom. 15:12; (*d*) of a spiritual awakening from lethargy, Eph. 5:14; (*e*) of resurrection from the dead: (1) of the resurrection of Christ, Matt. 17:9; 20:19; Mark 8:31; 9:9–10, 31; 10:34; Luke 18:33; 24:7, 46; John 20:9; Acts 2:24, 32; 10:41; 13:34; 17:3, 31; 1 Thess. 4:14; (2) of believers, John 6:39–40, 44, 54; 11:24; 1 Thess. 4:16; of unbelievers, Matt. 12:41. See LIFT, RAISE (up), STAND.

2. *exanistēmi* (ἐξανίστημι, 1817), a strengthened form of No. 1 (*ex*, i.e., *ek*, intensive), signifies "to raise up," Mark 12:19; Luke 20:28; intransitively, "to rise up," Acts 15:5.¶

3. *egeirō* (ἐγείρω, 1453) is frequently used in the NT in the sense of "raising" (active voice), or "rising" (middle and passive voices): (*a*) from sitting, lying, sickness, e.g., Matt. 2:14; 9:5, 7, 19; Jas. 5:15; Rev. 11:1; (*b*) of causing to appear, or, in the passive, appearing, or raising up so as to occupy a place in the midst of people, Matt. 3:9; 11:11; Mark 13:22; Acts 13:22. It is thus said of Christ in Acts 13:23; cf. No. 1, (*c*); (*c*) of rousing, stirring up, or "rising" against, Matt. 24:7; Mark 13:8; (*d*) of "raising" buildings," John 2:19–20; (*e*) of "raising or rising" from the dead: (1) of Christ, Matt. 16:21; and frequently elsewhere (but not in Phil., 2 Thess., 1 Tim., Titus, Jas., 2 Pet., 1, 2, 3 John, and Jude); (2) of Christ's "raising" the dead, Matt. 11:5; Mark 5:41; Luke 7:14; John 12:1, 9, 17; (3) of the act of the disciples, Matt.

---

* From *Notes on Thessalonians*, by Hogg and Vine, p. 142.

10:8; (4) of the resurrection of believers, Matt. 27:52; John 5:21; 1 Cor. 15:15–16, 29, 32, 35, 42–44, 52; 2 Cor. 1:9; 4:14; of unbelievers, Matt. 12:42 (cf. v. 41, No. 1).

Egeirō stands in contrast to *anistēmi* (when used with reference to resurrection) in this respect, that *egeirō* is frequently used both in the transitive sense of "raising up" and the intransitive of "rising," whereas *anistēmi* is comparatively infrequent in the transitive use. See AWAKE.

4. *diegeirō* (διεγείρω, 1326), a strengthened form of No. 3 (*dia*, "through," intensive), signifies "to rouse, to awaken from sleep." The active voice is not used intransitively. In Matt. 1:24, RV, "Joseph arose from his sleep," the passive participle is, lit., "being aroused." In Mark 4:39 (KJV, "he arose," RV, "he awoke"), the lit. rendering is "he being awakened." In John 6:18 the imperfect tense of the passive voice is used, and the rendering should be, "the sea was being aroused." See AWAKE, No. 2.

5. *ginomai* (γίνομαι, 1096), "to become, to take place," is sometimes suitably translated "arise"; e.g., Matt. 8:24; Mark 4:37, "there arose a great tempest." So of the arising of persecution, Matt. 13:21; Mark 4:17; this might be translated "taketh place"; of a tumult, Matt. 27:24, RV, "arising," for KJV, "made"; of a flood, Luke 6:48; a famine, 15:14; a questioning, John 3:25; a murmuring, Acts 6:1; a tribulation, 11:19 (RV); a stir in the city, 19:23; a dissension, 23:7; a great clamor, v. 9. See BECOME.

6. *anabainō* (ἀναβαίνω, 305), "to go up, to ascend," is once rendered "arise" in the RV, Luke 24:38, of reasonings in the heart; in Rev. 13:1, RV, "coming up," for KJV, "rise up," with reference to the beast; in 17:8, KJV, "ascend," for RV, "to come up"; in 19:3, RV, "goeth up," for KJV, "rose up." See CLIMB UP, COME, ENTER, GO, GROW, RISE, SPRING.

7. *sunephistēmi* (συνεφίστημι, 4911), "to rise up together" (*sun*, together, *epi*, "up," *histēmi*, "to stand"), is used in Acts 16:22, of the "rising up" of a multitude against Paul and Silas.¶

8. *eiserchomai* (εἰσέρχομαι, 1525), lit., "to go in" (*eis*, "in," *erchomai*, "to go"), "to enter," is once rendered "arose," metaphorically, with reference to a reasoning among the disciples which of them should be the greatest, Luke 9:46. See COME, ENTER, GO.

9. *anatellō* (ἀνατέλλω, 393), "to arise," is used especially of things in the natural creation, e.g., "the rising" of the sun, moon and stars; metaphorically, of light, in Matt. 4:16, "did spring up"; of the sun, Matt. 5:45; 13:6 (RV); Mark 4:6; Jas. 1:11; in Mark 16:2 the RV has

"when the sun was risen," keeping to the verb form, for the KJV, "at the rising of"; of a cloud, Luke 12:54; of the day-star, 2 Pet. 1:19; in Heb. 7:14 metaphorically, of the Incarnation of Christ: "Our Lord hath sprung out of Judah," more lit., "Our Lord hath arisen out of Judah," as of the rising of the light of the sun. See RISE, SPRING, UP.¶

Notes: (1) A corresponding noun, *anatolē*, signifies "the east," i.e., the place of the "sunrising."

(2) In Acts 27:14, the verb *ballō*, "to beat" (intransitive), is translated "arose" in the KJV; RV, "beat."

ARK

kibōtos (κιβωτός, 2787), "a wooden box, a chest," is used of (*a*) Noah's vessel, Matt. 24:38; Luke 17:27; Heb. 11:7; 1 Pet. 3:20; (*b*) the "ark" of the covenant in the tabernacle, Heb. 9:4; (*c*) the "ark" seen in vision in the heavenly temple, Rev. 11:19.¶

ARM (physical)

1. *ankalē* (ἀγκάλη, 43), used in the plural, in Luke 2:28, originally denoted "the curve, or the inner angle, of the arm." The word is derived from a term signifying "to bend, to curve"; the Eng. "angle" is connected.¶

Note: Enankalizomai (*en*, "in," and a verb akin to No. 1), "to take into the arms, to embrace," is used in Mark 9:36 and 10:16, of the tenderness of Christ towards little children.¶

2. *brachiōn* (βραχίων, 1023), "the shorter part of the arm, from the shoulder to the elbow," is used metaphorically to denote strength, power, and always in the NT of the power of God, Luke 1:51; John 12:38; Acts 13:17; frequently so in the OT, especially in Deuteronomy, the Psalms and Isaiah; see, e.g., Deut. 4:34; 5:15; Ps. 44:3; 71:18, where "strength" is, lit., "arm"; 77:15; Isa. 26:11, where "hand" is, lit., "arm"; 30:30; 40:10–11, etc.¶

ARMS (weapons), ARMOR, TO ARM

A. Nouns.

1. *hoplon* (ὅπλον, 3696), originally any tool or implement for preparing a thing, became used in the plural for "weapons of warfare." Once in the NT it is used of actual weapons, John 18:3; elsewhere, metaphorically, of (*a*) the members of the body as instruments of unrighteousness and as instruments of righteousness, Rom. 6:13; (*b*) the "armor" of light, Rom. 13:12; the "armor" of righteousness, 2 Cor. 6:7;

the weapons of the Christian's warfare, 2 Cor. 10:4.¶

2. *panoplia* (πανοπλία, 3833), (Eng., "panoply"), lit., "all armor, full armor," (*pas*, "all," *hoplon*, "a weapon"), is used (*a*) of literal "armor," Luke 11:22; (*b*) of the spiritual helps supplied by God for overcoming the temptations of the Devil, Eph. 6:11, 13. Among the Greeks the *panoplia* was the complete equipment used by heavily armed infantry.¶

B. Verbs.

1. *hoplizō* (ὁπλίζω, 3695), "to arm oneself," is used in 1 Pet. 4:1, in an exhortation "to arm" ourselves with the same mind as that of Christ in regard to His sufferings.¶

2. *kathoplizō* (καθοπλίζω, 2528) is an intensive form, "to furnish fully with arms," *kata*, "down," intensive, *hoplon*, "a weapon," Luke 11:21, lit., "a strong man fully armed."¶ In the Sept., Jer. 46:9.¶

ARMY

1. *strateuma* (στράτευμα, 4753) denotes (*a*) "an army" of any size, large or small, Matt. 22:7; Rev. 9:16; 19:14, 19 (twice); (*b*) "a company of soldiers," such as Herod's bodyguard, Luke 23:11 (RV, "soldiers"), or the soldiers of a garrison, Acts 23:10, 27 (RV, "the soldiers," for KJV, "an army"). See SOLDIER, WAR.¶

2. *stratopedon* (στρατόπεδον, 4760), from *stratos*, "a military host," *pedon*, "a plain," strictly denotes "an army encamped, a camp"; in Luke 21:20, of the soldiers which were to be encamped about Jerusalem in fulfillment of the Lord's prophecy concerning the destruction of the city; the phrase might be translated "by camps" (or encampments).¶

3. *parembolē* (παρεμβολή, 3925), lit., "a casting in among, an insertion" (*para*, "among," *ballō*, "to throw"), in the Macedonian dialect, was a military term. In the NT it denotes the distribution of troops in army formation, "armies," Heb. 11:34; a camp, as of the Israelites, Exod. 19:17; 29:14; 32:17; hence, in Heb. 13:11, 13, of Jerusalem, since the city was to the Jews what the camp in the wilderness had been to the Israelites; in Rev. 20:9, the "armies" or camp of the saints, at the close of the Millennium.

It also denoted a castle or barracks, Acts 21:34, 37; 22:24; 23:10, 16, 32.¶

For **AROUND** see *Note* †, p. 1

For **ARRAY** see **CLOTHE**, No. 6, **PUT**

ARRIVE

1. *katantaō* (καταντάω, 2658), "to come to, arrive at", is used (*a*) literally, of locality, Acts 16:1, "came to"; so 18:19, 24; 20:15 ("came"); 21:7; 25:13; 27:12 (KJV, "attain to," RV, "reach"); 28:13; (*b*) metaphorically, of attainment, Acts 26:7, "attain"; so Eph. 4:13; Phil. 3:11. In 1 Cor. 10:11 ("upon whom the ends of the ages are come," RV), the metaphor is apparently that of an inheritance as coming down or descending to an heir, the "ends" (*telē*) being the spiritual revenues (cf. Matt. 17:25, revenues derived from taxes, and Rom. 13:7, where the singular, *telos*, "custom," is used); the inheritance metaphor is again seen in 1 Cor. 14:36, of the coming (or descending) of the Word of God to the Corinthians. See ATTAIN.

2. *katapleō* (καταπλέω, 2668) denotes "to sail down" (*kata*, "down," *pleō*, "to sail"), i.e., from the high sea to the shore, Luke 8:26.¶

3. *paraginomai* (παραγίνομαι, 3854), lit., "to become near," hence, "to come on the scene," Matt. 3:1, of John the Baptist, is translated, "arrive" in the RV of 1 Cor. 16:3, for KJV, "come." See COME, GO, PRESENT.

4. *paraballō* (παραβάλλω, 3846), *para*, "alongside," *ballō*, "to throw," signifies, nautically, "touched at"; so the RV of Acts 20:15 (KJV, "arrived"); or, perhaps, to strike across, from one place to another. In Mark 4:30, some mss. have this verb (KJV, "compare"); the most authentic have *tithēmi*, to set forth (with the word "parable"). See COMPARE.

5. *phthanō* (φθάνω, 5348), "to anticipate, reach to," is translated "did arrive at," Rom. 9:31, RV, of Israel's failure to attain to the Law (KJV, "hath attained to"). See ATTAIN, COME, PRECEDE.

ART, ARTS

1. *technē* (τέχνη, 5078), "an art, handicraft, trade," is used in Acts 17:29, of the plastic art; in Acts 18:3, of a trade or craft (KJV, "occupation," RV, "trade"); in Rev. 18:22, "craft" (cf. *technitēs*, "a craftsman," Eng., "technical"). See CRAFT, OCCUPATION, TRADE.¶

2. *periergos* (περίεργος, 4021), lit., "a work about" (*peri*, "about," *ergon*, "a work"), hence, "busy about trifles," is used, in the plural, of things superfluous, "curious (or magical) arts," Acts 19:19; in 1 Tim. 5:13, "busybodies." See BUSYBODY.¶

For **AS** (and connected phrases) see *Note* †, p. 1

For **ASCEND** see **ARISE**, No. 6

ASHAMED (to be), SHAME

A. Verbs.

1. *aischunō* (αἰσχύνω, 153), from *aischos*, "shame," always used in the passive voice, signifies (*a*) "to have a feeling of fear or shame which prevents a person from doing a thing," e.g., Luke 16:3; (*b*) "the feeling of shame arising from something that has been done," e.g., 2 Cor. 10:8; Phil. 1:20; 1 John 2:28, of the possibility of being "ashamed" before the Lord Jesus at His judgment seat in His Parousia with His saints; in 1 Pet. 4:16, of being ashamed of suffering as a Christian.¶

2. *epaischunomai* (ἐπαισχύνομαι, 1870), a strengthened form of No. 1 (*epi*, "upon," intensive), is used only in the sense (*b*) in the preceding paragraph. It is said of being "ashamed" of persons, Mark 8:38; Luke 9:26; the gospel, Rom. 1:16; former evil doing, Rom. 6:21; "the testimony of our Lord," 2 Tim. 1:8; suffering for the gospel, v. 12; rendering assistance and comfort to one who is suffering for the gospel's sake, v. 16. It is used in Heb., of Christ in calling those who are sanctified His brethren, 2:11, and of God in His not being "ashamed" to be called the God of believers, 11:16.¶ In the Sept., in Job 34:19; Ps. 119:6; Isa. 1:29.¶

3. *kataischunō* (καταισχύνω, 2617), another strengthened form (*kata*, "down," intensive), is used (*a*) in the active voice, "to put to shame," e.g., Rom. 5:5; 1 Cor. 1:27 (KJV, "confound"); 11:4–5 ("dishonoreth"), and v. 22; (*b*) in the passive voice, Rom. 9:33; 10:11; 2 Cor. 7:14; 1 Pet. 2:6; 3:16. See CONFOUND, DISHONOR, SHAME.

4. *entrepō* (ἐντρέπω, 1788), "to put to shame," in the passive voice, to be ashamed, lit. means "to turn in" (*en*, "in," *trepō*, "to turn"), that is, to turn one upon himself and so produce a feeling of "shame," a wholesome "shame" which involves a change of conduct, 1 Cor. 4:14; 2 Thess. 3:14; Titus 2:8, the only places where it has this meaning. See also REGARD, REVERENCE.

B. Nouns.

1. *aischunē* (αἰσχύνην, 152), "shame," akin to A, No. 1, signifies (*a*) subjectively, the confusion of one who is "ashamed" of anything, a sense of "shame," Luke 14:9; those things which "shame" conceals, 2 Cor. 4:2; (*b*) objectively, ignominy, that which is visited on a person by the wicked, Heb. 12:2; that which should arise from guilt, Phil. 3:19; (*c*) concretely, a thing to be "ashamed" of, Rev. 3:18; Jude 13, where the word is in the plural, lit., "basenesses," "disgraces." See DISHONESTY.¶

2. *entropē* (ἐντροπή, 1791), akin to A, No. 4, lit., "a turning in upon oneself," producing a recoil from what is unseemly or vile, is used in 1 Cor. 6:5; 15:34. It is associated with *aischunē* in the Psalms, in the Sept., e.g., 35:26, where it follows *aischunē*, "let them be clothed with shame (*aischunē*) and confusion (*entropē*)"; 44:15, "all the day my shame is before me and the confusion of my face has covered me"; 69:19, "Thou knowest my reproach and my shame and my confusion"; so in 71:13. In 109:29 the words are in the opposite order.¶

Note: Aidōs, used in 1 Tim. 2:9, denotes "modesty, shamefastness" (the right spelling for the KJV, "shamefacedness"). In comparison with *aischunē, aidōs* is "the nobler word, and implies the nobler motive: in it is involved an innate moral repugnance to the doing of the dishonorable act, which moral repugnance scarcely or not at all exists in *aischunē*" (Trench, *Syn.* §xix). See SHAMEFASTNESS.¶

C. Adjectives.

1. *aischros* (αἰσχρός, 150), "base" (akin to No. 1), is used in 1 Cor. 11:6; 14:35; Eph. 5:12. See FILTHY B, No. 1. ¶Cf. *aischrotēs*, "filthiness," Eph. 5:4.¶

2. *anepaischuntos* (ἀνεπαίσχυντος, 422), an intensive adjective (*a*, negative, *n* euphonic, *epi*, "upon," intensive, *aischunē*, "shame"), "not ashamed, having no cause for shame," is used in 2 Tim. 2:15.¶

ASHES

A. Noun.

spodos (σποδός, 4700), "ashes", is found three times, twice in association with sackcloth, Matt. 11:21 and Luke 10:13, as tokens of grief (cf. Esth. 4:1, 3; Isa. 58:5; 61:3; Jer. 6:26; Jonah 3:6); of the ashes resulting from animal sacrifices, Heb. 9:13; in the OT, metaphorically, of one who describes himself as dust and "ashes," Gen. 18:27, etc.¶

B. Verb.

tephroō (τεφρόω, 5077), "to turn to ashes," is found in 2 Pet. 2:6, with reference to the destruction of Sodom and Gomorrah.¶

Notes: (1) *Tephra*, frequently used of the "ashes" of a funeral pile, is not found in the NT.

(2) The Hebrew verb, rendered "accept" in Ps. 20:3, "accept thy burnt sacrifice," signifies "to turn to ashes" (i.e., by sending fire from heaven). See also Exod. 27:3, and Num. 4:13, "shall take away the ashes."

For **ASHORE** (Acts 27:29) see **CAST,** A, No. 3

For **ASIDE** see **LAY**, No. 8, **TAKE,** No. 3, **TURN**, Nos. 3, 17, *Note* (1)

ASK

A. Verbs.

1. *aiteō* (αἰτέω, 154), "to ask," is to be distinguished from No. 2. *Aiteō* more frequently suggests the attitude of a suppliant, the petition of one who is lesser in position than he to whom the petition is made; e.g., in the case of men in asking something from God, Matt. 7:7; a child from a parent, Matt. 7:9–10; a subject from a king, Acts 12:20; priests and people from Pilate, Luke 23:23 (RV, "asking" for KJV, "requiring"); a beggar from a passer by, Acts 3:2. With reference to petitioning God, this verb is found in Paul's epistles in Eph. 3:20 and Col. 1:9; in James four times, 1:5–6; 4:2–3; in 1 John, five times, 3:22; 5:14, 15 (twice), 16. See BEG, CALL FOR, CRAVE, DESIRE, REQUIRE.

2. *erotaō* (ἐρωτάω, 2065) more frequently suggests that the petitioner is on a footing of equality or familiarity with the person whom he requests. It is used of a king in making request from another king, Luke 14:32; of the Pharisee who "desired" Christ that He would eat with him, an indication of the inferior conception he had of Christ, Luke 7:36; cf. 11:37; John 9:15; 18:19.

In this respect it is significant that the Lord Jesus never used *aiteō* in the matter of making request to the Father. "The consciousness of His equal dignity, of His potent and prevailing intercession, speaks out in this, that as often as He asks, or declares that He will ask anything of the Father, it is always *erotaō*, an asking, that is, upon equal terms, John 14:16; 16:26; 17:9, 15, 20, never *aiteō*, that He uses. Martha, on the contrary, plainly reveals her poor unworthy conception of His person, that . . . she ascribes that *aiteō* to Him which He never ascribes to Himself, John 11:22" (Trench, *Syn.* § xl).

In passages where both words are used, the distinction should be noticed, even if it cannot be adequately represented in English. In John 16:23, "in that day ye shall ask Me nothing," the verb is *erotaō*, whereas in the latter part of the verse, in the sentence, "If ye shall ask anything of the Father," the verb is *aiteō*. The distinction is brought out in the RV margin, which renders the former clause "Ye shall ask Me no question," and this meaning is confirmed by the fact that the disciples had been desirous of "asking" Him a question (*erotaō*, v. 19). If the Holy Spirit had been given, the time for "asking" questions from the Lord would have ceased. In John 14:14, where, not a question, but a request is made by the disciples, *aiteō*, is used.

Both verbs are found in 1 John 5:16: in the sentence "he shall ask, and God will give him life for them that sin not unto death," the verb is *aiteō*, but with regard to the sin unto death, in the sentence "not concerning this do I say that he shall make request," the verb is *erotaō*.

Later, the tendency was for *erotaō* to approximate to *aiteō*. See BESEECH, DESIRE, INTREAT, PRAY, REQUEST.

Note: In Matt. 19:17, the RV, following the most authentic mss., has "Why askest (*erotaō*) thou Me concerning that which is good?"

3. *eperotaō* (ἐπερωτάω, 1905), a strengthened form of No. 2 (*epi*, "in addition"), is frequently used in the synoptic Gospels, but only twice in the Gospel of John, 18:7, 21. In Rom. 10:20 it is rendered "asked of" (KJV, "asked after"). The more intensive character of the "asking" may be observed in Luke 2:46; 3:14; 6:9; 17:20; 20:21, 27, 40; 22:64; 23:3, 6, 9. In Matt. 16:1, it virtually signifies to demand (its meaning in later Greek). See DEMAND, DESIRE, QUESTION.

Note: For the corresponding noun *eperotēma*, see ANSWER.

4. *punthanomai* (πυνθάνομαι, 4441), to ask by way of enquiry, not by way of making a request for something, is found in the Gospels and the Acts, five times in the former, seven in the latter; in Matt. 2:4, KJV, "demanded," RV, "enquired," so Acts 21:33. See DEMAND, INQUIRE, UNDERSTAND.

5. *exetazō* (ἐξετάζω, 1833), "to search out" (*ek*, "out," intensive, *etazō*, "to examine"), is translated "ask," in John 21:12, KJV (RV, "inquire"); in Matt. 2:8, KJV, "search"; RV, "search out," expressing the intensive force of the verb, so Matt. 10:11 (KJV, "inquire"). See INQUIRE, SEARCH.¶

6. *lego* (λέγω, 3004), "to say," occasionally signifies "to ask," as of an inquiry, the reason being that *lego* is used for every variety of speaking, e.g., Acts 25:20, "I asked whether he would come to Jerusalem." See BID, BOAST, CALL, DESCRIBE, GIVE, NAME, PUT, *Note* (2), SAY, SPEAK, TELL, UTTER.

7. *anakrinō* (ἀνακρίνω, 350), "to judge," sometimes has the meaning to ask a question; e.g., 1 Cor. 10:25, 27. See DISCERN, EXAMINE, JUDGE, SEARCH.

Notes: (1) For *apaiteō*, Luke 6:30, see REQUIRE, No. 3. (2) In Luke 22:31, RV, *exaiteomai* is rendered "hath asked to have."¶

B. Noun.

aitēma (αἴτημα, 155), akin to No. 1, lit., "that which has been asked for," is used in Luke 23:24, RV, "what they asked for" (KJV, "required"); Phil. 4:6, "requests"; 1 John 5:15, "petitions." See PETITION, REQUEST, REQUIRE.¶

ASLEEP, SLEEP

A. Verbs.

1. *katheudō* (καθεύδω, 2518), "to go to sleep," is chiefly used of natural "sleep," and is found most frequently in the Gospels, especially Matthew and Luke. With reference to death it is found in the Lord's remark concerning Jairus' daughter, Matt. 9:24; Mark 5:39; Luke 8:52. In the epistles of Paul it is used as follows: (*a*) of natural "sleep," e.g., 1 Thess. 5:7; (*b*) of carnal indifference to spiritual things on the part of believers, Eph. 5:14; 1 Thess. 5:6, 10 (as in Mark 13:36), a condition of insensibility to divine things involving conformity to the world (cf. *hupnos* below).

2. *koimaomai* (κοιμάομαι, 2837) is used of natural "sleep," Matt. 28:13; Luke 22:45; John 11:12; Acts 12:6; of the death of the body, but only of such as are Christ's; yet never of Christ Himself, though He is "the firstfruits of them that have fallen asleep," 1 Cor. 15:20; of saints who departed before Christ came, Matt. 27:52; Acts 13:36; of Lazarus, while Christ was yet upon the earth, John 11:11; of believers since the Ascension, 1 Thess. 4:13–15, and Acts 7:60; 1 Cor. 7:39; 11:30; 15:6, 18, 51; 2 Pet. 3:4.¶

Note: "This metaphorical use of the word sleep is appropriate, because of the similarity in appearance between a sleeping body and a dead body; restfulness and peace normally characterize both. The object of the metaphor is to suggest that, as the sleeper does not cease to exist while his body sleeps, so the dead person continues to exist despite his absence from the region in which those who remain can communicate with him, and that, as sleep is known to be temporary, so the death of the body will be found to be. . . .

"That the body alone is in view in this metaphor is evident, (*a*) from the derivation of the word *koimaomai*, from *keimai*, to lie down (cf. *anastasis*, resurrection, from *ana*, 'up,' and *histēmi*, to cause to stand); cf. Isa. 14:8, where for 'laid down,' the Sept. has 'fallen asleep'; (*b*) from the fact that in the NT the word resurrection is used of the body alone; (*c*) from Dan. 12:2, where the physically dead are described as 'them that sleep (Sept. *katheudō*, as at 1 Thess. 5:6) in the dust of the earth,' language inapplicable to the spiritual part of man; moreover, when the body returns whence it came, Gen. 3:19, the spirit returns to God who gave it, Eccl. 12:7.

"When the physical frame of the Christian (the earthly house of our tabernacle, 2 Cor. 5:1) is dissolved and returns to the dust, the spiritual part of his highly complex being, the seat of personality, departs to be with Christ, Phil. 1:23. And since that state in which the believer, absent from the body, is at home with the Lord, 2 Cor. 5:6–9, is described as 'very far better' than the present state of joy in communion with God and of happy activity in His service, everywhere reflected in Paul's writings, it is evident the word 'sleep,' where applied to the departed Christians, is not intended to convey the idea that the spirit is unconscious. . . .

"The early Christians adopted the word *koimētērion* (which was used by the Greeks of a rest-house for strangers) for the place of interment of the bodies of their departed; thence the English word 'cemetery,' 'the sleeping place,' is derived."*

3. *exupnizo* (ἐξυπνίζω, 1852), "to awake" (*ek*, "out," *hupnos*, "sleep"), "to awake out of sleep," is used in John 11:11.¶ In the Sept., Judg. 16:14, 20; 1 Kings 3:15; Job 14:12.¶

4. *aphupnoō* (ἀφυπνόω, 879), "to fall asleep" (*apo*, "away"), is used of natural "sleep," Luke 8:23, of the Lord's falling "asleep" in the boat on the lake of Galilee.¶

B. Adjective.

exupnos (ἔξυπνος, 1853), Acts 16:27, signifies "out of sleep."¶

C. Noun.

hupnos (ὕπνος, 5278) is never used of death. In five places in the NT it is used of physical "sleep"; in Rom. 13:11, metaphorically, of a slumbering state of soul, i.e., of spiritual conformity to the world, out of which believers are warned to awake.

ASP

aspis (ἀσπίς, 785), "a small and very venomous serpent," the bite of which is fatal, unless the part affected is at once cut away, in Rom. 3:13 is said, metaphorically, of the conversation of the ungodly.¶

ASS

1. *onos* (ὄνος, 3688) is the usual word. *Onarion*, the diminutive of *onos*, "a young ass, or ass's colt," is used in John 12:14, together with *onos*.¶

2. *hupozugion* (ὑποζύγιον, 5268), lit., "under a yoke" (*hupo*, "under," *zugos*, "a yoke"), is used as an alternative description of the same animal, in Matt. 21:5, where both words are found together, "Behold, thy king cometh unto thee, meek and riding upon an ass (*onos*), and upon a colt the foal of an ass (*hupozugion*)." It was upon the colt that the Lord

* From *Notes on Thessalonians*, by Hogg and Vine. p. 172.

sat, John 12:14. In 2 Pet. 2:16, it is used of Balaam's "ass."¶

ASSASSIN

sikarios (σικάριος, 4607) is a Latin word (*sicarius*, "from" *sica*, "a dagger") denoting "one who carries a dagger or short sword under his clothing, an assassin," Acts 21:38, RV. Here it is used as a proper name (see the RV) of the Sicarii, "assassins," the fanatical Jewish faction which arose in Judea after Felix had rid the country of the robbers referred to by Josephus (Ant., XX). They mingled with the crowds at festivals and stabbed their political opponents unobserved (KJV, "murderers").¶

ASSAULT

A. Verb.

ephistēmi (ἐφίστημι, 2186), lit., "to stand over" (*epi*, "over," *histēmi*, "to stand"), signifies "to assault"; said in Acts 17:5, of those who attacked the house of Jason. For its usual meanings see COME (in, to, upon), HAND (at), INSTANT, PRESENT, STAND.

B. Noun.

hormē (ὁρμή, 3730), rendered "assault" in Acts 14:5, KJV; RV, "onset," corresponds to *hormaō*, "to rush." See IMPULSE, ONSET.¶

For ASSAY see TRY, No. 2

ASSEMBLE

1. *sunagō* (συνάγω, 4863), "to assemble" (*sun*, "together," *agō*, "to bring"), is used of the "gathering together" of people or things; in Luke 12:17–18, "bestow," with reference to the act of "gathering" one's goods; so in Luke 15:13, suggesting that the Prodigal, having "gathered" all his goods together, sold them off; in John 6:12, of "gathering" up fragments; in John 18:2, "resorted," with reference to the "assembling" of Christ with His disciples in the garden of Gethsemane, there in the passive voice (unsuitable, however, in an English translation). In Acts 11:26, the RV has "were gathered together (with the church)," for KJV, "assembled themselves" (possibly "they were hospitably entertained by"). The verb is not found in the most authentic mss. in Rev. 13:10. See BESTOW, GATHER, LEAD, TAKE, No. 29.

Note: Episunagō, "to gather together," is found only in the synoptic Gospels; twice of the "gathering" together of people, Mark 1:33; Luke 12:1; twice of the desire of the Lord to "gather" together the inhabitants of Jerusalem, Matt. 23:37; Luke 13:34; twice of His future act in "gathering" together His elect through the instrumentality of the angels, Matt. 24:31; Mark 13:27. See GATHER.¶

2. *sunalizō* (συναλίζω, 4871), "to gather together, to assemble," with the suggestion of a crowded meeting (*sun*, "with," *halizō*, "to crowd, or mass:" the corresponding adjective is *halēs*, "thronged"), is used in Acts 1:4. The meaning "to eat with," suggested by some, as if the word were derived from *hals*, "salt," is not to be accepted.¶

3. *sunerchomai* (συνέρχομαι, 4905), "to come together" (*sun*, "together," *erchomai*, "to come"), is once rendered "assemble," Mark 14:53, KJV. It is frequently used of "coming together," especially of the "gathering" of a local church, 1 Cor. 11:17–18, 20, 33–34; 14:23, 26; it is rendered "resorted" in Acts 16:13, KJV, where the RV adheres to the lit. rendering, "came together." See ACCOMPANY.

Notes: (1) In Acts 15:25, *ginomai*, "to become," is translated "having come to (one accord)," correcting the KJV, "being assembled with (one accord)."

(2) *Sunagōgē*, akin to A, No. 1, is, lit., "a place where people assemble." In Acts 13:43 the RV suitably has "synagogue," for the KJV "congregation," the building standing by metonymy for the people therein (cf. Matt. 10:17, etc.). In Jas. 2:2 (KJV, "assembly") the word is "synagogue" (RV). See SYNAGOGUE.

(3) *Episunagōgē*, akin to No. 1, *Note*, "an assembling together", is used in 2 Thess. 2:1, of the rapture of the saints into the air to meet the Lord, "our gathering together"; in Heb. 10:25, of the "gatherings" of believers on earth during the present period. See GATHERING.

ASSEMBLY

1. *ekklesia* (ἐκκλησία, 1577), from *ek*, "out of," and *klēsis*, "a calling" (*kaleō*, "to call"), was used among the Greeks of a body of citizens "gathered" to discuss the affairs of state, Acts 19:39. In the Sept. it is used to designate the "gathering" of Israel, summoned for any definite purpose, or a "gathering" regarded as representative of the whole nation. In Acts 7:38 it is used of Israel; in 19:32, 41, of a riotous mob. It has two applications to companies of Christians, (*a*) to the whole company of the redeemed throughout the present era, the company of which Christ said, "I will build My Church," Matt. 16:18, and which is further described as "the Church which is His Body," Eph. 1:22; 5:23, (*b*) in the singular number (e.g., Matt. 18:17, RV marg., "congregation"), to a company consisting of professed believers, e.g., Acts 20:28; 1 Cor. 1:2; Gal. 1:13; 1 Thess. 1:1;

2 Thess. 1:1; 1 Tim. 3:5, and in the plural, with reference to churches in a district.

There is an apparent exception in the RV of Acts 9:31, where, while the KJV has "churches," the singular seems to point to a district; but the reference is clearly to the church as it was in Jerusalem, from which it had just been scattered, 8:1. Again, in Rom. 16:23, that Gaius was the host of "the whole church," simply suggests that the "assembly" in Corinth had been accustomed to meet in his house, where also Paul was entertained. See CHURCH.

2. *panēguris* (πανήγυρις, 3831), from *pan*, "all," and *agora*, "any kind of assembly," denoted, among the Greeks, an assembly of the people in contrast to the council of national leaders, or a "gathering" of the people in honor of a god, or for some public festival, such as the Olympic games. The word is used in Heb. 12:23, coupled with the word "church," as applied to all believers who form the body of Christ.¶

3. *plēthos* (πλῆθος, 4128), "a multitude, the whole number," is translated "assembly" in Acts 23:7, RV. See BUNDLE, COMPANY, MULTITUDE.

Note: For *sunagōgē*, see ASSEMBLE, *Note* (2).

For **ASSENT** see **AGREE**, No. 2

For **ASSIST** see **HELP**, B, *Note*

ASSURANCE, ASSURE, ASSUREDLY

A. Nouns.

1. *pistis* (πίστις, 4102), "faith," has the secondary meaning of "an assurance or guarantee," e.g., Acts 17:31; by raising Christ from the dead, God has given "assurance" that the world will be judged by Him (the KJV margin, "offered faith" does not express the meaning). Cf. 1 Tim. 5:12, where "faith" means "pledge." See BELIEF, FAITH, FIDELITY.

2. *plērophoria* (πληροφορία, 4136), "a fullness, abundance," also means "full assurance, entire confidence"; lit., a "full-carrying" (*plēros*, "full," *pherō*, "to carry"). Some explain it as full fruitfulness (cf. RV, "fullness" in Heb. 6:11). In 1 Thess. 1:5 it describes the willingness and freedom of spirit enjoyed by those who brought the gospel to Thessalonica; in Col. 2:2, the freedom of mind and confidence resulting from an understanding in Christ; in Heb. 6:11 (KJV, "full assurance," RV, "fullness"), the engrossing effect of the expectation of the fulfillment of God's promises; in Heb. 10:22, the character of

the faith by which we are to draw near to God. See FULLNESS.¶

3. *hupostasis* (ὑπόστασις, 5287), lit., "a standing under, support" (*hupo*, "under," *histēmi*, "to stand"), hence, an "assurance," is so rendered in Heb. 11:1, RV, for KJV, "substance." It here may signify a title-deed, as giving a guarantee, or reality. See CONFIDENCE, PERSON, SUBSTANCE.

Note: In Acts 16:10, for the KJV (of *sumbibazomai*), "assuredly gathering," see CONCLUDE.

B. Verbs.

1. *pistoō* (πιστόω, 4104), "to trust or give assurance to" (cf. A, No. 1), has a secondary meaning, in the passive voice, "to be assured of," 2 Tim. 3:14.¶

2. *plērophoreō* (πληροφορέω, 4135), akin to A, No. 2, "to bring in full measure, to fulfill," also signifies "to be fully assured," Rom. 4:21, RV, of Abraham's faith. In 14:5 it is said of the apprehension of the will of God. So in Col. 4:12 in the best mss. In these three places it is used subjectively, with reference to an effect upon the mind. For its other and objective use, referring to things external, see FULFILL; see also BELIEVE, KNOW, PERSUADE, PROOF.¶ In the Sept., Eccl. 8:11.¶

3. *peithō* (πείθω, 3782), "to persuade," is rendered "assure" in 1 John 3:19 (marg., "persuade"), where the meaning is that of confidence toward God consequent upon loving in deed and in truth. See BELIEVE, CONFIDENCE, FRIEND, OBEY, PERSUADE, TRUST, YIELD.

C. Adverb.

asphalōs (ἀσφαλῶς, 806) means (*a*) "safely," Mark 14:44; Acts 16:23; (*b*) "assuredly," Acts 2:36; the knowledge there enjoined involves freedom from fear of contradiction, with an intimation of the impossibility of escape from the effects. See SAFELY.

For **ASTONISH** and **ASTONISHMENT** see **AMAZE** and **AMAZEMENT**

For **ASTRAY** see **ERR**

For **ASUNDER** see **BREAK, BURST, CUT, PART, PUT, REND**, and **SAW**

For **AT** see *Note* †, p. 1

For **ATHIRST** see **THIRST**

ATONEMENT

katallagē (καταλλαγή, 2643), translated "atonement" in the KJV of Rom. 5:11, signifies, not "atonement," but "reconciliation," as in the RV. See also Rom. 11:15; 2 Cor. 5:18–19.¶ So with the corresponding verb *katallassō*, see under RECONCILE. "Atonement" (the explanation of this English word as being "at-one-ment" is entirely fanciful) is frequently found in the OT. See, for instance, Leviticus, chapters 16 and 17. The corresponding NT words are *hilasmos*, "propitiation," 1 John 2:2; 4:10, and *hilastērion*, Rom. 3:25; Heb. 9:5, "mercy-seat," the covering of the ark of the covenant. These describe the means (in and through the person and work of the Lord Jesus Christ, in His death on the cross by the shedding of His blood in His vicarious sacrifice for sin) by which God shows mercy to sinners. See PROPITIATION.

ATTAIN

1. *katantaō* (καταντάω, 2658), a strengthened form of *antaō*, "to come opposite to," signifies "to reach, to arrive at." It is used in its local significance several times in the Acts, e.g., 27:12, RV, "could reach."

In its metaphorical sense of "attaining" to something it is used in three places: Acts 26:7, of the fulfillment of the promise of God made to the ancestors of Israel, to which promise the twelve tribes "hope to attain" (RV); in Eph. 4:13, of "attaining" to the unity of the faith and of the knowledge of the Son of God; in Phil. 3:11, of the paramount aims of the apostle's life, "if by any means," he says, "I might attain unto the resurrection from the dead," not the physical resurrection, which is assured to all believers hereafter, but to the present life of identification with Christ in His resurrection. For the metaphorical sense in 1 Cor. 10:11 and 14:36, see ARRIVE, A, No. 1. See also COME, No. 28.

2. *katalambanō* (καταλαμβάνω, 2638), "to seize, to apprehend," whether physically or mentally, is rendered "attain" in the sense of making something one's own, appropriating a thing, Rom. 9:30, said of the Gentiles, who through the gospel have "attained" to, or laid hold of, the righteousness which is of faith, in contrast to the present condition of Israel; in 1 Cor. 9:24, of securing a prize, RV, "attain," for KJV, "obtain." See APPREHEND.

3. *phthanō* (φθάνω, 5348), "to anticipate," also means "to reach, attain to a thing"; negatively of Israel (see ARRIVE, No. 5). The only other passage where it has this significance is Phil. 3:16, "we have attained." See COME, PREVENT.

4. *tunchanō* (τυγχάνω, 5177), "to reach, meet with," signifies "to attain to," in Luke 20:35, RV (for KJV, "obtain"). See CHANCE, ENJOY, OBTAIN.

Notes: (1) *Parakoloutheō*, rendered "attained" in 1 Tim. 4:6, KJV (RV, "hast followed"), does not signify attainment, but "following fully." It is an intensive form of *akoloutheō*, "to follow." So in 2 Tim. 3:10, RV, "didst follow" (KJV, "fully known"); "follow fully" would be suitable. In Mark 16:17 it is translated "follow"; in Luke 1:3, "having traced" (RV). See FOLLOW, KNOW, *Notes* (1), UNDERSTAND.¶

(2) *Lambanō*, incorrectly translated "attained" in the KJV of Phil. 3:12, means "obtained" (RV).

ATTEND, ATTENDANCE, ATTENDANT

A. Verbs.

1. *prosechō* (προσέχω, 4337), "to take heed, give heed," is said of the priests who "gave attendance at the altar," Heb. 7:13. It suggests devotion of thought and effort to a thing. In 1 Tim. 4:13 (in the exhortation regarding the public reading of the Scriptures), the RV translates it "give heed," for the KJV, "give attendance." In Acts 16:14, "to give heed" (for KJV, "attended"). See BEWARE, GIVE, No. 17, REGARD.

2. *proskstereō* (προσκαρτερέω, 4342), "to be steadfast," a strengthened form of *kartereō* (*pros*, "towards," intensive, *karteros*, "strong"), denotes to continue steadfastly in a thing and give unremitting care to it, e.g., Rom. 13:6, of rulers in the discharge of their functions. See CONTINUE, WAIT. In the Sept., Num. 13:21.¶

B. Adjective.

euparedros (εὐπάρεδρος, 2145v), lit., "sitting well beside" (*eu*, "well," *para*, "beside," *hedra*, "a seat"), i.e., sitting constantly by, and so applying oneself diligently to, anything, is used in 1 Cor. 7:35, with *pros*, "upon," "that ye may attend upon." Some mss. have *euprosedron*.¶

C. Noun.

hupēretēs (ὑπηρέτης, 5257), lit., "an underrower"; hence, "a servant," is rendered "attendant" in Luke 4:20 and Acts 13:5, RV. See MINISTER, OFFICER, SERVANT.

For **ATTENTIVE,** in the KJV of Luke 19:48, see **HANG,** No. 2

For **AUDIENCE** see **HEARING,** A, No. 1, B, No. 1

AUGHT

aught: See †, page 1. It is wrongly spelled "ought" in the KJV in some places, e.g., in John

4:33, "ought to eat" (there is no word in the original there for "ought").

AUSTERE

austēros (αὐστηρός, 840), akin to *auō*, "to dry up" (Eng., "austere"), primarily denotes "stringent to the taste," like new wine not matured by age, unripe fruit, etc.; hence, "harsh, severe," Luke 19:21–22.¶

Note: Synonymous with *austēros*, but to be distinguished from it, is *sklēros* (from *skellō*, "to be dry"). It was applied to that which lacks moisture, and so is rough and disageeable to the touch, and hence came to denote "harsh, stern, hard." It is used by Matthew to describe the unprofitable servant's remark concerning his master, in the parable corresponding to that in Luke 19 (see *austēros*, above). *Austēros* is derived from a word having to do with the taste, *sklēros*, "with the touch." *Austēros* is not necessarily a term of reproach, whereas *sklēros* is always so, and indicates a harsh, even inhuman, character. *Austēros* is "rather the exaggeration of a virtue pushed too far, than an absolute vice" (Trench, *Syn.* § xiv). *Sklēros* is used of the character of a man, Matt. 25:24; of a saying, John 6:60; of the difficulty and pain of kicking against the ox-goads, Acts 9:5; 26:14; of rough winds, Jas. 3:4 and of harsh speeches, Jude 15. See FIERCE, HARD.¶ Cf. *sklērotēs*, "hardness," *sklērunō*, "to harden," *sklērokardia*, "hardness of heart," and *sklērotrachēlos*, "stiff-necked."

AUTHOR

1. *aitios* (αἴτιος, 159), an adjective (cf. *aitia*, a cause), denotes "that which causes something." This and No. 2 are both translated "author" in Hebrews. *Aitios*, in Heb. 5:9, describes Christ as the "Author of eternal salvation unto all them that obey Him," signifying that Christ, exalted and glorified as our High Priest, on the ground of His finished work on earth, has become the personal mediating cause (RV, margin) of eternal salvation. It is difficult to find an adequate English equivalent to express the meaning here. Christ is not the merely formal cause of our salvation. He is the concrete and active cause of it. He has not merely caused or effected it, He is, as His name, "Jesus," implies, our salvation itself, Luke 2:30; 3:6.

2. *archēgos* (ἀρχηγός, 747), translated "Prince" in Acts 3:15 (marg., "Author") and 5:31, but "Author" in Heb. 2:10, RV, "Captain," RV marg., and KJV, and "Author" in 12:2, primarily signifies "one who takes a lead in, or provides the first occasion of, anything." In the Sept. it is used of the chief of a tribe or family, Num. 13:2 (RV, prince); of the "heads" of the

children of Israel, v. 3; a captain of the whole people, 14:4; in Micah 1:13, of Lachish as the leader of the sin of the daughter of Sion: there, as in Heb. 2:10, the word suggests a combination of the meaning of leader with that of the source from whence a thing proceeds. That Christ is the Prince of life signifies, as Chrysostom says, that "the life He had was not from another; the Prince or Author of life must be He who has life from Himself." But the word does not necessarily combine the idea of the source or originating cause with that of leader. In Heb. 12:2 where Christ is called the "Author and Perfecter of faith," He is represented as the one who takes precedence in faith and is thus the perfect exemplar of it. The pronoun "our" does not correspond to anything in the original, and may well be omitted. Christ in the days of His flesh trod undeviatingly the path of faith, and as the Perfecter has brought it to a perfect end in His own person. Thus He is the leader of all others who tread that path. See PRINCE.¶

Note: In 1 Cor. 14:33, the KJV, "the author," represents no word in the original; RV "a God of."

AUTHORITY

A. Nouns.

1. *exousia* (ἐξουσία, 1849) denotes "authority" (from the impersonal verb *exesti*, "it is lawful"). From the meaning of "leave or permission," or liberty of doing as one pleases, it passed to that of "the ability or strength with which one is endued," then to that of the "power of authority," the right to exercise power, e.g., Matt. 9:6; 21:23; 2 Cor. 10:8; or "the power of rule or government," the power of one whose will and commands must be obeyed by others, e.g., Matt. 28:18; John 17:2; Jude 25; Rev. 12:10; 17:13; more specifically of apostolic "authority," 2 Cor. 10:8; 13:10; the "power" of judicial decision, John 19:10; of "managing domestic affairs," Mark 13:34. By metonymy, or name-change (the substitution of a suggestive word for the name of the thing meant), it stands for "that which is subject to authority or rule," Luke 4:6 (RV, "authority," for the KJV "power"); or, as with the English "authority," "one who possesses authority, a ruler, magistrate," Rom. 13:1–3; Luke 12:11; Titus 3:1; or "a spiritual potentate," e.g., Eph. 3:10; 6:12; Col. 1:16; 2:10, 15; 1 Pet. 3:22. The RV usually translates it "authority."

In 1 Cor. 11:10 it is used of the veil with which a woman is required to cover herself in an assembly or church, as a sign of the Lord's "authority" over the church. See JURISDICTION, LIBERTY, POWER, RIGHT, STRENGTH.

2. *epitagē* (ἐπιταγή, 2003), an injunction (from *epi*, "upon," *tassō*, "to order"), is once rendered "authority," Titus 2:15 (RV marg., "commandment"). See COMMANDMENT.

Note: The corresponding verb is *epitassō*, "to command." See COMMAND.

3. *huperochē* (ὑπεροχή, 5247), primarily, "a projection, eminence," as a mountain peak, hence, metaphorically, "pre-eminence, superiority, excellency," is once rendered "authority," 1 Tim. 2:2, KJV (marg., "eminent place"), RV, "high place," of the position of magistrates; in 1 Cor. 2:1, "excellency" (of speech). Cf. *huperechō*, "to surpass." See EXCELLENCY.¶

4. *dunastēs* (δυνάστης, 1413), akin to *dunamis*, "power," (Eng., "dynasty,") signifies "a potentate, a high officer"; in Acts 8:27, of a high officer, it is rendered "of great authority"; in Luke 1:52, RV, "princes," (KJV, "the mighty"); in 1 Tim 6:15 it is said of God ("Potentate"). See MIGHTY, POTENTATE.¶

B. Verbs.

1. *exousiazō* (ἐξουσιάζω, 1850), akin to A, No. 1, signifies "to exercise power," Luke 22:25; 1 Cor. 6:12; 7:4 (twice). See POWER.¶

2. *katexousiazō* (κατεξουσιάζω, 2175), *kata*, "down," intensive, and No. 1, "to exercise authority upon," is used in Matt. 20:25, and Mark 10:42.¶

3. *authenteō* (αὐθεντέω, 831), from *autos*, "self," and a lost noun *hentēs*, probably signifying working (Eng., "authentic"), "to exercise authority on one's own account, to domineer over," is used in 1 Tim. 2:12, KJV, "to usurp authority," RV, "to have dominion." In the earlier usage of the word it signified one who with his own hand killed either others or himself. Later it came to denote one who acts on his own "authority"; hence, "to exercise authority, dominion." See DOMINION, *Note.*¶

AUTUMN

phthinopōrinos (φθινοπωρινός, 5352), an adjective signifying autumnal (from *phthinopōron*, "late autumn," from *phthinō*, "to waste away," or "wane," and *opōra*, "autumn"), is used in Jude 12, where unfruitful and worthless men are figuratively described as trees such as they are at the close of "autumn," fruitless and leafless (KJV, "trees whose fruit withereth").¶

AVAIL

ischuō (ἰσχύω, 2480) signifies (*a*) "to be strong in body, to be robust, in sound health," Matt. 9:12; Mark 2:17; (*b*) "to have power," as of the gospel, Acts 19:20; to prevail against, said of spiritual enemies, Rev. 12:8; of an evil spirit against exorcists, Acts 19:16; (*c*) "to be of force, to be effective, capable of producing results," Matt. 5:13 ("it is good for nothing"; lit., "it availeth nothing"); Gal. 5:6; in Heb. 9:17 it apparently has the meaning "to be valid" (RV, "for doth it ever avail . . .?", for KJV, "it is of no strength"). It is translated "avail" with reference to prayer, in Jas. 5:16; cf. the strengthened form *exischuō* in Eph. 3:18. See ABLE, CAN, GOOD, MAY, PREVAIL, STRENGTH, WHOLE, WORK.

AVENGE, AVENGER

A. Verb.

ekdikeō (ἐκδικέω, 1556), *ek*, "from," *dikē*, "justice," i.e., that which proceeds from justice, means (*a*) "to vindicate a person's right," (*b*) "to avenge a thing." With the meaning (*a*), it is used in the parable of the unjust judge, Luke 18:3, 5, of the "vindication" of the rights of the widow; with the meaning (*b*) it is used in Rev. 6:10 and 19:2, of the act of God in "avenging" the blood of the saints; in 2 Cor. 10:6, of the apostle's readiness to use his apostolic authority in punishing disobedience on the part of his readers; here the RV substitutes "avenge" for the KJV, "revenge"; in Rom. 12:19 of "avenging" oneself, against which the believer is warned.¶

Note: In Rev. 18:20, the KJV mistranslates *krinō* and *krima* "hath avenged you"; RV, "hath judged your judgment."

B. Nouns.

1. *ekdikos* (ἔκδικος, 1558), primarily, "without law," then, "one who exacts a penalty from a person, an avenger, a punisher," is used in Rom. 13:4 of a civil authority in the discharge of his function of executing wrath on the evildoer (KJV, wrongly, "revenger"); in 1 Thess. 4:6, of God as the avenger of the one who wrongs his brother, here particularly in the matter of adultery.¶

2. *ekdikēsis* (ἐκδίκησις, 1557), "vengeance," is used with the verb *poieō*, "to make," i.e., to avenge, in Luke 18:7-8; Acts 7:24; twice it is used in statements that "vengeance" belongs to God, Rom. 12:19; Heb. 10:30. In 2 Thess. 1:8 it is said of the act of divine justice which will be meted out to those who know not God and obey not the gospel, when the Lord comes in flaming fire at His second advent. In the divine exercise of judgment there is no element of vindictiveness, nothing by way of taking revenge. In Luke 21:22, it is used of the "days of vengeance" upon the Jewish people; in 1 Pet. 2:14, of civil governors as those who are sent of God "for vengeance on evildoers" (KJV, "punishment"); in 2 Cor. 7:11, of the "self-avenging" of believers, in their godly sorrow for wrong doing, RV, "avenging," for KJV, "revenge." See PUNISHMENT, VENGEANCE.¶

AVOID

1. *ekklinō* (ἐκκλίνω, 1578), "to turn away from, to turn aside," lit., "to bend out of" (*ek*, "out," *klinō*, "to bend"), is used in Rom. 3:12, of the sinful condition of mankind, KJV, "gone out of the way," RV, "turned aside"; in Rom. 16:17, of turning away from those who cause offenses and occasions of stumbling (KJV, "avoid"); in 1 Pet. 3:11 of turning away from evil (KJV, "eschew"). See ESCHEW, WAY.¶

2. *ektrepō* (ἐκτρέπω, 1624), lit., "to turn or twist out," is used in the passive voice in Heb. 12:13, "that which is lame be not turned out of the way" (or rather, "put out of joint"); in the sense of the middle voice (though passive in form) of turning aside, or turning away from, 2 Tim. 4:4 (KJV, "shall be turned unto fables," RV, "shall turn aside"); in 1 Tim. 1:6, of those who, having swerved from the faith, have turned aside unto vain talking; in 5:15, of those who have turned aside after Satan; in 6:20, RV, of "turning away from (KJV, 'avoiding') profane babblings and oppositions of the knowledge which is falsely so called." See TURN. In the Sept., Amos 5:8.¶

3. *paraiteomai* (παραιτέομαι, 3868), lit., "to ask aside" (*para*, "aside," *aiteō*, "to ask"), signifies (*a*) "to beg of (or from) another," Mark 15:6, in the most authentic mss.; (*b*) "to deprecate," (1) "to entreat (that) not," Heb. 12:19; (2) "to refuse, decline, avoid," 1 Tim. 4:7; 5:11; 2 Tim. 2:23; Titus 3:10 (see No. 4 for v. 9); Heb. 12:25; (*c*) "to beg off, ask to be excused," Luke 14:18–19 (some would put Heb. 12:25 here). See EXCUSE, INTREAT, REFUSE, REJECT.¶

4. *periistēmi* (περιΐστημι, 4026), in the active voice, means "to stand around" (*peri*, "around," *histēmi*, "to stand"), John 11:42; Acts 25:7; in the middle voice, "to turn oneself about," for the purpose of avoiding something, "to avoid, shun," said of profane babblings, 2 Tim. 2:16; of foolish questions, genealogies, strife, etc., Titus 3:9 (KJV, "avoid"). See SHUN, STAND.¶

5. *stellō* (στέλλω, 4724), "to place," sometimes signifies, in the middle voice, "to take care against a thing, to avoid," 2 Cor. 8:20; in 2 Thess. 3:6, "of withdrawing from a person." See WITHDRAW.¶

For AWAIT (KJV of Acts 9:24; 20:3, 19; 23:30) see PLOT

AWAKE

1. *egeirō* (ἐγείρω, 1453) is used, (*a*) in the active voice, of "arousing a person from sleep"; in Matt. 8:25 of the act of the disciples in awaking the Lord; in Acts 12:7, of the awaking of Peter, RV, "awake him"; (*b*) in the passive voice, with a middle significance, of the virgins, in "arousing themselves" from their slumber, Matt. 25:7; in Rom. 13:11, and Eph. 5:14, metaphorically, "of awaking from a state of moral sloth." See ARISE, LIFT, RAISE, REAR, RISE, STAND, TAKE.

2. *diegeirō* (διεγείρω, 1326) is used of "awaking from natural sleep," Matt. 1:24; Mark 4:38; of the act of the disciples in "awaking" the Lord, Luke 8:24 (cf. *egeirō*, in Matt. 8:25); metaphorically, "of arousing the mind," 2 Pet. 1:13; 3:1. See ARISE, RAISE, STIR UP.

3. *eknēphō* (ἐκνήφω, 1594), primarily, "to return to one's sense from drunkenness, to become sober," is so used in the Sept., e.g., Gen. 9:24; metaphorically, in Joel 1:5; Hab. 2:7; lit., in 2:19, of the words of an idolater to an image; in the NT in 1 Cor. 15:34, "Awake up righteously and sin not" (RV), suggesting a return to soberness of mind from the stupor consequent upon the influence of evil doctrine.¶

4. *exupnizō* (ἐξυπνίζω, 1852), from *ek*, "out of," and *hupnos*, "sleep," "to rouse a person out of sleep," is used metaphorically, in John 11:11.¶

5. *diagrēgoreō* (διαγρηγορέω, 1235), *dia*, intensive, *grēgoreō*, "to watch," is used in Luke 9:32, RV, "were fully awake." KJV "were awake."¶

For AWARE see KNOW, A, No. 1, end of 1st par.

AWAY

Note: This word is to be taken in connection with various verbs. The verb *airō*, "to seize, to lift up, take away," is translated "away with," in Luke 23:18; John 19:15; Acts 21:36; 22:22, implying a forcible removal for the purpose of putting to death. See BEAR, No. 9.

AWE

deos (δέος, 5399d), "awe," is so rendered in Heb. 12:28, RV; the previous word "reverence" represents the inferior reading *aidōs* (see SHAMEFASTNESS).

AXE

axinē (ἀξίνη, 513), "an axe," akin to *agnumi*, "to break," is found in Matt. 3:10, and Luke 3:9.¶

B

BABBLER, BABBLINGS

1. *spermologos* (σπερμολόγος, 4691), "a babbler," is used in Acts 17:18. Primarily an adjective, it came to be used as a noun signifying a crow, or some other bird, picking up seeds (*sperma*, "a seed," *legō*, "to collect"). Then it seems to have been used of a man accustomed to hang about the streets and markets, picking up scraps which fall from loads; hence a parasite, who lives at the expense of others, a hanger on.

Metaphorically it became used of a man who picks up scraps of information and retails them secondhand, a plagiarist, or of those who make a show, in unscientific style, of knowledge obtained from misunderstanding lectures. Prof. Ramsay points out that there does not seem to be any instance of the classical use of the word as a "babbler" or a mere talker. He finds in the word a piece of Athenian slang, applied to one who was outside any literary circle, an ignorant plagiarist. Other suggestions have been made, but without satisfactory evidence.¶

2. *kenophōnia* (κενοφωνία, 2757), "babbling" (from *kenos*, "empty," and *phonē*, "a sound"), signifies empty discussion, discussion on useless subjects, 1 Tim. 6:20 and 2 Tim. 2:16.¶

BABE

1. *brephos* (βρέφος, 1025) denotes (*a*) "an unborn child," as in Luke 1:41, 44; (*b*) "a newborn child, or an infant still older," Luke 2:12, 16; 18:15; Acts 7:19; 2 Tim. 3:15; 1 Pet. 2:2. See CHILD, INFANT.¶

2. *nēpios* (νήπιος, 3516), lit., "without the power of speech," denotes "a little child," the literal meaning having been lost in the general use of the word. It is used (*a*) of "infants," Matt. 21:16; (*b*) metaphorically, of the unsophisticated in mind and trustful in disposition, Matt. 11:25 and Luke 10:21, where it stands in contrast to the wise; of those who are possessed merely of natural knowledge, Rom. 2:20; of those who are carnal, and have not grown, as they should have done, in spiritual understanding and power, the spiritually immature, 1 Cor. 3:1, those who are so to speak partakers of milk, and "without experience of the word of righteousness," Heb. 5:13; of the Jews, who, while the Law was in force, were in a state corresponding to that of childhood, or minority, just as the word "infant" is used of a minor, in

English law, Gal. 4:3, "children"; of believers in an immature condition, impressionable and liable to be imposed upon instead of being in a state of spiritual maturity, Eph. 4:14, "children." "Immaturity" is always associated with this word. See CHILD, No. 7¶

Note: The corresponding verb, *nēpiazō*, is found in 1 Cor. 14:20, where believers are exhorted to be as "babes" (RV) in malice, unable to think or speak maliciously.¶

BACK (Noun)

nōtos (νῶτος, 3577), "the back," is derived from a root *nō*—, signifying "to bend, curve." It is used in Rom. 11:10.¶

BACK (Adverb), BACKSIDE, BACKWARD

1. *opisō* (ὀπίσω, 3694), connected with *hepomai*, "to follow," is used adverbially, of place, with the meaning "back," "backward," in the phrase *eis ta opisō*, lit., "unto the things behind," in Mark 13:16; Luke 9:62; 17:31; John 6:66; 18:6; 20:14. Cf. Phil. 3:13, "the things which are behind." See BEHIND.

2. *opisthen* (ὄπισθεν, 3693), "of place, behind, after," is rendered "backside" in Rev. 5:1, KJV (RV, "back"). See BEHIND.

BACKBITER, BACKBITING

katalalos (κατάλαλος, 2637), a "backbiter," and *katalalia* (καταλαλία, 2636), "backbiting," are formed from *kata*, "against," and *laleō*, "to speak." *Katalalos* is used in Rom. 1:30.¶ *Katalalia* is translated "evil speaking" in 1 Pet. 2:1, "backbiting" in 2 Cor. 12:20.¶

Note: The corresponding verb *katalaleō* the RV translates "speak against," in its five occurrences, Jas. 4:11 (three times); 1 Pet. 2:12, and 3:16; KJV, "speak evil," in all the passages except 1 Pet. 2:12.¶

For BADE see BID

BAD

1. *kakos* (κακός, 2556) indicates the lack in a person or thing of those qualities which should be possessed; it means "bad in character" (*a*) morally, by way of thinking, feeling or acting, e.g., Mark 7:21, "thoughts"; 1 Cor. 15:33, "company"; Col. 3:5, "desire"; 1 Tim. 6:10, "all kinds of evil"; 1 Pet. 3:9, "evil for evil"; (*b*) in the sense of what is injurious or

baneful, e.g., the tongue as "a restless evil," Jas. 3:8; "evil beasts," Titus 1:12; "harm," Acts 16:28; once it is translated "bad," 2 Cor. 5:10. It is the opposite of *agathos*, "good." See EVIL, HARM, ILL, NOISOME, WICKED.

2. *ponēros* (πονηρός, 4190), connected with *ponos*, "labor," expresses especially the "active form of evil," and is practically the same in meaning as (*b*), under No. 1. It is used, e.g., of thoughts, Matt. 15:19 (cf. *kakos*, in Mark 7:21); of speech, Matt. 5:11 (cf. *kakos*, in 1 Pet. 3:10); of acts, 2 Tim. 4:18. Where *kakos* and *ponēros* are put together, *kakos* is always put first and signifies "bad in character, base," *ponēros*, "bad in effect, malignant": see 1 Cor. 5:8, and Rev. 16:2. *Kakos* has a wider meaning, *ponēros* a stronger meaning. *Ponēros* alone is used of Satan and might well be translated "the malignant one," e.g., Matt. 5:37 and five times in 1 John (2:13–14; 3:12; 5:18–19, RV); of demons, e.g., Luke 7:21. Once it is translated "bad," Matt. 22:10. See EVIL, GRIEVOUS, HARM, LEWD, MALICIOUS, WICKED.

3. *sapros* (σαπρός, 4550), "corrupt, rotten" (akin to *sēpō*, "to rot"), primarily, of vegetable and animal substances, expresses what is of poor quality, unfit for use, putrid. It is said of a tree and its fruit, Matt. 7:17–18; 12:33; Luke 6:43; of certain fish, Matt. 13:48 (here translated "bad"); of defiling speech, Eph. 4:29. See CORRUPT.¶

BAG

1. *glōssokomon* (γλωσσόκομον, 1101), from *glōssa*, "a tongue," and *komeō*, "to tend," was, firstly, "a case" in which to keep the mouthpiece of wind instruments; secondly, "a small box" for any purpose, but especially a "casket or purse," to keep money in. It is used of the "bag" which Judas carried, John 12:6; 13:29; in the Sept. of 2 Chron. 24:8, 10, used of the "box" appointed by King Joash for offerings for the repair of the Temple.¶

2. *ballantion* (βαλλάντιον, 905), from *ballō*, "to cast," "a money-box or purse," is found in Luke's gospel, four times, 10:4; 12:33 (KJV, "bag"); 22:35–36. See PURSE.¶

Note: *Zōnē*, "a girdle or belt," also served as "a purse for money," Matt. 10:9; Mark 6:8. See GIRDLE.

BAGGAGE

episkeuazō (ἐπισκευάζω, 643v), "to furnish with things necessary"; in the middle voice, "to furnish for oneself"; it was used of equipping baggage animals for a journey; in Acts 21:15, RV, it is translated "we took up our baggage" (KJV, "we took up our carriages"). The form is

the 1st aorist participle, and lit. means "having made ready (the things that were necessary for the journey)."¶

Note: Some mss. have the verb *aposkeuazō*, which has the same meaning.

BALANCE

zugos (ζυγός, 2218), "a yoke," also has the meaning of "a pair of scales," Rev. 6:5. So the Sept. of Lev. 19:36; Isa. 40:12. See YOKE.¶

BAND

1. *speira* (σπεῖρα, 4686), primarily "anything round," and so "whatever might be wrapped round a thing, a twisted rope," came to mean "a body of men at arms," and was the equivalent of the Roman *manipulus*. It was also used for a larger body of men, a cohort, about 600 infantry, commanded by a tribune. It is confined to its military sense. See, e.g., Matt. 27:27, and corresponding passages.

2. *desmos* (δεσμός, 1199), "a band, fetter, anything for tying" (from *deō*, "to bind, fasten with chains, etc."), is sometimes translated "band," sometimes "bond"; "bands," in Luke 8:29; Acts 16:26; 22:30, KJV only. In the case of the deaf man who had an impediment in his speech, whom the Lord took aside, Mark 7:35, the KJV says "the string of his tongue was loosed"; the RV, more literally, "the bond of his tongue." See BOND, CHAIN, STRING.

3. *sundesmos* (σύνδεσμος, 4886), an intensive form of No. 2, denoting "that which binds firmly together," is used metaphorically of the joints and bands of the mystic body of Christ, Col. 2:19; otherwise in the following phrases, "the bond of iniquity," Acts 8:23; "the bond of peace," Eph. 4:3; "the bond of perfectness," Col. 3:14. See BOND.¶

4. *zeuktēria* (ζευκτηρία, 2202), "a bond" (connected with *zugos*, "a yoke"), is found once, of the rudder band of a ship, Acts 27:40.¶

BANDED

poieō sustrophēn (ποιέω συστροφήν, 4160, 4963), Acts 23:12, of the Jews who "banded together" with the intention of killing Paul, consists of the verb *poieō*, "to make," and the noun *sustrophē*, primarily "a twisting up together, a binding together"; then, "a secret combination, a conspiracy." Accordingly it might be translated "made a conspiracy." The noun is used elsewhere in 19:40. See CONCOURSE.¶

BANK, BANKERS

1. *trapeza* (τράπεζα, 5132), primarily "a table," denotes (*a*) an eating-table, e.g., Matt. 15:27; (*b*) food, etc. placed on "a table," Acts

6:2; 16:34; (c) "a feast, a banquet," 1 Cor. 10:21; (d) "the table or stand" of a money-changer, where he exchanged money for a fee, or dealt with loans and deposits, Matt. 21:12; Mark 11:15; Luke 19:23; John 2:15. See MEAT, TABLE.

2. trapezitēs (τραπεζίτης 5133), a "money-changer, broker, banker"; translated "bankers" in Matt. 25:27, RV (KJV, "exchangers").¶

Note: For charax, Luke 19:43, see TRENCH.

For BANQUETING see CAROUSINGS

BAPTISM, BAPTIST, BAPTIZE

A. Nouns.

1. baptisma (βάπτισμα, 908), "baptism," consisting of the processes of immersion, submersion and emergence (from baptō, "to dip"), is used (a) of John's "baptism," (b) of Christian "baptism," see B. below; (c) of the overwhelming afflictions and judgments to which the Lord voluntarily submitted on the cross, e.g., Luke 12:50; (d) of the sufferings His followers would experience, not of a vicarious character, but in fellowship with the sufferings of their Master. Some mss. have the word in Matt. 20:22–23; it is used in Mark 10:38–39, with this meaning.

2. baptismos (βαπτισμός, 909), as distinct from baptisma (the ordinance), is used of the "ceremonial washing of articles," Mark 7:4, 8, in some texts; Heb. 9:10; once in a general sense, Heb. 6:2.¶ See WASHING.

3. baptistēs (βαπτιστής, 910), "a baptist," is used only of John the Baptist, and only in the Synoptists, 14 times.

B. Verb.

baptizō (βαπτίζω, 907), "to baptize," primarily a frequentative form of baptō, "to dip," was used among the Greeks to signify the dyeing of a garment, or the drawing of water by dipping a vessel into another, etc. Plutarchus uses it of the drawing of wine by dipping the cup into the bowl (Alexis, 67) and Plato, metaphorically, of being overwhelmed with questions (Euthydemus, 277 D).

It is used in the NT in Luke 11:38 of washing oneself (as in 2 Kings 5:14, "dipped himself," Sept.); see also Isa. 21:4, lit., "lawlessness overwhelms me." In the early chapters of the four Gospels and in Acts 1:5; 11:16; 19:4, it is used of the rite performed by John the Baptist who called upon the people to repent that they might receive remission of sins. Those who obeyed came "confessing their sins," thus acknowledging their unfitness to be in the Messiah's coming kingdom. Distinct from this is the "baptism" enjoined by Christ, Matt. 28:19, a "baptism" to be undergone by believers, thus witnessing to their identification with Him in death, burial and resurrection, e.g., Acts 19:5; Rom. 6:3–4; 1 Cor. 1:13–17; 12:13; Gal. 3:27; Col. 2:12. The phrase in Matt. 28:19, "baptizing them into the Name" (RV; cf. Acts 8:16, RV), would indicate that the "baptized" person was closely bound to, or became the property of, the one into whose name he was "baptized."

In Acts 22:16 it is used in the middle voice, in the command given to Saul of Tarsus, "arise and be baptized," the significance of the middle voice form being "get thyself baptized." The experience of those who were in the ark at the time of the Flood was a figure or type of the facts of spiritual death, burial, and resurrection, Christian "baptism" being an antitupon, "a corresponding type," a "like figure," 1 Pet. 3:21. Likewise the nation of Israel was figuratively baptized when made to pass through the Red Sea under the cloud, 1 Cor. 10:2. The verb is used metaphorically also in two distinct senses: firstly, of "baptism" by the Holy Spirit, which took place on the Day of Pentecost; secondly, of the calamity which would come upon the nation of the Jews, a "baptism" of the fire of divine judgment for rejection of the will and word of God, Matt. 3:11; Luke 3:16.

BARBARIAN, BARBAROUS

barbaros (βάρβαρος, 915) properly meant "one whose speech is rude, or harsh"; the word is onomatopoeic, indicating in the sound the uncouth character represented by the repeated syllable "bar-bar." Hence it signified one who speaks a strange or foreign language. See 1 Cor. 14:11. It then came to denote any foreigner ignorant of the Greek language and culture. After the Persian war it acquired the sense of rudeness and brutality. In Acts 28:2, 4, it is used unreproachfully of the inhabitants of Malta, who were of Phoenician origin. So in Rom. 1:14, where it stands in distinction from Greeks, and in implied contrast to both Greeks and Jews. Cf. the contrasts in Col. 3:11, where all such distinctions are shown to be null and void in Christ. "Berber" stood similarly in the language of the Egyptians for all non-Egyptian peoples.¶

BARE (Adjective)

gumnos (γυμνός, 1131), "naked," is once translated "bare," 1 Cor. 15:37, where, used of grain, the meaning is made clearer by translating the phrase by "a bare grain," RV. See NAKED.

For BARE (Verb) see BEAR

BARLEY

A. Noun.

krithē (κριθή, 2915), "barley," is used in the plural in Rev. 6:6.¶

B. Adjective.

krithinos (κρίθινος, 2916) signifies "made of barley," John 6:9, 13.¶

BARN

apothēkē (ἀποθήκη, 596), lit., "a place where anything is stored" (Eng., "apothecary"), hence denoted a garner, granary, barn, Matt. 3:12; 6:26; 13:30; Luke 3:17; 12:18, 24. See also under GARNER.¶

Note: For *tameion*, "a storehouse, store-chamber," more especially "an inner chamber or secret room," Matt. 6:6; 24:26; Luke 12:3, 24, see CHAMBER.¶

BARREN

1. *steiros* (στεῖρος, 4723), from a root *ster*—meaning "hard, firm" (hence Eng., "sterile"), signifies "barren, not bearing children," and is used with the natural significance three times in the Gospel of Luke, 1:7, 36; 23:29; and with a spiritual significance in Gal. 4:27, in a quotation from Isa. 54:1. The circumstances of Sarah and Hagar, which Isaiah no doubt had in mind, are applied by the apostle to the contrast between the works of the Law and the promise by grace.¶

2. *argos* (ἀργός, 692), denoting "idle, barren, yielding no return, because of inactivity," is found in the best mss. in Jas. 2:20 (RV, "barren"); it is rendered "barren" in 2 Pet. 1:8, KJV, (RV, "idle"). In Matt. 12:36, the "idle word" means the word that is thoughtless or profitless. See IDLE, SLOW; cf. *katargeō*, under ABOLISH.

BASE, BASER

1. *agenēs* (ἀγενής, 36), "of low birth" (*a*, negative, *genos*, "family, race"), hence denoted "that which is of no reputation, of no account," 1 Cor. 1:28, "the base things of the world," i.e., those which are of no account or fame in the world's esteem. That the neuter plural of the adjective bears reference to persons is clear from verse 26.¶

2. *tapeinos* (ταπεινός, 5011), primarily "that which is low, and does not rise far from the ground," as in the Sept. of Ezek. 17:24, hence, metaphorically, signifies "lowly, of no degree." So the RV in 2 Cor. 10:1. Cf. Luke 1:52 and Jas. 1:9, "of low degree." Cf. *tapeinophrosunē*, "lowliness of mind," and *tapeinoō*, "to humble." See CAST, *Note* (7), HUMBLE, LOW, LOWLY.

3. *agoraios* (ἀγοραῖος, 60), translated in the KJV of Acts 17:5 "of the baser sort," RV, "of the rabble," signifies, lit., "relating to the market place"; hence, frequenting markets, and so sauntering about idly. It is also used of affairs usually transacted in the market-place, and hence of judicial assemblies, Acts 19:38, RV, "courts" (KJV, "law"); the margin in both RV and KJV has "court days are kept." See COURT.¶

BASKET, BASKETFUL

1. *kophinos* (κόφινος, 2894) was "a wicker basket," originally containing a certain measure of capacity, Matt. 14:20; 16:9; Mark 6:43 (RV, "basketfuls"); 8:19; Luke 9:17; 13:8 in some mss.; John 6:13.¶

2. *spuris* (σπυρίς, 4711), or *sphuris*, signifies "something round, twisted or folded together" (connected with *speira*, "anything rolled into a circle"; Eng., "sphere"); hence a reed basket, plaited, a capacious kind of hamper, sometimes large enough to hold a man, Matt. 15:37; 16:10; Mark 8:8, 20 (RV, "basketfuls"); Acts 9:25.¶

3. *sarganē* (σαργάνη, 4553) denotes (*a*) "a braided rope or band," (*b*) "a large basket made of ropes, or a wicker "basket" made of entwined twigs, 2 Cor. 11:33. That the "basket" in which Paul was let down from a window in Damascus is spoken of by Luke as a *spuris*, and by Paul himself as a *sarganē*, is quite consistent, the two terms being used for the same article. ¶

BASON

niptēr (νιπτήρ, 3537), the vessel into which the Lord poured water to wash the disciples' feet, was "a large ewer," John 13:5. The word is connected with the verb *niptō*, "to wash."¶

BASTARD

nothos (νόθος, 3541) denotes "an illegitimate child, one born out of lawful wedlock," Heb. 12:8.¶

BATHED

louō (λούω, 3068) signifies "to bathe or to wash." In John 13:10 the RV "bathed" is necessary to distinguish the act from the washing of feet. See WASH.

BATTLE

polemos (πόλεμος, 4171), "a war," is incorrectly rendered "battle" in the KJV of 1 Cor. 14:8; Rev. 9:7, 9; 16:14; 20:8; RV, invariably, "war."

BAY

kolpos (κόλπος, 2859), translated "bay" in the RV of Acts 27:39, is wider than a "creek" (KJV). Eng., "gulf," is connected. See BOSOM.

For **BE** see **BEING**

BEACH

aigialos (αἰγιαλός, 123), translated "shore" in the KJV in each place where it is used, Matt. 13:2, 48; John 21:4; Acts 21:5; 27:39–40, is always in the RV translated "beach." It is derived from a root signifying "to press, drive"; *aigis* denotes "a wind-storm."¶

BEAM

dokos (δοκός, 1385), "a beam," is perhaps etymologically connected with the root *dek*—, seen in the word *dechomai*, "to receive," "beams" being received at their ends into walls or pieces of timber. The Lord used it metaphorically, in contrast to a mote, "of a great fault, or vice," Matt. 7:3–5; Luke 6:41–42.¶

BEAR

(*in the sense of "carrying, supporting"*)
For the verb "to bear" in the sense of "begetting," see BEGET.

1. *bastazō* (βαστάζω, 941) signifies "to support as a burden." It is used with the meaning (*a*) "to take up," as in picking up anything, stones, John 10:31; (*b*) "to carry" something, Matt. 3:11; Mark 14:13; Luke 7:14; 22:10; Acts 3:2; 21:35; Rev. 17:7; "to carry" on one's person, Luke 10:4; Gal. 6:17; in one's body, Luke 11:27; "to bear" a name in testimony, Acts 9:15; metaphorically, of a root "bearing" branches, Rom. 11:18; (*c*) "to bear" a burden, whether physically, as of the cross, John 19:17, or metaphorically in respect of sufferings endured in the cause of Christ, Luke 14:27; Rev. 2:3; it is said of physical endurance, Matt. 20:12; of sufferings "borne" on behalf of others, Matt. 8:17; Rom. 15:1; Gal. 6:2; of spiritual truths not able to be "borne," John 16:12; of the refusal to endure evil men, Rev. 2:2; of religious regulations imposed on others, Acts 15:10; of the burden of the sentence of God to be executed in due time, Gal. 5:10; of the effect at the judgment seat of Christ, to be "borne" by the believer for failure in the matter of discharging the obligations of discipleship, Gal. 6:5; (*d*) to "bear" by way of carrying off, John 12:6; 20:15. See CARRY, TAKE.¶

2. *pherō* (φέρω, 5342), "to bring or bear," is translated in the RV by the latter verb in Luke 23:26; John 2:8 (twice); 12:24; 15:2 (twice); Heb. 13:13. See BRING, No. 1 and words there.

3. *anapherō* (ἀναφέρω, 399), No. 2, with *ana*, up, is used of "leading persons up to a higher place," and, in this respect, of the Lord's ascension, Luke 24:51. It is used twice of the Lord's propitiatory sacrifice, in His bearing sins on the cross, Heb. 9:28 and 1 Pet. 2:24; the KJV margin, "to the tree," is to be rejected. The KJV text, "on," and the RV "upon" express the phrase rightly. See BRING, CARRY, LEAD, OFFER.

4. *ekpherō* (ἐκφέρω, 1627), No. 2, with *ek*, "out," is used, literally, "of carrying something forth, or out," e.g., a garment, Luke 15:22; sick folk, Acts 5:15; a corpse, Acts 5:6, 9–10; of the impossibility of "carrying" anything out from this world at death, 1 Tim. 6:7. The most authentic mss. have this word in Mark 8:23, of the blind man, whom the Lord brought out of the village (RV). It is also used of the earth, in "bringing forth" produce, Heb. 6:8. See BRING, CARRY.¶

5. *peripherō* (περιφέρω, 4064), No. 2, with *peri*, "about," signifies "to carry about, or bear about," and is used literally, of carrying the sick, Mark 6:55, or of physical sufferings endured in fellowship with Christ, 2 Cor. 4:10; metaphorically, of being "carried" about by different evil doctrines, Eph. 4:14; Heb. 13:9; Jude 12. See CARRY.

6. *hupopherō* (ὑποφέρω, 5297), lit., "to bear up under," is best rendered by "endure," as 1 Cor. 10:13, RV, of enduring temptations; of "enduring" persecutions, 2 Tim. 3:11; grief, 1 Pet. 2:19. See ENDURE.¶

7. *phoreō* (φορέω, 5409), a frequentative form of *pherō*, is to be distinguished from it as denoting, not a simple act of bearing, but a continuous or habitual condition, e.g., of the civil authority in "bearing" the sword as symbolic of execution, Rom. 13:4; of a natural state of bodily existence in this life, spoken of as "the image of the earthy," and the spiritual body of the believer hereafter, "the image of the heavenly," 1 Cor. 15:49, the word "image" denoting the actual form and not a mere similitude. See WEAR.

8. *tropophoreō* (τροποφορέω, 5159), from *tropos*, "a manner," and *phoreō*, "to endure," is found in Acts 13:18, where some ancient authorities have the verb *trophophoreō*, "He bare them as a nursing father," (from *trophos*, "a feeder, a nurse," and *phoreō*, "to carry").¶

9. *airō* (αἴρω, 142) signifies (*a*) "to raise up, to lift, to take upon oneself and carry what has been raised, physically" (its most frequent use), or as applied to the mind, "to suspend, to keep in suspense," as in John 10:24, lit., "How long doth thou suspend our souls?"; (*b*) "to take away what is attached to anything, to remove," as of Christ, in taking (or "bearing," marg.) away the sin of the world, John 1:29; Christ "was manifested to take away sins," 1 John 3:5, where, not the nature of the Atonement is in

view, but its effect in the believer's life. See
CARRY, DOUBT, No. 6, LIFT, LOOSE, PUT, No. 17,
REMOVE, SUSPENSE, TAKE.

10. *poieō* (ποιέω, 4160), "to do," sometimes
means "to produce, bear," Luke 8:8; 13:9; Jas.
3:12 (KJV, "bear," RV, "yield"); Rev. 22:2. See
COMMIT, DO.

11. *stegō* (στέγω, 4722), primarily "to protect, or preserve by covering," hence means "to
keep off something which threatens, to bear up
against, to hold out against, and so to endure,
bear, forbear," 1 Cor. 9:12. The idea of supporting what is placed upon a thing is prominent in
1 Thess. 3:1, 5 ("forbear"), and 1 Cor. 13:7. See
FORBEAR and SUFFER.¶

12. *anechomai* (ἀνέχομαι, 430) signifies "to
hold up against a thing and so to bear with"
(*ana*, "up," and *echomai*, the middle voice of
echō, "to have, to hold"), e.g., Matt. 17:7; 1 Cor.
4:12; 2 Cor. 11:1, 4, 19–20; Heb. 13:22, etc.
See ENDURE, FORBEAR, SUFFER.

13. *metriopatheō* (μετριοπαθέω, 3356), "to
treat with mildness, or moderation, to bear
gently with" (*metrios*, "moderate," and *paschō*,
"to suffer"), is used in Heb. 5:2 (RV and KJV
marg.). The idea is that of not being unduly
disturbed by the faults and ignorance of others;
or rather perhaps of feeling in some measure, in
contrast to the full feeling with expressed in the
verb *sumpatheō* in 4:15, with reference to Christ
as the High Priest. See COMPASSION, No. 5.¶

14. *makrothumeō* (μακροθυμέω, 3114), "to
be long-tempered" (*makros*, "long," *thumos*,
"temper"), is translated "is longsuffering over"
in Luke 18:7, RV (KJV, "bear long with"). See
PATIENT, SUFFER.

Notes: (1) For "bear (or give) witness, see
WITNESS.

(2) For "bear up into," in Acts 27:15, see
FACE.

(3) In 1 Cor. 10:13 the adjective *anthrōpinos*,
"human" (from *anthrōpos*, "man") is translated
"is common to man," KJV (RV, "man can bear").

(4) For *karpophoreō*, "to bear fruit," e.g.,
Mark 4:20, (*karpos*, "fruit," and No. 7), KJV,
"bring forth," see FRUIT.

(5) In Acts 20:9, RV, *katapherō* is rendered
"borne down." See GIVE. No. 12.

BEAR (animal)

ark(t)os (ἄρκος, 715), "a bear," occurs in
Rev. 13:2.¶

BEAST

1. *zōon* (ζῶον, 2226) primarily denotes "a
living being" (*zōē*, "life"). The Eng., "animal,"
is the equivalent, stressing the fact of life as the
characteristic feature. In Heb. 13:11 the KJV and
the RV translate it "beasts" ("animals" would be
quite suitable). In 2 Pet. 2:12 and Jude 10, the
KJV has "beasts," the RV "creatures." In the
Apocalypse, where the word is found some 20
times, and always of those beings which stand
before the throne of God, who give glory and
honor and thanks to Him, 4:6, and act in perfect
harmony with His counsels, 5:14; 6:1–7, e.g.,
the word "beasts" is most unsuitable; the RV,
"living creatures," should always be used; it
gives to *zōon* its appropriate significance. See
CREATURE.

2. *thērion* (θηρίον, 2342), to be distinguished
from *zōon*, almost invariably denotes "a wild
beast." In Acts 28:4, "venomous beast" is used
of the viper which fastened on Paul's hand.
Zōon stresses the vital element, *thērion* the bestial. The idea of a "beast" of prey is not always
present. Once, in Heb. 12:20, it is used of the
animals in the camp of Israel, such, e.g., as were
appointed for sacrifice: But in the Sept. *thērion*
is never used of sacrificial animals; the word
ktēnos (see below) is reserved for these.

Thērion, in the sense of wild "beast," is used
in the Apocalypse for the two antichristian potentates who are destined to control the affairs
of the nations with Satanic power in the closing
period of the present era, 11:7; 13:1–18; 14:9,
11; 15:2; 16:2, 10, 13; 17:3–17; 19:19–20; 20:4,
10.

3. *ktēnos* (κτῆνος, 2934) primarily denotes
"property" (the connected verb *ktaomai* means
"to possess"); then, "property in flocks and
herds." In Scripture it signifies, (*a*) a "beast" of
burden, Luke 10:34; Acts 23:24, (*b*) "beasts" of
any sort, apart from those signified by *thērion*
(see above), 1 Cor. 15:39; Rev. 18:13, (*c*) animals for slaughter; this meaning is not found in
the NT, but is very frequent in the Sept.¶

4. *tetrapous* (τετράπους, 5074), "a four-
footed beast" (*tetra*, "four," and *pous*, "a foot")
is found in Acts 10:12; 11:6; Rom. 1:23.¶

5. *sphagion* (σφάγιον, 4968), from *sphazō*,
"to slay," denotes "a victim slaughtered for sacrifice, a slain beast," Acts 7:42, in a quotation
from Amos 5:25.¶

BEAT

1. *derō* (δέρω, 1194), from a root *der*—,
"skin" (*derma*, "a skin," cf. Eng., "dermatology"), primarily "to flay," then "to beat, thrash
or smite," is used of the treatment of the servants of the owner of the vineyard by the husbandmen, in the parable in Matt. 21:35; Mark
12:3, 5; Luke 20:10–11; of the treatment of
Christ, Luke 22:63, RV, "beat," for KJV,
"smote"; John 18:23; of the followers of Christ,
in the synagogues, Mark 13:9; Acts 22:19; of

the punishment of unfaithful servants, Luke 12:47–48; of the "beating" of apostles by the High Priest and the Council of the Sanhedrin, Acts 5:40; by magistrates, 16:37. The significance of flogging does not always attach to the word; it is used of the infliction of a single blow, John 18:23; 2 Cor. 11:20, and of "beating" the air, 1 Cor. 9:26. The usual meaning is that of "thrashing or cudgelling," and when used of a blow it indicates one of great violence. See SMITE.¶

2. *tuptō* (τύπτω, 5180), from a root *tup*—, meaning "a blow," (*tupos*, "a figure or print:" (Eng., "type") denotes "to smite, strike, or beat," usually not with the idea of giving a thrashing as with *derō*. It frequently signifies a "blow" of violence, and, when used in a continuous tense, indicates a series of "blows." In Matt. 27:30 the imperfect tense signifies that the soldiers kept on striking Christ on the head. So Mark 15:19. The most authentic mss. omit it in Luke 22:64. In that verse the word *paiō*, "to smite," is used of the treatment given to Christ (*derō* in the preceding verse). The imperfect tense of the verb is again used in Acts 18:17, of the beating given to Sosthenes. Cf. Acts 21:32, which has the present participle. It is used in the metaphorical sense of "wounding," in 1 Cor. 8:12. See SMITE, STRIKE, WOUND.

3. *rhabdizō* (ῥαβδίζω, 4463), "to beat with a rod, or stick, to cudgel," is the verbal form of *rhabdos*, "a rod, or staff," Acts 16:22; 2 Cor. 11:25.¶

4. *ballō* (Βάλλω, 906), "to throw or cast," is once rendered "beat," Acts 27:14 RV, of the tempestuous wind that "beat" down upon the ship. So the KJV margin. See CAST.

5. *epiballō* (ἐπιβάλλω, 1911), No. 4, with *epi*, "upon," "to cast upon, or lay hands upon," signifies to "beat" into, in Mark 4:37, of the action of the waves. See CAST, No. 7, FALL, No. 11, LAY, PUT, No. 8, STRETCH, THINK, No. 15.

6. *proskoptō* (προσκόπτω, 4350), "to stumble, to strike against" (*pros*, "to or against," *koptō*, "to strike"), is once used of a storm "beating" upon a house, Matt. 7:27. See DASH, STUMBLE, and cf. *proskomma* and *proskopē*, "a stumbling-block, offense."

7. *prospiptō* (προσπίπτω, 4363), "to fall upon" (*pros*, "to," *piptō*, "to fall"), is translated "beat" in Matt. 7:25; elsewhere, "to fall down at or before." See FALL.

prosrēgnumi (προσρήγνυμι, 4366), "to break upon," is translated "beat vehemently upon, or against" (*pros*, "upon," *rhēgnumi*, "to break"), in Luke 6:48–49, of the violent action of a flood (RV, "brake").¶

Note: In Luke 10:30, the phrase lit. rendered "inflicting blows," is translated "wounded" (KJV), RV, correctly, "beat."

BEAUTIFUL

1. *hōraios* (ὡραῖος, 5611) describes "that which is seasonable, produced at the right time," as of the prime of life, or the time when anything is at its loveliest and best (from *hōra*, "a season," a period fixed by natural laws and revolutions, and so the best season of the year). It is used of the outward appearance of whited sepulchres in contrast to the corruption within, Matt. 23:27; of the Jerusalem gate called "Beautiful," Acts 3:2, 10; of the feet of those that bring glad tidings, Rom. 10:15.¶

In the Sept. it is very frequent, and especially in Genesis and the Song of Solomon. In Genesis it is said of all the trees in the garden of Eden, 2:9, especially of the tree of the knowledge of good and evil, 3:6; of the countenances of Rebekah, 26:7, Rachel, 29:17 and Joseph, 39:6. It is used five times in the Song of Solomon, 1:16; 2:14; 4:3 and 6:3, 5.

2. *asteios* (ἀστεῖος, 791), connected with *astu*, "a city," was used primarily "of that which befitted the town, town-bred" (corresponding Eng. words are "polite," "polished," connected with *polis*, "a town"; cf. "urbane," from Lat., *urbs*, "a city"). Among Greek writers it is set in contrast to *agroikos*, "rustic," and *aischros*, "base," and was used, e.g., of clothing. It is found in the NT only of Moses, Acts 7:20, "(exceeding) fair," lit., "fair (to God)," and Heb. 11:23, "goodly" (KJV, "proper"). See FAIR, GOODLY, *Note*, PROPER.¶

Notes: (1) In the Sept. it is far less frequent than *hōraios*. It is said of Moses in Ex. 2:2; negatively, of Balaam's procedure in the sight of God, Num. 22:32; of Eglon in Jud. 3:17.

(2) *Asteios* belongs to the realm of art, *hōraios*, to that of nature. *Asteios* is used of that which is "beautiful" because it is elegant; *hōraios* describes that which is "beautiful" because it is, in its season, of natural excellence.

(3) *Kalos*, "good," describes that which is "beautiful" as being well proportioned in all its parts, or intrinsically excellent. See BETTER, FAIR, GOOD, etc.

For BECAME see BECOME

For BECAUSE see *Note* †, p. 1

BECKON

1. *neuō* (νεύω, 3506), lit., "to give a nod, to signify by a nod," is used in John 13:24, of Peter's beckoning to John to ask the Lord of

whom He had been speaking; in Acts 24:10, of the intimation given by Felix to Paul to speak.¶

2. *dianeuō* (διανεύω, 1269), "to express one's meaning by a sign" (No. 1, with *dia*, "through," used intensively), is said of the act of Zacharias, Luke 1:22 (RV, "continued making signs," for KJV, "beckoned"). In Sept., Ps. 35:19, "wink."¶

3. *kataneuō* (κατανεύω, 2656), No. 1, with *kata*, "down," intensive, is used of the fishermen-partners in Luke 5:7, "beckoned."¶

4. *kataseiō* (κατασείω, 2678), lit., "to shake down" (*kata*, "down," *seiō*, "to shake"), of shaking the hand, of waving, expresses a little more vigorously the act of "beckoning," Acts 12:17; 13:16; 19:33; 21:40. *Neuō* and its compounds have primary reference to a movement of the head; *kataseiō*, to that of the hand.¶

BECOME (to be fitting)

A. Verb.

prepō (πρέπω, 4241) means "to be conspicuous among a number, to be eminent, distinguished by a thing," hence, "to be becoming, seemly, fit." The adornment of good works "becometh women professing godliness," 1 Tim. 2:10. Those who minister the truth are to speak "the things which befit the sound doctrine," Titus 2:1. Christ, as a High Priest "became us," Heb. 7:26. In the impersonal sense, it signifies "it is fitting, it becometh," Matt. 3:15; 1 Cor. 11:13; Eph. 5:3; Heb. 2:10. See BEFIT, COMELY.¶

B. Adjective.

hieroprepēs (ἱεροπρεπής, 2412), from *hieros*, "sacred," with the adjectival form of *prepō*, denotes "suited to a sacred character, that which is befitting in persons, actions or things consecrated to God," Titus 2:3, RV, "reverent," KJV, "as becometh holiness," (marg., "holy women"). Trench (*Syn.* § xcii) distinguishes this word from *kosmios*, "modest," and *semnos*, "grave, honorable."¶

Notes: (1) The KJV translates the adverb *axiōs*, "as becometh," in Rom. 16:2; Phil. 1:27 (RV corrects to "worthily" and "worthy").

(2) *Ginomai*, "to become," is mentioned under various other headings.

(3) For "become of no effect," Gal. 5:4, KJV, RV, "severed from," see ABOLISH.

BED

1. *klinē* (κλίνη, 2825), akin to *klinō*, "to lean" (Eng., "recline, incline" etc.), "a bed," e.g., Mark 7:30, also denotes a "couch" for reclining at meals, Mark 4:21, or a "couch" for carrying the sick, Matt. 9:2, 6. The metaphorical phrase "to cast into a bed," Rev. 2:22, sig-

nifies to afflict with disease (or possibly, to lay on a bier). In Mark 7:4 the KJV curiously translates the word "tables" (marg., "beds"), RV, marg. only, "couches." See COUCH.

2. *klinarion* (κλινάριον, 2825*), a diminutive of No. 1, "a small bed," is used in Acts 5:15. Some mss. have *klinon*. See also No. 4. See COUCH.¶

3. *koitē* (κοίτη, 2845), primarily "a place for lying down" (connected with *keimai*, "to lie"), denotes a "bed," Luke 11:7; the marriage "bed," Heb. 13:4; in Rom. 13:13, it is used of sexual intercourse. By metonymy, the cause standing for the effect, it denotes conception, Rom. 9:10.¶

4. *krabbatos* (κράββατος, 2895), a Macedonian word (Lat. *grabatus*), is "a somewhat mean bed, pallet, or mattress for the poor," Mark 2:4, 9, 11–12; 6:55; John 5:8–11; Acts 5:15; 9:33. See also No. 2. See COUCH.¶

Note: The verb *strōnnuō* or *strōnnumi*, "to spread," signifies, in Acts 9:34, "to make a bed"; elsewhere it has its usual meaning. See FURNISH, SPREAD.

BEFALL

1. *ginomai* (γίνομαι, 1096), "to become," is rendered "befell" in Mark 5:16; "hath befallen" in Rom. 11:25, RV, for KJV, "is happened to"; so the RV in 2 Cor. 1:8; 2 Tim. 3:11.

2. *sumbainō* (συμβαίνω, 4819), lit., "to walk, or go together" (*sun*, "with," *bainō*, "to go"), is used of things which happen at the same time; hence, "to come to pass, befall," Acts 20:19. In 21:35, it is translated "so it was." See HAPPEN.

3. *sunantaō* (συναντάω, 4876), "to meet with" (*sun*, "with," *antaō*, "to meet"), is used much in the same way as *sumbainō*, of events which come to pass; "befall," Acts 20:22. See MEET.

Note: The phrase in Matt. 8:33, "what was befallen to them that were possessed with demons," is, lit., "the things of the demonized."

BEFIT, BEFITTING

1. *prepō* (πρέπω, 4241) is translated "befit" in Titus 2:1, RV (KJV, "become"). See BECOME.

2. *anēkō* (ἀνήκω, 433), primarily, "to have arrived at, reached to, pertained to," came to denote "what is due to a person, one's duty, what is befitting." It is used ethically in the NT; Eph. 5:4, RV, "are (not) befitting," for KJV, "are (not) convenient"; Col. 3:18, concerning the duty of wives towards husbands, RV, "as is fitting," for KJV, "as it is fit." In Philem. 8, the participle is used with the article, signifying "that which is befitting," RV (KJV, "that which

is convenient"). See CONVENIENT. For synonymous words see BECOME.¶

BEFORE, BEFORETIME

A. Adverbs.

1. *prōton* (πρῶτον, 4412), the neuter of the adjective *prōtos* (the superlative degree of *pro*, "before"), signifies "first, or at the first," (*a*) in order of time, e.g., Luke 10:5; John 18:13; 1 Cor. 15:46; 1 Thess. 4:16; 1 Tim. 3:10; (*b*) in enumerating various particulars, e.g., Rom. 3:2; 1 Cor. 11:18; 12:28; Heb. 7:2; Jas. 3:17. It is translated "before" in John 15:18. See CHIEFLY, FIRST.

2. *proteron* (πρότερον, 4386), the neuter of *proteros*, the comparative degree of *pro*, is always used of time, and signifies "aforetime, before," e.g., John 6:62; 9:8; 2 Cor. 1:15; Heb. 7:27; in Gal. 4:13, "the first time" (RV), lit., "the former time," i.e., the former of two previous visits; in Heb. 10:32 it is placed between the article and the noun, "the former days"; so in 1 Pet. 1:14, "the former lusts," i.e., the lusts formerly indulged. See FIRST, FORMER.

3. *prin* (πρίν, 4250), "before, formerly" (etymologically akin to *pro*, "before"), has the force of a conjunction, e.g., Matt. 1:18; 26:34, 75; John 14:29; Acts 7:2.

4. *emprosthen* (ἔμπροσθεν, 1715) is used of place or position only; adverbially, signifying "in front," Luke 19:28; Phil. 3:13; Rev. 4:6; as a preposition, e.g., Matt. 5:24; John 10:4; with the meaning "in the sight of a person," e.g., Matt. 5:16; 6:1; 17:2; Luke 19:27; John 12:37; 1 Thess. 2:19, RV, "before"; KJV, "in the presence of"; Rev. 19:10, RV, "before," especially in phrases signifying in the sight of God, as God wills, Matt. 11:26; 18:14 (lit., "a thing willed before your Father," RV, marg.); Luke 10:21; in the sense of "priority of rank or position or dignity," John 1:15, 30 (in some texts, v. 27); in an antagonistic sense, "against," Matt. 23:13 (RV, marg., "before").

5. *enantion* (ἐναντίον, 1726), from *en*, "in," and *anti*, "over against," the neuter of the adjective *enantios*, and virtually an adverb, is also used as a preposition signifying "in the presence of, in the sight of," Luke 20:26; Acts 7:10; 8:32; "in the judgment of," Luke 24:19.¶

6. *enanti* (ἔναντι, 1725), an adverb, used as a preposition, has meanings like those of No. 5, "before," Luke 1:8; "in the judgment of," Acts 8:21. Some texts have the word in Acts 7:10.¶

7. *apenanti* (ἀπέναντι, 561), *apo*, "from," with No. 6, denotes (*a*) "opposite," Matt. 27:61; (*b*) "in the sight of, before," Matt. 27:24; Acts 3:16; Rom. 3:18; (*c*) "against," Acts 17:7. See CONTRARY, PRESENCE.¶

8. *katenanti* (κατέναντι, 2713), *kata*, "down," with No. 6, lit., "down over against," is used (*a*) of locality, e.g., Mark 11:2; 13:3; Luke 19:30; (*b*) as "in the sight of," Rom. 4:17; in most mss. in 2 Cor. 2:17; 12:19.

9. *enōpion* (ἐνώπιον, 1799), from *en*, "in," and *ōps*, "the eye," is the neuter of the adjective *enōpios*, and is used prepositionally, (*a*) of place, that which is before or opposite a person, "towards which he turns his eyes," e.g., Luke 1:19; Acts 4:10; 6:6; Rev. 1:4; 4:10; 7:15; (*b*) in metaphorical phrases after verbs of motion, Luke 1:17; 12:9; Acts 9:15, etc.; signifying "in the mind or soul of persons," Luke 12:6; Acts 10:31; Rev. 16:19; (*c*) "in one's sight or hearing," Luke 24:43; John 20:30; 1 Tim. 6:12; metaphorically, Rom. 14:22; especially in Gal. 1:20; 1 Tim. 5:21; 6:13; 2 Tim. 2:14; 4:1; before, as "having a person present to the mind," Acts 2:25; Jas. 4:10; "in the judgment of a person," Luke 16:15; 24:11, RV, "in their sight," for KJV, "to"; Acts 4:19; Rom. 3:20; 12:17; 2 Cor. 8:21; 1 Tim. 2:3; "in the approving sight of God," Luke 1:75; Acts 7:46; 10:33; 2 Cor. 4:2; 7:12. See PRESENCE, SIGHT OF (in the).

10. *katenōpion* (κατενώπιον, 2714), *kata*, "against," with No. 9, signifies "right over against, opposite"; (*a*) of place, Jude 24; (*b*) before God as Judge, Eph. 1:4; Col. 1:22. See No. 8 (b).¶

B. Verb.

prouparchō (προυπάρχω, 4391), "to exist before, or be beforehand," is found in Luke 23:12, and Acts 8:9, "beforetime."¶ In the Sept., Job 42:18.¶

BEG, BEGGAR, BEGGARLY

A. Verbs.

1. *epaiteō* (ἐπαιτέω, 1871), a strengthened form of *aiteō*, is used in Luke 16:3.¶

2. *prosaiteō* (προσαιτέω, 4319), lit., "to ask besides" (*pros*, "towards," used intensively, and *aiteō*), "to ask earnestly, to importune, continue asking," is said of the blind beggar in John 9:8. In Mark 10:46 and Luke 18:35 certain mss. have this verb; the most authentic have *prosaitēs*, "a beggar," a word used in John 9:8, as well as the verb (see the RV).¶

Note: "Begged" in Matt. 27:58 and Luke 23:52, RV, "asked for," translates the verb *aiteō*; see ASK.

B. Adjective.

ptōchos (πτωχός, 4434), an adjective describing "one who crouches and cowers," is used as a noun, "a beggar" (from *ptōssō*, "to cower down or hide oneself for fear"), Luke 14:13, 21 ("poor"); 16:20, 22; as an adjective, "beggarly" in Gal. 4:9, i.e., poverty-stricken, powerless to enrich, metaphorically descriptive of the religion of the Jews.

While *prosaitēs* is descriptive of a "beggar," and stresses his "begging," *ptōchos* stresses his poverty-stricken condition. See POOR.

For BEGAN see BEGIN

BEGET, BEAR (of begetting), BORN

A. Verbs.

1. *gennaō* (γεννάω, 1080), "to beget," in the passive voice, "to be born," is chiefly used of men "begetting" children, Matt. 1:2–16; more rarely of women "begetting" children, Luke 1:13, 57, "brought forth" (for "delivered," in this v., see No. 4); 23:29; John 16:21, "is delivered of," and of the child, "is born" (for "is in travail" see No. 4). In Gal. 4:24, it is used allegorically, to contrast Jews under bondage to the Law, and spiritual Israel, KJV, "gendereth," RV, "bearing children," to contrast the natural birth of Ishmael and the supernatural birth of Isaac. In Matt. 1:20 it is used of conception, "that which is conceived in her." It is used of the act of God in the birth of Christ, Acts 13:33; Heb. 1:5; 5:5, quoted from Psalm 2:7, none of which indicate that Christ became the Son of God at His birth.

It is used metaphorically (*a*) in the writings of the apostle John, of the gracious act of God in conferring upon those who believe the nature and disposition of "children," imparting to them spiritual life, John 3:3, 5, 7; 1 John 2:29; 3:9; 4:7; 5:1, 4, 18; (*b*) of one who by means of preaching the gospel becomes the human instrument in the impartation of spiritual life, 1 Cor. 4:15; Philem. 10; (*c*) in 2 Pet. 2:12, with reference to the evil men whom the apostle is describing, the RV rightly has "born mere animals" (KJV, "natural brute beasts"); (*d*) in the sense of gendering strife, 2 Tim. 2:23. See A, No. 3, BRING, CONCEIVE, DELIVER, GENDER, SPRING.

2. *anagennaō* (ἀναγεννάω, 313), *ana*, "again, or from above," with No. 1, is found in 1 Pet. 1:3, 23.¶

Note: In John 3:3, 5, 7, the adverb *anōthen*, "anew, or from above," accompanies the simple verb *gennaō*. See ABOVE.

3. *apokueō* (ἀποκυέω, 616), "to give birth to, to bring forth" (from *kueō*, "to be pregnant"), is used metaphorically of spiritual birth by means of the Word of God, Jas. 1:18, and of death as the offspring of sin (v. 15; so in the best texts). See BRING, A, No. 30.¶

4. *tiktō* (τίκτω, 5088), "to bring forth," Luke 1:57; John 16:21; Heb. 11:11; Rev. 12:2, 4, or, "to be born," said of the Child, Matt. 2:2; Luke 2:11, is used metaphorically in Jas. 1:15, of lust

as bringing forth sin. See *apokueō*, above, used in the same verse. See BRING, DELIVER, TRAVAIL (be in).

B. Nouns.

1. *genos* (γένος, 1085), "a generation, kind, stock," is used in the dative case, with the article, to signify "by race," in Acts 18:2 and 24, RV, for the KJV, "born." See COUNTRYMEN, DIVERSITY, GENERATION, KIND, KINDRED, NATION, OFFSPRING, STOCK.

2. *ektrōma* (ἔκτρωμα, 1626) denotes "an abortion, an untimely birth"; from *ektitrōskō*, "to miscarry." In 1 Cor. 15:8 the apostle likens himself to "one born out of due time"; i.e., in point of time, inferior to the rest of the apostles, as an immature birth comes short of a mature one.¶

C. Adjectives.

1. *gennētos* (γεννητός, 1084), "born" (related to *gennaō*, verb No. 1), is used in Matt. 11:11 and Luke 7:28 in the phrase "born of women," a periphrasis for "men," and suggestive of frailty.¶

2. *artigennētos* (ἀρτιγέννητος, 738), "newborn" (*arti*, "newly, recently," and No. 1), is used in 1 Pet. 2:2.¶

Notes: (1) For *prōtotokos* see FIRSTBORN.

(2) For *monogenēs*, see ONLY BEGOTTEN.

For BEGGAR see BEG

BEGIN, BEGINNING, BEGINNER

A. Verbs.

1. *archomai* (ἄρχομαι, 756) denotes "to begin." In Luke 3:23 the present participle is used in a condensed expression, lit., "And Jesus Himself was beginning about thirty years." Some verb is to be supplied in English. The RV has "when He began to teach, was about thirty years of age." The meaning seems to be that He was about thirty years when He "began" His public career (cf. Acts 1:1). The KJV has "began to be about thirty years of age." In Acts 11:4 the RV suitably has "began, and expounded," instead of "from the beginning." See B, No. 1, below, and REIGN, RULE.

2. *enarchomai* (ἐνάρχομαι, 1728), lit., "to begin in" (*en*, "in," with No. 1), is used in Gal. 3:3 ("having begun in the Spirit"), to refer to the time of conversion; similarly in Phil. 1:6, "He which began a good work in you." The *en* may be taken in its literal sense in these places.¶

3. *proenarchomai* (προενάρχομαι, 4278), lit., "to begin in before" (*pro*, with No. 2), is used in 2 Cor. 8:6, "he had made a beginning before"; and in v. 10, "were the first to make a beginning" (RV).¶

4. *mellō* (μέλλω, 3195), "to be about to," is

rendered "begin" in the KJV of Rev. 10:7; RV suitably, "when he is about to sound." See COME, INTEND, MEAN, MIND, READY, SHALL, SHOULD, TARRY, WILL, WOULD.

Note: For "began to wax" in 1 Tim. 5:11, see WANTON, No. 2.

B. Noun.

archē (ἀρχή, 746) means "a beginning." The root *arch* primarily indicated what was of worth. Hence the verb *archō* meant "to be first," and *archōn* denoted "a ruler." So also arose the idea of "a beginning," the origin, the active cause, whether a person or thing, e.g., Col. 1:18. In Heb. 2:3 the phrase "having at the first been spoken" is, lit., "having received a beginning to be spoken." In 2 Thess. 2:13 ("God chose you from the beginning"), there is a well supported alternative reading, "chose you as first-fruits" (i.e., *aparchēn*, instead of *ap' archēs*). In Heb. 6:1, where the word is rendered "first principles," the original has "let us leave the word of the beginning of Christ," i.e., the doctrine of the elementary principles relating to Christ.

In John 8:25, Christ's reply to the question "Who art Thou?," "Even that which I have spoken unto you from the beginning," does not mean that He had told them before; He declares that He is consistently the unchanging expression of His own teaching and testimony from the first, the immutable embodiment of His doctrine. See CORNER, FIRST, MAGISTRATE, POWER, PRINCIPALITY, RULE.

Note: In the following passages the KJV faulty translations, "since the world began," etc. are rightly rendered in the RV by "before times eternal" and similar phrases, Rom. 16:25; Eph. 3:9; 2 Tim. 1:9; Titus 1:2. The alteration has not been made, however, in Luke 1:70; John 9:32; Acts 3:21; 15:18.

C. Adverb.

prōton (πρῶτον, 4412), the neuter of *prōtos* (the superlative degree of *proteros)*, "first, at the first," is rendered "at the beginning" in John 2:10, KJV, RV, "setteth on first." See BEFORE.

For BEGOTTEN see BEGET

BEGUILE

1. *apataō* (ἀπατάω, 538), "to deceive," is rendered "beguiled" in the RV of 1 Tim. 2:14. See No. 2.

2. *exapataō* (ἐξαπατάω, 1818), a strengthened form of No. 1, is rendered "beguile," 2 Cor. 11:3; the more adequate rendering would be "as the serpent thoroughly beguiled Eve." So in 1 Tim. 2:14, in the best mss., this stronger form is used of Satan's deception of Eve, lit.,

"thoroughly beguiled"; the simpler verb, No. 1, is used of Adam. In each of these passages the strengthened form is used. So of the influence of sin, Rom. 7:11 (RV, "beguile"); of self-deception, 1 Cor. 3:18 (RV, "deceive "); of evil men, who cause divisions, Rom. 16:18 (RV, "beguile"); of deceitful teachers, 2 Thess. 2:3 (RV, "beguile"). See DECEIVE.¶ In the Sept., Exod. 8:29.¶

3. *paralogizomai* (παραλογίζομαι, 3884), lit. and primarily, "to reckon wrong," hence means "to reason falsely" (*para*, "from, amiss," *logizomai*, "to reason") or "to deceive by false reasoning"; translated "delude" in Col. 2:4, RV (KJV, "beguile") and Jas. 1:22 (KJV, "deceive"). See DECEIVE, DELUDE.¶

4. *deleazō* (δελεάζω, 1185) originally meant "to catch by a bait" (from *delear*, "a bait"); hence "to beguile, entice by blandishments": in Jas. 1:14, "entice"; in 2 Pet. 2:14, KJV, "beguile"; in v. 18, KJV, "allure"; RV, "entice" in both. See ENTICE.¶

Note: In Col. 2:18, the verb *katabrabeuō*, "to give judgment against, condemn," is translated "beguile . . . of your reward," KJV; RV, "rob . . . of your prize." The verb was used of an umpire's decision against a racer; hence the translations (or paraphrases) in the Eng. versions. See ROB.

BEHALF

1. *meros* (μέρος, 3313), "a part," is translated "behalf" in the KJV of 2 Cor. 9:3 (RV, "respect") and 1 Pet. 4:16; here the most authentic texts have *onoma*, "a name"; hence RV, "in this name." See COAST, CRAFT, PART, PIECE, PORTION, RESPECT, SORT.

2. *huper* (ὑπέρ, 5228), "on behalf of," is to be distinguished from *anti*, "instead of." See *Note* †, p. 1.

BEHAVE, BEHAVIOR

A. Verbs.

1. *anastrephō* (ἀναστρέφω, 390), "to turn back, return" (*ana*, "back," *strephō*, "to turn"), hence, "to move about in a place, to sojourn," and, in the middle and passive voices, "to conduct oneself," indicating one's manner of life and character, is accordingly rendered "behave" in 1 Tim. 3:15, lit., "how it is necessary to behave," not referring merely to Timothy himself, but to all the members of the local church (see the whole epistle); in Eph. 2:3, KJV, "we had our conversation," RV, "we lived"; in 2 Cor. 1:12 "behaved ourselves," for KJV "have had our conversation." See ABIDE, etc.

2. *ginomai* (γίνομαι, 1096), "to become," is

rendered "behave" in 1 Thess. 2:10; lit., "we became among you" (cf. 1:5).

3. *atakteō* (ἀτακτέω, 812), lit., "to be disorderly" (*a*, negative, and *taxis*, "order"), "to lead a disorderly life," is rendered "behave disorderly" in 2 Thess. 3:7.¶ Cf. *ataktos*, "disorderly, unruly," and *ataktōs*, "disorderly."

4. *aschēmoneō* (ἀσχημονέω, 807), "to be unseemly" (*a*, negative, and *schēma*, "a form"), is used in 1 Cor. 7:36, "behave (himself) unseemly," i.e., so as to run the risk of bringing the virgin daughter into danger or disgrace, and in 13:5, "doth (not) behave itself unseemly."¶

B. Nouns.

1. *anastrophē* (ἀναστροφή, 391), lit., "a turning back" (cf. No. 1, above), is translated "manner of life," "living," etc. in the RV, for KJV, "conversation," Gal. 1:13; Eph. 4:22; 1 Tim. 4:12; Heb. 13:7; Jas. 3:13; 1 Pet. 1:15, 18; 2:1 ("behavior"); 3:1, 2, 16 (ditto); 2 Pet. 2:7; 3:11. see CONVERSATION, LIFE.¶

2. *katastēma* (κατάστημα, 2688), akin to *kathistēmi* (see APPOINT, No. 2), denotes "a condition, or constitution of anything, or deportment," Titus 2:3, "demeanor," RV, for KJV, "behavior." See DEMEANOR.¶

C. Adjective.

kosmios (κόσμιος, 2887), "orderly, modest," is translated "orderly" in 1 Tim. 3:2, RV, for KJV, "of good behavior." Both have "modest" in 1 Tim. 2:9. Cf. *kosmeō*, "to adorn," *kosmos*, "adornment."¶

BEHEAD

1. *apokephalizō* (ἀποκεφαλίζω, 607), *apo*, "from, off," *kephalē*, "a head," is found in Matt. 14:10; Mark 6:16, 27; Luke 9:9.¶

2. *pelekizō* (πελεκίζω, 3990) denotes "to cut with an axe" (from *pelekus*, "an axe"), Rev. 20:4.¶

BEHIND, COME BEHIND

A. Adverbs.

1. *opisthen* (ὄπισθεν, 3693), "behind," is used only of place, e.g., Matt. 9:20; Mark 5:27; Luke 8:44; Rev. 4:6; as a preposition, Matt. 15:23 ("after"), and Luke 23:26; in Rev. 5:1, RV, "on the back"; KJV, "backside." See BACK.¶

. 2. *opisō* (ὀπίσω, 3694), "after" (see BACK, adverb).

B. Verbs.

1. *hustereō* (ὑστερέω, 5302), "to come late, be behind," is translated "come behind," in 1 Cor. 1:7; "to be behind," 2 Cor. 11:5 and 12:11. See COME, No. 39, DESTITUTE, FAIL, LACK, NEED, B, *Note*, WANT, WORSE.

2. *hupomenō* (ὑπομένω, 5278), "to abide,

endure," is once rendered "tarry behind," Luke 2:43. See ABIDE.

Note: In 1 Thess. 3:1, the RV, "left behind" adequately expresses the verb *kataleipō*.

C. Noun.

husterēma (ὑστέρημα, 5303), akin to B. 1, denotes "that which is lacking," 1 Cor. 16:17; Phil. 2:30; Col. 1:24 (KJV, "that which is behind of the afflictions of Christ"), RV, "that which is lacking"; 1 Thess. 3:10. For the other meaning, "want," see LACK, PENURY, WANT.

BEHOLD, BEHELD

1. *horaō* (ὁράω, 3708), with its aorist form *eidon*, "to see" (in a few places the KJV uses the verb "to behold"), is said (*a*) of bodily vision, e.g., Mark 6:38; John 1:18, 46; (*b*) of mental perception, e.g., Rom. 15:21; Col. 2:18; (*c*) of taking heed, e.g., Matt. 8:4; 1 Thess. 5:15; (*d*) of experience, as of death, Luke 2:26; Heb. 11:5; life, John 3:36; corruption, Acts 2:27; (*e*) of caring for, Matt. 27:4; Acts 18:15 (here the form *opsomai* is used). See APPEAR, HEED, LOOK, PERCEIVE, SEE, SHEW.

2. *blepō* (βλέπω, 991) is also used of (*a*) bodily and (*b*) mental vision, (*a*) "to perceive," e.g., Matt. 13:13; (*b*) "to take heed," e.g., Mark 13:23, 33; it indicates greater vividness than *horaō*, expressing a more intent, earnest contemplation; in Luke 6:41, of "beholding" the mote in a brother's eye; Luke 24:12, of "beholding" the linen clothes in the empty tomb; Acts 1:9, of the gaze of the disciples when the Lord ascended. The greater earnestness is sometimes brought out by the rendering "regardest," Matt. 22:16. See BEWARE, HEED, LIE, LOOK, PERCEIVE, REGARD, SEE, SIGHT.

3. *emblepō* (ἐμβλέπω, 1689), from *en*, "in" (intensive), and No. 2, (not to be rendered literally), expresses "earnest looking," e.g., in the Lord's command to "behold" the birds of the heaven, with the object of learning lessons of faith from them, Matt. 6:26. See also 19:26; Mark 8:25; 10:21, 27; 14:67; Luke 20:17; 22:61; John 1:36; of the Lord's looking upon Peter, John 1:42; Acts 1:11; 22:11. See GAZE, LOOK, SEE.¶

4. *ide* and *idou* (ἴδε and ἰδού, 2396 and 2400) are imperative moods, active and middle voices, respectively, of *eidon*, "to see," calling attention to what may be seen or heard or mentally apprehended in any way. These are regularly rendered "behold." See especially the Gospels, Acts and the Apocalypse. See LO, SEE.

5. *epide* (ἔπιδε, 1896**), a strengthened form of No. 4 (with *epi*, "upon," prefixed), is used in Acts 4:29 of the entreaty made to the Lord to "behold" the threatenings of persecutors.¶

6. *theōreō* (θεωρέω, 2334), from *theōros*, "a spectator," is used of one who looks at a thing with interest and for a purpose, usually indicating the careful observation of details; this marks the distinction from No. 2; see, e.g., Mark 15:47; Luke 10:18; 23:35; John 20:6 (RV, "beholdeth," for KJV, "seeth"); so in verses 12 and 14; "consider," in Heb. 7:4. It is used of experience, in the sense of partaking of, in John 8:51; 17:24. See CONSIDER, LOOK, PERCEIVE, SEE. Cf. *theōria*, "sight," Luke 23:48, only.

7. *anatheōreō* (ἀναθεωρέω, 333), *ana*, "up" (intensive), and No. 6, "to view with interest, consider contemplatively," is translated "beheld," in Acts 17:23, RV, "observed"; "considering" in Heb. 13:7. See CONSIDER.¶

8. *theaomai* (θεάομαι, 2300), "to behold, view attentively, contemplate," had, in earlier Greek usage, the sense of a wondering regard. This idea was gradually lost. It signifies a more earnest contemplation than the ordinary verbs for "to see," "a careful and deliberate vision which interprets... its object," and is more frequently rendered "behold" in the RV than the KJV. Both translate it by "behold" in Luke 23:55 (of the sepulchre); "we beheld," in John 1:14, of the glory of the Son of God; "beheld," RV, in John 1:32; Acts 1:11; 1 John 1:1 (more than merely seeing); 4:12, 14. See LOOK, SEE.

9. *epopteuō* (ἐποπτεύω, 2029), from *epi*, "upon," and a form of *horaō*, "to see," is used of "witnessing as a spectator, or overseer," 1 Pet. 2:12; 3:2.¶

Note: The corresponding noun *epoptēs*, "an eye-witness," found in 2 Pet. 1:16, was used by the Greeks of those who had attained to the highest grade of certain mysteries, and the word is perhaps purposely used here of those who were at the transfiguration of Christ. See EYE-WITNESS.¶

10. *atenizō* (ἀτενίζω, 816) from *atenēs*, "strained, intent," denotes "to gaze upon," "beholding earnestly," or "steadfastly" in Acts 14:9; 23:1. See FASTEN, LOOK, SET, B, *Note* (5).

11. *katanoeō* (κατανοέω, 2657), a strengthened form of *noeō*, "to perceive," (*kata*, intensive), denotes "the action of the mind in apprehending certain facts about a thing"; hence, "to consider"; "behold," Acts 7:31–32; Jas. 1:23–24. See CONSIDER, DISCOVER, PERCEIVE.

12. *katoptrizō* (κατοπτρίζω, 2734), from *katoptron*, "a mirror" (*kata*, "down," *ōps*, "an eye or sight"), in the active voice, signifies "to make to reflect, to mirror"; in the middle voice, "to reflect as a mirror"; so the RV in 2 Cor. 3:18, for KJV, "beholding as in a glass." The whole

context in the 3rd chapter and the first part of the 4th bears out the RV.¶

Note: For *epeidon* (from *ephoraō*), Acts 4:29, see LOOK, No. 9. For *prooraō*, Acts 2:25, RV, "behold," see FORESEE.

BEHOVE

1. *opheilō* (ὀφείλω, 3784), "to owe," is once rendered "behove," Heb. 2:17; it indicates a necessity, owing to the nature of the matter under consideration; in this instance, the fulfillment of the justice and love of God, voluntarily exhibited in what Christ accomplished, that He might be a merciful and faithful High Priest. See BOUND, DEBT, DUE, DUTY, GUILTY, INDEBTED, MUST, NEED, OUGHT, OWE.

2. *dei* (δεῖ, 1163), "it is necessary," is rendered "behoved," in Luke 24:46; RV, (that the Christ) "should" (suffer). *Dei* expresses a logical necessity, *opheilō*, a moral obligation; cf. *chrē*, Jas. 3:10, "ought," which expresses a need resulting from the fitness of things (Trench, § cvii). See MEET, MUST, NEED, OUGHT.

BEING

When not part of another verb (usually the participle), or part of a phrase, this word translates one of the following:—

(*a*) the present participle of *eimi*, "to be," the verb of ordinary existence;

(*b*) the participle of *ginomai*, "to become," signifying origin or result;

(*c*) the present participle of *huparchō*, "to exist," which always involves a preexistent state, prior to the fact referred to, and a continuance of the state after the fact. Thus in Phil. 2:6, the phrase "who being (*huparchōn*) in the form of God," implies His preexistent deity, previous to His birth, and His continued deity afterwards.

In Acts 17:28 the phrase "we have our being" represents the present tense of the verb to be, "we are."

BELIAL

belial (βελίαλ, or βελίαρ, 955) is a word frequently used in the Old Testament, with various meanings, especially in the books of Samuel, where it is found nine times. See also Deut. 13:13; Jud. 19:22; 20:13; 1 Kings 21:10, 13; 2 Chron. 13:7. Its original meaning was either "worthlessness" or "hopeless ruin" (see the RV, margin). It also had the meanings of "extreme wickedness and destruction," the latter indicating the destiny of the former. In the period between the OT and the NT it came to be a proper name for Satan. There may be an indication of this in Nahum 1:15, where the word translated "the wicked one" is Belial.

The oldest form of the word is "Beliar," possibly from a phrase signifying "Lord of the forest," or perhaps simply a corruption of the form "Belial," due to harsh Syriac pronunciation. In the NT, in 2 Cor. 6:15, it is set in contrast to Christ and represents a personification of the system of impure worship connected especially with the cult of Aphrodite.¶

BELIEF, BELIEVE, BELIEVERS

A. Verbs.

1. *pisteuō* (πιστεύω, 4100), "to believe," also "to be persuaded of," and hence, "to place confidence in, to trust," signifies, in this sense of the word, reliance upon, not mere credence. It is most frequent in the writings of the apostle John, especially the Gospel. He does not use the noun (see below). For the Lord's first use of the verb, see 1:50. Of the writers of the Gospels, Matthew uses the verb ten times, Mark ten, Luke nine, John ninety-nine. In Acts 5:14 the present participle of the verb is translated "believers." See COMMIT, INTRUST, TRUST.

2. *peithō* (πείθω, 3982), "to persuade," in the middle and passive voices signifies "to suffer oneself to be persuaded," e.g., Luke 16:31; Heb. 13:18; it is sometimes translated "believe" in the RV, but not in Acts 17:4, RV, "were persuaded," and 27:11, "gave (more) heed"; in Acts 28:24, "believed." See AGREE, ASSURE, OBEY, PERSUADE, TRUST, YIELD.

Note: For *apisteō*, the negative of No. 1, and *apeitheō*, the negative of No. 2, see DISBELIEVE, DISOBEDIENT.

B. Noun.

pistis (πίστις, 4102), "faith," is translated "belief" in Rom. 10:17; 2 Thess. 2:13. Its chief significance is a conviction respecting God and His Word and the believer's relationship to Him. See ASSURANCE, FAITH, FIDELITY.

Note: In 1 Cor. 9:5 the word translated "believer" (RV), is *adelphē*, "a sister," so 7:15; Rom. 16:1; Jas. 2:15, used, in the spiritual sense, of one connected by the tie of the Christian faith.

C. Adjective.

pistos (πιστός, 4103), (a) in the active sense means "believing, trusting"; (b) in the passive sense, "trusty, faithful, trustworthy." It is translated "believer" in 2 Cor. 6:15; "them that believe" in 1 Tim. 4:12, RV (KJV, "believers "); in 1 Tim. 5:16, "if any woman that believeth," lit., "if any believing woman." So in 6:2, "believing masters." In 1 Pet. 1:21 the RV, following the most authentic mss., gives the noun form, "are believers in God" (KJV, "do believe in God"). In John 20:27 it is translated "believing." It is best understood with significance (a), above, e.g., in Gal. 3:9; Acts 16:1; 2 Cor. 6:15; Titus

1:6; it has significance (b), e.g., in 1 Thess. 5:24; 2 Thess. 3:3 (see *Notes on Thess.* p. 211, and *Gal.* p. 126, by Hogg and Vine). See FAITHFUL, SURE.

Notes: (1) The corresponding negative verb is *apisteō*, 2 Tim. 2:13, KJV, "believe not" RV, "are faithless," in contrast to the statement "He abideth faithful."

(2) The negative noun *apistia*, "unbelief," is used twice in Matthew (13:58; 17:20), three times in Mark (6:6; 9:24; 16:14), four times in Romans (3:3; 4:20; 11:20, 23); elsewhere in 1 Tim. 1:13 and Heb. 3:12, 19.¶

(3) The adjective *apistos* is translated "unbelievers" in 1 Cor. 6:6, and 2 Cor. 6:14; in v. 15, RV, "unbeliever" (KJV, "infidel"); so in 1 Tim. 5:8; "unbelieving" in 1 Cor. 7:12–15; 14:22–24; 2 Cor. 4:4; Titus 1:15; Rev. 21:8; "that believe not" in 1 Cor. 10:27. In the Gospels it is translated "faithless" in Matt. 17:17; Mark 9:19; Luke 9:41; John 20:27, but in Luke 12:46, RV, "unfaithful," KJV, "unbelievers." Once it is translated "incredible," Acts 26:8. See FAITHLESS, INCREDIBLE, UNBELIEVER.¶

(4) *Plērophoreō*, in Luke 1:1 (KJV, "are most surely believed," lit., "have had full course"), the RV renders "have been fulfilled." See FULFILL, KNOW, PERSUADE, PROOF.

BELLY

1. *koilia* (κοιλία, 2836), from *koilos*, "hollow" (Lat., *coelum*, "heaven," is connected), denotes the entire physical cavity, but most frequently was used to denote "the womb." In John 7:38 it stands metaphorically for the innermost part of man, the soul, the heart. See WOMB.

2. *gastēr* (γαστήρ, 1064), (cf. Eng., "gastritis"), is used much as No. 1, but in Titus 1:12, by synecdoche (a figure of speech in which the part is put for the whole, or vice versa), it is used to denote "gluttons," RV, for KJV, "bellies." See GLUTTON, WOMB.

BELONG

Note: This word represents (a) a phrase consisting of *eimi*, "to be," with or without a preposition and a noun, and usually best rendered, as in the RV, by the verb "to be," Mark 9:41, lit., "ye are of Christ"; Luke 23:7 and Heb. 5:14; cf. Rom. 12:19, "belongeth unto Me," RV; (b) a phrase consisting of the neuter plural of the definite article, either with the preposition *pros*, "unto," as in Luke 19:42, where the phrase "the things which belong unto peace" (RV) is, lit., "the (things) unto peace," or with the genitive case of the noun, as in 1 Cor. 7:32, KJV, "the things that belong to the Lord," RV, suitably, "the things of the Lord"; (*c*) a distinct verb, e.g., *metechō*, "to partake of, share in," Heb. 7:13 RV, "belongeth to (another tribe)," KJV, "pertaineth to."

BELOVED

A. Adjective.

agapētos (ἀγαπητός, 27), from *agapaō*, "to love," is used of Christ as loved by God, e.g., Matt. 3:17; of believers (ditto), Rom. 1:7; of believers, one of another, 1 Cor. 4:14; often, as a form of address, e.g., 1 Cor. 10:14. Whenever the KJV has "dearly beloved," the RV has "beloved"; so, "well beloved" in 3 John 1; in 1 John 2:7, KJV, "brethren" (*adelphos*), the RV has "beloved," according to the mss. which have *agapētos*. See DEAR.

B. Verb.

agapaō (ἀγαπάω, 25), in its perfect participle passive form, is translated "beloved" in Rom. 9:25; Eph. 1:6; Col. 3:12; 1 Thess. 1:4; 2 Thess. 2:13. In Jude 1 the best texts have this verb (RV); the KJV, "sanctified" follows those which have *hagiazō*. See LOVE.

Note: In Luke 9:35, the RV, translating from the most authentic mss., has "My chosen" (*eklegō*), for KJV, "beloved" (*agapētos*); so in Philem. 2, "sister" (*adelphē*).

BENEATH

katō (κάτω, 2736) signifies (*a*) "down, downwards," Matt. 4:6; Luke 4:9; John 8:6, 8; Acts 20:9; (*b*) "below, beneath," of place, Mark 14:66; the realms that lie below in contrast to heaven, John 8:23; the earth, as contrasted with the heavens, Acts 2:19; with *heōs*, "unto," Matt. 27:51; Mark 15:38. The comparative degree, *katōterō*, "under," is used in Matt. 2:16. See BOTTOM, UNDER.¶

BENEFIT, BENEFACTOR

1. *euergesia* (εὐεργεσία, 2108), lit., "good work" (*eu*, "well," *ergon*, "work"), is found in Acts 4:9, "good deed," and 1 Tim. 6:2, "benefit."¶

2. *euergetēs* (εὐεργέτης, 2110), "a benefactor," expresses the agent, Luke 22:25.¶

Note: Cf. *euergeteō*, "to do good."

3. *charis* (χάρις, 5485), "grace," is once rendered "benefit," 2 Cor. 1:15; it stresses the character of the "benefit," as the effect of the gracious disposition of the benefactor. See ACCEPTABLE, FAVOR, GRACE, LIBERALITY, PLEASURE, THANK.

4. *agathon* (ἀγαθόν, 18), the neuter of *agathos*, used as a noun in Philem. 14, is translated "benefit," KJV; RV, "goodness." See GOOD.

BENEVOLENCE

eunoia (εὔνοια, 2133), "good will" (*eu*, "well," *nous*, "the mind"), is rendered "benevolence" in 1 Cor. 7:3, KJV. The RV, following the texts which have *opheilēn* ("due"), has "her due," a more comprehensive expression; in Eph. 6:7, "good will."¶

BEREAVED, BEREFT

1. *aporphanizomai* (ἀπορφανίζομαι, 642), lit., "to be rendered an orphan" (*apo*, "from," with the thought of separation, and *orphanos*, "an orphan"), is used metaphorically in 1 Thess. 2:17 (KJV, "taken from"; RV, "bereaved"), in the sense of being "bereft" of the company of the saints through being compelled to leave them (cf. the similes in 7 and 11). The word has a wider meaning than that of being an orphan.¶

Note: The corresponding adjective, *orphanos*, is translated "desolate" in John 14:18 (KJV, "comfortless"); "fatherless" in Jas. 1:27; see DESOLATE, FATHERLESS.¶

2. *apostereō* (ἀποστερέω, 650), "to rob, defraud, deprive," is used in 1 Tim. 6:5, in the passive voice, of being deprived or "bereft" (of the truth), with reference to false teachers (KJV, "destitute"). See DEFRAUD, DESTITUTE, FRAUD.

BERYL

bērullos (βήρυλλος, 969), "beryl," is a precious stone of a sea-green color, Rev. 21:20 (cf. Exod. 28:20).¶

BESEECH

1. *parakaleō* (παρακαλέω, 3870), the most frequent word with this meaning, lit. denotes "to call to one's side," hence, "to call to one's aid." It is used for every kind of calling to a person which is meant to produce a particular effect, hence, with various meanings, such as "comfort, exhort, desire, call for," in addition to its significance "to beseech," which has a stronger force than *aiteō* (see ASK). See, e.g., the RV "besought" in Mark 5:18; Acts 8:31; 19:31; 1 Cor. 16:12. See CALL, No. 6, *Note* (2), COMFORT, DESIRE, EXHORT, INTREAT, PRAY.

2. *erōtaō* (ἐρωτάω, 2065), often translated by the verb "to beseech," in the Gospels, is elsewhere rendered "beseech" in 1 Thess. 4:1; 5:12; 2 Thess. 2:1; 2 John 5. See under ASK, No. 2.

3. *deomai* (δέομαι, 1189), "to desire, to long for," usually representing the word "need," is sometimes translated "beseech," e.g., Luke 5:12; Acts 21:39; 2 Cor. 10:2; Gal. 4:12. It is used of prayer to God, in Matt. 9:38; Luke 10:2; 21:36;

22:32; Acts 4:31; 8:22, 24; 10:2; Rom. 1:10; 1 Thess. 3:10. See PRAY, REQUEST.

Note: Proskuneō is wrongly rendered "besought" in the KJV marg. of Matt. 18:26. The word signifies "to worship."

BESET

euperistatos (εὐπερίστατος, 2139), used in Heb. 12:1, and translated "which doth so easily beset," lit. signifies "standing well (i.e., easily) around" (*eu*, "well," *peri*, "around," *statos*, "standing," i.e., easily encompassing). It describes sin as having advantage in favor of its prevailing.¶

BESIDE, BESIDES

1. *chōris* (χωρίς, 5565), "separately, apart from, besides," is translated "beside" in Matt. 14:21; 15:38; 2 Cor. 11:28. See APART, SEPARATE, WITHOUT.

2. *loipon* (λοιπόν, 3063) is rendered "besides" in 1 Cor. 1:16. See FINALLY.

Notes: (1) *Pareiserchomai*, in Rom. 5:20, signifies "to come in beside," i.e., of the Law, as coming in addition to sin committed previously apart from law, the prefix *par-* (i.e., *para*) denoting "beside" (the KJV, "entered" is inadequate); in Gal. 2:4 ("came in privily"). See COME.¶

(2) In Philem. 19, *prosopheilō* signifies "to owe in addition" (*pros*, "besides," and *opheilō*, "to owe"): "thou owest (to me even thine own self) besides."¶

(3) In 2 Pet. 1:5, the phrase, wrongly translated in the KJV, "beside this," means "for this very cause" (RV).

BESIDE ONESELF (to be)

1. *existēmi* (ἐξίστημι, 1839), primarily and lit. means "to put out of position, displace"; hence, (*a*) "to amaze," Luke 24:22 (for KJV, "make . . . astonished"); Acts 8:9, 11 (KJV, "bewitched"); or "to be amazed, astounded," Matt. 12:23; Mark 6:51; (*b*) "to be out of one's mind, to be beside oneself," Mark 3:21; 2 Cor. 5:13, in the latter of which it is contrasted with *sōphroneō*, "to be of a sound mind, sober." See AMAZE.

2. *mainomai* (μαίνομαι, 3105), "to be mad, to rave," is said of one who so speaks that he appears to be out of his mind, Acts 26:24, translated "thou art beside thyself," KJV; RV, "thou art mad." In v. 25; John 10:20; Acts 12:15; 1 Cor. 14:23, both versions use the verb to be mad. See MAD.¶

Note: For *paraphroneō*, 2 Cor. 11:23, RV, see FOOL, B, No. 2.

BEST

1. *prōtos* (πρῶτος, 4413) is one of two words translated "best" in the KJV, but the only one so rendered in the RV. In Luke 15:22 "the best (robe)" is, lit., "the first (robe)," i.e., chief, principal, first in rank or quality. See BEFORE, BEGINNING, CHIEF, FIRST, FORMER.

2. *meizōn* (μείζων, 3187), "greater," is translated "best" in 1 Cor. 12:31, "the best gifts," greater, not in quality, but in importance and value. It is the comparative degree of *megas*, "great"; the superlative, *megistos*, is used only in 2 Pet. 1:4. See ELDER, GREATER and MORE.

BESTOW

1. *didōmi* (δίδωμι, 1325), "to give," is rendered "bestow" in 1 John 3:1, the implied idea being that of giving freely. The KJV has it in 2 Cor. 8:1; the RV adheres to the lit. rendering, "the grace of God which hath been given in the churches of Macedonia." See ADVENTURE and especially GIVE.

2. *sunagō* (συνάγω, 4863), "to bring together" (*sun*, "together," *agō*, "to bring"), is used in the sense of "bestowing," or stowing, by the rich man who laid up his goods for himself, Luke 12:17–18. See ASSEMBLE, COME, GATHER, LEAD, RESORT, TAKE.

3. *kopiaō* (κοπιάω, 2872), (*a*) "to grow tired with toil," Matt. 11:28; John 4:6; Rev. 2:3, also means (*b*) "to bestow labor, work with toil," Rom. 16:6; Gal. 4:11; in John 4:38, KJV, "bestowed (no) labor," RV, "have (not) labored," and, in the same verse, KJV and RV, "labored." See LABOR, TOIL, WEARY.

4. *psōmizō* (ψωμίζω, 5595), primarily "to feed by putting little bits into the mouths of infants or animals," came to denote simply "to give out food, to feed," and is rendered by the phrase "bestow . . . to feed" in 1 Cor. 13:3; "feed," Rom. 12:20; there the person to be fed is mentioned; in 1 Cor. 13:3 the material to be given is specified, and the rendering "bestow . . . to feed" is necessary. See FEED.¶

5. *peritithēmi* (περιτίθημι, 4060), "to put around or on" (*peri*, "around," *tithēmi*, "to put"), is translated in 1 Cor. 12:23 (metaphorically) "bestow" (marg., "put on"). See PUT, SET, No. 5.

6. *charizomai* (χαρίζομαι, 5483), "to show favor, grant, bestow," is rendered "bestowed" in Luke 7:21, RV, for KJV, "gave." Here and in Gal. 3:18, the verb might be translated "graciously conferred." See DELIVER, FORGIVE, GIVE, GRANT.

Note: For "freely bestowed" see ACCEPT, A, *Note.*

BETRAY, BETRAYER

A. Verb.

paradidōmi (παραδίδωμι, 3860), "to betray" (*para*, "up," *didōmi*, "to give"), lit., "to give over," is used either (*a*) in the sense of delivering a person or thing to be kept by another, to commend, e.g., Acts 28:16; (*b*) to deliver to prison or judgment, e.g., Matt. 4:12; 1 Tim. 1:20; (*c*) to deliver over treacherously by way of "betrayal," Matt. 17:22 (RV, "delivered"); 26:16; John 6:64 etc.; (*d*) to hand on, deliver, e.g., 1 Cor. 11:23; (*e*) to allow of something being done, said of the ripening of fruit, Mark 4:29, RV, "is ripe" (marg., "alloweth"). See BRING, *Note* (4), CAST, COMMIT, DELIVER, GIVE, HAZARD, PUT (in prison), RECOMMEND.

B. Noun.

prodotēs (προδότης, 4273), "a betrayer" (akin to A), is translated "betrayers" in Acts 7:52; "traitor," "traitors," in Luke 6:16 and 2 Tim. 3:4. See TRAITOR.¶

BETROTH

mnēsteuō (μνηστεύω, 3423), in the active voice, signifies "to woo a woman and ask for her in marriage"; in the NT, only in the passive voice, "to be promised in marriage, to be betrothed," Matt. 1:18; Luke 1:27; 2:5, RV, "betrothed," (KJV, "espoused"). See ESPOUSED.¶

BETTER

1. *kreissōn* (κρείσσων, 2909), from *kratos*, "strong" (which denotes power in activity and effect), serves as the comparative degree of *agathos*, "good" (good or fair, intrinsically). *Kreissōn* is especially characteristic of the Epistle to the Hebrews, where it is used 12 times; it indicates what is (*a*) advantageous or useful, 1 Cor. 7:9, 38; 11:17; Heb. 11:40; 12:24; 2 Pet. 2:21; Phil. 1:23, where it is coupled with *mallon*, "more," and *pollō*, "much, by far," "very far better" (RV); (*b*) excellent, Heb. 1:4; 6:9; 7:7, 19, 22; 8:6; 9:23; 10:34; 11:16, 35.¶

2. *kalon... mallon* (καλὸν ... μᾶλλον), the neuter of *kalos*, with *mallon*, "more," is used in Mark 9:42, "it were better (lit., 'much better') for him if a great millstone were hanged about his neck." In verses 43, 45, 47, *kalos* is used alone (RV, "good," for KJV, "better").

Note: In Luke 5:39 the most authentic texts have *chrēstos*, "good," instead of the comparative, *chrēstoteros*, "better."

BETTER (be)

1. *diapherō* (διαφέρω, 1308), used (*a*) transitively, means "to carry through" or "about" (*dia*, "through," *pherō*, "to carry"), Mark 11:16

("carry... through "); Acts 13:49; 27:27 ("driven to and fro"); (*b*) intransitively, (1) "to differ," Rom. 2:18; Gal. 2:6; Phil. 1:10; (2) "to excel, be better," e.g., Matt. 6:26; 10:31 ("of more value"); 12:12; Luke 12:7, 24; 1 Cor. 15:41; Gal. 4:1; some would put Rom. 2:18 and Phil. 1:10 here (see marg.). See CARRY, DIFFER, DRIVE, EXCELLENT, MATTER (make), PUBLISH.¶

2. *perisseuō* (περισσεύω, 4052), "to be over or above (a number), to be more than enough, to be pre-eminent, superior," Matt. 5:20, is translated "are we the better," in 1 Cor. 8:8 (cf. 15:58; Rom. 15:13; 2 Cor. 3:9; 8:7; Phil. 1:9; Col. 2:7; 1 Thess. 4:1, 10). See ABOUND.

3. *lusiteleō* (λυσιτελέω, 3081) signifies "to indemnify, pay expenses, pay taxes" (from *luō*, "to loose," *telos*, "toll, custom"); hence, "to be useful, advantageous, to be better," Luke 17:2.¶

4. *huperechō* (ὑπερέχω, 5242) lit. means "to hold or have above" (*huper*, "above," *echō*, "to hold"); hence, metaphorically, to be superior to, to be better than, Phil. 2:3; 1 Pet. 2:13, "supreme," in reference to kings; in Rom. 13:1, "higher"; Phil. 3:8, "excellency," more strictly "the surpassing thing, (namely, the knowledge of Christ)"; in 4:7 "passeth." See EXCELLENCY, HIGHER, PASS, SUPREME.¶

Notes: (1) In Rom. 3:9 the RV rightly translates *proechō* (which there is used in the passive voice, not the middle) "are we in worse case than... ? ," i.e., "are we surpassed?" "are we at a disadvantage?" The question is, are the Jews, so far from being better off than the Gentiles, in such a position that their very privileges bring them into a greater disadvantage or condemnation than the Gentiles? The KJV "are we better" does not convey the meaning.

(2) *Sumpherō*, in Matt. 18:6, KJV, is translated "it were better for him," RV, "profitable." See Matt. 5:29–30 etc. See BRING, EXPEDIENT, GOOD, D, *Note* (2), PROFITABLE.

BETTERED (to be)

ōpheleō (ὠφελέω, 5623) in the active voice signifies "to help, to succor, to be of service"; in the passive "to receive help, to derive profit or advantage"; in Mark 5:26, "was (nothing) bettered," of the woman who had an issue of blood. See under ADVANTAGE, C, No. 1, and cf. A, Nos. 2, 3 and B.

BETWEEN

In addition to the prepositions *en* and *pros* (see *Note* †, p. 1), the following have this meaning:

1. *ana meson* (ἀνὰ μέσον, 303, 3349), lit., "up to the middle of," i.e., among, or in the midst of, hence, between, is used in 1 Cor. 6:5,

of those in the church able to decide between brother and brother, instead of their going to law with one another in the world's courts.

2. *metaxu* (μεταξύ, 3342), "in the midst, or between" (from *meta*, and *xun*, i.e., *sun*, "with"), is used as a preposition, (*a*) of mutual relation, Matt. 18:15; Acts 15:9; Rom. 2:15, RV, "one with another," lit., "between one another," for KJV, "the meanwhile"; (*b*) of place, Matt. 23:35; Luke 11:51; 16:26; Acts 12:6; (*c*) of time, "meanwhile," John 4:31. In Acts 13:42, the KJV marg. has "in the week between," the literal rendering. See WHILE.¶

Note: The phrase *ek meta* (*ek*, "out of," *meta*, "with") is translated "between ... and" in the KJV of John 3:25 (RV, "on the part of ... with").

BEWAIL

1. *klaiō* (κλαίω, 2799), "to wail," whether with tears or any external expression of grief, is regularly translated "weep" in the RV; once in the KJV it is rendered "bewail," Rev. 18:9. See WEEP.

Note: The associated noun is *klauthmos*, "weeping." Cf. *dakruō*, "to weep," John 11:35.¶

2. *koptō* (κόπτω, 2875), primarily, "to beat, smite"; then, "to cut off," Matt. 21:8; Mark 11:8, is used in the middle voice, of beating oneself, beating the breast, as a token of grief; hence, "to bewail," Matt. 11:17 (RV, "mourn," for KJV, "lament "); 24:30, "mourn"; Rev. 1:7 (RV, "mourn"; KJV, "wail"); in Luke 8:52; 23:27 "bewail"; in Rev. 18:9, "wail" (for KJV, "lament"). See CUT, MOURN.¶ Cf. *kopetos*, "lamentation," Acts 8:2.¶

3. *pentheō* (πενθέω, 3996) denotes "to lament, mourn," especially for the dead; in 2 Cor. 12:21, RV, "mourn" (KJV, "bewail"). See also Rev. 18:11, 15, 19. Cf. *penthos*, "mourning." See MOURN.

Notes: (1) *Thrēneō*, "to sing a dirge, to lament," is rendered "wail" in Matt. 11:17, RV; "mourned" in Luke 7:32; "to lament" in Luke 23:27 and John 16:20.¶ *Thrēnos*, "lamentation," occurs in Matt. 2:18.¶

(2) *Odurmos* from *oduromai*, "to wail" (a verb not found in the NT), denotes "mourning," Matt. 2:18 and 2 Cor. 7:7.¶

(3) Cf. *lupeomai*, "to grieve"; see also Trench, *Syn.* § lxv.

BEWARE

1. *blepō* (βλέπω, 991), "to see," is applied to mental vision, and is sometimes used by way of warning "to take heed" against an object, Mark 8:15; 12:38; Acts 13:40; Phil. 3:2 (three

times); in Col. 2:8, RV, "take heed," marg., "see whether." See BEHOLD.

2. *prosechō* (προσέχω, 4337), lit., "to hold to" (*pros*, "to," *echō*, "to have, to hold"), hence, "to turn one's mind or attention to a thing by being on one's guard against it," is translated "beware" in Matt. 7:15; 10:17; 16:6, 11–12; Luke 12:1; 20:46. See ATTEND, HEED, REGARD.

3. *phulassō* (φυλάσσω, 5442), "to guard, keep," is used, in the middle voice, of being "on one's guard against" (the middle v. stressing personal interest in the action), Luke 12:15, "beware of," RV, "keep yourselves from," as in Acts 21:25; in 2 Tim. 4:15, "be thou ware"; in 2 Pet. 3:17, "beware." See GUARD, KEEP, OBSERVE, SAVE.

BEWITCH

1. *baskainō* (βασκαίνω, 940), primarily, "to slander, to prate about anyone"; then "to bring evil on a person by feigned praise, or mislead by an evil eye, and so to charm, bewitch" (Eng., "fascinate" is connected), is used figuratively in Gal. 3:1, of leading into evil doctrine.¶

2. *existemi* (ἐξίστημι, 1839) is rendered "bewitch" in Acts 8:9, 11, KJV, concerning Simon the sorcerer; it does not mean "to bewitch," as in the case of the preceding verb, but "to confuse, amaze" (RV). See AMAZE, B. No. 1.

BEWRAY

Note: The word "bewrayeth," Matt. 26:73, is a translation of *poieō*, "to make," with *dēlos*, "manifest, evident"; lit., "maketh thee manifest."

BEYOND

In addition to the preposition *huper*, "over," rendered "beyond" in 2 Cor. 8:3, the following adverbs have this meaning:

1. *epekeina* (ἐπέκεινα, 1900), *epi*, "upon," and *ekeina*, "those," the word "parts" being understood, is used in Acts 7:43.¶

2. *peran* (πέραν, 4008), "on the other side, across," is used with the definite article, signifying the regions "beyond," the opposite shore, Matt. 8:18 etc. With verbs of going it denotes direction towards and "beyond" a place, e.g., John 10:40. It frequently indicates "beyond," of locality, without a verb of direction, Matt. 16:5; Mark 10:1, RV; John 1:28; 3:26. See FARTHER, SIDE.

Note: In 2 Cor. 10:14, the verb *huperekteinō*, "to stretch overmuch," is so rendered in the RV, for KJV, " ... beyond our measure."¶ In 2 Cor. 10:16 the adverb *huperekeina*, "beyond," is used as a preposition.

BID, BIDDEN, BADE, BID AGAIN

1. *kaleō* (καλέω, 2564), "to call," often means "to bid," in the sense of "invite," e.g., Matt. 22:3–4, 8, 9; Luke 14:7–10, 13, RV; Rev. 19:9, RV. See CALL, NAME, SURNAME.

2. *keleuō* (κελεύω, 2753), "to command," is translated "bid" in Matt. 14:28, only. See COMMAND, No. 5. Compare the synonym *entellō*, "to command."

3. *eipon* (εἶπον, 3004), used as the aorist tense of *legō*, "to speak, to say," sometimes has the meaning of "commanding, or bidding," and is translated "bid," or "bade," e.g., in Matt. 16:12; 23:3; Luke 10:40; 9:54, KJV, "command," RV, "bid"; Acts 11:12; "bidding," Acts 22:24, RV. See SAY, SPEAK.

4. *antikaleō* (ἀντικαλέω, 479), "to bid again, invite in turn," is found in Luke 14:12.¶

Notes: (1) *Legō*, "to say," is translated "bid" and "biddeth" in the KJV of 2 John 10, 11; RV, "give (him no greeting)," "giveth (him greeting)". See GREETING.

(2) In Matt. 1:24, *prostassō*, "to command," is translated "had bidden," KJV; RV, "commanded." See COMMAND.

BID FAREWELL

1. *apotassō* (ἀποτάσσω, 657) is used in the middle voice to signify "to bid adieu to a person." It primarily means "to set apart, separate" (*apo*, "from," *tassō*, "to set, arrange"); then, "to take leave of, to bid farewell to," Mark 6:46 (RV); Luke 9:61; "to give parting instructions to," Acts 18:18, 21; 2 Cor. 2:13; "to forsake, renounce," Luke 14:33. See FORSAKE, RENOUNCE, SEND, *Note* (2) at end.¶

2. *apaspazomai* (ἀπασπάζομαι, 575 and 782), "to bid farewell" (*apo*, "from," *aspazomai*, "to greet"), is used in Acts 21:6, KJV, "had taken our leave of"; RV, "bade ... farewell."¶

BIER

soros (σορός, 4673) originally denoted a receptacle for containing the bones of the dead, "a cinerary urn"; then "a coffin," Gen. 50:26; Job 21:32; then, "the funeral couch or bier" on which the Jews bore their dead to burial, Luke 7:14.¶

BILL

1. *biblion* (βιβλίον, 975), primarily "a small book, a scroll, or any sheet on which something has been written"; hence, in connection with *apostasion*, "divorce," signifies "a bill of divorcement," Matt. 19:7 (KJV, "writing"); Mark 10:4. See BOOK, SCROLL, WRITING.

2. *gramma* (γράμμα, 1121), from *graphō*, "to write" (Eng., "graph, graphic," etc.), in Luke 16:6, KJV, is translated "bill." It lit. signifies that which is drawn, a picture; hence, a written document; hence, a "bill," or bond, or note of hand, showing the amount of indebtedness. In the passage referred to the word is in the plural, indicating perhaps, but not necessarily, various "bills." The bonds mentioned in rabbinical writings, were formal, signed by witnesses and the Sanhedrin of three, or informal, when only the debtor signed. The latter were usually written on wax, and easily altered. See LEARNING, LETTER, SCRIPTURE, WRITING.

For **BILLOWS**, Luke 21; 25, RV, see **WAVE**

BIND, BINDING (see also BOUND)

1. *deō* (δέω, 1210), "to bind," is used (*a*) literally, of any sort of "binding," e.g., Acts 22:5; 24:27, (*b*) figuratively, of the Word of God, as not being "bound," 2 Tim. 2:9, i.e., its ministry, course and efficacy were not hindered by the bonds and imprisonment suffered by the apostle. A woman who was bent together, had been "bound" by Satan through the work of a demon, Luke 13:16. Paul speaks of himself, in Acts 20:22, as being "bound in the spirit," i.e., compelled by his convictions, under the constraining power of the Spirit of God, to go to Jerusalem. A wife is said to be "bound" to her husband, Rom. 7:2; 1 Cor. 7:39; and the husband to the wife, 1 Cor. 7:27. The Lord's words to the apostle Peter in Matt. 16:19, as to "binding," and to all the disciples in 18:18, signify, in the former case, that the apostle, by his ministry of the Word of Life, would keep unbelievers outside the kingdom of God, and admit those who believed. So with regard to 18:18, including the exercise of disciplinary measures in the sphere of the local church; the application of the rabbinical sense of forbidding is questionable. See BOND, KNIT, *Note*, TIE.

2. *perideō* (περιδέω, 4019), *peri*, "around," with No. 1, "to bind around," is used in John 11:44 of the napkin around the face of Lazarus.¶ Cf. Job 12:18, Sept.

3. *hupodeō* (ὑποδέω, 5265), *hupo*, "under," with No. 1, "to bind underneath," is used of binding of sandals, Acts 12:8; rendered "shod" in Mark 6:9 and Eph. 6:15. See SHOD.¶

4. *katadeō* (καταδέω, 2611), *kata*, "down," with No. 1, "to bind or tie down, or bind up," is used in Luke 10:34 of the act of the good Samaritan.¶

5. *sundeō* (συνδέω, 4887), *sun*, "together," and No. 1, "to bind together," implying associ-

ation, is used in Heb. 13:3 of those bound together in confinement.¶

6. *desmeō* or *desmeō* (δεσμεύω, 1195) signifies "to put in fetters or any kind of bond," Luke 8:29; Acts 22:4, or "to bind a burden upon a person," Matt. 23:4. The verb is connected with No. 1.¶

Notes: (1) Cf. *desmos*, "a band, bond, fetter," e.g., Luke 13:16, and *desmios*, "bound," Acts 25:14, KJV (RV, "a prisoner"); in Heb. 13:3, "them that are in bonds." See BOND, CHAIN, PRISONER, STRING.

(2) *Sundesmos* (see No. 5, above), "that which binds together," is translated "bands," in Col. 2:19. See BONDS.

7. *proteinō* (προτείνω, 4385), lit., "to stretch forth" (*pro*, "forth," *teinō*, "to stretch"), is used in Acts 22:25, KJV, "they bound"; RV, "they had tied (him) up," in reference to the preparations made for scourging, probably, to stretch the body forward, to make it tense for severer punishment. See TIE.¶

BIRD (Fowl)

1. *orneon* (ὄρνεον, 3732) is probably connected with a word signifying "to perceive, to hear"; Rev. 18:2; 19:17, 21. See FOWL. Cf. *ornis*, a hen.¶

2. *peteinon* (πετεινόν, 4071) signifies "that which is able to fly, winged." It is connected with *ptenon* signifying "feathered, winged," which is used in 1 Cor. 15:39. Cf. *petomai* and *petaomai*, "to fly." In the Gospels the RV always translates it "birds," e.g., Matt. 6:26; but "fowls" in Acts 10:12; 11:6. The KJV unsuitably has "fowls," in the Gospels, except Matt. 8:20; 13:32; Luke 9:58.

BIRTH

1. *gennēsis* (γέννησις, 1083), "a birth, begetting, producing" (related to *gennaō*, "to beget"), is used in Matt. 1:18 and Luke 1:14. Some mss. have *genesis*, "lineage, birth" (from *ginomai*, "to become").¶

2. *genetē* (γενετή, 1079), "a being born, or the hour of birth" (related to *genea*, "race, generation"), is connected with *ginomai*, "to become, to be born," and is used in John 9:1.¶

Notes (1) For *genesis* and *gennēma* see FRUIT, GENERATION, NATURE.

(2) In Gal. 4:19, *ōdinō*, "to have birth pangs," is rendered "travail in birth," KJV; RV, "am in travail." See Rev. 12:2.

BIRTHDAY

genesia (γενέσια, 1077), a neuter plural (akin to *genesis*, "lineage," from *ginomai*), primarily denoted "the festivities of a birthday, a

birthday feast," though among the Greeks it was also used of a festival in commemoration of a deceased friend. It is found in Matt. 14:6 and Mark 6:21. Some have regarded it as the day of the king's accession, but this meaning is not confirmed in Greek writings.¶

BIRTHRIGHT

prōtotokia (πρωτοτόκια, 4415), "a birthright" (from *prōtos*, "first," *tiktō*, "to beget"), is found in Heb. 12:16, with reference to Esau (cf. *prōtotokos*, firstborn). The "birthright" involved preeminence and authority, Gen. 27:29; 49:3. Another right was that of the double portion, Deut. 21:17; 1 Chron. 5:1–2. Connected with the "birthright" was the progenitorship of the Messiah. Esau transferred his "birthright" to Jacob for a paltry mess of pottage, profanely despising this last spiritual privilege, Gen. 25 and 27. In the history of the nation God occasionally set aside the "birthright," to show that the objects of His choice depended not on the will of the flesh, but on His own authority. Thus Isaac was preferred to Ishmael, Jacob to Esau, Joseph to Reuben, David to his elder brethren, Solomon to Adonijah. See FIRSTBORN.¶

BISHOP (Overseer)

1. *episkopos* (ἐπίσκοπος, 1985), lit., "an overseer" (*epi*, "over," *skopeō*, "to look or watch"), whence Eng. "bishop," which has precisely the same meaning, is found in Acts 20:28; Phil. 1:1; 1 Tim. 3:2; Titus 1:7; 1 Pet. 2:25. See OVERSEER.¶

Note: *Presbuteros*, "an elder," is another term for the same person as bishop or overseer. See Acts 20:17 with verse 28. The term "elder" indicates the mature spiritual experience and understanding of those so described; the term "bishop," or "overseer," indicates the character of the work undertaken. According to the divine will and appointment, as in the NT, there were to be "bishops" in every local church, Acts 14:23; 20:17; Phil. 1:1; Titus 1:5; Jas. 5:14. Where the singular is used, the passage is describing what a "bishop" should be, 1 Tim. 3:2; Titus 1:7. Christ Himself is spoken of as "the . . . Bishop of our souls," 1 Pet. 2:25. See ELDER.

2. *episkopē* (ἐπισκοπή, 1984), besides its meaning, "visitation," e.g., 1 Pet. 2:12 (cf. the Sept. of Exod. 3:16; Isa. 10:3; Jer. 10:15), is rendered "office," in Acts 1:20, RV (KJV, "bishoprick"); in 1 Tim. 3:1 "the office of a bishop," lit., "(if any one seeketh) overseership," there is no word representing office.

Note: The corresponding verb is *episkopeō*, which, in reference to the work of an overseer, is found in 1 Pet. 5:2, RV, "exercising the oversight," for KJV "taking the oversight." See OVER-SIGHT.

For BIT see BRIDLE

BITE

daknō (δάκνω, 1143), "to bite," in Gal. 5:15, "if ye bite and devour one another," is used metaphorically of wounding the soul, or rending with reproaches.¶

BITTER, BITTERLY, BITTERNESS

A. Adjective.

pikros (πικρός, 4089), from a root *pik—*, meaning "to cut, to prick," hence, lit., "pointed, sharp, keen, pungent to the sense of taste, smell, etc.," is found in Jas. 3:11, 14. In v. 11 it has its natural sense, with reference to water; in v. 14 it is used metaphorically of jealousy, RV.¶

B. Verb.

pikrainō (πικραίνω, 4087), related to A, signifies, in the active voice, "to be bitter," Col. 3:19, or "to embitter, irritate, or to make bitter," Rev. 10:9; the passive voice, "to be made bitter," is used in Rev. 8:11; 10:10.¶

C. Noun.

pikria (πικρία, 4088) denotes "bitterness." It is used in Acts 8:23, metaphorically, of a condition of extreme wickedness, "gall of bitterness" or "bitter gall"; in Rom. 3:14, of evil speaking; in Eph. 4:31, of "bitter" hatred; in Heb. 12:15, in the same sense, metaphorically, of a root of "bitterness," producing "bitter" fruit.¶

D. Adverb.

pikrōs (πικρῶς, 4090), "bitterly," is used of the poignant grief of Peter's weeping for his denial of Christ, Matt. 26:75; Luke 22:62.¶
Note: In the Sept., *pikris* (not in the NT), "a bitter herb," is used in Exod. 12:8; Num. 9:11.¶

BLACK, BLACKNESS

A. Adjective.

melas (μέλας, 3189), "black," Matt. 5:36; Rev. 6:5, 12, is derived from a root *mal—*, meaning "to be dirty"; hence Latin, *malus*, "bad." See INK.

B. Nouns.

1. *gnophos* (γνόφος, 1105), Heb. 12:18, "blackness, gloom," seems to have been associated with the idea of a tempest. It is related to *skotos*, "darkness," in that passage, and in the Sept. of Exod. 10:22; Deut. 4:11; Zeph. 1:15.¶

2. *zophos* (ζόφος, 2217), akin to No. 1, especially "the gloom of the regions of the lost," is used four times; 2 Pet. 2:4, "darkness" (RV); 2:17, RV, "blackness," for KJV, "mist"; Jude 6,

"darkness"; v. 13, "blackness," suggesting a kind of emanation. See DARKNESS, MIST.¶

For BLADE see GRASS

BLAME, BLAMELESS

A. Verb.

mōmaomai (μωμάομαι, 3469), "to find fault with, to blame, or calumniate," is used in 2 Cor. 6:3, of the ministry of the gospel; in 8:20, of the ministration of financial help.¶
Notes: (1) Cf. the synonymous verb, *memphomai*, "to find fault," Mark 7:2; Rom. 9:19; Heb. 8:8. See FAULT.¶
(2) In Gal. 2:11, *kataginōskō* is rightly rendered "stood condemned," RV, for KJV, "was to be blamed." See CONDEMN.

B. Adjectives.

1. *amōmos* (ἄμωμος, 299) : See BLEMISH, B.
2. *amōmētos* (ἀμώμητος, 298), translated in Phil. 2:15 "without blemish" (KJV, "without rebuke"), is rendered "blameless" in 2 Pet. 3:14 (KJV and RV).¶
3. *amemptos* (ἄμεμπτος, 273), related to *memphomai* (A, *Note*), is translated "unblameable" in 1 Thess. 3:13; "blameless," in Luke 1:6; Phil. 2:15; 3:6; "faultless" in Heb. 8:7. See FAULTLESS, UNBLAMEABLE.¶

"If *amōmos* is the 'unblemished,' *amemptos* is the 'unblamed.' ... Christ was *amōmos* in that there was in Him no spot or blemish, and He could say, 'Which of you convinceth (convicteth) Me of sin?' but in strictness of speech He was not *amemptos* (unblamed), nor is this epithet ever given to Him in the NT, seeing that He endured the contradiction of sinners against Himself, who slandered His footsteps and laid to His charge 'things that He knew not' (i.e., of which He was guiltless)." Trench, *Syn.* §103.

4. *anaitios* (ἀναίτιος, 338), "guiltless" (*a*, negative, *n*, euphonic, and *aitia*, "a charge"), is translated, "blameless" in the KJV of Matt. 12:5, "guiltless" in 12:7. The RV has "guiltless" in both places.¶ In the Sept., in Deut. 19:10, 13, and 21:8–9.¶ See GUILTLESS.

5. *anepilēptos* (ἀνεπίληπτος, 423), lit., "that cannot be laid hold of," hence, "not open to censure, irreproachable" (from *a*, negative, *n*, euphonic, and *epilambanō*, "to lay hold of"), is used in 1 Tim. 3:2; 5:7; 6:14 (in all three places the RV has "without reproach"; in the first two KJV, "blameless," in the last, "unrebukeable"; an alternative rendering would be "irreprehensible"). See REPROACH, UNREBUKEABLE.¶

6. *anenklētos* (ἀνέγκλητος, 410) signifies "that which cannot be called to account" (from *a*, negative, *n*, euphonic, and *enkaleō*, "to call in"), i.e., with nothing laid to one's charge (as

the result of public investigation), in 1 Cor. 1:8,
RV, "unreproveable," KJV, "blameless"; in Col.
1:22, KJV and RV, "unreproveable"; in 1 Tim.
3:10 and Titus 1:6–7, KJV and RV, "blameless."
It implies not merely acquittal, but the absence
of even a charge or accusation against a person.
This is to be the case with elders.¶

C. Adverb.

amemptōs (ἀμέμπτως, 274), in 1 Thess.
2:10, "unblameably"; in 5:23, "without blame,"
KJV, "blameless," is said of believers at the judgment-seat of Christ in His Parousia (His presence after His coming), as the outcome of
present witness and steadfastness. See B, No. 3,
above.¶

BLASPHEME, BLASPHEMY, BLASPHEMER, BLASPHEMOUS

A. Noun.

blasphēmia (βλασφημία, 988), either from
blax, "sluggish, stupid," or, probably, from
blaptō, "to injure," and *phēmē*, "speech," (Eng.
"blasphemy") is so translated thirteen times in
the RV, but "railing" in Matt. 15:19; Mark 7:22;
Eph. 4:31; Col. 3:8; 1 Tim. 6:4; Jude 9. The
word "blasphemy" is practically confined to
speech defamatory of the Divine Majesty. See
Note, below. See EVIL SPEAKING, RAILING.

B. Verb.

blasphēmeō (βλασφημέω, 987), "to blaspheme, rail at or revile," is used (*a*) in a general
way, of any contumelious speech, reviling, ca-
lumniating, railing at, etc., as of those who
railed at Christ, e.g., Matt. 27:39; Mark 15:29;
Luke 22:65 (RV, "reviling"); 23:39; (*b*) of those
who speak contemptuously of God or of sacred
things, e.g., Matt. 9:3; Mark 3:28; Rom. 2:24;
1 Tim. 1:20; 6:1; Rev. 13:6; 16:9, 11, 21; "hath
spoken blasphemy," Matt. 26:65; "rail at,"
2 Pet. 2:10; Jude 8, 10; "railing," 2 Pet. 2:12;
"slanderously reported," Rom. 3:8; "be evil spoken of," Rom. 14:16; 1 Cor. 10:30; 2 Pet. 2:2;
"speak evil of," Titus 3:2; 1 Pet. 4:4; "being
defamed," 1 Cor. 4:13. The verb (in the present
participial form) is translated "blasphemers" in
Acts 19:37; in Mark 2:7, "blasphemeth," RV, for
KJV, "speaketh blasphemies."
There is no noun in the original representing
the English "blasphemer." This is expressed
either by the verb, or by the adjective *blasphe-
mos*. See DEFAME, RAIL, REPORT, REVILE.

C. Adjective.

blasphēmos (βλάσφημος, 989), "abusive,
speaking evil," is translated "blasphemous," in
Acts 6:11, 13; "a blasphemer," 1 Tim. 1:13;
"railers," 2 Tim. 3:2, RV; "railing," 2 Pet. 2:11.
See RAIL.¶

Note: As to Christ's teaching concerning
"blasphemy" against the Holy Spirit, e.g., Matt.
12:32, that anyone, with the evidence of the
Lord's power before His eyes, should declare it
to be Satanic, exhibited a condition of heart
beyond divine illumination and therefore hopeless. Divine forgiveness would be inconsistent
with the moral nature of God. As to the Son of
Man, in his state of humiliation, there might be
misunderstanding, but not so with the Holy
Spirit's power demonstrated.

BLAZE ABROAD

diaphēmizō (διαφημίζω, 1310), "to spread
abroad" (*dia*, "throughout," *phēmizō*, "to
speak"), is so translated in the RV in Matt. 9:31;
28:15 (KJV, "commonly reported"); Mark 1:45
(KJV, "blaze abroad").¶

BLEMISH

A. Noun.

mōmos (μῶμος, 3470), akin to *mōmaomai*
(see BLAME, A), signifies (*a*) "a blemish" (Sept.
only); (*b*) "a shame, a moral disgrace," metaphorical of the licentious, 2 Pet. 2:13.¶

B. Adjective.

amōmos (ἄμωμος, 299), "without blemish";
is always so rendered in the RV, Eph. 1:4; 5:27;
Phil. 2:15; Col. 1:22; Heb. 9:14; 1 Pet. 1:19;
Jude 24; Rev. 14:5. This meaning is to be preferred to the various KJV renderings, "without
blame," Eph. 1:4, "unblameable," Col. 1:22,
"faultless," Jude 24, "without fault," Rev. 14:5.
The most authentic mss. have *amōmos*, "without blemish," in Phil. 2:15, for *amōmētos*,
"without rebuke."¶ In the Sept., in reference to
sacrifices, especially in Lev. and Num., the
Psalms and Ezek., "of blamelessness in character and conduct." See BLAME, FAULT.

BLESS, BLESSED, BLESSEDNESS, BLESSING

A. Verbs.

1. *eulogeō* (εὐλογέω, 2127), lit., "to speak
well of" (*eu*, "well," *logos*, "a word"), signifies,
(*a*) "to praise, to celebrate with praises," of that
which is addressed to God, acknowledging His
goodness, with desire for His glory, Luke 1:64;
2:28; 24:51, 53; Jas. 3:9; (*b*) "to invoke blessings upon a person," e.g., Luke 6:28; Rom.
12:14. The present participle passive, "blessed,
praised," is especially used of Christ in Matt.
21:9; 23:39, and the parallel passages; also in
John 12:13; (*c*) "to consecrate a thing with
solemn prayers, to ask God's blessing on a
thing," e.g., Luke 9:16; 1 Cor. 10:16; (*d*) "to
cause to prosper, to make happy, to bestow

blessings on," said of God, e.g., in Acts 3:26; Gal. 3:9; Eph. 1:3. Cf. the synonym *aineō*, "to praise." See PRAISE.

2. *eneulogeomai* (ἐνευλογέομαι, 1757), "to bless," is used in the passive voice, Acts 3:25, and Gal. 3:8. The prefix *en* apparently indicates the person on whom the blessing is conferred.¶

3. *makarizō* (μακαρίζω, 3106), from a root *mak*—, meaning "large, lengthy," found also in *makros*, "long," *mēkos*, "length," hence denotes "to pronounce happy, blessed," Luke 1:48 and Jas. 5:11. See HAPPY.¶

B. Adjectives.

1. *eulogētos* (εὐλογητός, 2128), akin to A, 1, means "blessed, praised"; it is applied only to God, Mark 14:61; Luke 1:68; Rom. 1:25; 9:5; 2 Cor. 1:3; 11:31; Eph. 1:3; 1 Pet. 1:3.¶ In the Sept. it is also applied to man, e.g., in Gen. 24:31; 26:29; Deut. 7:14; Judg. 17:2; Ruth 2:20; 1 Sam. 15:13.

2. *makarios* (μακάριος, 3107), akin to A, No. 3, is used in the beatitudes in Matt. 5 and Luke 6, and is especially frequent in the Gospel of Luke, and is found seven times in Revelation, 1:3; 14:13; 16:15; 19:9; 20:6; 22:7, 14. It is said of God twice, 1 Tim. 1:11; 6:15. In the beatitudes the Lord indicates not only the characters that are "blessed," but the nature of that which is the highest good.

C. Nouns.

1. *eulogia* (εὐλογία, 2129), akin to A, 1, lit., "good speaking, praise," is used of (*a*) God and Christ, Rev. 5:12–13; 7:12; (*b*) the invocation of blessings, benediction, Heb. 12:17; Jas. 3:10; (*c*) the giving of thanks, 1 Cor. 10:16; (*d*) a blessing, a benefit bestowed, Rom. 15:29; Gal. 3:14; Eph. 1:3; Heb. 6:7; of a monetary gift sent to needy believers, 2 Cor. 9:5–6; (*e*) in a bad sense, of fair speech, Rom. 16:18, RV, where it is joined with *chrēstologia*, "smooth speech," the latter relating to the substance, *eulogia* to the expression. See BOUNTY.¶

2. *makarismos* (μακαρισμός, 3109), akin to A, 3, "blessedness," indicates an ascription of blessing rather than a state; hence in Rom. 4:6, where the KJV renders it as a noun, "(describeth) the blessedness"; the RV rightly puts "(pronounceth) blessing." So v. 9. In Gal. 4:15 the KJV has "blessedness," RV, "gratulation." The Galatian believers had counted themselves happy when they heard and received the gospel. Had they lost that opinion? See GRATULATION.¶

Note: In Acts 13:34, *hosia*, lit., "holy things," is translated "mercies" (KJV), "blessings" (RV).

For **BLEW** see **BLOW**

BLIND, BLINDNESS

A. Verbs.

1. *tuphloō* (τυφλόω, 5186), "to blind" (from a root *tuph*—, "to burn, smoke"; cf. *tuphos*, "smoke"), is used metaphorically, of the dulling of the intellect, John 12:40; 2 Cor. 4:4; 1 John 2:11.¶

2. *pōroō* (πωρόω, 4456) signifies "to harden" (from *pōros*, "a thick skin, a hardening"); rendered "blinded," KJV, in Rom. 11:7 and 2 Cor. 3:14 (RV, "hardened"); cf. 4:4. See HARDEN.

B. Adjective.

tuphlos (τυφλός, 5185), "blind," is used both physically and metaphorically, chiefly in the Gospels; elsewhere four times; physically, Acts 13:11; metaphorically, Rom. 2:19; 2 Pet. 1:9; Rev. 3:17. The word is frequently used as a noun, signifying "a blind man."

C. Noun.

pōrosis (πώρωσις, 4457), akin to A. No. 2, primarily means "a covering with a callus," a "hardening," Rom. 11:25 and Eph. 4:18, RV, for KJV, "blindness"; Mark 3:5, RV, for KJV, "hardness." It is metaphorical of a dulled spiritual perception. See HARDNESS.¶

Note: In John 9:8, the most authentic mss. have *prosaitēs*, "a beggar," RV, instead of *tuphlos*, "blind."

BLINDFOLD

perikaluptō (περικαλύπτω, 4028) signifies "to blindfold" (*peri*, "around," *kaluptō*, "to hide"), Luke 22:64. See COVER, OVERLAY.

BLOOD

A. Nouns.

1. *haima* (αἷμα, 129), (hence Eng., prefix *haem*—), besides its natural meaning, stands, (*a*) in conjunction with *sarx*, "flesh," "flesh and blood," Matt. 16:17; 1 Cor. 15:50; Gal. 1:16; the original has the opposite order, blood and flesh, in Eph. 6:12 and Heb. 2:14; this phrase signifies, by *synecdoche*, "man, human beings." It stresses the limitations of humanity; the two are essential elements in man's physical being; "the life of the flesh is in the blood," Lev. 17:11; (*b*) for human generation, John 1:13; (*c*) for "blood" shed by violence, e.g., Matt. 23:35; Rev. 17:6; (*d*) for the "blood" of sacrificial victims, e.g., Heb. 9:7; of the "blood" of Christ, which betokens His death by the shedding of His "blood" in expiatory sacrifice; to drink His "blood" is to appropriate the saving effects of His expiatory death, John 6:53. As "the life of the flesh is in the blood," Lev. 17:11, and was forfeited by sin, life eternal can be imparted

only by the expiation made, in the giving up of the life by the sinless Savior.

2. *haimatekchusia* (αἱματεκχυσία, 130) denotes "shedding of blood," Heb. 9:22 (*haima*, "blood," *ekchunō*, "to pour out, shed").¶

B. Verb.

haimorrhoeō (αἱμορροέω, 131), from *haima*, "blood," *rheō*, "to flow" (Eng., "hemorrhage"), signifies "to suffer from a flow of blood," Matt. 9:20.¶

Notes: (1) In Mark 5:25 and Luke 8:43, different constructions are used, the translations respectively being "having a flowing of blood" and "being in (i.e., with) a flowing of blood."

(2) In Acts 17:26 (RV, "of one"; KJV, "of one blood"), the most authentic mss. do not contain the noun *haima*, "blood." So with the phrase "through His blood," in Col. 1:14.

(3) For "bloody flux" in Acts 28:8, KJV, see DYSENTERY (RV).

BLOT OUT

exaleiphō (ἐξαλείφω, 1813), from *ek*, "out," used intensively, and *aleiphō*, "to wipe," signifies "to wash, or to smear completely." Hence, metaphorically, in the sense of removal, "to wipe away, wipe off, obliterate"; Acts 3:19, of sins; Col. 2:14, of writing; Rev. 3:5, of a name in a book; Rev. 7:17; 21:4, of tears.¶

BLOW (Noun)

rhapisma (ῥάπισμα, 4475), (*a*) "a blow with a rod or staff," (*b*) "a blow with the hand, a slap or cuff," is found in three places; of the maltreatment of Christ by the officials or attendants of the high priest, Mark 14:65, RV, "received (according to the most authentic mss.) Him with blows of their hands," (KJV, "did strike Him with the palms of their hands"); that they received, or took, Him would indicate their rough handling of Him; John 18:22 and 19:3; in all three places the RV marg. gives the meaning (*a*), as to the use of a rod.¶

So with the corresponding verb *rhapizō*, in Matt. 26:67. The soldiers subsequently beat Him with a reed, 27:30, where *tuptō*, "to beat," is used; *rhapizō* occurs elsewhere in Matt. 5:39. See SMITE.¶

BLOW (Verb)

1. *pneō* (πνέω, 4154) signifies (*a*) "to blow," e.g., Matt. 7:25; John 3:8; in Acts 27:40 the present participle is used as a noun, lit., "to the blowing" (i.e., to the wind); (*b*) "to breathe." See BREATHE.

2. *hupopneō* (ὑποπνέω, 5285), *hupo*, "under" (indicating repression), and No. 1, denotes "to blow softly," Acts 27:13.¶

Note: In Acts 28:13, *epiginomai*, "to come on," is used of the springing up of a wind, KJV, "blew"; RV, "sprang up."

BOARD

sanis (σανίς, 4548) denotes "a plank, or board," Acts 27:44.¶

BOAST, BOASTER, BOASTFUL

A. Verbs.

1. *kauchaomai* (καυχάομαι, 2744), and its related words *katakauchaomai*, "to glory or boast" and the nouns *kauchēsis* and *kauchēma*, translated "boast," and "boasting," in the KJV, are always translated "glory," and "glorying" in the RV, e.g., 2 Cor. 10:15; 11:10, 17; Eph. 2:9. See GLORY.

2. *megalaucheō* (μεγαλαυχέω, 3166), from *megala*, "great things," and *aucheō*, "to lift up the neck," hence, "to boast," is found in some texts of Jas. 3:5. The most authentic mss. have the two words separated. It indicates any kind of haughty speech which stirs up strife or provokes others.¶

Note: In Acts 5:36, the verb *legō*, "to say," is rendered "boasting" in the KJV; "giving out" (RV).

B. Nouns.

1. *alazōn* (ἀλαζών, 213), "a boaster," Rom. 1:30 and 2 Tim. 3:2, KJV, "boasters," RV, "boastful," primarily signifies "a wanderer about the country" (from *alē*, "wandering"), "a vagabond"; hence, "an impostor."¶

2. *alazoneia* (ἀλαζονεία, 212), the practice of an *alazōn*, denotes quackery; hence, "arrogant display, or boastings," Jas. 4:16, RV, "vauntings"; in 1 John 2:16, RV, "vainglory"; KJV, "pride." See PRIDE, VAUNT.¶

Note: In 2 Cor. 9:4, *hupostasis*, "a support, substance," means "confidence" (RV); KJV, "confident boasting."

BOAT

1. *ploiarion* (πλοιάριον, 4142), "a skiff or small boat," is a diminutive of *ploion* (No. 2), Mark 3:9; 4:36; John 6:22 (but No. 2 in the 2nd part of the verse), 23 (here some texts have No. 2), 24; 21:8.¶

2. *ploion* (πλοῖον, 4143), KJV, "ship," is preferably translated "boat" (RV) in the gospels, where it is of frequent use; it is found 18 times in Acts, where, as in Jas. 3:4; Rev. 8:9; 18:19, it signifies a ship. See SHIP.

3. *skaphē* (σκάφη, 4627) is, lit., "anything dug or scooped out" (from *skaptō*, "to dig"), "as a trough, a tub, and hence a light boat, or skiff, a boat belonging to a larger vessel," Acts 27:16, 30, 32.¶

BODY, BODILY

A. Nouns.

1. *sōma* (σῶμα, 4983) is "the body as a whole, the instrument of life," whether of man living, e.g., Matt. 6:22, or dead, Matt. 27:52; or in resurrection, 1 Cor. 15:44; or of beasts, Heb. 13:11; of grain, 1 Cor. 15:37–38; of the heavenly hosts, 1 Cor. 15:40. In Rev. 18:13 it is translated "slaves." In its figurative uses the essential idea is preserved.

Sometimes the word stands, by *synecdoche*, for "the complete man," Matt. 5:29; 6:22; Rom. 12:1; Jas. 3:6; Rev. 18:13. Sometimes the person is identified with his or her "body," Acts 9:37; 13:36, and this is so even of the Lord Jesus, John 19:40 with 42. The "body" is not the man, for he himself can exist apart from his "body," 2 Cor. 12:2–3. The "body" is an essential part of the man and therefore the redeemed are not perfected till the resurrection, Heb. 11:40; no man in his final state will be without his "body," John 5:28–29; Rev. 20:13.

The word is also used for physical nature, as distinct from *pneuma*, "the spiritual nature," e.g., 1 Cor. 5:3, and from *psuchē*, "the soul," e.g., 1 Thess. 5:23. "*Sōma*, 'body,' and *pneuma*, 'spirit,' may be separated; *pneuma* and *psuchē*, 'soul,' can only be distinguished" (Cremer).

It is also used metaphorically, of the mystic body of Christ, with reference to the whole church, e.g., Eph. 1:23; Col. 1:18, 22, 24; also of a local church, 1 Cor. 12:27.

2. *chrōs* (χρώς, 5559) signifies "the surface of a body," especially of the human body, Acts 19:12, with reference to the handkerchiefs carried from Paul's body to the sick.¶

3. *ptōma* (πτῶμα, 4430) denotes, lit., "a fall" (akin to *piptō*, "to fall"); hence, "that which is fallen, a corpse," Matt. 14:12; 24:28, "carcase"; Mark 6:29; 15:45, "corpse"; Rev. 11:8–9, "dead bodies" (Gk., "carcase," but plural in the 2nd part of v. 9). See CARCASE, CORPSE.¶

B. Adjectives.

1. *sussōmos* (σύσσωμς, 4954), *sun*, "with," and A, No. 1., means "united in the same body," Eph. 3:6, of the church.¶

2. *sōmatikos* (σωματικός, 4984), "bodily," is used in Luke 3:22, of the Holy Spirit in taking a bodily shape; in 1 Tim. 4:8 of bodily exercise.¶

C. Adverb.

sōmatikōs (σωματικῶς, 4985), "bodily, corporeally," is used in Col. 2:9.¶

BOISTEROUS

Note: The KJV "boisterous" in Matt. 14:30 is a rendering of the word *ischuros*, "strong" (see margin); it is not in the most authentic mss.

BOLD, BOLDNESS, BOLDLY

A. Verbs.

1. *tharreō* (θαρρέω, 2292), a later form of *tharseō* (see CHEER, COMFORT), is connected with *therō*, "to be warm" (warmth of temperament being associated with confidence); hence, "to be confident, bold, courageous"; RV, invariably, "to be of good courage"; 2 Cor. 5:6, 8 (KJV, "to be confident"); 7:16 (KJV, "to have confidence"); 10:1–2 (KJV, "to be bold"); Heb. 13:6, KJV, "boldly"; RV, "with good courage" (lit., "being courageous"). See COURAGE.

2. *parrhēsiazomai* (παρρησιάζομαι, 3955), "to speak boldly, or freely," primarily had reference to speech (see B, below), but acquired the meaning of "being bold, or waxing bold," 1 Thess. 2:2; in Acts 13:46, RV, "spake out boldly" (the aorist participle here signifies "waxing bold"); Acts 9:27, 29, "preached boldly" (see also 18:26; 19:8); in 26:26, "speak freely." See FREELY.

3. *tolmaō* (τολμάω, 5111) signifies "to dare to do, or to bear, something terrible or difficult"; hence, "to be bold, to bear oneself boldy, deal boldly"; it is translated "be bold" in 2 Cor. 10:2, as contrasted with *tharreō* in verse 1, and the first line of verse 2, "shew courage" (see No. 1, above); in 10:12, RV, "are not bold to," for KJV, "dare not make ourselves of." *Tharreō* denotes confidence in one's own powers, and has reference to character; *tolmaō* denotes boldness in undertaking and has reference to manifestation (Thayer). See COURAGE, DARE.

4. *apotolmaō* (ἀποτολμάω, 662), *apo* (intensive), with No. 3, means "to be very bold, to speak out boldly," and is used in Rom. 10:20.¶

B. Noun.

parrhēsia (παρρησία, 3954), from *pas*, "all," *rhēsis*, "speech" (see A, No. 2), denotes (*a*), primarily, "freedom of speech, unreservedness of utterance," Acts 4:29, 31; 2 Cor. 3:12; 7:4; Philem. 8; or "to speak without ambiguity, plainly," John 10:24; or "without figures of speech," John 16:25; (*b*) "the absence of fear in speaking boldly; hence, confidence, cheerful courage, boldness, without any connection necessarily with speech"; the RV has "boldness" in the following; Acts 4:13; Eph. 3:12; 1 Tim. 3:13; Heb. 3:6; 4:16; 10:19, 35; 1 John 2:28; 3:21; 4:17; 5:14; (*c*) the deportment by which one becomes conspicuous, John 7:4; 11:54, acts

openly, or secures publicity, Col. 2:15. See CON-
FIDENCE, OPENLY, PLAINNESS.

C. Adverb.

tolmēroterōs (τολμηροτέρως, 5112), the
comparative degree of *tolmērōs*, means "the
more boldly," Rom. 15:15; in some texts, *tol-
mēroteron.* Cf. A, No. 3.¶ Cf. *tolmētēs*, "presumptuous"; RV, "daring," 2 Pet. 2:10.¶

BOND

1. *desmos* (δεσμός, 1199), from *deō*, "to
bind" (see BAND), is usually found in the plural,
either masculine or neuter; (*a*) it stands thus for
the actual "bonds" which bind a prisoner, as in
Luke 8:29; Acts 16:26; 20:23 (the only three
places where the neuter plural is used); 22:30;
(*b*) the masculine plural stands frequently in a
figurative sense for "a condition of imprisonment," Phil. 1:7, 13, i.e., "so that my captivity
became manifest as appointed for the cause of
Christ"; verses 14, 16; Col. 4:18; 2 Tim. 2:9;
Philem. 10, 13; Heb. 10:34.

In Mark 7:35 "the bond (KJV, string)" stands
metaphorically for "the infirmity which caused
an impediment in his speech." So in Luke
13:16, of the infirmity of the woman who was
bowed together. See BAND, CHAIN, STRING.

2. *desmios* (δέσμιος, 1198), "a binding," denotes "a prisoner," e.g., Acts 25:14, RV, for the
KJV, "in bonds"; Heb. 13:3, "them that are in
bonds." Paul speaks of himself as a prisoner of
Christ, Eph. 3:1; 2 Tim. 1:8; Philem. 1, 9; "in
the Lord," Eph. 4:1. See PRISONER.

3. *sundesmos* (σύνδεσμος, 4886), "that
which binds together" (*sun*, "with," and No. 1),
is said of "the bond of iniquity," Acts 8:23; "the
bond of peace," Eph. 4:3; "the bond of perfectness," Col. 3:14 (figurative of the ligaments of
the body); elsewhere; Col. 2:19, "bands," figuratively of the bands which unite the church, the
body of Christ. See BAND.¶

4. *halusis* (ἅλυσις, 254) denotes "a chain";
so the RV in Eph. 6:20, for KJV "bonds." See
CHAIN.

5. *gramma* (γράμμα, 1121), in Luke 16:6,
RV, means "a bill or note of hand." See BILL,
No. 2.

6. *cheirographon* (χειρόγραφον, 5498), "a
handwriting," is rendered "bond" in Col. 2:14,
RV.

BONDAGE

A. Noun.

douleia (δουλεία, 1397), akin to *deō*, "to
bind," primarily "the condition of being a
slave," came to denote any kind of bondage, as,
e.g., of the condition of creation, Rom. 8:21; of
that fallen condition of man himself which

makes him dread God, v. 15, and fear death,
Heb. 2:15; of the condition imposed by the
Mosaic Law, Gal. 4:24. See SERVE.

B. Verbs.

1. *douleuō* (δουλεύω, 1398), "to serve as a
slave, to be a slave, to be in bondage," is frequently used without any association of slavery,
e.g., Acts 20:19; Rom. 6:6; 7:6; 12:11; Gal.
5:13. See SERVE.

2. *douloō* (δουλόω, 1402), different from No.
1, in being transitive instead of intransitive, signifies "to make a slave of, to bring into bondage," Acts 7:6; 1 Cor. 9:19, RV; in the passive
voice, "to be brought under bondage," 2 Pet.
2:19; "to be held in bondage," Gal. 4:3 (lit.,
"were reduced to bondage"); Titus 2:3, "of
being enslaved to wine"; Rom. 6:18, "of service
to righteousness" (lit., "were made bondservants"). As with the purchased slave there were
no limitations either in the kind or the time of
service, so the life of the believer is to be lived
in continuous obedience to God. See ENSLAVED,
GIVE, SERVANT.

3. *doulagōgeō* (δουλαγωγέω, 1396), "to
bring into bondage" (from A, above, and *agō*,
"to bring"), is used in 1 Cor. 9:27, concerning
the body, RV, "bondage," for KJV, "subjection."¶

4. *katadouloō* (καταδουλόω, 2615), "to
bring into bondage," occurs in 2 Cor. 11:20;
Gal. 2:4.¶

BONDMAN, BONDMAID

doulos (δοῦλος, 1401), from *deō*, "to bind,"
"a slave," originally the lowest term in the scale
of servitude, came also to mean "one who gives
himself up to the will of another," e.g., 1 Cor.
7:23; Rom. 6:17, 20, and became the most
common and general word for "servant," as in
Matt. 8:9, without any idea of bondage. In
calling himself, however, a "bondslave of Jesus
Christ," e.g., Rom. 1:1, the apostle Paul intimates (1) that he had been formerly a "bondslave" of Satan, and (2) that, having been
bought by Christ, he was now a willing slave,
bound to his new Master. See SERVANT.

The feminine, *doulē*, signifies "a handmaid,"
Luke 1:38, 48; Acts 2:18.¶

paidiskē (παιδίσκη, 3814), "a young girl,
maiden," also denoted "a young female slave,
bondwoman, or handmaid." For the KJV,
"bondmaid" or "bondwoman," in Gal. 4:22–
23, 30–31, the RV has "handmaid." See DAM-
SEL, HANDMAID, MAID.

For **BONDSERVANT** see **SERVANT**

BONE

osteon (ὀστέον, 3747), probably from a word signifying strength, or firmness, sometimes denotes "hard substances other than bones," e.g., the stone or kernel of fruit. In the NT it always denotes "bones," Matt. 23:27; Luke 24:39; John 19:36; Heb. 11:22.¶

Note: As to Eph. 5:30, RV, "We are members of His body" (in contrast to the KJV), "the words that follow in the common text are an unintelligent gloss, in which unsuccessful endeavor is made to give greater distinctness to the Apostle's statement" (Westcott).

BOOK

1. *biblos* (βίβλος, 976) (Eng. "Bible") was the inner part, or rather the cellular substance, of the stem of the papyrus (Eng. "paper"). It came to denote the paper made from this bark in Egypt, and then a written "book," roll, or volume. It is used in referring to "books" of Scripture, the "book," or scroll, of Matthew's Gospel, Matt. 1:1; the Pentateuch, as the "book" of Moses, Mark 12:26; Isaiah, as "the book of the words of Isaiah," Luke 3:4; the Psalms, Luke 20:42 and Acts 1:20; "the prophets," Acts 7:42; to "the Book of Life," Phil. 4:3; Rev. 3:5; 20:15. Once only it is used of secular writings, Acts 19:19.¶

2. *biblion* (βιβλίον, 975), a diminutive of No. 1, had in Hellenistic Greek almost lost its diminutive force and was ousting *biblos* in ordinary use; it denotes "a scroll or a small book." It is used in Luke 4:17, 20, of the "book" of Isaiah; in John 20:30, of the Gospel of John; in Gal. 3:10 and Heb. 10:7, of the whole of the OT; in Heb. 9:19, of the "book" of Exodus; in Rev. 1:11; 22:7, 9–10, 18 (twice), 19, of the Apocalypse; in John 21:25 and 2 Tim. 4:13, of "books" in general; in Rev. 13:8; 17:8; 20:12; 21:27, of the "Book" of Life (see *Note,* below); in Rev. 20:12, of other "books" to be opened in the Day of Judgment, containing, it would seem, the record of human deeds. In Rev. 5:1–9 the "Book" represents the revelation of God's purposes and counsels concerning the world. So with the "little book" in Rev. 10:8. In 6:14 it is used of a scroll, the rolling up of which illustrates the removal of the heaven.

In Matt. 19:7 and Mark 10:4 the word is used of a bill of divorcement. See BILL.¶

Note: In Rev. 22:19, the most authentic mss. have *xulon,* "tree (of life)," instead of "*biblion.*"

3. *biblaridion* (βιβλαρίδιον, 974), another diminutive of No. 1, is always rendered "little book," in Rev. 10:2, 9–10. Some texts have it

also in verse 8, instead of *biblion* (but see beginning of No. 2).¶

BOON

dōrēma (δώρημα, 1434), translated "boon" in Jas. 1:17, RV, is thus distinguished, as the thing given, from the preceding word in the verse, *dosis,* "the act of giving" (KJV, "gift" in each case); elsewhere in Rom. 5:16. It is to be distinguished also from *dōron,* the usual word for a gift. See GIFT.¶

BORDER

1. *kraspedon* (κράσπεδον, 2899) was primarily "the extremity or prominent part of a thing, an edge"; hence "the fringe of a garment, or a little fringe," hanging down from the edge of the mantle or cloak. The Jews had these attached to their mantles to remind them of the Law, according to Num. 15:38–39; Deut. 22:12; Zech. 8:23.¶. This is the meaning in Matt. 23:5. In Matt. 9:20; 14:36; Mark 6:56; Luke 8:44, it is used of the border of Christ's garment (KJV "hem," in the first two places). See HEM.¶

2. *horion* (ὅριον, 3725), "the border of a country or district" (cf. Eng., "horizon"), is always used in the plural. The KJV has "coasts," but "borders" in Matt. 4:13; the RV always "borders," Matt. 2:16; 4:13; 8:34; 15:22, 39; 19:1; Mark 5:17; 7:31 (twice); 10:1; Acts 13:50. In some of these it signifies territory. See COAST.¶

3. *methorion* (μεθόριον, 3181**), *meta,* "with," and No. 2, similar in meaning, is found, in some mss., in Mark 7:24.¶ Cf. *horothesia,* under BOUND.

For BORN see BEGET

For BORNE see BEAR

BORROW

daneizō (δανείζω, 1155), in the active voice, signifies "to lend money," as in Luke 6:34–35; in the middle voice, "to have money lent to oneself, to borrow," Matt. 5:42.¶ Cf. *dan(e)ion,* "a debt," Matt. 18:27,¶ and *dan(e)istēs,* "a creditor," Luke 7:41.¶ See LEND.

BOSOM

kolpos (κόλπος, 2859) signifies (*a*) "the front of the body between the arms"; hence, to recline in the "bosom" was said of one who so reclined at table that his head covered, as it were, the "bosom" of the one next to him, John 13:23. Hence, figuratively, it is used of a place of blessedness with another, as with Abraham in paradise, Luke 16:22–23 (plural in v. 23), from the custom of reclining at table in the "bosom," a place of honor; of the Lord's eternal and essential relation with the Father, in all its blessedness and affection as intimated in the phrase, "The Only-begotten Son, which is in the bosom of the Father" (John 1:18); (b) "of the bosom of a garment, the hollow formed by the upper forepart of a loose garment, bound by a girdle and used for carrying or keeping things"; thus figuratively of repaying one liberally, Luke 6:38; cf. Isa. 65:6; Jer. 39:18; (c) "of an inlet of the sea," because of its shape, like a bosom, Acts 27:39. See BAY, CREEK.¶

For **BOTH** see *Note* †, p. 1

For **BOTTLE** see **SKIN**

BOTTOM, BOTTOMLESS

A. Adverb.

katō (κάτω, 2736); for this see BENEATH.

B. Adjective.

abussos (ἄβυσσος, 12), "bottomless" (from *a*, intensive, and *bussos*, "a depth"; akin to *bathus*, "deep"; Eng., "bath"), is used as a noun denoting the abyss (KJV, "bottomless pit"). It describes an immeasurable depth, the underworld, the lower regions, the abyss of Sheol. In Rom. 10:7, quoted from Deut. 30:13, the abyss (the abode of the lost dead) is substituted for the sea (the change in the quotation is due to the facts of the death and resurrection of Christ); the KJV has "deep" here and in Luke 8:31; the reference is to the lower regions as the abode of demons, out of which they can be let loose, Rev. 11:7; 17:8; it is found seven times in the Apocalypse, 9:1–2, 11; 11:7; 17:8; 20:1, 3; in 9:1, 2 the RV has "the pit of the abyss." See DEEP.¶

For **BOUGHT** see **BUY**

BOUND (Noun)

horothesia (ὁροθεσία, 3734), "the fixing of a boundary," rather than the boundary itself (from *horos*, "a boundary," and *tithēmi*, "to place"), is used in Acts 17:26, "bounds."¶

BOUND (to be)

(a) *of obligation*:

opheilō (ὀφείλω, 3784), "to owe, whether of a debt or any obligation," is translated "we are bound," in 2 Thess. 1:3 and 2:13 (the apostle expressing his obligation to give thanks for his readers). See BEHOVE.

Note: Dei, it is necessary (for which see MUST), expresses, not the obligation (as does

opheilō) but the certainty or inevitableness of what is bound to happen, e.g., John 3:15, "must be lifted up" (i.e., inevitably), and Acts 4:12, "wherein we must be saved" (i.e., there is a certainty of salvation).

(b) *of binding*:

perikeimai (περίκειμαι, 4029), lit., "to lie around" (*peri*, "around," *keimai*, "to lie"), "to be compassed," is used of binding fetters around a person, Acts 28:20; in Mark 9:42, and Luke 17:2, to hang about a person's neck; in Heb. 5:2, to compass about, metaphorically of infirmities; in 12:1, of those who have witness borne to their faith. See COMPASS, HANG.¶

Note: For "bound" in Acts 22:5; 24:27, see BIND, No. 1; for Acts 22:25, KJV, see BIND, No. 7; for Luke 8:29, see BIND, No. 6.

BOUNTY, BOUNTIFULLY

1. *eulogia* (εὐλογία, 2129), "a blessing," has the meaning of "bounty" in 2 Cor. 9:5, of the offering sent by the church at Corinth to their needy brethren in Judea.

Note: In the next verse the adverb "bountifully" is a translation of the phrase *ep' eulogiais*, lit., "with blessings" (RV marg.), that is, that blessings may accrue. See BLESSING.

2. *haplotēs* (ἁπλότης, 572), from *haplous*, "simple, single," is translated "bountifulness" in 2 Cor. 9:11, KJV; RV, "liberality" (marg., "singleness"); cf. 8:2; 9:13; from sincerity of mind springs "liberality." The thought of sincerity is present in Rom. 12:8; 2 Cor. 11:3; Eph. 6:5; Col. 3:22. See LIBERAL, SIMPLICITY, SINGLENESS.¶

3. *charis* (χάρις, 5485), "grace," is rendered, "bounty" in 1 Cor. 16:3, RV, (KJV, "liberality"), by metonymy for a material gift. See BENEFIT, No. 3.

4. *hadrotēs* (ἁδρότης, 100), lit., "fatness" (from *hadros*, "thick, well-grown"), is used of a monetary gift, in 2 Cor. 8:20, KJV, "abundance," RV, "bounty." ¶

BOW, BOWED (Verb)

1. *kamptō* (κάμπτω, 2578), "to bend," is used especially of bending the knees in religious veneration, Rom. 11:4; 14:11; Eph. 3:14; Phil. 2:10.¶

2. *sunkamptō* (συνκάμπτω, 4781) signifies "to bend completely together, to bend down by compulsory force," Rom. 11:10.¶

3. *sunkuptō* (συγκύπτω, 4794), "to bow together" (*sun*, "together with," *kuptō*, "to bow"), is said, in Luke 13:11, of the woman crippled with a physical infirmity.¶

4. *klinō* (κλίνω, 2827), "to incline, to bow down," is used of the women who in their fright

"bowed" their faces to the earth at the Lord's empty tomb, Luke 24:5; of the act of the Lord on the cross immediately before giving up His Spirit. What is indicated in the statement "He bowed His head," is not the helpless dropping of the head after death, but the deliberate putting of His head into a position of rest, John 19:30. The verb is deeply significant here. The Lord reversed the natural order. The same verb is used in His statement in Matt. 8:20 and Luke 9:58, "the Son of Man hath not where to lay His head." It is used, too, of the decline of day, Luke 9:12; 24:29; of turning enemies to flight, Heb. 11:34. See LAY, SPENT. No. 7, TURN, WEAR.¶

5. *tithēmi* (τίθημι, 5087), "to put, or place," is said of the soldiers who mockingly bowed their knees to Christ, Mark 15:19. See APPOINT.

Note: For *gonupeteō*, "to bow the knee," Matt. 27:29, see KNEEL.

BOW (Noun)

toxon (τόξον, 5115), "a bow," is used in Rev. 6:2. Cf. Hab. 3:8–9. The instrument is frequently mentioned in the Sept., especially in the Psalms.¶

BOWELS

splanchnon (σπλάγχνον, 4698), always in the plural, properly denotes "the physical organs of the intestines," and is once used in this respect, Acts 1:18 (for the use by Greeks and Hebrews, see AFFECTION, No. 2). The RV substitutes the following for the word "bowels": "affections," 2 Cor. 6:12; "affection," 2 Cor. 7:15; "tender mercies," Phil. 1:8; 2:1; "a heart (of compassion)," Col. 3:12; "heart," Philem. 12, 20; "hearts," Philem. 7; "compassion," 1 John 3:17. The word is rendered "tender" in the KJV and RV of Luke 1:78, in connection with the word "mercy." See AFFECTION, No. 2, COMPASSION, A, No. 2 and B, No. 2.¶

BOWL

phialē (φιάλη, 5357) (Eng., "phial") denotes "a bowl"; so the RV, for KJV, "vial," in Rev. 5:8; 15:7; 16:1–4, 8, 10, 12, 17; 17:1; 21:9; the word is suggestive of rapidity in the emptying of the contents. While the seals (ch. 6) give a general view of the events of the last "week" or "hebdomad," in the vision given to Daniel, Dan. 9:23–27, the "trumpets" refer to the judgments which, in a more or less extended period, are destined to fall especially, though not only, upon apostate Christendom and apostate Jews. The emptying of the "bowls" betokens the final series of judgments in which this exercise of the wrath of God is "finished" (Rev. 15:1, RV).

These are introduced by the 7th trumpet. See Rev. 11:15 and the successive order in v. 18, "the nations were wroth, and Thy wrath came . . ."; see also 6:17; 14:19, 20; 19:11–21.¶

BOX

alabastron (ἀλάβαστρον, 211), "an alabaster vessel," is translated in the KJV of Matt. 26:7; Mark 14:3; Luke 7:37, "box," RV, "cruse." The breaking refers to the seal, not to the box or cruse. See CRUSE.¶

BOY

pais (παῖς, 3816) denotes "a boy" (in contrast to *paidion*, a diminutive of *pais*, and to *teknon*, "a child"). With reference to Christ, instead of the KJV "child," the RV suitably translates otherwise as follows: Luke 2:43, "the boy Jesus"; Acts 4:27, 30, "Thy Holy Servant, Jesus." So in the case of others, Matt. 17:18 and Luke 9:42 ("boy"). See CHILD, MAID, MANSERVANT, SERVANT, SON, YOUNG MAN.

BRAIDED (KJV, BROIDED)

plegma (πλέγμα, 4117) signifies "what is woven" (from *plekō*, "to weave, plait"), whether a net or basket (Josephus uses it of the ark of bulrushes in which the infant Moses was laid), or of a web, plait, braid. It is used in 1 Tim. 2:9, of "braided hair," which the Vulgate signifies as "ringlets, curls."¶

Notes: (1) Cf. *emplokē*, 1 Pet. 3:3, "plaiting," i.e., intertwining the hair in ornament.¶

(2) "Broided" is to be distinguished from broidered, which means to adorn with needlework (not to plait).

For **BRAKE** see **BREAK**

For **BRAMBLE BUSH** see **BUSH**

BRANCH

1. *klados* (κλάδος, 2798), from *klaō*, "to break" (cf. *klasma*, "a broken piece"), properly a young tender shoot, "broken off" for grafting, is used for any kind of branch, Matt. 13:32; 21:8; 24:32; Mark 4:32; 13:28; Luke 13:19; the descendants of Israel, Rom. 11:16–19, 21.¶

2. *klēma* (κλῆμα, 2814), akin to *klaō*, "to break," denotes "a tender, flexible branch, especially the shoot of a vine, a vine sprout," John 15:2, 4–6.¶

3. *stoibas* or *stibas* (στοιβάς, 4746), from *steibō*, "to tread on," primarily denoted "a layer of leaves, reeds, twigs or straw, serving for a bed"; then "a branch full of leaves, soft foliage," which might be used in making a bed, or for treading upon, Mark 11:8.¶

4. *baion* (βαῖον, 902), of Egyptian origin, frequent in the papyri writings, denotes "a branch of the palm tree," John 12:13.¶

Note: Matthew, Mark and John each use a different word for "branch" in narrating Christ's entry into Jerusalem.

BRANDED

kaustēriazo (καυστηριάζω, 2743), "to burn in with a branding iron" (cf. Eng., "caustic"), is found, in the best mss., in 1 Tim. 4:2, RV "branded." Others have *kautēriazō* (from *kautērion*, "a branding-iron," Eng., "cauterize"), to mark by "branding," an act not quite so severe as that indicated by the former. The reference is to apostates whose consciences are "branded" with the effects of their sin. See SEARED.¶

Note: In the RV of Gal. 6:17, "branded" does not represent a word in the original; it serves to bring out the force of the apostle's metaphor of bearing in his body the *stigmata*, the marks, of the Lord Jesus. The reference is not to the branding of slaves, soldiers and criminals, but rather to the religious devotee, who "branded" himself with the mark of the god whom he specially worshipped. So Paul describes the physical marks due to the lictor's rods at Philippi and to the stones at Lystra, marks which, while not self-inflicted, betokened his devotion to Christ and his rejoicing therein.

BRASS, BRAZEN

1. *chalkos* (χαλκός, 5475), primarily, "copper," became used for metals in general, later was applied to bronze, a mixture of copper and tin, then, by metonymy, to any article made of these metals, e.g., money, Matt. 10:9; Mark 6:8; 12:41, or a sounding instrument, 1 Cor. 13:1, figurative of a person destitute of love. See Rev. 18:12. See MONEY.¶

2. *chalkeos* (χάλκεος, 5470), "made of brass or bronze," is used of idols, Rev. 9:20.¶

3. *chalkion* (χαλκίον, 5473) is used in Mark 7:4 of "brazen vessels."¶

4. *chalkolibanon* (χαλκολίβανον, 5474) is used of "white or shining copper or bronze," and describes the feet of the Lord, in Rev. 1:15 and 2:18.¶

5. *chalkeus* (χαλκεύς, 5471) denotes "a coppersmith," 2 Tim. 4:14.¶

BRAWLER

1. *paroinos* (πάροινος, 3943), an adjective, lit., "tarrying at wine" (*para*, "at," *oinos*, "wine"), "given to wine," 1 Tim. 3:3 and Titus 1:7, KJV, probably has the secondary sense, of the effects of wine-bibbing, viz., abusive brawling. Hence RV, "brawler." See WINE.¶

2. *amachos* (ἄμαχος, 269), an adjective, lit., "not fighting" (*a*, negative, *machē*, "a fight"), came to denote, metaphorically, "not contentious," 1 Tim. 3:3, and Titus 3:2, RV, for KJV, "not a brawler," "not brawlers." See CONTENTIOUS.¶

BREAD (Loaf)

1. *artos* (ἄρτος, 740), "bread" (perhaps derived from *arō*, "to fit together," or from a root *ar*—, "the earth"), signifies (*a*) "a small loaf or cake," composed of flour and water, and baked, in shape either oblong or round, and about as thick as the thumb; these were not cut, but broken and were consecrated to the Lord every Sabbath and called the "shewbread" (loaves of presentation), Matt. 12:4; when the "shewbread" was reinstituted by Nehemiah (Neh. 10:32) a poll-tax of 1/3 shekel was laid on the Jews, Matt. 17:24; (*b*) "the loaf at the Lord's Supper," e.g., Matt. 26:26 ("Jesus took a loaf," RV, marg.); the breaking of "bread" became the name for this institution, Acts 2:42; 20:7; 1 Cor. 10:16; 11:23; (*c*) "bread of any kind," Matt. 16:11; (*d*) metaphorically, "of Christ as the Bread of God, and of Life," John 6:33, 35; (*e*) "food in general," the necessities for the sustenance of life, Matt. 6:11; 2 Cor. 9:10, etc.

2. *azumos* (ἄζυμος, 106) denotes "unleavened bread," i.e., without any process of fermentation; hence, metaphorically, "of a holy, spiritual condition," 1 Cor. 5:7, and of "sincerity and truth" (v. 8). With the article it signifies the feast of unleavened bread, Matt. 26:17; Mark 14:1, 12; Luke 22:1, 7; Acts 12:3; 20:6.¶

For **BREADTH** see **BROAD**

BREAK, BREAKER, BREAKING, BRAKE

A. Verbs.

1. *klaō* or *klazō* (κλάω, 2806), "to break, to break off pieces," is used of "breaking bread," (*a*) of the Lord's act in providing for people, Matt. 14:19; 15:36; Mark 8:6, 19; (*b*) of the "breaking of bread" in the Lord's Supper, Matt. 26:26; Mark 14:22; Luke 22:19; Acts 20:7; 1 Cor. 10:16; 11:24; (*c*) of an ordinary meal, Acts 2:46; 20:11; 27:35; (*d*) of the Lord's act in giving evidence of His resurrection, Luke 24:30.¶

2. *ekklaō* (ἐκκλάω, 1575), *ek*, "off," and No. 1, "to break off," is used metaphorically of branches, Rom. 11:17, 19–20.¶

3. *kataklaō* (κατακλάω, 2622), *kata*, "down," and No. 1, is used in Mark 6:41 and

Luke 9:16, of Christ's "breaking" loaves for the multitudes.¶

4. *luō* (λύω, 3089), "to loosen," especially by way of deliverance, sometimes has the meaning of "breaking, destructively," e.g., of "breaking" commandments, not only infringing them, but loosing the force of them, rendering them not binding, Matt. 5:19; John 5:18; of "breaking" the Law of Moses, John 7:23; Scripture, John 10:35; of the "breaking up" of a ship, Acts 27:41; of the "breaking down" of the middle wall of partition, Eph. 2:14; of the marriage tie, 1 Cor. 7:27. See DESTROY, DISSOLVE, LOOSE, MELT, PUT, *Note* (5), UNLOOSE.

5. *suntribō* (συντρίβω, 4937), lit., "to rub together," and so "to shatter, shiver, break in pieces by crushing," is said of the bruising of a reed, Matt. 12:20 (No. 9 is used in the next clause); the "breaking" of fetters in pieces, Mark 5:4; the "breaking" of an alabaster cruse, Mark 14:3; an earthenware vessel, Rev. 2:27; of the physical bruising of a person possessed by a demon, Luke 9:39; concerning Christ, "a bone of Him shall not be broken," John 19:36; metaphorically of the crushed condition of a "broken-hearted" person, Luke 4:18 (KJV only); of the eventual crushing of Satan, Rom. 16:20. See BRUISE.¶ This verb is frequent in the Sept. in the passive voice, e.g., Ps. 51:17; Isa. 57:15, of a contrite heart, perhaps a figure of stones made smooth by being rubbed together in streams. Cf. *suntrimma*, "destruction."

6. *rhēgnumi* (ῥήγνυμι, 4486), "to tear, rend, as of garments, etc.," is translated "break" in the KJV, of Matt. 9:17, of wine-skins (RV, "burst"); as in Mark 2:22 and Luke 5:37.; "break forth" in Gal. 4:27. See BURST, REND, TEAR.

7. *diarrhēgnumi* (διαρρήγνυμι, 1284), *dia*, "through" (intensive), and No. 6, "to burst asunder, to rend, cleave," is said of the rending of garments, Matt. 26:65; Mark 14:63; Acts 14:14; of the "breaking" of a net, Luke 5:6; of fetters, 8:29. See REND.¶

8. *prosrhēgnumi* (προσρήγνυμι, 4366): see BEAT, No. 8.

9. *katagnumi* (κατάγνυμι, 2608), *kata*, "down" (intensive), and No. 6, is used of the "breaking" of a bruised reed, Matt. 12:20, and of the "breaking" of the legs of those who were crucified, John 19:31, 32, 33.¶

10. *sunthlaō* (συνθλάω, 4917), *sun*, "together" (intensive), and *thlaō*, "to break or crush, to break in pieces, to shatter," is used in Matt. 21:44 and Luke 20:18 of the physical effect of falling on a stone.¶

11. *sunthruptō* (συνθρύπτω, 4919), *sun*, and *thruptō*, "to crush, to break small, weaken," is

used metaphorically of "breaking" one's heart, Acts 21:13.¶

12. *schizō* (σχίζω, 4977), "to split, to rend open," is said of the veil of the temple, Matt. 27:51; the rending of rocks, Matt. 27:51; the rending of the heavens, Mark 1:10; a garment, Luke 5:36; John 19:24; a net, John 21:11; in the passive voice, metaphorically, of being divided into factions, Acts 14:4; 23:7. See DIVINE, *Note*, OPEN, REND, RENT.

Note: Cf. *schisma* (Eng., "schism"), said of the rent in a garment, Matt. 9:16. See DIVISION, RENT, SCHISM.

13. *diorussō* (διορύσσω, 1358), lit., "to dig through" (*dia*, "through," *orussō*, "to dig"), is used of the act of thieves in "breaking" into a house, Matt. 6:19, 20; 24:43; Luke 12:39.¶

14. *exorussō* (ἐξορύσσω, 1846), lit., "to dig out" (cf. No. 13), is used of the "breaking up" of part of a roof, Mark 2:4, and, in a vivid expression, of plucking out the eyes, Gal. 4:15. See PLUCK.¶

Note: For *aristaō*, "to break one's fast," see DINE.

B. Nouns.

1. *klasis* (κλάσις, 2800), "a breaking" (akin to A, No. 1), is used in Luke 24:35 and Acts 2:42, of the "breaking" of bread.¶

2. *klasma* (κλάσμα, 2801), "a broken piece, fragment," is always used of remnants of food, Matt. 14:20; 15:37 and corresponding passages. See PIECE.

3. *parabasis* (παράβασις, 3847), "a transgression" (*para*, "across," *bainō*, "to go"), is translated "breaking" in Rom. 2:23, KJV; RV, "transgression"; KJV and RV ditto in 4:15; 5:14; Gal. 3:19; 1 Tim. 2:14; Heb. 2:2; 9:15. See TRANSGRESSION.

4. *parabatēs* (παραβάτης, 3848), "a transgressor" (cf. No. 3), is translated "breaker," Rom. 2:25, KJV; RV, "transgressor." In v. 27 the KJV turns it into a verb, "dost transgress." See Gal. 2:18; Jas. 2:9, 11.¶

BREAST

1. *stēthos* (στῆθος, 4738), connected with *histēmi*, "to stand," i.e., that which stands out, is used of mourners in smiting the "breast," Luke 18:13; 23:48; of John in reclining on the "breast" of Christ, John 13:25; 21:20; of the "breasts" of the angels in Rev. 15:6.¶

2. *mastos* (μαστός, 3149), used in the plural, "paps," Luke 11:27; 23:29; Rev. 1:13, KJV, is preferably rendered "breasts," in the RV.¶

BREASTPLATE

thōrax (θώραξ, 2382), primarily, "the breast," denotes "a breastplate or corselet," consisting of two parts and protecting the body on both sides, from the neck to the middle. It is used metaphorically of righteousness, Eph. 6:14; of faith and love, 1 Thess. 5:8, with perhaps a suggestion of the two parts, front and back, which formed the coat of mail (an alternative term for the word in the NT sense); elsewhere in Rev. 9:9, 17.¶

BREATH, BREATHE

A. Nouns.

1. *pnoē* (πνοή, 4157), akin to *pneō*, "to blow," lit., "a blowing," signifies (*a*) "breath, the breath of life," Acts 17:25; (*b*) "wind," Acts 2:2. See WIND.¶

2. *pneuma* (πνεῦμα, 4151), "spirit," also denotes "breath," Rev. 11:11 and 13:15, RV. In 2 Thess. 2:8, the KJV has "spirit" for RV, "breath." See GHOST, LIFE, SPIRIT, WIND.

B. Verbs.

1. *empneō* (ἐμπνέω, 1709), lit., "to breathe in, or on," is used in Acts 9:1, indicating that threatening and slaughter were, so to speak, the elements from which Saul drew and expelled his breath.¶

2. *emphusaō* (ἐμφυσάω, 1720), "to breathe upon," is used of the symbolic act of the Lord Jesus in breathing upon His apostles the communication of the Holy Spirit, John 20:22.¶

BRIDE, BRIDECHAMBER, BRIDEGROOM

numphē (νύμφη, 3565) (Eng. "nymph") "a bride, or young wife," John 3:29; Rev. 18:23; 21:2, 9; 22:17, is probably connected with the Latin *nubō*, "to veil"; the "bride" was often adorned with embroidery and jewels (see Rev. 21:2), and was led veiled from her home to the "bridegroom." Hence the secondary meaning of "daughter-in-law," Matt. 10:35; Luke 12:53. See DAUGHTER-IN-LAW.¶ For the relationship between Christ and a local church, under this figure, see 2 Cor. 11:2; regarding the whole church, Eph. 5:23–32; Rev. 22:17.

numphios (νυμφίος, 3566), "a bridegroom," occurs fourteen times in the gospels, and in Rev. 18:23. "The friend of the bridegroom," John 3:29, is distinct from "the sons of the bridechamber" who were numerous. When John the Baptist speaks of "the friend of the Bridegroom," he uses language according to the customs of the Jews.

numphōn (νυμφών, 3567) signifies (*a*) "the room or dining hall in which the marriage ceremonies were held," Matt. 22:10; some mss. have *gamos*, "a wedding," here; (*b*) "the chamber containing the bridal bed," "the sons of the

bridechamber" being the friends of the bridegroom, who had the charge of providing what was necessary for the nuptials, Matt. 9:15; Mark 2:19; Luke 5:34.¶

BRIDLE

A. Noun.

chalinos (χαλινός, 5469), "a bridle," is used in Jas. 3:3 (KJV, "bits"), and Rev. 14:20. "The primitive bridle was simply a loop on the haltercord passed round the lower jaw of the horse. Hence in Ps. 32:9 the meaning is bridle and halter" (Hastings, *Bib. Dic.*).¶

B. Verb.

chalinagōgeō (χαλιναγωγέω, 5468), from *chalinos* and *agō*, "to lead," signifies "to lead by a bridle, to bridle, to hold in check, restrain"; it is used metaphorically of the tongue and of the body in Jas. 1:26 and 3:2.¶

BRIEFLY

di' oligōn (δι' ὀλίγων) lit. means "by few." In 1 Pet. 5:12 it signifies by means of few words, "briefly." The RV of Rom. 13:9 omits "briefly," the meaning being "it is summed up."¶

For BRIER see THISTLE

BRIGHT, BRIGHTNESS

A. Adjectives.

1. *phōteinos* (φωτεινός, 5460), "bright" (from *phōs*, "light"), is said of a cloud, Matt. 17:5; metaphorically of the body, Matt. 6:22, "full of light"; Luke 11:34, 36. See LIGHT.¶

2. *lampros* (λαμπρός, 2986), "shining, brilliant, bright," is used of the clothing of an angel, Acts 10:30 and Rev. 15:6; symbolically, of the clothing of the saints in glory, Rev. 19:8, RV, in the best texts (KJV, "white"); of Christ as the Morning Star, 22:16; of the water of life, 22:1, KJV, "clear." See CLEAR, GAY, GOODLY, GORGEOUS, WHITE.

Note: Cf. *lamprōs*, "sumptuously," Luke 16:19.¶

B. Nouns.

1. *lamprotēs* (λαμπρότης, 2987), "brightness," akin to A, No. 2, above, is found in Acts 26:13.¶

2. *apaugasma* (ἀπαύγασμα, 541), "a shining forth" (*apo*, "from," *augē*, "brightness"), of a light coming from a luminous body, is said of Christ in Heb. 1:3, KJV, "brightness," RV, "effulgence," i.e., shining forth (a more probable meaning than reflected brightness).¶

Note: Epiphaneia (ἐπιφάνεια), lit., "shining forth or upon," is rendered "brightness" in the KJV of 2 Thess. 2:8; RV, "manifestation." See APPEARING.

BRIM

anō (ἄνω, 507), "above, on high, in a higher place," in John 2:7 is used to denote the "brim" of a waterpot, lit., "up to above," i.e., "up to the higher parts," i.e., "the brim." See ABOVE, HIGH, UP.

BRIMSTONE

1. *theion* (θεῖον, 2303) originally denoted "fire from heaven." It is connected with sulphur. Places touched by lightning were called *theia*, and, as lightning leaves a sulphurous smell, and sulphur was used in pagan purifications, it received the name of *theion*, Luke 17:29; Rev. 9:17–18; 14:10; 19:20; 20:10; 21:8.¶

2. *theiōdēs* (θειώδης, 2306), akin to No. 1, signifies "brimstone-like, or consisting of brimstone," Rev. 9:17.¶

BRING, BRINGING, BROUGHT

A. Verbs.

1. *pherō* (φέρω, 5342), "to bear, or carry," is used also of "bearing or bringing forth fruit," Mark 4:8; John 15:5, etc. To bring is the most frequent meaning. See BEAR, CARRY, DRIVE, ENDURE, GO, LEAD, MOVE, REACH, RUSHING, UPHOLD.

Compounds of No. 1, translated by the verb "to bring," are as follows:

2. *anapherō* (ἀναφέρω, 399) denotes "to bring up," Matt. 17:1. See BEAR, No. 3.

3. *apopherō* (ἀποφέρω, 667), "to carry forth," is rendered "bring," in the KJV of 1 Cor. 16:3; Acts 19:12 (RV, "carried away"); some mss. have *epipherō* here. See CARRY.

4. *eispherō* (εἰσφέρω, 1533), denotes "to bring to," Acts 17:20; "to bring into," Luke 5:18, 19; 1 Tim. 6:7; Heb. 13:11. See LEAD, No. 11.

5. *ekpherō* (ἐκφέρω, 1627), "to bring forth." See BEAR, No. 4.

6. *epipherō* (ἐπιφέρω, 2018), signifies (*a*) "to bring upon, or to bring against," Jude 9; (*b*) "to impose, inflict, visit upon," Rom. 3:5. Some mss. have it in Acts 25:18 (for No. 1); some in Phil. 1:16 (RV, v. 17, "raise up," translating *egeirō*).¶

7. *propherō* (προφέρω, 4393) denotes "to bring forth," Luke 6:45, twice.¶

8. *prospherō* (προσφέρω, 4374) means (*a*) "to bring (in addition)," Matt. 25:20; "to bring unto," Matt. 5:23 (RV, "art offering"); Mark 10:13; (*b*) "to offer," Matt. 5:24. See DEAL WITH, DO, OFFER, PRESENT, PUT.

9. *sumpherō* (συμφέρω, 4851), "to bring together," has this meaning in Acts 19:19. See BETTER (be), EXPEDIENT, GOOD, PROFIT.

10. *ago* (ἄγω, 71), "to lead, to lead along, to bring," has the meaning "to bring" (besides its occurrences in the Gospels and Acts) in 1 Thess. 4:14, 2 Tim. 4:11, and Heb. 2:10. See CARRY, GO, KEEP, LEAD.

Compounds of this verb are:

11. *anagō* (ἀνάγω, 321), "to lead or bring up to," Luke 2:22; Acts 9:39 etc.; "to bring forth," Acts 12:4; "to bring again," Heb. 13:20; "to bring up again," Rom. 10:7. See DEPART, LAUNCH, LEAD, LOOSE, OFFER, TAKE UP, SAIL.

12. *apagō* (ἀπάγω, 520), "to lead away, bring forth, bring unto," Acts 23:17. See CARRY, DEATH, LEAD, TAKE.

13. *eisagō* (εἰσάγω, 1521), "to bring in, into," Luke 2:27 etc. See LEAD.

14. *exagō* (ἐξάγω, 1806), "to lead out, bring forth," Acts 5:19; 7:36, 40 etc. See FETCH, LEAD.

15. *epagō* (ἐπάγω, 1863), "to bring upon," Acts 5:28; 2 Pet. 2:1, 5.¶

16. *katagō* (κατάγω, 2609), "to bring down," Acts 9:30; 22:30; 23:15, 20; Rom. 10:6; "to bring forth," Acts 23:28; of boats, "to bring to land," Luke 5:11. See LAND, TOUCH.

17. *pareisagō* (παρεισάγω, 3919), "to bring in privily" (lit., "to bring in beside"), "to introduce secretly," 2 Pet. 2:1.¶

18. *proagō* (προάγω, 4254), "to bring or lead forth," e.g., Acts 12:6; 16:30; 25:26. See GO, No. 10.

19. *prosagō* (προσάγω, 4317), "to bring to, or unto," Acts 16:20; 1 Pet. 3:18. For Acts 27:27 see DRAW, (*B*), No. 3.¶

Other verbs are:

20. *komizō* (κομίζω, 2865), usually, "to receive, to bring in," Luke 7:37. See RECEIVE.

21. *parechō* (παρέχω, 3930), usually, "to offer, furnish, supply" (lit., "to have near"), "to bring, in the sense of supplying," Acts 16:16; 19:24. See DO, GIVE, KEEP, MINISTER, OFFER, SHEW, TROUBLE.

22. *apostrephō* (ἀποστρέφω, 654), "to turn, or put, back," is translated "brought back" in Matt. 27:3. See PERVERT, PUT, TURN.

23. *katabibazō* (καταβιβάζω, 2601), in the active voice, "to cause to go down," is used in the passive in the sense of "being brought down," Luke 10:15 (KJV, "thrust down"); "go down" in Matt. 11:23 (marg., "be brought down").¶

24. *sumbibazō* (συμβιβάζω, 4822), rendered "brought" in Acts 19:33.¶

25. *propempō* (προπέμπω, 4311), "to send forth, to bring on one's way," Acts 15:3; 20:38, RV; 21:5; Rom. 15:24; 1 Cor. 16:6, 11; 2 Cor. 1:16; Titus 3:13; 3 John 6. See ACCOMPANY, CONDUCT.¶

26. *blastanō* (βλαστάνω, 985), "to bud, spring up," translated "brought forth" (i.e., "caused to produce"), in Jas. 5:18. See BUD, SPRING.

27. *poieō* (ποιέω, 4160), "to make, to do," used of the bringing forth of fruit, Matt. 3:8, 10; 7:17, 18. See DO.

28. *ekballō* (ἐκβάλλω, 1544), "to cast out," used of bringing forth good and evil things from the heart, Matt. 12:35. See CAST, No. 5.

29. *tiktō* (τίκτω, 5088), "to beget, bring forth," Matt. 1:21, 23, 25; Jas. 1:15 (first part of verse, according to the best mss.); Rev. 12:5 (RV, "was delivered of"). See BEGET, BORN, DELIVER.

30. *apokueō* (ἀποκύεω, 616), "to bear young," "bringeth forth" in Jas. 1:15 (end of verse) and "brought forth," v. 18 (KJV, "begat"). See BEGET.¶

31. *gennaō* (γεννάω, 1080), "to beget," translated "brought forth" in Luke 1:57. See BEGET, A, No. 1.

32. *euphoreō* (εὐφορέω, 2164), "to bear well, be productive," "brought forth plentifully," Luke 12:16.¶ Cf. *karpophoreō*, Mark 4:20, RV "bear"; so, Col. 1:6.

33. *trephō* (τρέφω, 5142), "to rear, bring up," Luke 4:16. See FEED, NOURISH.

34. *anatrephō* (ἀνατρέφω, 397), "to nourish," Acts 7:20, 21; "brought up," Acts 22:3.¶

35. *ektrephō* (ἐκτρέφω, 1625), "to nourish," Eph. 5:29; "bring up," 6:4, KJV; RV, "nurture." See NURTURE.¶

36. *apangellō* (ἀπαγγέλλω, 518), "to announce," is translated "bring word" in Matt. 2:8, RV (the KJV unnecessarily adds "again"); 28:8. See DECLARE, REPORT, SHEW, TELL.

B. Noun.

epeisagōgē (ἐπεισαγωγή, 1898), lit., "a bringing in besides," is translated "a bringing in thereupon" in Heb. 7:19.¶

Notes: (1) In Mark 4:21, *erchomai*, "to come," is translated "is brought," lit., "(does a lamp) come."

(2) In Mark 13:9, the verb translated "be brought," KJV, is *histēmi*, "to stand" (RV); in Acts 27:24, *paristēmi*, "to stand before" (KJV, "be brought before").

(3) In Acts 5:36, *ginomai*, "to become," is rendered "came (to nought)," RV, for KJV, "were brought." So in 1 Cor. 15:54, "come to pass," for "shall be brought to pass."

(4) In Mark 4:29, *paradidōmi* is rendered "is ripe," RV and KJV marg., for KJV, "brought forth."

(5) In Matt. 1:11–12, 17, *metoikesia* signifies "a removal, or carrying away" (not "they were brought," v. 12, KJV).

(6) In Acts 13:1, *suntrophos* denotes "a foster-brother," RV (KJV, marg.).¶

(7) In 1 Cor. 4:17, for "bring you into remembrance" (RV, "put . . .), see REMEMBRANCE.

(8) In Luke 1:19, for RV, "bring you good tidings," and Acts 13:32, and Rom. 10:15 (end), see PREACH.

(9) In 1 Cor. 1:19, *atheteō*, "to reject" (RV), is rendered "bring to nothing" (KJV). See DESPISE, *Note* (1).

(10) For *katargeō*, "bring to nought," RV, "destroy," 1 Cor. 6:13, etc., see ABOLISH, DESTROY.

(11) For *eipon* in Matt. 2:13, KJV, "bring . . . word," see TELL.

(12) See also DESOLATION, No. 1, PERFECTION, B.

(13) For "bring into bondage" see BONDAGE, B.

(14) In Matt. 16:8 some mss. have *lambanō* (KJV, "ye have brought").

BROAD, BREADTH

A. Adjective.

euruchōros (εὐρύχωρος, 2149), from *eurus*, "broad," and *chōra*, "a place," signifies, lit., "(with) a broad place," i.e., "broad, spacious," Matt. 7:13.¶

B. Verb.

platunō (πλατύνω, 4115), connected with *plak*, "a flat, broad surface," signifies "to make broad"; said of phylacteries, Matt. 23:5; used figuratively in 2 Cor. 6:11, 13, "to be enlarged," in the ethical sense, of the heart.¶

C. Noun.

platos (πλάτος, 4114) denotes "breadth," Eph. 3:18; Rev. 20:9; 21:16 (twice).¶

For BROIDED see BRAIDED

For BROKEN see BREAK

For BROKENHEARTED see BREAK, A, No. 5

BROILED

optos (ὀπτός, 3702), "broiled" (from *optaō*, "to cook, roast"), is said of food prepared by fire, Luke 24:42.¶

BROOD

nossia (νοσσιά, 3555), primarily, "a nest," denotes "a brood," Luke 13:34. Some texts have *nossion* in the plural, as Matt. 23:37, "chicken."¶

BROOK

cheimarrhos (χείμαρρος, 5493), lit., "winter-flowing" (from *cheima*, "winter," and *rheō*, "to flow"), a stream which runs only in winter or when swollen with rains, a "brook," John 18:1.¶

BROTHER, BRETHREN, BROTHERHOOD, BROTHERLY

adelphos (ἀδελφός, 80) denotes "a brother, or near kinsman"; in the plural, "a community based on identity of origin or life." It is used of:—

(1) male children of the same parents, Matt, 1:2; 14:3; (2) male descendants of the same parents, Acts 7:23, 26; Heb. 7:5; (3) male children of the same mother, Matt. 13:55; 1 Cor. 9:5; Gal. 1:19; (4) people of the same nationality, Acts 3:17, 22; Rom. 9:3. With "men" (*anēr*, "male"), prefixed, it is used in addresses only, Acts 2:29, 37, etc.; (5) any man, a neighbor, Luke 10:29; Matt. 5:22; 7:3; (6) persons united by a common interest, Matt. 5:47; (7) persons united by a common calling, Rev. 22:9; (8) mankind, Matt. 25:40; Heb. 2:17; (9) the disciples, and so, by implication, all believers, Matt. 28:10; John 20:17; (10) believers, apart from sex, Matt. 23:8; Acts 1:15; Rom. 1:13; 1 Thess. 1:4; Rev. 19:10 (the word "sisters" is used of believers, only in 1 Tim. 5:2); (11) believers, with *anēr*, "male," prefixed, and with "or sister" added, 1 Cor. 7:14 (RV), 15; Jas. 2:15, male as distinct from female, Acts 1:16; 15:7, 13, but not 6:3.*

Notes: (1) Associated words are *adelphotēs*, primarily, "a brotherly relation," and so, the community possessed of this relation, "a brotherhood," 1 Pet. 2:17 (see 5:9, marg.)¶; *philadelphos, (phileō*, "to love," and *adelphos)*, "fond of one's brethren," 1 Pet. 3:8; "loving as brethren," RV¶; *philadelphia*, "brotherly love," Rom. 12:10; 1 Thess. 4:9; Heb. 13:1; "love of the brethren," 1 Pet. 1:22 and 2 Pet. 1:7, RV¶; *pseudadelphos*, "false brethren," 2 Cor. 11:26; Gal. 2:4.¶

(2) In Luke 6:16 and Acts 1:13, the RV has "son," for KJV, "brother."

(3) In Acts 13:1, for *suntrophos*, see BRING, B, Note (6).

For BROUGHT see BRING

* From *Notes on Thessalonians*, by Hogg and Vine, p. 32.

BROW

ophrus (ὀφρύς, 3790), "an eyebrow," stands for "the brow of a hill," Luke 4:29, from the resemblance to an eyebrow, i.e., a ridge with an overhanging bank.¶

BRUISE

1. *suntribō* (συντρίβω, 4937): see BREAK, A, No. 5.

2. *thrauō* (θραύω, 2352), "to smite through, shatter," is used in Luke 4:18, "them that are bruised," i.e., broken by calamity. ¶

BRUTE

alogos (ἄλογος, 249), translated "brute" in the KJV of 2 Pet. 2:12 and Jude 10, signifies "without reason," RV, though, as J. Hastings points out, "brute beasts" is not at all unsuitable, as "brute" is from Latin *brutus*, which means "dull, irrational"; in Acts 25:27 it is rendered "unreasonable." ¶

BUD

blastanō (βλαστάνω, 985), "to bud," is said of Aaron's rod, Heb. 9:14; "spring up," Matt. 13:26, and Mark 4:27; elsewhere, in Jas. 5:18. See BRING, No. 26, SPRING, No. 6.¶

BUFFET

1. *kolaphizō* (κολαφίζω, 2852) signifies "to strike with clenched hands, to buffet with the fist" (*kolaphos*, "a fist"), Matt. 26:67; Mark 14:65; 1 Cor. 4:11; 2 Cor. 12:7; 1 Pet. 2:20.¶

2. *hupōpiazō* (ὑπωπιάζω, 5299), lit., "to strike under the eye" (from *hupōpion*, "the part of the face below the eye"; *hupo*, "under," *ōps*, "an eye"), hence, to beat the face black and blue (to give a black eye), is used metaphorically, and translated "buffet" in 1 Cor. 9:27 (KJV, "keep under"), of Paul's suppressive treatment of his body, in order to keep himself spiritually fit (RV marg., "bruise"); so RV marg. in Luke 18:5, of the persistent widow, text, "wear out" (KJV, "weary"). See KEEP, WEAR, WEARY.¶

BUILD, BUILDER, BUILDING

A. Verbs.

1. *oikodomeō* (οἰκοδομέω, 3618), lit., "to build a house" (*oikos*, "a house," *domeō*, "to build"), hence, to build anything, e.g., Matt. 7:24; Luke 4:29; 6:48, RV, "well builded" (last clause of verse); John 2:20; is frequently used figuratively, e.g., Acts 20:32 (some mss. have No. 3 here); Gal. 2:18; especially of edifying, Acts 9:31; Rom. 15:20; 1 Cor. 10:23; 14:4; 1 Thess. 5:11 (RV). In 1 Cor. 8:10 it is translated

"emboldened" (marg., "builded up"). The participle with the article (equivalent to a noun) is rendered "builder," Matt. 21:42; Acts 4:11; 1 Pet. 2:7. See EDIFY, EMBOLDEN.

2. *anoikodomeō* (ἀνοικοδομέω, 456) signifies "to build again" (*ana*, "again"), Acts 15:16.¶

3. *epoikodomeō* (ἐποικοδομέω, 2026) signifies "to build upon" (*epi*, "upon"), 1 Cor. 3:10, 12, 14: Eph. 2:20; Jude 20; or up, Acts 20:32; Col. 2:7.¶

4. *sunoikodomeō* (συνοικοδομέω, 4925), "to build together" (*sun*, "with"), is used in Eph. 2:22, metaphorically, of the church, as a spiritual dwelling-place for God.¶

5. *kataskeuazō* (κατασκευάζω, 2680), "to prepare, establish, furnish," is rendered "builded" and "built" in Heb. 3:3–4. See MAKE, ORDAIN, PREPARE.

B. Nouns.

1. *oikodomē* (οἰκοδομή, 3619), "a building, or edification" (see A, No. 1), is used (*a*) literally, e.g., Matt. 24:1; Mark 13:1–2; (*b*) figuratively, e.g., Rom. 14:19 (lit., "the things of building up"); 15:2; of a local church as a spiritual building, 1 Cor. 3:9, or the whole church, the body of Christ, Eph. 2:21. It expresses the strengthening effect of teaching, 1 Cor. 14:3, 5, 12, 26; 2 Cor. 10:8; 12:19; 13:10, or other ministry, Eph. 4:12, 16, 29 (the idea conveyed is progress resulting from patient effort). It is also used of the believer's resurrection body, 2 Cor. 5:1. See EDIFICATION, EDIFY.¶

2. *endōmēsis* (ἐνδώμησις, 1739), "a thing built, structure" (*en*, "in," *dōmaō*, "to build"), is used of the wall of the heavenly city, Rev. 21:18 (some suggest that the word means "a fabric"; others, "a roofing or coping"; these interpretations are questionable; the probable significance is "a building").¶

3. *ktisis* (κτίσις, 2937), "a creation," is so translated in the RV of Heb. 9:11 (KJV "building,"). See CREATION, B, No. 1, CREATURE, ORDINANCE.

4. *technitēs* (τεχνίτης, 5079), "an artificer, one who does a thing by rules of art," is rendered "builder" in Heb. 11:10, marg., "architect," which gives the necessary contrast between this and the next noun in the verse. See CRAFTSMAN, No. 2.

For BULL see OX

BUNDLE

1. *desmē* (δέσμη, 1197), from *deō*, "to bind" (similarly, Eng. "bundle" is akin to "bind"), is used in Matt. 13:30.¶

2. *plēthos* (πλῆθος, 4128), "a great number" (akin to *pleō*, "to fill"), is the word for the "bundle of sticks" which Paul put on the fire, Acts 28:3. See COMPANY, MULTITUDE.

BURDEN, BURDENED, BURDENSOME

A. Nouns.

1. *baros* (βάρος, 922) denotes "a weight, anything pressing on one physically," Matt. 20:12, or "that makes a demand on one's resources," whether material, 1 Thess. 2:6 (to be burdensome), or spiritual, Gal. 6:2; Rev. 2:24, or religious, Acts 15:28. In one place it metaphorically describes the future state of believers as "an eternal weight of glory," 2 Cor. 4:17. See WEIGHT.¶

2. *phortion* (φορτίον, 5413), lit., "something carried" (from *pherō*, "to bear"), is always used metaphorically (except in Acts 27:10, of the lading of a ship); of that which, though "light," is involved in discipleship of Christ, Matt. 11:30; of tasks imposed by the scribes, Pharisees and lawyers, Matt. 23:4; Luke 11:46; of that which will be the result, at the judgment-seat of Christ, of each believer's work, Gal. 6:5.¶

Note: The difference between *phortion* and *baros* is, that *phortion* is simply "something to be borne," without reference to its weight, but *baros* always suggests what is "heavy or burdensome." Thus Christ speaks of His "burden" (*phortion*) as "light"; here *baros* would be inappropriate; but the "burden" of a transgressor is *baros*, "heavy." Contrast *baros* in Gal. 6:2, with *phortion* in v. 5.

3. *gomos* (γόμος, 1117), from a root *gem-*, signifying "full, or heavy," seen in *gemō*, "to be full," *gemizō*, "to fill," Lat. *gemo*, "to groan," denotes "the lading of freight of a ship," Acts 21:3, or "merchandise conveyed in a ship," and so "merchandise in general," Rev. 18:11–12. See MERCHANDISE.¶

B. Verbs.

1. *bareō* (βαρέω, 916), akin to A, No. 1, is used of the effect of drowsiness, "were heavy," Matt. 26:43; Mark 14:40; Luke 9:32; of the effects of gluttony, Luke 21:34 ("overcharged"); of the believer's present physical state in the body, 2 Cor. 5:4; of persecution, 2 Cor. 1:8; of a charge upon material resources, 1 Tim. 5:16 (RV). See CHARGE, HEAVY, PRESS.¶

2. *epibareō* (ἐπιβαρέω, 1912), *epi*, "upon" (intensive), "to burden heavily," is said of material resources, 1 Thess. 2:9 (RV); 2 Thess. 3:8, RV, "burden," KJV, "be chargeable to"; of the effect of spiritual admonition and discipline, 2 Cor. 2:5, RV, "press heavily," KJV, "overcharge." See CHARGEABLE, PRESS.¶

3. *katabareō* (καταβαρέω, 2599), "to weigh down" (*kata*, "down"), "overload," is used of material charges, in 2 Cor. 12:16.¶

4. *katanarkaō* (καταναρκάω, 2655), "to be a burden, to be burdensome," primarily signifies "to be numbed or torpid, to grow stiff" (*narkē* is the "torpedo or cramp fish," which benumbs anyone who touches it); hence, "to be idle to the detriment of another person" (like a useless limb), 2 Cor. 11:9; 12:13–14. See CHARGE-ABLE.¶

Note: For *thlipsis*, "distress, affliction," "burdened" (KJV of 2 Cor. 8:13), see AFFLICTION, B. No. 4.

C. Adjective.

abarēs (ἀβαρής, 4), "without weight" (*a,*) negative, and *baros*, "see" A, No. 1), is used in 2 Cor. 11:9, lit. "I kept myself burdensome-less."¶

BURIAL, BURY, BURYING

A. Nouns.

1. *entaphiasmos* (ἐνταφιασμός, 1780), lit., "an entombing" (from *en*, "in," *taphos*, "a tomb"), "burying," occurs in Mark 14:8; John 12:7. Cf. B.1.¶

2. *taphē* (ταφή, 5027), "a burial" (cf. No. 1, and Eng., "epitaph"), is found in Matt. 27:7, with *eis*, "unto," lit. "with a view to a burial (place) for strangers."¶

B. Verbs.

1. *entaphiazō* (ἐνταφιάζω, 1779), see A, No. 1, "to prepare a body for burial," is used of any provision for this purpose, Matt. 26:12; John 19:40.¶

2. *thaptō* (θάπτω, 2290) occurs in Matt. 8:21–22, and parallels in Luke; Matt. 14:12; Luke 16:22; Acts 2:29; 5:6, 9–10; of Christ's "burial," 1 Cor. 15:4.¶

3. *sunthaptō* (συνθάπτω, 4916), akin to A. 2, "to bury with, or together" (*sun*), is used in the metaphorical sense only, of the believer's identification with Christ in His "burial," as set forth in baptism, Rom. 6:4; Col. 2:12.¶

BURN, BURNING

A. Verbs.

1. *kaiō* (καίω, 2545), "to set fire to, to light"; in the passive voice, "to be lighted, to burn," Matt. 5:15; John 15:6; Heb. 12:18; Rev. 4:5; 8:8, 10; 19:20; 21:8; 1 Cor. 13:3, is used metaphorically of the heart, Luke 24:32; of spiritual light, Luke 12:35; John 5:35. See LIGHT.¶

2. *katakaiō* (κατακαίω, 2618), from *kata*, "down" (intensive), and No. 1, signifies "to burn up, burn utterly," as of chaff, Matt. 3:12; Luke 3:17; tares, Matt. 13:30, 40; the earth and its works, 2 Pet. 3:10; trees and grass, Rev. 8:7.

This form should be noted in Acts 19:19; 1 Cor. 3:15; Heb. 13:11; Rev. 17:16. In each place the full rendering "burn utterly" might be used, as in Rev. 18:8.¶

3. *ekkaiō* (ἐκκαίω, 1572), from *ek*, "out" (intensive), and No. 1, lit., "to burn out," in the passive voice, "to be kindled, burn up," is used of the lustful passions of men, Rom. 1:27.¶

4. *puroomai* (πυρόομαι, 4448), from *pur*, "fire, to glow with heat," is said of the feet of the Lord, in the vision in Rev. 1:15; it is translated "fiery" in Eph. 6:16 (of the darts of the evil one); used metaphorically of the emotions, in 1 Cor. 7:9; 2 Cor. 11:29; elsewhere literally, of the heavens, 2 Pet. 3:12; of gold, Rev. 3:18 (RV, "refined"). See FIERY, FIRE, TRY.¶

5. *empiprēmi* (ἐμπίπρημι, 1714), or *emprēthō*, "to burn up," occurs in Matt. 2:7.¶

B. Nouns.

1. *kausis* (καῦσις, 2740), akin to A, No. 1 (Eng., "caustic"), is found in Heb. 6:8, lit., "whose end is unto burning."¶ Cf. BRANDED.

2. *kausōn* (καύσων, 2742) is rendered "burning heat" in Jas. 1:11, KJV (RV, "scorching"). See HEAT.

3. *purōsis* (πύρωσις, 4451), akin to A. No. 4, is used literally in Rev. 18:9, 18; metaphorically in 1 Pet. 4:12, "fiery trial." See TRIAL.¶

BURNISHED

chalkolibanon (χαλκολίβανον, 5474): see BRASS.

BURNT (offering)

holokautōma (ὁλοκαύτωμα, 3646) denotes "a whole burnt offering" (*holos*, "whole," *kautos*, for *kaustos*, a verbal adjective from *kaiō*, "to burn"), i.e., "a victim," the whole of which is burned, as in Ex. 30:20; Lev. 5:12; 23:8, 25, 27. It is used in Mark 12:33, by the scribe who questioned the Lord as to the first commandment in the Law, and in Heb. 10:6, 8, RV, "whole burnt offerings." See OFFERING.¶

BURST (asunder)

1. *rhēgnumi* (ῥήγνυμι, 4486); see BREAK, A. No. 6.

2. *lakeō or laskō* (λάσκω, 2997), primarily, "to crack, or crash," denotes "to burst asunder with a crack, crack open" (always of making a noise), is used in Acts 1:18.¶

For BURY see BURIAL

BUSH

batos (βάτος, 942) denotes "a bramble bush," as in Luke 6:44. In Mark 12:26 and Luke 20:37 the phrase "in the place concerning the Bush" signifies in that part of the book of Exodus concerning it. See also Acts 7:30, 35.¶

BUSHEL

modios (μόδιος, 3426) was a dry measure containing about a peck, Matt. 5:15; Mark 4:21; Luke 11:33.¶

BUSINESS

A. Nouns.

1. *chreia* (χρεία, 5532), translated "business" in Acts 6:3, of the distribution of funds, signifies "a necessity, a need," and is used in this place concerning duty or business. See LACK, NECESSITY, NEED, USE, WANT.

2. *ergasia* (ἐργασία, 2039) denotes "a business," Acts 19:24, 25, RV, KJV, "gain" and "craft" (from *ergon*, "work"). See DILIGENCE.

B. Adjective.

idios (ἴδιος, 2398) expresses "what is one's own" (hence, Eng. "idiot," in a changed sense, lit., "a person with his own opinions"); the neuter plural with the article (*ta idia*) signifies "one's own things." In 1 Thess. 4:11, the noun is not expressed in the original but is supplied in the English versions by "business," "your own business." For the same phrase, otherwise expressed, see John 1:11, "His own (things)"; 16:32 and 19:27, "his own (home)"; Acts 21:6, "home." In Luke 2:49, the phrase "in My Father's house" (RV), "about My Father's business" (KJV), is, lit., "in the (things, the neuter plural of the article) of My Father." See ACQUAINTANCE, COMPANY, No. 8, DUE, HOME, OWN, PRIVATE, PROPER, SEVERAL.

Notes: (1) In the KJV of Rom. 16:2 *pragma* is translated "business," RV, "matter." See MATTER, THING, WORK.

(2) In Rom. 12:11 *spoudē*, translated "business" (KJV), signifies "diligence" (RV). See DILIGENCE.

BUSYBODY

A. Verb.

periergazomai (περιεργάζομαι, 4020), lit., "to be working round about, instead of at one's own business" (*peri*, "around," *ergon*, "work"), signifies to take more pains than enough about a thing, to waste one's labor, to be meddling with, or bustling about, other people's matters. This is found in 2 Thess. 3:11, where, following

the verb *ergazomai*, "to work," it forms a *paronomasia*. This may be produced in a free rendering: "some who are not busied in their own business, but are overbusied in that of others."¶

B. Adjective.

periergos (περίεργος, 4021), akin to A, denoting "taken up with trifles," is used of magic arts in Acts 19:19; "busybodies" in 1 Tim. 5:13, i.e., meddling in other persons' affairs. See CURIOUS.¶

C. Noun.

allotrioepiskopos (ἀλλοτριοεπίσκοπος, 244), from *allotrios*, "belonging to another person," and *episkopos*, "an overseer," translated "busybody" in the KJV of 1 Pet. 4:15, "meddler," RV, was a legal term for a charge brought against Christians as being hostile to civilized society, their purpose being to make Gentiles conform to Christian standards. Some explain it as a pryer into others' affairs. See MEDDLER.¶

BUY, BOUGHT

1. *agorazō* (ἀγοράζω, 59), primarily, "to frequent the market-place," the *agora*, hence "to do business there, to buy or sell," is used lit., e.g., in Matt. 14:15. Figuratively Christ is spoken of as having bought His redeemed, making them His property at the price of His blood (i.e., His death through the shedding of His blood in expiation for their sins), 1 Cor. 6:20; 7:23; 2 Pet. 2:1; see also Rev. 5:9; 14:3–4 (not as KJV, "redeemed"). *Agorazō* does not mean "to redeem." See REDEEM.

2. *ōneomai* (ὠνέομαι, 5608), "to buy, in contradistinction to selling," is used in Acts 7:16, of the purchase by Abraham of a burying place.¶

Note: In Jas. 4:13 (KJV) the verb *emporeuomai* (Eng., "emporium") is rendered "buy and sell." Its meaning is to trade, traffic, RV. It primarily denotes to travel, to go on a journey, then, to do so for traffic purposes; hence to trade; in 2 Pet. 2:3, "make merchandise of." See MERCHANDISE.¶

For BY See *Note* †, p. 1

Note: The phrase "by and by" in the KJV is in several places misleading. The three words *exautēs*, Mark 6:25, *euthus*, Matt. 13:21, and *eutheōs*, Luke 17:7; 21:9, mean "straightway," "immediately." See under these words.

C

CAGE

phulakē (φυλακή, 5438), from *phulassō*, "to guard," denotes (a) "a watching, keeping watch," Luke 2:8; (b) "persons keeping watch, a guard," Acts 12:10; (c) "a period during which watch is kept," e.g., Matt. 24:43; (d) "a prison, a hold." In Rev. 18:2, KJV, Babylon is described figuratively, first as a "hold" and then as a "cage" of every unclean and hateful bird (RV, "hold" in both clauses; marg., "prison"). The word is almost invariably translated "prison." See HOLD, IMPRISONMENT, PRISON, WARD, WATCH.

CALF

moschos (μόσχος, 3448) primarily denotes "anything young," whether plants or the off-spring of men or animals, the idea being that which is tender and delicate; hence "a calf, young bull, heifer," Luke 15:23, 27, 30; Heb. 9:12, 19; Rev. 4:7.¶

moschopoieō (μοσχοποιέω, 3447) signifies "to make a calf" (*moschos*, and *poieō*, "to make"), Acts 7:41.¶

CALL, CALLED, CALLING

A. Verbs.

1. *kaleō* (καλέω, 2564), derived from the root *kal—*, whence Eng. "call" and "clamor" (see B and C, below), is used (a) with a personal object, "to call anyone, invite, summon," e.g., Matt. 20:8; 25:14; it is used particularly of the divine call to partake of the blessings of redemption, e.g., Rom. 8:30; 1 Cor. 1:9; 1 Thess. 2:12; Heb. 9:15; cf. B and C, below; (b) of nomenclature or vocation, "to call by a name, to name"; in the passive voice, "to be called by a name, to bear a name." Thus it suggests either vocation or destination; the context determines which, e.g., Rom. 9:25–26; "surname," in Acts 15:37, KJV, is incorrect (RV, "was called"). See BID, NAME.

2. *eiskaleō* (εἰσκαλέω, 1528), lit., "to call in," hence, "to invite" (*eis*, "in," and No. 1), is found in Acts 10:23.¶

3. *epikaleō* (ἐπικαλέω, 1941), *epi*, "upon," and No. 1., denotes (a) "to surname"; (b) "to be called by a person's name"; hence it is used of being declared to be dedicated to a person, as to the Lord, Acts 15:17 (from Amos 9:12); Jas. 2:7; (c) "to call a person by a name by charging him with an offense," as the Pharisees charged Christ with doing His works by the help of Beelzebub, Matt. 10:25 (the most authentic reading has *epikaleō*, for *kaleō*); (d) "to call upon, invoke"; in the middle voice, "to call upon for oneself" (i.e., on one's behalf), Acts 7:59, or "to call upon a person as a witness," 2 Cor. 1:23, or to appeal to an authority, Acts 25:11, etc.; (e)"to call upon by way of adoration, making use of the Name of the Lord," Acts 2:21; Rom. 10:12–14; 2 Tim. 2:22. See APPEAL, SURNAME.

4. *metakaleō* (μετακαλέω, 3333), *meta*, implying "change," and No. 1, "to call from one place to another, to summon" (cf. the Sept. of Hos. 11:1), is used in the middle voice only, "to call for oneself, to send for, call hither," Acts 7:14; 10:32; 20:17; 24:25.¶

5. *proskaleō* (προσκαλέω, 4341), *pros*, "to," and No. 1, signifies (a) "to call to oneself, to bid to come"; it is used only in the middle voice, e.g., Matt. 10:1; Acts 5:40; Jas. 5:14; (b) "God's call to Gentiles through the gospel," Acts 2:39; (c) the divine call in entrusting men with the preaching of the gospel," Acts 13:2; 16:10.¶

6. *sunkaleō* (συγκαλέω, 4779) signifies "to call together," Mark 15:16; Luke 9:1; 15:6, 9; 23:13; Acts 5:21; 10:24; 28:17.¶

Notes: (1) *Enkaleō*, Acts 19:40, KJV, "called in question," signifies "to accuse," as always in the RV. See ACCUSE, IMPLEAD.

(2) *Parakaleō*, "to beseech, intreat," is rendered "have called for" in Acts 28:20, KJV; RV, "did intreat" (marg., "call for"). It is used only here with this meaning. See BESEECH.

7. *ait eō* (αἰτέω, 154), "to ask," is translated "called for" in Acts 16:29 ("he called for lights"). See ASK, A. No. 1.

Note: For the RV of Matt. 19:17 (KJV, "callest"), see ASK (A, No. 2, *Note*).

8. *phōneō* (φωνέω, 5455), "to sound" (Eng.,"phone"), is used of the crowing of a cock, e.g., Matt. 26:34; John 13:38; of "calling" out with a clear or loud voice, to cry out, e.g., Mark 1:26 (some mss. have *krazō* here); Acts 16:28; of "calling" to come to oneself, e.g., Matt. 20:32; Luke 19:15; of "calling" forth, as of Christ's call to Lazarus to come forth from the tomb, John 12:17; of inviting, e.g., Luke 14:12; of "calling" by name, with the implication of the pleasure taken in the possession of those "called," e.g., John 10:3; 13:13. See CROW, CRY.

9. *legō* (λέγω, 3004), "to speak," is used of all kinds of oral communication, e.g., "to call, to call by name," to surname, Matt. 1:16; 26:36;

John 4:5; 11:54; 15:15; Rev. 2:2, RV, "call themselves," etc. See ASK.

10. *epilegō* (ἐπιλέγω, 1951), *epi*, "upon," and No. 9, signifies "to call in addition," i.e., by another name besides that already intimated, John 5:2; for its other meaning in Acts 15:40, see CHOOSE.¶

11. *chrēmatizō* (χρηματίζω, 5337) occasionally means "to be called or named," Acts 11:26 (of the name "Christians") and Rom. 7:3, the only places where it has this meaning. Its primary significance, "to have business dealings with," led to this. They "were (publicly) called" Christians, because this was their chief business. See ADMONISH, REVEAL, SPEAK, WARN.

12. *eipon* (εἶπον, 3004), "to say, speak," means "to call by a certain appellation," John 10:35. See BID, No. 3.

13. *krinō* (κρίνω, 2919), "to judge," is translated "to call in question," in Acts 23:6; 24:21.

Notes: (1) For *onoma*, "a name," translated "called," KJV, in Luke 24:13, Acts 10:1, *onomazō*, "to name," translated "called," KJV, 1 Cor. 5:11, and *eponomazō*, "to surname," translated "art called," Rom. 2:17, see NAME and SURNAME.

(2) *Legō*, "to say," is rendered "calleth" in 1 Cor. 12:3, KJV, which the RV corrects to "saith"; what is meant is not calling Christ "Anathema," but making use of the phrase "Anathema Jesus," i.e., "Jesus is accursed."

(3) *Prosagoreuō*, Heb. 5:10, means "to be named." See NAME.¶

(4) *Metapempō*, rendered "call for," in Acts 10:5, KJV, and 11:13, signifies "to fetch," RV. See FETCH, SEND, No. 9.

(5) *Sunathroizō*, "to assemble," is translated "he called together," in the KJV of Acts 19:25; RV, "he gathered together."

(6) *Lambanō*, "to take or receive," is found with the noun *hupomnēsis*, "remembrance," in 2 Tim. 1:5; RV, "having been reminded" (lit., "having received remembrance"), for KJV, "when I call to remembrance."

(7) In Acts 10:15 and 11:9, *koinoō*, "to make common" (RV) is translated "call common" in the KJV.

(8) For *prosphōneō*, "to call unto," see SPEAK, No. 12.

B. Noun.

klēsis (κλῆσις, 2821), "a calling" (akin to A, No. 1), is always used in the NT of that "calling" the origin, nature and destiny of which are heavenly (the idea of invitation being implied); it is used especially of God's invitation to man to accept the benefits of salvation, Rom. 11:29; 1 Cor. 1:26; 7:20 (said there of the condition in which the "calling" finds one); Eph. 1:18, "His calling"; Phil. 3:14, the "high calling"; 2 Thess. 1:11 and 2 Pet. 1:10, "your calling"; 2 Tim. 1:9, a "holy calling"; Heb. 3:1, a "heavenly calling"; Eph. 4:1, "the calling wherewith ye were called"; 4:4, "in one hope of your calling." See VOCATION.¶

C. Adjective.

klētos (κλητός, 2822), "called, invited," is used, (a) "of the call of the gospel," Matt. 20:16; 22:14, not there "an effectual call," as in the Epistles, Rom. 1:1, 6–7; 8:28; 1 Cor. 1:2, 24; Jude 1; Rev. 17:14; in Rom. 1:7 and 1 Cor. 1:2 the meaning is "saints by calling"; (b) of "an appointment to apostleship," Rom. 1:1; 1 Cor. 1:1.¶

CALM

galēnē (γαλήνη, 1055) primarily signifies "calmness, cheerfulness" (from a root *gal*—, from which *gelaō*, "to smile," is also derived; hence the "calm" of the sea, the smiling ocean being a favorite metaphor of the poets), Matt. 8:26; Mark 4:39; Luke 8:24.¶

CALVARY

kranion (κρανίον, 2898), *kara*, "a head" (Eng., "cranium"), a diminutive of *kranon*, denotes "a skull" (Latin *calvaria*), Matt. 27:33; Mark 15:22; Luke 23:33; John 19:17. The corresponding Aramaic word is *Golgotha* (Heb. *gulgōleth*; see Judg. 9:53; 2 Kings 9:35).¶

For CAME see COME

CAMEL

kamēlos (κάμηλος, 2574), from a Hebrew word signifying "a bearer, carrier," is used in proverbs to indicate (a) "something almost or altogether impossible," Matt. 19:24, and parallel passages, (b) "the acts of a person who is careful not to sin in trivial details, but pays no heed to more important matters," Matt. 23:24.

For CAMP see ARMY

CAN (CANST, COULD, CANNOT)

1. *dunamai* (δύναμαι, 1410); see ABILITY, B, No. 1.

2. *ischuō* (ἰσχύω, 2480) is translated "I can do" in Phil. 4:13; see ABLE, B, No. 4.

3. *echō* (ἔχω, 2192), "to have," is translated "could" in Mark 14:8, lit., "she hath done what she had"; in Luke 14:14, for the KJV, "cannot," the RV has "they have not wherewith"; in Acts 4:14, "could say nothing against" is, lit., "had nothing to say against"; in Heb. 6:13, "he could swear" is, lit., "He had (by none greater) to swear." See ABLE, HAVE.

4. *ginōskō* (γινώσκω, 1097), "to know," is so rendered in the RV of Matt. 16:3, "ye know how to," for KJV, "ye can" (*dunamai* is used in the next sentence). This verb represents knowledge as the effect of experience. In Acts 21:37, for "canst thou speak Greek?" the RV has "dost . . ." See ALLOW, KNOW.

5. *oida* (οἶδα, Perf. of 1492), "to know by perception," is the word in Pilate's remark "make it as sure as ye can" (marg. "sure, as ye know"), Matt. 27:65. The phrases "cannot tell," "canst not tell," etc., are in the RV rendered "know not," etc., Matt. 21:27; Mark 11:33; Luke 20:7; John 3:8; 8:14; 16:18; 2 Cor. 12:2–3. See KNOW.

6. *esti* (ἐστί, 1510), meaning "it is," is translated "we cannot," in Heb. 9:5, lit., "it is not possible (now to speak)"; so in 1 Cor. 11:20; see margin.

7. *endechomai* (ἐνδέχομαι, 1735), "to accept, admit, allow of," is used impersonally in Luke 13:33, "it can (not) be," i.e., it is not admissible.¶

For CANDLE and CANDLESTICK see LAMP and LAMPSTAND

For CANKER see GANGRENE and RUST

CAPTAIN

1. *chiliarchos* (χιλίαρχος, 5506), denoting "a commander of 1000 soldiers" (from *chilios*, "a thousand," and *archō*, "to rule"), was the Greek word for the Persian vizier, and for the Roman military tribune, the commander of a Roman cohort, e.g., John 18:12; Acts 21:31–33, 37. One such commander was constantly in charge of the Roman garrison in Jerusalem. The word became used also for any military commander, e.g., a "captain" or "chief captain," Mark 6:21; Rev. 6:15; 19:18.

2. *stratēgos* (στρατηγός, 4755), originally the commander of an army (from *stratos*, "an army," and *agō*, "to lead"), came to denote "a civil commander, a governor" (Latin, *duumvir*), the highest magistrate, or any civil officer in chief command, Acts 16:20, 22, 35–36, 38; also the "chief captain" of the Temple, himself a Levite, having command of the Levites who kept guard in and around the Temple, Luke 22:4, 52; Acts 4:1; 5:24, 26. Cf. Jer. 20:1.¶

3. *archēgos* (ἀρχηγός, 747) : see AUTHOR (No. 2).

Note: In Acts 28:16 some mss. have the word *stratopedarchēs* (lit., "camp-commander"), which some take to denote a praetorian prefect, or commander of the praetorian cohorts, the Emperor's bodyguard, "the captain of the praetorian guard." There were two praetorian prefects, to whose custody prisoners sent bound to the Emperor were consigned. But the word probably means the commander of a detached corps connected with the commissariat and the general custody of prisoners.

CAPTIVE, CAPTIVITY

A. Nouns.

1. *aichmalōtos* (αἰχμάλωτος, 164), lit., "one taken by the spear" (from *aichmē*, "a spear," and *halōtos*, a verbal adjective, from *halōnai*, "to be captured"), hence denotes "a captive," Luke 4:18.¶

2. *aichmalōsia* (αἰχμαλωσία, 161), "captivity," the abstract noun in contrast to No. 1, the concrete, is found in Rev. 13:10 and Eph. 4:8, where "He led captivity captive" (marg., "a multitude of captives") seems to be an allusion to the triumphal procession by which a victory was celebrated, the "captives" taken forming part of the procession. See Judg. 5:12. The quotation is from Ps. 68:18, and probably is a forceful expression for Christ's victory, through His death, over the hostile powers of darkness. An alternative suggestion is that at His ascension Christ transferred the redeemed Old Testament saints from Sheol to His own presence in glory.¶

B. Verbs.

1. *aichmalōteuō* (αἰχμαλωτεύω, 162) signifies (a) "to be a prisoner of war," (b) "to make a prisoner of war." The latter meaning is the only one used in the NT, Eph. 4:8.¶

2. *aichmalōtizō* (αἰχμαλωτίζω, 163), practically synonymous with No. 1, denotes either "to lead away captive," Luke 21:24, or "to subjugate, to bring under control," said of the effect of the Law in one's members in bringing the person into captivity under the law of sin, Rom. 7:23; or of subjugating the thoughts to the obedience of Christ, 2 Cor. 10:5; or of those who took captive "silly women laden with sins," 2 Tim. 3:6.¶

3. *zōgreō* (ζωγρέω, 2221) lit. signifies "to take men alive" (from *zōos*, "alive," and *agreuō*, "to hunt or catch"), Luke 5:10 (marg. "take alive"), there of the effects of the work of the gospel; in 2 Tim. 2:26 it is said of the power of Satan to lead men astray. The verse should read "and that they may recover themselves out of the snare of the Devil (having been taken captive by him), unto the will of God." This is the probable meaning rather than "to take alive or for life." See CATCH.¶

CARCASE

1. *kōlon* (κῶλον, 2966) primarily denotes "a member of a body," especially the external and prominent members, particularly the feet, and so, a dead body (see, e.g., the Sept., in Lev. 26:30; Num. 14:29, 32; Isa. 66:24, etc.). The word is used in Heb. 3:17, from Num. 14:29, 32.¶

2. *ptōma* (πτῶμα, 4430): see BODY, No. 3.

CARE (noun and verb), CAREFUL, CAREFULLY, CAREFULNESS

A. Nouns.

1. *merimna* (μέριμνα, 3308), probably connected with *merizō*, "to draw in different directions, distract," hence signifies "that which causes this, a care, especially an anxious care," Matt. 13:22; Mark 4:19; Luke 8:14; 21:34; 2 Cor. 11:28 (RV, "anxiety for"); 1 Pet. 5:7 (RV, "anxiety"). See ANXIETY.¶
Note: The negative adjective *amerimnos* (*a*, negative) signifies "free from care," Matt. 28:14, RV, "we will . . . rid you of care," KJV, "we will . . . secure you" ("secure" lit. means "free from care"); 1 Cor. 7:32, KJV, "without carefulness."¶

2. *spoudē* (σπουδή, 4710), primarily "haste, zeal, diligence," hence means "earnest care, carefulness," 2 Cor. 7:11–12; 8:16 (RV, "earnest care," in each place). *Merimna* conveys the thought of anxiety, *spoudē*, of watchful interest and earnestness. See BUSINESS, DILIGENCE (A, No. 2), EARNESTNESS, FORWARDNESS, HASTE.

B. Verbs.

1. *merimnaō* (μεριμνάω, 3309), akin to A, No. 1, signifies "to be anxious about, to have a distracting care," e.g., Matt. 6:25, 28, RV, "be anxious," for KJV, "take thought"; 10:19; Luke 10:41 (RV, "anxious," for KJV, "careful"); 12:11 (RV, "anxious"); to be careful for, 1 Cor. 7:32–34; to have a care for, 1 Cor. 12:25; to care for, Phil. 2:20; "be anxious," Phil. 4:6, RV. See THOUGHT (to take).

2. *melei* (μέλει, 3199**), the third person sing. of *melō*, used impersonally, signifies that "something is an object of care," especially the care of forethought and interest, rather than anxiety, Matt. 22:16; Mark 4:38; 12:14; Luke 10:40; John 10:13; 12:6; Acts 18:17; 1 Cor. 9:9 (RV, "Is it for the oxen that God careth?" The KJV seriously misses the point. God does "care" for oxen, but there was a divinely designed significance in the OT passage, relating to the service of preachers of the gospel); 7:21; 1 Pet. 5:7.¶

3. *epimeleomai* (ἐπιμελέομαι, 1959) signifies "to take care of," involving forethought and

provision (*epi* indicating "the direction of the mind toward the object cared for"), Luke 10:34–35, of the Good Samaritan's care for the wounded man, and in 1 Tim. 3:5, of a bishop's (or overseer's) care of a church—a significant association of ideas.¶

4. *phrontizō* (φροντίζω, 5431), "to think, consider, be thoughtful" (from *phrēn*, "the mind"), is translated "be careful" in Titus 3:8.¶

5. *phroneō* (φρονέω, 5426), translated "be careful," in Phil. 4:10, KJV [RV, "(ye did) take thought"], has a much wider range of meaning than No. 5, and denotes to be minded, in whatever way. See AFFECTION, B, *Note* (1), MIND, REGARD, SAVOR, THINK, UNDERSTAND.
Note: *Episkopeō*, "to oversee," is rendered "looking carefully," in Heb. 12:15, RV. See OVERSIGHT.¶

C. Adverbs.

1. *akribōs* (ἀκριβῶς, 199), "carefully"; see ACCURATELY.
Note: For *akribesteron*, "more carefully," see EXACTLY.

2. *spoudaioterōs*, 4708, the comparative adverb corresponding to A, No. 2, signifies "the more diligently," Phil. 2:28, RV (KJV, "carefully").¶ The adverb *spoudaiōs* denotes "diligently," 2 Tim. 1:17 (some mss. have the comparative here); Titus 3:13; or "earnestly," Luke 7:4 (KJV, "instantly"). See also *spoudaios* and its comparative, in 2 Cor. 8:17, 22, RV, "earnest," "more earnest."¶

CARNAL, CARNALLY

1. *sarkikos* (σαρκικός, 4559), from *sarx*, "flesh," signifies (*a*) "having the nature of flesh," i.e., sensual, controlled by animal appetites, governed by human nature, instead of by the Spirit of God, 1 Cor. 3:3 (for v. 1, see below; same mss. have it in v. 4); having its seat in the animal nature, or excited by it, 1 Pet. 2:11, "fleshly"; or as the equivalent of "human," with the added idea of weakness, figuratively of the weapons of spiritual warfare, "of the flesh" (KJV, "carnal"), 2 Cor. 10:4; or with the idea of unspirituality, of human wisdom, "fleshly," 2 Cor. 1:12; (*b*) "pertaining to the flesh" (i.e., the body), Rom. 15:27; 1 Cor. 9:11.¶

2. *sarkinos* (σάρκινος, 4560), (*a*) "consisting of flesh," 2 Cor. 3:3, "tables that are hearts of flesh" (KJV, "fleshy tables of the heart"); (*b*) "pertaining to the natural, transient life of the body," Heb. 7:16, "a carnal commandment"; (*c*) given up to the flesh, i.e., with almost the same significance as *sarkikos*, above, Rom. 7:14, "I am carnal sold under sin"; 1 Cor. 3:1 (some texts have *sarkikos*, in both these places, and in those in (*a*) and (*b*), but textual evidence

is against it). It is difficult to discriminate between *sarkikos* and *sarkinos* in some passages. In regard to 1 Pet. 2:11, Trench (*Syn.* §lxxi, lxxii) says that *sarkikos* describes the lusts which have their source in man's corrupt and fallen nature, and the man is *sarkikos* who allows to the flesh a place which does not belong to it of right; in 1 Cor. 3:1 *sarkinos* is an accusation far less grave than *sarkikos* would have been. The Corinthian saints were making no progress, but they were not anti-spiritual in respect of the particular point with which the apostle was there dealing. In vv. 3–4, they are charged with being *sarkikos*. See FLESHLY, FLESHY.¶

CAROUSINGS

potos (πότοσ, 4224), lit., "a drinking," signifies not simply a banquet but "a drinking bout, a carousal," 1 Pet. 4:3 (RV, "carousings," KJV, "banquetings").¶ Synonymous is *kraipalē*, "surfeiting," Luke 21:34.¶

CARPENTER

tektōn (τέκτων, 5405) denotes any craftsman, but especially a worker in wood, a carpenter, Matt. 13:55; Mark 6:3.¶

For CARRIAGE see BAGGAGE

CARRY

1. *sunkomizō* (συγκομίζω, 4792), "to carry together, to help in carrying" (*sun*, "with," *komizō*, "to carry"), is used in Acts 8:2, RV, "buried," for KJV, "carried to his burial." The verb has also the meaning of "recovering or getting back a body."¶

2. *ekkomizō* (ἐκκομίζω, 1580), "to carry out," is found in Luke 7:12.¶

3. *pherō* (φέρω, 5342), "to bear, to bring," is translated "carry" only in John 21:18. See *Note* below.

4. *diapherō* (διαφέρω, 1308) has the meaning "to carry through" in Mark 11:16. See BETTER, DIFFER, DRIVE, EXCELLENT, MATTER, PUBLISH, VALUE.

5. *metatithēmi* (μετατίθημι, 3346), "to place among, put in another place" (*meta*, implying "change," and *tithēmi*, "to put"), has this latter meaning in Acts 7:16, "carried over." See CHANGE, REMOVE, TRANSLATE, TURN.

6. *apagō* (ἀπάγω, 520), "to lead away" (*apo*, "from," *agō*, "to lead"), is rendered "carried" in 1 Cor. 12:2, KJV (RV, "were led"). See BRING.

7. *sunapagō* (συναπάγω, 4879), "to carry away with" (*sun*, "with," and No. 6), is used in a bad sense, in Gal. 2:13 and 2 Pet. 3:17, "being

carried away with" (RV); in a good sense in Rom. 12:16; the RV marg. "be carried away with" is preferable to the text "condescend" (RV, and KJV), and to the KJV marg., "be contented (with mean things)." A suitable rendering would be "be led along with."¶

Notes: (1) For *pherō*, "to carry, or bring," *apopherō*, "to carry away," *peripherō*, "to carry about," *ekpherō*, "to carry forth," *anapherō*, "to carry up," *airō*, "to lift and carry away, to take away," *bastazō*, "to support, carry about," *agō*, "to lead or carry," *apagō*, "to carry away," see BEAR and BRING.

(2) For *elaunō*, rendered "carry" in 2 Pet. 2:17, see DRIVE.

CARRYING AWAY

A. Noun.

metoikesia (μετοικεσία, 3350), "a change of abode, or a carrying away by force" (*meta*, implying "change," *oikia*, "a dwelling"), is used only of the carrying away to Babylon, Matt. 1:11–12, 17.¶

B. Verb.

metoikizō (μετοικίζω, 3351), akin to A, is used of the removal of Abraham into Canaan, Acts 7:4, and of the carrying into Babylon, 7:43.¶

CASE

1. *aitia* (αἰτία, 156): see under ACCUSATION, A, No. 1.

2. *echō* (ἔχω, 2192), "to have," is idiomatically used in the sense of being in a case or condition, as with the infirm man at the pool of Bethesda, John 5:6, lit., "that he had already much time (in that case)."

Note: In Acts 25:14 the phrase in the original is "the things concerning Paul," KJV, "cause" (as if translating *aitia*); RV, "Festus laid Paul's case before the king."

3. *proechō* (προέχω, 4281), lit., "to have before," in the middle voice, Rom. 3:9, is rightly translated "are we in worse case?" (RV), as is borne out by the context. See BETTER (be), *Note* (1).¶

4. The preposition *en*, followed by the dative of the pronoun, lit., "in me," is translated in the RV, "in my case," in 1 Cor. 9:15; "unto me," in 1 Cor. 14:11 (marg. "in my case"). Similarly, in the plural, in 1 John 4:16, RV "in us" (marg., "in our case"); KJV, incorrectly, "to us."

Note: In Matt. 5:20 the strong double negative *ou mē* is translated "in no case" (KJV): RV, "in no wise."

CAST

A. Verbs.

1. *ballō* (βάλλω, 906), "to throw, hurl, in contrast to striking," is frequent in the four gospels and Revelation; elsewhere it is used only in Acts. In Matt. 5:30 some mss. have this verb (KJV, "should be cast"); the most authentic have *aperchomai*, "to go away," RV, "go." See ARISE, BEAT, DUNG, LAY, POUR, PUT, SEND, STRIKE, THROW, THRUST.

2. *rhiptō* (ῥίπτω, 4496) denotes "to throw with a sudden motion, to jerk, cast forth"; "cast down," Matt. 15:30 and 27:5; "thrown down," Luke 4:35; "thrown," 17:2 (KJV, "cast "); [*rhipteō* in Acts 22:23 (KJV, "cast off"), of the "casting" off of clothes (in the next sentence *ballō*, No. 1, is used of "casting" dust into the air)]; in 27:19 "cast out," of the tackling of a ship; in v. 29 "let go" (KJV, "cast"), of anchors; in Matt. 9:36, "scattered," said of sheep. See THROW, SCATTER.¶

3. *ekpiptō* (ἐκπίπτω, 1601), lit., "to fall out," is translated "be cast ashore," in Acts 27:29, RV, KJV, "have fallen upon." See EFFECT, FAIL, FALL, NOUGHT.

A number of compound verbs consisting of *ballō* or *rhiptō*, with prepositions prefixed, denote to cast, with a corresponding English preposition. Compounds of *ballō* are:

4. *apoballō* (ἀποβάλλω, 577), "to throw off from, to lay aside, to cast away," Mark 10:50; Heb. 10:35.¶

Note: Apobolē, "casting away" (akin to No. 4), is used of Israel in Rom. 11:15; elsewhere, Acts 27:22, "loss" (of life).¶

5. *ekballō* (ἐκβάλλω, 1544), "to cast out of, from, forth," is very frequent in the gospels and Acts; elsewhere, in Gal. 4:30; 3 John 10; in Jas. 2:25, "sent out"; in Rev. 11:2, "leave out" (marg., "cast without"). See BRING, No. 28, DRIVE, EXPEL, LEAVE, PLUCK, PULL, PUT, SEND, TAKE, THRUST.

6. *emballō* (ἐμβάλλω, 1685), "to cast into," is used in Luke 12:5.¶

7. *epiballō* (ἐπιβάλλω, 1911), "to cast on, or upon," is used in this sense in Mark 11:7 and 1 Cor. 7:35. See BEAT (No. 5), FALL, No. 11, LAY, PUT, No. 8, STRETCH.

8. *kataballō* (καταβάλλω, 2598) signifies "to cast down," 2 Cor. 4:9, KJV, "cast down," RV, "smitten down"; Heb. 6:1, "laying." See LAY.¶ Some mss. have this verb in Rev. 12:10 (for *ballō*).

9. *amphiballō* (ἀμφιβάλλω, 97 and 906), "to cast around," occurs Mark 1:16.¶

10. *periballō* (περιβάλλω, 4016), "to cast about, or around," is used in 23 of its 24 occur-

rences, of putting on garments, clothing, etc.; it is translated "cast about" in Mark 14:51; Acts 12:8; in Luke 19:43, used of "casting" up a bank or palisade against a city (see RV and marg.), KJV, "shall cast a trench about thee." See CLOTHE, No. 6, PUT.

Compounds of *rhiptō* are:

11. *aporiptō* (ἀπορίπτω, 641), "to cast off," Acts 27:43, of shipwrecked people in throwing themselves into the water.¶

12. *epiriptō* (ἐπιρίπτω, 1977), "to cast upon," (*a*) lit., "of casting garments on a colt," Luke 19:35; (*b*) figuratively, "of casting care upon God," 1 Pet. 5:7.¶

Other verbs are:

13. *apōtheō* (ἀπωθέω, 683), "to thrust away" (*apo*, "away," *ōtheō*, "to thrust"), in the NT used in the middle voice, signifying "to thrust from oneself, to cast off, by way of rejection," Acts 7:27, 39; 13:46; Rom. 11:1–2; 1 Tim. 1:19. See PUT and THRUST.¶

14. *kathaireō* (καθαιρέω, 2507), *kata*, "down," *haireō*, "to take, to cast down, demolish," in 2 Cor. 10:5, of strongholds and imaginations. See DESTROY, PULL, PUT, TAKE.

Note: The corresponding noun *kathairesis*, "a casting down," is so rendered in 2 Cor. 10:4 (KJV, "pulling down") and 13:10 (KJV, "destruction").

15. *dialogizomai* (διαλογίζομαι, 1260), "to reason" (*dia*, "through," *logizomai*, "to reason"), is translated "cast in (her) mind," Luke 1:29. See DISPUTE, MUSING, REASON, THINK.

16. *apotithēmi* (ἀποτίθημι, 659), "to put off, lay aside," denotes, in the middle voice, "to put off from oneself, cast off," used figuratively of works of darkness, Rom. 13:12, "let us cast off," (aorist tense, denoting a definite act). See LAY, No. 8, PUT, No. 5.

17. *ektithēmi* (ἐκτίθημι, 1260), "to expose, cast out" (*ek*, "out," *tithēmi*, "to put"), is said of a new-born child in Acts 7:21. In v. 19 "cast out" translates the phrase *poieō*, "to make," with *ekthetos*, "exposed," a verbal form of *ektithēmi*. See EXPOUND.

18. *periaireō* (περιαιρέω, 4014), "to take away," is used in Acts 27:40, as a nautical term, RV, "casting off," KJV, "taken up." See TAKE.

Notes: (1) For *zēmioō*, "cast away," Luke 9:25, see FORFEIT.

(2) For *katakrēmnizō*, Luke 4:29 (KJV, "cast down headlong"), see THROW.¶ (3) For *oneidizō*, Matt. 27:44 (KJV, "cast in one's teeth"), see REPROACH. (4) For *paradidōmi*, Matt. 4:12 (KJV, "cast into prison"), see DELIVER. (5) For *atheteō*, 1 Tim. 5:12 (KJV, "cast off"), see REJECT. (6) For *ekteinō*, Acts 27:30 (KJV, "cast

out"), see LAY No. 13. (7) For *tapeinos*, 2 Cor. 7:6 (KJV, "cast down"), see LOWLY.

B. Noun.

bole (βολή, 1000) denotes "a throw" (akin to *ballō*, "to throw"), and is used in Luke 22:21 in the phrase "a stone's cast," of the distance from which the Lord was parted from the disciples in the garden of Gethsemane.¶

Note: In Jas. 1:17, *aposkiasma* (from *aposkiazō*, "to cast a shadow"), is rendered "shadow that is cast," RV.¶

C. Adjective.

adokimos (ἀδόκιμος, 96) signifies not standing the test, rejected, (*a*), negative, and *dokimos*, "tested, approved"; it is said of things, e.g., the land, Heb. 6:8, "rejected," and of persons, Rom. 1:28, "reprobate"; 1 Cor. 9:27, KJV, "castaway," RV "rejected" (i.e., disapproved, and so rejected from present testimony, with loss of future reward); 2 Cor. 13:5–7, "reprobate" (sing. in RV in each verse), i.e., that will not stand the test; 2 Tim. 3:8, "reprobate (concerning the faith)," Titus 1:16, "reprobate." See REJECT, REPROBATE.¶

For **CASTLE** see **ARMY** (No. 3)

CATCH

1. *harpazō* (ἁρπάζω, 726), "to snatch or catch away," is said of the act of the Spirit of the Lord in regard to Philip in Acts 8:39; of Paul in being "caught" up to paradise, 2 Cor. 12:2, 4; of the rapture of the saints at the return of the Lord, 1 Thess. 4:17; of the rapture of the man child in the vision of Rev. 12:5. This verb conveys the idea of force suddenly exercised, as in Matt. 11:12, "take (it) by force"; 12:29, "spoil" (some mss. have *diarpazō* here); in 13:19, RV, "snatcheth"; for forceful seizure, see also John 6:15; 10:12, 28–29; Acts 23:10; in Jude 23, RV, "snatching." See PLUCK, PULL, SNATCH, TAKE (by force).¶

2. *lambanō* (λαμβάνω, 2983), "to receive," is once used of "catching" by fraud, circumventing, 2 Cor. 12:16. In Matt. 21:39 and Mark 12:3, RV "took," for KJV "caught." See ACCEPT, No. 4.

3. *agreuō* (ἀγρεύω, 4), "to take by hunting" (from *agra*, "a hunt, a catch"), is used metaphorically, of the Pharisees and Herodians in seeking to catch Christ in His talk, Mark 12:13.¶

4. *thēreuō* (θηρεύω, 2340), "to hunt or catch wild beasts" (*thērion*, "a wild beast"), is used by Luke of the same event as in No. 3, Luke 11:54.¶

5. *zōgreō* (ζωγρέω, 221), "to take alive": see CAPTIVE, B, No. 3.

6. *piazō* (πιάζω, 4084), "to capture": see APPREHEND, No. 2.

7. *sunarpazō* (συναρπάζω, 4884), *sun*, used intensively, and No. 1, "to snatch, to seize, to keep a firm grip of," is used only by Luke, and translated "caught" in the KJV of Luke 8:29, of demon-possession; in Acts 6:12, of the act of the elders and scribes in seizing Stephen, RV, more suitably, "seized." So in Acts 19:29. In 27:15, it is used of the effects of wind upon a ship. See SEIZE.¶

8. *sullambanō* (συλλαμβάνω, 4815), *sun*, and No. 2, "to seize," is used, similarly to No. 7, in Acts 26:21, of the act of the Jews in seizing Paul in the temple. See CONCEIVE, HELP, SEIZE, TAKE.

9. *epilambanō* (ἐπιλαμβάνω, 1949), "to lay hold" (*epi*, intensive, and No. 2), is translated "caught" in Acts 16:19, KJV; RV, "laid hold." See HOLD, TAKE.

CATTLE

1. *thremma* (θρέμμα, 2353), "whatever is fed or nourished" (from *trephō*, "to nourish, nurture, feed"), is found in John 4:12.¶

2. *ktēnos* (κτῆνος, 934), "cattle as property": see BEAST, No. 3.

Note: The verb *poimainō*, "to act as a shepherd" (*poimēn*), "to keep sheep," is translated "keeping sheep" in Luke 17:7, RV, for KJV, "feeding cattle."

CAUSE (Noun and Verb)

A. Nouns.

1. *aitia* (αἰτία, 156), "a cause": see ACCUSATION, A, No. 1.

2. *aition* (αἴτιον, 158), "a fault" (synonymous with No. 1, but more limited in scope), is translated "cause (of death)" in Luke 23:22; "cause" in Acts 19:40 (of a riot); "fault" in Luke 23:4, 14. See FAULT.¶

3. *logos* (λόγος, 3056), "a word spoken for any purpose," denotes, in one place, a cause or reason assigned, Matt. 5:32.

The following phrases are rendered by an English phrase containing the word "cause" (see WHEREFORE):

"For this cause."

1. *anti toutou* (ἀντί τούτου), lit., "instead of this," i.e., "for this cause," signifying the principle or motive, Eph. 5:31.

2. *dia touto* (διά τοῦτο), lit., "on account of this, for this cause," signifying the ground or reason, e.g., RV in Mark 12:24; John 1:31; 5:16, 18; 6:65; 7:22; 8:47; 12:18, 27, 39; Rom. 1:26; 4:16; 13:6; 1 Cor. 4:17; 11:10, 30; Eph. 1:15; Col. 1:9; 1 Thess. 2:13; 3:5, 7; 2 Thess. 2:11; 1 Tim. 1:16; Heb. 9:15; 1 John 3:1.

3. *heneken toutou* (ἕνεκεν τούτου), lit., "for the sake of this," therefore, "as a reason for," Matt. 19:5; Mark 10:7; *heneka toutōn*, "for the sake of these things," Acts 26:21; and *heneken tou*, "for the cause of the (one), etc.," 2 Cor. 7:12 (twice).

4. *charin toutou*, or *toutou charin* (τούτου χάριν), "for this cause," not simply as a reason, as in the preceding phrase, but in favor of, Eph. 3:1, 14; Titus 1:5.

"For this very cause."

auto touto (αὐτὸ τοῦτο), lit., "(as to) this very thing," 2 Pet. 1:5.

Notes: (1) This phrase often represents one containing *aitia* (see above).

(2) In John 18:37, *eis touto*, "unto this," denotes "unto this end," RV (KJV, "for this cause").

(3) For the phrase "for which cause" (*dio*), Rom. 15:22; 2 Cor. 4:16, see WHEREFORE, *Note* (2) (RV).

(4) In Phil. 2:18, *to auto*, is rendered "for the same cause," KJV; RV, "in the same manner."

"without a cause."

dōrean (δωρεάν, 1432), lit., "as a gift, gratis," (connected with *dōron*, "a gift"), is rendered "without a cause," John 15:25; "for nought," 2 Cor. 11:7; Gal. 2:21; 2 Thess. 3:8; "freely," Matt. 10:8; Rom. 3:24; Rev. 21:6; 22:17.¶

Notes: (1) *Eikē*, "in vain," "without a cause," Matt. 5:22 (KJV), is absent from the most authentic mss.

(2) For "cause," in Acts 25:14, KJV, see CASE.

(3) In 2 Cor. 5:13 (RV, "unto you"), the KJV has "for your cause."

B. Verbs.

1. *poieō* (ποιέω, 4160), "to do," is translated by the verb "to cause" in John 11:37; Acts 15:3; Rom. 16:17; Col. 4:16; Rev. 13:15–16. See DO.

2. *didōmi* (δίδωμι, 1325), "to give," is translated "cause" in 1 Cor. 9:12, RV, for KJV, "(lest we) should."

Notes: (1) In Matt. 5:32 the RV translates *poieō* "maketh (her an adulteress)": in Rev. 13:12, RV, "maketh," for KJV, "causeth."

(2) In 2 Cor. 9:11, *katergazomai*, "to work," is translated "causeth" in the KJV; RV, "worketh."

(3) In 2 Cor. 2:14, *thriambeuō* is rendered "causeth us to triumph," KJV; RV, "leadeth us in triumph," the metaphor being taken from the circumstances of the procession of a Roman "triumph."

CAVE

1. *opē* (ὀπή, 3692), perhaps from *ōps*, "sight," denotes "a hole, an opening," such as a

fissure in a rock, Heb. 11:38. In Jas. 3:11, the RV has "opening," of the orifice of a fountain (KJV, "place"). See PLACE.¶

2. *spēlaion* (σπήλαιον, 4693), "a grotto, cavern, den" (Lat., *spelunca)*, "cave," John 11:38, is said of the grave of Lazarus; in the RV in Heb. 11:38 and Rev. 6:15 (KJV, "dens"); in the Lord's rebuke concerning the defilement of the Temple, Matt. 21:13; Mark 11:17; Luke 19:46, "den" is used.¶

CEASE

A. Verbs.

1. *pauō* (παύω, 3973), "to stop, to make an end," is used chiefly in the middle voice in the NT, signifying "to come to an end, to take one's rest, a willing cessation" (in contrast to the passive voice which denotes a forced cessation), Luke 5:4, of a discourse; 8:24, of a storm; 11:1, of Christ's prayer; Acts 5:42, of teaching and preaching; 6:13, of speaking against; 13:10, of evil doing; 20:1, of an uproar; 20:31, of admonition; 21:32, of a scourging; 1 Cor. 13:8, of tongues; Eph. 1:16, of giving thanks; Col. 1:9, of prayer; Heb. 10:2, of sacrifices; 1 Pet. 4:1, of "ceasing" from sin. It is used in the active voice in 1 Pet. 3:10, "let him cause his tongue to cease from evil." See LEAVE, REFRAIN.¶

2. *dialeipō* (διαλείπω, 1257), lit., "to leave between," i.e., "to leave an interval, whether of space or time" (*dia*, "between," *leipō*, "to leave"); hence, "to intermit, desist, cease," in Luke 7:45 is used of the kissing of the Lord's feet.¶

3. *hēsuchazō* (ἡσυχάζω, 2270), "to be quiet, still, at rest," is said of Paul's friends in Caesarea, in "ceasing" to persuade him not to go to Jerusalem, Acts 21:14; it is used of silence (save in Luke 23:56 and 1 Thess. 4:11) in Luke 14:4 and Acts 11:18. See PEACE (hold one's), QUIET, REST.¶

4. *kopazō* (κοπάζω, 2869), "to cease through being spent with toil, to cease raging" (from *kopos*, "labor, toil," *kopiaō*, "to labor"), is said of the wind only, Matt. 14:32; Mark 4:39; 6:51.¶

5. *aphiēmi* (ἀφίημι, 863), "to let go," is translated "let us cease to" in Heb. 6:1, RV (marg., "leave ") for KJV, "leaving." See FORGIVE, LEAVE.

6. *katapauō* (καταπαύω, 2664), "to rest" (*kata*, "down," intensive, and No. 1), is so translated in Heb. 4:10, for the KJV "hath ceased." See REST, RESTRAIN.

Notes: (1) *katargeō*, "to render inactive, to bring to naught, to do away," is so rendered in Gal. 5:11, RV, for the KJV "ceased." See ABOLISH.

(2) *Akatapaustos*, "incessant, not to be set at rest" (from *a*, negative, *kata*, "down," *pauō*, "to cease"), is used in 2 Pet. 2:14, of those who "cannot cease" from sin, i.e., who cannot be restrained from sinning.¶

B. Adjective.

adialeiptos (ἀδιάλειπτος, 88), "unceasing" (from *a*, negative, *dia*, "through," *leipō*, "to leave"), is used of "incessant" heart pain, Rom. 9:2, KJV, "continual," RV, "unceasing," and in 2 Tim. 1:3, of remembrance in prayer; the meaning in each place is not that of unbroken continuity, but without the omission of any occasion. Cf. A, No. 2. See CONTINUAL.¶

C. Adverb.

adialeiptōs (ἀδιαλείπτως, 89), "unceasingly, without ceasing," is used with the same significance as the adjective, not of what is not interrupted, but of that which is constantly recurring; in Rom. 1:9 and 1 Thess. 5:17, of prayer; in 1 Thess. 1:3, of the remembrance of the work, labor and patience of saints; in 1 Thess. 2:13, of thanksgiving.¶

Note: Ektenēs, lit., "stretched out," signifies "earnest, fervent"; Acts 12:5, RV, for KJV, "without ceasing." See 1 Pet. 4:8, "fervent."¶

For CELESTIAL see HEAVEN, HEAVENLY, B, No. 2

CELL

oikēma (οἴκημα, 3612), lit., "a habitation" (akin to *oikeō*, "to dwell"), is euphemistically put for "a prison," in Acts 12:7, RV, "cell." See PRISON.¶

CELLAR

kruptē (κρυπτή, 2926)(Eng., "crypt"), "a covered way or vault" (akin to *kruptos*, "hidden, secret"), is used in Luke 11:33, of lighting a lamp and putting it "in a cellar," RV. See PLACE, *Note* (8).¶

CENSER

1. *thumiatērion* (θυμιατήριον, 2369), "a vessel for burning incense" (2 Chron. 26:19; Ezek. 8:11), is found in Heb. 9:4.¶

2. *libanōtos* (λιβανωτός, 3031) denotes "frankincense," the gum of the *libanos*, "the frankincense tree"; in a secondary sense, "a vessel in which to burn incense," Rev. 8:3, 5.¶

Note: No. 1 derives its significance from the act of burning (*thumiaō*); No. 2 from that which was burned in the vessel.

CENTURION

1. *hekatontarchos* (ἑκατόνταρχος, 1543), "a centurion," denotes a military officer commanding from 50 to 100 men, according to the size of the legion of which it was a part (*hekaton*, "a hundred," *archō*, "to rule"), e.g., Matt. 8:5, 8.

2. *hekatontarchēs* (ἑκατοντάρχης, 1543) has the same meaning as No. 1, e.g., Acts 10:1, 22. The Sept. has this word frequently, to denote "captains of hundreds."

3. *kenturiōn* (κεντυρίων, 2760) is a Greek transliteration of the Latin *centurio*, signifying practically the same as No. 1, Mark 15:39, 44–45. There were ten "centurions" to a cohort when the numbers were complete. There were several at Jerusalem under the chief captain mentioned in Acts 21:31.¶

CERTAIN, CERTAINTY, CERTAINLY, CERTIFY

A. Noun.

asphaleia (ἀσφάλεια, 803), primarily, "not liable to fall, steadfast, firm," hence denoting "safety," Acts 5:23, and 1 Thess. 5:3, has the further meaning, "certainty," Luke 1:4. See SAFETY.¶

B. Adjective.

asphalēs (ἀσφαλής, 804), safe, is translated "certainty," Acts 21:34; 22:30; "certain," Acts 25:26; "safe," Phil. 3:1; "sure," Heb. 6:19. See SAFE, SURE.¶

Notes: (1) *Dēlos*, "evident, visible," is translated "certain" in 1 Tim. 6:7, KJV. The most authentic mss. omit it.

(2) The rendering "certain," is frequently changed in the RV, or omitted, e.g., Luke 5:12; 8:22; Acts 23:17; Heb. 2:6; 4:4.

(3) The indefinite pronoun *tis* signifies "anyone, some one, a certain one"; the neuter, *ti*, "a certain thing," e.g., Matt. 20:20; Mark 14:51.

(4) In the KJV of Gal. 1:11, *gnōrizō* is rendered "certify," RV, "to make known."

(5) For "a certain island," Acts 27:16, see the RV, "small island."

(6) In 1 Cor. 4:11, the verb *astateō*, "to be unsettled, to lead a homeless life," is rendered "we ... have no certain dwelling place." The unsettlement conveyed by the word has suggested the meaning "we are vagabonds" or "we lead a vagabond life," a probable significance.¶

C. Adverbs.

1. *ontōs* (ὄντως, 3689), "really, actually, verily" (from *eimi*, "to be"), is translated "certainly" in Luke 23:47. See CLEAN, INDEED, TRUTH, VERILY.

2. *pantōs* (πάντωσ, 3843): see ALTOGETHER, B.

CHAFF

achuron (ἄχυρον, 892), "chaff, the stalk of the grain from which the kernels have been beaten out, or the straw broken up by a threshing machine," is found in Matt. 3:12 and Luke 3:17.¶

CHAIN

halusis (ἅλυσις, 254) denotes "a chain or bond for binding the body, or any part of it (the hands or feet)." Some derive the word from *a*, negative, and *luō*, "to loose," i.e., "not to be loosed"; others from a root connected with a word signifying "to restrain." It is used in Mark 5:3–4; Luke 8:29; Acts 12:6–7; 21:33; 28:20; Eph. 6:20; 2 Tim. 1:16; Rev. 20:1. See BOND.¶

Notes: (1) Some ancient authorities have *seira*, "a cord, rope, band, chain," in 2 Pet. 2:4, instead of *seiros*, "a cavern," RV, "pits."

(2) In Jude 6 the RV renders *desmos* by "bonds" (for the KJV "chains"). See BOND.¶

CHALCEDONY

chalkēdōn (χαλκηδών, 5472), the name of a gem, including several varieties, one of which resembles a cornelian, is "supposed to denote a green silicate of copper found in the mines near Chalcedon" (*Swete, on the Apocalypse*), Rev. 21:19.¶

CHAMBER (Store-chamber)

1. *tameion* (ταμεῖον, 5009) denotes, firstly, "a store-chamber," then, "any private room, secret chamber," Matt. 6:6; RV, "inner chamber" (KJV, "closet"); 24:26, "inner (KJV, secret) chambers"; Luke 12:3, RV, ditto, for KJV, "closets"; it is used in Luke 12:24 ("store-chamber") of birds.¶

2. *huperōon* (ὑπερῷον, 5253), the neuter of *huperōos*, "above," denotes "an upper room, upper chamber" (*huper*, "above"), Acts 1:13; 9:37, 39; 20:8. See ROOM.¶

CHAMBERING

koitē (κοίτη, 2845), primarily a place in which to lie down, hence, "a bed, especially the marriage bed," denotes, in Rom. 13:13, "illicit intercourse." See BED, CONCEIVE.

CHAMBERLAIN

ho epi tou koitōnos, lit., "the (one) over the bedchamber" (*epi*, "over," *koitōn*, "a bedchamber"), denotes "a chamberlain," an officer who had various duties in the houses of kings and nobles. The importance of the position is indi-

cated by the fact that the people of Tyre and Sidon sought the favor of Herod Agrippa through the mediation of Blastus, Acts 12:20.

Note: In Rom. 16:23, *oikonomos*, "a person who manages the domestic affairs of a family, in general, a manager, a steward," is translated "chamberlain" in the KJV, which the RV corrects to "treasurer."

CHANCE

1. *sunkuria* (συγκυρία, 4795), lit., "a meeting together with, a coincidence of circumstances, a happening," is translated "chance" in Luke 10:31. But concurrence of events is what the word signifies, rather than chance.¶

Note: Some texts have *tucha* here (from *tunchanō*, "to happen").

2. *ei tuchoi* (εἰ τύχοι, 5177), lit., "if it may happen" (*ei*, "if," *tunchanō*, "to happen"), signifies "it may chance," 1 Cor. 15:37.¶

CHANGE (Noun and Verb)

A. Noun.

metathesis (μετάθεσις, 3331), "a transposition, or a transference from one place to another" (from *meta*, implying "change," and *tithēmi*, "to put"), has the meaning of "change" in Heb. 7:12, in connection with the necessity of a "change" of the Law (or, as margin, law), if the priesthood is changed (see B, No. 3). It is rendered "translation" in 11:5, "removing" in 12:27. See REMOVING, TRANSLATION.¶

B. Verbs.

1. *allassō* (ἀλλάσσω, 236), "to make other than it is" (from *allos*, "another"), "to transform, change," is used (*a*) of the effect of the gospel upon the precepts of the Law, Acts 6:14; (*b*) of the effect, on the body of a believer, of Christ's return, 1 Cor. 15:51–52; (*c*) of the final renewal of the material creation, Heb. 1:12; (*d*) of a change in the apostle's mode of speaking (or dealing), Gal. 4:20. In Rom. 1:23 it has its other meaning, "to exchange."¶

2. *metallassō* (μεταλλάσσω, 3337), from *meta*, "implying change," and No. 1, "to change one thing for another, or into another," Rom. 1:25–26, is translated "exchange" in v. 25. See EXCHANGE.¶

3. *metatithēmi* (μετατίθημι, 3346), "to place differently, to change," (akin to A, above), is said of priesthood, Heb. 7:12. See CARRY, No. 5.

4. *metaballō* (μεταβάλλω, 3328), *meta*, as in No. 2, and *ballō*, "to throw," signifies "to turn quickly," or, in the middle voice, "to change one's mind," and is found in Acts 28:6.¶

Notes: (1) In Phil. 3:21, for the KJV rendering of *metaschēmatizō*, "change," the RV has "fashion anew"; in 2 Cor. 3:18 *metamorphoō* is rendered "change," in the KJV (RV, "transform").

(2) For *metanoia*, "a change of mind," see REPENTANCE.

CHANGER (Money-changer)

1. *kollubistēs* (κολλυβιστής, 2855), from *kollubos* (lit., "clipped"), "a small coin or rate of change" (*koloboō* signifies "to cut off, to clip, shorten," Matt. 24:22), denotes "a money-changer," lit., money-clipper, Matt. 21:12; Mark 11:15; John 2:15.¶

2. *kermatistēs* (κερματιστής, 2773), from *kermatizō* (not found in the NT), "to cut into small pieces, to make small change" (*kerma* signifies "a small coin," John 2:15; akin to *keirō*, "to cut short"). In the court of the Gentiles, in the temple precincts, were the seats of those who sold selected and approved animals for sacrifice, and other things. The magnitude of this traffic had introduced the bankers' or brokers' business, John 2:14.¶

CHARGE (Nouns, Adjective and Verbs), CHARGEABLE

A. Nouns.

(a) With the meaning of "an accusation."

1. *aitia* (αἰτία, 156), "a cause, accusation," is rendered "charges" in Acts 25:27 (KJV, "crimes"); cf. v. 18. See ACCUSATION, CAUSE.

2. *aitiōma* (αἰτίωμα, 157v), in some texts *aitiama*, denotes "a charge," Acts 25:7. See ACCUSATION, A, No. 2.

3. *enklēma* (ἔγκλημα, 1462): see ACCUSATION, A, No. 3.

(b) With the meaning of "something committed or bestowed."

4. *klēros* (κλῆρος, 2819), "a lot, allotment, heritage" (whence Eng. "clergy"), is translated in 1 Pet. 5:3, RV, "the charge allotted to you"; here the word is in the plural, lit., "charges." See INHERITANCE, LOT, PART.

5. *opsōnion* (ὀψώνιον, 3800), from *opson*, "meat," and *ōneomai*, "to buy," primarily signified whatever is brought to be eaten with bread, provisions, supplies for an army, soldier's pay, "charges," 1 Cor. 9:7, of the service of a soldier. It is rendered "wages" in Luke 3:14; Rom. 6:23; 2 Cor. 11:8. See WAGES.¶

6. *parangelia* (παραγγελία, 3852), "a proclamation, a command or commandment," is strictly used of commands received from a superior and transmitted to others. It is rendered "charge" in Acts 16:24; 1 Thess. 4:2, RV (where the word is in the plural); 1 Tim. 1:5 (RV) and v. 18. In Acts 5:28 the lit. meaning is "Did we

not charge you with a charge ?" See also COMMANDMENT, STRAITLY. Cf. C, No. 8, below.¶

B. Adjective.

adapanos (ἀδάπανος, 77), lit., "without expense" (*a*, negative, and *dapanē*, "expense, cost"), is used in 1 Cor. 9:18, "without charge" (of service in the gospel).¶

C. Verbs.

1. *diamarturomai* (διαμαρτύρομαι, 1263), a strengthened form of *marturomai* (*dia*, "through," intensive), is used in the middle voice; primarily it signifies to testify through and through, bear a solemn witness; hence, "to charge earnestly," 1 Tim. 5:21; 2 Tim. 2:14; 4:1. See TESTIFY, WITNESS.

2. *diastellomai* (διαστέλλομαι, 1291), lit., "to draw asunder" (*dia*, "asunder," *stellō*, "to draw"), signifies "to admonish, order, charge," Matt. 16:20; Mark 5:43; 7:36 (twice); 8:15; 9:9. In Acts 15:24 it is translated "gave commandment"; in Heb. 12:20, KJV, "commanded," RV, "enjoined." See COMMAND, *Note* (2).¶

3. *diatassō* (διατάσσω, 1299): see APPOINT, No. 6.

4. *embrimaomai* (ἐμβριμάομαι, 1690), from *en*, "in," intensive, and *brimē*, "strength," primarily signifies "to snort with anger, as of horses." Used of men it signifies "to fret, to be painfully moved"; then, "to express indignation against"; hence, "to rebuke sternly, to charge strictly," Matt. 9:30; Mark 1:43; it is rendered "murmured against" in Mark 14:5; "groaned" in John 11:33; "groaning" in v. 38. See GROAN, MURMUR.¶

5. *enkaleo* (ἐγκαλέω, 1458): see ACCUSE, B, No. 2.

6. *entellomai* (ἐντέλλομαι, 1781), to order, command, enjoin (from *en*, in, used intensively, and *teleō*, to fulfil), is translated by the verb to give charge, Matt. 4:6; 17:9 (AV); Luke 4:10. See COMMAND, ENJOIN.

7. *epitimaō* (ἐπιτιμάω, 2008) signifies (*a*) to put honour upon (*epi*, upon, *timē*, honour); (*b*) to adjudge, to find fault with, rebuke; hence to charge, or rather, to charge strictly (*epi*, intensive), e.g., Matt. 12:16; Mark 3:12, "charged much"; Mark 8:30; in 10:48, RV, "rebuked." See REBUKE.

8. *parangellō* (παραγγέλλω, 3853), lit., "to announce beside" (*para*, "beside," *angellō*, "to announce"), "to hand on an announcement from one to another," usually denotes "to command, to charge," Luke 5:14; 8:56; 1 Cor. 7:10 (KJV, "command"), "give charge," RV; 11:17, "in giving you this charge," RV; 1 Tim. 1:3; 6:13, RV, and 6:17. It is rendered by the verb "to charge" in the RV of Acts 1:4; 4:18; 5:28; 15:5;

1 Thess. 4:11. See Acts 5:28 under A, No. 6. See COMMAND, DECLARE.

9. *proaitiaomai* (προαιτιάομαι, 4256), "to accuse beforehand, to have already brought a charge" (*pro*, "before," *aitia*, "an accusation"), is used in Rom. 3:9, "we before laid to the charge."¶

10. *tēreō* (τηρέω, 5083), "to keep, to guard," is translated "to be kept in charge," in Acts 24:23; 25:4, RV (KJV, "kept"). See HOLD, KEEP, OBSERVE, PRESERVE, WATCH.

Notes: (1) *Martureō*, "to testify," translated "charged" in 1 Thess. 2:11, KJV, is found there in the most authentic mss. and translated "testifying" in the RV. (2) *Enorkizō*, "to adjure" (*en*, "in," used intensively, *horkos*, "an oath"), is translated "I adjure," in 1 Thess. 5:27, RV, for KJV, "I charge." Some mss. have *horkizō* here. (3) The following are translated by the verb "to charge or to be chargeable" in the KJV, but differently in the RV, and will be found under the word BURDEN: *bareō*, B, No. 1; *epibareō*, B, No. 2; *katanarkaō*, B, No. 5. (4) *Epitassō*, "to command," is so translated in Mark 9:25, RV, for the KJV, "charge." (5) *Dapanaō*, "to be at the expense of anything" (cf. B, above), is translated "be at charges," in Acts 21:24. See CONSUME, SPEND. (6) In 2 Tim. 4:16, *logizomai* is rendered "laid to (their) charge," KJV; RV, " . . . account." (7) In Acts 8:27, the RV translates the verb *eimi*, "to be," with *epi*, "over," "was over," KJV, "had the charge of." (8) In Acts 7:60 *histēmi*, "to cause to stand," is rendered "lay . . . to the charge."

CHARGER

pinax (πίναξ, 4094), primarily "a board or plank," came to denote various articles of wood; hence, "a wooden trencher, charger," Matt. 14:8, 11; Mark 6:25, 28; Luke 11:39. See PLATTER.¶

CHARIOT

1. *harma* (ἅρμα, 716), akin to *arariskō*, "to join," denotes "a war chariot with two wheels," Acts 8:28, 29, 38; Rev. 9:9.¶

2. *rhedē* (ῥέδη, 4480), "a wagon with four wheels," was chiefly used for traveling purposes, Rev. 18:13.¶

For CHARITY see LOVE

CHASTE

hagnos (ἁγνός, 53) signifies (*a*) "pure from every fault, immaculate," 2 Cor. 7:11 (KJV, "clear"); Phil. 4:8; 1 Tim. 5:22; Jas. 3:17; 1 John 3:3 (in all which the RV rendering is "pure"), and 1 Pet. 3:2, "chaste"; (*b*) "pure from carnality, modest," 2 Cor. 11:2, RV, "pure"; Titus 2:5, "chaste." See CLEAR, HOLY, PURE.¶

Note: Cf. *hagios*, "holy, as being free from admixture of evil"; *hosios*, "holy, as being free from defilement"; *eilikrinēs*, "pure, as being tested," lit., "judged by the sunlight"; *katharos*, "pure, as being cleansed."

CHASTEN, CHASTENING, CHASTISE, CHASTISEMENT

A. Verb.

paideuō (παιδεύω, 3811) primarily denotes "to train children," suggesting the broad idea of education (*pais*, "a child"), Acts 7:22; 22:3; see also Titus 2:12, "instructing" (RV), here of a training gracious and firm; grace, which brings salvation, employs means to give us full possession of it; hence, "to chastise," this being part of the training, whether (*a*) by correcting with words, reproving, and admonishing, 1 Tim. 1:20 (RV, "be taught"); 2 Tim. 2:25, or (*b*) by "chastening" by the infliction of evils and calamities, 1 Cor. 11:32; 2 Cor. 6:9; Heb. 12:6–7, 10; Rev. 3:19. The verb also has the meaning "to chastise with blows, to scourge," said of the command of a judge, Luke 23:16, 22. See CORRECTION, B, INSTRUCT, LEARN, TEACH, and cf. CHILD (Nos. 4 to 6).¶

B. Noun.

paideia (παιδεία, 3809) denotes "the training of a child, including instruction"; hence, "discipline, correction," "chastening," Eph. 6:4, RV (KJV, "nurture"), suggesting the Christian discipline that regulates character; so in Heb. 12:5, 7, 8 (in v. 8, KJV, "chastisement," the RV corrects to "chastening"); in 2 Tim. 3:16, "instruction." See INSTRUCTION, NURTURE.¶

CHEEK

siagōn (σιαγών, 4600) primarily denotes "the jaw, the jaw-bone"; hence "cheek," Matt. 5:39; Luke 6:29.¶

CHEER, CHEERFUL, CHEERFULLY, CHEERFULNESS

A. Verbs.

1. *euthumeō* (εὐθυμέω, 2114) signifies, in the active voice, "to put in good spirits, to make cheerful" (*eu*, "well," *thumos*, "mind or passion"); or, intransitively, "to be cheerful," Acts 27:22, 25; Jas. 5:13 (RV, "cheerful," for KJV, "merry"). See MERRY.¶

2. *tharseō* (θαρσέω, 2293), "to be of good courage, of good cheer" (*tharsos*, "courage, confidence"), is used only in the imperative mood, in the NT; "be of good cheer," Matt. 9:2, 22; 14:27; Mark 6:50; 10:49; Luke 8:48; John

16:33; Acts 23:11. See BOLD, A, No. 1, COM-
FORT, COURAGE.¶

B. Adjectives.

1. *euthumos* (εὔθυμος, 2115) means "of
good cheer" (see A, No. 1), Acts 27:36.¶

2. *hilaros* (ἱλαρός, 2431), from *hileōs*, "propitious," signifies that readiness of mind, that
joyousness, which is prompt to do anything;
hence, "cheerful" (Eng., "hilarious"), 2 Cor.
9:7, "God loveth a cheerful (hilarious) giver."¶

Note: In the Sept. the verb *hilarunō* translates
a Hebrew word meaning "to cause to shine," in
Ps. 104:15.¶

C. Adverb.

euthumōs (εὐθύμως, 2115*), cheerfully (see
A, No. 1), is found in the most authentic mss.,
in Acts 24:10, instead of the comparative degree, *euthumoteron.* ¶

D. Noun.

hilarotēs (ἱλαρότης, 2432), "cheerfulness"
(akin to B, No. 2), is used in Rom. 12:8, in
connection with showing mercy.¶

CHERISH

thalpō (θάλπω, 2282) primarily means "to
heat, to soften by heat"; then, "to keep warm,"
as of birds covering their young with their feathers, Deut. 22:6, Sept.; metaphorically, "to cherish with tender love, to foster with tender care,"
in Eph. 5:29 of Christ and the church; in
1 Thess. 2:7 of the care of the saints at Thessalonica by the apostle and his associates, as of a
nurse for her children.¶

CHERUBIM

cheroubim (χερουβίμ, 5502) are regarded
by some as the ideal representatives of redeemed animate creation. In the tabernacle and
Temple they were represented by the two
golden figures of two-winged living creatures.
They were all of one piece with the golden lid
of the ark of the covenant in the Holy of Holies,
signifying that the prospect of redeemed and
glorified creatures was bound up with the sacrifice of Christ.

This in itself would indicate that they represent redeemed human beings in union with
Christ, a union seen, figuratively, proceeding
out of the mercy seat. Their faces were towards
this mercy seat, suggesting a consciousness of
the means whereby union with Christ has been
produced.

The first reference to the "cherubim" is in
Gen. 3:24, which should read " . . . at the East
of the Garden of Eden He caused to dwell in a
tabernacle the cherubim, and the flaming sword
which turned itself to keep the way of the Tree
of Life." This was not simply to keep fallen

human beings out; the presence of the "cherubim" suggests that redeemed men, restored to
God on God's conditions, would have access to
the Tree of Life. (See Rev. 22:14).

Certain other references in the OT give clear
indication that angelic beings are upon occasion
in view, e.g., Ps. 18:10; Ezek. 28:4. So with the
vision of the cherubim in Ezek. 10:1–20; 11:22.
In the NT the word is found in Heb. 9:5, where
the reference is to the ark in the tabernacle, and
the thought is suggested of those who minister
to the manifestation of the glory of God.

We may perhaps conclude, therefore, that,
inasmuch as in the past and in the present
angelic beings have functioned and do function
administratively in the service of God, and that
redeemed man in the future is to act administratively in fellowship with Him, the "cherubim"
in Scripture represent one or other of these two
groups of created beings according to what is
set forth in the various passages relating to
them.¶

For CHICKEN see BROOD

CHIEF, CHIEFEST, CHIEFLY

A. Adjective.

prōtos (πρῶτος, 4413) denotes "the first,"
whether in time or place. It is translated "chief"
in Mark 6:21, RV, of men of Galilee; in Acts
13:50, of men in a city; in 28:7, of the "chief"
man in the island of Melita; in 17:4, of "chief"
women in a city; in 28:17, of Jews; in 1 Tim.
1:15–16, of a sinner. In the following, where
the KJV has "chief," or "chiefest," the RV renderings are different : Matt. 20:27 and Mark 10:44,
"first"; Luke 19:47 and Acts 25:2, "principal
men"; Acts 16:12, said of Philippi, "the first
(city) of the district," RV, for incorrect KJV, "the
chief city of that part of Macedonia." Amphi-
polis was the "chief" city of that part. *Prōtos*
here must mean the first in the direction in
which the apostle came. See BEGINNING, BE-
FORE, BEST, FIRST, FORMER.

B. Nouns.

1. *kephalaion* (κεφάλαιον, 2774), akin to
the adjective *kephalaios*, "belonging to the
head," and *kephalē*, "the head," denotes the
chief point or principal thing in a subject, Heb.
8:1, "the chief point is this" (KJV, "the sum");
elsewhere in Acts 22:28 (of principal, as to
money), "(a great) sum." See SUM.¶

Certain compound nouns involving the significance of chief, are as follows:

2. *archiereus* (ἀρχιερεύς, 749), "a chief
priest, high priest" (*archē*, "first," *hiereus*, "a
priest"), is frequent in the gospels, Acts and
Hebrews, but there only in the NT. It is used of

Christ, e.g., in Heb. 2:17; 3:1; of "chief" priests, including ex-high-priests and members of their families, e.g., Matt. 2:4; Mark 8:31.

3. *archipoimēn* (ἀρχιποίμην, 750), "a chief shepherd" (*archē*, "chief," *poimēn*, "a shepherd"), is said of Christ only, 1 Pet. 5:4. Modern Greeks use it of tribal chiefs.¶

4. *architelōnēs* (ἀρχιτελώνης, 754) denotes "a chief tax-collector, or publican," Luke 19:2.¶

5. *akrogōniaios* (ἀκρογωνιαῖος, 204) denotes "a chief corner-stone" (from *akros*, "highest, extreme," *gōnia*, "a corner, angle"), Eph. 2:20 and 1 Pet. 2:6.¶ In the Sept., Isa. 28:16.¶

6. *prōtokathedria* (πρωτοκαθεδρία, 4410), "a sitting in the first or chief seat" (*prōtos*, "first," *kathedra*, "a seat"), is found in Matt. 23:6; Mark 12:39; Luke 11:43; 20:46.¶

7. *prōtoklisia* (πρωτοκλισία, 4411), "the first reclining place, the chief place at table" (from *prōtos*, and *klisia*, "a company reclining at a meal"; cf. *klinō*, "to incline"), is found in Matt. 23:6; Mark 12:39 (as with No. 6); Luke 14:7–8; 20:46.¶

8. *chiliarchos* (χιλίαρχος, 5506) denotes "a chief captain": see CAPTAIN, No. 1.

9. *asiarchēs* ('ασιαρχής, 775), "an Asiarch," was one of certain officers elected by various cities in the province of Asia, whose function consisted in celebrating, partly at their own expense, the public games and festivals; in Acts 19:31, RV, the word is translated "chief officers of Asia" (KJV, "chief of Asia").

It seems probable, according to Prof. Ramsay, that they were "the high priests of the temples of the Imperial worship in various cities of Asia"; further, that "the Council of the Asiarchs sat at stated periods in the great cities alternately . . . and were probably assembled at Ephesus for such a purpose when they sent advice to St. Paul to consult his safety." A festival would have brought great crowds to the city.¶

10. *archōn* (ἄρχων, 758), "a ruler," is rendered "chief" in the KJV of Luke 14:1 (RV, "ruler"); "chief rulers," in John 12:42, RV, "rulers (of the people)," i.e., of members of the Sanhedrin; "chief," in Luke 11:15 (RV, "prince"), in reference to Beelzebub, the prince of demons. See MAGISTRATE, PRINCE, RULER.

11. *archisunagōgos* (ἀρχισυνάγωγος, 752), "a ruler of a synagogue," translated "chief ruler of the synagogue," in Acts 18:8, 17, KJV, was the administrative officer supervising the worship.

C. Verb.

hēgeomai (ἡγέομαι, 2233), "to lead the way, to preside, rule, be the chief," is used of the ambition "to be chief" among the disciples of Christ, Luke 22:26; of Paul as the "chief" speaker in gospel testimony at Lystra, Acts 14:12; of Judas and Silas, as chief (or rather, "leading") men among the brethren at Jerusalem, Acts 15:22. See ACCOUNT, COUNT, ESTEEM, GOVERNOR, JUDGE, SUPPOSE, THINK.

D. Adverbs.

1. *huperlian* (ὑπερλίαν, 5528 and 3029), "chiefest" (*huper*, "over," *lian*, "exceedingly, pre-eminently, very much"), is used in 2 Cor. 11:5; 12:11, of Paul's place among the apostles.¶

2. *malista* (μάλιστα, 3122), the superlative of *mala*, "very, very much," is rendered "chiefly" in 2 Pet. 2:10 and in the KJV of Phil. 4:22 (RV, "especially"). See ESPECIALLY, MOST.

Note: In Rom. 3:2, RV, the adverb *prōton* is translated "first of all" (KJV, "chiefly").

CHILD, CHILDREN, CHILD-BEARING, CHILDISH, CHILDLESS

1. *teknon* (τέκνον, 5043), "a child" (akin to *tiktō*, "to beget, bear"), is used in both the natural and the figurative senses. In contrast to *huios*, "son" (see below), it gives prominence to the fact of birth, whereas *huios* stresses the dignity and character of the relationship. Figuratively, *teknon* is used of "children" of (*a*) God, John 1:12; (*b*) light, Eph. 5:8; (*c*) obedience, 1 Pet. 1:14; (*d*) a promise, Rom. 9:8; Gal. 4:28; (*e*) the Devil, 1 John 3:10; (*f*) wrath, Eph. 2:3; (*g*) cursing, 2 Pet. 2:14; (*h*) spiritual relationship, 2 Tim. 2:1; Philem. 10. See DAUGHTER, SON.

2. *teknion* (τεκνίον, 5040), "a little child," a diminutive of No. 1, is used only figuratively in the NT, and always in the plural. It is found frequently in 1 John, see 2:1, 12, 28; 3:7, 18; 4:4; 5:21; elsewhere, once in John's Gospel, 13:33, once in Paul's epistles, Gal. 4:19. It is a term of affection by a teacher to his disciples under circumstances requiring a tender appeal, e.g., of Christ to the Twelve just before His death; the apostle John used it in warning believers against spiritual dangers; Paul, because of the deadly errors of Judaism assailing the Galatian churches. Cf. his use of *teknon* in Gal. 4:28.¶

3. *huios* (υἱός, 5207), "a son," is always so translated in the RV, except in the phrase "children of Israel," e.g., Matt. 27:9; and with reference to a foal, Matt. 21:5. The KJV does not discriminate between *teknon* and *huios*. In the First Epistle of John, the apostle reserves the word for the Son of God. See *teknia*, "little children" (above), and *tekna*, "children," in

John 1:12; 11:52. See *paidion* (below). For the other use of *huios*, indicating the quality of that with which it is connected, see SON.

4. *pais* (παῖς, 3816) signifies (*a*) "a child in relation to descent," (*b*) "a boy or girl in relation to age," (*c*) "a servant, attendant, maid, in relation to condition." As an instance of (*a*) see Matt. 21:15, "children," and Acts 20:12 (RV, "lad"). In regard to (*b*) the RV has "boy" in Matt. 17:18 and Luke 9:42. In Luke 2:43 it is used of the Lord Jesus. In regard to (*c*), see Matt. 8:6, 8, 13, etc. As to (*a*) note Matt. 2:16, RV, "male children. See MAID, MANSERVANT, SERVANT, SON, YOUNG MAN.

5. *paidion* (παιδίον, 3813), a diminutive of *pais*, signifies "a little or young child"; it is used of an infant just born, John 16:21; of a male child recently born, e.g., Matt. 2:8; Heb. 11:23; of a more advanced child, Mark 9:24; of a son, John 4:49; of a girl, Mark 5:39, 40, 41; in the plural, of "children," e.g., Matt. 14:21. It is used metaphorically of believers who are deficient in spiritual understanding, 1 Cor. 14:20, and in affectionate and familiar address by the Lord to His disciples, almost like the Eng., "lads," John 21:5; by the apostle John to the youngest believers in the family of God, 1 John 2:13, 18; there it is to be distinguished from *teknia*, which term he uses in addressing all his readers (vv. 1, 12, 28: see *teknia*, above). See DAMSEL.

Note: The adverb *paidiothen*, "from (or of) a child," is found in Mark 9:21.¶

6. *paidarion* (παιδάριον, 3808), another diminutive of *pais*, is used of "boys and girls," in Matt. 11:16 (the best texts have *paidiois* here), and a "lad," John 6:9; the tendency in colloquial Greek was to lose the diminutive character of the word.¶

7. *nēpios* (νήπιος, 3516), lit., "not-speaking" (from *nē*, a negative, and *epos*, a word is rendered "childish" in 1 Cor. 13:11: see BABE.

8. *monogenēs* (μονογενής, 3439), lit., "only-begotten," is translated "only child" in Luke 9:38. See ONLY, ONLY-BEGOTTEN.

9. *teknogonia* (τεκνογονία, 5042), *teknon* and a root *gen*—, whence *gennaō*, "to beget," denotes "bearing children," implying the duties of motherhood, 1 Tim. 2:15.¶

B. Verbs.

1. *nēpiazō* (νηπιάζω, 3515), "to be a babe," is used in 1 Cor. 14:20, "(in malice) be ye babes" (akin to No. 7, above).¶

2. *teknotropheō* (τεκνοτροφέω, 5044), "to rear young," *teknon*, and *trephō*, "to rear," signifies "to bring up children," 1 Tim. 5:10.¶

3. *teknogoneō* (τεκνογονέω, 5041), "to bear children" (*teknon*, and *gennaō*, "to beget"), see No. 9 above, is found in 1 Tim. 5:14.¶

C. Adjectives.

1. *enkuos* (ἔγκυος, 1471) denotes "great with child" (*en*, "in," and *kuō*, "to conceive"), Luke 2:5.¶

2. *philoteknos* (φιλότεκνος, 5388), from *phileō*, "to love," and *teknon*, signifies "loving one's children," Titus 2:4.¶

3. *ateknos* (ἄτεκνος, 815), from *a*, negative, and *teknon*, signifies "childless," Luke 20:28–30.¶

Notes: (1) For *brephos*, "a new born babe," always rendered "babe" or "babes" in the RV (KJV, "young children," Acts 7:19; "child," 2 Tim. 3:15), see under BABE.

(2) *Huiothesia*, "adoption of children," in the KJV of Eph. 1:5, is corrected to "adoption as sons" in the RV. See on ADOPTION.

CHOKE

1. *pnigō* (πνίγω, 4155) is used, in the passive voice, of "perishing by drowning," Mark 5:13; in the active, "to seize a person's throat, to throttle," Matt. 18:28. See THROAT.¶

2. *apopnigō* (ἀποπνίγω, 638), a strengthened form of No. 1 (*apo*, "from," intensive; cf. Eng., "to choke off"), is used metaphorically, of "thorns crowding out seed sown and preventing its growth," Matt. 13:7; Luke 8:7. It is Luke's word for "suffocation by drowning," Luke 8:33 (cf. Mark 5:13, above).¶

3. *sumpnigō* (συμπνίγω, 4846) gives the suggestion of "choking together" (*sun*, "with"), i.e., by crowding, Matt. 13:22; Mark 4:7, 19; Luke 8:14. It is used in Luke 8:42, of the crowd that thronged the Lord, almost, so to speak, to suffocation.¶

CHOICE, CHOOSE, CHOSEN

A. Verbs.

1. *eklegō* (ἐκλέγω, 1586), "to pick out, select," means, in the middle voice, "to choose for oneself," not necessarily implying the rejection of what is not chosen, but "choosing" with the subsidiary ideas of kindness or favor or love, Mark 13:20; Luke 6:13; 9:35 (RV); 10:42; 14:7; John 6:70; 13:18; 15:16, 19; Acts 1:2, 24; 6:5; 13:17; 15:22, 25; in 15:7 it is rendered "made choice"; 1 Cor. 1:27–28; Eph. 1:4; Jas. 2:5.¶

2. *epilegō* (ἐπιλέγω, 1951), in the middle voice, signifies "to choose," either in addition or in succession to another. It has this meaning in Acts 15:40, of Paul's choice of Silas. For its other meaning, "to call or name," John 5:2, see CALL.¶

3. *haireō* (αἱρέω, 138), "to take," is used in the middle voice only, in the sense of taking for oneself, choosing, 2 Thess. 2:13, of a "choice" made by God (as in Deut. 7:6–7; 26:18, Sept.);

in Phil. 1:22 and Heb. 11:25, of human "choice." Its special significance is to select rather by the act of taking, than by showing preference or favor.¶

4. *hairetizō* (αἱρετίζω, 140), akin to the verbal adjective *hairetos*, "that which may be taken" (see No. 3), signifies "to take," with the implication that what is taken is eligible or suitable; hence, "to choose," by reason of this suitability, Matt. 12:18, of God's delight in Christ as His "chosen."¶ It is frequent in the Sept., e.g., Gen. 30:20; Num. 14:8; Ps. 25:12; 119:30, 173; 132:13–14; Hos. 4:18; Hag. 2:23 ("he hath chosen the Canaanites"); Zech. 1:17; 2:12; Mal. 3:17.

5. *cheirotoneō* (χειροτονέω, 5500) : see APPOINT, No. 11.

6. *procheirotoneō* (προχειροτονέω, 4401) signifies "to choose before," Acts 10:41, where it is used of a choice made before by God.¶

Notes: (1) For *procheirizō* see APPOINT, No. 12.

(2) *Stratologeō*, in 2 Tim. 2:4 (KJV, "chosen to be a soldier"), signifies to enroll as a soldier (RV). See SOLDIER.

B. Adjective.

eklektos (ἐκλεκτός, 1588), akin to A, No. 1, signifies "chosen out, select," e.g., Matt. 22:14; Luke 23:35; Rom 16:13 (perhaps in the sense of "eminent"); Rev. 17:14. In 1 Pet. 2:4, 9, the RV translates it "elect." See ELECT.

C. Noun.

eklogē (ἐκλογή, 1589), akin to A, No. 1 and B, "a picking out, choosing" (Eng., "eclogue"), is translated "chosen" in Acts 9:15, lit., "he is a vessel of choice unto Me." In the six other places where this word is found it is translated "election." See ELECTION.

CHRIST

christos (χριστός, 5547), "anointed," translates, in the Sept., the word "Messiah," a term applied to the priests who were anointed with the holy oil, particularly the high priest, e.g., Lev. 4:3, 5, 16. The prophets are called *hoi christoi Theou*, "the anointed of God," Ps. 105:15. A king of Israel was described upon occasion as *christos tou Kuriou*, "the anointed of the Lord," 1 Sam. 2:10, 35; 2 Sam. 1:14; Ps. 2:2; 18:50; Hab. 3:13; the term is used even of Cyrus, Isa. 45:1.

The title *ho Christos*, "the Christ," is not used of Christ in the Sept. version of the inspired books of the OT. In the NT the word is frequently used with the article, of the Lord Jesus, as an appellative rather than a title, e.g., Matt. 2:4; Acts 2:31; without the article, Luke 2:11; 23:2; John 1:41. Three times the title was expressly accepted by the Lord Himself, Matt. 16:17; Mark 14:61–62; John 4:26.

It is added as an appellative to the proper name "Jesus," e.g., John 17:3, the only time when the Lord so spoke of Himself; Acts 9:34; 1 Cor. 3:11; 1 John 5:6. It is distinctly a proper name in many passages, whether with the article, e.g., Matt. 1:17; 11:2; Rom. 7:4; 9:5; 15:19; 1 Cor. 1:6, or without the article, Mark 9:41; Rom. 6:4; 8:9, 17; 1 Cor. 1:12; Gal. 2:16. The single title *Christos* is sometimes used without the article to signify the One who by His Holy Spirit and power indwells believers and molds their character in conformity to His likeness, Rom. 8:10; Gal. 2:20; 4:19; Eph. 3:17. As to the use or absence of the article, the title with the article specifies the Lord Jesus as "the Christ"; the title without the article stresses His character and His relationship with believers. Again, speaking generally, when the title is the subject of a sentence it has the article; when it forms part of the predicate the article is absent. See also JESUS.

CHRISTS (FALSE)

pseudochristos (ψευδόχριστος, 5580) denotes "one who falsely lays claim to the name and office of the Messiah," Matt. 24:24; Mark 13:22.¶ See *Note* under ANTICHRIST.

CHRISTIAN

christianos (χριστιανός, 5546), "Christian," a word formed after the Roman style, signifying an adherent of Jesus, was first applied to such by the Gentiles and is found in Acts 11:26; 26:28; 1 Pet. 4:16.

Though the word rendered "were called" in Acts 11:26 (see under CALL) might be used of a name adopted by oneself or given by others, the "Christians" do not seem to have adopted it for themselves in the times of the apostles. In 1 Pet. 4:16, the apostle is speaking from the point of view of the persecutor; cf. "as a thief," "as a murderer." Nor is it likely that the appellation was given by Jews. As applied by Gentiles there was no doubt an implication of scorn, as in Agrippa's statement in Acts 26:28. Tacitus, writing near the end of the first century, says, "The vulgar call them Christians. The author or origin of this denomination, Christus, had, in the reign of Tiberius, been executed by the procurator, Pontius Pilate" (Annals xv. 44). From the second century onward the term was accepted by believers as a title of honor.¶

CHRYSOLITE

chrusolithos (χρυσόλιθος, 5555), lit., "a gold stone" (*chrusos*, "gold," *lithos*, "a stone"), is the name of a precious stone of a gold color, now called "a topaz," Rev. 21:20 (see also Exod. 28:20 and Ezek. 28:13).¶

CHRYSOPRASUS

chrusoprasos (χρυσόπρασος, 5556), from (*chrusos*, "gold," and *prasos*, "a leek"), is a precious stone like a leek in color, a translucent, golden green. Pliny reckons it among the beryls. The word occurs in Rev. 21:20.¶

For **CHURCH** see **ASSEMBLY** and **CONGREGATION**

CINNAMON

kinnamōmon (κιννάμωμον, 2792) is derived from an Arabic word signifying "to emit a smell"; the substance was an ingredient in the holy oil for anointing, Ex. 30:23. See also Prov. 7:17 and Song of Sol. 4:14. In the NT it is found in Rev. 18:13. The cinnamon of the present day is the inner bark of an aromatic tree called *canella zeylanica.*¶

CIRCUIT

perierchomai (περιέρχομαι, 4022), "to go about" (*peri*, "about," *erchomai*, "to go"), is said of "navigating a ship under difficulty owing to contrary winds," Acts 28:13, RV, "we made a circuit," for KJV, "we fetched a compass." See COMPASS, STROLLING, WANDER.

CIRCUMCISION, UNCIRCUMCISION, CIRCUMCISE

A. Nouns.

1. *peritomē* (περιτομή, 4061), lit., "a cutting round, circumcision" (the verb is *peritemnō*), was a rite enjoined by God upon Abraham and his male descendants and dependents, as a sign of the covenant made with him, Gen. 17; Acts 7:8; Rom. 4:11. Hence Israelites termed Gentiles "the uncircumcised," Judg. 15:18; 2 Sam. 1:20. So in the NT, but without the suggestion of contempt, e.g., Rom. 2:26; Eph. 2:11.

The rite had a moral significance, Ex. 6:12, 30, where it is metaphorically applied to the lips; so to the ear, Jer. 6:10, and the heart, Deut. 30:6; Jer. 4:4. Cf. Jer. 9:25–26. It refers to the state of "circumcision," in Rom. 2:25–28; 3:1; 4:10; 1 Cor. 7:19; Gal. 5:6; 6:15; Col. 3:11.

"In the economy of grace no account is taken of any ordinance performed on the flesh; the old racial distinction is ignored in the preaching of the gospel, and faith is the sole condition upon which the favor of God in salvation is to be obtained, Rom. 10:11–13; 1 Cor. 7:19. See also Rom. 4:9–12."*

Upon the preaching of the gospel to, and the conversion of, Gentiles, a sect of Jewish believers arose who argued that the gospel, without the fulfillment of "circumcision," would make void the Law and make salvation impossible, Acts 15:1. Hence this party was known as "the circumcision," Acts 10:45; 11:2; Gal. 2:12; Col. 4:11; Titus 1:10 (the term being used by metonymy, the abstract being put for the concrete, as with the application of the word to Jews generally, Rom. 3:30; 4:9, 12; 15:8; Gal. 2:7–9; Eph. 2:11). It is used metaphorically and spiritually of believers with reference to the act, Col. 2:11 and Rom. 2:29; to the condition, Phil. 3:3.

The apostle Paul's defense of the truth, and his contention against this propaganda, form the main subject of the Galatian epistle. Cf. *katatomē*, "concision," Phil. 3:2. See CONCISION.

2. *akrobustia* (ἀκροβυστια, 203), "uncircumcision," is used (*a*) of the physical state, in contrast to the act of "circumcision," Acts 11:3 (lit., "having uncircumcision"); Rom. 2:25–26; 4:10–11 ("though they be in uncircumcision," RV), 12; 1 Cor. 7:18–19; Gal. 5:6; 6:15; Col. 3:11; (*b*) by metonymy, for Gentiles, e.g., Rom. 2:26–27; 3:30; 4:9; Gal. 2:7; Eph. 2:11; (*d*) in a metaphorical or transferred sense, of the moral condition in which the corrupt desires of the flesh still operate, Col. 2:13.¶

Note: In Rom. 4:11, the phrase "though they be in uncircumcision" translates the Greek phrase *di' akrobustias*, lit., "through uncircumcision"; here *dia* has the local sense of proceeding from and passing out.

B. Adjective.

aperitmētos (ἀπερίτμητος, 564), "uncircumcised" (*a*, negative, *peri*, "around," *temnō*, "to cut"), is used in Acts 7:51, metaphorically, of "heart and ears."¶

C. Verbs.

1. *peritemnō* (περιτέμνω, 4059), "to circumcise," is used (*a*) lit., e.g., Luke 1:59; 2:21; of receiving circumcision, Gal. 5:2–3; 6:13, RV; (*b*) metaphorically, of spiritual circumcision, Col. 2:11.

2. *epispaomai* (ἐπισπάομαι, 1986), lit., "to draw over, to become uncircumcised," as if to efface Judaism, appears in 1 Cor. 7:18.¶

For **CIRCUMSPECTLY** see **ACCURATELY**

---

* From *Notes on Galatians,* by Hogg and Vine, p.69.

CITIZEN, CITIZENSHIP

1. *politēs* (πολίτης, 4177), "a member of a city or state, or the inhabitant of a country or district," Luke 15:15, is used elsewhere in Luke 19:14; Acts 21:39, and, in the most authentic mss., in Heb. 8:11 (where some texts have *plēsion*, "a neighbor"). Apart from Heb. 8:11, the word occurs only in the writings of Luke (himself a Greek).¶

2. *sumpolitēs* (συμπολίτης, 4847), *sun*, "with," and No. 1, denotes "a fellow-citizen," i.e., possessing the same "citizenship," Eph. 2:19, used metaphorically in a spiritual sense.¶

3. *politeia* (πολιτεία, 4174) signifies (a) "the relation in which a citizen stands to the state, the condition of a citizen, citizenship," Acts 22:28, "with a great sum obtained I this citizenship" (KJV, "freedom"). While Paul's "citizenship" of Tarsus was not of advantage outside that city, yet his Roman "citizenship" availed throughout the Roman Empire and, besides private rights, included (1) exemption from all degrading punishments; (2) a right of appeal to the emperor after a sentence; (3) a right to be sent to Rome for trial before the emperor if charged with a capital offense. Paul's father might have obtained "citizenship" (1) by manumission; (2) as a reward of merit; (3) by purchase; the contrast implied in Acts 22:28 is perhaps against the last mentioned; (b) "a civil polity, the condition of a state, a commonwealth," said of Israel, Eph. 2:12. See COMMONWEALTH.¶

4. *politeuma* (πολίτευμα, 4175) signifies "the condition, or life, of a citizen, citizenship"; it is said of the heavenly status of believers, Phil. 3:20, "our citizenship (KJV, "conversation") is in Heaven." The RV marg. gives the alternative meaning, "commonwealth," i.e., community. See COMMONWEALTH, FREEDOM.¶

Note: Politeuō, Phil. 1:27, signifies "to be a *politēs*" (see No. 1), and is used in the middle voice, signifying, metaphorically, conduct characteristic of heavenly "citizenship," RV, "let your manner of life (KJV, "conversation") be worthy (marg., "behave as citizens worthily") of the gospel of Christ." In Acts 23:1 it is translated "I have lived." See CONVERSATION, LIVE.¶

CITY

polis (πόλις, 4172), primarily "a town enclosed with a wall" (perhaps from a root *plē—*, signifying "fullness," whence also the Latin *pleo*, "to fill," Eng., "polite, polish, politic, etc."), is used also of the heavenly Jerusalem, the abode and community of the redeemed, Heb. 11:10, 16; 12:22; 13:14. In the Apocalypse it signifies the visible capital of the heavenly kingdom, as destined to descend to earth in a coming age, e.g., Rev. 3:12; 21:2, 14, 19. By metonymy the word stands for the inhabitants, as in the English use, e.g., Matt. 8:34; 12:25; 21:10; Mark 1:33; Acts 13:44.

Note: In Acts 16:13, the most authentic mss. have *pulē*, "gate," RV, "without the gate."

CLAMOR

kraugē (κραυγή, 2906), an onomatopoeic word, imitating the raven's cry, akin to *krazō* and *kraugazō*, "to cry," denotes "an outcry," "clamor," Acts 23:9, RV; Eph. 4:31, where it signifies "the tumult of controversy." See CRY.

CLANGING

alalazō (ἀλαλάζω, 214), an onomatopoeic word, from the battle-cry, *alala*, is used of "raising the shout of battle," Josh. 6:20; hence, "to make a loud cry or shout," e.g., Ps. 47:1; "to wail," Jer. 29:2; in the NT, in Mark 5:38, of wailing mourners; in 1 Cor. 13:1, of the "clanging" of cymbals (KJV, "tinkling").¶

CLAY

pēlos (πηλός, 4081), "clay," especially such as was used by a mason or potter, is used of moist "clay," in John 9:6, 11, 14–15, in connection with Christ's healing the blind man; in Rom. 9:21, of potter's "clay," as to the potter's right over it as an illustration of the prerogatives of God in His dealings with men.¶

CLEAN, CLEANNESS, CLEANSE, CLEANSING

A. Adjective.

katharos (καθαρός, 2513), "free from impure admixture, without blemish, spotless," is used (a) physically, e.g., Matt. 23:26; 27:59; John 13:10 (where the Lord, speaking figuratively, teaches that one who has been entirely "cleansed," needs not radical renewal, but only to be "cleansed" from every sin into which he may fall); 15:3; Heb. 10:22; Rev. 15:6; 19:8, 14; 21:18, 21; (b) in a Levitical sense, Rom. 14:20; Titus 1:15, "pure"; (c) ethically, with the significance free from corrupt desire, from guilt, Matt. 5:8; John 13:10–11; Acts 20:26; 1 Tim. 1:5; 3:9; 2 Tim. 1:3; 2:22; Titus 1:15; Jas. 1:27; blameless, innocent (a rare meaning for this word), Acts 18:6; (d) in a combined Levitical and ethical sense ceremonially, Luke 11:41, "all things are clean unto you." See CLEAR, C, *Note* (2), PURE.¶

B. Verbs.

1. *katharizō* (καθαρίζω, 2511), akin to A, signifies (1) "to make clean, to cleanse" (*a*) from physical stains and dirt, as in the case of utensils, Matt. 23:25 (figuratively in verse 26); from disease, as of leprosy, Matt. 8:2; (*b*) in a moral sense, from the defilement of sin, Acts 15:9; 2 Cor. 7:1; Heb. 9:14; Jas. 4:8, "cleanse" from the guilt of sin, Eph. 5:26; 1 John 1:7; (2) "to pronounce clean in a Levitical sense," Mark 7:19, RV; Acts 10:15; 11:9; "to consecrate by cleansings," Heb. 9:22, 23; 10:2. See PURGE, PURIFY.

2. *diakatharizō* (διακαθαρίζω, 1245), "to cleanse thoroughly," is used in Matt. 3:12, RV.¶

Note: For *kathairō*, John 15:2, RV, see PURGE, No. 1. For *diakathairō*, Luke 3:17, RV, see PURGE, No. 3.

C. Nouns.

1. *katharismos* (καθαρισμός, 2512), akin to A, denotes "cleansing," (*a*) both the action and its results, in the Levitical sense, Mark 1:44; Luke 2:22, "purification"; 5:14, "cleansing"; John 2:6; 3:25, "purifying"; (*b*) in the moral sense, from sins, Heb. 1:3; 2 Pet. 1:9, RV, "cleansing." See PURGE, PURIFICATION, PURIFYING.¶

2. *katharotēs* (καθαρότης, 2514), akin to B, "cleanness, purity," is used in the Levitical sense in Heb. 9:13, RV, "cleanness." See PURIFY.¶

Note: In 2 Pet. 2:18, some inferior mss. have *ontōs*, "certainly" (KJV, "clean"), for *oligōs*, "scarcely" (RV, "just").

CLEAR, CLEARING, CLEARLY

A. Verb.

krustallizō (κρυσταλλίζω, 2929), "to shine like crystal, to be of crystalline brightness, or transparency," is found in Rev. 21:11, "clear as crystal." The verb may, however, have a transitive force, signifying "to crystallize or cause to become like crystal." In that case it would speak of Christ (since He is the "Lightgiver," see the preceding part of the verse), as the One who causes the saints to shine in His own likeness.¶

B. Adjective.

lampros (λαμπρός, 2986) is said of crystal, Rev. 22:1, KJV, "clear," RV, "bright. See BRIGHT, GAY, GOODLY, GORGEOUS, WHITE.

Note: The corresponding adverb *lamprōs* signifies "sumptuously."

C. Adverb.

tēlaugōs (τηλαυγῶς, 5081), from *tēle*, "afar," and *augē*, "radiance," signifies "conspicuously, or clearly," Mark 8:25, of the sight imparted by Christ to one who had been blind.¶ Some mss. have *dēlaugōs*, "clearly" (*dēlos*, "clear").

Notes: (1) In 2 Cor. 7:11, KJV, *hagnos* is rendered "clear." See PURE. (2) In Rev. 21:18, *katharos*, ("pure," RV) is rendered "clear," in the KJV. SEE CLEAN. (3) *Apologia* (Eng., "apology"), "a defense against an accusation," signifies, in 2 Cor. 7:11, a clearing of oneself. (4) For *diablepō*, "to see clearly," Matt. 7:5; Luke 6:42, and *kathoraō*, ditto, Rom. 1:20, see SEE.

CLEAVE, CLAVE

1. *kollaō* (κολλάω, 2853), "to join fast together, to glue, cement," is primarily said of metals and other materials (from *kolla*, "glue"). In the NT it is used only in the passive voice, with reflexive force, in the sense of "cleaving unto," as of cleaving to one's wife, Matt. 19:5; some mss. have the intensive verb No. 2, here; 1 Cor. 6:16–17, "joined." In the corresponding passage in Mark 10:7, the most authentic mss. omit the sentence. In Luke 10:11 it is used of the "cleaving" of dust to the feet; in Acts 5:13; 8:29; 9:26; 10:28; 17:34, in the sense of becoming associated with a person so as to company with him, or be on his side, said, in the last passage, of those in Athens who believed: in Rom. 12:9, ethically, of "cleaving" to that which is good. For its use in Rev. 18:5 see REACH (RV, marg. "clave together"). See COMPANY, JOIN.¶

2. *proskollaō* (προσκολλάω, 4347), in the passive voice, used reflexively, "to cleave unto," is found in Eph. 5:31 (KJV "joined to").

3. *prosmenō* (προσμένω, 4357), lit., "to abide with" (*pros,* "toward or with," and *menō,* "to abide"), is used of "cleaving" unto the Lord, Acts 11:23. See ABIDE.

CLEMENCY

epieikeia (ἐπιείκεια, 1932), "mildness, gentleness, kindness" (what Matthew Arnold has called "sweet reasonableness"), is translated "clemency" in Acts 24:4; elsewhere, in 2 Cor. 10:1, of the gentleness of Christ. See GENTLENESS.¶ Cf. *epieikēs* (see FORBEARANCE).

For **CLERK** see under **TOWNCLERK**

CLIMB UP

anabainō (ἀναβαίνω, 305), "to ascend," is used of climbing up, in Luke 19:4 and John 10:1. See ARISE.

CLOKE (Pretense)

1. *epikalumma* (ἐπικάλυμμα, 1942) is "a covering, a means of hiding" (*epi,* "upon," *kaluptō,* "to cover"); hence, "a pretext, a cloke, for wickedness," 1 Pet. 2:16.¶ In the Sept. it is used in Ex. 26:14; 39:21, "coverings"; 2 Sam. 17:19; Job 19:29, "deceit."¶

2. *prophasis* (πρόφασις, 4392), either from *pro*, "before," and *phainō*, "to cause to appear, shine," or, more probably, from *pro*, and *phēmi*, "to say," is rendered "cloke" (of covetousness) in 1 Thess. 2:5; "excuse" in John 15:22 (KJV "cloke"); "pretense" in Matt. 23:14; Mark 12: 40; Luke 20:47 (KJV "show"); Phil. 1:18; "color" in Acts 27: 30. It signifies the assuming of something so as to disguise one's real motives. See PRETENSE, SHOW.¶

CLOKE (Garment)

For the various words for garments see CLOTHING.

CLOSE (Verb)

1. *kammuō* (καμμύω, 2576), derived by syncope (i.e., shortening and assimilation of *t* to *m*) from *katamuō*, i.e., *kata*, "down," and *muō*, from a root *mu*—, pronounced by closing the lips, denotes "to close down"; hence, "to shut the eyes," Matt. 13:15 and Acts 28:27, in each place of the obstinacy of Jews in their opposition to the gospel.¶

2. *ptussō* (πτύσσω, 4428), "to fold, double up," is used of a scroll of parchment, Luke 4:20.¶ Cf. *anaptussō*, "to open up," v. 17.¶

Notes: (1) For "close-sealed," Rev. 5:1, see SEAL.

(2) In Luke 9:36, *sigaō*, "to be silent," is translated "they kept it close," KJV (RV, "they held their peace").

CLOSE (Adverb)

asson (ἆσσον, 788), the comparative degree of *anchi*, "near," is found in Acts 27:13, of sailing "close" by a place.¶

For CLOSET see CHAMBER

CLOTH

rhakos (ῥάκος, 4470) denotes "a ragged garment, or a piece of cloth torn off, a rag"; hence, a piece of undressed "cloth," Matt. 9:16; Mark 2:21.

Note: For other words, *othonion, sindon,* See LINEN, Nos. 1 and 3.¶

CLOTHE

1. *amphiennumi* (ἀμφιέννυμι, 294), "to put clothes round" (*amphi*, "around," *hennumi*, "to clothe"), "to invest," signifies, in the middle voice, to put clothing on oneself, e.g., Matt. 6:30; 11:8; Luke 7:25; 12:28.¶

2. *enduō* (ἐνδύω, 1746), (Eng., "endue"), signifies "to enter into, get into," as into clothes, "to put on," e.g., Mark 1:6; Luke 8:27 (in the best mss.); 24:49 (KJV, "endued"); 2 Cor. 5:3; Rev. 1:13; 19:14. See ARRAY, ENDUE, PUT ON.

3. *endiduskō* (ἐνδιδύσκω, 1737) has the same meaning as No. 2; the termination, —*skō* suggests the beginning or progress of the action. The verb is used in the middle voice in Luke 16:19 (of a rich man). Some mss. have it in 8:27, for No. 2 (of a demoniac). In Mark 15:17 the best texts have this verb (some have No. 2). See WEAR.¶

4. *ependuō* (ἐπενδύω, 1902), a strengthened form of No. 2, used in the middle voice, "to cause to be put on over, to be clothed upon," is found in 2 Cor. 5:2, 4, of the future spiritual body of the redeemed.¶

5. *himatizō* (ἱματίζω, 2439) means "to put on raiment" (see *himation*, below), Mark 5:15; Luke 8:35.¶

6. *periballō*, (περιβάλλω, 4016), "to cast around or about, to put on, array," or, in the middle and passive voices, "to clothe oneself," e.g., Matt. 25:36, 38, 43, is most frequent in the Apocalypse, where it is found some 12 times (see *peribolaion*, below). See CAST, No. 10, PUT, No. 9).

Note: The verb *enkomboomai*, "to gird oneself with a thing," in 1 Pet. 5:5, is rendered in the KJV, "be clothed with."

CLOTHING, CLOTHS, CLOTHES, CLOKE, COAT

1. *phelonēs*, or *phailonēs* (φαιλόνης, 534), probably by metathesis from *phainolēs* (Latin *paenula*), "a mantle," denotes a traveling "cloak" for protection against stormy weather, 2 Tim. 4:13. Some, however, regard it as a Cretan word for *chitōn*, "a tunic." It certainly was not an ecclesiastical vestment. The Syriac renders it a case for writings (some regard it as a book-cover), an explanation noted by Chrysostom, but improbable. It may have been "a light mantle like a cashmere dust-cloak, in which the books and parchments were wrapped" (Mackie in *Hastings' Dic. of the Bible*).¶

2. *himation* (ἱμάτιον, 2440), "an outer garment, a mantle, thrown over the *chitōn*." In the plural, "clothes" (the "cloke" and the tunic), e.g., Matt. 17:2; 26:65; 27:31, 35. See APPAREL, No. 2.

3. *chitōn* (χιτών, 5509) denotes "the inner vest or undergarment," and is to be distinguished, as such, from the *himation*. The distinction is made, for instance, in the Lord's command in Matt. 5:40: "If any man would go to law with thee, and take away thy coat (*chitōn*), let him have thy cloke (*himation*) also."

The order is reversed in Luke 6:29, and the difference lies in this, that in Matt. 5:40 the Lord is referring to a legal process, so the claimant is supposed to claim the inner garment, the less costly. The defendant is to be willing to let him have the more valuable one too. In the passage in Luke an act of violence is in view, and there is no mention of going to law. So the outer garment is the first one which would be seized.

When the soldiers had crucified Jesus they took His garments (*himation*, in the plural), His outer garments, and the "coat," the *chitōn*, the inner garment, which was without seam, woven from the top throughout, John 19:23. The outer garments were easily divisible among the four soldiers, but they could not divide the *chitōn* without splitting it, so they cast lots for it.

Dorcas was accustomed to make coats (*chitōn*) and garments (*himation*), Acts 9:39, that is, the close fitting undergarments and the long, flowing outer robes.

A person was said to be "naked" (*gumnos*), whether he was without clothing, or had thrown off his outer garment, e.g., his *ependutēs*, (No. 6, below), and was clad in a light undergarment, as was the case with Peter, in John 21:7. The high priest, in rending his clothes after the reply the Lord gave him in answer to his challenge, rent his undergarments (*chitōn*), the more forcibly to express his assumed horror and indignation, Mark 14:63. In Jude 23, "the garment spotted by the flesh" is the *chitōn*, the metaphor of the undergarment being appropriate; for it would be that which was brought into touch with the pollution of the flesh.

4. *himatismos* (ἱματισμός, 2441), in form a collective word, denoting "vesture, garments," is used generally of "costly or stately raiment," the apparel of kings, of officials, etc. See Luke 7:25, where "gorgeously apparelled" is, lit., "in gorgeous vesture." See also Acts 20:33 and 1 Tim. 2:9, "costly raiment." This is the word used of the Lord's white and dazzling raiment on the Mount of Transfiguration, Luke 9:29. It is also used of His *chitōn*, His undergarment (see note above), for which the soldiers cast lots, John 19:23–24, "vesture"; in Matt. 27:35 it is also translated vesture. See APPAREL, RAIMENT, VESTURE.¶

5. *enduma* (ἔνδυμα, 1742), akin to *enduō* (see CLOTHE, No. 2), denotes "anything put on, a garment of any kind." It was used of the clothing of ancient prophets, in token of their contempt of earthly splendor, 1 Kings 19:13; 2 Kings 1:8, RV; Zech. 13:4. In the NT it is similarly used of John the Baptist's raiment, Matt. 3:4; of raiment in general, Matt. 6:25, 28;

Luke 12:23; metaphorically, of sheep's clothing, Matt. 7:15; of a wedding garment, 22:11–12; of the raiment of the angel at the tomb of the Lord after His resurrection, 28:3. See GARMENT, RAIMENT.¶

6. *ependutēs* (ἐπενδύτης, 1903) denotes "an upper garment" (*epi*, "upon," *enduō*, "to clothe"). The word is found in John 21:7, where it apparently denotes a kind of linen frock, which fishermen wore when at their work. See No. 3.¶

7. *esthēs* (ἐσθής, 2066), "clothing," Acts 10:30; see APPAREL, No. 1.

8. *stolē* (στολή, 4749), (Eng., "stole"), denotes any "stately robe," a long garment reaching to the feet or with a train behind. It is used of the long clothing in which the scribes walked, making themselves conspicuous in the eyes of men, Mark 12:38; Luke 20:46; of the robe worn by the young man in the Lord's tomb, Mark 16:5; of the best or, rather, the chief robe, which was brought out for the returned prodigal, Luke 15:22; five times in the Apocalypse, as to glorified saints, 6:11; 7:9, 13–14; 22:14.¶ In the Sept. it is used of the holy garments of the priests, e.g., Exod. 28:2; 29:21; 31:10.

Notes: (1) *Peribolaion*, from *periballō*, "to throw around," lit., "that which is thrown around," was a wrap or mantle. It is used in 1 Cor. 11:15, of the hair of a woman which is given to her as a veil; in Heb. 1:12, of the earth and the heavens, which the Lord will roll up "as a mantle," RV, for KJV, "vesture." The other word in that verse rendered "garment," RV, is *himation*.¶

(2) *Endusis*, is "a putting on (of apparel)," 1 Pet. 3:3. Cf. No. 5.¶

(3) *Esthēsis*. See APPAREL, No. 1.

(4) The *chlamus* was a short "cloak" or robe, worn over the *chitōn* (No. 3), by emperors, kings, magistrates, military officers, etc. It is used of the scarlet robe with which Christ was arrayed in mockery by the soldiers in Pilate's Judgment Hall, Matt. 27:28, 31.

What was known as purple was a somewhat indefinite color. There is nothing contradictory about its being described by Mark and John as "purple," though Matthew speaks of it as "scarlet." The soldiers put it on the Lord in mockery of His Kingship.¶

(5) The *podērēs* was another sort of outer garment, reaching to the feet (from *pous*, "the foot," and *arō*, "to fasten"). It was one of the garments of the high priests, a robe (Hebrew, *chetoneth*), mentioned after the ephod in Exod. 28:4, etc. It is used in Ezek. 9:2, where instead of "linen" the Sept. reads "a long robe"; and in Zech. 3:4, "clothe ye him with a long robe"; in

the NT in Rev. 1:13, of the long garment in which the Lord is seen in vision amongst the seven golden lampstands. There, *podērēs* is described as "a garment down to the feet," indicative of His High Priestly character and acts.¶

(6) For *katastolē*, see APPAREL, No. 4.

CLOUD

1. *nephos* (νέφος, 3509) denotes "a cloudy, shapeless mass covering the heavens." Hence, metaphorically, of "a dense multitude, a throng," Heb. 12:1.¶

2. *nephelē* (νεφέλη, 3507), "a definitely shaped cloud, or masses of clouds possessing definite form," is used, besides the physical element, (*a*) of the "cloud" on the mount of transfiguration, Matt. 17:5; (*b*) of the "cloud" which covered Israel in the Red Sea, 1 Cor. 10:1–2; (*c*), of "clouds" seen in the Apocalyptic visions, Rev. 1:7; 10:1; 11:12; 14:14–16; (*d*), metaphorically in 2 Pet. 2:17, of the evil workers there mentioned; but RV, "and mists" (*homichlē*), according to the most authentic mss.

In 1 Thess. 4:17, the "clouds" referred to in connection with the rapture of the saints are probably the natural ones, as also in the case of those in connection with Christ's second advent to the earth. See Matt. 24:30; 26:64, and parallel passages. So at the Ascension, Acts 1:9.

CLOVEN

diamerizō (διαμερίζω, 1266), "to part asunder" (*dia*, "asunder," *meros*, "a part"), is translated "cloven" in the KJV of Acts 2:3, RV, "parting asunder." See DIVIDE, PART.

CLUSTER

botrus (βότρυς, 1009), "a cluster, or bunch, bunch of grapes," is found in Rev. 14:18.¶

Note: Cf. *staphulē*, "a bunch of grapes, the ripe cluster," stressing the grapes themselves, Matt. 7:16; Luke 6:44; Rev. 14:18.¶

COALS

1. *anthrax* (ἄνθραξ, 440), "a burning coal" (cf. Eng., "anthracite,") is used in the plural in Rom. 12:20, metaphorically in a proverbial expression, "thou shalt heap coals of fire on his head" (from Prov. 25:22), signifying retribution by kindness, i.e., that, by conferring a favor on your enemy, you recall the wrong he has done to you, so that he repents, with pain of heart.¶

2. *anthrakia* (ἀνθρακία, 439), akin to No. 1, is "a heap of burning coals, or a charcoal fire," John 18:18; 21:9.¶

COAST, COASTING

A. Noun.

horion (ὅριον, 3725), "a bound, boundary, limit, frontier" (akin to *horizō*, "to bound, limit"), is rendered "coasts" ten times in the KJV, but "borders" in Matt. 4:13, and is always translated "borders" in the RV. See BORDER.

B. Adjective.

paralios (παράλιος, 3882), "by the sea" (*para*, "by," *hals*, "salt"), hence denotes "a sea coast," Luke 6:17.¶ In the Sept., Gen. 49:13; Deut. 1:7; 33:19; Josh. 9:1; 11:3 (twice); Job 6:3; Isa. 9:1.

C. Verb.

paralegō (παραλέγω, 3881) is used, in the middle voice, as a nautical term, "to sail past," Acts 27:8, "coasting along"; v. 13, "sailed by."¶

Notes: (1) *Methorion (meta,* "with," and A), in Mark 7:24, is translated "borders." (2) The phrase "upon the sea coast," Matt. 4:13, KJV, translates *parathalassios (para,* "by," *thalassa,* "the sea"), RV, "by the sea."¶ (3) *Meros,* "a part," is translated "coasts" in Matt. 15:21; 16:13, KJV (RV, "parts,"); "country," RV, in Acts 19:1, KJV "coasts"; this refers to the high land in the interior of Asia Minor. See BEHALF, CRAFT, PART, PARTICULAR, PIECE, PORTION, RESPECT, SOMEWHAT, SORT. (4) *Chōra,* "a country," rendered "coasts" in Acts 26:20, KJV, is corrected in the RV to "country." See COUNTRY, FIELD, GROUND, LAND, REGION. (5) In Acts 27:2 the phrase in the RV, "on the coast of," translates the preposition *kata,* "along," and the complete clause, "unto the places on the coast of Asia," RV, is curiously condensed in the KJV to "by the coasts of Asia."

For **COAT** (*ependeutēs*) see **CLOTHING**

COCK, COCK-CROWING

1. *alektōr* (ἀλέκτωρ, 220), "a cock," perhaps connected with a Hebrew phrase for the oncoming of the light, is found in the passages concerning Peter's denial of the Lord, Matt. 26:34, 74–75; Mark 14:30, 68, 72; Luke 22:34, 60–61; John 13:38; 18:27.¶

2. *alektorophōnia* (ἀλεκτοροφωνία, 219) denotes "cock-crowing" (*alektōr,* and *phōnē,* "a sound"), Mark 13:35. There were two "cock-crowings," one after midnight, the other before dawn. In these watches the Jews followed the Roman method of dividing the night. The first "cock-crowing" was at the third watch of the night. That is the one mentioned in Mark 13:35. Mark mentions both; see 14:30. The latter, the second, is that referred to in the other Gospels

and is mentioned especially as "the cock-crowing."¶

COLD

A. Noun.
psuchos (ψύχος, 5592), "coldness, cold," appears in John 18:18; Acts 28:2; 2 Cor. 11:27.¶
B. Adjective.
psuchros (ψυχρός, 5593), "cool, fresh, cold, chilly" (fuller in expression than *psuchos*), is used in the natural sense in Matt. 10:42, "cold water"; metaphorically in Rev. 3:15–16.¶
C. Verb.
psuchō (ψύχω, 5594), "to breathe, blow, cool by blowing," passive voice, "grow cool," is used metaphorically in Matt. 24:12, in the sense of waning zeal or love.¶

COLLECTION

logia (λογία, 3048), akin to *legō*, "to collect," is used in 1 Cor. 16:1, 2; in the latter verse, KJV "gatherings," RV, "collections," as in v. 1. See GATHERING.¶

COLONY

kolōnia (κολωνία, 2862) transliterates the Latin *colonia*. Roman colonies belonged to three periods and classes, (*a*) those of the earlier republic before 100 B.C., which were simply centers of Roman influence in conquered territory; (*b*) agrarian "colonies," planted as places for the overflowing population of Rome; (*c*) military "colonies" during the time of the Civil wars and the Empire, for the settlement of disbanded soldiers. This third class was established by the *imperator*, who appointed a legate to exercise his authority. To this class Philippi belonged as mentioned in Acts 16:12, RV, "a Roman colony." They were watch towers of the Roman state and formed on the model of Rome itself. The full organization of Philippi as such was the work of Augustus, who, after the battle of Actium, 31 B.C., gave his soldiers lands in Italy and transferred most of the inhabitants there to other quarters including Philippi. These communities possessed the right of Roman freedom, and of holding the soil under Roman law, as well as exemption from poll-tax and tribute. Most Roman "colonies" were established on the coast.¶

For **COLOR** (Acts 27:30) see **CLOKE**

COLT

pōlos (πῶλος, 4454), "a foal," whether "colt or filly," had the general significance of "a young creature"; in Matt. 21:2, and parallel passages, "an ass's colt."

COME, CAME (see also COMING)

1. *erchomai* (ἔρχομαι, 2064), the most frequent verb, denoting either "to come, or to go," signifies the act, in contrast with *hēkō* (see No. 22, below), which stresses the arrival, as, e.g., "I am come and am here," John 8:42 and Heb. 10:9. See BRING, B, *Note* (1), FALL, GO, GROW, LIGHT, PASS, RESORT.

Compounds of this with prepositions are as follows (2 to 11):

2. *eiserchomai* (εἰσέρχομαι, 1525), "to come into, or to go into" (*eis*, "into"), e.g., Luke 17:7. See ENTER.

3. *exerchomai* (ἐξέρχομαι, 1831), "to come out, or go out or forth" (*ek*, "out"), e.g., Matt. 2:6. See DEPART, ESCAPE, GET, (*b*), No. 3, GO, *Note* (1) PROCEED, SPREAD.

4. *epanerchomai* (ἐπανέρχομαι, 1880), "to come back again, return" (*epi*, "on," *ana*, "again"), Luke 10:35; 19:15.¶

5. *dierchomai* (διέρχομαι, 1330), "to come or go through" (*dia*, "through"), e.g., Acts 9:38. See DEPART, GO, PASS, PIERCE, TRAVEL, WALK.

6. *eperchomai* (ἐπέρχομαι, 1904), "to come or go upon" (*epi*, "upon"), e.g., Luke 1:35; in Luke 21:26, used of "coming" events, suggesting their certainty; in Eph. 2:7, said of the "on-coming" of the ages; in Acts 14:19, of Jews coming to (lit., "upon") a place.

7. *katerchomai* (κατέρχομαι, 2718), "to come down" (*kata*, "down"), e.g., Luke 9:37. See DEPART, DESCEND, GO, *Note* (1), LAND.

8. *pareiserchomai* (παρεισέρχομαι, 3922), lit., "to come in" (*eis*) "beside or from the side" (*para*) so as to be present with, is used (*a*) in the literal sense, of the "coming" in of the Law in addition to sin, Rom. 5:20; (*b*) in Gal. 2:4, of false brethren, suggesting their "coming" in by stealth. See ENTER.¶

9. *parerchomai* (παρέρχομαι, 3928), *para*, "by or away"), signifies (*a*) "to come or go forth, or arrive," e.g., Luke 12:37; 17:7 (last part); Acts 24:7; (*b*) "to pass by," e.g., Luke 18:37; (*c*) "to neglect," e.g., Luke 11:42. See GO, PASS, TRANSGRESS.

10. *proserchomai* (προσέρχομαι, 4334) denotes "to come or go near to" (*pros*, "near to"), e.g., Matt. 4:3; Heb. 10:1, KJV, "comers," RV, "them that draw nigh." See CONSENT, DRAW, GO, *Note* (1).

11. *sunerchomai* (συνέρχομαι, 4905), "to come together" (*sun* "with"), e.g., John 18:20, is often translated by the verb "to assemble"; see the RV of 1 Cor. 11:20; 14:23. See ACCOMPANY, ASSEMBLE, COMPANY, GO WITH, RESORT.

Note: Aperchomai, "to come away or from," is differently translated in the RV; see, e.g., Mark

3:13 where it signifies that they went from the company or place where they were to Him; it usually denotes "to go away."

12. *ginomai* (γίνομαι, 1096) "to become," signifies a change of condition, state or place, e.g., Mark 4:35. In Acts 27:33, the verb is used with *mellō*, "to be about to," to signify the coming on of day.

13. *paraginomai* (παραγίνομαι, 3854), *para*, "near or by," denotes to "arrive, to be present," e.g., Matt. 2:1. See GO, PRESENT.

14. *sumparaginomai* (συμπαραγίνομαι, 4836), (*sun*, "with," *para*, "near"), "to come together," is used in Luke 23:48; 2 Tim. 4:16, lit., "stood at my side with me." See STAND.¶
Note: For "come by" in Acts 27:16, KJV, the RV suitably has "secure."
Compounds of the verb baino, "to go," are as follows (15 to 21):

15. *anabainō* (ἀναβαίνω, 305), "to come upon, to arrive in a place" (*ana*, "up or upon"), is translated "come into" in Acts 25:1. See ARISE, ASCEND, ENTER, GO, CLIMB, GROW, RISE, SPRING.

16. *epibainō* (ἐπιβαίνω, 1910), "to come to or into, or go upon," is rendered, in Acts 20:18, RV, "set foot in." See ENTER, GO, TAKE, *Note* (16).

17. *ekbainō* (ἐκβαίνω, 1543a), "to come or go out," appears in the best mss. in Heb. 11:15; KJV, "came out," RV, "went out."¶

18. *diabainō* (διαβαίνω, 1224), "to pass through," is translated "come over" in Acts 16:9; "pass" in Luke 16:26; "pass through" in Heb. 11:29. See PASS.¶

19. *katabainō* (καταβαίνω, 2597) signifies "to come down," e.g., Matt. 8:1. See DESCEND, FALL, GET, GO, STEP (down).

20. *sunanabainō* (συναναβαίνω, 4872), "to come up with" (*sun*, "with," *ana*, "up"), is used in Mark 15:41; Acts 13:31.¶

21. *embainō* (ἐμβαίνω, 1684), "to go into," is rendered, in Mark 5:18, KJV, "was come into," RV, "was entering." See ENTER, GET, GO, STEP.
Note: Apobainō, "to go away," is rendered, in the KJV of John 21:9, "were come to"; RV, "got out upon."

22. *hēkō* (ἥκω, 2240) means (*a*) "to come, to be present" (see above, on No. 1); (*b*) "to come upon, of time and events," Matt. 24:14; John 2:4; 2 Pet. 3:10; Rev. 18:8; (*c*) metaphorically, "to come upon one, of calamitous times, and evils," Matt. 23:36; Luke 19:43.

23. *aphikneomai* (ἀφικνέομαι, 864), "to arrive at a place," is used in Rom. 16:19, "come abroad" (of the obedience of the saints).¶

24. *chōreō* (χωρέω, 5562), lit., "to make

room (*chōra*, "a place") for another, and so to have place, receive," is rendered "come" (followed by "to repentance") in 2 Pet. 3:9; the meaning strictly is "have room (i.e., space of time) for repentance." See CONTAIN, GO, PLACE, ROOM. RECEIVE.

25. *eimi* (εἰμί, 1510), "to be," is, in the infinitive mood, rendered "come," in John 1:46 and in the future indicative "will come," in 2 Tim. 4:3.

26. *enistēmi* (ἐνίστημι, 1764), lit., "to stand in, or set in" (*en*, "in," *histēmi*, "to stand"), hence "to be present or to be imminent," is rendered "shall come" in 2 Tim. 3:1; it here expresses permanence, "shall settle in (upon you)." See AT HAND, PRESENT.

27. *ephistēmi* (ἐφίστημι, 2186) signifies "to stand by or over" (*epi*, "upon"), Luke 2:9, RV; Acts 12:7; "before," Acts 11:11; to come upon, Luke 20:1 (here with the idea of suddenness); Acts 4:1; 6:12; 23:27; 1 Thess. 5:3; "coming up," of the arrival of Anna at the Temple, Luke 2:38; "came up to (Him)," of Martha, Luke 10:40; "is come," 2 Tim. 4:6 (probably with the same idea as in Luke 20:1). The RV is significant in all these places. See ASSAULT, AT HAND, PRESENT, STAND.

28. *katantaō* (καταντάω, 2658) denotes (*a*) "to come to, or over against, a place, arrive," Acts 16:1; 18:19, 24; 20:15 (in 21:7 and 25:13, RV, "arrived"; in 27:12, "reach," for KJV, "attain to"); 28:13; (*b*) of things or events, "to arrive at a certain time, or come upon certain persons in the period of their lifetime," 1 Cor. 10:11; or "to come to persons" so that they partake of, as of the gospel, 1 Cor. 14:36. For the remaining instances, Acts 26:7; Eph. 4:13; Phil. 3:11, see ATTAIN.¶

29. *mellō* (μέλλω, 3195), "to be about (to do something)," often implying the necessity and therefore the certainty of what is to take place, is frequently rendered "to come," e.g., Matt. 3:7; 11:14; Eph. 1:21; 1 Tim. 4:8; 6:19; Heb. 2:5. See ALMOST, BEGIN, MEAN, MIND, SHALL, TARRY, WILL.

30. *paristēmi* (παρίστημι, 3936), "to stand by or near, to be at hand" (*para*, "near"), is translated "is come," of the arrival of harvest, Mark 4:29. See BRING, COMMEND, GIVE, PRESENT, PROVE, PROVIDE, SHOW, STAND, YIELD.

31. *pherō* (φέρω, 5342), "to bear, carry," is rendered "came," in the sense of being borne from a place, in 2 Pet. 1:17–18, 21. See BEAR, CARRY.

32. *phthanō* (φθάνω, 5348) denotes "to anticipate, to come sooner than expected," 1 Thess. 2:16, "is come upon," of divine wrath; cf. Rom. 9:31, "did not arrive at"; or to "come"

in a different manner from what was expected, Matt. 12:28, "come upon"; Luke 11:20, of the kingdom of God; so of coming to a place, 2 Cor. 10:14. See ATTAIN, PRECEDE, PREVENT.¶

Two of the compounds of the verb poreuomai, "to go, proceed," are translated "come," with a preposition or adverb:

33. *ekporeuō* (ἐκπορεύω, 1607), in the middle voice, "to come forth" (*ek*, "out of"), Mark 7:15, 20; John 5:29. See DEPART, GO, ISSUE, PROCEED.

34. *prosporeuomai* (προσπορεύομαι, 4365), in Mark 10:35, is translated "come near unto."¶

Notes: (1) No. 33 is rendered "proceed" in the RV of Mark 7:15, 20, 23 (KJV, "come"). (2) For *epiporeuomai*, in Luke 8:4, see RESORT.¶

35. *prosengizō* (προσεγγίζω, 4331) denotes "to come near" (*pros*, "to," *engizō*, "to be near, to approach"), Mark 2:4, used of those who tried to bring a palsied man to Christ.¶

36. *sumpleroō* (συμπληρόω, 4845), "to fill completely" (*sun*, "with," intensive), is used, in the passive voice, of time to be fulfilled or completed, Luke 9:51, "the days were well-nigh come"; Acts 2:1, "the day . . . was now come" (KJV "was fully come"). In Luke 8:23, it is used in the active voice, of the filling of a boat in a storm. See FILL.¶

37. *suntunchanō* (συντυγχάνω, 4940), "to meet with" (*sun*, "with," and *tunchanō*, "to reach"), is rendered "to come at" in Luke 8:19, (of the efforts of Christ's mother and brethren to get at Him through a crowd).¶

38. *kukloō* (κυκλόω, 2944), "to compass" (Eng., "cycle"), is translated "came round about," in John 10:24. See COMPASS, ROUND, STAND.

39. *hustereō* (ὑστερέω, 5302), "to be behind," is translated "to have come short," in Heb. 4:1. See BEHIND, B, No. 1.

Notes: (1) *Deuro*, "hither, here," is used (sometimes with verbs of motion) in the singular number, in calling a person to come, Matt. 19:21; Mark 10:21; Luke 18:22; John 11:43; Acts 7:3, 34; Rev. 17:1; 21:9. For its other meaning, "hitherto," Rom. 1:13, see HITHERTO.¶ It has a plural, *deute*, frequent in the gospels; elsewhere in Rev. 19:17. *In the following the RV has a different rendering:* (2) In Mark 14:8, *prolambanō*, "to anticipate, to be beforehand," KJV, "hath come aforehand to anoint My body," RV, "hath anointed My body aforehand." (3) In Acts 7:45, *diadechomai*, "to succeed one, to take the place of," KJV, "who came after," RV, "in their turn."¶ (4) In Luke 8:55, *epistrephō*, "to return to," KJV, "came again," RV, "returned." (5) In Acts 24:27, *lambanō*, with *diadochos*, "a successor," KJV, "came into the

room of," RV, "was succeeded by." (6) In Mark 9:23, for *episuntrechō*, "to come running together," see under RUN.¶ (7) In Acts 5:38, *kataluō*, "to destroy," KJV, "will come to nought," RV, "will be overthrown." (8) In John 12:35, *katalambanō*, "to seize," KJV, "come upon," RV, "overtake." (9) In 2 Cor. 11:28, *epistasis* (in some mss. *episustasis*), lit., "a standing together upon," hence, "a pressing upon," as of cares, KJV, "cometh upon," RV, "presseth upon." (10) In Acts 19:27, *erchomai*, "with" *eis apelegmon*, RV, "come into disrepute," KJV, "be set at nought." (11) For *pareimi*, John 7:6, see PRESENT, No. 1. (12) *Sunagō*, "to gather together," is always so rendered in RV, e.g., Matt. 27:62; Mark 7:1; Luke 22:66; Acts 13:44; 15:6; 20:7. See GATHER, No. 1. (13) For come to nought see NOUGHT. (14) For *eisporeuomai* see ENTER, No. 4. (15) For "was come again," Acts 22:17, KJV, see RETURN, No. 4. (16) For *engizō*, to come near, see APPROACH, NIGH.

For **COME BEHIND** see **BEHIND**

COMELINESS, COMELY

A. Noun.

euschēmosunē (εὐσχημοσύνη, 2157), "elegance of figure, gracefulness, comeliness" (*eu*, "well," *schēma*, "a form"), is found in this sense in 1 Cor. 12:23.

B. Adjective.

euschēmōn (εὐσχήμων, 2158), akin to A, "elegant in figure, well formed, graceful," is used in 1 Cor. 12:24, of parts of the body (see above); in 1 Cor. 7:35 RV, "(that which is) seemly," KJV, "comely"; "honourable," Mark 15:43; Acts 13:50; 17:12. See HONORABLE.¶

Note: In 1 Cor. 11:13, *prepō*, "to be becoming," is rendered in the KJV, "is it comely?" RV, "is it seemly?" See BECOME, SEEMLY.

COMFORT, COMFORTER, COMFORTLESS

A. Nouns.

1. *paraklēsis* (παράκλησις, 3874), means "a calling to one's side" (*para*, "beside," *kaleō*, "to call"); hence, either "an exhortation, or consolation, comfort," e.g., Luke 2:25 (here "looking for the consolation of Israel" is equivalent to waiting for the coming of the Messiah); 6:24; Acts 9:31; Rom. 15:4–5; 1 Cor. 14:3, "exhortation"; 2 Cor. 1:3, 4–7; 7:4, 7, 13; 2 Thess. 2:16; Philem. 7. In 2 Thess. 2:16 it combines encouragement with alleviation of grief. The RV changes "consolation" into "comfort," except in Luke 2:25; 6:24; Acts 15:31; in Heb. 6:18, "encouragement"; in Acts 4:36, "exhortation." RV

(KJV, consolation"). See CONSOLATION, ENCOURAGEMENT, EXHORTATION, INTREATY.

2. *paramuthia* (παραμυθία, 3889), primarily "a speaking closely to anyone" (*para*, "near," *muthos*, "speech"), hence denotes "consolation, comfort," with a greater degree of tenderness than No. 1, 1 Cor. 14:3.¶

3. *paramuthion* (παραμύθιον, 3890) has the same meaning as No. 2, the difference being that *paramuthia* stresses the process or progress of the act, *paramuthion* the instrument as used by the agent, Phil. 2:1.¶

4. *parēgoria* (παρηγορία, 3931), primarily "an addressing, address," hence denotes "a soothing, solace," Col. 4:11.¶ A verbal form of the word signifies medicines which allay irritation (Eng., "paregoric").

5. *paraklētos* (παράκλητος, 3875), lit., "called to one's side," i.e., to one's aid, is primarily a verbal adjective, and suggests the capability or adaptability for giving aid. It was used in a court of justice to denote a legal assistant, counsel for the defense, an advocate; then, generally, one who pleads another's cause, an intercessor, advocate, as in 1 John 2:1, of the Lord Jesus. In the widest sense, it signifies a "succorer, comforter." Christ was this to His disciples, by the implication of His word "another (*allos*, "another of the same sort," not *heteros*, "different") Comforter," when speaking of the Holy Spirit, John 14:16. In 14:26; 15:26; 16:7 He calls Him "the Comforter."¶ "Comforter" or "Consoler" corresponds to the name "*Menahem*," given by the Hebrews to the Messiah.

B. Verbs.

1. *parakaleō* (παρακαλέω, 3870) has the same variety of meanings as Noun, No. 1, above, e.g., Matt. 2:18; 1 Thess. 3:2, 7; 4:18. In 2 Cor. 13:11, it signifies "to be comforted" (so the RV). See BESEECH.

2. *sumparakaleō* (συμπαρακαλέω, 4837), *sun*, "with," and No. 1, signifies "to comfort together," Rom. 1:12.¶

3. *paramutheomai* (παραμυθέομαι, 3888), akin to Noun No. 2, "to soothe, console, encourage," is translated, in John 11:31, "comforted"; in v. 19, RV, "console." In 1 Thess. 2:11 and 5:14, RV, "encourage," as the sense there is that of stimulating to the earnest discharge of duties. See CONSOLE, ENCOURAGE.¶

4. *eupsucheō* (εὐψυχέω, 2174) signifies "to be of good comfort" (*eu*, "well," *psuchē*, "the soul"), Phil. 2:19.¶

Notes: (1) For the verb *tharseō*, "be of good comfort," see CHEER, No. 2.

(2) *Orphanos* is rendered "comfortless" in

John 14:18, KJV; RV, "desolate." See DESOLATE, FATHERLESS.

COMING (Noun)

1. *eisodos* (εἴσοδος, 1529), "an entrance" (*eis*, "in," *hodos*, "a way"), "an entering in," is once translated "coming," Acts 13:24, of the coming of Christ into the nation of Israel. For its meaning "entrance" see 1 Thess. 1:9; 2:1; Heb. 10:19; 2 Pet. 1:11. See ENTER, ENTRANCE.¶

2. *eleusis* (ἔλευσις, 1660), "a coming" (from *erchomai*, "to come"), is found in Acts 7:52.¶

3. *parousia* (παρουσία, 3952), lit., "a presence," *para*, "with," and *ousia*, "being" (from *eimi*, "to be"), denotes both an "arrival" and a consequent "presence with." For instance, in a papyrus letter a lady speaks of the necessity of her *parousia* in a place in order to attend to matters relating to her property there. Paul speaks of his *parousia* in Philippi, Phil. 2:12 (in contrast to his *apousia*, "his absence"; see ABSENCE). Other words denote "the arrival" (see *eisodos* and *eleusis*, above). *Parousia* is used to describe the presence of Christ with His disciples on the Mount of Transfiguration, 2 Pet. 1:16. When used of the return of Christ, at the rapture of the church, it signifies, not merely His momentary "coming" for His saints, but His presence with them from that moment until His revelation and manifestation to the world. In some passages the word gives prominence to the beginning of that period, the course of the period being implied, 1 Cor. 15:23; 1 Thess. 4:15; 5:23; 2 Thess. 2:1; Jas. 5:7–8; 2 Pet. 3:4. In some, the course is prominent, Matt. 24:3, 37; 1 Thess. 3:13; 1 John 2:28; in others the conclusion of the period, Matt. 24:27; 2 Thess. 2:8.

The word is also used of the Lawless One, the Man of Sin, his access to power and his doings in the world during his *parousia*, 2 Thess. 2:9. In addition to Phil. 2:12 (above), it is used in the same way of the apostle, or his companions, in 1 Cor. 16:17; 2 Cor. 7:6–7; 10:10; Phil. 1:26; of the Day of God, 2 Pet. 3:12. See PRESENCE.

Note: The word *apokalupsis*, rendered "coming" in 1 Cor. 1:7, KJV, denotes a "revelation" (RV). For a fuller treatment of *Parousia*, see *Notes on Thessalonians*, by Hogg and Vine, pp. 87–88.

COMMAND (Verbs)

1. *diatassō* (διατάσσω, 1299) signifies "to set in order, appoint, command," Matt. 11:1; Luke 8:55; 17:9–10; Acts 18:2; 23:31; "gave

order," 1 Cor. 16:1, RV. So in Acts 24:23, where it is in the middle voice. See APPOINT, No. 6.

2. *epō* (ἔπω, 2036) denotes "to speak" (connected with *eipon*, "to say"); hence, among various renderings, "to bid, command," Matt. 4:3; Mark 5:43; 8:7; Luke 4:3; 19:15. See BID.

Note: In 2 Cor. 4:6, the RV rightly has "said," followed by the quotation "Light shall shine out of darkness."

3. *entellō* (ἐντέλλω, 1781) signifies "to enjoin upon, to charge with"; it is used in the Middle Voice in the sense of commanding, Matt. 19:7; 28:20; Mark 10:3; 13:34; John 8:5; 15:14, 17; Acts 13:47; Heb. 9:20; 11:22, "gave commandment." See CHARGE, ENJOIN.

4. *epitassō* (ἐπιτάσσω, 2004) signifies to appoint over, put in charge (*epi*, "over," *tassō*, "to appoint"); then, "to put upon one as a duty, to enjoin," Mark 1:27; 6:27, 39; 9:25; Luke 4:36; 8:25, 31; 14:22; Acts 23:2; Philem. 8. See CHARGE, ENJOIN.¶

5. *keleuō* (κελεύω, 2753), "to urge, incite, order," suggests a stronger injunction than No. 6, Matt. 14:9, 19; 15:35; 18:25; 27:58, 64; Luke 18:40; Acts 4:15 (frequently in Acts, not subsequently in the NT). See BID.

6. *parangellō* (παραγγέλλω, 3853), "to announce beside" (*para*, "beside," *angellō*, "to announce"), "to pass on an announcement," hence denotes "to give the word, order, give a charge, command", e.g., Mark 6:8; Luke 8:29; 9:21; Acts 5:28; 2 Thess. 3:4, 6, 10, 12. See CHARGE, B, No. 8.

7. *prostassō* (προστάσσω, 4367) denotes "to arrange or set in order towards" (*pros*, "towards," *tassō*, "to arrange"); hence "to prescribe, give command," Matt. 1:24; 8:4; Mark 1:44; Luke 5:14; Acts 10:33, 48. For Matt. 21:6 see *Note* (3) below. See BID.¶

Notes: (1) In Rev. 9:4, *rheō*, "to speak," is translated "said" in the RV (KJV, "commanded"). (2) in Heb. 12:20 *diastellomai*, "to charge, enjoin" (so in the RV), is rendered "commanded" in the KJV. (3) in Matt. 21:6, the RV, translating *suntassō*, as in the best mss., has "appointed," KJV, "commanded."

COMMANDMENT

1. *diatagma* (διάταγμα, 1297) signifies "that which is imposed by decree or law," Heb. 11:23. It stresses the concrete character of the "commandment" more than *epitagē* (No. 4). Cf. COMMAND, No. 1. For the verb in v. 22 see No. 3 under COMMAND.¶

2. *entolē* (ἐντολή, 1785), akin to No. 3, above, denotes, in general, "an injunction, charge, precept, commandment." It is the most frequent term, and is used of moral and reli-

gious precepts, e.g., Matt. 5:19; it is frequent in the Gospels, especially that of John, and in his Epistles. See also, e.g., Acts 17:15; Rom. 7:8–13; 13:9; 1 Cor. 7:19; Eph. 2:15; Col. 4:10. See PRECEPT.

3. *entalma* (ἔνταλμα, 1778), akin to No. 2, marks more especially "the thing commanded, a commission"; in Matt. 15:9; Mark 7:7; Col. 2:22, RV, "precepts," KJV, "commandments." See PRECEPT.¶

4. *epitagē* (ἐπιταγή, 2003), akin to No. 4, above, stresses "the authoritativeness of the command"; it is used in Rom. 16:26; 1 Cor. 7:6, 25; 2 Cor. 8:8; 1 Tim. 1:1; Tit. 1:3; 2:15. See AUTHORITY.¶

Notes: (1) For *parangelia* (cf. *parangellō*, above), "a proclamation," see CHARGE. (2) In Rev. 22:14 the RV, "wash their robes" (for KJV, "do His commandments") follows the most authentic mss.

COMMEND, COMMENDATION

A. Verbs.

1. *epaineō* (ἐπαινέω, 1867), "to praise," is an intensive form of *aineō*, Luke 16:8. It is elsewhere translated by the verb "to praise," in the RV, Rom. 15:11; 1 Cor. 11:2, 17, 22. See LAUD, PRAISE.¶

2. *paradidōmi* (παραδίδωμι, 3860), lit., "to give or deliver over" (*para*, "over" *didōmi*, "to give"), is said of "commending," or "committing," servants of God to Him (KJV, "recommend"), Acts 14:26; 15:40. See BETRAY, BRING, B, *Note* (4), CAST, COMMIT, DELIVER, GIVE, HAZARD, PUT (in prison), RECOMMEND.

3. *paratithēmi* (παρατίθημι, 3908), lit., "to put near" (*para*, "near"), in the Middle Voice, denotes "to place with someone, entrust, commit." In the sense of commending, it is said (*a*) of the Lord Jesus in "commending" His spirit into the Father's hands, Luke 23:46; (*b*) of "commending" disciples to God, Acts 14:23; (*c*) of "commending" elders to God, Acts 20:32. See ALLEGE, COMMIT, PUT, No. 3, SET, No. 4. Cf. No. 2.

4. *paristēmi* (παρίστημι, 3936), lit., "to place near, set before," (*para*, "near," *histēmi*, "to set"), is used of "self-commendation," 1 Cor. 8:8. See ASSIST, BRING, COME, GIVE, PRESENT, PROVE, PROVIDE, SHOW, STAND, YIELD.

5. *sunistēmi* (συνίστημι, 4921), or *sunistanō* (συνιστάνω, 4921), lit., "to place together," denotes "to introduce one person to another, represent as worthy," e.g., Rom. 3:5; 5:8; 16:1; 2 Cor. 4:2; 6:4; 10:18; 12:11. In 2 Cor. 3:1; 5:12 and 10:12, the verb *sunistanō* is used. See APPROVE, CONSIST, MAKE, STAND.

B. Adjective.

sustatikos (συστατικός, 4956), akin to A, No. 5, lit., "placing together," hence, "commendatory," is used of letters of "commendation," 2 Cor. 3:1, lit., "commendatory letters."¶

COMMIT, COMMISSION

A. Verbs.

(I) *In the sense of "doing or practicing."*

1. *ergazomai* (ἐργάζομαι, 2038), to work, is translated by the verb "to commit" (of committing sin), in Jas. 2:9. This is a stronger expression than *poieō*, "to do," or *prassō*, "to practice" (Nos. 2 and 3). See DO, LABOR, MINISTER, TRADE, WORK.

2. *poieō* (ποιέω, 4160), "to do, cause, etc.," sometimes signifies "to commit, of any act, as of murder," Mark 15:7; sin, John 8:34; 2 Cor. 11:7; Jas. 5:15. See DO.

Note: In 1 John 3:4, 8, 9, the KJV wrongly has "commit" (an impossible meaning in v. 8); the RV rightly has "doeth," i.e., of a continuous habit, equivalent to *prassō*, "to practice." The committal of an act is not in view in that passage.

3. *prassō* (πράσσω, 4238), "to do, work, practice," is said of continuous action, or action not yet completed, Acts 25:11, 25; it is rendered "practice" in the RV, for the incorrect KJV "commit," in Rom. 1:32; 2:2. See DO, EXACT, KEEP, REQUIRE, USE.

(II) *In the sense of delivering or entrusting something to a person.*

1. *paradidōmi* (παραδίδωμι, 3860), "to give over," is often rendered by the verb "to commit," e.g., to prison, Acts 8:3; to the grace of God, Acts 14:26; to God, 1 Pet. 2:23; by God to pits of darkness, 2 Pet. 2:4. See COMMEND, No. 2.

2. *pisteuō* (πιστεύω, 4100) signifies "to entrust, commit to," Luke 16:11; 1 Tim. 1:11, "committed to (my) trust." See BELIEVE.

3. *tithēmi* (τίθημι, 5087), "to put, place," signifies, in the middle voice, "to put for oneself, assign, place in," 2 Cor. 5:19, "having committed (unto us)."

4. *paratithēmi* (παρατίθημι, 3908), see COMMEND, No. 3, signifies "to entrust, commit to one's charge," e.g., in Luke 12:48; 1 Tim. 1:18; 2 Tim. 2:2; 1 Pet. 4:19 (KJV, "commit the keeping").

Notes: (1) *Didōmi*, "to give," is rendered "committed" in the KJV of John 5:22 (RV, "given"). (2) For *porneuō* ("to commit fornication") see FORNICATION. (3) In Rom. 2:22, *hierosuleō*, "to rob temples," is so rendered in the RV, for KJV, "commit sacrilege." (4) In Acts 27:40, *eaō*, "to let, leave," is rendered in the RV,

"left (the anchors) in," for KJV, "committed themselves to."

B. Nouns.

1. *parathēkē* (παραθήκη, 3866), "a putting with, a deposit" (*para*, "with," *tithēmi*, "to put"), and its longer form, *parakatathēkē*, are found, the former in 2 Tim. 1:12, "that which He hath committed unto me," RV, marg., lit., "my deposit" (perhaps, "my deposit with Him"), the latter in 1 Tim. 6:20, where "guard that which is committed unto thee" is, lit., "guard the deposit," and 2 Tim. 1:14, "that good thing which was committed unto thee," i.e., the good deposit; RV, marg., "the good deposit."¶

2. *epitropē* (ἐπιτροπή, 2011) denotes "a turning over (to another), a referring of a thing to another" (*epi*, "over," *trepō*, "to turn"), and so a committal of full powers, "a commission," Acts 26:12.¶

COMMODIOUS (not)

aneuthetos (ἀνεύθετος, 428), "not commodious," lit., "not-well-placed" (from *a*, "not," *n*, euphonic, *eu*, "well," *thetos*, "from" *tithēmi*, "to put, place"), is found in Acts 27:12, where it is said of the haven at the place called Fair Havens.¶

COMMON, COMMONLY

A. Adjective.

koinos (κοινός, 2834) denotes (*a*) "common, belonging to several" (Lat., *communis*), said of things had in common, Acts 2:44; 4:32; of faith, Titus 1:4; of salvation, Jude 3; it stands in contrast to *idios*, "one's own"; (*b*) "ordinary, belonging to the generality, as distinct from what is peculiar to the few"; hence the application to religious practices of Gentiles in contrast with those of Jews; or of the ordinary people in contrast with those of the Pharisees; hence the meaning "unhallowed, profane," Levitically unclean (Lat., *profanus*), said of hands, Mark 7:2 (KJV, "defiled,") RV marg., "common"; of animals, ceremonially unclean, Acts 10:14; 11:8; of a man, 10:28; of meats, Rom. 14:14, "unclean"; of the blood of the covenant, as viewed by an apostate, Heb. 10:29, "unholy" (RV, marg., "common"); of everything unfit for the holy city, Rev. 21:27, RV, "unclean" (marg., "common"). Some mss. have the verb here. See DEFILED, UNCLEAN UNHOLY.¶

B. Verb.

koinoō (κοινόω, 2840), "to make, or count, common," has this meaning in Acts 10:15; 11:9. See DEFILE, POLLUTE, UNCLEAN.

Notes: (1) *Polus*, used of number, signifies "many, numerous"; used of space, it signifies "wide, far reaching"; hence, with the article it is said of a multitude as being numerous; it is translated "common" (people) in Mark 12:37 (see the RV, marg.). It does not, however, mean the ordinary folk, but the many folk. See ABUNDANT, GREAT, LONG, MANY, MUCH, PLENTY.

(2) *Ochlos* denotes "a crowd, a great multitude"; with the article it is translated "the common people," in John 12:9, 12 (RV, marg.). See COMPANY, CROWD, MULTITUDE, NUMBER, PEOPLE, PRESS.

(3) *Tunchanō*, "to happen," is used as an adjective in Acts 28:2, of the kindness shown by the people of Melita to the shipwrecked company; KJV, "(no) little"; RV, "(no) common"; the idea suggested by the verb is that which might happen anywhere or at all times; hence, "little, ordinary, or casual." See CHANCE, ENJOY, OBTAIN.

(4) In Matt. 27:27, what the KJV describes as "the common hall," is the praetorium, RV, "palace," the official residence of the Governor of a Province (marg., "praetorium").

(5) In Acts 5:18, *dēmosios* (KJV, "common," with reference to the prison) signifies "public," belonging to the people, *dēmos*, (RV, "public").

(6) In 1 Cor. 5:1, *holōs*, "altogether" (KJV, "commonly") means "actually" (RV).

(7) In Matt. 28:15, *diaphēmizō*, "to spread abroad" (as in the RV), is rendered in the KJV, "is commonly reported. See SPREAD, *Note* (5).

COMMONWEALTH

1. *politeia* (πολιτεία, 4174) : see CITIZENSHIP, No. 3.

2. *politeuma* (πολίτευμα, 4175) : see CITIZENSHIP, No. 4.

For **COMMOTION** see CONFUSION, TUMULT

COMMUNE

1. *dialaleō* (διαλαλέω, 1255) signifies "to speak with anyone" (*dia*, "by turns," *laleō*, "to speak"), Luke 6:11; in 1:65, "to talk over, to noise abroad." The idea that *laleō* and its compounds bear no reference to the word spoken or the sentiment, is unfounded. See NOISE.¶

2. *homileō* (ὁμιλέω, 3656), from *homos*, "together," signifies "to be in company, to associate with any one"; hence, "to have intercourse with," Luke 24:14 (RV, "communed"; KJV, "talked"), 15; Acts 24:26; in 20:11, "talked with." See TALK.¶

3. *sullaleō* (συλλαλέω, 4814), "to talk together," is translated "communed" in Luke 22:4, of the conspiracy of Judas with the chief priests. See CONFER, SPEAK, TALK.

Note: Laleō and its compounds, and the noun *lalia*, "speech," have a more dignified meaning in the Hellenistic Greek than "to chatter," its frequent meaning in earlier times.

COMMUNICATE, COMMUNICATION

A. Verbs.

1. *koinōneō* (κοινωνέω, 2841) is used in two senses, (*a*) "to have a share in," Rom. 15:27; 1 Tim. 5:22; Heb. 2:14; 1 Pet. 4:13; 2 John 11; (*b*) "to give a share to, go shares with," Rom. 12:13, RV, "communicating," for KJV, "distributing"; Gal. 6:6, "communicate"; Phil. 4:15, KJV, "did communicate," RV, "had fellowship with." See DISTRIBUTE, FELLOWSHIP, PARTAKE.¶

2. *sunkoinōneō* (συγκοινωνέω, 4790), "to share together with" (*sun* "and" No. 1), is translated "communicated with" in Phil. 4:14; "have fellowship with," Eph. 5:11; "be ... partakers of," Rev. 18:4 (RV, "have fellowship"). The thought is that of sharing with others what one has, in order to meet their needs. See FELLOWSHIP, B, No. 2, PARTAKE, B, No. 2.¶

Note: Anatithēmi, "to set forth," is rendered "laid before" in Gal. 2:2, RV, for KJV, "communicated unto"; in Acts 25:14, RV, "laid before," for KJV, "declared."¶

B. Nouns.

1. *koinōnia* (κοινωνία, 2842), akin to A (which see), is translated in Heb. 13:16 "to communicate," lit., "be not forgetful of good deed and of fellowship"; "fellowship" (KJV, "communication") in Philem. 6, RV. See COMMUNION.

2. *logos* (λόγος, 3056), "a word, that which is spoken" (*legō*, "to speak"), is used in the plural with reference to a conversation; "communication," Luke 24:17. Elsewhere with this significance the RV renders it "speech," Matt. 5:37; Eph. 4:29. See ACCOUNT.

Note: In Col. 3:8, where the KJV translates *aischrologia* by "filthy communication," the RV renders it "shameful speaking" (*aischros*, "base," *legō*, "to speak").

C. Adjective.

koinōnikos (κοινωνικός, 2843), akin to A, No. 1 and B, No. 1, means "apt, or ready, to communicate," 1 Tim. 6:18.¶

Note: Homilia, "a company, association, or intercourse with" (see COMMUNE, No. 2), is translated "company" in 1 Cor. 15:33, RV (KJV, "communications"); the word is in the plural, "evil companies," i.e., associations. See COMPANY, No. 6.¶

COMMUNION
A. Noun.
koinōnia (κοινωνία, 2842), "a having in common (*koinos*), partnership, fellowship" (see COMMUNICATE), denotes (*a*) the share which one has in anything, a participation, fellowship recognized and enjoyed; thus it is used of the common experiences and interests of Christian men, Acts 2:42; Gal. 2:9; of participation in the knowledge of the Son of God, 1 Cor. 1:9; of sharing in the realization of the effects of the blood (i.e., the death) of Christ and the body of Christ, as set forth by the emblems in the Lord's Supper, 1 Cor. 10:16; of participation in what is derived from the Holy Spirit, 2 Cor. 13:14 (RV, "communion"); Phil. 2:1; of participation in the sufferings of Christ, Phil. 3:10; of sharing in the resurrection life possessed in Christ, and so of fellowship with the Father and the Son, 1 John 1:3, 6–7; negatively, of the impossibility of "communion" between light and darkness, 2 Cor. 6:14; (*b*) fellowship manifested in acts, the practical effects of fellowship with God, wrought by the Holy Spirit in the lives of believers as the outcome of faith, Philem. 6, and finding expression in joint ministration to the needy, Rom. 15:26; 2 Cor. 8:4; 9:13; Heb. 13:16, and in the furtherance of the Gospel by gifts, Phil. 1:5. See COMMUNICATION, CONTRIBUTION, DISTRIBUTION, FELLOWSHIP.¶
B. Adjective.
koinōnos (κοινωνός, 2844), "having in common," is rendered "have communion with (the altar),"—the altar standing by metonymy for that which is associated with it—in 1 Cor. 10:18, RV (for KJV, "are partakers of"), and in v. 20, for KJV, "have fellowship with (demons)." See COMPANION.

COMPACTED
1. *sunistēmi* (συνίστημι, 4921), and transitively *sunistaō*, "to stand together" (*sun*, "with," *histēmi*, "to stand"), is rendered "compacted," in 2 Pet. 3:5, of the earth as formerly arranged by God in relation to the waters. See APPROVE, COMMEND, CONSIST, MAKE, STAND.

2. *sumbibazō* (συμβιβάζω, 4822), "to unite, to knit," is translated "compacted" in the KJV of Eph. 4:16 (RV, "knit together"), concerning the church as the body of Christ. See CONCLUDE, GATHER, INSTRUCT, KNIT, PROVE.

COMPANION
1. *sunekdēmos* (συνέκδημος, 4898), "a fellow-traveler" (*sun*, "with," *ek*, "from," *dēmos*, "people"; i.e., "away from one's people"), is used in Acts 19:29, of Paul's companions in

travel; in 2 Cor. 8:19, "travel with"; a closer rendering would be "(as) our fellow-traveler." See TRAVEL.¶

2. *koinōnos* (κοινωνός, 2844) is rendered "companions" in the KJV of Heb. 10:33 (RV "partakers"). So *sunkoinōnos* in Rev. 1:9, KJV, "companion"; RV, "partaker with you." See B, above, PARTAKER, PARTNER. Cf. COMMUNICATE.

3. *sunergos* (συνεργός, 4904), "a fellow-worker" (*sun*, "with," *ergon*, "work"), is translated in Phil. 2:25 "companion in labor," KJV (RV, "fellow-worker"). See HELPER, LABORER, WORKER.

COMPANY (Noun and Verb)
A. Nouns and Phrases.
1. *ochlos* (ὄχλος, 3793), "a throng of people, an irregular crowd," most usually "a disorganized throng"; in Acts 6:7, however, it is said of a company of the priests who believed; the word here indicates that they had not combined to bring this about. The RV usually translates this word "company" or "multitude." Cf. B, *Note* 3. See COMMON, CROWD, MULTITUDE, and Trench, *Syn.* §xcviii.

2. *sunodia* (συνοδία, 4923), lit., "a way or journey together" (*sun*, "with," *hodos*, "a way"), denotes, by metonymy, "a company of travelers"; in Luke 2:44, of the company from which Christ was missed by Joseph and Mary. (Eng., synod).¶

3. *sumposion* (συμπόσιον, 4849), lit. "denotes a drinking together (*sun*, "with," *pinō*, "to drink"), a drinking-party"; hence, by metonymy, "any table party or any company arranged as a party." In Mark 6:39 the noun is repeated, in the plural, by way of an adverbial and distributive phrase, *sumposia sumposia*, lit., "companies-companies" (i.e., by companies).¶

4. *klisia* (κλισία, 2828), akin to *klinō*, "to recline," primarily means "a place for lying down in, and hence a reclining company," for the same purpose as No. 3. It is found in the plural in Luke 9:14, corresponding to Mark's word *sumposia* (No. 3, above), signifying "companies reclining at a meal."¶

5. *plēthos* (πλῆθος, 4128), lit., "a fullness," hence denotes "a multitude, a large or full company," Luke 23:1; "a multitude," v. 27 (KJV, "a great company"). See BUNDLE, MULTITUDE.

6. *homilia* (ὁμιλία, 3657), "an association of people, those who are of the same company" (*homos*, "same"), is used in 1 Cor. 15:33, KJV, "(evil) communications"; RV, "(evil) company."¶

7. *homilos* (ὅμιλος, 3658), akin to No. 6, "a throng or crowd," is found, in some mss., in Rev. 18:17, "all the company in ships," KJV.

Homilos denotes the concrete; *homilia* is chiefly an abstract noun.¶

8. *idios* (ἴδιος, 2398) "one's own," is used in the plural with the article in Acts 4:23, to signify "their own (company)." See BUSINESS, B.

Notes: (1) The preposition *ex* (i.e., *ek*), "of," with the first personal pronoun in the genitive plural (*hēmōn*, "us"); signifies "of our company," lit., "of us," in Luke 24:22; so *ex autōn*, in Acts 15:22, "men out of their company," lit., "men out of them." (2) The phrase in Acts 13:13, *hoi peri Paulon*, lit., "the (ones) about Paul," signifies "Paul and his company." (3) *Murias*, a noun connected with the adjective *murios* ("numberless, infinite"), signifies "a myriad" (whence the English word), and is used hyperbolically, of vast numbers, e.g., Heb. 12:22, KJV, "an innumerable company"; RV, "innumerable hosts." (Contrast *murioi*, 10,000, Matt. 18:24). (4) In Acts 21:8, the phrase translated "that were of Paul's company" is absent from the best texts.

B. Verbs.

1. *sunanamignumi* (συναναμίγνυμι, 4874), lit., "to mix up with" (*sun*, "with," *ana*, "up," *mignumi*, "to mix, mingle"), signifies "to have, or keep, company with," 1 Cor. 5:9, 11; 2 Thess. 3:14.¶

2. *sunerchomai* (συνέρχομαι, 4905), "to come, or go, with," is rendered "have companied" in Acts 1:21. See COME, No. 11.

Notes: (1) *Aphorizō*, "to separate," is translated "separate (you) from (their) company," in Luke 6:22, the latter part being added in italics to supply the meaning of excommunication. See DIVIDE.

(2) *Kollaō*, "to join," is rendered "keep company," in Acts 10:28, KJV; RV, "join himself." See CLEAVE, JOIN.

(3) *Ochlopoieō*, lit., "to make a crowd" (*ochlos*, "a crowd," *poieō*, "to make"), is translated "gathered a company," in Acts 17:5, KJV; the RV corrects this to "gathering a crowd." See CROWD.¶

COMPARE, COMPARISON

1. *sunkrinō* (συγκρίνω, 4793) denotes (*a*) "to join fitly, to combine," 1 Cor. 2:13, either in the sense of combining spiritual things with spiritual, adapting the discourse to the subject, under the guidance of the Holy Spirit, or communicating spiritual things by spiritual things or words, or in the sense of interpreting spiritual things to spiritual men, RV and KJV, "comparing" (cf. the Sept. use, of interpreting dreams, etc. Gen. 40:8, 16, 22; 41:12, 15; Dan. 5:12); (*b*) "to place together; hence, judge or discriminate by comparison, compare, with or among," 2 Cor. 10:12 (thrice).¶

2. *paraballō* (παραβάλλω, 3846), "to place side by side, to set forth," and the noun *parabolē* (Eng., "parable"), occur in Mark 4:30, RV, "In what parable shall we set it forth?," KJV, "with what comparison shall we compare it?" See ARRIVE.

Note: The preposition *pros*, "towards," is sometimes used of mental direction, in the way of estimation, or comparison, as in the phrase "(worthy) to be compared," or "(worthy) in comparison with," Rom. 8:18.

COMPASS

1. *kukleuō* (κυκλεύω, 2944v) denotes "to encircle, surround," and is found in the best texts in John 10:24, "came round about," and Rev. 20:9, of a camp surrounded by foes; some mss. have No. 2 in each place.¶

2. *kukloō* (κυκλόω, 2944), (cf. Eng., "cycle"), signifies "to move in a circle, to compass about," as of a city "encompassed" by armies, Luke 21:20; Heb. 11:30; in Acts 14:20, "stood round about." See COME, No. 38, STAND.¶

3. *perikukloō* (περικυκλοω, 4033), *peri*, "about," with No. 2, is used in Luke 19:43, "shall compass . . . round."¶

4. *periagō* (περιάγω, 4013), "to lead about," 1 Cor. 9:5, or, intransitively, "to go about, to go up and down," is so used in Matt. 4:23; 9:35; Mark 6:6; Acts 13:11; "to compass regions," Matt. 23:15. See GO, LEAD. ¶

5. *perikeimai* (περίκειμαι, 4029), "to be encompassed": see BOUND (*b*), HANG.

6. *perierchomai* (περιέρχομαι, 4022), lit., "to go, or come, about" (*peri*, "about," *erchomai*, "to come"), is translated in Acts 28:13, KJV, "fetched a compass." See CIRCUIT.

COMPASSION, COMPASSIONATE
A. Verbs.

1. *oikteirō* (οἰκτείρω, 3627), "to have pity, a feeling of distress through the ills of others," is used of God's compassion, Rom. 9:15.¶

2. *splanchnizomai* (σπλαγχνίζομαι, 4697), "to be moved as to one's inwards (*splanchna*), to be moved with compassion, to yearn with compassion," is frequently recorded of Christ towards the multitude and towards individual sufferers, Matt. 9:36; 14:14; 15:32; 18:27; 20:34; Mark 1:41; 6:34; 8:2; 9:22 (of the appeal of a father for a demon-possessed son); Luke 7:13; 10:33; of the father in the parable of the Prodigal Son, 15:20. (Moulton and Milligan consider the verb to have been coined in the Jewish dispersion).¶

3. *sumpatheō* (συμπαθέω, 4834), "to suffer

with another (*sun*, 'with,' *paschō*, 'to suffer'), to be affected similarly" (Eng., "sympathy"), to have "compassion" upon, Heb. 10:34, of "compassionating" those in prison, is translated "be touched with" in Heb. 4:15, of Christ as the High Priest. See TOUCH.¶

4. *eleeō* (ἐλεέω, 1653), "to have mercy (*eleos*, "mercy"), to show kindness, by beneficence, or assistance," is translated "have compassion" in Matt. 18:33 (KJV); Mark 5:19 and Jude 22. See MERCY.

5. *metriopatheō* (μετριοπαθέω, 3356) is rendered "have compassion," in Heb. 5:2, KJV. See BEAR, No. 13.¶

B. Nouns.

1. *oiktirmos* (οἰκτιρμός, 3628), akin to A, No. 1, is used with *splanchna* (see below), "the viscera, the inward parts," as the seat of emotion, the "heart," Phil. 2:1; Col. 3:12, "a heart of compassion" (KJV, "bowels of mercies"). In Heb. 10:28 it is used with *chōris*, "without," (lit., "without compassions"). It is translated "mercies" in Rom. 12:1 and 2 Cor. 1:3. See MERCY.¶

2. *splanchnon* (σπλάγχνον, 4698), always used in the plural, is suitably rendered "compassion" in the RV of Col. 3:12 and 1 John 3:17; "compassions" in Phil. 2:1, Cf. A, No. 2. See BOWELS.

C. Adjective.

sumpathēs (συμπαθής, 4835) denotes suffering with, "compassionate," 1 Pet. 3:8, RV (KJV, "having compassion"). See A, No. 3.¶

COMPEL

1. *anankazō* (ἀναγκάζω, 315) denotes "to put constraint upon (from *anankē*, 'necessity'), to constrain, whether by threat, entreaty, force or persuasion"; Christ "constrained" the disciples to get into a boat, Matt. 14:22; Mark 6:45; the servants of the man who made a great supper were to constrain people to come in, Luke 14:23 (RV, "constrain"); Saul of Tarsus "strove" to make saints blaspheme, Acts 26:11, RV (KJV, "compelled"); Titus, though a Greek, was not "compelled" to be circumcised, Gal. 2:3, as Galatian converts were, 6:12, RV; Peter was "compelling" Gentiles to live as Jews, Gal. 2:14; Paul was "constrained" to appeal to Caesar, Acts 28:19, and was "compelled" by the church at Corinth to become foolish in speaking of himself, 2 Cor. 12:11. See CONSTRAIN.¶

2. *angareuō* (ἀγγαρεύω, 29), "to dispatch as an *angaros*" (a Persian courier kept at regular stages with power of impressing men into service), and hence, in general, "to impress into service," is used of "compelling" a person to go a mile, Matt. 5:41; of the impressing of Simon to bear Christ's cross, Matt. 27:32; Mark 15:21.¶

COMPLAINER, COMPLAINT

1. *mempsimoiros* (μεμψίμοιρος, 3202) denotes "one who complains," lit., "complaining of one's lot" (*memphomai*, "to blame," *moira*, "a fate, lot"); hence, "discontented, querulous, repining"; it is rendered "complainers" in Jude 16.¶

2. *momphē* (μομφή, 3437) denotes "blame" (akin to *memphomai*, see No. 1), "an occasion of complaint," Col. 3:13 (KJV, "quarrel"). See QUARREL.¶

3. *aitiōma* (αἰτίωμα, 157v), "a charge," is translated "complaints" in Acts 25:7, KJV. See CHARGE.¶

COMPLETE, COMPLETION, COMPLETELY

A. Verbs.

1. *epiteleō* (ἐπιτελζω, 2005), "to complete": see ACCOMPLISH, No. 4.

2. *exartizō* (ἐξαρτίδω, 1822), "to fit out" (*ek*, "out," intensive, *artos*, "a joint"; or from *artios*, perfect, lit., "exactly right"), is said of the equipment of the man of God, 2 Tim. 3:17, "furnished completely" (KJV, "throughly furnished"); elsewhere in Acts 21:5, "accomplished." Cf. B. See FURNISH.¶

3. *sunteleō* (συντελέω, 4931), "to end together, bring quite to an end" (*sun*, "together," intensive, *telos*, "an end"), is said (*a*) of the "completion" of a period of days, Luke 4:2; Acts 21:27; (*b*) of "completing" something; some mss. have it in Matt. 7:28, of the Lord, in ending His discourse (the best mss. have *teleō*, "to finish"); of God, in finishing a work, Rom. 9:28, in making a new covenant, Heb. 8:8, marg., "accomplish"; of the fulfillment of things foretold, Mark 13:4; of the Devil's temptation of the Lord, Luke 4:13. See END, FINISH, FULFILL, MAKE.¶

4. *plēroō* (πληρόω, 4137), "to fill" (in the passive voice, "to be made full"), is translated "complete" in the KJV of Col. 2:10 (RV, "made full"; cf. v. 9). See ACCOMPLISH.

5. *plerophoreō* (πληροφορέω, 4135), "to be fully assured," is translated "complete" in Col. 4:12. See ASSURED, B, No. 2.

B. Adjective.

artios (ἄρτιος, 739), "fitted, complete" (from *artos*, "a limb, joint"), is used in 2 Tim. 3:17, RV, "complete," KJV, "perfect. See PERFECT.¶

C. Noun.

apartismos (ἀπαρτισμός, 535) is rendered "complete" in Luke 14:28, RV.¶

For COMPREHEND see APPREHEND, John 1:5, KJV, and SUM UP

CONCEAL

parakaluptō (παρακαλύπτω, 3871), "to conceal thoroughly" (*para*, "beside," intensive, *kaluptō*, "to hide"), is found in Luke 9:45, of "concealing" from the disciples the fact of the delivering up of Christ.

CONCEITS

1. *en heautois* (ἐν ἑαυτοῖς), lit., "in yourselves," is used with *phronimos*, "wise," in Rom. 11:25, "(wise) in your own conceits (i.e., opinions)."

2. *par' heautois* (παρ' ἑαυτοῖς), (*para*, "with, in the estimation of"), in Rom. 12:16 has the same rendering as No. 1.

CONCEIVE

1. *gennaō* (γεννάω, 1080), "to conceive, beget": see BEGET, A, No. 1.

2. *sullambanō* (συλλαμβάνω, 4815), lit., "to take together" (*sun*, "with," *lambanō*, "to take or receive"), is used (*a*) of a woman, to "conceive," Luke 1:24, 31, 36; in the passive voice. Luke 2:21; (*b*) metaphorically, of the impulse of lust in the human heart, enticing to sin, Jas. 1:15. For its other meanings see CATCH, No. 8.

3. *tithēmi* (τίθημι, 5087), "to put, set," is used in Acts 5:4, of the sin of Ananias, in "conceiving" a lie in his heart.

Notes: (1) The phrase *echō*, "to have," with *koitē*, "a lying down, a bed," especially the marriage bed, denotes "to conceive," Rom. 9:10.¶

(2) The phrase *eis katabolēn*, lit., "for a casting down, or in," is used of conception in Heb. 11:11.¶

CONCERN (-ETH)

1. The neuter plural of the article ("the things"), with the genitive case of a noun, is used in 2 Cor. 11:30 of Paul's infirmity, "the things that concern my infirmity," lit., "the (things) of my infirmity."

2. The neuter singular of the article, with the preposition *peri*, "concerning," is used by the Lord in Luke 22:37, "that which concerneth," lit., "the (thing) concerning (Me)." The same construction is found in Luke 24:27; Acts 19:8; 28:31.

For CONCERNING see *Note* †, p. 1

CONCISION

katatomē (κατατομή, 2699), lit., "a cutting off" (*kata*, "down," *temnō*, "to cut"), "a mutilation," is a term found in Phil. 3:2, there used by the apostle, by a *paranomasia*, contemptuously, for the Jewish circumcision with its Judaistic influence, in contrast to the true spiritual circumcision.¶

CONCLUDE

sumbibazō (συμβιβάζω, 4822), lit., "to make to come together," is translated "concluding" in Acts 16:10, RV, for the KJV, "assuredly gathering." See COMPACTED, INSTRUCT, KNIT, PROVE.

Notes: (1) For *krinō*, "to judge, give judgment," rendered "concluded" in the KJV of Acts 21:25, RV, "giving judgment," see JUDGMENT.

(2) For *logizomai*, "to reckon," translated "conclude" in Rom. 3:28, KJV, RV, "reckon," see RECKON.

(3) For *sunkleiō*, "to shut up with," translated "concluded" in Rom. 11:32; Gal. 3:22, KJV, RV, "shut up," see INCLOSE, SHUT.

CONCORD

sumphōnēsis (συμφώνησις, 4857), lit., "a sounding together" (*sun*, "with," *phōnē*, "a sound"; Eng., "symphony"), is found in 2 Cor. 6:15, in the rhetorical question "what concord hath Christ with Belial?" See AGREE, A, No. 1.¶

CONCOURSE

suntrophē (συντροφή, 4963), "a turning together" (*sun*, "with," *trepō*, "to turn"), signifies (*a*) that which is rolled together; hence (*b*) a dense mass of people, concourse, Acts 19:40.¶ See BANDED.

For CONCUPISCENCE (KJV of Rom. 7:8; Col. 3:5; 1 Thess. 4:5) see COVET, DESIRE, LUST

CONDEMN, CONDEMNATION

A. Verbs.

1. *kataginōskō* (καταγινώσκω, 2607), "to know something against" (*kata*, "against," *ginōskō*, "to know by experience"), hence, "to think ill of, to condemn," is said, in Gal. 2:11, of Peter's conduct (RV, "stood condemned"), he being "self-condemned" as the result of an ex-

ercised and enlightened conscience, and "condemned" in the sight of others; so of "self-condemnation" due to an exercise of heart, 1 John 3:20–21. See BLAME.¶

2. *katadikazō* (καταδικάζω, 2613) signifies "to exercise right or law against anyone"; hence, "to pronounce judgment, to condemn" (*kata*, "down, or against," *dikē*, "justice"), Matt. 12:7, 37; Luke 6:37; Jas. 5:6.¶

3. *krinō* (κρίνω, 2919), "to distinguish, choose, give an opinion upon, judge," sometimes denotes "to condemn," e.g., Acts 13:27; Rom. 2:27; Jas. 5:9 (in the best mss.). Cf. No. 1, below. See CALL (No. 13), CONCLUDE, DECREE, DETERMINE, ESTEEM, JUDGE, LAW (go to), ORDAIN, SUE, THINK.

4. *katakrinō* (κατακρίνω, 2632), a strengthened form of No. 3, signifies "to give judgment against, pass sentence upon"; hence, "to condemn," implying (*a*) the fact of a crime, e.g., Rom. 2:1; 14:23; 2 Pet. 2:6; some mss. have it in Jas. 5:9; (*b*) the imputation of a crime, as in the "condemnation" of Christ by the Jews, Matt. 20:18; Mark 14:64. It is used metaphorically of "condemning" by a good example, Matt. 12:41–42; Luke 11:31–32; Heb. 11:7.

In Rom. 8:3, God's "condemnation" of sin is set forth in that Christ, His own Son, sent by Him to partake of human nature (sin apart) and to become an offering for sin, died under the judgment due to our sin.

B. Nouns.

1. *krima* (κρίμα, 2917) denotes (*a*) "the sentence pronounced, a verdict, a condemnation, the decision resulting from an investigation," e.g., Mark 12:40; Luke 23:40; 1 Tim. 3:6; Jude 4; (*b*) "the process of judgment leading to a decision," 1 Pet. 4:17 ("judgment"), where *krisis* (see No. 3, below) might be expected. In Luke 24:20, "to be condemned" translates the phrase *eis krima*, "unto condemnation" (i.e., unto the pronouncement of the sentence of "condemnation"). For the rendering "judgment," see, e.g., Rom. 11:33; 1 Cor. 11:34; Gal. 5:10; Jas. 3:1. In these (*a*) the process leading to a decision and (*b*) the pronouncement of the decision, the verdict, are to be distinguished. In 1 Cor. 6:7 the word means a matter for judgment, a lawsuit. See JUDGMENT.

2. *katakrima* (κατάκριμα, 2631), cf. No. 4, above, is "the sentence pronounced, the condemnation" with a suggestion of the punishment following; it is found in Rom. 5:16, 18; 8:1.¶

3. *krisis* (κρίσις, 2920) (*a*) denotes "the process of investigation, the act of distinguishing and separating" (as distinct from *krima*, see No. 1 above); hence "a judging, a passing of judg-

ment upon a person or thing"; it has a variety of meanings, such as judicial authority, John 5:22, 27; justice, Acts 8:33; Jas. 2:13; a tribunal, Matt. 5:21–22; a trial, John 5:24; 2 Pet. 2:4; a judgment, 2 Pet. 2:11; Jude 9; by metonymy, the standard of judgment, just dealing, Matt. 12:18, 20; 23:23; Luke 11:42; divine judgment executed, 2 Thess. 1:5; Rev. 16:7; (*b*) sometimes it has the meaning "condemnation," and is virtually equivalent to *krima* (*a*) ; see Matt. 23:33; John 3:19; Jas. 5:12, *hupo krisin*, "under judgment." See ACCUSATION, A (*Note*), DAMNATION, JUDGMENT.

Note: In John 9:39, "For judgment (*krima*) came I into this world," the meaning would appear to be, "for being judged" (as a touchstone for proving men's thoughts and characters), in contrast to 5:22, "hath given all judging (*krisis*) to the Son"; in Luke 24:20, "delivered Him up to be condemned to death," the latter phrase is, lit., "to a verdict (*krima*) of death" (which they themselves could not carry out); in Mark 12:40, "these shall receive greater condemnation" (*krima*), the phrase signifies a heavier verdict (against themselves).

4. *katakrisis* (κατάκρισις, 2633), a strengthened form of No. 3, denotes "a judgment against, condemnation," with the suggestion of the process leading to it, as of "the ministration of condemnation," 2 Cor. 3:9; in 7:3, "to condemn," more lit., "with a view to condemnation."¶

C. Adjectives.

1. *autokatakritos* (αὐτοκατάκριτος, 843), "self-condemned" (*auto*, "self," *katakrinō*, "to condemn"), i.e., on account of doing himself what he condemns in others, is used in Titus 3:11.¶

2. *akatagnōstos* (ἀκατάγνωστος, 176), akin to A, No. 1, with negative prefix, *a*, "not to be condemned," is said of sound speech, in Titus 2:8.¶

CONDESCEND

sunapagō (συναπάγω, 4879): see CARRY, No. 7.

CONDITIONS

Note: This translates the phrase *ta pros* in Luke 14:32, lit., "the (things) towards," i.e., the things relating to, or conditions of, (peace).

CONDUCT

A. Noun.

agōgē (ἀγωγή, 72), from *agō*, "to lead," properly denotes "a teaching"; then, figuratively, "a training, discipline," and so, the life led, a way or course of life, conduct, 2 Tim.

3:10, RV, "conduct"; KJV, "manner of life." See LIFE.¶

B. Verbs.

1. *kathistēmi* (καθίστημι, 2525), lit., "to stand down or set down" (*kata*, "down," *histēmi*, "to stand"), has, among its various meanings, "the significance of bringing to a certain place, conducting," Acts 17:15 (so the Sept. in Josh. 6:23; 1 Sam. 5:3; 2 Chron. 28:15). See APPOINT.

2. *propempō* (προπέμπω, 4311) signifies "to set forward, conduct": see ACCOMPANY, No. 4.

CONFER, CONFERENCE

1. *prosanatithēmi* (προσανατίθημι, 4323), lit., "to put before" (*pros*, "towards," *ana*, "up," and *tithēmi*, "to put"), i.e., "to lay a matter before others so as to obtain counsel or instruction," is used of Paul's refraining from consulting human beings, Gal. 1:16 (translated "imparted" in 2:6; KJV, "added ... in conference"). Cf. the shorter form *anatithēmi*, in 2:2, "laid before," the less intensive word being used there simply to signify the imparting of information, rather than conferring with others to seek advice. See ADD, IMPART.¶

2. *sullaleō* (συλλαλέω, 4814), "to speak together with" (*sun*, "with," *laleō*, "to speak"), is translated "conferred" in Acts 25:12; elsewhere of talking with Matt. 17:3; Mark 9:4; Luke 4:36; 9:30; "communed" in Luke 22:4. See COMMUNE, SPEAK, TALK.¶

3. *sumballō* (συμβάλλω, 4820), lit., "to throw together" (*sun*, "with," *ballō*, "to throw"), is used of "conversation, to discourse or consult together, confer," Acts 4:15. See ENCOUNTER, HELP, MEET WITH, PONDER.

Note: For the KJV, "conference" in Gal. 2:6, see No. 1, above.

CONFESS, CONFESSION

A. Verbs.

1. *homologeō* (ὁμολογέω, 3670), lit., "to speak the same thing" (*homos*, "same," *legō*, "to speak"), "to assent, accord, agree with," denotes, (*a*) "to confess, declare, admit," John 1:20; e.g., Acts 24:14; Heb. 11:13; (*b*) "to confess by way of admitting oneself guilty of what one is accused of, the result of inward conviction," 1 John 1:9; (*c*) "to declare openly by way of speaking out freely, such confession being the effect of deep conviction of facts," Matt. 7:23; 10:32 (twice) and Luke 12:8 (see next par.); John 9:22; 12:42; Acts 23:8; Rom. 10:9–10 ("confession is made"); 1 Tim. 6:12 (RV); Titus 1:16; 1 John 2:23; 4:2, 15; 2 John 7 (in John's epistle it is the necessary antithesis to Gnostic docetism); Rev. 3:5, in the best mss. (some

have No. 2 here); (*d*) "to confess by way of celebrating with praise," Heb. 13:15; (*e*) "to promise," Matt. 14:7.

In Matt. 10:32 and Luke 12:8 the construction of this verb with *en*, "in," followed by the dative case of the personal pronoun, has a special significance, namely, to "confess" in a person's name, the nature of the "confession" being determined by the context, the suggestion being to make a public "confession." Thus the statement, "every one ... who shall confess Me (lit., "in Me," i.e., in My case) before men, him (lit., "in him," i.e., in his case) will I also confess before My Father ...," conveys the thought of "confessing" allegiance to Christ as one's Master and Lord, and, on the other hand, of acknowledgment, on His part, of the faithful one as being His worshipper and servant, His loyal follower; this is appropriate to the original idea in *homologeō* of being identified in thought or language. See PROFESS, PROMISE, THANK.¶

2. *exomologeō* (ἐξομολογέω, 1843), *ek*, "out," intensive, and No. 1, and accordingly stronger than No. 1, "to confess forth," i.e., "freely, openly," is used (*a*) "of a public acknowledgment or confession of sins," Matt. 3:6; Mark 1:5; Acts 19:18; Jas. 5:16; (*b*) "to profess or acknowledge openly," Matt. 11:25 (translated "thank," but indicating the fuller idea); Phil. 2:11 (some mss. have it in Rev. 3:5: see No. 1); (*c*) "to confess by way of celebrating, giving praise," Rom. 14:11; 15:9. In Luke 10:21, it is translated "I thank," the true meaning being "I gladly acknowledge." In Luke 22:6 it signifies to consent (RV), for KJV, "promised." See CONSENT, PROMISE, THANK.¶

B. Noun.

homologia (ὁμολογία, 3671), akin to A, No. 1, denotes "confession, by acknowledgment of the truth," 2 Cor. 9:13; 1 Tim. 6:12–13; Heb. 3:1; 4:14; 10:23 (KJV, incorrectly, "profession," except in 1 Tim. 6:13).¶

Note: For the adverb *homologoumenōs*, confessedly, see CONTROVERSY.

CONFIDENCE (Noun, or Verb with "have"), CONFIDENT (-LY)

A. Nouns.

1. *pepoithēsis* (πεποίθησις, 4006), akin to *peithō*, B, No. 1 below, denotes "persuasion, assurance, confidence," 2 Cor. 1:15; 3:4, KJV, "trust"; 8:22; 10:2; Eph. 3:12; Phil. 3:4. See TRUST.¶

2. *hupostasis* (ὑπόστασις, 5287), lit., "a standing under" (*hupo*, "under," *stasis*, "a standing"), "that which stands, or is set, under, a foundation, beginning"; hence, the quality of

confidence which leads one to stand under, endure, or undertake anything, 2 Cor. 9:4; 11:17; Heb. 3:14. Twice in Heb. it signifies "substance," 1:3 (KJV, "Person") and 11:1. See SUBSTANCE.¶

3. *parrhēsia* (παρρησία, 3954), often rendered "confidence" in the KJV, is in all such instances rendered "boldness" in the RV, Acts 28:31; Heb. 3:6; 1 John 2:28; 3:21; 5:14. See BOLDNESS, OPENLY, PLAINNESS.

B. Verbs.

1. *peithō* (πείθω, 3982), "to persuade," or, intransitively, "to have confidence, to be confident" (cf. A, No. 1), has this meaning in the following, Rom. 2:19; 2 Cor. 2:3; Gal. 5:10; Phil. 1:6, 14 (RV, "being confident," for KJV, "waxing confident"), 25; 3:3–4; 2 Thess. 3:4; Philem. 21. See AGREE, ASSURE, BELIEVE, OBEY, PERSUADE, TRUST, YIELD.

2. *tharreō* (θαρρέω, 2292), "to be of good courage," is so translated in the RV of 2 Cor. 5:6; 7:16 (KJV, "to have confidence, or be confident"). See COURAGE.

Note: The adverb "confidently" is combined with the verb "affirm" to represent the verbs *diischurizomai*, Luke 22:59 and Acts 12:15, RV (KJV, "constantly affirmed"),¶, and *diabebaioomai*, 1 Tim. 1:7, KJV, "affirm," and Titus 3:8, KJV, "affirm constantly." See AFFIRM.¶

CONFIRM, CONFIRMATION
A. Verbs.

1. *bebaioō* (βεβαιόω, 950), "to make firm, establish, make secure" (the connected adjective *bebaios* signifies "stable, fast, firm"), is used of "confirming" a word, Mark 16:20; promises, Rom. 15:8; the testimony of Christ, 1 Cor. 1:6; the saints by the Lord Jesus Christ, 1 Cor. 1:8; the saints by God, 2 Cor. 1:21 ("stablisheth"); in faith, Col. 2:7; the salvation spoken through the Lord and "confirmed" by the apostles, Heb. 2:3; the heart by grace, Heb. 13:9 ("stablished").¶

2. *epistērizō* (ἐπιστηρίζω, 1991), "to make to lean upon, strengthen" (*epi*, "upon," *stērix*, "a prop, support"), is used of "confirming" souls, Acts 14:22; brethren, 15:32; churches, 15:41; disciples, 18:23, in some mss. ("stablishing," RV, "strengthening," KJV); the most authentic mss. have *stērizō* in 18:23. See STRENGTHEN.¶

3. *kuroō* (κυρόω, 2964), "to make valid, ratify, impart authority or influence" (from *kuros*, "might," *kurios*, "mighty, a head, as supreme in authority"), is used of spiritual love, 2 Cor. 2:8; a human covenant, Gal. 3:15.¶. In the Sept., see Gen. 23:20, e.g.

4. *prokuroō* (προκυρόω, 4300), *pro*, "before," and No. 3, "to confirm or ratify before," is said of the divine confirmation of a promise given originally to Abraham, Gen. 12, and "confirmed" by the vision of the furnace and torch, Gen. 15, by the birth of Isaac, Gen. 21, and by the oath of God, Gen. 22, all before the giving of the Law, Gal. 3:17.¶

5. *mesiteuō* (μεσιτεύω, 3315), "to act as a mediator, to interpose," is rendered "confirmed," in the KJV of Heb. 6:17 (marg., and RV, "interposed"). See INTERPOSED.¶

B. Noun.
bebaiōsis (βεβαίωσις, 951), akin to A, No. 1, is used in two senses (*a*) "of firmness, establishment," said of the "confirmation" of the gospel, Phil. 1:7; (*b*) "of authoritative validity imparted," said of the settlement of a dispute by an oath to produce confidence, Heb. 6:16. The word is found frequently in the papyri of the settlement of a business transaction.¶

CONFLICT (Noun)

1. *agōn* (ἀγών, 73), from *agō*, "to lead," signifies (*a*) "a place of assembly," especially the place where the Greeks assembled for the Olympic and Pythian games; (*b*) "a contest of athletes," metaphorically, 1 Tim. 6:12; 2 Tim. 4:7, "fight"; Heb. 12:1, "race"; hence, (*c*) "the inward conflict of the soul"; inward "conflict" is often the result, or the accompaniment, of outward "conflict," Phil. 1:30; 1 Thess. 2:2, implying a contest against spiritual foes, as well as human adversaries; so Col. 2:1, "conflict," KJV; RV, "(how greatly) I strive," lit., "how great a conflict I have." See CONTENTION, FIGHT, RACE.¶. Cf. *agōnizomai* (Eng., "agonize"), 1 Cor. 9:25 etc.

2. *athlēsis* (ἄθλησις, 119) denotes "a combat, contest of athletes"; hence, "a struggle, fight," Heb. 10:32, with reference to affliction. See FIGHT.¶ Cf. *athleō*, "to strive," 2 Tim. 2:5 (twice).¶

CONFORMED, CONFORMABLE
A. Verb.

summorphizō (συμμορφίζω, 4833v), "to make of like form with another person or thing, to render like" (*sun*, "with," *morphē*, "a form"), is found in Phil. 3:10 (in the passive participle of the verb), "becoming conformed" (or "growing into conformity") to the death of Christ, indicating the practical apprehension of the death of the carnal self, and fulfilling his share of the sufferings following upon the sufferings of Christ. Some texts have the alternative verb *summorphoō*, which has practically the same meaning.

B. Adjectives.

1. *summorphos* (σύμμορφος, 4832), akin to A, signifies "having the same form as another, conformed to"; (*a*) of the "conformity" of children of God "to the image of His Son," Rom. 8:29; (*b*), of their future physical "conformity" to His body of glory, Phil. 3:21. See FASHION.¶

2. *suschēmatizō* (συσχηματίζω, 4964), "to fashion or shape one thing like another," is translated "conformed" in Rom. 12:2, KJV; RV, "fashioned"; "fashioning" in 1 Pet. 1:14. This verb has more especial reference to that which is transitory, changeable, unstable; *summorphizō*, to that which is essential in character and thus complete or durable, not merely a form or outline. *Suschēmatizō* could not be used of inward transformation. See FASHION (*schēma*) and FORM (*morphē*).¶

CONFOUND, CONFUSE, CONFUSION

A. Nouns.

1. *akatastasia* (ἀκαταστασία, 181), "instability," (*a*, negative, *kata*, "down," *stasis*, "a standing"), denotes "a state of disorder, disturbance, confusion, tumult," 1 Cor. 14:33; Jas. 3:16, "revolution or anarchy"; translated "tumults" in Luke 21:9 (KJV, "commotions"); 2 Cor. 6:5; 12:20. See TUMULT.¶

2. *sunchusis* (σύγχυσις, 4799), "a pouring or mixing together" (*sun*, "with," *cheō*, "to pour"); hence "a disturbance, confusion, a tumultuous disorder, as of riotous persons," is found in Acts 19:29.¶

B. Verbs.

1. *suncheō* (συγχέω, 4797), or *sunchunnō* or *sunchunō* (the verb form of A., No. 2), lit., "to pour together, commingle," hence (said of persons), means "to trouble or confuse, to stir up," Acts 19:32 (said of the mind); "to be in confusion," 21:31, RV (KJV, "was in an uproar"); 21:27, "stirred up"; Acts 2:6; 9:22, "confounded." See STIR, UPROAR.¶

2. *kataischunō* (καταισχύνω, 2617), "to put to shame," is translated "confound" in 1 Cor. 1:27, and 1 Pet. 2:6, KJV (RV, "put to shame"). See ASHAMED, DISHONOR, SHAME.

CONFUTE

diakatelenchomai (διακατελέγχομαι, 1246), "to confute powerfully," is an intensive form of *elenchō*, "to convict" (*dia*, "through," *kata*, "down," both intensive), Acts 18:28, implying that "he met the opposing arguments in turn (*dia*), and brought them down to the ground (*kata*)." It carries also the thought that he brought home moral blame to them.

CONGREGATION

1. *ekklēsia* (ἐκκλησία, 1577) is translated "congregation" in Heb. 2:12, RV, instead of the usual rendering "church." See ASSEMBLY.

2. *sunagōgē* (συναγωγή, 4864) is translated "congregation" in Acts 13:43, KJV (RV, "synagogue"). See SYNAGOGUE.

CONQUER, CONQUEROR

1. *nikaō* (νικάω, 3528), "to overcome" (its usual meaning), is translated "conquering" and "to conquer" in Rev. 6:2. See OVERCOME, PREVAIL, VICTORY.

2. *hupernikaō* (ὑπενικάω, 5245), "to be more than conqueror" (*huper*, "over," and No. 1), "to gain a surpassing victory," is found in Rom. 8:37, lit., "we are hyper-conquerors," i.e., we are pre-eminently victorious.¶

CONSCIENCE

suneidēsis (συνείδησις, 4893), lit., "a knowing with" (*sun*, "with," *oida*, "to know"), i.e., "a co-knowledge (with oneself), the witness borne to one's conduct by conscience, that faculty by which we apprehend the will of God, as that which is designed to govern our lives"; hence (*a*) the sense of guiltiness before God; Heb. 10:2; (*b*) that process of thought which distinguishes what it considers morally good or bad, commending the good, condemning the bad, and so prompting to do the former, and avoid the latter; Rom. 2:15 (bearing witness with God's law); 9:1; 2 Cor. 1:12; acting in a certain way because "conscience" requires it, Rom. 13:5; so as not to cause scruples of "conscience" in another, 1 Cor. 10:28–29; not calling a thing in question unnecessarily, as if conscience demanded it, 1 Cor. 10:25, 27; "commending oneself to every man's conscience," 2 Cor. 4:2; cf. 5:11. There may be a "conscience" not strong enough to distinguish clearly between the lawful and the unlawful, 1 Cor. 8:7, 10, 12 (some regard consciousness as the meaning here). The phrase "conscience toward God," in 1 Pet. 2:19, signifies a "conscience" (or perhaps here, a consciousness) so controlled by the apprehension of God's presence, that the person realizes that griefs are to be borne in accordance with His will. Heb. 9:9 teaches that sacrifices under the Law could not so perfect a person that he could regard himself as free from guilt.

For various descriptions of "conscience" see Acts 23:1; 24:16; 1 Cor. 8:7; 1 Tim. 1:5, 19; 3:9; 4:2; 2 Tim. 1:3; Titus 1:15; Heb. 9:14; 10:22; 13:18; 1 Pet. 3:16, 21.¶

CONSECRATE

Note: In Heb. 7:28 the verb *teleioō* is translated "perfected" in the RV, for KJV, "consecrated"; so in 9:18 and 10:20, *enkainizō*, RV, "dedicated." See DEDICATE, PERFECT.

CONSENT

A. Verbs.

1. *exomologeō* (ἐξομολογέω, 1843), "to agree openly, to acknowledge outwardly, or fully" (*ex*, "for," *ek*, "out," intensive), is translated "consented" in the RV of Luke 22:6 (KJV, "promised"). See CONFESS, THANK.

2. *epineuō* (ἐπινεύω, 1962), lit. "signifies to nod to" (*epi*, "upon or to," *neuō*, "to nod"); hence, "to nod assent, to express approval, consent," Acts 18:20.

3. *proserchomai* (προσέρχομαι, 4334), "to come to," signifies "to consent," implying a coming to agreement with, in 1 Tim. 6:3. See COME, No. 10.

4. *sunkatatithēmi* (συγκατατίθημι, 4784), lit., "to put or lay down together with" (*sun*, "with," *kata*, "down," *tithēmi*, "to put"), was used of depositing one's vote in an urn; hence, "to vote for, agree with, consent to." It is said negatively of Joseph of Arimathaea, who had not "consented" to the counsel and deed of the Jews, Luke 23:51 (middle voice).¶

5. *sumphēmi* (σύμφημι, 4852), lit., "to speak with" (*sun*, "with," *phēmi*, "to speak"), hence, "to express agreement with," is used of "consenting" to the Law, agreeing that it is good, Rom. 7:16.¶

6. *suneudokeō* (συνευδοκέω, 4909), lit., "to think well with" (*sun*, "with," *eu*, "well," *dokeō*, "to think"), to take pleasure with others in anything, to approve of, to assent, is used in Luke 11:48, of "consenting" to the evil deeds of predecessors (KJV, "allow"); in Rom. 1:32, of "consenting" in doing evil; in Acts 8:1; 22:20, of "consenting" to the death of another. All these are cases of "consenting" to evil things. In 1 Cor. 7:12–13, it is used of an unbelieving wife's "consent" to dwell with her converted husband, and of an unbelieving husband's "consent" to dwell with a believing wife (KJV, "be pleased"; RV, "be content"). See ALLOW, CONTENT, PLEASE.¶

B. Phrases.

1. *apo mias*, lit., "from one," is found in Luke 14:18, some word like "consent" being implied; e.g., "with one consent."¶

2. *ek sumphōnou*, lit., "from (or by) agreement" (*sun*, "with," *phōnē*, "a sound"), i.e., "by consent," is found in 1 Cor. 7:5. Cf. AGREE.¶

CONSIDER

1. *eidon* (εἶδον, Aor. of 3708), used as the aorist tense of *horaō*, "to see," is translated "to consider" in Acts 15:6, of the gathering of the apostles and elders regarding the question of circumcision in relation to the gospel.

2. *suneidon* (συνεῖδον, 4894), *sun*, with, and No. 1, used as the aorist tense of *sunoraō*, to see with one view, to be aware, conscious, as the result of mental perception, is translated "considered" in Acts 12:12, of Peter's consideration of the circumstances of his deliverance from. See KNOW, PRIVY.

3. *katamanthanō* (καταμανθάνω, 2648), lit., "to learn thoroughly" (*kata*, "down," intensive, *manthanō*, "to learn"), hence, "to note accurately, consider well," is used in the Lord's exhortation to "consider" the lilies. Matt. 6:28.¶

4. *noeō* (νοέω, 3539), "to perceive with the mind" (*nous*), "think about, ponder," is translated "consider," only in Paul's exhortation to Timothy in 2 Tim. 2:7. See PERCEIVE, THINK, UNDERSTAND.

5. *katanoeō* (κατανοέω, 2657), "to perceive clearly" (*kata*, intensive, and No. 4), "to understand fully, consider closely," is used of not "considering" thoroughly the beam in one's own eye, Matt. 7:3 and Luke 6:41 (KJV, "perceivest"); of carefully "considering" the ravens, Luke 12:24; the lilies, v. 27; of Peter's full "consideration" of his vision, Acts 11:6; of Abraham's careful "consideration" of his own body, and Sarah's womb, as dead, and yet accepting by faith God's promise, Rom. 4:19 (RV); of "considering" fully the Apostle and High Priest of our confession, Heb. 3:1; of thoughtfully "considering" one another to provoke unto love and good works, Heb. 10:24. It is translated by the verbs "behold," Acts 7:31–32; Jas. 1:23–24; "perceive," Luke 20 :23; "discover," Acts 27:39. See BEHOLD, DISCOVER, PERCEIVE.¶

6. *logizomai* (λογίζομαι, 3049) signifies "to take account of," 2 Cor. 10:7 (RV, "consider," KJV, "think"), the only place where the RV translates it "consider." See ACCOUNT.

7. *theōreō* (θεωρέω, 2334): see BEHOLD, No. 6.

8. *anatheōreō* (ἀναθεωρέω, 333), "to consider carefully": see BEHOLD, No. 7.

9. *analogizomai* (ἀναλογίζομαι, 357),"to consider," occurs in Heb. 12:3.¶

Notes: (1) *Skopeō*, "to look," is translated "looking to" in Gal. 6:1, RV (KJV, "considering"). See HEED, LOOK, MARK. (2) *Suniēmi*, "to understand," is translated "considered" in Mark 6:52 (KJV), RV, "understood." (3) In John 11:50 (KJV, *dialogizomai*) the best texts have No. 6.

CONSIST

1. *eimi* (εἰμί, 1510), "to be," is rendered "consist" (lit., "is") in Luke 12:15.

2. *sunistēmi* (συνίστημι, 4921), *sun*, "with," *histēmi*, "to stand," denotes, in its intransitive sense, "to stand with or fall together, to be constituted, to be compact"; it is said of the universe as upheld by the Lord, Col. 1:17, lit., "by Him all things stand together," i.e., "consist" (the Latin *consisto*, "to stand together," is the exact equivalent of *sunistēmi*). See APPROVE, COMMEND, MAKE, STAND.

CONSOLATION, CONSOLE

A. Nouns.

1. *paraklēsis* (παράκλησις, 3874) is translated "consolation," in both KJV and RV, in Luke 2:25; 6:24; Acts 15:31; in 1 Cor. 14:3, KJV, "exhortation," RV, "comfort"; in the following the KJV has "consolation," the RV, "comfort," Rom. 15:5; 2 Cor. 1:6–7; 7:7; Phil. 2:1; 2 Thess. 2:16; Philem. 7; in Acts 4:36, RV, "exhortation"; in Heb. 6:18, RV, "encouragement." See COMFORT.

2. *paramuthia* (παραμυθία, 3889), "a comfort, consolation": see COMFORT, A, No. 2.

3. *paramuthion* (παραμύθιον, 3890), "an encouragement, consolation," Phil. 2:1, RV, in the phrase "consolation of love." See COMFORT, A, No. 3.

B. Verb.

paramutheomai (παραμυθέομαι, 3888), "to speak soothingly to," is translated "console," John 11:19, RV; in v. 31 "were comforting"; in 1 Thess. 2:11 and 5:14, KJV, "comforted" and "comfort," RV, "encouraged" and "encourage."

CONSORT (with)

prosklēroō (προσκληρόω, 4345), lit., "to assign by lot" (*pros*, "to," *klēros*, "a lot"), "to allot," is found in Acts 17:4, "consorted with," imparting to the passive voice (the form of the verb there) a middle voice significance, i.e., "they joined themselves to," or "threw in their lot with." The passive voice significance can be retained by translating (in the stricter sense of the word), "they were allotted" (i.e., by God) to Paul and Silas, as followers or disciples.¶

CONSPIRACY

sunōmosia (συνωμοσία, 4945) denotes, lit., "a swearing together" (*sun*, "with," *omnumi*, "to swear"), a "being leagued by oath, and so a conspiracy," Acts 23:13.¶

For **CONSTANTLY** see **AFFIRM**

CONSTRAIN, CONSTRAINT

A. Verbs.

1. *anankazō* (ἀναγκάζω, 315): see COMPEL, No. 1.

2. *parabiazomai* (παραβιάζομαι, 3849) primarily denotes "to employ force contrary to nature and right, to compel by using force" (*para*, "alongside," intensive, *biazō*, "to force"), and is used only of "constraining" by intreaty, as the two going to Emmaus did to Christ, Luke 24:29; as Lydia did to Paul and his companions, Acts 16:15.¶

3. *sunechō* (συνέχω, 4912), "to hold together, confine, secure, to hold fast" (*echō*, "to have or hold"), "to constrain," is said (*a*) of the effect of the word of the Lord upon Paul, Acts 18:5 (KJV, "was pressed in spirit," RV, "was constrained by the word"); of the effect of the love of Christ, 2 Cor. 5:14; (*b*) of being taken with a disease, Matt. 4:24; Luke 4:38; Acts 28:8; with fear, Luke 8:37; (*c*) of thronging or holding in a person, Luke 8:45; being straitened, Luke 12:50; being in a strait betwixt two, Phil. 1:23; keeping a city in on every side, Luke 19:43; keeping a tight hold on a person, as the men who seized the Lord Jesus did, after bringing Him into the High Priest's house, Luke 22:63; (*d*) of stopping the ears in refusal to listen, Acts 7:57. Luke uses the word nine times out of its twelve occurrences in the NT See HOLD, KEEP, No. (1), PRESS, SICK (lie), STOP, STRAIT (be in a), TAKEN (be), THRONG.¶

Note: The verb *echō*, "to have," with *anankē*, "a necessity," is translated "I was constrained," in Jude 3, RV (KJV, "it was needful").

B. Adverb.

anankastōs (ἀναγκαστῶς, 317), akin to A, No. 1, "by force, unwillingly, by constraint," is used in 1 Pet. 5:2.¶

CONSULT, CONSULTATION

A. Verbs.

1. *bouleuō* (βουλεύω, 1011), used in the middle voice, means (*a*) "to consult," Luke 14:31; (*b*) "to resolve," John 12:10, KJV, "consulted"; RV, "took counsel." See COUNSEL.

2. *sumbouleuō* (συμβουλεύω, 4823), "to take counsel together," is translated "consulted together," in Matt. 26:4, KJV (RV, "took counsel.") See COUNSEL.

B. Noun.

sumboulion (συμβούλιον, 4824), a word of the Graeco-Roman period (akin to A, No. 2), "counsel, advice," is translated "consultation" in Mark 15:1 (with *poieō*, "to make"), "to hold a consultation"; elsewhere "counsel" in the RV, except in Acts 25:12, where, by metonymy, it means a "council." See COUNCIL.

CONSUME

1. *analiskō* (ἀναλίσκω, 355), "to use up, spend up, especially in a bad sense, to destroy," is said of the destruction of persons, (*a*) literally, Luke 9:54 and the RV marg. of 2 Thess. 2:8 (text, "shall slay"); (*b*) metaphorically, Gal. 5:15 "(that) ye be not consumed (one of another)."¶

2. *katanaliskō* (καταναλίσκω, 2654), "to consume utterly, wholly" (*kata*, intensive), is said, in Heb. 12:29, of God as "a consuming fire."¶

3. *aphanizō* (ἀφανίζω, 853), lit., "to cause to disappear, put out of sight," came to mean "to do away with" (*a*, negative, *phainō*, "to cause to appear"), said of the destructive work of moth and rust, Matt. 6:19–20 (RV, "consume," KJV, "corrupt") . See CORRUPT, DISFIGURE, PERISH, VANISH.

Note: Dapanaō, "to expend, be at an expense," is translated "consume" in the KJV of Jas. 4:3 (RV, "spend"). See SPEND.

CONTAIN

1. *chōreō* (χωρέω, 5562) signifies (*a*), lit., "to give space, make room" (*chōra*, "a place"); hence, transitively, "to have space or room for a thing, to contain," said of the waterpots as "containing" a certain quantity, John 2:6; of a space large enough to hold a number of people, Mark 2:2; of the world as not possible of "containing" certain books, John 21:25; (*b*) "to go," Matt. 15:17; "to have place," John 8:37; "to come," 2 Pet. 3:9; (*c*) metaphorically, "of receiving with the mind," Matt. 19:11, 12; or "into the heart," 2 Cor. 7:2. See COME (No. 24), GO, PLACE, RECEIVE, ROOM. ¶

2. *periechō* (περιέχω, 4023), lit., "to have round" (*peri*, "around," *echō*, "to have"), means "to encompass, enclose, contain," as a writing contains details, 1 Pet. 2:6. Some mss. have it in Acts 23:25, lit., "having this form" (the most authentic have *echō*, "to have"). For the secondary meaning, "amazed" (KJV, "astonished"), Luke 5:9 (lit., "amazement encompassed," i.e., seized, him).¶

Notes: (1) The verb *allēgoreō* in Gal. 4:24, RV, is translated "contain an allegory" (KJV, "are an allegory"), i.e., they apply the facts of the narrative to illustrate principles. (2) In Eph. 2:15 "the law of commandments contained in ordinances" is, lit., "the law of commandments in ordinances." (3) In Rom. 2:14, the RV, translating literally, has "the things of the Law"; the KJV inserts the words "contained in." (4) In

1 Cor. 7:9, for the KJV, "if they cannot contain," see CONTINENCY.

For **CONTEMPTIBLE** see ACCOUNT No. 6

CONTEND (-ING)

1. *athleō* (ἀθλέω, 118), "to engage in a contest" (cf. Eng., "athlete"), "to contend in public games," is used in 2 Tim. 2:5, RV, "contend in the games," for the KJV, "strive for the masteries." See STRIVE.¶

Note: In 1 Cor. 9:25, the verb *agōnizomai*, "to strive," is used in the same connection, RV, "striveth in the games." Cf. No. 3.

2. *diakrinō* (διακρίνω, 1252), lit., "to separate throughout or wholly" (*dia*, "asunder," *krinō*, "to judge," from a root *kri*, meaning "separation"), then, to distinguish, decide, signifies, in the middle voice, "to separate oneself from, or to contend with," as did the circumcisionists with Peter, Acts 11:2; as did Michael with Satan, Jude 9. See RV marg. of v. 22, where the thought may be that of differing in opinion. See DIFFER, DISCERN, DOUBT, JUDGE, PARTIAL, STAGGER, WAVER.

3. *epagōnizomai* (ἐπαγωνίζομαι, 1864) signifies "to contend about a thing, as a combatant" (*epi*, "upon or about," intensive, *agōn*, "a contest"), "to contend earnestly," Jude 3. The word "earnestly" is added to convey the intensive force of the preposition.¶

CONTENT (to be), CONTENTMENT

A. Verb.

1. *arkeō* (ἀρκέω, 174) primarily signifies "to be sufficient, to be possessed of sufficient strength, to be strong, to be enough for a thing"; hence, "to defend, ward off"; in the middle voice, "to be satisfied, contented with," Luke 3:14, with wages; 1 Tim. 6:8, with food and raiment; Heb. 13:5, with "such things as ye have"; negatively of Diotrephes, in 3 John 10, "not content therewith." See ENOUGH, SUFFICE, SUFFICIENT.

2. *suneudokeō* (συνευδοκέω, 4909), in 1 Cor. 7:12–13, RV, signifies "to be content": see CONSENT, No. 6.

B. Adjectives.

1. *autarkēs* (αὐτάρκης, 842), as found in the papyri writings, means "sufficient in oneself" (*autos*, "self," *arkeō*, "see" A), "self-sufficient, adequate, needing no assistance"; hence, "content," Phil. 4:11.¶

2. *hikanos* (ἱκανός, 2425), "sufficient," used with *poieō*, "to do," in Mark 15:15, is translated

"to content (the multitude)," i.e., to do sufficient to satisfy them. See ABLE.

C. Noun.

autarkeia (αὐτάρκεια, 841), "contentment, satisfaction with what one has," is found in 1 Tim. 6:6. For its other meaning "sufficiency," in 2 Cor. 9:8, see SUFFICIENCY.¶

CONTENTION, CONTENTIOUS

A. Nouns.

1. *eris* (ἔρις, 2054), "strife, quarrel, especially rivalry, contention, wrangling," as in the church in Corinth, 1 Cor. 1:11, is translated "contentions" in Titus 3:9, KJV. See DEBATE, STRIFE, VARIANCE.

2. *paroxusmos* (παροξυσμός, 3948), (Eng., "paroxysm"), lit., "a sharpening," hence "a sharpening of the feeling, or action" (*para*, "beside," intensive, *oxus*, "sharp"), denotes an incitement, a sharp contention, Acts 15:39, the effect of irritation; elsewhere in Heb. 10:24, "provoke," unto love. See PROVOKE.¶

3. *philoneikia* (φιλονεικία, 5379), lit., "love of strife" (*phileō*, "to love," *neikos*, "strife"), signifies "eagerness to contend"; hence, a "contention," said of the disciples, Luke 22:24. Cf. B, 2.¶

B. Adjectives.

1. *amachos* (ἄμαχος, 269), lit., "not fighting" (*a*, negative, *machē*, "a fight, combat, quarrel"), primarily signifying "invincible," came to mean "not contentious," 1 Tim. 3:3, RV; Titus 3:2 (KJV, "not a brawler," "no brawlers").¶

2. *philoneikos* (φιλόνεικος, 5380), akin to A, No. 3, is used in 1 Cor. 11:16.¶ In the Sept., Ezek. 3:7, "stubborn."¶

Notes: (1) *Eritheia*, "contention," KJV, in Phil. 1:17, is translated "faction," in the RV. The phrase *hoi ex eritheias*, Rom. 2:8, lit., "those of strife," is rendered "contentious," in the KJV; RV, "factious." See FACTIOUS, STRIFE.

(2) For *agōn*, "a contest," "contention," 1 Thess. 2:2, KJV; "conflict, RV, see CONFLICT.

CONTINENCY

enkrateuomai (ἐγκρατεύομαι, 1467), *en*, "in," *kratos*, "power, strength," lit., "to have power over oneself," is rendered "(if they have not) continency" (i.e., are lacking in self-control), in 1 Cor. 7:9, RV; KJV, "can (not) contain"; in 9:25, "is temperate." See TEMPERATE.¶

CONTINUAL, CONTINUALLY (see also CONTINUE)

A. Adverbial Phrases.

1. *eis telos* (εἰς τέλος), lit., "unto (the) end," signifies "continual," in Luke 18:5, of the im-

portunate widow's applications to the unrighteous judge; see also Matt. 10:22; 24:13; Mark 13:13; John 13:1; 1 Thess. 2:16. Cf. *heōs telous*, lit., "until the end," 1 Cor. 1:8; 2 Cor. 1:13; ¶ *mechri telous*, ditto, Heb. 3:6, 14; ¶ *achri telous*, Heb. 6:11; Rev. 2:26.¶

2. *dia pantos* (διὰ παντός) is used of a "period throughout or during which anything is done"; it is said of the disciples' "continuance" in the Temple after the ascension of Christ, Luke 24:53; of the regular entrance of the priests into the first tabernacle, Heb. 9:6, RV (KJV "always"); of the constant sacrifice of praise enjoined upon believers, Heb. 13:15. See also Matt. 18:10; Mark 5:5; Acts 10:2; 24:16; Rom. 11:10; 2 Thess. 3:16, "at all times." See ALWAYS, No. 3, and Note under No. 3 below).¶

3. *eis to diēnekes* (εἰς τὸ διηνεκές), lit., "unto the carried-through" (*dia*, "through," *enenka*, "to carry"), i.e., unto (the) unbroken "continuance," is used of the continuous priesthood of Christ, Heb. 7:3, and of the "continual" offering of sacrifices under the Law, Heb. 10:1. It is translated "for ever," in Heb. 10:12, of the everlasting session of Christ at the right hand of God; and in 10:14, of the everlasting effects of His sacrifice upon "them that are sanctified." See EVER.¶

Note: No. 2 indicates that a certain thing is done frequently throughout a period; No. 3 stresses the unbroken continuity of what is mentioned.

B. Adjective.

adialeiptos (ἀδιάλειπτος, 88), "continual, unceasing": see CEASE, B.

CONTINUE, CONTINUANCE

1. *ginomai* (γίνομαι, 1096) signifies (*a*) "to begin to be" (suggesting origin); (*b*) "to become" (suggesting entrance on a new state); (*c*) "to come to pass" (suggesting effect); hence with the meaning (*c*) it is translated "continued" in Acts 19:10. See ARISE.

2. *diateleō* (διατελέω, 1300), "to bring through to an end" (*dia*, "through," *telos*, "an end"), "to finish fully" or, when used of time, "continue right through," is said of "continuing" fasting up to the time mentioned, Acts 27:33.¶

3. *menō* (μένω, 3306): see ABIDE. *Compounds of menō with this meaning, are as follows:*

4. *diamenō* (διαμένω, 1265), "to continue throughout," i.e., without interruption (No. 3 with *dia*, "through"), is said of the dumbness of Zacharias, Luke 1:22, KJV, "remained"; of the "continuance" of the disciples with Christ, Luke 22:28; of the permanency of the truth of the gospel with churches, Gal. 2:5; of the un-

changed course of things, 2 Pet. 3:4; of the eternal permanency of Christ, Heb. 1:11. See REMAIN.¶

5. *emmenō* (ἐμμένω, 1696), "to remain in" (*en*, "in"), is used of "abiding in a house," Acts 28:30 (in the best mss.); of "continuing" in the faith, Acts 14:22; in the Law, Gal. 3:10; in God's covenant, Heb. 8:9.¶

6. *epimenō* (ἐπιμένω, 1961), lit., "to remain on," i.e., in addition to (*epi*, "upon," and No. 3), "to continue long, still to abide," is used of "continuing" to ask, John 8:7; to knock, Acts 12:16; in the grace of God, 13:43; in sin, Rom. 6:1; in God's goodness, 11:22; in unbelief, 11:23 (KJV, "abide"); in the flesh, Phil. 1:24; in the faith, Col. 1:23; in doctrine, I Tim. 4:16; elsewhere of abiding in a place. See ABIDE, TARRY.

7. *paramenō* (παραμένω, 3887), "to remain by or near" (*para*, "beside," and No. 3), hence, "to continue or persevere in anything," is used of the inability of Levitical priests to "continue," Heb. 7:23; of persevering in the law of liberty, Jas. 1:25; it is translated "abide" in Phil. 1:25 (2nd clause, in the best mss.), RV [see *Note* (1)], and in 1 Cor. 16:6. See ABIDE.¶

8. *prosmenō* (προσμένω, 4357), "to remain with" (*pros*, "with," and No. 3), "to continue with a person," is said of the people with Christ, Matt. 15:32; Mark 8:2 (KJV, "been with"); of "continuing" in supplications and prayers, 1 Tim. 5:5. See ABIDE, CLEAVE (unto), TARRY.

9. *proskartereō* (προσκαρτερέω, 4342), lit., "to be strong towards" (*pros*, "towards," used intensively, and *kartereō*, "to be strong"), "to endure in, or persevere in, to be continually steadfast with a person or thing," is used of "continuing" in prayer with others, Acts 1:14; Rom. 12:12; Col. 4:2; in the apostles' teaching, Acts 2:42; in the Temple, 2:46 ("continuing steadfastly," RV), the adverb representing the intensive preposition; in prayer and the ministry, 6:4 (RV, "will continue steadfastly"); of Simon Magus with Philip, 8:13. In Mark 3:9 and Acts 10:7, it signifies "to wait on"; in Rom. 13:6, to attend "continually" upon. See ATTEND INSTANT, WAIT.¶

10. *dianuktereuō* (διανυκτερεύω, 1273), "to pass the night through" (*dia*, "through," *nux*, "a night"), "to continue all night," is found in Luke 6:12, of the Lord in spending all night in prayer.¶

Notes: (1) The following are translated by the verb "to continue," in the KJV, in the places mentioned: *diatribō*, "to tarry," (according to inferior mss.) John 11:54; Acts 15:35 (RV, "tarried"); *histēmi*, "to stand," Acts 26:22 (RV, "stand"); *kathizō*, "to sit down," Acts 18:11 (RV, "dwelt"); *parateinō*, "to extend, stretch," Acts

20:7 (RV, "prolonged"); *paramenō*, "to abide together with," Phil. 1:25, RV, "abide with"; the KJV, "continue," translating *sumparamenō* (in some mss.), marks the difference from the preceding *menō*. See ABIDE, No. 4.

(2) In Rom. 2:7, for KJV, "patient continuance," the RV has "patience" (lit., "according to patience").

(3) In Rev. 13:5 *poieō*, "to do," is rendered "to continue."

CONTRADICT, CONTRADICTION

A. Verb.

antilegō (ἀντιλέγω, 483), lit., "to speak against" (*anti*, "against," *legō*, "to speak"), is translated "contradict" in Acts 13:45. See ANSWER, GAINSAY, SPEAK (against).

B. Noun.

antilogia (ἀντιλογία, 485), akin to A, is translated "contradiction" in the KJV of Heb. 7:7; 12:3, "dispute," and "gainsaying." See DISPUTE, GAINSAY, STRIFE.

CONTRARIWISE

t'ounantion (τοὐναντίον, 5121), for *to enantion*, "the contrary, on the contrary or contrariwise," is used in 2 Cor. 2:7; Gal. 2:7; 1 Pet. 3:9.¶

CONTRARY

A. Verb.

antikeimai (ἀντίκειμαι, 480), "to be contrary" (*anti*, "against," *keimai*, "to lie"), Gal. 5:17; 1 Tim. 1:10. See ADVERSARY.

B. Prepositions.

1. *para* (παρά, 3844), "beside," has the meaning "contrary to" in Acts 18:13; Rom. 11:24; 16:17; "other than" in Gal. 1:8.

2. *apenanti* (ἀπέναντι, 561), lit., "from over against, opposite to" (*apo*, "from," *enantios*, "against"), is translated "contrary to" in Acts 17:7; "before" in Matt. 27:24; Rom. 3:18; "over against"; in Matt. 27:61; "in the presence of," in Acts 3:16.¶

Note: The most authentic mss. have *katenanti*, "over against," in Matt. 21:2.

C. Adjectives.

1. *enantios* (ἐναντίος, 1727), "over against" (*en*, "in," *antios*, "against"), is used primarily of place, Mark 15:39; of an opposing wind, Matt. 14:24; Mark 6:48; Acts 27:4; metaphorically, opposed as an adversary, antagonistic, Acts 26:9; 1 Thess. 2:15; Titus 2:8; Acts 28:17, "against."¶

2. *hupenantios* (ὑπεναντίος, 5227), *hupo*, "under," and No. 1, opposite to, is used of "that which is contrary to persons," Col. 2:14, and as

a noun, "adversaries," Heb. 10:27. See ADVER-SARY.¶

CONTRIBUTION

koinōnia (κοινωνία, 2842) is twice rendered "contribution," Rom. 15:26, and 2 Cor. 9:13, RV, (KJV, "distribution"). See COMMUNION.

CONTROVERSY (without)

homologoumenōs (ὁμολογουμένως, 3672), "confessedly, by common consent," akin to *homologeō*, "to confess" (*homos*, "same," *legō*, "to speak"), is rendered in 1 Tim. 3:16 "without controversy"; some translate it "confessedly." See CONFESS, A, No. 1, and B.¶

CONVENIENT, CONVENIENTLY

A. Adjective.

eukairos (εὔκαιρος, 2121), lit., "well-timed" (*eu*, "well," *kairos*, "a time, season"), hence signifies "timely, opportune, convenient"; it is said of a certain day, Mark 6:21; elsewhere, Heb. 4:16, "in time of need." See NEED.¶ Cf. *eukairia*, "opportunity," Matt. 26:16; Luke 22:6;¶ *eukaireō*, "to have opportunity," Mark 6:31; Acts 17:21 ("they spent their time," marg. "had leisure for nothing else"); 1 Cor. 16:12. See OPPORTUNITY, NEED, C, *Note*.¶

B. Adverb.

eukairōs (εὐκαίρως, 2122), "conveniently," Mark 14:11, is used elsewhere in 2 Tim. 4:2, "in season." ¶ See SEASON, C.

C. Verbs.

1. *anēkō* (ἀνήκω, 433) is rendered "befitting" in Eph. 5:4, for KJV, "convenient"; so in Philem. 8. See BEFIT.

2. *kathēkō* (καθήκω, 2520), "to be fitting," is so translated in Rom. 1:28, RV; KJV, "(not) convenient"; in Acts 22:22, "it is (not) fit." See FIT.¶

CONVERSATION

This word is not used in the RV, as it does not now express the meaning of the words so translated in the KJV. These are as follows:

A. Nouns.

1. *anastrophē* (ἀναστροφή, 391): see BE-HAVIOR, B, No. 1.

2. *tropos* (τρόπος, 5158), "a turning, a manner," is translated simply "be ye," RV in Heb. 13:5, instead of "let your conversation be." See MANNER, MEANS, WAY.

3. *politeuma* (πολίτευμα, 4175): see CITI-ZENSHIP, No. 4.

B. Verbs.

1. *anastrephō* (ἀναστρέφω, 390): see BE-HAVE, A, No. 1.

2. *politeuō* (πολιτεύω, 4176): see CITIZEN-SHIP, No. 4, *Note*.

CONVERT, CONVERSION

A. Verbs.

1. *strephō* (στρέφω, 4762), "to turn," is translated "be converted" in Matt. 18:3, KJV. See TURN.

2. *epistrephō* (ἐπιστρέφω, 1994), "to turn about, turn towards" (*epi*, "towards" and No. 1), is used transitively, and so rendered "convert" (of causing a person to turn) in Jas. 5:19–20. Elsewhere, where the KJV translates this verb, either in the middle voice and intransitive use, or the passive, the RV adheres to the middle voice significance, and translates by "turn again," Matt. 13:15; Mark 4:12; Luke 22:32; Acts 3:19; 28:27. See COME (again), *Note* (4), GO (again), RETURN, TURN.

B. Noun.

epistrophē (ἐπιστροφή, 1995), akin to A, No. 2, "a turning about, or round, conversion," is found in Acts 15:3. The word implies "a turning from and a turning to"; corresponding to these are repentance and faith; cf. "turned to God from idols" (1 Thess. 1:9). Divine grace is the efficient cause, human agency the responding effect.¶

CONVEY

ekneuō (ἐκνεύω, 1593), primarily, "to bend to one side, to turn aside"; then "to take oneself away, withdraw," is found in John 5:13, of Christ's "conveying" Himself away from one place to another. Some have regarded the verb as having the same meaning as *ekneō*, "to escape," as from peril, "slip away secretly"; but the Lord did not leave the place where He had healed the paralytic in order to escape danger, but to avoid the applause of the throng.¶

CONVICT (*including the* KJV, *"convince"*)

1. *elenchō* (ἐλέγχω, 1651) signifies (*a*) "to convict, confute, refute," usually with the suggestion of putting the convicted person to shame; see Matt. 18:15, where more than telling the offender his fault is in view; it is used of "convicting" of sin, John 8:46; 16:8; gainsayers in regard to the faith, Titus 1:9; transgressors of the Law, Jas. 2:9; some texts have the verb in John 8:9; (*b*) "to reprove," 1 Cor. 14:24, RV (for KJV, "convince"), for the unbeliever is there viewed as being reproved for, or "convicted" of, his sinful state; so in Luke 3:19; it is used of reproving works, John 3:20; Eph. 5:11, 13; 1 Tim. 5:20; 2 Tim. 4:2; Titus 1:13; 2:15; all

these speak of reproof by word of mouth. In Heb. 12:5 and Rev. 3:19, the word is used of reproving by action. See FAULT, REBUKE, REPROVE.¶

2. *exelenchō* (ἐξελέγχω, 1827), an intensive form of No. 1, "to convict thoroughly," is used of the Lord's future "conviction" of the ungodly, Jude 15.¶

Note: For *diakatelenchō*, "to confute powerfully in disputation," Acts 18:28 (KJV, "convinced"), see CONFUTE.¶

COOL

katapsuchō (καταψύχω, 2711), Luke 16:24, denotes "to cool off, make cool" (*kata*, "down," *psuchō*, "to cool").¶ In the Sept., Gen. 18:4.¶

For **COPPERSMITH** see under **BRASS**

COPY

hupodeigma (ὑπόδειγμα, 5262), from *hupo*, "under," *deiknumi*, "to show," properly denotes "what is shown below or privately"; it is translated "example," Heb. 8:5, KJV (RV, "copy"). It signifies (*a*) a sign suggestive of anything, the delineation or representation of a thing, and so, a figure, "copy"; in Heb. 9:23 the RV has "copies," for the KJV, "patterns"; (*b*) an example for imitation, John 13:15; Jas. 5:10; for warning, Heb. 4:11; 2 Pet. 2:6 (KJV "ensample"). See EXAMPLE, PATTERN. ¶

Note: Cf. *hupogrammos* (*hupo*, "under," *graphō*, "to write"), "an underwriting, a writing copy, an example," is used in 1 Pet. 2:21.

CORBAN

korban (κορβᾶν, 2878) signifies (*a*) "an offering," and was a Hebrew term for any sacrifice, whether by the shedding of blood or otherwise; (*b*) "a gift offered to God," Mark 7:11.¶ Jews were much addicted to rash vows; a saying of the rabbis was, "It is hard for the parents, but the law is clear, vows must be kept." The Sept. translates the word by *dōron*, "a gift." See *korbanas*, under TREASURY, Matt. 27:6.¶

CORD

schoinion (σχοινίον, 4979), "a cord or rope," a diminutive of *schoinos*, "a rush, bulrush," meant a "cord" made of rushes; it denotes (*a*) "a small cord," John 2:15 (plural), (*b*) "a rope," Acts 27:32. See ROPE.¶

CORN, CORNFIELD

1. *sitos* (σῖτος, 4621), "wheat, corn"; in the plural, "grain," is translated "corn" in Mark 4:28; "wheat," Matt. 3:12; 13:25, 29–30; Luke 3:17; 12:18 (some mss. have *genēmata*, "fruits," here); 16:7; 22:31; John 12:24; Acts 27:38; 1 Cor. 15:37; Rev. 6:6; 18:13. See WHEAT.¶

2. *sition* (σίτιον, 4621*), "corn, grain," a diminutive of No. 1, is found in Acts 7:12.¶

3. *sporimos* (σπόριμος, 4702), lit., "sown, or fit for sowing" (*speirō* "to sow, scatter seed"), denotes, in the plural, "sown fields, fields of grain, cornfields," Matt. 12:1, RV; Mark 2:23; Luke 6:1 (cf. *spora*, 1 Pet. 1:23,¶ and *sporos*, "seed").¶

4. *stachus* (στάχυς, 4719) means "an ear of grain," Matt. 12:1; Mark 2:23; 4:28; Luke 6:1. Cf. the name *Stachys* in Rom. 16:9.¶

Notes: (1) *Aloaō*, "to thresh," from *alōn*, "a threshing-floor," is translated "treadeth out (the) corn," in 1 Cor. 9:9–10 and 1 Tim. 5:18. Cf. THRESH, TREAD.¶

(2) *Kokkos*, "a grain" (its regular meaning), is translated "corn" in the KJV of John 12:24 (RV, "grain"). See GRAIN.

CORNER, CORNERSTONE

1. *gōnia* (γωνία, 1137), "an angle" (Eng., "coign"), signifies (*a*) "an external angle," as of the "corner" of a street, Matt. 6:5; or of a building, 21:42; Mark 12:10; Luke 20:17; Acts 4:11; 1 Pet. 2:7, "the corner stone or head-stone of the corner" (see below); or the four extreme limits of the earth, Rev. 7:1; 20:8; (*b*) "an internal corner," a secret place, Acts 26:26. See QUARTER.¶

2. *archē* (ἀρχή, 746), "a beginning" (its usual meaning), "first in time, order, or place," is used to denote the extremities or "corners" of a sheet, Acts 10:11; 11:5. See BEGINNING.

Note: For the adjective *akrogōniaios* (from *akros*, "extreme, highest," and No. 1), "a chief corner stone," see CHIEF. They were laid so as to give strength to the two walls with which they were connected. So Christ unites Jew and Gentile, Eph. 2:20; again, as one may carelessly stumble over the "corner stone," when turning the "corner," so Christ proved a stumbling stone to Jews, 1 Pet. 2:6.

CORPSE

ptoma (πτῶμα, 4430) : see BODY, No. 3.

CORRECT, CORRECTION, CORRECTOR, CORRECTING

A. Nouns.

1. *diorthōma* (διόρθωμα, 1357v) signifies "a reform, amendment, correction," lit., "a making straight" (*dia*, "through," *orthoō*, "to make straight"). In Acts 24:2, lit., "reformations come about (or take place, lit., 'become')," the RV has "evils are corrected," KJV, "worthy deeds are done"; there is no word for "worthy" or for "deeds" in the original. Some texts have *katorthōma*, which has the same meaning.¶ See *diorthōsis*, "reformation," Heb. 9:10.¶

2. *epanorthōsis* (ἐπανόρθωσις, 1882), lit., "a restoration to an upright or right state" (*epi*, "to," *ana*, "up, or again," and *orthoō*, see No. 1), hence, "correction," is used of the Scripture in 2 Tim. 3:16, referring to improvement of life and character.¶

3. *paideutēs* (παιδευτής, 3810) has two meanings, corresponding to the two meanings of the verb *paideuō* (see below) from which it is derived, (*a*) "a teacher, preceptor, corrector," Rom. 2:20 (KJV, "instructor"), (*b*) "a chastiser," Heb. 12:9, rendered "to chasten" (KJV, "which corrected"; lit., "chastisers"). See INSTRUCTOR.¶

B. Verb.

paideuō (παιδεύω, 381), "to train up a child" (*pais*), is rendered "correcting in 2 Tim. 2:25, RV, KJV, "instructing." See CHASTEN.

CORRUPT, verb and adjective. CORRUPTION, CORRUPTIBLE, INCORRUPTION, INCORRUPTIBLE

A. Verbs.

1. *kapēleuō* (καπηλεύω, 2585) primarily signifies "to be a retailer, to peddle, to huckster-ize" (from *kapēlos*, "an inn-keeper, a petty re-tailer, especially of wine, a huckster, peddler," in contrast to *emporos*, "a merchant"); hence, "to get base gain by dealing in anything," and so, more generally, "to do anything for sordid personal advantage." It is found in 2 Cor. 2:17, with reference to the ministry of the gospel. The significance can be best ascertained by com-parison and contrast with the verb *doloō* (δολόω) in 4:2 (likewise there only in the NT), "to handle deceitfully." The meanings are not identical. While both involve the deceitful deal-ing of adulterating the word of truth, *kapēleuō* has the broader significance of doing so in order to make dishonest gain. Those to whom the apostle refers in 2:17 are such as make mer-chandise of souls through covetousness (cf. Titus 1:11; 2 Pet. 2:3, 14–15; Jude 11, 16; Ezek. 13:19); accordingly "hucksterizing" would be

the most appropriate rendering in this passage, while "handling deceitfully" is the right mean-ing in 4:2. See Trench, *Syn.* §lxii.¶ In Isa. 1:22, the Sept. has "thy wine-merchants" (*kapēloi*, "hucksterizers").¶

2. *phtheirō* (φθείρω, 5351) signifies "to de-stroy by means of corrupting," and so "bringing into a worse state"; (*a*) with this significance it is used of the effect of evil company upon the manners of believers, and so of the effect of association with those who deny the truth and hold false doctrine, 1 Cor. 15:33 (this was a saying of the pagan poet Menander, which be-came a well known proverb); in 2 Cor. 7:2, of the effects of dishonorable dealing by bringing people to want (a charge made against the apostle); in 11:3, of the effects upon the minds (or thoughts) of believers by "corrupting" them "from the simplicity and the purity that is to-ward Christ"; in Eph. 4:22, intransitively, of the old nature in waxing "corrupt," "morally de-caying, on the way to final ruin" (Moule), "after the lusts of deceit"; in Rev. 19:2, metaphori-cally, of the Babylonish harlot, in "corrupting" the inhabitants of the earth by her false religion.

(*b*) With the significance of destroying, it is used of marring a local church by leading it away from that condition of holiness of life and purity of doctrine in which it should abide, 1 Cor. 3:17 (KJV, "defile"), and of God's retri-butive destruction of the offender who is guilty of this sin (id.); of the effects of the work of false and abominable teachers upon themselves, 2 Pet. 2:12 (some texts have *kataphtheirō*; KJV, "shall utterly perish"), and Jude 10 (KJV, "cor-rupt themselves." RV, marg., "are corrupted"). See DEFILE and DESTROY.¶

3. *diaphtheirō* (διαφθείρω, 1311), *dia*, "through," intensive, and No. 2, "to corrupt utterly, through and through," is said of men "corrupted in mind," whose wranglings result from the doctrines of false teachers, 1 Tim. 6:5 (the KJV wrongly renders it as an adjective, "corrupt"). It is translated "destroyeth" instead of "corrupteth," in the RV of Luke 12:33, of the work of a moth; in Rev. 8:9, of the effect of divine judgments hereafter upon navigation; in 11:18, of the divine retribution of destruction upon those who have destroyed the earth; in 2 Cor. 4:16 it is translated "is decaying," said of the human body. See DESTROY, PERISH.¶

4. *kataphtheirō* (καταφθείρω, 2704), *kata*, "down," intensive, and No. 2, is said of men who are reprobate concerning the faith, "cor-rupted in mind" (KJV, "corrupt"), 2 Tim. 3:8. For 2 Pet. 2:12, RV, "shall be destroyed," see No. 2.¶

5. *sēpō* (σήπω, 4595) signifies "to make cor-

rupt, to destroy"; in the passive voice with middle sense, "to become corrupt or rotten, to perish," said of riches, Jas. 5:2, of the gold and silver of the luxurious rich who have ground down their laborers. The verb is derived from a root signifying "to rot off, drop to pieces."¶

6. *aphanizō* (ἀφανίζω, 853): see CONSUME, No. 3.

B. Nouns.

1. *phthora* (φθορά, 5356), connected with *phtheirō*, No. 2, above, signifies "a bringing or being brought into an inferior or worse condition, a destruction or corruption." It is used (*a*) physically, (1), of the condition of creation, as under bondage, Rom. 8:21; (2) of the effect of the withdrawal of life, and so of the condition of the human body in burial, 1 Cor. 15:42; (3) by metonymy, of anything which is liable to "corruption," 1 Cor. 15:50; (4) of the physical effects of merely gratifying the natural desires and ministering to one's own needs or lusts, Gal. 6:8, to the flesh in contrast to the Spirit, "corruption" being antithetic to "eternal life"; (5) of that which is naturally short-lived and transient, Col. 2:22, "perish"; (*b*) of the death and decay of beasts, 2 Pet. 2:12, RV, "destroyed" (first part of verse; lit., "unto . . . destruction"); (*c*) ethically, with a moral significance, (1) of the effect of lusts, 2 Pet. 1:4; (2) of the effect upon themselves of the work of false and immoral teachers, 2 Pet. 2:12, RV, "destroying"; KJV, "corruption," and verse 19. See DESTROY, PERISH.¶

Note: There is nothing in any of these words suggesting or involving annihilation.

2. *diaphthora* (διαφθορά, 1312), an intensified form of No. 1, "utter or thorough corruption," referring in the NT to physical decomposition and decay, is used six times, five of which refer, negatively, to the body of God's "Holy One," after His death, which body, by reason of His absolute holiness, could not see "corruption," Acts 2:27, 31; 13:34–35, 37; once it is used of a human body, that of David, which, by contrast, saw "corruption," Acts 13:36.¶

3. *aphtharsia* (ἀφθαρσία, 861), "incorruption," *a*, negative, with A, No. 2, is used (*a*) of the resurrection body, 1 Cor. 15:42, 50, 53–54; (*b*) of a condition associated with glory and honor and life, including perhaps a moral significance, Rom. 2:7; 2 Tim. 1:10; this is wrongly translated "immortality" in the KJV; (*c*) of love to Christ, that which is sincere and undiminishing, Eph. 6:24 (translated "uncorruptness"). See IMMORTALITY, SINCERITY.¶

Note: For Titus 2:7 (where some texts have *aphtharsia*), see No. 4.

4. *aphthoria* (ἀφθορία, 5356d), similar to No. 3, "uncorruptness, free from (moral) taint," is said of doctrine, Titus 2:7 (some texts have *adiaphthoria*, the negative form of No. 2, above).¶

C. Adjectives.

1. *phthartos* (φθαρτός, 5349), "corruptible," akin to A, No. 2, is used (*a*) of man as being mortal, liable to decay (in contrast to God), Rom. 1:23; (*b*) of man's body as death-doomed, 1 Cor. 15:53–54; (*c*) of a crown of reward at the Greek games, 1 Cor. 9:25; (*d*) of silver and gold, as specimens or "corruptible" things, 1 Pet. 1:18; (*e*) of natural seed, 1 Pet. 1:23.¶

2. *apthartos* (ἄφθαρτος, 862), "not liable to corruption or decay, incorruptible" (*a*, negative, and A, No. 2), is used of (*a*) God, Rom. 1:23; 1 Tim 1:17 (KJV, "immortal"); (*b*) the raised dead, 1 Cor. 15:52; (*c*) rewards given to the saints hereafter, metaphorically described as a "crown," 1 Cor. 9:25; (*d*) the eternal inheritance of the saints, 1 Pet. 1:4; (*e*) the Word of God, as incorruptible" seed, 1 Pet. 1:23; (*f*) a meek and quiet spirit, metaphorically spoken of as "incorruptible" apparel, 1 Pet. 3:4. See IMMORTAL.¶

3. *sapros* (σαπρός, 4550), "corrupt," akin to *sēpō*, A, No. 5; see BAD, No. 3.

Note: (1) Trench, *Syn.* §lxviii, contrasts this with *amarantos*, and *amarantinos*, "unwithering, not fading away," 1 Pet. 1:4; 5:4. These are, however, distinct terms (see FADE) and are not strictly synonymous, though used in the same description of the heavenly inheritance.

COST, COSTLINESS, COSTLY

A. Nouns.

1. *dapanē* (δαπάνη, 1160), "expense, cost" (from *daptō*, "to tear"; from a root *dap*— meaning "to divide"), is found in Luke 14:28, in the Lord's illustration of counting the "cost" of becoming His disciple. Cf. *dapanaō*, "to spend," and its compounds, under CHARGE, SPEND.¶

2. *timiotēs* (τιμιότης, 5094), "costliness" (from *timios*, "valued at great price, precious"; see No. 3, below), is connected with *timē*, "honor, price," and used in Rev. 18:19, in reference to Babylon.¶

B. Adjectives.

1. *timios* (τίμιος, 5093), akin to A, No. 2, is translated "costly" in 1 Cor. 3:12, of "costly" stones, in a metaphorical sense (KJV, "precious"). Cf. Rev. 17:4; 18:12, 16; 21:19. See DEAR, HONORABLE, PRECIOUS, REPUTATION.

2. *polutelēs* (πολυτελής, 4185), primarily, "the very end or limit" (from *polus*, "much," *telos*, "revenue"), with reference to price, of highest "cost," very expensive, is said of spiken-

ard, Mark 14:3; raiment, 1 Tim. 2:9; metaphorically, of a meek and quiet spirit, 1 Pet. 3:4, "of great price"; cf. No. 1 and A, No. 2, above. See PRECIOUS, PRICE.¶

3. *polutimos* (πολύτιμος, 4186), lit., "of great value" (see A, No. 2 and B, No. 1), is used of a pearl, Matt. 13:46; of spikenard, John 12:3 (RV, "very precious," KJV "very costly"). See PRICE.¶ The comparative *polutimo (v.l.iō)teros*, "much more precious," is used in 1 Pet. 1:7.¶

COUCH

1. *klinidion* (κλινίδιον, 2826), "a small bed," a diminutive form of *klinē*, "a bed" (from *klinō*, "to incline, recline"), is used in Luke 5:19, 24 of the "bed" (*klinē*, in v. 18) on which the palsied man was brought. See BED.¶

2. *krabbatos* (κράββατος, 2895): see BED, No. 4.

COULD

1. *echō* (ἔχω, 2192), "to have," is rendered "could" in Mark 14:8, "she hath done what she could," lit., "she hath done what she had." See HAVE.

2. *ischuō* (ἰσχύω, 2480), "to have strength," is translated in Mark 14:37 "couldest thou not." See ABLE.

Notes: (1) *Emblepō* in Acts 22:11, lit., "I was not seeing," is translated "I could not see." See BEHOLD.

(2) See CAN, when not used as part of another verb.

COUNCIL, COUNCILLOR

1. *sumboulion* (συμβούλιον, 4824), "a uniting in counsel" (*sun*, "together," *boulē*, "counsel, advice"), denotes (*a*) "counsel" which is given, taken and acted upon, e.g., Matt. 12:14, RV, "took counsel," for KJV, "held a council"; 22:15; hence (*b*) "a council," an assembly of counsellors or persons in consultation, Acts 25:12, of the "council" with which Festus conferred concerning Paul. The governors and procurators of provinces had a board of advisers or assessors, with whom they took "counsel," before pronouncing judgment. See CONSULTATION.

2. *sunedrion* (συνέδριον, 4892), properly, "a settling together" (*sun*, "together," *hedra*, "a seat"), hence, (*a*) "any assembly or session of persons deliberating or adjusting," as in the Sept. of Ps. 26:4 (lit., "with a council of vanity"); Prov. 22:10; Jer. 15:17, etc.; in the NT, e.g., Matt. 10:17; Mark 13:9; John 11:47, in particular, it denoted (*b*) "the Sanhedrin," the Great Council at Jerusalem, consisting of 71 members, namely, prominent members of the families of the high priest, elders and scribes.

The Jews trace the origin of this to Num. 11:16. The more important causes came up before this tribunal. The Roman rulers of Judea permitted the Sanhedrin to try such cases, and even to pronounce sentence of death, with the condition that such a sentence should be valid only if confirmed by the Roman procurator. In John 11:47, it is used of a meeting of the Sanhedrin; in Acts 4:15, of the place of meeting.

3. *bouleutēs* (βουλευτής, 1010): Joseph of Arimathaea is described as "a councillor of honorable estate," Mark 15:43, RV; cf. Luke 23:50 (not as KJV, "counsellor").¶

COUNSEL. For COUNSELLOR see above.

A. Nouns.

1. *boulē* (βουλή, 1012): see under ADVICE.

2. *sumboulos* (σύμβουλος, 4825), "a councillor with," occurs in Rom.11:34.¶

B. Verbs.

1. *bouleuō* (βουλεύω, 1011), "to take counsel, to resolve," is used in the middle voice in the NT, "took counsel" in Acts 5:33, KJV (RV translates *boulomai*); both in 27:39; in Luke 14:31, RV "take counsel" (KJV, "consulteth"); in John 11:53, KJV and RV (so the best mss.); 12:10, RV, "took counsel," for KJV, "consulted"; in 2 Cor. 1:17 (twice), "purpose." See CONSULT, MINDED, PURPOSE.¶

2. *sumbouleuō* (συμβουλεύω, 4823), in the active voice, "to advise, to counsel," John 18:14, "gave counsel"; in Rev. 3:18, "I counsel"; in the middle voice, "to take counsel, consult," Matt. 26:4, RV, "took counsel together," for KJV, "consulted"; Acts 9:23, "took counsel" (RV adds "together"); in some mss. John 11:53. See CONSULT.¶

COUNT

1. *echō* (ἔχω, 2192), "to have, to hold"; then, "to hold in the mind, to regard, to count," has this significance in Matt. 14:5, "they counted Him as a prophet"; Philem. 17, "If then thou countest me a partner"; Mark 11:32, KJV, (RV, "hold"); Acts 20:24, KJV. See ABLE.

2. *hēgeomai* (ἡγέομαι, 2233), primarily, "to lead the way"; hence, "to lead before the mind, account," is found with this meaning in Phil. 2:3, RV (KJV, "esteem"); 2:6, RV (KJV, "thought"); 2:25 (KJV, "supposed"); Phil. 3:7–8; 2 Thess. 3:15; 1 Tim. 1:12; 6:1; Heb. 10:29; Jas. 1:2; Heb. 11:11 (KJV, "judged"); 2 Pet. 2:13; 3:9. See ACCOUNT.

3. *logizomai* (λογίζομαι, 3049), "to reckon," is rendered "count" in 2 Cor. 10:2, RV (KJV,

"think"); "counted" in the KJV of Rom. 2:26; 4:3, 5; 9:8 (RV, "reckoned").

4. *psēphizō* (ψηφίζω, 5585), akin to *psēphos*, "a stone," used in voting, occurs in Luke 14:28; Rev. 13:18.¶

5. *sumpsēphizō* (συμψηφίζω, 4860), "to count up," occurs in Acts 19:19.¶

Note: In Jas. 5:11, *makarizō*, "to pronounce blessed," is rendered "count ... happy," KJV (RV, "call ..."). For *kataxioō* see ACCOUNT, No. 5. For "descent is counted" see GENEALOGY.

COUNTENANCE

1. *opsis* (ὄψις, 3799): only Rev. 1:16 has "countenance." See APPEARANCE.

2. *prosōpon* (πρόσωπον, 4383) is translated "countenance" in Luke 9:29; Acts 2:28, and in the KJV of 2 Cor. 3:7 (RV, "face"). See APPEARANCE.

3. *eidea* (εἰδέα, 2397), akin to *eidon*, "to see": see APPEARANCE.

Notes: (1) In Acts 13:24 *prosōpon* is translated "before" (lit., "before the presence of His coming").

(2) *Skuthrōpos*, "of a sad countenance" (*skuthros*, "gloomy, sad," *ōps*, "an eye"), is used in Matt. 6:16 and Luke 24:17, "sad."

(3) *Stugnazō*, "to be or become hateful, gloomy, in aspect," is translated "his countenance fell," Mark 10:22, RV (KJV, "he was sad"). It is used of the heaven or sky in Matt. 16:3, "lowring." See LOWRING.¶

COUNTRY

A. Nouns.

1. *agros* (ἀγρός, 68) denotes "a field, especially a cultivated field"; hence, "the country" in contrast to the town (Eng., "agrarian, agriculture"), e.g., Mark 5:14; 6:36; 15:21; 16:12; Luke 8:34; 9:12 (plural, lit., "fields"); 23:26; a piece of ground, e.g., Mark 10:29; Acts 4:37. See FARM.

2. *patris* (πατρίς, 3968) primarily signifies "one's fatherland, native country, of one's own town," Matt. 13:54, 57; Mark 6:1, 4; Luke 4: 23–24; John 4:44; Heb. 11:14.¶

3. *chōra* (χώρα, 5561) properly denotes "the space lying between two limits or places"; accordingly it has a variety of meanings: "country," Matt. 2:12; 8:28; Mark 1:5, RV (KJV, "land"); 5:1, 10; Luke 2:8; 8:26; 15:13–14, RV (KJV, "land"), 15; 19:12; 21:21; Acts 10:39, RV (KJV, "land"); 12:20; 26:20, RV (KJV, "coasts"); 27:27; in Mark 6:55 (in the best mss.) and Acts 18:23, RV, "region." See COAST, FIELD, GROUND, LAND, REGION.

4. *perichōros* (περίχωρος, 4066), *peri*, "around," and No. 3, signifies "country round about," Luke 8:37; "country about," Luke 3:3, KJV (RV, "region round about"); in Matt. 14:35 and Luke 4:37, KJV, "country round about" (RV, "region round about"); Matt. 3:5; Mark 1:28; Luke 4:14; 7:17; Acts 14:6. See REGION.¶

5. *meros* (μέρος, 3313), "a part," is rendered "country" in Acts 19:1, RV.

Note: Some inferior mss. have No. 4 in Mark 6:55, for No. 3.

B. Adjectives.

1. *anōterikos* (ἀνωτερικός, 510), "upper," is used in the plural in Acts 19:1, to denote "upper regions," with KJV, "coast," RV, "country," i.e., the high central plateau, in contrast to the roundabout way by the river through the valley. See COAST.¶

2. *oreinos* (ὀρεινός, 3714), "hilly" (from *oros*, "a hill, mountain"), is translated "hill country" in Luke 1:39, 65.¶

C. Verb.

apodēmeō (ἀποδημέω, 589) signifies "to go or travel into a far country," lit., "to be away from one's people" (*apo*, "from," *dēmos*, "a people"), Matt. 21:33; 25:14; in v. 15 the verb is translated in the RV, "went on his journey" (KJV, "took his journey"); Mark 12:1; Luke 20:9, "went into another country," RV. In Luke 15:13 both versions translate by "took his journey" ("into a far country" being separately expressed); see JOURNEY.¶

Cf. *apodēmos*, lit., "away from one's own people, gone abroad," Mark 13:34.¶

Notes: (1) *Gē*, "earth, land," is translated "country" in the KJV of Matt. 9:31 and Acts 7:3; RV, "land." See LAND.

(2) *Genos*, "a race," is mistranslated "country" in the KJV of Acts 4:36 (RV, "by race"). See below.

COUNTRYMEN

1. *genos* (γένος, 1085) properly denotes "an offspring"; then, "a family"; then, "a race, nation; otherwise, a kind or species"; it is translated "countrymen," in 2 Cor. 11:26, in Paul's reference to his fellow-nationals; so in Gal. 1:14, RV, for KJV, "nation." See BEGET.

2. *sumphuletēs* (συμφυλέτης, 4853), lit., "a fellow-tribesman" (*sun*, "with," *phulē*, "a tribe, race, nation, people"), hence, one who is of the same people, a fellow-countryman, is found in 1 Thess. 2:14.¶

COUPLED

Note: The word "coupled" is inserted in italics in 1 Pet. 3:2, the more adequately to express the original, which is, lit., "your chaste behavior in fear."

COURAGE

A. Noun.

tharsos (θάρσος, 2294), akin to *thurseō*, "to be of good cheer," is found in Acts 28:15.¶

B. Verb.

tharreō (θαρρέω, 2292) is translated by some form of the verb "to be of good courage," in the RV in five of the six places where it is used: 2 Cor. 5:6, "being of good courage" (KJV, "we are . . . confident"); 5:8, "we are of good courage" (KJV, "we are confident"); 7:16, "I am of good courage" (KJV, "I have confidence"); 10:1, "I am of good courage" (KJV, "I am bold"); 10:2, "show courage" (KJV, "be bold"); Heb. 13:6, "with good courage," lit., "being of good courage" (KJV, "boldly"). See BOLD, CONFIDENCE.¶

Note: Tharreō is a later form of *tharseō*. Cf. *tolmaō*, "to be bold."

COURSE

A. Nouns.

1. *aiōn* (αἰών, 165), "an age" (see AGE), is sometimes wrongly spoken of as a "dispensation," which does not mean a period of time, but a mode of dealing. It is translated "course" in Eph. 2:2, "the course of this world," i.e., the cycle or present round of things. See AGE, ETERNAL, EVER, WORLD.

2. *dromos* (δρόμος, 1408), properly, "a running, a race" (from *edramon*, "to run"), hence, metaphorically, denotes "a career, course of occupation, or of life," viewed in a special aspect, Acts 13:25; 20:24; 2 Tim. 4:7.¶

3. *ephēmeria* (ἐφημερία, 2183), primarily, "daily service," as, e.g., in the Sept. of 2 Chron. 13:11 (from *epi*, "upon, or by," *hēmera*, "a day," Eng., "ephemeral"), hence denoted a "class," or "course," into which the priests were divided for the daily service in the Temple, each "class" serving for seven days (see 1 Chron. 9:25). In the NT it is used in Luke 1:5, 8.¶

Note: Cf. *ephēmeros*, "daily (food)," Jas. 2:15.¶

4. *trochos* (τροχός, 5164), "a wheel," is translated "wheel" in Jas. 3:6, RV, with metaphorical reference to the round of human activity (KJV, "course"), as a glowing axle would set on fire the whole wooden wheel.¶

B. Verb.

chōreō (χωρέω, 5562), "to make room for, to go forward," is rendered "hath not free course," in John 8:37, RV (KJV, "hath no place"). See COME, No. 24.

Notes: (1) Connected with *dromos*, A, No. 2, is *euthudromeō*, "to make (or run) a straight course" (*euthus*, "straight"), Acts 16:11 and 21:1.¶ (2) In 2 Thess. 3:1, *trechō*, "to run" (RV), is translated "have free course" (KJV).¶ (3) In 1 Cor. 14:27, *ana meros*, "by turn," "in turn" (RV), is rendered "by course" (KJV). (4) For *ploos*, "a sailing or voyage, course," Acts 21:7, KJV (RV, "voyage"), see VOYAGE.

COURT

1. *agoraios* (ἀγοραῖος, 60) is an adjective, "signifying pertaining to the *agora*, any place of public meeting, and especially where trials were held," Acts 19:38; the RV translates the sentence "the courts are open"; a more literal rendering is "court days are kept." In Acts 17:5 it is translated in the RV, "rabble"; KJV, "baser sort," lit., "frequenters of the markets." See BASER.¶

2. *aulē* (αὐλή, 833), primarily, "an uncovered space around a house, enclosed by a wall, where the stables were," hence was used to describe (*a*) "the courtyard of a house"; in the OT it is used of the "courts" of the tabernacle and Temple; in this sense it is found in the NT in Rev. 11:2; (*b*) "the courts in the dwellings of well-to-do folk," which usually had two, one exterior, between the door and the street (called the *proaulion*, or "porch," Mark 14:68.¶), the other, interior, surrounded by the buildings of the dwellings, as in Matt. 26:69 (in contrast to the room where the judges were sitting); Mark 14:66; Luke 22:55; KJV, "hall"; RV "court" gives the proper significance, Matt. 26:3, 58; Mark 14:54; 15:16 (RV, "Praetorium"); Luke 11:21; John 18:15. It is here to be distinguished from the Praetorium, translated "palace." See HALL, PALACE. For the other meaning "sheepfold," John 10:1, 16, see FOLD.¶

3. *basileion* (βασίλειον, 933), an adjective meaning "royal," signifies, in the neuter plural, "a royal palace," translated "kings' courts" in Luke 7:25; in the singular, 1 Pet. 2:9, "royal." See ROYAL.¶

COURTEOUS, COURTEOUSLY

A. Adjective.

tapeinophrōn (ταπεινόφρων), "lowly-minded," is used in 1 Pet. 3:8, "be courteous," KJV (RV, "humble-minded").¶

B. Adverbs.

1. *philophronōs* (φιλοφρόνως, 5390), lit., "friendly," or, more fully, "with friendly thoughtfulness" (*philos*, "friend," *phrēn*, "the mind"), is found in Acts 28:7, of the hospitality showed by Publius to Paul and his fellow-shipwrecked travelers.¶

Note: Some mss. have the corresponding adjective *philophrōn*, "courteous," in 1 Pet. 3:8; the most authentic mss. have *tapeinophrōn*, "humble-minded."

2. *philanthrōpōs* (φιλανθρώπως, 5364) is translated "courteously" in Acts 27:3, KJV; RV, "kindly" (Eng., "philanthropically"). See KINDLY.¶

COUSIN

1. *anepsios* (ἀνεψιός, 431), in Col. 4:10 denotes a "cousin" rather than a nephew (KJV, "sister's son"). "Cousin" is its meaning in various periods of Greek writers.¶ In this sense it is used in the Sept., in Num. 36:11.¶ In later writings it denotes a nephew; hence the KJV rendering. As Lightfoot says, there is no reason to suppose that the apostle would have used it in any other than its proper sense. We are to understand, therefore, that Mark was the cousin of Barnabas. See SISTER.

2. *sungenis* (συγγενίς, 4773v) in Luke 1:36 (so in the most authentic mss.) and *sungenēs* in v. 58 (plural), KJV, "cousin" and "cousins," respectively signify "kinswoman" and "kinsfolk," (RV); so the RV and KJV in 2:44 and 21:16. The word lit. signifies "born with," i.e., of the same stock, or descent; hence "kinsman, kindred." See KIN, KINSFOLK, KINSWOMAN.

COVENANT (Noun and Verb)
A. Noun.

diathēkē (διαθήκη, 1242) primarily signifies "a disposition of property by will or otherwise." In its use in the Sept., it is the rendering of a Hebrew word meaning a "covenant" or agreement (from a verb signifying "to cut or divide," in allusion to a sacrificial custom in connection with "covenant-making," e.g., Gen. 15:10, "divided" Jer. 34:18–19). In contradistinction to the English word "covenant" (lit., "a coming together"), which signifies a mutual undertaking between two parties or more, each binding himself to fulfill obligations, it does not in itself contain the idea of joint obligation, it mostly signifies an obligation undertaken by a single person. For instance, in Gal. 3:17 it is used as an alternative to a "promise" (vv. 16–18). God enjoined upon Abraham the rite of circumcision, but His promise to Abraham, here called a "covenant," was not conditional upon the observance of circumcision, though a penalty attached to its nonobservance.

"The NT uses of the word may be analyzed as follows: (*a*) a promise or undertaking, human or divine, Gal. 3:15; (*b*) a promise or undertaking on the part of God, Luke 1:72; Acts 3:25; Rom. 9:4; 11:27; Gal. 3:17; Eph. 2:12; Heb. 7:22; 8:6, 8, 10; 10:16; (*c*) an agreement, a mutual undertaking, between God and Israel, see Deut. 29–30 (described as a 'commandment,' Heb. 7:18, cf. v. 22); Heb. 8:9; 9:20; (*d*)

by metonymy, the token of the covenant, or promise, made to Abraham, Acts 7:8; (*e*) by metonymy, the record of the covenant, 2 Cor. 3:14; Heb. 9:4; cf. Rev. 11:19; (*f*) the basis, established by the death of Christ, on which the salvation of men is secured, Matt. 26:28; Mark 14:24; Luke 22:20; 1 Cor. 11:25; 2 Cor. 3:6; Heb. 10:29; 12:24; 13:20.

"This covenant is called the 'new,' Heb. 9:15, the 'second,' 8:7, the 'better,' 7:22. In Heb. 9:16–17, the translation is much disputed. There does not seem to be any sufficient reason for departing in these verses from the word used everywhere else. The English word 'Testament' is taken from the titles prefixed to the Latin Versions."*¶ See TESTAMENT.
B. Verb.

suntithēmi (συντίθημι, 4934), lit., "to put together," is used only in the middle voice in the NT, and, means "to determine, agree," John 9:22 and Acts 23:20; "to assent," Acts 24:9; "to covenant," Luke 22:5. See AGREE, ASSENT.¶

Note: In Matt. 26:15 the KJV translates *histēmi*, "to place (in the balances)," i.e., to weigh, "they covenanted with"; RV, "they weighed unto."

COVENANT-BREAKERS

asunthetos (ἀσύνθετος, 802), from *suntithēmi* (see above), with the negative prefix *a*, hence signifies "not covenant-keeping," i.e., refusing to abide by "covenants" made, "covenant-breaking," faithless, Rom. 1:31.¶ In the Sept. it is found in Jer. 3:8–11.¶ Cf. the corresponding verb, *asuntithēmi*, in the Sept. of Ps. 73:15, "to deal treacherously" (RV), and the noun *asunthesia*, "transgression, or covenant-breaking," e.g., Ezra 9:2, 4; 10:6.

Note: Trench, *Syn.* §lii, notes the distinction between *asunthetos* and *aspondos*, "implacable," the latter, in 2 Tim. 3:3 only, being derived from *spondē*, "a sacrificial libation," which accompanied treaty-making; hence, with the negative prefix *a*, "without a treaty or covenant," thus denoting a person who cannot be persuaded to enter into a "covenant." He points out that *asunthetos* presumes a state of peace interrupted by the unrighteous, *aspondos* a state of war, which the implacable refuse to terminate equitably. The words are clearly not synonymous.

COVER, COVERING
A. Verbs.

1. *kaluptō* (καλύπτω, 2572) signifies "to cover," Matt. 8:24; 10:26; Luke 8:16; 23:30;

---

* From *Notes on Galatians*, by Hogg and Vine, p. 144.

Jas. 5:20 (RV); 1 Pet. 4:8; to veil, in 2 Cor. 4:3 (RV; KJV, "hid"). See HIDE.¶

Note: Cf. the corresponding noun *kalumma,* "a veil," 2 Cor. 3:13–16. See VEIL.¶

2. *epikaluptō* (ἐπικαλύπτω, 1943), "to cover up or over" (*epi,* "over"), is used in Rom. 4:7, lit., "whose sins are covered over."¶ Cf. *epikalumma,* "a cloke," 1 Pet. 2:16.¶

3. *perikaluptō* (περικαλύπτω, 4028), "to cover around" (*peri,* "around"), e.g., the face, and so, to blindfold, is translated "cover" in Mark 14:65, "blindfold" in Luke 22:64. In Heb. 9:4, it signifies "to overlay." See BLINDFOLD, OVERLAY.

4. *sunkaluptō* (συγκαλύπτω, 4780), lit., "to cover together"; the *sun-,* however, is intensive, and the verb signifies "to cover wholly, to cover up," Luke 12:2.¶

5. *katakaluptō* (κατακαλύπτω, 2619), "to cover up" (*kata,* intensive), in the middle voice, "to cover oneself," is used in 1 Cor. 11:6–7 (RV, "veiled").¶

Note: In 1 Cor. 11:4, "having his head covered" is, lit., "having (something) down the head."

B. Nouns.

1. *peribolaion* (περιβόλαιον, 4018) lit. denotes "something thrown around" (*peri,* "around," *ballō,* "to throw"); hence, "a veil, covering," 1 Cor. 11:15 (marg.), or "a mantle around the body, a vesture," Heb. 1:12. See CLOTHING, Note (1), VESTURE.¶

2. *skepasma* (σκέπασμα, 4629), "a covering" (*skepazō,* "to cover"), strictly, "a roofing," then, "any kind of shelter or covering," is used in the plural in 1 Tim. 6:8 (KJV, "raiment"; RV, "covering").¶

COVET, COVETOUS, COVETOUSNESS

A. Verbs.

1. *epithumeō* (ἐπιθυμέω, 1937), "to fix the desire upon" (*epi,* "upon," used intensively, *thumos,* "passion"), whether things good or bad; hence, "to long for, lust after, covet," is used with the meaning "to covet evilly" in Acts 20:33, of "coveting money and apparel"; so in Rom. 7:7; 13:9. See DESIRE, FAIN, LUST.

2. *zēloō* (ζηλόω, 2206) is rendered "covet earnestly," in 1 Cor. 12:31, KJV; RV, "desire earnestly," as in 14:39 (KJV "covet"). See AFFECT, DESIRE, ENVY, JEALOUS, ZEALOUS.

3. *oregō* (ὀρέγω, 3713), "to stretch after," is rendered "covet after" in 1 Tim. 6:10, KJV; RV, "reaching after." See DESIRE, REACH.

B. Nouns.

1. *epithumētēs* (ἐπιθυμητής, 1938), "a luster after" (akin to A, No. 1), is translated in 1 Cor. 10:6, in verbal form, "should not lust after." See LUST.¶

2. *epithumia* (ἐπιθυμία, 1939) denotes "coveting," Rom. 7:7–8, RV; KJV, "lust" and "concupiscence"; the commandment here referred to convicted him of sinfulness in his desires for unlawful objects besides that of gain. See DESIRE, LUST.

3. *pleonexia* (πλεονεξία, 4124), "covetousness," lit., "a desire to have more" (*pleon,* "more," *echō,* "to have"), always in a bad sense, is used in a general way in Mark 7:22 (plural, lit., "covetings," i.e., various ways in which "covetousness" shows itself); Rom. 1:29; Eph. 5:3; 1 Thess. 2:5. Elsewhere it is used, (*a*) of material possessions, Luke 12:15; 2 Pet. 2:3; 2 Cor. 9:5 (RV, "extortion"), lit., "as (a matter of) extortion" i.e., a gift which betrays the giver's unwillingness to bestow what is due; (*b*) of sensuality, Eph. 4:19, "greediness"; Col. 3:5 (where it is called "idolatry"); 2 Pet. 2:14 (KJV, "covetous practices"). See EXTORTION.¶

Note: Cf. the corresponding verb *pleonekteō,* "to gain, take advantage of wrong." See ADVANTAGE, DEFRAUD, GAIN, B, *Note* (2), WRONG

C. Adjectives.

1. *pleonektēs* (πλεονέκτης, 4123), lit., "(eager) to have more" (see B, No. 3), i.e., to have what belongs to others; hence, "greedy of gain, covetous," 1 Cor. 5:10–11; 6:10; Eph. 5:5 ("covetous man").¶

2. *philarguros* (φιλάργυρος, 5366), lit., "money-loving," is rendered "covetous" in the KJV of Luke 16:14 and 2 Tim. 3:2; RV, "lovers of money," the wider and due significance.¶

3. *aphilarguros* (ἀφιλάργυρος, 866), No. 2, with negative prefix, is translated "without covetousness" in Heb. 13:5, KJV; RV, "free from the love of money." In 1 Tim. 3:3, the KJV has "not covetous," the RV, "no lover of money."

Note: Trench, *Syn.* §24, points out the main distinction between *pleonexia* and *philarguria* as being that between "covetousness" and avarice, the former having a much wider and deeper sense, being "the genus of which *philarguria* is the species." The "covetous" man is often cruel as well as grasping, while the avaricious man is simply miserly and stinting.

CRAFT, CRAFTSMAN

1. *technē* (τέχνη, 5078), "craft," Rev. 18:22: see ART.

2. *technitēs* (τεχνίτης, 5079), akin to No. 1, "an artificer, artisan, craftsman," is translated "craftsman" in Acts 19:24, 38 and Rev. 18:22.

It is found elsewhere in Heb. 11:10 "builder"; but this is practically the same as "maker" (*demiourgos*, the next noun in the verse; see No. 5, *Note*). Trench, *Syn*. §qv., suggests that *technitēs* brings out the artistic side of creation, viewing God as "moulding and fashioning ... the materials which He called into existence." This agrees with the usage of the word in the Sept. See BUILDER.¶

3. *ergasia* (ἐργασία, 2039): see DILIGENCE.

4. *homotechnos* (ὁμότεχνος, 3673), "one of the same trade" (from *homos*, "same," and *technē*, see No. 1), is used in Acts 18:3 (RV, "trade").¶ Cf. *architektōn*, "master-builder," 1 Cor. 3:10.¶

5. *meros* (μέρος, 3313), "a part, portion," is translated "craft" in Acts 19:27, KJV; "trade," RV (cf. *ergasia* in v. 25). See BEHALF, COAST, PART, PIECE, PORTION, RESPECT, SORT.

Note: Dēmiourgos, "a maker," properly signifies one who works for the people, or whose work stands forth to the public gaze (*dēmos*, "people," *ergon*, "work"), but this idea has been lost in the use of the word, which came to signify "a maker," Heb. 11:10. This has reference to the structure, No. 2 to the design. Cf. *ktistēs*, "a creator."¶

CRAFTINESS, CRAFTY

A. Noun.

panourgia (πανουργία, 3834), lit., "all-working," i.e., doing everything (*pan*, "all," *ergon*, "work"), hence, "unscrupulous conduct, craftiness," is always used in a bad sense in the NT, Luke 20:23; 1 Cor. 3:19; 2 Cor. 4:2; 11:3; Eph. 4:14, KJV, "cunning craftiness." See SUBTLETY. ¶ In the Sept. it is used in a good sense, Prov. 1:4; 8:5; indifferently in Num. 24:22 and Josh. 9:4.¶

B. Adjective.

panourgos (πανοῦργος, 3835), "cunning, crafty," is found in 2 Cor. 12:16, where the apostle is really quoting an accusation made against him by his detractors.¶ In the Sept. it is used in a good sense in Prov. 13:1; 28:2.¶

C. Noun.

dolos (δόλος, 1388), primarily, "a bait," hence, "fraud, guile, deceit," is rendered "craft" in the KJV of Mark 14:1 (RV "subtilty"). See DECEIT, GUILE, SUBTLETY.

CRAVE

Note: The word "crave," found in the KJV of Mark 15:43, translates the verb *aiteō*, "to ask" (RV, "asked for"). See ASK.

CREATE, CREATION, CREATOR, CREATURE

A. Verb.

ktizō (κτίζω, 2936), used among the Greeks to mean the founding of a place, a city or colony, signifies, in Scripture, "to create," always of the act of God, whether (*a*) in the natural creation, Mark 13:19; Rom. 1:25 (where the title "The Creator" translates the article with the aorist participle of the verb); 1 Cor. 11:9; Eph. 3:9; Col. 1:16; 1 Tim. 4:3; Rev. 4:11; 10:6, or (*b*) in the spiritual creation, Eph. 2:10, 15; 4:24; Col. 3:10. See MAKE.¶

B. Nouns.

1. *ktisis* (κτίσις, 2937), primarily "the act of creating," or "the creative act in process," has this meaning in Rom. 1:20 and Gal. 6:15. Like the English word "creation," it also signifies the product of the "creative" act, the "creature," as in Mark 16:15, RV; Rom. 1:25; 8:19; Col. 1:15 etc.; in Heb. 9:11, KJV, "building." In Mark 16:15 and Col. 1:23 its significance has special reference to mankind in general. As to its use in Gal. 6:15 and 2 Cor. 5:17, in the former, apparently, "the reference is to the creative act of God, whereby a man is introduced into the blessing of salvation, in contrast to circumcision done by human hands, which the Judaizers claimed was necessary to that end. In 2 Cor. 5:17 the reference is to what the believer is in Christ; in consequence of the creative act he has become a new creature."*

Ktisis is once used of human actions, 1 Pet. 2:13, "ordinance" (marg., "creation"). See BUILDING, ORDINANCE.

2. *ktisma* (κτίσμα, 2938) has the concrete sense, "the created thing, the creature, the product of the creative act," 1 Tim. 4:4; Jas. 1:18; Rev. 5:13; 8:9.¶

3. *ktistēs* (κτίστης, 2939), among the Greeks, the founder of a city, etc., denotes in Scripture "the Creator," 1 Pet. 4:19 (cf. Rom. 1:20, under B, No. 1, above).¶

Note: It is a significant confirmation of Rom. 1:20–21, that in all nonchristian Greek literature these words are never used by Greeks to convey the idea of a creator or of a creative act by any of their gods. The words are confined by them to the acts of human beings.

4. *zōon* (ζῶον, 2226), "a living creature": see BEAST.

For CREDITOR see LEND, LENDER

---

* From *Notes on Galatians*, by Hogg and Vine, p. 339.

For **CREEK** see **BAY**

CREEP, CREEPING, CREPT

A. Verbs.

1. *endunō* (ἐνδύνω, 1744), properly, "to envelop in" (*en*, "in," *dunō*, "to enter"), "to put on," as of a garment, has the secondary and intransitive significance of "creeping into, insinuating oneself into," and is found with this meaning in 2 Tim. 3:6. Cf. *enduō*, "to clothe."¶

2. *pareisdunō* (παρεισδύνω, 391), "to enter in by the side" (*para*, "beside," *eis*, "in"), to insinuate oneself into, by stealth, to creep in stealthily, is used in Jude 4.¶

B. Noun.

herpeton (ἑρπετόν, 2062) signifies "a creeping thing" (*herpō*, "to creep"; Eng., "serpent," Jas. 3:7 (RV, "creeping things," for KJV, "serpents," which form only one of this genus); it is set in contrast to quadrupeds and birds, Acts 10:12; 11:6; Rom. 1:23. See SERPENT.¶

For **CRIME** see **CHARGE**

For **CRIPPLE** see **HALT**

CROOKED

skolios (σκολιός, 4646), "curved, crooked," was especially used (*a*) of a way, Luke 3:5, with spiritual import (see Prov. 28:18, Sept.); it is set in contrast to *orthos* and *euthus*, "straight"; (*b*) metaphorically, of what is morally "crooked," perverse, froward, of people belonging to a particular generation, Acts 2:40 (KJV, "untoward"); Phil. 2:15; of tyrannical or unjust masters, 1 Pet. 2:18, "froward"; in this sense it is set in contrast to *agathos*, "good."¶

CROSS, CRUCIFY

A. Noun.

stauros (σταυρός, 4716) denotes, primarily, "an upright pale or stake." On such malefactors were nailed for execution. Both the noun and the verb *stauroō*, "to fasten to a stake or pale," are originally to be distinguished from the ecclesiastical form of a two beamed "cross." The shape of the latter had its origin in ancient Chaldea, and was used as the symbol of the god Tammuz (being in the shape of the mystic Tau, the initial of his name) in that country and in adjacent lands, including Egypt. By the middle of the 3rd cent. A.D. the churches had either departed from, or had travestied, certain doctrines of the Christian faith. In order to increase the prestige of the apostate ecclesiastical system pagans were received into the churches apart from regeneration by faith, and were permitted largely to retain their pagan signs and symbols. Hence the Tau or T, in its most frequent form, with the cross-piece lowered, was adopted to stand for the "cross" of Christ.

As for the Chi, or X, which Constantine declared he had seen in a vision leading him to champion the Christian faith, that letter was the initial of the word "Christ" and had nothing to do with "the Cross" (for *xulon*, "a timber beam, a tree," as used for the *stauros*, see under TREE).

The method of execution was borrowed by the Greeks and Romans from the Phoenicians. The *stauros* denotes (*a*) "the cross, or stake itself," e.g., Matt. 27:32; (*b*) "the crucifixion suffered," e.g., 1 Cor. 1:17–18, where "the word of the cross," RV, stands for the gospel; Gal. 5:11, where crucifixion is metaphorically used of the renunciation of the world, that characterizes the true Christian life; 6:12, 14; Eph. 2:16; Phil. 3:18.

The judicial custom by which the condemned person carried his stake to the place of execution, was applied by the Lord to those sufferings by which His faithful followers were to express their fellowship with Him, e.g., Matt. 10:38.

B. Verbs.

1. *stauroō* (σταυρόω, 4717) signifies (*a*) "the act of crucifixion," e.g., Matt. 20:19; (*b*) metaphorically, "the putting off of the flesh with its passions and lusts," a condition fulfilled in the case of those who are "of Christ Jesus," Gal. 5:24, RV; so of the relationship between the believer and the world, 6:14.

2. *sustauroō* (συσταυρόω, 4957), "to crucify with" (*su*-, "for," *sun*, "with"), is used (*a*) of actual "crucifixion" in company with another, Matt. 27:44; Mark 15:32; John 19:32; (*b*) metaphorically, of spiritual identification with Christ in His death, Rom. 6:6, and Gal. 2:20.¶

3. *anastauroō* (ἀνασταυρόω, 388) (*ana*, again) is used in Heb. 6:6 of Hebrew apostates, who as merely nominal Christians, in turning back to Judaism, were thereby virtually guilty of "crucifying" Christ again.¶

4. *prospēgnumi* (προσπήγνυμι, 4362), "to fix or fasten to anything" (*pros*, "to," *pēgnumi*, "to fix"), is used of the "crucifixion" of Christ, Acts 2:23.¶

CROSS (Verb)

diaperaō (διαπεράω, 1276), "to pass over, to cross over" (*dia*, "through," *peraō*, "to pass": akin to this are *peran*, "across," *peras*, "a boundary," Latin, *porta*, "a gate," Eng., "portal, port," etc.), is translated by the verb "to cross" in the RV, but differently in the KJV; in Matt. 9:1; Mark 5:21; 6:53 (KJV, "passed"); Matt.

14:34 (KJV, "were gone "); Luke 16:26 (KJV, "neither can they pass"); Acts 21:2 (KJV, "sailing "). See GO, PASS, SAIL.¶ In the Sept., Deut. 30:13; Isa. 23:2.¶

For the verb CROW (CREW) see CALL, A, No. 8

CROWD

A. Noun.

ochlos (ὄχλος, 3793), "a confused throng," is usually translated "multitude."

The RV translates it "crowd" (KJV, "press" in some) in Matt. 9:23, 25; Mark 2:4; 3:9; 5:27, 30; Luke 8:19; 19:3; Acts 21:34–35; 24:12, 18. See COMPANY, MULTITUDE, NUMBER, PEOPLE.

B. Verb.

ochlopoieō (ὀχλοποιέω, 3792), "to make a crowd" (A, with *poieō*, "to make"), is translated "gathered a crowd" in Acts 17:5, RV (KJV, "company").

CROWN (Noun and Verb)

A. Nouns.

1. *stephanos* (στέφανος, 4735), primarily, "that which surrounds, as a wall or crowd" (from *stephō*, "to encircle"), denotes (*a*) "the victor's crown," the symbol of triumph in the games or some such contest; hence, by metonymy, a reward or prize; (*b*) "a token of public honor" for distinguished service, military prowess, etc., or of nuptial joy, or festal gladness, especially at the parousia of kings. It was woven as a garland of oak, ivy, parsley, myrtle, or olive, or in imitation of these in gold. In some passages the reference to the games is clear, 1 Cor. 9:25; 2 Tim. 4:8 ("crown of righteousness"); it may be so in 1 Pet. 5:4, where the fadeless character of "the crown of glory" is set in contrast to the garlands of earth. In other passages it stands as an emblem of life, joy, reward and glory, Phil. 4:1; 1 Thess. 2:19; Jas. 1:12 ("crown of life "); Rev. 2:10 (ditto); 3:11; 4:4, 10: of triumph, 6:2; 9:7; 12:1; 14:14.

It is used of "the crown of thorns" which the soldiers plaited and put on Christ's head, Matt. 27:29; Mark 15:17; John 19:2, 5. At first sight this might be taken as an alternative for *diadēma*, "a kingly crown" (see below), but considering the blasphemous character of that masquerade, and the materials used, obviously *diadēma* would be quite unfitting and the only alternative was *stephanos* (see Trench *Syn.* §xxxii).¶

2. *diadēma* (διάδημα, 1238) is never used as *stephanos* is; it is always the symbol of kingly or imperial dignity, and is translated "diadem"

instead of "crown" in the RV, of the claims of the Dragon, Rev. 12:3; 13:1; 19:12. See DIADEM.¶

B. Verb.

stephanoō (στεφανόω, 4737), "to crown," conforms in meaning to *stephanos;* it is used of the reward of victory in the games, in 2 Tim. 2:5; of the glory and honor bestowed by God upon man in regard to his position in creation, Heb. 2:7; of the glory and honor bestowed upon the Lord Jesus in His exaltation, v. 9.¶

For CRUCIFY see CROSS

CRUMB

psichion (ψιχίον, 5589), "a small morsel," a diminutive of *psix*, "a bit, or crumb"; of bread or meat, it is used in Matt. 15:27 and Mark 7:28; some mss. have it in Luke 16:21.¶

CRUSE

alabastron (ἀλάβαστρον, 211) was a vessel for holding ointment or perfume; it derived its name from the alabaster stone, of which it was usually made. "Cruse," RV, is a more suitable rendering than "box"; Matt. 26:7; Mark 14:3; Luke 7:37.¶

CRUSH

apothlibō (ἀποθλίβω, 598), a strengthened form of *thlibō*, "to throng" (*apo*, intensive), is used in Luke 8:45, RV, "crush," for KJV, "press," of the multitude who were pressing around Christ (cf. the preceding word *sunechō*, "to press").¶ In the Sept., Num. 22:25.¶

CRY (Noun and Verb), CRYING

A. Nouns.

1. *kraugē* (κραυγή, 2906), an onomatopoeic word, is used in Matt. 25:6; Luke 1:42 (some mss. have *phōnē*); Acts 23:9, RV, "clamor"; Eph. 4:31, "clamor"; Heb. 5:7; Rev. 21:4, "crying." Some mss. have it in Rev. 14:18 (the most authentic have *phōnē*). See CLAMOR.¶

2. *boē* (βοή, 995), especially "a cry for help," an onomatopoeic word (cf. Eng., "boo"), connected with *boaō* (see B, No. 1), is found in Jas. 5:4.¶

B. Verbs.

1. *boaō* (βοάω, 994), akin to A, No. 2, signifies (*a*) "to raise a cry," whether of joy, Gal. 4:27, or vexation, Acts 8:7; (*b*) "to speak with a strong voice," Matt. 3:3; Mark 1:3; 15:34; Luke 3:4; 9:38 (some mss. have *anaboaō* here: see No. 2); John 1:23; Acts 17:6; 25:24 (some mss. have *epiboaō*, No. 3, here); (*c*) "to cry out for help," Luke 18:7, 38.¶ For Acts 21:34, see No. 8.

2. *anaboaō* (ἀναβοάω, 310), *ana*, "up," intensive, and No. 1, "to lift up the voice, cry out," is said of Christ at the moment of His death, a testimony to His supernatural power in giving up His life, Matt. 27:46; in some mss. in Mark 15:8, of the shouting of a multitude; in some mss. in Luke 9:38, of the "crying" out of a man in a company (see No. 1).¶

3. *epiboaō* (ἐπιβοάω, 1916), *epi*, "upon," intensive, and No. 1, "to cry out, exclaim vehemently," is used in some mss. in Acts 25:24 (see No. 1.¶)

4. *krazō* (κράζω, 2896), akin to A, No. 1, "to cry out," an onomatopoeic word, used especially of the "cry" of the raven; then, of any inarticulate cries, from fear, pain etc.; of the "cry" of a Canaanitish woman, Matt. 15:22 (so the best mss., instead of *kraugazō*); of the shouts of the children in the Temple, Matt. 21:15; of the people who shouted for Christ to be crucified, 27:23; Mark 15:13–14; of the "cry" of Christ on the Cross at the close of His sufferings, Matt. 27:50; Mark 15:39 (see No. 2, above).

In John's gospel it is used three times, out of the six, of Christ's utterances, 7:28, 37; 12:44. In the Acts it is not used of "cries" of distress, but chiefly of the shouts of opponents; in the Apocalypse, chiefly of the utterances of heavenly beings concerning earthly matters; in Rom. 8:15 and Gal. 4:6, of the appeal of believers to God the Father; in Rom. 9:27, of a prophecy concerning Israel; in Jas. 5:4, metaphorically, of hire kept back by fraud.

Note: A recent translator renders this verb in Matt. 27:50 "uttered a scream," an utterly deplorable mistranslation and a misrepresentation of the nature of the Lord's "cry."

5. *anakrazō* (ἀνακράζω, 349), *ana*, "up," intensive, and No. 4, signifies "to cry out loudly," Mark 1:23; 6:49; Luke 4:33; 8:28; 23:18.¶

6. *kraugazō* (κραυγάζω, 2905), a stronger form of No. 4, "to make a clamor or outcry" (A, No. 1), is used in Matt. 12:19, in a prophecy from Isaiah of Christ; in Luke 4:41 (in the best mss., instead of *krazō*); John 11:43; 12:13 (in the best mss.); 18:40; 19:6, 12, 15; Acts 22:23.¶

7. *phōneō* (φωνέω, 5455), "to utter a loud sound or cry," whether of animals, e.g., Matt. 26:34; or persons, Luke 8:8; 16:24; this is the word which Luke uses to describe the "cry" of the Lord at the close of His sufferings on the cross, Luke 23:46 (see under *anaboaō* and *krazō*, above); also, e.g., Acts 16:28; Rev. 14:18. See CALL, A, No. 8, CROW.

8. *epiphōneō* (ἐπιφωνέω, 2019), No. 7, with *epi*, "upon," or "against," signifies "to shout," either against, Luke 23:21; Acts 21:34 (in the best mss., No. 1); 22:24, or in acclamation, Acts 12:22. See SHOUT.¶

Note: For *aphiēmi*, Mark 15:37, See UTTER.

Comparing the various verbs, *kaleō*, denotes "to call out for any purpose," *boaō*, "to cry out as an expression of feeling," *krazō*, to cry out loudly." *Kaleō* suggests intelligence, *boaō*, sensibilities, *krazō*, instincts.

CRYSTAL

A. Noun.

krustallos (κρύσταλλος, 2930), from *kruos*, "ice," and hence properly anything congealed and transparent, denotes "crystal," a kind of precious stone, Rev. 4:6; 22:1. Rock crystal is pure quartz; it crystallizes in hexagonal prisms, each with a pyramidical apex.¶

B. Verb.

krustallizō (κρυσταλλίζω, 2929), "to be of crystalline brightness and transparency, to shine like crystal," is found in Rev. 21:11, where it is said of Christ as the "Light-giver" (*phōstēr*) of the heavenly city (not *phōs*, "light," RV and KJV). Possibly there the verb has a transitive force, "to transform into crystal splendor," as of the effect of Christ upon His saints.¶

CUBIT

pēchus (πῆχυς, 4083) denotes the forearm, i.e., the part between the hand and the elbow-joint; hence, "a measure of length," not from the wrist to the elbow, but from the tip of the middle finger to the elbow joint, i.e., about a foot and a half, or a little less than two feet, Matt. 6:27; Luke 12:25; John 21:8; Rev. 21:17.¶

CUMBER

1. *katargeō* (καταργέω, 2673), lit., "to reduce to idleness or inactivity" (*kata*, "down," and *argos*, "idle"), is once rendered "cumber," Luke 13:7. See ABOLISH.

2. *perispaō* (περισπάω, 4049), lit., "to draw around" (*peri*), "draw away, distract," is used in the passive voice in the sense of being over-occupied about a thing, to be "cumbered," Luke 10:40.¶

CUMMIN

kuminon (κύμινον, 2951) is an umbelliferous plant with aromatic seeds, used as a condiment, Matt. 23:23.

For the KJV **CUNNING** see **CRAFTINESS.** For **CUNNINGLY** see **DEVISED**

CUP

potērion (ποτήριον, 4221), a diminutive of *potēr*, denotes, primarily, a "drinking vessel"; hence, "a cup" (*a*) literal, as, e.g., in Matt. 10:42. The "cup" of blessing, 1 Cor. 10:16, is so named from the third (the fourth according to Edersheim) "cup" in the Jewish Passover feast, over which thanks and praise were given to God. This connection is not to be rejected on the ground that the church at Corinth was unfamiliar with Jewish customs. That the contrary was the case, see 5:7; (*b*) figurative, of one's lot or experience, joyous or sorrowful (frequent in the Psalms; cf. Ps. 116:18, "cup of salvation"); in the NT it is used most frequently of the sufferings of Christ, Matt. 20:22–23; 26:39; Mark 10:38–39; 14:36; Luke 22:42; John 18:11; also of the evil deeds of Babylon, Rev. 17:4; 18:6; of divine punishments to be inflicted, Rev. 14:10; 16:19. Cf. Ps. 11:6; 75:8; Isa. 51:17; Jer. 25:15; Ezek. 23:32–34; Zech. 12:2.

CURE (Noun and Verb)

A. Noun.

iasis (ἴασις, 2392), "a healing, a cure" (akin to *iaomai*, "to heal," and *iatros*, "a physician"), is used in the plural in Luke 13:32; in Acts 4:22, "healing"; in 4:30 with the preposition *eis*, "unto," lit., "unto healing," translated "heal." See HEALING.¶

B. Verb.

therapeuō (θεραπεύω, 2323), (Eng., "therapeutics," etc.), denotes (*a*) primarily, "to serve" (cf. *therapeia* and *therapōn*), Acts 17:25 (KJV, "worshiped"); then, (*b*) "to heal, restore to health, to cure"; it is usually translated "to heal," but "cure"in Matt. 17:16, 18; Luke 7:21; 9:1; John 5:10, Acts 28:9, RV. See HEAL, WORSHIP.

CURIOUS

Note: For the adjective *periergos*, "busy about trifles," see BUSYBODY: it is used of magic arts in Acts 19:19 (lit., "things that are around work," and thus superfluous), i.e., the arts of those who pry into forbidden things, with the aid of evil spirits. See also 1 Tim. 5:13, where the meaning is "inquisitive," prying into other people's affairs.¶

CURSE, CURSING (Noun and Verb), CURSED, ACCURSED

A. Nouns.

1. *ara* (ἀρά, 685), in its most usual meaning, "a malediction, cursing" (its other meaning is

"a prayer"), is used in Rom. 3:14 (often in the Sept.).¶

2. *katara* (κατάρα, 2671), *kata*, "down," intensive, and No. 1, denotes an "execration, imprecation, curse," uttered out of malevolence, Jas. 3:10; 2 Pet. 2:14; or pronounced by God in His righteous judgment, as upon a land doomed to barrenness, Heb. 6:8; upon those who seek for justification by obedience, in part or completely, to the Law, Gal. 3:10, 13; in this 13th verse it is used concretely of Christ, as having "become a curse" for us, i.e., by voluntarily undergoing on the cross the appointed penalty of the "curse." He thus was identified, on our behalf, with the doom of sin. Here, not the verb in the Sept. of Deut. 21:23 is used (see B, No. 3), but the concrete noun.¶

3. *anathema* (ἀνάθεμα, 33), transliterated from the Greek, is frequently used in the Sept., where it translates the Heb. *cherem*, "a thing devoted to God," whether (*a*) for His service, as the sacrifices, Lev. 27:28 (cf. *anathēma*, a votive offering, gift), or (*b*) for its destruction, as an idol, Deut. 7:26, or a city, Josh. 6:17. Later it acquired the more general meaning of "the disfavor of Jehovah," e.g., Zech. 14:11. This is the meaning in the NT. It is used of (*a*) the sentence pronounced, Acts 23:14 (lit., "cursed themselves with a curse"; see *anathematizō* below); (*b*) of the object on which "curse" is laid, "accursed"; in the following, the RV keeps to the word "anathema," Rom. 9:3; 1 Cor. 12:3; 16:22; Gal. 1:8–9, all of which the KJV renders by "accursed" except 1 Cor. 16:22, where it has "Anathema." In Gal. 1:8–9, the apostle declares in the strongest manner that the gospel he preached was the one and only way of salvation, and that to preach another was to nullify the death of Christ.¶

4. *katathema* (κατάθεμα, 2652), or, as in some mss., the longer form *katanathema*, is stronger than No. 3 (*kata*, intensive), and denotes, by metonymy, "an accursed thing" (the object "cursed" being put for the "curse" pronounced), Rev. 22:3.¶

B. Verbs.

1. *anathematizō* (ἀναθεματίζω, 332), akin to No. 3, signifies "to declare anathema," i.e., "devoted to destruction, accursed, to curse," Mark 14:71, or "to bind by a curse," Acts 23:12, 14, 21.¶

2. *katanathematizō* (καταναθεματίζω, 2653), a strengthened form of No. 1, denotes "to utter curses against," Matt. 26:74; cf. Mark's word concerning the same occasion (No. 1).¶

3. *kataraomai* (καταράομαι, 2672), akin to A, No. 2, primarily signifies "to pray against, to wish evil against a person or thing"; hence "to

curse," Matt. 25:41; Mark 11:21; Luke 6:28; Rom. 12:14; Jas. 3:9. Some mss. have it in Matt. 5:44.¶

4. *kakologeō* (κακολογέω, 2551), "to speak evil" (*kakos*, "evil," *legō*, "to speak"), is translated by the verb "to curse" in Matt. 15:4, and Mark 7:10, "to speak evil of father and mother," not necessarily "to curse," is what the Lord intended (RV). KJV and RV have the verb "to speak evil" in Mark 9:39 and Acts 19:9. See EVIL.

C. Adjectives.

1. *epikataratos* (ἐπικατάρατος, 1944), "cursed, accursed" (*epi*, "upon," and A, No. 2), is used in Gal. 3:10, 13.¶

2. *eparatos* (ἐπάρατος, 1883a), "accursed," is found, in the best mss., in John 7:49, RV, "accursed," instead of No. 1.

For CUSHION see PILLOW

CUSTOM (Usage), ACCUSTOM (Verb)

A. Nouns.

1. *ethos* (ἔθος, 1485) denotes (*a*) "a custom, usage, prescribed by law," Acts 6:14; 15:1; 25:16; "a rite or ceremony," Luke 2:42; (*b*) a "custom, habit, manner," Luke 22:39; John 19:40; Heb. 10:25 (KJV, "manner"). See MANNER, WONT.

2. *sunētheia* (συνήθεια, 4914), *sun*, "with," *ethos* (see No. 1), denotes (*a*) "an intercourse, intimacy," a meaning not found in the NT; (*b*) "a custom, customary usage," John 18:39; 1 Cor. 11:16; "or force of habit," 1 Cor. 8:7, RV, "being used to" (some mss. here have *suneidēsis*, "conscience"; whence KJV, "with conscience of").¶

B. Verbs.

1. *ethizō* (ἐθίζω, 1480), akin to A, No. 1, signifies "to accustom," or in the passive voice, "to be accustomed." In the participial form it is equivalent to a noun, "custom," Luke 2:27.¶

2. *ethō* (ἔθω, 1486), "to be accustomed," as in the case of No. 1, is used in the passive participle as a noun, signifying "a custom," Luke 4:16; Acts 17:2 (KJV, "manner"; RV, "custom"); in Matt. 17:15 and Mark 10:1, "was wont." See MANNER, WONT.¶

CUSTOM (Toll)

1. *telos* (τέλος, 5056), "an end, termination," whether of time or purpose, denotes, in its secondary significance, "what is paid for public ends, a toll, tax, custom," Matt. 17:25 (RV, "toll"); Rom. 13:7 (RV and KJV, "custom"). In Palestine the Herods of Galilee and Perea re-

ceived the "custom"; in Judea it was paid to the procurator for the Roman government. See END, FINALLY, UTTERMOST.

2. *telōnion* (τελώνιον, 5058) denotes "a custom-house," for the collection of the taxes, Matt. 9:9; Mark 2:14; Luke 5:27 (RV, "place of toll").

CUT

1. *koptō* (κόπτω, 2875) denotes "to cut by a blow," e.g., branches, Matt. 21:8; Mark 11:8. See BEWAIL, LAMENT, MOURN, WAIL.

2. *apokoptō* (ἀποκόπτω, 609), "to cut off, or cut away" (*apo*, "from," and No. 1), is used (*a*) literally, of members of the body, Mark 9:43, 45; John 18:10, 26; of ropes, Acts 27:32; (*b*) metaphorically, in the middle voice, of "cutting off oneself," to excommunicate, Gal. 5:12, of the Judaizing teachers, with a reference, no doubt, to circumcision.¶

3. *ekkoptō* (ἐκκόπτω, 1581), lit., "to cut or strike out" (*ek*, "out or off," and No. 1), "to cut down," is used (*a*) literally, Matt. 5:30 (in 3:10 and 7:19 and Luke 3:9, "hewn down"); 18:8; Luke 13:7, 9; (*b*) metaphorically, of "cutting off" from spiritual blessing, Rom. 11:22, 24; of depriving persons of an occasion for something, 2 Cor. 11:12. See HEW.¶

Note: In 1 Pet. 3:7 the best mss. have *enkoptō*, "to hinder"; some have *ekkoptō*.

4. *katakoptō* (κατακόπτω, 2629), lit., "to cut down, cut in pieces" (*kata*, "down," intensive), Mark 5:5, of the demoniac.¶

5. *diapriō* (διαπρίω, 1282) signifies "to saw asunder" (*dia*, "asunder," *priō*, "to saw"), "to divide by a saw" (as in 1 Chron. 20:3, Sept.), hence, metaphorically, "to be sawn through mentally, to be rent with vexation, to be cut to the heart," is used in Acts 5:33; 7:54.¶

6. *dichotomeō* (διχοτομέω, 1371), lit., "to cut into two parts" (*dicha*, "apart," *temnō*, "to cut," *tomē*, "a cutting"), Matt. 24:51, "to cut asunder," is used in Luke 12:46. Some take the reference to be to the mode of punishment by which criminals and captives were "cut" in two; others, on account of the fact that in these passages the delinquent is still surviving after the treatment, take the verb to denote "to cut up" by scourging, to scourge severely, the word being used figuratively.

As to Matt. 24:51, it has been remarked that the "cutting asunder" was an appropriate punishment for one who had lived a double life. In both passages the latter part of the sentence applies to retribution beyond this life.¶ In the Sept. the verb is used in Exod. 29:17 of the dividing of the ram as a whole burnt offering at the consecration of the priests.¶ The corresponding noun is found in Gen. 15:11, 17; Ex. 29:17; Lev. 1:8; Ezek. 24:4.¶

7. *suntemnō* (συντέμνω, 4932), lit., "to cut together" (*sun*, "with," *temnō*, "to cut"; the simple verb *temnō* is not found in the NT), signifies "to contract by cutting, to cut short"; thus, to bring to an end or accomplish speedily; it is said of a prophecy or decree, Rom. 9:28 (twice), from the Sept. of Isa. 10:23. See SHORT.¶

8. *aphaireō* (ἀφαιρέω, 851), "to take away, remove," is translated "cut off" in Mark 14:47, KJV, and Luke 22:50, and "smote off" in Matt. 26:51; RV, "struck off" in each place. See SMITE, TAKE.

CYMBAL

kumbalon (κύμβαλον, 2950), "a cymbal," was so called from its shape (akin to *kumbos*, "a hollow basin," *kumbē*, "a cup"), and was made of bronze, two being struck together, 1 Cor. 13:1.¶

D

DAILY (Adjective)

1. *epiousios* (ἐπιούσιος, 1967) is found in Matt. 6:11 and Luke 11:3. Some would derive the word from *epi*, "upon," and *eimi*, "to be," as if to signify "(bread) present," i.e., sufficient bread, but this formation is questionable. The same objection applies to the conjecture, that it is derived from *epi*, and *ousia*, and signifies "(bread) for sustenance." The more probable derivation is from *epi*, and *eimi*, "to go," (bread) for going on, i.e., for the morrow and after, or (bread) coming (for us). See the RV marg. This suits the added *sēmeron*, "to-day," i.e., the prayer is to be for bread that suffices for this day and next, so that the mind may conform to Christ's warning against anxiety for the morrow. Confirmation of this derivation is also to be found in the word *epiousē*, in the phrase "the next day," Acts 7:26; 16:11.¶

2. *ephēmeros* (ἐφήμερος, 2184) signifies "for the day" (*epi*, "upon, or for," *hēmera*, "a day," Eng., "ephemeral"), Jas. 2:15.¶

3. *kathēmerinos* (καθημερινός, 2522) means, lit., "according to" (*kata*) "the day" (*hēmera*), "day by day, daily," Acts 6:1.¶

Notes: The following phrases contain the word *hēmera*, "day," and are translated "daily" or otherwise: (*a*) *kath' hēmeran*, lit., "according to, or for, (the) day, or throughout the day," "day by day," e.g., Luke 11:3; Acts 3:2; 16:5; 1 Cor. 15:31; Heb. 7:27; (*b*) *hēmera kai hēmera*, lit., "day and day," "day by day," 2 Cor. 4:16; (*c*) *hēmeran ex hēmeras*, lit., "day from day," "from day to day," 2 Pet. 2:8; (*d*) *sēmeron*, "this day," or "today," used outside the Synoptists and the Acts, in 2 Cor. 3:14–15, eight times in Hebrews, and in Jas. 4:13; (*e*) *tēs sēmeron hēm-*

eras, "(unto) this very day," Rom. 11:8 (RV); (*f*) *tas hēmeras*, Luke 21:37, RV, "every day," for KJV, "in the daytime"; (*g*) *pasan hēmeran*, Acts 5:42, RV, "every day"; preceded by *kata* in Acts 17:17, RV, "every day"; (*h*) *kath' hekastēn hēmeran*, lit., "according to each day," Heb. 3:13, "day by day," RV.

DAINTY

liparos (λιπαρός, 3045) properly signifies "oily, or anointed with oil" (from *lipos*, "grease," connected with *aleiphō*, "to anoint"); it is said of things which pertain to delicate and sumptuous living; hence, "dainty," Rev. 18:14.¶ In the Sept., Judg. 3:29; Neh. 9:35; Isa. 30:23.¶

For DAMAGE see LOSS

For DAMNABLE, DAMNATION, and DAMNED see CONDEMNATION, DESTRUCTION, JUDGE, JUDGMENT

DAMSEL

1. *korasion* (κοράσιον, 2877), a diminutive of *korē*, "a girl," denotes "a little girl" (properly a colloquial word, often used disparagingly, but not so in later writers); in the NT it is used only in familiar conversation, Matt. 9:24–25 (KJV, "maid"); 14:11; Mark 5:41–42; 6:22, 28.¶

2. *paidion* (παιδίον, 3813), a diminutive of *pais*, denotes "a young child (male or female)" in the KJV of Mark 5:39–41 (1st line); the RV corrects "damsel" to "child," so as to distinguish between the narrative of facts, and the homely address to the little girl herself, in which, and in

the following sentence, *korasion* is used. (See No. 1). See CHILD.

3. *paidiskē* (παιδίσκη, 3814) denotes "a young girl, or a female slave"; "damsel," KJV, in John 18:17; Acts 12:13; 16:16; RV "maid" in each case. See BONDMAID, BONDWOMAN, MAID, MAIDEN.

DANCE

orcheō (ὀρχέω, 3738), (cf. Eng., "orchestra"), probably originally signified "to lift up," as of the feet; hence, "to leap with regularity of motion." It is always used in the middle voice, Matt. 11:17; 14:6; Mark 6:22; Luke 7:32. The performance by the daughter of Herodias is the only clear instance of artistic dancing, a form introduced from Greek customs.¶

DANCING

choros (χορός, 5525), (Eng., "chorus"), primarily denoted "an enclosure for dancing"; hence, "a company of dancers and singers." The supposition that the word is connected with *orcheō* by metathesis (i.e., change of place, of the letters *ch* and *o*) seems to be without foundation. The word is used in Luke 15:25.¶

DANGER, DANGEROUS

A. Verb.

kinduneuō (κινδυνεύω, 2793) properly signifies "to run a risk, face danger," but is used in the NT in the sense of "being in danger, jeopardy," Acts 19:27, 40. It is translated "were in jeopardy" in Luke 8:23, and "stand we in jeopardy," 1 Cor. 15:30.¶

Note: Kindunos, akin to A, "peril, danger," is always rendered "peril," Rom. 8:35 and 2 Cor. 11:26 (eight times).¶

B. Adjectives.

1. *enochos* (ἔνοχος, 1777), lit., "held in, contained in" (*en*, "in," *echō*, "to have, hold"), hence, "bound under obligation to, liable to, subject to," is used in the sense of being in "danger" of the penal effect of a misdeed, i.e., in a forensic sense, signifying the connection of a person with (*a*) his crime, "guilty of an eternal sin," Mark 3:29, RV; (*b*) the trial or tribunal, as a result of which sentence is passed, Matt. 5:21–22, "the judgment," "the council"; *enochos* here has the obsolete sense of control (J. Hastings); (*c*) the penalty itself, 5:22, "the hell of fire," and, with the translation "worthy" (KJV, "guilty"), of the punishment determined to be inflicted on Christ, Matt. 26:66 and Mark 14:64, "death"; (*d*) the person or thing against whom or which the offense is committed, 1 Cor. 11:27, "guilty," the crime being against "the body and blood of the Lord"; Jas. 2:10,

"guilty" of an offense against all the Law, because of a breach of one commandment.

Apart from the forensic sense, this adjective is used of the thing by which one is bound, "subject to" (bondage), in Heb. 2:15. See GUILTY, SUBJECT, WORTHY.¶

2. *episphalēs* (ἐπισφαλής, 2000), lit., "prone to fall" (*epi*, "upon," i.e., near upon, *sphallō*, "to fall"), hence, "insecure, dangerous," is used in Acts 27:9.¶

DARE, DARING, DURST

A. Verb.

tolmaō (τολμάω, 5111) signifies "to dare," (*a*) in the sense of not dreading or shunning through fear, Matt. 22:46; Mark 12:34; Mark 15:43, "boldly," lit., "having dared, went in"; Luke 20:40; John 21:12; Acts 5:13; 7:32; Rom. 15:18; 2 Cor. 10:2, RV, "show courage," (KJV, "be bold"); 10:12, RV, "are (not) bold"; 11:21; Phil. 1:14, "are bold"; Jude 9; (*b*) in the sense of bearing, enduring, bringing oneself to do a thing, Rom. 5:7; 1 Cor. 6:1.¶ Cf. *apotolmaō*, "to be very bold," Rom. 10:20.¶ See BOLD.

B. Adjective.

tolmētēs (τολμητής, 5113), akin to A, "daring," is used in 2 Pet. 2:10, RV, "daring" (KJV, "presumptuous"), "shameless and irreverent daring."¶

DARK, DARKEN, DARKLY, DARKNESS

A. Adjectives.

1. *skoteinos* (σκοτεινός, 4652), "full of darkness, or covered with darkness," is translated "dark" in Luke 11:36; "full of darkness," in Matt. 6:23 and Luke 11:34, where the physical condition is figurative of the moral. The group of *skot*-words is derived from a root *ska*—, meaning "to cover." The same root is to be found in *skēnē*, "a tent".¶

Note: Contrast *phōteinos*, "full of light," e.g., Matt. 6:22.

2. *auchmēros* (αὐχμηρός, 850), from *auchmos*, "drought produced by excessive heat," hence signifies "dry, murky, dark," 2 Pet. 1:19 (RV marg., "squalid"). No. 1 signifies "darkness" produced by covering; No. 2, "darkness" produced by being squalid or murky.¶

B. Nouns.

1. *skotia* (σκοτία, 4653) is used (*a*) of physical darkness, "dark," John 6:17, lit., "darkness had come on," and 20:1, lit., "darkness still being"; (*b*) of secrecy, in general, whether what is done therein is good or evil, Matt. 10:27; Luke 12:3; (*c*) of spiritual or moral "darkness," emblematic of sin, as a condition of moral or

spiritual depravity, Matt. 4:16; John 1:5; 8:12; 12:35, 46; 1 John 1:5; 2:8–9, 11.¶

2. *skotos* (σκότος, 4655), an older form than No. 1, grammatically masculine, is found in some mss. in Heb. 12:18.¶

3. *skotos* (σκότος, 4655), a neuter noun, frequent in the Sept., is used in the NT as the equivalent of No. 1; (*a*) of "physical darkness," Matt. 27:45; 2 Cor. 4:6; (*b*) of "intellectual darkness," Rom. 2:19 (cf. C, No. 1); (*c*) of "blindness," Acts 13:11; (*d*) by metonymy, of the "place of punishment," e.g., Matt. 8:12; 2 Pet. 2:17; Jude 13; (*e*) metaphorically, of "moral and spiritual darkness," e.g., Matt. 6:23; Luke 1:79; 11:35; John 3:19; Acts 26:18; 2 Cor. 6:14; Eph. 6:12; Col. 1:13; 1 Thess. 5:4–5; 1 Pet. 2:9; 1 John 1:6; (*f*) by metonymy, of "those who are in moral or spiritual darkness," Eph. 5:8; (*g*) of "evil works," Rom. 13:12; Eph. 5:11; (*h*) of the "evil powers that dominate the world," Luke 22:53; (*i*) "of secrecy" [as in No. 1, (*b*)]. While *skotos* is used more than twice as many times as *skotia* in the NT, the apostle John uses *skotos* only once, 1 John 1:6, but *skotia* 15 times out of the 18.

"With the exception of the significance of secrecy [No. 1, (*b*) and No. 3 (*i*)], darkness is always used in a bad sense. Moreover the different forms of darkness are so closely allied, being either cause and effect, or else concurrent effects of the same cause, that they cannot always be distinguished; 1 John 1:5; 2:8, e.g., are passages in which both spiritual and moral darkness are intended."*

4. *zophos* (ζόφος, 2217) denotes "the gloom of the nether world"; hence, "thick darkness, darkness that may be felt"; it is rendered "darkness" in Heb. 12:18; 2 Pet. 2:4 and Jude 6; in 2 Pet. 2:17, RV, "blackness," KJV, "mists"; in Jude 13, RV and KJV, "blackness." See BLACKNESS, B, Nos. 1 and 2, MIST.¶

C. Verbs.

1. *skotizō* (σκοτίζω, 4654), "to deprive of light, to make dark," is used in the NT in the passive voice only, (*a*) of the heavenly bodies, Matt. 24:29; Mark 13:24; Rev. 8:12; (*b*) metaphorically, of the mind, Rom. 1:21; 11:10; (some mss. have it in Luke 23:45).¶

2. *skotoō* (σκοτόω, 4656), "to darken," is used (*a*) of the heavenly bodies, Rev. 9:2; 16:10; (*b*) metaphorically, of the mind, Eph. 4:18.¶

Note: The phrase *en ainigmati*, lit., "in an enigma," is rendered "darkly" in 1 Cor. 13:12. *Ainigma* is akin to the verb *ainissomai*, "to hint obscurely." The allusion is to Num. 12:8 (Sept.),

"not in (*dia*, "by means of") dark speeches" (lit., "enigmas"); God's communications to Moses were not such as in the case of dreams, etc. After the same analogy, what we see and know now is seen "darkly" compared with the direct vision in the presence of God hereafter. The riddles of seeming obscurity in life will all be made clear.

DART

belos (βέλος, 956), akin to *ballō*, "to throw," denotes "a missile, an arrow, javelin, dart, etc.," Eph. 6:16 (see FIERY).¶ Cf. *bolē*, "a stone's throw or cast," Luke 22:41,¶; *bolizō*, "to sound" (to fathom the depth of water), Acts 27:28.¶

Note: The noun *bolis*, "a dart," is found in some texts in Heb. 12:20 (see KJV).¶

DASH

1. *proskoptō* (προσκόπτω, 4350) denotes "to beat upon or against, to strike against, dash against" (*pros*, "to or against," *koptō*, "to strike, beat"); hence, of the foot, to stumble, "dash" (KJV and RV), Matt. 4:6; Luke 4:11. See BEAT, STUMBLE.

2. *rhēgnumi* (ῥήγνυμι, 4486), "to tear, rend, break," is used of the action of a demon upon a human victim, Mark 9:18, "dasheth ... down," RV; (KJV, marg.; KJV, text, "teareth"); Luke 9:42, RV, "dashed ... down" (KJV, "threw ... down"). See BREAK, No. 6.

3. *edaphizō* (ἐδαφίζω, 1474), "to beat level with the earth," e.g., as a threshing floor (cf. *edaphos*, "the ground"), Luke 19:44; RV, "shall dash (thee) to the ground"; (KJV, "shall lay (thee) even with the ground"). See GROUND.¶

DAUGHTER, DAUGHTER-IN-LAW

1. *thugatēr* (θυγάτηρ, 2364), "a daughter," (etymologically, Eng., "daughter" is connected), is used of (*a*) the natural relationship (frequent in the gospels); (*b*) spiritual relationship to God, 2 Cor. 6:18, in the sense of the practical realization of acceptance with, and the approval of, God (cf. Isa. 43:6), the only place in the NT where it applies to spiritual relationship; (*c*) the inhabitants of a city or region, Matt. 21:5; John 12:15 ("of Zion"); cf. Isa. 37:22; Zeph. 3:14 (Sept.); (*d*) the women who followed Christ to Calvary, Luke 23:28; (*e*) women of Aaron's posterity, Luke 1:5; (*f*) a female descendant of Abraham, Luke 13:16.

2. *thugatrion* (θυγάτριον, 2365), a diminutive of No. 1, denotes "a little daughter," Mark 5:23; 7:25.¶

3. *parthenos* (παρθένος, 3933), "a maiden, virgin," e.g., Matt. 1:23, signifies a virgin-daugh-

ter in 1 Cor. 7:36–38 (RV); in Rev. 14:4, it is used of chaste persons. See VIRGIN.

4. *numphē* (νύμφη, 3565), (Eng., "nymph"), denotes "a bride," John 3:29; also "a daughter-in-law," Matt. 10:35; Luke 12:53. See BRIDE.

Note: In 1 Pet. 3:6, *teknon*, "a child," is translated "daughters" (KJV), "children" (RV).

DAWN

A. Verbs.

1. *augazō* (αὐγάζω, 826), "to shine," is used metaphorically of the light of dawn, in 2 Cor. 4:4 (some texts have *kataugazō*). Cf. *augē*, "brightness or break of day," Acts 20:11. The word formerly meant "to see clearly," and it is possible that this meaning was continued in general usage.¶

2. *diaugazō* (διαυγάζω, 1306) signifies "to shine through" (*dia*, "through," *augē*, "brightness"); it describes the breaking of daylight upon the darkness of night, metaphorically in 2 Pet. 1:19, of the shining of spiritual light into the heart. A probable reference is to the day to be ushered in at the second coming of Christ: "until the Day gleam through the present darkness, and the Light-bringer dawn in your hearts."¶

Note: Cf. *diaugēs*, "translucent, transparent," Rev. 21:21 (some texts have *diaphanēs*, "transparent").¶

3. *epiphōskō* (ἐπιφώσκω, 2020), "to grow light" (*epi*, "upon," *phōs*, "light"), in the sense of shining upon, is used in Matt. 28:1; in Luke 23:54, "drew on" (of the Sabbath-day); RV, marg., "began to dawn." See DRAW.¶

B. Noun.

orthros (ὄρθρος, 3722), "daybreak," denotes "at early dawn," Luke 24:1 (RV), "early in the morning" (KJV), and John 8:2 (KJV and RV); in Acts 5:21, RV, "about daybreak," for KJV, "early in the morning."¶

Note: Cf. *orthrios*, "early," in some texts in Luke 24:22;¶ *orthrinos*, a later form of *orthros*, in some mss. in Rev. 22:16;¶ *orthrizō*, "to do anything early in the morning," in Luke 21:38.¶

DAY

A. Nouns.

1. *hēmera* (ἡμέρα, 2250), "a day," is used of (*a*) the period of natural light, Gen. 1:5; Prov. 4:18; Mark 4:35; (*b*) the same, but figuratively, for a period of opportunity for service, John 9:4; Rom. 13:13; (*c*) one period of alternate light and darkness, Gen. 1:5; Mark 1:13; (*d*) a period of undefined length marked by certain characteristics, such as "the day of small things," Zech. 4:10; of perplexity and distress, Isa. 17:11; Obad. 12–14; of prosperity and of

adversity, Ecc. 7:14; of trial or testing, Ps. 95:8; of salvation, Isa. 49:8; 2 Cor. 6:2; cf. Luke 19:42; of evil, Eph. 6:13; of wrath and revelation of the judgments of God, Rom. 2:5; (*e*) an appointed time, Ecc. 8:6; Eph. 4:30; (*f*) a notable defeat in battle, etc., Isa. 9:4; Psa. 137:7; Ezek. 30:9; Hos. 1:11; (*g*) by metonymy = "when," "at the time when"; (1), of the past, Gen. 2:4; Num. 3:13; Deut. 4:10, (2), of the future, Gen. 2:17; Ruth 4:5; Matt. 24:50; Luke 1:20; (*h*) a judgment or doom, Job 18:20.* (*i*) of a time of life, Luke 1:17–18 ("years").

As the "day" throws light upon things that have been in darkness, the word is often associated with the passing of judgment upon circumstances. In 1 Cor. 4:3, "man's day," KJV, "man's judgement," RV, denotes mere human judgment upon matters ("man's" translates the adjective *anthrōpinos*, "human"), a judgment exercised in the present period of human rebellion against "God"; probably therefore "the Lord's Day," Rev. 1:10, or "the Day of the Lord" (where an adjective, *kuriakos*, is similarly used), is the day of His manifested judgment on the world.

The phrases "the day of Christ," Phil. 1:10; 2:16; "the day of Jesus Christ," 1:6; "the day of the Lord Jesus," 1 Cor. 5:5; 2 Cor. 1:14; "the day of our Lord Jesus Christ," 1 Cor. 1:8, denote the time of the Parousia of Christ with His saints, subsequent to the Rapture, 1 Thess. 4:16–17. In 2 Pet. 1:19 this is spoken of simply as "the day," (see DAY-STAR).

From these the phrase "the day of the Lord" is to be distinguished; in the OT it had reference to a time of the victorious interposition by God for the overthrow of the foes of Israel, e.g., Isa. 2:12; Amos 5:18; if Israel transgressed in the pride of their hearts, the Day of the Lord would be a time of darkness and judgment. For their foes, however, there would come "a great and terrible day of the Lord," Joel 2:31; Mal. 4:5. That period, still future, will see the complete overthrow of gentile power and the establishment of Messiah's kingdom, Isa. 13:9–11; 34:8; Dan. 2:34, 44; Obad. 15; cf. Isa. 61:2; John 8:56.

In the NT "the day of the Lord" is mentioned in 1 Thess. 5:2 and 2 Thess. 2:2, RV, where the apostle's warning is that the church at Thessalonica should not be deceived by thinking that "the Day of the Lord is now present." This period will not begin till the circumstances mentioned in verses 3 and 4 take place.

For the eventual development of the divine

---

* From *Notes on Thessalonians*, by Hogg and Vine, pp. 150–151.

purposes in relation to the human race see 2 Pet. 3:12, "the Day of God."

2. *augē* (αὐγή, 827), "brightness, bright, shining, as of the sun"; hence, "the beginning of daylight," is translated "break of day" in Acts 20 :11.¶

B. Adverb.

ennucha (ἔννυχα, 1773**), the neuter plural of *ennuchos*, used adverbially, lit., "in night" (*en*, "in," *nux*, "night," with *lian*, "very"), signifies "very early, yet in the night," "a great while before day," Mark 1:35.¶

Notes: (1) For phrases, see DAILY. (2) In Mark 6:35, the clause "the day was far spent" is, lit., "a much hour (i.e., a late hour) having become," or, perhaps, "many an hour having become," i.e., many hours having passed. In the end of the v., RV, "day," for KJV, "time." (3) In Mark 2:26, KJV, "in the days of," there is no word for "days" in the original; RV (from best mss.), "when"; in Acts 11:28, "in the days of." (4) In John 21:4, the adjective *prōios*, "at early morn," is translated "day" (RV, for KJV, "the morning"); see Matt. 27:1.¶ (5) In 2 Thess. 2:3, "that day shall not come" (KJV) translates nothing in the original; it is inserted to supply the sense (see the RV); cf. Luke 7:11 (RV, "soon afterwards"); 1 Cor. 4:13 (RV, "even until now").

(6) For "day following" see MORROW.

For **DAYBREAK** (RV, in Acts 5:21) see **DAWN, B**

DAYSPRING

anatolē (ἀνατολή, 395), lit., "a rising up" (cf. *anatellō*, "to cause to rise"), is used of the rising of the sun and stars; it chiefly means the east, as in Matt. 2:1, etc.; rendered "dayspring" in Luke 1:78. Its other meaning, "a shoot," is found in the Sept. in Jer. 23:5; Zech. 6:12. See also the margin of Luke 1:78, "branch." See EAST.

DAY-STAR

phōsphoros (φωσφόρος, 5459), (Eng., "phosphorus," lit., "light-bearing" *phōs*, "light," *pherō*, "to bear"), is used of the morning star, as the light-bringer, 2 Pet. 1:19, where it indicates the arising of the light of Christ as the personal fulfillment, in the hearts of believers, of the prophetic Scriptures concerning His coming to receive them to Himself.¶

DAZZLING

1. *astraptō* (ἀστράπτω, 797), "to flash forth, lighten," is said of lightning, Luke 17:24, and of

the apparel of the two men by the Lord's sepulchre, 24:4, KJV, "shining." See LIGHTEN, SHINE.¶

2. *exastraptō* (ἐξαστράπτω, 1823), a strengthened form of No. 1 (*ek*, out of), signifies "to flash like lightning, gleam, be radiant," in Luke 9:29 of the Lord's raiment at His transfiguration, RV, "dazzling"; KJV, "glistering."¶ In the Sept., Ezek. 1:4, 7; Nahum 3:3.¶

DEACON

diakonos (διάκονος, 1249), (Eng., "deacon"), primarily denotes a "servant," whether as doing servile work, or as an attendant rendering free service, without particular reference to its character. The word is probably connected with the verb *diōkō*, "to hasten after, pursue" (perhaps originally said of a runner). "It occurs in the NT of domestic servants, John 2:5, 9; the civil ruler, Rom. 13:4; Christ, Rom. 15:8; Gal. 2:17; the followers of Christ in relation to their Lord, John 12:26; Eph. 6:21; Col. 1:7; 4:7; the followers of Christ in relation to one another, Matt. 20:26; 23:11; Mark 9:35; 10:43; the servants of Christ in the work of preaching and teaching, 1 Cor. 3:5; 2 Cor. 3:6; 6:4; 11:23; Eph. 3:7; Col. 1:23, 25; 1 Thess. 3:2; 1 Tim. 4:6; those who serve in the churches, Rom. 16:1 (used of a woman here only in NT); Phil. 1:1; 1 Tim. 3:8, 12; false apostles, servants of Satan, 2 Cor. 11:15. Once *diakonos* is used where, apparently, angels are intended, Matt. 22:13; in v. 3, where men are intended, *doulos* is used."*

Diakonos is, generally speaking, to be distinguished from *doulos*, "a bondservant, slave"; *diakonos* views a servant in relationship to his work; *doulos* views him in relationship to his master. See, e.g., Matt. 22:2–14; those who bring in the guests (vv. 3–4, 6, 8, 10) are *douloi*; those who carry out the king's sentence (v. 13) are *diakonoi*.¶

Note: As to synonymous terms, *leitourgos* denotes "one who performs public duties"; *misthios* and *misthōtos*, "a hired servant"; *oiketēs*, "a household servant"; *hupēretēs*, "a subordinate official waiting on his superior" (originally an under-rower in a war-galley); *therapōn*, "one whose service is that of freedom and dignity." See MINISTER, SERVANT.

The so-called "seven deacons" in Acts 6 are not there mentioned by that name, though the kind of service in which they were engaged was of the character of that committed to such.

* From *Notes on Thessalonians,* by Hogg and Vine, p. 91.

DEAD

A. Noun and Adjective.

nekros (νεκρός, 3498) is used of (*a*) the death of the body, cf. Jas. 2:26, its most frequent sense: (*b*) the actual spiritual condition of unsaved men, Matt. 8:22; John 5:25; Eph. 2:1, 5; 5:14; Phil. 3:11; Col. 2:13; cf. Luke 15:24: (*c*) the ideal spiritual condition of believers in regard to sin, Rom. 6:11: (*d*) a church in declension, inasmuch as in that state it is inactive and barren, Rev. 3:1: (*e*) sin, which apart from law cannot produce a sense of guilt, Rom. 7:8: (*f*) the body of the believer in contrast to his spirit, Rom. 8:10: (*g*) the works of the Law, inasmuch as, however good in themselves, Rom. 7:13, they cannot produce life, Heb. 6:1; 9:14: (*h*) the faith that does not produce works, Jas. 2:17, 26; cf. v. 20.†

B. Verbs.

1. *nekroō* (νεκρόω, 3499), "to put to death," is used in the active voice in the sense of destroying the strength of, depriving of power, with reference to the evil desires which work in the body, Col. 3:5. In the passive voice it is used of Abraham's body as being "as good as dead," Rom. 4:19 with Heb. 11:12.¶

2. *thanatoō* (θανατόω, 2289), "to put to death:" see DEATH, C, No. 1.

DEADLY

1. *thanatēphoros* (θανατφρος, 2287), lit., "death-bearing, deadly" (*thanatos*, "death," *pherō*, "to bear"), is used in Jas. 3:8.¶ In the Sept., Num. 18:22; Job 33:23.¶

2. *thanasimos* (θανάσιμος, 2286), from *thanatos* (see No. 1), "belonging to death, or partaking of the nature of death," is used in Mark 16:18.¶

HALF DEAD

hēmithanēs (ἡμιθανής, 2253), from *hēmi*, "half," and *thnēskō*, "to die," is used in Luke 10:30.¶

DEADNESS

nekrōsis (νέκρωσις, 3500), "a putting to death" (cf. DEAD, A and B), is rendered "dying" in 2 Cor. 4:10; "deadness" in Rom. 4:19, i.e., the state of being virtually "dead."¶

DEAF

kōphos (κωφός, 2974), akin to *koptō*, "to beat," and *kopiaō*, "to be tired" (from a root *kop—*, "to cut"), signifies "blunted, dull," as of a weapon; hence, "blunted in tongue, dumb,"

† From *Notes on Thessalonians,* by Hogg and Vine, p. 143.

Matt. 9:32 etc.; "in hearing, deaf," Matt. 11:5; Mark 7:32, 37; 9:25; Luke 7:22. See DUMB.

For a GREAT DEAL see GREAT

DEAL

merizō (μερίζω, 3307) signifies "to divide into parts" (*meros*, "a portion, part"); hence, "to distribute, divide out, deal out to," translated "hath dealt" in Rom. 12:3. See DIFFERENCE, DISTRIBUTE, DIVINE.

DEAL WITH, HAVE DEALINGS WITH

1. *poieō* (ποιέω, 4160), "to do," used to describe almost any act, whether complete or repeated, like the Eng. "do," is translated to deal with, in Luke 2:48. In Luke 1:25, KJV, "hath dealt with (me)," the RV, adhering to the ordinary meaning, translates by "hath done unto (me)."

2. *prospherō* (προσφέρω, 4374), "to bring or bear to" (*pros*, "to," *pherō*, "to bear"), signifies, in the middle voice, to bear oneself towards any one, to deal with anyone in a certain manner, Heb. 12:7, "God dealeth with you." See BRING, OFFER, PRESENT.

3. *sunchraomai* (συγχράομαι, 4798), lit., "to use with" (*sun*, "with," *chraomai*, "to use"), "to have in joint use, and hence to have dealings with," is said, in John 4:9, of Jews and Samaritans.¶

Notes: (1) In Acts 25:24, *entunchanō*, "to fall in with, meet and talk with," and hence "to make suit to a person" by way of pleading with him, is translated "have dealt with" in the KJV; correctly in the RV, "have made suit to," of the Jews in appealing to Festus against Paul. See INTERCESSION.

(2) *Katasophizomai*, "to circumvent by fraud, conquer by subtle devices" (*kata*, "down," intensive, and *sophizō*, "to devise cleverly or cunningly"; cf. Eng., "sophist, sophistry"), is translated "dealt subtilly," in Acts 7:19, of Pharaoh's dealings with the Israelites.¶ This is the word in the Sept. of Ex. 1:10. See SUBTILLY.¶

(3) In 1 Thess. 2:11 the italicized phrase "we dealt with" (RV), has no corresponding word in the original, but is inserted in order to bring out the participial forms of the verbs "exhorting," "encouraging," "testifying," as showing the constant practice of the apostles at Thessalonica. The incompleteness of the sentence in the original illustrates the informal homeliness of the Epistle.

(4) In 2 Cor. 13:10, the verb *chraomai*, "to

use," is rendered, in the RV, "deal (sharply)," KJV, "use (sharpness)."

DEAR

1. *timios* (τίμιος, 5093), from *timē*, "honor, price," signifies (a), primarily, "accounted as of great price, precious, costly," 1 Cor. 3:12; Rev. 17:4; 18:12, 16; 21:19, and in the superlative degree, 18:12; 21:11; the comparative degree is found in 1 Pet. 1:7 (*polutimoteros*, in the most authentic mss., "much more precious"); (b) in the metaphorical sense, "held in honor, esteemed, very dear," Acts 5:34, "had in honor," RV (KJV, "had in reputation"); so in Heb. 13:4, RV, "let marriage be had in honor"; KJV, "is honorable"; Acts 20:24, "dear," negatively of Paul's estimate of his life; Jas. 5:7, "precious" (of fruit); 1 Pet. 1:19, "precious" (of the blood of Christ); 2 Pet. 1:4 (of God's promises). See COSTLY, HONORABLE, REPUTATION, PRECIOUS.¶ Cf. *timiōtes*, preciousness, Rev. 18:19.¶

2. *entimos* (ἔντιμος, 1784), "held in honor" (*timē*, see above), "precious, dear," is found in Luke 7:2, of the centurion's servant; 14:8, "more honorable"; Phil. 2:29, "honor" (KJV, "reputation"), of devoted servants of Christ; in 1 Pet. 2:4, 6, "precious," of stones, metaphorically. See HONORABLE, REPUTATION, PRECIOUS.¶

3. *agapētos* (ἀγαπητός, 27), from *agapē*, "love," signifies "beloved"; it is rendered "very dear" in 1 Thess. 2:8 (KJV, "dear"), of the affection of Paul and his fellow workers for the saints at Thessalonica; in Eph. 5:1 and Col. 1:7, KJV, "dear"; RV, "beloved." See BELOVED.

Note: In Col. 1:13, *agapē* is translated "dear" in the KJV; the RV, adhering to the noun, has "the Son of His love."

For DEARLY see BELOVED

For DEARTH see FAMINE

DEATH, DEATH-STROKE (See also DIE)

A. Nouns

1. *thanatos* (θάνατος, 2288), "death," is used in Scripture of:

(a) the separation of the soul (the spiritual part of man) from the body (the material part), the latter ceasing to function and turning to dust, e.g., John 11:13; Heb. 2:15; 5:7; 7:23. In Heb. 9:15, the KJV, "by means of death" is inadequate; the RV, "a death having taken place" is in keeping with the subject. In Rev. 13:3, 12, the RV, "death-stroke" (KJV, "deadly wound") is, lit., "the stroke of death":

(b) the separation of man from God; Adam

died on the day he disobeyed God, Gen. 2:17, and hence all mankind are born in the same spiritual condition, Rom. 5:12, 14, 17, 21, from which, however, those who believe in Christ are delivered, John 5:24; 1 John 3:14. "Death" is the opposite of life; it never denotes nonexistence. As spiritual life is "conscious existence in communion with God," so spiritual "death" is "conscious existence in separation from God."

"Death, in whichever of the above-mentioned senses it is used, is always, in Scripture, viewed as the penal consequence of sin, and since sinners alone are subject to death, Rom. 5:12, it was as the Bearer of sin that the Lord Jesus submitted thereto on the Cross, 1 Pet. 2:24. And while the physical death of the Lord Jesus was of the essence of His sacrifice, it was not the whole. The darkness symbolized, and His cry expressed, the fact that He was left alone in the Universe, He was 'forsaken;' cf. Matt. 27:45-46."*

2. *anairesis* (ἀναίρεσις, 336), another word for "death," lit. signifies "a taking up or off" (*ana*, "up," *airō*, "to take"), as of the taking of a life, or "putting to death"; it is found in Acts 8:1, of the murder of Stephen. Some mss. have it in 22:20. See *anaireō*, under KILL.¶ In the Sept., Num. 11:15; Judg. 15:17, "the lifting of the jawbone."¶

3. *teleutē* (τελευτή, 5054), "an end, limit" (cf. *telos*, see END), hence, "the end of life, death," is used of the "death" of Herod, Matt. 2:15.¶

B. Adjective.

epithanatios (ἐπιθανάτιος, 1935), "doomed to death" (*epi*, "upon," *thanatos*, A, No. 1), is said of the apostles, in 1 Cor. 4:9.¶

C. Verbs.

1. *thanatoō* (θανατόω, 2289), "to put to death" (akin to A, No. 1), in Matt. 10:21; Mark 13:12; Luke 21:16, is translated "shall ... cause (them) to be put to death," lit., "shall put (them) to death" (RV marg.). It is used of the death of Christ in Matt. 26:59; 27:1; Mark 14:55 and 1 Pet. 3:18. In Rom. 7:4 (passive voice) it is translated "ye ... were made dead," RV (for KJV, "are become"), with reference to the change from bondage to the Law to union with Christ; in 8:13, "mortify" (marg., "make to die"), of the act of the believer in regard to the deeds of the body; in 8:36, "are killed"; so in 2 Cor. 6:9. See KILL, MORTIFY.¶

2. *anaireō* (ἀναιρέω, 337), lit., "to take or lift up or away" (see A, No. 2), hence, "to put to death," is usually translated "to kill or slay";

* From *Notes on Thessalonians,* by Hogg and Vine, p. 134.

in two places "put to death," Luke 23:32; Acts 26:10. It is used 17 times, with this meaning, in Acts. See KILL, SLAY, TAKE.

3. *apagō* (ἀπάγω, 520), lit., "to lead away" (*apo*, "away," *agō*, "to lead"), is used especially in a judicial sense, "to put to death," e.g., Acts 12:19. See BRING, CARRY, LEAD, TAKE.

4. *apokteinō* (ἀποκτείνω, 615), "to kill," is so translated in the RV, for the KJV, "put to death," in Mark 14:1; Luke 18:33; in John 11:53; 12:10 and 18:31, RV, "put to death." See KILL, SLAY.

Note: The phrase *eschatōs echō*, lit., "to have extremely," i.e., "to be in extremity," *in extremis*, "at the last (gasp), to be at the point of death," is used in Mark 5:23.¶

For the KJV **DEBATE** (Rom. 1:29 and 2 Cor. 12:20) see **STRIFE**

DEBT

1. *opheilē* (ὀφειλή, 3782), "that which is owed" (see *Note,* below), is translated "debt" in Matt. 18:32; in the plural, "dues," Rom. 13:7; "(her) due," 1 Cor. 7:3, of conjugal duty: some texts here have *opheilomenēn* (*eunoian*) "due (benevolence)," KJV; the context confirms the RV. See DUE.¶

2. *opheilēma* (ὀφείλημα, 3783), a longer form of No. 1, expressing a "debt" more concretely, is used (*a*) literally, of that which is legally due, Rom. 4:4; (*b*) metaphorically, of sin as a "debt," because it demands expiation, and thus payment by way of punishment, Matt. 6:12.¶

3. *daneion* (δάνειον, 1156), "a loan" (akin to *danos*, "a gift"), is translated "debt" in Matt. 18:27 (RV, marg., "loan"), of the ten thousand talents debtor.¶ Cf. *daneizō*, "to lend," and *daneistēs*, "a money-lender, a creditor."

Note: In Matt. 18:30, *opheilō*, "to owe," is translated "debt" in the KJV (RV, "that which was due."). See DUE.

DEBTOR

1. *opheiletēs* (ὀφειλέτης, 3781), "one who owes anything to another," primarily in regard to money; in Matt. 18:24, "who owed" (lit., "one was brought, a debtor to him of ten thousand talents"). The slave could own property, and so become a "debtor" to his master, who might seize him for payment.

It is used metaphorically,

(*a*) of a person who is under an obligation, Rom. 1:14, of Paul, in the matter of preaching the gospel; in Rom. 8:12, of believers, to mortify the deeds of the body; in Rom. 15:27, of gentile

believers, to assist afflicted Jewish believers; in Gal. 5:3, of those who would be justified by circumcision, to do the whole Law: (*b*) of those who have not yet made amends to those whom they have injured, Matt. 6:12, "our debtors"; of some whose disaster was liable to be regarded as a due punishment, Luke 13:4 (RV, "offenders"; KJV, "sinners"; marg., "debtors").¶

2. *chreōpheiletēs* (χρεωφειλέτης, 5533), lit., "a debt-ower" (*chreos*, "a loan, a debt," and No. 1), is found in Luke 7:41, of the two "debtors" mentioned in the Lord's parable addressed to Simon the Pharisee, and in 16:5, of the "debtors" in the parable of the unrighteous steward. This parable indicates a system of credit in the matter of agriculture.¶ In the Sept., Job 31:37, "having taken nothing from the debtor"; Prov. 29:13, "when the creditor and the debtor meet together."¶ The word is more expressive than No. 1.

Note: In Matt. 23:16 *opheilō*, "to owe" (see DEBT), is translated "he is a debtor." The RV marg., keeping the verbal form, has "bound by his oath" (KJV, marg., "bound"). In the 18th verse the KJV, "he is guilty," means that he is under obligation to make amends for his misdeeds.

DECAY

1. *palaioō* (παλαιόω, 3822), "to make old" (*palaios*), is translated in Heb. 8:13, firstly, "hath made ... old," secondly (passive voice), RV "is becoming old" (KJV, "decayeth"); "wax old," Luke 12:33 and Heb. 1:11. See OLD.¶

2. *diaphtheirō* (διαφθείρω, 1311), "to destroy utterly," as used in 2 Cor. 4:16 (here in the passive voice, lit., "is being destroyed"), is rendered "is decaying" (RV, for KJV, "perish"). See CORRUPT, DESTROY.

DECEASE

A. Noun.

exodos (ἔξοδος, 1841), (Eng., "exodus"), lit. signifies "a way out" (*ex*, "out," *hodos*, "a way"); hence, "a departure," especially from life, "a decease"; in Luke 9:31, of the Lord's death, "which He was about to accomplish"; in 2 Pet. 1:15, of Peter's death (marg., "departure" in each case); "departure" in Heb. 11:22, RV. See DEPARTURE.¶

B. Verb.

teleutaō (τελευτάω, 5053), lit., "to end," is used intransitively and translated "deceased" in Matt. 22:25. See DEATH, A, No. 3, DIE.

DECEIT, DECEITFUL, DECEITFULLY, DECEITFULNESS, DECEIVE, DECEIVABLENESS

A. Nouns.

1. *apatē* (ἀπάτη, 539), "deceit or deceitfulness" (akin to *apataō*, "to cheat, deceive, beguile"), that which gives a false impression, whether by appearance, statement or influence, is said of riches, Matt. 13:22; Mark 4:19; of sin, Heb. 3:13. The phrase in Eph. 4:22, "deceitful lusts," KJV, "lusts of deceit," RV, signifies lusts excited by "deceit," of which "deceit" is the source of strength, not lusts "deceitful" in themselves. In 2 Thess. 2:10, "all deceit of unrighteousness," RV, signifies all manner of unscrupulous words and deeds designed to "deceive" (see Rev. 13:13–15). In Col. 2:8, "vain deceit" suggests that "deceit" is void of anything profitable.¶

Note: In 2 Pet. 2:13, the most authentic texts have "revelling in their love-feasts," RV (*agapais*), for KJV, "deceivings" (*apatais*).

2. *dolos* (δόλος, 1388), primarily "a bait, snare"; hence, "craft, deceit, guile," is translated "deceit" in Mark 7:22; Rom. 1:29. See CRAFT, GUILE, SUBTILTY.

Notes: (1) *Planē*, rendered "deceit" in 1 Thess. 2:3, KJV, signifies wandering (cf. Eng., "planet"), hence, "error" (RV), i.e., a wandering from the right path; in Eph. 4:14, "wiles of error," KJV, "to deceive." See DELUDE, ERROR.

(2) For *dolioō*, "to use deceit," see C, No. 4.

B. Adjective.

dolios (δόλιος, 1386), "deceitful," is used in 2 Cor. 11:13, of false apostles as "deceitful workers"; cf. A, No. 2 and *Note* (2).¶

C. Verbs.

1. *apataō* (ἀπατάω, 538), "to beguile, deceive" (see A, No. 1), is used (*a*) of those who "deceive" "with empty words," belittling the true character of the sins mentioned, Eph. 5:6; (*b*) of the fact that Adam was "not beguiled," 1 Tim. 2:14, RV (cf. what is said of Eve; see No. 2 below); (*c*) of the "self-deceit" of him who thinks himself religious, but bridles not his tongue, Jas. 1:26.¶

2. *exapataō* (ἐξαπατάω, 1818), *ek* (*ex*), intensive, and No. 1, signifies "to beguile thoroughly, to deceive wholly," 1 Tim. 2:14, RV. See BEGUILE.

3. *phrenapataō* (φρεναπατάω, 5422), lit., "to deceive in one's mind" (*phrēn*, "the mind," and No. 1), "to deceive by fancies" (Lightfoot), is used in Gal. 6:3, with reference to self-conceit, which is "self-deceit," a sin against common sense. Cf. Jas. 1:26 (above).¶

Note: Cf. *phrenapatēs*, No. 2, under DECEIVE.

4. *dolioō* (δολιόω, 1387), "to lure," as by a bait (see A, No. 2), is translated "have used deceit" in Rom. 3:13.¶

5. *doloō* (δολόω, 1389), a short form of No. 4, primarily signifies "to ensnare"; hence, "to corrupt," especially by mingling the truths of the Word of God with false doctrines or notions, and so handling it "deceitfully," 2 Cor. 4:2.¶ Cf. *kapēleuō*, "to corrupt by way of hucksterizing," 2:17.¶ For the difference between the words see CORRUPT, A, No. 1.

6. *planaō* (πλανάω, 4105), akin to *planē*, A, *Note* (1) (Eng., "planet"), in the passive form sometimes means "to go astray, wander," Matt. 18:12; 1 Pet. 2:25; Heb. 11:38; frequently active, "to deceive, by leading into error, to seduce," e.g., Matt. 24:4, 5, 11, 24; John 7:12, "leadeth astray," RV (cf. 1 John 3:7). In Rev. 12:9 the present participle is used with the definite article, as a title of the Devil, "the Deceiver," lit., "the deceiving one." Often it has the sense of "deceiving oneself," e.g., 1 Cor. 6:9; 15:33; Gal. 6:7; Jas. 1:16, "be not deceived," RV, "do not err," KJV. See ERR, LEAD (astray), SEDUCE, WANDER, WAY (be out of the).

7. *paralogizomai* (παραλογίζομαι, 3884); see BEGUILE, No. 3.

DECEIVER

1. *planos* (πλάνος, 4108) is, properly, an adjective, signifying "wandering, or leading astray, seducing," 1 Tim. 4:1, "seducing (spirits)"; used as a noun, it denotes an impostor of the vagabond type, and so any kind of "deceiver" or corrupter, Matt. 27:63; 2 Cor. 6:8; 2 John 7 (twice), in the last of which the accompanying definite article necessitates the translation "the deceiver," RV. See SEDUCE.¶

2. *phrenapatēs* (φρεναπάτης, 5423), akin to C, No. 3, under DECEIVE, lit., "a mind-deceiver," is used in Titus 1:10.¶

Note: For "the deceiver," in Rev. 12:9, see DECEIVE, C, No. 6.

DECENTLY

euschēmonōs (εὐσχημόνως, 2156) denotes "gracefully, becomingly, in a seemly manner" (*eu*, "well," *schēma*, "a form, figure"); "honestly," in Rom. 13:13 (marg., "decently"), in contrast to the shamefulness of gentile social life; in 1 Thess. 4:12, the contrast is to idleness and its concomitant evils and the resulting bad testimony to unbelievers; in 1 Cor. 14:40, "decently," where the contrast is to disorder in oral testimony in the churches. See HONESTLY.¶

Note: Cf. *euschēmosunē*, "comeliness," 1 Cor. 12:23,¶ and *euschēmōn*, "comely, honorable." See COMELY.

DECIDE, DECISION

A. Verb.

diakrinō (διακρίνω, 1252) primarily signifies "to make a distinction," hence, "to decide, especially judicially, to decide a dispute, to give judgment," 1 Cor. 6:5, KJV, "judge"; RV, "decide," where church members are warned against procuring decisions by litigation in the world's law courts. See CONTEND.

B. Nouns.

1. *diagnōsis* (διάγνωσις, 1233), transliterated in English, primarily denotes "a discrimination" (*dia*, "apart," *ginōskō*, "to know"), hence, "a judicial decision," which is its meaning in Acts 25:21, RV, "for the decision of the Emperor" (KJV, "hearing").¶

Note: Cf. *diaginōskō*, "to distinguish," Acts 23:15, "to judge" (KJV, "enquire"), or "determine," 24:22, RV (KJV, "know the uttermost of").¶

2. *diakrisis* (διάκρισις, 1253), "a distinguishing," and so "a decision" (see A), signifies "discerning" in 1 Cor. 12:10; Heb. 5:14, lit., "unto a discerning of good and evil" (translated "to discern"); in Rom. 14:1, "not to (doubtful) disputations" is more literally rendered in the margin "not for decisions (of doubts)." See DISCERN. Cf. JUDGE.¶ In the Sept., Job 37:16.¶

DECK (Verb)

chrusoō (χρυσόω, 5558), lit., "to gild with gold" (*chrusos*, "gold"), is used in Rev. 17:4; 18:16.¶

DECLARE, DECLARATION

A. Verbs.

1. *anangellō* (ἀναγγέλλω, 312) signifies "to announce, report, bring back tidings" (*ana*, "back," *angellō*, "to announce"). Possibly the *ana* carries the significance of upward, i.e., heavenly, as characteristic of the nature of the tidings. In the following, either the KJV or the RV translates the word by the verb "to declare"; in John 4:25, RV, "declare," KJV, "tell"; in 16:13–15, RV, "declare," KJV, "shew"; in Acts 15:4, RV, "rehearsed," KJV, "declared"; in 19:18, RV, "declaring," KJV, "shewed" (a reference, perhaps, to the destruction of their idols, in consequence of their new faith); in 20:20, RV, "declaring," KJV, "have shewed"; in 1 John 1:5, RV, "announce," KJV, "declare." See REHEARSE, REPORT, SHEW, SPEAK, TELL.

2. *apangellō* (ἀπαγγέλλω, 518) signifies "to announce or report from a person or place" (*apo*, "from"); hence, "to declare, publish"; it is rendered "declare" in Luke 8:47; Heb. 2:12; 1 John 1:3. It is very frequent in the Gospels

and Acts; elsewhere, other than the last two places mentioned, only in 1 Thess. 1:9 and 1 John 1:2. See BRING, A, No. 36.

3. *diangellō* (διαγγέλλω, 1229), lit., "to announce through," hence, "to declare fully, or far and wide" (*dia*, "through"), is translated "declaring" in Acts 21:26, RV (KJV, "to signify"); in Luke 9:60, RV, "publish abroad" (for KJV, "preach"), giving the verb its fuller significance; so in Rom. 9:17, for KJV, "declared." See PREACH, SIGNIFY.¶

4. *katangellō* (καταγγέλλω, 2605), lit., "to report down" (*kata*, intensive), is ordinarily translated "to preach"; "declare" in Acts 17:23, KJV (RV, "set forth"); in 1 Cor. 2:1, RV, "proclaiming," for KJV, "declaring." It is nowhere translated by "declare" in the RV. See PREACH, SHOW, SPEAK, TEACH.

5. *parangellō* (παραγγέλλω, 3853): see CHARGE, B, No. 8.

6. *diēgeomai* (διηγέομαι, 1334), "to conduct a narration through to the end" (*dia*, "through," intensive, *hegeomai*, "to lead"), hence denotes "to recount, to relate in full," Mark 5:16; Luke 8:39; 9:10; Acts 8:33; 9:27; 12:17; in Mark 9:9 and Heb. 11:32, "tell." See SHOW, TELL.¶

7. *ekdiēgeomai* (ἐκδιηγέομαι, 1555), properly, "to narrate in full," came to denote, "to tell, declare"; it is used in Acts 13:41; 15:3.¶

8. *exēgeomai* (ἐξηγέομαι, 1834), lit., "to lead out," signifies "to make known, rehearse, declare," Luke 24:35 (KJV, "told"; RV, rehearsed"); Acts 10:8; 15:12, 14; 21:19. In John 1:18, in the sentence "He hath declared Him," the other meaning of the verb is in view, to unfold in teaching, "to declare" by making known. See TELL.¶

9. *horizō* (ὁρίζω, 3724), "to mark off by boundaries," signifies "to determine," usually of time; in Rom. 1:4, Christ is said to have been "marked out" as the Son of God, by the fact of His resurrection; "declared" (RV, marg., "determined"). See DEFINE.

10. *dēloō* (δηλόω, 1213), "to make plain," is rendered "to declare" in 1 Cor. 1:11, KJV; 3:13; Col. 1:8. See SIGNIFY.

11. *phrazō* (φράζω, 5419), "to declare," occurs in Matt. 15:15 and (in some texts) in 13:36 (as KJV).

Note: For *gnōrizō*, "to make known," rendered "to declare" in John 17:26; 1 Cor. 15:1 and Col. 4:7, see KNOW, A, No. 8. For *emphanizō*, "to declare plainly," Heb. 11:14, KJV, see MANIFEST, A, No. 2. For *phaneroō*, see MANIFEST, B, No. 1. For *anatithēmi*, Acts 25:14, KJV, see COMMUNICATE. For "declare glad tidings" see TIDINGS.

B. Noun.

endeixis (ἔνδειξις, 1732), "a showing, pointing out" (*en*, "in," *deiknumi*, "to show"), is said of the "showing forth" of God's righteousness, in Rom. 3:25–26, KJV, "to declare"; RV, "to show," and "(for) the showing." In 2 Cor. 8:24, "proof"; Phil. 1:28, "an evident token." See SHOW, TOKEN.¶

Notes: (1) In Luke 1:1, *diēgēsis* is a "narrative" (RV), not a "declaration" (KJV).

(2) In 2 Cor. 8:19, "declaration" does not represent any word in the original.

DECREASE (Verb)

elattoō (ἐλαττόω, 1642) signifies "to make less or inferior, in quality, position or dignity"; "madest . . . lower" and "hast made . . . lower," in Heb. 2:7, 9. In John 3:30, it is used in the middle voice, in John the Baptist's "I must decrease," indicating the special interest he had in his own "decrease," i.e., in authority and popularity. See LOWER.¶

DECREE (Noun and Verb)

dogma (δόγμα, 1378), transliterated in English, primarily denoted "an opinion or judgment" (from *dokeō*, "to be of opinion"), hence, an "opinion expressed with authority, a doctrine, ordinance, decree"; "decree," Luke 2:1; Acts 16:4; 17:7; in the sense of ordinances, Eph. 2:15; Col. 2:14. See ORDINANCE.¶

Note: Krinō, "to determine," is translated "hath decreed" in 1 Cor. 7:37, KJV; RV, "hath determined."

DEDICATE, DEDICATION

A. Verb.

enkainizō (ἐγκαινίζω, 1457) primarily means "to make new, to renew" (*en*, "in," *kainos*, "new"), as in the Sept. of 2 Chron. 15:8; then, to initiate or "dedicate," Heb. 9:18, with reference to the first covenant, as not "dedicated" without blood; in 10:20, of Christ's "dedication" of the new and living way (KJV, "consecrated"; RV, "dedicated"). See CONSECRATE.¶ In the Sept. it has this meaning in Deut. 20:5; 2 Chron. 7:5; Isa. 16:11; 41:1; 45:16, "keep a feast (to Me)."

B. Noun.

enkainia (ἐγκαίνια, 1456), akin to A, frequent in the Sept., in the sense of "dedication," became used particularly for the annual eight days' feast beginning on the 25th of Chisleu (mid. of Dec.), instituted by Judas Maccabaeus, 164, B.C., to commemorate the cleansing of the Temple from the pollutions of Antiochus Epiphanes; hence it was called the Feast of the Dedication, John 10:22. This feast could be celebrated anywhere. The lighting of lamps was a prominent feature; hence the description "Feast of Lights." Westcott suggests that John 9:5 refers to this.¶

DEED, DEEDS

1. *ergon* (ἔργον, 2041) denotes "a work" (Eng., "work" is etymologically akin), "deed, act." When used in the sense of a "deed or act," the idea of "working" is stressed, e.g., Rom. 15:18; it frequently occurs in an ethical sense of human actions, good or bad, e.g., Matt. 23:3; 26:10; John 3:20–21; Rom. 2:7, 15; 1 Thess. 1:3; 2 Thess. 1:11, etc.; sometimes in a less concrete sense, e.g., Titus 1:16; Jas. 1:25 (RV, "that worketh," lit., "of work"). See LABOR, WORK.

2. *praxis* (πρᾶξις, 4234) denotes "a doing, transaction, a deed the action of which is looked upon as incomplete and in progress" (cf. *prassō*, "to practice"); in Matt. 16:27, RV, "deeds," for KJV, "works"; in Luke 23:51, "deed"; in v. 41, the verb is used [see *Note* (2) below]; Acts 19:18; Rom. 8:13; Col. 3:9. In Rom. 12:4 it denotes an "action," business, or function, translated "office." See OFFICE, WORK.¶

Note: Contrast *pragma*, "that which has been done, an accomplished act," e.g., Jas. 3:16, RV, "deed," KJV, "work."

3. *poiēsis* (ποίησις, 4162), "a doing" (akin to *poieō*, "to do"), is translated "deed" in Jas. 1:25, KJV, (RV, "doing").¶

Note: Cf. *poiēma*, "a work done," Rom. 1:20; Eph. 2:10.¶

4. *euergesia* (εὐεργεσία, 2108): see BENEFIT, No. 1.

Notes: (1) *Katergazomai*, "to work out, bring about something, to perpetrate a deed," is used with the neuter demonstrative pronoun *touto*, "this," in 1 Cor. 5:3, "hath (so) done this deed," KJV; RV, "hath (so) wrought this thing."

(2) *Prassō* (see No. 2), is used in Luke 23:41, with the neuter plural of the relative pronoun, "of our deeds"; lit., "(the things) which we practiced."

(3) In 2 Cor. 12:12 the phrase "mighty deeds" (RV, "mighty works") translates *dunameis*, "powers" (marg.). See WORK.

(4) In Acts 24:2, *diorthōma*, "a straightening," with *ginomai*, "to become," is translated in the KJV, "very worthy deeds are done," RV, "evils are corrected"; more lit., "reforms take place."¶ For the variant reading *katorthōma*, see CORRECTION, No. 1.

DEEM

huponoeō (ὑπονοέω, 5282), "to suppose, conjecture, surmise," is translated "deemed" in

Acts 27:27, KJV (RV, "surmised"); in 13:25, "think ye" (KJV); RV, "suppose ye"; in 25:18, "supposed." See SUPPOSE, THINK.¶

DEEP (Noun and Adjective), DEEPNESS, DEEPLY, DEPTH

A. Nouns.

1. *bathos* (βάθος, 899) is used (*a*) naturally, in Matt. 13:5, "deepness"; Mark 4:5, KJV, "depth," RV, "deepness"; Luke 5:4, of "deep" water; Rom. 8:39 (contrasted with *hupsōma*, "height"); (*b*) metaphorically, in Rom. 11:33, of God's wisdom and knowledge; in 1 Cor. 2:10, of God's counsels; in Eph. 3:18, of the dimensions of the sphere of the activities of God's counsels, and of the love of Christ which occupies that sphere; in 2 Cor. 8:2, of "deep" poverty; some mss. have it in Rev. 2:24.¶

2. *buthos* (βυθός, 1037), "a depth," is used in the NT only in the natural sense, of the sea 2 Cor. 11:25.¶

Notes: (1) Cf. *buthizō*, "to sink" (intransitive), middle voice, Luke 5:7; (transitive) "to drown," 1 Tim. 6:9.¶

(2) *Abussos*, (Eng., "abyss"), is translated "the deep" in Luke 8:31 and Rom. 10:7, KJV. See ABYSS, BOTTOM.

B. Adjective and Adverb.

bathus (βαθύς, 901), akin to A, No. 1, "deep," is said in John 4:11, of a well; in Acts 20:9, of sleep; in Rev. 2:24 the plural is used, of the "deep things," the evil designs and workings, of Satan.

Notes: (1) In Luke 24:1, some mss. have *batheos*, the genitive case, with *orthros*, "dawn"; the most authentic mss. have *batheōs*, "deeply," i.e., very early.

(2) In Mark 8:12, "He sighed deeply" represents *anastenazō*, "to fetch a deep-drawn sigh" (*ana*, "up," *stenazō*, "to sigh or groan"). See SIGH.¶

C. Verb.

bathunō (βαθύνω, 900), "to deepen, make deep," is used in Luke 6:48 (KJV, "digged deep"). The original has two separate verbs, *skaptō*, "to dig," and *bathunō;* the RV therefore has "digged and went deep."¶

DEFAME

dusphēmeō (δυσφημέω, 1418 and 5346), lit., "to speak injuriously" (from *dus—*, an inseparable prefix signifying "opposition, injury, etc.," and *phēmi*, "to speak"), is translated "defamed," 1 Cor. 4:13. Some mss. have *blasphēmeō*. See BLASPHEME.¶

DEFECT

hēttēma (ἥττημα, 2275), primarily "a lessening, a decrease, diminution," denotes "a loss." It is used of the "loss" sustained by the Jewish nation in that they had rejected God's testimonies and His Son and the gospel, Rom. 11:12, the reference being not only to national diminution but to spiritual "loss"; RV, "loss," for KJV, "diminishing." Here the contrasting word is *plērōma*, "fullness." In 1 Cor. 6:7 the reference is to the spiritual "loss" sustained by the church at Corinth because or their discord and their litigious ways in appealing to the world's judges. Here the RV has "defect" (marg. "loss"), for KJV, "fault." The preceding adverb "altogether" shows the comprehensiveness of the "defect"; the "loss" affected the whole church, and was "an utter detriment."

In the Sept. of Isa. 31:8 the word signifies the "loss" of a defeat, with reference to the overthrow of the Assyrians; lit. "his young men shall be for loss" (i.e., "tributary"). See DIMINISHING, FAULT, LOSS.¶

Note: Cf. *hēttaō*, "to make inferior," used in the passive voice, "to be overcome" (of spiritual defeat, 2 Pet. 2:20), and the adjective *hēttōn* or *hēssōn*, "less, worse."

DEFEND

amunō (ἀμύνω, 292), "to ward off," is used in the middle voice in Acts 7:24, of the assistance given by Moses to his fellow Israelite against an Egyptian (translated, "defended"). The middle voice indicates the special personal interest Moses had in the act.¶

DEFENSE

A. Noun.

apologia (ἀπολογία, 627), a speech made in defense. See ANSWER.

B. Verb.

apologeomai (ἀπολογέομαι, 626): see ANSWER, B, No. 4.

DEFER

anaballō (ἀναβάλλω, 306), lit., "to throw up" (*ana*, "up," *ballō*, "to throw"), hence "to postpone," is used in the middle voice in Acts 24:22, in the forensic sense of "deferring" the hearing of a case.¶

Note: Cf. *anabolē*, "a putting off, delay," Acts 25:17.¶

DEFILE, DEFILEMENT

A. Verbs.

1. *koinoō* (κοινόω, 2840) denotes (*a*) "to make common"; hence, in a ceremonial sense,

"to render unholy, unclean, to defile," Matt. 15:11, 18, 20; Mark 7:15, 18, 20, 23; Acts 21:28 (RV, "defiled"; KJV, "polluted"); Heb. 9:13 (RV, "them that have been defiled," KJV, "the unclean"); (b) "to count unclean," Acts 10:15; 11:9. In Rev. 21:27, some mss. have this verb, "defileth"; the most authentic have the adjective, koinos, "unclean." See CALL, COMMON.¶

2. miainō (μιαίνω, 3392), primarily, "to stain, to tinge or dye with another color," as in the staining of a glass, hence, "to pollute, contaminate, soil, defile," is used (a) of "ceremonial defilement," John 18:28; so in the Sept., in Lev. 22:5, 8; Num. 19:13, 20 etc.; (b) of "moral defilement," Titus 1:15 (twice); Heb. 12:15; "of moral and physical defilement," Jude 8. See B, Nos. 1 and 2.¶

3. molunō (μολύνω, 3435) properly denotes "to besmear," as with mud or filth, "to befoul." It is used in the figurative sense, of a conscience "defiled" by sin, 1 Cor. 8:7; of believers who have kept themselves (their "garments") from "defilement," Rev. 3:4, and of those who have not "soiled" themselves by adultery or fornication, Rev. 14:4.¶

Note: The difference between miainō and molunō is that the latter is not used in a ritual or ceremonial sense, as miainō is (Trench, Syn. §xxxi).

4. spiloō (σπιλόω, 4695), "to make a stain or spot," and so "to defile," is used in Jas. 3:6 of the "defiling" effects of an evil use of the tongue; in Jude 23, "spotted," with reference to moral "defilement." See SPOT.¶

Note: (1) Cf. spilos, "a spot, a moral blemish," Eph. 5:27; 2 Pet. 2:13;¶ aspilos, "without spot, spotless," 1 Tim. 6:14; Jas. 1:27; 1 Pet. 1:19; 2 Pet. 3:14; ¶ spilas, Jude 12, "hidden rocks," RV (KJV "spots," a late meaning, equivalent to spilos).¶

5. phtheirō (φθείρω, 5351): see CORRUPT, A, No. 2.

B. Nouns.

1. miasma (μίασμα, 3393), whence the Eng. word, denotes "defilement" (akin to A, No. 2), and is found in 2 Pet. 2:20, KJV, "pollutions," RV, "defilements," the vices of the ungodly which contaminate a person in his intercourse with the world.¶

2. miasmos (μιασμός, 3394), also akin to A, No. 2, primarily denotes "the act of defiling," the process, in contrast to the "defiling" thing (No. 1). It is found in 2 Pet. 2:10 (KJV, "uncleanness," RV, "defilement.")¶

3. molusmos (μολυσμός, 3436), akin to A, No. 3, denotes "defilement," in the sense of an action by which anything is "defiled," 2 Cor.

7:1.¶ Cf. the synonymous word spilos, A, No. 4, Note.

C. Adjective.

koinos (κοινός, 2839), akin to A, No. 1, common, and, from the idea of coming into contact with everything, "defiled," is used in the ceremonial sense in Mark 7:2; in v. 5, RV, "defiled," for KJV, "unwashen" (the verb is used in 7:15). See COMMON, UNCLEAN.

DEFINE

horizō (ὁρίζω, 3724), (Eng., "horizon"), primarily means "to mark out the boundaries of a place" (as in the Sept. of Num. 34:6; Josh. 13:27); hence "to determine, appoint." In Heb. 4:7, where the reference is to the time of God's invitation to enter into His rest, in contrast to Israel's failure to do so, the word may mean either the appointing of the day (i.e., the period), or the "defining" of the day, i.e., marking its limits. So the RV (KJV, "limiteth"). See DECLARE, DETERMINE, LIMIT, ORDAIN.

DEFRAUD

1. apostereō (ἀποστερέω, 650) signifies "to rob, despoil, defraud," Mark 10:19; 1 Cor. 6:8; 7:5 (of that which is due to the condition of natural relationship of husband and wife); in the middle voice, "to allow oneself to be defrauded," 1 Cor. 6:7; in the passive voice, "bereft," 1 Tim. 6:5, RV, with reference to the truth, with the suggestion of being retributively "robbed" of the truth, through the corrupt condition of the mind. Some mss. have this verb in Jas. 5:4 for aphustereō, "to keep back by fraud." See BEREFT, DESTITUTE, FRAUD.¶ In the Sept., Exod. 21:10; in some mss., Deut. 24:14.¶

2. pleonekteō (πλεονεκτέω, 4122), translated "defraud" in 1 Thess. 4:6, KJV (RV, "wrong"), the reference being to the latter part of the Tenth Commandment. See ADVANTAGE, C, No. 2.

DEGREE

bathmos (βαθμός, 898) denotes "a step," primarily of a threshold or stair, and is akin to bainō, "to go"; figuratively, "a standing, a stage in a career, position, degree," 1 Tim. 3:13, of faithful deacons.¶

Note: Tapeinos, "low, humble," whether in condition or mind, is translated "of low degree" in Luke 1:52 and Jas. 1:9.¶

DELAY

A. Verbs.

1. okneō (ὀκνέω, 3635), akin to oknos, "a shrinking, to be loath or slow to do a thing, to hesitate, delay," is used in Acts 9:38.¶ In the

Sept. in Num. 22:16, "do not delay"; Judg. 18:9.¶

2. *chronizō* (χρονίζω, 5549), from *chronos*, "time," lit. means "to while away time," i.e., by way of lingering, tarrying, "delaying"; "delayeth," Matt. 24:48; Luke 12:45; "tarried," Matt. 25:5; "tarried so long," Luke 1:21; "will (not) tarry," Heb. 10:37. See TARRY.¶

B. Noun.

anabolē (ἀναβολή, 311) lit. signifies "that which is thrown up" (*ana*, "up," *ballō*, "to throw"); hence "a delay," Acts 25:17. See DEFER.¶

Note: In Rev. 10:6, *chronos* is translated "delay" in RV marg., and is to be taken as the true meaning.

DELICACIES

Note: For *strēnos*, rendered "delicacies" in Rev. 18:3, KJV, denoting "wantonness" (RV), i.e., arrogant luxury, see WANTON.¶ Cf. the verb *strēniaō*, below, under DELICATELY.

DELICATELY (live)

A. Verbs.

truphaō (τρυφάω, 5171), from *thruptō*, "to enervate," signifies "to lead a voluptuous life, to give oneself up to pleasure," Jas. 5:5, RV, "ye have lived delicately"; KJV, "ye have lived in pleasure."¶

Notes: (1) Cf. *spatalaō*, from *spatalē*, "wantonness, to live riotously," used with A in Jas. 5:5, "ye have lived in pleasure" (RV, "have taken your . . ."); cf. 1 Tim. 5:6, of carnal women in the church, KJV, "liveth in pleasure," RV, "giveth herself to pleasure. See PLEASURE.¶

(2) Cf. also *strēniaō*, "to run riot," translated "lived deliciously," in Rev. 18:7, 9, KJV (RV, "waxed wanton" and "lived wantonly"). Cf. DELICACIES (above). See WANTON.¶ Cf. the intensive form *katastrēniaō*, "to wax utterly wanton," 1 Tim. 5:11.¶

(3) *Spatalaō* "might properly be laid to the charge of the prodigal, scattering his substance in riotous living, Luke 15:13; . . . *truphaō* to the charge of the rich man, faring sumptuously every day, Luke 16:19; *strēniaō* to Jeshurun, when, waxing fat, he kicked, Deut. 32:15" (Trench, *Syn.* §liv).

B. Noun.

truphē (τρυφή, 5172), akin to A, is used with *en*, in the phrase *en truphē*, "luxuriously," "delicately," Luke 7:25, and denotes effeminacy, softness; "to revel" in 2 Pet. 2:13 (KJV, "riot"), lit., "counting reveling in the day time a pleasure." See REVEL, RIOT.¶

Note: Entruphaō, "to revel luxuriously," is used in 2 Pet. 2:13, RV, "reveling" (KJV, "sporting themselves").¶

For **DELICIOUSLY,** Rev. 18:7, 9, KJV, see *Note* (1) above

DELIGHT IN

sunēdomai (συνήδομαι, 4913), lit., "to rejoice with (anyone), to delight in (a thing) with (others)," signifies "to delight with oneself inwardly in a thing," in Rom. 7:22.¶

Note: Cf. *hēdonē*, "desire, pleasure."

DELIVER, DELIVERANCE, DELIVERER

A. Verbs.

1. *didōmi* (δίδωμι, 1325), "to give," is translated "delivered" in Luke 7:15; RV, "gave"; so 19:13. See GIVE.

2. *anadidōmi* (ἀναδίδωμι, 325), *ana*, "up," and No. 1, "to deliver over, give up," is used of "delivering" the letter mentioned in Acts 23:33.¶

Note: For the different verb in Acts 15:30, see No. 4.

3. *apodidōmi* (ἀποδίδωμι, 591), *apo*, "from," and No. 1, lit., "to give away," hence, "to give back or up," is used in Pilate's command for the Lord's body to be "given up," Matt. 27:58; in the sense of "giving back," of the Lord's act in giving a healed boy back to his father, Luke 9:42. See GIVE, PAY, PAYMENT, PERFORM, RECOMPENSE, RENDER, REPAY, REQUITE, RESTORE, REWARD, SELL, YIELD.

4. *epididōmi* (ἐπιδίδωμι, 1929), lit., "to give upon or in addition," as from oneself to another, hence, "to deliver over," is used of the "delivering" of the roll of Isaiah to Christ in the synagogue, Luke 4:17; of the "delivering" of the epistle from the elders at Jerusalem to the church at Antioch, Acts 15:30. See DRIVE (let), GIVE, OFFER.

5. *paradidōmi* (παραδίδωμι, 3860), "to deliver over," in Rom. 6:17, RV, "that form of teaching whereunto ye were delivered," the figure being that of a mold which gives its shape to what is cast in it (not as the KJV). In Rom. 8:32 it is used of God in "delivering" His Son to expiatory death; so 4:25; see Mark 9:31; of Christ in "delivering" Himself up, Gal. 2:20; Eph. 5:2, 25. See BETRAY, A. In Mark 1:14, RV, it is used of "delivering" John the Baptist to prison. See PUT, No. 12.

6. *apallassō* (ἀπαλλάσσω, 525), lit., "to change from" (*apo*, "from," *allassō*, "to change"), "to free from, release," is translated "might deliver" in Heb. 2:15; in Luke 12:58, it

is used in a legal sense of being quit of a person, i.e., the opponent being appeased and withdrawing his suit. For its other meaning, "to depart," in Acts 19:12, see DEPART.¶

7. *eleutheroō* (ἐλευθερόω, 1659), "to set free," is translated "deliver" in Rom. 8:21. In six other places it is translated "make free," John 8:32, 36; Rom. 6:18, 22; 8:2; Gal. 5:1, RV, "set free." See FREE.¶

8. *exaireō* (ἐξαιρέω, 1807), lit., "to take out," denotes, in the middle voice, "to take out for oneself," hence, "to deliver, to rescue," the person who does so having a special interest in the result of his act. Thus it is used, in Gal. 1:4, of the act of God in "delivering" believers "out of this present evil world," the middle voice indicating His pleasure in the issue of their "deliverance." It signifies to "deliver" by rescuing from danger, in Acts 12:11; 23:27; 26:17; from bondage, Acts 7:10, 34. For its other meaning, "to pluck out of," Matt. 5:29; 18:9, see PLUCK.¶

9. *katargeō* (καταργέω, 2673): see ABOLISH.

10. *rhuomai* (ῥύομαι, 4506), "to rescue from, to preserve from," and so, "to deliver," the word by which it is regularly translated, is largely synonymous with *sōzō*, "to save," though the idea of "rescue from" is predominant in *rhuomai* (see Matt. 27:43), that of "preservation from," in *sōzō*. In Rom. 11:26 the present participle is used with the article, as a noun, "the Deliverer." This is the construction in 1 Thess. 1:10, where Christ is similarly spoken of. Here the KJV wrongly has "which delivered" (the tense is not past); RV, "which delivereth"; the translation might well be (as in Rom. 11:26), "our Deliverer," that is, from the retributive calamities with which God will visit men at the end of the present age. From that wrath believers are to be "delivered." The verb is used with *apo*, "away from," in Matt. 6:13; Luke 11:4 (in some mss.); so also in 11:4; Rom. 15:31; 2 Thess. 3:2; 2 Tim. 4:18; and with *ek*, "from, out of," in Luke 1:74; Rom. 7:24; 2 Cor. 1:10; Col. 1:13, from bondage; in 2 Pet. 2:9, from temptation; in 2 Tim. 3:11, from persecution; but *ek* is used of ills impending, in 2 Cor. 1:10; in 2 Tim. 4:17, *ek* indicates that the danger was more imminent than in v. 18, where *apo* is used. Accordingly the meaning "out of the midst of" cannot be pressed in 1 Thess. 1:10.¶

11. *charizomai* (χαρίζομαι, 5483), "to gratify, to do what is pleasing to anyone," is translated "deliver" in the KJV of Acts 25:11, 16; RV, "give up" (marg., "grant by favor," i.e., to give over to the Jews so as to gratify their wishes). See FORGIVE, GIVE, GRANT.

Note: For *gennaō* and *tiktō*, "to bear, to be delivered" (said of women at childbirth), see BEGET.

B. Nouns.

1. *apolutrōsis* (ἀπολύτρωσις, 629) denotes "redemption" (*apo*, "from," *lutron*, "a price of release"). In Heb. 11:35 it is translated "deliverance"; usually the release is effected by the payment of a ransom, or the required price, the *lutron* (ransom). See REDEMPTION.

2. *aphesis* (ἄφεσις, 859) denotes "a release, from bondage, imprisonment, etc." (the corresponding verb is *aphiēmi*, "to send away, let go"); in Luke 4:18 it is used of "liberation" from captivity (KJV, "deliverance," RV, "release"). See FORGIVENESS, REMISSION.

3. *lutrōtēs* (λυτρωτής, 3086), "a redeemer, one who releases" (see No. 1), is translated "deliverer" in Acts 7:35 (RV marg., "redeemer").¶

Note: See also DELIVER, A, No. 10.

C. Verbal Adjective.

ekdotos (ἔκδοτος, 1560), lit., "given up" (*ek*, "out of," *didōmi*, "to give"), "delivered up" (to enemies, or to the power or will of someone), is used of Christ in Acts 2:23.¶

DELUDE, DELUSION

A. Verb.

paralogizomai (παραλογίζομαι, 3884): see BEGUILE.

B. Noun.

planē (πλάνη, 4106), lit., "a wandering," whereby those who are led astray roam hither and thither, is always used in the NT, of mental straying, wrong opinion, error in morals or religion. In 2 Thess. 2:11, KJV, it is translated "delusion," RV, "error." See DECEIT, ERROR.

DEMAND

Note: For DEMAND (Matt. 2:4 and Acts 21:33), see INQUIRE; for its use in Luke 3:14 and 17:20, see under ASK.

DEMEANOR

katastēma (κατάστημα, 2688): see BEHAVIOR, B, No. 2.

DEMON, DEMONIAC

A. Nouns.

1. *daimōn* (δαίμων, 1142), "a demon," signified, among pagan Greeks, an inferior deity, whether good or bad. In the NT it denotes "an evil spirit." It is used in Matt. 8:31, mistranslated "devils."

Some would derive the word from a root *da*—, meaning "to distribute." More probably it is from a similar root *da*—, meaning "to know," and hence means "a knowing one."¶

2. *daimonion* (δαιμόνιον, 1140), not a diminutive of *daimōn*, No. 1, but the neuter of the adjective *daimonios*, pertaining to a demon, is also mistranslated "devil," "devils." In Acts 17:18, it denotes an inferior pagan deity. "Demons" are the spiritual agents acting in all idolatry. The idol itself is nothing, but every idol has a "demon" associated with it who induces idolatry, with its worship and sacrifices, 1 Cor. 10:20–21; Rev. 9:20; cf. Deut. 32:17; Isa. 13:21; 34:14; 65:3, 11. They disseminate errors among men, and seek to seduce believers, 1 Tim. 4:1. As seducing spirits they deceive men into the supposition that through mediums (those who have "familiar spirits," Lev. 20:6, 27, e.g.) they can converse with deceased human beings. Hence the destructive deception of spiritism, forbidden in Scripture, Lev. 19:31; Deut. 18:11; Isa. 8:19. "Demons" tremble before God, Jas. 2:19; they recognized Christ as Lord and as their future Judge, Matt. 8:29; Luke 4:41. Christ cast them out of human beings by His own power. His disciples did so in His name, and by exercising faith, e.g., Matt. 17:20.

Acting under Satan (cf. Rev. 16:13–14), "demons" are permitted to afflict with bodily disease, Luke 13:16. Being unclean they tempt human beings with unclean thoughts, Matt. 10:1; Mark 5:2; 7:25; Luke 8:27–29; Rev. 16:13; 18:2, e.g. They differ in degrees of wickedness, Matt. 12:45. They will instigate the rulers of the nations at the end of this age to make war against God and His Christ, Rev. 16:14. See DEVIL.

B. Verb.

daimonizomai (δαιμονίζομαι, 1139) signifies "to be possessed of a demon, to act under the control of a demon." Those who were thus afflicted expressed the mind and consciousness of the "demon" or "demons" indwelling them, e.g., Luke 8:28. The verb is found chiefly in Matt. and Mark; Matt. 4:24; 8:16, 28, 33; 9:32; 12:22; 15:22; Mark 1:32; 5:15–16, 18; elsewhere in Luke 8:36 and John 10:21, "him that hath a devil (demon)."¶

C. Adjective.

daimoniōdēs (δαιμονιώδης, 1141) signifies "proceeding from, or resembling, a demon, demoniacal"; see marg. of Jas. 3:15, RV (text, "devilish").¶

DEMONSTRATION

apodeixis (ἀπόδειξις, 585), lit., "a pointing out" (*apo*, "forth," *deiknumi*, "to show"), a "showing" or demonstrating by argument, is found in 1 Cor. 2:4, where the apostle speaks of a proof, a "showing" forth or display, by the operation of the Spirit of God in him, as affecting the hearts and lives of his hearers, in contrast to the attempted methods of proof by rhetorical arts and philosophic arguments.¶

DEN

spēlaion (σπήλαιον, 4693): see CAVE.

DENY

1. *arneomai* (ἀρνέομαι, 720) signifies (*a*) "to say... not, to contradict," e.g., Mark 14:70; John 1:20; 18:25, 27; 1 John 2:22; (*b*) "to deny" by way of disowning a person, as, e.g., the Lord Jesus as master, e.g., Matt. 10:33; Luke 12:9; John 13:38 (in the best mss.); 2 Tim. 2:12; or, on the other hand, of Christ Himself, "denying" that a person is His follower, Matt. 10:33; 2 Tim. 2:12; or to "deny" the Father and the Son, by apostatizing and by disseminating pernicious teachings, to "deny" Jesus Christ as master and Lord by immorality under a cloak of religion, 2 Pet. 2:1; Jude 4; (*c*) "to deny oneself," either in a good sense, by disregarding one's own interests, Luke 9:23, or in a bad sense, to prove false to oneself, to act quite unlike oneself, 2 Tim. 2:13; (*d*) to "abrogate, forsake, or renounce a thing," whether evil, Titus 2:12, or good, 1 Tim. 5:8; 2 Tim. 3:5; Rev. 2:13; 3:8; (*e*)"not to accept, to reject" something offered, Acts 3:14; 7:35, "refused"; Heb. 11:24, "refused." See REFUSE.

2. *aparneomai* (ἀπαρνέομαι, 533), a strengthened form of No. 1, with *apo*, "from," prefixed (Lat., *abnego*), means (*a*) "to deny utterly," to abjure, to affirm that one has no connection with a person, as in Peter's denial of Christ, Matt. 26:34–35, 75; Mark 14:30–31, 72; Luke 22:34, 61 (some mss. have it in John 13:38). This stronger form is used in the Lord's statements foretelling Peter's "denial," and in Peter's assurance of fidelity; the simple verb (No. 1) is used in all the records of his actual denial. The strengthened form is the verb used in the Lord's warning as to being "denied" in the presence of the angels, Luke 12:9; in the preceding clause, "he that denieth Me," the simple verb *arneomai* is used; the rendering therefore should be "he that denieth Me in the presence of men, shall be utterly denied in the presence of the angels of God"; (*b*) "to deny oneself" as a follower of Christ, Matt. 16:24; Mark 8:34; Luke 9:23.¶

3. *antilegō* (ἀντιλέγω, 483) means "to speak against, contradict." In Luke 20:27, the RV, "they which say that there is no resurrection," follows the texts which have the simple verb *legō;* for the KJV, which translates the verb *antilegō,* "which deny that there is any resurrec-

tion." See ANSWER, CONTRADICT, GAINSAY, SPEAK, No. 6.

DEPART

(a) *Compounds of agō.*

1. *anagō* (ἀνάγω, 321), lit., "to lead up" (*ana*, "up," *agō*, "to lead"), is used, in the middle voice, as a nautical term, signifying "to set sail, put to sea"; "to depart," Acts 27:12, KJV (RV, "put to sea"); 28:10 (RV, "sailed"); v. 11 (RV, "set sail"). Cf. *epanagō*, in Luke 5:3, to put out. See BRING, No. 11.

2. *paragō* (παράγω, 3855), used intransitively, means "to pass by" (*para*, "by, beside"), and is so translated everywhere in the Gospels, except in the KJV of Matt. 9:27, "departed"; RV, "passed by." Outside the Gospels it is used in its other meaning, "to pass away," 1 Cor. 7:31; 1 John 2:8 (RV), 17. See PASS.

3. *hupagō* (ὑπάγω, 5217), "to go," translated "depart" in Jas. 2:16, KJV, primarily and lit. meant "to lead under" (*hupo*, "under"); in its later use, it implied a "going," without noise or notice, or by stealth. In this passage the idea is perhaps that of a polite dismissal, "Go your ways." See GET, GO.

(b) *Compounds of erchomai.*

4. *aperchomai* (ἀπέρχομαι, 565), lit., "to come or go away" (*apo*), hence, "to set off, depart," e.g., Matt. 8:18, is frequent in the Gospels and Acts; Rev. 18:14, RV, "are gone." See COME, No. 11 (*Note*), GO, PASS.

5. *dierchomai* (διέρχομαι, 1330), "to come or go through, to pass through to a place," is translated "departed" in Acts 13:14, KJV; RV, "passing through"; elsewhere it is usually translated "pass through" or "go through." See COME, No. 5.

6. *exerchomai* (ἐξέρχομαι, 1831) denotes "to come out, or go out of, to go forth." It is frequently translated by the verb "to depart," e.g., Matt. 9:31; in Luke 4:42, for the KJV, "He departed and went (No. 8)," the RV has "He came out and went"; in 9:6 the KJV and RV agree. See COME, No. 3.

7. *katerchomai* (κατέρχομαι, 2718), "to come down" (its usual meaning), is translated "departed" in Acts 13:4, KJV (RV, "went down").

See COME, No. 7.

(c) *Poreuō and a compound.*

8. *poreuō* (πορεύω, 4198), akin to *poros*, "a passage," in the middle voice signifies "to go on one's way, to depart from one place to another." In some places, where the KJV has the verb "to depart," the RV translates by "to go one's way," e.g., Matt. 2:9, "went their way"; 11:7; 24:1, "was going on His way." In the following the

RV has the verb "to go," for the KJV "depart," Luke 4:42 (latter part of verse); 13:31; John 16:7; 2 Tim. 4:10. In Luke 21:8, "go (after)," is said of disciples or partisans. In some places both KJV and RV translate by the verb "to depart," e.g., Matt. 19:15; 25:41; Acts 5:41; Acts 22:21. This verb is to be distinguished from others signifying "to go." It is best rendered, as often as possible, "to go on one's way." See GO, JOURNEY, WALK.

9. *ekporeuō* (ἐκπορεύω, 1607), *ek*, "from," in the middle and passive, "to proceed from or forth," more expressive of a definite course than simply "to go forth," is translated "go forth," in Mark 6:11; "went out" in Matt. 20:29, RV (KJV, "departed"); both have "depart" in Acts 25:4. It is frequently translated by the verb "to proceed," and is often best so rendered, e.g., in Rev. 9:17–18, RV, for KJV, "issued." See COME, No. 33.

(d) *Compounds of chōreō.*

10. *anachōreō* (ἀναχωρέω, 402), "to go back, recede, retire" (*ana*, "back or up," *chōreō*, "to make room for, betake oneself," *chōros*, "a place"), is translated "departed" in Matt. 2:12–14; 4:12 (RV, "withdrew"); so in 14:13 and 15:21, but "departed" in 27:5; "withdrew" in John 6:15. In Matt. 2:22 the RV has "withdrew," which is preferable to the KJV, "turned aside." The most suitable translation wherever possible, is by the verb "to withdraw." See PLACE, B, No. 1, GO, No. 15, TURN, *Note* (1), WITHDRAW.

11. *apochōreō* (ἀποχωρέω, 672), "to depart from" (*apo*), is so translated in Matt. 7:23; Luke 9:39; Acts 13:13 (both KJV and RV). Some mss. have it in Luke 20:20.¶

12. *ekchōreō* (ἐκχωρέω, 1633) signifies "to depart out" (*ek*), "to leave a place," Luke 21:21.¶

(e) *Chōrizō and compounds.*

13. *chōrizō* (χωρίζω, 5563), "to put apart, separate," means, in the middle voice, "to separate oneself, to depart from," Acts 1:4; 18:1–2; in marital affairs, 1 Cor. 7:10–11, 15; "departed" (RV corrects to "was parted"), Philem. 15. The verb is also used in Matt. 19:6; Mark 10:9; Rom. 8:35, 39; Heb. 7:26. See PUT, No. 14, SEPARATE.¶

14. *apochōrizō* (ἀποχωρίζω, 673) signifies "to separate off" (*apo*); in the middle voice, "to depart from," Acts 15:39, KJV, "departed asunder"; RV, "parted asunder"; Rev. 6:14, RV, "was removed." See PART, REMOVE. ¶

15. *diachōrizō* (διαχωρίζω, 1316), lit., "to separate throughout" (*dia*), i.e., "completely," in the middle voice, "to separate oneself definitely

from," is used in Luke 9:33, RV, "were parting from."¶

(*f*) *Various other verbs.*

16. *analuō* (ἀναλύω, 360), lit., "to unloose, undo" (*ana*, "up, or again"), signifies "to depart," in the sense of "departing" from life, Phil. 1:23, a metaphor drawn from loosing moorings preparatory to setting sail, or, according to some, from breaking up an encampment, or from the unyoking of baggage animals. See DEPARTING, No. 1. In Luke 12:36, it has its other meaning, "to return." See RETURN.¶

17. *apoluō* (ἀπολύω, 630), "to loose from" (*apo*), in the middle voice, signifies "to depart," Luke 2:29; Acts 23:22, RV, "let go"; 28:25. See DISMISS.

18. *exeimi* (ἔξειμι, 1826), "to go out" (*ex*, "out," *eimi*, "to go"), is rendered "went out" in Acts 13:42; in 27:43, "got," of mariners getting to shore; in 17:15, "departed"; in 20:7, "to depart." See GET, GO.¶

19. *metairō* (μεταίρω, 3332), "to make a distinction, to remove, to lift away" (in its transitive sense), is used intransitively in the NT, signifying "to depart," and is said of Christ, in Matt. 13:53; 19:1. It could be well translated "removed."¶

20. *aphistēmi* (ἀφίστημι, 868), in the active voice, used transitively, signifies "to cause to depart, to cause to revolt," Acts 5:37; used intransitively, "to stand off, or aloof, or to depart from anyone," Luke 4:13; 13:27; Acts 5:38 ("refrain from"); 12:10; 15:38; 19:9; 22:29; 2 Cor. 12:8; metaphorically, "to fall away," 2 Tim. 2:19; in the middle voice, "to withdraw or absent oneself from," Luke 2:37; to "apostatize," Luke 8:13; 1 Tim. 4:1; Heb. 3:12, RV, "falling away." See DRAW (away), FALL, No. 14, REFRAIN, WITHDRAW.¶

21. *apallassō* (ἀπαλλάσσω, 525), lit., "to change from" (*apo*, "from," *allassō*, "to change"), is used once of "departing," said of the removal of diseases, Acts 19:12. In Heb. 2:15 it signifies "to deliver, release." In Luke 12:58, it is used in a legal sense, "to be quit of." See DELIVER.¶

22. *metabainō* (μεταβαίνω, 3327) is rendered "to depart" in Matt. 8:34; 11:1; 12:9; 15:29; John 7:3; 13:1; Acts 18:7.

DEPARTING, DEPARTURE

1. *analusis* (ἀνάλυσις, 359), "an unloosing" (as of things woven), "a dissolving into separate parts" (Eng., "analysis"), is once used of "departure from life," 2 Tim. 4:6, where the metaphor is either nautical, from loosing from moorings (thus used in Greek poetry), or mili-

tary, from breaking up an encampment; cf. *kataluō* in 2 Cor. 5:1 (cf. DEPART, No. 16).¶

2. *aphixis* (ἄφιξις, 867), most frequently "an arrival" (akin to *aphikneomas*, see COME), also signifies a "departure" (*apo*, "from," *hikneomai*, "to come": etymologically, to come far enough, reach; cf. *hikanos*, "sufficient"), the "departure" being regarded in relation to the end in view. Thus Paul speaks of his "departing," Acts 20:29.¶

3. *exodos* (ἔξοδος, 1841): see DECEASE.

DEPOSE

kathaireō (καθαιρέω, 2507) lit. signifies "to take down" (*kata*, "down," *haireō*, "to take"), the technical term for "removing a body after crucifixion," e.g., Mark 15:36; hence, "to pull down, demolish"; in Acts 19:27, according to the most authentic mss., the translation is (as the RV) "that she (Diana) should even be deposed from her magnificence" (possibly, in the partitive sense of the genitive, "destroyed from, or diminished in, somewhat of her magnificence"). See CAST, DESTROY, PULL, PUT, TAKE (down).

For **DEPOSIT** see **COMMIT**, B, No. 1

DEPTH

1. *bathos* (βάθος, 899): see DEEP.

2. *pelagos* (πέλαγος, 3989), "the sea," Acts 27:5, denotes also "the depth" (of the sea), Matt. 18:6. The word is most probably connected with a form of *plēssō*, "to strike," and *plēgē*, "a blow," suggestive of the tossing of the waves. Some would connect it with *plax*, "a level board," but this is improbable, and less applicable to the general usage of the word, which commonly denotes the sea in its restless character. See SEA.¶

For **DEPUTY** see **PROCONSUL**

DERIDE

Note: For *ekmuktērizō*, lit., "to turn up the nose at, to deride out and out," Luke 16:14; 23:35, see SCOFF.¶

DESCEND

1. *katabainō* (καταβαίνω, 2597), "to go down" (*kata*, "down," *bainō*, "to go"), used for various kinds of motion on the ground (e.g., going, walking, stepping), is usually translated "to descend." The RV uses the verb "to come down," for KJV, "descend," in Mark 15:32; Acts 24:1; Rev. 21:10. See COME, No. 19.

2. *katerchomai* (κατέρχομαι, 2718), "to come or go down," is translated "descendeth,"

in Jas. 3:15, KJV; RV, "cometh down." See COME, No. 7.

DESCENT

katabasis (κατάβασις, 2600) denotes "a going down," akin to No. 1 under DESCEND, "a way down," Luke 19:37.¶

Note: For "descent" (KJV in Heb. 7:3, 6), see GENEALOGY (the RV rendering).

DESCRIBE

1. *graphō* (γράφω, 1125), "to write," is rendered "describeth" in Rom. 10:5, KJV, "For Moses describeth the righteousness which is of the Law . . . "; this the RV corrects to "For Moses writeth that the man that doeth the righteousness which is of the Law . . . " See WRITE.

2. *legō,* (λέγω, 3004) "to say," is rendered "describeth" in Rom. 4:6, KJV, "David describeth the blessedness . . . "; this the RV corrects to, "David pronounceth blessing upon . . . " This might be regarded as the meaning, if David is considered as the human agent acting for God as the real pronouncer of blessing. Otherwise the verb *legō* is to be taken in its ordinary sense of "telling or relating"; especially as the blessedness (*makarismos*) is not an act, but a state of felicity resulting from God's act of justification.

DESERT (Noun and Adjective)

A. Noun.

eremia (ἐρημία, 2047), primarily "a solitude, an uninhabited place," in contrast to a town or village, is translated "deserts" in Heb. 11:38; "the wilderness" in Matt. 15:33, KJV, "a desert place," RV; so in Mark 8:4; "wilderness" in 2 Cor. 11:26. It does not always denote a barren region, void of vegetation; it is often used of a place uncultivated, but fit for pasturage. See WILDERNESS.¶

B. Adjective.

erēmos (ἔρημος, 2048), used as a noun, has the same meaning as *erēmia;* in Luke 5:16 and 8:29, RV, "deserts," for KJV, "wilderness"; in Matt. 24:26 and John 6:31, RV, "wilderness," for KJV, "desert." As an adjective, it denotes (*a*), with reference to persons, "deserted," desolate, deprived of the friends and kindred, e.g., of a woman deserted by a husband, Gal. 4:27; (*b*) so of a city, as Jerusalem, Matt. 23:38; or uninhabited places, "desert," e.g., Matt. 14:13, 15; Acts 8:26; in Mark 1:35, RV, "desert," for KJV, "solitary." See DESOLATE, WILDERNESS.

DESIRE (Noun and Verb), DESIROUS

A. Nouns.

1. *epithumia* (ἐπιθυμία, 1939), "a desire, craving, longing, mostly of evil desires," frequently translated "lust," is used in the following, of good "desires": of the Lord's "wish" concerning the last Passover, Luke 22:15; of Paul's "desire" to be with Christ, Phil. 1:23; of his "desire" to see the saints at Thessalonica again, 1 Thess. 2:17.

With regard to evil "desires," in Col. 3:5 the RV has "desire," for the KJV, "concupiscence"; in 1 Thess 4:5, RV, "lust," for KJV, "concupiscence"; there the preceding word *pathos* is translated "passion," RV, for KJV, "lust" (see AFFECTION); also in Col. 3:5 *pathos* and *epithumia* are associated, RV, "passion," for KJV, "inordinate affection." *Epithumia* is combined with *pathēma,* in Gal. 5:24; for the KJV, "affections and lusts," the RV has "passions, and the lusts thereof." *Epithumia* is the more comprehensive term, including all manner of "lusts and desires"; *pathēma* denotes suffering; in the passage in Gal. (l.c.) the sufferings are those produced by yielding to the flesh; *pathos* points more to the evil state from which "lusts" spring. Cf. *orexis,* "lust," Rom. 1:27. See CONCUPISCENCE, LUST, and Trench, *Syn.* §lxxxvii.

2. *eudokia* (εὐδοκία, 2107), lit., "good pleasure" (*eu,* "well," *dokeō,* "to seem"), implies a gracious purpose, a good object being in view, with the idea of a resolve, showing the willingness with which the resolve is made. It is often translated "good pleasure," e.g., Eph. 1:5, 9; Phil. 2:13; in Phil. 1:15, "good will"; in Rom. 10:1, "desire," (marg., "good pleasure"); in 2 Thess. 1:11, RV, "desire," KJV and RV, marg., "good pleasure."

It is used of God in Matt. 11:26 ("well pleasing," RV, for KJV, "seemed good"); Luke 2:14, RV, "men in whom He is well pleased," lit., "men of good pleasure" (the construction is objective); 10:21; Eph. 1:5, 9; Phil. 2:13. See PLEASURE, SEEM, WILL.¶

3. *epipothēsis* (ἐπιπόθησις, 1972), "an earnest desire, a longing for" (*epi,* "upon," intensive, *potheō,* "to desire"), is found in 2 Cor. 7:7, 11, KJV, "earnest desire," and "vehement desire"; RV, "longing" in both places. See LONGING.¶

4. *epipothia* (ἐπιποθία, 1974), with the same meaning as No. 3, is used in Rom. 15:23, RV, "longing," KJV, "great desire."¶ Cf. *epipothētos,* Phil. 4:1, "longed for" ¶, and *epipotheō,* "to long for" [see B, *Note* (4)]. See LONGING.

5. *thelēma* (θέλημα, 2307) denotes "a will,

that which is willed" (akin to B, No. 6). It is rendered "desires," in Eph. 2:3. See PLEASURE, WILL.

Note: In 1 Pet. 4:3, RV, *boulēma* is rendered "desire." See WILL.

B. Verbs.

1. *axioō* (ἀξιόω, 515), "to deem worthy," is translated "desire" in Acts 28:22, where a suitable rendering would be "We think it meet (or good) to hear of thee"; so in 15:38. See THINK.

2. *epithumeō* (ἐπιθυμέω, 1937), "to desire earnestly" (as with A, No. 1), stresses the inward impulse rather than the object desired. It is translated "to desire" in Luke 16:21; 17:22; 22:15; 1 Tim. 3:1; Heb. 6:11; 1 Pet. 1:12; Rev. 9:6. See COVET.

3. *erōtaō* (ἐρωτάω, 2065), in Luke 7:36 is translated "desired"; in 14:32, RV, "asketh," for KJV, "desireth"; so in John 12:21; Acts 16:39; 18:20; 23:20; in v. 18 "asked," for KJV, "prayed." See ASK.

4. *homeiromai, or himeiromai* (ὁμείρομαι, 2442), "to have a strong affection for, a yearning after," is found in 1 Thess. 2:8, "being affectionately desirous of you." It is probably derived from a root indicating remembrance.¶

5. *oregō* (ὀρέγω, 3713), "to reach or stretch out," is used only in the middle voice, signifying the mental effort of stretching oneself out for a thing, of longing after it, with stress upon the object desired (cf. No. 2); it is translated "desire" in Heb. 11:16; in 1 Tim. 3:1, RV, "seeketh," for KJV, "desireth"; in 1 Tim. 6:10, RV, "reached after," for KJV, "coveted after." In Heb. 11:16, a suitable rendering would be "reach after." See COVET, SEEK.¶ Cf. *orexis*, lust, Rom. 1:27.¶

6. *thelō* (θέλω, 2309),"to will, to wish," implying volition and purpose, frequently a determination, is most usually rendered "to will." It is translated "to desire" in the RV of the following: Matt. 9:13; 12:7; Mark 6:19; Luke 10:29; 14:28; 23:20; Acts 24:27; 25:9; Gal. 4:17; 1 Tim. 5:11; Heb. 12:17; 13:18. See DISPOSED, FORWARD, INTEND, LIST, LOVE, MEAN, PLEASED, RATHER, VOLUNTARY, WILL.

7. *boulomai* (βούλομαι, 1014), "to wish, to will deliberately," expresses more strongly than *thelō* (No. 6) the deliberate exercise of the will; it is translated "to desire" in the RV of the following: Acts 22:30; 23:38; 27:43; 28:18; 1 Tim. 2:8; 5:14; 6:9 and Jude 5. See DISPOSED, INTEND, LIST, MINDED, WILLING, WISH, WOULD.

8. *zēloō* (ζηλόω, 2206), "to have a zeal for, to be zealous towards," whether in a good or evil sense, the former in 1 Cor. 14:1, concerning spiritual gifts RV, "desire earnestly," KJV, "desire"; in an evil sense, in Jas. 4:2, RV, "covet," for KJV, "desire to have."

9. *aiteō* (αἰτέω, 154), "to ask," is rendered "to desire" in KJV, e.g., in Matt. 20:20; Luke 23:25 [RV, always "to ask (for)"].

10. *speudō* (σπεύδω, 4692) is translated "earnestly desiring" in 2 Pet. 3:12, RV. See HASTE.

Note: The following are translated by the verb "to desire" in the KJV.

(1) *Eperōtaō*, No. 3, with *epi*, intensive, "to ask, interrogate, inquire of, consult, or to demand of a person"; in Matt. 16:1, RV, "asked." See ASK. (2) *Zēteō*, "to seek"; in Matt. 12:46-47, RV, "seeking"; in Luke 9:9, RV, "sought." See ENDEAVOR, GO, *Note* (2), (*a*), INQUIRE, REQUIRE, SEEK. (3) *Epizēteō*, "to seek earnestly" (No. 2, with *epi*, intensive), in Acts 13:7, RV, "sought"; in Phil. 4:17, RV, "seek for" (twice). See INQUIRE, SEEK. (4) *Epipotheō*, "to long after, to lust"; in 2 Cor. 5:2, RV, "longing"; in 1 Thess. 3:6 and 2 Tim. 1:4, RV, "longing"; in 1 Pet. 2:2, RV, "long for." See A, Nos. 3-4. See LONG, LUST. (5) *Exaiteomai*, intensive of No. 9, occurs in Luke 22:31.¶ (6) For *parakaleō*, see BESEECH, EXHORT, INTREAT. (7) For "desirous of vain glory," see VAINGLORY.

DESOLATE (Verb and Adjective), DESOLATION

A. Verbs.

1. *erēmoō* (ἐρημόω, 2049) signifies "to make desolate, lay waste." From the primary sense of "making quiet" comes that of "making lonely." It is used only in the passive voice in the NT; in Rev. 17:16, "shall make desolate" is, lit., "shall make her desolated"; in 18:17, 19, "is made desolate"; in Matt. 12:25 and Luke 11:17, "is brought to desolation." See NOUGHT (come to).¶ Cf. DESERT.

2. *monoō* (μονόω, 3443), "to leave alone" (akin to *monos*, "alone"), is used in 1 Tim. 5:5, in the passive voice, but translated "desolate," lit., "was made desolate" or "left desolate."¶

B. Adjectives.

1. *erēmos* (ἔρημος, 2048) is translated "desolate" in the Lord's words against Jerusalem, Matt. 23:38; some mss. have it in Luke 13:35; in reference to the habitation of Judas, Acts 1:20, and to Sarah, from whom, being barren, her husband had turned, Gal. 4:27. See DESERT.

2. *orphanos* (ὀρφανός, 3737) (Eng., "orphan"; Lat., "*orbus*"), signifies "bereft of parents or of a father." In Jas. 1:27 it is translated "fatherless." It was also used in the general sense of being "friendless or desolate." In John 14:18 the Lord uses it of the relationship between Himself and His disciples, He having been their guide, teacher and protector; RV,

"desolate," KJV, "comfortless." Some mss. have the word in Mark 12:40. See FATHERLESS.¶

C. Noun.

erēmōsis (ἐρήμωσις, 2050), akin to A, No. 1, denotes "desolation," (*a*) in the sense of "making desolate," e.g., in the phrase "the abomination of desolation," Matt. 24:15; Mark 13:14; the genitive is objective, "the abomination that makes desolate"; (*b*) with stress upon the effect of the process, Luke 21:20, with reference to the "desolation" of Jerusalem.¶

DESPAIR

1. *exaporeō* (ἐξαπορέω, 1820) is used in the NT in the passive voice, with middle sense, "to be utterly without a way" (*ek*, "out of," intensive, *a*, negative, *poros*, "a way through"; cf. *poreuō*, "to go through"; (Eng., "ferry" is connected); "to be quite at a loss, without resource, in despair." It is used in 2 Cor. 1:8, with reference to life; in 4:8, in the sentence "perplexed, yet not unto (KJV, 'in') despair," the word "perplexed" translates the verb *aporeō*, and the phrase "unto despair" translates the intensive form *exaporeō*, a play on the words.¶ In the Sept., Ps. 88:15, where the translation is "having been lifted up, I was brought low and into despair."¶

2. *apelpizō* (ἀπελπίζω, 560), lit., "to hope away" (*apo*, "away from," *elpizō*, "to hope"), i.e., "to give up in despair, to despair," is used in Luke 6:35, RV, "nothing despairing," i.e., without anxiety as to the result, or not "despairing" of the recompense from God; this is probably the true meaning; KJV, "hoping for nothing again." The marg., "of no man," is to be rejected.¶

DESPISE, DESPISER

A. Verbs.

1. *exoutheneō* (ἐξουθενέω, 1848), "to make of no account" (*ex*, "out," *oudeis*, "nobody," alternatively written, *outheis*), "to regard as nothing, to despise utterly, to treat with contempt." This is usually translated to "set at nought," Luke 18:9, RV, KJV, "despised." So in Rom. 14:3. Both have "set at nought" in Luke 23:11; Acts 4:11; Rom. 14:10. Both have "despise" in 1 Cor. 16:11; Gal. 4:14, and 1 Thess. 5:20; in 2 Cor. 10:10, RV, "of no account," for KJV, "contemptible"; in 1 Cor. 1:28, KJV and RV, "despised." For the important rendering in 1 Cor. 6:4, RV, see ACCOUNT.¶

Note: In Mark 9:12 some mss. have this verb; the most authentic have the alternative spelling *exoudeneō*, "set at nought."

2. *kataphroneō* (καταφρονέω, 2706), lit., "to think down upon or against anyone" (*kata*, "down," *phrēn*, "the mind"), hence signifies "to think slightly of, to despise," Matt. 6:24; 18:10; Luke 16:13; Rom. 2:4; 1 Cor. 11:22; 1 Tim. 4:12; 6:2; Heb. 12:2; 2 Pet. 2:10.¶

3. *periphroneō* (περιφρονέω, 4065) lit. denotes "to think round a thing, to turn over in the mind"; hence, "to have thoughts beyond, to despise," Titus 2:15.¶

Notes: The following verbs, translated "to despise, etc." in the KJV, are given suitable meanings in the RV:

(1) *Atheteō*, lit., "to displace, to set aside," RV, "to reject," Luke 10:16; 1 Thess. 4:8; in 1 Tim. 5:12, "rejected," for KJV, "cast off"; in Heb. 10:28, "hath set at nought"; so Jude 8. See DISANNUL, REJECT, VOID, No. 2. (2) *Atimazō*, "to dishonor" (*a*, negative, *timē*, "honor"); in Jas. 2:6, RV, "have dishonored." See DISHONOR, ENTREAT, SHAME, C, No. 1, SHAMEFULLY. (3) *Oligōreō*, "to care little for, regard lightly" (*oligos*, "little"); in Heb. 12:5, RV, "regard lightly." See REGARD.¶ (4) The phrase *logizomai eis ouden* signifies "to reckon as nothing"; in the passive voice, "to be counted as nothing"; in Acts 19:27, RV, "be made of no account."

B. Adjective.

atimos (ἄτιμος, 820), "without honor," see Note (2), above, is translated as a verb in 1 Cor. 4:10, KJV, "are despised"; RV, "have dishonor," lit., "(we are) without honor"; "without honor" in Matt. 13:57; Mark 6:4. The comparative degree *atimoteros*, "less honorable," is used in 1 Cor. 12:23.¶

Note: Aphilagathos, "not loving the good" (*a*, negative, *phileō*, "to love," *agathos*, "good"), is used in 2 Tim. 3:3, KJV, "despisers of those that are good," RV, "no lovers of good." See LOVER.¶

C. Noun.

kataphronētēs (καταφρονητής, 2707), lit., "one who thinks down against," hence, "a despiser" (see A, No. 2), is found in Acts 13:41.¶ In the Sept., Hab. 1:5; 2:5 and Zeph. 3:4.¶

DESPITE, DESPITEFUL, DESPITEFULLY (use)

1. *enubrizō* (ἐνυβρίζω, 1796), "to treat insultingly, with contumely" (*en*, intensive, *hubrizō*, "to insult"; some connect it with *huper*, "above, over," Lat. *super*, which suggests the insulting disdain of one who considers himself superior), is translated "hath done despite" in Heb. 10:29.¶

Notes: (1) *Hubrizō*, "to insult, act with insolence," is translated "to use despitefully" in Acts 14:5, KJV; RV, "to entreat ... shamefully." See

(ENTREAT) SHAMEFULLY, (ENTREAT) SPITE-
FULLY, REPROACH, B, No. 2.

(2) The noun *hubristēs*, "a violent man," is
translated "despiteful" in Rom. 1:30, KJV; RV,
"insolent"; in 1 Tim. 1:13, "injurious."¶

2. *epēreazō* (ἐπηρεάζω, 1908), for which see
ACCUSE, B, No. 3, is found in some mss. in
Matt. 5:44, and translated "despitefully use,"
KJV (the RV follows the mss. which omit the
sentence). In the corresponding passage in Luke
6:28, the KJV and RV have "despitefully use"; in
1 Pet. 3:16, KJV, "falsely accuse," RV, "revile."
See ACCUSE, REVILE.¶

DESTITUTE (be, etc.)

1. *apostereō* (ἀποστερέω, 650): see DE-
FRAUD.

2. *hustereō* (ἱστερέω, 5302), primarily, "to
be behind, to be last," hence, "to lack, fail of,
come short of," is translated "being destitute"
in Heb. 11:37. See BEHIND, B, No. 1.

3. *leipō* (λείπω, 3007) signifies "to leave,
forsake"; in the passive voice, "to be left, forsaken, destitute"; in Jas. 2:15, KJV, "destitute,"
RV, "be in lack." See LACK, WANT.

DESTROY, DESTROYER, DESTRUCTION, DESTRUCTIVE

A. Verbs.

1. *apollumi* (ἀπόλλυμι, 622), a strengthened
form of *ollumi*, signifies "to destroy utterly"; in
middle voice, "to perish." The idea is not extinction but ruin, loss, not of being, but of well-
being. This is clear from its use, as, e.g., of the
marring of wine skins, Luke 5:37; of lost sheep,
i.e., lost to the shepherd, metaphorical of spiritual destitution, Luke 15:4, 6, etc.; the lost son,
15:24; of the perishing of food, John 6:27; of
gold, 1 Pet. 1:7. So of persons, Matt. 2:13, "destroy"; 8:25, "perish"; 22:7; 27:20; of the loss of
well-being in the case of the unsaved hereafter,
Matt. 10:28; Luke 13:3, 5; John 3:16 (v. 15 in
some mss.); 10:28; 17:12; Rom. 2:12; 1 Cor.
15:18; 2 Cor. 2:15, "are perishing"; 4:3;
2 Thess. 2:10; Jas. 4:12; 2 Pet. 3:9. Cf. B, II,
No. 1. See DIE, LOSE, MARRED, PERISH.

2. *katargeō* (καταργέω, 2673): see ABOLISH.

3. *kathaireō* (καθαιρέω, 2507), "to cast
down, pull down by force, etc.," is translated
"to destroy" in Acts 13:19. In Acts 19:27, KJV,
"should be destroyed," the RV suitably has
"should be deposed." See CAST, No. 13, PULL,
PUT, TAKE.

4. *luō* (λύω, 3089), "to loose, dissolve, sever,
break, demolish," is translated "destroy," in
1 John 3:8, of the works of the Devil. See
BREAK, A, No. 4.

5. *kataluō* (καταλύω, 2647), *kata*, "down,"
intensive, and No. 4, "to destroy utterly, to
overthrow completely," is rendered "destroy,"
in Matt. 5:17, twice, of the Law; Matt. 24:2;
26:61; 27:40; Mark 13:2; 14:58; 15:29; Luke
21:6, of the Temple; in Acts 6:14, of Jerusalem;
in Gal. 2:18, of the Law as a means of justification; in Rom. 14:20 (KJV, "destroy," RV,
"overthrow"), of the marring of a person's spiritual well-being (in v. 15 *apollumi*, No. 1, is used
in the same sense); in Acts 5:38 and 39 (RV,
"overthrow") of the failure of purposes; in
2 Cor. 5:1, of the death of the body ("dissolved"). See DISSOLVE, NOUGHT (come to),
OVERTHROW, THROW.

For its other meaning, "to lodge," see Luke
9:12 and 19:7. See GUEST, LODGE.¶

6. *olothreuō* (ὀλοθρεύω, 3645), "to destroy,"
especially in the sense of slaying, is found in
Heb. 11:28, where the RV translates the present
participle with the article by the noun "destroyer."¶ See B, below. The verb occurs frequently in the Sept., e.g., Ex. 12:23; Josh. 3:10;
7:25; Jer. 2:30; 5:6; 22:7.

7. *exolothreuō* (ἐξολοθρεύω, 1842), *ek*, "out
of" (intensive), and No. 6, "to destroy utterly,
to slay wholly," is found in Acts 3:23, RV, "utterly destroyed," referring to the "destruction"
of one who would refuse to hearken to the voice
of God through Christ.¶ This verb is far more
abundantly used in the Sept. than No. 6; it
occurs 35 times in Deut. 34 in Josh. 68 in the
Psalms.

8. *phtheirō* (φθείρω, 5351): see CORRUPT, A,
No. 2.

9. *diaphtheirō* (διαφθαίρω, 1311); See COR-
RUPT, A, No. 3.

Note: Portheō,"to ruin by laying waste, to
make havock of," is translated "destroyed" in
Acts 9:21, of the attacks upon the church in
Jerusalem by Saul of Tarsus; "wasted," in Gal.
1:13, with reference to the same; "destroyed" in
Gal. 1:23, where "the faith" is put by metonymy (one thing being put for another associated with it), for those who held the faith. In
each of these places the RV consistently translates by "made havock of." See HAVOC,
WASTE.¶

B. Nouns.

(I) (*Personal: DESTROYER*)

olothreutēs (ὀλοθρευτής, 3644), akin to A,
No. 6, "a destroyer," is found in 1 Cor. 10:10.¶

Note: For the construction in Heb. 11:28,
"the destroyer," see A, No. 6. Cf. *apolluōn*, in
Rev. 9:11, the present participle of *apollumi*, A,
No. 1, used as a proper noun.¶

(II) (*Abstract: DESTRUCTION*)

1. *apōleia* (ἀπώλεια, 684), akin to A,No. 1,

and likewise indicating "loss of well-being, not of being," is used (*a*) of things, signifying their waste, or ruin; of ointment, Matt. 26:8; Mark 14:4; of money, Acts 8:20 ("perish"); (*b*) of persons, signifying their spiritual and eternal perdition, Matt. 7:13; John 17:12; 2 Thess. 2:3, where "son of perdition" signifies the proper destiny of the person mentioned; metaphorically of men persistent in evil, Rom. 9:22, where "fitted" is in the middle voice, indicating that the vessels of wrath fitted themselves for "destruction"; of the adversaries of the Lord's people, Phil. 1:28 ("perdition"); of professing Christians, really enemies of the cross of Christ, Phil. 3:19 (RV, "perdition"); of those who are subjects of foolish and hurtful lusts, 1 Tim. 6:9 (for the preceding word "destruction" see No. 3, below); of professing Hebrew adherents who shrink back into unbelief, Heb. 10:39; of false teachers, 2 Pet. 2:1, 3; of ungodly men, 3:7; of those who wrest the Scriptures, 3:16; of the Beast, the final head of the revived Roman Empire, Rev. 17:8, 11; (*c*) of impersonal subjects, as heresies, 2 Pet. 2:1, where "destructive heresies" (RV; KJV, "damnable") is, lit., "heresies of destruction" (marg., "sects of perdition"); in v. 2 the most authentic mss. have *aselgeiais*, "lascivious," instead of *apōleiais*. See PERDITION, PERNICIOUS, WASTE.¶

2. *kathairesis* (καθαίρεσις, 2506), akin to A, No. 3, "a taking down, a pulling down," is used three times in 2 Cor.,"casting down" in the RV in each place; in 10:4 (KJV, "pulling down"); in 10:8 and 13:10 (KJV, "destruction"). See PULL.¶

3. *olethros* (ὄλοεθρος, 3639), "ruin, destruction," akin to A, No. 6, always translated "destruction," is used in 1 Cor. 5:5, of the effect upon the physical condition of an erring believer for the purpose of his spiritual profit; in 1 Thess. 5:3 and 2 Thess. 1:9, of the effect of the divine judgments upon men at the ushering in of the Day of the Lord and the revelation of the Lord Jesus; in 1 Tim. 6:9, of the consequences of the indulgence of the flesh, referring to physical "ruin" and possibly that of the whole being, the following word *apōleia* (see No. 1) stressing the final, eternal and irrevocable character of the "ruin".¶

4. *phthora* (φθορά, 5356), akin to A, No. 8, denotes "the destruction that comes with corruption." In 2 Pet. 2:12 it is used twice; for the KJV, "made to be taken and destroyed . . . shall utterly perish (*phtheirō*) in their own corruption," the RV has "to be taken and destroyed (lit., 'unto capture and destruction,' *phthora*) . . . shall in their destroying (*phthora*) surely be destroyed," taking the noun in the last clause in

the sense of their act of "destroying" others. See CORRUPT, CORRUPTION.

5. *suntrimma* (σύντριμμα, 4938), "a breaking in pieces, shattering" (the corresponding verb is *suntribō;* see under BREAK, BRUISE), hence, "ruin, destruction," is compounded of *sun*, "together," and *trimma*, "a rubbing or wearing away." The latter, and *tribō*, "to beat," are derived from a root, signifying "to rub, wear away"; hence Eng., "tribulation and trouble." It is used, metaphorically, of "destruction," in Rom. 3:16 (from Isa. 59:7), which, in a passage setting forth the sinful state of mankind in general, suggests the "wearing" process of the effects of cruelty.¶ The word is frequent in the Sept., especially in Isaiah and Jeremiah.

DETERMINE, DETERMINATE

1. *krinō* (κρίνω, 2919), primarily, "to separate," hence, "to be of opinion, approve, esteem," Rom. 14:5, also "to determine, resolve, decree," is used in this sense in Acts 3:13; 20:16; 25:25; 27:1; 1 Cor. 2:2; 2 Cor. 2:1; Titus 3:12. See CONDEMN, JUDGE, JUDGMENT, LAW, B, No. 2.

2. *horizō* (Ὁρίζω, 3724) denotes "to bound, to set a boundary" (Eng., "horizon"); hence, "to mark out definitely, determine"; it is translated "to determine" in Luke 22:22, of the foreordained pathway of Christ; Acts 11:29, of a "determination" to send relief; 17:26, where it is used of fixing the bounds of seasons. In Acts 2:23 the verb is translated "determinate," with reference to counsel. Here the verbal form might have been adhered to by the translation "determined"; that is to say, in the sense of "settled."

In Rom. 1:4 it is translated "declared," where the meaning is that Christ was marked out as the Son of God by His resurrection and that of others (see under DECLARE). In Acts 10:42 and 17:31 it has its other meaning of "ordain," that is, "to appoint by determined counsel." In Heb. 4:7, it is translated "limiteth," but preferably in the RV, "defineth," with reference to a certain period; here again it approaches its primary meaning of marking out the bounds of. See DECLARE, No. 9, LIMIT ORDAIN.¶

3. *proorizō* (προορίζω, 4309), *pro*, "beforehand," and No. 2, denotes "to mark out beforehand, to determine before, foreordain"; in Acts 4:28, KJV, "determined before," RV, "foreordained"; so the RV in 1 Cor. 2:7, KJV, "ordained"; in Rom. 8:29–30 and Eph. 1:5, 11, KJV, "predestinate," RV, "foreordain." See ORDAIN, *Note* (1), PREDESTINATE.¶

4. *epiluō* (ἐπιλύω, 1956), lit., "to loosen upon," denotes "to solve, expound," Mark 4:34; "to settle," as of a controversy, Acts 19:39, KJV,

"it shall be determined," RV, "it shall be settled. See EXPOUND, SETTLE.¶

5. *diaginōskō* (διαγινώσκω, 1231), besides its meaning "to ascertain exactly," Acts 23:15, was an Athenian law term signifying "to determine," so used in 24:22, RV, "determine"; KJV, "know the uttermost of."¶

6. *tassō* (τάσσω, 5021): see APPOINT, No. 5.

Note: Boulomai, "to be minded, to purpose," is translated "determined" in Acts 15:37; RV, "was minded." See MINDED, No. 2.

DEVICE

1. *enthumēsis* (ἐνθύμησις, 1761), "a cogitation, an inward reasoning" (generally, evil surmising or supposition), is formed from *en*, "in," and *thumos*, "strong feeling, passion" (cf. *thumoō*, in the middle voice, "to be wroth, furious"); Eng., "fume" is akin; the root, *thu*, signifies "to rush, rage." The word is translated "device" in Acts 17:29, of man's production of images; elsewhere, "thoughts," Matt. 9:4; 12:25; Heb. 4:12, where the accompanying word *ennoia* denotes inward intentions, See THOUGHT.¶

2. *noēma* (νόημα, 3540) denotes "thought, that which is thought out" (cf. *noeō*, "to understand"); hence, "a purpose, device"; translated "devices" in 2 Cor. 2:11; "minds" in 2 Cor. 3:14; 4:4; 11:3; in 2 Cor. 10:5, "thought"; in Phil. 4:7, KJV, "minds," RV, "thoughts." See MIND, THOUGHT.¶

DEVIL, DEVILISH

diabolos (διάβολος, 1228), "an accuser, a slanderer" (from *diaballō*, "to accuse, to malign"), is one of the names of Satan. From it the English word "Devil" is derived, and should be applied only to Satan, as a proper name. *Daimōn*, "a demon," is frequently, but wrongly, translated "devil"; it should always be translated "demon," as in the RV margin. There is one "Devil," there are many demons. Being the malignant enemy of God and man, he accuses man to God, Job 1:6–11; 2:1–5; Rev. 12:9, 10, and God to man, Gen. 3. He afflicts men with physical sufferings, Acts 10:38. Being himself sinful, 1 John 3:8, he instigated man to sin, Gen. 3, and tempts man to do evil, Eph. 4:27; 6:11, encouraging him thereto by deception, Eph. 2:2. Death having been brought into the world by sin, the "Devil" had the power of death, but Christ through His own death, has triumphed over him, and will bring him to nought, Heb. 2:14; his power over death is intimated in his struggle with Michael over the body of Moses, Jude 9. Judas, who gave himself over to the "Devil," was so identified with him, that the Lord described him as such, John 6:70 (see

13:2). As the "Devil" raised himself in pride against God and fell under condemnation, so believers are warned against similar sin, 1 Tim. 3:6; for them he lays snares, v. 7, seeking to devour them as a roaring lion, 1 Pet. 5:8; those who fall into his snare may be recovered therefrom unto the will of God, 2 Tim. 2:26, "having been taken captive by him (i.e., by the 'Devil')"; "by the Lord's servant" is an alternative, which some regard as confirmed by the use of *zōgreō* ("to catch alive") in Luke 5:10; but the general use is that of taking captive in the usual way. If believers resist he will flee from them, Jas. 4:7. His fury and malignity will be especially exercised at the end of the present age, Rev. 12:12. His doom is the lake of fire, Matt. 25:41; Rev. 20:10. The noun is applied to slanderers, false accusers, 1 Tim. 3:11; 2 Tim. 3:3; Titus 2:3.

Note: For "devilish," Jas. 3:17, see DEMON, C.

DEVISED (cunningly)

sophizō (σοφίζω, 4679), from *sophos*, "wise" (connected etymologically with *sophēs*, "tasty"), in the active voice signifies "to make wise," 2 Tim. 3:15 (so in the Sept. of Ps. 19:7, e.g., "making babes wise"; in 119:98, "Thou hast made me wiser than mine enemies"). In the middle voice it means (*a*) "to become wise"; it is not used thus in the NT, but is so found in the Sept., e.g., in Eccles. 2:15, 19; 7:17; (*b*) "to play the sophist, to devise cleverly"; it is used with this meaning in the passive voice in 2 Pet. 1:16, "cunningly devised fables." See WISE.¶

Note: Cf. *katasophizomai*, "to deal subtly. See DEAL WITH, *Note* (2).

DEVOTION

Note: For this word, in Acts 17:23, KJV, which translates *sebasma*, "devotions," marg., "gods that ye worship," RV, "objects of your worship," in 2 Thess. 2:4, "that is worshiped," see WORSHIP.¶ Cf. Acts 14:15, where, in translating *mataia*, the KJV has "vanities," the abstract for the concrete (RV, "vain things").

DEVOUR

1. *esthiō* (ἐσθίω, 2068) is a strengthened form of an old verb *edō*, from the root *ed*—, whence Lat., *edo*, Eng., "eat." The form *ephagon*, used as the 2nd aorist tense of this verb, is from the root *phag-*, "to eat up." It is translated "devour" in Heb. 10:27; elsewhere, by the verb "to eat." See EAT.

2. *katesthiō* and *kataphagō* (κατεσθίω and καταφάγω, 2719), *kata*, "down," intensive, and No. 1, signifies (*a*) "to consume by eating, to devour," said of birds, Matt. 13:4; Mark 4:4;

Luke 8:5; of the Dragon, Rev. 12:4; of a prophet, "eating" up a book, suggestive of spiritually "eating" and digesting its contents, Rev. 10:9 (cf. Ezek. 2:8; 3:1–3; Jer. 15:16); (*b*) metaphorically, "to squander, to waste," Luke 15:30; "to consume" one's physical powers by emotion, John 2:17; "to devour" by forcible appropriation, as of widows' property, Matt. 23:14 (KJV only); Mark 12:40; "to demand maintenance," as false apostles did to the church at Corinth, 2 Cor. 11:20; "to exploit or prey on one another," Gal. 5:15, where "bite . . . devour . . . consume" form a climax, the first two describing a process, the last the act of swallowing down; to "destroy" by fire, Rev. 11:5; 20:9. See EAT.¶

3. *katapinō* (καταπίνω, 2666), from *kata*, "down," intensive, *pinō*, "to drink," in 1 Pet. 5:8 is translated "devour," of Satan's activities against believers. The meaning "to swallow" is found in Matt. 23:24; 1 Cor. 15:54; 2 Cor. 2:7; 5:4; Heb. 11:29, RV (for KJV, "drowned"); Rev. 12:16. See SWALLOW.¶

DEVOUT

1. *eulabēs* (εὐλαβής, 2126), lit., "taking hold well" (*eu*, "well," *lambanō*, "to take hold"), primarily, "cautious," signifies in the NT, "careful as to the realization of the presence and claims of God, reverencing God, pious, devout"; in Luke 2:25 it is said of Simeon; in Acts 2:5, of certain Jews; in 8:2, of those who bore Stephen's body to burial; of Ananias, 22:12 (see No. 2). "In that mingled fear and love which, combined, constitute the piety of man toward God, the Old Testament placed its emphasis on the fear, the New places it on the love (though there was love in the fear of God's saints then, as there must be fear in their love now)," Trench, *Syn.,* §xlviii.¶

Note: Cf. the noun *eulabeia*, "reverence," and the verb *eulabeomai*, "to reverence."

2. *eusebēs* (εὐσεβής, 2152), from *eu*, "well," *sebomai*, "to reverence," the root *seb-* signifying "sacred awe," describes "reverence" exhibited especially in actions, reverence or awe well directed. Among the Greeks it was used, e.g., of practical piety towards parents. In the NT it is used of a pious attitude towards God, Acts 10:2, 7; (in some mss. in 22:12); "godly," in 2 Pet. 2:9. See GODLY.¶ In the Sept., Prov. 12:12; Isa. 24:16; 26:7; 32:8; Mic. 7:2.¶

Notes: (1) While *eulabēs* especially suggests the piety which characterizes the inner being, the soul, in its attitude towards God, *eusebēs* directs us rather to the energy which, directed by holy awe of God, finds expression in devoted activity.¶

(2) Cf. *theosebeia*, and *theosebēs*, which, by their very formation (*theos*, "God," and *sebomai*), express "reverence" towards God. See Trench (§xlviii).

3. *sebomai* (σέβομαι, 4576), "to feel awe," whether before God or man, "to worship," is translated "devout," in Acts 13:43, RV (KJV, "religious"); 13:50; 17:4, 17. See WORSHIP.

DIADEM

diadēma (διάδημα, 1238) is derived from *diadeō*, "to bind round." It was the kingly ornament for the head, and especially the blue band marked with white, used to bind on the turban or tiara of Persian kings. It was adopted by Alexander the Great and his successors. Among the Greeks and Romans it was the distinctive badge of royalty. Diocletian was the first Roman emperor to wear it constantly. The word is found in Rev. 12:3; 13:1; 19:12, in which passages it symbolizes the rule respectively of the Dragon, the Beast, and Christ.¶ In the Sept., Esth. 1:11; 2:17; in some mss. in 6:8 and 8:15; also in Isa. 62:3–4. For the distinction between this and *stephanos*, see CROWN.

DIE, DEAD (to be, become), DYING

1. *thnēskō* (θνήσκω, 2348), "to die" (in the perf. tense, "to be dead"), in the NT is always used of physical "death," except in 1 Tim. 5:6, where it is metaphorically used of the loss of spiritual life. The noun *thanatos*, and the verb *thanatoō* (below) are connected. The root of this group of words probably had the significance of the breathing out of the last breath. Cf. words under DEATH.

2. *apothnēskō* (ἀποθνήσκω, 599), lit., "to die off or out," is used (*a*) of the separation of the soul from the body, i.e., the natural "death" of human beings, e.g., Matt. 9:24; Rom. 7:2; by reason of descent from Adam, 1 Cor. 15:22; or of violent "death," whether of men or animals; with regard to the latter it is once translated "perished," Matt. 8:32; of vegetation, Jude 12; of seeds, John 12:24; 1 Cor. 15:36; it is used of "death" as a punishment in Israel under the Law, in Heb. 10:28; (*b*) of the separation of man from God; all who are descended from Adam not only "die" physically, owing to sin, see (*a*) above, but are naturally in the state of separation from God, 2 Cor. 5:14. From this believers are freed both now and eternally, John 6:50; 11:26, through the "death" of Christ, Rom. 5:8, e.g.; unbelievers, who "die" physically as such, remain in eternal separation from God, John 8:24. Believers have spiritually "died" to the Law as a means of life, Gal. 2:19; Col. 2:20; to sin, Rom. 6:2, and in general to

all spiritual association with the world and with that which pertained to their unregenerate state, Col. 3:3, because of their identification with the "death" of Christ, Rom. 6:8 (see No. 3, below). As life never means mere existence, so "death," the opposite of life, never means nonexistence. See PERISH.

3. *sunapothnēskō* (συναποθνήσκω, 4880), "to die with, to die together," is used of association in physical "death," Mark 14:31; in 2 Cor. 7:3, the apostle declares that his love to the saints makes separation impossible, whether in life or in "death." It is used once of association spiritually with Christ in His "death," 2 Tim. 2:11. See No. 2 (*b*).¶

4. *teleutaō* (τελευτάω, 5053), "to end" (from *telos*, "an end"), hence, "to end one's life," is used (*a*) of the "death" of the body, Matt. 2:19; 9:18; 15:4, where "die the death" means "surely die," RV, marg., lit., "let him end by death"; Mark 7:10; Matt. 22:25, "deceased"; Luke 7:2; John 11:39, some mss. have verb No. 1 here; Acts 2:29; 7:15; Heb. 11:22 (RV, "his end was nigh"); (*b*) of the gnawings of conscience in self reproach, under the symbol of a worm, Mark 9:48 (vv. 44 and 46, KJV). See DECEASE.¶

5. *koimaō* (κοιμάω, 2837), in the middle and passive voices, its only use in the NT, signifies "to fall asleep." It is connected etymologically with *keimai*, "to lie down," the root *ki*— signifying "to lie." Hence it is used metaphorically of "death," Matt. 27:52, etc. It is translated "be dead" in 1 Cor. 7:39. See ASLEEP.

6. *apoginomai* (ἀπογίνομαι, 581**), lit., "to be away from" (*apo*, "from," *ginomai*, "to be, become"; *apo* here signifies "separation"), is used in 1 Pet. 2:24 of the believer's attitude towards sin as the result of Christ's having borne our sins in His body on the tree; RV, "having died unto sins," the aorist or momentary tense, expressing an event in the past.¶

Note: Apollumi, "to destroy," is found in the middle voice in some mss. in John 18:14, and translated "die." The most authentic mss. have *apothnēskō* (No. 2, above).

DIFFER, DIFFERING, DIFFERENT, DIFFERENCE

A. Verbs.

1. *diapherō* (διαφέρω, 1308), lit., "to bear through, carry different ways," hence, "to be different from," is said of the stars, 1 Cor. 15:41; of a child under age in comparison with a servant, Gal. 4:1; in Phil. 1:10, marg., "things that differ," for "things that are excellent. See BETTER (be).

2. *merizō* (μερίζω, 3307) denotes "to divide"

(from *meros*, "a part": the root *mer*— indicates distribution, or measuring out, and is seen in *meris*, "a district"). In 1 Cor. 7:34 the perfect tense of the passive voice is translated "there is a difference." Some take the verb with what precedes, with reference to the married brother, and translate "he has been divided." See DEAL, DISTRIBUTE, DIVIDE, GIVE, PART.

3. *diakrinō* (διακρίνω, 1252), lit., "to separate throughout, to make a distinction," Acts 15:9, RV, is translated "to make to differ," in 1 Cor. 4:7. In Jude 22, where the middle voice is used, the KJV has "making a difference"; the RV, adopting the alternative reading, the accusative case, has "who are in doubt," a meaning found in Matt. 21:21; Mark 11:23; Acts 10:20; Rom. 14:23; Jas. 1:6; 2:4. See CONTEND.

B. Nouns.

1. *diairesis* (διαίρεσις, 1243) lit. signifies "to take asunder," from *dia*, "apart," and *haireō*, "to take" (Eng., "diaeresis," i.e., distinguishing two successive vowels as separate sounds); it is rendered in the KJV, "diversities" in 1 Cor. 12:4 and 6; "differences" in v. 5; RV, "diversities," in each place.¶

2. *diastolē* (διαστολή, 1293) signifies "a setting asunder" (*dia*, "asunder," *stellō*, "to set, place, arrange"), hence, "a distinction"; in Rom. 3:22 and 10:12, KJV, "difference"; RV, "distinction"; in 1 Cor. 14:7 it is used of the "distinction" in musical sounds.¶

C. Adjectives.

1. *diaphoros* (διάφορος, 1313), akin to A, No. 1, signifies "varying in kind, different, diverse." It is used of spiritual gifts, Rom. 12:6; of ceremonial washings, Heb. 9:10 ("divers"). See DIVERS, and for its other meaning, in Heb. 1:4; 8:6, see EXCELLENT.¶

2. *heteros* (ἕτερος, 2087), RV, "different," for KJV, "another," in Rom. 7:23; 2 Cor. 11:4; Gal. 1:6; cf. 1 Tim. 1:3; 6:3. See ANOTHER.

DIFFICULTY

molis (μόλις, 3433) signifies "with difficulty, hardly" (from *molos*, "toil"). In Luke 9:39, it is rendered "hardly," of the "difficulty" in the departure of a demon. In Acts 27:7, 8, 16, where the KJV has three different renderings, "scarce," "hardly," and "much work," respectively, the RV has "with difficulty" in each place. For its other meanings, "scarce, scarcely," see Acts 14:18; Rom. 5:7; 1 Pet. 4:18. See HARDLY, No. 3.¶

DIG, DIG DOWN

1. *orussō* (ὀρύσσω, 3736), "to dig, dig up soil, dig a pit," is said of a place for a winepress,

Matt. 21:33; Mark 12:1; of "digging" a pit for hiding something, Matt. 25:18.¶

Notes: (1) *Diorussō*, lit., "to dig through" (*dia*, "through"), is translated "to break through (or up)" in Matt. 6:19–20; 24:43; Luke 12:39. See BREAK.¶

(2) *Exorussō*, lit., "to dig out," is translated "to break up" in Mark 2:4; "to pluck out (the eyes)" in Gal. 4:15. See BREAK, PLUCK.¶

2. *skaptō* (σκάπτω, 4626), primarily, "to dig, by way of hollowing out," hence, denotes "to dig." The root *skap* is seen in *skapanē*, "a spade," *skapetos*, "a ditch," *skaphē*, "a boat," and in Eng., "scoop, skiff, and ship" (i.e., something hollowed out). The verb is found in Luke 6:48; 13:8; 16:3.¶

3. *kataskaptō* (κατασκάπτω, 2679), "to dig down" (*kata*, "down," and No. 2), is found in Rom. 11:3, of altars, and in some mss. in Acts 15:16, "ruins," lit., "the things dug down." Here the best texts have *katastrephō*, "to overthrow, overturn."¶

DIGNITY, DIGNITIES

doxa (δόξα, 1391) primarily denotes "an opinion, estimation, repute"; in the NT, always "good opinion, praise, honor, glory, an appearance commanding respect, magnificence, excellence, manifestation of glory"; hence, of angelic powers, in respect of their state as commanding recognition, "dignities," 2 Pet. 2:10; Jude 8. See GLORY, HONOR, PRAISE, WORSHIP.

DILIGENCE, DILIGENT, DILIGENTLY

A. Nouns.

1. *ergasia* (ἐργασία, 2039), (*a*) lit., "a working" (akin to *ergon*, "work"), is indicative of a process, in contrast to the concrete, *ergon*, e.g., Eph. 4:19, lit., "unto a working" (RV marg., "to make a trade of"); contrast *ergon* in v. 12; (*b*) "business," Acts 19:25, RV (for KJV, "craft"); or gain got by "work," Acts 16:16, 19; 19:24; (*c*) endeavor, pains, "diligence," Luke 12:58. See CRAFT, GAIN, WORK.¶

2. *spoudē* (σπουδή, 4710), "earnestness, zeal," or sometimes "the haste accompanying this," Mark 6:25; Luke 1:39, is translated "diligence" in Rom. 12:8; in v. 11, KJV, "business" (RV, "diligence"); in 2 Cor. 8:7, KJV, "diligence," RV, "earnestness"; both have "diligence" in Heb. 6:11; 2 Pet. 1:5; Jude 3; in 2 Cor. 7:11, 12, RV, "earnest care," KJV, "carefulness," and "care." See CARE.¶

B. Verbs.

1. *spoudazō* (σπουδάζω, 4704) has meanings corresponding to A, No. 2; it signifies "to hasten to do a thing, to exert oneself, endeavor, give diligence"; in Gal. 2:10, of remembering the poor, KJV, "was forward," RV, "was zealous"; in Eph. 4:3, of keeping the unity of the Spirit, KJV "endeavoring," RV, "giving diligence"; in 1 Thess. 2:17, of going to see friends, "endeavored"; in 2 Tim. 4:9; 4:21, "do thy diligence"; in the following the RV uses the verb "to give diligence": 2 Tim. 2:15, KJV, "study"; Titus 3:12, KJV, "be diligent"; Heb. 4:11, of keeping continuous Sabbath rest, KJV, "let us labor"; in 2 Pet. 1:10, of making our calling and election sure; in 2 Pet. 1:15, of enabling believers to call Scripture truth to remembrance, KJV, "endeavour"; in 2 Pet. 3:14, of being found in peace without fault and blameless, when the Lord comes, KJV, "be diligent." See ENDEAVOR, FORWARD, LABOR, STUDY, ZEALOUS.¶

2. *meletaō* (μελετάω, 3191), signifies "to care for, attend carefully" (from *meletē*, "care"); in 1 Tim. 4:15, KJV, "meditate," RV, "be diligent in"; in Acts 4:25, "imagine" (marg., "meditate"); in Mark 13:11, the most authentic mss. have *promerimnaō*. See IMAGINE, MEDITATE.¶

C. Adjectives.

1. *spoudaios* (σπουδαῖος, 4705), akin to A, No. 2 and B, No. 1, primarily signifies "in haste"; hence, diligent, earnest, zealous, 2 Cor. 8:22, KJV, "diligent, RV, "earnest." See EARNEST, FORWARD.¶ In the Sept., Ezek. 41:25, "stout (planks)."¶

2. *spoudaioteros* (σπουδαιότερος, 4707), the comparative degree of No. 1, 2 Cor. 8:22, KJV, "more diligent," RV, "more earnest"; in v. 17, KJV, "more forward," RV, "very earnest." See EARNEST; cf. FORWARD.¶

D. Adverbs.

1. *epimelōs* (ἐπιμελῶς, 1960), from *epi*, intensive, and an adverbial form of the impersonal verb *melei*, "it is a care" (cf. B, No. 2), signifies "carefully, diligently," Luke 15:8.¶

2. *pugmē* (πυγμή, 4435), the dative case of *pugmē*, "a fist," lit. means "with the fist" (one hand being rubbed with the clenched fist of the other), a metaphorical expression for "thoroughly," in contrast to what is superficial; Mark 7:3, RV and KJV marg., "diligently" (KJV, text, "oft"). It also signified "boxing" (not in the NT); cf. *puktēs* and *pugmachos*, "a boxer" (Lat., *pugnus* and *pugno*; Eng., "pugilist").¶ In the Sept., Exod. 21:18; Isa. 58:4.¶

3. *spoudaiōs* (σπουδαίως, 4709), "speedily, earnestly, diligently" (cf. the corresponding noun, verb and adjective above), is translated "earnestly" in the RV of Luke 7:4 (KJV, "instantly"); "diligently" in Titus 3:13. See INSTANTLY.

4. *spoudaioterōs* (σπουδαιοτέρως, 4708),

the comparative degree of No. 3, "more diligently," is used in Phil. 2:28, RV, "the more diligently" (KJV, "the more carefully"). See CAREFULLY.¶

Notes: (1) Some mss. have the neuter of the comparative adjective *spoudaioteron* in 2 Tim. 1:17. The most authentic texts have the adverb, No. 4.

(2) *Akribōs* (ἀκριβῶς, 199) means "accurately, exactly." The KJV translates it "diligently" in Matt. 2:8 and Acts 18:25; "perfectly" in 1 Thess. 5:2 (cf. Luke 1:3). See ACCURATELY, CAREFUL, CIRCUMSPECTLY, PERFECTLY.

DIMINISHING

hēttēma (ἥττημα, 2275): see DEFECT.

DINE, DINNER

A. Verb.

aristaō (ἀριστάω, 709), primarily, "to breakfast" (see B), was later used also with the meaning "to dine," e.g., Luke 11:37; in John 21:12, 15, RV, "break your fast," and "had broken their fast," for KJV, "dine"; obviously there it was the first meal in the day.¶ In the Sept., Gen. 43:25; 1 Sam. 14:24; 1 Chron. 13:7.¶

B. Noun.

ariston (ἄριστον, 712), primarily, "the first food," taken early in the morning before work; the meal in the Pharisee's house, in Luke 11:37, was a breakfast or early meal (see RV, marg.); the dinner was called *deipnon.* Later the breakfast was called *akratisma* (not in NT), and dinner, *ariston,* as in Matt. 22:4; Luke 11:38; 14:12.¶

DIP, DIPPED, DIPPETH

1. *baptō* (βάπτω, 911), "to immerse, dip" (derived from a root signifying "deep"), also signified "to dye," which is suggested in Rev. 19:13, of the Lord's garment "dipped (i.e., dyed) in blood" (RV, "sprinkled" translates the verb *rhantizō:* see SPRINKLED. It is elsewhere translated "to dip," Luke 16:24; John 13:26. Cf. the longer form *baptizō* (primarily a frequentative form). See BAPTIZE.¶

2. *embaptō* (ἐμβάπτω, 1686), *en,* "in," and No. 1, "to dip into," is used of the act of Judas in "dipping" his hand with that of Christ in the dish, Matt. 26:23; Mark 14:20.¶

DIRECT

kateuthunō (κατευθύνω, 2720), "to make straight" (*kata,* "down," intensive, *euthus,* "straight," *euthunō,* "to straighten"), is translated "guide" in Luke 1:79, of the Lord's "guidance" of the feet of His people; "direct," in 1 Thess. 3:11, of His "directing" the way of His

servants; in 2 Thess. 3:5, of His "directing" the hearts of His saints into the love of God. See GUIDE.¶

DISALLOW

apodokimazō (ἀποδοκιμάζω, 593), "to reject as the result of disapproval" (*apo,* "away from," *dokimazō,* "to approve"), is always translated "to reject," except in the KJV of 1 Pet. 2:4 and 7. See REJECT.

DISANNUL, DISANNULLING

A. Verbs.

1. *atheteō* (ἀθετέω, 114) signifies "to put as of no value" (*a,* negative, (*theton,* "what is placed," from *tithēmi,* "to put, place"); hence, (*a*) "to act towards anything as though it were annulled"; e.g., to deprive a law of its force by opinions or acts contrary to it, Gal. 3:15, KJV, "disannulleth," RV, "maketh void"; (*b*) "to thwart the efficacy of anything, to nullify, to frustrate it," Luke 7:30, "rejected"; 1 Cor. 1:19, "will I reject"; to make void, Gal. 2:21; to set at nought, Jude 8, RV (KJV, "despised"); the parallel passage, in 2 Pet. 2:10, has *kataphroneō.* In Mark 6:26, the thought is that of breaking faith with. See DESPISE, A, *Note* (1).

2. *akuroō* (ἀκυρόω, 208), "to deprive of authority" (*a,* negative, *kuros,* "force, authority"; cf. *kurios,* "a lord," *kuroō,* "to strengthen"), hence, "to make of none effect," Matt. 15:6; Mark 7:13, with reference to the commandment or word of God, RV, "to make void," is translated "disannul" in Gal. 3:17, of the inability of the Law to deprive of force God's covenant with Abraham. This verb stresses the effect of the act, while No. 1 stresses the attitude of the rejector. See VOID.¶

B. Noun.

athetēsis (ἀθέτησις, 115), akin to A, No. 1, "a setting aside, abolition," is translated "disannulling" in Heb. 7:18, with reference to a commandment; in 9:26 "to put away," with reference to sin, lit., "for a putting away." See PUTTING, *Note.*¶

DISBELIEVE

apisteō (ἀπιστέω, 569), "to be unbelieving" (*a,* negative, *pistis,* "faith"; cf. *apistos,* "unbelieving"), is translated "believed not," etc., in the KJV (except in 1 Pet. 2:7, "be disobedient"); "disbelieve" (or "disbelieved") in the RV, in Mark 16:11, 16; Luke 24:11, 41; Acts 28:24; "disbelieve" is the best rendering, implying that the unbeliever has had a full opportunity of believing and has rejected it; some mss. have *apeitheō,* "to be disobedient," in 1 Pet. 2:7; Rom. 3:3, RV, "were without faith"; 2 Tim.

2:13, RV, "are faithless. Cf. DISOBEDIENT, C. See BELIEVE.¶

DISCERN, DISCERNER, DISCERNMENT

A. Verbs.

1. *anakrinō* (ἀνακρίνω, 350), "to distinguish, or separate out so as to investigate (*krinō*) by looking throughout (*ana*, intensive) objects or particulars," hence signifies "to examine, scrutinize, question, to hold a preliminary judicial examination preceding the trial proper" (this first examination, implying more to follow, is often present in the nonlegal uses of the word), e.g., Luke 23:14; figuratively, in 1 Cor. 4:3; it is said of searching the Scriptures in Acts 17:11; of "discerning" or determining the excellence or defects of a person or thing, e.g., 1 Cor. 2:14, KJV, "discerned"; RV, "judged"; in 1 Cor. 10:27, "asking (no) question" (i.e., not raising the question as to whether the meat is the residue from an idolatrous sacrifice). Except in Luke 23:14, this word is found only in Acts and 1 Cor. See EXAMINE, JUDGE.

2. *diakrinō* (διακρίνω, 1252) signifies "to separate, discriminate"; then, "to learn by discriminating, to determine, decide." It is translated "discern" in Matt. 16:3, of discriminating between the varying conditions of the sky (see *dokimazō*, No. 3, below, in Luke 12:56), and in 1 Cor. 11:29, with reference to partaking of the bread and the cup of the Lord's Supper unworthily, by not "discerning" or discriminating what they represent; in v. 31, the RV has "discerned," for the KJV, "would judge," of trying oneself, "discerning" one's condition, and so judging any evil before the Lord; in 14:29, regarding oral testimony in a gathering of believers, it is used of "discerning" what is of the Holy Spirit, RV, "discern" (KJV, "judge"). See CONTEND, DECIDE, DIFFER, etc.

3. *dokimazō* (δοκιμάζω, 1381) signifies "to test, prove, scrutinize," so as "to decide." It is translated "discern" in the KJV of Luke 12:56; RV, "interpret" (marg., "prove"). See APPROVE.

B. Noun.

diakrisis (διάκρισις, 1253), cf. A, No. 2, "a distinguishing, a clear discrimination, discerning, judging," is translated "discernings" in 1 Cor. 12:10, of "discerning" spirits, judging by evidence whether they are evil or of God. In Heb. 5:14 the phrase consisting of *pros*, with this noun, lit., "towards a discerning," is translated "to discern," said of those who are capable of discriminating between good and evil. In Rom. 14:1 the word has its other sense of decision or judgment, and the phrase "doubtful disputations" is, lit., "judgments of reasonings" (marg., "not for decisions of doubts," i.e., not to act as a judge of the weak brother's scruples). See DECISION, B, No. 2.¶

Note: For "discernment," Phil. 1:19, see JUDGMENT, *Note* (4).

C. Adjective.

kritikos (κριτικός, 2924) signifies "that which relates to judging (*krinō*, "to judge"), fit for, or skilled in, judging" (Eng., "critical"), found in Heb. 4:12, of the Word of God as "quick to discern the thoughts and intents of the heart," (lit., "critical of, etc."), i.e., discriminating and passing judgment on the thoughts and feelings.¶

DISCHARGED

katargeō (καταργέω, 2673) means "to reduce to inactivity." "Discharged" is the RV translation of the word in Rom. 7:2 and 6 (KJV, "is loosed," and "are delivered"). In v. 2 the meaning is that the death of a woman's first husband makes void her status as a wife in the eyes of the Law; she is therefore "discharged" from the prohibition against remarrying; the prohibition is rendered ineffective in her case. So, in v. 6, with the believer in relation to the Law, he has been made dead to the Law as a means of justification and life. It is not the Law that has died (KJV), but the believer (see the RV), who has been "discharged," through being put to death, as to the old nature, in identification with the death of Christ, that he might have life in Christ. See ABOLISH.

DISCIPLE

A. Nouns.

1. *mathētēs* (μαθητής, 3101), lit., "a learner" (from *manthanō*, "to learn," from a root *math—*, indicating thought accompanied by endeavor), in contrast to *didaskalos*, "a teacher"; hence it denotes "one who follows one's teaching," as the "disciples" of John, Matt. 9:14; of the Pharisees, Matt. 22:16; of Moses, John 9:28; it is used of the "disciples" of Jesus (*a*) in a wide sense, of Jews who became His adherents, John 6:66; Luke 6:17, some being secretly so, John 19:38; (*b*) especially of the twelve apostles, Matt. 10:1; Luke 22:11, e.g.; (*c*) of all who manifest that they are His "disciples" by abiding in His Word, John 8:31; cf. 13:35; 15:8; (*d*) in the Acts, of those who believed upon Him and confessed Him, 6:1–2, 7; 14:20, 22, 28; 15:10; 19:1, etc.

A "disciple" was not only a pupil, but an adherent; hence they are spoken of as imitators of their teacher; cf. John 8:31; 15:8.

2. *mathētria* (μαθήτρια, 3102), "a female disciple," is said of Tabitha, Acts 9:36.¶

3. *summathētēs* (συμμαθητής, 4827) means "a fellow disciple" (*sun*, with, and No. 1), John 11:16.¶

Note: In Acts 1:15, the RV translates the mss. which have *adelphōn*, "brethren"; in 20:7, RV, "we," for KJV, "disciples."

B. Verb.

mathēteuō (μαθητεύω, 3100) is used in the active voice, intransitively, in some mss., in Matt. 27:57, in the sense of being the "disciple" of a person; here, however, the best mss. have the passive voice, lit., "had been made a disciple," as in Matt. 13:52, RV, "who hath been made a disciple." It is used in this transitive sense in the active voice in 28:19 and Acts 14:21.¶

DISCIPLINE

sōphronismos (σωφρονισμός, 4995), from *sōphrōn*, lit., "saving the mind," from *saos*, "contracted to" *sōs*, "safe" (cf. *sōzō*, "to save"), *phrēn*, "the mind," primarily, "an admonishing or calling to soundness of mind, or to self-control," is used in 2 Tim. 1:7, KJV, "a sound mind"; RV, "discipline." Cf. *sōphroneō* ("to be of sound mind"), *sōphronizō* ("to admonish"), *sōphronōs* ("soberly"), and *sōphrōn*, "of sound mind." See MIND.¶ Cf. CHASTISEMENT.

DISCOURAGE (-D)

athumeō (ἀθυμέω, 120), "to be disheartened, dispirited, discouraged" (*a*, negative, *thumos*, "spirit, courage," from the root *thu*, found in *thuō*, "to rush," denoting "feeling, passion"; hence Eng., "fume"), is found in Col. 3:21.¶

DISCOURSE

dialegomai (διαλέγομαι, 1256) primarily denotes "to ponder, resolve in one's mind" (*dia*, "through," *legō*, "to say"); then, "to converse, dispute, discuss, discourse with"; most frequently, "to reason or dispute with." In Heb. 12:5 the RV, "reasoneth with" is to be preferred to the KJV, "speaketh unto." The KJV translates it "preached," in Acts 20:7 and 9; this the RV corrects to "discoursed," lit., "dialogued," i.e., not by way of a sermon, but by a "discourse" of a more conversational character. See DISPUTE, PREACH, REASON, SPEAK. In the Sept., Exod. 6:27; Judg. 8:1; Isa. 63:1.

DISCOVER

Two verbs are translated by the verb "to discover," in the KJV. The RV translates differently in each case.

1. *anaphainō* (ἀναφαίνω, 398): see APPEAR, A, No. 3.

2. *katanoeō* (κατανοέω, 2657), "to perceive distinctly, discern clearly, descry," is translated "discovered" in Acts 27:39, KJV, of finding a bay with a creek (RV, "perceived"). See BEHOLD.

DISCREET, DISCREETLY

A. Adjective.

sōphrōn (σώφρων, 4998), "of sound mind, self-controlled" (for the derivation, see DISCIPLINE), is translated "sober-minded," in its four occurrences in the RV, 1 Tim. 3:2 (KJV, "sober"); Titus 1:8 (KJV, "ditto"); 2:2 (KJV, "temperate"); 2:5 (KJV, "discreet"). See SOBER, TEMPERATE.¶

B. Adverb.

nounechōs (νουνεχῶς, 3562), lit., "mind-possessing" (*nous*, "mind, understanding," *echō*, "to have"), hence denotes "discreetly, sensibly, prudently." Mark 12:34.¶

DISEASE, DISEASED (BE)

A. Nouns.

1. *astheneia* (ἀσθένεια, 769), lit., "lacking strength" (*a*, negative, *sthenos*, "strength"), "weakness, infirmity," is translated "diseases" in Matt. 8:17, RV, for KJV, "sicknesses," and in Acts 28:9. Its usual rendering is "infirmity" or "infirmities"; "sickness," in John 11:4. Cf. B, No. 1. See INFIRMITY, SICKNESS, WEAKNESS.

2. *malakia* (μαλακία, 3119) primarily denotes "softness" (cf. *malakos*, "soft," Matt. 11:8, etc.); hence, "debility, disease." It is found in Matthew only, 4:23; 9:35; 10:1.¶ It is frequent in the Sept., e.g., Gen. 42:4; 44:29; Deut. 7:15; 28:61; Isa. 38:9; 53:3.

3. *nosos* (νόσος, 3554), akin to Lat. *nocere*, "to injure" (Eng., "nosology"), is the regular word for "disease, sickness," Matt. 4:23; 8:17; 9:35; 10:1, RV, "disease," KJV, "sickness"; in Matt. 4:24; Mark 1:34; Luke 4:40; 6:17; 9:1; Acts 19:12, KJV and RV render it "diseases." In Luke 7:21, KJV has "infirmities." The most authentic mss. omit the word in Mark 3:15. See SICKNESS.¶

4. *nosēma* (νόσημα, 3553), an alternative form of No. 3, is found in some mss. in John 5:4.¶ Cf. *noseō*, "to dote about, have a diseased craving for," 1 Tim. 6:4.¶

B. Verbs.

1. *astheneō* (ἀσθενέω, 770), akin to A, No. 1, "to lack strength, to be weak, sick," is translated "were diseased" in John 6:2, KJV (RV, "were sick"). See IMPOTENT, SICK, WEAK.

2. *echō kakōs* (ἔχω κακῶς) lit., "to have badly," i.e., "to be ill or in an evil case," is used in Matt. 14:35 (KJV, "were diseased," RV, "were sick"); so in Mark 1:32; Luke 7:2. See SICK.¶

DISFIGURE

aphanizō (ἀφανίζω, 853) primarily means "to cause to disappear," hence (*a*) "to make unsightly, to disfigure," as of the face, Matt. 6:16; (*b*) "to cause to vanish away, consume," Matt. 6:19, 20; (*c*) in the passive voice, "to perish," Acts 13:41, or "to vanish away," Jas. 4:14. See CONSUME.¶

DISH

trublion (τρύβλιον, 5165) denotes "a bowl," somewhat deep, Matt. 26:23; Mark 14:20; among the Greeks it was a measure in medical prescriptions.¶

DISHONESTY

aischunē (αἰσχύνη, 152), "shame," so the RV in 2 Cor. 4:2 (for KJV, "dishonesty"), is elsewhere rendered "shame," Luke 14:9; Phil. 3:19; Heb. 12:2; Jude 13; Rev. 3:18. See SHAME.¶

DISHONOR

A. Noun.

atimia (ἀτιμία, 819), from *a*, negative, *timē*, "honor," denotes "dishonor, ignominy, disgrace," in Rom. 1:26, "vile passions" (RV), lit., 'passions of dishonor;' in Rom. 9:21, "dishonor," of vessels designed for meaner household purposes (in contrast to *timē*, "honor," as in 2 Tim. 2:20); in 1 Cor. 11:14, said of long hair, if worn by men, RV, "dishonor," for KJV, "shame," in contrast to *doxa*, glory, v. 15; so in 1 Cor. 15:43, of the "sowing" of the natural body, and in 2 Cor. 6:8, of the apostle Paul's ministry. In 2 Cor. 11:21 he uses it in self-disparagement, KJV, "reproach," RV, "disparagement." See DISPARAGEMENT, REPROACH, SHAME, VILE.

B. Adjective.

atimos (ἄτιμος, 820), akin to A: see DESPISE, B.

C. Verbs.

1. *atimazō* (ἀτιμάζω, 818) akin to A, signifies "to dishonour, treat shamefully, insult," whether in word, John 8:49, or deed, Mark 12:4; Luke 20:11, RV "handled (him) shamefully," (RV "entreated ... shamefully"); Rom. 1:24; 2:23, "dishonorest;" Jas. 2:6, RV, "ye have dishonored (the poor)," (KJV, "despised"); in the passive voice, to suffer dishonor, Acts 5:41 (KJV, "suffer shame"). See DESPISE, A, *Note* (2).

Note: Atimaō is found in some mss. in Mark 12:4.

2. *kataischunō* (καταισχύνω, 2617): see ASHAMED, No. 3.

DISMISS (-ED)

apoluō (ἀπολύω, 630), lit., "to loose from" *(apo,* "from," *luō,* "to loose"), is translated "dismiss" in Acts 15:30, 33, RV (KJV, "let go") and 19:41. See DEPART, DIVORCE, FORGIVE, GO, LIBERTY, LOOSE, PUT, No. 16, RELEASE, SEND.

DISOBEDIENCE, DISOBEDIENT

A. Nouns.

1. *apeitheia* (ἀπείθεια, 543), lit., "the condition of being unpersuadable" (*a*, negative, *peithō*, "to persuade"), denotes "obstinacy, obstinate rejection of the will of God"; hence, "disobedience"; Eph. 2:2; 5:6; Col. 3:6, and in the RV of Rom. 11:30, 32 and Heb. 4:6, 11 (for KJV, "unbelief"), speaking of Israel, past and present. See UNBELIEF.¶

2. *parakoē* (παρακοή, 3876), primarily, "hearing amiss" (*para*, "aside," *akouō*, "to hear"), hence signifies "a refusal to hear"; hence, "an act of disobedience," Rom. 5:19; 2 Cor. 10:6; Heb. 2:2. It is broadly to be distinguished from No. 1, as an act from a condition, though *parakoē* itself is the effect, in transgression, of the condition of failing or refusing to hear. Carelessness in attitude is the precursor of actual "disobedience." In the OT "disobedience" is frequently described as "a refusing to hear," e.g., Jer. 11:10; 35:17; cf. Acts 7:57. See Trench, *Syn.* §lxvi.¶

B. Adjective.

apeithēs (ἀπειθής, 545), akin to A, No. 1, signifies "unwilling to be persuaded, spurning belief, disobedient," Luke 1:17; Acts 26:19; Rom. 1:30; 2 Tim. 3:2; Titus 1:16; 3:3.¶

Note: In 1 Tim. 1:9 *anupotaktos*, "insubordinate, unsubjected" (*a*, negative, *n*, euphonic, *hupo*, "under," *tassō*, "to order"), is translated "disobedient" in the KJV; the RV has "unruly," as in Titus 1:6, 10; in Heb. 2:8, "not subject" (RV), "not put under" (KJV). See PUT, UNRULY.¶

C. Verb.

apeitheō (ἀπειθέω, 544), akin to A, No. 1, and B, "to refuse to be persuaded, to refuse belief, to be disobedient," is translated "disobedient," or by the verb "to be disobedient," in the RV of Acts 14:2 (KJV, "unbelieving"), and 19:9 (KJV, "believed not"); it is absent from the most authentic mss. in Acts 17:5; in John 3:36 "obeyeth not," RV (KJV, "believeth not"); in Rom. 2:8 "obey not"; in 10:21, "disobedient"; in 11:30, 31, "were disobedient" (KJV, "have not believed"); so in 15:31; Heb. 3:18; 11:31; in 1 Pet. 2:8, "disobedient"; so in 3:20; in 3:1 and 4:17, "obey not." In 2:7 the best mss. have *apisteō*, "to disbelieve." See OBEY, B, No. 4, UNBELIEVING.¶

DISORDERLY

A. Adjective.

ataktos (ἄτακτος, 813) signifies "not keeping order" (*a*, negative, *tassō*, "to put in order, arrange"); it was especially a military term, denoting "not keeping rank, insubordinate"; it is used in 1 Thess. 5:14, describing certain church members who manifested an insubordinate spirit, whether by excitability or officiousness or idleness. See UNRULY.¶

B. Adverb.

ataktōs (ἀτάκτως, 814) signifies "disorderly, with slackness" (like soldiers not keeping rank), 2 Thess. 3:6; in v. 11 it is said of those in the church who refused to work, and became busybodies (cf. 1 Tim. 5:13).¶

C. Verb.

atakteō (ἀτακτέω, 812) signifies "to be out of rank, out of one's place, undisciplined, to behave disorderly": in the military sense, "to break rank"; negatively in 2 Thess. 3:7, of the example set by the apostle and his fellow missionaries, in working for their bread while they were at Thessalonica so as not to burden the saints. See BEHAVE.¶

DISPARAGEMENT

For this RV translation of *atimia* in 2 Cor. 11:21, see DISHONOR, A.

DISPENSATION

oikonomia (οἰκονομία, 3622) primarily signifies "the management of a household or of household affairs" (*oikos*, "a house," *nomos*, "a law"); then the management or administration of the property of others, and so "a stewardship," Luke 16:2–4; elsewhere only in the epistles of Paul, who applies it (*a*) to the responsibility entrusted to him of preaching the gospel, 1 Cor. 9:17 (RV, "stewardship," KJV, "dispensation"); (*b*) to the stewardship committed to him "to fulfill the Word of God," the fulfillment being the unfolding of the completion of the divinely arranged and imparted cycle of truths which are consummated in the truth relating to the church as the body of Christ, Col. 1:25 (RV and KJV, "dispensation"); so in Eph. 3:2, of the grace of God given him as a stewardship ("dispensation") in regard to the same "mystery"; (*c*) in Eph. 1:10 and 3:9, it is used of the arrangement or administration by God, by which in "the fullness of the times" (or seasons) God will sum up all things in the heavens and on earth in Christ. In Eph. 3:9 some mss. have *koinōnia*, "fellowship," for *oikonomia*, "dispensation." In 1 Tim. 1:4 *oikonomia* may mean either a stewardship in the

sense of (*a*) above, or a "dispensation" in the sense of (*c*). The reading *oikodomia*, "edifying," in some mss., is not to be accepted. See STEWARDSHIP.¶

Note: A "dispensation" is not a period or epoch (a common, but erroneous, use of the word), but a mode of dealing, an arrangement, or administration of affairs. Cf. *oikonomos*, "a steward," and *oikonomeō*, "to be a steward."

DISPERSE, DISPERSION

A. Verbs.

1. *dialuō* (διαλύω, 1262), "to dissolve," is used in Acts 5:36 of the breaking up and dispersion of a company of men, RV, "dispersed," KJV, "scattered." See SCATTER.¶

2. *skorpizō* (σκορπίζω, 4650), "to scatter" (probably from a root, *skarp-*, signifying "to cut asunder," akin to *skorpios*, "a scorpion"), is used in Matt. 12:30; Luke 11:23; John 10:12; 16:32; in the RV of 2 Cor. 9:9, "scattered abroad" (KJV, "he hath dispersed abroad"), of one who liberally dispenses benefits. See SCATTER.¶

3. *diaskorpizō* (διασκορπίζω, 1287), *dia*, "through," and No. 2, signifies "to scatter abroad," in Matt. 26:31; Mark 14:27, metaphorically of sheep; in Luke 1:51, of the proud; in John 11:52, of the "scattering" of the children of God; in Acts 5:37, of the followers of Judas of Galilee (KJV, "were dispersed"); cf. No. 1, re v. 36; of "scattering" grain by winnowing, Matt. 25:24, 26; in Luke 15:13 and 16:1, it signifies "to waste." See SCATTER, STRAWED, WASTE.¶

4. *diaspeirō* (διασπείρω, 1289), "to scatter abroad" (*dia*, "through," *speirō*, "to sow"), is used in Acts 8:1, 4; 11:19.¶

B. Noun.

diaspora (διασπορά, 1290), akin to A, No. 4, "a scattering, a dispersion," was used of the Jews who from time to time had been scattered among the Gentiles, John 7:35; later with reference to Jews, so "scattered," who had professed, or actually embraced, the Christian faith, "the Dispersion," Jas. 1:1, RV; especially of believers who were converts from Judaism and "scattered" throughout certain districts, "sojourners of the Dispersion," 1 Pet. 1:1, RV.¶ In the Sept., of Israelites, "scattered" and exiled, e.g., Deut. 28:25; 30:4; Neh. 1:9.

DISPLEASED

1. *aganakteō* (ἀγανακτέω, 23), from *agan*, "much," and *achomai*, "to grieve," primarily meant "to feel a violent irritation, physically"; it was used, too, of the fermenting of wine; hence, metaphorically, "to show signs of grief,

to be displeased, to be grieved, vexed"; it is translated "sore displeased" in Matt. 21:15, KJV; "much displeased," in Mark 10:14, 41; the RV always renders it "to be moved with, or to have, indignation," as the KJV elsewhere, Matt. 20:24; 26:8; Mark 14:4; Luke 13:14. See INDIGNATION.¶

2. *prosochthizō* (προσοχθίζω, 4360), "to be wroth or displeased with" (*pros*, "toward," or "with," *ochtheō*, "to be sorely vexed"), is used in Heb. 3:10, 17 (KJV, "grieved"; RV, "displeased"). "Grieved" does not adequately express the righteous anger of God intimated in the passage. See GRIEVE.¶

3. *thumomacheō* (θυμομαχέω, 2371), lit., "to fight with great animosity" (*thumos*, "passion," *machomai*, "to fight"), hence, "to be very angry, to be highly displeased," is said of Herod's "displeasure" with the Tyrians and Sidonians, Acts 12:20.¶

DISPOSED (to be)

1. *boulomai* (βούλομαι, 1014), "to wish, to purpose, to will deliberately," indicating a predisposition acting through the deliberate will, is translated "was disposed" in Acts 18:27, KJV (RV, "was minded"). It expresses more strongly than *thelō* (No. 2) the deliberate exercise of the will. See DESIRE, B, No. 7.

2. *thelō* (θέλω, 2309) means "to will"; it signifies more especially the natural impulse or volition, and indicates a less formal or deliberate purpose than No. 1. It is translated "are disposed" in 1 Cor. 10:27.
See DESIRE, B, No. 6.

DISPOSITION

diatagē (διαταγή, 1296), an ordinance, e.g., Rom. 13:2 (cf. *diatassō*, "to appoint, ordain"), is rendered "disposition" in Acts 7:53; RV, "as it (the law) was ordained by angels" (marg., "as the ordinance of angels"; lit., "unto ordinances of angels"). Angels are mentioned in connection with the giving of the Law of Moses in Deut. 33:2. In Gal. 3:19 and Heb. 2:2 the purpose of the reference to them is to show the superiority of the gospel to the Law. In Acts 7:53 Stephen mentions the angels to stress the majesty of the Law. See ORDAIN, ORDINANCE.¶

DISPUTATION

1. *zētēsis* (ζήτησις, 2214) denotes, firstly, "a seeking" (*zēteō*, "to seek"), then, "a debate, dispute, questioning," Acts 15:2, 7 (some texts have *suzētēsis*, "reasoning," in both verses), RV, "questioning," for KJV, "disputation" and "disputing"; for John 3:25; Acts 25:20; 1 Tim. 1:4;

6:4; 2 Tim. 2:23; Titus 3:9, see QUESTION, QUESTIONING.¶

2. *dialogismos* (διαλογισμός, 1261) is translated "disputations" in Rom. 14:1. See below.

DISPUTE, DISPUTER, DISPUTING

A. Nouns.

1. *dialogismos* (διαλογισμός, 1261) denotes, primarily, "an inward reasoning, an opinion" (*dia*, "through," suggesting separation, *logismos*, "a reasoning"), e.g., Luke 2:35; 5:22; 6:8; then, "a deliberating, questioning," Luke 24:38; (more strongly) "a disputing," Phil. 2:14; 1 Tim. 2:8 (KJV, "doubtings"); in Rom. 14:1, "disputations"; marg., "(not for decisions) of doubts" (lit., "not unto discussions or doubts," which is perhaps a suitable rendering). Cf. *dialogizomai*, "to reason." See DOUBTING, IMAGINATION, REASONING, THOUGHT.

2. *logomachia* (λογομαχία, 3055) denotes "a dispute about words" (*logos*, "a word," *machē*, "a fight"), or about trivial things, 1 Tim. 6:4, RV, "disputes," KJV, "strifes." See STRIFE.¶

3. *diaparatribē* (διαπαρατριβή, 3859v) denotes "a constant or incessant wrangling" (*dia*, "through," *para*, "beside," *tribō*, "to wear out," suggesting the attrition or wearing effect of contention), 1 Tim. 6:5, RV, "wranglings," KJV, "perverse disputings." Some mss. have the word *paradiatribē*, in the opposite order of the prefixed prepositions. See WRANGLING.¶

4. *antilogia* (ἀντιλογία, 485) denotes "a gainsaying, contradiction" (*anti*, "against," *legō*, "to speak"), Heb. 6:16 (KJV, "strife," RV, "dispute,"); 7:7, "a gainsaying" (RV, "dispute"; KJV, "contradiction"); 12:3 (RV, "gainsaying"; KJV, "contradiction"); Jude 11 ("gainsaying"). See CONTRADICTION, B.¶

5. *suzētētēs* (συζητητής, 4804), from *sun*, "with," *zēteō*, "to seek," denotes "a disputer," 1 Cor. 1:20, where the reference is especially to a learned "disputant," a sophist.¶

B. Verbs.

1. *dialegomai* (διαλέγομαι, 1256), akin to A, No. 1, primarily signifies "to think different things with oneself, to ponder"; then, with other persons, "to converse, argue, dispute"; it is translated "to dispute" in Mark 9:34 (for v. 33, see No. 2), the RV and KJV "had disputed" is somewhat unsuitable here, for the delinquency was not that they had wrangled, but that they had reasoned upon the subject at all; in Acts 17:17, KJV (RV, "reasoned," as in the KJV of 18:4, 19); in 19:8–9 (RV, "reasoning"); in 24:12, "disputing"; in Jude 9, "disputed." See DISCOURSE.

2. *dialogizomai* (διαλογίζομαι, 1260), akin to A, No. 1, "to bring together different reasons, to reckon them up, to reason, discuss," in Mark 9:33 is translated "ye disputed among yourselves," KJV; RV, "were reasoning." See CAST, No. 15, REASON.

3. *suzēteō* (συζητέω, 4802), akin to A, No. 5, lit., "to seek or examine together," signifies "to discuss," but is translated "to dispute" in Acts 6:9, and 9:29; elsewhere only in Mark and Luke. See INQUIRE, QUESTION, REASON.

DISREPUTE

apelegmos (ἀπελεγμός, 557), from *apo*, "from," and *elenchō*, "to refute," denotes "censure, repudiation" (of something shown to be worthless), hence, "contempt," "disrepute," Acts 19:27, RV, "(come into) disrepute," for KJV, "(to be) set at nought." It is akin to *apelenchō*, "to convict, refute" (not in the NT), *elenchō*, "to convict," *elenxis*, "rebuke," and *elegmos*, "reproof." See NOUGHT.¶

For **DISSEMBLE** see DISSIMULATION

DISSENSION

stasis (στάσις, 4714), akin to *histēmi*, "to stand," denotes (*a*) "a standing, stability," Heb. 9:8, "(while as the first tabernacle) is yet standing"; (*b*) "an insurrection, uproar," Mark 15:7; Luke 23:19, 25; Acts 19:40; 24:5; (*c*) "a dissension," Acts 15:2; 23:7, 10. See INSURRECTION, SEDITION, STANDING, UPROAR.¶

DISSIMULATION, DISSEMBLE

A. Noun.

hupokrisis (ὑπόκρισις, 5272), primarily, "a reply," came to mean "the acting of a stage-player," because such answered one another in dialogue; hence the meaning "dissembling or pretense." It is translated "dissimulation" in Gal. 2:13 (see B). See HYPOCRISY.

B. Verb.

sunupokrinomai (συνυποκρίνομαι, 4942), *sun*, "with," *hupokrinomai*, akin to A, "to join in acting the hypocrite," in pretending to act from one motive, whereas another motive really inspires the act. So in Gal. 2:13, Peter with other believing Jews, in separating from believing Gentiles at Antioch, pretended that the motive was loyalty to the Law of Moses, whereas really it was fear of the Judaizers.¶

C. Adjective.

anupokritos (ἀνυπόκριτος, 505), from *a*, negative, *n*, euphonic, and an adjectival form corresponding to A, signifies "unfeigned"; it is

said of love, 2 Cor. 6:6; 1 Pet. 1:22; Rom. 12:9, KJV, "without dissimulation," RV, "without hypocrisy"; of faith, 1 Tim. 1:5; 2 Tim. 1:5, "unfeigned"; of the wisdom that is from above, Jas. 3:17, "without hypocrisy." See HYPOCRISY.¶

DISSOLVE

1. *luō* (λύω, 3089), "to loose," is used of the future demolition of the elements or heavenly bodies, 2 Pet. 3:10–12; in v. 10, KJV, "shall melt," RV, "shall be dissolved"; in verses 11–12, KJV and RV, "dissolved." See BREAK.

2. *kataluō* (καταλύω, 2647): see DESTROY, A, No. 5.

For **DISTINCTION** (*diastolē*) see DIFFERENCE

DISTRACTION (without)

aperispastōs (ἀπερισπάστως, 563), from *a*, negative, *perispaō*, "to draw around, draw away, distract" (see CUMBER), is found in 1 Cor. 7:35.¶

DISTRESS, DISTRESSED

A. Nouns.

1. *anankē* (ἀνάγκη, 318) denotes (*a*) "a necessity," imposed whether by external circumstances, e.g., Luke 23:17, or inward pressure, e.g., 1 Cor. 9:16; (*b*) "straits, distress," Luke 21:23 (in v. 25 "distress" translates No. 3); 1 Cor. 7:26; 1 Thess. 3:7; the last two refer to the lack of material things. See NECESSARY, NECESSITY, NEEDS.

2. *stenochōria* (στενοχωρία, 4730): see ANGUISH.

3. *sunochē* (συνοχή, 4928): see ANGUISH.

4. *thlipsis* (θλίψις, 2347): see AFFLICTION, B, No. 5.

B. Verbs.

1. *basanizō* (βασανίζω, 928), properly signifies "to test by rubbing on the touchstone" (*basanos*, "a touchstone"), then, "to question by applying torture"; hence "to vex, torment"; in the passive voice, "to be harassed, distressed"; it is said of men struggling in a boat against wind and waves, Matt. 14:24, RV, "distressed" (KJV, "tossed"); Mark 6:48, RV, "distressed" (KJV, "toiling"). See PAIN, TOIL, TORMENT, VEX.

2. *skullō* (σκύλλω, 4660) primarily signifies "to skin, to flay"; then "to rend, mangle"; hence, "to vex, trouble, annoy"; it is found in the most authentic mss. in Matt. 9:36, RV, "distressed" (of the multitudes who applied to the Lord for healing); KJV, "fainted," translating the alternative reading, *ekluō*, lit., "to loosen out." It is also used in Mark 5:35; Luke 7:6; 8:49. See TROUBLE.¶

3. *stenochōreō* (στενοχωρέω, 4729): see AN-GUISH.

4. *kataponeō* (καταπονέω, 2669), primarily, "to tire down with toil, exhaust with labor" (*kata*, "down," *ponos*, "labor"), hence signifies "to afflict, oppress"; in the passive voice, "to be oppressed, much distressed"; it is translated "oppressed" in Acts 7:24, and "sore distressed" in 2 Pet. 2:7, RV, (KJV, "vexed"). See OPPRESS, VEX.¶

DISTRIBUTE, DISTRIBUTION

A. Verbs.

1. *diadidōmi* (διαδίδωμι, 1239), lit., "to give through," (*dia*, "through," *didōmi*, "to give"), as from one to another, "to deal out," is said of "distributing" to the poor, Luke 18:22; Acts 4:35, "distribution was made," or to a company of people, John 6:11. It is translated "divideth" in Luke 11:22. In Rev. 17:13 the most authentic mss. have the verb *didōmi*, to give, instead of the longer form.¶

2. *merizō* (μερίζω, 3307) is translated "hath distributed" in 1 Cor. 7:17, and in the KJV of 2 Cor. 10:13, where, however, this rendering is unsuitable, as it is not a case of distributing among a number, but apportioning a measure to the apostle and his co-workers; hence the RV, "apportioned." See DIFFER, A, No. 2.

Note: Koinōneō, "to share in common with," is translated "distributing" in Rom. 12:13, KJV. The verb does not mean "to distribute"; hence RV, "communicating." Similarly *koinōnia*, "fellowship, communion," is translated "distribution" in 2 Cor. 9:13, KJV; RV, "contribution."

B. Adjective.

eumetadotos (εὐμετάδοτος, 2130), "ready to impart" (*eu*, "well," *meta*, "with," *didōmi*, "to give": see A, No. 1), is used in 1 Tim. 6:18, "ready to distribute."¶

DISTRICT

meris (μερίς, 3310) denotes "a part" (akin to *merizō*, DISTRIBUTE, A, No. 2), Luke 10:42; Acts 8:21; 2 Cor. 6:15; Col. 1:12 (lit., "unto the part," or share, of the inheritance). In Acts 16:12 the RV translates it "district," with reference to Macedonia. See PART.¶

DITCH

bothunos (βόθυνος, 999), any kind of "deep hole or pit" (probably connected with *bathos*, "deep"), is translated "ditch" in the KJV of Matt. 15:14 and Luke 6:39, RV, "pit" in each place, as in both versions of Matt. 12:11. See PIT.¶

DIVERS

A. Adjectives.

1. *diaphoros* (διάφορος, 1313) is rendered "divers" in Heb. 9:10. See DIFFER, C.

2. *poikilos* (ποικίλος, 4164) denotes "particolored, variegated" (*poikillō* means "to make gay": the root of the first syllable is *pik*—, found in Eng., "picture"), hence "divers," Matt. 4:24; Mark 1:34; Luke 4:40; 2 Tim. 3:6; Titus 3:3; Heb. 2:4 (RV, "manifold"); 13:9; Jas. 1:2 (RV, "manifold"); in 1 Pet. 1:6 and 4:10, "manifold," both KJV and RV. See MANIFOLD.¶

Notes: (1) Cf. *polupoikilos*, Eph. 3:10, "manifold" (lit., "much varied").

(2) The pronoun *tines*, "some" (the plural of *tis*, "someone"), is translated "divers" in the KJV of Mark 8:3 and Acts 19:9; RV, "some."

(3) In 1 Cor. 12:28, *genos*, in the plural, is rendered "divers kinds." See DIVERSITIES.

B. Adverb.

polutropōs (πολυτρόπως, 4187) means "in many ways" (*polus*, "much," *tropos*, "a manner, way"; Eng., "trope"), "in divers manners," Heb. 1:1.¶

Note: The phrase *kata topous*, lit., "throughout places" (*kata*, "down, or throughout," in a distributive sense, *topos*, "a place"), is translated "in divers places," in Matt. 24:7; Mark 13:8 and Luke 21:11.

DIVERSITY, DIVERSITIES

diairesis (διαίρεσις, 1243): See DIFFER, B, No. 1.

Note: Genos, "a kind, class, sort" (Eng., "genus"), is translated "diversities" in the KJV of 1 Cor. 12:28 (marg., "kinds"); RV, "divers kinds."

DIVIDE, DIVIDER, DIVIDING

A. Verbs.

1. *aphorizō* (ἀφορίζω, 873), lit., "to mark off by boundaries or limits" (*apo*, "from," *horizō*, "to determine, mark out"), denotes "to separate"; "divideth," Matt. 25:32, KJV; RV, "separateth," as in the preceding part of the verse. See SEPARATE, SEVER

2. *diaireō* (διαιρέω, 1244), lit., "to take asunder" (see DIFFER, B, No. 1), "to divide into parts, to distribute," is found in Luke 15:12 and 1 Cor. 12:11.¶

3. *diadidōmi* (διαδίδωμι, 1239): see DISTRIBUTE, A, No. 1.

4. *diakrinō* (διακρίνω, 1252), "to separate," discriminate, hence, "to be at variance with oneself, to be divided in one's mind," is rendered "divided" in Jas. 2:4, RV; KJV, "partial." See DISCERN.

5. *ginomai* (γίνομαι, 1096), "to become," is translated "was divided" in Rev. 16:19 (of "the great city"), lit., "became into three parts."

6. *merizō* (μερίζω, 3307), akin to *meros*, "a part, to part, divide into," in the middle voice means "to divide anything with another, to share with." The usual meaning is "to divide," Matt. 12:25, 26; Mark 3:24–26; 6:41; Luke 12:13 (middle voice); Rom. 12:3, "hath dealt"; 1 Cor. 1:13; Heb. 7:2, RV (KJV, "gave a part"). Elsewhere with other meanings, 1 Cor. 7:17, 34; 2 Cor. 10:13. See DEAL, DIFFER, A, No. 2, DISTRIBUTE, A, No. 2, GIVE.¶

7. *diamerizō* (διαμερίζω, 1266), *dia*, "through," and No. 6, "to divide through," i.e., "completely, to divide up," is translated "to divide" in Luke 11:17–18; 12:52–53; 22:17; "parted" in Matt. 27:35; Mark 15:24; Luke 23:34; John 19:24; Acts 2:45; in Acts 2:3, KJV, "cloven," RV, "parting asunder." See CLOVEN.¶

8. *orthotomeō* (ὀρθοτομέω, 3718), lit., "to cut straight" (*orthos*, "straight," *temnō*, "to cut"), is found in 2 Tim. 2:15, KJV, "rightly dividing," RV, "handling aright" (the word of truth); the meaning passed from the idea of cutting or "dividing," to the more general sense of "rightly dealing with a thing." What is intended here is not "dividing" Scripture from Scripture, but teaching Scripture accurately.¶ In the Sept., of directing one's paths, Prov. 3:6 and 11:5 ("righteousness traces out blameless paths").¶

Note: In Acts 13:19, the KJV, "He divided their land . . . by lot," represents the verb *kataklērodoteō*, from *kata*, suggesting "distribution," *klēros*, "a lot," *didōmi*, "to give." The most authentic mss. have *kataklēronomeō*, "to distribute," as an inheritance, from *klēronomia*, "an inheritance"; hence RV, "He gave them their land for an inheritance."¶ For *schizō*, Acts 14:4; 23:7, see BREAK, No. 12.

B. Nouns.

1. *meristēs* (μεριστής, 3312), "a divider," is found in Luke 12:14.¶

2. *merismos* (μερισμός, 3311), akin to No. 1, primarily denotes "a division, partition" (*meros*, "a part"); hence, (*a*) "a distribution," Heb. 2:4, "gifts" (marg. of RV, "distributions"); (*b*) "a dividing or separation," Heb. 4:12, "dividing" (KJV, "dividing asunder"). Some take this in the active sense, "as far as the cleaving asunder or separation of soul and spirit"; others in the passive sense, "as far as the division (i.e., the dividing line) between soul and spirit," i.e., where one differs from the other. The former seems more in keeping with the meaning of the word. See GIFT.¶

DIVINATION

puthōn (πύθων, 4436), (Eng., "python"), in Greek mythology was the name of the Pythian serpent or dragon, dwelling in Pytho, at the foot of mount Parnassus, guarding the oracle of Delphi, and slain by Apollo. Thence the name was transferred to Apollo himself. Later the word was applied to diviners or soothsayers, regarded as inspired by Apollo. Since demons are the agents inspiring idolatry, 1 Cor. 10:20, the young woman in Acts 16:16 was possessed by a demon instigating the cult of Apollo, and thus had "a spirit of divination."¶

DIVINE

A. Adjective.

theios (θεῖος, 2304), "divine" (from *theos*, "God"), is used of the power of God, 2 Pet. 1:3, and of His nature, v. 4, in each place, as that which proceeds from Himself. In Acts 17:29 it is used as a noun with the definite article, to denote "the Godhead," the Deity (i.e., the one true God). This word, instead of *theos*, was purposely used by the apostle in speaking to Greeks on Mars Hill, as in accordance with Greek usage. Cf. DIVINITY.¶ In the Sept., Exod. 31:3; 35:31; Job 27:3; 33:4; Prov. 2:17.¶

B. Noun.

latreia (λατρεία, 2999), akin to *latreuō*, "to serve," primarily, any service for hire, denotes in Scripture the service of God according to the requirements of the Levitical Law, Rom. 9:4; Heb. 9:1, 6, "divine service." It is used in the more general sense of service to God, in John 16:2; Rom. 12:1. See SERVICE.¶

DIVINITY

theiotēs (θειότης, 2305), difinity, the RV rendering in Rom. 1:20 (KJV, "Godhead"), is derived from *theios* (see DIVINE, A), and is to be distinguished from *theotēs*, in Col. 2:9, "Godhead." In Rom. 1:20 the apostle "is declaring how much of God may be known from the revelation of Himself which He has made in nature, from those vestiges of Himself which men may everywhere trace in the world around them. Yet it is not the personal God whom any man may learn to know by these aids; He can be known only by the revelation of Himself in His Son; . . . But in the second passage (Col. 2:9), Paul is declaring that in the Son there dwells all the fullness of absolute Godhead; they were no mere rays of Divine glory which gilded Him, lighting up His Person for a season and with a splendor not His own; but He was, and is, absolute and perfect God; and the apostle uses *theotēs* to express this essential and personal Godhead of the Son" (Trench, *Syn.* §ii). *Theotēs* indicates the "divine" essence of Godhood, the personality of God; *theiotēs*, the attributes of God, His "divine" nature and properties. See GODHEAD.¶

DIVISION

1. *diamerismos* (διαμερισμός, 1267), primarily, "a parting, distribution," denotes "a discussion, dissension, division or discord, breaking up as of family ties" (*dia*, "asunder," *meros*, "a part"), it is found in Luke 12:51, where it is contrasted with *eirēnē*, "peace." Cf. DIVIDE, A, No. 7.

2. *dichostasia* (διχοστασία, 1307), lit., "a standing apart" (*dichē*, "asunder, apart," *stasis*, "a standing"; the root *di*— indicating "division," is found in many words in various languages), is used in Rom. 16:17, where believers are enjoined to mark those who cause "division" and to turn away from them; and in Gal. 5:20, RV (KJV, "seditions"), where "divisions" are spoken of as "works of the flesh." Some mss. have this noun in 1 Cor. 3:3.¶

3. *schisma* (σχίσμα, 4978), (Eng., "schism"), denotes "a cleft, a rent," Matt. 9:16; Mark 2:21; then, metaphorically, "a division, dissension," John 7:43; 9:16; 10:19; 1 Cor. 1:10; 11:18; in 1 Cor. 12:25 it is translated "schism" (marg., "division"). The root is *skid*— seen in the corresponding verb *schizō*, "to cleave" (Lat. *scindo).* See SCHISM. Cf. *hairesis*, a sect.¶

DIVORCE, DIVORCEMENT

A. Verb.

apoluō (ἀπολύω, 630), "to let loose from, let go free" (*apo*, "from," *luō*, "to loose"), is translated "is divorced" in the KJV of Matt. 5:32 (RV, "is put away"); it is further used of "divorce" in Matt. 1:19; 19:3, 7–9; Mark 10:2, 4, 11; Luke 16:18. The Lord also used it of the case of a wife putting away her husband, Mark 10:12, a usage among Greeks and Romans, not among Jews. See DISMISS.

B. Noun.

apostasion (ἀποστάσιον, 647), primarily, "a defection," lit., "a standing off" (*apo*, "from," *stasis*, "a standing"; cf. *aphistēmi*, "to cause to withdraw"), denotes, in the NT, "a writing or bill of divorcement," Matt. 5:31; 19:7; Mark 10:4.¶ In Sept., Deut. 24:3; Isa. 50:1; Jer. 3:8.¶

DO, DONE

In English the verb "to do" serves the purpose of a large number of verbs, and has a large variety of meanings. It therefore translates a considerable number of Greek verbs. These, with their specific meanings, are as follows:

1. *poieō* (ποιέω, 4160) signifies (*a*) "to make," (*b*) "to do," i.e., to adopt a way of expressing by act the thoughts and feelings. It stands for a number of such acts, chiefly "to make, produce, create, cause," e.g., Matt. 17:4. See ABIDE, APPOINT, BEAR, BRING, CAUSE, COMMIT, CONTINUE, DEAL, EXECUTE, EXERCISE, FULFILL, GAIN, GIVE, HOLD, KEEP, MAKE, MEAN, OBSERVE, ORDAIN, PERFORM, PROVIDE, PURPOSE, PUT, SHOW, SHOOT FORTH, SPEND, TAKE, TARRY, WORK, YIELD.

2. *prassō* (πράσσω, 4238) signifies "to practice," though this is not always to be pressed. The apostle John, in his epistles, uses the continuous tenses of *poieō*, to indicate a practice, the habit of doing something, e.g., 1 John 3:4 (the KJV, "committeth" and "commit" in 1 John 3:8 and 9, e.g., is wrong; "doeth," RV, in the sense of practicing, is the meaning). He uses *prassō* twice in the Gospel, 3:20 and 5:29. The apostle Paul uses *prassō* in the sense of practicing, and the RV so renders the word in Rom. 1:32; 2:2, instead of KJV, "commit," though, strangely enough, the RV translates it "committed," instead of "practiced," in 2 Cor. 12:21.

Generally speaking, in Paul's epistles *poieō* denotes "an action complete in itself," while *prassō* denotes "a habit." The difference is seen in Rom. 1:32, RV. Again, *poieō* stresses the accomplishment, e.g., "perform," in Rom. 4:21; *prassō* stresses the process leading to the accomplishment, e.g., "doer," in 2:25. In Rom. 2:3 he who does, *poieō*, the things mentioned, is warned against judging those who practice them, *prassō*.

The distinction in John 3:20–21 is noticeable: "Every one that doeth (*prassō*, practiceth) ill . . . he that doeth (*poieō*) the truth." While we cannot draw the regular distinction, that *prassō* speaks of doing evil things, and *poieō* of doing good things, yet very often "where the words assume an ethical tinge, there is a tendency to use the verbs with this distinction" (Trench, *Syn.,* §xcvi). See COMMIT, EXACT, KEEP, REQUIRE, USE.

3. *ginomai* (γίνομαι, 1096), "to become," is sometimes translated "do" or "done," e.g., Luke 4:23, "done (at Capernaum)," followed by *poieō* in the next clause. In Matt. 21:42 and Mark 12:11, this verb is translated, in the KJV, "(the Lord's) doing"; RV, "this was from the Lord." See BECOME.

4. *ergazomai* (ἐργάζομαι, 2038) denotes "to work" (*ergon*, "work"). In Gal. 6:10 the RV renders it "let us work," for KJV, "let us do"; in

3 John 5, "thou doest." See COMMIT, LABOR, MINISTER, TRADE, WORK.

5. *katergazomai* (κατεργάζομαι, 2716), *kata* (intensive), is a more emphatic verb than No. 4. In Rom. 2:9 the RV has "worketh" for KJV, "doeth." In Rom. 7:15, 17, both translate it "I do" (RV marg., "work"); so in v. 20, "I that do." In 1 Cor. 5:3 the RV has "wrought," for KJV, "done." In Eph. 6:13 both render it "having done (all); more suitably, "having wrought" (all); the KJV marg. "having overcome" does not give the correct meaning. See CAUSE, B, *Note* (2), PERFORM, WORK, WROUGHT.

6. *ischuō* (ἰσχύω, 2480) signifies "to be strong, to prevail." It is translated "I can do," in Phil. 4:13. See ABLE, etc.

7. *parechō* (παρέχω, 3930) lit. means "to hold near" (*para*, "beside," and *echō*, "to have"), i.e., "to present, offer, supply." It is translated "do for" in Luke 7:4. See BRING, No. 21.

Notes: (1) In Phil. 2:13 *energeō*, "to work," is translated "to do," KJV; RV, "to work." (2) In Luke 13:32 *apoteleō*, "to complete, perform," is translated "I . . . do," KJV; RV, "I perform" (some mss. have *epiteleō* here). (3) In Acts 15:36, *echō*, "to have, to hold," sometimes used to express the condition in which a person is, how he is faring, is translated "(how) they do," KJV; RV, "how they fare." It is often used of a physical condition, e.g., Matt. 4:24 (see SICK). (4) In Acts 25:9 *katatithēmi*, "to deposit, or lay up, for future use, to lay up favor for oneself with a person," is translated "to do (the Jews a pleasure)," KJV; RV, "to gain (favor with the Jews)." (5) In John 16:2 *prospherō*, "to bring near, offer, present," is translated "doeth (service)," KJV; RV, "offereth (service)." (6) In Heb. 4:13 the phrase *hēmin ho logos*, rendered "(with whom) we have to do," is, lit., "(with whom is) the account to us." (7) In 1 Cor. 13:10, *katargeō*, "to render inactive, abolish," so is translated "shall be done away"; 2 Cor. 3:7, KJV, "was to be done away," RV, "was passing away"; v. 11. See ABOLISH, DESTROY. (8) For "done aforetime," Rom. 3:25, RV, see PAST. For "did," 2 Tim. 4:14, KJV, see SHOW, No. 3. For "do good" see GOOD.

For **DOING** see **DEED**, No. 3, **DO**, No. 3

DOCTOR

1. *didaskalos* (διδάσκαλος, 1320), a teacher (from *didaskō*, "to teach"), cf. *didaskalia*, "teaching, doctrine, instruction," is translated "doctors," with reference to the teachers of the Jewish religion, Luke 2:46. Cf. *paideutēs*, "a teacher". See MASTER, TEACHER.

2. *nomodidaskalos* (νομοδιδάσκαλος, 3547), "a teacher of the Law" (*nomos*, "a law," and No. 1), with reference to the teachers of the Mosaic Law, is used in the same sense as No. 1, Luke 5:17; Acts 5:34; also of those who went about among Christians, professing to be instructors of the Law, 1 Tim. 1:7. See TEACHER.¶ See under LAW.

DOCTRINE

1. *didachē* (διδαχή, 1322), akin to No. 1, under DOCTOR, denotes "teaching," either (*a*) that which is taught, e.g., Matt. 7:28, KJV, "doctrine," RV, "teaching"; Titus 1:9, RV; Rev. 2:14–15, 24, or (*b*) the act of teaching, instruction, e.g., Mark 4:2, KJV, "doctrine," RV, "teaching"; the RV has "the doctrine" in Rom. 16:17. See NOTE (1) below.

2. *didaskalia* (διδασκαλία, 1319) denotes, as No. 1 (from which, however, it is to be distinguished), (*a*) "that which is taught, doctrine," Matt. 15:9; Mark 7:7; Eph. 4:14; Col. 2:22; 1 Tim. 1:10; 4:1, 6; 6:1, 3; 2 Tim. 4:3; Titus 1:9 ("doctrine," in last part of verse: see also No. 1); 2:1, 10; (*b*) "teaching, instruction," Rom. 12:7, "teaching"; 15:4, "learning"; 1 Tim. 4:13, KJV, "doctrine," RV, "teaching"; v. 16, KJV, "the doctrine," RV, (correctly) "thy teaching; 5:17, KJV, "doctrine," RV "teaching"; 2 Tim. 3:10, 16 (ditto); Titus 2:7, "thy doctrine." Cf. No. 1, under DOCTOR. See LEARNING.¶

Notes: (I) Whereas *didachē* is used only twice in the Pastoral Epistles, 2 Tim. 4:2, and Titus 1:9, *didaskalia* occurs fifteen times. Both are used in the active and passive senses (i.e., the act of teaching and what is taught), the passive is predominant in *didachē*, the active in *didaskalia;* the former stresses the authority, the latter the act (Cremer). Apart from the apostle Paul, other writers make use of *didachē* only, save in Matt. 15:9 and Mark 7:7 (*didaskalia*).

(2) In Heb. 6:1, *logos*, "a word," is translated "doctrine," KJV; the RV margin gives the lit. rendering, "the word (of the beginning of Christ)," and, in the text, "the (first) principles (of Christ)."¶

DOER

poiētēs (ποιητής, 4163), akin to *poieō*, see DO, No. 1, signifies "a doer," Rom. 2:13; Jas. 1:22–23, 25; 4:11. Its meaning "poet" is found in Acts 17:28.¶

Notes: (1) For *prassō*, rendered "doer" in Rom. 2:25, see DO, No. 2.

(2) In 2 Tim. 2:9, *kakourgos* is rendered "evil doer" (RV, "malefactor").

DOG

1. *kuōn* (κύων, 2965) is used in two senses, (*a*) natural, Matt. 7:6; Luke 16:21; 2 Pet. 2:22; (*b*) metaphorical, Phil. 3:2; Rev. 22:15, of those whose moral impurity will exclude them from the New Jerusalem. The Jews used the term of Gentiles, under the idea of ceremonial impurity. Among the Greeks it was an epithet of impudence. Lat., *canis*, and Eng., "hound" are etymologically akin to it.¶

2. *kunarion* (κυνάριον, 2952), a diminutive of No. 1, "a little dog, a puppy," is used in Matt. 15:26-27; Mark 7:27, 28.¶

DOMINION (have . . . over)

A. Nouns.

1. *kratos* (κράτος, 2904), "force, strength, might," more especially "manifested power," is derived from a root *kra—*, "to perfect, to complete": "creator" is probably connected. It also signifies "dominion," and is so rendered frequently in doxologies, 1 Pet. 4:11; 5:11; Jude 25; Rev. 1:6; 5:13 (RV); in 1 Tim. 6:16, and Heb. 2:14 it is translated "power." See MIGHT, POWER, STRENGTH.

Note: Synonymous words are *bia*, "force," often oppressive, *dunamis*, "power," especially "inherent power"; *energeia*, "power" especially in exercise, operative power; *exousia*, primarily "liberty of action," then "authority" either delegated or arbitrary; *ischus*, "strength," especially physical, power as an endowment.

2. *kuriotēs* (κυριότης, 2963) denotes "lordship" (*kurios*, "a lord"), "power, dominion," whether angelic or human, Eph. 1:21; Col. 1:16; 2 Pet. 2:10 (RV, for KJV, "government"); Jude 8. In Eph. and Col. it indicates a grade in the angelic orders, in which it stands second.¶

B. Verbs.

1. *kurieuō* (κυριεύω, 2961), "to be lord over, rule over, have dominion over" (akin to A, No. 2), is used of (*a*) divine authority over men, Rom. 14:9, "might be Lord"; (*b*) human authority over men, Luke 22:25, "lordship," 1 Tim. 6:15, "lords" (RV, marg., "them that rule as lords"); (*c*) the permanent immunity of Christ from the "dominion" of death, Rom. 6:9; (*d*) the deliverance of the believer from the "dominion" of sin, Rom. 6:14; (*e*) the "dominion" of law over men, Rom. 7:1; (*f*) the "dominion" of a person over the faith of other believers, 2 Cor. 1:24 (RV, "lordship"). See LORD.¶

2. *katakurieuō* (κατακυριεύω, 2634), *kata*, "down" (intensive), and No. 1, "to exercise, or gain, dominion over, to lord it over," is used of (*a*) the "lordship" of gentile rulers, Matt. 20:25, KJV, "exercise dominion," RV, "lord it"; Mark 10:42, KJV, "exercise lordship," RV, "lord it"; (*b*) the power of demons over men, Acts 19:16, KJV, "overcame," RV, "mastered"; (*c*) of the evil of elders in "lording" it over the saints under their spiritual care, 1 Pet. 5:3. See LORDSHIP, OVERCOME.

Note: For *authenteō*, "to have dominion," 1 Tim. 2:12, RV, see AUTHORITY, No. 3.

DOOMED

For RV in 1 Cor. 4:9, see APPOINT (*Note* at end), DEATH, B.

DOOR

thura (θύρα, 2374), "a door, gate" (Eng., "door" is connected), is used (*a*) literally, e.g., Matt. 6:6; 27:60; (*b*) metaphorically, of Christ, John 10:7, 9; of faith, by acceptance of the gospel, Acts 14:27; of "openings" for preaching and teaching the Word of God, 1 Cor. 16:9; 2 Cor. 2:12; Col. 4:3; Rev. 3:8; of "entrance" into the Kingdom of God, Matt. 25:10; Luke 13:24-25; of Christ's "entrance" into a repentant believer's heart, Rev. 3:20; of the nearness of Christ's second advent, Matt. 24:33; Mark 13:29; cf. Jas. 5:9; of "access" to behold visions relative to the purposes of God, Rev. 4:1.

Note: For the phrase "that kept the door," *thurōros*, John 18:16-17 ("porter" in Mark 13:34; John 10:3), see PORTER.¶

DOTE

noseō (νοσέω, 3552) signifies "to be ill, to be ailing," whether in body or mind; hence, "to be taken with such a morbid interest in a thing as is tantamount to a disease, to dote," 1 Tim. 6:4 (marg., "sick"). The primary meaning of "dote" is to be foolish (cf. Jer. 50:36), the evident meaning of *noseō*, in this respect, is "to be unsound."¶

DOUBLE

A. Adjective.

diplous (διπλοῦς, 1362) denotes "twofold, double," 1 Tim. 5:17; Rev. 18:6 (twice).¶ The comparative degree *diploteron* (neuter) is used adverbially in Matt. 23:15, "twofold more."¶

B. Verb.

diploō (διπλόω, 1363) signifies "to double, to repay or render twofold," Rev. 18:6.¶

DOUBLE-MINDED

dipsuchos (δίψυχος, 1374) lit. means "two-souled" (*dis*, "twice," *psuchē*, "a soul"), hence, "double-minded," Jas. 1:8; 4:8.¶

DOUBLE–TONGUED

dilogos (δίλογος, 1351) primarily means "saying the same thing twice, or given to repetition" (*dis*, "twice," *logos*, "a word, or speech"); hence, "saying a thing to one person and giving a different view of it to another, double-tongued," 1 Tim. 3:8.¶

DOUBT (be in, make to), DOUBTFUL, DOUBTING

A. Verbs.

I. *aporeō* (ἀπορέω, 639), always used in the middle voice, lit. means "to be without a way" (*a*, negative, *poros*, "a way, transit"), "to be without resources, embarrassed, in doubt, perplexity, at a loss," as was Herod regarding John the Baptist, Mark 6:20 (RV, following the most authentic mss., "was much perplexed"); as the disciples were, regarding the Lord's betrayal, John 13:22, "doubting"; and regarding the absence of His body from the tomb, Luke 24:4, "were perplexed"; as was Festus, about the nature of the accusations brought against Paul, Acts 25:20, KJV "doubted," RV, "being perplexed"; as Paul was, in his experiences of trial, 2 Cor. 4:8, "perplexed," and, as to the attitude of the believers of the churches in Galatia towards Judaistic errors, Gal. 4:20, KJV, "I stand in doubt," RV, "I am perplexed." Perplexity is the main idea. See PERPLEX.¶ Cf. the noun *aporia*, "distress," Luke 21:25.¶

2. *diaporeō* (διαπορέω, 1280), *dia*, "asunder" (intensive), and No. 1, signifies "to be thoroughly perplexed," with a perplexity amounting to despair, Acts 2:12; 5:24 and 10:17, KJV, "were in doubt," "doubted," RV, "were (was) perplexed." See also Luke 9:7 (some mss. have it in Luke 24:4, where the most authentic have No. 1). See PERPLEX.¶

3. *diakrinō* (διακρίνω, 1252): see CONTEND and DIFFER, A, No. 2; in Acts 11:12, KJV, "nothing doubting," RV, "making no distinction"; in Jude 22, RV, "who are in doubt" (KJV, "making a difference," RV, marg., "while they dispute"); in Jas. 1:6, KJV, "wavereth," RV, "doubteth." This verb suggests, not so much weakness of faith, as lack of it (contrast, Nos. 4 and 5).

4. *distazō* (διστάζω, 1365), "to stand in two ways" (*dis*, "double," *stasis*, "a standing"), implying "uncertainty which way to take," is used in Matt. 14:31 and 28:17; said of believers whose faith is small. Cf. No. 5.¶

5. *meteōrizō* (μετεωρίζω, 3349), from *meteōros* (Eng., "meteor"), signifying "in mid air, raised on high," was primarily used of putting a ship out to sea, or of "raising" fortifications, or of the "rising" of the wind. In the Sept., it is used, e.g., in Micah 4:1, of the "exaltation" of the Lord's house; in Ezek. 10:16, of the "lifting" up of the wings of the cherubim; in Obad. 4, of the "mounting" up of the eagle; in the NT metaphorically, of "being anxious," through a "distracted" state of mind, of "wavering" between hope and fear, Luke 12:29, "neither be ye of doubtful mind" (KJV, marg., "live not in careful suspense"), addressed to those who have little faith. Cf. No. 4. The interpretation "do not exalt yourselves" is not in keeping with the context.¶

6. *psuchēn airō* (ψυχήν αἴρω), lit., "to raise the breath, or to lift the soul," signifies "to hold in suspense," RV of John 10:24 (KJV, "make us to doubt"), suggestive of "an objective suspense due to lack of light" (Warfield), through a failure of their expectations, rather than, subjectively, through unbelief. The meaning may thus be, "How long dost Thou raise our expectations without satisfying them?"

B. Noun.

dialogismos (διαλογισμός, 1261) expresses reasoning or questioning hesitation, 1 Tim. 2:8. See DISPUTE, A, No. 1.

Note: For KJV, "doubtful" in Rom. 14:1 see DECISION, B, No. 2.

DOUBT (No), DOUBTLESS

pantōs (πάντως, 3843): see ALTOGETHER, B.

Notes: (1) In 2 Cor. 12:1 the best texts have no word representing "doubtless." (2) In Luke 11:20, the particle *ara*, KJV, "no doubt," means "then" (RV). (3) In 1 Cor. 9:10 the conjunction *gar*, KJV, "no doubt," here means "assuredly," or "yea" (RV). (4) In Phil. 3:8, the opening phrase means "yea, verily," as RV. (5) In 1 Cor. 9:2, the RV, "at least," gives the right sense (not "doubtless").

DOVE, TURTLE-DOVE

1. *peristera* (περιστερά, 4058) denotes "a dove or pigeon," Matt. 3:16; 10:16 (indicating its proverbial harmlessness); 21:12; Mark 1:10; 11:15; Luke 2:24 ("pigeons"); 3:22; John 1:32; 2:14, 16.¶

2. *trugōn* (τρυγών, 5167) denotes "a turtle-dove" (from *truzō*, "to murmur, to coo"), Luke 2:24.¶

For **DOWN** see *Note* †, p. 1

DRAG

1. *surō* (σύρω, 4951), "to draw, drag, haul," is used of a net, John 21:8; of violently "dragging" persons along, Acts 8:3, "haling"; 14:19, RV, "dragged," KJV, "drew"; 17:6 (ditto); Rev.

12:4, KJV, "drew," RV, "draweth." See DRAW, HALE.¶

Note: Cf. the strengthened form *katasurō*, "to hale," used in Luke 12:58.¶

2. *helkuō* (or *helkō*) (ἑλκύω or ἕλκω, 1670), "to draw," differs from *surō*, as "drawing" does from violent "dragging." It is used of "drawing" a net, John 21:6, 11 (cf. No. 1, in v. 8); Trench remarks, "At vv. 6 and 11 *helkō* (or *helkuō*) is used; for there a *drawing* of the net to a certain point is intended; by the disciples to themselves in the ship, by Peter to himself upon the shore. But at v. 8 *helkō* gives place to *surō*: for nothing is there intended but the *dragging* of the net, which had been fastened to the ship, after it through the water" (*Syn.,* §xxi).

This less violent significance, usually present in *helkō*, but always absent from *surō*, is seen in the metaphorical use of *helkō*, to signify "drawing" by inward power, by divine impulse, John 6:44; 12:32. So in the Sept., e.g., Song of Sol. 1:4, and Jer. 31:3, "with lovingkindness have I drawn thee." It is used of a more vigorous action, in John 18:10, of "drawing" a sword; in Acts 16:19; 21:30, of forcibly "drawing" men to or from a place; so in Jas. 2:6, KJV, "draw," RV, "drag." See DRAW.¶

DRAGON

drakōn (δράκων, 1404) denoted "a mythical monster, a dragon"; also a large serpent, so called because of its keen power of sight (from a root *derk—,* signifying "to see"). Twelve times in the Apocalypse it is used of the Devil, 12:3–4, 7, 9, 13, 16–17; 13:2, 4, 11; 16:13; 20:2.¶

For **DRANK** see **DRINK**

DRAUGHT

1. *agra* (ἄγρα, 61), "a hunting, catching" (from *agō*, "to lead"), is used only in connection with fishing. In Luke 5:4 it signifies the act of catching fish; in v. 9 it stands for the catch itself.¶

2. *aphedrōn* (ἀφεδρών, 856), "a latrine, a sink, drain," is found in Matt. 15:17 and Mark 7:19.¶

For **DRAVE** and **DROVE** see **DRIVE**

DRAW (Away, Back, Nigh, On, Out, Up)

(A) In the sense of "dragging, pulling, or attracting":

1. *anabibazō* (ἀναβιβάζω, 307), a causal form of *anabainō*, "to go up," denotes, lit., "to make go up, cause to ascend" (*ana,* "up," *bi-*

bazō, "to cause to mount"), hence, "to draw a boat up on land," Matt. 13:48.¶

2. *helkō* (ἕλκω, 1670) is translated "to draw" in the KJV, of Acts 21:30 and Jas. 2:6; see DRAG, No. 2.

3. *surō* (σύρω, 4951): see DRAG, No. 1.

4. *spaō* (σπάω, 4685), "to draw or pull," is used, in the middle voice, of "drawing" a sword from its sheath, Mark 14:47; Acts 16:27.¶

5. *anaspaō* (ἀνασπάω, 385), *ana,* "up," and No. 4, "to draw up," is used of "drawing" up an animal out of a pit, Luke 14:5 (RV, "draw up"; KJV, "pull out"), and of the "drawing" up of the sheet into heaven, in the vision in Acts 11:10.¶

6. *apospaō* (ἀποσπάω, 645), *apo,* "from," and No. 4, "to draw away," lit., "to wrench away from," is used of a sword, Matt. 26:51; of "drawing" away disciples into error, Acts 20:30; of Christ's "withdrawal" from the disciples, in Gethsemane, Luke 22:41, KJV, "was withdrawn," RV, "was parted" (or "was reft away from them"); of "parting" from a company, Acts 21:1 (KJV, "were gotten," RV, "were parted"). See GET, PART.¶

7. *antleō* (ἀντλέω, 501) signified, primarily, "to draw out a ship's bilgewater, to bale or pump out" (from *antlos,* "bilge-water"), hence, "to draw water" in any way (*ana,* "up," and a root, *tel—,* "to lift, bear"), John 2:8–9; 4:7, 15.¶

Note: In John 4:11, "to draw with" translates the corresponding noun *antlēma,* "a bucket for drawing water by a rope."¶

8. *exelkō* (ἐξέλκω, 1828), *ek,* "out of," and No. 2, "to draw away, or lure forth," is used metaphorically in Jas. 1:14, of being "drawn away" by lust. As in hunting or fishing the game is "lured" from its haunt, so man's lust "allures" him from the safety of his self-restraint.¶

9. *anatassomai* (ἀνατάσσομαι, 392), "to arrange in order," is used in Luke 1:1; RV, "to draw up" (some interpret the word to mean to "bring together" from memory assisted by the Holy Spirit).¶

(B) In the sense of "approaching or withdrawing":

1. *engizō* (ἐγγίζω, 1448), "to come near, draw nigh" (akin to *engus,* "near"), is translated by the verb "draw near or nigh," in the RV, Luke 12:33, KJV, "approacheth"; Heb. 10:25, KJV, "approaching"; Luke 18:35; 19:29, 37; Acts 22:6, KJV, "was come nigh"; Luke 7:12, "came nigh"; Acts 9:3, "came near." See APPROACH.

2. *proserchomai* (προσέρχομαι, 4334) is translated "draw near" in Heb. 4:16; 7:25, RV, and 10:22, KJV and RV; in Acts 7:31, "drew near." See COME, GO.

3. *prosagō* (προσάγω, 4317), used transitively, "to bring to"; intransitively, "to draw near," is so rendered in Acts 27:27. See BRING.

4. *hupostellō* (ὑποστέλλω, 5288), "to draw back, withdraw," perhaps a metaphor from lowering a sail and so slackening the course, and hence of being remiss in holding the truth; in the active voice, rendered "drew back" in Gal. 2:12, RV (KJV, "withdrew"); in the middle, in Heb. 10:38, "shrink back" RV (KJV, "draw back"); the prefix *hupo*, "underneath," is here suggestive of stealth. In v. 39 the corresponding noun, *hupostolē*, is translated "of them that shrink back," RV; KJV, "draw back" (lit., "of shrinking back"). In Acts 20:20, 27, "shrank," RV. See KEEP, *Note* (6), SHRINK, SHUN, WITHDRAW.¶

5. *aphistēmi* (ἀφίστημι, 868): see DEPART, A, No. 20.

6. *ginomai* (γίνομαι, 1096), "to become, begin to be," is translated "drawing nigh," in John 6:19. See BECOME.

7. *epiphōskō* (ἐπιφώσκω, 2020), "to dawn" (lit., "to make to shine upon"), is said of the approach of the Sabbath, Luke 23:54 (marg., "began to dawn"); cf. Matt. 28:1.¶ See DAWN, A, No. 3.

Notes: (1) In Mark 6:53, *prosormizō*, "to bring a ship (or boat) to anchor, cast anchor, land at a place" (*pros*, "to," *hormizō*, "to moor, bring to anchorage"), is translated "moored to the shore," in the RV, for KJV, "drew."¶

(2) In Acts 19:33, where the most authentic mss. have *sumbibazō*, the RV translates it "brought" (marg., "instructed"), KJV, "draw out." Some mss. have *probibazō*, "to bring or drag forward." See BRING, No. 24.

DREAM (noun and verb), DREAMER

A. Nouns.

1. *onar* (ὄναρ, 3677) is "a vision in sleep," in distinction from a waking vision, Matt. 1:20; 2:12–13, 19, 22; 27:19.¶

2. *enupnion* (ἐνύπνιον, 1798), is, lit., "what appears in sleep" (*en*, "in," *hupnos*, "sleep"), an ordinary "dream," Acts 2:17. For synonymous nouns, see VISION.¶

B. Verb.

enupniazō (ἐνυπνιάζω, 1797), akin to A, No. 2, is used in Acts 2:17, in the passive voice, in a phrase (according to the most authentic mss.) which means "shall be given up to dream by dreams," translated "shall dream dreams"; metaphorically in Jude 8, of being given over to sensuous "dreamings," RV, KJV, "dreamers," and so defiling the flesh.¶

DRESSED

Note: This is the KJV translation of the passive of *geōrgeō*, Heb. 6:7, "to till the ground, to practice as a farmer"; RV, "is tilled." See TILL.¶

DRESSER

Note: For *ampelourgos*, "dresser," Luke 13:7, KJV (RV, "vine-dresser"), see VINEDRESSER.

For DRIED see DRY, B

DRIFT

pararheō (παραρέω, 3901), lit., "to flow past, glide by" (*para*, "by," *rheō*, "to flow"), is used in Heb. 2:1, where the significance is to find oneself "flowing" or "passing by," without giving due heed to a thing, here "the things that were heard," or perhaps the salvation of which they spoke; hence the RV, "lest haply we drift away from them," for KJV, "let them slip." The KJV marg. "run out as leaking vessels," does not give the meaning.¶ In the Sept., Prov. 3:21; Isa. 44:4.¶

DRINK (-ETH, -ER, -ING), DRANK

A. Nouns.

1. *poma* (πόμα, 4188), akin to B, No. 1, denotes "the thing drunk" (from a root *po—*, found in the Eng., "potion"; it is connected with the root *pi—*; see B, No. 3), 1 Cor. 10:4; Heb. 9:10.¶

2. *posis* (πόσις, 4213), akin to B, No. 1, suggests "the act of drinking," John 6:55 (where it is practically equivalent to No. 1); Rom. 14:17, "drinking," RV; Col. 2:16.¶

3. *sikera* (σίκερα, 4608) is "a strong, intoxicating drink," made from any sweet ingredients, whether grain, vegetables, or the juice of fruits, or a decoction of honey; "strong drink," Luke 1:15.¶ In the Sept., Lev. 10:9; Num. 6:3; 28:7; Deut. 14:26; 29:6; Isa. 5:11, 22; 24:9; 28:7; 29:9.

B. Verbs.

1. *pinō* (πίνω, 4095), "to drink," is used chiefly in the Gospels and in 1 Cor., whether literally (most frequently), or figuratively, (*a*) of "drinking" of the blood of Christ, in the sense of receiving eternal life, through His death, John 6:53–54, 56; (*b*) of "receiving" spiritually that which refreshes, strengthens and nourishes the soul, John 7:37; (*c*) of "deriving" spiritual life from Christ, John 4:14, as Israel did typically, 1 Cor. 10:4; (*d*) of "sharing" in the sufferings of Christ humanly inflicted, Matt. 20:22–23; Mark 10:38–39; (*e*) of "participating" in the abominations imparted by the corrupt religious and commercial systems emanating from Babylon,

Rev. 18:3; (*f*) of "receiving" divine judgment, through partaking unworthily of the Lord's Supper, 1 Cor. 11:29; (*g*) of "experiencing" the wrath of God, Rev. 14:10; 16:6; (*h*) of the earth's "receiving" the benefits of rain, Heb. 6:7.

2. *methuō* (μεθύω, 3184), from *methu*, "wine, to be drunk," is used in John 2:10 in the passive voice, and is translated in the RV, "have drunk freely"; KJV, "have well drunk." See DRUNK.

3. *potizō* (ποτίζω, 4222), "to give to drink, to make to drink," is used (*a*) in the material sense, in Matt. 10:42; 25:35, 37, 42 (here of "ministering" to those who belong to Christ and thus doing so virtually to Him); 27:48; Mark 9:41; 15:36; Luke 13:15 ("to watering"); Rom. 12:20; 1 Cor. 3:7–8; (*b*) figuratively, with reference to "teaching" of an elementary character, 1 Cor. 3:2, "I fed (you with milk)"; of "spiritual watering by teaching" the Word of God, 3:6; of being "provided" and "satisfied" by the power and blessing of the Spirit of God, 1 Cor. 12:13; of the effect upon the nations of "partaking" of the abominable mixture, provided by Babylon, of paganism with details of the Christian faith, Rev. 14:8. See FEED, WATER.¶

4. *sumpinō* (συμπίνω, 4844), "to drink together" (*sun*, "with," and B, No. 1), is found in Acts 10:41.¶

5. *hudropoteō* (ὑδροποτέω, 5202), "to drink water" (*hudōr*, "water," *poteō*, "to drink"), is found in 1 Tim. 5:23, RV, "be (no longer) a drinker of water."¶

DRIVE, DRIVEN, DRAVE, DROVE

1. *ekballō* (ἐκβάλλω, 1544) denotes, lit., "to cast forth," with the suggestion of force (*ek*, "out," *ballō*, "to cast"); hence "to drive out or forth." It is translated "driveth" in Mark 1:12, RV, "driveth forth." In John 2:15 for the KJV, "drove," the RV has "cast," the more usual translation. See CAST, No. 5.

2. *ekdiōkō* (ἐκδιώκω, 1559), "to chase away, drive out" (*ek*, "out," *diōkō*, "to pursue"), is used in 1 Thess. 2:15, RV, "drave out," KJV, "have persecuted." Some mss. have this verb for *diōkō*, in Luke 11:49.¶

3. *elaunō* (ἐλαύνω, 1643) signifies "to drive, impel, urge on." It is used of "rowing," Mark 6:48 and John 6:19; of the act of a demon upon a man, Luke 8:29; of the power of winds upon ships, Jas. 3:4; and of storms upon mists, 2 Pet. 2:17, KJV, "carried," RV, "driven." See also CARRY, *Note* (2), ROW.

4. *apelaunō* (ἀπελαύνω, 556), *apo*, "from," and No. 3, "to drive from," is used in Acts 18:16.¶

5. *exōtheō* (ἐξωθέω, 1856), "to thrust out" (*ek*, "out," *ōtheō*, "to push, thrust"), is translated "thrust" in Acts 7:45, RV (KJV, "drave"); in 27:39, of "driving" a storm-tossed ship ashore (RV, "drive," KJV, "thrust"). Cf. No. 6. See THRUST.¶

6. *pherō* (φέρω, 5342), "to bear," is translated "driven" in Acts 27:15, 17, of "being borne" in a storm-tossed ship. See BEAR, etc.

7. *diapherō* (διαφέρω, 1308), lit., "to bear through" (*dia*, "through," and No. 6), in Acts 27:27 signifies "to be borne hither and thither" (RV, "were driven to and fro"; KJV, "up and down"). See BETTER (be), No. 1.

8. *anemizō* (ἀνεμίζω, 416), "to drive by the wind" (*anemos*, "wind"), is used in Jas. 1:6.¶

(*Note:* For "let . . . drive," Acts 27:15, see GIVE, No. 3.

DROP (Noun)

thrombos (θρόμβος, 2361), "a large, thick drop of clotted blood" (etymologically akin to *trephō*, "to curdle"), is used in Luke 22:44, in the plural, in the narrative of the Lord's agony in Gethsemane.¶

DROPSY

hudrōpikos (ὑδρωπικός, 5203), "dropsical, suffering from dropsy" (*hudrops*, "dropsy"), is found in Luke 14:2, the only instance recorded of the healing of this disease by the Lord.¶

DROWN

1. *buthizō* (βυθίζω, 1036), "to plunge into the deep, to sink" (*buthos*, "bottom, the deep, the sea"), akin to *bathos*, "depth," and *abussos*, "bottomless," and Eng., "bath," is used in Luke 5:7 of the "sinking" of a boat; metaphorically in 1 Tim. 6:9, of the effect of foolish and hurtful lusts, which "drown men in destruction and perdition." See SINK.¶

2. *katapinō* (καταπίνω, 2666), lit., "to drink down" (*pinō*, "to drink," prefixed by *kata*, "down"), signifies "to swallow up" (RV, in Heb. 11:29, for KJV, "were drowned"). It is elsewhere translated by the verb "to swallow, or swallow up," except in 1 Pet. 5:8, "devour." See DEVOUR, No. 3, SWALLOW.

3. *katapontizō* (καταποντίζω, 2670), "to throw into the sea" (*kata*, "down," *pontos*, "the open sea"), in the passive voice, "to be sunk in, to be drowned," is translated "were drowned," in Matt. 18:6, KJV (RV, "should be sunk"); elsewhere in 14:30, "(beginning) to sink." See SINK.¶

DRUNK, (-EN, be), DRUNKARD, DRUNKENNESS

A. Verbs.

1. *methuō* (μεθύω, 3184) signifies "to be drunk with wine" (from *methu*, "mulled wine"; hence Eng., "mead, honey-wine"); originally it denoted simply "a pleasant drink." For John 2:10 see under DRINK. The verb is used of "being intoxicated" in Matt. 24:49; Acts 2:15; 1 Cor. 11:21; 1 Thess. 5:7*b;* metaphorically, of the effect upon men of partaking of the abominations of the Babylonish system, Rev. 17:2; of being in a state of mental "intoxication," through the shedding of men's blood profusely, v. 6.¶

2. *methuskō* (μέθύσκω, 3182) signifies "to make drunk, or to grow drunk" (an inceptive verb, marking the process or the state expressed in No. 1), "to become intoxicated," Luke 12:45; Eph. 5:18; 1 Thess. 5:7*a.*¶

B. Adjective.

methusos (μέθυσος, 3183), "drunken" (cf. No. 2), is used as noun, in the singular, in 1 Cor. 5:11, and in the plural, in 6:10, "drunkard," "drunkards."¶

C. Noun.

methē (μέθη, 3178), "strong drink" (akin to *methu*, "wine," see under A. 1, above), denotes "drunkenness, habitual intoxication," Luke 21:34; Rom. 13:13; Gal. 5:21.¶

DRY

A. Adjectives.

1. *xēros* (ξηρός, 3584) is used (*a*) naturally, of "dry" land, Heb. 11:29; or of land in general, Matt. 23:15, "land"; or of physical infirmity, "withered," Matt. 12:10; Mark 3:3; Luke 6:6, 8; John 5:3; (*b*) figuratively, in Luke 23:31, with reference to the spiritual "barrenness" of the Jews, in contrast to the character of the Lord. Cf. Ps. 1:3; Isa. 56:3; Ezek. 17:24; 20:47. See LAND, WITHERED.¶

2. *anudros* (ἄνυδρος, 504), "waterless" (*a*, negative, *n*, euphonic, *hudōr*, "water"), is rendered "dry" in Matt. 12:43, KJV, and Luke 11:24 (RV, "waterless"); "without water" in 2 Pet. 2:17 and Jude 12. See WATER. ¶

B. Verb.

xērainō (ξηραίνω, 3583), akin to A. 1, "to dry, dry up, make dry, wither," is translated "dried" (of physical infirmity), in Mark 5:29; of a tree, in the KJV of Mark 11:20 (RV, "withered away"); of water, in Rev. 16:12. It is translated "ripe" (RV, "overripe") in Rev. 14:15, of a harvest (used figuratively of the gathered nations against Jerusalem at the end of this age); "pi-

neth away," in Mark 9:18. See OVERRIPE, PINE AWAY, RIPE, WITHER.

DUE

A. Adjective.

idios (ἴδιος, 2398), "one's own," is applied to *kairos*, "a season," in Gal. 6:9, "in due season," i.e., in the season divinely appointed for the reaping. So in 1 Tim. 2:6, "the testimony to be borne in its own (KJV, 'due') times (seasons)"; 6:15, "in its own (*idios*) times (seasons)"; similarly in Titus 1:3. See BUSINESS, B.

Note: For *axios*, "the due reward," see REWARD, *Note* (1).

B. Verbs.

1. *opheilō* (ὀφείλω, 3784) signifies "to owe, to be indebted," especially financially, Matt. 18:30, RV, "that which was due"; 18:34, "all that was due." See BEHOVE, BOUND (to be).

2. *dei* (δεῖ, 1163), an impersonal verb signifying "it is necessary," is translated "was due" in Rom. 1:27, RV (KJV, "was meet"). See BEHOVE.

C. Noun.

opheilē (ὀφειλή, 3782), akin to B, No. 1, is rendered "dues" in Rom. 13:7. In 1 Cor. 7:3, RV, it is translated "her due" (the KJV, "due benevolence" follows another reading).

Notes: (1) In the phrases "in due season" in Matt. 24:45; Luke 12:42; Rom. 5:6 (lit., "according to time"), and "in due time," 1 Pet. 5:6, there is no word representing "due" in the original, and the phrases are, lit., "in season," "in time."

(2) For the phrase "born out of due time," in 1 Cor. 15:8, see BEGET, B, No. 2.

DULL

A. Adjective.

nōthros (νωθρός, 3576), "slow, sluggish, indolent, dull" (the etymology is uncertain), is translated "dull" in Heb. 5:11 (in connection with *akoē*, "hearing"; lit., "in hearings"); "sluggish, in 6:12. See SLOTHFUL, SLUGGISH.¶ In the Sept., Prov. 22:29.¶ Cf. *nōthrokardios*, "slow of heart" (*kardia*, "the heart"), Prov. 12:8.¶

Note: In Luke 24:25 "slow (of heart)" translates the synonymous word *bradus.* Of these Trench says (*Syn.* §civ), "*Bradus* differs from the words with which it is here brought into comparison, in that no moral fault or blame is necessarily involved in it; so far indeed is it from this, that of the three occasions on which it is used in the NT two are in honor; for to be 'slow' to evil things, to rash speaking, or to anger (Jas. 1:19, twice), is a grace, and not the contrary.... There is a deeper, more inborn sluggishness implied in *nōthros*, and this bound up as it were in the very life, more than in either of the other words of this group." Trench compares and contrasts *argos,* "idle," but this word is not strictly synonymous with the other two.¶

B. Adverb.

bareōs (βαρέως, 917), "heavily, with difficulty" (*barus,* "heavy"), is used with *akouō,* "to hear," in Matt. 13:15, and Acts 28:27 (from Isa. 6:10), lit., "to hear heavily, to be dull of hearing."¶ In the Sept., Gen. 31:35 (lit., "bear it not heavily"); Isa. 6:10.¶

DUMB

A. Adjectives.

1. *alalos* (ἄλαλος, 216), lit., "speechless" (*a,* negative, and *laleō,* "to speak"), is found in Mark 7:37; 9:17, 25.¶ In the Sept., Ps. 38:13.¶

2. *aphōnos* (ἄφωνος, 880), lit., "voiceless, or soundless" (*a,* negative, and *phōnē,* "a sound"), has reference to voice, Acts 8:32; 1 Cor. 12:2; 2 Pet. 2:16, while *alalos* has reference to words. In 1 Cor. 14:10 it is used metaphorically of the significance of voices or sounds, "without signification."¶ In the Sept. Isa. 53:7.¶

3. *kōphos* (κωφός, 2974) denotes "blunted or dulled"; see DEAF.

B. Verb.

siōpaō (σιωπάω, 4623), from *siōpē,* "silence, to be silent," is used of Zacharias' "dumbness," Luke 1:20. See PEACE (hold one's).

DUNG

1. *skubalon* (σκύβαλον, 4657) denotes "refuse," whether (*a*) "excrement," that which is cast out from the body, or (*b*) "the leavings of a feast," that which is thrown away from the table. Some have derived it from *kusibalon* (with *metathesis* of k and s), "thrown to dogs"; others connect it with a root meaning "shred." Judaizers counted gentile Christians as dogs, while they themselves were seated at God's banquet. The apostle, reversing the image, counts the Judaistic ordinances as refuse upon which their advocates feed, Phil. 3:8.¶

2. *koprion* (κόπριον, 2874d), "manure," Luke 13:8, used in the plural with *ballō,* "to throw," is translated by the verb "to dung." Some mss. have the accusative case of the noun *kopria,* "a dunghill." See below.¶

DUNGHILL

kopria (κοπρία, 2874), "a dunghill," is found in Luke 14:35.¶

For **DURE** see under **WHILE,** *Note* 1

For **DURING** see *Note* †, p. 1

For **DURST** see **DARE**

DUST

A. Nouns.

1. *chous,* or *choos* (χοῦς or χόος, 5522), from *cheō,* "to pour," primarily, "earth dug out, an earth heap," then, "loose earth or dust," is used in Mark 6:11 and Rev. 18:19.¶

2. *koniortos* (κονιορτός, 2868), "raised or flying dust" (*konia,* "dust," *ornumi,* "to stir up"), is found in Matt. 10:14; Luke 9:5; 10:11; Acts 13:51; 22:23.¶

B. Verb.

likmaō (λικμάω, 3039), primarily, "to winnow" (from *likmos,* "a winnowing-fan"), hence, "to scatter" as chaff or dust, is used in Matt. 21:44 and Luke 20:18, RV, "scatter as dust," KJV, "grind to powder." There are indications in the papyri writings that the word came to denote "to ruin, to destroy."¶

DUTY

opheilō (ὀφείλω, 3784), "to owe, to be indebted," is translated "it was our duty," in Luke 17:10, lit., "we owe (ought) to do"; so in Rom. 15:27, KJV, "their duty is": RV, "they owe it." See BEHOVE, BOUND.

DWELL, DWELLERS, DWELLING (place)

A. Verbs.

1. *oikeō* (οἰκέω, 3611), "to dwell" (from *oikos,* "a house"), "to inhabit as one's abode," is derived from the Sanskrit, *vic,* "a dwelling place" (the Eng. termination —"wick" is connected). It is used (*a*) of God as "dwelling" in light, 1 Tim. 6:16; (*b*) of the "indwelling" of the Spirit of God in the believer, Rom. 8:9, 11, or in a church, 1 Cor. 3:16; (*c*) of the "indwelling" of sin, Rom. 7:20; (*d*) of the absence of any good thing in the flesh of the believer, Rom. 7:18; (*e*) of the "dwelling" together of those who are married, 1 Cor. 7:12–13.¶

2. *katoikeō* (κατοικέω, 2730), *kata,* "down," and No. 1, the most frequent verb with this meaning, properly signifies "to settle down in a dwelling, to dwell fixedly in a place." Besides its literal sense, it is used of (*a*) the "indwelling" of the totality of the attributes and powers of the Godhead in Christ, Col. 1:19; 2:9; (*b*) the "indwelling" of Christ in the hearts of believers ("may make a home in your hearts"), Eph. 3:17; (*c*) the "dwelling" of Satan in a locality, Rev. 2:13; (*d*) the future "indwelling" of righteousness in the new heavens and earth, 2 Pet. 3:13. It is translated "dwellers" in Acts 1:19; 2:9; "inhabitants" in Rev. 17:2, KJV (RV, "they

that dwell"), "inhabiters" in Rev. 8:13 and 12:12, KJV (RV, "them that dwell").

Cf. the nouns *katoikēsis* (below), *katoikia*, "habitation," Acts 17:26¶; *katoikētērion*, "a habitation," Eph. 2:22; Rev. 18:2.¶ Contrast *paroikeō*, "to sojourn," the latter being temporary, the former permanent. See HABITATION, INHABITANT.

3. *katoikizō* (κατοικίζω, 2730d), "to cause to dwell," is said of the act of God concerning the Holy Spirit in Jas. 4:5, RV (some mss. have No. 2).¶

4. *enoikeō* (ἐνοικέω, 1774), lit., "to dwell in" (*en*, "in," and No. 1), is used, with a spiritual significance only, of (*a*) the "indwelling" of God in believers, 2 Cor. 6:16; (*b*) the "indwelling" of the Holy Spirit, Rom. 8:11; 2 Tim. 1:14; (*c*) the "indwelling" of the Word of Christ, Col. 3:16; (*d*) the "indwelling" of faith, 2 Tim. 1:5; (*e*) the "indwelling" of sin in the believer, Rom. 7:17.¶

5. *perioikeō* (περιοικέω, 4039), *peri*, "around," and No. 1, "to dwell around, be a neighbor," is used in Luke 1:65.¶ Cf. *perioikos*, "a neighbor," Luke 1:58.¶

6. *sunoikeō* (συνοικέω, 4924), *sun*, "with," and No. 1, "to dwell with," is used in 1 Pet. 3:7.¶

7. *enkatoikeō* (ἐγκατοικέω, 1460), *en*, "in," and No. 2, "to dwell among," is used in 2 Pet. 2:8.¶

8. *menō* (μένω, 3306), "to abide, remain," is translated "to dwell," in the KJV of John 1:38–39; 6:56; 14:10, 17; Acts 28:16. The RV adheres throughout to the verb "to abide." See ABIDE.

9. *skēnoō* (σκηνόω, 4637), "to pitch a tent" (*skēnē*), "to tabernacle," is translated "dwelt," in John 1:14, KJV, RV marg., "tabernacled"; in Rev. 7:15, KJV, "shall dwell," RV, "shall spread (His) tabernacle"; in Rev. 12:12; 13:6; 21:3, "dwell." See TABERNACLE.

10. *kataskēnoō* (κατασκηνόω, 2681), "to pitch one's tent" (*kata*, "down," *skēnē*, "a tent"), is translated "lodge" in Matt. 13:32; Mark 4:32; Luke 13:19; in Acts 2:26, RV, "dwell," KJV, "rest."¶

11. *embateuō* (ἐμβατεύω, 1687), primarily, "to step in, or on" (from *embainō*, "to enter"),

hence (*a*) "to frequent, dwell in," is used metaphorically in Col. 2:18, RV, "dwelling in" (marg., "taking his stand upon"); (*b*) with reference to the same passage, alternatively, "to invade, to enter on"; perhaps used in this passage as a technical term of the mystery religions, denoting the entrance of the initiated into the new life (KJV, "intruding into"). A suggested alternative reading involves the rendering "treading on air," i.e., indulging in vain speculations, but evidences in the papyri writings make the emendation unnecessary.¶

12. *kathēmai* (κάθημαι, 2521), "to sit down," is translated "dwell," in Luke 21:35. See SET, SIT.

13. *kathizō* (καθίζω, 2523), "to sit down," denotes "to dwell," in Acts 18:11 (RV, "dwelt," for KJV, "continued").

14. *astateō* (ἀστατέω, 790), "to wander about" (*a*, negative, *histēmi*, "to stand"), "to have no fixed dwelling-place," is used in 1 Cor. 4:11.¶ Cf. *akatastatos*, "unstable," Jas. 1:8; 3:8.¶; *akatastasia*, "revolution, confusion," e.g., 1 Cor. 14:33.

B. Nouns.

1. *paroikia* (παροικία, 3940) denotes "a sojourning," Acts 13:17, lit., "in the sojourning," translated "when they sojourned," RV (KJV, "dwelt as strangers"); in 1 Pet. 1:17, "sojourning."¶

2. *katoikēsis* (κατοίκησις, 2731), akin to A, No. 2, "a dwelling, a habitation," is used in Mark 5:3.¶

Note: Cf. *oikia*, and *oikos*, "a house," *oikēma*, "a prison," *katoikia*, "a habitation" (see A, No. 2).

3. *misthōma* (μίσθωμα, 3410), primarily, "a price, a hire" (akin to *misthos*, "wages, hire," and *misthoō*, "to let out for hire"), is used in Acts 28:30 to denote "a hired dwelling."¶

For DYING see DEADNESS

DYSENTERY

dusenterion (δυσεντέριον, 1420**), whence Eng., "dysentery," is so translated in Acts 28:8, RV, for KJV "bloody flux" (*enteron* denotes an "intestine").¶

E

In the following pages † indicates that the word referred to (preposition, conjunction, or particle) is not dealt with in this volume.

¶ indicates that all the NT occurrences of the Greek word under consideration are mentioned under the heading or sub-heading.

EACH, EACH MAN, EACH ONE

1. *hekastos* (ἕκαστος, 1538), "each" or "every," is used of any number separately, either (*a*) as an adjective qualifying a noun, e.g., Luke 6:44; John 19:23; Heb. 3:13, where "day by day," is, lit., "according to each day"; or, more emphatically with *heis*, "one," in Matt. 26:22; Luke 4:40; 16:5; Acts 2:3, 6; 20:31; 1 Cor. 12:18; Eph. 4:7, 16, RV, "each (several)," for KJV, "every"; Col. 4:6; 1 Thess. 2:11; 2 Thess. 1:3; (*b*) as a distributive pronoun, e.g., Acts 4:35; Rom. 2:6; Gal. 6:4; in Phil. 2:4, it is used in the plural; some mss. have it thus in Rev. 6:11. The repetition in Heb. 8:11 is noticeable, "every man" (i.e., everyone). Prefixed by the preposition *ana*, "apiece" (a colloquialism), it is used, with stress on the individuality, in Rev. 21:21, of the gates of the heavenly city, "each one of the several," RV; in Eph. 5:33, preceded by *kath' hena*, "by one," it signifies "each (one) his own."

2. The phrase *hen kath' hen*, lit., "one by one," is used in Rev. 4:8, "each one of them."

EACH OTHER

allēlōn (ἀλλήλων, 240), a reciprocal pronoun, preceded by the preposition *meta*, "with," signifies "with each other," Luke 23:12, RV, for KJV, "together." Similarly in 24:14 *pros allēlous*, where *pros* suggests greater intimacy. See ONE ANOTHER.

EAGLE

aetos (ἀετός, 105), "an eagle" (also a vulture), is perhaps connected with *aēmi*, "to blow," as of the wind, on account of its windlike flight. In Matt. 24:28 and Luke 17:37 the vultures are probably intended. The meaning seems to be that, as these birds of prey gather where the carcass is, so the judgments of God will descend upon the corrupt state of humanity. The figure of the "eagle" is used in Ezek. 17 to represent the great powers of Egypt and Babylon, as being employed to punish corrupt and faithless Israel. Cf. Job 39:30; Prov. 30:17. The "eagle" is mentioned elsewhere in the NT

in Rev. 4:7; 8:13 (RV); 12:14. There are eight species in Palestine.¶

EAR (of the body)

1. *ous* (οὖς, 3775), Latin *auris*, is used (*a*) of the physical organ, e.g., Luke 4:21; Acts 7:57; in Acts 11:22, in the plural with *akouō*, "to hear," lit., "was heard into the ears of someone," i.e., came to the knowledge of; similarly, in the singular, Matt. 10:27, in familiar private conversation; in Jas. 5:4 the phrase is used with *eiserchomai*, "to enter into"; in Luke 1:44, with *ginomai*, "to become, to come"; in Luke 12:3, with *lalein*, "to speak" and *pros*, "to"; (*b*) metaphorically, of the faculty of perceiving with the mind, understanding and knowing, Matt. 13:16; frequently with *akouō*, "to hear," e.g., Matt. 11:15; 13:9, 43; Rev. 2 and 3, at the close of each of the messages to the churches; in Matt. 13:15 and Acts 28:27, with *bareōs*, "heavily," of being slow to understand and obey; with a negative in Mark 8:18; Rom. 11:8; in Luke 9:44 the lit. meaning is "put those words into your ears," i.e., take them into your mind and keep them there; in Acts 7:51 it is used with *aperitmētos*, "uncircumcised." As seeing is metaphorically associated with conviction, so hearing is with obedience (*hupakoē*, lit., "hearing under"; the Eng., "obedience" is etymologically "hearing over against," i.e., with response in the hearer).

2. *ōtion* (ὠτίον, 5621), a diminutive of No. 1, but without the diminutive force, it being a common tendency in everyday speech to apply a diminutive form to most parts of the body, is used in Matt. 26:51; Mark 14:47 (in some mss.); Luke 22:51; John 18:10 (in some mss.) and v. 26, all with reference to the "ear" of Malchus.¶

Note: The most authentic mss. have the alternative diminutive *ōtarion*, in Mark 14:47 and John 18:10.¶

3. *akoē* (ἀκοή, 189), "hearing," akin to *akouō*, "to hear," denotes (*a*) the sense of "hearing," e.g., 1 Cor. 12:17; 2 Pet. 2:8; (*b*) that which is "heard," a report, e.g., Matt. 4:24; (*c*) the physical organ, Mark 7:35, standing for the sense of "hearing"; so in Luke 7:1, RV, for KJV, "audience"; Acts 17:20; 2 Tim. 4:3–4 (in v. 3, lit., "being tickled as to the ears"); (*d*) a message or teaching, John 12:38; Rom. 10:16–17; Gal. 3:2, 5; 1 Thess. 2:13; Heb. 4:2, RV, "(the word) of hearing," for KJV, "(the word) preached." See FAME, HEARING, PREACH, REPORT, RUMOR.

Note: In Matt. 28:14, the verb *akouō* is used with the preposition *epi*, "upon or before" (or *hupo*, "by," in some mss.), lit., "if this come to a hearing before the governor."

EAR (of corn)

stachus (στάχυς, 4719) is found in Matt. 12:1; Mark 2:23; 4:28 ("ear," twice); Luke 6:1. The first part of the word is derived from the root *sta*— found in parts of the verb *histēmi*, "to cause to stand." It is used as a proper name in Rom. 16:9.¶

EARLY

A. Noun.

orthros (ὄρθρος, 3722) denotes "daybreak, dawn" (cf. Lat. *orior*, "to rise"). Used with the adverb *batheōs*, "deeply," in Luke 24:1, it means "at early dawn" (RV). In John 8:2 it is used in the genitive case, *orthrou*, "at dawn," i.e., "early in the morning." In Acts 5:21, it is used with the article and preceded by the preposition *hupo*, "under," or about, lit., "about the dawn," "about daybreak," RV (for KJV, "early in the morning.").¶

B. Adjectives.

1. *orthrinos* (ὀρθρινός, 3720) "early," akin to A., is a later form of *orthrios*. It is found, in the most authentic mss., in Luke 24:22, of the women at the sepulchre, lit., "early ones" (some texts have the form *orthrios*, "at daybreak").¶

2. *prōimos* (πρώϊμος, 4406) or *proimos*, a longer and later form of *proios*, pertaining to the "morning," is formed from *prō*, "before" (cf. *prōtos*, "first"), and used in Jas. 5:7, of the early rain.¶

C. Adverb.

prōi (πρωΐ, 4404), "early in the day, at morn," is derived from *prō*, "before" (see B, No. 2, above). In Mark 16:2, KJV, it is translated "early in the morning"; in Mark 16:9 and John 18:28; 20:1, "early"; in Matt. 16:3; 20:1; 21:18; Mark 1:35; 11:20; 13:35; 15:1, "in the morning"; in Acts 28:23, "(from) morning." See MORNING.¶

Note: In Matt. 20:1, *hama*, "at once," is rendered "early."

EARNEST (Noun)

arrabōn (ἀρραβών, 728), originally, "earnest-money" deposited by the purchaser and forfeited if the purchase was not completed, was probably a Phoenician word, introduced into Greece. In general usage it came to denote "a pledge" or "earnest" of any sort; in the NT it is used only of that which is assured by God to believers; it is said of the Holy Spirit as the divine "pledge" of all their future blessedness,

2 Cor. 1:22; 5:5; in Eph. 1:14, particularly of their eternal inheritance.¶ In the Sept., Gen. 38:17-18, 20.¶ In modern Greek *arrabōna* is an "engagement ring."

EARNEST, EARNESTNESS, EARNESTLY

A. Noun.

spoude (σπουδή, 4710), akin to *speudō*, "to hasten," denotes "haste," Mark 6:25; Luke 1:39; hence, "earnestness," 2 Cor. 8:7, RV, for KJV, "diligence," and v. 8, for KJV, "forwardness"; in 7:12, "earnest care," for KJV, "care"; in 8:16, "earnest care." See BUSINESS, CARE, CAREFULNESS, DILIGENCE, FORWARDNESS, HASTE.

B. Adjective.

spoudaios (σπουδαῖος, 4705), akin to A,denotes "active, diligent, earnest," 2 Cor. 8:22 RV, "earnest," for KJV, "diligent"; in the latter part of the verse the comparative degree, *spoudaioteros*, is used, RV, "more earnest," for KJV, "more diligent"; in v. 17, RV, in the superlative sense, "very earnest," for KJV, "more forward." See DILIGENT, FORWARD.¶

C. Adverbs.

1. *ektenōs* (ἐκτενῶς, 1619), "earnestly" (*ek*, "out," *teinō*, "to stretch"; Eng., "tension," etc.), is used in Acts 12:5, "earnestly," RV, for KJV, "without ceasing" (some mss. have the adjective *ektenēs*, "earnest"); in 1 Pet. 1:22, "fervently." The idea suggested is that of not relaxing in effort, or acting in a right spirit. See FERVENTLY.¶

2. *ektenesteron* (ἐκτενέστερον, 1617), the comparative degree of No. 1, used as an adverb in this neuter form, denotes "more earnestly, fervently," Luke 22:44.¶

3. *spoudaiōs* (σπουδαίως, 4709), akin to B, signifies "with haste," or "with zeal, earnestly," Luke 7:4, RV, "earnestly," for KJV, "instantly"; in 2 Tim. 1:17, RV, and Titus 3:13, "diligently";¶ in Phil. 2:28, the comparative *spoudaioteros*, RV, "the more diligently," KJV, "the more carefully." See CAREFULLY, DILIGENTLY, INSTANTLY.¶

D. Adverbial Phrase.

en ekteneia (ἐν ἐκτενείᾳ), lit., "in earnestness," cf. C, No. 1, is translated "earnestly" in Acts 26:7, RV, for KJV, "instantly." See INSTANTLY.¶

Notes: (1) For the phrase "earnest expectation," Rom. 8:19 and Phil. 1:20, see EXPECTATION. (2) In 1 Cor. 12:31; 14:1, 39, *zēloō*, "to be zealous about," is translated "desire earnestly." See DESIRE. (3) In 2 Pet. 3:12, *speudō* is translated "earnestly desiring," for KJV, "hasting unto." See HASTEN. (4) In Jude 3, *epagōnizō*, "to contend earnestly," is so translated.¶ (5) In Jas. 5:17 the dative case of the noun *proseuchē* is translated "earnestly" (KJV), in connection with the corresponding verb, lit., "he prayed with prayer" (RV, "fervently"), implying persevering continuance in prayer with fervor. Cf., e.g., Ps. 40:1, lit., "in waiting I waited." See FERVENT. (6) *Atenizō*, akin to C, No. 1, "to fix the eyes upon, gaze upon," is translated "earnestly looked" in Luke 22:56, KJV (RV, "looking steadfastly"); in Acts 3:12, KJV, "look ye earnestly," RV, "fasten ye your eyes on"; in Acts 23:1, KJV, "earnestly beholding," RV, "looking steadfastly on." (7) In Heb. 2:1, *prosechō*, "to give heed," is used with the adverb *perissoterōs*, "more abundantly," to signify "to give the more earnest heed"; lit., "to give heed more exceedingly." For the verb see ATTEND, GIVE, No. 16, HEED, REGARD.

EARTH

1. *gē* (γῆ, 1093) denotes (*a*) "earth as arable land," e.g., Matt. 13:5, 8, 23; in 1 Cor. 15:47 it is said of the "earthly" material of which "the first man" was made, suggestive of frailty; (*b*) "the earth as a whole, the world," in contrast, whether to the heavens, e.g., Matt. 5:18, 35, or to heaven, the abode of God, e.g., Matt. 6:19, where the context suggests the "earth" as a place characterized by mutability and weakness; in Col. 3:2 the same contrast is presented by the word "above"; in John 3:31 (RV, "of the earth," for KJV, "earthly") it describes one whose origin and nature are "earthly" and whose speech is characterized thereby, in contrast with Christ as the One from heaven; in Col. 3:5 the physical members are said to be "upon the earth," as a sphere where, as potential instruments of moral evils, they are, by metonymy, spoken of as the evils themselves; (*c*) "the inhabited earth," e.g., Luke 21:35; Acts 1:8; 8:33; 10:12; 11:6; 17:26; 22:22; Heb. 11:13; Rev. 13:8. In the following the phrase "on the earth" signifies "among men," Luke 12:49; 18:8; John 17:4; (*d*) "a country, territory," e.g., Luke 4:25; John 3:22; (*e*) "the ground," e.g., Matt. 10:29; Mark 4:26, RV, "(upon the) earth," for KJV, "(into the) ground"; (*f*) "land," e.g., Mark 4:1; John 21:8–9, 11. Cf. Eng. words beginning with *ge*—, e.g., "geodetic," "geodesy," "geology," "geometry," "geography." See COUNTRY, GROUND, LAND, WORLD.

2. *oikoumenē* (οἰκουμένη, 3625), the present participle, passive voice, of *oikeō*, "to dwell, inhabit," denotes the "inhabited earth." It is translated "world" in every place where it has this significance, save in Luke 21:26, KJV, where it is translated "earth." See WORLD.

Note: For *epigeios*, translated "on earth" in Phil. 2:10, *ostrakinos*, "of earth," 2 Tim. 2:20, and *katachthonios*, "under the earth," Phil. 2:10,¶ see EARTHEN.

EARTHEN, EARTHLY, EARTHY

1. *ostrakinos* (ὀστράκινος, 3749) signifies "made of earthenware or clay" (from *ostrakon*, "baked clay, potsherd, shell"; akin to *osteon*, "a bone"), 2 Tim. 2:20, "of earth"; 2 Cor. 4:7, "earthen."¶

2. *epigeios* (ἐπίγειος, 1919), "on earth" (*epi*, "on," *gē*, "the earth"), is rendered "earthly" in John 3:12; 2 Cor. 5:1; Phil. 3:19; Jas. 3:15; in Phil. 2:10, "on earth," RV; "terrestrial" in 1 Cor. 15:40 (twice). See TERRESTRIAL.¶

3. *choïkos* (χοϊκός, 5517) denotes "earthy," made of earth, from *chous*, "soil, earth thrown down or heaped up," 1 Cor. 15:47–49.¶

4. *katachthonios* (καταχθόνιος, 2709), "under the earth, subterranean" (*kata*, "down," *chthōn*, "the ground," from a root signifying that which is deep), is used in Phil. 2:10.¶

EARTHQUAKE

seismos (σεισμός, 4578), "a shaking, a shock," from *seiō*, "to move to and fro, to shake," chiefly with the idea of concussion (Eng., "seismic," "seismology," "seismometry"), is used (*a*) of a "tempest" in the sea, Matt. 8:24; (*b*) of "earthquakes," Matt. 24:7; 27:54; 28:2; Mark 13:8; Luke 21:11; Acts 16:26; Rev. 6:12; 8:5; 11:13 (twice), 19; 16:18 (twice). See TEMPEST.¶

EASE, EASED

A. Verb.

anapauō (ἀναπαύω, 373) signifies "to cause or permit one to cease from any labor or movement" so as to recover strength. It implies previous toil and care. Its chief significance is that of taking, or causing to take, rest; it is used in the middle voice in Luke 12:19, "take (thine) ease," indicative of unnecessary, self-indulgent relaxation. In the papyri it is used technically, as an agricultural term. Cf. *anapausis*, "rest." See REFRESH, REST.

B. Noun.

anesis (ἄνεσις, 425) denotes "a letting loose, relaxation, easing"; it is connected with *aniēmi*, "to loosen, relax" (*ana*, "back," and *hiēmi*, "to send"). It signifies "rest," not from toil, but from endurance and suffering. Thus it is said (*a*) of a "less vigorous" condition in imprisonment, Acts 24:23, "indulgence," KJV, "liberty"; (*b*) "relief" from anxiety, 2 Cor. 2:13; 7:5, "relief" (KJV, "rest"); (*c*) "relief" from persecutions, 2 Thess. 1:7, "rest"; (*d*) of "relief" from the sufferings of poverty, 2 Cor. 8:13, "be eased," lit., "(that there should be) easing for others (trouble to you)." Cf. the synonymous word *anapausis*, "cessation or rest" (akin to A). See INDULGENCE, LIBERTY, RELIEF, REST.¶ In the Sept., 2 Chron. 23:15.¶

For EASILY see EASY

EAST

anatole (ἀνατολή, 395), primarily "a rising," as of the sun and stars, corresponds to *anatellō*, "to make to rise," or, intransitively, "to arise," which is also used of the sunlight, as well as of other objects in nature. In Luke 1:78 it is used metaphorically of Christ as "the Dayspring," the One through whom light came into the world, shining immediately into Israel, to dispel the darkness which was upon all nations. Cf. Mal. 4:2. Elsewhere it denotes the "east," as the quarter of the sun's rising, Matt. 2:1–2,9; 8:11; 24:27; Luke 13:29; Rev. 7:2; 16:12; 21:13. The "east" in general stands for that side of things upon which the rising of the sun gives light. In the heavenly city itself, Rev. 21:13, the reference to the "east" gate points to the outgoing of the influence of the city "eastward." See DAYSPRING.¶

EASTER

pascha (πάσχα, 3957), mistranslated "Easter" in Acts 12:4, KJV, denotes the Passover (RV). The phrase "after the Passover" signifies after the whole festival was at an end. The term "Easter" is not of Christian origin. It is another form of *Astarte*, one of the titles of the Chaldean goddess, the queen of heaven. The festival of Pasch held by Christians in post-apostolic times was a continuation of the Jewish feast, but was not instituted by Christ, nor was it connected with Lent. From this Pasch the pagan festival of "Easter" was quite distinct and was introduced into the apostate Western religion, as part of the attempt to adapt pagan festivals to Christianity. See PASSOVER.

EASY, EASIER, EASILY

1. *chrēstos* (χρηστός, 5543) primarily signifies "fit for use, able to be used" (akin to *chraomai*, "to use"), hence, "good, virtuous, mild, pleasant" (in contrast to what is hard, harsh, sharp, bitter). It is said (*a*) of the character of God as "kind, gracious," Luke 6:35; 1 Pet. 2:3; "good," Rom. 2:4, where the neuter of the adjective is used as a noun, "the goodness" (cf. the corresponding noun *chrēstotēs*, "goodness," in the same verse); of the yoke of Christ, Matt. 11:30, "easy" (a suitable rendering would be

"kindly"); (*c*) of believers, Eph. 4:32; (*d*) of things, as wine, Luke 5:39, RV, "good," for KJV, "better" (cf. Jer. 24:3, 5, of figs); (*e*) ethically, of manners, 1 Cor. 15:33. See GOOD, GRACIOUS, KIND.¶

2. *eukopōteros* (εὐκοπώτερος, 2123), the comparative degree of *eukopos*, "easy, with easy labor" (*eu*, "well," *kopos*, "labor"), hence, of that which is "easier to do," is found in the Synoptics only, Matt. 9:5; 19:24; Mark 2:9; 10:25; Luke 5:23; 16:17; 18:25.

Notes: (1) The adverb "easily" is included in the translation of *euperistatos* in Heb. 12:1, "easily beset," lit., "the easily besetting sin," probably a figure from a garment, "easily surrounding," and therefore easily entangling. See BESET. (2) In 1 Cor. 13:5, KJV, "is not easily provoked," there is no word in the original representing "easily"; RV, "is not provoked." (3) For "easy to be entreated" see INTREAT. For "easy to be understood" see UNDERSTAND.

EAT, EAT WITH, EATING

A. Verbs.

1. *esthiō* (ἐσθίω, 2068) signifies "to eat" (as distinct from *pinō*, "to drink"); it is a lengthened form from *edō* (Lat., *edō;* cf. Eng., "edible"); in Heb. 10:27, metaphorically, "devour"; it is said of the ordinary use of food and drink, 1 Cor. 9:7; 11:22; of partaking of food at table, e.g., Mark 2:16; of reveling, Matt. 24:49; Luke 12:45. Cf. the strengthened, form *katesthiō*, and the verb *sunesthiō*, below. See DEVOUR.

2. *phagō* (φάγω, 5315), "to eat, devour, consume," is obsolete in the present and other tenses, but supplies certain tenses which are wanting in No. 1, above. In Luke 8:55 the KJV has "(to give her) meat," the RV "(that something be given her) to eat." The idea that this verb combines both "eating" and "drinking," while No. 1 differentiates the one from the other, is not borne out in the NT. The word is very frequent in the Gospels and is used eleven times in 1 Cor. See also No. 3. See MEAT.

3. *trōgō* (τρώγω, 5176), primarily, "to gnaw, to chew," stresses the slow process; it is used metaphorically of the habit of spiritually feeding upon Christ, John 6:54, 56–58 (the aorists here do not indicate a definite act, but view a series of acts seen in perspective); of the constant custom of "eating" in certain company, John 13:18; of a practice unduly engrossing the world, Matt. 24:38.

In John 6, the change in the Lord's use from the verb *esthiō* (*phagō*) to the stronger verb *trōgō*, is noticeable. The more persistent the unbelief of His hearers, the more difficult His language and statements became. In vv. 49 to

53 the verb *phagō* is used; in 54, 58, *trōgō* (in v. 58 it is put into immediate contrast with *phagō*). The use of *trōgō* in Matt. 24:38 and John 13:18 is a witness against pressing into the meaning of the word the sense of munching or gnawing; it had largely lost this sense in its common usage.¶

4. *geuō* (γεύω, 1089), primarily, "to cause to taste, to give one a taste of," is used in the middle voice and denotes (*a*) "to taste," its usual meaning; (*b*) "to take food, to eat," Acts 10:10; 20:11; 23:14; the meaning to taste must not be pressed in these passages, the verb having acquired the more general meaning. As to whether Acts 20:11 refers to the Lord's Supper or to an ordinary meal, the addition of the words "and eaten" is perhaps a sufficient indication that the latter is referred to here, whereas v. 7, where the single phrase "to break bread" is used, refers to the Lord's Supper. A parallel instance is found in Acts 2:43, 46. In the former verse the phrase "the breaking of bread," unaccompanied by any word about taking food, clearly stands for the Lord's Supper; whereas in v. 46 the phrase "breaking bread at home" is immediately explained by "they did take their food," indicating their ordinary meals. See TASTE.

5. *bibrōskō* (βιβρώσκω, 977), "to eat," is derived from a root, *bor—,* "to devour" (likewise seen in the noun *brōma,* "food, meat"; cf. Eng., "carnivorous," "voracious," from Lat. *vorax*). This verb is found in John 6:13. The difference between this and *phagō,* No. 2, above, may be seen perhaps in the fact that whereas in the Lord's question to Philip in v. 5, *phagō* intimates nothing about a full supply, the verb *bibrōskō,* in v. 13, indicates that the people had been provided with a big meal, of which they had partaken eagerly.¶

6. *kataphagō* (καταφάγω, Aor. of 2719) signifies "to eat up" (*kata,* used intensively, and No. 2), John 2:17; Rev. 10:9–10; elsewhere it is translated "devour," as also is *katesthiō* (see No. 1). See DEVOUR.

7. *korennumi* (κορέννυμι, 2880), "to satiate, to satisfy," as with food, is used in the middle voice in Acts 27:38, "had eaten enough"; in 1 Cor. 4:8, "ye are filled." See FILL.¶

8. *sunesthiō* (συνεσθίω, 4906), "to eat with" (*sun,* "with," and No. 1), is found in Luke 15:2; Acts 10:41; 11:3; 1 Cor. 5:11; Gal. 2:12.¶

9. *nomēn echō* (νομὴν ἔχω) is a phrase consisting of the noun *nomē,* denoting (*a*) "pasturage," (*b*) "growth, increase," and *echō,* "to have." In John 10:9 the phrase signifies "to find pasture" (*a*). In 2 Tim. 2:17, with the meaning (*b*), the phrase is, lit., "will have growth," trans-

lated "will eat," i.e., "will spread like a gangrene." It is used in Greek writings, other than the NT, of the spread of a fire, and of ulcers. See PASTURE.¶

Note: The verb *metalambanō,* "to take a part or share of anything with others, to partake of, share," is translated "did eat," in Acts 2:46, corrected in the RV to "did take"; a still more suitable rendering would be "shared," the sharing of food being suggested; cf. *metadidōmi,* "to share," e.g., Luke 3:11.

B. Nouns.

1. *brōsis* (βρῶσις, 1035), akin to A,No. 5, denotes (*a*) "the act of eating," e.g., Rom. 14:17; said of rust, Matt. 6:19–20; or, more usually (*b*) "that which is eaten, food" (like *brōma,* "food"), "meat," John 4:32; 6:27, 55; Col. 2:16; Heb. 12:16 ("morsel of meat"); "food," 2 Cor. 9:10; "eating," 1 Cor. 8:4. See FOOD, MEAT, RUST.¶

2. *prosphagion* (προσφάγιον, 4371), primarily "a dainty or relish" (especially cooked fish), to be eaten with bread (*pros,* "to," and A, No. 2), then, "fish" in general, is used in John 21:5, "Have ye aught to eat?" (KJV, "have ye any meat?"). Moulton remarks that the evidences of the papyri are to the effect that *prosphagion,* "is not so broad a word as 'something to eat.' The apostles had left even loaves behind them once, Mark 8:14; they might well have left the 'relish' on this occasion. It would normally be fish; cf. Mark 6:38" (Gram. of NT Greek, Vol. 1, p. 170).¶

C. Adjective.

brōsimos (βρώσιμος, 1034), akin to A, No. 5, and B., signifying "eatable," is found in Luke 24:41, RV, appropriately, "to eat," for the KJV, "meat."¶ In the Sept., Lev. 19:23; Neh. 9:25; Ezek. 47:12.¶

EDGE, EDGED

A. Noun.

stoma (στόμα, 4750), the mouth (cf. Eng., "stomach," from *stomachos,* 1 Tim. 5:23), has a secondary and figurative meaning in reference to the "edge of a sharp instrument, as of a sword," Luke 21:24; Heb. 11:34 (cf. the Sept., e.g., Gen. 34:26; Judg. 18:27). See FACE, MOUTH.

B. Adjective.

distomos (δίστομος, 1366), lit., "doublemouthed" (*dis,* "twice," and A.), "two-edged," is used of a sword with two edges, Heb. 4:12; Rev. 1:16; 2:12.¶ In the Sept., Judg. 3:16; Psa. 149:6; Prov. 5:4.¶

EDIFICATION, EDIFY, EDIFYING

A. Noun.

oikodomē (οἰκοδομή, 3619) denotes (*a*) "the act of building" (*oikos*, "a home," and *demō*, "to build"); this is used only figuratively in the NT, in the sense of edification, the promotion of spiritual growth (lit., "the things of building up"), Rom. 14:19; 15:2; 1 Cor. 14:3, 5, 12, 26, e.g.; (*b*) "a building, edifice," whether material, Matt. 24:1, e.g., or figurative, of the future body of the believer, 2 Cor. 5:1, or of a local church, 1 Cor. 3:9, or the whole church, "the body of Christ," Eph. 2:21. See BUILDING.

B. Verb.

oikodomeō (οἰκοδομέω, 3618), lit., "to build a house" (see above), (*a*) usually signifies "to build," whether literally, or figuratively; the present participle, lit., "the (ones) building," is used as a noun, "the builders," in Matt. 21:42; Mark 12:10; Luke 20:17; Acts 4:11 (in some mss.; the most authentic have the noun *oikodomos;*) 1 Pet. 2:7; (*b*) is used metaphorically, in the sense of "edifying," promoting the spiritual growth and development of character of believers, by teaching or by example, suggesting such spiritual progress as the result of patient labor. It is said (1) of the effect of this upon local churches, Acts 9:31; 1 Cor. 14:4; (2) of the individual action of believers towards each other, 1 Cor. 8:1; 10:23; 14:17; 1 Thess. 5:11; (3) of an individual in regard to himself, 1 Cor. 14:4. In 1 Cor. 8:10, where it is translated "emboldened," the apostle uses it with pathetic irony, of the action of a brother in "building up" his brother who had a weak conscience, causing him to compromise his scruples; "strengthened," or "confirmed," would be suitable renderings. See BUILD, EMBOLDEN.

EFFECT (of none)

1. *akuroō* (ἀκυρόω, 208) signifies "to render void, deprive of force and authority" (from *a*, negative, and *kuros*, "might, authority"; *kurios*, "a lord," is from the same root), the opposite to *kuroō*, "to confirm" (see CONFIRM). It is used of making "void" the Word of God, Matt. 15:6; Mark 7:13 (KJV, "making of none effect"), and of the promise of God to Abraham as not being deprived of authority by the Law 430 years after, Gal. 3:17, "disannul." *Kuroō* is used in v. 15. See DISANNUL, VOID.¶

2. *katargeō* (καταργέω, 2673), "to reduce to inactivity, to render useless," is translated "to make of none effect," in Rom. 3:3, 31; 4:14; Gal. 3:17 (cf. *akuroō*, No. 1, in the same verse), and in the KJV of Gal. 5:4, RV, "ye are severed"

(from Christ). For the meaning and use of the word see ABOLISH and DESTROY.

3. *kenoō* (κενόω, 2758), "to make empty, to empty," is translated "should be made of none effect" in 1 Cor. 1:17, KJV (RV "made void"); it is used (*a*) of the Cross of Christ, there; (*b*) of Christ, in emptying Himself, Phil. 2:7; (*c*) of faith, Rom. 4:14; (*d*) of the apostle Paul's glorying in the gospel ministry, 1 Cor. 9:15; (*e*) of his glorying on behalf of the church at Corinth, 2 Cor. 9:3. See EMPTY, VAIN, VOID.¶

Note: In Rom. 9:6 the verb *ekpiptō*, lit., "to fall out of, as of a ship falling out of its course" (cf. the same word in Acts 27:17, "were driven"), is translated "hath taken none effect," KJV (RV, "hath come to nought"). See NOUGHT.

EFFECTUAL

A. Adjective.

energēs (ἐνεργής, 1756) denotes "active, powerful in action" (*en*, "in," *ergon*, "work"; Eng. "energy"; the word "work" is derived from the same root). It is translated "effectual" in 1 Cor. 16:9, of the door opened for the gospel in Ephesus, and made "effectual" in the results of entering it; and in Philem. 6, of the fellowship of Philemon's faith "in the knowledge of every good thing" (RV). In Heb. 4:12 it describes the Word of God as "active," RV (KJV, "powerful"), i.e., full of power to achieve results. See ACTIVE, POWERFUL.¶

B. Verb.

energeō (ἐνεργέω, 1754), "to put forth power, be operative, to work" (its usual meaning), is rendered by the verb "to work effectually," or "to be effectual," in the KJV of 2 Cor. 1:6; Gal. 2:8 and 1 Thess. 2:13; in each case the RV translates it by the simple verb "to work" (past tense, "wrought"). In Jas. 5:16 the RV omits the superfluous word "effectual," and translates the sentence "the supplication of a righteous man availeth much in its working," the verb being in the present participial form. Here the meaning may be "in its inworking," i.e., in the effect produced in the praying man, bringing him into line with the will of God, as in the case of Elijah. For a fuller treatment of the word, see WORK. See also DO, MIGHTY, SHEW, *Note* (11).

Note: The noun *energeia*, "working," is translated "effectual working," in the KJV of Eph. 3:7, and 4:16.

EFFEMINATE

malakos (μαλακός, 3120), "soft, soft to the touch" (Lat., *mollis*, Eng., "mollify," "emollient," etc.), is used (*a*) of raiment, Matt. 11:8 (twice); Luke 7:25; (*b*) metaphorically, in a bad sense, 1 Cor. 6:9, "effeminate," not simply of a male who practices forms of lewdness, but persons in general, who are guilty of addiction to sins of the flesh, voluptuous.¶

EFFULGENCE

apaugasma (ἀπαύγασμα, 541), "radiance, effulgence," is used of light shining from a luminous body (*apo*, "from," and *augē*, "brightness"). The word is found in Heb. 1:3, where it is used of the Son of God as "being the effulgence of His glory." The word "effulgence" exactly corresponds (in its Latin form) to *apaugasma*. The "glory" of God expresses all that He is in His nature and His actings and their manifestation. The Son, being one with the Father in Godhood, is in Himself, and ever was, the shining forth of the "glory," manifesting in Himself all that God is and does, all, for instance, that is involved in His being "the very image of His substance," and in His creative acts, His sustaining power, and in His making purification of sins, with all that pertains thereto and issues from it.¶

EGG

ōon (ᾠόν, 5609) denotes "an egg" (Lat., *ovum*), Luke 11:12.¶

EIGHT, EIGHTEEN, EIGHTH

oktō (ὀκτώ, 3638), "eight" (Lat., *octo, octavus;* cf. Eng., "octagon," "octave," "octavo," "October," etc.), is used in Luke 2:21; 9:28; John 20:26; Acts 9:33; 25:6; 1 Pet. 3:20; in composition with other numerals, *oktō kai deka*, lit., "eight and ten, eighteen," Luke 13:4, 11, 16; *triakonta kai oktō*, "thirty and eight," John 5:5.¶

ogdoos (ὄγδοος, 3590), "eighth" (connected with the preceding), is used in Luke 1:59; Acts 7:8; 2 Pet. 2:5; Rev. 17:11; 21:20.¶

oktaēmeros (ὀκταήμερος, 3637), an adjective, signifying an "eighth-day" person or thing, "eight days old" (*oktō*, and *hēmera*, "a day"), is used in Phil. 3:5. This, and similar numerical adjectives not found in the NT, indicate duration rather than intervals. The apostle shows by his being an "eighth-day" person as to circumcision, that his parents were neither Ishmaelites (circumcised in their thirteenth year) nor other Gentiles, converted to Judaism (circumcised on becoming Jews).¶

EITHER

ē (ἤ, 2228) is a disjunctive particle. One of its uses is to distinguish things which exclude each other, or one of which can take the place of another. It is translated "either" in Matt.

6:24; 12:33; Luke 16:13; Acts 17:21; 1 Cor. 14:6. The RV rightly omits it in Luke 6:42, and translates it by "or" in Luke 15:8; Phil. 3:12 and Jas. 3:12.

Note: The adverb *enteuthen*, denoting "hence," is repeated in the phrase rendered "on either side," (lit., "hence and hence") in John 19:18. The RV of Rev. 22:2 translates it "on this side," distinguishing it from *ekeithen*, "on that side"; the KJV, following another reading for the latter adverb, has "on either side." See HENCE.

ELDER, ELDEST

A. Adjectives.

1. *presbuteros* (πρεσβύτερος, 4245), an adjective, the comparative degree of *presbus*, "an old man, an elder," is used (*a*) of age, whether of the "elder" of two persons, Luke 15:25, or more, John 8:9, "the eldest"; or of a person advanced in life, a senior, Acts 2:17; in Heb. 11:2, the "elders" are the forefathers in Israel; so in Matt. 15:2; Mark 7:3, 5; the feminine of the adjective is used of "elder" women in the churches, 1 Tim. 5:2, not in respect of position but in seniority of age; (*b*) of rank or positions of responsibility, (1) among Gentiles, as in the Sept. of Gen. 50:7; Num. 22:7; (2) in the Jewish nation, firstly, those who were the heads or leaders of the tribes and families, as of the seventy who assisted Moses, Num. 11:16; Deut. 27:1, and those assembled by Solomon; secondly, members of the Sanhedrin, consisting of the chief priests, "elders" and scribes, learned in Jewish law, e.g., Matt. 16:21; 26:47; thirdly, those who managed public affairs in the various cities, Luke 7:3; (3) in the Christian churches, those who, being raised up and qualified by the work of the Holy Spirit, were appointed to have the spiritual care of, and to exercise oversight over, the churches. To these the term "bishops," *episkopoi*, or "overseers," is applied (see Acts 20, v. 17 with v. 28, and Titus 1:5 and 7), the latter term indicating the nature of their work, *presbuteroi* their maturity of spiritual experience. The divine arrangement seen throughout the NT was for a plurality of these to be appointed in each church, Acts 14:23; 20:17; Phil. 1:1; 1 Tim. 5:17; Titus 1:5. The duty of "elders" is described by the verb *episkopeō*. They were appointed according as they had given evidence of fulfilling the divine qualifications, Titus 1:6 to 9; cf. 1 Tim. 3:1–7 and 1 Pet. 5:2; (4) the twenty-four "elders" enthroned in heaven around the throne of God, Rev. 4:4, 10; 5:5–14; 7:11, 13; 11:16; 14:3; 19:4. The number twenty-four is representative of earthly conditions. The word "elder" is nowhere applied to angels. See OLD.

2. *sumpresbuteros* (συμπρεσβύτερος, 4850), "a fellow-elder" (*sun*, "with"), is used in 1 Pet. 5:1.¶

3. *meizōn* (μείζων, 3187), "greater," the comparative degree of *megas*, "great," is used of age, and translated "elder" in Rom. 9:12, with reference to Esau and Jacob. See GREATER, GREATEST, MORE.

B. Noun.

presbuterion (πρεσβυτέριον, 4244), "an assembly of aged men," denotes (*a*) the Council or Senate among the Jews, Luke 22:66; Acts 22:5; (*b*) the "elders" or bishops in a local church, 1 Tim. 4:14, "the presbytery." For their functions see A, No. 1, (3).

ELECT, ELECTED, ELECTION

A. Adjectives.

1. *eklektos* (ἐκλεκτός, 1588) lit. signifies "picked out, chosen" (*ek*, "from," *legō*, "to gather, pick out"), and is used of (*a*) Christ, the "chosen" of God, as the Messiah, Luke 23:35 (for the verb in 9:35 see *Note* below), and metaphorically as a "living Stone," "a chief corner Stone," 1 Pet. 2:4, 6; some mss. have it in John 1:34, instead of *huios*, "Son"; (*b*) angels, 1 Tim. 5:21, as "chosen" to be of especially high rank in administrative association with God, or as His messengers to human beings, doubtless in contrast to fallen angels (see 2 Pet. 2:4 and Jude 6); (*c*) believers (Jews or Gentiles), Matt. 24:22, 24, 31; Mark 13:20, 22, 27; Luke 18:7; Rom. 8:33; Col. 3:12; 2 Tim. 2:10; Titus 1:1; 1 Pet. 1:1; 2:9 (as a spiritual race); Matt. 20:16; 22:14 and Rev. 17:14, "chosen"; individual believers are so mentioned in Rom. 16:13; 2 John 1, 13.¶

Believers were "chosen" "before the foundation of the world" (cf. "before times eternal," 2 Tim. 1:9), in Christ, Eph. 1:4, to adoption, Eph. 1:5; good works, 2:10; conformity to Christ, Rom. 8:29; salvation from the delusions of the Antichrist and the doom of the deluded, 2 Thess. 2:13; eternal glory, Rom. 9:23.

The source of their "election" is God's grace, not human will, Eph. 1:4, 5; Rom. 9:11; 11:5. They are given by God the Father to Christ as the fruit of His death, all being foreknown and foreseen by God, John 17:6 and Rom. 8:29. While Christ's death was sufficient for all men, and is effective in the case of the "elect," yet men are treated as responsible, being capable of the will and power to choose. For the rendering "being chosen as firstfruits," an alternative reading in 2 Thess. 2:13, see FIRSTFRUITS. See CHOICE, B.

2. *suneklektos* (συνεκλεκτός, 4899) means "elect together with," 1 Pet. 5:13.¶

B. Noun.

eklogē (ἐκλογή, 1589) denotes "a picking out, selection" (Eng., "eclogue"), then, "that which is chosen"; in Acts 9:15, said of the "choice" of God of Saul of Tarsus, the phrase is, lit., "a vessel of choice." It is used four times in Romans; in 9:11, of Esau and Jacob, where the phrase "the purpose ... according to election" is virtually equivalent to "the electing purpose"; in 11:5, the "remnant according to the election of grace" refers to believing Jews, saved from among the unbelieving nation; so in v. 7; in v. 28, "the election" may mean either the "act of choosing" or the "chosen" ones; the context, speaking of the fathers, points to the former, the choice of the nation according to the covenant of promise. In 1 Thess. 1:4, "your election" refers not to the church collectively, but to the individuals constituting it; the apostle's assurance of their "election" gives the reason for his thanksgiving. Believers are to give "the more diligence to make their calling and election sure," by the exercise of the qualities and graces which make them fruitful in the knowledge of God, 2 Pet. 1:10.¶ For the corresponding verb *eklegomai*, see CHOOSE.

ELEMENTS

stoicheion (στοιχεῖον, 4747), used in the plural, primarily signifies any first things from which others in a series, or a composite whole, take their rise; the word denotes "an element, first principle" (from *stoichos*, "a row, rank, series"; cf. the verb *stoicheō*, "to walk or march in rank"; see WALK); it was used of the letters of the alphabet, as elements of speech. In the NT it is used of (*a*) the substance of the material world, 2 Pet. 3:10, 12; (*b*) the delusive speculations of gentile cults and of Jewish theories, treated as elementary principles, "the rudiments of the world," Col. 2:8, spoken of as "philosophy and vain deceit"; these were presented as superior to faith in Christ; at Colosse the worship of angels, mentioned in v. 18, is explicable by the supposition, held by both Jews and Gentiles in that district, that the constellations were either themselves animated heavenly beings, or were governed by them; (*c*) the rudimentary principles of religion, Jewish or Gentile, also described as "the rudiments of the world," Col. 2:20, and as "weak and beggarly rudiments," Gal. 4:3, 9, RV, constituting a yoke of bondage; (*d*) the "elementary" principles (the A.B.C.) of the OT, as a revelation from God, Heb. 5:12, RV, "rudiments," lit., "the rudiments of the beginning of the oracles of God," such as are taught to spiritual babes. See PRINCIPLES, RUDIMENTS.¶

ELEVEN, ELEVENTH

hendeka (ἕνδεκα, 1733), lit., "one ten" (Lat., *undecim*), is used only of the eleven apostles remaining after the death of Judas Iscariot, Matt. 28:16; Mark 16:14; Luke 24:9, 33; Acts 1:26; 2:14.¶

hendekatos (ἑνδέκατος, 1734), an adjective derived from the above, is found in Matt. 20:6, 9; Rev. 21:20.¶

ELOQUENT

logios (λόγιος, 3052), an adjective, from *logos*, "a word," primarily meant "learned, a man skilled in literature and the arts." In the KJV of Acts 18:24, it is translated "eloquent," said of Apollos; the RV is almost certainly right in translating it "learned." It was much more frequently used among the Greeks of one who was erudite than of one who was skilled in words. He had stores of "learning" and could use it convincingly.¶

ELSE

epei (ἐπεί, 1893), a conjunction, when used of cause, meaning "since," "otherwise," "for then," "because"; in an ellipsis, "else," as in 1 Cor. 7:14, where the ellipsis would be "if the unbelieving husband were not sanctified in the wife, your children would be unclean"; cf. Rom. 11:6, 22; 1 Cor. 5:10; Heb. 9:26. Sometimes it introduces a question, as in Rom. 3:6; 1. Cor. 14:16; 15:29; Heb. 10:2. It is translated "else" in 1 Cor. 14:16 and in the RV in Heb. 9:26 and 10:2, for KJV, "for then."

ELSEWHERE

allachou (ἀλλαχοῦ, 237v), connected with *allos*, "another," is used in Mark 1:38 (RV only).¶

For **EMBARK** (RV, in Acts 27:2) see **ABOARD**

EMBOLDEN

oikodomeō (οἰκοδομέω, 3618) is rendered "embolden" in 1 Cor. 8:10, in reference to blameworthy actions (see marg.), the delinquent being built up, so to speak, to do what is contrary to his conscience. See BUILD, EDIFICATION.

EMBRACE

1. *aspazomai* (ἀσπάζομαι, 782) lit. signifies "to draw to oneself"; hence, "to greet, salute, welcome," the ordinary meaning, e.g., in Rom. 16, where it is used 21 times. It also signifies "to bid farewell," e.g., Acts 20:1, RV, "took leave of" (KJV, "embraced"). A "salutation or farewell" was generally made by embracing and kissing (see Luke 10:4, which indicates the possibility of delay on the journey by frequent salutation). In Heb. 11:13 it is said of those who greeted the promises from afar, RV, "greeted," for KJV, "embraced." Cf. *aspasmos*, "a salutation." See GREET, LEAVE (take), SALUTE.

Note: In Acts 21:6 the most authentic texts have *apaspazomai (apo*, and No. 1), "to bid farewell."

2. *sumperilambanō* (συμπεριλαμβάνο, 4843), lit., "to take around with," (*sun*, "with" *peri*, "around," *lambanō*, "to take"), "to embrace," is used in Acts 20:10, in connection with Paul's recovery of Eutychus.¶ In the Sept., Ezra 5:3, "to enclose."¶

EMPEROR

sebastos (σεβαστός, 4575), "august, reverent," the masculine gender of an adjective (from *sebas*, "reverential awe"), became used as the title of the Roman emperor, Acts 25:21, 25, RV, for KJV, "Augustus"; then, taking its name from the emperor, it became a title of honor applied to certain legions or cohorts or battalions, marked for their valor, Acts 27:1.¶ Cf. *sebazomai*, "to worship," Rom. 1:25;¶ *sebasma*, "an object of worship," Acts 17:23; 2 Thess. 2:4.¶

EMERALD

A. Noun.

smaragdos (σμάραγδος, 4665) is a transparent stone of a light green color, occupying the first place in the second row on the high priest's breastplate, Exod. 28:18. Tyre imported it from Syria, Ezek. 27:16. It is one of the foundations of the heavenly Jerusalem, Rev. 21:19. The name was applied to other stones of a similar character, such as the carbuncle.¶

B. Adjective.

smaragdinos (σμαράγδινος, 4664), "emerald in character," descriptive of the rainbow round about the throne in Rev. 4:3, is used in the papyri to denote emerald green.¶

EMPTY

A. Verbs.

1. *kenoō* (κενόω, 2758), "to empty," is so translated in Phil. 2:7, RV, for KJV, "made ... of no reputation." The clauses which follow the verb are exegetical of its meaning, especially the phrases "the form of a servant," and "the likeness of men." Christ did not "empty" Himself of Godhood. He did not cease to be what He essentially and eternally was. The KJV, while not an exact translation, goes far to express the act of the Lord (see GIFFORD on the Incarna-

tion). For other occurrences of the word, see Rom. 4:14; 1 Cor. 1:17; 9:15; 2 Cor. 9:3.¶ In the Sept., Jer. 14:2; 15:9.¶

2. *scholazō* (σχολάζω, 4980), from *scholē*, "leisure," that for which leisure is employed, such as "a lecture" (hence, "the place where lectures are given"; Eng., "school"), is used of persons, to have time for anything and so to be occupied in, 1 Cor. 7:5; of things, to be unoccupied, empty, Matt. 12:44 (some mss. have it in Luke 11:25). See GIVE (oneself to).¶

B. Adjective.

kenos (κενός, 2756) expresses the "hollowness" of anything, the "absence" of that which otherwise might be possessed. It is used (*a*) literally, Mark 12:3; Luke 1:53; 20:10–11; (*b*) metaphorically, of imaginations, Acts 4:25; of words which convey erroneous teachings, Eph. 5:6; of deceit, Col. 2:8; of a person whose professed faith is not accompanied by works, Jas. 2:20; negatively, concerning the grace of God, 1 Cor. 15:10; of refusal to receive it, 2 Cor. 6:1; of faith, 1 Cor. 15:14; of preaching (id.); and other forms of Christian activity and labor, 1 Cor. 15:58; Gal. 2:2; Phil. 2:16; 1 Thess. 2:1; 3:5.¶ The synonymous word *mataios*, "vain," signifies "void" of result, it marks the aimlessness of anything. The vain (*kenos*) man in Jas. 2:20 is one who is "empty" of divinely imparted wisdom; in 1:26 the vain (*mataios*) religion is one that produces nothing profitable. *Kenos* stresses the absence of quality, *mataios*, the absence of useful aim or effect. Cf. the corresponding adverb *kenōs*, "in vain," in Jas. 4:5,¶ the noun *kenodoxia*, "vainglory," Phil. 2:3,¶ the adjective *kenodoxos*, "vainglorious," Gal. 5:26,¶ and the noun *kenophōnia*, "vain," or "empty," babblings, 1 Tim. 6:20; 2 Tim. 2:16.¶

For **EMULATION**, KJV (Rom. 11:14; Gal. 5:20) see **JEALOUSY**

ENABLE

endunamoō (ἐνδυναμόω, 1743), "to render strong" (*en*, "in," *dunamis*, "power"), is translated "enabled" in 1 Tim. 1:12, more lit., "instrengthened," "inwardly strengthened," suggesting strength in soul and purpose (cf. Phil. 4:13). See STRENGTH, STRONG. (In the Sept., Judg. 6:34; 1 Chron. 12:18; Ps. 52:7.¶)

ENACT

nomotheteō (νομοθετέω, 3549), "to ordain by law, to enact" (*nomos*, "a law," *tithēmi*, "to put"), is used in the passive voice, and rendered "enacted" in Heb. 8:6, RV, for KJV, "established"; in 7:11, used intransitively, it is ren-

dered "received the Law." See ESTABLISH, LAW.¶

For **ENCLOSE** see **INCLOSE**

ENCOUNTER

sumballō (συμβάλλω, 4820), lit., "to throw together" (*sun*, "with," *ballō*, "to throw"), is used of "encountering" in war, Luke 14:31, RV, "to encounter... (in war)," for KJV, "to make war against"; of meeting in order to discuss, in Acts 17:18, "encountered," of the philosophers in Athens and the apostle. See CONFER, HELP, MAKE, MEET, PONDER.

ENCOURAGE, ENCOURAGEMENT

A. Verbs.

1. *protrepō* (προτρέπω, 4389), "to urge forward, persuade," is used in Acts 18:27 in the middle voice, RV, "encouraged," indicating their particular interest in giving Apollos the "encouragement" mentioned; the KJV, "exhorting," wrongly connects the verb.¶

2. *paramutheomai* (παραμυθέομαι, 3888), from *para*, "with," and *muthos*, "counsel, advice," is translated "encouraging" in 1 Thess. 2:11, RV, and "encourage" in 5:14, RV, there signifying to stimulate to the discharge of the ordinary duties of life. In John 11:19, 31, it means "to comfort." See COMFORT.¶

Cf. the nouns *paramuthia*, 1 Cor. 14:3,¶ and *paramuthion*, Phil 2:1, "comfort."¶

B. Noun.

paraklēsis (παράκλησις, 3874), "a calling to one's aid" (*para*, "by the side," *kaleō*, "to call"), then, "an exhortation, encouragement," is translated "encouragement" in Heb. 6:18, RV, for KJV, "consolation"; it is akin to *parakaleō*, "to beseech or exhort, encourage, comfort," and *paraklētos*, "a paraclete or advocate." See COMFORT, CONSOLATION, EXHORTATION, INTREATY.

END, ENDING

A. Nouns.

1. *telos* (τέλος, 5056) signifies (*a*) "the limit," either at which a person or thing ceases to be what he or it was up to that point, or at which previous activities were ceased, 2 Cor. 3:13; 1 Pet. 4:7; (*b*) "the final issue or result" of a state or process, e.g., Luke 1:33; in Rom. 10:4, Christ is described as "the end of the Law unto righteousness to everyone that believeth"; this is best explained by Gal. 3:23–26; cf. Jas. 5:11; the following more especially point to the issue or fate of a thing, Matt. 26:58; Rom. 6:21; 2 Cor. 11:15; Phil. 3:19; Heb. 6:8; 1 Pet. 1:9; (*c*) "a fulfillment," Luke 22:37, KJV, "(have) an end"; (*d*) "the utmost degree" of an act, as of

the love of Christ towards His disciples, John 13:1; (e) "the aim or purpose" of a thing, 1 Tim. 1:5; (f) "the last" in a succession or series Rev. 1:8 (KJV, only, "ending"); 21:6; 22:13. See CONTINUAL, CUSTOM (Toll), FINALLY, UTTERMOST.

Note: The following phrases contain *telos* (the word itself coming under one or other of the above): *eis telos*, "unto the end," e.g., Matt. 10:22; 24:13; Luke 18:5, "continual"; John 13:1 (see above); 2 Cor. 3:13, "on the end" (RV); *heōs telous*, "unto the end," 1 Cor. 1:8; 2 Cor. 1:13;¶ *achri telous*, "even to the end" (a stronger expression than the preceding); Heb. 6:11; Rev. 2:26 (where "even" might well have been added);¶ *mechri telous*, with much the same meaning as *achri telous*, Heb. 3:6, 14.¶ See other expressions in the *Notes* after C.

2. *sunteleia* (συντέλεια, 4930) signifies "a bringing to completion together" (*sun* "with," *teleō*, "to complete," akin to No. 1), marking the "completion" or consummation of the various parts of a scheme. In Matt. 13:39–40, 49; 24:3; 28:20, the rendering "the end of the world" (KJV and RV, text) is misleading; the RV marg., "the consummation of the age," is correct. The word does not denote a termination, but the heading up of events to the appointed climax. *Aiōn* is not the world, but a period or epoch or era in which events take place. In Heb. 9:26, the word translated "world" (KJV) is in the plural, and the phrase is "'the consummation of the ages." It was at the heading up of all the various epochs appointed by divine counsels that Christ was manifested (i.e., in His Incarnation) "to put away sin by the sacrifice of Himself."¶

3. *peras* (πέρας, 4009), "a limit, boundary" (from *pera*, "beyond"), is used (a) of space, chiefly in the plural, Matt. 12:42, RV, "ends," for KJV, "uttermost parts"; so Luke 11:31 (KJV, "utmost"); Rom. 10:18 (KJV and RV, "ends"); (b) of the termination of something occurring in a period, Heb. 6:16, RV, "final," for KJV, "an end," said of strife. See UTTERMOST.¶

4. *ekbasis* (ἔκβασις, 1545) denotes "a way out" (*ek*, "out," *bainō*, "to go"), 1 Cor. 10:13, "way of escape"; or an issue, Heb. 13:7 (KJV, "end," RV, "issue"). See ISSUE.¶

B. Verbs.
1. *teleō* (τελέω, 5055), "to complete, finish, bring to an end," is translated "had made an end," in Matt. 11:1. See ACCOMPLISH.

2. *sunteleō* (συντελέω, 4931), cf. A, No. 2, signifies (a) "to bring to an end, finish completely" (*sun*, "together," imparting a perfective significance to *teleō*), Matt. 7:28 (in some mss.); Luke 4:2, 13; Acts 21:27, RV, "completed"; (b) "to bring to fulfillment," Mark 13:4; Rom. 9:28;

(c) "to effect, make," Heb. 8:8. See FINISH, FULFILL, MAKE.¶

3. *plēroō* (πληρόω, 4137), (a) "to fill," (b) "to fulfill, complete, end," is translated "had ended" in Luke 7:1; "were ended" (passive) in Acts 19:21 See ACCOMPLISH.

Note: In John 13:2, the verb *ginomai*, there signifying "to be in progress," and used in the present participle, is translated "during supper" (RV). A less authentic reading, is *genomenou*, "being ended" (KJV).

C. Adjective.
eschatos (ἔσχατος, 2078), "last, utmost, extreme," is used as a noun (a) of time, rendered "end" in Heb. 1:2, RV, "at the "end" of these days," i.e., at the "end" of the period under the Law, for KJV, "in these last days"; so in 1 Pet. 1:20, "at the end of the times." In 2 Pet. 2:20, the plural, *ta eschata*, lit., "the last things," is rendered "the latter end," KJV, (RV, "the last state"); the same phrase is used in Matt. 12:45; Luke 11:26; (b) of place, Acts 13:47, KJV, "ends (of the earth)," RV, "uttermost part. See LAST, LOWEST, UTTERMOST.

Notes: (1) In Matt. 28:1, *opse*, "late (in the evening)," is rendered "in the end (of)," KJV, RV, "late (on)." (2) In 1 Pet. 1:13, *teleiōs*, "perfectly," RV, is rendered "to the end," in KJV. (3) The phrase *eis touto*, lit., "unto this," signifies "to this end," John 18:37, RV (twice; KJV, "for this cause," in the second clause); so Mark 1:38; Acts 26:16; Rom. 14:9; 2 Cor. 2:9; 1 Tim. 4:10 (KJV, "therefore"); 1 Pet. 4:6; 1 John 3:8 (KJV, "for this purpose"). (4) *Eis*, "unto," followed by the article and the infinitive mood of a verb, signifies "to the end that ... " marking the aim of an action, Acts 7:19; Rom. 1:11; 4:16, 18; Eph. 1:12; 1 Thess. 3:13; 2 Thess. 1:5; 2:2, 6; 1 Pet. 3:7. In Luke 18:1, *pros*, "to," has the same construction and meaning. (5) The conjunction *hina*, "in order that," is sometimes rendered "to the end that," Eph. 3:17; 2 Thess. 3:14; Titus 3:8. (6) In Matt. 24:31, the prepositions *apo*, "from," and *heōs*, "unto," are used with the plural of *akros*, "highest, extreme," signifying "from one end ... to the other," lit., "from extremities ... to extremities."

ENDEAVOR

1. *spoudazō* (σπουδάζω, 4704), "to make haste, to be zealous," and hence, "to be diligent," is rendered "endeavoring" in Eph. 4:3, KJV; RV, "giving diligence." In 2 Pet. 1:15, KJV, "endeavor," RV, "give diligence." Both have "endeavored" in 1 Thess. 2:17. See DILIGENCE.

2. *zēteō* (ζητέω, 2212), "to seek after," is translated "endeavor" in Acts 16:10, KJV, RV,

"sought." See ABOUT (to be), DESIRE, INQUIRE, SEEK.

ENDLESS

1. *akatalutos* (ἀκατάλυτος, 179) denotes indissoluble (from *a*, negative, *kata*, "down," *luō*, "to loose"), Heb. 7:16, "endless"; see the RV, marg., i.e., a life which makes its possessor the holder of His priestly office for evermore.¶

2. *aperantos* (ἀπέραντος, 562), from *a*, negative and *perainō*, "to complete, finish," signifies "interminable, endless"; it is said of genealogies, 1 Tim. 1:4.¶ In the Sept., Job 36:26.¶

ENDUE

enduō (ἐνδύω, 1746), in the middle voice, "to put on oneself, be clothed with," is used metaphorically of power, Luke 24:49, RV, "clothed." See CLOTHE.

Note: In Jas. 3:13 the adjective *epistēmōn*, "knowing, skilled," is translated "endued with knowledge," KJV, RV, "understanding."¶

ENDURE, ENDURING

A. Verbs.

1. *menō* (μένω, 3306), "to abide," is rendered "to endure" in the KJV of John 6:27 and 1 Pet. 1:25 (RV, "abideth"); Heb. 10:34, KJV, "enduring (substance)," RV, "abiding." See ABIDE.

2. *hupomenō* (ὑπομένω, 5278), a strengthened form of No. 1, denotes "to abide under, to bear up courageously" (under suffering), Matt. 10:22; 24:13; Mark 13:13; Rom. 12:12, translated "patient"; 1 Cor. 13:7; 2 Tim. 2:10, 12 (KJV, "suffer"); Heb. 10:32; 12:2–3, 7; Jas. 1:12; 5:11; 1 Pet. 2:20, "ye shall take it patiently." It has its other significance, "to tarry, wait for, await," in Luke 2:43; Acts 17:14 (in some mss., Rom. 8:24).¶ Cf. B. See ABIDE, PATIENT, SUFFER, TARRY. Cf. *makrothumeō*, "to be longsuffering" (see No. 7).

3. *pherō* (φέρω, 5342), "to bear," is translated "endured" in Rom. 9:22 and Heb. 12:20. See BEAR.

4. *hupopherō* (ὑποφέρω, 5297), a strengthened form of No. 3, "to bear or carry," by being under, is said metaphorically of "enduring" temptation, 1 Cor. 10:13, KJV, "bear"; persecutions, 2 Tim. 3:11; griefs, 1 Pet. 2:19. See BEAR.¶

5. *anechō* (ἀνέχω, 430), "to hold up" (*ana*, "up," *echō*, "to hold or have"), always in the middle voice in the NT, is rendered "endure" in 2 Thess. 1:4, of persecutions and tribulations; in 2 Tim. 4:3, of sound doctrine. See BEAR.

6. *kartereō* (καρτερέω, 2594), "to be steadfast, patient," is used in Heb. 11:27, "endured,"

of Moses in relation to Egypt.¶ In the Sept., Job 2:9; Isa. 42:14.¶

7. *makrothumeō* (μακροθυμέω, 3114), "to be long-tempered" (*makros*, "long," *thumos*, "mind"), is rendered "patiently endured" in Heb. 6:15, said of Abraham. See B, below. See BEAR, LONGSUFFERING, PATIENCE, SUFFER.

Note: In 2 Tim. 2:9, *kakopatheō*, "to suffer evil" (*kakos*, "evil," *paschō*, "to suffer"), is translated "endure hardness," KJV; RV, "suffer hardship"; so in 4:5, KJV, "endure afflictions"; elsewhere in Jas. 5:13.¶ In 2 Tim. 2:3 the most authentic mss. have *sunkakopatheō*, "to suffer hardship with," as in 1:8.¶ See HARDSHIP, SUFFER.

B. Noun.

hupomonē (ὑπομονή, 5281), "patience," lit., "a remaining under" (akin to A, No. 2), is translated "patient enduring" in 2 Cor. 1:6, RV, for KJV, "enduring." Cf. *makrothumia*, "longsuffering" (akin to A, No. 7). See PATIENCE.

ENEMY

echthros (ἐχθρός, 2190), an adjective, primarily denoting "hated" or "hateful" (akin to *echthos*, "hate"; perhaps associated with *ektos*, "outside"), hence, in the active sense, denotes "hating, hostile"; it is used as a noun signifying an "enemy," adversary, and is said (*a*) of the Devil, Matt. 13:39; Luke 10:19; (*b*) of death, 1 Cor. 15:26; (*c*) of the professing believer who would be a friend of the world, thus making himself an enemy of God, Jas. 4:4; (*d*) of men who are opposed to Christ, Matt. 13:25, 28; 22:44; Mark 12:36; Luke 19:27; 20:43; Acts 2:35; Rom. 11:28; Phil. 3:18; Heb. 1:13; 10:13; or to His servants, Rev. 11:5, 12; to the nation of Israel, Luke 1:71, 74; 19:43; (*e*) of one who is opposed to righteousness, Acts 13:10; (*f*) of Israel in its alienation from God, Rom. 11:28; (*g*) of the unregenerate in their attitude toward God, Rom. 5:10; Col. 1:21; (*h*) of believers in their former state, 2 Thess. 3:15; (*i*) of foes, Matt. 5:43–44; 10:36; Luke 6:27, 35; Rom. 12:20; 1 Cor. 15:25; of the apostle Paul because he told converts "the truth," Gal. 4:16. See FOE. Cf. *echthra*, "enmity".¶

ENGRAFTED

Note: This is the KJV rendering of *emphutos*, Jas. 1:21, an adjective derived from *emphuō*, "to implant"; the RV has "implanted."¶ The metaphor is that of a seed rooting itself in the heart; cf. Matt. 13:21; 15:13; 1 Cor. 3:6, and the kindred word *sumphutos*, Rom. 6:5, "planted together" (*sun*, "with").¶ The KJV "engrafted" would translate the word *emphuteuton* (from *emphuteuō*, "to graft"), which is not found in the NT; it uses *enkentrizō* in Rom. 11. Cf. *ekphuō*, "to cause to grow out, put forth" (leaves), Matt. 24:32; Mark 13:28.

ENGRAVE

entupoō (ἐντυπόω, 1795), "to imprint, engrave" (*en*, "in," *tupos*, "a mark, impression, form, type"), is used of the "engraving" of the Law on the two stones, or tablets, 2 Cor. 3:7.¶ In the Sept., Exod. 36:39 (some texts have *ektupoō*).¶ See also GRAVEN.

ENJOIN

1. *entellomai* (ἐντέλλομαι, 1781) is translated "hath enjoined" in the KJV of Heb. 9:20. See COMMAND (RV).

2. *epitassō* (ἐπιτάσσω, 2004), lit., "to set or arrange over, to charge, command," is rendered "enjoin" in Philem. 8. See COMMAND. Cf. *keleuō*, "to order."

ENJOY

A. Verb.

tunchanō (τυγχάνω, 5177), used transitively, denotes "to hit upon, meet with"; then, "to reach, get, obtain"; it is translated "enjoy" (i.e., obtain to our satisfaction) in Acts 24:2. See CHANCE, COMMON, *Note* (3), OBTAIN.

B. Noun.

apolausis (ἀπόλαυσις, 619), "enjoyment" (from *apolauō*, "to take hold of, enjoy a thing"), suggests the advantage or pleasure to be obtained from a thing (from a root, *lab*— seen in *lambanō*, "to obtain"); it is used with the preposition *eis*, in 1 Tim. 6:17, lit., "unto enjoyment," rendered "to enjoy"; with *echō*, "to have," in Heb. 11:25, lit., "to have pleasure (of sin)," translated "to enjoy the pleasures." ¶ See PLEASURE.

ENLARGE

1. *megalunō* (μεγαλύνω, 3170) denotes "to make great" (from *megas*, "great"), Matt. 23:5, "enlarge"; 2 Cor. 10:15, KJV, "enlarged," RV, "magnified"; elsewhere in the KJV it is rendered by the verb "to magnify," except in Luke 1:58, KJV, "had showed great (mercy)," RV, "had magnified (His mercy); see Luke 1:46; Acts 5:13; 10:46; 19:17; Phil. 1:20. See MAGNIFY.¶

2. *platunō* (πλατύνω, 4115), "to make broad," from *platus*, "broad," is translated "enlarged" in 2 Cor. 6:11, 13 (metaphorically), "make broad," Matt. 23:5 (literally). From the primary sense of freedom comes that of the joy that results from it. See BROAD.¶ Cf. *platos*, "breadth," and *plateia*, "a street."

ENLIGHTEN

phōtizō (φωτίζω, 5461), from *phōs*, "light," (*a*), used intransitively, signifies "to give light, shine," Rev. 22:5; (*b*), used transitively, "to enlighten, illumine," is rendered "enlighten" in Eph. 1:18, metaphorically of spiritual "enlightenment"; so John 1:9, i.e., "lighting every man" (by reason of His coming); Eph. 3:9, "to make (all men) see" (RV marg., "to bring to light"); Heb. 6:4, "were enlightened"; 10:32, RV, "enlightened," KJV, "illuminated." See ILLUMINATED, LIGHT. Cf. *phōtismos*, "light," and *phōteinos*, "full of light."

ENMITY

echthra (ἔχθρα, 2189), from the adjective *echthros* (see ENEMY) is rendered "enmity" in Luke 23:12; Rom. 8:7; Eph. 2:15–16; Jas. 4:4; "enmities," Gal. 5:20, RV, for KJV, "hatred." It is the opposite of *agapē*, "love."¶

ENOUGH

A. Adjectives.

1. *arketos* (ἀρκετός, 713), "sufficient," akin to *arkeō* (see B, No. 1), is rendered "enough" in Matt. 10:25; "sufficient" in Matt. 6:34; "suffice" in 1 Pet. 4:3, lit., "(is) sufficient." See SUFFICE, SUFFICIENT.¶

2. *hikanos* (ἱκανός, 2425), "sufficient, competent, fit" (akin to *hikanō* and *hikō*, "to reach, attain" and *hikanoō*, "to make sufficient"), is translated "enough" in Luke 22:38, of the Lord's reply to Peter concerning the swords. See ABLE.

Note: In Luke 15:17 the verb *perisseuō*, "to have abundance," is translated "have enough and to spare." In Acts 27:38 the verb *korennumi*, "to satisfy," is translated "had eaten enough."

B. Verbs.

1. *arkeō* (ἀρκέω, 714), "to ward off"; hence, "to aid, assist"; then, "to be strong enough," i.e., "to suffice, to be enough" (cf. A, No. 1), is translated "be enough" in Matt. 25:9. See CONTENT.

2. *apechō* (ἀπέχω, 568), lit., "to hold off from, to have off or out" (*apo*, "from," *echō*, "to have"), i.e., "to have in full, to have received," is used impersonally in Mark 14:41, "it is enough," in the Lord's words to His slumbering disciples in Gethsemane. It is difficult, however, to find examples of this meaning in Greek usage of the word, and *apechō* may here refer, in its commercial significance, to Judas (who is mentioned immediately afterwards), with the meaning "he hath received" (his payment); cf. the same use in Matt. 6:2, 5, 16 (see Deissmann,

Light from the Ancient East, pp. 110ff.). See
ABSTAIN, HAVE, RECEIVE.

For ENQUIRE see INQUIRE

ENRICH

ploutizō (πλουτίζω, 4148), "to make rich"
(from *ploutos*, "wealth, riches"), is used metaphorically, of spiritual "riches," in 1 Cor. 1:5,
"ye were enriched"; 2 Cor. 6:10, "making rich";
2 Cor. 9:11, "being enriched." See RICH.¶

ENROLL, ENROLLMENT

A. Verb.

apographō (ἀπογράφω, 583) primarily signifies "to write out, to copy"; then, "to enroll,
to inscribe," as in a register. It is used of a
census, Luke 2:1, RV, "be enrolled," for KJV, "be
taxed"; in the middle voice, vv. 3, 5, to enroll
oneself, KJV, "be taxed." Confirmation that this
census (not taxation) was taken in the dominions of the Roman Empire is given by the
historians Tacitus and Suetonius. Augustus himself drew up a sort of Roman Doomsday Book,
a rationarium, afterwards epitomized into a
breviarium, to include the allied kingdoms, appointing twenty commissioners to draw up the
lists. In Heb. 12:23 the members of the church
of the firstborn are said to be "enrolled," RV.¶
  Note: For RV, 1 Tim. 5:9, *katalegō*, see TAKE,
Note (18); for RV, 2 Tim. 2:4, *stratologeō*, see
SOLDIER, B, *Note* (2).

B. Noun.

apographē (ἀπογραφή, 582) primarily denotes "a written copy," or, as a law term, "a
deposition"; then, "a register, census, enrollment," Luke 2:2; Acts 5:37, RV, for KJV, "taxing." Luke's accuracy has been vindicated, as
against the supposed inconsistency that as Quirinius was governor of Syria in A.D. 6, ten years
after the birth of Christ, the census, as "the first"
(RV), could not have taken place. At the time
mentioned by Luke, Cilicia, of which Quirinius
was governor, was separated from Cyprus and
joined to Syria. His later direct governorship of
Syria itself accounts for the specific inclusion of,
and reference to, his earlier connection with that
province. Justin Martyr, a native of Palestine,
writing in the middle of the 2nd century, asserts
thrice that Quirinius was present in Syria at the
time mentioned by Luke (see Apol., 1:34, 46;
Trypho 78). Noticeable, too, are the care and
accuracy taken by Luke in his historical details,
1:3, RV.
  As to charges made against Luke's accuracy,
Moulton and Milligan say as follows:— "The
deduction so long made ... about the census
apparently survives the demonstration that the

blunder lay only in our lack of information: the
microbe is not yet completely expelled. Possibly
the salutary process may be completed by our
latest inscriptional evidence that Quirinius was
a legate in Syria for census purposes in 8–6
B.C."¶

ENSAMPLE

  1. *tupos* (τύπος, 5179) primarily denoted "a
blow" (from a root *tup*—, seen also in *tuptō*, "to
strike"), hence, (*a*) an impression, the mark of
a "blow," John 20:25; (*b*) the "impress" of a
seal, the stamp made by a die, a figure, image,
Acts 7:43; (*c*) a "form" or mold, Rom. 6:17
(see RV); (*d*) the sense or substance of a letter,
Acts 23:25; (*e*) "an ensample," pattern, Acts
7:44; Heb. 8:5, "pattern"; in an ethical sense,
1 Cor. 10:6; Phil. 3:17; 1 Thess. 1:7; 2 Thess.
3:9; 1 Tim. 4:12, RV, "ensample"; Titus 2:7, RV,
"ensample," for KJV, "pattern"; 1 Pet. 5:3; in a
doctrinal sense, a type, Rom. 5:14. See EXAM-
PLE, FASHION, FIGURE, FORM, MANNER, PATTERN,
PRINT.¶
  2. *hupotupōsis* (ὑποτύπωσις, 5296), "an
outline, sketch," akin to *hupotupoō*, "to delineate," is used metaphorically to denote a
"pattern," an "ensample," 1 Tim. 1:16, RV, "ensample," for KJV, "pattern"; 2 Tim. 1:13, RV,
"pattern," for KJV, "form." See FORM, PAT-
TERN.¶
  3. *hupodeigma* (ὑπόδειγμα, 5262), lit., "that
which is shown" (from *hupo*, "under," and *deiknumi*, "to show"), hence, (*a*) "a figure, copy,"
Heb. 8:5, RV, "copy," for KJV, "example"; 9:23;
(*b*) "an example," whether for imitation, John
13:15; Jas. 5:10, or for warning, Heb. 4:11;
2 Pet. 2:6, RV, "example." See EXAMPLE, PAT-
TERN.¶

ENSLAVED

  douloō (δουλόω, 1402), "to make a slave
of," is rendered "enslaved" (to much wine) in
Titus 2:3, RV, for KJV, "given to." See BONDAGE.

ENSNARE

  pagideuō (παγιδεύω, 3802), "to entrap, lay
snares for" (from *pagis*, "anything which fixes
or grips," hence, "a snare"), is used in Matt.
22:15, of the efforts of the Pharisees to "entrap"
the Lord in His speech, KJV, "entangle." See
ENTANGLE.¶

For ENSUE see PURSUE

ENTANGLE

  1. *pagideuō* : see ENSNARE.
  2. *emplekō* (ἐμπλέκω, 1707), "to weave in"
(*en*, "in," *plekō*, "to weave"), hence, metaphor-

ically, to be involved, entangled in, is used in the passive voice in 2 Tim. 2:4, "entangleth himself"; 2 Pet. 2:20, "are entangled."¶ In the Sept., Prov. 28:18.¶

3. *enechō* (ἐνέχω, 1758), "to hold in," is said (*a*) of being "entangled" in a yoke of bondage, such as Judaism, Gal. 5:1. Some mss. have the word in 2 Thess. 1:4, the most authentic have *anechō*, "to endure"; (*b*) with the meaning to set oneself against, be urgent against, said of the plotting of Herodias against John the Baptist, Mark 6:19, RV, "set herself against," KJV, "had a quarrel against"; of the effort of the scribes and Pharisees to provoke the Lord to say something which would provide them with a ground of accusation against Him, Luke 11:53, RV, "to press upon," marg., "to set themselves vehemently against," KJV, "to urge."¶

ENTER, ENTERING, ENTRANCE

A. Verbs.

1. *eiserchomai* (εἰσέρχομαι, 1525), "to come into" (*eis*, "in," *erchomai*, "to come"), is frequently rendered "entered" in the RV for KJV, "went into," e.g., Matt. 9:25; 21:12; or "go in," e.g., Matt. 7:13; Luke 8:51; "go," Luke 18:25; "was coming in," Acts 10:25. See COME, No. 2, GO (*Notes*).

2. *suneiserchomai* (συνεισέρχομαι, 4897), "to enter together," is used in John 6:22 (in the best mss.; see No. 6) and 18:15.¶

3. *pareiserchomai* (παρεισέρχομαι, 3922), (*a*) "to come in beside" (*para*, "beside," and No. 1), is rendered "entered" in Rom. 5:20, KJV for RV, "came in beside," the meaning being that the Law entered in addition to sin; (*b*) "to enter" secretly, by stealth, Gal. 2:4, "came in privily," to accomplish the purposes of the circumcision party. See COME, No. 8.¶ Cf. *pareisduō* (or —*dunō*), Jude 4, "crept in privily."¶

4. *eisporeuomai* (εἰσπορεύομαι, 1531), "to go into," found only in the Synoptists and Acts, is translated "to enter," in the RV of Mark 1:21; 6:56; 11:2; Luke 8:16; 11:33 (KJV, "come in"); 19:30 (KJV, "at your entering"); 22:10; in the following the RV has the verb "to go," for the KJV, "to enter," Matt. 15:17; Mark 5:40; 7:15, 18–19; in Acts 28:30, "went," KJV, "came"; in 9:28, RV, "going," KJV, "coming"; in the following both KJV and RV have the verb "to enter," Mark 4:19; Luke 18:24 (in the best mss.); Acts 3:2; 8:3. See GO, No. 5.¶

5. *anabainō* (ἀναβαίνω, 305), "to go up" (*ana*, "up," *bainō*, "to go"), is translated "entered" in 1 Cor. 2:9, metaphorically, of "coming" into the mind. In John 21:3, the best mss. have No. 6. See ARISE, No. 6.

6. *embainō* (ἐμβαίνω, 1684), "to go in" (*en*,

"in"), is used only in the Gospels, of "entering" a boat, Matt. 8:23; 9:1; 13:2; 14:22, 32; 15:39; Mark 4:1; 5:18; 6:45; 8:10, 13; Luke 5:3; 8:22, 37; John 6:17, (in some mss., in v. 22), 24, RV, "got into the boats," for KJV, "took shipping"; 21:3 (some mss. have No. 5 here); Acts 21:6 (in the best mss.); of stepping into water, John 5:4 (RV omits the verb). See COME, No. 21, GET, No. 5, GO, *Note* (2), *m*, STEP, TAKE, *Note* (3).¶

7. *epibainō* (ἐπιβαίνω, 1910), "to go upon" (*epi*, "upon"), is used of "going" on board ship, Acts 21:2; 27:2, KJV, "entering into," RV, "embarking in." See ABOARD, COME, No. 16, SIT, *Note*.

8. *eiseimi* (εἴσειμι, 1524), "to go into" (*eis*, "into," *eimi*, "to go"), Acts 3:3; 21:18, 26, KJV, "entered"; Heb. 9:6, RV, "go in," for KJV, "went into." See GO, No. 12.¶

Notes: (1) *Erchomai*, "to come," is never translated "to enter," in the RV; in the KJV, Mark 1:29; Acts 18:7. (2) In 2 John 7, the most authentic mss. have the verb *exerchomai*, "gone forth," RV, for KJV (No. 1), "entered." (3) In Luke 16:16, *biazō*, "to force, to enter in violently," is so rendered in the RV, for KJV, "presseth."

B. Noun.

eisodos (εἴσοδος, 1529), lit., "a way in" (*eis*, "in," *hodos*, "a way"), "an entrance," is used (*a*) of the "coming" of Christ into the midst of the Jewish nation, Acts 13:24, RV marg., "entering in"; (*b*) of "entrance" upon gospel work in a locality, 1 Thess. 1:9; 2:1; (*c*) of the present "access" of believers into God's presence, Heb. 10:19, lit., "for entrance into"; (*d*) of their "entrance" into Christ's eternal Kingdom, 2 Pet. 1:11. See COMING.¶

ENTERTAIN

xenizō (ξενίζω, 3579) signifies (*a*) "to receive as a guest" (*xenos*, "a guest") rendered "entertained" in Acts 28:7, RV, for KJV, "lodged"; in Heb. 13:2, "have entertained"; (*b*) "to be astonished by the strangeness of a thing," Acts 17:20; 1 Pet. 4:4, 12. See LODGE, STRANGE (think).

Note: In Heb. 13:2 (first part), *philoxenia*, lit., "love of strangers" (*phileō*, "to love," and *xenos*, "a stranger or guest"), is translated "to show love to," RV, for KJV, "entertain." See HOSPITALITY.

ENTICE, ENTICING

A. Verb.

deleazō (δελεάζω, 1185), primarily, "to lure by a bait" (from *delear*, "a bait"), is used metaphorically in Jas. 1:14, of the "enticement" of lust; in 2 Pet. 2:14, of seducers, RV, "enticing," for KJV, "beguiling"; in v. 18, RV, "entice (in)," for KJV, "allure (through)."¶

B. Adjective.

peithos (πειθός, 3981), "apt to persuade" (from *peithō*, "to persuade"), is used in 1 Cor. 2:4, KJV, "enticing," RV, "persuasive."¶

Note: In Col. 2:4, *pithanologia*, "persuasive speech" (from *pithanos*, "persuasive, plausible," akin to the above, and *logos*, "speech"), is rendered "enticing" in the KJV (RV, "persuasiveness of.") It signifies the employment of plausible arguments, in contrast to demonstration.¶ Cf. *eulogia*, "fair speech," Rom. 16:18, i.e., "nice style."¶

ENTIRE

holoklēros (ὁλόκληρος, 3648), "complete, sound in every part" (*holos*, "whole," *klēros*, "a lot," i.e., with all that has fallen by lot), is used ethically in 1 Thess. 5:23, indicating that every grace present in Christ should be manifested in the believer; so Jas. 1:4.¶ In the Sept. the word is used, e.g., of a "full" week, Lev. 23:15; of altar stones unhewn, Deut. 27:6 and Josh. 8:31; of a "full-grown" vine tree, useless for work, Ezek. 15:5; of the "sound" condition of a sheep, Zech. 11:16.

The corresponding noun *holoklēria* is used in Acts 3:16, "perfect soundness."¶ The synonymous word *teleios*, used also in Jas. 1:4, "perfect," indicates the development of every grace into maturity.

The Heb. *shalom*, "peace," is derived from a root meaning "wholeness." See, e.g., Isa. 42:19, marg., "made perfect," for text, "at peace"; cf. 26:3. Cf. also Col. 1:28 with 2 Pet. 3:14.

For **ENTREAT,** to request, see **INTREAT;** for **ENTREATY** see **INTREATY**

ENTREAT ("to deal with, to treat")

Note: The distinction between this and the preceding word is maintained in the RV, which confines the initial "e" to the sense of "dealing with," or uses the verb "to treat."

chraomai (χράομαι, 5531) denotes (*a*) "to use" (of things); (*b*) "to use well or ill, to treat, deal with" (of persons); "treated (kindly)," Acts 27:3, RV, KJV, "(courteously) entreated." The remaining ten instances come under (*a*). See USE.

Note: In Luke 20:11, *atimazō*, "to dishonor" (*a*, negative, *timē*, "honor"), is translated "entreated shamefully," KJV (RV, "handled shamefully"). For *kakoucheō*, Heb. 11:37, RV, and *sunkakoucheomai*, Heb. 11:25, RV, see SUFFER, Nos. 6 and 7.

ENVY, ENVYING

A. Noun.

phthonos (φθόνος, 5355), "envy," is the feeling of displeasure produced by witnessing or hearing of the advantage or prosperity of others; this evil sense always attaches to this word, Matt. 27:18; Mark 15:10; Rom. 1:29; Gal. 5:21; Phil. 1:15; 1 Tim. 6:4; Titus 3:3; 1 Pet. 2:1; so in Jas. 4:5, where the question is rhetorical and strongly remonstrative, signifying that the Spirit (or spirit) which God made to dwell in us was certainly not so bestowed that we should be guilty of "envy." ¶

Note: Zēlos, "zeal or jealousy," translated "envy" in the KJV, in Acts 13:45; Rom. 13:13; 1 Cor. 3:3; 2 Cor. 12:20; Jas. 3:14, 16, is to be distinguished from *phthonos*, and, apart from the meanings "zeal" and "indignation," is always translated "jealousy" in the RV. The distinction lies in this, that "envy" desires to deprive another of what he has, "jealousy" desires to have the same or the same sort of thing for itself. See FERVENT, INDIGNATION, JEALOUSY, ZEAL.

B. Verbs.

1. *phthoneō* (φθονέω, 5354), "to envy" (akin to A.), is used in Gal. 5:26.¶

2. *zēloō* (ζηλόω, 2206) denotes "to be zealous, moved with jealousy," Acts 7:9 and 17:5, RV, "moved with jealousy" (KJV, "moved with envy"); both have "envieth" in 1 Cor. 13:4. See the *Note* under A. See AFFECT, COVET, DESIRE, JEALOUS, ZEALOUS.

EPHPHATHA

Note: Ephphatha is an Aramaic word signifying "to open," used in the imperative mood, "be opened," Mark 7:34; while the application in this case was to the ears, the tongue was remedially affected.

EPILEPTIC

selēniazō (σεληφιάζω, 4583), lit., "to be moon struck" (from *selēnē*, "the moon"), is used in the passive voice with active significance, RV, "epileptic," for KJV, "lunatick," Matt. 4:24; 17:15; the corresponding English word is "lunatic." Epilepsy was supposed to be influenced by the moon.¶

EPISTLE

epistolē (ἐπιστολή, 1992), primarily "a message" (from *epistellō*, "to send to"), hence, "a letter, an epistle," is used in the singular, e.g., Acts 15:30; in the plural, e.g., Acts 9:2; 2 Cor.

10:10. "Epistle is a less common word for a letter. A letter affords a writer more freedom, both in subject and expression, than does a formal treatise. A letter is usually occasional, that is, it is written in consequence of some circumstance which requires to be dealt with promptly. The style of a letter depends largely on the occasion that calls it forth."* "A broad line is to be drawn between the letter and the epistle. The one is essentially a spontaneous product dominated throughout by the image of the reader, his sympathies and interests, instinct also with the writer's own soul: it is virtually one half of an imaginary dialogue, the suppressed responses of the other party shaping the course of what is actually written. . . . the other has a general aim, addressing all and sundry whom it may concern: it is like a public speech and looks towards publication" (J. V. Bartlet, in *Hastings' Bib. Dic.*).

In 2 Pet. 3:16 the apostle includes the Epistles of Paul as part of the God-breathed Scriptures.

EQUAL, EQUALITY
A. Adjective.
isos (ἴσος, 2470), "the same in size, number, quality," etc., is translated "equal" in John 5:18; Phil. 2:6; in the latter the word is in the neuter plural, lit., "equalities"; "in the RV the words are translated 'on an equality with God,' instead of 'equal with God,' as in the KJV. The change is of great importance to the right interpretation of the whole passage. The rendering 'equal with God,' is evidently derived from the Latin Version. . . . It was apparently due at first to the fact that the Latin language had no adequate mode of representing the exact form and meaning of the Greek. The neuter plural denotes the various modes or states in which it was possible for the nature of Deity to exist and manifest itself as Divine."†

Note: Cf. *isotimos*, "equally precious," 2 Pet. 1:1;¶ *isopsuchos*, "of equal soul, like-minded," Phil. 2:20;¶ also Eng. words beginning with the prefix *iso*—.

B. Nouns.
1. *isotēs* (ἰσότης, 2471), "equality" (akin to A.), is translated "equality" in 2 Cor. 8:14, twice; in Col. 4:1, with the article, "that which is . . . equal," (lit., "the equality," as marg.), i.e., equity, fairness, what is equitable.¶ In the Sept., Job 36:29; Zech. 4:7.¶

2. *sunēlikiōtēs* (συνηλικιώτης, 4915) denotes "one of the same age, an equal in age" (*sun*, "with," *hēlikia*, "an age"), "a contempo-

rary," Gal. 1:14, RV, "of mine own age," for KJV "mine equals," the reference being to the apostle's good standing among his fellow students in the rabbinical schools; cf. Acts 22:3.¶

For **ERE** see *Note* †, p. 1

ERR
1. *planaō* (πλανάω, 4105), in the active voice, signifies "to cause to wander, lead astray, deceive" (*planē*, "a wandering"; cf. Eng., "planet"); in the passive voice, "to be led astray, to err." It is translated "err," in Matt. 22:29; Mark 12:24, 27; Heb. 3:10; Jas. 1:16 (KJV, "do not err," RV, "be not deceived"); 5:19. See DE-CEIVE, SEDUCE, WANDER, WAY, *Note* (5).

2. *apoplanaō* (ἀποπλανάω, 635), "to cause to wander away from, to lead astray from" (*apo*, "from," and No. 1), is used metaphorically of leading into error, Mark 13:22, KJV, "seduce," RV, "lead astray"; 1 Tim. 6:10, in the passive voice, KJV, "have erred," RV, "have been led astray." See SEDUCE.¶

3. *astocheō* (ἀστοχέω, 795), "to miss the mark, fail" (*a*, negative, *stochos*, "a mark"), is used only in the Pastoral Epistles, 1 Tim. 1:6, "having swerved"; 6:21 and 2 Tim. 2:18, "have erred." See SWERVE.¶

ERROR
1. *planē* (πλάνη, 4106), akin to *planaō* (see ERR, No. 1), "a wandering, a forsaking of the right path, see Jas. 5:20, whether in doctrine, 2 Pet. 3:17; 1 John 4:6, or in morals, Rom. 1:27; 2 Pet. 2:18; Jude 11, though, in Scripture, doctrine and morals are never divided by any sharp line. See also Matt. 27:64, where it is equivalent to 'fraud.'"* "Errors" in doctrine are not infrequently the effect of relaxed morality, and vice versa.

In Eph. 4:14 the RV has "wiles of error," for KJV, "they lie in wait to deceive"; in 1 Thess. 2:3, RV, "error," for KJV, "deceit"; in 2 Thess. 2:11, RV, "a working of error," for KJV, "strong delusion." See DECEIT.¶ Cf. *planētēs*, "a wandering," Jude 13,¶ and the adjective *planos*, "leading astray, deceiving, a deceiver."

2. *agnoēma* (ἀγνόημα, 51), "a sin of ignorance" (cf. *agnoia*, "ignorance," and *agnoeō*, "to be ignorant"), is used in the plural in Heb. 9:7.¶

ESCAPE
A. Verbs.
1. *pheugō* (φεύγω, 5343), "to flee" (Lat., *fuga*, "flight," etc.; cf. Eng., "fugitive, subter-

---

* From *Notes on Thessalonians,* by Hogg and Vine, p. 5.
† Gifford, *The Incarnation,* p. 20.

† From *Notes on Thesslonians,* by Hogg and Vine, p. 53.

fuge"), is rendered "escape" in Matt. 23:33; Heb. 11:34. See FLEE.

2. *apopheugō* (ἀποφεύγω, 668), "to flee away from" (*apo*, "from," and No. 1), is used in 2 Pet. 1:4; 2:18, 20.¶

3. *diapheugō* (διαφεύγω, 1309), lit., "to flee through," is used of the "escaping" of prisoners from a ship, Acts 27:42. For the word in v. 44, see No. 5.¶

4. *ekpheugō* (ἐκφεύγω, 1628), "to flee out of a place" (*ek*, "out of," and No. 1), is said of the "escape" of prisoners, Acts 16:27; of Sceva's sons, "fleeing" from the demoniac, 19:16; of Paul's escape from Damascus, 2 Cor. 11:33; elsewhere with reference to the judgments of God, Luke 21:36; Rom. 2:3; Heb. 2:3; 12:25; 1 Thess. 5:3. See FLEE.¶

5. *diasōzō* (διασώζω, 1295), in the active voice, "to bring safely through a danger" (*dia*, "through," intensive, *sōzō*, "to save"), to make completely whole, to heal, Luke 7:3; to bring "safe," Acts 23:24; "to save," 27:43; in the passive voice, Matt. 14:36, "were made whole"; 1 Pet. 3:20. It is also used in the passive voice, signifying "to escape," said of shipwrecked mariners, Acts 27:44; 28:1, 4. See HEAL, SAFE, SAVE.¶

Note: Exerchomai, "to come or go out of a place," is rendered, "He escaped," in John 10:39, KJV, an unsuitable translation, both in meaning and in regard to the circumstances of the Lord's departure from His would-be captors. The RV "went forth" is both accurate and appropriate to the dignity of the Lord's actions.

B. Noun.

ekbasis (ἔκβασις, 1545), "a way out" (*ek*, "out," *bainō*, "to go"), denotes (*a*) "an escape," 1 Cor. 10:13, used with the definite article and translated "the way of escape," as afforded by God in case of temptation; (*b*) "an issue or result," Heb. 13:7. See END, ISSUE.¶ Cf. *ekbainō*, "to go out," Heb. 11:15 (some mss. have *exerchomai*).¶

ESCHEW

ekklinō (ἐκκλίνω, 1578), "to turn aside" (*ek*, "from," *klinō*, "to turn, bend"), is used metaphorically (*a*) of leaving the right path, Rom. 3:12, RV, "turned aside," for KJV, "gone out of the way"; (*b*) of turning away from division-makers, and errorists, 16:17, RV, "turn away from"; (*c*) of turning away from evil, 1 Pet. 3:11, RV, "turn away from," KJV, "eschew." See AVOID, TURN.¶ In the Sept. the verb is frequently used of declining or swerving from God's ways, e.g., Job 23:11; Ps. 44:18; 119:51, 157.

ESPECIALLY

malista (μάλιστα, 3122), "most, most of all, above all," is the superlative of *mala*, "very much"; translated "especially" in Acts 26:3; Gal. 6:10; 1 Tim. 5:17; 2 Tim. 4:13; Phil. 4:22, RV (for KJV, "chiefly"); "specially," Acts 25:26; 1 Tim. 4:10; 5:8; Titus 1:10; Philem. 16; in Acts 20:38, "most of all." See CHIEFLY, MOST.

ESPOUSED

1. *harmozō* (ἁρμόζω, 718), "to fit, join" (from *harmos*, "a joint, joining"; the root *ar*—, signifying "to fit," is in evidence in various languages; cf. *arthron*, "a joint," *arithmos*, "a number," etc.), is used in the middle voice, of marrying or giving in marriage; in 2 Cor. 11:2 it is rendered "espoused," metaphorically of the relationship established between Christ and the local church, through the apostle's instrumentality. The thought may be that of "fitting" or "joining" to one husband, the middle voice expressing the apostle's interest or desire in doing so.¶

2. *mnēsteuō* (μνηστεύω, 3423), "to woo and win, to espouse or promise in marriage," is used in the passive voice in Matt. 1:18; Luke 1:27; 2:5, all with reference to the Virgin Mary, RV, "betrothed," for KJV, "espoused," in each case. See BETROTH.¶

ESTABLISH

1. *stērizō* (στηρίζω, 4741), "to fix, make fast, to set" (from *stērix*, "a prop"), is used of "establishing" or "stablishing" (i.e., the confirmation) of persons; the apostle Peter was called by the Lord to "establish" his brethren, Luke 22:32, translated "strengthen"; Paul desired to visit Rome that the saints might be "established," Rom. 1:11; cf. Acts 8:23; so with Timothy at Thessalonica, 1 Thess. 3:2; the "confirmation" of the saints is the work of God, Rom. 16:25, "to stablish (you)"; 1 Thess. 3:13, "stablish (your hearts)"; 2 Thess. 2:17, "stablish them (in every good work and word)"; 1 Pet. 5:10, "stablish"; the means used to effect the "confirmation" is the ministry of the Word of God, 2 Pet. 1:12, "are established (in the truth which is with you)"; James exhorts Christians to "stablish" their hearts, Jas. 5:8; cf. Rev. 3:2, RV.

The character of this "confirmation" may be learned from its use in Luke 9:51, "steadfastly set"; 16:26, "fixed," and in the Sept. in Exod. 17:12, "stayed up" (also from its strengthened form *epistērizō*, "to confirm," in Acts 14:22; 15:32, 41; in some mss. "to strengthen," in 18:23; see CONFIRM ¶). Neither the laying on of hands nor the impartation of the Holy Spirit is mentioned in the NT in connection with either of these words, or with the synonymous verb *bebaioō* (see 1 Cor. 1:8; 2 Cor. 1:21, etc.). See FIX, SET, STRENGTHEN.¶

2. *stereoō* (στερεόω, 4732), "to make firm, or solid" (akin to *stereos*, "hard, firm, solid"; cf. Eng., "stereotype"), is used only in Acts, (*a*) physically, 3:7, "received strength"; 3:16, "hath made strong"; (*b*) metaphorically, of establishment in the faith, 16:5, RV, "strengthened," for KJV, "established."¶

3. *histēmi* (ἵστημι, 2476), "to cause to stand," is translated "establish" in Rom. 3:31; 10:3; Heb. 10:9. See ABIDE, APPOINT, STAND, etc.

4. *bebaioō* (βεβαιόω, 950), "to confirm," is rendered "stablish," 2 Cor. 1:21; "stablished," Col. 2:7; "be established," Heb. 13:9. See CONFIRM.

5. *nomotheteō* (νομοθετέω, 3549): see ENACT.

ESTATE, STATE

1. *euschēmōn* (εὐσχήμων, 2158), signifying "elegant, graceful, comely" (*eu*, "well," *schēma*, "figure, fashion"), is used (*a*) in a moral sense, seemly, becoming, 1 Cor. 7:35; (*b*) in a physical sense, comely, 1 Cor. 12:24; (*c*) with reference to social degree, influential, a meaning developed in later Greek, and rendered of "honorable estate" in the RV of Mark 15:43; Acts 13:50; 17:12 (for KJV, "honorable"). See COMELY, HONORABLE.¶

2. *tapeinōsis* (ταπείνωσις, 5014) denotes "abasement, humiliation, low estate" (from *tapeinos*, "lowly"), Luke 1:48, "low estate"; Acts 8:33, "humiliation"; Phil. 3:21, RV, "of humiliation," for KJV, "vile"; Jas. 1:10, "is made low," lit., "in his low estate." See HUMILIATION, LOW, VILE. ¶

3. *hupsos* (ὕψος, 5311), signifying "height," is rendered "(in his) high estate," Jas. 1:9, RV, for KJV, "in that he is exalted"; "on high," Luke 1:78; 24:49; Eph. 4:8; "height," Eph. 3:18; Rev. 21:16. See EXALT, HEIGHT, HIGH.¶

Notes: (1) In Acts 22:5, *presbuterion*, "presbytery, a body of elders," is translated "estate of the elders," lit., "the presbytery," i.e., the Sanhedrin. (2) In Col. 4:7 the plural of the definite article with the preposition *kata*, and the singular personal pronoun with *panta*, "all," is rendered "all my state," KJV, RV, "all my affairs"; in v. 8 the preposition *peri*, with the personal pronoun, lit., "the things concerning us," is translated "our estate," i.e., "how we fare"; so in Phil. 2:19–20, "your state," i.e., "your condition." (3) In Mark 6:21 *prōtos*, lit., "first," is rendered "chief estates," KJV, RV, "the chief

men," i.e., the men to whom belongs the dignity. (4) In Rom. 12:16 *tapeinos*, in the plural with the article, lit., "the lowly," is translated "men of low estate," KJV, RV, "things that are lowly." (5) In Jude 6 *archē*, "principality," RV, KJV has "first estate," (6) For "last state" see LAST.

ESTEEM

1. *hēgeomai* (ἡγέομαι, 2233) signifies "to lead"; then, "to lead before the mind, to suppose, consider, esteem"; translated "esteem" in Phil. 2:3, KJV, RV, "counting"; in 1 Thess. 5:13, "esteem"; in Heb. 11:26, KJV, "esteeming," RV, "accounting."

2. *krinō* (κρίνω, 2919) signifies "to separate, choose"; then, "to approve, esteem"; translated "esteemeth" in Rom. 14:5 (twice), said of days; here the word "alike" (KJV) is rightly omitted in the RV, the meaning being that every day is especially regarded as sacred. See DETERMINE.

3. *logizomai* (λογίζομαι, 3049), "to reckon," is translated "esteemeth" in Rom. 14:14 (RV, "accounteth"). See ACCOUNT.

Notes: (1) In 1 Cor. 6:4, KJV, *exoutheneō*, "to set at nought," is rendered "are least esteemed"; the meaning is that judges in the world's tribunals have no place (are not of account) in the church. See ACCOUNT. (2) In the KJV marg. of 1 Pet. 2:17, *timaō*, "to honor," is rendered "esteem." (3) For "highly esteemed," Luke 16:15, KJV, see EXALT, B.

ETERNAL

1. *aiōn* (αἰών, 165), "an age," is translated "eternal" in Eph. 3:11, lit., "(purpose) of the ages" (marg.), and 1 Tim. 1:17, lit. "(king) of the ages" (marg.). See AGE.

2. *aiōnios* (αἰώνιος, 166) "describes duration, either undefined but not endless, as in Rom. 16:25; 2 Tim. 1:9; Titus 1:2; or undefined because endless as in Rom. 16:26, and the other sixty-six places in the NT.

"The predominant meaning of *aiōnios*, that in which it is used everywhere in the NT, save the places noted above, may be seen in 2 Cor. 4:18, where it is set in contrast with *proskairos*, lit., 'for a season,' and in Philem. 15, where only in the NT it is used without a noun. Moreover it is used of persons and things which are in their nature endless, as, e.g., of God, Rom. 16:26; of His power, 1 Tim. 6:16, and of His glory, 1 Pet. 5:10; of the Holy Spirit, Heb. 9:14; of the redemption effected by Christ, Heb. 9:12; and of the consequent salvation of men, 5:9, as well as of His future rule, 2 Pet. 1:11, which is elsewhere declared to be without end, Luke 1:33; of the life received by those who believe in Christ, John 3:16, concerning whom He said, 'they shall never perish,' 10:28, and of the resurrection body, 2 Cor. 5:1, elsewhere said to be 'immortal,' 1 Cor. 15:53, in which that life will be finally realized, Matt. 25:46; Titus 1:2.

"*Aiōnios* is also used of the sin that 'hath never forgiveness,' Mark 3:29, and of the judgment of God, from which there is no appeal, Heb. 6:2, and of the fire, which is one of its instruments, Matt. 18:8; 25:41; Jude 7, and which is elsewhere said to be 'unquenchable,' Mark 9:43.

"The use of *aiōnios* here shows that the punishment referred to in 2 Thess. 1:9, is not temporary, but final, and, accordingly, the phraseology shows that its purpose is not remedial but retributive."*

3. *aïdios* (ἀΐδιος, 126); see EVERLASTING.

EUNUCH

A. Noun.

eunouchos (εὐνοῦχος, 2135) denotes (*a*) "an emasculated man, a eunuch," Matt. 19:12; (*b*) in the 3rd instance in that verse, "one naturally incapacitated for, or voluntarily abstaining from, wedlock"; (*c*) one such, in a position of high authority in a court, "a chamberlain," Acts 8:27–39.¶

B. Verb.

eunouchizō (εὐνουχίζω, 2134), "to make a eunuch" (from A), is used in Matt. 19:12, as under (*b*) in A; and in the passive voice, "were made eunuchs," probably an allusion by the Lord to the fact that there were eunuchs in the courts of the Herods, as would be well known to His hearers.¶

EVANGELIST

euangelistēs (εὐαγγελιστής, 2099), lit., "a messenger of good" (*eu*, "well," *angelos*, "a messenger"), denotes a "preacher of the gospel," Acts 21:8; Eph. 4:11, which makes clear the distinctiveness of the function in the churches; 2 Tim. 4:5.¶ Cf. *euangelizō*, "to proclaim glad tidings," and *euangelion*, "good news, gospel." Missionaries are "evangelists," as being essentially preachers of the gospel.

EVEN (Noun), EVENING, EVENTIDE

A. Nouns.

1. *hespera* (ἑσπέρα, 2073), properly, the feminine of the adjective *hesperos*, "of, or at, evening, western" (Lat., *vesper*, Eng., "ves-

pers"), is used as a noun in Luke 24:29; Acts 4:3, "eventide"; 28:23. Some mss. have the word in 20:15, "in the evening (we touched)," instead of *hetera*, "next (day)."

2. *opsia* (ὀψία, 3798**), the feminine of the adjective *opsios*, "late," used as a noun, denoting "evening," with *hora*, "understood" (see No. 1), is found seven times in Matthew, five in Mark, two in John, and in these places only in the NT (some mss. have it in Mark 11:11, see B). The word really signifies the "late evening," the latter of the two "evenings" as reckoned by the Jews, the first from 3 p.m. to sunset, the latter after sunset; this is the usual meaning. It is used, however, of both, e.g., Mark 1:32 (cf. *opsimos*, "latter," said of rain, Jas. 5:7).

B. Adverb.

opse (ὀψέ, 3796), "long after, late, late in the day, at evening" (in contrast to *prōi*, "early," e.g., Matt. 20:1), is used practically as a noun in Mark 11:11, lit., "the hour being at eventide"; 11:19; 13:35; in Matt. 28:1 it is rendered "late on," RV, for KJV, "in the end of." Here, however, the meaning seems to be "after," a sense in which the word was used by late Greek writers. See LATE.¶ In the Sept., Gen. 24:11; Exod. 30:8; Jer. 2:23; Isa. 5:11.¶

Note: In Luke 12:38 some mss. have the adjective *hesperinos*, "of the evening" (see A, No. 1), lit., "in the evening watch."

EVEN (Adjective)

Notes: (1) In Luke 19:44 (KJV, "shall lay thee even with the ground"), there is no word representing "even"; the verb *edaphizō* signifies "to beat level" (like a threshing floor); hence, "to dash to the ground." See DASH.¶

(2) In Heb. 12:13 the adjective *orthos*, "straight," is rendered "even" in the KJV, marg.

EVEN (Adverb, etc.), EVEN AS, EVEN SO

1. *kai* (καί, 2532), a conjunction, is usually a mere connective, meaning "and"; it frequently, however, has an ascensive or climactic use, signifying "even," the thing that is added being out of the ordinary, and producing a climax. The determination of this meaning depends on the context. Examples are Matt. 5:46–47; Mark 1:27; Luke 6:33 (RV); 10:17; John 12:42; Gal. 2:13, 17, where "also" should be "even"; Eph. 5:12. Examples where the RV corrects the KJV "and" or "also," by substituting "even," are Luke 7:49; Acts 17:28; Heb. 11:11; in 1 John 4:3 the RV rightly omits "even."

When followed by "if" or "though," *kai* often signifies "even," e.g., Matt. 26:35; John

* From *Notes on Thessalonians,* by Hogg and Vine, pp. 232, 233.

8:14. So sometimes when preceded by "if," e.g., 1 Cor. 7:11, where "but and if" should be "but even if."

The epexegetic or explanatory use of *kai* followed by a noun in apposition, and meaning "namely," or "even" is comparatively rare. Winer's cautionary word needs heeding, that "this meaning has been introduced into too many passages" (Gram. of the NT, p. 546.). Some think it has this sense in John 3:5, "water, even the Spirit," and Gal. 6:16, "even the Israel of God."

2. *de* (δέ, 1161), usually signifying "but," is sometimes used for emphasis, signifying "even," e.g., Rom. 3:22; 9:30, "even the righteousness"; Phil. 2:8 (RV, "yea"). This is to be distinguished from No. 1.

3. *eti* (ἔτι, 2089), an adverb, "as yet, still," is rendered "even" in Luke 1:15.

4. *hōs* (ὥς, 5613), "as," in comparative sentences, is sometimes translated "even as," Matt. 15:28; Mark 4:36; Eph. 5:33; 1 Pet. 3:6 (KJV only); Jude 7.

5. *houtōs* (οὕτως, 3778), or *houtō*, "so, thus," is frequently rendered "even so," e.g., Matt. 7:17; 12:45; 18:14; 23:28; "so" in 1 Cor. 11:12 and 1 Thess. 2:4, RV.

6. *kathōs* (καθώς, 2531), "according as" (*kata*, "according to," and No. 4), is frequently translated "even as," e.g., Mark 11:6; Luke 1:2; 1 Thess. 5:11.

7. *hōsper* (ὥσπερ, 5618), No. 4, strengthened by *per*, is translated "even as" in Matt. 20:28.

8. *kathaper* (καθάπερ, 2509), "just as, even as," is rendered "even as" in Rom. 4:6; 9:13; 10:15; 12:4 (RV); 2 Cor. 3:18; 1 Thess. 3:6, 12; 4:5; Heb. 4:2; "according as," Rom. 11:8; elsewhere simply "as."

9. *nai* (ναί, 3483), a particle of strong affirmation, "yea, verily, even so," is rendered "even so" in the KJV, "yea" in the RV, in Matt. 11:26; Luke 10:21; Rev. 16:7; both KJV and RV have it in Rev. 1:7; the most authentic mss. omit it in 22:20. See SURELY, TRUTH, VERILY, YEA, YES.

10. *homōs* (ὅμως, 3676), "yet, nevertheless," is translated "even" in 1 Cor. 14:7 (KJV, "and even"); elsewhere John 12:42, "nevertheless"; Gal. 3:15, "yet" (i.e., "nevertheless," an example of hyperbaton, by which a word is placed out of its true position).¶

Notes: (1) In Rom. 1:26, there is no word representing "even" in the original. The KJV seems to have put it for the particle *te*, which simply annexes the statement to the preceding and does not require translation. (2) In 1 Thess. 2:18 the KJV renders the particle *men* by "even"; if translated, it signifies "indeed." (3) In 1 Cor.

12:2, *hōs* (see No. 4, above), followed by the particle *an*, means "howsoever" (RV, for KJV, "even as"). (4) In Matt. 23:37, "even as" translates the phrase *hon tropon*, lit., "(in) what manner." (5) In 1 Tim. 3:11, *hōsautōs*, a strengthened form of No. 4, "likewise, in like manner," is rendered "even so," KJV (RV, "in like manner"). (6) *K'agō*, for *kai egō*, means either "even I" or "even so I" or "I also." In John 10:15, the RV has "and I" for the KJV, "even so . . . I"; in 17:18 and 20:21, KJV and RV, "even so I"; in the following, *kágō* is preceded by *hōs*, or *kathōs*, "even as I," 1 Cor. 7:8; 10:33; "even as I also," 11:1; "as I also," Rev. 2:27. (7) In Luke 12:7 the RV renders *kai* by "very" (for KJV, "even the very"). (8) In John 6:57 *kákeinos* (for *kai ekeinos*, "also he"), is translated "he also," RV, for KJV, "even he." (9) In Eph. 1:10 there is no word in the original for "even." The RV expresses the stress on the pronoun by "in Him, I say."

EVER, FOR EVER, EVERMORE

A. Adverbs.

1. *pantote* (πάντοτε, 3842), "at all times, always" (akin to *pas*, "all"), is translated "ever" in Luke 15:31; John 18:20; 1 Thess. 4:17; 5:15; 2 Tim. 3:7; Heb. 7:25; "evermore" in John 6:34; in 1 Thess. 5:16, RV, "alway," for KJV, "evermore." It there means "on all occasions," as, e.g., in 1 Thess. 1:2; 3:6; 5:15; 2 Thess. 1:3, 11; 2:13. See ALWAYS.

2. *aei* (ἀεί, 104), "ever," is used (*a*) of continuous time, signifying "unceasingly, perpetually," Acts 7:51; 2 Cor. 4:11; 6:10; Titus 1:12; Heb. 3:10; (*b*) of successive occurrences, signifying "on every occasion," 1 Pet. 3:15; 2 Pet. 1:12. Some texts have the word in Mark 15:8. See ALWAYS.¶

Note: The adjective *diēnekēs*, "unbroken, continuous," is used in a phrase with *eis*, "unto," and the article, signifying "perpetually, for ever," Heb. 7:3; 10:1, 12, 14.¶

B. Phrases.

The following phrases are formed in connection with *aiōn*, "an age": they are idiomatic expressions betokening undefined periods and are not to be translated literally: (*a*) *eis aiōna*, lit., "unto an age," Jude 13, "for ever"; (*b*) *eis ton aiōna*, lit., "unto the age," "for ever" (or, with a negative, "never"), Matt. 21:19; Mark 3:29; 11:14; Luke 1:55; John 4:14; 6:51, 58; 8:35 (twice), 51–52; 10:28; 11:26; 12:34; 13:8; 14:16; 1 Cor. 8:13; 2 Cor. 9:9; Heb. 5:6; 6:20; 7:17, 21, 24, 28; 1 Pet. 1:25; 1 John 2:17; 2 John 2; (*c*) *eis tous aiōnas*, lit., "unto the ages," "for ever," Matt. 6:13 (KJV only); Luke 1:33; Rom. 1:25; 9:5; 11:36; 16:27 (some mss.

have the next phrase here); 2 Cor. 11:31; Heb. 13:8; (*d*) *eis tous aiōnas tōn aiōnōn*, lit. "unto the ages of the ages," "for ever and ever," or "for evermore," Gal. 1:5; Phil. 4:20; 1 Tim. 1:17; 2 Tim. 4:18; Heb. 13:21; 1 Pet. 4:11; 5:11 [(*c*) in some mss.]; Rev. 1:6 [(*c*) in some mss.]; 1:18, "for evermore"; 4:9–10; 5:13; 7:12; 10:6; 11:15; 15:7; 19:3; 20:10; 22:5; (*e*) *eis aiōnas aiōnōn*, lit., "unto ages of ages," "for ever and ever," Rev. 14:11; (*f*) *eis ton aiōna tou aiōnos*, lit., "unto the age of the age," "for ever and ever," Heb. 1:8; (*g*) *tou aiōnos tōn aiōnōn*, lit., "of the age of the ages," "for ever and ever," Eph. 3:21; (*h*) *eis pantas tous aiōnas*, lit., "unto all the ages," Jude 25 ("for evermore," RV; "ever," KJV); (*i*) *eis hēmeran aiōnos*, lit., "unto a day of an age," "for ever," 2 Pet. 3:18.

EVERLASTING

1. *aiōnios* (αἰώνιος, 166): see ETERNAL.

2. *aidios* (ἀΐδιος, 126) denotes "everlasting" (from *aei*, "ever"), Rom. 1:20, RV, "everlasting," for KJV, "eternal"; Jude 6, KJV and RV "everlasting." *Aiōnios*, should always be translated "eternal" and *aidios*, "everlasting." "While *aiōnios* ... negatives the end either of a space of time or of unmeasured time, and is used chiefly where something future is spoken of, *aidios* excludes interruption and lays stress upon permanence and unchangeableness" (Cremer).¶

EVERY, EVERYONE (MAN), EVERYTHING

1. *pas* (πᾶς, 3956) signifies (1) with nouns without the article, (*a*) "every one" of the class denoted by the noun connected with *pas*, e.g., Matt. 3:10, "every tree"; Mark 9:49, "every sacrifice"; see also John 2:10; Acts 2:43; Rom. 2:9; Eph. 1:21; 3:15; 2 Thess. 2:4; 2 Tim. 3:16, RV; (*b*) "any and every, of every kind, all manner of," e.g., Matt. 4:23; "especially with nouns denoting virtues or vices, emotions, condition, indicating every mode in which a quality manifests itself; or any object to which the idea conveyed by the noun belongs" (Grimm-Thayer). This is often translated "all," e.g., Acts 27:20; Rom. 15:14; 2 Cor. 10:6; Eph. 4:19, 31; Col. 4:12, "all the will of God," i.e., everything God wills; (2) without a noun, "every one, everything, every man" (i.e., person), e.g., Luke 16:16; or with a negative, "not everyone," e.g., Mark 9:49; with a participle and the article, equivalent to a relative clause, everyone who, e.g., 1 Cor. 9:25; Gal. 3:10, 13; 1 John 2:29; 3:3–4,6, 10, 15, rendered "whosoever." So in the neuter, 1 John 2:16; 5:4, often rendered "whatsoever"; governed by the preposition *en*,

"in," without a noun following, it signifies "in every matter, or condition," Phil. 4:6; 1 Thess. 5:18; "in every way or particular," 2 Cor. 4:8, translated "on every side"; so 2 Cor. 7:5; "in everything," Eph. 5:24; Phil. 4:12, lit., "in everything and (perhaps "even") in all things." See THOROUGHLY, WHOLE.

2. *hapas* (ἅπας, 537), a strengthened form of No. 1, signifies "all, the whole, altogether"; it is translated "every one" in Acts 5:16, where it occurs in the plural. In Mark 8:25, the KJV, "every man" translates the text with the masculine plural; the best mss. have the neuter plural, RV, "all things." See ALL, WHOLE.

3. *hekastos* (ἕκαστος, 1538): see EACH, No. 1. It is used with *heis*, "one," in Acts 2:6, "every man," and in Eph. 4:16, "each several (part)," for KJV, "every (part)." In Rev. 22:2 the most authentic mss. omit the numeral in the phrase "every month." It is preceded by *kath hena* (*kata*, "according to," *hena*, "one"), a strengthened phrase, in Eph. 5:33, KJV, "everyone ... in particular," RV, "severally, each one." The same kind of phrase with *ana*, "each," before the numeral, is used in Rev. 21:21, RV, "each one of the several (gates)," for KJV, "every several (gate)." See EACH, PARTICULAR, SEVERAL.

Notes: (1) The preposition *kata*, "down," is sometimes found governing a noun, in the sense of "every," e.g., Luke 2:41, "every year"; 16:19, "every day"; Heb. 9:25, "every year" (RV, "year by year"); so 10:3. This construction sometimes signifies "in every ...," e.g., Acts 14:23, "in every church"; 15:21, "in every city"; so 20:23; Titus 1:5; Acts 22:19, "in every synagogue" (plural); Acts 8:3 "(into) every house." In Luke 8:1 the phrase means "throughout every city," as in the KJV; in v. 4 "of every city," RV. In Acts 5:42 the RV renders *kat' oikon* "at home," for KJV, "in every house"; in 2:46, for KJV, "from house to house" (marg., "at home"). In Acts 15:21 (last part) the adjective *pas*, "all," is placed between the preposition and the noun for the sake of emphasis. In Acts 26:11, *kata*, followed by the plural of *pas* and the article before the noun, is rendered "in all the synagogues," RV, for KJV, "in every synagogue." The presence of the article confirms the RV. See SEVERALLY.

(2) In Matt. 20:9–10, the preposition *ana*, "upward" (used distributively), governing the noun *dēnarion*, is translated "every man (a penny)." There is no word for "every man," and an appropriate rendering would be "a penny apiece"; cf. Luke 9:14, "fifty each," RV; 10:1, "two and two"; John 2:6, "two or three ... apiece"; Rev. 4:8, "each ... six wings."

(3) The pronoun *tis*, "anyone," is rendered

"any" in Acts 2:45, RV, for the incorrect KJV, "every." In Mark 15:24, the interrogative form is rendered "what each (should take)" (KJV, "every man"), lit., "who (should take) what."

EVERYWHERE, EVERY QUARTER, EVERY SIDE

1. *pantachē* (πανταχῆ, 3837v), "everywhere," is used in Acts 21:28.¶

2. *pantachou* (πανταχοῦ, 3837), a variation of No. 1, is translated "everywhere" in Mark 1:28, RV, of the report throughout Galilee concerning Christ; in Mark 16:20, of preaching; Luke 9:6, of healing; Acts 17:30, of a divine command for repentance; 28:22, of disparagement of Christians; 1 Cor. 4:17, of apostolic teaching; in Acts 24:3, it is rendered "in all places."¶ In the Sept., Isa. 42:22.¶ See PLACE.

3. *pantothen* (παντόθεν, 3840) or *pantachothen*, "from all sides," is translated "from every quarter," Mark 1:45; in Luke 19:43, "on every side"; in Heb. 9:4, "round about."¶

Notes: (1) In Phil. 4:12, the phrase *en panti*, KJV, "everywhere," is corrected to "in everything," in the RV; in 2 Cor. 4:8, "on every side."

(2) In 1 Tim. 2:8, *en panti topō*, "in every place," RV, is translated "everywhere" in the KJV

EVERY WHIT

holos (ὅλος, 3650), "all, whole, complete," is rendered "every whit" in John 7:23; 13:10. See ALL.

For EVIDENCE (Heb. 11:1) see REPROOF, A

EVIDENT, EVIDENTLY

A. Adjectives.

1. *dēlos* (δῆλος, 1212), properly signifying "visible, clear to the mind, evident," is translated "evident" in Gal. 3:11 and 1 Cor. 15:27, RV (KJV, "manifest"); "bewrayeth," Matt. 26:73; "certain," 1 Tim. 6:7, KJV. Cf. *dēloō*, "to declare, signify." See BEWRAY, CERTAIN, MANIFEST.¶

2. *katadēlos* (κατάδηλος, 2612), a strengthened form of No. 1, "quite manifest, evident," is used in Heb. 7:15 (KJV, "more evident").¶ For the preceding verse see No. 3.

3. *prodēlos* (πρόδηλος, 4271), "manifest beforehand" (*pro*, "before," and No. 1), is used in Heb. 7:14 in the sense of "clearly evident." So in 1 Tim. 5:24–25, RV, "evident," for KJV, "open beforehand," and "manifest beforehand." The *pro* is somewhat intensive.¶

Note: Phaneros, "visible, manifest" (akin to *phainomai*, "to appear"), is synonymous with

the above, but is not translated "evident" in the NT. For "evident token" see TOKEN.

B. Adverb.

phanerōs (φανερῶς, 5320), manifestly (see note above), is rendered "openly" in Mark 1:45; "publicly" in John 7:10, RV (opposite to "in secret"); in Acts 10:3, RV, "openly," for KJV, "evidently." See OPENLY, PUBLICLY.¶

Note: For the KJV,"evidently," in Gal. 3:1, see OPENLY.

EVIL, EVIL-DOER

A. Adjectives.

1. *kakos* (κακός, 2556) stands for "whatever is evil in character, base," in distinction (wherever the distinction is observable) from *ponēros* (see No. 2), which indicates "what is evil in influence and effect, malignant." *Kakos* is the wider term and often covers the meaning of *ponēros*. *Kakos* is antithetic to *kalos*, "fair, advisable, good in character," and to *agathos*, "beneficial, useful, good in act"; hence it denotes what is useless, incapable, bad; *ponēros* is essentially antithetic to *chrēstos*, "kind, gracious, serviceable"; hence it denotes what is destructive, injurious, evil. As evidence that *ponēros* and *kakos* have much in common, though still not interchangeable, each is used of thoughts, cf. Matt. 15:19 with Mark 7:21; of speech, Matt. 5:11 with 1 Pet. 3:10; of actions, 2 Tim. 4:18 with 1 Thess. 5:15; of man, Matt. 18:32 with 24:48.

The use of *kakos* may be broadly divided as follows: (*a*) of what is morally or ethically "evil," whether of persons, e.g., Matt. 21:41; 24:48; Phil. 3:2; Rev. 2:2, or qualities, emotions, passions, deeds, e.g., Mark 7:21; John 18:23, 30; Rom. 1:30; 3:8; 7:19, 21; 13:4; 14:20; 16:19; 1 Cor. 13:5; 2 Cor. 13:7; 1 Thess. 5:15; 1 Tim. 6:10; 2 Tim. 4:14; 1 Pet. 3:9, 12; (*b*) of what is injurious, destructive, baneful, pernicious, e.g., Luke 16:25; Acts 16:28; 28:5; Titus 1:12; Jas. 3:8; Rev. 16:2, where *kakos* and *ponēros* come in that order, "noisome and grievous." See B, No. 3. For compounds of *kakos*, see below.

2. *ponēros* (πονηρός, 4190), akin to *ponos*, "labor, toil," denotes "evil that causes labor, pain, sorrow, malignant evil" (see No. 1); it is used (*a*) with the meaning bad, worthless, in the physical sense, Matt. 7:17–18; in the moral or ethical sense, "evil," wicked; of persons, e.g., Matt. 7:11; Luke 6:45; Acts 17:5; 2 Thess. 3:2; 2 Tim. 3:13; of "evil" spirits, e.g., Matt. 12:45; Luke 7:21; Acts 19:12–13, 15–16; of a generation, Matt. 12:39, 45; 16:4; Luke 11:29; of things, e.g., Matt. 5:11; 6:23; 20:15; Mark 7:22; Luke 11:34; John 3:19; 7:7; Acts 18:14; Gal.

1:4; Col. 1:21; 1 Tim. 6:4; 2 Tim. 4:18; Heb. 3:12; 10:22; Jas. 2:4; 4:16; 1 John 3:12; 2 John 11; 3 John 10; (b) with the meaning toilsome, painful, Eph. 5:16; 6:13; Rev. 16:2. Cf. *ponēria*, "iniquity, wickedness." For its use as a noun see B, No. 2.

3. *phaulos* (φαῦλος, 5337) primarily denotes "slight, trivial, blown about by every wind"; then, "mean, common, bad," in the sense of being worthless, paltry or contemptible, belonging to a low order of things; in John 5:29, those who have practiced "evil" things, RV, "ill" (*phaula*), are set in contrast to those who have done good things (*agatha*); the same contrast is presented in Rom. 9:11 and 2 Cor. 5:10, in each of which the most authentic mss. have *phaulos* for *kakos;* he who practices "evil" things (RV, "ill") hates the light, John 3:20; jealousy and strife are accompanied by "every vile deed," Jas. 3:16. It is used as a noun in Titus 2:8 (see B, No. 4). See BAD, ILL, VILE.¶

B. Nouns.

1. *kakia* (κακία, 2549), primarily, "badness" in quality (akin to A, No. 1), denotes (a) "wickedness, depravity, malignity," e.g., Acts 8:22, "wickedness"; Rom. 1:29, "maliciousness"; in Jas. 1:21, KJV, "naughtiness"; (b) "the evil of trouble, affliction," Matt. 6:34, only, and here alone translated "evil." See MALICE, MALICIOUSNESS, NAUGHTINESS, WICKEDNESS.

2. *ponēros* (πονηρός, 4190), the adjective (A, No. 2), is used as a noun, (a) of Satan as the "evil" one, Matt. 5:37; 6:13; 13:19, 38; Luke 11:4 (in some texts); John 17:15; Eph. 6:16; 2 Thess. 3:3; 1 John 2:13–14; 3:12; 5:18–19; (b) of human beings, Matt. 5:45; (probably v. 39); 13:49; 22:10; Luke 6:35; 1 Cor. 5:13; (c) neuter, "evil (things)," Matt. 9:4; 12:35; Mark 7:23; Luke 3:19; "that which is evil," Luke 6:45; Rom. 12:9; Acts 28:21, "harm."

3. *kakon* (κακόν, 2556), the neuter of A, No. 1, is used with the article, as a noun, e.g., Acts 23:9; Rom. 7:21; Heb. 5:14; in the plural, "evil things," e.g., 1 Cor. 10:6; 1 Tim. 6:10, "all kinds of evil," RV.

4. *phaulon* (φαῦλοθ, 5337), the neuter of A, No. 3, is used as a noun in Titus 2:8.

5. *kakopoios* (κακοποιός, 2555), properly th) masculine gender of the adjective, denotes an "evil-doer" (*kakon*, "evil," *poieō*, "to do"), 1 Pet. 2:12, 14; 4:15; in some mss. in 3:16 and John 18:30 (so the KJV).¶ For a synonymous word see *Note* (1). Cf. the verb below. In the Sept., Prov. 12:4; 24:19. See MALEFACTOR.¶

Notes: (1) *Kakourgos*, "an evil-worker" (*kakon*, "evil," *ergon*, "a work"), is translated "evil-doer" in 2 Tim. 2:9, KJV (RV, "malefactor"). Cf. Luke 23:32–33, 39.¶

(2) *Adikēma*, "an injustice" (a, negative, *dikaios*, "just"), is translated "evil-doing," in Acts 24:20, KJV, RV, "wrong-doing." See INIQUITY, WRONG.

C. Verbs.

1. *kakoō* (κακόω, 2559), "to ill-treat" (akin to A, No. 1), is rendered "to entreat evil" in Acts 7:6, 19; "made (them) evil affected," 14:2. See AFFECT, AFFLICT, HARM, HURT, VEX.

2. *kakopoieō* (κακοποιέω, 2554) signifies "to do evil" (cf. B, No. 5), Mark 3:4 (RV, "to do harm"); so, Luke 6:9; in 3 John 11, "doeth evil"; in 1 Pet. 3:17, "evil doing." See HARM.¶

Note: Cf. *kakologeō*, "to speak evil" (see CURSE, SPEAK); *kakopatheō*, "to endure evil" (see ENDURE, SUFFER); *kakopatheia*, "suffering affliction" (see SUFFER); *kakoucheō*, "to suffer adversity" (see SUFFER).

D. Adverb.

kakōs (κακῶς, 2560), "badly, evilly," akin to A, No. 1, is used in the physical sense, "to be sick," e.g., Matt. 4:24; Mark 1:32, 34; Luke 5:31 (see DISEASE). In Matt. 21:41 this adverb is used with the adjective, "He will miserably destroy those miserable men," more lit., "He will evilly destroy those men (evil as they are)," with stress on the adjective; (b) in the moral sense, "to speak evilly," John 18:23; Acts 23:5; "to ask evilly," Jas. 4:3. See AMISS, GRIEVOUSLY, SICK, SORE.

EVIL SPEAKING

1. *blasphēmia* (βλασφημία, 988) is translated "evil speaking" in Eph. 4:31, KJV (RV, "railing"). See BLASPHEMY.

2. *katalalia* (καταλαλία, 2636), "evil speaking," 1 Pet. 2:1; see BACKBITING.

EXACT (Verb)

1. *prassō* (πράσσω, 4238), "to do, to practice," also has the meaning of "transacting," or "managing in the matter of payment, to exact, to get money from a person," Luke 3:13 (RV, "extort"). Cf. the English idiom "to do a person in." This verb is rendered "required," in 19:23.

2. *sukophanteō* (συκοφαντέω, 4811), "to accuse falsely," Luke 3:14, has its other meaning, "to exact wrongfully," in 19:8. See ACCUSE.¶

EXACT, EXACTLY

akribesteron (ἀκριβέστερον, 197), the comparative degree of *akribōs*, "accurately, carefully," is used in Acts 18:26, KJV, "more perfectly," RV, "more carefully"; 23:15, KJV, "more perfectly," RV, "more exactly"; so v. 20; 24:22, KJV, "more perfect," RV, "more exact" (lit., "knowing more exactly"). See CAREFULLY, PERFECTLY. ¶

Cf. *akribeia*, "precision, exactness," Acts 22:3,¶ and *akriboō*, "to learn carefully, to enquire with exactness," Matt. 2:7, 16.¶

EXALT, EXALTED

A. Verbs.

1. *hupsoō* (ὑψόω, 5312), "to lift up" (akin to *hupsos*, "height"), is used (*a*) literally of the "lifting" up of Christ in His crucifixion, John 3:14; 8:28; 12:32, 34; illustratively, of the serpent of brass, John 3:14; (*b*) figuratively, of spiritual privileges bestowed on a city, Matt. 11:23; Luke 10:15; of "raising" to dignity and happiness, Luke 1:52; Acts 13:17; of haughty self-exaltation, and, contrastingly, of being "raised" to honor, as a result of self-humbling, Matt. 23:12; Luke 14:11; 18:14; of spiritual "uplifting" and revival, Jas. 4:10; 1 Pet. 5:6; of bringing into the blessings of salvation through the gospel, 2 Cor. 11:7; (*c*) with a combination of the literal and metaphorical, of the "exaltation" of Christ by God the Father, Acts 2:33; 5:31. See LIFT.¶

2. *huperupsoō* (ὑπερυψόω, 5251), "to exalt highly" (*huper*, "over," and No. 1), is used of Christ, as in No. 1, (*c*), in Phil. 2:9.¶

3. *epairō* (ἐπαίρω, 1869), "to lift up" (*epi*, "up," *airō*, "to raise"), is said (*a*) literally, of a sail, Acts 27:40; hands, Luke 24:50; 1 Tim. 2:8; heads, Luke 21:28; eyes, Matt. 17:8, etc.; (*b*) metaphorically, of "exalting" oneself, being "lifted up" with pride, 2 Cor. 10:5; 11:20. See LIFT.

4. *huperairō* (ὑπεραίρω, 5229), "to raise over" (*huper*, "above," and *airō*, see No. 3), is used in the middle voice, of "exalting" oneself exceedingly, 2 Cor. 12:7; 2 Thess. 2:4.¶

B. Adjective.

hupsēlos (ὑψηλός, 5308), "high, lofty," is used metaphorically in Luke 16:15, as a noun with the article, RV, "that which is exalted," KJV, "that which is highly esteemed." See ESTEEM, HIGH.

Note: For Jas. 1:9, RV, "in his high estate," see ESTATE, No. 3.

EXAMINATION, EXAMINE

A. Noun.

anakrisis (ἀνάκρισις, 351), from *ana*, "up or through," and *krinō*, "to distinguish," was a legal term among the Greeks, denoting the preliminary investigation for gathering evidence for the information of the judges, Acts 25:26.¶

B. Verbs.

1. *anakrinō* (ἀνακρίνω, 350), "to examine, investigate," is used (*a*) of searching or enquiry, Acts 17:11; 1 Cor. 9:3; 10:25, 27; (*b*) of reaching a result of the enquiry, judging, 1 Cor. 2:14–

15; 4:3–4; 14:24; (*c*) forensically, of examining by torture, Luke 23:14; Acts 4:9; 12:19; 24:8; 28:18. See ASK, DISCERN, JUDGE, SEARCH.¶

2. *anetazō* (ἀνετάζω, 426), "to examine judicially" (*ana*, "up," *etazō*, "to test"), is used in Acts 22:24, 29.¶ Cf. the synonymous verb *exetazō*, "to search" or "enquire carefully," Matt. 2:8; 10:11; John 21:12.¶

3. *dokimazō* (δοκιμάζω, 1381), "to prove, test, approve," is rendered "examine" in 1 Cor. 11:28, KJV (RV, "prove"). See APPROVE.

4. *peirazō* (πειράζω, 3985), "to tempt, try," is rendered "examine" in 2 Cor. 13:5, KJV (RV, "try"). See GO, PROVE, TEMPT, TRY.

EXAMPLE

A. Nouns.

1. *deigma* (δεῖγμα, 1164), primarily "a thing shown, a specimen" (akin to *deiknumi*, "to show"), denotes an "example" given as a warning, Jude 7.¶

Note: The corresponding word in 2 Pet. 2:6 is No. 2.

2. *hupodeigma* (ὑπόδειγμα, 5262): see ENSAMPLE, No. 3.

3. *tupos* (τύπος, 5179): see ENSAMPLE, No. 1.

4. *hupogrammos* (ὑπογραμμός, 5261), lit., "an under-writing" (from *hupographō*, "to write under, to trace letters" for copying by scholars); hence, "a writing-copy, an example," 1 Pet. 2:21, said of what Christ left for believers, by His sufferings (not expiatory, but exemplary), that they might "follow His steps."

B. Verbs.

1. *deigmatizō* (δειγματίζω, 1165), "to make a show of, to expose" (akin to A, No. 1), is translated "to make a public example," in Matt. 1:19 (some mss. have the strengthened form *paradeigmatizō* here; "put . . . to an open shame," Heb. 6:6,¶); in Col. 2:15, "made a show of."¶

2. *hupodeiknumi* (ὑποδείκνυμι, 5263), primarily, "to show secretly" (*hupo*, "under," *deiknumi*, "to show"), "to show by tracing out" (akin to A, No. 2); hence, "to teach, to show by example," Acts 20:35, RV, "I gave you an example," for KJV, "I showed you." Elsewhere, "to warn," Matt. 3:7; Luke 3:7; 12:5, RV, for KJV, "forewarn"; "to show," Luke 6:47; Acts 9:16. See FOREWARN, SHOW, WARN.¶

EXCEED, EXCEEDING, EXCEEDINGLY

A. Verbs.

1. *huperballō* (ὑπερβάλλω, 5235), "to throw over or beyond" (*huper*, "over," *ballō*,

"to throw"), is translated "exceeding" in 2 Cor. 9:14; Eph. 1:19; 2:7; "excelleth" (RV, "surpasseth") in 2 Cor. 3:10; "passeth" in Eph. 3:19 ("surpasseth" might be the meaning here). See EXCEL, SURPASS.¶ Cf. *huperbolē*, under EXCEL, B, No. 1.

2. *perisseuō* (περισσεύω, 4052), "to be over and above, over a certain number or measure, to abound, exceed," is translated "exceed" in Matt. 5:20; 2 Cor. 3:9. See ABUNDANCE, B, No. 1.

B. Adverbs and Adverbial Phrases.

1. *lian* (λίαν, 3029), "very, exceedingly," is translated "exceeding" in Matt. 2:16 (for v. 10, see No. 2); 4:8; 8:28; Mark 9:3; Luke 23:8. See GREATLY (GREAT), SORE, VERY.

2. *sphodra* (σφόδρα, 4970), properly the neuter plural of *sphodros*, "excessive, violent" (from a root indicating restlessness), signifies "very, very much, exceedingly," Matt. 2:10; 17:6, "sore"; 17:23; 18:31, RV, "exceeding," for KJV, "very"; 19:25; 26:22; 27:54, RV, "exceedingly" for KJV, "greatly"; Mark 16:4, "very"; Luke 18:23 (ditto); Acts 6:7, RV, "exceedingly," for KJV, "greatly"; Rev. 16:21. See GREATLY, SORE, VERY.¶

3. *sphodrōs* (σφοδρῶς, 4971), "exceedingly" (see No. 2), is used in Acts 27:18.¶

4. *perissōs* (περισσῶς, 4057) is used in Matt. 27:23, RV, "exceedingly," for KJV, "the more"; Mark 10:26, RV, "exceedingly," for KJV, "out of measure"; in Acts 26:11, "exceedingly." In Mark 15:14, the most authentic mss. have this word (RV, "exceedingly") for No. 5 (KJV, "the more exceedingly"). See MORE.¶

5. *perissoterōs* (περισσοτέρως, 4056), the comparative degree of No. 4, "abundantly, exceedingly" (akin to A, No. 2), Gal. 1:14, "more exceedingly"; 1 Thess. 2:17, RV, "the more exceedingly," for KJV, "the more abundantly; see ABUNDANCE, D, No. 2.

6. *huperekperissou* (ὑπερεκπερισσοῦ, 5528 and 1537 and 4053) denotes "superabundantly" (*huper*, "over," *ek*, "from," *perissos*, "abundant"); in 1 Thess. 3:10, "exceedingly"; Eph. 3:20, "exceeding abundantly."¶ Another form, *huperekperissōs* (*huper*, "and" *ek* and No. 4), is used in 1 Thess. 5:13 (in the best mss.), "exceeding highly."¶ Cf. the verb *huperperisseuō*, "to abound more exceedingly," Rom. 5:21; in 2 Cor. 7:4, "I overflow (with joy)," RV, for KJV, "I am exceeding (joyful). See ABUNDANT, D, No. 2.

Notes: (1) In Acts 7:20, the phrase "exceeding fair" (*asteios*) is, lit., "fair to God" (see marg.). (2) In Matt. 26:7, *barutimos* (*barus*, "weighty," *timē* "value"), is rendered "exceeding precious," RV, for KJV, "very precious." (3) In Mark 4:41,

"they feared exceedingly" is, lit., "they feared a great fear." See FEAR. (4) For other combinations of the adverb, see GLAD, GREAT, JOYFUL, SORROWFUL, SORRY.

EXCEL, EXCELLENCY, EXCELLENT

A. Verbs.

1. *huperballō* (ὑπερβάλλω, 5235), lit., "to throw over": see EXCEED, No. 1.

2. *perisseuō* (περισσεύω, 4052), "to be over and above," is rendered "abound in 1 Cor. 14:12, RV, for KJV, "excel." See ABUNDANCE, B, No. 1, and EXCEED, A, No. 2.

3. *huperechō* (ὑπερέχω, 5242), lit., "to have over" (*huper*, "over," *echō*, "to have"), is translated "excellency" in Phil. 3:8, "the surpassingness" (Moule); the phrase could be translated "the surpassing thing, which consists in the knowledge of Christ Jesus," and this is the probable meaning. This verb is used three times in Philippians, here and in 2:3; 4:7. See also Rom. 13:1; 1 Pet. 2:13. See BETTER, No. 4.¶

4. *diapherō* (διαφέρω, 1308), "to differ," is used in the neuter plural of the present participle with the article, in Phil. 1:10, "the things that are excellent" (marg., "the things that differ"), lit., "the excellent things." See DIFFER.

B. Nouns.

1. *huperbolē* (ὑπερβολή, 5236), lit., "a throwing beyond," hence, "a surpassing, an excellence," is translated "excellency" in 2 Cor. 4:7, KJV; RV, "exceeding greatness." It always betokens preeminence. It is used with *kata*, "according to," in the phrase *kath' huperbolēn*, signifying "beyond measure, exceedingly," Rom. 7:13, "exceeding sinful"; in 2 Cor. 1:8, RV, "exceedingly," for KJV, "out of measure"; in Gal. 1:13, "beyond measure"; in 1 Cor. 12:31, "more excellent." In 2 Cor. 4:17, there is an expanded phrase *kath' huperbolēn eis huperbolēn*, lit., "according to a surpassing unto a surpassing," RV, "more and more exceedingly," which corrects the KJV, "a far more exceeding"; the phrase refers to "worketh," showing the surpassing degree of its operation, and not to the noun "weight" (nor does it qualify, "eternal"). In 2 Cor. 12:7, the RV has "exceeding greatness," the KJV, "abundance." See ABUNDANCE.¶

2. *huperochē* (ὑπεροχή, 5247), akin to A, No. 3, strictly speaking, "the act of overhanging" (*huper*, and *echō*, "to hold") or "the thing which overhangs," hence, "superiority, preeminence," is translated "excellency (of speech)" in 1 Cor. 2:1; elsewhere, in 1 Tim. 2:2, RV, "high

place," for KJV, "authority." See AUTHORITY, PLACE.¶

Note: In 1 Pet. 2:9 RV renders *aretē* (virtue) "excellencies."

C. Adjectives.

1. *megaloprepēs* (μεγαλοπρεπής, 3169) signifies "magnificent, majestic, that which is becoming to a great man" (from *megas*, "great," and *prepō*, "to be fitting or becoming"), in 2 Pet. 1:17, "excellent."¶

2. *diaphorōteros* (διαφορώτερος, 1313*), comparative degree of *diaphoros*, "excellent," akin to A, No. 4, is used twice, in Heb. 1:4, "more excellent (name)," and 8:6, "more excellent (ministry)."¶ For the positive degree see Rom. 12:6; Heb. 9:10. See under DIFFER.¶

3. *pleiōn* (πλείων, 4119), "more, greater," the comparative degree of *polus*, "much," is translated "more excellent" in Heb. 11:4, of Abel's sacrifice; *pleiōn* is used sometimes of that which is superior by reason of inward worth, cf. 3:3, "more (honor)"; in Matt. 6:25, of the life in comparison with meat.

4. *kratistos* (κράτιστος, 2903), "mightiest, noblest, best," the superlative degree of *kratus*, "strong" (cf. *kratos*, "strength"), is used as a title of honor and respect, "most excellent," Luke 1:3 (Theophilus was quite possibly a man of high rank); Acts 23:26; 24:3 and 26:25, RV, for KJV, "most noble."¶

Note: The phrase *kath' huperbolēn* (for which see B, No. 1) is translated "more excellent" in 1 Cor. 12:31.

EXCEPT, EXCEPTED

Note: For the negative conjunctions *ean mē* and *ei mē*, see † p. 1.

1. *ektos* (ἐκτός, 1622), an adverb, lit., "outside," is used with *ei mē*, as an extended conjunction signifying "except"; so in 1 Cor. 14:5; in 15:2, RV, for KJV, "unless"; in 1 Tim. 5:19, RV, for KJV, "but." It has the force of a preposition in the sense of (*a*) "outside of," in 1 Cor. 6:18, "without; in 2 Cor. 12:2, "out of"; (*b*) "besides," except, in Acts 26:22, RV, "but," for KJV, "other than"; in 1 Cor. 15:27 "excepted." For its use as a noun see Matt. 23:26, "(the) outside." See OTHER, OUT OF, OUTSIDE, UNLESS, WITHOUT.¶

2. *parektos* (παρεκτός, 3924), a strengthened form of No. 1 (*para*, beside), is used (*a*) as an adverb, signifying "without," 2 Cor. 11:28; lit., "the things without," i.e., the things happening without; (*b*) as a preposition signifying "except"; in Matt. 5:32, "saving"; in Acts 26:29, "except."¶

Note: In Matt. 19:9, the KJV and RV, translating the mss. which have the negative *mē*, followed by *epi*, render it "except for." The authorities mentioned in the RV marg. have *parektos*, followed by *logou*, i.e., "saving for the cause of."

3. *plēn* (πλήν, 4133), an adverb, most frequently signifying "yet, howbeit," or "only," sometimes has the meaning "except (that)," "save (that)," Acts 20:23; Phil. 1:18, RV, "only that," for KJV, "notwithstanding." It is also used as a preposition, signifying "except, save," Mark 12:32, "but"; John 8:10, "but" (KJV only); Acts 8:1, "except"; Acts 15:28, "than"; 27:22, "but (only)."

EXCESS

1. *akrasia* (ἀκρασία, 192) lit. denotes "want of strength" (*a*, negative, *kratos*, "strength"), hence, "want of self-control, incontinence," Matt. 23:25, "excess"; 1 Cor. 7:5, "incontinency."¶ Cf. *akratēs*, "powerless, incontinent," 2 Tim. 3:3, RV, "without self-control."¶

2. *anachusis* (ἀνάχυσις, 401), lit., "a pouring out, overflowing" (akin to *anacheō*, "to pour out"), is used metaphorically in 1 Pet. 4:4, "excess," said of the riotous conduct described in v. 3.¶

Notes: (1) *Asōtia* denotes "prodigality, profligacy, riot" (from *a*, negative, and *sōzō*, "to save"); it is translated "riot" in Eph. 5:18, RV, for KJV, "excess"; in Titus 1:6 and 1 Pet. 4:4, "riot" in KJV and RV. See RIOT.¶ Cf. the adverb *asōtōs*, "wastefully," "in riotous living," Luke 15:13.¶ A synonymous noun is *aselgeia*, "lasciviousness, outrageous conduct, wanton violence."

(2) In 1 Pet. 4:3, *oinophlugia*, "drunkenness, debauchery" (*oinos*, "wine," *phluō*, "to bubble up, overflow"), is rendered "excess of wine," KJV (RV, "winebibbings").¶

EXCHANGE

A. Noun.

antallagma (ἀντάλλαγμα, 465), "the price received as an equivalent of, or in exchange for, an article, an exchange" (*anti*, "instead of," *allassō*, "to change," akin to *allos*, "another"), hence denotes the price at which the "exchange" is effected, Matt. 16:26; Mark 8:37.¶ Connected with this is the conception of atonement, as in the word *lutron*, "a ransom." Cf. *allagma* in the Sept., e.g., in Isa. 43:3.

B. Verb.

metallassō (μεταλλάσσω, 3337) denotes (*a*) "to exchange," *meta*, "with," implying change, and *allassō* (see A), Rom. 1:25, of "exchanging" the truth for a lie, RV, for KJV, "changed"; (*b*) "to change," v. 26, a different meaning from that in the preceding verse. See CHANGE.¶ In the Sept., Esth. 2:7, 20.¶

Note: In Luke 24:17, "what communications are these that ye have one with another?" the verb *antiballō*, "to throw in turn, to exchange," is used of conversation, lit., "what words are these that ye exchange one with another?"

For EXCHANGERS see BANKERS

EXCLUDE

ekkleiō (ἐκκλείω, 1576), "to shut out" (*ek*, "from," *kleiō*, "to shut"), is said of glorying in works as a means of justification, Rom. 3:27; of Gentiles, who by Judaism would be "excluded" from salvation and Christian fellowship, Gal. 4:17.¶

EXCUSE

A. Noun.

prophasis (πρόφασις, 4392), "a pretense, pretext" (from *pro*, "before," and *phēmi*, "to say"), is translated "excuse" in John 15:22, RV, for KJV, "cloke"; "cloke in 1 Thess. 2:5. KJV and RV. See CLOKE, PRETENCE, SHOW (Noun).

B. Adjective (*negative*).

anapologētos (ἀναπολόγητος, 379), "without excuse, inexcusable" (*a*, negative, *n*, euphonic, and *apologeomai*, see C, No. 1, below), is used, Rom. 1:20, "without excuse," of those who reject the revelation of God in creation; 2:1, RV, for KJV, "inexcusable," of the Jew who judges the Gentile.¶

C. Verbs.

1. *apologeomai* (ἀπολογέομαι, 626), lit., "to speak oneself off," hence "to plead for oneself," and so, in general, (*a*) "to defend," as before a tribunal; in Rom. 2:15, RV, "excusing them," means one "excusing" others (not themselves); the preceding phrase "one with another" signifies one person with another, not one thought with another; it may be paraphrased, "their thoughts with one another, condemning or else excusing one another"; conscience provides a moral standard by which men judge one another; (*b*) "to excuse" oneself, 2 Cor. 12:19; cf. B. See ANSWER.

2. *paraiteomai* (παραιτέομαι, 3868) is used in the sense of "begging off, asking to be excused or making an excuse," in Luke 14:18 (twice) and v. 19. In the first part of v. 18 the verb is used in the middle voice, "to make excuse" (acting in imagined self-interest); in the latter part and in v. 19 it is in the passive voice, "have me excused."

EXECUTE

1. *poieō* (ποιέω, 4160), "to do, to make," is thrice rendered "execute," of the Lord's authority and acts in "executing" judgment, (*a*) of His authority as the One to whom judgment is committed, John 5:27; (*b*) of the judgment which He will mete out to all transgressors at His second advent, Jude 15; (*c*) of the carrying out of His Word (not "work," as in the KJV) in the earth, especially regarding the nation of Israel, the mass being rejected, the remnant saved, Rom. 9:28. That He will "execute His Word finishing and cutting it short," is expressive of the summary and decisive character of His action. See DO.

2. *hierateuō* (ἱερατεύω, 2407), "to be a priest, to officiate as such," is translated "executed the priest's office," in Luke 1:8.¶ It occurs frequently in the Sept., and in inscriptions. Cf. *hierateuma*, "priesthood," 1 Pet. 2:5, 9,¶ *hierateia*, "a priest's office," Luke 1:9; Heb. 7:5,¶ *hiereus*, "a priest," and *hieros*, "sacred."

For EXECUTIONER, Mark 6:27, see GUARD, A, No. 2

EXERCISE

A. Verbs.

1. *gumnazō* (γυμνάζω, 1128) primarily signifies "to exercise naked" (from *gumnos*, "naked"); then, generally, "to exercise, to train the body or mind" (Eng., "gymnastic"), 1 Tim. 4:7, with a view to godliness; Heb. 5:14, of the senses, so as to discern good and evil; 12:11, of the effect of chastening, the spiritual "exercise" producing the fruit of righteousness; 2 Pet. 2:14, of certain evil teachers with hearts "exercised in covetousness," RV.¶

2. *askeō* (ἀσκέω, 778) signifies "to form by art, to adorn, to work up raw material with skill"; hence, in general, "to take pains, endeavor, exercise by training or discipline," with a view to a conscience void of offense, Acts 24:16.¶

3. *poieō* (ποιέω, 4160), "to do," is translated "exerciseth" in Rev. 13:12, said of the authority of the second "Beast." Cf. EXECUTE. See DO.

Notes: The following verbs contain in translation the word "exercise" but belong to other headings: *exousiazō*, "to exercise authority over," Luke 22:25 (*exousia*, "authority"); in the first part of this verse, the verb *kurieuō*, "to be lord," is translated "exercise lordship," KJV (RV, "have lordship"); *katexousiazō*, a strengthened form of the preceding (*kata*, "down," intensive), Matt. 20:25; Mark 10:42, "exercise authority" (in the first part of these verses the synonymous verb *katakurieuō*, is rendered "lord it," RV, for KJV, "exercise dominion," and "exercise lordship," respectively); *episkopeō*, "to look over or upon" (*epi*, "over," *skopeō*, "to look"), "to care for," 1 Pet. 5:2 (absent in some mss.), RV, "exercising the oversight," for KJV "taking, etc."

B. Noun.

gumnasia (γυμνασία, 1129) primarily denotes "gymnastic exercise" (akin to A, No. 1), 1 Tim. 4:8, where the immediate reference is probably not to mere physical training for games but to discipline of the body such as that to which the apostle refers in 1 Cor. 9:27, though there may be an allusion to the practices of asceticism.

EXHORT, EXHORTATION

A. Verbs.

1. *parakaleō* (παρακαλέω, 3870), primarily, "to call to a person" (*para*, "to the side," *kaleō*, "to call"), denotes (*a*) "to call on, entreat"; see BESEECH; (*b*) "to admonish, exhort, to urge" one to pursue some course of conduct (always prospective, looking to the future, in contrast to the meaning to comfort, which is retrospective, having to do with trial experienced), translated "exhort" in the RV of Phil. 4:2; 1 Thess. 4:10; Heb. 13:19, 22, for KJV, "beseech"; in 1 Tim. 5:1, for KJV, "intreat"; in 1 Thess. 5:11, for KJV, "comfort"; "exhorted" in 2 Cor. 8:6 and 12:18, for KJV, "desired"; in 1 Tim. 1:3, for KJV, "besought." See BESEECH.

2. *paraineō* (παραινέω, 3867), primarily, "to speak of near" (*para*, "near," and *aineō*, "to tell of, speak of,"), then, "to recommend"), hence, "to advise, exhort, warn," is used in Acts 27:9, "admonished," and v. 22, "I exhort." See ADMONISH.¶

3. *protrepō* (προτρέπω, 4389) lit., "to turn forward, propel" (*pro*, "before," *trepō*, "to turn"); hence, "to impel morally, to urge forward, encourage," is used in Acts 18:27, RV, "encouraged him" (Apollos), with reference to his going into Achaia; KJV, "exhorting the disciples"; while the encouragement was given to Apollos, a letter was written to the disciples in Achaia to receive him.¶

B. Noun.

paraklēsis (παράκλησις, 3874), akin to A, No. 1, primarily "a calling to one's side," and so "to one's aid," hence denotes (*a*) an appeal, "entreaty," 2 Cor. 8:4; (*b*) encouragement, "exhortation," e.g., Rom. 12:8; in Acts 4:36, RV, "exhortation," for KJV, "consolation"; (*c*) "consolation and comfort," e.g., Rom. 15:4. See COMFORT. Cf. *paraklētos*, "an advocate, comforter."

EXIST

huparchō (ὑπάρχω, 5225), primarily, "to make a beginning" (*hupo*, "under," *archē*, "a beginning"), denotes "to be, to be in existence," involving an "existence" or condition both previous to the circumstances mentioned and continuing after it. This is important in Phil. 2:6, concerning the deity of Christ. The phrase "being (existing) in the form (*morphē*, the essential and specific form and character) of God," carries with it the two facts of the antecedent Godhood of Christ, previous to His incarnation, and the continuance of His Godhood at and after the event of His Birth (see Gifford, on the Incarnation, pp. 11, sqq.). It is translated "exist" in 1 Cor. 11:18, RV, for KJV, "there be." Cf. Luke 16:14; 23:50; Acts 2:30; 3:2; 17:24; 22:3 etc. See BEING, GOODS, LIVE, POSSESS, SUBSTANCE.

EXORCIST

exorkistēs (ἐξορκιστής, 1845) denotes (*a*) "one who administers an oath"; (*b*) "an exorcist" (akin to *exorkizō*, "to adjure," from *orkos*, "an oath"), "one who employs a formula of conjuration for the expulsion of demons," Acts 19:13. The practice of "exorcism" was carried on by strolling Jews, who used their power in the recitation of particular names.¶

EXPECT, EXPECTATION

A. Verbs.

1. *ekdechomai* (ἐκδέχομαι, 1551), lit. and primarily, "to take or receive from" (*ek*, "from," *dechomai*, "to receive"), hence denotes "to await, expect," the only sense of the word in the NT; it suggests a reaching out in readiness to receive something; "expecting," Heb. 10:13; "expect," 1 Cor. 16:11, RV (KJV, "look for"); to wait for, John 5:3 (KJV only); Acts 17:16; 1 Cor. 11:33, RV (KJV, "tarry for"); Jas. 5:7; to wait, 1 Pet. 3:20 in some mss.; "looked for," Heb. 11:10. Cf. B, No. 1. See LOOK, TARRY, WAIT.¶

2. *prosdokaō* (προσδοκάω, 4328), "to watch toward, to look for, expect" (*pros*, "toward," *dokeō*, "to think": *dokaō* "does not exist"), is translated "expecting" in Matt. 24:50 and Luke 12:46, RV (KJV, "looketh for"); Luke 3:15, "were in expectation"; Acts 3:5, "expecting" (KJV and RV); 28:6 (twice), "expected that," RV (KJV, "looked when") and "when they were long in expectation" (KJV, "after they had looked a great while"). See LOOK, TARRY, WAIT.

B. Nouns.

1. *apokaradokia* (ἀποκαραδοκία, 603), primarily "a watching with outstretched head" (*apo*, "from," *kara*, "the head," and *dokeō*, "to

look, to watch"), signifies "strained expectancy, eager longing," the stretching forth of the head indicating an "expectation" of something from a certain place, Rom. 8:19 and Phil. 1:20. The prefix *apo* suggests "abstraction and absorption" (Lightfoot), i.e., abstraction from anything else that might engage the attention, and absorption in the object expected "till the fulfillment is realized" (Alford). The intensive character of the noun, in comparison with No. 2 (below), is clear from the contexts; in Rom. 8:19 it is said figuratively of the creation as waiting for the revealing of the sons of God ("waiting" translates the verb *apekdechomai*, a strengthened form of A, No. 1; see WAIT FOR). In Phil. 1:20 the apostle states it as his "earnest expectation" and hope, that, instead of being put to shame, Christ shall be magnified in his body, "whether by life, or by death," suggesting absorption in the person of Christ, abstraction from aught that hinders.¶

2. *prosdokia* (προσδοκία, 4329), "a watching for, expectation" (akin to A, No. 2, which see), is used in the NT only of the "expectation" of evil, Luke 21:26, RV, "expectation," KJV, "looking for," regarding impending calamities; Acts 12:11, "the expectation" of the execution of Peter.¶

3. *ekdochē* (ἐκδοχή, 1561), primarily "a receiving from," hence, "expectation" (akin to A, No. 1), is used in Heb. 10:27 (RV, "expectation"; KJV, "looking for"), of judgment.¶

EXPEDIENT

sumpherō (συμφέρω, 4851) signifies (*a*), transitively, lit., "to bring together," (*sun*, "with," *pherō*, "to bring"), Acts 19:19; (*b*) intransitively, "to be an advantage, profitable, expedient" (not merely 'convenient'); it is used mostly impersonally, "it is (it was) expedient"; so in Matt. 19:10, RV (negatively), KJV, "it is (not) good"; John 11:50; 16:7; 18:14; 1 Cor. 6:12; 10:23; 2 Cor. 8:10; 12:1; "it is profitable," Matt. 5:29–30; 18:6, RV; "was profitable," Acts 20:20; "to profit withal," 1 Cor. 12:7; in Heb. 12:10, used in the neuter of the present participle with the article as a noun, "for (our) profit." See PROFIT.¶

Cf. the adjective *sumphoros* (or *sumpheron*), "profitable," used with the article as a noun, 1 Cor. 7:35; 10:33.¶

For **EXPELLED**, Acts 13:50, KJV, see **CAST**, No. 5

EXPERIENCE (without), EXPERIMENT

1. *apeiros* (ἄπειροσ, 552), "without experience" (*a*, negative, *peira*, "a trial, experiment"), is used in Heb. 5:13, RV, "without experience," KJV, "unskillful," with reference to "the word of righteousness."¶ In the Sept., Num. 14:23, of youths; Jer. 2:6, of a land, "untried"; Zech. 11:15, of a shepherd.¶

2. *dokimē* (δοκιμή, 1382) means (*a*) "the process of proving"; it is rendered "experiment" in 2 Cor. 9:13, KJV, RV, "the proving (of you)"; in 8:2, KJV, "trial," RV, "proof"; (*b*) "the effect of proving, approval, approvedness," RV, "probation," Rom. 5:4 (twice), for KJV, "experience"; KJV and RV, "proof" in 2 Cor. 2:9; 13:3 and Phil. 2:22. See EXPERIENCE, PROOF.¶ Cf. *dokimos*, "approved," *dokimazō*, "to prove, approve"; see APPROVE.

EXPERT

gnōstēs (γνώστης, 1109), "one who knows" (akin to *ginōskō*, "to know"), denotes "an expert, a connoisseur," Acts 26:3.¶ Cf. *gnōstos*, "known."

EXPIRE

Note: In Acts 7:30, the KJV "were expired" translates the verb *plēroō*, "to fulfill" (RV). See FULFILL. In Rev. 20:7, the KJV "are expired" translates the verb *teleō*, "to finish" (RV). See FINISH.

EXPLAIN

diasapheō (διασαφέω, 1285), "to make clear, explain fully" (*dia* "through," intensive, and *saphēs*, "clear"), is translated "explain" in Matt. 13:36 RV (KJV, "declare") translates *phrazō;* in 18:31, "told," of the account of the unforgiving debtor's doings given by his fellow-servants. The preferable rendering would be "they made clear" or "they explained," suggesting a detailed explanation of the circumstances.¶

EXPOUND

1. *ektithēmi* (ἐκτίθημι, 1620), "to set out, expose" (*ek*, "out," *tithēmi*, "to place"), is used (*a*) literally, Acts 7:21; (*b*) metaphorically, in the middle voice, to set forth, "expound," of circumstances, Acts 11:4; of the way of God, 18:26; of the kingdom of God, 28:23.¶

2. *epiluō* (ἐπιλύω, 1956), primarily, "to loose, release," a strengthened form of *luō*, "to loose," signifies "to solve, explain, expound," Mark 4:34, "expounded"; in Acts 19:39, of settling a controversy, RV, "it shall be settled,"

for KJV, "it shall be determined." See DETERMINE.¶ Cf. *epilusis*, "an interpretation," 2 Pet. 1:20.¶

3. *diermēneuō* (διερμηνεύω, 1329), "to interpret fully" (*dia*, "through," intensive, *hermēneuō*, "to interpret"); (Eng., "hermeneutics"), is translated, "He expounded" in Luke 24:27, KJV, RV, "interpreted"; in Acts 9:36, "by interpretation," lit., "being interpreted"; see also 1 Cor. 12:30; 14:5, 13, 27. See INTERPRET.¶

For **EXPRESS,** Heb. 1:3, KJV, see **IMAGE,** No. 2

EXPRESSLY

rhētōs (ῥητῶς, 4490), meaning "in stated terms" (from *rhētos*, "stated, specified"; from *rheō*, or *erō*, "to say"; cf. *rhēma*, "a word"), is used in 1 Tim. 4:1, "expressly."¶

EXTORT, EXTORTION, EXTORTIONER

A. Verb.
prassō (πράσσω, 4238), "to practice," has the special meaning "extort" in Luke 3:13, RV (KJV, "exact"). In Luke 19:23 it is translated "required"; it may be that the master, in addressing the slothful servant, uses the word "extort" or "exact" (as in 3:13), in accordance with the character attributed to him by the servant.

B. Nouns.
1. *harpagē* (ἁρπαγή, 724) denotes "pillage, plundering, robbery, extortion" (akin to *harpazō*, "to seize, carry off by force," and *harpagmos*, "a thing seized, or the act of seizing"; from the root *arp*, seen in Eng., "rapacious"; an associated noun, with the same spelling, denoted a rake, or hook for drawing up a bucket); it is translated "extortion" in Matt. 23:25; Luke 11:39, RV, KJV, "ravening"; Heb. 10:34, "spoiling." See RAVENING, SPOILING.¶ Cf. C. below.

2. *pleonexia* (πλεονεξία, 4124), "covetousness, desire for advantage," is rendered "extortion" in 2 Cor. 9:5, RV (KJV and RV marg., "covetousness"). See COVET.

C. Adjective.
harpax (ἅρπαξ, 727), "rapacious" (akin to No. 1), is translated as a noun, "extortioners," in Luke 18:11; 1 Cor. 5:10–11; 6:10; in Matt. 7:15 "ravening" (of wolves).¶ In the Sept., Gen. 49:27.¶

EYE

1. *ophthalmos* (ὀφθαλμός, 3788), akin to *opsis*, "sight," probably from a root signifying "penetration, sharpness" (Curtius, Gk. Etym.) (cf. Eng., "ophthalmia," etc.). is used (*a*) of the physical organ, e.g., Matt. 5:38; of restoring sight, e.g., Matt. 20:33; of God's power of vision, Heb. 4:13; 1 Pet. 3:12; of Christ in vision, Rev. 1:14; 2:18; 19:12; of the Holy Spirit in the unity of Godhood with Christ, Rev. 5:6; (*b*) metaphorically, of ethical qualities, evil, Matt. 6:23; Mark 7:22 (by metonymy, for envy); singleness of motive, Matt. 6:22; Luke 11:34; as the instrument of evil desire, "the principal avenue of temptation," 1 John 2:16; of adultery, 2 Pet. 2:14; (*c*) metaphorically, of mental vision, Matt. 13:15; John 12:40; Rom. 11:8; Gal. 3:1, where the metaphor of the "evil eye" is altered to a different sense from that of bewitching (the posting up or placarding of an "eye" was used as a charm, to prevent mischief); by gospel-preaching Christ had been, so to speak, placarded before their "eyes"; the question may be paraphrased, "What evil teachers have been malignly fascinating you?"; Eph. 1:18, of the "eyes of the heart," as a means of knowledge.

2. *omma* (ὄμμα, 3659), "sight," is used in the plural in Matt. 20:34 (No. 1 is used in v. 33); Mark 8:23 (No. 1 is used in v. 25). The word is more poetical in usage than No. 1, and the writers may have changed the word with a view to distinguishing the simple desire of the blind man from the tender act of the Lord Himself.¶

3. *trumalia* (τρυμαλιά, 5168) is used of the "eye" of a needle, Mark 10:25 (from *trumē*, "a hole," *truō*, "to wear away").¶ Cf. *trēma*, "a hole, perforation," Matt. 19:24 (some texts have *trupēma*, "a hole," from *trupaō*, "to bore a hole") and Luke 18:25, as in the most authentic mss. (some texts have *trumalia* here).¶

EYE (with one)

monophthalmos (μονόφθαλμος, 3442), "one-eyed, deprived of one eye" (*monos*, "only," and No. 1, above), is used in the Lord's warning in Matt. 18:9; Mark 9:47.¶

EYE-SALVE

kollourion (κολλούριον, 2854), primarily a diminutive of *kollura*, and denoting "a coarse bread roll" (as in the Sept. of 1 Kings 12: after v. 24, lines 30, 32, 39; Eng. version, 14:3 ¶), hence an "eye-salve," shaped like a roll, Rev. 3:18, of the true knowledge of one's condition and of the claims of Christ. The word is doubtless an allusion to the Phrygian powder used by oculists in the famous medical school at Laodicea (Ramsay, *Cities and Bishoprics of Phrygia,* Vol. I, p. 52).

EYE–SERVICE

ophthalmodoulia (ὀφθαλμοδουλία, 3787) denotes "service performed only under the master's eye" (*ophthalmos*, "an eye," *doulos*, "a slave"), diligently performed when he is looking, but neglected in his absence, Eph. 6:6 and Col. 3:22.¶

EYEWITNESS

1. *autoptēs* (αὐτόπτης, 845) signifies "seeing with one's own eyes" (*autos*, "self," and a form, *optanō*, "to see"), Luke 1:2.¶

2. *epoptēs* (ἐπόπτης, 2030), primarily "an overseer" (*epi*, "over"), then, a "spectator, an eyewitness" of anything, is used in 2 Pet. 1:16 of those who were present at the transfiguration of Christ. Among the Greeks the word was used of those who had attained to the third grade, the highest, of the Eleusinian mysteries, a religious cult at Eleusis, with its worship, rites, festival and pilgrimages; this brotherhood was open to all Greeks.¶ In the Sept., Esth. 5:1, where it is used of God as the Overseer and Preserver of all things.¶ Cf. *epopteuō*, "to behold," 1 Pet. 2:12 and 3:2.¶

F

FABLE

muthos (μῦθος, 3454) primarily signifies "speech, conversation." The first syllable comes from a root *mu—*, signifying "to close, keep secret, be dumb"; whence, *muō*, "to close" (eyes, mouth) and *mustērion*, "a secret, a mystery"; hence, "a story, narrative, fable, fiction" (Eng., "myth"). The word is used of gnostic errors and of Jewish and profane fables and genealogies, in 1 Tim. 1:4; 4:7; 2 Tim. 4:4; Titus 1:14; of fiction, in 2 Pet. 1:16.¶

Muthos is to be contrasted with *alētheia*, "truth," and with *logos*, "a story, a narrative purporting to set forth facts," e.g., Matt. 28:15, a "saying" (i.e., an account, story, in which actually there is a falsification of facts); Luke 5:15, RV, "report."

FACE

1. *prosōpon* (πρόσωπον, 4383) denotes "the countenance," lit., "the part towards the eyes" (from *pros*, "towards," *ōps*, "the eye"), and is used (*a*) of the "face," Matt. 6:16–17; 2 Cor. 3:7, 2nd part (KJV, "countenance"); in 2 Cor. 10:7, in the RV, "things that are before your face" (KJV, "outward appearance"), the phrase is figurative of superficial judgment; (*b*) of the look, i.e., the "face," which by its various movements affords an index of inward thoughts and feelings, e.g., Luke 9:51, 53; 1 Pet. 3:12; (*c*) the presence of a person, the "face" being the noblest part, e.g., Acts 3:13, RV, "before the face of," KJV, "in the presence of"; 5:41, "presence"; 2 Cor. 2:10, "person"; 1 Thess. 2:17 (first part), "presence"; 2 Thess. 1:9, RV, "face," KJV, "presence"; Rev. 12:14, "face"; (*d*) the person himself, e.g., Gal. 1:22; 1 Thess. 2:17 (second part); (*e*) the appearance one presents by his wealth or poverty, his position or state, Matt. 22:16; Mark 12:14; Gal. 2:6; Jude 16; (*f*) the outward appearance of inanimate things, Matt. 16:3; Luke 12:56; 21:35; Acts 17:26.

"To spit in a person's face" was an expression of the utmost scorn and aversion, e.g., Matt. 26:67 (cf. 27:30; Mark 10:34; Luke 18:32). See APPEARANCE.

2. *opsis* (ὄψις, 3799) is primarily "the act of seeing"; then, (*a*) "the face"; of the body of Lazarus, John 11:44; of the "countenance" of Christ in a vision, Rev. 1:16; (*b*) the "outward appearance" of a person or thing, John 7:24. See APPEARANCE.¶

Note: The phrase "face to face" translates two phrases in Greek: (1) *kata prosōpon* (*kata*, "over against," and No. 1), Acts 25:16; (2) *stoma pros stoma*, lit., "mouth to mouth" (*stoma*, "a mouth"), 2 John 12; 3 John 14. See MOUTH. (3) For *antophthalmeō*, Acts 27:15, RV has "to face."

FACTION, FACTIOUS

erithia (or *—eia*) (ἐριθία, 2052) denotes "ambition, self-seeking, rivalry," self-will being an underlying idea in the word; hence it denotes "party-making." It is derived, not from *eris*, "strife," but from *erithos*, "a hireling"; hence the meaning of "seeking to win followers," "factions," so rendered in the RV of 2 Cor. 12:20, KJV, "strifes"; not improbably the meaning here is rivalries, or base ambitions (all the other words in the list express abstract ideas rather than factions); Gal. 5:20 (ditto); Phil. 1:17 (RV; KJV, v. 16, "contention"); 2:3 (KJV, "strife"); Jas. 3:14, 16 (ditto); in Rom. 2:8 it is translated as an adjective, "factious" (KJV, "contentious"). The order "strife, jealousy, wrath, faction," is the same in 2 Cor. 12:20 and Gal. 5:20. "Faction" is the fruit of jealousy.¶ Cf. the synonymous adjective *hairetikos*, Titus 3:10, causing division (marg., "factious"), not necessarily "heretical," in the sense of holding false doctrine.¶

FADE (away)

A. Verb.

marainō (μαραίνω, 3133) was used (*a*) to signify "to quench a fire," and in the passive voice, of the "dying out of a fire"; hence (*b*) in various relations, in the active voice, "to quench, waste, wear out"; in the passive, "to waste away," Jas. 1:11, of the "fading" away of a rich man, as illustrated by the flower of the field.¶ In the Sept., Job 15:30; 24:24.¶

B. Adjectives (negative).

1. *amarantos* (ἀμάραντος, 263), "unfading" (*a*, negative, and A, above), whence the "amaranth," an unfading flower, a symbol of perpetuity (see *Paradise Lost*, iii. 353), is used in 1 Pet. 1:4 of the believer's inheritance, "that fadeth not away." It is found in various writings in the language of the *Koinē*, e.g., on a gladiator's tomb; and as a proper name (Moulton and Milligan, Vocab.).¶

2. *amarantinos* (ἀμαράντινος, 262) primarily signifies "composed of amaranth" (see No. 1); hence, "unfading," 1 Pet. 5:4, of the crown of glory promised to faithful elders.¶ Cf. *rhodinos*, "made of roses" (*rhodon*, "a rose").

FAIL

A. Verbs.

1. *ekleipō* (ἐκλείπω, 1587), "to leave out" (*ek*, "out," *leipō*, "to leave"), used intransitively, means "to leave off, cease, fail"; it is said of the cessation of earthly life, Luke 16:9; of faith, 22:32; of the light of the sun, 23:45 (in the best mss.); of the years of Christ, Heb. 1:12.¶

2. *epileipō* (ἐπιλείπω, 1952), "not to suffice for a purpose" (*epi*, over), is said of insufficient time, in Heb. 11:32.¶

3. *piptō* (πίπτω, 4098), "to fall," is used of the law of God in its smallest detail, in the sense of losing its authority or ceasing to have force, Luke 16:17. In 1 Cor. 13:8 it is used of love (some mss. have *ekpiptō*, "to fall off"). See FALL.

Notes: (1) In 1 Cor. 13:8, *katargeō*, "to reduce to inactivity" (see ABOLISH), in the passive voice, "to be reduced to this condition, to be done away," is translated "shall fail," KJV. This,

however, misses the distinction between what has been previously said of love and what is here said of prophecies (see No. 3); the RV has "shall be done away"; so also as regards knowledge (same verse). (2) In Heb. 12:15, *hustereō*, "to come behind, fall short, miss," is rendered "fail" in the KJV, RV, "falleth short." (3) In Luke 21:26, *apopsuchō*, lit., "to breathe out life," hence, "to faint," is translated "hearts failing," in the KJV, RV, "fainting." See FAINT.¶

B. Adjective.

anekleiptos (ἀνέκλειπτος, 413), "unfailing" (*a*, negative, and A, No. 1), is rendered "that faileth not," in Luke 12:33.¶ In a Greek document dated A.D. 42, some contractors undertake to provide "unfailing" heat for a bath during the current year (Moulton and Milligan, Vocab.).¶

FAIN

1. *boulomai* (βούλομαι, 1014), "to will deliberately, wish, desire, be minded," implying the deliberate exercise of volition (contrast No. 3), is translated "would fain" in Philem. 13 (in the best mss.). See DISPOSED.

2. *epithumeō* (ἐπιθυμέω, 1937), "to set one's heart upon, desire," is translated "would fain" in Luke 15:16, of the Prodigal Son. See DESIRE.

3. *thelō* (θέλω, 2309), "to wish, to design to do anything," expresses the impulse of the will rather than the intention (see No. 1); the RV translates it "would fain" in Luke 13:31, of Herod's desire to kill Christ, KJV, "will (kill)"; in 1 Thess. 2:18, of the desire of the missionaries to return to the church in Thessalonica. See DISPOSED.

Note: In Acts 26:28, in Agrippa's statement to Paul, the RV rendering is "with but little persuasion thou wouldest fain make me a Christian." The lit. rendering is "with (or in) little (labor or time) thou art persuading me so as to make (me) a Christian." There is no verb for "wouldest" in the original, but it brings out the sense.

FAINT

1. *ekluō* (ἐκλύω, 1590) denotes (*a*) "to loose, release" (*ek*, "out," *luō*, "to loose"); (*b*) "to unloose," as a bow-string, "to relax," and so, "to enfeeble," and is used in the passive voice with the significance "to be faint, grow weary," (1) of the body, Matt. 15:32; (some mss. have it in 9:36); Mark 8:3; (2) of the soul, Gal. 6:9 (last clause), in discharging responsibilities in obedience to the Lord; in Heb. 12:3, of becoming weary in the strife against sin; in v. 5, under the chastening hand of God.¶ It expresses the opposite of *anazōnnumi*, "to gird up," 1 Pet. 1:13.¶

2. *enkakeō* or *ekkakeō* (ἐνκακέω, 1573), "to lack courage, lose heart, be fainthearted" (*en*, "in," *kakos*, "base"), is said of prayer, Luke 18:1; of gospel ministry, 2 Cor. 4:1, 16; of the effect of tribulation, Eph. 3:13; as to well doing, 2 Thess. 3:13, "be not weary" (KJV marg., "faint not"). Some mss. have this word in Gal. 6:9 (No. 1).¶

3. *kamnō* (κάμνω, 2577) primarily signified "to work"; then, as the effect of continued labor, "to be weary"; it is used in Heb. 12:3, of becoming "weary" (see also No. 1), RV, "wax not weary"; in Jas. 5:15, of sickness; some mss. have it in Rev. 2:3, KJV, "hast (not) fainted," RV, "grown weary." See SICK, WEARY.¶

Note: For *apopsuchō*, Luke 21:26, RV, see FAIL, *Note* (3).¶

FAINTHEARTED

oligopsuchos (ὀλιγόψυχος, 3642), lit., "small-souled" (*oligos*, "small," *psuchē*, "the soul"), denotes "despondent"; then, "fainthearted," 1 Thess. 5:14, RV, for the incorrect KJV, "feeble-minded." ¶ In the Sept., similarly, in a good sense, Isa. 57:15, "who giveth endurance to the fainthearted," for RV, "to revive the spirit of the humble"; in a bad sense, Prov. 18:14, "who can endure a fainthearted man?"

FAIR

1. *asteios* (ἀστεῖος, 791), lit., "of the city" (from *astu*, "a city"; like Lat. *urbanus*, from *urbs*, "a city"; Eng., "urbane"; similarly, "polite," from *polis*, "a town"), hence, "fair, elegant" (used in the papyri writings of clothing), is said of the external form of a child, Acts 7:20, of Moses "(exceeding) fair," lit., "fair to God"; Heb. 11:23 (RV, "goodly," KJV, "proper"). See BEAUTIFUL, GOODLY, *Note*.¶

2. *eudia* (εὐδία, 2105) denotes "fair weather," Matt. 16:2, from *eudios*, "calm"; from *eu*, "good," and *dios*, "divine," among the pagan Greeks, akin to the name for the god Zeus, or Jupiter. Some would derive *Dios* and the Latin *deus* (god) and *dies* (day) from a root meaning "bright." Cf. the Latin *sub divo*, "under a bright, open sky."¶

3. *kalos* (καλός, 2570), "beautiful, fair, in appearance," is used as part of the proper name, Fair Havens, Acts 27:8. See BETTER, GOOD.

Notes: (1) In Rom. 16:18 *eulogia*, which generally signifies "blessing," is used in its more literal sense, "fair speech," i.e., a fine style of utterance, giving the appearance of reasonableness.

(2) In Gal. 6:12 the verb *euprosōpeō*, "to look well," lit., "to be fair of face" (*eu*, "well," and *prosōpon*, "a face"), signifies "to make a fair or plausible show," used there metaphorically of making a display of religious zeal.¶

FAITH

pistis (πίστις, 4102), primarily, "firm persuasion," a conviction based upon hearing (akin to *peithō*, "to persuade"), is used in the NT always of "faith in God or Christ, or things spiritual."

The word is used of (*a*) trust, e.g., Rom. 3:25 [see *Note* (4) below]; 1 Cor. 2:5; 15:14, 17; 2 Cor. 1:24; Gal. 3:23 [see *Note* (5) below]; Phil. 1:25; 2:17; 1 Thess. 3:2; 2 Thess. 1:3; 3:2; (*b*) trust-worthiness, e.g., Matt. 23:23; Rom. 3:3, RV, "the faithfulness of God"; Gal. 5:22 (RV, "faithfulness"); Titus 2:10, "fidelity"; (*c*) by metonymy, what is believed, the contents of belief, the "faith," Acts 6:7; 14:22; Gal. 1:23; 3:25 [contrast 3:23, under (a)]; 6:10; Phil. 1:27; 1 Thess. 3:10; Jude 3, 20 (and perhaps 2 Thess. 3:2); (*d*) a ground for "faith," an assurance, Acts 17:31 (not as in KJV, marg., "offered faith"); (*e*) a pledge of fidelity, plighted "faith," 1 Tim. 5:12.

The main elements in "faith" in its relation to the invisible God, as distinct from "faith" in man, are especially brought out in the use of this noun and the corresponding verb, *pisteuō*; they are (1) a firm conviction, producing a full acknowledgement of God's revelation or truth, e.g., 2 Thess. 2:11–12; (2) a personal surrender to Him, John 1:12; (3) a conduct inspired by such surrender, 2 Cor. 5:7. Prominence is given to one or other of these elements according to the context. All this stands in contrast to belief in its purely natural exercise, which consists of an opinion held in good "faith" without necessary reference to its proof. The object of Abraham's "faith" was not God's promise (that was the occasion of its exercise); his "faith" rested on God Himself, Rom. 4:17, 20–21. See ASSURANCE, BELIEF, FAITHFULNESS, FIDELITY.

Notes: (1) In Heb. 10:23, *elpis*, "hope," is mistranslated "faith" in the KJV (RV, "hope"). (2) In Acts 6:8 the most authentic mss. have *charis*, "grace," RV, for *pistis*, "faith." (3) In Rom. 3:3, RV, *apistia*, is rendered "want of faith," for KJV, "unbelief" (so translated elsewhere). See UNBELIEF. The verb *apisteō* in that verse is rendered "were without faith," RV, for KJV, "did not believe." (4) In Rom. 3:25, the KJV wrongly links "faith" with "in His blood," as if "faith" is reposed in the blood (i.e., the death) of Christ; the *en* is instrumental; "faith" rests in the living Person; hence the RV rightly puts a comma after "through faith," and renders the next phrase "by His blood," which is to be connected with "a propitiation." Christ became a propitiation through His blood (i.e., His death in expiatory sacrifice for sin). (5) In Gal. 3:23, though the article stands before "faith" in the original, "faith" is here to be taken as under (*a*) above, and as in v. 22, and not as under (*c*), "the faith"; the article is simply that of renewed mention. (6) For the difference between the teaching of Paul and that of James, on "faith" and works, see *Notes on Galatians,* by Hogg and Vine, pp. 117–119.

FAITH (of little)

oligopistos (ὀλιγόπιστος, 3640), lit., "little of faith" (*oligos,* "little," *pistis,* "faith"), is used only by the Lord, and as a tender rebuke, for anxiety, Matt. 6:30 and Luke 12:28; for fear, Matt. 8:26; 14:31; 16:8.¶

FAITHFUL, FAITHFULLY, FAITHLESS

1. *pistos* (πιστός, 4103), a verbal adjective, akin to *peithō* (see FAITH), is used in two senses, (*a*) passive, "faithful, to be trusted, reliable," said of God, e.g., 1 Cor. 1:9; 10:13; 2 Cor. 1:18 (KJV, "true"); 2 Tim. 2:13; Heb. 10:23; 11:11; 1 Pet. 4:19; 1 John 1:9; of Christ, e.g., 2 Thess. 3:3; Heb. 2:17; 3:2; Rev. 1:5; 3:14; 19:11; of the words of God, e.g., Acts 13:34, "sure"; 1 Tim. 1:15; 3:1 (KJV, "true"); 4:9; 2 Tim. 2:11; Titus 1:9; 3:8; Rev. 21:5; 22:6; of servants of the Lord, Matt. 24:45; 25:21, 23; Acts 16:15; 1 Cor. 4:2, 17; 7:25; Eph. 6:21; Col. 1:7; 4:7, 9; 1 Tim. 1:12; 3:11; 2 Tim. 2:2; Heb. 3:5; 1 Pet. 5:12; 3 John 5; Rev. 2:13; 17:14; of believers, Eph. 1:1; Col. 1:2; (*b*) active, signifying "believing, trusting, relying," e.g., Acts 16:1 (feminine); 2 Cor. 6:15; Gal. 3:9 seems best taken in this respect, as the context lays stress upon Abraham's "faith" in God, rather than upon his "faithfulness." In John 20:27 the context requires the active sense, as the Lord is reproaching Thomas for his want of "faith." See No. 2.

With regard to believers, they are spoken of sometimes in the active sense, sometimes in the passive, i.e., sometimes as believers, sometimes as "faithful." See Lightfoot on Galatians, p. 155.

Note: In 3 John 5 the RV has "thou doest a faithful work," for KJV, "thou doest faithfully." The lit. rendering is "thou doest (*poieō*) a faithful thing, whatsoever thou workest (*ergazō*)." That would not do as a translation. To do a "faithful" work is to do what is worthy of a "faithful" man. The KJV gives a meaning but is not exact as a translation. Westcott suggests "thou makest sure (*piston*) whatsoever thou workest" (i.e., it will not lose its reward). The change between *poieō,* "to do," and *ergazō,* "to

work," must be maintained. Cf. Matt. 26:10 (*ergazō* and *ergon).*

2. *apistos* (ἄπιστος, 571) is used with meanings somewhat parallel to No. 1; (*a*) "untrustworthy" (*a,* negative, and No. 1), not worthy of confidence or belief, is said of things "incredible," Acts 26:8; (*b*) "unbelieving, distrustful," used as a noun, "unbeliever," Luke 12:46; 1 Tim. 5:8 (RV, for KJV, "infidel"); in Titus 1:15 and Rev. 21:8, "unbelieving"; "faithless" in Matt. 17:17; Mark 9:19; Luke 9:41; John 20:27. The word is most frequent in 1 and 2 Corinthians. See BELIEVE, INCREDIBLE, INFIDEL, UNBELIEVER, UNFAITHFUL. (In the Sept., Prov. 17:6; 28:25; Isa. 17:10.¶).

FAITHFULNESS

Note: This is not found in the KJV. The RV corrects the KJV "faith" to "faithfulness" in Rom. 3:3; Gal. 5:22. See FAITH.

FALL, FALLEN, FALLING, FELL

A. Nouns.

1. *ptōsis* (πτῶσις, 4431); "a fall" (akin to B, No. 1), is used (*a*) literally, of the "overthrow of a building," Matt. 7:27; (*b*) metaphorically, Luke 2:34, of the spiritual "fall" of those in Israel who would reject Christ; the word "again" in the KJV of the next clause is misleading; the "rising up" (RV) refers to those who would acknowledge and receive Him, a distinct class from those to whom the "fall" applies. The "fall" would be irretrievable, cf. (*a*); such a lapse as Peter's is not in view.¶

2. *paraptōma* (παράπτωμα, 3900), primarily "a false step, a blunder" (*para,* "aside," *piptō,* "to fall"), then "a lapse from uprightness, a sin, a moral trespass, misdeed," is translated "fall" in Rom. 11:11–12, of the sin and "downfall" of Israel in their refusal to acknowledge God's claims and His Christ; by reason of this the offer of salvation was made to Gentiles; cf. *ptaiō,* "to stumble," in v. 11. See FAULT, OFFENSE, SIN, TRESPASS.

3. *apostasia* (ἀποστασία, 646), "a defection, revolt, apostasy," is used in the NT of religious apostasy; in Acts 21:21, it is translated "to forsake," lit., "thou teachest apostasy from Moses." In 2 Thess. 2:3 "the falling away" signifies apostasy from the faith. In papyri documents it is used politically of rebels.¶ *Note:* For "mighty fall," Rev. 18:21, RV, see VIOLENCE.

B. Verbs.

1. *piptō* (πίπτω, 4098), "to fall," is used (*a*) of descent, to "fall" down from, e.g., Matt. 10:29; 13:4; (*b*) of a lot, Acts 1:26; (*c*) of "falling" under judgment, Jas. 5:12 (cf. Rev. 18:2, RV); (*d*) of persons in the act of prostra-

tion, to prostrate oneself, e.g., Matt. 17:6; John 18:6; Rev. 1:17; in homage and worship, e.g., Matt. 2:11; Mark 5:22; Rev. 5:14; 19:4; (e) of things, "falling" into ruin, or failing, e.g., Matt. 7:25; Luke 16:17, RV, "fall," for KJV, "fail"; Heb. 11:30; (f) of "falling" in judgment upon persons, as of the sun's heat, Rev. 7:16, RV, "strike," KJV, "light"; of a mist and darkness, Acts 13:11 (some mss. have *epipiptō*); (g) of persons, in "falling" morally or spiritually, Rom. 14:4; 1 Cor. 10:8, 12; Rev. 2:5 (some mss. have No. 3 here). See FAIL, LIGHT (upon), STRIKE.

2. *apopiptō* (ἀποπίπτω, 634), "to fall from" (*apo*, "from"), is used in Acts 9:18, of the scales which "fell" from the eyes of Saul of Tarsus.¶

3. *ekpiptō* (ἐκπίπτω, 1601), "to fall out of" (*ek*, "out," and No. 1), "is used in the NT, literally, of flowers that wither in the course of nature, Jas. 1:11; 1 Pet. 1:24; of a ship not under control, Acts 27:17, 26, 29, 32; of shackles loosed from a prisoner's wrist, 12:7; figuratively, of the Word of God (the expression of His purpose), which cannot "fall" away from the end to which it is set, Rom. 9:6; of the believer who is warned lest he "fall" away from the course in which he has been confirmed by the Word of God, 2 Pet. 3:17."* So of those who seek to be justified by law, Gal. 5:4, "ye are fallen away from grace." Some mss. have this verb in Mark 13:25, for No. 1; so in Rev. 2:5. See CAST, EFFECT.¶

4. *empiptō* (ἐμπίπτω, 1706), "to fall into, or among" (*en*, "in," and No. 1), is used (a) literally, Matt. 12:11; Luke 6:39 (some mss. have No. 1 here); 10:36; some mss. have it in 14:5; (b) metaphorically, into condemnation, 1 Tim. 3:6; reproach, 3:7; temptation and snare, 6:9; the hands of God in judgment, Heb. 10:31.¶

5. *epipiptō* (ἐπιπίπτω, 1968), "to fall upon" (*epi*, "upon," and No. 1), is used (a) literally, Mark 3:10, "pressed upon"; Acts 20:10, 37; (b) metaphorically, of fear, Luke 1:12; Acts 19:17; Rev. 11:11 (No. 1, in some mss.); reproaches, Rom. 15:3; of the Holy Spirit, Acts 8:16; 10:44; 11:15.

Note: Some mss. have this verb in John 13:25; Acts 10:10; 13:11. See PRESS.¶

6. *katapiptō* (καταπίπτω, 2667), "to fall down" (*kata*, "down," and No. 1), is used in Luke 8:6 (in the best mss.); Acts 26:14; 28:6.¶

7. *parapiptō* (παραπίπτω, 3895), akin to A, No. 2, properly, "to fall in one's way" (*para*, "by"), signifies "to fall away" (from adherence to the realities and facts of the faith), Heb. 6:6.¶

8. *peripiptō* (περιπίπτω, 4045), "to fall

around" (*peri*, "around"), hence signifies to "fall" in with, or among, to light upon, come across, Luke 10:30, "among (robbers)"; Acts 27:41, KJV, "falling into," RV, "lighting upon," a part of a shore; Jas. 1:2, into temptation (i.e., trials). See LIGHT (to l. upon).¶ In the Sept., Ruth 2:3; 2 Sam. 1:6; Prov. 11:5.¶

9. *prospiptō* (προσπίπτω, 4363), "to fall towards anything" (*pros*, "towards"), "to strike against," is said of "wind," Matt. 7:25; it also signifies to "fall" down at one's feet, "fall" prostrate before, Mark 3:11; 5:33; 7:25; Luke 5:8; 8:28, 47; Acts 16:29.¶

10. *hustereō* (ὑστερέω, 5302), "to come late, to be last, behind, inferior," is translated "falleth short" in Heb. 12:15, RV, for KJV, "fail," and "fall short" in Rom. 3:23, for KJV, "come short," which, in view of the preceding "have," is ambiguous, and might be taken as a past tense. See BEHIND.

11. *epiballō* (ἐπιβάλλω, 1911), "to cast upon" (*epi*, "on," *ballō*, "to throw"), also signifies to "fall" to one's share, Luke 15:12, "that falleth." The phrase is frequently found in the papyri documents as a technical formula. See CAST, A, No. 7.

12. *erchomai* (ἔρχομαι, 2064), "to come," is translated "have fallen out," in Phil. 1:12, of the issue of circumstances. See COME.

13. *ginomai* (γίνομαι, 1096), "to become," is translated "falling" (headlong) in Acts 1:18. See *Note* (1) below. See BECOME.

14. *aphistēmi* (ἀφίστημι, 868), when used intransitively, signifies "to stand off" (*apo*, "from," *histēmi*, "to stand"), "to withdraw from"; hence, "to fall away, to apostatize," 1 Tim. 4:1, RV, "shall fall away," for KJV, "shall depart"; Heb. 3:12, RV, "falling away." See DEPART, No. 20.

15. *parabainō* (παραβαίνω, 3845), "to transgress, fall" (*para*, "away, across," *bainō*, "to go"), is translated "fell away" in Acts 1:25, RV, for KJV, "by transgression fell." See TRANSGRESS.

16. *katabainō* (καταβαίνω, 2597) denotes "to come (or fall) down," Luke 22:44; in Rev. 16:21, "cometh down," RV. See COME, DESCEND.

Notes: (1) In Rev. 16:2, *ginomai*, "to become," is translated "it became," RV, for KJV, "there fell." (2) In 2 Pet. 1:10, *ptaiō*, "to stumble," is translated "stumble," RV, for KJV, "fall." (3) In Rom. 14:13, *skandalon*, "a snare, a means of doing wrong," is rendered "an occasion of falling," RV, for KJV "an occasion to fall." (4) *Koimaō*, in the middle voice, signifies "to fall asleep," Matt. 27:52, RV, "had fallen asleep," for KJV, "slept." See ASLEEP. (5) In Acts 27:34, *apollumi*, "to perish," is translated

---

* From *Notes on Galatians,* by Hogg and Vine, p. 242.

"shall ... perish," RV, for KJV, "shall ... fall." (6) In Jude 24 the adjective *aptaistos*, "without stumbling, sure footed" (*a*, negative, and *ptaiō*, "to stumble"), is translated "from stumbling," RV, for KJV, "from falling." (7) In Acts 1:18 the phrase *prēnēs*, headlong, with the aorist participle of *ginomai*, "to become," "falling headlong." lit., "having become headlong," is used of the suicide of Judas Iscariot. Some would render the word (it is a medical term) "swollen," (as connected with a form of the verb *pimprēmi*, "to burn"), indicating the condition of the body of certain suicides. (8) In Acts 20:9, KJV, *katapherō*, "to bear down," is translated "being fallen into" (RV, "borne down"), and then "he sunk down" (RV, ditto), the first of gradual oppression, the second (the aorist tense) of momentary effect. (9) In Acts 19:35 *diopetēs*, from *dios*, "heaven," *piptō*, "to fall," i.e., "fallen" from the sky, is rendered "image which fell down from Jupiter" (RV marg., "heaven").

FALSE, FALSEHOOD, FALSELY

A. Adjectives.

1. *pseudēs* (ψευδής, 5571), is used of "false witnesses," Acts 6:13; "false apostles," Rev. 2:2, RV, "false," KJV, "liars"; Rev. 21:8, "liars."¶

Note: For compound words with this adjective, see APOSTLE, BRETHREN, CHRIST, PROPHET, WITNESS.

2. *pseudōnumos* (ψευδώνυμος, 5581), "under a false name" (No. 1, and *onoma*, "a name"; Eng., "pseudonym"), is said of the knowledge professed by the propagandists of various heretical cults, 1 Tim. 6:20.¶

B. Noun.

pseudos (ψεῦδος, 5579), "a falsehood" (akin to A, No. 1), is so translated in Eph. 4:25, RV (KJV, "lying"); in 2 Thess. 2:9, "lying wonders" is lit. "wonders of falsehood," i.e., wonders calculated to deceive; it is elsewhere rendered "lie," John 8:44; Rom. 1:25; 2 Thess. 2:11; 1 John 2:21, 27; Rev. 14:5, RV; 21:27; 22:15. See GUILE, LIE. ¶

C. Verb.

pseudō (ψεύδω, 5574), "to deceive by lies," is used in the middle voice, translated "to say ... falsely," in Matt. 5:11; it is elsewhere rendered "to lie," Acts 5:3–4; Rom. 9:1; 2 Cor. 11:31; Gal. 1:20; Col. 3:9; 1 Tim. 2:7. See LIE.

FAME

A. Noun.

phēmē (φήμη, 5345) originally denoted "a divine voice, an oracle"; hence, "a saying or report" (akin to *phēmi*, "to say," from a root meaning "to shine, to be clear"; hence, Lat.,

fama, Eng., "fame"), is rendered "fame" in Matt. 9:26 and Luke 4:14.¶

Notes: (1) In Luke 5:15, RV, *logos*, "a word, report, account," is translated "report," for KJV, "fame." See REPORT. (2) *Akoē*, "a hearing," is translated "report" in the RV of Matt. 4:24; 14:1; Mark 1:28, for KJV, "fame." See EAR, No. 3. HEARING. (3) *Ēchos*, "a noise, report, sound," is translated "rumor," in the RV of Luke 4:37, for KJV, "fame"; "sound" in Acts 2:2; Heb. 12:19. See RUMOR, SOUND. ¶

B. Verb.

diaphēmizō (διαφημίζω, 1310) signifies "to spread abroad a matter," Matt. 28:15, RV; Mark 1:45, RV (from *dia*, "throughout," and *phēmi*, "to say"); hence, "to spread abroad one's fame," Matt. 9:31. All the passages under this heading relate to the testimony concerning Christ in the days of His flesh.¶

FAMILY

1. *oikos* (οἶκος, 3624) signifies (*a*) "a dwelling, a house" (akin to *oikeō*, to dwell); (*b*) "a household, family," translated "family" in 1 Tim. 5:4, RV, for KJV, "at home." See HOME, HOUSE, HOUSEHOLD, TEMPLE.

2. *patria* (πατριά, 3965), primarily "an ancestry, lineage," signifies in the NT "a family or tribe" (in the Sept. it is used of related people, in a sense wider than No. 1, but narrower than *phulē*, "a tribe," e.g., Exod. 12:3; Num. 32:28); it is used of the "family" of David, Luke 2:4, RV, for KJV, "lineage"; in the wider sense of "nationalities, races," Acts 3:25, RV, "families," for KJV, "kindreds"; in Eph. 3:15, RV, "every family," for KJV, "the whole family," the reference being to all those who are spiritually related to God the Father, He being the Author of their spiritual relationship to Him as His children, they being united to one another in "family" fellowship (*patria* is akin to *patēr*, "a father"); Luther's translation, "all who bear the name of children," is advocated by Cremer, p. 474. The phrase, however, is lit., "every family."¶ See KINDRED.¶

FAMINE

limos (λιμός, 3042) is translated "hunger" in Luke 15:17; 2 Cor. 11:27; elsewhere it signifies "a famine," and is so translated in each place in the RV; the KJV has the word "dearth" in Acts 7:11 and 11:28, and "hunger" in Rev. 6:8; the RV "famine" is preferable there; see Matt. 24:7; Mark 13:8; Luke 4:25; 15:14; 21:11; Rom. 8:35; Rev. 18:8. See HUNGER.¶

FAN

ptuon (πτύον, 4425) denotes "a winnowing shovel or fan," with which grain is thrown up against the wind, in order to separate the chaff, Matt. 3:12; Luke 3:17.¶

FAR

A. Adjective.

makros (μακρός, 3117) is used (*a*) of space and time, long, said of prayers (in some mss., Matt. 23:14), Mark 12:40; Luke 20:47; (*b*) of distance, "far, far" distant, Luke 15:13; 19:12. See LONG.¶

B. Adverbs.

1. *makran* (μακράν, 3112), properly a feminine form of the adjective above, denotes "a long way, far," (*a*) literally, Matt. 8:30, RV, "afar off." Luke 7:6; 15:20, RV, "afar off"; John 21:8; Acts 17:27; 22:21; (*b*) metaphorically, "far (from the kingdom of God)," Mark 12:34; in spiritual darkness, Acts 2:39; Eph. 2:13, 17. See AFAR.¶

2. *makrothen* (μακρόθεν, 3113), from "far" (akin to No. 1), Mark 8:3: see AFAR.

3. *porrō* (πόρρω, 4206) is used (*a*) literally, Luke 14:32, "a great way off"; the comparative degree *porrōteron*, "further," is used in 24:28; (*b*) metaphorically, of the heart in separation from God, Matt. 15:8; Mark 7:6. See FURTHER, WAY.¶ Cf. *porrōthen*, "afar off"; see AFAR.

Notes: (1) In Matt. 16:22, Peter's word to the Lord "be it far from Thee" translates the phrase *hileōs soi*, lit., "(God be) propitious to Thee," RV, marg., "God have mercy on Thee." Some would translate it "God avert this from Thee!" Others render it "God forbid!" Luther's translation is "spare Thyself." Lightfoot suggests "Nay, verily!" or "Away with the thought!" It was the vehement and impulsive utterance of Peter's horrified state of mind. *Hileōs* signifies "propitious, merciful," Heb. 8:12. See MERCY, C.¶ (2) In Luke 22:51, "thus far" translates the phrase *heōs toutou*, lit., "unto this." (3) In Gal. 6:14 the RV, "far be it" translates the phrase *mē genoito*, lit., "let it not be," elsewhere translated idiomatically "God forbid," e.g., Luke 20:16. See FORBID. (4) In Heb. 7:15 the KJV "far more" translates *perissoteron*, RV, "more abundantly"; see ABUNDANT. (5) In the following the verb *apodēmeō*, "to go abroad," is rendered, in the KJV, "to go into a far country," RV, "to go into another country," Matt. 21:33; 25:14; Mark 12:1; in Matt. 25:15, RV, "he went on his journey" (KJV, "took etc."). In Luke 15:13 the KJV and RV have "took (his) journey into a far country"; in Luke 20:9, RV, "another country," for KJV, "a far country."¶ The adjective *apodē-*

mos in Mark 13:34 is rendered in the KJV, "taking a far journey," RV, "sojourning in another country." See JOURNEY.¶ (6) In 2 Cor. 4:17 the phrase *kath' huperbolēn* is translated "more and more," RV, for KJV, "a far more." (7) In the following, *heōs*, used as a preposition, is translated "as far as" in the RV, for different words in the KJV; Acts 17:14, in the best mss., instead of *hōs*, which the KJV renders "as it were"; 17:15, "unto"; 23:23, "to." Both versions have "as far as" in 11:19, 22; in Luke 24:50, the RV has "until they were over against," for KJV, "as far as to." (8) In Rev. 14:20, the preposition *apo*, "from," is translated "as far as" in the RV, for KJV, "by the space of."

FARE, FAREWELL

1. *euphrainō* (εὐφραίνω, 2165), in the active voice, signifies "to cheer, gladden," 2 Cor. 2:2; in the passive, "to rejoice, make merry"; translated "faring sumptuously" in Luke 16:19, especially of food (RV, marg., "living in mirth and splendor"). See GLAD, MERRY, REJOICE.

2. *rhōnnumi* (ῥώννυμι, 4517), "to strengthen, to be strong," is used in the imperative mood as a formula at the end of letters, signifying "Farewell," Acts 15:29; some mss. have it in 23:30 (the RV omits it, as do most versions).¶

3. *echō* (ἔχω, 2192), "to have," is used idiomatically in Acts 15:36, RV, "(how) they fare," KJV, "how they do."

4. *chairō* (χαίρω, 5463), "to joy, rejoice, be glad," is used in the imperative mood in salutations, (*a*) on meeting, "Hail," e.g., Matt. 26:49; or with *legō*, "to say, to give a greeting," 2 John 11; in letters, "greeting," e.g., Acts 15:23; (*b*) at parting, the underlying thought being joy, 2 Cor. 13:11 (RV, marg., "rejoice"); (*c*) on other occasions, see the RV marg. in Phil. 3:1; 4:4. See GLAD, GREETING, No. 2, HAIL, JOY, JOYFULLY.

Note: As "farewell" is inadequate to express *chairō*, which always conveys the thought of joy or cheer, (*b*) properly comes under (*c*).

5. *apotassō* (ἀποτάσσω, 657) primarily denotes "to set apart"; then, in the middle voice, (*a*) "to take leave of, bid farewell to," Mark 6:46, "had taken leave of"; cf. Acts 18:18, 21; 2 Cor. 2:13 (in these three verses, the verb may signify to give final instructions to); Luke 9:61, "to bid farewell"; (*b*) "to forsake," Luke 14:33. In the papyri, besides saying goodbye, the stronger meaning is found of getting rid of a person (Moulton and Milligan). See FORSAKE, LEAVE (take), RENOUNCE, SEND (away).¶

Note: For *aspazomai*, "to bid farewell," see LEAVE (*c*), No. 2.

FARM

agros (ἀγρός, 68) denotes (*a*) "a field" (cf. Eng., "agriculture"), e.g., Matt. 6:28; (*b*) "the country," e.g., Mark 15:21, or, in the plural, "country places, farms," Mark 5:14; 6:36, 56; Luke 8:34; 9:12; (*c*) "a piece of ground," e.g., Mark 10:29; Acts 4:37; "a farm," Matt. 22:5. See COUNTRY, FIELD, GROUND, LAND.

Note: For the synonymous word *chōra*, "a country, land," see COUNTRY. Moulton and Milligan point out that *agros* is frequent in the Sept., and in the Synoptic Gospels, but that Luke uses *chōra* especially, and that possibly *agros* was a favorite word with translators from Hebrew and Aramaic.

For **FARTHER SIDE**, Mark 10:1, see **BEYOND**, No. 2

FARTHING

1. *assarion* (ἀσσάριον, 787), a diminutive of the Latin *as*, was one-tenth of a drachma, or one-sixteenth of a Roman *denarius*, i.e., about three farthings, Matt. 10:29; Luke 12:6.¶

2. *kodrantēs* (κοδράντης, 2835) was the Latin *quadrans*, "the fourth part of an *as*" (see No. 1), about two thirds of a farthing, Matt. 5:26; Mark 12:42.¶

FASHION

A. Nouns.

1. *eidos* (εἶδος, 1491), "that which is seen, an appearance," is translated "fashion" in Luke 9:29, of the Lord's countenance at the Transfiguration. See APPEARANCE, and *Note* under IMAGE, No. 1.

2. *prosōpon* (πρόσωπον, 4383), "the face, countenance," is translated "fashion" in Jas. 1:11, of the flower of grass. See COUNTENANCE. Cf. v. 24, "what manner of man," which translates *hopoios*, "of what sort."

3. *schēma* (σχῆμα, 4976), "a figure, fashion" (akin to *echō*, "to have"), is translated "fashion" in 1 Cor. 7:31, of the world, signifying that which comprises the manner of life, actions, etc. of humanity in general; in Phil. 2:8 it is used of the Lord in His being found "in fashion" as a man, and signifies what He was in the eyes of men, "the entire outwardly perceptible mode and shape of His existence, just as the preceding words *morphē*, "form," and *homoiōma*, "likeness," describe what He was in Himself as Man" (Gifford on the Incarnation, p. 44). "Men saw in Christ a human form, bearing, language, action, mode of life . . . in general the state and relations of a human being, so that in the entire mode of His appearance He made Himself known and was recognized as a man" (Meyer).

4. *tupos* (τύπος, 5179), "a type, figure, example," is translated "fashion" in the KJV of Acts 7:44, RV, "figure," said of the tabernacle. See ENSAMPLE.

B. Adverb.

houtōs (οὕτως, 3779), "thus, so, in this way," is rendered "on this fashion" in Mark 2:12. See EVEN, No. 5, LIKEWISE, MANNER, SO, THUS, WHAT.

C. Verbs.

1. *metaschēmatizō* (μετασχηματίζω, 3345), "to change in fashion or appearance" (*meta*, "after," here implying change, *schēma*, see A, No. 3), is rendered "shall fashion anew" in Phil. 3:21, RV; KJV, "shall change," of the bodies of believers as changed or raised at the Lord's return; in 2 Cor. 11:13, 14, 15, the RV uses the verb "to fashion oneself," for KJV, to transform, of Satan and his human ministers, false apostles; in 1 Cor. 4:6 it is used by way of a rhetorical device, with the significance of transferring by a figure. See CHANGE, TRANSFORM.¶

2. *suschēmatizō* (συσχηματίζω, 4964), "to give the same figure or appearance as, to conform to" (*sun*, "with," *schēma*, cf. No. 1), used in the passive voice, signifies "to fashion oneself, to be fashioned," Rom. 12:2, RV, "be not fashioned according to," for KJV, "be not conformed to"; 1 Pet. 1:14, "(not) fashioning yourselves." See CONFORMED.¶

Note: In Rom. 12:2 being outwardly "conformed" to the things of this age is contrasted with being "transformed" (or transfigured) inwardly by the renewal of the thoughts through the Holy Spirit's power. A similar distinction holds good in Phil. 3:21; the Lord will "fashion anew," or change outwardly, the body of our humiliation, and "conform" it in its nature (*summorphos*) to the body of His glory.

D. Adjective.

summorphos (σύμμορφος, 4832), "having like form with" (*sun*, "with," *morphē*, "form"), is used in Rom. 8:29 and Phil. 3:21 (KJV, "fashioned," RV, "conformed"). See CONFORM.¶

FAST, FASTING

A. Nouns.

1. *nēsteia* (νηστεία, 3521), "a fasting, fast" (from *nē*, a negative prefix, and *esthiō*, "to eat"), is used (*a*) of voluntary abstinence from food, Luke 2:37; Acts 14:23 (some mss. have it in Matt. 17:21 and Mark 9:29); "fasting" had become a common practice among Jews, and was continued among Christians; in Acts 27:9, "the Fast" refers to the Day of Atonement, Lev. 16:29; that time of the year would be one of

dangerous sailing; (b) of involuntary abstinence (perhaps voluntary is included), consequent upon trying circumstances, 2 Cor. 6:5; 11:27.¶

2. *nēstis* (νῆστις, 3523), "not eating" (see No. 1), "fasting," is used of lack of food, Matt. 15:32; Mark 8:3.¶

Note: Asitia, Acts 27:21, means "without food" (not through lack of supplies), i.e., abstinence from food. See ABSTINENCE, and cf. C, below.

B. Verb.

nēsteuō (νηστεύω, 3522), "to fast, to abstain from eating" (akin to A, Nos. 1 and 2), is used of voluntary "fasting," Matt.4:2; 6:16, 17, 18; 9:14, 15; Mark 2:18, 19, 20; Luke 5:33, 34, 35; 18:12; Acts 13:2, 3. Some of these passages show that teachers to whom scholars or disciples were attached gave them special instructions as to "fasting." Christ taught the need of purity and simplicity of motive.

The answers of Christ to the questions of the disciples of John and of the Pharisees reveal His whole purpose and method. No doubt He and His followers observed such a fast as that on the Day of Atonement, but He imposed no frequent "fasts" in addition. What He taught was suitable to the change of character and purpose which He designed for His disciples. His claim to be the Bridegroom, Matt. 9:15, and the reference there to the absence of "fasting," virtually involved a claim to be the Messiah (cf. Zech. 8:19).¶ Some mss. have the verb in Acts 10:30.

C. Adjective.

asitos (ἄσιτος, 777), "without food" (*a*, negative, *sitos*, "corn, food"), is used in Acts 27:33, "fasting." Cf. *asitia, Note* under A, No. 2.¶

FAST (to make)

asphalizō (ἀσφαλίζω, 805), "to make secure, safe, firm" (akin to *asphalēs*, "safe"), (*a*, negative, and *sphallō*, "to trip up"), is translated "make . . . fast," in Acts 16:24, of prisoners' feet in the stocks. In Matt. 27:64, 65, 66, it is rendered "to make sure." See SURE.¶

Note: For HOLD (fast) and STAND (fast), see HOLD and STAND, No. 7.

FASTEN

1. *atenizō* (ἀτενίζω, 816), from *atenēs*, "strained, intent," and *teinō*, "to stretch, strain" (from a root *ten—*, seen in Eng., "tension, tense," etc.), signifies "to look fixedly, gaze, fasten one's eyes upon," and is found twelve times in the writings of Luke (ten in the Acts), out of its fourteen occurrences. It always has a strongly intensive meaning, and is translated "to fasten the eyes upon" in the KJV and RV in Luke 4:20;

Acts 3:4; 11:6; so in the RV, where the KJV has different renderings, in Acts 6:15 (for KJV, "looking steadfastly"); 10:4 ("looked"); 13:9 ("set his eyes"); 14:9 ("steadfastly beholding"). In Acts 7:55, both have "looked up steadfastly." In the following the RV also varies the translation, Luke 22:56; Acts 1:10; 3:12; 23:1; 2 Cor. 3:7, 13. See BEHOLD, LOOK.¶

2. *kathaptō* (καθάπτω, 2510), "to fasten on, lay hold of, attack," is used of the serpent which fastened on Paul's hand, Acts 28:3.¶

FATHER

A. Noun.

patēr (πατήρ, 3962), from a root signifying "a nourisher, protector, upholder" (Lat., *pater*, Eng., "father," are akin), is used (*a*) of the nearest ancestor, e.g., Matt. 2:22; (*b*) of a more remote ancestor, the progenitor of the people, a "forefather," e.g., Matt. 3:9; 23:30; 1 Cor. 10:1; the patriarchs, 2 Pet. 3:4; (*c*) one advanced in the knowledge of Christ, 1 John 2:13; (*d*) metaphorically, of the originator of a family or company of persons animated by the same spirit as himself, as of Abraham, Rom. 4:11, 12, 16, 17, 18, or of Satan, John 8:38, 41, 44; (*e*) of one who, as a preacher of the gospel and a teacher, stands in a "father's" place, caring for his spiritual children, 1 Cor. 4:15 (not the same as a mere title of honor, which the Lord prohibited, Matt. 23:9); (*f*) of the members of the Sanhedrin, as of those who exercised religious authority over others, Acts 7:2; 22:1; (*g*) of God in relation to those who have been born anew (John 1:12, 13), and so are believers, Eph. 2:18; 4:6 (cf. 2 Cor. 6:18), and imitators of their "Father," Matt. 5:45, 48; 6:1, 4, 6, 8, 9, etc. Christ never associated Himself with them by using the personal pronoun "our"; He always used the singular, "My Father," His relationship being unoriginated and essential, whereas theirs is by grace and regeneration, e.g., Matt. 11:27; 25:34; John 20:17; Rev. 2:27; 3:5, 21; so the apostles spoke of God as the "Father" of the Lord Jesus Christ, e.g., Rom. 15:6; 2 Cor. 1:3; 11:31; Eph. 1:3; Heb. 1:5; 1 Pet. 1:3; Rev. 1:6; (*h*) of God, as the "Father" of lights, i.e., the Source or Giver of whatsoever provides illumination, physical and spiritual, Jas. 1:17; of mercies, 2 Cor. 1:3; of glory, Eph. 1:17; (*i*) of God, as Creator, Heb. 12:9 (cf. Zech. 12:1).

Note: Whereas the everlasting power and divinity of God are manifest in creation, His "Fatherhood" in spiritual relationship through faith is the subject of NT revelation, and waited for the presence on earth of the Son, Matt. 11:27; John 17:25. The spiritual relationship is not universal, John 8:42, 44 (cf. John 1:12 and Gal. 3:26).

B. Adjectives.

1. *patrōos* (πατρῷος, 3971) signifies "of one's fathers," or "received from one's fathers" (akin to A), Acts 22:3; 24:14; 28:17.¶ In the Sept., Prov. 27:10.¶

2. *patrikos* (πατρικός, 3967), "from one's fathers, or ancestors," is said of that which is handed down from one's "forefathers," Gal. 1:14.¶

3. *apatōr* (ἀπάτωρ, 540), "without father" (*a*, negative, and *patēr*), signifies, in Heb. 7:3, with no recorded genealogy.¶

4. *patroparadotos* (πατροπαράδοτος, 3970), "handed down from one's fathers" (*patēr*, and *paradidomi*, "to hand down"), is used in 1 Pet. 1:18.¶

FATHER-IN-LAW

pentheros (πενθερός, 3995), "a wife's father" (from a root signifying "a bond, union"), is found in John 18:13.¶

FATHERLESS

orphanos (ὀρφανός, 3737), properly, "an orphan," is rendered "fatherless" in Jas. 1:27; "desolate" in John 14:18, for KJV, "comfortless." See COMFORTLESS.¶

FATHOM

orguia (ὀργυιά, 3712), akin to *oregō*, "to stretch," is the length of the outstretched arms, about six feet, Acts 27:28 (twice).¶

FATLING, FATTED

1. *sitistos* (σιτιστός, 4619), "fattened," lit., "fed with grain" (from *siteuō*, "to feed, to fatten"), is used as a neuter plural noun, "fatlings," in Matt. 22:4.¶ Cf. *asitos*, under FASTING.

2. *siteutos* (σιτευτός, 4618), "fed" (with grain), denotes "fatted," Luke 15:23, 27, 30.¶

FATNESS

piotēs (πιότης, 4096), from *piōn*, "fat," from a root, *pi*—, signifying "swelling," is used metaphorically in Rom. 11:17. The gentile believer had become a sharer in the spiritual life and blessing bestowed by divine covenant upon Abraham and his descendants as set forth under the figure of "the root of (not 'and') the 'fatness' of the olive tree."¶

FAULT, FAULTLESS

A. Noun.

aition (αἴτιον, 158), properly the neuter of *aitios*, causative of, responsible for, is used as a noun, "a crime, a legal ground for punishment," translated "fault" in Luke 23:4, 14; in v. 22, "cause." See AUTHOR, CAUSE.

Notes: (1) For *aitia*, rendered "fault" in John 18:38; 19:4, 6, KJV (like *aition*, denoting "a ground for punishment"), see ACCUSATION, CAUSE, CHARGE. (2) For *hēttēma*, "a loss," translated "fault" in 1 Cor. 6:7, KJV, see DEFECT (RV). (3) For *paraptōma*, "a false step, a trespass," translated "fault" in Gal. 6:1, KJV, and "faults" in Jas. 5:16, KJV, see SIN, A, No. 2, *Note* (1), TRESPASS.

B. Adjective.

amemptos (ἄμεμπτος, 273), "without blame," is rendered "faultless," in Heb. 8:7. See BLAMELESS.

Note: For *anōmos*, "without blemish," rendered "faultless," i,e., without any shortcoming, in Jude 24, and "without fault" in Rev. 14:5, KJV, see BLEMISH.

C. Verbs.

1. *memphomai* (μέμφομαι, 3201), "to blame," is translated "to find fault" in Rom. 9:19 and Heb. 8:8. Some mss. have the verb in Mark 7:2. See BLAME.

2. *elenchō* (ἐλέγχω, 1651), "to convict, reprove, rebuke," is translated "shew (him) his fault" in Matt. 18:15. See CONVICT.

Note: In 1 Pet. 2:20, KJV, the verb *hamartanō*, "to sin" (strictly, to miss the mark) is rendered "for your faults." The RV corrects to "when ye sin (and are buffeted for it)."

FAVOR, FAVORED

A. Noun.

charis (χάρις, 5485) denotes (*a*) objectively, "grace in a person, graciousness," (*b*) subjectively, (1) "grace on the part of a giver, favor, kindness," (2) "a sense of favor received, thanks." It is rendered "favor" in Luke 1:30; 2:52; Acts 2:47; 7:10, 46; 24:27 and 25:9, RV (for KJV, "pleasure"); 25:3; see more fully under GRACE.

B. Verb.

charitoō (χαριτόω, 5487), akin to A, to endow with *charis*, primarily signified "to make graceful or gracious," and came to denote, in Hellenistic Greek, "to cause to find favor," Luke 1:28, "highly favored" (marg., "endued with grace"); in Eph. 1:6, it is translated "made . . . accepted," KJV, "freely bestowed," RV (lit., "graced"); it does not here mean to endue with grace. Grace implies more than favor; grace is a free gift, favor may be deserved or gained.¶

FEAR, FEARFUL, FEARFULNESS

A. Nouns.

1. *phobos* (φόβος, 5401) first had the meaning of "flight," that which is caused by being

scared; then, "that which may cause flight," (*a*) "fear, dread, terror," always with this significance in the four Gospels; also e.g., in Acts 2:43; 19:17; 1 Cor. 2:3; 1 Tim. 5:20 (lit., "may have fear"); Heb. 2:15; 1 John 4:18; Rev. 11:11; 18:10, 15; by metonymy, that which causes "fear," Rom. 13:3; 1 Pet. 3:14, RV, "(their) fear," KJV "(their) terror," an adaptation of the Sept. of Isa. 8:12, "fear not their fear"; hence some take it to mean, as there, "what they fear," but in view of Matt. 10:28, e.g., it seems best to understand it as that which is caused by the intimidation of adversaries; (*b*) "reverential fear," (1) of God, as a controlling motive of the life, in matters spiritual and moral, not a mere "fear" of His power and righteous retribution, but a wholesome dread of displeasing Him, a "fear" which banishes the terror that shrinks from His presence, Rom. 8:15, and which influences the disposition and attitude of one whose circumstances are guided by trust in God, through the indwelling Spirit of God, Acts 9:31; Rom. 3:18; 2 Cor. 7:1; Eph. 5:21 (RV, "the fear of Christ"); Phil. 2:12; 1 Pet. 1:17 (a comprehensive phrase: the reverential "fear" of God will inspire a constant carefulness in dealing with others in His "fear"); 3:2, 15; the association of "fear and trembling," as, e.g., in Phil. 2:12, has in the Sept. a much sterner import, e.g., Gen. 9:2; Exod. 15:16; Deut. 2:25; 11:25; Ps. 55:5; Isa. 19:16; (2) of superiors, e.g., Rom. 13:7; 1 Pet. 2:18. See TERROR.

2. *deilia* (δειλία, 1167), "fearfulness" (from *deos*, "fright"), is rightly rendered "fearfulness" in 2 Tim. 1:7, RV (for KJV, "fear "). That spirit is not given us of God. The word denotes "cowardice and timidity" and is never used in a good sense, as No. 1 is.¶ Cf. *deilos*, B, No. 2, below, and *deiliaō*, to be fearful (KJV, "afraid"), John 14:27.¶

3. *eulabeia* (εὐλάβεια, 2124) signifies, firstly, "caution"; then, "reverence, godly fear," Heb. 5:7; 12:28, in best mss., "reverence"; in general, "apprehension, but especially holy fear," "that mingled fear and love which, combined, constitute the piety of man toward God; the OT places its emphasis on the fear, the NT . . . on the love, though there was love in the fear of God's saints then, as there must be fear in their love now" (Trench, *Syn.* §xlviii).¶ In the Sept., Josh. 22:24; Prov. 28:14.¶

Note: In Luke 21:11, *phobētron* (akin to No. 1) denotes a terror, RV, "terrors," for KJV, "fearful sights," i.e., objects or instruments of terror.¶

B. Adjectives.

1. *phoberos* (φοβερός, 5398), "fearful" (akin to A, No. 1), is used only in the active sense in

the NT, i.e., causing "fear," terrible, Heb. 10:27, 31; 12:21, RV, "fearful," for KJV, "terrible."¶

2. *deilos* (δειλός, 1169), "cowardly" (see A, No. 2), "timid," is used in Matt. 8:26; Mark 4:40; Rev. 21:8 (here "the fearful" are first in the list of the transgressors).¶

3. *ekphobos* (ἔκφοβος, 1630) signifies "frightened outright" (*ek*, "out," intensive, and A, No. 1), Heb. 12:21 (with *eimi*, "I am"), "I exceedingly fear" (see No. 4); Mark 9:6, "sore afraid."¶

4. *entromos* (ἔντρομος, 1790), "trembling with fear" (*en*, "in," intensive, and *tremō*, "to tremble, quake"; Eng., "tremor," etc.), is used with *ginomai*, "to become," in Acts 7:32, "trembled"; 16:29, RV, "trembling for fear"; with *eimi*, "to be," in Heb. 12:21, "quake" (some mss. have *ektromos* here). See QUAKE, TREMBLE.¶ The distinction between No. 3 and No. 4, as in Heb. 12:21, would seem to be that *ekphobos* stresses the intensity of the "fear," *entromos* the inward effect, "I inwardly tremble (or quake)."

C. Adverb.

aphobōs (ἀφόβως, 880) denotes "without fear" (*a*, negative, and A, No. 1), and is said of serving the Lord, Luke 1:74; of being among the Lord's people as His servant, 1 Cor. 16:10; of ministering the Word of God, Phil. 1:14; of the evil of false spiritual shepherds, Jude 12.¶ In the Sept., Prov. 1:33.¶

D. Verbs.

1. *phobeō* (φοβέω, 5399), in earlier Greek, "to put to flight" (see A, No. 1), in the NT is always in the passive voice, with the meanings either (*a*) "to fear, be afraid," its most frequent use, e.g., Acts 23:10, according to the best mss. (see No. 2); or (*b*) "to show reverential fear" [see A, No. 1, (*b*)], (1) of men, Mark 6:20; Eph. 5:33, RV, "fear," for KJV, "reverence"; (2) of God, e.g., Acts 10:2, 22; 13:16, 26; Col. 3:22 (RV, "the Lord "); 1 Pet. 2:17; Rev. 14:7; 15:4; 19:5; (*a*) and (*b*) are combined in Luke 12:4, 5, where Christ warns His followers not to be afraid of men, but to "fear" God. See MARVEL, B, No. 1, *Note.*

2. *eulabeomai* (εὐλαβέομαι, 2125), "to be cautious, to beware" (see A, No. 3), signifies to act with the reverence produced by holy "fear," Heb. 11:7, "moved with godly fear."

Notes: (1) In Acts 23:10 some mss. have this verb with the meaning (*a*) under No. 1.

(2) In Luke 3:14, *diaseiō*, "to shake violently, to intimidate, to extort by violence, blackmail," is rendered "put no man in fear" in KJV marg. See VIOLENCE.

FEAST

A. Nouns.

1. *heortē* (ἑορτή, 1859), "a feast or festival," is used (*a*) especially of those of the Jews, and particularly of the Passover; the word is found mostly in John's gospel (seventeen times); apart from the Gospels it is used in this way only in Acts 18:21; (*b*) in a more general way, in Col. 2:16, KJV, "holy day," RV, "a feast day."

2. *deipnon* (δεῖπνον, 1173) denotes (*a*) "the chief meal of the day," dinner or supper, taken at or towards evening; in the plural "feasts," Matt. 23:6; Mark 6:21; 12:39; Luke 20:46; otherwise translated "supper," Luke 14:12, 16, 17, 24; John 12:2; 13:2, 4; 21:20; 1 Cor. 11:21 (of a social meal); (*b*) "the Lord's Supper," 1 Cor. 11:20; (*c*) "the supper or feast" which will celebrate the marriage of Christ with His spiritual Bride, at the inauguration of His Kingdom, Rev. 19:9; (*d*) figuratively, of that to which the birds of prey will be summoned after the overthrow of the enemies of the Lord at the termination of the war of Armageddon, 19:17 (cf. Ezek. 39:4, 17–20). See SUPPER.¶

3. *dochē* (δοχή, 1403), "a reception feast, a banquet" (from *dechomai*, "to receive"), Luke 5:29; 14:13 (not the same as No. 2; see v. 12).¶

4. *gamos* (γάμος, 1062), "a wedding," especially a wedding "feast" (akin to *gameō*, "to marry"); it is used in the plural in the following passages (the RV rightly has "marriage feast" for the KJV, "marriage," or "wedding"), Matt. 22:2, 3, 4, 9 (in verses 11, 12, it is used in the singular, in connection with the wedding garment); 25:10; Luke 12:36; 14:8; in the following it signifies a wedding itself, John 2:1, 2; Heb. 13:4; and figuratively in Rev. 19:7, of the marriage of the Lamb; in v. 9 it is used in connection with the supper, the wedding supper (or what in English is termed "breakfast"), not the wedding itself, as in v. 7.

5. *agapē* (ἀγάπη, 26), "love," is used in the plural in Jude 12, signifying "love feasts," RV (KJV, "feasts of charity"); in the corresponding passage, 2 Pet. 2:13, the most authentic mss. have the word *apatē*, in the plural, "deceivings."

Notes: (1) In 1 Cor. 10:27 the verb *kaleō*, "to call," in the sense of inviting to one's house, is translated "biddeth you (to a feast)"; in the most authentic texts there is no separate phrase representing "to a feast," as in some mss., *eis deipnon* (No. 2). (2) In Mark 14:2 and John 2:23 the KJV translates *heortē* (see No. 1) by "feast day" (RV, "feast"). (3) For the "Feast of the Dedication," John 10:22, see DEDICATION.

B. Verbs.

1. *heortazō* (ἑορτάζω, 1858), "to keep festival" (akin to A, No. 1) is translated "let us keep the feast," in 1 Cor. 5:8. This is not the Lord's Supper, nor the Passover, but has reference to the continuous life of the believer as a festival or holy-day (see KJV, margin), in freedom from "the leaven of malice and wickedness, but with the unleavened bread of sincerity and truth."¶

2. *suneuōcheō* (συνευωχέω, 4910), "to entertain sumptuously with," is used in the passive voice, denoting "to feast sumptuously with" (*sun*, "together," and *euōchia*, "good cheer"), "to revel with," translated "feast with" in 2 Pet. 2:13 and Jude 12.¶

FEEBLE

asthenēs (ἀσθενής, 772), "without strength" (*a*, negative, and *sthenos*, "strength"), is translated "feeble" in 1 Cor. 12:22, of members of the body. See IMPOTENT, SICK, STRENGTH, B, *Note* (5), WEAK.

Notes: (1) In Heb. 12:12 *paraluō*, "to weaken, enfeeble," in the passive voice, "to be enfeebled," as by a paralytic stroke, is translated "feeble" in the KJV (RV, "palsied"). (2) For "feeble-minded" in 1 Thess. 5:14, KJV, see FAINT-HEARTED.

FEED, FED

1. *boskō* (βόσκω, 1006), "to feed," is primarily used of a herdsman (from *boō*, "to nourish," the special function being to provide food; the root is *bo*, found in *botēr*, "a herdsman or herd," and *botanē*, "fodder, pasture"); its uses are (*a*) literal, Matt. 8:30; in v. 33, the RV corrects the KJV, "they that kept," to "they that fed," as in Mark 5:14 (KJV and RV) and Luke 8:34; in Mark 5:11 and Luke 8:32, "feeding"; Luke 15:15; (*b*) metaphorical, of spiritual ministry, John 21:15, 17 (see *Note* on No. 2). See KEEP.¶

2. *poimainō* (ποιμαίνω, 4165), "to act as a shepherd" (from *poimēn*, "a shepherd"), is used (*a*) literally, Luke 17:7, RV, "keeping sheep," for KJV, "feeding cattle"; 1 Cor. 9:7; (*b*) metaphorically, "to tend, to shepherd"; said of Christ, Matt. 2:6, RV, "shall be Shepherd of" (for KJV, "shall rule"); of those who act as spiritual shepherds under Him, John 21:16, RV, "tend" (for KJV "feed"); so 1 Pet. 5:2; Acts 20:28, "to feed" ("to tend" would have been a consistent rendering; a shepherd does not only "feed" his flock); of base shepherds, Jude 12. See RULE.

Note: In John 21:15, 16, 17, the Lord, addressing Peter, first uses No. 1, *boskō* (v. 15), then No. 2, *poimainō* (v. 16), and then returns to *boskō* (v. 17). These are not simply interchangeable (nor are other variations in His remarks); a study of the above notes will show this. Nor, again, is there a progression of ideas. The lesson to be learnt, as Trench points out (*Syn.* §xxv), is that, in the spiritual care of God's children, the "feeding" of the flock from the Word of God is the constant and regular necessity; it is to have the foremost place. The tending (which includes this) consists of other acts, of discipline, authority, restoration, material assistance of individuals, but they are incidental in comparison with the "feeding."

3. *trephō* (τρέφω, 5142) signifies (*a*) "to make to grow, bring up, rear," Luke 4:16, "brought up"; (*b*) "to nourish, feed," Matt. 6:26; 25:37; Luke 12:24; Acts 12:20; Rev. 12:6, 14; of a mother, "to give suck," Luke 23:29 (some mss. here have *thēlazō*, "to suckle"); "to fatten," as of fattening animals, Jas. 5:5, "ye have nourished (your hearts)." See BRING, A, No. 33.¶

4. *chortazō* (χορτάζω, 5526), "to feed, to fatten," is used (*a*) primarily of animals, Rev. 19:21; (*b*) of persons, to fill or satisfy with food. It is usually translated by the verb "to fill," but is once rendered "to be fed," in Luke 16:21, of Lazarus, in his desire for the crumbs (he could be well supplied with them) that fell from the rich man's table, a fact which throws light upon the utter waste that went on at the table of the latter. The crumbs that fell would provide no small meal. See FILL, SATISFY.

5. *psōmizō* (ψωμίζω, 5595) primarily denotes "to feed with morsels," as nurses do children; then, "to dole out or supply with food," Rom. 12:20; 1 Cor. 13:3.¶ Cf. *psōmion*, "a fragment, morsel," John 13:26, 27, 30 ("sop").¶

6. *potizō* (ποτίζω, 4222), to give to drink, is translated "I fed (you with milk)" in 1 Cor. 3:2. See DRINK, WATER.

FEEL, FEELING, FELT

1. *ginōskō* (γινώσκω, 1097), "to know, perceive," is translated "she felt (in her body)," of the woman with the issue of blood, Mark 5:29, i.e., she became aware of the fact. See KNOW.

2. *phroneō* (φρονέω, 5426), "to think, to be minded," is translated "I felt" in the RV of 1 Cor. 13:11 (for KJV, "I understood"). See CAREFUL.

3. *psēlaphaō* (ψηλαφάω, 5584), "to feel or grope about" (from *psaō*, "to touch"), expressing the motion of the hands over a surface, so as to "feel" it, is used (*a*) metaphorically, of seeking after God, Acts 17:27; (*b*) literally, of physical handling or touching, Luke 24:39 with 1 John 1:1; Heb. 12:18. See HANDLE, TOUCH.¶

4. *sumpatheō* (συμπαθέω, 4834), "to have a fellow-feeling for or with," is rendered "touched with the feeling of" in Heb. 4:15; "have compassion" in 10:34. See COMPASSION.¶

5. *apalgeō* (ἀπαλγέω, 524) signifies "to cease to feel pain for" (*apo*, "from," *algeō*, "to feel pain"; cf. Eng., "neuralgia"); hence, to be callous, "past feeling," insensible to honor and shame, Eph. 4:19.¶

Note: In Acts 28:5 *paschō*, "to suffer," is rendered "felt (no harm)," RV, "took," lit., "suffered no ill (effect)."

For FEET see FOOT

FEIGN, FEIGNED

A. Verb.

hupokrinomai (ὑποκρίνομαι, 5271) primarily denotes "to answer"; then, "to answer on the stage, play a part," and so, metaphorically, "to feign, pretend," Luke 20:20.¶ Cf. *hupokritēs*, "a hypocrite," and *hupokrisis*, "hypocrisy."

B. Adjective.

plastos (πλαστός, 4112) primarily denotes "formed, molded" (from *plassō*, to mold; Eng., "plastic"); then, metaphorically, "made up, fabricated, feigned," 2 Pet. 2:3.¶ Cf. *plasma*, "that which is molded," Rom. 9:20.¶

For FELL see FALL

FELLOW

1. *anēr* (ἀνήρ, 435) denotes "a man," in relation to his sex or age; in Acts 17:5 (plural) it is rendered "fellows," as more appropriate to the accompanying description of them. See HUSBAND, MAN, SIR.

2. *hetairos* (ἑταῖρος, 2083), "a companion, comrade," is translated "fellows" in Matt. 11:16 [where, however, the most authentic mss. have *heterois*, "(the) others"]. The word is used only by Matthew and is translated "friend"in 20:13; 22:12; 26:50. See FRIEND.¶

3. *metochos* (μέτοχος, 3353), properly an adjective, signifying "sharing in, partaking of," is translated "partners" in Luke 5:7; "partakers" in Heb. 3:1, 14; 6:4; 12:8; "fellows" in Heb. 1:9, of those who share in a heavenly calling, or have held, or will hold, a regal position in relation to the earthly, messianic kingdom. (Cf. *summetochos*, "fellow-partakers," in Eph. 3:6, RV). See PARTAKER, PARTNER.

Notes: (1) In Acts 24:5 *loimos*, "a plague, a pest," is rendered "a pestilent fellow." This is a sample of the strongest use of the epithet "fellow." (2) *Toioutos*, an adjective, "such a one," is often used as a noun, e.g., Acts 22:22, where it is translated "such a fellow." (3) *Houtos*, "this," is translated "this fellow" in the KJV of Luke 23:2 (RV, "this man"). So in John 9:29. Both versions have "this man," e.g., in Mark 2:7; John 6:52, in the same contemptuous sense.

(4) For the word in combination with various nouns see CITIZEN, DISCIPLE, ELDER, HEIR, HELPER, LABORER, MEMBER, PARTNER, PRISONER, SERVANT, SOLDIER, WORK, WORKER.

FELLOWSHIP

A. Nouns.

1. *koinōnia* (κοινωνία, 2842), (*a*) "communion, fellowship, sharing in common" (from *koinos*, "common"), is translated "communion" in 1 Cor. 10:16; Philem. 6, RV, "fellowship," for KJV, "communication"; it is most frequently translated "fellowship"; (*b*) "that which is the outcome of fellowship, a contribution," e.g., Rom. 15:26; 2 Cor. 8:4. See COMMUNION, CONTRIBUTION, etc.

Note: In Eph. 3:9, some mss. have *koinōnia*, instead of *oikonomia*, "dispensation," RV.

2. *metochē* (μετοχή, 3352), "partnership" (akin to No. 3, under FELLOW), is translated "fellowship" in 2 Cor. 6:14.¶ In the Sept., Ps. 122:3, "Jerusalem is built as a city whose fellowship is complete."¶ The word seems to have a more restricted sense than *koinōnia*. Cf. the verb form in Heb. 2:14.

3. *koinōnos* (κοινωνός, 2844) denotes "a partaker" or "partner" (akin to No. 1); in 1 Cor. 10:20 it is used with *ginomai*, "to become," "that ye should have communion with," RV (KJV, "fellowship with"). See COMPANION, PARTAKER, PARTNER.

B. Verbs.

1. *koinōneō* (κοινωνέω, 2841), "to have fellowship," is so translated in Phil. 4:15, RV, for KJV, "did communicate." See COMMUNICATE.

2. *sunkoinōneō* (συγκοινωνέω, 4790), "to have fellowship with or in" (*sun*, "with," and No. 1), is used in Eph. 5:11; Phil. 4:14, RV, "ye had fellowship," for KJV, "ye did communicate"; Rev. 18:4, RV, "have (no) fellowship with," for KJV, "be (not) partakers of." See COMMUNICATE, PARTAKER.¶

For **FELT** see **FEEL**

FEMALE

thēlus (θῆλυς, 2338), an adjective (from *thēlē*, "a breast"), is used in the form *thēlu* (grammatically neuter) as a noun, "female," in Matt. 19:4; Mark 10:6; Gal. 3:28; in the feminine form *thēleia*, in Rom. 1:26, "women"; v. 27 "woman." See WOMAN.¶

FERVENT, FERVENTLY

A. Adjective.

ektenēs (ἐκτενής, 1618) denotes "strained, stretched" (*ek*, "out," *teinō*, "to stretch"); hence, metaphorically, "fervent," 1 Pet. 4:8. Some mss. have it in Acts 12:5, for the adverb (see B).¶

Cf. *ekteneia* (with *en*), "intently, strenuously," in Acts 26:7, KJV, "instantly," RV, "earnestly." Cf. EARNEST.

B. Adverb.

ektenōs (ἐκτενῶς, 1619), "fervently" (akin to A), is said of love, in 1 Pet. 1:22; of prayer, in some mss., Acts 12:5 (see under A); for the comparative degree in Luke 22:44, see EARNESTLY.¶

C. Verb.

zeō (ζέω, 2204), "to be hot, to boil" (Eng. "zeal" is akin), is metaphorically used of "fervency" of spirit, Acts 18:25; Rom. 12:11.¶

Notes: (1) In Col. 4:12, the verb *agōnizomai*, "to strive," is translated "laboring fervently," KJV (RV, "striving"). (2) In 2 Cor. 7:7, the noun *zēlos*, "zeal" (akin to C.), is translated "fervent mind," KJV (RV, "zeal"). (3) In Jas. 5:17, "he prayed fervently" (KJV, "earnestly") translates the noun *proseuchē*, followed by the corresponding verb, lit., "he prayed with prayer." In v. 16 *deēsis*, "supplication," is so translated in the RV, for the KJV, "effectual fervent prayer." There is nothing in the original corresponding to the word "effectual." The phrase, including the verb *energeomai*, "to work in," is, lit., "the inworking supplication," suggesting a supplication consistent with inward conformity to the mind of God. (4) For "fervent heat" see HEAT, B.

FETCH

metapempō (μεταπέμπω, 3343), "to send after or for" (*meta*, "after," *pempō*, "to send"), in the middle voice, is translated "fetch" in the RV of Acts 10:5 and 11:13. See CALL.

Notes: (1) In Acts 16:37, the RV gives to *exagō*, "to bring out," the adequate meaning "let them ... bring us out," for the KJV, "let them fetch us out." "Fetch" is not sufficiently dignified for the just demand made. (2) For Acts 28:13, KJV, "fetched a compass," see CIRCUIT.

FETTER

pedē (πέδη, 3976), "a fetter" (akin to *peza*, "the instep," and *pous*, "a foot"; cf. Eng. prefix *ped*—), occurs in Mark 5:4 and Luke 8:29. Cf. FOOT.¶

FEVER (to be sick of)

A. Noun.

puretos (πυρετός, 4446), "feverish heat" (from *pur*, "fire"), hence, "a fever," occurs in Matt. 8:15; Mark 1:31; John 4:52; Acts 28:8; in Luke 4:38, with *megas*, "great, a high fever"; v. 39. Luke, as a physician, uses the medical distinction by which the ancients classified fevers into great and little.¶ In the Sept., Deut. 28:22.¶

B. Verb.

puressō (πυρέσσω, 4445) signifies "to be ill of a fever" (akin to A), Matt. 8:14; Mark 1:30.¶

FEW

A. Adjectives.

1. *oligos* (ὀλίγος, 3641), used of number, quantity, and size, denotes "few, little, small, slight," e.g., Matt. 7:14; 9:37; 15:34; 20:16; neuter plural, "a few things," Matt. 25:21, 23; Rev. 2:14 (20 in some mss.); in Eph. 3:3, the phrase *en oligō*, in brief, is translated "in a few words."

2. *brachus* (βραχύς, 1024) denotes (a) "short," in regard to time, e.g., Heb. 2:7; or distance, Acts 27:28; (b) "few," in regard to quantity, Heb. 13:22, in the phrase *dia bracheōn*, lit., "by means of few," i.e., "in few words." See LITTLE.

Note: In Luke 10:42, in the Lord's words to Martha, many ancient authorities provide the rendering, "but there is need of few things (neuter plural) or one."

B. Adverb.

suntomōs (συντόμως, 4935), "concisely, briefly, cut short" (from *suntemnō*, "to cut in pieces," *sun*, used intensively, *temnō*, "to cut"), occurs in the speech of Tertullus, Acts 24:4.¶

FICKLENESS

elaphria (ἐλαφρία, 1644) denotes lightness, levity, "fickleness," 2 Cor. 1:17, RV (for KJV, "lightness").¶ The corresponding adjective is *elaphros*, "light," Matt. 11:30; 2 Cor. 4:17.¶

FIDELITY

pistis (πίστις, 4102), "faith, faithfulness," is translated "fidelity" in Titus 2:10. See FAITH (b).

FIELD, CORNFIELD

1. *agros* (ἀγρός, 68), "a cultivated field," or "fields in the aggregate," e.g., Matt. 6:28; Mark 11:8 (some mss. here have *dendrōn*, "trees"); Luke 15:15. See FARM.

2. *chōra* (χώρα, 5561), (a) "a space, place," then, (b) "land, country, region," is translated "fields" in John 4:35; Jas. 5:4. See COUNTRY.

3. *chōrion* (χωρίον, 5564), a diminutive of No. 2, denotes (a) "a place, region," (b) "a piece of land, property," rendered "field" in Acts 1:18, 19. See LAND, PARCEL, PLACE, POSSESSION.

4. *sporimos* (σπόριμος, 4702) signifies "fit for sowing" (from *speirō*, "to sow"), and denotes "a cornfield," Matt. 12:1; Mark 2:23; Luke 6:1.¶ In the Sept., Gen. 1:29; Lev. 11:37.¶

FIERCE, FIERCENESS

A. Adjectives.

1. *anēmeros* (ἀνήμερος, 434) signifies "not tame, savage" (from *a*, negative, and *hēmeros*,

"gentle"), 2 Tim. 3:3. Epictetus describes those who forget God as their creator, as resembling lions, "wild, savage and fierce" (*anēmeroi*) (Moulton and Milligan, Greek Test. Vocab.).¶

2. *chalepos* (χαλεπός, 5467) "hard," (a) "hard to do or deal with, difficult, fierce," is said of the Gadarene demoniacs, Matt. 8:28; (b) "hard to bear, painful, grievous," said of the last times, 2 Tim. 3:1, RV, "grievous," for KJV, "perilous." See GRIEVOUS.¶

Notes: (1) In Jas. 3:4, *sklēros*, "hard, rough, violent," is said of winds, RV, "rough," for KJV, "fierce." (2) In Luke 23:5, the verb *epischuō*, "to make or grow stronger" (from *epi*, "over," intensive, and *ischus*, "strength"), is used metaphorically, "they were the more urgent," RV, for KJV, "the more fierce."¶

B. Nouns.

1. *thumos* (θυμός, 2372), "hot anger, wrath," is rendered "fierceness" in Rev. 16:19; 19:15, of the wrath of God. See ANGER(A, *Notes*), INDIGNATION, WRATH.

2. *zēlos* (ζῆλος, 2205), "zeal, jealousy," is rendered "fierceness" in Heb. 10:27, RV (of fire).

FIERY

puroō (πυρόω, 4448), "to set on fire, burn up" (from *pur*, "fire"), always used in the passive voice in the NT, is translated "fiery" in Eph. 6:16, metaphorically of the darts of the evil one; "fire-tipped" would perhaps bring out the verbal force of the word. The most ancient mss. have the article repeated, lit., "the darts of the evil one, the fiery (darts)," marking them as particularly destructive. Some mss. omit the repeated article. In ancient times, darts were often covered with burning material. See BURN, FIRE, TRY, *Note* (1).

Notes: (1) For Heb. 10:27, RV, see FIRE (cf. FIERCE, B, No. 2). (2) For *purōsis*, "a fiery trial," 1 Pet. 4:12, (lit., "a burning," as in Rev. 18:9, 18), "a refining, or trial by fire," see TRIAL.

FIFTEEN, FIFTEENTH

dekapente (δεκαπέντε, 1178), lit., "ten-five," occurs in John 11:18; Acts 27:28; Gal. 1:18.¶

Notes: (1) In Acts 7:14, "threescore and fifteen" translates a different numeral, lit., "seventy-five." This refers to all Joseph's kindred whom he sent for. There is no discrepancy between this and Gen. 46:26. The Sept. translations give the number as 75 in Gen. 46:27 and in Exod. 1:5, and this Stephen follows, being a Grecian Jew. (2) The corresponding ordinal numeral *pentekaidekatos*, "fifteenth" (lit., "five and tenth") is found In Luke 3:1, where Luke dates the reign of Tiberias from the period of his joint rule with Augustus.

FIFTH

pemptos (πέμπτος, 3991), akin to *pente*, "five," is found only in the Apocalypse, 6:9; 9:1; 16:10; 21:20.¶

FIFTY

pentēkonta (πεντήκοντα, 4004) is found in Luke 7:41; 16:6; John 8:57; 21:11; Acts 13:20; in Mark 6:40 with *kata* (in the most authentic mss.), according to, "by fifties"; in Luke 9:14, with *ana*, "up," used distributively, "fifty each," RV (Luke adds *hōsei*, "about").¶

FIG

1. *sukon* (σῦκον, 4810) denotes "the ripe fruit of a *sukē*, a fig-tree" (see below; cf. No. 2), Matt. 7:16; Mark 11:13; Luke 6:44; Jas. 3:12.¶

2. *olunthos* (ὄλυνθος, 3653) denotes "an unripe fig," which grows in winter and usually falls off in the spring, Rev. 6:13.¶ In the Sept., Song of Sol., 2:13.¶

FIG TREE

sukē or *sukea* (συκῆ, 4808), "a fig tree," is found in Matt. 21:19, 20, 21; 24:32; Mark 11:13, 20, 21; 13:28; Luke 13:6, 7; 21:29; John 1:48, 50; Jas. 3:12; Rev. 6:13 (see *sukon*, above).¶

Note: A "fig tree" with leaves must have young fruits already, or it will be barren for the season. The first figs ripen in late May or early June. The tree in Mark 11:13 should have had fruit, unripe indeed, but existing. In some lands "fig trees" bear the early fruit under the leaves and the later fruit above the leaves. In that case the leaves were a sign that there should have been fruit, unseen from a distance, underneath the leaves. The condemnation of this fig tree lay in the absence of any sign of fruit.

FIGHT

A. Nouns.

1. *agōn* (ἀγών, 73), akin to *agō*, "to lead," primarily "a gathering," then, "a place of assembly," and hence, "a contest, conflict," is translated "fight" in 1 Tim. 6:12; 2 Tim. 4:7. See CONFLICT.

2. *athlēsis* (ἄθλησις, 119) is translated "fight" in Heb. 10:32, KJV. See CONFLICT.¶

Note: In Heb. 11:34, *polemos*, "war," is translated "fight," KJV (RV, "war"); it is misrendered "battle" in the KJV of 1 Cor. 14:8; Rev. 9:7, 9; 16:14; 20:8.

B. Verbs.

1. *agōnizomai* (ἀγωνίζομαι, 75), from A, No. 1, denotes (*a*) "to contend" in the public games, 1 Cor. 9:25 ("striveth in the games," RV);

(*b*) "to fight, engage in conflict," John 18:36; (*c*) metaphorically, "to contend" perseveringly against opposition and temptation, 1 Tim. 6:12; 2 Tim. 4:7 (cf. A, No. 1; in regard to the meaning there, the evidence of *Koinē* inscriptions is against the idea of games-contests); to strive as in a contest for a prize, straining every nerve to attain to the object, Luke 13:24; to put forth every effort, involving toil, Col. 1:29; 1 Tim. 4:10 (some mss. have *oneidizomai* here, "to suffer reproach"); to wrestle earnestly in prayer, Col. 4:12 (cf. *sunagōnizomai*, Rom. 15:30). See LABOR, STRIVE.¶

2. *pukteuō* (πυκτεύω, 4438), "to box" (from *puktēs*, "a pugilist"), one of the events in the Olympic games, is translated "fight" in 1 Cor. 9:26.¶

3. *machomai* (μάχομαι, 3164), "to fight," is so rendered in Jas. 4:2 (cf. "fightings," v. 1, see below), and translated "strive" in 2 Tim. 2:24; "strove" in John 6:52; Acts 7:26. See STRIVE.¶

4. *thēriomacheō* (θηριομαχέω, 2341) signifies "to fight with wild beasts" (*thērion*, "a beast," and No. 3), 1 Cor. 15:32. Some think that the apostle was condemned to fight with wild beasts; if so, he would scarcely have omitted it from 2 Cor. 11:23–end. Moreover, he would have lost his status as a Roman citizen. Probably he uses the word figuratively of contending with ferocious men. Ignatius so uses it in his Ep. to the Romans.¶

Notes: (1) In Rev. 2:16 and 12:7, KJV, *polemeō*, "to war," is translated "to fight," RV, "will make war," "*going forth* to war," and "warred." (2) In Acts 23:9 some mss. have the verb *theomacheō*, "to fight against God." Cf. the corresponding adjective, below, under FIGHTING.

FIGHTING

A. Noun.

machē (μάχη, 3163), "a fight, strife" (akin to B, No. 3, under FIGHT), is always used in the plural in the NT, and translated "fightings" in 2 Cor. 7:5; Jas. 4:1; and Titus 3:9, RV (for KJV, "strivings"); "strifes in 2 Tim. 2:23. See STRIFE.¶

B. Adjective.

theomachos (θεομάχος, 2314), "fighting against God" (theos, "God," and A, occurs in Acts 5:39 (KJV, "to fight"), lit., "God-fighters."¶

FIGURE

1. *tupos* (τύπος, 5179), "a type, figure, pattern," is translated "figures" (i.e., representations of gods) in Acts 7:43; in the RV of v. 44 (for KJV, "fashion") and in Rom. 5:14, of Adam as a "figure" of Christ. See ENSAMPLE.

2. *antitupos* (ἀντίτυπος, 499), an adjective,

FIGURE 236 FILL, FILL UP

used as a noun, denotes, lit., "a striking back"; metaphorically, "resisting, adverse"; then, in a passive sense, "struck back"; in the NT metaphorically, "corresponding to," (a) a copy of an archetype (anti, "corresponding to, and No. 1), i.e., the event or person or circumstance corresponding to the type, Heb. 9:24, RV, "like in pattern" (KJV, "the figure of"), of the tabernacle, which, with its structure and appurtenances, was a pattern of that "holy place," "Heaven itself," "the true," into which Christ entered, "to appear before the face of God for us." The earthly tabernacle anticipatively represented what is now made good in Christ; it was a "figure" or "parable" (9:9), "for the time now present," RV, i.e., pointing to the present time, not "then present," KJV (see below); (b) "a corresponding type," 1 Pet. 3:21, said of baptism; the circumstances of the flood, the ark and its occupants, formed a type, and baptism forms "a corresponding type" (not an antitype), each setting forth the spiritual realities of the death, burial, and resurrection of believers in their identification with Christ. It is not a case of type and antitype, but of two types, that in Genesis, the type, and baptism, the corresponding type.¶

3. parabolē (παραβολή, 3850), "a casting or placing side by side" (para, "beside," ballō, "to throw") with a view to comparison or resemblance, a parable, is translated "figure" in the KJV of Heb. 9:9 (RV, "a parable for the time now present") and 11:19, where the return of Isaac was (parabolically, in the lit. sense of the term) figurative of resurrection (RV, "parable"). See No. 2 (a). See PARABLE.

Notes: (1) The synonymous noun hupotupōsis, "an example, pattern," 1 Tim. 1:16; 2 Tim. 1:13, denotes simply a delineation or outline.¶ (2) For metaschēmatizō, rendered "I have in a figure transferred" in 1 Cor. 4:6, where the fact stated is designed to change its application, i.e., from Paul and Apollos to circumstances in Corinth, see FASHION.

FILL, FILL UP

A. Verbs.

1. plēroō (πληρόω, 4137) denotes (I) "to make full, to fill to the full"; in the passive voice, "to be filled, made full"; it is used (1) of things: a net, Matt. 13:48; a building, John 12:3; Acts 2:2; a city, Acts 5:28; needs, Phil. 4:19, KJV, "supply," RV, "fulfill"; metaphorically, of valleys, Luke 3:5; figuratively, of a measure of iniquity, Matt. 23:32; (2) of persons: (a) of the members of the church, the body of Christ, as filled by Him, Eph. 1:23 ("all things in all the members"); 4:10; in 3:19, of their being filled "into" (eis), RV, "unto," KJV, "with" (all the

fullness of God); of their being "made full" in Him, Col. 2:10 (RV, for KJV, "complete"); (b) of Christ Himself: with wisdom, in the days of His flesh, Luke 2:40; with joy, in His return to the Father, Acts 2:28; (c) of believers: with the Spirit, Eph. 5:18; with joy, Acts 13:52; 2 Tim. 1:4; with joy and peace, Rom. 15:13; [from these are to be distinguished those passages which speak of joy as being fulfilled or completed, which come under FULFILL, John 3:29; 15:11 (RV); 16:24 (RV); Phil. 2:2; 1 John 1:4 (RV); 2 John 12 (RV)]; with knowledge, Rom. 15:14; with comfort, 2 Cor. 7:4; with the fruits of righteousness, Phil. 1:11 (Gk. "fruit"); with the knowledge of God's will, Col. 1:9; with abundance through material supplies by fellow believers, Phil. 4:18; (d) of the hearts of believers as the seat of emotion and volition, John 16:6 (sorrow); Acts 5:3 (deceitfulness); (e) of the unregenerate who refuse recognition of God, Rom. 1:29; (II) "to accomplish, complete, fulfill." See ACCOMPLISH, FULFILL.

2. anaplēroō (ἀναπληρόω, 378), "to fill up adequately, completely" (ana, "up," and No. 1), is twice translated by the verbs "to fill, to fill up," in 1 Cor. 14:16, RV (for KJV, "occupieth"), of a believer as a member of an assembly, who "fills" the position or condition (not one who "fills" it by assuming it) of being unable to understand the language of him who had the gift of tongues; in 1 Thess. 2:16, "to fill up their sins," of the Jews who persisted in their course of antagonism and unbelief. See FULFILL.

3. antanaplēroō (ἀνταναπληρόω, 466), "to fill up in turn (or on one's part"; anti, "corresponding to," and No. 2), is used in Col. 1:24, of the apostle's responsive devotion to Christ in "filling" up, or undertaking on his part a full share of, the sufferings which follow after the sufferings of Christ, and are experienced by the members of His Body, the church. "The point of the apostle's boast is that Christ, the sinless Master, should have left something for Paul, the unworthy servant, to suffer" (Lightfoot, on Col., p. 165).¶

4. sumplēroō (συμπληρόω, 4845), "to fill completely" (sun, "with," and No. 1), is used in the passive voice (a) of a boat filling with water, and, by metonymy, of the occupants themselves, Luke 8:23 (RV, "were filling"); (b) of "fulfilling," with regard to time, "when the days were well-nigh come," RV, for KJV, "when the time was come" (RV, marg., "were being fulfilled"), Luke 9:51; Acts 2:1, see RV, marg. See COME.¶ In the Sept. Jer. 25:12.¶

5. pimplēmi (πίμπλημι, 4130) and plēthō (πλήθω, 4130), lengthened forms of pleō, "to fill" (plēthō supplies certain tenses of pimplēmi),

is used (1) of things; boats, with fish, Luke 5:7; a sponge, with vinegar, Matt. 27:48 (some mss. have this verb in John 19:29); a city, with confusion, Acts 19:29; a wedding, with guests, Matt. 22:10; (2) of persons (only in Luke's writings): (*a*) with the Holy Spirit, Luke 1:15, 41, 67; Acts 2:4; 4:8, 31; 9:17; 13:9; (*b*) with emotions: wrath, Luke 4:28; fear, 5:26; madness, 6:11; wonder, amazement, Acts 3:10; jealousy, 5:17, RV, for KJV, "indignation," and 13:45 (KJV, "envy"). For its other significance, "to complete," see ACCOMPLISH.

6. *empiplēmi* (ἐμπίπλημι, 1705) or *emplēthō* (as in No. 5), "to fill full, to satisfy," is used (*a*) of "filling" the hungry, Luke 1:53; John 6:12; of the abundance of the rich, Luke 6:25; (*b*) metaphorically, of a company of friends, Rom. 15:24, RV, "satisfied," for KJV, "filled."¶

7. *empiplaō* (ἐμπιπλάω, 1705v), an alternative form of No. 6, is found in Acts 14:17, "filling (your hearts)," of God's provision for mankind.¶

8. *chortazō* (χορτάζω, 5526), "to fill or satisfy with food," e.g., Matt. 15:33; Phil. 4:12, is used metaphorically in Matt. 5:6; Luke 6:21. See FEED.

9. *gemizō* (γεμίζω, 1072), "to fill or load full," is used of a boat, Mark 4:37 (RV, "was filling"); a sponge, Mark 15:36 (cf. No. 5, Matt. 27:48); a house, Luke 14:23; the belly, Luke 15:16; waterpots, John 2:7; baskets, 6:13; bowls, with fire, Rev. 8:5; the temple, with smoke, 15:8.¶ Cf. *gemō*, "to be full." See FULL.

10. *korennumi* (κορέννυμι, 2880), "to satisfy" (akin to *koros*, "a surfeit"), is used metaphorically of spiritual things, in 1 Cor. 4:8, RV, "ye are filled"; in Acts 27:38, "had eaten enough," lit., "having being satisfied with food." See EAT, ENOUGH.¶

11. *mestoō* (μεστόω, 3325), "to fill full," from *mestos*, "full," is used of being "filled" with wine, Acts 2:13, RV, "are filled with."¶

B. Noun.

plērōma (πλήρωμα, 4138), fullness, has two meanings, (*a*) in the active sense, "that which fills up," a piece of undressed cloth on an old garment, Matt. 9:16; Mark 2:21, lit., "the filling" (RV, "that which should fill it up"), i.e., "the patch," which is probably the significance; (*b*) "that which has been completed, the fullness," e.g., Mark 8:20. See FULLNESS.

Notes: (1) In Rev. 18:6, KJV, *kerannumi*, "to mix," is incorrectly rendered "to fill full" (RV, to mingle). (2) In Rev. 15:1, KJV, *teleō*, "to finish, complete," is incorrectly rendered "filled up" (RV, "finished"); the contents of the seven bowls are not the sum total of the divine judgments; they form the termination of them; there are

many which precede (see previous chapters), which are likewise comprised under "the wrath of God," to be executed at the closing period of the present age, e.g., 6:17; 11:18; 14:10, 19.

FILTH

1. *perikatharma* (περικάθαρμα, 4027) denotes "offscouring, refuse" (lit., "cleanings," i.e., that which is thrown away in cleansing; from *perikathairō*, "to purify all around," i.e., completely, as in the Sept. of Deut. 18:10; Josh. 5:4.¶) It is once used in the Sept. (Prov. 21:18) as the price of expiation; among the Greeks the term was applied to victims sacrificed to make expiation; they also used it of criminals kept at the public expense, to be thrown into the sea, or otherwise killed, at the outbreak of a pestilence, etc. It is used in 1 Cor. 4:13 much in this sense (not of sacrificial victims), "the filth of the world," representing "the most abject and despicable men" (Grimm-Thayer), the scum or rubbish of humanity.¶

2. *rhupos* (ῥύπος, 4509) denotes "dirt, filth," 1 Pet. 3:21.¶ Cf. *rhuparia*, "filthiness" (see A, No. 2, below); *rhuparos*, "vile," Jas. 2:2; Rev. 22:11, in the best mss. (see B, No. 3, below);¶ *rhupoō*, "to make filthy," Rev. 22:11;¶ *rhupainō* (see D below).

FILTHINESS, FILTHY (to make)

A. Nouns.

1. *aischrotēs* (αἰσχρότης, 151), "baseness" (from *aischos*, "shame, disgrace"), is used in Eph, 5:4, of obscenity, all that is contrary to purity.¶

2. *rhuparia* (ῥυπαρία, 4507) denotes "dirt, filth" (cf. No. 2, under FILTH), and is used metaphorically of moral "defilement" in Jas. 1:21.¶

3. *molusmos* (μολυσμός, 3436), "a soiling, defilement," is used in 2 Cor. 7:1. See DEFILEMENT.¶

4. *aselgeia* (ἀσέλγεια, 766), "wantonness, licentiousness, lasciviousness," is translated "filthy (conversation)," in 2 Pet. 2:7, KJV; RV, "lascivious (life)." See LASCIVIOUSNESS, WANTONNESS.

Notes: (1) Broadly speaking, *aischrotēs* signifies "whatever is disgraceful"; *rhuparia*, "that which is characterized by moral impurity"; *molusmos*, "that which is defiling by soiling the clean"; *aselgeia*, "that which is an insolent disregard of decency." (2) In Col. 3:8 *aischrologia*, which denotes any kind of "base utterance," the utterance of an uncontrolled tongue, is rendered "filthy communication" in the KJV; but this is only part of what is included in the more comprehensive RV rendering, "shameful speaking."

In the papyri writings the word is used of "abuse." In general it seems to have been associated more frequently with "foul" or "filthy," rather than abusive, "speaking" (Moulton and Milligan).¶

B. Adjectives.

1. *aischros* (αἰσχρός, 150), "base, shameful" (akin to A, No. 1), is used of "base gain," "filthy (lucre)," Titus 1:11, and translated "shame" in 1 Cor. 11:6, with reference to a woman with shorn hair; in 14:35, of oral utterances of women in a church gathering (RV, "shameful"); in Eph. 5:12, of mentioning the base and bestial practices of those who live lascivious lives. See SHAME.¶

2. *aischrokerdēs* (αἰσχροκερδής, 146), "greedy of base gain" (No. 1, and *kerdos*, "gain"), is used in 1 Tim. 3:8 and Titus 1:7, "greedy of filthy lucre"; some mss. have it also in 1 Tim. 3:3.¶

3. *rhuparos* (ῥυπαρός, 4508), akin to A, No. 2 (see also FILTH, No. 2), "dirty," is said of shabby clothing, Jas. 2:2: metaphorically, of moral "defilement," Rev. 22:11 (in the best mss.).¶

Note: For *akathartos* see UNCLEAN, No. 1.

C. Adverb.

aischrokerdōs (αἰσχροκερδῶς, 147), "eagerness for base gain" (akin to B, No. 2), is used in 1 Pet. 5:2, "for filthy lucre."¶

D. Verb.

rhupainō (ῥυπαίνω, 4510v), "to make filthy, defile" (from A, No. 2), is used in the passive voice, in an ethical sense, in Rev. 22:11 (cf. B, No. 3, in the same verse), "let him be made filthy," RV. The tense (the aorist) marks the decisiveness of that which is decreed. Some texts have *rhupareuomai*, here, with the same meaning; some have *rhupoō*, in the middle voice, "to make oneself filthy."¶

FINAL, FINALLY

A. Nouns.

1. *peras* (πέρας, 4009), "a limit, end," is translated "final" in Heb. 6:16, RV, "an oath is final for confirmation" (the KJV connects the clauses differently). See END.

2. *telos* (τέλος, 5056), "an end," most frequently of the termination of something, is used with the article adverbially, meaning "finally" or "as to the end," i.e., as to the last detail, 1 Pet. 3:8. See END.

B. Adverb.

loipon (λοιπόν, 3063) is the neuter of the adjective *loipos*, remaining (which is used in its different genders as a noun, "the rest"), and is used either with the article or without, to signify "finally," lit., "for the rest." The apostle Paul uses it frequently in the concluding portion of his epistles, introducing practical exhortations, not necessarily implying that the letter is drawing to a close, but marking a transition in the subject-matter, as in Phil. 3:1, where the actual conclusion is for the time postponed and the farewell injunctions are resumed in 4:8. See also 1 Thess. 4:1 (KJV, "furthermore"); 2 Thess. 3:1.

FIND, FOUND

1. *heuriskō* (εὑρίσκω, 2147) denotes (*a*) "to find," either with previous search, e.g., Matt. 7:7, 8, or without, e.g., Matt. 27:32; in the passive voice, of Enoch's disappearance, Heb. 11:5; of mountains, Rev. 16:20; of Babylon and its occupants, 18:21, 22; (*b*) metaphorically, "to find out by enquiry," or "to learn, discover," e.g., Luke 19:48; John 18:38; 19:4, 6; Acts 4:21; 13:28; Rom. 7:10; Gal. 2:17, which indicates "the surprise of the Jew" who learned for the first time that before God he had no moral superiority over the Gentiles whom he superciliously dubbed "sinners," while he esteemed himself to be "righteous"; 1 Pet. 1:7; Rev. 5:4; (*c*) in the middle voice, "to find for oneself, gain, procure, obtain," e.g. Matt. 10:39; 11:29, "ye shall find (rest)"; Luke 1:30; Acts 7:46; 2 Tim. 1:18. See GET, OBTAIN.

2. *aneuriskō* (ἀνευρίσκω, 429), "to find out" (by search), "discover" (*ana*, "up," and No. 1), implying diligent searching, is used in Luke 2:16, of the shepherds in searching for and "finding" Mary and Joseph and the Child; in Acts 21:4, of Paul and his companions, in searching for and "finding" "the disciples" at Tyre (in v. 2, No. 1, is used).¶

3. *lambanō* (λαμβάνω, 2983), "to take, receive," is translated "finding (occasion)" in Rom. 7:11, RV (KJV, "taking"). See ACCEPT.

4. *katalambanō* (καταλαμβάνω, 2638), "to lay hold of," said of mental action, "to comprehend" by laying hold of or "finding" facts, is translated "I found," of Festus regarding charges made against Paul, Acts 25:25. See APPREHEND.

Notes: (1) For *sunanapauomai*, "to be refreshed in spirit," in Rom. 15:32, RV, "find rest with," see FIND, REFRESH. (2) In Rom. 7:18, there is no word in the original for "find." Hence the RV has "is not." (3) In Rom. 11:33, *anexichniastos*, untraceable, is rendered "past finding out," KJV, RV, "past tracing out" (*ichniazō*, "to track out"); in Eph. 3:8, "unsearchable." See TRACE, UNSEARCHABLE.¶

For **FINE** see **BRASS**, No. 4, **FLOUR, GOODLY**, *Note*, **LINEN**

FINGER

daktulos (δάκτυλος, 1147), Matt. 23:4; Mark 7:33; Luke 11:46; 16:24; John 8:6; 20:25, 27, is used metaphorically in Luke 11:20, for the power of God, the effects of which are made visible to men (cf. Matt. 12:28, "by the Spirit of God"; cf. also Exod. 8:19).¶

FINISH

1. *teleō* (τελέω, 5055), "to bring to an end" (*telos*, "an end"), in the passive voice, "to be finished," is translated by the verb "to finish" in Matt. 13:53; 19:1; 26:1; John 19:28, where the RV "are . . . finished" brings out the force of the perfect tense (the same word as in v. 30, "It is finished"), which is missed in the KJV; as Stier says, "the word was in His heart before He uttered it"; 2 Tim. 4:7; Rev. 10:7; 11:7; 20:3, RV, "should be finished" (KJV, "fulfilled"), 5, 7, RV, "finished" (KJV, "expired"). In Rev. 15:1 the verb is rightly translated "is finished," RV, see FILL, *Note* (2). In 15:8 the RV, "should be finished" corrects the KJV, "were fulfilled." See ACCOMPLISH.

2. *teleioō* (τελειόω, 5048), akin to the adjective *teleios*, "complete, perfect," and to No. 1, denotes "to bring to an end" in the sense of completing or perfecting, and is translated by the verb "to finish" in John 4:34; 5:36; 17:4; Acts 20:24. See CONSECRATE, FULFIL, PERFECT.

3. *ekteleō* (ἐκτελέω, 1615), lit., "to finish out," i.e., "completely" (*ek*, "out," intensive, and No. 1), is used in Luke 14:29, 30.¶

4. *epiteleō* (ἐπιτελέω, 2005), "to bring through to an end," is rendered "finish" in 2 Cor. 8:6, KJV (RV, "complete"). See ACCOMPLISH.

5. *sunteleō* (συντελέω, 4931), "to bring to fulfillment, to effect," is translated "finishing" (KJV, "will finish") in Rom. 9:28. See COMPLETE.

6. *dianuō* (διανύω, 1274) is translated "had finished," in Acts 21:7, of the voyage from Tyre to Ptolemais. As this is so short a journey, and this verb is intensive in meaning, some have suggested the rendering "but we having (thereby) completed our voyage (i.e., from Macedonia, 20:6), came from Tyre to Ptolemais." In late Greek writers, however, the verb is used with the meaning "to continue," and this is the probable sense here.¶

7. *ginomai* (γίνομαι, 1096), "to become, to come into existence," is translated "were finished" in Heb. 4:3, i.e., were brought to their predestined end.

Notes: (1) In Luke 14:28, *apartismos* denotes "a completion," and the phrase is, lit., "unto a completion." The KJV has "to finish" (RV, "to complete"). See COMPLETE.¶ (2) In Jas. 1:15 *apoteleō*, "to perfect," to bring to maturity, to become "fullgrown," RV (KJV, "is finished"), is said of the full development of sin. (3) In Heb. 12:2 the RV suitably translates *teleiōtēs* "perfecter," for KJV, "finisher."

FIRE

A. Nouns.

1. *pur* (πῦρ, 4442) (akin to which are No. 2, *pura*, and *puretos*, "a fever," Eng., "fire," etc.) is used (besides its ordinary natural significance):

(*a*) of the holiness of God, which consumes all that is inconsistent therewith, Heb. 10:27; 12:29; cf. Rev. 1:14; 2:18; 10:1; 15:2; 19:12; similarly of the holy angels as His ministers, Heb. 1:7; in Rev. 3:18 it is symbolic of that which tries the faith of saints, producing what will glorify the Lord:

(*b*) of the divine judgment, testing the deeds of believers, at the judgment seat of Christ, 1 Cor. 3:13 and 15:

(*c*) of the fire of divine judgment upon the rejectors of Christ, Matt. 3:11 (where a distinction is to be made between the baptism of the Holy Spirit at Pentecost and the "fire" of divine retribution; Acts 2:3 could not refer to baptism): Luke 3:16:

(*d*) of the judgments of God at the close of the present age previous to the establishment of the kingdom of Christ in the world, 2 Thess. 1:8; Rev. 18:8:

(*e*) of the "fire" of Hell, to be endured by the ungodly hereafter, Matt. 5:22; 13:42, 50; 18:8, 9; 25:41; Mark 9:43, 48; Luke 3:17:

(*f*) of human hostility both to the Jews and to Christ's followers, Luke 12:49:

(*g*) as illustrative of retributive judgment upon the luxurious and tyrannical rich, Jas. 5:3:

(*h*) of the future overthrow of the Babylonish religious system at the hands of the Beast and the nations under him, Rev. 17:16:

(*i*) of turning the heart of an enemy to repentance by repaying his unkindness by kindness, Rom. 12:20:

(*j*) of the tongue, as governed by a "fiery" disposition and as exercising a destructive influence over others, Jas. 3:6:

(*k*) as symbolic of the danger of destruction, Jude 23.

Note: See also under FLAME.

2. *pura* (πυρά, 4443), from No. 1, denotes "a heap of fuel" collected to be set on fire (hence Eng., "pyre"), Acts 28:2, 3.¶

Note: In Mark 14:54, the italicized phrase "of the fire" is added in the Eng. versions to indicate the light as coming from the "fire."

B. Adjective.

purinos (πύρινος, 4447), "fiery" (akin to A, No. 1), is translated "of fire" in Rev. 9:17.¶ In the Sept., Ezek. 28:14, 16.¶

C. Verbs.

1. *puroō* (πυρόω, 4448) is translated "being on fire" (middle voice) in 2 Pet. 3:12. See FIERY.

2. *phlogizō* (φλογίζω, 5394), "to set on fire, burn up," is used figuratively, in both active and passive voices, in Jas. 3:6, of the tongue, firstly, of its disastrous effects upon the whole round of the circumstances of life; secondly, of satanic agency in using the tongue for this purpose.¶

FIRKIN

metrētēs (μετρητής, 3355) is a liquid measure (akin to *metreō*, "to measure"), equivalent to one and a half Roman *amphoræ*, or about nine gallons, John 2:6.¶

FIRM

1. *bebaios* (βέβαιος, 949), "firm, steadfast, secure" (from *bainō*, "to go"), is translated "firm" in Heb. 3:6, of the maintenance of the boldness of the believer's hope, and in 3:14, RV, of "the beginning of our confidence" (KJV, "steadfast"). See STEADFAST, SURE.

2. *stereos* (στερεός, 4731), "solid, hard, stiff," is translated "firm" in 2 Tim. 2:19, RV, "the firm (foundation of God)," KJV, "(standeth) sure"; *stereos* is not part of the predicate; "solid (food)" in Heb. 5:12, 14, RV; "steadfast" in 1 Pet. 5:9. See SOLID, STEADFAST, STRONG.¶

Note: Cf. *stereoō*, "to make strong, establish," Acts 3:7, 16; 16:5, and *stereōma*, "steadfastness," Col. 2:5.¶

FIRST

A. Adjective.

prōtos (πρῶτος, 4413), the superlative degree of *pro*, "before," is used (I) "of time or place," (*a*) as a noun, e.g., Luke 14:18; Rev. 1:17; opposite to "the last," in the neuter plural, Matt. 12:45; Luke 11:26; 2 Pet. 2:20; in the neuter singular, opposite to "the second," Heb. 10:9; in 1 Cor. 15:3, *en prōtois*, lit., "in the first (things, or matters)" denotes "first of all"; (*b*) as an adjective, e.g., Mark 16:9, used with "day" understood, lit., "the first (day) of (i.e., after) the Sabbath," in which phrase the "of" is objective, not including the Sabbath, but following it (cf. B, No. 3); in John 20:4, 8; Rom. 10:19, e.g., equivalent to an English adverb; in John 1:15, lit., "first of me," i.e., "before me" (of superiority); (II) "of rank or dignity," see CHIEF. Cf. B, Nos. 3 and 4.

B. Adverbs.

1. *proteron* (πρότερον, 4386), the comparative degree of *pro* (see No. 1), "former, before," denotes "first" in Heb. 7:27; in 4:6, RV, "before" (KJV, "first"), speaking of Israel as having heard God's good tidings previously to the ministry of the Gospel; in Gal. 4:13, "I preached . . . unto you the first time" means on the former of his two previous visits.

2. *anōthen* (ἄνωθεν, 509), "from above," is rendered "from the first" in Luke 1:3, RV; it may mean "from their beginning, or source."

3. *prōtōs* (πρώτως, 4413), "firstly," is used in Acts 11:26, "first" (some mss. have No. 4 here).¶

4. *prōton* (πρῶτον, 4412), the neuter of the adjective *prōtos*, is used as an adverb, signifying "first, firstly," e.g., of time, Matt. 8:21; of order, Rom. 3:2 (KJV, "chiefly"); in John 7:51, RV, "except it first hear from himself" (the KJV, "before it hear him," follows the mss. which have No. 1).

C. Numeral.

mia (μία, 3391), a grammatically feminine form of *heis*, "one," is translated "first" in certain occurrences of the phrase "on the first day of the week," e.g., Luke 24:1; 1 Cor. 16:2; cf. A, and see DAY; also in Titus 3:10, of a "first" admonition to a heretical man. See ONE.

D. Noun.

archē (ἀρχή, 746), "a beginning," is translated "first" in Heb. 5:12, "of the first (principles of the oracles of God)," lit. "(the principles) of the beginning (of the oracles of God)"; in 6:1 "the first (principles) of Christ," lit., "(the account) of the beginning of Christ," i.e., the elementary teaching concerning Christ. In Acts 26:4, where the word is preceded by *apo*, "from," the KJV has "at the first," the RV, "from the beginning."

Notes: (1) In Jude 6 *archē* has the meaning "principality," as in the RV and the KJV margin.

(2) In 2 Cor. 8:12 *prokeimai*, "to be present," lit., "to lie beforehand" (*pro*, "before," *keimai*, "to lie"), RV renders "(if the readiness) is there," for KJV, "if there be first (a willing mind). See SET, A, No. 23.

FIRST-BEGOTTEN, FIRSTBORN

prōtotokos (πρωτότοκος, 4416), "firstborn" (from *prōtos*, "first," and *tiktō*, "to beget"), is used of Christ as born of the Virgin Mary, Luke 2:7; further, in His relationship to the Father, expressing His priority to, and preeminence over, creation, not in the sense of being the "first" to be born. It is used occasionally of superiority of position in the OT; see Exod. 4:22; Deut. 21:16, 17, the prohibition being against the evil of assigning the privileged position of the "firstborn" to one born subsequently to the "first" child.

The five passages in the NT relating to Christ may be set forth chronologically thus: (*a*) Col. 1:15, where His eternal relationship with the Father is in view, and the clause means both that He was the "Firstborn" before all creation and that He Himself produced creation (the genitive case being objective, as v. 16 makes clear); (*b*) Col. 1:18 and Rev. 1:5, in reference to His resurrection; (*c*) Rom. 8:29, His position in relationship to the church; (*d*) Heb. 1:6, RV, His second advent (the RV "when He again bringeth in," puts "again" in the right place, the contrast to His first advent, at His birth, being implied); cf. Ps. 89:27. The word is used in the plural, in Heb. 11:28, of the firstborn sons in the families of the Egyptians, and in 12:23, of the members of the Church.¶

Note: With (*a*) cf. John 1:30, "He was before me," lit., "He was first (*prōtos*) of me," i.e., "in regard to me," expressing all that is involved in His preexistence and priority.

FIRSTFRUIT(S)

aparchē (ἀπαρχή, 536) denotes, primarily, "an offering of firstfruits" (akin to *aparchomai*, "to make a beginning"; in sacrifices, "to offer firstfruits"). "Though the English word is plural in each of its occurrences save Rom. 11:16, the Greek word is always singular. Two Hebrew words are thus translated, one meaning the "chief" or "principal part," e.g., Num. 18:12; Prov. 3:9; the other, "the earliest ripe of the crop or of the tree," e.g., Exod. 23:16; Neh. 10:35; they are found together, e.g., in Exod. 23:19, "the first of the firstfruits."

"The term is applied in things spiritual, (*a*) to the presence of the Holy Spirit with the believer as the firstfruits of the full harvest of the Cross, Rom. 8:23; (*b*) to Christ Himself in resurrection in relation to all believers who have fallen asleep, 1 Cor. 15:20, 23; (*c*) to the earliest believers in a country in relation to those of their countrymen subsequently converted, Rom. 16:5; 1 Cor. 16:15; (*d*) to the believers of this age in relation to the whole of the redeemed, 2 Thess. 2:13 (see *Note* below) and Jas. 1:18. Cf. Rev. 14:4."¶*

Notes: (1) In Jas. 1:15 the qualifying phrase, "a kind of," may suggest a certain falling short, on the part of those mentioned, of what they might be. (2) In 2 Thess. 2:13, instead of *ap' archēs*, "from the beginning," there is an alter-

native reading, well supported, viz., *aparchēn*, "(God chose you) as firstfruits."

FISH

1. *ichthus* (ἰχθύς, 2486) denotes "a fish," Matt. 7:10; Mark 6:38, etc.; apart from the Gospels, only in 1 Cor. 15:39.

2. *ichthudion* (ἰχθύδιον, 2485) is a diminutive of No. 1, "a little fish," Matt. 15:34; Mark 8:7.¶

3. *opsarion* (ὀψάριον, 3795) is a diminutive of *opson*, "cooked meat," or "a relish, a dainty dish, especially of fish"; it denotes "a little fish," John 6:9, 11; 21:9, 10, 13.¶

FISH (Verb), FISHER, FISHERMAN

A. Noun.

halieus (ἁλιεύς, 231), "a fisherman, fisher" (from *hals*, "the sea"), occurs in Matt. 4:18, 19; Mark 1:16, 17; Luke 5:2.¶

B. Verb

halieuō (ἁλιεύω, 232), "to fish" (akin to A.), occurs in John 21:3.¶ In the Sept., Jer. 16:16.¶

FIT (Adjective and Verb), FITLY, FITTING

A. Adjectives.

1. *euthetos* (εὔθετος, 2111), "ready for use, fit, well adapted," lit., "well placed" (*eu*, "well," *tithēmi*, "to place"), is used (*a*) of persons, Luke 9:62, negatively, of one who is not fit for the kingdom of God; (*b*) of things, Luke 14:35, of salt that has lost its savor; rendered "meet" in Heb. 6:7, of herbs. See MEET.¶.

2. *arestos* (ἀρεστός, 701), "pleasing" (akin to *areskō*, "to please"), is translated "(it is not) fit," RV (KJV, "reason"), in Acts 6:2. See PLEASE, REASON.

B. Verbs.

1. *anēkō* (ἀνήκω, 433), properly, "to have come up to" (*ana*, "up," and *hēkō*, "to arrive"), is translated "is fitting," in Col. 3:18, RV. See BEFITTING.

2. *kathēkō* (καθήκω, 2520), "to come or reach down to" (*kata*, "down"), hence, "to befit, be proper," is translated "is (not fit)" in Acts 22:22; in Rom. 1:28, RV, "fitting" (KJV, "convenient"). See CONVENIENT.¶

3. *katartizō* (καταρτίζω, 2675), "to make fit, to equip, prepare" (*kata*, "down," *artos*, "a joint"), is rendered "fitted" in Rom. 9:22, of vessels of wrath; here the middle voice signifies that those referred to "fitted" themselves for destruction (as illustrated in the case of Pharaoh, the self-hardening of whose heart is accurately presented in the RV in the first part of the

---

* From *Notes on Thessalonians,* by Hogg and Vine, p. 271.

series of incidents in the Exodus narrative, which records Pharaoh's doings; only after repeated and persistent obstinacy on his part is it recorded that God hardened his heart.) See FRAME, JOIN, PERFECT, PREPARE, RESTORE.

4. *sunarmologeō* (συναρμολογέω, 4883), "to fit or frame together" (*sun*, "with," *harmos*, "a joint, in building," and *legō*, "to choose"), is used metaphorically of the various parts of the church as a building, Eph. 2:21, "fitly framed together"; also of the members of the church as the body of Christ, 4:16, RV, "fitly framed ... together."¶

FIVE, FIVE TIMES

pente (πέντε, 4002) is derived by some from words suggesting the fingers of a hand, or a fist. The word is frequent in the Gospels. *Pentakis*, "five times," is found in 2 Cor. 11:24;¶ *pentakosioi*, "five hundred," in Luke 7:41; 1 Cor. 15:6;¶ *pentakischilioi*, "five thousand" (*chilios*, "a thousand"), in Matt. 14:21; 16:9 and corresponding passages. See FIFTEENTH, FIFTH, FIFTY.

FIX

stērizō (στηρίζω, 4741), "to set forth, make fast, fix," is translated "fixed" in Luke 16:26, of the great gulf separating Hades or Sheol from the region called "Abraham's bosom." See ESTABLISH.

FLAME, FLAMING

phlox (φλόξ, 5395), akin to Lat. *fulgeō*, "to shine," is used apart from *pur*, "fire," in Luke 16:24; with *pur*, it signifies "a fiery flame," lit., "a flame of fire," Acts 7:30; 2 Thess. 1:8, where the fire is to be understood as the instrument of divine judgment; Heb. 1:7, where the meaning probably is that God makes His angels as active and powerful as a "flame" of fire; in Rev. 1:14; 2:18; 19:12, of the eyes of the Lord Jesus as emblematic of penetrating judgment, searching out evil.¶

FLATTERY (-ING)

kolakia (or *-eia*) (κολακία, 2850), akin to *kolakeuō*, "to flatter," is used in 1 Thess. 2:5 of "words of flattery" (RV), adopted as "a cloke of covetousness," i.e., words which "flattery" uses, not simply as an effort to give pleasure, but with motives of self-interest.¶

FLAX

linon (λίνον, 3043) primarily denotes "flax" (Eng., "linen"); then, that which is made of it, "a wick of a lamp," Matt. 12:20; several ancient mss. have the word in Rev. 15:6 (KJV only, "linen "). See LINEN.¶

FLEE, FLED

1. *pheugō* (φεύγω, 5343), "to flee from or away" (Lat., *fugio;* Eng., "fugitive," etc.), besides its literal significance, is used metaphorically, (*a*) transitively, of "fleeing" fornication, 1 Cor. 6:18; idolatry, 10:14; evil doctrine, questionings, disputes of words, envy, strife, railings, evil surmisings, wranglings, and the love of money, 1 Tim. 6:11; youthful lusts, 2 Tim. 2:22; (*b*) intransitively, of the "flight" of physical matter, Rev. 16:20; 20:11; of death, 9:6. See ESCAPE.

2. *ekpheugō* (ἐκφεύγω, 1628), "to flee away, escape" (*ek*, "from," and No. 1), is translated "fled" in Acts 16:27 (KJV only); 19:16. In Heb. 12:25 the best mss. have this verb instead of No. 1. See ESCAPE.

3. *katapheugō* (καταφεύγω, 2703), "to flee for refuge" (*kata*, used intensively, and No. 1), is used (*a*) literally in Acts 14:6; (*b*) metaphorically in Heb. 6:18, of "fleeing" for refuge to lay hold upon hope.¶

Note: For *apopheugō* and *diapheugō*, see ESCAPE.

FLESH

1. *sarx* (σάρξ, 4561) has a wider range of meaning in the NT than in the OT. Its uses in the NT may be analyzed as follows:

"(*a*) "the substance of the body," whether of beasts or of men, 1 Cor. 15:39; (*b*) "the human body," 2 Cor. 10:3a; Gal. 2:20; Phil. 1:22; (*c*) by synecdoche, of "mankind," in the totality of all that is essential to manhood, i.e., spirit, soul, and body, Matt. 24:22; John 1:13; Rom. 3:20; (*d*) by synecdoche, of "the holy humanity" of the Lord Jesus, in the totality of all that is essential to manhood, i.e., spirit, soul, and body, John 1:14; 1 Tim. 3:16; 1 John 4:2; 2 John 7; in Heb. 5:7, "the days of His flesh," i.e., His past life on earth in distinction from His present life in resurrection; (*e*) by synecdoche, for "the complete person," John 6:51–57; 2 Cor. 7:5; Jas. 5:3; (*f*) "the weaker element in human nature," Matt. 26:41; Rom. 6:19; 8:3a; (*g*) "the unregenerate state of men," Rom. 7:5; 8:8, 9; (*h*) "the seat of sin in man" (but this is not the same thing as in the body), 2 Pet. 2:18; 1 John 2:16; (*i*) "the lower and temporary element in the Christian," Gal. 3:3; 6:8, and in religious ordinances, Heb. 9:10; (*j*) "the natural attainments of men," 1 Cor. 1:26; 2 Cor. 10:2, 3b; (*k*) "circumstances," 1 Cor. 7:28; the externals of life, 2 Cor. 7:1; Eph. 6:5; Heb. 9:13; (*l*) by metonymy, "the outward and seeming," as contrasted with the spirit, the inward and real, John 6:63; 2 Cor. 5:16; (*m*) "natural relationship, consanguine," 1 Cor. 10:18; Gal. 4:23, or marital, Matt. 19:5."*

In Matt. 26:41; Rom. 8:4, 13; 1 Cor. 5:5; Gal. 6:8 (not the Holy Spirit, here), "flesh" is contrasted with spirit; in Rom. 2:28, 29, with heart and spirit; in Rom. 7:25, with the mind; cf. Col. 2:1, 5. It is coupled with the mind in Eph. 2:3, and with the spirit in 2 Cor. 7:1.

Note: In Col. 2:18 the noun *sarx* is used in the phrase "(by his) fleshly mind," lit., "by the mind of his flesh" [see (*h*) above], whereas the mind ought to be dominated by the Spirit.

2. *kreas* (κρέας, 2907) denotes "flesh" in the sense of meat. It is used in the plural in Rom. 14:21; 1 Cor. 8:13.¶

FLESHLY, FLESHY

1. *sarkikos* (σαρκικός, 4559), akin to No. 1, under FLESH, signifies (*a*) associated with or pertaining to, "the flesh, carnal," Rom. 15:27; 1 Cor. 9:11; (*b*) of "the nature of the flesh, sensual," translated "fleshly" in 2 Cor. 1:12, of wisdom; in 1 Pet. 2:11, of lusts; in 2 Cor. 10:4, negatively, of the weapons of the Christian's warfare, RV, "of the flesh" (KJV, "carnal"). See CARNAL.

2. *sarkinos* (σάρκινος, 4560) denotes "of the flesh, fleshly" (the termination—*inos* signifying the substance or material of a thing); in 2 Cor. 3:3, RV, "(tables that are hearts) of flesh," KJV, "fleshly (tables)," etc. See CARNAL.

Note: The adjectives "fleshly," "carnal" are contrasted with spiritual qualities in Rom. 7:14; 1 Cor. 3:1, 3, 4; 2 Cor. 1:12; Col. 2:18 (lit., "mind of flesh"). Speaking broadly, the carnal denotes the sinful element in man's nature, by reason of descent from Adam; the spiritual is that which comes by the regenerating operation of the Holy Spirit.

FLIGHT

A. Noun.

phugē (φυγή, 5437), akin to *pheugō* (see FLEE), is found in Matt. 24:20. Some inferior mss. have it in Mark 13:18.¶

B. Verb.

klinō (κλίνω, 2827), "to make to bend," is translated "turned to flight" in Heb. 11:34. See BOW.

FLOCK

1. *poimnē* (ποίμνη, 4167), akin to *poimēn*, "a shepherd," denotes "a flock" (properly, of sheep), Matt. 26:31; Luke 2:8; 1 Cor. 9:7; metaphorically, of Christ's followers, John 10:16,

RV, for the erroneous KJV, "fold." What characterizes Christ's sheep is listening to His voice, and the "flock" must be one as He is one.¶

2. *poimnion* (ποίμνιον, 4168), possibly a diminutive of No. 1, is used in the NT only metaphorically, of a group of Christ's disciples, Luke 12:32; of local churches cared for by elders, Acts 20:28, 29; 1 Pet. 5:2, 3.¶

FLOOD

A. Nouns.

1. *kataklusmos* (κατακλυσμός, 2627), "a deluge" (Eng., "cataclysm"), akin to *katakluzō*, "to inundate," 2 Pet. 3:6, is used of the "flood" in Noah's time, Matt. 24:38, 39; Luke 17:27; 2 Pet. 2:5.¶

2. *plēmmura* (πλήμμυρα, 4132), akin to *plēthō* and *pimplēmi*, "to fill, a flood of sea or river," the latter in Luke 6:48.¶ In the Sept., Job 40:18 (v. 23 in the EV).¶

3. *potamos* (ποταμός, 4215), "a river, stream, torrent," is translated "flood" in Matt. 7:25, 27; in Rev. 12:15, 16, KJV, "flood," RV, "river." See RIVER, WATER.

B. Adjective.

potamophorētos (ποταμοφόρητος, 4216) signifies "carried away by a stream or river" (A, No. 3, and *pherō*, "to carry"), Rev. 12:15, RV, "carried away by the stream" (KJV, "of the flood").¶

For **FLOOR** see **THRESHING-FLOOR**

FLOUR

semidalis (σεμίδαλις, 4585) denotes the "finest wheaten flour," Rev. 18:13.¶

For **FLOURISH** in Phil. 4:10, see **REVIVE**

FLOW

rheō (ῥέω, 4482), "to flow," is used figuratively in John 7:38 of the Holy Spirit, acting in and through the believer.¶

FLOWER

A. Noun.

anthos (ἄνθος, 438), "a blossom, flower" (used in certain names of flowers), occurs in Jas. 1:10, 11; 1 Pet. 1:24 (twice).¶

B. Adjective.

huperakmos (ὑπέρακμος, 5230), "past the bloom of youth" (from *huper*, "beyond," and *akmē*, "the highest point of anything," the full bloom of a flower: Eng., "acme"), is used in

1 Cor. 7:36, "past the flower of her age"; Lightfoot prefers the rendering "of full age."

For FLUX see DYSENTERY

FLUTE-PLAYERS

aulētēs (αὐλητής, 834), "a flute-player" (from *auleō*, "to play the flute"), occurs in Matt. 9:23 (KJV, "minstrel"), and Rev. 18:22 (KJV, "pipers"). In the papyri writings of the time the word is chiefly associated with religious matters (Moulton and Milligan, *Vocab.*). Cf. MINSTREL.¶

FLY

petomai (πέτομαι, 4072), "to fly" (the root of which is seen in *pteron* and *pterux*, "a wing," *ptilon*, "a feather," etc.), is confined to the Apocalypse, 4:7; 8:13; 12:14; 14:6; 19:17. Some mss. have the verb *petaomai*, a frequentative form.¶

FOAL

huios (υἱός, 5207), "a son," primarily signifying the relation of offspring to parent, is used of the "foal" of an ass in Matt. 21:5. See SON.

FOAM

A. Verbs.

1. *aphrizō* (ἀφρίζω, 875) denotes "to foam at the mouth" (akin to *aphros*, "foam"; see B.), Mark 9:18, 20.¶

2. *epaphrizō* (ἐπαφρίζω, 1890), "to foam out, or up" (*epi*, "up," and No. 1), is used metaphorically in Jude 13, of the impious libertines, who had crept in among the saints, and "foamed" out their own shame with swelling words. The metaphor is drawn from the refuse borne on the crest of waves and cast up on the beach.¶

B. Noun.

aphros (ἀφρός, 876), "foam," occurs in Luke 9:39, where it is used with the preposition *meta*, "with," lit., "(teareth him) with (accompanied by) foam." ¶

FOE

echthros (ἐχθρός, 2190), an adjective signifying "hated, hateful, or hostile," is used also as a noun denoting "an enemy," translated "foes" in Matt. 10:36 and the KJV of Acts 2:35. See ENEMY.

FOLD

aulē (αὐλή, 833) first signifies "an open courtyard" before a house; then, "an enclosure" in the open, "a sheepfold," John 10:1, 16. In the papyri "the word is extremely common, denoting the court attached to a house" (Moulton and Milligan, *Vocab.*). The "sheepfold" was usually surrounded by a stone wall, Numb. 32:16, preferably near a well, Exod. 2:16; Ps. 23:2, and often protected by a tower, 2 Chron. 26:10; Mic. 4:8. See COURT, HALL, PALACE.

Note: For the erroneous KJV rendering, "fold," of *poimnē*, "a flock," in John 10:16, see FLOCK.

For FOLD UP see ROLL, A, No. 4

For FOLK see IMPOTENT, B, SICK, B, No. 2

FOLLOW, FOLLOW AFTER

1. *akoloutheō* (ἀκολουθέω, 190), to be an *akolouthos*, "a follower," or "companion" (from the prefix *a*, here expressing "union, likeness," and *keleuthos*, "a way"; hence, "one going in the same way"), is used (*a*) frequently in the literal sense, e.g., Matt. 4:25; (*b*) metaphorically, of "discipleship," e.g., Mark 8:34; 9:38; 10:21. It is used 77 times in the Gospels, of "following" Christ, and only once otherwise, Mark 14:13.

2. *exakoloutheō* (ἐξακολουθέω, 1811), "to follow up, or out to the end" (*ek*, "out," used intensively, and No. 1), is used metaphorically, and only by the apostle Peter in his second epistle: in 1:16, of cunningly devised fables; 2:2, of lascivious doings; 2:15, of the way of Balaam.¶ In the Sept., Job 31:9; Is. 56:11; Jer. 2:2; Amos 2:4.¶

3. *epakoloutheō* (ἐπακολουθέω, 1872), "to follow after, close upon" (*epi*, "upon," and No. 1). is used of signs "following" the preaching of the gospel. Mark 16:20; of "following" good works, 1 Tim 5:10; of sins "following" after those who are guilty of them, 5:24; of "following" the steps of Christ, 1 Pet. 2:21.¶

4. *katakoloutheō* (κατακολουθέω, 2628), "to follow behind or intently after" (*kata*, "after," used intensively, and No. 1), is used of the women on their way to Christ's tomb, Luke 23:55; of the demon-possessed maid in Philippi in "following" the missionaries, Acts 16:17.¶

5. *parakoloutheō* (παρακολουθέω, 3877) lit. signifying "to follow close up, or side by side," hence, "to accompany, to conform to" (*para*, "beside," and No. 1), is used of signs accompanying "them that believe," Mark 16:17; of tracing the course of facts, Luke 1:3, RV; of "following" the good doctrine, 1 Tim. 4:6, RV (KJV, "attained"); similarly of "following" teaching so as to practice it, 2 Tim. 3:10, RV, "didst follow" (KJV, "hast fully known"). See ATTAIN, KNOW, TRACE, UNDERSTAND.¶

6. *sunakoloutheō* (συνακολουθέω, 4870),

"to follow along with, to accompany a leader" (*sun*, "with," and No. 1), is given its true rendering in the RV of Mark 5:37, "He suffered no man to follow with Him"; in 14:51, of the young man who "followed with" Christ (inferior mss. have No. 1 here); Luke 23:49, of the women who "followed with" Christ from Galilee.¶

7. *diōkō* (διώκω, 1377) denotes (*a*) "to drive away," Matt. 23:34; (*b*) "to pursue without hostility, to follow, follow after," said of righteousness, Rom. 9:30; the Law, 9:31; 12:13, hospitality ("given to") lit., "pursuing" (as one would a calling); the things which make for peace, 14:19; love, 1 Cor. 14:1; that which is good, 1 Thess. 5:15; righteousness, godliness, faith, love, patience, meekness, 1 Tim. 6:11; righteousness, faith, love, peace, 2 Tim. 2:22; peace and sanctification, Heb. 12:14; peace, 1 Pet. 3:11; (*c*) "to follow on" (used intransitively), Phil. 3:12, 14, RV, "I press on"; "follow after," is an inadequate meaning. See GIVE, PERSECUTE, PRESS, PURSUE.

8. *katadiōkō* (καταδιώκω, 2614), "to follow up or closely," with the determination to find (*kata*, "down," intensive, giving the idea of a hard, persistent search, and No. 7), Mark 1:36, "followed after (Him)," is said of the disciples in going to find the Lord who had gone into a desert place to pray.¶ The verb is found, e.g., in 1 Sam. 30:22; Ps. 23:6, and with hostile intent in Gen. 31:36.

9. *ginomai* (γίνομαι, 1096), "to become, to come into existence," is used in Rev. 8:17; 11:15, 19, in the sense of taking place after, translated "there followed." See BECOME.

10. *epeimi* (ἔπειμι, 1909 and 1510), "to come upon," or, of time, "to come on or after" (*epi*, "upon," and *eimi*, "to go"), is used in the present participle as an adjective, in reference to a day, in Acts 7:26; 16:11; 20:15; 21:18; a night, 23:11, RV, "following," in each place (KJV, "next").¶

Notes: (1) In Luke 13:33, the present participle, middle voice, of the verb *echō*, "to have, to be next," is used with the article, the word *hēmera*, "a day," being understood, signifying "the day following." (2) In John 1:43 and 6:22 the adverb *epaurion* with the article, "on the morrow," is translated "the day following" in the KJV. See MORROW. (3) In Acts 21:1 the adverb *hexēs*, in order, next, is translated "the day following" (KJV). (4) *Mimeomai*, "to imitate, be an imitator," is so translated always in the RV, where the KJV uses the verb "to follow"; it is always used in a good sense, 2 Thess. 3:7, 9; Heb. 13:7; 3 John 11. So with the nouns *mimētēs*, "an imitator," and *summimētēs*, "an

imitator together." See IMITATE, IMITATOR. (5) In Matt. 4:19, *deute*, "come hither," with *opisō*, "after," is translated "come ye after," RV (KJV, "follow"). (6) In Matt. 27:62, RV, the phrase *eimi meta*, "to be after," is translated "(which) is (the day) after" (KJV, "that followed"). (7) In 1 Pet. 1:11, the phrase *meta tauta*, lit., "after these things," is translated "that should follow," said of glories after the sufferings of Christ. (8) In Luke 22:49, the phrase *to esomenon*, lit. "the (thing) about to be" (from *eimi*, "to be"), is translated "what would follow." (9) In Acts 3:24, the adverb *kathexēs*, "successively, in order," is translated "(them) that followed after," i.e., those who succeeded (him), lit., "the (ones) successively (to him)." Cf. *Note* (3) above. See AFTERWARD.

FOLLY

anoia (ἄνοια, 454) lit. signifies "without understanding" (*a*, negative, *nous*, "mind"); hence, "folly," or, rather, "senselessness," 2 Tim. 3:9; in Luke 6:11 it denotes violent or mad rage, "madness." See MADNESS.¶ Cf. *anoētos*, "foolish."

Note: For *aphrosunē*, rendered "folly" in 2 Cor. 11:1, KJV, see FOOLISHNESS (RV).

FOOD

1. *trophē* (τροφή, 5160) denotes "nourishment, food" (akin to *trephō*, "to rear, nourish, feed"); it is used literally, in the Gospels, Acts and Jas. 2:15; metaphorically, in Heb. 5:12, 14, RV, "(solid) food," KJV, "(strong) meat," i.e., deeper subjects of the faith than that of elementary instruction. The word is always rendered "food" in the RV, where the KJV has "meat"; e.g., Matt. 3:4; 6:25; 10:10; 24:45; Luke 12:23; John 4:8; Acts 2:46, "did take their food," RV (KJV, "did eat their meat"); 9:19, "took food"; 27:33, 34, 36. The KJV also has "food" in Acts 14:17 and Jas. 2:15.¶

2. *diatrophē* (διατροφή, 1305), "sustenance, food," a strengthened form of No. 1 (*dia*, "through," suggesting a sufficient supply), is used in 1 Tim. 6:8.¶

3. *brōsis* (βρῶσις, 1035), "eating, the act of eating" (akin to *bibrōskō*, "to eat") is translated "food" in 2 Cor. 9:10. See EATING, MEAT, RUST.

4. *sitometrion* (σιτομέτριον, 4620), a measured "portion of food" (*sitos*, "corn," *metreō*, "to measure"), is used in Luke 12:42, RV.¶

5. *brōma* (βρῶμα, 1033), akin to No. 3, frequently translated "meat," and always so in the KJV except in Matt. 14:15, "victuals," is rendered "food" in the RV in Matt. 14:15; Luke 3:11; 9:13.

Note: For *asitia*, "without food," see ABSTINENCE.

FOOL, FOOLISH, FOOLISHLY, FOOLISHNESS

A. Adjectives.

1. *aphrōn* (ἄφρων, 878) signifies "without reason" (*a*, negative, *phrēn*, "the mind"), "want of mental sanity and sobriety, a reckless and inconsiderate habit of mind" (Hort), or "the lack of commonsense perception of the reality of things natural and spiritual ... or the imprudent ordering of one's life in regard to salvation" (G. Vos, in *Hastings' Bible Dic.*); it is mostly translated "foolish" or "foolish ones" in the RV; Luke 11:40; 12:20; Rom. 2:20; 1 Cor. 15:36; 2 Cor. 11:16 (twice), 19 (contrasted with *phronimos*, "prudent"); 12:6, 11; Eph. 5:17; 1 Pet. 2:15.¶

2. *anoētos* (ἀνόητος, 453) signifies "not understanding" (*a*, negative, *noeō*, "to perceive, understand"), not applying *nous*, "the mind," Luke 24:25; in Rom. 1:14 and Gal. 3:1, 3 it signifies "senseless," an unworthy lack of understanding; sometimes it carries a moral reproach (in contrast with *sōphrōn*, "sober-minded, self-controlled") and describes one who does not govern his lusts, Titus 3:3; in 1 Tim. 6:9 it is associated with evil desires, lusts. See UNWISE.¶

3. *mōros* (μωρός, 3474) primarily denotes "dull, sluggish" (from a root *muh*, "to be silly"); hence, "stupid, foolish"; it is used (*a*) of persons, Matt. 5:22, "Thou fool"; here the word means morally worthless, a scoundrel, a more serious reproach than "Raca"; the latter scorns a man's mind and calls him stupid; *mōros* scorns his heart and character; hence the Lord's more severe condemnation; in 7:26, "a foolish man"; 23:17, 19, "fools"; 25:2, 3, 8, "foolish"; in 1 Cor. 3:18, "a fool"; the apostle Paul uses it of himself and his fellow-workers, in 4:10, "fools" (i.e., in the eyes of opponents); (*b*) of things, 2 Tim. 2:23, "foolish and ignorant questionings"; so Titus 3:9; in 1 Cor. 1:25, "the foolishness of God," not *mōria*, "foolishness" as a personal quality (see C, No. 1), but adjectivally, that which is considered by the ignorant as a "foolish" policy or mode of dealing, lit., "the foolish (thing)"; so in v. 27, "the foolish (things) of the world."¶

4. *asunetos* (ἀσύνετος, 801) denotes "without discernment," or "understanding" (*a*, negative, *suniēmi*, "to understand"); hence "senseless," as in the RV of Rom. 1:21 (KJV, "foolish"), of the heart; in 10:19, KJV, "foolish," RV, "void of understanding." See UNDERSTANDING.

Note: For "fools," Eph. 5:15, see UNWISE, No. 3.

B. Verbs.

1. *mōrainō* (μωραίνω, 3471) is used (*a*) in the causal sense, "to make foolish," 1 Cor. 1:20; (*b*) in the passive sense, "to become foolish," Rom. 1:22; in Matt. 5:13 and Luke 14:34 it is said of salt that has lost its flavor, becoming tasteless. See SAVOUR.¶

2. *paraphroneō* (παραφρονέω, 3912), "to be beside oneself" (from *para*, "contrary to," and *phrēn*, "the mind"), "to be deranged," 2 Cor. 11:23, RV, "as one beside himself," for KJV, "as a fool."¶

C. Nouns.

1. *mōria* (μωρία, 3472) denotes "foolishness" (akin to A, No. 3 and B, No. 1), and is used in 1 Cor. 1:18, 21, 23; 2:14; 3:19.¶

2. *aphrosunē* (ἀφροσύνη, 877), "senselessness," is translated "foolishness" in Mark 7:22; 2 Cor. 11:1, 17, 21, "foolishness," RV (KJV, "folly" and "foolishly"). See FOLLY.¶

Note: Mōrologia denotes "foolish talking," Eph. 5:4. See TALKING.¶

FOOT, FEET

A. Nouns.

1. *pous* (πούς, 4228), besides its literal meaning, is used, by metonymy, of "a person in motion," Luke 1:79; Acts 5:9; Rom. 3:15; 10:15; Heb. 12:13. It is used in phrases expressing subjection, 1 Cor. 15:27, RV; of the humility and receptivity of discipleship, Luke 10:39; Acts 22:3; of obeisance and worship, e.g., Matt. 28:9; of scornful rejection, Matt. 10:14; Acts 13:51. Washing the "feet" of another betokened the humility of the service and the comfort of the guest, and was a feature of hospitality, Luke 7:38; John 13:5; 1 Tim. 5:10 (here figuratively).

Note: In Acts 7:5 *bēma*, "a step," is used with *podos*, the genitive case of *pous*, lit., "the step of a foot," i.e., "a foot breadth," what the "foot" can stand on, "(not so much as) to set his foot on."

2. *basis* (βάσις, 939), lit., "a step" (akin to *bainō*, "to go"), hence denotes that with which one steps, "a foot," and is used in the plural in Acts 3:7.¶

B. Adjectives.

1. *podērēs* (ποδήρης, 4158) signifies "reaching to the feet," from *pous*, and *arō*, "to fit" (akin to A, No. 1), and is said of a garment, Rev. 1:13.¶ In the Sept. it is used of the high priest's garment, e.g., Ex. 28:4.

2. *pezos* (πεζός, 3978), an adjective, "on foot," is used in one of its forms as an adverb in Matt. 14:13, and Mark 6:33, in each place signifying "by land," in contrast to "by sea."¶

Cf. *pezeuō*, "to go on foot," Acts 20:13, RV, "to go by land" (marg., "on foot").

Notes: (1) In Acts 20:18, the RV "set foot in" expresses more literally the verb *epibainō* (lit., "to go upon") than the KJV "came into." So again in 21:4 (some mss. have *anabainō* here). (2) In Luke 8:5, *katapateō*, "to tread down" (*kata*, "down," *pateō*, "to tread, trample"), is translated "was trodden under foot," RV (KJV, "was trodden down").

FOOTSTOOL

hupopodion (ὑποπόδιον, 5286), from *hupo*, "under," and *pous*, "a foot," is used (*a*) literally in Jas. 2:3, (*b*) metaphorically, of the earth as God's "footstool," Matt. 5:35; of the foes of the Lord, Matt. 22:44 (in some mss.); Mark 12:36, "underneath" (in some mss.); Luke 20:43; Acts 2:35; 7:49; Heb. 1:13; 10:13. The RV, adhering to the literal rendering, translates the phrase "the footstool of My (Thy, His) feet," for the KJV, "My (etc.) footstool," but in Matt. 22:44, "(till I put Thine enemies) underneath thy feet."¶

For **FOR** and **FORASMUCH** see *Note* †, p. 1

For **FORBADE** see **FORBID**

FORBEAR, FORBEARANCE

A. Verbs.

1. *anechō* (ἀνέχω, 430), "to hold up" (*ana*, "up," *echō*, "to have or hold"), is used in the middle voice in the NT, signifying "to bear with, endure"; it is rendered "forbearing (one another)" in Eph. 4:2 and Col. 3:13. See BEAR. Cf. B, No. 1, below.

2. *aniēmi* (ἀνίημι, 447), lit., "to send up or back" (*ana*, "up," *hiēmi*, "to send"), hence, "to relax, loosen," or, metaphorically, "to desist from," is translated "forbearing" (threatening) in Eph. 6:9 ("giving up your threatening," T. K. Abbott). See LEAVE, LOOSE.

3. *pheidomai* (φείδομαι, 5339), "to spare" (its usual meaning), "to refrain from doing something," is rendered "I forbear" in 2 Cor. 12:6. See SPARE.

4. *stegō* (στέγω, 4722) properly denotes "to protect by covering"; then, "to conceal"; then, by covering, "to bear up under"; it is translated "forbear" in 1 Thess. 3:1, 5. See BEAR.

Note: In 1 Cor. 9:6, the verb *ergazomai*, "to work," is used in the present infinitive, with a negative, and translated "to forbear working" (lit., "not working").

B. Noun.

anochē (ἀνοχή, 463), "a holding back" (akin to A, No. 1), denotes "forbearance," a

delay of punishment, Rom. 2:4; 3:25, in both places of God's "forbearance" with men; in the latter passage His "forbearance" is the ground, not of His forgiveness, but of His pretermission of sins, His withholding punishment. In 2:4 it represents a suspense of wrath which must eventually be exercised unless the sinner accepts God's conditions; in 3:25 it is connected with the passing over of sins in times past, previous to the atoning work of Christ.¶

Note: Cf. the noun *epieikeia*, Acts 24:4, "clemency"; 2 Cor. 10:1, "gentleness." Synonymous with this are *makrothumia*, "longsuffering," and *hupomonē*, "patience" (see Col. 1:11). *Anochē* and *makrothumia* are used together in Rom 2:4. See also Eph. 4:2 (where A, No. 1, is used in this combination). Trench (*Syn.*) and Abbott-Smith (*Lex.*) state that *hupononē* expresses patience with regard to adverse things, *makrothumia* patience with regard to antagonistic persons. It must be observed, however, that in Heb. 6:15 the verb *makrothumeō* is used of Abraham's patience under the pressure of trying circumstances (cf. also Jas. 5:7, 8). *Makrothumia* and *hupomonē* are often found together, e.g., 2 Cor. 6:4 and 6; 2 Tim. 3:10.

"Longsuffering is that quality of self-restraint in the face of provocation which does not hastily retaliate or promptly punish; it is the opposite of anger and is associated with mercy, and is used of God, Exod. 34:6, Sept.; Rom. 2:4; 1 Pet. 3:20. Patience is the quality that does not surrender to circumstances or succumb under trial; it is the opposite of despondency and is associated with hope, in 1 Thess. 1:3; it is not used of God."*

C. Adjectives.

1. *anexikakos* (ἀνεξίκακος, 420) denotes "patiently forbearing evil," lit., "patient of wrong," (from *anechō*, A, No. 1 and *kakos*, "evil"), "enduring"; it is rendered "forbearing" in 2 Tim. 2:24.¶

2. *epieikēs* (ἐπιεικής, 1933), an adjective (from *epi*, used intensively, and *eikos*, "reasonable"), is used as a noun with the article in Phil. 4:5, and translated "forbearance" in the RV; KJV, "moderation," RV, marg., "gentleness," "sweet reasonableness" (Matthew Arnold). See GENTLE.

FORBID, FORBADE

A. Verb.

kōluō (κωλύω, 2967), "to hinder, restrain, withhold, forbid" (akin to *kolos*, "docked, lopped, clipped"), is most usually translated "to

---

* From *Notes on Thessalonians,* by Hogg and Vine, pp. 183, 184.

forbid," often an inferior rendering to that of hindering or restraining, e.g., 1 Thess. 2:16; Luke 23:2; 2 Pet. 2:16, where the RV has "stayed"; in Acts 10:47 "forbid." In Luke 6:29, the RV has "withhold not (thy coat also)." See HINDER, KEEP, *Note* (7), STAY, SUFFER, A, *Note* (3), WITHHOLD, WITHSTAND, No. 1.

Notes: (1) The strengthened form *diakōluō* (*dia,* "through," used intensively) is used in Matt. 3:14, where, for the KJV, "forbad" the RV has "would have hindered him" ["forbad" is unsuitable with reference to the natural and persistent (*dia*) effort to prevent Christ from being baptized.]¶

(2) The phrase *mē genoito,* lit., "let it not be" (*mē,* negative, and *ginomai,* "to become"), is idiomatically translated "God forbid" in Luke 20:16; Rom. 3:4, 6, 31; 6:2, 15; 7:7, 13; 9:14; 11:1, 11; 1 Cor. 6:15; Gal. 2:17; 3:21, and in the KJV of 6:14; here the RV has "far be it from me (to glory)," which the American RV uses in the OT. In Paul's Epistles it is almost entirely used to express the apostle's repudiation of an inference which he apprehends may be drawn from his argument.

B. Adverb.

akolutōs (ἀκωλύτως, 209), "without hindrance" (*a,* negative, and A, No. 1, is translated "none forbidding him," in Acts 28:31. From the 2nd century A.D. onwards the word is found constantly in legal documents (Moulton and Milligan, Vocab., who draw attention to the triumphant note on which the word brings the Acts to a close).¶

FORCE

A. Adjective.

bebaios (βέβαιος, 949), "firm, secure," is translated "of force" (present usage would translate it "in force") in Heb. 9:17, of a testament, or covenant, in relation to a death. See FIRM.

B. Verb.

1. *harpazō* (ἁρπάζω, 726), "to snatch away, carry off by force," is used in the next sentence in Matt. 11:12, to that referred to under No. 1, "men of violence (KJV 'the violent') take it by force," the meaning being, as determined by the preceding clause, that those who are possessed of eagerness and zeal, instead of yielding to the opposition of religious foes, such as the scribes and Pharisees, press their way into the kingdom, so as to possess themselves of it. It is elsewhere similarly rendered in John 6:15, of those who attempted to seize the Lord, and in Acts 23:10, of the chief captain's command to the soldiers to rescue Paul. See CATCH, PLUCK, PULL. Cf. *diarpazō,* "to plunder," e.g., Matt. 12:29, and

sunarpazō, "to seize and carry away," e.g., Acts 6:12, and *harpax,* "rapacious, ravening," e.g., Matt. 7:15.

Notes: (1) *Biazō,* "to force" (from *bia,* "force"), is used in the passive voice in Matt. 11:12, of the kingdom of heaven as 'suffering violence;' so in Luke 16:16, "entereth violently into it," here in the middle voice, expressive of the special interest which the doer of the act has in what he is doing. This meaning is abundantly confirmed by the similar use in the papyri. Moulton and Milligan (*Vocab.*) remark that Luke's statement can be naturally rendered "everyone is entering it violently." See VIOLENCE.

(2) In Matt. 11:12, the corresponding noun, *biastēs,* "violence," is rendered "men of violence," RV (see No. 2). See VIOLENCE.

FOREFATHER

1. *progonos* (πρόγονος, 4269), an adjective, primarily denoting "born before" (*pro,* "before," and *ginomai,* "to become"), is used as a noun in the plural, 2 Tim. 1:3, "forefathers" (in 1 Tim. 5:4, "parents"). See PARENTS.¶

2. *propatōr* (προπάτωρ, 4253 and 3962), "a forefather" (*pro,* "before," *patēr,* "a father"), is used of Abraham in Rom. 4:1.¶

FOREGOING

proagō (προάγω, 4254), when used intransitively, signifies either to "lead the way," or "to go before, precede"; in Heb. 7:18, it is used of the commandment of the Law (v. 16), as preceding the bringing in of "a better hope" (RV, "foregoing"). See BRING, GO.

FOREHEAD

metōpon (μέτωπον, 3359), from *meta,* "with," and *ōps,* "an eye," occurs only in the Apocalypse, 7:3; 9:4; 13:16; 14:1, 9; 17:5; 20:4; 22:4.¶

FOREIGN, FOREIGNER

exō (ἔξω, 1854), an adverb, signifying "outside, without," is used in Acts 26:11, RV, "foreign," for KJV "strange," of cities beyond the limits of Palestine, lit., "unto (the) cities without," including Damascus. See FORTH, OUTWARD, STRANGE, WITHOUT.

Note: In Eph. 2:19, *paroikos,* lit., "dwelling near" (*para,* "near," *oikos,* a "dwelling"), denotes "an alien, a sojourner," in contrast to fellow-citizens, RV, "sojourners" (KJV, "foreigners"); in 1 Pet. 2:11, KJV, "strangers"; see also Acts 7:6, 29. See SOJOURNER, STRANGER. Cf. *allotrios,* e.g., Acts 7:6; Heb. 11:9, 34; *allophu-*

los, Acts 10:28;¶ *xenos*, Matt. 25:35, 38, 43; 27:7; Acts 17:21, etc.

FOREKNOW, FOREKNOWLEDGE

A. Verb.

proginōskō (προγινώσκω, 4267), "to know before" (*pro*, "before," *ginoskō*, "to know"), is used (*a*) of divine knowledge, concerning (1) Christ, 1 Pet. 1:20, RV, "foreknown" (KJV, "foreordained"); (2) Israel as God's earthly people, Rom. 11:2; (3) believers, Rom. 8:29; "the foreknowledge" of God is the basis of His foreordaining counsels; (*b*) of human knowledge, (1) of persons, Acts 26:5; (2) of facts, 2 Pet. 3:17.¶

B. Noun.

prognōsis (πρόγνωσις, 4268), "a foreknowledge" (akin to A.), is used only of divine "foreknowledge," Acts 2:23; 1 Pet. 1:2.¶ "Foreknowledge" is one aspect of omniscience; it is implied in God's warnings, promises and predictions. See Acts 15:18. God's "foreknowledge" involves His electing grace, but this does not preclude human will. He "foreknows" the exercise of faith which brings salvation. The apostle Paul stresses especially the actual purposes of God rather than the ground of the purposes, see, e.g., Gal. 1:16; Eph. 1:5, 11. The divine counsels will ever be unthwartable. Cf. FORESHEW.

For **FOREORDAIN** see **DETERMINE**, No. 3, **FOREKNOW**, A

For **FOREPART** see **FORESHIP**

FORERUNNER

prodromos (πρόδρομος, 4274), an adjective signifying "running forward, going in advance," is used as a noun, of "those who were sent before to take observations," acting as scouts, especially in military matters; or of "one sent before a king" to see that the way was prepared, Isa. 40:3; (cf. Luke 9:52; and, of John the Baptist, Matt. 11:10, etc). In the NT it is said of Christ in Heb. 6:20, as going in advance of His followers who are to be where He is, when He comes to receive them to Himself.¶ In the Sept., Num. 13:21, "forerunners (of the grape)"; Isa. 28:4, "an early (fig)."¶

FORESAIL

artemōn (ἀρτέμων, 736), from *artaō*, "to fasten to," is rendered "mainsail" in Acts 27:40, KJV; RV, "foresail." As to the particular kind of sail there mentioned, Sir William Ramsay, quoting from Juvenal concerning the entrance of a disabled ship into harbor by means of a prow-sail, indicates that the *artemōn* would be a sail set on the bow.¶

FORESEE, FORESEEN

1. *prooraō* (προοράω, 4308), with the aorist form *proeidon* (used to supply tenses lacking in *prooraō*), "to see before" (*pro*, "before," *horaō*, "to see"), is used with reference (*a*) to the past, of seeing a person before, Acts 21:29; (*b*) to the future, in the sense of "foreseeing" a person or thing, Acts 2:25, with reference to Christ and the Father, RV, "beheld" (here the middle voice is used).¶

2. *proeidon* (προεῖδον, 4275), an aorist tense form without a present, "to foresee," is used of David, as foreseeing Christ, in Acts 2:31, RV, "foreseeing" (KJV, "seeing before"); in Gal. 3:8, it is said of the Scripture, personified, personal activity being attributed to it by reason of its divine source (cf. v. 22). "What saith the Scripture?" was a common formula among the Rabbis.¶ In the Sept., Gen. 37:18; Ps. 16:8 (*prooraō*); 139:3.¶

3. *problepō* (προβλέπω, 4265), from *pro*, "before," and *blepō*, "to see, perceive," is translated "having provided" in Heb. 11:40 (middle voice), marg., "foreseen," which is the lit. meaning of the verb, as with Eng. "provide."¶ In the Sept., Ps. 37:13.¶

FORESHEW

prokatangellō (προκαταγγέλλω, 4293), "to announce beforehand" (*pro*, "before," *katangello*, "to proclaim"), is translated "foreshewed" in Acts 3:18, RV (KJV, "before had shewed"); in 7:52, KJV and RV, "shewed before."¶

FORESHIP

prōra (πρῶρα, 4408) denotes the forward part of a ship, "the prow," Acts 27:30; in v. 41 (KJV, "forepart") in contrast to *prumna*, "the stern."¶

FORETELL

prolegō (προλέγω, 4302), with the aorist form *proeipon*, and a perfect form *proeirēka* (from *proereō*), signifies (1) "to declare openly" or "plainly," or "to say" or "tell beforehand" (*pro*, "before," *legō*, "to say"), translated in 2 Cor. 13:2 (in the first sentence), RV, "I have said beforehand," KJV, "I told ... before"; in the next sentence, KJV, "I foretell," RV, "I do say beforehand" (marg., "plainly"); not prophecy is here in view, but a warning given before and repeated (see under FOREWARN); (2) "to speak before, of prophecy," as "foretelling" the future,

Mark 13:23, KJV, "have foretold," RV, "have told... beforehand"; Acts 1:16 (of the prophecy concerning Judas); Rom. 9:29; 2 Pet. 3:2; Jude 17; some inferior mss. have it in Heb. 10:15. See FOREWARN, SPEAK, TELL.

Note: In Acts 3:24 some mss. have *prokatangellō* (see FORESHEW); the most authentic have *katangellō*, RV, "told."

FOREWARN

prolegō (προλέγω, 4302), with verbal forms as mentioned above, is translated "I forewarn" and "I did forewarn," in the RV of Gal. 5:21, KJV, "I tell (you) before" and "I have told (you) in time past"; here, however, as in 2 Cor. 13:2 and 1 Thess. 3:4 (see below), the RV marg., "plainly" is to be preferred to "beforehand" or "before" (see under FORETELL); the meaning in Gal. 5:21 is not so much that Paul prophesied the result of the practice of the evils mentioned, but that he had told them before of the consequence and was now repeating his warning, as leaving no possible room for doubt or misunderstanding; in 1 Thess. 3:4, the subject told before was the affliction consequent upon the preaching of the Gospel; in 1 Thess. 4:6, "we forewarned," the warning was as to the consequences of whatsoever violates chastity.

Note: In Luke 12:5 the verb *hupodeiknumi*, "to shew, teach, make known," is translated "will warn" in the RV (KJV, "forewarn"). See EXAMPLE (B, No. 2), SHEW, WARN.

FORFEIT

zēmioō (ζημιόω, 2210), in the active voice, signifies "to damage"; in the passive, "to suffer loss, forfeit," Matt. 16:26 and Mark 8:36, of the "life," RV; KJV, and RV marg., "soul"; in each place the RV has "forfeit," for KJV, "lose"; Luke 9:25, "his own self" (RV, "forfeit," KJV, "be cast away"; here the preceding word "lose" translates *apollumi*, "to destroy"). What is in view here is the act of "forfeiting" what is of the greatest value, not the casting away by divine judgment, though that is involved, but losing or penalizing one's own self, with spiritual and eternal loss. The word is also used in 1 Cor. 3:15; 2 Cor. 7:9; Phil. 3:8. See CAST, LOSE, LOSS (suffer).¶

FORGET, FORGETFUL

A. Verbs.

1. *lanthanō* (λανθάνω, 2990), "to escape notice," is translated "they (wilfully) forget" in 2 Pet. 3:5, RV, lit., "this escapes them (i.e., their notice, wilfully on their part)," KJV, "they willingly are ignorant of"; in v. 8, RV, "forget not," lit., "let not this one thing escape you" (your

notice), KJV, "be not ignorant of." See HIDE, IGNORANT, UNAWARES.

2. *epilanthanomai* (ἐπιλανθάνομαι, 1950), "to forget, or neglect" (*epi*, "upon," used intensively, and No. 1), is said (*a*) negatively of God, indicating His remembrance of sparrows, Luke 12:6, and of the work and labor of love of His saints, Heb. 6:10; (*b*) of the disciples regarding taking bread, Matt. 16:5: Mark 8:14; (*c*) of Paul regarding "the things which are behind," Phil. 3:13; (*d*) of believers, as to showing love to strangers, Heb. 13:2, RV, and as to doing good and communicating, v. 16; (*e*) of a person who, after looking at himself in a mirror, forgets what kind of person he is, Jas. 1:24.¶

3. *eklanthanomai* (ἐκλανθάνομαι, 1585), "to forget utterly" (*ek*, "out," intensive), is used in the middle voice in Heb. 12:5, of "forgetting" an exhortation.¶

B. Nouns.

1. *lēthē* (λήθη, 3024), "forgetfulness" (from *lēthō*, "to forget," an old form of *lanthanō*, see A, No. 1; cf. Eng. "lethal," "lethargy," and the mythical river "Lethe," which was supposed to cause forgetfulness of the past to those who drank of it), is used with *lambanō*, "to take," in 2 Pet. 1:9, "having forgotten," lit., "having taken forgetfulness" (cf. 2 Tim. 1:5, lit., "having taken reminder"), a periphrastic expression for a single verb.¶

2. *epilēsmonē* (ἐπιλησμονή, 1953), "forgetfulness" (akin to A, No. 2), is used in Jas. 1:25, "a forgetful hearer," RV, "a hearer that forgetteth," lit., "a hearer of forgetfulness," i.e., a hearer characterized by "forgetfulness".¶

FORGIVE, FORGAVE, FORGIVENESS

A. Verbs.

1. *aphiēmi* (ἀφίημι, 863), primarily, "to send forth, send away" (*apo*, "from," *hiēmi*, "to send"), denotes, besides its other meanings, "to remit or forgive" (*a*) debts, Matt. 6:12; 18:27, 32, these being completely cancelled; (*b*) sins, e.g., Matt. 9:2, 5, 6; 12:31, 32; Acts 8:22 ("the thought of thine heart"); Rom. 4:7; Jas. 5:15; 1 John 1:9; 2:12. In this latter respect the verb, like its corresponding noun (below), firstly signifies the remission of the punishment due to sinful conduct, the deliverance of the sinner from the penalty divinely, and therefore righteously, imposed; secondly, it involves the complete removal of the cause of offense; such remission is based upon the vicarious and propitiatory sacrifice of Christ. In the OT atoning sacrifice and "forgiveness" are often associated, e.g., Lev. 4:20, 26. The verb is used in the NT

with reference to trespasses (*paraptōma*), e.g., Matt. 6:14, 15; sins (*hamartia*), e.g., Luke 5:20; debts (see above) (*opheilēma*), Matt. 6:12; (*opheilē*), 18:32; (*daneion*), 18:27; the thought (*dianoia*) of the heart, Acts 8:22. Cf. *kaluptō*, "to cover," 1 Pet. 4:8; Jas. 5:20; and *epikaluptō*, "to cover over," Rom. 4:7, representing the Hebrew words for "atonement."

Human "forgiveness" is to be strictly analogous to divine "forgiveness," e.g., Matt. 6:12. If certain conditions are fulfilled, there is no limitation to Christ's law of "forgiveness," Matt. 18:21, 22. The conditions are repentance and confession, Matt. 18:15–17; Luke 17:3.

As to limits to the possibility of divine "forgiveness," see Matt. 12:32, 2nd part (see BLASPHEMY) and 1 John 5:16 (see DEATH). See FORSAKE, LAY, *Note* (2) at end, LEAVE, LET, OMIT, PUT, No. 16, *Note*, REMIT, SEND, *Note*, (1), SUFFER, YIELD.

2. *charizomai* (χαρίζομαι, 5483), "to bestow a favor unconditionally," is used of the act of "forgiveness," whether divine, Eph. 4:32; Col. 2:13; 3:13; or human, Luke 7:42, 43 (debt); 2 Cor. 2:7, 10; 12:13; Eph. 4:32 (1st mention). Paul uses this word frequently, but No. 1 only, in Rom. 4:7, in this sense of the word. See DELIVER.

Note: Apoluō, "to let loose from" (*apo*, "from," *luō*, "to loose"), "to release," is translated "forgive," "ye shall be forgiven," Luke 6:37, KJV (RV, "release," "ye shall be released"), the reference being to setting a person free as a quasi-judicial act. The verb does not mean "to forgive." See DISMISS, RELEASE.

B. Noun.

aphesis (ἄφεσις, 859) denotes "a dismissal, release" (akin to A, No. 1); it is used of the remission of sins, and translated "forgiveness" in Mark 3:29; Eph. 1:7; Col. 1:14, and in the KJV of Acts 5:31; 13:38; 26:18, in each of which the RV has "remission." Eleven times it is followed by "of sins," and once by "of trespasses." It is never used of the remission of sins in the Sept., but is especially connected with the Year of Jubilee (Lev. 25:10, etc.). Cf. the RV of Luke 4:18, "release" (KJV, "liberty"). For the significance in connection with remission of sins and the propitiatory sacrifice of Christ, see A, No. 1. See DELIVERANCE, LIBERTY, RELEASE, REMISSION. Cf. the different word *paresis*, "a passing over, a remission," of sins committed under the old covenant, Rom. 3:25. The RV should be used here. This passing over, or by, was neither forgetting nor "forgiving"; it was rather a suspension of the just penalty; cf. Acts 17:30, "the times of ignorance God overlooked," RV; see also, e.g., Ps. 78:38.

FORM (Noun)

1. *morphē* (μορφή, 3444) denotes "the special or characteristic form or feature" of a person or thing; it is used with particular significance in the NT, only of Christ, in Phil. 2:6, 7, in the phrases "being in the form of God," and "taking the form of a servant." An excellent definition of the word is that of Gifford: "*morphē* is therefore properly the nature or essence, not in the abstract, but as actually subsisting in the individual, and retained as long as the individual itself exists.... Thus in the passage before us *morphē Theou* is the Divine nature actually and inseparably subsisting in the Person of Christ.... For the interpretation of 'the form of God' it is sufficient to say that (1) it includes the whole nature and essence of Deity, and is inseparable from them, since they could have no actual existence without it; and (2) that it does not include in itself anything 'accidental' or separable, such as particular modes of manifestation, or conditions of glory and majesty, which may at one time be attached to the 'form,' at another separated from it....

"The true meaning of *morphē* in the expression 'form of God' is confirmed by its recurrence in the corresponding phrase, 'form of a servant.' It is universally admitted that the two phrases are directly antithetical, and that 'form' must therefore have the same sense in both."[*]

The definition above mentioned applies to its use in Mark 16:12, as to the particular ways in which the Lord manifested Himself.¶

Note: For the synonymous word *schēma*, see FASHION. For the verb *morphoō*, see FORMED, No. 1, below.

2. *morphōsis* (μόρφωσις, 3446), "a form or outline," denotes, in the NT, "an image or impress, an outward semblance," Rom. 2:20, of knowledge of the truth; 2 Tim. 3:5, of godliness. It is thus to be distinguished from *morphē* (No. 1); it is used in almost the same sense as *schēma*, "fashion" (which see), but is not so purely the outward "form" as *schēma* is.¶

3. *tupos* (τύπος, 5179), "the representation or pattern" of anything (for which see ENSAMPLE), is rendered "form" in Rom. 6:17, "that form (or mold) of teaching whereunto ye were delivered," RV. The metaphor is that of a cast or frame into which molten material is poured so as to take its shape. The Gospel is the mould; those who are obedient to its teachings become conformed to Christ, whom it presents. In Acts 23:25, it is used of a letter, RV, "form" (KJV,

---

[*] From Gifford, "The Incarnation," pp. 16, 19, 39.

"manner"), with reference to the nature of the contents.

4. *eidos* (εἶδος, 1491), lit., "that which is seen" (*eidon*, "to see"), "an appearance or external form," is rendered "form" in the RV of Luke 3:22, of the Holy Spirit's appearance at the baptism of Christ; in John 5:37, in the Lord's testimony concerning the Father; in Luke 9:29 it is said of Christ Himself; it is translated "sight" in 2 Cor. 5:7, the Christian being guided by what he knows to be true, though unseen; in 1 Thess. 5:22 Christians are exhorted to abstain from "every form of evil," RV (the KJV, "appearance" is inadequate), i.e., from every kind of evil. See FASHION, SHAPE, SIGHT.¶

5. *hupotupōsis* (ὑποτύπωσις, 5296), "an outline, sketch" (akin to *hupotupoō*, "to delineate," *hupo*, "under," and No. 3), is used metaphorically to denote "a pattern, example," "form," in 2 Tim. 1:13, "of sound words" (RV, "pattern"); in 1 Tim. 1:16, "pattern" and "ensample." See ENSAMPLE.¶

FORMED

A. Verbs.

1. *morphoō* (μορφόω, 3445), like the noun (A, No. 1), refers, not to the external and transient, but to the inward and real; it is used in Gal. 4:19, expressing the necessity of a change in character and conduct to correspond with inward spiritual condition, so that there may be moral conformity to Christ.¶

Cf. *metamorphoō*, "to transform, transfigure," *summorphizō* and *suschematizō*, "to conform to."

2. *plassō* (πλάσσω, 4111), "to mold, to shape," was used of the artist who wrought in clay or wax (Eng., "plastic," "plasticity"), and occurs in Rom. 9:20; 1 Tim. 2:13.¶

B. Noun.

plasma (πλάσμα, 4110) denotes "anything molded or shaped into a form" (akin to A, No. 2), Rom. 9:20, "the thing formed."¶ Cf. the adjective *plastos*, "made up, fabricated, feigned," 2 Pet. 2:3.¶

FORMER

1. *prōtos* (πρῶτος, 4413*), "first," is translated "former" in Acts 1:1, of Luke's first treatise; in Rev. 21:4, RV, "first" (KJV, "former"). See BEFORE, FIRST.

2. *proteros* (πρότερος, 4387), "before, former," is translated "former" in Eph. 4:22; Heb. 10:32; 1 Pet. 1:14. See BEFORE.

FORNICATION, FORNICATOR

A. Nouns.

1. *porneia* (πορνεία, 4202) is used (*a*) of "illicit sexual intercourse," in John 8:41; Acts 15:20, 29; 21:25; 1 Cor. 5:1; 6:13, 18; 2 Cor. 12:21; Gal. 5:19; Eph. 5:3; Col. 3:5; 1 Thess. 4:3; Rev. 2:21; 9:21; in the plural in 1 Cor. 7:2; in Matt. 5:32 and 19:9 it stands for, or includes, adultery; it is distinguished from it in 15:19 and Mark 7:21; (*b*) metaphorically, of "the association of pagan idolatry with doctrines of, and professed adherence to, the Christian faith," Rev. 14:8; 17:2, 4; 18:3; 19:2; some suggest this as the sense in 2:21.¶

2. *pornos* (πόρνος, 4205) denotes "a man who indulges in fornication, a fornicator," 1 Cor. 5:9, 10, 11; 6:9; Eph. 5:5, RV; 1 Tim. 1:10, RV; Heb. 12:16; 13:4, RV; Rev. 21:8 and 22:15, RV (KJV, " whoremonger").¶

B. Verbs.

1. *porneuō* (πορνεύω, 4203) "to commit fornication," is used (*a*) literally, Mark 10:19; 1 Cor. 6:18; 10:8; Rev. 2:14, 20, see (*a*) and (*b*) above; (*b*) metaphorically, Rev. 17:2; 18:3, 9.¶

2. *ekporneuō* (ἐκπορνεύω, 1608), a strengthened form of No. 1 (*ek*, used intensively), "to give oneself up to fornication," implying excessive indulgence, Jude 7.¶

FORSAKE

A. Verbs.

1. *kataleipō* (καταλείπω, 2641), a strengthened form of *leipō*, "to leave," signifies (*a*) "to leave, to leave behind," e.g., Matt. 4:13; (*b*) "to leave remaining, reserve," e.g., Luke 10:40; (*c*) "to forsake," in the sense of abandoning, translated "to forsake" in the RV of Luke 5:28 and Acts 6:2; in Heb. 11:27 and 2 Pet. 2:15, KJV and RV In this sense it is translated "to leave," in Mark 10:7; 14:52; Luke 15:4; Eph. 5:31. See LEAVE, RESERVE.

2. *enkataleipō* (ἐγκαταλείπω, 1459), from *en*, "in," and No. 1, denotes (*a*) "to leave behind, among, leave surviving," Rom. 9:29; (*b*) "to forsake, abandon, leave in straits, or helpless," said by, or of, Christ, Matt. 27:46; Mark 15:34; Acts 2:27, 31 (No. 1 in some mss.); of men, 2 Cor. 4:9; 2 Tim. 4:10, 16; by God, Heb. 13:5; of things, by Christians (negatively), Heb. 10:25. See LEAVE.¶

3. *aphiēmi* (ἀφίημι, 863) sometimes has the significance of "forsaking," Mark 1:18; 14:50 (RV, "left "); so Luke 5:11. See FORGIVE.

4. *apotassō* (ἀποτάσσω, 657), primarily, "to set apart" (*apo*, off, "from," *tassō*, "to arrange"), is used in the middle voice, meaning (*a*) "to take leave of," e.g., Mark 6:46, (*b*) "to re-

nounce, forsake," Luke 14:33, KJV, "forsaketh," RV, "renounceth" ("all that he hath"). See BID FAREWELL, RENOUNCE, SEND, *Note* (2) at end, TAKE, *Note* (14).

B. Noun.

apostasia (ἀποστασία, 646), "an apostasy, defection, revolt," always in NT of religious defection, is translated "to forsake" in Acts 21:21, lit., "(thou teachest) apostasy (from Moses)"; in 2 Thess. 2:3, "falling away." See FALL.¶

For **FORSOMUCH** see † p. 1

FORSWEAR

epiorkeō (ἐπιορκέω, 1964) signifies "to swear falsely, to undo one's swearing, forswear oneself" (*epi*, "against," *orkos*, "an oath"), Matt. 5:33.¶ Cf. *epiorkos*, "a perjured person, a perjurer," 1 Tim. 1:10, "false swearers."¶

FORTH

exō (ἔξω, 1854), "outside, without" (from, *ek*, "out of, from"), frequently signifies "forth," especially after verbs of motion, e.g., John 11:43; 19:4, 13. See OUTWARD, STRANGE, WITHOUT.

Notes: (1) For the word "forth" in combination with various verbs, see, e.g., BREAK, BRING, COME, PUT. (2) In Matt. 26:16, the RV omits "forth," as the similar *apo tote*, "from then," simply means "from that time"; in the similar phrase "from that day forth," Matt. 22:46; John 11:53, there is no word in the original representing "forth." (3) In John 2:11 the RV rightly omits "forth."

FORTHWITH

1. *exautēs* (ἐξαυτῆς, 1824), "at once" (from, *ek*, "out of," and *autēs*, the genitive case of *autos*, "self or very," agreeing with "hour" understood, i.e., "from that very hour"), is translated "forthwith" in the RV in Mark 6:25 (KJV, "by and by"); Acts 10:33 (KJV, "immediately"); 11:11 (ditto); 21:32 (ditto); 23:30 (KJV, "straightway"); Phil. 2:23 (KJV, "presently"). The word is frequent in the period of the *koinē* Greek (see Preface). See IMMEDIATELY, PRESENTLY, STRAIGHTWAY.¶

2. *eutheōs* (εὐθέως, 2112), "at once, straightway" (from the adjective, *euthus*, "straight"), is translated "forthwith," in the KJV of Matt. 13:5; 26:49; (it occurs in some mss. in Mark 5:13; the RV omits it); Acts 12:10; 21:30 (RV, "straightway," in each place). See IMMEDIATELY, SHORTLY, STRAIGHTWAY.

3. *euthus* (εὐθύς, 2117), an alternative adverb to No. 2, is translated "forthwith" in the

KJV of Mark 1:29; 1:43 (in the best mss.), and John 19:34 (RV, "straightway"). See ANON, IMMEDIATELY, STRAIGHTWAY.¶

Note: Parachrēma, a synonymous word denoting "instantly, on the spot," is not translated "forthwith in KJV or RV. See IMMEDIATELY.

FORTY

tessarakonta (τεσσαράκοντα, 5062) is used in circumstances in Scripture which indicate the number as suggesting probation, separation or judgment, e.g., Matt. 4:2; Acts 1:3; Heb. 3:9, 17.

Note: Tessarakontaetēs, "forty years" (*etos*, "a year"), is found in Acts 7:23; 13:18.¶

FORWARD (be), FORWARDNESS

Notes: (1) The verb *thelō*, "to will, wish," is translated "to be forward," in the KJV of 2 Cor. 8:10, which the RV corrects to "to will." (2) In Gal. 2:10, *spoudazō*, "to be zealous," is so rendered in the RV (KJV, "I was forward"). (3) In 2 Cor. 8:17, the corresponding adjective *spoudaios*, "earnest," is so rendered in the RV (KJV, "forward"). So in v. 8, the noun *spoudē*, "earnestness," is thus rendered in the RV (KJV, "forwardness"). (4) In 9:2, RV, the noun *prothumia*, "readiness" (*pro*, "before," *thumos*, "impulse"), is so rendered (KJV, "forwardness of mind"). (5) For the combination of this word with verbs see GO, PUT, SET, STRETCH.

FOSTER-BROTHER

suntrophos (σύντροφος, 4939) primarily denotes "one nourished or brought up with another" (*sun*, "with," *trephō*, "to rear"); it is rendered "foster-brother" in Acts 13:1, RV. It has, however, been found in Hellenistic usage as a court term, signifying an intimate friend of a king (Deissmann), and this would seem to be the meaning regarding Manaen and Herod the Tetrarch.

FOUL

akathartos (ἀκάθαρτος, 169) denotes "unclean, impure" (*a*, negative, and *kathairō*, "to purify"), (*a*) ceremonially, e.g., Acts 10:14, 28; (*b*) morally, always, in the Gospels, of unclean spirits; it is translated "foul" in the KJV of Mark 9:25 and Rev. 18:2, but always "unclean" in the RV. Since the word primarily had a ceremonial significance, the moral significance is less prominent as applied to a spirit, than when *ponēros*, "wicked," is so applied. Cf. *akatharsia*, "uncleanness." See UNCLEAN.

Note: In Rev. 17:4 the best mss. have this word in the plural, RV, "the unclean things" (*akathartēs*, "filthiness," in some mss.).

FOUNDATION (to lay), FOUNDED

A. Nouns.

1. *themelios,* or *themelion* (θεμέλιος, 2310) is properly an adjective denoting "belonging to a foundation" (connected with *tithēmi,* "to place"). It is used (1) as a noun, with *lithos,* "a stone," understood, in Luke 6:48, 49; 14:29; Heb. 11:10; Rev. 21:14, 19; (2) as a neuter noun in Acts 16:26, and metaphorically, (*a*) of "the ministry of the gospel and the doctrines of the faith," Rom. 15:20; 1 Cor. 3:10, 11, 12; Eph. 2:20, where the "of" is not subjective (i.e., consisting of the apostles and prophets), but objective, (i.e., laid by the apostles, etc.); so in 2 Tim. 2:19, where "the foundation of God" is "the foundation laid by God," —not the Church (which is not a "foundation"), but Christ Himself, upon whom the saints are built; Heb. 6:1; (*b*) "of good works," 1 Tim. 6:19.¶

2. *katabolē* (καταβολή, 2602), lit., "a casting down," is used (*a*) of "conceiving seed," Heb. 11:11; (*b*) of "a foundation," as that which is laid down, or in the sense of founding; metaphorically, of "the foundation of the world"; in this respect two phrases are used, (1) "from the foundation of the world," Matt. 25:34 (in the most authentic mss. in 13:35 there is no phrase representing "of the world"); Luke 11:50; Heb. 4:3; 9:26; Rev. 13:8; 17:8; (2) "before the foundation of the world," John 17:24; Eph. 1:4; 1 Pet. 1:20. The latter phrase looks back to the past eternity.¶

B. Verb.

themelioō (θεμελιόω, 2311), "to lay a foundation, to found" (akin to A, No. 1), is used (*a*) literally, Matt. 7:25; Luke 6:48; Heb. 1:10; (*b*) metaphorically, Eph. 3:17, "grounded (in love)"; Col. 1:23 (ditto, "in the faith"); 1 Pet. 5:10, KJV, "settle." See GROUND, SETTLE.¶

FOUNTAIN

pēgē (πηγή, 4077), "a spring or fountain," is used of (*a*) "an artificial well," fed by a spring, John 4:6; (*b*) metaphorically (in contrast to such a well), "the indwelling Spirit of God," 4:14; (*c*) "springs," metaphorically in 2 Pet. 2:17, RV, for KJV, "wells"; (*d*) "natural fountains or springs," Jas. 3:11, 12; Rev. 8:10; 14:7; 16:4; (*e*) metaphorically, "eternal life and the future blessings accruing from it," Rev. 7:17; 21:6; (*f*) "a flow of blood," Mark 5:29.¶

FOUR (-TH), FOURTEEN (-TH), FOUR HUNDRED

tessares (τέσσαρες, 5064), "four," is not found in the NT outside the Gospels, the Acts and Apocalypse; in the last it is very frequent.

Tetartos, "fourth," is found in Matt. 14:25; Mark 6:48 and seven times in the Apocalypse; also in Acts 10:30, "four days ago," lit., "from a fourth day." *Dekatessares,* "fourteen" (lit., "ten-four"), is found in Matt. 1:17; 2 Cor. 12:2; Gal. 2:1;¶ *tessareskaidekatos,* "fourteenth" (lit., "four-and-tenth"), Acts 27:27, 33;¶ *tetrakosia,* "four hundred," Acts 5:36; 7:6; 13:20; Gal. 3:17.¶ In Acts 7:6 the 400 years refers to Abraham's descendants and to the sojourning and the bondage. This agrees with Gen. 15:13. In Exod. 12:40 the 430 years dates from the call of Abraham himself. Likewise the giving of the Law was 430 years from the promise in Gen. 12:3, which agrees with Gal. 3:17. In John 11:39 *tetartaios,* lit., "a fourth day (one)," is rendered "four days."

FOURFOLD

tetraploos (τετραπλόος, 5073), an adjective, is found in Luke 19:8.¶

FOURFOOTED

tetrapous (τετράπους, 5074), from *tetra,* "four" (used in compound words), and *pous,* "a foot," is used of "beasts," Acts 10:12; 11:6; Rom. 1:23.¶

FOURSCORE

ogdoēkonta (ὀγδοήκοντα, 3589), from *ogdoos,* "eighth," is found in Luke 2:37; 16:7.¶

FOURSQUARE

tetragōnos (τετράγωνος, 5068), "four-cornered" (from *tetra,* see above, and *gōnia,* "a corner, or angle"), is found in Rev. 21:16.¶

For FOWL see BIRD

FOX

alōpēx (ἀλώπηξ, 258) is found in Matt. 8:20; Luke 9:58; metaphorically, of Herod, in Luke 13:32.¶

For FRAGMENTS see PIECE, No. 4

FRAME (Verb)

1. *katartizō* (καταρτίζω, 2675), "to fit, to render complete," is translated "have been framed" in Heb. 11:3, of the worlds or ages. See FIT.

2. *sunarmologeō* (συναρμολογέω, 4883), "to fit or frame together" (*sun,* "with," *harmos,* "a joint," *legō,* "to choose"), is used metaphorically of the church as a spiritual temple, the parts being "fitly framed together," Eph. 2:21; as a body, 4:16, RV, "fitly framed," (for KJV, "fitly joined").¶

FRANKINCENSE

libanos (λίβανος, 2030), from a Semitic
verb signifying "to be white," is a vegetable
resin, bitter and glittering, obtained by incisions
in the bark of the *arbor thuris*, "the incense
tree," and especially imported through Arabia;
it was used for fumigation at sacrifices, Exod.
30:7, etc., or for perfume, Song of Sol., 3:6. The
Indian variety is called *looban*. It was among
the offerings brought by the wise men, Matt.
2:11. In Rev. 18:13 it is listed among the com-
modities of Babylon. The "incense" of Rev. 8:3
should be "frankincense." Cf. INCENSE.¶

FRANKLY

Note: In Luke 7:42, the verb *charizomai*, "to
forgive" (as a matter of grace), is rendered
"frankly forgave," so as to bring out the force
of the grace in the action. Older versions had
"forgave," and to this the RV returns.

FRAUD

aphustereō (ἀφυστερέω, 575 and 5302), "to
keep back, deprive" (*apo*, "from," *hustereō*, "to
be lacking"), is used in Jas. 5:4, "is kept back
by fraud" (some mss. have *apostereō*, "to defraud"). The word is found in a papyrus writing
of A.D. 42, of a bath insufficiently warmed
(Moulton and Milligan, *Vocab.*). The Law required the prompt payment of the laborer,
Deut. 24:15.¶

FREE, FREEDOM, FREELY, FREEMAN, FREEDMAN, FREEWOMAN

A. Adjective.

eleútheros (ἐλεύθερος, 1658), primarily of
"freedom to go wherever one likes," is used (*a*)
of "freedom from restraint and obligation" in
general, Matt. 17:26; Rom. 7:3; 1 Cor. 7:39, RV,
"free," of the second marriage of a woman; 9:1,
19; 1 Pet. 2:16; from the Law, Gal. 4:26; from
sin, John 8:36; with regard to righteousness,
Rom. 6:20 (i.e., righteousness laid no sort of
bond upon them, they had no relation to it); (*b*)
in a civil sense, "free" from bondage or slavery,
John 8:33; 1 Cor. 7:21, 22, 2nd part (for v. 22,
1st part, see C, No. 2); 12:13; Gal. 3:28; Eph.
6:8; Rev. 13:16; 19:18; as a noun, "freeman,"
Col. 3:11, RV; Rev. 6:15; "freewoman," Gal.
4:22, 23, 30, and v. 31. RV.¶

Notes: (1) In Matt. 15:6 and Mark 7:11, the
words "he shall be free," KJV, have nothing to
represent them in the Greek. (2) In Heb. 13:5,
RV, "be ye free from the love of money," is an
abbreviated rendering of the adjective *aphilarguros* ("not loving money") with the noun *tro-

pos, "turn (of mind)"; hence the marg., "let your
turn of mind be free, etc.," for KJV, "let your
conversation be without covetousness."

B. Verb.

eleutheroō (ἐλευθερόω, 1659), "to make
free" (akin to A), is used of deliverance from
(*a*) sin, John 8:32, 36; Rom. 6:18, 22; (*b*) the
Law, Rom. 8:2; Gal. 5:1 (see, however under
C); (*c*) the bondage of corruption, Rom. 8:21.
See DELIVER.¶

Note: In Rom. 6:7, the verb *dikaioō*, translated "is freed," signifies "to justify," as in the
RV, "is justified," i.e., in the legal sense; death
annuls all obligations. The death penalty which
Christ endured holds good for the believer,
through his identification with Christ in His
death; having been crucified as to his unregenerate nature, and justified from sin, he walks in
newness of life in Christ.

C. Nouns.

1. *eleutheria* (ἐλευθερία, 1657), "liberty"
(akin to A and B), is rendered "freedom" in
Gal. 5:1, "with freedom did Christ set us free."
The combination of the noun with the verb
stresses the completeness of the act, the aorist
(or point) tense indicating both its momentary
and comprehensive character; it was done once
for all. The RV margin "for freedom" gives perhaps the preferable meaning, i.e., "not to bring
us into another form of bondage did Christ
liberate us from that in which we were born,
but in order to make us free from bondage."
The word is twice rendered "freedom" in the
RV of Gal. 5:13 (KJV, "liberty"). The phraseology is that of manumission from slavery, which
among the Greeks was effected by a legal fiction, according to which the manumitted slave
was purchased by a god; as the slave could not
provide the money, the master paid it into the
temple treasury in the presence of the slave, a
document being drawn up containing the words
"for freedom." No one could enslave him again,
as he was the property of the god. Hence the
word *apeleutheros*, No. 2. The word is also
translated "freedom" in 1 Pet. 2:16, RV. In
2 Cor. 3:17 the word denotes "freedom" of access to the presence of God. See LIBERTY.

2. *apeleutheros* (ἀπελεύθερος, 558), "a freed
man" (*apo*, "from," and A), is used in 1 Cor.
7:22, "the Lord's freedman." See the illustration
above under No. 1. Here the fuller word brings
out the spiritual emancipation in contrast to the
natural "freedman."

Note: (1) In Acts 22:28, the word *politeia*,
rendered "freedom" (KJV), denotes citizenship,
as in the RV (see CITIZENSHIP); in the next sentence the Greek is, lit., "But I was even born";
the necessary word to be supplied is "Roman,"

from the previous verse; hence the RV, "But I am a Roman born." (2) For "free gift" (*charisma*), Rom. 5:15, 16; 6:23, see GIFT.

D. Adverb.

dōrean (δωρεάν, 1432), from *dōrea*, "a gift," is used as an adverb in the sense "freely," in Matt. 10:8; Rom 3:24; 2 Cor. 11:7 (RV, "for nought"); Rev. 21:6; 22:17. Here the prominent thought is the grace of the Giver. See CAUSE.

Notes: (1) In Acts 26:26 *parrhēsiazomai,* "to be bold in speech," is translated, "to speak freely." (2) In Acts 2:29 the noun *parrhēsia* with the preposition *meta,* "with," is rendered "freely," lit., "with free-spokenness." (3) For *charizomai,* "to give freely," Rom. 8:32; 1 Cor. 2:12, see GIVE. (4) In 2 Thess. 3:1, KJV, the verb *trechō,* "to run," is rendered "may have free course"; this the RV corrects to "may run." (5) For *charitoō,* "to bestow freely," Eph. 1:6, see ACCEPT, *Note.* (6) For "have drunk freely," John 2:10, RV, see DRINK, B, No. 2.

FREIGHT

ekbolē (ἐκβολή, 1546), lit., "a throwing out" (from *ekballō,* "to throw out"), denotes "a jettison, a throwing out of cargo," Acts 27:18, lit., "they made a throwing out," RV, "they began to throw the freight overboard," KJV, "they lightened the ship."¶ In the Sept., Exod. 11:1; Jonah 1:5.¶

For **FREQUENT,** 2 Cor. 11:23, see **ABUNDANT,** D

FRESH

neos (νέος, 3501), "new" (in respect of time, as distinct from *kainos,* "new," in respect of quality), is translated "fresh" in the RV of Matt. 9:17; Mark 2:22; Luke 5:38, with reference to wineskins. See NEW.

Note: Glukus, "sweet," is used in Jas. 3:11, 12 (in this verse, KJV, "fresh," RV, "sweet," as in both elsewhere); Rev. 10:9, 10. See SWEET.¶

FRIEND (make one's)

A. Nouns.

1. *philos* (φίλος, 5384), primarily an adjective, denoting "loved, dear, or friendly," became used as a noun, (*a*) masculine, Matt. 11:19; fourteen times in Luke (once feminine, 15:9); six in John; three in Acts; two in James, 2:23, "the friend of God"; 4:4, "a friend of the world"; 3 John 14 (twice); (*b*) feminine, Luke 15:9, "her friends."

2. *hetairos* (ἑταῖρος, 2083), "a comrade, companion, partner," is used as a term of kindly address in Matt. 20:13; 22:12; 26:50. This, as

expressing comradeship, is to be distinguished from No. 1, which is a term of endearment. Some mss. have the word in Matt. 11:16; the best have *heterois,* others, KJV and RV, "fellows." See FELLOW.

Notes: (1) The phrase *hoi para autou,* in Mark 3:21, "his friends," lit. means "the (ones) beside Him," i.e., those belonging to him. (2) In Mark 5:19, "thy friends" represents the phrase *hoi soi,* lit., "the (ones) to thee," i.e., "thine own."

B. Verb.

peithō (πείθω, 3982), "to persuade, influence," is rendered "having made ... their friend" in Acts 12:20, of the folks of Tyre and Sidon in winning the good will of Blastus, Herod's chamberlain, possibly with bribes. See ASSURE, B, No. 3.

FRIENDSHIP

philia (φιλία, 5373), akin to *philos,* "a friend" (see above), is rendered in Jas. 4:4, "the friendship (of the world)." It involves "the idea of loving as well as being loved" (Mayor); cf. the verb in John 15:19.¶

For **FRO** and **FROM** see † p. 1

FROG

batrachos (βάτραχος, 944) is mentioned in Rev. 16:13. Quacks were represented as "frogs" and were associated metaphorically with serpents.¶

For **FROWARD** see **CROOKED**

FRUIT (bear), FRUITFUL, UNFRUITFUL

A. Nouns.

1. *karpos* (καρπός, 2590), "fruit," is used (I) of the fruit of trees, fields, the earth, that which is produced by the inherent energy of a living organism, e.g., Matt. 7:17; Jas. 5:7, 18; plural, e.g., in Luke 12:17 [for the next verse, see *Note* (1) below] and 2 Tim. 2:6; of the human body, Luke 1:42; Acts 2:30; (II) metaphorically, (*a*) of works or deeds, "fruit" being the visible expression of power working inwardly and invisibly, the character of the "fruit" being evidence of the character of the power producing it, Matt. 7:16. As the visible expressions of hidden lusts are the works of the flesh, so the invisible power of the Holy Spirit in those who are brought into living union with Christ (John 15:2–8, 16) produces "the fruit of the Spirit," Gal. 5:22, the singular form suggesting the unity of the character of the Lord as reproduced in them, namely, "love, joy, peace, longsuffering,

kindness, goodness, faithfulness, meekness, temperance," all in contrast with the confused and often mutually antagonistic "works of the flesh." So in Phil. 1:11, marg., "fruit of righteousness." In Heb. 12:11, "the fruit of righteousness" is described as "peaceable fruit," the outward effect of divine chastening; "the fruit of righteousness is sown in peace," Jas. 3:18, i.e., the seed contains the fruit; those who make peace, produce a harvest of righteousness; in Eph. 5:9, "the fruit of the light" (RV, and see context) is seen in "goodness and righteousness and truth," as the expression of the union of the Christian with God (Father, Son and Holy Spirit); for God is good, Mark 10:18, the Son is "the righteous One," Acts 7:52, the Spirit is "the Spirit of truth," John 16:13; (b) of advantage, profit, consisting (1) of converts as the result of evangelistic ministry, John 4:36; Rom. 1:13; Phil. 1:22; (2) of sanctification, through deliverance from a life of sin and through service to God, Rom. 6:22, in contrast to (3) the absence of anything regarded as advantageous as the result of former sins, v. 21; (4) of the reward for ministration to servants of God, Phil. 4:17; (5) of the effect of making confession to God's Name by the sacrifice of praise, Heb. 13:15.

2. *genēma* (γένημα, 1096d), from *ginomai*, "to come into being," denotes "fruit" (a) as the produce of the earth, e.g., the vine; in the following the best mss. have this noun, Matt. 26:29; Mark 14:25; Luke 22:18; [12:18 in some mss.; see *Note* (1)]; (b) metaphorically, as "the fruits of ... righteousness" (i.e., of material ministrations to the needy), 2 Cor. 9:10.¶

Notes: (1) In Luke 12:18 some mss. have *gennēmata*, a mistake for *genēmata;* the best have *sitos*, "corn." (2) *Genēma* is to be distinguished from *gennēma*, "offspring" (from *gennaō*, "to beget"), Matt. 3:7; 12:34; 23:33; Luke 3:7.¶

3. *opōra* (ὀπώρα, 3703) primarily denotes "late summer or early autumn," i.e., late July, all August and early September. Since that is the time of "fruit-bearing," the word was used, by metonymy, for the "fruits" themselves, Rev. 18:14.¶

Note: Cf. *phthinopōrinos*, "autumnal," in Jude 12, "autumn trees," bearing no "fruit" when "fruit" should be expected.¶

B. Adjectives.

1. *karpophoros* (καρποφόρος, 2593) denotes "fruitful" (A, No. 1, and *pherō*, "to bear"), Acts 14:17.¶ Cf. C, below.

2. *akarpos* (ἄκαρπος, 175), "unfruitful" (a, negative, and A, No. 1), is used figuratively (a) of "the word of the Kingdom," rendered "un-fruitful" in the case of those influenced by the cares of the world and the deceitfulness of riches, Matt. 13:22; Mark 4:19; (b) of the understanding of one praying with a "tongue," which effected no profit to the church without an interpretation of it, 1 Cor. 14:14; (c) of the works of darkness, Eph. 5:11; (d) of believers who fail "to maintain good works," indicating the earning of one's living so as to do good works to others, Titus 3:14; of the effects of failing to supply in one's faith the qualities of virtue, knowledge, temperance, patience, godliness, love of the brethren, and love, 2 Pet. 1:8. In Jude 12 it is rendered "without fruit," of ungodly men, who oppose the gospel while pretending to uphold it, depicted as "autumn trees" (see *Note* under A, No. 3).¶ In the Sept., Jer. 2:6.¶

C. Verb.

karpophoreō (καρποφορέω, 2592), "to bear or bring forth fruit" (see B, No. 1), is used (a) in the natural sense, of the "fruit of the earth," Mark 4:28; (b) metaphorically, of conduct, or that which takes effect in conduct, Matt. 13:23; Mark 4:20; Luke 8:15; Rom. 7:4, 5 (the latter, of evil "fruit," borne "unto death," of activities resulting from a state of alienation from God); Col. 1:6 in the middle voice; Col. 1:10.¶

Note: For "bring forth fruit to perfection," Luke 8:14, see PERFECTION, B.

For **FRUSTRATE**, Gal. 2:21, see **VOID**

FULFILL, FULFILLING, FULFILLMENT

A. Verbs.

1. *plēroō* (πληρόω, 4137) signifies (1) "to fill" (see FILL); (2) "to fulfill, complete," (a) of time, e.g., Mark 1:15; Luke 21:24; John 7:8 (KJV, "full come"); Acts 7:23, RV, "he was well-nigh forty years old" (KJV, "was full" etc.), lit., "the time of forty years was fulfilled to him"; v. 30, KJV, "were expired"; 9:23; 24:27 (KJV, "after two years"; RV, "when two years were fulfilled"); (b) of number, Rev. 6:11; (c) of good pleasure, 2 Thess. 1:11; (d) of joy, Phil. 2:2; in the passive voice, "to be fulfilled," John 3:29 and 17:13; in the following the verb is rendered "fulfilled" in the RV, for the KJV, "full," John 15:11; 16:24; 1 John 1:4; 2 John 12; (e) of obedience, 2 Cor. 10:6; (f) of works, Rev. 3:2; (g) of the future Passover, Luke 22:16; (h) of sayings, prophecies, etc., e.g., Matt. 1:22 (twelve

times in Matt., two in Mark, four in Luke, eight in John, two in Acts); Jas. 2:23; in Col. 1:25 the word signifies to preach "fully," to complete the ministry of the Gospel appointed. See FILL.

2. *anaplēroō* (ἀναπληρόω, 378), "to fill up, fill completely" (*ana*, "up, up to," and No. 1), is used (*a*) of Isaiah's prophecy of Israel's rejection of God, fulfilled in the rejection of His Son, Matt. 13:14; (*b*) of the status of a person in a church, RV, "filleth the place," for KJV, "occupieth the room," 1 Cor. 14:16; (*c*) of an adequate supply of service, 1 Cor. 16:17, "supplied"; Phil. 2:30, "to supply"; (*d*) of sins, 1 Thess. 2:16; (*e*) of the law of Christ; Gal. 6:2. See FILL, OCCUPY, SUPPLY.¶

3. *teleō* (τελέω, 5055), "to end" (akin to *telos*, "an end"), signifies, among its various meanings, "to give effect to," and is translated "fulfill," of the Law, intentionally, Jas. 2:8, or unconsciously, Rom. 2:27; of the prophetic Scriptures concerning the death of Christ, Acts 13:29; prohibitively, of the lust of the flesh, Gal. 5:16. See ACCOMPLISH, FINISH.

Notes: (1) In regard to this word in Rev. 15:1 and 8, the RV, "finished," corrects the KJV, "filled up," and "fulfilled," as the judgments there indicated finish the whole series of those consisting of the wrath of God; so in 20:3, of the thousand years of the Millennium (cf. vv. 5, 7). (2) In 17:17, the RV has "should be accomplished," for KJV, "shall be fulfilled." (3) In Luke 22:37 the KJV has "be accomplished" (RV, "be fulfilled").

4. *sunteleō* (συντελέω, 4931), "to complete," is translated "fulfilled" in the KJV of Mark 13:4 (RV, "accomplished"). See COMPLETE.

5. *teleioō* (τελειόω, 5048), "to bring to an end, fulfill," is rendered "to fulfill," of days. Luke 2:43; of the Scripture, John 19:28. See FINISH.

6. *plērophoreō* (πληροφορέω, 4135), "to bring in full measure," from *pleroō* (see No. 1), and *phoreō*, "to bring"; hence, "to fulfill," of circumstances relating to Christ, Luke 1:1, RV, "have been fulfilled" (KJV "are most surely believed"); of evangelical ministry, 2 Tim. 4:5, "fulfill" (KJV, "make full proof"); so in v. 17, RV, "fully proclaimed" (KJV, "fully known"). See ASSURE, PERSUADE.

7. *ekplēroō* (ἐκπληρόω, 1603), a strengthened form of No. 1, occurs in Acts 13:33.¶

Notes: (1) *Poieō*, "to do," is so rendered in the RV, for KJV "fulfill," in Acts 13:22; Eph. 2:3; Rev. 17:17 [for the end of this verse see *Note* (2) under *teleō*, above]. (2) *Ginomai*, "to become, to take place," is rendered "fulfilled" in the KJV of Matt. 5:18; 24:34; Luke 21:32, RV, "accomplished," in each place.

B. Nouns.

1. *plērōma* (πλήρωμα, 4138) stands for the result of the action expressed in *pleroō*, "to fill." It is used to signify (*a*) "that which has been completed, the complement, fullness," e.g., John 1:16; Eph. 1:23; some suggest that the "fullness" here points to the body as the filled receptacle of the power of Christ (words terminating in —*ma* are frequently concrete in character; cf. *dikaiōma* in Rom. 5:18, act of righteousness); in Mark 8:20 the rendering "basketfuls" (RV) represents the plural of this word, lit., "the fulnesses of (how many baskets)"; (*b*) "that which fills up," Matt. 9:16; Mark 2:21 (see FILL); (*c*) "a filling up, fulfillment," Rom. 13:10, of the fulfilling of the Law. See FULLNESS (below).

2. *teleiōsis* (τελείωσις, 5058), a fulfillment, is so rendered in Luke 1:45, RV (KJV, "performance"). See PERFECTION.

FULL

A. Adjectives.

1. *plērēs* (πλήρης, 4134) denotes "full," (*a*) in the sense of "being filled," materially, Matt. 14:20; 15:37; Mark 8:19 (said of baskets "full" of bread crumbs); of leprosy, Luke 5:12; spiritually, of the Holy Spirit, Luke 4:1; Acts 6:3; 7:55; 11:24; grace and truth, John 1:14; faith, Acts 6:5; grace and power, 6:8; of the effects of spiritual life and qualities, seen in good works, Acts 9:36; in an evil sense, of guile and villany, Acts 13:10; wrath, 19:28; (*b*) in the sense of "being complete," "full corn in the ear," Mark 4:28; of a reward hereafter, 2 John 8.¶

2. *mestos* (μεστός, 3324) probably akin to a root signifying "to measure," hence conveys the sense of "having full measure," (*a*) of material things, a vessel, John 19:29; a net, 21:11; (*b*) metaphorically, of thoughts and feelings, exercised (1) in evil things, hypocrisy, Matt. 23:28; envy, murder, strife, deceit, malignity, Rom. 1:29; the utterances of the tongue, Jas. 3:8; adultery, 2 Pet. 2:14; (2) in virtues, goodness, Rom. 15:14; mercy, etc., Jas. 3:17.¶

B. Verb.

gemō (γέμω, 1073), "to be full, to be heavily laden with," was primarily used of a ship; it is chiefly used in the NT of evil contents, such as extortion and excess, Matt. 23:25; dead men's bones, v. 27; extortion and wickedness, Luke 11:39; cursing, Rom. 3:14; blasphemy, Rev. 17:3; abominations, v. 4; of divine judgments, 15:17; 21:9; (RV, "laden," KJV, "full"); of good things, 4:6, 8; 5:8.¶

Notes: (1) *Gemizō* (see FILL, A, No. 9) is always rendered "to fill" in RV (2) For Acts 2:13, KJV, see FILL, No. 11. (3) For "fullgrown,"

Heb. 5:14, RV, see AGE, No. 2; for Jas. 1:15, RV, see FINISH, *Note* (2).

FULLER

gnapheus (γναφεύς, 1102), akin to *knaptō*, "to card wool," denotes "a clothcarder, or dresser" (*gnaphos*, "the prickly teasel-cloth"; hence, "a carding comb"); it is used of the raiment of the Lord in Mark 9:3.¶

For **FULLGROWN** see **AGE, B, No. 2, FINISH,** *Note* (2)

For **FULLY** see **ASSURED, COME, KNOW, PERSUADE, PREACH, RIPE**

FULLNESS

plerōma (πλήρωμα, 4138) denotes "fullness," that of which a thing is "full"; it is thus used of the grace and truth manifested in Christ, John 1:16; of all His virtues and excellencies, Eph. 4:13; "the blessing of Christ," Rom. 15:29, RV (not as KJV); the conversion and restoration of Israel, Rom. 11:12; the completion of the number of Gentiles who receive blessing through the gospel, v. 25; the complete products of the earth, 1 Cor. 10:26; the end of an appointed period, Gal. 4:4; Eph. 1:10; God, in the completeness of His Being, Eph. 3:19; Col. 1:19; 2:9; the church as the complement of Christ, Eph. 1:23. In Mark 6:43, "basketfuls," RV, is, lit., "fullnesses of baskets." For Matt. 9:16; Mark 2:21 see FILL, (B); for 8:20 see FULFILL, B.

Note: For *plērophoria*, "fullness," Heb. 6:11, RV, see ASSURANCE.

FURLONG

stadion (στάδιον, 4712) denotes (*a*) "a stadium," i.e., a measure of length, 600 Greek feet, or one-eighth of a Roman mile, Matt. 14:24 (in the best mss.); Luke 24:13; John 6:19; 11:18; Rev. 14:20; 21:16; (*b*) "a race course," the length of the Olympic course, 1 Cor. 9:24.¶

FURNACE

kaminos (κάμινος, 2575), "an oven, furnace, kiln" (whence Lat. *caminus*, Eng., chimney), used for smelting, or for burning earthenware, occurs in Matt. 13:42, 50; Rev. 1:15; 9:2.¶

FURNISH

1. *strōnnumi* (στρώννυμι, 4766), or *strōn-nuō*, "to spread," is used of "furnishing a room," Mark 14:15; Luke 22:12; of "making a bed," Acts 9:34; in Matt. 21:8; Mark 11:8, "spread" (KJV, "strawed," twice). See SPREAD.¶

2. *exartizō* (ἐξαρτίζω, 1822), "to fit out, to prepare perfectly, to complete for a special purpose" (*ex*, "out," used intensively, and *artios*, "joined," *artos*, "a joint"), is used of "accomplishing" days, Acts 21:5, i.e., of "terminating" a space of time; of being "completely furnished," by means of the Scriptures, for spiritual service, 2 Tim. 3:17. See ACCOMPLISH.

3. *plēthō* (πλήθω, 4130), Matt. 21: 10, "furnished" RV, "filled." See FILL, No. 5.

FURTHER

1. *eti* (ἔτι, 2089), "yet, still, further," is used (*a*) of time, most usually translated "yet," e.g., Matt. 12:46; or negatively, "any more," "no more," e.g., Heb. 8:12; (*b*) of degree, translated "further," or "any further," Matt. 26:65; Mark 5:35; 14:63; Luke 22:71; Heb. 7:11; in Acts 21:28, RV, "moreover" (KJV, "further"). See LONGER, MORE, MOREOVER, STILL, THENCEFORTH, YET.

2. *porrōteron* (πορρώτερον, 4208), the comparative degree of *porrō*, "far off," signifies "further," Luke 24:28. See FAR.

Note: In Acts 27:28, *brachu*, "a little," is rendered "a little further," KJV (RV, "after a little space").

FURTHERANCE

Notes: (1) In Phil. 1:12, 25, KJV, *prokopē*, "a striking forward" (*pro*, "forward," *koptō*, "to cut"), is translated "furtherance"; "progress" in RV, as in 1 Tim. 4:15. Originally the word was used of a pioneer cutting his way through brushwood. See PROGRESS.¶ (2) In Phil. 1:5 the RV "(for your fellowship) in furtherance of the gospel," and in 2:22, "in furtherance of the Gospel," are, lit., "unto the Gospel."

FURTHERMORE

eita (εἶτα, 1534), which is chiefly used of time or enumerations, signifying "then" or "next," is once used in argument, signifying "furthermore," Heb. 12:9. See AFTERWARD, THEN.

Note: In 1 Thess. 4:1 the KJV "furthermore" translates the phrase *to loipon*, lit., "for the rest," RV, "finally." See FINALLY.

G

GAIN (Noun and Verb)

A. Nouns.

1. *ergasia* (ἐργασία, 2039) signifies (a) "work, working, performance" (from *ergon*, "work"), Eph. 4:19; in Luke 12:58, "diligence"; (b) "business or gain got by work," Acts 16:16, 19; in 19:24, 25, the RV adheres to the meaning "business" (KJV, "gain" and "craft"). See CRAFT, DILIGENCE.¶

2. *porismos* (πορισμός, 4200) primarily denotes "a providing" (akin to *porizō*, "to procure"), then, "a means of gain," 1 Tim. 6:5 (RV, "a way of gain"); 6:6.¶

3. *kerdos* (κέρδος, 2771), "gain" (akin to *kerdainō*, see below), occurs in Phil. 1:21; 3:7; Titus 1:11. See LUCRE.¶

B. Verbs.

1. *kerdainō* (κερδαίνω, 2770), akin to A, No. 3, signifies (I), literally, (a) "to gain something," Matt. 16:26; 25:16 (in the best mss.), 17, 20, 22; Mark 8:36; Luke 9:25; (b) "to get gain, make a profit," Jas. 4:13; (II), metaphorically, (a) "to win persons," said (1) of "gaining" an offending brother who by being told privately of his offense, and by accepting the representations, is won from alienation and from the consequences of his fault, Matt. 18:15; (2) of winning souls into the kingdom of God by the gospel, 1 Cor. 9:19, 20 (twice), 21, 22, or by godly conduct, 1 Pet. 3:1 (RV, "gained"); (3) of so practically appropriating Christ to oneself that He practically becomes the dominating power in and over one's whole being and circumstances, Phil. 3:8 (RV, "gain"); (b) "to gain things," said of getting injury and loss, Acts 27:21, RV, "gotten." See GET.¶

2. *diapragmateuomai* (διαπραγματεύομαι, 1281) signifies "to gain by trading," Luke 19:15 (from *dia*, "through," used intensively, and *pragmateuomai*, "to busy oneself, to be engaged in business").¶

3. *peripoieō* (περιποιέω, 4046), "to save for oneself, gain," is in the middle voice in the best mss. in Luke 17:33, RV, "gain." See PURCHASE.

Notes: (1) In Luke 19:16, KJV, *prosergazomai*, "to work out in addition," or "to earn in addition," is translated "gained" (RV, "made"); in v. 18 the verb *poieō*, "to make," is translated in the same way, the English verb "make" standing both for "earning" and for "producing." (2) In 2 Cor. 12:17, 18, *pleonekteō*, "to claim unduly, to overreach," is translated "make a gain of," KJV (RV, "take advantage of"). (3) For *er-*

gazomai, Rev. 18:17, RV, see TRADE. (4) In Acts 25:9, RV, *katatithēmi*, middle voice, "to lay up for oneself," is rendered "to gain."

GAINSAY, GAINSAYER, GAINSAYING

A. Verbs.

1. *antilegō* (ἀντιλέγω, 483), "to contradict, oppose," lit., "say against," is translated "gainsaying" in Rom. 10:21 and Titus 2:9, RV (KJV, "answering again"), of servants in regard to masters; in Titus 1:9 "gainsayers." Moulton and Milligan (*Vocab.*) illustrate from the papyri "the strong sense of *antilegō* in Rom. 10:21, "contradict," "oppose." See ANSWER, CONTRADICT.

2. *anteipon* (ἀντεῖπον, 483), which serves as an aorist tense of No. 1, is rendered "gainsay" in Luke 21:15; "say against" in Acts 4:14. See SAY.¶

B. Noun.

antilogia (ἀντιλογία, 485), akin to A, No. 1, is rendered "gainsaying," in Heb. 12:3, RV, and Jude 11. Opposition in act seems to be implied in these two places; though this sense has been questioned by some, it is confirmed by instances from the papyri (Moulton and Milligan, *Vocab.*). See CONTRADICTION, DISPUTE, STRIFE.

C. Adjective.

anantirrhētos (ἀναντίρρητος, 368), lit., "not to be spoken against" (a, negative, n, euphonic, *anti*, "against," *rhētos*, "spoken"), is rendered "cannot be gainsaid" in Acts 19:36, RV.¶

D. Adverb.

anantirrhētōs (ἀναντιρρήτως, 369), corresponding to C, is translated "without gainsaying" in Acts 10:29; it might be rendered "unquestioningly."¶

GALL

cholē (χολή, 5521), a word probably connected with *chloē*, "yellow," denotes "gall," (a) literal, Matt. 27:34 (cf. Ps. 69:21); some regard the word here as referring to myrrh, on account of Mark 15:23; (b) metaphorical, Acts 8:23, where "gall of bitterness" stands for extreme wickedness, productive of evil fruit.¶ In the OT it is used (a) of a plant characterized by bitterness (probably wormwood), Deut. 29:18; Hos. 10:4; Amos 6:12; (b) as the translation of the word *mererah*, "bitterness," Job. 13:26, e.g.; (c) as the translation of *rôsh*, "venom"; in Deut. 32:32 "(grapes) of gall." In Job 20:25, the gall bladder is referred to (the receptacle of bile). The ancients supposed that the poison of serpents lay in the gall (see Job 20:14).

For GAMES see CONTEND

GANGRENE

gangraina (γάγγραινα, 1044), "an eating sore," spreading corruption and producing mortification, is used, in 2 Tim. 2:17, of errorists in the church, who, pretending to give true spiritual food, produce spiritual gangrene (KJV, "canker," RV, "gangrene").¶

GARDEN

kēpos (κῆπος, 2779), "a garden," occurs in Luke 13:19, in one of the Lord's parables; in John 18:1, 26, of the garden of Gethsemane; in 19:41, of the garden near the place of the Lord's crucifixion.¶

GARDENER

kēpouros (κηπουρός, 2780), lit., "a gardenkeeper" (from *kēpos*, see above, and *ouros*, "a watcher"), occurs in John 20:15.¶

GARLAND

stemma (στέμμα, 4725) denotes "a wreath" (from *stephō*, "to put around, enwreath"), as used in sacrifices, Acts 14:13.¶

GARMENT

Note: For *himation*, the usual word for "garment," see CLOTHING, where see also *esthēsis* (translated "garments" in the KJV of Luke 24:4, RV, "apparel"), *enduma, chitōn*, and *stolē* (RV, "robe" in Mark 16:5). The fact of the wedding garment, *enduma* in Matt. 22, vv. 11, 12, indicates that persons of high rank showed their magnificence by providing the guests with festal garments. See APPAREL.

GARNER

apothēkē (ἀποθήκη, 596), "a storehouse, granary" (from *apo*, "away," and *tithēmi*, "to put"), is translated "garner" in Matt. 3:12 and Luke 3:17. See BARN.

GARNISH

kosmeō (κοσμέω, 2885) is translated by the verb "to garnish" in Matt. 12:44; 23:29; Luke 11:25; and in the KJV of Rev. 21:19. See ADORN.

For GARRISON see GUARD, B, No. 3

GATE

1. *pulē* (πύλη, 4439) is used (*a*) literally, for a larger sort of "gate," in the wall either of a city or palace or temple, Luke 7:12, of Nain (burying places were outside the "gates" of cities); Acts 3:10; 9:24; 12:10; Heb. 13:12; (*b*) metaphorically, of the "gates" at the entrances of the ways leading to life and to destruction, Matt. 7:13, 14; some mss. have *pulē*, for *thura*, "a door," in Luke 13:24 (see the RV); of the "gates" of Hades, Matt. 16:18, than which nothing was regarded as stronger. The importance and strength of "gates" made them viewed as synonymous with power. By metonymy, the "gates" stood for those who held government and administered justice there.¶

2. *pulōn* (πυλών, 4440), akin to No. 1, primarily signifies "a porch or vestibule," e.g., Matt. 26:71; Luke 16:20; Acts 10:17; 12:13, 14; then, the "gateway" or "gate tower" of a walled town, Acts 14:13; Rev. 21:12, 13, 15, 21, 25; 22:14.¶

Notes: (1) In Acts 3:2 *thura* denotes, not a "gate," but a "door," RV. See DOOR. (2) *Probatikos*, signifying "of, or belonging to, sheep," denotes a sheep "gate" in John 5:2, RV, and KJV marg. (3) The conjectural emendation which suggests the idea of "floods" for "gates" in Matt. 16:18 is not sufficiently substantiated to be accepted.

GATHER, GATHERING

A. Verbs.

1. *sunagō* (συνάγω, 4863), "to gather or bring together," is said of (*a*) persons, e.g., Matt. 2:4; (*b*) things, e.g., Matt. 13:30; in Luke 15:13 the idea is that of "gathering" his goods together for sale, i.e., "having sold off all." See ASSEMBLE, BESTOW, COME, RESORT.

2. *episunagō* (ἐπισυνάγω, 1996), "to gather together," suggesting stress upon the place at which the "gathering" is made (*epi*, "to"), is said of a hen and her chickens, Matt. 23:37; and so of the Lord's would-be protecting care of the people of Jerusalem, *id.*, and Luke 13:34; of the "gathering" together of the elect, Matt. 24:31; Mark 13:27; of the "gathering" together of a crowd, Mark 1:33; Luke 12:1.¶

3. *sullegō* (συλλέγω, 4816), "to collect, gather up or out" (*sun*, "with" *legō*, "to pick out"), is said of "gathering" grapes and figs, Matt. 7:16; Luke 6:44 (cf. No. 5); tares, Matt. 13:28, 29, 30, 40; good fish, 13:48; "all things that cause stumbling, and them that do iniquity," 13:41.¶

4. *sustrephō* (συστρέφω, 4962) signifies (*a*) "to twist together or roll into a mass" ("*sun*, together," *strephō*, "to turn"), said of the bundle of sticks "gathered" by Paul, Acts 28:3; (*b*) "to assemble or gather together" (possibly, to jour-

ney about together), of persons, Matt. 17:22 (in the best mss.), RV, marg.¶

5. *trugaō* (τρυγάω, 5166) signifies "to gather in," of harvest, vintage, ripe fruits (*trugē* denotes "fruit," etc., gathered in autumn), Luke 6:44, of grapes (last part of v.; for the previous clause, as to figs, see No. 3); metaphorically, of the clusters of "the vine of the earth," Rev. 14:18; of that from which they are "gathered," v. 19.¶

6. *athroizō* (ἀθροίζω, 119a) denotes "to assemble, gather together," Luke 24:33 (according to the best mss.); the word is akin to *athroos*, "assembled in crowds" (not found in the NT).¶

7. *sunathroizō* (συναθροίζω, 4867), *sun*, "together," and No. 6, signifies (*a*) "to gather together," Acts 19:25, RV (KJV, "called together"); in the passive voice, 12:12.¶

8. *epathroizō* (ἐπαθροίζω, 1865), "to assemble besides" (*epi*), said of multitudes, Luke 11:29, is rendered "were gathering together" (middle voice), RV (KJV, "were gathered thick together").¶

Notes: (1) In Eph. 1:10, KJV, the verb *anakephalaioō*, "to sum up, head up," is rendered "might gather together in one" (RV, "sum up"). (2) In Luke 8:4, KJV (*suneimi*, "to come together") as "were gathered together" (see RV). (4) For "assuredly gathering," see CONCLUDE.

B. Noun.

episunagōgē (ἐπισυναγωγή, 1997), "a gathering together," is used in 2 Thess. 2:1, of the "rapture" of the saints; for Heb. 10:25, see ASSEMBLE.

Note: For *logia*, 1 Cor. 16:2, KJV, see COLLECTION.

For GAY see GOODLY, A, *Note.*

For GAZE see BEHOLD, No. 3.

GAZINGSTOCK

theatrizō (θεατρίζω, 2301) signifies "to make a spectacle" (from *theatron*, "a theater, spectacle, show"); it is used in the passive voice in Heb. 10:33, "being made a gazingstock."¶

GEAR

skeuos (σκεῦος, 4632), "an implement, vessel, utensil," is used of the tackling or "gear" of a ship, Acts 27:17, RV (KJV, "sail").

For GENDER see BEGET, No. 1

GENEALOGY

A. Noun.

genealogia (γενεαλογία, 1076) is used in 1 Tim. 1:4 and Titus 3:9, with reference to such

"genealogies" as are found in Philo, Josephus and the book of Jubilees, by which Jews traced their descent from the patriarchs and their families, and perhaps also to Gnostic "genealogies" and orders of aeons and spirits. Amongst the Greeks, as well as other nations, mythological stories gathered round the birth and "genealogy" of their heroes. Probably Jewish "genealogical" tales crept into Christian communities. Hence the warnings to Timothy and Titus.¶

B. Verb.

genealogeō (γενεαλογέω, 1075), "to reckon or trace a genealogy" (from *genea*, "a race," and *legō*, "to choose, pick out"), is used, in the passive voice, of Melchizedek in Heb. 7:6, RV, "whose genealogy (KJV, 'descent') is not counted."¶

C. Adjective (*negative*).

agenealogētos (ἀγενεαλόγητος, 35), denoting "without recorded pedigree" (*a*, negative, and an adjectival form from B), is rendered "without genealogy" in Heb. 7:3. The narrative in Gen. 14 is so framed in facts and omissions as to foreshadow the person of Christ.¶

For GENERAL (Assembly) see ASSEMBLY, No. 2

GENERATION

1. *genea* (γενεά, 1074): see AGE, No. 2.

2. *genesis* (γένεσις, 1078) denotes "an origin, a lineage, or birth," translated "generation" in Matt. 1:1. See NATURAL, NATURE.

Notes: (1) For *gennēma*, translated "generation" in the KJV of Matt. 3:7; 12:34; 23:33; Luke 3:7, see OFFSPRING.¶ (2) For *genos*, translated "generation" in 1 Pet. 2:9, KJV, see KIND.

GENTILES

A. Nouns.

1. *ethnos* (ἔθνος, 1484), whence Eng., "heathen," denotes, firstly, "a multitude or company"; then, "a multitude of people of the same nature or genus, a nation, people"; it is used in the singular, of the Jews, e.g., Luke 7:5; 23:2; John 11:48, 50–52; in the plural, of nations (Heb., *goiim*) other than Israel, e.g., Matt. 4:15; Rom. 3:29; 11:11; 15:10; Gal. 2:8; occasionally it is used of gentile converts in distinction from Jews, e.g., Rom. 11:13; 16:4; Gal. 2:12, 14; Eph. 3:1.

2. *hellēn* (Ἕλλην, 1672) originally denoted the early descendants of Thessalian Hellas; then, Greeks as opposed to barbarians, Rom. 1:14. It became applied to such Gentiles as spoke the Greek language, e.g., Gal. 2:3; 3:28. Since that was the common medium of intercourse in the

Roman Empire, Greek and Gentile became more or less interchangeable terms. For this term the RV always adheres to the word "Greeks," e.g., John 7:35; Rom. 2:9, 10; 3:9; 1 Cor. 10:32, where the local church is distinguished from Jews and Gentiles; 12:13.

B. Adjective.

ethnikos (ἐθνικός, 1482) is used as noun, and translated "Gentiles" in the RV of Matt. 5:47; 6:7; "the Gentile" in 18:17 (KJV, "an heathen man"); "the Gentiles" in 3 John 7, KJV and RV.¶

C. Adverb.

ethnikōs (ἐθνικῶς, 1483), "in Gentile fashion, in the manner of Gentiles," is used in Gal. 2:14, "as do the Gentiles," RV.¶

Notes: (1) For the synonymous word *laos*, "a people," see PEOPLE. (2) When, under the new order of things introduced by the gospel the mystery of the church was made known, the word *ethnos* was often used in contrast to the local church, 1 Cor. 5:1; 10:20; 12:2; 1 Thess. 4:5; 1 Pet. 2:12.

GENTLE, GENTLENESS, GENTLY

A. Adjectives.

1. *epieikēs* (ἐπιεικής, 1933), from *epi*, "unto," and *eikos*, "likely," denotes "seemly, fitting"; hence, "equitable, fair, moderate, forbearing, not insisting on the letter of the law"; it expresses that considerateness that looks "humanely and reasonably at the facts of a case"; it is rendered "gentle" in 1 Tim. 3:3, RV (KJV, "patient"), in contrast to contentiousness; in Titus 3:2, "gentle," in association with meekness; in Jas 3:17, as a quality of the wisdom from above; in 1 Pet. 2:18, in association with the good; for the RV rendering "forbearance" in Phil. 4:5, RV, see FORBEARANCE. Cf. B. See PATIENT.¶ In the Sept., Esth. 8:13; Ps. 86:5.¶

2. *ēpios* (ἤπιος, 2261), "mild, gentle," was frequently used by Greek writers as characterizing a nurse with trying children or a teacher with refractory scholars, or of parents toward their children. In 1 Thess. 2:7, the apostle uses it of the conduct of himself and his fellow missionaries towards the converts at Thessalonica (cf. 2 Cor. 11:13, 20); in 2 Tim. 2:24, of the conduct requisite for a servant of the Lord.¶

B. Noun.

epieikeia (ἐπιείκεια, 1932), or *epieikia*, denotes "fairness, moderation, gentleness," "sweet reasonableness" (Matthew Arnold); it is said of Christ, 2 Cor. 10:1, where it is coupled with *praütēs*, "meekness"; for its meaning in Acts 24:4, see CLEMENCY.¶ Trench (*Syn.* §xlviii) considers that the ideas of equity and justice, which are essential to the meaning, do not adequately express it in English. In contrast with

praütēs ("meekness"), which is more especially a temperament or habit of mind, *epieikeia* expresses an active dealing with others.

Notes: (1) For *chrēstotēs*, "kindness, goodness of heart," rendered "gentleness" in Gal. 5:22, KJV, see KINDNESS. The corresponding adjective *chrēstos* is translated "good," "kind," "easy," "gracious."

(2) For *metriopatheō*, to bear gently with, Heb. 5:2, see BEAR, No. 13.

GET, GOT, GOTTEN

(a) *In the sense of acquiring:*

1. *heuriskō* (εὑρίσκω, 2147), "to find," is translated "get" in Luke 9:12, of victuals. See FIND.

2. *ktaomai* (κτάομαι, 2932), "to acquire, procure for oneself, gain," is rendered "get" in the RV of Matt. 10:9 and KJV marg. (KJV, text, "provide"); in Luke 18:12 (for KJV, "possess"). See OBTAIN, POSSESS, PROVIDE, PURCHASE.

3. *kerdainō* (κερδαίνω, 2770), "to gain," is rendered "have gotten" in Acts 27:21, RV (of injury and loss); the word is there used metaphorically, however, of avoiding, or saving oneself from. For the meaning, "to get gain," Jas. 4:13, see GAIN.

Notes: (1) For *pleonekteō*, "to get an advantage of" (KJV, in 2 Cor. 2:11; RV, "an advantage may be gained over,"), see ADVANTAGE. (2) In Rev. 15:2, KJV, *nikaō*, "to conquer, prevail over," is translated "had gotten the victory" (RV, "come victorious"). (3) In Rev. 3:17, RV, *plouteō*, "to become rich," is rendered "I have gotten riches."

(b) *In the sense of going:*

1. *exeimi* (ἔξειμι, 1826), "to go or come out," is used in Acts 27:43 of "getting" to land. See DEPART, GO, No. 23.

2. *hupagō* (ὑπάγω, 5217), "to go away, withdraw," is rendered "get," "get . . . hence," in Matt. 4:10; 16:23; Mark 8:33; some mss. have it in Luke 4:8. See DEPART, GO, No. 8.

3. *exerchomai* (ἐξέρχομαι, 1831), "to come or go out," is translated "get . . . out" in Luke 13:31; Acts 7:3; 22:18. See COME, No. 3, GO (*Notes*).

4. *katabainō* (καταβαίνω, 2597), "to descend," is translated "get . . . down," in Acts 10:20. See COME, No. 19.

5. *embainō* (ἐμβαίνω, 1684), "to enter," is translated "they got into" in John 6:24 (of boats), RV [KJV, "took (shipping)."]. See COME, No. 21.

6. *apobainō* (ἀποβαίνω, 576), "to go from," is translated "they got out" in John 21:9, RV (KJV, "were come to"). See COME, 21 (*Note*).

Note: In Acts 21:1, KJV, *apospaō*, "to withdraw or part from," is rendered "we had gotten (from)," RV, "had parted (from)." After the scene described at the end of ch. 20, it may well have the force of "being reft away" (or tearing themselves away) from them. Cf. the same verb in Luke 22:41 ("He was reft away from them"). See DRAW, PART, WITHDRAW.

For GHOST see SPIRIT

GHOST (give up the)

1. *ekpneō* (ἐκπνέω, 1606), lit., "to breathe out" (*ek*, "out," *pneō*, "to breathe"), "to expire," is used in the NT, without an object, "soul" or "life" being understood, Mark 15:37, 39, and Luke 23:46, of the death of Christ. In Matt. 27:50 and John 19:30, where different verbs are used, the act is expressed in a way which stresses it as of His own volition: in the former, "Jesus . . . yielded up His spirit (*pneuma*); in the latter, "He gave up His spirit."¶

2. *ekpsuchō* (ἐκψύχω, 1634), "to expire," lit., "to breathe out the soul (or life), to give up the ghost" (*ek*, "out," *psuchē*, "the soul"), is used in Acts 5:5, 10; 12:23.¶

GIFT, GIVING

1. *dōron* (δῶρον, 1435), akin to *didōmi*, "to give," is used (*a*) of "gifts" presented as an expression of honor, Matt. 2:11; (*b*) of "gifts" for the support of the temple and the needs of the poor, Matt. 15:5; Mark 7:11; Luke 21:1, 4; (*c*) of "gifts" offered to God, Matt. 5:23, 24; 8:4; 23:18, 19; Heb. 5:1; 8:3, 4; 9:9; 11:4; (*d*) of salvation by grace as the "gift" of God, Eph. 2:8; (*e*) of "presents" for mutual celebration of an occasion, Rev. 11:10. See OFFERING.¶

2. *dōrea* (δωρεά, 1431) denotes "a free gift," stressing its gratuitous character; it is always used in the NT of a spiritual or supernatural gift, John 4:10; Acts 8:20; 11:17; Rom. 5:15; 2 Cor. 9:15; Eph. 3:7; Heb. 6:4; in Eph. 4:7, "according to the measure of the gift of Christ," the "gift" is that given by Christ; in Acts 2:28, "the gift of the Holy Ghost," the clause is epexegetical, the "gift" being the Holy Ghost Himself; cf. 10:45; 11:17, and the phrase, "the gift of righteousness," Rom. 5:17. ¶

Note: For *dōrean*, a form of this noun, used adverbially, see FREELY.

3. *dōrēma* (δώρημα, 1434): see BOON.

4. *doma* (δόμα, 1390) lends greater stress to the concrete character of the "gift," than to its beneficent nature, Matt. 7:11; Luke 11:13; Eph. 4:8; Phil. 4:17.¶

5. *dosis* (δόσις, 1394) denotes, properly, "the act of giving," Phil. 4:15, euphemistically referring to "gifts" as a matter of debt and credit accounts; then, objectively, "a gift," Jas. 1:17 (1st mention; see BOON).¶

6. *charisma* (χάρισμα, 5486), "a gift of grace, a gift involving grace" (*charis*) on the part of God as the donor, is used (*a*) of His free bestowments upon sinners, Rom. 5:15, 16; 6:23; 11:29; (*b*) of His endowments upon believers by the operation of the Holy Spirit in the churches, Rom. 12:6; 1 Cor. 1:7; 12:4, 9, 28, 30, 31; 1 Tim. 4:14; 2 Tim. 1:6; 1 Pet. 4:10; (*c*) of that which is imparted through human instruction, Rom. 1:11; (*d*) of the natural "gift" of continence, consequent upon the grace of God as Creator, 1 Cor. 7:7; (*e*) of gracious deliverances granted in answer to the prayers of fellow believers, 2 Cor. 1:11.¶

Note: In the KJV of 2 Cor. 8:4 *charis*, "grace," is translated "gift." The RV, "in regard of this grace," adheres to the true meaning, as in v. 6.

7. *merismos* (μερισμός, 3311), "a dividing" (from *meros*, "a part"), is translated "gifts" in Heb. 2:4, "gifts of the Holy Ghost" (marg., "distributions"); in 4:12, "dividing." See DIVIDING.¶

Note: In the KJV of Luke 21:5 *anathēma*, "a votive offering," is translated "gifts" (RV, "offerings").¶

GIRD, GIRDED, GIRT (about, up)

1. *zōnnumi* (ζώννυμι, 2224), or *zōnnuō*, "to gird" in the middle voice, "to gird oneself," is used of the long garments worn in the east, John 21:18; Acts 12:8 (*perizōnnumi* in some mss.).¶

2. *anazōnnumi* (ἀναζώννυμι, 328), "to gird up" (*ana*, "up," and No. 1), is used metaphorically of the loins of the mind, 1 Pet. 1:13; cf. Luke 12:35 (see No. 4). The figure is taken from the circumstances of the Israelites as they ate the Passover in readiness for their journey, Exod. 12:11; the Christian is to have his mental powers alert in expectation of Christ's coming. The verb is in the middle voice, indicating the special interest the believer is to take in so doing.¶

3. *diazōnnumi* (διαζώννυμι, 1241), "to gird round," i.e., firmly (*dia*, "throughout," used intensively), is used of the Lord's act in "girding" Himself with a towel, John 13:4, 5, and of Peter's girding himself with his coat, 21:7.¶

4. *perizōnnumi* (περιζώννυμι, 4024), "to gird around or about," is used (*a*) literally, of "girding" oneself for service, Luke 12:37; 17:8; for rapidity of movement, Acts 12:8; (*b*) figuratively, of the condition for service on the part of the followers of Christ, Luke 12:35; Eph. 6:14; (*c*) emblematically, of Christ's priesthood, Rev. 1:13, indicative of majesty of attitude and

action, the middle voice suggesting the particular interest taken by Christ in "girding" Himself thus; so of the action of the angels mentioned in 15:6.¶

GIRDLE

zōnē (ζώνη, 2223), Eng., "zone," denotes "a belt or girdle," Matt. 3:4; Mark 1:6; Acts 21:11; Rev. 1:13; 15:6; it was often hollow, and hence served as a purse, Matt. 10:9; Mark 6:8.¶

GIVE

1. *didōmi* (δίδωμι, 1325), "to give," is used with various meanings according to the context; it is said, e.g., of seed "yielding fruit," Mark 4:7, 8; of "giving" (i.e., exercising) diligence, Luke 12:58; of "giving" lots, Acts 1:26, RV (KJV, "gave forth"); of "rendering" vengeance, 2 Thess. 1:8; of "striking or smiting" Christ, John 18:22 (lit., "gave a blow") and 19:3 (lit., "they gave Him blows"); of "putting" a ring on the hand, Luke 15:22; of Paul's "adventuring" himself into a place, Acts 19:31. (In Rev. 17:13 some mss. have *diadidōmi*, "to divide"). See ADVENTURE, BESTOW, No. 1, COMMIT, *Note* (1), DELIVER, GRANT, MAKE, MINISTER, OFFER, PUT, SET, SHEW, SUFFER, TAKE, UTTER, YIELD.

Note: In the following the RV gives the correct rendering: Acts 7:25, "was giving them deliverance" (KJV, "would deliver them"); Acts 10:40, "gave Him to be made manifest" (KJV, "shewed Him openly"); Rev. 13:14, 15, "it was given him" (KJV, "he had power").

2. *apodidōmi* (ἀποδίδωμι, 591) signifies "to give up or back, to restore, return, render what is due, to pay, give an account" (*apo*, "back," and No. 1), e.g., of an account. Matt. 5:26; 12:36; Luke 16:2; Acts. 19:40; Heb. 13:17; 1 Pet. 4:5; of wages, etc., e.g., Matt. 18:25–34; 20:8; of conjugal duty, 1 Cor. 7:3; of a witness, Acts 4:33; frequently of recompensing or rewarding, 1 Tim. 5:4; 2 Tim. 4:8, 14; 1 Pet. 3:9; Rev. 18:6; 22:12. In the middle voice it is used of "giving" up what is one's own; hence, "to sell," Acts 5:8; 7:9; Heb. 12:16. See DELIVER.

3. *epididōmi* (ἐπιδίδωμι, 1929) signifies (*a*) "to give by handing, to hand" (*epi*, "over"), e.g., Matt. 7:9, 10; Luke 4:17; 24:30, here of the Lord's act in "handing" the broken loaf to the two at Emmaus, an act which was the means of the revelation of Himself as the crucified and risen Lord; the simple verb, No. 1, is used of His "handing" the bread at the institution of the Lord's Supper, Matt. 26:26; Mark 14:22; Luke 22:19; this meaning of the verb *epididōmi* is found also in Acts 15:30, "they delivered"; (*b*) "to give in, give way," Acts 27:15, RV, "we gave way to it." See DELIVER.

4. *metadidōmi* (μεταδίδωμι, 3330), "to give a share of, impart" (*meta*, "with"), as distinct from "giving." The apostle Paul speaks of "sharing" some spiritual gift with Christians at Rome, Rom. 1:11, "that I may impart," and exhorts those who minister in things temporal, to do so as "sharing," and that generously, 12:8, "he that giveth"; so in Eph. 4:28; Luke 3:11; in 1 Thess. 2:8 he speaks of himself and his fellow missionaries as having been well pleased to impart to the converts both God's gospel and their own souls (i.e., so "sharing" those with them as to spend themselves and spend out their lives for them). See IMPART.¶

5. *paradidōmi* (παραδίδωμι, 3860), "to give or hand over," is said of "giving" up the ghost, John 19:30; of "giving" persons up to evil, Acts 7:42; Rom. 1:24, 26; of "giving" one's body to be burned, 1 Cor. 13:3; of Christ's "giving" Himself up to death, Gal. 2:20; Eph. 5:2, 25. See BETRAY, COMMIT, DELIVER.

6. *prodidōmi* (προδίδωμι, 4272), "to give before, or first" (*pro*, "before"), is found in Rom. 11:35.¶

7. *charizomai* (χαρίζομαι, 5483) primarily denotes "to show favor or kindness," as in Gal. 3:18, RV, "hath granted" (KJV, "gave"); then, to "give" freely, bestow graciously; in this sense it is used almost entirely of that which is "given" by God, Acts 27:24, "God hath granted thee all them that sail with thee" (RV); in Rom. 8:32, "shall ... freely give"; 1 Cor. 2:12, "are freely given"; Phil. 1:29, "it hath been granted" (said of believing on Christ and suffering for Him); 2:9, "hath given" (said of the name of Jesus as "given" by God); Philem. 22, "I shall be granted unto you" (RV). In Luke 7:21, it is said in regard to the blind, upon whom Christ "bestowed" sight (RV). The only exceptions, in this sense of the word, as to divinely imparted "gifts," are Acts 3:14, of the "granting" of Barabbas by Pilate to the Jews, and Acts 25:11, 16, of the "giving" up of a prisoner to his accusers or to execution. See DELIVER, FORGIVE, GRANT.

8. *parechō* (παρέχω, 3930), in the active voice, signifies "to afford, furnish, provide, supply" (lit., "to hold out or towards"; *para*, "near," *echō*, "to hold"); it is translated "hath given" in Acts 17:31; "giveth" in 1 Tim. 6:17 (in the sense of affording); in Col. 4:1, RV, "render" (KJV, "give"). See BRING, DO, KEEP, MINISTER, OFFER, RENDER, SHEW, TROUBLE.

9. *dōreō* (δωρέω, 143), akin to No. 1, and used in the middle voice, "to bestow, make a gift of," is translated in the RV by the verb "to grant," instead of the KJV, "to give," Mark 15:45; 2 Pet. 1:3, 4. See GRANT.¶

10. *aponemō* (ἀπονέμω, 632), "to assign, apportion" (*apo*, "away," *nemō*, "to distribute"), is rendered "giving" in 1 Pet. 3:7, of giving honor to the wife. In the papyri writings it is said of a prefect who "gives" to all their dues.¶ In the Sept., Deut. 4:19.¶

11. *poieō* (ποιέω, 4160), "to do," is used in Jude 3 of "giving" diligence (the middle voice indicating Jude's especial interest in his task).

12. *katapherō* (καταφέρω, 2702), "to bring down or against" (*kata*, "down"), said of an accusation in Acts 25:7 (in the best mss.), and of being "borne down" with sleep, 20:9, RV, is used of casting a ballot or "giving" a vote in 26:10. See FALL, *Note* (8), SINK.¶

13. *prostithēmi* (προστίθημι, 4369), lit., "to put in addition" (*pros*, "to," *tithēmi*, "to put"), "to give more," is translated "shall more be given," in Mark 4:24 (passive voice). See ADD.

14. *scholazō* (σχολάζω, 4980), "to be at leisure," hence, "to have time or opportunity for, to be occupied in," is said of "giving" oneself to prayer, 1 Cor. 7:5; of an "empty" house, "lying vacant," Matt. 12:44.¶

15. *legō* (λέγω, 3004), "to say," is rendered "giving out," of the self-advertisement of Simon Magus, Acts 8:9. See SAY.

16. *prosechō* (προσέχω, 4337), "to turn one's mind to, attend to," is used of "giving" oneself up to, 1 Tim. 3:8 (to wine); of "giving" heed to, Acts 8:6, 10, 11 (RV); 16:14 (RV); 1 Tim. 1:4; 4:1, 13 (RV); Titus 1:14; Heb. 2:1. See ATTEND.

17. *diōkō* (διώκω, 1377), "to pursue," is translated "given to" in Rom. 12:13, lit., "pursuing hospitality." See FOLLOW.

Notes: (1) In John 10:11, RV, *tithēmi*, "to put, lay down," is rendered "layeth down," for the KJV, "giveth." (2) For *pareispherō*, "to add," rendered "giving" in 2 Pet. 1:5, KJV, see ADD. (3) For *martureō*, "to bear witness" KJV "gave (record)" in 1 John 5:10, RV, "hath borne (witness)," see WITNESS. (4) For *chorēgeō* "to supply minister," rendered "giveth" (RV, "supplieth") in 1 Pet. 4:11, see MINISTER. (5) For *merizō*, "to divide into parts," rendered "gave a part" (RV, "divided") in Heb. 7:2, see DIVIDE. (6) For *paristēmi*, "to place by," rendered "give" in Matt. 26:53, KJV (RV, "send"), see SEND. (7) For *douloō*, in the passive voice, "to be enslaved," rendered "given to" in Titus 2:3, KJV, see ENSLAVE. (8) In 1 Tim. 4:15, the imperative mood of *eimi*, "to be," with *en*, "in," lit., "be in," is translated "give thyself wholly to." (9) In Luke 10:7, the phrase, lit., "the (things) by them," is rendered "such things as they give." (10) For *epikrinō*, see SENTENCE. (11) For *proskartereō*, "to give oneself continually," Acts

6:4, see CONTINUE. (12) See CHARGE, COMMANDMENT, DRINK, HOSPITALITY, LAW, LIGHT, MARRIAGE, PLACE, PLEASURE, SUCK, THANKS.

GIVER

dotēs (δότης, 1395), akin to *didomi*, "to give," is used in 2 Cor. 9:7 of him who gives cheerfully (hilariously) and is thereby loved of God.¶

GLAD (be, make), GLADLY

A. Verbs.

1. *chairō* (χαίρω, 5463) is the usual word for "rejoicing, being glad"; it is rendered by the verb "to be glad" in Mark 14:11; Luke 15:32; 22:5; 23:8; John 8:56; 11:15; 20:20; Acts 11:23; 13:48; in the following the RV has "to rejoice" for KJV, "to be glad," Rom. 16:19; 1 Cor. 16:17; 2 Cor. 13:9; 1 Pet. 4:13; Rev. 19:7. See FAREWELL, No. 4, GREETING, HAIL, JOY, REJOICE.

2. *agalliaō* (ἀγαλλιάω, 21), "to exult, rejoice greatly," is chiefly used in the middle voice (active in Luke 1:47; some mss. have the passive in John 5:35, "to be made glad"). In the OT, it is found abundantly in the Psalms, from 2:11 onward to 149:2, 5 (Sept.). It conveys the idea of jubilant exultation, spiritual "gladness," Matt. 5:12, "be exceeding glad," the Lord's command to His disciples; Luke 1:47, in Mary's song; 10:21, of Christ's exultation ("rejoiced"); cf. Acts 2:26, "(My tongue) was glad," KJV (RV, "rejoiced"); John 8:56, of Abraham; Acts 16:34, RV, "rejoiced greatly" (of the Philippian jailor); 1 Pet. 1:6, 8; 4:13 ("with exceeding joy"), of believers in general; in Rev. 19:7, RV, "be exceeding glad" (KJV, "rejoice"). See REJOICE.¶

3. *euphrainō* (εὐφραίνω, 2165), "to cheer, gladden," is rendered "maketh . . . glad" in 2 Cor. 2:2. See FARE, MERRY, REJOICE.

B. Adverbs.

1. *hēdeōs* (ἡδέως, 2234), "gladly" (from *hēdus*, "sweet"), is used in Mark 6:20; 12:37; 2 Cor. 11:19.¶

2. *hēdista* (ἥδιστα, 2236), the superlative degree of No. 1, "most gladly, most delightedly, with great relish," is rendered "most gladly" in 2 Cor. 12:9, and in v. 15 (RV; KJV, "very gladly").¶

3. *asmenōs* (ἀσμένως, 780), "with delight, delightedly, gladly," is found in Acts 21:17. It is absent from the best texts in 2:41 (see the RV).¶

GLADNESS

1. *chara* (χαρά, 5479), "joy, delight" (akin to A, No. 1 above), is rendered "gladness" in the KJV of Mark 4:16; Acts 12:14 and Phil. 2:29

(RV "joy", as elsewhere in both versions). See JOY.

2. *agalliasis* (ἀγαλλίασις, 20), "exultation, exuberant joy" (akin to A, No. 2), is translated "gladness" in Luke 1:14; Acts 2:6; Heb. 1:9; "joy" in Luke 1:44; "exceeding joy" in Jude 24. It indicates a more exultant "joy" than No. 1. In the Sept. this word is found chiefly in the Psalms, where it denotes "joy" in God's redemptive work, e.g., 30:5; 42:4; 45:7, 15. See JOY.

3. *euphrosunē* (εὐφροσύνη, 2167), "good cheer, joy, mirth, gladness of heart" (akin to A, No. 3), from *eu*, "well," and *phrēn*, "the mind," is rendered "gladness" in Acts 2:28, RV (KJV, "joy") and 14:17. See JOY.¶

GLASS, GLASSY

A. Nouns.

1. *hualos* (ὕαλος, 5194) primarily denoted anything transparent, e.g., a transparent stone or gem, hence, "a lens of crystal, a glass," Rev. 21:18, 21.¶

2. *esoptron* (ἔσοπτρον, 2072), "a mirror," is rendered "glass" in the KJV of 1 Cor. 13:12 and Jas. 1:23. See MIRROR.¶

Note: For the corresponding verb *katoptrizō* in 2 Cor. 3:18 (middle voice), see BEHOLD, No. 12.

B. Adjective.

hualinos (ὑάλινος, 5193) signifies "glassy, made of glass" (akin to A, No. 1), Rev. 4:6; 15:2 (twice), RV, "glassy."¶

For GLISTERING see DAZZLING and SHINE, No. 4

GLORIFY

1. *doxazō* (δοξάζω, 1392) primarily denotes "to suppose" (from *doxa*, "an opinion"); in the NT (*a*) "to magnify, extol, praise" (see *doxa* below), especially of "glorifying"; God, i.e., ascribing honor to Him, acknowledging Him as to His being, attributes and acts, i.e., His glory (see GLORY), e.g., Matt. 5:16; 9:8; 15:31; Rom. 15:6, 9; Gal. 1:24; 1 Pet. 4:16; the Word of the Lord, Acts 13:48; the Name of the Lord, Rev. 15:4; also of "glorifying" oneself, John 8:54; Rev. 18:7; (*b*) "to do honor to, to make glorious," e.g., Rom. 8:30; 2 Cor. 3:10; 1 Pet. 1:8, "full of glory," passive voice (lit., "glorified"); said of Christ, e.g., John 7:39; 8:54, RV, "glorifieth," for KJV, "honor" and "honoreth" (which would translate *timaō*, "to honor"); of the Father, e.g., John 13:31, 32; 21:19; 1 Pet. 4:11; of "glorifying" one's ministry, Rom. 11:13, RV, "glorify" (KJV, "magnify"); of a member of the

body, 1 Cor. 12:26, "be honored" (RV marg., "be glorified ").

"As the glory of God is the revelation and manifestation of all that He has and is . . . , it is said of a Self-revelation in which God manifests all the goodness that is His, John 12:28. So far as it is Christ through whom this is made manifest, He is said to glorify the Father, John 17:1, 4; or the Father is glorified in Him, 13:31; 14:13; and Christ's meaning is analogous when He says to His disciples, 'Herein is My Father glorified, that ye bear much fruit; and so shall ye be My disciples,' John 15:8. When *doxazō* is predicated of Christ . . . , it means simply that His innate glory is brought to light, is made manifest; cf. 11:4. So 7:39; 12:16, 23; 13:31; 17:1, 5. It is an act of God the Father in Him. . . . As the revelation of the Holy Spirit is connected with the glorification of Christ, Christ says regarding Him, 'He shall glorify Me,' 16:14" (Cremer).

2. *endoxazō* (ἐνδοξάζω, 1740), No. 1 prefixed by *en*, "in," signifies, in the passive voice, "to be glorified," i.e., to exhibit one's glory; it is said of God, regarding His saints in the future, 2 Thess. 1:10, and of the name of the Lord Jesus as "glorified" in them in the present, v. 12.¶

3. *sundoxazō* (συνδοξάζω, 4888), "to glorify together" (*sun*, "with"), is used in Rom. 8:17.¶

GLORY, GLORIOUS

A. Nouns.

1. *doxa* (δόξα, 1391), "glory" (from *dokeō*, "to seem"), primarily signifies an opinion, estimate, and hence, the honor resulting from a good opinion. It is used (I) (*a*) of the nature and acts of God in self-manifestation, i.e., what He essentially is and does, as exhibited in whatever way he reveals Himself in these respects, and particularly in the person of Christ, in whom essentially His "glory" has ever shone forth and ever will do, John 17:5, 24; Heb. 1:3; it was exhibited in the character and acts of Christ in the days of His flesh, John 1:14; John 2:11; at Cana both His grace and His power were manifested, and these constituted His "glory"; so also in the resurrection of Lazarus, 11:4, 40; the "glory" of God was exhibited in the resurrection of Christ, Rom. 6:4, and in His ascension and exaltation, 1 Pet. 1:21, likewise on the Mount of Transfiguration, 2 Pet. 1:17. In Rom. 1:23 His "everlasting power and Divinity" are spoken of as His "glory," i.e., His attributes and power as revealed through creation; in Rom. 3:23 the word denotes the manifested perfection of His character, especially His righteousness, of which all men fall short; in Col.

1:11 "the might of His glory" signifies the might which is characteristic of His "glory"; in Eph. 1:6, 12, 14, "the praise of the glory of His grace" and "the praise of His glory" signify the due acknowledgement of the exhibition of His attributes and ways; in Eph. 1:17, "the Father of glory" describes Him as the source from whom all divine splendor and perfection proceed in their manifestation, and to whom they belong; (b) of the character and ways of God as exhibited through Christ to and through believers, 2 Cor. 3:18 and 4:6; (c) of the state of blessedness into which believers are to enter hereafter through being brought into the likeness of Christ, e.g., Rom. 8:18, 21; Phil. 3:21 (RV, "the body of His glory"); 1 Pet. 5:1, 10; Rev. 21:11; (d) brightness or splendor, (1) supernatural, emanating from God (as in the shekinah "glory," in the pillar of cloud and in the Holy of Holies, e.g., Exod. 16:10; 25:22), Luke 2:9; Acts 22:11; Rom. 9:4; 2 Cor. 3:7; Jas. 2:1; in Titus 2:13 it is used of Christ's return, "the appearing of the glory of our great God and Savior Jesus Christ" (RV); cf. Phil. 3:21, above; (2) natural, as of the heavenly bodies, 1 Cor. 15:40, 41; (II) of good reputation, praise, honor, Luke 14:10 (RV, "glory," for KJV, "worship"); John 5:41 (RV, "glory," for KJV, "honor"); 7:18; 8:50; 12:43 (RV, "glory," for KJV, "praise"); 2 Cor. 6:8 (RV, "glory," for KJV "honor"); Phil. 3:19; Heb. 3:3; in 1 Cor. 11:7, of man as representing the authority of God, and of woman as rendering conspicuous the authority of man; in 1 Thess. 2:6, "glory" probably stands, by metonymy, for material gifts, an honorarium, since in human estimation "glory" is usually expressed in things material.

The word is used in ascriptions of praise to God, e.g., Luke 17:18; John 9:24, RV, "glory" (KJV, "praise"); Acts 12:23; as in doxologies (lit., "glory-words"), e.g., Luke 2:14; Rom. 11:36; 16:27; Gal. 1:5; Rev. 1:6. See DIGNITY, HONOR, PRAISE, WORSHIP.

2. kleos (κλέος, 2811), "good report, fame, renown," is used in 1 Pet. 2:20.¶ The word is derived from a root signifying "hearing"; hence, the meaning "reputation."

Note: In 2 Cor. 3:11 the phrase dia doxēs, "through (i.e., by means of) glory," is rendered "with glory" in the RV (KJV, "glorious"); in the same verse en doxē, "in glory" (RV), i.e., "accompanied by glory," is rendered "glorious" in the KJV. The first is said of the ministration of the Law, the second of that of the gospel.

B. Adjective.

endoxos (ἔνδοξος, 1741) signifies (a) "held in honor" (en, "in," doxa, "honor"), "of high repute," 1 Cor. 4:10, RV, "have glory" (KJV, "are

honorable"); (b) "splendid, glorious," said of apparel, Luke 7:25, "gorgeously"; of the works of Christ, 13:17; of the church, Eph. 5:27. See GORGEOUSLY, HONORABLE.¶

GLORY (to boast), GLORYING
A. Verbs.

1. kauchaomai (καυχάομαι, 2744), "to boast or glory," is always translated in the RV by the verb "to glory," where the KJV uses the verb "to boast" (see, e.g., Rom. 2:17, 23; 2 Cor. 7:14; 9:2; 10:8, 13, 15, 16); it is used (a) of "vainglorying," e.g., 1 Cor. 1:29; 3:21; 4:7; 2 Cor. 5:12; 11:12, 18; Eph. 2:9; (b) of "valid glorying," e.g., Rom. 5:2, "rejoice"; 5:3, 11 (RV, "rejoice"); 1 Cor. 1:31; 2 Cor. 9:2; 10:8; 12:9; Gal. 6:14; Phil. 3:3 and Jas. 1:9, RV, "glory" (KJV, "rejoice"). See BOAST, JOY, REJOICE.

2. katakauchaomai (κατακαυχάομαι, 2620), a strengthened form of No. 1 (kata, intensive), signifies "to boast against, exult over," Rom. 11:18, RV, "glory" (KJV, "boast"); Jas. 2:13, RV, "glorieth" (KJV, "rejoiceth"); 3:14, "glory (not)." See BOAST, REJOICE.¶

3. enkauchaomai (ἐνκαυχάομαι), en, "in," and No. 1, "to glory in," is found, in the most authentic mss., in 2 Thess. 1:4.¶

Note: Cf. perpereuomai, "to vaunt oneself, to be perperos, vainglorious," 1 Cor. 13:4.¶

B. Nouns.

1. kauchēma (καύχημα, 2745), akin to A, No. 1, denotes "that in which one glories, a matter or ground of glorying," Rom. 4:2 and Phil. 2:16, RV, "whereof to glory" (for Rom. 3:27, see No. 2); in the following the meaning is likewise "a ground of glorying": 1 Cor. 5:6; 9:15, "glorying," 16, "to glory of"; 2 Cor. 1:14, RV; 9:3, RV; Gal. 6:4, RV (KJV, "rejoicing"); Phil. 1:26 (ditto); Heb. 3:6 (ditto). In 2 Cor. 5:12 and 9:3 the word denotes the boast itself, yet as distinct from the act (see No. 2).¶

2. kauchēsis (καύχησις, 2746) denotes "the act of boasting," Rom. 3:27; 15:17, RV, "(my) glorying" (KJV, "whereof I may glory"); 1 Cor. 15:31, RV, "glorying"; 2 Cor. 1:12 (ditto); 7:4, 14 (KJV, "boasting"); 8:24; 11:10, and 17 (ditto); 1 Thess. 2:19 (KJV, "rejoicing"); Jas. 4:16 (ditto). The distinction between this and No. 1 is to be observed in 2 Cor. 8:24, speaking of the apostle's act of "glorying" in the liberality of the Corinthians, while in 9:3 he exhorts them not to rob him of the ground of his "glorying" (No. 1). Some take the word in 2 Cor. 1:12 (see above) as identical with No. 1, a boast, but there seems to be no reason for regarding it as different from its usual sense, No. 2.¶

Note: Cf. alazoneia (or -ia), "vainglory, ostentatious (or arrogant) display," Jas. 4:16 and

1 John 2:16,¶ and *alazōn*, "a boaster," Rom. 1:30 and 2 Tim. 3:2.¶

GLUTTON

gastēr (γαστήρ, 1064) denotes "a belly"; it is used in Titus 1:12, with the adjective *argos*, "idle," metaphorically, to signify a glutton, RV, "(idle) gluttons" [KJV "(slow) bellies"]; elsewhere, Luke 1:31. See WOMB.¶

GLUTTONOUS

phagos (φάγος, 5314), akin to *phagō*, "to eat," a form used for the aorist or past tense of *esthiō*, denotes "a glutton," Matt. 11:19; Luke 7:34.¶

GNASH, GNASHING

A. Verbs.

1. *bruchō* (βρύχω, 1031), primarily, "to bite or eat greedily" (akin to *brukō*, "to chew"), denotes "to grind or gnash with the teeth," Acts 7:54.¶

2. *trizō* (τρίζω, 5149), primarily used of the sounds of animals, "to chirp, cry, squeak," came to signify "to grind or gnash with the teeth," Mark 9:18.¶

B. Noun.

brugmos (βρυγμός, 1030), akin to A, No. 1, denotes "gnashing" ("of teeth" being added), Matt. 8:12; 13:42, 50; 22:13; 24:51; 25:30; Luke 13:28.¶

GNAT

kōnōps (κώνωψ, 2971) denotes "the wine-gnat or midge," which breeds in fermenting or evaporating wine, Matt. 23:24, where the KJV, "strain at" is corrected to "strain out," in the RV.¶

GNAW

masaomai or *massaomai* (μασάομαι, 3145) denotes "to bite or chew," Rev. 16:10.¶ In the Sept., Job. 30:4.¶

GO (WENT), GO ONWARD, etc.

1. *poreuomai* (πορεύομαι, 4198), "to go on one's way, to proceed from one place to another" (from *poros*, "a passage, a ford," Eng., "pore"), is always used in the middle voice in the NT and the Sept., and is the most frequent verb signifying "to go"; it is more distinctly used to indicate procedure or course than the verb *eimi*, "to go" (not found in the NT). It is often rendered "go thy (your) way," in Oriental usage the customary dismissal, marking the close of a case in court. Hence, in ordinary parlance, marking the end of a conversation, etc., e.g., Luke 7:22; 17:19; John 4:50; Acts 9:15; 24:25;

cf. Dan. 12:9; in Rom. 15:24 (1st part), RV, "go" (KJV, "take my journey"); in Acts 9:3 and 26:13, "journeyed" (KJV and RV). See DEPART, JOURNEY, WALK.

2. *paraporeuomai* (παραπορεύομαι, 3899) denotes "to go past, to pass by" (*para*, "by," and No. 1), Mark 2:23, KJV, "went (through)," RV, "was going (through)"; some mss. have No. 4 here. See PASS.

3. *proporeuomai* (προπορεύομαι, 4313), "to go before" (*pro*, and No. 1), is used in Luke 1:76 and Acts 7:40.¶

4. *diaporeuomai* (διαπορεύομαι, 1279), "to go through" (*dia*, "through," and No. 1), "to pass across," is translated "to go through," in Luke 6:1; 13:22, "went on His way through," RV; Acts 16:4; "going by" in Luke 18:36, RV (KJV, "pass by"); "in my journey" in Rom. 15:24 (2nd part). For Mark 2:23 see No. 2. See JOURNEY.

5. *eisporeuomai* (εἰσπορεύομαι, 1531), "to go in, enter," is never rendered by the verb "to come in," in the RV. See, e.g., Luke 11:33, "enter"; Acts 9:28, going in; 28:30, "went in." See ENTER.

6. *sumporeuomai* (συμπορεύομαι, 4848), "to go together with" (*sun*, "with"), is used in Mark 10:1, RV, "come together" (KJV, "resort"); Luke 7:11; 14:25; 24:15. See RESORT.¶

7. *agō* (ἄγω, 71), "to bring, lead," is used intransitively, signifying "let us go" (as if to say, "let us be leading on," with the point of departure especially in view), Matt. 26:46; Mark 1:38; 14:42; John 11:7, 15, 16; 14:31. See BRING.

8. *hupagō* (ὑπάγω, 5217), "to go away or to go slowly away, to depart, withdraw oneself," often with the idea of going without noise or notice (*hupo*, "under," and No. 7), is very frequent in the gospels; elsewhere it is used in Jas. 2:16; 1 John 2:11; Rev. 10:8; 13:10; 14:4; 16:1; 17:8, 11. It is frequently rendered "go your (thy) way." See DEPART.

9. *periagō* (περιάγω, 4013), "to lead about" (*peri*, "about," and No. 7), as in 1 Cor. 9:5, is used intransitively with the meaning "to go about"; "went about," Matt. 4:23; 9:35; Mark 6:6; Acts 13:11; in Matt. 23:15, "ye compass." See COMPASS, LEAD.¶

10. *proagō* (προάγω, 4254), "to lead forth," used intransitively signifies "to go before," usually of locality, e.g., Matt. 2:9; figuratively, in 1 Tim. 1:18, "went before" (RV, marg., "led the way to"), of the exercise of the gifts of prophecy which pointed to Timothy as one chosen by God for the service to be committed to him; in 5:24, of sins "going before unto judgment." In 2 John 9, where the best mss. have this verb

(instead of *parabainō*, "to transgress," KJV), the RV renders it "goeth onward" (marg., "taketh the lead"), of not abiding in the doctrine of Christ. Cf. Mal. 4:4. See BRING.

11. *apeimi* (ἄπειμι, 549), "to go away," is found in Acts 17:10.¶

12. *eiseimi* (εἴσειμι, 1524), "to go into, enter," is used in Acts 3:3; 21:18, 26; Heb. 9:6, RV, "go in" (KJV, "went . . . into"). See ENTER.¶

13. *metabainō* (μεταβαίνω, 3327), "to go or pass over from one place to another," is translated "go" in Luke 10:7. See DEPART.

14. *aperchomai* (ἀπέρχομαι, 565), "to go away" (*apo*, "from"), is chiefly used in the gospels; it signifies "to go aside" in Acts 4:15. See DEPART.

15. *anachōreō* (ἀναχωρέω, 402) signifies "to withdraw," often in the sense of avoiding danger, e.g., Acts 23:19, RV, "going aside" (KJV, "went . . . aside"). See DEPART.

16. *hupochōreō* (ὑποχωρέω, 5298), "to go back, retire" (*hupo*, "under," suggesting privacy), Luke 5:16; 9:10, KJV, "went aside" (RV, "withdrew apart"). See WITHDRAW.¶

17. *proerchomai* (προέρχομαι, 4281), "to go before, precede, go forward or farther" (*pro*, "before"), is used of (*a*) place, e.g., Matt. 26:39; Acts 12:10, "passed on through"; (*b*) time, Luke 1:17; Acts 20:5, 13; 2 Cor. 9:5. See OUTGO, PASS.

18. *epiduō* (ἐπιδύω, 1931) signifies "to go down," and is said of the sun in Eph. 4:26; i.e., put wrath away before sunset (see ANGER, A, *Note* (2). In the Sept., Deut. 24:15; Josh. 8:29; Jer. 15:9.¶

19. *sunkatabainō* (συνκαταβαίνω, 4782), "to go down with," is used in Acts 25:5.¶ In the Sept., Ps. 49:17.¶

20. *probainō* (προβαίνω, 4260), "to go on, forwards, advance," is used of locality, Matt. 4:21; Mark 1:19; for the metaphorical use with reference to age, Luke 1:7, 18; 2:36, see AGE, STRICKEN.¶

21. *apobainō* (ἀποβαίνω, 576), "to go away or from," is translated "had gone out," in Luke 5:2, i.e., disembarked. See COME, 21, *Note*, TURN.

22. *prosanabainō* (προσαναβαίνω, 4320), "to go up higher" (*pros*, "towards"), is used of moving to a couch of greater honor at a feast, Luke 14:10.¶

23. *exeimi* (ἔξειμι, 1826), "to go out," is so rendered in Acts 13:42. See DEPART, GET.

24. *sbennumi* (σβέννυμι, 4570), "to quench," is used in the passive voice, of the going out of the light of a torch or lamp, Matt. 25:8, "are going out" (RV). See QUENCH.

25. *teleō* (τελέω, 5055), "to finish," is ren-

dered "to go through or over" in Matt. 10:23, of "going through" the cities of Israel (KJV, marg., "end," or "finish"). See END, FINISH.

26. *diodeuō* (διοδεύω, 1353), "to travel throughout or along" (*dia*, "through," *hodos*, "a way"), is used in Luke 8:1, of "going throughout" (KJV) or "about through" (RV) cities and villages; of "passing through" towns, Acts 17:1. See PASS.

27. *apodēmeō* (ἀποδημέω, 589), "to be abroad," is translated "going into another country," in Matt. 25:14 (KJV, "traveling, etc."). See JOURNEY.

28. *anerchomai* (ἀνέρχομαι, 424), "to go up" (*ana*), occurs in John 6:3; Gal. 1:17, 18.¶

29. *perierchomai* (περιέρχομαι, 4022), "to go around, or about," is translated "going about" in 1 Tim. 5:13, RV (KJV, "wandering about"); "went about" in Heb. 11:37, RV (KJV, "wandered about"). See CIRCUIT.

30. *epicheireō* (ἐπιχειρέω, 2021), lit., "to put the hand to" (*epi*, "to," *cheir*, "the hand"), "to take in hand, undertake," occurs in Luke 1:1, "have taken in hand"; in Acts 9:29, "they went about"; in 19:13, "took upon them." See TAKE.¶

Notes: (1) The following verbs signify both "to come" and "to go," with prefixed prepositions accordingly, and are mentioned under the word COME: *erchomai* (No. 1); *eiserchomai* (No. 2); *exerchomai* (No. 3); *dierchomai* (No. 5); *katerchomai* (No. 7); Luke 17:7, *parerchomai* (No. 9); *proserchomai*, "go near," Acts 8:29 (No. 10); *sunerchomai*, "went with," Acts 9:39; 15:38; 21:16 (No. 11); *anabainō* (No. 15); *katabainō* (No. 19); *paraginomai*, Acts 23:16, KJV, "went," RV "entered" (No. 13); *ekporeuō* (No. 33); *chōreō*, Matt. 15:17, KJV, "goeth," RV, "passeth" (No. 24); *anabainō*, Luke 19:28, RV, "going up"; *ekbainō* (No. 17).

(2) In the following, the verbs mentioned, translated in the KJV by some form of the verb "to go," are rendered in the RV more precisely in accordance with their true meaning: (*a*) *zēteō*, "to seek," so the RV in John 7:19, 20; Acts 21:31; Rom. 10:3 (KJV, to go about); (*b*) *peirazō*, "to make an attempt," Acts 24:6, RV, "assayed" (KJV, "have gone about"); (*c*) *peiraō*, "to attempt," Acts 26:21, RV, "assayed" KJV, "went about"); (*d*) *epistrephō*, "to return," Acts 15:16, RV, "let us return" (KJV, "let us go again"); (*e*) *huperbainō*, "to overstep," 1 Thess. 4:6, RV, "transgress" (KJV, "go beyond"); (*f*) *diistēmi*, "to set apart, make an interval," Acts 27:28, RV, "(after) a space" (KJV, "had gone further"); (*g*) *suneiserchomai*, "to go in with," John 6:22 and 18:15, RV, "entered (in) with" (KJV, "went . . . with"); (*h*) *pherō*, in the middle voice, lit., "to

bear oneself along," Heb. 6:1, RV, "let us press on" (KJV, "let us go on"); (*i*) *ekklinō*, "to bend or turn away," Rom. 3:12, RV, "have turned aside" (KJV, "have gone out of the way"); (*j*) *diaperaō*, "to pass through, or across," Matt. 14:34, RV, "had crossed over" (KJV, "were gone over"); (*k*) *strateuomai*, "to serve in war," 1 Cor. 9:7, RV, "(what) soldier . . . serveth" (KJV, "goeth a warfare"); (*l*) *hodoiporeō*, "to be on a journey," Acts 10:9, RV, "as they were on their journey" (KJV, "as they went, etc."); (*m*) *embainō*, "to enter," Matt. 13:2 and Luke 8:22, RV, "entered" (KJV, "went into"); in v. 37 (KJV, "went up into"); (*n*) *apoluō*, "to set free," Luke 23:22 and John 19:12, RV, "release" (KJV, "let . . . go "); Acts 15:33, RV, "dismissed" (KJV, ditto); Acts 28:18, RV, "set at liberty" (KJV, ditto); (*o*) *epibainō*, "to go upon," Acts 21:4, RV, "set foot" (KJV, "go"); some mss. have *anabainō;* (*p*) *apangellō*, "to announce," Acts 12:17, RV, "tell" (KJV, "go shew"); (*q*) *aperchomai*, "to go away," Matt. 5:30, RV, "go" (KJV, "be cast"); some mss. have *ballō*, "to cast"; (*r*) *peripateō*, "to walk," Mark 12:38, RV, "walk" (KJV "go"); (*s*) for "gone by," Acts 14:16, RV, see PASS, No. 17.

GOAD

kentron (κέντρον, 2759), from *kenteō*, "to prick," denotes (*a*) "a sting," Rev. 9:10; metaphorically, of sin as the "sting" of death, 1 Cor. 15:55, 56; (*b*) "a goad," Acts 26:14, RV, "goad" (marg., "goads"), for KJV, "pricks" (in some mss. also in 9:5), said of the promptings and misgivings which Saul of Tarsus had resisted before conversion.¶

GOAL

skopos (σκοπός, 4649), primarily, "a watcher" (from *skopeō*, "to look at"; Eng., "scope"), denotes "a mark on which to fix the eye," and is used metaphorically of an aim or object in Phil. 3:14, RV, "goal" (KJV, "mark"). See MARK.

GOAT

1. *eriphos* (ἔριφος, 2056) denotes "a kid or goat," Matt. 25:32 (RV, marg., "kids"); Luke 15:29, "a kid"; some mss. have No. 2 here, indicating a sneer on the part of the elder son, that his father had never given him even a tiny kid.¶

2. *eriphion* (ἐρίφιον, 2055), a diminutive of No. 1, is used in Matt. 25:33. In v. 32 *eriphos* is purely figurative; in v. 33, where the application is made, though metaphorically, the change to the diminutive is suggestive of the contempt

which those so described bring upon themselves by their refusal to assist the needy.¶

3. *tragos* (τράγος, 5131) denotes "a he-goat," Heb. 9:12, 13, 19; 10:4, the male prefiguring the strength by which Christ laid down His own life in expiatory sacrifice.

GOATSKIN

Note: The adjective *aigeios* signifies "belonging to a goat" (from *aix*, "a goat"); it is used with *derma*, "a skin," in Heb. 11:37.

GOD

theos (θέος, 2316), (I) in the polytheism of the Greeks, denoted "a god or deity," e.g., Acts 14:11; 19:26; 28:6; 1 Cor. 8:5; Gal. 4:8.

(II) (*a*) Hence the word was appropriated by Jews and retained by Christians to denote "the one true God." In the Sept. *theos* translates (with few exceptions) the Hebrew words *Elohim* and *Jehovah*, the former indicating His power and preeminence, the latter His unoriginated, immutable, eternal and self-sustained existence.

In the NT, these and all the other divine attributes are predicated of Him. To Him are ascribed, e.g., His unity, or monism, e.g., Mark 12:29; 1 Tim. 2:5; self-existence, John 5:26; immutability, Jas. 1:17; eternity, Rom. 1:20; universality, Matt. 10:29; Acts 17:26–28; almighty power, Matt. 19:26; infinite knowledge, Acts 2:23; 15:18; Rom. 11:33; creative power, Rom. 11:36; 1 Cor. 8:6; Eph. 3:9; Rev. 4:11; 10:6; absolute holiness, 1 Pet. 1:15; 1 John 1:5; righteousness, John 17:25; faithfulness, 1 Cor. 1:9; 10:13; 1 Thess. 5:24; 2 Thess. 3:3; 1 John 1:9; love, 1 John 4:8, 16; mercy, Rom. 9:15, 18; truthfulness, Titus 1:2; Heb. 6:18. See GOOD, No. 1 (*b*).

(*b*) The divine attributes are likewise indicated or definitely predicated of Christ, e.g., Matt. 20:18–19; John 1:1–3; 1:18, RV, marg.; 5:22–29; 8:58; 14:6; 17:22–24; 20:28; Rom. 1:4; 9:5; Phil. 3:21; Col. 1:15; 2:3; Titus 2:13, RV; Heb. 1:3; 13:8; 1 John 5:20; Rev. 22:12, 13.

(*c*) Also of the Holy Spirit, e.g., Matt. 28:19; Luke 1:35; John 14:16; 15:26; 16:7–14; Rom. 8:9, 26; 1 Cor. 12:11; 2 Cor. 13:14.

(*d*) *Theos* is used (1) with the definite article, (2) without (i.e., as an anarthrous noun). "The English may or may not have need of the article in translation. But that point cuts no figure in the Greek idiom. Thus in Acts 27:23 ('the God whose I am,' RV) the article points out the special God whose Paul is, and is to be preserved in English. In the very next verse (*ho theos*) we in English do not need the article" (A. T. Robertson, *Gram. of Greek, NT*, p. 758).

As to this latter it is usual to employ the article with a proper name, when mentioned a second time. There are, of course, exceptions to this, as when the absence of the article serves to lay stress upon, or give precision to, the character or nature of what is expressed in the noun. A notable instance of this is in John 1:1, "and the Word was God"; here a double stress is on *theos*, by the absence of the article and by the emphatic position. To translate it literally, "a god was the Word," is entirely misleading. Moreover, that "the Word" is the subject of the sentence, exemplifies the rule that the subject is to be determined by its having the article when the predicate is anarthrous (without the article). In Rom. 7:22, in the phrase "the law of God," both nouns have the article; in v. 25, neither has the article. This is in accordance with a general rule that if two nouns are united by the genitive case (the "of" case), either both have the article, or both are without. Here, in the first instance, both nouns, "God" and "the law" are definite, whereas in v. 25 the word "God" is not simply titular; the absence of the article stresses His character as lawgiver.

Where two or more epithets are applied to the same person or thing, one article usually serves for both (the exceptions being when a second article lays stress upon different aspects of the same person or subject, e.g., Rev. 1:17). In Titus 2:13 the RV correctly has "our great God and Savior Jesus Christ." Moulton (*Prol.*, p. 84) shows, from papyri writings of the early Christian era, that among Greek-speaking Christians this was "a current formula" as applied to Christ. So in 2 Pet. 1:1 (cf. 1:11; 3:18).

In the following titles God is described by certain of His attributes; the God of glory, Acts 7:2; of peace, Rom. 15:33; 16:20; Phil. 4:9; 1 Thess. 5:23; Heb. 13:20; of love and peace, 2 Cor. 13:11; of patience and comfort, Rom. 15:5; of all comfort, 2 Cor. 1:3; of hope, Rom. 15:13; of all grace, 1 Pet. 5:10. These describe Him, not as in distinction from other persons, but as the source of all these blessings; hence the employment of the definite article. In such phrases as "the God of a person," e.g., Matt. 22:32, the expression marks the relationship in which the person stands to God and God to him.

(*e*) In the following the nominative case is used for the vocative, and always with the article; Mark 15:34; Luke 18:11, 13; John 20:28; (Acts 4:24 in some mss.); Heb. 1:8; 10:7.

(*f*) The phrase "the things of God" (translated literally or otherwise) stands for (1) His interests, Matt. 16:23; Mark 8:33; (2) His counsels, 1 Cor. 2:11; (3) things which are due to Him, Matt. 22:21; Mark 12:17; Luke 20:25. The phrase "things pertaining to God," Rom. 15:17; Heb. 2:17; 5:1, describes, in the Heb. passages, the sacrificial service of the priest; in the Rom. passage the gospel ministry as an offering to God.

(III) The word is used of divinely appointed judges in Israel, as representing God in His authority, John 10:34, quoted from Ps. 82:6, which indicates that God Himself sits in judgment on those whom He has appointed. The application of the term to the Devil, 2 Cor. 4:4, and the belly, Phil. 3:19, virtually places these instances under (I).

For GOD-SPEED see GREETING

GOD (without)

atheos (ἄθεος, 112), cf. Eng., "atheist," primarily signifies "godless" (*a*, negative), i.e., destitute of God; in Eph. 2:12 the phrase indicates, not only that the Gentiles were void of any true recognition of God, and hence became morally "godless" (Rom. 1:19–32) but that being given up by God, they were excluded from communion with God and from the privileges granted to Israel (see the context and cf. Gal. 4:8). As to pagan ideas, the popular cry against the early Christians was "away with the atheists" (see the account of the martyrdom of Polycarp, in Eusebius, *Eccles. Hist.* iv. 15, 19).¶

GODDESS

thea (θεά, 2299) is found in Acts 19:27 (in some mss. in vv. 35, 37).¶

For GODHEAD see DIVINE, DIVINITY

GODLINESS, GODLY

A. Nouns.

1. *eusebeia* (εὐσέβεια, 2150), from *eu*, "well," and *sebomai*, "to be devout," denotes that piety which, characterized by a Godward attitude, does that which is well-pleasing to Him. This and the corresponding verb and adverb (see below) are frequent in the Pastoral Epistles, but do not occur in previous epistles of Paul. The apostle Peter has the noun four times in his 2nd Epistle, 1:3, 6, 7; 3:11. Elsewhere it occurs in Acts 3:12; 1 Tim. 2:2; 3:16; 4:7, 8; 6:3, 5, 6, 11; 2 Tim. 3:5; Titus 1:1. In 1 Tim. 6:3 "the doctrine which is according to godliness" signifies that which is consistent with "godliness," in contrast to false teachings; in Titus 1:1, "the truth which is according to godliness" is that which is productive of "godli-

ness"; in 1 Tim. 3:16, "the mystery of godliness" is "godliness" as embodied in, and communicated through, the truths of the faith concerning Christ; in 2 Pet. 3:11, the word is in the plural, signifying acts of "godliness."¶

2. *theosebeia* (θεοσέβεια, 2317) denotes "the fear or reverence of God," from *theos*, "god," and *sebomai* (see No. 1), 1 Tim. 2:10.¶ Cf. the adjective *theosebēs*, "God-fearing," John 9:31.¶ In the Sept., Gen. 20:11 and Job 28:28.¶

Note: For *eulabeia*, "godly fear," Heb. 5:7; 12:28 see FEAR, A, No. 3; for *eulabeomai*, "to reverence," Heb. 11:7 ("for His godly fear") see FEAR, D, No. 2; for the verb *eusebeō*, "to show piety," 1 Tim. 5:4; "to worship," Acts 17:23, see PIETY and WORSHIP.¶

B. Adjective.
eusebēs (εὐσεβής, 2152), akin to A, No. 1, denotes "pious, devout, godly," indicating reverence manifested in actions; it is rendered "godly" in 2 Pet. 2:9. See DEVOUT.

C. Adverb.
eusebōs (εὐσεβῶς, 2153) denotes "piously, godly"; it is used with the verb "to live" (of manner of life) in 2 Tim. 3:12; Titus 2:12.¶

Notes: (1) In the following the word "godly" translates the genitive case of the noun *theos*, lit., "of God," 2 Cor. 1:12, KJV, "godly (sincerity)," RV, "(sincerity) of God"; 2 Cor. 11:2, "a godly jealousy," lit., "a jealousy of God" (RV, marg.); 1 Tim. 1:4, RV, "a dispensation of God" (*oikonomia*, in the best mss.), KJV, "godly edifying" (*oikodomē* lit., "an edifying of, i.e., by, God"). (2) In 2 Cor. 7:10, "godly (sorrow)," and in vv. 9 and 11, "after a godly sort," are in all three place, lit., "according to God." (3) In 3 John 6, where the KJV translates the adverb *axiōs*, with the noun *theos*, "after a godly sort," the RV rightly substitutes "worthily of God."

GODWARD
Note: This translates the phrase *pros ton theon*, lit., "toward God," in 2 Cor. 3:4, and 1 Thess. 1:8.

GOLD, GOLDEN
A. Nouns.
1. *chrusos* (χρυσός, 5557) is used (*a*) of "coin," Matt. 10:9; Jas. 5:3; (*b*) of "ornaments," Matt. 23:16, 17; Jas. 5:3 (perhaps both coin and ornaments); Rev. 18:12; some mss. have it instead of No. 2 in 1 Cor. 3:12; (*c*) of "images," Acts 17:29; (*d*) of "the metal in general," Matt. 2:11; Rev. 9:7 (some mss. have it in Rev. 18:16).¶

2. *chrusion* (χρυσίον, 5553), a diminutive of No. 1, is used (*a*) of "coin," primarily smaller than those in No. 1 (*a*), Acts 3:6; 20:33; 1 Pet.

1:18; (*b*) of "ornaments," 1 Pet. 3:3, and the following (in which some mss. have No. 1), 1 Tim. 2:9; Rev. 17:4; 18:16; (*c*) of "the metal in general," Heb. 9:4; 1 Pet. 1:7; Rev. 21:18, 21; metaphorically, (*d*) of "sound doctrine and its effects," 1 Cor. 3:12; (*e*) of "righteousness of life and conduct," Rev. 3:18.¶

B. Adjective.
chruseos (χρύσεος, 5552) denotes "golden," i.e., made of, or overlaid with, gold, 2 Tim. 2:20; Heb. 9:4, and fifteen times in the Apocalypse.

GOLD RING
chrusodaktulios (χρυσοδακτύλιος, 5554), an adjective denoting "with a gold ring" (*daktulos*, "a finger"), occurs in Jas. 2:2.¶

GOOD, GOODLY, GOODNESS
A. Adjectives.
1. *agathos* (ἀγαθός, 18) describes that which, being "good" in its character or constitution, is beneficial in its effect; it is used (*a*) of things physical, e.g., a tree, Matt. 7:17; ground, Luke 8:8; (*b*) in a moral sense, frequently of persons and things. God is essentially, absolutely and consummately "good," Matt. 19:17; Mark 10:18; Luke 18:19. To certain persons the word is applied in Matt. 20:15; 25:21, 23; Luke 19:17; 23:50; John 7:12; Acts 11:24; Titus 2:5; in a general application, Matt. 5:45; 12:35; Luke 6:45; Rom. 5:7; 1 Pet. 2:18.

The neuter of the adjective with the definite article signifies that which is "good," lit., "the good," as being morally honorable, pleasing to God, and therefore beneficial. Christians are to prove it, Rom. 12:2; to cleave to it, 12:9; to do it, 13:3; Gal. 6:10; 1 Pet. 3:11 (here, and here only, the article is absent); John 5:29 (here, the neuter plural is used, "the good things"); to work it, Rom. 2:10; Eph. 4:28; 6:8; to follow after it, 1 Thess. 5:15; to be zealous of it, 1 Pet. 3:13; to imitate it, 3 John 11; to overcome evil with it, Rom. 12:21. Governmental authorities are ministers of "good," i.e., that which is salutary, suited to the course of human affairs, Rom. 13:4. In Philem. 14, "thy goodness," RV (lit., "thy good"), means "thy benefit." As to Matt. 19:17, "why askest thou Me concerning that which is good?" the RV follows the most ancient mss.

The neuter plural is also used of material "goods," riches, etc., Luke 1:53; 12:18, 19; 16:25; Gal. 6:6 (of temporal supplies); in Rom. 10:15; Heb. 9:11; 10:1, the "good" things are the benefits provided through the sacrifice of Christ, in regard both to those conferred through the gospel and to those of the coming messianic kingdom. See further under No. 2. See BENEFIT, GOODS.

2. *kalos* (καλός, 2570) denotes that which is intrinsically "good," and so, "goodly, fair, beautiful," as (*a*) of that which is well adapted to its circumstances or ends, e.g., fruit, Matt. 3:10; a tree, 12:33; ground, 13:8, 23; fish, 13:48; the Law, Rom. 7:16; 1 Tim. 1:8; every creature of God, 1 Tim. 4:4; a faithful minister of Christ and the doctrine he teaches, 4:6; (*b*) of that which is ethically good, right, noble, honorable, e.g., Gal. 4:18; 1 Tim. 5:10, 25; 6:18; Titus 2:7, 14; 3:8, 14. The word does not occur in the Apocalypse, nor indeed after 1 Peter.

Christians are to "take thought for things honorable" (*kalos*), 2 Cor. 8:21, RV; to do that which is honorable, 13:7; not to be weary in well doing, Gal. 6:9; to hold fast "that which is good," 1 Thess. 5:21; to be zealous of good works, Titus 2:14; to maintain them, 3:8; to provoke to them, Heb. 10:24; to bear testimony by them, 1 Pet. 2:12.

Kalos and *agathos* occur together in Luke 8:15, an "honest" (*kalos*) heart, i.e., the attitude of which is right towards God; a "good" (*agathos*) heart, i.e., one that, instead of working ill to a neighbor, acts beneficially towards him. In Rom. 7:18, "in me . . . dwelleth no good thing" (*agathos*) signifies that in him is nothing capable of doing "good," and hence he lacks the power "to do that which is good" (*kalos*). In 1 Thess. 5:15, "follow after that which is good" (*agathos*), the "good" is that which is beneficial; in v. 21, "hold fast that which is good (*kalos*)," the "good" describes the intrinsic value of the teaching. See BETTER, FAIR HONEST, MEET, WORTHY.

3. *chrēstos* (χρηστός, 5543), said of things, "that which is pleasant," said of persons, "kindly, gracious," is rendered "good" in 1 Cor. 15:33, "goodness" in Rom. 2:4. See EASY.

Note: Lampros denotes "gay, bright," "goodly" in Jas. 2:2, KJV, (RV, "fine"); in 2:3, KJV, "gay"; in Rev. 18:14 (RV, "sumptuous"). See GORGEOUS, SUMPTUOUS. For *asteios*, "goodly," Heb. 11:23, RV, see BEAUTIFUL. For *hikanos*, Acts 18:18, KJV, "a good while" see WHILE. *Note* (16).

B. Nouns.

1. *chrēstotēs* (χρηστότης, 5544), akin to A, No. 3, denotes "goodness" (*a*) in the sense of what is upright, righteous, Rom. 3:12 (translated "good"); (*b*) in the sense of kindness of heart or act, said of God, Rom. 2:4; 11:22 (thrice); Eph. 2:7 ("kindness"); Titus 3:4 ("kindness"); said of believers and rendered "kindness," 2 Cor. 6:6; Col. 3:12; Gal. 5:22 (RV; KJV, "gentleness"). It signifies "not merely good-

ness as a quality, rather it is goodness in action, goodness expressing itself in deeds; yet not goodness expressing itself in indignation against sin, for it is contrasted with severity in Rom. 11:22, but in grace and tenderness and compassion."* See GENTLENESS, KINDNESS.¶

2. *agathōsunē* (ἀγαθωσύνη, 19), "goodness," signifies that moral quality which is described by the adjective *agathos* (see A, No. 1). It is used, in the NT, of regenerate persons, Rom. 15:14; Gal. 5:22; Eph. 5:9; 2 Thess. 1:11; in the last, the phrase "every desire of goodness" (RV; the addition of "His" in the KJV is an interpolation; there is no pronoun in the original) may be either subjective, i.e., desire characterized by "goodness," "good" desire, or objective, i.e., desire after "goodness," to be and do good.¶

Trench, following Jerome, distinguishes between *chrēstotēs* and *agathōsunē* in that the former describes the kindlier aspects of "goodness," the latter includes also the sterner qualities by which doing "good" to others is not necessarily by gentle means. He illustrates the latter by the act of Christ in cleansing the temple, Matt. 21:12, 13, and in denouncing the scribes and Pharisees, 23:13–29; but *chrēstotēs* by His dealings with the penitent woman, Luke 7:37–50. Lightfoot regards *chrēstotēs* as a kindly disposition towards others; *agathōsunē* as a kindly activity on their behalf.

J. A. Robertson (on Eph. 5:9) remarks that *agathōsunē* is "the kindlier, as *dikaiosunē* (righteousness) the sterner, element in the ideal character."

3. *eupoiia* (εὐποιΐα, 2140), "beneficence, doing good" (*eu*, "well," *poieō*, "to do"), is translated as a verb in Heb. 13:16, "to do good."¶

C. Adverbs.

1. *kalōs* (καλῶς, 2573), "well, finely," is used in some mss. in Matt. 5:44, with *poieō*, "to do," and translated "do good." In Jas. 2:3 it is rendered "in a good place" (KJV marg., "well" or "seemly"). See WELL.

2. *eu* (εὖ, 2095), "well," used with *poieō*, is translated "do . . . good" in Mark 14:7. See WELL.

D. Verbs (to do, or be, good).

1. *agathopoieō* (ἀγαθοποιέω, 15), from A, No. 1, and *poieō*, "to do," is used (*a*) in a general way, "to do well," 1 Pet. 2:15, 20; 3:6, 17; 3 John 11; (*b*) with pointed reference "to the benefit of another," Luke 6:9, 33, 35; in Mark 3:4 the parts of the word are separated in

---

* From *Notes on Galatians*, by Hogg and Vine, p. 292.

some mss. Some mss. have it in Acts 14:17, for No. 2.¶ Cf. the noun *agathopoiia*, "well-doing," 1 Pet. 4:19, and the adjective *agathopoios*, "doing well," 1 Pet. 2:14.

2. *agathourgeō* (ἀγαθουργέω, 14), for *agathoergeō*, "to do good" (from A, No. 1, and *ergon*, "a work"), is used in Acts 14:17 (in the best mss.; see No. 1), where it is said of God's beneficence towards man, and 1 Tim. 6:18, where it is enjoined upon the rich.¶

3. *euergeteō* (εὐεργετέω, 2109), "to bestow a benefit, to do good" (*eu*, "well," and a verbal form akin to *ergon*), is used in Acts 10:38.¶

Notes: (1) The verb *ischuō*, "to be strong" (*ischus*, "strength"), "to have efficacy, force or value," is said of salt in Matt. 5:13, negatively, "it is good for nothing." (2) In Matt. 19:10, KJV, *sumpherō*, "to be profitable, expedient" (*sun*, "together," *pherō*, "to bring"); is rendered with a negative "it is not good" (RV, "it is not expedient"). (3) In Mark 14:7, the two words *eu*, "well," and *poieō*, "to do," are in some mss. treated as one verb *eupoieō*, "to do good."

GOODMAN

oikodespotēs (οἰκοδεσπότης, 3617) denotes "the master of a house" (*oikos*, "a house," *despotēs*, "a master"), "a householder." It occurs only in the Synoptists, and there 12 times. It is rendered "goodman" in Luke 22:11, where "of the house" is put separately; in Matt. 20:11, where the KJV has "the goodman of the house" for the one word, the RV renders it by "householder," as in v. 1; in 24:43, "master"; so in Luke 12:39; in Mark 14:14, both have "the goodman of the house." See HOUSEHOLDER, MASTER.

GOODS

1. For the neuter plural of *agathos*, used as a noun, "goods," see Luke 12:18, 19, where alone this word is so rendered.

2. *huparxis* (ὕπαρξις, 5223), primarily, "subsistence," then, "substance, property, goods" (akin to *huparchō*, "to exist, be, belong to"), is translated "goods" in Acts 2:45; "possession." RV (KJV, "substance") in Heb. 10:34.¶

3. *bios* (βίος, 979), which denotes (*a*) "life, lifetime," (*b*) "livelihood, living, means of living," is translated "goods" in 1 John 3:17, RV (KJV, "good"). See LIFE, No. 2.

4. *skeuos* (σκεῦος, 4632), "a vessel," denotes "goods" in Matt. 12:29; Mark 3:27; Luke 17:31, RV (KJV, "stuff"). See VESSEL.

Notes: (1) The neuter plural of the present participle of *huparchō*, is used as a noun denoting "goods," in Matt. 24:47, KJV "his goods," RV, "that he hath"; "goods" in Matt. 25:14;

Luke 11:21; 16:1; 19:8; 1 Cor. 13:3; in Heb. 10:34 (1st part). (2) In Luke 6:30 "thy goods" translates the neuter plural of the possessive pronoun with the article, lit., "thy things," or possessions. (3) In Rev. 3:17, the KJV "I am ... increased with goods" translates the perfect tense of the verb *plouteō*, "to be rich"; RV, "I have gotten riches." (4) See SUBSTANCE.

GORGEOUS, GORGEOUSLY

lampros (λαμπρός, 2986), "bright, splendid," is rendered "gorgeous" in Luke 23:11, of the apparel in which Herod and his soldiers arrayed Christ. See BRIGHT.

Note: For the KJV, "gorgeously apparelled" in Luke 7:25, see GLORIOUS, B.

GOSPEL (Noun and Verb: to preach)

A. Noun.

euangelion (εὐαγγέλιον, 2098) originally denoted a reward for good tidings; later, the idea of reward dropped, and the word stood for "the good news" itself. The Eng. word "gospel," i.e. "good message," is the equivalent of *euangelion* (Eng., "evangel"). In the NT it denotes the "good tidings" of the kingdom of God and of salvation through Christ, to be received by faith, on the basis of His expiatory death, His burial, resurrection, and ascension, e.g., Acts 15:7; 20:24; 1 Pet. 4:17. Apart from those references and those in the gospels of Matthew and Mark, and Rev. 14:6, the noun is confined to Paul's epistles. The apostle uses it of two associated yet distinct things, (*a*) of the basic facts of the death, burial and resurrection of Christ, e.g., 1 Cor. 15:1–3; (*b*) of the interpretation of these facts, e.g., Rom. 2:16; Gal. 1:7, 11; 2:2; in (*a*) the "gospel" is viewed historically, in (*b*) doctrinally, with reference to the interpretation of the facts, as is sometimes indicated by the context.

The following phrases describe the subjects or nature or purport of the message; it is the "gospel" of God, Mark 1:14; Rom. 1:1; 15:16; 2 Cor. 11:7; 1 Thess. 2:2, 9; 1 Pet. 4:17; God, concerning His Son, Rom. 1:1–3; His Son, Rom. 1:9; Jesus Christ, the Son of God, Mark 1:1; our Lord Jesus, 2 Thess. 1:8; Christ, Rom. 15:19, etc.; the glory of Christ, 2 Cor. 4:4; the grace of God, Acts 20:24; the glory of the blessed God, 1 Tim. 1:11; your salvation, Eph. 1:13; peace, Eph. 6:15. Cf. also "the gospel of the Kingdom," Matt. 4:23; 9:35; 24:14; "an eternal gospel," Rev. 14:6.

In Gal. 2:14, "the truth of the gospel" denotes, not the true "gospel," but the true teaching of it, in contrast to perversions of it.

The following expressions are used in connection with the "gospel": (a) with regard to its testimony; (1) *kērussō*, "to preach it as a herald," e.g., Matt. 4:23; Gal. 2:2 (see PREACH); (2) *laleō*, "to speak," 1 Thess. 2:2; (3) *diamarturomai*, "to testify (thoroughly)," Acts 20:24; (4) *euangelizō*, "to preach," e.g., 1 Cor. 15:1; 2 Cor. 11:7; Gal. 1:11 (see B, No. 1 below); (5) *katangellō*, "to proclaim," 1 Cor. 9:14; (6) *douleuō eis*, "to serve unto" ("in furtherance of"), Phil. 2:22; (7) *sunathleō en*, "to labor with in," Phil. 4:3; (8) *hierourgeō*, "to minister," Rom. 15:16; (8) *plēroō*, "to preach fully," Rom. 15:19; (10) *sunkakopatheō*, "to suffer hardship with," 2 Tim. 1:8; (b) with regard to its reception or otherwise: (1) *dechomai*, "to receive," 2 Cor. 11:4; *hupakouō*, "to hearken to, or obey," Rom. 10:16; 2 Thess. 1:8; *pisteuō en*, "to believe in," Mark 1:15; *metastrephō*, "to pervert," Gal. 1:7.

Note: In connection with (a), the apostle's statement in 1 Cor. 9:23 is noticeable, "I do all things for the Gospel's sake, that I may be a joint partaker thereof," RV, for the incorrect KJV, "that I might be a partaker thereof with you."

B. Verbs.

1. *euangelizō* (εὐαγγελίζω, 2097), "to bring or announce glad tidings" (Eng., "evangelize"), is used (a) in the active voice in Rev. 10:7 ("declared") and 14:6 ("to proclaim," RV, KJV, "to preach"); (b) in the passive voice, of matters to be proclaimed as "glad tidings," Luke 16:16; Gal. 1:11; 1 Pet. 1:25; of persons to whom the proclamation is made, Matt. 11:5; Luke 7:22; Heb. 4:2, 6; 1 Pet. 4:6; (c) in the middle voice, especially of the message of salvation, with a personal object, either of the person preached, e.g., Acts 5:42; 11:20; Gal. 1:16, or, with a preposition, of the persons evangelized, e.g., Acts 13:32, "declare glad tidings"; Rom. 1:15; Gal. 1:8; with an impersonal object, e.g., "the word," Acts 8:4; "good tidings," 8:12; "the word of the Lord," 15:35; "the gospel," 1 Cor. 15:1; 2 Cor. 11:7; "the faith," Gal. 1:23; "peace," Eph. 2:17; "the unsearchable riches of Christ, 3:8. See PREACH, SHEW, TIDINGS.

2. *proeuangelizomai* (προευαγγελίζομαι, 4283), "to announce glad tidings beforehand," is used in Gal. 3:8.¶

Note: For other verbs see above.

For GOT and GOTTEN see GET

GOVERNMENT

kubernēsis (κυβέρνησις, 2941), from *kubernaō*, "to guide" (whence Eng., "govern"), denotes (a) "steering, pilotage"; (b) metaphorically, "governments or governings," said of those who act as guides in a local church, 1 Cor.

12:28.¶ Cf. *kubernētēs*, "a pilot," Acts 27:11; Rev. 18:17.¶

Note: For *kuriotēs*, "lordship, dominion," rendered "government" in 2 Pet. 2:10, KJV, see DOMINION.

GOVERNOR

A. Nouns.

1. *hēgemōn* (ἡγεμών, 2232) is a term used (a) for "rulers" generally, Mark 13:9; 1 Pet. 2:14; translated "princes" (i.e., leaders) in Matt. 2:6; (b) for the Roman procurators, referring, in the gospels to Pontius Pilate, e.g., Matt. 27:2; Luke 20:20 (so designated by Tacitus, *Annals*, xv. 44); to Felix, Acts 23:26. Technically the procurator was a financial official under a proconsul or propretor, for collecting the imperial revenues, but entrusted also with magisterial powers for decisions of questions relative to the revenues. In certain provinces, of which Judea was one (the procurator of which was dependent on the legate of Syria), he was the general administrator and supreme judge, with sole power of life and death. Such a governor was a person of high social standing. Felix, however, was an ex-slave, a freedman, and his appointment to Judea could not but be regarded by the Jews as an insult to the nation. The headquarters of the governor of Judea was Caesarea, which was made a garrison town. See PRINCE, RULER. For *anthupatos*, "a proconsul," see PROCONSUL.

2. *ethnarchēs* (ἐθνάρχης, 1481), "an ethnarch," lit. "a ruler of a nation" (*ethnos*, "a people," *archē*, "rule"), is translated "governor" in 2 Cor. 11:32; it describes normally the ruler of a nation possessed of separate laws and customs among those of a different race. Eventually it denoted a ruler of a province, superior to a tetrarch, but inferior to a king (e.g., Aretas).¶

3. *oikonomos* (οἰκονόμος, 3623), lit., "one who rules a house" (*oikos*, "a house," *nomos*, "a law"), Gal. 4:2, denotes a superior servant responsible for the family housekeeping, the direction of other servants, and the care of the children under age. See CHAMBERLAIN, STEWARD.

4. *architriklinos* (ἀρχιτρίκλινος, 755), from *archē*, "rule," and *triklinos*, "a room with three couches," denotes "the ruler of a feast," John 2:8, RV (KJV, "the governor of the feast"), a man appointed to see that the table and couches were duly placed and the courses arranged, and to taste the food and wine.¶

B. Verbs.

1. *hēgeomai* (ἡγέομαι, 2233), akin to A, No. 1, is used in the present participle to denote "a

governor," lit., "(one) governing," Matt. 2:6; Acts 7:10.

2. *hēgemoneuō* (ἡγεμονεύω, 2230), to be a *hēgemōn*, "to lead the way," came to signify to be "a governor of a province"; it is used of Quirinius, governor of Syria, Luke 2:2, rv (for the circumstances see under ENROLLMENT); of Pontius Pilate, governor of Judea, 3:1.¶ In the first clause of this verse the noun *hēgemonia*, "a rule or sovereignty," is translated "reign"; Eng., "hegemony."¶

Note. In Jas. 3:4, the verb *euthunō*, "to make or guide straight," is used in the present participle, as a noun, denoting the "steersman" (rv) or pilot of a vessel, kjv, "governor."

GRACE

1. *charis* (χάρις, 5485) has various uses, (*a*) objective, that which bestows or occasions pleasure, delight, or causes favorable regard; it is applied, e.g., to beauty, or gracefulness of person, Luke 2:40; act, 2 Cor. 8:6, or speech, Luke 4:22, rv, "words of grace" (kjv, "gracious words"); Col. 4:6; (*b*) subjective, (1) on the part of the bestower, the friendly disposition from which the kindly act proceeds, graciousness, loving-kindness, goodwill generally, e.g., Acts 7:10; especially with reference to the divine favor or "grace," e.g., Acts 14:26; in this respect there is stress on its freeness and universality, its spontaneous character, as in the case of God's redemptive mercy, and the pleasure or joy He designs for the recipient; thus it is set in contrast with debt, Rom. 4:4, 16, with works, 11:6, and with law, John 1:17; see also, e.g., Rom. 6:14, 15; Gal. 5:4; (2) on the part of the receiver, a sense of the favor bestowed, a feeling of gratitude, e.g., Rom. 6:17 ("thanks"); in this respect it sometimes signifies "to be thankful," e.g., Luke 17:9 ("doth he thank the servant?" lit., "hath he thanks to"); 1 Tim. 1:12; (*c*) in another objective sense, the effect of "grace," the spiritual state of those who have experienced its exercise, whether (1) a state of "grace," e.g., Rom. 5:2; 1 Pet. 5:12; 2 Pet. 3:18, or (2) a proof thereof in practical effects, deeds of "grace," e.g., 1 Cor. 16:3, rv, "bounty" (kjv, "liberality"); 2 Cor. 8:6, 19 (in 2 Cor. 9:8 it means the sum of earthly blessings); the power and equipment for ministry, e.g., Rom. 1:5; 12:6; 15:15; 1 Cor. 3:10; Gal. 2:9; Eph. 3:2, 7.

To be in favor with is to find "grace" with, e.g., Acts 2:47; hence it appears in this sense at the beginning and the end of several epistles, where the writer desires "grace" from God for the readers, e.g., Rom. 1:7; 1 Cor. 1:3; in this respect it is connected with the imperative mood of the word *chairō*, "to rejoice," a mode

of greeting among Greeks, e.g., Acts 15:23; Jas. 1:1 (marg.); 2 John 10, 11, rv, "greeting" (kjv, "God speed").

The fact that "grace" is received both from God the Father, 2 Cor. 1:12, and from Christ, Gal. 1:6; Rom. 5:15 (where both are mentioned), is a testimony to the deity of Christ. See also 2 Thess. 1:12, where the phrase "according to the grace of our God and the Lord Jesus Christ" is to be taken with each of the preceding clauses, "in you," "and ye in Him."

In Jas. 4:6, "But He giveth more grace" (Greek, "a greater grace," rv, marg.), the statement is to be taken in connection with the preceding verse, which contains two remonstrating, rhetorical questions, "Think ye that the Scripture speaketh in vain?" and "Doth the Spirit (the Holy Spirit) which He made to dwell in us long unto envying?" (see the rv). The implied answer to each is "it cannot be so." Accordingly, if those who are acting so flagrantly, as if it were so, will listen to the Scripture instead of letting it speak in vain, and will act so that the Holy Spirit may have His way within, God will give even "a greater grace," namely, all that follows from humbleness and from turning away from the world. See BENEFIT, BOUNTY, LIBERALITY, THANK.

Note: The corresponding verb *charitoō*, "to endue with divine favor or grace," is used in Luke 1:28, "highly favored" (marg., "endued with grace") and Eph. 1:6, kjv, "hath made ... accepted"; rv, "freely bestowed" (marg., "endued.").¶

2. *euprepeia* (εὐπρέπεια, 2143), "comeliness, goodly appearance," is said of the outward appearance of the flower of the grass, Jas. 1:11.¶

GRACIOUS

chrēstos (χρηστός, 5543) is rendered "gracious" in 1 Pet. 2:3, as an attribute of the Lord. See EASY, GOOD, KIND.

Note: Euphēmos, "fair-sounding" (*eu*, "well," *phēmē*, "a saying, or report"), "of good report," Phil. 4:8, is rendered "gracious" in the rv marg.

GRAFF, GRAFT (rv)

enkentrizō (ἐνκεντρίζω, 1461) denotes "to graft" in (*en*, in, *kentrizō*, to graft), to insert a slip of a cultivated tree into a wild one. In Rom. 11:17, 19, 23, 24, however, the metaphor is used "contrary to nature" (v. 24), of grafting a wild olive branch (the Gentile) into the good olive tree (the Jews); that unbelieving Jews (branches of the good tree) were broken off that Gentiles might be grafted in, afforded no occasion for glorying on the part of the latter. Jew and Gentile alike must enjoy the divine blessings by faith alone. So Jews who abide not in unbelief shall, as "the natural branches, be grafted into their own olive tree."¶

GRAIN

kokkos (κόκκος, 2848) denotes "a grain," Matt. 13:31; 17:20; Mark 4:31; Luke 13:19; 17:6; John 12:24 (KJV, "corn"); 1 Cor. 15:37 (where the RV has "a ... grain," to distinguish it from "grain" in general). See CORN.¶

GRANDCHILDREN

ekgonos (ἔκγονος, 1549**), an adjective, denoting "born of" (*ek*, "from," *ginomai*, "to become or be born"), was used as a noun, signifying "a child"; in the plural, descendants, "grand-children," 1 Tim. 5:4, RV (KJV, "nephews").¶

GRANDMOTHER

mammē (μάμμη, 3125), an onomatopoeic word, was primarily a child's name for its mother; later it denoted a "grandmother," 2 Tim. 1:5.¶

GRANT

1. *didōmi* (δίδωμι, 1325), "to give," is rendered "grant" in Mark 10:37; Luke 1:74; Acts 4:29; 11:18; 14:3. See GIVE.

2. *dōreō* (δωρέω, 1433), "to present, bestow" (akin to No. 1), is rendered "granted" in Mark 15:45, RV (KJV, "gave"); in 2 Pet. 1:3, 4, "hath granted," "He hath granted," RV (KJV, "hath given" and "are given"); in each place middle voice. See GIVE.¶

3. *charizomai* (χαρίζομαι, 5483) primarily signifies "to show favor or kindness" (akin to *charis*, see GRACE), Gal. 3:18, RV, "hath granted" (KJV, "gave"; it signifies more than "to give"); then, "to give freely, bestow," rendered "to grant" in Acts 3:14; 27:24, RV (KJV, "given"); Phil. 1:29, RV; Philem. 22, RV. See DELIVER.

GRAPE

staphulē (σταφυλή, 4718) denotes "a bunch of grapes, or a grape," Matt. 7:16; Luke 6:44; Rev. 14:18. It is to be distinguished from *omphax*, "an unripe grape" (not in NT), e.g., in the Sept. of Job 15:33, and from *botrus*, "a cluster," used together with *staphulē* in Rev. 14:18.¶

GRASS

chortos (χόρτος, 5528) primarily denoted "a feeding enclosure" (whence Latin *hortus*, "a garden"; Eng., "yard," and "garden"); then, "food," especially grass for feeding cattle; it is translated "grass" in Matt. 6:30; 14:19; Mark 6:39 (where "the green grass" is the first evidence of early spring); Luke 12:28; John 6:10; Jas. 1:10, 11; 1 Pet. 1:24; Rev. 8:7; 9:4; "blade" in Matt. 13:26; Mark 4:28; "hay" in 1 Cor. 3:12, used figuratively. In Palestine or Syria there are 90 genera and 243 species of grass.¶

GRATULATION

makarismos (μακαρισμός, 3108) denotes "a declaration of blessedness, a felicitation"; it is translated "gratulation" in Gal. 4:15, RV (KJV, "blessedness"); the Galatian converts had counted themselves happy when they heard and received the gospel from Paul; he asks them rhetorically what had become of that spirit which had animated them; the word is rendered "blessing" in Rom. 4:6, 9. See BLESSING, C, No. 2.¶

GRAVE (Noun)

1. *mnēmeion* (μνημεῖον, 3419) primarily denotes "a memorial" (akin to *mnaomai*, "to remember"), then, "a monument" (the significance of the word rendered "tombs," KJV, "sepulchres," in Luke 11:47), anything done to preserve the memory of things and persons; it usually denotes a tomb, and is translated either "tomb" or "sepulchre" or "grave." Apart from the Gospels, it is found only in Acts 13:29. Among the Hebrews it was generally a cavern, closed by a door or stone, often decorated. Cf. Matt. 23:29. See TOMB.

2. *mnēma* (μνῆμα, 3418), akin to No. 1, like which it signified "a memorial" or "record of a thing or a dead person," then "a sepulchral monument," and hence "a tomb"; it is rendered "graves" in the KJV of Rev. 11:9 (RV, "a tomb"); "tomb" or "tombs," Mark 5:3, 5 (some mss. have No. 1, as in 15:46, KJV, "sepulchre") and 16:2 (KJV, "sepulchre"); Luke 8:27; Acts 2:29 and 7:16 (KJV, "sepulchre"). See TOMB.

Note: In 1 Cor. 15:55, where some texts have "Hades," KJV, "grave," the most authentic have *thanatos*, "death."

GRAVE (Adjective)

semnos (σεμνός, 4586) first denoted "reverend, august, venerable" (akin to *sebomai*, "to reverence"); then, "serious, grave," whether of persons, 1 Tim. 3:8, 11 (deacons and their wives); Titus 2:2 (aged men); or things, Phil. 4:8, RV, "honorable" (marg., "reverend"), KJV, "honest." Trench (*Syn.* §xcii) points out that "grave" and "gravity" fail to cover the full meaning of their original; "the word we want is one in which the sense of gravity and dignity is combined." Cremer describes it as denoting what inspires reverence and awe, and says that *semnos* and *hosios*, "holy, consecrated," are only secondary designations of the conception of holiness. "The word points to seriousness of purpose and to self-respect in conduct" (Moule).¶ Cf. *semnotēs*, "gravity" (see below).

GRAVE-CLOTHES

keiria (κειρία, 2750) denotes, firstly, "a band" either for a bed girth, or bed sheets themselves (Sept. of Prov. 7:16.¶); then, "the swathings wrapped round a corpse"; it is used in the plural in John 11:44.¶

GRAVEN

charagma (χάραγμα, 5480), from *charassō*, "to engrave" (akin to *charaktēr*, "an impress," RV, marg., of Heb. 1:3), denotes (*a*) "a mark" or "stamp," e.g., Rev. 13:16, 17; 14:9, 11; 16:2; 19:20; 20:4; 15:2 in some mss.; (*b*) "a thing graven," Acts 17:29.¶

GRAVITY

semnotēs (σεμνότης, 4587) denotes "venerableness, dignity"; it is a necessary characteristic of the life and conduct of Christians, 1 Tim. 2:2, RV, "gravity" (KJV, "honesty"), a qualification of a bishop or overseer in a church, in regard to his children, 1 Tim. 3:4; a necessary characteristic of the teaching imparted by a servant of God, Titus 2:7.¶ Cf. the adjective *semnos*, under GRAVE.

GREAT

1. *megas* (μέγας, 3173) is used (*a*) of external form, size, measure, e.g., of a stone, Matt. 27:60; fish, John 21:11; (*b*) of degree and intensity, e.g., of fear, Mark 4:41; wind, John 6:18; Rev. 6:13, RV, "great" (KJV, "mighty"); of a circumstance, 1 Cor. 9:11; 2 Cor. 11:15; in Rev. 5:2, 12, the RV has "great" (KJV, "loud"), of a voice; (*c*) of rank, whether of persons, e.g., God, Titus 2:13; Christ as a "great Priest," Heb. 10:21, RV; Diana, Acts 19:27; Simon Magus, Acts 8:9 "(some) great one"; in the plural, "great ones," Matt. 20:25; Mark 10:42, those who hold positions of authority in gentile nations; or of things, e.g., a mystery, Eph. 5:32. Some mss. have it in Acts 8:8, of joy (see No. 2). See also *Note* (2) below. See GREATEST, HIGH, LOUD, MIGHTY, STRONG.

2. *polus* (πολύς, 4183), "much, many, great," is used of number, e.g., Luke 5:6; Acts 11:21; degree, e.g., of harvest, Matt. 9:37 [See *Note* (8)]; mercy, 1 Pet. 1:3, RV, "great" (KJV, "abundant"); glory, Matt. 24:30; joy, Philem. 7, RV, "much" (KJV, "great"); peace, Acts 24:2. The best mss. have it in Acts 8:8 (RV, "much"),

of joy. See ABUNDANT, COMMON, *Note* (1), LONG, MANY, MUCH, OFT, SORE, STRAITLY.

3. *hikanos* (ἱκανός, 2425), lit., "reaching to" (from *hikanō*, "to reach"), denotes "sufficient, competent, fit," and is sometimes rendered "great," e.g., of number (of people), Mark 10:46; of degree (of light), Acts 22:6. See ABLE, ENOUGH, GOOD, LARGE, LONG, MANY, MEET, MUCH, SECURITY, SUFFICIENT, WORTHY.

4. *hēlikos* (ἡλίκος, 2245) primarily denotes "as big as, as old as (akin to *hēlikia*, "an age"); then, as an indirect interrogation, "what, what size, how great, how small" (the context determines the meaning), said of a spiritual conflit, Col. 2:1, KJV, "what great (conflict) I have"; RV, "how greatly (I strive)"; of much wood as kindled by a little fire, Jas. 3:5 (twice in the best mss.), "how much (wood is kindled by) how small (a fire)," RV, said metaphorically of the use of the tongue. Some mss. have No. 4 in Gal. 6:11; the most authentic have No. 5.¶

5. *pēlikos* (πηλίκος, 4080), primarily a direct interrogative, "how large? how great?" is used in exclamations, indicating magnitude, like No. 4 (No. 6 indicates quantity), in Gal. 6:11, of letter characters (see No. 4, *Note*); in Heb. 7:4, metaphorically, of the distinguished character of Melchizedek.¶

6. *posos* (πόσος, 4214), an adjective of number, magnitude, degree etc., is rendered "how great" in Matt. 6:23. See MANY, MUCH.

7. *hosos* (ὅσος, 3745), "how much, how many," is used in the neuter plural to signify how great things, Mark 5:19, 20; Luke 8:39 (twice); Acts 9:16, KJV (RV, "how many things"); in Rev. 21:16 (in the best mss.), "as great as," RV (KJV, "as large as," said of length). See ALL, MANY, No. 5, WHATSOEVER.

8. *tosoutos* (τοσοῦτος, 5118), "so great, so many, so much," of quantity, size, etc., is rendered "so great," in Matt. 8:10, and Luke 7:9, of faith; Matt. 15:33, of a multitude; Heb. 12:1, of a cloud of witnesses; Rev. 18:17, of riches. See LARGE, LONG, MANY, MUCH.

9. *tēlikoutos* (τηλικοῦτος, 5082), "so great," is used in the NT of things only, a death, 2 Cor. 1:10; salvation, Heb. 2:3; ships, Jas. 3:4; an earthquake, Rev. 16:18, KJV, "so mighty," corrected in the RV to "so great." See MIGHTY.¶

Notes: (1) In Mark 7:36, "so much the more a great deal" translates a phrase lit. signifying "more abundantly"; in 10:48, "the more a great deal" translates a phrase lit. signifying "more by much." (2) For the noun *megistan*, in the plural, rendered "Lords" in the KJV of Mark 6:21, see LORD; in Rev. 6:15 and 18:23, see PRINCE. (3) In Luke 1:58, the verb *megalunō*, "to magnify, make great" (akin to No. 1), is rendered "had magnified (His mercy)," RV [KJV, "had shewed great (mercy)"]. (4) In Luke 10:13, the adverb *palai*, "of old, long ago," is so rendered in the RV (KJV, "a great while ago"). (5) In 2 Pet. 1:4, *megistos*, the superlative of *megas* (No. 1), said of the promises of God, is rendered "exceeding great."¶ (6) In Matt. 21:8, *pleistos*, the superlative of *polus* (No. 2), said of a multitude, is rendered "very great" in the KJV (RV, "the most part"). (7) In Rev. 21:10, the most authentic mss. omit "that great" [RV, "the holy (city)"]. (8) In Luke 10:2, the RV renders *polus* by "plenteous" (KJV, "great"). (9) In Mark 1:35, the adverb *lian*, exceedingly (see GREATLY), is rendered "a great while." See DAY, B. (10) In Luke 1:49 some texts have *megaleia*, "great things"; the best have No. 1.

GREATER

1. *meizōn* (μείζων, 3187) is the comparative degree of *megas* (see GREAT, No. 1), e.g., Matt. 11:11; in Matt. 13:32, the RV rightly has "greater than" (KJV, "the greatest among"); 23:17; in Luke 22:26, RV, "the greater (among you)" (KJV, "greatest"); in Jas. 3:1, RV, "the heavier (marg., greater) judgment" (KJV, "the greater condemnation"); it is used in the neuter plural in John 1:50, "greater things"; in 14:12, "greater works" (lit., "greater things"); in 1 Cor. 12:31, RV, "the greater," KJV, "the best". See GREATEST, No. 2.

Note: In Matt. 20:31, the neuter of *meizōn*, used as an adverb, is translated "the more." See MORE.

2. *meizoteros* (μειζότερος, 3186), a double comparative of *megas* (cf. No. 1, above), is used in 3 John 4, of joy.¶

3. *pleiōn* (πλείων, 4119), the comparative of *polus* (see GREAT, No. 2), is used (*a*) as an adjective, "greater, more," e.g., Acts 15:28; (*b*) as a noun, e.g., Matt. 12:41, "a greater (than Jonah)"; v. 42, "a greater (than Solomon)"; in these instances the neuter *pleion*, "something greater," is "a fixed or stereotyped form" of the word; in 1 Cor. 15:6, "the greater part" (masculine plural); (*c*) as an adverb, e.g., Matt. 5:20, lit., "(except your righteousness abound) more greatly (than of scribes and Pharisees)"; so 26:53, "more"; Luke 9:13. See ABOVE, LONGER, MANY, MORE, MOST, YET.

4. *perissoteros* (περισσότερος, 4055), the comparative of *perissos*, "over and above, abundant," signifies "more abundant, greater," e.g., of condemnation, Mark 12:40; Luke 20:47. See ABUNDANT, C, No. 2.

GREATEST

1. *megas* (μέγας, 3173), for which see GREAT, No. 1, is translated "the greatest," in Acts 8:10 and Heb. 8:11. The whole phrase, lit., "from small to great," is equivalent to the Eng. idiom "one and all." It is used in the Sept., e.g., in 1 Sam. 5:9: "God smote the people of Gath from the least to the greatest," ("both small and great"). So 1 Sam. 30:19; 2 Chron. 34:30, etc. See GREAT.

2. *meizōn* (μείζων, 3187), the comparative of No. 1, is sometimes translated "greatest"; besides the two cases given under GREATER, No. 1, where the RV corrects the KJV, "greatest" to "greater" (Matt. 13:32 and Luke 22:26), the RV itself has "greatest" for this comparative in the following, and relegates "greater" to the margin, Matt. 18:1, 4; 23:11; Mark 9:34; Luke 9:46; 22:24. See GREATER, MORE.

GREATLY

1. *lian* (λίαν, 3029), "very, exceedingly," is rendered "greatly" in Matt. 27:14, of wonder; 2 Tim. 4:15, of opposition; 2 John 4 and 3 John 3, of joy. See EXCEEDING, SORE, VERY.

2. *polus* (πολύς, 4183) is used in the neuter singular (*polu*) or the plural (*polla*), as an adverb; in the sing., e.g., Mark 12:27; in the plural, e.g., Mark 1:45, "much"; 5:23, "greatly" (RV, "much"); v. 38, KJV and RV, "greatly"; 1 Cor. 16:12 (RV, "much"). See LONG, MUCH.

Note: In Acts 28:6, KJV, *polu* is rendered "a great while" (RV, "long").

3. *megalōs* (μεγάλως, 3171), from *megas* (GREAT, No. 1), is used of rejoicing, Phil. 4:10.¶

4. *chara* (χαρά, 5479), "joy," is used in the dative case adverbially with the verb *chairō*, "to rejoice," in John 3:29, "rejoiceth greatly," lit., "rejoiceth with joy."

Notes: (1) For *sphodra*, RV, "exceedingly," in Matt. 27:54 and Acts 6:7, see EXCEED, B, No. 2. (2) In the following the RV omits "greatly," as the verbs are adequately translated without, Phil. 1:8; 1 Thess. 3:6; 2 Tim. 1:4. In the following the RV adds "greatly" to express the fuller force of the verb, Luke 1:29; Acts 16:34; 1 Pet. 1:8. (3) In 1 Pet. 1:6, "ye greatly rejoice," the adverb is not separately expressed, but is incorporated in the rendering of the verb *agalliaō*, "to rejoice much, to exult."

GREATNESS

1. *megethos* (μέγεθος, 3174), akin to *megas* (see GREAT, No. 1), is said of the power of God, in Eph. 1:19.¶

2. *huperbolē* (ὑπερβολή, 5236) denotes "ex-

ceeding greatness," 2 Cor. 4:7; 12:7. see EXCEL, B, No. 1.

For **GREEDILY** see **RUN,** No. 9

For **GREEDINESS** see **COVETOUSNESS,** B, No. 3

For **GREEDY** see **LUCRE**

GREEN

1. *chlōros* (χλωρός, 5515), akin to *chloē*, "tender foliage" (cf. the name "Chloe," 1 Cor. 1:11, and Eng., "chlorine"), denotes (*a*) "pale green," the color of young grass, Mark 6:39; Rev. 8:7; 9:4, "green thing"; hence, (*b*) "pale," Rev. 6:8, the color of the horse whose rider's name is Death. See PALE.¶

2. *hugros* (ύγρός, 5200) denotes "wet, moist" (the opposite of *xēros*, "dry"); said of wood, sappy, "green," Luke 23:31, i.e., if they thus by the fire of their wrath treated Christ, the guiltless, holy, the fruitful, what would be the fate of the perpetrators, who were like the dry wood, exposed to the fire of divine wrath.¶

GREET, GREETING

A. Verbs.

1. *aspazomai* (άσπάζομαι, 782) signifies "to greet, welcome," or "salute." In the KJV it is chiefly rendered by either of the verbs "to greet" or "to salute." "There is little doubt that the revisers have done wisely in giving 'salute' ... in the passages where KJV has 'greet.' For the cursory reader is sure to imagine a difference of Greek and of meaning when he finds, e.g., in Phil. 4:21, 'Salute every saint in Christ Jesus. The brethren which are with me greet you,' or in 3 John 14, 'Our friends salute thee. Greet the friends by name'" (Hastings, *Bible Dic.*). In Acts 25:13 the meaning virtually is "to pay his respects to."

In two passages the renderings vary otherwise; in Acts 20:1, of bidding farewell, KJV, "embraced them," RV, "took leave of them," or, as Ramsay translates it, "bade them farewell"; in Heb. 11:13, of welcoming promises, KJV, "embraced," RV, "greeted."

The verb is used as a technical term for conveying "greetings" at the close of a letter, often by an amanuensis, e.g., Rom. 16:22, the only instance of the use of the first person in this respect in the NT; see also 1 Cor. 16:19, 20; 2 Cor. 13:13; Phil. 4:22; Col. 4:10–15; 1 Thess. 5:26; 2 Tim. 4:21; Titus 3:15; Philem. 23; Heb. 13:24; 1 Pet. 5:13, 14; 2 John 13. This special use is largely illustrated in the papyri, one ex-

ample of this showing how keenly the absence of the greeting was felt. The papyri also illustrate the use of the addition "by name," when several persons are included in the greeting, as in 3 John 14 (Moulton and Milligan, *Vocab*). See EMBRACE, LEAVE, SALUTE.

2. *chairō* (χαίρω, 5463), "to rejoice," is thrice used as a formula of salutation in Acts 15:23, KJV, "send greeting," RV, "greeting"; so 23:26; Jas. 1:1. In 2 John 10, 11, the RV substitutes the phrase (to give) "greeting," for the KJV (to bid) "God speed." See FAREWELL, GLAD, HAIL, JOY, REJOICE.

B. Noun.

aspasmos (άσπασμός, 783), a salutation, is always so rendered in the RV; KJV, "greetings" in Matt. 23:7; Luke 11:43; 20:46; it is used (*a*) orally in those instances and in Mark 12:38; Luke 1:29, 41, 44; (*b*) in written salutations, 1 Cor. 16:21 (cf. A, No. 1, in v. 20); Col. 4:18; 2 Thess. 3:17.¶

GRIEF, GRIEVE

A. Noun.

lupē (λύπη, 3077) signifies "pain," of body or mind; it is used in the plural in 1 Pet. 2:19 only, RV, "griefs" (KJV, "grief"); here, however, it stands, by metonymy, for "things that cause sorrow, grievances"; hence Tyndale's rendering, "grief," for Wycliffe's "sorews"; everywhere else it is rendered "sorrow," except in Heb. 12:11, where it is translated "grievous" (lit., "of grief"). See HEAVINESS, SORROW.

B. Verbs.

1. *lupeō* (λύπέω, 3076), akin to A, denotes (*a*), in the active voice, "to cause pain, or grief, to distress, grieve," e.g., 2 Cor. 2:2 (twice, active and passive voices); v. 5 (twice), RV, "hath caused sorrow" (KJV, "have caused grief," and "grieved"); 7:8, "made (you) sorry"; Eph. 4:30, of grieving the Holy Spirit of God (as indwelling the believer); (*b*) in the passive voice, "to be grieved, to be made sorry, to be sorry, sorrowful," e.g., Matt. 14:9, RV, "(the king) was grieved" (KJV, "was sorry"); Mark 10:22, RV, "(went away) sorrowful" (KJV, "grieved"); John 21:17, "(Peter) was grieved"; Rom. 14:15, "(if ... thy brother) is grieved"; 2 Cor. 2:4, "(not that) ye should be made sorry," RV, KJV, "ye should be grieved." See HEAVINESS, SORROW, SORROWFUL, SORRY.

2. *sunlupeō* (συνλυπέω, 4818), or *sullupeō*, is used in the passive voice in Mark 3:5, "to be grieved" or afflicted together with a person, said of Christ's "grief" at the hardness of heart of those who criticized His healing on the Sabbath day; it here seems to suggest the sympathetic nature of His grief because of their self-injury.

Some suggest that the *sun* indicates the mingling of "grief" with His anger.¶

3. *stenazō* (στενάζω, 4727), "to groan" (of an inward, unexpressed feeling of sorrow), is translated "with grief" in Heb. 13:17 (marg. "groaning"). It is rendered "sighed" in Mark 7:34; "groan," in Rom. 8:23; 2 Cor. 5:2, 4; "murmur," in Jas. 5:9, RV (KJV, "grudge"). See GROAN, MURMUR, SIGH.¶

Notes: (1) *Diaponeō*, "to work out with labor," in the passive voice, "to be sore troubled," is rendered "being grieved" in Acts 4:2 and 16:18, KJV (RV, "sore troubled"). See TROUBLE.¶ In some mss., Mark 14:4. (2) *Prosochthizō*, "to be angry with," is rendered "was grieved" in Heb. 3:10, 17, KJV (RV, "was displeased). See DISPLEASE.¶

GRIEVOUS, GRIEVOUSLY

A. Adjectives.

1. *barus* (βαρύς, 926) denotes "heavy, burdensome"; it is always used metaphorically in the NT, and is translated "heavy" in Matt. 23:4, of Pharisaical ordinances; in the comparative degree "weightier," 23:23, of details of the law of God; "grievous," metaphorically of wolves, in Acts 20:29; of charges, 25:7; negatively of God's commandments, 1 John 5:3 (causing a burden on him who fulfills them); in 2 Cor. 10:10, "weighty," of Paul's letters. See HEAVY, WEIGHTY.¶

2. *ponēros* (πονηρός, 4190), "painful, bad," is translated "grievous" in Rev. 16:2, of a sore inflicted retributively. See BAD.

3. *dusbastaktos* (δυσβάστακτος, 1419), "hard to be borne" (from *dus*, an inseparable prefix, like Eng. "mis-," and "un-," indicating "difficulty, injuriousness, opposition," etc., and *bastazō*, "to bear"), is used in Luke 11:46 and, in some mss., in Matt. 23:4, "grievous to be borne"; in the latter the RV marg. has "many ancient authorities omit."¶

4. *chalepos* (χαλεπός, 5467), "hard," signifies (*a*) "hard to deal with," Matt. 8:28 (see FIERCE); (*b*) "hard to bear, grievous," 2 Tim. 3:1, RV, "grievous" (KJV, "perilous"), said of a characteristic of the last days of this age. See FIERCE.¶

Notes: (1) For the noun *lupē*, "grievous," in Heb. 12:11, see GRIEF. (2) In Phil. 3:1, the adjective *oknēros*, "shrinking," or "causing shrinking," hence, "tedious" (akin to *okneō*, "to shrink"), is rendered "irksome" in the RV (KJV, "grievous"); the apostle intimates that, not finding his message tedious, he has no hesitation in giving it. In Matt. 25:26 and Rom. 12:11, "slothful."¶

B. Adverbs.

1. *deinōs* (δεινῶς, 1171), akin to *deos*, "fear," signifies (*a*) "terribly," Matt. 8:6, "grievously (tormented)"; (*b*) "vehemently," Luke 11:53. See VEHEMENTLY.¶

2. *kakōs* (κακῶς, 2560), "badly, ill," is translated "grievously (vexed)," in Matt. 15:22. See AMISS, EVIL, MISERABLY, SORE.

Notes: (1) In Mark 9:20 and Luke 9:42, the RV renders the verb *susparassō* "tare (him) grievously," the adverb bringing out the intensive force of the prefix *su-* (i.e., *sun*); the meaning may be "threw violently to the ground." (2) In Matt. 17:15, the idiomatic phrase, consisting of No. 2 (above) with *echō*, "to have," (lit., "hath badly"), is rendered "suffereth grievously," RV (KJV, "is ... sore vexed").

GRIND

1. *alēthō* (ἀλήθω, 229) signifies "to grind at the mill," Matt. 24:41; Luke 17:35.¶ The Sept. has both the earlier form *aleō*, Isa. 47:2,¶, and the later one *alēthō*, used in the *Koinē* period, Num. 11:8; Judg. 16:21; Eccl. 12:3, 4.¶

2. *trizō* (τρίζω, 5149), primarily of animal sounds, "to chirp, cry," etc., is used of grinding the teeth, Mark 9:18, RV, "grindeth" (KJV, "gnasheth with"). See GNASH.¶

Note: In Matt. 21:44 and Luke 20:18, *likmaō*, "to winnow," as of grain, by throwing it up against the wind, to scatter the chaff and straw, hence has the meaning "to scatter," as chaff or dust, and is translated "will scatter ... as dust," RV (KJV, "will grind ... to powder"). In the Sept. it is used of being scattered by the wind or of sifting (cf. Amos 9:9). The use of the verb in the papyri writings suggests the meaning, "to ruin, destroy" (Deissmann).¶

GROAN, GROANING

A. Verbs.

1. *embrimaomai* (ἐμβριμάομαι, 1690), from *en*, "in," and *brimē*, "strength," is rendered "groaned" in John 11:33 (preferable to the RV marg., "He had indignation"); so in v. 38. The Lord was deeply moved doubtless with the combination of circumstances, present and in the immediate future. Indignation does not here seem to express His feelings. See CHARGE.

2. *stenazō* (στενάζω, 4727): see GRIEVE, B, No. 3.

3. *sustenazō* (συστενάζω, 4959), "to groan together" (*sun*, "with," and No. 2) is used of the Creation in Rom. 8:22. In v. 23, No. 2 is used.¶.

B. Noun.

stenagmos (στεναγμός, 4726), akin to A, No. 2, is used in Acts 7:34, in a quotation from

Exod. 3:7, but not from the Sept., which there has *kraugē*, "a cry"; the word is used, however, in Exod. 2:24; in Rom. 8:26, in the plural, of the intercessory groanings of the Holy Spirit.¶

GROSS (to wax)

pachunō (παχύνω, 3975), from *pachus*, "thick," signifies "to thicken, fatten"; in the passive voice, "to grow fat"; metaphorically said of the heart, to wax gross or dull, Matt. 13:15; Acts 28:27.¶

GROUND, GROUNDED

A. Nouns.

1. *gē* (γῆ, 1093), "the earth, land," etc., often denotes "the ground," e.g., Matt. 10:29; Mark 8:6. See EARTH.

2. *edaphos* (ἔδαφος, 1475), "a bottom, base," is used of the "ground" in Acts 22:7, suggestive of that which is level and hard.¶ Cf. B, No. 1, below.

3. *chōra* (χώρα, 5561), "land, country," is used of property, "ground," in Luke 12:16, "the ground (of a certain rich man)." See COUNTRY.

4. *chōrion* (χωρίον, 5564), a diminutive of No. 3, "a piece of land, a place, estate," is translated "parcel of ground" in John 4:5. See FIELD.

5. *hedraiōma* (ἑδραίωμα, 1477), "a support, bulwark, stay" (from *hedraios*, "steadfast, firm"; from *hedra*, "a seat"), is translated "ground" in 1 Tim. 3:15 (said of a local church); the RV marg., "stay" is preferable.¶
Notes: (1) In Mark 4:16 the RV rightly has "rocky places" (*petrōdēs*) for KJV, "stony ground." (2) In Acts 27:29, for the KJV, "rocks" the RV has "rocky ground," lit., "rough places," i.e., a rocky shore. (3) In Luke 14:18, *agros*, "a field," is translated "a piece of ground," KJV, RV, "a field." See FIELD.

B. Verbs.

1. *edaphizō* (ἐδαφίζω, 1474), akin to A, No. 2: see DASH.

2. *themelioō* (θεμελιόω, 2311) signifies "to lay the foundation of, to found" (akin to *themelios*, "a foundation"; from *tithēmi*, "to put"), and is rendered "grounded" in Eph. 3:17, said of the condition of believers with reference to the love of Christ; in Col. 1:23, of their continuance in the faith. See FOUND.

C. Adverb.

chamai (χαμαί, 5476) (akin to Lat., *humi*, "on the ground," and *homo*, "man"), signifies "on the ground," John 9:6, of the act of Christ in spitting on the "ground" before anointing the eyes of a blind man; in 18:6, "to the ground," of the fall of the rabble that had come to seize Christ in Gethsemane. ¶

GROW

1. *auxanō* (αὐξάνω, 837), "to grow or increase," of the growth of that which lives, naturally or spiritually, is used (*a*) transitively, signifying to make to increase, said of giving the increase, 1 Cor. 3:6, 7; 2 Cor. 9:10, the effect of the work of God, according to the analogy of His operations in nature; "to grow, become greater," e.g. of plants and fruit, Matt. 6:28; used in the passive voice in 13:32 and Mark 4:8, "increase"; in the active in Luke 12:27; 13:19; of the body, Luke 1:80; 2:40; of Christ, John 3:30, "increase"; of the work of the gospel of God, Acts 6:7, "increased"; 12:24; 19:20; of people, Acts 7:17; of faith, 2 Cor. 10:15 (passive voice), RV, "groweth" (KJV, "is increased"); of believers individually, Eph. 4:15; Col. 1:6, RV, 10 (passive voice), "increasing"; 1 Pet. 2:2; 2 Pet. 3:18; of the church, Col. 2:19; of churches, Eph. 2:21. See INCREASE.¶
Note: Cf. *auxēsis*, "increase," Eph. 4:16; Col. 2:19.¶

2. *ginomai* (γίνομαι, 1096), "to become or come to be," is translated "grow" in Acts 5:24, of the development of apostolic work. See ARISE, No. 5.
Notes: (1) In Matt. 21:19, for KJV, "let (no fruit) grow," the RV, more strictly, has "let there be (no fruit)." (2) In Heb. 11:24, *ginomai* is used with *megas*, "great," of Moses, lit., "had become great," RV, "had grown up" (KJV, "had come to years").

3. *erchomai* (ἔρχομαι, 2064), "to come or go," is translated "grew (worse)," in Mark 5:26. See COME, No. 1.

4. *anabainō* (ἀναβαίνω, 305), "to ascend," when used of plants, signifies "to grow up," Mark 4:7, 32; in 4:8, of seed, "growing up," RV, KJV, "that sprang up," (for the next word, "increasing," see No. 1). See ARISE, No. 6.

5. *mēkunomai* (μηκύνομαι, 3373), "to grow long, lengthen, extend" (from *mēkos*, "length"), is used of the "growth" of plants, in Mark 4:27.¶
Note: Three different words are used in Mark 4 of the "growth" of plants or seed, Nos. 1, 4, 5.

6. *huperauxanō* (ὑπεραυξάνω, 5232), "to increase beyond measure" (*huper*, "over," and No. 1), is used of faith and love, in their living and practical effects, 2 Thess. 1:3. Lightfoot compares this verb and the next in the verse (*pleonazō*, "to abound") in that the former implies "an internal, organic growth, as of a tree," the latter "a diffusive or expansive character, as of a flood irrigating the land."¶

7. *sunauxanō* (συναυξάνω, 4885), "to grow together," is in Matt. 13:30.¶

8. *phuō* (φύω, 5453), "to produce," is rendered "grew" (passive voice) in Luke 8:6. See SPRING.

9. *sumphuō* (συμφύω, 4855) is used in Luke 8:7, RV, "grow with."¶

For **GRUDGE** (Jas. 5:9), **GRIEVE**, B, No. 3, **GRUDGING** (1 Pet. 4:9) see **MURMUR**

GRUDGINGLY

Note: In 2 Cor. 9:7, the phrase *ek lupēs*, lit., "out of sorrow" (*ek*, "out of," or "from," *lupē*, "sorrow, grief"), is translated "grudgingly" (RV marg., "of sorrow"); the "grudging" regret is set in contrast to cheerfulness enjoined in giving, as is the reluctance expressed in "of necessity."

GUARD (Noun and Verb)

A. Nouns.

1. *koustōdia* (κουστωδία, 2892); "a guard," (Latin, *custodia;* Eng., "custodian"), is used of the soldiers who "guarded" Christ's sepulchre, Matt. 27:65, 66 and 28:11, and is translated "(ye have) a guard," "the guard (being with them)," and "(some of) the guard," RV, KJV, " . . . a watch," "(setting a) watch," and " . . . the watch." This was the Temple guard, stationed under a Roman officer in the tower of Antonia, and having charge of the high priestly vestments. Hence the significance of Pilate's words "Ye have a guard." See WATCH.¶

2. *spekoulatōr* (σπεκουλάτωρ, 4688), Latin, *speculator*, primarily denotes "a lookout officer," or "scout," but, under the emperors, "a member of the bodyguard"; these were employed as messengers, watchers and executioners; ten such officers were attached to each legion; such a guard was employed by Herod Antipas, Mark 6:27, RV, "a soldier of his guard" (KJV, "executioner").¶

3. *phulax* (φύλαξ, 5441), "a guard, keeper" (akin to *phulassō*, "to guard, keep"), is translated "keepers" in Acts 5:23; in 12:6, 19, RV, "guards" (KJV, "keepers"). See KEEPER.¶

Notes: (1) In Acts 28:16, some mss. have the sentence containing the word *stratopedarchēs*, "a captain of the guard." See CAPTAIN. (2) In Phil. 1:13, the noun *praitōrion*, the "praetorian guard," is so rendered in the RV (KJV, "palace").

B. Verbs.

1. *phulassō* (φυλάσσω, 5442), "to guard, watch, keep" (akin to A, No. 3), is rendered by the verb "to guard" in the RV (KJV, "to keep") of Luke 11:21; John 17:12; Acts 12:4; 28:16;

2 Thess. 3:3; 1 Tim. 6:20; 2 Tim. 1:12, 14; 1 John 5:21; Jude 24. In Luke 8:29, "was kept under guard," RV (KJV, "kept"). See BEWARE, KEEP, OBSERVE, PRESERVE, SAVE, WARE OF, WATCH.

2. *diaphulassō* (διαφυλάσσω, 1314), a strengthened form of No. 1 (*dia*, "through," used intensively), "to guard carefully, defend," is found in Luke 4:10 (from the Sept. of Ps. 91:11), RV, "to guard" (KJV, "to keep").¶

3. *phroureō* (φρουρέω, 5432), a military term, "to keep by guarding, to keep under guard," as with a garrison (*phrouros*, "a guard, or garrison"), is used, (*a*) of blocking up every way of escape, as in a siege; (*b*) of providing protection against the enemy, as a garrison does; see 2 Cor. 11:32, "guarded." KJV, "kept," i.e., kept the city, "with a garrison." It is used of the security of the Christian until the end, 1 Pet. 1:5, RV, "are guarded," and of the sense of that security that is his when he puts all his matters into the hand of God, Phil. 4:7, RV, "shall guard." In these passages the idea is not merely that of protection, but of inward garrisoning as by the Holy Spirit; in Gal. 3:23 ("were kept in ward"), it means rather a benevolent custody and watchful guardianship in view of worldwide idolatry (cf. Isa. 5:2). See KEEP.¶

GUARDIAN

epitropos (ἐπίτροπος, 2012), lit., "one to whose care something is committed" (*epi*, "upon," *trepō*, "to turn" or "direct"), is rendered "guardians" in Gal. 4:2, RV, KJV, "tutors" (in Matt. 20:8 and Luke 8:3, "steward").¶

"The corresponding verb, *epitrepō*, is translated "permit, give leave, suffer"; see 1 Cor. 14:34; 16:7; 1 Tim. 2:12, e.g., . . . An allied noun, *epitropē*, is translated "commission" in Acts 26:12 (¶) and refers to delegated authority over persons. This usage of cognate words suggests that the *epitropos* was a superior servant responsible for the persons composing the household, whether children or slaves."*

GUEST

anakeimai (ἀνάκειμαι, 345), "to recline at table," frequently rendered "to sit at meat," is used in its present participial form (lit., "reclining ones") as a noun denoting "guests," in Matt. 22:10, 11. See LEAN, LIE, SIT.

Note: For *kataluō*, "to unloose," rendered "to be a guest" in Luke 19:7, KJV, (RV, "to lodge"), see LODGE.

---

* From *Notes on Galatians,* by Hogg and Vine, p. 180.

GUEST–CHAMBER

kataluma (κατάλυμα, 2646), akin to *kataluō* (see *Note* above), signifies (*a*) "an inn, lodging-place," Luke 2:7; (*b*) "a guest-room," Mark 14:14; Luke 22:11. The word lit. signifies "a loosening down" (*kata*, "down," *luō*, "to loose"), used of the place where travelers and their beasts untied their packages, girdles and sandals. "In the East, no figure is more invested with chivalry than the guest. In his own right he cannot cross the threshold, but when once he is invited in, all do him honor and unite in rendering service; cf. Gen. 18:19; Judg. 19:9, 15." These two passages in the NT "concern a room in a private house, which the owner readily placed at the disposal of Jesus and His disciples for the celebration of the Passover ... At the festivals of Passover, Pentecost and Tabernacles the people were commanded to repair to Jerusalem; and it was a boast of the Rabbis that, notwithstanding the enormous crowds, no man could truthfully say to his fellow, 'I have not found a fire where to roast my paschal lamb in Jerusalem,' or 'I have not found a bed in Jerusalem to lie in,' or 'My lodging is too strait in Jerusalem'" (*Hastings, Bib. Dic.*, GUEST-CHAMBER and INN). See INN.¶

GUIDE (Noun and Verb)

A. Noun.

hodēgos (ὁδηγός, 3595), "a leader on the way" (*hodos*, "a way," *hēgeomai*, "to lead"), "a guide," is used (*a*) literally, in Acts 1:16; (*b*) figuratively, Matt. 15:14, RV, "guides" (KJV, "leaders"); Matt. 23:16, 24, "guides"; Rom. 2:19, "a guide." Cf. B, No. 1.¶

B. Verbs.

1. *hodēgeō* (ὁδηγέω, 3594), "to lead the way" (akin to A), is used (*a*) literally, RV, "guide" (KJV, "lead"), of "guiding" the blind, in Matt. 15:14; Luke 6:39; of "guiding" unto fountains of waters of life, Rev. 7:17; (*b*) figuratively, in John 16:13, of "guidance" into the truth by the Holy Spirit; in Acts 8:31, of the interpretation of Scripture. See LEAD.¶

2. *kateuthunō* (κατευθύνω, 2720), "to make straight," is said of "guiding" the feet into the way of peace, Luke 1:79. See DIRECT.

Notes: (1) In 1 Tim. 5:14, the RV rightly translates the verb *oikodespoteō* by "rule the household" (KJV, "guide the house"), the meaning being that of the management and direction of household affairs. See RULE.¶ (2) *Hēgeomai*, "to lead," in Heb. 13:7, 24, is rendered "that had the rule over" and "that have, etc.," more lit., "them that were (are) your leaders," or "guides."

GUILE

dolos (δόλος, 1388), "a bait, snare, deceit," is rendered "guile" in John 1:47, negatively of Nathanael; Acts 13:10, RV, KJV, "subtlety" (of Bar-Jesus); 2 Cor. 12:16, in a charge made against Paul by his detractors, of catching the Corinthian converts by "guile" (the apostle is apparently quoting the language of his critics); 1 Thess. 2:3, negatively, of the teaching of the apostle and his fellow missionaries; 1 Pet. 2:1, of that from which Christians are to be free; 2:22, of the guileless speech of Christ (cf. GUILE-LESS, No. 2); 3:10, of the necessity that the speech of Christians should be guileless. See also Matt. 26:4; Mark 7:22; 14:1. See CRAFT, DECEIT, SUBTLETY.¶

Note: In Rev. 14:5, some mss. have *dolos;* the most authentic have *pseudos*, a "lie."

GUILELESS (WITHOUT GUILE)

1. *adolos* (ἄδολος, 97), "without guile" (*a*, negative, and *dolos*, see GUILE), "pure, unadulterated," is used metaphorically of the teaching of the Word of God, 1 Pet. 2:2, RV. It is used in the papyri writings of seed, corn, wheat, oil, wine, etc.¶

2. *akakos* (ἄκακος, 172), lit., "without evil" (*a*, negative, *kakos*, "evil"), signifies "simple, guileless," Rom. 16:18, "simple," of believers (perhaps = unsuspecting, or, rather, innocent, free from admixture of evil); in Heb. 7:26, RV, "guileless" (KJV, "harmless"), the character of Christ (more lit., "free from evil").¶ Cf. Sept., Job 2:3; 8:20; Prov. 1:4; 14:15. See HARMLESS.

GUILTLESS

anaitios (ἀναίτιος, 338), "innocent, guiltless" (*a*, negative, *n*, euphonic, *aitia*, "a charge of crime"), is translated "blameless" in Matt. 12:5, KJV, "guiltless" in v. 7; RV, "guiltless" in each place. See BLAMELESS.¶

GUILTY (Adjective)

enochos (ἔνοχος, 1777), lit., "held in, bound by, liable to a charge or action at law": see DANGER.

Notes: (1) In Rom. 3:19, KJV, *hupodikos*, "brought to trial," lit., 'under judgment' (*hupo*, "under," *dikē*, "justice"), is incorrectly rendered "guilty"; RV, "under the judgement of." See JUDGMENT. (2) In Matt. 23:18, *opheilō*, "to owe, to be indebted, to fail in duty, be a delinquent," is misrendered "guilty" in the KJV; RV, "a debtor."

GULF

chasma (χάσμα, 5490), akin to *chaskō*, "to yawn" (Eng., "chasm"), is found in Luke 16:26.¶ In the Sept., 2 Sam. 18:17, two words are used with reference to Absalom's body, *bothunos* which signifies "a great pit," and *chasma*, "a yawning abyss, or precipice," with a deep pit at the bottom, into which the body was cast.¶

GUSH OUT

ekchunō, or *ekchunnō* (ἐκχύνω, 1632), a Hellenistic form of *ekcheō*, "to pour forth," is translated "gushed out" in Acts 1:18, of the bowels of Judas Iscariot. See POUR, RUN, SHED, SPILL.

H

For **HA** (Mark 15:29, RV) see **AH**

HABITATION

1. *oikētērion* (οἰκητήριον, 3613), "a habitation" (from *oikētēr*, "an inhabitant," and *oikos*, "a dwelling"), is used in Jude 6, of the heavenly region appointed by God as the dwelling place of angels; in 2 Cor. 5:2, RV, "habitation," KJV, "house," figuratively of the spiritual bodies of believers when raised or changed at the return of the Lord. See HOUSE.¶

2. *katoikētērion* (κατοικητήριον, 2732), (*kata*, "down," used intensively, and No. 1), implying more permanency than No. 1, is used in Eph. 2:22 of the church as the dwelling place of the Holy Spirit; in Rev. 18:2 of Babylon, figuratively, as the dwelling place of demons.¶

3. *katoikia* (κατοικία, 2733), "a settlement, colony, dwelling" (*kata*, and *oikos*, see above), is used in Acts 17:26, of the localities divinely appointed as the dwelling places of the nations.¶

4. *epaulis* (ἔπαυλις, 1886), "a farm, a dwelling" (*epi*, "upon," *aulis*, "a place in which to pass the night, a country house, cottage or cabin, a fold"), is used in Acts 1:20 of the habitation of Judas.¶

5. *skēnē* (σκηνή, 4633), akin to *skēnoō*, "to dwell in a tent or tabernacle," is rendered "habitations" in Luke 16:9, KJV (RV, "tabernacles") of the eternal dwelling places of the redeemed. See TABERNACLE.

6. *skēnōma* (σκήνωμα, 4638), "a booth," or "tent pitched" (akin to No. 5), is used of the Temple as God's dwelling, as that which David desired to build, Acts 7:46 (RV, "habitation," KJV, "tabernacle"); metaphorically of the body as a temporary tabernacle, 2 Pet. 1:13, 14.¶ See TABERNACLE.

HADES

hadēs (ᾅδης, 86), "the region of departed spirits of the lost" (but including the blessed dead in periods preceding the ascension of Christ). It has been thought by some that the word etymologically meant "the unseen" (from *a*, negative, and *eidō*, "to see"), but this derivation is questionable; a more probable derivation is from *hadō*, signifying "all-receiving." It corresponds to "Sheol" in the OT. In the KJV of the OT and NT; it has been unhappily rendered "hell," e.g., Ps. 16:10; or "the grave," e.g., Gen. 37:35; or "the pit," Num. 16:30, 33; in the NT the revisers have always used the rendering "hades"; in the OT, they have not been uniform in the translation, e.g. in Isa. 14:15 "hell" (marg., "Sheol"); usually they have "Sheol" in the text and "the grave" in the margin. It never denotes the grave, nor is it the permanent region of the lost; in point of time it is, for such, intermediate between decease and the doom of Gehenna. For the condition, see Luke 16:23–31.

The word is used four times in the Gospels, and always by the Lord, Matt. 11:23; 16:18; Luke 10:15; 16:23; it is used with reference to the soul of Christ, Acts 2:27, 31; Christ declares that He has the keys of it, Rev. 1:18; in Rev. 6:8 it is personified, with the signification of the temporary destiny of the doomed; it is to give up those who are therein, 20:13, and is to be cast into the lake of fire, v. 14.¶

Note: In 1 Cor. 15:55 the most authentic mss. have *thanatos*, "death," in the 2nd part of the verse, instead of "hades," which the KJV wrongly renders "grave" ("hell," in the marg.).

HAIL (Noun)

chalaza (χάλαζα, 5464), akin to *chalaō*, "to let loose, let fall," is always used as an instrument of divine judgment, and is found in the NT in Rev. 8:7; 11:19; 16:21.¶

HAIL (Verb)

chairō (χαίρω, 5463), "to rejoice," is used in the imperative mood, (*a*) as a salutation, only in the Gospels; in this respect it is rendered simply "hail," in mockery of Christ, Matt. 26:49; 27:29; Mark 15:18; John 19:3; (*b*) as a greeting, by the angel Gabriel to Mary, Luke 1:28, and, in the plural, by the Lord to the disciples after His resurrection, Matt 28:9.

HAIR

A. Nouns.
1. *thrix* (θρίξ, 2359) denotes the "hair," whether of beast, as of the camel's "hair" which formed the raiment of John the Baptist, Matt. 3:4; Mark 1:6; or of man. Regarding the latter (*a*) it is used to signify the minutest detail, as that which illustrates the exceeding care and protection bestowed by God upon His children, Matt. 10:30; Luke 12:7; 21:18; Acts 27:34; (*b*) as the Jews swore by the "hair," the Lord used the natural inability to make one "hair" white or black, as one of the reasons for abstinence from oaths, Matt. 5:36; (*c*) while long "hair" is a glory to a woman (see B), and to wear it loose or dishevelled is a dishonor, yet the woman who wiped Christ's feet with her "hair" (in place of the towel which Simon the Pharisee omitted to provide), despised the shame in her penitent devotion to the Lord (slaves were accustomed to wipe their masters' feet), Luke 7:38, 44 (RV, "hair"); see also John 11:2; 12:3; (*d*) the dazzling whiteness of the head and "hair" of the Son of Man in the vision of Rev. 1 (v. 14) is suggestive of the holiness and wisdom of "the Ancient of Days"; (*e*) the long "hair" of the spirit-beings described as locusts in Rev. 9:8 is perhaps indicative of their subjection to their satanic master (cf. 1 Cor. 11:10, RV); (*f*) Christian women are exhorted to refrain from adorning their "hair" for outward show, 1 Pet. 3:3.¶

Note: Goat's hair was used in tentmaking, as, e.g., in the case of Paul's occupation, Acts 18:3; the haircloth of Cilicia, his native province, was noted, being known in commerce as *cilicium*.

2. *komē* (κόμη, 2864) is used only of "human hair," but not in the NT of the ornamental. The word is found in 1 Cor. 11:15, where the context shows that the "covering" provided in the long "hair" of the woman is as a veil, a sign of subjection to authority, as indicated in the headships spoken of in vv. 1–10.¶

B. Verb.
komaō (κομάω, 2863) signifies "to let the hair grow long, to wear long hair," a glory to a

woman, a dishonor to a man (as taught by nature), 1 Cor. 11:14, 15.¶

C. Adjective.
trichinos (τρίχινος, 5155), akin to A, No. 1, signifies "hairy, made of hair," Rev. 6:12, lit., "hairy sackcloth." Cf. SACKCLOTH.¶

HALE (Verb)

1. *surō* (σύρω, 4951) "to drag, haul," is rendered "haling" in Acts 8:3, of taking to trial or punishment. See DRAG.

2. *katasurō* (κατασύρω, 2694), an intensive form of No. 1, lit., "to pull down" (*kata*), hence, "to drag away," is used in Luke 12:58, of haling a person before a judge.¶

HALF

hēmisus (ἥμισυς, 2255), an adjective, is used (*a*) as such in the neuter plural, in Luke 19:8, lit., "the halves (of my goods)"; (*b*) as a noun, in the neuter sing., "the half," Mark 6:23; "half (a time)," Rev. 12:14; "a half," 11:9, 11, RV.¶

For HALF-SHEKEL see SHEKEL

HALL

1. *aulē* (αὐλή, 833), "a court," most frequently the place where a governor dispensed justice, is rendered "hall" in Mark 15:16 and Luke 22:55, KJV (RV, "court"). See COURT, FOLD, PALACE.

2. *praitōrion* (πραιτώριον, 4232) is translated "common hall" in Matt. 27:27, KJV (RV, "palace"); "Praetorium" in Mark 15:16; "hall of judgment" or "judgment hall" in John 18:28, 33; 19:9; Acts 23:35 (RV, "palace," in each place); "praetorian guard," Phil. 1:13 (KJV, "palace"). See PALACE.¶

HALLELUJAH

hallēlouia (Ἀλληλουιά, 239) signifies "Praise ye Jah." It occurs as a short doxology in the Psalms, usually at the beginning, e.g., 111, 112, or the end, e.g., 104, 105, or both, e.g., 106, 135 (where it is also used in v. 3), 146–150. In the NT it is found in Rev. 19:1, 3, 4, 6, as the keynote in the song of the great multitude in heaven. "Alleluia," without the initial "H," is a misspelling.¶

HALLOW

hagiazō (ἁγιάζω, 37), "to make holy" (from *hagios*, "holy"), signifies to set apart for God, to sanctify, to make a person or thing the opposite of *koinos*, "common"; it is translated "Hallowed," with reference to the name of God the Father in the Lord's Prayer, Matt. 6:9; Luke 11:2. See SANCTIFY.

HALT

chōlos (χωλός, 5560), "lame," is translated "halt" in Matt. 18:8; Mark 9:45; John 5:3; in Acts 14:8, "cripple"; in Luke 14:21, KJV, "halt," RV, "lame"; elsewhere, "lame," Matt. 11:5; 15:30, 31; 21:14: Luke 7:22; 14:13; Acts 3:2; 8:7; Heb. 12:13; some mss. have it in Acts 3:11 (KJV, "the lame man"), RV, "he," translating *autou*, as in the best texts.¶

Note: For *kullos*, Matt. 18:8, RV, "halt, see MAIMED, No. 2.

HAND

cheir (χείρ, 5495), "the hand" (cf. Eng., "chiropody"), is used, besides its ordinary significance, (*a*) in the idiomatic phrases, "by the hand of," "at the hand of," etc., to signify "by the agency of," Acts 5:12; 7:35; 17:25; 14:3; Gal. 3:19 (cf. Lev. 26:46); Rev. 19:2; (*b*) metaphorically, for the power of God, e.g., Luke 1:66; 23:46; John 10:28, 29; Acts 11:21; 13:11; Heb. 1:10; 2:7; 10:31; (*c*) by metonymy, for power, e.g., Matt. 17:22; Luke 24:7; John 10:39; Acts 12:11.

AT HAND

A. Adverb.

engus (ἐγγύς, 1451), "near, nigh," frequently rendered "at hand," is used (*a*) of place, e.g., of the Lord's sepulchre, John 19:42, "nigh at hand"; (*b*) of time, e.g., Matt. 26:18; Luke 21:30, 31, RV, "nigh," KJV, "nigh at hand"; in Phil. 4:5, "the Lord is at hand," it is possible to regard the meaning as that either of (*a*) or (*b*); the following reasons may point to (*b*): (1) the subject of the preceding context has been the return of Christ, 3:20, 21; (2) the phrase is a translation of the Aramaic "Maranatha," 1 Cor. 16:22, a Christian watchword, and the use of the title "the Lord" is appropriate; (3) the similar use of the adverb in Rev. 1:3 and 22:10; (4) the similar use of the corresponding verb (see B) in Rom. 13:12; Heb. 10:25, "drawing nigh," RV; Jas. 5:8; cf. 1 Pet. 4:7. See NEAR, NIGH, READY.

B. Verb.

engizō (ἐγγίζω, 1448): See APPROACH, A.
Notes: (1) In 2 Thess. 2:2, KJV, the verb *enistēmi*, "to be present" (*en*, "in," *histēmi*, "to cause to stand"), is wrongly translated "is at hand"; the RV correctly renders it, "is (now) present"; the apostle is counteracting the error of the supposition that "the Day of the Lord" (RV), a period of divine and retributive judgments upon the world, had already begun.
(2) In 2 Tim. 4:6, KJV, the verb *ephistēmi*, "to stand by, to come to or upon" (*epi*, "upon,"

histēmi, "to make to stand"), is rendered "is at hand," of the apostle's departure from this life; the RV "is come" represent the vivid force of the statement, expressing suddenness or imminence.

HAND (lead by the)

A. Adjective.

cheiragōgos (χειραγωγός, 5497), lit., "a hand-leader" (*cheir*, "the hand," *agō*, "to lead"), is used as a noun (plural) in Acts 13:11, "some to lead him by the hand."¶

B. Verb.

cheiragōgeō (χειραγωγέω, 5496), "to lead by the hand," is used in Acts 9:8; 22:11.¶

HANDED DOWN

patroparadotos (πατροπαράδοτος, 3970), an adjective, denoting "handed down from one's fathers," is used in 1 Pet. 1:18, RV, for KJV, "*received* by tradition from your fathers" (from *patēr*, "a father," and *paradidōmi*, "to hand down").¶

HAND (with one's own)

autocheir (αὐτόχειρ, 849), a noun (*autos*, "self," *cheir*, "the hand"), is used in the plural in Acts 27:19, "with their own hands."¶

HAND (take in)

epicheireō (ἐπιχειρέω, 2021), "to put the hand to" (*epi*, "to," *cheir*, "the hand"), is rendered "have taken in hand" in Luke 1:1. See TAKE.

For **LAY HANDS ON** (*krateō* in Matt. 18:28; 21:46; *piazō* in John 8:20), see **HOLD** and **APPREHEND**

HANDS (made by, not made with)

1. *cheiropoiētos* (χειροποίητος, 5499), "made by hand," of human handiwork (*cheir*, and *poieō*, "to make"), is said of the temple in Jerusalem, Mark 14:58; temples in general, Acts 7:48 (RV, "houses"); 17:24; negatively, of the heavenly and spiritual tabernacle, Heb. 9:11; of the holy place in the earthly tabernacle, v. 24; of circumcision, Eph. 2:11.¶ In the Sept., of idols, Lev. 26:1, 30; Isa. 2:18; 10:11; 16:12; 19:1; 21:9; 31:7; 46:6.¶

2. *acheiropoiētos* (ἀχειροποίητος, 886), "not made by hands" (*a*, negative, and No. 1), is said of an earthly temple, Mark 14:58; of the resurrection body of believers, metaphorically as a house, 2 Cor. 5:1; metaphorically, of spiritual circumcision, Col. 2:11.¶ This word is not found in the Sept.

HANDKERCHIEF

soudarion (σουδάριον, 4676) a Latin word, *sudarium* (from *sudor*, "sweat"), denotes (*a*) "a cloth for wiping the face," etc., Luke 19:20; Acts 19:12; (*b*) "a headcovering for the dead," John 11:44; 20:7. See NAPKIN.¶

HANDLE

1. *psēlaphaō* (ψηλαφάω, 5584), "to feel, touch, handle," is rendered by the latter verb in Luke 24:39, in the Lord's invitation to the disciples to accept the evidence of His resurrection in His being bodily in their midst; in 1 John 1:1, in the apostle's testimony (against the gnostic error that Christ had been merely a phantom) that he and his fellow apostles had handled Him. See FEEL.

2. *thinganō* (θιγγάνω, 2345) signifies (*a*) "to touch, to handle" (though "to handle" is rather stronger than the actual significance compared with No 1). In Col. 2:21 the RV renders it "touch," and the first verb (*haptō*, "to lay hold of") "handle," i.e.,"handle not, nor taste, nor touch"; "touch" is the appropriate rendering; in Heb. 12:20 it is said of a beast's touching Mount Sinai; (*b*) "to touch by way of injuring," Heb. 11:28. See TOUCH.¶ In the Sept., Exod. 19:12.¶

Note: The shortened form found in the passages mentioned is an aorist (or point) tense of the verb.

3. *doloō* (δολόω, 1389), "to corrupt," is used in 2 Cor. 4:2, "handling (the Word of God) deceitfully," in the sense of using guile (*dolos*); the meaning approximates to that of adulterating (cf. *kapēleuō*, in 2:17).¶

4. *atimazō* (ἀτιμάζω, 818), "to dishonor, insult," is rendered "handled shamefully" in Mark 12:4. Some mss. have the alternative verb *atimaō*. See DESPISE, DISHONOR.

5. *orthotomeō* (ὀρθοτομέω, 3718), "to cut straight," as in road-making (*orthos*, "straight," *temnō*, "to cut"), is used metaphorically in 2 Tim. 2:15, of "handling aright (the word of truth)," RV (KJV, "rightly dividing"). The stress is on *orthos;* the Word of God is to be "handled" strictly along the lines of its teaching. If the metaphor is taken from plowing, cutting a straight furrow, the word would express a careful cultivation, the Word of God viewed as ground designed to give the best results from its ministry and in the life. See DIVIDE.¶ In the Sept., in Prov. 3:6 and 11:5, the knowledge of God's wisdom and the just dealing of the upright are enjoined as producing a straight walk in the life.¶

For **HANDMAID** and **HANDMAIDEN** see under **BONDMAN**

For **HANDWRITING** see **BOND**

HANG

1. *kremannumi* (κρεμάννυμι, 2910) is used (*a*) transitively in Acts 5:30; 10:39; in the passive voice, in Matt. 18:6, of a millstone about a neck, and in Luke 23:39, of the malefactors; (*b*) intransitively, in the middle voice, in Matt. 22:40, of the dependence of "the Law and the prophets" (i.e., that which they enjoin) upon the one great principle of love to God and one's neighbor (as a door "hangs" on a hinge, or as articles "hang" on a nail); in Acts 28:4, of the serpent "hanging" from Paul's hand; in Gal. 3:13 the word is used in a quotation from the Sept. of Deut. 21:23.¶

2. *ekkremannumi* (ἐκκρεμάννυμι, 1582), "to hang from, or upon" (*ek*, and No. 1), is used in the middle voice (*ekkremamai*) metaphorically in Luke 19:48, RV, "(the people all) 'hung' upon (Him, listening)," KJV, "were very attentive."¶ In the Sept., Gen. 44:30.¶

3. *pariēmi* (παρίημι, 3935) signifies (*a*) "to disregard, leave alone, leave undone," Luke 11:42 (some mss. have *aphiēmi*, here); (*b*) "to relax, loosen," and, in the passive voice, "to be relaxed, exhausted," said of hands that "hang" down in weakness, Heb. 12:12.¶

4. *perikeimai* (περίκειμαι, 4029) signifies "to lie round" (*peri*, "around," *keimai*, "to lie"); then, "to be hanged round," said of "a great millstone" (lit., "a millstone turned by an ass"), Mark 9:42, RV, and marg., to be "hung" round the neck of him who causes one of Christ's "little ones" to stumble; in Luke 17:2, "a millstone." See BOUND (to be).

5. *apanchō* (ἀπάγχω, 519) signifies "to strangle"; in the middle voice, to "hang" oneself, Matt. 27:5.¶ In the Sept. it is said of Ahithophel (2 Sam. 17:23).¶

HAPLY (if, lest)

1. *ei ara* (εἰ ἄρα) denotes "if therefore," "if accordingly" (i.e., if in these circumstances), e.g., Mark 11:13, of Christ and the fig tree (not "if perchance," but marking a correspondence in point of fact).

2. *ei arage* (εἰ ἄραγε) denotes "if in consequence," e.g., Acts 17:27, "if haply" they might feel after God, in consequence of seeking Him.

3. *mē pote* (μή ποτε, 3379), lit., "lest ever," "lest haply," e.g., Luke 14:29, of laying a foundation, with the possibility of being unable to

finish the building; Acts 5:39, of the possibility of being found fighting against God; Heb. 3:12, RV, "lest haply," of the possibility of having an evil heart of unbelief. The RV usually has "lest haply" (KJV "lest at any time"), e.g., Matt. 4:6; 5:25; 13:15; Mark 4:12; Luke 4:11; 21:34; Heb. 2:1; in Matt. 25:9, the RV has "peradventure"; in 2 Tim. 2:25, KJV and RV, have "if peradventure"; in John 7:26 the RV has "Can it be that," for the word "Do" in the KJV.

4. *mē pōs* (μή πως, 3381) denotes "lest in any way," "by any means," e.g., 2 Cor. 9:4, KJV, "lest haply," RV, "lest by any means."

5. *mē pou* (μή που) denotes "lest somehow"; the RV has "lest haply" in Acts 27:29 (some mss. have No. 4, here).

HAPPEN

1. *sumbainō* (συμβαίνω, 4819), lit., "to go or come together" (*sun*, "with," *bainō*, "to go"), signifies "to happen together," of things or events, Mark 10:32; Luke 24:14; Acts 3:10; 1 Cor. 10:11; 1 Pet. 4:12; 2 Pet. 2:22; "befell" in Acts 20:19; in Acts 21:35, "so it was." See BEFALL.¶

Notes: (1) In Phil. 1:12, the phrase *ta kat'* (i.e., *kata*) *eme*, lit., "the things relating to me," is rendered "the things *which happened* unto me." (2) In Luke 24:35, the phrase "the things *that happened* in the way," RV (KJV, "what things were done in the way"), is, lit., "the things in the way."

HAPPY, HAPPIER

A. Adjective.

makarios (μακάριος, 3107), "blessed, happy," is rendered "happy" in the RV, in two places only, as in the KJV, Acts 26:2 and Rom. 14:22 (where "blessed" would have done); also the comparative "happier" in 1 Cor. 7:40. Elsewhere the RV uses "blessed" for KJV "happy," e.g., John 13:17; 1 Pet. 3:14; 4:14. See BLESSED.

B. Verb.

makarizō (μακαρίζω, 3106), "to call blessed," Luke 1:48, is rendered "we count ... happy" in Jas. 5:11. See BLESSED.¶

HARD, HARDEN, HARDENING, HARDNESS

A. Adjectives.

1. *sklēros* (σκληρός, 4642), from *skellō*, "to dry," signifies "trying, exacting": see AUSTERE.

2. *duskolos* (δύσκολος, 1422) primarily means "hard to satisfy with food" (*dus*, a prefix like Eng., *un*— or *mis*—, indicating "difficulty, opposition, injuriousness," etc., the opposite of, *eu*, "well," and *kolon*, "food"); hence, "diffi-

cult," Mark 10:24, of the "difficulty," for those who trust in riches, to enter into the Kingdom of God.¶

B. Nouns.

1. *sklērotēs* (σκληρότης, 4643), akin to A, No. 1, is rendered "hardness" in Rom 2:5.¶

2. *pōrōsis* (πώρωσις, 4457) denotes "a hardening," a covering with a *pōros*, a kind of stone, indicating "a process" (from *pōroō*, C, No. 1), and is used metaphorically of dulled spiritual perception, Mark 3:5, RV, "at the hardening of their hearts"; Rom. 11:25, RV, "a hardening" (KJV, "blindness"), said of the state of Israel; Eph. 4:18, RV, "hardening," of the heart of Gentiles. See BLINDNESS.¶

Note: See also under HARDSHIP and HEART (hardness of).

C. Verbs.

1. *pōroō* (πωρόω, 4456), "to make hard, callous, to petrify" (akin to B, No. 2), is used metaphorically, of the heart, Mark 6:52; 8:17; John 12:40; of the mind (or thoughts), 2 Cor. 3:14, of those in Israel who refused the revealed will and ways of God in the gospel, as also in Rom. 11:7, RV, "hardened" (KJV, "blinded"), in both places. See BLINDNESS.¶

2. *sklērunō* (σκληρύνω, 4645), "to make dry or hard" (akin to A, No. 1 and B, No. 1), is used in Acts 19:9; in Rom. 9:18, illustrated by the case of Pharaoh, who first persistently "hardened" his heart (see the RV marg. of Ex. 7:13, 22; 8:19; text of v. 32 and 9:7), all producing the retributive "hardening" by God, after His much long-suffering, 9:12, etc.; in Heb. 3:8, 13, 15; 4:7, warnings against the "hardening" of the heart.¶

HARDLY

1. *duskolōs* (δυσκόλως, 1423), the adverbial form of HARD, A, No. 2, is used in Matt. 19:23; Mark 10:23; Luke 18:24 of the danger of riches.¶

2. *mogis* (μόγις, 3425), "with labor, pain, trouble" (akin to *mogos*, "toil"), is found in some mss. in Luke 9:39, instead of No. 3.¶

3. *molis* (μόλις, 3433), "with difficulty, scarcely, hardly" (akin to *molos*, "toil"), is used as an alternative for No. 2, and occurs in the most authentic mss. in Luke 9:39; it is rendered "hardly" in Acts 27:8, KJV. See DIFFICULTY.

HARDSHIP (to suffer)

1. *kakopatheō* (κακοπαθέω, 2553), "to suffer evil," is translated "suffer hardship" in three places in the RV, 2 Tim. 2:3 (in some mss.; see No. 2), KJV, "endure hardness"; 2:9; KJV, "suffer trouble"; 4:5, KJV, "endure affliction"; in Jas. 5:13, RV, "suffering" (KJV, "afflicted"). See AF-

FLICT, ENDURE, SUFFER.¶ In the Sept., Jonah 4:10.¶

2. *sunkakopatheō* (συγκακοπαθέω, 4777), "to suffer hardship with," is so rendered in 2 Tim. 1:8, RV, KJV, "be thou partaker of the afflictions" (of the gospel), and, in the best mss., in 2:3, "suffer hardship with me." See AFFLICTION, No. 3, *Note*.¶

HARLOT

pornē (πόρνη, 4204) "a prostitute, harlot" (from *pernēmi*, "to sell"), is used (*a*) literally, in Matt. 21:31, 32, of those who were the objects of the mercy shown by Christ; in Luke 15:30, of the life of the Prodigal; in 1 Cor. 6:15, 16, in a warning to the Corinthian church against the prevailing licentiousness which had made Corinth a byword; in Heb. 11:31 and Jas. 2:25, of Rahab; (*b*) metaphorically, of mystic Babylon, Rev. 17:1, 5 (KJV, "harlots"), 15, 16; 19:2, RV, for KJV, "whore."¶

HARM

A. Nouns.

1. *kakos* (κακός, 2556), "evil," is rendered "harm" in Acts 16:28; 28:5. See EVIL.

2. *ponēros* (πονηρός, 4190), "evil," generally of a more malignant sort than No. 1, is translated "harm" in Acts 28:21. See EVIL.

3. *atopos* (ἄτοπος, 824): see AMISS.

4. *hubris* (ὕβρις, 5196) primarily denotes "wantonness, insolence"; then, "an act of wanton violence, an outrage, injury," 2 Cor. 12:10, RV, "injuries," KJV, "reproaches" (more than reproach is conveyed by the term); metaphorically of a loss by sea, Acts 27:10, RV, "injury," KJV, "hurt," and v. 21, RV, "injury," KJV, "harm." See HURT, INJURY, REPROACH.¶

B. Verb.

1. *kakoō* (κακόω, 2559), "to do evil to a person" (akin to A, No. 1), is rendered "harm" in 1 Pet. 3:13, and in the RV of Acts 18:10 (KJV, "hurt"). See AFFECT, EVIL.

2. *kakopoieō* (κακοποιέω, 2554), "to do harm" (A, No. 1, and *poieō*, "to do"), is so rendered in the RV of Mark 3:4 and Luke 6:9 (KJV, "to do evil"), with reference to the moral character of what is done; in 1 Pet. 3:17, "evil doing"; 3 John 11, "doeth evil."¶

HARMLESS

1. *akeraios* (ἀκέραιος, 185), lit., "unmixed, with absence of foreign mixture" (from *a*, negative, and *kerannumi*, "to mix"), "pure," is used metaphorically in the NT of what is guileless, sincere, Matt. 10:16, "harmless" (marg., "simple"), i.e., with the simplicity of a single eye, discerning what is evil, and choosing only what

glorifies God; Rom. 16:19, "simple (unto that which is evil)," KJV marg., "harmless"; Phil. 2:15, "harmless," KJV marg., "sincere." The Greeks used it of wine unmixed with water, of unalloyed metal; in the papyri writings it is used of a loan the interest of which is guaranteed (Moulton and Milligan, *Vocab.*). Trench compares it and synonymous words as follows: "as the *akakos* (see No. 2, below) has no harmfulness in him, and the *adolos* no guile, so the *akeraios* no foreign mixture, and the *haplous* no folds" (*Syn.* §lvi). *Haplous* is said of the single eye, Matt. 6:22; Luke 11:34.¶

2. *akakos* (ἄκακος, 172), the negative of *kakos* (see HARM, A, No. 1), "void of evil," is rendered "harmless" in Heb. 7:26 (RV, "guileless"), of the character of Christ as a High Priest; in Rom. 16:18, RV, "innocent," KJV, "simple."¶

HARP

A. Noun.

kithara (κιθάρα, 2788), whence Eng., "guitar," denotes "a lyre" or "harp"; it is described by Josephus as an instrument of ten strings, played by a plectrum (a smaller instrument was played by the hand); it is mentioned in 1 Cor. 14:7; Rev. 5:8; 14:2; 15:2.¶

B. Verb.

kitharizō (κιθαρίζω, 2789) signifies "to play on the harp," 1 Cor. 14:7; Rev. 14:2.¶ In the Sept., Isa. 23:16.¶

HARPER

kitharōdos (κιθαρῳδός, 2790) denotes "one who plays and sings to the lyre" (from *kithara*, "a lyre," and *aoidos*, "a singer"), Rev. 14:2; 18:22.¶

HARVEST

therismos (θερισμός, 2326), akin to *therizō*, "to reap," is used (*a*) of "the act of harvesting," John 4:35; (*b*) "the time of harvest," figuratively, Matt. 13:30, 39; Mark 4:29; (*c*) "the crop," figuratively, Matt. 9:37, 38; Luke 10:2; Rev. 14:15. The beginning of "harvest" varied according to natural conditions, but took place on the average about the middle of April in the eastern lowlands of Palestine, in the latter part of the month in the coast plains and a little later in high districts. Barley "harvest" usually came first and then wheat. "Harvesting" lasted about seven weeks, and was the occasion of festivities.¶

HASTE, WITH HASTE, HASTILY

A. Noun.

spoudē (σπουδή, 4710) denotes (*a*) "haste, speed," accompanied by "with," Mark 6:25; Luke 1:39; (*b*) "zeal, diligence, earnestness": see BUSINESS, CARE, CAREFULNESS, DILIGENCE, FORWARDNESS.

B. Verb.

speudō (σπεύδω, 4692) denotes (*a*) intransitively, "to hasten," Luke 2:16, "with haste," lit., "(they came) hastening"; Luke 19:5, 6; Acts 20:16; 22:18; (*b*) transitively, "to desire earnestly," 2 Pet. 3:12, RV, "earnestly desiring" (marg., "hastening"), KJV, "hasting" (the day of God), i.e., in our practical fellowship with God as those who are appointed by Him as instruments through prayer and service for the accomplishment of His purposes, purposes which will be unthwartably fulfilled both in time and manner of accomplishment. In this way the earnest desire will find its fulfillment.¶

C. Adverb.

tacheōs (ταχέως, 5030), "quickly," is used in a warning to lay hands "hastily" on no man (with a suggestion of rashness), 1 Tim. 5:22, RV (KJV, "suddenly"); in John 11:31, RV, "(she rose up) quickly" (KJV, "hastily"). See QUICKLY, SHORTLY, SUDDENLY.

HATE, HATEFUL, HATER, HATRED

A. Verb.

miseō (μισέω, 3404), "to hate," is used especially (*a*) of malicious and unjustifiable feelings towards others, whether towards the innocent or by mutual animosity, e.g., Matt. 10:22; 24:10; Luke 6:22, 27; 19:14; John 3:20, of "hating" the light (metaphorically); 7:7; 15:18, 19, 23–25; Titus 3:3; 1 John 2:9, 11; 3:13, 15; 4:20; Rev. 18:2, where "hateful" translates the perfect participle passive voice of the verb, lit., "hated," or "having been hated"; (*b*) of a right feeling of aversion from what is evil; said of wrongdoing, Rom. 7:15; iniquity, Heb. 1:9; "the garment (figurative) spotted by the flesh," Jude 23; "the works of the Nicolaitans," Rev. 2:6 (and v. 15, in some mss.; see the KJV); (*c*) of relative preference for one thing over another, by way of expressing either aversion from, or disregard for, the claims of one person or thing relatively to those of another, Matt. 6:24, and Luke 16:13, as to the impossibility of serving two masters; Luke 14:26, as to the claims of parents relatively to those of Christ; John 12:25, of disregard for one's life relatively to the claims of Christ; Eph. 5:29, negatively, of one's flesh,

i.e. of one's own, and therefore a man's wife as one with him.

Note: In 1 John 3:15, he who "hates" his brother is called a murderer; for the sin lies in the inward disposition, of which the act is only the outward expression.

B. Adjective.

stugētos (στυγητός, 4767), "hateful" (from *stugeō*, "to hate," not found in the NT), is used in Titus 3:3.¶

C. Nouns.

1. *echthra* (ἔχθρα, 2189), "hatred": see ENMITY.

2. *theostugēs* (θεοστυγής, 2319), from *theos*, "God," and *stugeō* (see B), is used in Rom. 1:30, KJV, and RV, marg., "haters of God," RV, "hateful to God"; the former rendering is appropriate to what is expressed by the next words, "insolent," "haughty," but the RV text seems to give the true meaning. Lightfoot quotes from the Epistle of Clement of Rome, in confirmation of this, "those who practice these things are hateful to God."¶

HAUGHTY

huperēphanos (ὑπερήφανος, 5244), "showing oneself above others" (*huper*, "over," *phainomai*, "to appear"), though often denoting preeminent, is always used in the NT in the evil sense of "arrogant, disdainful, haughty"; it is rendered "haughty" in Rom. 1:30 and 2 Tim. 3:2, RV, KJV, "proud," but "proud" in both versions in Luke 1:51; Jas. 4:6; and 1 Pet. 5:5; in the last two it is set in opposition to *tapeinos*, "humble, lowly." Cf. the noun *huperēphania*, Mark 7:22, "pride".¶

HAVE

(*Note:* The following are distinct from the word when it is auxiliary to the tenses of other verbs.)

1. *echō* (ἔχω, 2192), the usual verb for "to have," is used with the following meanings: (*a*) "to hold, in the hand," etc., e.g., Rev. 1:16; 5:8; (*b*) "to hold fast, keep," Luke 19:20; metaphorically, of the mind and conduct, e.g., Mark 16:8; John 14:21; Rom. 1:28; 1 Tim. 3:9; 2 Tim. 1:13; (*c*) "to hold on, cling to, be next to," e.g., of accompaniment, Heb. 6:9, "things that accompany (salvation)," lit., "the things holding themselves of salvation" (RV, marg., "are near to"); of place, Mark 1:38, "next (towns)," lit., "towns holding nigh"; of time, e.g., Luke 13:33, "(the day) following," lit., "the holding (day)"; Acts 13:44; 20:15; 21:26; (*d*) "to hold, to count, consider, regard," e.g., Matt. 14:5; 21:46; Mark 11:32; Luke 14:18; Philem. 17; (*e*) "to involve," Heb. 10:35; Jas. 1:4; 1 John 4:18; (*f*) "to wear,"

of clothing, arms, etc., e.g., Matt. 3:4; 22:12; John 18:10; (*g*) "to be with child," of a woman, Mark 13:17; Rom. 9:10 (lit., "having conception"); (*h*) "to possess," the most frequent use, e.g., Matt. 8:20; 19:22; Acts 9:14; 1 Thess. 3:6; (*i*) of complaints, disputes, Matt. 5:23; Mark 11:25; Acts 24:19; Rev. 2:4, 20; (*j*) of ability, power, e.g., Luke 12:4; Acts 4:14 (lit., "had nothing to say"); (*k*) of necessity, e.g., Luke 12:50; Acts 23:17-19; (*l*) "to be in a certain condition," as, of readiness, Acts 21:12 (lit., "I have readily"); of illness, Matt. 4:24, "all that were sick" (lit., "that had themselves sickly"); Mark 5:23, "lieth (lit., "hath herself") at the point of death"; Mark 16:18, "they shall recover" (lit., "shall have themselves well"); John 4:52, "he began to amend" (lit., "he had himself better"); of evil works, 1 Tim. 5:25, "they that are otherwise," (lit., "the things having otherwise"); to be so, e.g., Acts 7:1, "are these things so?" (lit., "have these things thus?"); of time, Acts 24:25, "for this time" (lit., "the thing having now").

2. *apechō* (ἀπέχω, 568) denotes "to have in full, to have received" (*apo*, "from," and No. 1), Matt. 6:2, 5, 16, RV, "have received," for KJV, "have"; Luke 6:24, KJV and RV, "have received," but Phil. 4:18, "I have"; Philem. 15, "(that) thou shouldest have (him)" (KJV, "receive"). Deissmann, in *Light from the Ancient East*, and Moulton and Milligan (*Vocab. of Gk. Test.*) show that the verb was constantly used as a technical expression in drawing up a receipt. Consequently in the Sermon on the Mount we are led to understand 'they have received their reward' as 'they have signed the receipt of their reward: their right to receive their reward is realized, precisely as if they had already given a receipt for it.'"

Is there not a hint of this in Paul's word to Philemon concerning receiving Onesimus (v. 17)? Philemon would give the apostle a receipt for his payment in sending him. This is in keeping with the metaphorical terms of finance in vv. 18, 19. See ABSTAIN.

3. *ginomai* (γίνομαι, 1096), "to begin to be, come to pass, happen," is rendered "have" in Matt. 18:12; "had" in Acts 15:2; "shall have" in 1 Cor. 4:5, lit., "praise shall be," or come to pass. See BECOME.

4. *metalambanō* (μεταλαμβάνω, 3335), "to have," or "get a share of," is rendered "I have (a convenient season)," in Acts 24:25. See EAT, PARTAKE, RECEIVE, TAKE.

5. *huparchō* (ὑπάρχω, 5225), "to be in existence, to be ready, at hand," is translated by the verb "to have" in Acts 3:6, lit., "silver and gold is not to me" (in the next clause, "such as

I have," *echō* is used); 4:37, "having (land)," lit., "(land) being (to him)"; Matt. 19:21, "that (thou) hast," lit., "(things that) are (thine)," i.e., "thy belongings"; similarly Luke 12:33; 44; 14:33. See BEING.

6. *antiballō* (ἀντιβάλλω, 474), lit., "to throw in turn, exchange" (*anti*, "corresponding to," *ballō*, "to throw"), hence, metaphorically, "to exchange thoughts," is used in Luke 24:27, "ye have," i.e., "ye exchange."¶

7. *eimi* (εἰμί, 1510), "to be," is often used in its various forms with some case of the personal pronoun, to signify "to be to," or "of, a person," e.g., Matt. 19:27, "(what then) shall we have," lit., "what then shall be to us?"; Acts 21:23, "we have four men," lit., "there are to us, etc."

8. *enduō* (ἐνδύω, 1746), "to put on," is rendered "having on" in Eph. 6:14. See CLOTHE.

Notes: (1) In John 5:4 (in those mss. which contain the passage), *katechō*, "to hold fast," is used in the passive voice, in the phrase "whatsoever disease he had," lit., "(by whatsoever disease) he was held." (2) In Mark 12:22, in some mss., *lambanō*, "to take" or "receive," is translated "had," in the statement "the seven had her"; in Acts 25:16, RV, "have had" (KJV, "have"); in Heb. 11:36, "had." (3) In Matt. 27:19, "Have thou nothing to do with that righteous man" translates what is lit. "nothing to thee and that righteous man," the verb being omitted. Similarly with the phrase, "What have I to do with thee?" lit., "what (is) to me and thee?" Mark 5:7; Luke 8:28; John 2:4, where Westcott translates it "What is there to Me and to thee?"; Ellicott, "What is that to Me and to thee," i.e., "What is My concern and thine in the matter?" There is certainly nothing disparaging in the question. On the contrary, it answers what must have been the thought in Mary's heart, and suggests that while there is no obligation either on Him or her, yet the need is a case for rendering help. For the construction with the plural pronoun see Matt. 8:29; Mark 1:24; Luke 4:34. (4) In Heb. 4:13, "with whom we have to do" is, lit., "with whom (is) the account (*logos*) to us." (5) In Heb. 13:5, "such things as ye have" is, lit., "the (things) present." (6) In Mark 5:26, "all that she had" is, lit., "all the (things) with her." (7) For Luke 15:31, KJV, "all that I have," lit., "all my (things)," see RV. (8) For *eneimi*, Luke 11:41, "ye have," see WITHIN, *Note* (*h*).

HAVEN

limēn (λιμήν, 3040) is mentioned in Acts 27:8, "Fair Havens," and v. 12; for the first of these see FAIR. The first mention in the Bible is in Gen. 49:13 (see RV marg.).¶

HAVOC

1. *portheō* (πορθέω, 4199), "to destroy, ravage, lay waste," is used of the persecution inflicted by Saul of Tarsus on the church in Jerusalem, Acts 9:21, and Gal. 1:23, RV, "made havoc," for KJV, "destroyed"; Gal. 1:13, ditto, for KJV, "wasted." See DESTROY, *Note.*¶

2. *lumainomai* (λυμαίνομαι, 3075), "to maltreat, outrage" (*lumē*, "an outrage"), is translated "made havock" in Acts 8:3, KJV (RV, "laid waste.")¶

For HAY see GRASS

HAZARD

1. *paradidōmi* (παραδίδωμι, 3860), "to give over, deliver," signifies "to risk, to hazard," in Acts 15:26, of Barnabas and Paul, who "hazarded" their lives for the name of the Lord Jesus. See BETRAY.

2. *paraboleuomai* (παραβολεύομαι, 3851), lit., "to throw aside" (*para*, "aside," *ballō*, "to throw"), hence, "to expose oneself to danger, to hazard one's life," is said of Epaphroditus in Phil. 2:30, RV, "hazarding." Some mss. have *parabouleuomai* here, "to consult amiss," KJV, "not regarding."¶

HE

Note: This pronoun is generally part of the translation of a verb. Frequently it translates the article before nouns, adjectives, numerals, adverbs, prepositional phrases and the participial form of verbs. Apart from these it translates one of the following:

1. *autos* (αὐτός, 846), "he himself and no other," emphatic, e.g., Matt. 1:21, where the RV brings out the emphasis by the rendering "it is He"; 3:11 (last clause), where the repeated "He" brings out the emphasis; in some cases it can be marked only by a circumlocution which would not constitute a translation, e.g., 8:24; this use is very frequent, especially in the Gospels, the epistles of John and the Apocalypse; see also, e.g., Eph. 2:14; 4:11; 5:23, 27. See SAME, SELF, THIS, VERY.

2. *houtos* (οὗτος, 3778), "this, this person here," is always emphatic; it is used with this meaning, sometimes to refer to what precedes, e.g., Matt. 5:19, "he (shall be called great)"; John 6:46, "he (hath seen)"; often rendered "this," e.g., Rom. 9:9, or "this man," e.g., Matt. 27:58, RV; Jas. 1:25; "the same," e.g., Luke 9:48. See THAT, THIS, THESE.

3. *ekeinos* (ἐκεῖνος, 1565) denotes "that one, that person" (in contrast to No. 2); its use marks special distinction, favorable or unfavorable;

this form of emphasis should always be noted; e.g., John 2:21 "(But) He (spake)"; 5:19, "(what things soever) He (doeth)"; 7:11; 2 Cor. 10:18, lit., "for not he that commendeth himself, he (*ekeinos*) is approved"; 2 Tim. 2:13, "He (in contrast to "we") abideth faithful"; 1 John 3:3, "(even as) He (is pure)"; v. 5, "He (was manifested)"; v. 7, "He (is righteous)"; v. 16, "He laid down"; 4:17, "(as) He (is)." See OTHER, THAT, THIS.

Note: The indefinite pronoun *tis*, "anyone, any man," is rendered "he" in Acts 4:35, KJV (RV, rightly, "any one"); in Heb. 10:28, RV, "a man."

HE HIMSELF

1. *autos* (αὐτός, 846): see No. 1, above.

2. *heauton* (ἑαυτόν, 1438), "oneself, himself," a reflexive of No. 1, is rendered "he himself" in Luke 23:2 and Acts 25:4.

HE THAT

1. *hos* (ὅς, 3739), the relative pronoun "who," is sometimes rendered "he that," e.g., Matt. 10:38; with the particle *an*, expressing possibility, uncertainty or a condition, signifying "whosoever," Mark 3:29, KJV (RV, "whosoever"); 4:25 and 9:40 (with *an*, in the best mss.). See WHATSOEVER, WHICH, WHO, WHOSOEVER.

2. *hosge* (ὅσγε), "who even" (No. 1, and the particle *ge*), indicates a greater in regard to a less, Rom. 8:32, "He that (spared not)."

Notes: (1) In Rev. 13:10, *ei tis*, "if anyone," is rendered "if any man" in the RV, for KJV, "he that."

(2) In Matt. 23:12, *hostis*, No. 1, combined with the indefinite pronoun *tis* (see preceding note), is properly rendered "whosoever," RV, for KJV, "he that."

HEAD

kephalē (κεφαλή, 2776), besides its natural significance, is used (*a*) figuratively in Rom. 12:20, of heaping coals of fire on a "head" (see COALS); in Acts 18:6, "Your blood be upon your own heads," i.e., "your blood-guiltiness rest upon your own persons," a mode of expression frequent in the OT, and perhaps here directly connected with Ezek. 3:18, 20; 33:6, 8; see also Lev. 20:16; 2 Sam. 1:16; 1 Kings 2:37; (*b*) metaphorically, of the authority or direction of God in relation to Christ, of Christ in relation to believing men, of the husband in relation to the wife, 1 Cor. 11:3; of Christ in relation to the Church, Eph. 1:22; 4:15; 5:23; Col. 1:18; 2:19; of Christ in relation to principalities and powers, Col. 2:10. As to 1 Cor. 11:10, taken in connection with the context, the word "authority" probably stands, by metonymy, for a sign of authority (RV), the angels being witnesses of the preeminent relationship as established by God in the creation of man as just mentioned, with the spiritual significance regarding the position of Christ in relation to the Church; cf. Eph. 3:10; it is used of Christ as the foundation of the spiritual building set forth by the Temple, with its "corner stone," Matt. 21:42; symbolically also of the imperial rulers of the Roman power, as seen in the apocalyptic visions, Rev. 13:1, 3; 17:3, 7, 9.

HEAD (to wound in the)

kephalioō, or *kephalaioō* (κεφαλιόω, 2775), from *kephalion*, a diminutive of *kephalē*, usually meant "to sum up, to bring under heads"; in Mark 12:4 it is used for "wounding on the head," the only place where it has this meaning.¶

HEADLONG (to cast, to fall)

1. *katakrēmnizō* (κατακρημνίζω, 2630) signifies "to throw over a precipice" (*kata*, "down," *krēmnos*, "a steep bank," etc.), said of the purpose of the people of Nazareth to destroy Christ, Luke 4:29.¶

2. *prēnēs* (πρηνής, 4248), an adjective denoting "headlong, prone," is used with the verb *ginomai*, "to become," in Acts 1:18, of the death of Judas, "falling headlong"; various suggestions have been made as to the actual details; some ascribe to the word the meaning "swelling up."¶

HEADSTRONG (RV), HEADY (KJV)

propetēs (προπετής, 4312) lit. means "falling forwards" (from *pro*, "forwards," and *piptō*, "to fall"); it is used metaphorically to signify "precipitate, rash, reckless," and is said (a) of persons, 2 Tim. 3:4; "headstrong" is the appropriate rendering; (b) of things, Acts 19:36, RV, "(nothing) rash" (KJV, "rashly").¶

HEAL, HEALING

A. Verbs.

1. *therapeuō* (θεραπεύω, 2323) primarily signifies "to serve as a *therapōn*, an attendant"; then, "to care for the sick, to treat, cure, heal" (Eng., "therapeutics"). It is chiefly used in Matthew and Luke, once in John (5:10), and, after the Acts, only Rev. 13:3 and 12. See CURE.

2. *iaomai* (ἰάομαι, 2390), "to heal," is used (a) of physical treatment 22 times; in Matt. 15:28, KJV, "made whole," RV, "healed"; so in Acts 9:34; (b) figuratively, of spiritual "healing," Matt. 13:15; John 12:40; Acts 28:27; Heb.

12:13; 1 Pet. 2:24; possibly, Jas. 5:16 includes both (a) and (b); some mss. have the word, with sense (b), in Luke 4:18. Apart from this last, Luke, the physician, uses the word fifteen times. See WHOLE.

3. *sōzō* (σώζω, 4982), "to save," is translated by the verb "to heal" in the KJV of Mark 5:23 and Luke 8:36 (RV, "to make whole"; so KJV frequently); the idea is that of saving from disease and its effects. See SAVE.

4. *diasōzō* (διασώζω, 1295), "to save thoroughly" (*dia*, "through," and No. 3), is translated "heal" in Luke 7:3, KJV (RV, "save"). See ESCAPE.

B. Nouns.

1. *therapeia* (θεραπεία, 2322), akin to A, No. 1, primarily denotes "care, attention," Luke 12:42 (see HOUSEHOLD); then, "medical service, healing" (Eng., "therapy"), Luke 9:11; Rev. 22:2, of the effects of the leaves of the tree of life, perhaps here with the meaning "health."¶

2. *iama* (ἴαμα, 2386), akin to A, No. 2, formerly signified "a means of healing"; in the NT, "a healing" (the result of the act), used in the plural, in 1 Cor. 12:9, 28, 30, RV, "healings"; of divinely imparted gifts in the churches in apostolic times.¶

3. *iasis* (ἴασις, 2392), akin to A, No. 2, stresses the process as reaching completion, Luke 13:32, "cures," of the acts of Christ in the days of His flesh; Acts 4:22, 30, "to heal," lit. 'unto healing.'¶

HEALTH (to be in)

hugianiō (ὑγιαίνω, 5198) denotes "to be healthy, sound, in good health" (Eng., "hygiene"), rendered "mayest be in health," in 3 John 2; rendered "safe and sound" in Luke 15:27. See SAFE, D, No. 2, SOUND, WHOLE, B, No. 1.

Note: In Acts 27:34, *sōtēria*, "salvation, safety," is translated "health" in the KJV; the RV, gives the right meaning, "safety."

HEAP (to)

1. *sōreuō* (σωρεύω, 4987), "to heap one thing on another," is said of "heaping" coals of fire on the head, Rom. 12:20 (for the meaning see COALS); in 2 Tim. 3:6 it is used metaphorically of women "laden" (or overwhelmed) with sins. See LADEN.¶ In the Sept., Prov. 25:22.¶

2. *episōreuō* (ἐπισωρεύω, 2002), "to heap upon" or "together" (*epi*, "upon," and No. 1), is used metaphorically in 2 Tim. 4:3 of appropriating a number of teachers to suit the liking of those who do so. The reference may be to those who, like the Athenians, run about to

hear and follow those who proclaim new ideas of their own invention.¶

HEAR, HEARING

A. Verbs.

1. *akouō* (ἀκούω, 191), the usual word denoting "to hear," is used (*a*) intransitively, e.g., Matt. 11:15; Mark 4:23; (*b*) transitively when the object is expressed, sometimes in the accusative case, sometimes in the genitive. Thus in Acts 9:7, "hearing the voice," the noun "voice" is in the partitive genitive case [i.e., hearing (something) of], whereas in 22:9, "they heard not the voice," the construction is with the accusative. This removes the idea of any contradiction. The former indicates a "hearing" of the sound, the latter indicates the meaning or message of the voice (this they did not hear). "The former denotes the sensational perception, the latter (the accusative case) the thing perceived" (Cremer). In John 5:25, 28, the genitive case is used, indicating a "sensational perception" that the Lord's voice is sounding; in 3:8, of "hearing" the wind, the accusative is used, stressing "the thing perceived."

That God "hears" prayer signifies that He answers prayer, e.g., John 9:31; 1 John 5:14, 15. Sometimes the verb is used with *para* ("from beside"), e.g., John 1:40, "one of the two which heard John speak," lit., "heard from beside John," suggesting that he stood beside him; in John 8:26, 40, indicating the intimate fellowship of the Son with the Father; the same construction is used in Acts 10:22 and 2 Tim. 2:2, in the latter case, of the intimacy between Paul and Timothy. See HEARKEN.

2. *eisakouō* (εἰσακούω, 1522), "to listen to" (*eis*, to, and No. 1), has two meanings, (*a*) "to hear and to obey," 1 Cor. 14:21, "they will not hear"; (*b*) "to hear so as to answer," of God's answer to prayer, Matt. 6:7; Luke 1:13; Acts 10:31; Heb. 5:7.¶

3. *diakouō* (διακούω, 1251), "to hear through, hear fully" (*dia*, "through," and No. 1), is used technically, of "hearing" judicially, in Acts 23:35, of Felix in regard to the charges against Paul.¶ In the Sept., Deut. 1:16; Job 9:33.¶

4. *epakouō* (ἐπακούω, 1873), "to listen to, hear with favor, at or upon an occasion" (*epi*, "upon," and No. 1), is used in 2 Cor. 6:2 (RV, "hearken").¶

5. *epakroaomai* (ἐπακροάομαι, 1874), "to listen attentively to" (*epi*, used intensively, and a verb akin to No. 1), is used in Acts 16:25, "(the prisoners) were listening to (them)," RV, expressive of rapt attention.¶

6. *proakouō* (προακούω, 4257) signifies "to hear before" (*pro*), Col. 1:5, where Lightfoot suggests that the preposition contrasts what they heard before, the true gospel, with the false gospel of their recent teachers.¶

7. *parakouō* (παρακούω, 3878) primarily signifies "to overhear, hear amiss or imperfectly" (*para*, "beside, amiss," and No. 1); then (in the NT) "to hear without taking heed, to neglect to hear," Matt. 18:17 (twice); in Mark 5:36 the best mss. have this verb, which the RV renders "not heeding" (marg., "overhearing"); some mss. have No. 1, KJV, "hearing." It seems obvious that the Lord paid no attention to those from the ruler's house and their message that his daughter was dead.¶ Cf. the noun *parakoē*, "disobedience."

B. Nouns.

1. *akoē* (ἀκοή, 189), akin to A, No. 1, denotes (*a*) "the sense of hearing," 1 Cor. 12:17; 2 Pet. 2:8; a combination of verb and noun is used in phrases which have been termed Hebraic as they express somewhat literally an OT phraseology, e.g., "By hearing ye shall hear," Matt. 13:14; Acts 28:26, RV, a mode of expression conveying emphasis; (*b*) "the organ of hearing," Mark 7:35, "ears"; Luke 7:1, RV, "ears," for KJV, "audience"; Acts 17:20; 2 Tim. 4:3, 4; Heb. 5:11, "dull of hearing," lit., "dull as to ears"; (*c*) "a thing heard, a message or teaching," John 12:38, "report"; Rom. 10:16; 1 Thess. 2:13, "the word of the message," lit. "the word of hearing" (KJV, "which ye heard"); Heb. 4:2, "the word of hearing," RV, for KJV, "the word preached"; in a somewhat similar sense, "a rumor, report," Matt. 4:24; 14:1; Mark 1:28, KJV, "fame," RV, "report"; Matt. 24:6; Mark 13:7, "rumors (of wars)"; (*d*) "the receiving of a message," Rom. 10:17, something more than the mere sense of "hearing" [see (a)]; so with the phrase "the hearing of faith," Gal. 3:2, 5, which it seems better to understand so than under (*c*). See EAR, FAME, PREACH, REPORT, RUMOR.¶

Notes: (1) For *diagnōsis* (investigation, followed by decision), rendered "hearing" in Acts 25:21, KJV, see DECISION. (2) For the phrase to be dull of hearing, lit., "to hear heavily," Matt. 13:15; Acts 28:27, see DULL. (3) For *akroatērion*, "a place of hearing," Acts 25:23, see PLACE.¶

HEARER

akroatēs (ἀκροατής, 202), from *akroaomai*, "to listen," is used in Rom. 2:13, "of a law"; Jas. 1:22, 23, "of the word"; v. 25, "a (forgetful) hearer."¶

Note: In Eph. 4:29 and 2 Tim. 2:14, the verb

akouō, "to hear," is rendered "hearers" in the KJV (RV, "them that hear").

HEARKEN

1. *akouō* (ἀκούω, 191), "to hear," is rendered "hearken" in the KJV and RV, in Mark 4:3; Acts 4:19; 7:2; 15:13; Jas. 2:5; in the RV only, in Acts 3:22, 23; 13:16 (KJV, "give audience"); 15:12, "hearkened" (KJV "gave audience"). See HEAR, No. 1.

Note: In Acts 12:13, *hupakouō*, lit., "to hearken," with the idea of stillness, or attention (*hupo*, "under," *akouō*, "to hear"), signifies "to answer a knock at a door," RV, "to answer" (KJV, "to hearken"). See OBEY.

2. *epakouō* (ἐπακούω, 1873) denotes "to hearken to," 2 Cor. 6:2, RV (see HEAR, A, No. 4).¶

3. *enōtizomai* (ἐνωτίζομαι, 1801), "to give ear to, to hearken" (from *en*, "in," and *ous*, "an ear"), is used in Acts 2:14, in Peter's address to the men of Israel.¶

4. *peitharcheō* (πειθαρχέω, 3980), "to obey one in authority, be obedient" (*peithomai*, "to be persuaded," *archē*, "rule"), is translated "to hearken unto" in Acts 27:21, in Paul's reminder to the shipwrecked mariners that they should have given heed to his counsel. See OBEY.

HEART, HEARTILY

kardia (καρδία, 2588), "the heart" (Eng., "cardiac," etc.), the chief organ of physical life ("for the life of the flesh is in the blood," Lev. 17:11), occupies the most important place in the human system. By an easy transition the word came to stand for man's entire mental and moral activity, both the rational and the emotional elements. In other words, the heart is used figuratively for the hidden springs of the personal life. "The Bible describes human depravity as in the 'heart,' because sin is a principle which has its seat in the center of man's inward life, and then 'defiles' the whole circuit of his action, Matt. 15:19, 20. On the other hand, Scripture regards the heart as the sphere of Divine influence, Rom. 2:15; Acts 15:9.... The heart, as lying deep within, contains 'the hidden man,' 1 Pet. 3:4, the real man. It represents the true character but conceals it" (J. Laidlaw, in *Hastings' Bible Dic.*).

As to its usage in the NT it denotes (*a*) the seat of physical life, Acts 14:17; Jas. 5:5; (*b*) the seat of moral nature and spiritual life, the seat of grief, John 14:1; Rom. 9:2; 2 Cor. 2:4; joy, John 16:22; Eph. 5:19; the desires, Matt. 5:28; 2 Pet. 2:14; the affections, Luke 24:32; Acts 21:13; the perceptions, John 12:40; Eph. 4:18; the thoughts, Matt. 9:4; Heb. 4:12; the under-

standing, Matt. 13:15; Rom. 1:21; the reasoning powers, Mark 2:6; Luke 24:38; the imagination, Luke 1:51; conscience, Acts 2:37; 1 John 3:20; the intentions, Heb. 4:12, cf. 1 Pet. 4:1; purpose, Acts 11:23; 2 Cor. 9:7; the will, Rom. 6:17; Col. 3:15; faith, Mark 11:23; Rom. 10:10; Heb. 3:12.

The heart, in its moral significance in the OT, includes the emotions, the reason and the will.

2. *psuchē* (ψυχή, 5590), the soul, or life, is rendered "heart" in Eph. 6:6 (marg., "soul"), "doing the will of God from the heart." In Col. 3:23, a form of the word *psuchē* preceded by *ek*, from, lit., "from (the) soul," is rendered "heartily."

Notes: (1) The RV, "heart" is substituted for KJV, "bowels," in Col. 3:12; Philem. 7, 12, 20. (2) In 2 Cor. 3:3, the RV has "tables that are hearts of flesh," for KJV, "fleshy tables of the heart." (3) In Eph. 1:18, the best mss. have *kardia*, "(the eyes of your) heart"; some have *dianoia*, "understanding" (KJV). (4) In Heb. 8:10 and 10:16, the KJV has "in their hearts" and "into their hearts"; RV, "on their heart." (5) In Luke 21:26, where there is no word for "hearts" in the original, the RV has "men fainting (for fear)." (6) In 2 Cor. 7:2, the verb *chōreō*, to make room for, "receive" (KJV), is translated, or rather, interpreted, "open your hearts," RV, marg., "make room for (us)."

HEART (hardness of)

sklērokardia (σκληροκαρδία, 4641), "hardness of heart" (*sklēros*, "hard," and *kardia*), is used in Matt. 19:8; Mark 10:5; 16:14.¶ In the Sept., Deut. 10:16; Jer. 4:4.¶

HEART (knowing the)

kardiognōstēs (καρδιογνώστης, 2589), "a knower of hearts" (*kardia* and *ginōskō*, "to know"), is used in Acts 1:24; 15:8.¶

HEAT

A. Nouns.

1. *kausōn* (καύσων, 2742) denotes "a burning heat" (from *kaiō*, "to burn"; cf. Eng., "caustic," "cauterize"), Matt. 20:12; Luke 12:55 (KJV, "heat"), RV, in each place, "scorching heat" (marg. "hot wind"); in Jas. 1:11, "a burning heat," KJV, RV, "the scorching wind" like the sirocco. Cf. Amos 4:9, where the Sept. has *purōsis*, "burning" (*pur*, "fire"). See BURNING.

2. *kauma* (καῦμα, 2738), "heat" (akin to No. 1), signifies "the result of burning," or "the heat produced," Rev. 7:16; 16:9;¶ cf. *kaumatizō*, "to scorch," *kausis*, "burning," *kautēriazomai*, "to brand, sear."

3. *thermē* (θέρμη, 2329) denotes "warmth, heat," Acts 28:3 (Eng., "thermal," etc.).¶

B. Verb.

kausoō (καυσόω, 2741) was used as a medical term, of "a fever"; in the NT, "to burn with great heat" (akin to A, No. 1), said of the future destruction of the natural elements, 2 Pet. 3:10, 12, "with fervent heat," passive voice, lit., "being burned."¶

For HEATHEN see GENTILES

HEAVEN, HEAVENLY (-IES)

A. Nouns.

1. *ouranos* (οὐρανός, 3772), probably akin to *ornumi*, "to lift, to heave," is used in the NT (*a*) of "the aerial heavens," e.g., Matt. 6:26; 8:20; Acts 10:12; 11:6 (RV, "heaven," in each place, KJV, "air"); Jas. 5:18; (*b*) "the sidereal," e.g., Matt. 24:29, 35; Mark 13:25, 31; Heb. 11:12, RV, "heaven," KJV, "sky"; Rev. 6:14; 20:11; they, (*a*) and (*b*), were created by the Son of God, Heb. 1:10, as also by God the Father, Rev. 10:6; (*c*) "the eternal dwelling place of God," Matt. 5:16; 12:50; Rev. 3:12; 11:13; 16:11; 20:9. From thence the Son of God descended to become incarnate, John 3:13, 31; 6:38, 42. In His ascension Christ "passed through the heavens," Heb. 4:14, RV; He "ascended far above all the heavens," Eph. 4:10, and was "made higher than the heavens," Heb. 7:26; He "sat down on the right hand of the throne of the Majesty in the heavens," Heb. 8:1; He is "on the right hand of God," having gone into heaven, 1 Pet. 3:22. Since His ascension it is the scene of His present life and activity, e.g., Rom. 8:34; Heb. 9:24. From thence the Holy Spirit descended at Pentecost, 1 Pet. 1:12. It is the abode of the angels, e.g., Matt. 18:10; 22:30; cf. Rev. 3:5. Thither Paul was "caught up," whether in the body or out of the body, he knew not, 2 Cor. 12:2. It is to be the eternal dwelling place of the saints in resurrection glory, 2 Cor. 5:1. From thence Christ will descend to the air to receive His saints at the Rapture, 1 Thess. 4:16; Phil. 3:20, 21, and will subsequently come with His saints and with His holy angels at His second advent, Matt. 24:30; 2 Thess. 1:7. In the present life "heaven" is the region of the spiritual citizenship of believers, Phil. 3:20. The present "heavens," with the earth, are to pass away, 2 Pet. 3:10, "being on fire," v. 12 (see v. 7); Rev. 20:11, and new "heavens" and earth are to be created, 2 Pet. 3:13; Rev. 21:1, with Isa. 65:17, e.g.

In Luke 15:18, 21, "heaven" is used, by metonymy, for God. See AIR.

Notes: (1) For the phrase in Luke 11:13, see

Note on B, No. 2. (2) In Luke 11:2, the KJV, "as in heaven," translates a phrase found in some mss.

2. *mesouranēma* (μεσουράνημα, 3321) denotes "mid-heaven," or the midst of the heavens (*mesos*, "middle," and No. 1), Rev. 8:13; 14:6; 19:17.¶

B. Adjectives.

1. *ouranios* (οὐράνιος, 3770), signifying "of heaven, heavenly," corresponding to A, No. 1, is used (*a*) as an appellation of God the Father, Matt. 6:14, 26, 32, "your heavenly Father"; 15:13, "My heavenly Father"; (*b*) as descriptive of the holy angels, Luke 2:13; (*c*) of the vision seen by Paul, Acts 26:19.¶

2. *epouranios* (ἐπουράνιος, 2032), "heavenly," what pertains to, or is in, heaven (*epi*, in the sense of "pertaining to," not here, "above"), has meanings corresponding to some of the meanings of *ouranos*, A, No. 1. It is used (*a*) of God the Father, Matt. 18:35; (*b*) of the place where Christ "sitteth at the right hand of God" (i.e., in a position of divine authority), Eph. 1:20; and of the present position of believers in relationship to Christ, 2:6; where they possess "every spiritual blessing," 1:3; (*c*) of Christ as "the Second Man," and all those who are related to Him spiritually, 1 Cor. 15:48; (*d*) of those whose sphere of activity or existence is above, or in contrast to that of earth, of "principalities and powers," Eph. 3:10; of "spiritual hosts of wickedness," 6:12, RV, "in heavenly places," for KJV, "in high places"; (*e*) of the Holy Spirit, Heb. 6:4; (*f*) of "heavenly things," as the subjects of the teaching of Christ, John 3:12, and as consisting of the spiritual and "heavenly" sanctuary and "true tabernacle" and all that appertains thereto in relation to Christ and His sacrifice as antitypical of the earthly tabernacle and sacrifices under the Law, Heb. 8:5; 9:23; (*g*) of the "calling" of believers, Heb. 3:1; (*h*) of heaven as the abode of the saints, "a better country" than that of earth, Heb. 11:16, and of the spiritual Jerusalem, 12:22; (*i*) of the kingdom of Christ in its future manifestation, 2 Tim. 4:18; (*j*) of all beings and things, animate and inanimate, that are "above the earth," Phil. 2:10; (*k*) of the resurrection and glorified bodies of believers, 1 Cor. 15:49; (*l*) of the "heavenly orbs," 1 Cor. 15:40 ("celestial," twice, and so rendered here only).¶

Note: In connection with (*a*), the word "heavenly," used of God the Father in Luke 11:13, represents the phrase *ex ouranou*, "from heaven."

C. Adverb.

ouranothen (οὐρανόθεν, 3771), formed from A, No. 1, and denoting "from heaven," is used of (*a*) the aerial heaven, Acts 14:17; (*b*) heaven, as the uncreated sphere of God's abode, 26:13.¶

HEAVY, HEAVINESS

A. Nouns.

1. *lupē* (λύπη, 3077), "grief, sorrow," is rendered "heaviness" in the KJV of Rom. 9:2; 2 Cor. 2:1 (RV, "sorrow," in both places). See GRIEF, SORROW.

2. *katēpheia* (κατήφεια, 2726) probably denotes a downcast look, expressive of sorrow; hence, "dejection, heaviness"; it is used in Jas. 4:9.¶

B. Verbs.

1. *adēmoneō* (ἀδημονέω, 85), "to be troubled, much distressed," is used of the Lord's sorrow in Gethsemane, Matt. 26:37; Mark 14:33, KJV, "to be very heavy," RV, "to be sore troubled"; of Epaphroditus, because the saints at Philippi had received news of his sickness, Phil. 2:26, KJV, "was full of heaviness," RV, "was sore troubled." See TROUBLE, B, No. 12.¶

2. *lupeō* (λυπέω, 3076), "to distress, grieve" (akin to A, No. 1), is rendered "are in heaviness" in 1 Pet. 1:6, KJV (RV, "have been put to grief"); here, as frequently, it is in the passive voice. See GRIEF, SORROWFUL.

3. *bareō* (βαρέω, 916), always in the passive voice in the NT, is rendered "were heavy" in Matt. 26:43; Mark 14:40; Luke 9:32. See BURDEN.

Note: For "heavy laden," Matt. 11:28, see LADE, No. 3.

C. Adjective.

barus (βαρύς, 926), "heavy" (akin to B, No. 3), is so rendered in Matt. 23:4. See GRIEVOUS.

HEDGE

phragmos (φραγμός, 5418) denotes any sort of fence, hedge, palings or wall (akin to *phrassō*, "to fence in, stop"). It is used (*a*) in its literal sense, in Matt. 21:33, lit. "(he put) a hedge (around)"; Mark 12:1; Luke 14:23; (*b*) metaphorically, of the "partition" which separated Gentile from Jew, which was broken down by Christ through the efficacy of His expiatory sacrifice, Eph. 2:14.¶

HEED (to give, to take)

1. *blepō* (βλέπω, 991), "to look," see, usually implying more especially an intent, earnest contemplation, is rendered "take heed" in Matt. 24:4; Mark 4:24; 13:5, 9, 23, 33; Luke 8:18; 21:8; 1 Cor. 3:10; 8:9; 10:12; Gal. 5:15; Col. 2:8 (KJV, "beware"); 4:17; Heb. 3:12. See BEHOLD, BEWARE, LIE, LOOK, PERCEIVE, REGARD, SEE.

2. *horaō* (ὁράω, 3708), "to see," usually ex-

pressing the sense of vision, is rendered "take heed" in Matt. 16:6; 18:10, KJV (RV, "see"); Mark 8:15; Luke 12:15; Acts 22:26 (KJV only). See BEHOLD, SEE.

3. *prosechō* (προσέχω, 4337), lit., "to hold to," signifies "to turn to, turn one's attention to"; hence, "to give heed"; it is rendered "take heed" in Matt. 6:1; Luke 17:3; 21:34; Acts 5:35; 20:28; 2 Pet. 1:19; to give heed to, in Acts 8:6, 10; in v. 11 (KJV, "had regard to"); 16:14 (KJV, "attended unto"); 1 Tim. 1:4; 4:1, 13 (KJV, "give attendance to"); Titus 1:14; Heb. 2:1, lit., "to give heed more earnestly." See ATTEND, BEWARE, GIVE, REGARD.

4. *epechō* (ἐπέχω, 1907), lit., "to hold upon," then, "to direct towards, to give attention to," is rendered "gave heed," in Acts 3:5; "take heed," in 1 Tim. 4:16. See HOLD (forth), MARK, STAY.

Notes: (1) In Luke 11:35, KJV, *skopeō*, "to look," is translated "take heed (that)," RV, "look (whether)." (2) Nos. 2 and 3 are used together in Matt. 16:6; Nos. 2 and 1, in that order, in Mark 8:15; but in Luke 12:15 the RV rightly follows No. 2 by "keep yourselves from" (*phulassō*, "to guard"). (3) For the RV of Mark 5:36, "not heeding," see under HEAR, No. 7. (4) In Rom. 11:21 the KJV adds "take heed," because of a variant reading which introduces the clause by a conjunctive phrase signifying "lest."

HEEL

pterna (πτέρνα, 4418) is found in John 13:18, where the Lord quotes from Ps. 41:9; the metaphor is that of tripping up an antagonist in wrestling.¶ Cf. the verb in Gen. 27:36; Jer. 9:4; Hos. 12:3.

HEIFER

damalis (δάμαλις, 1151), etymologically "one of fit age to be tamed to the yoke" (*damaō*, "to tame"), occurs in Heb. 9:13, with reference to the "red heifer" of Num. 19.¶

HEIGHT

1. *hupsos* (ὕψος, 5311), "a summit, top," is translated "height" in Eph. 3:18, where it may refer either to "the love of Christ" or to "the fullness of God"; the two are really inseparable, for they who are filled into the fullness of God thereby enter appreciatively into the love of Christ, which "surpasseth knowledge"; in Rev. 21:16, of the measurement of the heavenly Jerusalem. See ESTATE, HIGH.

2. *hupsōma* (ὕψωμα, 5313), more concrete than No. 1, is used (*a*) of "a height," as a mountain or anything definitely termed a "height," Rom. 8:39 (metaphorically); (*b*) of "a high thing" lifted up as a barrier or in antago-

nistic exaltation, 2 Cor. 10:5. See HIGH.¶ Cf. *hupsoō*, "to exalt."

HEIR

A. Noun.

1. *klēronomos* (κληρονόμος, 2818) lit. denotes "one who obtains a lot or portion (*klēros*, "a lot," *nemomai*, "to possess"), especially of an inheritance. The NT usage may be analyzed as under: "(*a*) the person to whom property is to pass on the death of the owner, Matt. 21:38; Mark 12:7; Luke 20:14; Gal. 4:1; (*b*) one to whom something has been assigned by God, on possession of which, however, he has not yet entered, as Abraham, Rom. 4:13, 14; Heb. 6:17; Christ, Heb. 1:2; the poor saints, Jas. 2:5; (*c*) believers, inasmuch as they share in the new order of things to be ushered in at the return of Christ, Rom. 8:17; Gal. 3:29; 4:7; Titus 3:7; (*d*) one who receives something other than by merit, as Noah, Heb. 11:7."*¶

In the Sept., Judg. 18:7; 2 Sam. 14:7; Jer. 8:10; Mic. 1:15.¶

2. *sunklēronomos* (συγκληρονόμος, 4789), "a joint-heir, co-inheritor" (*sun*, "with," and No. 1), "is used of Isaac and Jacob as participants with Abraham in the promises of God, Heb. 11:9; of husband and wife who are also united in Christ, 1 Pet. 3:7; of Gentiles who believe, as participants in the gospel with Jews who believe, Eph. 3:6; and of all believers as prospective participants with Christ in His glory, as recompense for their participation in His sufferings, Rom. 8:17."*¶

B. Verb.

klēronomeō (κληρονομέω, 2816), "to be an heir to, to inherit" (see A, No. 1), is rendered "shall (not) inherit with" in Gal. 4:30, RV, KJV, "shall (not) be heir with"; in Heb. 1:14, RV, "shall inherit," KJV, "shall be heirs of." See INHERIT. Cf. *klēroomai*, "to be taken as an inheritance," *klēronomia*, "an inheritance," *klēros*, "a lot, an inheritance."

HELL

1. *geenna* (γέεννα, 1067) represents the Hebrew Gê-Hinnom (the valley of Tophet) and a corresponding Aramaic word; it is found twelve times in the NT, eleven of which are in the Synoptists, in every instance as uttered by the Lord Himself. He who says to his brother, Thou fool (see under FOOL), will be in danger of "the hell of fire," Matt. 5:22; it is better to pluck out (a metaphorical description of irrevocable law)

** From *Notes on Galatians,* by Hogg and Vine, pp. 177, 178.*
* ditto, p. 178.

an eye that causes its possessor to stumble, than that his "whole body be cast into hell," v. 29; similarly with the hand, v. 30; in Matt. 18:8, 9, the admonitions are repeated, with an additional mention of the foot; here, too, the warning concerns the person himself (for which obviously the "body" stands in chapt. 5); in v. 8, "the eternal fire" is mentioned as the doom, the character of the region standing for the region itself, the two being combined in the phrase "the hell of fire," v. 9. To the passage in Matt. 18, that in Mark 9:43–47, is parallel; here to the word "hell" are applied the extended descriptions "the unquenchable fire" and "where their worm dieth not and the fire is not quenched."

That God, "after He hath killed, hath power to cast into hell," is assigned as a reason why He should be feared with the fear that keeps from evil doing, Luke 12:5; the parallel passage to this in Matt. 10:28 declares, not the casting in, but the doom which follows, namely, the destruction (not the loss of being, but of well-being) of "both soul and body."

In Matt. 23 the Lord denounces the scribes and Pharisees, who in proselytizing a person "make him two-fold more a son of hell" than themselves (v. 15), the phrase here being expressive of moral characteristics, and declares the impossibility of their escaping "the judgment of hell," v. 33. In Jas. 3:6 "hell" is described as the source of the evil done by misuse of the tongue; here the word stands for the powers of darkness, whose characteristics and destiny are those of "hell."¶

For terms descriptive of "hell," see e.g., Matt. 13:42; 25:46; Phil. 3:19; 2 Thess. 1:9; Heb. 10:39; 2 Pet. 2:17; Jude 13; Rev. 2:11; 19:20; 20:6, 10, 14; 21:8.

Notes: (1) For the rendering "hell" as a translation of hades, corresponding to Sheol, wrongly rendered "the grave" and "hell," see HADES. (2) The verb *tartaroō*, translated "cast down to hell" in 2 Pet. 2:4, signifies to consign to Tartarus, which is neither Sheol nor hades nor hell, but the place where those angels whose special sin is referred to in that passage are confined "to be reserved unto judgment"; the region is described as "pits of darkness." RV¶

For HELM (Jas. 3:4) see RUDDER

HELMET

perikephalaia (περικεφαλαία, 4030), from *peri*, "around," and *kephalē*, "a head," is used figuratively in Eph. 6:17, with reference to salvation, and 1 Thess. 5:8, where it is described as "the hope of salvation." The head is not to be regarded here as standing for the seat of the intellect; the word is not so used elsewhere in Scripture. In Eph. 6:17 salvation is a present experience of the Lord's deliverance of believers as those who are engaged in spiritual conflict; in 1 Thess. 5:8, the hope is that of the Lord's return, which encourages the believer to resist the spirit of the age in which he lives.¶

HELP, HOLPEN

A. Nouns.

1. *antilēpsis* or *antilēmpsis* (ἀντίληψις, 484) properly signifies "a laying hold of, an exchange" (*anti*, "in exchange," or, in its local sense, "in front," and *lambanō*, "to take, lay hold of," so as to support); then, "a help" (akin to B, No. 1); it is mentioned in 1 Cor. 12:28, as one of the ministrations in the local church, by way of rendering assistance, perhaps especially of "help" ministered to the weak and needy. So Theophylact defines the injunction in 1 Thess. 5:14, "support the weak"; cf. Acts 20:35; not official functionaries are in view in the term "helps," but rather the functioning of those who, like the household of Stephanas, devote themselves to minister to the saints. Hort defines the ministration as "anything that would be done for poor or weak or outcast brethren."¶

2. *boētheia* (βοήθεια, 996), from *boē*, "a shout," and *theō*, "to run," denotes "help, succour," Heb. 4:16, lit., "(grace) unto (timely) help"; in Acts 27:17, where the plural is used, the term is nautical, "frapping."¶

3. *epikouria* (ἐπικουρία, 1947) strictly denotes such aid as is rendered by an *epikouros*, "an ally, an auxiliary"; Paul uses it in his testimony to Agrippa, "having therefore obtained the help that is from God," Acts 26:22, RV.¶

B. Verbs.

1. *antilambanō* (ἀντιλαμβάνω, 482), lit., "to take instead of, or in turn" (akin to A, No. 1), is used in the middle voice, and rendered "He hath holpen" in Luke 1:54; "to help," RV, "to support," KJV, in Acts 20:35; its other meaning, to partake of, is used of partaking of things, 1 Tim. 6:2, "that partake of," for KJV, "partakers of." See PARTAKE, SUPPORT. ¶

2. *sullambanō* (συλλαμβάνω, 4815), "to assist, take part with" (*sun*, "with," and *lambanō*), is used, in the middle voice, of rendering help in what others are doing, Luke 5:7, of bringing in a catch of fish; in Phil. 4:3, in an appeal to Synzygus ("yokefellow") to help Euōdia and Syntychē (v. 2). See CATCH, CONCEIVE.

3. *sunantilambanō* (συναντιλαμβάνω, 4878) signifies "to take hold with at the side for assistance" (*sun*, "with," and No. 1); hence, "to take a share in, help in bearing, to help in general."

It is used, in the middle voice, in Martha's request to the Lord to bid her sister help her, Luke 10:40; and of the ministry of the Holy Spirit in helping our infirmities, Rom. 8:26.¶ In the Sept., Exod. 18:22; Num. 11:17; Ps. 89:21.

4. *boētheō* (βοηθέω, 997), "to come to the aid of anyone, to succour" (akin to A, No. 2), is used in Matt. 15:25; Mark 9:22, 24; Acts 16:9; 21:28; 2 Cor. 6:2, "did I succour"; Heb. 2:18, "to succour"; Rev. 12:16.¶

5. *sumballō* (συμβάλλω, 4820), lit., "to throw together" (*sun*, "with," *ballō*, "to throw"), is used in the middle voice in Acts 18:27, of helping or benefiting believers by discussion or ministry of the Word of God. See CONFER, ENCOUNTER, MAKE (war), MEET, PONDER.

6. *sunupourgeō* (συνυπουργέω, 4943) denotes "to help together, join in helping, to serve with anyone as an underworker" (*sun*, "with," *hupourgeō*, "to serve"; *hupo*, "under," *ergon*, "work"); it is used in 2 Cor. 1:11.¶

7. *sunergeō* (συνεργέω, 4903), "to help in work, to co-operate, be a co-worker," is rendered "that helpeth with" in 1 Cor. 16:16. See WORK.

Note: Paristēmi, "to place beside" (*para*, "by," *histēmi*, "to cause to stand"), "to stand by, be at hand," is used of "standing up for help," in Rom. 16:2, "that ye assist," and 2 Tim. 4:17, "stood with." See BRING, COME, COMMEND, GIVE, PRESENT, PROVE, PROVIDE, SHEW, STAND, YIELD.

HELPER, FELLOW-HELPER

1. *boēthos* (βοηθός, 998), an adjective, akin to A, No. 2, and B, No. 4, under HELP, signifying "helping," is used as a noun in Heb. 13:6, of God as the helper of His saints.¶

2. *sunergos* (συνεργός, 4904), an adjective, akin to B, No. 7, under HELP, "a fellow worker," is translated "helper" in the KJV of Rom. 16:3, 9, RV, "fellow worker"; in 2 Cor. 1:24, KJV and RV, "helpers"; in 2 Cor. 8:23, KJV, "fellow helper," RV, "fellow worker"; so the plural in 3 John 8: See COMPANION, LABORER, etc.

For HEM see BORDER

HEN

ornis (ὄρνις, 3733), "a bird," is used, in the NT, only of a "hen," Matt. 23:37; Luke 13:34.¶

HENCE

1. *enthen* (ἔνθεν, 1782v) is found in the best mss. in Matt. 17:20; Luke 16:26.¶

2. *enteuthen* (ἐντεῦθεν, 1782), akin to No. 1, is used (*a*) of place, "hence," or "from hence,"

Luke 4:9; 13:31; John 2:16; 7:3; 14:31; 18:36; in John 19:18, "on either side (one)," lit., "hence and hence"; in Rev. 22:2, it is contrasted with *ekeithen*, "thence," RV, "on this side . . . on that" (KJV, "on either side"), lit. "hence . . . thence"; (*b*) causal; Jas. 4:1, "(come they not) hence," i.e., "owing to."¶

Notes: (1) For *makran*, "far hence," in Acts 22:21, see FAR. (2) In Acts 1:5, the phrase "not many days hence" is, lit., "not after (*meta*) many days."

HENCEFORTH (from, and negatives), HENCEFORWARD

Notes: (1) Positively, "henceforth" stands for the following: (*a*) *ap' arti* (i.e., *apo arti*), lit., "from now," e.g., Matt. 26:64; Luke 22:69; John 13:19, RV, and KJV marg., "from hence-forth"; Rev. 14:13 (where *aparti* is found as one word in the best mss.); (*b*) *to loipon*, lit., "(for) the remaining (time)," Heb. 10:13; *tou loipou*, Gal. 6:17; (*c*) *apo tou nun*, lit., "from the now," e.g., Luke 1:48; 5:10; 12:52; Acts 18:6; 2 Cor. 5:16 (1st part); (2) negatively, "henceforth . . . not" (or "no more") translates one or other of the negative adverbs *ouketi* and *mēketi*, "no longer," e.g., Acts 4:17, KJV, and RV, "hence-forth (to no man)"; in the following the RV has "no longer" for the KJV, "henceforth" (with a negative), John 15:15; Rom. 6:6; 2 Cor. 5:15; Eph. 4:17; in 2 Cor. 5:16 (last part), RV, "no more"; in Matt. 21:19 and Mark 11:14, "no (fruit . . .) henceforward"; KJV in the latter, "hereafter." See HEREAFTER.

For HER and HERSELF see the forms under HE

HERB

1. *lachanon* (λάχανον, 3001) denotes "a garden herb, a vegetable" (from *lachainō*, "to dig"), in contrast to wild plants, Matt. 13:32; Mark 4:32; Luke 11:42; Rom. 14:2.¶

2. *botanē* (βοτάνη, 1008) denotes "grass, fodder, herbs" (from *boskō*, "to feed"; cf. Eng., "botany"), Heb. 6:7.¶

HERD

agelē (ἀγέλη, 34), from *agō*, "to lead," is used, in the NT, only of swine, Matt. 8:30, 31, 32; Mark 5:11, 13; Luke 8:32, 33.¶

HERE

1. *hōde* (ὧδε, 5602), an adverb signifying (*a*) "here" (of place), e.g., Matt. 12:6; Mark 9:1; used with the neuter plural of the article, Col. 4:9, "(all) things (that are done) here," lit., "(all)

the (things) here"; in Matt. 24:23, *hōde* is used in both parts, hence the RV, "Lo, here (is the Christ, or) Here"; in Mark 13:21 *hōde* is fol-lowed by *ekei*, "there." The word is used meta-phorically in the sense of "in this circumstance," or connection, in 1 Cor. 4:2; Rev. 13:10, 18; 14:12; 17:9. See HITHER.

2. *enthade* (ἐνθάδε, 1759) has the same meanings as No. 1; "here" in Luke 24:41; Acts 16:28; 25:24. See HITHER (John 4:15, 16; Acts 25:17).¶

3. *autou* (αὐτοῦ, 847), the genitive case of *autos*, "self," signifies "just here" in Matt. 26:36. See THERE, No. 5.

HERE (to be, be present)

pareimi (πάρειμι, 3918), "to be by or beside or here" (*para*, "by," and *eimi*, "to be"), is rendered "to have been here" in Acts 24:19. See COME, PRESENT.

Note: For *sumpareimi*, "to be here present," see PRESENT.

HEREAFTER

Notes: (1) This adverb translates the phrase *meta tauta*, lit., "after these things," John 13:7; Rev. 1:19, and frequently in the Apocalypse, see 4:1 (twice); 7:9; 9:12; 15:5; 18:1; 19:1; 20:3. (2) For Matt. 26:64 and Luke 22:69 (KJV, "hereafter") see HENCEFORTH; for Mark 11:14 see HENCEFORWARD. (3) In John 14:30, *ouk eti* is rendered "no more" in the RV (KJV, "Here-after . . . not"). (4) In 1 Tim. 1:16, "hereafter" translates the verb *mellō*, "to be about to."

HEREBY

Notes: (1) This translates the phrase *en toutō*, lit., "in this," 1 Cor. 4:4; 1 John 2:3, 5; 3:16, 19, 24; 4:2, 13; 5:2 (RV, "hereby," KJV, "by this"). (2) In 1 John 4:6, KJV, *ek toutou*, lit., "out of this," i.e., in consequence of this, is rendered "hereby" (RV, "by this").¶

HEREIN

Note: This translates the phrase *en toutō*, "in this," in John 4:37; 9:30; 15:8; Acts 24:16; 2 Cor. 8:10; 1 John 4:9 (KJV, "in this"), 10, 17.¶

HEREOF

Notes: (1) This translates the word *hautē*, "this," the feminine of *houtos*, "this," in Matt. 9:26, lit., "this (fame)," KJV, and RV marg. (2) In Heb. 5:3, KJV, *dia tautēn*, lit., "by reason of (*dia*) this" (i.e., this infirmity), is rendered "her-eof"; the best texts have *autēn*, RV, "thereof."

HERESY

hairesis (αἵρεσις, 139) denotes (*a*) "a choosing, choice" (from *haireomai*, "to choose"); then, "that which is chosen," and hence, "an opinion," especially a self-willed opinion, which is substituted for submission to the power of truth, and leads to division and the formation of sects, Gal. 5:20 (marg., "parties"); such erroneous opinions are frequently the outcome of personal preference or the prospect of advantage; see 2 Pet. 2:1, where "destructive" (RV) signifies leading to ruin; some assign even this to (*b*); in the papyri the prevalent meaning is "choice" (Moulton and Milligan, *Vocab.*); (*b*) "a sect"; this secondary meaning, resulting from (*a*), is the dominating significance in the NT, Acts 5:17; 15:5; 24:5, 14; 26:5; 28:22; "heresies" in 1 Cor. 11:19 (see marg.). See SECT.¶

HERETICAL

hairetikos (αἱρετικός, 141), akin to the above, primarily denotes "capable of choosing" (*haireomai*); hence, "causing division by a party spirit, factious," Titus 3:10, RV, "heretical".¶

For HERETOFORE see SIN, C, No. 2

HEREUNTO

Note: This translates the phrase *eis touto*, lit., "unto this," in 1 Pet. 2:21.

For HEREWITH see TRADE, A, No. 2

HERITAGE

klēroō (κληρόω, 2820), primarily, "to cast lots" or "to choose by lot," then, "to assign a portion," is used in the passive voice in Eph. 1:11, "we were made a heritage," RV (KJV, "we have obtained an inheritance"). The RV is in agreement with such OT passages as Deut. 4:20, "a people of inheritance"; 9:29; 32:9; Ps. 16:6. The meaning "were chosen by lot," as in the Vulgate, and in 1 Sam. 14:41, indicating the freedom of election without human will (so Chrysostom and Augustine), is not suited to this passage.¶

HEW, HEW DOWN, HEWN

A. Verbs.

1. *ekkoptō* (ἐκκόπτω, 1581), "to cut out or down" (*ek*, "out of," *koptō*, "to cut"), is rendered "to hew down," of trees, Matt. 3:10; 7:19 (a similar testimony by John the Baptist and Christ); Luke 3:9. See CUT, HINDER.

2. *latomeō* (λατομέω, 2998) signifies "to hew out stones" (from *latomos*, "a stone-cutter"; *las*, "a stone," *temnō*, "to cut"), and is used of the sepulchre which Joseph of Arimathaea had "hewn" out of a rock for himself, where the body of the Lord was buried, Matt. 27:60; Mark 15:46.¶

B. Adjective.

laxeutos (λαξευτός, 2991) denotes "hewn in stone" (*las*, "a stone," *xeō*, "to scrape"; cf. A, No. 2), is used of Christ's tomb, in Luke 23:53.¶

HIDE, HID, HIDDEN

A. Verbs.

1. *kruptō* (κρύπτω, 2928), "to cover, conceal, keep secret" (Eng., "crypt," "cryptic," etc.), is used (*a*) in its physical significance, e.g., Matt. 5:14; 13:44; 25:18 (some mss. have No. 2); (*b*) metaphorically, e.g., Matt. 11:25 (some mss. have No. 2 here); 13:35, RV, "(things) hidden"; KJV, "(things) which have been kept secret"; Luke 18:34; 19:42; John 19:38, "secretly." See SECRET.

2. *apokruptō* (ἀποκρύπτω, 613), "to conceal from, to keep secret" (*apo*, "from," and No. 1), is used metaphorically, in Luke 10:21, of truths "hidden" from the wise and prudent and revealed to babes; 1 Cor. 2:7, of God's wisdom; Eph. 3:9, of the mystery of the unsearchable riches of Christ, revealed through the gospel; Col. 1:26, of the mystery associated with the preceding.¶

3. *enkruptō* (ἐγκρύπτω, 1470), "to hide in anything" (*en*, "in," and No. 1), is used in Matt. 13:33, of leaven "hidden" in meal.¶

4. *perikruptō* (περικρύπτω, 4032) signifies "to hide by placing something around, to conceal entirely, to keep hidden" (*peri*, "around," used intensively, and No. 1), Luke 1:24.¶

5. *kaluptō* (καλύπτω, 2572) signifies "to cover, conceal," so that no trace of it can be seen (hence somewhat distinct from No. 1): it is not translated "to hide" in the RV; in 2 Cor. 4:3 it is rendered "veiled," suitably continuing the subject of 3:13–18; in Jas. 5:20, "shall hide," KJV (RV, "shall cover"). See COVER.

6. *parakaluptō* (παρακαλύπτω, 3871), lit., "to cover with a veil," KJV, "hid," in Luke 9:45, "it was veiled from them"; see CONCEAL.¶

7. *lanthanō* (λανθάνω, 2990), "to escape notice, to be hidden from," is rendered "(could not) be hid" in Mark 7:24, of Christ; "was (not) hid," Luke 8:47, of the woman with the issue of blood; "is hidden," Acts 26:26, of the facts concerning Christ; the sentence might be rendered "none of these things has escaped the king's notice." See FORGET, UNAWARES.

B. Adjectives.

1. *kruptos* (κρυπτός, 2927), akin to A, No. 1, "hidden, secret," is translated "hid" in Matt.

10:26; Mark 4:22; Luke 8:17, RV, for KJV, "secret"; 12:2 (last part); in 1 Cor. 4:5, "hidden (things of darkness)"; 2 Cor. 4:2, "hidden (things of shame)"; 1 Pet. 3:4, "hidden (man of the heart)." See INWARDLY, SECRET.

2. *apokruphos* (ἀπόκρυφος, 614), "hidden away from" (corresponding to A, No. 2; cf. Eng., "apocryphal"), is translated, "made (KJV, kept) secret," in Mark 4:22; in Luke 8:17, RV, "secret," for KJV, "hid"; in Col. 2:3, RV, "hidden," KJV, "hid." See SECRET.¶

HIGH (from on, most), HIGHLY

A. Adjectives.

1. *hupsēlos* (ὑψηλός, 5308), "high, lofty," is used (*a*) naturally, of mountains, Matt. 4:8; 17:1; Mark 9:2; Rev. 21:10; of a wall, Rev. 21:12; (*b*) figuratively, of the arm of God, Acts 13:17; of heaven, "on high," plural, lit., "in high (places)," Heb. 1:3; (*c*) metaphorically, Luke 16:15, RV, "exalted" (KJV, "highly esteemed"); Rom. 11:20, in the best texts, "high-minded" [lit., "mind (not) high things"]; 12:16.¶

2. *hupsistos* (ὕψιστος, 5310), "most high," is a superlative degree, the positive not being in use; it is used of God in Luke 1:32, 35, 76; 6:35, in each of which the RV has "the most High," for KJV, "the highest"; KJV and RV in Mark 5:7; Luke 8:28; Acts 7:48; 16:17; Heb. 7:1. See HIGHEST (below).

3. *megas* (μέγας, 3173), "great," is translated "high" in John 19:31, of the Sabbath day at the Passover season; here the meaning is virtually equivalent to "holy." See GREAT.

Note: In Heb. 10:21, the RV rightly has "a great (priest)," KJV, "high." For "high places," Eph. 6:12, KJV, see HEAVENLY, B, No. 2.

B. Nouns.

1. *hupsos* (ὕψος, 5311), "height," is used with *ex* (*ek*) "from," in the phrase "on high," Luke 1:78; 24:49; with *eis*, "in" or "into," Eph. 4:8. See ESTATE, HEIGHT, No. 1.

2. *hupsōma* (ὕψωμα, 5313), "high thing," 2 Cor. 10:5; in Rom. 8:39, "height." See HEIGHT, No. 2.¶

C. Adverb.

anō (ἄνω, 507), "above, upward," is used in Phil. 3:14, of the "high calling of God in Christ Jesus," the prize of which is set before believers as their goal, lit., "calling upward" (RV, marg.), a preferable rendering to "heavenly calling." See ABOVE.

HIGHER

A. Adverb.

1. *anōteron* (ἀνώτερον, 511**), the neuter of *anōteros*, "higher," the comparative of *anō* (see C, under HIGH), is used as an adverb of

place in Luke 14:10; for the meaning "above," in Heb. 10:8, see ABOVE.¶

B. Verb.

huperechō (ὑπερέχω, 5242), lit., "to hold over anything," as being superior, is used metaphorically in Rom. 13:1, of rulers, as the "higher" powers; cf. 1 Pet. 2:13, "supreme." See BETTER, EXCELLENCY, PASS, SUPREME.

HIGHEST

hupsistos (ὕψιστος, 5310) is used in the plural in the phrase "in the highest," i.e., in the "highest" regions, the abode of God, Matt. 21:9; Mark 11:10; Luke omits the article, Luke 2:14; 19:38; for its use as a title of God, see HIGH, A, No. 2.

For HIGHLY see DISPLEASE, EXALT, EXCEEDING, FAVOR, THINK

HIGH-MINDED

1. *tuphoō* (τυφόω, 5187) properly means "to wrap in smoke" (from *tuphos*, "smoke"; metaphorically, for "conceit"); it is used in the passive voice, metaphorically in 1 Tim. 3:6, "puffed up," RV (KJV, "lifted up with pride"); so 6:4, KJV, "proud," and 2 Tim. 3:4, KJV, "high-minded." See PROUD, PUFF (up).¶ Cf. *tuphomai*, "to smoke," Matt. 12:20,¶ and *tuphōnikos*, "tempestuous" (with *anemos*, "wind," understood), Acts 27:14.¶

2. *hupsēlophroneō* (ὑψηλοφρονέω, 5309), "to be highminded," is used in 1 Tim. 6:17.¶

HIGHWAY, HIGHWAYSIDE

hodos (ὁδός, 3598), "a way, path, road," is rendered "highways" in Matt. 22:10; Luke 14:23; in Mark 10:46, RV, "way side," KJV, "highway side"; in Matt. 22:9, the word is used with *diexodoi* ("ways out through"), and the phrase is rightly rendered in the RV, "the partings of the highways" (i.e., the crossroads), KJV, "the highways." See WAY.

HILL

1. *oros* (ὄρος, 3735), "a hill or mountain," is translated "hill" in Matt. 5:14; Luke 4:29; "mountain" in Luke 9:37, RV, KJV, "hill" (of the mount of transfiguration) as in v. 28. See MOUNTAIN.

2. *oreinos* (ὀρεινός, 3714), an adjective meaning "mountainous, hilly," is used in the feminine, *oreinē*, as a noun, and rendered "hill country" in Luke 1:39, 65. See COUNTRY.¶

3. *bounos* (βουνός, 1015), "a mound, heap,

height," is translated "hill" in Luke 3:5; "hills" in 23:30.¶

Note: In Acts 17:22, KJV, *pagos* is translated "hill." "The Areopagus," RV, stands for the council (not hill) held near by.

For HIM and HIMSELF see HE

HINDER, HINDRANCE

A. Verbs.

1. *enkoptō* (ἐγκόπτω, 1465), lit., "to cut into" (*en*, "in," *koptō*, "to cut"), was used of "impeding" persons by breaking up the road, or by placing an obstacle sharply in the path; hence, metaphorically, of "detaining" a person unnecessarily, Acts 24:4; of "hindrances" in the way of reaching others, Rom. 15:22; or returning to them, 1 Thess. 2:18; of "hindering" progress in the Christian life, Gal. 5:7 (*anakoptō* in some mss.), where the significance virtually is "who broke up the road along which you were travelling so well?"; of "hindrances" to the prayers of husband and wife, through low standards of marital conduct, 1 Pet. 3:7 (*ekkoptō*, "to cut out, repulse," in some mss.).¶

2. *kōluō* (κωλύω, 2967), "to hinder, forbid, restrain," is translated "to hinder" in Luke 11:52; Acts 8:36; Rom. 1:13, RV (KJV,"was let"); Heb. 7:23, RV (KJV, "were not suffered"). See FORBID.

3. *diakōluō* (διακωλύω, 1254), a strengthened form of No. 2, "to hinder thoroughly," is used in Matt. 3:14, of John the Baptist's endeavor to "hinder" Christ from being baptized, KJV, "forbad," RV, "would have hindered," lit., "was hindering."¶

B. Noun.

enkopē (ἐγκοπή, 1464), "a hindrance," lit., "a cutting in," akin to A, No. 1, with corresponding significance, is used in 1 Cor. 9:12, with *didōmi*, "to give," RV, "(that) we may cause (no) hindrance," KJV, "(lest) we should hinder."¶

For HINDER (part) see STERN

HIRE, HIRED

A. Noun.

misthos (μισθός, 3408) denotes (*a*) "wages, hire," Matt. 20:8; Luke 10:7; Jas. 5:4; in 1 Tim. 5:18; 2 Pet. 2:13; Jude 11, RV, "hire" (KJV, "reward"); in 2 Pet. 2:15, RV, "hire" (KJV, "wages"). See REWARD.

B. Verb.

misthoō (μισθόω, 3409), "to let out for hire," is used in the middle voice, signifying "to hire, to engage the services of anyone by contract," Matt. 20:1, 7.¶

Note: In v. 9 there is no word for "hired" in the original.

HIRED HOUSE

misthōma (μίσθωμα, 3410), akin to A and B, above, primarily denotes "a hire," as in the Sept. of Deut. 23:18; Prov. 19:13; Ezek. 16:31, 34, 41, etc.; in the NT, it is used of "a hired dwelling," Acts 28:30.¶

HIRED SERVANT, HIRELING

1. *misthōtos* (μισθωτός, 3411), an adjective denoting "hired," is used as a noun, signifying "one who is hired," "hired servants," Mark 1:20; "hireling," John 10:12, 13; here, it expresses, not only one who has no real interest in his duty (that may or may not be present in its use in Mark 1:20, and in *misthios*, No. 2), but one who is unfaithful in the discharge of it; that sense attaches always to the word rendered "hireling."¶

2. *misthios* (μίσθιος, 3407), an adjective, akin to No. 1, and similarly signifying "a hired servant," is used in Luke 15:17, 19 (in some texts, v. 21). ¶

HIS, HIS OWN

Note: These translate (*a*) forms of pronouns under HE, No. 1 (a frequent use: in 1 Pet. 2:24, "His own self"); the form *autou*, "his," becomes emphatic when placed between the article and the noun, e.g., 1 Thess. 2:19; Titus 3:5; Heb. 2:4; also under HE, No. 3 (in which "his" is emphasized), e.g., John 5:47; 9:28; 1 Cor. 10:28; 2 Cor. 8:9; 2 Tim. 2:26; Titus 3:7; 2 Pet. 1:16; (*b*) *heautou*, "of himself, his own"; the RV rightly puts "his own," for the KJV, "his," in Luke 11:21; 14:26; Rom. 4:19; 5:8, "His own (love)"; 1 Cor. 7:37; Gal. 6:8; Eph. 5:28, 33; 1 Thess. 2:11, 12; 4:4; in Rev. 10:7 the change has not been made; it should read "his own servants"; (*c*) *idios*, "one's own," "his own," in the RV, in Matt. 22:5; John 5:18; 2 Pet. 2:16; in Matt. 25:15, it is rendered "his several"; in John 19:27, "his own home," lit., "his own things"; in 1 Tim. 6:15, RV, "its own (times)," referring to the future appearing of Christ; in Heb. 4:10 (end of verse), both KJV and RV have "his," where it should be "his own"; so in Acts 24:23, for KJV and RV, "his"; in 1 Cor. 7:7, RV, "his own," KJV, "his proper"; (*d*) in Acts 17:28, the genitive case of the definite article, "His (offspring)," lit., "of the" (i.e., the one referred to, namely, God).

HITHER

1. *hōde* (ὧδε, 5602), primarily an adverb of manner, then, of place, (*a*) of "motion" or "di-

rection towards a place," e.g., Matt. 8:29; Mark 11:3; Luke 9:41; John 6:25; (b) of "position"; see HERE, PLACE.

2. *enthade* (ἐνθάδε, 1759) has the same meaning as No. 1; "hither," John 4:15, 16; Acts 17:6; 25:17. See HERE.

Note: For *deuro*, "come hither," see COME, and HITHERTO, *Note* (2).

HITHERTO

Notes: (1) The phrase *heōs arti*, "until now," is rendered "hitherto" in John 16:24, KJV, and RV; in 5:17, RV, "even until now," which more definitely expresses the meaning than the KJV, "hitherto"; the rest of the Father and the Son having been broken by man's sin, they were engaged in the accomplishment of their counsels of grace with a view to redemption. (2) The phrase *achri tou deuro*, lit., "until the hither," or "the present," is used of time in Rom. 1:13, "hitherto." (3) In 1 Cor. 3:2, KJV, *oupō*, "not yet," is translated "hitherto ... not," RV, "not yet."

HOISE UP, HOIST UP

1. *airō* (αἴρω, 142), "to raise," is used of "hoisting up" a skiff, or little boat, before undergirding the ship, Acts 27:17, RV, "had hoisted up," for KJV, "had taken up." See AWAY, TAKE.

2. *epairō* (ἐπαίρω, 1869), "to raise up" (*epi*, "up," and No. 1), is used of "hoisting up" the foresail of a vessel, Acts 27:40, RV, "hoisting up." See EXALT, LIFT.

HOLD (Noun)

1. *tērēsis* (τήρησις, 5084), translated "hold" in Acts 4:3, KJV, "prison" in 5:18 (RV, "ward"), signifies (a) "a watching, guarding"; hence, "imprisonment, ward" (from *tēreō*, "to watch, keep"); the RV, has "ward" in both places; (b) "a keeping," as of commandments, 1 Cor. 7:19. See KEEPING, WARD.¶

2. *phulakē* (φυλακή, 5438), "a guarding" or "guard" (akin to *phulassō*, "to guard or watch"), also denotes "a prison, a hold," Rev. 18:2 (twice), RV, "hold" in both places, KJV, "cage," in the second (RV, marg., "prison," in both). See CAGE, IMPRISONMENT, PRISON.

HOLD (down, fast, forth, on, to, up), HELD, HOLDEN, (take) HOLD

1. *echō* (ἔχω, 2192), "to have or hold," is used of mental conception, "to consider, account," e.g., Matt. 21:26; of "steadfast adherence to faith, or the faith," e.g., 1 Tim. 1:19; 3:9; 2 Tim. 1:13. See HAVE.

2. *katechō* (κατέχω, 2722), "to hold firmly, hold fast" (*kata*, "down," and No. 1), is rendered "hold fast" in 1 Cor. 11:2, RV (KJV, "keep"); 1 Thess. 5:21; Heb. 3:6, 14 (RV); 10:23; "hold down," Rom. 1:18, RV, of unrighteous men who restrain the spread of truth by their unrighteousness, or, as RV marg., "who hold the truth in (or with) unrighteousness," contradicting their profession by their conduct (cf. 2:15, RV); in Rom. 7:6, RV, "holden," KJV, "held," of the Law as that which had "held" in bondage those who through faith in Christ were made dead to it as a means of life. See KEEP, MAKE (toward), POSSESS, RESTRAIN, RETAIN, SEIZE, STAY, TAKE.

3. *antechō* (ἀντέχω, 472), *anti*, "against, or to," and No. 1, signifies in the middle voice, (a) "to hold firmly to, cleave to," of "holding" or cleaving to a person, Matt. 6:24; Luke 16:13; of "holding" to the faithful word, Titus 1:9, RV, KJV, "holding fast"; (b) "to support," 1 Thess. 5:14 (the weak). See SUPPORT.¶

4. *sunechō* (συνέχω, 4912), *sun*, "with," intensive, and No. 1, is used of "holding" a prisoner, in Luke 22:63. See CONSTRAIN, KEEP, PRESS, STOP, STRAIT, STRAITENED, TAKE.

5. *epechō* (ἐπέχω, 1907) is used in Phil. 2:16, of "holding" forth the word of life (*epi*, "forth," and No. 1). See (give) HEED, (take) HEED, MARK, STAY.

6. *krateō* (κρατέω, 2902), "to be strong, mighty, to prevail," (1) is most frequently rendered "to lay or take hold on" (a) literally, e.g., Matt. 12:11; 14:3; 18:28 and 21:46, RV (KJV, "laid hands on"); 22:6, RV (KJV, "took"); 26:55, KJV (RV, "took"); 28:9, RV, "took hold of" (KJV, "held by"); Mark 3:21; 6:17; 12:12; 14:51; Acts 24:6, RV (KJV, "took"); Rev. 20:2; (b) metaphorically, of "laying hold of the hope of the Lord's return," Heb. 6:18; (2) also signifies "to hold" or "hold fast," i.e., firmly, (a), literally, Matt. 26:48, KJV (RV, "take"); Acts 3:11; Rev. 2:1; (b) metaphorically, of "holding fast a tradition or teaching," in an evil sense, Mark 7:3, 4, 8; Rev. 2:14, 15; in a good sense, 2 Thess. 2:15; Rev. 2:25; 3:11; of "holding" Christ, i.e., practically apprehending Him, as the head of His church, Col. 2:19; a confession, Heb. 4:14; the name of Christ, i.e., abiding by all that His name implies, Rev. 2:13; of restraint, Luke 24:16, "(their eyes) were holden"; of the winds, Rev. 7:1; of the impossibility of Christ's being "holden" of death, Acts 2:24. See KEEP, RETAIN (of sins), TAKE.

7. *epilambanō* (ἐπιλαμβάνω, 1949), "to lay hold of, to take hold of" (*epi*, "upon," *lambanō*, "to take"), with a special purpose, always in the middle voice, is so translated in Luke 20:20, 26,

of taking "hold" of Christ's words; in 23:26 and Acts 21:33, RV, of laying "hold" of persons; in 1 Tim. 6:12, 19, of laying "hold" on eternal life, i.e., practically appropriating all the benefits, privileges and responsibilities involved in the possession of it; in Heb. 2:16, RV "He taketh hold" (KJV "took on") perhaps to be viewed in connection with "deliver" (v. 15) and "succor" (v. 18). See APPREHEND CATCH, TAKE.

8. *tēreō* (τηρέω, 5083), akin to A, No. 1, under HOLD (Noun), "to watch over, keep, give heed to, observe," is rendered "hold fast" in Rev. 3:3, KJV (RV, "keep"). See KEEP, OBSERVE, RESERVE, WATCH.

9. *eimi* (εἰμί, 1510), "to be," is used in the imperfect tense, with the preposition, *sun*, "with," in the idiomatic phrase "held with," in Acts 14:4, lit., "were with."

Notes: (1) In Rom. 14:4, *histēmi*, "to cause to stand," in the passive voice, "to be made to stand," is used in both forms, the latter in the first part, RV, "he shall be made to stand" (KJV, "he shall be holden up"), the active voice in the second part, KJV, and RV, "to make stand." (2) In Matt. 12:14, RV, *lambanō*, "to take," is translated "took (counsel)," KJV, "held (a council)." (3) In Mark 15:1, some mss. have the verb *poieō*, "to make," rendered "held (a consultation)"; the most authentic have *hetoimazō*, "to prepare," also translated "held."

HOLE

1. *phōleos* (φωλεός, 5454), "a lair, burrow, den or hole," is used of foxes in Matt. 8:20 and Luke 9:58.¶

2. *opē* (ὀπή, 3692) is translated "holes" in Heb. 11:38, RV, KJV "caves." See CAVE, OPENING.

HOLINESS, HOLY, HOLILY

A. Nouns.

1. *hagiasmos* (ἁγιασμός, 38), translated "holiness" in the KJV of Rom. 6:19, 22; 1 Thess. 4:7; 1 Tim. 2:15; Heb. 12:14, is always rendered "sanctification" in the RV. It signifies (*a*) separation to God, 1 Cor. 1:30; 2 Thess. 2:13; 1 Pet. 1:2; (*b*) the resultant state, the conduct befitting those so separated, 1 Thess. 4:3, 4, 7, and the four other places mentioned above. "Sanctification" is thus the state predetermined by God for believers, into which in grace He calls them, and in which they begin their Christian course and so pursue it. Hence they are called "saints" (*hagioi*). See SANCTIFICATION.¶

Note: The corresponding verb *hagiazō* denotes "to set apart to God." See HALLOW, SANCTIFY.

2. *hagiōsunē* (ἁγιωσύνη, 42) denotes the manifestation of the quality of "holiness" in personal conduct; (*a*) it is used in Rom. 1:4, of the absolute "holiness" of Christ in the days of His flesh, which distinguished Him from all merely human beings; this (which is indicated in the phrase "the spirit of holiness") and (in vindication of it) His resurrection from the dead, marked Him out as (He was "declared to be") the Son of God; (*b*) believers are to be "perfecting holiness in the fear of God," 2 Cor. 7:1, i.e., bringing "holiness" to its predestined end, whereby (*c*) they may be found "unblameable in holiness" in the Parousia of Christ, 1 Thess. 3:13.¶

"In each place character is in view, perfect in the case of the Lord Jesus, growing toward perfection in the case of the Christian. Here the exercise of love is declared to be the means God uses to develop likeness to Christ in His children. The sentence may be paraphrased thus:— The Lord enable you more and more to spend your lives in the interests of others, in order that He may so establish you in Christian character now, that you may be vindicated from every charge that might possibly be brought against you at the Judgment-seat of Christ;' cf. 1 John 4:16, 17."*

3. *hagiotēs* (ἁγιότης, 41), "sanctity," the abstract quality of "holiness," is used (*a*) of God, Heb. 12:10; (*b*) of the manifestation of it in the conduct of the apostle Paul and his fellowlaborers, 2 Cor. 1:12 (in the best mss., for *haplotēs*).¶

4. *hosiotēs* (ὁσιότης, 3742) is to be distinguished from No. 3, as denoting that quality of "holiness" which is manifested in those who have regard equally to grace and truth; it involves a right relation to God; it is used in Luke 1:75 and Eph. 4:24, and in each place is associated with righteousness. ¶

Notes: (1) In Acts 3:12, the KJV translates *eusebeia*, by "holiness," RV, "godliness," as everywhere, the true meaning of the word. See GODLINESS. (2) In Titus 2:3, KJV, *hieroprepēs*, which denotes "suited to a sacred character, reverent," is rendered "as becometh holiness," RV, "reverent." See REVERENT.¶

B. Adjectives.

1. *hagios* (ἅγιος, 40), akin to A, Nos. 1 and 2, which are from the same root as *hagnos* (found in *hazō*, "to venerate"), fundamentally signifies "separated" (among the Greeks, dedicated to the gods), and hence, in Scripture in its moral and spiritual significance, separated from sin and therefore consecrated to God, sacred.

(*a*) It is predicated of God (as the absolutely

---

* From *Notes on Thessalonians,* by Hogg and Vine, pp. 108, 115.

"Holy" One, in His purity, majesty and glory): of the Father, e.g., Luke 1:49; John 17:11; 1 Pet. 1:15, 16; Rev. 4:8; 6:10; of the Son, e.g., Luke 1:35; Acts 3:14; 4:27, 30; 1 John 2:20; of the Spirit, e.g., Matt. 1:18 and frequently in all the Gospels, Acts, Romans, 1 and 2 Cor., Eph., 1 Thess.; also in 2 Tim. 1:14; Titus 3:5; 1 Pet. 1:12; 2 Pet. 1:21; Jude 20.

(b) It is used of men and things (see below) in so far as they are devoted to God. Indeed the quality, as attributed to God, is often presented in a way which involves divine demands upon the conduct of believers. These are called *hagioi*, "saints," i.e., "sanctified" or "holy" ones.

This sainthood is not an attainment, it is a state into which God in grace calls men; yet believers are called to sanctify themselves (consistently with their calling, 2 Tim. 1:9), cleansing themselves from all defilement, forsaking sin, living a "holy" manner of life, 1 Pet. 1:15; 2 Pet. 3:11, and experiencing fellowship with God in His holiness. The saints are thus figuratively spoken of as "a holy temple", 1 Cor. 3:17 (a local church); Eph. 2:21 (the whole Church), cp. 5:27; "a holy priesthood," 1 Pet. 2:5; "a holy nation," 2:9.

"It is evident that *hagios* and its kindred words ... express something more and higher than *hieros*, sacred, outwardly associated with God; ... something more than *semnos*, worthy, honorable; something more than *hagnos*, pure, free from defilement. *Hagios* is ... more comprehensive.... It is characteristically godlikeness" (G. B. Stevens, in Hastings' *Bib. Dic.*).

The adjective is also used of the outer part of the tabernacle, Heb. 9:2 (RV, "the holy place"); of the inner sanctuary, 9:3, RV, "the Holy of Holies"; 9:24, "a holy place," RV; v. 25 (plural), of the presence of God in heaven, where there are not two compartments as in the tabernacle, all being "the holy place"; 9:8, 12 (neuter plural); 10:19, "the holy place," RV (KJV, "the holiest," neut. plural), see SANCTUARY; of the city of Jerusalem, Rev. 11:2; its temple, Acts 6:13; of the faith, Jude 20; of the greetings of saints, 1 Cor. 16:20; of angels, e.g., Mark 8:38; of apostles and prophets, Eph. 3:5; of the future heavenly Jerusalem, Rev. 21:2, 10; 22:19.

2. *hosios* (ὅσιος, 3741), akin to A, No. 4, signifies "religiously right, holy," as opposed to what is unrighteous or polluted. It is commonly associated with righteousness (see A, No.4). It is used "of God, Rev. 15:4; 16:5; and of the body of the Lord Jesus, Acts 2:27; 13:35, citations from Ps. 16:10, Sept.; Heb. 7:26; and of certain promises made to David, which could be fulfilled only in the resurrection of the Lord Jesus, Acts 13:34. In 1 Tim. 2:8 and Titus 1:8,

it is used of the character of Christians.... In the Sept., *hosios* frequently represents the Hebrew word *chasid*, which varies in meaning between 'holy' and 'gracious,' or 'merciful;' cf. Ps. 16:10 with 145:17."*

Notes: (1) For Acts 13:34, see the RV and the KJV marg.; the RV in Rev. 16:5, "Thou Holy One," translates the most authentic mss. (KJV "and shalt be"). (2) For *hieros* (see No. 1), subserving a sacred purpose, translated "holy" in 2 Tim. 3:15, KJV (of the Scriptures), see SACRED.

C. Adverb.

hosiōs (ὁσίως, 3743), akin to A, No. 4, and B, No. 2, "holily," i.e., pure from evil conduct, and observant of God's will, is used in 1 Thess. 2:10, of the conduct of the apostle and his fellow missionaries.¶

D. Verb.

hagiazō (ἁγιάζω, 37), "to hallow, sanctify," in the passive voice, "to be made holy, be sanctified," is translated "let him be made holy" in Rev. 22:11, the aorist or point tense expressing the definiteness and completeness of the divine act; elsewhere it is rendered by the verb "to sanctify." See HALLOW, SANCTIFY.

For HOLY GHOST see under SPIRIT and HOLY, B, No. 1 (a)

HOLYDAY

heortē (ἑορτή, 1859) denotes "a feast, festival"; it is translated "a holy day" in the KJV of Col. 2:16; RV, "a feast day." See FEAST.

HOME, AT HOME (to be; workers)

A. Noun and Phrases.

1. *oikos* (οἶκος, 3624), "a house, dwelling," is used (a) with the preposition *eis*, "unto," with the meaning "to home," lit., "to a house," in Mark 8:3, RV, "to (their) home," KJV, "to (their own) houses"; so 8:26, "to (his) home"; Luke 15:6, "home," lit., "into the house"; (b) with the preposition *en*, "in," 1 Cor. 11:34, "(let him eat) at home"; 14:35, "(let them ask ...) at home"; (c) with the preposition *kata*, "down," Acts 2:46, "(breaking bread) at home," RV (KJV, "from house to house"); so in 5:42 (KJV, "in every house").

Notes: (1) In Mark 3:19, the KJV and RV marg., have "home," for the text "to a house"; the latter seems the more probable. See HOUSE. (2) In 1 Tim. 5:4, the phrase *ton idion oikon*, is rendered "at home," of the necessity that children should show piety there; RV, "towards their

---

* From *Notes on Thessalonians,* by Hogg and Vine, p. 64.

own family," the house being put by metonymy for the family.

2. The neuter plural of *idios*, "one's own," with the article, preceded by *eis*, "unto," lit., "unto one's own (things)," is translated "home" in Acts 21:6; in John 19:27, "unto his own home" ("home" being italicized).

Note: In John 16:32, this phrase is rendered "to his own" (of the predicted scattering of the disciples), KJV marg., "his own home"; cf. John 1:11, "His own things," RV, marg. (i.e., "His possessions").

For *oikia* in Matt. 8:6, KJV, "at home," see HOUSE.

3. In Luke 24:12 the reflexive pronoun *hauton* (in some mss. *heauton*), preceded by *pros*, to, is rendered "to his home," RV (lit., "to himself"), of the departure of Peter from the Lord's tomb; in John 20:10, the same construction is used, in the plural, of Peter and John on the same occasion, and rendered "unto their own home."

B. Adjective.

oikourgos (οἰκουργός, 3626), "working at home" (*oikos*, and a root of *ergon*, "work"), is used in Titus 2:5, "workers at home," RV, in the injunction given to elder women regarding the training of the young women. Some mss. have *oikouros*, "watching" or "keeping the home" (*oikos*, and *ouros*, "a keeper"), KJV, "keepers at home."¶

C. Verb.

endēmeō (ἐνδημέω, 1736), lit., "to be among one's people" (*en*, "in," *dēmos*, "people"; *endēmos*, "one who is in his own place or land"), is used metaphorically of the life on earth of believers, 2 Cor. 5:6, "at home (in the body)"; in v. 8 of the life in Heaven of the spirits of believers, after their decease, "at home (with the Lord)," RV (KJV, "present"); in v. 9, "at home" (KJV, "present") refers again to the life on earth. In each verse the verb is contrasted with *ekdēmeō*, "to be away from home, to be absent"; in v. 6, "we are absent," i.e., away from "home" (from the Lord); in v. 8, "to be absent" (i.e., away from the "home" of the body); so in v. 9, "absent." The implication in being "at home with the Lord" after death is a testimony against the doctrine of the unconsciousness of the spirit, when freed from the natural body.¶

HONEST, HONESTLY, HONESTY

A. Adjectives.

1. *kalos* (καλός, 2570), "good, admirable, becoming," has also the ethical meaning of what is "fair, right, honorable, of such conduct as deserves esteem"; it is translated "honest" [cf. Latin *honestus* (from *honos*, "honor")], which

has the same double meaning as "honest" in the KJV, namely, regarded with honor, honorable, and bringing honor, becoming; in Luke 8:15 (KJV, and RV), "an honest and good (*agathos*) heart"; Rom. 12:17; 2 Cor. 8:21 and 13:7, RV, "honorable" (KJV, "honest"), of things which are regarded with esteem; in 1 Pet. 2:12, of behavior, RV, "seemly," KJV, "honest" (i.e., becoming). See GOOD.

Note: In Titus 3:14, the RV and KJV margins give what is probably the accurate meaning, "(to profess) honest occupations" (KJV, "trades"); in the texts "(to maintain) good works."

2. *semnos* (σεμνός, 4586), "august, venerable," is rendered "honest" in Phil. 4:8, KJV (marg., "venerable"), RV, "honorable" (marg., "reverent"). Matthew Arnold suggests "nobly serious." See GRAVE.

Note: In Acts 6:3, "men of honest (RV, 'good') report" translates the passive voice of *martureō*, lit., "having had witness borne."

B. Adverbs.

1. *kalōs* (καλῶς, 2573), corresponding to A, No. 1, is used in Heb. 13:18, "honestly," i.e., honorably. See PLACE, C, *Note* (4), WELL.

2. *euschēmonōs* (εὐσχημόνως, 2156), "becomingly, decently," is rendered "honestly" in Rom. 13:13, where it is set in contrast with the confusion of gentile social life, and in 1 Thess. 4:12, of the manner of life of believers as a witness to "them that are without"; in 1 Cor. 14:40, "decently," in contrast with confusion in the churches. See DECENTLY.¶

C. Noun.

semnotēs (σεμνότης, 4587) denotes "gravity, dignified seriousness"; it is rendered "honesty" in the KJV of 1 Tim. 2:2, RV, "gravity." See GRAVITY.

HONEY

meli (μέλι, 3192) occurs with the adjective *agrios*, "wild," in Matt. 3:4; Mark 1:6; in Rev. 10:9, 10, as an example of sweetness.¶ As "honey" is liable to ferment, it was precluded from offerings to God, Lev. 2:11. The liquid "honey" mentioned in Ps. 19:10 and Prov. 16:24 is regarded as the best; a cruse of it was part of the present brought to Ahijah by Jeroboam's wife, 1 Kings 14:3.

HONEYCOMB

melissios (μελίσσιος, 3193), signifying "made by bees" from *melissa*, "a bee," is found, with *kerion*, "a comb," in some mss. in Luke 24:42.¶

HONOR (Noun and Verb)

A. Nouns.

1. *timē* (τιμή, 5092), primarily "a valuing," hence, objectively, (*a*) "a price paid or received," e.g., Matt. 27:6, 9; Acts 4:34; 5:2, 3; 7:16, RV, "price" (KJV, "sum"); 19:19; 1 Cor. 6:20; 7:23; (*b*) of "the preciousness of Christ" unto believers, 1 Pet. 2:7, RV, i.e., the honor and inestimable value of Christ as appropriated by believers, who are joined, as living stones, to Him the cornerstone; (*c*) in the sense of value, of human ordinances, valueless against the indulgence of the flesh, or, perhaps of no value in attempts at asceticism, Col. 2:23 (see extended note under INDULGENCE, No. 2); (*d*) "honor, esteem," (1) used in ascriptions of worship to God, 1 Tim. 1:17; 6:16; Rev. 4:9, 11; 5:13; 7:12; to Christ, 5:12, 13; (2) bestowed upon Christ by the Father, Heb. 2:9; 2 Pet. 1:17; (3) bestowed upon man, Heb. 2:7; (4) bestowed upon Aaronic priests, Heb. 5:4; (5) to be the reward hereafter of "the proof of faith" on the part of tried saints, 1 Pet. 1:7, RV; (6) used of the believer who as a vessel is "meet for the Master's use," 2 Tim. 2:21; (7) to be the reward of patience in well-doing, Rom. 2:7, and of working good (a perfect life to which man cannot attain, so as to be justified before God thereby), 2:10; (8) to be given to all to whom it is due, Rom. 13:7 (see 1 Pet. 2:17, under B, No. 1); (9) as an advantage to be given by believers one to another instead of claiming it for self, Rom. 12:10; (10) to be given to elders that rule well ("double honor"), 1 Tim. 5:17 (here the meaning may be an honorarium); (11) to be given by servants to their master, 1 Tim. 6:1; (12) to be given to wives by husbands, 1 Pet. 3:7; (13) said of the husband's use of the wife, in contrast to the exercise of the passion of lust, 1 Thess. 4:4 (some regard the "vessel" here as the believer's body); (14) of that bestowed upon; parts of the body, 1 Cor. 12:23, 24; (15) of that which belongs to the builder of a house in contrast to the house itself, Heb. 3:3; (16) of that which is not enjoyed by a prophet in his own country, John 4:44; (17) of that bestowed by the inhabitants of Melita upon Paul and his fellow-passengers, in gratitude for his benefits of healing, Acts 28:10; (18) of the festive honor to be possessed by nations, and brought into the Holy City, the heavenly Jerusalem, Rev. 21:26 (in some mss., v. 24); (19) of honor bestowed upon things inanimate, a potters' vessel, Rom. 9:21; 2 Tim. 2:20. See PRECIOUSNESS, PRICE, SUM, VALUE.¶

Note: For *entimos*, "in honor," see HONORABLE, No. 2.

2. *doxa* (δόξα, 1391), "glory," is translated "honor" in the KJV of John 5:41, 44 (twice); 8:54; 2 Cor. 6:8, and Rev. 19:7; the RV keeps to the word "glory," as the KJV everywhere else. See GLORY.

B. Verbs.

1. *timaō* (τιμάω, 5091), "to honor" (akin to A, No. 1), is used of (*a*) valuing Christ at a price, Matt. 27:9, cf. A, No. 1, (*a*); (*b*) "honoring" a person: (1) the "honor" done by Christ to the Father, John 8:49; (2) "honor" bestowed by the Father upon him who serves Christ, John 12:26; (3) the duty of all to "honor" the Son equally with the Father, 5:23; (4) the duty of children to "honor" their parents, Matt. 15:4; 19:19; Mark 7:10; 10:19; Luke 18:20; Eph. 6:2; (5) the duty of Christians to "honor" the king, and all men, 1 Pet. 2:17; (6) the respect and material assistance to be given to widows "that are widows indeed," 1 Tim. 5:3; (7) the "honor" done to Paul and his companions by the inhabitants of Melita, Acts 28:10; (8) mere lip profession of "honor" to God, Matt. 15:8; Mark 7:6.¶

2. *doxazō* (δοξάζω, 1392), "to glorify" (from *doxa*, A, No. 2), is rendered "honor" and "honoreth" in the KJV of John 8:54; in 1 Cor. 12:26, however, in reference to the members of the body, both KJV and RV have "honored" (RV marg., "glorified"). Everywhere else it is translated by some form of the verb "to glorify," "have glory," or "be made glorious," except in Rom. 11:13, "magnify," KJV. See GLORIFY.

HONORABLE, WITHOUT HONOR

1. *endoxos* (ἔνδοξος, 1741) denotes (*a*) "held in honor" (*en*, "in," *doxa*, "honor"; cf. HONOR, A, No. 2), "of high repute," 1 Cor. 4:10, KJV "(are) honorable," RV, "(have) glory," in contrast to *atimos*, "without honor" (see No. 6 below). See GLORIOUS, GORGEOUSLY.

2. *entimos* (ἔντιμος, 1784), lit., "in honor" (*en*, "in," *timē*, "honor": see HONOR, A, No. 1), is used of the centurion's servant in Luke 7:2, "dear" (RV marg., "precious . . . or honorable"); of self-sacrificing servants of the Lord, said of Epaphroditus, Phil. 2:29, RV "(hold such) in honor" (KJV, "in reputation"; marg., "honor such"); of Christ, as a precious stone, 1 Pet. 2:4, 6 (RV marg., "honorable"). Cf. *timios* in 1:7, 19; see No. 4.¶

The comparative degree, *entimoteros*, is used (in the best mss.) of degrees of honor attached to persons invited to a feast, a marriage feast, Luke 14:8, "a more honorable man." See PRECIOUS.¶

3. *euschēmōn* (εὐσχήμων, 2158) signifies "elegant, comely, of honorable position," KJV, "honorable," RV, "of honorable estate," Mark

15:43; Acts 13:50; 17:12; for other renderings in 1 Cor. 7:35 and 12:24 see COMELY, B.

4. *timios* (τίμιος, 5093), "precious, valuable, honorable" (akin to *timē*, "honor"; see No. 2), is used of marriage in Heb. 13:4, KJV, as a statement, "(marriage) is honorable (in all)," RV, as an exhortation, "let (marriage) be had in honor (among all)." See DEAR, PRECIOUS, REPUTATION.

5. *kalos* (καλός, 2570), "good, fair," is translated "honorable" in Rom. 12:17; 2 Cor. 8:21; 13:7, RV (KJV,"honest"). See GOOD, HONEST.

6. *atimos* (ἄτιμος, 820), without honor (*a*, negative, or privative, *timē*, "honor"), "despised," is translated "without honor" in Matt. 13:57; Mark 6:4; "dishonor" in 1 Cor. 4:10, RV (KJV, "despised"). See DESPISE.¶

The comparative degree *atimoteros* is used in the best mss. in 1 Cor. 12:23, "less honorable."¶

Note: For *semnos*, honorable, Phil. 4:8, RV, see GRAVE.

HOOK

ankistron (ἄγκιστρον, 44), "a fish-hook" (from *ankos*, "a bend"; Lat. *angulus*; Eng., "anchor" and "angle" are akin), is used in Matt. 17:27.¶ In the Sept., 2 Kings 19:28; Job 40:20; Isa. 19:8; Ezek. 32:3; Hab. 1:15.¶

HOPE (Noun and Verb), HOPE (for)

A. Noun.

elpis (ἐλπίς, 1680), in the NT, "favorable and confident expectation" (contrast the Sept. in Isa. 28:19, "an evil hope"). It has to do with the unseen and the future, Rom. 8:24, 25. "Hope" describes (*a*) the happy anticipation of good (the most frequent significance), e.g., Titus 1:2; 1 Pet. 1:21; (*b*) the ground upon which "hope" is based, Acts 16:19; Col. 1:27, "Christ in you the hope of glory"; (*c*) the object upon which the "hope" is fixed, e.g., 1 Tim. 1:1.

Various phrases are used with the word "hope," in Paul's epistles and speeches: (1) Acts 23:6, "the hope and resurrection of the dead"; this has been regarded as a hendiadys (one by means of two), i.e., the "hope" of the resurrection; but the *kai*, "and," is epexegetic, defining the "hope," namely, the resurrection; (2) Acts 26:6, 7, "the hope of the promise (i.e., the fulfillment of the promise) made unto the fathers"; (3) Gal. 5:5, "the hope of righteousness"; i.e., the believer's complete conformity to God's will, at the coming of Christ; (4) Col. 1:23, "the hope of the Gospel," i.e., the "hope" of the fulfillment of all the promises presented in the gospel; cf. 1:5; (5) Rom. 5:2, "(the) hope of the glory of God," i.e., as in Titus 2:13, "the blessed hope and appearing of the glory of our great

God and Savior Jesus Christ"; cf. Col. 1:27; (6) 1 Thess. 5:8, "the hope of salvation," i.e., of the rapture of believers, to take place at the opening of the Parousia of Christ; (7) Eph. 1:18, "the hope of His (God's) calling," i.e., the prospect before those who respond to His call in the gospel; (8) Eph. 4:4, "the hope of your calling," the same as (7), but regarded from the point of view of the called; (9) Titus 1:2, and 3:7, "the hope of eternal life," i.e., the full manifestation and realization of that life which is already the believer's possession; (10) Acts 28:20, "the hope of Israel," i.e., the expectation of the coming of the Messiah. See *Notes on Galatians* by Hogg and Vine, pp. 248, 249.

In Eph. 1:18; 2:12 and 4:4, the "hope" is objective. The objective and subjective use of the word need to be distinguished; in Rom. 15:4, e.g., the use is subjective.

In the NT three adjectives are descriptive of "hope": "good," 2 Thess. 2:16; "blessed," Titus 2:13; "living," 1 Pet. 1:3. To these may be added Heb. 7:19, "a better hope," i.e., additional to the commandment, which became disannulled (v. 18), a hope centered in a new priesthood.

In Rom. 15:13 God is spoken of as "the God of hope," i.e., He is the author, not the subject, of it. "Hope" is a factor in salvation, Rom. 8:24; it finds its expression in endurance under trial, which is the effect of waiting for the coming of Christ, 1 Thess. 1:3; it is "an anchor of the soul," staying it amidst the storms of this life, Heb. 6:18, 19; it is a purifying power, "every one that hath this hope set on Him (Christ) purifieth himself, even as He is pure," 1 John 3:3, RV (the apostle John's one mention of "hope").

The phrase "fullness of hope," Heb. 6:11, RV, expresses the completeness of its activity in the soul; cf. "fullness of faith," 10:22, and "of understanding," Col. 2:2 (RV, marg.).

B. Verbs.

1. *elpizō* (ἐλπίζω, 1679), "to hope," is not infrequently translated in the KJV, by the verb "to trust"; the RV adheres to some form of the verb "to hope," e.g., John 5:45, "Moses, on whom ye have set your hope"; 2 Cor. 1:10, "on whom we have set our hope"; so in 1 Tim. 4:10; 5:5; 6:17; see also, e.g., Matt. 12:21; Luke 24:21; Rom. 15:12, 24.

The verb is followed by three prepositions: (1) *eis*, rendered "on" in John 5:45 (as above); the meaning is really "in" as in 1 Pet. 3:5, "who hoped in God"; the "hope" is thus said to be directed to, and to center in, a person; (2) *epi*, "on," Rom. 15:12, "On Him shall the Gentiles hope," RV; so 1 Tim. 4:10; 5:5 (in the best mss.); 6:17, RV; this expresses the ground upon which "hope" rests; (3) *en*, "in," 1 Cor. 15:19, "we have hoped in Christ," RV, more lit., "we are (men) that have hoped in Christ," the preposition expresses that Christ is not simply the ground upon whom, but the sphere and element in whom, the "hope" is placed. The form of the verb (the perfect participle with the verb to be, lit., "are having hoped") stresses the character of those who "hope," more than the action; "hope" characterizes them, showing what sort of persons they are. See TRUST.

2. *proelpizō* (προελπίζω, 4276), "to hope before" (*pro*, "before," and No. 1), is found in Eph. 1:12.¶

3. *apelpizō* (ἀπελπίζω, 560), lit., "to hope from" (*apo*, and No, 1): see DESPAIR.

HORN

keras (κέρας, 2768), "a horn," is used in the plural, as the symbol of strength, (*a*) in the apocalyptic visions; (1) on the head of the Lamb as symbolic of Christ, Rev. 5:6; (2) on the heads of beasts as symbolic of national potentates, Rev. 12:3; 13:1, 11; 17:3,7, 12, 16 (cf. Dan.7:8; 8:9; Zech. 1:18, etc.); (3) at the corners of the golden altar, Rev. 9:13 (cf. Exod. 30:2; the horns were of one piece with the altar, as in the case of the brazen altar, 27:2, and were emblematic of the efficacy of the ministry connected with it); (*b*) metaphorically, in the singular, "a horn of salvation," Luke 1:69 (a frequent metaphor in the OT, e.g., Ps. 18:2; cf. 1 Sam. 2:10; Lam. 2:3).¶

HORSE

hippos (ἵππος, 2462), apart from the fifteen occurrences in the Apocalypse, occurs only in Jas. 3:3; in the Apocalypse "horses" are seen in visions in 6:2, 4, 5, 8; 9:7, 9, 17 (twice); 14:20; 19:11, 14, 19, 21; otherwise in 18:13; 19:18.¶

HORSEMEN

1. *hippeus* (ἱππεύς, 2460), "a horseman," is used in the plural in Acts 23:23, 32.¶

2. *hippikos* (ἱππικός, 2461**), an adjective signifying "of a horse" or "of horsemen, equestrian," is used as a noun denoting "cavalry," in Rev. 9:16, "horsemen," numbering "twice ten thousand times ten thousand," RV.¶

HOSANNA

hōsanna (ὡσαννά, 5614), in the Hebrew, means "save, we pray." The word seems to have become an utterance of praise rather than of prayer, though originally, probably, a cry for help. The people's cry at the Lord's triumphal entry into Jerusalem (Matt. 21:9, 15; Mark 11:9, 10; John 12:13) was taken from Ps. 118,

which was recited at the Feast of Tabernacles (see FEAST) in the great Hallel (Psalms 113 to 118) in responses with the priest, accompanied by the waving of palm and willow branches. "The last day of the feast" was called "the great Hosanna"; the boughs also were called "hosannas."¶

HOSPITALITY

A. Noun.

philoxenia (φιλοξενία, 5381), "love of strangers" (*philos*, "loving," *xenos*, "a stranger"), is used in Rom. 12:13; Heb. 13:2, lit. "(be not forgetful of) hospitality." See ENTERTAIN, *Note*.¶

B. Adjective.

philoxenos (φιλόξενος, 5382), "hospitable," occurs in 1 Tim. 3:2; Titus 1:8; 1 Pet. 4:9.¶

Note: For *xenodocheō*, 1 Tim. 5:10, see STRANGER, B.¶

HOST (of guests)

1. *xenos* (ξένος, 3581), in addition to the meaning "stranger," mentioned above under A, denotes one or other of the parties bound by ties of hospitality, (*a*) "the guest" (not in the NT), (*b*) "the host," Rom. 16:23.¶

2. *pandocheus* (πανδοχεύς, 3830), lit., "one who receives all" (*pas*, "all," *dechomai*, "to receive"), denotes "an innkeeper, host," Luke 10:35.¶

HOST (of angels, etc.)

stratia (στρατιά, 4756), "an army," is used of angels, Luke 2:13; of stars, Acts 7:42; some mss. have it instead of *strateia*, in 2 Cor. 10:4 ("warfare").¶ Cf. *strateuma*, "an army."

HOT

zestos (ζεστός, 2200), "boiling hot" (from *zeō*, "to boil, be hot, fervent"; cf. Eng., "zest"), is used, metaphorically, in Rev. 3:15, 16.¶

HOUR

hōra (ὥρα, 5610), whence Lat., *hora*, Eng., "hour," primarily denoted any time or period, expecially a season. In the NT it is used to denote (*a*) "a part of the day," especially a twelfth part of day or night, an "hour," e.g., Matt. 8:13; Acts 10:3, 9; 23:23; Rev. 9:15; in 1 Cor. 15:30, "every hour" stands for "all the time"; in some passages it expresses duration, e.g., Matt. 20:12; 26:40; Luke 22:59; inexactly, in such phrases as "for a season," John 5:35; 2 Cor. 7:8; "for an hour," Gal. 2:5; "for a short season," 1 Thess. 2:17, RV (KJV, "for a short time," lit., "for the time of an hour"); (*b*) "a period more or less extended," e.g., 1 John 2:18, "it is the last hour," RV; (c) "a definite point of time," e.g., Matt 26:45, "the hour is at hand"; Luke 1:10; 10:21; 14:17, lit., "at the hour of supper"; Acts 16:18; 22:13; Rev. 3:3; 11:13; 14:7; a point of time when an appointed action is to begin, Rev. 14:15; in Rom. 13:11, "it is high time," lit., "it is already an hour," indicating that a point of time has come later than would have been the case had responsibility been realized. In 1 Cor. 4:11, it indicates a point of time previous to which certain circumstances have existed.

Notes: (1) In 1 Cor. 8:7, KJV, "unto this hour," the phrase in the original is simply, "until now," as RV (2) In Rev. 8:1, *hēmiōron,* "half an hour" (*hēmi,* "half," and *hōra*), is used with *hōs,* "about," of a period of silence in Heaven after the opening of the 7th seal, a period corresponding to the time customarily spent in silent worship in the Temple during the burning of incense.¶

HOUSE

A. Nouns.

1. *oikos* (οἶκος, 3624) denotes (a) "a house, a dwelling," e.g., Matt. 9:6, 7; 11:8; it is used of the Tabernacle, as the House of God, Matt. 12:4, and the Temple similarly, e.g., Matt. 21:13; Luke 11:51, KJV, "temple," RV, "sanctuary"; John 2:16, 17; called by the Lord "your house" in Matt. 23:38 and Luke 13:35 (some take this as the city of Jerusalem); metaphorically of Israel as God's house, Heb. 3:2, 5, where "his house" is not Moses', but God's; of believers, similarly, v. 6, where Christ is spoken of as "over God's House" (the word "own" is rightly omitted in the RV); Heb. 10:21; 1 Pet. 2:5; 4:17; of the body, Matt. 12:44; Luke 11:24; (b) by metonymy, of the members of a household or family, e.g., Luke 10:5; Acts 7:10; 11:14; 1 Tim. 3:4, 5, 12; 2 Tim. 1:16; 4:19, RV (KJV, "household"); Titus 1:11 (plural); of a local church, 1 Tim. 3:15; of the descendants of Jacob (Israel) and David, e.g., Matt. 10:6; Luke 1:27, 33; Acts 2:36; 7:42. See HOME, A, No. 1. *Note* (1), HOUSEHOLD.

2. *oikia* (οἰκία, 3614) is akin to No. 1, and used much in the same way; in Attic law *oikos* denoted the whole estate, *oikia* stood for the dwelling only; this distinction was largely lost in later Greek. In the NT it denotes (a) "a house, a dwelling," e.g., Matt. 2:11; 5:15; 7:24–27; 2 Tim. 2:20; 2 John 10; it is not used of the Tabernacle or the Temple, as in the case of No. 1; (b) metaphorically, the heavenly abode, spoken of by the Lord as "My Father's house," John 14:2, the eternal dwelling place of believers; the body as the dwelling place of the soul,

2 Cor. 5:1; similarly the resurrection body of believers (*id.*); property, e.g., Mark 12:40; by metonymy, the inhabitants of a house, a household, e.g., Matt. 12:25; John 4:53; 1 Cor. 16:15. See HOUSEHOLD.

B. Adverb.

panoikei (πανοικεί, 3832) denotes "with all the house," Acts 16:34, i.e., "the household."¶

Notes: (1) In 2 Cor. 5:2, *oikētērion,* "a habitation" (see RV) is translated "house" in the KJV, of the resurrection body (cf. *oikia* in the preceding verse; see above). (2) In 1 Tim. 5:13, "from house to house" is, lit., "the houses." (3) For "in every house," Acts 5:42 (cf. 2:46), see HOME. (4) For "them which are of the house," 1 Cor. 1:11, KJV, see HOUSEHOLD.

For GOODMAN of the HOUSE see HOUSEHOLDER

For MASTER of the HOUSE see HOUSEHOLDER

HOUSEHOLD

A. Nouns.

1. *oikos* (οἶκος, 3624) is translated "household" in Acts 16:15; 1 Cor. 1:16; in the KJV of 2 Tim. 4:19 (RV, "house"). See HOUSE, No. 1.

2. *oikia* (οἰκία, 3614) is translated "household" in Phil. 4:22. See HOUSE, No. 2.

3. *oiketeia* (οἰκετεία, 3610d) denotes "a household of servants," Matt. 24:45 (some mss. have No. 4 here).¶

4. *therapeia* (θεραπεία, 2322), "service, care, attention," is also used in the collective sense of "a household," in Luke 12:42 (see No. 3). See HEALING.

Notes: (1) In Rom. 16:10, 11, the phrase "those of the household" translates a curtailed phrase in the original, lit., "the (persons) of (*ek,* 'consisting of') the (members of the household of)." (2) In 1 Cor. 1:11, "they which are of the household (KJV, house) of Chloe" is, lit., "the ... of Chloe," the Eng. translation being necessary to express the idiom.

B. Adjectives.

1. *oikeios* (οἰκεῖος, 3609), akin to A, No. 1, primarily signifies "of, or belonging to, a house," hence, "of persons, one's household, or kindred," as in 1 Tim. 5:8, RV, "household," KJV "house," marg., "kindred"; in Eph. 2:19, "the household of God" denotes the company of the redeemed; in Gal. 6:10, it is called "the household of the faith," RV. In these two cases *oikeios* is used in the same sense as those mentioned under *oikos* (A, No. 1).¶

2. *oikiakos* (οἰκιακός, 3615), from A, No. 2,

denotes "belonging to one's household, one's own"; it is used in Matt. 10:25, 36.¶

HOUSEHOLDER

A. Noun.

oikodespotēs (οἰκοδεσπότης, 3617), "a master of a house" (*oikos*, "a house," *despotēs*, "a master"), is rendered "master of the house" in Matt. 10:25; Luke 13:25, and 14:21, where the context shows that the authority of the "householder" is stressed; in Matt. 24:43 and Luke 12:39, the RV "master of the house" (KJV, "goodman of the house," does not give the exact meaning); "householder" is the rendering in both versions in Matt. 13:27, 52; 20:1; 21:33; so the RV in 20:11 (for KJV, "goodman of the house"); both have "goodman of the house" in Mark 14:14; in Luke 22:11, "goodman." See GOODMAN.¶

B. Verb.

oikodespoteō (οἰκοδεσποτέω, 3616), corresponding to A, "to rule a house," is used in 1 Tim. 5:14, RV, "rule the household" (KJV, "guide the house").¶

HOUSEHOLD-SERVANT

oiketēs (οἰκέτης, 3610), "a house-servant," is translated "household-servants" in Acts 10:7; elsewhere, "servant" or "servants," Luke 16:13; Rom. 14:4; 1 Pet. 2:18. See SERVANT.¶

HOUSETOP

dōma (δῶμα, 1430), akin to *demō*, "to build," denotes a housetop. The housetop was flat, and guarded by a low parapet wall (see Deut. 22:8). It was much frequented and used for various purposes, e.g., for proclamations, Matt. 10:27; Luke 12:3; for prayer, Acts 10:9. The house was often built round a court, across the top of which cords were fixed from the parapet walls for supporting a covering from the heat. The housetop could be reached by stairs outside the building; the paralytic in Luke 5:19 could be let down into the court or area by rolling back the covering. External flight from the housetop in time or danger is enjoined in Matt. 24:17; Mark 13:15; Luke 17:31.¶

For **HOW** and **HOWBEIT**, see † p. 1

For **HOW GREAT** see **GREAT**, Nos. 4, 5, 6

HOWL

ololuzō (ὀλολύζω, 3649), an onomatopoeic verb (expressing its significance in its sound), "to cry aloud" (the Sept. uses it to translate the Heb. *yālal*, e.g., Isa. 13:6; 15:3; Jer. 4:8; Ezek. 21:12; Lat., *ululare*, and Eng., howl are akin), was primarily used of crying aloud to the gods; it is found in Jas. 5:1 in an exhortation to the godless rich.¶

HUMBLE (Adjective and Verb)

A. Adjectives.

1. *tapeinos* (ταπεινός, 5011) primarily signifies "low-lying." It is used always in a good sense in the NT, metaphorically, to denote (*a*) "of low degree, brought low," Luke 1:52; Rom. 12:16, KJV, "(men) of low estate," RV, "(things that are) lowly" (i.e., of low degree); 2 Cor. 7:6, KJV, "cast down," RV, "lowly"; the preceding context shows that this occurrence belongs to (*a*); Jas. 1:9, "of low degree"; (*b*) humble in spirit, Matt. 11:29; 2 Cor. 10:1, RV, "lowly," KJV "base"; Jas. 4:6; 1 Pet. 5:5. See BASE, CAST, *Note* (7), DEGREE (*Note*), LOWLY.¶

2. *tapeinophrōn* (ταπεινόφρων), "humble-minded" (*phrēn*, "the mind"), 1 Pet. 3:8; see COURTEOUS.¶

B. Verb.

tapeinoō (ταπεινόω, 5013), akin to A, signifies "to make low," (*a*) literally, "of mountains and hills," Luke 3:5 (passive voice); (*b*) metaphorically, in the active voice, Matt. 18:4; 23:12 (2nd part); Luke 14:11 (2nd part); 18:14 (2nd part); 2 Cor. 11:7 ("abasing"); 12:21; Phil. 2:8; in the passive voice, Matt. 23:12 (1st part), RV, "shall be humbled," KJV, "shall be abased"; Luke 14:11 (ditto); 18:14 (ditto); Phil. 4:12, "to be abased"; in the passive, with middle voice sense, Jas. 4:10, "humble yourselves"; 1 Pet. 5:6 (ditto). See ABASE, LOW (to bring).¶

HUMBLENESS OF MIND, HUMILITY

tapeinophrosunē (ταπεινοφροσύνην, 5012), "lowliness of mind" (*tapeinos*, see A, above, under HUMBLE, and *phrēn*, "the mind"), is rendered "humility of mind" in Acts 20:19, KJV (RV, "lowliness of mind"); in Eph. 4:2, "lowliness"; in Phil. 2:3, "lowliness of mind"; in Col. 2:18, 23, of a false "humility"; in Col. 3:12, KJV, "humbleness of mind," RV, "humility"; 1 Pet. 5:5, "humility." See LOWLINESS.¶

HUMILIATION

tapeinōsis (ταπείνωσις, 5014), akin to *tapeinos* (see above), is rendered "low estate" in Luke 1:48; "humiliation," Acts 8:33; Phil. 3:21, RV "(the body of our) humiliation," KJV, "(our) vile (body)"; Jas. 1:10, where "in that he is made low," is, lit., "in his humiliation." See ESTATE, LOW.¶

HUNDRED, HUNDREDFOLD

1. *hekaton* (ἑκατόν, 1540), an indeclinable numeral, denotes "a hundred," e.g., Matt. 18:12, 28; it also signifies "a hundredfold," Matt. 13:8, 23, and the RV in the corresponding passage, Mark 4:8, 20 (for KJV, "hundred"), signifying the complete productiveness of sown seed. In the passage in Mark the phrase is, lit., "in thirty and in sixty and in a hundred." In Mark 6:40 it is used with the preposition *kata*, in the phrase "by hundreds." It is followed by other numerals in John 21:11; Acts 1:15; Rev. 7:4; 14:1, 3; 21:17.

2. *hekatontaplasiōn* (ἑκατονταπλασίων, 1542), an adjective, denotes "a hundredfold," Mark 10:30; Luke 8:8; the best mss. have it in Matt. 19:29 for *pollaplasiōn*, "many times more." See the RV margin.¶

For multiples of a hundred, see under the numerals TWO, THREE, etc. For "a hundred years," see YEARS.

HUNGER (Noun and Verb), HUNGERED, HUNGRY

A. Noun.

limos (λιμός, 3042) has the meanings "famine" and "hunger"; "hunger" in Luke 15:17; 2 Cor. 11:27; in Rev. 6:8, RV "famine" (KJV, "hunger"). See FAMINE.

B. Verb.

peinaō (πεινάω, 3983), "to hunger, be hungry, hungered," is used (*a*) literally, e.g., Matt. 4:2; 12:1; 21:18; Rom. 12:20; 1 Cor. 11:21, 34; Phil. 4:12; Rev. 7:16; Christ identifies Himself with His saints in speaking of Himself as suffering in their sufferings in this and other respects, Matt. 25:35, 42; (*b*) metaphorically, Matt. 5:6; Luke 6:21, 25; John 6:35.

C. Adjective.

prospeinos (πρόσπεινος, 4361) signifies "hungry" (*pros*, "intensive," *peina*, "hunger"), Acts 10:10, KJV, "very hungry," RV, "hungry."¶

HURT (Noun and Verb), HURTFUL

A. Noun.

hubris (ὕβρις, 5196) is rendered "hurt" in Acts 27:10, KJV only. See HARM.

B. Verbs.

1. *adikeō* (ἀδικέω, 91) signifies, intransitively, "to do wrong, do hurt, act unjustly" (*a*, negative, and *dikē*, "justice"), transitively, "to wrong, hurt or injure a person." It is translated "to hurt" in the following: (*a*), intransitively, Rev. 9:19; (*b*) transitively, Luke 10:19; Rev. 2:11 (passive); 6:6; 7:2, 3; 9:4, 10; 11:5. See INJURY, OFFENDER, UNJUST, UNRIGHTEOUSNESS, WRONG, WRONG-DOER.

2. *blaptō* (βλάπτω, 984) signifies "to injure, mar, do damage to," Mark 16:18, "shall (in no wise) hurt (them)"; Luke 4:35, "having done (him no) hurt," RV. *Adikeō* stresses the unrighteousness of the act, *blaptō* stresses the injury done.¶

3. *kakoō* (κακόω, 2559), "to do evil to anyone": see HARM.

C. Adjective.

blaberos (βλαβερός, 983), akin to B, No. 2, signifies "hurtful," 1 Tim. 6:9, said of lusts.¶ In the Sept., Prov. 10:26.¶

HUSBAND

A. Noun.

anēr (ἀνήρ, 435) denotes, in general, "a man, an adult male" (in contrast to *anthrōpos*, which generically denotes "a human being, male or female"); it is used of man in various relations, the context deciding the meaning; it signifies "a husband," e.g., Matt. 1:16, 19; Mark 10:12; Luke 2:36; 16:18; John 4:16, 17, 18; Rom. 7:23. See MAN.

B. Adjectives

1. *philandros* (φίλανδρος, 5362), primarily, "loving man," signifies "loving a husband," Titus 2:4, in instruction to young wives to love their husbands, lit., "(to be) lovers of their husbands."¶ The word occurs frequently in epitaphs.

2. *hupandros* (ὕπανδρος, 5220), lit., "under (i.e. subject to) a man," married, and therefore, according to Roman law under the legal authority of the husband, occurs in Rom. 7:2, "that hath a husband."¶

HUSBANDMAN

geōrgos (γεωργός, 1092), from *gē*, "land, ground," and *ergō* (or *erdō*), "to do" (Eng., "George"), denotes (*a*) "a husbandman," a tiller of the ground, 2 Tim. 2:6; Jas. 5:7; (*b*) "a vinedresser," Matt. 21:33–35, 38, 40, 41; Mark 12:1, 2, 7, 9; Luke 20:9, 10, 14, 16; John 15:1, where Christ speaks of the Father as the "Husbandman," Himself as the Vine, His disciples as the branches, the object being to bear much fruit, life in Christ producing the fruit of the Spirit, i.e., character and ways in conformity to Christ.¶

HUSBANDRY

geōrgion (γεώργιον, 1091), akin to the above, denotes "tillage, cultivation, husbandry," 1 Cor. 3:9, where the local church is described under this metaphor (KJV, marg., "tillage," RV, marg., "tilled land"), suggestive of the diligent toil of the apostle and his fellow missionaries, both in the ministry of the gospel, and the care of the church at Corinth; suggestive, too, of the effects in spiritual fruitfulness.¶ Cf. *geōrgeomai,* "to till the ground," Heb. 6:7.¶

HUSKS

keration (κεράτιον, 2769), "a little horn" (a diminutive of *keras,* "a horn"; see HORN), is used in the plural in Luke 15:16, of carob pods, given to swine, and translated "husks."¶

HYMN (Noun and Verb)

A. Noun.

humnos (ὕμνος, 5215) denotes "a song of praise addressed to God" (Eng., "hymn"), Eph. 5:19; Col. 3:16, in each of which the punctuation should probably be changed; in the former "speaking to one another" goes with the end of v. 18, and should be followed by a semicolon; similarly in Col. 3:16, the first part of the verse should end with the words "admonishing one another," where a semicolon should be placed.¶

Note: The *psalmos* denoted that which had a musical accompaniment; the *ōdē* (Eng., "ode") was the generic term for a song; hence the accompanying adjective "spiritual."

B. Verb.

humneō (ὑμνέω, 5214), akin to A, is used (*a*) transitively, Matt. 26:30; Mark 14:26, where the "hymn" was that part of the Hallel consisting of Psalms 113–118; (*b*) intransitively, where the verb itself is rendered "to sing praises" or "praise," Acts 16:25; Heb. 2:12. The Psalms are called, in general, "hymns," by Philo; Josephus calls them "songs and hymns."¶

HYPOCRISY

hupokrisis (ὑπόκρισις, 5272) primarily denotes "a reply, an answer" (akin to *hupokrinomai,* "to answer"); then, "play-acting," as the actors spoke in dialogue; hence, "pretence, hypocrisy"; it is translated "hypocrisy" in Matt. 23:28; Mark 12:15; Luke 12:1; 1 Tim. 4:2; the plural in 1 Pet. 2:1. For Gal. 2:13 and *anupokritos,* "without hypocrisy," in Jas. 3:17, see DISSIMULATION.¶

HYPOCRITE

hupokritēs (ὑποκριτής, 5273), corresponding to the above, primarily denotes "one who answers"; then, "a stage-actor"; it was a custom for Greek and Roman actors to speak in large masks with mechanical devices for augmenting the force of the voice; hence the word became used metaphorically of "a dissembler, a hypocrite." It is found only in the Synoptists, and always used by the Lord, fifteen times in Matthew; elsewhere, Mark 7:6; Luke 6:42; 11:44 (in some mss.); 12:56; 13:15.

HYSSOP

hussōpos (ὕσσωπος, 5301), a bunch of which was used in ritual sprinklings, is found in Heb. 9:19; in John 19:29 the reference is apparently to a branch or rod of "hyssop," upon which a sponge was put and offered to the Lord on the cross. The suggestion has been made that the word in the original may have been *hussos,* "a javelin"; there seems to be no valid reason for the supposition.¶

I

I

egō (ἐγώ, 1473) is the nominative case of the first personal pronoun. The pronoun, "I," however, generally forms a part of the verb itself in Greek; thus *luō* itself means "I loose," the pronoun being incorporated in the verb form. Where the pronoun *egō* is added to the verb, it is almost invariably, if not entirely, emphatic. The emphasis may not be so apparent in some instances, as e.g., Matt. 10:16, but even here it may be taken that something more of stress is present than if the pronoun were omitted. By far the greater number of instances are found in the Gospel of John, and there in the utterances of the Lord concerning Himself, e.g., 4:14, 26, 32, 38; 5:34, 36, 43, 45; 6:35, 40, 41, 48, 51 (twice), 63, 70; instances in the Epistles are Rom. 7:9, 14, 17, 20 (twice), 24, 25; there are more in that chapter than in any other outside the Gospel of John.

In other cases of the pronoun than the nominative, the pronoun is usually more necessary to the meaning, apart from any stress.

For *k'agō* (i.e., *kai egō*), see EVEN, *Note* (6).

IDLE

argos (ἀργός, 692) denotes "inactive, idle, unfruitful, barren" (*a*, negative, and *ergon,* "work"; cf. the verb *katargeō*, "to reduce to inactivity": see ABOLISH); it is used (*a*) literally, Matt. 20:3, 6; 1 Tim. 5:13 (twice); Titus 1:12, RV, "idle (gluttons)"; 2 Pet. 1:8, RV, "idle," KJV, "barren"; (*b*) metaphorically in the sense of "ineffective, worthless," as of a word, Matt. 12:36; of faith unaccompanied by works, Jas. 2:20 (some mss. have *nekra*, "dead").¶

For **IDLE TALES** (Luke 24:11, RV, "idle talk") see **TALK**

IDOL

eidōlon (εἴδωλον, 1497), primarily "a phantom or likeness" (from *eidos*, "an appearance," lit., "that which is seen"), or "an idea, fancy," denotes in the NT (*a*) "an idol," an image to represent a false god, Acts 7:41; 1 Cor. 12:2; Rev. 9:20; (*b*) "the false god" worshipped in an image, Acts 15:20; Rom. 2:22; 1 Cor. 8:4, 7; 10:19; 2 Cor. 6:16; 1 Thess. 1:9; 1 John 5:21.¶

"The corresponding Heb. word denotes 'vanity,' Jer. 14:22; 18:15; 'thing of nought,' Lev. 19:4, marg., cf. Eph. 4:17. Hence what represented a deity to the Gentiles, was to Paul a 'vain thing,' Acts 14:15; 'nothing in the world,' 1 Cor. 8:4; 10:19. Jeremiah calls the idol a 'scarecrow' ('pillar in a garden,' 10:5, marg.), and Isaiah, 44:9–20, etc., and Habakkuk, 2:18, 19 and the Psalmist, 115:4–8, etc., are all equally scathing. It is important to notice, however, that in each case the people of God are addressed. When he speaks to idolaters, Paul, knowing that no man is won by ridicule, adopts a different line, Acts 14:15–18; 17:16, 21–31."*

IDOLS (full of)

kateidōlos (κατείδωλος, 2712), an adjective denoting "full of idols" (*kata*, "throughout," and *eidōlon*), is said of Athens in Acts 17:16, RV, and KJV, marg. (KJV, "wholly given to idolatry").¶

IDOLS (offered to, sacrificed to)

1. *eidōlothutos* (εἰδωλόθυτος, 1494) is an adjective signifying "sacrificed to idols" (*eidōlon*, as above, and *thuō*, "to sacrifice"), Acts 15:29; 21:25; 1 Cor. 8:1, 4, 7, 10; 10:19 (in all these the RV substitutes "sacrificed" for the KJV); Rev. 2:14, 20 (in these the RV and KJV both have "sacrificed"). Some inferior mss. have this adjective in 1 Cor. 10:28; see No. 2. The flesh of the victims, after sacrifice, was eaten or sold.¶

* From *Notes on Thessalonians*, pp. 44, 45, by Hogg and Vine.

2. *hierothutos* (ἱερόθυτος), "offered in sacrifice" (*hieros*, "sacred," and *thuō*, "to sacrifice"), is found in the best mss. in 1 Cor. 10:28 (see No. 1).¶

IDOL'S TEMPLE

eidōlion (or *eidōleion*) (εἰδώλιον, 1493), an "idol's temple," is mentioned in 1 Cor. 8:10; feasting in the temple usually followed the sacrifice.¶

IDOLATER

eidōlolatrēs (εἰδωλολάτρη, 1496), an "idolater" (from *eidōlon*, and *latris*, "a hireling"), is found in 1 Cor. 5:10, 11; 6:9; 10:7; the warning is to believers against turning away from God to idolatry, whether "openly or secretly, consciously or unconsciously" (Cremer); Eph. 5:5; Rev. 21:8; 22:15.¶

IDOLATRY

eidōlolatria (or -*eia*) (εἰδωλολατρία, 1495), whence Eng., "idolatry," (from *eidōlon*, and *latreia*, "service"), is found in 1 Cor. 10:14; Gal. 5:20; Col. 3:5; and, in the plural, in 1 Pet. 4:3.¶

Heathen sacrifices were sacrificed to demons, 1 Cor. 10:19; there was a dire reality in the cup and table of demons and in the involved communion with demons. In Rom. 1:22–25, "idolatry," the sin of the mind against God (Eph. 2:3), and immorality, sins of the flesh, are associated, and are traced to lack of the acknowledgment of God and of gratitude to Him. An "idolater" is a slave to the depraved ideas his idols represent, Gal. 4:8, 9; and thereby, to divers lusts, Titus 3:3 (see *Notes on Thess.* by Hogg and Vine, p. 44).

For **IDOLATRY** (wholly given to) see **IDOLS** (full of)

IF: See † p. 1.

IGNORANCE, IGNORANT, IGNORANTLY

A. Nouns.

1. *agnoia* (ἄγνοια, 52), lit., "want of knowledge or perception" (akin to *agnoeō*, "to be ignorant"), denotes "ignorance" on the part of the Jews regarding Christ, Acts 3:17; of Gentiles in regard to God, 17:30; Eph. 4:18 (here including the idea of willful blindness: see Rom. 1:28, not the "ignorance" which mitigates guilt); 1 Pet. 1:14, of the former unregenerate condition of those who became believers (RV, "in *the time of* your ignorance").¶

2. *agnōsia* (ἀγνωσία, 56) denotes "igno-

rance" as directly opposed to *gnōsis*, which signifies "knowledge" as a result of observation and experience (*a*, negative, *ginōskō*, "to know"; cf. Eng., "agnostic"); 1 Cor. 15:34 ("no knowledge"); 1 Pet. 2:15. In both these passages reprehensible "ignorance" is suggested. See KNOWLEDGE.¶

3. *agnoēma* (ἀγνόημα, 51), "a sin of ignorance," occurs in Heb. 9:7, "errors" (RV marg., "ignorances").¶ For the corresponding verb in Heb. 5:2 see B, No. 1. What is especially in view in these passages is unwitting error. For Israel a sacrifice was appointed, greater in proportion to the culpability of the guilty, greater, for instance, for a priest or ruler than for a private person. Sins of "ignorance," being sins, must be expiated. A believer guilty of a sin of "ignorance" needs the efficacy of the expiatory sacrifice of Christ, and finds "grace to help." Yet, as the conscience of the believer receives enlightenment, what formerly may have been done in "ignorance" becomes a sin against the light and demands a special confession, to receive forgiveness, 1 John 1:8, 9.¶

4. *idiōtēs* (ἰδιώτης, 2399), primarily "a private person" in contrast to a state official, hence, "a person without professional knowledge, unskilled, uneducated, unlearned," is translated "unlearned" in 1 Cor. 14:16, 23, 24, of those who have no knowledge of the facts relating to the testimony borne in and by a local church; "rude" in 2 Cor. 11:6, of the apostle's mode of speech in the estimation of the Corinthians; "ignorant men," in Acts 4:13, of the speech of the apostle Peter and John in the estimation of the rulers, elders and scribes in Jerusalem.

While *agrammatoi* ("unlearned") may refer to their being unacquainted with rabbinical learning, *idiōtai* would signify "laymen," in contrast with the religious officials. See RUDE, UNLEARNED.¶

B. Verbs.

1. *agnoeō* (ἀγνοέω, 50), signifies (*a*) "to be ignorant, not to know," either intransitively, 1 Cor. 14:38 (in the 2nd occurrence in this verse, the RV text translates the active voice, the margin the passive); 1 Tim. 1:13, lit., "being ignorant (I did it)"; Heb. 5:2, "ignorant"; or transitively, 2 Pet. 2:12, KJV, "understand not," RV, "are ignorant (of)"; Acts 13:27, "knew (Him) not"; 17:23, RV, "(what ye worship) in ignorance," for KJV, "(whom ye) ignorantly (worship)," lit., "(what) not knowing (ye worship"; also rendered by the verb "to be ignorant that," or "to be ignorant of," Rom. 1:13; 10:3; 11:25; 1 Cor. 10:1; 12:1; 2 Cor. 1:8; 2:11; 1 Thess 4:13; to know not, Rom. 2:4; 6:3; 7:1; to be unknown (passive voice), 2 Cor. 6:9; Gal.

1:22; (*b*) "not to understand," Mark 9:32; Luke 9:45. See KNOW, UNDERSTAND.¶

2. *lanthanō* (λανθάνω, 2990); for 2 Pet. 3:5, 8, KJV, see FORGET.

Note: For adjectives see UNLEARNED.

ILL

kakos (κακός, 2556), "bad," is used in the neuter as a noun in Rom. 13:10, and translated "ill." See BAD.

Note: For *phaUlos*, John 5:29, RV, see EVIL, A, No. 3.

For **ILLUMINATED** (Heb. 10:32) see **ENLIGHTEN**

IMAGE

1. *eikōn* (εἰκών, 1504) denotes "an image"; the word involves the two ideas of representation and manifestation. "The idea of perfection does not lie in the word itself, but must be sought from the context" (Lightfoot); the following instances clearly show any distinction between the imperfect and the perfect likeness.

The word is used (1) of an "image" or a coin (not a mere likeness), Matt. 22:20; Mark 12:16; Luke 20:24; so of a statue or similar representation (more than a resemblance), Rom. 1:23; Rev. 13:14, 15 (thrice); 14:9, 11; 15:2; 16:2; 19:20; 20:4; of the descendants of Adam as bearing his image, 1 Cor. 15:49, each a representation derived from the prototype; (2) of subjects relative to things spiritual, Heb. 10:1, negatively of the Law as having "a shadow of the good things to come, not the very image of the things," i.e., not the essential and substantial form of them; the contrast has been likened to the difference between a statue and the shadow cast by it; (3) of the relations between God the Father, Christ, and man, (*a*) of man as he was created as being a visible representation of God, 1 Cor. 11:7, a being corresponding to the original; the condition of man as a fallen creature has not entirely effaced the "image"; he is still suitable to bear responsibility, he still has Godlike qualities, such as love of goodness and beauty, none of which are found in a mere animal; in the Fall man ceased to be a perfect vehicle for the representation of God; God's grace in Christ will yet accomplish more than what Adam lost; (*b*) of regenerate persons, in being moral representations of what God is, Col. 3:10; cf. Eph. 4:24; (*c*) of believers, in their glorified state, not merely as resembling Christ but representing Him, Rom. 8:29; 1 Cor. 15:49; here the perfection is the work of divine grace; believers are yet to represent, not something like

Him, but what He is in Himself, both in His spiritual body and in His moral character; (*d*) of Christ in relation to God, 2 Cor. 4:4, "the image of God," i.e., essentially and absolutely the perfect expression and representation of the Archetype, God the Father; in Col. 1:15, "the image of the invisible God" gives the additional thought suggested by the word "invisible," that Christ is the visible representation and manifestation of God to created beings; the likeness expressed in this manifestation is involved in the essential relations in the Godhead, and is therefore unique and perfect; "he that hath seen Me hath seen the Father," John 14:9. "The epithet 'invisible' . . . must not be confined to the apprehension of the bodily senses, but will include the cognizance of the inward eye also" (Lightfoot).¶

As to synonymous words, *homoiōma*, "likeness," stresses the resemblance to an archetype, though the resemblance may not be derived, whereas *eikōn* is a "derived likeness" (see LIKENESS); *eidos*, "a shape, form," is an appearance, "not necessarily based on reality" (see FORM); *skia*, is "a shadowed resemblance" (see SHADOW); *morphē* is "the form, as indicative of the inner being" (Abbott-Smith); see FORM. For *charaktēr*, see No. 2.

2. *charaktēr* (χαρακτήρ, 5481) denotes, firstly, "a tool for graving" (from *charassō*, "to cut into, to engross"; cf. Eng., "character," "characteristic"); then, "a stamp" or "impress," as on a coin or a seal, in which case the seal or die which makes an impression bears the "image" produced by it, and, *vice versa*, all the features of the "image" correspond respectively with those of the instrument producing it. In the NT it is used metaphorically in Heb. 1:3, of the Son of God as "the very image (marg., 'the impress') of His substance." RV. The phrase expresses the fact that the Son "is both personally distinct from, and yet literally equal to, Him of whose essence He is the adequate imprint" (Liddon). The Son of God is not merely his "image" (His *charaktēr*), He is the "image" or impress of His substance, or essence. It is the fact of complete similarity which this word stresses in comparison with those mentioned at the end of No. 1.¶ In the Sept., Lev. 13:28, "the mark (of the inflammation)."¶

"In John 1:1–3, Col. 1:15–17, and Heb. 1:2, 3, the special function of creating and upholding the universe is ascribed to Christ under His titles of Word, Image, and Son, respectively. The kind of Creatorship so predicated of Him is not that of a mere instrument or artificer in the formation of the world, but that of One 'by whom, in whom, and for whom' all things are made, and through whom they subsist. This implies the assertion of His true and absolute Godhood" (Laidlaw, in *Hastings' Bib. Dic.*).

Note: The similar word *charagma*, "a mark" (see GRAVEN and MARK), has the narrower meaning of "the thing impressed," without denoting the special characteristic of that which produces it, e.g., Rev. 13:16, 17. In Acts 17:29 the meaning is not "graven (*charagma*) by art," but "an engraved work of art."

IMAGINATION

1. *logismos* (λογισμός, 3053), "a reasoning, a thought" (akin to *logizomai*, "to count, reckon"), is translated "thoughts" in Rom. 2:15, suggestive of evil intent, not of mere reasonings; "imaginations" in 2 Cor. 10:5 (RV, marg., "reasonings," in each place). The word suggests the contemplation of actions as a result of the verdict of conscience. See THOUGHT.¶

2. *dialogismos* (διαλογισμός, 1261), *dia*, and No. 1, is rendered "imaginations" in Rom. 1:21, carrying with it the idea of evil purposes, RV, "reasonings"; it is most frequently translated "thoughts." See DISPUTE.

3. *dianoia* (διάνοια, 1271), strictly, "a thinking over," denotes "the faculty of thinking"; then, "of knowing"; hence, "the understanding," and in general, "the mind," and so, "the faculty of moral reflection"; it is rendered "imagination" in Luke 1:51, "the imagination of their heart" signifying their thoughts and ideas. See MIND, UNDERSTANDING.

IMAGINE

meletaō (μελετάω, 3191) signifies "to care for" (*meletē*, "care"); then, "to attend to," "be diligent in," 1 Tim. 4:15, RV, i.e., to practice as the result of devising or planning; thirdly, "to ponder," "imagine," Acts 4:25, RV, marg., "meditate." Some inferior mss. have it in Mark 13:11. See DILIGENT, MEDITATE. ¶

IMITATE, IMITATOR

A. Verb.

mimeomai (μιμέομαι, 3401), "a mimic, an actor" (Eng., "mime," etc.), is always translated "to imitate" in the RV, for KJV, "to follow," (*a*) of imitating the conduct of missionaries, 2 Thess. 3:7, 9; the faith of spiritual guides, Heb. 13:7; (*b*) that which is good, 3 John 11. The verb is always used in exhortations, and always in the continuous tense, suggesting a constant habit or practice. See FOLLOW.

B. Nouns.

1. *mimētēs* (μιμητής, 3402), akin to A, "an imitator," so the RV for KJV, "follower," is always used in a good sense in the NT. In 1 Cor.

4:16; 11:1; Eph. 5:1; Heb. 6:12, it is used in exhortations, accompanied by the verb *ginomai*, "to be, become," and in the continuous tense (see A) except in Heb. 6:12, where the aorist or momentary tense indicates a decisive act with permanent results; in 1 Thess. 1:6; 2:14, the accompanying verb is in the aorist tense, referring to the definite act of conversion in the past. These instances, coupled with the continuous tenses referred to, teach that what we became at conversion we must diligently continue to be thereafter. See FOLLOW, *Note* (4).¶

2. *summimētēs* (συμμιμητής, 4831) denotes "a fellow imitator" (*sun*, "with," and No. 1), Phil. 3:17, RV, "imitators together" (KJV, "followers together"). See FOLLOW, *Note* (4).¶

IMMEDIATELY

1. *parachrēma* (παραχρῆμα, 3916), lit., "with the matter (or business) itself" (*para*, "with," *chrēma*, "a business," or "event"), and so, "immediately," Matt. 21:19 (KJV, "presently"), 20; Luke 1:64; 4:39; 5:25; 8:44, 47, 55; 13:13; 18:43; 19:11; 22:60; Acts 3:7; 5:10; 12:23; 13:11; 16:26, 33; it is thus used by Luke only, save for the two instances in Matthew. See FORTHWITH. It is also rendered "presently," " soon," "straightway." ¶

2. *euthus* (εὐθύς, 2117): see FORTHWITH.

3. *eutheōs* (εὐθέως, 2112): ditto.

4. *exautēs* (ἐξαυτῆς, 1824): ditto.

IMMORTAL, IMMORTALITY

athanasia (ἀθανασία, 110), lit., "deathlessness" (*a*, negative, *thanatos*, "death"), is rendered "immortality" in 1 Cor. 15:53, 54, of the glorified body of the believer; 1 Tim. 6:16, of the nature of God. Moulton and Milligan (*Vocab.*) show that in early times the word had the wide connotation of freedom from death; they also quote Ramsay (*Luke the Physician*, p. 273), with reference to the use of the word in sepulchral epitaphs. In a papyrus writing of the sixth century, "a petitioner says that he will send up 'unceasing (*athanatous*)' hymns to the Lord Christ for the life of the man with whom he is pleading." In the NT, however, *athanasia* expresses more than deathlessness, it suggests the quality of the life enjoyed, as is clear from 2 Cor. 5:4; for the believer what is mortal is to be "swallowed up of life."¶

Note: The adjective *aphthartos*, translated "immortal" in 1 Tim. 1:17, KJV, does not bear that significance, it means "incorruptible." So with the noun *aphtharsia*, "incorruption," translated "immortality," in the KJV of Rom. 2:7 and 2 Tim. 1:10. See CORRUPT, B, No. 3, and C, No. 2.

IMMUTABLE, IMMUTABILITY

ametathetos (ἀμετάθετος, 276), an adjective signifying "immutable" (*a*, negative, *metatithēmi*, "to change"), Heb. 6:18, where the "two immutable things" are the promise and the oath. In v. 17 the word is used in the neuter with the article, as a noun, denoting "the immutability," with reference to God's counsel. Examples from the papyri show that the word was used as a technical term in connection with wills, "The connotation adds considerably to the force of Heb. 6:17 (and foll.)" (Moulton and Milligan).¶

IMPART

1. *prosanatithēmi* (προσανατίθμι, 4323) is used in the middle voice in the NT, in Gal. 1:16, "conferred," or "had recourse to," and 2:6, RV, "imparted." See CONFER.¶

2. *metadidōmi* (μεταδίδωμι, 3330): see GIVE, No. 4.

IMPEDIMENT

mogilalos (μογιλάλος, 3424) denotes "speaking with difficulty" (*mogis*, "hardly," *laleō*, "to talk"), "stammering," Mark 7:32; some mss. have *moggilalos*, "thick-voiced" (from *moggos*, "with a hoarse, hollow voice").¶ In the Sept., Isa. 35:6 "(the tongue) of stammerers."¶

IMPENITENT

ametanoētos (ἀμετανόητος, 279), lit., "without change of mind" (*a*, negative, *metanoeō*, "to change one's mind," *meta*, signifying "change," *nous*, "the mind"), is used in Rom. 2:5, "impenitent" (or "unrepentant").¶ Moulton and Milligan show from the papyri writings that the word is also used "in a passive sense, 'not affected by change of mind,' like *ametamelētos* in Rom. 11:29," "without repentance."

IMPLACABLE

aspondos (ἄσπονδος, 786) lit. denotes "without a libation" (*a*, negative, *spondē*, "a libation"), i.e., "without a truce," as a libation accompanied the making of treaties and compacts; then, "one who cannot be persuaded to enter into a covenant," "implacable," 2 Tim. 3:3 (KJV, "truce-breakers"). Some mss. have this word in Rom. 1:31.¶

Note: Trench (*Syn.* §lii) contrasts *aspondos* with *asunthetos; see *Note* under COVENANT-BREAKERS. *Aspondos* may signify "untrue to one's promise," *asunthetos* "not abiding by one's covenant, treacherous."

For **IMPLEAD** see **ACCUSE**, B, No. 2

IMPLANTED

emphutos (ἔμφυτος, 1721), "implanted," or "rooted" (from *emphuō*, "to implant"), is used in Jas. 1:21, RV, "implanted," for KJV, "engrafted," of the Word of God, as the "rooted word," i.e., a word whose property it is to root itself like a seed in the heart. "The KJV seems to identify it with *emphuteuton*, which however would be out of place here, since the word is sown, not grafted, in the heart" (Mayor).¶

IMPORTUNITY

anaidia (or *anaideia*) (ἀναιδία, 335) denotes "shamelessness, importunity" (*a*, negative, *n*, euphonic, and *aidōs*, "shame, modesty"), and is used in the Lord's illustration concerning the need of earnestness and perseverance in prayer, Luke 11:8. If shameless persistence can obtain a boon from a neighbor, then certainly earnest prayer will receive our Father's answer.¶

IMPOSED

epikeimai (ἐπίκειμαι, 1945) denotes "to be placed on, to lie on," (*a*) literally, as of the stone on the sepulchre of Lazarus, John 11:38; of the fish on the fire of coals, 21:9; (*b*) figuratively, of a tempest (to press upon), Acts 27:20; of a necessity laid upon the apostle Paul, 1 Cor. 9:16; of the pressure of the multitude upon Christ to hear Him, Luke 5:1, "pressed upon"; of the insistence of the chief priests, rulers and people that Christ should be crucified, Luke 23:23, "were instant"; of carnal ordinances "imposed" under the Law until a time of reformation, brought in through the High Priesthood of Christ, Heb. 9:10. See INSTANT, LIE, PRESS.¶

IMPOSSIBLE

A. Adjectives.

1. *adunatos* (ἀδύνατος, 102), from *a*, negative, and *dunatos*, "able, strong," is used (*a*) of persons, Acts 14:8, "impotent"; figuratively, Rom. 15:1, "weak"; (*b*) of things, "impossible," Matt. 19:26; Mark 10:27; Luke 18:27; Heb. 6:4, 18; 10:4; 11:6; in Rom. 8:3, "for what the Law could not do," is, more lit., "the inability of the law"; the meaning may be either "the weakness of the Law," or "that which was impossible for the Law"; the latter is perhaps preferable; literalism is ruled out here, but the sense is that the Law could neither justify nor impart life.¶

2. *anendektos* (ἀνένδεκτος, 418) signifies "inadmissible" (*a*, negative, *n*, euphonic, and *endechomai*, "to admit, allow"), Luke 17:1, of occasions of stumbling, where the meaning is "it cannot be but that they will come."¶

B. Verb.

adunateō (ἀδυνατέω, 101) signifies "to be impossible" (corresponding to A, No. 1), "unable"; in the NT it is used only of things, Matt. 17:20, "(nothing) shall be impossible (unto you)"; Luke 1:37. KJV "(with God nothing) shall be impossible"; RV, "(no word from God—a different construction in the best mss.) shall be void of power"; *rhēma* may mean either "word" or "thing" (i.e., fact).¶ In the Sept. the verb is always used of things and signifies either to be "impossible" or to be impotent, e.g., Gen. 18:14; Lev. 25:35, "he fail"; Deut. 17:8; Job 4:4, "feeble"; 42:2; Dan. 4:6; Zech. 8:6.

IMPOSTORS

goēs (γόης, 1114) primarily denotes "a wailer" (*goaō*, "to wail"); hence, from the howl in which spells were chanted, "a wizard, sorcerer, enchanter," and hence, "a juggler, cheat, impostor," rendered "impostors" in 2 Tim. 3:13, RV (KJV, "seducers"); possibly the false teachers referred to practiced magical arts; cf. v. 8.¶

IMPOTENT

A. Adjectives.

1. *adunatos* (ἀδύνατος, 102): see IMPOSSIBLE, A, No. 1.

2. *asthenēs* (ἀσθενής, 772), "without strength" (*a*, negative, *sthenos*, strength), is translated "impotent" in Acts 4:9. See FEEBLE, SICK, WEAK.

B. Verb.

astheneō (ἀσθενέω, 770), "to be without strength" (akin to A, No. 2), is translated "impotent folk" in John 5:3, KJV; cf. v. 7 (the present participle, lit., "being impotent"). See DISEASED, SICK, WEAK.

IMPRISON, IMPRISONMENT

A. Verb.

phulakizō (φυλακίζω, 5439), "to imprison," akin to *phulax*, "a guard, a keeper," and *phulassō*, "to guard," and B, below, is used in Acts 22:19.¶

B. Noun.

phulakē (φυλακή, 5438), besides its other meanings, denotes "imprisonment," in 2 Cor. 6:5 (plural) and Heb. 11:36. See CAGE.

IMPULSE

hormē (ὁρμή, 3730) denotes (*a*) "an impulse" or "violent motion," as of the steersman of a vessel, Jas. 3:4, RV, "impulse" (KJV omits);

(b) "an assault, onset," Acts 14:5. See AS-SAULT.¶

IMPUTE

1. *logizomai* (λογίζομαι, 3049), "to reckon, take into account," or, metaphorically, "to put down to a person's account," is never rendered in the RV by the verb "to impute." In the following, where the KJV has that rendering, the RV uses the verb "to reckon," which is far more suitable; Rom. 4:6, 8, 11, 22, 23, 24; 2 Cor. 5:19; Jas. 2:23. See ACCOUNT, and especially, in the above respect, RECKON.

2. *ellogaō*, or *-eō* (ἐλλογάω, 1677) (the *-ao* termination is the one found in the *Koinē*, the language covering the NT period), denotes "to charge to one's account, to lay to one's charge," and is translated "imputed" in Rom. 5:13, of sin as not being "imputed when there is no law." This principle is there applied to the fact that between Adam's transgression and the giving of the Law at Sinai, sin, though it was in the world, did not partake of the character of transgression; for there was no law. The law of conscience existed, but that is not in view in the passage, which deals with the fact of external commandments given by God. In Philem. 18 the verb is rendered "put (that) to (mine) account." See ACCOUNT.¶

For **IN** see †, p. 1

INASMUCH AS

1. *katho* (καθό, 2526), lit., "according to what" (*kata*, "according to," and *ho*, the neuter of the relative pronoun), is translated "inasmuch as" in 1 Pet. 4:13, KJV (RV, "insomuch as"); in Rom. 8:26, "as (we ought)"; in 2 Cor. 8:12, RV, "according as" (KJV, "according to that"). See INSOMUCH.¶

2. *eph'hoson* (ἐφ'ὅσον), lit., "upon how much" (*epi*, "upon," *hosos*, "how much"), is translated "inasmuch as" in Matt. 25:40, 45; Rom. 11:13.¶

3. *kathoti* (καθότι, 2530): see ACCORDING AS, No. 1.

4. *kath' hoson* (καθ' ὅσον), *kata*, "according to," and *hosos*, "how much," is translated "inasmuch as" in Heb. 3:3, KJV (RV, "by so much as"); 7:20; 9:27, RV (KJV, "as").

Note: In Phil. 1:7, the phrase "inasmuch as" translates the present participle of the verb *eimi*, "to be," lit., "(ye) being (all partakers)."

INCENSE (burn)

A. Noun.

thumiama (θυμίαμα, 2368) denotes "fragrant stuff for burning, incense" (from *thuō*, "to

offer in sacrifice"), Luke 1:10, 11; in the plural, Rev. 5:8 and 18:13, RV (KJV, "odors"); 8:3, 4, signifying "frankincense" here. In connection with the tabernacle, the "incense" was to be prepared from stacte, onycha, and galbanum, with pure frankincense, an equal weight of each; imitation for private use was forbidden, Exod. 30:34–38. See ODOR.¶ Cf. *thumiatērion*, "a censer," Heb. 9:4, and *libanos*, "frankincense," Rev. 18:13; see FRANKINCENSE.¶

B. Verb.

thumiaō (θυμιάω, 2370), "to burn incense" (see A), is found in Luke 1:9.¶

INCLOSE

sunkleiō (συγκλείω, 4788), "to shut together, shut in on all sides" (*sun*, "with," *kleiō*, "to shut"), is used of a catch of fish, Luke 5:6; metaphorically in Rom. 11:32, of God's dealings with Jew and Gentile, in that He has "shut up (KJV, concluded) all unto disobedience, that He might have mercy upon all." There is no intimation in this of universal salvation. The meaning, from the context, is that God has ordered that all should be convicted of disobedience without escape by human merit, that He might display His mercy, and has offered the gospel without national distinction, and that when Israel is restored, He will, in the resulting Millennium, show His mercy to all nations. The word "all" with reference to Israel, is to be viewed in the light of v. 26, and, in reference to the Gentiles, in the light of vv. 12–25; in Gal. 3:22, 23 ("the Scripture hath shut up all things under sin"), the apostle shows that, by the impossibility of being justified by keeping the Law, all, Jew and Gentile, are under sin, so that righteousness might be reckoned to all who believe. See CONCLUDE, SHUT. ¶

INCONTINENCY, INCONTINENT

A. Noun.

akrasia (ἀκρασία, 192) denotes "want of power" (*a*, negative, *kratos*, "power"); hence, "want of self-control, incontinency," 1 Cor. 7:5; in Matt. 23:25, "excess." See EXCESS.¶

B. Adjective.

akratēs (ἀκρατής, 193) denotes "powerless, impotent"; in a moral sense, unrestrained, "without self-control," 2 Tim. 3:3, RV (KJV, "incontinent"). See SELF-CONTROL.¶

For **INCORRUPTIBLE** and **INCORRUPTION**, see under **CORRUPT**

For the noun **INCREASE**, see **GROW**, No. 1, *Note*

INCREASE (Verb)

1. *auxanō* (αὐξάνω, 837): see GROW, No. 1.

2. *perisseuō* (περισσεύω, 4052), "to be over and above, to abound," is translated "increased" in Acts 16:5, of churches; "increase" in the KJV of 1 Thess. 4:10 (RV, "abound"). See ABOUND, under ABUNDANCE, B, No. 1.

3. *pleonazō* (πλεονάζω, 4121), "to make to abound," is translated "make (you) to increase" in 1 Thess. 3:12, with No. 2. See ABUNDANCE, B, No. 3.

4. *prokoptō* (προκόπτω, 4278) is translated by the verb "to increase" in Luke 2:52 and in the KJV of 2 Tim. 2:16 (RV, "will proceed further").

See ADVANCE, PROCEED.

5. *prostithēmi* (προστίθημι, 4369), "to put to, add to," is translated "increase" in Luke 17:5. See ADD, No. 2.

Note: For "increased in strength" see STRENGTH.

INCREDIBLE

apistos (ἄπιστος, 571) is once rendered "incredible," Acts 26:8, of the doctrine of resurrection; elsewhere it is used of persons, with the meaning "unbelieving." See BELIEF, C, *Note* (3).

INDEBTED (to be)

opheilō (ὀφείλω, 3784) "to owe, to be a debtor," is translated "is indebted" in Luke 11:4. Luke does not draw a parallel between our forgiving and God's; he speaks of God's forgiving sins, of our forgiving "debts," moral debts, probably not excluding material debts. Matthew speaks of our sins as *opheilēmata*, "debts," and uses parallel terms. Ellicott and others suggest that Luke used a term more adapted to the minds of gentile readers. The inspired language provides us with both, as intended by the Lord.

INDEED

1. *men* (μέν, 3303), a conjunctive particle (originally a form of *mēn*, "verily, truly," found in Heb. 6:14.¶), usually related to an adversative conjunction or particle, like *de*, in the following clause, which is placed in opposition to it. Frequently it is untranslatable; sometimes it is rendered "indeed," e.g., Matt. 3:11; 13:32; 17:11, RV (KJV, "truly"); 20:23; 26:41; (some mss. have it in Mark 1:8); Mark 9:12, RV (KJV, "verily").

2. *alēthēs* (ἀληθής, 227), "true," is rendered "indeed" in John 6:55 (twice), see RV marg.; some mss. have No. 3 here.

3. *alēthōs* (ἀληθῶς, 230), "truly" (from No. 2), is translated "indeed" in John 1:47; 4:42; 8:31.

4. *ontōs* (ὄντως, 3689), an adverb from *ōn*, the present participle of *eimi*, "to be," denotes "really, actually"; it is translated "indeed" in Mark 11:32 (RV, "verily"); Luke 24:34; John 8:36; 1 Cor. 14:25, RV (KJV "of a truth"); 1 Tim. 5:3, 5, 16; 6:15, RV, where some mss. have *aiōnios*, "eternal" (KJV); in Gal. 3:21, "verily."

5. *kai gar* (καί γάρ) signifies "and in fact," "for also" (*kai*, "and," or "even," or "also"; *gar*, "for"; *gar* always comes after the first word in the sentence); it is translated "For indeed" in the RV of Acts 19:40; 2 Cor. 5:4; 1 Thess. 4:10 (KJV, "and indeed"); KJV and RV in Phil. 2:27. This phrase has a confirmatory sense, rather than a modifying effect, e.g., Matt. 15:27, RV, "for even," instead of the KJV "yet"; the woman confirms that her own position as a Gentile "dog" brings privilege, "for indeed the dogs, etc."

6. *oude gar* (οὐδέ γάρ), "for neither," is rendered "neither indeed" in Rom. 8:7.

7. *alla kai* (ἀλλὰ καί), "but even," or "but also," is rendered "nay indeed" in 2 Cor. 11:1, RV (KJV, "and indeed"; RV marg., "but indeed").

8. *kai* (καί, 2532), preceded by the particle *ge*, "at least, ever," is rendered "indeed" in Gal. 3:4, RV (KJV, "yet"). *Kai* alone is rendered "indeed" in Phil. 4:10, RV (KJV, "also").

9. *ei mēti* (εἰ μήτι), "if not indeed," is rendered "unless indeed" in 2 Cor. 13:5, RV (KJV, "except").

INDIGNATION

A. Noun.

aganaktēsis (ἀγανάκτησις, 24) is rendered "indignation" in 2 Cor. 7:11. See ANGER, A, *Note* (3).¶

Notes: (1) *Orgē*, "wrath," is translated "indignation" in Rev. 14:10, KJV; RV, "anger." See ANGER, A, No. 1. (2) For *thumos*, see ANGER, A, *Notes* (1) and (2). (3) In Acts 5:17, the KJV translates *zēlos* by "indignation" (RV "jealousy"); in Heb. 10:27, KJV, "indignation" (RV, "fierceness"; marg., "jealousy"). See JEALOUSY.

B. Verb.

aganakteō (ἀγανακτέω, 23), "to be indignant, to be moved with indignation" (from *agan*, "much," *achomai*, "to grieve"), is translated "were moved with indignation" of the ten disciples against James and John, Matt. 20:24; in Mark 10:41, RV (KJV, "they began to be much displeased"); in Matt. 21:15, of the chief priests and scribes, against Christ and the children, RV, "they were moved with indignation" (KJV, "they were sore displeased"); in 26:8, of the disciples against the woman who anointed

Christ's feet, "they had indignation"; so Mark 14:4; in Mark 10:14, of Christ, against the disciples, for rebuking the children, "He was moved with indignation," RV (KJV, "he was much displeased"); in Luke 13:14, of the ruler of the synagogue against Christ for healing on the Sabbath, "being moved with indignation," RV, KJV, "(answered) with indignation." See ANGER, B, *Note* (3).¶

INDULGENCE

1. *anesis* (ἄνεσις, 425), "a loosening, relaxation of strain" (akin to *aniēmi*, "to relax, loosen"), is translated "indulgence" in Acts 24:23, RV (KJV, "liberty"), in the command of Felix to the centurion, to moderate restrictions upon Paul. The papyri and inscriptions illustrate the use of the word as denoting relief (Moulton and Milligan, *Vocab.*) In the NT it always carries the thought of relief from tribulation or persecution; so 2 Thess. 1:7, "rest"; in 2 Cor. 2:13 and 7:5 it is rendered "relief," RV (KJV, "rest"); in 8:13, "eased." Josephus speaks of the rest or relief (*anesis*) from plowing and tillage, given to the land in the Year of Jubilee. See EASE, LIBERTY, RELIEF, REST.¶

2. *plēsmonē* (πλησμονή, 4140), "a filling up, satiety" (akin to *pimplēmi*, "to fill"), is translated "indulgence (of the flesh)" in Col. 2:23, RV (KJV, "satisfying"). Lightfoot translates the passage "yet not really of any value to remedy indulgence of the flesh." A possible meaning is, "of no value in attempts at asceticism." Some regard it as indicating that the ascetic treatment of the body is not of any honor to the satisfaction of the flesh (the reasonable demands of the body): this interpretation is unlikely. The following paraphrase well presents the contrast between the asceticism which "practically treats the body as an enemy, and the Pauline view which treats it as a potential instrument of a righteous life": ordinances, "which in fact have a specious look of wisdom (where there is no true wisdom), by the employment of self-chosen acts of religion and humility (and) by treating the body with brutality instead of treating it with due respect, with a view to meeting and providing against over-indulgence of the flesh" (Parry, in the *Camb. Greek Test.*).¶

For INEXCUSABLE see EXCUSE

For INFALLIBLE see PROOF

For INFANT see BABE

INFERIOR

hēttaomai, or *hēssaomai* (ἡττάομαι, 2274), "to be less or inferior," is used in the passive voice, and translated "ye were made inferior," in 2 Cor. 12:13, RV, for KJV, "ye were inferior," i.e., were treated with less consideration than other churches, through his independence in not receiving gifts from them. In 2 Pet. 2:19, 20 it signifies to be overcome, in the sense of being subdued and enslaved. See OVERCOME.¶ Cf. *hēssōn*, "less," 2 Cor. 12:15; in 1 Cor. 11:17, "worse";¶ *hēttēma*, "a loss, a spiritual defect," Rom. 11:12; 1 Cor. 6:7.¶ Also *elattoō*, "to decrease, make lower," John 3:30; Heb. 2:7, 9.¶

For INFIDEL (RV, UNBELIEVER), see BELIEF, C, *Note* (3)

INFIRMITY

1. *astheneia* (ἀσθένεια, 769), lit., "want of strength" (*a*, negative, *sthenos*, "strength"), "weakness," indicating inability to produce results, is most frequently translated "infirmity," or "infirmities"; in Rom. 8:26, the RV has "infirmity" (KJV, "infirmities"); in 2 Cor. 12:5, 9, 10, "weaknesses" and in 11:30, "weakness" (KJV, "infirmities"); in Luke 13:11 the phrase "a spirit of infirmity" attributes her curvature directly to satanic agency. The connected phraseology is indicative of trained medical knowledge on the part of the writer.

2. *asthenēma* (ἀσθένημα, 771), akin to No. 1, is found in the plural in Rom. 15:1, "infirmities," i.e., those scruples which arise through weakness of faith. The strong must support the infirmities of the weak (*adunatos*) by submitting to self-restraint.¶

Note: In Luke 7:21, KJV, *nosos*, "a disease," is translated "infirmities" (RV, "diseases").

INFLICTED

Note: This is inserted in 2 Cor. 2:6 to complete the sentence; there is no corresponding word in the original, which lit. reads "this punishment, the (one) by the majority."

INFORM

1. *emphanizō* (ἐμφανίζω, 1718), "to manifest, exhibit," in the middle and passive voices, "to appear, also signifies to declare, make known," and is translated "informed" in Acts 24:1; 25:2, 15. For all the occurrences of the word see APPEAR, A, No. 5.

2. *katēcheō* (κατηχέω, 2727) primarily denotes "to resound" (*kata*, "down," *ēchos* "a sound"); then, "to sound down the ears, to teach by word of mouth, instruct, inform"

(Eng., "catechize, catechumen"); it is rendered, in the passive voice, by the verb "to inform," in Acts 21:21, 24. Here it is used of the large numbers of Jewish believers at Jerusalem whose zeal for the Law had been stirred by information of accusations made against the Apostle Paul, as to certain anti-Mosaic teaching he was supposed to have given the Jews. See INSTRUCT, TEACH.

For INHABITANTS, INHABITERS, see DWELL, A, No. 2

INHERIT, INHERITANCE

A. Verbs.

1. *klēronomeō* (κληρονομέω, 2816) strictly means "to receive by lot" (*klēros*, "a lot," *nemomai*, "to possess"); then, in a more general sense, "to possess oneself of, to receive as one's own, to obtain." The following list shows how in the NT the idea of inheriting broadens out to include all spiritual good provided through and in Christ, and particularly all that is contained in the hope grounded on the promises of God.

The verb is used of the following objects:

"(*a*) birthright, that into the possession of which one enters in virtue of sonship, not because of a price paid or of a task accomplished, Gal. 4:30; Heb. 1:4; 12:17:

(*b*) that which is received as a gift, in contrast with that which is received as the reward of law-keeping, Heb. 1:14; 6:12 ("through," i.e., "through experiences that called for the exercise of faith and patience,' but not 'on the ground of the exercise of faith and patience.'):

(*c*) that which is received on condition of obedience to certain precepts, 1 Pet. 3:9, and of faithfulness to God amidst opposition, Rev. 21:7:

(*d*) the reward of that condition of soul which forbears retaliation and self-vindication, and expresses itself in gentleness of behavior. . ., Matt. 5:5. The phrase "inherit the earth," or "land," occur several times in OT. See especially Ps. 37:11, 22:

(*e*) the reward (in the coming age, Mark 10:30) of the acknowledgment of the paramountcy of the claims of Christ, Matt. 19:29. In the three accounts given of this incident, see Mark 10:17–31, Luke 18:18–30, the words of the question put to the Lord are, in Matthew, "that I may have," in Mark and Luke, "that I may inherit." In the report of the Lord's word to Peter in reply to his subsequent question, Matthew has "inherit eternal life," while Mark and Luke have "receive eternal life." It seems to follow that the meaning of the word "inherit"

is here ruled by the words "receive" and "have," with which it is interchanged in each of the three Gospels, i.e., the less common word "inherit" is to be regarded as equivalent to the more common words "receive" and "have." Cf. Luke 10:25:

(*f*) the reward of those who have shown kindness to the "brethren" of the Lord in their distress, Matt. 25:34:

(*g*) the kingdom of God, which the morally corrupt cannot "inherit," 1 Cor. 6:9, 10, the "inheritance" of which is likewise impossible to the present physical constitution of man, 1 Cor. 15:50:

(*h*) incorruption, impossible of "inheritance" by corruption, 1 Cor. 15:50."*

See HEIR.¶

Note: In regard to (*e*), the word clearly signifies entrance into eternal life without any previous title; it will not bear the implication that a child of God may be divested of his "inheritance" by the loss of his right of succession.

2. *klēroō* (κληρόω, 2820) is used in the passive voice in Eph. 1:11, KJV, "we have obtained an inheritance"; RV, "we were made a heritage." See HERITAGE.¶

B. Nouns.

1 *klēronomia* (κληρονομία, 2817), "a lot" (see A), properly "an inherited property, an inheritance." "It is always rendered inheritance in NT, but only in a few cases in the Gospels has it the meaning ordinarily attached to that word in English, i.e., that into possession of which the heir enters only on the death of an ancestor. The NT usage may be set out as follows: (*a*) that property in real estate which in ordinary course passes from father to son on the death of the former, Matt. 21:38; Mark 12:7; Luke 12:13; 20:14; (*b*) a portion of an estate made the substance of a gift, Acts 7:5; Gal. 3:18, which also is to be included under (*c*); (*c*) the prospective condition and possessions of the believer in the new order of things to be ushered in at the return of Christ, Acts 20:32; Eph. 1:14; 5:5; Col. 3:24; Heb. 9:15; 1 Pet. 1:4; (*d*) what the believer will be to God in that age, Eph. 1:18."†

Note: In Gal. 3:18, "if the inheritance is of the Law," the word "inheritance" stands for "the title to the inheritance."

2. *klēros* (κλῆρος, 2819), (whence Eng., "clergy"), denotes (*a*) "a lot," given or cast (the latter as a means of obtaining divine direction),

---

* From *Notes on Galatians,* by Hogg and Vine, pp. 286–289.

† From *Notes on Galatians,* by Hogg and Vine, pp. 146–147.

Matt. 27:35; Mark 15:24; Luke 23:24; John 19:24; Acts 1:26; (b) "a person's share" in anything, Acts 1:17, RV, "portion" (KJV, "part"); 8:21, "lot"; (c) "a charge" (lit., "charges") "allotted," to elders, 1 Pet. 5:3, RV [KJV, "(God's) heritage"]; the figure is from portions of lands allotted to be cultivated; (d) "an inheritance," as in No. 1 (c); Acts 26:18; Col. 1:12. See CHARGE, A, No. 4, LOT(S), PART, PORTION.¶

INIQUITY

1. *anomia* (ἀνομία, 458), lit., "lawlessness" (*a*, negative, *nomos*, "law"), is used in a way which indicates the meaning as being lawlessness or wickedness. Its usual rendering in the NT is "iniquity," which lit. means unrighteousness. It occurs very frequently in the Sept., especially in the Psalms, where it is found about 70 times. It is used (*a*) of iniquity in general, Matt. 7:23; 13:41; 23:28; 24:12; Rom. 6:19 (twice); 2 Cor. 6:14, RV, "iniquity" (KJV, "unrighteousness"); 2 Thess. 2:3, in some mss.; the KJV and RV follow those which have *hamartia*, "(man of) sin"; 2:7, RV, "lawlessness" (KJV, "iniquity"); Titus 2:14; Heb. 1:9; 1 John 3:4 (twice), RV, "(doeth) ... lawlessness" and "lawlessness" (KJV, "transgresseth the law" and "transgression of the law"); (*b*) in the plural, of acts or manifestations of lawlessness, Rom. 4:7; Heb. 10:17 (some inferior mss. have it in 8:12, for the word *hamartia*). See LAWLESSNESS, TRANSGRESSION, UNRIGHTEOUSNESS.¶

Note: In the phrase "man of sin," 2 Thess. 2:3, the word suggests the idea of contempt of Divine law, since the Antichrist will deny the existence of God.

2. *adikia* (ἀδικία, 93) denotes "unrighteousness," lit., "unrightness" (*a*, negative, *dikē*, "right"), a condition of not being right, whether with God, according to the standard of His holiness and righteousness, or with man, according to the standard of what man knows to be right by his conscience. In Luke 16:8 and 18:6, the phrases lit. are, "the steward of unrighteousness" and "the judge of injustice," the subjective genitive describing their character; in 18:6 the meaning is "injustice" and so perhaps in Rom. 9:14. The word is usually translated "unrighteousness," but is rendered "iniquity" in Luke 13:27; Acts 1:18; 8:23; 1 Cor. 13:6, KJV (RV, "unrighteousness"); so in 2 Tim. 2:19; Jas. 3:6.

3. *adikēma* (ἀδίκημα, 92) denotes "a wrong, injury, misdeed" (akin to No. 2; from *adikeō*, "to do wrong"), the concrete act, in contrast to the general meaning of No. 2, and translated "a matter of wrong," in Acts 18:14; "wrong-

doing," 24:20 (KJV, "evil-doing"); "iniquities," Rev. 18:5. See EVIL, WRONG.¶

4. *ponēria* (πονηρία, 4189), akin to *poneō*, "to toil" (cf. *ponēros*, "bad, worthless"; see BAD), denotes "wickedness," and is so translated in Matt. 22:18; Mark 7:22 (plural); Luke 11:39; Rom. 1:29; 1 Cor. 5:8; Eph. 6:12; in Acts 3:26, "iniquities." See WICKEDNESS.¶ Cf. *kakia*, "evil."

5. *paranomia* (παρανομία, 3892), "law-breaking" (*para*, "against," *nomos*, "law"), denotes "transgression," so rendered in 2 Pet. 2:16, for KJV, "iniquity."¶

INJURE, INJURIOUS, INJURY

A. Verb.

adikeō (ἀδικέω, 91), akin to Nos. 2 and 3, under INIQUITY, is usually translated either "to hurt," or by some form of the verb "to do wrong." In the KJV of Gal. 4:12, it is rendered "ye have (not) injured me," which the RV corrects, both in tense and meaning, to "ye did (me no) wrong." See HURT.

B. Adjective.

hubristēs (ὑβριστής, 5197), "a violent, insolent man" (akin to C), is translated "insolent" in Rom. 1:30, RV, for KJV, "despiteful"; in 1 Tim. 1:13, "injurious." See DESPITEFUL, INSOLENT.¶

C. Noun.

hubris (ὕβρις, 5196): see HARM, A, No. 4.

INK

melan (μέλαν, 3188), the neuter of the adjective *melas*, "black" (see Matt. 5:36; Rev. 6:5, 12), denotes "ink," 2 Cor. 3:3; 2 John 12; 3 John 13.¶

INN

1. *kataluma* (κατάλυμα, 2646): see GUEST-CHAMBER.

2. *pandocheion* (πανδοχεῖον, 3829), lit., "a place where all are received" (*pas*, "all," *dechomai*, "to receive"), denotes "a house for the reception of strangers," a *caravanserai*, translated "inn," in Luke 10:34, in the parable of the good samaritan. Cattle and beasts of burden could be sheltered there, and this word must thereby be distinguished from No. 1.¶ Cf. *pandocheus* in the next verse, "(the) host."¶

INNER

1. *esō* (ἔσω, 2080), an adverb connected with *eis*, "into," is translated "inner" in the KJV of Eph. 3:16 (RV, "inward"); after verbs of motion, it denotes "into," Mark 15:16; after verbs of rest, "within." See WITHIN.

2. *esōteros* (ἐσώτερος, 2082), the compara-

tive degree of No. 1, denotes "inner," Acts 16:24 (of a prison); Heb. 6:19, with the article, and practically as a noun, "that which is within (the veil)," lit., "the inner (of the veil)."¶ Cf. Eng., esoteric.

Note: For "inner chamber(s)" see CHAMBER, No. 1.

INNOCENT

1. *athōos* (ἀθῶος, 121) primarily denotes "unpunished" (*a*, negative, *thōē*, "a penalty"); then, "innocent," Matt. 27:4, "innocent blood," i.e., the blood of an "innocent" person, the word "blood" being used both by synecdoche (a part standing for the whole), and by metonymy (one thing standing for another), i.e., for death by execution (some mss. have *dikaion*, "righteous"); v. 24, where Pilate speaks of himself as "innocent."¶

2. *akakos* (ἄκακος, 172), lit., "not bad" (*a*, negative, *kakos*, "bad"), denotes "guileless, innocent," Rom. 16:18, RV, "innocent" (KJV, "simple"); "harmless" in Heb. 7:26. See HARMLESS.¶

INNUMERABLE

1. *anarithmētos* (ἀναρίθμητος, 382), *a*, negative, *n*, euphonic, *arithmeō* "to number," is used in Heb. 11:12.¶

2. *murias* (μυριάς, 3461) denotes either "ten thousand," or, "indefinitely, a myriad, a numberless host," in the plural, Acts 19:19; lit. "five ten-thousands," Rev. 5:11; 9:16; in the following, used of vast numbers, Luke 12:1, KJV, "an innumerable multitude," RV, "the many thousands" (RV marg., "the myriads"); Acts 21:20, "thousands"; Heb. 12:22, "innumerable hosts"; Jude 14, "ten thousands" (RV, marg., in each place, "myriads"). See COMPANY, THOUSANDS.¶ Cf. the adjective *murios*, "ten thousand," Matt. 18:24; 1 Cor. 4:15; 14:19.¶

For INORDINATE see AFFECTION, No. 1

INQUIRE, INQUIRY (make)

A. Verbs.

1. *punthanomai* (πυνθάνομαι, 4441), "to inquire," is translated "inquired" in Matt. 2:4, and Acts 21:33, RV (KJV, "demanded"); in Luke 15:26; 18:36 and Acts 4:7 (KJV, "asked"); "inquired" (KJV, "inquired") in John 4:52; "inquire" (KJV, "inquire") in Acts 23:20; in Acts 23:34 it denotes "to learn by inquiry," KJV, and RV, "when (he) understood"; elsewhere it is rendered by the verb "to ask," Acts 10:18, 29; 23:19. See ASK, UNDERSTAND.¶

2. *zēteō* (ζητέω, 2212), "to seek," is rendered "inquire" in John 16:19; "inquire . . . for" in Acts 9:11. See ABOUT, B, *Note,* DESIRE, ENDEAVOR, GO, *Note* (2), *a,* REQUIRE, SEEK.

3. *dierōtaō* (διερωτάω, 1331), "to find by inquiry, to inquire through to the end" (*dia*, intensive, *erōtaō*, "to ask"), is used in Acts 10:17.¶

4. *exetazō* (ἐξετάζω, 1833), "to examine, seek out, inquire thoroughly," is translated "inquire" in Matt. 10:11, KJV (RV, "search out"); in John 21:12, "durst inquire," RV [KJV, "(durst) ask"]; in Matt. 2:8, RV, "search out" (KJV, "search"). See ASK, SEARCH.¶

Notes: (1) *Epizēteō*, "to seek after or for" (*epi*, "after," *zēteō*, "to seek"), is rendered "inquire" in Acts 19:39, KJV (RV, "seek"). (2) *Sunzēteō*, "to search" or "examine together," is rendered "to inquire" in Luke 22:23, KJV (RV, "to question"). (3) *Ekzēteō*, "to seek out, search after," is rendered "have inquired" in 1 Pet. 1:10, KJV (RV, "sought"). (4) *Diaginōskō*, "to ascertain exactly," or "to determine," is rendered "inquire" in Acts 23:15, KJV (RV, "judge"). (5) *Akriboō*, "to learn by diligent or exact inquiry," is rendered "inquired diligently" and "had diligently inquired" respectively, in Matt. 2:7, 16, KJV (RV, "learned carefully," and "had carefully learned"). (6) In 2 Cor. 8:23, the words "any inquire" are inserted to complete the meaning, lit., "whether about Titus."

B. Noun.

zētēsis (ζήτησις, 2214) primarily denotes "a search"; then, "an inquiry, a questioning, debate"; it forms part of a phrase translated by the verb "to inquire," in Acts 25:20, RV, "how to inquire," lit. "(being perplexed as to) the inquiry." See QUESTION.

INSCRIPTION

epigraphō (ἐπιγράφω, 1924), "to write upon, inscribe" (*epi*, "upon," *graphō*, "to write"), is usually rendered by the verb "to write upon, over, or in," Mark 15:26; Heb. 8:10; 10:16; Rev. 21:12; it is translated by a noun phrase in Acts 17:23, "(with this) inscription," lit., "(on which) had been inscribed."¶ Cf. the noun *epigraphē*, "a superscription."

INSIDE

1. *entos* (ἐντός, 1787), an adverb denoting "within," or "among," is once used with the article, as a noun, of "the inside (of the cup and of the platter)," Matt. 23:26, RV (KJV, "that which is within etc."); elsewhere, Luke 17:21. See WITHIN.¶

2. *esōthen* (ἔσωθεν, 2081), an adverb denoting "from within," or "within," is used with the

article, as a noun, of the inner being, the secret intents of the heart, which, the Lord declared, God made, as well as the visible physical frame, Luke 11:40. In v. 39, it is rendered "inward part." See INWARD, WITHIN.

INSOLENT

hubristēs (ὑβριστής, 5197), "violent, injurious, insolent," is rendered "insolent" in Rom. 1:30, RV (KJV, "despiteful"). See DESPITEFUL, INJURIOUS.

INSOMUCH THAT, or AS

1. *hōste* (ὥστε, 5620), a consecutive particle, is used with the meaning "insomuch that," or "so that," or "that," to express the effect or result of anything, e.g., Matt. 8:24; 13:54; 15:31; 27:14; Acts 1:19 (KJV, "insomuch as"); 5:15; 19:12 (KJV, "so that"); 2 Cor. 1:8; Gal. 2:13. See WHEREFORE.

2. *eis to* (εἰς τό, 2526), lit., "unto the," followed by the infinitive mood, is sometimes used of result, and is rendered "insomuch that" in 2 Cor. 8:6.

3. *katho* (καθό) is translated "insomuch as" in 1 Pet. 4:13, RV (KJV, "inasmuch as"). See INASMUCH.

INSPIRATION OF GOD, INSPIRED OF GOD

theopneustos (θεόπνευστος, 2315), "inspired by God" (*Theos*, "God," *pneō*, "to breathe"), is used in 2 Tim. 3:16, of the Scriptures as distinct from non-inspired writings. Wycliffe, Tyndale, Coverdale and the Great Bible have the rendering "inspired of God."¶

INSTANT, BE INSTANT, INSTANTLY

A. Verbs.

1. *epikeimai* (ἐπίκειμαι, 1945), "to lie" or "press upon," is rendered "they were instant" in Luke 23:23 (Amer. RV, "they were urgent"). See IMPOSE.

2. *ephistēmi* (ἐφίστημι, 2186), "to set upon or by," is used in the NT intransitively, either in the middle voice, or in certain tenses of the active, signifying "to stand by, be present, be at hand, come on or upon," and is translated "be instant" in 2 Tim. 4:2. See ASSAULT, COME, etc.

Note: For *proskartereō*, in Rom. 12:12, KJV, rendered "continuing instant," RV, "steadfastly," see CONTINUE, No. 9.

B. Noun.

Note: The word *hōra*, "an hour," is translated "instant" in Luke 2:38, KJV; the RV renders it "hour." See HOUR.

C. Adverb.

spoudaiōs (σπουδαίως, 4709), "earnestly, diligently," is rendered "instantly" in Luke 7:4, KJV (RV, "earnestly"). See EARNEST.

Note: For the phrase *en ekteneia*, rendered "instantly" in Acts 26:7, KJV, see EARNEST, D.

INSTRUCT, INSTRUCTION, INSTRUCTOR

A. Verbs.

1. *katēcheō* (κατηχέω, 2727), "to teach orally, inform, instruct," is translated by the verb "to instruct" in Luke 1:4; Acts 18:25 (RV marg., "taught by word of mouth"); Rom. 2:18; 1 Cor. 14:19, RV (KJV, "teach"). See INFORM, TEACH.

2. *paideuō* (παιδεύω, 3811), "to train children, teach," is rendered "was instructed," in Acts 7:22, RV (KJV, "learned"); "instructing" in 2 Tim. 2:25, KJV (RV, "correcting"); Titus 2:12, RV, "instructing" (KJV, "teaching"). The verb is used of the family discipline, as in Heb. 12:6, 7, 10; cf. 1 Cor. 11:32; 2 Cor. 6:9; Rev. 3:19. In 1 Tim. 1:20 (passive voice) it is translated "might be taught," RV (KJV, "may learn"), but, "however the passage is to be understood, it is clear that not the impartation of knowledge but severe discipline is intended. In Luke 23:16, 22, Pilate, since he had declared the Lord guiltless of the charge brought against Him, and hence could not punish Him, weakly offered, as a concession to the Jews, to 'chastise, *paideuō*, Him, and let Him go.'"*

This sense of *paideuō* is confirmed by Heb. 12:6, where it is joined (in a quotation from the Sept. of Prov. 3:12) with "to lash or scourge." Cf. the scene in the *Pilgrim's Progress* where a shining one with a whip of small cords "chastised sore" the pilgrims foolishly caught in the net of the flatterer and said to them, "As many as I love I rebuke and chasten" (*paideuō*). See CORRECT, TEACH.¶

3. *mathēteuō* (μαθητεύω, 3100), used transitively, "to make a disciple," is translated "which is instructed" in Matt. 13:52, KJV (RV, "who hath been made a disciple"). See DISCIPLE.

4. *mueō* (μυέω), "to initiate into the mysteries," is used in the passive voice, in Phil. 4:12, KJV, "I am instructed," RV, "have I learned the secret." See LEARN.¶

5. *probibazō* (προβιβάζω, 4264), "to lead forward, lead on" (the causal of *probainō*, "to go forward"; *pro*, "forward," *bibazō*, "to lift up"), is used in the passive voice In Matt. 14:8, and translated, KJV, "being before instructed,"

---

* From *Notes on Galatians*, by Hogg and Vine, p. 165.

RV, "being put forward." Some mss. have it in Acts 19:33, instead of No. 6.¶

6. *sumbibazō* (συμβιβάζω, 4822), "to join, knit, unite" (*sun*, "with"), then, "to compare," and so, "to prove," hence, "to teach, instruct," is so rendered in 1 Cor. 2:16; it is found in the best mss. in Acts 19:33 (RV marg., "instructed"). See COMPACTED, CONCLUDE, KNIT TOGETHER, PROVE.

B. Nouns.
(INSTRUCTION)

paideia (παιδεία, 3809), "training, instruction," is translated "instruction" in 2 Tim. 3:16. See CHASTEN.

(INSTRUCTOR)

1. *paidagōgos* (παιδαγωγός, 3807), "a guide," or "guardian" or "trainer of boys," lit., "a child-leader" (*pais*, "a boy, or child," *agō*, "to lead"), "a tutor," is translated "instructors" in 1 Cor. 4:15, KJV (RV, "tutors"); here the thought is that of pastors rather than teachers; in Gal. 3:24, 25, KJV, "schoolmaster" (RV, "tutor,"), but here the idea of instruction is absent. "In this and allied words the idea is that of training, discipline, not of impartation of knowledge. The *paidagōgos* was not the instructor of the child; he exercised a general supervision over him and was responsible for his moral and physical well-being. Thus understood, *paidagōgos* is appropriately used with 'kept in ward' and 'shut up,' whereas to understand it as equivalent to 'teacher' introduce; an idea entirely foreign to the passage, and throws the Apostle's argument into confusion."*¶ Cf. *epitropos*, "a steward, guardian, tutor."

2. *paideutēs* (παιδευτής, 3810), akin to A, No. 2, denotes (*a*) "an instructor, a teacher," Rom. 2:20, KJV, "an instructor" (RV, "a corrector"); (*b*) "one who disciplines, corrects, chastens," Heb. 12:9, RV, "to chasten" [KJV, "which corrected" (lit., "correctors")]. In (*a*) the discipline of the school is in view; in (*b*) that of the family. See CORRECTOR.¶ Cf. *epitropos*, "a steward, guardian, tutor."

INSTRUMENTS

hoplon (ὅπλον, 3696), "a tool, instrument, weapon," is used metaphorically in Rom. 6:13 of the members of the body as "instruments" (marg., "weapons"), negatively, of unrighteousness, positively, of righteousness. The metaphor is probably military (cf. v. 23, "wages," i.e., soldiers' pay); Moule renders it "implements"; "weapons" seems to be the meaning. See ARMOR, WEAPONS.

---

* From *Notes on Galatians*, by Hogg and Vine, pp. 163, 164.

INSURRECTION

A. Nouns.

1. *stasis* (στάσις, 4714), akin to *histēmi*, "to make to stand," denotes (*a*) primarily, "a standing or place," Heb. 9:8; (*b*) "an insurrection, sedition," translated "insurrection" in Mark 15:7; "insurrections" in Acts 24:5, RV (KJV, "sedition"); in Luke 23:19, 25 (KJV "sedition"), "riot," Acts 19:40, RV (KJV, "uproar"); (*c*) "a dissension," Acts 15:2; in Acts 23:7, 10, "dissension." See DISSENSION.¶

2. *stasiastēs* (στασιαστής, 4955v) denotes "a rebel, revolutionist, one who stirs up sedition" (from *stasiazō*, "to stir up sedition"), Mark 15:7, "had made insurrection." Some mss. have *sustasiastēs*, a fellow-rioter, a fellow-mover of sedition, KJV, "had made insurrection with (him)."¶

B. Verb.

katephistēmi (κατεφίστημι, 2721) signifies "to rise up against" (lit., "to cause to stand forth against," *kata*, "against," *epi*, "forth," *histēmi*, "to cause to stand"), Acts 18:12, KJV, "made insurrection" (RV, "rose up against")."¶

INTEND

1. *boulomai* (βούλομαι, 1014), "to will, wish, desire, purpose" (expressing a fixed resolve, the deliberate exercise of volition), is translated "intend" in Acts 5:28, and "intending" in 12:4. See DESIRE.

2. *thelō* (θέλω, 2309), "to will, be willing, desire" (less strong, and more frequent than No. 1), is translated "intending" in Luke 14:28, KJV (RV, "desiring"). See DESIRE.

3. *mellō* (μέλλω, 3195), "to be about to do a thing," indicating simply the formation of a design, is translated "intend" in Acts 5:35, KJV (RV, "are about"); "intending," in Acts 20:7, RV (KJV, "ready"); 20:13 (1st part); in the 2nd part of the v., RV, "intending" (KJV, "minding").

INTENT

1. *ennoia* (ἔννοια, 1771), primarily "a thinking, idea, consideration," denotes "purpose, intention, design" (*en*, in, *nous*, mind); it is rendered "intents" in Heb. 4:12; "mind," in 1 Pet. 4:1 (RV, marg., "thought"). See MIND.¶ Cf. *Enthumēsis*, "thought" (see DEVICE).

2. *logos* (λόγος, 3056), "a word, account, etc.," sometimes denotes "a reason, cause, intent," e.g., Matt. 5:32, "cause"; it is rendered "intent" in Acts 10:29. See CAUSE.

Notes: (1) The phrase *eis touto*, lit., "unto this," i.e., "for this purpose," is rendered "for this (KJV, 'that') intent" in Acts 9:21, RV (2) The phrase *eis to*, "unto the," followed by a verb in the infinitive mood, is translated "to the intent" in 1 Cor. 10:6. (3) The phrase *pros ti*, lit., "in reference to what," is rendered "for what intent" in John 13:28. (4) In John 11:15 the conjunction *hina*, "to the end that," is translated "to the intent," and in Eph. 3:10, "to the intent that."

INTERCESSIONS

A. Noun.

enteuxis (ἔντευξις, 1783) primarily denotes "a lighting upon, meeting with" (akin to B); then, "a conversation"; hence, "a petition," a meaning frequent in the papyri; it is a technical term for approaching a king, and so for approaching God in "intercession"; it is rendered "prayer" in 1 Tim. 4:5; in the plural in 2:1 (i.e., seeking the presence and hearing of God on behalf of others).¶ For the synonymous words, *proseuchē, deēsis*, see PRAYER.

B. Verbs.

1. *entunchanō* (ἐντυγχάνω, 1793), primarily "to fall in with, meet with in order to converse"; then, "to make petition," especially "to make intercession, plead with a person," either for or against others; (*a*) against, Acts 25:24, "made suit to (me)," RV [KJV, "have dealt with (me)"], i.e., against Paul; in Rom. 11:2, of Elijah in "pleading" with God, RV (KJV, "maketh intercession to"), against Israel; (*b*) for, in Rom. 8:27, of the intercessory work of the Holy Spirit for the saints; v. 34, of the similar intercessory work of Christ; so Heb. 7:25. See DEAL WITH, PLEAD, SUIT.¶

2. *huperentunchanō* (ὑπερεντυγχάνω, 5241), "to make a petition" or "intercede on behalf of another" (*huper*, "on behalf of," and No. 1), is used in Rom. 8:26 of the work of the Holy Spirit in making "intercession" (see No. 1, v. 27).¶

INTEREST

tokos (τόκος, 5110), primarily "a bringing forth, birth" (from *tiktō*, "to beget"), then, "an offspring," is used metaphorically of the produce of money lent out, "interest," usury, Matt. 25:27; Luke 19:23. See USURY.¶

INTERPOSED

mesiteuō (μεσιτεύω, 3315), "to mediate, give surety" (akin to *mesitēs*, "a mediator"), is translated "interposed" in Heb. 6:17, RV. See CONFIRM, No. 5.¶

INTERPRET, INTERPRETATION, INTERPRETER

A. Verbs.

1. *hermēneuō* (ἑρμηνεύω, 2059), (cf. *Hermēs*, the Greek name of the pagan god Mercury, who was regarded as the messenger of the gods), denotes "to explain, interpret" (Eng., "hermeneutics"), and is used of explaining the meaning of words in a different language, John 1:38 (in some mss.), see No. 3; 9:7 ("Siloam," interpreted as "sent"); Heb. 7:2 (Melchizedec, "by interpretation," lit., "being interpreted," King of righteousness).¶

2. *diermēneuō* (διερμηνεύω, 1329), a strengthened form of No. 1 (*dia*, "through," used intensively), signifies "to interpret fully, to explain." In Luke 24:27, it is used of Christ in interpreting to the two on the way to Emmaus "in all the Scriptures the things concerning Himself," RV, "interpreted" (KJV, "expounded"); in Acts 9:36, it is rendered "is by interpretation," lit., "being interpreted" (of Tabitha, as meaning Dorcas); in 1 Cor. 12:30 and 14:5, 13, 27, it is used with reference to the temporary gift of tongues in the churches; this gift was inferior in character to that of prophesying unless he who spoke in a "tongue" interpreted his words, 14:5; he was, indeed, to pray that he might interpret, v. 13; only two, or at the most three, were to use the gift in a gathering, and that "in turn" (RV); one was to interpret; in the absence of an interpreter, the gift was not to be exercised, v. 27. See EXPOUND.¶

3. *methermēneuō* (μεθερμηνεύω, 3177), "to change or translate from one language to another (*meta*, implying change, and No. 1), to interpret," is always used in the passive voice in the NT, "being interpreted," of interpreting the names, Immanuel, Matt. 1:23; Golgotha, Mark 15:22; Barnabas, Acts 4:36; in Acts 13:8, of Elymas, the verb is rendered "is ... by interpretation," lit., "is interpreted"; it is used of interpreting or translating sentences in Mark 5:41; 15:34; in the best mss., John 1:38 (Rabbi, interpreted as "Master"); v. 41 (Messiah, interpreted as "Christ"); see No. 1.¶

B. Nouns.

(INTERPRETATION)

1. *hermēneia* (or -*ia*) (ἑρμηνία, 2058), akin to A, No. 1, is used in 1 Cor. 12:10; 14:26 (see A, No. 2).¶

2. *epilusis* (ἐπίλυσις, 1955), from *epiluō*, "to loose, solve, explain," denotes "a solution, explanation," lit., "a release" (*epi*, "up," *luō*, "to loose"), 2 Pet. 1:20, "(of private) interpretation"; i.e., the writers of Scripture did not put their own construction upon the "God-breathed" words they wrote.¶ *Note:* For "hard of interpretation," Heb. 5:11, RV, see UTTER, *Note* (1).

(INTERPRETER)

diermēneutēs (διερμηνευτής, 1328), lit., "a

thorough interpreter" (cf. A, No. 2), is used in 1 Cor. 14:28 (some mss. have *hermēneutēs*).¶

INTERROGATION

eperōtēma (ἐπερώτημα, 1906), primarily a question or inquiry, denotes "a demand or appeal"; it is found in 1 Pet. 3:21, RV, "interrogation" (KJV, "answer"). See ANSWER, *Note*. Some take the word to indicate that baptism affords a good conscience, an appeal against the accuser.¶

For **INTO** see †, p. 1

INTREAT, INTREATY
A. Verbs.

1. *erōtaō* (ἐρωτάω, 2065), "to ask, beseech," is rendered "intreat," e.g., in Phil. 4:3, KJV (RV, "beseech"). See ASK.

2. *parakaleō* (παρακαλέω, 3870), "to beseech, comfort, exhort," is rendered by the verb "to intreat" in Luke 8:31, RV, "intreated" (KJV, "besought"); 15:28; Acts 9:38, RV, "intreating" (KJV, "desiring"); 28:20, RV (KJV, "called for"); 1 Cor. 4:13; 2 Cor. 9:5, RV (KJV, "exhort"); 10:1, RV (KJV, "beseech"); 1 Tim. 5:1, KJV (RV, "exhort"). See BESEECH.

3. *paraiteomai* (παραιτέομαι, 3868), "to ask to be excused, to beg," etc., is rendered "intreated" in Heb. 12:19, See AVOID.

B. Adjective.

eupeithēs (εὐπειθής, 2138), "ready to obey" (*eu*, "well," *peithomai*, "to obey, to be persuaded"), "compliant," is translated "easy to be intreated" in Jas. 3:17, said of the wisdom that is from above.¶

C. Noun.

paraklēsis (παράκλησις, 3874), "an appeal, a comfort, exhortation," etc., is translated "intreaty" in 2 Cor. 8:4.

For **INTRUDE** (Col. 2:18) see **DWELL**, A, No. 11

INTRUST

pisteuō (πιστεύω, 4100), "to believe," also means "to entrust," and in the active voice is translated "to commit," in Luke 16:11; John 2:24; in the passive voice, "to be intrusted with," Rom. 3:2, RV, "they were intrusted with" (KJV, "unto them were committed"), of Israel and the oracles of God; 1 Cor. 9:17, RV, "I have ... intrusted to me" (KJV, "is committed unto me"), of Paul and the stewardship of the gospel; so Gal. 2:7; Titus 1:3; in 1 Thess. 2:4, where he associates with himself his fellow mis-

sionaries, RV, "to be intrusted with" (KJV, "to be put in trust with"). See BELIEVE, COMMIT.

INVENTORS

epheuretēs (ἐφευρετής, 2182), "an inventor, contriver" (akin to *epheuriskō*, "to find out"; *epi*, "on," used intensively, *heuriskō*, "to find"), occurs in the plural in Rom. 1:30.¶

INVISIBLE

aoratos (ἀόρατος, 517), lit., "unseen" (*a*, negative, *horaō*, "to see"), is translated "invisible" in Rom. 1:20, of the power and divinity of God; of God Himself, Col. 1:15; 1 Tim. 1:17; Heb. 11:27; of things unseen, Col. 1:16.¶ In the Sept., Gen. 1:2; Isa. 45:3, "unseen (treasures)." ¶

INWARD (man, part), INWARDLY

1. *esō* (ἔσω, 2080), "within, inward," is used adjectively in Rom. 7:22, "(the) inward (man)"; 2 Cor. 4:16, with "man" expressed in the preceding clause, but not repeated in the original, "(our) inward (man)" (some mss. have *esōthen*, "from within"); Eph. 3:16, RV, "(the) inward (man)" (KJV, "inner"). See INNER, WITHIN.

2. *esōthen* (ἔσωθεν, 2081) is used in Luke 11:39, as a noun with the article, "part" being understood, "(your) inward part"; in Matt. 7:15 it has its normal use as an adverb, "inwardly." See WITHIN.

Note: In Rom. 2:29 the phrase *en tō kruptō*, lit., "in (the) secret, or hidden" ("part" being understood) is rendered "inwardly," said of a spiritual Jew, in contrast to the one who is merely naturally circumcised and so is one outwardly. See HIDE, SECRET.

IRKSOME

oknēros (ὀκνηρός, 3636), "shrinking, timid" (from *okneō*, "to shrink, delay"), is used negatively in Phil. 3:1, RV, "irksome" (KJV, "grievous"), i.e., "I do not hesitate"; in Matt. 25:26, and Rom. 12:11, "slothful." See GRIEVOUS, SLOTHFUL.¶

IRON
A. Noun.

sidēros (σίδηρος, 4604), "iron," occurs in Rev. 18:12.¶

B. Adjective.

sidēreos (σιδήρεος, 4603), "of iron," occurs in Acts 12:10, of an iron gate; "of iron," Rev. 2:27; 9:9; 12:5; 19:15.¶

ISLAND, ISLE

1. *nēsos* (νῆσος, 3520), "an island," occurs in Acts 13:6; 27:26; 28:1, 7, 9, 11; Rev. 1:9; 6:14; 16:20.¶

2. *nēsion* (νησίον, 3519), a diminutive of No. 1, "a small island," occurs in Acts 27:16, Cauda, RV.¶

ISSUE

A. Nouns.

1. *ekbasis* (ἔκβασις, 1545), "a way out," "way of escape," 1 Cor. 10:13 (*ek*, "out," *bainō*, "to go"), is rendered "issue" in Heb. 13:7, RV, for KJV, "end," regarding the manner of life of deceased spiritual guides. See END.¶

2. *rhusis* (ῥύσις, 4511), "a flowing" (akin to *rheō*, "to flow"), "an issue," is used in Mark 5:25; Luke 8:43, 44.¶

Note: In Matt. 22:25, KJV, *sperma*, "seed," is translated "issue" (RV, "seed").

B. Verb.

ekporeuō (ἐκπορεύω, 1607), "to cause to go forth" (*ek*, "out," *poreuō*, "to cause to go"), is used in the middle voice in Rev. 9:17, 18, of the coming forth of fire, smoke and brimstone from the mouths of the symbolic horses in a vision, KJV, "issued" (the RV renders it by the verb "to proceed"). See COME, DEPART, GO, PROCEED.

IT

Note: The pronouns used are the same, in their neuter forms, as Nos. 1, 2, 3 under HE.

ITCHING

knēthō (κνήθω, 2833), "to scratch, tickle," is used in the passive voice, metaphorically, of an eagerness to hear, in 2 Tim. 4:3, lit., "itched (as to the hearing)," of those who, not enduring sound doctrine, heap to themselves teachers.¶

ITSELF

Note: The pronouns used are the same in their neuter forms, as those under HIMSELF.

IVORY

elephantinos (ἐλεφάντινος, 1661), an adjective from *elephas* (whence Eng., elephant), signifies "of ivory," Rev. 18:12.¶

J

JACINTH

A. Noun.

huakinthos (ὑάκινθος, 5192) primarily denoted "a hyacinth," probably the dark blue iris; then, "a precious stone," most likely the sapphire, Rev. 21:20.¶

B. Adjective.

huakinthinos (ὑακίνθινος, 5191) signifies "hyacinthine," perhaps primarily having the color of the hyacinth. Some regard its color as that of the martagon lily, a dusky red. According to Swete, the word in Rev. 9:17 is "doubtless meant to describe the blue smoke of a sulphurous flame."¶

JAILER

desmophulax (δεσμοφύλαξ, 1200), "a prison keeper, jailer" (*desmos*, "a band," *phulax*, "a guard, keeper"), occurs in Acts 16:23, 27, 36.¶

For **JANGLING** (1 Tim. 1:6, KJV) see **TALKING** (vain)

JASPER

iaspis (ἴασπις, 2393), a Phoenician word (cf. Heb. *yāsh'pheh*, e.g., Exod. 28:20; 39:16), seems to have denoted a translucent stone of various colors, especially that of fire, Rev. 4:3; 21:11, 18, 19. The sardius and the jasper, of similar color, were the first and last stones on the breastplate of the high priest, Ex. 28:17, 20.¶

JEALOUS, JEALOUSY

A. Noun.

zēlos (ζῆλος, 2205), "zeal, jealousy," is rendered "jealousy" in the RV (KJV, "envying") in Rom. 13:13; 1 Cor. 3:3; Jas. 3:14, 16; in 2 Cor. 12:20 (KJV, "envyings"); in Gal. 5:20, RV "jealousies" (KJV, "emulations"); in Acts 5:17 (KJV, "indignation"); in 13:45 (KJV, "envy"); in 2 Cor. 11:2 it is used in the phrase "with a godly jealousy," lit., "with a jealousy of God" (RV, marg.). See ENVY.

B. Verbs.

1. *zēloō* (ζηλόω, 2206), akin to A, "to be jealous, to burn with jealousy" (otherwise, to

seek or desire eagerly), is rendered "moved with jealousy," in Acts 7:9 and 17:5, RV (KJV, "moved with envy"); in 1 Cor. 13:4, "envieth (not)," KJV and RV; in Jas. 4:2, RV marg., "are jealous" (text "covet;" KJV, "desire to have"). See AFFECT, *Note,* DESIRE.

2. *parazēloō* (παραζηλόω, 3863), "to provoke to jealousy" (*para,* "beside," used intensively, and No. 1), is found in Rom. 10:19 and 11:11, of God's dealings with Israel through his merciful dealings with Gentiles; in 11:14, RV, "I may provoke to jealousy" (KJV, ". . . emulation"), of the apostle's evangelical ministry to Gentiles with a view to stirring his fellow nationals to a sense of their need and responsibilities regarding the gospel; in 1 Cor. 10:22, of the provocation of God on the part of believers who compromise their divine relationship by partaking of the table of demons; in Gal 5:20, of the works of the flesh.¶

For JEOPARDY see DANGER

JESTING

eutrapelia (εὐτραπελία, 2160) properly denotes "wit, facetiousness, versatility" (lit., "easily turning," from *eu,* "well," *trepō,* "to turn"). It was used in the literal sense to describe the quick movements of apes and persons. Pericles speaks of the Athenians of his day (430 B.C.) as distinguished by a happy and gracious "flexibility." In the next century Aristotle uses it of "versatility" in the give and take of social intercourse, quick repartee. In the sixth century, B.C., the poet Pindar speaks of one Jason as never using a word of "vain lightness," a meaning approaching its latest use. Its meaning certainly deteriorated, and it came to denote "coarse jesting, ribaldry," as in Eph. 5:4, where it follows *mōrologia,* "foolish talking."¶

JESUS

iēsous (Ἰησοῦς, 2424) is a transliteration of the Heb. "Joshua," meaning "Jehovah is salvation," i.e., "is the Savior," "a common name among the Jews, e.g., Ex. 17:9; Luke 3:29 (RV); Col. 4:11. It was given to the Son of God in Incarnation as His personal name, in obedience to the command of an angel to Joseph, the husband of His Mother, Mary, shortly before He was born, Matt. 1:21. By it He is spoken of throughout the Gospel narratives generally, but not without exception, as in Mark 16:19, 20; Luke 7:13, and a dozen other places in that Gospel, and a few in John.

"'Jesus Christ' occurs only in Matt. 1:1, 18; 16:21, marg.; Mark 1:1; John 1:17; 17:3. In Acts the name 'Jesus' is found frequently. 'Lord Jesus' is the normal usage, as in Acts 8:16; 19:5, 17; see also the reports of the words of Stephen, 7:59, of Ananias, 9:17, and of Paul, 16:31; though both Peter, 10:36, and Paul, 16:18, also used 'Jesus Christ.'

"In the Epistles of James, Peter, John and Jude, the personal name is not once found alone, but in Rev. eight times (RV), 1:9; 12:17; 14:12; 17:6; 19:10 (twice); 20:4; 22:16.

"In the Epistles of Paul 'Jesus' appears alone just thirteen times, and in the Hebrews eight times; in the latter the title 'Lord' is added once only, at 13:20. In the Epistles of James, Peter, John, and Jude, men who had companied with the Lord in the days of His flesh, 'Jesus Christ' is the invariable order (in the RV) of the Name and Title, for this was the order of their experience; as 'Jesus' they knew Him first, that He was Messiah they learnt finally in His resurrection. But Paul came to know Him first in the glory of heaven, Acts 9:1–6, and his experience being thus the reverse of theirs, the reverse order, 'Christ Jesus,' is of frequent occurrence in his letters, but, with the exception of Acts 24:24, does not occur elsewhere in the RV.

"In Paul's letters the order is always in harmony with the context. Thus 'Christ Jesus' describes the Exalted One who emptied Himself, Phil. 2:5, and testifies to His pre-existence; 'Jesus Christ' describes the despised and rejected One Who was afterwards glorified, Phil. 2:11, and testifies to His resurrection. 'Christ Jesus' suggests His grace, 'Jesus Christ' suggests His glory."*

JEW(-S) (live as do the), JEWESS, JEWISH, JEWRY, JEWS' RELIGION

A. Adjectives.

1. *ioudaios* (Ἰουδαῖος, 2453) is used (*a*) adjectivally, with the lit. meaning, "Jewish," sometimes with the addition of *anēr,* "a man," Acts 10:28; 22:3; in 21:39 with *anthrōpos,* in some mss. (a man in the generic sense); other mss. omit the phrase here; in 13:6, lit., "a Jewish false-prophet"; in John 3:22, with the word *chōra,* "land" or "country," signifying "Judean," lit., "Judean country"; used by metonymy for the people of the country; (*b*) as a noun, "a Jew, Jews," e.g., Matt. 2:2; Mark 7:3. The name "Jew" is primarily tribal (from Judah). It is first found in 2 Kings 16:6, as distinct from Israel, of the northern kingdom. After the Captivity it was chiefly used to distin-

---

* From *Notes on Thessalonians,* by Hogg and Vine, pp. 26, 29.

guish the race from Gentiles, e.g., John 2:6; Acts 14:1; Gal. 2:15, where it denotes Christians of "Jewish" race; it distinguishes Jews from Samaritans, in John 4:9; from proselytes, in Acts 2:10. The word is most frequent in John's gospel and the Acts; in the former "it especially denotes the typical representatives of Jewish thought contrasted with believers in Christ ... or with other Jews of less pronounced opinions, e.g., John 3:25; 5:10; 7:13; 9:22" (Lukyn Williams, in *Hastings' Bib. Dic.*); such representatives were found, generally, in opposition to Christ; in the Acts they are chiefly those who opposed the apostles and the gospel. In Rom. 2:28, 29 the word is used of ideal "Jews," i.e., "Jews" in spiritual reality, believers, whether "Jews" or Gentiles by natural birth. The feminine, "Jewess," is found in Acts 16:1; 24:24.

It also denotes Judea, e.g., Matt. 2:1; Luke 1:5; John 4:3, the word "country" being understood [cf. (*a*) above]. In Luke 23:5 and John 7:1, where the KJV has "Jewry," the RV translates it as usual, "Judea."

2. *ioudaikos* ('Ιουδαϊκός, 2451) denotes "Jewish," Titus 1:14.¶

B. Noun.

ioudaismos ('Ιουδαϊσμός, 2454), "Judaism," denotes "the Jews' religion," Gal. 1:13, 14, and stands, not for their religious beliefs, but for their religious practices, not as instituted by God, but as developed and extended from these by the traditions of the Pharisees and scribes. In the Apocrypha it denotes comprehensively "the Government, laws, institutions and religion of the Jews."¶

C. Verb.

ioudaizo ('Ιουδαΐζω, 2450), lit., "to Judaize," i.e., to conform to "Jewish" religious practices and manners, is translated "to live as do the Jews," in Gal. 2:14.¶

D. Adverb.

ioudaikos ('Ιουδαϊκῶς, 2452), "in Jewish fashion," is translated "as do the Jews," in Gal. 2:14.¶

JEWELS

chrusion (χρυσίον, 5553), "gold," is used of ornaments in 1 Pet. 3:3, RV, "jewels." See GOLD, No. 2.

JOIN

1. *kollao* (κολλάω, 2853), primarily, "to glue or cement together," then, generally, "to unite, to join firmly," is used in the passive voice signifying "to join oneself to, to be joined to," Luke 15:15; Acts 5:13; 8:29; 9:26; 10:28, RV (KJV, "to keep company with"); 1 Cor. 6:16, 17;

elsewhere, "to cleave to," Luke 10:11; Acts 17:34; Rom. 12:9. See CLEAVE. ¶

2. *proskollao* (προσκολλάω, 4347), "to stick to," a strengthened form of No. 1, with *pros*, "to," intensive, is used in the passive voice, reflexively, in a metaphorical sense, with the meanings (*a*) "to join oneself to," in Acts 5:36; (*b*) "to cleave to," of the husband with regard to the wife, Matt. 19:5; Mark 10:7; in Eph. 5:31, RV, "shall cleave to" (KJV, "shall be joined to"). See CLEAVE.¶

3. *su(n)zeugnumi* (συνζεύγνυμι, 4801), "to yoke together" (*sun*, "with," *zugos*, "a yoke"), is used metaphorically of union in wedlock, in Matt. 19:6; Mark 10:9.¶

4. *sunomoreo* (συνομορέω, 4927), "to border on," is used of a house as being contiguous with a synagogue, in Acts 18:7, "joined hard to."¶

Notes: (1) In 1 Cor. 1:10, *katartizo*, "to render complete, to perfect" (*kata*, "down," intensive, and *artios*, "complete, jointed"), "to restore," is translated "be perfectly joined together," KJV (RV, "be perfected together"); see FIT. (2) In Eph. 4:16, *sunarmologeo*, "to fit" or "frame together," is translated "fitly joined together," KJV (RV, "fitly framed ... together"); cf. 2:21.¶

JOINT

1. *harmos* (ἁρμός, 719), "a joining, joint" (akin to *harmozo*, "to fit, join"), is found in Heb. 4:12, figuratively (with the word "marrow") of the inward moral and spiritual being of man, as just previously expressed literally in the phrase "soul and spirit."¶

2. *haphe* (ἁφή, 860), "a ligature, joint" (akin to *hapto*, "to fit, to fasten"), occurs in Eph. 4:16 and Col. 2:19.¶

For JOINT-HEIR see HEIR

JOT

iota (ἰῶτα, 2503), from the Heb. *yod*, the smallest Hebrew letter, is mentioned by the Lord in Matt. 5:18 (together with *keraia*, "a little horn, a tittle, the point or extremity" which distinguishes certain Hebrew letters from others), to express the fact that not a single item of the Law will pass away or remain unfulfilled.¶

JOURNEY (Noun and Verb), JOURNEYINGS

A. Nouns.

1. *hodos* (ὁδός, 3598), "a way, path, road," used of a traveler's way, a "journey," is rendered "journey" in Matt. 10:13; Mark 6:8; Luke 2:44, "a day's journey" (probably to Beeroth, six

miles north of Jerusalem); 9:3; 11:6; Acts 1:12, "a Sabbath day's journey," i.e., the journey which a Jew was allowed to take on the Sabbath, viz., about 2,000 yards or cubits (estimates vary). The regulation was not a Mosaic enactment, but a rabbinical tradition, based upon an exposition of Exod. 16:29, and a comparison of the width of the suburb of a Levitical city as enjoined in Num. 35:4, 5, and the distance between the ark and the people at the crossing of the Jordan, Josh. 3:4. In regard to Acts 1:12, there is no discrepancy between this and Luke 24:50, where the RV rightly translates by "over against Bethany," which does not fix the exact spot of the Ascension. See HIGHWAY, WAY.

2. *hodoiporia* (ὁδοιπορία, 3597), "a wayfaring, journeying" (No. 1, and *poros*, "a way, a passage"), is used of the Lord's journey to Samaria, John 4:6, and of Paul's "journeyings," 2 Cor. 11:26. Cf. B, No. 3.

Note: In Luke 13:22 the noun *poreia*, "a journey, a going" (cf. *poros*, No. 2, above), is used with the verb *poieō*, "to make," with the meaning "to journey," lit., "making (for Himself, middle voice) a way", "journeying." In Jas. 1:11, "ways." See WAY.¶

B. Verbs.

1. *poreuomai* (πορεύομαι, 4198) is used in the middle voice in the NT, signifying "to go, proceed, go on one's way"; it is translated by the verb "to journey" in Acts 9:3; 22:6, "as I made (my) journey"; 26:13; Rom. 15:24 (1st part), KJV, "I take my journey," RV, "I go" (for the 2nd part, "in my journey," see No. 2). See GO, No. 1.

2. *diaporeuō* (διαπορεύω, 1279), "to carry over," used in the passive voice with the meaning 'to pass by, to journey through," is translated "in my journey," in Rom. 15:24, lit., "journeying through"; in Luke 18:36, RV, "going by" (KJV "pass by"). See GO, No. 4.

3. *hodoiporeō* (ὁδοιπορέω, 3596), "to travel, journey" (akin to A, No. 2), is found in Acts 10:9.¶

4. *hodeuō* (ὁδεύω, 3593), "to be on the way, journey" (from *hodos*, "a way"), the simplest form of the verbs denoting "to journey," is used in the parable of the good samaritan, Luke 10:33.¶

5. *sunodeuō* (συνοδεύω, 4922), *sun*, "with," and No. 4, "to journey with," occurs in Acts 9:7.¶ In the Sept., Zech. 8:21.¶

6. *euodoō* (εὐοδόω, 2137), "to help on one's way" (*eu*, "well," and *hodos*), is used in the passive voice with the meaning "to have a prosperous journey"; so the KJV of Rom. 1:10; the RV, "I may be prospered" rightly expresses the

metaphorical use which the verb acquired, without reference to a "journey"; see 1 Cor. 16:2; 3 John 2.¶

7. *propempō* (προπέμπω, 4311), "to send before or forth" (*pro*, "before," *pempō*, "to send"), also means "to set forward on a journey, to escort"; in 1 Cor. 16:6, "may set (me) forward on my journey," RV [KJV, "may bring (me) etc."]; so Titus 3:13, and 3 John 6. See ACCOMPANY, CONDUCT, WAY.

8. *apodēmeō* (ἀποδημέω, 589) denotes "to go on a journey to another country, go abroad," Matt. 21:33; 25:14, 15; Mark 12:1; Luke 15:13; 20:9. See COUNTRY.¶

Note: For the adjective *apodēmos*, Mark 13:34, KJV, "taking a far journey," RV, "sojourning in another country," see COUNTRY.

JOY (Noun and Verb), JOYFULNESS, JOYFULLY, JOYOUS

A. Nouns.

1. *chara* (χαρά, 5479), "joy, delight" (akin to *chairō*, "to rejoice"), is found frequently in Matthew and Luke, and especially in John, once in Mark (4:16, RV, "joy," KJV, "gladness"); it is absent from 1 Cor. (though the verb is used three times), but is frequent in 2 Cor., where the noun is used five times (for 7:4, RV, see *Note* below), and the verb eight times, suggestive of the apostle's relief in comparison with the circumstances of the 1st Epistle; in Col. 1:11, KJV, "joyfulness," RV, "joy." The word is sometimes used, by metonymy, of the occasion or cause of "joy," Luke 2:10 (lit., "I announce to you a great joy"); in 2 Cor. 1:15, in some mss., for *charis*, "benefit"; Phil. 4:1, where the readers are called the apostle's "joy"; so 1 Thess. 2:19, 20; Heb. 12:2, of the object of Christ's "joy"; Jas. 1:2, where it is connected with falling into trials; perhaps also in Matt. 25:21, 23, where some regard it as signifying, concretely, the circumstances attending cooperation in the authority of the Lord. See also the *Note* following No. 3.

Note: In Heb. 12:11, "joyous" represents the phrase *meta*, "with," followed by *chara*, lit., "with joy." So in 10:34, "joyfully"; in 2 Cor. 7:4 the noun is used with the middle voice of *huperperisseuō*, "to abound more exceedingly," and translated "(I overflow) with joy," RV (KJV, "I am exceeding joyful").

2. *agalliasis* (ἀγαλλίασις, 20), "exultation, exuberant joy." Cf. B, No. 3, below. See GLADNESS.

3. *euphrosunē* (εὐφροσύνη, 2167) is ren-

dered "joy" in the KJV of Acts 2:28, RV, "gladness," as in 14:17. See GLADNESS.¶

Note: "Joy" is associated with life, e.g., 1 Thess. 3:8, 9. Experiences of sorrow prepare for, and enlarge, the capacity for "joy," e.g., John 16:20; Rom. 5:3, 4; 2 Cor. 7:4; 8:2; Heb. 10:34; Jas. 1:2. Persecution for Christ's sake enhances "joy," e.g., Matt. 5:11, 12; Acts 5:41. Other sources of "joy" are faith, Rom. 15:13; Phil. 1:25; hope, Rom. 5:2 (*kauchaomai*, see B, No. 2); 12:12 (*chairō*, see B, No. 1); the "joy" of others, 12:15, which is distinctive of Christian sympathy. Cf. 1 Thess. 3:9. In the OT and the NT God Himself is the ground and object of the believer's "joy," e.g., Ps. 35:9; 43:4; Isa. 61:10; Luke 1:47; Rom. 5:11; Phil. 3:1; 4:4.

B. Verbs.

1. *chairō* (χαίρω, 5463), "to rejoice, be glad," is translated "joyfully" in Luke 19:6, lit., "rejoicing"; "we joyed," 2 Cor. 7:13; "I joy," Phil. 2:17; "do ye joy," 2:18; "joying," Col. 2:5; "we joy," 1 Thess. 3:9. It is contrasted with weeping and sorrow, e.g., in John 16:20, 22; Rom. 12:15; 1 Cor. 7:30 (cf. Ps. 30:5). See FAREWELL, GLAD, GREETING, HAIL, REJOICE.

2. *kauchaomai* (καυχάομαι, 2744), "to boast, glory, exult," is rendered "we joy," in Rom. 5:11, KJV (RV, "we rejoice"). It would have been an advantage to translate this word distinctively by the verbs "to glory" or "to exult."

3. *agalliaō* (ἀγαλλιάω, 21), "to exult, rejoice greatly," is translated "with exceeding joy" in 1 Pet. 4:13 (middle voice), lit., "(ye rejoice, *chairō*) exulting." Cf. A, No. 2. See GLAD, REJOICE.

4. *oninēmi* (ὀνίνημι, 3685), "to benefit, profit," in the middle voice, "to have profit, derive benefit," is translated "let me have joy" in Philem. 20 (RV marg., "help"); the apostle is doubtless continuing his credit and debit metaphors and using the verb in the sense of "profit."¶

JUDGE (Noun and Verb)

A. Nouns.

1. *kritēs* (κριτής, 2923), "a judge" (from *krino*, see B, No. 1), is used (*a*) of God, Heb. 12:23, where the order in the original is "to a Judge who is God of all"; this is really the significance; it suggests that He who is the Judge of His people is at the same time their God; that is the order in 10:30; the word is also used of God in Jas. 4:12, RV; (*b*) of Christ, Acts 10:42; 2 Tim. 4:8; Jas. 5:9; (*c*) of a ruler in Israel in the times of the Judges, Acts 13:20; (*d*) of a Roman procurator, Acts 24:10; (*e*) of those whose conduct provides a standard of "judg-

ing," Matt. 12:27; Luke 11:19; (*f*) in the forensic sense, of one who tries and decides a case, Matt. 5:25 (twice); Luke 12:14 (some mss. have No. 2 here); 12:58 (twice); 18:2; 18:6 (lit., "the judge of unrighteousness," expressing subjectively his character); Acts 18:15; (*g*) of one who passes, or arrogates to himself, judgment on anything, Jas. 2:4 (see the RV); 4:11.

2. *dikastēs* (δικαστής, 1348) denotes "a judge" (from *dikē*, "right, a judicial hearing, justice"; akin to *dikazo*, "to judge"), Acts 7:27, 35; some mss. have it in Luke 12:14 (see No. 1); while *dikastēs* is a forensic term, *kritēs* "gives prominence to the mental process" (Thayer). At Athens the *dikastēs* acted as a juryman, the *kritēs* being the presiding "judge."¶

B. Verbs.

1. *krinō* (κρίνω, 2919) primarily denotes "to separate, select, choose"; hence, "to determine," and so "to judge, pronounce judgment." "The uses of this verb in the NT may be analyzed as follows: (*a*) to assume the office of a judge, Matt. 7:1; John 3:17; (*b*) to undergo process of trial, John 3:18; 16:11; 18:31; Jas. 2:12; (*c*) to give sentence, Acts 15:19; 16:4; 21:25; (*d*) to condemn, John 12:48; Acts 13:27; Rom. 2:27; (*e*) to execute judgment upon, 2 Thess. 2:12; Acts 7:7; (*f*) to be involved in a lawsuit, whether as plaintiff, Matt. 5:40; 1 Cor. 6:1; or as defendant, Acts 23:6; (*g*) to administer affairs, to govern, Matt. 19:28; cf. Judg. 3:10; (*h*) to form an opinion, Luke 7:43; John 7:24; Acts 4:19; Rom. 14:5; (*i*) to make a resolve, Acts 3:13; 20:16; 1 Cor. 2:2"*

See CALL, No. 13, CONCLUDE, CONDEMN, DECREE, DETERMINE, ESTEEM, LAW (go to), ORDAIN, SENTENCE, THINK.

Note: In Acts 21:25, the RV has "giving judgement" (KJV, "concluded"); see JUDGMENT, *Note* (5).

2. *anakrinō* (ἀνακρίνω, 350), "to examine, investigate, question" (*ana*, "up," and No. 1), is rendered "judged" in 1 Cor. 2:14, RV (KJV, "are ... discerned;" RV marg., "examined"), said of the things of the Spirit of God; in v. 15, "judgeth" (RV marg., "examineth"), said of the exercise of a discerning "judgment" of all things as to their true value, by one who is spiritual; in the same verse, "is judged (of no man)," RV marg., "examined", i.e., the merely natural mind cannot estimate the motives of the spiritual; in 4:3, "I should be judged," i.e., as to examining and passing sentence on the fulfillment or nonfulfillment of the apostle's stewardship; so in the same verse, "I judge (not mine

---

* From *Notes on Thessalonians* by Hogg and Vine, p. 267.

own self)," and in v. 4 "(he that) judgeth (me is the Lord)"; in 14:24, "he is judged (of all)," i.e., the light of the heart-searching testimony of the assembly probes the conscience of the unregenerate, sifting him judicially. See ASK, No. 7, DISCERN, A, No. 1.

3. *diakrinō* (διακρίνω, 1252) denotes "to separate throughout" (*dia*, and No. 1), "discriminate, discern," and hence, "to decide, to judge" (also "to contend, to hesitate, to doubt"); it is rendered "to judge" in 1 Cor. 6:5, in the sense of arbitrating; in 11:31 (1st part), the RV has "(if we) discerned (ourselves)," KJV "(if we would) judge" (*krinō*, No. 1, is used in the 2nd part); so in 14:29, RV, "discern" (KJV, "judge"). See DECIDE, A, DISCERN, A. No. 2.

Notes: (1) In 1 Cor. 6:2 (last clause) "to judge" represents the noun *kritērion*, which denotes "a tribunal, a law court," and the meaning thus is "are ye unworthy of sitting upon tribunals of least importance?" (see RV marg.), i.e., to "judge" matters of smallest importance. Some would render it "cases," but there is no clear instance elsewhere of this meaning. See JUDGMENT SEAT. (2) In Heb. 11:11, the verb *hēgeomai*, "to consider, think, account," is rendered "she judged (Him faithful)," KJV (RV, "she counted"). See COUNT, No. 2.

JUDGMENT

1. *krisis* (κρίσις, 2920) primarily denotes "a separating," then, "a decision, judgment," most frequently in a forensic sense, and especially of divine "judgment." For the variety of its meanings, with references, see CONDEMNATION, B, No. 3.

Notes: (1) The Holy Spirit, the Lord said, would convict the world of (*peri*, "in respect of"), i.e., of the actuality of, God's "judgment," John 16:8, 11. Cf. 2 Thess. 1:5. (2) In Rom. 2:5 the word *dikaiokrisia*, "righteous judgment," combines the adjective *dikaios*, "righteous," with *krisis*, the two words which are used separately in 2 Thess. 1:5.¶

2. *krima* (κρίμα, 2917) denotes the result of the action signified by the verb *krinō*, "to judge"; for its general significance see CONDEMNATION, B, No. 1: it is used (*a*) of a decision passed on the faults of others, Matt. 7:2; (*b*) of "judgment" by man upon Christ, Luke 24:20; (*c*) of God's "judgment" upon men, e.g., Rom. 2:2, 3; 3:8; 5:16; 11:33; 13:2; 1 Cor 11:29; Gal. 5:10; Heb. 6:2; Jas. 3:1; through Christ, e.g., John 9:39; (*d*) of the right of "judgment," Rev. 20:4; (*e*) of a lawsuit, 1 Cor. 6:7.

3. *hēmera* (ἡμέρα, 2250), "a day," is translated "judgment" in 1 Cor. 4:3, where "man's judgment" (lit., "man's day," marg.) is used of

the present period in which man's mere "judgment" is exercised, a period of human rebellion against God. The adjective *anthrōpinos*, "human, belonging to man" (*anthrōpos*), is doubtless set in contrast here to *kuriakos*, "belonging to the Lord" (*kurios*, "a lord"), which is used in the phrase "the Day of the Lord," in Rev. 1:10, "The Lord's Day," a period of divine judgments. See DAY.

4. *gnōmē* (γνώμη, 1106), primarily "a means of knowing" (akin to *ginōskō*, "to know"), came to denote "a mind, understanding"; hence (*a*) "a purpose," Acts 20:3, lit., "(it was his) purpose"; (*b*) "a royal purpose, a decree," Rev. 17:17, RV, "mind" (KJV, "will"); (*c*) "judgment, opinion," 1 Cor. 1:10, "(in the same) judgment"; Rev. 17:13, "mind"; (*d*) "counsel, advice," 1 Cor. 7:25, "(I give my) judgment;" 7:40, "(after my) judgment"; Philem. 14, mind. See MIND, PURPOSE, WILL.¶

Notes: (1) In 1 Cor. 6:4, KJV, *kritērion*, "a tribunal," is rendered "judgments" (RV, "to judge," marg., "tribunals"). See JUDGE, B, No. 3, Note (1). (2) In Rom. 1:32, KJV, *dikaiōma*, "an ordinance, righteous act," is translated "judgment" (RV "ordinance"); in Rev. 15:4, "judgments" (RV, "righteous acts"). (3) In Acts 25:15, KJV, *katadikē*, "a sentence, condemnation," is translated "judgment" (RV, "sentence"). Some mss. have *dikē*. See SENTENCE. (4) In Phil. 1:9, KJV, *aisthēsis*, "perception, discernment," is translated "judgment" (RV, "discernment"). (5) In Acts 21:25, in the record of the decree from the apostles and elders at Jerusalem to the churches of the Gentiles, the verb *krinō* (see JUDGE, B, No. 1), is translated "giving judgment," RV (KJV, "concluded").

B. Adjective.

hupodikos (ὑπόδικος, 5267), "brought to trial, answerable to" (*hupo*, "under," *dikē*, "justice"), Rom. 3:19, is translated "under the judgment," RV (KJV, "guilty").¶

HALL OF JUDGMENT, JUDGMENT HALL, see HALL

JUDGMENT SEAT

1. *bēma* (βῆμα, 968), primarily, "a step, a pace" (akin to *bainō*, "to go"), as in Acts 7:5, translated "to set (his foot) on," lit., "footroom," was used to denote a raised place or platform, reached by steps, originally that at Athens in the Pnyx Hill, where was the place of assembly; from the platform orations were made. The word became used for a tribune, two of which were provided in the law courts of Greece, one for the accuser and one for the defendant; it was applied to the tribunal of a

Roman magistrate or ruler, Matt. 27:19; John 19:13; Acts 12:21, translated "throne"; 18:12, 16, 17; 25:6, 10, 17.

In two passages the word is used of the divine tribunal before which all believers are hereafter to stand. In Rom. 14:10 it is called "The judgement seat of God," RV (KJV, "of Christ"), according to the most authentic mss. The same tribunal is called "the judgment seat of Christ," 2 Cor. 5:10, to whom the Father has given all judgment, John 5:22, 27. At this *bēma* believers are to be made manifest, that each may "receive the things done in (or through) the body," according to what he has done, "whether it be good or bad." There they will receive rewards for their faithfulness to the Lord. For all that has been contrary in their lives to His will they will suffer loss, 1 Cor. 3:15. This judgment seat is to be distinguished from the premillennial, earthly throne of Christ, Matt. 25:31, and the postmillennial "Great White Throne," Rev. 20:11, at which only "the dead" will appear. The judgment seat of Christ will be a tribunal held "in His Parousia," i.e., His presence with His saints after His return to receive them to Himself.¶

2. *kritērion* (κριτήριον, 2922) primarily "a means of judging" (akin to *krinō,* "to judge": Eng., "criterion"), then, a tribunal, law court, or "lawsuit," 1 Cor. 6:2 (last clause), for which see JUDGE, B, No. 3, Note (1); 6:4, for which see JUDGMENT, Note (1) at end; Jas. 2:6.¶

JURISDICTION

exousia (ἐξουσία, 1849), "power, authority," is used, by metonymy, to denote "jurisdiction," in Luke 23:7. For the different meanings of the word and other instances of its use by metonymy, see AUTHORITY, A, No. 1.

JUST, JUSTLY

A. Adjectives.

1. *dikaios* (δίκαιος, 1342) was first used of persons observant of *dikē,* "custom, rule, right," especially in the fulfillment of duties towards gods and men, and of things that were in accordance with right. The Eng. word "righteous" was formerly spelt "rightwise," i.e., (in a) straight way. In the NT it denotes "righteous," a state of being right, or right conduct, judged whether by the divine standard, or according to human standards, of what is right. Said of God, it designates the perfect agreement between His nature and His acts (in which He is the standard for all men). See RIGHTEOUSNESS. It is used (1) in the broad sense, of persons: (*a*) of God, e.g., John 17:25; Rom. 3:26; 1 John 1:9; 2:29; 3:7; (*b*) of Christ, e.g., Acts 3:14; 7:52; 22:14; 2 Tim.

4:8; 1 Pet. 3:18; 1 John 2:1; (*c*) of men, Matt. 1:19; Luke 1:6; Rom. 1:17; 2:13; 5:7. (2) of things; blood (metaphorical), Matt. 23:35; Christ's judgment, John 5:30; any circumstance, fact or deed, Matt. 20:4 (v. 7, in some mss.); Luke 12:57; Acts 4:19; Eph. 6:1; Phil. 1:7; 4:8; Col. 4:1; 2 Thess. 1:6; "the commandment" (the Law), Rom. 7:12; works, 1 John 3:12; the ways of God, Rev. 15:3. See RIGHTEOUS.

2. *endikos* (ἔνδικος, 1738), "just, righteous" (*en,* "in," *dike,* "right"), is said of the condemnation of those who say "Let us do evil, that good may come," Rom. 3:8; of the recompense of reward of transgressions under the Law, Heb. 2:2.¶

Note: As to the distinction between No. 1 and No. 2, "*dikaios* characterizes the subject so far as he or it is (so to speak) one with *dikē,* right; *endikos,* so far as he occupies a due relation to *dikē; . . .* in Rom. 3:8 *endikos* presupposes that which has been decided righteously, which leads to the just sentence" (Cremer).

B. Adverb.

dikaiōs (δικαίως, 1346), "justly, righteously, in accordance with what is right," is said (*a*) of God's judgment, 1 Pet. 2:23; (*b*) of men, Luke 23:41, "justly;" 1 Cor. 15:34, RV, "righteously" (KJV, "to righteousness"); 1 Thess. 2:10, RV, "righteously;" Titus 2:12.¶

JUSTICE

dikē (δίκη, 1349), primarily "custom, usage," came to denote "what is right"; then, "a judicial hearing"; hence, "the execution of a sentence," "punishment," 2 Thess. 1:9, RV; Jude 7, "punishment," RV (KJV, "vengeance"). In Acts 28:4 (KJV, "vengeance") it is personified and denotes the goddess Justice or Nemesis (Lat., *Justitia*), who the Melita folk supposed was about to inflict the punishment of death upon Paul by means of the viper. See PUNISHMENT, VENGEANCE.¶

JUSTIFICATION, JUSTIFIER, JUSTIFY

A. Nouns.

1. *dikaiōsis* (δικαίωσις, 1347) denotes "the act of pronouncing righteous, justification, acquittal"; its precise meaning is determined by that of the verb *dikaioō,* "to justify" (see B); it is used twice in the Ep. to the Romans, and there alone in the NT, signifying the establishment of a person as just by acquittal from guilt. In Rom. 4:25 the phrase "for our justification," is, lit., "because of our justification" (parallel to the preceding clause "for our trespasses," i.e., because of trespasses committed), and means,

not with a view to our "justification," but because all that was necessary on God's part for our "justification" had been effected in the death of Christ. On this account He was raised from the dead. The propitiation being perfect and complete, His resurrection was the confirmatory counterpart. In 5:18, "justification of life" means "justification which results in life" (cf. v. 21). That God "justifies" the believing sinner on the ground of Christ's death, involves His free gift of life. On the distinction between *dikaiōsis* and *dikaiōma*, see below.¶ In the Sept., Lev. 24:22.¶

2. *dikaiōma* (δικαίωμα, 1345) has three distinct meanings, and seems best described comprehensively as "a concrete expression of righteousness"; it is a declaration that a person or thing is righteous, and hence, broadly speaking, it represents the expression and effect of *dikaiōsis* (No. 1). It signifies (a) "an ordinance," Luke 1:6; Rom. 1:32, RV, "ordinance," i.e., what God has declared to be right, referring to His decree of retribution (KJV, "judgment"); Rom. 2:26, RV, "ordinances of the Law" (i.e., righteous requirements enjoined by the Law); so 8:4, "ordinance of the Law," i.e., collectively, the precepts of the Law, all that it demands as right; in Heb. 9:1, 10, ordinances connected with the tabernacle ritual; (b) "a sentence of acquittal," by which God acquits men of their guilt, on the conditions (1) of His grace in Christ, through His expiatory sacrifice, (2) the acceptance of Christ by faith, Rom. 5:16; (c) "a righteous act," Rom. 5:18, "(through one) act of righteousness," RV, not the act of "justification," nor the righteous character of Christ (as suggested by the KJV: *dikaiōma* does not signify character, as does *dikaiosunē*, righteousness), but the death of Christ, as an act accomplished consistently with God's character and counsels; this is clear as being in antithesis to the "one trespass" in the preceding statement. Some take the word here as meaning a decree of righteousness, as in v. 16; the death of Christ could indeed be regarded as fulfilling such a decree, but as the apostle's argument proceeds, the word, as is frequently the case, passes from one shade of meaning to another, and here stands not for a decree, but an act; so in Rev. 15:4, RV, "righteous acts" (KJV, "judgments"), and 19:8, "righteous acts (of the saints)" (KJV, "righteousness").¶

Note: For *dikaiosunē*, always translated "righteousness," see RIGHTEOUSNESS.

B. Verb.

dikaioō (δικαιόω, 1344) primarily, "to deem to be right," signifies, in the NT, (a) "to show to be right or righteous"; in the passive voice, to be justified, Matt. 11:19; Luke 7:35; Rom. 3:4; 1 Tim. 3:16; (b) "to declare to be righteous, to pronounce righteous," (1) by man, concerning God, Luke 7:29 (see Rom. 3:4, above); concerning himself, Luke 10:29; 16:15; (2) by God concerning men, who are declared to be righteous before Him on certain conditions laid down by Him.

Ideally the complete fulfillment of the law of God would provide a basis of "justification" in His sight, Rom. 2:13. But no such case has occurred in mere human experience, and therefore no one can be "justified" on this ground, Rom. 3:9–20; Gal. 2:16; 3:10, 11; 5:4. From this negative presentation in Rom. 3, the apostle proceeds to show that, consistently with God's own righteous character, and with a view to its manifestation, He is, through Christ, as "a propitiation . . . by (*en*, "instrumental") His blood," 3:25, RV, "the Justifier of him that hath faith in Jesus" (v. 26), "justification" being the legal and formal acquittal from guilt by God as Judge, the pronouncement of the sinner as righteous, who believes on the Lord Jesus Christ. In v. 24, "being justified" is in the present continuous tense, indicating the constant process of "justification" in the succession of those who believe and are "justified." In 5:1, "being justified" is in the aorist, or point, tense, indicating the definite time at which each person, upon the exercise of faith, was justified. In 8:1, "justification" is presented as "no condemnation." That "justification" is in view here is confirmed by the preceding chapters and by verse 34. In 3:26, the word rendered "Justifier" is the present participle of the verb, lit., "justifying"; similarly in 8:33 (where the article is used), "God that justifieth," is, more lit., "God is the (One) justifying," with stress upon the word "God."

"Justification" is primarily and gratuitously by faith, subsequently and evidentially by works. In regard to "justification" by works, the so-called contradiction between James and the apostle Paul is only apparent. There is harmony in the different views of the subject. Paul has in mind Abraham's attitude toward God, his acceptance of God's word. This was a matter known only to God. The Romans epistle is occupied with the effect of this Godward attitude, not upon Abraham's character or actions, but upon the contrast between faith and the lack of it, namely, unbelief, cf. Rom. 11:20. James (2:21–26) is occupied with the contrast between faith that is real and faith that is false, a faith barren and dead, which is not faith at all.

Again, the two writers have before them different epochs in Abraham's life—Paul, the event recorded in Gen. 15, James, that in Gen. 22. Contrast the words "believed" in Gen. 15:6 and "obeyed" in 22:18.

Further, the two writers use the words "faith" and "works" in somewhat different senses. With Paul, faith is acceptance of God's word; with James, it is acceptance of the truth of certain statements about God, (v. 19), which may fail to affect one's conduct. Faith, as dealt with by Paul, results in acceptance with God., i.e., "justification," and is bound to manifest itself. If

not, as James says "Can that faith save him?" (v. 14). With Paul, works are dead works; with James they are life works. The works of which Paul speaks could be quite independent of faith: those referred to by James can be wrought only where faith is real, and they will attest its reality.

So with righteousness, or "justification": Paul is occupied with a right relationship with God, James, with right conduct. Paul testifies that the ungodly can be "justified" by faith, James that only the right-doer is "justified." See also under RIGHTEOUS, RIGHTEOUSNESS.

K

KEEP, KEEPING (Noun)

A. Verbs.

1. *tēreō* (τηρέω, 5083) denotes (a) "to watch over, preserve, keep, watch," e.g., Acts 12:5, 6; 16:23; in 25:21, RV (1st part), "kept" (KJV, "reserved"); the present participle is translated "keepers" in Matt. 28:4, lit. "the keeping (ones)"; it is used of the "keeping" power of God the Father and Christ, exercised over His people, John 17:11, 12, 15; 1 Thess. 5:23, "preserved"; 1 John 5:18, where "He that was begotten of God," RV, is said of Christ as the Keeper ("keepeth him," RV, for KJV, "keepeth himself"); Jude 1, RV, "kept for Jesus Christ" (KJV, "preserved in Jesus Christ"); Rev. 3:10; of their inheritance, 1 Pet. 1:4 ("reserved"); of judicial reservation by God in view of future doom, 2 Pet. 2:4, 9, 17; 3:7; Jude 6, 13; of "keeping" the faith, 2 Tim. 4:7; the unity of the Spirit, Eph. 4:3; oneself, 2 Cor. 11:9; 1 Tim. 5:22; Jas. 1:27; figuratively, one's garments, Rev. 16:15; (b) "to observe, to give heed to," as of keeping commandments, etc., e.g., Matt. 19:17; John 14:15; 15:10; 17:6; Jas. 2:10; 1 John 2:3, 4, 5; 3:22, 24; 5:2 (in some mss.), 3; Rev. 1:3; 2:26; 3:8, 10; 12:17; 14:12; 22:7, 9. See RESERVE.

2. *diatēreō* (διατηρέω, 1301), "to keep carefully" (*dia*, intensive, and No. 1), is said of "the mother of Jesus," in keeping His sayings in her heart, Luke 2:51, and of the command of the apostles and elders in Jerusalem to gentile converts in the churches to "keep" themselves from the evils mentioned in Acts 15:29.¶

3. *suntēreō* (συντηρέω, 4933) denotes "to preserve, keep safe, keep close" (*sun*, "together with," used intensively, and No. 1), in Luke

2:19, as in v. 51 (see No. 2, above), of the mother of Jesus in regard to the words of the shepherds; in Mark 6:20 it is used of Herod's preservation of John the Baptist from Herodias, RV, "kept (him) safe," KJV, "observed (him)" (marg., "kept"); in Matt. 9:17 (in some mss., Luke 5:38), of the preservation of wineskins. See OBSERVE, PRESERVE.¶

4. *phulassō* (φυλάσσω, 5442) denotes (a) "to guard, watch, keep watch," e.g., Luke 2:8; in the passive voice, 8:29; (b) "to keep by way of protection," e.g., Luke 11:21; John 12:25; 17:12 (2nd part; No. 1 in 1st part and in v. 11); (c) metaphorically, "to keep a law precept," etc., e.g., Matt. 19:20 and Luke 18:21, "have observed"; Luke 11:28; John 12:47 (in the best mss.); Acts 7:53; 16:4; 21:24; Rom. 2:26; Gal. 6:13; 1 Tim. 5:21 ("observe"); in the middle voice, Mark 10:20 ("have observed"); (d) in the middle voice, "to keep oneself from," Acts 21:25; elsewhere translated by the verb "to beware." See BEWARE, No. 3, GUARD, B, No. 1.

5. *diaphulassō* (διαφυλάσσω, 1314), an intensive form of No. 4, "to guard thoroughly"; see GUARD.

6. *phroureō* (φρουρέω, 5432), "to keep with a military guard," e.g., Gal. 3:23, RV, "kept in ward"; see GUARD, B, No. 3.

7. *poieō* (ποιέω, 4160), "to do, make," signifies "to keep," in Matt. 26:18, in the Lord's statement, "I will keep the passover;" so in Acts 18:21, in some mss.; in John 7:19, where the KJV has "keepeth (the law)," the RV adheres to the usual meaning "doeth."

8. *echō* (ἔχω, 2192), "to have, to hold," is rendered "I kept" in Luke 19:20, RV (KJV, "I

have kept"), of "keeping" a pound laid up in a napkin. See HAVE.

9. *krateō* (κρατέω, 2902), "to be strong, get possession of, hold fast," is used in Mark 9:10, "(and) they kept (the saying)," i.e., they held fast to the Lord's command to refrain from telling what they had seen in the mount of Transfiguration. See HOLD.

10. *nosphizō* (νοσφίζω, 3557), "to set apart, remove," signifies, in the middle voice, "to set apart for oneself, to purloin," and is rendered "purloining" in Titus 2:10; "kept back" (and "keep") in Acts 5:2, 3, of the act of Ananias and his wife in "retaining" part of the price of the land.¶

11. *sunechō* (συνέχω, 4912), "to hold together," is translated "shall . . . keep (thee) in," in Luke 19:43. See also *Note* (8), below. See CONSTRAIN.

Notes: (1) In Acts 22:2, KJV, *parechō*, "to afford, give, cause," is rendered "kept (the more silence)," RV, "were (the more quiet)." (2) In Matt. 14:6 some mss. have the verb *agō*, "to lead, hold" (of a feast), of "keeping" Herod's birthday; the most authentic have *ginomai*, "to become, take place"; hence the RV, "when Herod's birthday came." The verb *agō* is used in Acts 19:38 of "keeping" certain occasions, as of the holding of law courts, RV "(the courts) are open," KJV marg., "court days are kept"; Moulton and Milligan illustrate from the papyri the use of the adjective *agoraios*, in the plural with *hēmerai*, "days," understood, in regard to certain market days; certain court days are what are indicated here. The conjecture that the meaning is "courts are now being held" (*sunodoi* being understood as meetings of the court instead of "days") is scarcely so appropriate to the circumstances. (3) In Matt. 8:33, *boskō*, "to feed" (swine, etc.), is translated "(they that) fed," RV for KJV "(they that) kept." (4) In Acts 9:33, *katakeimai*, "to lie down," is used with *epi*, "upon," with the meaning "to keep one's bed" (see LIE, No. 2). (5) In Rom. 2:25, *prassō*, "to do" (continuously), "to practice," is rendered "be a doer of," RV (KJV, "keep"). (6) In Acts 20:20, *hupostellō*, "to shrink, draw back from," is translated "I shrank (not)" (middle voice), RV, KJV, "I kept back (nothing)." (7) In Acts 27:43, *kōluō*, "to hinder," is translated "stayed (them from)," RV, KJV, "kept (them from)." (8) In Luke 8:15 and 1 Cor. 11:2, *katechō*, "to hold fast" (a strengthened form of *echō*, No. 8), is translated "hold fast," RV, KJV, "keep;" in 15:2, RV, "hold fast," KJV, "keep in memory." (9) For "keep secret," see SECRET. (10) For "keep under," see BUFFET. (11) *Paratithēmi* is rendered "commit the keeping" in 1 Pet. 4:19,

KJV, (12) For "keep the feast" see FEAST, B, No. 2.

B. Noun.

tērēsis (τήρησις, 5084), akin to A, No. 1, denotes (*a*) "a watching," and hence, "imprisonment, prison," Acts 4:3 and 5:18, "ward," RV (KJV, "hold" and "prison"); (*b*) "keeping," 1 Cor. 7:19. See HOLD, PRISON.¶

KEEPER

phulax (φύλαξ, 5441), akin to A, No. 4, above, "a guard": see GUARD.

Note: For *tēreō*, in Matt. 28:4, see A, No. 1, above.

KEY

kleis (κλείς, 2807), "a key," is used metaphorically (*a*) of "the keys of the kingdom of heaven," which the Lord committed to Peter, Matt. 16:19, by which he would open the door of faith, as he did to Jews at Pentecost, and to Gentiles in the person of Cornelius, acting as one commissioned by Christ, through the power of the Holy Spirit; he had precedence over his fellow disciples, not in authority, but in the matter of time, on the ground of his confession of Christ (v. 16); equal authority was committed to them (18:18); (*b*) of "the key of knowledge," Luke 11:52, i.e., knowledge of the revealed will of God, by which men entered into the life that pleases God; this the religious leaders of the Jews had presumptuously "taken away," so that they neither entered in themselves, nor permitted their hearers to do so; (*c*) of "the keys of death and of Hades," Rev. 1:18, RV (see HADES), indicative of the authority of the Lord over the bodies and souls of men; (*d*) of "the key of David," Rev. 3:7, a reference to Isa. 22:22, speaking of the deposition of Shebna and the investiture of Eliakim, in terms evidently messianic, the metaphor being that of the right of entrance upon administrative authority; the mention of David is symbolic of complete sovereignty; (*e*) of "the key of the pit of the abyss," Rev. 9:1; here the symbolism is that of competent authority; the pit represents a shaft or deep entrance into the region (see ABYSS), from whence issued smoke, symbolic of blinding delusion; (*f*) of "the key of the abyss," Rev. 20:1; this is to be distinguished from (*e*): the symbolism is that of the complete supremacy of God over the region of the lost, in which, by angelic agency, Satan is destined to be confined for a thousand years.¶

KICK

laktizō (λακτίζω, 2979), "to kick" (from *lax*, an adverb signifying "with the foot"), is used in Acts 26:14 (some mss. have it in 9:5).

For KID see GOAT

KILL

1. *apokteinō* (ἀποκτείνω, 615), "to kill," is used (*a*) physically, e.g., Matt. 10:28; 14:5, "put . . . to death," similarly rendered in John 18:31; often of Christ's death; in Rev. 2:13, RV, "was killed" (KJV, "was slain"); 9:15, RV, "kill" (KJV,"slay"); 11:13, RV,"were killed" (KJV, "were slain"); so in 19:21; (*b*) metaphorically, Rom. 7:11, of the power of sin, which is personified, as "finding occasion, through the commandment," and inflicting deception and spiritual death, i.e., separation from God, realized through the presentation of the commandment to conscience, breaking in upon the fancied state of freedom; the argument shows the power of the Law, not to deliver from sin, but to enhance its sinfulness; in 2 Cor. 3:6, "the letter killeth," signifies not the literal meaning of Scripture as contrasted with the spiritual, but the power of the Law to bring home the knowledge of guilt and its punishment; in Eph. 2:16 "having slain the enmity" describes the work of Christ through His death in annulling the enmity, "the Law" (v. 15), between Jew and Gentile, reconciling regenerate Jew and Gentile to God in spiritual unity "in one body." See DEATH, C, No. 4, SLAY.

2. *anaireō* (ἀναιρέω, 337) denotes (*a*) "to take up" (*ana*, "up," *haireō*, "to take"), said of Pharaoh's daughter, in "taking up" Moses, Acts 7:21; (*b*) "to take away" in the sense of removing, Heb. 10:9, of the legal appointment of sacrifices, to bring in the will of God in the sacrificial offering of the death of Christ; (*c*) "to kill," used physically only (not metaphorically as in No. 1), e.g., Luke 22:2; in 2 Thess. 2:8, instead of the future tense of this verb, some texts (followed by RV marg.) read the future of *analiskō*, "to consume." See DEATH, C, No. 2, SLAY.

3. *thuō* (θύω, 2380) primarily denotes "to offer firstfruits to a god"; then (*a*) "to sacrifice by slaying a victim," Acts 14:13, 18, to do sacrifice; 1 Cor. 10:20, to sacrifice; 1 Cor. 5:7, "hath been sacrificed," of the death of Christ as our Passover; (*b*) "to slay, kill," Matt. 22:4; Mark 14:12; Luke 15:23, 27, 30; 22:7; John 10:10; Acts 10:13; 11:7.¶

4. *phoneuō* (φονεύω, 5407), "to murder," akin to *phoneus*, "a murderer," is always rendered by the verb "to kill" (except in Matt. 19:18, KJV, "do . . . murder," and in Matt. 23:35, KJV and RV, "ye slew"); Matt. 5:21 (twice); 23:31; Mark 10:19; Luke 18:20; Rom. 13:9; Jas. 2:11 (twice); 4:2; 5:6.¶

5. *thanatoō* (θανατόω, 2289), "to put to death" (from *thanatos*, "death"), is translated "are killed" in Rom. 8:36; "killed" in 2 Cor. 6:9. See DEATH, C, No. 1.

6. *diacheirizō* (διαχειρίζω, 1315), primarily, "to have in hand, manage" (*cheir*, "the hand"), is used in the middle voice, in the sense of "laying hands on" with a view to "kill," or of actually "killing," Acts 5:30, "ye slew"; 26:21, "to kill." See SLAY.¶

7. *sphazō*, or *sphattō* (σφάζω, 4969), "to slay, to slaughter," especially victims for sacrifice, is most frequently translated by the verb "to slay"; so the RV in Rev. 6:4 (KJV, "should kill"); in 13:3, RV, "smitten unto death" (KJV, "wounded"). See SLAY, WOUND. Cf. *katasphazō*, "to kill off," Luke 19:27;¶ *sphagē*, "slaughter," e.g., Acts 8:32, and *sphagion*, "a victim for slaughter," Acts 7:42.¶

KIN, KINSFOLK, KINSMAN, KINSWOMAN

A. Adjective.

sungenēs (συγγενής, 4773), primarily denoting "congenital, natural, innate" (*sun*, "with," *genos*, "a family, race, offspring"), then, "akin to," is used as a noun, denoting (*a*) of "family relationship, kin, a kinsman, kinsfolk(s)," Luke 1:58, RV, "kinsfolk" (KJV, "cousins"); 14:12; 21:16; John 18:26; Acts 10:24; (*b*) of "tribal or racial kinship, fellow nationals," Rom. 9:3; 16:7, 11, 21.¶

B. Nouns.

1. *sungenis* (συγγενίς, 4773v), a late feminine form of A (some mss. have *sungenēs*), denotes "a kinswoman," Luke 1:36, RV, "kinswoman" (KJV, "cousin"). Cf. *sungeneia* (see KINDRED).¶

2. *sungeneus* (συγγενεύς, 4773**), an alternative form of A, is used in Mark 6:4, "kin," and Luke 2:44, "kinsfolk."¶

KIND (Noun)

1. *genos* (γένος, 1085), akin to *ginomai*, "to become," denotes (*a*) "a family," Acts 4:6, "kindred;" 7:13, RV, "race" (KJV, "kindred"); 13:26, "stock"; (*b*) "an offspring," Acts 17:28; Rev. 22:16; (*c*) "a nation, a race," Mark 7:26, RV, "race" (KJV, "nation"); Acts 4:36, RV "(a man of Cyprus) by race," KJV, "of the country (of Cyprus);" *genos* does not mean "a country;" the word here signifies "parentage" (Jews had

settled in Cyprus from, or even before, the reign of Alexander the Great); 7:19, RV, "race" (KJV, "kindred"); 18:2, 24, RV, "by race" (KJV, "born"); 2 Cor. 11:26, "countrymen"; Gal. 1:14, RV, "countrymen" (KJV, "nation"); Phil. 3:5, "stock"; 1 Pet. 2:9, RV, "race" (KJV, "generation"); (d) "a kind, sort, class," Matt. 13:47, "kind"; in some mss. in 17:21, KJV, "kind;" Mark 9:29, "kind"; 1 Cor. 12:10, 28, "kinds" (KJV, "diversities"); 14:10 (ditto).¶ See BEGET, B.

2. *phusis* (φύσις, 5449) among its various meanings denotes "the nature, the natural constitution or power of a person or thing," and is translated "kind" in Jas. 3:7 (twice), "kind" (of beasts etc.), and "(man)kind," lit., "human kind." See NATURE, NATURAL.

Notes: (1) The indefinite pronoun *tis*, "some, a certain, one," is used adjectively with the noun *aparchē*, "firstfruits," in Jas. 1:18, "a kind of." (2) In 1 Cor. 15:37, RV, "some other kind" (KJV, "some other grain") translates a phrase which, lit. rendered, is "some (one) of the rest (*loipos*)." (3) In 2 Cor. 6:13, "(for a recompense) in like kind," RV, (KJV, "in the same"), is, lit., "(as to) the same (recompense)."

KIND (Adjective), KIND (be), KINDLY, KINDNESS

A. Adjectives.

1. *chrēstos* (χρηστός, 5543), "serviceable, good, pleasant" (of things), "good, gracious, kind" (of persons), is translated "kind" in Luke 6:35, of God; in Eph. 4:32, enjoined upon believers. See BETTER, EASY, GOOD, GOODNESS, GRACIOUS.

2. *agathos* (ἀγαθός, 18), "good," is translated "kind" in Titus 2:5, RV. See GOOD.

B. Verb.

chrēsteuomai (χρηστεύομαι, 5541), akin to A, No. 1, "to be kind," is said of love, 1 Cor. 13:4.¶

C. Nouns.

1. *chrēstotēs* (χρηστότης, 5544), akin to A, No. 1, and B, used of "goodness of heart, kindness," is translated "kindness" in 2 Cor. 6:6; Gal. 5:22, RV (KJV, "gentleness"); Eph. 2:7; Col. 3:12; Titus 3:4. See GOODNESS.

2. *philanthrōpia* (φιλανθρωπία, 5363), from *philos*, "loving," *anthrōpos*, "man" (Eng., "philanthropy"), denotes "kindness," and is so translated in Acts 28:2, of that which was shown by the inhabitants of Melita to the shipwrecked voyagers; in Titus 3:4, of the "kindness" of God, translated "(His) love toward man." See LOVE.¶

D. Adverb.

philanthrōpōs (φιλανθρώπως, 5364), akin to C, No. 2, "humanely, kindly," is translated "kindly" in Acts 27:3 (KJV, "courteously"). See COURTEOUSLY.¶

KINDLE

1. *haptō* (ἅπτω, 681), properly, "to fasten to," is used in Acts 28:2 (in the most authentic mss., some mss. have No. 3), of "kindling a fire." See No. 2.

Note: Haptō is used of "lighting a lamp," in Luke 8:16; 11:33; 15:8. For the middle voice see TOUCH.

2. *periaptō* (περιάπτω, 4012 and 681), properly, "to tie about, attach" (*peri*, "around," and No. 1), is used of "lighting" a fire in the midst of a court in Luke 22:55 (some mss. have No. 1).¶

3. *anaptō* (ἀνάπτω, 381), "to light up" (*ana*, "up," and No. 1), is used (a) literally, in Jas. 3:5, "kindleth"; (b) metaphorically, in the passive voice, in Luke 12:49, of the "kindling" of the fire of hostility; see FIRE, A (f). For Acts 28:2, see No. 1, above.¶

KINDRED

1. *sungeneia* (συνγένεια, 4772) primarily denotes "kinship"; then, "kinsfolk, kindred" (cf. *sungenēs*, "a kinsman"; see KIN), Luke 1:61; Acts 7:3, 14.¶

2. *genos* (γένος, 1085); see KIND (Noun), No. 1.

Notes: (1) *Phulē*, "a tribe," rendered "kindreds" in the KJV of Rev. 1:7; 7:9; 11:9; 13:7, "kindred" in 5:9; 14:6, and elsewhere, "tribe," "tribes," is always translated by the latter in the RV. See TRIBE. (2) For *patria*, rendered "kindreds" Acts 3:25, KJV, see FAMILY.

KING

A. Noun.

basileus (βασιλεύς, 935), "a king" (cf. Eng., "Basil"), e.g., Matt. 1:6, is used of the Roman emperor in 1 Pet. 2:13, 17 (a command of general application); this reference to the emperor is illustrated frequently in the *Koinē* (see Preface to this volume); of Herod the Tetrarch (used by courtesy), Matt. 14:9; of Christ, as the "King" of the Jews, e.g., Matt. 2:2; 27:11, 29, 37; as the "King" of Israel, Mark 15:32; John 1:49; 12:13; as "King of kings," Rev. 17:14; 19:16; as "the King" in judging nations and men at the establishment of the millennial kingdom, Matt. 25:34, 40; of God, "the great King," Matt. 5:35; "the King eternal, incorruptible, invisible," 1 Tim. 1:17; "King of kings," 1 Tim. 6:15, see *Note* (2) below; "King of the ages," Rev. 15:3,

RV (KJV, "saints"). Christ's "kingship" was predicted in the OT, e.g., Ps. 2:6, and in the NT, e.g., Luke 1:32, 33; He came as such, e.g., Matt. 2:2; John 18:37; was rejected and died as such, Luke 19:14; Matt. 27:37; is now a "King" Priest, after the order of Melchizedek, Heb. 5:6; 7:1, 17; and will reign for ever and ever, Rev. 11:15.

Notes: (1) In Rev. 1:6 and 5:10, the most authentic mss. have the word *basileia,* "kingdom," instead of the plural of *basileus,* KJV, "kings;" RV, "a kingdom (to be priests)," and "a kingdom (and priests)." The kingdom was conditionally offered by God to Israel, that they should be to Him "a kingdom of priests," Exod. 19:6, the entire nation fulfilling priestly worship and service. Their failure to fulfill His covenant resulted in the selection of the Aaronic priesthood. The bringing in of the new and better covenant of grace has constituted all believers a spiritual kingdom, a holy and royal priesthood, 1 Pet. 2:5, 9. (2) In 1 Tim. 6:15, the word "kings" translates the present participle of the verb *basileuō,* "to be king, to have kingship," lit., "of (those) who are kings." See REIGN, (3) Deissmann has shown that the title "king of kings" was "in very early eastern history a decoration of great monarchs and also a divine title" (*Light from the Ancient East,* pp. 367ff.). Moulton and Milligan illustrate the use of the title among the Persians, from documents discovered in Media.

B. Adjectives.

1. *basileios* (βασίλειος, 934), denoting "royal," as in 1 Pet. 2:9, is used in the plural, of the courts or palaces of kings, Luke 7:25, "kings' courts"; a possible meaning is "among royal courtiers or persons."¶

2. *basilikos* (βασιλικός, 937), "royal, belonging to a king," is used in Acts 12:20 with "country" understood, "their country was fed from the king's," lit., "the royal (country)." See NOBLEMAN, ROYAL.

KINGDOM

basileia (βασιλεία, 932) is primarily an abstract noun, denoting "sovereignty, royal power, dominion," e.g., Rev. 17:18, translated "(which) reigneth," lit., "hath a kingdom" (RV marg.); then, by metonymy, a concrete noun, denoting the territory or people over whom a king rules, e.g., Matt. 4:8; Mark 3:24. It is used especially of the "kingdom" of God and of Christ.

"The Kingdom of God is (*a*) the sphere of God's rule, Ps. 22:28; 145:13; Dan. 4:25; Luke 1:52; Rom. 13:1, 2. Since, however, this earth is the scene of universal rebellion against God, e.g., Luke 4:5, 6; 1 John 5:19; Rev. 11:15–18,

the "kingdom" of God is (*b*) the sphere in which, at any given time, His rule is acknowledged. God has not relinquished His sovereignty in the face of rebellion, demoniac and human, but has declared His purpose to establish it, Dan. 2:44; 7:14; 1 Cor. 15:24, 25. Meantime, seeking willing obedience, He gave His law to a nation and appointed kings to administer His "kingdom" over it, 1 Chron. 28:5. Israel, however, though declaring still a nominal allegiance shared in the common rebellion, Isa. 1:2–4, and, after they had rejected the Son of God, John 1:11 (cf. Matt. 21:33–43), were "cast away," Rom. 11:15, 20, 25. Henceforth God calls upon men everywhere, without distinction of race or nationality, to submit voluntarily to His rule. Thus the "kingdom" is said to be "in mystery" now, Mark 4:11, that is, it does not come within the range of the natural powers of observation, Luke 17:20, but is spiritually discerned, John 3:3 (cf. 1 Cor. 2:14). When, hereafter, God asserts His rule universally, then the "kingdom" will be in glory, that is, it will be manifest to all; cf. Matt. 25:31–34; Phil. 2:9–11; 2 Tim. 4:1, 18.

"Thus, speaking generally, references to the Kingdom fall into two classes, the first, in which it is viewed as present and involving suffering for those who enter it, 2 Thess. 1:5; the second, in which it is viewed as future and is associated with reward, Matt. 25:34, and glory, 13:43. See also Acts 14:22.

"The fundamental principle of the Kingdom is declared in the words of the Lord spoken in the midst of a company of Pharisees, "the Kingdom of God is in the midst of you," Luke 17:21, marg., that is, where the King is, there is the Kingdom. Thus at the present time and so far as this earth is concerned, where the King is and where His rule is acknowledged, is, first, in the heart of the individual believer, Acts 4:19; Eph. 3:17; 1 Pet. 3:15; and then in the churches of God, 1 Cor. 12:3, 5, 11; 14:37; cf. Col. 1:27, where for "in" read "among."

"Now, the King and His rule being refused, those who enter the Kingdom of God are brought into conflict with all who disown its allegiance, as well as with the desire for ease, and the dislike of suffering and unpopularity, natural to all. On the other hand, subjects of the Kingdom are the objects of the care of God, Matt. 6:33, and of the rejected King, Heb. 13:5.

"Entrance into the Kingdom of God is by the new birth, Matt. 18:3; John 3:5, for nothing that a man may be by nature, or can attain to by any form of self-culture, avails in the spiritual realm. And as the new nature, received in the new birth, is made evident by obedience, it is further said that only such as do the will of God shall enter into His Kingdom, Matt. 7:21, where, however, the context shows that the reference is to the future, as in 2 Pet. 1:10, 11. Cf. also 1 Cor. 6:9, 10; Gal. 5:21; Eph. 5:5.

"The expression 'Kingdom of God' occurs four times in Matthew, 'Kingdom of the Heavens' usually taking its place. The latter (cf. Dan. 4:26) does not occur elsewhere in NT, but see 2 Tim. 4:18, "His heavenly Kingdom." . . . This Kingdom is identical with the Kingdom of the Father (cf. Matt. 26:29 with Mark 14:25), and with the Kingdom of the Son (cf. Luke 22:30). Thus there is but one Kingdom, variously described: of the Son of Man, Matt. 13:41; of Jesus, Rev. 1:9; of Christ Jesus, 2 Tim. 4:1; "of Christ and God," Eph. 5:5; "of our Lord, and of His Christ," Rev. 11:15; "of our God, and the authority of His Christ," 12:10; "of the Son of His love," Col. 1:13.

"Concerning the future, the Lord taught His disciples to pray, "Thy Kingdom come," Matt. 6:10, where the verb is in the point tense, precluding the notion of gradual progress and development, and implying a sudden catastrophe as declared in 2 Thess. 2:8.

"Concerning the present, that a man is of the Kingdom of God is not shown in the punctilious observance of ordinances, which are external and material, but in the deeper matters of the heart, which are spiritual and essential, viz., "righteousness, and peace, and joy in the Holy Spirit," Rom. 14:17."*

"With regard to the expressions "the Kingdom of God" and the "Kingdom of the Heavens," while they are often used interchangeably, it does not follow that in every case they mean exactly the same and are quite identical.

"The Apostle Paul often speaks of the Kingdom of God, not dispensationally but morally, e.g., in Rom. 14:17; 1 Cor. 4:20, but never so of the Kingdom of Heaven. 'God' is not the equivalent of 'the heavens.' He is everywhere and above all dispensations, whereas 'the heavens' are distinguished from the earth, until the Kingdom comes in judgment and power and glory (Rev. 11:15, RV) when rule in heaven and on earth will be one.

"While, then, the sphere of the Kingdom of God and the Kingdom of Heaven are at times identical, yet the one term cannot be used indiscriminately for the other. In the 'Kingdom of Heaven' (32 times in Matt.), heaven is in antithesis to earth, and the phrase is limited to the Kingdom in its earthly aspect for the time being,

and is used only dispensationally and in connection with Israel. In the 'Kingdom of God', in its broader aspect, God is in antithesis to 'man' or 'the world,' and the term signifies the entire sphere of God's rule and action in relation to the world. It has a moral and spiritual force and is a general term for the Kingdom at any time. The Kingdom of Heaven is always the Kingdom of God, but the Kingdom of God is not limited to the Kingdom of Heaven, until in their final form, they become identical; e.g., Rev. 11:15, RV; John 3:5; Rev. 12:10." (An Extract).

For KINSFOLK and KINSMAN see KIN

KISS (Noun and Verb)

A. Noun.

philēma (φίλημα, 5370), "a kiss" (akin to B), Luke 7:45; 22:48, was a token of Christian brotherhood, whether by way of welcome or farewell, "a holy kiss," Rom. 16:16; 1 Cor. 16:20; 2 Cor. 13:12; 1 Thess. 5:26, "holy" (hagios), as free from anything inconsistent with their calling as saints (hagioi); "a kiss of love," 1 Pet. 5:14. There was to be an absence of formality and hypocrisy, a freedom from prejudice arising from social distinctions, from discrimination against the poor, from partiality towards the well-to-do. In the churches masters and servants would thus salute one another without any attitude of condescension on the one part or disrespect on the other. The "kiss" took place thus between persons of the same sex. In the "Apostolic Constitutions," a writing compiled in the 4th century, A.D., there is a reference to the custom whereby men sat on one side of the room where a meeting was held, and women on the other side of the room (as is frequently the case still in parts of Europe and Asia), and the men are bidden to salute the men, and the women the women, with "the kiss of the Lord."¶

B. Verbs.

1. phileō (φιλέω, 5368), "to love," signifies "to kiss," in Matt. 26:48; Mark 14:44; Luke 22:47.

2. kataphileō (καταφιλέω, 2705) denotes "to kiss fervently" (kata, intensive, and No. 1); the stronger force of this verb has been called in question, but the change from phileō to kataphileō in Matt. 26:49 and Mark 14:45 can scarcely be without significance, and the act of the traitor was almost certainly more demonstrative than the simple kiss of salutation. So with the kiss of genuine devotion, Luke 7:38, 45; 15:20; Acts 20:37, in each of which this verb is used.¶

* From Notes on Thessalonians by Hogg and Vine, pp. 68–70.

KNEE

gonu (γόνυ, 1119) "a knee" (Latin, *genu*), is used (*a*) metaphorically in Heb. 12:12, where the duty enjoined is that of "courageous self-recovery in God's strength;" (*b*) literally, of the attitude of a suppliant, Luke 5:8; Eph. 3:14; of veneration, Rom. 11:4; 14:11; Phil. 2:10; in mockery, Mark 15:19. See KNEEL.

KNEEL

1. *gonupeteō* (γονυπετέω, 1120) denotes "to bow the knees, kneel," from *gonu* (see above) and *piptō*, "to fall prostrate," the act of one imploring aid, Matt. 17:14; Mark 1:40; of one expressing reverence and honor, Mark 10:17; in mockery, Matt. 27:29.¶

2. A phrase consisting of *tithēmi*, "to put," with *gonata*, the plural of *gonu*, "the knee" (see above), signifies "to kneel," and is always used of an attitude of prayer, Luke 22:41 (lit., "placing the knees"); Acts 7:60; 9:40; 20:36; 21:5.¶

KNIT TOGETHER

sumbibazō (συμβιβάζω, 4822) signifies "to cause to coalesce, to join or knit together," Eph. 4:16, RV, "knit together" (KJV, "compacted)"; Col. 2:2, where some would assign the alternative meaning, "to instruct," as, e.g., in 1 Cor. 2:16; in Col. 2:19, "knit together," it is said of the church, as the body of which Christ is the Head. See COMPACTED.

Note: In Acts 10:11 some mss. have the verb *deō*, "to bind," translated "knit," of the four corners of the sheet in Peter's vision. The RV "let down" translates the verb *kathiēmi*, found in the best texts.

KNOCK

krouō (κρούω, 2925), "to strike, knock," is used in the NT of "knocking" at a door, (*a*) literally, Luke 12:36; Acts 12:13, 16; (*b*) figuratively, Matt. 7:7, 8; Luke 11:9, 10 (of importunity in dealing with God); 13:25; Rev. 3:20.¶

KNOW, KNOWN, KNOWLEDGE, UNKNOWN

A. Verbs.

1. *ginōskō* (γινώσκω, 1097) signifies "to be taking in knowledge, to come to know, recognize, understand," or "to understand completely," e.g., Mark 13:28, 29; John 13:12; 15:18; 21:17; 2 Cor. 8:9; Heb. 10:34; 1 John 2:5; 4:2, 6 (twice), 7, 13; 5:2, 20; in its past tenses it frequently means "to know in the sense of realizing," the aorist or point tense usually indicating definiteness, Matt. 13:11; Mark 7:24; John 7:26; in 10:38 "that ye may know (aorist tense) and understand, (present tense)"; 19:4; Acts 1:7; 17:19; Rom. 1:21; 1 Cor. 2:11 (2nd part), 14; 2 Cor. 2:4; Eph. 3:19; 6:22; Phil. 2:19; 3:10; 1 Thess. 3:5; 2 Tim. 2:19; Jas. 2:20; 1 John 2:13 (twice), 14; 3:6; 4:8; 2 John 1; Rev. 2:24; 3:3, 9. In the passive voice, it often signifies "to become known," e.g., Matt. 10:26; Phil. 4:5. In the sense of complete and absolute understanding on God's part, it is used, e.g., in Luke 16:15; John 10:15 (of the Son as well as the Father); 1 Cor. 3:20. In Luke 12:46, KJV, it is rendered "he is . . . aware."

In the NT *ginōskō* frequently indicates a relation between the person "knowing" and the object known; in this respect, what is "known" is of value or importance to the one who knows, and hence the establishment of the relationship, e.g., especially of God's "knowledge," 1 Cor. 8:3, "if any man love God, the same is known of Him"; Gal. 4:9, "to be known of God"; here the "knowing" suggests approval and bears the meaning "to be approved"; so in 2 Tim. 2:19; cf. John 10:14, 27; Gen. 18:19; Nah. 1:7; the relationship implied may involve remedial chastisement, Amos 3:2. The same idea of appreciation as well as "knowledge" underlies several statements concerning the "knowledge" of God and His truth on the part of believers, e.g., John 8:32; 14:20, 31; 17:3; Gal. 4:9 (1st part); 1 John 2:3 13, 14; 4:6, 8, 16; 5:20; such "knowledge" is obtained, not by mere intellectual activity, but by operation of the Holy Spirit consequent upon acceptance of Christ. Nor is such "knowledge" marked by finality; see e.g., 2 Pet. 3:18; Hos. 6:3, RV

The verb is also used to convey the thought of connection or union, as between man and woman, Matt. 1:25; Luke 1:34.

2. *oida* (οἶδα, Perf. of 1492), from the same root as *eidon*, "to see," is a perfect tense with a present meaning, signifying, primarily, "to have seen or perceived"; hence, "to know, to have knowledge of," whether absolutely, as in divine knowledge, e.g., Matt. 6:8, 32; John 6:6, 64; 8:14; 11:42; 13:11; 18:4; 2 Cor. 11:31; 2 Pet. 2:9; Rev. 2:2, 9, 13, 19; 3:1, 8, 15; or in the case of human "knowledge," to know from observation, e.g., 1 Thess. 1:4, 5; 2:1; 2 Thess. 3:7.

The differences between *ginōskō* (No. 1) and *oida* demand consideration: (*a*) *ginōskō*, frequently suggests inception or progress in "knowledge," while *oida* suggests fullness of "knowledge," e.g., John 8:55, "ye have not known Him" (*ginōskō*), i.e., begun to "know," "but I know Him" (*oida*), i.e., "know Him perfectly"; 13:7, "What I do thou knowest not now," i.e. Peter did not yet perceive (*oida*) its significance, "but thou shalt understand," i.e., "get to know (*ginōskō*), hereafter"; 14:7, "If ye had known Me" (*ginōskō*), i.e., "had definitely come to know Me," "ye would have known My Father also" (*oida*), i.e., "would have had perception of": "from henceforth ye know Him" (*ginōskō*), i.e., having unconsciously been coming to the Father, as the One who was in Him, they would now consciously be in the constant and progressive experience of "knowing" Him; in Mark 4:13, "Know ye not (*oida*) this parable? and how shall ye know (*ginōskō*) all the parables?" (RV), i.e., "Do ye not understand this parable? How shall ye come to perceive all . . ." the intimation being that the first parable is a leading and testing one; (*b*) while *ginōskō* frequently implies an active relation between the one who "knows" and the person or thing "known" (see No. 1, above), *oida* expresses the fact that the object has simply come within the scope of the "knower's" perception; thus in Matt. 7:23 "I never knew you" (*ginōskō*) suggests "I have never been in approving connection with you," whereas in 25:12, "I know you not" (*oida*) suggests "you stand in no relation to Me."

3. *epiginōskō* (ἐπιγινώσκω, 1921) denotes (*a*) "to observe, fully perceive, notice attentively, discern, recognize" (*epi*, "upon," and No. 1); it suggests generally a directive, a more special, recognition of the object "known" than does No. 1; it also may suggest advanced "knowledge" or special appreciation; thus, in Rom. 1:32, "knowing the ordinance of God" (*epiginōskō*) means "knowing full well," whereas in verse 21 "knowing God" (*ginōskō*) simply suggests that they could not avoid the perception. Sometimes *epiginōskō* implies a special participation in the object "known," and gives greater weight to what is stated; thus in John 8:32, "ye shall know the truth," *ginōskō* is used, whereas in 1 Tim. 4:3, "them that believe and know the truth," *epiginōskō* lays stress on participation in the truth. Cf. the stronger statement in Col. 1:6 (*epiginōskō*) with that in 2 Cor. 8:9 (*ginōskō*), and the two verbs in 1 Cor. 13:12, "now I know in part (*ginōskō*); but then shall I know (*piginōskō*) even as also I have been known (*epiginōskō*)," "a knowledge" which perfectly unites the subject with the object; (*b*) "to discover, ascertain, determine," e.g., Luke 7:37; 23:7; Acts 9:30; 19:34; 22:29; 28:1; in 24:11 the best mss. have this verb instead of No. 1; hence the RV, "take knowledge." J. Armitage Robinson (on Ephesians) points out that *epignōsis* is "knowledge directed towards a particular object, perceiving, discerning," whereas

gnōsis is knowledge in the abstract. See AC-KNOWLEDGE.

4. *proginōskō* (προγινώσκω, 4267), "to know beforehand," is used (*a*) of the divine "foreknowledge" concerning believers, Rom. 8:29; Israel, 11:2; Christ as the Lamb of God, 1 Pet. 1:20, RV, "foreknown" (KJV, "foreordained"); (*b*) of human previous "knowledge," of a person, Acts 26:5, RV, "having knowledge of" (KJV, "which knew"); of facts, 2 Pet. 3:17. See FOREKNOW.¶

5. *epistamai* (ἐπίσταμαι, 1987), "to know, know of, understand" (probably an old middle voice form of *ephistēmi*, "to set over"), is used in Mark 14:68, "understand," which follows *oida* "I (neither) know"; most frequently in the Acts, 10:28; 15:7; 18:25; 19:15, 25; 20:18; 22:19; 24:10; 26:26; elsewhere, 1 Tim. 6:4; Heb. 11:8; Jas. 4:14; Jude 10. See UNDER-STAND.¶

6. *sunoida* (σύνοιδα, 4923), *sun*, "with," and No. 2, a perfect tense with a present meaning, denotes (*a*) "to share the knowledge of, be privy to," Acts 5:2; (*b*) "to be conscious of," especially of guilty consciousness, 1 Cor. 4:4, "I know nothing against (KJV, by) myself." The verb is connected with *suneidon*, found in Acts 12:12; 14:6 (in the best texts). See CONSIDER, PRIVY, WARE. ¶

7. *agnoeō* (ἀγνοέω, 50), "not to know, to be ignorant": see IGNORANT.

8. *gnōrizō* (γνωρίζω, 1107) signifies (*a*) "to come to know, discover, know," Phil. 1:22, "I wot (not)," i.e., "I know not," "I have not come to know" (the RV, marg. renders it, as under (*b*), "I do not make known"); (*b*) "to make known," whether (I) communicating things before "unknown," Luke 2:15, 17; in the latter some mss. have the verb *diagnōrizō* (hence the KJV, "made known abroad)"; John 15:15, "I have made known"; 17:26; Acts 2:28; 7:13 (1st part), see *Note* (3) below; Rom. 9:22, 23; 16:26 (passive voice); 2 Cor. 8:1, "we make known (to you)," RV, KJV, "we do (you) to wit"; Eph. 1:9; 3:3, 5, 10 (all three in the passive voice); 6:19, 21; Col. 1:27; 4:7, 9, "shall make known" (KJV, "shall declare"); 2 Pet. 1:16; or (II) reasserting things already "known," 1 Cor. 12:3, "I give (you) to understand" (the apostle reaffirms what they knew); 15:1, of the gospel; Gal. 1:11 (he reminds them of what they well knew, the ground of his claim to apostleship); Phil. 4:6 (passive voice), of requests to God. See CERTIFY, DE-CLARE (*Note*), UNDERSTAND, WIT, WOT. ¶

Notes: (1) In 2 Tim. 3:10, KJV, *parakoloutheō*, "to follow closely, follow as a standard of conduct," is translated "hast fully known" (RV, "didst follow"). See FOLLOW. (2) In 2 Tim.

4:17, KJV, *plērophoreō*, "to fulfill, accomplish," is translated "might be fully known" (RV, "might be fully proclaimed"). See FULFILL. (3) In Acts 7:13, some mss. have the verb *anagnōrizō*, "to make oneself known," "was made known," instead of No. 8 (which see).¶ (4) In Acts 7:13 (2nd part) the KJV, "was made known" translates the phrase *phaneros ginomai*, "to become manifest" (RV, "became manifest"). See MANIFEST. (5) For *diagnōrizō*, "to make known," in Luke 2:17, see No. 8. (6) For *diaginōskō*, in Acts 24:22, "I will know the uttermost of," see DETERMINE, No. 5.

B. Adjectives.

1. *gnōstos* (γνωστός, 1110), a later form of *gnōtos* (from No. 1), most frequently denotes "known"; it is used ten times in the Acts, always with that meaning (save in 4:16, where it means "notable"); twice in the Gospel of John, 18:15, 16; in Luke 2:44 and 23:49 it denotes "acquaintance"; elsewhere only in Rom. 1:19, "(that which) may be known (of God)," lit., "the knowable of God," referring to the physical universe, in the creation of which God has made Himself "knowable," that is, by the exercise of man's natural faculties, without such supernatural revelations as those given to Israel. See ACQUAINTANCE.

2. *phaneros* (φανερός, 5318), "visible, manifest," is translated "known" in Matt. 12:16 and Mark 3:12. See APPEAR, MANIFEST, OPENLY, OUTWARDLY.

3. *epistēmōn* (ἐπιστήμων, 1990), akin to A, No. 5, "knowing, skilled," is used in Jas. 3:13, KJV, "endued with knowledge" (RV "understanding").¶

4. *agnōstos* (ἄγνωστος, 57), the negative of No. 1, "unknown," is found in Acts 17:23.¶

C. Nouns.

1. *gnōsis* (γνῶσις, 1108), primarily "a seeking to know, an enquiry, investigation" (akin to A, No. 1), denotes, in the NT, "knowledge," especially of spiritual truth; it is used (*a*) absolutely, in Luke 11:52; Rom. 2:20; 15:14; 1 Cor.

1:5; 8:1 (twice), 7, 10, 11; 13:2, 8; 14:6; 2 Cor. 6:6; 8:7; 11:6; Eph. 3:19; Col. 2:3; 1 Pet. 3:7; 2 Pet. 1:5, 6; (*b*) with an object: in respect of (1) God, 2 Cor. 2:14; 10:5; (2) the glory of God, 2 Cor. 4:6; (3) Christ Jesus, Phil. 3:8; 2 Pet. 3:18; (4) salvation, Luke 1:77; (*c*) subjectively, of God's "knowledge," Rom. 11:33; the word of "knowledge," 1 Cor. 12:8; "knowledge" falsely so called, 1 Tim. 6:20.¶

2. *epignōsis* (ἐπίγνωσις, 1922), akin to A, No. 3, denotes "exact or full knowledge, discernment, recognition," and is a strengthened form of No. 1, expressing a fuller or a full "knowledge," a greater participation by the "knower" in the object "known," thus more powerfully influencing him. It is not found in the Gospels and Acts. Paul uses it 15 times (16 if Heb. 10:26 is included) out of the 20 occurrences; Peter 4 times, all in his 2nd Epistle. Contrast Rom. 1:28 (*epignōsis*) with the simple verb in v. 21. "In all the four Epistles of the first Roman captivity it is an element in the Apostle's opening prayer for his correspondents' well-being, Phil. 1:9; Eph. 1:17; Col. 1:9; Philem. 6" (Lightfoot).

It is used with reference to God in Rom. 1:28; 10:2; Eph. 1:17; Col. 1:10; 2 Pet. 1:3; God and Christ, 2 Pet. 1:2; Christ, Eph. 4:13; 2 Pet. 1:8; 2:20; the will of the Lord, Col. 1:9; every good thing, Philem. 6, RV (KJV, "acknowledging"); the truth, 1 Tim. 2:4; 2 Tim. 2:25, RV; 3:7; Titus 1:1, RV; the mystery of God. Col. 2:2, RV, "(that they) may know" (KJV, "to the acknowledgment of"), lit., "into a full knowledge." It is used without the mention of an object in Phil. 1:9; Col. 3:10, RV, "(renewed) unto knowledge." See ACKNOWLEDGE.¶

3. *agnōsia* (ἀγνωσία, 56), the negative of No. 1, "ignorance," is rendered "no knowledge" in 1 Cor. 15:34, RV (KJV, "not the knowledge"); in 1 Pet. 2:15, ignorance. See IGNORANCE.¶

Note: In Eph. 3:4, KJV, *sunesis*, "understanding," is translated "knowledge"; RV, "understanding." For *kardiognōstēs* see p. 297.

L

LABOR (Noun and Verb)

A. Nouns.

1. *kopos* (κόπος, 2873) primarily denotes "a striking, beating" (akin to *koptō*, "to strike, cut"); then, "toil resulting in weariness, laborious toil, trouble"; it is translated "labor" or "labors" in John 4:38; 1 Cor. 3:8; 15:58; 2 Cor. 6:5; 10:15; 11:23, 27, RV, "labor" (KJV, "weariness"); 1 Thess. 1:3; 2:9; 3:5; 2 Thess. 3:8; (in some mss., Heb. 6:10); Rev. 2:2 (RV "toil"); 14:13. In the following the noun is used as the object of the verb *parechō*, "to afford, give, cause," the phrase being rendered "to trouble," lit., "to cause toil or trouble," to embarrass a person by giving occasion for anxiety, as some disciples did to the woman with the ointment, perturbing her spirit by their criticisms, Matt. 26:10; Mark 14:6; or by distracting attention or disturbing a person's rest, as the importunate friend did, Luke 11:7; 18:5; in Gal. 6:17, "let no man trouble me," the apostle refuses, in the form of a peremptory prohibition, to allow himself to be distracted further by the Judaizers, through their proclamation of a false gospel and by their malicious attacks upon himself.¶

2. *ponos* (πόνος, 4192) denotes (*a*) "labors, toil," Col. 4:13, in the best mss. (some have *zēlos*, "zeal," KJV); (*b*) "the consequence of toil," viz., distress, suffering, pain, Rev. 16:10, 11; 21:4. See PAIN.¶

Notes: (1) In Phil. 1:22, KJV, *ergon*, "work," is translated "labor" (RV, "work"); work refers to what is done, and may be easy and pleasant; *kopos* suggests the doing, and the pains taken therein. (2) A synonymous word is *mochthos*, "toil, hardship, distress," 2 Cor. 11:27; 1 Thess. 2:9; 2 Thess. 3:8.¶

B. Verbs.

1. *kopiaō* (κοπιάω, 2872), akin to A, No. 1, has the two different meanings (*a*) "growing weary," (*b*) "toiling"; it is sometimes translated "to bestow labor" (see under BESTOW, No. 3). It is translated by the verb "to labor" in Matt. 11:28; John 4:38 (2nd part); Acts 20:35; Rom. 16:12 (twice); 1 Cor. 15:10; 16:16; Eph. 4:28; Phil. 2:16; Col. 1:29; 1 Thess. 5:12; 1 Tim. 4:10; 5:17; 2 Tim. 2:6; Rev. 2:3; 1 Cor. 4:12, RV, "toil" (KJV, "labor"). See TOIL.

2. *cheimazō* (χειμάζω, 5492), from *cheima*, "winter cold," primarily, "to expose to winter cold," signifies "to drive with a storm"; in the passive voice, "to be driven with storm, to be tempest-tossed," Acts 27:18, RV, "as (we) la-bored with the storm" (KJV, "being ... tossed with a tempest").¶

3. *sunathleō* (συναθλέω, 4866), "to contend along with a person" (*sun*, "with," *athleō*, "to contend"), is said in Phil. 4:3 of two women who "labored with" the apostle in the gospel; in 1:27, RV, "striving (for)," marg., "with," KJV, "striving together (for). See STRIVE.¶

Notes: (1) In John 6:27 and 1 Thess. 2:9, KJV, *ergazomai*, "to work," is translated respectively "labor" and "laboring" (RV, "working"). It is used of manual work here and in 4:11 and Eph. 4:28; of work for Christ in general, in 1 Cor. 16:10. See COMMIT. (2) In Heb. 4:11, KJV, *spoudazō*, "to be diligent," is translated "let us labor" (RV, "let us give diligence"). (3) In Col. 4:12, KJV, *agōnizomai*, "to strive, wrestle," is translated "laboring fervently" (RV, and KJV, marg., "striving"). (4) In 2 Cor. 5:9, KJV, *philotimeomai*, "to seek after honor," and hence, "to be ambitious," is translated "we labor," marg., "endeavor" (RV, "we make it our aim," marg., "are ambitious"); cf. Rom. 15:20; 1 Thess. 4:11, RV, marg.¶

LABORER, FELLOW LABORER

ergatēs (ἐργάτης, 2040), akin to *ergazomai*, "to work," and *ergon*, "work," denotes (*a*) a field laborer, a husbandman," Matt. 9:37, 38; 20:1, 2, 8; Luke 10:2 (twice); Jas. 5:4; (*b*) "a workman, laborer," in a general sense, Matt. 10:10; Luke 10:7; Acts 19:25; 1 Tim. 5:18; it is used (*c*) of false apostles and evil teachers, 2 Cor. 11:13; Phil. 3:2; (*d*) of a servant of Christ, 2 Tim. 2:15; (*e*) of evildoers, Luke 13:27.¶

Note: In the KJV of Philem. 1 and 24, *sunergos*, "a fellow worker," is translated "fellow laborer," RV, "fellow worker"; in Phil. 4:3, the plural, RV, "fellow workers;" in Phil. 2:25, KJV, "companion in labor," RV, "fellow worker"; in 1 Cor. 3:9, KJV, "laborers together (with God)," RV, "God's fellowworkers," i.e., fellow workers belonging to and serving God; in 3 John 8, KJV, "fellow helpers" (to the truth), RV, "fellow workers (with the truth)," i.e., acting together with the truth as an operating power; in 1 Thess. 3:2, some ancient authorities have the clause "fellow worker (with God)," RV, marg.; it is absent from the most authentic mss. See HELPER.

LACK, LACKING

A. Noun.

husterēma (ὑστέρημα, 5303) denotes (*a*) "that which is lacking, deficiency, shortcoming" (akin to *hustereō*, "to be behind, in want"), 1 Cor. 16:17; Phil. 2:30; Col. 1:24, RV, "that which is lacking" [KJV, "that which is behind" (of the afflictions of Christ)], where the reference is not to the vicarious sufferings of Christ, but to those which He endured previously, and those which must be endured by His faithful servants; 1 Thess. 3:10, where "that which is lacking" means that which Paul had not been able to impart to them, owing to the interruption of his spiritual instruction among them; (*b*) "need, want, poverty," Luke 21:4, RV, "want" (KJV, "penury"); 2 Cor. 8:14 (twice) "want;" 9:12, "wants" (KJV, "want"); 11:9, RV, "(the measure of my) want" [KJV, "that which was lacking (to me)"]. See BEHIND, PENURY, WANT.¶

Note: In 1 Thess. 4:12, KJV, *chreia*, "need," is translated "lack" (RV, "need"). See NEED.

B. Adjective.

endeēs (ἐνδεής, 1729), from *endeō*, "to lack," signifies "needy, in want," translated "that lacked" in Acts 4:34.¶

C. Verbs.

1. *hustereō* (ὑστερέω, 5302), akin to A, "to come or be behind," is used in the sense of "lacking" certain things, Matt. 19:20; Mark 10:21 ("one thing"; cf. No. 3 in Luke 18:22); Luke 22:35; in the sense of being inferior, 1 Cor. 12:24 (middle voice). Elsewhere it is translated in various ways; see BEHIND, B, No. 1, COME, No. 39, DESTITUTE, FAIL, *Note* (2), NEED, WANT, WORSE.

2. *elattoneō* (ἐλαττονέω, 1641), "to be less" (from *elattōn*, "less"), is translated "had no lack," 2 Cor. 8:15 (quoted from the Sept. of Exod. 16:18), the circumstance of the gathering of the manna being applied to the equalizing nature of cause and effect in the matter of supplying the wants of the needy.¶

3. *leipō* (λείπω, 3007), "to leave," denotes (*a*) transitively, in the passive voice, "to be left behind, to lack," Jas. 1:4, "ye may be lacking in (nothing)," RV (KJV, "wanting"); v. 5, "lacketh" (KJV, "lack"); 2:15, RV, "be . . . in lack" (KJV, "be . . . destitute"); (*b*) intransitively, active voice, Luke 18:22, "(one thing thou) lackest," is, lit., "(one thing) is lacking (to thee)"; Titus 1:5, "(the things) that were wanting"; 3:13, "(that nothing) be wanting." See DESTITUTE, WANTING.¶

Note: In 2 Pet. 1:9, "he that lacketh" translates a phrase the lit. rendering of which is "(he to whom these things) are not present" (*pareimi*, "to be present").

For **LAD,** in John 6:9, see **CHILD,** A, No. 6

LADE, LADEN

1. *sōreuō* (σωρεύω, 4987) signifies (*a*) "to heap on" (from *sōros*, "a heap," not in the NT; in the Sept., e.g., Josh. 7:26; 8:29; 2 Sam. 18:17; 2 Chron. 31:6–9), Rom. 12:20, of coals of fire; 2 Tim. 3:6, said of silly women ("womanlings") "laden" with sins. See HEAP.¶ In the Sept., Prov. 25:22.¶

2. *gemō* (γέμω, 1073), "to be full," is translated "laden" in Rev. 21:9, RV. See FULL.

3. *phortizō* (φορτίζω, 5412), "to load" (akin to *pherō*, "to bear"), is used in the active voice in Luke 11:46, "ye lade"; in the passive voice, metaphorically, in Matt. 11:28, "heavy laden." See BURDEN.¶ In the Sept., Ezek. 16:33.¶

Note: In Acts 28:10, KJV, *epitithēmi*, "to put on" (*epi*, "on," *tithēmi*, "to put"), is translated "they laded (us) with," RV, "they put on (board)."

LADING

phortion (φορτίον, 5413), "a burden, load" (a diminutive of *phortos*, "a load," from *pherō*, "to bear"), is used of the cargo of a ship, Acts 27:10, "lading," (some mss. have *phortos*). See BURDEN, A, No. 2.

LADY

kuria (κυρία, 2959) is the person addressed in 2 John 1 and 5. Not improbably it is a proper name (Eng., "Cyria"), in spite of the fact that the full form of address in v. 1 is not quite in accord, in the original, with those in v. 13 and in 3 John 1. The suggestion that the church is addressed is most unlikely. Possibly the person is one who had a special relation with the local church.¶

For **LAID** see **LAY**

LAKE

limnē (λίμνη, 3041), "a lake," is used (*a*) in the Gospels, only by Luke, of the Sea of Galilee, Luke 5:2; 8:22, 23, 33, called Gennesaret in 5:1 (Matthew and Mark use *thalassa*, "a sea"); (*b*) of the "lake" of fire, Rev. 19:20; 20:10, 14, 15; 21:8.¶

LAMA

lama (λαμά, 2982) is the Hebrew word for "Why?" (the variant *lema* is the Aramaic form), Matt. 27:46; Mark 15:34.¶

LAMB

1. *arēn* (ἀρήν, 704), a noun the nominative case of which is found only in early times, occurs in Luke 10:3. In normal usage it was replaced by *arnion* (No. 2), of which it is the equivalent.¶

2. *arnion* (ἀρνίον, 721) is a diminutive in form, but the diminutive force is not to be pressed (see *Note* under No. 3). The general tendency in the vernacular was to use nouns in *-ion* freely, apart from their diminutive significance. It is used only by the apostle John, (*a*) in the plural, in the Lord's command to Peter, John 21:15, with symbolic reference to young converts; (*b*) elsewhere, in the singular, in the Apocalypse, some 28 times, of Christ as the "Lamb" of God, the symbolism having reference to His character and His vicarious Sacrifice, as the basis both of redemption and of divine vengeance. He is seen in the position of sovereign glory and honor, e.g., 7:17, which He shares equally with the Father, 22:1, 3, the center of angelic beings and of the redeemed and the object of their veneration, e.g. 5:6, 8, 12, 13; 15:3, the Leader and Shepherd of His saints, e.g., 7:17, 14:4, the Head of his spiritual bride, e.g., 21:9, the luminary of the heavenly and eternal city, 21:23, the One to whom all judgment is committed, e.g., 6:1, 16; 13:8, the Conqueror of the foes of God and His people, 17:14; the song that celebrates the triumph of those who "gain the victory over the Beast," is the song of Moses . . . and the song of the Lamb, 15:3. His sacrifice, the efficacy of which avails for those who accept the salvation thereby provided, forms the ground of the execution of divine wrath for the rejector, and the defier of God, 14:10; (*c*) in the description of the second "Beast," Rev. 13:11, seen in the vision "like a lamb," suggestive of his acting in the capacity of a false messiah, a travesty of the true. For the use in the Sept. see *Note* under No. 3.

3. *amnos* (ἀμνός, 286), "a lamb," is used figuratively of Christ, in John 1:29, 36, with the article, pointing Him out as the expected One, the One to be well known as the personal fulfillment and embodiment of all that had been indicated in the OT, the One by whose sacrifice deliverance from divine judgment was to be obtained; in Acts 8:32 (from the Sept. of Is. 53:7) and 1 Pet. 1:19, the absence of the article stresses the nature and character of His sacrifice

as set forth in the symbolism. The reference in each case is to the lamb of God's providing, Gen. 22:8, and the Paschal lamb of God's appointment for sacrifice in Israel, e.g., Ex. 12:5, 14, 27 (cf. 1 Cor. 5:7).¶

Note: The contrast between *arnion* and *amnos* does not lie in the diminutive character of the former as compared with the latter. As has been pointed out under No. 2, *arnion* lost its diminutive force. The contrast lies in the manner in which Christ is presented in the two respects. The use of *amnos* points directly to the fact, the nature and character of His sacrifice; *arnion* (only in the Apocalypse) presents Him, on the ground, indeed, of His sacrifice, but in His acquired majesty, dignity, honor, authority and power.

In the Sept. *arnion* is used in Ps. 114:4, 6; in Jer. 11:19, with the adjective *akakos*, "innocent"; in Jer. 27:45, "lambs." There is nothing in these passages to suggest a contrast between a "lamb" in the general sense of the term and the diminutive; the contrast is between "lambs" and sheep. Elsewhere in the Sept. *amnos* is in general used some 100 times in connection with "lambs" for sacrifice.

For **LAME** see **HALT**

For **LAMENT** and **LAMENTATION** see **BEWAIL**

LAMP

1. *lampas* (λαμπάς, 2985) denotes "a torch" (akin to *lampō*, "to shine"), frequently fed, like a "lamp," with oil from a little vessel used for the purpose (the *angeion* of Matt. 25:4); they held little oil and would frequently need replenishing. Rutherford (*The New Phrynichus*) points out that it became used as the equivalent of *luchnos* (No. 2), as in the parable of the ten virgins, Matt. 25:1, 3, 4, 7, 8; John 18:3, "torches"; Acts 20:8, "lights"; Rev. 4:5; 8:10 (RV, "torch," KJV, "lamp"). See *Note* below.¶ Cf. *phanos*, "a torch," John 18:3 (translated "lanterns").¶

2. *luchnos* (λύχνος, 3088) frequently mistranslated "candle," is a portable "lamp" usually set on a stand (see LAMPSTAND); the word is used literally, Matt. 5:15; Mark 4:21; Luke 8:16; 11:33, 36; 15:8; Rev. 18:23; 22:5; (*b*) metaphorically, of Christ as the Lamb, Rev. 21:23, RV, "lamp" (KJV, "light"); of John the Baptist, John 5:35, RV, "the lamp" (KJV, "a . . . light"); of the eye, Matt. 6:22, and Luke 11:34, RV, "lamp"; of spiritual readiness, Luke 12:35,

RV, "lamps"; of "the word of prophecy," 2 Pet. 1:19, RV, "lamp." See LIGHT.¶

"In rendering *luchnos* and *lampas* our translators have scarcely made the most of the words at their command. Had they rendered *lampas* by 'torch' not once only (John 18:3), but always, this would have left 'lamp,' now wrongly appropriated by *lampas*, disengaged. Altogether dismissing 'candle,' they might then have rendered *luchnos* by 'lamp' wherever it occurs. At present there are so many occasions where 'candle' would manifestly be inappropriate, and where, therefore, they are obliged to fall back on 'light,' that the distinction between *phōs* and *luchnos* nearly, if not quite, disappears in our Version. The advantages of such a re-distribution of the words would be many. In the first place, it would be more accurate. *Luchnos* is not a 'candle' ('*candela,*' from '*candeo,*' the white wax light, and then any kind of taper), but a hand-lamp, fed with oil. Neither is *lampas* a 'lamp,' but a 'torch'" (Trench *Syn.*, §xlvi).

Note: There is no mention of a candle in the original either in the OT or in the NT. The figure of that which feeds upon its own substance to provide its light would be utterly inappropriate. A lamp is supplied by oil, which in its symbolism is figurative of the Holy Spirit.

LAMPSTAND

luchnia (λυχνία, 3087) is mistranslated "candlestick" in every occurrence in the KJV and in certain places in the RV; the RV has "stand" in Matt. 5:15; Mark 4:21; Luke 8:16; 11:33; "candlestick" in Heb. 9:2; Rev. 1:12, 13, 20 (twice); 2:1, 5; 11:4; the RV marg., gives "lampstands" in the passages in Rev., but not in Heb. 9:2.¶

LAND

A. Nouns.

1. *gē* (γῆ, 1093), in one of its usages, denotes (*a*) "land" as distinct from sea or other water, e.g., Mark 4:1; 6:47; Luke 5:3; John 6:21; (*b*) "land" as subject to cultivation, e.g., Luke 14:35 (see GROUND); (*c*) "land" as describing a country or region, e.g., Matt. 2:20, 21; 4:15; Luke 4:25; in 23:44, RV, "(the whole) land," KJV, "(all the) earth"; Acts 7:29; Heb. 11:9, RV, "a land (not his own)," KJV "a (strange) country;" Jude 5. In Acts 7:11 the KJV follows a reading of the noun with the definite article which necessitates the insertion of "land." See EARTH.

2. *chōra* (χώρα, 5561) is used with the meaning "land," (*a*) of a country, region, e.g., Mark 1:5; Luke 15:14; sometimes translated "region," e.g., Matt. 4:16; Luke 3:1; Acts 8:1;

13:49; 16:6; (*b*) of property, Luke 12:16, "ground." See COUNTRY, A, No. 3.

3. *chōrion* (χωρίον, 5564), a diminutive of No. 2, in form, but not in meaning, is translated "land" in the sense of property, in Acts 4:34; 5:3, 8; 28:7, RV, "lands" (KJV, "possessions "). See FIELD, GROUND, A, No. 4, PLACE, POSSESSION.

4. *agros* (ἀγρός, 68), "a field," or "piece of ground," or "the country" as distinct from the town, is translated "lands" in Matt. 19:29; Mark 10:29, 30; Acts 4:37 (cf. No. 3 in v. 34). See COUNTRY, A, No. 1, FARM, FIELD, GROUND.

B. Adjective.

xēros (ξηρός, 3584), "dry," "dry land," Matt. 23:15 (*gē,* "land," being understood); Heb. 11:29: see DRY.

Note: In Luke 4:26, the RV, "in the land (of)" and KJV, "a city (of)," represent no word in the original, but give the sense of the phrase.

C. Verb.

katerchomai (κατέρχομαι, 2718), "to come down, or go down, descend," is used of coming to port by ship, in Acts 18:22, "landed"; 21:3 (ditto); 27:5, "came to." See COME, No. 7, GO, *Note* (1).

Notes: (1) In Acts 28:12, RV, *katagō,* "to bring down," used as a nautical term in the passive voice, is translated "touching" (KJV, "landing"). (2) In Acts 21:3, some mss. have the verb *katagō,* with reference to Cyprus. (3) In Acts 20:13, *pezeuō,* "to travel by land" or "on foot" (*pezos,* "on foot"; *pous,* "a foot"), is translated "to go by land," RV, KJV, "to go afoot," and RV marg., "to go on foot."¶

LANE

rhumē (ῥύμη, 4505) in earlier Greek meant "the force or rush or swing of a moving body"; in later times, "a narrow road, lane or street"; it is translated "lanes" in Luke 14:21; "streets" in Matt. 6:2; "street" in Acts 9:11; 12:10. See STREET.¶ In the Sept., Isa. 15:3.¶

LANGUAGE

dialektos (διάλεκτος, 1258), primarily "a conversation, discourse" (akin to *dialegomai,* "to discourse or discuss"), came to denote "the language or dialect of a country or district"; in the KJV and RV of Acts 2:6 it is translated "language"; in the following the RV retains "language," for KJV, "tongue," Acts 1:19; 2:8; 21:40; 22:2; 26:14. See TONGUE.¶ In the Sept., Esth. 9:26.¶

LANTERN

phanos (φανός, 5322) denotes either "a torch" or "a lantern" (from *phainō,* "to cause to shine, to give light"), John 18:3, where it is distinguished from *lampas* (see LAMP, No. 1); it was "a link or torch consisting of strips of resinous wood tied together" (Rutherford). "Torch" would seem to be the meaning.¶

LARGE

1. *megas* (μέγας, 3173), "great, large, of physical magnitude," is translated "large" in Mark 14:15 and Luke 22:12, of the upper room. See GREAT, No. 1.

2. *hikanos* (ἱκανός, 2425), of persons, denotes "sufficient, competent, fit"; of things, "sufficient, enough, much, many (so of time)"; it is translated "large" in Matt. 28:12, of money. See ABLE, C, No. 2.

3. *pēlikos* (πηλίκος, 4080), "how large," is used of letters of the alphabet, characters in writing, Gal. 6:11, "with how large (letters)"; it is said of personal greatness in Heb. 7:4. See GREAT, No. 5.¶

LASCIVIOUS, LASCIVIOUSNESS

aselgeia (ἀσέλγεια, 766) denotes "excess, licentiousness, absence of restraint, indecency, wantonness"; "lasciviousness" in Mark 7:22, one of the evils that proceed from the heart; in 2 Cor. 12:21, one of the evils of which some in the church at Corinth had been guilty; in Gal. 5:19, classed among the works of the flesh; in Eph. 4:19, among the sins of the unregenerate who are "past feeling"; so in 1 Pet. 4:3; in Jude 4, of that into which the grace of God had been turned by ungodly men; it is translated "wantonness" in Rom. 13:13, one of the sins against which believers are warned; in 2 Pet. 2:2, according to the best mss., "lascivious (doings)," RV (the KJV "pernicious ways" follows those texts which have *apōleiais*); in v. 7, RV, "lascivious (life)," KJV, "filthy (conversation)," of the people of Sodom and Gomorrah; in 2:18, RV, "lasciviousness" (KJV, "wantonness"), practiced by the same persons as mentioned in Jude. The prominent idea is shameless conduct. Some have derived the word from *a*, negative, and *selgē*, "a city in Pisidia." Others, with similar improbability, trace it to *a*, negative, and *selgō*, or *thelgō*, "to charm." See WANTONNESS.¶

LAST

A. Adjective.

eschatos (ἔσχατος, 2078), "last, utmost, extreme," is used (*a*) of place, e.g., Luke 14:9, 10, "lowest;" Acts 1:8 and 13:47, "uttermost part;" (*b*) of rank, e.g., Mark 9:35; (*c*) of time, relating either to persons or things, e.g., Matt. 5:26, "the last (farthing)," RV (KJV, "uttermost"); Matt. 20:8, 12, 14; Mark 12:6, 22; 1 Cor. 4:9, of

apostles as "last" in the program of a spectacular display; 1 Cor. 15:45, "the last Adam"; Rev. 2:19; of the "last" state of persons, Matt. 12:45, neuter plural, lit., "the last (things)"; so Luke 11:26; 2 Pet. 2:20, RV, "the last state" (KJV, "the latter end"); of Christ as the Eternal One, Rev. 1:17 (in some mss. v. 11); 2:8; 22:13; in eschatological phrases as follows: (*a*) "the last day," a comprehensive term including both the time of the resurrection of the redeemed, John 6:39, 40, 44, 54 and 11:24, and the ulterior time of the judgment of the unregenerate, at the Great White Throne, John 12:48; (*b*) "the last days," Acts 2:17, a period relative to the supernatural manifestation of the Holy Spirit at Pentecost and the resumption of the divine interpositions in the affairs of the world at the end of the present age, before "the great and notable Day of the Lord," which will usher in the messianic kingdom; (*c*) in 2 Tim. 3:1, "the last days" refers to the close of the present age of world conditions; (*d*) in Jas. 5:3, the phrase "in the last days" (RV) refers both to the period preceding the Roman overthrow of the city and the land in A.D. 70, and to the closing part of the age in consummating acts of gentile persecution including "the time of Jacob's trouble" (cf. verses 7, 8); (*e*) in 1 Pet. 1:5, "the last time" refers to the time of the Lord's second advent; (*f*) in 1 John 2:18,"the last hour" (RV) and, in Jude 18, "the last time" signify the present age previous to the Second Advent.

Notes: (1) In Heb. 1:2, RV, "at the end of these days" (KJV, "in these last days"), the reference is to the close of the period of the testimony of the prophets under the Law, terminating with the presence of Christ and His redemptive sacrifice and its effects, the perfect tense "hath spoken" indicating the continued effects of the message embodied in the risen Christ; so in 1 Pet. 1:20, RV, "at the end of the times" (KJV, "in these last times").

B. Adverb.

husteron (ὕστερον, 5305), the neuter of the adjective *husteros*, is used as an adverb signifying "afterwards, later," see AFTER, No. 5. Cf. the adjective, under LATER.

Note: In Phil. 4:10 the particle *pote*, "sometime," used after *ēdē*, "now, already," to signify "now at length," is so rendered in the RV, KJV, "(now) at the last."

LATCHET

himas (ἱμάς, 2438) denotes "a thong, strap," whether for binding prisoners, Acts 22:25, "(the) thongs" (for scourging; see BIND, No. 7), or for fastening sandals, Mark 1:7; Luke 3:16; John 1:27. "Among the Orientals everything connected with the feet and shoes is defiled and debasing, and the stooping to unfasten the dusty latchet is the most insignificant in such service" (Mackie, in *Hastings' Bib. Dic.*).¶

LATE

opse (ὀψέ, 3796), an adverb of time, besides its meaning "at evening" or "at eventide," denotes "late in, or on," Matt. 28:1, RV, "late on (the Sabbath day)" (KJV, "in the end of"); it came also to denote "late after," which seems to be the meaning here. See EVENING.

Note: In John 11:8, KJV, "*nun*, now," is translated "of late" (RV, "but now").

LATELY

prosphatōs (προσφάτως, 4373) denotes "recently, lately," from the adjective *prosphatos*, "new, fresh, recent"; primarily, "newly slain," Heb. 10:20 (*phatos*, "slain"), is also found in Acts 18:2.¶ In the Sept., Deut. 24:5; Ezek. 11:3.¶

LATER

husteros (ὕστερος, 5306) denotes "later" or "latter" and is used in 1 Tim. 4:1, RV, "in later (times)," KJV, "in (the) latter (times)." Several mss. have it in Matt. 21:31, "the former," for *prōtos*, "the first."¶

LATIN

rhōmaisti (ῥωμαϊστί, 4515), an adverb, "in Latin," occurs in John 19:20, lit., "in Roman."¶

Note: In Luke 23:38, some mss. have the adjective *Rhomaikos*, "of Latin," agreeing with "letters."

LATTER

opsimos (ὄψιμος, 3797), akin to *opse* and *opsios* (see LATE), denotes "late," or "latter," and is used of "the latter rain" in Jas. 5:7 (the most authentic mss. omit *huetos*, "rain"; some have *karpos*, "fruit"); this rain falls in March and April, just before the harvest, in contrast to the early rain, in October.¶ In the Sept., Deut. 11:14; Prov. 16:15; Jer. 5:24; Hos. 6:3; Joel 2:23; Zech. 10:1.¶

Note: For "latter" (*husteros*) in the KJV of 1 Tim. 4:1 see LATER, and for 2 Pet. 2:20 see LAST.

For **LAUD** (Rom. 15:11, KJV) see **PRAISE**, B, No. 1

LAUGH, LAUGH TO SCORN

1. *gelaō* (γελάω, 1070), "to laugh," is found in Luke 6:21, 25. This signifies loud laughter in contrast to demonstrative weeping.¶

2. *katagelaō* (καταγελάω, 2606) denotes "to laugh scornfully at," more emphatic than No. 1 (*kata*, "down," used intensively, and No. 1), and signifies derisive laughter, Matt. 9:24; Mark 5:40; Luke 8:53.¶ Cf. *ekmuktērizō*, "to deride."

Note: The laughter of incredulity, as in Gen. 17:17 and 18:12, is not mentioned in the NT.

LAUGHTER

gelōs (γέλως, 1071) denotes "laughter," Jas. 4:9.¶ This corresponds to the kind of "laughter" mentioned above (see LAUGH, No. 1).

LAUNCH

1. *anagō* (ἀνάγω, 321), "to bring up" (*ana*, "up," *agō*, "to lead"), is used in the middle voice as a nautical term signifying "to put to sea"; it is translated "launch forth" in Luke 8:22; "set sail" in Acts 13:13, RV (KJV, "loosed"); similarly in 16:11; in 18:21, for KJV, "sailed"; similarly in 20:3, 13; in 21:1, RV, "set sail," (KJV, "launched"), and in v. 2, for KJV, "set forth"; in 27:2 and 4 the RV has the verb "to put to sea," for KJV "to launch"; in v. 12 for KJV, "depart"; in v. 21, RV, "set sail" (KJV, "loosed"); in 28:10, 11, "sailed" and "set sail" (KJV, "departed"). See BRING, DEPART, LEAD, LOOSE, OFFER, PUT, SAIL, SET.

2. *epanagō* (ἐπανάγω, 1877), "to lead up upon" (*epi*, "upon," and No. 1), is used as a nautical term with *ploion*, "a ship," understood, denoting "to put out to sea," translated in Luke 5:3, "put out," RV (KJV, "thrust out"); in v. 4, for KJV, "launch." For the nonnautical significance "to return," see Matt. 21:18. See PUT, RETURN, THRUST.¶ In the Sept., Zech. 4:12, "that communicate with (the golden oil vessels)."

LAW

A. Nouns.

1. *nomos* (νόμος, 3551), akin to *nemō*, "to divide out, distribute," primarily meant "that which is assigned"; hence, "usage, custom," and then, "law, law as prescribed by custom, or by statute"; the word *ēthos*, "custom," was retained for unwritten "law," while *nomos* became the established name for "law" as decreed by a state and set up as the standard for the administration of justice.

In the NT it is used (*a*) of "law" in general, e.g., Rom. 2:12, 13, "a law" (RV), expressing a general principle relating to "law"; v. 14, last part; 3:27, "By what manner of law?" i.e., "by what sort of principle (has the glorying been excluded)?"; 4:15 (last part); 5:13, referring to the period between Adam's trespass and the giving of the Law; 7:1 (1st part, RV marg., "law"); against those graces which constitute the fruit of the Spirit "there is no law," Gal. 5:23; "the ostensible aim of the law is to restrain the evil tendencies natural to man in his fallen estate; yet in experience law finds itself not merely ineffective, it actually provokes those tendencies to greater activity. The intention of the gift of the Spirit is to constrain the believer to a life in which the natural tendencies shall have no place, and to produce in him their direct contraries. Law, therefore, has nothing to say against the fruit of the Spirit; hence the believer is not only not under law, ver. 18, the law finds no scope in his life, inasmuch as, and in so far as, he is led by the Spirit;"*

(b) of a force or influence impelling to action, Rom. 7:21, 23 (1st part), "a different law," RV;

(c) of the Mosaic Law, the "law" of Sinai, (1) with the definite article, e.g., Matt. 5:18; John 1:17; Rom. 2:15, 18, 20, 26, 27; 3:19; 4:15; 7:4, 7, 14, 16, 22; 8:3, 4, 7; Gal. 3:10, 12, 19, 21, 24; 5:3; Eph. 2:15; Phil. 3:6; 1 Tim. 1:8; Heb. 7:19; Jas. 2:9; (2) without the article, thus stressing the Mosaic Law in its quality as "law," e.g., Rom. 2:14 (1st part); 5:20; 7:9, where the stress in the quality lies in this, that "the commandment which was unto (i.e., which he thought would be a means of) life," he found to be "unto (i.e., to have the effect of revealing his actual state of) death"; 10:4; 1 Cor. 9:20; Gal. 2:16, 19, 21; 3:2, 5, 10 (1st part), 11, 18, 23; 4:4, 5, 21 (1st part); 5:4, 18; 6:13; Phil. 3:5, 9; Heb. 7:16; 9:19; Jas. 2:11; 4:11; (in regard to the statement in Gal. 2:16, that "a man is not justified by the works of the Law," the absence of the article before nomos indicates the assertion of a principle, "by obedience to law," but evidently the Mosaic Law is in view. Here the apostle is maintaining that submission to circumcision entails the obligation to do the whole "Law." Circumcision belongs to the ceremonial part of the "Law," but, while the Mosaic Law is actually divisible into the ceremonial and the moral, no such distinction is made or even assumed in Scripture. The statement maintains the freedom of the believer from the "law" of Moses in its totality as a means of justification);

(d) by metonymy, of the books which contain the "law," (1) of the Pentateuch, e.g., Matt.

5:17; 12:5; Luke 16:16; 24:44; John 1:45; Rom. 3:21; Gal. 3:10; (2) of the Psalms, John 10:34; 15:25; of the Psalms, Isaiah, Ezekiel and Daniel, 12:34; the Psalms and Isaiah, Rom. 3:19 (with vv. 10–18); Isaiah, 1 Cor. 14:21; from all this it may be inferred that "the law" in the most comprehensive sense was an alternative title to "The Scriptures."

The following phrases specify "laws" of various kinds; (a) "the law of Christ," Gal. 6:2, i.e., either given by Him (as in the Sermon on the Mount and in John 13:14, 15; 15:4), or the "law" or principle by which Christ Himself lived (Matt. 20:28; John 13:1); these are not actual alternatives, for the "law" imposed by Christ was always that by which He Himself lived in the "days of His flesh." He confirmed the "Law" as being of divine authority (cf. Matt. 5:18); yet He presented a higher standard of life than perfunctory obedience to the current legal rendering of the "Law," a standard which, without annulling the "Law," He embodied in His own character and life (see, e.g., Matt. 5:21–48; this breach with legalism is especially seen in regard to the ritual or ceremonial part of the "Law" in its wide scope); He showed Himself superior to all human interpretations of it; (b) "a law of faith," Rom. 3:27, i.e., a principle which demands only faith on man's part; (c) "the law of my mind," Rom. 7:23, that principle which governs the new nature in virtue of the new birth; (d) "the law of sin," Rom. 7:23, the principle by which sin exerts its influence and power despite the desire to do what is right; "of sin and death," 8:2, death being the effect; (e) "the law of liberty," Jas. 1:25; 2:12, a term comprehensive of all the Scriptures, not a "law" of compulsion enforced from without, but meeting with ready obedience through the desire and delight of the renewed being who is subject to it; into it he looks, and in its teaching he delights; he is "under law (ennomos, "in law," implying union and subjection) to Christ," 1 Cor. 9:21; cf., e.g., Ps. 119:32, 45, 97; 2 Cor. 3:17; (f) "the royal law," Jas. 2:8, i.e., the "law" of love, royal in the majesty of its power, the "law" upon which all others hang, Matt. 22:34–40; Rom. 13:8; Gal. 5:14; (g) "the law of the Spirit of life," Rom. 8:2, i.e., the animating principle by which the Holy Spirit acts as the imparter of life (cf. John 6:63); (h) "a law of righteousness," Rom. 9:31, i.e., a general principle presenting righteousness as the object and outcome of keeping a "law," particularly the "Law" of Moses (cf. Gal. 3:21); (i) "the law of a carnal commandment," Heb. 7:16, i.e., the "law" respecting the Aaronic priesthood, which appointed men conditioned by the circum-

---

* From *Notes on Galatians*, by Hogg and Vine, p. 298.

stances and limitations of the flesh. In the Epistle to the Hebrews the "Law" is treated of especially in regard to the contrast between the Priesthood of Christ and that established under the "law" of Moses, and in regard to access to God and to worship. In these respects the "Law" "made nothing perfect," 7:19. There was "a disannulling of a foregoing commandment ... and a bringing in of a better hope." This is established under the "new Covenant," a covenant instituted on the basis of "better promises," 8:6.

Notes: (1) In Gal. 5:3, the statement that to receive circumcision constitutes a man a debtor to do "the whole Law," views the "Law" as made up of separate commands, each essential to the whole, and predicates the unity of the "Law"; in v. 14, the statement that "the whole law" is fulfilled in the one commandment concerning love, views the separate commandments as combined to make a complete "law." (2) In Rom. 8:3, "what the law could not do," is lit., "the inability (*adunaton*, the neuter of the adjective *adunatos*, 'unable,' used as a noun) of the Law"; this may mean either "the weakness of the Law" or "that which was impossible for the Law"; the latter is preferable; the significance is the same in effect; the "Law" could neither give freedom from condemnation nor impart life. (3) For the difference between the teaching of Paul and that of James in regard to the "Law," see under JUSTIFICATION. (4) For Acts 19:38, KJV, "the law is open" (RV, "courts," etc.) see COURT, No. 1. (5) For *nomodidaskaloi*, "doctors of the law", Luke 5:17, singular in Acts 5:34, "teachers of the law," 1 Tim. 1:7, see DOCTOR.

2. *nomothesia* (νομοθεσία, 3548) denotes "legislation, lawgiving" (No. 1, and *tithēmi*, "to place, to put"), Rom. 9:4, "(the) giving of the law." Cf. B, No. 1.¶

B. Verbs.

1. *nomotheteō* (νομοθετέω, 3549), (*a*) used intransitively, signifies "to make laws" (cf. A, No. 2, above); in the passive voice, "to be furnished with laws," Heb. 7:11, "received the law," lit., "was furnished with (the) law"; (*b*) used transitively, it signifies "to ordain by law, to enact"; in the passive voice, Heb. 8:6. See ENACT.¶

2. *krinō* (κρίνω, 2919), "to esteem, judge," etc., signifies "to go to law," and is so used in the middle voice in Matt. 5:40, RV, "go to law" (KJV, "sue ... at the law"); 1 Cor. 6:1, 6. See ESTEEM.

Note: In 1 Cor. 6:7, the KJV, "go to law," is a rendering of the phrase *echō krimata*, "to have lawsuits," as in the RV.

3. *paranomeō* (παρανομέω, 3891), "to transgress law" (*para*, "contrary to," and *nomos*), is used in the present participle in Acts 23:3, and translated "contrary to the law," lit., "transgressing the law."¶

C. Adjectives.

1. *nomikos* (νομικός, 3544) denotes "relating to law"; in Titus 3:9 it is translated "about the law," describing "fightings" (KJV, "strivings"); see LAWYER.

2. *ennomos* (ἔννομος, 1772), (*a*) "lawful, legal," lit., "in law" (*en*, "in," and *nomos*), or, strictly, "what is within the range of law," is translated "lawful" in Acts 19:39, KJV (RV, "regular"), of the legal tribunals in Ephesus; (*b*) "under law" (RV), in relation to Christ, 1 Cor. 9:21, where it is contrasted with *anomos* (see No. 3 below); the word as used by the apostle suggests not merely the condition of being under "law," but the intimacy of a relation established in the loyalty of a will devoted to his Master. See LAWFUL.

3. *anomos* (ἄνομος, 459) signifies "without law" (*a*, negative) and has this meaning in 1 Cor. 9:21 (four times). See LAWLESS, TRANSGRESSOR, UNLAWFUL, WICKED.

D. Adverb.

anomōs (ἀνόμως, 460), "without law" (the adverbial form of C, No. 3), is used in Rom. 2:12 (twice), where "(have sinned) without law" means in the absence of some specifically revealed "law," like the "law" of Sinai; "(shall perish) without law" predicates that the absence of such a "law" will not prevent their doom; the "law" of conscience is not in view here. The succeeding phrase "under law" is lit., "in law," not the same as the adjective *ennomos* (C, No. 2), but two distinct words.¶

LAWFUL, LAWFULLY

A. Verb.

exesti (ἔξεστι, 1832), an impersonal verb, signifying "it is permitted, it is lawful" (or interrogatively, "is it lawful?"), occurs most frequently in the synoptic Gospels and the Acts; elsewhere in John 5:10; 18:31; 1 Cor. 6:12; 10:23; 2 Cor. 12:4; in Acts 2:29, it is rendered "let me (speak)," lit., "it being permitted"; in the KJV of 8:37, "thou mayest," lit., "it is permitted;" 16:21; in 21:37, "may I," lit., "is it permitted?" See LET, MAY.

Note: For *ennomos*, see C, No. 2, (under LAW).

B. Adverb.

nomimōs (νομίμως, 3545), "lawfully," is used in 1 Tim. 1:8, "the Law is good, if a man use it lawfully," i.e., agreeably to its design; the meaning here is that, while no one can be justified or obtain eternal life through its instrumentality, the believer is to have it in his heart and to fulfill its requirements; walking "not after the flesh but after the spirit," Rom. 8:4, he will "use it lawfully." In 2 Tim. 2:5 it is used of contending in the games and adhering to the rules.¶

LAWGIVER

nomothetēs (νομοθέτης, 3550), "a law-giver" (see LAW, A, No. 2, and B, No. 1), occurs in Jas. 4:12, of God, as the sole "Lawgiver"; therefore, to criticize the Law is to presume to take His place, with the presumption of enacting a better law.¶

LAWLESS, LAWLESSNESS

A. Adjective.

anomos (ἄνομος, 459), "without law," also denotes "lawless," and is so rendered in the RV of Acts 2:23, "lawless (men)," marg., "(men) without the law," KJV, "wicked (hands);" 2 Thess. 2:8, "the lawless one" (KJV, "that wicked"), of the man of sin (v. 4); in 2 Pet. 2:8, of deeds (KJV, "unlawful"), where the thought is not simply that of doing what is unlawful, but of flagrant defiance of the known will of God. See LAW, C, No. 3.

B. Noun.

anomia (ἀνομία, 458), "lawlessness," akin to A, is most frequently translated "iniquity;" in 2 Thess. 2:7, RV, "lawlessness" (KJV, "iniquity"); "the mystery of lawlessness" is not recognized by the world, for it does not consist merely in confusion and disorder (see A); the display of "lawlessness" by the "lawless" one (v. 8) will be the effect of the attempt by the powers of darkness to overthrow the divine government. In 1 John 3:4, the RV adheres to the real meaning of the word, "every one that doeth sin (a practice, not the committal of an act) doeth also lawlessness: and sin is lawlessness." This definition of sin sets forth its essential character as the rejection of the law, or will, of God and the substitution of the will of self. See INIQUITY and synonymous words.

LAWYER

nomikos (νομικός, 3544), an adjective, "learned in the law" (see Titus 3:9, under LAW, C, No. 1), is used as a noun, "a lawyer," Matt. 22:35; Luke 7:30; 10:25; 11:45, 46, 52 (v. 53 in some mss.); 14:3; Titus 3:13, where Zenas is so named. As there is no evidence that he was one skilled in Roman jurisprudence, the term may be regarded in the usual NT sense as applying to one skilled in the Mosaic Law.¶

The usual name for a scribe is *grammateus*, a man of letters; for a doctor of the law, *nomodi-*

daskalos (see DOCTOR). "A comparison of Luke 5:17 with v. 21 and Mark 2:6 and Matt. 9:3 shows that the three terms were used synonymously, and did not denote three distinct classes. The scribes were originally simply men of letters, students of Scripture, and the name first given to them contains in itself no reference to the law; in course of time, however, they devoted themselves mainly, though by no means exclusively, to the study of the law. They became jurists rather than theologians, and received names which of themselves called attention to that fact. Some would doubtless devote themselves more to one branch of activity than to another; but a 'lawyer' might also be a 'doctor,' and the case of Gamaliel shows that a 'doctor' might also be a member of the Sanhedrin, Acts 5:34" (Eaton, in *Hastings' Bib. Dic.*).

LAY

1. *tithēmi* (τίθημι, 5087), "to put, place, set," frequently signifies "to lay," and is used of (*a*) "laying" a corpse in a tomb, Matt. 27:60; Mark 6:29; 15:47; 16:6; Luke 23:53, 55; John 11:34; 19:41, 42; 20:2, 13, 15; Acts 7:16; 13:29; Rev. 11:9, RV, "to be laid" (KJV, "to be put"); in an upper chamber, Acts 9:37; (*b*) "laying" the sick in a place, Mark 6:56; Luke 5:18; Acts 3:2; 5:15; (*c*) "laying" money at the apostles' feet, Acts 4:35, 37; 5:2; (*d*) Christ's "laying" His hands upon children, Mark 10:16, RV, "laying" (KJV, "put"); upon John, Rev. 1:17 (in the best mss.); (*e*) "laying" down one's life, (1) of Christ, John 10:11, RV, "layeth down" (KJV, "giveth"); vv. 17, 18 (twice); 1 John 3:16; (2) of Peter for Christ's sake, John 13:37, 38; (3) of Christ's followers, on behalf of others, 1 John 3:16; (4) of anyone, for his friends, John 15:13; (*f*) "laying" up sayings in one's heart, Luke 1:66 (middle voice, in the sense of "for themselves"); in 9:44, of letting Christ's words "sink" (middle voice, in the sense of "for oneself"; KJV, "sink down") into the ears; (*g*) "laying" a foundation (1) literally, Luke 6:48; 14:29; (2) metaphorically, of Christ in relation to an assembly, 1 Cor. 3:10, 11; (*h*) in "laying" Christ as a "stone of stumbling" for Israel, Rom. 9:33; (*i*) Christ's "laying" aside His garments, John 13:4; (*j*) Christians, in "laying" money in store for the help of the needy, 1 Cor. 16:2 (lit., "let him put"); (*k*) "depositing" money, Luke 19:21, 22. See APPOINT.

2. *katatithēmi* (κατατίθημι, 2698), "to lay down" (*kata*), is used in Mark 15:46 of the act of Joseph of Arimathaea in "laying" Christ's body in the tomb (some mss. have No. 1 here). See DO, *Note* (4), SHEW.

3. *ballō* (βάλλω, 906), "to cast, throw, place,

put," is used in the passive voice signifying "to be laid," e.g., Mark 7:30; Luke 16:20; for Matt. 8:14, RV, "lying" (KJV, "laid") and 9:2, see LIE, No. (3). See CAST.

4. *epiballō* (ἐπιβάλλω, 1911), "to lay upon," is used of seizing men, to imprison them, Acts 4:3. See CAST.

5. *kataballō* (καταβάλλω, 2598), "to cast down" (*kata*), is used metaphorically in Heb. 6:1, in the middle voice, negatively, "of laying" a foundation of certain doctrines. See CAST.

6. *klinō* (κλίνω, 2827), "to make to bend, to bow," or "to make to lean, to rest," is used in Matt. 8:20 and Luke 9:58, in the Lord's statement, "the Son of man hath not where to lay His head"; it is significant that this verb is used in John 19:30 of the Lord's act at the moment of His death in placing His head into a position of rest, not a helpless drooping of the head as in all other cases of crucifixion. He reversed the natural order, by first reclining His head (indicative of His submission to His Father's will), and then "giving up His spirit." The rest He found not on earth in contrast to His creatures the foxes and birds, He found in this consummating act on the cross. See BOW.

7. *anaklinō* (ἀνακλίνω, 347), "to lay down, make to recline" (in the passive voice, "to lie back, recline"), is used in Luke 2:7, of the act of the Virgin Mary in "laying" her Child in a manger. See SIT.

8. *apotithēmi* (ἀποτίθημι, 659), "to put off from oneself" (*apo*, "from," and No. 1), always in the middle voice in the NT, is used metaphorically in Heb. 12:1, "laying aside (every weight);" in Jas. 1:21, KJV, "lay apart," RV, "putting away"; in Acts 7:58 of "laying" down garments, after taking them off, for the purpose of stoning Stephen. See CAST, PUT.

9. *hupotithēmi* (ὑποτίθημι, 5294), "to place under, lay down" (*hupo*, "under," and No. 1), is used metaphorically in Rom. 16:4, of risking one's life, "laid down" (their own necks). In the middle voice in 1 Tim. 4:6 it is used of "putting" persons in mind, RV, (KJV, "in remembrance"). See REMEMBRANCE.¶

10. *epitithēmi* (ἐπιτίθημι, 2007), "to add to, lay upon," etc., is used of "laying" hands on the sick, for healing, Matt. 9:18; 19:13, RV, "lay" (KJV, "put"); 19:15; Mark 5:23; 6:5; 7:32; 8:23, RV, "laid" (KJV, "put"); so in v. 25; 16:18; Luke 4:40; 13:13; Acts 6:6; 8:17, 19; 9:12 and 17, RV, "laying" (KJV, "putting"); 13:3; 19:6; 28:8; in some mss. in Rev. 1:17, see No. 1, (*d*); of "laying" hands on a person by way of public recognition, 1 Tim. 5:22; of a shepherd's "laying" a sheep on his shoulders, Luke 15:5; of "laying" the cross on Christ's shoulders, Luke

23:26; of "laying" on stripes, Acts 16:23; wood on a fire, 28:3; metaphorically, of "laying" burden's on men's shoulders, Matt. 23:4; similarly of "giving" injunctions, Acts 15:28 (cf. "put . . . upon" in v. 10). See LADE, PUT, SET, SURNAME, WOUND.

11. *anatithēmi* (ἀνατίθημι, 394), "to put up or before" (*ana*), is used in the middle voice of "laying" a case before an authority, Acts 25:14, RV, "laid before," for KJV, "declared unto"; of "setting forth" a matter for consideration, Gal. 2:2, RV, "laid before (them the gospel)," for KJV, "communicated unto." See COMMUNICATE, DECLARE.¶

12. *prostithēmi* (προστίθημι, 4369), "to put to, add," is used in the passive voice in Acts 13:36, "was laid" (unto his fathers), of the burial of David. See ADD, No. 2.

13. *ekteinō* (ἐκτείνω, 1614), "to stretch out or forth," especially of the hand, is used of "laying" out anchors from a vessel, in Acts 27:30, RV, "lay out" (KJV, "cast . . . out"). See CAST, *Notes*, STRETCH.

14. *keimai* (κεῖμαι, 2749), "to be laid, to lie," is used as the passive voice of *tithēmi*, "to put," and is translated by some part of the verb "to be laid" in Matt. 3:10 and Luke 3:9, of an axe; Luke 12:19, of goods; John 21:9, where the verb has been omitted from the translation, after the words "a fire of coals" (for *epikeimai*, of the fish, see No. 15); 1 Cor. 3:11, of Christ, as a foundation. See APPOINT, LIE, MADE (be), SET.

Notes: (1) In Luke 23:53, the RV has "had lain" (intransitive: see LIE), for KJV, "was laid." (2) In Luke 24:12, some mss. have the verb, with reference to the linen cloths (the clause is absent in the best mss.); the translation should be "lying," not as KJV, "laid." (3) In John 11:41, the verb is not found in the best mss.

15. *epikeimai* (ἐπίκειμαι, 1945), "to be placed, to lie on" (*epi*, "upon," and No. 14), is translated by the verb "to be laid upon," in John 21:9, of a fish; in 1 Cor. 9:16, of necessity. See IMPOSED, INSTANT, LIE, PRESS.

16. *apokeimai* (ἀπόκειμαι, 606), "to be laid away, or up," is used of money in a napkin, Luke 19:20; metaphorically, of a hope, Col. 1:5; the crown of righteousness, 2 Tim. 4:8. In Heb. 9:27, said of physical death, it is translated "it is appointed" (RV marg., "laid up"). See APPOINT.¶

17. *thēsaurizō* (θησαυρίζω, 2343), "to lay up, store up" (akin to *thēsauros*, "a treasury, a storehouse, a treasure"), is used of "laying" up treasures, on earth, Matt. 6:19; in Heaven, v. 20; in the last days, Jas. 5:3, RV, "ye have laid up your treasure" (KJV, "ye have heaped treasure

together"); in Luke 12:21, "that layeth up treasure (for himself)"; in 1 Cor. 16:2, of money for needy ones (here the present participle is translated "in store," lit. "treasuring" or "storing," the "laying by" translating the preceding verb *tithēmi*, see No. 1); in 2 Cor. 12:14, negatively, of children for parents; metaphorically, of "laying" up wrath, Rom. 2:5, "treasurest up." In 2 Pet. 3:7 the passive voice is used of the heavens and earth as "stored up" for fire, RV (marg., "stored" with fire), KJV, "kept in store." See STORE, TREASURE.¶

18. *trachēlizō* (τραχηλίζω, 5136), "to seize and twist the neck" (from *trachēlos*, "the throat"), was used of wrestlers, in the sense of taking by the throat. The word is found in Heb. 4:13, "laid open," RV (KJV, "opened"). The literal sense of the word seems to be "with the head thrown back and the throat exposed." Various suggestions have been made as to the precise significance of the word in this passage. Some have considered that the metaphor is from the manner of treating victims about to be sacrificed. Little help, however, can be derived from these considerations. The context serves to explain the meaning and the RV rendering is satisfactory.¶

Notes: (1) In Acts 25:7, KJV, *pherō*, "to bear, bring," is rendered "laid ... (complaints)," RV, "bringing ... (charges)." (2) In Mark 7:8, KJV, *aphiēmi*, "to leave," is translated "laying aside" (RV, "ye leave"). (3) For *epilambanō*, "to lay hold," see HOLD, No. 7.

For LAY WAIT see LIE IN WAIT

For LAYING (Acts 9:24) see PLOT

LAY WASTE

lumainomai (λυμαίνομαι, 3075), "to maltreat, to outrage" (from *lumē*, "a brutal outrage"), is translated "laid waste" (the church), in Acts 8:3, RV (KJV, "made havoc of").¶

LAYING ON

epithesis (ἐπίθεσις, 1936), "a laying on" (*epi*, "on," *tithēmi*, "to put"), is used in the NT (*a*) of the "laying" on of hands by the apostles, accompanied by the impartation of the Holy Spirit in outward demonstration, in the cases of those in Samaria who had believed, Acts 8:18; such supernatural manifestations were signs especially intended to give witness to Jews as to the facts of Christ and the faith; they were thus temporary; there is no record of their continuance after the time and circumstances narrated in Acts 19 (in v. 6 of which the corresponding verb *epitithēmi* is used; see below), nor was the gift delegated by the apostles to others (see LAY, Nos. 1 and 10); (*b*) of the similar act by the elders of a church on occasions when a member of a church was set apart for a particular work, having given evidence of qualifications necessary for it, as in the case of Timothy, 1 Tim. 4:14; of the impartation of a spiritual gift through the laying on of the hands of the apostle Paul, 2 Tim. 1:6, RV, "laying" (KJV, "putting"); cf. the verb *epitithēmi* in Acts 6:6, on the appointment of the seven, and in the case of Barnabas and Saul, 13:3; also in 19:6; (*c*) in Heb. 6:2, the doctrine of the "laying" on of hands refers to the act enjoined upon an Israelite in connection, e.g., with the peace offerings, Lev. 3:2, 8, 13; 4:29, 33; upon the priests in connection with the sin offering, 4:4; 16:21; upon the elders, 4:15; upon a ruler, 4:24.¶

The principle underlying the act was that of identification on the part of him who did it with the animal or person upon whom the hands were laid. In the Sept., 2 Chron. 25:27; Ezek. 23:11.¶

Note: For the "laying" of Christ's hands on the sick, see LAY, No. 10.

LEAD, LED

1. *agō* (ἄγω, 71), "to bear, bring, carry, lead," is translated by the verb "to lead," e.g., in Mark 13:11; Luke 4:1; 4:9, RV; 4:29; 22:54; 23:1, KJV only; 23:32; John 18:28 (present tense, RV); Acts 8:32; metaphorically in Rom. 2:4, of the goodness of God; 8:14 and Gal. 5:18, of the Spirit of God; 1 Cor. 12:2, of the powers of darkness instigating to idolatry; 2 Tim. 3:6, of divers lusts (in some mss., *aichmalōteuō*). In Luke 24:21 *agō* is used of the passing (or spending) of a day, and translated "it is (now the third day)"; here the verb is probably to be taken impersonally, according to idiomatic usage, in the sense "there is passing the third day." See BRING, No. 10, KEEP, *Note* (2).

2. *anagō* (ἀνάγω, 321), "to lead up" (*ana*, "up"), is used of Christ in being "led" up by the Spirit into the wilderness, Matt. 4:1; Luke 4:5 (KJV, "taking up"); by the elders of the people into their council, Luke 22:66, "led away." See BRING, No. 11.

3. *apagō* (ἀπάγω, 520), "to lead away" (*apo*, "away"), is used of a way "leading" to destruction, Matt. 7:13; to life, v. 14; of those who "led" Christ away from Gethsemane, Mark 14:44; in some mss., John 18:13,to Annas (the best mss. have No. 1 here); to Caiaphas, Matt. 26:57; Mark 14:53; to Pilate, Matt. 27:2; to the Praetorium, Mark 15:16; to crucifixion, Matt. 27:31; Luke 23:26; in some mss. John 19:16; of "leading" an animal away to watering,

Luke 13:15; of being "led" away to idolatry, 1 Cor. 12:2, RV, "led away" (KJV, "carried away"). Some mss. have it in Acts 24:7 (KJV, "took away"). It is translated "bring" in 23:17. In 12:19 it signifies "to put to death." See BRING, No. 12, DEATH, C, No. 3.¶

4. *periagō* (περιάγω, 4013), used transitively, denotes "to lead about," 1 Cor. 9:5. For the intransitive use, see GO, No. 9.

5. *pherō* (φέρω, 5342), "to bear, carry," is used metaphorically of a gate, as "leading" to a city, Acts 12:10. See BRING, No. 1.

6. *hodēgeō* (ὁδηγέω, 3594), "to lead the way": see GUIDE, B, No. 1.

7. *eisagō* (εἰσάγω, 1521), "to bring into," is translated "to be led into" in Acts 21:37, KJV (RV, "to be brought into"). See BRING, A, No. 13.

8. *sunapagō* (συναπάγω, 4879), always in the passive voice, "to be carried or led away with," is translated "being led away with" in 2 Pet. 3:17, KJV (RV, "being carried away with"). See CARRY.

9. *exagō* (ἐξάγω, 1806), "to lead out," is rendered by the verb "to lead, out or forth," in Mark 15:20 (in some mss. in 8:23, the best have *ekpherō*, "to bring out)"; Luke 24:50; John 10:3; Acts 7:36, 40 (KJV "brought"), and 13:17, RV; Acts 21:38; Heb. 8:9. See BRING, No. 14.

10. *anapherō* (ἀναφέρω, 399), "to carry or lead up," is translated "leadeth . . . up" in the KJV of Mark 9:2 (RV "bringeth . . . up"). See BRING, No. 2.

11. *eispherō* (εἰσφέρω, 1533), "to bring in, or into," is translated "lead (us not) into," in Matt. 6:13 and Luke 11:4 (RV, "bring . . . into"), of temptation. See BRING, No. 4.

12. *planaō* (πλανάω, 4105), "to lead astray" (akin to *planē*, "a wandering"), is translated "lead . . . astray," metaphorically, in Matt. 24:4, 5, 11 and Mark 13:5, 6 (KJV, "deceive").

13. *apoplanaō* (ἀποπλανάω, 635), "to cause to go astray" (*apo*, "away from," and No. 12), is used metaphorically of "leading into error," Mark 13:22, RV, "lead astray" (KJV, "seduce"); passive voice in 1 Tim. 6:10 (KJV, "erred").¶

Notes: (1) In Rev. 13:10, some mss. have *sunagō*, "to bring together," translated "leadeth (into captivity)," KJV and RV marg. (RV text, "is for"). (2) For the verb *diagō*, "to lead a life," 1 Tim. 2:2, see LIVE, No. 7. (3) For *thriambeuō*, to "lead in triumph," 2 Cor. 2:14, RV, see TRIUMPH. (4) See also HAND (lead by the).

For **LEADERS** (Matt. 15:14) see **GUIDE**

LEAF

phullon (φύλλον, 5444), "a leaf" (originally *phulion*, Lat., *folium;* Eng., "folio," "foliaceous," "foliage," "foliate," "folious," etc.), is found in Matt. 21:19; 24:32; Mark 11:13 (twice); 13:28; Rev. 22:2.¶

LEAN

1. *anakeimai* (ἀνάκειμαι, 345), "to be laid up, to lie," is used of reclining at table, and translated "leaning (on Jesus' bosom)" in the KJV of John 13:23, RV, "reclining" (for v. 25 see No. 2). In v. 28, it is translated "at the table," lit., "of (those) reclining." See GUEST, RECLINE, SIT, TABLE (at the).

2. *anapiptō* (ἀναπίπτω, 377), lit., "to fall back" (*ana*, "back," *piptō*, "to fall"), is used of reclining at a repast and translated "leaning back, (as he was, on Jesus' breast)" in John 13:25, RV (the KJV follows the mss. which have *epipiptō*, and renders it "lying"); in 21:20, "leaned back," the apostle's reminder of the same event in his experience. See SIT.

LEAP

1. *hallomai* (ἅλλομαι, 242), "to leap" (akin to *halma*, "a leap"), is used (*a*) metaphorically, of the "springing" up of water, John 4:14; (*b*) literally, of the "leaping" of healed cripples, Acts 3:8 (2nd part); 14:10.¶

2. *skirtaō* (σκιρτάω, 4640), "to leap," is found in Luke 1:41, 44 and 6:23, there translated "leap for joy"; in 1:44 the words "for joy" are expressed separately.¶

3. *exallomai* (ἐξάλλομαι, 1814), "to leap up" (lit., "out," *ek*, and No. 1), is said in Acts 3:8 (1st part) of the cripple healed by Peter (cf. No. 1, above). ¶

4. *ephallomai* (ἐφάλλομαι, 2177), "to leap upon" (*epi*, "upon," and No. 1), is said of the demoniac in Acts 19:16.¶

LEARN, LEARNED (be)

1. *manthanō* (μανθάνω, 3129) denotes (*a*) "to learn" (akin to *mathētēs*, "a disciple"), "to increase one's knowledge," or "be increased in knowledge," frequently "to learn by inquiry, or observation," e.g., Matt. 9:13; 11:29; 24:32; Mark 13:28; John 7:15; Rom. 16:17; 1 Cor. 4:6; 14:35; Phil. 4:9; 2 Tim. 3:14; Rev. 14:3; said of "learning" Christ, Eph. 4:20, not simply the doctrine of Christ, but Christ Himself, a process not merely of getting to know the person but of so applying the knowledge as to walk differently from the rest of the Gentiles; (*b*) "to ascertain," Acts 23:27, RV, "learned" (KJV, "understood"); Gal. 3:2, "This only would

I learn from you," perhaps with a tinge of irony in the enquiry, the answer to which would settle the question of the validity of the new Judaistic gospel they were receiving; (c) "to learn by use and practice, to acquire the habit of, be accustomed to," e.g., Phil. 4:11; 1 Tim. 5:4, 13; Titus 3:14; Heb. 5:8. See UNDERSTAND.

2. *ginōskō* (γινώσκω, 1097), "to know by observation and experience," is translated "to learn," in the RV of Mark 15:45; John 12:9. See ALLOW.

3. *akriboō* (ἀκριβόω, 198), "to learn carefully," is so translated in Matt. 2:7, 16, RV (KJV, "diligently enquired").¶

4. *mueō* (μυέω, 3453), "to initiate into mysteries," is translated "I have learned the secret" (passive voice, perfect tense) in Phil. 4:12, RV (KJV, "I am instructed"). See INSTRUCT.¶

Note: Paideuō, "to teach, instruct, train," is translated "instructed" in Acts 7:22, RV (KJV, "learned"); in 1 Tim. 1:20, "(that) they might be taught," KJV, "(that) they may learn."

LEARNING (Noun)

1. *gramma* (γράμμα, 1121), "a letter," is used in the plural in Acts 26:24, with the meaning "learning": "(thy much) learning (doth turn thee to madness)," RV, possibly an allusion to the Jewish Scriptures, to which the apostle had been appealing; in John 7:15, "(How knoweth this Man) letters" (KJV marg., "learning"), the succeeding phrase "not having learned" is illustrated in the papyri, where it indicates inability to write. See BILL.

2. *didaskalia* (διδασκαλία, 1319), "teaching, instruction" (akin to *didaskō*, "to teach"), is translated "learning" in Rom. 15:4. See DOCTRINE.

LEAST

1. *elachistos* (ἐλάχιστος, 1646), "least," is a superlative degree formed from the word *elachus*, "little," the place of which was taken by *mikros* (the comparative degree being *elassōn*, "less"); it is used of (a) size, Jas. 3:4; (b) amount; of the management of affairs, Luke 16:10 (twice); 19:17, "very little"; (c) importance, 1 Cor. 6:2, "smallest (matters)"; (d) authority: of commandments, Matt. 5:19; (e) estimation, as to persons, Matt. 5:19 (2nd part); 25:40, 45; 1 Cor. 15:9; as to a town, Matt. 2:6; as to activities or operations, Luke 12:26; 1 Cor. 4:3, "a very small thing."¶

2. *elachistoteros* (ἐλαχιστότερος, 1647), a comparative degree formed from No. 1, is used in Eph. 3:8, "less than the least."¶

3. *mikros* (μικρός, 3398), "small, little," is translated "the least" in Acts 8:10 and Heb.

8:11, with reference to rank or influence. See LITTLE, A, No. 1.

4. *mikroteros* (μικρότερος, 3398), the comparative of No. 3, is used of (a) size, Matt. 13:32, KJV, "the least," RV, "less;" Mark 4:31 [cf. No. 1 (a)]; (b) estimation, Matt. 11:11 and Luke 7:28, KJV, "least," RV, "but little," marg., "lesser" (in the kingdom of heaven), those in the kingdom itself being less than John the Baptist [cf. No. 1 (e)]; Luke 9:48. See LESS.¶

Notes: (1) In 1 Cor. 6:4, KJV, *exoutheneō*, in the passive voice, "to be of no account," is translated "is least esteemed" (RV, "are of no account"); see ACCOUNT. (2) In Luke 19:42, the adverbial phrase *kai ge*, "at least," is found in some mss.; the RV follows those in which it is absent. (3) In 1 Cor. 9:2, KJV, the phrase *alla ge* is rendered "doubtless;" RV, "at least." (4) In Acts 5:15, the phrase *k'an* (for *kai ean*, "even if") denotes "at the least."

LEATHER, LEATHERN

dermatinos (δερμάτινος, 1193) denotes "of skin, leather" (from *derma*, "skin, hide of beasts," akin to *derō*, "to flay"; whence Eng., "derm," "dermal," "dermatology"); it is translated "leather" in Matt. 3:4, of John the Baptist's girdle; in Mark 1:6, RV (KJV, "of a skin"). See SKIN.¶

LEAVE, LEFT

(a) *In the sense of leaving, abandoning, forsaking.*

1. *aphiēmi* (ἀφίημι, 863), *apo*, "from," and *hiēmi*, "to send," has three chief meanings, (a) "to send forth, let go, forgive"; (b) "to let, suffer, permit"; (c) "to leave, leave alone, forsake, neglect." It is translated by the verb "to leave" (c), in Matt. 4:11; 4:20, 22, and parallel passages; 5:24; 8:15, and parallel passages; 8:22, RV, "leave (the dead)," KJV, "let," and the parallel passage; 13:36, RV, "left (the multitude)," KJV, "sent . . . away"; 18:12; 19:27, and parallel passages, RV, "we have left" (KJV, "we have forsaken"); so v. 29; 22:22, 25; 23:23, RV, "have left undone" (KJV, "have omitted," in the 1st part, "leave undone" in the second); 23:38, and the parallel passage; 24:2, 40, 41, and parallel passages; 26:56, RV, "left"; Mark 1:18, "left"; 1:31; 7:8, RV, "ye leave"; 8:13; 10:28, 29; 12:12, 19–22; 13:34; Luke 10:30; 11:42 (in some mss.); Luke 12:39, RV "have left," KJV "have suffered" (No. 9 in Matt. 24:43); John 4:3, 28, 52; 8:29; 10:12; 14:18, 27; 16:28, 32; Rom. 1:27; 1 Cor. 7:11, RV, "leave" (KJV "put away"); 7:13 (KJV and RV); Heb 2:8; 6:1; Rev. 2:4. See FORGIVE.

2. *aniēmi* (ἀνίημι, 447), *ana*, "back" and

hiēmi, "to send," denotes "to let go, loosen, forbear"; it is translated "I will (never) leave (thee)" in Heb. 13:5. See FORBEAR.

3. *kataleipō* (καταλείπω, 2641), "to leave behind" (*kata*, "down," *leipō*, "to leave"), is everywhere rendered by the verb "to leave" except in the following: the KJV of Rom. 11:4, "I have reserved" (RV, "I have left"); Heb. 11:27, "he forsook"; 2 Pet. 2:15, KJV, "have forsaken," RV, "forsaking." See FORSAKE, RESERVE.

4. *apoleipō* (ἀπολείπω, 620), "to leave behind" (*apo*, "from"), is used (*a*) in the active voice, of "leaving" behind a cloak, 2 Tim. 4:13; a person, 2 Tim. 4:20; of "abandoning" a principality (by angels), Jude 6, RV; (*b*) in the passive voice, "to be reserved, to remain," Heb. 4:6, 9; 10:26. See REMAIN, No. 3.¶ In the papyri it is used as a technical term in wills (Moulton and Milligan, *Vocab.*).

5. *enkataleipo* (ἐγκαταλείπω, 1459), lit., "to leave behind in" (*en*, "in," and No. 3), signifies (*a*) "to leave behind," Rom. 9:29, "a seed"; (*b*) "to abandon, forsake," translated by the verb "to leave" in Acts 2:27, 31 (in some mss., No. 3) of the soul of Christ; in the following, by the verb "to forsake," Matt. 27:46; Mark 15:34; 2 Cor. 4:9; 2 Tim. 4:10, 16; Heb. 10:25; 13:5 (see No. 2 in the same v.). See FORSAKE.¶

6. *hupoleipō* (ὑπολείπω, 5275), "to leave remaining"; lit., "to leave under" (*hupo*), is used in the passive voice in Rom. 11:3, of a survivor.¶

7. *perileipō* (περιλείπω, 4035), "to leave over," is used in the passive voice in 1 Thess. 4:15, 17, RV, "that are left" (KJV, "that remain"), lit., "left over," i.e., the living believers at the Lord's return. See REMAIN.¶

8. *pauō* (παύω, 3973), "to make to cease," is used in the middle voice, signifying "to cease, leave off," and is translated "had left" in Luke 5:4; "left" in Acts 21:32; elsewhere, "to cease." See CEASE.

9. *eaō* (ἐάω, 1439) signifies (*a*) "to let, permit, suffer," e.g., Matt. 24:43; (*b*) "to leave," Acts 23:32, of "leaving" horsemen; 27:40, of "leaving" anchors in the sea, RV [KJV, "committed (themselves)"]. See COMMIT, SUFFER.

10. *hupolimpanō* (ὑπολιμπάνω, 5277), *limpanō* being a late form for *leipō*, "to leave," is used in 1 Pet. 2:21, "leaving (us an example)."¶

11. *perisseuō* (περισσεύω, 4052), "to be over and above" (the number), hence, "to be or remain over," is translated "was left," in Matt. 15:37, KJV (RV, "remained over," as in 14:20; Luke 9:17; John 6:12 and v. 13, where the KJV adds "and above"), of the broken fragments after the feeding of the multitudes. See ABOUND.

Note: The corresponding noun, *perisseuma*, "that which is over and above," is used in the plural in Mark 8:8, RV, "(of broken pieces) that remained over," KJV, "(of the broken meat) that was left," lit., "of fragments of broken pieces." See REMAIN.

12. *ekballō* (ἐκβάλλω, 1544), "to cast out" (*ek*, "from," *ballō*, "to cast"), "to drive out," is used in the sense of "rejecting" or "leaving out," in Rev. 11:2, as to the measuring of the court of the Temple (marg., "cast without"). See CAST, No. 5.

(*b*) *In the sense of giving leave.*

epitrepō (ἐπιτρέπω, 2010) lit. denotes "to turn to" (*epi*, "upon, to," *trepō*, "to turn"), and so (*a*) "to commit, entrust" (not in NT); (*b*) "to permit, give leave, send," of Christ's permission to the unclean spirits to enter the swine, Mark 5:13; in Luke 8:32, RV, "give ... leave," "gave ... leave" (KJV, "suffer" and "suffered"); in John 19:38, of Pilate's permission to Joseph to take away the body of the Lord; in Acts 21:39, of Paul's request to the chief captain to permit him to address the people, RV, "give ... leave" (for KJV, "suffer"); in 21:40, "he had given him leave" (KJV, " ... licence "). See LET, LIBERTY, LICENCE, PERMIT, SUFFER.

(*c*) *In the sense of taking leave of, bidding farewell to.*

1. *apotassō* (ἀποτάσσω, 657), used in the middle voice in the NT, lit. signifies "to arrange oneself off" (*apo*, "from," *tassō*, "to arrange"); hence, "to take leave of," Mark 6:46, RV, "had taken leave of" (KJV, "had sent ... away"); Acts 18:18; 18:21, RV, "taking his leave of" (KJV, "bade ... farewell"); 2 Cor. 2:13; in Luke 9:61, "to bid farewell"; in Luke 14:33 it has its other meaning "renouncing" (KJV, "forsaking"). See FAREWELL, FORSAKE, RENOUNCE.¶

2. *apaspazomai* (ἀπασπάζομαι), "to embrace, salute, take leave of" (*apo*, "from," *aspazomai*, "to salute"), is used in Acts 21:6, KJV, "when we had taken our leave" (RV, "bade ... farewell"). Some mss. have the simple verb *aspazomai*.¶

LEAVEN (Noun and Verb)

A. Noun.

zumē (ζύμη, 2219), "leaven, sour dough, in a high state of fermentation," was used in general in making bread. It required time to fulfill the process. Hence, when food was required at short notice, unleavened cakes were used, e.g., Gen. 18:6; 19:3; Exod. 12:8. The Israelites were forbidden to use "leaven" for seven days at the time of Passover, that they might be reminded that the Lord brought them out of Egypt "in haste," Deut. 16:3, with Exod. 12:11; the unleavened bread, insipid in taste, reminding them, too, of their afflictions, and of the need of self-judgment, is called "the bread of affliction." "Leaven" was forbidden in all offerings to the Lord by fire, Lev. 2:11; 6:17. Being bred of corruption and spreading through the mass of that in which it is mixed, and therefore symbolizing the pervasive character of evil, "leaven" was utterly inconsistent in offerings which typified the propitiatory sacrifice of Christ.

In the OT "leaven" is not used in a metaphorical sense. In the NT it is used (*a*) metaphorically (1) of corrupt doctrine, Matt. 13:33 and Luke 13:21, of error as mixed with the truth (there is no valid reason for regarding the symbol here differently from its application elsewhere in the NT); Matt. 16:6, 11; Mark 8:15 (1st part); Luke 12:1; that the kingdom of heaven is likened to "leaven," does not mean that the kingdom is "leaven." The same statement, as made in other parables, shows that it is the whole parable which constitutes the similitude of the kingdom; the history of Christendom confirms the fact that the pure meal of the doctrine of Christ has been adulterated with error; (2) of corrupt practices, Mark 8:15 (2nd part), the reference to the Herodians being especially applied to their irreligion; 1 Cor. 5:7, 8; (*b*) literally, in Matt. 16:12, and in the general statements in 1 Cor. 5:6 and Gal. 5:9, where the implied applications are to corrupt practice and corrupt doctrine respectively.¶

B. Verb.

zumoō (ζυμόω, 2220) signifies "to leaven, to act as leaven," passive voice in Matt. 13:33 and Luke 13:21; active voice in 1 Cor. 5:6 and Gal. 5:9.¶

For **LED** see **LEAD**

LEE

Note: This forms part of the RV rendering of two verbs, (1) *hupopleō*, "to sail under" (i.e., under the lee of), from *hupo*, "under," *pleō*, "to sail," Acts 27:4, 7 (KJV, "sailed under");¶ (2) *hupotrechō*, "to run in under" (in navigation), "to run under the lee of" (*hupo*, and a form *hupodramōn*, used as an aorist participle of the verb), Acts 27:16, RV, "running under the lee of" (KJV, "running under"). See RUN, SAIL.¶

For **LEFT** (Verb) see **LEAVE**

LEFT (Adjective)

1. *aristeros* (ἀριστερός, 710), is used (*a*) of the "left" hand, in Matt. 6:3, the word "hand" being understood; in connection with the armor of righteousness, in 2 Cor. 6:7, "(on the right hand and) on the left," lit., "(of the weapons . . . the right and) the left"; (*b*) in the phrase "on the left," formed by *ex* (for *ek*), "from," and the genitive plural of this adjective, Mark 10:37 (some mss. have No. 2 here); Luke 23:33.¶

2. *euōnumos* (εὐώνυμος, 2176), lit., "of good name," or "omen" (*eu*, "well," *onoma*, "a name"), a word adopted to avoid the ill-omen attaching to the "left" (omens from the "left" being unlucky, but a good name being desired for them, cf. *aristeros*, lit., "better of two," euphemistic for the ill-omened *laios* and *skaios;* cf., too, the Eng., "sinister," from the Latin word meaning "left"), is used euphemistically for No. 1, either (*a*) simply as an adjective in Rev. 10:2, of the "left" foot; in Acts 21:3, "on the left" (lit., "left"); or (*b*) with the preposition *ex* (for *ek*), signifying "on the left hand," Matt. 20:21, 23; 25:33, 41; 27:38; Mark 10:40 (for v. 37, in some mss., see No. 1); 15:27.¶

LEG

skelos (σκέλος, 4628), "the leg from the hip downwards," is used only of the breaking of the "legs" of the crucified malefactors, to hasten their death, John 19:31–33 (a customary act, not carried out in the case of Christ, in fulfillment of Exod. 12:46; Num. 9:12). The practice was known as *skelokopia* (from *koptō*, "to strike"), or, in Latin, *crurifragium* (from *crus*, "a leg," and *frango*, "to break").¶

LEGION

legiōn (λεγιών, 3003), otherwise spelled *legeōn*, "a legion," occurs in Matt. 26:53, of angels; in Mark 5:9, 15, and Luke 8:30, of demons. Among the Romans a "legion" was primarily a chosen (*lego*, "to choose") body of soldiers divided into ten cohorts, and numbering from 4,200 to 6,000 men (Gk. *speira*, see BAND). In the time of our Lord it formed a complete army of infantry and cavalry, of upwards of 5,000 men. The "legions" were not brought into Judea till the outbreak of the Jewish war (A.D. 66), as they were previously employed in the frontier provinces of the Empire. Accordingly in its NT use the word has its other and more general significance "of a large number."¶

LEISURE (to have)

eukaireō (εὐκαιρέω, 2119), "to have leisure or opportunity" (*eu*, "well," *kairos*, "a time or season"), is translated "they had . . . leisure" in Mark 6:31; in Acts 17:21, "spent their time" (RV, marg., "had leisure for"); in 1 Cor. 16:12, "he shall have opportunity," RV (KJV, " . . . convenient time"). See CONVENIENT, OPPORTUNITY,

SPEND.¶ This verb differs from *scholazō*, "to have leisure"; it stresses the opportunity of doing something, whereas *scholazō* stresses the "leisure" for engaging in it, e.g., 1 Cor. 7:5, "(that) ye may give yourselves to."

LEND, LENDER

A. Verbs.

1. *daneizō* (δανείζω, 1155v) is translated "to lend" in Luke 6:34, 35: see BORROW.

2. *kichrēmi* (κίχρημι, 5531v), or *chraō* (χράω, 5531), "to lend," is used in the aorist (or "point") tense, active voice, in Luke 11:5, in the request, "lend me three loaves." The radical sense of the verb is "to furnish what is needful" (akin to *chreia*, which means both "use" and "need," and to *chrē*, "it is needful"). Hence it is distinct from No. 1, the basic idea of which is to "lend" on security or return.¶

B. Noun.

danistēs or *daneistēs* (δανειστής, 1157) denotes a moneylender (akin to A, No. 1), translated "lender" in Luke 7:41, RV (KJV, "creditor").¶ In the Sept., 2 Kings 4:1; Ps. 109:11; Prov. 29:13.¶

LENGTH

mēkos (μῆκος, 3372), "length," from the same root as *makros*, "long" (see FAR, LONG), occurs in Eph. 3:18 and Rev. 21:16 (twice).¶

LENGTH (at)

pote (ποτέ, 4218) is translated "at length" in Rom. 1:10, where the whole phrase "if by any means now at length" suggests not only ardent desire but the existence of difficulties for a considerable time. See AFORETIME.

LEOPARD

pardalis (πάρδαλις, 3917) denotes "a leopard or a panther," an animal characterized by swiftness of movement and sudden spring, in Dan. 7:6 symbolic of the activities of Alexander the Great, and the formation of the Grecian kingdom, the third seen in the vision there recorded. In Rev. 13:2 the imperial power, described there also as a "beast," is seen to concentrate in himself the characteristics of those mentioned in Dan. 7.¶

LEPER

lepros (λεπρός, 3015), an adjective, primarily used of "psoriasis," characterized by an eruption of rough, scaly patches; later, "leprous," but chiefly used as a noun, "a leper," Matt. 8:2; 10:8; 11:5; Mark 1:40; Luke 4:27; 7:22; 17:12; especially of Simon, mentioned in Matt. 26:6; Mark 14:3.¶

LEPROSY

lepra (λέπρα, 3014), akin to *lepros* (above), is mentioned in Matt. 8:3; Mark 1:42; Luke 5:12, 13.¶ In the removal of other maladies the verb "to heal" (*iaomai*) is used, but in the removal of "leprosy," the verb "to cleanse" (*katharizō*), save in the statement concerning the Samaritan, Luke 17:15, "when he saw that he was healed." Matt. 10:8 and Luke 4:27 indicate that the disease was common in the nation. Only twelve cases are recorded in the NT, but these are especially selected. For the Lord's commands to the leper mentioned in Matthew 8 and to the ten in Luke 17, see Lev. 14:2–32.

LESS

1. *elassōn* (ἐλάσσων, 1640) serves as a comparative degree of *mikros*, "little" (see LEAST), and denotes "less" in (*a*) quality, as of wine, John 2:10, "worse;" (*b*) age, Rom. 9:12, "younger"; 1 Tim. 5:9, "under" neuter, adverbially); (*c*) rank, Heb. 7:7. See UNDER, WORSE, YOUNG.¶

2. *mikroteros* (μικρότερος, 3398), the comparative of *mikros*, is translated "less" in Matt. 13:32, RV (KJV, "least"), and Mark 4:31. See LEAST.

3. *hēssōn* (ἥσσων, 2276), "inferior," is used in the neuter adverbially in 2 Cor. 12:15, "the less." See WORSE.

LEST

1. *mē* (μή, 3361), a negative particle, often used as a conjunction, is frequently translated "lest," e.g., Mark 13:36 (in v. 5, RV, "that no," for KJV, "lest"); Acts 13:40; 23:10.

2. *hina mē* (ἵνα μή), "in order that not," is rendered "lest," e.g., in Matt. 17:27; in some instances the RV renders the phrase "that ... not," e.g., Luke 8:12, or "that ... no," 1 Cor. 9:12 (KJV, "lest").

3. *mēpote* or *mē pote* (μήποτε, 3379) denotes "lest ever, lest perhaps, lest at any time," e.g., Matt. 4:6; "lest haply," Matt. 7:6, RV (KJV, "lest"), and in 13:15 (KJV, "lest at any time"); in 25:9, RV, "peradventure" (KJV, "lest"). The RV does not translate this simply by "lest," as in the KJV; see further, e.g., in Matt. 27:64; Mark 14:2; Luke 12:58; the addition of *pote* requires the fuller rendering.

Note: In Luke 14:29, the conjunctive phrase *hina mēpote*, "lest haply," is used.

4. *mēpōs*, or *mē pōs* (μήπως, 3381), used as a conjunction, denotes "lest somehow, lest haply, lest by any means," e.g., 2 Cor. 2:7, RV, "lest by any means" (KJV, "lest perhaps"); so

12:20 (twice) and Gal. 4:11 (KJV, "lest"); in 1 Thess. 3:5 (KJV, "lest by some means").

5. *mēpou*, or *mē pou* (μήπου, 3361 and 4225), "lest perhaps," is used in Acts 27:29, RV, "lest haply" (KJV, "lest").

Note: In 2 Cor. 4:4, KJV, the phrase *eis* ("unto") *to* ("the") *mē* ("not"), i.e., "in order that... not," is rendered "lest (the light)... should"; RV, "that (the light)... should not."

LET (alone, go)

1. *aphiēmi* (ἀφίημι, 863), for the meanings of which see LEAVE, No. 1, frequently denotes "to let, suffer, permit," e.g., Matt. 5:40 (translated "let... have"); 7:4; 13:30; 15:14; 27:49 and Mark 15:36, RV, "let be," probably short for "let us see" (Moulton and Milligan, *Vocab.*); Mark 7:27; 11:6 ("let... go"); 14:6 ("let... alone"); so Luke 13:8; John 11:48; in Acts 5:38 (where some mss. have *eaō*, "to permit, let, suffer"); in John 11:44 and 18:8 ("let"); 1 Cor. 7:11, 12, RV, "let... leave," KJV, "let... put away"; 7:13 ("let... leave").

2. *epitrepō* (ἐπιτρέπω, 2010), for the meanings of which see LEAVE (*b*), is translated "let (me)" in Luke 9:61, KJV, RV, "suffer (me)."

3. *apoluō* (ἀπολύω, 630) signifies "to set free, release, loose" (*apo*, "from," *luō*, "to loose"), e.g., Luke 13:12; John 19:10; forgive, Luke 6:37; to release, dismiss, send away, translated "to let go," e.g., in Luke 14:4; in some mss. 22:68; in Luke 23:22, John 19:12 and Acts 3:13, KJV, "let... go" (RV, "release"); in Acts 4:21, "they let... go"; in v. 23 (passive voice), "being let go"; 5:40; in 15:33, KJV, "let go" (RV, "dismissed"); 16:35, 36; 17:9; in 23:22, RV, "let... go" (KJV, "let... depart"); in 28:18, KJV, "let... go" (RV, "set... at liberty"). See DISMISS.

4. *eaō* (ἐάω, 1439), "to let," occurs in Acts 27:32. See SUFFER.

Note: In Acts 2:29, the impersonal verb *exesti*, "it is permitted, it is lawful," is rendered "let me," KJV (RV and KJV, marg., "I may").

For **LET** (KJV in Rom. 1:13 and 2 Thess. 2:7) see **HINDER** and **RESTAIN**

LET DOWN

1. *kathiēmi* (καθίημι, 2524), "to send," or "let down" (*kata*, "down," *hiēmi*, "to send"), is translated "to let down," with reference to (*a*) the paralytic in Luke 5:19; (*b*) Saul of Tarsus, Acts 9:25; (*c*) the great sheet in Peter's vision, 10:11 and 11:5.¶

2. *chalaō* (χαλάω, 5465), "to slacken, loosen, let loose," denotes in the NT, "to let down, to lower"; it is used with reference to (*a*) the paralytic, in Mark 2:4, cf. No. 1 (*a*); (*b*) Saul of Tarsus, Acts 9:25, "lowering" [see also No. 1 (*b*)]; 2 Cor. 11:33, "was I let down" (passive voice); (*c*) nets, Luke 5:4, 5 (in the latter, RV, "nets"; KJV, "net"); (*d*) the gear of a ship, Acts 27:17, RV, "they lowered (the gear)," KJV, "they strake (sail)"; (*e*) a ship's boat, v. 30, RV, "lowered" (KJV, "let down"). See LOWER, STRIKE.¶

LET OUT

ekdidōmi (ἐκδίδωμι, 1554), primarily, "to give out, give up, surrender" (*ek*, "out, from," *didōmi*, "to give"), denotes "to let out for hire"; in the NT it is used, in the middle voice, with the meaning "to let out to one's advantage," in the parable of the husbandman and his vineyard, Matt. 21:33, 41; Mark 12:1; Luke 20:9, KJV, "let... forth"; RV, "let... out."¶

LETTER

1. *gramma* (γράμμα, 1121) primarily denotes "that which is traced or drawn, a picture"; then, "that which is written," (*a*) "a character, letter of the alphabet," 2 Cor. 3:7; "written," lit., "(in) letters"; Gal. 6:11; here the reference is not to the length of the epistle (Paul never uses *gramma*, either in the singular or the plural of his epistles; of these he uses *epistolē*, No. 2), but to the size of the characters written by his own hand (probably from this verse to the end, as the use of the past tense, "I have written," is, according to Greek idiom, the equivalent of our "I am writing"). Moreover, the word for "letters" is here in the dative case, *grammasin*, "with (how large) letters"; (*b*) "a writing, a written document, a bond" (KJV, "bill") Luke 16:6, 7; (*c*) "a letter, by way of correspondence," Acts 28:21; (*d*) the Scriptures of the OT, 2 Tim. 3:15; (*e*) "learning," John 7:15, "letters"; Acts 26:24, "(much) learning" (lit., "many letters"); in the papyri an illiterate person is often spoken of as one who does not know "letters," "which never means anything else than inability to write" (Moulton and Milligan); (*f*) "the letter," the written commandments of the Word of God, in contrast to the inward operation of the Holy Spirit under the New Covenant, Rom. 2:27, 29; 7:6; 2 Cor. 3:6; (*g*) "the books of Moses," John 5:47.¶

2. *epistolē* (ἐπιστολή, 1992): see EPISTLE.

For **LEVEL** see **PLACE,** *Note* (4)

For **LEWD** and **LEWDNESS** see **VILE** and **VILLANY**

LIAR

A. Nouns.

pseustēs (ψεύστης, 5583), "a liar," occurs in John 8:44, 55; Rom. 3:4; 1 Tim. 1:10; Titus 1:12; 1 John 1:10; 2:4, 22; 4:20; 5:10.¶

B. Adjective.

pseudēs (ψευδής, 5571), "lying, false" (Eng., "pseudo-"), rendered "false" in Acts 6:13 and in the RV of Rev. 2:2 (KJV, "liars"), is used as a noun, "liars," in Rev. 21:8. See FALSE.¶

Note: Many compound nouns are formed by the prefix *pseudo-*: see, e.g., APOSTLES, BRETHREN, CHRISTS, PROPHETS, TEACHERS, WITNESS.

LIBERAL, LIBERALITY, LIBERALLY

A. Noun.

1. *haplotēs* (ἁπλοτής, 572) denotes (*a*) "simplicity, sincerity, unaffectedness" (from *haplous*, "single, simple," in contrast to *diplous*, "double"), Rom. 12:8, "simplicity"; 2 Cor. 11:3 (in some mss. in 1:12); Eph. 6:5 and Col. 3:22, singleness"; (*b*) "simplicity as manifested in generous giving," "liberality," 2 Cor. 8:2; 9:11 (KJV, "bountifulness," RV marg., "singleness"); 9:13 (KJV, "liberal"). See BOUNTY, No. 2.¶

2. *charis* (χάρις, 5485) is rendered "liberality" in 1 Cor. 16:3, KJV. See BOUNTY, No. 3.

B. Adverb.

haplōs (ἁπλῶς, 574), "liberally, with singleness of heart," is used in Jas. 1:5 of God as the gracious and "liberal" Giver. The word may be taken either (*a*) in a logical sense, signifying unconditionally, simply, or (*b*) in a moral sense, generously; for the double meaning compare A, No. 1.¶ On this passage Hort writes as follows: "Later writers comprehend under the one word the whole magnanimous and honorable type of character in which singleness of mind is the central feature."

LIBERTY

A. Nouns.

1. *anesis* (ἄνεσις, 425), "a loosening, relaxation," is translated "liberty" in Acts 24:23, KJV. See INDULGENCE.

2. *aphesis* (ἄφεσις, 859), "dismissal, release, forgiveness," is rendered "liberty" in the KJV of Luke 4:18, RV, "release." See FORGIVENESS.

3. *eleutheria* (ἐλευθερία, 1657): see FREEDOM.

4. *exousia* (ἐξουσία, 1849), "authority, right," is rendered "liberty" in 1 Cor. 8:9 (marg., "power"), "this liberty of yours," or "this right which you assert." See AUTHORITY.

B. Adjective.

eleutheros (ἐλεύθερος, 1658) is rendered "at liberty" in 1 Cor. 7:39, KJV (RV "free"). See FREE.

C. Verbs.

1. *apoluō* (ἀπολύω, 630), for the meanings of which see LET, No. 3, is translated "to set at liberty" in Acts 26:32 and Heb. 13:23. See DISMISS.

2. *apostellō* (ἀποστέλλω, 649), "to send away," is translated "to set at liberty" in Luke 4:18. See SEND.

Note: In Acts 27:3, KJV, *epitrepō* is rendered "gave . . . liberty" (RV "gave . . . leave"). See LEAVE (*b*).

For **LICENCE** (in Acts 21:40 and 25:16, KJV) see **LEAVE** (*b*) and **OPPORTUNITY**, A, No. 3

LICK

epileichō (ἐπιλείχω, 1952a), "to lick over" (*epi*, "over," *leichō*, "to lick"), is said of the dogs in Luke 16:21. Some mss. have *apoleichō*, "to lick off."¶

LIE (falsehood: Noun and Verb)

A. Nouns.

1. *pseudos* (ψεῦδος, 5579), "a falsehood, lie" (see also under LIAR), is translated "lie" in John 8:44 (lit., "the lie"); Rom. 1:25, where it stands by metonymy for an idol, as, e.g., in Isa. 44:20; Jer. 10:14; 13:25; Amos 2:4 (plural); 2 Thess. 2:11, with special reference to the lie of v. 4, that man is God (cf. Gen. 3:5); 1 John 2:21, 27; Rev. 21:27; 22:15; in Eph. 4:25, KJV "lying," RV, "falsehood," the practice; in Rev. 14:5, RV, "lie." (some mss. have *dolos*, "guile," KJV); 2 Thess. 2:9, where "lying wonders" is, lit., "wonders of falsehood," i.e., wonders calculated to deceive (cf. Rev. 13:13–15), the purpose being to deceive people into the acknowledgement of the spurious claim to deity on the part of the Man of Sin.¶

Note: In Rom. 1:25 the "lie" or idol is the outcome of pagan religion; in 1 John 2:21, 22 the "lie" is the denial that Jesus is the Christ; in 2 Thess. 2:11 the "lie" is the claim of the Man of Sin.

2. *pseusma* (ψεῦσμα, 5582), "a falsehood," or "an acted lie," Rom. 3:7, where "my lie" is not idolatry, but either the universal false attitude of man toward God or that with which his detractors charged the apostle; the former seems to be the meaning.¶

B. Adjectives.

1. *pseudologos* (ψευδολόγος, 5573) denotes "speaking falsely" (*pseudēs*, "false," *logos*, "a word") in 1 Tim. 4:2, where the adjective is translated "that speak lies," RV (KJV, "speaking lies") and is applied to "demons," the actual utterances being by their human agents.¶

2. *apseudēs* (ἀψευδής, 893) denotes "free from falsehood" (*a*, negative, *pseudēs*, "false"), truthful, Titus 1:2, of God, "who cannot lie."¶

C. Verb.

pseudō (ψεύδω, 5574), "to deceive by lies" (always in the middle voice in the NT), is used (*a*) absolutely, in Matt. 5:11, "falsely," lit., "lying" (KJV, marg.); Rom. 9:1; 2 Cor. 11:31; Gal. 1:20; Col. 3:9 (where the verb is followed by the preposition *eis*, "to"); 1 Tim. 2:7; Heb. 6:18; Jas. 3:14 (where it is followed by the preposition *kata*, "against"); 1 John 1:6; Rev. 3:9; (*b*) transitively, with a direct object (without a preposition following), Acts 5:3 (with the accusative case), "to lie to (the Holy Ghost)," RV marg., "deceive"; v. 4 (with the dative case) "thou hast (not) lied (unto men, but unto God)."¶

LIE (to lie down, on, upon)

1. *keimai* (κεῖμαι, 2749), "to be laid, to lie," used as the passive voice of *tithēmi*, "to lay" (see LAY, No. 14), is said (*a*) of the Child Jesus, Luke 2:12, 16; (*b*) of the dead body of the Lord, Matt. 28:6; John 20:12; in Luke 23:53, "had ... lain," RV, KJV, "was laid" [see LAY, No. 14, *Note* (1)], in the tomb as hitherto empty; (*c*) of the linen cloths, John 20:5, 6, 7; (*d*) figuratively of a veil as "lying" upon the hearts of the Jews, 2 Cor. 3:15, RV, "lieth" (KJV, "is"); (*e*) metaphorically, of the world as "lying" in the evil one, 1 John 5:19, RV; (*f*) of the heavenly city, Rev. 21:16. For other instances in which the rendering is in the passive voice, see LAY, No. 14. See APPOINT.

2. *katakeimai* (κατάκειμαι, 2621), "to lie down" (*kata*, "down," and No. 1), is used of the sick, Mark 1:30; 2:4; Luke 5:25; John 5:3, 6; Acts 28:8; in Acts 9:33 it is rendered "had kept (his bed)," lit., "lying (on a bed)." See SIT.

3. *ballō* (βάλλω, 906), "to throw, cast," is used in the passive voice, with reference to the sick, with the meaning "to be laid, to lie," in Matt. 8:6, "(my servant) lieth (in the house)," lit., "is laid"; 8:14, "lying," RV, (KJV, "laid"); 9:2, "lying (on a bed)." See CAST.

4. *epikeimai* (ἐπίκειμαι, 1945), "to lie upon, be laid upon," is translated with this meaning, intransitively in John 11:38 and Acts 27:20; transitively, in the passive voice, in John 21:9 and 1 Cor. 9:16. See IMPOSED.

Notes: (1) In Mark 5:40, some mss. have the verb *anakeimai*, "to be laid up," translated "was lying," KJV. In the most authentic the word is absent. (2) In Acts 27:12, KJV, *blepō*, "to look," is rendered "lieth," of the situation of the haven Phoenix (KJV, Phenice); RV, "looketh." (3) In John 11:17, KJV, the verb *echō*, "to have, to hold," used with *en*, "in," signifying "to be in a certain condition," is translated "had *lain*" (RV, "*had been*"). (4) In John 13:25, *anapiptō*, lit., to fall back (some mss. have *epipiptō*, lit., "to fall upon," hence the KJV, "lying"), is used of John's position at the table, RV, "leaning back (... on Jesus' breast)."

LIE IN WAIT

A. Verb.

enedreuō (ἐνεδρεύω, 1748), "to lie in wait for, to lay wait for" (from *en*, "in," and *hedra*, "a seat," cf. B), occurs in Luke 11:54, "laying wait for"; Acts 23:21, "there lie in wait for."¶

Note: In Acts 23:30, the word *epiboulē*, "a plot," necessitates the RV "(that there would be) a plot." For Eph. 4:14, KJV, see WILES.

B. Noun.

enedra or *enedron* (ἐνέδρα, 1747, 1749), akin to A, "a lying in wait, an ambush," occurs in Acts 23:16 (where some mss. have the form *enedron*); 25:3, "laying wait," lit., "making an ambush."¶ In the Sept., Josh. 8:7, 9; Ps. 10:8.¶

LIFE, LIVING, LIFETIME, LIFE-GIVING

A. Nouns.

1. *zōē* (ζωή, 2222) (Eng., "zoo," "zoology") is used in the NT "of life as a principle, life in the absolute sense, life as God has it, that which the Father has in Himself, and which He gave to the Incarnate Son to have in Himself, John 5:26, and which the Son manifested in the world, 1 John 1:2. From this life man has become alienated in consequence of the Fall, Eph. 4:18, and of this life men become partakers through faith in the Lord Jesus Christ, John 3:15, who becomes its Author to all such as trust in Him, Acts 3:15, and who is therefore said to be 'the life' of the believer, Col. 3:4, for the life that He gives He maintains, John 6:35, 63. Eternal life is the present actual possession of the believer because of his relationship with Christ, John 5:24; 1 John 3:14, and that it will one day extend its domain to the sphere of the body is assured by the Resurrection of Christ, 2 Cor. 5:4; 2 Tim. 1:10. This life is not merely a principle of power and mobility, however, for it has moral associations which are inseparable from it, as of holiness and righteousness. Death

and sin, life and holiness, are frequently contrasted in the Scriptures.

"*Zōē* is also used of that which is the common possession of all animals and men by nature, Acts 17:25; 1 John 5:16, and of the present sojourn of man upon the earth with reference to its duration, Luke 16:25; 1 Cor. 15:19; 1 Tim. 4:8; 1 Pet. 3:10. 'This life' is a term equivalent to 'the gospel,' 'the faith,' 'Christianity,' Acts 5:20."*

Death came through sin, Rom. 5:12, which is rebellion against God. Sin thus involved the forfeiting of the "life." "The life of the flesh is in the blood," Lev. 17:11. Therefore the impartation of "life" to the sinner must be by a death caused by the shedding of that element which is the life of the flesh. "It is the blood that maketh atonement by reason of the life" (*id.*, RV). The separation from God caused by the forfeiting of the "life" could be removed only by a sacrifice in which the victim and the offerer became identified. This which was appointed in the typical offerings in Israel received its full accomplishment in the voluntary sacrifice of Christ. The shedding of the blood in the language of Scripture involves the taking or the giving of the "life." Since Christ had no sins of his own to die for, His death was voluntary and vicarious, John 10:15 with Isa. 53:5, 10, 12; 2 Cor. 5:21. In His sacrifice He endured the divine judgment due to man's sin. By this means the believer becomes identified with Him in His deathless "life," through His resurrection, and enjoys conscious and eternal fellowship with God.

2. *bios* (βίος, 979) (cf. Eng. words beginning with *biō*), is used in three respects (*a*) of "the period or duration of life," e.g., in the KJV of 1 Pet. 4:3, "the time past of our life" (the RV follows the mss. which omit "of our life"); Luke 8:14; 2 Tim. 2:4; (*b*) of "the manner of life, life in regard to its moral conduct," 1 Tim. 2:2; 1 John 2:16; (*c*) of "the means of life, livelihood, maintenance, living," Mark 12:44; Luke 8:43; 15:12, 30; 21:4; 1 John 3:17, "goods," RV (KJV, "good"). See GOODS.¶

Note: "While *zōē* is 'life' intensive ... *bios* is 'life' extensive.... In *bios*, used as manner of 'life,' there is an ethical sense often inhering which, in classical Greek at least, *zōē* does not possess." In Scripture *zōē* is "the nobler word, expressing as it continually does, all of highest and best which the saints possess in God" (Trench, *Syn.* §xxvii).

3. *psuchē* (ψυχή, 5590), besides its meanings, "heart, mind, soul," denotes "life" in two chief respects, (*a*) "breath of life, the natural life," e.g., Matt. 2:20; 6:25; Mark 10:45; Luke 12:22; Acts 20:10; Rev. 8:9; 12:11 (cf. Lev. 17:11; Esth. 8:11); (*b*) "the seat of personality," e.g., Luke 9:24, explained in v. 25 as "own self." See list under SOUL. See also HEART, MIND.

Notes: (1) "Speaking generally, *psuchē*, is the individual life, the living being, whereas *zōē*, is the life of that being, cf. Ps. 66:9, 'God ... which holdeth our soul (*psuchē*) in life (*zōē*),' and John 10:10, 'I came that they may have life (*zōē*),' with v. 11, 'The Good Shepherd layeth down His life (*psuchē*) for the sheep.'"† (2) In Rev. 13:15, KJV, *pneuma*, "breath," is translated "life" (RV, "breath"). (3) In 2 Cor. 1:8, "we despaired even of life," the verb *zaō*, "to live," is used in the infinitive mood, as a noun, and translated "life" (lit., "living"). In Heb. 2:15 the infinitive mood of the same verb is translated "lifetime."

4. *biōsis* (βίωσις, 981), from *bioō*, "to spend one's life, to live," denotes "a manner of life," Acts 26:4.¶

5. *agōgē* (ἀγωγή, 72), "a manner of life," 2 Tim. 3:10; see CONDUCT.

6. *anastrophe* (ἀναστροφή, 391), "behavior, conduct," is translated "manner of life" (KJV "conversation") in the RV of Gal. 1:13; 1 Tim. 4:12; 1 Pet. 1:18; 3:16; "living," in 1 Pet. 1:15. See BEHAVIOR.

B. Adjectives.

1. *biōtikos* (βιωτικός, 982), "pertaining to life" (*bios*), is translated "of this life," in Luke 21:34, with reference to cares; in 1 Cor. 6:3, "(things) that pertain to this life," and v. 4, "(things) pertaining to this life," i.e., matters of this world, concerning which Christians at Corinth were engaged in public lawsuits one with another; such matters were to be regarded as relatively unimportant in view of the great tribunals to come under the jurisdiction of saints hereafter. Moulton and Milligan (*Vocab.*) illustrate the word from phrases in the papyri, e.g., "business (documents)"; "business concerning my livelihood"; "(stories) of ordinary life."¶

2. *apsuchos* (ἄψυχος, 895) denotes "lifeless, inanimate" (*a*, negative, and *psuchē*, see A, No. 3), "without life," 1 Cor. 14:7.¶

C. Verb.

zōopoieō (ζωοποιέω, 2227), "to make alive, cause to live, quicken" (from *zōē*, "life," and *poieō*, "to make"), is used as follows:

"(*a*) of God as the bestower of every kind of life in the universe, 1 Tim. 6:13 (*zōogoneō*, to

---

* From *Notes on Galatians*, by Hogg and Vine. pp. 324–325.

† From *Notes on Thessalonians*, by Hogg and Vine, p. 325.

preserve alive, is the alternative reading adopted by most editors; see LIVE, No. 6), and, particularly, of resurrection life, John 5:21; Rom. 4:17; (*b*) of Christ, who also is the bestower of resurrection life, John 5:21 (2nd part); 1 Cor. 15:45; cf. v. 22; (*c*) of the resurrection of Christ in "the body of His glory," 1 Pet. 3:18; (*d*) of the power of reproduction inherent in seed, which presents a certain analogy with resurrection, 1 Cor. 15:36; (*e*) of the 'changing,' or 'fashioning anew,' of the bodies of the living, which corresponds with, and takes place at the same time as, the resurrection of the dead in Christ, Rom. 8:11; (*f*) of the impartation of spiritual life, and the communication of spiritual sustenance generally, John 6:63; 2 Cor. 3:6; Gal. 3:21."¶* See QUICKEN, and cf. *sunzōopoieō*, "to quicken together with," Eph. 2:5 and Col. 2:13.¶

Notes: (1) For the verb *diagō*, "to lead a life," see LIVE, No. 7. (2) For *politeuō*, in Phil. 1:27, RV, "let your manner of life be," see LIVE, No. 8.

LIFT

1. *egeirō* (ἐγείρω, 1453), "to awaken, raise up," is used in Matt. 12:11, of "lifting" a sheep out of a pit. In the following the RV has "raised" for KJV, "lifted": Mark 1:31; 9:27; Acts 3:7. See ARISE, AWAKE, RAISE.

2. *airō* (αἴρω, 142) signifies (*a*) "to raise, take up, lift, draw up," (*b*) "to bear, carry," (*c*) "to take or carry away." It is used of "lifting" up the voice, Luke 17:13; Acts 4:24; eyes, John 11:41; hand, Rev. 10:5. See AWAY, BEAR, CARRY, DOUBT, A, No. 6, LOOSE, PUT, No. 17, REMOVE, TAKE.

3. *epairō* (ἐπαίρω, 1869), "to lift up, raise" (*epi*, "upon," and No. 2), is used of "lifting" up the eyes, Matt. 17:8; Luke 6:20; 16:23; 18:13; John 4:35; 6:5; 17:1; the head, Luke 21:28; the hands, Luke 24:50; 1 Tim. 2:8; the voice, Luke 11:27; Acts 2:14; 14:11; 22:22; a foresail, Acts 27:40 ("hoisting," RV); metaphorically, of the heel, John 13:18, as of one "lifting" up the foot before kicking; the expression indicates contempt and violence; in the passive voice, Acts 1:9, of Christ's ascension, "was taken up"; 2 Cor. 10:5, "is exalted" (with pride); 11:20, "exalteth himself." See EXALT, HOIST, TAKE.¶

4. *hupsoō* (ὑψόω, 5312), "to lift or raise up" (akin to *hupsos*, "height"), is rendered by the verb "to lift up" in John 3:14, of the brazen serpent; of Christ in crucifixion (*id.*), and 8:28; 12:32, 34; metaphorically, "to exalt, lift up,"

e.g., Jas. 4:10, KJV, "shall lift . . . up," RV, "shall exalt." See EXALT.

5. *anistēmi* (ἀνίστημι, 450), "to raise up" (*ana*, "up," *histēmi*, "to cause to stand"), is translated "lifted (her) up," in Acts 9:41, KJV; RV, "raised (her) up." See ARISE, RAISE.

6. *anorthoō* (ἀνορθόω, 461), "to set upright" (*ana*, "up," *orthos*, "straight"), is used of "lifting" up "hands that hang down," Heb. 12:12; of setting up a building, restoring ruins, Acts 15:16 (cf., e.g., 2 Sam. 7:13, 16; 1 Chron. 17:12; Jer. 10:12; often so used in the papyri); of the healing of the woman with a spirit of infirmity, Luke 13:13, "was made straight" (for v. 11, see No. 7). See SET, STRAIGHT.¶

7. *anakuptō* (ἀνακύπτω, 352), "to lift oneself up," is used (*a*) of the body, Luke 13:11; John 8:7, 10; (*b*) metaphorically, of the mind, to look up, to be elated, Luke 21:28 (followed by No. 3, "lift up"); an instance is found in the papyri in which a person speaks of the impossibility of ever looking up again in a certain place, for very shame (Moulton and Milligan, *Vocab.*).¶ In the Sept., Job 10:15.¶

LIGHT, Noun, and Verb (bring to, give), LIGHTEN

A. Nouns.

1. *phōs* (φῶς, 5457), akin to *phaō*, "to give light" (from roots *pha—* and *phan—*, expressing "light as seen by the eye," and, metaphorically, as "reaching the mind," whence *phainō*, "to make to appear," *phaneros*, "evident," etc.); cf. Eng., "phosphorus" (lit., "light-bearing"). "Primarily light is a luminous emanation, probably of force, from certain bodies, which enables the eye to discern form and color. Light requires an organ adapted for its reception (Matt. 6:22). Where the eye is absent, or where it has become impaired from any cause, light is useless. Man, naturally, is incapable of receiving spiritual light inasmuch as he lacks the capacity for spiritual things, 1 Cor. 2:14. Hence believers are called 'sons of light,' Luke 16:8, not merely because they have received a revelation from God, but because in the New Birth they have received the spiritual capacity for it.

"Apart from natural phenomena, light is used in Scripture of (*a*) the glory of God's dwelling-place, 1 Tim. 6:16; (*b*) the nature of God, 1 John 1:5; (*c*) the impartiality of God, Jas. 1:17; (*d*) the favor of God, Ps. 4:6; of the King, Prov. 16:15; of an influential man, Job 29:24; (*e*)God, as the illuminator of His people, Isa. 60:19, 20; (*f*) the Lord Jesus as the illuminator of men, John 1:4, 5, 9; 3:19; 8:12; 9:5; 12:35, 36, 46; Acts 13:47; (*g*) thc illuminating power

---

of the Scriptures, Ps. 119:105; and of the judgments and commandments of God, Isa. 51:4; Prov. 6:23, cf. Ps. 43:3; (h) the guidance of God, Job 29:3; Ps. 112:4; Isa. 58:10; and, ironically, of the guidance of man, Rom. 2:19; (i) salvation, 1 Pet. 2:9; (j) righteousness, Rom. 13:12; 2 Cor. 11:14, 15; 1 John 2:9, 10; (k) witness for God, Matt. 5:14, 16; John 5:35; (l) prosperity and general well-being, Esth. 8:16; Job 18:18; Isa. 58:8–10."*

2. *phōstēr* (φωστήρ, 5458) denotes "a luminary, light," or "light-giver"; it is used figuratively of believers, as shining in the spiritual darkness of the world, Phil. 2:15; in Rev. 21:11 it is used of Christ as the "Light" reflected in and shining through the heavenly city (cf. v. 23).¶ In the Sept., Gen. 1:14, 16.¶

3. *phōtismos* (φωτισμός, 5462), "an illumination, light," is used metaphorically in 2 Cor. 4:4, of the "light" of the gospel, and in v. 6, of the knowledge of the glory of God.¶ In the Sept., Job 3:9; Ps. 27:1; 44:3; 78:14; 90:8; 139:11.¶

4. *phengos* (φέγγος, 5338), "brightness, luster," is used of the "light" of the moon, Matt. 24:29; Mark 13:24; of a lamp, Luke 11:33 (some mss. have *phōs*, here).¶

5. *luchnos* (λύχνος, 3088), "a hand-lamp": see LAMP.

6. *lampas* (λαμπάς, 2985), "a torch": see LAMP.

B. Verbs.

1. *phōtizō* (φωτίζω, 5461), used (a) intransitively, signifies "to shine, give light," Rev. 22:5; (b) transitively, (1) "to illumine, to light, enlighten, to be lightened," Luke 11:36; Rev. 21:23; in the passive voice, Rev. 18:1; metaphorically, of spiritual enlightenment, John 1:9; Eph. 1:18; 3:9, "to make . . . see;" Heb. 6:4; 10:32, "ye were enlightened," RV (KJV, " . . . illuminated"); (2) "to bring to light," 1 Cor. 4:5 (of God's act in the future); 2 Tim. 1:10 (of God's act in the past). See ENLIGHTEN, ILLUMINATE.¶

2. *epiphauskō* (ἐπιφαύσκω, 2017), or possibly *epiphauō*, "to shine forth," is rendered "shall give . . . light," in Eph. 5:14, KJV (RV, "shall shine upon"), of the glory of Christ, illumining the believer who fulfills the conditions, so that being guided by His "light" he reflects His character. See SHINE.¶ Cf. *epiphōskō*, "to dawn" (really a variant form of *epiphauskō*).

3. *lampō* (λάμπω, 2989), "to give the light of a torch," is rendered "giveth light" in Matt. 5:15, KJV (RV, "shineth"). See SHINE.

4. *epiphainō* (ἐπιφαίνω, 2014), transitively, "to show forth" (*epi*, "upon," *phainō*, "to cause to shine"), is used intransitively and metaphorically in Luke 1:79, and rendered "to give light," KJV (RV, "to shine upon"). See APPEAR, SHINE.

5. *haptō* (ἅπτω, 681), "to kindle a fire" and so give "light": see KINDLE, No. 1, Note.

6. *kaiō* (καίω, 2545), "to burn," is translated "do (men) light" in Matt. 5:15. See BURN.

7. *astraptō* (ἀστράπτω, 797), "to flash forth, lighten as lightning" (akin to *astrapē*, "lightning"), occurs in Luke 17:24; 24:4 (KJV "shining;" RV, "dazzling"). See DAZZLING.

Note: In Luke 2:32, KJV, the noun *apokalupsis*, "an unveiling, revelation," preceded by *eis*, "unto, with a view to," is rendered "to lighten" (RV, "for revelation"; marg., "(the) unveiling"). See REVELATION.

C. Adjective.

phōteinos (φωτεινός, 5460), from *phōs* (A, No. 1), "bright," is rendered "full of light" in Matt. 6:22; Luke 11:34, 36 (twice), figuratively, of the single-mindedness of the eye, which acts as the lamp of the body; in Matt. 17:5, "bright," of a cloud. See BRIGHT.¶

LIGHT (to light upon)

Notes: (1) In Matt. 3:16, KJV, *erchomai*, "to come," is translated "lighting"; RV, "coming." (2) In Rev. 7:16. KJV, *piptō*, "to fall," is translated "shall . . . light" (RV, "shall . . . strike"). See STRIKE. (3) For Acts 27:41, RV, see FALL, B, No. 8.

LIGHT, LIGHTEN (as to weight)

A. Adjective.

elaphros (ἐλαφρός, 1645), "light in weight, easy to bear," is used of the burden imparted by Christ, Matt. 11:30; of affliction, 2 Cor. 4:17.¶

B. Verb.

kouphizō (κουφίζω, 2893), "to make light, lighten" (the adjective *kouphos*, not in NT, denotes "slight, light, empty"), is used of "lightening" the ship, in Acts 27:38.

Note: For the phrase in v. 18, KJV, "they lightened the ship," See FREIGHT.

C. Noun.

elaphria (ἐλαφρία, 1644), "lightness," 2 Cor. 1:17, KJV: see FICKLENESS.

LIGHT OF (make), LIGHTLY

ameleō (ἀμελέω, 272) denotes "to be careless, not to care" (a, negative, and *melei*, an impersonal verb, signifying "it is a care": see CARE), Matt. 22:5, "they made light of (it)," lit., "making light of (it)," aorist participle, indicating the definiteness of their decision. See NEGLECT, NEGLIGENT, REGARD.

* From *Notes on Thessalonians,* by Hogg and Vine, pp. 159, 160.

Note: In Mark 9:39, KJV, the adverb *tachu*, "quickly," is translated "lightly" (RV, "quickly"). See QUICKLY.

LIGHTNING

astrapē (ἀστραπή, 796) denotes (*a*) "lightning" (akin to LIGHT, B, No. 7), Matt. 24:27; 28:3; Luke 10:18; 17:24; in the plural, Rev. 4:5; 8:5; 11:19; 16:18; (*b*) "bright shining," or "shining brightness," Luke 11:36. See SHINING.¶

LIKE, LIKE (as to, unto), (be) LIKE, (make) LIKE, LIKE (things), LIKEN

A. Adjectives.

1. *homoios* (ὅμοιος, 3664), "like, resembling, such as, the same as," is used (*a*) of appearance or form, John 9:9; Rev. 1:13, 15; 2:18; 4:3 (twice), 6, 7; 9:7 (twice), 10, 19; 11:1; 13:2, 11; 14:14; (*b*) of ability, condition, nature, Matt. 22:39; Acts 17:29; Gal. 5:21, "such like," lit., "and the (things) similar to these"; 1 John 3:2; Rev. 13:4; 18:18; 21:11, 18; (*c*) of comparison in parables, Matt. 13:31, 33, 44, 45, 47; 20:1; Luke 13:18, 19, 21; (*d*) of action, thought, etc., Matt. 11:16; 13:52; Luke 6:47, 48, 49; 7:31, 32; 12:36; John 8:55; Jude 7.¶

2. *isos* (ἴσος, 2470), "equal" (the same in size, quality, etc.), is translated "like," of the gift of the Spirit, Acts 11:17. See EQUAL, MUCH (AS).

3. *paromoios* (παρόμοιος, 3946), "much like" (*para*, "beside," and No. 1), is used in Mark 7:13, in the neuter plural, "(many such) like things."¶

B. Verbs.

1. *homoioō* (ὁμοιόω, 3666), "to make like" (akin to A, No. 1), is used (*a*) especially in the parables, with the significance of comparing, "likening," or, in the passive voice, "being likened," Matt. 7:24, 26; 11:16; 13:24; 18:23; 22:2 (RV, "likened"); 25:1; Mark 4:30; Luke 7:31; 13:18, RV, "liken" (KJV, "resemble"); v. 20; in several of these instances the point of resemblance is not a specific detail, but the whole circumstances of the parable; (*b*) of making "like," or, in the passive voice, of being made or becoming "like," Matt. 6:8; Acts 14:11, "in the likeness of (men)," lit., "being made like" (aorist participle, passive); Rom. 9:29; Heb. 2:17, of Christ in being "made like" unto His brethren, i.e., in partaking of human nature, apart from sin (cf. v. 14).¶

2. *eoika* (ἔοικα, 1503v), a perfect tense with a present meaning (from an obsolete present, *eikō*), denotes "to be like, to resemble," Jas. 1:6, 23.¶ In the Sept., Job 6:3, 25.¶

3. *paromoiazō* (παρομοιάζω, 3945), "to be like" (from *para*, "by," and a verbal form from

homoios, A, No. 1), is used in Matt. 23:27 (perhaps with intensive force), in the Lord's comparison of the scribes and Pharisees to whitened sepulchres.¶

4. *aphomoioō* (ἀφομοιόω, 871), "to make like" (*apo*, "from," and No. 1), is used in Heb. 7:3, of Melchizedek as "made like" the Son of God, i.e., in the facts related and withheld in the Genesis record.¶

Note: For the KJV of Rom. 1:23, "made like," see LIKENESS, No. 1.

C. Adverbs.

1. *hōs* (ὡς, 5613), used as a relative adverb of manner, means "as, like as," etc. and is translated "like," e.g., in Matt. 6:29; Mark 4:31; Luke 12:27; in Acts 3:22 and 7:37 (see RV, marg.); in 8:32 (2nd part), RV, "as" (KJV, "like"); Rev. 2:18, RV (the rendering should have been "as" here); 18:21, RV, "as it were" (KJV, "like"); 21:11, 2nd part (ditto).

2. *hōsper* (ὥσπερ, 5618), "just as," is rendered "like as" in Rom. 6:4.

Notes: (1) In Heb. 4:15, the phrase *kath'homoiotēta* (*kata*, "according to," *homoiotēs*, "a likeness," i.e., "after the similitude"), is rendered "like as," in the statement that Christ has been tempted in all points "like as we are, yet without sin"; this may mean either "according to the likeness of our temptations," or "in accordance with His likeness to us." (2) In the following the most authentic mss. have *hōs*, "as," for *hōsei*, "like," in the KJV; Mark 1:10; Luke 3:22; John 1:32; Rev. 1:14. (3) In John 7:46, KJV, the combination of the adverb *houtōs*, thus, with *hōs*, "as," is translated "like," RV "(never man) so (spake)." (4) For "in like manner" see MANNER. (5) In 1 Thess. 2:14, KJV, *ta auta*, "the same (things)," is translated "like (things)," RV, "the same (things)."

For (DID NOT) LIKE, Rom. 1:28, KJV, see REFUSE; No. 3

LIKEMINDED

1. *isopsuchos* (ἰσόψυχος, 2473), lit., "of equal soul" (*isos*, "equal," *psuchē*, "the soul"), is rendered "likeminded" in Phil. 2:20.¶ In the Sept., Ps. 55:13.¶

2. *homophrōn* (ὁμόφρων, 3675), (*homos*, "the same," *phrēn*, "the mind"), occurs in 1 Pet. 3:8, RV, "likeminded" (KJV, "of one mind").

Note: In Rom. 15:5; Phil. 2:2, *phroneō to auto*, "to think the same thing," is translated, KJV, "be likeminded" (RV, "be of the same mind").

LIKENESS, LIKENESS OF (in the)

1. *homoiōma* (ὁμοίωμα, 3667) denotes "that which is made like something, a resemblance," (*a*) in the concrete sense, Rev. 9:7, "shapes" (RV, marg., "likenesses"); (*b*) in the abstract sense, Rom. 1:23, RV, "(for) the likeness (of an image)"; the KJV translates it as a verb, "(into an image) made like to"; the association here of the two words *homoiōma* and *eikōn* (see IMAGE) serves to enhance the contrast between the idol and "the glory of the incorruptible God," and is expressive of contempt; in 5:14, "(the) likeness of Adam's transgression" (KJV, "similitude"); in 6:5, "(the) likeness (of His death); in 8:3, "(the) likeness (of sinful flesh); in Phil. 2:7, "the likeness of men." "The expression 'likeness of men' does not of itself imply, still less does it exclude or diminish, the reality of the nature which Christ assumed. That . . . is declared in the words 'form of a servant.' 'Paul justly says *in the likeness of men*, because, in fact, Christ, although certainly perfect Man (Rom. 5:15; 1 Cor. 15:21; 1 Tim. 2:5), was, by reason of the Divine nature present in Him, not simply and merely man . . . but the Incarnate Son of God'" (Gifford, quoting Meyer). See SHAPE.¶ Cf. LIKE, B, (*b*).

2. *homoiōsis* (ὁμοίωσις, 3669), "a making like," is translated "likeness" in Jas. 3:9, RV (KJV, "similitude").¶

3. *homoiotēs* (ὁμοιότης, 3665) is translated "likeness" in Heb. 7:15, RV (KJV, "similitude").

4. *antitupon* (ἀντίτυπον, 499) is rendered "after a true likeness," in 1 Pet. 3:21, RV (marg., "in the antitype"). See FIGURE, No. 2.

LIKEWISE

1. *homoiōs* (ὁμοίως, 3668), "in like manner" (from the adjective *homoios*, see LIKE, A, No. 1), is rendered "likewise" in the KJV of Matt. 22:26; 27:41, Luke 10:32; 16:25; John 5:19; Jas. 2:25; 1 Pet. 3:1, 7; Jude 8; Rev. 8:12 (in all these the RV has "in like manner"); in the following, KJV and RV have "likewise"; Matt. 26:35; Luke 5:33; 6:31; 10:37; 17:28, 31; 22:36; John 6:11; 21:13; Rom. 1:27; 1 Pet. 5:5.¶ See MANNER, SO.

2. *hōsautōs* (ὡσαύτως, 5615), a strengthened form of *hōs*, "as," denotes "in like manner, just so, likewise"; it is sometimes translated "likewise," e.g., Matt. 20:5; 21:30.

3. *kai* (καί, 2532), "and, even," is translated "likewise" in the KJV and RV of Matt. 20:10 (last *kai* in the verse), more lit., "even they"; elsewhere the RV has "also," for the KJV, "likewise," Matt. 18:35; 24:33; Luke 3:14; 17:10; 19:19; 21:31; Acts 3:24; 1 Cor. 14:9; Col. 4:16;

1 Pet. 4:1; in Matt. 21:24, the KJV has "in like wise" (RV, "likewise").

4. *paraplēsiōs* (παραπλησίως, 3898), from *para*, "beside," and the adjective *plēsios*, "near" (akin to the adverb *pelas*, "near, hard by"), is used in Heb. 2:14, KJV, "likewise" (RV, "in like manner"), expressing the true humanity of Christ in partaking of flesh and blood.¶

Notes: (1) In Matt. 17:12 and Rom. 6:11, KJV, the adverb *houtōs*, "thus, so," is translated "likewise" (RV, "so"); in Luke 15:7 and 10, KJV, "likewise," RV, "even so"; in Luke 14:33, KJV, followed by *oun*, "therefore," it is rendered "so likewise" (RV, "so therefore").

LILY

krinon (κρίνον, 2918) occurs in Matt. 6:28 and Luke 12:27; in the former the Lord speaks of "the lilies of the field"; the "lily" referred to was a flower of rich color, probably including the gladiolus and iris species. The former "grow among the grain, often overtopping it and illuminating the broad fields with their various shades of pinkish purple to deep violet purple and blue. . . . Anyone who has stood among the wheat fields of Galilee . . . will see at once the appropriateness of our Savior's allusion. They all have a reedy stem, which, when dry, would make such fuel as is used in the ovens. The beautiful irises . . . have gorgeous flowers, and would suit our Savior's comparison even better than the above. But they are plants of pasture grounds and swamps, and seldom found in grain fields. If, however, we understand by 'lilies of the field' simply wild lilies, these would also be included in the expression. Our Savior's comparison would then be like a 'composite photograph,' a reference to all the splendid colors and beautiful shapes of the numerous wild plants comprehended under the name 'lily'" (G. E. Post, in *Hastings' Bib. Dic.*).

For **LIMIT,** in Heb. 4:7, KJV, see **DEFINE**

For **LINE** see **PROVINCE,** No. 2

For **LINEAGE** in Luke 2:4, KJV, see **FAMILY**

LINEN, LINEN CLOTH, FINE LINEN

1. *sindōn* (σινδών, 4616) was "a fine linen cloth, an article of domestic manufacture" (Prov. 31:24) used (*a*) as a garment or wrap, the "linen cloth" of Mark 14:51, 52; (*b*) as shrouds or winding sheets, Matt. 27:59; Mark

15:46, RV, "linen cloth," for KJV, "linen"; Luke 23:53 (ditto).¶ In the Sept., Judg. 14:12, "(thirty) sheets"; Prov. 31:24 (see above).¶ The Mishna (the great collection of legal decisions by the ancient Rabbis) records that the material was sometimes used for curtains.

2. *linon* (λίνον, 3043) denotes (*a*) "flax," Matt. 12:20; (*b*) "linen," in Rev. 15:6, KJV; the best texts have *lithos*, "stone," RV. See FLAX.

3. *othonion* (ὀθόνιον, 3608), "a piece of fine linen," is used in the plural, of the strips of cloth with which the body of the Lord was bound, after being wrapped in the *sindōn*, Luke 24:12; John 19:40; 20:5, 6, 7.¶ In the Sept., Judg. 14:13, "changes of raiment"; Hos. 2:5, 9.¶ The word is a diminutive of *othonē*, "a sheet" (see SHEET).

4. *bussos* (βύσσος, 1040), "fine linen," made from a special species of flax, a word of Aramean origin, used especially for the Syrian *byssus* (Arab. *bûs* is still used for native "linen"). Cf. Heb. *bûs*, in all OT passages quoted here, except Ezek. 27:7; Syriac *bûsâ* In Luke 16:19. It is the material mentioned in 1 Chron. 4:21, wrought by the house of Ashbea; 15:27, *bussinos*, No. 5 (David's robe); 2 Chron. 3:14, *bussos* (the veil of the Temple); 5:12, *bussinos* (the clothing of the Levite singers); Esth. 1:6 (the cords of the hangings in the king's garden); 8:15 (Mordecai's dress); Ezek. 27:7 (*bussos*, in Syrian trade with Tyre). In the NT, Luke 16:19, the clothing of the "rich man."¶

5. *bussinos* (βύσσινος, 1039), an adjective formed from No. 4, denoting "made of fine linen." This is used of the clothing of the mystic Babylon, Rev. 18:12, 16, and of the suitable attire of the Lamb's wife, 19:8, 14, figuratively describing "the righteous acts of the saints." The presumption of Babylon is conspicuous in that she arrays herself in that which alone befits the bride of Christ.¶ For examples of the use in the Sept. see No. 4.

LINGER

argeō (ἀργέω, 691), "to be idle, to linger" (akin to *argos*, "idle": see *katargeō*, under ABOLISH), is used negatively regarding the judgment of the persons mentioned in 2 Pet. 2:3.¶ In the Sept., Ezra 4:24; Eccles. 12:3.¶

LION

leōn (λέων, 3023) occurs in 2 Tim. 4:17, probably figurative of the imminent peril of death, the figure being represented by the whole phrase, not by the word "lion" alone; some suppose the reference to be to the lions of the amphitheater; the Greek commentators regarded the "lion" as Nero; others understand it

to be Satan. The language not improbably recalls that of Ps. 22:21 and Dan. 6:20. The word is used metaphorically, too, in Rev. 5:5, where Christ is called "the Lion of the tribe of Judah." Elsewhere it has the literal meaning, Heb. 11:33; 1 Pet. 5:8; Rev. 4:7; 9:8, 17; 10:3; 13:2.¶ Taking the OT and NT occurrences the allusions are to the three great features of the "lion," (1) its majesty and strength, indicative of royalty, e.g., Prov. 30:30, (2) its courage, e.g., Prov. 28:1, (3) its cruelty, e.g., Ps. 22:13.

LIP

cheilos (χεῖλος, 5491) is used (*a*) of the organ of speech, Matt. 15:8 and Mark 7:6, where "honoring with the lips," besides meaning empty words, may have reference to a Jewish custom of putting to the mouth the tassel of the tallith (the woollen scarf wound round the head and neck during prayer), as a sign of acceptance of the Law from the heart; Rom. 3:13; 1 Cor. 14:21 (from Isa. 28:11, 12, speaking of the Assyrian foe as God's message to disobedient Israel); Heb. 13:15; 1 Pet. 3:10; (*b*) metaphorically, of "the brink or edge of things," as of the sea shore, Heb. 11:12, lit., "the shore (of the sea)."¶

LIST (Verb)

1. *thelō* (θέλω, 2309), "to will, wish," is translated by the verb "to list" in Matt. 17:12; Mark 9:13; John 3:8. See DESIRE, B, No. 6.

2. *boulomai* (βούλομαι, 1014), "to will, be minded," is translated "listeth" in Jas. 3:4 (RV, "willeth"). See DESIRE, B, No. 7.

LITTLE

A. Adjectives.

1. *mikros* (μικρός, 3398), "little, small" (the opposite of *megas*, "great"), is used (*a*) of persons, with regard to (1) station, or age, in the singular, Mark 15:40, of James "the less" (RV marg., "little"), possibly referring to age; Luke 19:3; in the plural, "little" ones, Matt. 18:6, 10, 14; Mark 9:42; (2) rank or influence, e.g., Matt. 10:42 (see context); Acts 8:10; 26:22, "small," as in Rev. 11:18; 13:16; 19:5, 18; 20:12; (*b*) of things, with regard to (1) size, e.g., Jas. 3:5 (some mss. have No. 2 here); (2) quantity, Luke 12:32; 1 Cor. 5:6; Gal. 5:9; Rev. 3:8; (3) time, John 7:33; 12:35; Rev. 6:11; 20:3. See B, No. 1. See LEAST, SMALL.

2. *oligos* (ὀλίγος 3641), "little, few" (the opposite of *polus*, "much"), is translated "short" in Rev. 12:12; in the neut. sing., e.g., 2 Cor. 8:15. For Jas. 3:5, see No. 1. See FEW, SHORT, SMALL.

3. *brachus* (βραχύς, 1024), "short," is used

to some extent adverbially of (*a*) time, with the preposition *meta*, "after," Luke 22:58, "(after) a little while"; in Acts 5:34, without a preposition, RV, "a little while" (KJV, "a little space"); in Heb. 2:7, 9, "a little" (KJV marg. in v. 7, and RV marg., in both, "a little while"), where the writer transfers to time what the Sept. in Ps. 8:5 says of rank; (*b*) of quantity, John 6:7; in Heb. 13:22, preceded by the preposition *dia*, "by means of," and with *logōn*, "words" (genitive plural) understood, "(in) few words"; (*c*) of distance, Acts 27:28, RV, "a little space" (KJV, "a little further"). See FEW, FURTHER, SPACE.¶

4. *elachistos* (ἐλάχιστος, 1646), which serves as the superlative of No. 1, is translated "a very little" in Luke 19:17. See LEAST.

Note: For *mikroteros*, "but little," see LEAST, No. 4.

B. Adverbs.

1. *mikron* (μικρόν, 3397), the neuter of A, No. 1, is used adverbially (*a*) of distance, Matt. 26:39; Mark 14:35; (*b*) of quantity, 2 Cor. 11:1, 16; (*c*) of time, Matt. 26:73, "a while"; Mark 14:70; John 13:33, "a little while"; 14:19; 16:16–9; Heb. 10:37, with the repeated *hoson*, "how very," lit., "a little while, how little, how little!" See WHILE.¶

2. *oligon* (ὀλίγον, 3641**), the neuter of A, No. 2, is used adverbially of (*a*) time, Mark 6:31, "a while;" 1 Pet. 1:6, RV, "a little while (KJV, "a season"); 5:10, RV, "a little while" (KJV, "a while"); Rev. 17:10, RV, "a little while" (KJV, "a short space"); (*b*) space, Mark 1:19; Luke 5:3; (*c*) extent, with the preposition *pros*, "for," in 1 Tim. 4:8, RV, "(for) a little" (KJV, and RV marg., "little"), where, while the phrase might refer to duration (as KJV marg.), yet the antithesis "for all things" clearly indicates extent, i.e., "physical training is profitable towards few objects in life." See BRIEFLY, FEW, SEASON, C, *Note*.

3. *metriōs* (μετρίως, 3357), moderately, occurs in Acts 20:12, "a little."¶

For **(NO) LITTLE** see **COMMON**, B, *Note* (3)

LIVE

1. *zaō* (ζάω, 2198), "to live, be alive," is used in the NT of "(*a*) God, Matt. 16:16; John 6:57; Rom. 14:11; (*b*) the Son in Incarnation, John 6:57; (*c*) the Son in Resurrection, John 14:19; Acts 1:3; Rom. 6:10; 2 Cor. 13:4; Heb. 7:8; (*d*) spiritual life, John 6:57; Rom. 1:17; 8:13*b*; Gal. 2:19, 20; Heb. 12:9; (*e*) the present state of departed saints, Luke 20:38; 1 Pet. 4:6; (*f*) the hope of resurrection, 1 Pet. 1:3; (*g*) the resurrection of believers, 1 Thess. 5:10; John 5:25; Rev.

20:4, and of unbelievers, v. 5, cf. v. 13; (*h*) the way of access to God through the Lord Jesus Christ, Heb. 10:20; (*i*) the manifestation of divine power in support of divine authority, 2 Cor. 13:4*b*; cf. 12:10, and 1 Cor. 5:5; (*j*) bread, figurative of the Lord Jesus, John 6:51; (*k*) a stone, figurative of the Lord Jesus, 1 Pet. 2:4; (*l*) water, figurative of the Holy Spirit, John 4:10; 7:38; (*m*) a sacrifice, figurative of the believer, Rom. 12:1; (*n*) stones, figurative of the believer, 1 Pet. 2:5; (*o*) the oracles, *logion*, Acts 7:38, and word, *logos*, Heb. 4:12; 1 Pet. 1:23, of God; (*p*) the physical life of men, 1 Thess. 4:15; Matt. 27:63; Acts 25:24; Rom. 14:9; Phil. 1:21 (in the infinitive mood used as a noun, with the article, 'living'), 22; 1 Pet. 4:5; (*q*) the maintenance of physical life, Matt. 4:4; 1 Cor. 9:14; (*r*) the duration of physical life, Heb. 2:15; (*s*) the enjoyment of physical life, 1 Thess. 3:8; (*t*) the recovery of physical life from the power of disease, Mark 5:23; John 4:50; (*u*) the recovery of physical life from the power of death, Matt. 9:18; Acts 9:41; Rev. 20:5; (*v*) the course, conduct, and character of men, (1) good, Acts 26:5; 2 Tim. 3:12; Titus 2:12; (2) evil, Luke 15:13; Rom. 6:2; 8:13*a*; 2 Cor. 5:15*b*; Col. 3:7; (3) undefined, Rom. 7:9; 14:7; Gal. 2:14; (*w*) restoration after alienation, Luke 15:32.

"*Note:* In 1 Thess. 5:10, to live means to experience that change, 1 Cor. 15:51, which is to be the portion of all in Christ who will be alive upon the earth at the Parousia of the Lord Jesus, cf. John 11:25, and which corresponds to the resurrection of those who had previously died in Christ, 1 Cor. 15:52–54.

"2. *sunzaō* (συνζάω, 4800), "to live together with" (*sun*, "with," and *zao*, "to live"), may be included with *zao* in the above analysis as follows: (*g*) Rom. 6:8; 2 Tim. 2:11; (*s*), 2 Cor. 7:3.¶

"3. *anazaō* (ἀναζάω, 326) *ana*, "again," and *zao*, denotes "to live again," "to revive," Luke 15:24; cf. (*w*) in list above, and Rom. 7:9, to manifest activity again."¶*

Note: Zaō is translated "quick" (i.e., "living") in Acts 10:42; 2 Tim. 4:1; 1 Pet. 4:5; in Heb. 4:12, KJV (RV, "living").

4. *bioō* (βιόω, 980), "to spend life, to pass one's life," is used in 1 Pet. 4:2.¶

5. *anastrephō* (ἀναστρέφω, 390), used metaphorically, in the middle voice, "to conduct oneself, behave, live," is translated "to live," in Heb. 13:18 ("honestly"); in 2 Pet. 2:18 ("in error"). See ABIDE, BEHAVE, etc.

6. *zōogoneō* (ζωογονέω, 2225) denotes "to

---

* From *Notes on Thessalonians*, by Hogg and Vine, pp. 173, 174.

preserve alive" (from *zōos*, "alive," and *ginomai*, "to come to be, become, be made"); in Luke 17:33, "shall preserve (it)," i.e., his life, RV marg., "save (it) alive"; cf. the parallels *sōzō*, "to save," in Matt. 16:25, and *phulassō*, "to keep," in John 12:25; in Acts 7:19, "live," negatively of the efforts of Pharaoh to destroy the babes in Israel; in 1 Tim. 6:13, according to the best mss. (some have *zōopoieō*, "to cause to live"), "quickeneth" (RV, marg., "preserveth ... alive," the preferable rendering). See PRESERVE, QUICKEN.¶

7. *diagō* (διάγω, 1236) is used of time in the sense of passing a life, 1 Tim. 2:2, "(that) we may lead (a tranquil and quiet, RV) life"; Tit. 3:3, "living (in malice and envy)."¶

8. *politeuō* (πολιτεύω, 4176), "to be a citizen (*politēs*), to live as a citizen," is used metaphorically of conduct as in accordance with the characteristics of the heavenly community; in Acts 23:1, "I have lived"; in Phil. 1:27, "let your manner of life (KJV, conversation) be." See CITIZENSHIP, No. 4, *Note.*¶

9. *huparchō* (ὑπάρχω, 5225), "to be in existence, to be," is translated "live (delicately)" in Luke 7:25. See BEING.

Note: In 1 Cor. 9:13, KJV, *esthiō*, "to eat," is translated "live of." In Tim. 5:6 the KJV renders *spatalaō* "liveth in pleasure."

LIVE LONG

makrochronios (μακροχρόνιος, 3118), an adjective denoting "of long duration, long-lived" (*makros*, "long," *chronos*, "time"), is used in Eph. 6:3, "(that thou mayest) live long," lit., "(that thou mayest be) long-lived."¶ In the Sept., Ex. 20:12; Deut. 4:40; 5:16; 17:20.¶

LIVELY

Note: This is the KJV translation of the present participle of the verb; *zaō*, "to live," in three passages, in each of which the RV has "living," Acts 7:38; 1 Pet. 1:3; 2:5.

For **LIVING** see **BEHAVIOR**, B, No. 1, **LIFE**, Nos. 2, 6, and **LIVE**, No. 3, *Note*

For **LIVING CREATURES** see **BEAST**

LO!

1. *ide* (ἴδε, 2396), an aorist or point tense, marking a definite point of time, of the imperative mood of *eidon*, "to see" (taken as part of *horaō*, "to see"), is used as an interjection, addressed either to one or many persons, e.g.,

Matt. 25:20, 22, 25; John 1:29, 36, 47; Gal. 5:2, the only occurrence outside Matthew, Mark and John. See BEHOLD, SEE.

2. *idou* (ἰδού, 2400) a similar tense of No. 1, but in the middle voice, e.g., Matt. 1:20, 23; very frequent in the Synoptists and Acts and the Apocalypse.

For **LOAF** see **BREAD**

LOCUST

akris (ἀκρίς, 200) occurs in Matt. 3:4 and Mark 1:6, of the animals themselves, as forming part of the diet of John the Baptist; they are used as food; the Arabs stew them with butter, after removing the head, legs and wings. In Rev. 9:3, 7, they appear as monsters representing satanic agencies, let loose by divine judgments inflicted upon men for five months, the time of the natural life of the "locust." For the character of the judgment see the whole passage.¶

LODGE, LODGING

A. Verbs.

1. *aulizomai* (αὐλίζομαι, 835), properly, "to lodge in a courtyard" (*aulē*, See COURT, No. 2), then, "to lodge in the open," denotes, in the NT, "to pass the night, to lodge anywhere," Matt. 21:17; Luke 21:37, RV, "lodged" (KJV, "abode").¶ See the metaphorical use in the Sept. and the Heb. of Ps. 30:5, "(weeping) may come in to lodge (at even)," i.e., as a passing stranger. See ABIDE.

2. *kataskēnoō* (κατασκηνόω, 2681) "to pitch one's tent" (*kata*, "down," *skēnē*, "a tent"), is rendered "to lodge," of birds, in Matt. 13:32; Mark 4:32; Luke 13:19. In Acts 2:26, it is used of the body of the Lord in the tomb, as dwelling in hope, RV, "shall dwell" (marg., "tabernacle"), KJV, "shall rest." See DWELL, REST.¶ Cf. *kataskēnōsis*, "a roosting place."

3. *kataluō* (καταλύω, 2647), in one of its meanings, signifies "to unloose" (*kata*, "down," *luō*, "to loose"), "unyoke," as of horses, etc., hence intransitively, "to take up one's quarters, to lodge," Luke 9:12; 19:7, RV, "to lodge" (KJV, "to be a guest"). See COME, *Note* (7) (come to nought), DESTROY, DISSOLVE, OVERTHROW, THROW. Cf. *kataluma*, "a guest chamber, inn."

4. *xenizō* (ξενίζω, 3579), "to receive as a guest" (*xenos*, "a guest, stranger"), "to entertain, lodge," is used in the active voice in Acts 10:23; 28:7, RV, "entertained" (KJV, "lodged"); Heb. 13:2, "have entertained"; in the passive voice, Acts 10:6 (lit., "he is entertained"), 18, 32; 21:16. Its other meaning, "to think strange," is found in 1 Pet. 4:4, 12. See ENTERTAIN, STRANGE.

B. Noun.

xenia (ξενία, 3578), akin to A, No. 4, denotes (*a*) "hospitality, entertainment," Philem. 22; (*b*) by metonymy, "a place of entertainment, a lodging-place," Acts 28:23 (some put Philem. 22 under this section).¶

For **LOFT,** Acts 20:9, see **STORY**

LOINS

osphus (ὀσφύς, 3751) is used (*a*) in the natural sense in Matt. 3:4; Mark 1:6; (*b*) as "the seat of generative power," Heb. 7:5, 10; metaphorically in Acts 2:30; (*c*) metaphorically, (1) of girding the "loins" in readiness for active service for the Lord, Luke 12:35; (2) the same, with truth, Eph. 6:14, i.e., bracing up oneself so as to maintain perfect sincerity and reality as the counteractive in Christian character against hypocrisy and falsehood; (3) of girding the "loins" of the mind, 1 Pet. 1:13, RV, "girding," suggestive of the alertness necessary for sobriety and for setting one's hope perfectly on "the grace to be brought . . . at the revelation of Jesus Christ" (the present participle, "girding," is introductory to the rest of the verse).¶

LONG (Adjective and Adverb)

A. Adjectives.

1. *makros* (μακρός, 3117) is used of "long prayers" (Matt. 23:14, in some mss.), Mark 12:40; Luke 20:47. It denotes "far" in Luke 15:13; 19:12. See FAR.¶

2. *hikanos* (ἱκανός, 2425), "sufficient, much, long," is used with *chronos*, "time," in Luke 8:27; in 20:9 and 23:8 (KJV, "season") the plural is used, lit., "long times"; Acts 8:11; 14:3. See ABLE (ABILITY), C, No. 2, MANY, MUCH.

3. *polus* (πολύς, 4183), "much," is used with *chronos*, "time," in Matt. 25:19; John 5:6; in Acts 27:21, with *asitia*, KJV, "long abstinence," RV, "long without food." See COMMON, *Note* (1).

4. *tosoutos* (τοσοῦτος, 5118), "so long," is used with *chronos* in John 14:9 and Heb. 4:7.

5. *posos* (πόσος, 4214), "how much," is used with *chronos*, in Mark 9:21, "how long time," RV (KJV, "how long ago").

6. *hosos* (ὅσος, 3745), "how much, so much," is used after the preposition *epi* (*eph'*), and as an adjective qualifying *chronos*, signifying "for so long time," in Rom. 7:1; 1 Cor. 7:39; Gal. 4:1; see also B, No. 4.

Notes: (1) In Acts 14:28, KJV, the adjective *oligos*, "little," with the negative *ou*, "not," and qualifying *chronos*, is rendered "long time;" RV, "no little (time)." (2) For the comparative adjective, *pleiōn*, see LONGER, B.

B. Adverbs.

1. *polus* (πολύς, 4183), in one or other of its neuter forms, singular or plural, is used (*a*) of degree, "greatly, much, many," e.g., Mark 1:45; (*b*) of time, e.g., Acts 27:14. Cf. A, No. 3. See GREAT, MUCH, OFT, SORE, STRAITLY, WHILE.

2. *eph' hikanon* (ἐφ' ἱκανόν), lit., "unto much (time)," is rendered "a long while" in Acts 20:11. Cf. A, No. 2.

3. *heōs pote* (ἕως πότε), lit., "until when?" signifies "how long?" Matt. 17:17 (twice); Mark 9:19 (twice); Luke 9:41; John 10:24; Rev. 6:10.

4. *eph' hoson* (ἐφ' ὅσον) signifies "so long as, as long as" (*epi*, "upon," *hosos*, "how much"), Matt. 9:15; Mark 2:19; 2 Pet. 1:13. See INASMUCH, No. 2.

Notes: (1) For the adverb LONGER, see below. (2) In 2 Pet. 2:3, KJV, the adverb *ekpalai*, "from of old," RV (*ek*, "from," *palai*, "of old, formerly"), is translated "of a long time."

LONG (Verb), LONG (after, for), LONGING

A. Verb.

epipotheō (ἐπιποθέω, 1971), "to long for greatly" (a strengthened form of *potheō*, "to long for," not found in the NT), is translated "I long," in Rom. 1:11; in 2 Cor. 5:2, RV, "longing" (KJV, "earnestly desiring"); in 1 Thess. 3:6 and 2 Tim. 1:4, RV, "longing" (KJV, "desiring greatly"); to long after, in 2 Cor. 9:14; Phil. 1:8; 2:26; to long for, in 1 Pet. 2:2, RV (KJV, "desire"); Jas. 4:5, RV, "long." See DESIRE.¶

B. Adjective.

epipothētos (ἐπιπόθητος, 1973), akin to A, and an intensive form of *pothētos*, "desired, greatly desired," "longed for," is used in Phil. 4:1.¶

C. Nouns.

1. *epipothia* (ἐπιποθία, 1974), "a longing" (akin to A and B), is found in Rom. 15:23, RV, "longing" (KJV, "great desire"). See DESIRE.¶

2. *epipothēsis* (ἐπιπόθησις, 1972), "a longing" (perhaps stressing the process more than No. 1), is found in 2 Cor. 7:7, RV, "longing" (KJV, "earnest desire"); 7:11, RV, "longing" (KJV, "vehement desire").¶

LONGER

A. Adverbs.

1. *eti* (ἔτι, 2089), "yet, as yet, still," is translated "longer" in Luke 16:2 (with separate negative); "any longer" in Rom. 6:2. See ALSO, EVEN, FURTHER, MORE, MOREOVER, STILL, THENCEFORTH, YET.

2. *ouketi* (οὐκέτι, 3765), "no more, no longer" (*ou*, "not," *k*, euphonic, and No. 1), is

rendered "no longer" in the RV of Mark 7:12 (KJV, "no more"); John 15:15, RV (KJV, "henceforth not"); Rom. 14:15, RV (KJV, "now... not"); Gal. 2:20, RV (KJV, "yet not"); Gal. 3:25; 4:7 (KJV, "no more"); Philem. 16 (KJV, "not now"). See HENCEFORTH, MORE, NOW, YET.

3. *mēketi* (μηκέτι, 3371) also means "no more, no longer," but generally suggests what is a matter of thought or supposition, whereas No. 1 refers to what is a matter of fact. It is rendered "any longer" in Acts 25:24; "no longer," in Mark 2:2, RV, "no longer (room)," KJV, "no (room);" 2 Cor. 5:15, RV (KJV, "not henceforth"); Eph. 4:14, RV (KJV, "no more"); 4:17, RV (KJV, "henceforth... not"); 1 Thess. 3:1, 5; 1 Tim. 5:23; 1 Pet. 4:2. See (negatively) HENCEFORTH, HENCEFORWARD, HEREAFTER, NO MORE.

4. *pleion* (πλεῖον, 4119), the neuter of *pleiōn*, "more," the comparative degree of *polu*, "much," is rendered "longer" in Acts 20:9, RV (KJV "long").

B. Adjective.

pleiōn (πλείων, 4119), "more," (cf. A, No. 4), is used with *chronos*, "time," in Acts 18:20, "a longer time," RV (KJV, "longer").

LONGSUFFERING (Noun and Verb)

A. Noun.

makrothumia (μακρουμία, 3115), "forbearance, patience, longsuffering" (*makros*, "long," *thumos*, "temper"), is usually rendered "longsuffering," Rom. 2:4; 9:22; 2 Cor. 6:6; Gal. 5:22; Eph. 4:2; Col. 1:11; 3:12; 1 Tim. 1:16; 2 Tim. 3:10; 4:2; 1 Pet. 3:20; 2 Pet. 3:15; "patience" in Heb. 6:12 and Jas. 5:10. See PATIENCE, and *Note* under FORBEAR.¶

B. Verb.

makrothumeō (μακροθυμέω, 3114), akin to A, "to be patient, longsuffering, to bear with," lit., "to be long-tempered," is rendered by the verb "to be longsuffering" in Luke 18:7, RV (KJV, "bear long"); in 1 Thess. 5:14, RV (KJV, "be patient"); so in Jas. 5:7, 8; in 2 Pet. 3:9, KJV and RV, "is longsuffering. See BEAR, No. 14, ENDURE, PATIENT, SUFFER.

Note: "Longsuffering is that quality of self-restraint in the face of provocation which does not hastily retaliate or promptly punish; it is the opposite of anger, and is associated with mercy, and is used of God, Ex. 34:6 (Sept.); Rom. 2:4; 1 Pet. 3:20. Patience is the quality that does not surrender to circumstances or succumb under trial; it is the opposite of despondency and is associated with hope, 1 Thess. 1:3; it is not used of God."*

* From *Notes on Thessalonians,* by Hogg and Vine, pp. 183, 184.

LOOK

A. Verbs.

1. *blepō* (βλέπω, 991), primarily, "to have sight, to see," then, "observe, discern, perceive," frequently implying special contemplation (cf. No. 4), is rendered by the verb "to look" in Luke 9:62, "looking (back)"; John 13:22 "(the disciples) looked (one on another)"; Acts 1:9, RV, "were looking" (KJV, "beheld"); 3:4, "look (on us)"; 27:12, RV, looking," KJV, "that lieth (towards)," of the haven Phenix; Eph. 5:15, RV, "look (therefore carefully how ye walk)," KJV, "see (that ye walk circumspectly)"; Rev. 11:9 and 18:9, RV, "look upon" (KJV, "shall see"). See BEHOLD.

2. *anablepō* (ἀναβλέπω, 308), denotes (*a*) "to look up" (*ana*, "up," and No. 1), e.g., Matt. 14:19; Mark 8:24 (in some mss. v. 25); (*b*) "to recover sight," e.g., Matt. 11:5; 20:34, RV, "received their sight"; John 9:11. See SIGHT. Cf. *anablepsis*, "recovering of sight," Luke 4:18.

3. *periblepō* (περιβλέπω, 4017), "to look about, or round about, on" (*peri*, "around," and No. 1), is used in the middle voice, Mark 3:5, 34; 5:32; 9:8; 10:23; 11:11; Luke 6:10.¶

4. *apoblepō* (ἀποβλέπω, 578) signifies "to look away from" (*apo*) all else at one object; hence, "to look steadfastly," Heb. 11:26, RV, "he looked" (KJV, "he had respect").¶ Cf. No. 8.

5. *emblepō* (ἐμβλέπω, 1689), to look at (*en*, in, and No. 1), is translated "to look upon" in Mark 10:27; 14:67; Luke 22:61; John 1:36. This verb implies a close, penetrating "look," as distinguished from Nos. 6 and 9. See BEHOLD, No. 3, GAZE, SEE, No. 6.

6. *epiblepō* (ἐπιβλέπω, 1914), "to look upon" (*epi*, "upon"), is used in the NT of favorable regard, Luke 1:48, RV, "he hath looked upon" (KJV, "hath regarded"), of the low estate of the Virgin Mary; in 9:38, in a request to the Lord to "look" upon an afflicted son; in Jas. 2:3, RV, "ye have regard" (KJV, "... respect"), of having a partial regard for the well-to-do. See REGARD, RESPECT.¶

7. *eidon* (εἶδον, 3708), used as the aorist tense of *horaō*, "to see," in various senses, is translated "to look," in the KJV of John 7:52, RV, "see;" Rev. 4:1 (RV, "I saw"); so in 6:8; 14:1, 14 (as in KJV of v. 6), and 15:5. See BEHOLD, CONSIDER, HEED, No. 2, PERCEIVE, SEE, SHEW.

8. *aphoraō* (ἀφοράω, 872), "to look away from one thing so as to see another" (*apo*, "from," and No. 7), "to concentrate the gaze upon," occurs in Phil. 2:23, "I shall see;" Heb. 12:2, "looking."¶

9. *epeidon* (ἐπεῖδον, 1896) denotes "to look

upon" (*epi*, "upon"), (*a*) favorably, Luke 1:25; (*b*) unfavorably, in Acts 4:29.¶

10. *parakuptō* (παρακύπτω, 3879), lit. and primarily, "to stoop sideways" *para*, "aside," *kuptō*, "to bend forward"), denotes "to stoop to look into," Luke 24:12, "stooping and looking in" (KJV, "stooping down"); John 20:5, 11; metaphorically in Jas. 1:25, of "looking" into the perfect law of liberty; in 1 Pet. 1:12 of things which the angels desire "to look" into.¶

11. *anakuptō* (ἀνακύπτω, 352), "to lift oneself up" (*ana*, "up"), is translated "look up" in Luke 21:28, of being elated in joyous expectation (followed by *epairō*, "to lift up"). See LIFT.

12. *skopeō* (σκοπέω, 4648), "to look at, consider" (Eng., "scope"), implying mental consideration, is rendered "while we look . . . at" in 2 Cor. 4:18; "looking to" (KJV, "on") in Phil. 2:4. See HEED, MARK.

13. *episkopeō* (ἐπισκοπέω, 1983), lit., "to look upon" (*epi*, and No. 12), is rendered "looking carefully" in Heb. 12:15, RV (KJV, "looking diligently"), *epi* being probably intensive here; in 1 Pet. 5:2, "to exercise the oversight, to visit, care for." See OVERSIGHT.¶

14. *episkeptomai* (ἐπισκέπτομαι, 1980), a later form of No. 13, "to visit," has the meaning of "seeking out," and is rendered "look ye out" in Acts 6:3. See VISIT.

15. *atenizō* (ἀτενίζω, 816), "to look fixedly, gaze," is translated "looking steadfastly" in Luke 22:56, RV (KJV, " . . . earnestly"); in Acts 1:10, "looking steadfastly;" in 3:12, KJV, "look . . . earnestly" (RV, "fasten ye your eyes," as in 3:4 and 11:6); so in the RV of 6:15; 10:4; 13:9; 14:9; in 7:55, "looked up steadfastly;" in 23:1, "looking steadfastly on" (KJV, "earnestly beholding"); in 2 Cor, 3:7, RV, "look steadfastly" (KJV, "steadfastly behold"); in 3:13, RV, ditto (KJV, "steadfastly look"). In Luke 4:20, "were fastened" (*ophthalmoi*, "eyes," being used separately). See BEHOLD, No. 10.¶

16. *theaomai* (θεάομαι, 2300), "to behold" (of careful contemplation), is translated "look" in John 4:35, of "looking" on the fields; in 1 John 1:1, KJV (RV, "we beheld"), of the apostles' personal experiences of Christ in the days of His flesh, and the facts of His Godhood and Manhood. See BEHOLD, No. 8.

17. *theōreō* (θεωρέω, 2334), "to look at, gaze at, behold," is translated "looking on" in Mark 15:40, KJV (RV, "beholding"). See BEHOLD, No. 6.

B. Noun.

horasis (ὅρασις, 3706), akin to A, No. 7, denotes (*a*) a vision (so the associated noun *horama*, e.g., Acts 7:31; *horasis* signifies especially the act of seeing, *horama* that which is

seen), Acts 2:17; Rev. 9:17; (*b*) an appearance, Rev. 4:3, translated "to look upon" (twice in the RV; In the second instance the KJV has "in sight").¶

LOOK (for), LOOKING (after, for)

A. Verbs.

1. *prosdokaō* (προσδοκάω, 4328), "to await, expect" (*pros*, "to" or "towards," *dokeō*, "to think, be of opinion"), is translated "to look for," e.g., in Matt. 11:3; 2 Pet. 3:12, 13, 14; the RV renders it by the verb "to expect, to be in expectation," in some instances, as does the KJV in Luke 3:15; Acts 3:5, See EXPECT.

2. *prosdechomai* (προσδέχομαι, 4327), "to receive favorably," also means "to expect," and is rendered "to look for," e.g., in Luke 2:38; 23:51; Acts 24:15, RV (KJV, "allow"); Titus 2:13; Jude 21. See ACCEPT, A, No. 3, ALLOW, No. 4.

3. *ekdechomai* (ἐκδέχομαι, 1551), primarily "to receive from another," hence, "to expect, to await," is translated "he looked for" in Heb. 11:10; in 1 Cor. 16:11, KJV, "I look for" (RV, "I expect"). See EXPECT, No. 1.

Notes: (1) In Phil. 3:20 and Heb. 9:28, KJV, *apekdechomai* (the verb in the preceding No. extended by *apo*, "from"), "to await" or "expect eagerly," is translated "look for" (RV, "wait for"; so KJV everywhere else). See WAIT. (2) In Acts 28:6, KJV, *prosdokaō*, "to expect," is translated "they looked" (RV, "they expected"), and "they had looked" (RV, "they were long in expectation").

B. Nouns.

1. *prosdokia* (προσδοκία, 4329); akin to A, No. 1, is translated "a looking after" in Luke 21:26, KJV ("expectation," as in Acts 12:11, KJV and RV). See EXPECTATION.¶

2. *ekdochē* (ἐκδοχή, 1561), akin to A, No. 3, is translated "looking for" in Heb. 10:27, KJV. See EXPECTATION.¶

LOOK (to)

1. *blepō* (βλέπω, 991), "to look" (see LOOK, No. 1), has the meaning of "taking heed, looking to oneself," in 2 John 8. See HEED.

2. *horaō* (ὁράω, 3708), "to see" (see LOOK, No. 7), has the meaning of "seeing to" or "caring for a thing" in Matt. 27:4, "see (thou to it);" in Acts 18:15, "look to it (yourselves)"; the future (sing. *opsei*, plural, *opsesthe*), is used for the tense which is wanting in *horaō*, and stands for the imperative.

LOOSE

A. Verbs.

1. *luō* (λύω, 3089) denotes (*a*) "to loose, unbind, release," (1) of things, e.g., in Acts 7:33, RV, "loose (the shoes)," KJV, "put off"; Mark 1:7; (2) of animals, e.g., Matt. 21:2; (3) of persons, e.g., John 11:44; Acts 22:30; (4) of Satan, Rev. 20:3, 7, and angels, Rev. 9:14, 15; (5) metaphorically, of one diseased, Luke 13:16; of the marriage tie, 1 Cor. 7:27; of release from sins, Rev. 1:5 (in the most authentic mss.); (*b*) "to loosen, break up, dismiss, dissolve, destroy"; in this sense it is translated "to loose" in Acts 2:24, of the pains of death; in Rev. 5:2, of the seals of a roll. See BREAK, DESTROY, DISSOLVE, MELT, PUT (off), UNLOOSE.

2. *apoluō* (ἀπολύω, 630), *apo*, "from," and No. 1, denotes (*a*) "to set free, release," translated "loosed" in Luke 13:12, of deliverance from an infirmity; in Matt. 18:27, KJV, "loosed" (RV, "released"), of a debtor; (*b*) "to let go, dismiss," e.g., Matt. 14:15, 22. See DEPART, DISMISS, DIVORCE, FORGIVE, LET (go), LIBERTY, PUT (away), RELEASE, SEND (away).

3. *aniēmi* (ἀνίημι, 447), "to send back" (*ana*, "back," *hiēmi*, "to send"), "to leave, forbear," is translated "to loose," in Acts 16:26, of the "loosening" of bonds; 27:40, rudder bands. Elsewhere, Eph. 6:9; Heb. 13:5. See FORBEAR, LEAVE.¶

4. *anagō* (ἀνάγω, 321): see LAUNCH.

Notes: (1) In Acts 27:13, KJV, *airō*, "to lift," is translated "loosing (thence)" (RV, "they weighed anchor"). (2) For *katargeō*, translated "she is loosed" in Rom. 7:2, KJV (RV "discharged"), see ABOLISH.

B. Noun.

lusis (λύσις, 3080), "a loosening" (akin to A, No. 1), 1 Cor. 7:27, of divorce, is translated "to be loosed," lit., "loosing." In the second part of the verse the verb *luō* is used.¶ In the Sept., Eccl. 8:1, with the meaning "interpretation."¶

LORD, LORDSHIP

A. Nouns.

1. *kurios* (κύριος, 2962), properly an adjective, signifying "having power" (*kuros*) or "authority," is used as a noun, variously translated in the NT, " 'Lord,' 'master,' 'Master,' 'owner,' 'Sir,' a title of wide significance, occurring in each book of the NT save Titus and the Epistles of John. It is used (*a*) of an owner, as in Luke 19:33, cf. Matt. 20:8; Acts 16:16; Gal. 4:1; or of one who has the disposal of anything, as the Sabbath, Matt. 12:8; (*b*) of a master, i.e., one to whom service is due on any ground, Matt. 6:24; 24:50; Eph. 6:5; (*c*) of an Emperor or King,

Acts 25:26; Rev. 17:14; (*d*) of idols, ironically, 1 Cor. 8:5, cf. Isa. 26:13; (*e*) as a title of respect addressed to a father, Matt. 21:30, a husband, 1 Pet. 3:6, a master, Matt. 13:27; Luke 13:8, a ruler, Matt. 27:63, an angel, Acts 10:4; Rev. 7:14; (*f*) as a title of courtesy addressed to a stranger, John 12:21; 20:15; Acts 16:30; from the outset of His ministry this was a common form of address to the Lord Jesus, alike by the people, Matt. 8:2; John 4:11, and by His disciples, Matt. 8:25; Luke 5:8; John 6:68; (*g*) *kurios* is the Sept. and NT representative of Heb. Jehovah ('LORD' in Eng. versions), see Matt. 4:7; Jas. 5:11, e.g., of *adon*, Lord, Matt. 22:44, and of *Adonay*, Lord, 1:22; it also occurs for *Elohim*, God, 1 Pet. 1:25.

"Thus the usage of the word in the NT follows two main lines: *one—a—f*, customary and general, the other, *g*, peculiar to the Jews, and drawn from the Greek translation of the OT.

"Christ Himself assumed the title, Matt. 7:21, 22; 9:38; 22:41–45; Mark 5:19 (cf. Ps. 66:16; the parallel passage, Luke 8:39, has 'God'); Luke 19:31; John 13:13, apparently intending it in the higher senses of its current use, and at the same time suggesting its OT associations.

"His purpose did not become clear to the disciples until after His resurrection, and the revelation of His Deity consequent thereon. Thomas, when he realized the significance of the presence of a mortal wound in the body of a living man, immediately joined with it the absolute title of Deity, saying, 'My Lord and my God,' John 20:28. Thereafter, except in Acts 10:4 and Rev. 7:14, there is no record that *kurios* was ever again used by believers in addressing any save God and the Lord Jesus; cf. Acts 2:47 with 4:29, 30.

"How soon and how completely the lower meaning had been superseded is seen in Peter's declaration in his first sermon after the resurrection, 'God hath made Him—Lord,' Acts 2:36, and that in the house of Cornelius, 'He is Lord of all,' 10:36; cf. Deut. 10:14; Matt. 11:25; Acts 17:24. In his writings the implications of his early teaching are confirmed and developed. Thus Ps. 34:8, 'O taste and see that Jehovah is good,' is applied to the Lord Jesus, 1 Pet. 2:3, and 'Jehovah of Hosts, Him shall ye sanctify,' Isa. 8:13, becomes 'sanctify in your hearts Christ as Lord,' 3:15.

"So also James who uses *kurios* alike of God, 1:7 (cf. v. 5); 3:9; 4:15; 5:4, 10, 11, and of the Lord Jesus, 1:1 (where the possibility that *kai* is intended epexegetically, i.e. = even, cf. 1 Thess. 3:11, should not be overlooked); 2:1 (lit., 'our Lord Jesus Christ of glory,' cf. Ps. 24:7; 29:3; Acts 7:2; 1 Cor. 2:8); 5:7, 8, while the language of 4:10; 5:15, is equally applicable to either.

"Jude, v. 4, speaks of 'our only—Lord, Jesus Christ,' and immediately, v. 5, uses 'Lord' of God (see the remarkable marg. here), as he does later, vv. 9, 14.

"Paul ordinarily uses *kurios* of the Lord Jesus, 1 Cor. 1:3, e.g., but also on occasion, of God, in quotations from the OT, 1 Cor. 3:20, e.g., and in his own words, 1 Cor. 3:5, cf. v. 10. It is equally appropriate to either in 1 Cor. 7:25; 2 Cor. 3:16; 8:21; 1 Thess. 4:6, and if 1 Cor. 11:32 is to be interpreted by 10:21, 22, the Lord Jesus is intended, but if by Heb. 12:5–9, then *kurios* here also = God. 1 Tim. 6:15, 16 is probably to be understood of the Lord Jesus, cf. Rev. 17:14.

"Though John does not use 'Lord' in his Epistles, and though, like the other Evangelists, he ordinarily uses the personal Name in his narrative, yet he occasionally speaks of Him as 'the Lord,' John 4:1; 6:23; 11:2; 20:20; 21:12.

"The full significance of this association of Jesus with God under the one appellation, 'Lord,' is seen when it is remembered that these men belonged to the only monotheistic race in the world. To associate with the Creator one known to be a creature, however exalted, though possible to Pagan philosophers, was quite impossible to a Jew.

"It is not recorded that in the days of His flesh any of His disciples either addressed the Lord, or spoke of Him, by His personal Name. Where Paul has occasion to refer to the facts of the gospel history he speaks of what the Lord Jesus said, Acts 20:35, and did, 1 Cor. 11:23, and suffered, 1 Thess. 2:15; 5:9, 10. It is our Lord Jesus who is coming, 1 Thess. 2:19, etc. In prayer also the title is given, 3:11; Eph. 1:3; the sinner is invited to believe on the Lord Jesus, Acts 16:31; 20:21, and the saint to look to the Lord Jesus for deliverance, Rom. 7:24, 25, and in the few exceptional cases in which the personal Name stands alone a reason is always discernible in the immediate context.

"The title 'Lord,' as given to the Savior, in its full significance rests upon the resurrection, Acts 2:36; Rom. 10:9; 14:9, and is realized only in the Holy Spirit, 1 Cor. 12:3."*

2. *despotēs* (δεσπότης, 1203), "a master, lord, one who possesses supreme authority," is used in personal address to God in Luke 2:29; Acts 4:24; Rev. 6:10; with reference to Christ, 2 Pet. 2:1; Jude 4; elsewhere it is translated

"master," "masters," 1 Tim. 6:1, 2; 2 Tim. 2:21 (of Christ); Titus 2:9; 1 Pet. 2:18. See MASTER.¶

Note: For *rabboni*, rendered "Lord" in the KJV of Mark 10:51, see RABBONI.

3. *megistan* (μεγιστάν, 3175**), akin to *megistos*, "greatest," the superlative degree of *megas*, "great," denotes "chief men, nobles"; it is rendered "lords" in Mark 6:21, of nobles in Herod's entourage; "princes" in Rev. 6:15 and 18:23, RV (KJV, "great men").¶

B. Verbs.

1. *kurieuō* (κυριεύω, 2961) denotes "to be lord of, to exercise lordship over," Luke 22:25; Rom. 6:9, 14; 7:1; 14:9; 2 Cor. 1:24; 1 Tim. 6:15; see DOMINION, B, No. 1.¶

2. *katakurieuō* (κατακυριεύω, 2634), a strengthened form of No. 1, is rendered "lording it" in 1 Pet. 5:3, RV: see DOMINION, B, No. 2.

C. Adjective.

kuriakos (κυριακός, 2960), from *kurios* (A, No. 1), signifies "pertaining to a lord or master"; "lordly" is not a legitimate rendering for its use in the NT, where it is used only of Christ; in 1 Cor. 11:20, of the Lord's Supper, or the Supper of the Lord (see FEAST); in Rev. 1:10, of the Day of the Lord (see DAY, No. 1).¶

LOSE, (suffer) LOSS, LOST

1. *apollumi* (ἀπόλλυμι, 622) signifies (I) In the active voice, (*a*) "to destroy, destroy utterly, kill," e.g., Matt. 10:28; Mark 1:24; 9:22; (*b*) "to lose utterly," e.g., Matt. 10:42, of "losing" a reward; Luke 15:4 (1st part), of "losing" a sheep; Luke 9:25, of "losing" oneself (of the "loss" of well-being hereafter); metaphorically, John 6:39, of failing to save; 18:9, of Christ's not "losing" His own; (II) in the middle voice, (*a*) "to perish," of things, e.g., John 6:12 "(that nothing) be lost"; of persons, e.g., Matt. 8:25, "we perish;" of the "loss" of eternal life, usually (always in the RV) translated to perish, John 3:16; 17:12, KJV, "is lost," RV, "perished"; 2 Cor. 4:3, "are perishing," KJV, "are lost" (see PERISH); (*b*) "to be lost," e.g., Luke 15:4 (2nd part), "which is lost"; metaphorically, from the relation between shepherd and flock, of spiritual destitution and alienation from God, Matt. 10:6, "(the) lost (sheep)" of the house of Israel; Luke 19:10 (the perfect tense translated "lost" is here intransitive). See DESTROY.

2. *zēmioō* (ζημιόω, 2210), "to damage" (akin to *zēmia*, "damage," e.g., Acts 27:10, 21), is used in the NT, in the passive voice, signifying "to suffer loss, forfeit, lose," Matt. 16:26; Mark 8:36, of losing one's soul or life; Luke 9:25, RV, "forfeit (his own self)," KJV, "be cast away" (for the preceding verb see No. 1); 1 Cor. 3:15, "he shall suffer loss," i.e., at the Judgment-Seat of

---

* From *Notes on Thessalonians,* by Hogg and Vine, p. 25.

Christ (see v. 13 with 2 Cor. 5:10); 2 Cor. 7:9, "(that) ye might suffer loss," RV (KJV, "might receive damage"); though the apostle did regret the necessity of making them sorry by his letter, he rejoiced that they were made sorry after a godly sort, and that they thus suffered no spiritual loss, which they would have done had their sorrow been otherwise than after a godly manner; in Phil. 3:8, "I suffered the loss (of all things)," RV, i.e., of all things which he formerly counted gain (especially those in verses 5 and 6, to which the article before "all things" points). See CAST, FORFEIT.¶

LOSS

1. *zēmia* (ζημία, 2209), akin to No. 2, above, is used in Acts 27:10, RV, "loss" (KJV, "damage"); v. 21, KJV and RV, "loss," of ship and cargo; in Phil. 3:7, 8 of the apostle's estimate of the things which he formerly valued, and of all things on account of "the excellency of the knowledge of Christ Jesus."¶

2. *apobolē* (ἀποβολή, 580), lit., "casting away" (*apo*, "away," *ballō*, "to cast"), is translated "loss" in Acts 27:22; in Rom. 11:15, "casting away," of the temporary exclusion of the nation of Israel from its position of divine favor, involving the reconciling of the world (i.e., the provision made through the gospel, which brings the world within the scope of reconciliation).¶

3. *hēttēma* (ἥττημα, 2275) denotes "a defect, loss," Rom. 11:12, RV, "loss," KJV, "diminishing" (for the meaning of which in regard to Israel see No. 2); 1 Cor. 6:7, RV, "defect" (KJV, "fault"). See DEFECT.

Note: For "suffer loss" see LOSE, No. 2.

LOT, LOTS

A. Noun.

klēros (κλῆρος, 2819) denotes (*a*) an object used in casting or drawing lots, which consisted of bits, or small tablets, of wood or stone (the probable derivation is from *klaō*, "to break"); these were sometimes inscribed with the names of persons, and were put into a receptacle or a garment ("a lap," Prov. 16:33), from which they were cast, after being shaken together; he whose "lot" first fell out was the one chosen. The method was employed in a variety of circumstances, e.g., of dividing or assigning property, Matt. 27:35; Mark 15:24; Luke 23:34; John 19:24 (cf., e.g., Num. 26:55); of appointing to office, Acts 1:26 (cf., e.g., 1 Sam. 10:20); for other occurrences in the OT, see, e.g., Josh. 7:14 (the earliest instance in Scripture); Lev. 16:7–10; Esth. 3:7; 9:24; (*b*) "what is obtained by lot, an allotted portion," e.g., of the ministry allotted

to the apostles, Acts 1:17, RV, "portion," marg., "lot" (KJV, "part"); in some mss. v. 25, KJV, "part" (the RV follows those which have *topos*, "place"); Acts 8:21; it is also used like *klēronomia*, "an inheritance," in Acts 26:18, of what God has in grace assigned to the sanctified; so Col. 1:12; in 1 Pet. 5:3 it is used of those the spiritual care of, and charge over, whom is assigned to elders, RV, "the charge allotted to you" (plural, lit., "the charges"), KJV, "(God's) heritage." From *klēros* the word "clergy" is derived (a transposition in the application of the term). See CHARGE, No. 4.¶

B. Verb.

lanchanō (λαγχάνω, 2975) denotes (*a*) "to draw lots," John 19:24; (*b*) "to obtain by lot, to obtain," Luke 1:9, "his lot was," lit., "he received by lot," i.e., by divine appointment; Acts 1:17, of the portion "allotted" by the Lord to His apostles in their ministry (cf. A, above); 2 Pet. 1:1, "that have obtained (a like precious faith)," i.e., by its being "allotted" to them, not by acquiring it for themselves, but by divine grace (an act independent of human control, as in the casting of "lots"). See OBTAIN.¶

Note: For divide by lot see DIVIDE.

LOUD

megas (μέγας, 3173), "great," is used, besides other meanings, of intensity, as, e.g., of the force of a voice, e.g., Matt. 27:46, 50; in the following the RV has "great" for the KJV, "loud," Rev. 5:2, 12; 6:10; 7:2, 10; 8:13; 10:3; 12:10; 14:7, 9, 15, 18. See GREAT.

LOVE (Noun and Verb)

A. Verbs.

1. *agapaō* (ἀγαπάω, 25) and the corresponding noun *agapē* (B, No. 1 below) present "the characteristic word of Christianity, and since the Spirit of revelation has used it to express ideas previously unknown, inquiry into its use, whether in Greek literature or in the Septuagint, throws but little light upon its distinctive meaning in the NT. Cf., however, Lev. 19:18; Deut. 6:5.

"*Agapē* and *agapaō* are used in the NT (*a*) to describe the attitude of God toward His Son, John 17:26; the human race, generally, John 3:16; Rom 5:8; and to such as believe on the Lord Jesus Christ, particularly, John 14:21; (*b*) to convey His will to His children concerning their attitude one toward another, John 13:34, and toward all men, 1 Thess. 3:12; 1 Cor. 16:14; 2 Pet. 1:7; (*c*) to express the essential nature of God, 1 John 4:8.

"Love can be known only from the actions it prompts. God's love is seen in the gift of His

Son, 1 John 4:9, 10. But obviously this is not the love of complacency, or affection, that is, it was not drawn out by any excellency in its objects, Rom. 5:8. It was an exercise of the divine will in deliberate choice, made without assignable cause save that which lies in the nature of God Himself, Cf. Deut. 7:7, 8.

"Love had its perfect expression among men in the Lord Jesus Christ, 2 Cor. 5:14; Eph. 2:4; 3:19; 5:2; Christian love is the fruit of His Spirit in the Christian, Gal. 5:22.

"Christian love has God for its primary object, and expresses itself first of all in implicit obedience to His commandments, John 14:15, 21, 23; 15:10; 1 John 2:5; 5:3; 2 John 6. Self-will, that is, self-pleasing, is the negation of love to God.

"Christian love, whether exercised toward the brethren, or toward men generally, is not an impulse from the feelings, it does not always run with the natural inclinations, nor does it spend itself only upon those for whom some affinity is discovered. Love seeks the welfare of all, Rom. 15:2, and works no ill to any, 13:8–10; love seeks opportunity to do good to 'all men, and especially toward them that are of the household of the faith,' Gal. 6:10. See further 1 Cor. 13 and Col. 3:12–14."*

In respect of *agapaō* as used of God, it expresses the deep and constant "love" and interest of a perfect Being towards entirely unworthy objects, producing and fostering a reverential "love" in them towards the Giver, and a practical "love" towards those who are partakers of the same, and a desire to help others to seek the Giver. See BELOVED.

2. *phileō* (φιλέω, 5368) is to be distinguished from *agapaō* in this, that *phileō* more nearly represents "tender affection." The two words are used for the "love" of the Father for the Son, John 3:35 (No. 1), and 5:20 (No. 2); for the believer, 14:21 (No. 1) and 16:27 (No. 2); both, of Christ's "love" for a certain disciple, 13:23 (No. 1), and 20:2 (No. 2). Yet the distinction between the two verbs remains, and they are never used indiscriminately in the same passage; if each is used with reference to the same objects, as just mentioned, each word retains its distinctive and essential character.

Phileō is never used in a command to men to "love" God; it is, however, used as a warning in 1 Cor. 16:22; *agapaō* is used instead, e.g., Matt. 22:37; Luke 10:27; Rom. 8:28; 1 Cor. 8:3; 1 Pet. 1:8; 1 John 4:21. The distinction between the two verbs finds a conspicuous instance in

the narrative of John 21:15–17. The context itself indicates that *agapaō* in the first two questions suggests the "love" that values and esteems (cf. Rev. 12:11). It is an unselfish "love," ready to serve. The use of *phileō* in Peter's answers and the Lord's third question, conveys the thought of cherishing the Object above all else, of manifesting an affection characterized by constancy, from the motive of the highest veneration. See also Trench, *Syn.*, §xii.

Again, to "love" (*phileō*) life, from an undue desire to preserve it, forgetful of the real object of living, meets with the Lord's reproof, John 12:25. On the contrary, to "love" life (*agapaō*) as used in 1 Pet. 3:10, is to consult the true interests of living. Here the word *phileō* would be quite inappropriate.

Note: In Mark 12:38, KJV, *thelō*, "to wish," is translated "love" (RV, "desire").

B. Nouns.

1. *agapē* (ἀγάπη, 26), the significance of which has been pointed out in connection with A, No. 1, is always rendered "love" in the RV where the KJV has "charity," a rendering nowhere used in the RV; in Rom. 14:15, where the KJV has "charitably," the RV, adhering to the translation of the noun, has "in love."

Note: In the two statements in 1 John 4:8 and 16, "God is love," both are used to enjoin the exercise of "love" on the part of believers. While the former introduces a declaration of the mode in which God's love has been manifested (vv. 9, 10), the second introduces a statement of the identification of believers with God in character, and the issue at the Judgment Seat hereafter (v. 17), an identification represented ideally in the sentence "as He is, so are we in this world."

2. *philanthrōpia* (φιλανθρωπία, 5363) denotes, lit., "love for man" (*phileō* and *anthrōpos*, "man"); hence, "kindness," Acts 28:2; in Titus 3:4, "(His) love toward man."¶ Cf. the adverb *philanthrōpōs*, "humanely, kindly," Acts 27:3.¶ See KINDNESS.

Note: For *philarguria*, "love of money," 1 Tim. 6:10, see MONEY (love of). For *philadelphia*, see BROTHER, *Note* (1).

LOVE FEASTS

agapē (ἀγάπη, 26) is used in the plural in Jude 12, and in some mss. in 2 Pet. 2:13; RV marg., "many ancient authorities read 'deceivings,'" (*apatais*); so the KJV. These love feasts arose from the common meals of the early churches (cf. 1 Cor. 11:21). They may have had this origin in the private meals of Jewish households, with the addition of the observance of the Lord's Supper. There were, however, similar

* From *Notes on Thessalonians,* by Hogg and Vine, p. 105.

common meals among the pagan religious brotherhoods. The evil dealt with at Corinth (l.c.) became enhanced by the presence of immoral persons, who degraded the feasts into wanton banquets, as mentioned in 2 Pet. and Jude. In later times the *agapē* became detached from the Lord's Supper.

LOVELY

prosphilēs (προσφιλής, 4375), "pleasing, agreeable, lovely" (*pros*, "toward," *phileō*, "to love"), occurs in Phil. 4:8.¶ In the Sept., Esth. 5:1 (3rd sentence).¶

LOVER

This is combined with other words, forming compound adjectives as follows:

1. *philotheos* (φιλόθεος, 5377), "a lover of God," 2 Tim. 3:4.¶

2. *philoxenos* (φιλόξενος, 5382), "loving strangers" (*xenia*, "hospitality"), translated "a lover of hospitality" in Titus 1:8, KJV (RV, "given to h."); elsewhere, in 1 Tim. 3:2; 1 Pet. 4:9. See HOSPITALITY.¶

3. *philagathos* (φιλάγαθος, 5358), "loving that which is good" (*agathos*), Titus 1:8, "a lover of good," RV.¶

Note: The negative *aphilagathos* is found in 2 Tim. 3:3, "no lovers of good."¶

4. *philarguros* (φιλάργυρος, 5366), "loving money" (*arguros*, "silver"), translated "lovers of money" in Luke 16:14; 2 Tim. 3:2, RV (KJV, "covetous"). See COVETOUS.¶

5. *philautos* (φίλαυτος, 5367), "loving oneself," 2 Tim. 3:2, RV.¶

6. *philēdonos* (φιλήδονος, 5369), "loving pleasure" (*hēdonē*, "pleasure"), 2 Tim. 3:4, "lovers of pleasure."¶

Note: For "loving warmly," Rom. 12:10, see AFFECTION, B, No. 2.¶ For *aphilarguros*, "no lover of money," 1 Tim. 3:3, RV, and Heb. 13:5, RV, see COVETOUS.¶

LOW (to bring, to make), LOW (estate, degree)

A. Verb.

tapeinoō (ταπεινόω, 5013), "to bring low, to humble," is translated "shall be brought low" in Luke 3:5. See HUMBLE.

B. Adjective.

tapeinos (ταπεινός, 5011) denotes "of low degree or estate," Rom. 12:16, "things that are lowly," RV (KJV, "men of low estate"). See BASE, DEGREE, ESTATE, HUMBLE, LOWLY.

C. Noun.

tapeinōsis (ταπείνωσις, 5014), "abasement, humiliation, low estate," is translated "low es-

tate" in Luke 1:48; in Jas. 1:10, "that he is made low," lit., "in his abasement." See HUMILIATION.

LOWER (Adjective, and Verb, to make), LOWEST

A. Adjectives.

1. *katōteros* (κατώτερος, 2737), the comparative degree of *katō*, "beneath," is used in Eph. 4:9, of Christ's descent into "the lower parts of the earth"; two of the various interpretations of this phrase are (1) that the earth is in view in contrast to heaven, (2) that the region is that of hades, the Sheol of the OT. Inasmuch as the passage is describing the effects not merely of the Incarnation but of the death and resurrection of Christ, the second interpretation is to be accepted; cf., e.g., Ps. 16:10; 63:9; where the Sept. has the superlative; 139:15; Acts 2:31. Moreover, as Westcott says, it is most unlikely that the phrase would be used to describe the earth. The word *merē* (plural of *meros*), "parts," would have no force in such a meaning.¶

2. *eschatos* (ἔσχατος, 2078), "last, utmost, lowest," is rendered "lowest" in Luke 14:9, 10, of the "lowest" place at a meal. See LAST.

B. Verb.

elattoō (ἐλαττόω, 1642) denotes "to make less" (*elattōn*, "less"), and is used in the active voice in Heb. 2:7, "Thou madest (Him) . . . lower," and in the passive in v. 9, "was made . . . lower," and John 3:30, "(I must) decrease," (lit., "be made less").¶

LOWER (Verb, to let down) see LET DOWN, No. 2 (*d*)

LOWLINESS, LOWLY

A. Noun.

tapeinophrosunē (ταπεινοφροσύνη, 5012), "lowliness of mind, humbleness," is translated "lowliness" or "lowliness of mind" in Acts 20:19, RV; Eph. 4:2; Phil. 2:3. See HUMBLENESS OF MIND.

B. Adjective.

tapeinos (ταπεινός, 5011), "low, lowly": see HUMBLE and LOW, B.

LOWRING (to be)

stugnazō (στυγνάζω, 4768), "to have a gloomy, somber appearance" (akin to *stugnos*, "somber, gloomy," from a root *stug*—, "to hate"; cf. *stugētos*, "hateful," Titus 3:3), is said of the human countenance, Mark 10:22, RV, "his countenance fell" (KJV, "he was sad"); of the sky, Matt. 16:3, "lowring." See COUNTE-

NANCE, *Note* (3).¶ In the Sept., Ezek. 27:35; 28:19; 32:10.¶

LUCRE (filthy)

A. Noun.

kerdos (κέρδος, 2771), "gain" (cf. *kerdainō*, "to gain, get gain"), is translated "gain" in Phil. 1:21 and 3:7; "lucre" in Titus 1:11 (preceded by *aischros*, "filthy"). See GAIN.¶

B. Adjective.

aischrokerdēs (αἰσχροκερδής, 146) denotes "greedy of base gains" (*aischros*, and A, as above), 1 Tim. 3:8, "greedy of filthy lucre"; so the RV in Titus 1:7, KJV, "given to) filthy lucre." In some mss. 1 Tim 3:3.¶

aischrokerdōs (αἰσχροκερδῶς, 147) denotes "from eagerness for base gain," 1 Pet. 5:2, "for filthy lucre."¶

LUKEWARM

chliaros (χλιαρός, 5513), "tepid, warm" (akin to *chliō*, "to become warm," not found in the NT or Sept.), is used metaphorically in Rev. 3:16, of the state of the Laodicean church, which afforded no refreshment to the Lord, such as is ministered naturally by either cold or hot water.¶

LUMP

phurama (φύραμα, 5445) denotes "that which is mixed or kneaded" (*phuraō*, "to mix"); hence, "a lump," either of dough, Rom. 11:16 (cf. Num. 15:21); 1 Cor. 5:6, 7; Gal. 5:9 (see under LEAVEN); of potter's clay, Rom. 9:21.¶

For LUNATIC see EPILEPTIC

LUST (Noun and Verb)

A. Nouns.

1. *epithumia* (ἐπιθυμία, 1939) denotes "strong desire" of any kind, the various kinds being frequently specified by some adjective (see below). The word is used of a good desire in Luke 22:15; Phil. 1:23, and 1 Thess. 2:17 only. Everywhere else it has a bad sense. In Rom. 6:12 the injunction against letting sin reign in our mortal body to obey the "lust" thereof, refers to those evil desires which are ready to express themselves in bodily activity. They are equally the "lusts" of the flesh, Rom. 13:14; Gal. 5:16, 24; Eph. 2:3; 2 Pet. 2:18; 1 John 2:16, a phrase which describes the emotions of the soul, the natural tendency towards things evil. Such "lusts" are not necessarily base and immoral, they may be refined in character, but are evil if inconsistent with the will of God.

Other descriptions besides those already mentioned are:—"of the mind," Eph. 2:3; "evil (desire)," Col. 3:5; "the passion of," 1 Thess. 4:5, RV; "foolish and hurtful," 1 Tim. 6:9; "youthful," 2 Tim. 2:22; "divers," 2 Tim. 3:6 and Titus 3:3; "their own," 2 Tim. 4:3; 2 Pet. 3:3; Jude 16; "worldly," Titus 2:12; "his own," Jas. 1:14; "your former," 1 Pet. 1:14, RV; "fleshly," 2:11; "of men," 4:2; "of defilement," 2 Pet. 2:10; "of the eyes," 1 John 2:16; of the world ("thereof"), v. 17; "their own ungodly," Jude 18. In Rev. 18:14 "(the fruits) which thy soul lusted after" is, lit., "of thy soul's lust." See DESIRE, A, No. 1 (where associated words are noted).

2. *orexis* (ὄρεξις, 3715), lit., "a reaching" or "stretching after" (akin to *oregomai*, "to stretch oneself out, reach after"), a general term for every kind of desire, is used in Rom. 1:27, "lust."¶

3. *hēdonē* (ἡδονή, 2237), "pleasure," is translated "lusts," in the KJV of Jas. 4:1, 3 (RV, "pleasures"). See PLEASURE.

Note: In 1 Thess. 4:5, KJV, *pathos*, "passion" (RV, "passion"), is translated "lust," which is the better rendering of the next word *epithumia*, rendered "concupiscence." *Pathos* is described by Trench as "the diseased condition out of which *epithumia* springs." In 1 Cor. 12:6: *epithumētēs*, a luster after, is rendered "to lust."

B. Verb.

epithumeō (ἐπιθυμέω, 1937), akin to A, No. 1, has the same twofold meaning as the noun, namely (*a*) "to desire," used of the Holy Spirit against the flesh, Gal. 5:17 (see below); of the Lord Jesus, Luke 22:15, "I have desired;" of the holy angels, 1 Pet. 1:12; of good men, for good things, Matt. 13:17; 1 Tim. 3:1; Heb. 6:11; of men, for things without moral quality, Luke 15:16; 16:21; 17:22; Rev. 9:6; (*b*) of "evil desires," in respect of which it is translated "to lust" in Matt. 5:28; 1 Cor. 10:6; Gal. 5:17 (1st part; see below); Jas. 4:2; to covet, Acts 20:23; Rom. 7:7; 13:9. See COVET, DESIRE, B, No. 2.¶

Notes: (1) In Gal. 5:17, in the statement, "the flesh lusteth against the Spirit, and the Spirit against the flesh," the Holy Spirit is intended, as in the preceding verse. To walk by the Spirit involves the opposition here referred to. The verb "lusteth" is not repeated in the second part of the statement, but must in some way be supplied. Since in modern English the word "lust" is used exclusively in a bad sense, it is unsuitable as a translation of *epithumeō*, where the word is used in a good sense. As the rendering "desire" is used of the Lord Jesus (as mentioned above), it may be best so understood here in respect of the Holy Spirit.

(2) In James 4:5 the RV translates correctly in giving two questions, each of a rhetorical

character, asked by way of remonstrance. The first draws attention to the fact that it is impossible for the Scripture to speak in vain; the second to the impossibility that the Holy Spirit, whom God has caused to dwell in the believer, should "long (unto envying)," *epipotheō* (KJV,

"lust"). Here again, not the human spirit is in view, but the Spirit of God; cf. 1 Cor. 6:19. See LONG.

For **LYING** (falsehood) see **LIE,** and for **LYING** (in wait) see **LIE IN WAIT**

M

MAD, MADNESS
A. Verbs.

1. *mainomai* (μαίνομαι, 3105), "to rage, be mad," is translated by the verb "to be mad" in John 10:20; Acts 12:15; 26:24, 25; 1 Cor. 14:23; see BESIDE ONESELF, No. 2.

2. *emmainomai* (ἐμμαίνομαι, 1693), an intensive form of No. 1, prefixed by *en*, "in," implying "fierce rage, to be furious against"; it is rendered "being exceedingly mad" in Acts 26:11 (cf. 9:1).¶

B. Nouns.

1. *mania* (μανία, 3130), akin to A, and transliterated into English, denotes "frenzy, madness," Acts 26:24 "(thy much learning doth turn thee to) madness," RV; KJV, "(doth make thee) mad."¶

2. *anoia* (ἄνοια, 454), lit., "without understanding" (*a*, negative, *nous*, "mind, understanding"), denotes "folly," 2 Tim. 3:9, and this finding its expression in violent rage, Luke 6:11. See FOLLY.¶

3. *paraphronia* (παραφρονία, 3913), "madness" (from *para*, "contrary to," and *phrēn*, "the mind"), is used in 2 Pet. 2:16.¶ Cf. *paraphroneō*, 2 Cor. 11:23, "I speak like one distraught."¶

MADE (be)
A. Verbs.

1. *ginomai* (γίνομαι, 1096), "to become," is sometimes translated by the passive voice of the verb to make, e.g., Matt. 9:16; John 1:3 (three times), 10; 8:33; Rom. 11:9; 1 Cor. 1:30; 3:13; 4:9, 13; Eph. 2:13; 3:7; Phil. 2:7 (but RV marg., "becoming"); Col. 1:23, 25; Heb. 5:5; 6:4; 7:12, 16, 21, 26; 11:3; Jas. 3:9; 1 Pet. 2:7. In many places the RV translates otherwise, and chiefly by the verb to become, e.g., Matt. 25:6, "there is"; 27:24, "was arising"; John 1:14, "became"; John 2:9, "become"; Rom. 1:3, "born"; 2:25, "is become"; 10:20, "became"; Gal. 3:13, "hav-

ing become"; 4:4, "born" (twice); Heb. 3:14, "are become"; 7:22, "hath . . . become."

2. *keimai* (κεῖμαι, 2749), "to lie," is sometimes used as the passive voice of *tithēmi*, "to put"; it is translated "is (not) made" in 1 Tim. 1:9, of the Law, where a suitable rendering would be "is (not) enacted."

Notes: (1) In 2 Pet. 2:12, KJV, the verb *gennaō*, "to beget," in the passive voice, to be born, is translated "made" (RV, "born"). (2) In Luke 3:5, KJV (3rd statement), the future tense of *eimi*, "to be," is translated "shall be made" (RV, "shall become"); in the next sentence there is nothing in the original representing "*shall be* made". (3) In Acts 16:13, KJV, the infinitive mood of *eimi*, "to be," is translated "to be made" (of prayer), RV, "there was (a place of prayer)." (4) For the translation of words in which the Eng. "made" forms a part of another verb, see under those words, e.g., CONFESSION, KNOWN, LIKE, LOW, PAYMENT, RICH, SUBJECT.

B. Noun.

poiēma (ποίημα, 4161), whence Eng., "poem," denotes "that which is made" (from *poieō*, "to do, make"), Rom. 1:20, "the things that are made"; Eph. 2:10, "(His) workmanship."¶

MAGISTRATE

1. *stratēgos* (στρατηγός, 4755), besides its application to "the captain of the Temple" (see CAPTAIN), denotes "a magistrate or governor," Acts 16:20, 22, 35, 36, 38. These were, in Latin terminology, the *duumviri* or *praetores*, so called in towns which were Roman colonies. They were attended by lictors or "sergeants," who executed their orders. In the circumstances of Acts 16 they exceeded their powers, in giving orders for Roman citizens to be scourged; hence they became suppliants. See CAPTAIN.

2. *archōn* (ἄρχων, 758), "a ruler," denotes, in Luke 12:58, "a local authority, a magistrate,"

acting in the capacity of one who received complaints, and possessing higher authority than the judge, to whom the "magistrate" remits the case. See CHIEF, PRINCE, RULER.

Notes: (1) In Luke 12:11, KJV, *archē,* "a beginning, rule, principality," is translated "magistrates"; the word, however, denotes "rulers" in general: hence the RV, "rulers." (2) For the KJV of Titus 3:1, "to obey magistrates," see OBEY, B, No. 3.

MAGNIFICENCE

megaleiotēs (μεγαλειότης, 3168) denotes "splendor, magnificence" (from *megaleios,* "magnificent," mighty," Acts 2:11, *megas,* "great"), translated "magnificence" in Acts 19:27, of the splendor of the goddess Diana. In Luke 9:43, RV (KJV, "mighty power"); in 2 Pet. 1:16, "majesty." In the papyri writings it is frequent as a ceremonial title.¶

MAGNIFY

megalunō (μεγαλύνω, 3170), "to make great" (*megas*), is translated "to magnify" in Luke 1:46; in v. 58, RV, "had magnified (His mercy)," KJV, "had shewed great (mercy)"; Acts 5:13; 10:46; 19:17; 2 Cor. 10:15, RV (KJV, "we shall be enlarged"), i.e., by their faith in its practical effect he will be so assisted as to enlarge the scope of his gospel ministry and carry its message to regions beyond them; in Phil. 1:20, of the "magnifying" of Christ by him in his body, i.e., in all his activities and ways. In Matt. 23:5, it signifies "to enlarge." See ENLARGE.¶

Note: In Rom. 11:13, KJV, the verb *doxazō,* "to glorify," is translated "I magnify (my office)," RV, "I glorify (my ministry)." See GLORIFY.

MAID, MAIDEN, MAIDSERVANT

1. *pais* (παῖς, 3816), "a child," denotes "a maid" or "maiden" in Luke 8:51 and 54, RV, "maiden" in both places. See CHILD, MANSERVANT, SERVANT, SON, YOUNG MAN.

2. *paidiskē* (παιδίσκη, 3814), a diminutive of No. 1, is translated "maid," "maids," in the KJV and RV in Mark 14:66, 69; Luke 22:56; in the RV (KJV, "damsel"), in Matt. 26:69; John 18:17; Acts 12:13; 16:16; in Luke 12:45, "maidservants" (KJV "maidens"); in Gal. 4:22, 23, 30, 31, RV, "handmaid" (KJV, "bondmaid" or "bondwoman"). See BONDMAID, DAMSEL.¶

3. *korasion* (κοράσιον, 2877), a colloquial, familiar term, is translated "maid" in Matt. 9:24, 25, KJV (RV, "damsel"). See DAMSEL, No. 1.

MAIMED

1. *anapēros,* or *anapeiros* (ἀνάπηρος, 376), "crippled, maimed" (from *ana,* "up," and *pēros,* "disabled in a limb"), is found in Luke 14:13, 21.¶

2. *kullos* (κυλλός, 2948) denotes "crooked, crippled" (akin to *kuliō,* "to roll"); in Matt. 15:30, 31, translated "maimed"; so in 18:8, KJV (RV, "halt") and Mark 9:43 (KJV and RV). See HALT.¶

For MAINSAIL see FORESAIL

MAINTAIN

proistēmi (προΐστημι, 4291), "to preside, rule," also means "to maintain," Titus 3:8 and 14, "to maintain (good works)," RV marg., "profess honest occupations" (KJV, marg.... "trades"). The usage of the phrase *kala erga* (good works) in the Pastoral Epistles is decisive for the rendering "good works," here. See OVER (to be), RULE.

MAJESTY

1. *megaleiotēs* (μεγαλειότης, 3168): see MAGNIFICENCE.

2. *megalōsunē* (μεγαλωσύνη, 3172), from *megas,* "great," denotes "greatness, majesty"; it is used of God the Father, signifying His greatness and dignity, in Heb. 1:3, "the Majesty (on high)," and 8:1, "the Majesty (in the Heavens)"; and in an ascription of praise acknowledging the attributes of God in Jude 25.¶

MAKE

1. *poieō* (ποιέω, 4160), "to do, to make," is used in the latter sense (*a*) of constructing or producing anything, of the creative acts of God, e.g., Matt. 19:4 (2nd part); Acts 17:24; of the acts of human beings, e.g., Matt. 17:4; Acts 9:39; (*b*) with nouns denoting a state or condition, to be the author of, to cause, e.g., peace, Eph. 2:15; Jas. 3:18; stumbling blocks, Rom. 16:17; (*c*) with nouns involving the idea of action (or of something accomplished by action), so as to express the idea of the verb more forcibly (the middle voice is commonly used in this respect, suggesting the action as being of special interest to the doer); for the active voice see, e.g., Mark 2:23, of "making" one's way, where the idea is not that the disciples "made" a path through the standing corn, but simply that they went, the phrase being equivalent to going, "(they began) as they went (to pluck the ears)"; other instances of the active are Rev. 13:13, 14; 16:14; 19:20; for the middle voice (the dynamic or subjective middle), see, e.g.,

John 14:23, "will make Our abode"; in Acts 20:24, "none of these things move me," lit., "I make account of none of these things"; 25:17, "I made no delay," RV; Rom. 15:26; Eph. 4:16; Heb. 1:2; 2 Pet. 1:10; (d) to "make" ready or prepare, e.g., a dinner, Luke 14:12; a supper, John 12:2; (e) to acquire, provide a thing for oneself, Matt. 25:16; Luke 19:18; (f) to render or "make" one or oneself anything, or cause a person or thing to become something, e.g., Matt. 4:19; 12:16, "make (Him known)"; John 5:11, 15, to "make" whole; 16:2, lit., "they shall make (you put out of the synagogue)"; Eph. 2:14; Heb. 1:7; to change one thing into another, Matt. 21:13; John 2:16; 4:46; 1 Cor. 6:15; (g) to constitute one anything, e.g., Acts 2:36; (h) to declare one or oneself anything, John 5:18, "making (Himself equal with God)"; 8:53; 10:33; 19:7, 12; 1 John 1:10; 5:10; (i) to "make" one do a thing, e.g., Luke 5:34; John 6:10; Rev. 3:9. See DO, No. 1, and other renderings there.

2. tithemi (τίθημι, 5087), "to put," is used in the same way as No. 1 (f), Matt. 22:44; Mark 12:36; Luke 20:43; Acts 2:35; 1 Cor. 9:18 (of making the gospel without charge); Heb. 1:13; 10:13; 2 Pet. 2:6; as No. 1 (g), Acts 20:28; Rom. 4:17. See APPOINT, No. 3.

3. diatithemi (διατίθημι, 1303), "to covenant," is rendered "I will make" (the noun diathēkē, "a covenant," being expressed additionally), in the middle voice, in Acts 3:25; Heb. 8:10 and 10:16, lit., "I will covenant" (see RV, marg.). See APPOINT, No. 4.

4. kathistēmi (καθίστημι, 2525), "to set down, set in order, appoint," is used in the same way as No. 1 (g) in Acts 7:10, 27, 35; Heb. 7:28, KJV (RV, "appointeth"); as No. 1 (f) in Rom. 5:19 (twice). See APPOINT, No. 2.

5. sunistēmi (συνίστημι, 4921), "to commend, prove, establish," is used in Gal. 2:18, much as in No. 1 (g), "I make myself (a transgressor)," i.e., "I constitute (or prove) myself, etc." See APPROVE, No. 2.

6. didōmi (δίδωμι, 1325), "to give," is used in 2 Thess. 3:9 in much the same sense as No. 1 (g), "to make (ourselves an ensample)"; in Rev. 3:9 (1st part), RV, "I will give," the sense is virtually the same as poieō in the 2nd part of the verse, see No. 1 (i). See GIVE.

7. epiteleō (ἐπιτελέω, 2005), "to complete," is translated "to make" in Heb. 8:5 (1st part), RV marg., "complete" [in the 2nd part No. 1 is used in sense (a)]. See ACCOMPLISH.

8. sunteleō (συντελέω, 4931), "to end, fulfill," is translated "I will make" in Heb. 8:8, said of the New Covenant. See END.

9. eimi (εἰμί, 1510), "to be," is translated "make" in Mark 12:42, lit., "which is (a farthing)."

10. prospoieō (προσποιέω, 4364), primarily, "to claim," is used in the middle voice with the meaning "to make as if," in Luke 24:28, of the Lord's action regarding the two on the way to Emmaus.¶ In the Sept., 1 Sam. 21:13; Job 19:14.¶

11. katechō (κατέχω, 2722), "to hold fast" (kata, "down," intensive, echō, "to hold"), is used of "making" for a place, in Acts 27:40, RV, "they made for" (KJV, "they made toward"). See HOLD.

12. prokatartizō (προκαταρτίζω, 4294), "to render fit" ("fitted"; artos, "a joint") "beforehand," is used in 2 Cor. 9:5, "to make up beforehand."¶

Notes: (1) In Heb. 9:2, KJV, kataskeuazō, "to prepare," is translated "made" (RV, "prepared"). (2) In Eph. 2:15, KJV, ktizō, "to create," is translated "make" (RV, "create"). (3) In Acts 26:16, KJV, procheirizō, "to determine, choose," is translated "make" (RV, "appoint"). (4) In Gal. 3:16, KJV, erō, "to speak," is translated "were ... made" (RV, "were ... spoken"). (5) In Luke 14:31, KJV, sumballō, "to meet with," in hostile sense, is rendered in combination with the phrase eis polemon, "in war," "to make war"; RV, "to encounter (in war)." (6) In Rom. 14:19 "the things which make for peace" is, lit., "the things of peace." (7) In Acts 22:1 the verb "I make" represents no word in the original, lit., "hear now my defense unto you." (8) The Eng. verb "to make" forms with many other verbs a rendering of single Greek verbs which are given under the respective headings. (9) For "made," Luke 19:16, RV, see GAIN, Note (1).

MAKER

dēmiourgos (δημιουργός, 1217), lit., "one who works for the people" (from dēmos, "people," ergon, "work"; an ancient inscription speaks of the magistrates of Tarsus as dēmiourgoi: the word was formerly used thus regarding several towns in Greece; it is also found used of an artist), came to denote, in general usage, a builder or "maker," and is used of God as the "Maker" of the heavenly city, Heb. 11:10. In that passage the first word of the two, technitēs, denotes "an architect, designer," the second, dēmiourgos, is the actual Framer; the city is the archetype of the earthly one which God chose for His earthly people.¶ Cf. ktistēs, "creator."

MALE

arsēn or arrēn (ἄρσην, 730) is translated "men" in Rom. 1:27 (three times); "man child" in Rev. 12:5 (v. 13 in some mss.); "male" in

Matt. 19:4; Mark 10:6; Luke 2:23; Gal. 3:28, "(there can be no) male (and female),", RV, i.e., sex distinction does not obtain in Christ; sex is no barrier either to salvation or the development of Christian graces. See MAN.¶

MALEFACTOR

1. *kakourgos* (κακοῦργος, 2557), an adjective, lit., "evil-working" (*kakos*, "evil," *ergon*, "work"), is used as a noun, translated "malefactor(-s)" in Luke 23:32, 33, 39, and in the RV in 2 Tim. 2:9 (KJV, "evil doer"). See EVIL, B, *Note* (1). In the Sept., Prov. 21:15.¶

2. *kakopoios* (κακοποιός, 2555), an adjective, lit., "doing evil," is used in 1 Pet. 2:12, 14; 3:16 (in some mss.); 4:15. See EVIL, B, No. 5.¶

MALICE, MALICIOUSNESS, MALICIOUS

kakia (κακία, 2549), "badness in quality" (the opposite of *aretē*, "excellence"), "the vicious character generally" (Lightfoot), is translated "malice" in 1 Cor. 5:8; 14:20; Eph. 4:31; Col. 3:8; Titus 3:3; 1 Pet. 2:1, KJV (RV, "wickedness"; marg., "malice"); "maliciousness" in Rom. 1:29; in 1 Pet. 2:16, KJV (RV, "wickedness"; marg., "malice"). Elsewhere, Matt. 6:34; Acts 8:22; Jas. 1:21 (RV marg., "malice"). See EVIL, B, No. 1.¶

Note: In 2 John 10, KJV, *poneros*, "evil, wicked" (see EVIL, A. No. 2) is translated "malicious" (RV, "wicked").

MALIGNITY

kakoētheia (κακοήθεια, 2550), lit., "bad manner or character" (*kakos*, "bad," *ēthos*, "manner"), hence, "an evil disposition" that tends to put the worst construction on everything, "malice, malevolence, craftiness," occurs in Rom. 1:29, as the accompaniment of *dolos*, "guile."¶

MAMMON

mamōnas (μαμωνᾶς, 3126), a common Aramaic word for "riches," akin to a Hebrew word signifying "to be firm, steadfast" (whence "Amen"), hence, "that which is to be trusted"; Gesenius regards it as derived from a Heb. word signifying "treasure" (Gen. 43:23); it is personified in Matt. 6:24; Luke 16:9, 11, 13.¶

MAN (see also MEN)

1. *anthrōpos* (ἄνθρωπος, 444) is used (*a*) generally, of "a human being, male or female," without reference to sex or nationality, e.g., Matt. 4:4; 12:35; John 2:25; (*b*) in distinction from God, e.g., Matt. 19:6; John 10:33; Gal.

1:11; Col. 3:23; (*c*) in distinction from animals, etc., e.g., Luke 5:10; (*d*) sometimes, in the plural, of "men and women," people, e.g., Matt. 5:13, 16; in Mark 11:2 and 1 Tim. 6:16, lit., "no one of men"; (*e*) in some instances with a suggestion of human frailty and imperfection, e.g., 1 Cor. 2:5; Acts 14:15 (2nd part); (*f*) in the phrase translated "after man," "after the manner of men," "as a man" (KJV), lit. "according to (*kata*) man," is used only by the apostle Paul, of "(1) the practices of fallen humanity, 1 Cor. 3:3; (2) anything of human origin, Gal. 1:11; (3) the laws that govern the administration of justice among men, Rom. 3:5; (4) the standard generally accepted among men, Gal. 3:15; (5) an illustration not drawn from Scripture, 1 Cor. 9:8; (6) probably = 'to use a figurative expression' (see KJV, marg.), i.e., to speak evil of men with whom he had contended at Ephesus as 'beasts' (cf. 1 Cor. 4:6), 1 Cor. 15:32; Lightfoot prefers 'from worldly motives'; but the other interpretation, No. (4), seems to make better sense. See also Rom. 6:19, where, however, the Greek is slightly different, *anthrōpinos*, 'pertaining to mankind'; the meaning is as Nos. (5) and (6)."*

(*g*) in the phrase "the inward man," the regenerate person's spiritual nature personified, the inner self of the believer, Rom. 7:22, as approving of the law of God; in Eph. 3:16, as the sphere of the renewing power of the Holy Spirit; in 2 Cor. 4:16 (where *anthrōpos* is not repeated), in contrast to "the outward man," the physical frame, the "man" as cognizable by the senses; the "inward" man is identical with "the hidden man of the heart," 1 Pet. 3:4.

(*h*) in the expressions "the old man," "the new man," which are confined to Paul's epistles, the former standing for the unregenerate nature personified as the former self of a believer, which, having been crucified with Christ, Rom. 6:6, is to be apprehended practically as such, and to be "put off," Eph. 4:22; Col. 3:9, being the source and seat of sin; the latter, "the new man," standing for the new nature personified as the believer's regenerate self, a nature "created in righteousness and holiness of truth," Eph. 4:24, and having been "put on" at regeneration, Col. 3:10; being "renewed after the image of Him that created him," it is to be "put on" in practical apprehension of these facts.

(*i*) often joined with another noun, e.g., Matt. 11:19, lit., "a man, a glutton"; 13:52, lit., "a man, a householder"; 18:23, "a certain king," lit., "a man, a king."

---

* From *Notes on Galatians*, by Hogg and Vine, p. 139.

(*j*) as equivalent simply to "a person," or "one," whether "man" or woman, e.g., Acts 19:16; Rom. 3:28; Gal. 2:16; Jas. 1:19; 2:24; 3:8 (like the pronoun *tis*, "someone"; *tis* is rendered "man" in Matt. 8:28); or, again (as *tis* sometimes signifies), "a man," e.g., Matt. 17:14; Luke 13:19.

(*k*) definitely, with the article, of some particular person, Matt. 12:13; Mark 3:3, 5; or with the demonstrative pronoun and the article, e.g., Matt. 12:45; Luke 14:30. For the phrase "the Son of man" see SON OF MAN. For "the man of sin," 2 Thess. 2:3, see INIQUITY, No. 1.

(*l*) in the phrase "the man of God," 2 Tim. 3:17, not used as an official designation, nor denoting a special class of believers, it specifies what every believer should be, namely, a person whose life and conduct represent the mind of God and fulfill His will; so in 1 Tim 6:11, "O man of God." Some regard this in the OT sense as of a prophet acting in a distinctive character, possessed of divine authority; but the context is of such a general character as to confirm the more extended designation here.

Notes: (1) In Gal. 3:28, the RV adds the italicized word "man" ("ye all are one *man* in Christ Jesus"), in accordance with Eph. 2:15, which speaks of Jew and Gentile as becoming "one new man" in Christ. The figure is closely analogous to that of "the body." In these two passages "one" is masculine, i.e., "one person"; in John 10:30; 11:52; 17:21, 22, 23, "one" is neuter, "one thing," as in 1 Cor. 3:8; 11:5. The first two, in Gal. 3 and Eph. 2, express vital union, present and eternal; in John 17 the union is moral, a process in course of accomplishment. (2) For *philanthrōpia*, Titus 3:4, "(His) love toward man," see KIND, C, No. 2.

(3) In Rev. 9:20, the RV translates the genitive plural of *anthrōpos* with the article, "mankind" (KJV, "the men"); it might have been rendered "(the rest) of men."

2. *anēr* (ἀνήρ, 435) is never used of the female sex; it stands (*a*) in distinction from a woman, Acts 8:12; 1 Tim. 2:12; as a husband, Matt. 1:16; John 4:16; Rom. 7:2; Titus 1:6; (*b*) as distinct from a boy or infant, 1 Cor. 13:11; metaphorically in Eph. 4:13; (*c*) in conjunction with an adjective or noun, e.g., Luke 5:8, lit., "a man, a sinner"; 24:19, lit., "a man, a prophet"; often in terms of address, e.g., Acts 1:16; 13:15, 26; 15:7, 13, lit., "men, brethren"; with gentilic or local names (virtually a title of honor), e.g., Acts 2:14; 22:3, lit., "Judean men," "a Judean man"; 3:12; 5:35, lit., "Israelite men"; 17:22, "Athenian men"; 19:35, lit., "Ephesian men"; in Acts 14:15 it is used in addressing a company of "men," without any descriptive term. In this verse, however, the distinction between *anēr* and *anthrōpos* (2nd part) is noticeable; the use of the latter comes under No. 1 (*e*); (*d*) in general, "a man, a male person" (used like the pronoun *tis*, No. 3), "a man" (i.e., a certain "man"), e.g., Luke 8:41; in the plural, Acts 6:11.

3. *tis* (τις, 5100), "some one, a certain one," is rendered "a man," "a certain man," e.g., in Matt. 22:24; Mark 8:4, KJV (RV, "one"); 12:19; John 3:3, 5; 6:50; 14:23; 15:6, 13; Acts 13:41, KJV (RV, "one"); 1 Cor. 4:2; 1 Tim. 1:8; 2 Tim. 2:5, 21; Jas. 2:14, 18; 1 Pet. 2:19; 1 John 4:20.

4. *arrēn* and *arsēn* (ἄρσην, 730): see MALE.

5. *teleios* (τέλειος, 5046), perfect, is translated "men" in 1 Cor. 14:20, RV marg., "of full age," KJV marg., "perfect, or, of a ripe age." See PERFECT.

Note: In many cases the word "man" is combined with an adjective to translate one word in the original. These will be found under various other headings.

For MAN CHILD see MALE

MAN'S, OF MAN, MANKIND (see also MEN)

anthrōpinos (ἀνθρώπινος, 442), "human, belonging to man" (from *anthrōpos*, see MAN, No. 1), is used (*a*) of man's wisdom, in 1 Cor. 2:13 (some mss. have it in v. 4, where indeed it is implied; see, however, the RV); (*b*) of "man's judgement," 1 Cor. 4:3 (marg., "day": see DAY); (*c*) of "mankind," Jas. 3:7, lit., "the human nature," RV marg. (KJV marg., "nature of man"); (*d*) of human ordinance, 1 Pet. 2:13; Moulton and Milligan show from the papyri how strongly antithetic to the divine use of the word is in this respect; (*e*) of temptation, 1 Cor. 10:13, RV, "such as man can bear" (KJV, "such as is common to man"), i.e., such as must and does come to "men"; (*f*) of "men's" hands, Acts 17:25; (*g*) in the phrase "after the manner of men," Rom. 6:19.¶

Notes: (1) In Luke 16:12, KJV, *allotrios*, "belonging to another" (*allos*, "another"), here used as a pronoun, is translated "another man's" (RV, "another's"); so, as an adjective, in Rom. 14:4; 15:20; 2 Cor. 10:15, 16 (in this last the RV omits "man"). (2) In Acts 27:22 there is no word representing "man's"; the RV has "of life." (3) In Rom. 5:17, the RV rightly has "the trespass of the one," for KJV, "one man's offense."

MANGER

phatnē (φάτνη, 5336), "a manger," Luke 2:7, 12, 16, also denotes "a stall," 13:15.¶ So in the Sept., the word denoted not only a "manger" but, by metonymy, the stall or crib (Prov. 14:4) containing the "manger."

MANIFEST (Adjective and Verb)

A. Adjectives.

1. *emphanēs* (ἐμφανής, 1717), manifest (akin to *emphainō*, "to show in, to exhibit"; *en*, "in," *phainō*, "to cause to shine"), is used (*a*) literally in Acts 10:40, RV "(gave Him to be made) manifest"; (*b*) metaphorically in Rom. 10:20, "(I was made) manifest." See OPENLY.¶ Cf. B, No. 2.

2. *phaneros* (φανερός, 5318), "open to sight, visible, manifest" (the root *phan*—, signifying "shining," exists also in No. 1), is translated "manifest" in Luke 8:17; Acts 4:16; 7:13, RV (KJV, "known"); Rom. 1:19; 1 Cor. 3:13; 11:19; 14:25; Gal. 5:19; Phil. 1:13; 1 Tim. 4:15 (KJV, "appear"); 1 John 3:10. See APPEAR, B, *Note* (2), KNOW, B, No. 2, OPENLY, OUTWARDLY.

3. *aphanēs* (ἀφανής, 852) denotes "unseen, hidden," Heb. 4:13, "not manifest" (*a*, negative, and *phainō*).¶ In the Sept., Neh. 4:8; Job 24:20.¶

Notes: (1) In 1 Cor. 15:27, KJV *dēlos*, "evident," is translated "manifest" (RV, "evident"). (2) So with *ekdēlos*, 2 Tim. 3:9, an intensive form of *dēlos*, signifying "quite evident."¶ (3) In 1 Tim. 5:25, KJV, *prodēlos*, "evident beforehand, clearly evident," is translated "manifest beforehand" (RV, "evident"); see EVIDENT. (4) For "manifest token," see TOKEN.

B. Verbs.

1. *phaneroō* (φανερόω, 5319), "to make visible, clear, manifest," known (akin to A, No. 2), is used especially in the writings of the apostles John and Paul), occurring 9 times in the Gospel, 9 times in 1 John, 2 in Rev.; in the Pauline Epistles (including Heb.) 24 times; in the other Gospels, only in Mark, 3 times; elsewhere in 1 Pet. 1:20; 5:4.

The true meaning is "to uncover, lay bare, reveal." The following are variations in the rendering, which should be noted: Mark 16:12, 14 (RV, "was manifested," KJV, "appeared"); John 21:1 (RV, "manifested," KJV, "shewed"; cf. v. 14); Rom. 1:19 (RV, "manifested," KJV, "hath shewed"); 2 Cor. 3:3 (RV, "being made manifest," KJV, "are manifestly declared"); 2 Cor. 5:10; 7:12 and Rev. 3:18 (RV, "be made manifest," KJV, "appear"); 2 Cor. 11:6 (RV, "we have made it manifest," KJV, "we have been throughly made manifest"); Col. 1:26 (RV, "hath it been manifested," KJV, "is made manifest"); 3:4 (RV, "be manifested," KJV, "appear"; so 1 Pet. 5:4); 1 Tim. 3:16 (RV, "was manifested," KJV, "was manifest"); 2 Tim. 1:10 (RV,

"hath... been manifested," KJV, "is... made manifest"; cf. Rom. 16:26; 2 Cor. 4:10, 11; 1 Pet. 1:20); Heb. 9:26 (RV, "hath He been manifested," KJV, "hath He appeared"); 1 John 2:28; 3:2 (RV, "is... made manifest," KJV, "doth appear"). See APPEAR, A, No. 4.

2. *emphanizō* (ἐμφανίζω, 1718), akin to A, No. 1, is translated "to manifest, make manifest," in John 14:21, 22; Heb. 11:14, RV; see APPEAR, A, No. 5.

Note: For the adverb *phanerōs*, "manifestly," see EVIDENTLY, OPENLY.

MANIFESTATION

phanerōsis (φανέρωσις, 5321), "a manifestation" (akin to *phaneros* and *phaneroō;* see MANIFEST), occurs in 1 Cor. 12:7 and 2 Cor. 4:2.¶

Note: In Rom. 8:19, KJV, *apokalupsis*, "an uncovering, laying bare, revealing, revelation," is translated "manifestation" (RV, "revealing"). See REVELATION.

MANIFOLD

1. *poikilos* (ποικίλος, 4164), "varied," is translated "manifold" in 1 Pet. 1:6; 4:10 and in Jas. 1:2, RV (KJV, "divers"). See DIVERS, A, No. 2.

2. *polupoikilos* (πολυποίκιλος, 4182), "much varied" (*polus*, "much," and No. 1), is said of the wisdom of God, in Eph. 3:10.¶

3. *pollaplasiōn* (πολλαπλασίων, 4179), "many times more" (from *polus*, "much"), occurs in Luke 18:30, "manifold more," and in many ancient authorities in Matt. 19:29 (RV, marg.; some editions in text); KJV and RV text, "a hundredfold," translating *hekatontaplasiona*.¶

For **MANKIND** see **MAN**, No. 1, *Note* (3), **MAN'S** (c), **ABUSERS**

MANNA

manna (μάννα, 3131), the supernaturally provided food for Israel during their wilderness journey (for details see Exod. 16 and Num. 11). The Hebrew equivalent is given in Exod. 16:15, RV marg., *"man hu."* The translations are, RV, "what is it?"; KJV and RV marg., "it is manna." It is described in Ps. 78:24, 25 as "the corn of heaven" and "the bread of the mighty," RV text and KJV marg. ("angels' food," KJV text), and in 1 Cor. 10:3, as "spiritual meat." The vessel appointed to contain it as a perpetual memorial, was of gold, Heb. 9:4, with Exod. 16:33. The Lord speaks of it as being typical of Himself, the true Bread from Heaven, imparting eternal life and sustenance to those who by faith partake spiritually of Him, John 6:31–35. The "hidden manna" is promised as one of the rewards of the overcomer, Rev. 2:17; it is thus suggestive of the moral excellence of Christ in His life on earth, hid from the eyes of men, by whom He was "despised and rejected"; the path of the overcomer is a reflex of His life.

None of the natural substances called "manna" is to be identified with that which God provided for Israel.¶

MANNER

A. Nouns.

1. ethos (ἔθος, 1485), "a habit, custom" (akin to the verb ethō, "to be accustomed"), is always translated "custom" in the RV ("manner" in the KJV of John 19:40; Acts 15:1; 25:16; Heb. 10:25). See CUSTOM, No. 1.

2. ēthos (ἦθος, 2239), primarily "a haunt, abode," then, "a custom, manner," occurs in the plural in 1 Cor. 15:33, i.e., ethical conduct, morals.¶

3. tropos (τρόπος, 5158), "a turning, fashion, manner, character, way of life," is translated "manner" in Acts 1:11, with reference to the Lord's ascension and return; in Jude 7, of the similarity of the evil of those mentioned in vv. 6 and 7. See CONVERSATION, MEANS, WAY.

Note: In Acts 15:11, the phrase kath' hon tropon, "according to what manner," is translated "in like manner as," RV (KJV, "even as").

4. tupos (τύπος, 5179), "a mark or impress," is translated "manner" in Acts 23:25. See FORM, No. 3.

5. akribeia (ἀκρίβεια, 195), "exactness, precision" (akin to akribēs, "exact, careful"; see akriboō, "to inquire carefully," and akribōs, "carefully"), occurs in Acts 22:3, RV, "strict manner" (KJV, "perfect manner").¶

Notes: (1) The verb ethō, "to be accustomed," has a perfect tense eiōtha, with a present meaning, the neuter of the participle of which, eiōthos, used with the article, signifies "custom," Luke 4:16. In Acts 17:2 the KJV translates it "manner" (RV, "custom"). See CUSTOM, WONT. (2) For agōgē, in 2 Tim. 3:10, KJV, "manner of life" (RV, "conduct") see CONDUCT. (3) For anastrophē, "manner of life," see LIFE, A, No. 6; cf. LIVE, No. 5. Agōgē suggests conduct according to one's leading; anastrophē, conduct as one goes about and mingles with others.

B. Adjectives and Pronouns.

1. potapos (ποταπός, 4217), primarily, "from what country," then, "of what sort," is rendered "what manner of man." Matt. 8:27: so 2 Pet. 3:11; Mark 13:1 (twice); Luke 1:29; 7:39; 1 John 3:1.¶

2. poios (ποῖος, 4169), "of what sort," is translated "by what manner of (death)" in John 21:19, RV, (KJV, "by what"); in Acts 7:49, "what manner of (house)"; Rom. 3:27, "what manner of law"; 1 Cor. 15:35, "what manner of body."

3. hoios (οἷος, 3634), a relative pronoun, signifying "what sort of or manner of," is translated by the latter phrase in 1 Thess. 1:5; some mss. have it in Luke 9:55, as in KJV; the RV follows those in which it is absent.

4. hopoios (ὁποῖος, 3697) is rendered "what manner of" in 1 Thess. 1:9; Jas. 1:24. See SORT, A.

C. Adverbs.

1. polutropōs (πολυτρόπως, 4187), lit., "much turning" (polus, "much," tropos, "a turning"), "in many ways (or manners)," is rendered "in divers manners" in Heb. 1:1.¶

2. houtōs or houtō (οὕτως, 3779), "thus, in this way," is rendered "after this manner" in Matt. 6:9; 1 Pet. 3:5; Rev. 11:5. See SO, THUS.

3. hōsautōs (ὡσαύτως, 5615), a strengthened form of hōs, "thus," signifies "just so, likewise, in like manner," e.g., 1 Tim. 2:9; in the following the RV has "in like manner," for KJV, "likewise"; Mark 14:31; Luke 22:20; Rom. 8:26; 1 Tim. 3:8; 5:25; in Luke 20:31 the RV has "likewise," KJV, "in like manner." See LIKEWISE.

4. homoiōs (ὁμοίως, 3668), akin to the adjective homoios, "like," signifies in "like manner, equally"; in the following the RV has "in like manner" for KJV, "likewise"; Matt. 27:41; Mark 4:16; 15:31; Luke 10:32; 13:3; 16:25; John 5:19; (Heb. 9:21); Jas. 2:25; 1 Pet. 3:1, 7; Rev. 8:12; in Rev. 2:15 the KJV "which thing I hate" translates a variant reading (ho misō). See LIKEWISE, SO.

5. pōs (πῶς, 4459), how, is translated "after what manner" in Acts 20:18. See MEANS.

Note: For paraplēsiōs, Heb. 2:14, RV, see LIKEWISE, No. 4.

D. Preposition.

kata (κατά, 2596), "according to," is translated "after the manner" in John 2:6, i.e., "in accordance with"; in Rom. 3:5; 1 Cor. 3:3; 9:8, RV, "after the manner of" (KJV, "as").

E. Verb.

tropophoreō (τροποφορέω, 5159), "to bear another's manners," is translated "suffered He (their) manners" in Acts 13:18. For this and the alternative reading see BEAR, No. 8.¶

Notes: (1) In the following the phrase kata tauta, or kata ta auta, lit., "according to the same things," is translated "in (the) like (RV, same) manner," Luke 6:23; v. 26, RV (KJV, "so"); 17:30, RV, "after the same manner" (KJV, "even thus"). (2) In Phil. 2:18 the phrase to . . . auto, lit., "the same (thing)," used adverbially, is translated "in the same manner," RV (KJV, "for the same cause"). (3) In Mark 13:29, KJV, *kai*, "also" (so RV), is translated "in like manner." (4) In Acts 15:23 some mss. have the demonstrative pronoun *tode* used adverbially and rendered "after this manner" (KJV). The RV, adhering to the mss. in which it is absent, inserts the word "*thus*" in italics. (5) In Acts 25:20 a phrase lit. rendered "(as to) the inquiry concerning these things" (or according to some mss. "this person," whether "Jesus" or "Paul," v. 19), is translated "of such manner of questions," KJV (RV, "how to inquire concerning these things"). (6) In Luke 1:66, KJV, *ara*, "then" (so RV), is rendered freely "(what) manner." (7) In Luke 24:17, KJV, the pronoun *tis*, "who, what," in the plural (RV, "what") is translated "what manner of"; similarly, in the singular in Mark 4:41; Luke 8:25 (RV, "who"); John 7:36. (8) In Gal. 2:14, KJV, the adverb *ethnikōs*, "in gentile fashion" (*ethnos*, "a nation": in the plural, "Gentiles or nations"), is translated "after the manner of Gentiles" (RV, "as do"). (9) In Matt. 12:31; Luke 11:42; Rev. 18:12, KJV, *pas*, "every" (so RV), is translated "all manner."

MANSERVANT

pais (παῖς, 3816), "a child, boy, youth," also means "a servant, attendant"; in Luke 12:45 it is used in the plural "menservants," in contrast to *paidiskē*, "a maidservant." See CHILD, No. 4.

MANSIONS

monē (μονή, 3438), primarily "a staying, abiding" (akin to *menō*, "to abide"), denotes an "abode" (Eng., "manor," "manse," etc.), translated "mansions" in John 14:2; "abode" in v. 23. There is nothing in the word to indicate separate compartments in heaven; neither does it suggest temporary resting places on the road.¶

MANSLAYERS

androphonos (ἀνδροφόνος, 409), from *anēr*, "a man," and *phoneus*, "a murderer," occurs in the plural in 1 Tim. 1:9.¶

MANTLE

peribolaion (περιβόλαιον, 4018), lit., "that which is thrown around," is translated "mantle" in Heb. 1:12, RV (KJV, "vesture.") See COVERING, VEIL.

MANY

1. *polus* (πολύς, 4183), "much, many, great," is used especially of number when its significance is "many," e.g., Matt. 8:30; 9:10; 13:17; so the RV of Matt. 12:15, where some mss. follow the word by *ochloi*, "multitudes";

1 Cor. 12:12; Rev. 1:15; it is more frequently used as a noun, "many (persons)," e.g., Matt. 3:7; 7:22; 22:14; with the article, "the many," e.g., Matt. 24:12, RV; Mark 9:26, RV, "the more part" (KJV "many"); Rom. 5:15, 19 (twice), RV; 12:5; 1 Cor. 10:17; v. 33, RV; so 2 Cor. 2:17; in 1 Cor. 11:30, RV, "not a few." In Luke 12:47 it is translated "many stripes," the noun being understood. See GREAT, MUCH.

Notes: (1) In Luke 23:8 some mss. have *polla*, "many things," though it is absent from the most authentic; see the RV. (2) In Mark 6:20 the RV, following the mss. which have *aporeō*, "to be perplexed," translates *polla* by "much"; some mss. have *poieō*, "to do"; hence KJV, "did many things." (3) In Gal. 4:27 the plural of *polus*, with *mallon*, "more," is translated "more" in the RV (KJV, "many more"), lit., "many are the children of the desolate more than of her that, etc.," the phrase implying that both should have many children, but the desolate more than the other. (4) In John 7:40 there is no word in the original representing "some" or "many."

2. *pleiōn* (πλείων, 4119), "more, greater," the comparative of No. 1, is translated "many" in Acts 2:40; 13:31; 21:10; 24:17; 25:14; 27:20; 28:23 (KJV; RV, "in great number"); with the article, "most," RV (or rather, "the more part"), Acts 19:32; 1 Cor. 10:5, and Phil. 1:14 (for KJV, "many," an important change); in 2 Cor. 2:6, RV, "the many" (marg., "the more"); so 4:15; in 9:2, "very many" (marg., "the more part"); Heb. 7:23, RV, "many in number" (KJV, "many"). See GREATER, MORE.

3. *hikanos* (ἱκανός, 2425), "sufficient," when used of number sometimes signifies "many," suggesting a sufficient number, (*a*) with nouns, Luke 8:32; 23:9; Acts 9:23, 43; 20:8; 27:7; (*b*) absolutely, some noun being understood, e.g., Acts 12:12; 14:21; 19:19; 1 Cor. 11:30. See ABLE, C, No. 2.

4. *hosos* (ὅσος, 3745), "how much, how many, how great, as much as, as many as," is translated "as many as," e.g., in Matt. 14:36; Mark 3:10; Luke 9:5, RV (KJV, "whosoever"); Acts 2:39; in 9:16, RV, "how many things" (KJV, "how great things"); in Rom. 6:3 the RV renders it by "all we who" (KJV, "so many of us as"), a necessary alteration, not singling out some believers from others, as if some were not baptized, but implying what was recognized as true of all (see Acts 18:8); in 2 Cor. 1:20, RV, "how many soever be" (KJV, "all"). See ALL, C.

5. *posos* (πόσος, 4214), "how much, how great, how many," has the last meaning in Matt. 15:34; 16:9, 10; 27:13 ("how many things"); Mark 6:38; 8:5, 19, 20; 15:4 ("how many things"); Luke 15:17; Acts 21:20. See GREAT.

6. *tosoutos* (τοσοῦτος, 5118), "so great, so much, so many," (*a*) qualifying a noun, is rendered "these many (years)" in Luke 15:29; "so many," John 12:37; 1 Cor. 14:10; (*b*) without a noun, John 6:9; 21:11; Gal. 3:4, "so many things." See GREAT.

Note: In John 17:2, KJV, the neuter of *pas*, "all," followed by the neuter of the relative pronoun "what," and then by the plural of the personal pronoun, is translated "to as many as" (RV, "whatsoever . . . to them").

MARAN-ATHA

maran-atha (μαρὰν ἀθά, 3134), an expression used in 1 Cor. 16:22, is the Greek spelling for two Aramaic words, formerly supposed by some to be an imprecatory utterance or "a curse reinforced by a prayer," an idea contrary to the intimations conveyed by its use in early Christian documents, e.g., "The Teaching of the Apostles," a document of the beginning of the 2nd cent., and in the "Apostolic Constitutions" (vii. 26), where it is used as follows: "Gather us all together into Thy Kingdom which Thou hast prepared. Maranatha, Hosanna to the Son of David; blessed is He that cometh, etc."

The first part, ending in 'n,' signifies "Lord"; as to the second part, the Fathers regarded it as a past tense, "has come." Modern expositors take it as equivalent to a present, "cometh," or future, "will come." Certain Aramaic scholars regard the last part as consisting of *tha,* and regard the phrase as an ejaculation, "Our Lord, come," or "O Lord, come." The character of the context, however, indicates that the apostle is making a statement rather than expressing a desire or uttering a prayer.

As to the reason why it was used, most probably it was a current ejaculation among early Christians, as embodying the consummation of their desires.

"At first the title *Marana* or *Maran*, used in speaking to and of Christ was no more than the respectful designation of the Teacher on the part of the disciples." After His resurrection they used the title of or to Him as applied to God, "but it must here be remembered that the Aramaic-speaking Jews did not, save exceptionally, designate God as 'Lord'; so that in the 'Hebraist' section of the Jewish Christians the expression 'our Lord' (*Marana*) was used in reference to Christ only" (Dalman, *The Words of Jesus*).¶

MARBLE

marmaros (μάρμαρος, 3139) primarily denoted any "glistering stone" (from *mainō,* "to glisten"); hence, "marble," Rev. 18:12.¶

MARINERS

nautēs (ναύτης, 3492), "a seaman, mariner, sailor" (from *naus,* "a ship," Eng., "nautical"), is translated "sailors" in Acts 27:27, 30, RV (KJV, "shipmen"); in Rev. 18:17, RV, "mariners" (KJV, "sailors").¶

MARK (Noun)

1. *charagma* (χάραγμα, 5480) denotes "a stamp, impress," translated "mark" in Rev. 13:16, 17, etc. See GRAVEN.

2. *stigma* (στίγμα, 4742) denotes "a tattooed mark" or "a mark burnt in, a brand" (akin to *stizō,* "to prick"), translated "marks" in Gal. 6:17.¶ "It is probable that the apostle refers to the physical sufferings he had endured since he began to proclaim Jesus as Messiah and Lord [e.g., at Lystra and Philippi]. It is probable, too, that this reference to his scars was intended to set off the insistence of the Judaizers upon a body-mark which cost them nothing. Over against the circumcision they demanded as a proof of obedience to the law he set the indelible tokens, sustained in his own body, of his loyalty to the Lord Jesus. As to the origin of the figure, it was indeed customary for a master to brand his slaves, but this language does not suggest that the apostle had been branded by His Master. Soldiers and criminals also were branded on occasion; but to neither of these is the case of Paul as here described analogous. The religious devotee branded himself with the peculiar mark of the god whose cult he affected; so was Paul branded with the marks of his devotion to the Lord Jesus. It is true such markings were forbidden by the law, Lev. 19:28, but then Paul had not inflicted these on himself.

"The marks of Jesus cannot be taken to be the marks which the Lord bears in His body in consequence of the Crucifixion; they were different in character."*

3. *skopos* (σκοπός, 4649), primarily "a watcher, watchman" (as in the Sept., e.g., Ezek. 3:17), then, "a mark on which to fix the eye" (akin to *skopeō,* "to look at"), is used metaphorically in Phil. 3:14, of "an aim or object," RV, "goal." See GOAL.¶

MARK (Verb)

1. *epechō* (ἐπέχω, 1907), lit., "to hold upon" (*epi,* "upon," *echō,* "to hold"), signifies (like *parechō*) "to hold out," Phil. 2:16, of the word of life; then, "to hold one's mind towards, to observe," translated "marked" in Luke 14:7, of

---

* From *Notes on Galatians,* by Hogg and Vine, p. 344.

the Lord's observance of those who chose the chief seats. See HEED, HOLD, STAY.

2. *skopeō* (σκοπέω, 4648), "to look at, behold, watch, contemplate," (akin to *skopos*, "a mark," see Noun above), is used metaphorically of "looking to," and translated "mark" in Rom. 16:17, of a warning against those who cause divisions, and in Phil. 3:17, of observing those who walked after the example of the apostle and his fellow workers, so as to follow their ways. See HEED, *Note* (1), LOOK.

MARKET, MARKETPLACE

agora (ἀγορά, 58), primarily "an assembly," or, in general, "an open space in a town" (akin to *ageirō*, "to bring together"), became applied, according to papyri evidences, to a variety of things, e.g., "a judicial assembly," "a market," or even "supplies, provisions" (Moulton and Milligan, *Vocab.*). In the NT it denotes "a place of assembly, a public place or forum, a marketplace." A variety of circumstances, connected with it as a public gathering place, is mentioned, e.g., business dealings such as the hiring of laborers, Matt. 20:3; the buying and selling of goods, Mark 7:4 (involving risk of pollution); the games of children, Matt. 11:16; Luke 7:32; exchange of greetings, Matt. 23:7; Mark 12:38; Luke 11:43; 20:46; the holding of trials, Acts 16:19; public discussions, Acts 17:17. Mark 6:56 records the bringing of the sick there. The word always carries with it the idea of publicity, in contrast to private circumstances.

The RV always translates it "marketplace" or in the plural. The KJV sometimes changes the rendering to "markets" and translates it "streets" in Mark 6:56. See STREET.¶

MARRED

Note: In Mark 2:22, *apollumi*, "to destroy, perish," is found in the most authentic mss. as applying both to the wine and the wine skins, RV, "perisheth"; the KJV follows the mss. which tell of the wine being "spilled" (*ekcheō*, "to pour out"), and the skins (KJV, "bottles") being "marred." See DESTROY, No. 1.

MARRIAGE (give in), MARRY

A. Noun.

gamos (γάμος, 1062), "a marriage, wedding," or "wedding feast," is used to denote (*a*) the ceremony and its proceedings, including the "marriage feast," John 2:1, 2; of the "marriage ceremony" only, figuratively, Rev. 19:7, as distinct from the "marriage feast" (v. 9); (*b*) "the marriage feast," RV in Matt. 22:2–4, 9; in v. 8, 10, "wedding;" in 25:10, RV "marriage feast;" so Luke 12:36; 14:8; in Matt. 22:11, 12, the

"wedding garment" is, lit., "a garment of a wedding." In Rev. 19, where, under the figure of a "marriage," the union of Christ, as the Lamb of God, with His heavenly bride is so described, the marriage itself takes place in heaven during the Parousia, v. 7 (the aorist or point tense indicating an accomplished fact; the bride is called "His wife"); the "marriage feast" or supper is to take place on earth, after the Second Advent, v. 9. That Christ is spoken of as the Lamb points to His atoning sacrifice as the ground upon which the spiritual union takes place. The background of the phraseology lies in the OT description of the relation of God to Israel, e.g., Isa. 54:4,ff.; Ezek. 16:7,ff.; Hos. 2:19; (*c*) "marriage" in general, including the "married" state, which is to be "had in honor," Heb. 13:4, RV¶

Note: Among the Jews the "marriage supper" took place in the husband's house and was the great social event in the family life. Large hospitality, and resentment at the refusal of an invitation, are indicated in Matt. 22:1–14. The "marriage" in Cana exhibits the way in which a "marriage feast" was conducted in humbler homes. Special honor attached to the male friends of the bridegroom, "the sons of the bridechamber," Matt. 9:15, RV (see BRIDECHAMBER). At the close the parents conducted the bride to the nuptial chamber (cf. Judg. 15:1)

B. Verbs.

1. *gameō* (γαμέω, 1060), "to marry" (akin to A), is used (*a*) of "the man," Matt. 5:32; 19:9, 10; 22:25 (RV; KJV, "married a wife"); v. 30; 24:38; Mark 6:17; 10:11; 12:25; Luke 14:20; 16:18; 17:27, RV, "married" (KJV, "married wives"); 20:34, 35; 1 Cor. 7:28 (1st part); v. 33; (*b*) of "the woman," in the active voice, Mark 10:12; 1 Cor. 7:28 (last part); ver. 34; 1 Tim. 5:11, 14; in the passive voice, 1 Cor. 7:39; (*c*) of "both sexes," 1 Cor. 7:9, 10, 36; 1 Tim. 4:3.¶

2. *gamizō* (γαμίζω, 1061v), "to give in marriage," is used in the passive voice in Matt. 22:30 (2nd clause), some mss. have No. 5 here; Mark 12:25 (No. 3 in some mss.); Luke 17:27 (No. 5 in some mss.); 20:35 (last word), passive (Nos. 3 and 4 in some mss.); in the active voice Matt. 24:38 (Nos. 3 and 5 in some mss.); further, of giving a daughter in "marriage," 1 Cor. 7:38 (twice), RV (No. 5 in some mss.), which, on the whole, may be taken as the meaning. In this part of the Epistle, the apostle was answering a number of questions on matters about which the church at Corinth had written to him, and in this particular matter the formal transition from "marriage" in general to the subject of giving a daughter in "marriage," is simple.

Eastern customs naturally would involve the inclusion of the latter in the inquiry and the reply.¶

3. *gamiskō* (γαμίσκω, 1061), an alternative for No. 2, Luke 20:34 (some mss. have No. 4); in some mss. in Mark 12:25; Luke 20:35.¶

4. *ekgamiskō* (ἐκγαμίσκω, 1548), "to give out in marriage" (*ek*, "out," and No. 3): see Nos. 2 and 3.

5. *ekgamizō* (ἐκγαμίζω, 1547), an alternative for No. 4: see Nos. 2 and 3.¶

6. *epigambreuō* (ἐπιγαμβρεύω, 1918), "to take to wife after" (*epi*, "upon," *gambros*, "a connection by marriage"), signifies "to marry" (of a deceased husband's next of kin, Matt. 22:24).¶ Cf. Gen. 38:8.

Note: In Rom. 7:3 (twice) and v. 4, KJV, *ginomai*, "to become" (here, "to become another man's"), is translated "be married" (RV, "be joined").

MARROW

muelos (μυελός, 3452), "marrow," occurs in Heb. 4:12, where, by a natural metaphor, the phraseology changes from the material to the spiritual.¶

For MARTYR see WITNESS

MARVEL (Noun and Verb), MARVELLOUS

A. Noun.

thauma (θαῦμα, 2295), "a wonder" (akin to *theaomai*, "to gaze in wonder"), is found in the most authentic mss. in 2 Cor. 11:14 (some mss. have the adjective *thaumastos*: see C, below), "(no) marvel"; in Rev. 17:6, RV, "wonder" (KJV, "admiration"), said of John's astonishment at the vision of the woman described as Babylon the Great.¶ In the Sept., Job 17:8; 18:20; in some mss., 20:8 and 21:5.¶ Cf. *teras*, "a wonder"; *sēmeion*, "a sign"; *thambos*, "wonder"; *ekstasis*, "amazement."

B. Verbs.

1. *thaumazō* (θαυμάζω, 2296) signifies "to wonder at, marvel" (akin to A); the following are RV differences from the KJV: Luke 2:33, "were marveling" for "marveled"; Luke 8:25 and 11:14, "marveled" for "wondered"; 9:43, "were marveling" for "wondered"; 2 Thess. 1:10, "marveled at" for "admired" (of the person of Christ at the time of the shining forth of His Parousia, at the Second Advent). See WONDER.

Note: In Matt. 9:8, KJV translates this verb; RV, *phobeō*, "were afraid."

2. *ekthaumazō* (ἐκθαυμάζω, 1537 and

2296), a strengthened form of No. 1 (*ek*, intensive), is found in the best mss. in Mark 12:17, RV, "wondered greatly" (some mss. have No. 1).¶

C. Adjective.

thaumastos (θαυμαστός, 2298), "marvellous" (akin to A and B), is said (*a*) of the Lord's doing in making the rejected Stone the Head of the corner, Matt. 21:42; Mark 12:11; (*b*) of the erstwhile blind man's astonishment that the Pharisees knew not from whence Christ had come, and yet He had given him sight, John 9:30, RV, "the marvel," KJV, "a marvellous thing"; (*c*) of the spiritual light into which believers are brought, 1 Pet. 2:9; (*d*) of the vision of the seven angels having the seven last plagues, Rev. 15:1; (*e*) of the works of God, 15:3.¶

MASTER (Noun and Verb)

A. Nouns.

1. *didaskalos* (διδάσκαλος, 1320), "a teacher" (from *didaskō*, "to teach"), is frequently rendered "Master" in the four Gospels, as a title of address to Christ, e.g., Matt. 8:19; Mark 4:38 (there are more instances in Luke than in the other Gospels); John 1:38, where it interprets "Rabbi"; 20:16, where it interprets "Rabboni." It is used by Christ of Himself in Matt. 23:8 (see No. 6) and John 13:13–14; by others concerning Him, Matt. 17:24; 26:18; Mark 5:35; 14:14; Luke 8:49; 22:11; John 11:28. In John 3:10, the Lord uses it in addressing Nicodemus, RV, "the teacher" (KJV, "a master"), where the article does not specify a particular "teacher," but designates the member of a class; for the class see Luke 2:46, "the doctors" (RV, marg., "teachers"). It is used of the relation of a disciple to his "master," in Matt. 10:24, 25; Luke 6:40. It is not translated "masters" in the rest of the NT, save in the KJV of Jas. 3:1 "(be not many) masters," where obviously the RV "teachers" is the meaning. See TEACHER.

2. *kurios* (κύριος, 2962), "a lord, one who exercises power," is translated "masters" in Matt. 6:24; 15:27; Mark 13:35; Luke 16:13; Acts 16:16, 19; Rom. 14:4, KJV (RV, "lord"); Eph. 6:5, 9 (twice), the 2nd time of Christ; so in Col. 3:22; 4:1. See LORD.

3. *despotēs* (δεσπότης, 1203), one who has "absolute ownership and uncontrolled power," is translated "masters" in 1 Tim. 6:1, 2; Titus 2:9; 1 Pet. 2:18; of Christ, 2 Tim. 2:21; 2 Pet. 2:1, RV (for KJV, "Lord"); in Jude 4, RV, it is applied to Christ "(our only) Master (and Lord, Jesus Christ)," KJV "(the only) Lord (God)"; in Rev. 6:10, RV, in an address to God, "O Master"

(KJV, "O Lord"). It is rendered "Lord" in Luke 2:29 and Acts 4:24. See LORD.¶

Note: For "master of the house," see GOODMAN.

4. *rabbei* (ῥαββεί, 4461) was an Aramaic word signifying "my master," a title of respectful address to Jewish teachers.

"The Aramaic word *rabbei*, transliterated into Greek, is explicitly recognized as the common form of address to Christ, Matt. 26:25 (cf., however, v. 22, *kurios*); 26:49; Mark 9:5, but Matt. 17:4, *kurios*" (Dalman, *The Words of Jesus*).

In the following the RV has "Rabbi" for KJV "Master"; Matt. 26:25, 49; Mark 9:5; 11:21; 14:45; John 4:31; 9:2; 11:8. In other passages the KJV has "Rabbi," Matt. 23:7–8; John 1:38, 49; 3:2, 26; 6:25.¶

Note: The form *Rabbounei (Rabboni)*, in Mark 10:51, is retained in the RV (for KJV, "Lord"); in John 20:16, in both KJV and RV. This title is said to be Galilean; hence it would be natural in the lips of a woman of Magdala. It does not differ materially from "Rabbi."¶

5. *epistatēs* (ἐπιστάτης, 1988) denotes "a chief, a commander, overseer master." It is used by the disciples in addressing the Lord, in recognition of His authority rather than His instruction (Nos. 1 and 6); it occurs only in Luke 5:5; 8:24, 45; 9:33, 49; 17:13.¶ In the Sept., 2 Kings 25:19; 2 Chron. 31:12; Jer. 36:26; 52:25.¶

Note: "The form *epistata* . . . alongside of the commoner *didaskale* is . . . a Greek synonym for the latter, and both are to be traced back to the Aramaic *rabbei*." Christ forbade His disciples to allow themselves to be called *rabbi*, "on the ground that He alone was their Master, Matt. 23:8. In reference to Himself the designation was expressive of the real relation between them. The form of address 'Good Master' He, however, refused to allow, Mark 10:17, 18 . . . in the mouth of the speaker it was mere insolent flattery . . . the Lord was unwilling that anyone should thoughtlessly deal with such an epithet; and here, as always, the honor due to the Father was the first consideration with Him. . . . The primitive community never ventured to call Jesus 'Our Teacher' after He had been exalted to the Throne of God. The title *rabbi*, expressing the relation of the disciple to the teacher, vanished from use; and there remained only the designation *maran*, the servant's appropriate acknowledgement of his Lord" (Dalman).

6. *kathēgetēs* (καθηγητής, 2519), properly "a guide" (akin to *kathēgeomai*, "to go before, guide"; *kata*, "down," *hēgeomai*, "to guide"), denotes "a master, a teacher," Matt. 23:10

(twice); some mss. have it in v. 8, where the most authentic have No. 1.¶

7. *kubernētēs* (κυβερνήτης, 2942), "the pilot or steersman of a ship," or, metaphorically, "a guide or governor" (akin to *kubernaō*, "to guide": Eng., "govern" is connected; cf. *kubernēsis*, "a steering, pilotage," 1 Cor. 12:28, "governments"), is translated "master" in Acts 27:11; "shipmaster" in Rev. 18:17.¶ In the Sept., Prov. 23:34; Ezek. 27:8, 27–28.¶

B. Verb.

katakurieuō (κατακυριεύω, 2634), "to exercise lordship" (*kata*, "down upon," *kurios*, "a lord"), is translated "mastered" in Acts 19:16, RV, of the action of the evil spirit on the sons of Sceva (KJV, "overcame"). In translating the word *amphoterōn* by its primary meaning, "both," the RV describes the incident as referring to two only. It has been shown, however, that in the period of the *Koinē* (see Foreword) *amphoteroi*, "both," was no longer restricted to two persons. Ramsay ascribes the abruptness of the word here to the vivid narrative of an eye witness. See DOMINION, LORD, LORDSHIP.

MASTERBUILDER

architektōn (ἀρχιτέκτων, 753), from *archē*, "rule, beginning," and *tektōn*, "an artificer" (whence Eng., "architect"), "a principal artificer," is used figuratively by the apostle in 1 Cor. 3:10, of his work in laying the foundation of the local church in Corinth, inasmuch as the inception of the spiritual work there devolved upon him. The examples from the papyri and from inscriptions, as illustrated by Moulton and Milligan, show that the word had a wider application than our "architect," and confirm the rendering "masterbuilder" in this passage, which is of course borne out by the context.¶

MATTER, MATTERS

1. *logos* (λόγος, 3056), "a word, speech, discourse, account," hence also "that which is spoken of, a matter, affair, thing," is translated "matter" in Mark 1:45; Acts 8:21; 15:6; 19:38; in the RV of Phil. 4:15, "in the matter of" (KJV, "concerning"). See ACCOUNT.

2. *pragma* (πρᾶγμα, 4229), akin to *prassō*, "to do," denotes (*a*) "that which has been done, a deed," translated "matters" in Luke 1:1, RV (KJV, "things"); "matter" in 2 Cor. 7:11; (*b*) "that which is being done, an affair," translated "matter" in Rom. 16:2, RV (KJV, "business"); 1 Cor. 6:1, in a forensic sense, "a lawsuit" (frequently found with this meaning in the papyri); 1 Thess. 4:6, "in the matter," i.e., the "matter" under consideration, which, as the preceding

words show, is here the sin of adultery. See BUSINESS, B, *Note* (1), THING.

3. *enklēma* (ἔγκλημα, 1462), "an accusation, charge," Acts 25:16, RV, "matter laid against him"; elsewhere, Acts 23:29, "charge"; see ACCUSATION, A, No. 3.¶

Notes: (1) In Gal. 2:6, the statement "it maketh no matter" translates the verb *diapherō*, "to bear asunder, make a difference," with *ouden*, "nothing," used adverbially, i.e., "it makes no difference (to me)"; his commission from the Lord relieved him of responsibility to the authority of the apostles. (2) In 1 Cor. 9:11, RV, the neuter of the adjective *megas*, "great," is translated "a great matter" (KJV, "a great thing"). (3) In Jas. 3:5, KJV, *hulē*, "a wood, forest," is translated "a matter" (RV, and KJV marg., "wood"). In older English the word "matter" actually meant "wood" (like its Latin original, *materia*). (4) In Acts 17:32, the KJV adds "*matter*" to the pronoun "this," RV, "(concerning) this." (5) In 2 Cor. 8:19, RV, the phrase, lit., "in this grace" is translated "in the matter of (KJV, with) this grace." (6) In 2 Cor. 8:20, RV, the phrase, lit., "in this bounty" is translated "in the matter of this bounty" (KJV, "in this abundance"). (7) In 2 Cor. 9:5, the phrase, lit., "as a bounty" is amplified to "as a matter of bounty." (8) For 1 Pet. 4:15 see BUSYBODY. See also OTHER, THIS, THESE, WEIGHTIER, WRONG.

MAY, MAYEST, MIGHT

1. *dunamai* (δύναμαι, 1410), "to be able, have power," whether by personal ability, permission, or opportunity, is sometimes rendered "may" or "might," e.g., Matt. 26:9; Mark 14:5; Acts 17:19; 1 Thess. 2:6. In the following the RV substitutes "can," "canst," "couldst," for the KJV, e.g., Matt. 26:42; Mark 4:32; 14:7; Luke 16:2; Acts 24:11; 25:11; 27:12; 1 Cor. 7:21; 14:31 (here the alteration is especially important, as not permission for all to prophesy, but ability to do so, is the meaning); Eph. 3:4. In the following the RV substitutes the verb "to be able," Acts 19:40; 24:8; Rev. 13:17. See ABLE, B, No. 1.

2. *exesti* (ἔξεστι, 1832), "it is permitted, lawful" (*eimi*, "to be," prefixed by *ek*, "from"), is rendered "(I) may" in Acts 2:29, RV [KJV, "let (me)"]; in Acts 21:37, "may (I)," lit., "is it permitted (me to speak)?" Some mss. have it in 8:37, "thou mayest" (KJV). See LAWFUL.

3. *isos* (ἴσος, 2481), "equally" (from the adjective *isos*, "equal"), is translated "it may be" in Luke 20:13 (i.e., "perhaps").¶

4. *tunchanō* (τυγχάνω, 5177), "to meet with, reach, obtain," denotes, intransitively, "to happen, chance, befall"; used impersonally with

the conjunction *ei*, "if," it signifies "it may be," "perhaps," e.g., 1 Cor. 14:10; 15:37, "it may chance"; 16:6.

Notes: (1) In Matt. 8:28, KJV, *ischuō*, "to have strength, be strong, be well able," is translated "might" (RV, "could"). (2) "May," "might," sometimes translate the prepositional phrase *eis*, "unto," with the definite article, followed by the infinitive mood of some verb, expressing purpose, e.g., Acts 3:19, "may be blotted out," lit., "unto the blotting out of"; Rom. 3:26, "that he might be," lit., "unto his being"; so 8:29; 2 Cor. 1:4, "that we may be able," lit., "unto our being able"; Eph. 1:18, "that ye may know," lit., "unto your knowing"; Acts 7:19; Rom. 1:11; 4:16; 12:2; 15:13; Phil. 1: 10; 1 Thess. 3:10, 13; 2 Thess. 1:5; 2:6, 10; Heb. 12:10. In Luke 20:20 the best mss. have *hōste*, "so as to," RV, as, e.g., in 1 Pet. 1:21. Sometimes the article with the infinitive mood without a preceding preposition, expresses result, e.g., Luke 21:22; Acts 26:18 (twice), "that they may turn," RV; cf. Rom. 6:6; 11:10; 1 Cor. 10:13; Phil. 3:10, "that I may know"; Jas. 5:17.

(3) The phrases "may be," "might be," are frequently the rendering of the verb "to be," in the subjunctive or optative moods, preceded by a conjunction introducing a condition, or expressing a wish or purpose, e.g., Matt. 6:4; John 14:3; 17:11. Sometimes the phrase translates simply the infinitive mood of the verb *eimi*, "to be," e.g., Luke 8:38, lit., "to be (with Him)"; so the RV in 2 Cor. 5:9; in 2 Cor. 9:5, "that (the same) might be," lit., "(the same) to be."

(4) In Heb. 7:9 the phrase *hōs* ("so") *epos* ("a word") *eipein* ("to say"), i.e., lit., "so to say a word" is an idiom, translated in the RV, "so to say" (KJV, "if I may so say"); the Eng. equivalent is "one might almost say."

ME

Notes: (1) The pronoun, whether alone or with some English preposition, e.g., "of, to, for, in," translates one or other of the oblique cases of *ego*, "I." (2) In Philem. 13 the reflexive pronoun *emauton*, "myself," is translated "me," governed by the preposition *pros*, with, lit., "with myself." (3) In Titus 1:3, for the KJV, "is committed unto me," the RV has "I was intrusted." (4) In Phil. 2:23, "how it will go with me," is, lit., "the (things) concerning me." (5) The phrase *en emoi*, "in me," is used (*a*) instrumentally (*en*, instrumental, "by" or "through"), e.g., 2 Cor. 13:3; (*b*) subjectively, "within me," e.g., Gal. 2:20; (*c*) objectively, "in my case," e.g., 1 Cor. 9:15; 14:11; Gal. 1:16, 24; 1 Tim. 1:16. (6) In Luke 22:19 the possessive pronoun *emos*, "my," is rendered "of Me," lit., "(into) My (remembrance)."

MEAL

aleuron (ἄλευρον, 224), "meal" (akin to *aleuō*, "to grind," and therefore, lit., "what is ground"), occurs in Matt. 13:33; Luke 13:21.¶

MEAN (Adjective)

asēmos (ἄσημος, 767), lit., "without mark" (*a*, negative, *sēma*, "a mark"), i.e., "undistinguished, obscure," was applied by the apostle Paul negatively, to his native city, Tarsus, Acts 21:39.¶ Moulton and Milligan (*Vocab.*) have a note as follows: "This word occurs perpetually in the papyri to denote a man who is 'not distinguished' from his neighbors by the convenient scars on eyebrow or arm or right shin, which identify so many individuals in formal documents." Deissmann suggests that the word may have been the technical term for "uncircumcised," among the Greek Egyptians. In another papyrus document a pair of silver bracelets are described as of "unstamped" (*asēmos*) silver.

MEAN (Verb)

1. *eimi* (εἰμί, 1510), "to be," in certain of its forms, has an explicative force, signifying "to denote, to import," e.g., Matt. 9:13; 12:7, "(what this) meaneth," lit. "(what this) is"; Luke 18:36, "meant" (lit., "might be"); Acts 10:17, "might mean," RV (lit., "might be"); in Luke 15:26 the RV keeps to the verb "to be," "(what these things) might be" (KJV, "meant"). In Acts 2:12 the verb "to be" is preceded by *thelō*, "to will," and the phrase is translated "(what) meaneth (this)," lit., "(what) does (this) will to be?" in 17:20, lit., "(what do these things) will to be?"

2. *legō* (λέγω, 3004), "to say," sometimes has the significance of "meaning" something; so the RV in 1 Cor. 1:12; KJV, "(this) I say." *Notes:* (1) In Acts 27:2, KJV, *mellō*, "to be about to," is translated "meaning" (RV, "was about to"), with reference to the ship (according to the best mss.). (2) In Acts 21:13, KJV, *poieō*, "to do," is translated "(what) mean ye (to weep)"; RV, "(what) do ye, (weeping)." (3) The abbreviated original in 2 Cor. 8:13 is rendered by the italicized additions, KJV, "*I mean* (not)," RV, "*I say* (not) *this*." Cf. the RV italics in Mark 6:2.

MEANING

dunamis (δύναμις, 1411), "power, force," is used of the significance or force of what is spoken, 1 Cor. 14:11. See MIGHT, POWER.

MEANS (by all, by any, etc.)

1. *pantōs* (πάντως, 3843), an adverb from *pas*, "all," denoting "wholly, altogether, entirely," is used in 1 Cor. 9:22, "by all means." When the apostle says, "I am become all things to all men, that I may by all means save some," he is simply speaking of his accommodating himself to various human conditions consistently with fidelity to the truth, with no unscriptural compliance with men, but in the exercise of self denial; "by all means" refers to the preceding context from v. 18, and stresses his desire to be used in the salvation of some. It is found in Acts 21:22, RV, "certainly." Some mss. have the word in this sense in Acts 18:21 (KJV). See ALTOGETHER, B, No. 1.

2. *pōs* (πως, 4458), "at all, somehow, in any way," is used after the conjunction (*a*) *ei*, "if," meaning "if by any means," e.g., Acts 27:12; Rom. 1:10; 11:14; Phil. 3:11; (*b*) *mē*, "lest, lest by any means," e.g., 1 Cor. 8:9; 9:27; 2 Cor. 2:7, RV (KJV, "perhaps"); 9:4, RV (KJV, "haply"); 11:3; 12:20, RV; Gal. 2:2; 4:11, RV (KJV, "lest"); 1 Thess. 3:5 (KJV, "lest by some means").

3. *ek* (ἐκ, 1537), "out of, from, by," suggesting "the source from which something is done," is sometimes rendered "by means of," e.g., Luke 16:9, RV, "by means of (the mammon of unrighteousness)"; KJV, "of"; 2 Cor. 1:11, "by (the) means of (many)."

4. *dia* (διά, 1223), "by, by means of," when followed by the genitive case, is instrumental, e.g., 2 Pet. 3:6, RV, "by which means" (KJV, "whereby").

5. *pōs* (πῶς, 4459), an interrogative adverb (different from No. 2), "how, in what way," Luke 8:36, KJV, "by what means," RV, "how"; so John 9:21; cf. *Note* (4) below.

Notes: (1) In Luke 5:18 the KJV adds the word "*means*" in italics. (2) The word *tropos*, "a manner, way," is sometimes used in a prepositional phrase, e.g., 2 Thess. 2:3, KJV, "by any means," RV, "in any wise," lit., "in any manner"; 3:16, KJV, "by all means," RV, "in all ways," lit., "in every manner." (3) The double negative *ou mē*, i.e., "no not," "not at all," is translated "by no means," Matt. 5:26; in Luke 10:19, "by any means," KJV (RV, "in any wise"); Luke 12:59, RV, "by no means" (KJV, "not"). (4) In Acts 4:9, the phrase *en*, "in" or "by," with *tini* (from *tis*, "who"), lit., "in whom" (RV, marg.), is translated "by what means." (5) In Heb. 9:15, RV, the verb *ginomai*, "to come to be, become, take place," used in its 2nd aorist participle, is rightly translated "(a death) having taken place"; KJV, "by means of (death)." (6) In Rev. 13:14, RV, *dia*, followed by the accusative case, is rightly translated "by reason of," i.e., "on account of" (KJV, wrongly, "by *the means of*").

For MEANWHILE see WHILE

MEASURE (Noun and Verb)

A. Nouns.

1. *metron* (μέτρον, 3358) denotes (I) "that which is used for measuring, a measure," (*a*) of "a vessel," figuratively, Matt. 23:32; Luke 6:38 (twice); in John 3:34, with the preposition *ek*, "(He giveth not the Spirit) by measure," RV (which is a necessary correction; the italicized words "*unto him*," KJV, detract from the meaning). Not only had Christ the Holy Spirit without "measure," but God so gives the Spirit through Him to others. It is the ascended Christ who gives the Spirit to those who receive His testimony and set their seal to this, that God is true. The Holy Spirit is imparted neither by degrees, nor in portions, as if He were merely an influence, He is bestowed personally upon each believer, at the time of the New Birth; (*b*) of "a graduated rod or rule for measuring," figuratively, Matt. 7:2; Mark 4:24; literally, Rev. 21:15 (in the best mss.; see the RV); v. 17; (II) "that which is measured, a determined extent, a portion measured off," Rom. 12:3; 2 Cor. 10:13 (twice); Eph. 4:7, "(according to the) measure (of the gift of Christ)"; the gift of grace is "measured" and given according to the will of Christ; whatever the endowment, His is the bestowment and the adjustment; v. 13, "the measure (of the stature of the fullness of Christ)," the standard of spiritual stature being the fullness which is essentially Christ's; v. 16, "(according to the working in due) measure (of each several part)," i.e., according to the effectual working of the ministration rendered in due "measure" by every part.¶

2. *meros* (μέρος, 3313), "a part, portion," is used with the preposition *apo*, "from," with the meaning "in some measure," Rom. 15:15, RV (KJV, " . . . sort"). See COAST, PART.

3. *saton* (σάτον, 4568) is a Hebrew dry measure (Heb., *seah*), about a peck and a half, Matt. 13:33; Luke 13:21; "three measures" would be the quantity for a baking (cf. Gen. 18:6; Judg. 6:19; 1 Sam. 1:24; the "ephah" of the last two passages was equal to three *sata*).¶

4. *koros* (κόρος, 2884) denotes a *cor*, the largest Hebrew dry measure (ten *ephahs*), containing about 11 bushels, Luke 16:7; the hundred "measures" amounted to a very considerable quantity.¶

5. *batos* (βάτος, 943) denotes a *bath*, a Jewish liquid measure (the equivalent of an *ephah*), containing between 8 and 9 gallons, Luke 16:6.¶

6. *choinix* (χοῖνιξ, 5518), a dry "measure" of rather less than a quart, about "as much as would support a person of moderate appetite for a day," occurs in Rev. 6:6 (twice). Usually eight *choinixes* could be bought for a *denarius* (about 9 1/2d.); this passage predicts circumstances in which the *denarius* is the price of one *choenix*.¶ In the Sept., Ezek. 45:10, 11, where it represents the Heb. *ephah* and *bath*.¶

Notes: (1) In 2 Cor. 10:14, KJV, *huperekteinō*, "to stretch out overmuch," is translated "we stretch (not ourselves) beyond measure," (RV " . . . overmuch)." (2) In 2 Cor. 11:9, RV, *prosanaplēroō*, "to fill up by adding to, to supply fully," is translated "supplied the measure" (KJV, "supplied"). See SUPPLY. (3) For the phrases in the KJV, "beyond measure," Gal. 1:13; "out of measure," 2 Cor. 1:8, see ABUNDANCE, A, No. 4, EXCEL, B. (4) In Mark 6:51, some mss. have the phrase *ek perissou*, "beyond measure" (KJV). (5) For the phrase "be exalted above measure," 2 Cor. 12:7, KJV, see EXALT, A, No. 4.

B. Adverbs.

1. *huperballontōs* (ὑπερβαλλόντως, 5234), "beyond measure" (*huper*, "over, beyond," *ballō*, "to throw"; for the verb *huperballō*, see EXCEEDING), is rendered "above measure" in 2 Cor. 11:23.¶

2. *perissōs* (περισσῶς, 4057), Mark 10:26; see EXCEED, B, No. 4.

3. *huperperissōs* (ὑπερπερισσῶς, 5249), Mark 7:37: see ABUNDANCE D, No. 3.¶

C. Adjective.

ametros (ἄμετρος, 280), "without measure" (*a*, negative, and A, No. 1), is used in the neuter plural in an adverbial phrase in 2 Cor. 10:13, 15, *eis ta ametra*, lit., "unto the (things) without measure," RV, "(we will not glory) beyond our measure"; KJV, "(we will not boast) of things without measure," referring to the sphere divinely appointed for the apostle as to his gospel ministry; this had reached to Corinth, and by the increase of the faith of the church there, would extend to regions beyond. His opponents had no scruples about intruding into the spheres of other men's work.¶

D. Verbs.

1. *metreō* (μετρέω, 3354), "to measure" (akin to A, No. 1), is used (*a*) of space, number, value, etc., Rev. 11:1, 2; 21:15, 16, 17; metaphorically, 2 Cor. 10:12; (*b*) in the sense of "measuring" out, giving by "measure," Matt. 7:2, "ye mete" (some mss. have No. 2); Mark 4:24; in some mss. in Luke 6:38 (see No. 2).¶

2. *antimetreō* (ἀντιμετρέω, 488), "to measure in return" (*anti*, "back, in return" and No.

1), is used in the passive voice, and found in some mss. in Matt. 7:2 (the most authentic have No. 1); in Luke 6:38 the most authentic have this verb.¶ It is not found in the Sept.

MEAT

1. *brōma* (βρῶμα, 1033), "food" (akin to *bibrōskō*, "to eat," John 6:13¶), solid food in contrast to milk, is translated "food" in Matt. 14:15, RV (KJV, "victuals"); "meats," Mark 7:19; 1 Cor. 6:13 (twice); 1 Tim. 4:3; Heb. 9:10; 13:9; "meat," John 4:34; Rom. 14:15 (twice), 20; 1 Cor. 3:2; 8:8, 13; 10:3; "food," RV, for KJV, "meat," Luke 3:11; 9:13.¶

2. *brōsis* (βρῶσις, 1035), akin to No. 1, denotes (*a*) "the act of eating," 1 Cor. 8:4 (see EAT); (*b*) "food," translated "meat" in John 4:32 (for v. 34, see No. 1); 6:27 (twice, the second time metaphorically, of spiritual food); 6:55, RV, marg., "(true) meat"; Rom. 14:17, KJV, "meat," RV, "eating"; Col. 2:16; in Heb. 12:16, RV, "mess of meat," KJV, "morsel of meat"; in 2 Cor. 9:10, "food"; in Matt. 6:19, 20, "rust." See EAT, EATING, B.¶

3. *brōsimos* (βρώσιμος, 1034), "eatable," Luke 24:41, KJV, "any meat" (RV, "anything to eat"). See EAT, C.¶

4. *trophē* (τροφή, 5160), "nourishment, food," is translated "meat" in the KJV (RV "food") except in two instances. See FOOD, No. 1.

5. *phagō* (φάγω, 5315), "to eat," is used as a noun, in the infinitive mood, and translated "meat" in Matt. 25:35, 42 (lit., "to eat"); in Luke 8:55 the RV translates it literally, "to eat" (KJV, "meat"). See EAT, No. 2.

6. *trapeza* (τράπεζα, 5132), "a table" (Eng., "trapeze"), is used, by metonymy, of "the food on the table," in Acts 16:34 (RV, marg., "a table") and translated "meat"; cf. "table" in Rom. 11:9; 1 Cor. 10:21. See TABLE.

Notes: (1) For *prosphagion*, John 21:5, KJV, "any meat," see EAT, B, No. 2. (2) In Luke 12:42, *sitometrion* denotes "a measured portion of food" (*sitos,* "food," *metrios,* "within measure"). (3) In Matt. 15:37 and Mark 8:8, the KJV translates the plural of *klasma*, "a broken piece" (from *klaō*, "to break"), "broken meat" (RV, "broken pieces"). (4) In John 12:2, RV, *anakeimai*, "to recline at table," is translated "sat at meat" (KJV, "sat at the table"); in Mark 6:26, RV, according to the best mss., "sat at meat," some have *sunanakeimai* (KJV, "sat with him"); in Mark 6:22, RV, *sunanakeimai*, "to recline at table together," is translated "that sat at meat with him." (5) In Acts 15:29, KJV, the neuter plural of *eidōlothutos*, "sacrificed to idols," is translated "meats offered to idols" (RV,

"things . . . ," as elsewhere in the KJV). See IDOLS (offered to). (6) For *kataklinō*, "to sit down to (recline at) meat," see SIT, No. 7.

MEDIATOR

mesitēs (μεσίτης, 3316), lit., "a go-between" (from *mesos,* "middle," and *eimi,* "to go"), is used in two ways in the NT, (*a*) "one who mediates" between two parties with a view to producing peace, as in 1 Tim. 2:5, though more than mere "mediatorship" is in view, for the salvation of men necessitated that the Mediator should Himself possess the nature and attributes of Him towards whom He acts, and should likewise participate in the nature of those for whom He acts (sin apart); only by being possessed both of deity and humanity could He comprehend the claims of the one and the needs of the other; further, the claims and the needs could be met only by One who, Himself being proved sinless, would offer Himself an expiatory sacrifice on behalf of men; (*b*) "one who acts as a guarantee" so as to secure something which otherwise would not be obtained. Thus in Heb. 8:6; 9:15; 12:24 Christ is the Surety of "the better covenant," "the new covenant," guaranteeing its terms for His people.

In Gal. 3:19 Moses is spoken of as a "mediator," and the statement is made that "a mediator is not a mediator of one," v. 20, that is, of one party. Here the contrast is between the promise given to Abraham and the giving of the Law. The Law was a covenant enacted between God and the Jewish people, requiring fulfillment by both parties. But with the promise to Abraham, all the obligations were assumed by God, which is implied in the statement, "but God is one."¶ In the Sept., Job 9:33, "daysman."¶

MEDITATE

1. *meletaō* (μελετάω, 3191), primarily, "to care for" (akin to *meletē*, "care"; cf. *melei*, "it is a care"), denotes (*a*) "to attend to, practice," 1 Tim. 4:15, RV, "be diligent in" (KJV, "meditate upon"); to practice is the prevalent sense of the word, and the context is not against this significance in the RV rendering; some mss. have it in Mark 13:11; (*b*) "to ponder, imagine," Acts 4:25. See IMAGINE.¶

2. *promeletaō* (προμελετάω, 4304), "to premeditate," is used in Luke 21:14.¶

Note: In the corresponding passage in Mark 13:11, the most authentic mss. have the verb *promerimnaō*, "to be anxious beforehand" (RV); see No. 1.

For MEDDLER see BUSYBODY

MEEK, MEEKNESS

A. Adjective.

praüs or *praos* (πραΰς, 4239) denotes "gentle, mild, meek"; for its significance see the corresponding noun, below, B. Christ uses it of His own disposition, Matt. 11:29; He gives it in the third of His Beatitudes, 5:5; it is said of Him as the King Messiah, 21:5, from Zech. 9:9; it is an adornment of the Christian profession, 1 Pet. 3:4.¶ Cf. *ēpios*, "gentle, of a soothing disposition," 1 Thess. 2:7; 2 Tim. 2:24.¶

B. Nouns.

1. *praütēs*, or *praotes*, an earlier form, (πραΰτης, 4240) denotes "meekness." In its use in Scripture, in which it has a fuller, deeper significance than in nonscriptural Greek writings, it consists not in a person's "outward behavior only; nor yet in his relations to his fellow-men; as little in his mere natural disposition. Rather it is an inwrought grace of the soul; and the exercises of it are first and chiefly towards God. It is that temper of spirit in which we accept His dealings with us as good, and therefore without disputing or resisting; it is closely linked with the word *tapeinophrosunē* [humility], and follows directly upon it, Eph. 4:2; Col. 3:12; cf. the adjectives in the Sept. of Zeph. 3:12, "meek and lowly"; ... it is only the humble heart which is also the meek, and which, as such, does not fight against God and more or less struggle and contend with Him. This meekness, however, being first of all a meekness before God, is also such in the face of men, even of evil men, out of a sense that these, with the insults and injuries which they may inflict, are permitted and employed by Him for the chastening and purifying of His elect" (Trench, *Syn.* §xlii). In Gal. 5:23 it is associated with *enkrateia*, "self-control."

The meaning of *praütēs* "is not readily expressed in English, for the terms meekness, mildness, commonly used, suggest weakness and pusillanimity to a greater or less extent, whereas *praütēs* does nothing of the kind. Nevertheless, it is difficult to find a rendering less open to objection than 'meekness'; 'gentleness' has been suggested, but as *praütēs* describes a condition of mind and heart, and as 'gentleness' is appropriate rather to actions, this word is no better than that used in both English Versions. It must be clearly understood, therefore, that the meekness manifested by the Lord and commended to the believer is the fruit of power. The common assumption is that when a man is meek it is because he cannot help himself; but the Lord was 'meek' because he had the infinite resources of God at His command.

Described negatively, meekness is the opposite to self-assertiveness and self-interest; it is equanimity of spirit that is neither elated nor cast down, simply because it is not occupied with self at all.

"In 2 Cor. 10:1 the apostle appeals to the 'meekness ... of Christ.' Christians are charged to show 'all meekness toward all men,' Titus 3:2, for meekness becomes 'God's elect,' Col. 3:12. To this virtue the 'man of God' is urged; he is to 'follow after meekness' for his own sake, 1 Tim. 6:11 (the best texts have No. 2 here, however), and in his service, and more especially in his dealings with the 'ignorant and erring,' he is to exhibit 'a spirit of meekness,' 1 Cor. 4:21, and Gal. 6:1; even 'they that oppose themselves' are to be corrected in meekness, 2 Tim. 2:25. James exhorts his 'beloved brethren' to 'receive with meekness the implanted word,' 1:21. Peter enjoins 'meekness' in setting forth the grounds of the Christian hope, 3:15."*¶

2. *praüpathia* (πραϋπαθία), "a meek disposition, meekness" (*praus*, "meek," *paschō*, "to suffer"), is found in the best texts in 1 Tim. 6:11.¶

MEET (Adjective and Verb)

A. Adjectives.

1. *axios* (ἄξιος, 514) has the meaning of being of "weight, value, worth"; also "befitting, becoming, right on the ground of fitness," e.g., Matt. 3:8, KJV, "meet" (RV, "worthy"); so Acts 26:20; Luke 3:8 ("worthy"); 23:41 ("due reward"). See REWARD, WORTHY.

2. *hikanos* (ἱκανός, 2425), "sufficient, competent, fit," is translated "meet" in 1 Cor. 15:9. See ENOUGH, SUFFICIENT.

3. *kalos* (καλός, 2570), "good," is translated "meet" in Matt. 15:26 and Mark 7:27. See GOOD.

4. *euthetos* (εὔθετος, 2111), "well-placed," is translated "meet" in Heb. 6:7: see FIT.

Note: In Phil. 1:7 and 2 Pet. 1:13, KJV, *dikaios*, "just," is translated "meet" (RV, "right"). For "meet ... for use," 2 Tim. 2:21, see USE, *Note*.

B. Verbs.

1. *dei* (δεῖ, 1163), an impersonal verb, "it is necessary, one must," is translated "it was meet," in Luke 15:32; in Rom. 1:27, KJV, "was meet" (RV, "was due"). See DUE, B, No. 2.

2. *hikanoō* (ἱκανόω, 2427), "to render fit, meet, to make sufficient," is translated "hath made ... meet" in Col. 1:12; in 2 Cor. 3:6, RV,

---

* From *Notes on Galatians,* by Hogg and Vine, pp. 294, 295.

"made ... sufficient" (KJV, "hath made ... able"). See ABLE.¶

MEET (Verb), MEET WITH, MET

A. Verbs.

1. *apantaō* (ἀπαντάω, 528), "to go to meet, to meet" (*apo*, "from," *antaō*, "to meet with, come face to face with"), is used in Mark 14:13 and Luke 17:12. Some mss. have this verb for No. 3 in Matt. 28:9; Mark 5:2; Luke 14:31; John 4:51; Acts 16:16.¶

2. *sunantaō* (συναντάω, 4876), "to meet with," lit., "to meet together with" (*sun*, "with," and *antaō*, see No. 1), is used in Luke 9:37 (in v. 18, in some mss.); 22:10; Acts 10:25; Heb. 7:1, 10; metaphorically in Acts 20:22 ("shall befall"). See BEFALL.¶

3. *hupantaō* (ὑπαντάω, 5221), "to go to meet, to meet," has the same meaning as No. 1, and is used in Matt. 8:28; Luke 8:27; John 11:20, 30, and, in the most authentic mss., in Matt. 28:9; Mark 5:2; Luke 14:31 (of meeting in battle); John 4:51; 12:18 and Acts 16:16 (see No. 1).¶

4. *paratunchanō* (παρατυγχάνω, 3909), "to happen to be near or present, to chance to be by" (*para*, "beside, near," *tunchanō*, "to happen"), occurs in Acts 17:17, "met with (him)."¶

5. *sumballō* (συμβάλλω, 4820), "to confer, to fall in with, meet with," is translated "met" in Acts 20:14, RV (KJV, "met with"), of the apostle Paul's "meeting" his companions at Assos. See CONFER, No. 3.

B. Nouns.

1. *hupantēsis* (ὑπάντησις, 5222), "a going to meet" (akin to A, No. 3), preceded by the preposition *eis*, "unto," lit., "unto a meeting," translated "to meet," is found in John 12:13, and in the most authentic mss. in Matt. 8:34 (see No. 3) and 25:1 (see No. 2).¶

2. *apantēsis* (ἀπάντησις, 529), "a meeting" (akin to A, No. 1), occurs in Matt. 25:6 (in some mss. in v. 1, and in 27:32, in some mss.); Acts 28:15; 1 Thess. 4:17. It is used in the papyri of a newly arriving magistrate. "It seems that the special idea of the word was the official welcome of a newly arrived dignitary" (Moulton, *Greek Test. Gram.* Vol. I, p. 14).¶

3. *sunantēsis* (συνάντησις, 4877), "a coming to meet with" (akin to A, No. 2), is found in some mss. in Matt. 8:34, of the coming out of all the people of a city to meet the Lord (see No. 1).¶

MELODY (Verb)

psallō (ψάλλω, 5567), primarily "to twitch, twang," then, "to play a stringed instrument with the fingers," and hence, in the Sept., "to sing with a harp, sing psalms," denotes, in the NT, "to sing a hymn, sing praise"; in Eph. 5:19, "making melody" (for the preceding word *adō*, see SING). Elsewhere it is rendered "sing," Rom. 15:9; 1 Cor. 14:15; in Jas. 5:13, RV, "let him sing praise" (KJV, "let him sing psalms"). See SING.¶

MELT

tēkō (τήκω, 5080), "to melt, melt down," is used in the passive voice in 2 Pet. 3:12, "shall melt" (lit., "shall be melted"), of the elements (Eng., "thaw" is etymologically connected).¶

Note: In verse 10, the KJV "shall melt" represents the verb *luō*, "to loosen, dissolve" (RV, "shall be dissolved," passive voice); so in vv. 11–12.

MEMBER

melos (μέλος, 3196), "a limb of the body," is used (*a*) literally, Matt. 5:29–30; Rom. 6:13 (twice), 19 (twice); 7:5, 23 (twice); 12:4 (twice); 1 Cor. 12:12 (twice), 14, 18–20, 22, 25–26 (twice); Jas. 3:5, 6; 4:1; in Col. 3:5, "mortify therefore your members which are upon the earth"; since our bodies and their "members" belong to the earth, and are the instruments of sin, they are referred to as such (cf. Matt. 5:29–30; Rom. 7:5, 23, mentioned above); the putting to death is not physical, but ethical; as the physical "members" have distinct individualities, so those evils, of which the physical "members" are agents, are by analogy regarded as examples of the way in which the "members" work if not put to death; this is not precisely the same as "the old man," v. 9, i.e., the old nature, though there is a connection; (*b*) metaphorically, "of believers as members of Christ," 1 Cor. 6:15 (1st part); of one another, Rom. 12:5 (as with the natural illustration, so with the spiritual analogy, there is not only vital unity, and harmony in operation, but diversity, all being essential to effectivity; the unity is not due to external organization but to common and vital union in Christ); there is stress in v. 5 upon "many" and "in Christ" and "members;" 1 Cor. 12:27 (of the "members" of a local church as a body); Eph. 4:25 (of the "members" of the whole Church as the mystical body of Christ); in 1 Cor. 6:15 (2nd part), of one who practices fornication.¶

MEMORIAL

mnēmosunon (μνημόσυνον, 3422) denotes "a memorial," that which keeps alive the memory of someone or something (from *mnēmōn*, "mindful"), Matt. 26:13; Mark 14:9; Acts 10:4.¶

For **MEMORY** (keep in) see **KEEP**, *Note* (8)

MEN

Notes: (1) For this plural see the nouns under MAN. (2) For *anthrōpinos*, e.g., Rom. 6:19, "after the manner of men," see MAN'S, No. 1. (3) For the phrase *kat' anthrōpon*, "after the manner of men," see MAN, No. 1 (*f*). (4) The phrase "quit you like men," 1 Cor. 16:13, translates the verb *andrizō*, in the middle voice, "to play the man" (a verb illustrated in the papyri). (5) See also ALL, GOOD, GREAT, LOW (estate), THESE, (of) WAR.

MEN-PLEASERS

anthrōpareskos (ἀνθρωπάρεσκος, 441), an adjective signifying "studying to please men" (*anthrōpos*, "man," *areskō*, "to please"), designates, "not simply one who is pleasing to men . . . , but one who endeavors to please men and not God" (Cremer). It is used in Eph. 6:6 and Col. 3:22.¶ In the Sept., Ps. 53:5.¶

MENSERVANTS

pais (παῖς, 3816), for the meanings of which see CHILD, No. 4, is translated "menservants" in Luke 12:45.

MEN-STEALERS

andrapodistēs (ἀνδραποδιστής, 405), "a slave dealer, kidnapper," from *andrapodon*, "a slave captured in war," a word found in the plural in the papyri, e.g., in a catalogue of property and in combination with *tetrapoda*, "four-footed things" (*andrapodon, anēr*, "a man," *pous*, "a foot"); *andrapodon* "was never an ordinary word for slave; it was too brutally obvious a reminder of the principle which made quadruped and human chattels differ only in the number of their legs" (Moulton and Milligan, *Vocab.*). The verb *andrapodizō* supplied the noun "with the like odious meaning," which appears in 1 Tim. 1:10.¶

MEND

katartizō (καταρτίζω, 2675), from *kata*, "down," intensive and *artios*, "fit," has three meanings, (*a*) "to mend, repair," Matt. 4:21; Mark 1:19, of nets; (*b*) "to complete, furnish completely, equip, prepare," Luke 6:40; Rom. 9:22; Heb. 11:3 and in the middle voice, Matt. 21:16; Heb. 10:5; (*c*) "ethically, to prepare, perfect," Gal. 6:1; 1 Thess. 3:10; 1 Pet. 5:10; Heb. 13:21; and in the passive voice, 1 Cor. 1:10; 2 Cor. 13:11. See FIT, FRAME, JOIN, PERFECT, PREPARE, RESTORE.¶

MENTION (Noun and Verb)

A. Noun.

mneia (μνεία, 3417), "remembrance, mention" (akin to *mimnēskō*, "to remind, remember"), is always used in connection with prayer, and translated "mention" in Rom. 1:9; Eph. 1:16; 1 Thess. 1:2; Philem. 4, in each of which it is preceded by the verb to make; "remembrance" in Phil. 1:3; 1 Thess. 3:6; 2 Tim. 1:3. Some mss. have it in Rom. 12:13, instead of *chreiais*, "necessities." See REMEMBRANCE.¶ Cf. *mnēmē*, "memory, remembrance," 2 Pet. 1:15.¶

B. Verb.

mnēmoneuō (μνημονεύω, 3421), which most usually means "to call to mind, remember," signifies "to make mention of," in Heb. 11:22. See REMEMBER.

MERCHANDISE (Noun, and Verb, to make)

A. Nouns.

1. *emporia* (ἐμπορία, 1711) denotes "commerce, business, trade" [akin to No. 2, and to *emporos*, "one on a journey" (*en*, "in," *poros*, "a journey"), "a merchant"], occurs in Matt. 22:5.¶

2. *emporion* (ἐμπόριον, 1712) denotes "a trading place, exchange" (Eng., "emporium"), John 2:16, "(a house) of merchandise."¶

3. *gomos* (γόμος, 1117) is translated "merchandise" in Rev. 18:11, 12: see BURDEN, A, No. 3.

B. Verb.

emporeuomai (ἐμπορεύομαι, 1710) primarily signifies "to travel," especially for business; then, "to traffic, trade," Jas. 4:13; then, "to make a gain of, make merchandise of," 2 Pet. 2:3.¶

MERCHANT

emporos (ἔμπορος, 1713) denotes "a person on a journey" (*poros*, "a journey"), "a passenger on shipboard"; then, "a merchant," Matt. 13:45; Rev. 18:3, 11, 15, 23.¶

MERCIFUL (Adjective, and Verb, to be), MERCY (Noun, and Verb, to have, etc.)

A. Nouns.

1. *eleos* (ἔλεος, 1656) "is the outward manifestation of pity; it assumes need on the part of him who receives it, and resources adequate to meet the need on the part of him who shows it. It is used (*a*) of God, who is rich in mercy, Eph. 2:4, and who has provided salvation for all men, Titus 3:5, for Jews, Luke 1:72, and Gentiles, Rom. 15:9. He is merciful to those who fear

him, Luke 1:50, for they also are compassed with infirmity, and He alone can succor them. Hence they are to pray boldly for mercy, Heb. 4:16, and if for themselves, it is seemly that they should ask for mercy for one another, Gal. 6:16; 1 Tim. 1:2. When God brings His salvation to its issue at the Coming of Christ, His people will obtain His mercy, 2 Tim. 1:16; Jude 21; (b) of men; for since God is merciful to them, He would have them show mercy to one another, Matt. 9:13; 12:7; 23:23; Luke 10:37; Jas. 2:13.

"Wherever the words mercy and peace are found together they occur in that order, except in Gal. 6:16. Mercy is the act of God, peace is the resulting experience in the heart of man. Grace describes God's attitude toward the law-breaker and the rebel; mercy is His attitude toward those who are in distress."*

"In the order of the manifestation of God's purposes of salvation grace must go before mercy . . . only the forgiven may be blessed. . . . From this it follows that in each of the apostolic salutations where these words occur, grace precedes mercy, 1 Tim. 1:2; 2 Tim. 1:2; Titus 1:4 (in some mss.); 2 John 3" (Trench, *Syn.* §xlvii).

2. *oiktirmos* (οἰκτιρμός, 3628), "pity, compassion for the ills of others," is used (a) of God, Who is "the Father of mercies," 2 Cor. 1:3; His "mercies" are the ground upon which believers are to present their bodies a living sacrifice, holy, acceptable to God, as their reasonable service, Rom. 12:1; under the Law he who set it at nought died without compassion, Heb. 10:28; (b) of men; believers are to feel and exhibit compassions one toward another, Phil. 2:1, RV "compassions," and Col. 3:12, RV "(a heart) of compassion"; in these two places the word is preceded by No. 3, rendered "tender mercies" in the former, and "a heart" in the latter, RV¶

3. *splanchnon* (σπλάγχνον, 4698), "affections, the heart," always in the plural in the NT, has reference to "feelings of kindness, goodwill, pity," Phil. 2:1, RV, "tender mercies;" see AFFECTION, No. 2, and BOWELS.

Note: In Acts. 13:34 the phrase, lit., "the holy things, the faithful things (of David)" is translated, "the holy and sure blessings," RV; the KJV, following the mss. in which the words "holy and" are absent, has "the sure mercies," but notices the full phrase in the margin.

B. Verbs.

1. *eleeō* (ἐλεέω, 1653), akin to A, No. 1, signifies, in general, "to feel sympathy with the misery of another," and especially sympathy

manifested in act, (a) in the active voice, "to have pity or mercy on, to show mercy" to, e.g., Matt. 9:27; 15:22; 17:15; 18:33; 20:30, 31 (three times in Mark, four in Luke); Rom. 9:15, 16, 18; 11:32; 12:8; Phil. 2:27; Jude 22, 23; (b) in the passive voice, "to have pity or mercy shown one, to obtain mercy," Matt. 5:7; Rom. 11:30, 31; 1 Cor. 7:25; 2 Cor. 4:1; 1 Tim. 1:13, 16; 1 Pet. 2:10.

2. *oikteirō* (οἰκτείρω, 3627), akin to A, No. 2, "to have pity on" (from *oiktos*, "pity": *oi*, an exclamation, = oh!), occurs in Rom. 9:15 (twice), where it follows No. 1 (twice); the point established there and in Exod. 33:19, from the Sept. of which it is quoted, is that the "mercy" and compassion shown by God are determined by nothing external to His attributes. Speaking generally *oikteirō* is a stronger term than *eleeō.*¶

3. *hilaskomai* (ἱλάσκομαι, 2433) in profane Greek meant "to conciliate, appease, propitiate, cause the gods to be reconciled"; their goodwill was not regarded as their natural condition, but as something to be earned. The heathen believed their gods to be naturally alienated in feeling from man. In the NT the word never means to conciliate God; it signifies (a) "to be propitious, merciful," Luke 18:13, in the prayer of the publican; (b) "to expiate, make propitiation for," Heb. 2:17, "make propitiation."

That God is not of Himself already alienated from man, see John 3:16. His attitude toward the sinner does not need to be changed by his efforts. With regard to his sin, an expiation is necessary, consistently with God's holiness and for His righteousness' sake, and that expiation His grace and love have provided in the atoning sacrifice of His Son; man, himself a sinner, justly exposed to God's wrath (John 3:36), could never find an expiation. As Lightfoot says, "when the NT writers speak at length on the subject of Divine wrath, the hostility is represented, not as on the part of God, but of men." Through that which God has accomplished in Christ, by His death, man, on becoming regenerate, escapes the merited wrath of God. The making of this expiation [(b) above], with its effect in the mercy of God (a) is what is expressed in *hilaskomai.*¶ The Sept. uses the compound verb *exilaskomai*, e.g., Gen. 32:20; Exod. 30:10, 15, 16; 32:30, and frequently in Lev. and Num. See PROPITIATION.

C. Adjectives.

1. *eleēmōn* (ἐλεήμων, 1655), "merciful," akin to A, No. 1, not simply possessed of pity but actively compassionate, is used of Christ as a High Priest, Heb. 2:17, and of those who are like God, Matt. 5:7 (cf. Luke 6:35, 36, where

* From *Notes on Galatians*, by Hogg and Vine, pp. 340, 341.

the RV, "sons" is to be read, as representing characteristics resembling those of their Father).¶

2. *oiktirmōn* (οἰκτίρμων, 3629) "pitiful, compassionate for the ills of others," a stronger term than No. 1 (akin to A, No. 2), is used twice in Luke 6:36, "merciful" (of the character of God, to be expressed in His people); Jas. 5:11, RV, "merciful," KJV, "of tender mercy."¶

3. *hileōs* (ἵλεως, 2436), "propitious, merciful" (akin to B, No. 3), was used in profane Greek just as in the case of the verb (which see). There is nothing of this in the use of the word in Scripture. The quality expressed by it there essentially appertains to God, though man is undeserving of it. It is used only of God, Heb. 8:12; in Matt. 16:22, "Be it far from Thee" (Peter's word to Christ) may have the meaning given in the RV marg., "(God) have mercy on Thee," lit., "propitious to Thee" (KJV marg., "Pity Thyself")¶ Cf. the Sept., 2 Sam. 20:20; 23:17.

4. *aneleos* or *anileōs* (ἀνέλεος or ἀνίλεως, 448), "unmerciful, merciless" (*a*, negative, *n*, euphonic, and A, No. 2, or C, No. 3), occurs in Jas. 2:13, said of judgment on him who shows no "mercy."¶

MERCY SEAT

hilastērion (ἱλαστήριον, 2435), "the lid or cover of the ark of the covenant," signifies the Propitiatory, so called on account of the expiation made once a year on the great Day of Atonement, Heb. 9:5. For the formation see Exod. 25:17–21. The Heb. word is *kapporeth*, "the cover," a meaning connected with the covering or removal of sin (Ps. 32:1) by means of expiatory sacrifice. This mercy seat, together with the ark, is spoken of as the footstool of God, 1 Chron. 28:2; cf. Ps. 99:5; 132:7. The Lord promised to be present upon it and to commune with Moses "from above the mercy seat, from between the two cherubim," Exod. 25:22 (see CHERUBIM). In the Sept. the word *epithēma*, which itself means "a cover," is added to *hilastērion; epithēma* was simply a translation of *kapporeth;* accordingly, *hilastērion*, not having this meaning, and being essentially connected with propitiation, was added. Eventually *hilastērion* stood for both. In 1 Chron. 28:11 the Holy of Holies is called "the House of the Kapporeth" (see RV, marg.).

Through His voluntary expiatory sacrifice in the shedding of His blood, under divine judgment upon sin, and through His resurrection, Christ has become the Mercy Seat for His people. See Rom. 3:25, and see PROPITIATION, B, No. 1.¶

MERRY (to be, to make)

1. *euphrainō* (εὐφραίνω, 2165), in the active voice, "to cheer, make glad," 2 Cor. 2:2, is used everywhere else in the passive voice, signifying, "to be happy, rejoice, make merry," and translated "to be merry" in Luke 12:19; 15:23, 24, 29, 32; in 16:19, "fared (sumptuously)"; in Rev. 11:10, "make merry." See FARE, GLAD, REJOICE.

2. *euthumeō* (εὐθυμέω, 2114), from *eu*, "well," and *thumos*, "the soul," as the principle of feeling, especially strong feeling, signifies "to make cheerful"; it is used intransitively in the NT, "to be of good cheer," Acts 27:22, 25; in Jas. 5:13, RV, "is (any) cheerful?" (KJV, "... merry?"). See CHEER.¶

MESS

brōsis (βρῶσις, 1035), "eating, food," is translated "mess of meat" in Heb. 12:16, RV (KJV, "morsel of meat"). See FOOD, MEAT, No. 2.

MESSAGE

1. *angelia* (ἀγγελία, 31), akin to *angellō*, "to bring a message, proclaim," denotes a "message, proclamation, news," 1 John 1:5 [some mss. have *epangelia:* see *Note* (1)]; 1 John 3:11, where the word is more precisely defined (by being followed by the conjunction "that," expressing the purpose that we should love one another) as being virtually equivalent to an order.¶

Notes: (1) *Epangelia* (*epi*, "upon," and No. 1), "a promise," is found in some mss. in 1 John 1:5, "message" (see No. 1). See PROMISE. (2) In Luke 19:14, KJV, *presbeia*, is translated "a message"; RV, "an ambassage," as in 14:32. See AMBASSAGE.¶

2. *akoē* (ἀκοή, 189), "hearing," also denotes "the thing heard, a message"; in 1 Thess. 2:13, it is associated with *logos*, "a word," lit., "the word of hearing" (RV marg.), RV, "the word of the message," KJV, "the word ... which ye heard"; so in Heb. 4:2, RV, "the word of hearing" (KJV, "the word preached"). See HEARING.

3. *kērugma* (κήρυγμα, 2782), "that which is proclaimed by a herald, a proclamation, preaching," is translated "the message" in Titus 1:3, RV (KJV, "preaching"). See PREACHING.

MESSENGER

1. *angelos* (ἄγγελος, 32), "a messenger, an angel, one sent," is translated "messenger," of John the Baptist, Matt. 11:10; Mark 1:2; Luke 7:27; in the plural, of John's "messengers," 7:24; of those whom Christ sent before Him when on His journey to Jerusalem, 9:52; of

Paul's "thorn in the flesh," "a messenger of Satan," 2 Cor. 12:7; of the spies as received by Rahab, Jas. 2:25. See ANGEL.

2. *apostolos* (ἀπόστολος, 652), "an apostle," is translated "messengers" in 2 Cor. 8:23 regarding Titus and "the other brethren," whom Paul describes to the church at Corinth as "messengers of the churches," in respect of offerings from those in Macedonia for the needy in Judea; in Phil. 2:25, of Epaphroditus as the "messenger" of the church at Philippi to the apostle in ministering to his need; RV marg. in each case, "apostle." See APOSTLE.

For METE see MEASURE

For MID see MIDST

MIDDAY

Note: In Acts 26:13, "at midday" translates the adjective *mesos*, "middle," and the noun *hēmera*, "a day," in a combined adverbial phrase. See MIDST.

For MIDDLE see WALL

MIDNIGHT

mesonuktion (μεσονύκτιον, 3317), an adjective denoting "at, or of, midnight," is used as a noun in Mark 13:35; Luke 11:5; Acts 16:25; 20:7.¶

Note: In Matt. 25:6 "at midnight" translates the adjective *mesos*, and noun *nux*, "night," in the combined adverbial phrase. In Acts 27:27 "about midnight" translates an adverbial phrase consisting of *kata*, "towards," followed by *mesos*, "middle" and *nux*, "night," with the article, lit., "towards (the) middle of the night." See MIDST.

MIDST

A. Adjective and Adverb.

mesos (μέσος, 3319), an adjective denoting "middle, in the middle or midst," is used in the following, in which the English requires a phrase, and the adjectival rendering must be avoided: Luke 22:55, "Peter sat in the midst of them," lit., "a middle one of (them)"; Luke 23:45, of the rending of the veil "in the midst"; here the adjective idiomatically belongs to the verb "was rent," and is not to be taken literally, as if it meant "the middle veil"; John 1:26, "in the midst of you (standeth One)," RV (lit., "a middle One"); Acts 1:18, where the necessity of avoiding the lit. rendering is obvious. Cf. the phrases "at midday," "at midnight" (see MIDDAY, MIDNIGHT, above).

Notes: (1) *Mesos* is used adverbially, in prepositional phrases, (a) *ana m.*, e.g., 1 Cor. 6:5, "between"; Matt. 13:25, "among"; Rev. 7:17, "in the midst"; (b) *dia m.*, e.g., Luke 4:30; 17:11, "through the midst"; (c) *en m.*, Luke 10:3, RV, "in the midst," KJV, "among"; so 22:27; 1 Thess. 2:7; with the article after *en*, e.g., Matt. 14:6, RV, "in the midst," KJV, "before"; (d) *eis m.*, Mark 14:60, "in the midst"; with the article, e.g., Mark 3:3, "forth" (lit., "into the midst"); (e) *ek m.*, "out of the way," lit., "out of the midst," Col. 2:14; 2 Thess. 2:7, where, however, removal is not necessarily in view; there is no accompanying verb signifying removal, as in each of the other occurrences of the phrase; with the article, e.g., 1 Cor. 5:2; 2 Cor. 6:17; see WAY; (f) *kata m.*, Acts 27:27, "about mid(night)."

(2) The neuter, *meson*, is used adverbially in Matt. 14:24, in some mss., "in the midst (of the waves)"; in Phil. 2:15 in the best mss. (where some mss. have *en m.* . . .). (3) For Rev. 8:13, see HEAVEN, A, No. 2.

B. Verb.

mesoō (μεσόω, 3322), "to be in the middle," is used of time in John 7:14, translated "when it was . . . the midst (of the feast)," lit., "(the feast) being in the middle."¶

MIGHT (Noun), MIGHTY, MIGHTILY, MIGHTIER

A. Nouns.

1. *dunamis* (δύναμις, 1411), "power," (a) used relatively, denotes "inherent ability, capability, ability to perform anything," e.g., Matt. 25:15, "ability"; Acts 3:12, "power"; 2 Thess. 1:7, RV, "(angels) of His power" (KJV, "mighty"); Heb. 11:11, RV, "power" (KJV, "strength"); see ABILITY; (b) used absolutely, denotes (1) "power to work, to carry something into effect," e.g., Luke 24:49; (2) "power in action," e.g., Rom. 1:16; 1 Cor. 1:18; it is translated "might" in the KJV of Eph. 1:21 (RV, "power"); so 3:16; Col. 1:11 (1st clause); 2 Pet. 2:11; in Rom. 15:19, KJV, this noun is rendered "mighty"; RV, "(in the) power of signs." The RV consistently avoids the rendering "might" for *dunamis;* the usual rendering is "power." Under this heading comes the rendering "mighty works," e.g., Matt. 7:22, RV (KJV, "wonderful works"); 11:20–23; singular number in Mark 6:5; in Matt. 14:2 and Mark 6:14 the RV has "powers"; in 2 Cor. 12:12, RV, "mighty works" (KJV, "mighty deeds"). See MIRACLE, especially POWER.

Note: Dunamis, "power," is to be distinguished from *exousia,* "the right to exercise power." See DOMINION, *Note.*

2. *ischus* (ἰσχύς, 2479) denotes "might, strength, power," (*a*) inherent and in action as used of God, Eph. 1:19, RV, "(the strength, *kratos*, of His) might," KJV, "(His mighty) power," i.e., power (over external things) exercised by strength; Eph. 6:10, "of His might"; 2 Thess. 1:9, RV, "(from the glory) of His might" (KJV "power"); Rev. 5:12, RV, "might" (KJV, "strength"); 7:12, "might"; (*b*) as an endowment, said (1) of angels, 2 Pet. 2:11; here the order is No. 2 and No. 1, RV, "might and power," which better expresses the distinction than the KJV, "power and might"; in some mss. in Rev. 18:2 it is said of the voice of an angel [see E, (*c*)]; the most authentic mss. have the adjective *ischuros*, "mighty"; (2) of men, Mark 12:30, 33; Luke 10:27 (RV and KJV, "strength," in all three verses); 1 Pet. 4:11, RV, "strength" (KJV, "ability": this belongs rather to No. 1). Either "strength" or "might" expresses the true significance of *ischus*. See ABILITY, POWER, STRENGTH.¶

Notes: (1) In Luke 9:43, KJV, *megaleiotēs*, "greatness, majesty," is translated "mighty power" (RV, "majesty"). (2) Cf. *kratos* (see POWER).

B. Adjectives.

1. *dunatos* (δυνατός, 1415), "powerful, mighty" (akin to A, No. 1), is used, with that significance, (1) of God, Luke 1:49, "mighty"; Rom. 9:22, "power" (here the neuter of the adjective is used with the article, as a noun, equivalent to *dunamis*); frequently with the meaning "able" (see ABLE, C, No. 1); (2) of Christ, regarded as a prophet, Luke 24:19 ("in deed and word"); (3) of men: Moses, Acts 7:22 ("in his words and works"); Apollos, 18:24, "in the Scriptures"; of those possessed of natural power, 1 Cor. 1:26; of those possessed of spiritual power, 2 Cor. 10:4. For the shades of meaning in the translation "strong," see Rom. 15:1; 2 Cor. 12:10; 13:9. For Rev. 6:15, see No. 2, below; see STRONG. See also POSSIBLE.

2. *ischuros* (ἰσχυρός, 2478), "strong, mighty" (akin to A, No. 2, and with corresponding adjectival significance), is usually translated "strong"; "mighty" in Luke 15:14 (of a famine); Rev. 19:6 (of thunders); 19:18 (of men): in the following, where the KJV has "mighty," the RV substitutes "strong," 1 Cor. 1:27; Rev. 6:15 (KJV, "mighty men"); 18:10, 21; Heb. 11:34, RV, "(waxed) mighty" (KJV, "valiant"). See BOISTEROUS, POWERFUL, STRONG (where the word is analyzed).

3. *ischuroteros* (ἰσχυρότερος, 2478*), "stronger, mightier," the comparative degree of No. 2, is translated "mightier" in Matt. 3:11;

Mark 1:7; Luke 3:16; "stronger" in Luke 11:22; 1 Cor. 1:25; 10:22. See STRONG.¶

4. *biaios* (βίαιος, 972), "violent" (from *bia*, "force, violence, strength," found in Acts 5:26; 21:35; 24:7; 27:41¶), occurs in Acts 2:2, of wind.¶

5. *krataios* (κραταιός, 2900), "strong, mighty" (akin to *kratos*, "strength," relative and manifested power: see MIGHTILY, below), is found in 1 Pet. 5:6, of the "mighty" hand of God.¶

6. *megaleios* (μεγαλεῖος, 3167) is rendered "mighty" in Acts 2:11, RV See WONDERFUL, *Note* (2).

Notes: (1) In Luke 1:52, KJV, *dunastēs*, "a potentate, prince," is translated "mighty" (RV, "princes"). (2) In Rev. 6:13, KJV, *megas*, "great," is translated "mighty" (RV, "great"), of a wind. (3) In Rev. 16:18, KJV, *tēlikoutos*, "so great" (when said of things), is translated "so mighty" (RV, "so great"), of an earthquake.

C. Verb.

dunateō (δυνατέω, 1414), "to be powerful" (akin to A, No. 1 and B, No. 1), is found in the most authentic mss. in Rom. 14:4 (some have *dunatos*, B, No. 1), RV "(the Lord) hath power," KJV, "(God) is able"; similarly, as regard mss., in 2 Cor. 9:8, where the RV and KJV have "(God) is able"; in 2 Cor. 13:3, KJV, "is mighty," RV, "is powerful" (according to the general significance of *dunamis*).¶

Note: In Gal. 2:8, KJV, *energeō*, "to work, work in" (*en*, "in," *ergon*, "work"), is first translated "wrought effectually," then "was mighty in" (RV, "wrought for," in both places; the probable meaning is "in me"). See EFFECTUAL, WORK.

D. Adverb.

eutonōs (εὐτόνως, 2159), "vigorously, vehemently" (*eu*, "well," *teinō*, "to stretch"), is translated "mightily" in Acts 18:28, KJV, of the power of Apollos in "confuting" the Jews (RV, "powerfully"); in Luke 23:10 it is rendered "vehemently." See POWERFUL, VEHEMENTLY.¶ In the Sept., Josh. 6:7, "(let them sound) loudly."¶

E. Phrases.

The following phrases signify "mightily:" (*a*) *en dunamei*, Col. 1:29, of the inward power of God's working, lit., "in power," as RV marg. (*en*, "in," and A, No. 1); (*b*) *kata kratos*, Acts 19:20, of the increase of the word of the Lord in a place, lit, "according to might"; (*c*) in Rev. 18:2 some mss. have *en ischui*, lit., "in strength" (*en*, "in," and A, No. 2), of the voice of an angel.

MILE

milion (μίλιον, 3400), "a Roman mile," a word of Latin origin (1680 yards), is used in Matt. 5:41.¶

MILK

gala (γάλα, 1051) is used (*a*) literally, 1 Cor. 9:7; (*b*) metaphorically, of rudimentary spiritual teaching, 1 Cor. 3:2; Heb. 5:12, 13; 1 Pet. 2:2; here the meaning largely depends upon the significance of the word *logikos*, which the KJV renders "of the word," RV "spiritual." While *logos* denotes "a word," the adjective *logikos* is never used with the meaning assigned to it in the KJV, nor does the context in 1:23 compel this meaning. While it is true that the Word of God, like "milk," nourishes the soul, and this is involved in the exhortation, the only other occurrence in the NT is Rom. 12:1, where it is translated "reasonable," i.e., rational, intelligent (service), in contrast to the offering of an irrational animal; so here the nourishment may be understood as of that spiritually rational nature which, acting through the regenerate mind, develops spiritual growth. God's Word is not given so that it is impossible to understand it, or that it requires a special class of men to interpret it; its character is such that the Holy Spirit who gave it can unfold its truths even to the young convert. Cf. 1 John 2:27.¶

MILL

mulōn (μύλων, 3459) denotes "a mill house," where the millstone is, Matt. 24:41; some mss. have *mulos* (see next word).¶ In the Sept., Jer. 52:11, "grinding house" (lit., "house of a mill").¶

MILLSTONE

A. Noun.

mulos (μύλος, 3458) denotes "a handmill," consisting of two circular stones, one above the other, the lower being fixed. From the center of the lower a wooden pin passes through a hole in the upper, into which the grain is thrown, escaping as flour between the stones and falling on a prepared material below them. The handle is inserted into the upper stone near the circumference. Small stones could be turned by one woman (millgrinding was a work deemed fit only for women and slaves; cf. Judg. 16:21); larger ones were turned by two (cf. Matt. 24:41, under MILL), or more.

Still larger ones were turned by an ass (*onikos*), Matt. 18:6, RV, "a great millstone" (marg., "a millstone turned by an ass"), indicating the immediate and overwhelming drowning of one who causes one young believer to stumble; Mark 9:42 (where some mss. have *lithos mulikos*, "a stone of a mill," as in Luke 17:2); Rev. 18:22 (some mss. have it in v. 21, see below).¶

B. Adjectives.

1. *mulikos* (μυλικός, 3457), "of a mill," occurs in Luke 17:2 (see above).¶

2. *mulinos* (μύλινος, 3458(v)), "made of millstone," is used with *lithos*, "a stone"; and with the adjective *megas*, "great," in the best mss. in Rev. 18:21 (some have the word *mulos;* see A).¶

MIND (Noun and Verb)

A. Nouns.

1. *nous* (νοῦς, 3563), "mind," denotes, speaking generally, the seat of reflective consciousness, comprising the faculties of perception and understanding, and those of feeling, judging and determining.

Its use in the NT may be analyzed as follows: it denotes (*a*) the faculty of knowing, the seat of the understanding, Luke 24:45; Rom. 1:28; 14:5; 1 Cor. 14:15, 19; Eph. 4:17; Phil. 4:7; Col. 2:18; 1 Tim. 6:5; 2 Tim. 3:8; Titus 1:15; Rev. 13:18; 17:9; (*b*) counsels, purpose, Rom. 11:34 (of the "mind" of God); 12:2; 1 Cor. 1:10; 2:16, twice (1) of the thoughts and counsels of God, (2) of Christ, a testimony to His Godhood; Eph. 4:23; (*c*) the new nature, which belongs to the believer by reason of the new birth, Rom. 7:23, 25, where it is contrasted with "the flesh," the principle of evil which dominates fallen man. Under (*b*) may come 2 Thess. 2:2, where it stands for the determination to be steadfast amidst afflictions, through the confident expectation of the day of rest and recompense mentioned in the first chapter.¶

2. *dianoia* (διάνοια, 1271), lit. "a thinking through, or over, a meditation, reflecting," signifies (*a*) like No. 1, "the faculty of knowing, understanding, or moral reflection," (1) with an evil significance, a consciousness characterized by a perverted moral impulse, Eph. 2:3 (plural); 4:18; (2) with a good significance, the faculty renewed by the Holy Spirit, Matt. 22:37; Mark 12:30; Luke 10:27; Heb. 8:10; 10:16; 1 Pet. 1:13; 1 John 5:20; (*b*) "sentiment, disposition" (not as a function but as a product); (1) in an evil sense, Luke 1:51, "imagination"; Col. 1:21; (2) in a good sense, 2 Pet. 3:1.¶

3. *ennoia* (ἔννοια, 1771), "an idea, notion, intent," is rendered "mind" in 1 Pet. 4:1; see INTENT.

4. *noēma* (νόημα, 3540), "thought, design," is rendered "minds" in 2 Cor. 3:14; 4:4; 11:3; Phil. 4:7; see DEVICE, No. 2.

5. *gnōmē* (γνώμη, 1106), "a purpose, judg-

ment, opinion," is translated "mind" in Philem. 14 and Rev. 17:13. See JUDGMENT, No. 4.

6. *phronēma* (φρόνημα, 5427) denotes "what one has in the mind, the thought" (the content of the process expressed in *phroneō*, "to have in mind, to think"); or "an object of thought"; in Rom. 8:6 (KJV, "to be carnally minded" and "to be spiritually minded"), the RV, adhering to the use of the noun, renders by "the mind of the flesh," in vv. 6 and 7, and "the mind of the spirit," in v. 6. In v. 27 the word is used of the "mind" of the Holy Spirit.¶

Notes: (1) This word is to be distinguished from *phronēsis*, which denotes "an understanding, leading to right action, prudence," Luke 1:17; Eph. 1:8.¶ (2) In three places, Acts 14:2; Phil. 1:27; Heb. 12:3, the KJV translates *psuchē*, "the soul," by "mind" (RV, "soul").

B. Verbs.

1. *phroneō* (φρονέω, 5426) signifies (*a*) "to think, to be minded in a certain way"; (*b*) "to think of, be mindful of." It implies moral interest or reflection, not mere unreasoning opinion. Under (*a*) it is rendered by the verb "to mind" in the following: Rom. 8:5,"(they that are after the flesh) do mind (the things of the flesh)"; 12:16, "be of (the same) mind," lit., "minding the same," and "set (not) your mind on," RV, KJV, "mind (not)"; 15:5, "to be of (the same) mind," RV, (KJV, "to be like-minded"); so the RV in 2 Cor. 13:11, KJV, "be of (one) mind"; Gal. 5:10, "ye will be (none otherwise) minded"; Phil. 1:7, RV, "to be (thus) minded," KJV, "to think (this)"; 2:2, RV, "be of (the same) mind," KJV, "be likeminded," and "being . . . of (one) mind," lit., "minding (the one thing)"; 2:5, RV, "have (this) mind," KJV, "let (this) mind be," lit., "mind this"; 3:15, "let us . . . be (thus) minded," and "(if) . . . ye are (otherwise) minded" (some mss. have the verb in v. 16); 3:19, "(who) mind (earthly things)"; 4:2, "be of (the same) mind"; Col. 3:2, RV and KJV marg., "set your mind," lit., "mind (the things above)," KJV, "set your affection." See CAREFUL, B, 6, REGARD, SAVOR, THINK, UNDERSTAND.

2. *anamimnēskō* (ἀναμιμνήσκω, 363), "to remind, call to remembrance" (*ana*, "up," *mimnēskō*, "to remind"), is translated "called to mind," in Mark 14:72 (passive voice). See REMEMBRANCE.

Note: The lengthened form *epanamimnēskō* is used in Rom. 15:15, KJV, "putting (you) in mind"; RV, "putting (you) again (*epi*) in remembrance."¶

3. *hupomimnēskō* (ὑπομιμνήσκω, 5279), "to cause one to remember, put one in mind" (*hupo*, "under"), is translated "put (them) in

mind" in Titus 3:1. See REMEMBER, REMEMBRANCE.

4. *hupotithēmi* (ὑποτίθημι, 5294), lit., "to place under" (*hupo*, "under," *tithēmi*, "to place"), "to lay down" (of risking the life, Rom. 16:4), also denotes "to suggest, put into one's mind," 1 Tim. 4:6, RV, "put . . . in mind" (KJV, "put . . . in remembrance"). See LAY.¶

5. *sōphroneō* (σωφρονέω, 4993) signifies (*a*) "to be of sound mind," or "in one's right mind, sober-minded" (*sōzō*, "to save," *phrēn*, "the mind"), Mark 5:15 and Luke 8:35, "in his right mind"; 2 Cor. 5:13, RV, "we are of sober mind" (KJV, "we be sober"); (*b*) "to be temperate, self-controlled," Titus 2:6, "to be sober-minded"; 1 Pet. 4:7, RV, "be ye . . . of sound mind" (KJV, "be ye sober"). See also Rom. 12:3. See SOBER.¶

Note: In Acts 20:13, KJV, *mellō*, "to be about to, to intend," is translated "minding" (RV, "intending"). See INTEND.

C. Adjective.

homophrōn (ὁμόφρων, 3675), "agreeing, of one mind" (*homos*, "same," *phrēn*, "the mind"), is used in 1 Pet. 3:8.¶

Notes: (1) For the noun *sōphronismos*, in 2 Tim. 1:7, see DISCIPLINE.¶ (2) In Rom. 15:6, KJV, the adverb *homothumadon*, "of one accord," is translated "with one mind" (RV, "of one accord"). See ACCORD. (3) See also CAST, CHANGE, DOUBTFUL, FERVENT, FORWARDNESS, HUMBLENESS, HUMILITY, LOWLINESS, READINESS, READY, WILLING.

MINDED

1. *phroneō* (φρονέω, 5426): see MIND, B, No. 1.

2. *boulomai* (βούλομαι, 1014), "to wish, will, desire, purpose" (akin to *boulē*, "counsel, purpose"), is translated "was minded" in Matt. 1:19; Acts 15:37, RV (KJV, "determined"); 18:27, RV (KJV, "was disposed"); 19:30, RV (KJV, "would have"); 5:33, RV, "were minded" (KJV, "took counsel"); 18:15, RV, "I am (not) minded (to be)," KJV, "I will (be no)"; Heb. 6:17, "being minded," RV (KJV, "willing"), said of God. See COUNSEL.

3. *bouleuō* (βουλεύω, 1011), "to take counsel," is translated "to be minded" in Acts 27:39; 2 Cor. 1:17, middle voice in each case. See COUNSEL, B, No. 1.

Note: For the noun *phronēma* in Rom. 8:6, see MIND, A, No. 6.

MINDFUL OF (to be)

1. *mimnēskō* (μιμνήσκω, 5403), the tenses of which are from the older verb *mnaomai*, signifies "to remind"; but in the middle voice,

"to remember, to be mindful of," in the sense of caring for, e.g., Heb. 2:6, "Thou art mindful"; in 13:3, "remember"; in 2 Tim. 1:4, RV, "remembering" (KJV, "being mindful of"); so in 2 Pet. 3:2. See REMEMBER.

2. *mnēmoneuō* (μνημονεύω, 3421), "to call to mind, remember," is rendered "they had been mindful" in Heb. 11:15. See MENTION, B, REMEMBER.

For MINE, MINE OWN (self), see MY

MINGLE

1. *mignumi* (μίγνυμι, 3396), "to mix, mingle" (from a root *mik;* Eng., "mix" is akin), is always in the NT translated "to mingle," Matt. 27:34; Luke 13:1; Rev. 8:7; 15:2.¶

2. *kerannumi* (κεράννυμι, 2767), "to mix, to mingle," chiefly of the diluting of wine, implies "a mixing of two things, so that they are blended and form a compound, as in wine and water, whereas *mignumi* (No. 1) implies a mixing without such composition, as in two sorts of grain" (Liddell and Scott, *Lex.*). It is used in Rev. 18:6 (twice); in 14:10, RV, "prepared" (marg., "mingled"; KJV, "poured out"), lit., "mingled," followed by *akratos*, "unmixed, pure" (*a*, negative, and *kratos*, an adjective, from this verb *kerannumi*), the two together forming an oxymoron, the combination in one phrase of two terms that are ordinarily contradictory.¶

Note: For the verb *smurnizō*, "to mingle with myrrh," Mark 15:23, see MYRRH.¶

MINISTER (Noun and Verb)

A. Nouns.

1. *diakonos* (διάκονος, 1249), "a servant, attendant, minister, deacon," is translated "minister" in Mark 10:43; Rom. 13:4 (twice); 15:8; 1 Cor. 3:5; 2 Cor. 3:6; 6:4; 11:15 (twice); Gal. 2:17; Eph. 6:21; Col. 1:7, 23, 25; 4:7; 1 Thess. 3:2; 1 Tim. 4:6. See DEACON.

2. *leitourgos* (λειτουργός, 3011) denoted among the Greeks, firstly, "one who discharged a public office at his own expense," then, in general, "a public servant, minister." In the NT it is used (*a*) of Christ, as a "Minister of the sanctuary" (in the Heavens), Heb. 8:2; (*b*) of angels, Heb. 1:7 (Ps. 104:4); (*c*) of the apostle Paul, in his evangelical ministry, fulfilling it as a serving priest, Rom. 15:16; that he used it figuratively and not in an ecclesiastical sense, is obvious from the context; (*d*) of Epaphroditus, as ministering to Paul's needs on behalf of the church at Philippi, Phil. 2:25; here, representa-

tive service is in view; (*e*) of earthly rulers, who though they do not all act consciously as servants of God, yet discharge functions which are the ordinance of God, Rom. 13:6.¶

3. *hupēretēs* (ὑπηρέτης, 5257), properly "an under rower" (*hupo*, "under," *eretēs*, "a rower"), as distinguished from *nautēs*, "a seaman" (a meaning which lapsed from the word), hence came to denote "any subordinate acting under another's direction"; in Luke 4:20, RV, "attendant," KJV, "minister" it signifies the attendant at the synagogue service; in Acts 13:5, it is said of John Mark, RV, "attendant," KJV, "minister;" in Acts 26:16, "a minister," it is said of Paul as a servant of Christ in the gospel; so in 1 Cor. 4:1, where the apostle associates others with himself, as Apollos and Cephas, as "ministers of Christ." See ATTEND, C, OFFICER.

Note: Other synonymous nouns are *doulos*, "a bondservant"; *oiketēs*, "a household servant"; *misthios*, "a hired servant"; *misthōtos* (ditto); *pais*, "a boy, a household servant." For all these see SERVANT. Speaking broadly, *diakonos* views a servant in relation to his work; *doulos*, in relation to his master; *hupēretēs*, in relation to his superior; *leitourgos*, in relation to public service.

B. Verbs.

1. *diakoneō* (διακονέω, 1247), akin to A, No. 1, signifies "to be a servant, attendant, to serve, wait upon, minister." In the following it is translated "to minister," except where "to serve" is mentioned: it is used (*a*) with a general significance, e.g., Matt. 4:11; 20:28; Mark 1:13; 10:45; John 12:26 ("serve," twice); Acts 19:22; Philem. 13; (*b*) of waiting at table, "ministering" to the guests, Matt. 8:15; Luke 4:39; 8:3; 12:37; 17:8, "serve"; 22:26, "serve," v. 27, "serveth," twice; the 2nd instance, concerning the Lord, may come under (*a*); so of women preparing food, etc., Mark 1:31; Luke 10:40, "serve"; John 12:2, "served"; (*c*) of relieving one's necessities, supplying the necessaries of life, Matt. 25:44; 27:55; Mark 15:41; Acts 6:2, "serve"; Rom. 15:25; Heb. 6:10; more definitely in connection with such service in a local church, 1 Tim. 3:10, 13 [there is nothing in the original representing the word "office"; RV, "let them serve as deacons," "they that have served (well) as deacons"]; (*d*) of attending, in a more general way, to anything that may serve another's interests, as of the work of an amanuensis, 2 Cor. 3:3 (metaphorical): of the conveyance of material gifts for assisting the needy, 2 Cor. 8:19, 20, RV, "is ministered" (KJV, "is administered"); of a variety of forms of service, 2 Tim. 1:18; of the testimony of the OT prophets, 1 Pet. 1:12; of the ministry of believers one to

another in various ways, 1 Pet. 4:10, 11 (not here of discharging ecclesiastical functions).¶

Note: In Heb. 1:14, KJV (2nd part), the phrase *eis diakonian* is translated "to minister," RV, "to do service," lit., "for service"; for the noun "ministering" in the 1st part, see MINISTERING, B.

2. *leitourgeō* (λειτουργέω, 3008), (akin to A, No. 2), in classical Greek, signified at Athens "to supply public offices at one's own cost, to render public service to the State"; hence, generally, "to do service," said, e.g., of service to the gods. In the NT (see *Note* below) it is used (*a*) of the prophets and teachers in the church at Antioch, who "ministered to the Lord," Acts 13:2; (*b*) of the duty of churches of the Gentiles to "minister" in "carnal things" to the poor Jewish saints at Jerusalem, in view of the fact that the former had "been made partakers" of the "spiritual things" of the latter, Rom. 15:27; (*c*) of the official service of priests and Levites under the Law, Heb. 10:11 (in the Sept., e.g., Exod. 29:30; Num. 16:9).¶

Note: The synonymous verb *latreuō* (properly, "to serve for hire"), which is used in the Sept. of the service of both priests and people (e.g., Exod. 4:3; Deut. 10:12, and in the NT, e.g., Heb. 8:5), and, in the NT, of Christians in general, e.g., Rev. 22:3, is to be distinguished from *leitourgeō*, which has to do with the fulfillment of an office, the discharge of a function, something of a representative character (Eng., "liturgy").

3. *hupēreteō* (ὑπηρετέω, 5256), "to do the service of a *hupēretēs*" (see A, No. 3), properly, "to serve as a rower on a ship," is used (*a*) of David, as serving the counsel of God in his own generation, Acts 13:36, RV, expressive of the lowly character of his service for God; (*b*) of Paul's toil in working with his hands, and his readiness to avoid any pose of ecclesiastical superiority, Acts 20:34; (*c*) of the service permitted to Paul's friends to render to him, 24:23.¶

4. *hierourgeō* (ἱερουργέω, 2418), "to minister in priestly service" (akin to *hierourgos*, "a sacrificing priest," a word not found in the Sept. or NT: from *hieros*, "sacred," and *ergon*, "work"), is used by Paul metaphorically of his ministry of the Gospel, Rom. 15:16; the offering connected with his priestly ministry is "the offering up of the Gentiles," i.e., the presentation by gentile converts of themselves to God.¶ The apostle uses words proper to the priestly and Levitical ritual, to explain metaphorically his own priestly service. Cf. *prosphora*, "offering up," and *leitourgos*, in the same verse.

5. *parechō* (παρέχω, 3930), "to furnish, pro-

vide, supply," is translated "minister" in 1 Tim. 1:4, of the effect of "fables and endless genealogies." See BRING, A, No. 21.

6. *ergazomai* (ἐργάζομαι, 2038), "to work, work out, perform," is translated "minister" in 1 Cor. 9:13; the verb is frequently used of business, or employment, and here the phrase means "those employed in sacred things" or "those who are assiduous in priestly functions." See COMMIT, A, No. 1.

Notes: (1) The verb *chorēgeō*, rendered "minister" in the KJV of 2 Cor. 9:10, and the strengthened form *epichorēgeō*, rendered by the same verb in the KJV of 2 Cor. 9:10; Gal. 3:5; Col. 2:19; 2 Pet. 1:11, in v. 5, "add," are always translated "to supply" in the RV. Both verbs suggest an abundant supply, and are used of material or of spiritual provision. See SUPPLY. (2) In Eph. 4:29, KJV, *didōmi*, "to give," is translated "minister" (RV, "give").

MINISTERING, MINISTRATION, MINISTRY

A. Nouns.

1. *diakonia* (διακονία, 1248), "the office and work of a *diakonos*" (see MINISTER, A, No. 1), "service, ministry," is used (*a*) of domestic duties, Luke 10:40; (*b*) of religious and spiritual "ministration," (1) of apostolic "ministry," e.g., Acts 1:17, 25; 6:4; 12:25; 21:19; Rom. 11:13, RV (KJV, "office"); (2) of the service of believers, e.g., Acts 6:1; Rom. 12:7; 1 Cor. 12:5, RV, "ministrations" (KJV, "administrations"); 1 Cor. 16:15; 2 Cor. 8:4; 9:1, 12, RV, "ministration"; v. 13; Eph. 4:12, RV, "ministering" (KJV, "the ministry," not in the sense of an ecclesiastical function); 2 Tim. 4:11, RV, "(for) ministering"; collectively of a local church, Acts 11:29, "relief" (RV marg. "for ministry"); Rev. 2:19, RV, "ministry" (KJV, "service"); of Paul's service on behalf of poor saints, Rom. 15:31; (3) of the "ministry" of the Holy Spirit in the gospel, 2 Cor. 3:8; (4) of the "ministry" of angels, Heb. 1:14, RV, "to do service" (KJV, "to minister"); (5) of the work of the gospel, in general, e.g., 2 Cor. 3:9, "of righteousness;" 5:18, "of reconciliation"; (6) of the general "ministry" of a servant of the Lord in preaching and teaching, Acts 20:24; 2 Cor. 4:1; 6:3; 11:8; 1 Tim. 1:12, RV, "(to His) service"; 2 Tim. 4:5; undefined in Col. 4:17; (7) of the Law, as a "ministration" of death, 2 Cor. 3:7; of condemnation, 3:9.¶

2. *leitourgia* (λειτουργία, 3009), akin to *leitourgos* (see MINISTER, A, No. 2), to which the meanings of *leitourgia* correspond, is used in the NT of "sacred ministrations," (*a*) priestly, Luke 1:23; Heb. 8:6; 9:21; (*b*) figuratively, of

the practical faith of the members of the church at Philippi regarded as priestly sacrifice, upon which the apostle's lifeblood might be poured out as a libation, Phil. 2:17; (c) of the "ministration" of believers one to another, regarded as priestly service, 2 Cor. 9:12; Phil. 2:30. See SERVICE.¶

B. Adjective.

leitourgikos (λειτουργικός, 3010), "of or pertaining to service, ministering," is used in Heb. 1:14, of angels as "ministering spirits" (for the word "do service" in the next clause, see A, No. 1).¶ In the Sept., Exod. 31:10; 39:13; Num. 4:12, 26; 7:5; 2 Chron. 24:14.¶

MINSTREL

mousikos (μουσικός, 3451) is found in Rev. 18:22, RV, "minstrels" (KJV, "musicians"); inasmuch as other instrumentalists are mentioned, some word like "minstrels" is necessary to make the distinction, hence the RV; Bengel and others translate it "singers." Primarily the word denoted "devoted to the Muses" (the nine goddesses who presided over the principal departments of letters), and was used of anyone devoted to or skilled in arts and sciences, or "learned."¶

MINT

hēduosmon (ἡδύοσμον, 2238), an adjective denoting sweet-smelling (hēdus, "sweet," osmē, "a smell"), is used as a neuter noun signifying "mint," Matt. 23:23; Luke 11:42.¶

MIRACLE

1. dunamis (δύναμις, 1411), "power, inherent ability," is used of works of a supernatural origin and character, such as could not be produced by natural agents and means. It is translated "miracles" in the RV and KJV in Acts 8:13 (where variant readings give the words in different order); 19:11; 1 Cor. 12:10, 28, 29; Gal. 3:5; KJV only, in Acts 2:22 (RV, "mighty works"); Heb. 2:4 (RV, "powers"). In Gal. 3:5, the word may be taken in its widest sense, to include "miracles" both physical and moral. See MIGHT, A, No. 1, POWER, WORK.

2. sēmeion (σημεῖον, 4592), "a sign, mark, token" (akin to sēmainō, "to give a sign"; sēma, "a sign"), is used of "miracles" and wonders as signs of divine authority; it is translated "miracles" in the RV and KJV of Luke 23:8; Acts 4:16, 22; most usually it is given its more appropriate meaning "sign," "signs," e.g., Matt. 12:38, 39, and in every occurrence in the Synoptists, except Luke 23:8; in the following passages in John's Gospel the RV substitutes "sign" or "signs" for the KJV, "miracle or miracles"; 2:11,

23; 3:2; 4:54; 6:2, 14, 26; 7:31; 9:16; 10:41; 11:47; 12:18, 37; the KJV also has "signs" elsewhere in this Gospel; in Acts, RV, "signs," KJV, "miracles," in 6:8; 8:6; 15:12; elsewhere only in Rev. 13:14; 16:14; 19:20. See SIGN, TOKEN, WONDER.

MIRE

borboros (βόρβορος, 1004), "mud, filth," occurs in 2 Pet. 2:22.¶ In the Sept., Jer. 38:6 (twice), of the "mire" in the dungeon into which Jeremiah was cast.¶

MIRROR

esoptron (ἔσοπτρον, 2072), rendered "glass" in the KJV, is used of any surface sufficiently smooth and regular to reflect rays of light uniformly, and thus produce images of objects which actually in front of it appear to the eye as if they were behind it. "Mirrors" in Biblical times were, it seems, metallic; hence the RV adopts the more general term "mirror"; in 1 Cor. 13:12, spiritual knowledge in this life is represented metaphorically as an image dimly perceived in a "mirror"; in Jas. 1:23, the "law of liberty" is figuratively compared to a "mirror"; the hearer who obeys not is like a person who, having looked into the "mirror," forgets the reflected image after turning away; he who obeys is like one who gazes into the "mirror" and retains in his soul the image of what he should be.¶

Note: For the verb katoptrizō, "to reflect as a mirror" (some regard it as meaning "beholding in a mirror"), in 2 Cor. 3:18, see BEHOLD, No. 12.

For MISCHIEF, Acts 13:10, see VILLANY

MISERABLE, MISERABLY, MISERY

A. Adjectives.

1. eleeinos (ἐλεεινός, 1652), "pitiable, miserable" (from eleos, "mercy, pity"; see MERCY), is used in Rev. 3:17, in the Lord's description of the church at Laodicea; here the idea is probably that of a combination of "misery" and pitiableness.¶

Note: For the comparative degree eleeinoteros, rendered "most pitiable" in 1 Cor. 15:19, RV (KJV, "most miserable"), see PITIABLE.

2. kakos (κακός, 2556), "bad, evil," is translated "miserable" in Matt. 21:41, RV (KJV, "wicked"). See BAD.

B. Adverb.

kakōs (κακῶς, 2560), "badly, ill," is translated "miserably" in Matt. 21:41 (see A, No. 2). Adhering to the meaning "evil," and giving the designed stress, the sentence may be rendered, "evil (as they are) he will evilly destroy them."

C. Noun.

talaipōria (ταλαιπωρία, 5004), "hardship, suffering, distress" (akin to *talaipōros*, "wretched," Rom. 7:24; Rev. 3:17,¶ and to *talaipōreō*, in the middle voice, "to afflict oneself," in Jas. 4:9, "be afflicted"¶), is used as an abstract noun, "misery," in Rom. 3:16; as a concrete noun, "miseries," in Jas. 5:1.¶

MIST

1. *achlus* (ἀχλύς, 887), "a mist," especially a dimness of the eyes, is used in Acts 13:11. "In the single place of its NT use it attests the accuracy in the selection of words, and not least of medical words, which 'the beloved physician' so often displays. For him it expresses the mist of darkness ... which fell on the sorcerer Elymas, being the outward and visible sign of the inward spiritual darkness which would be his portion for a while in punishment for his resistance to the truth" (Trench, *Syn.*, §c).¶

2. *homichlē* (ὁμίχλη, 3658a), "a mist" (not so thick as *nephos* and *nephelē*, "a cloud"), occurs in 2 Pet. 2:17 (1st part), RV, "mists"; some mss. have *nephelai*, "clouds" (KJV).¶

3. *zophos* (ζόφος, 2217) is rendered "mist" in the KJV of 2 Pet. 2:17 (2nd part), RV, "blackness"; "murkiness" would be a suitable rendering. For this and other synonymous terms see BLACKNESS, DARKNESS.

MITE

lepton (λεπτόν, 3016), the neuter of the adjective *leptos*, signifying, firstly, "peeled," then, "fine, thin, small, light," became used as a noun, denoting a small copper coin, often mentioned in the Mishna as proverbially the smallest Jewish coin. It was valued at 1/8th of the Roman *as*, and the 1/128th part of the *denarius:* its legal value was about one third of an English farthing; Mark 12:42 lit. reads "two *lepta*, which make a *kodrantēs* (a *quadrans*)"; in Luke 12:59 "the last *lepton*" corresponds in effect to Matt. 5:26, "the uttermost *kodrantēs*," "farthing"; elsewhere Luke 21:2; see FARTHING.¶

MIXED (with)

Note: In Heb. 4:2, KJV, *sunkerannumi*, lit., "to mix with" (*sun*, "with," *kerannumi*, see MINGLE, No. 2), is so translated; RV, "were (not) united (by faith) with" [KJV, "(not) being mixed ... in],

as said of persons; in 1 Cor. 12:24 "hath tempered." See TEMPER TOGETHER.¶

MIXTURE

migma (μίγμα, 3395), "a mixture" (akin to *mignumi*, "to mix, mingle": see MINGLE, No. 1), occurs in John 19:39 (some mss. have *heligma*, "a roll").¶

Note: In Rev. 14:10, KJV, *akratos* (*a*, negative, and *kerannumi*, "to mingle") is translated "without mixture" (RV, "unmixed").¶ In the Sept., Ps. 75:8; Jer. 32:1.¶

MOCK, MOCKER, MOCKING

A. Verbs.

1. *empaizō* (ἐμπαίζω, 1702), a compound of *paizō*, "to play like a child" (*pais*), "to sport, jest," prefixed by *en*, "in" or "at," is used only in the Synoptists, and, in every instance, of the "mockery" of Christ, except in Matt. 2:16 (there in the sense of deluding, or deceiving, of Herod by the wise men) and in Luke 14:29, of ridicule cast upon the one who after laying a foundation of a tower is unable to finish it. The word is used (*a*) prophetically by the Lord, of His impending sufferings, Matt. 20:19; Mark 10:34; Luke 18:32; (*b*) of the actual insults inflicted upon Him by the men who had taken Him from Gethsemane, Luke 22:63; by Herod and his soldiers, Luke 23:11; by the soldiers of the governor, Matt. 27:29, 31; Mark 15:20; Luke 23:36; by the chief priests, Matt. 27:41; Mark 15:31.¶

2. *muktērizō* (μυκτηρίζω, 3456), from *muktēr*, "the nose," hence, "to turn up the nose at, sneer at, treat with contempt," is used in the passive voice in Gal. 6:7, where the statement "God is not mocked" does not mean that men do not mock Him (see Prov. 1:30, where the Sept. has the same verb); the apostle vividly contrasts the essential difference between God and man. It is impossible to impose upon Him who discerns the thoughts and intents of the heart. ¶

Note: Ekmuktērizō, a strengthened form of the above, "to scoff at," is used in Luke 16:14 and 23:35 (RV, "scoffed at"; KJV, "derided"). See DERIDE, SCOFF.¶

3. *chleuazō* (χλευάζω, 5512), "to jest, mock, jeer at" (from *chleuē*, "a jest"), is said of the ridicule of some of the Athenian philosophers at the apostle's testimony concerning the resurrection of the dead, Acts 17:32.¶

4. *diachleuazō* (διαχλευάζω, 1223 and 5512), an intensive form of No. 3, "to scoff at," whether by gesture or word, is said of those who jeered at the testimony given on the Day of Pentecost, Acts 2:13 (some mss. have No. 3).¶

B. Nouns.

1. *empaiktēs* (ἐμπαίκτης, 1703), "a mocker" (akin to A, No. 1), is used in 2 Pet. 3:3, RV, "mockers". (KJV, "scoffers"); Jude 18, RV and KJV, "mockers."¶ In the Sept., Isa. 3:4.¶

2. *empaigmos* (ἐμπαιγμός, 1701), the act of the *empaiktēs*, "a mocking," is used in Heb. 11:36, "mockings."¶ In the Sept., Ps. 38:7; Ezek. 22:4.¶

3. *empaigmonē* (ἐμπαιγμονή, 1702d), an abstract noun, "mockery," is used in 2 Pet. 3:3 (some mss. omit it, as in KJV): (see also No. 1, above).¶

For **MODERATION**, Phil. 4:5, KJV, see **FORBEARANCE**, C, No. 2

MODEST

kosmios (κόσμιος, 2887), "orderly, well-arranged, decent, modest" (akin to *kosmos*, in its primary sense as "harmonious arrangement, adornment"; cf. *kosmikos*, of the world, which is related to *kosmos* in its secondary sense as the world), is used in 1 Tim. 2:9 of the apparel with which Christian women are to adorn themselves; in 3:2 (RV, "orderly;" KJV, "of good behavior"), of one of the qualifications essential for a bishop or overseer. "The well-ordering is not of dress and demeanor only, but of the inner life, uttering indeed and expressing itself in the outward conversation" (Trench, *Syn.*, §xcii).¶ In the Sept., Eccl. 12:9.¶

MOISTURE

ikmas (ἰκμάς, 2429), "moisture" (probably from an Indo-European root *sik*— indicating "wet"), is used in Luke 8:6.¶ In the Sept., Job 26:14; Jer. 17:8.¶

MOMENT

A. Nouns.

1. *atomos* (ἄτομος, 823) lit. means "indivisible" (from *a*, negative, and *temnō*, "to cut"; Eng., "atom"); hence it denotes "a moment," 1 Cor. 15:52.¶

2. *stigmē* (στιγμή, 4743), "a prick, a point" (akin to *stizō*, "to prick"), is used metaphorically in Luke 4:5, of a "moment," with *chronos*, "a moment (of time)."¶

Note: It is to be distinguished from *stigma*, "a mark" or "brand," Gal. 6:17, which is, however, also connected with *stizō*.

B. Adverb.

parautika (παραυτίκα, 3910), the equivalent of *parauta*, immediately (not in the NT), i.e., *para auta*, with *ta pragmata* understood, "at the same circumstances," is used adjectivally in 2 Cor. 4:17 and translated "which is but for a moment"; the meaning is not, however, simply that of brief duration, but that which is present with us now or immediate (*para*, "beside, with"), in contrast to the future glory; the clause is, lit., "for the present lightness (i.e., 'light burden,' the adjective *elaphron*, 'light,' being used as a noun) of (our) affliction."¶ This meaning is confirmed by its use in the Sept. of Ps. 70:3, "(let them be turned back) immediately," where the rendering could not be "for a moment."¶

MONEY

1. *argurion* (ἀργύριον, 694), properly, "a piece of silver," denotes (*a*) "silver," e.g., Acts 3:6; (*b*) a "silver coin," often in the plural, "pieces of silver," e.g., Matt. 26:15; so 28:12, where the meaning is "many, (*hikanos*) pieces of silver"; (*c*) "money"; it has this meaning in Matt. 25:18, 27; 28:15; Mark 14:11; Luke 9:3; 19:15, 23; 22:5; Acts 8:20 (here the RV has "silver").

Note: In Acts 7:16, for the KJV, "(a sum of) money," the RV has "(a price in) silver." See SILVER.

2. *chrēma* (χρῆμα, 5536), lit., "a thing that one uses" (akin to *chraomai*, "to use"), hence, (*a*) "wealth, riches," Mark 10:23, 24; Luke 18:24; (*b*) "money," Acts 4:37, singular number, "a sum of money"; plural in 8:18, 20; 24:26.¶ See RICHES.

3. *chalkos* (χαλκός, 5475), "copper," is used, by metonymy, of "copper coin," translated "money," in Mark 6:8; 12:41. See BRASS.

4. *kerma* (κέρμα, 2772), primarily "a slice" (akin to *keirō*, "to cut short"), hence, "a small coin, change," is used in the plural in John 2:15, "the changers' money," probably considerable heaps of small coins.¶

5. *nomisma* (νόμισμα, 3546), primarily "that which is established by custom" (*nomos*, "a custom, law"), hence, "the current coin of a state, currency," is found in Matt. 22:19, "(tribute) money."¶ In the Sept., Neh. 7:71.¶

Note: In Matt. 17:27, KJV, *statēr* ("a coin," estimated at a little over three shillings, equivalent to four *drachmae*, the temple-tax for two persons), is translated "piece of money" (RV, "shekel"). See SHEKEL.¶

For **MONEY-CHANGER**, **CHANGER OF MONEY**, see **CHANGER**

MONEY (love of)

philarguria (φιλαργυρία, 5365), from *phileō*, "to love," and *arguros*, "silver," occurs in

1 Tim. 6:10 (cf. *philarguros*, "covetous, avaricious"). Trench contrasts this with *pleonexia*, "covetousness." See under COVET, COVETOUSNESS.¶

MONTH, MONTHS

1. *mēn* (μήν, 3376), connected with *mēnē*, "the moon," akin to a Sanskrit root *mā*—, "to measure" (the Sanskrit *māsa* denotes both moon and month, cf., e.g., Lat. *mensis*, Eng., "moon" and "month," the moon being in early times the measure of the "month"). The interval between the 17th day of the second "month" (Gen. 7:11) and the 17th day of the seventh "month," is said to be 150 days (8:3, 4), i.e., five months of 30 days each; hence the year would be 360 days (cf. Dan. 7:25; 9:27; 12:7 with Rev. 11:2–3; 12:6, 14; 13:5; whence we conclude that 3 ½ years or 42 months = 1260 days, i.e., one year = 60 days); this was the length of the old Egyptian year; later, five days were added to correspond to the solar year. The Hebrew year was as nearly solar as was compatible with its commencement, coinciding with the new moon, or first day of the "month." This was a regular feast day, Num. 10:10; 28:11–14; the Passover coincided with the full moon (the 14th of the month Abib: see PASSOVER).

Except in Gal. 4:10; Jas. 5:17; Rev. 9:5, 10, 15; 11:2; 13:5; 22:2, the word is found only in Luke's writings, Luke 1:24, 26, 36, 56; 4:25; Acts 7:20; 18:11; 19:8; 20:3; 28:11, examples of Luke's care as to accuracy of detail.¶

2. *trimēnos* (τρίμηνος, 5150**), an adjective, denoting "of three months" (*tri*, "for" *treis*, "three," and No. 1), is used as a noun, a space of three "months," in Heb. 11:23.¶

3. *tetramēnos* (τετράμηνος, 5072**), an adjective, denoting of four "months" (*tetra*, for *tessares*, "four," and No. 1), is used as a noun in John 4:35 (where *chronos*, "time," may be understood).¶

MOON

1. *selēnē* (σελήνη, 4582), from *selas*, "brightness" (the Heb. words are *yarēach*, "wandering," and *lebānāh*, "white"), occurs in Matt. 24:29; Mark 13:24; Luke 21:25; Acts 2:20; 1 Cor. 15:41; Rev. 6:12; 8:12; 12:1; 21:23. In Rev. 12:1, "the moon under her feet" is suggestive of derived authority, just as her being clothed with the sun is suggestive of supreme authority; everything in the symbolism of the passage centers in Israel. In 6:12 the similar symbolism of the sun and "moon" is suggestive of the supreme authority over the world, and of derived authority, at the time of the execution

of divine judgments upon nations at the close of the present age.¶

2. *neomēnia* (νεομηνία, 3561), or *noumēniua*, denoting "a new moon" (*neos*, "new," *mēn*, "a month": see MONTH), is used in Col. 2:16, of a Jewish festival.¶ Judaistic tradition added special features in the liturgy of the synagogue in connection with the observance of the first day of the month, the new "moon" time.

In the OT the RV has "new moon" for KJV, "month" in Num. 29:6; 1 Sam. 20:27; Hos. 5:7. For the connection with feast days see Lev. 23:24; Num. 10:10; 29:1; Ps. 81:3.

For MOOR see DRAW, B, *Note* (1)

MORE

A. Adverbs.

1. *mallon* (μᾶλλον, 3123), the comparative degree of *mala*, "very, very much," is used (*a*) of increase, "more," with qualifying words, with *pollǭ*, "much," e.g., Mark 10:48, "the more (a great deal)"; Rom. 5:15, 17, "(much) more"; Phil. 2:12 (ditto); with *posǭ*, "how much," e.g., Luke 12:24; Rom. 11:12; with *tosoutǭ*, "by so much," Heb. 10:25; (*b*) without a qualifying word, by way of comparison, "the more," e.g., Luke 5:15, "so much the more"; John 5:18, "the more"; Acts 5:14 (ditto); Phil. 1:9; 1 Thess. 4:1, 10, "more and more"; 2 Pet. 1:10, RV, "the more" (KJV, "the rather"); in Acts 20:35, by a periphrasis, it is translated "more (blessed)"; in Gal. 4:27, "more (than)," lit., "rather (than)"; (*c*) with qualifying words, similarly to (*a*), e.g., Mark 7:36. See RATHER.

2. *eti* (ἔτι, 2089), "yet, as yet, still," used of degree is translated "more" in Matt. 18:16, "(one or two) more"; Heb. 8:12 and 10:17,"(will I remember no) more"; 10:2, "(no) more (conscience)"; 11:32, "(what shall I) more (say)?" Rev. 3:12, "(he shall go out thence no) more"; 7:16, "(no) more" and "any more;" 9:12, KJV "more" (RV, "hereafter"); 18:21–23, "(no) more" "any more" (5 times); 20:3, "(no) more"; 21:1, 4 (twice); 22:3. See ALSO, No. 2.

3. *ouketi* (οὐκέτι, 3765), *ouk*, "not," and No. 2, combined in one word, is translated "no more," e.g., in Matt. 19:6; Luke 15:19, 21; Acts 20:25, 38; Eph. 2:19. See HENCEFORTH, HEREAFTER, LONGER, NOW, *Note* (2).

4. *perissoteron* (περισσότερον, 4054), the neuter of the comparative degree of *perissos*, "more abundant," is used a an adverb, "more," e.g., Luke 12:4; 2 Cor. 10:8, KJV (RV, "abundantly"); Heb. 7:15, RV, "more abundantly" (KJV, "far more"). See ABUNDANTLY, C, No. 2.

Note: For the corresponding adverbs *perissōs*

and *perissoterōs*, see ABUNDANTLY, EXCEED-INGLY.

5. *meizon* (μεῖζον, 3187), the neuter of *meizōn*, "greater," the comparative degree of *megas*, "great," is used as an adverb, and translated "the more" in Matt. 20:31. See GREATER.

6. *huper* (ὑπέρ, 5228), a preposition, "over, above," etc., is used as an adverb in 2 Cor. 11:23, "(I) more."

7. *hoson* (ὅσον), neuter of *hosos*, "how much," is used adverbially in Mark 7:36 (1st part), "the more."

B. Adjectives (*some with adverbial uses*).

1. *pleiōn* (πλείων, 4119), the comparative degree of *polus*, "much," is used (*a*) as an adjective, e.g., John 15:2; Acts 24:11, RV, "(not) more (than)" (KJV, "yet but"); Heb. 3:3; (*b*) as a noun, or with a noun understood, e.g., Matt. 20:10; Mark 12:43; Acts 19:32 and 27:12, "the more part"; 1 Cor. 9:19; (*c*) as an adverb, Matt. 5:20, "shall exceed," lit., "(shall abound) more (than)"; 26:53; Luke 9:13. See ABOVE, No. 3, *Note*, GREATER.

2. *perissos* (περισσός, 4053), "more than sufficient, over and above, abundant" (a popular substitute for No. 3), is translated "more," e.g., in Matt. 5:37 47. In John 10:10 the neuter form is rendered "more abundantly," KJV, RV, "abundantly" (marg., "abundance").

3. *perissoteros* (περισσότερος, 4055), the comparative degree of No. 2, is translated "much more (than a prophet)" in Matt. 11:9, RV (KJV, "more"); in Luke 7:26 both RV and KJV have "much more." See ABUNDANT, C.

Notes: (1) In Matt. 25:20 (2nd part), KJV, *allos*, "other" (so the RV), is translated "more." (2) In Jas. 4:6, KJV, the adjective *meizōn*, "greater" (see A, No. 5, above), is translated "more (grace)" (RV marg. "a greater grace"). See GRACE (at end). (3) Various uses of the word "more" occur in connection with other words, especially in the comparative degree. The phrase "more than" translates certain prepositions and particles: in Rom. 1:25, KJV, *para*, "beside, compared with," is translated "more than" (RV, "rather than"): cf. Rom. 12:3 *huper*, "over, above," "more than," in Matt. 10:37 (twice); in Philem. 21, KJV, "more than" (RV, "beyond"). In Mark 14:5, KJV, *epanō*, "above," is translated "more than" (RV, "above"). In Luke 15:7 the particle *ē*, "than," is necessarily rendered "more than"; cf. Luke 17:2 and 1 Cor. 14:19, "rather than." In Mark 8:14, the conjunction *ei*, "if," with the negative *mē*, lit., "if not," signifying "except," is translated "more than (one loaf)."

MOREOVER

1. *eti* (ἔτι, 2089), "yet, as yet, still," is translated "moreover" in Acts 2:26; in 21:28, RV (KJV, "further"); Heb. 11:36. See MORE, A, No. 2.

2. *kai* (καί, 2532), and, is translated "moreover" in Acts 24:6; in the KJV, where the RV has "and," Acts 19:26.

3. *de* (δέ, 1161), a particle signifying "and" or "but," is translated "moreover" in Matt. 18:15, KJV (RV, "and"); Acts 11:12 (RV, "and"); Rom. 5:20, KJV (RV, "but"); 8:30 ("and"); 1 Cor. 15:1 (RV, "now"); 2 Cor. 1:23 (RV, "but"); 2 Pet. 1:15 (RV, "yea").

4. *alla kai* (ἀλλὰ καί), "but also, yea even," is translated "moreover" in Luke 24:22, RV (KJV, "yea, and"); in 16:21, KJV, "moreover" (RV, "yea, even").

5. *de kai* (δὲ καί), "but also," is translated "moreover" in 1 Tim. 3:7.

6. *kai ... de* (καὶ ... δέ) is translated "moreover" in Heb. 9:21.

7. *loipon* (λοιπόν, 3063), the neuter of the adjective *loipos*, "the rest," used adverbially, most usually rendered "finally," is translated "moreover" in 1 Cor. 4:2 (some mss. have *ho de loipon*, lit., "but what is left," KJV, "moreover," for *hōde loipon*, "here, moreover," as in the RV). See FINALLY.

Note: In 1 Cor. 10:1, KJV, *gar*, "for," is translated "moreover" (RV, "for"); the RV is important here, as it introduces a reason for what has preceded in ch. 9, whereas "moreover" may indicate that a new subject is being introduced; this incorrect rendering tends somewhat to dissociate the two passages, whereas *gar* connects them intimately.

MORNING (in the, early in the)

A. Adjectives.

1. *prōios* (πρώϊος, 4405), "early, at early morn" (from *pro*, "before"), is used as a noun in the feminine form *prōïa*, "morning" in Matt. 27:1 and John 21:4 (in some mss. in Matt. 21:18 and John 18:28, for B, No. 1, which see). Its adjectival force is retained by regarding it as qualifying the noun *hōra*, "an hour," i.e., "at an early hour."¶

2. *prōïnos* (πρώϊνος, 4407), a later form of No. 1, qualifies *astēr*, "star," in Rev. 2:28 and 22:16 (where some mss. have No. 3). That Christ will give to the overcomer "the morning star" indicates a special interest for such in Himself, as He thus describes Himself in the later passage. For Israel He will appear as "the sun of righteousness"; as the "morning" Star

which precedes He will appear for the rapture of the church.¶

3. *orthrinos* or *orthrios* (ὀρθρινός, 3721), "pertaining to dawn or morning," in some mss. in Rev. 22:16 (see No. 2); see DAWN, B, *Note*.

B. Adverb.

prōï (πρωΐ, 4404), "early," is translated "in the morning" in Matt. 16:3; 20:1 (with *hama*, "early"); 21:18; Mark 1:35; 11:20; 13:35; 15:1; "early" in Mark 16:2 (with *lian*, "very"; KJV, "early in the morning"); 16:9; Matt. 21:18 and John 18:28 (in the best texts for A, No. 1); 20:1; Acts 28:23 (with *apo*, "from").¶

C. Noun.

orthros (ὄρθρος, 3722) denotes "daybreak, dawn," Luke 24:1; John 8:2; Acts 5:21; see DAWN, B.¶

D. Verb.

orthrizō (ὀρθρίζω, 3719), "to do anything early in the morning," is translated "came early in the morning," in Luke 21:38.¶

MORROW

1. *aurion* (αὔριον, 839), an adverb denoting "tomorrow," is used (*a*) with this meaning in Matt. 6:30; Luke 12:28; 13:32, 33; Acts 23:15 (in some mss.), 20; 25:22; 1 Cor. 15:32; Jas. 4:13; (*b*) with the word *hēmera*, "day," understood (occurring thus in the papyri), translated as a noun,"(the) morrow," Matt. 6:34 (twice); Luke 10:35; Acts 4:3 (KJV, "next day"); 4:5; Jas. 4:14.¶

2. *epaurion* (ἐπαύριον, 1887), epi, "upon," and No. 1, is used as in (*b*) above; the RV always translates it "on (the) morrow"; in the following the KJV has "(the) next day," Matt. 27:62; John 1:29, 35 ("the next day after"); 12:12; Acts 14:20; 21:8; 25:6; "(the) day following," John 1:43; 6:22; "the morrow after," Acts 10:24.

Note: In Acts 25:17, KJV, the adverb *hexēs*, "next, successively, in order," is translated "on (the) morrow." See NEXT.

For MORSEL see MEAT, No. 2

MORTAL, MORTALITY

thnētos (θνητός, 2349), "subject or liable to death, mortal" (akin to *thnēskō*, "to die"), occurs in Rom. 6:12, of the body, where it is called "mortal," not simply because it is liable to death, but because it is the organ in and through which death carries on its death-producing activities; in 8:11, the stress is on the liability to death, and the quickening is not reinvigoration but the impartation of life at the time of the Rapture, as in 1 Cor. 15:53, 54 and 2 Cor. 5:4 (RV, "what is mortal"; KJV, "mortality"); in 2 Cor. 4:11, it is applied to the flesh,

which stands, not simply for the body, but the body as that which consists of the element of decay, and is thereby death-doomed. Christ's followers are in this life delivered unto death, that His life may be manifested in that which naturally is the seat of decay and death. That which is subject to suffering is that in which the power of Him who suffered here is most manifested.¶

MORTIFY

1. *thanatoō* (θανατόω, 2289), "to put to death" (from *thanatos*, "death," akin to *thnētos*, "mortal," see above), is translated "mortify" in Rom. 8:13 (Amer. RV, "put to death"); in 7:4, "ye were made dead" (passive voice), betokens the act of God on the believer, through the death of Christ; here in 8:13 it is the act of the believer himself, as being responsible to answer to God's act, and to put to death "the deeds of the body." See DEATH, C, No. 1.

2. *nekroō* (νεκρόω, 3499), "to make dead" (from *nekros*, see DEAD, A), is used figuratively in Col. 3:5 and translated "mortify" (Amer. RV, "put to death"). See DEAD, B, No. 1.

MOST

1. *pleion* (πλεῖον, 4119), the neuter of *pleiōn*, "more," is used adverbially and translated "most" (of degree) in Luke 7:42 (without the article); in v. 43 (with the article, "the most"); 1 Cor. 10:5, RV, "most" (KJV, "many"); Phil. 1:14 (ditto). See MORE.

2. *pleistos* (πλεῖστος, 4118), the superlative degree of *polus*, is used (*a*) as an adjective in Matt. 11:20; 21:8, RV, "(the) most part of" (KJV, "a very great"); (*b*) in the neuter, with the article, adverbially, "at the most," 1 Cor. 14:27; (*c*) as an elative (i.e., intensively) in Mark 4:1 (in the best mss.; some have *polus*), "a very great (multitude)."

3. *malista* (μάλιστα, 3122), an adverb, the superlative of *mala*, "very," is translated "most of all" in Acts 20:38. See ESPECIALLY.

Note: For combinations in the translation of other words, see BELIEVE, C, *Note* (4), EXCELLENT, GLADLY, HIGH, STRAITEST.

MOTE

karphos (κάρφος, 2595), "a small, dry stalk, a twig, a bit of dried stick" (from *karphō*, "to dry up"), or "a tiny straw or bit of wool," such as might fly into the eye, is used metaphorically of a minor fault, Matt. 7:3, 4, 5; Luke 6:41, 42 (twice), in contrast with *dokos*, "a beam supporting the roof of a building" (see BEAM).¶ In the Sept., Gen. 8:11.¶

MOTH

sēs (σής, 4597) denotes "a clothes moth," Matt. 6:19, 20; Luke 12:33.¶ In Job 4:19 "crushed before the moth" alludes apparently to the fact that woolen materials, riddled by the larvae of "moths," become so fragile that a touch demolishes them. In Job 27:18 "He buildeth his house as a moth" alludes to the frail covering which a larval "moth" constructs out of the material which it consumes. The rendering "spider" (marg.) seems an attempt to explain a difficulty.

MOTH-EATEN

sētobrōtos (σητόβρωτος, 4598), from *sēs*, "a moth," and *bibrōskō*, "to eat," is used in Jas. 5:2.¶ In the Sept. Job 13:28.¶

MOTHER

1. *mētēr* (μήτηρ, 3384) is used (*a*) of the natural relationship, e.g., Matt. 1:18; 2 Tim. 1:5; (*b*) figuratively, (1) of "one who takes the place of a mother," Matt. 12:49, 50; Mark 3:34, 35; John 19:27; Rom. 16:13; 1 Tim. 5:2; (2) of "the heavenly and spiritual Jerusalem," Gal. 4:26, which is "free" (not bound by law imposed externally, as under the Law of Moses), "which is our mother" (RV), i.e., of Christians, the metropolis, mother-city, used allegorically, just as the capital of a country is "the seat of its government, the center of its activities, and the place where the national characteristics are most fully expressed"; (3) symbolically, of "Babylon," Rev. 17:5, as the source from which has proceeded the religious harlotry of mingling pagan rites and doctrines with the Christian faith.

Note: In Mark 16:1 the article, followed by the genitive case of the name "James," the word "mother" being omitted, is an idiomatic mode of expressing the phrase "the mother of James."

2. *mētrolǭas*, or *mētralǭas* (μητραλῴας, 3389) denotes "a matricide" (No. 1, and *aloiaō*, to smite); 1 Tim. 1:9, "murderers of mothers"; it probably has, however, the broader meaning of "smiters" (RV, marg.), as in instances elsewhere than the NT.¶

3. *amētōr* (ἀμήτωρ, 282), "without a mother" (*a*, negative, and No. 1), is used in Heb. 7:3, of the Genesis record of Melchizedek, certain details concerning him being purposely omitted, in order to conform the description to facts about Christ as the Son of God. The word has been found in this sense in the writings of Euripides the dramatist and Herodotus the historian. See also under FATHER.¶

MOTHER-IN-LAW

penthera (πενθερά, 3994), the feminine of *pentheros* ("a father-in-law"), occurs in Matt. 8:14; 10:35; Mark 1:30; Luke 4:38; 12:53 (twice).¶

For **MOTION**, Rom. 7:5, KJV, see **PASSION**

MOUNT, MOUNTAIN

oros (ὄρος, 3735) is used (*a*) without specification, e.g., Luke 3:5 (distinct from *bounos*, "a hill," see HILL, No. 3); John 4:20; (*b*) of "the Mount of Transfiguration," Matt. 17:1, 9; Mark 9:2, 9; Luke 9:28, 37 (KJV, "hill"); 2 Pet. 1:18; (*c*) of "Zion," Heb. 12:22; Rev. 14:1; (*d*) of "Sinai," Acts 7:30, 38; Gal. 4:24, 25; Heb. 8:5; 12:20; (*e*) of "the Mount of Olives," Matt. 21:1; 24:3; Mark 11:1; 13:3; Luke 19:29, 37; 22:39; John 8:1; Acts 1:12; (*f*) of "the hill districts as distinct from the lowlands," especially of the hills above the Sea of Galilee, e.g., Matt. 5:1; 8:1; 18:12; Mark 5:5; (*g*) of "the mountains on the east of Jordan" and "those in the land of Ammon" and "the region of Petra," etc., Matt. 24:16; Mark 13:14; Luke 21:21; (*h*) proverbially, "of overcoming difficulties, or accomplishing great things," 1 Cor. 13:2; cf. Matt. 17:20; 21:21; Mark 11:23; (*i*) symbolically, of "a series of the imperial potentates of the Roman dominion, past and future," Rev. 17:9. See HILL.

MOURN, MOURNING

A. Verbs.

1. *koptō* (κόπτω, 2875), "to cut or beat," used in the middle voice of "beating the breast or head in mourning" (cf. Luke 23:27), is translated "shall mourn" in Matt. 24:30. See BEWAIL, No. 2, CUT, WAIL.

2. *pentheō* (πενθέω, 3996), "to mourn for, lament," is used (*a*) of mourning in general, Matt. 5:4; 9:15; Luke 6:25; (*b*) of sorrow for the death of a loved one, Mark 16:10; (*c*) of "mourning" for the overthrow of Babylon and the Babylonish system, Rev. 18:11, 15, RV, "mourning" (KJV, "wailing"); v. 19 (ditto); (*d*) of sorrow for sin or for condoning it, Jas. 4:9; 1 Cor. 5:2; (*e*) of grief for those in a local church who show no repentance for evil committed, 2 Cor. 12:21, RV, "mourn" (KJV, "bewail"). See BEWAIL, No. 3.¶

3. *thrēneō* (θρηνέω, 2354), "to lament, wail" (akin to *thrēnos*, "a lamentation, a dirge"), is used (*a*) in a general sense, of the disciples during the absence of the Lord, John 16:20, "lament"; (*b*) of those who sorrowed for the sufferings and the impending crucifixion of the

Lord, Luke 23:27, "lamented"; the preceding word is *koptō* (No. 1); (*c*) of "mourning" as for the dead, Matt. 11:17, RV, "wailed" (KJV, "have mourned"); Luke 7:32 (ditto). See BE-WAIL, *Note* (1).¶

Notes: (1) Trench points out that *pentheō* is often joined with *klaiō*, "to weep," 2 Sam. 19:1; Mark 16:10; Jas. 4:9; Rev. 18:15, indicating that *pentheō* is used especially of external manifestation of grief (as with *koptō* and *thrēneō*), in contrast to *lupeomai*, which may be used of inward grief (*Syn.* §xlv); though in Classical Greek *pentheō* was used of grief without violent manifestations (Grimm-Thayer). (2) Among the well-to-do it was common to hire professional mourners (men and women), who accompanied the dead body to the grave with formal music and the singing of dirges. At the death of Jairus' daughter male flute players were present, Matt. 9:23 (see, however, Jer. 9:17).

B. Nouns.

1. *odurmos* (ὀδυρμός, 3602), "lamentation, mourning," is translated "mourning" in Matt. 2:18 and 2 Cor. 7:7: see BEWAIL, *Note* (2).¶

2. *penthos* (πένθος, 3997), akin to A, No. 2, "mourning," is used in Jas. 4:9; Rev. 18:7 (twice), RV, "mourning" (KJV, "sorrow"); v. 8, "mourning"; 21:4, RV, "mourning" (KJV, "sorrow"). See SORROW.¶

MOUTH

A. Noun.

stoma (στόμα, 4750), akin to *stomachos* (which originally meant "a throat, gullet"), is used (*a*) of "the mouth" of man, e.g., Matt. 15:11; of animals, e.g., Matt. 17:27; 2 Tim. 4:17 (figurative); Heb. 11:33; Jas. 3:3; Rev. 13:2 (2nd occurrence); (*b*) figuratively of "inanimate things," of the "edge" of a sword, Luke 21:24; Heb. 11:34; of the earth, Rev. 12:16; (*c*) figuratively, of the "mouth," as the organ of speech, (1) of Christ's words, e.g., Matt. 13:35; Luke 11:54; Acts 8:32; 22:14; 1 Pet. 2:22; (2) of human, e.g., Matt. 18:16; 21:16; Luke 1:64; Rev. 14:5; as emanating from the heart, Matt. 12:34; Rom. 10:8, 9; of prophetic ministry through the Holy Spirit, Luke 1:70; Acts 1:16; 3:18; 4:25; of the destructive policy of two world potentates at the end of this age, Rev. 13:2, 5, 6; 16:13 (twice); of shameful speaking, Eph. 4:29 and Col. 3:8; (3) of the Devil speaking as a dragon or serpent, Rev. 12:15, 16; 16:13; (*d*) figuratively, in the phrase "face to face" (lit., "mouth to mouth"), 2 John 12; 3 John 14; (*e*) metaphorically, of "the utterances of the Lord, in judgment," 2 Thess. 2:8; Rev. 1:16; 2:16; 19:15, 21; of His judgment

upon a local church for its lukewarmness, Rev. 3:16; (*f*) by metonymy, for "speech," Matt. 18:16; Luke 19:22; 21:15; 2 Cor. 13:1.

Note: In Acts 15:27, *logos*, "a word," is translated "word of mouth," RV (KJV, "mouth," marg., "word").

B. Verb.

epistomizō (ἐπιστομίζω, 1993), "to bridle" (*epi*, "upon," and A), is used metaphorically of "stopping the mouth, putting to silence," Titus 1:11.¶ Cf. *phrassō*, "to stop, close," said of stopping the "mouths" of men, in Rom. 3:19. See STOP.

MOVE, MOVED, MOVER, MOVING, UNMOVEABLE

A. Verbs.

1. *kineō* (κινέω, 2795), "to set in motion, move" (hence, e.g., Eng. "kinematics," "kinetics," "cinema"), is used (*a*) of wagging the head, Matt. 27:39; Mark 15:29; (*b*) of the general activity of the human being, Acts 17:28; (*c*) of the "moving" of mountains, Rev. 6:14, in the sense of removing, as in Rev. 2:5, of removing a lampstand (there figuratively of causing a local church to be discontinued); (*d*) figuratively, of exciting, stirring up feelings and passions, Acts 21:30 (passive voice); 24:5, "a mover"; (*e*) of "moving burdens," Matt. 23:4. See REMOVE, WAG.¶ Cf. *sunkineo*, "to stir up," Acts 6:12.¶

2. *metakineō* (μετακινέω, 3334), in the active voice, "to move something away" (not in the NT; in the Sept., e.g., Deut. 19:14; Isa. 54:10); in the middle voice, "to remove oneself, shift" translated in the passive in Col. 1:23, "be . . . not moved away (from the hope of the gospel)."¶

3. *seiō* (σείω, 4579), "to shake, move to and fro," usually of violent concussion (Eng., "seismic," "seismograph," "seismology"), is said (*a*) of the earth as destined to be shaken by God, Heb. 12:26; (*b*) of a local convulsion of the earth, at the death of Christ, Matt. 27:51, "did quake"; (*c*) of a fig tree, Rev. 6:13; (*d*) metaphorically, to stir up with fear or some other emotion, Matt. 21:10, of the people of a city; 28:4, of the keepers or watchers, at the Lord's tomb, RV, "did quake" (KJV, "did shake").¶

4. *saleuō* (σαλεύω, 4531), "to shake," properly of the action of stormy wind, then, "to render insecure, stir up," is rendered "I should (not) be moved" in Acts 2:25, in the sense of being cast down or shaken from a sense of security and happiness, said of Christ, in a quotation from Ps. 16:8. See SHAKE, STIR (up).

5. *sainō* (σαίνω, 4525), properly, of dogs,

"to wag the tail, fawn"; hence, metaphorically of persons, "to disturb, disquiet," 1 Thess. 3:3, passive voice, "(that no man) be moved (by these afflictions)." Some have suggested the primary meaning, "to be wheedled, befooled, by pleasing utterances"; but Greek interpreters regard it as synonymous with No. 3, or with *tarassō*, "to disturb," and this is confirmed by the contrast with "establish" in v. 2, and "stand fast" in v. 8. A variant reading gives the verb *siainesthai*, "to be disheartened, unnerved."¶

6. *pherō* (φέρω, 5342), "to bear, carry," is rendered "being moved" in 2 Pet. 1:21, signifying that they were "borne along," or impelled, by the Holy Spirit's power, not acting according to their own wills, or simply expressing their own thoughts, but expressing the mind of God in words provided and ministered by Him.

Notes: (1) In Mark 15:11, KJV, *anaseiō*, "to shake to and fro, stir up," is translated "moved" (RV, "stirred up," as in Luke 23:5, KJV and RV).¶ (2) In Acts 20:24 some mss. have a phrase translated "none of these things move me." The text for which there is most support gives the rendering "but I hold not my life of any account, as dear unto myself." Field suggests a reading, the translation of which is, "neither make I account of anything, nor think my life dear unto myself." (3) In 1 Cor. 15:34, for the more literal KJV, "I speak this to your shame," the RV has "I speak this to move you to shame." (4) For "moved with godly fear" see FEAR, D, No. 2. (5) See also COMPASSION, ENVY, FEAR, INDIGNATION.

B. Adjectives.

1. *asaleutos* (ἀσάλευτος, 761), "unmoved, immoveable" (from *a*, negative, and A, No. 4), is translated "unmoveable" in Acts 27:41; "which cannot be moved" in Heb. 12:28, KJV (RV, "that cannot be shaken").¶ In the Sept., Exod. 13:16; Deut. 6:8; 11:18.¶

2. *ametakinētos* (ἀμετακίνητος, 277), "firm, immoveable" (*a*, negative, and A, No. 2), is used in 1 Cor. 15:58.¶

C. Noun.

kinēsis (κίνησις, 2796), "a moving" (akin to A, No. 1), is found in John 5:3 (in many ancient authorities, RV, marg.), of the "moving" of the water at the pool of Bethesda.¶

MOW

amaō (ἀμάω, 270), "to mow," is translated "mowed" in Jas. 5:4, RV (KJV, "have reaped down"). "The cognate words seem to show that the sense of cutting or mowing was original, and that of gathering-in secondary" (Liddell and Scott, *Lex.*).¶

MUCH

1. *polus* (πολύς, 4183) is used (*a*) as an adjective of degree, e.g., Matt. 13:5, "much (earth)"; Acts 26:24, "much (learning)"; in v. 29, in the answer to Agrippa's "with but little persuasion," some texts have *pollō* (some *megalō*, "with great"), RV, "(whether with little or) with much"; of number, e.g., Mark 5:24, RV, "a great (multitude)," KJV, "much (people)"; so Luke 7:11; John 12:12; Rev. 19:1, etc.; (*b*) in the neuter singular form (*polu*), as a noun, e.g., Luke 16:10 (twice); in the plural (*polla*), e.g., Rom. 16:6, 12, "(labored) much," lit., "many things"; (*c*) adverbially, in the neuter singular, e.g., Acts 18:27; James 5:16; Matt. 26:9 (a genitive of price); in the plural, e.g., Mark 5:43, RV, "much" (KJV, "straitly"); Mark 9:26, RV, "much" (KJV, "sore"); John 14:30; and with the article, Acts 26:24; Rom. 15:22; 1 Cor. 16:19; Rev. 5:4. See GREAT.

2. *hikanos* (ἱκανός, 2425), "enough, much, many," is translated "much," e.g., in Luke 7:12 (in some mss. Acts 5:37; see the RV); Acts 11:24, 26; 19:26; 27:9. See ABLE, ENOUGH, A, No. 2, GREAT, LARGE, MANY, MEET, SECURITY, SORE, SUFFICIENT, WORTHY.

Notes: (1) For "much more," "so much the more," see MORE. (2) In John 12:9, the RV has "the common people" for "much people." (3) In Acts 27:16, KJV, *ischuō*, "to be able," with *molis*, "scarcely," is translated "had much work" (RV, "were able, with difficulty"). (4) In Luke 19:15, KJV, the pronoun *ti*, "what" (RV), is translated "how much." (5) The adjective *tosoutos*, "so great, so much," is translated "so much (bread)," in Matt. 15:33, plural, RV, "so many (loaves)"; in the genitive case, of price, in Acts 5:8, "for so much"; in the dative case, of degree, in Heb. 1:4, RV, "by so much" (KJV, "so much"); so in Heb. 10:25; in Heb. 7:22 "by so much" translates the phrase *kata tosouto;* in Rev. 18:7, "so much." (6) See DISPLEASED, EXHORTATION, PERPLEX, SPEAKING, WORK.

MUCH (AS)

Notes: (1) In Luke 6:34 the phrase *ta isa*, lit., "the equivalent (things)," is translated "as much" (of lending, to receive back the equivalent). (2) In Rom. 1:15, the phrase *to kat' eme*, lit., "the (thing) according to me," signifies "as much as in me is"; cf. the KJV marg. in 1 Pet. 5:2 [lit., "the (extent) in, or among, you"; the text takes the word "flock" as understood, the marg. regards the phrase as adverbially idiomatic]; in Rom. 12:18 "as much as in you lieth" translates a similar phrase, lit., "the (extent) out of you." (3) In Heb. 12:20, KJV, *kai ean* (contracted to *k'an*), "if even" (RV), is translated "and if so much as." (4) The negatives *oude* and *mēde*, "not even" (RV) are translated "not so much as" in the KJV in Mark 2:2; Luke 6:3 and 1 Cor. 5:1; in the following the RV and KJV translate them "not so much as," Mark 3:20 (some mss. have *mēte*, with the same meaning); Acts 19:2; in Mark 6:31 "no (leisure) so much as." (5) In Rom. 3:12, *heōs*, "as far as, even unto," is translated "so much as" in the RV; the KJV supplies nothing actually corresponding to it. (6) In John 6:11 *hosos* denotes "as much as."

MULTIPLY

1. *plēthunō* (πληθύνω, 4129), used (*a*) transitively, denotes "to cause to increase, to multiply," 2 Cor. 9:10; Heb. 6:14 (twice); in the passive voice, "to be multiplied," Matt. 24:12, RV, "(iniquity) shall be multiplied" (KJV, "shall abound"); Acts 6:7; 7:17; 9:31; 12:24; 1 Pet. 1:2; 2 Pet. 1:2; Jude 2; (*b*) intransitively it denotes "to be multiplying," Acts 6:1, RV, "was multiplying" (KJV, "was multiplied"). See ABUNDANCE, B, No. 5.¶

2. *pleonazō* (πλεονάζω, 4121), used intransitively, "to abound," is translated "being multiplied" in the RV of 2 Cor. 4:15 (KJV, "abundant"); the active voice, aorist tense, here would be more accurately rendered "having superabounded" or "superabounding" or "multiplying." See ABUNDANCE, B, No. 3.

MULTITUDE

1. *ochlos* (ὄχλος, 3793) is used frequently in the four Gospels and the Acts; elsewhere only in Rev. 7:9; 17:15; 19:1, 6; it denotes (*a*) "a crowd or multitude of persons, a throng," e.g., Matt. 14:14, 15; 15:33; often in the plural, e.g., Matt. 4:25; 5:1; with *polus*, "much" or "great," it signifies "a great multitude," e.g., Matt. 20:29, or "the common people," Mark 12:37, perhaps preferably "the mass of the people." Field supports the meaning in the text, but either rendering is suitable. The mass of the people was attracted to Him (for the statement "heard Him gladly" cf. what is said in Mark 6:20 of Herod Antipas concerning John the Baptist); in John 12:9, "the common people," RV, stands in contrast with their leaders (v. 10); Acts 24:12, RV, "crowd"; (*b*) "the populace, an unorganized multitude," in contrast to *dēmos*, "the people as a body politic," e.g., Matt. 14:5; 21:26; John 7:12 (2nd part); (*c*) in a more general sense, "a multitude or company," e.g., Luke 6:17, RV, "a (great) multitude (of His disciples)," KJV, "the company"; Acts 1:15, "a multitude (of persons)," RV, KJV, "the number (of names)"; Acts

24:18, RV, "crowd" (KJV, "multitude"). See COMPANY, No. 1, NUMBER.

2. *plēthos* (πλῆθος, 4128), lit., "a fullness," hence, "a large company, a multitude," is used (*a*) of things: of fish, Luke 5:6; John 21:6; of sticks ("bundle"), Acts 28:3; of stars and of sand, Heb. 11:12; of sins, Jas. 5:20; 1 Pet. 4:8; (*b*) of persons, (1) a "multitude": of people, e.g., Mark 3:7, 8; Luke 6:17; John 5:3; Acts 14:1; of angels, Luke 2:13; (2) with the article, the whole number, the "multitude," the populace, e.g., Luke 1:10; 8:37; Acts 5:16; 19:9; 23:7; a particular company, e.g., of disciples, Luke 19:37; Acts 4:32; 6:2, 5; 15:30; of elders, priests, and scribes, 23:7; of the apostles and the elders of the Church in Jerusalem, Acts 15:12. See ASSEMBLY, No. 3, BUNDLE, No. 2, COMPANY, No. 5.

Note: In Luke 12:1. KJV, the phrase, lit., "the myriads of the multitude" is translated "an innumerable multitude of people" (where "people" translates No. 1, above), RV, "the many thousands of the multitude" (where "multitude" translates No. 1).

MURDER

phonos (φόνος, 5408) is used (*a*) of a special act, Mark 15:7; Luke 23:19, 25; (*b*) in the plural, of "murders" in general, Matt. 15:19; Mark 7:21 (Gal. 5:21, in some inferior mss.); Rev. 9:21; in the singular, Rom. 1:29; (*c*) in the sense of "slaughter," Heb. 11:37, "they were slain with the sword," lit., "(they died by) slaughter (of the sword)"; in Acts 9:1, "slaughter." See SLAUGHTER.¶

Note: In Matt. 19:18, KJV, *phoneuō*, "to kill" (akin to *phoneus*, see below), is translated "thou shalt do (no) murder" (RV, "thou shalt (not) kill"). See KILL, SLAY.

MURDERER

1. *phoneus* (φονεύς, 5406), akin to *phoneuō* and *phonos* (see above), is used (*a*) in a general sense, in the singular, 1 Pet. 4:15; in the plural, Rev. 21:8; 22:15; (*b*) of those guilty of particular acts, Matt. 22:7; Acts 3:14, lit. "a man (*anēr*), a murderer"; 7:52; 28:4.¶

2. *anthropoktonos* (ἀνθρωποκτόνος, 443), an adjective, lit., "manslaying," used as a noun, "a manslayer, murderer" (*anthrōpos*, "a man," *kteinō*, "to slay"), is used of Satan, John 8:44; of one who hates his brother, and who, being a "murderer," has not eternal life, 1 John 3:15 (twice).¶

3. *patroloas* (or *patral-*) (πατρολῴας, 3964) "a murderer of one's father," occurs in 1 Tim. 1:9.¶

Note: For *sikarios*, in the plural, "murderers,"

in Acts 21:38, see ASSASSIN.¶ See MOTHER, No. 2.

MURMUR, MURMURING

A. Verbs.

1. *gonguzō* (γογγύζω, 1111), "to mutter, murmur, grumble, say anything in a low tone" (Eng., "gong"), an onomatopoeic word, representing the significance by the sound of the word, as in the word "murmur" itself, is used of the laborers in the parable of the householder, Matt. 20:11; of the scribes and Pharisees, against Christ, Luke 5:30; of the Jews, John 6:41, 43; of the disciples, 6:61; of the people, 7:32 (of debating secretly); of the Israelites, 1 Cor. 10:10 (twice), where it is also used in a warning to believers.¶ In the papyri it is used of the "murmuring" of a gang of workmen; also in a remark interposed, while the Emperor (late 2nd cent. A.D.) was interviewing a rebel, that the Romans were then "murmuring" (Moulton and Milligan, *Vocab.*).

2. *diagonguzō* (διαγογγύζω, 1234), lit., "to murmur through" (*dia*, i.e., "through a whole crowd," or "among themselves"), is always used of indignant complaining, Luke 15:2; 19:7.¶

3. *embrimaomai* (ἐμβριμάομαι, 1690) is rendered "murmured against" in Mark 14:5; it expresses indignant displeasure: see CHARGE, C, No. 4.

Note: For *stenazō*, Jas. 5:9, RV, "murmur," see GRIEVE, No. 3.

B. Noun.

gongusmos (γογγυσμός, 1112), "a murmuring, muttering" (akin to A, No. 1), is used (*a*) in the sense of secret debate among people, John 7:12 (as with the verb in v. 32); (*b*) of displeasure or complaining (more privately than in public), said of Grecian Jewish converts against Hebrews, Acts 6:1; in general admonitions, Phil. 2:14; 1 Pet. 4:9, RV, "murmuring" (KJV, "grudging").¶

MURMURER

gongustēs (γογγυστής, 1113), "a murmurer" (akin to A, No. 1, and B, above), "one who complains," is used in Jude 16, especially perhaps of utterances against God (see v. 15).¶

For **MUSING** (*dialogizomai*, in Luke 3:15, KJV) see **REASON (Verb)**

MUSIC

sumphōnia (συμφωνία, 4858), lit., "a sounding together" (Eng., "symphony"), occurs in Luke 15:25.¶ In the Sept., Dan. 3:5, 7, 10, 15, for Aramaic *sumphônyâ* (not in v. 7), itself a loan

word from the Greek; translated "dulcimer" (RV, marg., "bagpipe").¶

For **MUSICIAN,** Rev. 18:22, KJV, see **MINSTREL**

MUST

1. *dei* (δεῖ, 1163) an impersonal verb, signifying "it is necessary" or "one must," "one ought," is found most frequently in the Gospels, Acts and the Apocalypse, and is used (*a*) of a necessity lying in the nature of the case e.g., John 3:30; 2 Tim. 2:6; (*b*) of necessity brought about by circumstances, e.g., Matt. 26:35, RV, "must," KJV, "should"; John 4:4; Acts 27:21, "should"; 2 Cor. 11:30; in the case of Christ, by reason of the Father's will, e.g., Luke 2:49; 19:5; (*c*) of necessity as to what is required that something may be brought about, e.g., Luke 12:12, "ought"; John 3:7; Acts 9:6; 1 Cor. 11:19; Heb. 9:26; (*d*) of a necessity of law, duty, equity, e.g., Matt. 18:33, "shouldest"; 23:23, "ought"; Luke 15:32, "it was meet"; Acts 15:5, "it is needful" (RV); Rom. 1:27, RV, "was due," KJV, "was meet" (of a recompense due by the law of God); frequently requiring the rendering "ought," e.g., Rom. 8:26; 12:3; 1 Cor. 8:2; (*e*) of necessity arising from the determinate will and counsel of God, e.g., Matt. 17:10; 24:6; 26:54; 1 Cor. 15:53, especially regarding the salvation of men through the death, resurrection and ascension of Christ, e.g., John 3:14; Acts 3:21; 4:12. See BEHOVE, No. 2 (where see the differences in the meanings of synonymous words), MEET, NEED, NEEDFUL, OUGHT, SHOULD.

2. *opheilō* (ὀφείλω, 3784), "to owe," is rendered "must... needs" in I Cor. 5:10. See BEHOVE, No. 1.

Notes: (1) In Mark 14:49, KJV, the conjunction *hina* with the subjunctive mood, "in order that," is represented by "must" (RV, "that... might"). (2) In Heb. 13:17, KJV, the future participle of *apodidōmi*, "to give," is translated "they that must give" (RV, "they that shall give"). (3) In 2 Pet. 1:14, KJV, the verb "to be," with *apothesis*, "a putting off," is translated "I must put off," RV, "(the) putting off... cometh," lit., "is (swift)." (4) Sometimes the infinitive mood of a verb, with or without the article, is necessarily rendered by a phrase involving the word "must," e.g., 1 Pet. 4:17, KJV, "must (begin)"; or "should," Heb. 4:6, RV, "should" (KJV "must"). (5) Sometimes the subjunctive mood of a verb, used as a deliberative, is rendered "must," etc., John 6:28, "(what) must (we do)," RV (KJV, "shall").

MUSTARD

sinapi (σίναπι, 4615), a word of Egyptian origin, is translated "mustard seed" in the NT. "The conditions to be fulfilled by the mustard are that it should be a familiar plant, with a very small seed, Matt. 17:20; Luke 17:6, sown in the earth, growing larger than garden herbs, Matt. 13:31, having large branches, Mark 4:31,... attractive to birds, Luke 13:19 [RV, '(became) a tree']. The cultivated mustard is *sinapis nigra.* The seed is well known for its minuteness. The mustards are annuals, reproduced with extraordinary rapidity... In fat soil they often attain a height of 10 or 12 feet, and have branches which attract passing birds" (A. E. Post, in *Hastings' Bib. Dic.*).¶

The correct RV translation in Matt. 13:32, "greater than the herbs," for the KJV, "greatest among herbs" (the "mustard" is not a herb), should be noted.

As the parable indicates, Christendom presents a sort of Christianity that has become conformed to the principles and ways of the world, and the world has favored this debased Christianity. Contrast the testimony of the NT, e.g., in John 17:14; Gal. 6:14; 1 Pet. 2:11; 1 John 3:1.

MUTUAL

Note: This is the KJV rendering of the phrase *en allēlois* in Rom. 1:12, translated in the RV, "each of us by the other's (faith)." See OTHER, No. 5.

MUZZLE

phimoō (φιμόω, 5392), "to close the mouth with a muzzle" (*phimos*), is used (*a*) of "muzzling" the ox when it treads out the corn, 1 Cor. 9:9, KJV, "muzzle the mouth of," RV, "muzzle," and 1 Tim. 5:18, with the lesson that those upon whom spiritual labor is bestowed should not refrain from ministering to the material needs of those who labor on their behalf; (*b*) metaphorically, of putting to silence, or subduing to stillness, Matt. 22:12, 34; Mark 1:25; 4:39; Luke 4:35; 1 Pet. 2:15. See PEACE (hold), SILENCE.¶

MY (MINE)

emos (ἐμός, 1699), a possessive adjective of the first person, often used as a possessive pronoun with greater emphasis than the oblique forms of *ego* (see below), a measure of stress which should always be observed; it denotes (I) subjectively, (*a*) "what I possess," e.g., John 4:34; 7:16 (1st part); 13:35; 1 Cor. 16:21; Gal. 6:11; Col. 4:18 (1st clause); as a pronoun, absolutely (i.e., not as an adjective), e.g., Matt. 20:15; 25:27; Luke 15:31, RV, "(all that is) mine," KJV, "(all that) I have"; John 16:14, 15; 17:10; (*b*) "proceeding from me," e.g. Mark 8:38; John 7:16 (2nd part); 8:37 (here the repetition of the article with the pronoun, after the article with the noun, lends special stress to the pronoun; more lit., "the word, that which is mine"); so in John 15:12. Such instances are to be distinguished from the less emphatic order where the pronoun comes between the article and the noun, as in John 7:16, already mentioned; (*c*) in the phrase "it is mine" (i.e., "it rests with me"), e.g., Matt. 20:23; Mark 10:40; (II) objectively, "pertaining or relating to me": (*a*) "appointed for me," e.g., John 7:6, "My time" (with the repeated article and special stress just referred to); (*b*) equivalent to an objective genitive ("of me") e.g., Luke 22:19, "(in remembrance) of Me" (lit., "in My remembrance"); so 1 Cor. 11:24.

Notes: (1) This pronoun frequently translates oblique forms of the first personal pronoun *ego*, "I," e.g., "of me, to me." These instances are usually unemphatic, always less so than those under *emos* (above). (2) For "my affairs" and "my state" see AFFAIR, *Notes*. (3) In Matt. 26:12, "for My burial" translates a phrase consisting of the preposition *pros* ("towards") governing the article with the infinitive mood, aorist tense, of *entaphiazō*, "to bury," followed by the personal pronoun "Me," as the object, where the infinitive is virtually a noun, lit., "towards the burying (of) Me." (4) In 1 Tim. 1:11, "was committed to my trust" is, lit., "(with) which I was entrusted" (*pisteuō*, "to entrust").

MYRRH

A. Noun.

smurna (σμύρνα, 4666), whence the name "Smyrna," a word of Semitic origin, Heb., *mōr*, from a root meaning "bitter," is a gum resin from a shrubby tree, which grows in Yemen and neighboring regions of Africa; the fruit is smooth and somewhat larger than a pea. The color of myrrh varies from pale reddish-yellow to reddish-brown or red. The taste is bitter, and the substance astringent, acting as an antiseptic and a stimulant. It was used as a perfume, Ps. 45:8, where the language is symbolic of the graces of the Messiah; Prov. 7:17; Song of Sol. 1:13; 5:5; it was one of the ingredients of the "holy anointing oil" for the priests, Ex. 30:23 (RV, "flowing myrrh"); it was used also for the purification of women, Esth. 2:12; for embalming, John 19:39; as an anodyne see B); it was one of the gifts of the Magi, Matt. 2:11.¶

B. Verb.

smurnizō (σμυρνίζω, 4669) is used transitively in the NT, with the meaning "to mingle or drug with myrrh," Mark 15:23; the mixture was doubtless offered to deaden the pain (Matthew's word "gall" suggests that "myrrh" was not the only ingredient). Christ refused to partake of any such means of alleviation; He would retain all His mental power for the complete fulfillment of the Father's will.¶

MYSELF

1. *emautou* (ἐμαυτοῦ, 1683), a reflexive pronoun, of the first person, lit., "of myself," is used (*a*) frequently after various prepositions, e.g., *hupo*, "under," Matt. 8:9; Luke 7:8; RV, "under myself"; *peri*, "concerning," John 5:31; 8:14, 18; Acts 24:10; *apo*, "from," John 5:30; 7:17, RV, "from" (KJV, "of," which is ambiguous); so v. 28; 8:28, 42; 10:18; 14:10 (RV, "from"); *pros*, "unto," John 12:32, RV, "unto Myself"; 14:3; Philem. 13, "with me"; *eis*, "to," 1 Cor. 4:6; *huper*, "on behalf of," 2 Cor. 12:5; *ek (ex)*, "out of," or "from," John 12:49, RV, "from Myself"; (*b*) as the direct object of a verb, Luke 7:7; John 8:54; 14:21; 17:19; Acts 26:2; 1 Cor. 4:3; 9:19; 2 Cor. 11:7, 9; Gal. 2:18; Phil. 3:13; (*c*) in other oblique cases of the pronoun, without a preposition, e.g., Acts 20:24, "unto" (or to); 26:9, "with" (or "to"); Rom. 11:4, RV, "for" (KJV, "to"); 1 Cor. 4:4, RV, "against myself" (KJV, inaccurately, "by"); in all these instances the pronoun is in the dative case; in 1 Cor. 10:33, "mine own" (the genitive case); in 1 Cor. 7:7, "I myself" (the accusative case).¶

2. *autos* (αὐτός, 846), "self" (*a*) with *egō*, "I," "I myself," Luke 24:39; Acts 10:26; Rom. 7:25; 9:3; 2 Cor. 10:1; 12:13; (*b*) without the personal pronoun, Acts 24:16 (as the subject of a verb); in the nominative case, Acts 25:22; 1 Cor. 9:27; Phil. 2:24; in the genitive case, Rom. 16:2, RV, "of mine own self."

MYSTERY

mustērion (μυστήριον, 3466), primarily that which is known to the *mustēs*, "the initiated" (from *mueō*, "to initiate into the mysteries"; cf. Phil. 4:12, *mueomai*, "I have learned the secret," RV). In the NT it denotes, not the mysterious (as with the Eng. word), but that which, being outside the range of unassisted natural apprehension, can be made known only by divine revelation, and is made known in a manner and at a time appointed by God, and to those only

who are illumined by His Spirit. In the ordinary sense a "mystery" implies knowledge withheld; its Scriptural significance is truth revealed. Hence the terms especially associated with the subject are "made known," "manifested," "revealed," "preached," "understand," "dispensation." The definition given above may be best illustrated by the following passage: "the mystery which hath been hid from all ages and generations: but now hath it been manifested to His saints" (Col. 1:26, RV). "It is used of:

"(*a*) spiritual truth generally, as revealed in the gospel, 1 Cor. 13:2; 14:2 [cf. 1 Tim. 3:9]. Among the ancient Greeks 'the mysteries' were religious rites and ceremonies practiced by secret societies into which any one who so desired might be received. Those who were initiated into these 'mysteries' became possessors of certain knowledge, which was not imparted to the uninitiated, and were called 'the perfected,' cf. 1 Cor. 2:6–16 where the Apostle has these 'mysteries' in mind and presents the gospel in contrast thereto; here 'the perfected' are, of course, the believers, who alone can perceive the things revealed; (*b*) Christ, who is God Himself revealed under the conditions of human life, Col. 2:2; 4:3, and submitting even to death, 1 Cor. 2:1 [in some mss., for *marturion*, testimony], 7, but raised from among the dead, 1 Tim. 3:16, that the will of God to coordinate the universe in Him, and subject it to Him, might in due time be accomplished, Eph. 1:9 (cf. Rev. 10:7), as is declared in the gospel Rom 16:25; Eph. 6:19; (*c*) the Church, which is Christ's Body, i.e., the union of redeemed men with God in Christ, Eph. 5:32 [cf. Col. 1:27]; (*d*) the rapture into the presence of Christ of those members of the Church which is His Body who shall be alive on the earth at His Parousia, 1 Cor. 15:51; (*e*) the operation of those hidden forces that either retard or accelerate the Kingdom of Heaven (i.e., of God), Matt. 13:11; Mark 4:11; (*f*) the cause of the present condition of Israel, Rom. 11:25; (*g*) the spirit of disobedience to God, 2 Thess. 2:7; Rev. 17:5, 7; cf. Eph. 2:2."*

To these may be added (*h*) the seven local churches, and their angels, seen in symbolism, Rev. 1:20; (*i*) the ways of God in grace, Eph. 3:9. The word is used in a comprehensive way in 1 Cor. 4:1.†

---

* From *Notes on Thessalonians,* by Hogg and Vine, pp. 256, 257.

† See *The Twelve Mysteries of Scripture,* by Vine.

N

NAIL (Noun and Verb)

A. Noun.

hēlos (ἧλος, 2247) occurs in the remarks of Thomas regarding the print of the nails used in Christ's crucifixion, John 20:25.¶

B. Verb.

proseloō (προσηλόω, 4338), "to nail to" (*pros*, "to," and a verbal form of A), is used in Col. 2:14, in which the figure of a bond (ordinances of the Law) is first described as cancelled, and then removed; the idea in the verb itself is not that of the cancellation, to which the taking out of the way was subsequent, but of nailing up the removed thing in triumph to the cross. The death of Christ not only rendered the Law useless as a means of salvation, but gave public demonstration that it was so.¶

NAKED (Adjective and Verb), NAKEDNESS

A. Adjective.

gumnos (γυμνός, 1131) signifies (*a*) "unclothed," Mark 14:52; in v. 51 it is used as a noun ("*his*" and "*body*" being italicized); (*b*) "scantily or poorly clad," Matt. 25:36, 38, 43, 44; Acts 19:16 (with torn garments); Jas. 2:15; (*c*) "clad in the undergarment only" (the outer being laid aside), John 21:7 (see CLOTHING); (*d*) metaphorically, (1) of "a bare seed," 1 Cor. 15:37; (2) of "the soul without the body," 2 Cor. 5:3; (3) of "things exposed to the all-seeing eye of God," Heb. 4:13; (4) of "the carnal condition of a local church," Rev. 3:17; (5) of "the similar state of an individual," 16:15; (*b*) of "the desolation of religious Babylon," 17:16.¶

B. Verb.

gumniteuō (γυμνιτεύω, 1130), "to be naked or scantily clad" (akin to A), is used in 1 Cor. 4:11. In the *Koinē* writings (see Preface to Vol. 1) it is used of being light-armed.¶

C. Noun.

gumnotēs (γυμνότης, 1132), "nakedness" (akin to A), is used (*a*) of "want of sufficient clothing," Rom. 8:35; 2 Cor. 11:27; (*b*) metaphorically, of "the nakedness of the body," said of the condition of a local church, Rev. 3:18.¶

NAME

A. Noun.

onoma (ὄνομα, 3686) is used (*I*) in general of the "name" by which a person or thing is called, e.g., Mark 3:16, 17, "(He) surnamed," lit., "(He added) the name"; 14:32, lit., "(of which) the name (was)"; Luke 1:63; John 18:10; sometimes translated "named," e.g., Luke 1:5, "named (Zacharias)," lit., "by name"; in the same verse, "named (Elizabeth)," lit., "the name of her," an elliptical phrase, with "was" understood; Acts 8:9, RV, "by name," 10:1; the "name" is put for the reality in Rev. 3:1; in Phil. 2:9, the "Name" represents "the title and dignity" of the Lord, as in Eph. 1:21 and Heb. 1:4;

(II) for all that a "name" implies, of authority, character, rank, majesty, power, excellence, etc., of everything that the "name" covers: (*a*) of the "Name" of God as expressing His attributes, etc., e.g., Matt. 6:9; Luke 1:49; John 12:28; 17:6, 26; Rom.15:9; 1 Tim. 6:1; Heb. 13:15; Rev. 13:6; (*b*) of the "Name" of Christ, e.g., Matt. 10:22; 19:29; John 1:12; 2:23; 3:18; Acts 26:9; Rom. 1:5; Jas. 2:7; 1 John 3:23; 3 John 7; Rev. 2:13; 3:8; also the phrases rendered "in the name"; these may be analyzed as follows: (1) representing the authority of Christ, e.g., Matt. 18:5 (with *epi*, "on the ground of My authority"); so Matt. 24:5 (falsely) and parallel passages; as substantiated by the Father, John 14:26; 16:23 (last clause), RV; (2) in the power of (with *en*, "in"), e.g., Mark 16:17; Luke 10:17; Acts 3:6; 4:10; 16:18; Jas. 5:14; (3) in acknowledgement or confession of, e.g., Acts 4:12; 8:16; 9:27, 28; (4) in recognition of the authority of (sometimes combined with the thought of relying or resting on), Matt. 18:20; cf. 28:19; Acts 8:16; 9:2 (*eis*, "into"); John 14:13; 15:16; Eph. 5:20; Col. 3:17; (5) owing to the fact that one is called by Christ's "Name" or is identified with Him, e.g. 1 Pet. 4:14 (with *en*, "in"); with *heneken*, "for the sake of," e.g., Matt. 19:29; with *dia*, "on account of," Matt. 10:22; 24:9; Mark 13:13; Luke 21:17; John 15:21; 1 John 2:12; Rev. 2:3 (for 1 Pet. 4:16, see *Note* below);

(III) as standing, by metonymy, for "persons," Acts 1:15; Rev. 3:4; 11:13 (RV, "persons").

Note: In Mark 9:41, the use of the phrase *en* with the dative case of *onoma* (as in the best mss.) suggests the idea of "by reason of" or "on the ground of" (i.e., "because ye are My disciples"); 1 Pet. 4:16, RV, "in this Name" (KJV, "on this behalf"), may be taken in the same way.

B. Verbs.

1. *onomazō* (ὀνομάζω, 3687) denotes (*a*) "to name," "mention," or "address by name," Acts 19:13, RV, "to name" (KJV, "to call"); in the passive voice, Rom. 15:20; Eph. 1:21; 5:3; to

make mention of the "Name" of the Lord in praise and worship, 2 Tim. 2:19; (*b*) "to name, call, give a name to," Luke 6:13, 14; passive voice, 1 Cor. 5:11, RV, "is named" (KJV, "is called"); Eph. 3:15 (some mss. have the verb in this sense in Mark 3:14 and 1 Cor. 5:1). See CALL, *Note* (1).¶

2. *eponomazō* (ἐπονομάζω, 2028), "to call by a name, surname" (*epi*, "on," and No. 1), is used in Rom. 2:17, passive voice, RV, "bearest the name of" (KJV, "art called"). See CALL, *Note* (1).¶

3. *prosagoreuō* (προσαγορεύω, 4316) primarily denotes "to address, greet, salute"; hence, "to call by name," Heb. 5:10, RV, "named (of God a High Priest)" (KJV, "called"), expressing the formal ascription of the title to Him whose it is; "called" does not adequately express the significance. Some suggest the meaning "addressed," but this is doubtful. The reference is to Ps. 110:4, a prophecy confirmed at the Ascension.¶ In the Sept., Deut. 23:6.¶

4. *kaleō* (καλέω, 2564), "to call," is translated "named" in Acts 7:58, RV (KJV, "whose name was"). See CALL, No. 1 (*b*).

Notes: (1) In Luke 19:2, KJV, *kaleō*, "to call" (with the dative case of *onoma*, "by name"), is translated "named" (RV, "called by name"); in Luke 2:21, KJV, the verb alone is rendered "named" (RV, "called"). (2) In Matt. 9:9 and Mark 15:7, KJV, the verb *legō*, "to speak, to call by name," is rendered "named" (RV, "called"). See CALL, No. 9.

NAMELY

Notes: (1) In Rom. 13:9, the preposition *en*, "in," with the article, lit., "in the," is translated "namely." (2) In 1 Cor. 7:26 the RV, "*namely*," and KJV, "*I say*," do not translate anything in the original, but serve to reintroduce the phrase "that this is good."

NAPKIN

soudarion (σουδάριον, 4676), for which see HANDKERCHIEF, is translated "napkin" in Luke 19:20; John 11:44; 20:7. In Luke 19:20 the reference may be to a towel or any kind of linen cloth or even a sort of headdress, any of which might be used for concealing money.

NARRATIVE

diēgēsis (διήγησις, 1335), translated "a declaration" in the KJV of Luke 1:1, denotes a "narrative," RV (akin to *diēgeomai*, "to set out in detail, recount, describe"). See DECLARE, B, *Note* (1).¶ In the Sept., Judg. 7:15; Hab. 2:6.¶

NARROW

A. Adjective.

stenos (στενός, 4728), from a root *sten-*, seen in *stenazō*, "to groan," *stenagmos*, "groaning" (Eng., "stenography," lit., "narrow writing"), is used figuratively in Matt. 7:13, 14, of the gate which provides the entrance to eternal life, "narrow" because it runs counter to natural inclinations, and "the way" is similarly characterized; so in Luke 13:24 (where the more intensive word *agōnizomai*, "strive," is used); RV, "narrow" (KJV, "strait") in each place. Cf. *stenochōreō*, "to be straitened," and *stenochōria*, "narrowness, anguish, distress." ¶

B. Verb.

thlibō (θλίβω, 2346), "to press," is translated "narrow" in Matt. 7:14, KJV, lit., "narrowed" (RV, "straitened"; the verb is in the perfect participle, passive voice), i.e., hemmed in, like a mountain gorge; the way is rendered "narrow" by the divine conditions, which make it impossible for any to enter who think the entrance depends upon self-merit, or who still incline towards sin, or desire to continue in evil. See AFFLICT, No. 4.

NATION

1. *ethnos* (ἔθνος, 1484), originally "a multitude," denotes (*a*) "a nation" or "people," e.g., Matt. 24:7; Acts 10:35; the Jewish people, e.g., Luke 7:5; 23:2; John 11:48, 50–52; Acts 10:22; 24:2, 10, 17; in Matt. 21:43, the reference is to Israel in its restored condition; (*b*) in the plural, "the nations" as distinct from Israel. See GENTILES.

2. *genos* (γένος, 1085), "a race": see KIND (Noun).

3. *allophulos* (ἀλλόφυλος, 246), "foreign, of another race" (*allos*, "another," *phulon*, "a tribe"), is used in Acts 10:28, "one of another nation."¶

Note: For Phil. 2:15, *genea* (KJV, "nation," RV, "generation"), see AGE.

NATURAL, NATURALLY

A. Adjectives.

1. *phusikos* (φυσικός, 5446) originally signifying "produced by nature, inborn," from *phusis*, "nature" (see below), cf. Eng., "physical," "physics," etc., denotes (*a*) "according to nature," Rom. 1:26, 27; (*b*) "governed by mere natural instincts," 2 Pet. 2:12, RV, "(born) mere animals," KJV and RV marg., "natural (brute beasts)."¶

2. *psuchikos* (ψυχικός, 5591), "belonging to the *psuchē*, soul" (as the lower part of the immaterial in man), "natural, physical," describes

the man in Adam and what pertains to him (set in contrast to *pneumatikos*, "spiritual"), 1 Cor. 2:14; 15:44 (twice), 46 (in the latter used as a noun); Jas. 3:15, "sensual" (RV marg., "natural" or "animal"), here relating perhaps more especially to the mind, a wisdom in accordance with, or springing from, the corrupt desires and affections; so in Jude 19.¶

B. Noun.

genesis (γένεσις, 1078), "birth," is used in Jas. 1:23, of the "natural face," lit., "the face of his birth," "what God made him to be" (Hort). See GENERATION, NATURE, No. 2.

Note: In Rom. 11:21, 24 the preposition *kata*, "according to," with the noun *phusis*, "nature," is translated "natural," of branches, metaphorically describing members of the nation of Israel.

C. Adverb.

phusikōs (φυσικῶς, 5447), "naturally, by nature" (akin to A, No. 1), is used in Jude 10.¶

Note: In Phil. 2:20, KJV, *gnēsiōs*, "sincerely, honorably, truly" (from the adjective *gnēsios*, "true, sincere, genuine"; see, e.g., Phil. 4:3), is translated "naturally" (RV, "truly;" marg., "genuinely").¶

NATURE

1. *phusis* (φύσις, 5449), from *phuō*, "to bring forth, produce," signifies (*a*) "the nature" (i.e., the natural powers or constitution) of a person or thing, Eph. 2:3; Jas. 3:7 ("kind"); 2 Pet. 1:4; (*b*) "origin, birth," Rom. 2:27, one who by birth is a Gentile, uncircumcised, in contrast to one who, though circumcised, has become spiritually uncircumcised by his iniquity; Gal. 2:15; (*c*) "the regular law or order of nature," Rom. 1:26, against "nature" (*para*, "against"); 2:14, adverbially, "by nature" (for 11:21, 24, see NATURAL, Note); 1 Cor. 11:14; Gal. 4:8, "by nature (are no gods)," here "nature" is the emphatic word, and the phrase includes demons, men regarded as deified, and idols; these are gods only in name (the negative, *mē*, denies not simply that they were gods, but the possibility that they could be).¶

2. *genesis* (γένεσις, 1078) is used in the phrase in Jas. 3:6, "the wheel of nature," RV (marg., "birth"). Some regard this as the course of birth or of creation, or the course of man's "nature" according to its original divine purpose; Mayor (on the Ep. of James) regards *trochos* here as a wheel, "which, catching fire from the glowing axle, is compared to the widespreading mischief done by the tongue," and shows that "the fully developed meaning" of *genesis* denotes "the incessant change of life ... the sphere of this earthly life, meaning all that is contained in our life." The significance, then,

would appear to be the whole round of human life and activity. Moulton and Milligan illustrate it in this sense from the papyri. See NATURAL, B.

For NAUGHTINESS, Jas. 1:21, KJV, see WICKEDNESS

NAY

1. *ou* (οὐ, 3756), "no, not," expressing a negation absolutely, is rendered "nay," e.g., in Matt. 5:37; 13:29; John 7:12, KJV (RV, "not so"); Acts 16:37; 2 Cor. 1:17–19; Jas. 5:12.

2. *ouchi* (οὐχί, 3780), a strengthened form of No. 1, is used, e.g., in Luke 12:51; 13:3, 5; 16:30; Rom. 3:27.

3. *alla* (ἀλλά, 235), "but," to mark contrast or opposition, is rendered "nay" in Rom. 3:31, RV, "nay" (KJV, "yea"); in 7:7, RV, "howbeit" (KJV, "nay"); 8:37; 1 Cor. 3:2, RV; 6:8; 12:22; in Heb. 3:16, RV, "nay" (KJV, "howbeit").

4. *menounge* (μενοῦνγε, 3304), (i.e., *men oun ge*), "nay rather," is rendered "nay but" in Rom. 9:20 (in Rom. 10:18 and Phil. 3:8, "yea verily," KJV, "yea doubtless"). See YEA.¶

NEAR (Adverb), NEAR (come, draw), NEARER

A. Adverbs.

1. *engus* (ἐγγύς, 1451), "near, nigh," is used (*a*) of place, e.g., Luke 19:11, "nigh"; John 3:23; 11:54, "near"; 6:19, 23, "nigh"; metaphorically in Rom. 10:8; Eph. 2:13, 17, "nigh"; (*b*) of time, e.g., Matt. 24:32–33, "nigh"; so Luke 21:30–31; as a preposition, Heb. 6:8, "nigh unto (a curse)," and 8:13, "nigh unto (vanishing away)." See HAND (at), NIGH, READY.

2. *enguteron* (ἐγγύτερον, 1452), the comparative degree of No. 1, and the neuter of the adjective *enguteros*, used adverbially, occurs in Rom. 13:11.¶

3. *plēsion* (πλησίον, 4139), "near, close by, neighboring" (the neuter of the adjective *plēsios*, used as an adverb), occurs in John 4:5. See NEIGHBOR.

B. Adjective.

anankaios (ἀναγκαῖος, 316), "necessary," is used, in a secondary sense, of persons connected by bonds of nature or friendship, with the meaning "intimate," in Acts 10:24, "(his) near (friends)"; it is found in this sense in the papyri. See NECESSARY, NEEDFUL.

C. Verbs.

1. *engizō* (ἐγγίζω, 1448), transitively, "to bring near" (not in NT; in the Sept., e.g., Gen. 48:10; Isa. 5:8); intransitively, "to draw near,"

e.g., Matt. 21:34; Luke 18:40; 19:41, RV, "draw nigh"; see APPROACH, A.

2. *proserchomai* (προσέρχομαι, 4334), "to come to, go to," is translated "drew near" in Acts 7:31 and Heb. 10:22. See COME, No. 10.

3. *prosagō* (προσάγω, 4317) is used (*a*) transitively, "to bring," Acts 16:20; 1 Pet. 3:18; (*b*) intransitively, "to draw near," in the latter sense in Acts 27:27.¶

NECESSARY

1. *anankaios* (ἀναγκαῖος, 316), "necessary" (from *anankē*, "necessity"; see below), is so rendered in Acts 13:46; 1 Cor. 12:22; 2 Cor. 9:5; Phil. 2:25; Titus 3:14; Heb. 8:3, RV (KJV, "of necessity"); for Acts 10:24, "near friends," see NEAR, B.¶

2. *anankē* (ἀνάγκη, 318), "a necessity" (see No. 1), is rendered "(it was) necessary" in Heb. 9:23, lit., "it was a necessity." See DISTRESS, A, No. 1.

3. *epanankēs* (ἐπανάγκης, 1876), an adjective akin to the preceding, with *epi*, used intensively, found only in the neuter form, is used as an adverb signifying "of necessity" and translated as an adjective in Acts 15:28, "necessary," lit., "(things) of necessity."¶

Note: For the KJV of Acts 28:10 see NEED, A, No. 1.

NECESSITY (-TIES)

I. *anankē* (ἀνάγκη, 318) signifies (*a*) "a necessity," what must needs be (see NEEDS), translated "necessity" (in some mss. in Luke 23:17) in 1 Cor. 7:37; 9:16; 2 Cor. 9:7 (with *ek* "out of"); Philem. 14 (with *kata*, "according to"); Heb. 7:12; 9:16; (*b*) "distress, pain," translated "necessities" in 2 Cor. 6:4; 12:10. See DISTRESS, No. 1, and the synonymous words there, and NEEDS, NEEDFUL (also CONSTRAIN, *Note*).

2. *chreia* (χρεία, 5532), "a need," and almost always so translated, is used in the plural in Acts 20:34, "necessities"; Rom. 12:13, RV (KJV, "necessity"); in Phil. 4:16, KJV, "necessity," RV, "need." See NEED, NEEDFUL.

NECK

trachēlos (τράχηλος, 5137) is used (*a*) literally, Matt. 18:6; Mark 9:42; Luke 17:2; of "embracing," Luke 15:20; Acts 20:37; (*b*) metaphorically, in Acts 15:10, of "putting a yoke upon"; Rom. 16:4, singular in the original, "(laid down their) neck," indicating the figurative use of the term rather than the literal. Prisca and Aquila in some way had risked their lives for the apostle (the phrase is found with this significance in the papyri).¶

NEED, NEEDS, NEEDFUL
A. Nouns.

1. *chreia* (χρεία, 5532) denotes "a need," in such expressions as "there is a need"; or "to have need of" something, e.g., Matt. 3:14; 6:8; 9:12, RV, "(have no) need," KJV, "need (not)," the RV adheres to the noun form; so in 14:16; Mark 14:63; Luke 5:31; 22:71; Eph. 4:28; 1 Thess. 4:9; in the following, however, both RV and KJV use the verb form, "to need" (whereas the original has the verb *echō*, "to have," with the noun *chreia* as the object, as in the instances just mentioned): Luke 15:7; John 2:25; 13:10; 16:30; 1 Thess. 1:8; 1 John 2:27; Rev. 22:5; in all these the verb "to have" could well have been expressed in the translation.

In Luke 10:42 it is translated "needful," where the "one thing" is surely not one dish, or one person, but is to be explained according to Matt. 6:33 and 16:26. In Eph. 4:29, for the KJV, "(to) the use (of edifying)," the RV more accurately has "(for edifying) as the need may be," marg., "the building up of the need," i.e., "to supply that which needed in each case"; so Westcott, who adds "The need represents a gap in the life which the wise word 'builds up,' fills up solidly and surely." In Phil. 4:19 the RV has "every need of yours" (KJV, "all your need"); in 1 Thess. 4:12, RV, "need" (KJV, "lack"); in Acts 28:10, RV, "(such things) as we needed" (KJV, "as were necessary"), lit., "the things for the needs (plural)." See BUSINESS, A, No. 1, LACK, NECESSITY, USE, WANT.

2. *anankē* (ἀνάγκη, 318), "a necessity, need," is translated "it must needs be" in Matt. 18:7, with the verb "to be" understood (according to the best mss.); in Luke 14:18, "I must needs" translates the verb *echō*, "to have," with this noun as the object, lit., "I have need"; in Rom. 13:5 "(ye) must needs," lit., "(it is) necessary (to be subject)." See NECESSARY, No. 2, NECESSITY, No. 1. See also DISTRESS.

B. Verbs.

1. *chrēzō* (χρήζω, 5535), "to need, to have need of" (akin to *chrē*, "it is necessary, fitting"), is used in Matt. 6:32; Luke 11:8; 12:30; Rom. 16:2, RV, "may have need" (KJV, "hath need"); 2 Cor. 3:1.¶

2. *dei* (δεῖ, 1163), an impersonal verb, signifying "it is necessary," is rendered "must needs" in Mark 13:7; John 4:4; Acts 1:16, KJV (RV, "it was needful"); 17:3, KJV (RV, "it behoved"); (in some mss. in Acts 21:22); 2 Cor. 11:30; 12:1; in Acts 15:5, "it was needful."

3. *deon* (δέον, 1163**), the neuter of the present participle of No. 2, is used as a noun, signifying "that which is needful, due, proper,"

in 1 Pet. 1:6, with the meaning "need," "(if) need (be)," with the verb to be understood. See OUGHT.

4. *prosdeomai* (προσδέομαι, 4326), "to want besides, to need in addition" (*pros*, "besides," *deomai*, "to want"), is used in Acts 17:25, "(as though) He needed (anything)"; the literal sense of *pros* is not to be stressed.¶ In the Sept., Prov. 12:9, "lacking (bread)."¶

5. *opheilō* (ὀφείλω, 3784), "to owe, be bound, obliged to do something," is translated "must ye needs," in 1 Cor. 5:10; in 7:36 it is used impersonally, signifying "it is due," and followed by the infinitive mood of *ginomai*, "to become, to occur, come about," lit. "it is due to become," translated "(if) need (so) require." See BEHOVE, BOUND, DEBT, DUE, DUTY, GUILTY, INDEBTED, MUST, OUGHT, OWE.

Note: In Phil. 4:12, KJV, *hustereō*, "to come short, fail, to be in want," is translated "to suffer need" (RV, "to be in want"). See BEHIND.

C. Adjectives.

1. *anankaioteros* (ἀναγκαιότερος, 316*), the comparative degree of *anankaios*, "necessary," is translated "more needful" in Phil. 1:24. See NECESSARY, No. 1.

2. *epitēdeios* (ἐπιτήδειος, 2006), primarily, "suitable, convenient," then, "useful, necessary," is translated "needful" in Jas. 2:16, neuter plural, "necessaries."¶ In the Sept., 1 Chron. 28:2, "suitable."¶

Note: In Heb. 4:16 *eukairos*, "timely, seasonable," qualifying the noun *boētheia*, "help," is translated "time of need," lit., "for opportune help." See CONVENIENT.

NEEDLE

1. *rhaphis* (ῥαφίς, 4476), from *rhaptō*, "to sew," occurs in Matt. 19:24; Mark 10:25.¶

2. *belonē* (βελόνη, 956d), akin to *belos*, "a dart," denotes a sharp point, hence, "a needle," Luke 18:25 (some mss. have No. 1).¶

Note: The idea of applying "the needle's eye" to small gates seems to be a modern one; there is no ancient trace of it. The Lord's object in the statement is to express human impossibility and there is no need to endeavor to soften the difficulty by taking the needle to mean anything more than the ordinary instrument. Mackie points out *(Hastings' Bib. Dic.)* that "an attempt is sometimes made to explain the words as a reference to the small door, a little over 2 feet square, in the large heavy gate of a walled city. This mars the figure without materially altering the meaning, and receives no justification from the language and traditions of Palestine."

NEGLECT, NEGLIGENT

1. *ameleō* (ἀμελέω, 272) denotes (*a*) "to be careless, not to care" (*a*, negative, *melei*, "it is a care"; from *melō*, "to care, to be a care"), Matt. 22:5, "made light of"; (*b*) "to be careless of, neglect," 1 Tim. 4:14; Heb. 2:3; 8:9, "I regarded (them) not." See LIGHT OF (make), REGARD.¶ (In the Sept., Jer. 4:17; 38:32.¶)

2. *paratheōreō* (παραθεωρέω, 3865), primarily, "to examine side by side, compare" (*para*, "beside," *theōreō*, "to look at"), hence, "to overlook, to neglect," is used in Acts 6:1, of the "neglect" of widows in the daily ministration in Jerusalem.¶

Note: In 2 Pet. 1:12, some mss. have No. 1, hence the KJV, "I will not be negligent;" the RV follows those which have the future tense of *mellō*, "to be ready." See READY. For "neglect to hear" see HEAR, No. 7.

For **NEGLECTING** (Col. 2:23) see **SEVERITY**

NEIGHBOR

1. *geitōn* (γείτων, 1069), lit., "one living in the same land," denotes "a neighbor," always plural in the NT, Luke 14:12; 15:6, 9; John 9:8.¶

2. *perioikos* (περίοικος, 4040), an adjective, lit., "dwelling around" (*peri*, "around," *oikos*, "a dwelling"), is used as a noun in Luke 1:58, "neighbors."¶

3. *plēsion* (πλησίον, 4139), the neuter of the adjective *plēsios* (from *pelas*, "near"), is used as an adverb accompanied by the article, lit., "the (one) near"; hence, one's "neighbor"; see refs. below.

This and Nos. 1 and 2 have a wider range of meaning than that of the Eng. word "neighbor." There were no farmhouses scattered over the agricultural areas of Palestine; the populations, gathered in villages, went to and fro to their toil. Hence domestic life was touched at every point by a wide circle of neighborhood. The terms for neighbor were therefore of a very comprehensive scope. This may be seen from the chief characteristics of the privileges and duties of neighborhood as set forth in Scripture, (*a*) its helpfulness, e.g., Prov. 27:10; Luke 10:36; (*b*) its intimacy, e.g., Luke 15:6, 9 (see No. 1); Heb. 8:11; (*c*) its sincerity and sanctity, e.g., Ex. 22:7, 10; Prov. 3:29; 14:21; Rom. 13:10; 15:2; Eph. 4:25; Jas. 4:12. The NT quotes and expands the command in Lev. 19:18, "to love one's neighbor as oneself"; see, e.g., Matt. 5:43; 19:19; 22:39; Mark 12:31, 33; Luke 10:27; Gal. 5:14; Jas. 2:8. See also Acts 7:27.

Note: In Rom. 13:8, for *heteron,* "another," RV has "his neighbor."

NEIGHBORHOOD

Note: This, in Acts 28:7, RV, translates a phrase consisting of the dative plural of the article followed by *peri,* "around," governed by the preposition *en,* "in," "in the neighborhood of (that place)," KJV, "in the (same quarters)," lit., "in the (parts) around (that place)."

For **NEITHER** See †, p. 1

For **NEITHER AT ANY TIME,** Luke 15:29, see **NEVER**

For **NEPHEWS** see **GRANDCHILDREN**

NEST

kataskēnōsis (κατασκήνωσις, 2682), properly "an encamping, taking up one's quarters," then, "a lodging, abode" (*kata,* "down over," *skēnē,* "a tent"), is used of birds' "nests" in Matt. 8:20 and Luke 9:58.¶ In the Sept., 1 Chron. 28:2, "the building"; Ezek. 37:27, "(My) tabernacle."¶

The word *nossia,* signifying "a brood," Luke 13:34, used in the Sept. to denote a "nest," e.g., in Deut. 22:6; 32:11, signifies the actual receptacle built by birds in which to lay their eggs (having special reference to the prospective brood); but the word *kataskēnōsis,* used by the Lord, denotes "a resting or roosting place." This lends force to His comparison. Not only was He without a home, He had not even a lodging place (cf. *kataskēnoō,* "to lodge," e.g., Matt. 13:32; Acts 2:26, RV marg., "shall tabernacle"; see LODGE).

NET

1. *amphiblēstron* (ἀμφίβληστρον, 293), lit., "something thrown around" (*amphi,* "around," *ballō,* "to throw"), denotes "a casting net," a somewhat small "net," cast over the shoulder, spreading out in a circle and made to sink by weights, Matt. 4:18 (in some mss. in Mark 1:16: the best have the verb *amphiballō* alone).¶

2. *diktuon* (δίκτυον, 1350), a general term for a "net" (from an old verb *dikō,* "to cast": akin to *diskos,* "a quoit"), occurs in Matt. 4:20–21; Mark 1:18–19; Luke 5:2, 4–6; John 21:6, 8, 11 (twice).¶ In the Sept. it was used for a "net" for catching birds, Prov. 1:17, in other ways, e.g., figuratively of a snare, Job 18:8; Prov. 29:5.

3. *sagēnē* (σαγήνη, 4522) denotes "a drag-net, a seine"; two modes were employed with this, either by its being let down into the water and drawn together in a narrowing circle, and then into the boat, or as a semicircle drawn to the shore, Matt. 13:47, where Nos. 1 and 2 would not have suited so well. The Greek historian Herodotus uses the corresponding verb *sagēneuō* of a device by which the Persians are said to have cleared a conquered island of its inhabitants.¶

NEVER

1. *oudepote* (οὐδέποτε, 3763), from *oude,* "not even," and *pote,* "at any time," is used in definite negative statements, e.g., Matt. 7:23; 1 Cor. 13:8; Heb. 10:1, 11, or questions, e.g., Matt. 21:16, 42; in Luke 15:29 (1st part), RV, "never" (KJV, "neither . . . at any time"); KJV and RV, "never" (2nd part).

2. *mēdepote* (μηδέποτε, 3368), virtually the same as No. 1, the negative *mē,* however, conveying a less strong declarative negation, 2 Tim. 3:7.¶

3. *oudepō* (οὐδέπω, 3764), "not yet," is translated "never (man) yet" in John 19:41 ("man" representing the idiomatically used negative pronoun *oudeis,* "no one"); some mss. have it in Luke 23:53, instead of *oupō,* "not yet."

Notes: (1) In Mark 14:21, KJV, the negative particle *ouk,* "not," is translated "never" (RV, "not"); the negative particle *mē,* "not" (which suggests nonexistence when the existence was after all possible, or even probable, in contrast to *ou,* which implies nonexistence absolutely), is translated "never" in John 7:15, KJV and RV (2) The phrase *eis ton aiona,* "for ever" (not to be rendered literally, "unto the age," see ETERNAL), preceded by the double negative *ou mē,* denotes "never," John 4:14; 8:51–52; 10:28; 11:26; 13:8; so, preceded by *ouk,* "not," in Mark 3:29. (3) In 2 Pet. 1:10, "never" is the translation of *ou mē pote,* i.e., "by no means ever"; so with the double negative followed by the extended word *pōpote,* i.e., "by no means not even at any time," John 6:35 (2nd part). (4) *Pōpote* follows *oudeis,* "no one," in the dative case ("to no man") in John 8:33, RV, "never yet" (KJV, "never"); so in Luke 19:30, where *oudeis* is in the nominative case, RV, "no man ever yet" (KJV, "yet never man").

For **NEVERTHELESS** see †, 1. 9

NEW

1. *kainos* (καινός, 2537) denotes "new," of that which is unaccustomed or unused, not "new" in time, recent, but "new" as to form or

quality, of different nature from what is contrasted as old. "'The new tongues,' *kainos*, of Mark 16:17 are the 'other tongues,' *heteros*, of Acts 2:4. These languages, however, were 'new' and 'different,' not in the sense that they had never been heard before, or that they were new to the hearers, for it is plain from v. 8 that this is not the case; they were new languages to the speakers, different from those in which they were accustomed to speak.

"The new things that the Gospel brings for present obedience and realization are: a new covenant, Matt. 26:28 in some texts; a new commandment, John 13:34; a new creative act, Gal. 6:15; a new creation, 2 Cor. 5:17; a new man, i.e., a new character of manhood, spiritual and moral, after the pattern of Christ, Eph. 4:24; a new man, i.e., 'the Church which is His (Christ's) body,' Eph. 2:15.

"The new things that are to be received and enjoyed hereafter are: a new name, the believer's, Rev. 2:17; a new name, the Lord's, Rev. 3:12; a new song, Rev. 5:9; a new Heaven and a new Earth, Rev. 21:1; the new Jerusalem, Rev. 3:12; 21:2; 'And He that sitteth on the Throne said, Behold, I make all things new,' Rev. 21:5"*

Kainos is translated "fresh" in the RV of Matt. 9:17; Mark 2:22 (in the best texts) and Luke 5:38, of wineskins. Cf. *kainotēs*, "newness" (below).

2. *neos* (νέος, 3501) signifies "new" in respect of time, that which is recent; it is used of the young, and so translated, especially the comparative degree "younger"; accordingly what is *neos* may be a reproduction of the old in quality or character. *Neos* and *kainos* are sometimes used of the same thing, but there is a difference, as already indicated. Thus the "new man" in Eph. 2:15 (*kainos*) is "new" in differing in character; so in 4:24 (see No. 1); but the "new man" in Col. 3:10 (*neos*) stresses the fact of the believer's "new" experience, recently begun, and still proceeding. "The old man in him . . . dates as far back as Adam; a new man has been born, who therefore is fitly so called" [i.e., *neos*], Trench, *Syn.* §lx. The "New" Covenant in Heb. 12:24 is "new" (*neos*) compared with the Mosaic, nearly fifteen hundred years before; it is "new" (*kainos*) compared with the Mosaic, which is old in character, ineffective, 8:8, 13; 9:15.

The "new" wine of Matt. 9:17; Mark 2:22; Luke 5:37–39, is *neos*, as being of recent production; the "new" wine of the kingdom, Matt.

26:29; Mark 14:25, is *kainos*, since it will be of a different character from that of this world. The rendering "new" (*neos*) is elsewhere used metaphorically in 1 Cor. 5:7, "a new lump." See YOUNG, YOUNGER.

3. *prosphatos* (πρόσφατος, 4732), originally signifying "freshly slain," acquired the general sense of "new," as applied to flowers, oil, misfortune, etc. It is used in Heb. 10:20 of the "living way" which Christ "dedicated for us . . . through the veil . . . His flesh" (which stands for His expiatory death by the offering of His body, v. 10).¶ In the Sept., Num. 6:3; Deut. 32:17; Ps. 81:9; Eccl. 1:9.¶ Cf. the adverb *prosphatōs*, "lately, recently," Acts 18:2.¶

Note: In Matt. 9:16 and Mark 2:21, KJV, *agnaphos* is translated "new" (RV, "undressed"). Moulton and Milligan give an instance in the papyri of its use in respect of a "new white shirt." See UNDRESSED.¶

For **NEWBORN,** 1 Pet. 2:2, see **BEGET,** C, No. 2

NEWNESS

kainotēs (καινότης, 2538), akin to *kainos*, is used in the phrases (*a*) "newness of life," Rom. 6:4, i.e., life of a new quality (see NEW, No. 1); the believer, being a new creation (2 Cor. 5:17), is to behave himself consistently with this in contrast to his former manner of life; (*b*) "newness of the spirit," RV, Rom. 7:6, said of the believer's manner of serving the Lord. While the phrase stands for the new life of the quickened spirit of the believer, it is impossible to dissociate this (in an objective sense) from the operation of the Holy Spirit, by whose power the service is rendered.¶

NEXT

1. *hexēs* (ἑξῆς, 1836), an adverb (akin to *echō*, "to have") denoting "in order, successively, next," is used adjectively, qualifying the noun "day" in Luke 9:37; Acts 21:1, RV, "next" (KJV, "following"); 25:17, RV, "next" (KJV, "on the morrow"); in 27:18, with *hēmera*, "day," understood; in Luke 7:11, in the best mss., with the word *chronos*, "time," understood, "soon afterwards" (marg., "on the next day," according to some ancient authorities). See AFTER, FOLLOW, *Note* (3), MORROW.

2. *metaxu* (μεταξύ, 3342) signifies "between, next," in Acts 13:42. See BETWEEN, No. 2.

3. *echō* (ἔχω, 2192), "to have," in the middle voice, sometimes signifies "to be next to," said of towns, in Mark 1:38; of a day, Acts 21:26; in

---

* From *Notes on Galatians,* by Hogg and Vine, pp. 337, 338.

20:15 (2nd part), *hēmera*, "day," is unexpressed. See HAVE.

4. *erchomai* (ἔρχομαι, 2064), "to come," is used in the present participle in Acts 13:44, "(the) next (sabbath)." See COME.

Note: In Acts 7:26, KJV, *epeimi*, "to come on or after," used with *hēmera*, "day," is translated "next" (RV, "following"); so with *hēmera*, understood, Acts 16:11; 20:15 (1st part); in 21:18, RV and KJV, "following."

NEXT DAY

Notes: (1) For *aurion*, "tomorrow," translated "next day" in Acts 4:3, and *epaurion*, "on the morrow," Matt. 27:62; John 1:29, 35; 12:12; Acts 14:20; 25:6, see MORROW. (2) For *echō*, Acts 20:15, see NEXT, No. 3. (3) For *epeimi*, without the noun *hēmera*, "day," see NEXT (end of *Note*). (4) In Acts 20:15 (mid. of verse) *heteros*, "other," signifies "next," with *hēmera*, understood. (5) In Acts 28:13 (end of v.) the adjective *deuteraios*, second, is used in the masculine plural adverbially, signifying "the second (day)," RV, KJV, "the next (day)."

NIGH

A. Adverbs.

1. *engus* (ἐγγύς, 1451), "nigh" or "near," is translated in both ways in Matt. 24:32-33 and Mark 13:28-29, KJV (RV, "nigh" in both); in Acts 1:12, with *echon*, present participle neuter of *echō*, "to have," RV, "nigh unto . . . off" (KJV, "from"). See NEAR, No. 1.

2. *paraplēsion* (παραπλήσιον, 3897), the neuter of the adjective *paraplēsios, para*, "beside," *plēsios*, "near, nearly resembling," is translated "nigh unto," with reference to death, in Phil. 2:27.¶

B. Verb.

engizō (ἐγγίζω, 1448): see APPROACH.

C. Preposition.

para (παρά, 3844), "beside, alongside of," is translated "nigh unto" in Matt. 15:29; in Mark 5:21, RV, "by" (KJV, "nigh unto").

Note: In Mark 5:11, KJV, *pros*, "towards, on the side of," is translated "nigh unto (the mountain)," RV, "on the (mountain) side"; the swine were not simply "near" the mountain.

NIGHT (by, in the)

nux (νύξ, 3571) is used (I) literally, (*a*) of "the alternating natural period to that of the day," e.g., Matt. 4:2; 12:40; 2 Tim. 1:3; Rev. 4:8; (*b*) of "the period of the absence of light," the time in which something takes place, e.g., Matt. 2:14 (27:64, in some mss.); Luke 2:8; John 3:2 (7:50, in some mss.); Acts 5:19; 9:25; (*c*) of "point of time," e.g., Matt. 14:27 (in some

mss.), 30; Luke 12:20; Acts 27:23; (*d*) of "duration of time," e.g., Luke 2:37; 5:5; Acts 20:31; 26:7 (note the difference in the phrase in Mark 4:27); (II) metaphorically, (*a*) of "the period of man's alienation from God," Rom. 13:12; 1 Thess. 5:5, lit., "not of night," where "of" means 'belonging to;' cf. "of the Way," Acts 9:2; "of shrinking back" and "of faith," Heb. 10:39, marg.; (*b*) of "death," as the time when work ceases, John 9:4.

NIGHT AND A DAY (A)

nuchthēmeros (νυχθήμερος, 3574), an adjective denoting "lasting a night and a day" (from *nux*, "night," and *hēmera*, "a day"), is used in 2 Cor. 11:25, in the neuter gender, as a noun, the object of the verb *poieō*, to do, lit., 'I have done a night-and-a-day.'¶

NINE

ennea (ἐννέα, 1767) is found in Luke 17:17, and in connection with "ninety" (see below).¶

NINETY

enenēkonta, or *ennēn*—(ἐνενήκοντα, 1767d) is found in Matt. 18:12-13; Luke 15:4, 7.¶

NINTH

enatos, or *enn*—(ἔνατος, 1766) is found in reference (*a*) to "the ninth hour" (3 o'clock, p.m.) in Matt. 20:5; 27:45-46; Mark 15:33-34; Luke 23:44; Acts 3:1; 10:3, 30; (*b*) to "the topaz" as the "ninth" foundation of the city wall in the symbolic vision in Rev. 21 (v. 20).¶

For **NO** see †, p. 1.

NO LONGER, NO MORE

1. *ouketi* (οὐκέτι, 3765), a negative adverb of time, signifies "no longer, no more" (*ou*, "not," *k*, euphonic, *eti* "longer"), denying absolutely and directly, e.g., Matt. 19:6; John 4:42, "now . . . not"; 6:66; Acts 20:25, 38; 2 Cor. 1:23, KJV, "not as yet"; Eph. 2:19; with another negative, to strengthen the negation, e.g., Matt. 22:46; Mark 14:25; 15:5, RV, "no more (anything)," KJV, "yet . . . no (thing)"; Acts 8:39; Rev. 18:11, 14.

2. *mēketi* (μηκέτι, 3371), with the same meaning as No. 1, but generally expressing a prohibition, e.g., Matt. 21:19; John 5:14; Rom. 14:13; Eph. 4:28; 1 Tim. 5:23; 1 Pet. 4:2; indicating some condition expressed or implied, e.g., 1 Thess. 3:5; or nonexistence, when the existence might have been possible under certain conditions, e.g., Mark 1:45; 2:2, RV, "no longer" (KJV, "no"). See HENCEFORTH.

Notes: (1) The double negative *ou mē*, "by no

means, in no wise," followed by *eti*, "longer, still, yet," is rendered "no more" in Heb. 8:12; 10:17; Rev. 3:12. (2) In John 15:4, KJV, *houtōs*, "so," followed by *oude*, "neither," is translated "no more" (RV, "so neither").

NO MAN, NO ONE, NEITHER ANY MAN

Note: Oudeis and *mēdeis*, "no one, no man," are related to one another in much the same way as indicated above under *ouketi* and *mēketi*. Instances of *oudeis* are Matt. 6:24; 9:16; 24:36 (RV, "no one"); John 1:18; 3:2, 13, 32; 14:6 and 16:22 (RV, "no one"); 2 Cor. 7:2 (thrice); Heb. 12:14; 1 John 4:12; Rev. 2:17, RV, "no one"; so 5:3–4; 19:12; in 3:7–8 and 15:8 (RV,"none"); in 7:9 and 14:3, "no man." In all these cases "man" stands for "person." The spelling *outheis* occurs occasionally in the mss.; Westcott and Hort adopt it in 2 Cor. 11:8, in the genitive case *outhenos*.

Instances of *mēdeis* are Matt. 8:4 (almost all those in the Synoptists are cases of prohibition or admonition); Acts 9:7; Rom. 12:17; 1 Cor. 3:18, 21; Gal. 6:17; Eph. 5:6; Col. 2:18; 1 Thess. 3:3; 1 Tim. 4:12; Rev. 3:11, RV, "no one."

Notes: (1) In some mss. the negative *mē* and the indefinite pronoun *tis*, "some one, anyone," appear as one word, *mētis* (always separated in the best mss.), e.g., Matt. 8:28, "no man"; so in 1 Cor. 16:11; 2 Cor. 11:16; 2 Thess. 2:3. The words are separated also in Matt. 24:4; 2 Cor. 8:20 (RV, "any man," after "avoiding"); Rev. 13:17. These instances represent either impossibility or prohibition (see under NO LONGER, No. 2); contrast *ouch* (i.e., *ou*)... *tis* in Heb. 5:4, "no man (taketh)," where a direct negative statement is made. (2) In 2 Cor. 11:10 the negative *ou*, "not," is translated "no man" (KJV marg. "not"); in 1 Cor. 4:6, e.g., the negative *mē* is translated "no one"; in Rom. 14:13, the negative *mē*, used in an admonition, is translated "no man."

NO WISE (in), ANYWISE (in)

1. *ou mē* (οὐ μή), a double negative, strongly expressing a negation, is translated "in no wise" in Matt. 5:18, 20, RV (KJV, "in no case"); 10:42; Luke 18:17; John 6:37; Acts 13:41; Rev. 21:27; in Matt. 13:14 (twice, RV; KJV, "not"); so in Mark 9:1; Luke 9:27; John 4:48; Acts 28:26 (twice); 1 Thess. 4:15; in Luke 10:19, RV "(nothing)... in any wise" (KJV, "by any means").

Note: In 2 Thess. 2:3, RV, "(no man)... in any wise" (KJV, "by any means"), the double negative is *mē*... *mēdena*.

2. *oudamōs* (οὐδαμῶς, 3760), akin to the adjective *oudamos*, "not even one" (not in the NT), denotes "by no means, in no wise," Matt. 2:6.¶

3. *ou pantōs* (οὐ πάντως), lit., "not altogether," i.e., "wholly not" (from *pas*, "all"), is rendered "in no wise" in Rom. 3:9.

Note: In Luke 13:11 the phrase *eis to panteles*, lit., "unto the complete end" (*pas*, "all," *telos*, "an end"), i.e., "completely, utterly," preceded by the negative *mē*, is translated "in no wise" ("who was utterly unable to lift herself up"). Cf. Heb. 7:25, where the same phrase is used without a negative, signifying "to the uttermost."

For ON THIS WISE see THUS (*b*)

NOBLE

1. *eugenēs* (εὐγενής, 2104), an adjective, lit., "well born" (*eu*, "well," and *genos*, "a family, race"), (*a*) signifies "noble," 1 Cor. 1:26; (*b*) is used with *anthrōpos*, "a man," i.e., "a nobleman," in Luke 19:12.¶ In the Sept., Job 1:3.¶

2. *eugenesteros* (εὐγενέστερος, 2104*), the comparative degree of No. 1, occurs in Acts 17:11, "more noble," i.e., "more noble-minded."¶

3. *kratistos* (κράτιστος, 2903) is translated "most noble" in the KJV of Acts 24:3 and 26:25 (RV, "most excellent"), See EXCELLENT.

NOBLEMAN

basilikos (βασιλικός, 937), an adjective, "royal, belonging to a king" (*basileus*), is used of the command, "thou shalt love thy neighbor as thyself," "the royal law," Jas. 2:8; this may mean a law which covers or governs other laws and therefore has a specially regal character (as Hort suggests), or beause it is made by a King (a meaning which Deissmann assigns) with whom there is no respect of persons; it is used with the pronoun *tis*, "a certain one," in John 4:46, 49, of a courtier, one in the service of a king, "a nobleman" (some mss. have the noun *basiliskos*, "a petty king," in these two verses). It is used of a country in Acts 12:20, "the king's (country)," and of royal apparel in v. 21. See KING, ROYAL.¶

Note: For *eugenēs* in Luke 19:12, see NOBLE, No. 1.

NOISE

A. Adverb.

rhoizēdon (ῥοιζηδόν, 4500), from *rhoizos*, "the whistling of an arrow," signifies "with rushing sound," as of roaring flames, and is used in 2 Pet. 3:10, of the future passing away of the heavens.¶

B. Verbs.

1. *akouō* (ἀκούω, 191), "to hear," is translated "it was noised" in Mark 2:1 (passive voice), of the rapid spread of the information that Christ was "in the house" in Capernaum. See HEAR.

2. *dialaleō* (διαλαλέω, 1255), lit., "to speak through," is rendered "were noised abroad" in Luke 1:65. See COMMUNE.

Notes: (1) In Rev. 6:1, KJV, *phōnē*, "a voice" or "sound," is translated "noise" (RV, "voice"); it is used with *ginomai* in Acts 2:6, KJV, "(this) was noised abroad," RV, "(this) sound was heard." (2) In Matt. 9:23, KJV, *thorubeō*, "to make a tumult or uproar," in the middle voice, as in Mark 5:39 and Acts 20:10, is translated "making a noise" (RV, "making a tumult"). See ADO, TROUBLE, TUMULT, UPROAR.

NOISOME

kakos (κακός, 2556), "evil," is translated "noisome" in Rev. 16:2. See BAD.

For NONE see NO MAN

NOON

mesēmbria (μεσημβρία, 3314), lit., "middle-day" (*mesos*, "middle," and *hēmera*, "a day"), signifies (*a*) "noon," Acts 22:6; (*b*) "the south," Acts 8:26.¶

For NOR see †, p. 1

NORTH

borras (βορρᾶς, 1005), primarily Boreas, the North Wind, came to denote the "north" (cf. "Borealis"), Luke 13:29; Rev. 21:13.¶

NORTH EAST, NORTH WEST

chōros (χῶρος, 5566), Lat., *corus*, the Latin name for "the north-west wind," hence, "the north-west," occurs in Acts 27:12, KJV, RV, "(north-east and) south-east," as the N.W. wind blows towards the S.E.¶

Note: In the same v., *lips*, "the south-west (lit., 'Libyan') wind," hence, "the south-west" (so KJV), is rendered "north-east" in RV, as the S.W. wind blows towards the N.E. The difficulty is that Lutro (commonly identified with Phoenix) faces E., not W. But there is a harbor opposite Lutro which does look S.W. and N.W., bearing the name Phineka (RV marg. renders the whole phrase literally). This seems the best solution.

For NOT see †, p. 1

NOTABLE, OF NOTE

1. *gnōstos* (γνωστός, 1110), an adjective, signifying "known" (from *ginōskō*, "to know"), is used (*a*) as an adjective, most usually translated "known," whether of facts, e.g., Acts 1:19; 2:14; 4:10; or persons, John 18:15-16; it denotes "notable" in Acts 4:16, of a miracle; (*b*) as a noun, "acquaintance," Luke 2:44 and 23:49. See ACQUAINTANCE, KNOWN.

2. *episēmos* (ἐπίσημος, 1978) primarily meant "bearing a mark," e.g., of money, "stamped, coined," (from *epi*, "upon," and *sēma*, "a mark, a sign"; cf. *sēmainō*, "to give a sign, signify, indicate," and *sēmeioō*, "to note"; see below); it is used in the NT, metaphorically, (*a*) in a good sense, Rom. 16:7, "of note, illustrious," said of Andronicus and Junias; (*b*) in a bad sense, Matt. 27:16, "notable," of the prisoner Barabbas.¶ In the Sept., Gen. 30:42; Esth. 5:4; 8:13, toward the end of the verse, "a distinct (day)".¶

3. *epiphanēs* (ἐπιφανής, 2016), "illustrious, renowned, notable" (akin to *epiphainō*, "to show forth, appear"; Eng., "epiphany"), is translated "notable" in Acts 2:20, of the great Day of the Lord. The appropriateness of this word (compared with Nos. 1 and 2) to that future occasion is obvious.¶

NOTE (Verb)

sēmeioō (σημειόω, 4593), from *sēmeion*, "a sign, token," signifies "to mark, to note," in the middle voice, "to note for oneself," and is so used in 2 Thess. 3:14, in an injunction to take cautionary note of one who refuses obedience to the apostle's word by the Epistle.¶ In the Sept. Ps. 5:6.¶

NOTHING

1. *ouden* (οὐδέν, 3762), the neuter of *oudeis*, "no one," occurs, e.g., in Matt. 5:13; 10:26; 23:16; adverbially, e.g., in Matt. 27:24; 2 Cor. 12:11 (1st part), "in nothing"; 1 Tim. 4:4; in the dative case, after *en*, "in," Phil. 1:20. Westcott and Hort adopt the spelling *outhen* in Luke 22:35; 23:14; Acts 15:9; 19:27; 26:26; 1 Cor. 13:2.

2. *mēden* (μηδέν, 3367), the neuter of *mēdeis*, "no one," is related to No. 1, in the same way as the masculine genders are; so with the negatives *ou* and *mē*, "not," in all their usage and connections (see under NO MAN). Thus it is found, not in direct negative statements, as with No. 1, but in warnings, prohibitions, etc., e.g., Matt. 27:19; Acts 19:36; in expressions conveying certain impossibilities, e.g., Acts 4:21; comparisons, e.g., 2 Cor. 6:10; intimating a sup-

position to the contrary, 1 Tim. 6:4; adverbially, e.g., 2 Cor. 11:5, "not a whit." Westcott and Hort adopt the spelling *mēthen* in Acts 27:33.

3. *ou* (οὐ, 3756), "not," is translated "nothing" in Luke 8:17; 11:6; 1 Cor. 9:16; 2 Cor. 8:15 (in each case, an absolute and direct negative).

4. *mē* (μή, 3361), "not," is translated "nothing" in John 6:39 in a clause expressing purpose; in the KJV of Luke 7:42 (RV, "not"), in a temporal clause.

5. *ou . . . ti* (οὐ . . . τί), followed by the subjunctive mood, "(have) nothing (to eat)," lit., "(they have) not what (they should eat)," in Matt. 15:32 (in some mss. in Mark 6:36); Mark 8:2; the phrase conveys more stress than the simple negative (No. 3).

6. *mē . . . ti* (μὴ . . . τί), followed by the subjunctive mood, "(they had) nothing (to eat)," RV, "(having) nothing (to eat)," KJV, lit., "not (having) what (they should eat)," in Mark 8:1; the negative is *mē* here because it is attached to a participle, "having"; whereas in No. 5 the negative *ou* is attached to the indicative mood, "they have."

7. *mē ti* (μή τι), lit., "not anything," not used in simple, direct negations (see under NO MAN), occurs in John 6:12 in a clause of purpose; in 1 Cor. 4:5, in a prohibition.

8. *oude ti* (οὐδέ τι), "not even anything," is found in 1 Tim. 6:7 (2nd part); it is a more forceful expression than the simple *ouden* in the 1st part of the verse, as if to say, "it is a fact that we brought nothing into the world, and most certainly we can carry out not even the slightest thing, whatever we may have possessed."

Notes: (1) For "nothing" in Luke 1:37, KJV see WORD, No. 2 (RV). (2) In John 11:49 the double negative *ouk* ("not") . . . *ouden* ("nothing") is translated "nothing at all." (3) In Acts 11:8 *pan*, "everything," with *oudepote*, "not even ever," is rendered "nothing . . . ever," RV, KJV, "nothing . . . at any time." (4) In 1 Cor. 1:19, KJV, *atheteō*, "to set aside, make void, reject," is translated "I will bring to nothing" (RV, "will I reject").

For NOTICE BEFORE, 2 Cor. 9:5, KJV, see AFOREPROMISED

NOTWITHSTANDING

Note: This is the KJV rendering of (1) *alla*, "but," in Rev. 2:20 (RV, "but"); (2) *plēn*, "howbeit, yet, except that," in Luke 10:11, 20, and Phil. 1:18 (RV, "only that"); in 4:14, KJV, "notwithstanding" (RV, "howbeit").

NOUGHT (for, bring to, come to, set at)

A. Pronoun.
ouden (οὐδέν, 3762), "nothing" (the neuter of *oudeis*, no one), is translated "nought" in Acts 5:36. See NOTHING.

B. Adverb.
dōrean (δωρεάν, 1432), "freely, as a gift," is translated "for nought" in Gal. 2:21, RV (KJV, "in vain"); in 2 Thess. 3:8, in a denial by the apostle that he lived on the hospitality of others at Thessalonica. See FREELY.

C. Verbs.
1. *katargeō* (καταργέω, 2673) is used in 1 Cor. 1:28, "(that) He might bring to nought"; 1 Cor. 2:6 (passive voice in the original); 1 Cor. 6:13, RV, "will bring to nought" (KJV "will destroy"); so 2 Thess. 2:8 and Heb. 2:14. See ABOLISH.

2. *exoutheneō* (ἐξουθενέω, 1848), "to set at nought, treat with utter contempt, despise," is translated "set at nought" in Luke 18:9, RV (KJV, "despised"); in 23:11, "set (Him) at nought"; "was set at nought" in Acts 4:11; in Rom. 14:3, RV, "set at nought" (KJV, "despise"); v. 10, "set at nought." See ACCOUNT, DESPISE.

3. *exoudeneō* or *exoudenoō* (ἐξουδενέω, 1847) has the same meaning as No. 2, and is virtually the same word (*outhen* being another form of *ouden*, "nothing"), i.e., "to treat as nothing" (*ex*, intensive), and is translated "be set at nought" in Mark 9:12.¶

4. *ekpiptō* (ἐκπίπτω, 1601), "to fall out," is used in Rom. 9:6 in the sense of falling from its place, failing, of the word of God, RV, "hath come to nought" (KJV, "hath taken none effect"). See FALL.

5. *atheteō* (ἀθετέω, 114), "to set aside, reject," is translated "set at nought" in Heb. 10:28, RV (KJV, "despised"); so Jude 8. See NOTHING, *Note* (4).

Notes: (1) In Acts 5:38, KJV, *kataluō*, lit., "to loosen down," hence, "to overthrow," is translated "it will come to nought" (RV, "it will be overthrown"). See DESTROY. (2) In Rev. 18:17, KJV, *erēmoō*, "to make desolate," is translated "is come to nought" (RV, "is made desolate"). See DESOLATE. (3) In Acts 19:27, KJV, the accusative case of *apelegmos*, "confutation, disrepute," preceded by the verb *erchomai*, "to come," and *eis*, "unto" or "into," is translated "be set at nought" (RV, "come into disrepute"). See DISREPUTE.¶

NOURISH, NOURISHMENT

1. *trephō* (τρέφω, 5142), "to rear, feed, nourish," is translated by the verb "to nourish" in

Jas. 5:5 (of luxurious living); Rev. 12:14 (of God's care for Israel against its enemies); so v. 6, RV (KJV, "feed"); in Acts 12:20, RV, "was fed" (KJV, "was nourished"). See FEED.

2. *anatrephō* (ἀνατρέφω, 397), "to nurse, bring up" (*ana*, "up," and No. 1), is translated "nourished" in Acts 7:20 (KJV, "nourished up"); in 21, "nourished," KJV and RV. See BRING.

3. *ektrephō* (ἐκτρέφω, 1625), *ek*, "from, out of," and No. 1, primarily used of children, "to nurture, rear," is translated "nurture" of the care of one's own flesh, Eph. 5:29, and in Eph. 6:4, RV (KJV, "bring . . . up"). See BRING.¶

4. *entrephō* (ἐντρέφω, 1789), "to train up, nurture," is used metaphorically, in the passive voice, in 1 Tim. 4:6, of being "nourished" in the faith.¶

For NOURISHMENT MINISTERED, Col. 2:19, see SUPPLY

NOVICE

neophutos (νεόφυτος, 3504), an adjective, lit., "newly-planted" (from *neos*, "new," and *phuō*, "to bring forth, produce"), denotes "a new convert, neophyte, novice," 1 Tim. 3:6, of one who by inexperience is unfitted to act as a bishop or overseer in a church.¶ In the Sept., Job 14:9; Ps. 128:3; 144:12; Isa. 5:7.¶

NOW

A. Adverbs.

1. *nun* (νῦν, 3568) is used (*a*) of time, the immediate present, whether in contrast to the past, e.g., John 4:18; Acts 7:52, or to the future, e.g., John 12:27; Rom. 11:31; sometimes with the article, singular or plural, e.g., Acts 4:29; 5:38; (*b*) of logical sequence, often partaking also of the character of (*a*), "now therefore, now however," as it is, e.g., Luke 11:39; John 8:40; 9:41; 15:22, 24; 1 Cor. 5:11, RV marg., "as it is."

Note: Under (*a*) comes the phrase in 2 Cor. 8:14, with *kairos*, "a time," all governed by *en*, "in," or "at," KJV, "now at this time" (RV, "at this present time").

2. *nuni* (νυνί, 3570), a strengthened form of No. 1, is used (*a*) of time, e.g., Acts 22:1 (in the best mss.); 24:13; Rom. 6:22; 15:23, 25; (*b*) with logical import, e.g., Rom. 7:17; 1 Cor. 13:13, which some regard as temporal (*a*); but if this is the significance, "the clause means, 'but faith, hope, love, are our abiding possession now in this present life.' The objection to this rendering is that the whole course of thought has been to contrast the things which last only

for the present time with the things which survive. And the main contrast so far has been between love and the special [then] present activity of prophecy, tongues, knowledge. There is something of disappointment, and even of bathos, in putting as a climax to these contrasts the statement that in this present state faith, hope, love abide; that is no more than can be said of [the then existing] prophecies, tongues and knowledge. If there is to be a true climax the 'abiding' must cover the future as well as the present state. And that involves as a consequence that *nuni* must be taken in its logical meaning, i.e., 'as things are,' 'taking all into account' . . . This logical sense of *nuni* . . . is enforced by the dominant note of the whole passage" (R. St. John Parry, in the *Camb. Greek Test.*).

It is certain that love will continue eternally; and hope will not cease at the Parousia of Christ, for hope will ever look forward to the accomplishment of God's eternal purposes, a hope characterized by absolute assurance; and where hope is in exercise faith is its concomitant. Faith will not be lost in sight.

3. *ēdē* (ἤδη, 2235) denotes "already, now already," "the subjective present, with a suggested reference to some other time, or to some expectation" (Thayer), e.g., Matt. 3:10; 14:24; Luke 11:7; John 6:17; Rom. 1:10; 4:19; 13:11; Phil. 4:10.

4. *arti* (ἄρτι, 737), expressing "coincidence," and denoting "strictly present time," signifies "just now, this moment," in contrast (*a*) to the past, e.g., Matt 11:12; John 2:10; 9:19, 25; 13:33; Gal 1:9–10; (*b*) to the future, e.g., John 13:37; 16:12, 31; 1 Cor. 13:12 (cf. No. 2 in v. 13); 2 Thess. 2:7; 1 Pet. 1:6, 8; (*c*) sometimes without necessary reference to either, e.g., Matt. 3:15; 9:18; 26:53; Gal. 4:20; Rev. 12:10.

5. *aparti* (ἀπάρτι, 534), sometimes written separately, *ap'arti*, i.e., *apo*, "from," and No. 4, denotes "from now, henceforth," John 13:19; 14:7; Rev. 14:13. See HENCEFORTH.¶

6. *loipon* (λοιπόν, 3063), the neuter of *loipos*, "the rest, from now," is used adverbially with the article and translated "now" in Mark 14:41.

B. Conjunctions and Particles.

1. *oun* (οὖν, 3767), "therefore, so then," is sometimes used in continuing a narrative, e.g., Acts 1:18; 1 Cor. 9:25; or resuming it after a digression, usually rendered "therefore," e.g., Acts 11:19; 25:1, RV (KJV, "now"). In the following it is absent from the best mss., Mark 12:20; Luke 10:36; John 16:19; 18:24; 19:29.

Note: In 2 Cor. 5:20 *oun* is simply "therefore," as in RV (KJV, "now then").

2. *de* (δέ, 1161), "but, and, now," often implying an antithesis, is rendered "now" in John 19:23; 1 Cor. 10:11; 15:50; Gal. 1:20; Eph. 4:9; in Acts 27:9 (1st part), RV, "and" (KJV, "now"); in Gal. 4:1, RV, "but" (KJV "now").

3. *dē* (δή, 1211), a consecutive particle, giving stress to the word or words to which it is attached, sometimes with hardly any exact Eng. equivalent, is translated "now" in Luke 2:15, in the words of the shepherds; in Acts 15:36, RV (KJV, "and"). Some mss. have it in 2 Cor. 12:1; see RV marg.

Notes: (1) In 1 Cor. 4:7, KJV, B, No. 2, followed by *kai*, and, is translated "now" (RV, "but"). (2) In Rom. 14:15 and Philem. 16, KJV, *ouketi*, "no longer," is translated "now . . . not" and "not now" (RV, "no longer"); cf. John 4:42 and 21:6, "now . . . not." (3) The particle *ara*, "then," expressing a more informal inference than *oun* (B, No. 1 above), is often in Paul's epistles coupled with *oun*, the phrase meaning "so then," as KJV and RV in Rom. 7:3, 25; 9:16; 14:12; in RV only (KJV, "therefore"), Rom. 5:18; 8:12; 9:18; 14:19; Gal. 6:10; 1 Thess. 5:6; 2 Thess. 2:15. In Eph. 2:19 the KJV renders it "now therefore." (4) In 1 Tim. 1:4, the RV *"so do I now"* (KJV, *"so do"*) is added to complete the sentence. (5) In Heb. 9:9, RV, the perfect participle of *enistēmi*, "to be present," is translated "(the time) *now* present" (KJV, "then present," which misses the meaning). See COME, (AT) HAND, PRESENT.

NUMBER

A. Nouns.

1. *arithmos* (ἀριθμός, 706), number, "a number" (Eng., "arithmetic," etc.), occurs in Luke 22:3; John 6:10; Rom. 9:27; elsewhere five times in Acts, ten times in the Apocalypse.

2. *ochlos* (ὄχλος, 3793), "a multitude," is translated "number" in Luke 6:17, RV (KJV, "multitude"); in Mark 10:46 and Acts 1:15 the renderings are reversed. See COMMON, COMPANY, CROWD MULTITUDE, PEOPLE.

B. Verbs.

1. *arithmeō* (ἀριθμέω, 705), akin to A, is found in Matt. 10:30; Luke 12:7; Rev. 7:9.¶

2. *katarithmeō* (καταριθμέω, 2674), "to number" or "count among" (*kata*, and No. 1), is used in Acts 1:17.¶

3. *enkrinō* (ἐγκρίνω, 1469), "to reckon among" (*en*, "in," *krinō*, "to judge or reckon"), is translated "to number . . . (ourselves) with" in 2 Cor. 10:12 (RV marg., "to judge ourselves among or . . . with"), of the apostle's dissociation of himself and his fellow missionaries from those who commended themselves.¶

4. *sunkatapsēphizō* (συγκαταψηφίζω, 4785), "to vote or reckon (one) a place among" (*sun*, "with" or "among," *kata*, "down," and *psēphizō*, "to count or vote," originally with pebbles, *psēphos*, "a pebble"), is used of the "numbering" of Matthias with the eleven apostles, Acts 1:26.¶

Notes: (1) Some mss. have verse 28 in Mark 15 (KJV), where *logizomai*, "to reckon," is translated "He was numbered." (2) For *katalegō* 1 Tim. 5:9 (KJV, "let . . . be taken into the number"), see TAKE, *Note* (18). (3) In Mark 5:13 see the italicized words in RV. (4) In Heb. 7:23, RV, the adjective *pleiōn*, "more, many," is translated "many in number" (KJV, "many"); in Acts 28:23, RV, "a great number" (KJV, "many").

NURSE

trophos (τροφός, 5162), translated "nurse" in 1 Thess. 2:7, there denotes a "nursing" mother, as is clear from the statement "cherisheth her own children"; this is also confirmed by the word *ēpios*, "gentle" (in the same verse), which was commonly used of the kindness of parents towards children. Cf. *trephō*, "to bring up" (see NOURISH).

For NURTURE (Eph. 6:4) see CHASTENING

O

OATH

1. *horkos* (ὅρκος, 3727) is primarily equivalent to *herkos*, "a fence, an enclosure, that which restrains a person"; hence, "an oath." The Lord's command in Matt. 5:33 was a condemnation of the minute and arbitrary restrictions imposed by the scribes and Pharisees in the matter of adjurations, by which God's Name was profaned. The injunction is repeated in Jas. 5:12. The language of the apostle Paul, e.g., in Gal. 1:20 and 1 Thess. 5:27 was not inconsistent with Christ's prohibition, read in the light of its context. Contrast the "oaths" mentioned in Matt. 14:7, 9; 26:72; Mark 6:26.

Heb. 6:16 refers to the confirmation of a compact among men, guaranteeing the discharge of liabilities; in their disputes "the oath is final for confirmation." This is referred to in order to illustrate the greater subject of God's "oath" to Abraham, confirming His promise; cf. Luke 1:73; Acts 2:30.¶ Cf. the verbs *horkizō*, and *exorkizō*, under ADJURE.

2. *horkōmosia* (ὁρκωμοσία, 3728) denotes "an affirmation on oath" (from No. 1 and *omnumi*, "to swear"). This is used in Heb. 7:20–21 (twice), 28, of the establishment of the Priesthood of Christ, the Son of God, appointed a Priest after the order of Melchizedek, and "perfected for evermore."¶ In the Sept., Ezek. 17:18, 19.¶

Note: For *anathematizō* in Acts 23:21, KJV, "have bound (themselves) with an oath," see CURSE.

OBEDIENCE, OBEDIENT, OBEY

A. Nouns.

1. *hupakoē* (ὑπακοή, 5218), "obedience" (*hupo*, "under," *akouō*, "to hear"), is used (*a*) in general, Rom. 6:16 (1st part), RV, "(unto) obedience," KJV, "(to) obey"; here "obedience" is not personified, as in the next part of the verse, "servants . . . of obedience" [see (*c*)], but is simply shown to be the effect of the presentation mentioned; (*b*) of the fulfillment of apostolic counsels, 2 Cor. 7:15; 10:6; Philem. 21; (*c*) of the fulfillment of God's claims or commands, Rom. 1:5 and 16:26, "obedience of faith," which grammatically might be objective, to the faith (marg.), or subjective, as in the text. Since faith is one of the main subjects of the Epistle, and is the initial act of obedience in the new life, as well as an essential characteristic thereof, the text rendering is to be preferred; Rom. 6:16

(2nd part); 15:18, RV "(for) the obedience," KJV, "(to make) obedient"; 16:19; 1 Pet. 1:2, 14, RV, "(children of) obedience," i.e., characterized by "obedience," KJV, "obedient (children)"; v. 22, RV, "obedience (to the truth)," KJV, "obeying (the truth)"; (*d*) of "obedience" to Christ (objective), 2 Cor. 10:5; (*e*) of Christ's "obedience," Rom. 5:19 (referring to His death; cf. Phil. 2:8); Heb. 5:8, which refers to His delighted experience in constant "obedience" to the Father's will (not to be understood in the sense that He learned to obey).¶

2. *hupotagē* (ὑποταγή, 5292), subjection (*hupo*, "under," *tassō*, "to order"), is translated "obedience" in 2 Cor. 9:13, RV (KJV, "subjection"). See SUBJECTION.

B. Verbs.

1. *hupakouō* (ὑπακούω, 5219), "to listen, attend" (as in Acts 12:13), and so, "to submit, to obey," is used of "obedience" (*a*) to God, Heb. 5:9; 11:8; (*b*) to Christ, by natural elements, Matt. 8:27; Mark 1:27; 4:41; Luke 8:25; (*c*) to disciples of Christ, Luke 17:6; (*d*) to the faith, Acts 6:7; the gospel, Rom. 10:16; 2 Thess. 1:8; Christian doctrine, Rom. 6:17 (as to a form or mold of teaching); (*e*) to apostolic injunctions, Phil. 2:12; 2 Thess. 3:14; (*f*) to Abraham by Sarah, 1 Pet. 3:6; (*g*) to parents by children, Eph. 6:1; Col. 3:20; (*h*) to masters by servants, Eph. 6:5; Col. 3:22; (*i*) to sin, Rom. 6:12; (*j*) in general, Rom. 6:16.¶

2. *peithō* (πείθω, 3982), "to persuade, to win over," in the passive and middle voices, "to be persuaded, to listen to, to obey," is so used with this meaning, in the middle voice, e.g., in Acts 5:36–37 (in v. 40, passive voice, "they agreed"); Rom. 2:8; Gal. 5:7; Heb. 13:17; Jas. 3:3. The "obedience" suggested is not by submission to authority, but resulting from persuasion.

"*Peithō* and *pisteuō*, 'to trust,' are closely related etymologically; the difference in meaning is that the former implies the obedience that is produced by the latter, cf. Heb. 3:18–19, where the disobedience of the Israelites is said to be the evidence of their unbelief. Faith is of the heart, invisible to men; obedience is of the conduct and may be observed. When a man obeys God he gives the only possible evidence that in his heart he believes God. Of course it is persuasion of the truth that results in faith (we believe because we are persuaded that the thing is true, a thing does not become true because it is believed), but *peithō*, in NT suggests an actual and outward result of the inward persuasion and consequent faith."* See ASSURANCE, B, No. 3.

3. *peitharcheō* (πειθαρχέω, 3980), "to obey one in authority" (No. 2, and *archē*, "rule"), is translated "obey" in Acts 5:29, 32; "to be obedient," Titus 3:1, RV (KJV, "to obey magistrates"); in Acts 27:21, "hearkened." See HEARKEN.¶

4. *apeitheō* (ἀπειθέω, 544), "to disobey, be disobedient" (*a*, negative, and No. 2), is translated "obey not" in Rom. 2:8; 1 Pet. 3:1; 4:17. See DISOBEDIENT.

Note: In 1 Cor. 14:34, KJV, *hupotassō*, "to be in subjection" (RV), is translated "to be under obedience"; so Titus 2:5, RV, "being in subjection" (KJV, "obedient"); and v. 9, RV (KJV, "to be obedient"). See SUBJECTION.

C. Adjective.
hupēkoos (ὑπήκοος, 5255), "obedient" (akin to A, No. 1), "giving ear, subject," occurs in Acts 7:39, RV, "(would not be) obedient," KJV, "(would not) obey"; 2 Cor. 2:9; Phil. 2:8, where the RV *"even"* is useful as making clear that the "obedience" was not to death but to the Father.¶

For the verb **OBJECT**, Acts 24:19, see **ACCUSATION**, B, No. 4

For **OBJECTS**, RV, in Acts 17:23, see **WORSHIP**

OBSERVATION, OBSERVE
A. Noun.
paratērēsis (παρατήρησις, 3907), "attentive watching" (akin to *paratēreō*, "to observe"), is used in Luke 17:20, of the manner in which the kingdom of God (i.e., the operation of the spiritual kingdom in the hearts of men) does not come, "in such a manner that it can be watched with the eyes" (Grimm-Thayer), or, as KJV marg., "with outward show."¶

B. Verbs.
1. *anatheōreō* (ἀναθεωρέω, 333), "to observe carefully, consider well" (*ana*, "up," intensive, and *theōreō*, "to behold"), is used in Acts 17:23, RV, "observed" (of Paul's notice of the objects of Athenian worship), and Heb. 13:7, "considering." See BEHOLD.¶

2. *tēreō* (τηρέω, 5083): see KEEP, No. 1.

3. *suntēreō* (συντηρέω, 4933): see KEEP, No. 3.

4. *paratēreō* (παρατηρέω, 3906), "to watch closely, observe narrowly" (*para*, used inten-

sively, and No. 2), is translated "ye observe" in Gal. 4:10, where the middle voice suggests that their religious observance of days, etc. was not from disinterested motives, but with a view to their own advantage. See WATCH. Cf. *phroneō* ("to think"), "regardeth" in Rom. 14:6, where the subject is connected with the above, though the motive differs.

5. *phulassō* (φυλάσσω, 5442): see KEEP, No. 4.

6. *poieō* (ποιέω, 4160), "to do," is translated "to observe" in Acts 16:21. See DO.

OBTAIN, OBTAINING
A. Verbs.
1. *tunchanō* (τυγχάνω, 5177), "to meet with, light upon," also signifies "to obtain, attain to, reach, get" (with regard to things), translated "to obtain" in Acts 26:22, of "the help that is from God"; 2 Tim. 2:10, of "the salvation which is in Christ Jesus with eternal glory"; Heb. 8:6, of the ministry obtained by Christ; 11:35, of "a better resurrection." See CHANCE.

2. *epitunchanō* (ἐπιτυγχάνω, 2013), primarily, "to light upon" (*epi*, "upon," and No. 1), denotes "to obtain," Rom. 11:7 (twice); Heb. 6:15; 11:33; Jas. 4:2.¶

3. *lanchanō* (λαγχάνω, 2975), "to obtain by lot," is translated "that have obtained" in 2 Pet. 1:1; in Acts 1:17, KJV, "had obtained" (RV, "received"), with *klēros*, "a lot" or "portion." See LOTS.

4. *ktaomai* (κτάομαι, 2932), "to procure for oneself, get, gain, acquire," is translated "obtained" in Acts 1:18, RV (KJV, "purchased"); 8:20, RV (KJV, "may be purchased"); 22:28. See POSSESS, PROVIDE, PURCHASE.

5. *krateō* (κρατέω, 2902), "to be strong," also means "to get possession of, obtain," e.g., in Acts 27:13, "they had obtained (their purpose)." See HOLD.

6. *lambanō* (λαμβάνω, 2983), "to take, to receive," is translated by the verb "to obtain" in 1 Cor. 9:25; Phil. 3:12, RV, "(not that) I have (already) obtained" (contrast *katantaō*, "to attain," v. 11); Moule translates it "not that I have already received," i.e., the prize; the verb does not signify "to attain"; Heb. 4:16, KJV, "obtain." See ACCEPT, No. 4.

7. *heuriskō* (εὑρίσκω, 2147) denotes "to find"; in the middle voice, "to find for oneself, to procure, get, obtain," with the suggestion of accomplishing the end which had been in view; so in Heb. 9:12, "having obtained (eternal redemption)."

Notes: (1) In 1 Cor. 9:24, KJV, *katalambanō*, a strengthened form of No. 6 (*kata*, used intensively), is translated "obtain" (RV, "attain"). (2)

In Heb. 11:2, 4, 39, KJV, *martureō*, "to bear witness," and in the passive voice, "to have witness borne to one," is translated "to obtain" a good report, or "to obtain" witness (RV, "had witness borne"). See WITNESS. (3) For the KJV of Heb. 1:4, "He hath by inheritance obtained" (RV, "He hath inherited"), and of Eph. 1:11, see INHERIT. (4) For the phrase "to obtain mercy," the passive voice of *eleeō* in Matt. 5:7; Rom. 11:30–31; 1 Cor. 7:25; 2 Cor. 4:1 (RV); 1 Tim. 1:13, 16; 1 Pet. 2:10 (twice), see MERCY.

B. Noun.

peripoiēsis (περιποίησις, 4047), lit., "a making around" (*peri*, "around," *poieō*, "to do or make"), denotes (*a*) "the act of obtaining" anything, as of salvation in its completeness, 1 Thess. 5:9; 2 Thess. 2:14; (*b*) "a thing acquired, an acquisition, possession," Eph. 1:14, RV, "(*God's* own) possession" [some would put this under (*a*)]; so 1 Pet. 2:9, RV, KJV, "a peculiar (people);" cf. Isa. 43:21; (*c*) preservation; this may be the meaning in Heb. 10:39, "saving" (RV marg., "gaining"); cf. the corresponding verb in Luke 17:33 (in the best texts), "preserve."¶ In the Sept. the noun has the meaning (*b*) in Hag. 2:10 and Mal. 3:17, (*c*) in 2 Chron. 14:13.¶

OCCASION

aphormē (ἀφορμή, 874), properly "a starting point," was used to denote "a base of operations in war." In the NT it occurs as follows: "(*a*) the Law provided sin with a base of operations for its attack upon the soul, Rom. 7:8, 11; (*b*) the irreproachable conduct of the Apostle provided his friends with a base of operations against his detractors, 2 Cor. 5:12; (*c*) by refusing temporal support at Corinth he deprived these detractors of their base of operations against him, 2 Cor. 11:12; (*d*) Christian freedom is not to provide a base of operations for the flesh, Gal. 5:13; (*e*) unguarded behavior on the part of young widows (and the same is true or all believers) would provide Satan with a base of operations against the faith, 1 Tim. 5:14."*¶

The word is found frequently in the papyri with meanings which illustrate those in the NT. In the Sept., Prov. 9:9; Ezek. 5:7.¶

Notes: (1) For the RV renderings "occasion (or 'occasions') of stumbling," "occasion of falling," see FALLING, B, *Note* (3), OFFENSE. (2) In 2 Cor. 8:8, KJV, the phrase "by occasion of" translates the preposition *dia*, "through, by means of" (RV, "through").

For **OCCUPATION,** Acts 18:3, KJV, see **TRADE**

Notes: The phrase "of like occupation" in Acts 19:25 translates the phrase *peri* ("about") *ta* ("the") *toiauta* ("such things"), i.e., lit., "(occupied) about such things."

OCCUPY

peripateō (περιπατέω, 4043), "to walk," is sometimes used of the state in which one is living, or of that to which a person is given, e.g., Heb. 13:9, "(meats, wherein they that) occupied themselves," RV (marg., "walked"; KJV,"have been occupied"), i.e., exercising themselves about different kinds of food, regarding some as lawful, others as unlawful (referring especially to matters of the ceremonial details of the law).

Notes: (1) For "occupy," in the KJV of Luke 19:13, see TRADE. (2) For "occupieth," in the KJV of 1 Cor. 14:16, see FILL, No. 2.

ODOR

osmē (ὀσμή, 3744), "a smell, an odor" (akin to *ozō*, "to smell"), is translated "odor" in John 12:3; it is used metaphorically in Eph. 5:2, RV, "an odor (of a sweet smell)," KJV, "(a sweet smelling) savor," of the effects Godward of the sacrifice of Christ; in Phil. 4:18 of the effect of sacrifice, on the part of those in the church at Philippi, who sent material assistance to the apostle in his imprisonment. The word is translated "savor" in 2 Cor. 2:14, 16 (twice).¶

Note: For *thumiama*, "incense," translated "odors" in the KJV of Rev. 5:8 (RV, "incense"), see INCENSE. For *amōmon* (quoted in RV marg. in the Latinized form *amomum*) in Rev. 18:13, see SPICE.

OF

Note: (1) In addition to the rendering of a number of prepositions, "of" translates the genitive case of nouns, with various shades of meaning. Of these the subjective and objective are mentioned here, which need careful distinction. Thus the phrase "the love of God," e.g., in 1 John 2:5 and 3:16, is subjective, signifying "God's love"; in 1 John 5:3, it is objective, signifying our love to God. Again, "the witness of God," e.g., 1 John 5:9, is subjective, signifying the witness which God Himself has given; in Rev. 1:2, 9, and 19:10, e.g., "the testimony of Jesus" is objective, signifying the testimony borne to Him. In the KJV "the faith of" is sometimes ambiguous; with reference to Christ it is objective, i.e., faith in Him, not His own faith, in the following passages in which the RV, "in" gives the correct meaning; Rom. 3:22; Gal.

---

* From *Notes on Galatians,* by Hogg and Vine, p. 269.

2:16 (twice), 20, RV, "I live in faith, the faith which is in the Son of God"; 3:22; Eph. 3:12; Phil. 3:9 (cf. Col. 2:12, "faith in the working of God"). In Eph. 2:20, "the foundation of the apostles and prophets" is subjective, i.e., the foundation laid by the apostles and prophets ("other foundation can no man lay than . . . Jesus Christ," 1 Cor. 3:11). (2) In the KJV of John 16:13, "He shall not speak of Himself," the preposition is *apo*, "from," as in the RV; the Spirit of God often speaks of Himself in Scripture, the Lord's assurance was that the Holy Spirit would not be the source of His utterances. So with regard to Christ's utterances, John 7:17, RV, "I speak from (*apo*) Myself": and 14:10. (3) In John 6:46; 15:15; 17:7; Acts 17:9, the RV, "from" is to be observed, as rightly translating *para* (KJV, "of"). (4) The following are instances in which "of" translates *ek*, or *ex*, "out of, from," Matt. 21:25 (RV, "from"); 1 Cor. 1:30; 15:6; 2 Cor. 5:1 (RV, "from"); Jas. 4:1. (5) In the following, *peri*, "concerning," is so translated in the RV (for KJV, "of"), e.g., Acts 5:24; 1 Cor. 1:11; 1 John 1:1 (the RV is important); cf. John 16:8. (6) *Epi*, "over," is so translated in Matt. 18:13, RV; "concerning" in Acts 4:9. (7) *Huper*, "on behalf of," is so rendered in 2 Cor. 7:4, RV (KJV, "of"); (8) For *hupo*, "by," see the RV of Matt. 1:22; 2:16; 11:27; Luke 9:7; Acts 15:4; 1 Cor. 14:24; 2 Cor. 8:19; Phil. 3:12. (9) For other prepositions, etc., see †, p. 1.

For **OFF** see †, p. 1

OFFENCE (OFFENSE)

A. Nouns.

1. *skandalon* (σκάνδαλον, 4625) originally was "the name of the part of a trap to which the bait is attached, hence, the trap or snare itself, as in Rom. 11:9, RV, 'stumblingblock,' quoted from Psa. 69:22, and in Rev. 2:14, for Balaam's device was rather a trap for Israel than a stumblingblock to them, and in Matt. 16:23, for in Peter's words the Lord perceived a snare laid for Him by Satan.

"In NT *skandalon* is always used metaphorically, and ordinarily of anything that arouses prejudice, or becomes a hindrance to others, or causes them to fall by the way. Sometimes the hindrance is in itself good, and those stumbled by it are the wicked."*

Thus it is used (*a*) of Christ in Rom. 9:33, "(a rock) of offense"; so 1 Pet. 2:8; 1 Cor. 1:23 (KJV and RV, "stumblingblock"), and of His cross, Gal. 5:11 (RV, ditto); of the "table" pro-

* From *Notes on Galations,* by Hogg and Vine, p. 262.

vided by God for Israel, Rom. 11:9 (see above); (*b*) of that which is evil, e.g., Matt. 13:41, RV, "things that cause stumbling" (KJV, "things that offend"), lit., "all stumblingblocks"; 18:7, RV, "occasions of stumbling" and "occasion"; Luke 17:1 (ditto); Rom. 14:13, RV, "an occasion of falling" (KJV, "an occasion to fall"), said of such a use of Christian liberty as proves a hindrance to another; 16:17, RV, "occasions of stumbling," said of the teaching of things contrary to sound doctrine; 1 John 2:10, "occasion of stumbling," of the absence of this in the case of one who loves his brother and thereby abides in the light. Love, then, is the best safeguard against the woes pronounced by the Lord upon those who cause others to stumble. See FALL, B, *Note* (3).¶ Cf. the Sept. in Hos. 4:17, "Ephraim partaking with idols hath laid stumblingblocks in his own path."

2. *proskomma* (πρόσκομμα, 4348), "an obstacle against which one may dash his foot" (akin to *proskoptō*, "to stumble" or "cause to stumble"; *pros*, "to or against," *koptō*, "to strike"), is translated "offense" in Rom. 14:20, in v. 13, "a stumblingblock," of the spiritual hindrance to another by a selfish use of liberty (cf. No. 1 in the same verse); so in 1 Cor. 8:9. It is used of Christ, in Rom. 9:32–33, RV, "(a stone) of stumbling," and 1 Pet. 2:8, where the KJV also has this rendering.¶ Cf. the Sept. in Ex. 23:33, "these (the gods of the Canaanites) will be an offense (stumblingblock) unto thee."

3. *proskopē* (προσκοπή, 4349), like No. 2, and formed from the same combination, occurs in 2 Cor. 6:3, RV, "occasion of stumbling" (KJV, "offense"), something which leads others into error or sin.¶ Cf. the Sept. in Prov. 16:18, "a haughty spirit (becomes) a stumblingblock" (i.e., to oneself).

Notes: (1) In the KJV of Rom. 4:25; 5:15 (twice), 16–18, 20, *paraptōma*, "a trespass," is translated "offense." See TRESPASS. (2) In 2 Cor. 11:7, KJV, *hamartia*, a sin, is translated "an offense." See SIN.

B. Adjective.

aproskopos (ἀπρόσκοπος, 677), akin to A, No. 3, with *a*, negative, prefixed, is used (*a*) in the active sense, "not causing to stumble," in 1 Cor. 10:32, metaphorically of "refraining from doing anything to lead astray" either Jews or Greeks or the church of God (i.e., the local church), RV, "no occasion of stumbling" (KJV, "none offense"); (*b*) in the passive sense, "blameless, without stumbling," Acts 24:16, "(a conscience) void of offense;" Phil. 1:10, "void of (KJV, without) offense." The adjective is found occasionally in the papyri writings.¶

OFFEND

skandalizō (σκανδαλίζω, 4624), from *skandalon* (OFFENSE, No. 1), signifies "to put a snare or stumblingblock in the way," always metaphorically in the NT, in the same ways as the noun, which see. It is used 14 times in Matthew, 8 in Mark, twice in Luke, twice in John; elsewhere in 1 Cor. 8:13 (twice) and 2 Cor. 11:29. It is absent in the most authentic mss. in Rom. 14:21. The RV renders it by the verb "to stumble," or "cause to stumble," in every place save the following, where it uses the verb "to offend," Matt. 13:57; 15:12; 26:31, 33; Mark 6:3; 14:27, 29.

Notes: (1) In Jas. 2:10; 3:2 (twice), KJV, *ptaiō*, "to stumble," is translated "offend;" see FALL, STUMBLE. (2) In Acts 25:8, KJV, *hamartanō*, "to sin," is translated "have I offended;" see SIN.

OFFENDER

opheiletēs (ὀφειλέτης, 3781), "a debtor," is translated "offenders" in Luke 13:4, RV (RV and KJV marg., "debtors;" KJV, "sinners"). See DEBTOR.

Note: In Acts 25:11, KJV, *adikeō*, "to do wrong," is translated "be an offender" (RV, "am a wrong-doer").

OFFER, OFFERING

A. Verbs.

1. *prospherō* (προσφέρω, 4374), primarily, "to bring to" (*pros*, "to," *pherō*, "to bring"), also denotes "to offer," (*a*) of the sacrifice of Christ Himself, Heb. 8:3; of Christ in virtue of his High Priesthood (RV, "this *high priest*"; KJV, "this man"); 9:14, 25 (negative), 28; 10:12; (*b*) of offerings under, or according to, the Law, e.g., Matt. 8:4; Mark 1:44; Acts 7:42; 21:26; Heb. 5:1, 3; 8:3; 9:7, 9; 10:1-2, 8, 11; (*c*) of "offerings" previous to the Law, Heb. 11:4, 17 (of Isaac by Abraham); (*d*) of gifts "offered" to Christ, Matt. 2:11, RV, "offered" (KJV, "presented unto"); (*e*) of prayers "offered" by Christ, Heb. 5:7; (*f*) of the vinegar "offered" to Him in mockery by the soldiers at the cross, Luke 23:36; (*g*) of the slaughter of disciples by persecutors, who think they are "offering" service to God, John 16:2, RV (KJV, "doeth"); (*h*) of money "offered" by Simon the sorcerer, Acts 8:18. See BRING, A, No. 8, DEAL WITH, No. 2.

2. *anapherō* (ἀναφέρω, 399), primarily, "to lead" or "carry up" (*ana*), also denotes "to offer," (*a*) of Christ's sacrifice, Heb. 7:27; (*b*) of sacrifices under the Law, Heb. 7:27; (*c*) of such previous to the Law, Jas. 2:21 (of Isaac by Abraham); (*d*) of praise, Heb. 13:15; (*e*) of

spiritual sacrifices in general, 1 Pet. 2:5. See BEAR, No. 3, BRING, A, No. 2.

3. *didomi* (δίδωμι, 1325), to give, is translated "to offer" in Luke 2:24; in Rev. 8:3, KJV, "offer" (RV, "add;" marg., "give"). See GIVE.

4. *parechō* (παρέχω, 3930), "to furnish, offer, present, supply," is used in Luke 6:29, of "offering" the other cheek to be smitten after receiving a similar insult; for the KJV marg., in Acts 17:31, see ASSURANCE, A, No. 1. See BRING, A, No. 21.

5. *spendō* (σπένδω, 4689), "to pour out as a drink offering, make a libation," is used figuratively in the passive voice in Phil. 2:17, "offered" (RV marg., "poured out as a drink offering"; KJV marg., "poured forth"). In 2 Tim. 4:6, "I am already being offered," RV (marg., "poured out as a drink-offering"), the apostle is referring to his approaching death, upon the sacrifice of his ministry.¶ This use of the word is exemplified in the papyri writings.

Notes: (1) In Luke 11:12, KJV *epididōmi*, "to give" (*epi*, "over," in the sense of "instead of," and No. 3), is translated "will he offer" (RV, and KJV marg., "will he give"). (2) In Acts 7:41, KJV, *anagō*, "to lead up" or "bring up," is rendered "offered" (RV, "brought"). (3) In Acts 15:29; 21:25 and 1 Cor. 8:1, 4, 10; 10:19, KJV, *eidōlothutos*, "sacrificed to idols," is translated "offered to idols" (*thuō* denotes "to sacrifice"). See SACRIFICE.

B. Nouns.

1. *prosphora* (προσφορά, 4376), lit., "a bringing to" (akin to A, No. 1), hence an "offering," in the NT a sacrificial "offering," (*a*) of Christ's sacrifice, Eph. 5:2; Heb. 10:10 (of His body); 10:14; negatively, of there being no repetition, 10:18; (*b*) of "offerings" under, or according to, the Law, Acts 21:26; Heb. 10:5, 8; (*c*) of gifts in kind conveyed to needy Jews, Acts 24:17; (*d*) of the presentation of believers themselves (saved from among the Gentiles) to God, Rom. 15:16.¶

2. *holokautōma* (ὁλοκαύτωμα, 3646), "a burnt offering": see BURNT.

3. *anathēma* (ἀνάθημα, 334) denotes "a gift set up in a temple, a votive offering" (*ana*, "up," *tithēmi*, "to place"), Luke 21:5, RV "offerings" (KJV, "gifts")¶ Cf. *anathema* (see CURSE).

Notes: (1) In Luke 21:4, KJV, the plural of *dōron*, "a gift," is translated "offerings" (RV, "gifts"). (2) In Rom. 8:3 and Heb. 13:11, the RV, "as an offering" is added to complete the sacrificial meaning of *peri*.

OFFICE

A. Nouns.

1. *praxis* (πρᾶξις, 4234), "a doing, deed" (akin to *prassō*, "to do or practice"), also denotes "an acting" or "function," translated "office" in Rom. 12:4. See DEED.

2. *hierateia* (ἱερατεία, 2405), or *hieratia*, denotes "a priests's office," Luke 1:9; Heb. 7:5, RV, "priest's office" (KJV "office of the priesthood"). ¶

B. Verb.

hierateuō (ἱερατεύω, 2407), "to officiate as a priest" (akin to A, No. 2), is translated "he executed the priest's office" in Luke 1:8. The word is frequent in inscriptions.¶

Notes: (1) In Rom. 11:13, KJV, *diakonia*, "a ministry," is translated "office" (RV, "ministry"). (2) In Acts 1:20, RV, *episkopē*, "an overseership," is translated "office" (marg., "overseership"; KJV, "bishopric"). (3) In 1 Tim. 3:1, the word "office," in the phrase "the office of a bishop," has nothing to represent it in the original; the RV marg. gives "overseer" for "bishop," and the phrase lit. is "overseership"; so in vv. 10, 13, where the KJV has "use (and 'used') the office of a deacon," the RV rightly omits "office," and translates the verb *diakoneō*, "to serve," "let them serve as deacons" and "(they that) have served (well) as deacons."

OFFICER

1. *hupēretēs* (ὑπηρέτης, 5257), for the original of which see MINISTER, A, No. 3, is translated "officer," with the following applications, (a) to a magistrate's attendant, Matt. 5:25; (b) to officers of the synagogue, or officers or bailiffs of the Sanhedrin, Matt. 26:58; Mark 14:54, 65; John 7:32, 45–46; 18:3, 12, 18, 22; 19:6; Acts 5:22, 26. See MINISTER, SERVANT.

2. *praktōr* (πράκτωρ, 4233), lit., "one who does," or "accomplishes" (akin to *prassō*, "to do"), was used in Athens of one who exacts payment, a collector (the word is frequently used in the papyri of a public accountant); hence, in general, a court "officer," an attendant in a court of justice (so Deissmann); the word is used in Luke 12:58 (twice).¶ In the Sept., Isa. 3:12.¶

OFFSCOURING

peripsēma (περίψημα, 4067), "that which is wiped off" (akin to *peripsaō*, "to wipe off all round"; *peri*, "around," *psaō*, "to wipe"), hence, "offscouring," is used metaphorically in 1 Cor. 4:13. This and the synonymous word *perikatharma*, "refuse, rubbish," "were used especially of condemned criminals of the lowest classes, who were sacrificed as expiatory offerings . . . because of their degraded life" (Lightfoot).¶

OFFSPRING

1. *gennēma* (γέννημα, 1081), akin to *gennaō*, "to beget," denotes "the offspring of men and animals," Matt. 3:7; 12:34; 23:33; Luke 3:7, RV, "offspring" (KJV, "generation"). See FRUIT.¶

2. *genos* (γένος, 1085), "a race, family" (akin to *ginomai*, "to become"), denotes "an offspring," Acts 17:28, 29; Rev. 22:16. See GENERATION, KIND.

OFT, OFTEN, OFTENER, OFTENTIMES, OFT-TIMES

A. Adverbs.

1. *pollakis* (πολλάκις, 4178), akin to *polus*, "much, many," is variously translated, e.g., "oft-times," Matt. 17:15 (KJV, "oft," 2nd part); "many times," 2 Cor. 8:22, RV (KJV, "oftentimes"); "oft," 2 Cor. 11:23; "often" (v. 26).

2. *polla* (πολλά, 4183**), the neuter plural of *polus*, is translated "oft" in Matt. 9:14; some ancient authorities omit it here (see RV marg.); in Rom. 15:22, with the article, RV, "these many times" (KJV, "much").

3. *posakis* (ποσάκις, 4212), an interrogative numeral adverb, "how many times, how oft (or often)?" occurs in Matt. 18:21; 23:37; Luke 13:34.¶

4. *hosakis* (ὁσάκις, 3740), a relative adverb, "as often" (or oft) as, 1 Cor. 11:25–26; Rev. 11:6.¶

5. *pukna* (πυκνά, 4437), the neuter plural of *puknos* (see B), used adverbially, is translated "often" in Luke 5:33.

6. *puknoteron* (πυκνότερον, 4437*), the neuter singular of the comparative degree of *puknos* (cf. No. 5, and see B), "very often," or "so much the oftener," Acts 24:26, "the oftener."¶

Notes: (1) In Luke 8:29, the phrase *pollois chronois*, lit., "many times," is translated "oftentimes" (RV marg., "of a long time"). (2) For the rendering "oft" in Mark 7:3, see DILIGENTLY, D, No. 2.

B. Adjective.

puknos (πυκνός, 4437) primarily signifies "close, compact, solid"; hence, "frequent, often," 1 Tim. 5:23. Cf. A, Nos. 5 and 6.

OIL

elaion (ἔλαιον, 1637), "olive oil," is mentioned over 200 times in the Bible. Different kinds were known in Palestine. The "pure," RV (KJV, "beaten"), mentioned in Exod. 27:20; 29:40; Lev. 24:2; Num. 28:5 (now known as virgin oil), extracted by pressure, without heat, is called "golden" in Zech. 4:12. There were also inferior kinds. In the NT the uses mentioned were (*a*) for lamps, in which the "oil" is a symbol of the Holy Spirit, Matt. 25:3–4, 8; (*b*) as a medicinal agent, for healing, Luke 10:34; (*c*) for anointing at feasts, Luke 7:46; (*d*) on festive occasions, Heb. 1:9, where the reference is probably to the consecration of kings; (*e*) as an accompaniment of miraculous power, Mark 6:13, or of the prayer of faith, Jas. 5:14. For its general use in commerce, see Luke 16:6; Rev. 6:6; 18:13.¶

OINTMENT

muron (μύρον, 3464), a word derived by the ancients from *murō*, "to flow," or from *murra*, "myrrh-oil" (it is probably of foreign origin; see MYRRH). The "ointment" is mentioned in the NT in connection with the anointing of the Lord on the occasions recorded in Matt. 26:7, 9, 12; Mark 14:3–4; Luke 7:37–38, 46; John 11:2; 12:3 (twice), 5. The alabaster cruse mentioned in the passages in Matthew, Mark and Luke was the best of its kind, and the spikenard was one of the costliest of perfumes. "Ointments" were used in preparing a body for burial, Luke 23:56 ("ointments"). Of the act of the woman mentioned in Matt. 26:6–13, the Lord said, "she did it to prepare Me for burial"; her devotion led her to antedate the customary ritual after death, by showing both her affection and her understanding of what was impending. For the use of the various kinds of "ointments" as articles of commerce, see Rev. 18:13.¶

OLD

A. Adjectives.

1. *archaios* (ἀρχαῖος, 744), "original, ancient" (from *archē*, "a beginning": Eng., "archaic," "archaeology," etc.), is used (*a*) of persons belonging to a former age,"(to) them of old time," Matt. 5:21, 33, RV; in some mss. v. 27; the RV rendering is right; not ancient teachers are in view; what was said to them of old time was "to be both recognized in its significance and estimated in its temporary limitations, Christ intending His words to be regarded not as an abrogation, but a deepening and fulfilling" (Cremer); of prophets, Luke 9:8, 19; (*b*) of time long gone by, Acts 15:21; (*c*) of days gone by in a person's experience, Acts 15:7, "a good while ago," lit., "from old (days)," i.e., from the first days onward in the sense of originality, not age; (*d*) of Mnason, "an early disciple," Acts 21:16, RV, not referring to age, but to his being one of the first who had accepted the gospel from the beginning of its proclamation;

(*e*) of things which are "old" in relation to the new, earlier things in contrast to things present, 2 Cor. 5:17, i.e., of what characterized and conditioned the time previous to conversion in a believer's experience, RV, "they are become new," i.e., they have taken on a new complexion and are viewed in an entirely different way; (*f*) of the world (i.e., the inhabitants of the world) just previous to the Flood, 2 Pet. 2:5; (*g*) of the Devil, as "that old serpent," Rev. 12:9; 20:2, "old," not in age, but as characterized for a long period by the evils indicated.¶

Note: For the difference between this and No. 2, see below.

2. *palaios* (παλαιός, 3820), akin to C, No. 1 (Eng., "paleontology," etc.), "of what is of long duration, old in years," etc., a garment, wine (in contrast to *neos;* see NEW), Matt. 9:16–17; Mark 2:21–22 (twice); Luke 5:36–37, 39 (twice); of the treasures of divine truth, Matt. 13:52 (compared with *kainos:* see NEW); of what belongs to the past, e.g., the believer's former self before his conversion, his "old man," "old" because it has been superseded by that which is new, Rom. 6:6; Eph. 4:22 (in contrast to *kainos*); Col. 3:9 (in contrast to *neos*); of the covenant in connection with the Law, 2 Cor. 3:14; of leaven, metaphorical of moral evil, 1 Cor. 5:7, 8 (in contrast to *neos*); of that which was given long ago and remains in force, an "old" commandment, 1 John 2:7 (twice), that which was familiar and well known in contrast to that which is fresh (*kainos*).¶

Note: Palaios denotes "old," "without the reference to beginning and origin contained in *archaios*" (Abbott-Smith), a distinction observed in the papyri (Moulton and Milligan). While sometimes any difference seems almost indistinguishable, yet "it is evident that wherever an emphasis is desired to be laid on the reaching back to a beginning, whatever that beginning may be, *archaios* will be preferred (e.g., of Satan, Rev. 12:9; 20:2, see No. 1). That which . . . is old in the sense of more or less worn out . . . is always *palaios*" (Trench).

3. *presbuteros* (πρεσβύερος, 4245), "older, elder," is used in the plural, as a noun, in Acts 2:17, "old men." See ELDER.

B. Nouns.

1. *gerōn* (γέρων, 1088) denotes "an old man" (from the same root comes Eng., "gray"), John 3:4.¶

2. *presbutēs* (πρεσβύτης, 4246), "an old man," Luke 1:18, is translated "aged" in Titus 2:2; Philem. 9 (for this, however, see the RV marg. See AGED.

3. *gēras* (γῆρας, 1094), "old age," occurs in Luke 1:36.¶

Note: Augustine (quoted by Trench, §cvii, 2) speaks of the distinction observed among Greeks, that *presbutēs* conveys the suggestion of gravity.

C. Adverbs.

1. *palai* (πάλαι, 3819) denotes "long ago, of old," Heb. 1:1, RV, "of old time" (KJV, "in time past"); in Jude 4, "of old"; it is used as an adjective in 2 Pet. 1:9, "(his) old (sins)," lit., "his sins of old." See WHILE.

2. *ekpalai* (ἔκπαλαι, 1597), "from of old, for a long time" (*ek*, "from," and No. 1), occurs in 2 Pet. 2:3, RV, "from of old" (KJV, "of a long time"); 3:5. See LONG, B, *Note* (2).

Note: In 1 Pet. 3:5, KJV, the particle *pote*, "once, formerly, ever, sometime," is translated "in the old time" (RV, "aforetime"); in 2 Pet. 1:21, "in old time" (RV, "ever"), KJV marg., "at any time."

D. Verbs.

1. *palaioō* (παλαιόω, 3822), akin to A, No. 2, denotes, in the active voice, "to make or declare old," Heb. 8:13 (1st part); in the passive voice, "to become old," of things worn out by time and use, Luke 12:33; Heb. 1:11, "shall wax old," lit., "shall be made old," i.e., worn out; in 8:13 (2nd part), RV, "is becoming old" (KJV "decayeth"); here and in the 1st part of the verse, the verb may have the meaning "to abrogate"; for the next verb in the verse, see No. 2.¶

2. *gēraskō* (γηράσκω, 1095), from *gēras*, "old age" (akin to B, No. 1), "to grow old," is translated "thou shalt be old," in John 21:18; "waxeth aged," Heb. 8:13, RV (KJV, "waxeth old").¶

Notes: (1) In John 8:57, *echō*, "to have," is used with "fifty years" as the object, signifying, "Thou art (not yet fifty years) old," lit., "Thou hast not yet fifty years." (2) In Mark 5:42, RV, the verb *eimi*, "to be," with the phrase "of twelve years" is translated "was ... old" (KJV, "was *of the age* of").

OLDNESS

palaiotēs (παλαιότης, 3821), from *palaios* (see A, No. 2, above), occurs in Rom. 7:6, of "the letter," i.e., "the law," with its rules of conduct, mere outward conformity to which has yielded place in the believer's service to a response to the inward operation of the Holy Spirit. The word is contrasted with *kainotēs*, "newness."¶

OLD WIVES'

graōdēs (γραώδης, 1126), an adjective, signifying "old-womanish" (from *graus*, "an old woman"), is said of fables, in 1 Tim. 4:7.¶

OLIVES (OLIVE BERRIES), OLIVE TREE

1. *elaia* (ἐλαία, 1636) denotes (*a*) "an olive tree," Rom. 11:17, 24; Rev. 11:4 (plural); the Mount of Olives was so called from the numerous olive trees there, and indicates the importance attached to such; the Mount is mentioned in the NT in connection only with the Lord's life on earth, Matt. 21:1; 24:3; 26:30; Mark 11:1; 13:3; 14:26; Luke 19:37; 22:39; John 8:1; (*b*) "an olive," Jas. 3:12, RV (KJV, "olive berries").¶

2. *elaiōn* (ἐλαιών, 1638), "an olive grove" or "olive garden," the ending—*ōn*, as in this class of noun, here indicates "a place set with trees of the kind designated by the primitive" (Thayer); hence it is applied to the Mount of Olives, Luke 19:29; 21:37; Acts 1:12 ("Olivet"): in the first two of these and in Mark 11:1, some mss. have the form of the noun as in No. 1.¶

3. *kallielaios* (καλλιέλαιος, 2565), "the garden olive" (from *kallos*, "beauty," and No. 1), occurs in Rom. 11:24, "a good olive tree."¶

4. *agrielaios* (ἀγριέλαιος, 65), an adjective (from *agrios*, "growing in the fields, wild," and No. 1), denoting "of the wild olive," is used as a noun in Rom. 11:17, 24, "a wild olive tree" (RV, in the latter verse).¶

For **OMITTED** (Matt. 23:23, KJV) see **LEAVE** (undone), No. 1

For **OMNIPOTENT** (Rev. 19:6) see **ALMIGHTY**

For **ON** see †, p. 1

ONCE (at; for all)

1. *hapax* (ἅπαξ, 530) denotes (*a*) "once, one time," 2 Cor. 11:25; Heb. 9:7, 26–27; 12:26–27; in the phrase "once and again," lit., "once and twice," Phil. 4:16; 1 Thess. 2:18; (*b*) "once for all," of what is of perpetual validity, not requiring repetition, Heb. 6:4; 9:28; 10:2; 1 Pet. 3:18; Jude 3, RV, "once for all" (KJV, "once"); v. 5 (ditto); in some mss. 1 Pet. 3:20 (so the KJV).¶

2. *ephapax* (ἐφάπαξ, 2178), a strengthened form of No. 1 (*epi*, "upon"), signifies (*a*) "once for all," Rom. 6:10; Heb. 7:27, RV (KJV, "once"); 9:12 (ditto); 10:10; (*b*) "at once," 1 Cor. 15:6.¶

3. *pote* (ποτέ, 4218) denotes "once upon a time, formerly, sometime," e.g., Rom. 7:9; Gal. 1:23, 1st part, RV, "once" (KJV, "in times past"); 2nd part, KJV and RV, "once"; Gal. 2:6, RV marg., "what they once were" (to be preferred

to the text, "whatsoever they were"), the reference probably being to the association of the twelve apostles with the Lord during His ministry on earth; upon this their partisans based their claim for the exclusive authority of these apostles, which Paul vigorously repudiated; in Eph. 5:8, RV, "once" (KJV, "sometimes"). See AFORETIME, LAST, LENGTH (at), TIME (past).

Note: In Luke 23:18, KJV, *pamplēthei*, denoting "with the whole multitude" (*pas*, "all," *plēthos*, "a multitude"), is rendered "all at once," RV, "all together").¶

ONE

A. Numeral.

heis (εἷς, 1520), the first cardinal numeral, masculine (feminine and neuter nominative forms are *mia* and *hen*, respectively), is used to signify (1) (*a*) "one" in contrast to many, e.g., Matt. 25:15; Rom. 5:18, RV, "(through) one (trespass)," i.e., Adam's transgression, in contrast to the "one act of righteousness," i.e., the death of Christ (not as KJV, "the offense of one," and "the righteousness of one"); (*b*) metaphorically, "union" and "concord," e.g., John 10:30; 11:52; 17:11, 21–22; Rom. 12:4–5; Phil. 1:27; (2) emphatically, (*a*) a single ("one"), to the exclusion of others, e.g., Matt. 21:24; Rom. 3:10; 1 Cor. 9:24; 1 Tim. 2:5 (twice); (*b*) "one, alone," e.g., Mark 2:7, RV (KJV, "only"); 10:18; Luke 18:19; (*c*) "one and the same," e.g., Rom. 3:30, RV, "God is one," i.e., there is not "one" God for the Jew and one for the Gentile; cf. Gal. 3:20, which means that in a promise there is no other party; 1 Cor. 3:8; 11:5; 12:11; 1 John 5:8 (lit., "and the three are into one," i.e., united in "one" and the same witness); (3) a certain "one," in the same sense as the indefinite pronoun *tis* (see B, No. 1), e.g., Matt. 8:19, RV, "a (scribe)," marg., "one (scribe)," KJV, "a certain (scribe)"; 19:16, "one;" in Rev. 8:13, RV marg., "one (eagle)"; *heis tis* are used together in Luke 22:50; John 11:49; this occurs frequently in the papyri (Moulton, *Prol.*, p. 96); (4) distributively, with *hekastos*, "each," i.e., "every one," e.g., Luke 4:40; Acts 2:6, "every man" (lit., "every one"); in the sense of "one . . . and one," e.g., John 20:12; or "one" . . . followed by *allos* or *heteros*, "the other," e.g., Matt. 6:24; or by a second *heis*, e.g., Matt. 24:40, RV, "one"; John 20:12; in Rom. 12:5 *heis* is preceded by *kata (kath')* in the sense of "severally (members) one (of another)," RV (KJV, "every one . . . one"); cf. Mark 14:19; in 1 Thess. 5:11 the phrase in the 2nd part, "each other," RV (KJV, "one another"), is, lit., "one the one"; (5) as an ordinal number, equivalent to *prōtos*, "first," in the phrase "the first day of the week,"

lit. and idiomatically, "one of sabbaths," signifying "the first day after the sabbath," e.g., Matt. 28:1; Mark 16:2; Acts 20:7; 1 Cor. 16:2. Moulton remarks on the tendency for certain cardinal numerals to replace ordinals (*Prol.,* p. 96).

B. Pronouns.

1. *tis* (τις, 5100), an indefinite pronoun signifying "a certain one, some one, any one, one" (the neuter form *ti* denotes "a certain thing"), is used (*a*) like a noun, e.g., Acts 5:25; 19:32; 21:34; 1 Cor. 3:4; or with the meaning "someone," e.g., Acts 8:31, RV, "some one" (KJV, "some man"); Rom. 5:7; (*b*) as an adjective; see CERTAIN, *Note* (3), SOME.

2. *hos* (ὅς, 3739), as a relative pronoun, signifies "who"; as a demonstrative pronoun, "this," or "the one" in contrast with "the other," or "another," e.g., Rom. 14:2, KJV (RV, "one man"); 1 Cor. 12:8.

Notes: (1) The RV often substitutes "one" for "man," e.g., Matt. 17:8 (*oudeis*, "no one"); 1 Cor. 3:21 (i.e., "no person"); 1 Cor. 15:35; 1 Thess. 5:15; 2 Tim. 4:16; 1 John 2:27; 3:3. (2) The pronoun *houtos* is sometimes translated "this one," e.g., Luke 7:8. (3) In 1 Pet. 3:8, KJV, *homophrōn*, "likeminded" (RV), is translated "of one mind" (lit., "of the same mind"). (4) In Acts 7:26, "at one," is, lit., "unto peace" (see PEACE). (5) For "every one" in Acts 5:16 see EVERY, No. 2. (6) In Mark 9:26 *nekros*, "dead," is translated "one dead." (7) In Acts 2:1 "in one place" translates *epi to auto*, lit., "to the same," which may mean "for the same (purpose)"; in 1 Cor. 11:20 and 14:23, the RV translates it "together." (8) In Mark 1:7, KJV, the article *ho*, "the," is rendered "one" (RV, "he that"). (9) In Mark 7:14, KJV, the plural of *pas*, "all" (so RV), is translated "every one"; in Matt. 5:28, KJV, *pas*, with the article, is translated "whosoever" (RV "every one who"). (10) In Acts 1:24, KJV, "whether" is, lit., and as the RV, "the one whom." (11) In 2 Thess. 2:7, the article is rendered "one that," RV (KJV, "he who").

See also ACCORD, CONSENT, B, No. 1, END, C, *Note* (6), EYE (with one), GREAT, HOLY, LITTLE, MIND, NATION, WICKED.

ONE ANOTHER or ONE . . . ANOTHER, ONE . . . THE OTHER

Notes: (1) This translates a number of words and phrases, (*a*) *allēlōn*, a reciprocal pronoun in the genitive plural, signifying "of, or from, one another" (akin to *allos*, "another"), e.g., Matt. 25:32; John 13:22; Acts 15:39; 19:38; 1 Cor. 7:5; Gal. 5:17; the accusative *allēlous* denotes "one another," e.g., Acts 7:26, lit., "why do ye wrong one another?"; 2 Thess. 1:3, RV; in Eph.

4:32 and Col. 3:13, e.g., RV, "each other"; in 1 Thess. 5:15, "one (toward) another," RV; the dative *allēlois* denotes "one to another," e.g., Luke 7:32; (*b*) different forms of the plural of *heautou*, "of himself," used as a reciprocal pronoun, e.g., Eph. 5:19, RV, "one to another" (KJV, and RV marg., "to yourselves"); see also *Note* (5); (*c*) *allos pros allon*, "one to another," Acts 2:12; (*d*) *allos . . . heteros*, 1 Cor. 12:8 (for the difference between *allos* and *heteros*, see ANOTHER); (*e*) *hos men . . . hos de* (in various forms of the pronoun), lit., "this indeed . . . but that," e.g., Luke 23:33; Rom. 9:21; 14:5; 1 Cor. 11:21; 2 Cor. 2:16; Phil. 1:16–17; (*f*) *heteros . . . heteros*, "one . . . another," 1 Cor. 15:40. (2) In Matt. 24:2; Mark 13:2; Luke 19:44, and 21:6, "one (stone upon) another" is, lit., "stone upon stone." (3) In Heb. 10:25, *"one another"* is necessarily added in English to complete the sense of *parakaleō*, "to exhort." (4) In 1 Pet. 3:8, KJV, "one of another" represents nothing in the original (the RV, "compassionate" sufficiently translates the adjective *sumpathēs*: see COMPASSION, C.). (5) In Mark 9:10, KJV, *pros heautous*, "among yourselves" (RV), is translated "one with another." (6) In 1 Tim. 5:21, KJV, the accusative case of *prosklisis*, "partiality," preceded by *kata*, "according to," is translated "preferring one before another" (RV, "prejudice"; marg., "preference," lit., "according to partiality").

ONLY

A. Adjectives.

1. *monos* (μόνος, 3441), "alone, solitary," is translated "only," e.g., in Matt. 4:10; 12:4; 17:8; 1 Cor. 9:6; 14:36; Phil. 4:15; Col. 4:11; 2 John 1; it is used as an attribute of God in John 5:44; 17:3; Rom. 16:27; 1 Tim. 1:17; 1 Tim. 6:15–16; Jude 4, 25; Rev. 15:4. See ALONE, A.

2. *monogenēs* (μονογενής, 3439), "only begotten" (No. 1 and *genos*, "offspring"), has the meaning "only," of human offspring, in Luke 7:12; 8:42; 9:38; the term is one of endearment, as well as of singleness. For Heb. 11:17 see ONLY BEGOTTEN.

B. Adverbs.

1. *monon* (μόνον, 3441), the neuter of A, No. 1, "only, exclusively," is translated "only," e.g., in Matt. 5:47; 8:8; John 5:18; 11:52; 12:9; 13:9; frequently in Acts, Romans and Galatians. See ALONE, B, No. 1.

2. *plēn* (πλήν, 4133), "howbeit, except that," is translated "only that" in the RV of Phil. 1:18 (KJV, "notwithstanding"); "only" in 3:16 (KJV, "nevertheless").

Notes: (1) In Mark 2:7, KJV, *heis*, "one" (so RV), is translated "only"; in Jas. 4:12, RV, "one only" (KJV, "one"). (2) For "only that" in Acts 21:25, KJV, see the RV. (3) The conjunction *ei*, "if," with the negative *mē*, "not," is translated "but only" in Luke 4:26, RV (KJV, "save"); 4:27 (KJV, "saving"); "only" in 1 Cor. 7:17 (KJV, "but"); in some mss. in Acts 21:25 (KJV "save only").

ONLY BEGOTTEN

monogenēs (μονογενής, 3439) is used five times, all in the writings of the apostle John, of Christ as the Son of God; it is translated "only begotten" in Heb. 11:17 of the relationship of Isaac to Abraham.

With reference to Christ, the phrase "the only begotten from the Father," John 1:14, RV (see also the marg.), indicates that as the Son of God He was the sole representative of the Being and character of the One who sent Him. In the original the definite article is omitted both before "only begotten" and before "Father," and its absence in each case serves to lay stress upon the characteristics referred to in the terms used. The apostle's object is to demonstrate what sort of glory it was that he and his fellow apostles had seen. That he is not merely making a comparison with earthly relationships is indicated by *para*, "from." The glory was that of a unique relationship and the word "begotten" does not imply a beginning of His Sonship. It suggests relationship indeed, but must be distinguished from generation as applied to man.

We can only rightly understand the term "the only begotten" when used of the Son, in the sense of unoriginated relationship. "The begetting is not an event of time, however remote, but a fact irrespective of time. The Christ did not *become*, but necessarily and eternally *is* the Son. He, a Person, possesses every attribute of pure Godhood. This necessitates eternity, absolute being; in this respect He is not 'after' the Father" (Moule). The expression also suggests the thought of the deepest affection, as in the case of the OT word *yachid*, variously rendered, "only one," Gen. 22:2, 12; "only son," Jer. 6:26; Amos 8:10; Zech. 12:10; "only beloved," Prov. 4:3, and "darling," Ps. 22:20; 35:17.

In John 1:18 the clause "the only begotten son, which is in the bosom of the Father," expresses both His eternal union with the Father in the Godhead and the ineffable intimacy and love between them, the Son sharing all the Father's counsels and enjoying all His affections. Another reading is *monogenēs Theos*, "God only-begotten." In John 3:16 the statement, "God so loved the world that He gave His only begotten son," must not be taken to mean that Christ became the only begotten son by incarnation. The value and the greatness of the gift lay in the Sonship of Him who was given. His Sonship was not the effect of His being given. In John 3:18 the phrase "the name of the only begotten son of God" lays stress upon the full revelation of God's character and will, His love and grace, as conveyed in the name of One who, being in a unique relationship to Him, was provided by Him as the object of faith. In 1 John 4:9 the statement "God hath sent His only begotten son into the world" does not mean that God sent out into the world one who at His birth in Bethlehem had become His Son. Cf. the parallel statement, "God sent forth the Spirit of His Son," Gal. 4:6, RV, which could not mean that God sent forth One who became His Spirit when He sent Him.¶

For **ONSET**, Acts 14:5, RV, see **ASSAULT** and **IMPULSE**

For **ONWARD**, 2 John 9, RV, see **GO**, No. 10

OPEN, OPENING (for OPENLY, see below)

A. Verbs.

1. *anoigō* (ἀνοίγω, 455) is used (1) transitively, (*a*) literally, of "a door or gate," e.g., Acts 5:19; graves, Matt. 27:52; a sepulchre, Rom. 3:13; a book, e.g., Luke 4:17 (some mss. have No. 4); Rev. 5:2–5; 10:8; the seals of a roll, e.g., Rev. 5:9; 6:1; the eyes, Acts 9:40; the mouth of a fish, Matt. 17:27; "the pit of the abyss," Rev. 9:2, RV; heaven and the heavens, Matt. 3:16; Luke 3:21; Acts 10:11 (for 7:56, see No. 2); Rev. 19:11; "the temple of the tabernacle of the testimony in heaven," Rev. 15:5; by metonymy, for that which contained treasures, Matt. 2:11; (*b*) metaphorically, e.g., Matt. 7:7–8; 25:11; Rev. 3:7; Hebraistically, "to open the mouth," of beginning to speak, e.g., Matt. 5:2; 13:35; Acts 8:32, 35; 10:34; 18:14; Rev. 13:6 (cf., e.g., Num. 22:28; Job. 3:1; Isa. 50:5); and of recovering speech, Luke 1:64; of the earth "opening," Rev. 12:16; of the "opening" of the eyes, Acts 26:18; the ears, Mark 7:35 (in the best mss.; some have No. 2); (2) intransitively (perfect tense, active, in the Greek), (*a*) literally, of "the heaven," John 1:51, RV, "opened;" (*b*) metaphorically, of "speaking freely," 2 Cor. 6:11.

2. *dianoigō* (διανοίγω, 1272), "to open up completely" (*dia*, "through," intensive, and No. 1), is used (*a*) literally, Luke 2:23; Acts 7:56, in the best mss.; (*b*) metaphorically, of the eyes, Mark 7:34; Luke 24:31; of the Scriptures, v. 32 and Acts 17:3; of the mind, Luke 24:45, RV

(KJV, "understanding"); of the heart, Acts 16:14.¶

3. *agō* (ἄγω, 71), "to lead," or "to keep or spend a day," is so used in Acts 19:38: see KEEP, *Note* (2).

4. *anaptussō* (ἀναπτύσσω, 380), "to unroll" (*ana*, "back," *ptussō*, "to roll"), is found in some mss. in Luke 4:17 (of the roll of Isaiah), and translated "He had opened" (KJV); see No. 1.¶

Notes: (1) For Heb. 4:13, "laid open," RV (KJV, "opened") see LAY, No. 18. (2) In 2 Cor. 3:18, KJV, *anakaluptō*, "to unveil," is translated "open" (RV, "unveiled," which consistently continues the metaphor of the veil upon the heart of Israel). (3) In Mark 1:10, KJV, *schizō*, "to rend" or "split," is translated "opened," of the heavens, RV, "rent asunder," KJV marg., "cloven, or, rent." (4) For *prodēlos*, in 1 Tim.5:24, KJV, "open beforehand," see EVIDENT, A, No. 3. (5) For "be opened" See EPHPHATHA. (6) For "open (your hearts)," 2 Cor. 7:2, RV, see RECEIVE, No. 18.

B. Nouns.

1. *anoixis* (ἄνοιξις, 457), "an opening" (akin to A, No. 1), is used in Eph. 6:19, metaphorically of the "opening" of the mouth as in A, No. 1 (2), (*b*).¶

2. *opē* (ὀπή, 3692), "an opening, a hole," is used in Jas. 3:11, of the orifice of a fountain: see CAVE, HOLE, PLACE.

OPENLY

1. *parrhēsia* (παρρησία, 3954), "freedom of speech, boldness," is used adverbially in the dative case and translated "openly" in Mark 8:32, of a saying of Christ; in John 7:13, of a public statement; in 11:54, of Christ's public appearance; in 7:26 and 18:20, of His public testimony; preceded by the preposition *en*, "in," John 7:4, lit., "in boldness" (cf. v. 10, RV, "publicly"). See BOLD, B.

2. *phanerōs* (φανερῶς, 5318), manifestly, openly: see EVIDENT, B.

Notes: (1) In Gal. 3:1, "openly set forth" translates the verb *prographō*, lit., "to write before," as of the OT, Rom. 15:4 (cf. Jude 4), and of a previous letter, Eph. 3:3. In Gal. 3:1, however, "it is probably used in another sense, unexampled in the Scriptures but not uncommon in the language of the day, = 'proclaimed,' 'placarded,' as a magistrate proclaimed the fact that an execution had been carried out, placarding his proclamation in a public place. The Apostle carries on his metaphor of the 'evil eye;' as a preventive of such mischief it was common to post up charms on the walls of houses, a glance at which was supposed to counteract any evil influence to which a person may have been subjected. 'Notwithstanding,' he says, in effect, 'that the fact that Christ had been crucified was placarded before your very eyes in our preaching, you have allowed yourselves to be ... fascinated by the enemies of the Cross of Christ, when you had only to look at Him to escape their malignant influence;' cf. the interesting and instructive parallel in Num. 21:9."* (2) In some mss. in Matt. 6:4, 6, 18, the phrase *en tǭ phanerǭ*, lit., "in the manifest," is found (KJV, "openly"); see the RV (3) For *emphanēs*, rendered "openly" in Acts 10:40, KJV, see MANIFEST. (4) In Acts 16:37, KJV, the dative case of the adjective *dēmosios*, "belonging to the people" (*dēmos*, "a people"), "public" (so RV), used adverbially, is translated "openly"; in 18:28 and 20:20, "publicly." For the adjective itself, "public," see Acts 5:18. See PUBLIC.¶

For OPERATION see WORKING

OPPORTUNITY (lack)

A. Nouns.

1. *kairos* (καιρός, 2540), primarily, "a due measure," is used of "a fixed and definite period, a time, season," and is translated "opportunity" in Gal. 6:10 and Heb. 11:15. See SEASON, TIME, WHILE.

2. *eukairia* (εὐκαιρία, 2120), "a fitting time, opportunity" (*eu*, "well," and No. 1), occurs in Matt. 26:16 and Luke 22:6.¶ Cf. *eukairos*, "seasonable"; see CONVENIENT.

3. *topos* (τόπος, 5117), "a place," is translated "opportunity" in Acts 25:16, RV (KJV, "licence"). See PLACE, ROOM.

B. Verbs.

1. *eukaireō* (εὐκαιρέω, 2119), "to have time or leisure" (akin to A, No. 2), is translated "he shall have opportunity" in 1 Cor. 16:12, RV (KJV, "convenient time"). See LEISURE.

2. *akaireomai* (ἀκαιρέομαι, 170), "to have no opportunity" (*a*, negative, and *kairos*, "season"), occurs in Phil. 4:10.¶

OPPOSE

1. *antikeimai* (ἀντίκειμαι, 480) : see ADVERSARY, B.

2. *antitassō* (ἀντιτάσσω, 498) is used in the middle voice in the sense of setting oneself against (*anti*, "against," *tassō*, "to order, set"), "opposing oneself to," Acts 18:6; elsewhere rendered by the verb "to resist," Rom. 13:2; Jas. 4:6; 5:6; 1 Pet. 5:5. See RESIST.¶

3. *antidiatithēmi* (ἀντιδιατίθημι, 475) signifies "to place oneself in opposition, oppose"

(anti, "against," *dia*, "through," intensive, *tithēmi*, "to place"), 2 Tim. 2:25. The KJV and RV translate this as a middle voice, "them (KJV, 'those') that oppose themselves." Field (*Notes on the Trans. of the NT*) points out that in the only other known instance of the verb it is passive. The sense is practically the same if it is rendered "those who are opposed."¶

OPPOSITIONS

antithesis (ἀντίθεσις, 477), "a contrary position" (*anti*, "against," *tithēmi*, "to place"; Eng., "antithesis"), occurs in 1 Tim. 6:20.¶

OPPRESS

1. *katadunasteuō* (καταδυναστεύω, 2616), "to exercise power over" (*kata*, "down," *dunastēs*, "a potentate": *dunamai*, "to have power"), "to oppress," is used, in the passive voice, in Acts 10:38; in the active, in Jas. 2:6.¶

2. *kataponeō* (καταπονέω, 2669) : see DISTRESS, B, No. 4.

For OR see †, p. 1

ORACLE

logion (λόγιον, 3051), a diminutive of *logos*, "a word, narrative, statement," denotes "a divine response or utterance, an oracle"; it is used of (*a*) the contents of the Mosaic Law, Acts 7:38; (*b*) all the written utterances of God through OT writers, Rom. 3:2; (*c*) the substance of Christian doctrine, Heb. 5:12; (*d*) the utterances of God through Christian teachers, 1 Pet. 4:11.¶

Note: Divine "oracles" were given by means of the breastplate of the high priest, in connection with the service of the tabernacle, and the Sept. uses the associated word *logeion* in Exod. 28:15, to describe the breastplate.

ORATION

dēmēgoreō (δημηγορέω, 1215), from *dēmos*, "the people" and *agoreuō*, "to speak in the public assembly, to deliver an oration," occurs in Acts 12:21.¶

ORATOR

rhētōr (ῥήτωρ, 4489), from an obsolete present tense, *rheō*, "to say" (cf. Eng., "rhetoric"), denotes "a public speaker, an orator," Acts 24:1, of Tertullus. Such a person, distinct from the professional lawyer, was hired, as a professional speaker, to make a skillful presentation of a case in court. His training was not legal but rhetorical.¶

* From *Notes on Galatians*, by Hogg and Vine, pp. 106, 107.

ORDAIN

1. *tithēmi* (τίθημι, 5087), to put : see AP-POINT, No. 3.

2. *kathistēmi* (καθίστημι, 2525), from *kata*, "down," or "over against," and *histēmi*, "to cause to stand, to set," is translated "to ordain" in the KJV of Titus 1:5; Heb. 5:1; 8:3. See APPOINT, No. 2.

3. *tassō* (τάσσω, 5021) is translated "to ordain," in Acts 13:48 and Rom. 13:1. See AP-POINT, No. 5.

4. *diatassō* (διατάσσω, 1299) is translated "to ordain" in 1 Cor. 7:17; 9:14; Gal. 3:19, the last in the sense of "administered." Cf. *diatagē*, under DISPOSITION. See APPOINT, No. 6.

5. *horizō* (ὁρίζω, 3724) is twice used of Christ as divinely "ordained" to be the Judge of men, Acts 10:42; 17:31. See DETERMINE, No. 2.

6. *krinō* (κρίνω, 2919), "to divide, separate, decide, judge," is translated "ordained" in Acts 16:4, of the decrees by the apostles and elders in Jerusalem. See JUDGE.

Notes: (1) In 1 Cor. 2:7, KJV, *proorizō*, "to foreordain" (see RV) is translated "ordained." See DETERMINE, No. 3. (2) In Mark 3:14, KJV, *poieō*, "to make," is translated "ordained" (RV, "appointed"). (3) In Heb. 9:6, KJV, *kataskeuazō*, "to prepare" (so RV), is translated "were . . . ordained. See PREPARE. (4) In Acts 14:23, KJV, *cheirotoneō*, "to appoint" (RV), is translated "they had ordained." See APPOINT, No. 11. (5) In Eph. 2:10, KJV, *proetoimazō*, "to prepare before," is translated "hath before ordained" (RV, "afore prepared"); see PREPARE. (6) In Jude 4, KJV, *prographō*, lit., "to write before," is translated "were before . . . ordained" (RV, "were . . . set forth"). See SET (forth). (7) In Acts 1:22, KJV, *ginomai*, "to become," is translated "be ordained" (RV, "become"). (8) In Rom. 7:10, KJV, *"ordained"* represents no word in the original (see RV).

ORDER (Noun and Verb)

A. Nouns.

1. *taxis* (τάξις, 5010), "an arranging, arrangement, order" (akin to *tassō*, "to arrange, draw up in order"), is used in Luke 1:8 of the fixed succession of the course of the priests; of due "order," in contrast to confusion, in the gatherings of a local church, 1 Cor. 14:40; of the general condition of such, Col. 2:5 (some give it a military significance here); of the divinely appointed character or nature of a priesthood, of Melchizedek, as foreshadowing that of Christ, Heb. 5:6, 10; 6:20; 7:11 (where also the character of the Aaronic priesthood is set in contrast); 7:17 (in some mss., v. 21).¶

2. *tagma* (τάγμα, 5001), a more concrete form of No. 1, signifying "that which has been arranged in order," was especially a military term, denoting "a company"; it is used metaphorically in 1 Cor. 15:23 of the various classes of those who have part in the first resurrection.¶

B. Verbs.

1. *anatassomai* (ἀνατάσσομαι, 392), "to arrange in order" (*ana*, "up," and the middle voice of *tassō*, "to arrange"), is used in Luke 1:1, KJV, "to set forth in order" (RV, "to draw up"); the probable meaning is to bring together and so arrange details in "order."¶

2. *diatassō* (διατάσσω, 1299), "to appoint, arrange, charge, give orders to," is used, in the middle voice, in Acts 24:23, "gave order" (RV); 1 Cor. 11:34, "will I set in order"; in the active voice, in 1 Cor. 16:1, "I gave order" (RV). See COMMAND, No. 1.

3. *epidiorthoō* (ἐπιδιορθόω, 1930), "to set in order" (*epi*, "upon," *dia*, "through, intensive," and *orthos*, "straight"), is used in Titus 1:5, in the sense of setting right again what was defective, a commission to Titus, not to add to what the apostle himself had done, but to restore what had fallen into disorder since the apostle had labored in Crete; this is suggested by the *epi*.¶

C. Adverb.

kathexēs (καθεξῆς, 2517) is translated "in order" in Luke 1:3; Acts 11:4, RV (KJV, "by order"); Acts 18:23. See AFTERWARD, No. 3.

Note: In 2 Cor. 11:32, RV, the phrase "in order to" (as with the KJV, "desirous to") represents nothing in the original: the infinitive mood of the verb *piazō* expresses the purpose, viz., "to take."

ORDERLY

kosmios (κόσμιος, 2887), an adjective signifying "decent, modest, orderly" (akin to *kosmos*, "order, adornment"), is translated "modest" in 1 Tim. 2:9; "orderly" in 3:2, RV (KJV, "of good behavior"). See MODEST.¶

Note: For *stoicheō*, in Acts 21:24, "thou walkest orderly," see WALK.

ORDINANCE

A. Nouns.

1. *dikaiōma* (δικαίωμα, 1345) : see JUSTIFICATION, No. 2.

2. *diatagē* (διαταγή, 1296) is translated "ordinances" in Rom. 13:2. See DISPOSITION.

3. *dogma* (δόγμα, 1378) is translated "ordinances" in Eph. 2:15 and Col. 2:14. See DE-CREE.

4. *ktisis* (κτίσις, 2937), "a creation, creature," is translated "ordinance" in 1 Pet. 2:13. See CREATE, B, No. 1.

Note: In 1 Cor. 11:2, KJV, *paradosis*, "a tradition" (marg., and RV, "traditions"), is translated "ordinances." See TRADITION.

B. Verb.

dogmatizō (δογματίζω, 1379), akin to A, No. 3, "to decree," signifies, in the middle voice, "to subject oneself to an ordinance," Col. 2:20.¶ In the Sept., Esth. 3:9; in some texts, Dan. 2:13, 15.¶

OTHER

1. *allos* (ἄλλος, 243) indicates numeral distinction of objects of similar character, and is used (*a*) absolutely, e.g., Matt. 20:3 (plural); (*b*) attached to a noun, e.g., Matt. 21:36; (*c*) with the article, e.g., Matt. 5:39; 1 Cor. 14:29 (plural, RV); in Matt. 13:5; Luke 9:19; John 9:9, e.g., RV, "others" (KJV, "some"); in Matt. 25:20, RV, "other" (KJV, "beside them ... more"). See AN-OTHER, MORE, B, *Note* (1), SOME.

2. *heteros* (ἕτερος, 2087) indicates either numerical distinction, e.g., Luke 4:43; 5:7; or generic distinction, different in character, etc., e.g., Luke 9:29, "(the fashion of His countenance) was altered," lit., "became other"; 23:32, "two others, (malefactors)," RV, where the plural serves to make the necessary distinction between them and Christ; Acts 2:4; 19:39 ("other matters"); 1 Cor. 14:21, KJV, "other" (RV, "strange"); 2 Cor. 11:4 (2nd and 3rd parts, RV, "different"; in the 1st clause, *allos*, "another"). For the distinction between this and No. 1, see under ANOTHER.

3. *loipos* (λοιπός, 3062**) signifies "remaining, the rest." It is translated "other," or "others," e.g., in Matt. 25:11; Mark 4:19; Luke 18:9; 24:10 (in v. 9, "the rest"); but in Luke 8:10; Acts 28:9; Rom. 1:13; 1 Cor. 9:5; Eph. 2:3; 1 Thess. 4:13; 5:6; 1 Tim. 5:20, e.g., the RV renders this word "the rest" (KJV, "other" or "others"); in Eph. 4:17, some mss. have *loipa*, neuter plural, KJV, "other (Gentiles)"; see the RV See REMNANT, REST (the).

4. *allotrios* (ἀλλότριος, 245), "belonging to another, not one's own," is translated "other men's" in 2 Cor. 10:15; 1 Tim. 5:22; in Heb. 9:25, RV, "not his own" (KJV, "of others"). See ALIEN, MAN'S, *Note* (1), STRANGE, STRANGER.

5. *allēlōn* (ἀλλήλων, 240), in Rom. 1:12, used in the dative case, is translated in the RV "(each of us by the) other's" (KJV, "mutual"); the accusative is translated "other" in Phil. 2:3. See MUTUAL and ONE ANOTHER.

6. *heis* (εἷς, 1520), "one," is sometimes translated "other" when expressing the second of a pair, e.g., Matt. 24:40, KJV (RV, "one"), See ONE, A (4).

7. *ekeinos* (ἐκεῖνος, 1565), signifying "that one," implying remoteness as compared with *houtos*, "this," is translated "the other," e.g., in Matt. 23:23; Luke 11:42; 18:14.

Notes: (1) In Acts 26:22, KJV, *ouden ektos*, lit., "nothing besides" is translated "none other things" (RV, "nothing but"). (2) The plural of the definite article is translated "others" in Acts 17:32; in Jude 23, KJV, "others" (RV, "some"). (3) In Luke 24:1, the plural of *tis*, "a certain one," is found in some mss., and translated "certain others" in the KJV.

For OTHER SIDE and OTHER WAY see SIDE and WAY

OTHERWISE

1. *allos* (ἄλλος, 243) is used, in its neuter form, *allo*, in Gal. 5:10, lit., "another thing," with the meaning "otherwise." See OTHER, No. 1.

2. *allōs* (ἀλλῶς, 247), the adverb corresponding to No. 1, is translated "otherwise" in 1 Tim. 5:25; the contrast is not with works that are not good (No. 3 would signify that), but with good works which are not evident.¶

3. *heterōs* (ἑτέρως, 2088) is used in Phil. 3:15, "otherwise (minded)," i.e., "differently minded."¶ Contrast No. 2, and for the corresponding difference between the adjectives *allos* and *heteros*, see ANOTHER.

4. *epei* (ἐπεί, 1893), when used of time, means "since" or "when"; used of cause, it means "since, because"; used elliptically it means "otherwise" or "else"; "otherwise" in Rom. 11:6 (the 2nd part of the v. is absent from the most authentic mss.); v. 22; in Heb. 9:17, KJV, "otherwise (it is of no strength at all)," RV, "for (doth it ever avail?)." See ELSE.

Note: The phrase *ei*, "if," *de*, "but," *mēge*, "not indeed," i.e., "but if not indeed," is translated "otherwise" in the KJV of Matt. 6:1; Luke 5:36 (RV, "else," in each place); in 2 Cor. 11:16, KJV, "if otherwise" (RV, "but if *ye do* "). See also TEACH.

For the pronoun OUGHT (KJV) see AUGHT

OUGHT (Verb)

1. *dei* (δεῖ, 1163) denotes "it is necessary," "one must"; in Luke 24:26, KJV, "ought" (RV "behoved it"); the neuter of the present participle, used as a noun, is translated "things which

they ought (not)" in 1 Tim. 5:13; in Acts 19:36, "ye ought" (see NEED). See MUST, No. 1.

2. *opheilō* (ὀφείλω, 3784), "to owe," is translated "ought," with various personal pronouns, in John 13:14; 19:7; Acts 17:29; Rom. 15:1; Heb. 5:3, KJV (RV, "he is bound"); 5:12; 1 John 3:16; 4:11; 3 John 8; with other subjects in 1 Cor. 11:7, 10; 2 Cor. 12:14; Eph. 5:28; 1 John 2:6. See BEHOVE, OWE, etc.

3. *chrē* (χρή, 5534), an impersonal verb (akin to *chraomai*, "to use"), occurs in Jas. 3:10, "(these things) ought (not so to be)," lit., "it is not befitting, these things so to be."¶

OUR, OURS

Notes: (1) This usually translates *hēmōn*, the genitive of *hēmeis*, "we," lit., "of us," e.g., Matt. 6:9, 11–12. It is translated "ours," e.g., in Mark 12:7; Luke 20:14; 1 Cor. 1:2; 2 Cor. 1:14. (2) In 1 John 4:17, the phrase *meta hēmōn*, rendered "our (love)" in the KJV, is accurately translated in the RV "(herein is love made perfect) with us," i.e., divine love in Christ finds its expression in "our" manifestation of it to others. (3) In Luke 17:5, "increase our faith" is, lit., "add faith to us." (4) In Luke 24:22, "of our company" is, lit., "from among us." (5) *Hēmeteros*, a possessive pronoun, more emphatic than *hēmeis*, is used in Luke 16:12, in the best mss. (some have *humeteros*, "your own"); Acts 2:11; 24:6, in some mss.; 26:5; 2 Tim. 4:15; Titus 3:14, "ours"; 1 John 1:3; 2:2, "ours." (6) In Luke 23:41, "of our deeds," is, lit., "of what things we practiced." (7) In 1 Cor. 9:10, "for our sake," RV (twice), is, lit., "on account of us."

OUR OWN

1. *heautōn* (ἑαυτῶν, 1438) is sometimes used as a reflexive pronoun of the 1st person plural, signifying "our own selves," translated "our own" in 1 Thess. 2:8, lit., "(the souls) of ourselves."

2. *idios* (ἴδιος, 2398), "one's own," signifies "our own" in Acts 3:12; 1 Cor. 4:12; in Acts 2:8, with *hēmōn*, forming a strong possessive, lit., "each in his own language of us."

OURSELVES

Notes: (1) This translates (a) *autoi*, the plural of *autos*, "self," used emphatically either alone, e.g., John 4:42; Rom. 8:23 (1st part); 2 Cor. 1:4 (last part); 1:9, RV, "we ourselves" (1st part); or joined with the plural pronouns, e.g., *hēmeis*, "we," Rom. 8:23 (2nd part); (b) the plural *hemeis* alone, e.g., Titus 3:3; in 2 Cor. 4:7, RV, *ex hēmōn*, is translated "from ourselves" (KJV, "of us"); (c) *heautōn*, governed by the preposition *apo*, "from," e.g., 2 Cor. 3:5 (1st part), lit., "from ourselves" ("of ourselves," in the text); (d) *heautis*, the dative case of (c), e.g., Rom. 15:1; governed by *en*, "in," 2 Cor. 1:9 (1st part); by *epi*, "on" (2nd part). (e) *heautous*, the accusative case, e.g., Acts 23:14; 2 Cor. 3:1; 4:2, 5. (2) In Acts 6:4, KJV, *proskartereō*, "to continue steadfastly" (RV), is translated "give ourselves continually." (3) In 2 Cor. 10:12, KJV, *enkrinō*, "to number" (RV), is translated "to make ourselves of the number."

OUT, OUT OF

Notes: (1) The preposition *ek* (or *ex*), which frequently signifies "out of" or "from the midst of," has a variety of meanings, among which is "from," as virtually equivalent to *apo*, "away from," e.g., 2 Cor. 1:10, "who delivered us out of so great a death, and will deliver"; since death was not actually experienced, but was impending, *ek* here does not signify "out of the midst of." In Acts 12:7 it is used in the statement "his chains fell off from his hands." In Matt. 17:9 it is used of descending from a mountain, not "out of"; "we are not to suppose that they had been in a cave" (Dr. A. T. Robertson, *Gram. of the Greek NT*). In 1 Thess. 1:10, "even Jesus, which delivereth us from the wrath to come," RV, the question whether *ek* here means "out of the midst of" or "away from," is to be determined by some statement of Scripture where the subject is specifically mentioned; this is provided, e.g., in 5:9, the context of which makes clear that believers are to be delivered from (not "out of") the divine wrath to be executed on the nations at the end of the present age. (2) For the phrase *ek mesou*, "out of the way," see MIDST, *Note* (1), (e). (3) In Luke 8:4, KJV, the phrase *kata polin* is translated "out of every city" (RV, "of every city," to be taken in connection with "they"). (4) *Ektos*, "outside of," is translated "out of" in 2 Cor. 12:2; in 12:3 the best mss. have *chōris*, "apart from," RV (KJV, *ektos*, "out of"). (4) For other prepositions, and adverbs, see † p. 1.

OUTER

exōteros (ἐξώτερος, 1857), the comparative degree of *exō*, "without," is used of the "outer" darkness, Matt. 8:12; 22:13; 25:30.¶

OUTGO

proerchomai (προέρχομαι, 4281), "to go forward, go in advance, outgo," is used of time in Mark 6:33, "outwent," of the people who in their eagerness reached a spot earlier than Christ and His disciples. See GO, No. 17.

OUTRUN

protrechō (προτρέχω, 4390), primarily, "to run forward" (*pro*, "forward" or "before," *trechō*, "to run"), is used with *tachion*, "more quickly," in John 20:4, "outran," RV (KJV, "did outrun"), lit., "ran forward more quickly"; in Luke 19:4, "he ran on before," RV (KJV, "ran before"). See RUN.¶ In the Sept., 1 Sam. 8:11; in some texts, Job 41:13, "destruction runneth before him," in the Eng. versions, v. 22.¶

OUTSIDE

1. *exōthen* (ἔξωθεν, 1855), an adverb formed from *exō*, "without," properly signifies "from without," Mark 7:18 (in v. 15 it is used as a preposition); with the article it is equivalent to a noun, "the outside," Matt. 23:25 (for v. 27, see OUTWARD, No. 2); Luke 11:39; in v. 40, RV, "the outside" (KJV, "that which is without"). See OUTWARD, OUTWARDLY, WITHOUT.

2. *ektos* (ἐκτός, 1622) is once used with the article, "the outside," Matt. 23:26. See EXCEPT, No. 1.

OUTWARD, OUTWARDLY

1. *exō* (ἔξω, 1854), "without," is used metaphorically of the physical frame, "the outward man," 2 Cor. 4:16. See WITHOUT.

2. *exōthen* (ἔξωθεν, 1855) is translated "outward" in Matt. 23:27 (RV, "outwardly"); it is used with the article, adjectively, in 1 Pet. 3:3, of "outward" adorning. See OUTSIDE, No. 1.

Notes: (1) The phrase *en tō phanerō*, lit., "in the open" ("manifest"), is rendered "outwardly" in Rom. 2:28. (2) For "with outward show," KJV, marg., Luke 17:20, see OBSERVATION. (3) For the KJV, of 2 Cor. 10:7, "outward appearance," see FACE, No. 1.

OVEN

klibanos (κλίβανος, 2823) is mentioned in Matt. 6:30 and Luke 12:28. The form of "oven" commonly in use in the east indicates the kind in use as mentioned in Scripture. A hole is sunk in the ground about 3 feet deep and somewhat less in diameter. The walls are plastered with cement. A fire is kindled inside, the fuel being grass, or dry twigs, which heat the oven rapidly and blacken it with smoke and soot (see Lam. 5:10). When sufficiently heated the surface is wiped, and the dough is molded into broad thin loaves, placed one at a time on the wall of the "oven" to fit its concave inner circle. The baking takes a few seconds. Such ovens are usually outside the house, and often the same "oven" serves for several families (Lev. 26:26). An "oven" of this sort is doubtless referred to in Ex. 8:3 (see *Hastings, Bib. Dic.*).¶

For **OVER, OVER AGAINST** see *Note* †, p. 1

OVER (to be, to have)

1. *proistēmi* (προίστημι, 4291), lit., "to stand before," hence "to lead, to direct, attend to," is translated "rule," with reference to the family, in 1 Tim. 3:4–5, 12; with reference to the church, in Rom. 12:8; 1 Thess. 5:12, "are over;" 1 Tim. 5:17, In Titus 3:8, 14, it signifies "to maintain." See MAINTAIN.¶

2. *pleonazō* (πλεονάζω, 4121), used intransitively, signifies "to abound, to superabound"; in 2 Cor. 8:15 it is used with the negative *ou*, "had nothing over," lit., "had not more" (*pleon*, the comparative degree of *polus*, "much").

For **OVERBOARD**, Acts 27:18, RV, see **FREIGHT**, and, in 27:43, RV, see **CAST**, No. 11.

OVERCHARGE

1. *bareō* (βαρέω, 916), or *barunō*, is rendered "overcharged" in Luke 21:34. See BURDEN, B, No. 1.

2. *epibareō* (ἐπιβαρέω, 1912) is rendered "overcharge" in 2 Cor. 2:5, KJV. See BURDEN, B, No. 2, and PRESS.

OVERCOME

1. *nikaō* (νικάω, 3528) is used (*a*) of God, Rom. 3:4 (a law term), RV, "mightest prevail"; (*b*) of Christ, John 16:33; Rev. 3:21; 5:5; 17:14; (*c*) of His followers, Rom. 12:21 (2nd part); 1 John 2:13–14; 4:4; 5:4–5; Rev. 2:7, 11, 17, 26; 3:5, 12, 21; 12:11; 15:2; 21:7; (*d*) of faith, 1 John 5:4; (*e*) of evil (passive voice), Rom. 12:21; (*f*) of predicted human potentates, Rev. 6:2; 11:7; 13:7.¶

2. *hēttaomai* (ἡττάομαι, 2274), "to be made inferior, be enslaved," is rendered "is (are) overcome," in 2 Pet. 2:19–20. See INFERIOR.

3. *katakurieuō* (κατακυριεύω, 2634) is translated "overcome" in Acts 19:16; see MASTER, B.

OVERFLOW, OVERFLOWING

A. Verbs.

1. *huperperisseuō* (ὑπερπερισσεύω, 5248), "to abound more exceedingly," Rom. 5:20, is used in the middle voice in 2 Cor. 7:4, RV, "I overflow (with joy)," KJV, "I am exceeding (joyful)." See ABUNDANCE, B, No. 2.

2. *katakluzō* (κατακλύζω, 2626), "to inun-

date, deluge" (*kata*, "down," *kluzō*, "to wash" or "dash over," said, e.g., of the sea), is used in the passive voice in 2 Pet. 3:6, of the Flood.¶

B. Noun.

perisseia (περισσεία, 4050) is translated "overflowing" in Jas. 1:21, RV. See ABUNDANCE, A, No. 2.

OVERLAY

perikaluptō (περικαλύπτω, 4028) denotes "to cover around, cover up or over"; it is translated "overlaid" in Heb. 9:4. See BLINDFOLD, COVER.

OVERLOOK

hupereidon (ὑπερεῖδον, 5237), "to overlook" (an aorist form), is used in Acts 17:30, RV (KJV, "winked at"), i.e., God bore with them without interposing by way of punishment, though the debasing tendencies of idolatry necessarily developed themselves.¶

OVERMUCH

perissoteros (περισσότερος, 4055), the comparative degree of *perissos*, "abundant," is translated "overmuch" in 2 Cor. 2:7. See ABUNDANCE, C, No. 2.

Notes: (1) In 2 Cor. 10:14, RV, the verb *huperekteinō*, "to stretch out over," is translated "we stretch (not ourselves) overmuch" (KJV, . . . beyond *our measure*"). See STRETCH.¶ (2) In 2 Cor. 12:7 (twice), RV, *huperairō*, in the middle voice, "to uplift oneself," is translated "I should (not) be exalted overmuch," KJV, " . . . above measure." See EXALT.

OVERRIPE

xērainō (ξηραίνω, 3583) denotes "to dry up, wither," translated in Rev. 14:15, "overripe," RV (KJV, "ripe"), said figuratively of the harvest of the earth, symbolizing the condition of the world, political, especially connected with Israel (Joel 3:9, 14), and religious, comprehensive of the whole scene of Christendom (Matt. 13:38). See DRY.

For OVERSEER see BISHOP

OVERSHADOW

1. *episkiazō* (ἐπισκιάζω, 1982), "to throw a shadow upon" (*epi*, "over," *skia*, "a shadow"), "to overshadow," is used (*a*) of the bright cloud at the Transfiguration, Matt. 17:5; Mark 9:7; Luke 9:34; (*b*) metaphorically of the power of "the Most High" upon the Virgin Mary, Luke 1:35; (*c*) of the apostle Peter's shadow upon the sick, Acts 5:15.¶

2. *kataskiazō* (κατασκιάζω, 2683), lit., "to

shadow down," is used of the "overshadowing" (RV) of the cherubim of glory above the mercy seat, Heb. 9:5 (KJV, "shadowing").¶

OVERSIGHT (exercise, take)

episkopeō (ἐπισκοπέω, 1983), lit., "to look upon" (*epi*, "upon," *skopeō*, "to look at, contemplate"), is found in 1 Pet. 5:2 (some ancient authorities omit it), "exercising the oversight," RV (KJV, "taking . . ."); "exercising" is the right rendering; the word does not imply the entrance upon such responsibility, but the fulfillment of it. It is not a matter of assuming a position, but of the discharge of the duties. The word is found elsewhere in Heb. 12:15, "looking carefully," RV. See LOOK.¶ Cf. *episkopē* in 1 Tim. 3:1 (see BISHOP, No. 2).

OVERTAKE

1. *katalambanō* (καταλαμβάνω, 2638), "to lay hold of," has the significance of "overtaking," metaphorically, in John 12:35 (RV, "overtake," KJV, "come upon") and 1 Thess. 5:4. See APPREHEND, No. 1.

2. *prolambanō* (προλαμβάνω, 4301), "to anticipate" (*pro*, "before," *lambanō*, "to take"), is used of the act of Mary, in Mark 14:8 [see COME, *Note* (2)]; of forestalling the less favored at a social meal, 1 Cor. 11:21; of being "overtaken" in any trespass, Gal. 6:1, where the meaning is not that of detecting a person in the act, but of his being caught by the trespass, through his being off his guard (see 5:21 and contrast the premeditated practice of evil in 5:26). The modern Greek version is "even if a man, through lack of circumspection, should fall into any sin." See TAKE.¶

OVERTHROW (Noun and Verb)

A. Noun.

katastrophē (καταστροφή, 2692), lit., "a turning down" (*kata*, "down," *strophē*, "a turning"; Eng., "catastrophe"), is used (*a*) literally, 2 Pet. 2:6; (*b*) metaphorically, 2 Tim. 2:14, "subverting," i.e., the "overthrowing" of faith.¶ Cf. *kathairesis*, "a pulling down," 2 Cor. 10:4, 8; 13:10.¶

B. Verbs.

1. *katastrephō* (καταστρέφω, 2690), akin to A, lit. and primarily, "to turn down" or "turn over," as, e.g., the soil, denotes to "overturn, overthrow," Matt. 21:12; Mark 11:15; in Acts 15:16, passive voice, "ruins," lit., "the overthrown (things) of it" (some mss. have *kataskaptō*, "to dig down"). See RUIN.¶

2. *anastrephō* (ἀναστρέφω, 390) is found in some mss. in John 2:15 (see No. 3). See ABIDE, No. 8.

3. *anatrepō* (ἀνατρέπω, 396), lit., "to turn up or over" (*ana*, "up," *trepō*, "to turn"), "to upset," is used (*a*) literally, in the most authentic mss., in John 2:15 (see No. 2); (*b*) metaphorically, in 2 Tim. 2:18, "overthrow (the faith of some);" in Titus 1:11, RV, "overthrow (whole houses)," KJV, "subvert . . . ," i.e., households. Moulton and Milligan (*Vocab.*) give an apt illustration from a 2nd cent. papyrus, of the complete upsetting of a family by the riotous conduct of a member.¶

4. *kataluō* (καταλύω, 2647), lit., "to loosen down," signifies "to overthrow" in Acts 5:38, RV, "it will be overthrown" (KJV, "it will come to nought"); Rom. 14:20, RV, "overthrow" (KJV, "destroy"). See DESTROY.

5. *katastrōnnumi* (καταστρώννυμι, 2693), primarily, "to strew" or "spread over" (*kata*, "down," *strōnnumi*, or *strōnnuō*, "to spread"), then, "to overthrow," has this meaning in 1 Cor. 10:5, "they were overthrown."¶ In the Sept., Num. 14:16; Job 12:23.¶

OWE

A. Verbs.

1. *opheilō* (ὀφείλω, 3784), "to owe, to be a debtor" (in the passive voice, "to be owed, to be due"), is translated by the verb "to owe" in Matt. 18:28 (twice); Luke 7:41; 16:5, 7; Rom. 13:8; in 15:27, RV, "they (gentile converts) owe it" (KJV, "it is their duty"); Philem. 18. See BEHOVE, DEBT, DUE, DUTY, GUILTY, INDEBTED, MUST, NEED, OUGHT.

2. *prosopheilō* (προσοφείλω, 4359), "to owe besides" (*pros*, "in addition," and No. 1), is used in Philem. 19, "thou owest (to me even thine own self) besides," i.e., "thou owest me already as much as Onesimus' debt, and in addition even thyself" (not "thou owest me much more").

B. Noun.

opheiletēs (ὀφειλέτης, 3781), "a debtor" (akin to A, No. 1), is translated "which owed" in Matt. 18:24, lit., "a debtor (of ten thousand talents)." See DEBTOR.

OWN (Adjective)

Notes: (1) *Gnēsios*, primarily, "lawfully begotten," and hence "true, genuine," is translated "own" in the KJV of 1 Tim. 1:2 and Titus 1:4 (RV, "true"). See SINCERITY, TRUE. (2) In Acts 5:4, "was it not thine own?" is, lit., "did it not remain (*menō*) to thee?" (3) In Jude 6 (1st part), KJV, *heautōn*, "of themselves," "their own" (RV), is rendered "their"; in the 2nd part, RV, *idios*, one's own, is translated "their proper" (KJV, "their own"). (4) In Gal. 1:14, RV, *sunēlikiōtēs*, is rendered "of mine own age" (KJV, "my equals"; marg., "equals in years").¶ (5) For "its own" in 1 Tim. 2:6, RV, see DUE, A. (6) For association with other words see ACCORD, BUSINESS, COMPANY, CONCEITS, COUNTRY.

OWNER

1. *kurios* (κύριος, 2962), "one having power" (*kuros*) or "authority, a lord, master," signifies "an owner" in Luke 19:33. See LORD, MASTER, SIR.

2. *nauklēros* (ναύκληρος, 3490), "a ship owner" (*naus*, "a ship," *klēros*, "a lot"), "a shipmaster," occurs in Acts 27:11, "(the) owner of the ship."¶

OWNETH

Note: In Acts 21:11, "that owneth this girdle," is lit., "whose is (*esti*) this girdle."

OX

1. *bous* (βοῦς, 1016) denotes an "ox" or "a cow," Luke 13:15; 14:5, 19; John 2:14–15; 1 Cor. 9:9 (twice); 1 Tim. 5:18.¶

2. *tauros* (ταῦρος, 5022), Latin *taurus*, is translated "oxen" in Matt. 22:4 and Acts 14:13; "bulls" in Heb. 9:13 and 10:4.¶

P

PAIN (Noun and Verb)

A. Nouns.

1. *ponos* (πόνος, 4192) is translated "pain" in Rev. 16:10; 21:4; "pains" in 16:11. See LABOR.

2. *ōdin* (ὠδίν, 5604), "a birth pang, travail pain," is rendered "travail," metaphorically, in Matt. 24:8 and Mark 13:8, RV (KJV, "sorrows"); by way of comparison, in 1 Thess. 5:3; translated "pains (of death)," Acts 2:24 (RV, "pangs"). See SORROW, TRAVAIL.¶ Cf. *ōdinō*, "to travail in birth."

B. Verb.

basanizō (βασανίζω, 928) primarily signifies "to rub on the touchstone, to put to the test" (from *basanos*, "a touchstone," a dark stone used in testing metals); hence, "to examine by torture," and, in general, "to distress"; in Rev. 12:2, "in pain," RV (KJV, "pained"), in connection with parturition. See TORMENT. (In the Sept., 1 Sam. 5:3.¶).

Note: For Rom. 8:22, "travaileth in pain together," see TRAVAIL,

For **PAINFULNESS** (2 Cor. 11:27, KJV) see **TRAVAIL**

PAIR

zeugos (ζεῦγος, 2201), "a yoke" (akin to *zeugnumi*, "to yoke"), is used (*a*) of beasts, Luke 14:19; (*b*) of a pair of anything; in Luke 2:24, of turtledoves. See YOKE.¶

Note: In Rev. 6:5, KJV, *zugos*, a yoke (akin to *zeugos*), is translated "a pair of balances" (RV, "a balance"). See BALANCE, YOKE.

PALACE

1. *aulē* (αὐλή, 833), "a court, dwelling, palace": see COURT.

2. *praitōrion* (πραιτώριον, 4232) signified originally "a general's (praetor's) tent." Then it was applied to "the council of army officers"; then to "the official residence of the governor of a province"; finally, to "the imperial bodyguard." In the KJV the word appears only once, Mark 15:16, "the hall, called Praetorium" (RV, "within the court which is the Praetorium," marg., "palace"); in the Greek of the NT it also occurs in Matt. 27:27, KJV, "the common hall," marg., "the governor's house"; RV, "palace," see marg.; John 18:28 (twice), KJV, "the hall of judgment"; and "judgment hall," marg., "Pilate's house," RV, "palace"; 18:33 and 19:9, KJV, "judgment hall," RV, "palace," see marg.; so in Acts 23:35; in Phil. 1:13, KJV, "in all the palace," marg., "Caesar's court," RV, "throughout the whole praetorian guard," marg., "in the whole Praetorium."

"In the Gospels the term denotes the official residence in Jerusalem of the Roman governor, and the various translations of it in our versions arose from a desire either to indicate the special purpose for which that residence was used on the occasion in question, or to explain what particular building was intended. But whatever building the governor occupied was the Praetorium. It is most probable that in Jerusalem he resided in the well-known palace of Herod.... Pilate's residence has been identified with the castle of Antonia, which was occupied by the regular garrison. The probability is that it was the same as Herod's palace. Herod's palace in Caesarea was used as the Praetorium there, and the expression in Acts 23:35, marg., 'Herod's praetorium,' is abbreviated from 'the praetorium of Herod's palace.'" (*Hastings' Bib. Dic.*).

In Phil. 1:13, marg., "the whole Praetorium" has been variously explained. It has been spoken of as "the palace," in connection with 4:22, where allusion is made to believers who belong to Caesar's household. Others have understood it of the barracks of the "praetorian" guard, but Lightfoot shows that this use of the word cannot be established, neither can it be regarded as referring to the barracks of the "palace" guard. The phrase "and to all the rest" in 1:13 indicates that persons are meant. Mommsen, followed by Ramsay (*St. Paul the Traveller*, p. 357) regards it as improbable that the apostle was committed to the "praetorian" guard and holds the view that Julius the centurion, who brought Paul to Rome, belonged to a corps drafted from legions in the provinces, whose duty it was to supervise the corn supply and perform police service, and that Julius probably delivered his prisoners to the commander of his corps. Eventually Paul's case came before the praetorian council, which is the "praetorium" alluded to by the apostle, and the phrase "to all the rest" refers to the audience of the trial.¶

Note: Some scholars, believing that this epistle was written during an Ephesian imprisonment, take the "Praetorium" here to be the residence in Ephesus of the proconsul of the province of Asia, and "Caesar's household" to be the local imperial civil service (Deissmann etc.).

PALE

chlōros (χλωρός, 5515), "pale green," is translated "pale" (of a horse) in Rev. 6:8, symbolizing death. See GREEN.

PALM (of the hand)

Note: For *rhapizō*, "to strike with a rod or with the palm of the hand," Matt. 26:67 (cf. 5:39), see SMITE.¶ For *rhapisma*, "a blow," with *didōmi*, "to give," translated "did strike (and, struck) ... with the palm of his hand" (KJV, in Mark 14:65; John 18:22), see BLOW.

PALM (palm tree)

phoinix (φοῖνιξ, 5404) denotes "the date palm"; it is used of "palm" trees in John 12:13, from which branches were taken; of the branches themselves in Rev. 7:9.¶ The "palm" gave its name to Phoenicia and to Phoenix in

Crete, Acts 27:12, RV. Jericho was the city of "palm trees," Deut. 34:3; Judg. 1:16; 3:13; 2 Chron. 28:15. They were plentiful there in the time of Christ.

PALSY (sick of)

A. Adjective.

paralutikos (παραλυτικός, 3885), "paralytic, sick of the palsy," is found in Matt. 4:24 (RV, "palsied"); 8:6; 9:2 (twice), 6; Mark 2:3, 4, 5, 9, 10; in some mss. Luke 5:24 (see B).¶

B. Verb

paraluō (παραλύω, 3886), lit., "to loose from the side," hence, "to set free," is used in the passive voice of "being enfeebled by a paralytic stroke, palsied," Luke 5:18, RV, "palsied" (KJV, "taken with a palsy"); 5:24 (ditto), in the best mss.; Acts 8:7 (ditto); 9:33, RV, "he was palsied" (KJV, "was sick of the palsy"); Heb. 12:12, RV, "palsied (knees)," KJV, "feeble." See FEEBLE.¶

For **PANGS**, Acts 2:24, RV, see **PAIN**

For **PAPS** see **BREAST**

PAPER

chartēs (χάρτης, 5489), "a sheet of paper made of strips of papyrus" (whence Eng., "paper"), Eng., "chart," "charter," etc.; the word is used in 2 John 12.¶ The papyrus reed grew in ancient times in great profusion in the Nile and was used as a material for writing. From Egypt its use spread to other countries and it was the universal material for writing in general in Greece and Italy during the most flourishing periods of their literature.

The pith of the stem of the plant was cut into thin strips, placed side by side to form a sheath. Another layer was laid upon this at right angles to it. The two layers were united by moisture and pressure and frequently with the addition of glue. The sheets, after being dried and polished, were ready for use. Normally, the writing is on that side of the papyrus on which the fibers lie horizontally, parallel to the length of the roll, but where the material was scarce the writer used the other side also (cf. Rev. 5:1). Papyrus continued to be used until the seventh cent., A.D., when the conquest of Egypt by the Arabs led to the disuse of the material for literary purposes and the use of vellum till the 12th century.

PARABLE

1. *parabolē* (παραβολή, 3850) lit. denotes "a placing beside" (akin to *paraballō*, "to throw" or "lay beside, to compare"). It signifies "a placing of one thing beside another" with a view to comparison (some consider that the thought of comparison is not necessarily contained in the word). In the NT it is found outside the gospels, only in Heb. 9:9 and 11:19. It is generally used of a somewhat lengthy utterance or narrative drawn from nature or human circumstances, the object of which is to set forth a spiritual lesson, e.g., those in Matt. 13 and Synoptic parallels; sometimes it is used of a short saying or proverb, e.g., Matt. 15:15; Mark 3:23; 7:17; Luke 4:23; 5:36; 6:39. It is the lesson that is of value; the hearer must catch the analogy if he is to be instructed (this is true also of a proverb). Such a narrative or saying, dealing with earthly things with a spiritual meaning, is distinct from a fable, which attributes to things what does not belong to them in nature.

Christ's "parables" most frequently convey truths connected with the subject of the kingdom of God. His withholding the meaning from His hearers as He did from the multitudes, Matt. 13:34, was a divine judgment upon the unworthy.

Two dangers are to be avoided in seeking to interpret the "parables" in Scripture, that of ignoring the important features, and that of trying to make all the details mean something.

2. *paroimia* (παροιμία, 3942) denotes "a wayside saying" (from *paroimos*, "by the way"), "a byword," "maxim," or "problem," 2 Pet. 2:22. The word is sometimes spoken of as a "parable," John 10:6, i.e., a figurative discourse (RV marg., "proverb"); see also 16:25, 29, where the word is rendered "proverbs" (marg. "parables") and "proverb."¶

PARADISE

paradeisos (παράδεισος, 3857) is an Oriental word, first used by the historian Xenophon, denoting "the parks of Persian kings and nobles." It is of Persian origin (Old Pers. *pairidaeza*, akin to Gk. *peri*, "around," and *teichos*, "a wall") whence it passed into Greek. See the Sept., e.g., in Neh. 2:8; Eccl. 2:5; Song of Sol. 4:13. The Sept. translators used it of the garden of Eden, Gen. 2:8, and in other respects, e.g., Num. 24:6; Isa. 1:30; Jer. 29:5; Ezek. 31:8–9.

In Luke 23:43, the promise of the Lord to the repentant robber was fulfilled the same day; Christ, at His death, having committed His spirit to the Father, went in spirit immediately into Heaven itself, the dwelling place of God (the Lord's mention of the place as "paradise" must have been a great comfort to the malefactor; to the oriental mind it expressed the sum total of blessedness). Thither the apostle Paul was caught up, 2 Cor. 12:4, spoken of as "the third heaven" (v. 3 does not introduce a different vision), beyond the heavens of the natural creation (see Heb. 4:14, RV, with reference to the Ascension). The same region is mentioned in Rev. 2:7, where the "tree of life," the figurative antitype of that in Eden, held out to the overcomer, is spoken of as being in "the Paradise of God" (RV), marg., "garden," as in Gen. 2:8.¶

For **PARCEL** see **GROUND**, No. 4

PARCHMENT

membrana (μεμβράνα, 3200) is a Latin word, properly an adjective, from *membrum*, "a limb," but denoting "skin, parchment." The Eng. word "parchment" is a form of *pergamena*, an adjective signifying "of Pergamum," the city in Asia Minor where "parchment" was either invented or brought into use. The word *membrana* is found in 2 Tim. 4:13, where Timothy is asked to bring to the apostle "the books, especially the parchments." The writing material was prepared from the skin of the sheep or goat. The skins were first soaked in lime for the purpose of removing the hair, and then shaved, washed, dried, stretched and ground or smoothed with fine chalk or lime and pumice stone. The finest kind is called "vellum," and is made from the skins of calves or kids.¶

PARENTS

1. *goneus* (γονεύς, 1118), "a begetter, a father" (akin to *ginomai*, "to come into being, become"), is used in the plural in the NT, Matt. 10:21; Mark 13:12; six times in Luke (in Luke 2:43, RV, "His parents," KJV, "Joseph and His mother"); six in John; elsewhere, Rom. 1:30; 2 Cor. 12:14 (twice); Eph. 6:1; Col. 3:20; 2 Tim. 3:2.¶

2. *progonos* (πρόγονος, 4269), an adjective signifying "born before" (*pro*, before, and *ginomai*, see No. 1), is used as a noun, in the plural, (a) of ancestors, "forefathers," 2 Tim. 1:3; (b) of living "parents," 1 Tim. 5:4. See FOREFATHER.¶

3. *patēr* (πατήρ, 3962), "a father," is used in Heb. 11:23, in the plural, of both father and mother, the "parents" of Moses. See FATHER.

PART (Noun, a portion; Verb, to give or divide, partake)

A. Nouns.

1. *meros* (μέρος, 3313) denotes (a) "a part, portion," of the whole, e.g., John 13:8; Rev. 20:6; 22:19; hence, "a lot" or "destiny," e.g., Rev. 21:8; in Matt. 24:51 and Luke 12:46, "portion"; (b) "a part" as opposite to the whole,

e.g., Luke 11:36; John 19:23; 21:6, "side"; Acts 5:2; 23:6; Eph. 4:16; Rev. 16:19; a party, Acts 23:9; the divisions of a province, e.g., Matt. 2:22; Acts 2:10; the regions belonging to a city, e.g., Matt. 15:21, RV, "parts" (KJV, "coasts"); 16:13 (ditto); Mark 8:10, KJV and RV, "parts"; "the lower parts of the earth," Eph. 4:9; this phrase means the regions beneath the earth (see LOWER, A, No. 1); (c) "a class," or "category" (with *en*, in, "in respect of"), Col. 2:16; "in this respect," 2 Cor. 3:10; 9:3, RV (KJV, "in this behalf"). See BEHALF, COAST, CRAFT, PIECE, PORTION, RESPECT.

2. *meris* (μερίς, 3310) denotes (a) "a part" or "portion," Luke 10:42; Acts 8:21; 2 Cor. 6:15 (RV, "portion"); in Col. 1:12, "partakers," lit., "unto the part of"; (b) "a district" or "division," Acts 16:12, RV, "district" (KJV, "part"). See DISTRICT, PARTAKER.¶

3. *klima* (κλίμα, 2824), primarily "an incline, slope" (Eng., "clime, climate"), is used of "a region," Rom. 15:23, KJV, "parts" (RV, "regions"); 2 Cor. 11:10, KJV and RV, "regions"; Gal. 1:21 (ditto). See REGION.¶

4. *eschatos* (ἔσχατος, 2078), an adjective signifying "last, utmost, extreme," is often used as a noun; in Acts 13:47, RV, "uttermost part" (KJV, "ends"). See END, LAST, LOWEST, UTTERMOST.

5. *topos* (τόπος, 5117), "a place," is translated "parts" in Acts 16:3, RV (KJV, "quarters"). See PLACE, etc.

6. The plural of the article, followed first by the particle *men*, "indeed," and then by *de*, "but," is translated "part . . . and part" in Acts 14:4.

7. *peras* (πέρας, 4009), "an end, boundary," is translated "utmost parts" in the KJV of Matt. 12:42 and Luke 11:31. See END, A, No. 3.

Notes: (1) *Meros* is used with certain prepositions in adverbial phrases, (a) with *ana*, used distributively, 1 Cor. 14:27, "in turn," RV, KJV, "by course"; (b) with *kata*, "according to," Heb. 9:5, RV, "severally" (KJV, "particularly"); (c) with *apo*, "from," "in part," Rom. 11:25; 2 Cor. 1:14; 2:5 (see also MEASURE); (d) with *ek*, "from," 1 Cor. 13:9, 10, 12; in 1 Cor. 12:27, RV, "severally," marg., "each in his part" (KJV, "in particular"). (2) In Mark 4:38 and Acts 27:41, KJV, *prumna*, "a stern," is translated "hinder part" (RV, "stern"). (3) In Acts 1:17, KJV, *klēros*, "a lot," is translated "part" (RV, "portion"; marg., "lot"), of that portion allotted to Judas in the ministry of the Twelve. See INHERITANCE, LOT. (4) In Acts 1:25, where the best mss. have *topos*, "a place," RV, "(to take) the place (in this ministry)," some texts have *klēros*, which the KJV translates "part." (5) In Mark 9:40, KJV, the preposition *huper*, "on behalf of," is translated "on (our) part," RV, "for (us)." (6) In 1 Pet. 4:14, KJV, "on (their) part," "on (your) part," represents the preposition *kata*, "according to," followed by the personal pronouns; the statements are not found in the most authentic mss. (7) In Acts 9:32, KJV, the phrase *dia pantōn*, lit., "through all," is rendered "throughout all *quarters*" (RV, "throughout all parts"). (8) In 1 Cor. 12:23, the RV has "*parts*" for "*members*"; KJV and RV have "*parts*" in the end of the verse; see also v. 24. (9) In 2 Cor. 10:16, the RV translates the neuter plural of the article "the parts" (KJV, "the *regions*"). (10) For "inward part" see INWARD.

B. Verbs.

1. *merizō* (μερίζω, 3307), "to divide, to distribute" (akin to A, No. 1), is translated "divided (KJV, gave) a... part" in Heb. 7:2, RV. See DEAL.

2. *metechō* (μετέχω, 3348), "to partake of, share in," Heb. 2:14: see PARTAKE.

3. *paraginomai* (παραγίνομαι, 3854), "to be beside, support" (*para*, "beside," *ginomai*, "to become"), is rendered "took (my) part" in 2 Tim. 4:16 (KJV, "stood with"); some mss. have *sunparaginomai*. See COME, No. 13, GO, PRESENT (to be).

Notes: (1) In Rev. 6:8, *tetartos*, "a fourth," is rendered "the fourth part." (2) See GREATER, HINDER, INWARD, MORE, TENTH, THIRD, UTMOST, UTTERMOST.

PART (Verb, to separate)

1. *diamerizō* (διαμερίζω, 1266), "to part among, to distribute," is translated by the verb "to part" (*a*) in the middle voice, with reference to the Lord's garments, Matt. 27:35, 1st part (in some mss., 2nd part); Mark 15:24; Luke 23:34; John 19:24; (*b*) in the active voice, of "the proceeds of the sale of possessions and goods," Acts 2:45; (*c*) in the passive voice in Acts 2:3, of the "parting asunder" (RV) of tongues like fire (KJV, "cloven"). See CLOVEN, DIVIDE, No. 7.

2. *diistēmi* (διΐστημι, 1339), "to set apart, separate" (*dia*, "apart," *histēmi*, "to cause to stand"), is used in the active voice in Luke 24:51, RV, "He parted (from them)," KJV, "was parted." See GO, SPACE.

3. *apospaō* (ἀποσπάω, 645), "to draw off" or "tear away," is used in the passive voice in Luke 22:41, RV, "He was parted" (KJV, "was withdrawn"), lit. "He was torn away," indicating the reluctance with which Christ parted from the loving sympathy of the disciples. Moulton and Milligan suggest that the ordinary use of the verb does not encourage this stronger meaning, but since the simpler meaning is not

found in the NT, except in Acts 21:1, and since the idea of withdrawal is expressed in Matt. by *anachōreō*, Luke may have used *apospaō* here in the stronger sense. See DRAW, A, No. 6.

4. *chōrizō* (χωρίζω, 5563), in Philem. 15, RV, "parted": see DEPART, No. 13.

5. *apochōrizō* (ἀποχωρίζω, 673), "to part from," Acts 15:39, RV; see DEPART, No. 14.

PARTAKE, PARTAKER

A. Nouns.

1. *koinōnos* (κοινωνός, 2844), an adjective, signifying "having in common" (*koinos*, "common"), is used as a noun, denoting "a companion, partner, partaker," translated "partakers" in Matt. 23:30; 1 Cor. 10:18, KJV (see COMMUNION, B); 2 Cor. 1:7; Heb. 10:33, RV (see COMPANION, No. 2); 2 Pet. 1:4; "partaker" in 1 Pet. 5:1. See PARTNER.

2. *sunkoinōnos* (συγκοινωνός, 4791) denotes "partaking jointly with" (*sun*, and No. 1), Rom. 11:17, RV, "(didst become) partaker with them" (KJV, "partakest"); 1 Cor. 9:23, RV, "a joint partaker," i.e., with the gospel, as cooperating in its activity; the KJV misplaces the "with" by attaching it to the superfluous italicized pronoun "*you*"; Phil. 1:7, "partakers with (me of grace)," RV, and KJV marg.; not as KJV text, "partakers (of my grace)"; Rev. 1:9, "partaker with (you in the tribulation, etc.)," KJV, "companion." See COMPANION.¶

3. *metochos* (μέτοχος, 3353): see FELLOW, No. 3, PARTNER.

4. *summetochos* (συμμέτοχος, 4830), "partaking together with" (*sun*, "with," and No. 3), is used as a noun, a joint partaker, Eph. 3:6, RV, "fellow partakers" (KJV, "partakers"); in 5:7, RV and KJV, "partakers."¶

Notes: (1) For *antilambanō*, "to partake of," rendered "partakers" in 1 Tim. 6:2, KJV, see B, No. 4. (2) For the phrase "to be partakers," Col. 1:12, see PART, A, No. 2.

B. Verbs.

1. *koinōneō* (κοινωνέω, 2841), "to have a share of, to share with, take part in" (akin to A, No. 1), is translated "to be partaker of" in 1 Tim. 5:22; Heb. 2:14 (1st part), KJV, "are partakers of," RV, "are sharers in" (for the 2nd part see No. 3); 1 Pet. 4:13; 2 John 11, RV, "partaketh in" (KJV, "is partaker of"); in the passive voice in Rom. 15:27. See COMMUNICATE, DISTRIBUTE.

2. *sunkoinōneō* (συγκοινωνέω, 4790): see FELLOWSHIP, B, No. 2.

3. *metechō* (μετέχω, 3348), "to partake of, share in" (*meta*, "with," *echō*, "to have"), akin to A, No. 3, is translated "of partaking" in 1 Cor. 9:10, RV (KJV, "be partaker of"); "par-

take of" in 9:12, RV (KJV, "be partakers of"); so in 10:17, 21; in v. 30 "partake"; in Heb. 2:14, the KJV "took part of" is awkward; Christ "partook of" flesh and blood, RV; cf. No. 1 in this verse; in Heb. 5:13, metaphorically, of receiving elementary spiritual teaching, RV, "partaketh of (milk)," KJV, "useth"; in Heb. 7:13, it is said of Christ (the antitype of Melchizedek) as "belonging to" (so RV) or "partaking of" (RV marg.) another tribe than that of Levi (KJV, "pertaineth to"). See PERTAIN, USE.¶ See PARTNER, *Note*.

4. *antilambanō* (ἀντιλαμβάνω, 482), "to take hold of, to lay hold of" something before one, has the meaning "to partake of" in 1 Tim. 6:2, RV, "partake of," marg., "lay hold of," KJV, "are . . . partakers of" (*anti*, "in return for," *lambanō*, "to take or receive"); the benefit mentioned as "partaken" of by the masters would seem to be the improved quality of the service rendered; the benefit of redemption is not in view here. See HELP.

5. *metalambanō* (μεταλαμβάνω, 3335), "to have, or get, a share of," is translated "to be partaker (or partakers) of" in 2 Tim. 2:6 and Heb. 12:10. See EAT, HAVE, RECEIVE, TAKE.

6. *summerizō* (συμμερίζω, 4829), primarily, "to distribute in shares" (*sun*, "with," *meros*, "a part"), in the middle voice, "to have a share in," is used in 1 Cor. 9:13, KJV, "are partakers with (the altar)," RV, "have their portion with," i.e., they feed with others on that which, having been sacrificed, has been placed upon an altar; so the believer feeds upon Christ (who is the altar in Heb. 13:10).¶

PARTIAL, PARTIALITY

A. Verb.

diakrinō (διακρίνω, 1252), "to separate, distinguish, discern, judge, decide" (*dia*, "asunder," *krinō*, "to judge"), also came to mean "to be divided in one's mind, to hesitate, doubt," and had this significance in Hellenistic Greek (though not so found in the Sept.). For the KJV, "are ye (not) partial" in Jas. 2:4, see DIVIDE, No. 4. "'This meaning seems to have had its beginning in near proximity to Christianity.' It arises very naturally out of the general sense of making distinctions" (Moulton and Milligan).

B. Noun.

prosklisis (πρόσκλισις, 4346) denotes "inclination" (*pros*, "towards," *klinō*, "to lean"); it is used with *kata* in 1 Tim. 5:21, lit., "according to partiality."¶

C. Adjective.

adiakritos (ἀδιάκριτος, 87) primarily signifies "not to be parted" (*a*, negative, and an adjectival form akin to A), hence, "without uncertainty," or "indecision," Jas. 3:17, KJV,

"without partiality" (marg. "wrangling"), RV, "without variance" (marg., "Or, doubtfulness Or, partiality"). See VARIANCE.¶ In the Sept., Prov. 25:1.¶

For PARTICULAR and PARTICULARLY see EVERY, No. 3, SEVERALLY

Note: In Acts 21:19, for the KJV "particularly" the RV has "one by one," translating the phrase. lit., "according to each one."

For PARTING see HIGHWAY

PARTITION

phragmos (φραγμός, 5418), primarily "a fencing" in (akin to *phrassō*, "to fence in, stop, close"), is used metaphorically in Eph. 2:14, of "the middle wall of partition"; "the partition" is epexegetic of "the middle wall," namely, the "partition" between Jew and Gentile. J. A. Robinson suggests that Paul had in mind the barrier between the outer and inner courts of the Temple, notices fixed to which warned Gentiles not to proceed further on pain of death (see Josephus, *Antiq.* xv. 11. 5; *B. J.* v. 5. 2; vi. 2. 4; cf. Acts 21:29). See HEDGE.

PARTLY

Notes: (1) In the statement "I partly believe it," 1 Cor. 11:18, "partly" represents the phrase "*meros* (part) *ti* (some)," used adverbially, i.e., "in some part," "in some measure," (2) In Heb. 10:33, "partly . . . partly" is a translation of the antithetic phrases "*touto men*," ("this indeed,") and "*touto de*," ("but this,"), i.e., "on the one hand . . . and on the other hand."

PARTNER

1. *koinōnos* (κοινωνός, 2844), an adjective, signifying "having in common" (*koinos*), is used as a noun, "partners" in Luke 5:10, "partner" in 2 Cor. 8:23; Philem. 17 (in spiritual life and business). See COMMUNION, B, COMPANION, No. 2, PARTAKER.

2. *metochos* (μέτοχος, 3353), an adjective, signifying "having with, sharing," is used as a noun, "partners" in Luke 5:7. See FELLOW, PARTAKER.

Note: Koinōnos stresses the fact of having something in common, *metochos*, "the fact of sharing"; the latter is less thorough in effect than the former.

PASS, COME TO PASS (see *Notes* below)

1. *parerchomai* (παρέρχομαι, 3928), from *para*, "by," *erchomai*, "to come" or "go," denotes (I), literally, "to pass, pass by," (*a*) of persons, Matt. 8:28; Mark 6:48; Luke 18:37; Acts 16:8; (*b*) of things, Matt. 26:39, 42; of time, Matt. 14:15; Mark 14:35; Acts 27:9, KJV, "past" (RV, "gone by"); 1 Pet. 4:3; (II), metaphorically, (*a*) "to pass away, to perish," Matt. 5:18; 24:34, 35; Mark 13:30, 31; Luke 16:17; 21:32, 33; 2 Cor. 5:17; Jas. 1:10; 2 Pet. 3:10; (*b*) "to pass by, disregard, neglect, pass over," Luke 11:42; 15:29, "transgressed." For the meaning "to come forth or come," see Luke 12:37; 17:7, RV (Acts 24:7 in some mss.). See COME, No. 9.¶

2. *dierchomai* (διέρχομαι, 1330) denotes "to pass through or over," (*a*) of persons, e.g., Matt. 12:43, RV, "passeth (KJV, walketh) through"; Mark 4:35, KJV, "pass (RV, go) over"; Luke 19:1, 4; Heb. 4:14, RV, "passed through" (KJV "into"); Christ "passed through" the created heavens to the throne of God; (*b*) of things, e.g., Matt. 19:24, "to go through"; Luke 2:35, "shall pierce through" (metaphorically of a sword). See COME, No. 5.

3. *aperchomai* (ἀπέρχομαι, 565), "to go away," is rendered "to pass" in Rev. 9:12; 11:14; "passed away" in Rev. 21:4. See DEPART, No. 4.

4. *proerchomai* (προέρχομαι, 4281), "to go forward," is translated "passed on" in Acts 12:10. See GO.

5. *antiparerchomai* (ἀντιπαρέρχομαι, 492), denotes "to pass by opposite to" (*anti*, "over against," and No. 1), Luke 10:31, 32.¶

6. *diabainō* (διαβαίνω, 1224), "to step across, cross over," is translated "to pass" in Luke 16:26 (of "passing" across the fixed gulf: for the KJV in the 2nd part of the v., see No. 13); in Heb. 11:29, "passed through." See COME, No. 18.

7. *metabainō* (μεταβαίνω, 3327), "to pass over from one place to another" (*meta*, implying change), is translated "we have passed out of" (KJV, "from") in 1 John 3:14, RV, as to the change from death to life. See REMOVE, No. 1.

8. *anastrephō* (ἀναστρέφω, 390), lit., "to turn back" (*ana*, "back," *strephō*, "to turn"), in the middle voice, "to conduct oneself, behave, live," is translated "pass (the time)" in 1 Pet. 1:17. See ABIDE, No. 8.

9. *paragō* (παράγω, 3855), "to pass by, pass away," in Matt. 9:9, RV, "passed by" (KJV, "forth"), is used in the middle voice in 1 John 2:8, RV, "is passing away" (KJV, "is past"), of

the "passing" of spiritual darkness through the light of the gospel, and in v. 17 of the world. See DEPART, No. 2.

10. *paraporeuomai* (παραπορεύομαι, 3899), primarily, "to go beside, accompany" (*para*, "beside," *poreuomai*, "to proceed"), denotes "to go past, pass by," Matt. 27:39; Mark 9:30, "passed through" (some mss. have *poreuomai*); 11:20; 15:29; in Mark 2:23, "going ... through." See GO.¶

11. *diaporeuomai* (διαπορεύομαι, 1279), "to pass across, journey through," is used in the middle voice, translated "pass by" in Luke 18:36, KJV, RV, "going by." See GO.

12. *huperballō* (ὑπερβάλλω, 5235), in Eph. 3:19, "passeth": see EXCEED, A, No. 1.

13. *huperechō* (ὑπερέχω, 5242), "passeth" in Phil. 4:7: see BETTER (be), No. 4.

14. *diaperaō* (διαπεράω, 1276), "to pass over, cross over" (used in Luke 16:26, 2nd part: see No. 6): see CROSS.

15. *diodeuō* (διοδεύω, 1353), "to travel through, or along" (*dia*, "through," *hodos* "a way"), is translated "they had passed through" in Acts 17:1, lit., "having passed through"; in Luke 8:1, "He went about," RV (KJV, "throughout").¶

16. *chōreō* (χωρέω, 5562), used intransitively, signifies "to make room, retire, pass"; in Matt. 15:17, RV, "passeth (into the belly)," KJV, "goeth." See COME, No. 24.

17. *katargeō* (καταργέω, 2673) is translated "was passing away" in 2 Cor. 3:7 (KJV, "was to be done away"); "passeth away" in 3:11, RV (KJV, "is done away"). See ABOLISH.

18. *paroichomai* (παροίχομαι, 3944), "to have passed by, to be gone by," is used in Acts 14:16, of past generations, KJV, "(in times) past," RV, "(in the generations) gone by."¶

Notes: (1) *Ginomai*, "to become, take place," is often translated "to come to pass"; frequently in the Synoptic Gospels and Acts (note the RV of Luke 24:21); elsewhere in John 13:19; 14:22, RV, "(what) is come to pass ... ?" KJV, "(how) is it ... ?"; 14:29 (twice); 1 Thess. 3:4; Rev. 1:1. (2) In Acts 2:17, 21; 3:23 and Rom. 9:26, the KJV translates the future of *eimi*, "to be," "it shall come to pass" (RV, "it shall be"). (3) In Acts 5:15, KJV, *erchomai*, "to come," is translated "passing by" (RV, "came by"). (4) For the KJV, "passing" in Acts 27:8, see COASTING, C. (5) In Mark 6:35, KJV, "the time is far passed" (RV, "the day is .. far spent") is, lit., "the hour is much (*polus*)." (6) For *huperakmos* in 1 Cor. 7:36, RV, "past the flower of her age," see FLOWER.

PASSING OVER

paresis (πάρεσις, 3929), primarily "a letting go, dismissal" (akin to *pariēmi*, "to let alone, loosen"), denotes "a passing by" or "praetermission (of sin)," "a suspension of judgment," or "withholding of punishment," Rom. 3:25, RV, "passing over" (KJV, "remission"), with reference to sins committed previously to the propitiatory sacrifice of Christ, the "passing by" not being a matter of divine disregard but of forbearance.¶

PASSION

A. Nouns.

1. *pathēma* (πάθημα, 3804), "a suffering" or "a passive emotion," is translated "passions" in Rom. 7:5, RV, "(sinful) passions," KJV, "motions," and Gal. 5:24, RV; see AFFECTION, A, No. 3, AFFLICT, B, No. 3.

2. *pathos* (πάθος, 3806): see AFFECTION, A, No. 1.

B. Verb.

paschō (πάσχω, 3958), "to suffer," is used as a noun, in the aorist infinitive with the article, and translated "passion" in Acts 1:3, of the suffering of Christ at Calvary. See SUFFER.

C. Adjective.

homoiopathēs (ὁμοιπαθής, 3663), "of like feelings or affections" (*homoios*, "like," and A, No. 2; Eng., "homeopathy"), is rendered "of like passions" in Acts 14:15 (RV marg., "nature"); in Jas. 5:17, RV, ditto (KJV, "subject to like passions").¶

PASSOVER

pascha (πάσχα, 3957), the Greek spelling of the Aramaic word for the Passover, from the Hebrew *pāsach*, "to pass over, to spare," a feast instituted by God in commemoration of the deliverance of Israel from Egypt, and anticipatory of the expiatory sacrifice of Christ. The word signifies (I) "the Passover Feast," e.g., Matt. 26:2; John 2:13, 23; 6:4; 11:55; 12:1; 13:1; 18:39; 19:14; Acts 12:4; Heb. 11:28; (II) by metonymy, (*a*) "the Paschal Supper," Matt. 26:18, 19; Mark 14:16; Luke 22:8, 13; (*b*) "the Paschal lamb," e.g., Mark 14:12 (cf. Exod. 12:21); Luke 22:7; (*c*) "Christ Himself," 1 Cor. 5:7.

PAST

A. Verbs.

1. *ginomai* (γίνομαι, 1096), "to become, come to pass," is translated "was past" in Luke 9:36, KJV, and RV marg. (RV, "came"), of the voice of God the Father at the Transfiguration; "is past," 2 Tim. 2:18.

2. *diaginomai* (διαγίνομαι, 1230), *dia*, "through," a stronger form than No. 1, used of time, denotes "to intervene, elapse, pass," Mark 16:1, "was past"; Acts 25:13, RV, "were passed"; 27:9, "was spent."¶

3. *proginomai* (προγίνομαι, 4266), "to happen before" (*pro*, before, and No. 1), is used in Rom. 3:25, KJV, "that are past" (RV, "done aforetime"), of sins committed in times previous to the atoning sacrifice of Christ (see PASSING OVER).¶

Note: For the past tense of the verb "to pass," see PASS, e.g., Nos. 1 and 17.

B. Particle.

pote (ποτέ, 4218), "once, formerly, sometime," is translated "in time (or times) past," in Rom. 11:30; Gal. 1:13; v. 23, KJV (RV, "once"); Eph. 2:2, 11 (RV, "aforetime"); v. 3 (RV, "once"); Philem. 11 (RV, "aforetime"); 1 Pet. 2:10.

PASTOR

poimēn (ποιμήν, 4166), "a shepherd, one who tends herds or flocks" (not merely one who feeds them), is used metaphorically of Christian "pastors," Eph. 4:11. "Pastors" guide as well as feed the flock; cf. Acts 20:28, which, with v. 17, indicates that this was the service committed to elders (overseers or bishops); so also in 1 Pet. 5:1, 2, "tend the flock . . . exercising the oversight," RV; this involves tender care and vigilant superintendence. See SHEPHERD.

PASTURE

nomē (νομή, 3542) denotes (*a*) "pasture, pasturage," figuratively in John 10:9; (*b*) "grazing, feeding," figuratively in 2 Tim. 2:17, of the doctrines of false teachers, lit., "their word will have feeding as a gangrene." See EAT.¶

PATH

1. *tribos* (τρίβος, 5147), "a beaten track" (akin to *tribō*, "to rub, wear down"), "a path," is used in Matt. 3:3; Mark 1:3; Luke 3:4.¶

2. *trochia* (τροχία, 5163), "the track of a wheel" (*trochos*, "a wheel"; *trechō*, "to run"), hence, "a track, path," is used figuratively in Heb. 12:13.¶ In the Sept., Prov. 2:15; 4:11, 26, 27; 5:6, 21; in some texts, Ezek. 27:19.¶

PATIENCE, PATIENT, PATIENTLY

A. Nouns.

1. *hupomonē* (ὑπομονή, 5281), lit., "an abiding under" (*hupo*, "under," *menō*, "to abide"), is almost invariably rendered "patience." "Patience, which grows only in trial, Jas. 1:3, may be passive, i.e., = "endurance," as, (*a*) in trials, generally, Luke 21:19 (which is to be

understood by Matt. 24:13); cf. Rom. 12:12; Jas. 1:12; (b) in trials incident to service in the gospel, 2 Cor. 6:4; 12:12; 2 Tim. 3:10; (c) under chastisement, which is trial viewed as coming from the hand of God our Father, Heb. 12:7; (d) under undeserved affliction, 1 Pet. 2:20; or active, i.e. = "persistence, perseverance," as (e) in well doing, Rom. 2:7 (KJV, "patient continuance"); (f) in fruit bearing, Luke 8:15; (g) in running the appointed race, Heb. 12:1.

"Patience perfects Christian character, Jas. 1:4, and fellowship in the patience of Christ is therefore the condition upon which believers are to be admitted to reign with Him, 2 Tim. 2:12; Rev. 1:9. For this patience believers are 'strengthened with all power,' Col. 1:11, 'through His Spirit in the inward man,' Eph. 3:16.

"In 2 Thess. 3:5, the phrase 'the patience of Christ,' RV, is possible of three interpretations, (a) the patient waiting for Christ, so KJV paraphrases the words, (b) that they might be patient in their sufferings as Christ was in His, see Heb. 12:2, (c) that since Christ is 'expecting till His enemies be made the footstool of His feet,' Heb. 10:13, so they might be patient also in their hopes of His triumph and their deliverance. While a too rigid exegesis is to be avoided, it may, perhaps, be permissible to paraphrase: 'the Lord teach and enable you to love as God loves, and to be patient as Christ is patient.'"*

In Rev. 3:10, "the word of My patience" is the word which tells of Christ's patience, and its effects in producing "patience" on the part of those who are His (see above on 2 Thess. 3:5).

2. makrothumia (μακροθυμία, 3115), "longsuffering" (see B, No. 2), is rendered "patience" in Heb. 6:12; Jas. 5:10; see LONGSUFFERING.

B. Verbs.

1. hupomenō (ὑπομένω, 5278), akin to A, No. 1, (a) used intransitively, means "to tarry behind, still abide," Luke 2:43; Acts 17:14; (b) transitively, "to wait for," Rom. 8:24 (in some mss.), "to bear patiently, endure," translated "patient" (present participle) in Rom. 12:12; "ye take it patiently," 1 Pet. 2:20 (twice). See also under A, No. 1.

2. makrothumeō (μακροθυμέω, 3114), akin to A, No. 2, "to be long-tempered," is translated "to have patience," or "to be patient," in Matt. 18:26, 29; 1 Thess. 5:14, KJV (RV, "be longsuffering"); Jas. 5:7 (1st part, "be patient"; 2nd part, RV, "being patient," KJV, "hath long patience"); in Heb. 6:15, RV, "having (KJV, after he had) patiently endured." See LONGSUFFERING.

C. Adjectives.

Notes: (1) For epieikēs, translated "patient" in 1 Tim. 3:3, KJV, see GENTLE. (2) For anexikakos, translated "patient" in 2 Tim. 2:24, KJV, see FORBEAR.¶

D. Adverb.

makrothumōs (μακροθύμως, 3116), akin to A, No. 2, and B, No. 2, denotes "patiently," Acts 26:3.¶

PATRIARCH

patriarchēs (πατριάρχης, 3966), from patria, "a family," and archō, "to rule," is found in Acts 2:29; 7:8, 9; Heb. 7:4.¶ In the Sept., 1 Chron. 24:31; 27:22; 2 Chron. 19:8; 23:20; 26:12.¶

PATTERN

A. Nouns.

1. tupos (τύπος, 5179) is translated "pattern" in Titus 2:7, KJV; Heb. 8:5 (KJV and RV). See ENSAMPLE.

2. hupotupōsis (ὑποτύπωσις, 5296) is translated "pattern" in 1 Tim. 1:16, KJV; 2 Tim. 1:13, RV. See ENSAMPLE, FORM.¶

3. hupodeigma (ὑπόδειγμα, 5262) is translated "patterns" in Heb. 9:23, KJV. See COPY.

B. Adjective.

antitupos (ἀντίτυπος, 499) is translated "like in pattern" in Heb. 9:24, RV. See FIGURE, No. 2.

PAVEMENT

lithostrōtos (λιθόστρωτος, 3038), an adjective, denoting "paved with stones" (lithos, "a stone," and strōnnuō, "to spread"), especially of tessellated work, is used as a noun in John 19:13, of a place near the Praetorium in Jerusalem, called Gabbatha, a Greek transliteration of an Aramaic word.¶ In the Sept., 2 Chron. 7:3; Esth. 1:6; Song of Sol. 3:10.¶

PAY (Verb), PAYMENT

1. apodidōmi (ἀποδίδωμι, 591), "to give back, to render what is due, to pay," used of various obligations in this respect, is translated "to pay, to make payment," in Matt. 5:26; 18:25 (twice), 26, 28, 29, 30, 34; 20:8, RV (KJV, "give"). See DELIVER.

2. teleō (τελέω, 5055), "to bring to an end, complete, fulfill," has the meaning "to pay" in Matt. 17:24 and Rom. 13:6. See ACCOMPLISH.

Notes: (1) In Matt. 23:23, KJV, apodekatoō, "to tithe," is translated "ye pay tithe" (RV, "ye tithe"). (2) In Heb. 7:9, dekatoō (passive voice),

---

* From *Notes on Thessalonians* by Hogg and Vine, pp. 222, 285.

"to pay tithe," is translated "hath paid tithes," RV (perfect tense). See TITHE.

PEACE, PEACEABLE, PEACEABLY

N. Noun.

eirēnē (εἰρήνη, 1515) "occurs in each of the books of the NT, save 1 John and save in Acts 7:26 ['(at) one again'] it is translated "peace" in the RV. It describes (a) harmonious relationships between men, Matt. 10:34; Rom. 14:19; (b) between nations, Luke 14:32; Acts 12:20; Rev. 6:4; (c) friendliness, Acts 15:33; 1 Cor. 16:11; Heb. 11:31; (d) freedom from molestation, Luke 11:21; 19:42; Acts 9:31 (RV, 'peace,' KJV, 'rest'); 16:36; (e) order, in the State, Acts 24:2 (RV, 'peace,' KJV, 'quietness'); in the churches, 1 Cor. 14:33; (f) the harmonized relationships between God and man, accomplished through the gospel, Acts 10:36; Eph. 2:17; (g) the sense of rest and contentment consequent thereon, Matt. 10:13; Mark 5:34; Luke 1:79; 2:29; John 14:27; Rom. 1:7; 3:17; 8:6; in certain passages this idea is not distinguishable from the last, Rom. 5:1."*

"The God of peace" is a title used in Rom. 15:33; 16:20; Phil. 4:9; 1 Thess. 5:23; Heb. 13:20; cf. 1 Cor. 14:33; 2 Cor. 13:11. The corresponding Heb. word *shalom* primarily signifies "wholeness": see its use in Josh. 8:31, "unhewn"; Ruth 2:12, "full"; Neh. 6:15, "finished"; Isa. 42:19, marg., "made perfect." Hence there is a close connection between the title in 1 Thess. 5:23 and the word *holoklēros*, "entire," in that verse. In the Sept. *shalom* is often rendered by *sōtēria*, "salvation, e.g., Gen. 26:31; 41:16; hence the "peace-offering" is called the "salvation offering." Cf. Luke 7:50; 8:48. In 2 Thess. 3:16, the title "the Lord of peace" is best understood as referring to the Lord Jesus. In Acts 7:26, "would have set them at one" is, lit., "was reconciling them (conative imperfect tense, expressing an earnest effort) into peace."

B. Verbs.

1. *eirēneuō* (εἰρηνεύω, 1514), primarily, "to bring to peace, reconcile," denotes in the NT, "to keep peace or to be at peace": in Mark 9:50, RV, the Lord bids the disciples "be at peace" with one another, gently rebuking their ambitious desires; in Rom. 12:18 (RV, "be at peace," KJV, "live peaceably") the limitation "if it be possible, as much as in you lieth," seems due to the phrase "with all men," but is not intended to excuse any evasion of the obligation imposed by the command; in 2 Cor. 13:11 it is rendered

"live in peace," a general exhortation to believers; in 1 Thess. 5:13, "be at peace (among yourselves)."¶

2. *eirēnopoieō* (εἰρηνοποιέω, 1517), "to make peace" (*eirēnē*, and *poieō*, "to make"), is used in Col. 1:20.¶ In the Sept., Prov. 10:10.¶

C. Adjective.

eirēnikos (εἰρηνικός, 1516), akin to A, denotes "peaceful." It is used (a) of the fruit of righteousness, Heb. 12:11, "peaceable" (or "peaceful") because it is produced in communion with God the Father, through His chastening; (b) of "the wisdom that is from above," Jas. 3:17.¶

Note: In 1 Tim. 2:2, KJV, *hēsuchios*, "quiet," is translated "peaceable" (RV, "quiet").

PEACE (hold one's)

1. *sigaō* (σιγάω, 4601) signifies (a), used intransitively, "to be silent" (from *sigē*, "silence"), translated "to hold one's peace," in Luke 9:36; 18:39; 20:26; Acts 12:17; 15:13 (in v. 12, "kept silence"; similarly rendered in 1 Cor. 14:28, 30, KJV, "hold his peace," 34); (b) used transitively, "to keep secret"; in the passive voice, "to be kept secret," Rom. 16:25, RV, "hath been kept in silence." See SECRET, SILENCE.

2. *siōpaō* (σιωπάω, 4623), "to be silent or still, to keep silence" (from *siōpē*, "silence"), is translated "to hold one's peace," in Matt. 20:31; 26:63; Mark 3:4; 9:34; 10:48; 14:61; Luke 19:40; Acts 18:9; in the Lord's command to the sea, in Mark 4:39, it is translated "peace" (for the next word "be still" see No. 4); in Luke 1:20, RV, "thou shalt be silent" (KJV, "dumb"). See DUMB, B.¶

3. *hēsuchazō* (ἡσυχάζω, 2270) signifies "to be still"; it is used of holding one's "peace," being silent, Luke 14:4; Acts 11:18; 21:14, "we ceased." See CEASE, A, No. 3, QUIET.

4. *phimoō* (φιμόω, 5392), "to muzzle," is used metaphorically in the passive voice, in Mark 1:25 and Luke 4:35, "hold thy peace"; in Mark 4:39, "be still." See MUZZLE.

PEACEMAKER

eirēnopoios (εἰρηνοποιός, 1518), an adjective signifying peace making (*eirēnē*, and *poieō*, "to make"), is used in Matt. 5:9, "peacemakers." Cf. PEACE, B, No. 2.¶

PEARL

margaritēs (μαργαρίτης, 3135), "a pearl" (Eng., Margaret), occurs in Matt. 7:6 (proverbially and figuratively); 13:45, 46; 1 Tim. 2:9; Rev. 17:4; 18:12, 16; 21:21 (twice).¶

---

* From *Notes on Thessalonians* by Hogg and Vine, p. 154.

For PECULIAR see POSSESSION, B, No. 3, and C

PEN

kalamos (κάλαμος, 2563), "a reed, reed pipe, flute, staff, measuring rod," is used of a "writing-reed" or "pen" in 3 John 13. This was used on papyrus. Different instruments were used on different materials; the *kalamos* may have been used also on leather. "Metal pens in the form of a reed or quill have been found in the so-called Grave of Aristotle at Eretria." See REED.

PENCE, PENNY, PENNYWORTH

dēnarion (δηνάριον, 1220), a Roman coin, a *denarius*, a little less than the value of the Greek *drachmē* (see PIECE), now estimated as amounting to about 9 1/2d. in the time of our Lord, occurs in the singular, e.g., Matt. 20:2; 22:19; Mark 12:15; Rev. 6:6; in the plural, e.g., Matt. 18:28; Mark 14:5; Luke 7:41; 10:35; John 12:5; "pennyworth" in Mark 6:37 and John 6:7, lit., "(loaves of two hundred) pence." Considering the actual value, "shilling" would have been a more accurate translation, as proposed by the American translators, retaining "penny" for the *as*, and "farthing" for the *quadrans*.

PENTECOST

pentēkostos (πεντηκοστός, 4005), an adjective denoting "fiftieth," is used as a noun, with "day" understood, i.e., the "fiftieth" day after the Passover, counting from the second day of the Feast, Acts 2:1; 20:16; 1 Cor. 16:8.¶ For the divine instructions to Israel see Exod. 23:16; 34:22; Lev.23:15–21; Num. 28:26–31; Deut. 16:9–11.

For PENURY (Luke 21:4, KJV, RV, "want") see LACK

PEOPLE

1. *laos* (λαός, 2992) is used of (a) "the people at large," especially of people assembled, e.g., Matt. 27:25; Luke 1:21; 3:15; Acts 4:27; (b) "a people of the same race and language," e.g., Rev. 5:9; in the plural, e.g., Luke 2:31; Rom. 15:11; Rev. 7:9; 11:9; especially of Israel, e.g., Matt. 2:6; 4:23; John 11:50; Acts 4:8; Heb. 2:17; in distinction from their rulers and priests, e.g., Matt. 26:5; Luke 20:19; Heb. 5:3; in distinction from Gentiles, e.g., Acts 26:17, 23; Rom. 15:10; (c) of Christians as the people of God, e.g., Acts 15:14; Titus 2:14; Heb. 4:9; 1 Pet. 2:9.

2. *ochlos* (ὄχλος, 3793), "a crowd, throng": see CROWD, MULTITUDE.

3. *dēmos* (δῆμος, 1218), "the common people, the people generally" (Eng., "demagogue," "democracy," etc.), especially the mass of the "people" assembled in a public place, Acts 12:22; 17:5; 19:30, 33.¶

4. *ethnos* (ἔθνος, 1484) denotes (a) "a nation," e.g., Matt. 24:7; Acts 10:35; "the Jewish people," e.g., Luke 7:5; Acts 10:22; 28:19; (b) in the plural, "the rest of mankind" in distinction from Israel or the Jews, e.g., Matt. 4:15; Acts 28:28; (c) "the people of a city," Acts 8:9; (d) gentile Christians, e.g., Rom. 10:19; 11:13; 15:27; Gal. 2:14. See GENTILES, NATION.

5. *anthrōpos* (ἄνθρωπος, 444), "man," without distinction of sex (cf. *anēr*, "a male"), is translated "people" in John 6:10, RV (KJV, "men").

PERADVENTURE

A. Adverb.

tacha (τάχα, 5029), primarily "quickly" (from *tachus*, "quick"), signifies "peradventure" in Rom. 5:7; in Philem. 15, "perhaps." See PERHAPS.¶

B. Conjunction.

mēpote (μήποτε, 3379), often written as two words, usually signifies "lest ever, lest haply, haply"; in indirect questions, "if haply" or "whether haply," e.g., Luke 3:15, RV; in Matt. 25:9, RV, "peradventure" (KJV, "lest"); "if peradventure," in 2 Tim. 2:25. See HAPLY.

PERCEIVE

1. *ginōskō* (γινώσκω, 1097), "to know by experience and observation," is translated "to perceive" in Matt. 12:15, RV (KJV, "knew"); 16:8; 21:45; 22:18; 26:10, RV, (KJV, "understood"); Mark 8:17; 12:12 and 15:10, RV (KJV, "knew"); so Luke 9:11; 18:34; in Luke 7:39, RV (KJV, "known"); 20:19 (cf. No. 7 in v. 23); John 6:15; 8:27, RV (KJV, "understood"); 16:19, RV (KJV, "knew"); Acts 23:6; Gal. 2:9; in 1 John 3:16, KJV, "perceive" (RV, "know," perfect tense, lit., "we have perceived," and therefore "know"). See KNOW.

2. *epiginōskō* (ἐπιγινώσκω, 1921), a strengthened form of No. 1, "to gain a full knowledge of, to become fully acquainted with," is translated "to perceive" in Mark 5:30, RV (KJV, "knowing"); Luke 1:22; 5:22; Acts 19:34, RV (KJV, "knew"). See ACKNOWLEDGE, KNOW.

3. *eidon* (εἶδον, Aor. of 3708) (akin to *oida*, "to know"), an aorist form used to supply that tense of *horaō*, "to see," is translated "to perceive" in Matt. 13:14; Mark 4:12; Acts 28:26;

in Luke 9:47, KJV (RV, "saw"); in Acts 14:9, KJV, "perceiving" (RV, "seeing"). See BEHOLD, No. 1.

4. *theōreō* (θεωρέω, 2334), "to be a spectator of, look at, discern," is translated "to perceive" in John 4:19 (indicating the woman's earnest contemplation of the Lord); so Acts 17:22; in John 12:19, RV, "behold" (KJV, "perceive ye"). See BEHOLD, No. 6.

5. *aisthanomai* (αἰσθάνομαι, 143), "to perceive, to notice, understand," is used in Luke 9:45, RV, "(that they should not) perceive," KJV, "(that) they perceived . . . (not)."¶

6. *noeō* (νοέω, 3539), "to perceive with the mind, to understand," is translated "to perceive" in Matt. 15:17, RV (KJV, "understand"); so 16:9, 11; John 12:40; Rom. 1:20; Eph. 3:4; in Mark 7:18 and 8:17, KJV and RV, "perceive." See CONSIDER, No. 4.

7. *katanoeō* (κατανοέω, 2657), a strengthened form of No. 6, "to take note of, consider carefully," is translated "to perceive" in Luke 6:41, KJV (RV, "considerest"); 20:23; Acts 27:39, RV (KJV, "discovered"). See BEHOLD, No. 11.

8. *katalambanō* (καταλαμβάνω, 2638), "to lay hold of, apprehend, comprehend," is translated "to perceive" in Acts 4:13; 10:34. See APPREHEND, No. 1.

Notes: (1) In Mark 12:28 the best mss. have *oida*, "to know" (so RV), for *eidon*, "to see, perceive" (KJV). (2) In Acts 8:23, KJV, *horaō*, "to see," is translated "I perceive" (RV, "I see"). (3) In 2 Cor. 7:8, KJV, *blepō*, "to look at, consider, see," is translated "I perceive" (RV, "I see"). (4) In Acts 23:29, KJV, *heuriskō*, "to find," is translated "perceived" (RV, "found").

For **PERDITION** see **DESTRUCTION**, No. 1

PERFECT (Adjective and Verb), PERFECTLY

A. Adjectives.

1. *teleios* (τέλειος, 5049) signifies "having reached its end" (*telos*), "finished, complete, perfect." It is used (I) of persons, (*a*) primarily of physical development, then, with ethical import, "fully grown, mature," 1 Cor. 2:6; 14:20 ("men"; marg., "of full age"); Eph. 4:13; Phil. 3:15; Col. 1:28; 4:12; in Heb. 5:14, RV, "fullgrown" (marg., "perfect"), KJV, "of full age" (marg., "perfect"); (*b*) "complete," conveying the idea of goodness without necessary reference to maturity or what is expressed under (*a*), Matt. 5:48; 19:21; Jas. 1:4 (2nd part); 3:2. It is used thus of God in Matt. 5:48; (II) of "things, complete, perfect," Rom. 12:2; 1 Cor. 13:10

(referring to the complete revelation of God's will and ways, whether in the completed Scriptures or in the hereafter); Jas. 1:4 (of the work of patience); v. 25; 1 John 4:18.¶

2. *teleioteros* (τελειότερος, 5046*), the comparative degree of No. 1, is used in Heb. 9:11, of the very presence of God.¶

3. *artios* (ἄρτιος, 739) is translated "perfect" in 2 Tim. 3:17: see COMPLETE, B.

B. Verbs.

1. *teleioō* (τελειόω, 5048), "to bring to an end by completing or perfecting," is used (I) of "accomplishing" (see FINISH, FULFILL); (II) of "bringing to completeness," (*a*) of persons: of Christ's assured completion of His earthly course, in the accomplishment of the Father's will, the successive stages culminating in His death, Luke 13:32; Heb. 2:10, to make Him "perfect," legally and officially, for all that He would be to His people on the ground of His sacrifice; cf. 5:9; 7:28, RV, "perfected" (KJV, "consecrated"); of His saints, John 17:23, RV, "perfected" (KJV, "made perfect"); Phil. 3:12; Heb. 10:14; 11:40 (of resurrection glory); 12:23 (of the departed saints); 1 John 4:18; of former priests (negatively), Heb. 9:9; similarly of Israelites under the Aaronic priesthood, 10:1; (*b*) of things, Heb. 7:19 (of the ineffectiveness of the Law); Jas. 2:22 (of faith made "perfect" by works); 1 John 2:5, of the love of God operating through him who keeps His word; 4:12, of the love of God in the case of those who love one another; 4:17, of the love of God as "made perfect with" (RV) those who abide in God, giving them to be possessed of the very character of God, by reason of which "as He is, even so are they in this world."

2. *epiteleō* (ἐπιτελέω, 2005), "to bring through to the end" (*epi*, intensive, in the sense of "fully," and *teleō*, "to complete"), is used in the middle voice in Gal. 3:3, "are ye (now) perfected," continuous present tense, indicating a process, lit., "are ye now perfecting yourselves"; in 2 Cor. 7:1, "perfecting (holiness)"; in Phil. 1:6, RV, "will perfect (it)," KJV, "will perform." See ACCOMPLISH, No. 4.

3. *katartizō* (καταρτίζω, 2675), "to render fit, complete" (*artios*), "is used of mending nets, Matt. 4:21; Mark 1:19, and is translated 're-store' in Gal. 6:1. It does not necessarily imply, however, that that to which it is applied has been damaged, though it may do so, as in these passages; it signifies, rather, right ordering and arrangement, Heb. 11:3, 'framed;' it points out the path of progress, as in Matt. 21:16; Luke 6:40; cf. 2 Cor. 13:9; Eph. 4:12, where corresponding nouns occur. It indicates the close relationship between character and destiny,

Rom. 9:22, 'fitted.' It expresses the pastor's desire for the flock, in prayer, Heb. 13:21, and in exhortation, 1 Cor. 1:10, RV, 'perfected' (KJV, 'perfectly joined'); 2 Cor. 13:11, as well as his conviction of God's purpose for them, 1 Pet. 5:10. It is used of the Incarnation of the Word in Heb. 10:5, 'prepare,' quoted from Ps. 40:6 (Sept.), where it is apparently intended to describe the unique creative act involved in the Virgin Birth, Luke 1:35. In 1 Thess. 3:10 it means to supply what is necessary, as the succeeding words show."* See FIT, B, No. 3.¶

Note: Cf. *exartizō*, rendered "furnished completely," in 2 Tim. 3:17, RV; see ACCOMPLISH, No. 1.

C. Adverbs.

1. *akribōs* (ἀκριβῶς, 199), accurately, is translated "perfectly" in 1 Thess. 5:2, where it suggests that Paul and his companions were careful ministers of the Word. See ACCURATELY, and see *Note* (2) below.

2. *akribesteron* (ἀκριβέστερον, 197), the comparative degree of No. 1, Acts 18:26; 23:15: see CAREFULLY, EXACTLY.

3. *teleiōs* (τελείως, 5049), "perfectly," is so translated in 1 Pet. 1:13, RV (KJV, "to the end"), of setting one's hope on coming grace. See END.¶

Notes: (1) In Rev. 3:2, KJV, *plēroō*, "to fulfill," is translated "perfect" (RV, "fulfilled"). (2) For the adverb *akribōs* in Luke 1:3, KJV, see ACCURATELY; in Acts 24:22, KJV, see EXACT. (3) For the noun *akribeia* in Acts 22:3, see MANNER.

PERFECTION, PERFECTING (noun), PERFECTNESS

A. Nouns.

1. *katartisis* (κατάρτισις, 2676), "a making fit," is used figuratively in an ethical sense in 2 Cor. 13:9, RV, "perfecting" (KJV, "perfection"), implying a process leading to consummation (akin to *katartizō*, see PERFECT, B, No. 3).¶

2. *katartismos* (καταρτισμός, 2677) denotes, in much the same way as No. 1, "a fitting or preparing fully," Eph. 4:12.¶

3. *teleiōsis* (τελείωσις, 5050) denotes "a fulfillment, completion, perfection, an end accomplished as the effect of a process," Heb. 7:11; in Luke 1:45, RV, "fulfillment" (KJV, "performance"). ¶

4. *teleiotēs* (τελειότης, 5047) denotes much the same as No. 3, but stressing perhaps the actual accomplishment of the end in view, Col.

3:14, "perfectness"; Heb. 6:1, "perfection."¶ In the Sept., Judg. 9:16, 19; Prov. 11:3; Jer. 2:2.¶

B. Verb.

telesphoreō (τελεσφορέω, 5052), "to bring to a completion" or "an end in view" (*telos*, "an end," *pherō*, "to bear"), is said of plants, Luke 8:14.¶

PERFORM, PERFORMANCE

1. *teleō* (τελέω, 5055), "to finish," is translated "performed" in Luke 2:39, KJV: see ACCOMPLISH, No. 3.

2. *apoteleō* (ἀποτελέω, 658), "to bring to an end, accomplish," is translated "I perform" in Luke 13:32, RV (KJV, "I do"); some mss. have No. 3; in Jas. 1:15, it is used of sin, "fullgrown" RV (KJV, "finished"). See FINISH, *Note* 2.¶

3. *epiteleō* (ἐπιτελέω, 2005), Rom. 15:28, KJV, "performed" (RV, "accomplished"); 2 Cor. 8:11, KJV, "perform" (RV, "complete"); Phil. 1:6, KJV, "perform" (RV, "perfect"): see ACCOMPLISH, No. 4.

4. *poieō* (ποιέω, 4160), "to do," is translated "to perform" in Rom. 4:21; in Luke 1:72, KJV (RV, "to show"). See SHEW.

5. *apodidōmi* (ἀποδίδωμι, 591), "to give back, or in full," is translated "thou . . . shalt perform" in Matt. 5:33. See DELIVER. No. 3.

Notes: (1) In Rom. 7:18, KJV, *katergazomai*, "to work," is translated "to perform" (RV, "to do"; marg., "work"). (2) In Luke 1:20, KJV, *ginomai*, "to come to pass" (RV), is translated "shall be performed." (3) For "performance" in Luke 1:45, see FULFILLMENT.

PERHAPS

1. *tacha* (τάχα, 5029) is translated "perhaps" in Philem. 15. See PERADVENTURE.

2. *ara* (ἄρα, 686), a particle, "then," sometimes marking a result about which some uncertainty is felt, is translated "perhaps" in Acts 8:22.

Note: In 2 Cor. 2:7, KJV, *pōs*, "anyhow," "by any means" (RV), is translated "perhaps."

For PERIL, see DANGER, *Note:*
PERILOUS see GRIEVOUS

PERISH

1. *apollumi* (ἀπόλλυμι, 622), "to destroy," signifies, in the middle voice, "to perish," and is thus used (*a*) of things, e.g., Matt. 5:29, 30; Luke 5:37; Acts 27:34, RV, "perish" (in some texts *piptō*, "to fall," as KJV); Heb. 1:11; 2 Pet. 3:6; Rev. 18:14 (2nd part), RV, "perished" (in some texts *aperchomai*, "to depart," as KJV); (*b*) of persons, e.g., Matt. 8:25; John 3:(15), 16;

10:28; 17:12, RV, "perished" (KJV, "is lost"); Rom. 2:12; 1 Cor. 1:18, lit., "the perishing," where the perfective force of the verb implies the completion of the process of destruction (Moulton, *Proleg.*, p. 114); 8:11; 15:18; 2 Pet. 3:9; Jude 11. For the meaning of the word see DESTROY, No. 1.

2. *sunapollumi* (συναπόλλυμι, 4881), in the middle voice, denotes "to perish together" (*sun*, "with," and No. 1), Heb. 11:31.¶

3. *apothnēskō* (ἀποθνήσκω, 599), "to die"; in Matt. 8:32 "perished." See DIE, No. 2.

4. *aphanizō* (ἀφανίζω, 853), "to make unseen" (*a*, negative, *phainō*, "to cause to appear"), in the passive voice, is translated "perish" in Acts 13:41 (RV, marg., "vanish away"). See DISFIGURE.

5. *diaphtheirō* (διαφθείρω, 1311), "to corrupt," is rendered "perish" in 2 Cor. 4:16, KJV (RV, "is decaying"). See CORRUPT, No. 3, DECAY.

Notes: (1) In Acts 8:20, "(thy money) perish" is a translation of a phrase, lit, "be unto destruction," *apōleia;* see DESTRUCTION, B, (II), No. 1. (2) In Col. 2:22, "to perish" is a translation of the phrase *eis pthoran,* lit., "unto corruption"; see CORRUPT, B, No. 1. (3) For "shall utterly perish," in 2 Pet. 2:12, KJV, see CORRUPT, B, No. 1 (b).

For PERJURED PERSON see FORSWEAR

PERMISSION

sungnōmē (συγγνώμη, 4774), lit., "a joint opinion, mind or understanding" (*sun*, "with," *gnōmē*, "an opinion"), "a fellow feeling," hence, "a concession, allowance," is translated "permission," in contrast to "commandment," in 1 Cor. 7:6.¶

PERMIT

epitrepō (ἐπιτρέπω, 2010), lit., "to turn to" (*epi*, "to," *trepō*, "to turn"), "to entrust," signifies "to permit," Acts 26:1; 1 Cor. 14:34; 1 Cor. 16:7; 1 Tim. 2:12, RV "permit" (KJV,"suffer"); Heb. 6:3. See LEAVE.

For PERNICIOUS, 2 Pet. 2:2, KJV, see LASCIVIOUS

PERPLEX, PERPLEXITY

A. Verbs

1. *aporeō* (ἀπορέω, 639) is rendered "perplexed" in 2 Cor. 4:8, and in the most authentic mss. in Luke 24:4; see DOUBT, A, No. 1.

2. *diaporeō* (διαπορέω, 1280), "was much perplexed" in Luke 9:7; see DOUBT, A, No. 2.

B. Noun.

aporia (ἀπορία, 640), akin to A, No. 1, is translated "perplexity" in Luke 21:25 (lit., "at a loss for a way," *a*, negative, *poros*, "a way, resource"), of the distress of nations, finding no solution to their embarrassments; papyri illustrations are in the sense of being at one's wit's end, at a loss how to proceed, without resources.¶

PERSECUTE, PERSECUTION

A. Verbs.

1. *diōkō* (διώκω, 1377) has the meanings (*a*) "to put to flight, drive away," (*b*) "to pursue," whence the meaning "to persecute," Matt. 5:10–12, 44; 10:23; 23:34; Luke 11:49 (No. 2 in some mss.); 21:12; John 5:16; 15:20 (twice); Acts 7:52; 9:4, 5, and similar passages; Rom. 12:14; 1 Cor. 4:12; 15:9; 2 Cor. 4:9, KJV (RV, "pursued"); Gal. 1:13, 23; 4:29; Gal. 5:11, RV, "am . . . persecuted" (KJV, "suffer persecution"); so 6:12; Phil. 3:6; 2 Tim. 3:12, "shall suffer persecution"; Rev. 12:13. See FOLLOW, PURSUE.

2. *ekdiōkō* (ἐκδιώκω, 1559), *ek*, "out," and No. 1, is used in 1 Thess. 2:15, KJV, "persecuted" (RV, "drove out"). See also No. 1. See DRIVE, No. 2.¶

B. Noun.

diōgmos (διωγμός, 1375), akin to A, No. 1, occurs in Matt. 13:21; Mark 4:17; 10:30; Acts 8:1; 13:50; Rom. 8:35; 2 Cor. 12:10; 2 Thess. 1:4; 2 Tim. 3:11, twice (for v. 12, see A, No. 1).¶ In the Sept., Prov. 11:19; Lam. 3:19.¶

Note: In Acts 11:19, KJV, *thlipsis*, "tribulation" (RV), is translated "persecution."

PERSECUTOR

diōktēs (διώκτης, 1376), akin to *diōkō* (see above), occurs in 1 Tim. 1:13.¶

PERSEVERANCE

proskarterēsis (προσκαρτέρησις, 4343) occurs in Eph. 6:18. Cf. the verb (and the formation) under ATTEND, No. 2.¶

PERSON

1. *prosōpon* (πρόσωπον, 4383), for the meaning of which see APPEARANCE, No. 2, is translated "person" or "persons" in Matt. 22:16; Mark 12:14; Luke 20:21; 2 Cor. 1:11; 2 Cor. 2:10; Gal. 2:6; Jude 16, lit., "(admiring, or showing respect of, RV) persons."

2. *anthrōpos* (ἄνθρωπος, 444), a generic name for man, is translated "persons" in Rev. 11:13, RV (KJV, "men").

Notes: (1) In Heb. 1:3, KJV, *hupostasis*, "substance," is translated "person"; see SUBSTANCE. (2) In Matt. 27:24, RV, *toutou*, "of this . . .

(man)," is translated "of this . . . person" (KJV). (3) In Philem. 12, the pronoun *autos*, "he," placed in a position of strong emphasis, is translated "in his own person," RV, stressing the fact that in spite of the apostle's inclination to retain Onesimus, he has sent him, as being, so to speak, "his very heart," instead of adopting some other method. (4) In 1 Cor. 5:13, KJV, the adjective *ponēros*, "wicked," used as a noun, is translated "wicked person" (RV, " . . . man"). (5) In 2 Pet. 2:5, KJV, *ogdoos*, "eighth," is translated "the (lit., 'an') eighth *person*" (RV, "with seven others"). (*b*) Various adjectives are used with the word "persons," e.g., "devout, perjured, profane."

PERSONS (respect of)
A. Nouns.
1. *prosōpolēmptēs* (προσωπολήμπτης, 4381) denotes "a respecter of persons" (*prosōpon*, "a face" or "person," *lambanō*, "to lay hold of"), Acts 10:34.¶

2. *prosōpolēmpsia* (in inferior texts without the letter m) (προσωπολημψία, 4382) denotes "respect of persons, partiality" (akin to No. 1), the fault of one who, when responsible to give judgment, has respect to the position, rank, popularity, or circumstances of men, instead of their intrinsic conditions, preferring the rich and powerful to those who are not so, Rom. 2:11; Eph. 6:9; Col. 3:25; Jas. 2:1.¶
B. Verb.
prosōpolēmpteō (προσωπολημπτέω, 4380), "to have respect of persons" (see above), occurs in Jas. 2:9.¶

C. Adverb.
aprosōpolēmptōs (ἀπροσωπολήμυπτως, 678), "without respect of persons, impartially" (*a*, negative), occurs in 1 Pet. 1:17.¶

PERSUADE
1. *peithō* (πείθω, 3982) in the active voice, signifies "to apply persuasion, to prevail upon or win over, to persuade," bringing about a change of mind by the influence of reason or moral considerations, e.g., in Matt. 27:20; 28:14; Acts 13:43; 19:8; in the passive voice, "to be persuaded, believe" (see BELIEVE, No. 2, and OBEY), e.g., Luke 16:31; 20:6; Acts 17:4, RV (KJV, "believed"); 21:14; 26:26; Rom. 8:38; 14:14; 15:14; 2 Tim. 1:5, 12; Heb. 6:9; 11:13, in some mss.; 13:18, RV (KJV, "trust"). See ASSURANCE, B, No. 3.
Note: For Acts 26:28, KJV, "thou persuadest," see FAIN, *Note*.
2. *anapeithō* (ἀναπείθω, 374), "to persuade, induce," in an evil sense (*ana*, "back," and No.

1), is used in Acts 18:13.¶ In the Sept., Jer. 29:8.¶
Note: For *plērophoreō*, rendered "being fully persuaded," in Rom. 4:21 and 14:5, KJV, see ASSURANCE, B, No. 2.

PERSUASIVE, PERSUASIVENESS
A. Adjective.
peithos (πειθός, 3981), an adjective (akin to *peithō*), not found elsewhere, is translated "persuasive" in 1 Cor. 2:4, RV (KJV, "enticing"); see ENTICE, B.¶
B. Noun.
pithanologia (πιθανολογία, 4086), "persuasiveness of speech," is used in Col. 2:4, RV. See ENTICE, B, *Note*.¶

PERSUASION
peismonē (πεισμονή, 3988), akin to *peithō*, is used in Gal. 5:8, where the meaning is "this influence that has won you over, or that seems likely to do so"; the use of *peithō*, in the sense of "to obey," in v. 7, suggests a play upon words here.¶

PERTAIN TO
metechō (μετέχω, 3348), Heb. 7:13, KJV; see BELONG, *Note* (*c*), PARTAKE, B, No. 3.
Notes: (1) In Rom. 15:17, the phrase *ta pros*, lit., "the (things) towards" is translated "things pertaining to," RV (KJV, "those things which pertain to"); in Heb. 2:17 and 5:1, RV and KJV, "things pertaining to." (2) In Acts 1:3, KJV, the phrase *ta peri*, "the (things) concerning" (RV), is translated "the things pertaining to." (3) In Rom. 9:4, the RV rightly translates the relative pronoun *hōn*, lit., "of whom" from *hos*, "who"), by "whose is" (KJV, "to whom *pertaineth*"). (4) In Rom. 4:1, KJV, *kata*, "according to" (RV), is translated "as pertaining to." (5) For 1 Cor. 6:3, 4, see LIFE, B, No. 1.

PERVERSE, PERVERT
1. *apostrephō* (ἀποστρέφω, 654), "to turn away" (*apo*, "from," *strephō*, "to turn"), is used metaphorically in the sense of "perverting" in Luke 23:14 (cf. No. 2 in v. 2). See BRING, No. 22.
2. *diastrephō* (διαστρέφω, 1294), "to distort, twist" (*dia*, "through," and *strephō*), is translated "to pervert" in Luke 23:2 (cf. No. 1 in v. 14); Acts 13:10 [in v. 8, "to turn aside" (KJV, "away")]; in the perfect participle, passive voice, it is translated "perverse," lit., "turned aside, corrupted," in Matt. 17:17; Luke 9:41; Acts 20:30; Phil. 2:15.¶
3. *metastrephō* (μεταστρέφω, 3344), "to transform into something of an opposite char-

acter" (*meta*, signifying "a change," and *strephō*,) as the Judaizers sought to "pervert the gospel of Christ," Gal. 1:7; cf. "the sun shall be turned into darkness," Acts 2:20; laughter into mourning and joy to heaviness, Jas. 4:9. See TURN.¶

4. *ekstrephō* (ἐκστρέφω, 1612), "to turn inside out" (*ek*, "out"), "to change entirely," is used metaphorically in Titus 3:11, RV, "is perverted" (KJV, "is subverted"). See SUBVERT.¶

Note: For "perverse disputings," 1 Tim. 6:5, KJV, see DISPUTE, A, No. 3.

PESTILENCE, PESTILENT FELLOW

loimos (λοιμός, 3061), "a pestilence, any deadly infectious malady," is used in the plural in Luke 21:11 (in some mss., Matt. 24:7); in Acts 24:5, metaphorically, "a pestilent fellow." See FELLOW.¶

PETITION

aitēma (αἴτημα, 155), from *aiteō*, "to ask" is rendered "petitions" in 1 John 5:15: see ASK, B, and cf. the distinction between A, Nos. 1 and 2.¶ Cf. *deēsis* (see PRAYER).

PHARISEES

pharisaios (φαρισαῖος, 5330), from an Aramaic word *peras* (found in Dan. 5:28), signifying "to separate," owing to a different manner of life from that of the general public. The "Pharisees" and Sadducees appear as distinct parties in the latter half of the 2nd cent. B.C., though they represent tendencies traceable much earlier in Jewish history, tendencies which became pronounced after the return from Babylon (537 B.C.). The immediate progenitors of the two parties were, respectively, the Hasidaeans and the Hellenizers; the latter, the antecedents of the Sadducees, aimed at removing Judaism from its narrowness and sharing in the advantages of Greek life and culture. The Hasidaeans, a transcription of the Hebrew *chasidim*, i.e., "pious ones," were a society of men zealous for religion, who acted under the guidance of the scribes, in opposition to the godless Hellenizing party; they scrupled to oppose the legitimate high priest even when he was on the Greek side. Thus the Hellenizers were a political sect, while the Hasidaeans, whose fundamental principle was complete separation from non-Jewish elements, were the strictly legal party among the Jews, and were ultimately the more popular and influential party. In their zeal for the Law they almost deified it and their attitude became merely external, formal, and mechani-

cal. They laid stress, not upon the righteousness of an action, but upon its formal correctness. Consequently their opposition to Christ was inevitable; His manner of life and teaching was essentially a condemnation of theirs; hence His denunciation of them, e.g., Matt. 6:2, 5, 16; 15:7 and chapter 23.

While the Jews continued to be divided into these two parties, the spread of the testimony of the gospel must have produced what in the public eye seemed to be a new sect, and in the extensive development which took place at Antioch, Acts 11:19–26, the name "Christians" seems to have become a popular term applied to the disciples as a sect, the primary cause, however, being their witness to Christ (see CALL, A, No. 11). The opposition of both "Pharisees" and Sadducees (still mutually antagonistic, Acts 23:6–10) against the new "sect" continued unabated during apostolic times.

PHILOSOPHER

philosophos (φιλόσοφος, 5386), lit., "loving wisdom" (*philos*, "loving," *sophia*, "wisdom"), occurs in Acts 17:18.¶

PHILOSOPHY

philosophia (φιλοσοφία, 5385) denotes "the love and pursuit of wisdom," hence, "philosophy," the investigation of truth and nature; in Col. 2:8, the so-called "philosophy" of false teachers. "Though essentially Greek as a name and as an idea, it had found its way into Jewish circles ... Josephus speaks of the three Jewish sects as three 'philosophies' ... It is worth observing that this word, which to the Greeks denoted the highest effort of the intellect, occurs here alone in Paul's writings ... the Gospel had deposed the term as inadequate to the higher standard whether of knowledge or of practice, which it had introduced" (Lightfoot).¶

PHYLACTERY

phulaktērion (φυλακτήριον, 5440), primarily "an outpost," or "fortification" (*phulax*, "a guard"), then, "any kind of safeguard," became used especially to denote "an amulet." In the NT it denotes a prayer fillet, "a phylactery," a small strip of parchment, with portions of the Law written on it; it was fastened by a leather strap either to the forehead or to the left arm over against the heart, to remind the wearer of the duty of keeping the commandments of God in the head and in the heart; cf. Ex. 13:16; Deut. 6:8; 11:18. It was supposed to have potency as a charm against evils and demons. The Pharisees broadened their "phylacteries" to render conspicuous their superior eagerness to be mindful of God's Law, Matt. 23:5.¶

PHYSICIAN

iatros (ἰατρός, 2395), akin to *iaomai*, "to heal," "a physician," occurs in Matt. 9:12; Mark 2:17; 5:26; Luke 4:23; 5:31 (in some mss., 8:43); Col. 4:14.¶

PIECE

1. *epiblēma* (ἐπίβλημα, 1915) primarily denotes "that which is thrown over, a cover" (*epi*, "over," *ballō*, "to throw"); then, "that which is put on, or sewed on, to cover a rent, a patch," Matt. 9:16; Mark 2:21; in the next sentence, RV, "that which should fill" (KJV, "the new piece that filled"), there is no word representing "piece" (lit., "the filling," *plērōma*); see FILL, B; Luke 5:36.¶

2. *drachmē* (δραχμή, 1406), a *drachma*, firstly, "an Attic weight," as much as one can hold in the hand (connected with *drassomai*, "to grasp with the hand, lay hold of," 1 Cor. 3:19), then, "a coin," nearly equal to the Roman *denarius* (see PENNY), is translated "pieces of silver" in Luke 15:8, 1st part; "piece," 2nd part and v. 9.¶

3. *meros* (μέρος, 3313), "a part," is translated "a piece (of a broiled fish)" in Luke 24:42. See BEHALF, PART.

4. *klasma* (κλάσμα, 2801), "a broken piece" (from *klaō*, "to break") is used of the broken pieces from the feeding of the multitudes, RV, "broken pieces," KJV, "fragments," Matt. 14:20; Mark 6:43; 8:19, 20; Luke 9:17; John 6:12, 13; in Matt. 15:37 and Mark 8:8, RV, "broken pieces" (KJV, "broken meat").¶

5. *argurion* (ἀργύριον, 694), which frequently denotes "money," also represents "a silver coin," of the value of a shekel or *tetradrachmon* (four times the *drachmē*, see No. 2); it is used in the plural in Matt. 26:15; 27:3–9. In Acts 19:19, "fifty thousand pieces of silver," is, lit., "fifty thousand of silver" (probably drachmas). See MONEY, SILVER.

Notes: (1) In Acts 27:44, for KJV, "*broken pieces,*" the RV translates *epi* ("on") *tinōn* ("certain things") *tōn* ("the," i.e., "those namely") by "on *other* things"; there is no word in the original representing "pieces." (2) For the phrase "to break to (in) pieces," Matt. 21:44, RV, and Mark 5:4, see BREAK, A, Nos. 10 and 5 respectively. (3) In Luke 14:18, KJV, *agros*, "a field" (RV), is translated "a piece of ground." (4) In Matt. 17:27, KJV, *statēr*, "a shekel" (RV), a *tetradrachmon* (see No. 5, above), is translated "a piece of money."

PIERCE

1. *diikneomai* (διικνέομαι, 1338), "to go through, penetrate" (*dia*, "through," *ikneomai*, "to go"), is used of the power of the Word of God, in Heb. 4:12, "piercing."¶ In the Sept., Ex. 26:28.¶

2. *dierchomai* (διέρχομαι, 1330), "to go through," is translated "shall pierce through" in Luke 2:35. See COME, No. 5.

3. *ekkenteō* (ἐκκεντέω, 1574), primarily, "to prick out" (*ek*, "out," *kenteō*, "to prick"), signifies "to pierce," John 19:37; Rev. 1:7.¶

4. *nussō* (νύσσω, 3572), "to pierce" or "pierce through," often of inflicting severe or deadly wounds, is used of the piercing of the side of Christ, John 19:34 (in some mss., Matt. 27:49).¶

5. *peripeirō* (περιπείρω, 4044), "to put on a spit," hence, "to pierce," is used metaphorically in 1 Tim. 6:10, of torturing one's soul with many sorrows, "have pierced (themselves) through."¶

PIETY (to shew)

eusebeō (εὐσεβέω, 2151), "to reverence, to show piety" towards any to whom dutiful regard is due (akin to *eusebēs*, "pious, godly, devout"), is used in 1 Tim. 5:4 of the obligation on the part of children and grandchildren (RV) to express in a practical way their dutifulness "towards their own family"; in Acts 17:23 of worshiping God. See WORSHIP.¶

For PIGEON see DOVE, No. 1

PILGRIM

parepidēmos (παρεπίδημος, 3927), an adjective signifying "sojourning in a strange place, away from one's own people" (*para*, "from," expressing a contrary condition, and *epidēmeō*, "to sojourn"; *dēmos*, "a people"), is used of OT saints, Heb. 11:13, "pilgrims" (coupled with *xenos*, "a foreigner"); of Christians, 1 Pet. 1:1, "sojourners (of the Dispersion)," RV; 2:11, "pilgrims" (coupled with *paroikos*, "an alien, sojourner"); the word is thus used metaphorically of those to whom Heaven is their own country, and who are sojourners on earth.¶

PILLAR

stulos (στύλος, 4769), "a column supporting the weight of a building," is used (*a*) metaphorically, of those who bear responsibility in the churches, as of the elders in the church at Jerusalem, Gal. 2:9; of a local church as to its responsibility, in a collective capacity, to maintain the doctrines of the faith by teaching and practice, 1 Tim. 3:15; some would attach this and the next words to the statement in v. 16; the connection in the Eng. versions seems preferable; (b) figuratively in Rev. 3:12, indicating a firm and permanent position in the spiritual, heavenly and eternal Temple of God; (c) illustratively, of the feet of the angel in the vision in Rev. 10:1, seen as flames rising like columns of fire indicative of holiness and consuming power, and thus reflecting the glory of Christ as depicted in 1:15; cf. Ezek. 1:7.¶

PILLOW

proskephalaion (προσκεφάλαιον, 4344) denotes "a pillow, a cushion for the head" (*pros*, "to, *kephalē*, "a head"), Mark 4:38 (RV, "cushion").¶ In the Sept., Ezek. 13:18.¶

PINE AWAY

xērainō (ξηραίνω, 3583), "to dry up, wither," is rendered "pineth away" in Mark 9:18. See DRY.

PINNACLE

pterugion (πτερύγιον, 4419) denotes (a) "a little wing" (diminutive of *pterux*, "a wing"); (b) "anything like a wing, a turret, battlement," of the temple in Jerusalem, Matt. 4:5 and Luke 4:9 (of the *hieron*, "the entire precincts," or parts of the main building, as distinct from the *naos*, "the sanctuary"). This "wing" has been regarded (1) as the apex of the sanctuary, (2) the top of Solomon's porch, (3) the top of the Royal Portico, which Josephus describes as of tremendous height (*Antiq.* xv. 11.5).¶ It is used in the Sept. of the fins of fishes, e.g., Lev. 11:9–12; of the part of a dress, hanging down in the form of a wing, Ruth 3:9; 1 Sam. 24:5.

PIPE (Noun and Verb)

A. Noun.

aulos (αὐλός, 836), "a wind instrument," e.g., "a flute" (connected with *aēmi*, "to blow"), occurs in 1 Cor. 14:7.¶

B. Verb.

auleō (αὐλέω, 832), "to play on an *aulos*," is used in Matt. 11:17; Luke 7:32; 1 Cor. 14:7 (2nd part).¶

For **PIPERS**, Rev. 18:22, KJV, see **FLUTE PLAYERS**

PIT

1. *phrear* (φρέαρ, 5421), "a well, dug for water" (distinct from *pēgē*, "a fountain"), denotes "a pit" in Rev. 9:1, 2, RV, "the pit (of the abyss)," "the pit," i.e., the shaft leading down to the abyss, KJV, "(bottomless) pit"; in Luke 14:5, RV, well (KJV, "pit"); in John 4:11, 12, "well." See WELL.¶

2. *bothunos* (βόθυνος, 999) is rendered "pit" in Matt. 12:11: see DITCH.

3. *abussos* (ἄβυσσος, 12): see BOTTOMLESS, B.

4. *hupolēnion* (ὑπολήνιον, 5276) denotes "a vessel or trough beneath a winepress," to receive the juice, Mark 12:1, RV, "a pit for the winepress" (KJV, "a place for . . . the wine-fat").¶

Note: For "pits," 2 Pet. 2:4, RV, see CHAIN *Note* (1).

PITCH (Verb)

pēgnumi (πήγνυμι, 4078), "to make fast, to fix" (cf. *prospēgnumi*, Acts 2:23, of crucifixion), is used of "pitching" a tent; in Heb. 8:2, of the "true tabernacle," the heavenly and spiritual, which "the Lord pitched."¶

PITCHER

keramion (κεράμιον, 2765), "an earthen vessel" (*keramos*, "potter's clay"), "a jar" or "jug," occurs in Mark 14:13; Luke 22:10.¶

PITIABLE (most)

eleeinoteros (ἐλεεινότερας, 1652*), the comparative degree of *eleeinos*, "miserable, pitiable" (*eleos*, "pity"), is used in 1 Cor. 15:19, "most pitiable" (RV), lit., "more pitiable than all men." See MISERABLE.¶

PITIFUL, PITY

1. *polusplanchnos* (πολύσπλαγχνος, 4184) denotes "very pitiful" or "full of pity" (*polus*, "much," *splanchnon*, "the heart"; in the plural, "the affections"), occurs in Jas. 5:11, RV, "full of pity."¶

2. *eusplanchnos* (εὔσπλαγχνος, 2155), "compassionate, tenderhearted," lit., "of good heartedness" (*eu*, "well," and *splanchnon*), is translated "pitiful" in 1 Pet. 3:8, KJV, RV, "tenderhearted," as in Eph. 4:32.¶

PLACE (Noun, Verb, Adverb)

A. Nouns.

1. *topos* (τόπος, 5117), (Eng., "topic," "topography," etc.,) is used of "a region" or "locality," frequently in the Gospels and Acts; in Luke 2:7 and 14:22, "room"; of a place which a person or thing occupies, a couch at table, e.g., Luke 14:9, 10, RV, "place" (KJV, "room"); of the destiny of Judas Iscariot, Acts 1:25; of the condition of the "unlearned" or nongifted in a church gathering, 1 Cor. 14:16, RV, "place"; the sheath of a sword, Matt. 26:52; a place in a book, Luke 4:17; see also Rev. 2:5; 6:14; 12:8;

metaphorically, of "condition, occasion, opportunity" Acts 25:16, RV, "opportunity" (KJV, "license"); Rom. 12:19; Eph. 4:27. See OPPORTUNITY, ROOM.

2. *chōrion* (χωρίον, 5564), "a region" (a diminutive of *chōra*, "a land, country"), is used of Gethsemane, Matt. 26:36; Mark 14:32. See FIELD.

3. *huperochē* (ὑπεροχή, 5247), "high place," 1 Tim. 2:2: see AUTHORITY, No. 3.

4. *periochē* (περιοχή, 4042), primarily "a circumference, compass" (*peri*, "around," *echō*, "to have"), hence denotes "a portion circumscribed," that which is contained, and in reference to a writing or book, "a portion or passage of its contents," Acts 8:32, "(the) place."¶

5. *akroatērion* (ἀκροατήριον, 201) denotes "a place of audience" (*akroaomai*, "to listen"), Acts 25:23, "place of hearing."¶

6. *prōtoklisia* (πρωτοκλισία, 4411): see CHIEF, B, No. 7.

Notes: (1) For *opē*, "a hole," Jas. 3:11, KJV, "place," see OPENING: see also CAVE. (2) For "place of toll," Matt. 9:9; Mark 2:14, see CUSTOM (TOLL), No. 2. (3) In Heb. 4:5 "in this place" is, lit., "in this," i.e., "in this (passage)." (4) In Luke 6:17, RV, *topos*, with *pedinos*, "level," is translated "level place" (KJV, "plain"). (5) For *amphodon*, rendered "a place where two ways met," Mark 11:4 (RV, "the open street"), see STREET.¶ (6) For *erēmia*, "a desert place," see DESERT, A. (7) In 1 Cor. 11:20 and 14:23, KJV, the phrase *epi to auto*, lit., "to the same," is translated "into one place," RV, "together"; perhaps = "in assembly." (8) For "secret place," Luke 11:33, KJV, see CELLAR. (9) For "place of prayer," Acts 16:13, RV, see PRAYER. (10) For Phil. 1:13 (KJV, "in all other places"), RV, "to all the rest," see PALACE. (11) For "rocky places," Mark 4:16, see ROCKY.

B. Verbs.

1. *anachōreō* (ἀναχωρέω, 402), "to withdraw" (*ana*, "back," *chōreō*, "to make room, retire"), is translated "give place" in Matt. 9:24. See DEPART, No. 10.

2. *eikō* (εἴκω, 1502), "to yield, give way," is rendered "gave place" in Gal. 2:5.¶

3. *ginomai* (γίνομαι, 1096), "to become, take place," is translated "(a death) having taken place" in Heb. 9:15, RV, KJV, "by means of (death)," referring, not to the circumstances of a testamentary disposition, but to the sacrifice of Christ as the basis of the New Covenant.

Note: For *chōreō* in John 8:37, KJV, "hath . . . place," see COURSE, B.

C. Adverbs, etc.

1. *hōde* (ὧδε, 5602), "here, hither," is translated "to ('unto,' RV) this place" in Luke 23:5. See HERE.

2. *pantachou* (πανταχοῦ, 3837), "everywhere," is translated "in all places" in Acts 24:3. See EVERYWHERE, No. 2.

Notes: (1) For "in divers places," Matt. 24:7, etc., see DIVERS, B, *Note*. (2) In the following the RV gives the correct meaning: in Mark 6:10, *ekeithen*, "thence" (KJV, "from that place"); in Heb. 2:6 and 4:4, *pou*, "somewhere" (KJV, "in a certain place"); in Matt. 12:6, *hōde*, "here" (KJV, "in this place"); in Mark 6:10, *hopou ean*, "wheresoever" (KJV, "in what place soever"). (3) The adjective *entopios*, "of that place," occurs in Acts 21:12.¶ (4) In Jas. 2:3 *kalōs*, "well" (KJV, marg.), is rendered "in a good place." See DWELLING, HEAVENLY, HOLY, MARKET, SKULL, STEEP, YONDER.

PLAGUE

I. *mastix* (μάστιξ, 3148), "a whip, scourge," Acts 22:24, "by scourging"; Heb. 11:36, "scourgings," is used metaphorically of "disease" or "suffering," Mark 3:10; 5:29, 34; Luke 7:21. See SCOURGING.¶

2. *plēgē* (πληγή, 4127), "a stripe, wound" (akin to *plēssō*, "to smite"), is used metaphorically of a calamity, "a plague," Rev. 9:20; 11:6; 15:1, 6, 8; 16:9, 21 (twice); 18:4, 8; 21:9; 22:18. See STRIPE, WOUND.

For **PLAIN** (Noun) see **PLACE, A,** *Note* (4)

PLAIN (Adverb), PLAINLY, PLAINNESS

1. *orthōs* (ὀρθῶς, 3723), "rightly" (from *orthos*, "straight"), is translated "plain," in Mark 7:35, of restored speech. See RIGHTLY.

2. *parrhēsia* (παρρησία, 3954), "boldness," is used adverbially in its dative case and rendered "plainly" in John 10:24; 11:14; 16:25; 16:29 (with *en*, lit., "in plainness"). See BOLD, B, where see also "plainness of speech," 2 Cor. 3:12, RV.

PLAIT

plekō (πλέκω, 4120), "to weave, twist, plait," is used of the crown of thorns inflicted on Christ, Matt. 27:29; Mark 15:17; John 19:2.¶

For **PLAITING** (of the hair) see **BRAIDED,** *Note* (1)

For **PLANK** see **BOARD**

PLANT (Noun, Verb, Adjective)

A. Noun.

phuteia (φυτεία, 5451), firstly, "a planting," then "that which is planted, a plant" (from *phuō*, "to bring forth, spring up, grow," *phuton*, "a plant"), occurs in Matt. 15:13.¶ In the Sept., 2 Kings 19:29; Ezek. 17:7; Mic. 1:6.¶

B. Verb.

phuteuō (φυτεύω, 5452), "to plant," is used (*a*) literally, Matt. 21:33; Mark 12:1; Luke 13:6; 17:6, 28; 20:9; 1 Cor. 9:7; (*b*) metaphorically, Matt. 15:13; 1 Cor. 3:6, 7, 8.¶

C. Adjective.

sumphutos (σύμφυτος, 4854), firstly, "congenital, innate" (from *sumphuō*, "to make to grow together"), then, "planted" or "grown along with, united with," Rom. 6:5, KJV, "planted together," RV, "united with *Him*," indicating the union of the believer with Christ in experiencing spiritually "the likeness of His death." See UNITED.¶ Cf. *emphutos*, Jas. 1:21, RV, "implanted" (marg., "inborn"). See EN-GRAFTED.

PLATTER

1. *paropsis* (παροψίς, 3953), firstly, "a side dish of dainties" (*para*, "beside," *opson*, "cooked"); then, "the dish itself," Matt. 23:25; v. 26, in some mss.¶

2. *pinax* (πίναξ, 4094) is translated "platter" in Luke 11:39; see CHARGER.

PLAY

paizō (παίζω, 3815), properly, "to play as a child" (*pais*), hence denotes "to play" as in dancing and making merry, 1 Cor. 10:7.¶ Cf. *empaizō*, "to mock."

PLEAD

entunchanō (ἐντυγχάνω, 1793), "to make petition," is used of the "pleading" of Elijah against Israel, Rom. 11:2, RV, "pleadeth with" (KJV, "maketh intercession to"). See DEAL WITH, INTERCESSIONS.

PLEASE, PLEASING (Noun), WELL-PLEASING, PLEASURE

A. Verbs.

1. *areskō* (ἀρέσκω, 700) signifies (*a*) "to be pleasing to, be acceptable to," Matt. 14:6; Mark 6:22; Acts 6:5; Rom. 8:8; 15:2; 1 Cor. 7:32–34; Gal. 1:10; 1 Thess. 2:15; 4:1 (where the preceding *kai*, "and," is epexegetical, "even," explaining the "walking," i.e., Christian manner of life, as "pleasing" God; in Gen. 5:22, where the Hebrew has "Enoch walked with God," the Sept. has "Enoch pleased God"; cf. Mic. 6:8;

Heb. 11:5); 2 Tim. 2:4; (*b*) "to endeavor to please," and so, "to render service," doing so evilly in one's own interests, Rom. 15:1, which Christ did not, v. 3; or unselfishly, 1 Cor. 10:33; 1 Thess. 2:4. This sense of the word is illustrated by Moulton and Milligan (*Vocab.*) from numerous inscriptions, especially describing "those who have proved themselves of use to the commonwealth."¶

2. *euaresteō* (εὐαρεστέω, 2100) signifies "to be well-pleasing" (*eu*, "well," and a form akin to No. 1); in the active voice, Heb. 11:5, RV, "he had been "well-pleasing" (unto God)," KJV, "he pleased"; so v. 6; in the passive voice, Heb. 13:16.¶

3. *eudokeō* (εὐδοκέω, 2106) signifies (*a*) "to be well pleased, to think it good" [*eu*, "well," and *dokeō*, see *Note* (1) below], not merely an understanding of what is right and good as in *dokeō*, but stressing the willingness and freedom of an intention or resolve regarding what is good, e.g., Luke 12:32, "it is (your Father's) good pleasure"; so Rom. 15:26, 27, RV; 1 Cor. 1:21; Gal. 1:15; Col. 1:19; 1 Thess. 2:8, RV, "we were well pleased" (KJV, "we were willing"); this meaning is frequently found in the papyri in legal documents; (*b*) "to be well pleased with," or "take pleasure in," e.g., Matt. 3:17; 12:18; 17:5; 1 Cor. 10:5; 2 Cor. 12:10; 2 Thess. 2:12; Heb. 10:6, 8, 38; 2 Pet. 1:17.

4. *thelō* (θέλω, 2309), "to will, wish, desire," is translated "it pleased (Him)" in 1 Cor. 12:18; 15:38, RV. See DESIRE, B, No. 6.

5. *spatalaō* (σπαταλάω, 4684), "to live riotously," is translated "giveth herself to pleasure" in 1 Tim. 5:6, RV (KJV, "liveth in pleasure"); "taken your pleasure" in Jas. 5:5, KJV, "been wanton."¶

Notes: (1) In Acts 15:22, KJV, *dokeō*, "to seem good to" (RV), is translated "it pleased" (in some mss., v. 34); in Heb. 12:10, KJV, "(after their own) pleasure," RV,"(as) seemed good (to them)." (2) For *suneudokeō*, rendered "have pleasure in" in Rom. 1:32, KJV, see CONSENT, No. 6. (3) For *truphaō*, rendered "lived in pleasure" in Jas. 5:5 KJV, see DELICATELY.

B. Adjectives.

1. *arestos* (ἀρεστός, 701) denotes "pleasing, agreeable," John 8:29, RV, "(the things that are) pleasing," KJV, "(those things that) please"; KJV and RV in 1 John 3:22; in Acts 6:2, "fit" (RV marg., "pleasing"); 12:3, "it pleased," lit., "it was pleasing." See FIT.¶

2. *euarestos* (εὐάρεστος, 2101), eu, "well," and No. 1, is translated "well-pleasing" in the RV except in Rom. 12:1, 2 (see marg., however). See ACCEPT, B, No. 4.

C. Noun.

areskeia (or *-ia*) (ἀρεσκεία, 699), a "pleasing," a giving pleasure, Col. 1:10, of the purpose Godward of a walk worthy of the Lord (cf. 1 Thess. 4:1). It was used frequently in a bad sense in classical writers. Moulton and Milligan illustrate from the papyri its use in a favorable sense, and Deissmann (*Bible Studies*) from an inscription.¶ In the Sept., Prov. 31:30.¶

PLEASURE

A. Nouns.

1. *hēdonē* (ἡδονή, 2237), "pleasure," is used of the gratification of the natural desire or sinful desires (akin to *hēdomai*, "to be glad," and *hēdeōs*, "gladly"), Luke 8:14; Titus 3:3; Jas. 4:1, 3, RV, "pleasures" (KJV, "lusts"); in the singular, 2 Pet. 2:13. See LUST.¶

2. *eudokia* (εὐδοκία, 2107), "good pleasure" (akin to *eudokeō*, PLEASE, No. 3), Eph. 1:5, 9; Phil. 2:13; 2 Thess. 1:11. See DESIRE, A, No. 2.

3. *apolausis* (ἀπόλαυσις, 619), "enjoyment," is used with *echō*, "to have," and rendered "enjoy the pleasures" (lit., "pleasure") in Heb. 11:25. See ENJOY.

Notes: (1) In Rev. 4:11, KJV, *thelēma*, "a will," is translated "(for Thy) pleasure," RV, "(because of Thy) will." (2) For *charis*, translated "pleasure" in the KJV of Acts 24:27 and 25:9, see FAVOR, A.

B. Adjective.

philēdonos (φιλήδονος, 5369), "loving pleasure" (*philos*, "loving," and A, No. 1), occurs in 2 Tim. 3:4, RV, "lovers of pleasure" (KJV, " . . . pleasures"). See LOVER.¶

Note: In 1 Tim. 5:6 the RV renders *spatalaō* "giveth herself to pleasure."

PLENTEOUS

polus (πολύς, 4183), "much," is rendered "plenteous" in Matt. 9:37, of a harvest of souls, and Luke 10:2, RV (KJV, "great"). See GREAT.

PLENTIFULLY

Note: This translates the prefix *eu* ("well") of the verb *euphoreō*, "to produce well," in Luke 12:16, "brought forth plentifully."¶

PLOT

epiboulē (ἐπιβουλή, 1917), lit., "a plan against" (*epi*, "against," *boulē*, "a counsel, plan"), is translated "plot" in the RV (KJV, "laying await" and "lying in wait") in Acts 9:24; 20:3, 19; 23:30.¶

PLOUGH, PLOW

A. Noun.

arotron (ἄροτρον, 723), from *aroō*, "to plough," occurs in Luke 9:62.¶

B. Verb.

arotriaō (ἀροτριάω, 722), akin to A, a later form of *aroō*, "to plow," occurs in Luke 17:7 and 1 Cor. 9:10.¶

PLUCK (out)

1. *tillō* (τίλλω, 5089) is used of "plucking off ears of corn," Matt. 12:1; Mark 2:23; Luke 6:1.¶ In the Sept., Isa. 18:7.¶

2. *harpazō* (ἁρπάζω, 726), "to seize, snatch," is rendered "pluck" in John 10:28, 29, KJV, RV, "snatch." For the meaning, see CATCH, No. 1.

3. *exaireō* (ἐξαιρέω, 1807), "to take out" (*ex* for *ek*, "out," *haireō*, "to take"), is translated "pluck out," of the eye as the occasion of sin, in Matt. 5:29; 18:9, indicating that, with determination and promptitude, we are to strike at the root of unholy inclinations, ridding ourselves of whatever would stimulate them. Cf. *Note* (2) below. See DELIVER, No. 8.

4. *exorussō* (ἐξορύσσω, 1846), "to dig out or up," is rendered "ye would have plucked out (your eyes)" in Gal. 4:15, an indication of their feelings of gratitude to, and love for, the apostle. The metaphor affords no real ground for the supposition of a reference to some weakness of his sight, and certainly not to the result of his temporary blindness at his conversion, the recovery from which must have been as complete as the infliction. There would be some reason for such an inference had the pronoun "ye" been stressed; but the stress is on the word "eyes"; their devotion prompted a readiness to part with their most treasured possession on his behalf. For Mark 2:4 see BREAK, No. 14, DIG, No. 1, *Note* (2).¶ In the Sept., 1 Sam. 11:2; Prov. 29:22.¶

5. *ekrizoō* (ἐκριζόω, 1610), "to pluck up by the roots" (*ek*, "out," *rhiza*, "a root"), is so translated in Jude 12 (figuratively), and in the KJV in Luke 17:6, RV, "rooted up"; "root up," Matt. 13:29; "shall be rooted up," 15:13. See ROOT.¶

Notes: (1) In Mark 5:4, KJV, *diaspaō*, "to rend asunder" (RV), is translated "plucked asunder," said of chains. (2) In Mark 9:47, KJV, *ekballō*, "to cast out" (RV), is translated "pluck . . . out." Cf. No. 3, above.

POET

poiētēs (ποιητής, 4163), primarily "a maker," later "a doer" (*poieō* "to make, to do"), was used, in classical Greek, of "an author," especially a "poet"; so Acts 17:28. See DOER.

POINT, POINTS

A. Phrases.

Notes: (1) In Heb. 4:15, "in all points" represents the phrase *kata* with the neuter plural of *pas*, "all," lit., "according to all (things)." (2) "To be at the point of death" is a translation (*a*) of the verb *mellō*, "to be about," with *teleutaō*, "to end one's life, die," Luke 7:2; see DIE, No. 4; (*b*) of *mellō* with *apothnēskō*, "to die," John 4:47; (*c*) of the phrase mentioned under DEATH, C, *Note*. (3) In Jas. 2:10, *en heni* (the dative case of *heis*, "one"), lit., "in one," is rendered "in one *point.*"

B. Noun.

kephalaion (κεφάλαιον, 2774), the neuter of the adjective *kephalaios*, "of the head," is used as a noun, signifying (*a*) "a sum, amount, of money," Acts 22:28; (*b*) "a chief point," Heb. 8:1, not the summing up of the subject, as the KJV suggests, for the subject was far from being finished in the Epistle; on the contrary, in all that was being set forth by the writer "the chief point" consisted in the fact that believers have "a High Priest" of the character already described. See SUM.¶

C. Verb.

dēloō (δηλόω, 1213), "to make plain" (*dēlos*, "evident"), is translated "did point unto" in 1 Pet. 1:11, RV (KJV, "did signify"), of the operation of "the Spirit of Christ" in the prophets of the Old Testament in "pointing" on to the time and its characteristics, of the sufferings of Christ and subsequent glories. See SHEW, SIGNIFY.

POISON

ios (ἰός, 2447) denotes "something active" as (*a*) "rust," as acting on metals, affecting their nature, Jas. 5:3; (*b*) "poison," as of asps, acting destructively on living tissues, figuratively of the evil use of the lips as the organs of speech, Rom. 3:13; so of the tongue, Jas. 3:8.¶

For **POLLUTE** see **DEFILE**, A, No. 1

POLLUTION

alisgēma (ἀλίσγημα, 234), akin to a late verb *alisgeō*, "to pollute," denotes "a pollution, contamination," Acts 15:20, "pollutions of idols," i.e., all the contaminating associations connected with idolatry including meats from sacrifices offered to idols.¶

Note: For *miasma*, KJV, "pollutions," in 2 Pet. 2:20, see DEFILEMENT, B, No. 1.¶

POMP

phantasia (φαντασία, 5325), as a philosophic term, denoted "an imagination"; then, "an appearance," like *phantasma*, "an apparition"; later, "a show, display, pomp" (Eng., "phantasy"), Acts 25:23.¶ In the Sept., Hab. 2:18; 3:10; Zech. 10:1.¶

PONDER

sumballō (συμβάλλω, 4820), "to throw together, confer," etc., has the meaning "to ponder," i.e., "to put one thing with another in considering circumstances," in Luke 2:19. See CONFER.

POOL

kolumbēthra (κολυμβήθρα, 2861) denotes "a swimming pool" (akin to *kolumbaō*, "to swim," Acts 27:43), John 5:2 (v. 4 in some mss.), 7; 9:7 (v. 11 in some mss.).¶

POOR

A. Adjectives.

1. *ptōchos* (πτωχός, 4434), for which see BEG, B, has the broad sense of "poor," (*a*) literally, e.g., Matt. 11:5; 26:9, 11; Luke 21:3 (with stress on the word, "a conspicuously poor widow"); John 12:5, 6, 8; 13:29; Jas. 2:2, 3, 6; the "poor" are constantly the subjects of injunctions to assist them, Matt. 19:21; Mark 10:21; Luke 14:13, 21; 18:22; Rom. 15:26; Gal. 2:10; (*b*) metaphorically, Matt. 5:3; Luke 6:20; Rev. 3:17.

2. *penichros* (πενιχρός, 3998), akin to B, "needy, poor," is used of the widow in Luke 21:2 (cf. No. 1, of the same woman, in v. 3); it is used frequently in the papyri.¶ In the Sept., Ex. 22:25; Prov. 28:15; 29:7.¶

B. Noun.

penēs (πένης, 3993), "a laborer "(akin to *penomai*, "to work for one's daily bread"), is translated "poor" in 2 Cor. 9:9.¶

C. Verb.

ptōcheuō (πτωχεύω, 4433), "to be poor as a beggar" (akin to A, No. 1), "to be destitute," is said of Christ in 2 Cor. 8:9.¶

PORCH

1. *stoa* (στοά, 4745), "a portico," is used (*a*) of the "porches" at the pool of Bethesda, John 5:2; (*b*) of the covered colonnade in the Temple, called Solomon's "porch," John 10:23; Acts 3:11; 5:12 a portico on the eastern side of the temple; this and the other "porches" existent in the time of Christ were almost certainly due to Herod's restoration. Cf. *Stoics* (Acts 17:18), "philosophers of the porch."¶

2. *pulōn* (πυλών, 4440), akin to *pulē*, "a gate" (Eng., "pylon"), is used of "a doorway, porch or vestibule" of a house or palace, Matt. 26:71. In the parallel passage Mark 14:68, No. 3 is used, and *pulōn* doubtless stands in Matt. 26 for *proaulion*. See GATE, No. 2.

3. *proaulion* (προαύλιον, 4259), "the exterior court" or "vestibule," between the door and the street, in the houses of well-to-do folk, Mark 14:68, "porch" (RV marg., "forecourt").¶

PORTER

thurōros (θυρωρός, 2377), "a door-keeper" (*thura*, "a door," *ouros*, "a guardian"), is translated "porter" in Mark 13:34; John 10:3; it is used of a female in John 18:16, 17, translated "(her) that kept the door."¶ In the Sept., 2 Sam. 4:6; 2 Kings 7:11; Ezek. 44:11.¶

PORTION

A. Nouns.

1. *meros* (μέρος, 3313), "a part," is translated "portion" in Matt. 24:51; Luke 12:46; 15:12. See PART.

2. *klēros* (κλῆρος, 2819), "a lot," is translated "portion" in Acts 1:17, RV. See CHARGE, INHERITANCE, LOT.

3. *meris* (μερίς, 3310), "a part," is translated "portion" in 2 Cor. 6:15, RV. See PART.

Note: For "portion of food," Luke 12:42, RV, see FOOD, No. 4.

B. Verb.

summerizō (συμμερίζω, 4829), "to have a part with" (akin to A, No. 3), is translated "have their portion with" in 1 Cor. 9:13. RV. See PARTAKER.¶

C. Adverb

polumerōs (πολυμερῶς, 4181) signifies "in many parts" or "portions" (*polus*, "many," and A, No. 1), Heb. 1:1, RV (KJV, "at sundry times").¶

POSSESS, POSSESSION

A. Verbs.

1. *katechō* (κατέχω, 2722), "to hold fast, hold back," signifies "to possess," in 1 Cor. 7:30 and 2 Cor. 6:10. See HOLD.

2. *ktaomai* (κτάομαι, 2932), "to procure for oneself, acquire, obtain," hence, "to possess" (akin to B, No. 1), has this meaning in Luke 18:12 and 1 Thess. 4:4; in Luke 21:19, RV, "ye shall win" (KJV, "possess ye"), where the probable meaning is "ye shall gain the mastery over your souls," i.e., instead of giving way to adverse circumstances. See OBTAIN.

3. *huparchō* (ὑπάρχω, 5225), "to be in existence," and, in a secondary sense, "to belong to," is used with this meaning in the neuter plural of the present participle with the article signifying one's "possessions," "the things which he possesseth," Luke 12:15; Acts 4:32; in Heb. 10:34, RV, "possessions" (KJV, "goods"); cf. B, No. 4. See GOODS.

4. *daimonizomai* (δαιμονίζομαι, 1139), "to be possessed of a demon or demons": see DEMON, B.

Note: In Acts 8:7 and 16:16, KJV, *echō*, "have," is translated "to be possessed of," in the sense of No. 4, above, RV, "had" and "having."

B. Nouns.

1. *ktēma* (κτῆμα, 2933), akin to A, No. 2, denotes "a possession, property," Matt. 19:22; Mark 10:22; Acts 2:45; 5:1.¶

2. *kataschesis* (κατάσχεσις, 2697), primarily "a holding back" (akin to A, No. 1), then, "a holding fast," denotes "a possession," Acts 7:5, or "taking possession," v. 45, with the article, lit., "in the (i.e., their) taking possession."¶

3. *peripoiēsis* (περιποίησις, 4047), "an obtaining, an acquisition," is translated "(*God's* own) possession" in Eph. 1:14, RV, which may mean "acquisition," KJV, "purchased possession"; 1 Pet. 2:9, RV, "*God's* own possession," KJV, "a peculiar (people)." See OBTAIN.

4. *huparxis* (ὕπαρξις, 5223), primarily "subsistence" (akin to A, No. 3), later denoted "substance, property, possession" in Heb. 10:34, RV (KJV, "substance"). See GOODS, SUBSTANCE.

Note: In Acts 28:7, KJV, *chōria*, "lands" (RV), is translated "possessions."

C. Adjective.

periousios (περιούσιος, 4041), "of one's own possession, one's own," qualifies the noun *laos*, "people," in Titus 2:14, KJV, "peculiar," see RV.¶ In the Sept., Ex. 19:5; 23:22; Deut. 7:6; 14:2; 26:18.¶

POSSESSOR

ktētōr (κτήτωρ, 2935), "a possessor, an owner" (akin to *ktaomai*, see POSSESS, No. 2), occurs in Acts 4:34.¶

POSSIBLE

A. Adjective.

dunatos (δυνατός, 1415), "strong, mighty, powerful, able (to do)," in its neuter form signifies "possible," Matt. 19:26; 24:24; 26:39; Mark 9:23; 10:27; 13:22; 14:35, 36; Luke 18:27; Acts 2:24; 20:16 (27:39, in some mss.; *dunamai*, "to be able," in the most authentic, RV, "they could"); Rom. 12:18; Gal. 4:15. See ABLE.

B. Verb.

eimi (εἰμί, 1510), "to be," is used in the third person singular, impersonally, with the meaning "it is possible," negatively in 1 Cor. 11:20, RV,

(KJV, "it is not"), and Heb. 9:5, "we cannot," lit., "it is not possible."

Note: For Heb. 10:4, KJV, "it is not possible," see IMPOSSIBLE.

POT

1. *xestēs* (ξέστης, 3582) was a Sicilian corruption of the Latin liquid measure *sextarius*, about a pint; in Mark 7:4 (v. 8 also in some mss.) it denotes "a pitcher," of wood or stone.¶

2. *stamnos* (στάμνος, 4713), primarily "an earthen jar" for racking off wine, hence, "any kind of jar," occurs in Heb. 9:4.¶

For **POTENTATE,** used of God, 1 Tim. 6:15, see **AUTHORITY,** No. 4

POTTER

A. Noun.

kerameus (κεραμεύς, 2763), "a potter" (from *kerannumi*, "to mix," akin to *keramos*, "potter's clay"), is used (*a*) in connection with the "potter's field," Matt. 27:7, 10; (*b*) illustratively of the "potter's" right over the clay, Rom. 9:21, where the introductory "or" suggests the alternatives that either there must be a recognition of the absolute discretion and power of God, or a denial that the "potter" has power over the clay. There is no suggestion of the creation of sinful beings, or of the creation of any simply in order to punish them. What the passage sets forth is God's right to deal with sinful beings according to His own counsel.¶

B. Adjective.

keramikos (κεραμικός, 2764) denotes "of (or made by) a potter" (Eng., "ceramic"), "earthen," Rev. 2:27.¶

POUND

1. *litra* (λίτρα, 3046) was a Sicilian coin, the equivalent of a Latin *libra* or *as* (whence the metric unit, "liter"); in the NT it is used as a measure of weight, a pound, John 12:3; 19:39.¶

2. *mna* (μνᾶ, 3414), a Semitic word, both "a weight" and "a sum of money," 100 shekels (cf. 1 Kings 10:17, *maneh;* Dan. 5:25, 26, *mene*), in Attic Greek 100 *drachmai*, in weight about 15 oz., in value near about L/4 Is. 3d. (see PIECE), occurs in Luke 19:13, 16 (twice), 18 (twice), 20, 24 (twice), 25.¶

POUR

1. *ballō* (βάλλω, 906), "to throw," is used of "pouring" liquids, Matt. 26:12, RV, marg., "cast" (of ointment); John 13:5 (of water). See CAST, No. 1.

2. *katacheō* (καταχέω, 2708), "to pour down upon" (*kata*, "down," *cheō*, "to pour"), is used in Matt. 26:7 (cf. No. 1 in v. 12) and Mark 14:3, of ointment.¶

3. *ekcheō* (ἐκχέω, 1632), "to pour out" (*ek*, "out"), is used (*a*) of Christ's act as to the changers' money, John 2:15; (*b*) of the Holy Spirit, Acts 2:17, 18, 33, RV, "He hath poured forth" (KJV, " . . . shed forth"); Titus 3:6, RV, "poured out" (KJV, "shed"); (*c*) of the emptying of the contents of the bowls (KJV, "vials") of divine wrath, Rev. 16: 1–4, 8, 10, 12, 17; (*d*) of the shedding of the blood of saints by the foes of God, Rev. 16:6, RV, "poured out" (KJV, "shed"); some mss. have it in Acts 22:20. See RUN, SHED, SPILL.

4. *ekchunō* (ἐκχύνω, 1632) or *ekchunnō*, a Hellenistic form of No. 3, is used of the blood of Christ, Luke 22:20, RV "is poured out" (KJV, "is shed"); of the Holy Spirit, Acts 10:45. See GUSH OUT, RUN, SHED, SPILL.

5. *epicheō* (ἐπιχέω, 2022), "to pour upon" (*epi*), is used in Luke 10:34, of the oil and wine used by the good Samaritan on the wounds of him who had fallen among robbers.¶

Note: For the KJV, "poured out" in Rev. 14:10 (RV, "prepared"), see MINGLE, No. 2.

POVERTY

ptōcheia (πτωχεία, 4432), "destitution" (akin to *ptōcheuō*, see POOR), is used of the "poverty" which Christ voluntarily experienced on our behalf, 2 Cor. 8:9; of the destitute condition of saints in Judea, v. 2; of the condition of the church in Smyrna, Rev. 2:9, where the word is used in a general sense. Cf. synonymous words under POOR.¶

For **POWDER** see **GRIND**

POWER (Noun, and Verb, to have, bring under)

A. Nouns.

1. *dunamis* (δύναμις, 1411), for the different meanings of which see ABILITY, MIGHT, is sometimes used, by metonymy, of persons and things, e.g., (*a*) of God, Matt. 26:64; Mark 14:62; (*b*) of angels, e.g., perhaps in Eph. 1:21, RV, "power," KJV, "might" (cf. Rom. 8:38; 1 Pet. 3:22); (*c*) of that which manifests God's "power": Christ, 1 Cor. 1:24; the gospel, Rom. 1:16; (*d*) of mighty works (RV, marg., "power" or "powers"), e.g., Mark 6:5, "mighty work"; so 9:39, RV (KJV, "miracle"); Acts 2:22 (ditto); 8:13, "miracles"; 2 Cor. 12:12, RV, "mighty works" (KJV, "mighty deeds").

Note: For different meanings of synonymous terms, see *Note* under DOMINION, A, No. 1.

2. *exousia* (ἐξουσία, 1849) denotes "freedom of action, right to act"; used of God, it is absolute, unrestricted, e.g., Luke 12:5 (RV marg., "authority"); in Acts 1:7 "right of disposal" is what is indicated; used of men, authority is delegated. Angelic beings are called "powers" in Eph. 3:10 (cf. 1:21); 6:12; Col. 1:16; 2:15 (cf. 2:10). See AUTHORITY, No. 1, see also PRINCIPALITY.

3. *ischus* (ἰσχύς, 2479), "ability, force, strength," is nowhere translated "power" in the RV (KJV in 2 Thess. 1:9). See ABILITY, No. 2.

4. *kratos* (κράτος, 2904) is translated "power" in the RV and KJV in 1 Tim. 6:16; Heb. 2:14; in Eph. 1:19 (last part); 6:10, KJV, "power" (RV, "strength"): see DOMINION, A, No. 1, STRENGTH, A, No. 3.

5. *dunaton* (δυνατόν, 1415**), the neuter of the adjective *dunatos*, "powerful" (akin to No. 1), is used as a noun with the article in Rom. 9:22, "(to make His) power (known)." See ABLE.

6. *archē* (ἀρχή, 746), "a beginning, rule," is translated "power" in Luke 20:20, KJV (RV, "rule"). See BEGINNING, B.

B. Verb.

exousiazō (ἐξουσιάζω, 1850), "to exercise authority" (akin to A, No. 2), is used (*a*) in the active voice, Luke 22:25, RV, "have authority" (KJV, "exercise authority"), of the "power" of rulers; 1 Cor. 7:4 (twice), of marital relations and conditions; (*b*) in the passive voice, 1 Cor. 6:12, to be brought under the "power" of a thing; here, this verb and the preceding one connected with it, *exesti*, present a *paronomasia*, which Lightfoot brings out as follows: "All are within my power; but I will not put myself under the power of any one of all things." See AUTHORITY, B, No. 1.¶

Notes: (1) In Rev. 13:14, 15, KJV, *didōmi*, "to give," is translated "(he) had power"; RV, "it was given (him)" and "it was given *unto him*"; the KJV misses the force of the permissive will of God in the actings of the Beast. (2) In Rom. 16:25, KJV, *dunamai*, "to be able," is translated "that is of power" (RV, "that is able"). See ABLE. (3) The subject of power in Scripture may be viewed under the following heads: (*a*) its original source, in the Persons in the Godhead; (*b*) its exercise by God in creation, its preservation and its government; (*c*) special manifestations of divine "power," past, present and future; (*d*) "power" existent in created beings, other than man, and in inanimate nature; (*e*) committed to man, and misused by him; (*f*) committed to those who, on becoming believers, were "em-powered" by the Spirit of God, are indwelt by Him, and will exercise it hereafter for God's glory.

POWERFUL, POWERFULLY

A. Adjectives.

1. *energēs* (ἐνεργής, 1756): see ACTIVE.

2. *ischuros* (ἰσχυρός, 2478), "strong, mighty," akin to *ischus* (see POWER, A, No. 3), is translated "powerful" in 2 Cor. 10:10, KJV (RV, "strong"). See STRONG.

B. Adverb.

eutonōs (εὐτόνως, 2159) signifies "vigorously, vehemently" (*eu*, "well," *teinō*, "to stretch"), Luke 23:10, "vehemently," of the accusation of the chief priests and scribes against Christ; Acts 18:28, RV, "powerfully" (KJV, "mightily"), of Apollos in confuting Jews.¶ In the Sept., Josh. 6:8.¶

Note: For "is powerful," 2 Cor. 13:3, RV, see MIGHTY, C.

For PRACTICES see COVETOUS, B, No. 3

PRACTICE

prassō (πράσσω, 4238) is translated by the verb "to practice" in the RV in the following passages (the KJV nowhere renders the verb thus): John 3:20 (marg.); 5:29 (marg.); Acts 19:19; Rom. 1:32 (twice); 2:1, 2, 3; 7:15, 19; Gal. 5:21. See DO, No. 2.

For PRAETORIUM and PRAETORIAN GUARD see PALACE

PRAISE

A. Nouns.

1. *ainos* (αἶνος, 136), primarily "a tale, narration," came to denote "praise"; in the NT only of praise to God, Matt. 21:16; Luke 18:43.¶

2. *epainos* (ἔπαινος, 1868), a strengthened form of No. 1 (*epi*, upon), denotes "approbation, commendation, praise"; it is used (*a*) of those on account of, and by reason of, whom as God's heritage, "praise" is to be ascribed to God, in respect of His glory (the exhibition of His character and operations), Eph. 1:12; in v. 14, of the whole company, the church, viewed as "*God's* own possession" (RV); in v. 6, with particular reference to the glory of His grace towards them; in Phil. 1:11, as the result of "the fruits of righteousness" manifested in them through the power of Christ; (*b*) of "praise" bestowed by God, upon the Jew spiritually (Judah = "praise"), Rom. 2:29; bestowed upon

believers hereafter at the judgment seat of Christ, 1 Cor. 4:5 (where the definite article indicates that the "praise" will be exactly in accordance with each person's actions); as the issue of present trials, "at the revelation of Jesus Christ," 1 Pet. 1:7; (c) of whatsoever is "praiseworthy," Phil. 4:8; (d) of the approbation by churches of those who labor faithfully in the ministry of the gospel, 2 Cor. 8:18; (e) of the approbation of well-doers by human rulers, Rom. 13:3; 1 Pet. 2:14.¶

3. *ainesis* (αἴνεσις, 133), "praise" (akin to No. 1), is found in Heb. 13:15, where it is metaphorically represented as a sacrificial offering.¶

Notes: (1) In 1 Pet. 2:9, KJV, *arētē*, "virtue, excellence," is translated "praises" (RV, "excellencies"). (2) In the following the KJV translates *doxa*, "glory," by "praise" (RV, "glory"); John 9:24, where "give glory to God" signifies "confess thy sins" (cf. Josh. 7:19, indicating the genuine confession of facts in one's life which gives glory to God); 12:43 (twice); 1 Pet. 4:11.

B. Verbs

1. *aineō* (αἰνέω, 134), "to speak in praise of, to praise" (akin to A, No. 1), is always used of "praise" to God, (a) by angels, Luke 2:13; (b) by men, Luke 2:?; 19:37; 24:53; Acts 2:20, 47; 3:8, 9; Rom. 15:11 (No. 2 In some texts); Rev. 19:5.¶

2. *epaineō* (ἐπαινέω, 1867), akin to A, No. 2, is rendered "praise," 1 Cor. 11:2, 17, 22: see COMMEND, No. 1.

3. *humneō* (ὑμνέω, 5214) denotes (a) transitively, "to sing, to laud, sing to the praise of" (Eng., "hymn"), Acts 16:25, KJV, "sang praises" (RV, "singing hymns"); Heb. 2:12, RV, "will I sing (Thy) praise," KJV, "will I sing praise (unto Thee)," lit., "I will hymn Thee"; (b) intransitively, "to sing," Matt. 26:30; Mark 14:26, in both places of the singing of the paschal hymns (Ps. 113–118, and 136), called by Jews the Great Hallel.¶

4. *psallō* (ψάλλω, 5567), primarily, "to twitch" or "twang" (as a bowstring, etc.), then, "to play" (a stringed instrument with the fingers), in the Sept., to sing psalms, denotes, in the NT, to sing a hymn, sing "praise"; in Jas. 5:13, RV, "sing praise" (KJV, "sing psalms"). See MELODY, SING.

5. *exomologeō* (ἐξομολογέω, 1843) in Rom. 15:9, RV, "will I give praise" (KJV, and RV marg., "I will confess"): see CONFESS, A, No. 2 (c).

Note: In Luke 1:64, KJV, *eulogeō*, "to bless," is translated "praised" (RV, "blessing").

PRATE

phluareō (φλυαρέω, 5396) signifies "to talk nonsense" (from *phluō*, "to babble"; cf. the adjective *phluaros*, "babbling, garrulous, tattlers," 1 Tim. 5:13), "to raise false accusations," 3 John 10.¶

PRAY, PRAYER

A. Verbs.

1. *euchomai* (εὔχομαι, 2172), "to pray (to God)," is used with this meaning in 2 Cor. 13:7; v. 9, RV, "pray" (KJV, "wish"); Jas. 5:16; 3 John 2, RV, "pray" (KJV, wish). Even when the RV and KJV translate by "I would," Acts 26:29, or "wished for," Acts 27:29 (RV, marg., "prayed"), or "could wish," Rom. 9:3 (RV, marg., "could pray"), the indication is that "prayer" is involved.¶

2. *proseuchomai* (προσεύχομαι, 4336), "to pray," is always used of "prayer" to God, and is the most frequent word in this respect, especially in the Synoptists and Acts, once in Romans, 8:26; in Ephesians, 6:18; in Philippians, 1:9; in 1 Timothy, 2:8; in Hebrews, 13:18; in Jude, v. 20. For the injunction in 1 Thess. 5:17, see CEASE, C.

3. *erōtaō* (ἐρωτάω, 2065), "to ask," is translated by the verb to pray in Luke 14:18, 19; 16:27; John 4:31; 14:16; 16:26; 17:9, 15, 20; in Acts 23:18, RV, "asked" (KJV "prayed"); in 1 John 5:16, RV, "should make request" (KJV "shall pray"). See ASK, A, No. 2.

4. *deomai* (δέομαι, 1189), "to desire," in 2 Cor. 5:20; 8:4, RV, "beseech" (KJV, "pray"): see BESEECH, No. 3.

Notes: (1) *Parakaleō*, "to call to one's aid," is rendered by the verb "to pray" in the KJV in the following: Matt. 26:53 (RV, "beseech"); so Mark 5:17, 18; Acts 16:9; in 24:4, RV, "intreat"; in 27:34, RV, "beseech." See BESEECH, No. 1. (2) In 1 Thess. 5:23 and 2 Tim. 4:16, there is no word in the original for "I pray," see the RV.

B. Nouns.

1. *euchē* (εὐχή, 2171), akin to A, No. 1, denotes "a prayer," Jas. 5:15; "a vow," Acts 18:18 and 21:23. See vow.¶

2. *proseuchē* (προσευχή, 4335), akin to A, No. 2, denotes (a) "prayer" (to God), the most frequent term, e.g., Matt. 21:22; Luke 6:12, where the phrase is not to be taken literally as if it meant, "the prayer of God" (subjective genitive), but objectively, "prayer to God." In Jas. 5:17, "He prayed fervently," RV, is, lit., "he prayed with prayer" (a Hebraistic form); in the following the word is used with No. 3: Eph. 6:18; Phil. 4:6; 1 Tim. 2:1; 5:5; (b) "a place of

prayer," Acts 16:13, 16, a place outside the city wall, RV.

3. deēsis (δέησις, 1162), primarily "a wanting, a need" (akin to A, No. 4), then, "an asking, entreaty, supplication," in the NT is always addressed to God and always rendered "supplication" or "supplications" in the RV; in the KJV "prayer," or "prayers," in Luke 1:13; 2:37; 5:33; Rom. 10:1; 2 Cor. 1:11; 9:14; Phil. 1:4 (in the 2nd part, "request"); 1:19; 2 Tim. 1:3; Heb. 5:7; Jas. 5:16; 1 Pet. 3:12.

4. enteuxis (ἔντευξις, 1783) is translated "prayer" in 1 Tim. 4:5; see INTERCESSION.

Notes: (1) *Proseuchē* is used of "prayer" in general; *deēsis* stresses the sense of need; it is used sometimes of request from man to man.

(2) In the papyri *enteuxis* is the regular word for a petition to a superior. For the synonymous word *aitēma* see PETITION; for *hiketēria*, Heb. 5:7, see SUPPLICATION.

(3) "Prayer is properly addressed to God the Father Matt. 6:6; John 16:23; Eph. 1:17; 3:14, and the Son, Acts 7:59; 2 Cor 12:8; but in no instance in the NT is prayer addressed to the Holy Spirit distinctively, for whereas the Father is in Heaven, Matt. 6:9, and the Son is at His right hand, Rom. 8:34, the Holy Spirit is in and with the believers, John 14:16, 17.

"Prayer is to be offered in the Name of the Lord Jesus, John 14:13, that is, the prayer must accord with His character, and must be presented in the same spirit of dependence and submission that marked Him, Matt. 11:26; Luke 22:42.

"The Holy Spirit, being the sole interpreter of the needs of the human heart, makes His intercession therein; and inasmuch as prayer is impossible to man apart from His help, Rom. 8:26, believers are exhorted to pray at all seasons in the Spirit, Eph. 6:18; cf. Jude 20, and Jas. 5:16, the last clause of which should probably be read 'the inwrought [i.e., by the Holy Spirit] supplication of righteous man availeth much' (or 'greatly prevails' *ischuō*, as in Acts 19:16, 20).

"None the less on this account is the understanding to be engaged in prayer, 1 Cor. 14:15, and the will, Col. 4:12; Acts 12:5 (where 'earnestly' is, lit., 'stretched out') and so in Luke 22:44.

"Faith is essential to prayer, Matt. 21:22; Mark 11:24; Jas. 1:5–8, for faith is the recognition of, and the committal of ourselves and our matters to, the faithfulness of God.

"Where the Jews were numerous, as at Thessalonica, they had usually a Synagogue, Acts 17:1; where they were few, as at Philippi, they had merely a *proseuchē*, or 'place of prayer,' of

much smaller dimensions, and commonly built by a river for the sake of the water necessary to the preliminary ablutions prescribed by Rabbinic tradition, Acts 16:13, 16."*

PREACH, PREACHING

A. Verbs.

1. *euangelizō* (εὐαγγελίζω, 2097) is almost always used of "the good news" concerning the Son of God as proclaimed in the gospel [exceptions are e.g., Luke 1:19; 1 Thess. 3:6, in which the phrase "to bring (or show) good (or glad) tidings" does not refer to the gospel]; Gal. 1:8 (2nd part). With reference to the gospel the phrase "to bring, or declare, good, or glad, tidings" is used in Acts 13:32; Rom. 10:15; Heb. 4:2.

In Luke 4:18 the RV "to preach good tidings" gives the correct quotation from Isaiah, rather than the KJV "to preach the Gospel." In the Sept. the verb is used of any message intended to cheer the hearers, e.g. 1 Sam. 31:9; 2 Sam. 1:20. See GOSPEL, B, No. 1.

2. *kērussō* (κηρύσσω, 2784) signifies (a) "to be a herald," or, in general, "to proclaim," e.g., Matt. 3:1; Mark 1:45, "publish"; in Luke 4:18, RV, "to proclaim," KJV, "to preach"; so verse 19; Luke 12:3; Acts 10:37; Rom. 2:21; Rev. 5:2. In 1 Pet. 3:19 the probable reference is, not to glad tidings (which there is no real evidence that Noah preached, nor is there evidence that the spirits of antediluvian people are actually "in prison"), but to the act of Christ after His resurrection in proclaiming His victory to fallen angelic spirits; (b) "to preach the gospel as a herald," e.g., Matt. 24:14; Mark 13:10, RV, "be preached" (KJV, "be published"); 14:9; 16:15, 20; Luke 8:1; 9:2; 24:47; Acts 8:5; 19:13; 28:31; Rom. 10:14, present participle, lit., "(one) preaching," "a preacher"; 10:15 (1st part); 1 Cor. 1:23; 15:11, 12; 2 Cor. 1:19; 4:5; 11:4; Gal. 2:2; Phil. 1:15; Col. 1:23; 1 Thess. 2:9; 1 Tim. 3:16; (c) "to preach the word," 2 Tim. 4:2 (of the ministry of the Scriptures, with special reference to the gospel). See PROCLAIM, PUBLISH.

3. *proeuangelizomai* (προευαγγελίζομαι, 4283): see GOSPEL, B, No. 2.

4. *prokērussō* (προκηρύσσω, 4296), lit., "to proclaim as a herald" (*pro*, before, and No. 2), is used in Acts 13:24, "had first preached." Some mss. have the verb in Acts 3:20; for the best see APPOINT, No. 12.¶

5. *parrhēsiazomai* (παρρησιάζομαι, 3955), "to be bold in speech," is translated "to preach

---

* From *Notes on Thessalonians* by Hogg and Vine, pp. 189, 190.

boldly" in Acts 9:27 (2nd part); in v. 29, RV (KJV, "he spake boldly"). See BOLD, A, No. 2.

Notes: (1) For *diangellō*, translated "preach" in Luke 9:60, see DECLARE, A, No. 3. (2) *Katangellō*, "to proclaim," is always so translated in the RV; the KJV renders it by "to preach" in Acts 4:2; 13:5, 38; 15:36; 17:3, 13; 1 Cor. 9:14; Col. 1:28. (3) *Laleō*, "to speak," is translated "preached," Mark 2:2, KJV, "preached" (RV, "spake"); in Acts 8:25, 1st part, KJV (RV, "spoken"); so in 13:42 and 14:25; "preaching" in Acts 11:19, KJV, but what is indicated here is not a formal "preaching" by the believers scattered from Jerusalem, but a general testimony to all with whom they came into contact; in 16:6, RV, "to speak" (KJV, "to preach"). (4) For *dialegomai*, in KJV of Acts 20:7, 9, see DISCOURSE. (5) For KJV, "preached" in Heb. 4:2 (2nd part), see HEARING. (6) In Rom. 15:19 *plēroō*, "to fulfill" (RV, marg.), is rendered "I have fully preached."

B. Nouns.

kērugma (κήρυγμα, 2782), "a proclamation by a herald" (akin to A, No. 2), denotes "a message, a preaching" (the substance of what is "preached" as distinct from the act of "preaching"), Matt. 12:41; Luke 11:32; Rom. 16:25; 1 Cor. 1:21; 2:4; 15:14; in 2 Tim. 4:17 and Titus 1:3, RV, "message," marg., "proclamation," KJV, "preaching." See MESSAGE.¶ In the Sept., 2 Chron. 30:5; Prov. 9:3; Jonah 3:2.¶

Note: In 1 Cor. 1:18, KJV, *logos*, "a word," is translated "preaching," RV, "the word (of the Cross)," i.e., not the act of "preaching," but the substance of the testimony, all that God has made known concerning the subject. For Heb. 4:2, KJV, see HEAR, B, No. 1.

PREACHER

kērux (κῆρυξ, 2783), "a herald" (akin to A, No. 2 and B, above), is used (*a*) of the "preacher" of the gospel, 1 Tim. 2:7; 2 Tim. 1:11; (*b*) of Noah, as a "preacher" of righteousness, 2 Pet. 2:5.¶

Notes: (1) For "a preacher," in Rom. 10:14, where the verb *kērussō* is used, see PREACH, A, No. 2. (2) *Kērux* indicates the "preacher" as giving a proclamation; *euangelistēs* points to his message as glad tidings; *apostolos* suggests his relationship to Him by whom he is sent.

PRECEDE

phthanō (φθάνω, 5348), "to anticipate, to come sooner," is translated "shall (in no wise) precede" in 1 Thess. 4:15, RV (KJV, "prevent"), i.e., "shall in no wise obtain any advantage over" (the verb does not convey the thought of a mere succession of one event after another);

the apostle, in reassuring the bereaved concerning their departed fellow believers, declares that, as to any advantage, the dead in Christ will "rise first." See ATTAIN, No. 3, COME, No. 32.

PRECEPT

1. *entolē* (ἐντολή, 1785), "a commandment," is translated "precept" in Mark 10:5 (RV, "commandment"); so Heb. 9:19. See COMMANDMENT, No. 2.

2. *entalma* (ἔνταλμα, 1778) is always translated "precepts" in the RV; see COMMANDMENT, No. 3.

PRECIOUS, PRECIOUSNESS

1. *timios* (τίμιος, 5093), translated "precious," e.g., in Jas. 5:7; 1 Pet. 1:19; 2 Pet. 1:4; in 1 Cor. 3:12, KJV (RV, "costly"): see COSTLY, B, No. 1 DEAR, No. 1.

2. *entimos* (ἔντιμος, 1784), "precious," 1 Pet. 2:4, 6: see DEAR, No. 2.

3. *polutelēs* (πολυτελής, 4185), "very expensive," translated "very precious" in Mark 14:3, KJV (RV, "very costly"): see COSTLY, B, No. 2.

4. *polutimos* (πολύτιμος, 4186), "of great value"; comparative degree in 1 Pet. 1:7; see COSTLY, B, No. 3, DEAR, No. 1 (for a less authentic reading).

5. *barutimos* (βαρύτιμος, 927), "of great value, exceeding precious" (*barus*, "weighty," *timē*, value), is used in Matt. 26:7.¶

6. *isotimos* (ἰσότιμος, 2472), "of equal value, held in equal honor" (*isos*, "equal," and *timē*), is used in 2 Pet. 1:1, "a like precious (faith)," RV (marg., "an equally precious").¶

Note: In 1 Pet. 2:7, KJV, the noun *timē*, is translated "precious" (RV, "preciousness"). See HONOR, No. 1.

PREDESTINATE

proorizō (προορίζω, 4309): see DETERMINE.

Note: This verb is to be distinguished from *proginōskō*, "to foreknow"; the latter has special reference to the persons foreknown by God; *proorizō* has special reference to that to which the subjects of His foreknowledge are "predestinated." See FOREKNOW, A and B.

PREEMINENCE (to have the)

1. *prōteuō* (πρωτεύω, 4409), "to be first" (*prōtos*), "to be preeminent," is used of Christ in relation to the Church, Col. 1:18.¶

2. *philoprōteuō* (φιλοπρωτεύω, 5383), lit., "to love to be preeminent" (*philos*, "loving"), "to strive to be first," is said of Diotrephes, 3 John 9.¶

PREFER, PREFERRING

proēgeomai (προηγέομαι, 4285), "to go before and lead," is used in Rom. 12:10, in the sense of taking the lead in showing deference one to another, "(in honor) preferring one another."¶

Notes: (1) In John 1:15, 30, KJV, *ginomai*, "to become," is translated "is preferred" (RV, "is become"); some mss. have it again in v. 27. (2) For *prokrima*, 1 Tim. 5:21 (KJV, "preferring one before another"), see PREJUDICE.

PREJUDICE

prokrima (πρόκριμα, 4299) denotes "prejudging" (akin to *prokrinō*, "to judge beforehand"), 1 Tim. 5:21, RV, "prejudice" (marg., "preference"), preferring one person, another being put aside, by unfavorable judgment due to partiality.¶

PREMEDITATE

Note: This is the KJV rendering of *meletaō*, "to care for," which occurs in some mss. in Mark 13:11, "(neither) do ye premeditate." It is absent from the best mss. See IMAGINE.

PREPARATION, PREPARE, PREPARED

A. Nouns.

1. *hetoimasia* (ἑτοιμασία, 2091) denotes (*a*) "readiness," (*b*) "preparation"; it is found in Eph. 6:15, of having the feet shod with the "preparation" of the gospel of peace; it also has the meaning of firm footing (foundation), as in the Sept. of Ps. 89:14 (RV, "foundation"); if that is the meaning in Eph. 6:15, the gospel itself is to be the firm footing of the believer, his walk being worthy of it and therefore a testimony in regard to it. See READY.¶

2. *paraskeuē* (παρασκευή, 3904) denotes "preparation, equipment." The day on which Christ died is called "the Preparation" in Mark 15:42 and John 19:31; in John 19:42 "the Jews' Preparation," RV; in 19:14 it is described as "the Preparation of the Passover"; in Luke 23:54, RV, "the day of the Preparation (and the Sabbath drew on)." The same day is in view in Matt. 27:62, where the events recorded took place on "the day after the Preparation" (RV). The reference would be to the 6th day of the week. The title arose from the need of preparing food etc. for the Sabbath. Apparently it was first applied only to the afternoon of the 6th day; later, to the whole day. In regard to the phraseology in John 19:14, many hold this to indicate the "preparation" for the paschal feast. It probably means "the Preparation day," and

thus falls in line with the Synoptic Gospels. In modern Greek and ecclesiastical Latin, *Parasceve* = Friday.¶

B. Verbs.

1. *hetoimazō* (ἑτοιμάζω, 2090), "to prepare, make ready," is used (I) absolutely, e.g., Mark 14:15; Luke 9:52; (II) with an object, e.g., (*a*) of those things which are ordained (1) by God, such as future positions of authority, Matt. 20:23; the coming Kingdom, 25:34; salvation personified in Christ, Luke 2:31; future blessings, 1 Cor. 2:9; a city, Heb. 11:16; a place of refuge for the Jewish remnant, Rev. 12:6; Divine judgments on the world, Rev. 8:6; 9:7, 15; 16:12; eternal fire, for the Devil and his angels, Matt. 25:41; (2) by Christ: a place in Heaven for His followers, John 14:2, 3; (*b*) of human "preparation" for the Lord, e.g., Matt. 3:3; 26:17, 19; Luke 1:17 ("make ready"), 76; 3:4, KJV (RV, "make ye ready"); 9:52 ("to make ready"); 23:56; Rev. 19:7; 21:2; in 2 Tim. 2:21, of "preparation" of oneself for "every good work"; (*c*) of human "preparations" for human objects, e.g., Luke 12:20, RV, "thou hast prepared" (KJV, "provided"); Acts 23:23; Philem. 22.

2. *katartizō* (καταρτίζω, 2675), "to furnish completely, prepare," is translated "didst Thou prepare" in Heb. 10:5 (KJV, "hast Thou prepared"), of the body of the Lord Jesus. See FIT, B, No. 3.

3. *kataskeuazō* (κατασκευάζω, 2680), "to prepare, make ready" (*kata*, used intensively, *skeuē*, "equipment"), is so translated in Matt. 11:10; Mark 1:2; Luke 1:17; 7:27; Heb. 9:2, RV (KJV, "made"); 9:6, RV (KJV, "were ... ordained"); 11:7; 1 Pet. 3:20. See BUILD, No. 5.

4. *paraskeuazō* (παρασκευάζω, 3903), "to prepare, make ready" (*para*, "beside"), is used of making ready a meal, Acts 10:10: in the middle voice, of "preparing" oneself for war, 1 Cor. 14:8, RV; in the passive voice, of "preparing" an offering for the needy, 2 Cor. 9:2, "hath been prepared," RV (KJV, "was ready"); v. 3, "ye may be prepared," RV (KJV, "ye may be ready"). See READY.¶

5. *proetoimazō* (προετοιμάζω, 4282), "to prepare beforehand" (*pro*, "before," and No. 1), is used of good works which God "afore prepared," for fulfillment by believers, Eph. 2:10, RV (KJV, "hath before ordained," marg., "prepared"); of "vessels of mercy," as "afore prepared" by God "unto glory," Rom. 9:23. See ORDAIN.¶

Notes: (I) Etymologically, the difference between *hetoimazō* and *paraskeuazō*, is that the former is connected with what is real (*etumos*) or ready, the latter with *skeuos*, an article ready to hand, an implement, vessel. (2) In Mark 14:15, KJV, *hetoimos*, "ready," is translated "prepared" (RV, "ready"). It is absent in some mss. See READY.

For **PRESBYTERY** see **ELDER,** A and B

PRESENCE

A. Nouns.

1. *prosōpon* (πρόσωπον, 4383): see FACE, No. 1 (also APPEARANCE, No. 2).

2. *parousia* (παρουσία, 3952): see COMING (Noun), No. 3.

B. Adverbs and Prepositions.

1. *emprosthen* (ἔμπροσθεν, 1715): see BEFORE, A, No. 4.

2. *enōpion* (ἐνώπιον, 1799) is translated "in the presence of" in Luke 1:19; 13:26; 14:10; 15:10; John 20:30; Rev. 14:10 (twice); in 1 Cor. 1:29 KJV, "in His presence" (RV, "before God"): see BEFORE, A, No. 9.

3. *katenōpion* (κατενώπιον, 2714), *kata*, "down," and No. 2, "in the very presence of," is translated "before the presence of" in Jude 24. See BEFORE, A, No. 10.

4. *apenanti* (ἀπέναντι, 561), "over against, opposite to," is translated "in the presence of" in Acts 3:16. See BEFORE, A, No. 7.

PRESENT (to be)

A. Verbs.

1. *pareimi* (πάρειμι, 3918) signifies (*a*) "to be by, at hand or present," of persons, e.g., Luke 13:1; Acts 10:33; 24:19; 1 Cor. 5:3; 2 Cor. 10:2, 11; Gal. 4:18, 20; of things, John 7:6, of a particular season in the Lord's life on earth, "is (not yet) come," or "is not yet at hand"; Heb. 12:11, of chastening "(for the) present" (the neuter of the present participle, used as a noun); in 13:5 "such things as ye have" is, lit., "the things that are present"; 2 Pet. 1:12, of the truth "(which) is with (you)" (not as KJV, "the present truth," as if of special doctrines applicable to a particular time); in v. 9 "he that lacketh" is lit., "to whom are not present"; (*b*) "to have arrived or come," Matt. 26:50, "thou art come," RV; John 11:28; Acts 10:21; Col. 1:6.

2. *enistēmi* (ἐνίστημι, 1764), "to set in," or, in the middle voice and perfect tense of the active voice, "to stand in, be present," is used of the present in contrast with the past, Heb. 9:9, where the RV correctly has "(for the time) *now* present" (for the incorrect KJV, "then present"); in contrast to the future, Rom. 8:38; 1 Cor. 3:22; Gal. 1:4, "present"; 1 Cor. 7:26, where "the present distress" is set in contrast to both

the past and the future; 2 Thess. 2:2, where the RV, "is *now* present" gives the correct meaning (KJV, incorrectly, "is at hand"); the saints at Thessalonica, owing to their heavy afflictions, were possessed of the idea that "the day of the Lord," RV (not as KJV, "the day of Christ"), had begun; this mistake the apostle corrects; 2 Tim. 3:1, "shall come." See COME, No. 26.¶

3. *ephistēmi* (ἐφίστημι, 2186), "to set over, stand over," is translated "present" in Acts 28:2. See ASSAULT, A, COME, No. 27.

4. *paraginomai* (παραγίνομαι, 3854), "to be beside" (*para*, "by," *ginomai*, "to become"), is translated "were present" in Acts 21:18. See COME, No. 13.

5. *parakeimai* (παράκειμαι, 3873), "to lie beside" (*para*, and *keimai*, "to lie"), "to be near," is translated "is present" in Rom. 7:18, 21.¶

6. *sumpareimi* (συμπάρειμι, 4840), "to be present with" (*sun*, with, and No. 1), is used in Acts 25:24.¶

B. Adverbs.

1. *arti* (ἄρτι, 737), "just, just now, this moment," is rendered "(this) present (hour)" in 1 Cor. 4:11; in 1 Cor. 15:6, RV, "now" (KJV, "this present"). See NOW.

2. *nun* (νῦν, 3568), "now," is translated "present," with reference to this age or period ("world"), in Rom. 8:18; 11:5; 2 Tim. 4:10; Titus 2:12. See HENCEFORTH, NOW.

Notes: (1) *Endēmeō*, "to be at home," is so rendered in 2 Cor. 5:6 (KJV and RV); in vv. 8, 9, RV, "at home" (KJV, "present"). See HOME. (2) In John 14:25, KJV, *menō*, "to abide," is translated "being present" (RV, "abiding"). (3) In Luke 5:17 the RV has "with Him," for KJV, italicized, "*present.*"

PRESENT (Verb)

1. *paristēmi* (παρίστημι, 3936) denotes, when used transitively, "to place beside" (*para*, "by," *histēmi*, "to set"), "to present," e.g., Luke 2:22; Acts 1:3, "He shewed (Himself)"; 9:41; 23:33; Rom. 6:13 (2nd part), RV, "present," KJV, "yield"; so 6:19 (twice); 12:1; 2 Cor. 4:14; 11:2; Eph. 5:27; Col. 1:22, 28; 2 Tim. 2:15, RV (KJV, "shew"). See SHEW.

2. *paristanō* (παριστάνω, 3936), a late present form of No. 1, is used in Rom. 6:13 (1st part) and v. 16, RV, "present" (KJV, "yield").

Notes: (1) In Jude 24, KJV, *histēmi*, "to cause to stand, to set," is translated "to present" (RV, "to set"). (2) In Matt. 2:11, KJV, *prospherō*, "to offer," is translated "presented" (RV, "offered").

For **PRESENTLY** see **FORTHWITH,** No. 1, and **IMMEDIATELY,** No. 1

PRESERVE

1. *tēreō* (τηρέω, 5083) is translated "to preserve" in 1 Thess. 5:23, where the verb is in the singular number, as the threefold subject, "spirit and soul and body," is regarded as the unit, constituting the person. The aorist or "point" tense regards the continuous "preservation" of the believer as a single, complete act, without reference to the time occupied in its accomplishment; in Jude 1, KJV (RV, "kept"). See KEEP, No. 1.

2. *suntēreō* (συντηρέω, 4933): see KEEP, No. 3.

3. *zōogoneō* (ζωογονέω, 2225), "to preserve alive": see LIVE, No. 6.

4. *phulassō* (φυλάσσω, 5442), "to guard, protect, preserve," is translated "preserved" in 2 Pet. 2:5, RV (KJV, "saved"). See GUARD.

Note: In 2 Tim. 4:18, KJV, *sōzō*, "to save," is translated "will preserve" (RV, "will save").

For PRESS (Noun) see CROWD, A

PRESS (Verb)

A. Verbs.

1. *thlibō* (θλίβω, 2346), "to press, distress, trouble," is translated "pressed" in 2 Cor. 4:8, RV (KJV, "troubled"). See AFFLICT, No. 4.

2. *apothlibō* (ἀποθλίβω, 598), translated "press" in Luke 8:45 (end): see CRUSH.

3. *biazo* (βιάζω, 971), in the middle voice, "to press violently" or "force one's way into," is translated "presseth" in Luke 16:16, KJV, RV, "entereth violently," a meaning confirmed by the papyri. Moulton and Milligan also quote a passage from D. S. Sharp's *Epictetus and the NT*, speaking of "those who (try to) force their way in"; the verb suggests forceful endeavor. See ENTER, *Note* (3), VIOLENCE, B, No. 2.

4. *sunechō* (συνέχω, 4912): for the significance of this in Acts 18:5, "was constrained by the word," RV, i.e., Paul felt the urge of the word of his testimony to the Jews in Corinth, see CONSTRAIN, No. 3. It is used with No. 1 in Luke 8:45, RV, "press" (KJV, "throng").

5. *enechō* (ἐρέχω, 1758), lit., "to hold in," also signifies "to set oneself against, be urgent against," as the scribes and Pharisees were regarding Christ, Luke 11:53, RV, "to press upon," marg., "set themselves vehemently against" (KJV, "to urge"). See ENTANGLE, No. 3.

6. *epikeimai* (ἐπίκειμαι, 1945), "to lie upon, press upon," is rendered "pressed upon" in Luke 5:1. See IMPOSED.

7. *epipiptō* (ἐπιπίπτω, 1968), "to fall upon," is rendered "pressed upon" in Mark 3:10. See FALL, B, No. 5.

8. *bareō* (βαρέω, 916), "to weigh down, burden," is rendered "we were pressed" in 2 Cor. 1:8, KJV (RV, "we were weighed down"). See BURDEN, B, No. 1.

9. *epibareō* (ἐπιβαρέω, 1912), 2 Cor. 2:5, RV, "I press (not) too heavily" (KJV, "overcharge"). See BURDEN, B, No. 2, OVERCHARGE.

10. *piezō* (πιέζω, 4085), "to press down together," is used in Luke 6:38, "pressed down," of the character of the measure given in return for giving.¶ In the Sept., Mic. 6:15.¶

11. *diōkō* (διώκω, 1377), "to pursue," is used as a metaphor from the footrace, in Phil. 3:12, 14, of "speeding on earnestly," RV, "I press on." See FOLLOW, No. 7.

12. *pherō* (φέρω, 5342), "to bear, carry," is used in the passive voice in Heb. 6:1, "let us . . . press on," RV, lit., "let us be borne on" (KJV, "go on"). See GO, *Note* (2), (*h*).

B. Noun.

epistasis (ἐπίστασις, 1999v), primarily "a stopping, halting" (as of soldiers), then, "an incursion, onset, rush, pressure" (akin to *ephistēmi*, "to set upon"), is so used in 2 Cor. 11:28, "(that which) presseth upon (me)," KJV, "cometh upon," lit., "(the daily) pressure (upon me)"; some have taken the word in its other meaning "attention," which perhaps is accounted for by the variant reading of the pronoun (*mou*, "my", instead of *moi*, "to me, upon me"), but that does not adequately describe the "pressure" or onset due to the constant call upon the apostle for all kinds of help, advice, counsel, exhortation, decisions as to difficulties, disputes, etc. Cf. the other occurrence of the word in Acts 24:12, "stirring up," RV (KJV, "raising"), lit. "making a stir" (in some mss., *episustasis*). See COME, *Notes* at end (9).¶

For PRESUMPTUOUS see DARING, B

PRETENSE

prophasis (πρόφασις, 4392): see CLOKE (Pretense), No. 2.

PREVAIL

1. *ischuō* (ἰσχύω, 2480), "to be strong, powerful," is translated "to prevail" in Acts 19:16, 20; Rev. 12:8. See ABLE, B, No. 4.

2. *katischuō* (κατισχύω, 2729), "to be strong against" (*kata*, "against," and No. 1), is used in Matt. 16:18, negatively of the gates of hades; in Luke 21:36 (in the most authentic mss.; some have *kataxioō*, "to count worthy"; see KJV), of "prevailing" to escape judgments at the close of this age; in Luke 23:23, of the voices

of the chief priests, rulers and people against Pilate regarding the crucifixion of Christ.¶

3. *ōpheleō* (ὠφελέω, 5623), "to benefit, do good, profit," is translated "prevailed" in Matt. 27:24, RV (KJV, "could prevail"), of the conclusion formed by Pilate concerning the determination of the chief priests, elders and people. The meaning of the verb with the negative is better expressed by the phrase "he would do no good"; so in John 12:19, "ye prevail (nothing)," lit., "ye are doing no good." See ADVANTAGE, BETTERED, PROFIT.

4. *nikaō* (νικάω, 3528), "to conquer, prevail," is used as a law term in Rom. 3:4, "(that) Thou ... mightest prevail [KJV, 'overcome'] (when Thou comest into judgment)"; that the righteousness of the judge's verdict compels an acknowledgement on the part of the accused, is inevitable where God is the judge. God's promises to Israel provided no guarantee that an unrepentant Jew would escape doom. In Rev. 5:5, KJV, "hath prevailed" (RV, "hath overcome"). See CONQUER, No. 1.

For **PREVENT**, 1 Thess. 4:15, KJV, see **PRECEDE**: Matt. 17:25, KJV, see **SPEAK** No. 11

PRICE

A. Noun.

timē (τιμή, 5092) denotes "a valuing," hence, objectively, (a) "price paid or received," Matt. 27:6, 9; Acts 4:34 (plural); 5:2, 3; 7:16, RV, "price (in silver)," KJV, "sum (of money)"; 19:19 (plural); 1 Cor. 6:20; 7:23; (b) "value, honor, preciousness." See HONOR, PRECIOUSNESS.

B. Verb.

timaō (τιμάω, 5091), "to fix the value, to price," is translated "was priced" and "did price" in the RV of Matt. 27:9 (KJV, "was valued" and "did value"). See HONOR.

C. Adjectives

1. *polutelēs* (πολυτελής, 4185), "of great price," 1 Pet. 3:4: see COST, B, No. 2.

2. *polutimos* (πολύτιμος, 4186), "of great price," Matt. 13:46: see COST, B, No. 3.

For **PRICK** (Noun) see **GOAD**

PRICK (Verb)

katanussō (κατανύσσω, 2660), primarily, "to strike or prick violently, to stun," is used of strong emotion, in Acts 2:37 (passive voice), "they were pricked (in their heart)."¶ Cf. *katanuxis*, "stupor, torpor of mind," Rom. 11:8.¶

PRIDE

A. Nouns.

1. *alazonia* (or —*eia*) (ἀλαζονία, 212) is translated "pride" in 1 John 2:16, KJV. See BOAST, B, No. 2, VAINGLORY.

2. *huperēphania* (ὑπερηφανία, 5243), "pride," Mark 7:22: see HAUGHTY.¶

B. Verb.

tuphoō (τυφόω, 5187), "lifted up with pride," 1 Tim. 3:6, KJV (RV, "puffed up"). See HIGH-MINDED.

PRIEST

1. *hiereus* (ἱερεύς, 2409), "one who offers sacrifice and has the charge of things pertaining thereto," is used (a) of a "priest" of the pagan god Zeus, Acts 14:13; (b) of Jewish "priests," e.g., Matt. 8:4; 12:4, 5; Luke 1:5, where allusion is made to the 24 courses of "priests" appointed for service in the Temple (cf. 1 Chron. 24:4ff.); John 1:19; Heb. 8:4; (c) of believers, Rev. 1:6; 5:10; 20:6. Israel was primarily designed as a nation to be a kingdom of "priests," offering service to God, e.g., Ex. 19:6; the Israelites having renounced their obligations, Ex. 20:19, the Aaronic priesthood was selected for the purpose, till Christ came to fulfil His ministry in offering up Himself; since then the Jewish priesthood has been abrogated, to be resumed nationally, on behalf of Gentiles, in the millennial kingdom, Is. 61:6; 66:21. Meanwhile all believers, from Jews and Gentiles, are constituted "a kingdom of priests," Rev. 1:6 (see above), "a holy priesthood," 1 Pet. 2:5, and "royal," v. 9. The NT knows nothing of a sacerdotal class in contrast to the laity; all believers are commanded to offer the sacrifices mentioned in Rom. 12:1; Phil. 2:17; 4:18; Heb. 13:15, 16; 1 Pet. 2:5; (d) of Christ, Heb. 5:6; 7:11, 15, 17, 21; 8:4 (negatively); (e) of Melchizedek, as the foreshadower of Christ, Heb. 7:1, 3.

2. *archiereus* (ἀρχιερεύς, 749) designates (a) "the high priests" of the Levitical order, frequently called "chief priests" in the NT, and including "ex-high priests" and members of "high priestly" families, e.g., Matt. 2:4; 16:21; 20:18; 21:15; in the singular, a "high priest," e.g., Abiathar, Mark 2:26; Annas and Caiaphas, Luke 3:2, where the RV rightly has "in the high priesthood of A. and C." (cf. Acts 4:6). As to the combination of the two in this respect, Annas was the "high priest" from A.D. 7–14, and, by the time referred to, had been deposed for some years; his son-in-law, Caiaphas, the fourth "high priest" since his deposition, was appointed about A.D. 24. That Annas was still called the "high priest" is explained by the facts

(1) that by the Mosaic law the high priesthood was held for life, Num. 35:25; his deposition was the capricious act of the Roman procurator, but he would still be regarded legally and religiously as "high priest" by the Jews; (2) that he probably still held the office of deputy-president of the Sanhedrin (cf. 2 Kings 25:18); (3) that he was a man whose age, wealth and family connections gave him a preponderant influence, by which he held the real sacerdotal power; indeed at this time the high priesthood was in the hands of a clique of some half dozen families; the language of the writers of the gospels is in accordance with this, in attributing the high priesthood rather to a caste than a person; (4) the "high priests" were at that period mere puppets of Roman authorities who deposed them at will, with the result that the title was used more loosely than in former days.

The divine institution of the priesthood culminated in the "high priest," it being his duty to represent the whole people, e.g., Lev. 4:15, 16; ch. 16. The characteristics of the Aaronic "high priests" are enumerated in Heb. 5:1–4; 8:3; 9:7, 25; in some mss., 10:11 (RV, marg.); 13:11.

(b) Christ is set forth in this respect in the Ep. to the Hebrews, where He is spoken of as "a high priest," 4:15; 5:5, 10; 6:20; 7:26; 8:1, 3 (RV); 9:11; "a great high priest," 4:14; "a great priest," 10:21; "a merciful and faithful high priest," 2:17; "the Apostle and high priest of our confession," 3:1, RV; "a high priest after the order of Melchizedek," 5:10. One of the great objects of this Epistle is to set forth the superiority of Christ's High Priesthood as being of an order different from and higher than the Aaronic, in that He is the Son of God (see especially 7:28), with a priesthood of the Melchizedek order. Seven outstanding features of His priesthood are stressed, (1) its character, 5:6, 10; (2) His commission, 5:4, 5; (3) His preparation, 2:17; 10:5; (4) His sacrifice, 8:3; 9:12, 14, 27, 28; 10:4–12; (5) His sanctuary, 4:14; 8:2; 9:11, 12, 24; 10:12, 19; (6) His ministry, 2:18; 4:15; 7:25; 8:6; 9:15, 24; (7) its effects, 2:15; 4:16; 6:19, 20; 7:16, 25; 9:14, 28; 10:14–17, 22, 39; 12:1; 13:13–17.

Note: In Acts 4:6 the adjective *hieratikos*, "high priestly," is translated "of the high priest."

PRIESTHOOD, PRIEST'S OFFICE

A. Nouns.

1. *hierateuma* (ἱεράτευμα, 2406) denotes "a priesthood" (akin to *hierateuō*, see below), "a body of priests," consisting of all believers, the whole church (not a special order from among them), called "a holy priesthood," 1 Pet. 2:5; "a royal priesthood," v. 9; the former term is asso-

ciated with offering spiritual sacrifices, the latter with the royal dignity of showing forth the Lord's excellencies (RV).¶ In the Sept., Exod. 19:6; 23:22.¶

2. *hierōsunē* (ἱερωσύνη, 2420), "a priesthood," signifies the office, quality, rank and ministry of "a priest," Heb. 7:11, 12, 24, where the contrasts between the Levitical "priesthood" and that of Christ are set forth.¶ In the Sept., 1 Chron. 29:22.¶

3. *hierateia* (ἱερατεία, 2405), "a priesthood," denotes the priest's office, Luke 1:9; Heb. 7:5, RV, "priest's office."¶

B. Verb.

hierateuō (ἱερατεύω, 2407) signifies "to officiate as a priest," Luke 1:8, "he executed the priest's office."¶

PRINCE

1. *archēgos* (ἀρχηγός, 747), primarily an adjective signifying "originating, beginning," is used as a noun, denoting "a founder, author, prince or leader," Acts 3:15, "Prince" (marg., "Author"); 5:31; see AUTHOR, No. 2.

2. *archōn* (ἄρχων, 758), the present participle of the verb *archō*, "to rule"; denotes "a ruler, a prince." It is used as follows ("p" denoting "prince," or "princes"; "r," "ruler" or "rulers"): (a) of Christ, as "the Ruler (KJV, Prince) of the kings of the earth," Rev. 1:5; (b) of rulers of nations, Matt. 20:25, RV, "r," KJV, "p"; Acts 4:26, "r"; 7:27, "r"; 7:35, "r" (twice); (c) of judges and magistrates, Acts 16:19, "r"; Rom. 13:3, "r"; (d) of members of the Sanhedrin, Luke 14:1, RV, "r" (KJV, "chief"); 23:13, 35, "r"; so 24:20; John 3:1; 7:26, 48; 12:42, RV, "r" (KJV, "chief r."); "r" in Acts 3:17; 4:5, 8; 13:27; 14:5; (e) of rulers of synagogues, Matt. 9:18, 23, "r"; so Luke 8:41; 18:18; (f) of the Devil, as "prince" of this world, John 12:31; 14:30; 16:11; of the power of the air, Eph. 2:2, "the air" being that sphere in which the inhabitants of the world live and which, through the rebellious and godless condition of humanity, constitutes the seat of his authority; (g) of Beelzebub, the "prince" of the demons, Matt. 9:24; 12:24; Mark 3:22; Luke 11:15. See CHIEF, B, No. 10.¶

3. *hēgemōn* (ἡγεμών, 2232), "a leader, ruler," is translated "princes" (i.e., leaders) in Matt. 2:6: see GOVERNOR, A, No. 1.

Note: For *megistan*, Rev. 6:15; 18:23, RV, "princes," see LORD, No. 3.

PRINCIPAL

prōtos (πρῶτος, 4413), "first," is translated "principal men" in the RV of Luke 19:47 and Acts 25:2. See CHIEF, A.

Note: In Acts 25:23 the phrase *kat' exochēn*,

lit., "according to eminence," is translated "principal (men)"; *exochē*, primarily a projection (akin to *exechō*, "to stand out"), is used here metaphorically of eminence.¶ In the Sept., Job 39:28.¶

PRINCIPALITY ·

archē (ἀρχή, 746), "beginning, government, rule," is used of supramundane beings who exercise rule, called "principalities"; (*a*) of holy angels, Eph. 3:10, the church in its formation being to them the great expression of "the manifold (or "much-varied") wisdom of God"; Col. 1:16; (*b*) of evil angels, Rom. 8:38; Col. 2:15, some would put this under (*a*), but see SPOIL, B, No. 4; (*a*) and (*b*) are indicated in Col. 2:10. In Eph. 1:21, the RV renders it "rule" (KJV, "principality") and in Titus 3:1, "rulers" (KJV, "principalities"). In Jude 6, RV, it signifies, not the first estate of fallen angels (as KJV), but their authoritative power, "their own" indicating that which had been assigned to them by God, which they left, aspiring to prohibited conditions. See BEGIN, B.

PRINCIPLES

1. *archē* (ἀρχή, 746), "beginning," is used in Heb. 6:1, in its relative significance, of the beginning of the thing spoken of; here "the first principles of Christ," lit., "the account (or word) of the beginning of Christ," denotes the teaching relating to the elementary facts concerning Christ. See BEGIN, B.

2. *stoicheion* (στοιχεῖον, 4747) is translated "principles" in Heb. 5:12. See ELEMENTS.

PRINT

tupos (τύπος, 5179), for which see ENSAMPLE, No. 1, is translated "print" in John 20:25 (twice), of the marks made by the nails in the hands of Christ.

PRISON, PRISON-HOUSE

1. *desmōtērion* (δεσμωτήριον, 1201), "a place of bonds" (from *desmos*, "a bond," *deō*, "to bind"), "a prison," occurs in Matt. 11:2; in Acts 5:21, 23 and 16:26, RV, "prison house" (KJV, "prison").¶

2. *phulakē* (φυλακή, 5438), for the various meanings of which see CAGE, denotes a "prison," e.g., Matt. 14:10; Mark 6:17; Acts 5:19; 2 Cor. 11:23; in 2 Cor. 6:5 and Heb. 11:36 it stands for the condition of imprisonment; in Rev. 2:10; 18:2, "hold" (twice, RV, marg., "prison"; in the 2nd case, KJV, "cage"); 20:7.

3. *tērēsis* (τήρησις, 5084), "a watching, keeping," then "a place of keeping" is translated "prison" in Acts 5:18 KJV (RV "ward"). See KEEPING, B.

Notes: (1) For *oikēma* in Acts 12:7, KJV, "prison," see CELL. (2) In Matt. 4:12, KJV, *paradidōmi*, "to betray, deliver up," is translated "was cast into prison" (RV, "was delivered up"); see BETRAY. In Mark 1:14, KJV, "was put in prison," RV, as in Matt. 4:12; see PUT, No. 12.

For **PRISON KEEPER** see **JAILOR**

PRISONER

1. *desmios* (δέσμιος, 1198), an adjective, primarily denotes "binding, bound," then, as a noun, "the person bound, a captive, prisoner" (akin to *deō*, "to bind"), Matt. 27:15, 16; Mark 15:6; Acts 16:25, 27; 23:18; 25:14, RV (KJV, "in bonds"), 27; 28:16, 17; Eph. 3:1; 4:1; 2 Tim. 1:8; Philem. 1, 9; in Heb. 10:34 and 13:3, "in bonds." See BOND, No. 2.¶

Note: The prison at Jerusalem (Acts 5) was controlled by the priests and probably attached to the high priest's palace, or the Temple. Paul was imprisoned at Jerusalem in the fort Antonia, Acts 23:10; at Caesarea, in Herod's Praetorium, 23:35; probably his final imprisonment in Rome was in the Tullianum dungeon.

2. *desmōtēs* (δεσμώτης, 1202), akin to No. 1, occurs in Acts 27:1, 42.¶

3. *sunaichmalōtos* (συναιχμάλωτος, 4869), "a fellow prisoner," primarily "one of fellow captives in war" (from *aichmē*, "a spear," and *haliskomai*, "to be taken"), is used by Paul of Andronicus and Junias, Rom. 16:7; of Epaphras, Philem. 23; of Aristarchus, Col. 4:10, on which Lightfoot remarks that probably his relations with the apostle in Rome excited suspicion and led to a temporary confinement, or that he voluntarily shared his captivity by living with him.¶

PRIVATE, PRIVATELY

A. Adjective.

idios (ἴδιος, 2398), one's own, is translated "private" in 2 Pet. 1:20 (see under INTERPRETATION). See BUSINESS, B.

B. Adverbial Phrase.

kat' idian (κατ' ἰδίαν) is translated "privately" in Matt. 24:3; Mark 4:34, RV (KJV, "when they were alone"); 6:32 (KJV only); 7:33, RV; 9:28; 13:3; Luke 10:23; Acts 23:19; Gal. 2:2. Contrast 2:14.

PRIVILY

lathra (λάθρα, 2977), "secretly, covertly" (from a root *lath*— indicating "unnoticed, unknown," seen in *lanthanō*, "to escape notice," *lēthē*, "forgetfulness"), is translated "privily" in

Matt. 1:19; 2:7; Acts 16:37; "secretly" in John 11:28 (in some mss., Mark 5:33). See SE-CRETLY.¶

Note: In Gal. 2:4, *pareisaktos*, an adjective (akin to *pareisagō*, lit., "to bring in beside," i.e., "secretly," from *para*, "by the side," *eis*, "into," *agō*, "to bring"), is used, "privily brought in," RV (KJV, "unawares, etc."), i.e., as spies or traitors. Strabo, a Greek historian contemporary with Paul, uses the word of enemies introduced secretly into a city by traitors within.¶ In the same verse the verb *pareiserchomai* (see COME, No. 8) is translated "came in privily," of the same Judaizers, brought in by the circumcision party to fulfill the design of establishing the ceremonial law, and thus to accomplish the overthrow of the faith; cf. in Jude 4 the verb *pareisduō* (or—*dunō*), "to slip in secretly, steal in," RV, "crept in privily" (KJV, " . . . unawares"). See CREEP, No. 2.

PRIVY

sunoida (σύνοιδα, 4862 and Perf. of 1492): see KNOW, No. 6

PRIZE

1. *brabeion* (βραβεῖον, 1017), "a prize bestowed in connection with the games" (akin to *brabeus*, "an umpire," and *brabeuō*, "to decide, arbitrate," "rule," Col. 3:15), 1 Cor. 9:24, is used metaphorically of "the reward" to be obtained hereafter by the faithful believer, Phil. 3:14; the preposition *eis*, "unto," indicates the position of the goal. The "prize" is not "the high calling," but will be bestowed in virtue of, and relation to, it, the heavenly calling, Heb. 3:1, which belongs to all believers and directs their minds and aspirations heavenward; for the "prize" see especially 2 Tim. 4:7, 8.¶

2. *harpagmos* (ἁρπαγμός, 725), akin to *harpazō*, "to seize, carry off by force," is found in Phil. 2:6, "(counted it not) a prize," RV (marg., "a thing to be grasped"), KJV, "(thought it not) robbery"; it may have two meanings, (*a*) in the active sense, "the act of seizing, robbery," a meaning in accordance with a rule connected with its formation; (*b*) in the passive sense, "a thing held as a prize." The subject is capably treated by Gifford in "*The Incarnation*," pp. 28, 36, from which the following is quoted:

"In order to express the meaning of the clause quite clearly, a slight alteration is required in the RV, 'Counted it not a prize to be on an equality with God.' The form 'to be' is ambiguous and easily lends itself to the erroneous notion that to be on equality with God was something to be acquired in the future. The rendering 'counted it not a prize that He was on

an equality with God,' is quite as accurate and more free from ambiguity. . . . Assuming, as we now may, that the equality was something which Christ possessed prior to His Incarnation, and then for a time resigned we have . . . to choose between two meanings of the word *harpagmos* (1) with the active sense 'robbery' or 'usurpation' we get the following meaning: 'Who *because* He was subsisting in the essential form of God, did not regard it as any usurpation that He was on an equality of glory and majesty with God, *but yet* emptied Himself of that co-equal glory. . . .' (2) The passive sense gives a different meaning to the passage: 'Who *though* He was subsisting in the essential form of God, *yet* did not regard His being on an equality of glory and majesty with God as a prize and a treasure to be held fast, *but* emptied himself thereof."

After reviewing the arguments *pro* and *con* Gifford takes the latter to be the right meaning, as conveying the purpose of the passage "to set forth Christ as the supreme example of humility and self-renunciation."

Note: For *katabrabeuō* (*kata*, "down," and *brabeuō*, see No. 1), translated "rob (you) of your prize," Col. 2:18, see BEGUILE, Note.

For **PROBATION**, RV in Rom. 5:4, see **EXPERIENCE**, No. 2

PROCEED

1. *ekporeuomai* (ἐκπορεύομαι, 1607), "to go forth," is translated "to proceed out of" in Matt. 4:4; 15:11, RV; 15:18; Mark 7:15, RV; 7:20, RV; 7:21; 7:23, RV; Luke 4:22; John 15:26; Eph. 4:29; Rev. 1:16, RV; 4:5; 9:17, 18, RV (KJV, "issued"); 11:5; 19:15, RV; 19:21, KJV (RV, "came forth"); 22:1. See COME, No. 33, GO, *Note* (1).

2. *exerchomai* (ἐξέρχομαι, 1831) is translated "proceed" in Matt. 15:19, KJV (RV, "come forth"); John 8:42, RV, "came forth"; Jas. 3:10. The verb "to proceed" is not so suitable. See COME, No. 3.

3. *prokoptō* (προκόπτω, 4298), lit., "to cut forward (a way)," is translated "will proceed" in 2 Tim. 2:16, RV (KJV, "will increase") and "shall proceed" (both versions) in 3:9. See IN-CREASE.

4. *prostithēmi* (προστίθημι, 4369), "to put to, to add," is translated "proceeded" in Acts 12:3 (a Hebraism). See ADD, No. 2.

PROCLAIM

1. *kērussō* (κηρύσσω, 2784) is translated "to proclaim" in the RV, for KJV, "to preach," in

Matt. 10:27; Luke 4:19; Acts 8:5; 9:20. See PREACH, No. 2.

2. *katangellō* (καταγγέλλω, 2605), "to declare, proclaim," is translated "to proclaim" in the RV, for KJV, to "show," in Acts 16:17; 26:23; 1 Cor. 11:26, where the verb makes clear that the partaking of the elements at the Lord's Supper is a "proclamation" (an evangel) of the Lord's death; in Rom. 1:8, for KJV, "spoken of"; in 1 Cor. 2:1, for KJV, "declaring." See also PREACH, *Note* (2), and DECLARE, A, No. 4.

3. *plērophoreō* (πληροφορέω, 4135), "to bring in full measure" (*plērēs*, "full," *pherō*, "to bring"), hence, "to fulfill, accomplish," is translated "might be fully proclaimed," in 2 Tim. 4:17, RV, with *kērugma*, marg., "proclamation" (KJV"... known"). See ASSURE, B, No. 2, BELIEVE, C, *Note* (4), FULFILL, No. 6, KNOW, *Note* (2), PERSUADE, No. 2, *Note*, PROOF.

PROCONSUL

anthupatos (ἀνθύπατος, 446), from *anti*, "instead of," and *hupatos*, "supreme," denotes "a consul, one acting in place of a consul, a proconsul, the governor of a senatorial province" (i.e., one which had no standing army). The "proconsuls" were of two classes, (*a*) ex-consuls, the rulers of the provinces of Asia and Africa, who were therefore "proconsuls" (*b*) those who were ex-pretors or "proconsuls" of other senatorial provinces (a pretor being virtually the same as a consul). To the former belonged the "proconsuls" at Ephesus, Acts 19:38 (KJV, "deputies"); to the latter, Sergius Paulus in Cyprus, Acts 13:7, 8, 12, and Gallio at Corinth, 18:12. In the NT times Egypt was governed by a prefect. Provinces in which a standing army was kept were governed by an imperial legate (e.g., Quirinius in Syria, Luke 2:2): see GOVERNOR, A, No. 1.¶

Note: Anthupateō, "to be proconsul," is in some texts in Acts 18:12.

PROFANE (Adjective and Verb)

A. Adjective.

bebēlos (βέβηλος, 952), primarily, "permitted to be trodden, accessible" (from *bainō*, "to go," whence *bēlos*, "a threshold"), hence, "unhallowed, profane" (opposite to *hieros*, "sacred"), is used of (*a*) persons, 1 Tim. 1:9; Heb. 12:16; (*b*) things, 1 Tim. 4:7; 6:20; 2 Tim. 2:16. "The natural antagonism between the profane and the holy or divine grew into a moral antagonism.... Accordingly *bebēlos* is that which lacks all relationship or affinity to God" (Cremer, who compares *koinos*, "common," in the sense of ritual uncleanness).¶

B. Verb.

bebēloō (βεβηλόω, 953), primarily, "to cross the threshold" (akin to A, which see), hence, "to profane, pollute," occurs in Matt. 12:5 and Acts 24:6 (the latter as in 21:28, 29: cf. DEFILE, A, No. 1, PARTITION).¶

PROFESS, PROFESSION

A. Verbs.

1. *epangellō* (ἐπαγγέλλω, 1861), "to announce, proclaim, profess," is rendered "to profess" in 1 Tim. 2:10, of godliness, and 6:21, of "the knowledge ... falsely so called." See PROMISE.

2. *homologeō* (ὁμολογέω, 3670) is translated "to profess" in Matt. 7:23 and Titus 1:16; in 1 Tim. 6:12, KJV (RV, "confess"). See CONFESS.

3. *phaskō* (φάσκω, 5335), "to affirm, assert": see AFFIRM, No. 3.

B. Noun.

homologia (ὁμολογία, 3671), akin to A, No. 2, "confession," is translated "profession" and "professed" in the KJV only. See CONFESS.

PROFIT (Noun and Verb), PROFITABLE, PROFITING

A. Nouns.

1. *ōpheleia* (ὠφέλεια, 5622) primarily denotes "assistance"; then, "advantage, benefit,"; "profit," in Rom. 3:1. See ADVANTAGE, No. 3.

2. *ophelos* (ὄφελος, 3786), "profit" in Jas. 2:14, 16: see ADVANTAGE, No. 2.

3. *sumpheron* (συμφέρον, 4851d), the neuter form of the present participle of *sumpherō* (see B, No. 1), is used as a noun with the article in Heb. 12:10, "(for our) profit"; in some mss. in 1 Cor. 7:35 and 10:33 (see No. 4); in 1 Cor. 12:7, preceded by *pros*, "with a view to, towards," translated "to profit withal," lit., "towards the profiting."¶

4. *sumphoros* (σύμφορος, 4851d), akin to No. 3, an adjective, signifying "profitable, useful, expedient," is used as a noun, and found in the best texts, with the article, in 1 Cor. 7:35 (see No. 3) and 10:33 (1st part), the word being understood in the 2nd part.¶

5. *prokopē* (προκοπή, 4297), translated "profiting" in 1 Tim. 4:15, KJV (RV, "progress"); see FURTHERANCE.

B. Verbs.

1. *sumpherō* (συμφέρω, 4851), "to be profitable," Matt. 5:29, 30; Acts 20:20: see EXPEDIENT.

2. *ōpheleō* (ὠφελέω, 5623), akin to A, No. 1, is translated "to profit" in Matt. 15:5; 16:26; Mark 7:11; 8:36; Luke 9:25, RV; John 6:63;

Rom. 2:25; 1 Cor. 13:3; 14:6; Gal. 5:2; Heb. 4:2; 13:9. See ADVANTAGE, BETTERED, PREVAIL.

3. *prokoptō* (προκόπτω, 4298) is translated "I profited" in Gal. 1:14, KJV. See ADVANCE.

C. Adjectives.

1. *chrēsimos* (χρήσιμος, 5539), "useful" (akin to *chraomai*, "to use"), is translated as a noun in 2 Tim. 2:14, "to (no) profit," lit., "to (nothing) profitable."¶

2. *euchrēstos* (εὔχρηστος, 2173), "useful, serviceable" (*eu*, "well," *chrēstos*, "serviceable," akin to *chraomai*, see No. 1), is used in Philem. 11, "profitable," in contrast to *achrēstos*, "unprofitable" (*a*, negative), with a delightful play upon the name "Onesimus," signifying "profitable" (from *onēsis*, "profit"), a common name among slaves. Perhaps the prefix *eu* should have been brought out by some rendering like "very profitable," "very serviceable," the suggestion being that whereas the runaway slave had done great disservice to Philemon, now after his conversion, in devotedly serving the apostle in his confinement, he had thereby already become particularly serviceable to Philemon himself, considering that the latter would have most willingly rendered service to Paul, had it been possible. Onesimus, who had belied his name, was now true to it on behalf of his erstwhile master, who also owed his conversion to the apostle.

It is translated "meet for (the master's) use" in 2 Tim. 2:21; "useful" in 4:11, RV (KJV, "profitable"). See USEFUL.¶ In the Sept., Prov. 31:13.¶

3. *ōphelimos* (ὠφέλιμος, 5624), "useful, profitable" (akin to B, No. 2), is translated "profitable" in 1 Tim. 4:8, both times in the RV (KJV, "profiteth" in the 1st part), of physical exercise, and of godliness; in 2 Tim. 3:16 of the God-breathed Scriptures; in Titus 3:8, of maintaining good works.¶

PROGRESS

prokopē (προκοπή, 4297) is translated "progress" in Phil. 1:12, 25 and 1 Tim. 4:15: see FURTHERANCE.¶

PROLONG

parateinō (παρατείνω, 3905), "to stretch out along" (*para*, "along," *teinō*, "to stretch"), is translated "prolonged" in Acts 20:7, RV, of Paul's discourse: see CONTINUE, *Note* (1).¶

PROMISE (Noun and Verb)

A. Noun.

1. *epangelia* (ἐπαγγελία, 1860), primarily a law term, denoting "a summons" (*epi*, "upon," *angellō*, "to proclaim, announce"), also meant "an undertaking to do or give something, a promise." Except in Acts 23:21 it is used only of the "promises" of God. It frequently stands for the thing "promised," and so signifies a gift graciously bestowed, not a pledge secured by negotiation; thus, in Gal. 3:14, "the promise of the Spirit" denotes "the promised Spirit": cf. Luke 24:49; Acts 2:33 and Eph. 1:13; so in Heb. 9:15, "the promise of the eternal inheritance" is "the promised eternal inheritance." On the other hand, in Acts 1:4, "the promise of the Father," is the "promise" made by the Father.

In Gal. 3:16, the plural "promises" is used because the one "promise" to Abraham was variously repeated (Gen. 12:1–3; 13:14–17; 15:18; 17:1–14; 22:15–18), and because it contained the germ of all subsequent "promises"; cf. Rom. 9:4; Heb. 6:12; 7:6; 8:6; 11:17. Gal. 3 is occupied with showing that the "promise" was conditional upon faith and not upon the fulfillment of the Law. The Law was later than, and inferior to, the "promise," and did not annul it, v. 21; cf. 4:23, 28. Again, in Eph. 2:12, "the covenants of the promise" does not indicate different covenants, but a covenant often renewed, all centering in Christ as the "promised" Messiah-Redeemer, and comprising the blessings to be bestowed through Him.

In 2 Cor. 1:20 the plural is used of every "promise" made by God: cf. Heb. 11:33; in 7:6, of special "promises" mentioned. For other applications of the word, see, e.g., Eph. 6:2; 1 Tim. 4:8; 2 Tim. 1:1; Heb. 4:1; 2 Pet. 3:4, 9; in 1 John 1:5 some mss. have this word, instead of *angelia*, "message."

The occurrences of the word in relation to Christ and what centers in Him, may be arranged under the headings (1) the contents of the "promise," e.g., Acts 26:6; Rom. 4:20; 1 John 2:25; (2) the heirs, e.g., Rom. 9:8; 15:8; Gal. 3:29; Heb. 11:9; (3) the conditions, e.g., Rom. 4:13, 14; Gal. 3:14–22; Heb. 10:36.

2. *epangelma* (ἐπάγγελμα, 1862) denotes "a promise made," 2 Pet. 1:4; 3:13.¶

B. Verbs.

1. *epangellō* (ἐπαγγέλλω, 1861), "to announce, proclaim," has in the NT the two meanings "to profess" and "to promise," each used in the middle voice; "to promise" (*a*) of "promises" of God, Acts 7:5; Rom. 4:21; in Gal. 3:19, passive voice; Titus 1:2; Heb. 6:13; 10:23; 11:11; 12:26; Jas. 1:12; 2:5; 1 John 2:25; (*b*) made by men, Mark 14:11; 2 Pet. 2:19. See PROFESS.

2. *proepangellō* (προεπαγγέλλω, 4279), in the middle voice, "to promise before" *pro*, and No. 1), occurs in Rom. 1:2; 2 Cor. 9:5. See AFOREPROMISED.¶

3. *homologeō* (ὁμολογέω, 3670), "to agree, confess," signifies "to promise" in Matt. 14:7. See CONFESS.

Note: For *exomologeō* in Luke 22:6, see CONSENT, No. 1.

PRONOUNCE

legō (λέγω, 3004), "to say, declare," is rendered "pronounceth (blessing)" in Rom. 4:6, RV, which necessarily repeats the verb in v. 9 (it is absent from the original), for KJV, "*cometh*" (italicized). See ASK, A, No. 6, DESCRIBE, No. 2, SAY.

PROOF

1. *dokimē* (δοκιμή, 1382): see EXPERIENCE, No. 2.

2. *dokimion* (δοκίμιον, 1383), "a test, a proof," is rendered "proof" in Jas. 1:3, RV (KJV, "trying"); it is regarded by some as equivalent to *dokimeion*, "a crucible, a test"; it is the neuter form of the adjective *dokimios*, used as a noun, which has been taken to denote the means by which a man is tested and "proved" (Mayor), in the same sense as *dokimē* (No. 1) in 2 Cor. 8:2; the same phrase is used in 1 Pet. 1:7, RV, "the proof (of your faith)," KJV, "the trial"; where the meaning probably is "that which is approved [i.e., as genuine] in your faith"; this interpretation, which was suggested by Hort, and may hold good for Jas. 1:3, has been confirmed from the papyri by Deissmann (*Bible Studies*, p. 259ff.). Moulton and Milligan (*Vocab.*) give additional instances.¶

3. *endeixis* (ἔνδειξις, 1732): see DECLARE, B. Cf. the synonymous word *endeigma*, "a token," 2 Thess. 1:5, which refers rather to the thing "proved," while *endeixis* points to the act of "proving."

4. *tekmērion* (τεκμήριον, 5039), "a sure sign, a positive proof" (from *tekmar*, "a mark, sign"), occurs in Acts 1:3, RV, "proofs" (KJV, "infallible proofs"; a "proof" does not require to be described as infallible, the adjective is superfluous).¶

Note: For the KJV in 2 Tim. 4:5, "make full proof," RV, "fulfill" (*plērophoreō*), see FULFILL.

PROPER

1. *asteios* (ἀστεῖος, 791) is translated "proper" in Heb. 11:23, RV, "goodly": see BEAUTIFUL, No. 2.

2. *idios* (ἴδιος, 2398), "one's own," is found in some mss. in Acts 1:19, KJV, "proper"; in 1 Cor. 7:7, RV, "own" (KJV, "proper"); in Jude 6, RV, "their proper (habitation)," KJV, "their own."

PROPHECY, PROPHESY, PROPHESYING

A. Noun.

prophēteia (προφητεία, 4394) signifies "the speaking forth of the mind and counsel of God" (*pro*, "forth," *phēmi*, "to speak": see PROPHET); in the NT it is used (*a*) of the gift, e.g., Rom. 12:6; 1 Cor. 12:10; 13:2; (*b*) either of the exercise of the gift or of that which is "prophesied," e.g., Matt. 13:14; 1 Cor. 13:8; 14:6, 22 and 1 Thess. 5:20, "prophesying (s)"; 1 Tim. 1:18; 4:14; 2 Pet. 1:20, 21; Rev. 1:3; 11:6; 19:10; 22:7, 10, 18, 19.¶

"Though much of OT prophecy was purely predictive, see Micah 5:2, e.g., and cf. John 11:51, prophecy is not necessarily, nor even primarily, fore-telling. It is the declaration of that which cannot be known by natural means, Matt. 26:68, it is the forth-telling of the will of God, whether with reference to the past, the present, or the future, see Gen. 20:7; Deut. 18:18; Rev. 10:11; 11:3....

"In such passages as 1 Cor. 12:28; Eph. 2:20, the 'prophets' are placed after the 'Apostles,' since not the prophets of Israel are intended, but the 'gifts' of the ascended Lord, Eph. 4:8, 11; cf. Acts 13:1; ...; the purpose of their ministry was to edify, to comfort, and to encourage the believers, 1 Cor. 14:3, while its effect upon unbelievers was to show that the secrets of a man's heart are known to God, to convict of sin, and to constrain to worship, vv. 24, 25.

"With the completion of the canon of Scripture prophecy apparently passed away, 1 Cor. 13:8, 9. In his measure the teacher has taken the place of the prophet, cf. the significant change in 2 Pet. 2:1. The difference is that, whereas the message of the prophet was a direct revelation of the mind of God for the occasion, the message of the teacher is gathered from the completed revelation contained in the Scriptures."*

B. Adjective.

prophētikos (προφητικός, 4397), "of or relating to prophecy," or "proceeding from a prophet, prophetic," is used of the OT Scriptures, Rom. 16:26, "of the prophets," lit., "(by) prophetic (Scriptures)"; 2 Pet. 1:19, "the word of prophecy (*made* more sure)," i.e., confirmed by the person and work of Christ (KJV, "a more sure, etc."), lit., "the prophetic word."¶

C. Verb.

prophēteuō (προφητεύω, 4395), "to be a prophet, to prophesy," is used (*a*) with the pri-

---

* From *Notes on Thessalonians* by Hogg and Vine, pp. 196, 197.

mary meaning of telling forth the divine counsels, e.g., Matt. 7:22; 26:68; 1 Cor. 11:4, 5; 13:9; 14:1, 3–5, 24, 31, 39; Rev. 11:3; (b) of foretelling the future, e.g., Matt. 15:7; John 11:51; 1 Pet. 1:10; Jude 14.

PROPHET

1. *prophētēs* (προφήτης, 4396), "one who speaks forth or openly" (see PROPHECY, A), "a proclaimer of a divine message," denoted among the Greeks an interpreter of the oracles of the gods.

In the Sept. it is the translation of the word *rôeh*, "a seer"; 1 Sam. 9:9, indicating that the "prophet" was one who had immediate intercourse with God. It also translates the word *nābhî*, meaning "either one in whom the message from God springs forth" or "one to whom anything is secretly communicated." Hence, in general, "the prophet" was one upon whom the Spirit of God rested, Num. 11:17–29, one, to whom and through whom God speaks, Num. 12:2; Amos 3:7, 8. In the case of the OT prophets their messages were very largely the proclamation of the divine purposes of salvation and glory to be accomplished in the future; the "prophesying" of the NT "prophets" was both a preaching of the divine counsels of grace already accomplished and the foretelling of the purposes of God in the future.

In the NT the word is used (a) of "the OT prophets," e.g., Matt. 5:12; Mark 6:15; Luke 4:27; John 8:52; Rom. 11:3; (b) of "prophets in general," e.g., Matt. 10:41; 21:46; Mark 6:4; (c) of "John the Baptist," Matt. 21:26; Luke 1:76; (d) of "prophets in the churches," e.g., Acts 13:1; 15:32; 21:10; 1 Cor. 12:28, 29; 14:29, 32, 37; Eph. 2:20; 3:5; 4:11; (e) of "Christ, as the aforepromised Prophet," e.g., John 1:21; 6:14; 7:40; Acts 3:22; 7:37, or, without the article, and, without reference to the Old Testament, Mark 6:15, Luke 7:16; in Luke 24:19 it is used with *anēr*, "a man"; John 4:19; 9:17; (f) of "two witnesses" yet to be raised up for special purposes, Rev. 11:10, 18; (g) of "the Cretan poet Epimenides," Titus 1:12; (h) by metonymy, of "the writings of prophets," e.g., Luke 24:27; Acts 8:28.

2. *pseudoprophētēs* (ψευδοπροφήτης, 5578), "a false prophet," is used of such (a) in OT times, Luke 6:26; 2 Pet. 2:1; (b) in the present period since Pentecost, Matt. 7:15; 24:11, 24; Mark 13:22; Acts 13:6; 1 John 4:1; (c) with reference to a false "prophet" destined to arise as the supporter of the "Beast" at the close of this age, Rev. 16:13; 19:20; 20:10 (himself described as "another beast," 13:11).¶

PROPHETESS

prophētis (προφῆτις, 4398), the feminine of *prophētēs* (see above), is used of Anna, Luke 2:36; of the self-assumed title of "the woman Jezebel" in Rev. 2:20.¶

PROPITIATION

A. Verb.

hilaskomai (ἱλάσκομαι, 2433) was used amongst the Greeks with the significance "to make the gods propitious, to appease, propitiate," inasmuch as their good will was not conceived as their natural attitude, but something to be earned first. This use of the word is foreign to the Greek Bible, with respect to God, whether in the Sept. or in the NT. It is never used of any act whereby man brings God into a favorable attitude or gracious disposition. It is God who is "propitiated" by the vindication of His holy and righteous character, whereby, through the provision He has made in the vicarious and expiatory sacrifice of Christ, He has so dealt with sin that He can show mercy to the believing sinner in the removal of his guilt and the remission of his sins.

Thus in Luke 18:13 it signifies "to be propitious" or "merciful to" (with the person as the object of the verb), and in Heb. 2:17 "to expiate, to make propitiation for" (the object of the verb being sins); here the RV, "to make propitiation" is an important correction of the KJV, "to make reconciliation." Through the "propitiatory" sacrifice of Christ, he who believes upon Him is by God's own act delivered from justly deserved wrath, and comes under the covenant of grace. Never is God said to be reconciled, a fact itself indicative that the enmity exists on man's part alone, and that it is man who needs to be reconciled to God, and not God to man. God is always the same and, since He is Himself immutable, His relative attitude does change towards those who change. He can act differently towards those who come to Him by faith, and solely on the ground of the "propitiatory" sacrifice of Christ, not because He has changed, but because He ever acts according to His unchanging righteousness.

The expiatory work of the Cross is therefore the means whereby the barrier which sin interposes between God and man is broken down. By the giving up of His sinless life sacrificially, Christ annuls the power of sin to separate between God and the believer.

In the OT the Hebrew verb *kaphar* is connected with *kopher*, "a covering" (see MERCY SEAT), and is used in connection with the burnt offering, e.g., Lev. 1:4; 14:20; 16:24, the guilt offering, e.g., Lev. 5:16, 18, the sin offering, e.g., Lev. 4:20, 26, 31, 35, the sin offering and burnt offering together, e.g., Lev. 5:10; 9:7, the meal offering and peace offering, e.g., Ezek. 45:15, 17, as well as in other respects. It is used of the ram offered at the consecration of the high priest, Ex. 29:33, and of the blood which God gave upon the altar to make "propitiation" for the souls of the people, and that because "the life of the flesh is in the blood," Lev. 17:11, and "it is the blood that maketh atonement by reason of the life" (RV). Man has forfeited his life on account of sin and God has provided the one and only way whereby eternal life could be bestowed, namely, by the voluntary laying down of His life by His Son, under divine retribution. Of this the former sacrifices appointed by God were foreshadowings.

B. Nouns.

1. *hilastērion* (ἱλαστήριον, 2435), akin to A, is regarded as the neuter of an adjective signifying "propitiatory." In the Sept. it is used adjectivally in connection with *epithēma*, "a cover," in Exod. 25:17 and 37:6, of the lid of the ark (see MERCY SEAT), but it is used as a noun (without *epithēma*), of locality, in Exod. 25:18, 19, 20, 21, 22; 31:7; 35:12; 37:7, 8, 9; Lev. 16:2, 13, 14, 15; Num. 7:89, and this is its use in Heb. 9:5.

Elsewhere in the NT it occurs in Rom. 3:25, where it is used of Christ Himself; the RV text and punctuation in this verse are important: "whom God set forth *to be* a propitiation, through faith, by His blood." The phrase "by His blood" is to be taken in immediate connection with "propitiation." Christ, through His expiatory death, is the personal means by whom God shows the mercy of His justifying grace to the sinner who believes. His "blood" stands for the voluntary giving up of His life, by the shedding of His blood in expiatory sacrifice, under divine judgment righteously due to us as sinners, faith being the sole condition on man's part.

Note: "By metonymy, 'blood' is sometimes put for 'death,' inasmuch as, blood being essential to life, Lev. 17:11, when the blood is shed life is given up, that is, death takes place. The fundamental principle on which God deals with sinners is expressed in the words 'apart from shedding of blood,' i.e., unless a death takes place, 'there is no remission' of sins, Heb. 9:22.

"But whereas the essential of the type lay in the fact that blood was shed, the essential of the antitype lies in this, that the blood shed was that of Christ. Hence, in connection with Jewish sacrifices, 'the blood' is mentioned without reference to the victim from which it flowed, but in connection with the great antitypical sacrifice of the NT the words 'the blood' never stand alone; the One Who shed the blood is invariably specified, for it is the Person that gives value to the work; the saving efficacy of the Death depends entirely upon the fact that He Who died was the Son of God."*

2. *hilasmos* (ἱλασμός, 2434), akin to *hileōs* ("merciful, propitious"), signifies "an expiation, a means whereby sin is covered and remitted." It is used in the NT of Christ Himself as "the propitiation," in 1 John 2:2 and 4:10, signifying that He Himself, through the expiatory sacrifice of His death, is the personal means by whom God shows mercy to the sinner who believes on Christ as the One thus provided. In the former passage He is described as "the propitiation for our sins; and not for ours only, but also for the whole world." The italicized addition in the KJV, "*the sins of,*" gives a wrong interpretation. What is indicated is that provision is made for the whole world, so that no one is, by divine predetermination, excluded from the scope of God's mercy; the efficacy of the "propitiation," however, is made actual for those who believe. In 4:10, the fact that God "sent His Son to be the propitiation for our sins," is shown to be the great expression of God's love toward man, and the reason why Christians should love one another.¶ In the Sept., Lev. 25:9; Num. 5:8; 1 Chron. 28:20; Ps. 130:4; Ezek. 44:27; Amos 8:14.¶

PROPORTION

analogia (ἀναλογία, 356), Cf. Eng., "analogy," signified in classical Greek "the right relation, the coincidence or agreement existing or demanded according to the standard of the several relations, not agreement as equality" (Cremer). It is used in Rom. 12:6, where "let us prophesy according to the proportion of our faith," RV, recalls v. 3. It is a warning against going beyond what God has given and faith receives. This meaning, rather than the other rendering, "according to the analogy of the faith," is in keeping with the context. The word *analogia* is not to be rendered literally. "Proportion" here represents its true meaning. The fact that there is a definite article before "faith" in the original does not necessarily afford an intimation that the faith, the body of Christian doctrine, is here in view. The presence of the definite article is due to the fact that faith is an abstract noun. The meaning "the faith" is not relevant to the context.¶

---

* From *Notes on Thessalonians* by Hogg and Vine, p. 168.

PROSELYTE

prosēlutos (προσήλυτος, 4339), akin to *proserchomai*, "to come to," primarily signifies "one who has arrived, a stranger"; in the NT it is used of converts to Judaism, or foreign converts to the Jewish religion, Matt. 23:15; Acts 2:10; 6:5; 13:43.¶ There seems to be no connection necessarily with Palestine, for in Acts 2:10 and 13:43 it is used of those who lived abroad. Cf. the Sept., e.g., in Exod. 22:21; 23:9; Deut. 10:19, of the "stranger" living among the children of Israel.

PROSPER

euodoō (εὐοδόω, 2137), "to help on one's way" (*eu*, "well," *hodos*, "a way or journey"), is used in the passive voice signifying "to have a prosperous journey," Rom. 1:10; metaphorically, "to prosper, be prospered," 1 Cor. 16:2, RV, "(as) he may prosper," KJV, "(as God) hath prospered (him)," lit., "in whatever he may be prospered," i.e., in material things; the continuous tense suggests the successive circumstances of varying prosperity as week follows week; in 3 John 2, of the "prosperity" of physical and spiritual health.¶

PROTEST

Note: In 1 Cor. 15:31, "I protest by" is a rendering of *nē*, a particle of strong affirmation used in oaths.¶ In the Sept., Gen. 42:15, 16.¶

PROUD

huperēphanos (ὑπερήφανος, 5244) signifies "showing oneself above others, preeminent" (*huper*, "above," *phainomai*, "to appear, be manifest"); it is always used in Scripture in the bad sense of "arrogant, disdainful, proud," Luke 1:51; Rom. 1:30; 2 Tim. 3:2; Jas. 4:6; 1 Pet. 5:5.¶

Note: For the KJV renderings of the verb *tuphoō*, in 1 Tim. 3:6; 6:4; 2 Tim. 3:4, see HIGHMINDED.

PROVE

A. Verbs.

1. *dokimazō* (δοκιμάζω, 1381), "to test, prove," with the expectation of approving, is translated "to prove" in Luke 14:19; Rom. 12:2; 1 Cor. 3:13, RV (KJV, "shall try"); 11:28, RV (KJV, "examine"); 2 Cor. 8:8, 22; 13:5; Gal. 6:4; Eph. 5:10; 1 Thess. 2:4 (2nd part), RV (KJV, "trieth"); 5:21; 1 Tim. 3:10; in some mss., Heb. 3:9 (the most authentic have the noun *dokimasia*, "a proving"¶); 1 Pet. 1:7, RV (KJV, "tried"); 1 John 4:1, RV (KJV, "try"). See APPROVE.

2. *apodeiknumi* (ἀποδείκνυμι, 584), "to show forth," signifies "to prove" in Acts 25:7. See APPROVE, No. 3.

3. *paristēmi* (παρίστημι, 3936), "to present," signifies "to prove" in Acts 24:13. See COMMEND, No. 4.

4. *peirazō* (πειράζω, 3985), "to try," either in the sense of attempting, e.g., Acts 16:7, or of testing, is rendered "to prove" in John 6:6. See EXAMINE, TEMPT.

5. *sumbibazō* (συμβιβάζω, 4822), "to join together," signifies "to prove" in Acts 9:22. See COMPACTED, No. 2.

6. *sunistēmi* or *sunistanō* (συνίστημι, 4921), "to commend, to prove," is translated "I prove (myself a transgressor)" in Gal. 2:18 (KJV, "I make"). See COMMEND.

B. Noun.

peirasmos (πειρασμός, 3986), (*a*) "a trying, testing," (*b*) "a temptation," is used in sense (*a*) in 1 Pet. 4:12, with the preposition *pros*, "towards" or "with a view to," RV, "to prove" (KJV, "to try"), lit., "for a testing." See TEMPTATION.

Notes: (1) In Luke 10:36, RV, *ginomai*, "to become, come to be," is translated "proved (neighbor)," KJV, "was . . ."; so in Heb. 2:2. (2) In Rom. 3:9, KJV, *proaitiaomai*, "to accuse beforehand," is translated "we have before proved" (marg., "charged"); for the RV, see CHARGE, C, No. 9.

For **PROVERB** see **PARABLE**, No. 2

PROVIDE, PROVIDENCE, PROVISION

A. Verbs.

1. *hetoimazō* (ἑτοιμάζω, 2090), "to prepare," is translated "hast provided" in Luke 12:20, KJV. See PREPARE.

2. *ktaomai* (κτάομαι, 2932), "to get, to gain," is rendered "provide" in Matt. 10:9. See OBTAIN, POSSESS.

3. *paristēmi* (παρίστημι, 3936), "to present," signifies "to provide" in Acts 23:24. See COMMEND, PROVE, No. 3.

4. *problepō* (προβλέπω, 4265), "to foresee," is translated "having provided" in Heb. 11:40. See FORESEE.¶

5. *pronoeō* (προνοέω, 4306), "to take thought for, provide," is translated "provide . . . for" in 1 Tim. 5:8; in Rom. 12:17 and 2 Cor. 8:21, RV, to take thought for (KJV, "to provide").¶

Note: In Luke 12:33, KJV, *poieō*, "to make" (RV), is translated "provide."

B. Noun.

pronoia (πρόνοια, 4307), "forethought" (*pro*, "before," *noeō*, "to think"), is translated "providence" in Acts 24:2; "provision" in Rom. 13:14.¶

PROVINCE

1. *eparcheia*, or -*ia* (ἐπαρχεία, 1885) was a technical term for the administrative divisions of the Roman Empire. The original meaning was the district within which a magistrate, whether consul or pretor, exercised supreme authority. The word *provincia* acquired its later meaning when Sardinia and Sicily were added to the Roman territories, 227 B.C. On the establishment of the empire the proconsular power over all "provinces" was vested in the emperor. Two "provinces," Asia and Africa, were consular, i.e., held by ex-consuls; the rest were praetorian. Certain small "provinces," e.g. Judea and Cappadocia, were governed by procurators. They were usually districts recently added to the empire and not thoroughly Romanized. Judea was so governed in the intervals between the rule of native kings; ultimately it was incorporated in the "province" of Syria. The "province" mentioned in Acts 23:34 and 25:1 was assigned to the jurisdiction of an *eparchos*, "a prefect or governor" (cf. GOVERNOR, PROCONSUL).¶ In the Sept., Esth. 4:11.¶

2. *kanōn* (κανών, 2583) originally denoted "a straight rod," used as a ruler or measuring instrument, or, in rare instances, "the beam of a balance," the secondary notion being either (*a*) of keeping anything straight, as of a rod used in weaving, or (*b*) of testing straightness, as a carpenter's rule; hence its metaphorical use to express what serves "to measure or determine" anything. By a common transition in the meaning of words, "that which measures," was used for "what was measured"; thus a certain space at Olympia was called a *kanōn*. So in music, a canon is a composition in which a given melody is the model for the formation of all the parts. In general the word thus came to serve for anything regulating the actions of men, as a standard or principle. In Gal. 6:16, those who "walk by this rule (*kanōn*)" are those who make what is stated in vv. 14 and 15 their guiding line in the matter of salvation through faith in Christ alone, apart from works, whether following the principle themselves or teaching it to others. In 2 Cor. 10:13, 15, 16, it is translated "province," RV (KJV, "rule" and "line of things"; marg., "line"; RV marg., "limit" or "measuring rod.") Here it signifies the limits of the responsibility in gospel service as measured and appointed by God.¶

For **PROVING** (*elenchos*) see **REPROOF, A**

PROVOCATION, PROVOKE

A. Nouns.

1. *parapikrasmos* (παραπικρασμός, 3894), from *para*, "amiss" or "from," used intensively, and *pikrainō*, "to make bitter" (*pikros*, "sharp, bitter"), "provocation," occurs in Heb. 3:8, 15.¶ In the Sept., Ps. 95:8.¶

2. *paroxusmos* (παροξυσμός, 3948) denotes "a stimulation" (Eng., "paroxysm"), (cf. B, No. 2): in Heb. 10:24, "to provoke," lit., "unto a stimulation (of love)." See CONTENTION, No. 2.

B. Verbs.

1. *parapikrainō* (παραπικραίνω, 3893), "to embitter, provoke" (akin to A, No. 1), occurs in Heb. 3:16.¶

2. *paroxunō* (παροξύνω, 3947), primarily, "to sharpen" (akin to A, No. 2), is used metaphorically, signifying "to rouse to anger, to provoke," in the passive voice, in Acts 17:16, RV, "was provoked" (KJV, "was stirred"); in 1 Cor. 13:5, RV, "is not provoked" (the word "easily" in KJV, represents no word in the original). See STIR.¶

3. *erethizō* (ἐρεθίζω, 2042), "to excite, stir up, provoke," is used (*a*) in a good sense in 2 Cor. 9:2, KJV, "hath provoked," RV, "hath stirred up"; (*b*) in an evil sense in Col. 3:21, "provoke." See STIR.¶

4. *parorgizō* (παροργίζω, 3949), "to provoke to wrath": see ANGER, B, No. 2.

5. *parazēloō* (παραζηλόω, 3863), "to provoke to jealousy": see JEALOUSY.

6. *apostomatizō* (ἀποστοματίζω, 653) in classical Greek meant "to speak from memory, to dictate to a pupil" (*apo*, "from," *stoma*, "a mouth"); in later Greek, "to catechize"; in Luke 11:53, "to provoke (Him) to speak."¶

7. *prokaleō* (προκαλέω, 4292), "to call forth," as to a contest, hence "to stir up what is evil in another," occurs in the middle voice in Gal. 5:26.¶

PRUDENCE, PRUDENT

A. Nouns.

1. *phronēsis* (φρόνησις, 5428), akin to *phroneō*, "to have understanding" (*phrēn*, "the mind"), denotes "practical wisdom, prudence in the management of affairs." It is translated "wisdom" in Luke 1:17; "prudence" in Eph. 1:8. See WISDOM.¶

2. *sunesis* (σύνεσις, 4907), "understanding," is rendered "prudence" in 1 Cor. 1:19, RV (KJV, "understanding"); it suggests quickness of apprehension, the penetrating consideration which

precedes action. Cf. B, in the same verse. See KNOWLEDGE, UNDERSTANDING.

B. Adjective.

sunetos (συνετός, 4908) signifies "intelligent, sagacious, understanding" (akin to *suniēmi*, "to perceive"), translated "prudent" in Matt. 11:25, KJV (RV, "understanding"); Luke 10:21 (ditto); Acts 13:7, RV, "(a man) of understanding"; in 1 Cor. 1:19, "prudent," RV and KJV.¶ Cf. *asunetos*, "without understanding."

PSALM

psalmos (ψαλμός, 5568) primarily denoted "a striking or twitching with the fingers (on musical strings)"; then, "a sacred song, sung to musical accompaniment, a psalm." It is used (*a*) of the OT book of "Psalms," Luke 20:42; 24:44; Acts 1:20; (*b*) of a particular "psalm," Acts 13:33 (cf. v. 35); (*c*) of "psalms" in general, 1 Cor. 14:26; Eph. 5:19; Col. 3:16.¶

Note: For *psallō*, rendered "let him sing psalms" in Jas. 5:13, see MELODY, SING.

PUBLIC, PUBLICLY

A. Adjective.

dēmosios (δημόσιος, 1219), "belonging to the people" (*dēmos*, "the people"), is translated "public" in Acts 5:18, RV, "public (ward)", KJV, "common (prison)."

B. Adverbs.

phanerōs (φανερῶς, 5320): see OPENLY, No. 2.

Note: For a form of *dēmosios* used as an adverb, "publicly," see OPENLY, *Note* (4).

PUBLICAN

telōnēs (τελώνης, 5057) primarily denoted "a farmer of the tax" (from *telos*, "toll, custom, tax"), then, as in the NT, a subsequent subordinate of such, who collected taxes in some district, "a tax gatherer"; such were naturally hated intensely by the people; they are classed with "sinners," Matt. 9:10, 11; 11:9; Mark 2:15, 16; Luke 5:30; 7:34; 15:1; with harlots, Matt. 21:31, 32; with "the Gentile," Matt. 18:17; some mss. have it in Matt. 5:47, the best have *ethnikoi*, "Gentiles." See also Matt. 5:46; 10:3; Luke 3:12; 5:27, 29; 7:29; 18:10, 11, 13.¶

Note: For *architelōnēs*, "a chief publican," see CHIEF, B, No. 4.

PUBLISH

1. *kērussō* (κηρύσσω, 2784), "to be a herald, to proclaim, preach," is translated "to publish" in Mark 1:45; 5:20; 7:36; 13:10, KJV (RV, "preached"); Luke 8:39. See PREACH, PROCLAIM.

2. *diapherō* (διαφέρω, 1308), "to bear through," is translated "was published" in Acts 13:49, KJV (RV, "was spread abroad"). See BETTER (be), No. 1.

3. *ginomai* (γίνομαι, 1096), "to become, come to be," is translated "was published" in Acts 10:37, lit., "came to be."

4. *diangellō* (διαγγέλλω, 1229), "to publish abroad," is so translated in Luke 9:60, RV (KJV, "preach"), and Rom. 9:17. See DECLARE, A, No. 3.

PUFF (up)

1. *phusioō* (φυσιόω, 5448), "to puff up, blow up, inflate" (from *phusa*, "bellows"), is used metaphorically in the NT, in the sense of being "puffed" up with pride, 1 Cor. 4:6, 18, 19; 5:2; 8:1; 13:4; Col. 2:18.¶

2. *tuphoō* (τυφόω, 5187) is always rendered "to puff up" in the RV. See HIGH-MINDED, PROUD.

PULL (down)

kathaireō (καθαιρέω, 2507), "to take down," is translated "I will pull down" in Luke 12:18. See DESTROY, No. 3.

Notes: (1) In Jude 23, KJV, *harpazō*, "to seize, snatch away," is rendered "pulling ... out." See SNATCH. (2) In Acts 23:10, KJV, *diaspaō*, "to rend or tear asunder," is translated "should have been pulled in pieces" (RV, "should be torn in pieces"). (3) *Ekballō*, "to cast out," is translated "to pull out" in Matt. 7:4 and Luke 6:42 (twice), KJV (RV, "cast out"). See CAST, No. 5. (4) For *anaspaō*, rendered "pull out" in Luke 14:5, KJV, see DRAW, No. 5. (5) For *kathairesis*, "a casting down," 2 Cor. 10:4, see CAST, A, No. 14, Note.

PUNISH

1. *kolazō* (κολάζω, 2849) primarily denotes "to curtail, prune, dock" (from *kolos*, "docked"); then, "to check, restrain, punish"; it is used in the middle voice in Acts 4:21; passive voice in 2 Pet. 2:9, KJV, "to be punished" (RV, "under punishment," lit., "being punished"), a futurative present tense.¶

2. *timōreō* (τιμωρέω, 5097), primarily, "to help," then, "to avenge" (from *timē*, "value, honor," and *ouros*, "a guardian"), i.e., "to help" by redressing injuries, is used in the active voice in Acts 26:11, RV, "punishing" (KJV, "I punished"); passive voice in 22:5, lit., "(that) they may be punished." Cf. No. 5, below.¶

Note: For 2 Thess. 1:9, "shall suffer punishment," RV, see JUSTICE. See SUFFER, *Note* (10).

PUNISHMENT

1. *ekdikēsis* (ἐκδίκησις, 1557): for 1 Pet. 2:14, KJV, "punishment" (RV, "vengeance"), see AVENGE, B, No. 2.

2. *epitimia* (ἐπιτιμία, 2009) in the NT denotes "penalty, punishment," 2 Cor. 2:6.¶ Originally it signified the enjoyment of the rights and privileges of citizenship; then it became used of the estimate (*timē*) fixed by a judge on the infringement of such rights, and hence, in general, a "penalty."

3. *kolasis* (κόλασις, 2851), akin to *kolazō* (PUNISH, No. 1), "punishment," is used in Matt. 25:46, "(eternal) punishment," and 1 John 4:18, "(fear hath) punishment," RV (KJV, "torment"), which there describes a process, not merely an effect; this kind of fear is expelled by perfect love; where God's love is being perfected in us, it gives no room for the fear of meeting with His reprobation; the "punishment" referred to is the immediate consequence of the sense of sin, not a holy awe but a slavish fear, the negation of the enjoyment of love.¶

4. *dikē* (δίκη, 1349), "justice," or "the execution of a sentence," is translated "punishment" in Jude 7, RV (KJV, "vengeance"). See JUSTICE.

5. *timōria* (τιμωρία, 5098), primarily "help" (see PUNISH, No. 2), denotes "vengeance, punishment," Heb. 10:29.¶

Note: The distinction, sometimes suggested, between No. 3 as being disciplinary, with special reference to the sufferer, and No. 5, as being penal, with reference to the satisfaction of him who inflicts it, cannot be maintained in the *Koinē* Greek of NT times.

PURCHASE

1. *ktaomai* (κτάομαι, 2932): see OBTAIN, A, No. 4.

2. *peripoieō* (περιποιέω, 4046) signifies "to gain" or "get for oneself, purchase"; middle voice in Acts 20:28 and 1 Tim. 3:13 (RV "gain"); see GAIN.

3. *agorazō* (ἀγοράζω, 59) is rendered "to purchase" in the RV of Rev. 5:9; 14:3, 4. See BUY, No. 1.

Note: For *peripoiēsis*, "purchased possession," Eph. 1:14, see POSSESSION.

PURE, PURENESS, PURITY

A. Adjectives.

1. *hagnos* (ἁγνός, 53), "pure from defilement, not contaminated" (from the same root as *hagios*, "holy"), is rendered "pure" in Phil. 4:8; 1 Tim. 5:22; Jas. 3:17; 1 John 3:3; see CHASTE.

2. *katharos* (καθαρός, 2513), "pure," as being cleansed, e.g., Matt. 5:8; 1 Tim. 1:5; 3:9; 2 Tim. 1:3; 2:22; Titus 1:15; Heb. 10:22; Jas. 1:27; 1 Pet. 1:22; Rev. 15:6; 21:18; 22:1 (in some mss.). See CHASTE, Note, CLEAN, A.

Note: In 1 Pet. 1:22 the KJV, "with a pure heart," follows those mss. which have this adjective (RV, "from the heart").

3. *eilikrinēs* (εἰλικρινής, 1506) signifies "unalloyed, pure"; (*a*) it was used of unmixed substances; (*b*) in the NT it is used of moral and ethical "purity," Phil. 1:10, "sincere"; so the RV in 2 Pet. 3:1 (KJV, "pure"). Some regard the etymological meaning as "tested by the sunlight" (Cremer).¶ See CHASTE, Note, SINCERE.

Note: Wine mixed with water may be *hagnos*, "not being contaminated"; it is not *katharos*, when there is the admixture of any element even though the latter is "pure" in itself.

B. Nouns.

1. *hagnotēs* (ἁγνότης, 54), the state of being *hagnos* (A, No. 1), occurs in 2 Cor. 6:6, "pureness"; 11:3, in the best mss., "(and the) purity," RV.¶

2. *hagneia* (ἁγνεία, 47), synonymous with No. 1, "purity," occurs in 1 Tim. 4:12; 5:2, where it denotes the chastity which excludes all impurity of spirit, manner, or act.¶

PURGE

1. *kathairō* (καθαίρω, 2508), akin to *katharos* (see PURE, A, No. 2), "to cleanse," is used of pruning, John 15:2, KJV, "purgeth" (RV, "cleanseth").¶ In the Sept., 2 Sam. 4:6; Isa. 28:27; Jer. 38:28.¶

2. *ekkathairō* (ἐκκαθαίρω, 1571), "to cleanse out, cleanse thoroughly," is said of "purging" out leaven, 1 Cor. 5:7; in 2 Tim. 2:21, of "purging" oneself from those who utter "profane babblings," vv. 16–18.¶

3. *diakathairō* (διακαθαίρω, 1223 and 2508), "to cleanse thoroughly," is translated "will throughly purge" in Luke 3:17, KJV (RV, "thoroughly to cleanse"; less authentic mss. have No. 5).¶

4. *kathakizō* (καθαρίζω, 2511), "to cleanse, make clean," is translated "purging (all meats)," in Mark 7:19, KJV, RV, "making (all meats) clean"; Heb. 9:14, KJV, "purge" (RV, "cleanse"); so 9:22 (for v. 23, see PURIFY) and 10:2. See CLEAN, B, No. 1.

5. *diakatharizō* (διακαθαρίζω, 1245), "to cleanse thoroughly," is translated "will throughly purge" in Matt. 3:12, KJV. See CLEAN, B, No. 2. Cf. the synonymous verb No. 3.¶

Notes: (1) For Heb. 1:3, KJV, "had purged," see PURIFICATION. (2) For the KJV rendering of the noun *katharismos*, "cleansing," "that he was purged," see CLEAN, C, No. 1.

PURIFICATION, PURIFY, PURIFYING

A. Nouns.

1. *katharismos* (καθαρισμός, 2512) is rendered "a cleansing" (akin to No. 4, above), Mark 1:44; Luke 5:14; in Heb. 1:3, RV, "purification."

2. *katharotēs* (καθαρότης, 2514), "cleansing," Heb. 9:13. See CLEAN, C, No. 2.¶

3. *hagnismos* (ἁγνισμός, 49) denotes "a ceremonial purification," Acts 21:26, for the circumstances of which with reference to the vow of a Nazirite (RV), see Num. 6:9–13.¶

B. Verbs.

1. *hagnizō* (ἁγνίζω, 48), akin to *hagnos*, "pure" (see CHASTE), "to purify, cleanse from defilement," is used of "purifying" (*a*) ceremonially, John 11:55; Acts 21:24, 26 (cf. No. 3 above); 24:18; (*b*) morally, the heart, Jas. 4:8; the soul, 1 Pet. 1:22; oneself, 1 John 3:3.¶

2. *katharizō* (καθαρίζω, 2511), "to cleanse, make free from admixture," is translated "to purify" in Acts 15:9, KJV (RV, "cleansing"); Titus 2:14; Heb. 9:23, KJV (RV, "cleansed"). See CLEAN, B, No. 1.

PURLOIN

nosphizō (νοσφίζω, 3557) is translated "purloining" in Titus 2:10. See KEEP, A, No. 10.

PURPLE

A. Noun.

porphura (πορφύρα, 4209) originally denoted the "purple-fish," then, "purple dye" (extracted from certain shell fish): hence, "a purple garment," Mark 15:17, 20; Luke 16:19; Rev. 18:12.¶

B. Adjective.

porphureos (πορφύρεος, 4210), "purple, a reddish purple," is used of the robe put in mockery on Christ, John 19:2, 5; in Rev. 17:4 (in the best texts; some have No. 1); 18:16, as a noun (with *himation*, "a garment," understood).¶

PURPLE (seller of)

porphuropōlis (πορφυρόπωλις, 4211) denotes "a seller of purple fabrics" (from *porphura*, and *pōleō*, "to sell"), Acts 16:14.¶

PURPOSE (Noun and Verb)

A. Nouns.

1. *boulēma* (βούλημα, 1013), "a purpose or will" (akin to *boulomai*, "to will, wish, purpose"), "a deliberate intention," occurs in Acts 27:43, "purpose"; Rom. 9:19, "will"; 1 Pet. 4:3, in the best mss. (some have *thelēma*), KJV, "will," RV, "desire." See WILL.¶

2. *prothesis* (πρόθεσις, 4286), "a setting forth" (used of the "showbread"), "a purpose" (akin to B, No. 3), is used (*a*) of the "purposes of God," Rom. 8:28; 9:11; Eph. 1:11; 3:11; 2 Tim. 1:9; (*b*) of "human purposes," as to things material, Acts 27:13; spiritual, Acts 11:23; 2 Tim. 3:10. See SHEWBREAD.

3. *gnōmē* (γνώμη, 1106), "an opinion, purpose, judgment," is used in the genitive case with *ginomai*, "to come to be," in Acts 20:3, "he purposed," KJV (RV, "he determined"), lit., "he came to be of purpose."

Notes: The following phrases are translated with the word "purpose": (*a*) *eis auto touto*, "for this same (or very) purpose," lit., "unto this same (thing)," Rom. 9:17; Eph. 6:22; Col. 4:8; (*b*) *eis touto*, "for this purpose," Acts 26:16, KJV (RV, "to this end"), lit., "unto this"; so 1 John 3:8; (*c*) *eis ti*, "to what purpose," Matt. 26:8, lit., "unto what"; Mark 14:4, RV, "to what purpose" (KJV, "why").

B. Verbs.

1. *bouleuō* (βουλεύω, 1011), "to take counsel, resolve," always in the middle voice in the NT, "to take counsel with oneself," to determine with oneself, is translated "I purpose" in 2 Cor. 1:17 (twice). See COUNSEL, B, No. 1.

2. *tithēmi* (τίθημι, 5087), "to put, place," is used in the middle voice in Acts 19:21, "purposed," in the sense of resolving.

3. *protithēmi* (προτίθημι, 4388), "to set before, set forth" (*pro*, "before," and No. 2, akin to A, No. 2), is used in Rom. 3:25, "set forth," RV marg., "purposed," KJV marg., "foreordained," middle voice, which lays stress upon the personal interest which God had in so doing; either meaning, "to set forth" or "to purpose," would convey a scriptural view, but the context bears out the former as being intended here; in Rom. 1:13, "I purposed"; Eph. 1:9, "He purposed (in Him)," RV. See SET.¶

4. *poieō* (ποιέω, 4160), "to make," is translated "He purposed" in Eph. 3:11 (for the noun *prothesis*, in the same verse, see A, No. 2). See DO, No. 1.

5. *proaireō* (προαιρέω, 4255), "to bring forth or forward," or, in the middle voice, "to take by choice, prefer, purpose," is translated "He hath purposed" in 2 Cor. 9:7, RV (KJV, "he purposed").¶

For PURSE see BAG, No. 2 and *Note*

PURSUE

diōkō (διώκω, 1377), "to put to flight, pursue, persecute," is rendered "to pursue" in 2 Cor. 4:9, RV (KJV, "persecute"), and is used metaphorically of "seeking eagerly" after peace in 1 Pet. 3:11, RV (KJV, "ensue"). See FOLLOW.

PUT

1. *tithēmi* (τίθημι, 5087), "to place, lay, set, put," is translated "to put" in Matt. 5:15; 12:18; in Matt. 22:44, RV, "put (underneath Thy feet)"; Mark 4:21 (1st part), in the 2nd part, RV, "put" (in some texts, No. 4, KJV, "set"); 10:16, KJV (RV, "laying"); Luke 8:16 (1st part); 2nd part, RV (KJV, "setteth"); 11:33; John 19:19; Acts 1:7, KJV (RV, "set"); 4:3; 5:18, 25; 12:4; Rom. 14:13; 1 Cor. 15:25; 2 Cor. 3:13; 1 Tim. 1:12, KJV (RV, "appointing"); Rev. 11:9, KJV (RV, "laid"). See APPOINT, No. 3.

2. *perititithēmi* (περιτίθημι, 4060), "to put around or on" (*peri*, "around," and No. 1), is so used in Matt. 27:28; Mark 15:17, RV, "put on" (KJV, " . . . about"); 15:36; John 19:29. See BESTOW, No. 5.

3. *paratithēmi* (παρατίθημι, 3908), "to set before" (*para*, "beside" or "before"), is rendered "to put forth" (of a parable) in Matt. 13:24, 31, KJV (RV, "set before"). See SET.

4. *epitithēmi* (ἐπιτίθημι, 2007), "to put on, upon," is so rendered in Matt. 19:13, KJV (RV, "lay"); so Mark 7:32; 8:25 (some mss. have No. 1, here); Matt. 21:7; 27:29; John 9:15; 19:2 (1st part); Acts 9:12 (RV, "laying . . . on "); 15:10. See ADD, No. 1.

5. *apotithēmi* (ἀποτίθημι, 659), always in the middle voice in the NT, "to put off (*apo*) from oneself," is rendered "to put away" in the RV in the following: Eph. 4:22 (KJV, "put off"); Col. 3:8 (KJV, ditto); Eph. 4:25; Jas. 1:21 (KJV, "laying apart"); 1 Pet. 2:1 (KJV, "laying aside"). See CAST, No. 16.

6. *ballō* (βάλλω, 906), "to throw, cast, put," is translated "to put," in Matt. 9:17 (twice); 25:27; 27:6; Mark 2:22; 7:33; Luke 5:37; John 5:7; 12:6; 13:2 (of "putting" into the heart by the Devil); 18:11 (of "putting" up a sword); 20:25 (RV twice, KJV, "put" and "thrust"); v. 27, RV; Jas. 3:3; Rev. 2:24 (RV, "cast"). See CAST, No. 1.

Note: blēteos, 992 (a gerundive form from *ballō*), meaning "(that which) one must put," is found in Luke 5:38, and, in some mss., Mark 2:22.¶

7. *ekballō* (ἐκβάλλω, 1544), "to cast out," is translated "to put forth or out" in Matt. 9:25; Mark 5:40 (Luke 8:54 in some mss.); John 10:4; Acts 9:40. See CAST, No. 5.

8. *epiballō* (ἐπιβάλλω, 1911), "to put to or unto," is so translated in Matt. 9:16; Luke 5:36; 9:62; in Acts 12:1, RV, "put forth (his hands)," KJV, "stretched forth." See CAST, No. 7.

9. *periballō* (περιβάλλω, 4016), "to put or throw around," is translated "put on" in John 19:2, KJV (RV, "arrayed . . . in"). See CAST, No. 10, CLOTHE, No. 6.

10. *proballō* (προβάλλω, 4261), "to put forward," is so used in Acts 19:33. See SHOOT FORTH.

11. *didōmi* (δίδωμι, 1325), "to give," is rendered "to put" in Luke 15:22, of the ring on the returned Prodigal's finger; 2 Cor. 8:16 and Rev. 17:17, of "putting" into the heart by God; Heb. 8:10, of laws into the mind (KJV, marg., "give"); 10:16, of laws on (RV; KJV, "into") the heart. See GIVE.

12. *paradidōmi* (παραδίδωμι, 3860), "to give or hand over," is rendered "put in prison" in Mark 1:14, KJV (RV, "delivered up"). See BETRAY.

13. *poieō* (ποιέω, 4160), "to do, make," is translated "to put" (with *exō*, "forth") in Acts 5:34, lit., "do (them) outside."

14. *chōrizō* (χωρίζω, 5563), "to separate, divide" (cf. *chōris*, "apart, separate from"), is translated "to put asunder" in Matt. 19:6; Mark 10:9, of "putting" away a wife.

15. *ekphuō* (ἐκφύω, 1631), "to cause to grow out, put forth" (*ek*, "out," *phuō*, "to bring forth, produce, beget"), is used of the leaves of a tree, Matt. 24:32; Mark 13:28, "putteth forth."¶

16. *apoluō* (ἀπολύω, 630), "to set free, let go," is rendered "to put away" in reference to one who is betrothed, Matt. 1:19; a wife, 5:31, 32 (twice; in 2nd part, RV; KJV, "is divorced"); 19:3, 7, 8, 9 (twice); Mark 10:2, 4, 11, 12; Luke 16:18 (twice). See DISMISS.

Note: In 1 Cor. 7:11, 12, KJV, *aphiēmi*, "to send away," is translated "to put away" (RV, "leave"), of the act of the husband toward the wife; in v. 13, "leave," of the act of the wife toward the husband.

17. *airō* (αἴρω, 142), "to take up, remove," is rendered "put away," of bitterness, wrath, anger, clamor, railing and malice, Eph. 4:31; in 1 Cor. 5:2 of the divine effects of church discipline. See BEAR, No. 9.

18. *exairō* (ἐξαίρω, 1808), "to put away from the midst of" (*ek*, "from," and No. 17), is used of church discipline, 1 Cor. 5:13.¶

19. *katargeō* (καταργέω, 2673) is rendered "I put away" in 1 Cor. 13:11; in 15:24, KJV, "shall have put down" (RV, "abolished"). See ABOLISH.

20. *kathaireō* (καθαιρέω, 2507), "to take

down, put down," is rendered "He hath put down" in Luke 1:52. See CAST, A, No. 14.

21. *apostellō* (ἀποστέλλω, 649), "to send forth" (*apo*, "from or forth," *stellō*, "to send"), is said of using the sickle, Mark 4:29, RV, "he putteth forth," marg., "sendeth forth" (KJV, "putteth in"). See SEND, SET.

22. *apekduō* (ἀπεκδύω, 554), "to strip off clothes or arms," is used in the middle voice in the NT, Col. 2:15, RV, "having put off from Himself," (KJV, "having spoiled"); in 3:9, "ye have put off," of "the old man" (see MAN). See SPOIL.¶

23. *methistēmi* or *methistanō* (μεθίστημι, 3179), "to change, remove" (*meta*, implying "change," *histēmi*, "to cause to stand"), is used of "putting" a man out of his stewardship, Luke 16:4 (passive voice). See REMOVE, TRANSLATE, TURN (away).

24. *anagō* (ἀνάγω, 321), "to lead or bring up," is used nautically of "putting" out to sea, Acts 27:2, 4, RV. See LAUNCH.

25. *epanagō* (ἐπανάγω, 1877), "to bring up or back," is used in the same sense as No. 24, in Luke 5:3, 4. See LAUNCH.

26. *enduō* (ἐνδύω, 1746), used in the middle voice, of "putting" on oneself, or on another, is translated "to put on" (*a*) literally, Matt. 6:25; 27:31; Mark 6:9; 15:20; Luke 12:22; 15:22; (*b*) metaphorically, of "putting" on the armor of light, Rom. 13:12; the Lord Jesus Christ, 13:14; Christ, Gal. 3:27; incorruption and immortality (said of the body of the believer), 1 Cor. 15:53, 54; the new man, Eph. 4:24; Col. 3:10; the whole armor of God, Eph. 6:11; the breastplate of righteousness, 6:14, RV; the breastplate of faith and love, 1 Thess. 5:8; various Christian qualities, Col. 3:12. See CLOTHE, No. 2.

27. *embibazō* (ἐμβιβάζω, 1688), "to put in" (*en*, "in," *bibazō*, not found in the NT), is used of "putting" persons on board ship, Acts 27:6.¶ In the Sept., 2 Kings 9:28; Prov. 4:11.¶

28. *probibazō* (προβιβάζω, 4264), "to put forward," hence, "to induce, incite," is rendered "being put forward" in Matt. 14:8, RV (KJV, "being before instructed").¶ In the Sept., Exod. 35:34; Deut. 6:7.¶

29. *apostrephō* (ἀποστρέφω, 654), "to turn away, remove, return," is used of "putting" up again a sword into its sheath, Matt. 26:52. See BRING, A, No. 22.

Notes: (1) *Ekteinō*, "to stretch forth" (always so translated in the RV, save in Acts 27:30, "lay out," of anchors), is rendered "to put forth" in the KJV of Matt. 8:3; Mark 1:41; Luke 5:13. (2)

In Luke 14:7, KJV, *legō*, "to speak" (see RV), is translated "He put forth." (3) In Acts 13:46, KJV, *apōtheō*, "to thrust away" (RV), is rendered "put . . . from"; in 1 Tim. 1:19, KJV, "having put away" (RV, "having thrust from"), middle voice in each; so in Acts 7:27, KJV and RV, "thrust away." See CAST, No. 13, THRUST. (4) For "to put away" in Heb. 9:26, see PUTTING, *Note* (below). (5) In Acts 7:33, KJV, *luō*, "to loose" (RV), is translated "put off." See LOOSE. (6) For the KJV of *hupotassō*, "put under" in 1 Cor. 15:27, 28; Eph. 1:22; Heb. 2:8, see SUBJECT, and for the connected negative adjective *anupotaktos*, rendered "not put under" in Heb. 2:8, KJV, see DISOBEDIENT, B, (Note). (7) In John 19:29, KJV, *prospherō*, "to bring to," is translated "they put it to (His mouth)," RV, "they brought it . . ." (8) For *anamimnēskō*, "to put in remembrance," 1 Cor. 4:17, RV, see REMEMBRANCE. (9) For *apokteinō*, "to kill," rendered "put to death" in Mark 14:1, etc., see DEATH, C, No. 4. (10) For 1 Thess. 2:4, KJV, "to be put in trust," see ENTRUST. (11) For the phrase "put . . . to . . . account" in Philem. 18, see ACCOUNT, A, No. 2. (12) In Acts 15:9, KJV, *diakrinō*, "to make a distinction" (RV), is translated "put (no) difference." (13) In Matt. 9:16, KJV, *plērōma*, "the fullness or filling," is rendered "(that) which is put in to fill it up," RV, "(that) which should fill it up." See FILL. (14) For *paradeigmatizō*, "to put to an open shame," Heb. 6:6, see SHAME. (15) For *phimoō*, "to put to silence," see SILENCE. (16) For "I will put My trust," Heb. 2:13, see TRUST.

PUTTING

1. *endusis* (ἔνδυσις, 1745), "a putting on" (akin to *enduō*, PUT, No. 26), is used of apparel, 1 Pet. 3:3.¶ In the Sept., Esth. 5:1; Job 41:4.¶

2. *epithesis* (ἐπίθεσις, 1936), "a putting on" (akin to *epitithēmi*, PUT, No. 4), is used of the "putting" or laying on of hands; in 2 Tim. 1:6, RV, "laying" (KJV, "putting "). See LAYING ON.

3. *apothesis* (ἀπόθεσις, 595) "a putting off or away" (akin to *apotithēmi*, PUT, No. 5), is used metaphorically in 1 Pet. 3:21, of the "putting" away of the filth of the flesh; in 2 Pet. 1:14, RV, of "the putting off" of the body (as a tabernacle) at death (KJV, "I must put off").¶

4. *apekdusis* (ἀπέκδυσις, 555), "a putting off, stripping off" (akin to *apekduō*, PUT, No. 22), is used in Col. 2:11, of "the body of the flesh" (RV, an important rendering).¶

Note: For *athetēsis*, "a putting away," translated "to put away" in Heb. 9:26, lit., "(unto) a setting aside," see DISANNUL, B.¶

Q

QUAKE

1. *entromos* (ἔντρομος, 1790), an adjective signifying "trembling with fear" (*en*, "in," *tremō*, "to tremble"), is used with *eimi*, "to be," in Heb. 12:21 (some mss. have *ektromos*, with the same meaning), "I quake," lit., "I am trembling." It is used with *ginomai*, "to become," in Acts 7:32, "trembled," lit., "became trembling," and 16:29, RV, "trembling for fear" (KJV, "came trembling"). See TREMBLE.¶

2. *seiō* (σείω, 4579), "did quake," Matt. 27:51, and 28:4, RV (KJV, "did shake"). See MOVE, No. 3, SHAKE, TREMBLE.

For QUARREL see COMPLAINT, No. 2, and SET, No. 15, Mark 6:19, RV

QUARTER

pantothen (πάντοθεν, 3840), "from all sides," is translated "from every quarter" in Mark 1:45. See EVERY SIDE, ROUND ABOUT.

Notes: (1) In Rev. 20:8, KJV, *gōnia*, "an angle, corner," is rendered "quarter" (RV, "corner"). (2) In Acts 16:3, KJV, *topois*, "parts" (RV) is translated "quarters." (3) In Acts 9:32 the phrase *dia pantōn*, lit., "throughout all," is rendered "throughout all parts," RV (*meros*, "a part," being understood), KJV, "throughout all *quarters*." (4) For "quarters" in Acts 28:7, KJV, see NEIGHBORHOOD.

QUATERNION

tetradion (τετράδιον, 5069), "a group of four" (*tetra—*, "four"), occurs in Acts 12:4. A "quaternion" was a set of four men occupied in the work of a guard, two soldiers being chained to the prisoner and two keeping watch; alternatively one of the four watched while the other three slept. The night was divided into four watches of three hours each; there would be one "quaternion" for each watch by day and by night.¶ Cf. the "guard" in Matt. 27:65 and 28:11.

QUEEN

basilissa (βασίλισσα, 938), the feminine of *basileus*, "a king," is used (*a*) of the "Queen of Sheba," Matt. 12:42; Luke 11:31; of "Candace," Acts 8:27; (*b*) metaphorically, of "Babylon," Rev. 18:7.¶

QUENCH, UNQUENCHABLE

A. Verb.

sbennumi (σβέννυμι, 4570) is used (*a*) of "quenching" fire or things on fire, Matt. 12:20, quoted from Isa. 42:3, figurative of the condition of the feeble; Heb. 11:34; in the passive voice, Matt. 25:8, of torches (see LAMP), RV, "are going out," lit., "are being quenched"; of the retributive doom hereafter of sin unrepented of and unremitted in this life, Mark 9:48 (in some mss. in vv. 44, 46); (*b*) metaphorically, of "quenching" the fire-tipped darts of the evil one, Eph. 6:16; of "quenching" the Spirit, by hindering His operations in oral testimony in the church gatherings of believers, 1 Thess. 5:19. "The peace, order, and edification of the saints were evidence of the ministry of the Spirit among them, 1 Cor. 14:26, 32, 33, 40, but if, through ignorance of His ways, or through failure to recognize, or refusal to submit to, them, or through impatience with the ignorance or self-will of others, the Spirit were quenched, these happy results would be absent. For there was always the danger that the impulses of the flesh might usurp the place of the energy of the Spirit in the assembly, and the endeavor to restrain this evil by natural means would have the effect of hindering His ministry also. Apparently then, this injunction was intended to warn believers against the substitution of a mechanical order for the restraints of the Spirit."*¶ Cf. Song of Sol. 8:7.

B. Adjective.

asbestos (ἄσβεστος, 762), "not quenched" (*a*, negative, and A), is used of the doom of persons described figuratively as "chaff," Matt. 3:12 and Luke 3:17, "unquenchable"; of the fire of Gehenna (see HELL), Mark 9:43, RV, "unquenchable fire" (in some mss. v. 45).¶ In the Sept., Job 20:26.¶

QUESTION (Noun and Verb), QUESTIONING

A. Nouns.

1. *zētēsis* (ζήτησις, 2214), primarily "a seeking, search" (*zēteō*, "to seek"), for which see DISPUTATION, is used in John 3:25; Acts 25:20, RV, "(being perplexed) how to inquire (concerning these things)," KJV "(because I doubted of such manner) of questions," lit., "being perplexed as to the inquiry (or discussion) concern-

---

* From *Notes on Thessalonians*, by Hogg and Vine, p. 196.

ing these things"; in 1 Tim. 1:4 (in some mss.); 6:4; 2 Tim. 2:23; Titus 3:9. See INQUIRY.

2. *zētēma* (ζήτημα, 2213), synonymous with No. 1, but, generally speaking, suggesting in a more concrete form the subject of an inquiry, occurs in Acts 15:2; 18:15; 23:29; 25:19; 26:3.¶

3. *logos* (λόγος, 3056), "a word," is translated "question" in Matt. 21:24 (KJV, "thing"); in Mark 11:29 (RV, marg., "word") and Luke 20:3, KJV, "one thing:" there is no word in the original for "one," hence the RV, "a question."

4. *ekzētēsis* (ἐκζήτησις, 1537 and 2214), "a questioning," is found in the best texts in 1 Tim. 1:4 (see RV); cf. No. 1.¶

Notes: (1) In Matt. 22:41, there is no word in the original for "question." (2) For *suzētēsis* or *sunzētēsis*, "a questioning together" (*sun*, "with"), see DISPUTATION. (3) In Acts 19:40, KJV, *enkaleō*, "to bring a charge against," is translated "to be called in question" (RV, "to be accused").

B. Verbs.

1. *suzēteō* (συζητέω, 4802) or *sunzēteō*, "to search together" (cf. Note, above), "to discuss, dispute," is translated "to question" (or "question with or together") in Mark 1:27; 8:11; 9:10, 14, 16; 12:28, RV (KJV, "reasoning together"); Luke 22:23, RV (KJV, "inquire"); 24:15, RV (KJV, "reasoned"). See DISPUTE, B, No. 3, INQUIRE, REASON.

2. *eperōtaō* (ἐπερωτάω, 1905), "to ask," is translated "asked . . . a question," in Matt. 22:35, 41; in Luke 2:46, "asking . . . questions"; "questioned" in Luke 23:9. See ASK, A, No. 3.

For QUICK, see DISCERN, C, LIVE, No. 3, *Note*

QUICKEN

1. *zōopoieō* (ζωοποιέω, 2227), "to make alive": see LIFE, C.

2. *zōogoneō* (ζωογονέω, 2225), "to endue with life, produce alive, preserve alive": see LIVE, No. 6.

3. *suzōopoieō* (συζωοποιέω, 4806) or *sunzōopoieō*, "to quicken together with, make alive with" (*sun*, "with" and No. 1), is used in Eph. 2:5; Col. 2:13, of the spiritual life with Christ, imparted to believers at their conversion.¶

QUICKLY

1. *tachu* (ταχύ, 5035), the neuter of *tachus*, "swift, quick," signifies "quickly," Matt. 5:25; 28:7, 8; Mark 9:39, RV (KJV, "lightly"); Luke 15:22; John 11:29; Rev. 2:16 (v. 5 in some mss.); 3:11; 11:14; 22:7, 12, 20. See LIGHTLY.¶

2. *tacheion* (τάχειον, 5032), the comparative

degree of No. 1, is translated "quickly" in John 13:27; "out(ran)" in 20:4, RV, lit., "(ran before) more quickly (than Peter)"; "shortly" in 1 Tim. 3:14 and Heb. 13:23; in 13:19, "(the) sooner." See SHORTLY.¶

3. *tacheōs* (ταχέως, 5030), akin to No. 1, is translated "quickly" in Luke 14:21; 16:6; John 11:31, RV; "shortly" in 1 Cor. 4:19; Phil. 2:19, 24; 2 Tim 4:9; with a suggestion of rashness in the following, Gal. 1:6, RV, "quickly" (KJV, "soon"); 2 Thess. 2:2; and 1 Tim. 5:22, "hastily," (KJV, "suddenly"). See HASTILY, C.¶

4. *en tachei* (ἐν τάχει), lit., "in, or with, swiftness, with speed" (*en*, "in," and the dative case of *tachos*, "speed"), is translated "quickly" in Acts 12:7; 22:18; "speedily" in Luke 18:8; "shortly" in Acts 25:4; Rom. 16:20; 1 Tim. 3:14 in some texts; Rev. 1:1; 22:6. In the last two places, "with speed" is probably the meaning. See SHORTLY, SPEEDILY.¶

QUICKSANDS

Note: This is the KJV rendering in Acts 27:17 of *Surtis*, "Syrtis" (RV). The Syrtes, Major and Minor, lie on the north coast of Africa, between the headlands of Tunis and Barca. They have been regarded as dangerous to mariners from very early times, both from the character of the sands and from the crosscurrents of the adjoining waters. In the voyage described in this chapter the vessel had left the shelter of the island of Cauda and was drifting before the N.E. wind Euraquilo. The mariners might well fear that they would be driven on the Syrtes on the leeward of their course. The changing character of the tempest, however, drove them into the sea of Adria.¶

QUIET, QUIETNESS

A. Adjectives.

1. *ēremos* (ἤρεμος, 2263), "quiet, tranquil," occurs in 1 Tim. 2:2, RV, "tranquil" (KJV, "quiet"); it indicates tranquillity arising from without.¶

2. *hēsuchios* (ἡσύχιος, 2272) has much the same meaning as No. 1, but indicates "tranquillity arising from within," causing no disturbance to others. It is translated "quiet" in 1 Tim. 2:2, RV (KJV, "peaceable"); "quiet" in 1 Pet. 3:4, where it is associated with "meek," and is to characterize the spirit or disposition. See PEACEABLE.¶

B. Verbs.

1. *hēsuchazō* (ἡσυχάζω, 2270), akin to A, No, 2, "to be still, to live quietly": see CEASE, A, No. 3.¶

2. *katastellō* (καταστέλλω, 2687) denotes "to quiet": see APPEASE.

B. Verbs.

1. *hēsuchazō* (ήσυχάζω, 2270), akin to A, No, 2, "to be still, to live quietly": see CEASE, A, No. 3.¶

2. *katastellō* (καταστέλλω, 2687) denotes "to quiet": see APPEASE.

C. Nouns.

1. *eirēnē* (εἰρήνη, 1515), "peace," is translated "quietness" in Acts 24:2, KJV (RV, "peace"). See PEACE (*e*).

2. *hēsuchia* (ήσυχία, 2271), akin to A, No. 2, and B. No. 1, denotes "quietness," 2 Thess. 3:12; it is so translated in the RV of 1 Tim. 2:11, 12 (KJV, "silence"); in Acts 22:2, RV, "(they were the more) quiet," KJV, "(they kept the more) silence," lit., "they kept quietness the more."¶

QUIT

1. *apallassō* (ἀπαλλάσσω, 525), "to free from," is used in the passive voice in Luke 12:58, RV, "to be quit" (KJV, "to be delivered"). See DELIVER, A, No. 6.

2. *andrizō* (ἀνδρίζω, 407) signifies "to make a man of" (*anēr*, "a man"); in the middle voice, in 1 Cor. 16:13, "to play the man," "quit you like men."¶

R

RABBI

rabbei or *rabbi* (ῥαββεί, 4461), from a word *rab*, primarily denoting "master" in contrast to a slave; this with the added pronominal suffix signified "my master" and was a title of respect by which teachers were addressed. The suffix soon lost its specific force, and in the NT the word is used as courteous title of address. It is applied to Christ in Matt. 26:25, 49; Mark 9:5; 11:21; 14:45; John 1:38 (where it is interpreted as *didaskalos*, "master," marg., "teacher" (see also "Rabboni" in John 20:16); v. 49; 3:2; 4:31; 6:25; 9:2; 11:8; to John the Baptist in John 3:26. In Matt. 23:7, 8 Christ forbids his disciples to covet or use it. In the latter verse it is again explained as *didaskalos*, "master" (some mss. have *kathēgētēs*, "a guide").¶

RABBONI

rabbounei or *rabbōni* (ῥαββουνεί, 4462), formed in a similar way to the above, was an Aramaic form of a title almost entirely applied to the president of the Sanhedrin, if such was a descendant of Hillel. It was even more respectful than Rabbi, and signified "My great master"; in its use in the NT the pronominal force of the suffix is apparently retained (contrast Rabbi above); it is found in Mark 10:51 in the best texts, RV, "Rabboni" (KJV, "Lord"), addressed to Christ by blind Bartimaeus, and in John 20:16 by Mary Magdalene, where it is interpreted by *didaskalos*, "Master" (marg., "Teacher").¶

For **RABBLE** see **COURT**, No. 1

RACA

raka (ῥακά, 4469) is an Aramaic word akin to the Heb. *rêq*, "empty," the first *a* being due to a Galilean change. In the KJV of 1611 it was spelled *racha;* in the edition of 1638, *raca*. It was a word of utter contempt, signifying "empty," intellectually rather than morally, "empty-headed," like Abimelech's hirelings, Judg. 9:4, and the "vain" man of Jas. 2:20. As condemned by Christ, Matt. 5:22, it was worse than being angry, inasmuch as an outrageous utterance is worse than a feeling unexpressed or somewhat controlled in expression; it does not indicate such a loss of self-control as the word rendered "fool," a godless, moral reprobate.¶

For **RACE** (kindred) see **KIND**

RACE (contest)

1. *agōn* (ἀγών, 73) is translated "race" in Heb. 12:1, one of the modes of athletic contest, this being the secondary meaning of the word. See CONFLICT.

2. *stadion* (στάδιον, 4712), "a stadium," denotes a "racecourse," 1 Cor. 9:24. The stadium (about 600 Greek feet or 1/8 of a Roman mile) was the length of the Olympic course. See FURLONG.

Note: No. 1 signifies the "race" itself; No. 2 the "course."

RAGE, RAGING

A. Verb.

phruassō (φρυάσσω, 5433) was primarily used of "the snorting, neighing and prancing of horses"; hence, metaphorically, of "the haughtiness and insolence of men," Acts 4:25.¶ In the Sept., Ps. 2:1.¶

B. Noun.

kludōn (κλύδων, 2830), "a billow, surge" (akin to *kluzō*, "to wash over," said of the sea; cf. *kludōnizomai*, "to be tossed by the waves," Eph. 4:14), is translated "raging" in Luke 8:24; in Jas. 1:6, RV, "surge" (KJV, "wave").¶

Note: In Jude 13, KJV, the adjective *agrios*, "wild," is translated "raging" (RV, "wild"). See WILD.

RAIL, RAILER, RAILING

A. Verb.

blasphēmeō (βλασφημέω, 987), "to blaspheme, rail, revile" (for the meanings of which see BLASPHEME), is translated "to rail at, or on," in Matt. 27:39, RV (KJV, "reviled"); Mark 15:29; Luke 23:39; 2 Pet. 2:10, RV (KJV, "to speak evil of"); 2:12, RV (KJV, "speak evil of"). Cf. *loidoreō*, "to revile" (see REVILE), and B, No. 2 and C, No. 2.

B. Nouns.

1. *blasphēmia* (βλασφημία, 988) is translated "railings" in Matt. 15:19, RV; 1 Tim. 6:4, KJV and RV; "railing" in Mark 7:22, RV; Col. 3:8, RV; Jude 9, KJV and RV, lit., "judgment of railing"; in Eph. 4:31, RV (KJV, "evil speaking"). See BLASPHEMY.

2. *loidoria* (λοιδορία, 3059), "abuse, railing, reviling," is rendered "reviling" in the RV, 1 Pet. 3:9 (twice); in 1 Tim. 5:14, KJV marg., "for their reviling." See REVILE, C.¶

C. Adjectives.

1. *blasphēmos* (βλάσφημος, 989), akin to A, and B, No. 1; see BLASPHEME, C.

2. *loidoros* (λοίδορος, 3060), an adjective denoting "reviling, railing" (akin to B, No. 2), is used as a noun, "a railer," 1 Cor. 5:11. See REVILE.

RAIMENT

Notes: (1) For *himation*, rendered "raiment" in Matt. 17:2, KJV (RV, "garments"), so Matt. 27:31; Mark 9:3; Luke 23:34; John 19:24; Acts 22:20; Rev. 3:5, 18; 4:4; KJV and RV, Acts 18:6, see CLOTHING, No. 2 and ROBE. *Himatismos* is rendered "raiment" in Luke 9:29; *enduma* in Matt. 3:4; 6:25, 28; 28:3 and Luke 12:23. For *esthēs*, translated "raiment" in Jas. 2:2 (2nd part), KJV, see APPAREL. (2) For *skepasma*, "a covering," rendered "raiment" in 1 Tim. 6:8, KJV, see COVER, B, No. 2.

RAIN (Noun and Verb)

A. Nouns.

1. *huetos* (ὑετός, 5205), from *huō*, "to rain," is used especially, but not entirely, of "showers," and is found in Acts 14:17; 28:2; Heb. 6:7; Jas. 5:7 (see EARLY AND LATTER); 5:18; Rev. 11:6 (see B).¶

2. *brochē* (βροχή, 1028), akin to B, below, lit., "a wetting," hence, "rain," is used in Matt. 7:25, 27.¶ In the Sept., Ps. 68:9; 105:32.¶ It is found in the papyri in connection with irrigation in Egypt (Deissmann, *Light from the Ancient East*).

B. Verb.

brechō (βρέχω, 1026), akin to A, No. 2, signifies (*a*) "to wet," Luke 7:38, 44, RV (KJV, to wash); (*b*) "to send rain," Matt. 5:45; to rain, Luke 17:29 (of fire and brimstone); Jas. 5:17, used impersonally (twice); Rev. 11:6, where *huetos* (A, No. 1) is used as the subject, lit., "(that) rain rain (not)."¶

RAINBOW

iris (ἶρις, 2463), whence Eng., "iris," the flower, describes the "rainbow" seen in the heavenly vision, "round about the throne, like an emerald to look upon," Rev. 4:3, emblematic of the fact that, in the exercise of God's absolute sovereignty and perfect counsels, He will remember His covenant concerning the earth (Gen. 9:9–17); in Rev. 10:1, "the rainbow," RV, the definite article suggests a connection with the scene in 4:3; here it rests upon the head of an angel who declares that "there shall be delay no longer" (v. 6, RV marg., the actual meaning); the mercy to be shown to the earth must be preceded by the execution of divine judgments upon the nations who defy God and His Christ. Cf. Ezek. 1:28.¶

RAISE (up)

1. *egeirō* (ἐγείρω, 1453), for the various meanings of which see ARISE, No. 3, is used (*a*) of "raising" the dead, active and passive voices, e.g. of the resurrection of Christ, Matt. 16:21; 17:23; 20:19, RV; 26:32, RV; "(after) I am raised up" (KJV, " . . . risen again"); Luke 9:22; 20:37; John 2:19; Acts 3:15; 4:10 [not 5:30, see (*c*) below]; 10:40 [not 13:23 in the best texts, see (*c*) below]; 13:30, 37; Rom. 4:24, 25; 6:4, 9; 7:4; 8:11 (twice); 8:34, RV; 10:9; 1 Cor. 6:14 (1st part); 15:13, 14, RV; 15:15 (twice), 16, 17; 15:20, RV; 2 Cor. 4:14; Gal. 1:1; Eph. 1:20; Col. 2:12; 1 Thess. 1:10; 1 Pet. 1:21; in 2 Tim. 2:8, RV, "risen"; (*b*) of the raising of human beings, Matt. 10:8; 11:5; Matt. 27:52, RV (KJV, "arose"); Mark 12:26, RV; Luke 7:22; John

5:21; 12:1, 9, 17; Acts 26:8; 1 Cor. 15:29 and 32, RV; 15:35, 42, 43 (twice), 44, 52; 2 Cor. 1:9; 4:14; Heb. 11:19; (c) of "raising" up a person to occupy a place in the midst of a people, said of Christ, Acts 5:30; in 13:23, KJV only (the best texts have *agō*, to bring, RV, "hath . . . brought"); of David, Acts 13:22 (for v. 33 see No. 2); (d) metaphorically, of a horn of salvation, Luke 1:69; (e) of children, from stones, by creative power, Luke 3:8; (f) of the Temple, as the Jews thought, John 2:20, RV, "wilt Thou raise (it) up" (KJV, "rear"); (g) of "lifting" up a person, from physical infirmity, Mark 1:31, RV, "raised . . . up" (KJV, "lifted"); so 9:27; Acts 3:7; 10:26, RV (KJV, "took"); Jas. 5:15, "shall raise . . . up"; (h) metaphorically, of "raising" up affliction, Phil. 1:17, RV (in the best texts; the KJV, v. 16, following those which have *epipherō*, has "to add"). See AWAKE, No. 1.

2. *anistēmi* (ἀνίστημι, 450), for the various applications of which see ARISE, No. 1, is translated "to raise or raise up," (a) of the resurrection of the dead by Christ, John 6:39, 40, 44, 54; (b) of the resurrection of Christ from the dead, Acts 2:24 (for v. 30 see RV, *kathizō*, "to set," as in the best texts); 2:32; 13:34, see (c) below; Acts 17:31; (c) of "raising" up a person to occupy a place in the midst of a nation, said of Christ, Acts 3:26; 7:37; 13:33, RV, "raised up Jesus," not here by resurrection from the dead, as the superfluous "again" of the KJV would suggest; this is confirmed by the latter part of the verse, which explains the "raising" up as being by way of His incarnation, and by the contrast in v. 34, where stress is laid upon His being "raised" from the dead, the same verb being used: (d) of "raising" up seed, Matt. 22:24; (e) of being "raised" from natural sleep, Matt. 1:24, KJV, "being raised" (RV, "arose"); here some mss. have *diegeirō*, "to arouse completely"; see ARISE, No. 4.

Note: For the contrast between No. 1 and No. 2 see ARISE, No. 3 (parag. 2).

3. *exegeirō* (ἐξεγείρω, 1825), *ek*, "out of," and No. 1, is used (a) of the "resurrection" of believers, 1 Cor. 6:14 [2nd part; see No. 1 (a) for the 1st part]; (b) of "raising" a person to public position, Rom. 9:17, "did I raise thee up," RV, said of Pharaoh.¶

4. *exanistēmi* (ἐξανίστημι, 1817), *ek*, "out of," and No. 2, is used of "raising" up seed, Mark 12:19; Luke 20:28; elsewhere, Acts 15:5, "to rise up." See RISE.¶

5. *sunegeirō* (συνεγείρω, 4891), "to raise together" (*sun*, "with," and No. 1), is used of the believer's spiritual resurrection with Christ. Eph. 2:6; passive voice in Col. 2:12, RV, "ye

were . . . raised (with Him)," KJV, "ye are risen"; so 3:1. See RISE.

Notes: (1) In Acts 13:50, KJV, *epegeirō*, "to rouse up, excite," is translated "raised" (RV, "stirred up," as in KJV and RV in 14:2). (2) In Acts 24:12, *poieō*, to make, is used With *epistasis*, a collection of people, and translated "stirring up (a crowd)," RV, lit., 'making a collection (of a crowd)'; some mss. have *episustasis*, a riotous throng, KJV, "raising up (the people)." (3) In Heb. 11:35, KJV, the noun *anastasis*, a resurrection, preceded by *ex* (i.e., *ek*), "out of, or by," instrumental, is translated "raised to life again" (a paraphrase), RV, "by a resurrection."

For RAN see RUN

RANKS

prasia (πρασιά, 4237), "a garden bed or plot" (probably from *prason*, "a leek"), is used metaphorically in Mark 6:40 of "ranks" of persons arranged in orderly groups.¶

RANSOM

1. *lutron* (λύτρον, 3083), lit., "a means of loosing" (from *luō*, "to loose"), occurs frequently in the Sept., where it is always used to signify "equivalence." Thus it is used of the "ransom" for a life, e.g., Exod. 21:30, of the redemption price of a slave, e.g., Lev. 19:20, of land, 25:24, of the price of a captive, Isa. 45:13. In the NT it occurs in Matt. 20:28 and Mark 10:45, where it is used of Christ's gift of Himself as "a ransom for many." Some interpreters have regarded the "ransom" price as being paid to Satan; others, to an impersonal power such as death, or evil, or "that ultimate necessity which has made the whole course of things what it has been." Such ideas are largely conjectural, the result of an attempt to press the details of certain Old Testament illustrations beyond the actual statements of New Testament doctrines.

That Christ gave up His life in expiatory sacrifice under God's judgment upon sin and thus provided a "ransom" whereby those who receive Him on this ground obtain deliverance from the penalty due to sin, is what Scripture teaches. What the Lord states in the two passages mentioned involves this essential character of His death. In these passages the preposition is *anti*, which has a vicarious significance, indicating that the "ransom" holds good for those who, accepting it as such, no longer remain in death since Christ suffered death in their stead. The change of preposition in 1 Tim. 2:6, where the word *antilutron*, a substitutionary "ransom," is used, is significant. There the preposition is *huper*, "on behalf of," and the statement is made that He "gave Himself a ransom for all," indicating that the "ransom" was provisionally universal, while being of a vicarious character. Thus the three passages consistently show that while the provision was universal, for Christ died for all men, yet it is actual for those only who accept God's conditions, and who are described in the Gospel statements as "the many." The giving of His life was the giving of His entire person, and while His death under divine judgment was alone expiatory, it cannot be dissociated from the character of His life which, being sinless, gave virtue to His death and was a testimony to the fact that His death must be of a vicarious nature.¶

2. *antilutron* (ἀντίλυτρον, 487), 1 Tim. 2:6. See under No. 1.¶

For **RASH, RASHLY** see **HEADSTRONG**

RATHER

A. Adverb.

mallon (μᾶλλον, 3123), the comparative degree of *mala*, "very, very much," is frequently translated "rather," e.g., Matt. 10:6, 28; 1 Cor. 14:1, 5; sometimes followed by "than," with a connecting particle, e.g., Matt. 18:13 ("more than"); or without, e.g., John 3:19; Acts 4:19, RV (KJV, "more"); in 1 Cor. 9:12, KJV, "rather" (RV, "yet more"); 12:22, RV, "rather" (KJV, "more"); 2 Cor. 3:9 (ditto); Philem. 16 (ditto); in 2 Pet. 1:10, KJV, "the rather" (RV, "the more"). See MORE.

B. Verb.

thelō (θέλω, 2309), "to will, wish," is translated "I had rather" in 1 Cor. 14:19. See DESIRE, B, No. 6.

C. Preposition.

para (παρά, 3844), "beyond, in comparison with," is translated "rather than" in Rom. 1:25, RV (KJV, "more than"; marg., "rather").

D. Conjunction.

alla (ἀλλά, 235), "but, on the contrary," is translated "and rather" in Luke 17:8.

Notes: (1) In Heb. 13:19, KJV, *perissoterōs*, "the more exceedingly" (RV), is translated "the rather." (2) In Luke 11:41 and 12:31, KJV, *plēn*, an adverb signifying "yet, howbeit," is translated "rather" (RV, "howbeit"). (3) In Rom. 3:8, KJV, the negative particle *mē*, "not," is translated with "*rather*" in italics (RV, "why not"). (4) In Luke 10:20, KJV, "rather rejoice," there is no word in the original for "rather" (see the RV).

RAVEN

korax (κόραξ, 2876), "a raven" (perhaps onomatopoeic, representing the sound), occurs in the plural in Luke 12:24. The Heb. *oreb* and the Arabic *ghurab* are from roots meaning "to be black"; the Arabic root also has the idea of leaving home. Hence the evil omen attached to the bird. It is the first bird mentioned in the Bible, Gen. 8:7. Christ used the "ravens" to illustrate and enforce the lesson of God's provision and care.¶

RAVENING

A. Adjective.

harpax (ἅρπαξ, 727), an adjective signifying "rapacious," is translated "ravening" (of wolves) in Matt. 7:15: see EXTORT, C.

B. Noun.

harpagē (ἁρπαγή, 724) is translated "ravening" in Luke 11:39, KJV: see EXTORT, B, No. 1.

REACH

1. *akoloutheō* (ἀκολουθέω, 190), "to follow," is translated "have reached," in Rev. 18:5, of the sins of Babylon. Some mss. have the verb *kollaomai*, "to cleave together," RV, marg.; see FOLLOW.

2. *oregō* (ὀρέγω, 3713), "to reach or stretch out," is rendered "reached after" in 1 Tim. 6:10, RV; see DESIRE, B, No. 5.

3. *pherō* (φέρω, 5342), "to bear, carry," is used of "reaching" forth the hand in John 20:27 (twice). See BEAR, No. 2.

4. *ephikneomai* (ἐφικνέομαι, 2185), "to come to, reach," is used in 2 Cor. 10:13, 14.¶

5. *katantaō* (καταντάω, 2658), "to come to a place," is translated "reach" in Acts 27:12, RV (KJV, "attain to"). See COME, No. 28.

Note: In Phil. 3:13, KJV, *epekteinō*, in the middle voice, "to stretch forward," is translated "reaching forth" (RV, "stretching forward").

READ, READING

A. Verb.

anaginōskō (ἀναγινώσκω, 314), primarily, "to know certainly, to know again, recognize" (*ana*, "again," *ginōskō*, "to know"), is used of "reading" written characters, e.g., Matt. 12:3, 5; 21:16; 24:15; of the private "reading" of Scripture, Acts 8:28, 30, 32; of the public "reading" of Scripture, Luke 4:16; Acts 13:27; 15:21; 2 Cor. 3:15; Col. 4:16 (thrice); 1 Thess. 5:27; Rev. 1:3. In 2 Cor. 1:13 there is a purposive play upon words; firstly, "we write none other things unto you, than what ye read (*anaginōskō*)" signifies that there is no hidden or mysterious meaning in his epistles; whatever doubts may have arisen and been expressed in this respect, he means what he says; then follows the similar verb *epiginōskō*, "to acknowledge," "or even acknowledge, and I hope ye will acknowledge unto the end." The *paronomasia* can hardly be reproduced in English. Similarly, in 3:2 the verb *ginōskō*, "to know," and *anaginōskō*, "to read," are put in that order, and metaphorically applied to the church at Corinth as being an epistle, a message to the world, written by the apostle and his fellow missionaries, through their ministry of the gospel and the consequent change in the lives of the converts, an epistle "known and read of all men." For other instances of *paronomasia* see, e.g., Rom. 12:3, *phroneō, huperphroneō, sōphroneō;* 1 Cor. 2:13, 14, *sunkrinō, anakrinō;* 2 Thess. 3:11, *ergazomai,* and *periergazomai;* 1 Cor. 7:31, *chraomai* and *katachraomai;* 11:31, *diakrinō* and *krinō;* 12:2, *agō* and *apagō;* Phil. 3:2, 3, *katatomē* and *peritomē.*

B. Noun.

anagnōsis (ἀνάγνωσις, 320) in nonbiblical Greek denoted "recognition" or "a survey" (the latter found in the papyri); then, "reading"; in the NT the public "reading" of Scripture, Acts 13:15; 2 Cor. 3:14; 1 Tim. 4:13, where the context makes clear that the reference is to the care required in reading the Scriptures to a company, a duty ever requiring the exhortation "take heed." Later, readers in churches were called *anagnōstai.*¶ In the Sept., Neh. 8:8.¶

READINESS

1. *prothumia* (προθυμία, 4288), "eagerness, willingness, readiness" (*pro*, "forward," *thumos*, "mind, disposition," akin to *prothumos*, READY, A, No. 2), is translated "readiness of mind" in Acts 17:11, "readiness" in 2 Cor. 8:11; in v. 12, RV (KJV, "a willing mind"); in v. 19, RV "(our) readiness," KJV, "(your) ready mind"; in 9:2, RV, "readiness" (KJV, "forwardness of ... mind"; see FORWARDNESS, *Note* (4).¶

2. *hetoimos* (ἕτοιμος, 2092), an adjective (see READY, A, No. 1), is used with *echō*, "to have," and *en*, "in," idiomatically, as a noun in 2 Cor 10:6, RV, "being in readiness" (KJV, "having in readiness"), of the apostle's aim for the church to be obedient to Christ. Cf. READY, C.

READY

A. Adjectives.

1. *hetoimos* (ἕτοιμος, 2092), "prepared, ready" (akin to *hetoimasia*, "preparation"), is used (*a*) of persons, Matt. 24:44; 25:10; Luke 12:40; 22:33; Acts 23:15, 21 (for 2 Cor. 10:6, see above); Titus 3:1; 1 Pet. 3:15; (*b*) of things,

Matt. 22:4 (2nd part), 8; Mark 14:15, RV, "ready" (KJV, "prepared"); Luke 14:17; John 7:6; 2 Cor. 9:5; 10:16, RV, "things ready" (KJV, "things made ready"); 1 Pet. 1:5. See PREPARE, No. 5, *Note* (2).¶

2. *prothumos* (πρόθυμος, 4289), "predisposed, willing" (akin to *prothumia*, see READINESS), is translated "ready" in Rom. 1:15, expressive of willingness, eagerness: in Mark 14:38, RV, "willing" (KJV, "ready"); in Matt. 26:41. "willing." See WILLING.¶

B. Verbs.

1. *mellō* (μέλλω, 3195), "to be about to," is translated "to be ready" in 2 Pet. 1:12, RV, where the future indicates that the apostle will be prepared, as in the past and the present, to remind his readers of the truths they know (some mss. have *ouk amelēsō*, "I will not be negligent," KJV; cf., however, v. 15. Field, in *Notes on the Translation of the NT*, suggests that the true reading is *melēsō*, the future of *melō*, "to be a care, or an object of care"); in Rev. 3:2, RV, "were ready" (some texts have the present tense, as in the KJV). Elsewhere, where the KJV has the rendering to be ready, the RV gives renderings in accordance with the usual significance as follows: Luke 7:2, "was ... at the point of"; Acts 20:7, "intending"; Rev. 12:4, "about (to)."

2. *hetoimazō* (ἑτοιμάζω, 2090), "make ready": see PREPARE, B, No. 1.

3. *paraskeuazō* (παρασκευάζω, 3903), "to prepare, make ready": see PREPARE, B, No. 4. *Note:* On the difference between No. 2 and No. 3, see PREPARE, *Note* (1) under No. 5.

C. Adverb.

hetoimōs (ἑτοίμως, 2093) "readily" (akin to A, No. 1), is used with *echō*, "to have," lit., "to have readily," i.e., "to be in readiness, to be ready," Acts 21:13; 2 Cor. 12:14; 1 Pet. 4:5.¶

Notes: (1) In Heb. 8:13, KJV, *engus*, "near," is translated "ready" (RV, "nigh"). See NIGH. (2) For "ready to distribute," 1 Tim. 6:18, see DISTRIBUTE, B. (3) In 2 Tim. 4:6, KJV, *spendomai*, "I am being offered," RV, with *ēdē*, "already," is translated "I am now ready to be offered." See OFFER. (4) In 1 Pet. 5:2 *prothumōs*, "willingly, with alacrity," is rendered "of a ready mind."¶

REAP

therizō (θερίζω, 2325), "to reap" (akin to *theros*, "summer, harvest"), is used (*a*) literally, Matt. 6:26; 25:24, 26; Luke 12:24; 19:21, 22; Jas. 5:4 (2nd part), KJV, "have reaped"; (*b*) figuratively or in proverbial expressions, John 4:36 (twice), 37, 38, with immediate reference to bringing Samaritans into the kingdom of God, in regard to which the disciples would enjoy the fruits of what Christ Himself had been doing in Samaria; the Lord's words are, however, of a general application in respect of such service; in 1 Cor. 9:11, with reference to the right of the apostle and his fellow missionaries to receive material assistance from the church, a right which he forbore to exercise; in 2 Cor. 9:6 (twice), with reference to rendering material help to the needy, either "sparingly" or "bountifully," the "reaping" being proportionate to the sowing; in Gal. 6:7, 8 (twice), of "reaping" corruption, with special reference, according to the context, to that which is naturally shortlived transient (though the statement applies to every form of sowing to the flesh), and of "reaping" eternal life (characteristics and moral qualities being in view), as a result of sowing "to the Spirit," the reference probably being to the new nature of the believer, which is, however, under the controlling power of the Holy Spirit, v. 9, the "reaping" (the effect of well doing) being accomplished, to a limited extent, in this life, but in complete fulfillment at and beyond the judgment seat of Christ; diligence or laxity here will then produce proportionate results; in Rev. 14:15 (twice), 16, figurative of the discriminating judgment divinely to be fulfilled at the close of this age, when the wheat will be separated from the tares (see Matt. 13:30).¶

For **REAP DOWN**, Jas. 5:4, see **MOW**

REAPER

theristēs (θεριστής, 2327), "a reaper" (akin to *therizō*, see above), is used of angels in Matt. 13:30, 39.¶

For **REAR UP**, John 2:20, see **RAISE**, No. 1 (f)

REASON (Noun)

logos (λόγος, 3056), "a word," etc., has also the significance of "the inward thought itself, a reckoning, a regard, a reason," translated "reason" in Acts 18:14, in the phrase "reason would," *kata logon*, lit., "according to reason (I would bear with you)"; in 1 Pet. 3:15, "a reason (concerning the hope that is in you)." See WORD.

Note: In Acts 6:2, KJV, the adjective *arestos*, "pleasing, agreeable," is translated "reason" (RV, "fit," marg., "pleasing"). See FIT, No. 2.

For the prepositions rendered **BY REASON OF** see †, p. 1

REASON (Verb)

1. *dialogizomai* (διαλογίζομαι, 1260), "to bring together different reasons and reckon them up, to reason," is used in the NT (*a*) chiefly of thoughts and considerations which are more or less objectionable, e.g., of the disciples who "reasoned" together, through a mistaken view of Christ's teaching regarding leaven, Matt. 16:7, 8 and Mark 8:16, 17; of their "reasoning" as to who was the greatest among them, Mark 9:33, RV, "were ye reasoning," KJV, "ye disputed" (for v. 34, see DISPUTE); of the scribes and Pharisees in criticizing Christ's claim to forgive sins, Mark 2:6, 8 (twice) and Luke 5:21, 22; of the chief priests and elders in considering how to answer Christ's question regarding John's baptism, Matt. 21:25; Mark 11:31 (some mss. have *logizomai*, here, which is nowhere else rendered "to reason"); of the wicked husbandmen, and their purpose to murder the heir and seize his inheritance, Luke 20:14; of the rich man who "reasoned" within himself, RV (KJV, "thought"), as to where to bestow his fruits, Luke 12:17 (some mss. have it in John 11:50, the best have *logizomai;* see ACCOUNT, No. 4); (*b*) of considerations not objectionable, Luke 1:29, "cast in (her) mind"; 3:15, RV, and KJV, marg., "reasoned" (KJV, "mused"). See CAST, No. 15, DISPUTE, B, No. 2.¶

2. *dialegomai* (διαλέγομαι, 1256), "to think different things with oneself, to ponder," then, "to dispute with others," is translated "to reason" in Acts 17:2, KJV and RV; 17:17, RV; 18:4, 19, KJV and RV; 19:8, 9, RV; 24:25, KJV and RV; Heb. 12:5, RV, "reasoneth (with you)," KJV, "speaketh (unto you)." See DISPUTE, B, No. 1.

3. *sullogizomai* (συλλογίζομαι, 4817), "to compute" (*sun*, "with," and *logizomai;* cf. Eng., "syllogism"), also denotes "to reason," and is so rendered in Luke 20:5.¶

4. *suzēteō* (συζητέω, 4802), "to seek or examine together" (*sun*, "with," *zēteō*, "to seek"), "to discuss," is translated "reasoning" in Mark 12:28, KJV (RV, "questioning"); similarly in Luke 24:15. See DISPUTE, B, No. 3.

REASONABLE

logikos (λογικός, 3050), pertaining to "the reasoning faculty, reasonable, rational," is used in Rom. 12:1, of the service (*latreia*) to be rendered by believers in presenting their bodies "a living sacrifice, holy, acceptable to God." The sacrifice is to be intelligent, in contrast to those offered by ritual and compulsion; the presentation is to be in accordance with the spiritual intelligence of those who are new creatures in

Christ and are mindful of "the mercies of God." For the significance of the word in 1 Pet. 2:2, see under MILK.¶

REASONING

dialogismos (διαλογισμός, 1261), "a thought, reasoning, inward questioning" [akin to *dialogizomai*, see REASON (Verb), No. 1], is translated "reasoning" or "reasonings" in Luke 5:22, RV (KJV, "thoughts"); 9:46; v. 47, RV (KJV, "thoughts"); 24:38 (KJV, "thoughts"); Rom. 1:21 (KJV, "imaginations"); 1 Cor. 3:20 (KJV, "thoughts"). See DISPUTE, A, No. 1.

Note: In those mss. which contain Acts 28:29, occurs *suzētēsis*, "a disputation," which is translated "reasoning" (KJV).¶

REBUKE (Verb and Noun)

A. Verbs.

1. *epitimaō* (ἐπιτιμάω, 2008), primarily, "to put honor upon," then, "to adjudge," hence signifies "to rebuke." Except for 2 Tim. 4:2 and Jude 9, it is confined in the NT to the Synoptic Gospels, where it is frequently used of the Lord's rebukes to (*a*) evil spirits, e.g., Matt. 17:18; Mark 1:25; 9:25; Luke 4:35, 41; 9:42; (*b*) winds, Matt. 8:26; Mark 4:39; Luke 8:24; (*c*) fever, Luke 4:39; (*d*) disciples, Mark 8:33; Luke 9:55; contrast Luke 19:39. For rebukes by others see Matt. 16:22; 19:13; 20:31; Mark 8:32; 10:13; 10:48, RV, "rebuked" (KJV, "charged"); Luke 17:3; 18:15, 39; 23:40. See CHARGE, C, No. 7.

2. *elenchō* (ἐλέγχω, 1651), "to convict, refute, reprove," is translated "to rebuke" in the KJV of the following (the RV always has the verb "to reprove"): 1 Tim. 5:20; Titus 1:13; 2:15; Heb. 12:5; Rev. 3:19. See CONVICT, No. 1.

Note: While *epitimaō* signifies simply "a rebuke" which may be either undeserved, Matt. 16:22, or ineffectual, Luke 23:40, *elenchō* implies a "rebuke" which carries conviction.

3. *epiplēssō* (ἐπιπλήσσω, 1969), "to strike at" (*epi*, "upon" or "at," *plēssō*, "to strike, smite"), hence, "to rebuke," is used in the injunction against "rebuking" an elder, 1 Tim. 5:1.¶

Note: In Phil. 2:15, the best texts have *amōmos*, "without blemish" (*a*, negative, *mōmos*, "a blemish, a moral disgrace"), RV, "without blemish"; some mss. have *amōmētos* (*a*, negative, and *mōmaomai*, "to blame"), KJV, "without rebuke." Contrast *amemptos* in the same verse, "blameless on account of absence of inconsistency" or "ground of reproof," whereas *amōmos* indicates "absence of stain or blemish." We may have blemish, with freedom from blame.

B. Noun.

elenxis (ἔλεγξις, 1649), akin to A, No. 2, denotes "rebuke"; in 2 Pet. 2:16, it is used with *echō*, "to have," and translated "he was rebuked," lit., "he had rebuke."¶ In the Sept., Job 21:4, "reproof"; 23:2, "pleading."¶

For RECEIPT see CUSTOM (Toll), No. 2

RECEIVE, RECEIVING

A. Verbs.

1. *lambanō* (λαμβάνω, 2983) denotes either "to take" or "to receive," (I) literally, (*a*) without an object, in contrast to asking, e.g., Matt. 7:8; Mark 11:24, RV, "have received" (the original has no object); (*b*) in contrast to giving, e.g., Matt. 10:8; Acts 20:35; (*c*) with objects, whether things, e.g., Mark 10:30; Luke 18:30, in the best mss. (some have No. 4); John 13:30; Acts 9:19, RV, "took" (KJV, "received"); 1 Cor. 9:25, RV, "receive" (KJV, "obtain"); or persons, e.g., John 6:21; 13:20; 16:14, RV, "take"; 2 John 10; in Mark 14:65, RV, "received (Him with blows of their hands)"; this has been styled a vulgarism; (II) metaphorically, of the word of God, Matt. 13:20; Mark 4:16; the sayings of Christ, John 12:48; the witness of Christ, John 3:11; a hundredfold in this life, and eternal life in the world to come, Mark 10:30; mercy, Heb. 4:16, RV, "may receive" (KJV, "may obtain"); a person (*prosōpon*, see FACE), Luke 20:21, "acceptest," and Gal. 2:6, "accepteth," an expression used in the OT either in the sense of being gracious or kind to a person, e.g., Gen. 19:21; 32:20, or (negatively) in the sense of being impartial, e.g., Lev. 19:15; Deut. 10:17; this latter is the meaning in the two NT passages just mentioned. See ACCEPT, A, No. 4, TAKE, etc.

Lambanō and *prosōpon* are combined in the nouns *prosōpolēmpsia*, "respect of persons," and *prosōpolēmptēs*, "respecter of persons," and in the verb *prosōpolēmptō*, "to have respect of persons": see PERSON.

2. *paralambanō* (παραλαμβάνω, 3880), "to receive from another" (*para*, "from beside"), or "to take," signifies "to receive," e.g., in Mark 7:4; John 1:11; 14:3; 1 Cor. 11:23; 15:1, 3; Gal. 1:9, 12; Phil. 4:9; Col. 2:6; 4:17; 1 Thess. 2:13 (1st part); 4:1; 2 Thess. 3:6; Heb. 12:28. See TAKE.

3. *analambanō* (ἀναλαμβάνω, 353), "to take up" (*ana*), "to take to oneself, receive," is rendered "to receive" in Mark 16:19; Acts 1:2, 11, 22, RV, "He was received up" (KJV, "taken"); 10:16; 1 Tim. 3:16. See TAKE.

4. *apolambanō* (ἀπολαμβάνω, 618) signifies "to receive from another," (*a*) to "receive" as one's due (for Luke 18:30, see No. 1); Luke 23:41; Rom. 1:27; Col. 3:24; 2 John 8; (*b*) without the indication of what is due, Luke 16:25; Gal. 4:5 (in some mss. 3 John 8, for No. 7); (*c*) to receive back, Luke 6:34 (twice); 15:27. For its other meaning, "to take apart," Mark 7:33, see TAKE.¶

5. *proslambanō* (προσλαμβάνω, 4355) denotes "to take to oneself" (*pros*, "to") or "to receive," always in the middle voice, signifying a special interest on the part of the receiver, suggesting a welcome, Acts 28:2; Rom. 14:1, 3; 15:7; Philem. 12 (in some mss.; the best omit it); v. 17. See TAKE.

6. *metalambanō* (μεταλαμβάνω, 3335), "to have or get a share of, partake of" (*meta*, with), is rendered "receiveth" in Heb. 6:7. See EAT, HAVE, PARTAKE, TAKE. In the Sept., Esth. 5:1.¶

7. *hupolambanō* (ὑπολαμβάνω, 5274), "to take or bear up" (*hupo*, "under"), "to receive," is rendered "received" in Acts 1:9, of the cloud at the Ascension; in 3 John 8, RV, "welcome" (KJV, "receive"). See ANSWER, B, No. 3, SUPPOSE, WELCOME.

8. *dechomai* (δέχομαι, 1209), "to receive by deliberate and ready reception of what is offered," is used of (*a*) taking with the hand, taking hold, taking hold of or up, e.g., Luke 2:28, RV, "he received (Him)," KJV, "took he (Him) up"; 16:6, 7; 22:17; Eph. 6:17; (*b*) "receiving," said of a place "receiving" a person, of Christ into the Heavens, Acts 3:21; or of persons in giving access to someone as a visitor, e.g., John 4:45; 2 Cor. 7:15; Gal. 4:14; Col. 4:10; by way of giving hospitality, etc., e.g., Matt. 10:14, 40 (four times), 41 (twice); 18:5; Mark 6:11; 9:37; Luke 9:5, 48, 53; 10:8, 10; 16:4; v. 9, of reception, "into the eternal tabernacles," said of followers of Christ who have used "the mammon of unrighteousness" to render assistance to ("make . . . friends of") others; of Rahab's reception of the spies, Heb. 11:31; of the reception, by the Lord, of the spirit of a departing believer, Acts 7:59; of "receiving" a gift, 2 Cor. 8:4 (in some mss.; RV follows those which omit it); of the favorable reception of testimony and teaching, etc., Luke 8:13; Acts 8:14; 11:1; 17:11; 1 Cor. 2:14; 2 Cor. 8:17; 1 Thess. 1:6; 2:13, where *paralambanō* (No. 2) is used in the 1st part, "ye received," *dechomai* in the 2nd part, "ye accepted," RV (KJV, "received"), the former refers to the ear, the latter, adding the idea of appropriation, to the heart; Jas. 1:21; in 2 Thess. 2:10, "the love of the truth," i.e., love for the truth; cf. Matt. 11:14, "if ye are willing to receive it," an elliptical

construction frequent in Greek writings; of "receiving," by way of bearing with, enduring, 2 Cor. 11:16; of "receiving" by way of getting, Acts 22:5; 28:21; of becoming partaker of benefits, Mark 10:15; Luke 18:17; Acts 7:38; 2 Cor. 6:1; 11:4 (last clause "did accept": cf. *lambanō* in previous clauses); Phil. 4:18.¶

Note: There is a certain distinction between *lambanō* and *dechomai* (more pronounced in the earlier, classical use), in that in many instances *lambanō* suggests a self-prompted taking, whereas *dechomai* more frequently indicates "a welcoming or an appropriating reception" (Grimm-Thayer).

9. *anadechomai* (ἀναδέχομαι, 324), "to receive gladly," is used in Acts 28:7, of the reception by Publius of the shipwrecked company in Melita; in Heb. 11:17, of Abraham's reception of God's promises, RV, "gladly (*ana*, "up," regarded as intensive) received." Moulton and Milligan point out the frequency of this verb in the papyri in the legal sense of taking the responsibility of something, becoming security for, undertaking, and say "The predominance of this meaning suggests its application in Heb. 11:17. The statement that Abraham had 'undertaken,' 'assumed the responsibility of,' the promises, would not perhaps be alien to the thought." The responsibility would surely be that of his faith in "receiving" the promises. In Classical Greek it had the meaning of "receiving," and it is a little difficult to attach any other sense to the circumstances, save perhaps that Abraham's faith undertook to exercise the assurance of the fulfillment of the promises.¶

10. *apodechomai* (ἀποδέχομαι, 588), "to welcome, to accept gladly" (*apo*, "from"), "to receive without reserve," is used (*a*) literally, Luke 8:40, RV, "welcomed"; 9:11 (in the best texts, some have No. 8); Acts 18:27; 21:17; 28:30; (*b*) metaphorically, Acts 2:41; 24:3, "we accept," in the sense of acknowledging, the term being used in a tone of respect. See ACCEPT, A No. 2.¶

11. *eisdechomai* (εἰσδέχομαι, 1523), "to receive into" (*eis*), is used only in 2 Cor. 6:17, where the verb does not signify "to accept," but "to admit" (as antithetic to "come ye out," and combining Isa. 52:11 with Zeph. 3:20).¶

12. *epidechomai* (ἐπιδέχομαι, 1926), lit., "to accept besides" (*epi*, "upon"), "to accept" (found in the papyri, of accepting the terms of a lease), is used in the sense of accepting in 3 John 9; in v. 10, in the sense of "receiving" with hospitality, in each verse said negatively concerning Diotrephes.¶

13. *paradechomai* (παραδέχομαι, 3858), "to receive or admit with approval" (*para*, "be-

side"), is used (*a*) of persons, Acts 15:4 (in some texts, No. 10); Heb. 12:6; (*b*) of things, Mark 4:20, KJV, "receive" (RV, "accept"); Acts 16:21; 22:18; 1 Tim. 5:9.¶ In the Sept., Ex. 23:1; Prov. 3:12.¶

14. *prosdechomai* (προσδέχομαι, 4327), "to receive to oneself, to receive favorably," also "to look for, wait for," is used of "receiving" in Luke 15:2; Rom. 16:2; Phil. 2:29. See ACCEPT, A, No. 3, ALLOW, LOOK (for), TAKE, WAIT.

15. *hupodechomai* (ὑποδέχομαι, 5264) denotes "to receive under one's roof" (*hupo*, "under"), "receive as a guest, entertain hospitably," Luke 10:38; 19:6; Acts 17:7; Jas. 2:25.¶

16. *komizō* (κομίζω, 2865) denotes "to bear, carry," e.g., Luke 7:37; in the middle voice, "to bear for oneself," hence (*a*) "to receive," Heb. 10:36; 11:13 (in the best texts; some have *lambanō*, No. 1), 39; 1 Pet. 1:9; 5:4; in some texts in 2 Pet. 2:13 (in the best mss. *adikeomai*, "suffering wrong," RV); (*b*) "to receive back, recover," Matt. 25:27; Heb. 11:19; metaphorically, of requital, 2 Cor. 5:10; Col. 3:25, of "receiving back again" by the believer at the judgment seat of Christ hereafter, for wrong done in this life; Eph. 6:8, of "receiving," on the same occasion, "whatsoever good thing each one doeth," RV; see BRING, No. 20.¶

17. *apechō* (ἀπέχω, 568) denotes (*a*) transitively, "to have in full, to have received"; so the RV in Matt. 6:2, 5, 16 (for KJV, "they have"); Luke 6:24, KJV, and RV; in all these instances the present tense (to which the KJV incorrectly adheres in the Matt. 6 verses) has a perfective force, consequent upon the combination with the prefix *apo* ("from"), not that it stands for the perfect tense, but that it views the action in its accomplished result; so in Phil. 4:18, where the KJV and RV translate it "I have"; in Philem. 15, "(that) thou shouldest have (him for ever)," KJV, "shouldest receive"; see HAVE, No. 2, and the reference to illustrations from the papyri of the use of the verb in receipts; (*b*) intransitively, "to be away, distant," used with *porrō*, "far," Matt. 15:8; Mark 7:6; with *makran*, "far off, afar," Luke 7:6; 15:20; without an accompanying adverb, Luke 24:13, "which was from." See ABSTAIN, ENOUGH, HAVE.

18. *chōreō* (χωρέω, 5562), "to give space, make room for" (*chōra*, "a place"), is used metaphorically, of "receiving" with the mind, Matt. 19:11, 12; into the heart, 2 Cor. 7:2, RV, "open your hearts," marg., "make room" (KJV, "receive"). See COME, No. 24, CONTAIN, No. 1, COURSE, B.

19. *lanchanō* (λαγχάνω, 2975), "to obtain by lot," is translated "received" in Acts 1:17, RV (KJV, "had obtained"). See LOT.

Notes: (1) In Mark 2:2, KJV, *chōreō* is translated "there was (no) room to receive" [RV, "there was (no longer) room (for)]." (2) In Rev. 13:16, KJV, *didōmi* is translated "to receive" (marg., "to give them"), RV, "(that) there be given (them)." (3) In 2 Cor. 7:9, KJV, *zēmioō*, "to suffer loss" (RV), is translated "ye might receive damage." (4) In Luke 7:22, RV, *anablepō*, "to recover sight," is translated "receive their sight" (KJV, "see"). (5) For "received (RV, 'hath taken') tithes," Heb. 7:6, see TITHE. (6) For *eleeō*, in the passive voice, 2 Cor. 4:1, KJV, "having received mercy" (RV, "obtained"), see MERCY. (7) For *patroparadotos*, in 1 Pet. 1:18, KJV, "*received* by tradition from your fathers," see HANDED DOWN. (8) In the KJV of Matt. 13:19, 20, 22, 23, *speirō*, "to sow seed," is translated "received seed"; see SOW.

B. Nouns

1. *lēpsis* or *lēmpsis* (λῆμψις, 3028), "a receiving" (akin to *lambanō*, A, No. 1), is used in Phil. 4:15.¶ In the Sept., Prov. 15:27, 29.¶

2. *analē(m)psis* (ἀνάλημψις, 354), "a taking up" (*ana*, "up," and No. 1), is used in Luke 9:51 with reference to Christ's ascension; "that He should be received up" is, lit., "of the receiving up (of Him)."¶

3. *metalē(m)psis* (μετάλημψις, 3336), "a participation, taking, receiving," is used in 1 Tim. 4:3, in connection with food, "to be received," lit., "with a view to (*eis*) reception."¶

4. *proslē(m)psis* (πρόσλημψις, 4356), *pros*, "to," and No. 1, is used in Rom. 11:15, of the restoration of Israel.¶

RECKON, RECKONING

1. *logizomai* (λογίζομαι, 3049) is properly used (*a*) of "numerical calculation," e.g., Luke 22:37; (*b*) metaphorically, "by a reckoning of characteristics or reasons, to take into account," Rom. 2:26, "shall . . . be reckoned," RV (KJV, "counted"), of "reckoning" uncircumcision for circumcision by God's estimate in contrast to that of the Jew regarding his own condition (v. 3); in 4:3, 5, 6, 9, 11, 22, 23, 24, of "reckoning" faith for righteousness, or "reckoning" righteousness to persons, in all of which the RV uses the verb "to reckon" instead of the KJV "to count or to impute"; in v. 4 the subject is treated by way of contrast between grace and debt, which latter involves the "reckoning" of a reward for works; what is owed as a debt cannot be "reckoned" as a favor, but the faith of Abraham and his spiritual children sets them outside the category of those who seek to be justified by self-effort, and, *vice versa*, the latter are excluded from the grace of righteousness bestowed on the sole condition of faith; so in Gal.

3:6 (RV, "was reckoned," KJV, "was accounted"); since Abraham, like all the natural descendants of Adam, was a sinner, he was destitute of righteousness in the sight of God; if, then, his relationship with God was to be rectified (i.e., if he was to be justified before God), the rectification could not be brought about by works of merit on his part; in Jas. 2:23, RV, "reckoned," the subject is viewed from a different standpoint (see under JUSTIFICATION, B, last four paragraphs); for other instances of "reckoning" in this respect see Rom. 9:8, RV, "are reckoned" (KJV, "are counted"); 2 Cor. 5:19, RV, "(not) reckoning (trespasses)," KJV, "imputing"; (c) "to consider, calculate," translated "to reckon" in Rom. 6:11; 8:36; 2 Cor. 10:11, RV, "let (such a one) reckon (this)"; (d) "to suppose, judge, deem," translated "to reckon" in Rom. 2:3, "reckonest thou (this)," RV (KJV, "thinkest"); 3:28 (KJV, "we conclude"); 8:18; 2 Cor. 11:5 (KJV, "I suppose"); see ACCOUNT, A, No. 4, CONSIDER, No. 6, COUNT, No. 3, SUPPOSE; (e) "to purpose, decide," 2 Cor. 10:2, RV, "count" (KJV, "think"); see COUNT, No. 3.

2. legō (λέγω, 3004), "to say, speak," also has the meaning "to gather, reckon, account," used in this sense in Heb. 7:11, RV, "be reckoned" (KJV, "be called"). See ASK, A, No. 6.

3. sunairō (συναίρω, 4868), "to take up together" (sun, "with," airō, "to take"), is used with the noun logos, "an account," signifying "to settle accounts," Matt. 18:23, RV, "make a reckoning" (KJV, "take account"); v. 24, KJV and RV, "to reckon" (logos being understood); 25:19, RV, "maketh a reckoning" (KJV, "reckoneth"). This phrase occurs not infrequently in the papyri in the sense of settling accounts (see Deissmann, Light from the Ancient East, 118).¶ In the Sept. the verb occurs in its literal sense in Exod. 23:5, "thou shalt help to raise" (lit., "raise with").¶

RECLINE

anakeimai (ἀνάκειμαι, 345), lit., and in classical usage, "to be laid up, laid," denotes, in the NT, "to recline at table"; it is translated "reclining" in John 13:23, RV (KJV, "leaning"); cf. anapiptō in v. 25, RV, "leaning back." See also v. 12, marg. See LEAN, SIT, TABLE (at the)

For RECOMMEND, Acts 14:26; 15:40, KJV, see COMMEND, No. 2

RECOMPENCE, RECOMPENSE

A. Nouns.

1. antapodoma (ἀνταπόδομα, 468), akin to antapodidōmi, "to recompense" (see below), lit., "a giving back in return" (anti, "in return," apo, back, didōmi, "to give"), a requital, recompence, is used (a) in a favorable sense, Luke 14:12; (b) in an unfavorable sense, Rom. 11:9, indicating that the present condition of the Jewish nation is the retributive effect of their transgressions, on account of which that which was designed as a blessing ("their table") has become a means of judgment.¶

2. antapodosis (ἀνταπόδοσις, 469), derived, like No. 1, from antapodidōmi, is rendered "recompense" in Col. 3:24, RV (KJV, "reward").¶

3. antimisthia (ἀντιμισθία, 489), "a reward, requital" (anti, "in return," misthos, "wages, hire"), is used (a) in a good sense, 2 Cor. 6:13; (b) in a bad sense, Rom. 1:27.¶

4. misthapodosia (μισθαποδοσία, 3405), "a payment of wages" (from misthos, see No. 3, and apodidōmi, B, No. 2), "a recompence," is used (a) of reward, Heb. 10:35; 11:26; (b) of punishment, Heb. 2:2.¶ Cf. misthapodotēs, "a rewarder," Heb. 11:6.¶

B. Verbs.

1. antapodidōmi (ἀνταποδίδωμι, 467), akin to A, No. 1 and No. 2, "to give back as an equivalent, to requite, recompense" (the anti expressing the idea of a complete return), is translated "render" in 1 Thess. 3:9, here only in the NT of thanksgiving to God (cf. the Sept. of Ps. 116:12); elsewhere it is used of "recompense," "whether between men (but in that case only of good, not of evil, see No. 2 in 1 Thess. 5:15), Luke 14:14 a, cf. the corresponding noun in v. 12; or between God and evil-doers, Rom. 12:19, RV (KJV, "repay"); Heb. 10:30, cf. the noun in Rom. 11:9; or between God and those who do well, Luke 14:14 b; Rom. 11:35, cf. the noun in Col. 3:24; in 2 Thess. 1:6 both reward and retribution are in view."*¶

2. apodidōmi (ἀποδίδωμι, 591), "to give up or back, restore, return," is translated "shall recompense" in the RV of Matt. 6:4, 6, 18 (KJV, "shall reward"); in Rom. 12:17, KJV, "recompense" (RV, "render"); in 1 Thess. 5:15, "render," See DELIVER, GIVE, PAY, PERFORM, RENDER, REPAY, REQUITE, RESTORE, REWARD, SELL, YIELD.

RECONCILE, RECONCILIATION

A. Verbs.

1. katallassō (καταλλάσσω, 2644) properly denotes "to change, exchange" (especially of money); hence, of persons, "to change from enmity to friendship, to reconcile." With regard to the relationship between God and man, the

use of this and connected words shows that primarily "reconciliation" is what God accomplishes, exercising His grace towards sinful man on the ground of the death of Christ in propitiatory sacrifice under the judgment due to sin, 2 Cor. 5:19, where both the verb and the noun are used (cf. No. 2, in Col. 1:21). By reason of this men in their sinful condition and alienation from God are invited to be "reconciled" to Him; that is to say, to change their attitude, and accept the provision God has made, whereby their sins can be remitted and they themselves be justified in His sight in Christ.

Rom. 5:10 expresses this in another way: "For if, while we were enemies, we were reconciled to God through the death of His Son ... "; that we were "enemies" not only expresses man's hostile attitude to God but signifies that until this change of attitude takes place men are under condemnation, exposed to God's wrath. The death of His Son is the means of the removal of this, and thus we "receive the reconciliation," v. 11, RV. This stresses the attitude of God's favor toward us. The KJV rendering "atonement" is incorrect. Atonement is the offering itself of Christ under divine judgment upon sin. We do not receive atonement. What we do receive is the result, namely, "reconciliation."

The removal of God's wrath does not contravene His immutability. He always acts according to His unchanging righteousness and lovingkindness, and it is because He changes not that His relative attitude does change towards those who change. All His acts show that He is Light and Love. Anger, where there is no personal element, is a sign of moral health if, and if only, it is accompanied by grief. There can be truest love along with righteous indignation, Mark 3:5, but love and enmity cannot exist together. It is important to distinguish "wrath" and "hostility." The change in God's relative attitude toward those who receive the "reconciliation" only proves His real unchangeableness. Not once is God said to be "reconciled." The enmity is alone on our part. It was we who needed to be "reconciled" to God, not God to us, and it is propitiation, which His righteousness and mercy have provided, that makes the "reconciliation" possible to those who receive it.

When the writers of the NT speak upon the subject of the wrath of God, "the hostility is represented not as on the part of God, but of man. And this is the reason why the apostle never uses *diallassō* [a word used only in Matt. 5:24, in the NT] in this connection, but always *katallassō*, because the former word denotes mutual concession after mutual hostility [frequently exemplified in the Sept.], an idea absent from *katallassō*" (Lightfoot, *Notes on the Epistles of Paul*, p. 288).

The subject finds its great unfolding in 2 Cor. 5:18–20, which states that God "reconciled us (believers) to Himself through Christ," and that "the ministry of reconciliation" consists in this, "that God was in Christ reconciling the world unto Himself." The insertion of a comma in the KJV after the word "Christ" is misleading; the doctrine stated here is not that God was in Christ (the unity of the Godhead is not here in view), but that what God has done in the matter of reconciliation He has done in Christ, and this is based upon the fact that "Him who knew no sin He made to be sin on our behalf; that we might become the righteousness of God in Him." On this ground the command to men is "be ye reconciled to God."

The verb is used elsewhere in 1 Cor. 7:11, of a woman returning to her husband.¶

2. *apokatallassō* (ἀποκαταλλάσσω, 604), "to reconcile completely" (*apo*, from, and No. 1), a stronger form of No. 1, "to change from one condition to another," so as to remove all enmity and leave no impediment to unity and peace, is used in Eph. 2:16, of the "reconciliation" of believing Jew and Gentile "in one body unto God through the Cross"; in Col. 1:21 not the union of Jew and Gentile is in view, but the change wrought in the individual believer from alienation and enmity, on account of evil works, to "reconciliation" with God; in v. 20 the word is used of the divine purpose to "reconcile" through Christ "all things unto Himself ... whether things upon the earth, or things in the heavens," the basis of the change being the peace effected "through the blood of His Cross." It is the divine purpose, on the ground of the work of Christ accomplished on the cross, to bring the whole universe, except rebellious angels and unbelieving man, into full accord with the mind of God, Eph. 1:10. Things "under the earth," Phil. 2:10, are subdued, not "reconciled."¶

3. *diallassō* (διαλλάσσω, 1259), "to effect an alteration, to exchange," and hence, "to reconcile," in cases of mutual hostility yielding to mutual concession, and thus differing from No. 1 (under which see Lightfoot's remarks), is used in the passive voice in Matt. 5:24, which illustrates the point. There is no such idea as "making it up" where God and man are concerned.¶

B. Noun.

katallagē (καταλλαγή, 2643), akin to A, No. 1, primarily "an exchange," denotes "reconciliation," a change on the part of one party, induced by an action on the part of another; in the NT, the "reconciliation" of men to God by His grace and love in Christ. The word is used in Rom. 5:11 and 11:15. The occasioning cause of the world-wide proclamation of "reconciliation" through the gospel, was the casting away (partially and temporarily) of Israel. A new relationship Godward is offered to the Gentiles in the gospel. The word also occurs in 2 Cor. 5:18, 19, where "the ministry of reconciliation" and "the word of reconciliation" are not the ministry of teaching the doctrine of expiation, but that of beseeching men to be "reconciled" to God on the ground of what God has wrought in Christ. See No. 1, above.¶

Note: In the OT in some passages the KJV incorrectly has "reconciliation," the RV rightly changes the translation to "atonement," e.g., Lev. 8:15; Ezek. 45:20, RV, "make atonement for" (KJV, "reconcile").

For RECONCILIATION (MAKE), Heb. 2:17, KJV, see PROPITIATION

For RECORD (KJV) see TESTIFY, No. 3, TESTIMONY, No. 2

RECOVER

1. *sōzō* (σώζω, 4982), "to save," is sometimes used of "healing" or "restoration to health," the latter in John 11:12, RV, "he will recover," marg., "be saved" (KJV, "he shall do well"). See HEAL, PRESERVE, SAVE, WHOLE.

2. *ananēphō* (ἀνανήφω, 366), "to return to soberness," as from a state of delirium or drunkenness (*ana*, "back," or "again," *nēphō*, "to be sober, to be wary"), is used in 2 Tim. 2:26, "may recover themselves" (RV marg., "return to soberness," KJV marg., "awake"), said of those who, opposing the truth through accepting perversions of it, fall into the snare of the Devil, becoming intoxicated with error; for these "recovery" is possible only by "repentance unto the knowledge of the truth." For a translation of the verse see CAPTIVE, B, No. 3.¶

Notes: (1) For "recovering of sight," Luke 4:18, see SIGHT. (2) In Mark 16:18, the phrase *echō kalōs*, lit., "to have well," i.e., "to be well," is rendered "they shall recover."

RED

A. Adjectives.

1. *purrhos* (πυρρός, 4450) denotes "fire-colored" (*pur*, "fire"), hence, "fiery red," Rev. 6:4; 12:3, in the latter passage said of the Dragon, indicative of the cruelty of the Devil.¶

2. *eruthros* (ἐρυθρός, 2063) denotes "red" (the ordinary color); the root *rudh*— is seen, e.g., in the Latin *rufus*, Eng., "ruby," "ruddy," "rust," etc. It is applied to the Red Sea, Acts 7:36; Heb. 11:29.¶ The origin of the name is uncertain; it has been regarded as due, e.g., to the color of the corals which cover the Red Sea bed or line its shores, or to the tinge of the mountains which border it, or to the light of the sky upon its waters.

B. Verb.

purrhazō (πυρράζω, 4449), "to be fiery red" (akin to A, No. 1), is used of the sky, Matt. 16:2, 3.¶ In the Sept., *purrhizō*, Lev. 13:19, 42, 43, 49; 14:37.¶

REDEEM, REDEMPTION

A. Verbs.

1. *exagorazō* (ἐξαγοράζω, 1805), a strengthened form of *agorazō*, "to buy" (see BUY, No. 1), denotes "to buy out" (*ex* for *ek*), especially of purchasing a slave with a view to his freedom. It is used metaphorically (*a*) in Gal. 3:13 and 4:5, of the deliverance by Christ of Christian Jews from the Law and its curse; what is said of *lutron* (RANSOM, No. 1) is true of this verb and of *agorazō*, as to the death of Christ, that Scripture does not say to whom the price was paid; the various suggestions made are purely speculative; (*b*) in the middle voice, "to buy up for oneself," Eph. 5:16 and Col. 4:5, of "buying up the opportunity" (RV marg.; text, "redeeming the time," where "time" is *kairos*, "a season," a time in which something is seasonable), i.e., making the most of every opportunity, turning each to the best advantage since none can be recalled if missed.¶

Note: In Rev. 5:9; 14:3, 4, KJV, *agorazō*, "to purchase" (RV) is translated "redeemed." See PURCHASE.

2. *lutroō* (λυτρόω, 3084), "to release on receipt of ransom" (akin to *lutron*, "a ransom"), is used in the middle voice, signifying "to release by paying a ransom price, to redeem" (*a*) in the natural sense of delivering, Luke 24:21, of setting Israel free from the Roman yoke; (*b*) in a spiritual sense, Titus 2:14, of the work of Christ in "redeeming" men "from all iniquity" (*anomia*, "lawlessness," the bondage of self-will which rejects the will of God); 1 Pet. 1:18 (passive voice), "ye were redeemed," from a vain manner of life, i.e., from bondage to tradition. In both instances the death of Christ is stated as the means of "redemption."¶

Note: While both No. 1 and No. 2 are translated "to redeem," *exagorazō* does not signify the actual "redemption," but the price paid with a view to it, *lutroō* signifies the actual "deliverance," the setting at liberty.

B. Nouns.

1. *lutrōsis* (λύτρωσις, 3085), "a redemption" (akin to A, No. 2), is used (*a*) in the general sense of "deliverance," of the nation of Israel, Luke 1:68 RV, "wrought redemption"; 2:38; (*b*) of "the redemptive work" of Christ, Heb. 9:12, bringing deliverance through His death, from the guilt and power of sin.¶ In the Sept., Lev. 25:29, 48; Num. 18:16; Judg. 1:15; Ps. 49:8; 111:9; 130:7; Isa. 63:4.¶

2. *apolutrōsis* (ἀπολύτρωσις, 629), a strengthened form of No. 1, lit., "a releasing, for (i.e., on payment of) a ransom." It is used of (*a*) "deliverance" from physical torture, Heb. 11:35, see DELIVER, B, No. 1; (*b*) the deliverance of the people of God at the coming of Christ with His glorified saints, "in a cloud with power and great glory," Luke 21:28, a "redemption" to be accomplished at the "outshining of His Parousia," 2 Thess. 2:8, i.e., at His second advent; (*c*) forgiveness and justification, "redemption" as the result of expiation, deliverance from the guilt of sins, Rom. 3:24, "through the redemption that is in Christ Jesus"; Eph. 1:7, defined as "the forgiveness of our trespasses," RV; so Col. 1:14, "the forgiveness of our sins," indicating both the liberation from the guilt and doom of sin and the introduction into a life of liberty, "newness of life" (Rom. 6:4); Heb. 9:15, "for the redemption of the transgressions that were under the first covenant," RV, here "redemption of" is equivalent to "redemption from," the genitive case being used of the object from which the "redemption" is effected, not from the consequence of the transgressions, but from the transgressions themselves; (*d*) the deliverance of the believer from the presence and power of sin, and of his body from bondage to corruption, at the coming (the Parousia in its inception) of the Lord Jesus, Rom. 8:23; 1 Cor. 1:30; Eph. 1:14; 4:30.¶ See also PROPITIATION.

For REDOUND, 2 Cor. 4:15 (RV, "abound"), see ABUNDANCE, B, No. 1 (*c*)

REED

kalamos (κάλαμος, 2563) denotes (*a*) "the reed" mentioned in Matt. 11:7; 12:20; Luke 7:24, the same as the Heb., *qāneh* (among the various reeds in the OT), e.g., Isa. 42:3, from which Matt. 12:20 is quoted (cf. Job 40:21; Ezek. 29:6, "a reed with jointed, hollow stalk"); (*b*) "a reed staff, staff," Matt. 27:29, 30, 48; Mark 15:19, 36 (cf. *rhabdos*, "a rod"; in 2 Kings 18:21, *rhabdos kalaminē*); (*c*) "a measuring reed

or rod," Rev. 11:1; 21:15, 16; (*d*) "a writing reed, a pen," 3 John 13; see PEN.¶

REFINED

puroomai (πυρόομαι, 4448), "to burn," is translated "refined," as of metals, in Rev. 1:15 and 3:18, RV (KJV, "burned," and "tried"). See BURN, No. 4.

For REFLECTING, 2 Cor. 3:18, RV, see BEHOLD, No. 12

REFORMATION

diorthōsis (διόρθωσις, 1357), properly, "a making straight" (*dia*, "through," *orthos*, "straight"; cf. *diorthōma* in Acts 24:2; see CORRECTION, No. 1), denotes a "reformation" or reforming, Heb. 9:10; the word has the meaning either (*a*) of a right arrangement, right ordering, or, more usually, (*b*) of restoration, amendment, bringing right again; what is here indicated is a time when the imperfect, the inadequate, would be superseded by a better order of things, and hence the meaning (*a*) seems to be the right one; it is thus to be distinguished from that of Acts 24:2, mentioned above.¶ The word is used in the papyri in the other sense of the rectification of things, whether by payments or manner of life.

REFRAIN

1. *pauō* (παύω, 3973), "to stop," is used in the active voice in the sense of "making to cease, restraining" in 1 Pet. 3:10, of causing the tongue to refrain from evil; elsewhere in the middle voice, see CEASE, No. 1.

2. *aphistēmi* (ἀφίστημι, 868), "to cause to depart," is used intransitively, in the sense of "departing from, refraining from," Acts 5:38. See DEPART, No. 20.

REFRESH, REFRESHING

A. Verbs.

1. *anapauō* (ἀναπαύω, 373), "to give intermission from labor, to give rest, refresh" (*ana*, "back," *pauō*, "to cause to cease"), is translated "to refresh" in 1 Cor. 16:18; 2 Cor. 7:13; Philem. 7, 20. See REST.

2. *sunanapauomai* (συναναπαύομαι, 4875), "to lie down, to rest with" (*sun*, "with," and No. 1 in the middle voice), is used metaphorically of being "refreshed" in spirit with others, in Rom. 15:32, KJV, "may with (you) be refreshed" (RV, " . . . find rest").¶ In the Sept., Isa. 11:6.¶

3. *anapsuchō* (ἀναψύχω, 404), "to make cool, refresh" (*ana*, "back," *psuchō*, "to cool"),

is used in 2 Tim. 1:16 (cf. B).¶ In the papyri it is used of "taking relaxation."

Note: In Acts 27:3, the verb *tunchanō,* "to obtain or receive," with the object *epimeleia,* "care," is translated "to refresh himself" (RV, marg., "to receive attention," i.e., to enjoy the kind attention of his friends).

B. Noun.

anapsuxis (ἀνάψυξις, 403), "a refreshing" (akin to A, No. 3), occurs in Acts 3:19.¶ In the Sept., Ex. 8:15.¶ In the papyri it is used of "obtaining relief."

For REFUGE see FLEE, No. 3

REFUSE (Verb)

1. *arneomai* (ἀρνέομαι, 720), "to deny, renounce, reject," in late Greek came to signify "to refuse to acknowledge, to disown," and is translated "to refuse" in Acts 7:35; Heb. 11:24. See DENY, No. 1.

2. *paraiteomai* (παραιτέομαι, 3868), for the various meanings of which see AVOID, No. 3, denotes "to refuse" in Acts 25:11; 1 Tim. 4:7; 5:11; 2 Tim. 2:23, RV (KJV, "avoid"); Titus 3:10, RV (marg., "avoid"; KJV, "reject"); Heb. 12:25 (twice), perhaps in the sense of "begging off." See EXCUSE, INTREAT, REJECT.

3. *dokimazō* (δοκιμάζω, 1381), "to prove, to approve," used with a negative in Rom. 1:28, is translated "they refused," RV (KJV, "they did not like"); RV marg., "did not approve." See APPROVE, No. 1.

Notes: (1) For *parakouō,* "to refuse to hear," RV in Matt. 18:17 (twice), see HEAR, A, No. 7. (2) In 1 Tim. 4:4, KJV, *apoblētos,* "rejected" (RV), is translated "refused." See REJECT.

REGARD

1. *blepō* (βλέπω, 991), "to behold, look, perceive, see," has the sense of "regarding" by way of partiality, in Matt. 22:16 and Mark 12:14. See BEHOLD, No. 2.

2. *entrepō* (ἐντρέπω, 1788), "to turn about" (*en,* "in," *trepō,* "to turn"), is metaphorically used of "putting to shame," e.g., 1 Cor. 4:14; in the middle voice, "to reverence, regard," translated "regard" in Luke 18:2, 4. See ASHAMED, REVERENCE, SHAME.

3. *phroneō* (φρονέω, 5426), "to think, set the mind on," implying moral interest and reflection, is translated "to regard" in Rom. 14:6 (twice); the second part in the KJV represents an interpolation and is not part of the original. The Scripture does not speak of not "regarding" a day. See CARE, B, No. 6, MIND, SAVOR, THINK, UNDERSTAND.

4. *epiblepō* (ἐπιβλέπω, 1914), "to look

upon" (*epi,* "upon," and No. 1), in the NT "to look on with favor," is used in Luke 1:48, KJV, "hath regarded" (RV, "hath looked upon"); in Jas. 2:3, RV, "ye have regard to" (KJV, "ye have respect to"). See LOOK, No. 6, RESPECT.

5. *oligōreō* (ὀλιγωρέω, 3643) denotes "to think little of" (*oligos,* "little," *ōra,* "care"), "to regard lightly," Heb. 12:5, RV (KJV, "despise"). See DESPISE, *Note* (3).¶ In the Sept., Prov. 3:11.¶

6. *prosechō* (προσέχω, 4337), "to take or give heed," is translated "they had regard" in Acts 8:11, KJV (RV, "they gave heed"). See ATTEND, No. 1.

7. *ameleō* (ἀμελέω, 272), "not to care," is translated "I regarded . . . not" in Heb. 8:9. See NEGLECT.

Notes: (1) In Gal. 6:4, RV, *eis,* "into," is translated "in regard of (himself)," KJV, "in"; so in 2 Cor. 10:16; Eph. 5:32. (2) In Rom. 6:20, the dative case of *dikaiosunē,* "righteousness," signifies, not "from righteousness," KJV, but "in regard of righteousness," RV, lit., "free to righteousness"; i.e., righteousness laid no sort of bond upon them, they had no relation to it in any way. (3) In 2 Cor. 8:4 the accusative case of *charis* and *koinōnia* is, in the best texts, used absolutely, i.e., not as the objects of an expressed verb; hence the RV, "in regard to" (KJV, "that we would receive," where the verb is the result of a supplementary gloss). (4) For "not regarding" in Phil. 2:30, KJV (RV, "hazarding"), see HAZARD, No. 2.

REGENERATION

palingenesia (παλινγενεσία, 3824) "new birth" (*palin,* "again," *genesis,* "birth"), is used of "spiritual regeneration," Titus 3:5, involving the communication of a new life, the two operating powers to produce which are "the word of truth," Jas. 1:18; 1 Pet. 1:23, and the Holy Spirit, John 3:5, 6; the *loutron,* "the laver, the washing," is explained in Eph. 5:26, "having cleansed it by the washing (*loutron*) of water with the word."

The new birth and "regeneration" do not represent successive stages in spiritual experience, they refer to the same event but view it in different aspects. The new birth stresses the communication of spiritual life in contrast to antecedent spiritual death; "regeneration" stresses the inception of a new state of things in contrast with the old; hence the connection of the use of the word with its application to Israel, in Matt. 19:28. Some regard the *kai* in Titus 3:5 as epexegetic, "even"; but, as Scripture marks two distinct yet associated operating powers, there is not sufficient ground for this interpretation. See under EVEN.

In Matt. 19:28 the word is used, in the Lord's discourse, in the wider sense, of the "restoration of all things" (Acts 3:21, RV), when, as a result of the second advent of Christ, Jehovah "sets His King upon His holy hill of Zion" (Ps. 2:6), and Israel, now in apostasy, is restored to its destined status, in the recognition and under the benign sovereignty of its Messiah. Thereby will be accomplished the deliverance of the world from the power and deception of Satan and from the despotic and antichristian rulers of the nations. This restitution will not in the coming millennial age be universally a return to the pristine condition of Edenic innocence previous to the Fall, but it will fulfill the establishment of God's covenant with Abraham concerning his descendants, a veritable rebirth of the nation, involving the peace and prosperity of the Gentiles. That the worldwide subjection to the authority of Christ will not mean the entire banishment of evil, is clear from Rev. 20:7, 8. Only in the new heavens and earth, "wherein dwelleth righteousness," will sin and evil be entirely absent.¶

REGION

1. chōra (χώρα, 5561), "a space lying between two limits, a country, land," is translated "region" in Matt. 4:16; Luke 3:1; Acts 8:1; 13:49; 16:6; 18:23, RV. In the last three passages it has the technical sense of a subdivision of a Roman province, Lat. regio; as also No. 2 in Acts 14:6. See COUNTRY, No. 3.

2. perichōros (περίχωρος, 4066), "a country or region round about" peri), is translated "region round about" in Matt. 3:5; 14:35, RV; Mark 1:28 (in some mss. Mark 6:55); Luke 3:3, RV; 4:14; 4:37, RV; 7:17; Acts 14:6 (see No. 1). See COUNTRY, No. 4.

3. klima (κλίμα, 2824), "an inqlination, slope," is translated "regions" in Rom. 15:23 RV; 2 Cor. 11:10; Gal. 1:21. See PART, A, No. 3.¶

Note: For "regions beyond," 2 Cor. 10:16, KJV, see PART, A. *Note* (9).

REGRET

A. Verb.

metamelomai (μεταμέλομαι, 3338), "to regret, to repent one," is translated "to regret" in 2 Cor. 7:8, RV (twice), KJV, "repent." See REPENT.

B. Adjective.

ametameletos (ἀμεταμέλητος, 278), "not repented of" (a, negative, and A), is translated "which bringeth no regret" in 2 Cor. 7:10, RV,

said of repentance (KJV, "not to be repented of"); elsewhere, in Rom. 11:29. See REPENT.¶

For **REGULAR,** Acts 19:39, RV, see LAW, C, No. 2

REHEARSE

1. anangellō (ἀναγγέλλω, 312), "to bring back word" (ana, "back," angellō, "to announce"), is translated "to rehearse" in Acts 14:27; 15:4, RV. See ANNOUNCE.

2. exēgeomai (ἐξηγέομαι, 1834), primarily, "to lead, show the way," is used metaphorically with the meaning "to unfold, declare, narrate," and is translated "to rehearse" in the RV of Luke 24:35; Acts 10:8; 15:12, and 14, RV. See DECLARE, No. 8.

Note: In Acts 11:4, the KJV translates the middle voice of archō, "to begin," "rehearsed... from the beginning," RV, "began, (and)."

REIGN (Verb and Noun)

1. basileuō (βασιλεύω, 936), "to reign," is used (I) literally, (a) of God, Rev. 11:17; 19:6, in each of which the aorist tense (in the latter, translated "reigneth") is "ingressive," stressing the point of entrance; (b) of Christ, Luke 1:33; 1 Cor. 15:25; Rev. 11:15; as rejected by the Jews, Luke 19:14, 27; (c) of the saints, hereafter, 1 Cor. 4:8 (2nd part), where the apostle, casting a reflection upon the untimely exercise of authority on the part of the church at Corinth, anticipates the due time for it in the future (see No. 2); Rev. 5:10; 20:4, where the aorist tense is not simply of a "point" character, but "constative," that is, regarding a whole action as having occurred, without distinguishing any steps in its progress (in this instance the aspect is future); v. 6; 22:5; (d) of earthly potentates, Matt. 2:22; 1 Tim. 6:15, where "kings" is, lit., "them that reign"; (II) metaphorically, (a) of believers, Rom. 5:17, where "shall reign in life" indicates the activity of life in fellowship with Christ in His sovereign power, reaching its fullness hereafter; 1 Cor. 4:8 (1st part), of the carnal pride that laid claim to a power not to be exercised until hereafter; (b) of divine grace, Rom. 5:21; (c) of sin, Rom. 5:21; 6:12; (d) of death, Rom. 5:14, 17.¶

2. sumbasileuō (συμβασιλεύω, 4821), "to reign together with" (sun, "with," and No. 1), is used of the future "reign" of believers together and with Christ in the kingdom of God in manifestation, 1 Cor. 4:8 (3rd part); of those who endure 2 Tim. 2:12, cf. Rev. 20:6.¶

Notes: (1) In Rom. 15:12, KJV, archō, "to

rule" (RV, is translated "to reign." (2) In Rev. 17:18, *echō*, "to have," with *basileia*, "a kingdom," is translated "reigneth," lit., "hath a kingdom," suggestive of a distinction between the sovereignty of mystic Babylon and that of ordinary sovereigns.

(3) In Luke 3:1, *hēgemonia*, "rule," is rendered "reign."¶

REINS

nephros (νεφρός, 3510), "a kidney" (Eng., "nephritis," etc.), usually in the plural, is used metaphorically of "the will and the affections," Rev. 2:23, "reins" (cf. Ps. 7:9; Jer. 11:20; 17:10; 20:12). The feelings and emotions were regarded as having their seat in the "kidneys."¶

REJECT

A. Verbs.

1. *apodokimazō* (ἀποδοκιμάζω, 593), "to reject" as the result of examination and disapproval (*apo*, "away from," *dokimazō*, "to approve"), is used (*a*) of the "rejection" of Christ by the elders and chief priests of the Jews, Matt. 21:42; Mark 8:31; 12:10; Luke 9:22; 20:17; 1 Pet. 2:4, 7 (KJV, "disallowed"); by the Jewish people, Luke 17:25; (*b*) of the "rejection" of Esau from inheriting "the blessing," Heb. 12:17. See DISALLOW.¶ Cf. and contrast *exoutheneō*, Acts 4:11. See DESPISE.

2. *atheteō* (ἀθετέω, 114), properly, "to do away" with what has been laid down, to make *atheton* (i.e., "without place," *a*, negative, *tithēmi*, "to place"), hence, besides its meanings "to set aside, make void, nullify, disannul," signifies "to reject"; in Mark 6:26, regarding Herod's pledge to Salome, it almost certainly has the meaning "to break faith with" (cf. the Sept. of Jer. 12:6, and Lam. 1:2, "dealt treacherously"). Moulton and Milligan illustrate this meaning from the papyri. Field suggests "disappoint." In Mark 7:9 "ye reject (the commandment)" means "ye set aside"; in Luke 7:30, "ye reject" may have the meaning of "nullifying or making void the counsel of God"; in Luke 10:16 (four times), "rejecteth," RV (KJV, "despiseth"); "rejecteth" in John 12:48; "reject" in 1 Cor. 1:19 (KJV, "bring to nothing"); 1 Thess. 4:8, "to despise," where the reference is to the charges in v. 2; in 1 Tim. 5:12 RV, "have rejected" (KJV, "have cast off"). See DESPISE, *Notes* (1), DISANNUL, No. 1.

3. *ekptuō* (ἐκπτύω, 1609), "to spit out" (*ek*, "out," and *ptuō*, "to spit"), i.e., "to abominate, loathe," is used in Gal. 4:14, "rejected" (marg., "spat out"), where the sentence is elliptical: "although my disease repelled you, you did not refuse to hear my message."¶

4. *paraiteomai* (παραιτέομαι, 3868), besides the meanings "to beg from another," Mark 15:6 (in the best texts); "to entreat that . . . not," Heb. 12:19; "to beg off, ask to be excused," Luke 14:18, 19; 12:25 (see REFUSE, No. 2), is translated to reject in Titus 3:10, KJV. See EXCUSE, INTREAT, REFUSE.

B. Adjectives.

1. *adokimos* (ἀδόκιμος, 96), "not standing the test" (see CAST, C), is translated "rejected" in 1 Cor. 9:27, RV; Heb. 6:8, KJV and RV. See REPROBATE.

2. *apoblētos* (ἀπόβλητος, 579), lit., "cast away" (*apo*, "from," *ballō*, "to throw"), occurs in 1 Tim. 4:4, RV, "rejected" (KJV, "refused"). See REFUSE.¶

REJOICE

1. *chairō* (χαίρω, 5463), "to rejoice," is most frequently so translated. As to this verb, the following are grounds and occasions for "rejoicing," on the part of believers: in the Lord, Phil. 3:1; 4:4; His incarnation, Luke 1:14; His power, Luke 13:17; His presence with the Father, John 14:28; His presence with them, John 16:22; 20:20; His ultimate triumph, 8:56; hearing the gospel, Acts 13:48; their salvation, Acts 8:39; receiving the Lord, Luke 19:6; their enrollment in Heaven, Luke 10:20; their liberty in Christ, Acts 15:31; their hope, Rom. 12:12 (cf. Rom. 5:2; Rev. 19:7); their prospect of reward, Matt. 5:12; the obedience and godly conduct of fellow believers, Rom. 16:19, RV, "I rejoice" (KJV, "I am glad"); 2 Cor. 7:7, 9; 13:9; Col. 2:5; 1 Thess. 3:9; 2 John 4; 3 John 3; the proclamation of Christ, Phil. 1:18; the gospel harvest, John 4:36; suffering with Christ, Acts 5:41; 1 Pet. 4:13; suffering in the cause of the gospel, 2 Cor. 13:9 (1st part); Phil. 2:17 (1st part); Col. 1:24; in persecutions, trials and afflictions, Matt. 5:12; Luke 6:23; 2 Cor. 6:10; the manifestation of grace, Acts 11:23; meeting with fellow believers, 1 Cor. 16:17, RV, "I rejoice"; Phil. 2:28; receiving tokens of love and fellowship, Phil. 4:10; the "rejoicing" of others, Rom. 12:15; 2 Cor. 7:13; learning of the well-being of others, 2 Cor. 7:16. See FAREWELL, GLAD, GREETING, etc.

2. *sunchairō* (συγχαίρω, 4796), "to rejoice with" (*sun*, and No. 1), is used of "rejoicing" together in the recovery of what was lost, Luke 15:6, 9; in suffering in the cause of the gospel, Phil. 2:17 (2nd part), 18; in the joy of another, Luke 1:58; in the honor of fellow believers, 1 Cor. 12:26; in the triumph of the truth, 1 Cor. 13:6, RV, "rejoiceth with."¶

3. *agalliaō* (ἀγαλλιάω, 21), "to rejoice greatly, to exult," is used, (I) in the active voice,

of "rejoicing" in God, Luke 1:47; in faith in Christ, 1 Pet. 1:8, RV (middle voice in some mss.), "ye rejoice greatly"; in the event of the marriage of the Lamb, Rev. 19:7, "be exceeding glad," RV; (II) in the middle voice, (a) of "rejoicing" in persecutions, Matt. 5:12 (2nd part); in the light of testimony for God, John 5:35; in salvation received through the gospel, Acts 16:34, "he rejoiced greatly," RV; in salvation ready to be revealed, 1 Pet. 1:6; at the revelation of His glory, 1 Pet. 4:13, "with exeeding joy," lit., "ye may rejoice (see No. 1) exulting"; (b) of Christ's "rejoicing" (greatly) "in the Holy Spirit," Luke 10:21, RV; said of His praise, as foretold in Ps. 16:9, quoted in Acts 2:26 (which follows the Sept., "My tongue"); (c) of Abraham's "rejoicing," by faith, to see Christ's day, John 8:56.¶

4. *euphrainō* (εὐφραίνω, 2165), in the active voice, "to cheer, gladden" (*eu*, "well," *phrēn*, "the mind"), signifies in the passive voice "to rejoice, make merry"; it is translated "to rejoice" in Acts 2:26, RV, "was glad," KJV, "did ... rejoice," of the heart of Christ as foretold in Ps. 16:9 [cf. No. 3, II (b)]; in Acts 7:41, of Israel's idolatry; in Rom. 15:10 (quoted from the Sept. of Deut. 32:43, where it is a command to the Gentiles to "rejoice" with the Jews in their future deliverance by Christ from all their foes, at the establishment of the messianic kingdom) the apostle applies it to the effects of the gospel; in Gal. 4:27 (touching the barrenness of Sarah as referred to in Isa. 54:1, and there pointing to the ultimate restoration of Israel to God's favor, cf. 51:2), the word is applied to the effects of the gospel, in that the progeny of grace would greatly exceed the number of those who had acknowledged allegiance to the Law; grace and faith are fruitful, law and works are barren as a means of salvation; in Rev. 12:12, it is used in a call to the heavens to "rejoice" at the casting out of Satan and the inauguration of the Kingdom of God in manifestation and the authority of His Christ; in 18:20, of a call to heaven, saints, apostles, prophets, to "rejoice" in the destruction of Babylon. See GLAD, No. 3, MERRY, No. 1.

5. *kauchaomai* (καυχάομαι, 2744), "to boast, to glory," is rendered "to rejoice," (a) Rom. 5:2, in hope of the glory of God; (b) 5:3, RV (KJV "glory"), in tribulation; (c) 5:11, RV (KJV, "we joy"), in God; (d) Phil. 3:3, RV, "glory" (KJV, "rejoice") in Christ Jesus; (e) Jas. 1:9 (RV, "glory," KJV, "rejoice"), the brother of low degree in his high estate; the rich brother in being made low; (f) Jas. 4:16, of evil glorying. See GLORY (to boast).

Notes: (1) In Jas. 2:13, KJV, *katakauchaomai*,

"to glory, boast against," is translated "rejoiceth against" (RV, "glorieth against"). See GLORY (to boast), A, No. 2. (2) The nouns *kauchēma*, *kauchēsis*, signifying "glorying, boasting," are always so rendered in the RV, where the KJV has "rejoicing," the former in 2 Cor. 1:14; Gal. 6:4; Phil. 1:26; 2:16; Heb. 3:6; the latter in 1 Cor. 15:31; 2 Cor. 1:12; 1 Thess. 2:19; Jas. 4:16. See GLORY, B, Nos. 1 and 2.

RELEASE

apoluō (ἀπολύω, 630), "to loose from," is translated "to release" in Matt. 18:27, RV (KJV, "loosed"); 27:15, 17, 21, 26; Mark 15:6, 9, 11, 15; Luke 6:37 (twice), RV (KJV, "forgive" and "ye shall be forgiven"); 23:16 (v. 17, in some mss.), 18, 20, 25; 23:22, RV (KJV, "let ... go"); John 18:39 (twice); 19:10; in 19:12, in the 1st part, KJV and RV; in the 2nd part, RV, "release" (KJV, "let ... go"); so in Acts 3:13. See DEPART, DISMISS.

Note: For *aphesis*, "release," Luke 4:18, RV, see DELIVERANCE.

RELIEF

1. *diakonia* (διακονία, 1248), "ministry," is translated "relief" in Acts 11:29 [RV, marg., "for (*eis*) ministry"].

2. *anesis* (ἄνεσις, 425), "a loosening, relaxation" (akin to *aniēmi*, "to send away, let go, loosen"), is translated "relief" in 2 Cor. 2:13 and 7:5 (KJV, "rest"). See REST.

RELIEVE

eparkeō (ἐπαρκέω, 1884) signifies "to be strong enough for," and so either "to ward off," or "to aid, to relieve" (a strengthened form of *arkeō*, which has the same three meanings, *epi* being intensive); it is used in 1 Tim. 5:10, 16 (twice).¶

RELIGION

1. *thrēskeia* (θρησκεία, 2356) signifies "religion" in its external aspect (akin to *thrēskos*, see below), "religious worship," especially the ceremonial service of "religion"; it is used of the "religion" of the Jews, Acts 26:5; of the "worshiping" of angels, Col. 2:18, which they themselves repudiate (Rev. 22:8, 9); "there was an officious parade of humility in selecting these lower beings as intercessors rather than appealing directly to the Throne of Grace" (Lightfoot); in Jas. 1:26, 27 the writer purposely uses the word to set in contrast to that which is unreal and deceptive, and the "pure religion" which consists in visiting "the fatherless and widows in their affliction," and in keeping oneself "unspotted from the world." He is "not herein affirm-

ing ... these offices to be the sum total, nor yet the great essentials, of true religion, but declares them to be the body, the *thrēskeia*, of which godliness, or the love of God, is the informing soul" (Trench).¶

2. *deisidaimonia* (δεισιδαιμονία, 1175) primarily denotes "fear of the gods" (from *deidō*, "to fear," *daimōn*, "a pagan deity," Eng., "demon"), regarded whether as a religious attitude, or, in its usual meaning, with a condemnatory or contemptuous significance, "superstition." That is how Festus regarded the Jews' "religion," Acts 25:19, KJV and RV marg., "superstition" (RV, "religion"). See RELIGIOUS, *Note* (1), and under SUPERSTITIOUS.¶

Notes: (1) *Thrēskeia* is external, *theosebeia* is the reverential worship of God (see GODLINESS), *eusebeia* is piety (see GODLINESS), *eulabeia* the devotedness arising from godly fear (see FEAR). (2) For "the Jews' religion," Gal. 1:13, 14, see JEWS, B.

RELIGIOUS

thrēskos (θρῆσκος, 2357), "religious, careful of the externals of divine service," akin to *thrēskeia* (see above), is used in Jas. 1:26.¶

Notes: (1) For *deisidaimōn*, Acts 17:22, RV, marg., "religious," see SUPERSTITIOUS. (2) For "religious (proselytes)," KJV in Acts 13:43, see DEVOUT, No. 3.

REMAIN

1. *menō* (μένω, 3306), "to stay, abide," is frequently rendered "to remain," e.g., Matt. 11:23; Luke 10:7; John 1:33, KJV (RV, "abiding"); 9:41 (in 15:11, the best texts have the verb to be, see RV); 15:16, KJV (RV, "abide"); 19:31; Acts 5:4 (twice), RV, "whiles it remained, did it (not) remain (thine own)?"; 27:41; 1 Cor. 7:11; 15:6; 2 Cor. 3:11, 14; 9:9, KJV (RV, "abideth"); Heb. 12:27; 1 John 3:9. See ABIDE.

2. *diamenō* (διαμένω, 1265), "to remain throughout" (*dia*, "through," and No. 1), is translated "to remain" in Luke 1:22; Heb. 1:11, KJV (RV, "Thou continuest"). See CONTINUE, No. 4.

3. *apoleipō* (ἀπολείπω, 620), in the passive voice, "to be reserved, to remain," is translated "remaineth" in Heb. 4:6, 9; 10:26. See LEAVE, No. 4.

4. *perileipō* (περιλείπω, 4035), "to leave over," used in the middle voice, is translated "remain" in 1 Thess. 4:15, 17, KJV (RV, "are left"), where it stands for the living believers at the coming (the beginning of the Parousia) of Christ.¶

5. *perisseuō* (περισσεύω, 4052), "to abound, to be over and above, to remain over," is ren-

dered "(that which) remained over" in Matt. 14:20, RV; and Luke 9:17, RV (KJV, "remained"); John 6:12, 13 (KJV, " ... over and above"). See ABUNDANCE, B, No. 1.

Notes: (1) In Mark 8:8, *perisseuma*, "an abundance," is used in the plural, RV, "(of broken pieces) that remained over" (KJV "that was left"). (2) In 1 Cor. 7:29, KJV, *to loipon*, lit., "(as to) what is left," "(as for) the rest," is translated "it remaineth" (RV, "henceforth"); in Rev. 3:2, *ta loipa*, the plural, "the things that remain."

REMEMBER, REMEMBRANCE, REMINDED

A. Verbs.

1. *mimnēskō* (μιμνήσκω, 3403), from the older form *mnaomai*, in the active voice signifies "to remind"; in the middle voice, "to remind oneself of," hence, "to remember, to be mindful of"; the later form is found only in the present tense, in Heb. 2:6, "are mindful of," and 13:3, "remember"; the perfect tense in 1 Cor. 11:2 and in 2 Tim. 1:4 (RV, "remembering," KJV, "being mindful of"), is used with a present meaning. RV variations from the KJV are, in Luke 1:54, RV, "that He might remember" (KJV, "in remembrance of"); 2 Pet. 3:2, "remember" (KJV, "be mindful of"); Rev. 16:19 (passive voice), "was remembered" (KJV, "came in remembrance"). The passive voice is used also in Acts 10:31, KJV and RV, "are had in remembrance." See MINDFUL OF (to be).

2. *mnēmoneuō* (μνημονεύω, 3421) signifies "to call to mind, remember"; it is used absolutely in Mark 8:18; everywhere else it has an object, (*a*) persons, Luke 17:32; Gal. 2:10; 2 Tim. 2:8, where the RV rightly has "remember Jesus Christ, risen from the dead"; Paul was not reminding Timothy (nor did he need to) that Christ was raised from the dead (KJV), what was needful for him was to "remember" (to keep in mind) the One who rose, the Source and Supplier of all his requirements; (*b*) things, e.g., Matt. 16:9; John 15:20; 16:21; Acts 20:35; Col. 4:18; 1 Thess. 1:3; 2:9; Heb. 11:15, "had been mindful of"; 13:7; Rev. 18:5; (*c*) a clause, representing a circumstance, etc., John 16:4; Acts 20:31; Eph. 2:11; 2 Thess. 2:5; Rev. 2:5; 3:3; in Heb. 11:22 it signifies "to make mention of." See MENTION.¶

3. *anamimnēskō* (ἀναμιμνήσκω, 363), *ana*, "back," and No. 1, signifies in the active voice "to remind, call to one's mind," 1 Cor. 4:17, "put (KJV, bring) ... into remembrance"; so 2 Tim. 1:6; in the passive voice, "to remember, call to (one's own) mind," Mark 11:21, "calling to remembrance"; 14:72, "called to mind";

2 Cor. 7:15, "remembereth"; Heb. 10:32, "call to remembrance."¶

4. *hupomimnēskō* (ὑπομιμνήσκω, 5279) signifies "to cause one to remember, put one in mind of" (*hupo*, "under," often implying suggestion, and No. 1), John 14:26, "shall . . . bring . . . to (your) remembrance"; 2 Tim. 2:14, "put . . . in remembrance"; Titus 3:1, "put . . . in mind"; 3 John 10, RV, "I will bring to remembrance" (KJV, "I will remember"); Jude 5, "to put . . . in remembrance." In Luke 22:61 it is used in the passive voice, "(Peter) remembered," lit., "was put in mind."¶

5. *epanamimnēskō* (ἐπαναμιμνήσκω, 1878), "to remind again" (*epi*, "upon," and No. 3), is used in Rom. 15:15, RV, "putting (you) again in remembrance," KJV, "putting (you) in mind." See MIND.¶

Note: In 1 Tim. 4:6, KJV, *hupotithēmi*, "to lay under, to suggest," is translated "put . . . in remembrance" (RV, "put . . . in mind"). See MIND.

B. Nouns.

1. *anamnēsis* (ἀνάμνησις, 364), "a remembrance" (*ana*, "up," or "again," and A, No. 1), is used (*a*) in Christ's command in the institution of the Lord's Supper, Luke 22:19; 1 Cor. 11:24, 25, not "in memory of" but in an affectionate calling of the Person Himself to mind; (*b*) of the "remembrance" of sins, Heb. 10:3, RV, "a remembrance" (KJV, "a remembrance again"; but the prefix *ana* does not here signify "again"); what is indicated, in regard to the sacrifices under the Law, is not simply an external bringing to "remembrance," but an awakening of mind.¶ In the Sept., Lev. 24:7; Num. 10:10; Pss. 38 and 70, Titles.¶

2. *hupomnēsis* (ὑπόμνησις, 5280) denotes "a reminding, a reminder"; in 2 Tim. 1:5 it is used with *lambanō*, "to receive," lit., "having received a reminder," RV, "having been reminded" (KJV, "when I call to remembrance"); in 2 Pet. 1:13 and 3:1, "remembrance."¶

Note: A distinction has been drawn between Nos. 1 and 2, in that *anamnēsis* indicates an unassisted recalling, *hupomnēsis*, a "remembrance" prompted by another.

3. *mneia* (μνεία, 3417) denotes "a remembrance," or "a mention." See MENTION.

4. *mnēmē* (μνήμη, 3420) denotes "a memory" (akin to *mnaomai*, A, No. 1), "remembrance, mention," 2 Pet. 1:15, "remembrance"; here, however, it is used with *poieō*, "to make" (middle voice), and some suggest that the meaning is "to make mention."¶

REMISSION, REMIT

A. Nouns.

1. *aphesis* (ἄφεσις, 859), "a dismissal, release" (from *aphiēmi*, B), is used of the forgiveness of sins and translated "remission" in Matt. 26:28; Mark 1:4; Luke 1:77; 3:3; 24:47; Acts 2:38; 5:31 (KJV, "forgiveness"); 10:43; 13:38, RV (KJV, "forgiveness"); 26:18 (ditto); Heb. 9:22; 10:18. See FORGIVE, B, and A, No. 1.

2. *paresis* (πάρεσις, 3929), "a passing by of debt or sin," Rom. 3:25, KJV, "remission" (RV and KJV marg., "passing over"). See PASSING OVER.¶

Note: No. 2 is a matter of forbearance, No. 1 a matter of grace.

B. Verb.

aphiēmi (ἀφίημι, 863), "to send away" (akin to A, No. 1), is translated "to remit" in John 20:23 (twice), KJV (RV, "to forgive"). Scripture makes clear that the Lord's words could not have been intended to bestow the exercise of absolution, which Scripture declares is the prerogative of God alone. There is no instance in the NT of this act on the part of the apostles. The words are to be understood in a "declarative" sense; the statement has regard to the effects of their ministry of the gospel, with its twofold effects of "remission" or retention. They could not, nor could anyone subsequently, forgive sins, any more than that Joseph actually restored the butler to his office and hanged the baker (Gen. 41:13), or any more than that the prophets actually accomplished things when they declared that they were about to be done (Jer. 1:10; Ezek. 43:3). See FORGIVE, No. 1.

REMNANT

1. *loipos* (λοιπός, 3062**), an adjective (akin to *leipō*, "to leave") signifying "remaining," is used as a noun and translated "the rest" in the RV, where the KJV has "the remnant," Matt. 22:6; Rev. 11:13; 12:17; 19:21. See OTHER, RESIDUE, REST (the).

2. *leimma* (λεῖμμα, 3005), "that which is left" (akin to *leipō*, "to leave"), "a remnant," is used in Rom. 11:5, "there is a remnant," more lit., "there has come to be a remnant," i.e., there is a spiritual "remnant" saved by the gospel from the midst of apostate Israel. While in one sense there has been and is a considerable number, yet, compared with the whole nation, past and present, the "remnant" is small, and as such is an evidence of God's electing grace (see v. 4).¶ In the Sept., 2 Kings 19:4.¶

3. *hupoleimma* (ὑπόλειμμα, 5259 and 3005), *hupo*, "under," signifying "diminution," and No. 2, is used in Rom. 9:27: some mss.

have *kataleimma*, which has virtually the same meaning (*kata*, "down, behind"), "a remnant," where the contrast is drawn between the number of Israel as a whole, and the small number in it of those who are saved through the gospel. The quotation is chiefly from the Sept. of Isa. 10:22, 23, with a modification recalling Hosea 1:10, especially with regard to the word "number." The return of the "remnant" is indicated in the name "Shear-Jashub," see Isa. 7:3, marg. The primary reference was to the return of a remnant from captivity to their own land and to God Himself; here the application is to the effects of the gospel. There is stress on the word "remnant."¶

REMOVE, REMOVING

A. Verbs.

1. *metabainō* (μεταβαίνω, 3327), "to pass over from one place to another" (*meta*, implying "change," and *bainō*, "to go"), is translated "to remove" in Matt. 17:20 (twice). See PASS, No. 7.

2. *methistēmi* (μεθίστημι, 3179) is used transitively in the sense of causing "to remove," in Acts 13:22, of the "removing" of King Saul, by bringing about his death; in 1 Cor. 13:2, of "removing" mountains. See PUT, No. 23, TRANSLATE, TURN.

3. *metatithēmi* (μετατίθημι, 3346), "to remove a person or thing from one place to another" (*meta*, implying "change," *tithēmi*, "to put"), e.g., Acts 7:16, "were carried over," signifies, in the middle voice, "to change oneself," and is so used in Gal. 1:6 "(I marvel that) ye are ... removing," RV (not as KJV, "removed"); the present tense suggests that the defection of the Galatians from the truth was not yet complete and would continue unless they changed their views. The middle voice indicates that they were themselves responsible for their declension, rather than the Judaizers who had influenced them. See CARRY, No. 5.

4. *parapherō* (παραφέρω, 3911), lit., "to bring to or before" (*para*, "beside," *pherō*, "to carry"), "to take or carry away," is translated "remove" in the Lord's prayer in Gethsemane, Mark 14:36, RV (KJV, "take away"); Luke 22:42. See TAKE. In the Sept., 1 Sam. 21:13.¶

5. *metoikizō* (μετοικίζω, 3351), "to remove to a new abode, cause to migrate" (*meta*, implying "change," *oikos*, "a dwelling place"), is translated "removed" in Acts 7:4; "I will carry ... away" (v. 43). See CARRYING AWAY, B.

6. *apochōrizō* (ἀποχωρίζω, 673), "to separate, part asunder," is used in the passive voice in Rev. 6:14, "(the heaven) was removed," RV (KJV, "departed"). See DEPART, No. 14.

Notes: (1) In Matt. 21:21 and Mark 11:23, *airō*, "to lift, take up," is translated "be thou removed" (RV, "be thou taken up"). (2) In Rev. 2:5, KJV, *kineō*, "to move" (RV), is translated "will remove." See MOVE.

B. Noun.

metathesis (μετάθεσις, 3331), "change of position" (transliterated in Eng., "metathesis," a transposition of the letter of a word), from *meta*, implying "change," and *tithēmi*, "to place," is used only in Hebrews and translated "removing" in 12:27; "translation" in 11:5; "change" in 7:12. See CHANGE, A.¶

REND, RENT (Verb and Noun)

A. Verbs.

1. *rhēgnumi* (ῥήγνυμι, 4486), "to tear, rend," is translated "to rend" in Matt. 7:6, of swine. See BREAK, A, No. 6.

2. *diarrhēssō*, or *diarēssō* (διαρήσσω, 1284), a late form of *diarrhēgnumi*, "to break asunder, rend" (*dia*, "through," and No. 1), is used of "rending" one's garments, Matt. 26:65; Mark 14:63; Acts 14:14. See BREAK, A, No. 7.

3. *perirrhēgnumi*, or *perirēgnumi* (περιρήγνυμι, 4048), "to tear off all round" (*peri*, "around"), is said of garments in Acts 16:22.¶

4. *schizō* (σχίζω, 4977), "to split, rend open," translated "to rend" in Matt. 27:51 (twice); Mark 1:10, RV, "rent asunder" (KJV, "open"); 15:38; Luke 5:36, RV, "rendeth (from)"; the KJV follows the mss. which omit it in the 1st part of this verse; 23:45; John 19:24; 21:11, RV, "rent" (KJV, "broken"), of a net. See BREAK, A, No. 12.

5. *diaspaō* (διασπάω, 1288), "to tear asunder," is translated "rent asunder" in Mark 5:4, RV (KJV, "plucked asunder"); for Acts 23:10, see TEAR.¶

Note: In Mark 9:26, KJV, *sparassō*, "to tear" (RV), is rendered "rent." See TEAR.

B. Noun.

schisma (σχίσμα, 4978), "a rent, division" (akin to A, No. 4), signifies a "rent" in wineskins in Matt. 9:16; Mark 2:21. See DIVISION, No. 3.

RENDER

1. *apodidōmi* (ἀποδίδωμι, 591), "to give up or back," is translated "to render," (*a*) of righteous acts, (1) human, Matt. 21:41; 22:21; Mark 12:17; Luke 16:2, RV (KJV, "give"); Luke 20:25; Rom. 13:7; 1 Cor. 7:3; (2) divine, Matt. 16:27, RV, "shall render" (KJV, "shall reward"), an important RV change; Rom. 2:6; 2 Tim. 4:14, RV (KJV, "reward"); Rev. 18:6 (ditto); 22:12, RV (KJV, "give"); (*b*) of unrighteous acts, Rom. 12:17, RV (KJV, "recompense"); 1 Thess. 5:15;

1 Pet. 3:9. See DELIVER, A, No. 3, RECOMPENSE, B, No. 2.

2. *antapodidōmi* (ἀνταποδίδωμι, 467), "to give in return for," is translated "render" in 1 Thess. 3:9. See RECOMPENSE, REPAY.

3. *parechō* (παρέχω, 3930), "to furnish, provide, supply," is translated "render" in Col. 4:1, RV (KJV, "give"), of what is due from masters to servants. See GIVE, No. 8.

4. *didōmi* (δίδωμι, 1325), "to give," is translated "rendering" in 2 Thess. 1:8, RV (KJV, "taking"), of the divine execution of vengeance at the revelation of Christ from heaven hereafter. See GIVE, No. 1.

RENEW, RENEWING (Verb and Noun)

A. Verbs.

1. *anakainoō* (ἀνακαινόω, 341), "to make new" (*ana*, "back" or "again," *kainos*, "new," not recent but different), "to renew," is used in the passive voice in 2 Cor. 4:16, of the daily renewal of "the inward man" (in contrast to the physical frame), i.e., of the "renewal" of spiritual power; in Col. 3:10, of "the new man" (in contrast to the old unregenerate nature), which "is being renewed unto knowledge," RV (cf. No. 3 in Eph. 4:23), i.e., the true knowledge in Christ, as opposed to heretical teachings.¶ *Note:* This word has not been found elsewhere in Greek writings as yet, though No. 2 is, which would prevent the supposition that the apostle coined a new word.

2. *anakainizō* (ἀνακαινίζω, 340) is a variant form of No. 1, used in Heb. 6:6, of the impossibility of "renewing" to repentance those Jews who professedly adhered to the Christian faith, if, after their experiences of it (not actual possession of its regenerating effects), they apostatized into their former Judaism.¶ In the Sept., 2 Chron. 15:8; Ps. 39:2; 103:5; 104:30; Lam. 5:21.¶

3. *ananeoō* (ἀνανεόω, 365), "to renew, make young" (*ana*, as in No. 1, and *neos*, "recent," not different), is used in Eph. 4:23, "be renewed (in the spirit of your mind)." The "renewal" here mentioned is not that of the mind itself in its natural powers of memory, judgment and perception, but "the spirit of the mind," which, under the controlling power of the indwelling Holy Spirit, directs its bent and energies Godward in the enjoyment of "fellowship with the Father and with His Son, Jesus Christ," and of the fulfillment of the will of God.¶ The word is frequent in inscriptions and in the papyri.

B. Noun.

anakainōsis (ἀνακαίνωσις, 342), akin to A, No. 1, "a renewal," is used in Rom. 12:2, "the renewing (of your mind)," i.e., the adjustment of the moral and spiritual vision and thinking to the mind of God, which is designed to have a transforming effect upon the life; in Titus 3:5, where "the renewing of the Holy Spirit" is not a fresh bestowment of the Spirit, but a revival of His power, developing the Christian life; this passage stresses the continual operation of the indwelling Spirit of God; the Romans passage stresses the willing response on the part of the believer.¶

RENOUNCE

1. *apeipon* (ἀπεῖπον, 550), lit., "to tell from" (*apo*, "from," *eipon*, an aorist form used to supply parts of *legō*, "to say"), signifies "to renounce," 2 Cor. 4:2 (middle voice), of disowning "the hidden things of shame."¶ In the Sept. of 1 Kings 11:2 it signifies "to forbid," a meaning found in the papyri. The meaning "to renounce" may therefore carry with it the thought of forbidding the approach of the things disowned.

2. *apotassō* (ἀποτάσσω, 657), "to set apart, to appoint," a meaning found in the papyri (*apo*, from, *tassō*, "to arrange"), is used in the middle voice in the sense either of "taking leave of," e.g., Acts 18:18, or "forsaking," Luke 14:33, RV, "renounceth" (KJV "forsaketh"). See FORSAKE, LEAVE.

REPAY

1. *apodidōmi* (ἀποδίδωμι, 591), "to give back," is translated "I will repay" in Luke 10:35. See DELIVER, A, No. 3, RECOMPENSE, B, No. 2, RENDER, No. 1.

2. *antapodidōmi* (ἀνταποδίδωμι, 467), "to give in return for," is translated "I will repay" in Rom. 12:19, KJV (RV, "I will recompense"). See RECOMPENSE, B, No. 1, RENDER, No. 2.

3. *apotinō* or *apotiō* (ἀποτίνω, 661), signifying "to pay off" (*apo*, "off," *tinō*, "to pay a fine"), is used in Philem. 19, of Paul's promise to "repay" whatever Onesimus owed Philemon, or to whatever extent the runaway slave had wronged his master.¶ The verb is very common in the papyri, e.g., in a contract of apprenticeship the father has to pay a forfeit for each day of the son's absence from work. Moulton and Milligan, who draw this and other illustrations in the way of "repayment," point out that "this verb is stronger than *apodidōmi* (No. 1), and carries with it the idea of "repayment" by way of a fine or punishment, a fact which lends emphasis to its use in Philem. 19."

REPENT, REPENTANCE

A. Verbs.

1. *metanoeō* (μετανοέω, 3340), lit., "to perceive afterwards" (*meta*, "after," implying "change," *noeō*, "to perceive"; *nous*, "the mind, the seat of moral reflection"), in contrast to *pronoeō*, "to perceive beforehand," hence signifies "to change one's mind or purpose," always, in the NT, involving a change for the better, an amendment, and always, except in Luke 17:3, 4, of "repentance" from sin. The word is found in the Synoptic Gospels (in Luke, nine times), in Acts five times, in the Apocalypse twelve times, eight in the messages to the churches, 2:5 (twice), 16, 21 (twice), RV, "she willeth not to repent" (2nd part); 3:3, 19 (the only churches in those chapters which contain no exhortation in this respect are those at Smyrna and Philadelphia); elsewhere only in 2 Cor. 12:21. See also the general *Note* below.

2. *metamelomai* (μεταμέλομαι, 3338), *meta*, as in No. 1, and *melō*, "to care for," is used in the passive voice with middle voice sense, signifying "to regret, to repent oneself," Matt. 21:29, RV, "repented himself"; v. 32, RV, "ye did (not) repent yourselves" (KJV, "ye repented not"); 27:3, "repented himself"; 2 Cor. 7:8 (twice), RV, "regret" in each case; Heb. 7:21, where alone in the NT it is said (negatively) of God.¶

B. Adjective.

ametamelētos (ἀμεταμέλητος, 278), "not repented of, unregretted" (*a*, negative, and a verbal adjective of A, No. 2), signifies "without change of purpose"; it is said (*a*) of God in regard to his "gifts and calling," Rom. 11:29; (*b*) of man, 2 Cor. 7:10, RV, "[repentance (*metanoia*, see C)] ... which bringeth no regret" (KJV, "not to be repented of"); the difference between *metanoia* and *metamelomai*, illustrated here, is briefly expressed in the contrast between "repentance" and "regret."¶

C. Noun.

metanoia (μετάνοια, 3341), "afterthought, change of mind, repentance," corresponds in meaning to A, No. 1, and is used of "repentance" from sin or evil, except in Heb. 12:17, where the word "repentance" seems to mean, not simply a change of Isaac's mind, but such a change as would reverse the effects of his own previous state of mind. Esau's birthright-bargain could not be recalled; it involved an irretrievable loss.

As regards "repentance" from sin, (*a*) the requirement by God on man's part is set forth, e.g., in Matt. 3:8; Luke 3:8; Acts 20:21; 26:20; (*b*) the mercy of God in giving "repentance" or leading men to it is set forth, e.g., in Acts 5:31; 11:18; Rom. 2:4; 2 Tim. 2:25. The most authentic mss. omit the word in Matt. 9:13 and Mark 2:17, as in the RV.

Note: In the OT, "repentance" with reference to sin is not so prominent as that change of mind or purpose, out of pity for those who have been affected by one's action, or in whom the results of the action have not fulfilled expectations, a "repentance" attributed both to God and to man, e.g., Gen. 6:6; Exod. 32:14 (that this does not imply anything contrary to God's immutability, but that the aspect of His mind is changed toward an object that has itself changed, see under RECONCILE).

In the NT the subject chiefly has reference to "repentance" from sin, and this change of mind involves both a turning from sin and a turning to God. The parable of the Prodigal Son is an outstanding illustration of this. Christ began His ministry with a call to "repentance," Matt. 4:17, but the call is addressed, not as in the OT to the nation, but to the individual. In the Gospel of John, as distinct from the Synoptic Gospels, referred to above, "repentance" is not mentioned, even in connection with John the Baptist's preaching; in John's gospel and 1st epistle the effects are stressed, e.g., in the new birth, and, generally, in the active turning from sin to God by the exercise of faith (John 3:3; 9:38; 1 John 1:9), as in the NT in general.

REPETITIONS (use vain)

battalogeō or *battologeō* (βατταλογέω, 945), "to repeat idly," is used in Matt. 6:7, "use (not) vain repetitions"; the meaning "to stammer" is scarcely to be associated with this word. The word is probably from an Aramaic phrase and onomatopoeic in character. The rendering of the Sinaitic Syriac is "Do not be saying *battalatha*, idle things," i.e., meaningless and mechanically repeated phrases, the reference being to pagan (not Jewish) modes of prayer. *Battalos*, "the Gabbler," was a nickname for Demosthenes, the great orator, assigned to him by his rivals.¶

REPLY

antapokrinomai (ἀνταποκρίνομαι, 470) is translated "repliest against" in Rom. 9:20 (*anti*, "against," *apokrinomai*, "to answer"); in Luke 14:6, "answer again." See ANSWER, B, No. 2.¶

REPORT (Noun and Verb)

A. Nouns.

1. *akoē* (ἀκοή, 189), "a hearing," is translated "report" in John 12:38 and Rom. 10:16,

and in the RV of Matt. 4:24; 14:1; Mark 1:28. See HEARING, B, No. 1.

2. *euphēmia* (εὐφημία, 2162), "a good report, good reputation" (*eu*, "well," *phēmē* "a saying or report"), is used in 2 Cor. 6:8. Contrast No. 3.¶

3. *dusphēmia* (δυσφημία, 1426), "evil-speaking, defamation" (*dus*-, an inseparable prefix, the opposite to *eu*, "well," see No. 2), is used in 2 Cor. 6:8.¶

4. *logos* (λόγος, 3056), "a word," is translated "report," i.e., "a story, narrative"; in Luke 5:15 (KJV, "fame"); 7:17 (KJV, "rumor"); Acts 11:22 (KJV, "tidings"). See WORD.

Note: For *marturia*, rendered "report" in 1 Tim. 3:7, KJV, see TESTIMONY, WITNESS.

B. Adjective.

euphēmos (εὔφημος, 2613), akin to A, No. 2, primarily, "uttering words or sounds of good omen," then, "avoiding ill-omened words," and hence "fair-sounding," "of good report," is so rendered in Phil. 4:8.¶

C. Verbs.

1. *martureō* (μαρτυρέω, 3140), "to be a witness, bear witness, testify," signifies, in the passive voice, "to be well testified of, to have a good report," Acts 6:3, "of good (KJV, honest) report," lit., "being well testified of"; 10:22; 16:2; 22:12; 1 Tim. 5:10; in Heb. 11:2, 39, KJV, "obtained a good report" (RV, "had witness borne to them"); in 3 John 12, KJV, "hath good report" (RV, "hath the witness"), lit., "witness hath been borne." See TESTIFY, WITNESS.

2. *apangellō* (ἀπαγγέλλω, 518), "to report" (*apo*, "from," *angellō*, "to give a message"), "announce, declare" (by a messenger, speaker, or writer), is translated "reported" in Acts 4:23; 16:36, RV (KJV, "told"); v. 38 (some mss. have No. 3; KJV, "told"); "report" in 1 Cor. 14:25, KJV (RV, "declaring"); 1 Thess. 1:9, RV, "report" (KJV, "shew"); so Acts 28:21. See DECLARE, No. 2.

3. *anangellō* (ἀναγγέλλω, 312), "to bring back word," in later Greek came to have the same meaning as No. 2, "to announce, declare"; it is translated "are reported" in 1 Pet. 1:12, KJV (RV, "have been announced"). See DECLARE, No. 1.

4. *akouō* (ἀκούω, 191), "to hear," is used in the passive voice, impersonally, in 1 Cor. 5:1, lit., "it is heard" or "there is heard," translated "it is reported." See HEAR.

5. *blasphēmeō* (βλασφημέω, 987), "to speak slanderously, impiously, profanely" (*blaptō*, "to injure," and *phēmē*, "a saying"), is translated "we be slanderously reported" in Rom. 3:8 (passive voice). See BLASPHEME, B.

Note: In Matt. 28:15, KJV, *diaphēmizō*, "to

spread abroad" (*dia*, "throughout," *phēmē*, "a saying, report"), is translated "is commonly reported" (RV, "was spread abroad"). See BLAZE ABROAD.

REPROACH (Noun and Verb), REPROACHFULLY

A. Nouns.

1. *oneidismos* (ὀνειδισμός, 3680), "a reproach, defamation," is used in Rom. 15:3; 1 Tim. 3:7; Heb. 10:33; 11:26; 13:13.¶

2. *oneidos* (ὄνειδος, 3681), akin to No. 1, is used in Luke 1:25 in the concrete sense of "a matter of reproach, a disgrace."¶ To have no children was, in the Jewish mind, more than a misfortune, it might carry the implication that this was a divine punishment for some secret sin. Cf. Gen. 30:1; 1 Sam. 1:6–10.

3. *atimia* (ἀτιμία, 819), "dishonor," is translated "reproach" in 2 Cor. 11:21, KJV (RV, "disparagement"). See DISHONOR, SHAME, VILE.

Note: In 2 Cor. 12:10, KJV, *hubris*, "insolence, injury," is translated "reproaches" (RV, "injuries"). See HARM.

B. Verbs.

1. *oneidizō* (ὀνειδίζω, 3679), akin to A, Nos. 1 and 2, signifies (*a*), in the active voice, "to reproach, upbraid," Matt. 5:11, RV, "shall reproach" (KJV, "shall revile"); 11:20, "to upbraid"; 27:44, RV, "cast ... reproach" [KJV, "cast ... in (His) teeth"]; Mark 15:32 RV, "reproached" (KJV, "reviled"); 16:14 "upbraided"; Luke 6:22 "shall reproach"; Rom. 15:3; Jas. 1:5, "upbraideth"; (*b*) in the passive voice, "to suffer reproach, be reproached," 1 Tim. 4:10 (in some mss. in the 2nd part); 1 Pet. 4:14.¶

2. *hubrizō* (ὑβρίζω, 5195), akin to *hubris* (see A, Note), used transitively, denotes "to outrage, insult, treat insolently"; it is translated "Thou reproachest" in Luke 11:45. The word is much stronger than "to reproach"; the significance is "Thou insultest (even us)," i.e., who are superior to ordinary Pharisees. The lawyer's imputation was unjust; Christ's rebuke was not *hubris*, "insult." What He actually said was by way of "reproach" (*oneidizō*). See DESPITEFULLY.

Notes: (1) For *anepilēptos*, "without reproach," RV, in 1 Tim. 3:2; 5:7; 6:14, see BLAMELESS, B No. 5. (2) In 1 Tim. 5:14, KJV, *loidoria*, "reviling" (RV), used in the genitive case with *charin*, "in respect of," "for," is translated "reproachfully" (RV, "for reviling"). Cf. *loidoreō*, "to revile." See RAILING.

REPROBATE

adokimos (ἀδόκιμος, 96), signifying "not standing the test, rejected" (*a*, negative, *doki*-

mos, "approved"), was primarily applied to metals (cf. Isa. 1:22); it is used always in the NT in a passive sense, (*a*) of things, Heb. 6:8, "rejected," of land that bears thorns and thistles; (*b*) of persons, Rom. 1:28, of a "reprobate mind," a mind of which God cannot approve, and which must be rejected by Him, the effect of refusing "to have God in *their* knowledge"; in 1 Cor. 9:27 (for which see CAST, REJECTED); 2 Cor. 13:5, 6, 7, where the RV rightly translates the adjective "reprobate" (KJV, "reprobates"), here the reference is to the great test as to whether Christ is in a person; in 2 Tim. 3:8 of those "reprobate concerning the faith," i.e., men whose moral sense is perverted and whose minds are beclouded with their own speculations; in Titus 1:16, of the defiled, who are "unto every good work reprobate," i.e., if they are put to the test in regard to any good work (in contrast to their profession), they can only be rejected.¶ In the Sept., Prov. 25:4; Isa. 1:22.¶

REPROOF, REPROVE

A. Noun.

elegmos (ἐλεγμός, 1650v), "a reproof" (akin to B), is found in the best texts in 2 Tim. 3:16 (some mss. have *elenchos*, which denotes "a proof, proving, test," as in Heb. 11:1, "proving," RV marg., "test").¶ Cf. *elenxis*, "rebuke," 2 Pet. 2:16 (lit., "had rebuke").¶

B. Verb.

elenchō (ἐλέγχω, 1651), "to convict, rebuke, reprove," is translated "to reprove" in Luke 3:19; John 3:20, RV marg., "convicted"; the real meaning here is "exposed" (KJV marg., "discovered"); Eph. 5:11, 13, where "to expose" is again the significance; in John 16:8, KJV, "will reprove" (RV, "will convict"); in 1 Cor. 14:24, RV, "reproved" (KJV, "convinced"); in the following the RV has "to reprove," for KJV, "to rebuke," 1 Tim. 5:20; Titus 2:15; Heb. 12:5; Rev. 3:19; for synonymous words see CONVICT and REBUKE.

REPUTATION, REPUTE

dokeō (δοκέω, 1380) signifies (*a*) "to be of opinion" (akin to *doxa*, "an opinion"), "to suppose," e.g., Luke 12:51; 13:2 (see SUPPOSE); (*b*) "to seem, to be reputed"; in Gal. 2:2, RV, "who were of repute" (KJV, "which were of reputation"); in 2:6 (twice), and 9, RV, "were reputed" and "were of repute" (KJV, "seemed"); in each case the present participle of the verb with the article is used, lit., "(well) thought of" by them, persons held in consideration; in v. 6, RV, "(those) who were reputed to be somewhat" (KJV, "who seemed to be somewhat"); so v. 9, where there is no irony [cf. the rendering "are

accounted" in Mark 10:42 (i.e., not rulers nominally)], Paul recognized that James, Cephas, and John were, as they were "reputed" by the church at Jerusalem, its responsible guides; (*c*) impersonally, "to think, to seem good." See SEEM and THINK.

The first meaning, "to suppose," implies a subjective opinion based on thought; the second meaning, exemplified in the Galatians passages, expresses, from the standpoint of the observer, his own judgment about a matter (Trench, *Syn.*, §lxxx).

Notes: (1) In Acts 5:34, KJV, *timios*, "honored, had in honor" (RV), is translated "had in reputation." (2) In Phil. 2:29, KJV, *entimos*, "honorable," with *echō*, "to have," i.e., "to hold in honor," is translated "hold . . . in reputation" (RV, "hold . . . in honor"). (3) For *kenoō*, in Phil. 2:7, KJV, "made (Himself) of no reputation," see EMPTY.

REQUEST (Noun and Verb)

A. Nouns.

1. *aitēma* (αἴτημα, 155) denotes "that which has been asked for" (akin to *aiteō*, "to ask"); in Luke 23:24, RV, "what they asked for" (KJV, "as they required"), lit., "their request (should be done, *ginomai*)"; in Phil. 4:6, "requests"; in 1 John 5:15, "petitions." See PETITION, REQUIRE.¶

2. *deēsis* (δέησις, 1162), "an asking, entreaty, supplication," is translated "request" in Phil. 1:4, KJV (RV, "supplication"). See PRAYER, SUPPLICATION.

B. Verbs.

1. *deomai* (δέομαι, 1189), akin to A, No. 2, "to beseech, pray, request," is translated "to make request" in Rom. 1:10. See BESEECH, No. 3.

2. *aiteō* (αἰτέω, 154), "to ask," is translated "to make request" in Col. 1:9, RV (KJV, "to desire"). See ASK, No. 1.

3. *erōtaō* (ἐρωτάω, 2065), "to ask," is translated "to make request" in 1 John 5:16. See ASK, No. 2 and remarks on the difference between Nos. 1 and 2.

REQUIRE

1. *zēteō* (ζητέω, 2212), "to seek, seek after," also signifies "to require, demand," "shall be required," Luke 12:48; in 1 Cor. 4:2, "it is required (in stewards)." See DESIRE, *Note* (2), ENDEAVOR, GO, *Note* (2) (*a*), SEEK.

2. *ekzēteō* (ἐκζητέω, 1567), "to seek out" (*ek*, "out," and No. 1), also denotes "to demand, require," Luke 11:50, 51, of executing vengeance for the slaughter of the prophets (cf. 2 Sam. 4:11; Ezek. 3:18). See SEEK.

3. *apaiteō* (ἀπαιτέω, 523), "to ask back, demand back" (*apo*, "from," or "back," *aiteō*, "to ask"), is translated "shall be required" in Luke 12:20, lit. "do they require," in the impersonal sense; elsewhere, Luke 6:30, "to ask again."¶ It is used in the papyri frequently in the sense of "demanding, making demands."

4. *prassō* (πράσσω, 4238), "to do, practice, perform," is used financially in the sense of "exacting" payment, in Luke 19:23. See EXTORT, A.

Notes: (1) In Luke 23:23, KJV, *aiteō*, "to ask" (middle voice) is translated "requiring" (RV, "asking'); so in 1 Cor. 1:22 (active voice), KJV, "require" (RV, "ask"). (2) In Luke 23:24, KJV, the noun *aitēma* (see REQUEST), "that which is asked for," is translated "as they required" (RV, "what they asked for"). (3) In 1 Cor. 7:36 the rendering "need so requireth" (RV) represents the phrase *houtōs* ("thus") *opheilei* ("it ought") *genesthai* ("to become," i.e., "to be done").

REQUITE

amoibē (ἀμοιβή, 287), "a requital, recompence" (akin to *ameibomai*, "to repay," not found in the NT), is used with the verb *apodidōmi*, "to render," in 1 Tim. 5:4, and translated "to requite."¶ This use is illustrated in the papyri by way of making a return, conferring a benefaction in return for something (Moulton and Milligan).

RESCUE

exaireō (ἐξαιρέω, 1807), "to take out" (*ek*, "from," *haireō*, "to take"), is used of "delivering" from persons and circumstances, and translated "rescued" in Acts 23:27. See DELIVER, No. 8, PLUCK.

For RESEMBLE, Luke 13:18, KJV, see LIKEN, B, No. 1.

RESERVE

tēreō (τηρέω, 5083), "to guard, keep, preserve, give heed to," is translated "to reserve," (*a*) with a happy issue, 1 Pet. 1:4; (*b*) with a retributive issue, 2 Pet. 2:4; v. 9, KJV (RV, "keep"); 2:17; 3:7; Jude 6, KJV (RV, "hath kept"); v. 13; (*c*) with the possibility either of deliverance or execution, Acts 25:21, KJV (RV, "kept"). See KEEP.

Note: In Rom. 11:4, KJV, *kataleipō*, "to leave behind, leave remaining," is translated "I have reserved" (RV, "I have left"). See LEAVE.

RESIDUE

kataloipos (κατάλοιπος, 2645), an adjective denoting "left remaining" (*kata*, "after, behind," *leipō*, "to leave"), akin to the verb in the *Note* above, is translated "residue" in Acts 15:17, from the Sept. of Amos 9:12.¶

Note: In Mark 16:13, KJV, the plural of *loipos*, "left," is translated "residue" (RV, "rest").

RESIST

1. *anthistēmi* (ἀνθίστημι, 436), "to set against" (*anti*, "against," *histēmi*, "to cause to stand"), used in the middle (or passive) voice and in the intransitive 2nd aorist and perfect active, signifying "to withstand, oppose, resist," is translated "to resist" in Matt. 5:39; Acts 6:10, KJV (RV, "withstand"); Rom. 9:19, KJV (RV, "withstandeth"); 13:2 (2nd and 3rd parts; for 1st part, see No. 3), KJV (RV, "withstandeth" and "withstand"); Gal. 2:11, RV (KJV, "withstood"); 2 Tim. 3:8 (2nd part), KJV (RV, "withstand"); Jas. 4:7; 1 Pet. 5:9, KJV (RV, "withstand"); "to withstand" in Acts 13:8; Eph. 6:13; 2 Tim. 3:8 (1st part); 4:15.¶

2. *antikathistēmi* (ἀντικαθίστημι, 478), "to stand firm against" (*anti*, "against," *kathistēmi*, "to set down," *kata*), is translated "ye have (not) resisted" in Heb. 12:4.¶ In the Sept., Deut. 31:21; Josh. 5:7; Mic. 2:8.¶

3. *antitassō* (ἀντιτάσσω, 498), *anti*, "against," *tassō*, "to arrange," originally a military term, "to range in battle against," and frequently so found in the papyri, is used in the middle voice signifying "to set oneself against, resist," (*a*) of men, Acts 18:6, "opposed themselves"; elsewhere "to resist," of resisting human potentates, Rom. 13:2; (*b*) of God, Jas. 4:6; 5:6, negatively, of leaving persistent evildoers to pursue their self-determined course, with eventual retribution; 1 Pet. 5:5. See OPPOSE.¶

4. *antipiptō* (ἀντιπίπτω, 496), lit., and primarily, "to fall against or upon" (*anti*, "against," *piptō*, "to fall"), then, "to strive against, resist," is used in Acts 7:51 of "resisting" the Holy Spirit.¶

RESOLVE

ginōskō (γινώσκω, 1097), "to come to know, perceive, realize," is used in the 2nd aorist tense in Luke 16:4. "I am resolved," expressing the definiteness of the steward's realization, and his consequent determination of his course of action. See KNOW.

RESORT

1. *erchomai* (ἔρχομαι, 2064), "to come," is translated "resorted" in Mark 2:13; in John 10:41 (RV, "came"). See COME, No. 1.

2. *epiporeuomai* (ἐπιπορεύομαι, 1975), "to travel or journey to a place" (*epi*, "to," *poreuomai*, "to go"), is translated "resorted" in Luke 8:4, RV (KJV, "were come").¶

3. *sunagō* (συνάγω, 4863), "to gather or bring together" (*sun*, "with," *agō*, "to bring"), in the passive voice, "to be gathered or come together," is translated "resorted" in John 18:2 (the aorist tense expressing repeated action viewed cumulatively). See ASSEMBLE, GATHER, LEAD, *Note* (1).

Notes: (1) In the KJV of John 18:20 and Acts 16:13, *sunerchomai*, "to come together" (RV), is translated "to resort." (2) In Mark 10:1, KJV, *sumporeuomai*, "to come together" (RV), is translated "resort."

RESPECT (Noun and Verb)

A. Noun.

meros (μέρος, 3313), "a part," has occasionally the meaning of "a class" or "category," and, used in the dative case with *en*, "in," signifies "in respect of," 2 Cor. 3:10, "in (this) respect"; 9:3, RV, KJV, "in (this) behalf"; Col. 2:16, "in respect of (a feast day)."

B. Verbs.

1. *apoblepō* (ἀποβλέπω, 578), "to look away from all else at one object" (*apo*, "from"), hence, "to look steadfastly," is translated "he had respect" in Heb. 11:26, KJV (RV, "looked"). See LOOK.

2. *epiblepō* (ἐπιβλέπω, 1914), "to look upon" (*epi*), is translated "have respect" in Jas. 2:3 (RV "regard"); see LOOK, No. 6.

Notes: (1) The following prepositions are translated "in respect of": *peri*, "concerning," in John 16:8, RV; *epi*, "upon, over," in Heb. 11:4, RV; marg., "over (his gifts)"; *kata*, "in regard to," in Phil. 4:11. (2) For "respect of persons" and "respecter of persons" see PERSON.

REST (Noun and Verb)

A. Nouns.

1. *anapausis* (ἀνάπαυσις, 372), "cessation, refreshment, rest" (*ana*, "up," *pauō*, "to make to cease"), the constant word in the Sept. for the Sabbath "rest," is used in Matt. 11:29; here the contrast seems to be to the burdens imposed by the Pharisees. Christ's "rest" is not a "rest" from work, but in work, "not the rest of inactivity but of the harmonious working of all the faculties and affections—of will, heart, imagination, conscience—because each has found in God the ideal sphere for its satisfaction and development" (J. Patrick, in *Hastings' Bib. Dic.*); it occurs also in Matt. 12:43; Luke 11:24; Rev. 4:8, RV, "(they have no) rest" [KJV, "(they)

rest (not)"], where the noun is the object of the verb *echō*, "to have"; so in 14:11.¶

2. *katapausis* (κατάπαυσις, 2663), in classical Greek, denotes "a causing to cease" or "putting to rest"; in the NT, "rest, repose"; it is used (*a*) of God's "rest," Acts 7:49; Heb. 3:11, 18; 4:1, 3 (twice), RV (1st part), "that rest" (the KJV, "rest," is ambiguous), 5, 11; (*b*) in a general statement, applicable to God and man, 4:10.¶

3. *anesis* (ἄνεσις, 425), for the significance of which see EASE, B, is translated "rest" in 2 Cor. 2:13, KJV (RV, "relief"); 7:5 (ditto); in 2 Thess. 1:7, the subject is not the "rest" to be granted to the saints, but the divine retribution on their persecutors; hence the phrase "and to you that are afflicted rest with us," is an incidental extension of the idea of recompense, and is to be read parenthetically. The time is not that at which the saints will be relieved of persecution, as in 1 Thess. 4:15–17, when the Parousia of Christ begins, but that at which the persecutors will be punished, namely, at the epiphany (or out-shining) of His Parousia (2 Thess. 2:8). For similar parentheses characteristic of epistolary writings see v. 10; 1 Thess. 1:6; 2:15, 16.

4. *sabbatismos* (σαββατισμός, 4520), "a Sabbath-keeping," is used in Heb. 4:9, RV, "a sabbath rest," KJV marg., "a keeping of a sabbath" (akin to *sabbatizō*, "to keep the Sabbath," used, e.g., in Exod. 16:30, not in the NT); here the sabbath-keeping is the perpetual sabbath "rest" to be enjoyed uninterruptedly by believers in their fellowship with the Father and the Son, in contrast to the weekly Sabbath under the Law. Because this sabbath "rest" is the "rest" of God Himself, 4:10, its full fruition is yet future, though believers now enter into it. In whatever way they enter into divine "rest," that which they enjoy is involved in an indissoluble relation with God.¶

5. *koimēsis* (κοίμησις, 2838), "a resting, reclining" (akin to *keimai*, "to lie"), is used in John 11:13, of natural sleep, translated "taking rest," RV.¶

Note: In Acts 9:31, KJV, *eirēnē*, "peace" (RV), is translated "rest."

B. Verbs.

1. *anapauō* (ἀναπαύω, 373), akin to A, No. 1, in the active voice, signifies "to give intermission from labor, to give rest, to refresh," Matt. 11:28; 1 Cor. 16:18, "have refreshed"; Philem. 20, "refresh"; passive voice, "to be rested, refreshed," 2 Cor. 7:13, "was refreshed"; Philem. 7, "are refreshed"; in the middle voice, "to take or enjoy rest," Matt. 26:45; Mark 6:31; 14:41; Luke 12:19, "take thine ease"; 1 Pet. 4:14; Rev. 6:11; 14:13. See REFRESH.¶ In the papyri it is found as an agricultural term, e.g., of giving

land "rest" by sowing light crops upon it. In inscriptions it is found on gravestones of Christians, followed by the date of death (Moulton and Milligan).

2. *katapauō* (καταπαύω, 2664), akin to A, No. 2, used transitively, signifies "to cause to cease, restrain," Acts 14:18; "to cause to rest," Heb. 4:8; intransitively, "to rest," Heb. 4:4, 10. See CEASE, A, No. 6, RESTRAIN.¶

3. *episkēnoō* (ἐπισκηνόω, 1981), "to spread a tabernacle over" (*epi*, "upon," *skēnē*, "a tent"), is used metaphorically in 2 Cor. 12:9, "may rest upon (me)," RV, marg., "cover," "spread a tabernacle over."¶

4. *kataskēnoō* (κατασκηνόω, 2681), "to pitch one's tent, lodge," is translated "shall rest," in Acts 2:26, KJV (RV, "shall dwell"). See LODGE.

5. *hēsuchazō* (ἡσυχάζω, 2270), "to be still, to rest from labor,'" is translated "they rested" in Luke 23:56. See PEACE (hold one's), No. 3.

6. *epanapauō* (ἐπαναπαύω, 1879), "to cause to rest," is used in the middle voice, metaphorically, signifying "to rest upon" (*epi*, "upon," and No. 1), in Luke 10:6 and Rom. 2:17.¶

Note: For "find rest" Rom. 15:32, RV, see REFRESH, No. 2.

REST (the)

1. *loipos* (λοιπός, 3062**), "remaining" (for which see REMNANT), is frequently used to mean "the rest," and is generally so translated in the RV (KJV, "others" in Luke 8:10; Acts 28:9; Eph. 2:3; 1 Thess. 4:13; 5:6; 1 Tim. 5:20; KJV, "other" in Luke 18:11; Acts 17:9; Rom. 1:13; 2 Cor. 12:13; 13:2; Gal. 2:13; Phil. 1:13; 4:3); the neut. plur., lit., "remaining things," is used in Luke 12:26; 1 Cor. 11:34.

2. *epiloipos* (ἐπίλοιπος, 1954), signifying "still left, left over" (*epi*, "over," and No. 1), is used in the neuter with the article in 1 Pet. 4:2, "the rest (of your time)."¶

For RESTITUTION see RESTORATION

RESTLESS

akatastatos (ἀκατάστατος, 182), "unsettled, unstable, disorderly" (*a*, negative, *kathistēmi*, "to set in order"), is translated "unstable" in Jas. 1:8; "restless" in 3:8, RV [in the latter, the KJV "unruly" represents the word *akataschetos*, signifying "that cannot be restrained" (*a*, negative, *katechō*, "to hold down, restrain"). In the Sept., Job 31:11¶]. See UNRULY, UNSTABLE.¶ In the Sept., Isa. 54:11.¶

RESTORATION

apokatastasis (ἀποκατάστασις, 605), from *apo*, "back, again," *kathistēmi*, "to set in order," is used in Acts 3:21, RV, "restoration" (KJV, "restitution"). See under REGENERATION, concerning Israel in its regenerated state hereafter. In the papyri it is used of a temple cell of a goddess, a "repair" of a public way, the "restoration" of estates to rightful owners, a "balancing" of accounts. Apart from papyri illustrations the word is found in an Egyptian reference to a consummating agreement of the world's cyclical periods, an idea somewhat similar to that in the Acts passage (Moulton and Milligan).¶

RESTORE

1. *apodidōmi* (ἀποδίδωμι, 591), "to give back," is translated "I restore" in Luke 19:8. See DELIVER, A, No. 3.

2. *apokathistēmi* or the alternative form *apokathistanō* (ἀποκαθίστημι, 600) is used (*a*) of "restoration" to a former condition of health, Matt. 12:13; Mark 3:5; 8:25; Luke 6:10; (*b*) of the divine "restoration" of Israel and conditions affected by it, including the renewal of the covenant broken by them, Matt. 17:11; Mark 9:12; Acts 1:6; (*c*) of "giving" or "bringing" a person back, Heb. 13:19.¶ In the papyri it is used of financial restitution, of making good the breaking of a stone by a workman by his substituting another, of the reclamation of land, etc. (Moulton and Milligan).

3. *katartizō* (καταρτίζω, 2675), "to mend, to furnish completely," is translated "restore" in Gal. 6:1, metaphorically, of the "restoration," by those who are spiritual, of one overtaken in a trespass, such a one being as a dislocated member of the spiritual body. The tense is the continuous present, suggesting the necessity for patience and perseverance in the process. See FIT, MEND, PERFECT.

RESTRAIN

1. *katapauō* (καταπαύω, 2664); See REST, B, No. 2.

2. *katechō* (κατέχω, 2722), "to hold fast or down," is translated "restraineth" in 2 Thess. 2:6 and 7. In v. 6 lawlessness is spoken of as being "restrained" in its development: in v. 7 "one that restraineth" is, lit., "the restrainer" (the article with the present participle, "the restraining one"); this may refer to an individual, as in the similar construction in 1 Thess. 3:5, "the tempter" (cf. 1:10, lit., "the Deliverer"); or to a number of persons presenting the same characteristics, just as "the believer" stands for all believers, e.g., Rom. 9:33; 1 John 5:10. V. 6

speaks of a principle, v. 7 of the principle as embodied in a person or series of persons; cf. what is said of "the power" in Rom. 13:3, 4, a phrase representing all such rulers. Probably such powers, i.e., "constituted governments," are the "restraining" influence here intimated (specifications being designedly withheld). For an extended exposition see *Notes on Thessalonians*, by Hogg and Vine, pp. 254–261.

RESURRECTION

1. *anastasis* (ἀνάστασις, 386) denotes (I) "a raising up," or "rising" (*ana*, "up," and *histēmi*, "to cause to stand"), Luke 2:34, "the rising up"; the KJV "again" obscures the meaning; the Child would be like a stone against which many in Israel would stumble while many others would find in its strength and firmness a means of their salvation and spiritual life; (II) of "resurrection" from the dead, (*a*) of Christ, Acts 1:22; 2:31; 4:33; Rom. 1:4; 6:5; Phil. 3:10; 1 Pet. 1:3; 3:21; by metonymy, of Christ as the Author of "resurrection," John 11:25; (*b*) of those who are Christ's at His Parousia (see COMING), Luke 14:14, "the resurrection of the just"; Luke 20:33, 35, 36; John 5:29 (1st part); "the resurrection of life"; 11:24; Acts 23:6; 24:15 (1st part); 1 Cor. 15:21, 42; 2 Tim. 2:18; Heb. 11:35 (2nd part), see RAISE, *Note* (3); Rev. 20:5, "the first resurrection"; hence the insertion of "is" stands for the completion of this "resurrection," of which Christ was "the firstfruits"; 20:6; (*c*) of "the rest of the dead," after the Millennium (cf. Rev. 20:5); John 5:29 (2nd part), "the resurrection of judgment"; Acts 24:15 (2nd part), "of the unjust"; (*d*) of those who were raised in more immediate connection with Christ's "resurrection," and thus had part already in the first "resurrection," Acts 26:23 and Rom. 1:4 (in each of which "dead" is plural; see Matt. 27:52); (*e*) of the "resurrection" spoken of in general terms, Matt. 22:23; Mark 12:18; Luke 20:27; Acts 4:2; 17:18; 23:8; 24:21; 1 Cor. 15:12, 13; Heb. 6:2; (*f*) of those who were raised in OT times, to die again, Heb. 11:35 (1st part), lit., "out of resurrection."¶

2. *exanastasis* (ἐξανάστασις, 1815), ek, "from" or "out of," and No. 1, Phil. 3:11, followed by *ek*, lit., "the out-resurrection from among the dead." For the significance of this see ATTAIN, No. 1.¶

3. *egersis* (ἔγερσις, 1454), "a rousing" (akin to *egeirō*, "to arouse, to raise"), is used of the "resurrection" of Christ, in Matt. 27:53.¶

RETAIN

krateō (κρατέω, 2902), "to be strong, obtain, hold, hold fast," is translated "to retain," of sins,

John 20:23 (twice); see on REMIT. See HOLD, KEEP, OBTAIN, TAKE.

Notes: (1) In Philem. 13, KJV, *katechō*, "to hold fast, hold back, detain," is translated "to retain" (RV, to keep). (2) In Rom. 1:28, KJV, *echō*, "to have" (RV), is translated "to retain."

RETURN

1. *analuō* (ἀναλύω, 360), "to depart" in Phil. 1:23, signifies "to return" in Luke 12:36, used in a simile of the "return" of a lord for his servants after a marriage feast (RV). See DEPART, No. 16.¶

2. *anastrephō* (ἀναστρέφω, 390), "to turn back," is translated "to return" in Acts 5:22 and 15:16. See ABIDE, BEHAVE.

3. *epistrephō* (ἐπιστρέφω, 1994), "to turn about," or "towards," is translated "to return" in Matt. 12:44; 24:18; Mark 13:16, RV (KJV, "turn back again"); Luke 2:39; 8:55, RV (KJV, "came again"); 17:31; Acts 15:36, RV (KJV, "go again"). See CONVERT, A, No. 2, TURN.

4. *hupostrephō* (ὑποστρέφω, 5290), "to turn behind," or "back" (*hupo*, "under"), is translated "to return" (in some texts in Mark 14:40) in Luke 1:56; 2:20, 43; v. 45, RV (KJV, "turned back again"); 4:1, 14; 7:10; 8:37; 10:17; 11:24, KJV (RV, "I will turn back"); 17:18; 19:12; 23:48, 56; Acts 1:12; 12:25; 13:13; 13:34; 20:3; 21:6; 22:17, RV (KJV, "was come again"); 23:32; Gal. 1:17; Heb. 7:1. See TURN (back).

5. *anakamptō* (ἀνακάμπτω, 344), "to turn or bend back," occurs in Matt. 2:12; Luke 10:6 (i.e., as if it was unsaid); Acts 18:21; Heb. 11:15.¶

6. *epanagō* (ἐπανάγω, 1877), "to bring up or back" (primarily a nautical term for "putting to sea"; see LAUNCH, PUT), is used intransitively, in Matt. 21:18, "He returned."

Note: In Luke 19:15, KJV, *epanerchomai*, "to come back again" (RV) is translated "returned." See COME, No. 4.

REVEAL

1. *apokaluptō* (ἀποκαλύπτω, 601) signifies "to uncover, unveil" (*apo*, "from," *kaluptō*, "to cover"); both verbs are used in Matt. 10:26; in Luke 12:2, *apokaluptō* is set in contrast to *sunkaluptō*, "to cover up, cover completely." "The NT occurrences of this word fall under two heads, subjective and objective. The subjective use is that in which something is presented to the mind directly, as, (*a*) the meaning of the acts of God, Matt. 11:25; Luke 10:21; (*b*) the secret of the Person of the Lord Jesus, Matt. 16:17; John 12:38; (*c*) the character of God as Father, Matt. 11:27; Luke 10:22; (*d*) the will of God for the conduct of His children, Phil. 3:15;

(e) the mind of God to the prophets of Israel, 1 Pet. 1:12, and of the Church, 1 Cor. 14:30; Eph. 3:5.

"The objective use is that in which something is presented to the senses, sight or hearing, as, referring to the past, (f) the truth declared to men in the gospel, Rom. 1:17; 1 Cor. 2:10; Gal. 3:23; (g) the Person of Christ to Paul on the way to Damascus, Gal. 1:16; (h) thoughts before hidden in the heart, Luke 2:35; referring to the future, (i) the coming in glory of the Lord Jesus, Luke 17:30; (j) the salvation and glory that await the believer, Rom. 8:18; 1 Pet. 1:5; 5:1; (k) the true value of service, 1 Cor. 3:13; (l) the wrath of God (at the Cross, against sin, and, at the revelation of the Lord Jesus, against the sinner), Rom. 1:18; (m) the Lawless One, 2 Thess. 2:3, 6, 8."*¶

2. chrēmatizō (χρηματίζω, 5537), "to give divine admonition, instruction, revelation," is translated "it had been revealed," in Luke 2:26. See ADMONITION, B, No. 3, CALL.

REVELATION

apokalupsis (ἀποκάλυψις, 602), "an uncovering" (akin to apokaluptō; see above), "is used in the NT of (a) the drawing away by Christ of the veil of darkness covering the Gentiles, Luke 2:32; cf. Isa. 25:7; (b) 'the mystery,' the purpose of God in this age, Rom. 16:25; Eph. 3:3; (c) the communication of the knowledge of God to the soul, Eph. 1:17; (d) an expression of the mind of God for the instruction of the church, 1 Cor. 14:6, 26, for the instruction of the Apostle Paul, 2 Cor. 12:1, 7; Gal. 1:12, and for his guidance, Gal. 2:2; (e) the Lord Jesus Christ, to the saints at His Parousia, 1 Cor. 1:7, RV (KJV, 'coming'); 1 Pet. 1:7, RV (KJV, 'appearing'), 13; 4:13; (f) the Lord Jesus Christ when He comes to dispense the judgments of God, 2 Thess. 1:7; cf. Rom. 2:5; (g) the saints, to the creation, in association with Christ in His glorious reign, Rom. 8:19, RV, 'revealing' (KJV, 'manifestation'); (h) the symbolic forecast of the final judgments of God, Rev. 1:1 (hence the Greek title of the book, transliterated 'Apocalypse' and translated 'Revelation')."* See APPEARING, COMING, LIGHTEN, B, Note, MANIFESTATION.¶

REVEL, REVELING

1. truphē (τρυφή, 5172), "luxuriousness, daintiness, reveling," is translated freely by the verb "to revel" in 2 Pet. 2:13, RV (KJV, "to riot"), lit., "counting reveling in the daytime a

pleasure." In Luke 7:25 it is used with en, "in," and translated "delicately." See DELICATELY, RIOT.¶

2. kōmos (κῶμος, 2970), "a revel, carousal," the concomitant and consequence of drunkenness, is used in the plural, Rom. 13:13, translated by the singular, RV, "reveling" (KJV, "rioting"); Gal. 5:21 and 1 Pet. 4:3, "revelings." See RIOT.¶

Note: For entruphaō, 2 Pet. 2:13, RV, "to revel," see SPORTING.

For REVENGE and REVENGER see AVENGE and AVENGER

REVERENCE (Noun and Verb)

A. Verbs.

1. entrepō (ἐντρέπω, 1788), lit., "to turn in" (i.e., upon oneself), "to put to shame," denotes, when used in the passive voice, "to feel respect for, to show deference to, to reverence," Matt. 21:37; Mark 12:6; Luke 20:13; Heb. 12:9. See ASHAMED, A, No. 4, REGARD.

2. phobeō (φοβέω, 5399), "to fear," is used in the passive voice in the NT; in Eph. 5:33 of reverential fear on the part of a wife for a husband, KJV, "reverence" (RV, "fear"). See FEAR, D, No. 1.

B. Noun

eulabeia (εὐλάβεια, 2124), "caution, reverence," is translated "reverence" in Heb. 12:28 (1st part in the best mss; some have aidōs). See FEAR.

REVERENT

hieroprepēs (ἱεροπρεπής, 2412), "suited to a sacred character, reverend" (hieros, "sacred," prepō, "to be fitting"), is translated "reverent" in Titus 2:3, RV (KJV, "as becometh holiness"). See BECOME, B.¶

REVILE, REVILING, REVILER

A. Verbs.

1. loidoreō (λοιδορέω, 3058) denotes "to abuse, revile," John 9:28; Acts 23:4; 1 Cor. 4:12; 1 Pet. 2:23 (1st clause).¶

2. oneidizō (ὀνειδίζω, 3679), "to reproach, upbraid," is translated "to revile" in Matt. 5:11, KJV, and Mark 15:32 (RV, "reproach"). See REPROACH.

3. blasphēmeō (βλασφημέω, 987), "to speak profanely, rail at," is translated "reviled" in Matt. 27:39, KJV (RV, "railed on"); Luke 22:65, RV, "reviling" (KJV, "blasphemously").

4. antiloidoreō (ἀντιλοιδορέω, 486), "to revile back or again" (anti, and No. 1), is found in 1 Pet. 2:23 (2nd clause).¶

---

* From Notes on Galatians, by Hogg and Vine, pp. 41, 42.
* From Notes on Thessalonians, by Hogg and Vine, pp. 228, 229.

Note: For *epēreazō*, 1 Pet. 3:16, RV, "revile," see ACCUSE, B, No. 3.

B. Adjective.

loidoros (λοίδορος, 3060), akin to A, No. 1, "abusive, railing, reviling," is used as a noun, 1 Cor. 5:11, RV, "a reviler" (KJV "a railer"); 6:10, "revilers."¶ In the Sept., Prov. 25:24; 26:21; 27:15.¶

C. Noun.

loidoria (λοιδορία, 3059), akin to A, No. 1, and B, "abuse, railing," is used in 1 Tim. 5:14, RV, "for (*charin*, 'for the sake of') reviling" (KJV, "to speak reproachfully"—a paraphrase); 1 Pet. 3:9 (twice), RV, "reviling" (KJV, "railing"). See RAIL, B.¶

REVIVE

1. *anathallō* (ἀναθάλλω, 330), "to flourish anew" (*ana*, "again, anew," *thallō*, "to flourish or blossom"), hence, "to revive," is used metaphorically in Phil. 4:10, RV, "ye have revived (your thought for me)," KJV, "(your care of me) hath flourished again."¶ In the Sept., Ps. 28:7; Ezek. 17:24; Hos. 8:9.¶

2. *anazaō* (ἀναζάω, 326), "to live again" (*ana*, "and" *zaō*, "to live"), "to regain life," is used of moral "revival," Luke 15:24, "is alive again"; (*b*) of sin, Rom. 7:9, "revived," lit., "lived again" i.e., it sprang into activity, manifesting the evil inherent in it; here sin is personified, by way of contrast to the man himself. Some mss. have it in Rom. 14:9, for *zaō*, as in the RV, which italicizes "*again*."¶

REWARD (Noun and Verb)

A. Noun.

misthos (μισθός, 3408), primarily "wages, hire," and then, generally, "reward," (*a*) received in this life, Matt. 5:46; 6:2, 5, 16; Rom. 4:4; 1 Cor. 9:17, 18; of evil "rewards," Acts 1:18; see also HIRE; (*b*) to be received hereafter, Matt. 5:12; 10:41 (twice), 42; Mark 9:41; Luke 6:23, 35; 1 Cor. 3:8, 14; 2 John 8; Rev. 11:18; 22:12. See WAGES.

Notes: (1) In Luke 23:41, *axios*, "worthy, befitting," used in the plur., is rendered "the due reward," lit., "things worthy." (2) For *antapodosis*, rendered "reward" in Col. 3:24, KJV, see RECOMPENSE. (3) For *katabrabeuō*, "to rob of a reward," Col. 2:18, see BEGUILE, Note, and ROB.

B. Verb.

apodidōmi (ἀποδίδωμι, 591), "to give back," is nowhere translated "to reward" in the RV; KJV, Matt. 6:4, 6, 18 (see RECOMPENSE, B, No. 2); Matt. 16:27; 2 Tim. 4:14; Rev. 18:6 (see RENDER).

REWARDER

misthapodotēs (μισθαποδότης, 3406), "one who pays wages" (*misthos*, "wages," *apo*, "back," *didōmi*, "to give"), is used by metonymy in Heb. 11:6, of God, as the "Rewarder" of those who "seek after Him" (RV).¶ Cf. *misthapodosia*, "recompence."

RICH, RICHES, RICHLY, RICH MAN

A. Adjective.

plousios (πλούσιος, 4145), akin to B, C, No. 1, "rich, wealthy," is used (I) literally, (*a*) adjectivally (with a noun expressed separately) in Matt. 27:57; Luke 12:16; 14:12; 16:1, 19; (without a noun), 18:23; 19:2; (*b*) as a noun, singular, a "rich" man (the noun not being expressed), Matt. 19:23, 24; Mark 10:25; 12:41; Luke 16:21, 22; 18:25; Jas. 1:10, 11, "the rich," "the rich (man)"; plural, Mark 12:41, lit., "rich (ones)"; Luke 6:24 (ditto); 21:1; 1 Tim. 6:17, "(them that are) rich," lit., "(the) rich"; Jas. 2:6, RV, "the rich"; 5:1, RV, "ye rich"; Rev. 6:15 and 13:16, RV, "the rich"; (II) metaphorically, of God, Eph. 2:4 ("in mercy"); of Christ, 2 Cor. 8:9; of believers, Jas. 2:5, RV, "(*to be*) rich (in faith)"; Rev. 2:9, of spiritual "enrichment" generally; 3:17, of a false sense of "enrichment."¶

B. Verbs.

1. *plouteō* (πλουτέω, 4147), "to be rich," in the aorist or point tense, "to become rich," is used (*a*) literally, Luke 1:53, "the rich," present participle, lit., "(ones or those) being rich"; 1 Tim. 6:9, 18; Rev. 18:3, 15, 19 (all three in the aorist tense); (*b*) metaphorically, of Christ, Rom. 10:12 (the passage stresses the fact that Christ is Lord; see v. 9, and the RV); of the "enrichment" of believers through His poverty, 2 Cor. 8:9 (the aorist tense expressing completeness, with permanent results); so in Rev. 3:18, where the spiritual "enrichment" is conditional upon righteousness of life and conduct (see GOLD, No. 2); of a false sense of "enrichment," 1 Cor. 4:8 (aorist), RV, "ye are become rich" (KJV, "ye are rich"); Rev. 3:17 (perfect tense, RV, "I . . . have gotten riches," KJV, "I am . . . increased with goods"), see GOODS, *Note* (3); of not being "rich" toward God, Luke 12:21.¶

2. *ploutizō* (πλουτίζω, 4148), "to make rich, enrich," is rendered "making (many) rich" in 2 Cor. 6:10 (metaphorical of "enriching" spiritually). See ENRICH.

C. Nouns

1. *ploutos* (πλοῦτος, 4149) is used in the singular (I) of material "riches," used evilly, Matt. 13:22; Mark 4:19; Luke 8:14; 1 Tim. 6:17; Jas. 5:2; Rev. 18:17; (II) of spiritual and

moral "riches," (a) possessed by God and exercised towards men, Rom. 2:4, "of His goodness and forbearance and longsuffering"; 9:23 and Eph. 3:16, "of His glory" (i.e., of its manifestation in grace towards believers); Rom. 11:33, of His wisdom and knowledge; Eph. 1:7 and 2:7, "of His grace"; 1:18, "of the glory of His inheritance in the saints"; 3:8, "of Christ"; Phil. 4:19, "in glory in Christ Jesus," RV; Col. 1:27, "of the glory of this mystery... Christ in you, the hope of glory"; (b) to be ascribed to Christ, Rev, 5:12; (c) of the effects of the gospel upon the Gentiles, Rom. 11:12 (twice); (d) of the full assurance of understanding in regard to the mystery of God, even Christ, Col. 2:2, RV; (e) of the liberality of the churches of Macedonia, 2 Cor. 8:2 (where "the riches" stands for the spiritual and moral value of their liberality); (f) of "the reproach of Christ" in contrast to this world's treasures, Heb. 11:26.¶

2. *chrēma* (χρῆμα, 5536), "what one uses or needs" (*chraomai*, "to use"), "a matter, business," hence denotes "riches," Mark 10:23, 24; Luke 18:24; see MONEY, No. 2.

D. Adverb.

plousiōs (πλουσίως, 4146), "richly, abundantly," akin to A, is used in Col. 3:16; 1 Tim. 6:17; Titus 3:6, RV, "richly" (KJV, "abundantly"); 2 Pet. 1:11 (ditto).¶

For **RID** see **CARE**, A, No. 1, Note

RIDE

epibainō (ἐπιβαίνω, 1910), "to go upon" (*epi*, "upon," *bainō*, "to go"), is used of Christ's "riding" into Jerusalem, Matt. 21:5, RV, "riding" (KJV, "sitting"). See COME, No. 16.

RIGHT (opp. to left), RIGHT HAND, RIGHT SIDE

dexios (δεξιός, 1188), an adjective, used (a) of "the right" as opposite to the left, e.g., Matt. 5:29, 30; Rev. 10:5, RV, "right hand"; in connection with armor (figuratively), 2 Cor. 6:7; with *en*, followed by the dative plural, Mark 16:5; with *ek*, and the genitive plural, e.g., Matt. 25:33, 34; Luke 1:11; (b) of giving the "right hand" of fellowship, Gal. 2:9, betokening the public expression of approval by leaders at Jerusalem of the course pursued by Paul and Barnabas among the Gentiles; the act was often the sign of a pledge, e.g., 2 Kings 10:15; 1 Chron. 29:24, marg.; Ezra 10:19; Ezek. 17:18; figuratively, Lam. 5:6; it is often so used in the papyri; (c) metaphorically of "power" or "authority," Acts 2:33; with *ek*, signifying "on," followed by the genitive plural, Matt. 26:64;

Mark 14:62; Heb. 1:13; (d) similarly of "a place of honor in the messianic kingdom," Matt. 20:21; Mark 10:37.

RIGHT (not wrong—Noun and Adjective), RIGHTLY

A. Noun.

exousia (ἐξουσία, 1849), "authority, power," is translated "right" in the RV, for KJV, "power," in John 1:12; Rom. 9:21; 1 Cor. 9:4, 5, 6, 12 (twice), 18; 2 Thess. 3:9, where the "right" is that of being maintained by those among whom the ministers of the gospel had labored, a "right" possessed in virtue of the "authority" given them by Christ, Heb. 13:10; Rev. 22:14.

Exousia first denotes "freedom to act" and then "authority for the action." This is first true of God, Acts 1:7. It was exercised by the Son of God, as from, and in conjunction with, the Father when the Lord was upon earth, in the days of His flesh, Matt. 9:6; John 10:18, as well as in resurrection, Matt. 28:18; John 17:2. All others hold their freedom to act from God (though some of them have abused it), whether angels, Eph. 1:21, or human potentates, Rom. 13:1. Satan offered to delegate his authority over earthly kingdoms to Christ, Luke 4:6, who, though conscious of His "right" to it, refused, awaiting the divinely appointed time. See AUTHORITY, No. 1, and for various synonyms see DOMINION, No. 1, Note.

B. Adjectives.

1. *dikaios* (δίκαιος, 1342), "just, righteous, that which is in accordance with" *dikē*, "rule, right, justice," is translated "right" in Matt. 20:4; v. 7, KJV only (RV omits, according to the most authentic mss., the clause having been inserted from v. 4, to the detriment of the narrative); Luke 12:57; Acts 4:19; Eph. 6:1; Phil. 1:7, RV (KJV, "meet"); 2 Pet. 1:13 (KJV, "meet"). See JUST, RIGHTEOUS.

2. *euthus* (εὐθύς, 2117), "straight," hence, metaphorically, "right," is so rendered in Acts 8:21, of the heart; 13:10, of the ways of the Lord; 2 Pet. 2:15. See STRAIGHT.

C. Adverb.

orthōs (ὀρθῶς, 3723), "rightly" (akin to *orthos*, "straight, direct"), is translated "plain" in Mark 7:35; in Luke 7:43 and 20:21, "rightly"; in Luke 10:28, "right."¶

Notes: (1) For "right mind" see MIND, B, No. 5. (2) For the KJV, "rightly" in 2 Tim. 2:15, see DIVIDE, A, No. 8.

RIGHTEOUS, RIGHTEOUSLY

A. Adjective.

dikaios (δίκαιος, 1342) signifies "just," without prejudice or partiality, e.g., of the judgment of God, 2 Thess. 1:5, 6; of His judgments, Rev. 16:7; 19:2; of His character as Judge, 2 Tim. 4:8; Rev. 16:5; of His ways and doings, Rev. 15:3. See further under JUST, A, No. 1, RIGHT, B, No. 1.

In the following the RV substitutes "righteous" for the KJV "just"; Matt. 1:19; 13:49; 27:19, 24; Mark 6:20; Luke 2:25; 15:7; 20:20; 23:50; John 5:30; Acts 3:14; 7:52; 10:22; 22:14; Rom. 1:17; 7:12; Gal. 3:11; Heb. 10:38; Jas. 5:6; 1 Pet. 3:18; 2 Pet. 2:7; 1 John 1:9; Rev. 15:3.

B. Adverb.

dikaiōs (δικαίως, 1346) is translated "righteously" in 1 Cor. 15:34, RV, "(awake up) righteously," KJV, "(awake to) righteousness"; 1 Thess. 2:10, RV (KJV, "justly"); Titus 2:12; 1 Pet. 2:23. See JUSTLY.

Notes: (1) In Rev. 22:11 the best texts have *dikaiosunē*, "righteousness," with *poieō*, "to do," RV, "let him do righteousness"; the KJV follows those which have the passive voice of *dikaioō* and renders it "let him be righteous," lit., "let him be made righteous." (2) *Dikaiokrisia*, "righteous judgment" (*dikaios*, and *krisis*), occurs in Rom. 2:5.¶

RIGHTEOUSNESS

1. *dikaiosunē* (δικαιοσύνη, 1343) is "the character or quality of being right or just"; it was formerly spelled "rightwiseness," which clearly expresses the meaning. It is used to denote an attribute of God, e.g., Rom. 3:5, the context of which shows that "the righteousness of God" means essentially the same as His faithfulness, or truthfulness, that which is consistent with His own nature and promises; Rom. 3:25, 26 speaks of His "righteousness" as exhibited in the death of Christ, which is sufficient to show men that God is neither indifferent to sin nor regards it lightly. On the contrary, it demonstrates that quality of holiness in Him which must find expression in His condemnation of sin.

"*Dikaiosunē* is found in the sayings of the Lord Jesus, (*a*) of whatever is right or just in itself, whatever conforms to the revealed will of God, Matt. 5:6, 10, 20; John 16:8, 10; (*b*) whatever has been appointed by God to be acknowledged and obeyed by man, Matt. 3:15; 21:32; (*c*) the sum total of the requirements of God, Matt. 6:33; (*d*) religious duties, Matt. 6:1 (distinguished as almsgiving, man's duty to his neighbor, vv. 2–4, prayer, his duty to God, vv. 5–15, fasting, the duty of self-control, vv. 16–18).

"In the preaching of the apostles recorded in Acts the word has the same general meaning.

So also in Jas. 1:20; 3:18, in both Epp. of Peter, 1st John and the Revelation. In 2 Pet. 1:1, 'the righteousness of our God and Savior Jesus Christ,' is the righteous dealing of God with sin and with sinners on the ground of the death of Christ. 'Word of righteousness,' Heb. 5:13, is probably the gospel, and the Scriptures as containing the gospel, wherein is declared the righteousness of God in all its aspects.

"This meaning of *dikaiosunē*, right action, is frequent also in Paul's writings, as in all five of its occurrences in Rom. 6; Eph. 6:14, etc. But for the most part he uses it of that gracious gift of God to men whereby all who believe on the Lord Jesus Christ are brought into right relationship with God. This righteousness is unattainable by obedience to any law, or by any merit of man's own, or any other condition than that of faith in Christ.... The man who trusts in Christ becomes 'the righteousness of God in Him,' 2 Cor. 5:21, i.e., becomes in Christ all that God requires a man to be, all that he could never be in himself. Because Abraham accepted the Word of God, making it his own by that act of the mind and spirit which is called faith, and, as the sequel showed, submitting himself to its control, therefore God accepted him as one who fulfilled the whole of His requirements, Rom. 4:3....

"Righteousness is not said to be imputed to the believer save in the sense that faith is imputed ('reckoned' is the better word) for righteousness. It is clear that in Rom. 4:6, 11, 'righteousness reckoned' must be understood in the light of the context, 'faith reckoned for righteousness,' vv. 3, 5, 9, 22. 'For' in these places is *eis*, which does not mean 'instead of,' but 'with a view to.' The faith thus exercised brings the soul into vital union with God in Christ, and inevitably produces righteousness of life, that is, conformity to the will of God."*

2. *dikaiōma* (δικαίωμα, 1345) is the concrete expression of "righteousness": see JUSTIFICATION, A, No. 2.

Note: In Heb. 1:8, KJV, *euthutēs*, "straightness, uprightness" (akin to *euthus*, "straight, right"), is translated "righteousness" (RV, "uprightness"; KJV, marg., "rightness, or straightness").

RING

daktulios (δακτύλιος, 1146), "a finger ring," occurs in Luke 15:22.¶

Note: Chrusodaktulios, an adjective signifying "with a gold ring," "a gold-ringed (person),"

---

* From *Notes on Galatians,* by Hogg and Vine, pp. 246, 247.

from *chrusos*, "gold," and *daktulos*, "a finger," occurs in Jas. 2:2.¶

RINGLEADER

prōtostatēs (πρωτοστάτης, 4414), "one who stands first" (*prōtos*, "first," *histēmi*, "to cause to stand"), was used of soldiers, one who stands in the front rank; hence, metaphorically, "a leader," Acts 24:5.¶

RIOT, RIOTING, RIOTOUS, RIOTOUSLY

A. Nouns.

1. *asōtia* (ἀσωτία, 810), "prodigality, a wastefulness, profligacy" (*a*, negative, *sōzō*, "to save"), is rendered "riot" in Eph. 5:18, RV (KJV, "excess"); Titus 1:6 and 1 Pet. 4:4 (KJV and RV, "riot"). The corresponding verb is found in a papyrus writing, telling of "riotous living" (like the adverb *asōtōs*, see B).¶ In the Sept., Prov. 28:7.¶ Cf. the synonymous word *aselgeia* (under LASCIVIOUSNESS).

2. *kōmos* (κῶμος, 2970), "a revel," is rendered "rioting" in Rom. 13:13, KJV; see REVEL.

3. *truphē* (τρυφή, 5172), "luxuriousness," is rendered "riot" in 2 Pet. 2:13, KJV; see DELICATELY, REVEL.

4. *stasis* (στάσις, 4714), primarily "a standing" (akin to *histēmi*, "to cause to ("stand"), then "an insurrection," is translated "riot" in Acts 19:40 RV (KJV, "uproar"). See DISSENSION, INSURRECTION, SEDITION, UPROAR.

B. Adverb.

asōtōs (ἀσώτως, 811), "wastefully" (akin to A, No. 1), is translated "with riotous living" in Luke 15:13; though the word does not necessarily signify "dissolutely," the parable narrative makes clear that this is the meaning here.¶ In the Sept., Prov. 7:11.¶

Note: The verb *ekchunō*, a Hellenistic form of *ekcheō* (though the form actually used is the regular classical aorist passive of *ekcheō*), "to pour out, shed," is translated "ran riotously" in Jude 11, RV (KJV, "ran greedily"); see POUR, SHED.

RIPE (to be fully)

1. *akmazō* (ἀκμάζω, 187), "to be at the prime" (akin to *akmē*, "a point"), "to be ripe," is translated "are fully ripe" in Rev. 14:18.¶

2. *xērainō* (ξηραίνω, 3583), "to dry up, wither," is used of "ripened" crops in Rev. 14:15, RV, "overripe," KJV, "ripe" (marg., "dried"). See DRY, B, OVERRIPE, WITHER.

3. *paradidōmi* (παραδίδωμι, 3860), "to give over, commit, deliver," etc., also signifies "to permit"; in Mark 4:29, of the "ripe" condition

of corn, RV, and KJV marg., "is ripe"; RV marg., "alloweth" (the nearest rendering); KJV, "is brought forth."

RISE, RISING

Notes: (1) For the various verbs *anistēmi*, *exanistēmi*, *egeirō*, *anabainō*, *anatellō*, *sunephistēmi*, see under ARISE. (2) For the KJV, "should rise" in Acts 26:23, see RESURRECTION. (3) *Exanistēmi*, transitively, "to raise up" (*ek*, "out, from, out of"), is used intransitively in Acts 15:5, "there rose up," i.e., from the midst of a gathered company. See RAISE. (4) For the KJV and RV of *sunegeirō*, "to raise together with," and in the passive voice in Col. 2:12; 3:1, RAISE. (5) For the word "rising," which is used to translate the verbs *anatellō* in Mark 16:2, and *anistēmi*, in Mark 9:10, see under ARISE, Nos. 9 and 1 respectively. (6) For *katephistēmi* Acts 18:12, RV, see INSURRECTION, B. (7) *Epanistamai*, "to rise up against," occurs in Matt. 10:21; Mark 13:12.¶ (8) *Anastasis*, is rendered "rising up" in Luke 2:34, RV.

RIVER

potamos (ποταμός, 4215) denotes (*a*) "a stream," Luke 6:48, 49; (*b*) "a flood or floods," Matt. 7:25, 27; (*c*) "a river," natural, Matt. 3:6, RV; Mark 1:5; Acts 16:13; 2 Cor. 11:26, RV (KJV, "waters"); Rev. 8:10; 9:14; 16:4, 12; symbolical, Rev. 12:15 (1st part), RV, "river" (KJV, "flood"); so v. 16; 22:1, 2 (cf. Gen. 2:10; Ezek. 47); figuratively, John 7:38, "the effects of the operation of the Holy Spirit in and through the believer." See FLOOD, WATER.¶

Note: For *potamophorētos* in Rev. 12:15, see FLOOD, B.

ROAR, ROARING

A. Verbs.

1. *mukaomai* (μυκάομαι, 3455), properly of oxen, an onomatopoeic word, "to low, bellow," is used of a lion, Rev. 10:3.¶

2. *ōruomai* (ὠρύομαι, 5612), "to howl" or "roar," onomatopoeic, of animals or men, is used of a lion, 1 Pet. 5:8, as a simile of Satan.¶

B. Noun.

ēchos (ἦχος, 2279), "a noise" or "sound" (Eng., "echo"), is used of the "roaring" of the sea in Luke 21:25, in the best mss., "for the roaring (of the sea and the billows)," RV; some mss. have the present participle of *ēcheō*, "to sound," KJV, "(the sea and the waves) roaring. See RUMOR, SOUND.

ROB

1. *sulaō* (συλάω, 4813), "to plunder, spoil," is translated "I robbed" in 2 Cor. 11:8.¶ Cf. *sulagōgeō*, "to make spoil of," Col. 2:8.¶

2. *katabrabeuō* (καταβραβεύω, 2603), "to give judgment against, to condemn" (*kata*, "against," and *brabeus*, "an umpire"; cf. *brabeion*, "a prize in the games," 1 Cor. 9:24; Phil. 3:14, and *brabeuō*, "to act as an umpire, arbitrate," Col. 3:15), occurs in Col. 2:18, RV, "let (no man) rob (you) of your prize" (KJV, " . . . beguile . . . of your reward"), said of false teachers who would frustrate the faithful adherence of the believers to the truth, causing them to lose their reward. Another rendering closer to the proper meaning of the word, as given above, is "let no man decide for or against you" (i.e., without any notion of a prize); this suitably follows the word "judge" in v. 16, i.e., "do not give yourselves up to the judgment and decision of any man" (KJV, marg., "judge against").¶

ROBBER

1. *lēstēs* (λῃστής, 3027), "a robber, brigand" (akin to *leia*, "booty"), "one who plunders openly and by violence" (in contrast to *kleptēs*, "a thief," see below), is always translated "robber" or "robbers" in the RV, as the KJV in John 10:1, 8; 18:40; 2 Cor. 11:26; the KJV has "thief" or "thieves" in Matt. 21:13, and parallel passages; 26:55, and parallel passages; 27:38, 44 and Mark 15:27; Luke 10:30, 36; but "thief" is the meaning of *kleptēs*. See THIEF.

2. *hierosulos* (ἱερόσυλος, 2417), an adjective signifying "robbing temples" (*hieron*, "a temple," and *sulaō*, "to rob"), is found in Acts 19:37.¶ Cf. *hierosuleō*, "to rob a temple," Rom. 2:22, KJV, "commit sacrilege."¶

For ROBBERY see PRIZE

ROBE

1. *stolē* (στολή, 4749), for which see CLOTHING, No. 8, is translated "robe" in Mark 16:5, RV (KJV, "garment"); "long robes" in Luke 20:46.

2. *chlamus* (χλαμύς, 5511), "a cloak," is translated "robe" in Matt. 27:28, 31. See CLOTHING, *Note* (4).¶

3. *himation* (ἱμάτιον, 2440) is translated "robe" in the KJV of John 19:2, 5 (RV, "garment"). See APPAREL, No. 2, CLOTHING, No. 2, GARMENT.

4. *esthēs* (ἐσθής, 2066), "apparel," is translated "robe" in Luke 23:11 (RV, "apparel"). See APPAREL, No. 1.

ROCK

1. *petra* (πέτρα, 4073) denotes "a mass of rock," as distinct from *petros*, "a detached stone or boulder," or a stone that might be thrown or easily moved. For the nature of *petra*, see Matt. 7:24, 25; 27:51, 60; Mark 15:46; Luke 6:48 (twice), a type of a sure foundation (here the true reading is as in the RV, "because it had been well builded"); Rev. 6:15, 16 (cf. Isa. 2:19,ff.; Hos. 10:8); Luke 8:6, 13, used illustratively; 1 Cor. 10:4 (twice), figuratively, of Christ; in Rom. 9:33 and 1 Pet. 2:8, metaphorically, of Christ; in Matt. 16:18, metaphorically, of Christ and the testimony concerning Him; here the distinction between *petra*, concerning the Lord Himself, and *Petros*, the apostle, is clear (see above).¶

2. *spilas* (σπιλάς, 4694), "a rock or reef," over which the sea dashes, is used in Jude 12, "hidden rocks," RV, metaphorical of men whose conduct is a danger to others.¶ A late meaning ascribed to it is that of "spots," (KJV), but that rendering seems to have been influenced by the parallel passage in 2 Pet. 2:13, where *spiloi*, "spots," occurs.

ROCKY

petrōdēs (πετρώδης, 4075), "rock-like" (*petra*, "a rock," *eidos*, "a form, appearance"), is used of "rock" underlying shallow soil, Matt. 13:5, 20, RV, "the rocky places" (KJV, "stony places"); Mark 4:5, RV, "the rocky ground" (KJV, "stony ground"); v. 16, RV, "rocky places" (KJV, "stony ground").¶

Note: In Acts 27:29, KJV, the phrase *tracheis topoi*, lit., "rough places," is translated "rocks" (RV, "rocky ground").

ROD

A. Noun.

rhabdos (ῥάβδος, 4464), "a staff, rod, scepter," is used (*a*) of Aaron's "rod," Heb. 9:4; (*b*) a staff used on a journey, Matt. 10:10, RV, "staff" (KJV, "staves"); so Luke 9:3; Mark 6:8, "staff"; Heb. 11:21, "staff"; (*c*) a ruler's staff, a "scepter," Heb. 1:8 (twice); elsewhere a "rod," Rev. 2:27; 12:5; 19:15; (*d*) a "rod" for chastisement (figuratively), 1 Cor. 4:21; (*e*) a measuring "rod," Rev. 11:1. See STAFF.¶

B. Verb.

rhabdizō (ῥαβδίζω, 4463), "to beat with a rod," is used in Acts 16:22, RV, "to beat . . . with rods"; 2 Cor. 11:25. The "rods" were those of the Roman lictors or "sergeants" (*rhabdouchoi*, lit., "rodbearers"); the Roman beating with "rods" is distinct from the Jewish infliction of stripes.¶ In the Sept., Jud., 6:11; Ruth 2:17.¶

Cf. Matt. 26:67, RV marg.; John 18:22 (KJV marg., and RV marg.); 19:3, RV marg.; see SMITE.

ROLL (Noun and Verb)

A. Verbs.

1. *apokuliō* or *apokulizō* (ἀποκυλίω, 617), "to roll away" (*apo*, "from," *kuliō*, "to roll"; cf. Eng., "cylinder," etc.), is used of the sepulchre stone, Matt. 28:2; Mark 16:3 (v. 4 in some mss.; see No. 2); Luke 24:2.¶ In the Sept., Gen. 29:3, 8, 10.¶

2. *anakuliō* (ἀνακυλίω, 303 and 2947), "to roll up or back" (*ana*), is found in the best texts, in Mark 16:4 (see No. 1).¶

3. *proskuliō* (προσκυλίω, 4351), "to roll up or to" (*pros*), is used in Matt. 27:60; Mark 15:46, of the sepulchre stone.¶

4. *heilissō, or helissō* (ἑλίσσω, 1507), "to roll," or "roll up," is used (*a*) of the "rolling" up of a mantle, illustratively of the heavens, Heb. 1:12, RV; (*b*) of the "rolling" up of a scroll, Rev. 6:14, illustratively of the removing of the heaven.¶

5. *entulissō* (ἐντυλίσσω, 1794), "to wrap up, roll round or about," is translated "rolled up" in John 20:7, RV, of the cloth or "napkin" that had been wrapped around the head of the Lord before burial. Both the RV and the KJV, "wrapped together," might suggest that this cloth had been "rolled" or wrapped up and put in a certain part of the tomb at the Lord's resurrection, whereas, as with the body wrappings, the head cloth was lying as it had been "rolled" round His head, an evidence, to those who looked into the tomb, of the fact of His resurrection without any disturbance of the wrappings either by friend or foe or when the change took place. It is followed by *en*, "in," and translated "wrapped" in Matt. 27:59, a meaning and construction which Moulton and Milligan illustrate from the papyri; in Luke 23:53 it is followed by the dative of the noun *sindōn*, "linen cloth," used instrumentally. See WRAP.¶

B. Noun.

kephalis (κεφαλίς, 2777), lit., "a little head" (a diminutive of *kephalē*, "a head"; Lat., *capitulum*, a diminutive of *caput*), hence, "a capital of a column," then, "a roll" (of a book), occurs in Heb. 10:7, RV, "in the roll" (KJV, "in the volume"), lit., "in the heading of the scroll" (from Ps. 40:7).¶

ROMAN

rhōmaios ('Ρωμαῖος, 4514) occurs in John 11:48; Acts 2:10, RV, "from Rome" (KJV, "of Rome"); 16:21, 37, 38; 22:25, 26, 27, 29;

23:27; 25:16; 28:17.¶ For a note on Roman citizenship see CITIZEN, No. 3.

ROOF

stegē (στέγη, 4721), "a covering" (*stegō*, "to cover"), denotes "a roof," Mark 2:4; said of entering a house, Matt. 8:8; Luke 7:6.¶

ROOM

A. Nouns.

1. *topos* (τόπος, 5117), "a place," is translated "room" in Luke 2:7 and 14:22, i.e., "place"; in the KJV in Luke 14:9, 10, RV, "place" (of a couch at a feast); of a position or condition which a person occupies, 1 Cor. 14:16 (RV, "place"). See OPPORTUNITY, PLACE.

2. *prōtoklisia* (πρωτοκλισία, 4411), "the chief reclining place at table," is rendered "uppermost rooms," in Matt. 23:6, KJV (RV, "chief place"); in Mark 12:39, "uppermost rooms," KJV (RV, "chief places"); in Luke 14:7, "chief rooms," KJV (RV, "chief seats"); in v. 8, KJV, "highest room" (RV, "chief seat"); in 20:46, KJV, "highest seats" (RV, "chief seats"). See CHIEF, B, No. 7, PLACE, No. 5.¶

3. *anagaion or anōgeon* (ἀνάγαιον, 508), "an upper room" (*ana*, "above," *gē*, "ground"), occurs in Mark 14:15; Luke 22:12, "a chamber," often over a porch, or connected with the roof, where meals were taken and privacy obtained.¶

4. *huperōon* (ὑπερῷον, 5253), the neuter of the adjective *huperōos*, "upper" (from *huper*, "above"), used as a noun, denoted in classical Greek "an upper story" or "room" where the women resided; in the Sept. and the NT, "an upper chamber, a roof-chamber," built on the flat "roof" of the house, Acts 1:13, RV, "upper chamber" (KJV "upper room"); see CHAMBER, No. 2.

B. Verb.

chōreō (χωρέω, 5562), "to make room," is translated "there was ... room" in Mark 2:2. See CONTAIN, No. 1

C. Preposition.

anti (ἀντί, 473), "in place of, instead of," is translated "in the room of" in Matt. 2:22.

Notes: (1) In Luke 12:17, KJV, *pou*, "anywhere" or "where," with a negative, is translated "no room" (RV, "not where"). (2) In Acts 24:27, KJV, *diadochos*, "a successor," with *lambanō*, "to receive," is translated "came into (Felix') room," RV, "(Felix) was succeeded by." *Diadochos* often meant a deputy, a temporary successor."¶

ROOT

A. Noun.

rhiza (ῥίζα, 4491) is used (*a*) in the natural sense, Matt. 3:10; 13:6, 21; Mark 4:6, 17; 11:20; Luke 3:9; 8:13; (*b*) metaphorically (1) of "cause, origin, source," said of persons, ancestors, Rom. 11:16, 17, 18 (twice); of things, evils, 1 Tim. 6:10, RV, of the love of money as a "root" of all "kinds of evil" (marg., "evils"; KJV, "evil"); bitterness, Heb. 12:15; (2) of that which springs from a "root," a shoot, said of offspring, Rom. 15:12; Rev. 5:5; 22:16.¶

B. Verbs.

1. *rhizoō* (ῥιζόω, 4492), "to cause to take root," is used metaphorically in the passive voice in Eph. 3:17, of being "rooted" in love; Col. 2:7, in Christ, i.e., in the sense of being firmly planted, or established.¶ In the Sept., Isa. 40:24; Jer. 12:2.¶

2. *ekrizoō* (ἐκριζόω, 1610), "to root out or up" (*ek*, "out," and No. 1), is rendered "to root up" in Matt. 13:29; 15:13; see PLUCK.

ROPE

schoinion (σχοινίον, 4979), a diminutive of *schoinos*, "a rush," is used of the small cords of which Christ made a scourge, John 2:15; of the "ropes" of a boat, Acts 27:32. See CORD.¶

For **ROSE** see **RISE**

ROUGH

1. *sklēros* (σκληρός, 4672), "hard," is translated "rough" in Jas. 3:4, RV, of winds (KJV, "fierce"). See AUSTERE, FIERCE, *Note* (1).

2. *trachus* (τραχύς, 5138), "rough, uneven," is used of paths, Luke 3:5; of rocky places, Acts 27:29. See ROCKY.¶

ROUND, ROUND ABOUT

1. *kuklothen* (κυκλόθεν, 2943), from *kuklos*, "a circle, ring" (Eng., "cycle," etc.), occurs in Rev. 4:3, 4; in v. 8, RV, "round about," with reference to the eyes.¶

2. *pantothen* (πάντοθεν, 3840), "on all sides" (from *pas*, "all"), is translated "round about" in Heb. 9:4. See EVERYWHERE, No. 3.

3. *perix* (πέριξ, 4038), from the preposition *peri*, "around," occurs in Acts 5:16, "round about" (of cities).¶

4. *kuklō* (κύκλῳ, 2945), the dative case of the noun *kuklos*, "a ring," is used as an adverb, and translated "round about" in Mark 3:34, KJV (RV, "round"); 6:6, 36; Luke 9:12; Rom. 15:19; Rev. 4:6; 7:11.¶

Note: For combinations with other words see, e.g., COME, No. 38, COUNTRY, A, No. 6, A, No. 4, DWELL, No. 5, GO, No. 9, HEDGE, LOOK, A, No. 3, REGION, SHINE, STAND, B, No. 5.

ROUSE

exupnos (ἔξυπνος, 1853), "roused out of sleep" (*ek*, "out of," *hupnos*, "sleep"), occurs in Acts 16:27.¶ Cf. *exupnizō*, AWAKE, No. 4.

ROW (Verb)

elaunō (ἐλαύνω, 1643), "to drive," is used of "rowing" or sailing a boat, Mark 6:48; John 6:19. See DRIVE.

ROYAL

1. *basileios* (βασίλειος, 934), from *basileus*, "a king," is used in 1 Pet. 2:9 of the priesthood consisting of all believers.¶ Cf. Luke 7:25, for which see COURT, No. 3. In the Sept., Ex. 19:6; 23:22; Deut. 3:10.¶

2. *basilikos* (βασιλικός, 937), "belonging to a king," is translated "royal" in Acts 12:21; Jas. 2:8. See KING B, No. 2 NOBLEMAN.

RUB

psōchō (ψώχω, 5597), "to rub, to rub to pieces," is used in Luke 6:1.¶

RUDDER

pēdalion (πηδάλιον, 4079), "a rudder" (akin to *pēdos*, "the blade of an oar"), occurs in Jas. 3:4, RV, "rudder" (KJV, "helm"), and Acts 27:40, plural, RV, "(the bands of) the rudders," KJV, "the rudder (bands)."¶

The *pēdalia* were actually steering paddles, two of which were used as "rudders" in ancient ships.

RUDE

idiōtēs (ἰδιώτης, 2399), for which see IGNORANT, No. 4, is translated "rude" in 2 Cor. 11:6.

RUDIMENTS

stoicheion (στοιχεῖον, 4747), "one of a row or series," is translated "rudiments" in the RV of Gal. 4:3, 9; Heb. 5:12, and the KJV and RV of Col. 2:8, 20. See ELEMENTS.

RUE

pēganon (πήγανον, 4076), a shrubby plant with yellow flowers and a heavy smell, cultivated for medicinal purposes, is mentioned in Luke 11:42.¶

RUIN

1. *rhēgma* (ῥῆγμα, 4485), akin to *rhēgnumi*, "to break," denotes "a cleavage, fracture" (so in the Sept., e.g., 1 Kings 11:30, 31); by meto-

nymy, that which is broken, "a ruin," Luke 6:49.¶

2. *katestrammena* (κατεστραμμένα, 2690**), the neuter plural, perfect participle, passive, of *katastrephō*, "to overturn," is translated "ruins" in Acts 15:16; cf. DIG, No. 3. See OVERTHROW.

RULE (Noun and Verb)

A. Nouns.

1. *archē* (ἀρχή, 746), "a beginning," etc., denotes "rule," Luke 20:20, RV, "rule" (KJV, "power"); 1 Cor. 15:24; Eph. 1:21, RV, "rule" (KJV, "principality"). See BEGINNING, B.

2. *kanōn* (κανών, 2583) is translated "rule" in the KJV of 2 Cor. 10:13, 15; in Gal. 6:16, KJV and RV; in Phil. 3:16, KJV (RV, in italics): see PROVINCE, No. 2.

B. Verbs.

1. *archō* (ἄρχω, 756), (akin to A, No. 1), in the active voice denotes "to rule," Mark 10:42 and Rom. 15:12, RV, "to rule" (KJV, "to reign"). See BEGIN, A, No. 1.

2. *oikodespoteō* (οἰκοδεσποτέω, 3616), from *oikos*, "a house," and *despotēs*, "a master," signifies "to rule the household"; so the RV in 1 Tim. 5:14 (KJV, "guide the house"). See GUIDE, B, *Note* (1).¶ Cf. *oikodespotēs*, "a householder."

3. *proistēmi* (προΐστημι, 4291), lit., "to stand before," hence, "to lead, attend to" (indicating care and diligence), is translated "to rule" (middle voice), with reference to a local church, in Rom. 12:8; perfect active in 1 Tim. 5:17; with reference to a family, 1 Tim. 3:4 and 12 (middle voice); v. 5 (2nd aorist, active). See MAINTAIN.

4. *hēgeomai* (ἡγέομαι, 2233), "to lead," is translated "to rule" in Heb. 13:7, 17, 24 (KJV marg., in the first two, "are the guides" and "guide."

5. *poimaino* (ποιμαίνω, 4165), "to act as a shepherd, tend flocks," is translated "to rule" in Rev. 2:27; 12:5; 19:15, all indicating that the governing power exercised by the Shepherd is to be of a firm character; in Matt. 2:6, KJV, "shall rule" (RV, "shall be shepherd of"). See FEED.

6. *brabeuō* (βραβεύω, 1018), properly, "to act as an umpire" (*brabeus*), hence, generally, "to arbitrate, decide," Col. 3:15, "rule" (RV, marg., "arbitrate"), representing "the peace of Christ" (RV) as deciding all matters in the hearts of believers; some regard the meaning as that of simply directing, controlling, "ruling."¶ Cf. *katabrabeuō;* see ROB.

RULER

1. *archōn* (ἄρχων, 758), "a ruler, chief, prince," is translated "rulers," e.g., in 1 Cor. 2:6, 8, RV (KJV, "princes"); "ruler," Rev. 1:5 (KJV, "prince"). See MAGISTRATE, PRINCE, No. 2.

2. *archē* (ἀρχή, 746), "a rule, sovereignty," is rendered "rulers" in Luke 12:11, RV (KJV, "magistrates"). See BEGINNING.

3. *kosmokratōr* (κοσμοκράτωρ, 2888) denotes "a ruler of this world" (contrast *pantokratōr*, "almighty"). In Greek literature, in Orphic hymns, etc., and in rabbinic writings, it signifies a "ruler" of the whole world, a world lord. In the NT it is used in Eph. 6:12, "the world rulers (of this darkness)," RV, KJV, "the rulers (of the darkness) of this world." The context ("not against flesh and blood") shows that not earthly potentates are indicated, but spirit powers, who, under the permissive will of God, and in consequence of human sin, exercise satanic and therefore antagonistic authority over the world in its present condition of spiritual darkness and alienation from God. The suggested rendering "the rulers of this dark world" is ambiguous and not phraseologically requisite. Cf. John 12:31; 14:30; 16:11; 2 Cor. 4:4.¶

4. *politarchēs* (πολιτάρχης, 4173), "a ruler of a city" (*polis*, "a city," *archō*, "to rule"), "a politarch," is used in Acts 17:6, 8, of the magistrates in Thessalonica, before whom the Jews, with a mob of market idlers, dragged Jason and other converts, under the charge of showing hospitality to Paul and Silas, and of treasonable designs against the emperor. Thessalonica was a "free" city and the citizens could choose their own politarchs. The accuracy of Luke has been vindicated by the use of the term, for while classical authors use the terms *poliarchos* and *politarchos* of similar "rulers," the form used by Luke is supported by inscriptions discovered at Thessalonica, one of which mentions Sosipater, Secundus, and Gaius among the politarchs, names occurring as those of Paul's companions. Prof. Burton of Chicago, in a paper on "The Politarchs," has recorded 17 inscriptions which attest their existence, thirteen of which belong to Macedonia and five presumably to Thessalonica itself, illustrating the influence of Rome in the municipal organization of the place.¶

5. *architriklinos* (ἀρχιτρίκλινος, 755) denotes "the superintendent of a banquet," whose duty lay in arranging the tables and food (*archē*, "ruler," *triklinos*, lit., "a room with three couches"), John 2:8, 9.¶

Notes: (1) In Mark 13:9 and Luke 21:12, KJV, *hēgemōn*, "a leader, a governor of a province," is translated "ruler" (RV, "governor"). See GOV-

ERNOR, PRINCE, No. 3. (2) For "ruler" of the synagogue, see SYNAGOGUE. (3) In Matt. 24:45, KJV, *kathistēmi*, "to appoint," is translated "hath made ruler" (RV, "hath set"); so in v. 47; 25:21, 23; Luke 12:42, 44.

RUMOR

1. *akoē* (ἀκοή, 189), "a hearing," is translated "rumor" in Matt. 24:6; Mark 13:7. See HEARING, B, No. 1.

2. *ēchos* (ἦχος, 2279), "a noise, sound," is translated "rumor" in Luke 4:37, RV (KJV, "fame"). See ROAR, SOUND.

Note: In Luke 7:17, KJV, *logos*, "a word," is translated "rumor" (RV, "report").

RUN, RAN

1. *trechō* (τρέχω, 5143), "to run," is used (*a*) literally, e.g., Matt. 27:48 (*dramōn*, an aorist participle, from an obsolete verb *dramō*, but supplying certain forms absent from *trechō*, lit., "having run, running," expressive of the decisiveness of the act); the same form in the indicative mood is used, e.g., in Matt. 28:8; in the Gospels the literal meaning alone is used; elsewhere in 1 Cor. 9:24 (twice in 1st part); Rev. 9:9, KJV, "running" (RV, "rushing"); (*b*) metaphorically, from the illustration of "runners" in a race, of either swiftness or effort to attain an end, Rom. 9:16, indicating that salvation is not due to human effort, but to God's sovereign right to exercise mercy; 1 Cor. 9:24 (2nd part), and v. 26, of persevering activity in the Christian course with a view to obtaining the reward; so Heb. 12:1; in Gal. 2:2 (1st part), RV, "(lest) I should be running," continuous present tense, referring to the activity of the special service of his mission to Jerusalem; (2nd part), "had run," aorist tense, expressive of the continuous past, referring to the activity of his antagonism to the Judaizing teachers at Antioch, and his consent to submit the case to the judgment of the church in Jerusalem; in 5:7 of the erstwhile faithful course doctrinally of the Galatian believers; in Phil. 2:16, of the apostle's manner of life among the Philippian believers; in 2 Thess. 3:1, of the free and rapid progress of "the word of the Lord."

2. *prostrechō* (προστρέχω, 4370), "to run to" (*pros*, "to," and No. 1), is used in Mark 9:15; 10:17; Acts 8:30.¶

3. *peritrechō* (περιτρέχω, 4063), "to run about" (*peri* "around," and No. 1), is used in Mark 6:55, RV, "ran round about" (KJV, "ran through").¶

4. *suntrechō* (συντρέχω, 4936), "to run together with" (*sun*, "with"), is used (*a*) literally, Mark 6:33; Acts 3:11; (*b*) metaphorically, 1 Pet.

4:4, of "running" a course of evil with others.¶ In the Sept., Ps. 50:18.¶

5. *protrechō* (προτρέχω, 4390), "to run before," Luke 19:4: see OUTRUN.

6. *eistrechō* (εἰστρέχω, 1532), "to run in" (*eis*, "in"), occurs in Acts 12:14.¶

7. *hupotrechō* (ὑποτρέχω, 5295), "to run under" (*hupo*, "under"), is used nautically in Acts 27:16.¶

8. *episuntrechō* (ἐπισυντρέχω, 1998), "to run together again" (*epi*, "upon, or again," and No. 4), occurs in Mark 9:25.¶

9. *ekchunnō or ekchunō* (ἐκχύννω, 1632), "to shed," is translated "ran riotously" in Jude 11, RV (KJV, "ran greedily"). See RIOTOUSLY, Note. See SHED, SPILL.

10. *huperekchunnō* (ὑπερεκχύννω, 5240), a late form of *huperekcheō*, "to overflow," is rendered "running over" in Luke 6:38.¶

11. *epikellō or epokellō* (ἐπικέλλω, 2207), "to drive upon," is used in Acts 27:41 of "running" a ship ashore.¶

Notes: (1) *Hormaō*, "to set in motion, urge on," but intransitively, "to hasten on, rush," is always translated "to rush" in the RV; KJV, "ran violently," Matt. 8:32; Mark 5:13; Luke 8:33; "ran," Acts 7:57; "rushed", 19:29. See RUSH.¶ (2) In Acts 21:30, *sundromē*, "a running together," with *ginomai*, "to become, take place," is translated "ran together," lit., "a running together took place." (3) In Matt. 9:17, KJV, *ekcheō*, "to pour out," used in the passive voice (RV, "is spilled"), is translated "runneth out." (4) In Acts 14:14, RV, *ekpēdaō*, "to spring forth," is translated "sprang forth" (this verb is found in the papyri); the KJV, "ran in" translates the mss. which have *eispēdaō*, "to spring in." (5) *Katatrechō*, "to run down," occurs in Acts 21:32.¶

RUSH, RUSHING

1. *hormaō* (ὁρμάω, 3729), for which see RUN, *Note* (1), with refs., is akin to *hormē* (see ASSAULT) and *hormēma*, "a rushing" (see VIOLENCE).

2. *pherō* (φέρω, 5342), "to bear," is used in the present participle, passive voice, in Acts 2:2, and translated "rushing," RV, "the rushing (of a mighty wind)," KJV "a rushing (mighty wind)" lit "a violent wind borne (along)."

3. *trechō* (τρέχω, 5143), "to run," is translated "rushing (to war)" in Rev. 9:9, RV, KJV, "running (to battle)."

RUST (Noun and Verb)

A. Nouns.

1. *brōsis* (βρῶσις, 1035), "an eating" (akin to *bibrōskō*, "to eat"), is used metaphorically to

denote "rust" in Matt. 6:19, 20. See EAT, B, No. 1, FOOD, MEAT, MORSEL.

2. *ios* (ἰός, 2447), "poison," denotes "rust" in Jas. 5:3. See POISON.

B. Verb.

katioō (κατιόω, 2728), an intensive form of *ioō*, "to poison" (akin to A, No. 2), strength-ened by *kata*, "down," "to rust over," and in the passive voice, "to become rusted over," occurs in Jas. 5:3, RV, "are rusted" (KJV, "are cankered").¶ Cf. *gangraina*, "a gangrene," 2 Tim. 2:17, RV.¶

S

SABACHTHANI

sabachthanei (σαβαχθανεί, 4518), an Aramaic word signifying "Thou hast forsaken Me," is recorded as part of the utterance of Christ on the cross, Matt. 27:46; Mark 15:34, a quotation from Ps. 22:1. Recently proposed renderings which differ from those of the KJV and RV have not been sufficiently established to require acceptance.

SABAOTH

sabaōth (σαβαώθ, 4519) is the transliteration of a Hebrew word which denotes "hosts" or "armies," Rom. 9:29; Jas. 5:4.¶ While the word "hosts" probably had special reference to angels, the title "the LORD of hosts" became used to designate Him as the One who is supreme over all the innumerable hosts of spiritual agencies, or of what are described as "the armies of heaven." Eventually it was used as equivalent to "the LORD all-sovereign." In the prophetical books of the OT the Sept. sometimes has *Kurios Sabaōth* as the equivalent of "the LORD of hosts," sometimes *Kurios Pantokratōr,* in Job, it uses *Pantokratōr* to render the Hebrew divine title *Shadday* (see AL-MIGHTY).

SABBATH

1. *sabbaton* (σάββατον, 4521) or *sabbata*: the latter, the plural form, was transliterated from the Aramaic word, which was mistaken for a plural; hence the singular, *sabbaton*, was formed from it. The root means "to cease, desist" (Heb., *shābath;* cf. Arab., *sabata*, "to intercept, interrupt"); the doubled *b* has an intensive force, implying a complete cessation or a making to cease, probably the former. The idea is not that of relaxation or refreshment, but cessation from activity.

The observation of the seventh day of the week, enjoined upon Israel, was a sign between God and His earthly people, based upon the fact that after the six days of creative operations He rested, Exod. 31:16, 17, with 20:8–11. The OT regulations were developed and systematized to such an extent that they became a burden upon the people (who otherwise rejoiced in the rest provided) and a byword for absurd extravagance. Two treatises of the Mishna (the *Shabbāth* and *Ērūbin*) are entirely occupied with regulations for the observance; so with the discussions in the Gemara, on rabbinical opinions. The effect upon current opinion explains the antagonism roused by the Lord's cures wrought on the "Sabbath," e.g., Matt. 12:9–13; John 5:5–16, and explains the fact that on a "Sabbath" the sick were brought to be healed after sunset, e.g., Mark 1:32. According to rabbinical ideas, the disciples, by plucking ears of corn (Matt. 12:1; Mark 2:23), and rubbing them (Luke 6:1), broke the "sabbath" in two respects; for to pluck was to reap, and to rub was to thresh. The Lord's attitude towards the "sabbath" was by way of freeing it from these vexatious traditional accretions by which it was made an end in itself, instead of a means to an end (Mark 2:27).

In the Epistles the only direct mentions are in Col. 2:16, "a sabbath day," RV (which rightly has the singular, see 1st parag., above), where it is listed among things that were "a shadow of the things to come" (i.e., of the age introduced at Pentecost), and in Heb. 4:4–11, where the perpetual *sabbatismos* is appointed for believers (see REST); inferential references are in Rom. 14:5 and Gal. 4:9–11. For the first three centuries of the Christian era the first day of the week was never confounded with the "sabbath"; the confusion of the Jewish and Christian institutions was due to declension from apostolic teaching.

Notes: (1) In Matt. 12:1 and 11, where the plural is used, the KJV (as the RV) rightly has the singular, "the sabbath day"; in v. 5 the KJV has the plural (see above). Where the singular is used the RV omits the word "day," v. 2; 24:20; Mark 6:2; Luke 6:1 ("on a sabbath"); 14:3; John 9:14 ("it was the sabbath on the day when . . ."). As to the use or omission of the article the omission does not always require the rendering "a sabbath"; it is absent, e.g., in Matt. 12:2. (2) In Acts 16:13, "on the sabbath day," is, lit., "on the day of the sabbath" (plural). (3) For Matt. 28:1, see LATE. (4) For "the first day of the week" see ONE, A, (5).

2. *prosabbaton* (προσάββατον, 4315) signifies "the day before the sabbath" (*pro*, "before," and No. 1), Mark 15:42; some mss. have *prin*, "before," with *sabbaton* separately).¶

SACKCLOTH

sakkos (σάκκος, 4526), "a warm material woven from goat's or camel's hair," and hence of a dark color, Rev. 6:12; Jerome renders it *saccus cilicinus* (being made from the hair of the black goat of Cilicia; the Romans called it *cilicium*); cf. Isa. 50:3; it was also used for saddlecloths, Josh. 9:4; also for making sacks, e.g., Gen. 42:25, and for garments worn as expressing mourning or penitence, Matt. 11:21; Luke 10:13, or for purposes of prophetic testimony, Rev. 11:3.¶

SACRED

hieros (ἱερός, 2413) denotes "consecrated to God," e.g., the Scriptures, 2 Tim. 3:15, RV, "sacred" (KJV "holy"); it is used as a noun in the neuter plural in 1 Cor. 9:13, RV, "sacred things" (KJV, "holy things").¶ The neuter singular, *hieron*, denotes "a temple." See TEMPLE. For a comparison of this and synonymous terms see HOLY, B, No. 1 (*b*) and *Note* (2).

SACRIFICE (Noun and Verb)

A. Noun.

thusia (θυσία, 2378) primarily denotes "the act of offering"; then, objectively, "that which is offered" (*a*) of idolatrous "sacrifice," Acts 7:41; (*b*) of animal or other "sacrifices," as offered under the Law, Matt. 9:13; 12:7; Mark 9:49; 12:33; Luke 2:24; 13:1; Acts 7:42; 1 Cor. 10:18; Heb. 5:1; 7:27 (RV, plural); 8:3; 9:9; 10:1, 5, 8 (RV, plural), 11; 11:4; (*c*) of Christ, in His "sacrifice" on the cross, Eph. 5:2; Heb. 9:23, where the plural antitypically comprehends the various forms of Levitical "sacrifices" in their typical character; 9:26; 10:12, 26; (*d*) metaphorically, (1) of the body of the believer, presented to God as a living "sacrifice," Rom. 12:1; (2) of faith, Phil. 2:17; (3) of material assistance rendered to servants of God, Phil. 4:18; (4) of praise, Heb. 13:15; (5) of doing good to others and communicating with their needs, Heb. 13:16; (6) of spiritual "sacrifices" in general, offered by believers as a holy priesthood, 1 Pet. 2:5.¶

B. Verb.

thuō (θύω, 2380) is used of "sacrificing by slaying a victim," (*a*) of the "sacrifice" of Christ, 1 Cor. 5:7, RV, "hath been sacrificed" (KJV, "is sacrificed"); (*b*) of the Passover "sacrifice," Mark 14:12, RV, "they sacrificed" (KJV, "they killed"); Luke 22:7, RV, "(must) be sacrificed," KJV, "(must) be killed"; (*c*) of idolatrous "sacrifices," Acts 14:13, 18; 1 Cor. 10:20 (twice). See KILL, No. 3.

Note: For *eidōlothutos*, "sacrificed to idols," see IDOLS (offered to), No. 1.

For SACRILEGE see ROBBER, No. 2, Rom. 2:22

For SAD see COUNTENANCE

For SADDUCEES see under PHARISEES

SAFE, SAFELY, SAFETY

A. Adjective.

asphalēs (ἀσφαλής, 804), "certain, secure, safe" (from *a*, negative, and *sphallō*, "to trip up"), is translated "safe" in Phil. 3:1. See CERTAIN, B.

B. Nouns.

1. *asphaleia* (ἀσφάλεια, 803), "certainty, safety" (akin to A), is translated "safety" in Acts 5:23; 1 Thess. 5:3. See CERTAIN, A.

2. *sōtēria* (σωτηρία, 4991), "salvation," is translated "safety" in Acts 27:34, RV (KJV, "health"). See HEALTH, *Note*.

C. Adverb.

asphalōs (ἀσφαλῶς, 806), "safely" (akin to A, and B, No. 1), is so rendered in Mark 14:44 and Acts 16:23. See ASSURANCE, C. In the Sept., Gen. 34:25.¶

D. Verbs.

1. *diasōzō* (διασώζω, 1295), "to bring safely through danger," and, in the passive voice, "to come safe through" (*dia*, "through," *sōzō*, "to save"), is translated "bring safe" in Acts 23:24; "escaped safe" in 27:44. See ESCAPE, HEAL, SAVE, WHOLE.

2. *hugiainō* (ὑγιαίνω, 5198), "to be sound, healthy" (Eng., "hygiene," etc.), is translated "safe and sound" in Luke 15:27, lit., "being healthy." See HEALTH, SOUND, WHOLE.

For SAIL (Noun, Acts 27:17, KJV) see GEAR

SAIL (Verb)

1. *pleō* (πλέω, 4126), "to sail," occurs in Luke 8:23; Acts 21:3; 27:2, 6, 24; Rev. 18:17, RV, "saileth" (for the KJV see COMPANY, A, No. 7).¶

2. *apopleō* (ἀποπλέω, 636), "to sail away" (*apo*, "from," and No. 1), occurs in Acts 13:4; 14:26; 20:15; 27:1.¶

3. *ekpleō* (ἐκπλέω, 1602), "to sail from or thence" (*ek*, "from"), occurs in Acts 15:39; 18:18; 20:6.¶

4. *parapleō* (παραπλέω, 3896), "to sail by" (*para*), occurs in Acts 20:16.¶

5. *diapleō* (διαπλέω, 1277), "to sail across" (*dia*, "through"), occurs in Acts 27:5.¶

6. *hupopleō* (ὑποπλέω, 5284), "to sail under" (*hupo*), i.e., "under the lee of," occurs in Acts 27:4, 7.¶

7. *anagō* (ἀνάγω, 321), "to lead up," is used of "putting to sea," Acts 13:13; 16:11; 18:21; 20:3, 13; 21:1; 27:21; 28:10, 11; see LAUNCH.

8. *paralegō* (παραλέγω, 3881), "to lay beside" (*para*), is used in the middle voice, of "sailing past" in Acts 27:8, RV, "coasting along" (KJV, "passing"); v. 13, RV, "sailed along" (KJV, "sailed").¶

9. *diaperaō* (διαπεράω, 1276), "to cross over," is translated "sailing over" in Acts 21:2, KJV (RV, "crossing over"). See PASS.

10. *braduploeō* (βραδυπλοέω, 1020), "to sail slowly" (*bradus*, "slow," *plous*, "a voyage"), occurs in Acts 27:7.¶

For SAILING see VOYAGE

For SAILORS see MARINERS

SAINT(S)

hagios (ἅγιος, 40), for the meaning and use of which see HOLY, B, No. 1, is used as a noun in the singular in Phil. 4:21, where *pas*, "every," is used with it. In the plural, as used of believers, it designates all such and is not applied merely to persons of exceptional holiness, or to those who, having died, were characterized by exceptional acts of "saintliness." See especially 2 Thess. 1:10, where "His saints" are also described as "them that believed," i.e., the whole number of the redeemed. They are called "holy ones" in Jude 14, RV. For the term as applied to the Holy Spirit see HOLY SPIRIT. See also SANCTIFY.

Notes: (1) In Rev. 15:3 the RV follows those texts which have *aiōnōn*, "ages," and assigns the reading *ethnōn*, "nations," to the margin; the KJV translates those which have the inferior reading *hagiōn*, "saints," and puts "nations" and

"ages" in the margin. (2) In Rev. 18:20, the best texts have *hagioi* and *apostoloi*, each with the article, each being preceeded by *kai*, "and," RV, "and ye saints, and ye apostles"; the KJV, "and ye holy apostles" follows those mss. from which the 2nd *kai* and the article are absent. (3) In Rev. 22:21, the RV follows those mss. which have *hagiōn*, with the article,"(with) the saints"; the KJV those which simply have *pantōn*, "all," but adds "you" (RV, marg., "with all").

For SAKE (for the) see †, p. 1

SALT (Noun, Adjective and Verb), SALTNESS

A. Noun.

halas (ἅλας, 251), a late form of *hals* (found in some mss. in Mark 9:49), is used (*a*) literally in Matt. 5:13 (2nd part); Mark 9:50 (1st part, twice); Luke 14:34 (twice); (*b*) metaphorically, of "believers," Matt. 5:13 (1st part); of their "character and condition," Mark 9:50 (2nd part); of "wisdom" exhibited in their speech, Col. 4:6.¶

Being possessed of purifying, perpetuating and antiseptic qualities, "salt" became emblematic of fidelity and friendship among eastern nations. To eat of a person's "salt" and so to share his hospitality is still regarded thus among the Arabs. So in Scripture, it is an emblem of the covenant between God and His people, Num. 18:19; 2 Chron. 13:5; so again when the Lord says "Have salt in yourselves, and be at peace one with another" (Mark 9:50). In the Lord's teaching it is also symbolic of that spiritual health and vigor essential to Christian virtue and counteractive of the corruption that is in the world, e.g., Matt. 5:13, see (*b*) above. Food is seasoned with "salt" (see B); every meal offering was to contain it, and it was to be offered with all offerings presented by Israelites, as emblematic of the holiness of Christ, and as betokening the reconciliation provided for man by God on the ground of the death of Christ, Lev. 2:13. To refuse God's provision in Christ and the efficacy of His expiatory sacrifice is to expose oneself to the doom of being "salted with fire," Mark 9:49.

While "salt" is used to fertilize soil, excess of it on the ground produces sterility (e.g., Deut. 29:23; Judg. 9:45; Jer. 17:6; Zeph. 2:9).

B. Verb.

halizō (ἁλίζω, 233), akin to A, signifies "to sprinkle" or "to season with salt," Matt. 5:13; Mark 9:49 (see under A).¶ Cf. SAVOR, B.

C. Adjectives.

1. *halukos* (ἁλυκός, 252) occurs in Jas. 3:12, "salt (water)."¶

2. *analos* (ἄναλος, 358) denotes "saltless" (*a*, negative, *n*, euphonic, and A), insipid, Mark 9:50, "have lost its saltness," lit., "have become (*ginomai*) saltless (*analos*)"; cf. *mōrainō* in Luke 14:34 (see SAVOR, B).

For SALUTATION and SALUTE see GREET

SALVATION

A. Nouns.

1. *sōtēria* (σωτηρία, 4991) denotes "deliverance, preservation, salvation." "Salvation" is used in the NT (*a*) of material and temporal deliverance from danger and apprehension, (1) national, Luke 1:69, 71; Acts 7:25, RV marg., "salvation" (text, "deliverance"); (2) personal, as from the sea, Acts 27:34; RV, "safety" (KJV, "health"); prison, Phil. 1:19; the flood, Heb. 11:7; (*b*) of the spiritual and eternal deliverance granted immediately by God to those who accept His conditions of repentance and faith in the Lord Jesus, in whom alone it is to be obtained, Acts 4:12, and upon confession of Him as Lord, Rom. 10:10; for this purpose the gospel is the saving instrument, Rom. 1:16; Eph. 1:13 (see further under SAVE); (*c*) of the present experience of God's power to deliver from the bondage of sin, e.g., Phil. 2:12, where the special, though not the entire, reference is to the maintenance of peace and harmony; 1 Pet. 1:9; this present experience on the part of believers is virtually equivalent to sanctification; for this purpose, God is able to make them wise, 2 Tim. 3:15; they are not to neglect it, Heb. 2:3; (*d*) of the future deliverance of believers at the Parousia of Christ for His saints, a salvation which is the object of their confident hope, e.g., Rom. 13:11; 1 Thess. 5:8, and v. 9, where "salvation" is assured to them, as being deliverance from the wrath of God destined to be executed upon the ungodly at the end of this age (see 1 Thess. 1:10; 2 Thess. 2:13; Heb. 1:14; 9:28; 1 Pet. 1:5; 2 Pet. 3:15; (*e*) of the deliverance of the nation of Israel at the second advent of Christ at the time of "the epiphany (or shining forth) of His Parousia" (2 Thess. 2:8); Luke 1:71; Rev. 12:10; (*f*) inclusively, to sum up all the blessings bestowed by God on men in Christ through the Holy Spirit, e.g., 2 Cor. 6:2; Heb. 5:9; 1 Pet. 1:9, 10; Jude 3; (*g*) occasionally, as standing virtually for the Savior, e.g., Luke 19:9; cf. John 4:22 (see SAVIOR); (*h*) in ascriptions of praise to God, Rev. 7:10, and as that which it is His prerogative to bestow, 19:1 (RV).

2. *sōtērion* (σωτήριον, 4992), the neuter of the adjective (see B), is used as a noun in Luke 2:30; 3:6, in each of which it virtually stands for the Savior, as in No. 1 (*g*); in Acts 28:28, as in No. 1 (*b*); in Eph. 6:17, where the hope of "salvation" [see No. 1 (*d*)] is metaphorically described as "a helmet."¶

B. Adjective.

sōtērios (σωτήριος, 4992**), "saving, bringing salvation," describes the grace of God, in Titus 2:11.¶

SAME

1. *autos* (αὐτός, 846) denotes "the same" when preceded by the article, and either with a noun following, e.g., Mark 14:39; Phil 1:30; 1 Cor. 12:4, or without, e.g., Matt. 5:46, 47; Rom. 2:1; Phil. 2:2; 3:1; Heb. 1:12; 13:8. It is thus to be distinguished from uses as a personal and a reflexive pronoun.

2. *houtos* (οὗτος, 3778), "this" (person or thing), or "he" (and the feminine and neuter forms), is sometimes translated "the same," e.g., John 3:2, 26; 7:18; Jas. 3:2; sometimes the RV translates it by "this" or "these," e.g., John 12:21, "these" (KJV, "the same"); 2 Cor. 8:6, "this" (KJV, "the same").

SANCTIFICATION, SANCTIFY

A. Noun.

hagiasmos (ἁγιασμός, 38), "sanctification," is used of (*a*) separation to God, 1 Cor. 1:30; 2 Thess. 2:13; 1 Pet. 1:2; (*b*) the course of life befitting those so separated, 1 Thess. 4:3, 4, 7; Rom. 6:19, 22; 1 Tim. 2:15; Heb. 12:14.¶ "Sanctification is that relationship with God into which men enter by faith in Christ, Acts 26:18; 1 Cor. 6:11, and to which their sole title is the death of Christ, Eph. 5:25, 26; Col. 1:22; Heb. 10:10, 29; 13:12.

"Sanctification is also used in NT of the separation of the believer from evil things and ways. This sanctification is God's will for the believer, 1 Thess. 4:3, and His purpose in calling him by the gospel, v. 7; it must be learned from God, v. 4, as He teaches it by His Word, John 17:17, 19; cf. Ps. 17:4; 119:9, and it must be pursued by the believer, earnestly and undeviatingly, 1 Tim. 2:15; Heb. 12:14. For the holy character, *hagiōsunē*, 1 Thess. 3:13, is not vicarious, i.e., it cannot be transferred or imputed, it is an individual possession, built up, little by little, as the result of obedience to the Word of God, and of following the example of Christ, Matt. 11:29; John 13:15; Eph. 4:20; Phil. 2:5, in the power of the Holy Spirit, Rom. 8:13; Eph. 3:16.

"The Holy Spirit is the Agent in sanctification, Rom. 15:16; 2 Thess. 2:13; 1 Pet. 1:2; cf. 1 Cor. 6:11.... The sanctification of the Spirit is associated with the choice, or election, of God; it is a Divine act preceding the acceptance of the Gospel by the individual."*

For synonymous words see HOLINESS.

B. Verb.

hagiazō (ἁγιάζω, 37), "to sanctify," "is used of (*a*) the gold adorning the Temple and of the gift laid on the altar, Matt. 23:17, 19; (*b*) food, 1 Tim. 4:5; (*c*) the unbelieving spouse of a believer, 1 Cor. 7:14; (*d*) the ceremonial cleansing of the Israelites, Heb. 9:13; (*e*) the Father's Name, Luke 11:2; (*f*) the consecration of the Son by the Father, John 10:36; (*g*) the Lord Jesus devoting Himself to the redemption of His people, John 17:19; (*h*) the setting apart of the believer for God, Acts 20:32; cf. Rom. 15:16; (*i*) the effect on the believer of the Death of Christ, Heb. 10:10, said of God, and 2:11; 13:12, said of the Lord Jesus; (*j*) the separation of the believer from the world in his behavior— by the Father through the Word, John 17:17, 19; (*k*) the believer who turns away from such things as dishonor God and His gospel, 2 Tim. 2:21; (*l*) the acknowledgment of the Lordship of Christ, 1 Pet. 3:15.

"Since every believer is sanctified in Christ Jesus, 1 Cor. 1:2, cf. Heb. 10:10, a common NT designation of all believers is 'saints,' *hagioi*, i.e., 'sanctified' or 'holy ones.' Thus sainthood, or sanctification, is not an attainment, it is the state into which God, in grace, calls sinful men, and in which they begin their course as Christians, Col. 3:12; Heb. 3:1."†

SANCTUARY

hagion (ἅγιον, 39), the neuter of the adjective *hagios*, "holy," is used of those structures which are set apart to God, (*a*) of "the tabernacle" in the wilderness, Heb. 9:1, RV, "its sanctuary, *a sanctuary* of this world" (KJV, "a worldly sanctuary"); in v. 2 the outer part is called "the Holy place," RV (KJV, "the sanctuary"); here the neuter plural *hagia* is used, as in v. 3.

Speaking of the absence of the article, Westcott says "The anarthrous form Ἅγια (literally *Holies*) in this sense appears to be unique, as also ἅγια ἁγίων below, if indeed the reading

---

is correct. Perhaps it is chosen to fix attention on the character of the sanctuary as in other cases. The plural suggests the idea of the sanctuary with all its parts: cf. Moulton-Winer, p. 220." In their margin, Westcott and Hort prefix the article *ta* to *hagia* in vv. 2 and 3. In v. 3 the inner part is called "the Holy of holies," RV (KJV, "the holiest of all"); in v. 8, "the holy place" (KJV, "the holiest of all"), lit., "(the way) of the holiest"; in v. 24 "a holy place," RV (KJV, "the holy places"), neuter plural; so in v. 25, "the holy place" (KJV and RV), and in 13:11, RV, "the holy place" (KJV, "the sanctuary"); in all these there is no separate word *topos*, "place," as of the Temple in Matt. 24:15; (*b*) of "Heaven itself," i.e., the immediate presence of God and His throne, Heb. 8:2, "the sanctuary" (RV, marg., "holy things"); the neut. plur. with the article points to the text as being right, in view of 9:24, 25 and 13:11 (see above), exegetically designated "the true tabernacle"; neut. plur. in 9:12, "the holy place"; so 10:19, RV (KJV, "the holiest"; there are no separate compartments in the antitypical and heavenly sanctuary), into which believers have "boldness to enter" by faith.¶

2. *naos* (ναός, 3485) is used of the inner part of the Temple in Jerusalem, in Matt. 23:35, RV, "sanctuary." See TEMPLE.

SAND

ammos (ἄμμος, 285), "sand" or "sandy ground," describes (*a*) an insecure foundation, Matt. 7:26; (*b*) numberlessness, vastness, Rom. 9:27; Heb. 11:12; Rev. 20:8; (*c*) symbolically in Rev. 13:1, RV, the position taken up by the Dragon (not, as in the KJV, by John), in view of the rising of the Beast out of the sea (emblematic of the restless condition of nations; see SEA).¶

SANDAL

sandalion (σανδάλιον, 4547), a diminutive of *sandalon*, probably a Persian word, Mark 6:9; Acts 12:8. The "sandal" usually had a wooden sole bound on by straps round the instep and ankle.¶

SAPPHIRE

sappheiros (σάπφειρος, 4552) is mentioned in Rev. 21:19 (RV, marg., "*lapis lazuli*") as the second of the foundations of the wall of the heavenly Jerusalem (cf. Isa. 54:11).¶ It was one of the stones in the high priest's breastplate, Exod. 28:18; 39:11; as an intimation of its value see Job 28:16; Ezek. 28:13. See also Exod. 24:10; Ezek. 1:26; 10:1. The "sapphire" has various shades of blue and ranks next in hardness to the diamond.

SARDIUS, SARDINE (KJV)

sardion or *sardinos* (σάρδιον, 4555) denotes "the sardian stone." *Sardius* is the word in the best texts in Rev. 4:3 (RV, "a sardius"), where it formed part of the symbolic appearance of the Lord on His throne, setting forth His glory and majesty in view of the judgment to follow. There are two special varieties, one a yellowish brown, the other a transparent red (like a cornelian). The beauty of the stone, its transparent brilliance, the high polish of which it is susceptible, made it a favorite among the ancients. It forms the sixth foundation of the wall of the heavenly Jerusalem, Rev. 21:20.¶

SARDONYX

sardonux (σαρδόνυξ, 4557), a name which indicates the formation of the gem, a layer of sard, and a layer of onyx, marked by the red of the sard and the white of the onyx. It was used among the Romans both for cameos and for signets. It forms the fifth foundation of the wall of the heavenly Jerusalem, Rev. 21:20.¶

SATAN

satanas (Σατανᾶς, 4567), a Greek form derived from the Aramaic (Heb., *Sātān*), "an adversary," is used (*a*) of an angel of Jehovah in Num. 22:22 (the first occurrence of the Word in the OT); (*b*) of men, e.g., 1 Sam. 29:4; Ps. 38:20; 71:13; four in Ps. 109; (*c*) of "Satan," the Devil, some seventeen or eighteen times in the OT; in Zech. 3:1, where the name receives its interpretation, "to be (his) adversary," RV (see marg.; KJV, "to resist him").

In the NT the word is always used of "Satan," the adversary (*a*) of God and Christ, e.g., Matt. 4:10; 12:26; Mark 1:13; 3:23, 26; 4:15; Luke 4:8 (in some mss.); 11:18; 22:3; John 13:27; (*b*) of His people, e.g., Luke 22:31; Acts 5:3; Rom. 16:20; 1 Cor. 5:5; 7:5; 2 Cor. 2:11; 11:14; 12:7; 1 Thess. 2:18; 1 Tim. 1:20; 5:15; Rev. 2:9, 13 (twice), 24; 3:9; (*c*) of mankind, Luke 13:16; Acts 26:18; 2 Thess. 2:9; Rev. 12:9; 20:7.

His doom, sealed at the Cross, is foretold in its stages in Luke 10:18; Rev. 20:2, 10. Believers are assured of victory over him, Rom. 16:20.

The appellation was given by the Lord to Peter, as a "Satan-like" man, on the occasion when he endeavored to dissuade Him from death, Matt. 16:23; Mark 8:33.¶

"Satan" is not simply the personification of evil influences in the heart, for he tempted Christ, in whose heart no evil thought could

ever have arisen (John 14:30; 2 Cor. 5:21; Heb. 4:15); moreover his personality is asserted in both the OT and the NT, and especially in the latter, whereas if the OT language was intended to be figurative, the NT would have made this evident. See DEVIL.

SATISFY

1. *chortazō* (χορτάζω, 5526), "to fill or satisfy with food," is translated "satisfy" in Mark 8:4, KJV (RV, "to fill"). See FILL, No. 8.

2. *empiplēmi* or *emplēthō* (ἐμπίπλημι, 1705), "to fill up, fill full, satisfy" (*en*, "in," *pimplēmi* or *plēthō*, "to fill"), is used metaphorically in Rom. 15:24, of taking one's fill of the company of others, RV, "I shall have been satisfied" (KJV, "I be . . . filled"). See FILL, No. 6.

For **SATISFYING**, Col. 2:23, KJV, see **INDULGENCE**

For **SAVE** (Preposition) see †, p.1

SAVE, SAVING

A. Verbs.

1. *sōzō* (σώζω, 4982), "to save," is used (as with the noun *sōtēria*, "salvation") (*a*) of material and temporal deliverance from danger, suffering, etc., e.g., Matt. 8:25; Mark 13:20; Luke 23:35; John 12:27; 1 Tim. 2:15; 2 Tim. 4:18 (KJV, "preserve"); Jude 5; from sickness, Matt. 9:22, "made . . . whole" (RV, marg., "saved"); so Mark 5:34; Luke 8:48; Jas. 5:15; (*b*) of the spiritual and eternal salvation granted immediately by God to those who believe on the Lord Jesus Christ, e.g., Acts 2:47, RV "(those that) were being saved"; 16:31; Rom. 8:24, RV, "were we saved"; Eph. 2:5, 8; 1 Tim. 2:4; 2 Tim. 1:9; Titus 3:5; of human agency in this, Rom. 11:14; 1 Cor. 7:16; 9:22; (*c*) of the present experiences of God's power to deliver from the bondage of sin, e.g., Matt. 1:21; Rom. 5:10; 1 Cor. 15:2; Heb. 7:25; Jas. 1:21; 1 Pet. 3:21; of human agency in this, 1 Tim. 4:16; (*d*) of the future deliverance of believers at the second coming of Christ for His saints, being deliverance from the wrath of God to be executed upon the ungodly at the close of this age and from eternal doom, e.g., Rom. 5:9; (*e*) of the deliverance of the nation of Israel at the second advent of Christ, e.g., Rom. 11:26; (*f*) inclusively for all the blessings bestowed by God on men in Christ, e.g., Luke 19:10; John 10:9; 1 Cor. 10:33; 1 Tim. 1:15; (*g*) of those who endure to the end of the time of the Great Tribulation, Matt. 10:22; Mark 13:13; (*h*) of the individual believer, who, though losing his reward at the judgment seat

of Christ hereafter, will not lose his salvation, 1 Cor. 3:15; 5:5; (*i*) of the deliverance of the nations at the Millennium, Rev. 21:24 (in some mss.). See SALVATION.

2. *diasōzō* (διασώζω 1295), "to bring safely through" (*dia*, "through," and No. 1), is used (*a*) of the healing of the sick by the Lord, Matt. 14:36, RV, "were made whole" (KJV adds "perfectly"); Luke 7:3; (*b*) of bringing "safe" to a destination, Acts 23:24; (*c*) of keeping a person "safe," 27:43; (*d*) of escaping through the perils of shipwreck, 27:44; 28:1, 4, passive voice; (*e*) through the Flood, 1 Pet. 3:20. See ESCAPE, WHOLE.¶

Note: In 2 Pet. 2:5, KJV, *phulassō*, "to guard, keep, preserve," is translated "saved" (RV, "preserved"). In Luke 17:33 some mss. have *sōzō* (KJV, "save"), for the RV: see GAIN, B, No. 3. For "save alive," Luke 17:33, RV, see LIVE, No. 6.

B. Noun.

peripoiēsis (περιποίησις, 4047), (*a*) "preservation," (*b*) "acquiring or gaining something," is used in this latter sense in Heb. 10:39, translated "saving" (RV marg., "gaining"); the reference here is to salvation in its completeness. See OBTAIN, POSSESSION.

Note: In Heb. 11:7 *sōtēria* is rendered saving. See SALVATION.

SAVING (Preposition)

parektos (παρεκτός, 3924), used as a preposition, denotes "saving," Matt. 5:32 (in some mss., 19:9). See EXCEPT.¶

Note: In Luke 4:27 and Rev. 2:17, KJV, *ei mē* (lit., "if not"), is translated "saving" (RV, "but only" and "but").

SAVIOR

sōtēr (σωτήρ, 4990), "a savior, deliverer, preserver," is used (*a*) of God, Luke 1:47; 1 Tim. 1:1; 2:3; 4:10 (in the sense of "preserver," since He gives "to all life and breath and all things"); Titus 1:3; 2:10; 3:4; Jude 25; (*b*) of Christ, Luke 2:11; John 4:42; Acts 5:31; 13:23 (of Israel); Eph. 5:23 (the sustainer and preserver of the church, His "body"); Phil. 3:20 (at His return to receive the Church to Himself); 2 Tim. 1:10 (with reference to His incarnation, "the days of His flesh"); Titus 1:4 (a title shared, in the context, with God the Father); 2:13, RV, "our great God and Savior Jesus Christ," the pronoun "our," at the beginning of the whole clause, includes all the titles; Titus 3:6; 2 Pet. 1:1, "our God and Savior Jesus Christ; RV, where the pronoun "our," coming immediately in connection with "God," involves the inclusion of both titles as referring to Christ, just as in the parallel in v. 11, "our Lord and Savior

Jesus Christ" (KJV and RV); these passages are therefore a testimony to His deity; 2 Pet. 2:20; 3:2, 18; 1 John 4:14.¶

SAVOR (Noun and Verb)

A. Nouns.

1. *euōdia* (εὐωδία, 2175), "fragrance" (*eu*, "well," *ozō*, "to smell"), is used metaphorically (*a*) of those who in the testimony of the gospel are to God "a sweet savor of Christ," 2 Cor. 2:15; (*b*) of the giving up of His life by Christ for us, an offering and a sacrifice to God for an odor (*osmē*, see No. 2) of "a sweet smell," Eph. 5:2, RV [KJV, "a sweet smelling (savor)"]; (*c*) of material assistance sent to Paul from the church at Philippi "(an odor) of a sweet smell," Phil. 4:18. In all three instances the fragrance is that which ascends to God through the person, and as a result of the sacrifice, of Christ.¶

2. *osmē* (ὀσμή, 3744), "a smell, odor" (from *ozō*, "to smell"; Eng., "ozone"), is translated "odor" in John 12:3; it is used elsewhere in connection with No. 1, in the three passages mentioned, as of an odor accompanying an acceptable sacrifice; in 2 Cor. 2:14, 16 (twice), of the "savor" of the knowledge of Christ through Gospel testimony, in the case of the perishing "a savor from death unto death," as of that which arises from what is dead (the spiritual condition of the unregenerate); in the case of the saved "a savor from life unto life," as from that which arises from what is instinct with life (the spiritual condition of the regenerate); in Eph. 5:2, "a (sweetsmelling) savor"; in Phil. 4:18, "an odor (of a sweet smell)"; cf. No. 1. See ODOR.¶

B. Verb.

mōrainō (μωραίνω, 3471), primarily, "to be foolish," is used of salt that has lost its "savor," Matt. 5:13; Luke 14:34. See FOOLISH, B, No. 1.

Note: In the KJV of Matt. 16:23 and Mark 8:33, *phroneō*, "to think, to mind," is translated "thou savorest" (RV, "thou mindest").

SAW ASUNDER

prizō or *priō* (πρίζω, 4249), "to saw asunder," occurs in Heb. 11:37. Some have seen here a reference to the tradition of Isaiah's martyrdom under Manasseh.¶ In the Sept., Amos 1:3.¶ Cf. *diapriō*, "to cut to the heart," Acts 5:33; 7:54.¶

SAY

1. *legō* (λέγω, 3004), primarily, "to pick out, gather," chiefly denotes "to say, speak, affirm," whether of actual speech, e.g., Matt. 11:17, or of unspoken thought, e.g., Matt. 3:9, or of a message in writing, e.g., 2 Cor. 8:8. The 2nd

aorist form *eipon* is used to supply that tense, which is lacking in *legō*.

Concerning the phrase "he answered and said," it is a well known peculiarity of Hebrew narrative style that a speech is introduced, not simply by "and he said," but by prefixing "and he answered" (*apokrinomai*, with *eipon*). In Matt. 14:27, "saying," and Mark 6:50, "and saith," emphasis is perhaps laid on the fact that the Lord, hitherto silent as He moved over the lake, then addressed His disciples. That the phrase sometimes occurs where no explicit question has preceded (e.g., Matt. 11:25; 17:4; 28:5; Mark 11:14; 12:35; Luke 13:15; 14:3; John 5:17, 19), illustrates the use of the Hebrew idiom.

Note: A characteristic of *legō* is that it refers to the purport or sentiment of what is said as well as the connection of the words; this is illustrated in Heb. 8:1, RV, "(in the things which) we are saying," KJV, "(which) we have spoken." In comparison with *laleō* (No. 2), *legō* refers especially to the substance of what is "said," *laleō*, to the words conveying the utterance; see, e.g., John 12:49, "what I should say (*legō*, in the 2nd aorist subjunctive form *eipō*), and what I should speak (*laleō*)"; v. 50, "even as the Father hath said (*legō*, in the perfect form *eirēke*) unto Me, so I speak" (*laleō*); cf. 1 Cor. 14:34, "saith (*legō*) the law"; v. 35, "to speak" (*laleō*). Sometimes *laleō* signifies the utterance, as opposed to silence, *legō* declares what is "said"; e.g., Rom. 3:19, "what things soever the law saith (*legō*), it speaketh (*laleō*) to them that are under the law"; see also Mark 6:50; Luke 24:6. In the NT *laleō* never has the meaning "to chatter."

2. *laleō* (λαλέω, 2980), "to speak," is sometimes translated "to say"; in the following where the KJV renders it thus, the RV alters it to the verb "to speak," e.g., John 8:25 (3rd part), 26; 16:6; 18:20 (2nd part), 21 (1st part); Acts 3:22 (2nd part); 1 Cor. 9:8 (1st part); Heb. 5:5; in the following the RV uses the verb "to say," John 16:18; Acts 23:18 (2nd part); 26:22 (2nd part); Heb. 11:18. See *Note* above, and SPEAK, TALK, TELL, UTTER.

3. *phēmi* (φημί, 5346), "to declare, say," (*a*) is frequently used in quoting the words of another, e.g., Matt. 13:29; 26:61; (*b*) is interjected into the recorded words, e.g., Acts 23:35; (*c*) is used impersonally, 2 Cor. 10:10.

4. *eirō* (εἴρω, Fut. of 3004), an obsolete verb, has the future tense *ereō*, used, e.g., in Matt. 7:4; Luke 4:23 (2nd part); 13:25 (last part); Rom. 3:5; 4:1; 6:1; 7:7 (1st part); 8:31; 9:14, 19, 20, 30; 11:19; 1 Cor. 15:35; 2 Cor. 12:6; Jas. 2:18. The perfect is used, e.g., in John 12:50; see No.

1, Note. The 1st aorist passive, "it was said," is used in Rom. 9:12, 26; Rev. 6:11. See SPEAK, No. 13.

5. *proeipon* (προεῖπον, 4302) and *proereō*, "to say before," used as aorist and future respectively of *prolegō (pro*, "before," and No. 1), is used (*a*) of prophecy, e.g., Rom. 9:29; "to tell before," Matt. 24:25; Mark 13:23; "were spoken before," 2 Pet. 3:2; Jude 17; (*b*) of "saying" before, 2 Cor. 7:3; 13:2, RV (KJV, "to tell before" and "foretell"); Gal. 1:9; 5:21; in 1 Thess. 4:6, "we forewarned," RV. See FORETELL, FOREWARN, TELL.

6. *anteipon* (ἀντεῖπον, 473 and Aor. of 3004), "to say against" (*anti*, "against," and No. 1), is so rendered in Acts 4:14. See GAINSAY.

Notes: (1) *Phaskō*, "to affirm, assert," is translated "saying" in Acts 24:9, KJV (RV, "affirming"), and Rev. 2:2 in some mss. (KJV). See AFFIRM, No. 3. (2) In Acts 2:14, KJV, *apophthengomai*, "to speak forth" (RV), is rendered "said." (3) The phrase *tout' esti* (i.e., *touto esti*), "that is," is so translated in Matt. 27:46, RV (KJV, "that is to say"); so Acts 1:19; in Heb. 9:11 and 10:20, KJV and RV, "that is to say"; in Mark 7:11 the phrase is *ho esti*, lit., "which is"; the phrase *ho legetai*, lit., "which is said," John 1:38 and 20:16, is rendered "which is to say." (4) In Luke 7:40 and Acts 13:15, the imperative mood of *eipon* and *legō*, respectively, is rendered "say on." (5) In Mark 6:22, KJV, *autēs*, "herself," RV, is rendered "the said." (6) In Heb. 5:11, "we have many things to say" is, lit., "much (*polus*) is the word (or discourse, *logos*) for us."

SAYING

1. *logos* (λόγος, 3056), "a word," as embodying a conception or idea, denotes among its various meanings, "a saying, statement or declaration," uttered (*a*) by God; RV, "word" or "words" (KJV, "saying"), e.g., in John 8:55; Rom. 3:4; Rev. 19:9; 22:6, 7, 9, 10; (*b*) by Christ, e.g., Mark 8:32; 9:10; 10:22; Luke 9:28; John 6:60; 21:23; the RV appropriately substitutes "word" or "words" for KJV, "saying" or "sayings," especially in John's gospel e.g. 7:36, 40; 8:51, 52; 10:19; 14:24; 15:20; 18:9, 32; 19:13; (*c*) by an angel, Luke 1:29; (*d*) by OT prophets, John 12:38 (RV, "word") Rom. 13:9 (ditto); 1 Cor. 15:54; (*e*) by the apostle Paul in the Pastoral Epp., 1 Tim. 1:15; 3:1; 4:9; 2 Tim. 2:11; Titus 3:8; (*f*) by other men, Mark 7:29; Acts 7:29; John 4:37 (in general). See ACCOUNT, and especially WORD.

2. *rhēma* (ῥῆμα, 4487), "that which is said, a word," is rendered "saying" or "sayings" in

Mark 9:32; Luke 1:65; 2:17, 50, 51; 7:1; 9:45 (twice); 18:34. See WORD.

Note: In Acts 14:18, "with these sayings" is, lit., "saying (*legō*) these things." For *lalia*, "saying," John 4:42, KJV, see SPEECH, No. 2.

SCALE

lepis (λεπίς, 3013), from *lepō*, "to peel," occurs in Acts 9:18.¶

For SCARCE, SCARCELY see DIFFICULTY

SCARLET

kokkinos (κόκκινος, 2847) is derived from *kokkos*, used of the "berries" (clusters of the eggs of an insect) collected from the *ilex coccifera;* the color, however, is obtained from the cochineal insect, which attaches itself to the leaves and twigs of the coccifera oak; another species is raised on the leaves of the *cactus ficus.* The Arabic name for this insect is *qírmíz*, whence the word "crimson." It is used (*a*) of "scarlet" wool, Heb. 9:19; cf., in connection with the cleansing of a leper, Lev. 14:4, 6, "scarlet"; with the offering of the red heifer, Num. 19:6; (*b*) of the robe put on Christ by the soldiers, Matt. 27:28; (*c*) of the "beast" seen in symbolic vision in Rev. 17:3, "scarlet-colored"; (*d*) of the clothing of the "woman" as seen sitting on the "beast," 17:4; (*e*) of part of the merchandise of Babylon, 18:12; (*f*) figuratively, of the glory of the city itself, 18:16; the neuter is used in the last three instances.¶

SCATTER

A. Verbs.

1. *skorpizō* (σκορπίζω, 4650) is used in Matt. 12:30; Luke 11:23; John 10:12; 16:32; 2 Cor. 9:9, RV. See DISPERSE, No. 2.¶

2. *diaskorpizō* (διασκορπίζω, 1287), "to scatter abroad," is rendered "to scatter" in Matt. 25:24, 26, RV (KJV, "strawed"); 26:31; Mark 14:27; Luke 1:51; John 11:52; Acts 5:37, RV. See DISPERSE, No. 3.

3. *diaspeirō* (διασπείρω, 1289), "to scatter abroad" (*dia*, "throughout," *speirō*, "to sow seed"), is used in Acts 8:1, 4; 11:19, all of the church in Jerusalem "scattered" through persecution; the word in general is suggestive of the effects of the "scattering" in the sowing of the spiritual seed of the Word of life. See DISPERSE, No. 4.¶

4. *rhiptō* (ῥίπτω, 4496), "to throw, cast, hurl, to be cast down, prostrate," is used in Matt. 9:36 of people who were "scattered" as sheep without a shepherd. See CAST, No. 2, THROW.

5. *likmaō* (λικμάω, 3039), "to winnow" (*likmos*, "a winnowing fan"), is rendered "will scatter ... as dust" in Matt. 21:44 and Luke 20:18, RV (KJV, "will grind ... to powder"). See GRIND, Note.¶

6. *dialuō* (διαλύω, 1262), "to dissolve," is translated "scattered" in Acts 5:36, KJV; see DISPERSE, No. 1.¶

B. Noun.

diaspora (διασπορά, 1290), "a dispersion," is rendered "scattered abroad" in Jas. 1:1, KJV; "scattered" in 1 Pet. 1:1, KJV; see DISPERSION, B.

For SCEPTRE see ROD

SCHISM

schisma (σχίσμα, 4978), "a rent, division," is translated "schism" in 1 Cor. 12:25, metaphorically of the contrary condition to that which God has designed for a local church in "tempering the body together" (v. 24), the members having "the same care one for another" ("the same" being emphatic). See DIVISION, No. 3, RENT.

SCHOOL

scholē (σχολή, 4981) (whence Eng., "school") primarily denotes "leisure," then, "that for which leisure was employed, a disputation, lecture"; hence, by metonymy, "the place where lectures are delivered, a school," Acts 19:9.¶

For SCHOOLMASTER, Gal. 3:24, 25, see INSTRUCTOR, B, No. 1

SCIENCE

gnōsis (γνῶσις, 1108) is translated "science" in the KJV of 1 Tim. 6:20; the word simply means "knowledge" (RV), where the reference is to the teaching of the Gnostics (lit., "the knowers") "falsely called knowledge." Science in the modern sense of the word, viz., the investigation, discovery, and classification of secondary laws, is unknown in Scripture. See KNOW, C, No. 1.

SCOFF

ekmuktērizō (ἐκμυκτηρίζω, 1592), "to hold up the nose in derision at" (*ek*, "from," used intensively, *muktērizō*, "to mock"; from *muktēr*, "the nose"), is translated "scoffed at" in Luke 16:14, RV (KJV, "derided"), of the Pharisees in their derision of Christ on account of His teaching; in 23:35 (ditto), of the mockery of Christ on the cross by the rulers of the people.¶ In the Sept., Ps. 2:4; 22:7; 35:16.¶

For **SCOFFERS**, 2 Pet. 3:3, KJV, see
MOCKERS

SCORCH, SCORCHING
A. Verb.
kaumatizō (καυματίζω, 2739), "to scorch"
(from *kauma*, "heat"), is used (*a*) of seed that
had not much earth, Matt. 13:6; Mark 4:6; (*b*)
of men, stricken retributively by the sun's heat,
Rev. 16:8, 9.¶
B. Noun.
kausōn (καύσων, 2742), "burning heat"
(akin to *kaiō*, "to burn"), is translated "scorching heat" in Matt. 20:12 (KJV, "heat"); Luke
12:55 (ditto); in Jas. 1:11, RV, "scorching wind"
(KJV,"burning heat"), here the reference is to a
hot wind from the east (cf. Job 1:19). See
HEAT.¶ In the Sept., Job 27:21; Jer. 18:17; 51:1;
Ezek. 17:10; 19:12; Hos. 12:1; 13:15; Jonah
4:8.¶

For **SCORN** see **LAUGH**

SCORPION
skorpios (σκορπίος, 4651), akin to *skorpizō*,
"to scatter" (which see), is a small animal (the
largest of the several species is 6 in. long) like a
lobster, but with a long tail, at the end of which
is its venomous sting; the pain, the position of
the sting, and the effect are mentioned in Rev.
9:3, 5, 10. The Lord's rhetorical question as to
the provision of a "scorpion" instead of an egg,
Luke 11:12, is, firstly, an allusion to the egg-like
shape of the creature when at rest; secondly, an
indication of the abhorrence with which it is
regarded. In Luke 10:19, the Lord's assurance
to the disciples of the authority given them by
Him to tread upon serpents and scorpions conveys the thought of victory over spiritually antagonistic forces, the powers of darkness, as is
shown by His reference to the "power of the
enemy" and by the context in vv. 17, 20.¶

SCOURGE (Noun and Verb)
A. Noun.
phragellion (φραγέλλιον, 5416), "a whip"
(from Latin, *flagellum*), is used of the "scourge"
of small cords which the Lord made and employed before cleansing the Temple, John 2:15.
However He actually used it, the whip was in
itself a sign of authority and judgment.¶
B. Verbs.
1. *phragelloō* (φραγελλόω, 5417) (akin to
A: Latin, *flagello;* Eng., "flagellate"), is the word
used in Matt. 27:26, and Mark 15:15, of the
"scourging" endured by Christ and administered by the order of Pilate. Under the Roman

method of "scourging," the person was stripped
and tied in a bending posture to a pillar, or
stretched on a frame. The "scourge" was made
of leather thongs, weighted with sharp pieces of
bone or lead, which tore the flesh of both the
back and the breast (cf. Ps. 22:17). Eusebius
(*Chron.*) records his having witnessed the suffering of martyrs who died under this treatment.¶
Note: In John 19:1 the "scourging" of Christ
is described by Verb No. 2, as also in His
prophecy of His sufferings, Matt. 20:19; Mark
10:34; Luke 18:33. In Acts 22:25 the similar
punishment about to be administered to Paul is
described by Verb No. 3 (the "scourging" of
Roman citizens was prohibited by the Porcian
law of 197, B.C.).
2. *mastigoō* (μαστιγόω, 3146), akin to *mastix* (see below), is used (*a*) as mentioned under
No. 1; (*b*) of Jewish "scourgings," Matt. 10:17
and 23:34; (*c*) metaphorically, in Heb. 12:6, of
the "chastening" by the Lord administered in
love to His spiritual sons.¶
Note: The Jewish method of "scourging," as
described in the Mishna, was by the use of three
thongs of leather, the offender receiving thirteen
stripes on the bare breast and thirteen on each
shoulder, the "forty stripes save one," as administered to Paul five times (2 Cor. 11:24). See
also SCOURGINGS (below).
3. *mastizō* (μαστίζω, 3147), akin to No. 2,
occurs in Acts 22:25 (see No. 1, above).¶ In the
Sept., Num. 22:25.¶

SCOURGING (-S)
mastix (μάστιξ, 3148), "a whip, scourge," is
used (*a*) with the meaning "scourging," in Acts
22:24, of the Roman method (see above, B, No.
1, Note); (*b*) in Heb. 11:36, of the "sufferings"
of saints in the OT times. Among the Hebrews
the usual mode, legal and domestic, was that of
beating with a rod (see 2 Cor. 11:25); (*c*) metaphorically, of "disease" or "suffering": see
PLAGUE, No. 1.

SCRIBE (-S)
grammateus (γραμματεύς, 1122), from
gramma, "a writing," denotes "a scribe, a man
of letters, a teacher of the law"; the "scribes"
are mentioned frequently in the Synoptists, especially in connection with the Pharisees, with
whom they virtually formed one party (see
Luke 5:21), sometimes with the chief priests,
e.g., Matt. 2:4; Mark 8:31; 10:33; 11:18, 27;
Luke 9:22. They are mentioned only once in
John's gospel, 8:3, three times in the Acts, 4:5;
6:12; 23:9; elsewhere only in 1 Cor. 1:20, in the
singular. They were considered naturally qualified to teach in the synagogues, Mark 1:22.

They were ambitious of honor, e.g., Matt. 23:5–11, which they demanded especially from their pupils, and which was readily granted them, as well as by the people generally. Like Ezra (Ezra 7:12), the "scribes" were found originally among the priests and Levites. The priests being the official interpreters of the Law, the "scribes" ere long became an independent company; though they never held political power, they became leaders of the people.

Their functions regarding the Law were to teach it, develop it, and use it in connection with the Sanhedrin and various local courts. They also occupied themselves with the sacred writings both historical and didactic. They attached the utmost importance to ascetic elements, by which the nation was especially separated from the Gentiles. In their regime piety was reduced to external formalism. Only that was of value which was governed by external precept. Life under them became a burden; they themselves sought to evade certain of their own precepts, Matt. 23:16,ff.; Luke 11:46; by their traditions the Law, instead of being a help in moral and spiritual life, became an instrument for preventing true access to God, Luke 11:52. Hence the Lord's stern denunciations of them and the Pharisees (see PHARISEES).

Note: The word *grammateus* is used of the town "clerk" in Ephesus, Acts 19:35.

For SCRIP see WALLET

SCRIPTURE

1. *graphē* (γραφή, 1124), akin to *graphō*, "to write" (Eng., "graph," "graphic," etc.), primarily denotes "a drawing, painting"; then "a writing," (*a*) of the OT Scriptures, (1) in the plural, the whole, e.g., Matt. 21:42; 22:29; John 5:39; Acts 17:11; 18:24; Rom. 1:2, where "the prophets" comprises the OT writers in general; 15:4; 16:26, lit., "prophetic writings," expressing the character of all the Scriptures; (2) in the singular in reference to a particular passage, e.g., Mark 12:10; Luke 4:21; John 2:22; 10:35 (though applicable to all); 19:24, 28, 36, 37; 20:9; Acts 1:16; 8:32, 35; Rom. 4:3; 9:17; 10:11; 11:2; Gal. 3:8, 22; 4:30; 1 Tim. 5:18, where the 2nd quotation is from Luke 10:7, from which it may be inferred that the apostle included Luke's gospel as "Scripture" alike with Deuteronomy, from which the first quotation is taken; in reference to the whole, e.g. Jas. 4:5 (see RV, a separate rhetorical question from the one which follows); in 2 Pet. 1:20, "no prophecy of Scripture," a description of all, with special application to the OT in the next verse; (*b*) of the OT Scriptures (those accepted by the

Jews as canonical) and all those of the NT which were to be accepted by Christians as authoritative, 2 Tim. 3:16; these latter were to be discriminated from the many forged epistles and other religious "writings" already produced and circulated in Timothy's time. Such discrimination would be directed by the fact that "every Scripture," characterized by inspiration of God, would be profitable for the purposes mentioned; so the RV. The KJV states truth concerning the completed canon of Scripture, but that was not complete when the apostle wrote to Timothy.

The Scriptures are frequently personified by the NT writers (as by the Jews, John 7:42), (*a*) as speaking with divine authority, e.g., John 19:37; Rom. 4:3; 9:17, where the Scripture is said to speak to Pharaoh, giving the message actually sent previously by God to him through Moses; Jas. 4:5 (see above); (*b*) as possessed of the sentient quality of foresight, and the active power of preaching, Gal. 3:8, where the Scripture mentioned was written more than four centuries after the words were spoken. The Scripture, in such a case, stands for its divine Author with an intimation that it remains perpetually characterized as the living voice of God. This divine agency is again illustrated in Gal. 3:22 (cf. v. 10 and Matt. 11:13).

2. *gramma* (γράμμα, 1121), "a letter of the alphabet," etc. is used of the Holy Scriptures in 2 Tim. 3:15. For the various uses of this word see LETTER.

SCROLL

biblion (βιβλίον, 975), the diminutive of *biblos*, "a book," is used in Rev. 6:14, of "a scroll," the rolling up of which illustrates the removal of the heaven. See BOOK, No. 2.

SEA

A. Nouns.

1. *thalassa* (θάλασσα, 2281) is used (*a*) chiefly literally, e.g., "the Red Sea," Acts 7:36; 1 Cor. 10:1; Heb. 11:29; the "sea" of Galilee or Tiberias, Matt. 4:18; 15:29; Mark 6:48, 49, where the acts of Christ testified to His deity; John 6:1; 21:1; in general, e.g., Luke 17:2; Acts 4:24; Rom. 9:27; Rev. 16:3; 18:17; 20:8, 13; 21:1; in combination with No. 2, Matt. 18:6; (*b*) metaphorically, of "the ungodly men" described in Jude 13 (cf. Isa. 57:20); (*c*) symbolically, in the apocalyptic vision of "a glassy sea like unto crystal,'" Rev. 4:6, emblematic of the fixed purity and holiness of all that appertains to the authority and judicial dealings of God; in 15:2, the same, "mingled with fire," and, standing by it (RV) or on it (KJV and RV marg.), those

who had "come victorious from the beast" (ch. 13); of the wild and restless condition of nations, Rev. 13:1 (see 17:1, 15), where "he stood" (RV) refers to the dragon, not John (KJV); from the midst of this state arises the beast, symbolic of the final gentile power dominating the federated nations of the Roman world (see Dan., chs. 2, 7, etc.).

Note: For the change from "the sea" in Deut. 30:13, to "the abyss" in Rom. 10:7, see BOTTOM, B.

2. *pelagos* (πέλαγος, 3989), "the deep sea, the deep," is translated "the depth" in Matt. 18:6, and is used of the "Sea of Cilicia" in Acts 27:5. See DEPTH, No. 2.¶ *Pelagos* signifies "the vast expanse of open water," *thalassa*, "the sea as contrasted with the land" (Trench, *Syn.*, §xiii).

B. Adjectives.

1. *enalios* (ἐνάλιος, 1724), "in the sea," lit., "of, or belonging to, the salt water" (from *hals*, "salt"), occurs in Jas. 3:7.¶

2. *paralios* (παράλιος, 3882), "by the sea," Luke 6:17: see COAST.¶

3. *parathalassios* (παραθαλάσσιος, 3864), "by the sea," Matt. 4:13, see COAST, *Note* 2.¶

4. *dithalassos* (διθάλασσος, 1337) primarily signifies "divided into two seas" (*dis*, "twice," and *thalassa*); then, "dividing the sea," as of a reef or rocky projection running out into the "sea," Acts 27:41.¶

SEAL (Noun and Verb)

A. Noun.

sphragis (σφραγίς, 4973) denotes (*a*) "a seal" or "signet," Rev. 7:2, "the seal of the living God," an emblem of ownership and security, here combined with that of destination (as in Ezek. 9:4), the persons to be "sealed" being secured from destruction and marked for reward; (*b*) "the impression" of a "seal" or signet, (1) literal, a "seal" on a book or roll, combining with the ideas of security and destination those of secrecy and postponement of disclosures, Rev. 5:1, 2, 5, 9; 6:1, 3, 5, 7, 9, 12; 8:1; (2) metaphorical, Rom. 4:11, said of "circumcision," as an authentication of the righteousness of Abraham's faith, and an external attestation of the covenant made with him by God; the rabbis called circumcision "the seal of Abraham"; in 1 Cor. 9:2, of converts as a "seal" or authentication of Paul's apostleship; in 2 Tim. 2:19, "the firm foundation of God standeth, having this seal, The Lord knoweth them that are His," RV, indicating ownership, authentication, security and destination, "and, Let every one that nameth the Name of the Lord depart from unrighteousness," indicating a ratification

on the part of the believer of the determining counsel of God concerning him; Rev. 9:4 distinguishes those who will be found without the "seal" of God on their foreheads [see (*a*) above and B, No. 1].¶

B. Verbs.

1. *sphragizō* (σφραγίζω, 4972), "to seal" (akin to A), is used to indicate (*a*) security and permanency (attempted but impossible), Matt. 27:66; on the contrary, of the doom of Satan, fixed and certain, Rev. 20:3, RV, "sealed it over"; (*b*) in Rom. 15:28, "when ... I have ... sealed to them this fruit," the formal ratification of the ministry of the churches of the Gentiles in Greece and Galatia to needy saints in Judea, by Paul's faithful delivery of the gifts to them; this material help was the fruit of his spiritual ministry to the Gentiles, who on their part were bringing forth the fruit of their having shared with them in spiritual things; the metaphor stresses the sacred formalities of the transaction (Deissmann illustrates this from the papyri of Fayyum, in which the "sealing" of sacks guarantees the full complement of the contents); (*c*) secrecy and security and the postponement of disclosure, Rev. 10:4; in a negative command, 22:10; (*d*) ownership and security, together with destination, Rev. 7:3, 4, 5 (as with the noun in v. 2; see A); the same three indications are conveyed in Eph. 1:13, in the metaphor of the "sealing" of believers by the gift of the Holy Spirit, upon believing (i.e., at the time of their regeneration, not after a lapse of time in their spiritual life, "having also believed"—not as KJV, "after that ye believed"—; the aorist participle marks the definiteness and completeness of the act of faith); the idea of destination is stressed by the phrase "the Holy Spirit of promise" (see also v. 14); so 4:30, "ye were sealed unto the day of redemption"; so in 2 Cor. 1:22, where the middle voice intimates the special interest of the Sealer in His act; (*e*) authentication by the believer (by receiving the witness of the Son) of the fact that "God is true," John 3:33; authentication by God in sealing the Son as the Giver of eternal life (with perhaps a figurative allusion to the impress of a mark upon loaves), 6:27.¶

Note: In Rev. 7, after the 5th verse (first part) the original does not repeat the mention of the "sealing" except in v. 8 (last part) (hence the omission in the RV).

2. *katasphragizō* (κατασφραγίζω, 2696), No. 1, strengthened by *kata*, intensive, is used of the "book" seen in the vision in Rev. 5:1, RV, "close sealed (with seven seals)," the successive opening of which discloses the events destined

to take place throughout the period covered by chapters 6 to 19.¶ In the Sept., Job 9:7; 37:7.¶

SEAM (without)

araphos or arrhaphos (ἄραφος, 729) denotes "without seam" (*a*, negative, and *rhaptō*, "to sew"), John 19:23.¶

SEARCH

1. *eraunaō* or *ereunaō*, an earlier form, (ἐραυνάω, 2045), "to search, examine," is used (*a*) of God, as "searching" the heart, Rom. 8:27; (*b*) of Christ, similarly, Rev. 2:23; (*c*) of the Holy Spirit, as "searching" all things, 1 Cor. 2:10, acting in the spirit of the believer; (*d*) of the OT prophets, as "searching" their own writings concerning matters foretold of Christ, testified by the Spirit of Christ in them, 1 Pet. 1:11 (cf. No. 2); (*e*) of the Jews, as commanded by the Lord to "search" the Scriptures, John 5:39, KJV, and RV marg., "search," RV text, "ye search," either is possible grammatically; (*f*) of Nicodemus as commanded similarly by the chief priests and Pharisees, John 7:52.¶

2. *exeraunaō* (ἐξεραυνάω, 1830), a strengthened form of No. 1 (*ek*, or *ex*, "out"), "to search out," is used in 1 Pet. 1:10, "searched diligently"; cf. No. 1 (*d*).¶

3. *exetazō* (ἐξετάζω, 1833), "to examine closely, inquire carefully" (from *etazō*, "to examine"), occurs in Matt. 2:8, RV, "search out"; so Matt. 10:11, RV: see INQUIRE, No. 4.

Note: For *anakrinō*, rendered "searched" in Acts 17:11, KJV, see EXAMINE.

For SEARED see BRANDED

SEASON (Noun)

A. Nouns.

1. *kairos* (καιρός, 2540), primarily, "due measure, fitness, proportion," is used in the NT to signify "a season, a time, a period" possessed of certain characteristics, frequently rendered "time" or "times"; in the following the RV substitutes "season" for the KJV "time," thus distinguishing the meaning from *chronos* (see No. 2): Matt. 11:25; 12:1; 14:1; 21:34; Mark 11:13; Acts 3:19; 7:20; 17:26; Rom. 3:26; 5:6; 9:9; 13:11; 1 Cor. 7:5; Gal. 4:10; 1 Thess. 2:17, lit., "for a season (of an hour)"; 2 Thess. 2:6; in Eph. 6:18, "at all seasons" (KJV, "always"); in Titus 1:3, "His own seasons" (marg., "its"; KJV, "in due times"); in the preceding clause *chronos* is used.

The characteristics of a period are exemplified in the use of the term with regard, e.g., to harvest, Matt. 13:30; reaping, Gal. 6:9; punishment, Matt. 8:29; discharging duties, Luke 12:42; opportunity for doing anything, whether good, e.g., Matt. 26:18; Gal. 6:10 ("opportunity"); Eph. 5:16; or evil, e.g., Rev. 12:12; the fulfillment of prophecy, Luke 1:20; Acts 3:19; 1 Pet. 1:11; a time suitable for a purpose, Luke 4:13, lit., "until a season"; 2 Cor. 6:2; see further under No. 2. See ALWAYS, *Note,* OPPORTUNITY, TIME, WHILE.

2. *chronos* (χρόνος, 5550), whence Eng. words beginning with "chron"—, denotes "a space of time," whether long or short: (*a*) it implies duration, whether longer, e.g., Acts 1:21, "(all the) time"; Acts 13:18; 20:18, RV, "(all the) time" (KJV, "at all seasons"); or shorter, e.g., Luke 4:5; (*b*) it sometimes refers to the date of an occurrence, whether past, e.g., Matt. 2:7, or future, e.g., Acts 3:21; 7:17.

Broadly speaking, *chronos* expresses the duration of a period, *kairos* stresses it as marked by certain features; thus in Acts 1:7, "the Father has set within His own authority" both the times (*chronos*), the lengths of the periods, and the "seasons" (*kairos*), epochs characterized by certain events; in 1 Thess. 5:1, "times" refers to the length of the interval before the Parousia takes place (the presence of Christ with the saints when He comes to receive them to Himself at the Rapture), and to the length of time the Parousia will occupy; "seasons" refers to the special features of the period before, during, and after the Parousia.

Chronos marks quantity, *kairos*, quality. Sometimes the distinction between the two words is not sharply defined as, e.g., in 2 Tim. 4:6, though even here the apostle's "departure" signalizes the time (*kairos*). The words occur together in the Sept. only in Dan. 2:21 and Eccl. 3:1. *Chronos* is rendered "season" in Acts 19:22, KJV (RV, "a while"); 20:18 (RV, "all the time," see above); Rev. 6:11, KJV (RV, "time"); so 20:3. In Luke 23:8 it is used with *hikanos* in the plural, RV, "(of a long) time," more lit., "(for a sufficient number) of times."

In Rev. 10:6 *chronos* has the meaning "delay" (RV, marg.), an important rendering for the understanding of the passage (the word being akin to *chronizō*, "to take time, to linger, delay," Matt. 24:48; Luke 12:45). See DELAY, B, *Note,* SPACE, TIME, WHILE.

3. *hōra* (ὥρα, 5610), "an hour," is translated "season" in John 5:35; 2 Cor. 7:8; Philem. 15: see HOUR.

B. Adjective.

proskairos (πρόσκαιρος, 4340), "temporary, transient," is rendered "for a season" in Heb. 11:25. See TEMPORAL, TIME, WHILE.

C. Adverbs.

1. *akairōs* (ἀκαίρως, 171) denotes "out of season, unseasonably" (akin to *akairos*, "unseasonable," *a*, negative, and A, No. 1), 2 Tim. 4:2.¶

2. *eukairōs* (εὐκαίρως, 2122), "in season" (*eu*, "well"), 2 Tim. 4:2; it occurs also in Mark 14:11, "conveniently."¶

Note: For *oligon*, 1 Pet. 1:6, KJV, "for a season," see WHILE.

SEASON (Verb)

artuō (ἀρτύω, 741), "to arrange, make ready" (cf. *artios*, "fitted"), is used of "seasoning," Mark 9:50; Luke 14:34; Col. 4:6.¶

SEAT (Noun and Verb)

A. Nouns.

1. *kathedra* (καθέδρα, 2515), from *kata*, "down," and *hedra*, "a seat," denotes "a seat" (Eng., "cathedral"), "a chair," Matt. 21:12; Mark 11:15; of teachers, Matt. 23:2.¶

2. *prōtokathedria* (πρωτοκαθεδρία, 4410), "the first seat," Matt. 23:6; Mark 12:39; Luke 11:43; 20:46; see CHIEF, No. 6. Cf. ROOM.¶

Note: For *thronos*, sometimes translated "seat" in the KJV, see THRONE.

B. Verb.

kathēmai (κάθημαι, 2521), "to sit, be seated," is translated "shall . . . be seated" in Luke 22:69, RV; "is seated," Col. 3:1, RV (KJV, "shall . . . sit" and "sitteth"). See SIT.

SECOND, SECONDARILY, SECONDLY

1. *deuteros* (δεύτερος, 1208) denotes "second in order" with or without the idea of time, e.g., Matt. 22:26, 39; 2 Cor. 1:15; Rev. 2:11; in Rev. 14:8, RV only ("a second angel"); it is used in the neuter, *deuteron*, adverbially, signifying a "second" time, e.g., John 3:4; 21:16; Acts 7:13; Rev. 19:3, RV (KJV, "again"); Jude 5, "afterward" (RV, marg., "the second time"); used with *ek* ("of") idiomatically, the preposition signifying "for (the second time)," Mark 14:72; John 9:24 and Acts 11:9, RV (KJV, "again"); Heb. 9:28; in 1 Cor. 12:28, KJV, "secondarily," RV, "secondly."

Note: In Acts 13:33 some mss. have *prōtos*, "(in the) first (psalm)"; the 1st and 2nd Psalms were originally one, forming a prologue to the whole book; hence the numbering in the Sept.

2. *deuteraios* (δευτεραῖος, 1206), an adjective with an adverbial sense (from No. 1), is used in Acts 28:13, RV, "on the second day" (KJV, "the next day"), lit., "second day (persons we came)."¶

Note: In Luke 6:1, the KJV translates those mss. which have *deuteroprōtos*, lit., "second-first," said of a sabbath (see RV marg.).¶

SECRET, SECRETLY

A. Adjectives.

1. *kruptos* (κρυπτός, 2927), "secret, hidden" (akin to *kruptō*, "to hide"), Eng., "crypt," "cryptic," etc., is used as an adjective and rendered "secret" in Luke 8:17, KJV (RV, "hid"); in the neuter, with *en*, "in," as an adverbial phrase, "in secret," with the article, Matt. 6:4, 6 (twice in each v.); without the article, John 7:4, 10; 18:20; in the neuter plural, with the article, "the secrets (of men)," Rom. 2:16; of the heart, 1 Cor. 14:25; in Luke 11:33, KJV, "a secret place" (RV, "cellar"). See CELLAR, HIDDEN, INWARDLY.

2. *apokruphos* (ἀπόκρυφος, 614) (whence "Apocrypha"), "hidden," is translated "kept secret" in Mark 4:22, KJV (RV, "made secret"); "secret" in Luke 8:17, RV (KJV, "hid"). See HIDE, B, No. 2.

3. *kruphaios* (κρυφαῖος, 2928d) occurs in the best mss. in Matt. 6:18 (twice; some have No. 1).¶

B. Adverbs.

1. *kruphē* (κρυφῇ, 2931), akin to A, No. 1, "secretly, in secret," is used in Eph. 5:12.¶

2. *lathra* (λάθρα, 2977), akin to *lanthanō*, "to escape notice, be hidden," is translated "secretly" in John 11:28. See PRIVILY.

C. Verb.

kruptō (κρύπτω, 2928), "to hide," is translated "secretly" in John 19:38 [perfect participle, passive voice, lit., "(but) having been hidden"], referring to Nicodemus as having been a "secret" disciple of Christ; in Matt. 13:35, KJV, it is translated "kept secret" (RV, "hidden").

Notes: (1) For *tameion*, translated "secret chambers" in Matt. 24:26, see CHAMBER, No. 1. (2) For the KJV rendering of *sigaō*, in Rom. 16:25, "kept secret," see PEACE (hold one's), No. 2, and SILENCE. (3) For "I have learned the secret," see LEARN, No. 4.

SECT

hairesis (αἵρεσις, 139), "a choosing," is translated "sect" throughout the Acts, except in 24:14, KJV, "heresy" (RV, "sect"); it properly denotes a predilection either for a particular truth, or for a perversion of one, generally with the expectation of personal advantage; hence, a division and the formation of a party or "sect" in contrast to the uniting power of "the truth," held *in toto;* "a sect" is a division developed and brought to an issue; the order "divisions, heresies" (marg. "parties") in "the works of the flesh" in Gal. 5:19–21 is suggestive of this. See HERESY.

SECURE (Verb)

perikratēs (περικρατής, 4031), an adjective, signifies "having full command of" (*peri*, "around, about," *krateō*, "to be strong, to rule"); it is used with *ginomai*, "to become," in Acts 27:16, RV, "to secure (the boat)," KJV, "to come by."¶

Note: In Matt. 28:14, KJV, *amerimnos*, "without anxiety," with *poieō*, "to make," is translated "we will . . . secure (you)," RV, "we will . . . rid (you) of care." The Eng. "secure" is derived from the Latin *se*, "free from," and *cura*, "care." See CARE.

SECURITY

hikanos (ἱκανός, 2425), "sufficient," is used in its neuter form with the article, as a noun, in Acts 17:9, "(when they had taken) security," i.e., satisfaction, lit., "the sufficient." The use of *hikanos* in this construction is a Latinism in Greek. See Moulton, *Proleg.*, p. 20. Probably the bond given to the authorities by Jason and his friends included an undertaking that Paul would not return to Thessalonica. Any efforts to have the bond cancelled were unsuccessful; hence the reference to the hindrance by Satan (1 Thess. 2:18). See ABLE, C, No. 2.

SEDITION

A. Nouns.

1. *stasis* (στάσις, 4714), "a dissension, an insurrection," is translated "sedition" in Acts 24:5, KJV (RV, "insurrections"). See DISSENSION, INSURRECTION.

2. *dichostasia* (διχοστασία, 1370), lit., "a standing apart" (*dicha*, "asunder, apart," *stasis*, "a standing"), hence "a dissension, division," is translated "seditions" in Gal. 5:20, KJV. See DIVISION, No. 2.

B. Verb.

anastatoō (ἀναστατόω, 387), "to excite, unsettle," or "to stir up to sedition," is so translated in Acts 21:38, RV (KJV, "madest an uproar"); in 17:6, "have turned (the world) upside down," i.e., "causing tumults"; in Gal. 5:12, RV, "unsettle" (KJV, "trouble"), i.e., by false teaching (here in the continuous present tense, lit., "those who are unsettling you"). The word was supposed not to have been used in profane authors. It has been found, however, in several of the papyri writings. See TURN, UNSETTLE.¶

SEDUCE, SEDUCING

A. Verbs.

1. *planaō* (πλανάω, 4105), "to cause to wander, lead astray," is translated "to seduce" in 1 John 2:26, KJV (RV, "lead . . . astray"); in Rev. 2:20, "to seduce." See DECEIT, C, No. 6.

2. *apoplanaō* (ἀποπλανάω, 635) is translated "seduce" in Mark 13:22 (RV, "lead astray"); see LEAD, No. 13.

B. Adjective.

planos (πλάνος, 4108), akin to A, lit., "wandering," then, "deceiving," is translated "seducing" in 1 Tim. 4:1. See DECEIVER, No. 1.

For SEDUCERS see IMPOSTORS

SEE, SEEING

A. Verbs.

1. *blepō* (βλέπω, 991), "to have sight," is used of bodily vision, e.g., Matt. 11:4; and mental, e.g., Matt. 13:13, 14; it is said of God the Father in Matt. 6:4, 6, 18; of Christ as "seeing" what the Father doeth, John 5:19. It especially stresses the thought of the person who "sees." For the various uses see BEHOLD, No. 2; see *Note* below.

2. *horaō* (ὁράω, 3708), with the form *eidon*, serving for its aorist tense, and *opsomai*, for its future tense (middle voice), denotes "to see," of bodily vision, e.g., John 6:36; and mental, e.g., Matt. 8:4; it is said of Christ as "seeing" the Father, John 6:46, and of what He had "seen" with the Father, 8:38. It especially indicates the direction of the thought to the object "seen." See BEHOLD, No. 1.

Note: "*Horaō* and *blepō* both denote the physical act: *horaō*, in general, *blepō*, the single look; *horaō* gives prominence to the discerning mind, *blepō* to the particular mood or point. When the physical side recedes, *horaō* denotes perception in general (as resulting principally from vision) . . . *Blepō*, on the other hand, when its physical side recedes, gets a purely outward sense, look (open, incline) towards [as of a situation]" (Schmidt, Grimm-Thayer).

3. *aphoraō* (ἀφοράω, 872), with *apeidon* serving as the aorist tense, "to look away from one thing so as to see another" (*apo*, "from," and No. 2), as in Heb. 12:2, simply means "to see" in Phil. 2:23.¶

4. *kathoraō* (καθοράω, 2529), lit., "to look down" (*kata*, and No. 2), denotes "to discern clearly," Rom. 1:20, "are clearly seen."¶ In the Sept., Num. 24:2; Job 10:4; 39:26.¶

5. *diablepō* (διαβλέπω, 1227), "to see clearly" (*dia*, "through," and No. 1), is used in Matt. 7:5; Luke 6:42; in Mark 8:25, RV, "he

looked steadfastly" (No. 6 is used in the next clause; No. 1 in v. 24, and No. 2 in the last part).¶

6. *emblepō* (ἐμβλέπω, 1689), "to look at" (*en*, "in," and No. 1), used of earnestly looking, is translated "saw" in Mark 8:25 (last part); "could (not) see" in Acts 22:11. See BEHOLD, No. 3.

7. *anablepō* (ἀναβλέπω, 308), "to look up," is translated "see," of the blind, in Luke 7:22, KJV (RV, "receive their sight"). See SIGHT.

8. *theaomai* (θεάομαι, 2300), "to view attentively, to see with admiration, desire, or regard," stresses more especially the action of the person beholding, as with No. 1, in contrast to No. 2; it is used in Matt. 11:7 (RV, "to behold"), while *idein*, the infinitive of *eidon* (see under No. 2), is used in the questions in the next two verses; in verse 7 the interest in the onlooker is stressed, in vv. 8, 9, the attention is especially directed to the object "seen." The verb is translated "to see" in the KJV and RV of Matt. 6:1; Mark 16:11, 14; John 6:5; Acts 8:18 (in some mss.); 21:27; Rom. 15:24; elsewhere, for the KJV, "to see," the RV uses the verb "to behold," bringing out its force more suitably. See BEHOLD, No. 8.

9. *theōreō* (θεωρέω, 2334) denotes "to be a spectator of," indicating the careful perusal of details in the object; it points especially, as in No. 1, to the action of the person beholding, e.g., Matt. 28:1; the RV frequently renders it by "to behold," for the KJV, "to see," e.g., John 14:17, 19; 16:10, 16, 17, 19. The difference between this verb and Nos. 1 and 2 is brought out in John 20:5, 6, 8; in v. 5 *blepō* is used of John's sight of the linen cloths in the tomb, without his entering in; he "saw" at a glance the Lord was not there; in v. 6 the closer contemplation by Peter is expressed in the verb *theōreō*. But in v. 8 the grasping by John of the significance of the undisturbed cloths is denoted by *eidon* (see No. 2, and see WRAP).

10. *muōpazō* (μυωπάζω, 3467), "to be short-sighted" (*muō*, "to shut," *ōps*, "the eye"; cf. Eng., "myopy," "myopic": the root *mu* signifies a sound made with closed lips, e.g., in the words "mutter," "mute"), occurs in 2 Pet. 1:9, RV, "seeing only what is near" (KJV, "and cannot see afar off"); this does not contradict the preceding word "blind," it qualifies it; he of whom it is true is blind in that he cannot discern spiritual things, he is near-sighted in that he is occupied in regarding worldly affairs.¶

11. *phainō* (φαίνω, 5316), "to cause to appear," and in the passive voice, "to appear, be manifest," is rendered "(that) they may be seen" in Matt. 6:5; "it was (never so) seen," 9:33. See APPEAR.

Notes: (1) For *ide* and *idou*, regularly rendered "behold" in the RV, see BEHOLD, No. 4. (2) For *optanō*, in Acts 1:3, KJV, "being seen," see APPEAR, A, No. 7. (3) For *historeō*, in Gal. 1:18, KJV, "to see," see VISIT. (4) For *prooraō*, and *proeidon*, "to see before," see FORESEE. (5) For "make . . . see" see ENLIGHTEN.

B. Noun.

blemma (βλέμμα, 990), primarily, "a look, a glance" (akin to A, No. 1), denotes "sight," 2 Pet. 2:8, rendered "seeing"; some interpret it as meaning "look"; Moulton and Milligan illustrate it thus from the papyri; it seems difficult, however, to take the next word "hearing" (in the similar construction) in this way.¶

SEED

1. *sperma* (σπέρμα, 4690), akin to *speirō*, "to sow" (Eng., "sperm," "spermatic," etc.), has the following usages, (*a*) agricultural and botanical, e.g., Matt. 13:24, 27, 32 (for the KJV of vv. 19, 20, 22, 23, see SOW, as in the RV); 1 Cor. 15:38; 2 Cor. 9:10; (*b*) physiological, Heb. 11:11; (*c*) metaphorical and by metonymy for "offspring, posterity," (1) of natural offspring, e.g., Matt. 22:24, 25, RV, "seed" (KJV, "issue"); John 7:42; 8:33, 37; Acts 3:25; Rom. 1:3; 4:13, 16, 18; 9:7 (twice), 8, 29; 11:1; 2 Cor. 11:22; Heb. 2:16; 11:18; Rev. 12:17; Gal. 3:16, 19, 29; in the 16th v., "He saith not, And to seeds, as of many; but as of one, And to thy seed, which is Christ," quoted from the Sept. of Gen. 13:15 and 17:7, 8, there is especial stress on the word "seed," as referring to an individual (here, Christ) in fulfillment of the promises to Abraham—a unique use of the singular. While the plural form "seeds," neither in Hebrew nor in Greek, would have been natural any more than in English (it is not so used in Scripture of human offspring; its plural occurrence is in 1 Sam. 8:15, of crops), yet if the divine intention had been to refer to Abraham's natural descendants, another word could have been chosen in the plural, such as "children"; all such words were, however, set aside, "seed" being selected as one that could be used in the singular, with the purpose of showing that the "seed" was Messiah. Some of the rabbis had even regarded "seed," e.g., in Gen. 4:25 and Isa. 53:10, as referring to the Coming One. Descendants were given to Abraham by other than natural means, so that through him Messiah might come, and the point of the apostle's argument is that since the fulfillment of the promises of God is secured alone by Christ, they only who are "in Christ" can receive them; (2) of spiritual offspring, Rom. 4:16, 18; 9:8; here "the children of the promise are reckoned for a seed"

points, firstly, to Isaac's birth as being not according to the ordinary course of nature but by divine promise, and, secondly, by analogy, to the fact that all believers are children of God by spiritual birth; Gal. 3:29.

As to 1 John 3:9, "his seed abideth in him," it is possible to understand this as meaning that children of God (His "seed") abide in Him, and do not go on doing (practicing) sin (the verb "to commit" does not represent the original in this passage). Alternatively, the "seed" signifies the principle of spiritual life as imparted to the believer, which abides in him without possibility of removal or extinction; the child of God remains eternally related to Christ, he who lives in sin has never become so related, he has not the principle of life in him. This meaning suits the context and the general tenor of the Epistle.

2. *sporos* (σπόρος, 4703), akin to No. 1, properly "a sowing," denotes "seed sown," (*a*) natural, Mark 4:26, 27; Luke 8:5, 11 (the natural being figuratively applied to the Word of God); 2 Cor. 9:10 (1st part); (*b*) metaphorically of material help to the needy, 2 Cor. 9:10 (2nd part), RV, "(your) seed for sowing" (KJV, "seed sown").¶

3. *spora* (σπορά, 4701), akin to No. 1, and like No. 2, "a sowing, seedtime," denotes "seed sown," 1 Pet. 1:23, of human offspring.¶ In the Sept., 2 Kings 19:29.¶

For SEEING, SEEING THAT
(conjunction), see †, p. 1

SEEK

1. *zēteō* (ζητέω, 2212) signifies (*a*) "to seek, to seek for," e.g., Matt. 7:7, 8; 13:45; Luke 24:5; John 6:24; of plotting against a person's life, Matt. 2:20; Acts 21:31; Rom. 11:3; metaphorically, to "seek" by thinking, to "seek" how to do something, or what to obtain, e.g., Mark 11:18; Luke 12:29; to "seek" to ascertain a meaning, John 16:19, "do ye inquire"; to "seek" God, Acts 17:27, RV; Rom. 10:20; (*b*) "to seek or strive after, endeavor, to desire," e.g., Matt. 12:46, 47, RV, "seeking" (KJV, "desiring"); Luke 9:9, RV, "sought" (KJV, "desired"); John 7:19, RV, "seek ye" (KJV, "go ye about"); so v. 20; Rom. 10:3, RV, "seeking" (KJV, "going about"); of "seeking" the kingdom of God and His righteousness, in the sense of coveting earnestly, striving after, Matt. 6:33; "the things that are above," Col. 3:1; peace, 1 Pet. 3:11; (*c*) "to require or demand," e.g., Mark 8:12; Luke 11:29 (some mss. have No. 4); 1 Cor. 4:2, "it is required"; 2 Cor. 13:3, "ye seek." See ABOUT, B,

Note, DESIRE, B, *Note* (2), ENDEAVOR, GO, *Note* (2) (*a*), INQUIRE, REQUIRE.

2. *anazēteō* (ἀναζητέω, 327), "to seek carefully" (*ana,* "up," used intensively, and No. 1), is used of searching for human beings, difficulty in the effort being implied Luke 2:44, 45 (some mss. have No. 1 in the latter v.); Acts 11:25; numerous illustrations of this particular meaning in the papyri are given by Moulton and Milligan.¶ In the Sept., Job 3:4; 10:6.¶

3. *ekzēteō* (ἐκζητέω, 1567) signifies (*a*) "to seek out (*ek*) or after, to search for"; e.g., God, Rom. 3:11; the Lord, Acts 15:17; in Heb. 11:6, RV, "seek after" (KJV, "diligently seek"); 12:17, RV, "sought diligently" (KJV, "sought carefully"); 1 Pet. 1:10, RV, "sought" (KJV, "have inquired"), followed by *exeraunaō,* "to search diligently"; (*b*) "to require or demand," Luke 11:50, 51. See INQUIRE, *Note* (3), REQUIRE.¶

4. *epizēteō* (ἐπιζητέω, 1934), "to seek after" (directive, *epi,* "towards") is always rendered in the RV, by some form of the verb "to seek," Acts 13:7, "sought" (KJV, "desired"); 19:39, "seek" (KJV, "inquire"); Phil. 4:17, "seek for" (KJV, "desire"), twice; elsewhere, Matt. 6:32; 12:39; 16:4; Mark 8:12 (in some texts); Luke 12:30; Acts 12:19; Rom. 11:7; Heb. 11:14; 13:14. See DESIRE, INQUIRE.¶

5. *oregō* (ὀρέγω, 3713), "to reach out, or after," used in the middle voice is translated "seeketh" in 1 Tim. 3:1, RV, of "seeking overseership" (KJV, "desireth"). See DESIRE, No. 5.

Note: For the RV renderings of *zēloō,* in Gal. 4:17, 18, "they zealously seek," "ye may seek," "to be zealously sought," see AFFECT, *Note,* and ZEALOUS.

SEEM

dokeō (δοκέω, 1380) denotes (*a*) "to be of opinion" (akin to *doxa,* "opinion"), e.g., Luke 8:18, RV, "thinketh" (KJV, "seemeth"); so 1 Cor. 3:18; to think, suppose, Jas. 1:26, RV, "thinketh himself" (KJV, "seem"); see SUPPOSE, THINK; (*b*) "to seem, to be reputed," e.g., Acts 17:18; 1 Cor. 11:16; 12:22; 2 Cor. 10:9; Heb. 4:1; 12:11; for Gal. 2:2, 6, 9, see REPUTE; (*c*) impersonally (1) to think (see THINK), (2) to "seem" good, Luke 1:3; Acts 15:22, RV, "it seemed good" (KJV, "it pleased"); 15:25, 28 (v. 34 in some mss.); in Heb. 12:10, the neuter of the present participle is used with the article, lit., "the (thing) seeming good," RV, "(as) seemed good," KJV, "after (their own) pleasure." See ACCOUNT, No. 1.

Notes: In Matt. 11:26 and Luke 10:21, *eudokia,* "good pleasure, satisfaction" (*eu,* "well," and *dokeō*), is used with *ginomai,* "to become," and translated "it seemed good," KJV (RV, "it was well-pleasing"). (2) In Luke 24:11, KJV, *phainō*, "to appear" (passive voice), is translated "seemed" (RV, "appeared").

For SEEMLY, RV, see COMELY, B, and *Note* (2)

Note: In 1 Pet. 2:12, RV, *kalos*, "good, fair," is rendered "seemly."

SEIZE

1. *sullambanō* (συλλαμβάνω, 4815), lit., "to take together" (*sun*, "with," *lambanō*, "to take or lay hold of"), chiefly signifies "to seize as a prisoner"; in the following the RV substitutes the more suitable and forceful verb, "to seize," for KJV, "to take": Matt. 26:55; Mark 14:48; Luke 22:54; John 18:12; Acts 12:3; 23:27; 26:21; in Acts 1:16, RV and KJV, "took." See CATCH, No. 8, CONCEIVE, HELP.

2. *sunarpazō* (συναρπάζω, 4884) is translated "seized" in the RV of Luke 8:29; Acts 6:12; 19:29; see CATCH, No. 7.

Note: In Matt. 21:38, the best texts have *echō*, "to have" ("to take," RV); some have *katechō*, "to lay hold of" (KJV, "seize on").

SELF, SELVES

1. *automatos* (αὐτόματος, 844), "of oneself" (Eng., "automatic," "automaton," etc.), is used in Mark 4:28; Acts 12:10. See ACCORD, B, No. 2.¶

2. *autos* (αὐτός, 846), "he," also means "self," in the reflexive pronouns "myself, thyself, himself," etc. (see, e.g., HE), expressing distinction, exclusion, etc.; it is usually emphatic in the nominative case, e.g., Luke 6:42; 11:4; John 18:28; Rom. 8:16, RV, "Himself."

Note: In John 16:27, "the Father Himself (*autos*)," Field (*Notes on the Translation of the NT*) remarks that *autos* stands for *automatos*.

For SELF-CONDEMNED see CONDEMN, C, No. 1

SELF-CONTROL (without)

akratēs (ἀκρατής, 193), "powerless" (*a*, negative, *kratos*, "strength"), is rendered "without self-control," in 2 Tim. 3:3, RV; see INCONTINENT.¶

SELFSAME

Notes: (1) In 2 Cor. 5:5, KJV, *auto touto*, "this thing itself," "this very thing," RV, is rendered "the selfsame"; in 2 Cor. 7:11, RV and KJV, "this selfsame thing." (2) In Matt. 8:13, KJV, *ekeinos*, with the article, "that," RV, is rendered "that selfsame." (3) In 1 Cor. 12:11, KJV, the article

with *autos*, "the same," RV, is rendered "the selfsame."

SELF-WILLED

authadēs (αὐθάδης, 829), "self-pleasing" (*autos*, "self," *hēdomai*, "to please"), denotes one who, dominated by self-interest, and inconsiderate of others, arrogantly asserts his own will, "self-willed," Titus 1:7; 2 Pet. 2:10 (the opposite of *epieikēs*, "gentle," e.g., 1 Tim. 3:3), "one so far overvaluing any determination at which he has himself once arrived that he will not be removed from it" (Trench, who compares and contrasts *philautos*, "loving self, selfish"; *Syn.* §xciii).¶ In the Sept., Gen. 49:3, 7; Prov. 21:24.¶

SELL

1. *pōleō* (πωλέω, 4453), "to exchange or barter, to sell," is used in the latter sense in the NT, six times in Matthew, three in Mark, six in Luke; in John only in connection with the cleansing of the Temple by the Lord, 2:14, 16; in Acts only in connection with the disposing of property for distribution among the community of believers, 4:34, 37; 5:1; elsewhere, 1 Cor. 10:25; Rev. 13:17.

2. *pipraskō* (πιπράσκω, 4097), from an earlier form, *peraō*, "to carry across the sea for the purpose of selling or to export," is used (*a*) literally, Matt. 13:46; 18:25; 26:9; Mark 14:5; John 12:5; Acts 2:45; 4:34; 5:4; (*b*) metaphorically, Rom. 7:14, "sold under sin," i.e., as fully under the domination of sin as a slave is under his master; the statement evinces an utter dissatisfaction with such a condition; it expresses, not the condemnation of the unregenerate state, but the evil of bondage to a corrupt nature, involving the futility of making use of the Law as a means of deliverance.¶

3. *apodidōmi* (ἀποδίδωμι, 591), "to give up or back," also means, in the middle voice, "to give up of one's own will"; hence, "to sell"; it is so used in Peter's question to Sapphira as to "selling" the land, Acts 5:8; of the act of Joseph's brothers, 7:9; of Esau's act in "selling" his birthright, Heb. 12:16.

Note: In Jas. 4:13, KJV, *emporeuomai*, "to trade" (RV), is rendered "buy and sell."

For SELLER see PURPLE

SENATE

gerousia (γερουσία, 1087), "a council of elders" (from *gerōn*, "an old man," a term which early assumed a political sense among the Greeks, the notion of age being merged in that of dignity), is used in Acts 5:21, apparently epexegetically of the preceding word *sunedrion*, "council," the Sanhedrin.¶

SEND

1. *apostellō* (ἀποστέλλω, 649), lit., "to send forth" (*apo*, "from"), akin to *apostolos*, "an apostle," denotes (*a*) "to send on service, or with a commission." (1) of persons; Christ, sent by the Father, Matt. 10:40; 15:24; 21:37; Mark 9:37; 12:6; Luke 4:18, 43; 9:48; 10:16; John 3:17; 5:36, 38; 6:29, 57; 7:29; 8:42; 10:36; 11:42; 17:3, 8, 18 (1st part), 21, 23, 25; 20:21; Acts 3:20 (future); 3:26; 1 John 4:9, 10, 14; the Holy Spirit, Luke 24:49 (in some texts; see No. 3); 1 Pet. 1:12; Rev. 5:6; Moses, Acts 7:35; John the Baptist, John 1:6; 3:28; disciples and apostles, e.g., Matt. 10:16; Mark 11:1; Luke 22:8; John 4:38; 17:18 (2nd part); Acts 26:17; servants, e.g., Matt. 21:34; Luke 20:10; officers and officials, Mark 6:27; John 7:32; Acts 16:35; messengers, e.g., Acts 10:8, 17, 20; 15:27; evangelists, Rom. 10:15; angels, e.g., Matt. 24:31; Mark 13:27; Luke 1:19, 26; Heb. 1:14; Rev. 1:1; 22:6; demons, Mark 5:10; (2) of things, e.g., Matt. 21:3; Mark 4:29, RV, marg., "sendeth forth," text, "putteth forth" (KJV, " . . . in"); Acts 10:36; 11:30; 28:28; (*b*) "to send away, dismiss," e.g., Mark 8:26; 12:3; Luke 4:18, "to set (at liberty)." See *Note* below, No. 2.

2. *pempō* (πέμπω, 3992), "to send," is used (*a*) of persons: Christ, by the Father, Luke 20:13; John 4:34; 5:23, 24, 30, 37; 6:38, 39, (40), 44; 7:16, 18, 28, 33; 8:16, 18, 26, 29; 9:4; 12:44, 45, 49; 13:20 (2nd part); 14:24; 15:21; 16:5; Rom. 8:3; the Holy Spirit, John 14:26; 15:26; 16:7; Elijah, Luke 4:26; John the Baptist, John 1:33; disciples and apostles, e.g., Matt. 11:2; John 20:21; servants, e.g., Luke 20:11, 12; officials, Matt. 14:10; messengers, e.g., Acts 10:5, 32, 33; 15:22, 25; 2 Cor. 9:3; Eph. 6:22; Phil. 2:19, 23, 25; 1 Thess. 3:2, 5; Titus 3:12; a prisoner, Acts 25:25, 27; potentates, by God, 1 Pet. 2:14; an angel, Rev. 22:16; demons, Mark 5:12; (*b*) of things, Acts 11:29; Phil. 4:16; 2 Thess. 2:11; Rev. 1:11; 11:10; 14:15, 18, RV, "send forth" (KJV, "thrust in").

Notes: (1) *Pempō* is a more general term than *apostellō*; *apostellō* usually "suggests official or authoritative sending" (Thayer). A comparison of the usages mentioned above shows how nearly (in some cases practically quite) interchangeably they are used, and yet on close consideration the distinction just mentioned is discernible; in the Gospel of John, cf. *pempō* in 5:23, 24, 30, 37, *apostellō* in 5:33, 36, 38; *pempō* in 6:38, 39, 44, *apostellō* in 6:29, 57; the two are not used simply for the sake of variety of expression. *Pempō* is not used in the Lord's

prayer in ch. 17, whereas *apostellō* is used six times.

(2) The "sending" of the Son by the Father was from the glory which He had with the Father into the world, by way of the Incarnation, not a "sending" out into the world after His birth, as if denoting His mission among and His manifestation to the people. "Hofmann, in support of his view that Jesus is called the Son of God only in virtue of His being born of man, vainly urges that the simple accusative after *apostellō* also denotes what the Person is or becomes by being sent. What he states is true but only when the name of the object spoken of is chosen to correspond with the purposed mission, as e.g., in Mark 1:2; Luke 14:32; 19:14. We can no more say, 'God sent Jesus that He should be His Son' than we can render 'he sent his servants,' Matt. 21:34, in this manner. That the Sonship of Christ is anterior to His mission to the world . . . is clear from John 16:28; cf. especially also the double accusative in 1 John 4:14, 'the Father sent the Son the Savior of the world.' The expression that Jesus is sent by God denotes the mission which He has to fulfill and the authority which backs Him" (Cremer, *Lexicon of NT Greek*).

3. *exapostellō* (ἐξαποστέλλω, 1821) denotes (*a*) "to send forth": of the Son by God the Father, Gal. 4:4; of the Holy Spirit, 4:6; Luke 24:49 in the best texts (some have No. 1); an angel, Acts 12:11; the ancestors of Israel, Acts 7:12; Paul to the Gentiles, 22:21; of the word of salvation, 13:26 (some mss. have No. 1); (*b*) "to send away," Luke 1:53; 20:10, 11; Acts 9:30; 11:22; 17:14.¶

4. *anapempō* (ἀναπέμπω, 375) denotes (*a*) "to send up" (*ana*, "up," and No. 2), to a higher authority, Luke 23:7, 15; Acts 25:21 (in the best texts; some have No. 2); this meaning is confirmed by examples from the papyri (Moulton and Milligan), by Deissmann (*Bible Studies*, p. 229); see also Field, *Notes on the Trans. of the NT;* (*b*) "to send back," Luke 23:11; Philem. 12.¶

5. *ekpempō* (ἐκπέμπω, 1599) denotes "to send forth" (*ek*, "out of"), Acts 13:4, "being sent forth"; 17:10, "sent away."¶

6. *ballō* (βάλλω, 906), "to cast, throw," is translated "to send (peace)" in Matt. 10:34 (twice), (RV, marg., "cast"). See CAST.

7. *ekballō* (ἐκβάλλω, 1544), "to cast out," or "send out," is translated "sent out" in Mark 1:43, RV (KJV, "sent away"), and in KJV and RV in Jas. 2:25. See CAST, No. 5.

8. *apoluō* (ἀπολύω, 630), "to set free, to let go," is translated "to send away" in Matt. 14:15, 22, 23; Mark 6:36, 45; 8:3, 9; Luke 8:38; Acts

13:3, where the "sending" is not that of commissioning, but of letting go, intimating that they would gladly have retained them (contrast *ekpempō*, the act of commissioning by the Holy Spirit in v. 4).

9. *metapempō* (μεταπέμπω, 3343), "to send after or for, fetch" (*meta*, "after"), is used only in the Acts; in the middle voice, translated "to send for" in 10:22, 29 (2nd part: passive voice in the 1st part); 20:1, RV only (some texts have *proskaleō*); 24:24, 26; 25:3; in 10:5 and 11:13, RV, "fetch." See FETCH.¶

10. *bruō* (βρύω, 1032), "to be full to bursting," was used of the earth in producing vegetation, of plants in putting forth buds; in Jas. 3:11 it is said of springs gushing with water, "(doth the fountain) send forth . . . ?"¶

11. *sunapostellō* (συναποστέλλω, 4882), "to send along with," is used in 2 Cor. 12:18.¶ In the Sept., Ex. 33:2, 12.¶

12. *sunpempō* (συνπέμπω, 4842), "to send along with," is used in 2 Cor. 8:18, 22.¶

Notes: (1) In Matt. 13:36, KJV, *aphiēmi*, "to leave," is translated "He sent . . . away" (RV, "He left"); so in Mark 4:36, KJV, "they had sent away," RV, "leaving." (2) In Mark 6:46, *apotassomai*, "to take leave of" (RV) is translated "He had sent . . . away." (3) In John 13:16 *apostolos* is rendered "one (KJV, he) that is sent," RV marg., "an apostle." (4) *Paristēmi* is rendered "send" in Matt. 26:53, RV

For SENSELESS see FOOLISH, No. 4

SENSES

aisthētērion (αἰσθητήριον, 145), "sense, the faculty of perception, the organ of sense" (akin to *aisthanomai*, "to perceive"), is used in Heb. 5:14, "senses," the capacities for spiritual apprehension.¶ In the Sept., Jer. 4:19, "(I am pained . . . in the) sensitive powers (of my heart)."¶

For SENSUAL see NATURAL, A, No. 2

SENTENCE

A. Nouns.

1. *krima* (κρίμα, 2917), "a judgment," a decision passed on the faults of others, is used especially of God's judgment upon men, and translated "sentence" in 2 Pet. 2:3, RV (KJV, "judgment"). See JUDGMENT, No. 2.

2. *katadikē* (καταδίκη, 2613d), "a judicial sentence, condemnation," is translated "sen-

tence" in Acts 25:15, RV (KJV, "judgment"); some mss. have *dikē*.¶

3. *apokrima* (ἀπόκριμα, 610) is translated "sentence" in 2 Cor. 1:9, KJV (RV, "answer"). See ANSWER, No. 2.¶

B. Verbs.

1. *krinō* (κρίνω, 2919), "to judge, to adjudge," is translated "(my) sentence is" in Acts 15:19, KJV, RV, "(my) judgment is," lit., "I (*egō*, emphatic) judge," introducing the substance or draft of a resolution. See JUDGE, B, No. 1.

2. *epikrinō* (ἐπικρινω, 1948), "to give sentence," is used in Luke 23:24.¶

SEPARATE

A. Verbs.

1. *aphorizō* (ἀφορίζω, 873), "to mark off by bounds" (*apo*, "from," *horizō*, "to determine"; *horos*, "a limit"), "to separate," is used of "(*a*) the Divine action in setting men apart for the work of the gospel, Rom. 1:1; Gal. 1:15; (*b*) the Divine judgment upon men, Matt. 13:49; 25:32; (*c*) the separation of Christians from unbelievers, Acts 19:9; 2 Cor. 6:17; (*d*) the separation of believers by unbelievers, Luke 6:22; (*e*) the withdrawal of Christians from their brethren, Gal. 2:12. In (*c*) is described what the Christian must do, in (*d*) what he must be prepared to suffer, and in (*e*) what he must avoid."¶*

2. *chōrizō* (χωρίζω, 5563), "to put asunder, separate," is translated "to separate" in Rom. 8:35, 39; in the middle voice, "to separate oneself, depart" (see DEPART); in the passive voice in Heb. 7:26, RV, "separated" (KJV, "separate"), the verb here relates to the resurrection of Christ, not, as KJV indicates, to the fact of His holiness in the days of His flesh; the list is progressive in this respect that the first three qualities apply to His sinlessness, the next to His resurrection, the last to His ascension. See PUT, No. 14.

3. *apodiorizō* (ἀποδιορίζω, 592), "to mark off" (*apo*, "from," *dia*, "asunder," *horizō*, "to limit"), hence denotes metaphorically to make "separations," Jude 19, RV (KJV, "separate themselves"), of persons who make divisions (in contrast with v. 20); there is no pronoun in the original representing "themselves."¶

B. Preposition.

chōris (χωρίς, 5565), "apart from, without" (cf. *aneu*, "without," a rarer word than this), is translated "separate from" in Eph. 2:12 (KJV, "without"). See APART, BESIDE, WITHOUT.

For SEPARATIONS see No. 3, above

---

* From *Notes on Galatians*, by Hogg and Vine, p. 83.

SEPULCHRE

1. *taphos* (τάφος, 5028), akin to *thaptō*, "to bury," originally "a burial," then, "a place for burial, a tomb," occurs in Matt. 23:27; v. 29, RV (KJV, "tombs"); 27:61, 64, 66; 28:1; metaphorically, Rom. 3:13.¶

2 and 3. *mnēma* (μνῆμα) and *mnēmeion* (μνημεῖον): see GRAVE.

SERGEANT (-S)

rhabdouchos (ῥαβδοῦχος, 4465), "a rod bearer" (*rhabdos*, "a rod," *echō*, "to hold"), one who carries a staff of office, was, firstly, an umpire or judge, later, a Roman lictor, Acts 16:35, 38. The duty of these officials was to attend Roman magistrates to execute their orders, especially administering punishment by scourging or beheading; they carried as their sign of office the *fasces* (whence "Fascist"), a bundle of rods with an axe inserted. At Philippi they acted under the *stratēgoi* or *pretors* (see MAGISTRATE, No. 1.)¶

SERPENT

1. *ophis* (ὄφις, 3789): the characteristics of the "serpent" as alluded to in Scripture are mostly evil (though Matt. 10:16 refers to its caution in avoiding danger); its treachery, Gen. 49:17; 2 Cor. 11:3; its venom, Ps. 58:4; 1 Cor. 10:9; Rev. 9:19; its skulking, Job 26:13; its murderous proclivities, e.g., Ps. 58:4; Prov. 23:32; Eccl. 10:8, 11; Amos 5:19; Mark 16:18; Luke 10:19; the Lord used the word metaphorically of the scribes and Pharisees, Matt. 23:33 (cf. *echidna*, "viper," in Matt. 3:7; 12:34). The general aspects of its evil character are intimated in the Lord's rhetorical question in Matt. 7:10 and Luke 11:11. Its characteristics are concentrated in the archadversary of God and man, the Devil, metaphorically described as the serpent, 2 Cor. 11:3; Rev. 12:9, 14, 15; 20:2. The brazen "serpent" lifted up by Moses was symbolical of the means of salvation provided by God, in Christ and His vicarious death under the divine judgment upon sin, John 3:14. While the living "serpent" symbolizes sin in its origin, hatefulness, and deadly effect, the brazen "serpent" symbolized the bearing away of the curse and the judgment of sin; the metal was itself figurative of the righteousness of God's judgment.¶

2. *herpeton* (ἑρπετόν, 2062), "a creeping thing" (from *herpō*, "to creep"), "a reptile," is rendered "serpents" in Jas. 3:7, KJV (RV, "creeping things," as elsewhere). See CREEP, B.

SERVANT

A. Nouns.

1. *doulos* (δοῦλος, 1401), an adjective, signifying "in bondage," Rom. 6:19 (neuter plural, agreeing with *melē*, "members"), is used as a noun, and as the most common and general word for "servant," frequently indicating subjection without the idea of bondage; it is used (*a*) of natural conditions, e.g., Matt. 8:9; 1 Cor. 7:21, 22 (1st part); Eph. 6:5; Col. 4:1; 1 Tim. 6:1; frequently in the four Gospels; (*b*) metaphorically of spiritual, moral and ethical conditions: "servants" (1) of God, e.g., Acts 16:17; Titus 1:1; 1 Pet. 2:16; Rev. 7:3; 15:3; the perfect example being Christ Himself, Phil. 2:7; (2) of Christ, e.g., Rom. 1:1; 1 Cor. 7:22 (2nd part); Gal. 1:10; Eph. 6:6; Phil. 1:1; Col. 4:12; Jas. 1:1; 2 Pet. 1:1; Jude 1; (3) of sin, John 8:34 (RV, "bondservants"); Rom. 6:17, 20; (4) of corruption, 2 Pet. 2:19 (RV, "bondservants"); cf. the verb *douloō* (see B). See BONDMAN.

2. *diakonos* (διάκονος, 1249), for which see DEACON and *Note* there on synonymous words, is translated "servant" or "servants" in Matt. 22:13 (RV marg., "ministers"); 23:11 (RV marg., ditto); Mark 9:35, KJV (RV, "minister"); John 2:5, 9; 12:26; Rom. 16:1.

3. *pais* (παῖς, 3816), for which see CHILD, No. 4, also denotes "an attendant"; it is translated "servant" (*a*) of natural conditions, in Matt. 8:6, 8, 13; 14:2; Luke 7:7 ("menservants" in 12:45); 15:26; (*b*) of spiritual relation to God, (1) of Israel, Luke 1:54; (2) of David, Luke 1:69; Acts 4:25; (3) of Christ, so declared by God the Father, Matt. 12:18; spoken of in prayer, Acts 4:27, 30, RV (KJV, "child"); the argument advanced by Dalman for the rendering "Child" in these passages, is not sufficiently valid as against the RV, "Servant" in Acts 4, and the KJV and RV in Matt. 12 (cf., e.g., the use of *pais* in the Sept. of Gen. 41:38; Jer. 36:24). The Matt. 12 passage by direct quotation, and the Acts 4 passages by implication, refer to the ideal "Servant of Jehovah" (Sept., *pais Kuriou*), of Isa. 42:1 and following passages, thus identifying the Servant with the Lord Jesus; for the same identification, cf. Acts 8:35.

4. *oiketēs* (οἰκέτης, 3610), "a house servant" (*oikeō*, "to dwell," *oikos*, "a house"), is translated "servant" in Luke 16:13 (RV marg., "household servant"); so Rom. 14:4 and 1 Pet. 2:18; in Acts 10:7, KJV and RV, "household servants." ¶

5. *hupēretēs* (ὑπηρέτης, 5257), for which see MINISTER, No. 3, and OFFICER, is translated "servants" in the KJV of Matt. 26:58; Mark 14:65

(RV, "officers"); in John 18:36, KJV and RV (RV, marg., "officers").

6. *therapōn* (θεράπων, 2324), akin to *therapeuō*, "to serve, to heal, an attendant, servant," is a term of dignity and freedom, used of Moses in Heb. 3:5.¶

7. *sundoulos* (σύνδουλος, 4889), "a fellow servant," is used (*a*) of natural conditions, Matt. 18:28, 29, 31, 33; 24:49; (*b*) of "servants" of the same divine Lord, Col. 1:7; 4:7; Rev. 6:11; of angels, Rev. 19:10; 22:9.¶

Note: For *misthios* and *misthōtos*, see HIRED SERVANT.

B. Verb.

douloō (δουλόω, 1402), "to enslave, to bring into bondage" (akin to A, No. 1), e.g., 1 Cor. 9:19, RV, "I brought (myself) under bondage (to all)," KJV, "I made myself servant," denotes in the passive voice, "to be brought into bondage, to become a slave or servant," rendered "ye became servants (of righteousness)" in Rom. 6:18; "being . . . become servants (to God)," v. 22. See BONDAGE, B, No. 2.

SERVE

1. *diakoneō* (διακονέω, 1247), "to minister" (akin to *diakonos*, No. 2, above), "to render any kind of service," is translated "to serve," e.g., in Luke 10:40; 12:37; 17:8; 22:26, 27 (twice); see MINISTER, B, No. 1.

2. *douleuō* (δουλεύω, 1398), "to serve as a *doulos*" (No. 1, above), is used (*a*) of serving God (and the impossibility of serving mammon also), Matt. 6:24 and Luke 16:13; Rom. 7:6; in the gospel, Phil. 2:22; (*b*) Christ, Acts 20:19; Rom. 12:11; 14:18; 16:18; Eph. 6:7; Col. 3:24; (*c*) the law of God, Rom. 7:25; (*d*) one another, Gal. 5:13, RV, "be servants to" (KJV, "serve"); (*e*) a father, Luke 15:29 (with a suggestion of acting as a slave); (*f*) earthly masters, Matt. 6:24; Luke 16:13; 1 Tim. 6:2, RV, "serve"; (*g*) the younger by the elder, Rom. 9:12; (*h*) of being in bondage to a nation, Acts 7:7; Gal. 4:25, to the Romans, actually, though also spiritually to Judaizers; (*i*) to idols, Gal. 4:8, RV, "were in bondage" (KJV, "did service"); (*j*) to "the weak and beggarly rudiments," v. 9 (RV), "to be in bondage" (aorist tense in the best texts, suggesting "to enter into bondage"), i.e., to the religion of the Gentiles ("rudiments" being used in v. 3 of the religion of the Jews); (*k*) sin, Rom. 6:6, RV, "be in bondage" (KJV, "serve"); (*l*) "divers lusts and pleasures," Titus 3:3; (*m*) negatively, to any man—a proud and thoughtless denial by the Jews, John 8:33.¶

3. *latreuō* (λατρεύω, 3000), primarily "to work for hire" (akin to *latris*, "a hired servant"), signifies (1) to worship, (2) to "serve"; in the latter sense it is used of service (*a*) to God, Matt. 4:10; Luke 1:74 ("without fear"); 4:8; Acts 7:7; 24:14, RV, "serve" (KJV, "worship"); 26:7; 27:23; Rom. 1:9 ("with my spirit"); 2 Tim. 1:3; Heb. 9:14; 12:28, KJV, "we may serve," RV, "we may offer service"; Rev. 7:15; (*b*) to God and Christ ("the Lamb"), Rev. 22:3; (*c*) in the tabernacle, Heb. 8:5, RV; 13:10; (*d*) to "the host of heaven," Acts 7:42, RV, "to serve" (KJV, "to worship"); (*e*) to "the creature," instead of the Creator, Rom. 1:25, of idolatry: see WORSHIP.

Note: In Luke 2:37 the RV has "worshiping," for KJV, "served"; in Heb. 9:9, "the worshiper," for KJV, "that did the service."

4. *hupēreteō* (ὑπηρετέω, 5256), for which see MINISTER. B, No. 3, is translated "to serve" in Acts 13:36; there is a contrast intimated between the service of David, lasting for only a generation, and the eternal character of Christ's ministry as the One who not having seen corruption was raised from the dead.

SERVICE, SERVING

1. *diakonia* (διακονία, 1248) is rendered "service" in Rom. 15:31, KJV; "serving" in Luke 10:40. See MINISTRY, A, No. 1.

2. *leitourgia* (λειτουργία, 3009) is rendered "service" in 2 Cor. 9:12; Phil. 2:17, 30. See MINISTRY, A, No. 2.

3. *latreia* (λατρεία, 2999), akin to *latreuō* (see No. 3, above), primarily "hired service," is used (*a*) of the "service" of God in connection with the tabernacle, Rom. 9:4; Heb. 9:1, "divine service"; v. 6, plural, RV, "services" (KJV, "service", and, in italics, "*of God*"); (*b*) of the intelligent "service" of believers in presenting their bodies to God, a living sacrifice, Rom. 12:1, RV marg., "worship"; (*c*) of imagined "service" to God by persecutors of Christ's followers, John 16:2.¶

Note: For "soldier on service," 2 Tim. 2:3, RV, see SOLDIER, B.

SET

A. Verbs.

1. *histēmi* (ἵστημι, 2476), "to cause to stand," is translated "to set" in Matt. 4:5 (aorist tense in the best texts; some have the present, as in KJV); 18:2; 25:33; Mark 9:36; Luke 4:9; 9:47; John 8:3; Acts 4:7; 5:27; 6:6; v. 13, "set up"; 22:30; in Jude 24, RV, "to set" (KJV, "to present"). See ABIDE, No. 10.

2. *kathistēmi* (καθίστημι, 2525), lit., "to set down" (*kata*, "down," and No. 1), "to appoint, constitute," is translated "to set" in Matt. 24:45, 47; 25:21, 23, RV (KJV, "made"); so Luke 12:42,

44; it is found in some mss. in Heb. 2:7, and translated "set over" (KJV). See APPOINT, No. 2.

3. *tithēmi* (τίθημι, 5087), "to put, to place," is translated "to set" in Acts 1:7, of times and seasons (KJV, "put"); Acts 13:47; Rev. 10:2; "setteth on" (of wine) in John 2:10, RV (KJV, "doth set forth"); in the KJV of Mark 4:21 (2nd part) and in Luke 8:16 it is rendered "set" (RV, "put"), of a lamp (some texts have No. 6 in both). In Mark 4:30 it is used of "setting" forth by parable the teaching concerning the kingdom of God, RV, "shall we set (it) forth" (KJV, "compare"). See APPOINT, No. 3.

4. *paratithēmi* (παρατίθημι, 3908), "to place beside" (*para*, "beside," and No. 3), "to set forth," of a parable, Matt. 13:24, RV (KJV, "put forth"); "to set before," of food, Mark 6:41; 8:6 (twice), 7; Luke 9:16; 10:8; 11:6; Acts 16:34; 1 Cor. 10:27. See ALLEGE, No. 1, PUT, No. 3.

5. *peritithēmi* (περιτίθημι, 4060), "to place or put around" (*peri*, "around," and No. 3), is translated "to set about" (of a hedge) in Mark 12:1. See BESTOW, No. 5, PUT.

6. *epitithēmi* (ἐπιτίθημι, 2007), "to put, set or lay upon," is used of the placing over the head of Christ on the cross "His accusation," Matt. 27:37, "set up"; of attacking a person, Acts 18:10, "shall set on." See ADD, No. 1.

7. *protithēmi* (προτίθημι, 4388), "to set before" (*pro*, "before," and No. 3), is used in the middle voice, translated "set forth," of Christ, in Rom. 3:25 (RV marg., "purposed"). See PURPOSE, B, No. 3.

8. *didōmi* (δίδωμι, 1325), "to give," is translated "I have set before" in Rev. 3:8 (RV marg., "given"). See GIVE.

9. *kathizō* (καθίζω, 2523), used transitively, signifies "to cause to sit down, set, appoint," translated "to set" in Acts 2:30, RV (KJV, incorrectly, "to sit"); in 1 Cor. 6:4, of appointing, i.e., obtaining the services of, judges in lawcourts; in Eph. 1:20, RV, "made (Him) to sit" (KJV, "set").
Note: In Heb. 8:1, *kathizō* is used intransitively, RV, "sat down" (KJV, "is set"); so in 12:2, RV, "hath sat down" (KJV, "is set down"); Rev. 3:21, RV, "I . . . sat down" (KJV, "am set down"). So *epikathizō* in Matt. 21:7 (last part), RV, "He sat" [some mss. have the plural in a transitive sense, KJV, "they set (Him)]." See SIT, No. 8.

10. *tassō* (τάσσω, 5021), "to arrange, assign, order," is translated "set (under authority)" in Luke 7:8. In 1 Cor. 16:15, RV, "have set (themselves)," KJV, "addicted." See APPOINT, No. 5.

11. *anatassomai* (ἀνατάσσομαι, 392), "to arrange in order, draw up in order" (*ana*, "up," and the middle voice of No. 10), occurs in Luke

1:1, KJV, "to set forth in order," RV, "to draw up." See DRAW, No. 9.¶

12. *dunō* (δύνω, 1416), "to sink into," is used of the "setting" of the sun, Mark 1:32, "did set"; Luke 4:40, "was setting." The sun, moon and stars were conceived of as sinking into the sea when they set.¶

13. *sunallassō* (συναλλάσσω, 4862, 236), "to reconcile" (*sun*, "together," *allassō*, "to change or exchange"), is translated "he . . . would have set (them at one, lit., 'into peace') again" in Acts 7:26 (the imperfect tense being conative, expressing an attempt); some mss. have *sunelaunō*, "to drive together, force together."¶

14. *katangellō* (καταγγέλλω, 2605), "to declare, proclaim," is translated "set forth" in Acts 16:21, RV (KJV, "teach"); "set I forth" in Acts 17:23, RV (KJV, "declare I"). See DECLARE, No. 4.

15. *enechō* (ἐνέχω, 1758), "to hold in," has a secondary significance of "setting oneself against a person," "being urgent against," Mark 6:19; Luke 11:53 (RV, marg.). See ENTANGLE, No. 3, QUARREL, URGE.

16. *propempō* (προπέμπω, 4311), lit., "to send forward" (*pro*, "forward," *pempō*, "to send"), is translated "set forward" in Titus 3:13, RV (KJV, "bring") and in 3 John 6, RV (KJV, "bring forward"), of practical assistance to servants of God in their journeys. See ACCOMPANY, No. 4.

17. *apodeiknumi* (ἀποδείκνυμι, 584), "to show forth, declare," is translated "set forth" in 1 Cor. 4:9, here, a technical term, used for exhibiting gladiators in an arena, "last of all" referring to the grand finale, to make the most thrilling sport for the spectators (cf. 15:32); prophets and others had preceded the apostles in the spectacle; in 2 Thess. 2:4 it is used of the man of sin, who will "set (himself) forth (as God)," KJV, "showing." Elsewhere Acts 2:22; 25:7. See APPROVE, PROVE.¶ The word is frequently used in the papyri of the proclamation of the accession of a king or the appointment of an official. Cf. *apodeixis*, "demonstration," 1 Cor. 2:4.¶

18. *epibibazō* (ἐπιβιβάζω, 1913), "to place upon," is used of causing persons to mount animals for riding, Luke 10:34; 19:35; Acts 23:24.¶

19. *stērizō* (στηρίζω, 4741), "to fix, establish," is rendered "He steadfastly set (His face)" in Luke 9:51. See ESTABLISH, No. 1.

20. *anorthoō* (ἀνορθόω, 461), "to set straight, set up" (*ana*, "up," *orthos*, "straight"), is used in Acts 15:16 in God's promise to "set" up the fallen tabernacle (*skēnē*, "tent") of

David. The word is used in the papyri of rearing buildings again. See LIFT, No. 6, STRAIGHT.

21. *keimai* (κεῖμαι, 2749), "to lie, to be laid" (used as the passive voice of *tithēmi*, No. 3), is translated "to be set," e.g., in Matt. 5:14 (of a city); Luke 2:34 (of Christ); John 2:6 (of water-pots); 19:29 (of a vessel of vinegar); Phil. 1:16, RV (v. 17, KJV) (of the apostle Paul); Rev. 4:2 (of the throne in heaven). See APPOINT, LAY, LIE.

22. *anakeimai* (ἀνάκειμαι, 345), "to be laid up" (*ana* "up"), "to recline at a meal," is so used in John 6:11, "(to them) that were set down." See LEAN, LIE, *Note* (1) SIT, No. 3.

23. *prokeimai* (πρόκειμαι, 4295) signifies (*a*) "to be set before" (*pro*, "before," and No. 21), and is so rendered in Heb. 6:18 of the hope of the believer; 12:1, of the Christian race; v. 2, of the joy "set" before Christ in the days of His flesh and at His death; (*b*) "to be set forth," said of Sodom and Gomorrah, in Jude 7. It is used elsewhere in 2 Cor. 8:12, for which see FIRST, D, *Note* (2).¶

24. *prographō* (προγράφω, 4270), "to write before," is translated "were set forth (unto this condemnation)" in Jude 4, RV (KJV, "ordained"); the evil teachers were "designated of old for this judgment" (cf. 2 Pet. 2:3). For the meaning of this verb in Gal. 3:1, RV, "openly set forth," see OPENLY, No. 2, *Note*. See WRITE.

B. Adjective.

taktos (τακτός, 5002), an adjective (from *tassō*, A, No. 10), "ordered, fixed, set," is said of an appointed day, in Acts 12:21.¶ In the Sept., Job 12:5.¶

Notes: (1) For "to set at liberty" (*apoluō* and *apostellō*), see LIBERTY. (2) In Acts 21:2, KJV, *anagō*, "to set sail" (RV), is translated "set forth"; see LAUNCH. (3) In Luke 22:55, KJV, *sunkathizō*, "to sit down together" (RV), is translated "were set down together." See SIT, No. 10. (4) For Acts 7:5, "to set his foot on," see FOOT, A, No. 1, *Note*. (5) In Acts 13:9, KJV, *atenizō*, "to look fixedly, gaze," is rendered "set his eyes on" (RV, "fastened his eyes on"). See FASTEN, No. 1. (6) In Matt. 27:19, KJV, *kathēmai*, "to sit," is rendered "he was set down" (RV, "he was sitting"). See SIT, No. 1. (7) In John 13:12, (KJV, *anapiptō*, "to recline at table," is translated "was set down" (RV, "sat down"; marg., "reclined"). See RECLINE. (8) In Matt. 27:66 there is no word in the Greek representing the KJV "setting"; the RV has "the guard being with them," lit., "with (*meta*) the guard." (9) The verb is combined with other words, e.g., AFFECTION, FIRE, MIND, NOUGHT, ORDER, SEAL, UPROAR, VARIANCE.

SETTER FORTH

katangeleus (καταγγελεύς, 2604), "a proclaimer, herald" (akin to *katangellō*, "to proclaim"), is used in Acts 17:18, "a setter forth (of strange gods)." It is found in inscriptions in connection with proclamations made in public places.¶

SETTLE

tithēmi (τίθημι, 5087), "to put, place," is translated "settle (it therefore in your hearts)" in Luke 21:14, active voice in the best texts (some have the middle), the aorist tense signifying complete decision, i.e., "resolve" (not "consider"); cf. Acts 5:4, "to conceive in the heart," and contrast Luke 1:66, "to lay up" (both have aorist tense, middle voice). See APPOINT, No. 3.

Notes: (1) In 1 Pet. 5:10, some texts have *themelioō*, "to lay a foundation," used metaphorically, and translated "settle," KJV. (2) In Col. 1:23, KJV, *hedraios*, lit., "seated" (*hedra*, "a seat"), is translated "settled" (RV, "steadfast"). (3) For *epiluō* see DETERMINE, No. 4.

SEVEN

hepta (ἑπτά, 2033), whence Eng. words beginning with "hept"—, corresponds to the Heb. *sheba'* (which is akin to *sāba'*, signifying "to be full, abundant"), sometimes used as an expression of fullness, e.g., Ruth 4:15: it generally expresses completeness, and is used most frequently in the Apocalypse; it is not found in the Gospel of John, nor between the Acts and the Apocalypse, except in Heb. 11:30 (in Rom. 11:4 the numeral is *heptakischilioi*, "seven thousand"); in Matt. 22:26 it is translated "seventh" (marg., "seven").

Note: In 2 Pet. 2:5, RV, "Noah with seven others" is a translation into idiomatic English of the Greek idiom "Noah the eighth *person*" (so KJV, translating literally). See EIGHTH.

SEVENTH

hebdomos (ἕβδομος, 1442) occurs in John 4:52; Heb. 4:4 (twice); Jude 14; Rev. 8:1; 10:7; 11:15; 16:17; 21:20.¶

SEVEN TIMES

heptakis (ἑπτάκις, 2034) occurs in Matt. 18:21, 22; Luke 17:4 (twice).¶

SEVENTY

hebdomēkonta (ἑβδομήκοντα, 1440) occurs in Luke 10:1, 17; in Acts 7:14 it precedes *pente*, "five," lit., "seventy-five," rendered "threescore and fifteen"; for the details see FIFTEEN, *Note*

(1); in 23:23 it is translated "threescore and ten"; in 27:37 it precedes *hex*, "six," lit., "seventy-six," rendered "threescore and sixteen."¶

SEVENTY TIMES

hebdomēkontakis (ἑβδομηκοντάκις, 1441) occurs in Matt. 18:22, where it is followed by *hepta*, "seven," "seventy times seven"; RV marg. has "seventy times and seven," which many have regarded as the meaning; cf. Gen. 4:24 (Winer, in Winer-Moulton, *Gram.*, p. 314, remarks that while this would be the strict meaning, it "would not suit the passage"; his translator, W. F. Moulton, in a footnote, expresses the opinion that it would. So also J. H. Moulton, *Prol.*, p. 98, says: "A definite *allusion* to the Genesis story is highly probable: Jesus pointedly sets against the natural man's craving for seventy-sevenfold revenge the spiritual man's ambition to exercise the privilege of seventy-sevenfold forgiveness").

The Lord's reply "until seventy times seven" was indicative of completeness, the absence of any limit, and was designed to turn away Peter's mind from a merely numerical standard. God's forgiveness is limitless; so should man's be.¶

SEVER

1. *katargeō* (καταργέω, 2673), lit., "to reduce to inactivity" (see ABOLISH, where all the occurrences are given), is rendered "ye are severed (from Christ)" in Gal. 5:4, RV; the aorist tense indicates that point of time at which there was an acceptance of the Judaistic doctrines; to those who accepted these Christ would be of no profit, they were as branches severed from the tree.

2. *aphorizō* (ἀφορίζω, 873), "to separate from," is used of the work of the angels at the end of this age, in "severing" the wicked from among the righteous, Matt. 13:49, a premillennial act quite distinct from the rapture of the Church as set forth in 1 Thess. 4. See DIVIDE, No. 1.

SEVERAL

idios (ἴδιος, 2398), "one's own," is translated "several (ability)," in Matt. 25:15.

Note: For Rev. 21:21, "the several gates," RV, see EVERY, No. 3.

SEVERALLY

idiq (ἰδίᾳ, 2398**), the dative case, feminine, of *idios* (see above), is used adverbially, signifying "severally," in 1 Cor. 12:11.

Notes: (1) In Rom. 12:5, *kata (kath')* followed by the numeral *heis*, "one," and preceded by the article, signifies "severally," RV (KJV, "every one"). Cf. EVERY, *Note* (1). (2) In 1 Cor. 12:27, RV, the phrase *ek merous*, lit., "out of a part" (*meros*), is rendered "severally" (KJV, "in particular"). (3) In Heb. 9:5, RV, the phrase *kata meros*, lit., "according to a part," is rendered "severally." (4) For Eph. 5:33, RV, "severally," see EVERY, No. 3.

SEVERITY

1. *apotomia* (ἀποτομία, 663), "steepness, sharpness" (*apo*, "off," *temnō*, "to cut"; *tomē*, "a cutting"), is used metaphorically in Rom. 11:22 (twice) of "the severity of God," which lies in His temporary retributive dealings with Israel.¶ In the papyri it is used of exacting to the full the provisions of a statute. Cf. the adverb *apotomōs*, "sharply" (which see).

2. *apheidia* (ἀφειδία, 857), primarily "extravagance" (*a*, negative, *pheidomai*, "to spare"), hence, "unsparing treatment, severity," is used in Col. 2:23, RV, "severity (to the body)," KJV, "neglecting of" (marg., "punishing, not sparing"); here it refers to ascetic discipline; it was often used among the Greeks of courageous exposure to hardship and danger.¶

SEW

epiraptō or *epirrhaptō* (ἐπιράπτω, 1976) (*epi*, "upon," *rhaptō*, "to sew or stitch"), is used in Mark 2:21.¶

SHADOW (Noun)

1. *skia* (σκιά, 4639) is used (*a*) of "a shadow," caused by the interception of light, Mark 4:32, Acts 5:15; metaphorically of the darkness and spiritual death of ignorance, Matt. 4:16; Luke 1:79; (*b*) of "the image" or "outline" cast by an object, Col. 2:17, of ceremonies under the Law; of the tabernacle and its appurtenances and offerings, Heb. 8:5; of these as appointed under the Law, Heb. 10:1.¶

2. *aposkiasma* (ἀποσκίασμα, 644), "a shadow," is rendered "shadow that is cast" in Jas. 1:17, RV; the KJV makes no distinction between this and No. 1. The probable significance of this word is "overshadowing" or "shadowing-over" (which *apo* may indicate), and this with the genitive case of *tropē*, "turning," yields the meaning "shadowing-over of mutability" implying an alternation of "shadow" and light; of this there are two alternative explanations, namely, "overshadowing" (1) not caused by mutability in God, or (2) caused by change in others, i.e., "no changes in this lower world can cast a shadow on the unchanging Fount of light" [Mayor, who further remarks, "The meaning of the passage will then be, 'God is

alike incapable of change (*parallagē*) and incapable of being changed by the action of others'"].

For **SHADOWING**, Heb. 9:5, KJV, see **OVERSHADOW**

SHAKE

1. *saleuō* (σαλεύω, 4531), "to agitate, shake," primarily of the action of stormy winds, waves, etc., is used (*a*) literally, of a reed, Matt. 11:7; Luke 7:24; a vessel, "shaken" in filling, Luke 6:38; a building, Luke 6:48; Acts 4:31; 16:26; the natural forces of the heavens and heavenly bodies, Matt. 24:29; Mark 13:25; Luke 21:26; the earth, Heb. 12:26, "shook"; (*b*) metaphorically, (1) of "shaking" so as to make insecure, Heb. 12:27 (twice); (2) of casting down from a sense of security, Acts 2:25, "I should (not) be moved"; (3) to stir up (a crowd), Acts 17:13; (4) to unsettle, 2 Thess. 2:2, "(to the end that) ye be not (quickly) shaken (from your mind)," i.e., from their settled conviction and the purpose of heart begotten by it, as to the return of Christ before the Day of the Lord begins; the metaphor may be taken from the loosening of a ship from its moorings by a storm. See MOVE, STIR.¶

2. *seiō* (σείω, 4579), "to shake to and fro," is rendered "to shake" in Matt. 28:4, KJV; Heb. 12:26, KJV; Rev. 6:13, KJV and RV; see MOVE, No. 3.

3. *apotinassō* (ἀποτινάσσω, 660), "to shake off" (*apo*, "from," *tinassō*, "to shake"), is used in Luke 9:5, of dust from the feet; Acts 28:5, of a viper from the hand.¶ In the Sept., Judg. 16:20; 1 Sam 10:2; Lam. 2:7.¶

4. *ektinassō* (ἐκτινάσσω, 1621), "to shake out," is used of "shaking off" the dust from the feet, Matt. 10:14; Mark 6:11; Acts 13:51; of "shaking out" one's raiment, Acts 18:6.¶

SHALL

mellō (μέλλω, 3195), "to be about (to be or do)," is used of purpose, certainty, compulsion or necessity. It is rendered simply by "shall" or "should" (which frequently represent elsewhere part of the future tense of the verb) in the following (the RV sometimes translates differently, as noted): Matt. 16:27 (1st part), lit., "is about to come"; 17:12, 22; 20:22, RV, "am about"; 24:6; Mark 13:4 (2nd part), RV, "are about"; Luke 9:44; 21:7 (2nd part), RV, "are about"; v. 36; Acts 23:3; 24:15; 26:2, RV, "I am (to)"; Rom. 4:24; 8:13 (1st part), RV, "must"; v. 18; 2 Tim. 4:1; Heb. 1:14; 10:27; Jas. 2:12, RV, "are to"; 1 Pet. 5:1; Rev. 1:19; 2:10 (1st and 2nd parts), RV, "art about," "is about"; 3:10, RV,

"is (to)"; 17:8 (1st part), RV, "is about." See ABOUT, B.

Notes: (1) The use of "shall, shalt," is frequently part of the rendering of a future tense of a verb. (2) The phrase "it shall come to pass" is the rendering of the future tense of *eimi*, "to be," in Acts 2:17, 21; 3:23; Rom. 9:26.

SHAMBLES

makellon (μάκελλον, 3111), a term of late Greek borrowed from the Latin *macellum*, denotes a "meat market," translated "shambles" in 1 Cor. 10:25. The word is found in the *koinē*, or vernacular Greek covering the time of the NT, illustrating this passage (see Deissmann, *Light from the Ancient East*, 274). A plan, drawn by Lietzmann, of a forum in Pompeii, shows both the slaughterhouse and the meat shop next to the chapel of Caesar. Some of the meat which had been used for sacrificial purposes was afterwards sold in the markets. The apostle enjoins upon the believer to enter into no inquiry, so as to avoid the troubling of conscience (contrast v. 28).¶

SHAME (Noun, and Verb)

A. Nouns.

1. *atimia* (ἀτιμία, 819) signifies (*a*) "shame, disgrace," Rom 1:26, "vile (passions)," RV, lit., "(passions) of shame"; 1 Cor. 11:14; (*b*) "dishonor," e.g., 2 Tim. 2:20, where the idea of disgrace or "shame" does not attach to the use of the word; the meaning is that while in a great house some vessels are designed for purposes of honor, others have no particular honor (*timē*) attached to their use (the prefix *a* simply negatives the idea of honor). See DISHONOR.

2. *aischunē* (αἰσχύνη, 152): See ASHAMED, B, No. 1.

3. *entropē* (ἐντροπή, 1791), 1 Cor. 6:5 and 15:34. See ASHAMED, B, No. 2.¶

4. *aschēmosunē* (ἀσχημοσύνη, 808) denotes (*a*) "unseemliness," Rom. 1:27, RV (KJV, "that which is unseemly"); (*b*) "shame, nakedness," Rev. 16:15, a euphemism for No. 2.¶

B. Adjective.

aischros (αἰσχρός, 150), "base, shameful" (akin to *aischos*, "shame"), of that which is opposed to modesty or purity, is translated as a noun in 1 Cor. 11:6; 14:35, KJV (RV, "shameful"); Eph. 5:12; in Titus 1:11, "filthy (lucre)," lit., "shameful (gain)." See FILTHY.¶

C. Verbs.

1. *atimazō* (ἀτιμάζω, 818), "to dishonor, put to shame" (akin to A, No. 1): see DISHONOR, C, No. 1.

2. *entrepō* (ἐντρέπω, 1788), lit., "to turn in upon, to put to shame" (akin to A, No. 3), is

translated "to shame (you)" in 1 Cor. 4:14. See ASHAMED, A, No. 4.

3. *kataischunō* (καταισχύνω, 2617), "to put to shame" (*kata*, perhaps signifying "utterly"), is translated "ye . . . shame (them)" in 1 Cor. 11:22, KJV, RV, "ye . . . put (them) to shame." See ASHAMED, A, No. 3.

4. *paradeigmatizō* (παραδειγματίζω, 3856) signifies "to set forth as an example" (*para*, "beside," *deiknumi*, "to show"), and is used in Heb. 6:6 of those Jews, who, though attracted to, and closely associated with, the Christian faith, without having experienced more than a tasting of the heavenly gift and partaking of the Holy Ghost (not actually receiving Him), were tempted to apostatize to Judaism, and, thereby crucifying the Son of God a second time, would "put Him to an open shame." So were criminals exposed.¶ In the Sept., Num. 25:4; Jer. 13:22; Ezek. 28:17.¶

SHAMEFASTNESS (KJV, SHAMEFACEDNESS)

aidōs (αἰδώς, 127), "a sense of shame, modesty," is used regarding the demeanor of women in the church, 1 Tim. 2:9 (some mss. have it in Heb. 12:28 for *deos*, "awe": here only in NT). "Shamefastness is that modesty which is 'fast' or rooted in the character . . . The change to 'shamefacedness' is the more to be regretted because shamefacedness . . . has come rather to describe an awkward diffidence, such as we sometimes call sheepishness" (Davies; *Bible English*, p. 12).

As to *aidōs* and *aischunē* (see ASHAMED, B, No. 1), *aidōs* is more objective, having regard to others; it is the stronger word. "*Aidōs* would always restrain a good man from an unworthy act, *aischunē* would sometimes restrain a bad one" (Trench, *Syn.* §xix, xx).

SHAMEFULLY (ENTREAT)

Note: This forms part of the rendering of (*a*) *atimazō*, Mark 12:4, Luke 20:11, see DISHONOR, C, No. 1, ENTREAT, Note, HANDLE, No. 4; (*b*) *hubrizō*, "to insult," Acts 14:5, RV; 1 Thess. 2:2, "were (RV, having been) shamefully entreated." See SPITEFULLY.

SHAPE

1. *eidos* (εἶδος, 1491), rendered "shape" in the KJV of Luke 3:22 and John 5:37: see FORM, No. 4.

2. *homoiōma* (ὁμοίωμα, 3667), rendered "shapes" in Rev. 9:7: see LIKENESS, No. 1.

For **SHARERS** (Heb. 2:14) see **PARTAKE**, B, No. 1.

SHARP, SHARPER, SHARPLY, SHARPNESS

A. Adjectives.

1. *oxus* (ὀξύς, 3691) denotes (*a*) "sharp" (Eng., "oxy—)," said of a sword, Rev. 1:16; 2:12; 19:15; of a sickle, 14:14, 17, 18 (twice); (*b*) of motion, "swift," Rom. 3:15. See SWIFT.¶

2. *tomos* (τομός, 5114*), akin to *temnō*, "to cut" [Eng., "(ana)tomy," etc.], is used metaphorically in the comparative degree, *tomōteros*, in Heb. 4:12, of the Word of God.¶

B. Adverb.

apotomōs (ἀποτόμως, 664) signifies "abruptly, curtly," lit., "in a manner that cuts" (*apo*, "from," *temnō*, "to cut," hence "sharply, severely," 2 Cor. 13:10, RV, "(that I may not . . . deal) sharply," KJV, "(use) sharpness"; the pronoun "you" is to be understood, i.e., "that I may not use (or deal with) . . . sharply"; Titus 1:13, of rebuking.¶ Cf. *apotomia*, "severity."

SHAVE

xuraō (ξυράω, 3587), a late form of *xureō*, or *xurō*, from *xuron*, "a razor," occurs in Acts 21:24 (middle voice), in connection with a vow (Num. 6:2–18; cf. Acts 18:18: see SHEAR); 1 Cor. 11:5, 6 (2nd part in each).¶

SHE

Note: The words under HE in their feminine forms are used for this pronoun.

SHEAR, SHEARER, SHORN

keirō (κείρω, 2751) is used (*a*) of "shearing sheep," Acts 8:32, "shearer," lit., "the (one) shearing": (*b*) in the middle voice, "to have one's hair cut off, be shorn," Acts 18:18; 1 Cor. 11:6 (twice; cf. *xuraō*, "to shave"; see above).¶

SHEATH

thēkē (θήκη, 2336), "a place to put something in" (akin to *tithēmi*, "to put"), "a receptacle, chest, case," is used of the "sheath" of a sword, John 18:11.¶

SHED

1. *ekcheō* (ἐκχέω, 1632), "to pour out," is translated "to shed" or "to shed forth" in Acts 2:33; Titus 3:6, KJV; of "shedding" blood in murder, Rom. 3:15. See POUR, No. 3.

2. *ekchunō*, or *ekchunnō* (ἐκχύνω, 1632), a later form of No. 1, is used of the voluntary giving up of His life by Christ through the "shedding" of His blood in crucifixion as an atoning sacrifice, Matt. 26:28; Mark 14:24; Luke 22:20, KJV, "is shed," RV, "is poured out";

these passages do not refer to the effect of the piercing of His side (which took place after His death); of the murder of servants of God, Matt. 23:35; Luke 11:50; Acts 22:20 (in the best texts; others have No. 1); of the love of God in the hearts of believers through the Holy Spirit, Rom. 5:5. For the "pouring out" of the Holy Spirit, Acts 10:45, see POUR, No. 4. (The form in the last two passages might equally well come from No. 1, above.) See GUSH OUT, RUN, SPILL.

SHEEP

1. *probaton*(πρόβατον, 4263), from *probainō*, "to go forward," i.e., of the movement of quadrupeds, was used among the Greeks of small cattle, sheep and goats; in the NT, of "sheep" only (*a*) naturally, e.g., Matt. 12:11, 12; (*b*) metaphorically, of those who belong to the Lord, the lost ones of the house of Israel, Matt. 10:6; of those who are under the care of the Good Shepherd, e.g., Matt. 26:31; John 10:1, lit., "the fold of the sheep," and vv. 2–27; 21:16, 17 in some texts; Heb. 13:20; of those who in a future day, at the introduction of the millennial kingdom, have shown kindness to His persecuted earthly people in their great tribulation, Matt. 25:33; of the clothing of false shepherds, Matt. 7:15; (*c*) figuratively, by way of simile, of Christ, Acts 8:32; of the disciples, e.g., Matt. 10:16; of true followers of Christ in general, Rom. 8:36; of the former wayward condition of those who had come under His Shepherd care, 1 Pet. 2:25; of the multitudes who sought the help of Christ in the days of His flesh, Matt. 9:36; Mark 6:34.

2. *probation* (προβάτιον, 4263*), a diminutive of No. 1, "a little sheep," is found in the best texts in John 21:16, 17 (some have No. 1); distinct from *arnia*, "lambs" (v. 15), but used as a term of endearment.¶

Note: For "keeping sheep," Luke 17:7, RV, see CATTLE.

For SHEEPFOLD see FOLD

SHEEP GATE, SHEEP MARKET

probatikos (προβατικος, 4262), an adjective, used in the grammatically feminine form, in John 5:2, to agree with *pulē*, "a gate," understood, RV, "sheep *gate*" (not with *agora*, "a market," KJV, "sheep *market*").¶ In the Sept., Neh. 3:1, 32; 12:39.¶ This "sheep gate" was near the Temple; the sacrifices for the Temple probably entered by it.

SHEEPSKIN

mēlōtē (μηλωτή, 3374), from *mēlon*, "a sheep or goat," occurs in Heb. 11:37.¶ In the Sept., 1 Kings 19:13, 19; 2 Kings 2:8, 13, 14.¶

SHEET

othonē (ὀθόνη, 3607) primarily denoted "fine linen," later, "a sheet," Acts 10:11; 11:5.¶ Cf. *othonion*, "linen."

SHEKEL, HALF SHEKEL

1. *statēr* (στατήρ, 4715), a *tetradrachmon* or four *drachmae*, originally 224 grains, in Tyrian currency, but reduced in weight somewhat by the time recorded in Matt. 17:24; the value was about three shillings, and would pay the Temple tax for two persons, Matt. 17:27, RV, "shekel" (KJV, "a piece of money"); in some mss., 26:16; see MONEY, *Note*.¶

2. *didrachmon* (δίδραχμον, 1323), "a half-shekel" (i.e., *dis*, "twice," *drachmē*, "a drachma," the coin mentioned in Luke 15:8, 9), was the amount of the tribute in the 1st cent., A.D., due from every adult Jew for the maintenance of the Temple services, Matt. 17:24 (twice).¶ This was based on Exod. 30:13, 24 (see also 38:24–26; Lev. 5:15; 27:3, 25; Num. 3:47, 50; 7:13ff.; 18:16).

SHEPHERD

poimēn (ποιμήν, 4166) is used (*a*) in its natural significance, Matt. 9:36; 25:32; Mark 6:34; Luke 2:8, 15, 18, 20; John 10:2, 12; (*b*) metaphorically of Christ, Matt. 26:31; Mark 14:27; John 10:11, 14, 16; Heb. 13:20; 1 Pet. 2:25; (*c*) metaphorically of those who act as pastors in the churches, Eph. 4:11.¶ See PASTOR.

For CHIEF SHEPHERD see CHIEF, B, No. 3

SHEW (SHOW)

1. *deiknumi*, or *deiknuō*, (δείκνυμι, 1166) denotes (*a*) "to show, exhibit," e.g., Matt. 4:8; 8:4; John 5:20; 20:20; 1 Tim. 6:15; (*b*) "to show by making known," Matt. 16:21; Luke 24:40; John 14:8, 9; Acts 10:28; 1 Cor. 12:31; Rev. 1:1; 4:1; 22:6; (*c*) "to show by way of proving," Jas. 2:18; 3:13.

2. *anadeiknumi* (ἀναδείκνυμι, 322) signifies (*a*) "to lift up and show, show forth, declare" (*ana*, "up," and No. 1), Acts 1:24; (*b*) to "appoint," Luke 10:1. See APPOINT, No. 14.¶

3. *endeiknumi* (ἐνδείκνυμι, 1731) signifies (1) "to show forth, prove" (middle voice), said (*a*) of God as to His power, Rom. 9:17; His

wrath, 9:22; the exceeding riches of His grace, Eph. 2:7; (b) of Christ, as to His longsuffering, 1 Tim. 1:16; (c) of Gentiles, as to "the work of the Law written in their hearts," Rom. 2:15; (d) of believers, as to the proof of their love, 2 Cor. 8:24; all good fidelity, Titus 2:10; meekness, 3:2; love toward God's Name, Heb. 6:10; diligence in ministering to the saints, v. 11; (2) "to manifest by evil acts," 2 Tim. 4:14, "did (me much evil)," marg., "showed."¶

4. *epideiknumi* (ἐπιδείκνυμι, 1925), *epi*, "upon," intensive, and No. 1, signifies (a) "to exhibit, display," Matt. 16:1; 22:19; 24:1; Luke 17:14 (in some mss. 24:40; No. 1 in the best texts); in the middle voice, "to display," with a special interest in one's own action, Acts 9:39; (b) "to point out, prove, demonstrate," Acts 18:28; Heb. 6:17.¶

5. *hupodeiknumi* (ὑποδείκνυμι, 5263), primarily, "to show secretly (*hupo*, 'under'), or by tracing out," hence, "to make known, warn," is translated "to show" in Luke 6:47; Acts 9:16; in 20:35, KJV (RV, "I gave . . . an example"). See EXAMPLE, WARN.

6. *poieō* (ποιέω, 4160), "to make, to do," is translated, "He hath showed" in Luke 1:51; "to show (mercy)," v. 72, RV (KJV, "perform"); "showed (mercy)," 10:37; John 6:30, KJV, "showest Thou," RV, "doest Thou (for a sign)"; Acts 7:36, KJV, "showed," RV, "wrought"; Jas. 2:13, "showed (no mercy)"; in Mark 13:22 in the best texts (some have *didōmi*), "shall show (signs)." See DO, No. 1.

7. *mēnuō* (μηνύω, 3377), "to disclose, make known" (what was secret), is rendered "to show" in Luke 20:37; 1 Cor. 10:28; in a forensic sense, John 11:57; Acts 23:30, RV (KJV, "it was told"). See TELL.¶

8. *paristēmi* (παρίστημι, 3936), "to show," in Acts 1:3; 2 Tim. 2:15 (KJV): see PRESENT, No. 1.

9. *parechō* (παρέχω, 3930), "to afford, give, show," etc., in the active voice, is translated "showed" in Acts 28:2; in the middle voice, "showing" in Titus 2:7 (1st part). See BRING, No. 21.

10. *exangellō* (ἐξαγγέλλω, 1804), "to tell out, proclaim abroad, to publish completely" (*ek*, or *ex*, "out," *angellō*, "to proclaim"), is rendered "show forth" in 1 Pet. 2:9; it indicates a complete proclamation (verbs compounded with *ek* often suggest what is to be done fully).¶

11. *didōmi* (δίδωμι, 1325), "to give," is rendered "to show" in Matt. 24:24. See also No. 6.

Notes: The KJV translates the following words by the verb "to show" in the passages indicated. The RV gives the better renderings: (1) *apodeiknumi* ("to demonstrate"), 2 Thess. 2:4, "setting (himself) forth," see SET, No. 17; (2) *anangellō* ("to declare"), Matt. 11:4, "tell"; John 16:13–15, "declare"; 16:25, "shall tell"; Acts 19:18 and 20:20, "declaring"; (3) *katangellō*, Acts 16:17; 26:23; 1 Cor. 11:26, "proclaim"; in the last passage the partaking of the elements at the Lord's Supper is not a "showing forth" of His death, but a proclamation of it; (4) *phaneroō*, John 7:4; 21:1 (twice), 14; Rom. 1:19, "to manifest"; (5) *dēloō*, ("to make plain"), 2 Pet. 1:14, "signify"; (6) *diēgeomai* ("to recount"), Luke 8:39, "declare"; (7) *emphanizō* ("to manifest"), Acts 23:22, "hast signified"; (8) *euangelizō*, Luke 1:19, "to bring glad tidings"; (9) *katatithēmi* ("to lay up"), Acts 24:27, "to gain"; (10) *legō* ("to tell"), 1 Cor. 15:51, "I tell"; (11) *energeō*, Matt. 14:2 and Mark 6:14, "work"; (12) *ōphthē* (lit., "was seen"), Acts 7:26, "He appeared"; (13) *ginomai* ("to become"), Acts 4:22, "was wrought"; (14) in Acts 10:40, *emphanēs*, "manifest," with *didōmi*, "to give," and *ginomai*, "to become," gave . . . to be made manifest" (KJV "showed . . . openly"); (15) *apangellō* ("to announce"), Matt. 11:4, "tell"; 12:18, "declare"; 28:11, "told"; Luke 14:21, "told"; Acts 26:20, "declared"; 28:21, "report"; 1 Thess. 1:9, "report"; 1 John 1:2, "declare"; (16) In Luke 1:58, KJV, *megalunō*, to magnify (RV), is rendered "shewed great." (17) See also SHEWING.

For SHEW BEFORE see FORESHEW

SHEWBREAD

Note: The phrase rendered "the shewbread" is formed by the combination of the nouns *prothesis*, "a setting forth" (*pro*, "before," *tithēmi*, "to place") and *artos*, "a loaf" (in the plural), each with the article, Matt. 12:4; Mark 2:26 and Luke 6:4, lit., "the loaves of the setting forth"; in Heb. 9:2, lit., "the setting forth of the loaves."¶ The corresponding OT phrases are lit., "bread of the face," Exod. 25:30, i.e., the presence, referring to the Presence of God (cf. Isa. 63:9 with Exod. 33:14, 15); "the bread of ordering," 1 Chron. 9:32, marg. In Num. 4:7 it is called "the continual bread"; in 1 Sam. 21:4, 6, "holy bread" (KJV, "hallowed"). In the Sept. of 1 Kings 7:48, it is called "the bread of the offering" (*prosphora*, "a bearing towards"). The twelve loaves, representing the tribes of Israel, were set in order every Sabbath day before the Lord, "on the behalf of the children," Lev. 24:8, RV (marg., and KJV, "from"), "an everlasting covenant." The loaves symbolized the fact that on the basis of the sacrificial atonement of the

Cross, believers are accepted before God, and nourished by Him in the person of Christ. The showbread was partaken of by the priests, as representatives of the nation. Priesthood now being coextensive with all who belong to Christ, 1 Pet. 2:5, 9, He, the Living Bread, is the nourishment of all, and where He is, there, representatively, they are.

SHEWING

anadeixis (ἀνάδειξις, 323), "a shewing forth" (*ana*, "up or forth," and *deiknumi*, "to show"), is translated "showing" in Luke 1:80.¶
Note: For "showing," Rom. 3:25, 26, RV, see DECLARE, B.

SHIELD

thureos (θυρεός, 2375) formerly meant "a stone for closing the entrance of a cave"; then, "a shield," large and oblong, protecting every part of the soldier; the word is used metaphorically of faith, Eph. 6:16, which the believer is to take up "in (*en* in the original) all" (all that has just been mentioned), i.e., as affecting the whole of his activities.¶

SHINE, SHINING

A. Verbs.

1. *phainō* (φαίνω, 5316), "to cause to appear," denotes, in the active voice, "to give light, shine," John 1:5; 5:35; in Matt. 24:27, passive voice; so Phil. 2:15, RV, "ye are seen" (for KJV, "ye shine"); 2 Pet. 1:19 (active); so 1 John 2:8; Rev. 1:16; in 8:12 and 18:23 (passive); 21:23 (active). See APPEAR.

2. *epiphainō* (ἐπιφαίνω, 2014), "to shine upon" (*epi*, "upon," and No. 1), is so translated in Luke 1:79, RV (KJV, "to give light"). See APPEAR, No. 2.

3. *lampō* (λάμπω, 2989), "to shine as a torch," occurs in Matt. 5:15, 16; 17:2; Luke 17:24; Acts 12:7; 2 Cor. 4:6 (twice).¶: see LIGHT, B, No. 3.

4. *stilbō* (στίλβω, 4744), "to shine, glisten," is used in Mark 9:3 of the garments of Christ at His transfiguration, RV, "glistering," KJV, "shining."¶ Cf. *exastraptō*, "dazzling," in Luke 9:29, RV.

5. *eklampō* (ἐκλάμπω, 1584), "to shine forth" (*ek*, "out" and No. 3), is used in Matt. 13:43, of the future shining "forth" of the righteous "in the Kingdom of their Father."¶

6. *perilampō* (περιλάμπω, 4034), "to shine around" (*peri*, "around," and No. 3), is used in Luke 2:9, "shone round about," of the glory of the Lord; so in Acts 26:13, of the light from Heaven upon Saul of Tarsus.¶

7. *periastraptō* (περιαστράπτω, 4015), "to flash around, shine round about" (*peri*, and *astrapē*, "shining brightness"), is used in Acts 9:3 and 22:6 of the same circumstance as in 26:13 (No. 6).¶

8. *epiphauskō* or *epiphauō* (ἐπιφαύσκω, 2017), "to shine forth," is used figuratively of Christ upon the slumbering believer who awakes and arises from among the dead, Eph. 5:14, RV, "shall shine upon thee" (KJV, "shall give thee light").¶

B. Noun.

astrapē (ἀστραπή, 796) denotes (*a*) "lightning," (*b*) "bright shining," of a lamp, Luke 11:36. See LIGHTNING. Cf. No. 7, above, and *Note* (1) below.
Notes: (1) In Luke 24:4, KJV, *astraptō*, "to lighten," is translated "shining" (RV, "dazzling"). (2) In 2 Cor. 4:4, KJV, *augazō*, "to shine forth," is translated "shine" (RV, "dawn").¶

SHIP, SHIPPING

1. *ploion* (πλοῖον, 4143), akin to *pleō*, "to sail," a boat or a ship, always rendered appropriately "boat" in the RV in the Gospels; "ship" in the Acts; elsewhere, Jas. 3:4; Rev. 8:9; 18:17 (in some mss.), 19. See BOAT, No. 2.

2. *ploiarion* (πλοιάριον, 4142), a diminutive form of No. 1, is translated "ship" in the KJV of Mark 3:9; 4:36 and John 21:8; "(took) shipping" in John 6:24, KJV, RV "(got into the) boats." See BOAT, No. 1.

3. *naus* (ναῦς, 3491) denotes "a ship" (Lat. *navis*, Eng. "nautical," "naval," etc.), Acts 27:41.¶ *Naus*, in classical Greek the ordinary word for a "ship," survived in Hellenistic Greek only as a literary word, but disappeared from popular speech (Moulton, *Proleg.*, p. 25). Blass (*Philology of the Gospels*, p. 186) thinks the solitary Lucan use of *naus* was due to a reminiscence of the Homeric phrase for beaching a "ship."
Note: For *epibainō*, Acts 21:6, "we took ship," see TAKE, *Note* (16).

For OWNER OF THE SHIP see OWNER, No. 2

For SHIPMEN see MARINERS

For SHIPMASTER see MASTER, A, No. 7

SHIPWRECK

nauageō (ναυαγέω, 3489) signifies (*a*) literally, "to suffer shipwreck" (*naus*, "a ship," *agnumi*, "to break"), 2 Cor. 11:25; (*b*) metaphorically, "to make shipwreck," 1 Tim.

1:19, "concerning the faith," as the result of thrusting away a good conscience (both verbs in this v. are in the aorist tense, signifying the definiteness of the acts).¶

For **SHIVERS** (Rev. 2:27) see **BREAK**, A, No. 5

For **SHOD** see **BIND**, No. 3

SHOE

hupodēma (ὑπόδημα, 5266) denotes "a sole bound under the foot" (*hupo*, "under," *deō*, "to bind"; cf. *hupodeō*, "to bind under"), "a sandal," always translated "shoes," e.g., Matt. 3:11; 10:10; Mark 1:7.

SHOOT FORTH

proballō (προβάλλω, 4261), lit., "to throw before," is used of "the putting forth of leaves, blossom, fruit," said of trees in general, Luke 21:30, "shoot forth." See PUT (forward), Acts 19:33.¶

Note: In Mark 4:32, KJV, *poieō*, "to do, make," is rendered "shooteth out," RV, "putteth out."

For **SHORE** see **BEACH** and **LIP**

For **SHORT** (Adjective and Adverb) see **LITTLE**, A, No 2 and B, No. 2

Note: In 1 Thess. 2:17, "a short season," is lit., "a season of an hour" (*hōra;* see HOUR, SEASON, No. 1.

SHORT (come, cut), SHORTEN

1. *koloboō* (κολοβόω, 2856) denotes "to cut off, amputate" (*kolobos*, "docked"); hence, "to curtail, shorten," said of the "shortening" by God of the time of the great tribulation, Matt. 24:22 (twice); Mark 13:20 (twice).¶ In the Sept., 2 Sam. 4:12.¶

2. *sustellō* (συστέλλω, 4958) denotes (*a*) "to draw together" (*sun*, "together," *stellō*, "to bring, gather"), "to contract, shorten," 1 Cor. 7:29, RV, "(the time) is shortened" (KJV, " . . . is short"); the coming of the Lord is always to be regarded as nigh for the believer, who is to be in constant expectation of His return, and thus is to keep himself from being the slave of earthly conditions and life's relationships; (*b*) "to wrap up," of enshrouding a body for burial, Acts 5:6, RV, "they wrapped (KJV, wound) . . . up."¶

3. *suntemnō* (συντέμνω, 4933), primarily, "to cut in pieces" (*sun*, "together," *temnō*, "to cut"), then, "to cut down, cut short," is used metaphorically in Rom. 9:28 (twice in some

texts), "the Lord will execute His word (*logos*, not "work," as KJV) upon the earth, finishing it and cutting it short," i.e., in the fullfillment of His judgments pronounced upon Israel, a remnant only being saved; the "cutting short" of His word is suggestive of the summary and decisive character of the divine act.¶

Note: For *hustereō*, "to come short, fall short," see FALL, No. 10.

SHORTLY

1. *eutheōs* (εὐθέως, 2112), "straightway, directly," is translated "shortly" in 3 John 14. The general use of the word suggests something sooner than "shortly." See FORTHWITH, STRAIGHTWAY.

2. *tacheōs* (ταχέως, 5030): see QUICKLY, No. 3.

3. *tacheion* (τάχειον, 5032): see QUICKLY, No. 2.

4. *en tachei* (ἐν τάχει): see QUICKLY, No. 4.

Note: In 2 Pet. 1:14, KJV, *tachinos*, an adjective denoting "swift" (akin to the above), is translated "shortly" (RV, "swiftly"), lit., "the putting off of my tabernacle is swift" (i.e., in its approach). Cf. 2:1.

SHOULD

Note: This is frequently part of the translation of the tense of a verb. Otherwise it translates the following:

1. *mellō* (μέλλω, 3195), "to be about to" (for the significance of which see SHALL), e.g., Mark 10:32, RV, "were to"; Luke 19:11, RV, "was to"; "should" in 22:23; 24:21; John 6:71; 7:39, RV, "were to"; 11:51; 12:4, 33; 18:32; Acts 11:28; 23:27, RV, "was about (to be slain)"; 1 Thess. 3:4, RV, "are to"; Rev. 6:11. See ABOUT, B.

2. *dei* (δεῖ, 1163), "it needs, it should," e.g., Matt. 18:33; Acts 27:21: see MUST.

Note: In 1 Cor. 9:10, KJV, *opheilō*, "to owe," is rendered "should" (RV, "ought to").

SHOULDER

ōmos (ὦμος, 5606) occurs in Matt. 23:4 and Luke 15:5, and is suggestive (as in the latter passage) of strength and safety.¶

SHOUT (Noun and Verb)

A. Noun.

keleusma (κέλευσμα, 2752), "a call, summons, shout of command" (akin to *keleuō*, "to command"), is used in 1 Thess. 4:16 of the "shout" with which (*en*, "in," denoting the attendant circumstances) the Lord will descend from heaven at the time of the rapture of the saints (those who have fallen asleep, and the living) to meet Him in the air. The "shout" is not here said to be His actual voice, though this indeed will be so (John 5:28).¶ In the Sept., Prov. 30:27, "(the locusts ... at the) word of command (march in rank)."¶

B. Verb.

epiphōneō (ἐπιφωνέω, 2019), "to call out" (*epi*, "upon," *phōneō*, "to utter a sound"), is translated "shouted" in Acts 12:22, RV (KJV, "gave a shout"). See CRY, B, No. 8.

SHOW (Noun)

logos (λόγος, 3056), "a word," is sometimes used of mere talk, the talk which one occasions; hence, "repute, reputation"; this seems to be the meaning in Col. 2:23, translated "a show (KJV 'show') of wisdom," i.e., "a reputation for wisdom," rather than "appearance, reason," etc. See WORD.

Note: In Luke 20:47, KJV, *prophasis*, "a pretense" (RV), is translated "show." See CLOKE (Pretense), No. 2.

SHOW (make a)

1. *deigmatizō* (δειγματίζω, 1165), "to make a show of, expose," is used in Col. 2:15 of Christ's act regarding the principalities and powers, displaying them "as a victor displays his captives or trophies in a triumphal procession" (Lightfoot). Some regard the meaning as being that He showed the angelic beings in their true inferiority (see under TRIUMPH). For its other occurrence, Matt. 1:19, see EXAMPLE, B, No. 1.¶

2. *euprosōpeō* (εὐπροσωπέω, 2146) denotes "to look well, make a fair show" (*eu*, "well," *prosōpon*, "a face"), and is used in Gal. 6:12, "to make a fair show (in the flesh)," i.e., "to make a display of religious zeal." Deissmann illustrates the metaphorical use of this word from the papyri in *Light from the Ancient East*, p. 96.¶

Note: For *paratērēsis*, KJV marg. in Luke 17:20, "outward show," see OBSERVATION.¶

For SHOW (Verb) see SHEW

SHOWER

ombros (ὄμβρος, 3655) denotes a "heavy shower, a storm of rain," Luke 12:54.¶

For SHRANK and SHRINK see DRAW (B), No. 4

SHRINE

naos (ναός, 3485), "the inmost part of a temple, a shrine," is used in the plural in Acts

19:24, of the silver models of the pagan "shrine" in which the image of Diana (Greek Artemis) was preserved. The models were large or small, and were signs of wealth and devotion on the part of purchasers. The variety of forms connected with the embellishment of the image provided "no little business" for the silversmiths. See TEMPLE.

SHUDDER

phrissō (φρίσσω, 5425), primarily, "to be rough, to bristle," then, "to shiver, shudder, tremble," is said of demons, Jas. 2:19, RV, "shudder" (KJV, "tremble").¶ Cf. Matt. 8:29, indicating a cognizance of their appointed doom.

For SHUN see AVOID, No. 4, and DRAW, (B), No. 4

SHUT, SHUT UP

1. *kleiō* (κλείω, 2808) is used (*a*) of things material, Matt. 6:6; 25:10; Luke 11:7; John 20:19, 26; Acts 5:23; 21:30; Rev. 20:3; figuratively, 21:25; (*b*) metaphorically, of the kingdom of heaven, Matt. 23:13; of heaven, with consequences of famine, Luke 4:25; Rev. 11:6; of compassion, 1 John 3:17, RV (KJV, "bowels *of compassion*"); of the blessings accruing from the promises of God regarding David, Rev. 3:7; of a door for testimony, 3:8.¶

2. *apokleiō* (ἀποκλείω, 608), "to shut fast" (*apo*, away from, and No. 1), is used in Luke 13:25, expressing the impossibility of entrance after the closing.¶

3. *katakleiō* (κατακλείω, 2623), lit., "to shut down" (the *kata* has, however, an intensive use), signifies "to shut up in confinement," Luke 3:20; Acts 26:10.¶ In the Sept., Jer. 32:3.¶

4. *sunkleiō* (συγκλείω, 4788): see ENCLOSE.

SICK, SICKLY, SICKNESS

A. Verbs.

1. *astheneō* (ἀσθενέω, 770), lit., "to be weak, feeble" (*a*, negative, *sthenos*, "strength"), is translated "to be sick," e.g., in Matt. 10:8, "(the) sick"; 25:36; v. 39 in the best texts (some have B, No. 1); Mark 6:56; Luke 4:40; 7:10 (RV omits the word); 9:2; John 4:46; 5:3, RV (KJV, "impotent folk"); v. 7; 6:2, RV (KJV, "were diseased"); 11:1–3, 6; Acts 9:37; 19:12; Phil. 2:26, 27; 2 Tim. 4:20; Jas. 5:14. See DISEASED, B, No. 1, IMPOTENT, and, especially, WEAK.

2. *kamnō* (κάμνω, 2577), primarily, "to work," hence, from the effect of constant work, "to be weary," Heb. 12:3, is rendered "(him) that is sick," in Jas. 5:15, RV, KJV "(the) sick."

The choice of this verb instead of the repetition of No. 1 (v. 14, see above), is suggestive of the common accompaniment of "sickness," weariness of mind (which is the meaning of this verb), which not infrequently hinders physical recovery; hence this special cause is here intimated in the general idea of "sickness." In some mss. it occurs in Rev. 2:3.¶ In the Sept., Job 10:1; 17:2.¶

3. *sunechō* (συνέχω, 4912), "to hold in, hold fast," is used, in the passive voice, of "being seized or afflicted by ills," Acts 28:8, "sick" (of the father of Publius, cf. Matt. 4:24; Luke 4:38, "taken with"). See CONSTRAIN, No. 3.

Notes: (1) *Noseō*, "to be sick," is used metaphorically of mental ailment, in 1 Tim. 6:4, "doting" (marg., "sick"). (2) The adverb *kakōs*, "evilly ill," with *echō*, "to hold, to have," is rendered "to be sick," in Matt. 4:24, RV, "that were sick"; 8:16; 9:12; 14:35 and Mark 1:32, RV (KJV, "diseased"); 1:34; 2:17; 6:55; Luke 5:31; 7:2. (3) For "sick of the palsy," Luke 5:24; Acts 9:33, see PALSY (sick of).

B. Adjectives.

1. *asthenēs* (ἀσθενής, 772), lit., "without strength," hence, "feeble, weak," is used of "bodily debility," Matt. 25:43 (for v. 39, see A, No. 1), 44; some texts have it in Luke 9:2 (the best omit it, the meaning being "to heal" in general); 10:9; Acts 5:15, 16; in 4:9 it is rendered "impotent." See FEEBLE, IMPOTENT, WEAK.

2. *arrhōstos* (ἄρρωστος, 732), "feeble, sickly" (*a*, negative, *rhōnnumi*, "to be strong"), is translated "sick" in Matt. 14:14; Mark 16:18; "sick folk" in Mark 6:5; "that were sick" in 6:13; "sickly" in 1 Cor. 11:30, here also of the physical state.¶ In the Sept., 1 Kings 14:5; Mal. 1:8.¶

C. Nouns.

1. *astheneia* (ἀσθένεια, 769), "weakness, sickness" (akin to A, No. 1 and B, No. 1), is translated "sickness" in John 11:4. See DISEASE, No. 1, INFIRMITY, WEAKNESS.

2. *nosos* (νόσος, 3554): see DISEASE, No. 3.

SICKLE

drepanon (δρέπανον, 1407), "a pruning hook, a sickle" (akin to *drepō*, "to pluck"), occurs in Mark 4:29; Rev. 14:14, 15, 16, 17, 18 (twice), 19.¶

SIDE

A. Noun.

pleura (πλευρά, 4125), "a side" (cf. Eng., "pleurisy"), is used of the "side" of Christ, into which the spear was thrust, John 19:34; 20:20,

25, 27 (some mss. have it in Matt. 27:49; see RV marg.); elsewhere, in Acts 12:7.¶

B. Adverb.

peran (πέραν, 4008), an adverb, signifying "beyond, on the other side," is used (*a*) as a preposition and translated "on the other side of," e.g., in Mark 5:1; Luke 8:22; John 6:1, RV; 6:22, 25; (*b*) as a noun with the article, e.g., Matt. 8:18, 28; 14:22; 16:5. See BEYOND, No. 2.

Notes: (1) In Luke 9:47, the preposition *para*, "by the side of," with the dative case of the pronoun *heautou*, is rendered "by His side," RV (KJV, "by Him"). (2) See also EITHER, EVERYWHERE, No. 3 HIGHWAY, RIGHT.

SIFT

siniazō (σινιάζω, 4617), "to winnow, sift" (*sinion*, "a sieve"), is used figuratively in Luke 22:31.¶

SIGH

1. *stenazō* (στενάζω, 4727), "to groan," is translated "He sighed" in Mark 7:34. See GRIEF, GROAN.

2. *anastenazō* (ἀναστενάζω, 389), "to sigh deeply" (*ana*, "up," suggesting "deep drawn," and No. 1), occurs in Mark 8:12.¶ In the Sept., Lam. 1:4.¶

SIGHT

A. Nouns.

1. *eidos* (εἶδος, 1491) is translated. "sight" in 2 Cor. 5:7; see APPEARANCE, No. 1.

2. *theōria* (θεωρία, 2335) denotes "a spectacle, a sight" (akin to *theōreō*, to gaze, behold"; see BEHOLD), in Luke 23:48.¶

3. *horama* (ὅραμα, 3705), "that which is seen" (akin to *horaō*, "to see"), besides its meaning, "a vision, appearance," denotes "a sight," in Acts 7:31. See VISION.

4. *ophthalmos* (ὀφθαλμός, 3788) "an eye" (Eng. "ophthalmic," etc.) in Acts 1:9 is translated "sight" (plur. lit., "eyes"). See EYE.

5. *anablepsis* (ἀνάβλεψις, 309) denotes "recovering of sight" (*ana*, "again," *blepō*, "to see"), Luke 4:18.¶ In the Sept., Isa. 61:1.¶

Notes: (1) For *horasis* (akin to No. 3), translated "in sight" in Rev. 4:3, KJV (RV, "to look upon"), see LOOK, B. (2) In Luke 7:21, the infinitive mood of *blepō*, "to see," is used as a noun, "(He bestowed, KJV, 'gave') sight." In Acts 9:9 it is used in the present participle with *mē*, "not," "without sight" (lit., "not seeing"). (3) In Heb. 12:21 *phantazomai*, "to make visible," is used in the present participle as a noun, with the article, "(the) sight."¶ (4) In Luke 21:11, KJV, *phobētron* (or *phobēthron*), plur., is translated "fearful sights" (RV, "terrors").¶

B. Verb.

anablepō (ἀναβλέπω, 308), "to look up," also denotes "to receive or recover sight" (akin to A, No. 5), e.g., Matt. 11:5; 20:34; Mark 10:51, 52; Luke 18:41–43; John 9:11, 15, 18 (twice); Acts 9:12, 17, 18; 22:13.

SIGHT OF (in the)

1. *enōpion* (ἐνώπιον, 1799), for which see BEFORE, No. 9, is translated "in the sight of" in the RV (for KJV, "before") in Luke 12:6; 15:18; 16:15; Acts 7:46; 10:33; 19:19; 1 Tim. 5:4, 21; 2 Tim. 2:14; 4:1; Rev. 13:12. The RV is more appropriate in most passages, as giving the real significance of the word.

2. *katenōpion* (κατενώπιον, 2714), see BEFORE, No. 10, is translated "in the sight of" in 2 Cor. 2:17 (in some texts); Col. 1:22, KJV.

3. *emprosthen* (ἔμπροσθεν, 1715), see BEFORE, No. 4, is translated "in the sight of" in Matt. 11:26; Luke 10:21; 1 Thess. 1:3, KJV.

4. *enantion* (ἐναντίον, 1726), see BEFORE, No. 5, is translated "in the sight of" in Acts 7:10.

5. *enanti* (ἔναντι, 1725), see BEFORE, No. 6, is translated "in the sight of" in Acts 8:21, KJV.

6. *katenanti* (κατέναντι, 2713), see BEFORE, No. 8, is found in the best texts in 2 Cor. 12:19, "in the sight of," RV, and in 2:17.

SIGN

1. *sēmeion* (σημεῖον, 4592), "a sign, mark, indication, token," is used (*a*) of that which distinguished a person or thing from others, e.g., Matt. 26:48; Luke 2:12; Rom. 4:11; 2 Cor. 12:12 (1st part); 2 Thess. 3:17, "token," i.e., his autograph attesting the authenticity of his letters; (*b*) of a "sign" as a warning or admonition, e.g., Matt. 12:39, "the sign of (i.e., consisting of) the prophet Jonas"; 16:4; Luke 2:34; 11:29, 30; (*c*) of miraculous acts (1) as tokens of divine authority and power, e.g., Matt. 12:38, 39 (1st part); John 2:11, RV, "signs"; 3:2 (ditto); 4:54, "(the second) sign," RV; 10:41 (ditto); 20:30; in 1 Cor. 1:22, "the Jews ask for signs," RV, indicates that the Apostles were met with the same demand from Jews as Christ had been: "signs were vouchsafed in plenty, signs of God's power and love, but these were not the signs which they sought.... They wanted signs of an outward Messianic Kingdom, of temporal triumph, of material greatness for the chosen people.... With such cravings the Gospel of a 'crucified Messiah' was to them a stumblingblock indeed" (Lightfoot); 1 Cor. 14:22; (2) by demons, Rev. 16:14; (3) by false teachers or prophets, indications of assumed authority, e.g., Matt. 24:24; Mark 13:22; (4) by Satan through his special

agents, 2 Thess. 2:9; Rev. 13:13, 14; 19:20; (*d*) of tokens portending future events, e. g., Matt. 24:3, where "the sign of the Son of Man" signifies, subjectively, that the Son of Man is Himself the "sign" of what He is about to do; Mark 13:4; Luke 21:7, 11, 25; Acts 2:19; Rev. 12:1, RV; 12:3, RV; 15:1.

"Signs" confirmatory of what God had accomplished in the atoning sacrifice of Christ, His resurrection and ascension, and of the sending of the Holy Spirit, were given to the Jews for their recognition, as at Pentecost, and supernatural acts by apostolic ministry, as well as by the supernatural operations in the churches, such as the gift of tongues and prophesyings; there is no record of the continuance of these latter after the circumstances recorded in Acts 19:1–20.

2. *parasēmos* (παράσημος, 3902), an adjective meaning "marked at the side" (*para*, "beside," *sēma*, "a mark"), is used in Acts 28:11 as a noun denoting the figurehead of a vessel.¶

SIGNS (to make)

enneuō (ἐννεύω, 1770), "to nod to" (*en*, "in," *neuō*, "to nod"), denotes "to make a sign to" in Luke 1:62.¶ In the Sept., Prov. 6:13; 10:10.¶

Note: For *dianeuō*, Luke 1:22, RV, see BECKON, No. 2.

For SIGNIFICATION, 1 Cor. 14:10, see DUMB, No. 2

SIGNIFY

1. *sēmainō* (σημαίνω, 4591), "to give a sign, indicate" (*sēma*, "a sign": cf. SIGN, No. 1), "to signify," is so translated in John 12:33; 18:32; 21:19; Acts 11:28; 25:27; Rev. 1:1, where perhaps the suggestion is that of expressing by signs.¶

2. *dēloō* (δηλόω, 1213), "to make plain" (*dēlos*, "evident"), is translated "to signify" in 1 Cor. 1:11, RV, "it hath been signified" (KJV, "declared"); Heb. 9:8; 12:27; 1 Pet. 1:11, KJV (RV, "point unto"); 2 Pet. 1:14, RV, "signified" (KJV, "hath showed"). See POINT (unto).

3. *emphanizō* (ἐμφανίζω, 1718), "to manifest, make known," is translated "signify" in Acts 23:15; v. 22, RV (KJV, "hath showed"). See APPEAR, No. 5.

Note: In Acts 21:26, KJV, *diangellō*, "to announce," is rendered "to signify" (RV, "declaring").

SILENCE

A. Noun.

sigē (σιγή, 4602) occurs in Acts 21:40; Rev. 8:1, where the "silence" is introductory to the judgments following the opening of the seventh seal.¶

Note: For *hēsuchia*, KJV, "silence," in Acts 22:2 and 1 Tim. 2:11, 12, see QUIETNESS.

B. Verbs.

1. *phimoō* (φιμόω, 5392), "to muzzle," is rendered "to put to silence" in Matt. 22:34; 1 Pet. 2:15. See MUZZLE, PEACE (hold), SPEECHLESS, STILL.

2. *sigaō* (σιγάω, 4601), "to be silent": see PEACE (hold), No. 1.

For SILENT, Luke 1:20, RV, see DUMB, B

SILK

sērikos or *sirikos* (σιρικός, 4596), "silken," an adjective derived from the *Sēres*, a people of India, who seem to have produced "silk" originally as a marketable commodity, is used as a noun with the article, denoting "silken fabric," Rev. 18:12.¶

For SILLY, 2 Tim. 3:6, see WOMAN, No. 2

SILVER

A. Nouns.

1. *argurion* (ἀργύριον, 694) is rendered "silver" in Acts 3:6; 8:20, RV (KJV, "money"); 20:33; 1 Cor. 3:12 (metaphorical); 1 Pet. 1:18. See MONEY, PIECE.

2. *arguros* (ἄργυρος, 696), akin to *argos*, "shining," denotes "silver." In each occurrence in the NT it follows the mention of gold, Matt. 10:9; Acts 17:29; Jas. 5:3; Rev. 18:12.¶

Note: For *drachmē*, Luke 15:8, see PIECE.

B. Adjective.

argureos (ἀργύρεος, 693) signifies "made of silver," Acts 19:24; 2 Tim. 2:20; Rev. 9:20.¶

SILVERSMITH

argurokopos (ἀργυροκόπος, 695), from *arguros* (see above) and *koptō*, "to beat," occurs in Acts 19:24.¶ In the Sept., Judg. 17:4; Jer. 6:29.¶

SIMILITUDE

Note: For *homoiōma*, rendered "similitude" in Rom. 5:14, KJV, see LIKENESS, No. 1. For *homoiotēs*, "similitude" in Heb. 7:15 KJV, see LIKE, C, *Note* (1), and LIKENESS, No. 3. For *homoiōsis*, "similitude" in Jas. 3:9, KJV, see LIKENESS, No. 2.

For SIMPLE see GUILELESS, No. 2, and HARMLESS

For SIMPLICITY see LIBERALITY

SIN (Noun and Verb)

A. Nouns.

1. *hamartia* (ἀμαρτία, 266) is, lit., "a missing of the mark," but this etymological meaning is largely lost sight of in the NT. It is the most comprehensive term for moral obliquity. It is used of "sin" as (*a*) a principle or source of action, or an inward element producing acts, e.g., Rom. 3:9; 5:12, 13, 20; 6:1, 2; 7:7 (abstract for concrete); 7:8 (twice), 9, 11, 13, "sin, that it might be shown to be sin," i.e., "sin became death to me, that it might be exposed in its heinous character": in the last clause, "sin might become exceeding sinful," i.e., through the holiness of the Law, the true nature of sin was designed to be manifested to the conscience;

(*b*) a governing principle or power, e.g., Rom. 6:6, "(the body) of sin," here "sin" is spoken of as an organized power, acting through the members of the body, though the seat of "sin" is in the will (the body is the organic instrument); in the next clause, and in other passages, as follows, this governing principle is personified, e.g., Rom. 5:21; 6:12, 14, 17; 7:11, 14, 17, 20, 23, 25; 8:2; 1 Cor. 15:56; Heb. 3:13; 11:25; 12:4; Jas. 1:15 (2nd part);

(*c*) a generic term (distinct from specific terms such as No. 2 yet sometimes inclusive of concrete wrong doing, e.g., John 8:21, 34, 46; 9:41; 15:22, 24; 19:11); in Rom. 8:3, "God, sending His own Son in the likeness of sinful flesh," lit., "flesh of sin," the flesh stands for the body, the instrument of indwelling "sin" [Christ, preexistently the Son of God, assumed human flesh, "of the substance of the Virgin Mary"; the reality of incarnation was His, without taint of sin (for *homoiōma*, "likeness," see LIKENESS)], and *as an offering* for sin," i.e., "a sin offering" (so the Sept., e.g., in Lev. 4:32; 5:6, 7, 8, 9), "condemned sin in the flesh," i.e., Christ, having taken human nature, "sin" apart (Heb. 4:15), and having lived a sinless life, died under the condemnation and judgment due to our "sin"; for the generic sense see further, e.g., Heb. 9:26; 10:6, 8, 18; 13:11; 1 John 1:7, 8; 3:4 (1st part; in the 2nd part, "sin" is defined as "lawlessness," RV), 8, 9; in these verses the KJV use of the verb to commit is misleading; not the committal of an act is in view, but a continuous course of "sin," as indicated by the RV, "doeth." The apostle's use of the present tense of *poieō*, "to do," virtually expresses the meaning of *prassō*, "to practice," which John does not use (it is not infrequent in this sense in Paul's Epp., e.g., Rom. 1:32, RV; 2:1; Gal. 5:21; Phil. 4:9);

1 Pet. 4:1 (singular in the best texts), lit., "has been made to cease from sin," i.e., as a result of suffering in the flesh, the mortifying of our members, and of obedience to a Savior who suffered in flesh. Such no longer lives in the flesh, "to the lusts of men, but to the will of God"; sometimes the word is used as virtually equivalent to a condition of "sin," e.g., John 1:29, "the sin (not sins) of the world"; 1 Cor. 15:17; or a course of "sin," characterized by continuous acts, e.g., 1 Thess. 2:16; in 1 John 5:16 (2nd part) the RV marg., is probably to be preferred, "there is sin unto death," not a special act of "sin," but the state or condition producing acts; in v. 17, "all unrighteousness is sin" is not a definition of "sin" (as in 3:4), it gives a specification of the term in its generic sense;

(d) a sinful deed, an act of "sin," e.g., Matt. 12:31; Acts 7:60; Jas. 1:15 (1st part); 2:9; 4:17; 5:15, 20; 1 John 5:16 (1st part).

Notes: (1) Christ is predicated as having been without "sin" in every respect, e.g., (a), (b), (c) above, 2 Cor. 5:21 (1st part); 1 John 3:5; John 14:30; (d) John 8:46; Heb. 4:15; 1 Pet. 2:22. (2) In Heb. 9:28 (2nd part) the reference is to a "sin" offering. (3) In 2 Cor. 5:21, "Him ... He made to be sin" indicates that God dealt with Him as He must deal with "sin," and that Christ fulfilled what was typified in the guilt offering. (4) For the phrase "man of sin" in 2 Thess. 2:3, see INIQUITY, No. 1.

2. *hamartēma* (ἁμάρτημα, 265), akin to No. 1, denotes "an act of disobedience to divine law" [as distinct from No. 1 (a), (b), (c)]; plural in Mark 3:28; Rom. 3:25; 2 Pet. 1:9, in some texts; sing. in Mark 3:29 (some mss. have *krisis*, KJV, "damnation"); 1 Cor. 6:18.¶

Notes: (1) For *paraptōma*, rendered "sins" in the KJV in Eph. 1:7; 2:5; Col. 2:13 (RV, "trespass"), see TRESPASS. In Jas. 5:16, the best texts have No. 1 (RV, "sins"). (2) For synonymous terms see DISOBEDIENCE, ERROR, FAULT, INIQUITY, TRANSGRESSION, UNGODLINESS.

B. Adjective.

anamartētos (ἀναμάρτητος, 361), "without sin" (a, negative, n, euphonic, and C, No. 1), is found in John 8:7.¶ In the Sept., Deut. 29:19.¶

C. Verbs.

1. *hamartanō* (ἁμαρτάνω, 264), lit., "to miss the mark," is used in the NT (a) of "sinning" against God, (1) by angels, 2 Pet. 2:4; (2) by man, Matt. 27:4; Luke 15:18, 21 (heaven standing, by metonymy, for God); John 5:14; 8:11; 9:2, 3; Rom. 2:12 (twice); 3:23; 5:12, 14, 16; 6:15; 1 Cor. 7:28 (twice), 36; 15:34; Eph. 4:26; 1 Tim. 5:20; Titus 3:11; Heb. 3:17; 10:26; 1 John 1:10; in 2:1 (twice), the aorist tense in each place, referring to an act of "sin"; on the

contrary, in 3:6 (twice), 8, 9, the present tense indicates, not the committal of an act, but the continuous practice of "sin" [see on A, No. 1 (c)]; in 5:16 (twice) the present tense indicates the condition resulting from an act, "unto death" signifying "tending towards death"; (b) against Christ, 1 Cor. 8:12; (c) against man, (1) a brother, Matt. 18:15, RV, "sin" (KJV, "trespass"); v. 21; Luke 17:3, 4, RV, "sin" (KJV, "trespass"); 1 Cor. 8:12; (2) in Luke 15:18, 21, against the father by the Prodigal Son, "in thy sight" being suggestive of befitting reverence; (d) against Jewish law, the Temple, and Caesar, Acts 25:8, RV, "sinned" (KJV, "offended"); (e) against one's own body, by fornication, 1 Cor. 6:18; (f) against earthly masters by servants, 1 Pet. 2:20, RV, "(when) ye sin (and are buffeted for it)," KJV, "(when ye be buffeted) for your faults," lit., "having sinned."¶

2. *proamartanō* (προαμαρτάνω, 4258), "to sin previously" (*pro*, "before," and No. 1), occurs in 2 Cor. 12:21; 13:2, RV in each place, "have sinned heretofore" (so KJV in the 2nd; in the 1st, "have sinned already").¶

For **SINCE** see †, p. 1

SINCERE, SINCERELY, SINCERITY

A. Adjectives.

1. *adolos* (ἄδολος, 97), "guileless, pure," is translated "sincere" in 1 Pet. 2:2, KJV, "without guile," RV. See GUILELESS, No. 1.

2. *gnēsios* (γνήσιος, 1103), "true, genuine, sincere," is used in the neuter, as a noun, with the article, signifying "sincerity," 2 Cor. 8:8 (of love). See OWN, TRUE.

3. *eilikrinēs* (εἰλικρινής, 1506), see PURE, A, No. 3.

B. Adverb.

hagnōs (ἁγνῶς, 55) denotes "with pure motives," akin to words under PURE, A, No. 1, and B, Nos. 1 and 2, and is rendered "sincerely" in Phil. 1:17, RV (v. 16, KJV).¶

C. Noun.

eilikrinia (or —*eia*) (εἰλικρινία, 1505), akin to A, No. 3 denotes "sincerity, purity"; it is described metaphorically in 1 Cor. 5:8 as "unleavened (bread)"; in 2 Cor. 1:12, "sincerity (of God)," RV, KJV, "(godly) sincerity," it describes a quality possessed by God, as that which is to characterize the conduct of believers; in 2 Cor. 2:17 it is used of the rightful ministry of the Scriptures.¶

Notes: (1) For 2 Cor. 8:8, see A, No. 2. (2) In Eph. 6:24, KJV, *aphtharsia*, "incorruption," is translated "sincerity" (RV, "uncorruptness," KJV marg., "incorruption"); some inferior mss. have it in Titus 2:7, KJV; the RV follows those in which it is absent.

SINFUL

hamartōlos (ἁμαρτωλός, 268), an adjective, akin to *hamartanō*, "to sin," is used as an adjective, "sinful" in Mark 8:38; Luke 5:8; 19:7 (lit., "a sinful man"); 24:7; John 9:16, and 24 (lit., "a man sinful"); Rom. 7:13, for which see SIN, A, No. 1 (*a*). Elsewhere it is used as a noun: see SINNER. The noun is frequently found in a common phrase in sepulchral epitaphs in the S.W. of Asia Minor, with the threat against any desecrator of the tomb, "let him be as a sinner before the subterranean gods" (Moulton and Milligan).

Notes: (1) In Rom. 8:3, "sinful flesh" is, lit., "flesh of sin" (RV marg.): see SIN, No. 1 (*c*). (2) For the RV of Rom. 7:5, "sinful passions," see PASSION, No. 1.

SING, SINGING

1. *adō* (ᾄδω, 103) is used always of "praise to God," (*a*) intransitively, Eph. 5:19; Col. 3:16; (*b*) transitively, Rev. 5:9; 14:3; 15:3.¶

2. *psallō* (ψάλλω, 5567): see MELODY.

3. *humneō* (ὑμνέω, 5214): see HYMN, B.

SINGLE

haplous (ἁπλοῦς, 573), "simple, single," is used in a moral sense in Matt. 6:22 and Luke 11:34, said of the eye; "singleness" of purpose keeps us from the snare of having a double treasure and consequently a divided heart.¶ The papyri provide instances of its use in other than the moral sense, e.g., of a marriage dowry, to be repaid pure and simple by a husband (Moulton and Milligan). In the Sept., Prov. 11:25.¶

SINGLENESS

1. *aphelotēs* (ἀφελότης, 858) denotes "simplicity," Acts 2:46, "singleness," for which Moulton and Milligan, from papyri examples, suggest "unworldly simplicity"; the idea here is that of an unalloyed benevolence expressed in act.¶

2. *haplotēs* (ἁπλότης, 572): see BOUNTY, No. 2.

SINK

1. *buthizō* (βυθίζω, 1036) is used literally in Luke 5:7. See DROWN, No. 1.

2. *katapontizō* (καταποντίζω, 2670) is translated "to sink" in Matt. 14:30 (passive voice). See DROWN, No. 3.

3. *tithēmi* (τίθημι, 5087), "to put," is ren-

dered "let . . . sink" in Luke 9:44, RV ("let . . . sink down," KJV). See APPOINT, LAY.

Note: In Acts 20:9 (2nd part), KJV, *kataspherō*, "to bear down," is translated "he sunk down" (RV, "being borne down"); in the 1st part it is rendered "being fallen," KJV, "borne down," RV.

SINNER

hamartōlos (ἁμαρτωλός, 268), lit., "one who misses the mark" (a meaning not to be pressed), is an adjective, most frequently used as a noun (see SINFUL); it is the most usual term to describe the fallen condition of men; it is applicable to all men, Rom. 5:8, 19. In the Synoptic Gospels the word is used not infrequently, by the Pharisees, of publicans (tax collectors) and women of ill repute, e.g., "a woman which was in the city, a sinner," Luke 7:37; "a man that is a sinner," 19:7. In Gal. 2:15, in the clause "not sinners of the Gentiles," the apostle is taking the Judaizers on their own ground, ironically reminding them of their claim to moral superiority over Gentiles; he proceeds to show that the Jews are equally sinners with Gentiles.

Note: In Luke 13:4, KJV, *opheiletēs*, "a debtor," is translated "sinners" (RV, "offenders"; RV and KJV marg., "debtors").

SIR(-S)

1. *kurios* (κύριος, 2962): see LORD.

2. *anēr* (ἀνήρ, 435), "a man," is translated "sirs" in Acts 7:26; 14:15; 19:25; 27:10, 21, 25. See MAN.

Note: In John 21:5 the KJV marg. has "sirs" for *paidia*, "children."

SISTER

adelphē (ἀδελφή, 79) is used (*a*) of natural relationship, e.g., Matt. 19:29; of the "sisters" of Christ, the children of Joseph and Mary after the virgin birth of Christ, e.g., Matt. 13:56; (*b*) of "spiritual kinship" with Christ, an affinity marked by the fulfillment of the will of the Father, Matt. 12:50; Mark 3:35; of spiritual relationship based upon faith in Christ, Rom. 16:1; 1 Cor. 7:15; 9:5, KJV and RV marg.; Jas. 2:15; Philem. 2, RV.

Note: In Col. 4:10, KJV, *anepsios* (cf. Lat., *nepos*, whence Eng., "nephew"), "a cousin" (so, RV), is translated "sister's son." See COUSIN.¶

SIT

1. *kathēmai* (κάθημαι, 2521) is used (*a*) of the natural posture, e.g., Matt. 9:9, most frequently in the Apocalypse, some 32 times; frequently in the Gospels and Acts; elsewhere only in 1 Cor. 14:30; Jas. 2:3 (twice); and of Christ's

position of authority on the throne of God, Col. 3:1, KJV, "sitteth" (RV, "is, seated"); Heb. 1:13 (cf. Matt. 22:44; 26:64 and parallel passages in Mark and Luke, and Acts 2:34); often as antecedent or successive to, or accompanying, another act (in no case a superfluous expression), e.g., Matt. 15:29; 27:36; Mark 2:14; 4:1; (b) metaphorically in Matt. 4:16 (twice); Luke 1:79; of inhabiting a place (translated "dwell"), Luke 21:35; Rev. 14:6, RV marg., "sit" (in the best texts: some have katoikeō, "to dwell"). See DWELL.

2. sunkathēmai (συγκάθημαι, 4775), "to sit with" (sun, "with," and No. 1), occurs in Mark 14:54; Acts 26:30.¶ In the Sept., Ps. 101:6, "dwell."¶

3. anakeimai (ἀνάκειμαι, 345), "to recline at table" (ana, "up," keimai, "to lie"), is rendered "to sit at meat" in Matt. 9:10 (RV, marg., "reclined"); 26:7; 26:20, RV, "He was sitting at meat" (KJV, "He sat down"); Mark 16:14; in some mss. Luke 7:37 (see No. 5); 22:27 (twice); in Mark 14:18, "sat"; in John 6:11, "were set down"; John 12:2 in the best texts (see No. 4). See GUEST, LEAN, LIE, Note (1), SET, No. 22, TABLE (at the).

4. sunanakeimai (συνανάκειμαι, 4873), "to recline at table with or together" (sun, and No. 3), "to sit at meat or at table with," occurs in Matt. 9:10, "sat down"; 14:9; Mark 2:15, RV, "sat down with" (KJV, "sat ... together with"); 6:22; Luke 7:49; 14:10, 15; John 12:2 (in some texts).¶

5. katakeimai (κατάκειμαι, 2621), "to lie down" (kata, "down," and keimai, cf. No. 3), is used of "reclining at a meal," Mark 2:15; 14:3; Luke 5:29, RV, "were sitting at meat" (KJV, "sat down"); 7:37 (in the best texts); 1 Cor. 8:10. See KEEP, LIE.

6. anaklinō (ἀνακλίνω, 347), "to cause to recline, make to sit down," is used in the active voice, in Luke 12:37 (also in 2:7, of "laying" the infant Christ in the manger); in the passive, Matt. 8:11; 14:19; Mark 6:39 (in the best texts); in some texts, Luke 7:36 and 9:15 (see No. 7); 13:29. See LAY.¶

7. kataklinō (κατακλίνω, 2625) is used only in connection with meals, (a) in the active voice, "to make recline," Luke 9:14, 15 (in the best texts); in the passive voice, "to recline," Luke 7:36 (in the best texts), "sat down to meat"; 14:8; 24:30 (RV, "had sat down ... to meat").¶

8. kathizō (καθίζω, 2523) is used (a) transitively, "to make sit down," Acts 2:30 (see also SET, No. 9); (b) intransitively, "to sit down," e.g., Matt. 5:1, RV, "when (He) had sat down" (KJV, "was set"); 19:28; 20:21, 23; 23:2; 25:31;

26:36; Mark 11:2, 7; 12:41; Luke 14:28, 31; 16:6; John 19:13; Acts 2:3 (of the tongues of fire); 8:31; 1 Cor. 10:7; 2 Thess. 2:4, "he sitteth," aorist tense, i.e., "he takes his seat" (as, e.g., in Mark 16:19); Rev. 3:21 (twice), RV, "to sit down" and "sat down"; 20:4.

9. parakathezomai (παρακαθέζομαι, 3869v), "to sit down beside" (para), in a passive voice form, occurs in the best mss. in Luke 10:39.¶ Some texts have the verb parakathizō, "to set beside," active form in middle sense.

10. sunkathizō (συγκαθίζω, 4776) denotes (a) transitively, "to make to sit together," Eph. 2:6; (b) intransitively, Luke 22:55, RV, "had sat down together" (KJV, "were set down").¶

11. anakathizō (ἀνακαθίζω, 339), "to set up," is used intransitively, "to sit up," of two who were raised from the dead, Luke 7:15; Acts 9:40.¶

12. anapiptō (ἀναπίπτω, 377), "to fall back" (ana, "back," piptō, "to fall"), denotes, in the NT, "to recline for a repast," Matt. 15:35; Mark 6:40; 8:6; Luke 11:37; 14:10; 17:7; 22:14; John 6:10 (twice); 13:12; in John 13:25 and 21:20 it is used of leaning on the bosom of Christ. See LEAN.¶ In the Sept., Gen. 49:9.¶

13. kathezomai (καθέζομαι, 2516), "to sit (down)," is used in Matt. 26:55; Luke 2:46; John 4:6; 11:20; 20:12; Acts 6:15.¶

Note: For epibainō, "sitting upon," Matt. 21:5, KJV, see RIDE.

SIX

hex (ἕξ, 1803), whence Eng. prefix, "hex"-, is used separately from other numerals in Matt. 17:1; Mark 9:2; Luke 4:25; 13:14; John 2:6; 12:1; Acts 11:12; 18:11; Jas. 5:17; Rev. 4:8. It sometimes suggests incompleteness, in comparison with the perfect number seven.

Notes: (1) In combination with tessarakonta, "forty," it occurs in John 2:20; with hebdomēkonta, "seventy," Acts 27:37, "(two hundred) threescore and sixteen." (2) It forms the first syllable of hexēkonta, "sixty" (see below) and hexakosioi, "six hundred," Rev. 13:18 (see SIXTY, Note); 14:20.

SIXTH

hektos (ἕκτος, 1623) is used (a) of a month, Luke 1:26, 36; (b) an hour, Matt. 20:5; 27:45 and parallel passages; John 4:6; (c) an angel, Rev. 9:13, 14; 16:12; (d) a seal of a roll, in vision, Rev. 6:12; (e) of the "sixth" precious stone, the sardius, in the foundations of the wall of the heavenly Jerusalem, Rev. 21:20.

SIXTY, SIXTYFOLD

hexēkonta (ἑξήκοντα, 1835) occurs in Matt. 13:8, RV (KJV, "sixty-fold"); 13:23; Mark 4:8, where the RV and KJV reverse the translation, as in Matt. 13:8, while in Mark 4:20 the RV has "sixtyfold," KJV, "sixty"; in Rev. 13:18, RV,"sixty" (KJV, "threescore"). It is rendered "threescore" in Luke 24:13; 1 Tim. 5:9; Rev. 11:3; 12:6.¶

Note: In Rev. 13:18, the number of the "Beast," the human potentate destined to rule with satanic power the ten-kingdom league at the end of this age, is given as "six hundred and sixty and six" (RV), and described as "the number of (a) man." The number is suggestive of the acme of the pride of fallen man, the fullest development of man under direct satanic control, and standing in contrast to "seven" as the number of completeness and perfection.

SKIN

askos (ἀσκός, 779), "a leather bottle, wineskin," occurs in Matt. 9:17 (four times); Mark 2:22 (four times); Luke 5:37 (three times), 38; in each place, RV, "wineskins" or "skins," for KJV, "bottles." A whole goatskin, for example, would be used with the apertures bound up, and when filled, tied at the neck. They were tanned with acacia bark and left hairy on the outside. New wines, by fermenting, would rend old skins (cf. Josh. 9:13; Job 32:19). Hung in the smoke to dry, the skin-bottles become shriveled (see Ps. 119:83).¶

Note: For "(a girdle) of a skin," Mark 1:6, see LEATHERN.

SKULL

kranion (κρανίον, 2898), Lat., *cranium* (akin to *kara*, "the head"), is used of the scene of the Crucifixion, Matt. 27:33; Mark 15:22; John 19:17; in Luke 23:33, RV, "(the place which is called) The skull," KJV, "Calvary" (from Latin *calvaria*, "a skull": marg., "the place of a skull"). The locality has been identified by the traces of the resemblance of the hill to a "skull".¶ In the Sept., Judg. 9:53; 2 Kings 9:35.¶

For SKY see HEAVEN

SLACK (Verb), SLACKNESS

A. Verb.

bradunō (βραδύνω, 1019), used intransitively signifies "to be slow, to tarry" (*bradus*, "slow"), said negatively of God, 2 Pet. 3:9, "is (not) slack"; in 1 Tim. 3:15, translated "(if) I

tarry." See TARRY.¶ In the Sept., Gen. 43:10; Deut. 7:10; Isa. 46:13.¶

B. Noun.

bradutēs (βραδυτής, 1022), "slowness" (akin to A), is rendered "slackness" in 2 Pet. 3:9.¶

SLANDERER

diabolos (διάβολος, 1228), an adjective, "slanderous, accusing falsely," is used as a noun, translated "slanderers" in 1 Tim. 3:11, where the reference is to those who are given to finding fault with the demeanor and conduct of others, and spreading their innuendos and criticisms in the church; in 2 Tim. 3:3, RV (KJV, "false accusers"); Titus 2:3 (ditto): see ACCUSER, DEVIL.

For SLANDEROUSLY see REPORT, C, No. 5

SLAUGHTER

1. *sphagē* (σφαγή, 4967) is used in two quotations from the Sept., Acts 8:32 from Isa. 53:7, and Rom. 8:36 from Ps. 44:22; in the latter the quotation is set in a strain of triumph, the passage quoted being an utterance of sorrow. In Jas. 5:5 there is an allusion to Jer. 12:3, the luxurious rich, getting wealth by injustice, spending it on their pleasures, are "fattening themselves like sheep unconscious of their doom."¶

2. *kopē* (κοπή, 2871), "a stroke" (akin to *koptō*, "to strike, to cut"), signifies "a smiting in battle," in Heb. 7:1.¶ In the Sept., Gen. 14:17; Deut. 28:25; Josh. 10:20.¶

3. *phonos* (φόνος, 5408), "a killing, murder," is rendered "slaughter" in Acts 9:1; see MURDER.

SLAVE

sōma (σῶμα, 4983), "a body," is translated "slaves" in Rev. 18:13 (RV and KJV marg., "bodies"), an intimation of the unrighteous control over the bodily activities of "slaves"; the next word "souls" stands for the whole being. See BODY.

SLAY, SLAIN, SLEW

1. *apokteinō* (ἀποκτείνω, 615), the usual word for "to kill," is so translated in the RV wherever possible (e.g., for KJV, "to slay," in Luke 11:49; Acts 7:52; Rev. 2:13; 9:15; 11:13; 19:21); in the following the verb "to kill" would not be appropriate, Rom. 7:11, "slew," metaphorically of sin, as using the commandment; Eph. 2:16, "having slain," said metaphorically of the enmity between Jew and Gentile. See KILL, No. 1.

Note: Some mss. have it in John 5:16 (KJV, "to slay").

2. *anaireō* (ἀναιρέω, 337), "to take away, destroy, kill," is rendered "to slay" in Matt. 2:16; Acts 2:23; 5:33, 36; 9:29, KJV (RV, "to kill"); 10:39; 13:28; 22:20; 23:15, RV; in 2 Thess. 2:8 the best texts have this verb (for *analiskō*, "to consume," KJV and RV marg.); hence the RV, "shall slay," of the destruction of the man of sin. See KILL, No. 2.

3. *sphazō* or *sphattō* (σφάττω, 4969), "to slay," especially of victims for sacrifice (akin to *sphagē*: see SLAUGHTER), is used (*a*) of taking human life, 1 John 3:12 (twice); Rev. 6:4, RV, "slay" (KJV, "kill"); in 13:3, probably of assassination, RV, "smitten (unto death)," KJV, "wounded (to death)," RV marg., "slain;" 18:24; (*b*) of Christ, as the Lamb of sacrifice, Rev. 5:6, 9, 12; 6:9; 13:8. See KILL, No. 7.¶

4. *kataphazō* (κατασφάζω, 2695V), "to kill off" (*kata*, used intensively, and No. 3), is used in Luke 19:27.¶. In the Sept., Ezek. 16:40; Zech. 11:5.¶

5. *diacheirizō* (διαχειρίζω, 1315), "to lay hands on, kill," is translated "slew" in Acts 5:30. See KILL, No. 6.

6. *phoneuō* (φονεύω, 5407), "to kill, to murder," is rendered "ye slew" in Matt. 23:35. See KILL, No. 4.

Note: For *thuō*, Acts 11:7, KJV, "slay" (RV, "kill"), see KILL, No. 3.

For SLAIN BEASTS see BEAST, No. 5

For SLEEP see ASLEEP

SLEIGHT

kubia (or *-eia*) (κυβία, 2940) denotes "dice playing" (from *kubos*, "a cube, a die as used in gaming"); hence, metaphorically, "trickery, sleight," Eph. 4:14. The Eng. word is connected with "sly" ("not with slight").¶

For SLIP see DRIFT

SLOTHFUL

1. *nōthros* (νωθρός, 3576), "indolent, sluggish," is rendered "slothful" in Heb. 6:12, KJV, See DULL, and synonymous words there, and SLUGGISH.

2. *oknēros* (ὀκνηρός, 3636), "shrinking, irksome," is translated "slothful" in Matt. 25:26, and Rom. 12:11, where "in diligence not slothful," RV, might be rendered "not flagging in zeal." See GRIEVOUS, *Note* (2).

SLOW

bradus (βραδύς, 1021) is used twice in Jas. 1:19, in an exhortation to "be slow to speak" and "slow to wrath"; in Luke 24:25, metaphorically of the understanding.¶

Note: For "slow" (*argos*) in Titus 1:12, see IDLE.

For SLOWLY (sailed) see SAIL, No. 10

SLUGGISH

nōthros (νωθρός, 3576), for which see SLOTHFUL, is translated "sluggish" in Heb. 6:12, RV; here it is set in contrast to confident and constant hope; in 5:11 ("dull") to vigorous growth in knowledge. See DULL.¶

For SLUMBER (Noun) see STUPOR

SLUMBER (Verb)

nustazō (νυστάζω, 3573) denotes "to nod in sleep" (akin to *neuō*, "to nod"), "fall asleep," and is used (*a*) of natural slumber, Matt. 25:5; (*b*) metaphorically in 2 Pet. 2:3, negatively, of the destruction awaiting false teachers.¶

SMALL

1. *mikros* (μικρός, 3398), "little, small" (of age, quantity, size, space), is translated "small" in Acts 26:22; Rev. 11:18; 13:16; 19:5, 18; 20:12. See LITTLE.

2. *oligos* (ὀλίγος, 3641), "little, small" (of amount, number, time), is translated "small" in Acts 12:18; 15:2; 19:23; v. 24; KJV (RV, "little"); 27:20.

Notes: (1) For "very small" and "smallest" see LEAST. (2) For combinations with other words, see CORD, FISH, ISLAND.

For SMELL see SAVOR

SMELLING

osphrēsis (ὄσφρησις, 3750) denotes "the sense of smell," 1 Cor. 12:17, "smelling."¶

SMITE

1. *patassō* (πατάσσω, 3960), "to strike, smite," is used (I) literally, of giving a blow with the hand, or fist or a weapon, Matt. 26:51, RV, "smote" (KJV, "struck"); Luke 22:49, 50; Acts 7:24; 12:7; (II) metaphorically, (*a*) of judgment meted out to Christ, Matt. 26:31; Mark 14:27; (*b*) of the infliction of disease, by an angel, Acts 12:23; of plagues to be inflicted upon men by two divinely appointed witnesses, Rev. 11:6; (*c*) of judgment to be executed by Christ upon the

nations, Rev. 19:15, the instrument being His Word, described as a sword.¶

2. *tuptō* (τύπτω, 5180), "to strike, smite, beat," is rendered "to smite" in Matt. 24:49, KJV (RV, "beat"); 27:30; Mark 15:19; Luke 6:29; 18:13; in some texts in 22:64 (1st part: RV omits; for the 2nd part see No. 3); 23:48; Acts 23:2, 3 (twice). See BEAT, No. 2.

3. *paiō* (παίω, 3817) signifies "to strike or smite" (*a*) with the hand or fist, Matt. 26:68; Luke 22:64 (see No. 2); (*b*) with a sword, Mark 14:47; John 18:10, KJV (RV, "struck"); (*c*) with a sting, Rev. 9:5, "striketh."¶

4. *derō* (δέρω, 1194), "to flay, to beat," akin to *derma*, "skin," is translated "to smite" in Luke 22:63, KJV (RV, "beat"); John 18:23; 2 Cor. 11:20. See BEAT, No. 1.

5. *plēssō* (πλήσσω, 4141), akin to *plēgē*, "a plague, stripe, wound," is used figuratively of the effect upon sun, moon and stars, after the sounding of the trumpet by the fourth angel, in the series of divine judgments upon the world hereafter, Rev. 8:12.¶

6. *rhapizō* (ῥαπίζω, 4474), primarily "to strike with a rod" (*rhapis*, "a rod"), then, "to strike the face with the palm of the hand or the clenched fist," is used in Matt. 5:39; 26:67, where the marg. of KJV and RV has "with rods." Cf. *rhapisma*, *Note* (2), below.¶

7. *kataballō* (καταβάλλω, 2598), "to cast down," is translated "smitten down" in 2 Cor. 4:9, RV. See CAST, No. 8.

8. *proskoptō* (προσκόπτω, 4350), "to beat upon," is translated "smote upon" in Matt. 7:27. See BEAT, No. 6.

9. *sphazō* (σφάζω, 4969), "to slay," is translated "smitten unto death" in Rev. 13:3; see KILL, SLAY.

Notes: (1) In Matt. 26:51, KJV, *aphaireō*, "to take away, take off," is translated "smote off" (RV, "struck off"). (2) The noun *rhapisma*, "a blow," in the plural, as the object of *didōmi*, "to give," in John 19:3 is translated "smote (Him) with their hands" (RV, "struck, etc."), lit., "gave ... blows" (RV marg., "with rods"); in 18:22 (where the phrase is used with the singular of the noun) the RV renders it "struck ... with his hand" (KJV, "struck ... with the palm of his hand"), marg. of both, "with a rod."

The same word is used in Mark 14:65, "(received Him) with blows (of their hands)", RV [KJV, "did strike Him with the palms (of their hands)," RV margin, "strokes of rods"]. See BLOW (Noun).¶ Cf. No. 6, above, Matt. 26:67.

SMOKE (Noun and Verb)

A. Noun.

kapnos (καπνός, 2586), "smoke," occurs in Acts 2:19 and 12 times in the Apocalypse.¶

B. Verb.

tuphō (τύφω, 5188), "to raise a smoke" [akin to *tuphos*, "smoke" (not in the NT), and *tuphoō*, "to puff up with pride," see HIGH-MINDED], is used in the passive voice in Matt. 12:20, "smoking (flax)," lit., "caused to smoke," of the wick of a lamp which has ceased to burn clearly, figurative of mere nominal religiousness without the Spirit's power.¶ The Sept. uses the verb *kapnizō* (akin to A).

SMOOTH

leois (λεῖος, 3006), "smooth," occurs in Luke 3:5, figurative of the change in Israel from self-righteousness, pride and other forms of evil, to repentance, humility and submission.¶ In the Sept., Gen. 27:11; 1 Sam. 17:40; Prov. 2:20; 12:13; 26:23; Isa. 40:4.¶

Note: Chrēstologia (*chrēstos*, "good," *legō*, "to speak") is rendered "smooth ... (speech)," in Rom. 16:18, RV (KJV, "good words").¶

SNARE

1. *pagis* (παγίς, 3803), "a trap, a snare" (akin to *pēgnumi*, "to fix," and *pagideuō*, "to ensnare," which see), is used metaphorically of (*a*) the allurements to evil by which the Devil "ensnares" one, 1 Tim. 3:7; 2 Tim. 2:26; (*b*) seductions to evil, which "ensnare" those who "desire to be rich," 1 Tim. 6:9; (*c*) the evil brought by Israel upon themselves by which the special privileges divinely granted them and centering in Christ, became a "snare" to them, their rejection of Christ and the Gospel being the retributive effect of their apostasy, Rom. 11:9; (*d*) of the sudden judgments of God to come upon those whose hearts are "overcharged with surfeiting, and drunkenness, and cares of this life," Luke 21:34 (v. 35 in KJV).¶

2. *brochos* (βρόχος, 1029), "a noose, slip-knot, halter," is used metaphorically in 1 Cor. 7:35, "a snare" (RV, marg., "constraint," "noose").¶ In the Sept., Prov. 6:5; 7:21; 22:25.¶

SNATCH

harpazō (ἁρπάζω, 726), "to snatch," is translated "to snatch" in the RV only, in Matt. 13:19, KJV, "catcheth away"; John 10:12, KJV, "catcheth"; 10:28, 29, KJV, "pluck"; Jude 23, KJV, "pulling." See CATCH, No. 1.

SNOW

chiōn (χιών, 5510) occurs in Matt. 28:3; Rev. 1:14. Some mss. have it in Mark 9:3 (KJV).¶

SO

Notes: (1) *Houtōs* or *houtō*, "thus," is the usual word (see THUS). (2) Some form of *houtos*, "this," is sometimes rendered "so," e.g., Acts 23:7; Rom. 12:20. (3) It translates *homoiōs*, "likewise," e.g., in Luke 5:10; *oun*, "therefore," e.g., John 4:40, 53. (4) For "so many as," see MANY; for "so much as," see MUCH. (5) *Sumbainō*, when used of events, signifies "to come to pass, happen"; in Acts 21:35 it is rendered "so it was." See BEFALL, HAPPEN. (6) In 1 Pet. 3:17, *thelō*, "to will," is translated "should so will," lit., "willeth." (7) In 2 Cor. 12:16, the imperative mood, 3rd person singular, of *eimi*, "to be," is used impersonally, and signifies "be it so." (8) In Heb. 7:9 *epos*, "a word," is used in a phrase rendered "so to say"; see WORD, *Note* (1). (9) In 1 Tim. 3:11, *hōsautōs*, "likewise," is translated "even so." (10) *Hōs*, as, is rendered "so" in Heb. 3:11 (RV, "as"). For association with other words see †, p. 1.

SOBER, SOBERLY, SOBERMINDED

A. Adjective.

sōphrōn (σώφρων, 4998) denotes "of sound mind" (*sōzō*, "to save," *phrēn*, "the mind"); hence, "self-controlled, soberminded," always rendered "sober-minded" in the RV; in 1 Tim. 3:2 and Titus 1:8, KJV, "sober"; in Titus 2:2, KJV, "temperate"; in 2:5, KJV, "discreet."¶

Note: For *nēphalios* (akin to B, No. 1), translated "sober" in 1 Tim. 3:11; Titus 2:2, see TEMPERATE.

B. Verbs.

1. *nēphō* (νήφω, 3525) signifies "to be free from the influence of intoxicants"; in the NT, metaphorically, it does not in itself imply watchfulness, but is used in association with it, 1 Thess. 5:6, 8; 2 Tim. 4:5; 1 Pet. 1:13; 4:7, RV (KJV, "watch"); 5:8.¶ Cf. *eknēphō* and *ananēphō*, under AWAKE, No. 3 and *Note*.

2. *sōphroneō* (σωφρονέω, 4993), akin to A, is rendered "to think soberly," Rom. 12:3; "to be sober," 2 Cor. 5:13; "to be soberminded," Titus 2:6; in 1 Pet. 4:7, KJV "be ye sober" (RV, "of sound mind"); see MIND, B, No. 5.

3. *sōphronizō* (σωφρονίζω, 4994) denotes "to cause to be of sound mind, to recall to one's senses"; in Titus 2:4, RV, it is rendered "they may train" (KJV, "they may teach . . . to be sober," marg., "wise"); "train" expresses the

meaning more adequately; the training would involve the cultivation of sound judgment and prudence.¶

C. Adverb.

sōphronōs (σωφρόνως, 4996), akin to A and B, Nos. 2 and 3, "soberly," occurs in Titus 2:12; it suggests the exercise of that self-restraint that governs all passions and desires, enabling the believer to be conformed to the mind of Christ.¶

Note: For the phrase "to think soberly," see B, No. 2.

SOBERNESS, SOBRIETY

sōphrosunē (σωφροσύνη, 4997) denotes "soundness of mind" (see SOBER, A), Acts 26:25, "soberness"; 1 Tim. 2:9, 15, "sobriety"; "sound judgment" practically expresses the meaning; "it is that habitual inner self-government, with its constant rein on all the passions and desires, which would hinder the temptation to these from arising, or at all events from arising in such strength as would overbear the checks and barriers which *aidōs* (shamefastness) opposed to it" (Trench *Syn.* §xx, end).¶

For SOFT see EFFEMINATE

For SOFTLY see BLOW (Verb), No. 2

SOJOURN, SOJOURNER, SOJOURNING

A. Verbs.

1. *paroikeō* (παροικέω, 3939) denotes "to dwell beside, among or by" (*para*, "beside," *oikeō*, "to dwell"); then, "to dwell in a place as a *paroikos*, a stranger" (see below), Luke 24:18, RV, "Dost thou (alone) sojourn . . . ?" [marg., "Dost thou sojourn (alone)" is preferable], KJV, "art thou (only) a stranger?" (*monos*, "alone," is an adjective, not an adverb); in Heb. 11:9, RV, "he became a sojourner" (KJV, "he sojourned"), the RV gives the force of the aorist tense.¶

2. *epidēmeō* (ἐπιδημέω, 1927) is rendered "to sojourn" in Acts 17:21, RV.

B. Adjectives.

1. *paroikos* (πάροικος, 3941), an adjective, akin to A, No. 1, lit., "dwelling near" (see above), then, "foreign, alien" (found with this meaning in inscriptions), hence, as a noun, "a sojourner," is used with *eimi*, "to be," in Acts 7:6, "should sojourn," lit., "should be a sojourner"; in 7:29, RV, "sojourner" (KJV, "stranger"); in Eph. 2:19, RV, "sojourners" (KJV, "foreigners"), the preceding word rendered "strangers"

is *xenos;* in 1 Pet. 2:11, RV, ditto (KJV, "strangers").¶

2. *apodēmos* (ἀπόδημος, 590), "gone abroad" (*apo,* "from," *dēmos,* "people"), signifies "sojourning in another country," Mark 13:34, RV (KJV, "taking a far journey").¶

3. *parepidēmos* (παρεπίδημος, 3927), "sojourning in a strange place," is used as a noun, denoting "a sojourner, an exile," 1 Pet. 1:1, RV, "sojourners" (KJV, "strangers"). See PILGRIM.¶

C. Noun.

paroikia (παροικία, 3940), "a sojourning" (akin to A and B, Nos. 1), occurs in Acts 13:17, rendered "they sojourned," RV, KJV, "dwelt as strangers," lit., "in the sojourning"; in 1 Pet. 1:17, "sojourning."¶

SOLDIER

A. Nouns.

1. *stratiōtēs* (στρατιώτης, 4757), "a soldier," is used (*a*) in the natural sense, e.g., Matt. 8:9; 27:27; 28:12; Mark 15:16; Luke 7:8; 23:36; six times in John; thirteen times in Acts; not again in the NT; (*b*) metaphorically of one who endures hardship in the cause of Christ, 2 Tim. 2:3.

2. *strateuma* (στράτευμα, 4753), "an army," is used to denote "a company of soldiers" in Acts 23:10; in v. 27, RV, "the soldiers," KJV, "an army"; in Luke 23:11 (plural), RV, "soldiers," KJV, "men of war." See ARMY.

3. *sustratiōtēs* (συστρατιώτης, 4961), "a fellow-soldier" (*sun,* "with," and No. 1), is used metaphorically in Phil. 2:25 and Philem. 2, of fellowship in Christian service.¶

B. Verb.

strateuō (στρατεύω, 4754), always in the middle voice in the NT, is used (*a*) literally of "serving as a soldier," Luke 3:14, "soldiers" (RV, marg., "soldiers on service," present participle); 1 Cor. 9:7, RV, "(what) soldier . . . serveth," KJV, "(who) goeth a warfare"; 2 Tim. 2:4, RV, "soldier on service," KJV, "man that warreth," lit., "serving as a soldier"; (*b*) metaphorically, of "spiritual conflict": see WAR.

Notes: (1) For *spekoulatōr,* Mark 6:27, RV, "soldier of his guard," see GUARD.¶ (2) In 2 Tim. 2:4 *stratologeō* is rendered "hath chosen (him) to be a soldier," KJV (RV, "enrolled (him) as a soldier").¶

SOLID

stereos (στερεός, 4731), for which see FIRM, No. 2, has the meaning "solid" in Heb. 5:12, 14, of food (KJV, "strong"). As "solid" food requires more powerful digestive organs than are possessed by a babe, so a fuller knowledge of Christ (especially here with reference to His

Melchizedek priesthood) required that exercise of spiritual intelligence which is derived from the practical appropriation of what had already been received.

For **SOLITARY,** Mark 1:35, KJV, see **DESERT, B**

SOME, SOMEONE, SOMETHING, SOMEWHAT

Notes: (1) Various forms of the article and certain pronouns, followed by the particles *men* and *de* denote "some." These are not enumerated here. (2) The indefinite pronoun *tis* in its singular or plural forms, frequently means "some," "some one" (translated "some man," in the KJV, e.g., of Acts 8:31; 1 Cor. 15:35), or "somebody," Luke 8:46; the neuter plural denotes "some things" in 2 Pet. 3:16; the singular denotes "something," e.g., Luke 11:54; John 13:29 (2nd part); Acts 3:5; 23:18; Gal. 6:3, where the meaning is "anything," as in 2:6, "somewhat." It is translated "somewhat," in the more indefinite sense, in Luke 7:40; Acts 23:20; 25:26; 2 Cor. 10:8; Heb. 8:3. See also ONE, B, No. 1. (3) *Meros,* "a part, a measure," preceded by the preposition *apo,* "from," is translated "in some measure" in Rom. 15:15, RV (KJV, "in some sort"), and v. 24 (KJV, "somewhat"). (4) In the following *alloi,* "others" ("some" in the KJV), is translated "others" in the RV, Matt. 13:5, 7; Mark 4:7 ("other"); 8:28; Luke 9:19; John 9:9. Followed by a correlative expression it denotes "some," e.g., Acts 19:32; 21:34; see OTHER, No. 1.

For **SOMETIMES** see **TIME**

SOMEWHERE

pou (πού, 4225), a particle, signifies "somewhere" in Heb. 2:6 and 4:4, RV (KJV, "in a certain place"); the writer avoids mentioning the place to add stress to his testimony. See HAPLY, No. 5, VERILY.

SON

huios (υἱός, 5207) primarily signifies the relation of offspring to parent (see John 9:18–20; Gal. 4:30). It is often used metaphorically of prominent moral characteristics (see below). "It is used in the NT of (*a*) male offspring, Gal. 4:30; (*b*) legitimate, as opposed to illegitimate offspring, Heb. 12:8; (*c*) descendants, without reference to sex, Rom. 9:27; (*d*) friends attending a wedding, Matt. 9:15; (*e*) those who enjoy certain privileges, Acts 3:25; (*f*) those who act in a certain way, whether evil, Matt. 23:31, or good, Gal. 3:7; (*g*) those who manifest a certain character, whether evil, Acts 13:10; Eph. 2:2, or good, Luke 6:35; Acts 4:36; Rom. 8:14; (*h*) the destiny that corresponds with the character, whether evil, Matt. 23:15; John 17:12; 2 Thess. 2:3, or good, Luke 20:36; (*i*) the dignity of the relationship with God whereinto men are brought by the Holy Spirit when they believe on the Lord Jesus Christ, Rom. 8:19; Gal. 3:26. . . .

"The Apostle John does not use *huios*, 'son,' of the believer, he reserves that title for the Lord; but he does use *teknon*, 'child,' as in his Gospel, 1:12; 1 John 3:1, 2; Rev. 21:7 (*huios*) is a quotation from 2 Sam. 7:14.

"The Lord Jesus used *huios* in a very significant way, as in Matt. 5:9, 'Blessed are the peacemakers, for they shall be called the sons of God,' and vv. 44, 45, 'Love your enemies, and pray for them that persecute you; that ye may be (become) sons of your Father which is in heaven.' The disciples were to do these things, not in order that they might become children of God, but that, being children (note 'your Father' throughout), they might make the fact manifest in their character, might 'become sons.' See also 2 Cor. 6:17, 18.

"As to moral characteristics, the following phrases are used: (*a*) sons of God, Matt. 5:9, 45; Luke 6:35; (*b*) sons of the light, Luke 16:8; John 12:36; (*c*) sons of the day, 1 Thess. 5:5; (*d*) sons of peace, Luke 10:6; (*e*) sons of this world, Luke 16:8; (*f*) sons of disobedience, Eph. 2:2; (*g*) sons of the evil one, Matt. 13:38, cf. 'of the Devil,' Acts 13:10; (*h*) son of perdition, John 17:12; 2 Thess. 2:3. It is also used to describe characteristics other than moral, as: (*i*) sons of the resurrection, Luke 20:36; (*j*) sons of the Kingdom, Matt. 8:12; 13:38; (*k*) sons of the bridechamber, Mark 2:19; (*l*) sons of exhortation, Acts 4:36; (*m*) sons of thunder, Boanerges, Mark 3:17."*

Notes: (1) For the synonyms *teknon* and *teknion* see under CHILD. The difference between believers as "children of God" and as "sons of God" is brought out in Rom. 8:14–21. The Spirit bears witness with their spirit that they are "children of God," and, as such, they are His heirs and joint-heirs with Christ. This stresses the fact of their spiritual birth (vv. 16, 17). On the other hand, "as many as are led by the Spirit of God, these are sons of God," i.e., "these and no other." Their conduct gives evidence of the dignity of their relationship and their likeness to His character. (2) *Pais* is ren-

dered "son" in John 4:51. For Acts 13:13, 26 see below.

The Son of God

In this title the word "Son" is used sometimes (*a*) of relationship, sometimes (*b*) of the expression of character. "Thus, e.g., when the disciples so addressed Him, Matt. 14:33; 16:16; John 1:49, when the centurion so spoke of Him, Matt. 27:54, they probably meant that (*b*) He was a manifestation of God in human form. But in such passages as Luke 1:32, 35; Acts 13:33, which refer to the humanity of the Lord Jesus, . . . the word is used in sense (*a*).

"The Lord Jesus Himself used the full title on occasion, John 5:25; 9:35 [some mss. have 'the Son of Man'; see RV marg.]; 11:4, and on the more frequent occasions on which He spoke of Himself as 'the Son,' the words are to be understood as an abbreviation of 'the Son of God,' not of 'the Son of Man'; this latter He always expressed in full; see Luke 10:22; John 5:19, etc.

"John uses both the longer and shorter forms of the title in his Gospel, see 3:16–18; 20:31, e.g., and in his Epistles; cf. Rev. 2:18. So does the writer of Hebrews, 1:2; 4:14; 6:6, etc. An eternal relation subsisting between the Son and the Father in the Godhead is to be understood. That is to say, the Son of God, in His eternal relationship with the Father, is not so entitled because He at any time began to derive His being from the Father (in which case He could not be co-eternal with the Father), but because He is and ever has been the expression of what the Father is; cf. John 14:9, 'he that hath seen Me hath seen the Father.' The words of Heb. 1:3, 'Who being the effulgence of His (God's) glory, and the very image of His (God's) substance' are a definition of what is meant by 'Son of God.' Thus absolute Godhead, not Godhead in a secondary or derived sense, is intended in the title."†

Other titles of Christ as the "Son of God" are: "His Son," 1 Thess. 1:10 (in Acts 13:13, 26, RV, *pais* is rendered "servant"); "His own Son," Rom. 8:32; "My beloved Son," Matt. 3:17; "His Only Begotten Son," John 3:16; "the Son of His love," Col. 1:13.

"The Son is the eternal object of the Father's love, John 17:24, and the sole Revealer of the Father's character, John 1:14; Heb. 1:3. The words, 'Father' and 'Son,' are never in the NT so used as to suggest that the Father existed before the Son; the Prologue to the Gospel according to John distinctly asserts that the

---

* From *Notes on Galatians*, by Hogg and Vine, pp. 167–169, and on *Thessalonians*, pp. 158, 159.

† From *Notes on Galatians*, by Hogg and Vine, pp. 99, 100.

Word existed 'in the beginning,' and that this Word is the Son, Who 'became flesh and dwelt among us.'"*

In addressing the Father in His prayer in John 17 He says, "Thou lovedst Me before the foundation of the world." Accordingly in the timeless past the Father and the "Son" existed in that relationship, a relationship of love, as well as of absolute Deity. In this passage the "Son" gives evidence that there was no more powerful plea in the Father's estimation than that coeternal love existing between the Father and Himself.

The declaration "Thou art My Son, this day have I begotten Thee," Ps. 2:7, quoted in Acts 13:33; Heb. 1:5; 5:5, refers to the birth of Christ, not to His resurrection. In Acts 13:33 the verb "raise up" is used of the raising up of a person to occupy a special position in the nation, as of David in verse 22 (so of Christ as a Prophet in 3:22 and 7:37). The word "again" in the KJV in v. 33 represents nothing in the original. The RV rightly omits it. In v. 34 the statement as to the resurrection of Christ receives the greater stress in this respect through the emphatic contrast to that in v. 33 as to His being raised up in the nation, a stress imparted by the added words "from the dead." Accordingly v. 33 speaks of His incarnation, v. 34 of His resurrection.

In Heb. 1:5, that the declaration refers to the Birth is confirmed by the contrast in verse 6. Here the word "again" is rightly placed in the RV, "when He again bringeth in the Firstborn into the world." This points on to His second advent, which is set in contrast to His first advent, when God brought His Firstborn into the world the first time (see FIRSTBORN).†

So again in Heb. 5:5, where the High Priesthood of Christ is shown to fulfill all that was foreshadowed in the Levitical priesthood, the passage stresses the facts of His humanity, the days of His flesh, His perfect obedience and His sufferings.

Son of Man

In the NT this is a designation of Christ, almost entirely confined to the Gospels. Elsewhere it is found in Acts 7:56, the only occasion where a disciple applied it to the Lord and in Rev. 1:13; 14:14 (see below).

"Son of Man" is the title Christ used of Himself; John 12:34 is not an exception, for the

quotation by the multitude was from His own statement. The title is found especially in the Synoptic Gospels. The occurrences in John's gospel, 1:51; 3:13, 14; 5:27; 6:27, 53, 62; 8:28 (9:35 in some texts); 12:23, 34 (twice); 13:31, are not parallel to those in the Synoptic Gospels. In the latter the use of the title falls into two groups, (a) those in which it refers to Christ's humanity, His earthly work, sufferings and death, e.g., Matt. 8:20; 11:19; 12:40; 26:2, 24; (b) those which refer to His glory in resurrection and to that of His future advent, e.g., Matt. 10:23; 13:41; 16:27, 28; 17:9; 24:27, 30 (twice), 37, 39, 44.

While it is a messianic title it is evident that the Lord applied it to Himself in a distinctive way, for it indicates more than Messiahship, even universal headship on the part of One who is Man. It therefore stresses His manhood, manhood of a unique order in comparison with all other men, for He is declared to be of heaven, 1 Cor. 15:47, and even while here below, was "the Son of Man, which is in Heaven," John 3:13. As the "Son of Man" He must be appropriated spiritually as a condition of possessing eternal life, John 6:53. In His death, as in His life, the glory of His Manhood was displayed in the absolute obedience and submission to the will of the Father (12:23; 13:31), and, in view of this, all judgment has been committed to Him, who will judge in full understanding experimentally of human conditions, sin apart, and will exercise the judgment as sharing the nature of those judged, John 5:22, 27. Not only is He man, but He is "Son of Man," not by human generation but, according to the Semitic usage of the expression, partaking of the characteristics (sin apart) of manhood belonging to the category of mankind. Twice in the Apocalypse, 1:13 and 14:14, He is described as "One like unto a Son of man," RV (KJV, " ... the Son of Man"), cf. Dan. 7:13. He who was thus seen was indeed the "Son of Man," but the absence of the article in the original serves to stress what morally characterizes Him as such. Accordingly in these passages He is revealed, not as the Person known by the title, but as the One who is qualified to act as the Judge of all men. He is the same Person as in the days of His flesh, still continuing His humanity with His Deity. The phrase "like unto" serves to distinguish Him as there seen in His glory and majesty in contrast to the days of His humiliation.

SONG

ō̧dē (ᾠδή, 5603), "an ode, song," is always used in the NT (as in the Sept.), in praise of God or Christ; in Eph. 5:19 and Col. 3:16 the

---

* From *Notes on Thessalonians*, by Hogg and Vine. pp. 46, 47.

† The Western text of Luke 3:22 reads "Thou art My Son, this day have I begotten Thee," instead of "Thou art My beloved Son, in Thee I am well pleased." There is probably some connection between this and those early heresies which taught that our Lord's deity began at His baptism.

adjective "spiritual" is added, because the word in itself is generic and might be used of songs anything but spiritual; in Rev. 5:9 and 14:3 (1st part) the descriptive word is "new" (*kainos*, "new," in reference to character and form: see NEW), a "song," the significance of which was confined to those mentioned (v. 3, and 2nd part); in 15:3 (twice), "the song of Moses ... and the song of the Lamb," the former as celebrating the deliverance of God's people by His power, the latter as celebrating redemption by atoning sacrifice.¶

For **SOON** see **IMMEDIATELY,** No. 1 and **QUICKLY,** No. 3.

For **AS SOON AS** see †, p. 1

For **SOONER** see **QUICKLY,** No. 2

SOOTHSAYING

manteuomai (μαντεύομαι, 3132), "to divine, practice divination" (from *mantis*, "a seer, diviner"), occurs in Acts 16:16.¶ The word is allied to *mainomai*, "to rave," and *mania*, "fury" displayed by those who were possessed by the evil spirit (represented by the pagan god or goddess) while delivering their oracular messages. Trench (*Syn.* §vi) draws a distinction between this verb and *prophēteuō*, not only as to their meanings, but as to the fact of the single occurrence of *manteuomai* in the NT, contrasted with the frequency of *prophēteuō*, exemplifying the avoidance by NT writers of words the employment of which "would tend to break down the distinction between heathenism and revealed religion."

SOP

psōmion (ψωμίον, 5596), a diminutive of *psōmos*, "a morsel," denotes "a fragment, a sop" (akin to *psōmizō;* see FEED), John 13:26 (twice), 27, 30. It had no connection with the modern meaning of "sop," something given to pacify (as in the classical expression "a sop to Cerberus").¶

SORCERER

1. *magos* (μάγος, 3097), (*a*) "one of a Median caste, a magician": see WISE; (*b*) "a wizard, sorcerer, a pretender to magic powers, a professor of the arts of witchcraft," Acts 13:6, 8, where Bar-Jesus was the Jewish name, Elymas, an Arabic word meaning "wise." Hence the name Magus, "the magician," originally applied to Persian priests. In the Sept., only in Dan. 2:2, 10, of the "enchanters," RV (KJV, "astrologers"),

of Babylon. The superior Greek version of Daniel by Theodotion has it also at 1:20; 2:27; 4:7; 5:7, 11, 15.¶

2. *pharmakos* (φαρμακός, 5333), an adjective signifying "devoted to magical arts," is used as a noun, "a sorcerer," especially one who uses drugs, potions, spells, enchantments, Rev. 21:8, in the best texts (some have *pharmakeus*), and 22:15.¶

SORCERY

A. Nouns.

1. *pharmakia* (or *-eia*) (φαρμακία, 5331) (Eng., "pharmacy," etc.) primarily signified "the use of medicine, drugs, spells"; then, "poisoning"; then, "sorcery," Gal. 5:20, RV, "sorcery" (KJV, "witchcraft"), mentioned as one of "the works of the flesh." See also Rev. 9:21; 18:23.¶ In the Sept., Ex. 7:11, 22; 8:7, 18; Isa. 47:9, 12.¶ In "sorcery," the use of drugs, whether simple or potent, was generally accompanied by incantations and appeals to occult powers, with the provision of various charms, amulets, etc., professedly designed to keep the applicant or patient from the attention and power of demons, but actually to impress the applicant with the mysterious resources and powers of the sorcerer.

2. *magia* (or *-eia*) (μαγία, 3095), "the magic art," is used in the plural in Acts 8:11, "sorceries" (see SORCERER, No. 1).¶

B. Verb.

mageuō (μαγεύω, 3096), akin to A, No. 2, "to practice magic," Acts 8:9, "used sorcery," is used as in A, No. 2, of Simon Magnus.¶

SORE (Noun, Adjective, Adverb), SORER

A. Noun.

helkos (ἕλκος, 1668), "a sore" or "ulcer" (primarily a wound), occurs in Luke 16:21; Rev. 16:2, 11.¶

B. Verb.

helkoō (ἑλκόω, 1669), "to wound, to ulcerate," is used in the passive voice, signifying "to suffer from sores," to be "full of sores," Luke 16:20 (perfect participle).¶

C. Adjectives.

1. *hikanos* (ἱκανός, 2425), used of things, occasionally denotes "much," translated "sore" in Acts 20:37, lit., "there was much weeping of all." See ABLE, C, No. 2.

2. *cheirōn* (χείρων, 5501), "worse" (used as a comparative degree of *kakos*, "evil"), occurs in Heb. 10:29, "sorer." See WORSE.

D. Adverbs.

1. *lian* (λίαν, 3029), "very, exceedingly," is translated "sore" in Mark 6:51 (of amazement). See EXCEED, B, No. 1.

2. *sphodra* (σφόδρα, 4970), "very, very much," is translated "sore" in Matt. 17:6 (of fear). See GREATLY, *Note* (1).

Notes: (1) For the KJV, "sore vexed" in Matt. 17:15, see GRIEVOUSLY, B, No. 2, *Note* (2). (2) In Luke 2:9 *megas*, "great," is used with *phobos*, "fear," as the object of the verb "to fear," "(they were) sore (afraid)," lit., "(they feared) a great (fear)." (3) In Mark 9:26, KJV, *polla*, "much" (RV), the neuter plur. of *polus*, used as an adverb, is translated "sore." (4) In Matt. 21:15, *aganakteō*, "to be moved with indignation" (RV), is translated "they were sore displeased." (5) For the RV, "sore troubled," Matt. 26:37 and Mark 14:33 (KJV, "very heavy"), see TROUBLE, B, No. 12. (6) For KJV, "were sore amazed" in Mark 14:33, see AMAZE, B, No. 4. (7) In Luke 9:39, RV, *suntribō*, "to break, bruise," is rendered "bruiseth sorely." See BREAK, A, No. 5. (8) In Mark 9:6, *ekphobos* is rendered "sore afraid."

SORROW (Noun and Verb), SORROWFUL

A. Nouns.

1. *lupē* (λύπη, 3077), "grief, sorrow," is translated "sorrow" in Luke 22:45; John 16:6, 20–22; Rom. 9:2, RV (KJV, "heaviness"); 2 Cor. 2:1, RV; 2:3, 7; 7:10 (twice); Phil. 2:27 (twice). See GRIEF.

2. *odunē* (ὀδύνη, 3601), "pain, consuming grief, distress," whether of body or mind, is used of the latter, Rom. 9:2, RV, "pain"; 1 Tim. 6:10.¶

3. *ōdin* (ὠδίν, 5604), "a birth-pang, travail, pain," "sorrows," Matt. 24:8; Mark 13:8; see PAIN, A, No. 2.

4. *penthos* (πένθος, 3997), "mourning," "sorrow," Rev. 18:7 (twice); 21:4: see MOURN.

B. Verbs.

1. *lupeō* (λυπέω, 3076), akin to A, No. 1: see GRIEF, B, No. 1, SORRY, A (below).

2. *odunaō* (ὀδυνάω, 3600), "to cause pain" (akin to A, No. 2), is used in the middle voice in Luke 2:48; Acts 20:38: see ANGUISH, B, No. 3.

C. Adjectives.

1. *perilupos* (περίλυπος, 4036), "very sad, deeply grieved" (*peri*, intensive), is used in Matt. 26:38 and Mark 14:34, "exceeding sorrowful"; Mark 6:26; Luke 18:23 (v. 24 in some mss.).¶

2. *alupos* (ἄλυπος, 253) denotes "free from grief" (*a*, negative, *lupē*, "grief"), comparative

degree in Phil. 2:28, "less sorrowful," their joy would mean the removal of a burden from his heart.¶

SORRY

A. Verb.

lupeō (λυπέω, 3076) is rendered "to be sorry" (passive voice) in Matt. 14:9, KJV (RV, "grieved"); 17:23; 18:31; 2 Cor. 2:2 [1st part, active voice, "make sorry" (as in 7:8, twice); 2nd part, passive]; 2:4, RV, "made sorry"; 9:9 and 11, RV, "ye were made sorry." See GRIEVE, B, No. 1.

B. Adjective.

perilupos (περίλυπος, 4036) is translated "exceeding sorry" in Mark 6:26: see SORROWFUL, C, No. 1.

SORT

A. Adjective.

hopoios (ὁποῖος, 3697), "of what sort," is so rendered in 1 Cor. 3:13. See MANNER, SUCH AS, WHAT.

B. Noun.

meros (μέρος, 3313), "a part," is used with *apo*, "from," in Rom. 15:15 and rendered "(in some) sort," KJV (RV, " . . . measure"). See BEHALF.

Note: See BASE, No. 3, GODLY, C, *Notes* (2) and (3).

For SOUGHT see SEEK

SOUL

psuchē (ψυχή, 5590) denotes "the breath, the breath of life," then "the soul," in its various meanings. The NT uses "may be analyzed approximately as follows:

(*a*) the natural life of the body, Matt. 2:20; Luke 12:22; Acts 20:10; Rev. 8:9; 12:11; cf. Lev. 17:11; 2 Sam. 14:7; Esth. 8:11; (*b*) the immaterial, invisible part of man, Matt. 10:28; Acts 2:27; cf. 1 Kings 17:21; (*c*) the disembodied (or "unclothed" or "naked," 2 Cor. 5:3, 4) man, Rev. 6:9; (*d*) the seat of personality, Luke 9:24, explained as = "own self," v. 25; Heb. 6:19; 10:39; cf. Isa. 53:10 with 1 Tim. 2:6; (*e*) the seat of the sentient element in man, that by which he perceives, reflects, feels, desires, Matt. 11:29; Luke 1:46; 2:35; Acts 14:2, 22; cf. Ps. 84:2; 139:14; Isa. 26:9; (*f*) the seat of will and purpose, Matt. 22:37; Acts 4:32; Eph. 6:6; Phil. 1:27; Heb. 12:3; cf. Num. 21:4; Deut. 11:13; (*g*) the seat of appetite, Rev. 18:14; cf. Ps. 107:9; Prov. 6:30; Isa. 5:14 ("desire"); 29:8; (*h*) persons, individuals, Acts 2:41, 43; Rom. 2:9; Jas. 5:20; 1 Pet. 3:20; 2 Pet. 2:14; cf. Gen. 12:5; 14:21 ("persons"); Lev. 4:2 ('any one'); Ezek.

27:13; of dead bodies, Num. 6:6, lit., "dead soul"; and of animals, Lev. 24:18, lit., "soul for soul"; (i) the equivalent of the personal pronoun, used for emphasis and effect:— 1st person, John 10:24 ("us"); Heb. 10:38; cf. Gen. 12:13; Num. 23:10; Jud. 16:30; Ps. 120:2 ("me"); 2nd person, 2 Cor. 12:15; Heb. 13:17; Jas. 1:21; 1 Pet. 1:9; 2:25; cf. Lev. 17:11; 26:15; 1 Sam. 1:26; 3rd person, 1 Pet. 4:19; 2 Pet. 2:8; cf. Exod. 30:12; Job 32:2, Heb. "soul," Sept. "self"; (j) an animate creature, human or other, 1 Cor. 15:45; Rev. 16:3; cf. Gen. 1:24; 2:7, 19; (k) "the inward man," the seat of the new life, Luke 21:19 (cf. Matt. 10:39); 1 Pet. 2:11; 3 John 2.

"With (j) compare a-psuchos, "soulless, inanimate," 1 Cor. 14:7.¶

"With (f) compare di-psuchos, "two-souled," Jas. 1:8; 4:8;¶ oligo psuchos, "feeble-souled," 1 Thess. 5:14;¶ iso-psuchos, "like-souled," Phil. 2:20;¶ sum-psuchos, "joint-souled" ("with. one accord"), Phil. 2:2.¶

"The language of Heb. 4:12 suggests the extreme difficulty of distinguishing between the soul and the spirit, alike in their nature and in their activities. Generally speaking the spirit is the higher, the soul the lower element. The spirit may be recognized as the life principle bestowed on man by God, the soul as the resulting life constituted in the individual, the body being the material organism animated by soul and spirit. . . .

"Body and soul are the constituents of the man according to Matt. 6:25; 10:28; Luke 12:20; Acts 20:10; body and spirit according to Luke 8:55; 1 Cor. 5:3; 7:34; Jas. 2:26. In Matt. 26:38 the emotions are associated with the soul, in John 13:21 with the spirit; cf. also Ps. 42:11 with 1 Kings 21:5. In Ps. 35:9 the soul rejoices in God, in Luke 1:47 the spirit.

"Apparently, then, the relationships may be thus summed up 'Sōma, body, and pneuma, spirit, may be separated, pneuma and psuchē, soul, can only be distinguished' (Cremer)."*

SOUND (Noun and Verb)

A. Nouns.

1. phōnē (φωνή, 5456), most frequently "a voice," is translated "sound" in Matt. 24:31 (KJV marg., "voice"); John 3:8, KJV (RV, "voice"); so 1 Cor. 14:7 (1st part), 8; Rev. 1:15; 18:22 (2nd part, RV, "voice"); KJV and RV in 9:9 (twice); in Acts 2:6, RV, "(this) sound (was heard)," KJV, "(this) was noised abroad."

2. echos (ἦχος, 2279), "a noise, a sound of

any sort" (Eng., "echo"), is translated "sound" in Acts 2:2; Heb. 12:19. See ROARING, B, RUMOR.

3. phthongos (φθόγγος, 5353), akin to phthengomai, "to utter a voice," occurs in Rom. 10:18; 1 Cor. 14:7.¶ In the Sept., Ps. 19:4.¶

B. Verbs.

1. echeō (ἠχέω, 2278), akin to A, No. 2, occurs in 1 Cor. 13:1, "sounding (brass)"; in some mss., Luke 21:25. See ROARING.¶

2. exēcheō (ἐξηχέω, 1837), "to sound forth as a trumpet" or "thunder" (ex, "out," and No. 1), is used in 1 Thess. 1:8, "sounded forth," passive voice, lit., "has been sounded out."¶ In the Sept., Joel 3:14.¶

3. salpizō (σαλπίζω, 4537), "to sound a trumpet" (salpinx), occurs in Matt. 6:2; 1 Cor. 15:52, "the trumpet shall sound"; Rev. 8:6–8, 10, 12, 13; 9:1, 13; 10:7; 11:15.¶

4. bolizō (βολίζω, 1001), "to heave the lead" (bolis, "that which is thrown or hurled," akin to ballō, "to throw"; sounding-lead), to take soundings, occurs in Acts 27:28 (twice).¶

Note: In Luke 1:44, KJV, ginomai, "to become," is rendered "sounded" (RV, "came").

SOUND (Adjective), BE SOUND

A. Adjective.

hugiēs (ὑγιής, 5199), "whole, healthy," is used metaphorically of "sound speech," Titus 2:8. See WHOLE.

B. Verb.

hugiainō (ὑγιαίνω, 5198), "to be healthy, sound in health" (Eng., "hygiene," etc.), translated "safe and sound" in Luke 15:27, is used metaphorically of doctrine, 1 Tim. 1:10; 2 Tim. 4:3; Titus 1:9; 2:1; of words, 1 Tim. 6:3, RV (KJV, "wholesome," RV marg., "healthful"); 2 Tim. 1:13; "in the faith," Titus 1:13 (RV marg., "healthy"); "in faith," Titus 2:2 (RV marg., ditto).

Note: For "sound mind" in 2 Tim. 1:7, KJV, see DISCIPLINE; in 1 Pet. 4:7 (KJV, "sober"), see MIND, B, No. 5.

SOUNDNESS

holoklēria (ὁλοκληρία, 3647), "completeness, soundness" (akin to holoklēros, see ENTIRE), occurs in Acts 3:16.¶ In the Sept., Isa. 1:6.¶

SOUTH, SOUTH WIND

notos (νότος, 3558) denotes (a) "the south wind," Luke 12:55; Acts 27:13; 28:13; (b) "south," as a direction, Luke 13:29; Rev. 21:13; (c) "the South," as a region, Matt. 12:42; Luke 11:31.¶

Note: For mesēmbria, Acts 8:26, see NOON.

---

* From Notes on Thessalonians, by Hogg and Vine, pp. 205–207.

SOUTHWEST

lips (λίψ, 3047), lit., "Libyan," denotes "the S.W. wind," Acts 27:12, "(looking) northeast (and southeast)," RV, lit., "(looking down) the southwest wind (and down the northwest wind)"; to look down a wind was to look in the direction in which it blows. A S.W. wind blows towards the N.E.; the aspect of the haven answers to this. See also under NORTHEAST, NORTHWEST.¶

SOW (Noun)

hus (ὑς, 5300), "swine" (masc. or fem.), is used in the fem. in 2 Pet. 2:22.¶

SOW (Verb), SOWER

speirō (σπείρω, 4687), "to sow seed," is used (1) literally, especially in the Synoptic Gospels; elsewhere, 1 Cor. 15:36, 37; 2 Cor. 9:10, "the sower"; (2) metaphorically, (*a*) in proverbial sayings, e.g., Matt. 13:3, 4; Luke 19:21, 22; John 4:37; 2 Cor. 9:6; (*b*) in the interpretation of parables, e.g., Matt. 13:19–23 (in these vv., RV, "was sown," for KJV, "received seed"); (*c*) otherwise as follows: of "sowing" spiritual things in preaching and teaching, 1 Cor. 9:11; of the interment of the bodies of deceased believers, 1 Cor. 15:42–44; of ministering to the necessities of others in things temporal (the harvest being proportionate to the "sowing"), 2 Cor. 9:6, 10 (see above); of "sowing" to the flesh, Gal. 6:7, 8 ("that" in v. 7 is emphatic, "that and that only," what was actually "sown"); in v. 8, *eis*, "unto," signifies "in the interests of"; of the "fruit of righteousness" by peacemakers, Jas. 3:18.

SPACE

A. Noun.

diastēma (διάστημα, 1292), "an interval, space" (akin to B), is used of time in Acts 5:7.¶

B. Verb.

diistēmi (διΐστημι, 1339), "to set apart, separate" (*dia*, "apart," *histēmi*, "to cause to stand"), see A, is rendered "after the space of" in Luke 22:59; in Acts 27:28, with *brachu*, "a little," RV, "after a little space" (KJV, "when they had gone a little further"). See PART.

Notes: (1) In Acts 15:33 and Rev. 2:21, KJV, *chronos*, "time" (RV), is translated "space." (2) In Acts 19:8 and 10, *epi*, "for or during" (of time), is translated "for the space of"; in 19:34, "about the space of." (3) In Acts 5:34, KJV, *brachu* (the neuter of *brachus*, "short"), used adverbially, is translated "a little space" (RV " . . . while"). (4) In Gal. 2:1, *dia*, "through," is rendered "after the space of," RV, stressing the

length of the period mentioned (KJV, "after," which would represent the preposition *meta*). (5) In Jas. 5:17 there is no word in the original representing the phrase "by the space of," KJV (RV, "for"). (6) In Rev. 14:20, KJV, *apo*, "away from," is translated "by the space of" (RV, "as far as"). (7) In Rev. 17:10, KJV, *oligon*, "a little while" (RV), is rendered "a short space."

SPARE, SPARINGLY

A. Verb.

pheidomai (φείδομαι, 5339), "to spare," i.e., "to forego" the infliction of that evil or retribution which was designed, is used with a negative in Acts 20:29; Rom. 8:32; 11:21 (twice); 2 Cor. 13:2; 2 Pet. 2:4, 5; positively, in 1 Cor. 7:28; 2 Cor. 1:3; rendered "forbear" in 2 Cor. 12:6. See FORBEAR.¶

Note: In Luke 15:17, *perisseuō*, "to abound, have abundance," is translated "have enough and to spare."

B. Adverb.

pheidomenōs (φειδομένως, 5340), akin to A, "sparingly," occurs in 2 Cor. 9:6 (twice), of sowing and reaping.¶

SPARROW

strouthion (στρουθίον, 4765), a diminutive of *strouthos*, "a sparrow," occurs in Matt. 10:29, 31; Luke 12:6, 7.¶

SPEAK

1. *legō* (λέγω, 3004), "to say, speak": see SAY, No. 1.

2. *laleō* (λαλέω, 2980), for which see SAY, No. 2, is used several times in 1 Cor. 14; the command prohibiting women from speaking in a church gathering, vv. 34, 35, is regarded by some as an injunction against chattering, a meaning which is absent from the use of the verb everywhere else in the NT; it is to be understood in the same sense as in vv. 2, 3–6, 9, 11, 13, 18, 19, 21, 23, 27–29, 39.

3. *proslaleō* (προσλαλέω, 4354), "to speak to or with" (*pros*, "to," and No. 2), is used in Acts 13:43 and 28:20.¶

4. *phthengomai* (φθέγγομαι, 5350), "to utter a sound or voice," is translated "to speak" in Acts 4:18: 2 Pet. 2:16; in 2:18, KJV, "speak" (RV, "utter").

5. *apophthengomai* (ἀποφθέγγομαι, 669), "to speak forth" (*apo*, "forth," and No. 4), is so rendered in Acts 2:14, RV (KJV, "said"), and 26:25; in 2:2 it denotes to give utterance.¶

6. *antilegō* (ἀντιλέγω, 483), "to speak against," is so rendered in Luke 2:34; John 19:12; Acts 13:45, KJV (RV, "contradicted"); 28:19, 22. See CONTRADICT, GAINSAY.

7. *katalaleō* (καταλαλέω, 2635), synonymous with No. 6 (*kata*, "against," and No. 2), is always translated "to speak against" in the RV. See BACKBITER, *Note.*

8. *kakologeō* (κακολογέω, 2551), "to speak evil": see CURSE, B, No. 4.

9. *sullaleō* (συλλαλέω, 4814), "to speak together" (*sun*, "with," and No. 2), is rendered "spake together" in Luke 4:36, RV. See COMMUNE, No. 3, CONFER, No. 2, TALK.

10. *proeipon* (προεῖπον, 4302), "to speak or say before" (a 2nd aorist tense from an obsolete present), is rendered "to speak before" in Acts 1:16; 2 Pet. 3:2; Jude 17. See FORETELL.

11. *prophthanō* (προφθάνω, 4399), "to anticipate" (an extension, by *pro*, "before," of *phthanō*, which has the same meaning), is rendered "spake first" in Matt. 17:25, RV (KJV, "prevented").¶

12. *prosphōneō* (προσφωνέω, 4377), "to address, call to," is rendered "spake unto" (or "to") in Luke 23:20; Acts 21:40; 22:2; "to call unto" (or "to") in Matt. 11:16; Luke 6:13; 7:32; 13:12.¶

13. *eirō* (εἴρω, Fut. of 3004), for which see SAY, No. 4, has a 1st aorist, passive participle *rhēthen*, "spoken" or "spoken of," used in Matt. 1:22; 2:15, 17, 23; 3:3; 4:14; 8:17; 12:17; 13:35; 21:4; 22:31; 24:15; 27:9 (in some texts in 27:35 and Mark 13:14).

Notes: (1) In Heb. 12:5, KJV, *dialegomai*, "to discuss, to reason," is translated "speaketh" (RV, "reasoneth"). (2) In Heb. 12:25, KJV *chrēmatizō*, "to warn, instruct," is translated "spake" (RV, "warned"): see ADMONISH. (3) In Eph. 4:31, KJV, *blasphēmia* is translated "evil speaking": see RAILING. (4) In Heb. 12:19, *prostithēmi*, "to put to, add," used with *logos*, "a word," is rendered "(that no word) more should be spoken," RV [KJV, "(that) the word should (not) be spoken (to them) any more"]. (5) In Acts 26:24, KJV, *apologeomai*, "to make a defense" (RV), is rendered "spake for himself." See ANSWER, B, No. 4. (6) In Rom. 15:21, KJV, *anangellō*, "to bring back word" (RV, "tidings . . . came"), is translated "he was . . . spoken of." (7) For "is spoken of" in Rom. 1:8, KJV, see PROCLAIM, No. 2. (8) For "spake out" in Luke 1:42, KJV, see VOICE, *Note.* (9) In Gal. 4:15, there is no verb in the original for the KJV, "ye spake of" (see RV). (10) For "spoken against" in Acts 19:36 see GAINSAY, C. (11) For "speak reproachfully," 1 Tim. 5:14, see REVILE, C. (12) In Acts 21:3, KJV, *ginōskō* is translated "speak," RV, "know."

SPEAKER (chief)

Note: In Acts 14:12 the verb *hēgeomai*, "to lead the way, be the chief," is used in the present participle with the article (together equivalent to a noun), followed by the genitive case of *logos*, "speech," with the article, the phrase being rendered "the chief speaker," lit., "the leader of the discourse." See CHIEF, C.

SPEAKING (evil, much)

polulogia (πολυλογία, 4180), "loquacity," "much speaking" (*polus*, "much," *logos*, "speech"), is used in Matt. 6:7.¶ In the Sept., Prov. 10:19.¶

Note: For "evil speaking(s)," in Eph. 4:31, see RAILING; in 1 Pet. 2:1, see BACKBITING. For "shameful speaking" see COMMUNICATION, B, *Note.*

SPEAR

lonchē (λόγχη, 3057), primarily "a spearhead," then, "a lance or spear," occurs in John 19:34; some texts have it in Matt. 27:49¶ As to John 19:29, there is an old conjecture, mentioned by Field (*Notes on the Trans. of the NT*), to the effect that the sponge was put on a spear (*hussos*, "a javelin," the Roman *pilum*, instead of *hussōpos*, "hyssop").

SPEARMAN

dexiolabos (δεξιολάβος, 1187), from *dexios*, "the right (hand)," and *lambanō*, "to lay hold of," is used in the plural in Acts 23:23, "spearmen." Some texts have *dexiobolos*, "one who throws with his right hand" (*ballō*, "to throw"), "right-handed slingers."¶

SPECIAL

Note: Tuchōn, the 2nd aorist participle of *tunchanō*, "to happen, meet with, chance," is used with a negative signifying "not common or ordinary, special," Acts 19:11; so in 28:2. See COMMON, B, *Note* (3).

For SPECIALLY see ESPECIALLY

SPECTACLE

theatron (θέατρον, 2302), akin to *theaomai*, "to behold," denotes (*a*) "a theater" (used also as a place of assembly), Acts 19:29, 31; (*b*) "a spectacle, a show," metaphorically in 1 Cor. 4:9. See THEATER.¶

SPEECH

1. *logos* (λόγος, 3056), akin to *legō* (SPEAK, No. 1), most frequently rendered "word" (for an analysis see WORD), signifies "speech," as follows: (*a*) "discourse," e.g., Luke 20:20, RV, "speech" (KJV, "words"); Acts 14:12 (see SPEAKER); 20:7; 1 Cor. 2:1, 4; 4:19, KJV (RV, "word"); 2 Cor. 10:10; (*b*) "the faculty of

speech," e.g., 2 Cor. 11:6; (c) "the manner of speech," e.g., Matt. 5:37, RV, "speech" (KJV, "communication"); Col. 4:6; (d) "manner of instruction," Titus 2:8; 1 Cor. 14:9, RV (KJV, "words"); Eph. 4:29, RV (KJV, "communication"). See SAYING.

2. *lalia* (λαλιά, 2981), akin to *laleō* (SPEAK, No. 2), denotes "talk, speech," (a) of "a dialect," Matt. 26:73; Mark 14:70; (b) "utterances," John 4:42, RV, "speaking" (KJV, "saying"); 8:43.¶

3. *eulogia* (εὐλογία, 2129) has the meaning "fair speaking, flattering speech" in Rom. 16:18, RV, "fair speech" (KJV, "fair speeches"). See BLESSING, C, No. 1.

4. *chrēstologia* (χρηστολογία, 5542), which has a similar meaning to No. 3, occurs with it in Rom. 16:18 [RV, "smooth . . . (speech)"]. See SMOOTH, *Note*.¶

Notes: (1) For "persuasiveness of speech," Col. 2:4, RV, see PERSUASIVE, B. (2) In Acts 14:11 "the speech of Lycaonia" translates the adverb *Lukaonisti.* Lycaonia was a large country in the center and south of the plateau of Asia Minor; the villages retained the native language, but cities like Lystra probably had a Seleucid tone in their laws and customs (Ramsay on Galatians).

SPEECHLESS

1. *eneos* (or *enneos*) (ἐνεός, 1769), "dumb, speechless," occurs in Acts 9:7.¶ In the Sept., Prov. 17:28; Isa. 56:10.¶

2. *kōphos* (κωφός), which means either "deaf" or "dumb" (see DEAF), is translated "speechless" in Luke 1:22.

Note: For *phimoō*, translated "he was speechless" in Matt. 22:12, see MUZZLE, SILENCE.

SPEED, SPEEDILY

Notes: (1) In Acts 17:15 "with all speed" is the rendering of the phrase *hōs*, "as," *tachista*, "most speedily" (the superlative of *tachu*, "speedily"), i.e., "as speedily as possible." (2) For "speedily," *en tachei*, in Luke 18:8, see QUICKLY, No. 4. (3) For "God speed" see GREETING, A, No. 2.

SPEND, SPENT

1. *dapanaō* (δαπανάω, 1159) denotes (a) "to expend, spend," Mark 5:26 [for Acts 21:24 see CHARGE, *Note* (5)]: 2 Cor. 12:15 (1st part: for "be spent," see No. 2); (b) "to consume, squander," Luke 15:14; Jas. 4:3. See CONSUME, *Note*.¶

2. *ekdapanaō* (ἐκδαπανάω, 1550), lit., "to spend out" (*ek*), an intensive form of No. 1, "to spend entirely," is used in 2 Cor. 12:15, in the

passive voice, with reflexive significance, "to spend oneself out (for others)," "will . . . be spent," RV marg., "spent out" (see No. 1).¶

3. *prosdapanaō* (προσδαπανάω, 4325), "to spend besides" (*pros*, and No. 1), is used in Luke 10:35, "thou spendest more."¶

4. *prosanaliskō* (προσαναλίσκω, 4321), "to spend besides," a strengthened form of *analiskō*, "to expend, consume" (see CONSUME, No. 1), occurs in most texts in Luke 8:43.¶

5. *diaginomai* (διαγίνομαι, 1230), used of time, "to intervene, elapse," is rendered "was spent" in Acts 27:9. See PAST.

6. *prokoptō* (προκόπτω, 4298), "to cut forward a way, advance," is translated "is far spent," in Rom. 13:12, said metaphorically of "the night," the whole period of man's alienation from God. Though the tense is the aorist, it must not be rendered "was far spent," as if it referred, e.g., to Christ's first advent. The aorist is here perfective. See ADVANCE.

7. *klinō* (κλίνω, 2827), "to lean, decline," is said of the decline of day in Luke 24:29, "is (now) far spent," lit., "has declined." See BOW (Verb).

8. *ginomai* (γίνομαι, 1096), "to become, occur," is rendered "was far spent" in Mark 6:35, lit., "much hour (i.e., many an hour) having taken place."

9. *poieō* (ποιέω, 4160), "to do," is translated "have spent (*but* one hour)," in Matt. 20:12, RV (KJV, "have wrought") lit., as in the Eng. idiom, "have done one hour"; so in Acts 20:3, RV, "when he had spent (lit., 'had done') three months" (KJV, "abode").

10. *eukaireō* (εὐκαιρέω, 2119), "to have leisure or devote one's leisure to," is translated "spent their time," in Acts 17:21. See LEISURE.

11. *chronotribeō* (χρονοτριβέω, 5551), "to spend time" (*chronos*, "time," *tribō*, "to rub, to wear out"), occurs in Acts 20:16.¶

Note: Polus, much, is rendered "far spent" twice in Mark 6:35, RV.

SPEW (KJV, SPUE)

emeō (ἐμέω, 1692), "to vomit" (cf. Eng., "emetic"), is used in Rev. 3:16, figuratively of the Lord's utter abhorrence of the condition of the church at Laodicea.¶ In the Sept., Isa. 19:14.¶

SPICE(S)

1. *arōma* (ἄρωμα, 759), "spice," occurs in Mark 16:1, RV "spices" (KJV, "sweet spice"); Luke 23:56; 24:1; John 19:40.¶ A papyrus document has it in a list of articles for a sacrifice.

2. *amōmon* (ἄμωμον, 298a), *amomum*, probably a word of Semitic origin, a fragrant

plant of India, is translated "spice" in Rev. 18:13, RV (KJV, "odors").¶

SPIKENARD

nardos (νάρδος, 3487) is derived, through the Semitic languages (Heb. *nērd*, Syriac *nardin*), from the Sanskrit *nalada*, "a fragrant oil," procured from the stem of an Indian plant. The Arabs call it the "Indian spike." The adjective *pistikos* is attached to it in the NT, Mark 14:3; John 12:3; *pistikos*, if taken as an ordinary Greek word, would signify "genuine." There is evidence, however, that it was regarded as a technical term. It has been suggested that the original reading was *pistakēs*, i.e., the *Pistacia Terebinthus*, which grows in Cyprus, Syria, Palestine, etc., and yields a resin of very fragrant odor, and in such inconsiderable quantities as to be very costly. "Nard was frequently mixed with aromatic ingredients . . . so when scented with the fragrant resin of the *pistakē* it would quite well be called *nardos pistakēs*" (E. N. Bennett, in the *Classical Review* for 1890, Vol. iv, p. 319). The oil used for the anointing of the Lord's head was worth about L/12, and must have been of the most valuable kind.¶ In the Sept., Song of Sol. 1:12; 4:13, 14.¶

SPILL

ekchunnō (or *ekchunō*,) (ἐκχύννω, 1632), "to pour out, shed," is rendered "be spilled" in Luke 5:37. See POUR, SHED.

Note: Some texts have *ekcheō* in Mark 2:22 (so KJV). The form in Luke 5:37 might also come from *ekcheō*.

SPIN

nēthō (νήθω, 3514), "to spin," is found in Matt. 6:28 and Luke 12:27, of the lilies of the field (see LILY).¶

SPIRIT

pneuma (πνεῦμα, 4151) primarily denotes "the wind" (akin to *pneō*, "to breathe, blow"); also "breath"; then, especially "the spirit," which, like the wind, is invisible, immaterial and powerful. The NT uses of the word may be analyzed approximately as follows:

"(*a*) the wind, John 3:8 (where marg. is, perhaps, to be preferred); Heb. 1:7; cf. Amos 4:13, Sept.; (*b*) the breath, 2 Thess. 2:8; Rev. 11:11; 13:15; cf. Job 12:10, Sept.; (*c*) the immaterial, invisible part of man, Luke 8:55; Acts 7:59; 1 Cor. 5:5; Jas. 2:26; cf. Eccl. 12:7, Sept.; (*d*) the disembodied (or 'unclothed,' or 'naked,' 2 Cor. 5:3, 4) man, Luke 24:37, 39; Heb. 12:23; 1 Pet. 4:6; (*e*) the resurrection body, 1 Cor. 15:45; 1 Tim. 3:16; 1 Pet. 3:18; (*f*) the sentient

element in man, that by which he perceives, reflects, feels, desires, Matt. 5:3; 26:41; Mark 2:8; Luke 1:47, 80; Acts 17:16; 20:22; 1 Cor. 2:11; 5:3, 4; 14:4, 15; 2 Cor. 7:1; cf. Gen. 26:35; Isa. 26:9; Ezek. 13:3; Dan. 7:15; (*g*) purpose, aim, 2 Cor. 12:18; Phil. 1:27; Eph. 4:23; Rev. 19:10; cf. Ezra 1:5; Ps. 78:8; Dan. 5:12; (*h*) the equivalent of the personal pronoun, used for emphasis and effect: 1st person, 1 Cor. 16:18; cf. Gen. 6:3; 2nd person, 2 Tim. 4:22; Philem. 25; cf. Ps. 139:7; 3rd person, 2 Cor. 7:13; cf. Isa. 40:13; (*i*) character, Luke 1:17; Rom. 1:4; cf. Num. 14:24; (*j*) moral qualities and activities: bad, as of bondage, as of a slave, Rom. 8:15; cf. Isa. 61:3; stupor, Rom. 11:8; cf. Isa. 29:10; timidity, 2 Tim. 1:7; cf. Josh. 5:1; good, as of adoption, i.e., liberty as of a son, Rom. 8:15; cf. Ps. 51:12; meekness, 1 Cor. 4:21; cf. Prov. 16:19; faith, 2 Cor. 4:13; quietness, 1 Pet. 3:4; cf. Prov. 14:29; (*k*) the Holy Spirit, e.g., Matt. 4:1 (see below); Luke 4:18; (*l*) 'the inward man' (an expression used only of the believer, Rom. 7:22; 2 Cor. 4:16; Eph. 3:16); the new life, Rom. 8:4–6, 10, 16; Heb. 12:9; cf. Ps. 51:10; (*m*) unclean spirits, demons, Matt. 8:16; Luke 4:33; 1 Pet. 3:19; cf. 1 Sam. 18:10; (*n*) angels, Heb. 1:14; cf. Acts 12:15; (*o*) divine gift for service, 1 Cor. 14:12, 32; (*p*) by metonymy, those who claim to be depositories of these gifts, 2 Thess. 2:2; 1 John 4:1–3; (*q*) the significance, as contrasted with the form, of words, or of a rite, John 6:63; Rom. 2:29; 7:6; 2 Cor. 3:6; (*r*) a vision, Rev. 1:10; 4:2; 17:3; 21:10."*

Notes: (1) For *phantasma*, rendered "spirit," Matt. 14:26; Mark 6:49, KJV, see APPARITION. (2) For the distinction between "spirit" and "soul," see under SOUL, last three paragraphs.

The Holy Spirit

The "Holy Spirit" is spoken of under various titles in the NT ("Spirit" and "Ghost" are renderings of the same word, *pneuma;* the advantage of the rendering "Spirit" is that it can always be used, whereas "Ghost" always requires the word "Holy" prefixed.) In the following list the omission of the definite article marks its omission in the original (concerning this see below): "Spirit, Matt. 22:43; Eternal Spirit, Heb. 9:14; the Spirit, Matt. 4:1; Holy Spirit, Matt. 1:18; the Holy Spirit, Matt. 28:19; the Spirit, the Holy, Matt. 12:32; the Spirit of promise, the Holy, Eph. 1:13; Spirit of God, Rom. 8:9; Spirit of (the) living God, 2 Cor. 3:3; the Spirit of God, 1 Cor. 2:11; the Spirit of our God, 1 Cor. 6:11; the Spirit of God, the Holy,

---

* From *Notes on Thessalonians,* by Hogg and Vine, pp. 204, 205.

Eph. 4:30; the Spirit of glory and of God, 1 Pet. 4:14; the Spirit of Him that raised up Jesus from the dead (i.e., God), Rom. 8:11; the Spirit of your Father, Matt. 10:20; the Spirit of His Son, Gal. 4:6; Spirit of (the) Lord, Acts 8:39; the Spirit of (the) Lord, Acts 5:9; (the) Lord, (the) Spirit, 2 Cor. 3:18; the Spirit of Jesus, Acts 16:7; Spirit of Christ, Rom. 8:9; the Spirit of Jesus Christ, Phil. 1:19; Spirit of adoption, Rom. 8:15; the Spirit of truth, John 14:17; the Spirit of life, Rom. 8:2; the Spirit of grace, Heb. 10:29."†

The use or absence of the article in the original where the "Holy Spirit" is spoken of cannot always be decided by grammatical rules, nor can the presence or absence of the article alone determine whether the reference is to the "Holy Spirit." Examples where the Person is meant when the article is absent are Matt. 22:43 (the article is used in Mark 12:36); Acts 4:25, RV (absent in some texts); 19:2, 6; Rom. 14:17; 1 Cor. 2:4; Gal. 5:25 (twice); 1 Pet. 1:2. Sometimes the absence is to be accounted for by the fact that *Pneuma* (like *Theos*) is substantially a proper name, e.g., in John 7:39. As a general rule the article is present where the subject of the teaching is the Personality of the Holy Spirit, e.g., John 14:26, where He is spoken of in distinction from the Father and the Son. See also 15:26 and cf. Luke 3:22.

In Gal. 3:3, in the phrase "having begun in the Spirit," it is difficult to say whether the reference is to the "Holy Spirit" or to the quickened spirit of the believer; that it possibly refers to the latter is not to be determined by the absence of the article, but by the contrast with "the flesh"; on the other hand, the contrast may be between the "Holy Spirit" who in the believer sets His seal on the perfect work of Christ, and the flesh which seeks to better itself by works of its own. There is no preposition before either noun, and if the reference is to the quickened spirit it cannot be dissociated from the operation of the "Holy Spirit." In Gal. 4:29 the phrase "after the Spirit" signifies "by supernatural power," in contrast to "after the flesh," i.e., "by natural power," and the reference must be to the "Holy Spirit"; so in 5:17.

The full title with the article before both *pneuma* and *hagios* (the "resumptive" use of the article), lit., "the Spirit the Holy," stresses the character of the Person, e.g., Matt. 12:32; Mark 3:29; 12:36; 13:11; Luke 2:26; 10:21 (RV); John 14:26; Acts 1:16; 5:3; 7:51; 10:44, 47; 13:2;

15:28; 19:6; 20:23, 28; 21:11; 28:25; Eph. 4:30; Heb. 3:7; 9:8; 10:15.

The Personality of the Spirit is emphasized at the expense of strict grammatical procedure in John 14:26; 15:26; 16:8, 13, 14, where the emphatic pronoun *ekeinos*, "He," is used of Him in the masculine, whereas the noun *pneuma* is neuter in Greek, while the corresponding word in Aramaic, the language in which our Lord probably spoke, is feminine (*rûchâ*, cf. Heb. *rûach*). The rendering "itself" in Rom. 8:16, 26, due to the Greek gender, is corrected to "Himself" in the RV.

The subject of the "Holy Spirit" in the NT may be considered as to His divine attributes; His distinct Personality in the Godhead; His operation in connection with the Lord Jesus in His birth, His life, His baptism, His death; His operations in the world; in the church; His having been sent at Pentecost by the Father and by Christ; His operations in the individual believer; in local churches; His operations in the production of Holy Scripture; His work in the world, etc.

SPIRITUAL

A. Adjective.

pneumatikos (πνευματικός, 4152) "always connotes the ideas of invisibility and of power. It does not occur in the Sept. nor in the Gospels; it is in fact an after-Pentecost word. In the NT it is used as follows: (*a*) the angelic hosts, lower than God but higher in the scale of being than man in his natural state, are 'spiritual hosts,' Eph. 6:12; (*b*) things that have their origin with God, and which, therefore, are in harmony with His character, as His law is, are 'spiritual,' Rom. 7:14; (*c*) 'spiritual' is prefixed to the material type in order to indicate that what the type sets forth, not the type itself, is intended, 1 Cor. 10:3, 4; (*d*) the purposes of God revealed in the gospel by the Holy Spirit, 1 Cor. 2:13a, and the words in which that revelation is expressed, are 'spiritual,' 13b, matching, or combining, spiritual things with spiritual words [or, alternatively, 'interpreting spiritual things to spiritual men,' see (*e*) below]; 'spiritual songs' are songs of which the burden is the things revealed by the Spirit, Eph. 5:19; Col. 3:16; 'spiritual wisdom and understanding' is wisdom in, and understanding of, those things, Col. 1:9; (*e*) men in Christ who walk so as to please God are 'spiritual,' Gal. 6:1; 1 Cor. 2:13b [but see (*d*) above], 15; 3:1; 14:37; (*f*) the whole company of those who believe in Christ is a 'spiritual house,' 1 Pet. 2:5a; (*g*) the blessings that accrue to regenerate men at this present time are called 'spiritualities,' Rom. 15:27; 1 Cor. 9:11; 'spiri-

---

† From *Notes on Galatians*, by Hogg and Vine, p. 193.

tual blessings,' Eph. 1:3; 'spiritual gifts,' Rom. 1:11; (h) the activities Godward of regenerate men are 'spiritual sacrifices,' 1 Pet. 2:5b; their appointed activities in the churches are also called 'spiritual gifts,' lit., 'spiritualities,' 1 Cor. 12:1; 14:1; (i) the resurrection body of the dead in Christ is 'spiritual,' i.e., such as is suited to the heavenly environment, 1 Cor. 15:44; (j) all that is produced and maintained among men by the operations of the Spirit of God is 'spiritual,' 1 Cor. 15:46. . . .

"The spiritual man is one who walks by the Spirit both in the sense of Gal. 5:16 and in that of 5:25, and who himself manifests the fruit of the Spirit in his own ways. . . .

"According to the Scriptures, the 'spiritual' state of soul is normal for the believer, but to this state all believers do not attain, nor when it is attained is it always maintained. Thus the apostle, in 1 Cor. 3:1–3, suggests a contrast between this spiritual state and that of the babe in Christ, i.e., of the man who because of immaturity and inexperience has not yet reached spirituality, and that of the man who by permitting jealousy, and the strife to which jealousy always leads, has lost it. The spiritual state is reached by diligence in the Word of God and in prayer; it is maintained by obedience and self-judgment. Such as are led by the Spirit are spiritual, but, of course, spirituality is not a fixed or absolute condition, it admits of growth; indeed growth in 'the grace and knowledge of our Lord and Savior Jesus Christ,' 2 Pet. 3:18, is evidence of true spirituality."*

B. Adverb.

pneumatikōs (πνευματικῶς, 4153), "spiritually," occurs in 1 Cor. 2:14, with the meaning as (j) above, and Rev. 11:8, with the meaning as in (c). Some mss. have it in 1 Cor. 2:13.¶

Notes: (1) In Rom. 8:6, the RV rightly renders the noun pneuma "(the mind) of the spirit," KJV, "spiritual (mind)." (2) In 1 Cor. 14:12 the plural of pneuma, "spirits," RV, marg., stands for "spiritual gifts" (text). (3) In 1 Pet. 2:2, the RV renders logikos "spiritual."

SPIT

1. ptuō (πτύω, 4429), "to spit," occurs in Mark 7:33; 8:23; John 9:6.¶ In the Sept., Num. 12:14.¶

2. emptuō (ἐμπτύω, 1716), "to spit upon" (en, "in," and No. 1), occurs in Matt. 26:67; 27:30; Mark 10:34; 14:65; 15:19; Luke 18:32.¶ In the Sept., Num. 12:14, in some texts; Deut. 25:9.¶

* From Notes on Galatians, by Hogg and Vine, pp. 308–319.

SPITEFULLY (ENTREAT)

hubrizō (ὑβρίζω, 5195), used transitively, denotes "to outrage, treat insolently"; "to entreat shamefully" in Matt. 22:6, RV (KJV, "spitefully"); so in Luke 18:32, RV; in Acts 14:5 (KJV, "use despitefully"); in 1 Thess. 2:2, KJV and RV; in Luke 11:45, "reproachest." See DESPITEFULLY, ENTREAT, REPROACH, SHAMEFULLY.¶

SPITTLE

ptusma (πτύσμα, 4427), akin to ptuō, "to spit," occurs in John 9:6.¶

SPOIL (Noun and Verb), SPOILING

A. Nouns.

1. skulon (σκῦλον, 4661), used in the plural, denotes "arms stripped from a foe"; "spoils" in Luke 11:22.¶

2. akrothinion (ἀκροθίνιον, 205), primarily "the top of a heap" (akros, "highest, top," and this, "a heap), hence "firstfruit offerings," and in war "the choicest spoils," Heb. 7:4.¶

3. harpagē (ἁρπαγή, 724), "pillage," is rendered "spoiling" in Heb. 10:34. See EXTORT, B, No. 1.

B. Verbs.

1. diarpazō (διαρπάζω, 1283), "to plunder," is found in Matt. 12:29, 2nd part (the 1st has harpazō, in the best texts), lit., "(then) he will completely (dia, intensive) spoil (his house)"; Mark 3:27 (twice).¶

2. harpazō (ἁρπάζω, 726), "to seize, snatch away," is rendered "spoil" in Matt. 12:29a (see No. 1). See CATCH, No. 1.

3. sulagōgeō (συλαγωγέω, 4812), "to carry off as spoil, lead captive" (sulē, "spoil," agō, "to lead"), is rendered "maketh spoil of" in Col. 2:8, RV (KJV, "spoil"), rather "carry you off as spoil." The false teacher, through his "philosophy and vain deceit," would carry them off as so much booty.¶

4. apekduō (ἀπεκδύω, 554), in the middle voice is translated "having spoiled" in Col. 2:15, KJV, RV, "having put off from Himself (the principalities and the powers)." These are regarded by some as the unsinning angels, because they are mentioned twice before in the Epistle (1:16; 2:10). It is also argued that the verb apekduō, rendered "having put off from Himself," in 2:15, is used in a somewhat different sense in 3:9. Such representations do not form a sufficiently cogent reason for regarding the principalities and the powers here mentioned as those of light, rather than those of darkness.

Others think that the reference is to the holy angels, which were in attendance at the giving of the Law (Acts 7:53; Gal. 3:19), and that

Christ wrought His work on the cross, without any such attendance; or, again, that, even apart from the Law and its circumstances, the Lord stripped Himself of those who usually ministered to Him, as, e.g., in the wilderness and in the garden of Gethsemane.

The exposition given by Lightfoot and others seems to be the right one. There is no doubt that Satan and his hosts gathered together to attack the soul of Christ, while He was enduring, in propitiatory sacrifice, the judgment due to our sins, and fulfilling the great work of redemption. There is an intimation of this in Ps. 22:21, "Save Me from the lion's mouth; yea, from the horns of the wild-oxen" (cf. vv. 12, 13). Doubtless the powers of darkness gathered against the Lord at that time, fiercely assaulting Him to the utmost of their power. He Himself had said, "This is your hour, and the power of darkness" (Luke 22:53). The metaphor of putting off from Himself these powers need not be pressed to the extent of regarding them as a garment clinging about Him. It seems to stand simply as a vivid description of His repulsion of their attack and of the power by which He completely overthrew them.

SPONGE

spongos (σπόγγος, 4699) was the medium by which vinegar was carried to the mouth of Christ on the cross, Matt. 27:48; Mark 15:36; John 19:29.¶

SPORTING

entruphaō (ἐντρυφάω, 1792) occurs in 2 Pet. 2:13 (RV, "revel").

SPOT (Noun and Verb)
A. Nouns.
1. *spilos* (σπῖλος, 4696), "a spot or stain," is used metaphorically (*a*) of moral blemish, Eph. 5:27; (*b*) of lascivious and riotous persons, 2 Pet. 2:13.¶

2. *spilas* (σπιλάς, 4694) is rendered "spots" in Jude 12, KJV: see ROCK, No. 2.

B. Verb.
spiloō (σπιλόω, 4695), akin to A, No. 1, is used in Jude 23, in the clause "hating even the garment spotted by the flesh," the garment representing that which, being brought into contact with the polluting element of the flesh, becomes defiled: see CLOTHING, No. 3 (last par.). See DEFILE, No. 4.

C. Adjective.
aspilos (ἄσπιλος, 784), "unspotted, unstained" (*a*, negative, and A), is used of a lamb, 1 Pet. 1:19; metaphorically, of keeping a commandment without alteration and in the fulfill-

ment of it, 1 Tim. 6:14; of the believer in regard to the world, Jas. 1:27, and free from all defilement in the sight of God, 2 Pet. 3:14.¶

Note: For *amōmos*, in Heb. 9:14, KJV, see BLEMISH, B.

SPREAD

1. *strōnnuō* or *strōnnumi* (στρωννύω, 4766), "to spread," is so rendered in Matt. 21:8, RV, twice; Mark 11:8, RV, once. See FURNISH.

2. *hupostrōnnuō* (ὑποστρωννύω, 5291), "to spread under" (*hupo*), of clothes, is used in Luke 19:36.¶

3. *dianemō* (διανέμω, 1268), "to distribute," is used in the passive voice in Acts 4:17, "spread," lit., "be spread about" (*dia*).¶ In the Sept., Deut. 29:26, "to assign" or "divide" (concerning the worship of other gods).¶

4. *diapherō* (διαφέρω, 1308), "to carry about, spread abroad": see PUBLISH, No. 2; for other meanings of the word see BETTER (be), No. 1.

5. *ekpetannumi* (ἐκπετάννυμι, 1600), "to spread out" (as a sail), is rendered "did I spread out" in Rom. 10:21, RV (KJV, "I have stretched forth").¶

Notes: (1) In Mark 1:28 and 1 Thess. 1:8, KJV, *exerchomai*, "to go out or forth" (RV), is rendered "to spread abroad." (2) In Mark 6:14, KJV, *ginomai*, "to become," with *phaneros*, "manifest," is translated "had spread abroad" (RV, "had become known"). (3) In 2 Cor. 8:18, the RV "*is spread*" (KJV, "*is*") represents nothing in the original. (4) For RV, "spread His tabernacle over," Rev. 7:15, see DWELL, No. 9. (5) For Mark 1:45, see BLAZE ABROAD.

SPRING (Noun and Verb)
A. Verbs.
1. *ginomai* (γίνομαι, 1096), "to become," is used in the best texts in Heb. 11:12, "sprang" (some have *gennaō*, in the passive voice, rendered in the same way).

2. *anatellō* (ἀνατέλλω, 393), "to arise," is rendered by the verb "to spring," or "spring up," in Matt. 4:16 and Heb. 7:14. See ARISE, No. 9.

3. *exanatellō* (ἐξανατέλλω, 1816), *ek* or *ex*, "out," and No. 2, is used of the "springing" up of seeds, Matt. 13:5; Mark 4:5 (No. 7 in v. 8).¶

4. *phuō* (φύω, 5453), used transitively, "to bring forth, produce," denotes, in the passive voice, "to spring up, grow," of seed, Luke 8:6, 8, KJV, "was sprung up" and "sprang up" (RV, "grew"); in the active voice, intransitively, in Heb. 12:15, of a root of bitterness. See GROW.¶

5. *sumphuō* (συμφύω, 4855), "to cause to grow together" (*sun*, "with," and No. 4), occurs

in Luke 8:7, RV, "grew with," KJV, "sprang up with."¶

6. *blastanō* (βλαστάνω, 985), "to sprout," is rendered "to spring up" in Matt. 13:26, of tare blades, and Mark 4:27, of seed. See BRING, A, No. 26, BUD.

7. *anabainō* (ἀναβαίνω, 305), "to go up," is rendered "sprang up" in Matt. 13:7, KJV, of thorns, and Mark 4:8, of seed (RV, "grew up").See GROW, No. 4.

8. *hallomai* (ἅλλομαι, 242), "to leap, spring," is rendered "springing up," of well water, in John 4:14, figurative of the Holy Spirit in the believer. See LEAP.

9. *eispēdaō* (εἰσπηδάω, 1530), "to spring" or "leap in," occurs in Acts 16:29, "sprang in."¶ In the Sept., Amos 5:19.¶

10. *ekpēdaō* (ἐκπηδάω, 1600a), "to spring forth," occurs in Acts 14:14, in the best texts. See RUN, *Note* (4).

B. Noun.

pēgē (πηγή, 4077) is rendered "springs" in 2 Pet. 2:17, RV: see FOUNTAIN.

Note: For *epiginomai*, Acts 28:13, see BLOW (verb).

SPRINKLE, SPRINKLING

A. Verb.

rhantizō (ῥαντίζω, 4472), "to sprinkle" (a later form of *rhainō*), is used in the active voice in Heb. 9:13, of "sprinkling" with blood the unclean, a token of the efficacy of the expiatory sacrifice of Christ, His blood signifying the giving up of His life in the shedding of His blood (cf. 9:22) under divine judgment upon sin (the voluntary act to be distinguished from that which took place after His death in the piercing of His side); so again in vv. 19, 21 (see B); in Heb. 10:22, passive voice, of the purging (on the ground of the same efficacy) of the hearts of believers from an evil conscience. This application of the blood of Christ is necessary for believers, in respect of their committal of sins, which on that ground receive forgiveness, 1 John 1:9. In Mark 7:4, the verb is found in the middle voice "in some ancient authorities" (RV marg.) instead of *baptizō*. In Rev. 19:13, the RV, "sprinkled" follows those texts which have *rhantizō* (marg., "some anc. auth. read 'dipped in.'" *baptō*; so Nestle's text).¶ This requires mention as a variant text in Rev. 19:13 under DIP.

B. Nouns.

1. *rhantismos* (ῥαντισμός, 4473), "sprinkling," akin to A, is used of the "sprinkling" of the blood of Christ, in Heb. 12:24 and 1 Pet. 1:2, an allusion to the use of the blood of sacrifices, appointed for Israel, typical of the sacrifice of Christ (see under A).¶

2. *proschusis* (πρόσχυσις, 4378), "a pouring or sprinkling upon," occurs in Heb. 11:28, of the "sprinkling" of the blood of the Passover lamb.¶

For SPUE see SPEW

SPY (Noun and Verb)

A. Nouns.

1. *enkathetos* (ἐγκάθετος, 1455), an adjective denoting "suborned to lie in wait" (*en*, "in," *kathiēmi*, "to send down"), is used as a noun in Luke 20:20, "spies."¶ In the Sept., Job. 19:12; 31:9.¶

2. *kataskopos* (κατάσκοπος, 2685) denotes "a spy" (*kata*, "down," signifying "closely," and *skopeō*, "to view"), Heb. 11:31.¶

B. Verb.

kataskopeō (κατασκοπέω, 2684), "to view closely" (akin to A, No. 2), "spy out, search out" with a view to overthrowing, is used in Gal. 2:4.¶ In the Sept., 2 Sam. 10:3; 1 Chron. 19:3.¶

For STABLISH see ESTABLISH

STAFF, STAVES

1. *rhabdos* (ῥάβδος, 4464), rendered "staff" or "staves" in Matt. 10:10, parallel passages, and Heb. 11:21: see ROD.

2. *xulon* (ξύλον, 3586), "wood," then, "anything made of wood," e.g., "a cudgel" or "staff," is rendered "staves" in Matt. 26:47, 55 and parallel passages. See STOCKS, TREE, WOOD.

For STAGGER see WAVER

STAIR

anabathmos (ἀναβαθμός, 304), "an ascent" (akin to *anabainō*, "to go up"), denotes "a flight of stairs," Acts 21:35, 40. These were probably the steps leading down from the castle of Antonia to the Temple. (See Josephus, *B.J.*, v., 5, 8.)¶ In the Sept., it is used, e.g., in the titles of the Songs of Ascents, Ps. 120–134.

For STALL see MANGER

STANCH

histēmi (ἵστημι, 2476), transitively, "to cause to stand," is used intransitively ("to stand still") in Luke 8:44, translated "stanched." See STAND.

STAND (Noun and Verb), STANDING, STOOD

A. Noun.

luchnia (λυχνία, 3087), "a lampstand," is translated "stand" in Matt. 5:15 and parallel passages (KJV, "candlestick"). See LAMPSTAND.

B. Verbs.

1. *histēmi* (ἵστημι, 2476), (*a*) transitively, denotes "to cause to stand, to set"; in the passive voice, "to be made to stand," e.g., Matt. 2:9, lit., "was made to stand"; so Luke 11:18; 19:8 (Col. 4:12 in some mss.); in Rev. 13:1 the RV follows the best texts, "he stood" (not as KJV, "I stood"); the reference is to the Dragon. In the middle voice, "to take one's stand, place oneself," e.g., Rev. 18:15; (*b*) intransitively, in the 2nd aorist and perfect active, "to stand, stand by, stand still," e.g., Matt. 6:5; 20:32, "stood still"; in Luke 6:8, "stand forth" and "stood forth"; metaphorically, "to stand firm," John 8:44 (negatively), in the truth (see No. 7); Rom. 5:2, in grace; 1 Cor. 15:1, in the gospel; Rom. 11:20, "by thy faith," RV; 2 Cor. 1:24, "by faith" (marg., "by your faith"); of steadfastness, 1 Cor. 7:37; Eph. 6:11, 13, 14; Col. 4:12 [some mss. have the passive, see (*a*)]. See APPOINT, ESTABLISH, SET.

2. *anistēmi* (ἀνίστημι, 450), "to raise," intransitively, "to rise," is translated "to stand up" in Matt. 12:41, RV; Mark 14:60; Luke 4:16; 10:25; Acts 1:15; 5:34; 10:26; 11:28; 13:16; in 14:10, "stand upright." See ARISE, No. 1.

3. *ephistēmi* (ἐφίστημι, 2186) (*epi*, "upon," and No. 1), used intransitively, denotes "to stand upon or by, be present," Luke 2:9 and Acts 12:7, "stood by," RV (KJV, "came upon"); Luke 4:39, "stood over"; 24:4 and Acts 23:11, "stood by"; Acts 10:17, "stood"; 22:13, "standing by (me)," RV; so v. 20, KJV and RV. See ASSAULT, COME, No. 27, HAND (AT), B *Note* (2), INSTANT, PRESENT.

4. *paristēmi* (παρίστημι, 3936), intransitively, denotes "to stand by or beside" (*para*, "by," and No. 1), Mark 14:47, 69, 70; 15:35, 39 (RV, "stood by"); Luke 19:24; John 18:22; 19:26; Acts 1:10; 9:39; 23:2, 4; 27:23; in 27:24, "stand before"; in 4:10, "doth . . . stand here"; in Luke 1:19, "stand"; Rom. 14:10, "we shall . . . stand before" (middle voice); 2 Tim. 4:17, RV, "stood by" (KJV, " . . . with"). See COMMEND, No. 4.

5. *periistēmi* (περιίστημι, 4026), intransitively, "to stand around" (*peri*), is so used in John 11:42; Acts 25:7. See AVOID, No. 4.

6. *sunistēmi* (συνίστημι, 4921), intransitively, denotes "to stand with" (*sun*), Luke 9:32; for 2 Pet. 3:5, KJV, "standing," see COMPACTED,

No. 1: for other meanings see APPROVE, A, No. 2.

7. *stēkō* (στήκω, 4739), a late present tense from *hestēka*, the perfect of *histēmi*, is used (*a*) literally, Mark 3:31; 11:25; John 1:26, in the best texts (in some texts Rev. 12:4); (*b*) figuratively, Rom. 14:4, where the context indicates the meaning "standeth upright" rather than that of acquittal; of "standing fast," 1 Cor. 16:13, "in the faith," i.e., by adherence to it; Gal. 5:1, in freedom from legal bondage; Phil. 1:27, "in one spirit"; Phil. 4:1 and 1 Thess. 3:8, "in the Lord," i.e., in the willing subjection to His authority; 2 Thess. 2:15, in the apostle's teaching; some mss. have it in John 8:44, the most authentic have *histēmi*, RV, "stood" (KJV, "abode").¶

8. *menō* (μένω, 3306), "to abide, remain," is rendered "might stand," in Rom. 9:11, of the purpose of God, i.e., might abide for the permanent recognition of its true character. See ABIDE, No. 1.

9. *kukloō* (κυκλόω, 2944), "stood round about," Acts 14:20: see COMPASS, No. 2.

Notes: (1) In Mark 3:3, *egeirō*, "to raise," followed by the phrase *eis to meson*, "into the midst," is translated "stand forth." (2) In 2 Tim. 4:16, KJV, *paraginomai* (in some texts, *sumparaginomai*), "to come up to assist," is rendered "stood with (me)," RV, "took (my) part." (3) In Heb. 9:8, RV, "is . . . standing" (KJV, "was . . . standing") represents the phrase *echō*, "to have," *stasis*, "a standing," lit., "has a standing." (4) For "stand . . . in jeopardy" see DANGER.

STAR

1. *astēr* (ἀστήρ, 792), "a star," Matt. 2:2–10; 24:29; Mark 13:25; 1 Cor. 15:41; Rev. 6:13; 8:10–12; 9:1; 12:1, 4, is used metaphorically, (*a*) of Christ, as "the morning star," figurative of the approach of the day when He will appear as the "sun of righteousness," to govern the earth in peace, an event to be preceded by the rapture of the Church, Rev. 2:28; 22:16, the promise of the former to the overcomer being suggestive of some special personal interest in Himself and His authority; (*b*) of the angels of the seven churches, Rev. 1:16, 20; 2:1; 3:1; (*c*) of certain false teachers, described as "wandering stars," Jude 13, as if the "stars," intended for light and guidance, became the means of deceit by irregular movements.¶

2. *astron* (ἄστρον, 798), practically the same as No. 1, is used (*a*) in the sing. in Acts 7:43, "the star of the god Rephan," RV, the symbol or "figure," probably of Saturn, worshiped as a god, apparently the same as Chiun in Amos 5:26 (Rephan being the Egyptian deity corre-

sponding to Saturn, Chiun the Assyrian); (b) in the plur., Luke 21:25; Acts 27:20; Heb. 11:12.¶

For **STATE** see **ESTATE,** *Notes*

For **STATURE** see **AGE,** A, No. 3

For **STAVES** see **STAFF**

STAY

1. *katechō* (κατέχω, 2722), "to hold fast, hold back," is used in the sense of detaining in Luke 4:42, "would have stayed (Him)," RV. See HOLD.

2. *epechō* (ἐπέχω, 1907) has the meaning "to wait in a place, to stay," in Acts 19:22. See HEED, HOLD, MARK.

3. *kōluō* (κωλύω, 2967), "to hinder," is rendered "stayed" in Acts 27:43, RV (KJV, "kept"); so in 2 Pet. 2:16, RV (KJV, "forbad"). See HINDER.

For **STEADFAST** see **STEDFAST**

STEAL

kleptō (κλέπτω, 2813), "to steal," akin to *kleptēs*, "a thief" (cf. Eng., "kleptomania"), occurs in Matt. 6:19, 20; 19:18; 27:64; 28:13; Mark 10:19; Luke 18:20; John 10:10; Rom. 2:21 (twice); 13:9; Eph. 4:28 (twice).¶

STEDFAST, STEDFASTLY, STEDFASTNESS

A. Adjectives.

1. *bebaios* (βέβαιος, 949), "firm, secure" (akin to *bainō*, "to go"), is translated "steadfast" in 2 Cor. 1:7; Heb. 2:2; 3:14, KJV (RV, "firm"); 6:19. See FIRM, FORCE, SURE.

2. *hedraios* (ἑδραῖος, 1476) primarily denotes "seated" (*hedra*, "a seat"); hence, "steadfast," metaphorical of moral fixity, 1 Cor. 7:37; 15:58; Col. 1:23, RV (KJV, "settled").¶

3. *stereos* (στερεός, 4731), firm, is rendered "steadfast" in 1 Pet. 5:9. See FIRM, No. 2.

B. Nouns.

1. *stereōma* (στερέωμα, 4733), primarily "a support, foundation," denotes "strength, steadfastness," Col. 2:5.¶ In the Sept., in Gen. 1:6, and Ezek. 1:22, it is used of the firmament, which was believed to be a solid canopy. The corresponding Heb. word *rāqîa'* means "expanse," from *rāqa'*, "to spread out."

2. *stērigmos* (στηριγμός, 4740), "a setting firmly, supporting," then "fixedness, steadfastness" (akin to *stērizō*, "to establish"), is used in 2 Pet. 3:17.¶

Note: For STEADFASTLY see BEHOLD, No. 10,

CONTINUE, No. 9, FASTEN, No. 1, LOOK, No. 15, SET, No. 19.

STEEP

krēmnos (κρημνός, 2911), "a steep bank" (akin to *kremannumi*, "to hang"), occurs in Matt. 8:32; Mark 5:13; Luke 8:33, RV, "the steep" (KJV, "a steep place").¶ In the Sept., 2 Chron. 25:12.¶

For **STEERSMAN** see **GOVERNOR,** B, *Note*

STEP (Noun and Verb)

A. Noun.

ichnos (ἴχνος, 2487), "a footstep, a track," is used metaphorically of the "steps" (a) of Christ's conduct, 1 Pet. 2:21; (b) of Abraham's faith, Rom. 4:12; (c) of identical conduct in carrying on the work of the gospel, 2 Cor. 12:18.¶

B. Verb.

katabainō (καταβαίνω, 2597), "to go, or come, down," is translated "steppeth down" in John 5:7. See COME, No. 19.

Note: Many ancient authorities have the passage in the KJV in John 5:4, which contains *embainō*, rendered "stepped in." See COME, No. 21.

STERN

prumna (πρύμνα, 4403), the feminine form of the adjective *prumnos*, "hindmost," is rendered "stern" in Acts 27:29; and in the RV in v. 41 and Mark 4:38. See PART, A, *Note* (2).¶

STEWARD, STEWARDSHIP

A. Nouns.

1. *oikonomos* (οἰκονόμος, 3623) primarily denoted "the manager of a household or estate" (*oikos*, "a house," *nemō*, "to arrange"), "a steward" (such were usually slaves or freedmen), Luke 12:42; 16:1, 3, 8; 1 Cor. 4:2; Gal. 4:2, RV (KJV, "governors"); in Rom. 16:23, the "treasurer" (RV) of a city (see CHAMBERLAIN, *Note*); it is used metaphorically, in the wider sense, of a "steward" in general, (a) of preachers of the gospel and teachers of the Word of God, 1 Cor. 4:1; (b) of elders or bishops in churches, Titus 1:7; (c) of believers generally, 1 Pet. 4:10.¶

2. *epitropos* (ἐπίτροπος, 2012) is rendered "steward" in Matt. 20:8; Luke 8:3: see GUARDIAN.

3. *oikonomia* (οἰκονομία, 3622) is rendered "stewardship" in Luke 16:2, 3, 4, and in the RV in 1 Cor. 9:17: see DISPENSATION.

B. Verb.

oikonomeō (οἰκονομέω, 3621), akin to A, Nos. 1 and 3, signifies "to be a house steward," Luke 16:2.¶ In the Sept., Ps. 112:5.¶

STICK

phruganon (φρύγανον, 5434) denotes "a dry stick" (from *phrugō*, "to parch"); in the plural, "brushwood," Acts 28:3.¶

STICK FAST

ereidō (ἐρείδω, 2043), primarily "to prop, fix firmly," is used intransitively in Acts 27:41 of a ship driving ashore, RV, "struck."¶

STIFFNECKED

sklērotrachēlos (σκληροτράχηλος, 4644), from *sklēros*, "harsh, hard," *trachēlos*, "a neck," is used metaphorically in Acts 7:51.¶

STILL (Verb)

phimoō (φιμόω, 5392), in the passive voice, is rendered "be still" in Mark 4:39: see MUZZLE.

STILL (Adverb)

eti (ἔτι, 2089), "yet, as yet, still," is translated "still" in the RV in 1 Cor. 12:31; 2 Cor. 1:10; Gal. 1:10 and 5:11; KJV and RV in Rev. 22:11 (four times), where the word indicates the permanent character, condition and destiny of the unrighteous and the filthy, the righteous and the holy (for the verbs see the RV); in John 11:30, the best mss. have the word; so RV (KJV omits).

Note: For combinations see ABIDE, IGNORANCE, B, No. 1, STAND.

For STING see GOAD

STINK

ozō (ὄζω, 3605), "to emit a smell" (cf. Eng., "ozone"), occurs in John 11:39.¶ In the Sept., Ex. 8:14.¶

STIR, STIR UP (Noun and Verb)

A. Noun.

tarachos (τάραχος, 5017), akin to *tarachē*, "trouble," and *tarassō*, "to trouble," is rendered "stir" in Acts 12:18; 19:23.¶

B. Verbs.

1. *anazōpureō* (ἀναζωπυρέω, 329) denotes "to kindle afresh," or "keep in full flame" (*ana*, "up," or "again," *zōos*, "alive," *pur*, "fire"), and is used metaphorically in 2 Tim. 1:6, where "the gift of God" is regarded as a fire capable of dying out through neglect.¶ The verb was in common use in the vernacular of the time.

2. *epegeirō* (ἐπεγείρω, 1892), "stirred up" in Acts 14:2. See RAISE.

3. *diegeirō* (διεγείρω, 1326), "stir up" in 2 Pet. 1:13; 3:1: see ARISE, No. 4.

4. *seiō* (σείω, 4579), "to move to and fro," is rendered "was stirred" in Matt. 21:10, RV (KJV, "was moved"). See MOVE, QUAKE, SHAKE.

5. *anaseiō* (ἀνασείω, 383) primarily denotes "to shake back or out, move to and fro"; then, "to stir up," used metaphorically in Mark 15:11, RV, "stirred . . . up" (KJV, "moved"), and Luke 3:14; 23:5.¶

6. *saleuō* (σαλεύω, 4531), "stirred up" in Acts 17:13: see SHAKE.

7. *parotrunō* (παροτρύνω, 3951), from *para*, used intensively, beyond measure, and *otrunō*, "to urge on, rouse," occurs in Acts 13:50, "stirred up."¶

8. *sunkineō* (συγκινέω, 4787), "to move together" (*sun*, "together," *kineō*, "to move"), "to stir up, excite," is used metaphorically in Acts 6:12.¶

9. *suncheō* (συνχέω, 4797), "to pour together," is used metaphorically in Acts 21:27, "stirred up." See CONFOUND, B, No. 1.

10. *paroxunō* (παροξύνω, 3947), "stirred" in Acts 17:16: see PROVOKE, No. 2.

11. *erethizō* (ἐρεθίζω, 2042), "hath stirred" in 2 Cor. 9:2, RV. See PROVOKE, No. 3.

12. *anastatoō* (ἀναστατόω, 387), "to excite, unsettle" (akin to *anistēmi*, "to raise up," and *anastasis*, "a raising"), is used (*a*) of "stirring up" to sedition, and tumult, Acts 17:6, "turned . . . upside down"; 21:38, RV, "stirred up to sedition," KJV, "madest an uproar"; (*b*) "to upset" by false teaching, Gal. 5:12, RV, "unsettle" (KJV, "trouble").¶

Note: In Acts 24:12, *poieō*, "to make," with *epistasis*, "a stopping" (in some texts *episustasis*), signifies "to collect" (a crowd), KJV, "raising up (the people)," RV, "stirring up (a crowd)." See COME, *Note* (9).

For STOCK see KIND

STOCKS

xulon (ξύλον, 3586), "wood," is used of "stocks" in Acts 16:24. See STAFF, TREE, WOOD.

STOMACH

stomachos (στόμαχος, 4751), properly "a mouth, an opening," akin to *stoma*, "a mouth," denotes "the stomach" in 1 Tim. 5:23.¶

STONE (Noun, Verb, and Adjective)

A. Nouns.

1. *lithos* (λίθος, 3037) is used (I) literally, of (*a*) the "stones" of the ground, e.g., Matt. 4:3, 6; 7:9; (*b*) "tombstones," e.g., Matt. 27:60, 66; (*c*) "building stones," e.g., Matt. 21:42; (*d*) "a

millstone," Luke 17:2; cf. Rev. 18:21 (see MILL-STONE); (e) the "tables (or tablets)" of the Law, 2 Cor. 3:7; (f) "idol images," Acts 17:29; (g) the "treasures" of commercial Babylon, Rev. 18:12, 16; (II) metaphorically, of (a) Christ, Rom. 9:33; 1 Pet. 2:4, 6, 8; (b) believers, 1 Pet. 2:5; (c) spiritual edification by scriptural teaching, 1 Cor. 3:12; (d) the adornment of the foundations of the wall of the spiritual and heavenly Jerusalem, Rev. 21:19; (e) the adornment of the seven angels in Rev. 15:6, RV (so the best texts; some have *linon*, "linen," KJV); (f) the adornment of religious Babylon, Rev. 17:4; (III) figuratively, of Christ, Rev. 4:3; 21:11, where "light" stands for "Light-giver" (*phōstēr*).

2. *psēphos* (ψῆφος, 5586), "a smooth stone, a pebble," worn smooth as by water, or polished (akin to *psaō*, "to rub"), denotes (a) by metonymy, a vote (from the use of "pebbles" for this purpose; cf. *psēphizō*, "to count"), Acts 26:10, RV (KJV, "voice"); (b) a (white) "stone" to be given to the overcomer in the church at Pergamum, Rev. 2:17 (twice); a white "stone" was often used in the social life and judicial customs of the ancients; festal days were noted by a white "stone," days of calamity by a black; in the courts a white "stone" indicated acquittal, a black condemnation. A host's appreciation of a special guest was indicated by a white "stone" with the name or a message written on it; this is probably the allusion here.¶

Note: In John 1:42 *petros* stands for the proper name, Peter, as the RV (KJV, "a stone"; marg., "Peter"); *petros* denotes "a piece of a rock, a detached stone or boulder," in contrast to *petra*, "a mass of rock." See ROCK.

B. Verbs.

1. *lithoboleō* (λιθοβολέω, 3036), "to pelt with stones" (A, No. 1, and *ballō*, "to throw"), "to stone to death," occurs in Matt. 21:35; 23:37; Luke 13:34 (John 8:5 in some mss.: see No. 2); Acts 7:58, 59; 14:5; Heb. 12:20.¶

2. *lithazō* (λιθάζω, 3034), "to stone," virtually equivalent to No. 1, but not stressing the casting, occurs in John 8:5 (in the most authentic mss.); 10:31–33; 11:8; Acts 5:26; 14:19; 2 Cor. 11:25; Heb. 11:37.¶

3. *katalithazō* (καταλιθάζω, 2642), an intensive form of No. 2, "to cast stones at," occurs in Luke 20:6.¶

C. Adjective.

lithinos (λίθινος, 3035), "of stone" (akin to A, No. 1), occurs in John 2:6; 2 Cor. 3:3; Rev. 9:20.¶

For **STONY** see **ROCKY**

STOOP

1. *kuptō* (κύπτω, 2955), "to bow the head, stoop down," occurs in Mark 1:7; John 8:6, 8.¶

2. *parakuptō* (παρακύπτω, 3879) is rendered "to stoop down" in Luke 24:12; John 20:5, 11, RV, "stooping and looking in": see LOOK, No. 10.

STOP

1. *phrassō* (φράσσω, 5420), "to fence in" (akin to *phragmos*, "a fence"), "close, stop," is used (a) metaphorically, in Rom. 3:19, of "preventing" all excuse from Jew and Gentile, as sinners; in 2 Cor. 11:10, lit., "this boasting shall not be stopped to me"; passive voice in both; (b) physically, of the mouths of lions, Heb. 11:33 (active voice).¶

2. *sunechō* (συνέχω, 4912), "to hold together," is rendered "stopped (their ears)" in Acts 7:57. See HOLD.

3. *epistomizō* (ἐπιστομίζω, 1993), "to stop the mouth," Titus 1:11: see MOUTH, B.¶

STORE (Verb)

1. *thēsaurizō* (θησαυρίζω, 2343), "to lay up, store up," is rendered "in store" (lit., "storing"), with a view to help a special case of need, 1 Cor. 16:2; said of the heavens and earth in 2 Pet. 3:7, RV, "have been stored up (for fire)," marg., "stored (with fire)," KJV, "kept in store (reserved unto fire)." See LAY, No. 17, TREASURE.

2. *apothēsaurizō* (ἀποθησαυρίζω, 597), "to treasure up, store away" (*apo*), is used in 1 Tim. 6:19, of "laying up in store" a good foundation for the hereafter by being rich in good works.¶

For **STOREHOUSE, STORECHAMBER**, see **CHAMBER**

STORM

lailaps (λαῖλαψ, 2978), "a hurricane, whirlwind," is rendered "storm" in Mark 4:37; Luke 8:23; 2 Pet. 2:17, RV (KJV, "tempest"). See TEMPEST.¶

STORY

tristegos (τρίστεγος, 5152), an adjective denoting "of three stories" (*treis*, "three," *stegē*, "a roof"), occurs in Acts 20:9 (with *oikēma*, "a dwelling," understood), RV, "the third story" (KJV, "the third loft").¶

STRAIGHT

A. Adjectives.

1. *euthus* (εὐθύς, 2117), "direct, straight, right," is translated "straight," figuratively, of

the paths of the Lord, Matt. 3:3; Mark 1:3; Luke 3:4; in v. 5 of the rectification of the crooked, with reference to moral transformation; in Acts 9:11, the name of a street in Damascus, still one of the principal thoroughfares. See RIGHT.

2. *orthos* (ὀρθός, 3717), used of height, denotes "upright," Acts 14:10; of line of direction, figuratively, said of paths of righteousness, Heb. 12:13.¶

B. Verbs.

1. *euthunō* (εὐθύνω, 2116), akin to A, No. 1, is used of the directing of a ship by the steersman, Jas. 3:4 (see GOVERNOR, B, *Note*); metaphorically, of making "straight" the way of the Lord, John 1:23.¶

2. *anorthoō* (ἀνορθόω, 461), "to set up, make straight": see LIFT, No. 6.

For **STRAIGHT COURSE,** see **COURSE,** B, *Note* (1)

For **STRAIGHTWAY** see **FORTHWITH,** Nos. 1, 2, 3, and **IMMEDIATELY,** No. 1

STRAIN OUT

diülizō (διϋλίζω, 1368), primarily denotes "to strain thoroughly" (*dia*, "through," intensive, *hulizō*, "to strain"), then, "to strain out," as through a sieve or strainer, as in the case of wine, so as to remove the unclean midge, Matt. 23:24, RV (KJV, "strain at").¶ In the Sept., Amos 6:6.¶

For the Adjective **STRAIT** see **NARROW**

STRAIT (be in a), STRAITENED

1. *sunechō* (συνέχω, 4912), "to hold together, constrain," is translated "I am in a strait" in Phil. 1:23 (passive voice), i.e., being restricted on both sides, under a pressure which prevents a definite choice; so in Luke 12:50, "(how) am I straitened," i.e., pressed in. See CONSTRAIN, A, No. 3.

2. *stenochōreō* (στενοχωρέω, 4729), "to be pressed for room" (*stenos*, "narrow," *chōros*, "a space"), is rendered "to be straitened" in 2 Cor. 4:8, RV (KJV, "distressed"); 6:12 (twice). See ANGUISH, B, No. 1.¶

3. *thlibō* (θλίβω, 2346), for which see AFFLICT, No. 4, is used in the perfect participle passive of "a narrowed way," in Matt. 7:14, RV, "straitened," KJV, "narrow," of the way "that leadeth unto life," i.e., hemmed in like a narrow gorge between rocks.

STRAITEST

akribestatos (ἀκριβέστατος, 196), the superlative degree of *akribēs*, "accurate, exact" (cf. *akribōs*, see ACCURATELY and associated words there), occurs in Acts 26:5, "the straitest (sect)," RV (KJV, "most straitest").¶

STRAITLY

Notes: (1) For *polla*, KJV, "straitly" in Mark 3:12; 5:43, see MUCH (RV). (2) In Acts 4:17 some mss. have *apeilē*, "a threat," with *apeilō* (middle voice), lit., "let us threaten them with a threat," KJV, "let us straitly threaten"; the best texts omit the noun (so RV). Moulton and Milligan (*Vocab.*), arguing for the presence of the noun, consider that it "clearly reflects the literal rendering of a Semitic original reported to Luke from an eye-witness—was it Paul?" (3) A similar construction, *parangellō* with the noun *parangelia*, occurs in Acts 5:28, "we straitly charged you," lit., "we charged you with a charge." See CHARGE, A, No. 6. (4) For *embrimaomai*, KJV, "charge straitly" (RV, "strictly") in Matt. 9:30; Mark 1:43, see CHARGE, C, No. 4.

For **STRAKE,** Acts 27:17, KJV (RV, "lowered"), see **LET DOWN,** No. 2.

STRANGE

A. Adjectives.

1. *xenos* (ξένος, 3581) denotes (*a*) "foreign, alien," Acts 17:18, of gods; Heb. 13:9, of doctrines; (*b*) "unusual," 1 Pet. 4:12, 2nd part, of the fiery trial of persecution (for 1st part, see B). See STRANGER.

2. *allotrios* (ἀλλότριος, 245) denotes (*a*) "belonging to another" (*allos*), see MAN'S, *Note* (1); (*b*) "alien, foreign, strange," Acts 7:6; Heb. 11:9, KJV, RV, "(a *land*) not his own." See ALIEN, STRANGER.

3. *paradoxos* (παράδοξος, 3861), "contrary to received opinion" (*para*, "beside," *doxa*, "opinion"; Eng. "paradox," "-ical"), is rendered "strange things" in Luke 5:26.¶

4. *exō* (ἔξω, 1845), outside, is rendered "strange" in Acts 26:11, KJV: see FOREIGN.

Note: In 1 Cor. 14:21 (1st part), RV, *heteroglōssos*, signifying "of a different tongue" (*heteros*, "another," *glōssa*, "a tongue") is translated "of strange (KJV, other) tongues."¶

B. Verb.

xenizō (ξενίζω, 3579) denotes "to think something strange," 1 Pet. 4:4, 12, passive voice, i.e., "they are surprised," and "be (not) surprised"; in Acts 17:20, the present participle, active, is rendered "strange," i.e., "surprising." See ENTERTAIN, LODGE.

STRANGER

A. Adjectives (used as nouns).

1. *xenos* (ξένος, 3581) "strange" (see No. 1 above), denotes "a stranger, foreigner," Matt. 25:35, 38, 43, 44; 27:7; Acts 17:21; Eph. 2:12, 19; Heb. 11:13; 3 John 5.

2. *allotrios* (ἀλλότριος, 245), "strangers," Matt. 17:25, 26; John 10:5 (twice): see No. 2, above.

3. *allogenēs* (ἀλλογενής, 241) (*allos*, "another," *genos*, "a race") occurs in Luke 17:18, of a Samaritan. Moulton and Milligan illustrate the use of the word by the inscription on the Temple barrier, "let no foreigner enter within the screen and enclosure surrounding the sanctuary"; according to Mommsen this inscription was cut by the Romans: cf. PARTITION.¶

Notes: (1) For *paroikos*, in KJV, see SOJOURN, B, No. 1. For *parepidēmos*, in KJV, see PILGRIM. (2) The pronoun *heteros*, "other," is translated "strangers" in 1 Cor. 14:21 (2nd part), RV (KJV, "other"); cf. STRANGE, A, Note.

B. Verb.

xenodocheō (ξενοδοχέω, 3580), "to receive strangers" (*xenos*, No. 1, above, and *dechomai*, "to receive"), occurs in 1 Tim. 5:10, RV, "(if) she hath used hospitality to strangers," KJV, "(if) she have lodged strangers."¶

Note: For *epidēmeō*, in KJV, see SOJOURNER, A, No. 2. For *paroikeō*, in KJV, see SOJOURN, A, No. 1.

C. Noun.

philoxenia (φιλοξενία, 5381), "love of strangers," occurs in Rom. 12:13, "hospitality," and Heb. 13:2, RV, "to show love unto strangers," KJV, "to entertain strangers." See ENTERTAIN, Note.¶

Note: For *paroikia* in Acts 13:17, see SOJOURN, C.

STRANGLED

pniktos (πνικτός, 4156), from *pnigō*, "to choke," occurs in Acts 15:20, 29; 21:25, of the flesh of animals killed by strangling, without shedding their blood (see, e.g., Lev. 17:13, 14).¶

For STRAWED see FURNISH and SCATTER, No. 2

For STREAM see RIVER

STREET

1. *plateia* (πλατεῖα, 4113), grammatically the feminine of *platus*, "broad," is used as a noun (*hodos*, "a way," being understood, i.e., "a broad way"), "a street," Matt. 6:5; 12:19 (in some texts, Mark 6:56); Luke 10:10; 13:26; 14:21; Acts 5:15; Rev. 11:8; 21:21; 22:2.¶

2. *amphodon* (ἄμφοδον, 296), properly "a way around" (*amphi*, "around," *hodos*, "a way"), occurs in Mark 11:4, RV, "the open street" (KJV, "where two ways met").¶

Note: For *rhumē*, see LANE. For *agora*, see MARKET.

STRENGTH, STRENGTHEN

A. Nouns.

1. *dunamis* (δύναμις, 1411) is rendered "strength" in the RV and KJV of Rev. 1:16; elsewhere the RV gives the word its more appropriate meaning "power," for KJV, "strength," 1 Cor. 15:56; 2 Cor. 1:8; 12:9; Heb. 11:11; Rev. 3:8; 12:10. See ABILITY, No. 1, POWER, No. 1.

2. *ischus* (ἰσχύς, 2479), "ability, strength," is rendered "strength" in Mark 12:30, 33; Luke 10:27; in Rev. 5:12, KJV (RV, "might"). See ABILITY, No. 2, MIGHT.

3. *kratos* (κράτος, 2904), "force, might," is rendered "strength" in Luke 1:51, RV and KJV; RV, "strength" (KJV, "power") in Eph. 1:19 and 6:10. See DOMINION, No. 1, POWER, No. 4.

Note: In Rev. 17:13, KJV, *exousia*, "freedom of action," is rendered "strength" (RV, "authority").

B. Verbs.

1. *dunamoō* (δυναμόω, 1412), "to strengthen," occurs in Col. 1:11, and in the best texts in Heb. 11:34, "were made strong" (some have No. 2); some have it in Eph. 6:10 (the best have No. 2).¶ In the Sept., Ps. 52:7; 68:28; Eccl. 10:10; Dan. 9:27.¶

2. *endunamoō* (ἐνδυναμόω, 1743), "to make strong," is rendered "increased... in strength" in Acts 9:22; "to strengthen" in Phil. 4:13; 2 Tim. 2:1, RV, "be strengthened"; 4:17. See ENABLE, STRONG, B.

3. *ischuō* (ἰσχύω, 2480), akin to A, No. 2, "to have strength," is so rendered in Mark 5:4, RV (KJV, "could"); in Luke 16:3, RV, "I have not strength to" (KJV, "I cannot"). See AVAIL.

4. *enischuō* (ἐνισχύω, 1765), akin to A, No. 2, a strengthened form of No. 3, is used in Luke 22:43 and Acts 9:19.¶

5. *krataioō* (κραταιόω, 2901), "to strengthen," is rendered "to be strengthened" in Eph. 3:16. See STRONG, B.

6. *sthenoō* (σθενόω, 4599), from *sthenos*, "strength," occurs in 1 Pet. 5:10, in a series of future tenses, according to the best texts, thus constituting divine promises.¶

Notes: (1) For *ischuō*, Heb. 9:17, see AVAIL. (2) For *stērizō*, Luke 22:32, see ESTABLISH, No. 1. (3) For *stereoō*, Acts 3:7, see ESTABLISH, No. 2. (4) *Epistērizō* is found in some texts in Acts

18:23, KJV, "strengthening." See CONFIRM, A, No. 2, ESTABLISH, No. 1. (5) For "without strength," Rom. 5:6, KJV, see WEAK.

STRETCH

1. *ekteinō* (ἐκτείνω, 1614), "to stretch out or forth," is so rendered in Matt. 12:13 (twice), 49; 14:31; 26:51; Mark 3:5 (twice); Luke 6:10; in Matt. 8:3; Mark 1:41 and Luke 5:13, RV (KJV, "put forth"); Luke 22:53; John 21:18; Acts 4:30; 26:1. For Acts 27:30 see LAY, No. 13.¶

2. *epekteinō* (ἐπεκτείνω, 1901), an intensive form of No. 1 (*epi*, "forth"), is used in Phil. 3:13, RV, "stretching forward" (KJV, "reaching forth"), a metaphor probably from the foot race (rather than the chariot race), so Lightfoot, who quotes Bengel's paraphrase, "the eye goes before and draws on the hand, the hand goes before and draws on the foot."¶

3. *huperekteinō* (ὑπερκτείνω, 5239), "to stretch out beyond" (*huper*, "over," and No. 1), occurs in 2 Cor. 10:14, RV, "we stretch (not) . . . overmuch" (KJV, " . . . beyond *our measure*").¶

Note: For *ekpetannumi*, Rom. 10:21, see SPREAD, No. 5. For *epiballō*, Acts 12:1, see PUT, No. 8.

STRICKEN (in years)

probainō (προβαίνω, 4260), "to go forward," is used metaphorically of age, in Luke 1:7, 18, with the phrases "in their (her) days," translated "well stricken in years" (see marg.); in 2:36, "of a great age" (marg., "advanced in many days"). See GO, No. 20.

For STRICT, RV, see MANNER, A, No. 5. For STRICTLY, RV, see STRAITLY

STRIFE

1. *eris* (ἔρις, 2054), "strife, contention," is the expression of "enmity," Rom. 1:29, RV, "strife" (KJV, "debate"); 13:13; 1 Cor. 1:11, "contentions" (RV and KJV); 3:3; 2 Cor. 12:20, RV, "strife" (KJV, "debates"); Gal. 5:20, RV, "strife" (KJV, "variance"); Phil. 1:15; 1 Tim. 6:4; Titus 3:9, RV, "strifes" (KJV, "contentions"). See CONTENTION, A, No. 1.¶

2. *erithia* (or *-eia*) (ἐριθία, 2052): see FACTION.

3. *antilogia* (ἀντιλογία, 485), "strife," Heb. 6:16, KJV: see DISPUTE, A, No. 4.

4. *machē* (μάχη, 3163), "strifes," 2 Tim. 2:23: see FIGHTING, A.

5. *philoneikia* (φιλονεικία, 5379), "strife," Luke 22:24, KJV: see CONTENTION, A, No. 3.¶

6. *logomachia* (λογομαχία, 3055), "strife of words," 1 Tim. 6:4: see DISPUTE, A, No. 2.¶

STRIKE

Notes: (1) In Rev. 7:16, *piptō*, "to fall," is rendered "strike" in the RV, KJV, "light (on)." (2) In Acts 27:41, *ereidō*, "to fix firmly," is used of a ship driving ashore, RV, "struck" (KJV, "stuck fast").¶ (3) For *paiō*, "to smite," Rev. 9:5, KJV, "striketh," see SMITE, No. 3. (4) For *patassō*, "to smite," Matt. 26:51, KJV, "struck," see SMITE, No. 1. (5) For *chalaō*, "to let go," Acts 27:17, KJV, "strake," see LET DOWN, No. 2. (6) In Luke 22:64 some mss. have *tuptō*, "to beat," imperfect tense, "they were beating." (7) For *rhapizō*, Matt. 26:67, and *rhapisma*, Mark 14:65, see BLOW, SMITE, No. 6 and *Note* (2). Some mss. have *ballō*, "struck."

STRIKER

plēktēs (πλήκτης, 4131), "a striker, a brawler" (akin to *plēssō*, "to strike," smite), occurs in 1 Tim. 3:3; Titus 1:7.¶

For STRING see BOND, No. 1

STRIP

ekduō (ἐκδύω, 1562), "to take off, strip off," is used especially of clothes, and rendered "to strip" in Matt. 27:28 (some mss. have *enduō*, "to clothe"), and Luke 10:30; to take off, Matt. 27:31; Mark 15:20; figuratively, 2 Cor. 5:4, "unclothed" (middle voice), of putting off the body at death (the believer's state of being unclothed does not refer to the body in the grave but to the spirit, which awaits the "body of glory" at the resurrection).¶

STRIPE

1. *mōlōps* (μώλωψ, 3468), "a bruise, a wound from a stripe," is used in 1 Pet. 2:24 (from the Sept. of Isa. 53:5), lit., in the original, "by whose bruise," not referring to Christ's scourging, but figurative of the stroke of divine judgment administered vicariously to Him on the cross (a comforting reminder to these Christian servants, who were not infrequently buffeted, v. 20, by their masters).¶

2. *plēgē* (πληγή, 4127), "a blow, stripe, wound" (akin to *plēssō*, "to strike," and *plēktēs*, "a striker"), is rendered "stripes" in Luke 12:48 (the noun is omitted in the original in v. 47 and the 2nd part of v. 48); Acts 16:23, 33; 2 Cor. 6:5; 11:23. See PLAGUE, WOUND.

STRIVE

1. *agōnizomai* (ἀγωνίζομαι, 75), "to contend" (Eng., "agonize"), is rendered "to strive"

in Luke 13:24; 1 Cor. 9:25; Col. 1:29; 4:12, RV (KJV, "laboring fervently"). In 1 Tim. 4:10, the best texts have this verb (RV, "strive") for *oneidizomai*, "to suffer reproach," KJV; see FIGHT, B, No. 1.

2. *machomai* (μάχομαι, 3164), "to fight, to quarrel, dispute," is rendered "to strive" in John 6:52; Acts 7:26; 2 Tim. 2:24. See FIGHT, B, No. 3.

3. *diamachomai* (διαμάχομαι, 1264), "to struggle against" (*dia*, intensive, and No. 2), is used of "contending" in an argument, Acts 23:9, "strove."¶

4. *erizō* (ἐρίζω, 2051), "to wrangle, strive" (*eris*, "strife"), is used in Matt. 12:19.¶

5. *logomacheō* (λογομαχέω, 3054), "to strive about words" (*logos*, "a word," and No. 2), is used in 2 Tim. 2:14.¶

6. *antagōnizomai* (ἀνταγωνίζομαι, 464), "to struggle against" (*anti*), is used in Heb. 12:4, "striving against."¶

7. *sunagōnizomai* (συναγωνίζομαι, 4865), "to strive together with" (*sun*), is used in Rom. 15:30.¶

8. *sunathleō* (συναθλέω, 4866), "to strive together," Phil. 1:27: see LABOR, B, No. 3.

Notes: (1) In 2 Tim. 2:5, KJV, *athleō*, "to contend in games, wrestle" (*athlos*, "a contest"), is rendered "strive." See CONTEND. (2) For *philotimeomai*, Rom. 15:20, see AIM.

For **STRIVINGS**, Titus 3:9, KJV, see **FIGHTING**

STROLLING

perierchomai (περιέρχομαι, 4022), "to go about," as an itinerant (*peri*, "around," *erchomai*, "to go"), is used of certain Jews in Acts 19:13, RV, "strolling" (KJV, "vagabond"). See COMPASS, No. 6, WANDER.

STRONG, STRONGER

A. Adjectives.

1. *dunatos* (δυνατός, 1415), "powerful, mighty," is translated "strong," in Rom. 15:1, where the "strong" are those referred to in ch. 14, in contrast to "the weak in faith," those who have scruples in regard to eating meat and the observance of days; 2 Cor. 12:10, where the strength lies in bearing sufferings in the realization that the endurance is for Christ's sake; 2 Cor. 13:9, where "ye are strong" implies the good spiritual condition which the apostle desires for the church at Corinth in having nothing requiring his exercise of discipline (contrast No. 2 in 1 Cor. 4:10). See ABLE, C, No. 1, MIGHTY, POSSIBLE, POWER.

2. *ischuros* (ἰσχυρός, 2478), "strong, mighty," is used of (*a*) persons: (1) God, Rev. 18:8; (2) angels, Rev. 5:2; 10:1; 18:21; (3) men, Matt. 12:29 (twice) and parallel passages; Heb. 11:34, KJV, "valiant" (RV, "mighty"); Rev. 6:15 (in the best texts; some have No. 1); 19:18, "mighty"; metaphorically, (4) the church at Corinth, 1 Cor. 4:10, where the apostle reproaches them ironically with their unspiritual and self-complacent condition; (5) of young men in Christ spiritually strong, through the Word of God, to overcome the evil one, 1 John 2:14; of (*b*) things: (1) wind, Matt. 14:30 (in some mss.), "boisterous"; (2) famine, Luke 15:14; (3) things in the mere human estimate, 1 Cor. 1:27; (4) Paul's letters, 2 Cor. 10:10; (5) the Lord's crying and tears, Heb. 5:7; (6) consolation, 6:18; (7) the voice of an angel, Rev. 18:2 (in the best texts; some have *megas*, "great"); (8) Babylon, Rev. 18:10; (9) thunderings, Rev. 19:6. See BOISTEROUS, MIGHTY.

3. *ischuroteros* (ἰσχυρότερος, 2478*), the comparative degree of No. 2, is used (*a*) of Christ, Matt. 3:11; Mark 1:7; Luke 3:16; (*b*) of "the weakness of God," as men without understanding regard it, 1 Cor. 1:25; (*c*) of a man of superior physical strength, Luke 11:22; (*d*) in 1 Cor. 10:22, in a rhetorical question, implying the impossibility of escaping the jealousy of God when it is kindled.¶

Notes: (1) For "strong delusion," 2 Thess. 2:11, KJV, see ERROR, No. 1. (2) For "strong (meat)," Heb. 5:12, 14, KJV, see SOLID.

B. Verbs.

1. *endunamoō* (ἐνδυναμόω, 1743), "to make strong" (*en*, "in," *dunamis*, "power"), "to strengthen," is rendered "waxed strong" in Rom. 4:20, RV (KJV, "was strong"); "be strong," Eph. 6:10; "were made strong," Heb. 11:34. See ENABLE, STRENGTH, B, No. 2.

2. *krataioō* (κραταιόω, 2901), "to strengthen" (akin to *kratos*, "strength"), is rendered (*a*) "to wax strong," Luke 1:80; 2:40; "be strong," 1 Cor. 16:13, lit., "be strengthened"; "to be strengthened," Eph. 3:16 (passive voice in each place). See STRENGTHEN.¶

3. *stereoō* (στερεόω, 4732): see ESTABLISH, No. 2.

STRONGHOLDS

ochurōma (ὀχύρωμα, 3794), "a stronghold, fortress" (akin to *ochuroō*, "to make firm"), is used metaphorically in 2 Cor. 10:4, of those things in which mere human confidence is imposed.¶

STUBBLE

kalamē (καλάμη, 2562), "a stalk of corn," denotes "straw" or "stubble"; in 1 Cor. 3:12, metaphorically of the effect of the most worthless form of unprofitable doctrine, in the lives and conduct of those in a church who are the subjects of such teaching; the teachings received and the persons who receive them are associated; the latter are "the doctrine exhibited in concrete form" (Lightfoot).¶

For STUCK see STICK

STUDY

Notes: For *philotimeomai,* "study," 1 Thess. 4:11, see AIM. For *spoudazō,* 2 Tim. 2:15, KJV, see DILIGENCE, B, No. 1.

For STUFF, Luke 17:31, KJV, see GOODS, No. 4

STUMBLE

1. *proskoptō* (προσκόπτω, 4350), "to strike against," is used of "stumbling," (*a*) physically, John 11:9, 10; (*b*) metaphorically, (1) of Israel in regard to Christ, whose Person, teaching, and atoning death, and the gospel relating thereto, were contrary to all their ideas as to the means of righteousness before God, Rom. 9:32; 1 Pet. 2:8; (2) of a brother in the Lord in acting against the dictates of his conscience, Rom. 14:21. See BEAT, No. 6.

2. *ptaiō* (πταίω, 4417), "to cause to stumble," signifies, intransitively, "to stumble," used metaphorically in Rom. 11:11, in the sense (*b*) (1) in No. 1; with moral significance in Jas. 2:10 and 3:2 (twice), RV, "stumble" (KJV, "offend"); in 2 Pet. 1:10, RV, "stumble" (KJV, "fall").¶

Note: For *aptaistos,* "from stumbling," Jude 24, RV, see FALL, B, *Note* (6).

For STUMBLING, STUMBLING BLOCK, STUMBLING-STONE, see OFFENSE, A, Nos. 1, 2, 3 and B

STUPOR

katanuxis (κατάνυξις, 2659), "a pricking" (akin to *katanussō,* "to strike" or "prick violently," Acts 2:37), is used in Rom. 11:8, RV, "stupor" (KJV, "slumber"). It is suggested that this meaning arose from the influence of the verb *katanustazō,* "to nod" or "fall asleep" (Field, *Notes on the Translation of the NT*). Evidently what is signified is the dulling of the spiritual sense.¶ In the Sept., Ps. 60:3; Isa. 29:10.¶

SUBDUE

katagōnizomai (καταγωνίζομαι, 2610), primarily, "to struggle against" (*kata,* "against," *agōn,* "a contest"), came to signify "to conquer," Heb. 11:33, "subdued."¶

Note: For *hupotassō,* KJV, "to subdue," in 1 Cor. 15:28 and Phil. 3:21, see SUBJECT.

SUBJECT, SUBJECTION (Verb, Adjective, Noun)

A. Verb.

hupotassō (ὑποτάσσω, 5293), primarily a military term, "to rank under" (*hupo,* "under," *tassō,* "to arrange"), denotes (*a*) "to put in subjection, to subject," Rom. 8:20 (twice); in the following, the RV, has to subject for KJV, "to put under," 1 Cor. 15:27 (thrice), 28 (3rd clause); Eph. 1:22; Heb. 2:8 (4th clause); in 1 Cor. 15:28 (1st clause), for KJV "be subdued"; in Phil. 3:21, for KJV, "subdue"; in Heb. 2:5, KJV, "hath . . . put in subjection"; (*b*) in the middle or passive voice, to subject oneself, to obey, be subject to, Luke 2:51; 10:17, 20; Rom. 8:7; 10:3, RV, "did (not) subject themselves" [KJV, "have (not) submitted themselves"]; 13:1, 5; 1 Cor. 14:34, RV, "be in subjection" (KJV, "be under obedience"); 15:28 (2nd clause); 16:16 RV, "be in subjection" (KJV, "submit, etc."); so Col. 3:18; Eph. 5:21, RV, "subjecting yourselves" (KJV, "submitting, etc."); v. 22, RV in italics, according to the best texts; v. 24, "is subject"; Titus 2:5, 9, RV, "be in subjection" (KJV, "be obedient"); 3:1, RV, "to be in subjection" (KJV, "to be subject"); Heb. 12:9, "be in subjection"; Jas. 4:7, RV, "be subject" (KJV, "submit yourselves"); so 1 Pet. 2:13; v. 18, RV, "be in subjection"; so 3:1, KJV and RV; v. 5, similarly; 3:22, "being made subject"; 5:5, RV, "be subject" (KJV, "submit yourselves"); in some texts in the 2nd part, as KJV. See OBEDIENT, SUBMIT.

Note: For *doulagōgeō,* 1 Cor. 9:27, KJV, "bring into subjection," see BONDAGE, B, No. 3. For *anupotaktos,* "not subject," Heb. 2:8, see DISOBEDIENT, B, Note.

B. Adjective.

enochos (ἔνοχος, 1777), "held in, bound by," in Heb. 2:15, "subject to": see DANGER, B, No. 1.

Note: For "subject to like passions," Jas. 5:17, KJV, see PASSION.

C. Noun.

hupotagē (ὑποταγή, 5292), "subjection," occurs in 2 Cor. 9:13; Gal. 2:5; 1 Tim. 2:11; 3:4.¶

SUBMIT

hupeikō (ὑπείκω, 5226), "to retire, withdraw" (*hupo*, under, *eikō*, "to yield"), hence, "to yield, submit," is used metaphorically in Heb. 13:17, of "submitting" to spiritual guides in the churches.¶

Note: For *hupotassō*, see SUBJECT, A.

SUBORN

hupoballō (ὑποβάλλω, 5260), "to throw or put under, to subject," denoted "to suggest, whisper, prompt"; hence, "to instigate," translated "suborned" in Acts 6:11. To "suborn" in the legal sense is to procure a person who will take a false oath. The idea of making suggestions is probably present in this use of the word.¶

SUBSTANCE

1. *ousia* (οὐσία, 3776), derived from a present participial form of *eimi*, "to be," denotes "substance, property," Luke 15:12, 13, RV, "substance," KJV, "goods" and "substance."¶

2. *huparchonta* (ὑπάρχοντα, 5224), the neuter plural of the present participle of *huparchō*, "to be in existence," is used as a noun with the article, signifying one's "goods," and translated "substance" in Luke 8:3. See GOODS, POSSESS, A, No. 3.

3. *huparxis* (ὕπαρξις, 5223), existence (akin to No. 2), possession: see POSSESS, B, No. 4.

4. *hupostasis* (ὑπόστασις, 5287), for which see CONFIDENCE, A No. 2, is translated "substance" (*a*) in Heb. 1:3, of Christ as "the very image" of God's "substance"; here the word has the meaning of the real nature of that to which reference is made in contrast to the outward manifestation (see the preceding clause); it speaks of the divine essence of God existent and expressed in the revelation of His Son. The KJV, "person" is an anachronism; the word was not so rendered till the 4th cent. Most of the earlier Eng. versions have "substance"; (*b*) in Heb. 11:1 it has the meaning of "confidence, assurance" (RV), marg., "the giving substance to," KJV, "substance," something that could not equally be expressed by *elpis*, "hope."

SUBTLY

katasophizomai (κατασοφίζομαι, 2686), "to deal subtly" (from *kata*, "against, under," *sophos*, "wise, subtle," used in the Sept. in 2 Sam. 13:3, of Jonadab), occurs in Acts 7:19.¶ In the Sept., Ex. 1:10.¶

SUBTLETY

Note: For *dolos*, Matt. 26:4; Acts 13:10, see GUILE. For *panourgia*, 2 Cor. 11:3, see CRAFTINESS.

SUBVERT, SUBVERTING

A. Verb.

anaskeuazō (ἀνασκευάζω, 384), primarily, "to pack up baggage" (*ana*, "up," *skeuos*, "a vessel"), hence, from a military point of view, "to dismantle a town, to plunder," is used metaphorically in Acts 15:24, of unsettling or "subverting" the souls of believers. In the papyri it is used of going bankrupt.¶

Note: For *anatrepō*, Titus 1:11, see OVERTHROW, B, No. 3. For *ekstrephō*, Titus 3:11, see PERVERT, No. 4.

B. Noun.

katastrophē (καταστροφή, 2692), "an overthrow," 2 Pet. 2:6 (Eng., "catastrophe"), is rendered "subverting" in 2 Tim. 2:14. See OVERTHROW.¶

For **SUCCEED,** Acts 24:27, RV, see **ROOM,** *Note* (2)

For **SUCCOR** see **HELP,** B, No. 4

SUCCORER

prostatis (προστάτις, 4368), a feminine form of *prostatēs*, denotes "a protectress, patroness"; it is used metaphorically of Phoebe in Rom. 16:2. It is a word of dignity, evidently chosen instead of others which might have been used (see, e.g., under HELPER), and indicates the high esteem with which she was regarded, as one who had been a protectress of many. *Prostatēs* was the title of a citizen in Athens, who had the responsibility of seeing to the welfare of resident aliens who were without civic rights. Among the Jews it signified a wealthy patron of the community.¶

For **SUCH** see †, p. 1

SUCH AS

Notes: (1) In Acts 2:47, KJV, the article with the present participle, passive, of *sōzō*, "to save," lit., "the (ones), i.e., those, being saved," is translated "such as (should be saved)"; the RV, "those that (were being saved)," gives the correct meaning, marking the kind of persons who were added to the company; (2) "such as" is a rendering of certain relative pronouns: *hoios*, "what sort of," e.g., Matt. 24:21; 2 Cor. 12:20 (twice); Rev. 16:18; *hostis*, "whoever," e.g., Mark 4:20; *hopoios*, "of what sort," preceded by *toioutos*, "of such a sort," Acts 26:29; (3) *deina*, Matt. 26:18, denotes "such a one" (whom one cannot, or will not, name).¶ (4) In Heb. 13:5, "such things as ye have" represents the phrase *ta paronta*, "the (things) present" (present participle of *pareimi*); (5) in Luke 11:41, *ta enonta*, KJV, "such things as ye have," lit., "the (things) within" (*eneimi*, "to be in"), RV, "those things which are within" (KJV marg., "as you are able," RV, marg., "ye can"), perhaps signifying not outward things such as lustrations, but "what things ye have within your cups and platters," i.e., "your possessions."

SUCK (GIVE SUCK), SUCKLING

thēlazō (θηλάζω, 2337), from *thēlē*, "a breast," is used (*a*) of the mother, "to suckle," Matt. 24:19; Mark 13:17; Luke 21:23; in some texts in 23:29 (the best have *trephō*); (*b*) of the young, "to suck," Matt. 21:16, "sucklings"; Luke 11:27.¶

SUDDEN, SUDDENLY

A. Adjective.

aiphnidios (αἰφνίδιος, 160), "sudden," occurs in 1 Thess. 5:3, where it has the place of emphasis at the beginning of the sentence, as *olethros*, "destruction," which the adjective qualifies, has at the end; in Luke 21:34, it is used adverbially, RV, "suddenly" (KJV, "unawares"). See UNAWARES.¶

B. Adverbs.

1. *aphnō* (ἄφνω, 869), "suddenly," occurs in Acts 2:2; 16:26; 28:6.¶

2. *exaiphnēs* (ἐξαίφνης, 1810), a strengthened form, akin to No. 1, occurs in Mark 13:36; Luke 2:13; 9:39; Acts 9:3; 22:6.¶

3. *exapina* (ἐξάπινα, 1819), a later form of No. 2, occurs in Mark 9:8.¶

Note: For *tacheōs* in 1 Tim. 5:22, KJV, "suddenly," RV, "hastily," see QUICKLY, No. 3.

For SUE see LAW, B, No. 2

SUFFER

A. Verbs.

(*a*) *to permit*

1. *eaō* (ἐάω, 1439), "to let, permit," is translated "to suffer" in Matt. 24:43; Luke 4:41; 22:51; Acts 14:16; 16:7; 19:30; 28:4; 1 Cor. 10:13. See LEAVE (*a*) No. 9, LET, No. 4.

2. *proseaō* (προσεάω, 4330), "to permit further" (*pros*, and No. 1), occurs in Acts 27:7.¶

3. *epitrepō* (ἐπιτρέπω, 2010), for which see LEAVE, (*b*), is rendered "to suffer" in KJV and RV in Matt. 8:21; Mark 10:4; Luke 9:59; Acts 28:16; RV only, Luke 9:61 (KJV, "let"); KJV only,

Acts 21:39; in some texts, Matt. 8:31, KJV only. See LIBERTY, C, Note, PERMIT.

4. *aphiēmi* (ἀφίημι, 863), "to send away," signifies "to permit, suffer," in Matt. 3:15 (twice); Matt. 19:14; 23:13; Mark 1:34; 5:19, 37; 10:14; 11:16; Luke 8:51; 12:39, KJV (RV, "left"); 18:16; John 12:7, RV, KJV and RV marg., "let (her) alone"; Rev. 11:9. See FORGIVE.

Notes: (1) In Acts 2:27 and 13:35, KJV, *didōmi*, "to give" (RV), is rendered "to suffer." (2) In 1 Cor. 6:7, KJV, *apostereō*, in the passive voice, is rendered "*suffer yourselves to* be defrauded" (RV, "be defrauded"). (3) For *kōluō* in Heb. 7:23, KJV, "were not suffered," see HINDER.

(*b*) *to endure suffering*

1. *anechō* (ἀνέχω, 430), in the middle voice, "to bear with," is rendered "to suffer" in Matt. 17:17 and parallel passages; KJV only, 1 Cor. 4:12 (RV, "endure"); 2 Cor. 11:19, 20 and Heb. 13:22 (RV, "bear with"). See BEAR, ENDURE.

2. *paschō* (πάσχω, 3958), "to suffer," is used (I) of the "sufferings" of Christ (*a*) at the hands of men, e.g., Matt. 16:21; 17:12; 1 Pet. 2:23; (*b*) in His expiatory and vicarious sacrifice for sin, Heb. 9:26; 13:12; 1 Pet. 2:21; 3:18; 4:1; (*c*) including both (*a*) and (*b*), Luke 22:15; 24:26, 46; Acts 1:3, "passion"; 3:18; 17:3; Heb. 5:8; (*d*) by the antagonism of the evil one, Heb. 2:18; (II) of human "suffering "(*a*) of followers of Christ, Acts 9:16; 2 Cor. 1:6; Gal. 3:4; Phil. 1:29; 1 Thess. 2:14; 2 Thess. 1:5; 2 Tim. 1:12; 1 Pet. 3:14, 17; 5:10; Rev. 2:10; in identification with Christ in His crucifixion, as the spiritual ideal to be realized, 1 Pet. 4:1; in a wrong way, 4:15; (*b*) of others, physically, as the result of demoniacal power, Matt. 17:15, RV, "suffereth (grievously)," KJV, "is (sore) vexed"; cf. Mark 5:26; in a dream, Matt. 27:19; through maltreatment, Luke 13:2; 1 Pet. 2:19, 20; by a serpent (negatively), Acts 28:5, RV, "took" (KJV, "felt:" see FEEL, *Note*); (*c*) of the effect upon the whole body through the "suffering" of one member, 1 Cor. 12:26, with application to a church.

3. *propaschō* (προπάσχω, 4310), "to suffer before" (*pro*, and No. 2), occurs in 1 Thess. 2:2.¶

4. *sumpaschō* (συμπάσχω, 4841), "to suffer with" (*sun*, and No. 2), is used in Rom. 8:17 of "suffering" with Christ; in 1 Cor. 12:26 of joint "suffering" in the members of the body.¶

5. *hupechō* (ὑπέχω, 5254), "to hold under" (*hupo*, "under," *echō*, "to have or hold"), is used metaphorically in Jude 7 of "suffering" punishment.¶ In the Sept., Ps. 89:50; Lam. 5:7.¶

6. *kakoucheō* (κακουχέω, 2558), "to ill-treat" (*kakos*, "evil," and *echō*, "to have"), is used in the passive voice in Heb. 11:37, RV,

"evil entreated" (KJV, "tormented"); in 13:3, RV, "are evil entreated" (KJV, "suffer adversity").¶

7. *sunkakoucheomai* (συγκακουχέομαι, 4778), "to endure adversity with," is used in Heb. 11:25 (*sun*, "with," and No. 6), RV, "to be evil entreated with," KJV, "to suffer affliction with."¶

8. *makrothumeō* (μακροθυμέω, 3114) is rendered "suffereth long" in 1 Cor. 13:4. See PATIENCE.

9. *adikeō* (ἀδικέω, 91), "to do wrong, injustice" (*a*, negative, *dikē*, "right"), is used in the passive voice in 2 Pet. 2:13, RV, "suffering wrong" (some texts have *komizō*, "to receive," KJV); there is a play upon words here which may be brought out thus, "being defrauded (of the wages of fraud)," a use of the verb illustrated in the papyri. See HURT.

Notes: (1) In 1 Cor. 9:12, KJV, *stegō*, "to bear up under," is translated "suffer" (RV, "bear"); see BEAR, No. 11. (2) For *hupomenō*, rendered "to suffer" in 2 Tim. 2:12, see ENDURE, No. 2. (3) For "suffer hardship, suffer trouble," see HARDSHIP, Nos. 1 and 2. (4) For "suffer need," Phil. 4:12, see WANT. (5) For "suffer loss," 2 Cor. 7:9, RV, see LOSE, No. 2. (6) For "suffer persecution," see PERSECUTION. (7) For "suffer shipwreck," see SHIPWRECK. (8) For *tropophoreō* in Acts 13:18, "suffered . . . manners," see MANNER, E. (9) For "suffereth violence," *biazō*, see FORCE, B, No. 1, VIOLENCE, B, No. 2. (10) In 2 Thess. 1:9, RV, *tinō*, "to pay a penalty," is rendered "shall suffer (punishment)."¶

B. Adjective.

pathētos (παθητός, 3805), akin to *paschō*, denotes "one who has suffered," or "subject to suffering," or "destined to suffer"; it is used in the last sense of the "suffering" of Christ, Acts 26:23.¶

SUFFERING

pathēma (πάθημα, 3804) is rendered "sufferings" in the RV (KJV, "afflictions") in 2 Tim. 3:11; Heb. 10:32; 1 Pet. 5:9; in Gal. 5:24, "passions" (KJV, "affections"). See AFFLICTION, B, No. 3.

Note: For *kakopatheia*, Jas. 5:10, RV, "suffering," see AFFLICTION, B, No. 1.

SUFFICE, SUFFICIENT

A. Verbs.

1. *arkeō* (ἀρκέω, 714), "to suffice," is rendered "is sufficient" in John 6:7; 2 Cor. 12:9; "it sufficeth" in John 14:8. See CONTENT, ENOUGH.

Note: For 1 Pet. 4:3, see B, No. 2.

2. *hikanoō* (ἱκανόω, 2427), "to make sufficient, render fit," is translated "made (us) suffi-

cient" in 2 Cor. 3:6, RV (KJV, "hath made . . . able"). See ABLE, B, No. 6, *Note.*

B. Adjectives.

1. *hikanos* (ἱκανός, 2425), akin to A, No. 2, "enough, sufficient, fit," etc. is translated "sufficient" in 2 Cor. 2:6, 16; 3:5. See ABLE, C, No. 2.

2. *arketos* (ἀρκετός, 713), akin to A, No. 1, used with *eimi*, "to be," is translated "may suffice" in 1 Pet. 4:3. See ENOUGH, A, No. 1.

SUFFICIENCY

1. *autarkeia* (αὐτάρκεια, 841) (*autos*, "self," *arkeō*, see A, above; Eng., "autarchy"), "contentment," 1 Tim. 6:6, is rendered "sufficiency" in 2 Cor. 9:8.¶

2. *hikanotēs* (ἱκανότης, 2426) is rendered "sufficiency" in 2 Cor. 3:5.¶

For SUIT (make), Acts 25:24, RV, see DEAL WITH, *Note* (1)

SUM (Noun), SUM UP

A. Noun.

Note: For *kephalaion*, Acts 22:28; Heb. 8:1, see POINT, B.¶ For *timē*, Acts 7:16, see PRICE, A.

B. Verb.

anakephalaioō (ἀνακεφαλαιόω, 346), "to sum up, gather up" (*ana*, "up," *kephalē*, "a head"), "to present as a whole," is used in the passive voice in Rom. 13:9, RV, "summed up" (KJV, "briefly comprehended"), i.e., the one commandment expresses all that the Law enjoins, and to obey this one is to fulfil the Law (cf. Gal. 5:14); middle voice in Eph. 1:10, RV, "sum up" (KJV, "gather together"), of God's purpose to "sum up" all things in the heavens and on the earth in Christ, a consummation extending beyond the limits of the church, though the latter is to be a factor in its realization.¶

SUMMER

theros (θέρος, 2330), akin to *therō*, "to heat," occurs in Matt. 24:32; Mark 13:28; Luke 21:30.¶

SUMPTUOUS, SUMPTUOUSLY

A. Adjective.

lampros (λαμπρός, 2986), "bright," is rendered "sumptuous" in Rev. 18:14, RV See BRIGHT, GOODLY, *Note.*

B. Adverb.

lamprōs (λαμπρῶς, 2988), the corresponding adverb, is used in Luke 16:19, "sumptuously."¶

SUN

hēlios (ἥλιος, 2246), whence Eng. prefix "helio—," is used (*a*) as a means of the natural benefits of light and heat, e.g., Matt. 5:45, and power, Rev. 1:16; (*b*) of its qualities of brightness and glory, e.g., Matt. 13:43; 17:2; Acts 26:13; 1 Cor. 15:41; Rev. 10:1; 12:1; (*c*) as a means of destruction, e.g., Matt. 13:6; Jas. 1:11; of physical misery, Rev. 7:16; (*d*) as a means of judgment, e.g., Matt. 24:29; Mark 13:24; Luke 21:25; 23:45; Acts 2:20; Rev. 6:12; 8:12; 9:2; 16:8.

Note: In Rev. 7:2 and 16:12, *anatolē*, "rising," used with *hēlios*, is translated "sunrising," RV (KJV, "east").

For SUNDER (Asunder) see CUT, No. 6

For SUNDRY see PORTION, C

SUP

deipneō (δειπνέω, 1172), "to sup" (said of taking the chief meal of the day), occurs in Luke 17:8; 22:20 (in the best texts), lit., "(the) supping"; so 1 Cor. 11:25; metaphorically in Rev. 3:20, of spiritual communion between Christ and the faithful believer.¶

For SUPERFLUITY see ABUNDANCE, A, No. 2, B, No. 1

SUPERFLUOUS

perissos (περισσός, 4053), "abundant, more than sufficient," is translated "superfluous" in 2 Cor. 9:1. See ABUNDANT, C, No. 1, ADVANTAGE, MORE, B, No. 2.

SUPERSCRIPTION

epigraphē (ἐπιγραφή, 1923), lit., "an overwriting" (*epi*, "over," *graphō*, "to write") (the meaning of the anglicized Latin word "superscription"), denotes "an inscription, a title." On Roman coins the emperor's name was inscribed, Matt. 22:20; Mark 12:16; Luke 20:24. In the Roman Empire, in the case of a criminal on his way to execution, a board on which was inscribed the cause of his condemnation, was carried before him or hung round his neck; the inscription was termed a "title" (*titlos*). The four Evangelists state that at the crucifixion of Christ the title was affixed to the cross, Mark (15:26) and Luke (23:38) call it a "superscription"; Mark says it was "written over" (*epigraphō*, the corresponding verb). Matthew calls it "His accusation"; John calls it "a title" (a technical term). The wording varies: the essential words

are the same, and the variation serves to authenticate the narratives, showing that there was no consultation leading to an agreement as to the details. See further under TITLE.¶

For SUPERSTITION see RELIGION

SUPERSTITIOUS

deisidaimōn (δεισιδαίμων, 1175), "reverent to the deity" (*deidō*, "to fear"; *daimōn*, "a demon," or "pagan god"), occurs in Acts 17:22 in the comparative degree, rendered "somewhat superstitious," RV (KJV, "too superstitious"), a meaning which the word sometimes has; others, according to its comparative form, advocate the meaning "more religious (than others)," "quite religious" (cf. the noun in 25:19). This is supported by Ramsay, who renders it "more than others respectful of what is divine"; so Deissmann in *Light from the Ancient East*, and others. It also agrees with the meaning found in Greek writers; the context too suggests that the adjective is used in a good sense; perhaps, after all, with kindly ambiguity (Grimm-Thayer). An ancient epitaph has it in the sense of "reverent" (Moulton and Milligan).¶

SUPPER

deipnon (δεῖπνον, 1173) denotes "a supper" or "feast" (for an analysis of the uses see FEAST, No. 2). In John 13:2 the RV, following certain texts, has "during supper" (KJV, "supper being ended").

Note: For "supper" in Luke 22:20 see SUP.

SUPPLICATION

1. *deēsis* (δέησις, 1162) is always translated "supplication," or the plural, in the RV. See PRAYER, B, No. 3.

2. *hiketēria* (ἱκετηρία, 2428) is the feminine form of the adjective *hiketērios*, denoting "of a suppliant," and used as a noun, formerly "an olive branch" carried by a suppliant (*hiketēs*), then later, "a supplication," used with No. 1 in Heb. 5:7.¶ In the Sept., Job 40:22 (Eng. Vers. 41:3).¶

SUPPLY (Noun and Verb)

A. Verbs.

1. *chorēgeō* (χορηγέω, 5524) primarily, among the Greeks, signified "to lead a stage chorus or dance" (*choros*, and *hēgeomai*, "to lead"), then, "to defray the expenses of a chorus"; hence, later, metaphorically, "to supply," 2 Cor. 9:10 (2nd part; see also No. 2), RV, "supply" (KJV "minister"); 1 Pet. 4:11, RV, "supplieth" (KJV, "giveth"). See GIVE, *Note* (4), MINISTER, B, *Note* (1).¶

2. *epichorēgeō* (ἐπιχορηγέω, 2023), "to supply fully, abundantly" (a strengthened form of No. 1), is rendered "to supply" in the RV of 2 Cor. 9:10 (1st part) and Gal. 3:5 (for KJV, "to minister"), where the present continuous tense speaks of the work of the Holy Spirit in all His ministrations to believers individually and collectively; in Col. 2:19, RV, "being supplied" (KJV, "having nourishment ministered"), of the work of Christ as the Head of the church His body; in 2 Pet. 1:5, "supply" (KJV, "add"); in v. 11, "shall be ... supplied" (KJV, "shall be ministered"), of the reward hereafter which those are to receive, in regard to positions in the kingdom of God, for their fulfillment here of the conditions mentioned.¶

Note: In 2 Cor. 9:10 (see Nos. 1 and 2 above) the stronger verb No. 2 is used where the will and capacity to receive are in view.

3. *anaplēroō* (ἀναπληρόω, 378), "to fill up, fulfill," is rendered "to supply" in 1 Cor. 16:17 and Phil. 2:30. See FILL, FULFILL, OCCUPY.

4. *prosanaplēroō* (προσαναπληρόω, 4322), "to fill up by adding to, to supply fully" (*pros*, "to," and No. 3), is translated "supplieth" in 2 Cor. 9:12, KJV (RV, "filleth up the measure of"); in 11:9, RV and KJV, "supplied."¶

Note: In Phil. 4:19, KJV, *plēroō*, to fulfill (RV), is rendered "shall supply."

B. Noun.

epichorēgia (ἐπιχορηγία, 2024), "a full supply," occurs in Eph. 4:16, "supplieth," lit., "by the supply of every joint," metaphorically of the members of the church, the body of which Christ is the Head, and Phil. 1:19, "the supply (of the Spirit of Jesus Christ)," i.e., "the bountiful supply"; here "of the Spirit" may be taken either in the subjective sense, the Giver, or the objective, the Gift.¶

SUPPORT

Notes: (1) In Acts 20:35, KJV, *antilambanomai*, "to help" (RV), is translated "support." See HELP, B, No. 1. (2) In 1 Thess. 5:14, *antechomai* signifies "to support": see HOLD, No. 3.

SUPPOSE

1. *nomizō* (νομίζω, 3543), "to consider, suppose, think," is rendered "to suppose" in Matt. 20:10; Luke 2:34; 3:23; Acts 7:25; 14:19; 16:27; 21:29; 1 Tim. 6:5; in 1 Cor. 7:26, KJV (RV, "I think"); in Acts 16:13, the RV adheres to the meaning "to suppose," "(where) we supposed (there was a place of prayer)"; this word also signifies "to practice a custom" (*nomos*) and is commonly so used by Greek writers. Hence the KJV, "was wont (to be made)"; it is rendered

"to think" in Matt. 5:17; 10:34; Acts 8:20; 17:29; 1 Cor. 7:36. See THINK.¶

2. *dokeō* (δοκέω, 1380), "to be of opinion," is translated "to suppose" in Mark 6:49; Luke 24:37; John 20:15; Acts 27:13; in the following, KJV "suppose," RV, "think," Luke 12:51; 13:2; Heb. 10:29. It is most frequently rendered "to think," always in Matthew; always in John, except 11:31, "supposing," RV [where the best texts have this verb (for *legō*, KJV, "saying")], and 20:15 (see above).

3. *hupolambanō* (ὑπολαμβάνω, 5274), when used of mental action, signifies "to suppose," Luke 7:43, and Acts 2:15. See ANSWER, RECEIVE.

4. *huponoeō* (ὑπονοέω, 5282), "to suspect, to conjecture," is translated "suppose ye" in Acts 13:25, RV (KJV, "think ye"); "I supposed" in 25:18. See DEEM.

5. *oiomai* or *oimai* (οἴομαι, 3633) signifies "to expect, imagine, suppose"; it is rendered "to suppose" in John 21:25; Phil. 1:17, RV (KJV, v. 16, "thinking"); "think" in Jas. 1:7. See THINK.¶

Notes: (1) In 2 Cor. 11:5, KJV, *logizomai*, "to reckon" (RV), is rendered "I suppose"; so in 1 Pet. 5:12, KJV, RV, "(as) I account (him)"; Silvanus was not supposed by Peter to be faithful, he was "reckoned" or regarded so. (2) In Phil. 2:25, KJV, *hēgeomai*, "to reckon," deem, is rendered "I supposed" (RV, "I counted").

SUPREME

huperechō (ὑπερέχω, 5242), "to be superior, to excel," is translated "supreme" in 1 Pet. 2:13: see EXCEL, No. 3.

SURE

A. Adjectives.

1. *asphalēs* (ἀσφαλής, 804), "safe," is translated "sure" in Heb. 6:19. See CERTAIN, B.

2. *bebaios* (βέβαιος, 949), "firm, steadfast," is used of (*a*) God's promise to Abraham, Rom. 4:16; (*b*) the believer's hope, Heb. 6:19, "steadfast"; (*c*) the hope of spiritual leaders regarding the welfare of converts, 2 Cor. 1:7, "steadfast"; (*d*) the glorying of the hope, Heb. 3:6, "firm"; (*e*) the beginning of our confidence, 3:14, RV, "firm" (KJV, "steadfast"); (*f*) the Law given at Sinai, Heb. 2:2, "steadfast"; (*g*) the testament (or covenant) fulfilled after a death, 9:17, "of force"; (*h*) the calling and election of believers, 2 Pet. 1:10, to be made "sure" by the fulfillment of the injunctions in vv. 5–7; (*i*) the word of prophecy, "*made* more sure," 2 Pet. 1:19, RV, KJV, "a more sure (word of prophecy)"; what is meant is not a comparison between the prophecies of the OT and NT, but that the former

have been confirmed in the person of Christ (vv. 16–18). See FIRM.¶

3. *pistos* (πιστός, 4103), "faithful," is translated "sure" in Acts 13:34. See FAITHFUL.

Note: In 2 Tim. 2:19, KJV, *stereos*, "firm," is translated "sure," and connected with "standeth," RV, "the firm (foundation of God standeth)," i.e., "however much the faith may be misrepresented or denied, the firm foundation of God's knowledge and truth, with its separating power, remains."

B. Verb.

asphalizō (ἀσφαλίζω, 805), "to make safe or sure" (akin to A, No. 1), is rendered "to make sure" in Matt. 27:64, 65, 66, of the sepulchre of Christ; elsewhere, Acts 16:24, of making feet fast in the stocks. See FAST.¶

Note: In the KJV of John 16:30; Rom. 2:2 and 15:29, the verb *oida*, "to know," is translated "to be sure" (RV, in each place, "to know"). So with *ginōskō*, "to know," in John 6:69. For the difference between the verbs see KNOW.

SURELY

Notes: (1) In the KJV of Matt. 26:73; Mark 14:70; John 17:8, *alēthōs*, "truly," is rendered "surely" (RV, "of a truth"); so *pantōs*, "at all events, altogether," in Luke 4:23 (RV, "doubtless"), and *nai*, "yea," in Rev. 22:20 (RV, "yea"). (2) In Heb. 6:14, "surely" represents the phrase *ei mēn* (so the best texts; some have *ē mēn*). (3) For Luke 1:1, KJV, see BELIEVE, C, *Note* (4). (4) For "surely" in 2 Pet. 2:12, RV, see CORRUPT, A, No. 2 (*b*).

SURETY (Noun)

enguos (ἔγγυος, 1450) primarily signifies "bail," the bail who personally answers for anyone, whether with his life or his property (to be distinguished from *mesitēs*, "a mediator"); it is used in Heb. 7:22, "(by so much also hath Jesus become) the Surety (of a better covenant)," referring to the abiding and unchanging character of His Melchizedek priesthood, by reason of which His suretyship is established by God's oath (vv. 20, 21). As the Surety, He is the personal guarantee of the terms of the new and better covenant, secured on the ground of His perfect sacrifice (v. 27).¶

For **SURETY** (of a), Acts 12:11, KJV, see **TRUE**, D, No. 1

SURFEITING

kraipalē (κραιπάλη, 2897) signifies "the giddiness and headache resulting from excessive wine-bibbing, a drunken nausea," "surfeiting,"

Luke 21:34.¶ Trench (*Syn.* §lxi) distinguishes this and the synonymous words, *methē*, "drunkenness," *oinophlugia*, "wine-bibbing" (KJV, "excess of wine," 1 Pet. 4:3), *kōmos*, "revelling."

For **SURGE**, Jas. 1:6, RV, see **RAGE** and **WAVE**

For **SURMISE, SURMISINGS,** see **DEEM**

SURNAME

epikaleō (ἐπικαλέω, 1941), "to put a name upon" (*epi*, "upon," *kaleō*, "to call"), "to surname," is used in this sense in the passive voice, in some texts in Matt. 10:3 (it is absent in the best); in Luke 22:3, in some texts (the best have *kaleō*, "to call"); Acts 1:23; 4:36; 10:5, 18, 32; 11:13; 12:12, 25; in some texts, 15:22 (the best have *kaleō*).

Notes: (1) In Mark 3:16, 17, "He surnamed" is a translation of *epitithēmi*, "to put upon, to add to," with *onoma*, "a name," as the object. (2) In Acts 15:37, KJV, *kaleō*, "to call "(RV, "called"), is rendered "whose surname was." (3) The verb *eponomazō*, translated "bearest the name" in Rom. 2:17, RV, finds a literal correspondence in the word "surname" (*epi*, "upon," = *sur*), and had this significance in Classical Greek.¶

For **SURPASS**, 2 Cor. 3:10, see **EXCEED**, A, No. 1

For **SUSPENSE** (hold in) see **DOUBT**, No. 6

SUSTENANCE

chortasma (χόρτασμα, 5527), "fodder" (akin to *chortazō*, "to feed, fill," see FEED, No. 4), is used in the plural in Acts 7:11, "sustenance."¶ In the Sept., Gen. 24:25, 32; 42:27; 43:24; Deut. 11:15; Jud. 19:19.¶

SWADDLING CLOTHES

sparganoō (σπαργανόω, 4683), "to swathe" (from *sparganon*, "a swathing band"), signifies "to wrap in swaddling clothes" in Luke 2:7, 12. The idea that the word means "rags" is without foundation.¶ In the Sept., Job 38:9; Ezek. 16:4.¶

SWALLOW (Verb)

katapinō (καταπίνω, 2666), "to drink down" (*kata*, and *pinō*, "to drink"), "to swallow," is used with this meaning (*a*) physically, but figuratively, Matt. 23:24; Rev. 12:16;

(*b*)metaphorically, in the passive voice, of death (by victory), 1 Cor. 15:54; of being overwhelmed by sorrow, 2 Cor. 2:7; of the mortal body (by life), 5:4. See DEVOUR, No. 3, DROWN, No. 2.

SWEAR, SWORN

omnumi (ὄμνυμι) or *omnuō* (ὀμνύω, 3660) is used of "affirming or denying by an oath," e.g., Matt. 26:74; Mark 6:23; Luke 1:73; Heb. 3:11, 18; 4:3; 7:21; accompanied by that by which one swears, e.g., Matt. 5:34, 36; 23:16; Heb. 6:13, 16; Jas. 5:12; Rev. 10:6. Cf. ADJURE.

Note: For "false swearers," 1 Tim. 1:10, see FORSWEAR.

SWEAT

hidrōs (ἱδρώς, 2402) is used in Luke 22:44.¶ In the Sept., Gen. 3:19.¶

SWEEP

saroō (σαρόω, 4563) occurs in Matt. 12:44; Luke 11:25; 15:8.¶

SWEET

glukus (γλυκύς, 1099) (cf. Eng., "glycerine," "glucose"), occurs in Jas. 3:11, 12 (KJV, "fresh" in this verse); Rev. 10:9, 10.¶

For SWEET SMELLING see SAVOR, No. 1

SWELL, SWOLLEN

pimprēmi (πίμπρημι, 4092), primarily, "to blow, to burn," later came to denote "to cause to swell," and, in the middle voice, "to become swollen," Acts 28:6.¶ In the Sept., Num. 5:21, 22, 27.¶

Note: Some, connecting the word *prēnēs* in Acts 1:18 with *pimprēmi*, give it the meaning "swelling up": see HEADLONG.

SWELLING

1. *phusiōsis* (φυσίωσις, 5450) denotes "a puffing up, swelling with pride" (akin to *phusioō*, "to puff up"), 2 Cor. 12:20, "swellings."¶

2. *huperonkos* (ὑπέρογκος, 5246), an adjective denoting "of excessive weight or size," is used metaphorically in the sense of "immoderate," especially of arrogant speech, in the neuter plural, virtually as a noun, 2 Pet. 2:18; Jude 16, "great swelling words," doubtless with reference to gnostic phraseology.¶

SWERVE

astocheō (ἀστοχέω, 795), "to miss the mark," is translated "having swerved" in 1 Tim.

1:6. See ERR, No. 3. Moulton and Milligan illustrate the use of the verb from the papyri, e.g., of a man in extravagant terms bewailing the loss of a pet fighting cock, "(I am distraught, for my cock) has failed (me)."

SWIFT, SWIFTLY

1. *oxus* (ὀξύς, 3691) denotes "swift" in Rom. 3:15. See SHARP.

2. *tachus* (ταχύς, 5036), "swift, speedy," is used in Jas. 1:19.¶ Cf. *tacheōs, tachu* and *tacheion,* "quickly," *tachos,* "quickness, speed."

3. *tachinos* (ταχινός, 5031), a poetical and late form of No. 2, "of swift approach," is used in 2 Pet. 1:14, RV, "swiftly" (KJV, "shortly"), lit., "(the putting off of my tabernacle is) swift," i.e., "imminent"; in 2:1, "swift (destruction)."¶ In the Sept., Prov. 1:16; Isa. 59:7; Hab. 1:6.¶

SWIM

1. *kolumbaō* (κολυμβάω, 2860), "to dive, plunge, into the sea," hence, "to swim," occurs in Acts 27:43.¶ Cf. *kolumbēthra,* "a pool."

2. *ekkolumbaō* (ἐκκολυμβάω, 1579), "to swim out of" (*ek*), occurs in Acts 27:42.¶

SWINE

choiros (χοῖρος, 5519), "a swine," is used in the plural, in the Synoptic Gospels only, Matt. 7:6; 8:30, 31, 32; Mark 5:11–13, 16; Luke 8:32, 33; Luke 15:15, 16. It does not occur in the OT¶

SWORD

1. *machaira* (μάχαιρα, 3162), "a short sword or dagger" (distinct from No. 2), e.g., Matt. 26:47, 51, 52 and parallel passages; Luke 21:24; 22:38, possibly "a knife" (Field, *Notes on the Translation of the NT*); Heb. 4:12 (see TWO-EDGED); metaphorically and by metonymy, (*a*) for ordinary violence, or dissensions, that destroy peace, Matt. 10:34; (*b*) as the instrument of a magistrate or judge, e.g., Rom. 13:4; (*c*) of the Word of God, "the sword of the Spirit," probing the conscience, subduing the impulses to sin, Eph. 6:17.

2. *rhomphaia* (ῥομφαία, 4501), a word of somewhat doubtful origin, denoted "a Thracian weapon of large size," whether a sword or spear is not certain, but usually longer than No. 1; it occurs (*a*) literally in Rev. 6:8; (*b*) metaphorically, as the instrument of anguish, Luke 2:35; of judgment, Rev. 1:16; 2:12, 16; 19:15, 21, probably figurative of the Lord's judicial utterances.¶

SYCAMINE

sukaminos (συκάμινος, 4807) occurs in Luke 17:6.¶ It is generally recognized as the black mulberry, with fruit like blackberries. The leaves are too tough for silkworms and thus are unlike the white mulberry. Neither kind is the same as the mulberry of 2 Sam. 5:23, 24, etc. The town Haifa was called Sycaminopolis, from the name of the tree.

SYCAMORE

sukomorea (συκομορέα, 4809) occurs in Luke 19:4.¶ This tree is of the fig species, with leaves like the mulberry and fruit like the fig. It is somewhat less in height than the sycamine and spreads to cover an area from 60 to 80 feet in diameter. It is often planted by the roadside, and was suitable for the purpose of Zacchaeus. Seated on the lowest branch he was easily within speaking distance of Christ.

SYNAGOGUE

sunagōgē (συναγωγή, 4864), properly "a bringing together" (*sun*, "together," *agō*, "to bring"), denoted (*a*) "a gathering of things, a collection," then, of "persons, an assembling, of Jewish religious gatherings," e.g., Acts 9:2; an assembly of Christian Jews, Jas. 2:2, RV, "synagogue" (KJV, marg.; text, "assembly"); a company dominated by the power and activity of Satan, Rev. 2:9; 3:9; (*b*) by metonymy, "the building" in which the gathering is held, e.g. Matt. 6:2; Mark 1:21. The origin of the Jewish "synagogue" is probably to be assigned to the time of the Babylonian exile. Having no temple,

the Jews assembled on the Sabbath to hear the Law read, and the practice continued in various buildings after the return. Cf. Ps. 74:8.

SYNAGOGUE (put out of the)

aposunagōgos (ἀποσυνάγωγος, 656), an adjective denoting "expelled from the congregation, excommunicated," is used (*a*) with *ginomai*, "to become, be made," John 9:22; 12:42; (*b*) with *poieō*, "to make," John 16:2. This excommunication involved prohibition not only from attendance at the "synagogue," but from all fellowship with Israelites.¶

SYNAGOGUE (ruler of the)

archisunagōgos (ἀρχισυνάγωγος, 752) denotes "the administrative official," with the duty of preserving order and inviting persons to read or speak in the assembly, Mark 5:22, 35, 36, 38; Luke 8:49; 13:14; Acts 13:15; "chief ruler" (KJV) in Acts 18:8, 17.¶

Note: In Luke 8:41, "ruler of the synagogue" represents *archōn*, "ruler," followed by the genitive case of the article and *sunagōgē*.

SYROPHOENICIAN

surophoinikissa or *surophunissa* (Συροφοινίκισσα, 4949) occurs in Mark 7:26 as the national name of a woman called "a Canaanitish woman" in Matt. 15:22, i.e., not a Jewess but a descendant of the early inhabitants of the coastland of Phoenicia. The word probably denoted a Syrian residing in Phoenicia proper.¶ There is a tradition that the woman's name was Justa and her daughter Bernice (*Clementine Homilies*, ii:19; iii:73). In Acts 21:2, 3, the two parts of the term are used interchangeably.

T

TABERNACLE

1. *skēnē* (σκηνή, 4633), "a tent, booth, tabernacle," is used of (*a*) tents as dwellings, Matt. 17:4; Mark 9:5; Luke 9:33; Heb. 11:9, KJV, "tabernacles" (RV, "tents"); (*b*) the Mosaic tabernacle, Acts 7:44; Heb. 8:5; 9:1 (in some mss.); 9:8, 21, termed "the tent of meeting," RV (i.e., where the people were called to meet God), a preferable description to "the tabernacle of the congregation," as in the KJV in the OT; the outer part, 9:2, 6; the inner sanctuary, 9:3; (*c*) the heavenly prototype, Heb. 8:2; 9:11; Rev. 13:6;

15:5; 21:3 (of its future descent); (*d*) the eternal abodes of the saints, Luke 16:9, RV, "tabernacles" (KJV, "habitations"); (*e*) the Temple in Jerusalem, as continuing the service of the tabernacle, Heb. 13:10; (*f*) the house of David, i.e., metaphorically of his people, Acts 15:16; (*g*) the portable shrine of the god Moloch, Acts 7:43.¶

2. *skēnos* (σκῆνος, 4636), the equivalent of No. 1, is used metaphorically of the body as the "tabernacle" of the soul, 2 Cor. 5:1, 4.¶

3. *skēnōma* (σκήνωμα, 4638) occurs in Acts 7:46; 2 Pet. 1:13, 14; see HABITATION, No. 6.¶

4. *skēnopēgia* (σκηνοπηγία, 4634), properly "the setting up of tents or dwellings" (No. 1, and *pēgnumi*, "to fix"), represents the word "tabernacles" in "the feast of tabernacles," John 7:2.¶ This feast, one of the three Pilgrimage Feasts in Israel, is called "the feast of ingathering" in Exod. 23:16; 34:22; it took place at the end of the year, and all males were to attend at the "tabernacle" with their offerings. In Lev. 23:34; Deut. 16:13, 16; 31:10; 2 Chron. 8:13; Ezra 3:4 (cf. Neh. 8:14–18), it is called "the feast of tabernacles" (or "booths," *sukkôth*), and was appointed for seven days at Jerusalem from the 15th to the 22nd Tishri (approximately October), to remind the people that their fathers dwelt in these in the wilderness journeys. Cf. Num. 29:15–38, especially v. 35–38, for the regulations of the eighth or "last day, the great day of the feast" (John 7:37).

Note: For *skēnoō*, "to spread a tabernacle over," Rev. 7:15, RV, see DWELL, No. 9.

TABLE

1. *trapeza* (τράπεζα, 5132) is used of (*a*) "a dining table," Matt. 15:27; Mark 7:28; Luke 16:21; 22:21, 30; (*b*) "the table of shewbread," Heb. 9:2; (*c*) by metonymy, of "what is provided on the table" (the word being used of that with which it is associated), Acts 16:34; Rom. 11:9 (figurative of the special privileges granted to Israel and centering in Christ); 1 Cor. 10:21 (twice), "the Lord's table," denoting all that is provided for believers in Christ on the ground of His death (and thus expressing something more comprehensive than the Lord's Supper); "the table of demons," denoting all that is partaken of by idolaters as the result of the influence of demons in connection with their sacrifices; (*d*) "a moneychanger's table," Matt. 21:12; Mark 11:15; John 2:15; (*e*) "a bank," Luke 19:23 (cf. *trapezitēs*: see BANKERS); (*f*) by metonymy for "the distribution of money," Acts 6:2. See BANK.¶

2. *plax* (πλάξ, 4109) primarily denotes "anything flat and broad," hence, "a flat stone, a tablet," 2 Cor. 3:3 (twice); Heb. 9:4.¶

Note: Some texts have the word *klinē*, "a couch," in Mark 7:4 (KJV, "tables").

TABLE (at the)

anakeimai (ἀνάκειμαι, 345), "to recline at a meal table," is rendered "sat at the table" in John 12:2, KJV, RV, "sat at meat" (some texts have *sunanakeimai*); "sat," of course does not express the actual attitude; in John 13:23, RV, "at the table reclining"; KJV, "leaning"; in 13:28, "at the table" (KJV and RV), lit., "of (those) reclining."

For TABLET see WRITING TABLET

TACKLING

skeuē (σκευή, 4631) denotes "gear, equipment, tackling" (of a ship), Acts 27:19.¶

TAIL

oura (οὐρά, 3769), "the tail of an animal," occurs in Rev. 9:10 (twice), 19; 12:4.¶

TAKE

1. *lambanō* (λαμβάνω, 2983), "to take, lay hold of," besides its literal sense, e.g., Matt. 5:40; 26:26, 27, is used metaphorically, of fear, in "taking" hold of people, Luke 7:16, RV (KJV, "came ... on"); of sin in "finding (occasion)," RV (KJV, "taking"), Rom. 7:8, 11, where sin is viewed as the corrupt source of action, an inward element using the commandment to produce evil effects; of the power of temptation, 1 Cor. 10:13; of "taking" an example, Jas. 5:10; of "taking" peace from the earth, Rev. 6:4; of Christ in "taking" the form of a servant, Phil. 2:7; of "taking" rightful power (by the Lord, hereafter), Rev. 11:17. See ACCEPT, No. 4.

2. *analambanō* (ἀναλαμβάνω, 353) signifies (*a*) "to take up" (*ana*), e.g., Acts 1:2, 11, 22 (RV, "received"); (*b*) "to take to oneself," Acts 7:43; or "to one's company," 20:13, 14; 23:31; 2 Tim. 4:11; of "taking up spiritual armor," Eph. 6:13, 16. See RECEIVE.

3. *apolambanō* (ἀπολαμβάνω, 618), besides its common meaning, "to receive," denotes "to take apart or aside," Mark 7:33, middle voice. It is frequent in the papyri, and, in the sense of separation or drawing aside, is illustrated in a message of sorrow, concerning the nonarrival of one who with others had been "shut up" as recluses in a temple (Moulton and Milligan, *Vocab.*). See RECEIVE.

4. *epilambanō* (ἐπιλαμβάνω, 1949), in the middle voice, "to lay hold of, take hold of," is used literally, e.g., Mark 8:23; Luke 9:47; 14:4; metaphorically, e.g., Heb. 8:9, "(I) took them (by the hand)": for other instances in each respect see HOLD, No. 7.

5. *katalambanō* (καταλαμβάνω, 2638), "to lay hold of," is rendered "to take," in Mark 9:18; John 8:3, 4. See APPREHEND.

6. *metalambanō* (μεταλαμβάνω, 3335), "to get, or have, a share of," is rendered "to take (food)" in Acts 2:46, RV (KJV, "did eat," see EAT, Note); 27:33, i.e., "to share it together." See HAVE, PARTAKE, RECEIVE.

7. *paralambanō* (παραλαμβάνω, 3880), besides its meaning "to receive," denotes "to take to (or with) oneself," of "taking" a wife,

e.g., Matt. 1:20, 24; of "taking" a person or persons with one, e.g., Matt. 2:13, 14, 20, 21; 4:5, 8; of demons, 12:45; of Christ and His disciples, 17:1; 20:17; Mark 9:2; 10:32; 14:33; of witnesses, Matt. 18:16; of the removal of persons from the earth in judgment, when "the Son of Man is revealed," Matt. 24:40, 41; Luke 17:34, 35 (cf. the means of the removal of corruption, in v. 37); of the "taking" of Christ by the soldiers for scourging, Matt. 27:27, RV, and to crucifixion, John 19:16; see also Acts 15:39; 16:33; 21:24, 26, 32; 23:18. See RECEIVE.

8. *sumparalambanō* (συμπαραλαμβάνω, 4838), *sun*, "with," and No. 7, denotes "to take along with oneself," as a companion, Acts 12:25; 15:37, 38; Gal. 2:1.¶

9. *proslambanō* (προσλαμβάνω, 4355), "to take to oneself" (*pros*), is used of food, Acts 27:33–36; of persons, of Peter's act toward Christ, Matt. 16:22; Mark 8:32; for evil purposes, Acts 17:5; for good purposes, 18:26. See RECEIVE.

10. *prolambanō* (προλαμβάνω, 4301) is rendered "to take before" in 1 Cor. 11:21. See COME, *Note* (2) at end, OVERTAKE.

11. *sullambanō* (συλλαμβάνω, 4815), "to seize, take," is rendered "to take" in Matt. 26:55 and Mark 14:48, KJV (RV, "seize"); Luke 5:9; Acts 1:16; in 12:3 and 23:27, KJV (RV, "seize"). See CATCH, CONCEIVE, HELP.

12. *airō* (αἴρω, 142), "to lift, carry, take up or away," occurs very frequently with its literal meanings. In John 1:29 it is used of Christ as "the Lamb of God, which taketh away the sin of the world," not the sins, but sin, that which has existed from the time of the Fall, and in regard to which God has had judicial dealings with the world; through the expiatory sacrifice of Christ the sin of the world will be replaced by everlasting righteousness; cf. the plural, "sins", in 1 John 3:5. Righteous judgment was "taken away" from Christ at human tribunals, and His life, while voluntarily given by Himself (John 10:17, 18), was "taken (from the earth)," Acts 8:33 (quoted from the Sept. of Isa. 53:8). In John 15:2 it is used in the Lord's statement, "Every branch in Me that beareth not fruit, He taketh it away." This does not contemplate members of the "body" of Christ, but those who (just as a graft which being inserted, does not "abide" or "strike") are merely professed followers, giving only the appearance of being joined to the parent stem.

The Law described in Col. 2:14 as "the bond written in ordinances that was against us," Christ "took" out of the way at His cross. In 1 Cor. 5:2, *airō* is used in the best texts (some have No. 14), of the divine judgment which would have been exercised in "taking away" from the church the incestuous delinquent, had they mourned before God. See AWAY, BEAR, No. 9, etc.

13. *apairō* (ἀπαίρω, 522), "to lift off" (*apo*, "from," and No. 12), is used, in the passive voice, of Christ, metaphorically as the Bridegroom of His followers, Matt. 9:15; Mark 2:20; Luke 5:35.¶

14. *exairō* (ἐξαίρω, 1808), "to take away," is used of "putting away" a person in church discipline, 1 Cor. 5:13; for this verb as a variant reading in v. 2, see No. 12.¶

15. *epairō* (ἐπαίρω, 1869), "to lift, raise," is used in the passive voice and rendered "He was taken up" in Acts 1:9. See EXALT, HOIST, LIFT.

16. *anaireō* (ἀναιρέω, 337), "to take up" (*ana*, "up," and *haireō*, "to take"), is used of Pharaoh's daughter in "taking up" the infant Moses, Acts 7:21; of God's act in "taking away" the typical animal sacrifices under the Law, Heb. 10:9. See DEATH, C, No. 2, KILL, SLAY.

17. *aphaireō* (ἀφαιρέω, 851), "to take away" (*apo*), is used with this meaning in Luke 1:25; 10:42; 16:3; Rom. 11:27, of the "removal" of the sins of Israel; Heb. 10:4, of the impossibility of the "removal" of sins by offerings under the Law; in Rev. 22:19 (twice). See CUT, No. 8.

18. *kathaireō* (καθαιρέω, 2507), "to take down" (*kata*), besides its meaning of "putting down by force," was the technical term for the "removal" of the body after crucifixion, Mark 15:36, 46; Luke 23:53; Acts 13:29. See CAST, No. 14.

19. *periaireō* (περιαιρέω, 4014), "to take away that which surrounds" (*peri*, "around"), is used (*a*) literally, of "casting off" anchors, Acts 27:40, RV (KJV, "having taken up"); 28:13 in some texts, for *perierchomai*, "to make a circuit"; (*b*) metaphorically, of "taking away" the veil off the hearts of Israel, 2 Cor. 3:16; of hope of rescue, Acts 27:20; of sins (negatively), Heb. 10:11.¶

20. *dechomai* (δέχομαι, 1209), "to receive," is rendered "take (thy bond, RV, KJV, bill)" in Luke 16:6, 7; "take (the helmet of salvation)," Eph. 6:17, suggesting a heartiness in the "taking." See ACCEPT, No. 1, RECEIVE.

21. *prosdechomai* (προσδέχομαι, 4327), "to receive favorably," is rendered "took" in Heb. 10:34. See ACCEPT, No. 3.

22. *krateō* (κρατέω, 2902), "to take hold of, get possession of," is translated "to take" in Matt. 9:25; 22:6; 26:4; Mark 1:31; 5:41; 9:27; 14:1, 44, 46, 49; Luke 8:54; Acts 24:6. See HOLD, No. 6.

23. *drassomai* (δράσσομαι, 1405), "to grasp

with the hand, take hold of," is used metaphorically in 1 Cor. 3:19, "taketh (the wise in their craftiness)."¶

24. *didōmi* (δίδωμι, 1325), "to give," found in the best texts in Mark 3:6, is rendered "took (counsel)"; some have *poieō*, "to make."

25. *katechō* (κατέχω, 2722), "to hold," is rendered "to take (the lowest place)" in Luke 14:9. See HOLD.

26. *piazō* (πιάζω, 4084), "to lay or take hold of forcefully," is always rendered "to take" in the RV. See APPREHEND, No. 2.

27. *parapherō* (παραφέρω, 3911), "to bear away" (*para*, "aside," *pherō*, "to bear"), "remove," is rendered "take away" in Mark 14:36, KJV, RV, "remove," as in Luke 22:42. See REMOVE.¶

28. *echō* (ἔχω, 2192), "to have, to hold," is used in Matt. 21:46 in the sense of regarding a person as something, "they took (Him) for (a prophet)." See HAVE.

29. *sunagō* (συνάγω, 4863), "to bring together," is used of "taking" a person into one's house receiving hospitality, "took . . . in," Matt. 25:35, 38, 43; so in Acts 11:26, RV, "were gathered together," KJV, "assembled"; perhaps the meaning is "they were entertained." See ASSEMBLE, BESTOW, GATHER.

30. *ekduō* (ἐκδύω, 1562), "to take off a garment from a person," is so rendered with reference to the soldiers' treatment of Christ, Matt. 27:31; Mark 15:20. See STRIP.

31. *ekballō* (ἐκβάλλω, 1544) has the meaning "to bring or take out" in Luke 10:35, "took out (two pence)," a word perhaps chosen to express the wholeheartedness of the act (lit., "to throw out"). See CAST, No. 5.

32. *bastazō* (βαστάζω, 941), "to bear, lift," is used of "taking up" stones, John 10:31. As to Matt. 3:11, Moulton and Milligan supply evidences from the vernacular that the word signified "to take off" (the sandals), which confirms Mark's word *luō*, "to unloose" (1:7). See BEAR, No. 1.

33. *epicheireō* (ἐπιχειρέω, 2021), "to take in hand" (*epi*, "upon," *cheir*, "the hand"), "to attempt, take upon oneself," is rendered "have taken in hand," Luke 1:1; "took upon (them)," Acts 19:13. See GO, No. 30.

34. *ginomai* (γίνομαι, 1096), "to become, to come to be," is rendered "he be taken" in 2 Thess. 2:7, lit., "(until) he, or it, become" (for a treatment of the whole passage see *Notes on Thess.* by Hogg and Vine).

Notes: (1) For *sunairō* in Matt. 18:23, see RECKON. (2) Some texts have *apagō*, "to take away," in Acts 24:7. (3) In John 6:24, KJV, *embainō*, "to enter," is rendered "took (ship-

ping)," RV, "got into (the boats)." (4) In 2 Thess. 1:8, KJV, *didōmi*, "to give" (RV "rendering"), is translated "taking." (5) In Rom. 3:5, KJV, *epipherō*, "to bring against," is rendered "taketh (vengeance)," RV, "visiteth (with wrath)." (6) In Luke 4:5, KJV, *anagō*, "to lead up" (RV, "led"), is rendered "took up." (7) In Acts 10:26, KJV, *egeirō*, "to raise" (RV), is rendered "took . . . up." (8) For "taking up" baggage, Acts 21:15, see BAGGAGE. (9) For "taken from" in 1 Thess. 2:17, KJV, see BEREAVED, No. 1. (10) *Sunechō* is translated "taken with" in Matt. 4:24; Luke 4:38; 8:37. See HOLDEN. (11) In 2 Pet. 2:12 "to be taken" translates the phrase *eis halōsin*, lit., "for capture" (*halōsis*, "a taking"). (12) In 1 Pet. 2:20, *hupomenō*, "to endure," is rendered "ye take . . . patiently." (13) In Matt. 11:12; John 6:15; Acts 23:10 *harpazō* (see CATCH) is rendered "take . . . by force." (14) For *apotassomai*, "to take leave of," see LEAVE, (*c*) No. 1. (15) For *apaspazomai*, rendered "to take leave of" in Acts 21:6, KJV, see LEAVE, (*c*) No. 2. (16) In Acts 21:6 some mss. have *epibainō*, KJV, "we took ship" (RV, *embainō*, "we went on board"): cf. *Note* (3), above. (17) For "untaken" in 2 Cor. 3:14 see UNLIFTED. (18) In 1 Tim. 5:9, KJV, *katalegō* is rendered "to take into the number" (RV, "be enrolled").¶ (19) For "take . . . to record" see TESTIFY. See also CARE, HEED, JOURNEY, THOUGHT (to take).

TALENT

A. Noun.

talanton (τάλαντον, 5007), originally "a balance," then, "a talent in weight," was hence "a sum of money" in gold or silver equivalent to a "talent." The Jewish "talent" contained 3,000 shekels of the sanctuary, e.g., Ex. 30:13 (about 114 lbs.). In NT times the "talent" was not a weight of silver, but the Roman-Attic "talent," comprising 6,000 denarii or drachmas, and equal to about L/240. It is mentioned in Matthew only, 18:24; 25:15, 16, 20 (twice in the best texts), 22 (thrice), 24, 25, 28 (twice). In 18:24 the vastness of the sum, 10,000 talents (L/2,400,000), indicates the impossibility of man's clearing himself, by his own efforts, of the guilt which lies upon him before God.¶

Note: That the "talent" denoted "something weighed" has provided the meaning of the Eng. word as "a gift or ability," especially under the influence of the parable of the talents (Matt. 25:14–30).

B. Adjective.

talantiaios (ταλαντιαῖος, 5006) denotes "of a talent's weight," Rev. 16:21.¶

For TALES see TALK

TALITHA

taleitha or *talitha* (ταλειθά, 5008), an Aramaic feminine meaning "maiden," Mark 5:41, has been variously transliterated in the NT Greek mss. *Koumi* or *Koum* (Heb. and Aram., *qûm*, "arise"), which follows, is interpreted by, "I say unto thee, arise." *Koum* is the better attested word; so in the Talmud, where this imperative occurs "seven times in one page" (Edersheim, *Life and Times of Jesus*, i, p. 631).¶

TALK (Noun and Verb)

A. Nouns.

1. *logos* (λόγος, 3056), a word, is translated "talk" in Matt. 22:15; Mark 12:13. See ACCOUNT, B.

2. *lēros* (λῆρος, 3026) denotes "foolish talk, nonsense," Luke 24:11, RV, "idle talk" (KJV, "idle tales").¶

B. Verbs.

1. *laleō* (λαλέω, 2980), "to speak, say," is always translated "to speak" in the RV, where the KJV renders it by "to talk," Matt. 12:46; Mark 6:50; Luke 24:32; John 4:27 (twice); 9:37; 14:30; Acts 26:31; Rev. 4:1; 17:1; 21:9, 15. The RV rendering is preferable; the idea of "chat" or "chatter" is entirely foreign to the NT, and should never be regarded as the meaning in 1 Cor. 14:34, 35. See COMMUNE, *Note,* SAY, No. 1, *Note,* and No. 2, SPEAK.

2. *sullaleō* (συλλαλέω, 4814), "to speak with" (*sun*), is translated "to talk with," Matt. 17:3; Mark 9:4; Luke 9:30. See CONFER, No. 2.

3. *homileō* (ὁμιλέω, 3656), "to be in company with, consort with" (*homilos*, "a throng"; *homilia*, "company"), hence, "to converse with," is rendered "to talk with," Acts 20:11. See COMMUNE, No. 2.

4. *sunomileō* (συνομιλέω, 4926), "to converse, talk with," occurs in Acts 10:27.¶

TALKERS (vain)

mataiologos (ματαιολόγος, 3151), an adjective denoting "talking idly" (*mataios*, "vain, idle," *legō*, "to speak"), is used as a noun (plural) in Titus 1:10.¶

TALKING (vain, foolish)

1. *mataiologia* (ματαιολογία, 3150), a noun corresponding to the above, is used in 1 Tim. 1:6, RV, "vain talking" (KJV, "vain jangling").¶

2. *mōrologia* (μωρολογία, 3473), from *mōros*, "foolish, dull, stupid," and *legō*, is used in Eph. 5:4; it denotes more than mere idle "talk." Trench describes it as "that 'talk of fools'

which is foolishness and sin together" (*Syn.* §xxxiv).¶

TAME

damazō (δαμάζω, 1150), "to subdue, tame," is used (*a*) naturally in Mark 5:4 and Jas. 3:7 (twice); (*b*) metaphorically, of the tongue, in Jas. 3:8.¶ In the Sept., Dan. 2:40.¶

TANNER

burseus (βυρσεύς, 1038), "a tanner" (from *bursa*, "a hide"), occurs in Acts 9:43; 10:6, 32.¶

For TARE (Verb) see TEAR

TARES

zizanion (ζιζάνιον, 2215) is a kind of darnel, the commonest of the four species, being the bearded, growing in the grain fields, as tall as wheat and barley, and resembling wheat in appearance. It was credited among the Jews with being degenerate wheat. The rabbis called it "bastard." The seeds are poisonous to man and herbivorous animals, producing sleepiness, nausea, convulsions and even death (they are harmless to poultry). The plants can be separated out, but the custom, as in the parable, is to leave the cleaning out till near the time of harvest, Matt. 13:25–27, 29, 30, 36, 38, 40.¶ The Lord describes the tares as "the sons of the evil *one*"; false teachings are indissociable from their propagandists. For the Lord's reference to the Kingdom see KINGDOM.

TARRY

1. *menō* (μένω, 3306), "to abide," is translated by the verb "to abide," in the RV, for KJV, "to tarry," in Matt. 26:38; Mark 14:34; Luke 24:29; John 4:40; Acts 9:43; 18:20; the RV retains the verb "to tarry" in John 21:22, 23; in Acts 20:5, KJV, "tarried" (RV, "were waiting"). Some mss. have it in Acts 20:15 (KJV, "tarried"). See ABIDE.

2. *epimenō* (ἐπιμένω, 1961), to abide, continue, a strengthened form of No. 1, is translated "to tarry" in Acts 10:48; 21:4, 10; 28:12, 14; 1 Cor. 16:7, 8; Gal. 1:18, RV (KJV, "abode"). See ABIDE, No. 2.

3. *hupomenō* (ὑπομένω, 5278), "to endure," is rendered "tarried behind" in Luke 2:43. See ENDURE, No. 2.

4. *prosmenō* (προσμένω, 4357), "to abide still, continue," is translated "tarried" in Acts 18:18, suggesting patience and steadfastness in remaining after the circumstances which preceded; in 1 Tim. 1:3, RV, "to tarry" (KJV, "to abide still"). See ABIDE, No. 6.

5. *diatribō* (διατρίβω, 1304), for which see

ABIDE, No. 7, is invariably rendered "to tarry," in the RV; KJV, twice, John 3:22; Acts 25:6; "continued" in John 11:54; Acts 15:35; "abode," Acts 12:19; 14:3, 28; 20:6; "abiding," 16:12; "had been," 25:14.¶

6. *chronizō* (χρονίζω, 5549), "to spend or while away time"; "to tarry," Matt. 25:5; Luke 1:21; Heb. 10:37. See DELAY, No. 2.

7. *bradunō* (βραδύνω, 1019), "to be slow" (*bradus*, "slow"), is rendered "I tarry long," 1 Tim. 3:15; "is . . . slack," 2 Pet. 3:9.¶

8. *kathizō* (καθίζω, 2523), "to make to sit down," or, intransitively, "to sit down," is translated "tarry ye" in Luke 24:49. See SIT.

9. *mellō* (μέλλω, 3195), "to be about to," is rendered "(why) tarriest thou?" in Acts 22:16. See ABOUT, B.

10. *ekdechomai* (ἐκδέχομαι, 1551), "to expect, await" (*ek*, "from," *dechomai*, "to receive"), is translated "tarry" in 1 Cor. 11:33, KJV (RV, "wait"). See EXPECT, LOOK, WAIT.

Notes: (1) In Acts 27:33, KJV, *prosdokaō*, "to wait, look for," is translated "have tarried" (RV, "wait"). (2) In Acts 15:33, *poieō*, "to make or do," is used with *chronos*, "time," KJV, "they had tarried a space," RV, "they had spent some time."

TASTE

geuō (γεύω, 1089), "to make to taste," is used in the middle voice, signifying "to taste" (*a*) naturally, Matt. 27:34; Luke 14:24; John 2:9; Col. 2:21; (*b*) metaphorically, of Christ's "tasting" death, implying His personal experience in voluntarily undergoing death, Heb. 2:9; of believers (negatively) as to "tasting" of death, Matt. 16:28; Mark 9:1; Luke 9:27; John 8:52; of "tasting" the heavenly gift (different from receiving it), Heb. 6:4; "the good word of God, and the powers of the age to come," 6:5; "that the Lord is gracious," 1 Pet. 2:3. See EAT.

TATTLER

phluaros (φλύαρος, 5397), "babbling, garrulous" (from *phluō*, "to babble": cf. *phluareō*, "to prate against"), is translated "tattlers" in 1 Tim. 5:13.¶

TAUGHT (Adjective)

1. *didaktos* (διδακτός, 1318), primarily "what can be taught," then, "taught," is used (*a*) of persons, John 6:45; (*b*) of things, 1 Cor. 2:13 (twice), "(not in words which man's wisdom) teacheth, (but which the Spirit) teacheth," lit., "(not in words) taught (of man's wisdom, but) taught (of the Spirit)."¶

2. *theodidaktos* (θεοδίδακτος, 2312), "God-taught" (*Theos*, "God," and No. 1), occurs in

1 Thess. 4:9, lit., "God-taught (persons)"; while the missionaries had "taught" the converts to love one another, God had Himself been their Teacher. Cf. John 6:45 (see No. 1).¶

For TAXED, TAXING see ENROLL, ENROLMENT

TEACH

A. Verbs.

1. *didaskō* (διδάσκω, 1321) is used (*a*) absolutely, "to give instruction," e.g., Matt. 4:23; 9:35; Rom. 12:7; 1 Cor. 4:17; 1 Tim. 2:12; 4:11; (*b*) transitively, with an object, whether persons, e.g., Matt. 5:2; 7:29, and frequently in the Gospels and Acts, or things "taught," e.g., Matt. 15:9; 22:16; Acts 15:35; 18:11; both persons and things, e.g., John 14:26; Rev. 2:14, 20.

2. *paideuō* (παιδεύω, 3811), "to instruct and train": see INSTRUCT, No. 2.

3. *katecheō* (κατηχέω, 2727), for which see INFORM, No. 2, INSTRUCT, No. 1, is rendered "to teach" in 1 Cor. 14:19, KJV (RV, "instruct"); Gal. 6:6 (twice).

4. *heterodidaskaleō* (ἑτεροδιδασκαλέω, 2085), "to teach a different doctrine" (*heteros*, "different," to be distinguished from *allos*, "another of the same kind": see ANOTHER), is used in 1 Tim. 1:3; 6:3, RV, KJV, "teach (no) other doctrine" and "teach otherwise," of what is contrary to the faith.¶

Notes: (1) For *mathēteuō*, "to teach," in the KJV of Matt. 28:19; Acts 14:21, see DISCIPLE, B. (2) In Acts 16:21, KJV, *katangellō*, "to declare, preach," is rendered "teach" (RV, "set forth"). (3) For "teacheth" in 1 Cor. 2:13, see TAUGHT, No. 1 (*b*).

B. Adjective.

didaktikos (διδακτικός, 1317), "skilled in teaching" (akin to No. 1 above: Eng., "didactic"), is translated "apt to teach" in 1 Tim. 3:2; 2 Tim. 2:24.¶

TEACHER, FALSE TEACHERS

1. *didaskalos* (διδάσκαλος, 1320) is rendered "teacher" or "teachers" in Matt. 23:8, by Christ, of Himself; in John 3:2 of Christ; of Nicodemus in Israel, 3:10, RV; of "teachers" of the truth in the churches, Acts 13:1; 1 Cor. 12:28, 29; Eph. 4:11; Heb. 5:12; Jas. 3:1, RV; by Paul of his work among the churches, 1 Tim. 2:7; 2 Tim. 1:11; of "teachers," wrongfully chosen by those who have "itching ears," 2 Tim. 4:3. See MASTER, RABBI.

2. *kalodidaskalos* (καλοδιδάσκαλος, 2567) denotes "a teacher of what is good" (*kalos*), Titus 2:3.¶

3. *pseudodidaskalos* (ψευδοδιδάσκαλος, 5572), "a false teacher," occurs in the plural in 2 Pet. 2:1.¶

For **TEACHING** (Noun) see **DOCTRINE,** Nos. 1 and 2

TEARS

dakruon or *dakru* (δάκρυον, 1144), akin to *dakruō*, "to weep," is used in the plural, Mark 9:24; Luke 7:38, 44 (with the sense of washing therewith the Lord's feet); Acts 20:19, 31; 2 Cor. 2:4; 2 Tim. 1:4; Heb. 5:7; 12:17; Rev. 7:17; 21:4.¶

TEAR, TORN

1. *sparassō* (σπαράσσω, 4682), denotes "to tear, rend, convulse," Mark 1:26; 9:20 (in some mss.), 26, RV, "having ... torn" (KJV, "rent"); Luke 9:39.¶ In the Sept., 2 Sam. 22:8, of the foundations of heaven; Jer. 4:18, of the heart.¶

2. *susparassō* (συσπαράσσω, 4952), "to tear violently" (*sun*, "with," intensive), "convulse completely," a strengthened form of No. 1, is used in Mark 9:20, in the best texts (some have No. 1); Luke 9:42.¶

3. *diaspaō* (διασπάω, 1288), "to break or tear asunder," is translated "should be torn in pieces" in Acts 23:10, RV (KJV, " ... pulled ... "). See REND, No. 5.

4. *rhēgnumi* (ῥήγνυμι, 4486), "to break," is rendered "teareth" in Mark 9:18, KJV (RV, "dasheth ... down"). See HINDER, No. 1.

TEDIOUS (to be)

enkoptō (ἐνκόπτω, 1465), "to hinder," is rendered "to be tedious" in Acts 24:4, of detaining a person unnecessarily. See HINDER, No. 1.

For TEETH see TOOTH

TELL

1. *legō* (λέγω, 3004) and the 2nd aorist form *eipon*, used to supply this tense in *legō*, are frequently translated "to tell," e.g., Matt. 2:13, RV, "I tell," KJV, "I bring (thee) word"; 10:27. See SAY, No. 1.

2. *laleō* (λαλέω, 2980), for which see SAY, No. 2, is usually rendered "to speak," in the RV (for KJV, "to tell"), e.g., Matt. 26:13; Luke 1:45; 2:17, 18, 20; Acts 11:14; 27:25; but RV and KJV, "to tell" in John 8:40; Acts 9:6; 22:10.

3. *eklaleō* (ἐκλαλέω, 1583), "to speak out" (*ek*), is translated "tell" in Acts 23:22.¶

4. *eirō* (εἴρω, Fut. of 3004), for which see SAY, No. 4, is rendered "to tell" in Matt. 21:24; Mark 11:29; John 14:29; Rev. 17:7.

5. *apangellō* (ἀπαγγέλλω, 518), "to announce, declare, report" (usually as a messenger), is frequently rendered "to tell," e.g., Matt. 8:33; 14:12. See BRING, No. 36.

6. *anangellō* (ἀναγγέλλω, 312), "to bring back word, announce," is sometimes rendered "to tell," e.g., John 5:15; 2 Cor. 7:7. See DECLARE, No. 1.

7. *diēgeomai* (διηγέομαι, 1334), for which see DECLARE, No. 6, is rendered "to tell," in the KJV and RV, in Mark 9:9; Heb. 11:32.

8. *exēgeomai* (ἐξηγέομαι, 1834), for which see DECLARE, No. 8, is translated "told" in Luke 24:35, KJV (RV, "rehearsed").

9. *diasapheō* (διασαφέω, 1285), "to make clear" (*dia*, "throughout," *saphēs*, "clear"), explain fully, is translated "told" in Matt. 18:31. See EXPLAIN.

10. *mēnuō* (μηνύω, 3377) is rendered "told" in Acts 23:30, KJV: see show, No. 7.

11. *proeirō* (*prolegō*) (προείρω, 4280v), "to tell before," is so rendered in Matt. 24:25: see FORETELL, FOREWARN.

Note: In the following, *oida*, "to know," is translated "tell" in the KJV (RV, "know"), Matt. 21:27; Mark 11:33; Luke 20:7; John 3:8; 8:14; 16:18; 2 Cor. 12:2.

TEMPER TOGETHER

sunkerannumi (συγκεράννυμι, 4786), "to mix or blend together," is used in 1 Cor. 12:24, of the combining of the members of the human body into an organic structure, as illustrative of the members of a local church (see v. 27, where there is no definite article in the original). See MIXED (with).

TEMPERANCE, TEMPERATE

A. Noun.

enkrateia (ἐγκράτεια, 1466), from *kratos*, "strength," occurs in Acts 24:25; Gal. 5:23; 2 Pet. 1:6 (twice), in all of which it is rendered "temperance"; the RV marg., "self-control" is the preferable rendering, as "temperance" is now limited to one form of self-control; the various powers bestowed by God upon man are capable of abuse; the right use demands the controlling power of the will under the operation of the Spirit of God; in Acts 24:25 the word follows "righteousness," which represents God's claims, self-control being man's response thereto; in 2 Pet. 1:6, it follows "knowledge," suggesting that what is learned requires to be put into practice.¶

B. Adjectives.

1. *enkratēs* (ἐγκρατής, 1468), akin to A, denotes "exercising self-control," rendered "temperate" in Titus 1:8.¶

2. *nēphalios* (νηφάλιος, 3524), for which see SOBER, is translated "temperate" in 1 Tim. 3:2, RV (KJV, "vigilant"); in 3:11 and Titus 2:2, RV (KJV, "sober").¶

Note: In Titus 2:2, KJV, *sōphrōn*, "sober," is rendered "temperate" (RV, "soberminded").

C. Verb.

enkrateuomai (ἐγκρατεύομαι, 1467), akin to A and B, No. 1, rendered "is temperate" in 1 Cor. 9:25, is used figuratively of the rigid self-control practiced by athletes with a view to gaining the prize. See CONTINENCY.

TEMPEST

1. *thuella* (θύελλα, 2366), "a hurricane, cyclone, whirlwind" (akin to *thuō*, "to slay," and *thumos*, "wrath"), is used in Heb. 12:18.¶ In the Sept., Ex. 10:22; Deut. 4:11; 5:22.¶

2. *seismos* (σεισμός, 4578), "a shaking" (Eng., "seismic," etc.), is used of a "tempest" in Matt. 8:24. See EARTHQUAKE.

3. *cheimōn* (χειμών, 5494), "winter, a winter storm," hence, in general, "a tempest," is so rendered in Acts 27:20. See WEATHER, WINTER.

4. *lailaps* (λαῖλαψ, 2978), "a tempest," 2 Pet. 2:17, KJV: see STORM.

Note: For "tossed with a tempest," Acts 27:18, KJV, see LABOR, B, No. 2.

TEMPESTUOUS

tuphōnikos (τυφωνικός, 5189), from *tuphōn*, "a hurricane, typhoon," is translated "tempestuous" in Acts 27:14.¶

TEMPLE

1. *hieron* (ἱερόν, 2411), the neuter of the adjective *hieros*, "sacred," is used as a noun denoting "a sacred place, a temple," that of Artemis (Diana), Acts 19:27; that in Jerusalem, Mark 11:11, signifying the entire building with its precincts, or some part thereof, as distinct from the *naos*, "the inner sanctuary" (see No. 2); apart from the Gospels and Acts, it is mentioned only in 1 Cor. 9:13. Christ taught in one of the courts, to which all the people had access. *Hieron* is never used figuratively. The Temple mentioned in the Gospels and Acts was begun by Herod in 20 B.C., and destroyed by the Romans in A.D. 70.

2. *naos* (ναός, 3485), "a shrine or sanctuary," was used (*a*) among the heathen, to denote the shrine containing the idol, Acts 17:24; 19:24 (in the latter, miniatures); (*b*) among the Jews, the sanctuary in the "Temple," into which only the priests could lawfully enter, e.g., Luke 1:9, 21, 22; Christ, as being of the tribe of Judah, and thus not being a priest while upon the earth (Heb. 7:13, 14; 8:4), did not enter the *naos*; for

2 Thess. 2:4 see *Note* (below); (*c*) by Christ metaphorically, of His own physical body, John 2:19, 21; (*d*) in apostolic teaching, metaphorically, (1) of the church, the mystical body of Christ, Eph. 2:21; (2) of a local church, 1 Cor. 3:16, 17; 2 Cor. 6:16; (3) of the present body of the individual believer, 1 Cor. 6:19; (4) of the "Temple" seen in visions in the Apocalypse, 3:12; 7:15; 11:19; 14:15, 17; 15:5, 6, 8; 16:1, 17; (5) of the Lord God Almighty and the Lamb, as the "Temple" of the new and heavenly Jerusalem, Rev. 21:22. See SANCTUARY and HOLY, B (*b*), par. 4.

Notes: (1) The "temple" mentioned in 2 Thess. 2:4 (*naos*), as the seat of the Man of Sin, has been regarded in different ways. The weight of Scripture evidence is in favor of the view that it refers to a literal "temple" in Jerusalem, to be reconstructed in the future (cf. Dan. 11:31 and 12:11, with Matt. 24:15). For a fuller examination of the passage, see *Notes on Thessalonians,* by Hogg and Vine, pp. 250–252. (2) For *oikos*, rendered "temple," Luke 11:51, KJV, see HOUSE, No. 1.

TEMPLE KEEPER

neōkoros (νεωκόρος, 3511), Acts 19:35, RV, and KJV marg., "temple keeper" (KJV, "worshiper"), is used in profane Greek of "one who has charge of a temple." Coin inscriptions show that it was an honorary title given to certain cities, especially in Asia Minor, where the cult of some god or of a deified human potentate had been established, here to Ephesus in respect of the goddess Artemis. Apparently the imperial cult also existed at Ephesus. Josephus applies the word to Jews as worshipers, but this is not the meaning in Acts 19.¶

TEMPORAL

proskairos (πρόσκαιρος, 4340), "for a season" (*pros*, "for," *kairos*, "a season"), is rendered "temporal" in 2 Cor. 4:18. See SEASON, WHILE.

TEMPT

A. Verbs.

1. *peirazō* (πειράζω, 3985) signifies (1) "to try, attempt, assay" (see TRY); (2) "to test, try, prove," in a good sense, said of Christ and of believers, Heb. 2:18, where the context shows that the temptation was the cause of suffering to Him, and only suffering, not a drawing away to sin, so that believers have the sympathy of Christ as their High Priest in the suffering which sin occasions to those who are in the enjoyment of communion with God; so in the similar passage in 4:15; in all the temptations which Christ

endured, there was nothing within Him that answered to sin. There was no sinful infirmity in Him. While He was truly man, and His divine nature was not in any way inconsistent with His Manhood, there was nothing in Him such as is produced in us by the sinful nature which belongs to us; in Heb. 11:37, of the testing of OT saints; in 1 Cor. 10:13, where the meaning has a wide scope, the verb is used of "testing" as permitted by God, and of the believer as one who should be in the realization of his own helplessness and his dependence upon God (see PROVE, TRY); in a bad sense, "to tempt" (a) of attempts to ensnare Christ in His speech, e.g., Matt. 16:1; 19:3; 22:18, 35, and parallel passages; John 8:6; (b) of temptations to sin, e.g., Gal. 6:1, where one who would restore an erring brother is not to act as his judge, but as being one with him in liability to sin, with the possibility of finding himself in similar circumstances, Jas. 1:13, 14 (see note below); of temptations mentioned as coming from the Devil, Matt. 4:1; and parallel passages; 1 Cor. 7:5; 1 Thess. 3:5 (see TEMPTER); (c) of trying or challenging God, Acts 15:10; 1 Cor. 10:9 (2nd part); Heb. 3:9; the Holy Spirit, Acts 5:9: cf. No. 2.

Note: *"James 1:13–15 seems to contradict other statements of Scripture in two respects, saying (a) that 'God cannot be tempted with evil,' and (b) that 'He Himself tempteth no man.' But God tempted, or tried, Abraham, Heb. 11:17, and the Israelites tempted, or tried, God, 1 Cor. 10:9. V. 14, however, makes it plain that, whereas in these cases the temptation or trial, came from without, James refers to temptation, or trial, arising within, from uncontrolled appetites and from evil passions, cf. Mark 7:20–23. But though such temptation does not proceed from God, yet does God regard His people while they endure it, and by it tests and approves them."

2. *ekpeirazō* (ἐκπειράζω, 1598), an intensive form of the foregoing, is used in much the same way as No. 1 (2) (c), in Christ's quotation from Deut. 6:16, in reply to the Devil, Matt. 4:7; Luke 4:12; so in 1 Cor. 10:9, RV, "the Lord" (KJV, "Christ"); of the lawyer who "tempted" Christ, Luke 10:25.¶ In the Sept., Deut. 6:16; 8:2, 16; Ps. 78:18.¶ Cf. *dokimazō* (see PROVE).

B. Adjective.

apeirastos (ἀπείραστος, 551), "untempted, untried" (a, negative, and A, No. 1), occurs in Jas. 1:13, with *eimi*, "to be," "cannot be tempted," "untemptable" (Mayor).¶

* From *Notes on Thessalonians,* by Hogg and Vine, p. 97.

TEMPTATION

peirasmos (πειρασμός, 3986), akin to A, above, is used of (1) "trials" with a beneficial purpose and effect, (a) of "trials" or "temptations," divinely permitted or sent, Luke 22:28; Acts 20:19; Jas. 1:2; 1 Pet. 1:6; 4:12, RV, "to prove," KJV, "to try"; 2 Pet. 2:9 (singular); Rev. 3:10, RV, "trial" (KJV, "temptation"); in Jas. 1:12, "temptation" apparently has meanings (1) and (2) combined (see below), and is used in the widest sense; (b) with a good or neutral significance, Gal. 4:14, of Paul's physical infirmity, "a temptation" to the Galatian converts, of such a kind as to arouse feelings of natural repugnance; (c) of "trials" of a varied character, Matt. 6:13 and Luke 11:4, where believers are commanded to pray not to be led into such by forces beyond their own control; Matt. 26:41; Mark 14:38; Luke 22:40, 46, where they are commanded to watch and pray against entering into "temptations" by their own carelessness or disobedience; in all such cases God provides "the way of escape," 1 Cor. 10:13 (where *peirasmos* occurs twice). (2) Of "trial" definitely designed to lead to wrong doing, "temptation," Luke 4:13; 8:13; 1 Tim. 6:9; (3) of "trying" or challenging God, by men, Heb. 3:8.¶

TEMPTER

Note: The present participle of *peirazō*, "to tempt," preceded by the article, lit., "the (one) tempting," is used as a noun, describing the Devil in this character, Matt. 4:3; 1 Thess. 3:5.¶

TEN

deka (δέκα, 1176), whence the Eng. prefix "deca–," is regarded by some as the measure of human responsibility, e.g., Luke 19:13, 17; Rev. 2:10; it is used in a figurative setting in Rev. 12:3; 13:1; 17:3, 7, 12, 16.

Notes: (1) In Acts 23:23, *hebdomēkonta,* "seventy," is translated "threescore and ten." (2) For "ten thousand" see THOUSAND.

For TEND, John 21:16; 1 Pet. 5:2, RV, see FEED, No. 2

TENDER

hapalos (ἁπαλός, 527), "soft, tender," is used of the branch of a tree, Matt. 24:32; Mark 13:28.¶

Note: For Luke 1:78, "tender mercy"; Phil. 1:8; 2:1 "tender mercies," see BOWELS.

For TENDERHEARTED see PITIFUL, No. 2

TENTH

1. *dekatos* (δέκατος, 1182), an adjective from *deka*, "ten," occurs in John 1:39; Rev. 11:13; 21:20.¶

2. *dekatē* (δεκάτη, 1181), grammatically the feminine form of No. 1, with *meris*, "a part," understood, is used as a noun, translated "a tenth part" in Heb. 7:2, "a tenth," v. 4; "tithes" in vv. 8, 9.¶

For **TENTS** see **TABERNACLE,** No. 1

TENTMAKERS

skēnopoios (σκηνοποιός, 4635), an adjective, "tentmaking" (*skēnē*, "a tent," *poieō*, "to make"), is used as a noun in Acts 18:3.¶

TERM (appointed)

prothesmios (προθέσμιος, 4287), an adjective denoting "appointed beforehand" (*pro*, "before," *tithēmi*, "to put, appoint": see APPOINT No. 3, *Note*), is used as a noun, *prothesmia* (grammatically feminine, with *hēmera*, "a day," understood), as in Greek law, "a day appointed before," Gal. 4:2, RV, "the term appointed," i.e., "a stipulated date" (KJV, "the time appointed").¶

TERRESTRIAL

epigeios (ἐπίγειος, 1919), "on earth, earthly" (*epi*, "on," *gē*, "the earth"), is rendered "terrestrial" in 1 Cor. 15:40 (twice), in contrast to *epouranios*, "heavenly." See EARTHLY, No. 2.

For **TERRIBLE,** Heb. 12:21, see **FEARFUL,** B, No. 1

TERRIFY

A. Verbs.
1. *ptoeō* (πτοέω, 4422), "to terrify," is used in the passive voice, Luke 21:9; 24:37.¶

2. *ekphobeō* (ἐκφοβέω, 1629), "to frighten away" (*ek*, "out," *phobos*, "fear"), occurs in 2 Cor. 10:9.¶

3. *pturō* (πτύρω, 4426), "to scare," Phil. 1:28: see AFFRIGHTED, B, No. 1.¶

B. Adjective.
emphobos (ἔμφοβος, 1719), "terrified," is so rendered in the RV of Acts 24:25. See TREMBLE.

TERROR

1. *phobos* (φόβος, 5401), "fear," is rendered "terror" in Rom. 13:3; in 2 Cor. 5:11 and 1 Pet. 3:14, KJV (RV, "fear"). See FEAR, No. 1.

2. *phobētron* (φόβητρον, 5400), "that which causes fright, a terror," is translated "terrors" in Luke 21:11, RV (KJV, "fearful sights").¶ See FEAR, A, *Note*. For *ptoēsis*, See AMAZEMENT.

For **TESTAMENT** see **COVENANT**

TESTATOR

diatithēmi (διατίθημι, 1303), "to arrange, dispose," is used only in the middle voice in the NT; in Heb. 9:16, 17, the present participle with the article, lit., "the (one) making a testament (or covenant)," virtually a noun, "the testator" (the covenanting one); it is used of "making a covenant" in 8:10 and 10:16 and Acts 3:25. In "covenant-making," the sacrifice of a victim was customary (Gen. 15:10; Jer. 34:18, 19). He who "made a covenant" did so at the cost of a life. While the terminology in Heb. 9:16, 17 has the appearance of being appropriate to the circumstances of making a will, there is excellent reason for adhering to the meaning "covenant-making." The rendering "the death of the testator" would make Christ a Testator, which He was not. He did not die simply that the terms of a testamentary disposition might be fulfilled for the heirs. Here He who is "the Mediator of a new covenant" (v. 15) is Himself the Victim whose death was necessary. The idea of "making a will" destroys the argument of v. 18. In spite of various advocacies of the idea of a will, the weight of evidence is confirmatory of what Hatch, in *Essays in Biblical Greek*, p. 48, says: "There can be little doubt that the word (*diathēkē*) must be invariably taken in this sense of 'covenant' in the NT, and especially in a book ... so impregnated with the language of the Sept. as the Epistle to the Hebrews" (see also Westcott, and W. F. Moulton). We may render somewhat literally thus: 'For where a covenant (is), a death (is) necessary to be brought in of the one covenanting; for a covenant over dead ones (victims) is sure, since never has it force when the one covenanting lives' [Christ being especially in view]. The writer is speaking from a Jewish point of view, not from that of the Greeks. "To adduce the fact that in the case of wills the death of the testator is the condition of validity, is, of course, no proof at all that a death is necessary to make a covenant valid.... To support his argument, proving the necessity of Christ's death, the writer adduces the general law that he who makes a covenant does so at the expense of life" (Marcus Dods). See APPOINT, MAKE.

TESTIFY

1. *martureō* (μαρτυρέω, 3140), for which see WITNESS, is frequently rendered "to bear witness, to witness," in the RV, where KJV ren-

ders it "to testify," John 2:25; 3:11, 32; 5:39; 15:26; 21:24; 1 Cor. 15:15; Heb. 7:17; 11:4; 1 John 4:14; 5:9; 3 John 3. In the following, however, the RV, like the KJV, has the rendering "to testify," John 4:39, 44; 7:7; 13:21; Acts 26:5; Rev. 22:16, 18, 20.

2. *epimartureō* (ἐπιμαρτυρέω, 1957), "to bear witness to" (a strengthened form of No. 1), is rendered "testifying" in 1 Pet. 5:12.¶

3. *marturomai* (μαρτύρομαι, 3143), primarily, "to summon as witness," then, "to bear witness" (sometimes with the suggestion of solemn protestation), is rendered "to testify" in Acts 20:26, RV (KJV, "I take ... to record"); 26:22, in the best texts (some have No. 1), RV; Gal. 5:3; Eph. 4:17; 1 Thess. 2:11, in the best texts (some have No. 1), RV, "testifying" (KJV, "charged").¶

4. *diamarturomai* (διαμαρτύρομαι, 1263), "to testify or protest solemnly," an intensive form of No. 3, is translated "to testify" in Luke 16:28; Acts 2:40; 8:25; 10:42; 18:5; 20:21, 23, 24; 23:11; 28:23; 1 Thess. 4:6; Heb. 2:6; "to charge" in 1 Tim. 5:21; 2 Tim. 2:14; 4:1.¶

5. *promarturomai* (προμαρτύρομαι, 4303), "to testify beforehand," occurs in 1 Pet. 1:11, where the pronoun "it" should be "He" (the "it" being due to the grammatically neuter form of *pneuma;* the personality of the Holy Spirit requires the masculine pronoun).¶

Note: In Rev. 22:18 some texts have *summartureō,* "to bear witness with." See WITNESS.

TESTIMONY

1. *marturion* (μαρτύριον, 3142), "a testimony, witness," is almost entirely translated "testimony" in both KJV and RV. The only place where both have "witness" is Acts 4:33. In Acts 7:44 and Jas. 5:3, the RV has "testimony" (KJV, "witness").

In 2 Thess. 1:10, "our testimony unto you," RV, refers to the fact that the missionaries, besides proclaiming the truths of the gospel, had borne witness to the power of these truths. *Kērugma,* "the thing preached, the message," is objective, having especially to do with the effect on the hearers; *marturion* is mainly subjective, having to do especially with the preacher's personal experience. In 1 Tim. 2:6 the RV is important, "the testimony (i.e., of the gospel) *to be borne* in its own times," i.e., in the times divinely appointed for it, namely, the present age, from Pentecost till the church is complete. In Rev. 15:5, in the phrase, "the temple of the tabernacle of the testimony in Heaven," the "testimony" is the witness to the rights of God, denied and refused on earth, but about to be vindicated by the exercise of the judgments

under the pouring forth of the seven bowls or vials of divine retribution. See WITNESS.

2. *marturia* (μαρτυρία, 3141), "witness, evidence, testimony," is almost always rendered "witness" in the RV (for KJV, "testimony" in John 3:32, 33; 5:34; 8:17; 21:24, and always for KJV, "record," e.g., 1 John 5:10, 11), except in Acts 22:18 and in the Apocalypse, where both, with one exception, have "testimony," 1:2, 9; 6:9; 11:7; 12:11, 17; 19:10 (twice); 20:4 (KJV, "witness"). In 19:10, "the testimony of Jesus" is objective, the "testimony" or witness given to Him (cf. 1:2, 9; as to those who will bear it, see Rev. 12:17, RV). The statement "the testimony of Jesus is the spirit of prophecy," is to be understood in the light, e.g., of the "testimony" concerning Christ and Israel in the Psalms, which will be used by the godly Jewish remnant in the coming time of "Jacob's Trouble." All such "testimony" centers in and points to Christ. See WITNESS.

TETRARCH

A. Noun.

tetraarchēs or *tetrarchēs* (τετραάρχης, 5076) denotes "one of four rulers" (*tetra,* "four," *archē,* "rule"), properly, "the governor of the fourth part of a region"; hence, "a dependent princeling," or "any petty ruler" subordinate to kings or ethnarchs; in the NT, Herod Antipas, Matt. 14:1; Luke 3:19; 9:7; Acts 13:1.¶

B. Verb.

tetraarcheō or *tetrarcheō* (τετρααρχέω, 5075), "to be a tetrarch," occurs in Luke 3:1 (thrice), of Herod Antipas, his brother Philip and Lysanias. Antipas and Philip each inherited a fourth part of his father's dominions. Inscriptions bear witness to the accuracy of Luke's details.¶

For **THAN** see †, p. 1

THANK, THANKS (Noun and Verb), THANKFUL, THANKFULNESS, THANKSGIVING, THANKWORTHY

A. Nouns.

1. *charis* (χάρις, 5485), for the meanings of which see GRACE, No. 1, is rendered "thank" in Luke 6:32, 33, 34; in 17:9, "doth he thank" is lit., "hath he thanks to"; it is rendered "thanks (be to God)" in Rom. 6:17, RV (KJV, "God be thanked"); "thanks" in 1 Cor. 15:57; in 1 Tim. 1:12 and 2 Tim. 1:3, "I thank" is, lit., "I have thanks"; "thankworthy," 1 Pet. 2:19, KJV (RV, "acceptable"). See ACCEPT, D, No. 2.

2. *eucharistia* (εὐχαριστία, 2169), *eu,*

"well," *charizomai*, "to give freely" (Eng., "eucharist"), denotes (*a*) "gratitude," "thankfulness," Acts 24:3; (*b*) "giving of thanks, thanksgiving," 1 Cor. 14:16; 2 Cor. 4:15; 9:11, 12 (plur.); Eph. 5:4; Phil. 4:6; Col. 2:7; 4:2; 1 Thess. 3:9 ("thanks"); 1 Tim. 2:1 (plur.); 4:3, 4; Rev. 4:9, "thanks"; 7:12.¶

B. Verbs.

1. *eucharisteō* (εὐχαριστέω, 2168), akin to A, No. 2, "to give thanks," (*a*) is said of Christ, Matt. 15:36; 26:27; Mark 8:6; 14:23; Luke 22:17, 19; John 6:11, 23; 11:41; 1 Cor. 11:24; (*b*) of the Pharisee in Luke 18:11 in his self-complacent prayer; (*c*) is used by Paul at the beginning of all his epistles, except 2 Cor. (see, however, *eulogētos* in 1:3), Gal., 1 Tim., 2 Tim. (see, however, *charin echō*, 1:3), and Titus, (1) for his readers, Rom. 1:8; Eph. 1:16; Col. 1:3; 1 Thess. 1:2; 2 Thess. 1:3 (cf. 2:13); virtually so in Philem. 4; (2) for fellowship shown, Phil. 1:3; (3) for God's gifts to them, 1 Cor. 1:4; (*d*) is recorded (1) of Paul elsewhere, Acts 27:35; 28:15; Rom. 7:25; 1 Cor. 1:14; 14:18; (2) of Paul and others, Rom. 16:4; 1 Thess. 2:13; of himself, representatively, as a practice, 1 Cor. 10:30; (3) of others, Luke 17:16; Rom. 14:6 (twice); 1 Cor. 14:17; Rev. 11:17; (*e*) is used in admonitions to the saints, the Name of the Lord Jesus suggesting His character and example, Eph. 5:20; Col. 1:12; 3:17; 1 Thess. 5:18; (*f*) as the expression of a purpose, 2 Cor. 1:11, RV; (*g*) negatively of the ungodly, Rom. 1:21.¶ "Thanksgiving" is the expression of joy Godward, and is therefore the fruit of the Spirit (Gal. 5:22); believers are encouraged to abound in it (e.g., Col. 2:7, and see C, below).

2. *exomologeō* (ἐξομολογέω, 1843), in the middle voice, signifies "to make acknowledgment," whether of sins (to confess), or in the honor of a person, as in Rom. 14:11; 15:9 (in some mss. in Rev. 3:5); this is the significance in the Lord's address to the Father, "I thank (Thee)," in Matt. 11:25 and Luke 10:21, the meaning being "I make thankful confession" or "I make acknowledgment with praise." See CONFESS, No. 2, CONSENT, PROMISE.

3. *anthomologeomai* (ἀνθομολογέομαι, 437), "to acknowledge fully, to celebrate fully (*anti*) in praise with thanksgiving," is used of Anna in Luke 2:38.¶

Note: For *homologeō*, rendered "giving thanks" in Heb. 13:15 (RV, "make confession"), See CONFESS, A, No. 1 (*d*).

C. Adjective.

eucharistos (εὐχάριστος, 2170), primarily, "gracious, agreeable" (as in the Sept., Prov. 11:16, of a wife, who brings glory to her husband¶), then "grateful, thankful," is so used in Col. 3:15.¶

For **THAT** (Conjunction, etc.) see †, p. 1

For **THAT** (Demonstrative Pronoun), see **THIS**

THEATER

theatron (θέατρον, 2302), "a theater," was used also as "a place of assembly," Acts 19:29, 31; in 1 Cor. 4:9 it is used of "a show" or "spectacle." See SPECTACLE.¶

THEE

Note: This translates the oblique forms of the pronoun *su*, "thou." In 2 Tim. 4:11, it translates the reflexive pronoun *seautou*, "thyself."

THEFT

1. *klopē* (κλοπή, 2829), akin to *kleptō*, "to steal," is used in the plural in Matt. 15:19; Mark 7:22.¶

2. *klemma* (κλέμμα, 2809), "a thing stolen," and so, "a theft," is used in the plural in Rev. 9:21.¶ In the Sept., Gen. 31:39; Ex. 22:3, 4.¶

THEIR, THEIRS

Note: These pronouns are the rendering of (1) *autōn*, the genitive plur. of *autos*, "he," e.g., Matt. 2:12; (2) *heautōn*, "of themselves," the genitive plur. of *heautou*, "of himself," e.g., Matt. 8:22; Rom. 16:4, 18, "their own"; or the accusative plur. *heautous*, e.g., 2 Cor. 8:5, "their own selves" (for John 20:10, see HOME, A, No. 3); (3) *idious*, the accusative plur. of *idios*, "one's own," e.g., 1 Cor. 14:35, "their own"; (4) *toutōn*, lit., "of these," the gen. plur. of *houtos*, "this," Rom. 11:30, "their (disobedience)"; (5) *ekeinōn*, the gen. plur. of *ekeinos*, "that one" (emphatic), e.g., 2 Cor. 8:14 (twice), "their," lit., "of those"; 2 Tim. 3:9, "theirs."

THEM, THEMSELVES

Note: These translate the plural, in various forms, of (1) *autos* [see (1) above], e.g., Matt. 3:7; (2) *heatou* [see (2) above], e.g., Matt. 15:30; (3) *houtos* (*toutous*) [see (4) above], e.g., Acts 21:24; (4) *ekeinos* [see (5) above], e.g., Matt. 13:11. Regarding *allēlōn*, "of one another," and its other forms, the RV substitutes "one another" for the KJV "themselves" in Mark 8:16; 9:34; Luke 4:36; John 6:52; 11:56; 16:17; 19:24; Acts 26:31; 28:4; Rom. 2:15, but adheres to the rendering "themselves" in Mark 15:31; Acts 4:15; 28:25.

THEN

1. *tote* (τότε, 5119), a demonstrative adverb of time, denoting "at that time," is used (*a*) of concurrent events, e.g., Matt. 2:17; Gal. 4:8, "at that time"; v. 29, "then"; 2 Pet. 3:6,"(the world) that then was," lit., "(the) then (world)"; (*b*) of consequent events, "then, thereupon," e.g., Matt. 2:7; Luke 11:26; 16:16, "[from (KJV, "since")] that time"; John 11:14; Acts 17:14; (*c*) of things future, e.g., Matt. 7:23; 24:30 (twice), 40; eight times in ch. 25; 1 Cor. 4:5; Gal. 6:4; 1 Thess. 5:3; 2 Thess. 2:8. It occurs 90 times in Matthew, more than in all the rest of the NT together.

2. *eita* (εἶτα, 1534) denotes sequence (*a*) "of time, then, next," Mark 4:17, RV, "then"; 4:28, in some texts; 8:25, RV, "then" (KJV, "after that"); Luke 8:12; John 13:5; 19:27; 20:27; in some texts in 1 Cor. 12:28; 1 Cor. 15:5, 7, 24; 1 Tim. 2:13; 3:10; Jas. 1:15; (*b*) In argument, Heb. 12:9, "furthermore."¶

3. *epeita* (ἔπειτα, 1899) "thereupon, thereafter," then (in some texts, Mark 7:5; *kai*, "and," in the best); Luke 16:7; John 11:7; 1 Cor. 12:28, RV, "then" (KJV, "after that"); 15:6 and 7 (ditto); v. 23, RV, KJV, "afterward" (No. 2 in v. 24); v. 46 (ditto); Gal. 1:18; v. 21, RV (KJV, "afterwards"); 2:1; 1 Thess. 4:17; Heb. 7:2, RV (KJV, "after that"); v. 27, Jas. 3:17, 4:14. See AFTER.¶

4. *loipon* (λοιπόν, 3063), "finally, for the rest," the neuter of *loipos*, "(the) rest," used adverbially, is rendered "then" in Acts 27:20, KJV (RV, "now.").

5. *oun* (οὖν, 3767), a particle expressing sequence or consequence, is rendered "then," e.g., Matt. 22:43; 27:22; Luke 11:13.

6. *oukoun* (οὐκοῦν, 3766), an adverb formed from *ouk*, "not," *oun*, "therefore," with the negative element dropped, meaning "so then," is used in John 18:37.¶

Notes: (1) In James 2:24, where in some texts the inferential particle *toinun*, "therefore," occurs, the KJV renders it by "then" (RV follows the superior mss. which omit it). (2) For conjunctions (*ara*, "so"; *de*, "but"; *gar* "for"; *kai*, "and"; *te*, "and"), sometimes translated "then," see †, p. 1.

THENCE (from)

ekeithen (ἐκεῖθεν, 1564) is used (*a*) of place, e.g., Matt. 4:21, "from thence"; 5:26; in Acts 20:13, "there"; often preceded by *kai*, written *kakeithen*, e.g., Mark 9:30 and Luke 11:53 (in the best texts); Acts 7:4; 14:26; (*b*) of time, Acts 13:21, "and afterward." See AFTER.

Note: In Acts 28:13, *hothen*, "from whence," is translated "from thence."

THENCEFORTH

eti (ἔτι, 2089), "yet, still, further," is rendered "thenceforth" in Matt. 5:13.

Notes: (1) In Luke 13:9, RV, the phrase *eis to mellon*, lit., "unto the about to be" (*mellō*, "to be about to"), is translated "thenceforth" (KJV, "after that"). (2) In John 19:12, KJV, *ek toutou*, "from this," is translated "from thenceforth" (RV, "upon this").

THERE, THITHER

1. *ekei* (ἐκεῖ, 1563) signifies (*a*) "there," e.g., Matt. 2:13, frequently in the Gospels; (*b*) "thither," e.g., Luke 17:37; in Rom. 15:24, "thitherward."

2. *ekeise* (ἐκεῖσε, 1566), properly, "thither," signifies "there" in Acts 21:3; 22:5.¶ In the Sept., Job 39:29.¶

3. *ekeithen* (ἐκεῖθεν, 1564), "thence," is rendered "there" in Acts 20:13. See THENCE.

4. *enthade* (ἐνθάδε, 1759), "here, hither," is rendered "there" in Acts 10:18. See HERE, HITHER.

5. *autou* (αὐτοῦ, 847), the genitive case, neuter, of *autos*, he, lit., "of it," is used as an adverb, "there," in Acts 18:19; 21:4 (in some texts in 15:34). See HERE.

Notes: (1) In Luke 24:18 and Acts 9:38, "there" translates the phrase *en autē*, "in it." (2) In John 21:9, "there" is used to translate the verb *keimai.* (3) In Matt. 24:23 (2nd part), KJV, *hōde*, "here" (RV), is translated "there." (4) In Acts 17:21, "there" forms part of the translation of *epidēmeō*, "to sojourn," "sojourning there," RV ("which were there," KJV).

THEREABOUT

Note: The phrase *peri toutou*, "concerning this," is rendered "thereabout" in Luke 24:4.

THEREAT

Note: The phrase *di'autēs*, lit., "by (*dia*) it," is rendered "thereat" in Matt. 7:13, KJV (RV, "thereby").

THEREBY

Notes: (1) *Di'autēs* (see above) occurs in Matt. 7:13; John 11:4; Heb. 12:11. (2) *Dia tautēs*, "by means of this, thereby," occurs in Heb. 12:15; 13:2. (3) *En autē*, "in, or by, it," is rendered "thereby" in Rom. 10:5; *en autō* in Eph. 2:16 (some texts have *en heautō*, "in Himself"); 1 Pet. 2:2.

For **THEREFORE** see †, p. 1

THEREIN, THEREINTO, THEREOF, THEREON, THEREOUT, THERETO, THEREUNTO, THEREUPON, THEREWITH

Note: These translate various phrases consisting of a preposition with forms of either the personal pronoun *autos,* "he," or the demonstrative *houtos,* "this."

For THESE see THIS

THEY, THEY THEMSELVES

Note: When not forming part of the translation of the 3rd pers., plur. of a verb, (1) these translate the plural of the pronouns under HE, in their various forms, *autos, houtos, ekeinos, heautou.* (2) In Acts 5:16, *hoitines,* the plural of *hostis,* "anyone who," is translated "they"; so in 23:14, translated "and they"; in 17:11, "in that they" (some texts have it in Matt. 25:3). (3) Sometimes the plural of the article is rendered "they," e.g., Phil. 4:22; Heb. 13:24; in 1 Cor. 11:19, "they which are (approved)" is, lit., "the approved"; in Gal. 2:6, "they ... (who were of repute)," RV.

For THICK see GATHER, A, No. 8

THIEF, THIEVES

1. *kleptēs* (κλέπτης, 2812) is used (*a*) literally, Matt. 6:19, 20; 24:43; Luke 12:33, 39; John 10:1, 10; 12:6; 1 Cor. 6:10; 1 Pet. 4:15; (*b*) metaphorically of "false teachers," John 10:8; (*c*) figuratively, (1) of the personal coming of Christ, in a warning to a local church, with most of its members possessed of mere outward profession and defiled by the world, Rev. 3:3; in retributive intervention to overthrow the foes of God, 16:15; (2) of the Day of the Lord, in divine judgment upon the world, 2 Pet. 3:10 and 1 Thess. 5:2, 4; in v. 2, according to the order in the original "the word 'night' is not to be read with 'the day of the Lord,' but with 'thief,' i.e., there is no reference to the time of the coming, only to the manner of it. To avoid ambiguity the phrase may be paraphrased, 'so comes as a thief in the night comes.' The use of the present tense instead of the future emphasizes the certainty of the coming.... The unexpectedness of the coming of the thief, and the unpreparedness of those to whom he comes, are the essential elements in the figure; cf. the entirely different figure used in Matt. 25:1–13."¶*

* From *Notes on Thessalonians,* by Hogg and Vine, pp. 153, 154.

2. *lēstēs* (λῃστής, 3027) is frequently rendered "thieves" in the KJV, e.g., Matt. 21:13. See ROBBER.

THIGH

mēros (μηρός, 3382) occurs in Rev. 19:16; Christ appears there in the manifestation of His judicial capacity and action hereafter as the executor of divine vengeance upon the foes of God; His name is spoken of figuratively as being upon His "thigh" (where the sword would be worn; cf. Ps. 45:3), emblematic of His strength to tread down His foes, His action being the exhibition of His divine attributes of righteousness and power.¶

For THINE see THY

THING(S)

1. *logos* (λόγος, 3056), "a word, an account," etc., is translated "thing" in Matt. 21:24, KJV (1st part), and Luke 20:3, KJV, RV, "question" (in Matt. 21:24, 2nd part, "these things" translates *tauta,* the neut. plur. of *houtos,* "this"); Luke 1:4; Acts 5:24, KJV (RV, "words") See ACCOUNT.

2. *pragma* (πρᾶγμα, 4229), for which see MATTER, No. 2, is translated "thing" in Matt. 18:19, as part of the word "anything," lit., "every thing"; Luke 1:1, KJV only; Acts 5:4; in Heb. 6:18; 10:1, and 11:1, "things." See BUSINESS, MATTER, WORK.

3. *rhēma* (ῥῆμα, 4487), "a saying, word," is translated "thing" in Luke 2:15; v. 19, KJV (RV, "saying"); in Acts 5:32, "things." See SAYING.

Notes: (1) The neuter sing. and plur. of the article are frequently rendered "the thing" and "the things"; so with *tauta,* "these things," the neut. plur. of *houtos,* "this." (2) So in the case of the neut. plur. of certain pronouns and adjectives without nouns, e.g., "all," "base," "heavenly," "which." (3) When "thing" represents a separate word in the original, it is a translation of one or other of Nos. 1, 2, 3, above. (4) In Phil. 2:10, *"things"* is added in italics to express the meaning of the three adjectives.

THINK

1. *dokeō* (δοκέω, 1380), "to suppose, to think, to form an opinion," which may be either right or wrong, is sometimes rendered "to think," e.g., Matt. 3:9; 6:7; see ACCOUNT, No. 1, SUPPOSE, No. 2.

2. *hēgeomai* (ἡγέομαι, 2233), for which see ACCOUNT, No. 3, is rendered "to think" in Acts 26:2; 2 Cor. 9:5, "I thought"; Phil. 2:6, KJV (RV, "counted"); 2 Pet. 1:13.

3. *noeō* (νοέω, 3539), "to perceive, under-

stand, apprehend," is rendered "think" in Eph. 3:20. See PERCEIVE, UNDERSTAND.

4. *huponoeō* (ὑπονοέω, 5282), "to suppose, surmise" (*hupo*, "under," and No. 3), is rendered "to think" in Acts 13:25, KJV (RV, "suppose"). See DEEM.

5. *logizomai* (λογίζομαι, 3049), "to reckon," is rendered "to think," in Rom. 2:3, KJV (RV, "reckonest"); 1 Cor. 13:5, KJV, RV, "taketh (not) account of," i.e., love does not reckon up or calculatingly consider the evil done to it (something more than refraining from imputing motives); 13:11, "I thought"; in the following, for the KJV, "to think," in 2 Cor. 3:5, RV, "to account"; 10:2 (twice), "count"; 10:7, "consider"; 10:11, "reckon"; 12:6, "account." In Phil. 4:8, "think on (these things)," it signifies "make those things the subjects of your thoughtful consideration," or "carefully reflect on them" (RV marg., "take account of"). See ACCOUNT, A, No. 4.

6. *nomizō* (νομίζω, 3543), to suppose, is sometimes rendered to think, e.g., Matt. 5:17. See SUPPOSE, No. 1.

7. *phroneō* (φρονέω, 5426), "to be minded in a certain way" (*phrēn*, "the mind"), is rendered "to think," in Rom. 12:3 (2nd and 3rd occurrences), RV, "not to think of himself more highly (*huperphroneō*, see No. 13) than he ought to think (*phroneō*); but so to think (*phroneō*) as to think soberly [*sōphroneō*, see *Note* (3)]"; the play on words may be expressed by a literal rendering somewhat as follows: "not to over-think beyond what it behoves him to think, but to think unto sober-thinking"; in 1 Cor. 4:6, some inferior texts have this verb, hence the KJV "to think"; in the best texts, it is absent, hence the RV, puts "*go*" in italics; lit., the sentence is "that ye might learn the (i.e., the rule) not beyond what things have been written." The saying appears to be proverbial, perhaps a rabbinical adage. Since, however, *graphō*, "to write," was a current term for framing a law or an agreement (so Deissmann, *Bible Studies*, and Moulton and Milligan, *Vocab.*), it is quite possible that the apostle's meaning is "not to go beyond the terms of a teacher's commission, thinking more of himself than the character of his commission allows"; this accords with the context and the whole passage, 3:1–4:5. In Phil. 1:7, KJV, "to think" (RV, "to be... minded"). See AFFECTION, B, *Note* (1) and list there.

8. *oiomai* or *oimai* (οἴομαι, 3633), "to imagine," is rendered "I suppose" in John 21:25; "thinking" in Phil. 1:17, RV (v. 16, KJV, "supposing"); "let (not that man) think," Jas. 1:7. See SUPPOSE.¶

9. *phainō* (φαίνω, 5316), in the passive voice, "to appear," is rendered "(what) think (ye)" in Mark 14:64, lit., "what does it appear to you?" See APPEAR, No. 1.

10. *eudokeō* (εὐδοκέω, 2106), "to be well-pleasing," is rendered "we thought it good" in 1 Thess. 3:1. See PLEASE.

11. *axioō* (ἀξιόω, 515), "to regard as worthy" (*axios*), "to deem it suitable," is rendered "thought (not) good" in Acts 15:38. See WORTHY, B.

12. *enthumeomai* (ἐνθυμέομαι, 1760), "to reflect on, ponder," is used in Matt. 1:20; 9:4: see No. 14. Cf. *enthumēsis*, "consideration" (see THOUGHT).¶

13. *huperphroneō* (ὑπερφρονέω, 5252), "to be overproud, high-minded," occurs in Rom. 12:3, rendered "to think of himself more highly." See No. 7.¶

14. *dienthumeomai* (διενθυμέομαι, 1223 and 1760), "to consider deeply" (*dia*, "through," and No. 12), is used of Peter in Acts 10:19, in the best texts (some have No. 12).¶

15. *epiballō* (ἐπιβάλλω, 1911), "to throw oneself upon," is used metaphorically in Mark 14:72, "when he thought thereon (he wept)," lit., "thinking thereon," but "to think" is an exceptional sense of the word (see BEAT, CAST, LAY, PUT); hence various suggestions have been made. Field, following others, adopts the meaning "putting (his garment) over (his head)," as an expression of grief. Others regard it as having here the same meaning as *archomai*, "to begin" (at an early period, indeed, *archomai* was substituted in the text for the authentic *epiballō*); Moulton confirms this from a papyrus writing. Another suggestion is to understand it as with *dianoian*, mind, i.e., "casting his mind thereon."

Notes: (1) In Acts 26:8, KJV, *krinō*, "to judge, reckon," is translated "should it be thought" (RV, "is it judged"). (2) In Luke 12:17, KJV, *dialogizomai*, "to reason" (RV, "reasoned"), is translated "thought." (3) In Rom. 12:3, *sōphroneō*, "to think soberly," RV, is, lit., "unto sober thinking," the infinitive mood of the verb being used as a noun (KJV marg., "to sobriety"): Cf. No. 7. See SOBER, B, No. 2.

THIRD, THIRDLY

tritos (τρίτος, 5154) is used (*a*) as a noun, e.g., Luke 20:12, 31; in Rev. 8:7–12 and 9:15, 18, "the third part," lit., "the third"; (*b*) as an adverb, with the article, "the third time," e.g., Mark 14:41; John 21:17 (twice); without the article, lit., "a third time," e.g., John 21:14; 2 Cor. 12:14; 13:1; in enumerations, in Matt. 26:44, with *ek*, "from," lit., "from the third time" (the *ek* indicates the point of departure, especially in a succession of events, cf. John 9:24; 2 Pet. 2:8); absolutely, in the accusative neuter, in 1 Cor. 12:28, "thirdly"; (c) as an adjective (its primary use), e.g., in the phrase "the third heaven," 2 Cor. 12:2 [cf. HEAVEN, A, No. 1 (c), PARADISE]; in the phrase "the third hour," Matt. 20:3; Mark 15:25; Acts 2:15 (". . . of the day"); 23:23 (". . . of the night"); in a phrase with *hēmera*, "a day," "on the third day" (i.e., "the next day but one"), e.g., Matt. 16:21; Luke 24:46; Acts 10:40; in this connection the idiom "three days and three nights," Matt. 12:40, is explained by ref. to 1 Sam. 30:12, 13, and Esth. 4:16 with 5:1; in Mark 9:31 and 10:34, the RV, "after three days," follows the texts which have this phrase, the KJV, "the third day," those which have the same phrase as in Matt. 16:21, etc.

Note: For "third story," Acts 20:9, RV, see STORY.

THIRST (Noun and Verb), THIRSTY (to be), ATHIRST

A. Noun.

dipsos (δίψος, 1373), "thirst" (cf. Eng., "dipsomania"), occurs in 2 Cor. 11:27.¶

B. Verb.

dipsaō (διψάω, 1372) is used (a) in the natural sense, e.g., Matt. 25:35, 37, 42; in v. 44, "athirst" (lit., "thirsting"); John 4:13, 15; 19:28; Rom. 12:20; 1 Cor. 4:11; Rev. 7:16; (b) figuratively, of spiritual "thirst," Matt. 5:6; John 4:14; 6:35; 7:37; in Rev. 21:6 and 22:17, "that is athirst."

THIRTY, THIRTYFOLD

triakonta (τριάκοντα, 5144) is usually rendered "thirty," e.g., Matt. 13:23; "thirtyfold," in Matt. 13:8, KJV only; in Mark 4:8, RV only; in Mark 4:20, KJV and RV.

THIS, THESE

Note: The singular and plural translate various forms of the following: (1) *houtos*, which is used (a) as a noun, "this one," followed by no noun, e.g., Matt. 3:17; translated in Luke 2:34, "this *child*"; in 1 Cor. 5:3, RV, "this thing." (KJV, "this deed"); for "this fellow" see FELLOW, *Note* (3); in Acts 17:32 the RV rightly omits "*matter*"; in Heb. 4:5 "*place*" is italicized; it is frequently rendered "this man," e.g., Matt. 9:3; John 6:52; "of this sort," 2 Tim. 3:6, KJV (RV, "of these"); (b) as an adjective with a noun, either with the article and before it, e.g., Matt. 12:32, or after the noun (which is preceded by the article), e.g., Matt. 3:9 and 4:3, "these stones"; or without the article often forming a

predicate, e.g., John 2:11; 2 Cor. 13:1; (2) *ekeinos*, "that one," rendered "this" in Matt. 24:43; (3) *autos*; "he," rendered "this" in Matt. 11:14, lit., "he"; in John 12:7, KJV (RV, "it"); in the feminine, Luke 13:16; (4) the article *ho*, Matt. 21:21 (*to*, the neuter), KJV (RV, "what"); in Rom. 13:9 (1st part); Gal. 5:14; Heb. 12:27, the article *to* is virtually equivalent to "the following."

The demonstrative pronouns THAT and the plural THOSE translate the same pronouns (1), (2), (3) mentioned above. In Heb. 7:21, KJV, "those" translates the article, which requires the RV, "they."

THISTLE

tribolos (τρίβολος, 5146) occurs in Matt. 7:16 and Heb. 6:8 (KJV, "briers").¶ In the Sept., Gen. 3:18; 2 Sam. 12:31; Prov. 22:5; Hos. 10:8.¶ Cf. THORNS.

For THITHER, THITHERWARD see THERE

Note: In John 7:34, 36, KJV, *hopou*, "where" (RV) is amplified by the italicized word "*thither*."

For THONG see LATCHET

THORN, THORNS (of)

A. Nouns.

1. *akantha* (ἄκανθα, 173), "a brier, a thorn" (from *akē*, "a point"), is always used in the plural in the NT, Matt. 7:16 and parallel passage in Luke 6:44; Matt. 13:7 (twice), 22 and parallels in Mark and Luke; in Matt. 27:29 and John 19:2, of the crown of "thorns" placed on Christ's head (see also B) in mock imitation of the garlands worn by emperors. They were the effects of the divine curse on the ground (Gen. 3:18; contrast Isa. 55:13). The "thorns" of the crown plaited by the soldiers, are usually identified with those of the *Zizyphus spina Christi*, some 20 feet high or more, fringing the Jordan and abundant in Palestine; its twigs are flexible. Another species, however, the Arabian *qundaul*, crowns of which are plaited and sold in Jerusalem as representatives of Christ's crown, seems likely to be the one referred to. The branches are easily woven and adapted to the torture intended. The word *akantha* occurs also in Heb. 6:8.¶

2. *skolops* (σκόλοψ, 4647) originally denoted "anything pointed," e.g., "a stake"; in Hellenistic vernacular, "a thorn" (so the Sept., in Num. 33:55; Ezek. 28:24; Hos. 2:6¶), 2 Cor. 12:7, of the apostle's "thorn in the flesh"; his

language indicates that it was physical, painful, humiliating; it was also the effect of divinely permitted Satanic antagonism; the verbs rendered "that I should (not) be exalted overmuch" (RV) and "to buffet" are in the present tense, signifying recurrent action, indicating a constantly repeated attack. Lightfoot interprets it as "a stake driven through the flesh," and Ramsay agrees with this. Most commentators adhere to the rendering "thorn." Field says "there is no doubt that the Alexandrine use of *skolops* for thorn is here intended, and that the ordinary meaning of 'stake' must be rejected." What is stressed is not the metaphorical size, but the acuteness of the suffering and its effects. Attempts to connect this with the circumstances of Acts 14:19 and Gal. 4:13 are speculative.¶

B. Adjective.

akanthinos (ἀκάνθινος, 174), "of thorns" (from A, No. 1), is used in Mark 15:17 and John 19:5.¶ In the Sept., Isa. 34:13.¶

THOROUGHLY (THROUGHLY)

Note: This is usually part of the translation of a verb, e.g., CLEANSE, FURNISH, PURGE. In 2 Cor. 11:6, the phrase *en panti*, "in everything," RV, is translated "throughly" in the KJV.

For THOSE see THIS (last part of *Note*)

THOU

Note: Frequently this forms part of the translation of a verb in the 2nd person, singular. Otherwise it translates (*a*) the pronoun *su*, used for emphasis or contrast, e.g., John 1:19, 21 (twice), 25, 42 (twice); 8:5, 13, 25, 33, 48, 52, 53; Acts 9:5; in addressing a person or place, e.g., Matt. 2:6; Luke 1:76; John 17:5; perhaps also in the phrase *su eipas*, "thou hast said," e.g., Matt. 26:64 (sometimes without emphasis, e.g., Acts 13:33); (*b*) in the oblique cases, e.g., the dative *soi*, lit., "to thee," e.g., Matt. 17:25, "what thinkest thou?" (lit., "what does it seem to thee?"); (*c*) *autos*, "self," e.g., Luke 6:42; Acts 21:24, "thou thyself"; (*d*) the reflexive pronoun, *seauton*, Rom. 2:19, "thou thyself."

For THOUGH see †, p. 1

For THOUGHT (Verb) see THINK

THOUGHT (Noun)

1. *epinoia* (ἐπίνοια, 1963), "a thought by way of a design" (akin to *epinoeō*, "to contrive," *epi*, intensive, *noeō*, "to consider"), is used in Acts 8:22.¶ In the Sept., Jer. 20:10.¶

2. *noēma* (νόημα, 3540), "a purpose, device of the mind" (akin to *noeō*, see No. 1), is rendered "thought" in 2 Cor. 10:5, "thoughts" in Phil. 4:7, RV: see DEVICE, No. 2.

3. *dianoēma* (διανόημα, 1270), "a thought," occurs in Luke 11:17, where the sense is that of "machinations."¶

4. *enthumēsis* (ἐνθύμησις, 1761), is translated "thoughts" in Matt. 9:4; 12:25; Heb. 4:12: see DEVICE, No. 1.

5. *logismos* (λογισμός, 3053) is translated "thoughts" in Rom. 2:15: see IMAGINATION, No. 1.

6. *dialogismos* (διαλογισμός, 1261), "reasoning," is translated "thoughts" in Matt. 15:19; Mark 7:21; Luke 2:35; 6:8; in 5:22, KJV, RV, "reasonings"; in 9:47, KJV, RV, "reasoning," and 24:38, KJV, RV, "reasonings"; so 1 Cor. 3:20; in Luke 9:46, KJV and RV, "reasoning"; "thoughts" in Jas. 2:4, KJV and RV. See DISPUTE, IMAGINATION, REASONING.

THOUGHT (to take)

1. *merimnaō* (μεριμνάω, 3309) denotes "to be anxious, careful." For the KJV, "to take thought," the RV substitutes "to be anxious" in Matt. 6:25, 27, 28, 31, 34; 10:19; Luke 12:11, 22, 25, 26, See CARE, B, No. 1.

2. *promerimnaō* (προμεριμνάω, 4305), "to be anxious beforehand," occurs in Mark 13:11.¶

3. *phroneō* (φρονέω, 5426): for Phil. 4:10, RV, "ye did take thought," see CARE, B, No. 6.

4. *pronoeō* (προνοέω, 4306), "to provide," is rendered "to take thought" in Rom. 12:17 and 2 Cor. 8:21. See PROVIDE.

THOUSAND (-S)

1. *chilioi* (χίλιοι, 5507), "a thousand," occurs in 2 Pet. 3:8; Rev. 11:3; 12:6; 14:20; 20:2–7.¶

2. *chilias* (χιλιάς, 5505), "one thousand," is always used in the plural, *chiliades*, but translated in the sing. everywhere, except in the phrase "thousands of thousands," Rev. 5:11.

Notes: (1) The following compounds of No. 1 represent different multiples of a thousand: *dischilioi*, 2,000, Mark 5:13;¶ *trischilioi*, 3,000, Acts 2:41;¶ *tetrakischilioi*, 4,000, Matt. 15:38; 16:10; Mark 8:9, 20; Acts 21:38;¶ *pentakischilioi*, 5,000, Matt. 14:21; 16:9; Mark 6:44; 18:19; Luke 9:14; John 6:10;¶ *heptakischilioi*, 7,000, Rom. 11:4.¶ (2) *Murias*, "a myriad, a vast number," "many thousands," Luke 12:1, RV; Acts 21:20; it also denotes 10,000, Acts 19:19, lit., "five ten-thousands"; Jude 14, "ten thousands"; in Rev. 5:11 "ten thousand times ten thousand" is, lit., "myriads of myriads"; in Rev. 9:16 the best texts, *dismuriades muriadōn*, "twice ten thousand times ten thousand" RV (KJV, "two hundred thousand thousand"): see INNUMERABLE. (3) *Murioi* (the plur. of *murios*), an adjective signifying "numberless," is used in this indefinite sense in 1 Cor. 4:15 and 14:19; it also denotes the definite number "ten thousand," Matt. 18:24.¶

THREATEN

1. *apeileō* (ἀπειλέω, 546) is used of Christ, negatively, in 1 Pet. 2:23; in the middle voice, Acts 4:17, where some texts have the noun *apeilē* in addition, hence the KJV, "let us straitly threaten," lit., "let us threaten . . . with threatening" (see THREATENING).¶ (See also STRAITLY.)

2. *prosapeileō* (προσαπειλέω, 4324), "to threaten further" (*pros*, and No. 1), occurs in the middle voice in Acts 4:21.¶

THREATENING

apeilē (ἀπειλή, 547), akin to *apeileō* (see above), occurs in Acts 4:29 (in some mss. v. 17); 9:1; Eph. 6:9.¶

THREE

treis (τρεῖς, 5143) is regarded by many as a number sometimes symbolically indicating fullness of testimony or manifestation, as in the three persons in the Godhead, cf. 1 Tim. 5:19; Heb. 10:28; the mention in 1 John 5:7 is in a verse which forms no part of the original; no Greek ms. earlier than the 14th century contained it; no version earlier than the 5th cent. in any other language contains it, nor is it quoted by any of the Greek or Latin "Fathers" in their writings on the Trinity. That there are those who bear witness in Heaven is not borne out by any other Scripture. It must be regarded as the interpolation of a copyist.

In Mark 9:31 and 10:34 the best texts have *meta treis hemeras*, "after three days," which idiomatically expresses the same thing as *tę̄ tritę̄ hēmerą*, "on the third day," which some texts have here, as, e.g., the phrase "the third day" in Matt. 17:23; 20:19; Luke 9:22; 18:33, where the repetition of the article lends stress to the number, lit., "the day the third"; 24:7, 46; Acts 10:40. For THREE TIMES see THRICE.

THREE HUNDRED

triakosioi (τριακοσιοι, 5145) occurs in Mark 14:5 and John 12:5.¶

For **THREESCORE** see **SIXTY** and **SEVENTY**

For **THREE THOUSAND** see **THOUSAND**

THRESH

aloaō (ἀλοάω, 248), "to thresh," is so rendered in 1 Cor. 9:10; in v. 9 and 1 Tim. 5:18, "that treadeth out the corn."¶

THRESHING FLOOR

halōn (ἅλων, 257), "a threshing floor," is so translated in Matt. 3:12, and Luke 3:17, RV (KJV, "floor"), perhaps by metonymy for the grain.¶

For **THREW** see **THROW**

THRICE

tris (τρίς, 5151) occurs in Matt. 26:34, 75 and parallel passages; in Acts 10:16 and 11:10, preceded by *epi*, "up to"; 2 Cor. 11:25 (twice); 12:8.

THROAT (Noun), to take by the (Verb)

A. Noun.
larunx (λάρυγξ, 2995), "a throat" (Eng., "larynx"), is used metaphorically of "speech" in Rom. 3:13.¶

B. Verb.
pnigō (πνίγω, 4155), "to choke," is rendered "took . . . by the throat" in Matt. 18:28. See CHOKE, No. 1.

THRONE

1. *thronos* (θρόνος, 2362), "a throne, a seat of authority," is used of the "throne" (*a*) of God, e.g., Heb. 4:16, "the throne of grace," i.e., from which grace proceeds; 8:1; 12:2; Rev. 1:4; 3:21 (2nd part); 4:2 (twice); 5:1; frequently in Rev.; in 20:12, in the best texts, "the throne" (some have *Theos*, "God," KJV); cf. 21:3; Matt. 5:34; 23:22; Acts 7:49; (*b*) of Christ, e.g. Heb. 1:8; Rev 3:21 (1st part); 22:3; His seat of authority in the Millennium, Matt. 19:28 (1st part); (*c*) by metonymy for angelic powers, Col. 1:16; (*d*) of the Apostles in millennial authority, Matt. 19:28 (2nd part); Luke 22:30; (*e*) of the elders in the heavenly vision, Rev. 4:4 (2nd and 3rd parts), RV, "thrones" (KJV, "seats"); so 11:16; (*f*) of David, Luke 1:32; Acts 2:30; (*g*) of Satan, Rev. 2:13, RV, "throne" (KJV, "seat"); (*h*) of "the beast," the final and federal head of the revived Roman Empire, Rev. 13:2; 16:10.

2. *bēma* (βῆμα, 968), for which see JUDGMENT SEAT, is used of the throne or tribunal of Herod, Acts 12:21.

THRONG (Verb)

1. *thlibō* (θλίβω, 2346), "to press," is rendered "throng," Mark 3:9. See AFFLICT, No. 4.

2. *sunthlibō* (συνθλίβω, 4918), "to press together," on all sides (*sun*, "together," and No. 1), a strengthened form, is used in Mark 5:24, 31.¶

3. *sumpnigō* (συμπνίγω, 4846), "to choke," is used of "thronging" by a crowd, Luke 8:42. See CHOKE, No. 3.

Note: For *sunechō*, "to hold together, press together," Luke 8:45 (KJV, "throng"), see PRESS.

For **THROUGH** and **THROUGHOUT** see †, p. 1

For **THROUGHLY** see **THOROUGHLY**

THROW

1. *ballō* (βάλλω, 906), "to cast, to throw," is rendered "to throw" in Mark 12:42, KJV (RV, "cast"); so Acts 22:23 (2nd part); "to throw down," Rev. 18:21 (2nd part), KJV (RV, "cast down"). See CAST, No. 1.

2. *rhiptō* (ῥίπτω, 4496), "to hurl, throw, throw off," is rendered "had thrown ... down" in Luke 4:35, RV (KJV, "had thrown"). See CAST, No. 2.

3. *katakrēmnizō* (κατακρημνίζω, 2630), "to throw over a precipice" (*krēmnos*), "cast down headlong," is rendered "throw ... down" in Luke 4:29 (KJV, "cast ... down headlong").¶

4. *kataluō* (καταλύω, 2647), lit., "to loosen down," is rendered "to throw down" (of the stones of the Temple) in Matt. 24:2 and parallel passages. See DESTROY, No. 5.

THRUST

1. *ballō* (βάλλω, 906), for which cf. THROW, No. 1, is rendered "to thrust" in John 20:25, 27, KJV (RV, "put"); Acts 16:24, KJV (RV, "cast"); so Rev. 14:16, 19. See CAST, No. 1.

2. *ekballō* (ἐκβάλλω, 1544), "to cast out," is rendered "thrust ... out" in Luke 4:29, KJV (RV, "cast ... forth"); so 13:28 and Acts 16:37. See CAST, No. 5.

3. *apōtheō* (ἀπωθέω, 638), "to thrust away," is used in the middle voice, "to thrust away from oneself," and translated "thrust away" in Acts 7:27, 39; "thrust ... from," 13:46, RV (KJV, "put ... from"); "having thrust from them," 1 Tim. 1:19, RV (KJV, "having put away"). See CAST, No. 13.

4. *katatoxeuō* (κατατοξεύω, 2700), "to strike down with an arrow, shoot dead," occurs in Heb. 12:20 in some mss. (in a quotation from Ex. 19:13, Sept.).¶

Notes: (1) In Matt. 11:23 and Luke 10:15 the best texts have *katabainō*, "to go down" (RV), instead of *katabibazō*, in the passive voice, "to be thrust down or brought down" (KJV). (2) In Acts 27:39, KJV, *exōtheō*, "to drive out," is rendered "to thrust in," RV, "drive (the ship) upon (it [i.e., the beach])." (3) In Rev. 14:15, 18, KJV, *pempō*, to send (RV, "send forth"), is translated "thrust in." (4) For Luke 5:3, KJV, see LAUNCH, No. 2.

THUNDER, THUNDERING

brontē (βροντή, 1027): in Mark 3:17 "sons of thunder" is the interpretation of Boanērges, the name applied by the Lord to James and John; their fiery disposition is seen in 9:38 and Luke 9:54; perhaps in the case of James it led to his execution. The name and its interpretation have caused much difficulty; some suggest the meaning "the twins." It is however most probably the equivalent of the Aramaic *benê regesh*, "sons of tumult"; the latter of the two words was no doubt used of "thunder" in Palestinian Aramaic; hence the meaning "the sons of thunder"; the cognate Hebrew word *ragash*, "to rage," is used in Ps. 2:1 and there only. In John 12:29 *brontē* is used with *ginomai*, "to take place," and rendered "it had thundered"; lit., "there was thunder"; elsewhere, Rev. 4:5; 6:1; 8:5; 10:3, 4; 11:19; 14:2; 16:18; 19:6.¶

THUS

houtōs or *houtō* (οὕτως, 3779), "in this way, so, thus," is used (*a*) with reference to what precedes, e.g., Luke 1:25; 2:48; (*b*) with reference to what follows, e.g., Luke 19:31, rendered "on this wise," in Matt. 1:18; John 21:1, and before quotations, Acts 7:6; 13:34; Rom. 10:6, KJV (RV, "thus"); Heb. 4:4; (*c*) marking intensity, rendered "so," e.g., Gal. 1:6; Heb. 12:21; Rev. 16:18; (*d*) in comparisons, rendered "so," e.g., Luke 11:30; Rom. 5:15. See FASHION, B, LIKEWISE, *Note* (1), MANNER, C, No. 2, SO, *Note* (1).

Notes: (1) *Touto*, the neuter of *houtos*, "this," is translated "thus" in 2 Cor. 1:17; 5:14; Phil. 3:15; the neuter plural, *tauta*, "these things," e.g., in Luke 18:11; 19:28; John 9:6; 11:43; 13:21; 20:14; Acts 19:41. (2) *Tade*, these things (the neuter plural of *hode*, "this"), is translated "thus" in Acts 21:11. (3) In Luke 17:30, KJV, *kata tauta*, lit., "according to these things," is rendered "thus" (RV, "after the same manner," follows the reading *kata ta auta*, lit., "according to the same things").

THY, THINE, THINE OWN, THYSELF

Note: These are translations of (1) the possessive pronoun *sos*, and its inflections, e.g., Matt. 7:3 (1st part); it is used as a noun with the article, in the phrases *to son*, "that which is thine," Matt. 20:14; 25:25, "thine own"; *hoi soi*, "thy friends," Mark 5:19; *ta sa*, "thy goods," Luke 6:30, lit., "the thine"; (2) one of the oblique cases of *su*, "thou"; *sou*, "of thee," e.g., Matt. 1:20; 7:3 (2nd part), "thine own"; *soi*, "to thee," e.g., Mark 5:9; with *menō*, "to remain," Acts 5:4 (1st part), "thine own," lit., "remain to thee"; in Matt. 26:18, *pros se*, "at thy house," lit., "with thee"; (3) *seauton*, "(as) thyself," Rom. 13:9; *seautou*, "of thyself," e.g., Matt. 4:6; *seautō*, "to thyself," Acts 16:28; (4) *heautou* (with *apo*, "from"), John 18:34, "of thyself," lit., "from thyself"; (5) *autos*, "self," is sometimes used for "thyself," e.g., Luke 6:42.

THYINE (WOOD)

thuïnos (θύϊνος, 2367) is akin to *thuia*, or *thua*, an African aromatic and coniferous tree; in Rev. 18:12 it describes a wood which formed part of the merchandise of Babylon; it was valued by Greeks and Romans for tables, being hard, durable and fragrant (KJV marg., "sweet").¶

TIDINGS

A. Noun.

phasis (φάσις, 5334), akin to *phēmi*, "to speak," denotes "information," especially against fraud or other delinquency, and is rendered "tidings" in Acts 21:31.¶

Note: In Acts 11:22, KJV, *logos*, "a word, a report" (RV), is rendered "tidings."

B. Verbs.

1. *euangelizō* (εὐαγγελίζω, 2097) is used of any message designed to cheer those who receive it; it is rendered "to bring, declare, preach," or "show good or glad tidings," e.g., Luke 1:19; 2:10; 3:18, RV; 4:43, RV; 7:22, RV; 8:1; Acts 8:12 and 10:36, RV; 14:15, RV; in 1 Thess. 3:6, "brought us glad (KJV, good) tidings"; in Heb. 4:2, RV, "we have had good tidings preached"; similarly, 4:6; in 1 Pet. 1:25 *rhēma*, "a word," is coupled with this verb, "the word of good tidings which was preached," RV (KJV, "the word which by the gospel is preached"). See PREACH, A, No. 1.

2. *anangellō* (ἀναγγέλλω, 312), "to announce, declare," is rendered "(no) tidings... came," in Rom. 15:21, RV, KJV, "was (not) spoken of." See TELL.

TIE

1. *deō* (δέω, 1210), "to bind," is rendered "to tie" in Matt. 21:2; Mark 11:2, 4; Luke 19:30. See BIND.

2. *proteinō* (προτείνω, 4385), "to stretch out or forth," is used of preparations for scourging, Acts 22:25, RV, "had tied (him) up" (KJV, "bound").¶

TILES, TILING

keramos (κέραμος, 2766), "potter's clay," or "an earthen vessel," denotes in the plural "tiles" in Luke 5:19, RV, KJV, "tiling."¶ In the Sept., 2 Sam. 17:28.¶

For TILL (Conjunction) see †, p. 1

TILL (Verb)

geōrgeō (γεωργέω, 1090), "to till the ground," is used in the passive voice in Heb. 6:7, RV, "it is tilled" (KJV, "... dressed").¶ Moulton and Milligan point out that, agriculture being the principal industry in Egypt, this word and its cognates (*geōrgion*, see HUSBANDRY, and *geōrgos*, see HUSBANDMAN) are very common in the papyri with reference to the cultivation of private allotments and the crown lands.

TIME

A. Nouns.

1. *chronos* (χρόνος, 5550) denotes "a space of time," whether short, e.g., Matt. 2:7; Luke 4:5, or long, e.g., Luke 8:27; 20:9; or a succession of "times," shorter, e.g., Acts 20:18, or longer, e.g., Rom. 16:25, RV, "times eternal"; or duration of "time," e.g., Mark 2:19, 2nd part, RV, "while" (KJV, "as long as"), lit., "for whatever time." For a fuller treatment see SEASON, A, No. 2.

2. *kairos* (καιρός, 2540), primarily "due measure, due proportion," when used of "time," signified "a fixed or definite period, a season," sometimes an opportune or seasonable "time," e.g., Rom. 5:6, RV, "season"; Gal. 6:10, "opportunity." In Mark 10:30 and Luke 18:30, "this time" (*kairos*), i.e., "in this lifetime," is contrasted with "the coming age." In 1 Thess. 5:1, "the times and the seasons," "times" (*chronos*) refers to the duration of the interval previous to the Parousia of Christ and the length of "time" it will occupy (see COMING, No. 3), as well as other periods; "seasons" refers to the characteristics of these periods. See SEASON, A, No. 1, and the contrasts between *chronos* and *kairos* under SEASON, A, No. 2.

3. *hōra* (ὥρα, 5610), primarily, "any time or

period fixed by nature," is translated "time" in Matt. 14:15; Luke 14:17; Rom. 13:11, "high time"; in the following the RV renders it "hour," for KJV, "time," Matt. 18:1; Luke 1:10; John 16:2, 4, 25; 1 John 2:18 (twice); Rev. 14:15; in Mark 6:35, RV, "day"; in 1 Thess. 2:17, RV, "a short (season)," lit., "(the season, KJV, 'time') of an hour." See HOUR.

B. Adverbs.

1. *pōpote* (πώποτε, 4455), "ever yet," is rendered "at any time" in John 1:18; 5:37; 1 John 4:12. For Luke 15:29 see *Note* (14) below. See NEVER.

2. *ēdē* (ἤδη, 2235), "already, now," is translated "by this time" in John 11:39. See ALREADY.

3. *palai* (πάλαι, 3819), "long ago, of old," is rendered "of old time" in Heb. 1:1 (KJV, "in time past"). See OLD.

Notes: (1) In Luke 9:51 and Acts 8:1, KJV, *hēmera*, "a day," is translated "time," in the former, plural, RV, "the days"; in Luke 23:7 (plural), RV "(in these) days," KJV, "(at that) time." (2) In 1 Tim. 6:19 the phrase *eis to mellon*, lit., "unto the about-to-be," i.e., "for the impending (time)," is rendered "against the time to come." (3) In 1 Cor. 16:12, KJV, *nun*, "now" (RV), is rendered "at this time"; in Acts 24:25, the phrase *to nun echon*, lit., "the now having," is rendered "at this time" (the verb is adjectival); the phrase is more expressive than the simple "now." Cf. *heōs tou nun*, "until now," Matt. 24:21 and Mark 13:19, RV, KJV, "unto (this time)." (4) For *polumerōs*, strangely rendered "at sundry times," in Heb. 1:1, KJV, see PORTION, C. (5) For "long time," see LONG. (6) For "nothing ... at any time," see NOTHING, *Note* (3). (7) For *proskairos*, rendered "for a time" in Mark 4:17, KJV, see SEASON, WHILE. (8) In Matt., *apo tote*, "from that time," lit., "from then," occurs thrice, 4:17; 16:21; 26:16; in Luke 16:16, RV (KJV, "since that time"); in John 6:66, KJV, "from that time" translates *ek toutou*, lit., "from, or out of, this," RV, "upon this." (9) In Luke 4:27, the preposition *epi* signifies "in the time of." (10) For *genea*, rendered "times" in Acts 14:16, "time" in 15:21, see AGE, No. 2 (RV, "generations"). (11) For "at every time," 2 Pet. 1:15, RV, see ALWAYS, No. 2. (12) For "in time of need," Heb. 4:16, see CONVENIENT, and NEED, C, Note. (13) In Heb. 2:1, *pote* signifies "at any time"; in 1 Pet. 3:5, "in the old time"; in 2 Pet. 1:21, "in old time." See PAST. In the following where the KJV has "sometimes" the RV has "once" in Eph. 2:13 and 5:8; "aforetime" in Titus 3:3. (14) In Luke 15:29, KJV, *oudepote*, "never," is rendered "neither ... at any time" (RV, "never"). (15) For *eukaireō,* "to spend

time," Acts 17:21, see SPEND, No. 10. (16) For *chronotribeō*, "to spend time," see SPEND, No. 11. (17) For *prolegō*, rendered "told ... in time past," in Gal. 5:21, KJV, see FOREWARN. (18) In Luke 12:1, "in the mean time" is a rendering of the phrase *en hois*, lit., "in which (things or circumstances)." (19) In Rev. 5:11 there is no word representing "times": see THOUSAND, *Note* (2). (20) In Gal. 4:2 *prothesmios* (in its feminine form, with *hēmera*, "day," understood) is rendered "time appointed" (see APPOINT, No. 3 and Note, TERM).

For TINKLING see CLANGING

TIP

akron (ἄκρον, 206), "the top, an extremity," is translated "tip" in Luke 16:24. See END, C, *Note* (6), TOP.

For TITHES (Noun) see TENTH, No. 2

TITHE (Verb)

1. *dekatoō* (δεκατόω, 1183), from *dekatos*, "tenth", in the active voice denotes "to take tithes of," Heb. 7:6, RV, "hath taken (KJV, received) tithes"; in the passive, "to pay tithes," 7:9, RV, "hath paid (KJV, 'payed') tithes."¶ In the Sept., Neh. 10:37.¶

2. *apodekatoō* (ἀποδεκατόω, 586) denotes (*a*) "to tithe" (*apo*, "from," *dekatos*, "tenth"), Matt. 23:23 (KJV, "pay tithe of"); Luke 11:42; in Luke 18:12 (where the best texts have the alternative form *apodekateuō*), "I give tithes"; (*b*) "to exact tithes" from Heb. 7:5.¶

3. *apodekateuō* (ἀποδεκατεύω, 586v), "to give tithes," in Luke 18:12 (some texts have No. 2).¶

Note: Heb. 7:4–9 shows the superiority of the Melchizedek priesthood to the Levitical, in that (1) Abraham, the ancestor of the Levites, paid "tithes" to Melchizedek (Gen. 14:20); (2) Melchizedek, whose genealogy is outside that of the Levites, took "tithes" of Abraham, the recipient himself of the divine promises; (3) whereas death is the natural lot of those who receive "tithes," the death of Melchizedek is not recorded; (4) the Levites who received "tithes" virtually paid them through Abraham to Melchizedek.

TITLE

titlos (τίτλος, 5102), from Latin *titulus*, is used of the inscription above the cross of Christ, John 19:19, 20. See SUPERSCRIPTION.¶

TITTLE

keraia or *kerea* (κεραία, 2762), "a little horn" (*keras*, "a horn"), was used to denote the small stroke distinguishing one Hebrew letter from another. The rabbis attached great importance to these; hence the significance of the Lord's statements in Matt. 5:18 and Luke 16:17, charging the Pharisees with hypocrisy, because, while professing the most scrupulous reverence to the Law, they violated its spirit.

Grammarians used the word to denote the accents in Greek words.¶

For **TO** see †, p. 1

TODAY, THIS DAY

sēmeron (σήμερον, 4594), an adverb (the Attic form is *tēmeron*), akin to *hēmera*, a day, with the prefix *t* originally representing a pronoun. It is used frequently in Matthew, Luke and Acts; in the last it is always rendered "this day"; also in Heb. 1:5, and the RV of 5:5 (KJV, "to day") in the same quotation; "today" in 3:7, 13, 15; 4:7 (twice); 13:8; also Jas. 4:13.

The clause containing *sēmeron* is sometimes introduced by the conjunction *hoti*, "that," e.g., Mark 14:30; Luke 4:21; 19:9; sometimes without the conjunction, e.g., Luke 22:34; 23:43, where "today" is to be attached to the next statement, "shalt thou be with Me"; there are no grammatical reasons for the insistence that the connection must be with the statement "Verily I say unto thee," nor is such an idea necessitated by examples from either the Sept. or the NT; the connection given in the KJV and RV is right.

In Rom. 11:8 and 2 Cor. 3:14, 15, the lit. rendering is "unto the today day," the emphasis being brought out by the RV, "unto (until) this very day."

In Heb. 4:7, the "today" of Ps. 95:7 is evidently designed to extend to the present period of the Christian faith.

TOGETHER

1. *homou* (ὁμοῦ, 3674), used in connection with place, in John 21:2; Acts 2:1 (in the best texts), RV, "together" (KJV, "with one accord," translating the inferior reading *homothumadon*: see ACCORD, A), is used without the idea of place in John 4:36; 20:4.¶

2. *hama* (ἅμα, 260), "at once," is translated "together" in Rom. 3:12; 1 Thess. 4:17; 5:10. See EARLY, *Note*, WITHAL.

Notes: (1) For *pamplēthei*, Luke 23:18, RV, see ONCE, *Note*. (2) In 1 Thess. 5:11, KJV, *allēlous*, "one another" (RV), is rendered "yourselves together"; in Luke 23:12, KJV, *meta allēlōn*, lit., "with one another," is rendered "together" (RV, "with each other"); so in Luke 24:14, KJV, *pros allēlous*, RV, "with each other." (3) In the following, "together" translates the phrase *epi to auto*, lit., "to (upon, or for) the same," Matt. 22:34; Luke 17:35; Acts 1:15; 2:44 (3:1, in some texts); 4:26; 1 Cor. 7:5; 14:23, RV: see PLACE, A, *Note* (7). (4) In Acts 14:1, it translates *kata to auto*, "at the same"; it may mean "in the same way" (i.e., as they had entered the synagogue at Pisidian Antioch). (5) In many cases "together" forms part of another word.

TOIL (Verb and Noun)

A. Verbs.

1. *kopiaō* (κοπιάω, 2872), "to be weary, to labor," is rendered "to toil" in Matt. 6:28; Luke 5:5 (12:27, in some mss.); in 1 Cor. 4:12, RV (KJV, "we labor"). See LABOR.

2. *basanizō* (βασανίζω, 928), primarily, "to rub on the touchstone, to put to the test," then, "to examine by torture" (*basanos*, "touchstone, torment"), hence denotes "to torture, torment, distress"; in the passive voice it is rendered "toiling" in Mark 6:48, KJV (RV, "distressed"). See PAIN, TORMENT, VEX.

B. Noun.

kopos (κόπος, 2873), "labor, trouble," is rendered "toil" in Rev. 2:2, RV (KJV, "labor"). See LABOR.

TOKEN

1. *sēmeion* (σημεῖον, 4592), "a sign, token or indication," is translated "token" in 2 Thess. 3:17, of writing of the closing salutations, the apostle using the pen himself instead of his amanuensis, his autograph attesting the authenticity of his Epistles. See MIRACLE, SIGN.

2. *sussēmon* (σύσσημον, 4953), "a fixed sign or signal, agreed upon with others" (*sun*, "with"), is used in Mark 14:44, "a token."¶ In the Sept., Judg. 20:38, 40; Isa. 5:26; 49:22; 62:10.¶

3. *endeigma* (ἔνδειγμα, 1730), "a plain token, a proof" (akin to *endeiknumi*, "to point out, prove"), is used in 2 Thess. 1:5 "a manifest token," said of the patient endurance and faith of the persecuted saints at Thessalonica, affording proof to themselves of their new life, and a guarantee of the vindication by God of both Himself and them (see No. 4, *Note*).¶

4. *endeixis* (ἔνδειξις, 1732), "a pointing out, showing forth," is rendered "evident token" in Phil. 1:28. See DECLARE, B, PROOF. Cf. *apodeixis*, 1 Cor. 2:4.

Note: No. 4 refers to the act or process of

proving, No. 3 to the thing proved. While the two passages, Phil. 1:28 and 2 Thess. 1:5, contain similar ideas, *endeigma* indicates the "token" as acknowledged by those referred to; *endeixis* points more especially to the inherent veracity of the "token."

TOLERABLE

anektos (ἀνεκτός, 414) (akin to *anechō*, in the middle voice, "to endure," see ENDURE, No. 5) is used in its comparative form, *anektoteros*, in Matt. 10:15; 11:22, 24; Luke 10:12, 14; some texts have it in Mark 6:11.¶

For TOLL see CUSTOM (Toll)

TOMB

1. *mnēmeion* (μνημεῖον, 3419) is almost invariably rendered "tomb" or "tombs" in the RV, never "grave," sometimes "sepulchre"; in the KJV, "tomb" in Matt. 8:28; 27:60; Mark 5:2; 6:29. See GRAVE No. 1, SEPULCHRE.

2. *mnēma* (μνῆμα, 3418), rendered "tombs" in Mark 5:3, 5; Luke 8:27: see GRAVE, No. 2, SEPULCHRE.

3. *taphos* (τάφος, 5028), akin to *thaptō*, "to bury," is translated "tombs" in Matt. 23:29; elsewhere "sepulchre." See SEPULCHRE.

TOMORROW

aurion (αὔριον, 839) is used either without the article, e.g., Matt. 6:30; 1 Cor. 15:32; Jas. 4:13; or with the article in the feminine form, to agree with *hēmera*, "day," e.g., Matt. 6:34; Acts 4:3, RV, "the morrow" (KJV, "next day"); Jas. 4:14; preceded by *epi*, "on," e.g., Luke 10:35; Acts 4:5.

TONGUE (-S)

A. Nouns.

1. *glōssa* (γλῶσσα, 1100) is used of (1) the "tongues ... like as of fire" which appeared at Pentecost; (2) "the tongue," as an organ of speech, e.g., Mark 7:33; Rom. 3:13; 14:11; 1 Cor. 14:9; Phil. 2:11; Jas. 1:26; 3:5, 6, 8; 1 Pet. 3:10; 1 John 3:18; Rev. 16:10; (3) (*a*) "a language," coupled with *phulē*, "a tribe," *laos*, "a people," *ethnos*, "a nation," seven times in the Apocalypse, 5:9; 7:9; 10:11; 11:9; 13:7; 14:6; 17:15; (*b*) "the supernatural gift of speaking in another language without its having been learnt"; in Acts 2:4–13 the circumstances are recorded from the viewpoint of the hearers; to those in whose language the utterances were made it appeared as a supernatural phenomenon; to others, the stammering of drunkards; what was uttered was not addressed primarily to the audience but consisted in recounting "the

mighty works of God"; cf. 2:46; in 1 Cor., chapters 12 and 14, the use of the gift of "tongues" is mentioned as exercised in the gatherings of local churches; 12:10 speaks of the gift in general terms, and couples with it that of "the interpretation of tongues"; chapt. 14 gives instruction concerning the use of the gift, the paramount object being the edification of the church; unless the "tongue" was interpreted the speaker would speak "not unto men, but unto God," v. 2; he would edify himself alone, v. 4, unless he interpreted, v. 5, in which case his interpretation would be of the same value as the superior gift of prophesying, as he would edify the church, vv. 4–6; he must pray that he may interpret, v. 13; if there were no interpreter, he must keep silence, v. 28, for all things were to be done "unto edifying," v. 26. "If I come ... speaking with tongues, what shall I profit you," says the apostle (expressing the great object in all oral ministry), "unless I speak to you either by way of revelation, or of knowledge, or of prophesying, or of teaching?" (v. 6). "Tongues" were for a sign, not to believers, but to unbelievers, v. 22, and especially to unbelieving Jews (see v. 21): cf. the passages in the Acts.

There is no evidence of the continuance of this gift after apostolic times nor indeed in the later times of the apostles themselves; this provides confirmation of the fulfillment in this way of 1 Cor. 13:8, that this gift would cease in the churches, just as would "prophecies" and "knowledge" in the sense of knowledge received by immediate supernatural power (cf. 14:6). The completion of the Holy Scriptures has provided the churches with all that is necessary for individual and collective guidance, instruction, and edification.

2. *dialektos* (διάλεκτος, 1258), "language" (Eng., "dialect"), is rendered "tongue" in the KJV of Acts 1:19; 2:6, 8; 21:40; 22:2; 26:14. See LANGUAGE.¶

B. Adjective.

heteroglōssos (ἑτερόγλωσσος, 2084) is rendered "strange tongues" in 1 Cor. 14:21, RV (*heteros*, "another of a different sort"—see ANOTHER— and A, No. 1), KJV, "other tongues."¶

C. Adverb.

hebraisti (or *ebraisti*, Westcott and Hort) (Ἑβραϊστί, 1447) denotes (*a*) "in Hebrew," Rev. 9:11, RV (KJV, "in the Hebrew tongue"); so 16:16; (*b*) in the Aramaic vernacular of Palestine, John 5:2, KJV, "in the Hebrew tongue" (RV, "in Hebrew"); in 19:13, 17, KJV, "in the Hebrew" (RV, "in Hebrew"); in v. 20, KJV and RV, "in Hebrew"; in 20:16, RV only, "in Hebrew (Rabboni)."¶

Note: Cf. *Hellēnisti*, "in Greek," John 19:20,

RV; Acts 21:37, "Greek."¶ See also *Rhōmaisti*, under LATIN.

TOOTH, TEETH

odous (ὀδούς, 3599) is used in the sing. in Matt. 5:38 (twice); elsewhere in the plural, of "the gnashing of teeth," the gnashing being expressive of anguish and indignation, Matt. 8:12; 13:42, 50; 22:13; 24:51; 25:30; Mark 9:18; Luke 13:28; Acts 7:54; in Rev. 9:8, of the beings seen in a vision and described as locusts.¶

TOP

A. Noun.

akron (ἄκρον, 206), for which see TIP, is used of Jacob's staff, Heb. 11:21.

B. Phrases.

Note: In Matt. 27:51 and Mark 15:38, *apo anōthen*, "from the top" (lit., "from above"), is used of the upper part of the Temple veil. In John 19:23, the different phrase *ek tōn anōthen* is used of the weaving of the Lord's garment (the *chitōn:* see CLOTHING), lit., "from the parts above."

TOPAZ

topazion (τοπάζιον, 5116) is mentioned in Rev. 21:20, as the ninth of the foundation stones of the wall of the heavenly Jerusalem; the stone is of a yellow color (though there are topazes of other colors) and is almost as hard as the diamond. It has the power of double refraction, and when heated or rubbed becomes electric.¶ In the Sept., Ex. 28:17; 39:10; Job 28:19; Ps. 119:127, "(gold and) topaz"; Ezek. 28:13.¶

TORCH

lampas (λαμπάς, 2985), "a torch," is used in the plur. and translated "torches" in John 18:3; in Rev. 8:10, RV, "torch" (KJV, "lamp"). See LAMP.

TORMENT (Noun and Verb)

A. Nouns.

1. *basanismos* (βασανισμός, 929), akin to *basanizō* (see TOIL, No. 2), is used of divine judgments in Rev. 9:5; 14:11; 18:7, 10, 15.¶

2. *basanos* (βάσανος, 931), primarily "a touchstone," employed in testing metals, hence, "torment," is used (*a*) of physical diseases, Matt. 4:24: (*b*) of a condition of retribution in Hades, Luke 16:23, 28.¶

Note: In 1 John 4:18, KJV, *kolasis*, "punishment" (RV), is rendered "torment." See PUNISHMENT, No. 3.

B. Verbs.

1. *basanizō* (βασανίζω, 928), for which see TOIL, No. 2, is translated "to torment," (*a*) of

sickness, Matt. 8:6; (*b*) of the doom of evil spirits, Mark 5:7; Luke 8:28; (*c*) of retributive judgments upon impenitent mankind at the close of this age, Rev. 9:5; 11:10; (*d*) upon those who worship the Beast and his image and receive the mark of his name, 14:10; (*e*) of the doom of Satan and his agents, 20:10.

2. *kakoucheō* (κακουχέω, 2558), "to treat evilly," in the passive voice is translated "tormented" in Heb. 11:37, KJV (RV, "evil entreated"). See SUFFER, No. 6.

3. *odunao* (ὀδυνάω, 3600), for which see ANGUISH, B, No. 3, in the passive voice is rendered "I am (thou art) tormented" in Luke 16:24, 25, KJV.

TORMENTOR

basanistēs (βασανιστής, 930), properly, "a torturer" (akin to *basanizō*, see TORMENT, B), "one who elicits information by torture," is used of jailors, Matt. 18:34.¶

TORTURE (Verb)

tumpanizō (τυμπανίζω, 5178) primarily denotes "to beat a drum" (*tumpanon*, "a kettledrum," Eng., "tympanal," "tympanitis," "tympanum"), hence, "to torture by beating, to beat to death," Heb. 11:35.¶ In the Sept., 1 Sam. 21:13, "(David) drummed (upon the doors of the city)."¶ The tympanum as an instrument of "torture" seems to have been a wheel-shaped frame upon which criminals were stretched and beaten with clubs or thongs.

TOSS

1. *rhipizō* (ῥιπίζω, 4494), primarily "to fan a fire" (*rhipis*, "a fan," cf. *rhipē*, "twinkling"), then, "to make a breeze," is used in the passive voice in Jas. 1:6, "tossed," of the raising of waves by the wind.¶

2. *kludōnizomai* (κλυδωνίζομαι, 2831) signifies "to be tossed by billows" (*kludōn*, "a billow"); metaphorically, in Eph. 4:14, of an unsettled condition of mind influenced and agitated by one false teaching and another, and characterized by that immaturity which lacks the firm conviction begotten by the truth.¶ In the Sept., Isa. 57:20.¶

Note: For "being . . . tossed," Acts 27:18, See LABOR, B, No. 2.

TOUCH (Verb)

1. *haptō* (ἅπτω, 681), primarily, "to fasten to," hence, of fire, "to kindle," denotes, in the middle voice (*a*) "to touch," e.g., Matt. 8:3, 15; 9:20, 21, 29; (*b*) "to cling to, lay hold of," John 20:17; here the Lord's prohibition as to clinging to Him was indicative of the fact that commu-

nion with Him would, after His ascension, be by faith, through the Spirit; (c) "to have carnal intercourse with a woman," 1 Cor. 7:1; (d) "to have fellowship and association with unbelievers," 2 Cor. 6:17; (e) (negatively) "to adhere to certain Levitical and ceremonial ordinances," in order to avoid contracting external defilement, or to practice rigorous asceticism, all such abstentions being of "no value against the indulgence of the flesh," Col. 2:21, KJV (RV, "handle"); (f) "to assault," in order to sever the vital union between Christ and the believer, said of the attack of the Evil One, 1 John 5:18. See HANDLE, No. 2, KINDLE, LIGHT.

2. thinganō (θιγγάνω, 2345), "to touch," a lighter term than No. 1, though Heb. 11:28 approximates to it, in expressing the action of the Destroyer of the Egyptian firstborn; in Heb. 12:20 it signifies "to touch," and is not to be interpreted by Ps. 104:32, "He toucheth (No. 1 in the Sept.) the hills and they smoke"; in Col. 2:21, RV (KJV, "handle"). See HANDLE, No. 2.¶

3. prospsauō (προσψαύω, 4379), "to touch upon, to touch slightly," occurs in Luke 11:46.¶

4. psēlaphaō (ψηλαφάω, 5584), "to feel, to handle," is rendered "that might be touched" in Heb. 12:18. See FEEL, No. 3, HANDLE, No. 1.

5. katagō (κατάγω, 2609), "to bring down," is used of bringing a ship to land in Acts 27:3. See BRING No. 16.

6. sumpatheō (συμπαθέω, 4834), for which see COMPASSION, A, No. 3, is rendered "be touched with" in Heb. 4:15.

7. paraballō (παραβάλλω, 3846), for which see ARRIVE, No. 4, COMPARE, No. 2, is rendered "touched at" in Acts 20:15, RV.

For **TOUCHING** (Preposition) see †, p. 1

For **TOWARD** (Preposition), see †, p. 1

TOWEL

lention (λέντιον, 3012) denotes "a linen cloth or towel" (Lat., linteum), as used by the Lord, John 13:4, 5; it was commonly used by servants in a household.¶

TOWER

purgos (πύργος, 4444) is used of "a watchtower in a vineyard," Matt. 21:33; Mark 12:1; probably, too, in Luke 14:28 (cf. Isa. 5:2); in Luke 13:4, of the "tower in Siloam," the modern Silwan, which is built on a steep escarpment of rock.¶

TOWN

1. kōmopolis (κωμόπολις, 2969) denotes "a country town," Mark 1:38, "a large village" usually without walls.¶

2. kōmē (κώμη, 2968), "a village," or "country town without walls." The RV always renders this "village" or "villages," KJV, "town" or "towns," Matt. 10:11; Mark 8:23, 26 (twice), 27; Luke 5:17; 9:6, 12; John 7:42; 11:1, 30. See VILLAGE.

TOWN CLERK

grammateus (γραμματεύς, 1122), "a writer, scribe," is used in Acts 19:35 of a state "clerk," an important official, variously designated, according to inscriptions found in Graeco-Asiatic cities. He was responsible for the form of decrees first approved by the Senate, then sent for approval in the popular assembly, in which he often presided. The decrees having been passed, he sealed them with the public seal in the presence of witnesses. Such an assembly frequently met in the theater. The Roman administration viewed any irregular or unruly assembly as a grave and even capital offense, as tending to strengthen among the people the consciousness of their power and the desire to exercise it. In the circumstances at Ephesus the town clerk feared that he might himself be held responsible for the irregular gathering. See SCRIBE.

TRACE

A. Verb.

parakoloutheō (παρακολουθέω, 3877), "to follow up," is used of investigating or "tracing" a course of events, Luke 1:3, where the writer, humbly differentiating himself from those who possessed an essential apostolic qualification, declares that he "traced the course of all things" (RV) about which he was writing (KJV, "having had... understanding, etc."). See FOLLOW, No. 5.

B. Adjective.

anexichniastos (ἀνεξιχνίαστος, 421) signifies "that cannot be traced out" (a, negative, ex, for ek, "out," ichnos, "a track"), is rendered "past tracing out" in Rom. 11:33, RV (KJV, "past finding out"); in Eph. 3:8, "unsearchable." See FIND, Note (3), UNSEARCHABLE.¶ In the Sept., Job 5:9; 9:10; 34:24.¶

TRADE (Noun and Verb)

A. Verbs.

1. ergazomai (ἐργάζομαι, 2038), "to work," is rendered "traded" in Matt. 25:16; in Rev. 18:17, KJV, "trade," RV, "gain their living." See

COMMIT, DO, LABOR, B, *Note* (1), MINISTER, WORK.

2. *pragmateuomai* (πραγματεύομαι, 4231) is rendered "trade ye" in Luke 19:13, RV, which adds "*herewith*": see OCCUPY.¶

3. *diapragmateuomai* (διαπραγματεύομαι, 1281), "to accomplish by traffic, to gain by trading," occurs in Luke 19:15.¶

4. *emporeuomai* (ἐμπορεύομαι, 1710) is rendered "trade" in Jas. 4:13, RV: see BUY, *Note, MERCHANDISE, B.*

B. Nouns.

1. *technē* (τέχνη, 5078), "an art" (Eng., "technique," "technical"), is used in Acts 18:3 (2nd part) of a "trade," RV (KJV, "occupation"). For the 1st part see *Note* below. See ART.

2. *meros* (μέρος, 3313), "a portion," is used of "a trade" in Acts 19:27. See CRAFT, No. 5.

Note: For the adjective *homotechnos*, "of the same trade," Acts 18:3, 1st part, RV, see CRAFT, No. 4.¶

TRADITION

paradosis (παράδοσις, 3862), "a handing down or on" (akin to *paradidōmi*, "to hand over, deliver"), denotes "a tradition," and hence, by metonymy, (*a*) "the teachings of the rabbis," interpretations of the Law, which were thereby made void in practice, Matt. 15:2, 3, 6; Mark 7:3, 5, 8, 9, 13; Gal. 1:14; Col. 2:8; (*b*) of "apostolic teaching," 1 Cor. 11:2, RV, "traditions" (KJV, "ordinances"), of instructions concerning the gatherings of believers (instructions of wider scope than ordinances in the limited sense); in 2 Thess. 2:15, of Christian doctrine in general, where the apostle's use of the word constitutes a denial that what he preached originated with himself, and a claim for its divine authority (cf. *paralambanō*, "to receive," 1 Cor. 11:23; 15:3); in 2 Thess. 3:6, it is used of instructions concerning everyday conduct.¶

For **TRAIN**, Titus 2:4, RV, see **SOBER**, B, No. 3

TRAITOR

prodotēs (προδότης, 4273) denotes "a betrayer, traitor"; the latter term is assigned to Judas, virtually as a title, in Luke 6:16; in 2 Tim. 3:4 it occurs in a list of evil characters, foretold as abounding in the last days. See BETRAY, B.

TRAMPLE

katapateō (καταπατέω, 2662), "to tread down, trample under foot," is rendered "trample" in Matt. 7:6. See TREAD, No. 2.

TRANCE

ekstasis (ἔκστασις, 1611), for which see AMAZE, A, No. 1, denotes "a trance" in Acts 10:10; 11:5; 22:17, a condition in which ordinary consciousness and the perception of natural circumstances were withheld, and the soul was susceptible only to the vision imparted by God.

For **TRANQUIL**, 1 Tim. 2:2, RV, see **QUIET**, No. 1

For **TRANSFER** (in a figure) see **FASHION**, C, No. 1, and **FIGURE**, *Note* (2).

TRANSFIGURE

metamorphoō (μεταμορφόω, 3339), "to change into another form" (*meta*, implying change, and *morphē*, "form:" see FORM, No. 1), is used in the passive voice (*a*) of Christ's "transfiguration," Matt. 17:2; Mark 9:2; Luke (in 9:29) avoids this term, which might have suggested to gentile readers the metamorphoses of heathen gods, and uses the phrase *egeneto heteron*, "was altered", lit., "became (*ginomai*) different (*heteros*)"; (*b*) of believers, Rom. 12:2, "be ye transformed," the obligation being to undergo a complete change which, under the power of God, will find expression in character and conduct; *morphē* lays stress on the inward change, *schēma* (see the preceding verb in that verse, *suschēmatizō*) lays stress on the outward (see FASHION, No. 3, FORM, No. 2); the present continuous tenses indicate a process; 2 Cor. 3:18 describes believers as being "transformed (RV) into the same image" (i.e., of Christ in all His moral excellencies), the change being effected by the Holy Spirit.¶

TRANSFORM

1. *metamorphoō* (μεταμορφόω, 3339) is rendered "transformed" in Rom. 12:2: see TRANSFIGURE.

2. *metaschēmatizō* (μετασχηματίζω, 3345) in the passive voice is rendered "to be transformed" in the KJV of 2 Cor. 11:13, 14, 15: see FASHION, C, No. 1.

TRANSGRESS, TRANSGRESSION

A. Verbs.

1. *parabainō* (παραβαίνω, 3845), lit., "to go aside" (*para*), hence "to go beyond," is chiefly used metaphorically of "transgressing" the tradition of the elders, Matt. 15:2; the commandment of God, 15:3; in Acts 1:25, of Judas, KJV, "by transgression fell" (RV, "fell away"); in

2 John 9 some texts have this verb (KJV, "transgresseth"), the best have *proagō* (see GO, No. 10).¶

2. *huperbainō* (ὑπερβαίνω, 5233), lit., "to go over" (*huper*), used metaphorically and rendered "transgress" in 1 Thess. 4:6 (KJV, "go beyond"), i.e., of "overstepping" the limits separating chastity from licentiousness, sanctification from sin.¶.

3. *parerchomai* (παρέρχομαι, 3928), "to come by" (*para*, "by," *erchomai*, "to come"), "pass over," and hence, metaphorically, "to transgress," is so used in Luke 15:29. See COME, No. 9, PASS.

B. Nouns.

1. *parabasis* (παράβασις, 3847), akin to A, No. 1, primarily "a going aside," then, "an overstepping," is used metaphorically to denote "transgression" (always of a breach of law): (*a*) of Adam, Rom. 5:14; (*b*) of Eve, 1 Tim. 2:14; (*c*) negatively, where there is no law, since "transgression" implies the violation of law, none having been enacted between Adam's "transgression" and those under the Law, Rom. 4:15; (*d*) of "transgressions" of the Law, Gal. 3:19, where the statement "it was added because of transgressions" is best understood according to Rom. 4:15; 5:13 and 5:20; the Law does not make men sinners, but makes them "transgressors"; hence sin becomes "exceeding sinful," Rom. 7:7, 13. Conscience thus had a standard external to itself; by the Law men are taught their inability to yield complete obedience to God, that thereby they may become convinced of their need of a Savior; in Rom. 2:23, RV, "transgression (of the Law)," KJV, "breaking (the Law)"; Heb. 2:2; 9:15.¶

2. *paranomia* (παρανομία, 3892), "law-breaking" (*para*, "contrary to," *nomos*, "law"), is rendered "transgression" in 2 Pet. 2:16, RV (KJV, "iniquity").¶

Note: In 1 John 3:4 (1st part), KJV, *poieō*, "to do," with *anomia*, "lawlessness," is rendered "transgresseth ... the law" (RV, "doeth ... lawlessness"); in the 2nd part *anomia* alone is rendered "transgression of the law," KJV (RV, "lawlessness").

TRANSGRESSOR

1. *parabatēs* (παραβάτης, 3848), lit. and primarily, "one who stands beside," then, "one who oversteps the prescribed limit, a transgressor" (akin to *parabainō*, "to transgress," see above); so Rom. 2:25, RV (KJV, "a breaker"); v. 27, RV, "a transgressor" (KJV, "dost transgress"); Gal. 2:18; Jas. 2:9, 11.¶

Note: Hamartōlos, "a sinner, one who misses the mark," is applicable to all men without

distinction; *parabatēs* stresses the positive side of sin, and is applicable to those who received the Law.

2. *anomos* (ἄνομος, 459), "without law" (*a-*, negative), is translated "transgressors" in Luke 22:37 (in some texts, Mark 15:28), in a quotation from Isa. 53:12. See LAW, C, No. 3, LAWLESS, A.

TRANSLATE, TRANSLATION

A. Verbs.

1. *methistēmi* or *methistanō* (μεθίστημι, 3179), "to change, remove" (*meta*, implying "change," *histēmi*, "to cause to stand"), is rendered "hath translated" in Col. 1:13. See PUT, REMOVE, TURN (away).

2. *metatithēmi* (μετατίθημι, 3346), "to transfer to another place" (*meta*, see above, *tithēmi*, "to put"), is rendered "to translate" in Heb. 11:5 (twice). See CARRY, CHANGE, REMOVE, TURN.

B. Noun.

metathesis (μετάθεσις, 3331), "a change of position" (akin to A, No. 2), is rendered "translation" in Heb. 11:5. See CHANGE, REMOVING.

For TRANSPARENT, Rev. 21:21, see DAWN, A, No. 2, *Note*

TRAP

thēra (θήρα, 2339) denotes "a hunting, chase," then, "a prey"; hence, figuratively, of "preparing destruction by a net or trap," Rom. 11:9.¶

TRAVAIL (Noun and Verb)

A. Nouns.

1. *mochthos* (μόχθος, 3449), "labor, involving painful effort," is rendered "travail" in 2 Cor. 11:27, RV (KJV, "painfulness"); in 1 Thess. 2:9 and 2 Thess. 3:8 it stresses the toil involved in the work.¶

2. *ōdin* (ὠδίν, 5604), a birth pang, "travail pain," is used illustratively in 1 Thess. 5:3 of the calamities which are to come upon men at the beginning of the Day of the Lord; the figure used suggests the inevitableness of the catastrophe. See PAIN, No. 2, SORROW.

B. Verbs.

1. *ōdinō* (ὠδίνων, 5605), akin to A, No. 2, is used negatively in Gal. 4:27, "(thou) that travailest (not)," quoted from Isa. 54:1; the apostle applies the circumstances of Sarah and Hagar (which doubtless Isaiah was recalling) to show that, whereas the promise by grace had temporarily been replaced by the works of the Law (see Gal. 3:17), this was now reversed, and, in

the fulfillment of the promise to Abraham, the number of those saved by the gospel would far exceed those who owned allegiance to the Law. Isa. 54 has primary reference to the future prosperity of Israel restored to God's favor, but frequently the principles underlying events recorded in the OT extend beyond their immediate application.

In 4:19 the apostle uses it metaphorically of a second travailing on his part regarding the churches of Galatia; his first was for their deliverance from idolatry (v. 8), now it was for their deliverance from bondage to Judaism. There is no suggestion here of a second regeneration necessitated by defection. There is a hint of reproach, as if he was enquiring whether they had ever heard of a mother experiencing second birth pangs for her children.

In Rev. 12:2 the woman is figurative of Israel; the circumstances of her birth pangs are mentioned in Isa. 66:7 (see also Micah 5:2, 3). Historically the natural order is reversed. The Manchild, Christ, was brought forth at His first advent; the travail is destined to take place in "the time of Jacob's trouble," the "great tribulation," Matt. 24:21; Rev. 7:14. The object in 12:2 in referring to the birth of Christ is to connect Him with His earthly people Israel in their future time of trouble, from which the godly remnant, the nucleus of the restored nation, is to be delivered (Jer. 30:7).¶

2. *sunōdinō* (συνωδίνω, 4944), "to be in travail together," is used metaphorically in Rom. 8:22, of the whole creation.¶

3. *tikto* (τίκτω, 5088), "to beget," is rendered "travail" in John 16:21.

For TRAVEL (companions in), Acts 19:29, and TRAVEL WITH, 2 Cor. 8:19, see COMPANION, No. 1.

TRAVEL

dierchomai (διέρχομαι, 1330), "to go or pass through," is translated "travelled" in Acts 11:19. See COME, No. 5.

Note: For *apodēmeō*, rendered "travelling" in Matt. 25:14, KJV, see GO, No. 27.

TREAD, TRODE, TRODDEN

1. *pateō* (πατέω, 3961) is used (*a*) intransitively and figuratively, of "treading" upon serpents, Luke 10:19; (*b*) transitively, of "treading" on, down or under, of the desecration of Jerusalem by its foes, Luke 21:24; Rev. 11:2; of the avenging, by the Lord in Person hereafter, of this desecration and of the persecution of the Jews, in divine retribution, metaphorically spoken of as the "treading" of the winepress of God's wrath, Rev. 14:20; 19:15 (cf. Isa. 63:2, 3).¶

2. *katapateō* (καταπατέω, 2662), "to tread down, trample under foot," is used (*a*) literally, Matt. 5:13; 7:6; Luke 8:5; 12:1; (*b*) metaphorically, of "treading under foot" the Son of God, Heb. 10:29, i.e., turning away from Him, to indulge in willful sin.¶

For TREADING out the corn, see THRESH

TREASURE (Noun and Verb)

A. Nouns.

1. *thēsauros* (θησαυρός, 2344) denotes (1) "a place of safe keeping" (possibly akin to *tithēmi*, "to put"), (*a*) "a casket," Matt. 2:11; (*b*) "a storehouse," Matt. 13:52; used metaphorically of the heart, Matt. 12:35, twice (RV, "out of his treasure"); Luke 6:45; (2) "a treasure," Matt. 6:19, 20, 21; 13:44; Luke 12:33, 34; Heb. 11:26; "treasure" (in heaven or the heavens), Matt. 19:21; Mark 10:21; Luke 18:22; in these expressions (which are virtually equivalent to that in Matt. 6:1, "with your Father which is in Heaven") the promise does not simply refer to the present life, but looks likewise to the hereafter; in 2 Cor. 4:7 it is used of "the light of the knowledge of the glory of God in the face of Jesus Christ," descriptive of the gospel, as deposited in the earthen vessels of the persons who proclaim it (cf. v. 4); in Col. 2:3, of the wisdom and knowledge hidden in Christ.¶

2. *gaza* (γάζα, 1047), a Persian word, signifying "royal treasure," occurs in Acts 8:27.¶

B. Verb.

thēsaurizō (θησαυρίζω, 2343), akin to A, No. 1, is used metaphorically in Rom. 2:5 of "treasuring up wrath." See LAY, No. 17.

For TREASURER see CHAMBERLAIN, *Note*

TREASURY

1. *gazophulakion* (γαζοφυλάκιον, 1049), from *gaza*, "a treasure," *phulakē*, "a guard," is used by Josephus for a special room in the women's court in the Temple in which gold and silver bullion was kept. This seems to be referred to in John 8:20; in Mark 12:41 (twice), 43 and Luke 21:1 it is used of the trumpet-shaped or ram's-horn-shaped chests, into which the temple offerings of the people were cast. There were 13 chests, six for such gifts in general, seven for distinct purposes.¶

2. *korbanas* (κορβανᾶς, 2878), signifying

"the place of gifts," denoted the Temple "treasury," Matt. 27:6. See CORBAN.¶

For **TREATED**, Acts 27:3, RV, see **ENTREAT** (to deal with)

TREATISE

logos (λόγος, 3056), a word, denotes "a treatise or written narrative" in Acts 1:1. See WORD.

TREE

1. *dendron* (δένδρον, 1186), "a living, growing tree" (cf. Eng., "rhododendron," lit., "rose tree"), known by the fruit it produces, Matt. 12:33; Luke 6:44; certain qualities are mentioned in the NT; "a good tree," Matt. 7:17, 18; 12:33; Luke 6:43; "a corrupt tree" (ditto); in Jude 12, metaphorically, of evil teachers, "autumn trees (KJV, 'trees whose fruit withereth') without fruit, twice dead, plucked up by the roots," RV; in Luke 13:19 in some texts, "a great tree," KJV (RV, "a tree"); for this and Matt. 13:32 see MUSTARD; in Luke 21:29 "the fig tree" is illustrative of Israel, "all the trees" indicating gentile nations.

2. *xulon* (ξύλον, 3586) "wood, a piece of wood, anything made of wood" (see STAFF, STOCKS), is used, with the rendering "tree," (*a*) in Luke 23:31, where "the green tree" refers either to Christ, figuratively of all His living power and excellencies, or to the life of the Jewish people while still inhabiting their land, in contrast to "the dry," a figure fulfilled in the horrors of the Roman massacre and devastation in A.D. 70 (cf. the Lord's parable in Luke 13:6–9; see Ezek. 20:47, and cf. 21:3); (*b*) of "the cross," the tree being the *stauros*, the upright pale or stake to which Romans nailed those who were thus to be executed, Acts 5:30; 10:39; 13:29; Gal. 3:13; 1 Pet. 2:24; (*c*) of "the tree of life," Rev. 2:7; 22:2 (twice), 14, 19, RV, KJV, "book." See WOOD.

TREMBLE, TREMBLING

A. Verbs.

1. *tremō* (τρέμω, 5141), "to tremble, especially with fear," is used in Mark 5:33; Luke 8:47 (Acts 9:6, in some mss.); 2 Pet. 2:10, RV, "they tremble (not)," KJV, "they are (not) afraid."¶

2. *seiō* (σείω, 4579), "to move to and fro, shake," is rendered "will I make to tremble" in Heb. 12:26, RV (KJV, "I shake"). See QUAKE, SHAKE.

Notes: (1) For *phrissō* in Jas. 2:19, KJV, "tremble," see SHUDDER. (2) For the adjective

entromos, "trembling," Acts 7:32; 16:29, RV, "trembling for fear," see QUAKE, No. 1. (3) The adjective *emphobos*, used with *ginomai*, "to become," is rendered "trembled" in Acts 24:25 (RV, "was terrified"); in Luke 24:5, RV, "they were affrighted," KJV, "they were afraid." See AFFRIGHTED, A.

B. Noun.

tromos (τρόμος, 5156), "a trembling" (akin to A, No. 1), occurs in Mark 16:8, RV, "trembling (. . . had come upon them)"; 1 Cor. 2:3; 2 Cor. 7:15; Eph. 6:5; Phil. 2:12.¶

TRENCH

charax (χάραξ, 5482), primarily "a pointed stake," hence, "a palisade or rampart," is rendered "trench" in Luke 19:43, KJV (RV, "bank," marg., "palisade"). In A.D. 70, Titus, the Roman general, surrounded Jerusalem with a palisaded mound (Tyndale, *l.c.*, renders it "mound"). The Jews in one of their sorties destroyed this *charax*, after which Titus surrounded the city with a wall of masonry.¶

TRESPASS (Noun and Verb)

A. Noun.

paraptōma (παράπτωμα, 3900), primarily "a false step, a blunder" (akin to *parapiptō*, "to fall away," Heb. 6:6), lit., "a fall beside," used ethically, denotes "a trespass," a deviation, from uprightness and truth, Matt. 6:14, 15 (twice); 18:35, in some mss.; Mark 11:25, 26; in Romans the RV substitutes "trespass" and "trespasses" for KJV, "offense" and "offenses," 4:25, "for (i.e., because of) our trespasses"; 5:15 (twice), where the trespass is that of Adam (in contrast to the free gift of righteousness, v. 17, a contrast in the nature and the effects); 5:16, where "of many trespasses" expresses a contrast of quantity; the condemnation resulted from one "trespass," the free gift is "of (*ek*, expressing the origin, and throwing stress upon God's justifying grace in Christ) many trespasses"; v. 17, introducing a contrast between legal effects and those of divine grace; v. 18, where the RV, "through one trespass," is contrasted with "one act of righteousness"; this is important, the difference is not between one man's "trespass" and Christ's righteousness (as KJV), but between two acts, that of Adam's "trespass" and the vicarious death of Christ; v. 20 [cf. TRANSGRESSION, B, No. 1 (*d*)]; in 2 Cor. 5:19, KJV and RV, "trespasses"; in Eph. 1:7, RV, "trespasses" (KJV, "sins"); in 2:1, RV, "(dead through your) trespasses," KJV, "(dead in) trespasses"; 2:5, RV, "(dead through our) trespasses," KJV, "(dead in) sins"; so Col 2:13 (1st part); in the 2nd part, KJV and RV, "trespasses."

In Gal. 6:1, RV, "(in any) trespass" (KJV, "fault"), the reference is to "the works of the flesh" (5:19), and the thought is that of the believer's being found off his guard, the "trespass" taking advantage of him; in Jas. 5:16, KJV, "faults" (RV, "sins" translates the word *hamartias*, which is found in the best texts), auricular confession to a priest is not in view here or anywhere else in Scripture; the command is comprehensive, and speaks either of the acknowledgment of sin where one has wronged another, or of the unburdening of a troubled conscience to a godly brother whose prayers will be efficacious, or of open confession before the church.

In Rom. 11:11, 12, the word is used of Israel's "fall," i.e., their deviation from obedience to God and from the fulfillment of His will (to be distinguished from the verb *ptaiō*, "fall," in the 1st part of v. 11, which indicates the impossibility of recovery). See FALL, A, No. 2.¶

B. Verb.

hamartanō (ἁμαρτάνω, 264) "to sin," is translated "to trespass," in the KJV of Matt. 18:15, and Luke 17:3, 4 (RV, "to sin").

Note: For the different meanings of words describing sin, see SIN. *Paraptōma*, and *hamartēma* ("a sinful deed") are closely associated, with regard to their primary meanings: *parabasis* seems to be a stronger term, as the breach of a known law (see TRANSGRESSION).

TRIAL

1. *dokimē* (δοκιμή, 1382), for which see EXPERIENCE, No. 2, is rendered "trial" in 2 Cor. 8:2, KJV (RV, "proof").

2. *peira* (πεῖρα, 3984), "a making trial, an experiment," is used with *lambanō*, "to receive or take," in Heb. 11:29, rendered "assaying," and v. 36, in the sense of "having experience of" (akin to *peiraō*, "to assay, to try"), "had trial."¶ In the Sept., Deut. 28:56.¶

3. *peirasmos* (πειρασμός, 3986), akin to No. 2, is rendered "trials" in Acts 20:19, RV. See TEMPTATION.

4. *purōsis* (πύρωσις, 4451), akin to *puroō*, "to set on fire," signifies (*a*) "a burning"; (*b*) "a refining," metaphorically in 1 Pet. 4:12, "fiery trial," or rather "trial by fire," referring to the refining of gold (1:7). See BURNING.

Note: For *dokimion*, rendered "trial" in 1 Pet. 1:7, KJV, see PROOF, No. 2.

TRIBE (-S)

1. *phulē* (φυλή, 5443), "a company of people united by kinship or habitation, a clan, tribe," is used (*a*) of the peoples of the earth, Matt. 24:30; in the following the RV has "tribe(-s)" for KJV, "kindred(-s)," Rev. 1:7; 5:9; 7:9; 11:9; 13:7; 14:6; (*b*) of the "tribes" of Israel, Matt. 19:28; Luke 2:36; 22:30; Acts 13:21; Rom. 11:1; Phil. 3:5; Heb. 7:13, 14; Jas. 1:1; Rev. 5:5; 7:4–8; 21:12.¶

2. *dōdekaphulos* (δωδεκάφυλος, 1429), an adjective signifying "of twelve tribes" (*dōdeka*, "twelve," and No. 1), used as a noun in the neuter, occurs in Acts 26:7.¶

TRIBULATION

thlipsis (θλῖψις, 2347), for which see AFFLICTION, B, No. 4, is translated "tribulation" in the RV (for KJV, "affliction") in Mark 4:17; 13:19; plural in 2 Thess. 1:4, KJV, "tribulations," RV, "afflictions"; in Acts 14:22 "many tribulations" (KJV, "much tribulation"); in Matt. 24:9, "unto tribulation" (KJV, "to be afflicted"); in 2 Cor. 1:4; 7:4; 2 Thess. 1:6, KJV, "tribulation" for RV, "affliction"; RV and KJV, "tribulation(-s)," e.g., in Rom. 2:9; 5:3 (twice); 8:35; 12:12; Eph. 3:13; Rev. 1:9; 2:9, 10, 22.

In Rev. 7:14, "the great tribulation," RV, lit., "the tribulation, the great one" (not as KJV, without the article), is not that in which all saints share; it indicates a definite period spoken of by the Lord in Matt. 24:21, 29; Mark 13:19, 24, where the time is mentioned as preceding His second advent, and as a period in which the Jewish nation, restored to Palestine in unbelief by gentile instrumentality, will suffer an unprecedented outburst of fury on the part of the antichristian powers confederate under the Man of Sin (2 Thess. 2:10–12; cf. Rev. 12:13–17); in this tribulation gentile witnesses for God will share (Rev. 7:9), but it will be distinctly "the time of Jacob's trouble" (Jer. 30:7); its beginning is signalized by the setting up of the "abomination of desolation" (Matt. 24:15; Mark 13:14, with Dan. 11:31; 12:11).

Note: For the verb *thlibō*, in the passive voice rendered "suffer tribulation" in 1 Thess. 3:4, KJV (RV, "suffer affliction"), see AFFLICT, No. 4.

TRIBUTE

1. *phoros* (φόρος, 5411), akin to *pherō*, "to bring," denotes "tribute" paid by a subjugated nation, Luke 20:22; 23:2; Rom. 13:6, 7.¶

2. *kēnsos* (κῆνσος, 2778), Lat. and Eng., "census," denotes "a poll tax," Matt. 17:25; 22:17, 19; Mark. 12:14.¶

3. *didrachmon* (δίδραχμον, 1323), "the half-shekel," is rendered "tribute" in Matt. 17:24 (twice): see SHEKEL, No. 2.¶

TRIM

kosmeō (κοσμέω, 2885), "to arrange, adorn," is used of "trimming" lamps, Matt. 25:7. See ADORN, GARNISH.

TRIUMPH

thriambeuō (θριαμβεύω, 2358) denotes (*a*) "to lead in triumph," used of a conqueror with reference to the vanquished, 2 Cor. 2:14. Theodoret paraphrases it "He leads us about here and there and displays us to all the world." This is in agreement with evidences from various sources. Those who are led are not captives exposed to humiliation, but are displayed as the glory and devoted subjects of Him who leads (see the context). This is so even if there is a reference to a Roman "triumph." On such occasions the general's sons, with various officers, rode behind his chariot (Livy, xlv. 40). But there is no necessary reference here to a Roman "triumph" (Field, in *Notes on the Trans. of the NT*). The main thought is that of the display, "in Christ" being the sphere; its evidences are the effects of gospel testimony.

In Col. 2:15 the circumstances and subjects are quite different, and relate to Christ's victory over spiritual foes at the time of His death; accordingly the reference may be to the triumphant display of the defeated.¶

For TRODE see TREAD

TROUBLE (Noun and Verb)

A. Noun.

thlipsis (θλῖψις, 2347), for which see AFFLICTION, No. 4, and TRIBULATION, is rendered "trouble" in the KJV of 1 Cor. 7:28 (RV, "tribulation"); 2 Cor. 1:4 (2nd clause), 8 (RV, "affliction").

Note: In some mss. *tarachē*, "an agitation, disturbance, trouble," is found in Mark 13:8 (plur.) and John 5:4 (RV omits).¶

B. Verbs.

1. *tarassō* (ταράσσω, 5015), akin to *tarachē* (A, Note), is used (1) in a physical sense, John 5:7 (in some mss. v. 4), (2) metaphorically, (*a*) of the soul and spirit of the Lord, John 11:33, where the true rendering is "He troubled Himself"; (*b*) of the hearts of disciples, 14:1, 27; (*c*) of the minds of those in fear or perplexity, Matt. 2:3; 14:26; Mark 6:50; Luke 1:12; 24:38; 1 Pet. 3:14; (*d*) of subverting the souls of believers, by evil doctrine, Acts 15:24; Gal. 1:7; 5:10; (*e*) of stirring up a crowd, Acts 17:8; v. 13 in the best texts, "troubling (the multitudes)," RV.¶

2. *diatarassō* (διαταράσσω, 1298), "to agi-

tate greatly" (*dia*, "throughout," and No. 1), is used of the Virgin Mary, Luke 1:29.¶

3. *ektarassō* (ἐκτράσσω, 1613), "to throw into great trouble, agitate," is used in Acts 16:20, "do exceedingly trouble (our city)."¶ In the Sept., Ps. 18:4; 88:16.¶

4. *thlibō* (θλίβω, 2346), "to afflict," is rendered "to trouble" in the KJV, e.g., 2 Cor. 4:8 (RV, "pressed"); 7:5, but never in the RV: see AFFLICT, No. 4, PRESS, STRAITENED, TRIBULATION.

5. *enochleō* (ἐνοχλέω, 1776), from *en*, "in," *ochlos*, "a throng, crowd," is used in Heb. 12:15 of a root of bitterness; in Luke 6:18 (in the best texts; some have *ochleō*), RV, "were troubled" (KJV, "were vexed").¶

6. *parenochleō* (παρενοχλέω, 3926), "to annoy concerning anything" (*para*, and No. 5), occurs in Acts 15:19, "we trouble (not them)."¶

7. *skullō* (σκύλλω, 4660), primarily "to flay," hence, "to vex, annoy" ("there was a time when the Greek, in thus speaking, compared his trouble to the pains of flaying alive," Moulton, *Proleg.*, p. 89), is used in the active voice in Mark 5:35; Luke 8:49; in the passive voice, Matt. 9:36, in the best texts, RV, "they were distressed" (some have *ekluō*, KJV, "they fainted"); in the middle voice, Luke 7:6, "trouble (not thyself)."¶ The word is frequent in the papyri.

8. *anastatoō* (ἀναστατόω, 387) is rendered "trouble" in Gal. 5:12, KJV: see STIR, No. 12, TURN, No. 15, UPROAR.

9. *thorubeō* (θορυβέω, 2350), akin to *thorubos*, "a tumult," in the middle voice, "to make an uproar," is rendered "trouble not yourselves" in Acts 20:10, KJV. See ADO, TUMULT.

10. *throeō* (θροέω, 2360), "to make an outcry" (*throos*, "a tumult"), is used in the passive voice, Matt. 24:6; Mark 13:7; Luke 24:37; 2 Thess. 2:2.¶ In the Sept., Song of Sol. 5:4.¶

11. *thorubazō* (θορυβάζω, 2351d), "to disturb, to trouble" (akin to No. 9), is used in Luke 10:41, in the best texts (in some, *turbazō*, with the same meaning).¶

12. *adēmoneō* (ἀδημονέω, 85), "to be much troubled, distressed" (perhaps from *a*, negative, and *dēmōn*, "knowing," the compound therefore originally suggesting bewilderment), is translated "sore troubled" in Matt. 26:37 and Mark 14:33, RV (KJV, "very heavy"); so the RV in Phil. 2:26 (KJV, "full of heaviness"); Lightfoot renders it "distressed," a meaning borne out in the papyri. See HEAVY.¶

13. *diaponeō* (διαπονέω, 1278) denotes "to work out with toil," hence, "to be sore troubled"; so the RV in Acts 4:2 and 16:18 (KJV, "grieved"); Mark 14:4 in some texts.¶

Notes: (1) The noun *kopos*, "a striking, beating," then, "laborious toil, trouble," used with *parechō*, "to furnish, to supply," is rendered "to trouble" (lit., "to give trouble to"), in Matt. 26:10; Mark 14:6; Luke 11:7; 18:5; Gal. 6:17; the meaning is to embarrass a person by distracting his attention, or to give occasion for anxiety. In the last passage the apostle expresses his determination not to allow the Judaizing teachers to distract him any further. See LABOR, A, No. 1. (2) For "suffer trouble" in 2 Tim. 2:9, see HARDSHIP.

TROW

Note: Some mss. have *dokeō*, "to think," in Luke 17:9, KJV, "I trow (not)."

For TRUCE BREAKERS see IMPLACABLE

TRUE, TRULY, TRUTH

A. Adjectives.

1. *alēthēs* (ἀληθής, 227), primarily, "unconcealed, manifest" (*a*, negative, *lēthō*, "to forget," = *lanthanō*, "to escape notice"), hence, actual, "true to fact," is used (*a*) of persons, "truthful," Matt. 22:16; Mark 12:14; John 3:33; 7:18; 8:26; Rom. 3:4; 2 Cor. 6:8; (*b*) of things, "true," conforming to reality, John 4:18, "truly," lit., "true"; 5:31, 32; in the best texts, 6:55 (twice), "indeed"; 8:13, 14 (v. 16 in some texts: see No. 2), 17; 10:41; 19:35; 21:24; Acts 12:9; Phil. 4:8; Titus 1:13; 1 Pet. 5:12; 2 Pet. 2:22; 1 John 2:8, 27; 3 John 12.¶

2. *alēthinos* (ἀληθινός, 228), akin to No. 1, denotes "true" in the sense of real, ideal, genuine; it is used (*a*) of God, John 7:28 (cf. No. 1 in 7:18, above); 17:3; 1 Thess. 1:9; Rev. 6:10; these declare that God fulfills the meaning of His Name; He is "very God," in distinction from all other gods, false gods (*alēthēs*, see John 3:33 in No. 1, signifies that He is veracious, "true" to His utterances, He cannot lie); (*b*) of Christ, John 1:9; 6:32; 15:1; 1 John 2:8; 5:20 (thrice); Rev. 3:7, 14; 19:11; His judgment, John 8:16 (in the best texts, instead of No. 1); (*c*) God's words, John 4:37; Rev. 19:9; 21:5; 22:6; the last three are equivalent to No. 1; (*d*) His ways, Rev. 15:3; (*e*) His judgments, Rev. 16:7; 19:2; (*f*) His riches, Luke 16:11; (*g*) His worshipers, John 4:23; (*h*) their hearts, Heb. 10:22; (*i*) the witness of the apostle John, John 19:35; (*j*) the spiritual, antitypical tabernacle, Heb. 8:2; 9:24, not that the wilderness tabernacle was false, but that it was a weak and earthly copy of the heavenly.¶

Note: "*Alēthinos* is related to *alēthēs* as form

to contents or substances; *alēthēs* denotes the reality of the thing, *alēthinos* defines the relation of the conception to the thing to which it corresponds = genuine" (Cremer).

3. *gnēsios* (γνήσιος, 1103), primarily "lawfully begotten" (akin to *ginomai*, "to become"), hence, "true, genuine, sincere," is used in the apostle's exhortation to his "true yoke-fellow" in Phil. 4:3. See OWN, SINCERITY.

Note: In the KJV of 2 Cor. 1:18 and 1 Tim. 3:1, *pistos*, "faithful" (RV), is translated "true."

B. Verb.

alētheuō (ἀληθεύω, 226) signifies "to deal faithfully or truly with anyone" (cf. Gen. 42:16, Sept., "whether ye deal truly or no"), Eph. 4:15, "speaking the truth"; Gal. 3:16, "I tell (you) the truth," where probably the apostle is referring to the contents of his epistle.¶

C. Noun.

alētheia (ἀλήθεια, 225), "truth," is used (*a*) objectively, signifying "the reality lying at the basis of an appearance; the manifested, veritable essence of a matter" (Cremer), e.g., Rom. 9:1; 2 Cor. 11:10; especially of Christian doctrine, e.g., Gal. 2:5, where "the truth of the Gospel" denotes the "true" teaching of the Gospel, in contrast to perversions of it; Rom. 1:25, where "the truth of God" may be "the truth concerning God" or "God whose existence is a verity"; but in Rom 15:8 "the truth of God" is indicative of His faithfulness in the fulfillment of His promises as exhibited in Christ; the word has an absolute force in John 14:6; 17:17; 18:37, 38; in Eph. 4:21, where the RV, "even as truth is in Jesus," gives the correct rendering, the meaning is not merely ethical "truth," but "truth" in all its fullness and scope, as embodied in Him; He was the perfect expression of the truth; this is virtually equivalent to His statement in John 14:6; (*b*) subjectively, "truthfulness," "truth," not merely verbal, but sincerity and integrity of character, John 8:44; 3 John 3, RV; (*c*) in phrases, e.g., "in truth" (*epi*, "on the basis of"), Mark 12:14; Luke 20:21; with *en*, "in," 2 Cor. 6:7; Col. 1:6; 1 Tim. 2:7, RV (KJV, "in . . . verity"); 1 John 3:18; 2 John 1, 3, 4.

Note: In Matt. 15:27, KJV, *nai*, "yea" (RV), is translated "truth."

D. Adverbs.

1. *alēthōs* (ἀληθῶς, 230), "truly, surely," is rendered "of a truth" in Matt. 14:33; 26:73 and Mark 14:70, R.V, (KJV, "surely"); Luke 9:27; 12:44; 21:3; John 6:14; 7:40; 17:8, RV, "of a truth" (KJV, "surely"); Acts 12:11, RV (KJV, "of a surety"); "in truth," 1 Thess. 2:13; "truly," Matt. 27:54; Mark 15:39. See INDEED, No. 3.

2. *gnēsiōs* (γνησίως, 1104), "sincerely, honorably" (akin to A, No. 3), is rendered "truly"

(marg., "genuinely") in Phil, 2:20 (KJV, "naturally").¶

Notes: (1) The particles *ara, men,* and *de* are sometimes rendered "truly" in the KJV, but are differently rendered in the RV. (2) In 1 Cor. 14:25, KJV, *ontōs* (RV, "indeed") is rendered "of a truth." See CERTAIN, C, No. 1, INDEED, No. 4. (3) In John 20:30, KJV, the particle *oun,* therefore (RV), is rendered "truly."

TRUMP, TRUMPET

A. Noun.

salpinx (σάλπιγξ, 4536) is used (1) of the natural instrument, 1 Cor. 14:8; (2) of the supernatural accompaniment of divine interpositions, (*a*) at Sinai, Heb. 12:19; (*b*) of the acts of angels at the second advent of Christ, Matt. 24:31; (*c*) of their acts in the period of divine judgments preceding this, Rev. 8:2, 6, 13; 9:14; (*d*) of a summons to John to the presence of God, Rev. 1:10; 4:1; (*e*) of the act of the Lord in raising from the dead the saints who have fallen asleep and changing the bodies of those who are living, at the Rapture of all to meet Him in the air, 1 Cor. 15:52, where "the last trump" is a military allusion, familiar to Greek readers, and has no connection with the series in Rev. 8:6 to 11:15; there is a possible allusion to Num. 10:2–6, with reference to the same event, 1 Thess. 4:16, "the (lit., a) trump of God" (the absence of the article suggests the meaning "a trumpet such as is used in God's service").¶

B. Verb.

salpizō (σαλπίζω, 4537), "to sound a trumpet," Matt. 6:2; as in (2) (*c*) above, Rev. 8:6, 7, 8, 10, 12, 13; 9:1, 13; 10:7; 11:15; as in (2) (*e*) 1 Cor. 15:52.¶

TRUMPETER

salpistēs (σαλπιστής, 4538) occurs in Rev. 18:22.¶

TRUST (Noun and Verb)

A. Noun.

pepoithēsis (πεποίθησις, 4006) is rendered "trust" in 2 Cor. 3:4, KJV; see CONFIDENCE, No. 1.

B. Verbs.

1. *peithō* (πείθω, 3982), intransitively, in the perfect and pluperfect active, "to have confidence, trust," is rendered "to trust" in Matt. 27:43; Mark 10:24; Luke 11:22; 18:9; 2 Cor. 1:9; 10:7; Phil, 2:24; 3:4, KJV (RV, "to have confidence"); Heb. 2:13; in the present middle, Heb. 13:18, KJV (RV, "are persuaded"). See AGREE, No. 5, PERSUADE.

2. *pisteuō* (πιστεύω, 4100), "to entrust," or, in the passive voice, "to be entrusted with," is rendered "to commit to one's trust," in Luke 16:11; 1 Tim 1:11; "to be put in trust with," 1 Thess. 2:4, KJV (RV, "to be intrusted").

Note: Wherever *elpizō,* "to hope," is translated "to trust" in the KJV, the RV substitutes "to hope." So *proelpizō,* "to hope before." See HOPE.

For TRUTH see TRUE

TRY, TRIED

1. *dokimazō* (δοκιμάζω, 1381) is rendered "to try" in the KJV in 1 Cor. 3:13; 1 Thess. 2:4; 1 Pet. 1:7; 1 John 4:1: see PROVE, No. 1.

2. *peirazō* (πειράζω, 3985) is rendered "to try" in Heb. 11:17; Rev. 2:2, 10; 3:10. In Acts 16:7 it is rendered "assayed"; in 24:6, RV, "assayed" (KJV, "hath gone about"): see GO, *Note* (2) (*b*). See EXAMINE, PROVE, TEMPT. Cf. *peiraō* in Acts 26:21, RV, "assayed" (KJV, "went about"); see GO, *Note* (2) (*c*).

Notes: (1) In Rev. 3:18, KJV, *puroō,* in the passive voice, "to be purified by fire" (RV, "refined"), is rendered "tried." (2) For *dokimion,* Jas. 1:3, KJV, "trying," see PROOF. (3) For *dokimos,* Jas. 1:12, KJV, "tried," see APPROVED. (4) In 1 Pet. 4:12, KJV, the phrase *pros peirasmon,* lit., "for trial," i.e., "for testing," is rendered "to try (you)," RV, "to prove (you)."

TUMULT

1. *akatastasia* (ἀκαταστασία, 181) is rendered "tumults" in Luke 21:9, RV; 2 Cor. 6:5; 12:20. See CONFOUND, A, No. 1.

2. *thorubos* (θόρυβος, 2351), "a noise, uproar, tumult," is rendered "tumult" in Matt. 27:24 and Mark 5:38; in Matt. 26:5, RV (KJV, "uproar"), so in Mark 14:2; in Acts 20:1, "uproar," KJV and RV; in 24:18, "tumult"; in 21:34, KJV, "tumult" (RV, "uproar").¶

Note: For *thorubeō,* RV, "to make a tumult," see NOISE, *Note* (2).

TURN

1. *strephō* (στρέφω, 4762) denotes (1) in the active voice, (*a*) "to turn" (something), Matt. 5:39; (*b*) "to bring back," Matt. 27:3 (in the best texts; some have No. 2); (*c*) reflexively, "to turn oneself, to turn the back to people," said of God, Acts 7:42; (*d*) "to turn one thing into another," Rev. 11:6 (the only place where this word occurs after the Acts); (2) in the passive voice, (*a*) used reflexively, "to turn oneself," e.g. Matt. 7:6; John 20:14, 16; (*b*) metaphorically, Matt. 18:3, RV, "(except) ye turn" (KJV, " . . . be converted"); John 12:40 (in the best texts; some have No. 4). See CONVERT, A, No. 1.

2. *apostrephō* (ἀποστρέφω, 654) denotes (*a*)

"to cause to turn away (*apo*), to remove," Rom. 11:26; 2 Tim. 4:4 (1st clause); metaphorically, "to turn away from allegiance, pervert," Luke 23:14; (*b*) "to make to return, put back," Matt. 26:52; (*c*) in the passive voice, used reflexively, "to turn oneself away from," Matt. 5:42; 2 Tim. 1:15; Titus 1:14; Heb. 12:25; in the active voice, Acts 3:26. See PERVERT, PUT.¶

3. *diastrephō* (διαστρέφω, 1294), "to distort" (*dia*, "asunder"), is rendered "to turn aside," RV (KJV, " . . . away"), in Acts 13:8. See PERVERT, No. 2.

4. *epistrephō* (ἐπιστρέφω, 1994) is used (*a*) transitively, "to make to turn towards" (*epi*), Luke 1:16, 17; Jas 5:19, 20 (to convert); (*b*) intransitively, "to turn oneself round," e.g., in the passive voice, Mark 5:30 (see RETURN); in the active voice, Matt. 13:15, RV, "turn again" (KJV, "be converted"); Acts 11:21; 14:15; 15:19; 1 Thess. 1:9, "ye turned," the aorist tense indicating an immediate and decisive change, consequent upon a deliberate choice; conversion is a voluntary act in response to the presentation of truth. See CONVERT.

5. *metastrephō* (μεταστρέφω, 3344) signifies, in the passive voice, "to be turned" (of a change into something different, *meta*) in Acts 2:20 and Jas. 4:9: see PERVERT, No. 3.

6. *hupostrephō* (ὑποστρέφω, 5290) is used intransitively of "turning back, behind" (*hupo*), e.g., Luke 17:15, "turned back"; in 2:45, RV, "returned": see RETURN.

7. *apobainō* (ἀποβαίνω, 576), "to go from," is used metaphorically of events, "to issue, turn out," Luke 21:13; Phil. 1:19. See GO, No. 21.

8. *metagō* (μετάγω, 3329), "to move from one side to another," is rendered "to turn about" in Jas. 3:3, 4.¶

9. *metatithēmi* (μετατίθημι, 3346), "to change," is translated "turning (the grace of God)" in Jude 4. See CARRY, CHANGE, REMOVE, TRANSLATE.

10. *anakamptō* (ἀνακάμπτω, 344), *ana*, "back," *kamptō*, "to bend," is rendered "shall turn . . . again," in Luke 10:6. See RETURN.

11. *ektrepō* (ἐκτρέπω, 1624), "to cause to turn aside" (*ek*, "from," *trepō*, "to turn"), is used in the passive voice, with middle sense, in 1 Tim. 1:6; 5:15; 6:20, RV, "turning away" (KJV, "avoiding"); 2 Tim. 4:4 (2nd clause); Heb. 12:13, "be (not) turned out of the way" (RV, marg., "put out of joint"); some adhere to the meaning "to turn aside, go astray"; the interpretation depends on the antithesis which follows, "but rather be healed" (RV), which is not the antithesis to "turning aside" or being "turned" out of the way; accordingly the marg. is to be

preferred (the verb is often used medically).¶ In the Sept., Amos 5:8.¶

12. *apotrepō* (ἀποτρέπω, 665), "to cause to turn away" (*apo*), is used in the middle voice in 2 Tim. 3:5.¶

13. *peritrepō* (περιτρέπω, 4062), "to turn about" (*peri*), is rendered "doth turn (thee to madness)" in Acts 26:24, RV, KJV, "doth make (thee mad)."¶

14. *methistēmi* (μεθίστημι, 3179) is used metaphorically in Acts 19:26, "turned away (much people)." See PUT, REMOVE, TRANSLATE.

15. *anastatoō* (ἀναστατόω, 387), "to stir up, excite, unsettle" (*ana*, "up," *histēmi*, "to cause to stand"), is rendered "have turned (the world) upside down" in Acts 17:6. See TROUBLE, UPROAR.

16. *ginomai* (γίνομαι, 1096), "to become," is rendered "shall be turned" in John 16:20 (of sorrow into joy).

17. *ekklinō* (ἐκκλίνω, 1578), "to turn aside" (*ek*, "from," *klinō*, "to lean"), is rendered "have . . . turned aside" in Rom. 3:12 (KJV, "are . . . gone out of the way"); 16:17, RV, "turn away" (KJV, "avoid"); 1 Pet. 3:11, RV, ditto (KJV, "eschew").¶

18. *diadechomai* (διαδέχομαι, 1237), "to receive through another, to receive in turn" (*dia*, "through," *dechomai*, "to receive"), occurs in Acts 7:45, RV, "in their turn . . . when they entered" (KJV, "that came after"); the meaning here is "having received (it) after," i.e., as from Moses under Joshua's leadership. In the papyri the word is used similarly of visiting as deputy (see also Field, *Notes on the Trans. of the NT*, 116).¶

Notes: (1) In Matt. 2:22, KJV, *anachōreō*, "to retire, withdraw," is rendered "turned aside" (RV, "withdrew"). (2) For "turned to flight," *klinō*, Heb. 11:34, see FLIGHT, B. (3) For the phrase "by turn" in 1 Cor. 14:27 see COURSE, B, *Note* (3).

TURNING

tropē (τροπή, 5157), used especially of the revolution of the heavenly orbs (akin to *trepō*, "to turn"), occurs in Jas. 1:17, "(neither shadow) that is cast by turning," RV (KJV, "of turning"). For a more detailed treatment of the passage, see SHADOW, No. 2.¶

For TURTLEDOVE see DOVE

For TUTOR see GUARDIAN and INSTRUCTOR, No. 1.

TWAIN, TWO

duo (δύο, 1417) is rendered "twain" in Matt. 5:41; 19:5, 6; 21:31; 27:21, 51; Mark 10:8 (twice); 15:38; in 1 Cor. 6:16 and Eph. 5:31, RV (KJV, "two"); Eph. 2:15; in Rev. 19:20, RV (KJV, "both").

Notes: (1) In the following phrases the numeral is used distributively: (*a*) *ana duo*, "two apiece," John 2:6 (in some mss., Luke 9:3); in Luke 10:1, "two and two" ("by twos"); (*b*) *kata duo*, "by two," 1 Cor. 14:27; (*c*) *duo duo*, "by two and two," lit., "two (and) two," Mark 6:7 (not a Hebraism; the form of expression is used in the papyri); (*d*) *eis duo*, "into two," "in twain," Matt. 27:51 and Mark 15:38 (see above). (2) In Luke 17:34 *duo* stands for "two men"; in v. 35 for "two women."

TWELFTH

dōdekatos (δωδέκατος, 1428) occurs in Rev. 21:20.¶

TWELVE

dōdeka (δώδεκα, 1427) is used frequently in the Gospels for the twelve apostles, and in Acts 6:2; 1 Cor. 15:5; Rev. 21:14b; of the tribes of Israel, Matt. 19:28; Luke 22:30; Jas. 1:1; Rev. 21:12c (cf. 7:5–8; 12:1); in various details relating to the heavenly Jerusalem, Rev. 21:12–21; 22:2. The number in general is regarded as suggestive of divine administration.

TWENTY

eikosi (εἴκοσι, 1501) occurs in Luke 14:31; John 6:19; Acts 1:15; 27:28; 1 Cor. 10:8; of the "four and twenty" elders, in Rev. 4:4 (twice), 10; 5:8; 11:16; 19:4 (combined in one numeral with *tessares*, "four," in some mss.).¶

TWICE

dis (δίς, 1364) occurs in Mark 14:30, 72; Luke 18:12; Jude 12; combined with *muriades*, "ten thousand," in Rev. 9:16; rendered "again" in Phil. 4:16 and 1 Thess. 2:18. See AGAIN.¶

TWINKLING

rhipē (ῥιπή, 4493), akin to *rhiptō*, "to hurl," was used of any rapid movement, e.g., the throw of a javelin, the rush of wind or flame; in 1 Cor. 15:52 of the "twinkling" of an eye.¶

For TWO see TWAIN

TWO-EDGED

distomos (δίστομος, 1366), lit., "two-mouthed" (*dis*, and *stoma*, "a mouth"), was used of rivers and branching roads; in the NT of swords, Heb. 4:12; Rev. 1:16; 2:12, RV, "two-edged" (KJV, "with two edges").¶ In the Sept., Judg. 3:16; Ps. 149:6; Prov. 5:4.¶

For TWOFOLD MORE see DOUBLE

TWO HUNDRED

diakosioi (διακόσιοι, 1250) occurs in Mark 6:37; John 6:7; 21:8; Acts 23:23 (twice); 27:37, "two hundred (threescore and sixteen)"; Rev. 11:3, "(a thousand) two hundred (and threescore)"; so 12:6.¶

Note: In Acts 27:37, some ancient authorities read "about threescore and sixteen souls" (RV, margin). The confusion was quite natural when the word *diakosioi* was not written in full but represented by one Greek letter. The larger number is by no means improbable: Josephus sailed for Rome in A.D. 63 in a ship which had 600 on board (*Life*, ch. 3).

For TWO THOUSAND see THOUSAND, *Note* (1)

U

For UNAPPROACHABLE, 1 Tim. 6:16, RV, see APPROACH, B

UNAWARES

Notes: (1) In Heb. 13:2, *lanthanō*, "to escape notice," is used with the aorist participle of *xenizō*, "to entertain," signifying "entertained . . . unawares" (an idiomatic usage common in classical Greek). (2) For *aiphnidios*, "unawares," in Luke 21:34, KJV, see SUDDENLY. (3) In Gal. 2:4, KJV, *pareisaktos*, "brought in secretly," is rendered "unawares brought in." See PRIVILY, *Note:* cf. BRING, No. 17.¶ (4) In

Jude 4, KJV, *pareisdunō*, "to slip in secretly," is rendered "crept in unawares." See CREEP, A, No. 2.¶.

UNBELIEF

1. *apistia* (ἀπιστία, 570), "unbelief" 12 times, but see BELIEF, C, *Note* (2) for references.

2. *apeitheta* (ἀπείθεια, 543) is always rendered "disobedience" in the RV; in Rom. 11:30, 32 and Heb. 4:6, 11, KJV, "unbelief." See DISOBEDIENCE, A, No. 1.

UNBELIEVER

apistos (ἄπιστος, 571), an adjective, is used as a noun, rendered "unbeliever" in 2 Cor. 6:15 and 1 Tim. 5:8, RV; plural in 1 Cor. 6:6 and 2 Cor. 6:14; KJV only, Luke 12:46 (RV, "unfaithful"). See BELIEF, C, *Note* (3) FAITHLESS, INCREDIBLE.

UNBELIEVING

A. Adjective.

apistos (ἄπιστος, 571): see BELIEF, C, *Note* (3).

B. Verb.

apeitheō (ἀπειθέω, 544): see DISBELIEVE, DISOBEDIENT, C.

UNBLAMEABLE, UNBLAMEABLY

A. Adjectives.

1. *amemptos* (ἄμεμπτος, 273), "unblameable" (from *a*, negative, and *memphomai*, "to find fault"), is so rendered in 1 Thess. 3:13, i.e., "free from all valid charge." See BLAME, B, No. 3.

2. *amōmos* (ἄμωμος, 299): see BLEMISH, B.

B. Adverb.

amemptōs (ἀμέμπτως, 274) is used in 1 Thess. 2:10, "unblameably," signifying that no charge could be maintained, whatever charges might be made. See BLAME, C.

For UNCEASING see CEASE, B. For UNCEASINGLY, RV, in Rom. 1:9, see CEASE, C

UNCERTAIN, UNCERTAINLY, UNCERTAINTY

A. Adjective.

adēlos (ἄδηλος, 82) denotes (*a*) "unseen"; with the article, translated "which appear not" (*a*, negative, *dēlos*, "evident"), Luke 11:44; (*b*) "uncertain, indistinct," 1 Cor. 14:8.¶ In the Sept., Ps. 51:6.¶

B. Adverb.

adēlōs (ἀδήλως, 84), "uncertainly" (akin to A), occurs in 1 Cor. 9:26.¶

C. Noun.

adēlotēs (ἀδηλότης, 83), "uncertainty" (akin to A and B), occurs in 1 Tim. 6:17, "(the) uncertainty (of riches)," RV (the KJV translates it as an adjective, "uncertain"), i.e., riches the special character of which is their "uncertainty"; the Greek phrase is a rhetorical way of stressing the noun "riches"; when a genitive (here "of riches") precedes the governing noun (here "uncertainty") the genitive receives emphasis.¶

UNCHANGEABLE

aparabatos (ἀπαράβατος, 531) is used of the priesthood of Christ, in Heb. 7:24, "unchangeable," "unalterable, inviolable," RV, marg. (a meaning found in the papyri); the more literal meaning in KJV and RV margins, "that doth not pass from one to another," is not to be preferred. This active meaning is not only untenable, and contrary to the constant usage of the word, but does not adequately fit with either the preceding or the succeeding context.¶

For UNCIRCUMCISED and UNCIRCUMCISION see CIRCUMCISION

UNCLEAN

A. Adjectives.

1. *akathartos* (ἀκάθαρτος, 169), "unclean, impure" (*a*, negative, *kathairo*, "to purify"), is used (*a*) of "unclean" spirits, frequently in the Synoptists, not in John's gospel; in Acts 5:16; 8:7; Rev. 16:13; 18:2a (in the 2nd clause the birds are apparently figurative of destructive satanic agencies); (*b*) ceremonially, Acts 10:14, 28; 11:8; 1 Cor. 7:14; (*c*) morally, 2 Cor. 6:17, including (*b*), RV; "no unclean thing"; Eph. 5:5; Rev. 17:4, RV, "the unclean things" (KJV follows the text which have the noun *akathartēs*, "the filthiness").

2. *koinos* (κοινός, 2839), "common," is translated "unclean" in Rom. 14:14 (thrice); in Rev. 21:27, RV (KJV, "that defileth," follows the inferior texts which have the verb *koinoō*: see B). See COMMON, DEFILE, C, UNHOLY, No. 2.

B. Verb.

koinoō (κοινόω, 2840), to make *koinos*, "to defile," is translated "unclean" in Heb. 9:13, KJV, where the perfect participle, passive, is used with the article, hence the RV, "them that have been defiled." See DEFILE, A, No. 1.

C. Noun.

akatharsia (ἀκαθαρσία, 167), akin to A, No. 1, denotes "uncleanness," (*a*) physical, Matt. 23:27 (instances in the papyri speak of tenants keeping houses in good condition); (*b*) moral, Rom. 1:24; 6:19; 2 Cor. 12:21; Gal. 5:19; Eph. 4:19; 5:3; Col. 3:5; 1 Thess. 2:3 (suggestive of the fact that sensuality and evil doctrine are frequently associated); 4:7.¶

Note: In 2 Pet. 2:10, KJV, *miasmos*, "a defilement," is rendered "uncleanness"; see DEFILEMENT, B, No. 2.¶

For UNCLOTHED see STRIP

UNCOMELY

aschēmōn (ἀσχήμων, 809), "shapeless" (*a*, negative, *schēma*, "a form"), the opposite of *euschēmōn*, "comely," is used in 1 Cor. 12:23.¶ In the Sept., Gen. 34:7; Deut. 24:3.¶

Note: For the verb *aschēmoneō*, rendered "to behave oneself uncomely" in 1 Cor. 7:36, KJV, see BEHAVE, No. 4.

UNCONDEMNED

akatakritos (ἀκατάκριτος, 178), rendered "uncondemned" in Acts 16:37; 22:25 (*a*, negative, *katakrinō*, "to condemn"), properly means "without trial, not yet tried." Sir W. M. Ramsay points out that the apostle, in claiming his rights, would probably use the Roman phrase *re incognita*, i.e., "without investigating our case" (*The Cities of St. Paul*, p. 225).¶

For UNCORRUPTIBLE see CORRUPT, C, No. 2. For UNCORRUPTNESS, see CORRUPT, B, No. 4

UNCOVER

apostegazō (ἀποστεγάζω, 648) signifies "to unroof" (*apo*, from, *stegē*, "a roof"), Mark 2:4.¶

For UNCOVERED, 1 Cor. 11:5, 13, see UNVEILED

For UNCTION see ANOINT, B

UNDEFILED

amiantos (ἀμίαντος, 283), "undefiled, free from contamination" (*a*, negative, *miainō*, "to defile"), is used (*a*) of Christ, Heb. 7:26; (*b*) of pure religion, Jas. 1:27; (*c*) of the eternal inheritance of believers, 1 Pet. 1:4; (*d*) of the marriage bed as requiring to be free from unlawful sexual intercourse, Heb. 13:4.¶

UNDER, UNDERNEATH

1. *hupokatō* (ὑποκάτω, 5270), an adverb signifying "under," is used as a preposition and rendered "under" in Mark 6:11; 7:28; Luke 8:16; Heb. 2:8; Rev. 5:3, 13; 6:9; 12:1; "under-

neath" in Matt. 22:44, RV (Mark 12:36 in some mss.); John 1:50, RV (KJV, "under").¶

2. *katōterō* (κατωτέρω, 2736), the comparative degree of *katō*, "below, beneath," occurs in Matt. 2:16, "under."

3. *elasson* (ἔλασσον, 1640), the neuter of the adjective *elassōn*, "less," is used adverbially in 1 Tim. 5:9, "under" (or "less than"). See LESS.

Notes: (1) The preposition *epi*, "upon," is rendered "under" in Heb. 7:11; 9:15; 10:28, KJV (RV, "on *the word of*"). (2) The preposition *en*, "in," is rendered "under" in Matt. 7:6; Rom. 3:19 (1st part). (3) The usual preposition is *hupo*.

UNDERGIRD

hupozōnnumi (ὑποζώννυμι, 5269), *hupo*, "under," *zōnnumi*, "to gird," is used of frapping a ship, Acts 27:17, bracing the timbers of a vessel by means of strong ropes.¶

UNDERSTAND, UNDERSTOOD

A. Verbs.

1. *suniēmi* (συνίημι, 4920), primarily, "to bring or set together," is used metaphorically of "perceiving, understanding, uniting" (*sun*), so to speak, the perception with what is perceived, e.g., Matt. 13:13–15, 19, 23, 51; 15:10; 16:12; 17:13, and similar passages in Mark and Luke; Acts 7:25 (twice); 28:26, 27; in Rom. 3:11, the present participle, with the article, is used as a noun, lit., "there is not the understanding (one)," in a moral and spiritual sense; Rom. 15:21; 2 Cor. 10:12, RV, "are (without) understanding," KJV, "are (not) wise"; Eph. 5:17, RV, "understand." See CONSIDER, *Note* (2).

2. *noeō* (νοέω, 3539), "to perceive with the mind," as distinct from perception by feeling, is so used in Matt. 15:17, KJV, "understand," RV, "perceive"; 16:9, 11; 24:15 (here rather perhaps in the sense of considering) and parallels in Mark (not in Luke); John 12:40; Rom. 1:20; 1 Tim. 1:7; Heb. 11:3; in Eph. 3:4, KJV, "may understand" (RV, "can perceive"); 3:20, "think"; 2 Tim. 2:7, "consider," See CONSIDER, No. 4.¶

3. *ginōskō* (γινώσκω, 1097), "to know, to come to know," is translated "to understand" in the KJV in Matt. 26:10 and John 8:27 (RV, "to perceive"); KJV and RV in John 8:43; 10:6; 10:38, RV (in some texts *pisteuō*, KJV, "believe"); KJV and RV in 12:16; 13:7 RV, KJV, "know" (see *Note* under KNOW, No. 2); Acts 8:30; in Phil. 1:12, KJV, RV, "know" (in some texts, Acts 24:11, KJV). See KNOW, No. 1.

4. *epistamai* (ἐπίσταμαι, 1987), "to know well," is rendered "to understand" in Mark 14:68; Jude 10, RV, 2nd clause (KJV, "know"). See KNOW, No. 5.

5. *punthanomai* (πυνθάνομαι, 4441), "to inquire," is rendered "to understand" in Acts 23:34. See INQUIRE.

6. *gnōrizō* (γνωρίζω, 1107), "to make known," is rendered "I give . . . to understand" in 1 Cor. 12:3. See KNOW, No. 8.

7. *agnoeō* (ἀγνοέω, 50), "to be ignorant," is rendered "they understood not" in Mark 9:32; Luke 9:45; in 2 Pet. 2:12, KJV, RV, "they are ignorant of." See IGNORANT, B, No. 1.

Notes: (1) In 1 Cor. 13:2, KJV, *oida*, "to know, to perceive," is rendered "understand" (RV, "know"); so in 14:16. (2) For *manthanō*, rendered "understand in Acts 23:27, KJV, see LEARN, No. 1. (3) In 1 Cor. 13:11, KJV, *phroneō*, "to be minded," is rendered "I understood" (RV, "I felt"). (4) For *parakoloutheō*, Luke 1:3, KJV, "have perfect understanding of," see TRACE.

B. Adjectives.

1 *eusēmos* (εὔσημος, 2154) primarily denotes "conspicuous" or "glorious" (as in Ps. 81:3, Sept.; EV, "solemn"¶), then, "distinct, clear to understanding," 1 Cor. 14:9, "easy to be understood" (KJV, marg., "significant"). ¶

2. *dusnoētos* (δυσνόητος, 1425), "hard to be understood" (*dus*, a prefix like Eng., "mis– or un–," and A, No. 2), occurs in 2 Pet. 3:16.¶

UNDERSTANDING

A. Nouns.

1. *nous* (νοῦς, 3563), for which see MIND, No. 1, is translated "understanding" in Luke 24:45, KJV (RV, "mind"); 1 Cor. 14:14, 15 (twice), 19; Phil. 4:7; Rev. 13:18.

2. *sunesis* (σύνεσις, 4907), akin to *suniēmi*, "to set together, to understand," denotes (*a*) "the understanding, the mind or intelligence," Mark 12:33; (*b*) "understanding, reflective thought," Luke 2:47; 1 Cor. 1:19, RV, "prudence"; Eph. 3:4, RV (KJV, "knowledge"); Col. 1:9; 2:2; 2 Tim. 2:7¶ See PRUDENCE, No. 2.

3. *dianoia* (διάνοια, 1271), for which see MIND, No. 2, is rendered "understanding" in Eph. 4:18; 1 John 5:20 (in some texts, Eph. 1:18, KJV, for *kardia*, "heart," RV).

B. Adjective.

asunetos (ἀσύνετος, 801), "without understanding or discernment" (*a*, negative, *sunetos*, "intelligent, understanding"), is translated "without understanding" in Matt. 15:16; Mark 7:18; Rom. 1:31; 10:19, RV, "void of understanding" (KJV, "foolish"); in Rom. 1:21, RV, "senseless" (KJV, "foolish").¶

Note: In 1 Cor. 14:20, KJV, *phrēn*, "the mind," is translated "understanding" (twice), RV, "mind."

For **UNDONE** (leave) see **LEAVE,** No. 1

UNDRESSED

agnaphos (ἄγναφος, 46), "uncarded" (*a*, negative, *knaptō*, "to card wool"), is rendered "undressed," of cloth, in Matt. 9:16 and Mark 2:21, RV (KJV, "new").¶

For **UNEQUALLY** see **YOKED**

UNFAITHFUL

apistos (ἄπιστος, 571), "unbelieving, faithless," is translated "unfaithful" in Luke 12:46, RV (KJV, "unbelievers"). See BELIEF, C, *Note* (3), FAITHLESS, INCREDIBLE.

For **UNFEIGNED** see **DISSIMULATION,** C

For **UNFRUITFUL** see **FRUIT,** B, No. 2

UNGODLINESS, UNGODLY

A. Noun.

asebeia (ἀσέβεια, 763), "impiety, ungodliness," is used of (*a*) general impiety, Rom. 1:18; 11:26; 2 Tim. 2:16; Titus 2:12; (*b*) "ungodly" deeds, Jude 15, RV, "works of ungodliness"; (*c*) of lusts or desires after evil things, Jude 18. It is the opposite of *eusebeia*, "godliness."¶

Note: Anomia is disregard for, or defiance of, God's laws; *asebeia* is the same attitude towards God's Person.

B. Adjective.

asebēs (ἀσεβής, 765), "impious, ungodly" (akin to A), "without reverence for God," not merely irreligious, but acting in contravention of God's demands, Rom. 4:5; 5:6; 1 Tim. 1:9; 1 Pet. 4:18; 2 Pet. 2:5 (v. 6 in some mss.); 3:7; Jude 4, 15 (twice).¶

C. Verb.

asebeō (ἀσεβέω, 764), akin to A and B, signifies (*a*) "to be or live ungodly," 2 Pet. 2:6; (*b*) "to commit ungodly deeds," Jude 15.¶

UNHOLY

1. *anosios* (ἀνόσιος, 462) (*a*, negative, *n*, euphonic, *hosios*, "holy"), "unholy, profane," occurs in 1 Tim. 1:9; 2 Tim. 3:2.¶ Cf. HOLY. In the Sept., Ezek. 22:9.¶

2. *koinon* (κοινόν, 2839), the neut. of *koinos*, "common," is translated "an unholy thing" in Heb. 10:29. See COMMON, DEFILE, C, UNCLEAN, A, No. 2.

For **UNITED**, Rom. 6:5, RV, see **PLANT**, C; in Heb. 4:2, see **MIXED** (with), *Note*

UNITY

henotēs (ἑνότης, 1775), from *hen*, the neuter of *heis*, "one," is used in Eph. 4:3, 13.¶

UNJUST

adikos (ἄδικος, 94), "not in conformity with *dikē*, 'right,'" is rendered "unjust" in the KJV and RV in Matt. 5:45; Luke 18:11; Acts 24:15; elsewhere for the KJV "unjust" the RV has "unrighteous." See UNRIGHTEOUS.

Note: For *adikeō*, "to be unrighteous," or "do unrighteousness," Rev. 22:11, RV, and *adikia*, "unrighteous," Luke 16:8 and 18:6, RV, see UNRIGHTEOUSNESS.

For **UNKNOWN** see **IGNORANCE**, B, No. 1, and **KNOW**, B, No. 4

UNLADE

apophortizō (ἀποφορτίζω, 670), "to discharge a cargo" (*apo*, "from," *phortizō*, "to load"), is used in Acts 21:3.¶

UNLAWFUL

athemitos (ἀθέμιτος, 111), a late form for *athemistos* (*themis*, "custom, right"; in classical Greek, "divine law"), "contrary to what is right," is rendered "an unlawful thing" (neuter) in Acts 10:28; in 1 Pet. 4:3, "abominable."¶

Note: For 2 Pet. 2:8, KJV, see LAWLESS.

UNLEARNED

1. *agrammatos* (ἀγράμματος, 62), lit., "unlettered" (*grammata*, "letters": *graphō*, "to write"), Acts 4:13, is explained by Grimm-Thayer as meaning "unversed in the learning of the Jewish schools"; in the papyri, however, it occurs very frequently in a formula used by one who signs for another who cannot write, which suggests that the rulers, elders and scribes regarded the apostles as "unlettered" (Moulton and Milligan).¶

2. *amathēs* (ἀμαθής, 261), "unlearned" (*manthanō*, "to learn"), is translated "unlearned" in 2 Pet. 3:16, KJV (RV, "ignorant").¶

3. *apaideutos* (ἀπαίδευτος, 521), "uninstructed" (*paideuō*, "to train, teach"), is translated "unlearned" in 2 Tim. 2:23, KJV (RV, "ignorant").¶

Note: For *idiōtēs*, rendered "unlearned" in 1 Cor. 14:16, 23, 24, see IGNORANT, No. 4.

For **UNLEAVENED** see **BREAD**, No. 2

For **UNLESS** see **EXCEPT**

UNLIFTED

anakaluptō (ἀνακαλύπτω, 343), "to uncover, unveil," used in 2 Cor. 3:14 with the negative *mē*, "not," is rendered "unlifted," RV, KJV, "untaken away" (a paraphrase rather than translation); the RV marg., "remaineth, it not being revealed that it is done away," is not to be preferred. The best rendering seems to be, "the veil remains unlifted (for it is in Christ that it is done away)." Judaism does not recognize the vanishing of the glory of the Law as a means of life, under God's grace in Christ. In 3:18 the RV, "unveiled (face)" (KJV, "open"), continues the metaphor of the veil (vv. 13–17), referring to hindrances to the perception of spiritual realities, hindrances removed in the unveiling.¶

UNLOOSE

luō (λύω, 3089), "to loose," is rendered "to unloose" in Mark 1:7; Luke 3:16; John 1:27; in Acts 13:25, RV: see LOOSE.

UNMARRIED

agamos (ἄγαμος, 22), *a*, negative, *gameō*, "to marry," occurs in 1 Cor. 7:8, 11, 32, 34.¶

UNMERCIFUL

aneleēmōn (ἀνελεήμων, 415), "without mercy" (*a*, negative, *n*, euphonic, *eleēmōn*, "merciful"), occurs in Rom. 1:31.¶

For **UNMIXED**, Rev. 14:10, RV, see **MIXTURE**, *Note*

For **UNMOVABLE**, Acts 27:41, see **MOVE**, B, No. 1; in 1 Cor. 15:58, **MOVE**, B, No. 2

UNPREPARED

aparaskeuastos (ἀπαρασκεύαστος, 532), from *a*, negative, and *paraskeuazō* (see PREPARE, B, No. 4), occurs in 2 Cor. 9:4.¶

UNPROFITABLE, UNPROFITABLENESS

A. Adjectives.

1. *achreios* (ἀχρεῖος, 888), "useless" (*chreia*, "use"), "unprofitable," occurs in Matt. 25:30 and Luke 17:10.¶ In the Sept., 2 Sam. 6:22.¶

2. *achrēstos* (ἄχρηστος, 890), "unprofitable, unserviceable" (*chrēstos*, "serviceable"), is said of Onesimus, Philem. 11, antithetically to *eu-*

chrēstos, "profitable," with a play on the name of the converted slave (from *onēsis*, "profit").¶

Note: Achreios is more distinctly negative than *achrēstos*, which suggests positively hurtful.

3. *alusitelēs* (ἀλυσιτελής, 255), "not advantageous, not making good the expense involved" (*lusitelēs*, "useful"), occurs in Heb. 13:17.¶

4. *anōphelēs* (ἀνωφελής, 512), "not beneficial or serviceable" (*a*, negative, *n*, euphonic, *ōpheleō*, "to do good, to benefit"), is rendered "unprofitable" in Titus 3:9; in the neuter, used as a noun, "unprofitableness," Heb. 7:18, said of the Law as not accomplishing that which the "better hope" could alone bring.¶ In the Sept., Prov. 28:3; Isa. 44:10; Jer. 2:8.¶

B. Verb.

achreoō, or *achreioō* (ἀχρεόω, 889), akin to A, No. 1, "to make useless," occurs in Rom. 3:12, in the passive voice, rendered "they have . . . become unprofitable."¶

For **UNQUENCHABLE** see **QUENCH**

UNREASONABLE

1. *alogos* (ἄλογος, 249), "without reason, irrational," is rendered "unreasonable" in Acts 25:27. See BRUTE.

2. *atopos* (ἄτοπος, 824), lit., "out of place" (*topos*, "a place"), is translated "unreasonable" in 2 Thess. 3:2, where the meaning intended seems to be "perverse, truculent." See AMISS.

For **UNREBUKEABLE** see **BLAME**, B, No. 5

UNRIGHTEOUS

adikos (ἄδικος, 94), not conforming to *dikē*, "right," is translated "unrighteous" in Luke 16:10 (twice), RV, 11; Rom. 3:5; 1 Cor. 6:1, RV; 6:9; Heb. 6:10; 1 Pet. 3:18, RV; 2 Pet. 2:9, RV: see UNJUST.

UNRIGHTEOUSNESS

A. Noun.

adikia (ἀδικία, 93) denotes (*a*) "injustice," Luke 18:6, lit., "the judge of injustice"; Rom. 9:14; (*b*) "unrighteousness, iniquity," e.g., Luke 16:8, lit., "the steward of unrighteousness," RV marg., i.e., characterized by "unrighteousness"; Rom. 1:18, 29; 2:8; 3:5; 6:13; 1 Cor. 13:6, RV, "unrighteousness"; 2 Thess. 2:10, "[with all (lit., 'in every) deceit'] of unrighteousness," i.e., deceit such as "unrighteousness" uses, and that in every variety; Antichrist and his ministers will

not be restrained by any scruple from words or deeds calculated to deceive; 2 Thess. 2:12, of those who have pleasure in it, not an intellectual but a moral evil; distaste for truth is the precursor of the rejection of it; 2 Tim. 2:19, RV; 1 John 1:9, which includes (*c*); (*c*) "a deed or deeds violating law and justice" (virtually the same as *adikēma*, "an unrighteous act"), e.g., Luke 13:27, "iniquity"; 2 Cor. 12:13, "wrong," the wrong of depriving another of what is his own, here ironically of a favor; Heb. 8:12, 1st clause, "iniquities," lit., "unrighteousnesses" (plural, not as KJV); 2 Pet. 2:13, 15, RV, "wrongdoing," KJV, "unrighteousness"; 1 John 5:17. See INIQUITY.

Notes: (1) In 2 Cor. 6:14, KJV, *anomia*, "lawlessness," is translated "unrighteousness" (RV, "iniquity"). (2) *Adikia* is the comprehensive term for wrong, or wrongdoing, as between persons; *anomia*, "lawlessness," is the rejection of divine law, or wrong committed against it.

B. Verb.

adikeō (ἀδικέω, 91), "to do wrong," is rendered in Rev. 22:11, RV, firstly, "he that is unrighteous," lit., "the doer of unrighteousness" (present participle of the verb, with the article), secondly, "let him do unrighteousness (still)," the retributive and permanent effect of a persistent course of unrighteous-doing (KJV, "he that is unjust, let him be unjust"). See HURT, OFFENDER, Note, WRONG.

For **UNRIPE, UNTIMELY,** see **FIG**, No. 2

UNRULY

1. *anupotaktos* (ἀνυπότακτος, 506), "not subject to rule" (*a*, negative, *n*, euphonic, *hupotassō*, "to put in subjection"), is used (*a*) of things, Heb. 2:8, RV, "not subject" (KJV, "not put under"); (*b*) of persons, "unruly," 1 Tim. 1:9, RV (KJV, "disobedient"); Titus 1:6, 10. See DISOBEDIENT, B, *Note*.¶

2. *ataktos* (ἄτακτος, 814) is rendered "unruly" in 1 Thess. 5:14, KJV (marg. and RV, "disorderly"). See DISORDERLY, A.¶

Note: In Jas. 3:8, some texts have *akataschetos*, "that cannot be restrained," KJV, "unruly": see RESTLESS.¶

UNSEARCHABLE

1. *anexeraunētos*, or *anexereunētos* (ἀνεξεραύνητος, 419), *a*, negative, *n*, euphonic, *ex* (*ek*), "out," *eraunaō*, "to search, examine," is used in Rom. 11:33, of the judgments of God.¶

2. *anexichniastos* (ἀνεξιχνίαστος, 421), with the same prefixes as in No. 1, and an

adjectival form akin to *ichneuō*, "to trace out" (*ichnos*, "a footprint, a track"), is translated "unsearchable" in Eph. 3:8, of the riches of Christ; in Rom. 11:33, "past tracing out," of the ways of the Lord (cf. No. 1, in the same verse). The ways of God are the outworkings of His judgment. Of the two questions in v. 34, the first seems to have reference to No. 1, the second to No. 2. See FIND, *Note* (3), TRACE.¶

UNSEEMLINESS, UNSEEMLY

aschēmosunē (ἀσχημοσύνη, 808), from *aschēmōn*, "unseemly," is rendered "unseemliness" in Rom. 1:27, RV: see SHAME, No. 4.

Note: For "behave . . . unseemly" see BEHAVE, No. 4.

For UNSETTLE, Gal. 5:12, RV, see STIR, No. 12

For UNSKILLFUL, Heb. 5:13, see EXPERIENCE, No. 1

UNSPEAKABLE

1. *anekdiēgētos* (ἀνεκδιήγητος, 411) denotes "inexpressible" (*a*, negative, *n*, euphonic, *ekdiēgeomai*, "to declare, relate"), 2 Cor. 9:15, "unspeakable" (of the gift of God); regarding the various explanations of the gift, it seems most suitable to view it as the gift of His Son.¶

2. *aneklalētos* (ἀνεκλάλητος, 412) denotes "unable to be told out" (*eklaleō*, "to speak out"), 1 Pet. 1:8, of the believer's joy.¶

3. *arrhētos* (ἄρρητος, 731), primarily, "unspoken" (*a*, negative, *rhētos*, "spoken"), denotes "unspeakable," 2 Cor. 12:4, of the words heard by Paul when caught up into paradise.¶ The word is common in sacred inscriptions especially in connection with the Greek Mysteries; hence Moulton and Milligan suggest the meaning "words too sacred to be uttered."

For UNSPOTTED see SPOT, C

UNSTABLE, UNSTEADFAST

1. *astēriktos* (ἀστήρικτος, 793), *a*, negative, *stērizō*, "to fix," is used in 2 Pet. 2:14; 3:16, KJV, "unstable," RV, "unsteadfast."¶

2. *akatastatos* (ἀκατάστατος, 182), from *kathistēmi*, "to set in order," is rendered "unstable" in Jas. 1:8: see RESTLESS.

For UNTAKEN AWAY, 2 Cor. 3:14, KJV, see UNLIFTED

UNTHANKFUL

acharistos (ἀχάριστος, 884) denotes "ungrateful, thankless" (*charis*, "thanks"), Luke 6:35; 2 Tim. 3:2.¶

For UNTIL and UNTO see †, p. 1

For UNTIMELY see FIG, No. 2

For UNTOWARD see CROOKED

UNVEILED

akatakaluptos (ἀκατακάλυπτος, 177), "uncovered" (*a*, negative, *katakaluptō*, "to cover"), is used in 1 Cor. 11:5, 13, RV, "unveiled," with reference to the injunction forbidding women to be "unveiled" in a church gathering.¶ Whatever the character of the covering, it is to be on her head as "a sign of authority" (v. 10), RV, the meaning of which is indicated in v. 3 in the matter of headships, and the reasons for which are given in vv. 7–9, and in the phrase "because of the angels," intimating their witness of, and interest in, that which betokens the headship of Christ. The injunctions were neither Jewish, which required men to be veiled in prayer, nor Greek, by which men and women were alike "unveiled." The apostle's instructions were "the commandment of the Lord" (14:37) and were for all the churches (vv. 33, 34).

Note: For the verb *anakaluptō*, rendered "unveiled" in 2 Cor. 3:18, RV, see UNLIFTED (2nd ref.).

UNWASHED

aniptos (ἄνιπτος, 449), "unwashed" (*a*, negative, *niptō*, "to wash"), occurs in Matt. 15:20; Mark 7:2 (v. 5 in some mss.).¶

UNWILLING

Note: "I am unwilling" is the RV rendering of *thelō*, "to will," with the negative *ou*, in 3 John 13 (KJV, "I will not").

UNWISE

1. *anoētos* (ἀνόητος, 453) is translated "unwise" in Rom. 1:14, KJV; see FOOLISH, No. 2.

2. *aphrōn* (ἄφρων, 878) is translated "unwise" in Eph. 5:17, KJV; see FOOLISH, No. 1.

3. *asophos* (ἄσοφος, 781), *a*, negative, is rendered "unwise" in Eph. 5:15, RV (KJV, "fools").¶

UNWORTHILY, UNWORTHY

A. Adverb.

anaxiōs (ἀναξίως, 371) is used in 1 Cor. 11:27, of partaking of the Lord's Supper "unworthily," i.e., treating it as a common meal, the bread and cup as common things, not apprehending their solemn symbolic import. In the best texts the word is not found in v. 29 (see RV).¶

B. Adjective.

anaxios (ἀνάξιος, 370), *a*, negative, *n*, euphonic, *axios*, "worthy," is used in 1 Cor. 6:2. In modern Greek it signifies "incapable."¶

Note: In Acts 13:46, "unworthy" represents the adjective *axios*, preceded by the negative *ouk*.

UP

Notes: (1) In Matt. 13:6 and Mark 4:6, KJV, *anatellō*, "to rise" (of the sun), is rendered "was up." See RISE. (2) The adverb is used with numerous Eng. verbs to translate single Greek verbs. In John 11:41 and Heb. 12:15, however, the adverb *anō*, "up," is used separately: see ABOVE, BRIM, HIGH.

For UPBRAID see REPROACH, B, No. 1

UPHOLD

pherō (φέρω, 5342), "to bear, carry, uphold," is rendered "upholding" in Heb. 1:3. See BEAR.

For UPON see †, p. 1

For UPPER see CHAMBER, COUNTRY, B, No. 1, ROOM

UPPERMOST

Note: In Luke 11:43 *prōtokathedria*, "a chief seat," is translated "uppermost seats," KJV (RV, "chief seats"). In Matt. 23:6 and Mark 12:39, KJV, *prōtoklisia*, "a chief place," is translated "uppermost rooms" (RV, "chief place" and "chief places"). See CHIEF, B, Nos. 6 and 7.

For UPRIGHT see STRAIGHT, No. 2; UPRIGHTLY see WALK, No. 6

UPRIGHTNESS

euthutēs (εὐθύτης, 2118), from *euthus*, "straight," is rendered "uprightness" in Heb. 1:8, RV, KJV, "righteousness," marg., "rightness," or, "straightness."¶

For UPROAR (Noun), *thorubos*, see TUMULT, and for *stasis* see RIOT

UPROAR (Verbs)

thorubeō (θορυβέω, 2350), used in the middle voice, denotes "to make a noise or uproar," or, transitively, in the active voice, "to trouble, throw into confusion," Acts 17:5. See ADO, NOISE, TROUBLE.

Note: For *suncheō*, "to confuse," Acts 21:31 (KJV, "was in an uproar"), see CONFUSION; for *anastatoō*, Acts 21:38 (KJV, "madest an uproar"), see STIR UP.

For UPSIDE DOWN see TURN, No. 15

URGE

Notes: (1) In Acts 13:50, KJV, *parotrunō*, "to urge on" (RV), is rendered "stirred up."¶ (2) In Acts 13:43, *peithō*, "to persuade," is rendered "urged," RV (KJV, "persuaded"). (3) For *enechō*, rendered "to urge" in Luke 11:53, KJV, see ENTANGLE, No. 3.

US

The oblique cases of *hēmeis*, "we," are the genitive *hēmōn*, "of us," the dative *hēmin*, "to us," the accusative *hēmas*, "us." When the nominative *hēmeis* is used, it is always emphatic, e.g., John 11:16, "(let) us (go)"; lit., "we, let us go"; 1 Thess. 5:8, "let us ... be sober," lit., "we ... let us be sober." Sometimes the oblique cases are governed by prepositions.

USE (Noun), USEFUL

1. *hexis* (ἕξις, 1838), akin to *echō*, "to have," denotes "habit, experience," "use," Heb. 5:14.¶

2. *chreia* (χρεία, 5532), "need," is translated "uses" in Titus 3:14; in Eph. 4:29, KJV, "(for the) use (of edifying)," RV, "(as the) need (may be)." See NECESSITY, NEED.

3. *chrēsis* (χρῆσις, 5540), "use" (akin to *chraomai*, "to use"), occurs in Rom. 1:26, 27.¶

Notes: (1) In 2 Tim. 2:21, the adjective *euchrēstos*, "useful, serviceable" (*eu*, "well," *chraomai*, "to use"), is translated "meet for ... use"; in 4:11, "useful," RV (KJV, "profitable"); in Philem. 11, "profitable." See PROFITABLE, B, No. 2.¶ (2) In 1 Cor. 8:7 the best texts have the noun *sunētheia*, RV, "being used," lit., "by the custom (of the idol)," i.e., by being associated. See CUSTOM. In the Sept., Prov. 31:13.¶ Contrast *achrēstos*, "unprofitable," Philem. 11.¶

USE (Verb)

1. *chraomai* (χράομαι, 5531), from *chrē*, "it is necessary," denotes (*a*) "to use," Acts 27:17; 1 Cor. 7:21, where "use it rather" means "use your bondservice rather"; 7:31, where "they

that use (this world)" is followed by the strengthened form *katachraomai*, rendered "abusing," or "using to the full" (RV, marg.); 9:12, 15; 2 Cor. 1:17; 3:12; 13:10; 1 Tim. 1:8, of "using" the Law lawfully, i.e., agreeably to its designs; 1 Tim. 5:23; (*b*) "deal with," Acts 27:3. See ENTREAT (to treat). Cf. the active *chraō* (or *kichrēmi*), "to lend," Luke 11:5. See LEND.¶

2. *echō* (ἔχω, 2192), "to have," is rendered "using" in 1 Pet. 2:16 (marg., "having"); see HAVE.

3. *anastrephō* (ἀναστρέφω, 390) chiefly denotes "to behave, to live in a certain manner," rendered "(were so) used" in Heb. 10:33 (passive voice); the verb, however, does not mean "to treat or use"; here it has the significance of "living amidst sufferings, reproaches," etc. See ABIDE, BEHAVE, LIVE, OVERTHROW, PASS, RETURN.

Notes: (1) In Acts 19:19, KJV, *prassō*, "to practice" (RV), is rendered "used." (2) For Heb. 5:13, KJV, "useth (milk)," see PARTAKE, B, No. 3. (3) In 1 Thess. 2:5, "were we found using" is the rendering of the verb *ginomai*, "to become," with the preposition *en*, "in," governing the noun, "words (or speech) [of flattery]"; this idiomatic phrase signifies "to be engaged in, to resort to." A rendering close to the meaning of the Greek is "for neither at any time did we fall into the use of flattering speech"; cf. 1 Tim. 2:14, "fallen into transgression." (4) "To use" is combined in Eng. with other words, e.g., DECEIT, DESPITEFULLY, HOSPITALITY, REPETITIONS.

USING

apochrēsis (ἀπόχρησις, 671), a strengthened form of *chrēsis*, "a using," and signifying "a misuse" (akin to *apochraomai*, "to use to the full, abuse"), is translated "using" in Col. 2:22; the clause may be rendered "by their using up." "The unusual word was chosen for its expressiveness; the *chrēsis* here was an *apochrēsis;* the things could not be used without rendering them unfit for further use" (Lightfoot).¶

For USURP see AUTHORITY, B, No. 3

USURY

Note: The RV, "interest," Matt. 25:27; Luke 19:23, is the preferable rendering of *tokos* here. See INTEREST.¶

For UTMOST PART see END, A, No. 3

UTTER

1. *laleō* (λαλέω, 2980), "to speak," is rendered "to utter" in 2 Cor. 12:4 and Rev. 10:3, 4 (twice). See PREACH, SAY, SPEAK, TALK, TELL.

2. *ereugomai* (ἐρεύγομαι, 2044), primarily, "to spit or spue out," or, of oxen, "to bellow, roar," hence, "to speak aloud, utter," occurs in Matt. 13:35.¶ This affords an example of the tendency for certain words to become softened in force in late Greek.

3. *aphiēmi* (ἀφίημι, 863), "to send forth," is used of "uttering" a cry, Mark 15:37, of Christ's final "utterance" on the cross, RV, "uttered" (KJV, "cried"). See FORGIVE, LAY, *Note* (2), LEAVE, LET, OMITTED, PUT, REMIT, SUFFER, YIELD.

4. *didōmi* (δίδωμι, 1325), "to give," is translated "utter" in 1 Cor. 14:9. See GIVE.

5. *phthengomai* (φθέγγομαι, 5350), "to utter a sound or voice," is translated "uttering" in 2 Pet. 2:18, RV: see SPEAK, No. 4.

Notes: (1) In Rom. 8:26, *alalētos*, "inexpressible" (*a*, negative, *laleō*, "to speak"), is rendered "which cannot be uttered."¶ (2) In Heb. 5:11, KJV, *dusermēneutos*, followed by *legō*, "to speak," [translated "hard of interpretation" (RV), *dus* (whence "dys-" in Eng., "dyspeptic," etc.), a prefix like Eng., "un-," or "mis-," and *hermēneuō*, "to interpret"], is rendered "hard to be uttered."¶

UTTERANCE

logos (λόγος, 3056), "a word," is translated "utterance" in 1 Cor. 1:5; 2 Cor. 8:7; Eph. 6:19. See WORD.

Notes: (1) In Col. 4:3, KJV, *logos* is rendered "(a door) of utterance." (2) For *apophthengomai*, rendered "utterance" in Acts 2:4, see SPEAK, No. 5.

For UTTERLY, 1 Cor. 6:7, see ACTUALLY; 2 Pet. 2:12, see CORRUPT, A, No. 2 (*b*)

UTTERMOST

1. *panteles* (παντελές, 3838), the neuter of the adjective *pantelēs*, "complete, perfect," used with *eis to* ("unto the"), is translated "to the uttermost" in Heb. 7:25, where the meaning may be "finally"; in Luke 13:11 (negatively), "in no wise."¶

2. *telos* (τέλος, 5056), "an end," is rendered "the uttermost" in 1 Thess. 2:16, said of divine wrath upon the Jews, referring to the prophecy of Deut. 28:15–68; the nation as such, will yet, however, be delivered (Rom. 11:26; cf. Jer. 30:4–11). The full phrase is *eis telos*, "to the

uttermost," which is probably the meaning in John 13:1, "to the end."

Notes: (1) For "uttermost (farthing)," Matt. 5:26, KJV, see LAST. For "uttermost in Acts 24:22, see DETERMINE, No. 5. (2) For "uttermost part (-s)", see END, A, No. 3 (*a*) and C (*b*).

V

For **VAGABOND** see **STROLLING**

For **VAIL** see **VEIL**

VAIN, IN VAIN, VAINLY

A. Adjectives.

1. *kenos* (κενός, 2756), "empty," with special reference to quality, is translated "vain" (as an adjective) in Acts 4:25; 1 Cor. 15:10, 14 (twice); Eph. 5:6; Col. 2:8; Jas. 2:20; in the following the neuter, *kenon*, follows the preposition *eis*, "in," and denotes "in vain," 2 Cor. 6:1; Gal. 2:2; Phil. 2:16 (twice); 1 Thess. 3:5. See EMPTY, B, where the applications are enumerated.

2. *mataios* (μάταιος, 3152), "void of result," is used of (*a*) idolatrous practices, Acts 14:15, RV, "vain things" (KJV, "vanities"); (*b*) the thoughts of the wise, 1 Cor. 3:20; (*c*) faith, if Christ is not risen, 1 Cor. 15:17; (*d*) questionings, strifes, etc., Titus 3:9; (*e*) religion, with an unbridled tongue, Jas. 1:26; (*f*) manner of life, 1 Pet. 1:18.¶ For the contrast between No. 1 and No. 2 see EMPTY.

Note: For *mataiologoi*, Titus 1:10, see TALKERS (vain).¶

B. Verbs.

1. *mataioō* (ματαιόω, 3154), "to make vain, or foolish," corresponding in meaning to A, No. 2, occurs in Rom. 1:21, "became vain."¶

2. *kenoō* (κενόω, 2758), "to empty," corresponding to A, No. 1, is translated "should be in vain" in 2 Cor. 9:3, KJV. See EFFECT, EMPTY, VOID.

C. Adverbs.

1. *matēn* (μάτην, 3155), properly the accusative case of *matē*, "a fault, a folly," signifies "in vain, to no purpose," Matt. 15:9; Mark 7:7.¶

2. *dōrean* (δωρεάν, 1432), the accusative of *dōrea*, "a gift," is used adverbially, denoting (*a*) "freely" (see FREE, D); (*b*) "uselessly," "in vain," Gal. 2:21, KJV (RV, "for nought"). See CAUSE, A, under *"without a cause."*

3. *eikē* (εἰκῆ, 1500) denotes (*a*) "without cause," "vainly," Col. 2:18; (*b*) "to no purpose," "in vain," Rom. 13:4; Gal. 3:4 (twice); 4:11. See CAUSE, A, *Note* (1), under *"without a cause."*

VAINGLORY, VAINGLORIOUS

A Nouns.

1. *kenodoxia* (κενοδοξία, 2754), from *kenos*, "vain, empty," *doxa*, "glory," is used in Phil. 2:3.¶

2. *alazoneia*, or -*ia* (ἀλαζονεία, 212) denotes "boastfulness, vaunting," translated "vainglory" in 1 John 2:16, RV (KJV, "pride"); in Jas. 4:16, RV, "vauntings" (KJV, "boastings"). Cf. *alazōn*, "a boaster."¶

B. Adjective.

kenodoxos (κενόδοξος, 2755), akin to A, No. 1, is rendered "vainglorious" in Gal. 5:26, RV (KJV, "desirous of vain glory").¶

For **VALIANT** see **MIGHTY**, B, No. 2, **STRONG**, No. 2 (*a*) (3)

VALLEY

pharanx (φάραγξ, 5327) denotes "a ravine or valley," sometimes figurative of "a condition of loneliness and danger" (cf. Ps. 23:4); the word occurs in Luke 3:5 (from the Sept. of Isa. 40:4).¶

VALUE

A. Verb.

diapherō (διαφέρω, 1308), used intransitively, means "to differ, to excel," hence "to be of more value," Matt. 6:26, RV, "are (not) ye of (much) more value" (KJV, "better"); 12:12 and Luke 12:24, ditto; Matt. 10:31; Luke 12:7. See BETTER (be), CARRY, No. 4, DIFFER, DRIVE, No. 7, EXCELLENT, MATTER, *Note* (1), PUBLISH, No. 2.

Note: For *timaō*, rendered "to value" in Matt. 27:9 (twice), KJV, see PRICE.

B. Noun.

timē (τιμή, 5092) denotes "a valuing, a price, honor"; in Col. 2:23, RV, "(not of any) value (against the indulgence of the flesh)" [KJV, "(not in any) honor . . . "], i.e., the ordinances enjoined by human tradition are not of any value to prevent (*pros*, "against"; cf. Acts 26:14) indulgence of the flesh. See HONOR, PRECIOUS, PRICE, SUM.

VANISH, VANISHING

A. Verb.

aphanizō (ἀφανίζω, 853), "to render unseen," is translated "vanisheth away" in Jas. 4:14 (passive voice, lit., "is made to disappear"). See CONSUME, DISFIGURE, PERISH.

Note: In 1 Cor. 13:8, KJV, *katargeō*, "to abolish," is rendered "it shall vanish away" (RV, " . . . be done away"). See ABOLISH.

B. Noun.

aphanismos (ἀφανισμός, 854), *a*, negative, *phainō*, "to cause to appear" (akin to A), occurs in Heb. 8:13, RV, "(nigh unto) vanishing away"; the word is suggestive of abolition.¶

Note: In Luke 24:31, the adjective *aphantos* (akin to A and B), "invisible," used with *ginomai*, "to become," and followed by *apo*, "from," with the plural personal pronoun, is rendered "He vanished out of their sight" (KJV, marg., "He ceased to be seen of them"), lit., "He became invisible from them."¶

VANITY

mataiotēs (ματαιότης, 3153), "emptiness as to results," akin to *mataios* (see EMPTY, VAIN), is used (*a*) of the creation, Rom. 8:20, as failing of the results designed, owing to sin; (*b*) of the mind which governs the manner of life of the Gentiles, Eph. 4:17; (*c*) of the "great swelling *words*" of false teachers, 2 Pet. 2:18.¶

Note: For *mataios*, in the neut. plur. in Acts 14:15, "vanities," see VAIN, A, No. 2 (*a*).

VAPOR

atmis (ἀτμίς, 822) is used of "smoke," Acts 2:19; figuratively of human life, Jas. 4:14.¶

VARIABLENESS, VARIATION

parallagē (παραλλαγή, 3883) denotes, in general, "a change" (Eng., "parallax," the difference between the directions of a body as seen from two different points), "a transmission" from one condition to another; it occurs in Jas. 1:17, RV, "variation" (KJV, "variableness"); the reference may be to the sun, which "varies" its position in the sky.¶ In the Sept., 2 Kings 9:20.¶

VARIANCE

dichazō (διχάζω, 1369), "to cut apart, divide in two," is used metaphorically in Matt. 10:35, "to set at variance."¶

Notes: (1) In Gal. 5:20, KJV, *eris*, "strife" (RV), is rendered "variance." (2) For *adiakritos*, Jas. 3:17, RV, "without variance" (marg., "doubtfulness, or partiality"), KJV, "without partiality" (marg., "without wrangling"), see PARTIAL.¶

VAUNT (ONESELF)

perpereuomai (περπερεύομαι, 4068), "to boast or vaunt oneself" (from *perperos*, "vainglorious, braggart," not in the NT), is used in 1 Cor. 13:4, negatively of love.¶

For VAUNTINGS see VAINGLORY

For VEHEMENT see DESIRE, A, No. 3

VEHEMENTLY

1. *deinōs* (δεινῶς, 1171), for which see GRIEVOUS, B, No. 1, is rendered "vehemently" in Luke 11:53.

2. *eutonōs* (εὐτόνως, 2159), vigorously, is translated "vehemently" in Luke 23:10, of accusations against Christ. See MIGHTY, D.

3. *ekperissōs* (ἐκπερισσῶς, 1537 and 4053), formed from *ek*, "out of," and the adverb *perissōs*, "exceedingly, the more," is found in Mark 14:31, in the best texts (some have *ek perissou*, the genitive case of the adjective *perissos*, "more"), RV, "exceeding vehemently" (KJV, "the more vehemently"), of Peter's protestation of loyalty; the RV gives the better rendering.¶

Note: For "brake (KJV, 'beat') vehemently," Luke 6:48, 49, see BEAT, No. 8.

VEIL

1. *katapetasma* (καταπέτασμα, 2665), lit., "that which is spread out" (*petannumi*) "before" (*kata*), hence, "a veil," is used (*a*) of the inner "veil" of the tabernacle, Heb. 6:19; 9:3; (*b*) of the corresponding "veil" in the Temple, Matt. 27:51; Mark 15:38; Luke 23:45; (*c*) metaphorically of the "flesh" of Christ, Heb. 10:20, i.e., His body which He gave up to be crucified, thus by His expiatory death providing a means of the spiritual access of believers, the "new and living way," into the presence of God.¶

2. *kalumma* (κάλυμμα, 2571), "a covering," is used (*a*) of the "veil" which Moses put over his face when descending Mount Sinai, thus preventing Israel from beholding the glory, 2 Cor. 3:13; (*b*) metaphorically of the spiritually darkened vision suffered retributively by Israel, until the conversion of the nation to their Messiah takes place, vv. 14, 15, 16. See under UNLIFTED.¶

3. *peribolaion* (περιβόλαιον, 4018), ren-

dered "a veil" in the KJV marg. of 1 Cor. 11:15: see COVER, B, No. 1, VESTURE.¶

VENGEANCE

ekdikēsis (ἐκδίκησις, 1557), lit., "(that which proceeds) out of justice," not, as often with human "vengeance," out of a sense of injury or merely out of a feeling of indignation. The word is most frequently used of divine "vengeance," e.g., Rom. 12:19; Heb. 10:30. For a complete list see AVENGE, B, No. 2. The judgments of God are holy and right (Rev. 16:7), and free from any element of self-gratification or vindictiveness.

Notes: (1) *Dikē*, "justice," is translated "vengeance" in the KJV of Acts 28:4 and Jude 7: see JUSTICE. (2) In Rom. 3:5, KJV, *orgē*, "wrath" (RV), is rendered "vengeance": see ANGER, WRATH.

For VENOMOUS see BEAST, No. 2

VERILY

1. *alēthōs* (ἀληθῶς, 230), "truly" (akin to *alētheia*, "truth"), is translated "verily" in 1 John 2:5. See INDEED, No. 3, SURELY, TRULY.

2. *amēn* (ἀμήν, 281), the transliteration of a Heb. word = "truth," is usually translated "verily" in the four Gospels; in John's gospel the Lord introduces a solemn pronouncement by the repeated word "verily, verily" twenty-five times. See AMEN.

3. *ontōs* (ὄντως, 3689), "really" (connected with *eimi*, "to be"), is rendered "verily" in Mark 11:32, RV, and Gal. 3:21. See INDEED, No. 4.

Notes: (1) In Acts 16:37, *gar*, "for," is translated "verily." (2) In Heb. 2:16, *dēpou* (in some texts *dē pou*), a particle meaning "of course, we know," is rendered "verily."¶ (3) In Luke 11:51, KJV, *nai*, "yea" (RV), is translated "verily." (4) The particle *men* (see INDEED, No. 1) is rendered "verily," e.g., in 1 Cor. 5:3; 14:17; Heb. 12:10; in the KJV, Heb. 3:5; 7:5, 18; 1 Pet. 1:20; in Acts 26:9 it is combined with *oun* ("therefore"): see YEA, No. 4.

For VERITY, 1 Tim. 2:7, KJV, see TRUTH

VERY

Notes: (1) When "very" forms part of the translation of numerous other words (e.g., act, bold, many, precious, sorrowful, well), there is no separate word in the original. (2) For *sphodra*, "exceedingly," sometimes rendered "very" in the KJV, see EXCEEDING, B, No. 2. (3) Occasionally one of the forms of the pronoun

autos, "self, same," is translated "very"; the RV rendering is sometimes "himself," etc., e.g., 1 Thess. 5:23, "(The God of peace) Himself"; see, however, John 14:11, "(the) very (works)"; Rom. 13:6 and Phil. 1:6, "(this) very (thing)"; Heb. 10:1, "(the) very (image)"; and the RV, "very" (KJV, "same") in Luke 12:12; 20:19; 24:13, 33; Acts 16:18; Rom. 9:17; Eph. 6:22. (4) Sometimes it translates the conjunction *kai*, in the sense of "even," e.g., Matt. 10:30; in 24:24, KJV, "very" (RV, "even"); Luke 12:59. (5) In Philem. 12, RV, "my very" translates the possessive pronoun *emos* (in the neuter plural, *ema*) used with emphasis. (6) In Mark 8:1 some texts have *pampollou*, "very great," KJV (from *pas*, "all," *polus*, "much"), RV, "a great (*pollou*) multitude" (after *palin*, "again"). (7) For "very great" in Matt. 21:8 see GREAT, *Note* (6). (8) The adverb *lian* is translated "very" in Mark 16:2; 2 Cor. 11:5; 12:11. See EXCEEDING, B, No. 1.

VESSEL

1. *skeuos* (σκεῦος, 4632) is used (*a*) of "a vessel or implement" of various kinds, Mark 11:16; Luke 8:16; John 19:29; Acts 10:11, 16; 11:5; 27:17 (a sail); Rom. 9:21; 2 Tim. 2:20; Heb. 9:21; Rev. 2:27; 18:12; (*b*) of "goods or household stuff," Matt. 12:29 and Mark 3:27, "goods"; Luke 17:31, RV, "goods" (KJV, "stuff"); (*c*) of "persons," (1) for the service of God, Acts 9:15, "a (chosen) vessel"; 2 Tim. 2:21, "a vessel (unto honor)"; (2) the "subjects" of divine wrath, Rom. 9:22; (3) the "subjects" of divine mercy, Rom. 9:23; (4) the human frame, 2 Cor. 4:7; perhaps 1 Thess. 4:4; (5) a husband and wife, 1 Pet. 3:7; of the wife, probably, 1 Thess. 4:4; while the exhortation to each one "to possess himself of his own vessel in sanctification and honor" is regarded by some as referring to the believer's body [cf. Rom. 6:13; 1 Cor. 9:27; see No. (4)], the view that the "vessel" signifies the wife, and that the reference is to the sanctified maintenance of the married state, is supported by the facts that in 1 Pet. 3:7 the same word *timē*, "honor," is used with regard to the wife; again in Heb. 13:4, *timios*, "honorable" (RV, "in honor") is used in regard to marriage; further, the preceding command in 1 Thess. 4 is against fornication, and the succeeding one (v. 6) is against adultery.¶ In Ruth 4:10, Sept., *ktaomai*, "to possess," is used of a wife.

2. *angos* (ἄγγος, 30d) denotes "a jar" or "pail," Matt. 13:48, in the best texts (some have No. 3). It is used, in an inscription, of a cinerary urn.¶

3. *angeion* (ἀγγεῖον, 30) denotes "a small

vessel" (a diminutive of No. 2), e.g., for carrying oil, Matt. 25:4.¶

Note: For *phaulos,* Jas. 3:16, RV, see EVIL, A, No. 3.

VESTURE

1. *himation* (ἱμάτιον, 2440), "an outer garment," is rendered "vesture" in Rev. 19:13, 16, KJV (RV, "garment"). See APPAREL, No. 2.

2. *himatismos* (ἱματισμός, 2441), used of "clothing in general," is translated "vesture" in Matt. 27:35, KJV, in a quotation from Ps. 22:18 (RV, following the better texts, omits the quotation); in John 19:24, KJV and RV; see CLOTHING, No. 4.

3. *peribolaion* (περιβόλαιον, 4018) is translated "vesture" in Heb. 1:12, KJV (RV, "mantle"). See COVER, B, No. 1.

VEX

1. *ochleō* (ὀχλέω, 3791), "to disturb, trouble," is used in the passive voice, of being "troubled" by evil spirits, Acts 5:16.¶

2. *basanizō* (βασανίζω, 928), "to torment," is translated "vexed" in 2 Pet. 2:8. See TORMENT.

Notes: (1) In Luke 6:18, the best texts have *enochleō,* RV, "troubled." See TROUBLE, B, No. 5. (2) In 2 Pet. 2:7, KJV, *kataponeō,* "to wear down with toil," is translated "vexed." See DISTRESS, B, No. 4. (3) In Acts 12:1, KJV, *kakoō,* "to afflict" (RV), is translated "to vex." See AFFLICT, No. 1. (4) For Matt. 17:15, KJV, "vexed," see GRIEVOUSLY, B, *Note* (2).

For VIAL see BOWL

VICTORY, VICTORIOUS

A. Nouns.

1. *nikē* (νίκη, 3529), "victory," is used in 1 John 5:4.¶

2. *nikos* (νῖκος, 3534), a later form of No. 1, is used in Matt. 12:20; 1 Cor. 15:54, 55, 57.¶

B. Verb.

nikaō (νικάω, 3528), "to conquer, overcome," is translated "(them) that come victorious (from)" in Rev. 15:2, RV (KJV, "that had gotten the victory"). See CONQUER, OVERCOME, PREVAIL.

VICTUALS

episitismos (ἐπισιτισμός, 1979), "provisions, food" (*epi,* "upon," *sitizō,* "to feed, nourish"; *sitos,* "food"), is translated "victuals" in Luke 9:12.¶

Note: In Matt. 14:15, KJV, *brōma,* "food, meat," is translated "victuals" (RV, "food"). See MEAT.

For VIGILANT, 1 Tim. 3:2, see TEMPERATE; 1 Pet. 5:8, see WATCHFUL

VILE

A. Noun.

atimia (ἀτιμία, 819), "dishonor," is translated "vile" in Rom. 1:26, RV, marg., "(passions) of dishonor." See DISHONOR.

B. Adjectives.

1. *rhuparos* (ῥυπαρός, 4508), "filthy, dirty," is used (*a*) literally, of old shabby clothing, Jas. 2:2, "vile"; (*b*) metaphorically, of moral defilement, Rev. 22:11 (in the best texts).¶ In the Sept., Zech. 3:3, 4.¶

2. *poneros* (πονηρός, 4190), "evil," is translated "vile" in Acts 17:5, RV (KJV, "lewd"). See BAD, EVIL.

Note: For "vile" in the KJV of Phil. 3:21, see HUMILIATION.

VILLAGE

kōmē (κώμη, 2968), "a village," or "country town," primarily as distinct from a walled town, occurs in the Gospels; elsewhere only in Acts 8:25. The difference between *polis,* "a city," and *kōmē,* is maintained in the NT, as in Josephus. Among the Greeks the point of the distinction was not that of size or fortification, but of constitution and land. In the OT the city and the village are regularly distinguished. The Mishna makes the three distinctions, a large city, a city, and a village.

The RV always substitutes "village(-s)" for KJV, "town(-s)," Matt. 10:11; Mark 8:23, 26, 27; Luke 5:17; 9:6, 12; John 7:42; 11:1, 30. See TOWN.

VILLANY

1. *rhadiourgia* (ῥᾳδιουργία, 4468) lit. and primarily denotes "ease in working" (*rhadios,* "easy," *ergon,* "work"), "easiness, laziness"; hence "recklessness, wickedness," Acts 13:10, RV, "villany," KJV, "mischief."¶ In the papyri it is used of "theft."

2. *rhadiourgēma* (ῥᾳδιούργημα, 4467), "a reckless act" (akin to No. 1), occurs in Acts 18:14, RV, "villany" (KJV, "lewdness").¶

VINE, VINTAGE

ampelos (ἄμπελος, 288) is used (*a*) lit., e.g., Matt. 26:29 and parallel passages; Jas. 3:12; (*b*) figuratively, (1) of Christ, John 15:1, 4, 5; (2) of His enemies, Rev. 14:18, 19, "the vine of the earth" (RV, "vintage" in v. 19), probably figurative of the remaining mass of apostate Christendom.¶

VINEDRESSER

ampelourgos (ἀμπελουργός, 289), "a worker in a vineyard" (from *ampelos*, "a vine," and *ergon*), is rendered "vinedresser" in Luke 13:7, RV (KJV, "dresser of the vineyard").¶

VINEGAR

oxos (ὄξος, 3690), akin to *oxus*, "sharp," denotes "sour wine," the ordinary drink of laborers and common soldiers; it is used in the four Gospels of the "vinegar" offered to the Lord at His crucifixion. In Matt. 27:34 the best texts have *oinos*, "wine" (RV). Some have *oxos* (KJV, "vinegar"), but Mark 15:23 (KJV and RV) confirms the RV in the passage in Matthew. This, which the soldiers offered before crucifying, was refused by Him, as it was designed to alleviate His sufferings; the "vinegar" is mentioned in Mark 15:36; so Luke 23:36, and John 19:29, 30.¶ In the Sept., Num. 6:3; Ruth 2:14; Ps. 69:21; Prov. 25:20.¶

VINEYARD

ampelōn (ἀμπελών, 290) is used 22 times in the Synoptic Gospels; elsewhere in 1 Cor. 9:7.

VIOLENCE, VIOLENT, VIOLENTLY

A. Nouns.

1. *bia* (βία, 970) denotes "force, violence," said of men, Acts 5:26; 21:35; 24:7; of waves, 27:41.¶

2. *hormēma* (ὅρμημα, 3731), "a rush" (akin to *hormaō*, "to urge on, to rush"), is used of the fall of Babylon, Rev. 18:21, KJV, "violence," RV, "mighty fall."¶

3. *biastēs* (βιαστής, 973), "a forceful or violent man," is used in Matt. 11:12. See FORCE, B, No. 1, *Note*.¶

Note: In Heb. 11:34, KJV, *dunamis*, "power" (RV), is rendered "violence."

B. Verbs.

1. *diaseiō* (διασείω, 1286), "to shake violently," is used in Luke 3:14, "do violence," including intimidation.¶ In the Sept., Job 4:14.¶

2. *biazō* (βιάζω, 971), in the passive voice, is rendered "suffereth violence" in Matt. 11:12; see FORCE, B, Nos. 1 and 2. Some, e.g., Cremer (*Lexicon*) and Dalman (*Words of Jesus*, pp. 139,ff.), hold that the reference is to the antagonism of the enemies of the kingdom, but Luke 16:16 (middle voice: RV, "entereth violently") indicates the meaning as referring to those who make an effort to enter the kingdom in spite of violent opposition: see PRESS, A, No. 3.¶

Note: For *hormaō*, rendered "ran violently," in Matt. 8:32 and parallels, see RUN, RUSH.

VIPER

echidna (ἔχιδνα, 2191) is probably a generic term for "poisonous snakes." It is rendered "viper" in the NT, (*a*) of the actual creature, Acts 28:3; (*b*) metaphorically in Matt. 3:7; 12:34; 23:33; Luke 3:7.¶

VIRGIN

parthenos (παρθένος, 3933) is used (*a*) of "the Virgin Mary," Matt. 1:23; Luke 1:27; (*b*) of the ten "virgins" in the parable, Matt. 25:1, 7, 11; (*c*) of the "daughters" of Philip the evangelist, Acts 21:9; (*d*) those concerning whom the apostle Paul gives instructions regarding marriage, 1 Cor. 7:25, 28, 34; in vv. 36, 37, 38, the subject passes to that of "virgin *daughters*" (RV), which almost certainly formed one of the subjects upon which the church at Corinth sent for instructions from the apostle; one difficulty was relative to the discredit which might be brought upon a father (or guardian), if he allowed his daughter or ward to grow old unmarried. The interpretation that this passage refers to a man and woman already in some kind of relation by way of a spiritual marriage and living together in a vow of virginity and celibacy, is untenable if only in view of the phraseology of the passage; (*e*) figuratively, of "a local church" in its relation to Christ, 2 Cor. 11:2; (*f*) metaphorically of "chaste persons," Rev. 14:4.¶

VIRGINITY

parthenia (παρθενία, 3932), akin to the above, occurs in Luke 2:36.¶ In the Sept., Jer. 3:4.¶

VIRTUE

aretē (ἀρετή, 703) properly denotes whatever procures preeminent estimation for a person or thing; hence, "intrinsic eminence, moral goodness, virtue," (*a*) of God, 1 Pet. 2:9, "excellencies" (KJV, "praises"); here the original and general sense seems to be blended with the impression made on others, i.e., renown, excellence or praise (Hort); in 2 Pet. 1:3, "(by His own glory and) virtue," RV (instrumental dative), i.e., the manifestation of His divine power; this significance is frequently illustrated in the papyri and was evidently common in current Greek speech; (*b*) of any particular moral excellence, Phil. 4:8; 2 Pet. 1:5 (twice), where virtue is enjoined as an essential quality in the exercise of faith, RV, "(in your faith supply) virtue."¶

Note: In the KJV of Mark 5:30; Luke 6:19;

8:46, *dunamis,* "power" (RV), is rendered "virtue."

VISIBLE

horatos (ὁρατός, 3707), from *horaō,* "to see," occurs in Col. 1:16.¶

VISION

1. *horama* (ὅραμα, 3705), "that which is seen" (*horaō*), denotes (*a*) "a spectacle, sight," Matt. 17:9; Acts 7:31 ("sight"); (*b*) "an appearance, vision," Acts 9:10 (v. 12 in some mss.); 10:3, 17, 19; 11:5; 12:9; 16:9, 10; 18:9.¶

2. *horasis* (ὅρασις, 3706), "sense of sight," is rendered "visions" in Acts 2:17; Rev. 9:17. See LOOK, B.

3. *optasia* (ὀπτασία, 3701) (a late form of *opsis,* "the act of seeing"), from *optanō,* "to see, a coming into view," denotes a "vision" in Luke 1:22; 24:23; Acts 26:19; 2 Cor. 12:1.¶

VISIT

1. *episkeptomai* (ἐπισκέπτομαι, 1980), primarily, "to inspect" (a late form of *episkopeō,* "to look upon, care for, exercise oversight"), signifies (*a*) "to visit" with help, of the act of God, Luke 1:68, 78; 7:16; Acts 15:14; Heb. 2:6; (*b*) "to visit" the sick and afflicted, Matt. 25:36, 43; Jas. 1:27; (*c*) "to go and see," "pay a visit to," Acts 7:23; 15:36; (*d*) "to look out" certain men for a purpose, Acts 6:3. See LOOK.¶

Note: In the Sept., "to visit with punishment," e.g., Ps. 89:32; Jer. 9:25.

2. *historeō* (ἱστορέω, 2477), from *histōr,* "one learned in anything," denotes "to visit" in order to become acquainted with, Gal. 1:18, RV, "visit" (KJV, "see"), RV marg., "become acquainted with."¶

3. *epipherō* (ἐπιφέρω, 2018), for which see BRING, No. 6, is rendered "visiteth (with wrath)" in Rom. 3:5, RV, KJV, "taketh (vengeance)."

VISITATION

episkopē (ἐπισκοπή, 1984), for which see BISHOP, No. 2, denotes "a visitation," whether in mercy, Luke 19:44, or in judgment, 1 Pet. 2:12.

For VOCATION, Eph. 4:1, see CALL, B

VOICE

phōnē (φωνή, 5456), "a sound," is used of the voice (*a*) of God, Matt. 3:17; John 5:37; 12:28, 30; Acts 7:31; 10:13, 15; 11:7, 9; Heb. 3:7, 15; 4:7; 12:19, 26; 2 Pet. 1:17, 18; Rev. 18:4; 21:3; (*b*) of Christ, (1) in the days of His flesh, Matt. 12:19 (negatively); John 3:29; 5:25; 10:3, 4, 16, 27; 11:43; 18:37; (2) on the cross, Matt. 27:46, and parallel passages; (3) from heaven, Acts 9:4, 7; 22:7, 9, 14; 26:14; Rev. 1:10, 12 (here, by metonymy, of the speaker), 15; 3:20; (4) at the resurrection "to life," John 5:28; 1 Thess. 4:16, where "the voice of the archangel" is, lit., "a voice of an archangel," and probably refers to the Lord's voice as being of an archangelic character; (5) at the resurrection to judgment, John 5:28 [not the same event as (4)]; (*c*) of human beings on earth, e.g., Matt. 2:18; 3:3; Luke 1:42, in some texts, KJV, "voice", and frequently in the Synoptists; (*d*) of angels, Rev. 5:11, and frequently in the Apocalypse; (*e*) of the redeemed in heaven, e.g., Rev. 6:10; 18:22; 19:1, 5; (*f*) of a pagan god, Acts 12:22; (*g*) of things, e.g., wind, John 3:8, RV, "voice" (KJV, "sound"). See SOUND.

Notes: (1) In Luke 1:42 (1st part), KJV, *anaphōneō,* "to lift up one's voice," is rendered "spake out," RV, "lifted up (her) voice." (2) In Acts 26:10, KJV, "I gave my voice" (RV, " . . . vote"): see STONE, No. 2.

VOID

1. *kenoō* (κενόω, 2758), "to empty, make of no effect," is rendered "to make void," in Rom. 4:14; 1 Cor. 1:17, RV; 9:15; 2 Cor. 9:3, RV. See EFFECT (of none), No. 3, EMPTY, VAIN, B, No. 2.

2. *atheteō* (ἀθετέω, 114), for which see DISANNUL, No. 1, is rendered "to make void" in Gal. 2:21, RV (KJV, "frustrate"); 3:15, RV.

3. *akuroō* (ἀκυρόω, 208), for which see DISANNUL, No. 2, is rendered "to make void" in Matt. 15:6; Mark 7:13, RV.

Notes: (1) In Rom. 3:31, KJV, *katargeō* is translated "to make void." See ABOLISH, EFFECT (of none), No. 2. (2) See also IMPOSSIBLE, B, OFFENSE, UNDERSTANDING.

For VOLUME see ROLL, B

VOLUNTARY

Note: In Col. 2:18, *thelō* (for which see DESIRE, B, No. 6) is rendered "(in a) voluntary (humility)," present participle, i.e., "being a voluntary (in humility)," KJV marg., RV marg., "of his own mere will (by humility)," *en,* "in," being rendered as instrumental; what was of one's own mere will, with the speciousness of humility, would mean his being robbed of his prize.

VOMIT

exerama (ἐξέραμα, 1829), "a vomit" (from *exeraō,* "to disgorge"), occurs in 2 Pet. 2:22.¶

For **VOTE**, Acts 26:10, RV, see
STONE, No. 2

VOUCHSAFE

homologeō (ὁμολογέω, 3670), "to agree," is found in the best texts in Acts 7:17, and rendered "vouchsafed," RV, with reference to God's promise to Abraham; some mss. have *ōmosen*, "swore" (*omnumi*, "to swear"), as in KJV. See CONFESS, PROFESS, PROMISE, THANKS, B, *Note*.

VOW

euchē (εὐχή, 2171) denotes also "a vow," Acts 18:18; 21:23, with reference to the "vow" of the Nazirite (wrongly spelt Nazarite), see Num. 6, RV; in Jas. 5:15, "prayer." See PRAYER.¶

VOYAGE

ploos or *plous* (πλόος, 4144) is rendered "a voyage" (*pleō*, "to sail") in Acts 27:10 (KJV and RV); in 21:7, RV (KJV, "course"); in 27:9, RV (KJV, "sailing"). See COURSE, B, *Note* (4).¶

W

WAG

kineō (κινέω, 2795), "to move," is used of those who mocked the Lord at His crucifixion, nodding their heads in the direction of the cross as if sneering at this supposed ending of His career, Matt. 27:39; Mark 15:29. Cf. 2 Kings 19:21; Job 16:4; Ps. 22:7; 109:25; Isa. 37:22. See MOVE, No. 1.

WAGES

1. *opsōnion* (ὀψώνιον, 3800), for which see CHARGE, A, No. 5, denotes (*a*) "soldiers' pay," Luke 3:14; 1 Cor. 9:7 ("charges"); (*b*) in general, "hire, wages of any sort," used metaphorically, Rom. 6:23, of sin; 2 Cor. 11:8, of material support which Paul received from some of the churches which he had established and to which he ministered in spiritual things; their support partly maintained him at Corinth, where he forebore to receive such assistance (vv. 9, 10).¶
2. *misthos* (μισθός, 3408), "hire," is rendered "wages" in John 4:36; in 2 Pet. 2:15, KJV (RV, "hire"). See HIRE, A.

WAIL, WAILING

Notes: (1) For *alalazō*, rendered "to wail" in Mark 5:38, see CLANGING. (2) For *koptō*, rendered "to wail" in Rev. 1:7, KJV (RV, "shall mourn") and 18:9, RV, "wail" (KJV, "lament"), see BEWAIL. (3) For *pentheō*, rendered "to wail" in Rev. 18:15, 19, KJV, see MOURN. (4) For *klauthmos*, rendered "wailing" in Matt. 13:42, 50, KJV, see WEEP. (5) In Matt. 11:17 and Luke 7:32, KJV, *thrēneō*, "to wail" (RV), is rendered "to mourn." See BEWAIL, *Note* (1), MOURN.

WAIT

1. *ekdechomai* (ἐκδέχομαι, 1551), for which see EXPECT, No. 1, is rendered "to wait" in John 5:3, KJV; Acts 17:16; 1 Cor. 11:33, RV.
2. *apekdechomai* (ἀπεκδέχομαι, 553), "to await or expect eagerly," is rendered "to wait for" in Rom. 8:19, 23, 25; 1 Cor. 1:7; Gal. 5:5; Phil 3:20, RV (KJV, "look for"); Heb. 9:28, RV (KJV, "look for"), here "them that wait" represents believers in general, not a section of them; 1 Pet. 3:20 (in the best texts; some have No. 1). See LOOK (for), *Note* (1).¶
3. *prosdechomai* (προσδέχομαι, 4327), "to look for" with a view to favorable reception, is rendered "to wait for" in Mark 15:43; Luke 2:25; 12:36; 23:51. See LOOK (for), No. 2.
4. *prosdokaō* (προσδοκάω, 4328), "to await," is rendered "to wait for" in Luke 1:21; 8:40; Acts 10:24; in 27:33, RV "ye wait" (KJV, "have tarried"). See LOOK (for), No. 1.
5. *anamenō* (ἀναμένω, 362), "to wait for" (*ana*, "up," used intensively, and *menō*, "to abide"), is used in 1 Thess. 1:10, of "waiting" for the Son of God from heaven; the word carries with it the suggestion of "waiting" with patience and confident expectancy.¶
6. *perimenō* (περιμένω, 4037), "to await an event," is used in Acts 1:4, of "waiting" for the Holy Spirit, "the promise of the Father."¶ In the Sept., Gen. 49:18.¶
7. *proskartereō* (προσκαρτερέω, 4342), to continue steadfastly, is rendered "to wait on," in Mark 3:9 and Acts 10:7. See CONTINUE, No. 9 (in the Sept., Num. 13:21¶).
8. *paredreuō* (παρεδρεύω, 3917a), "to sit constantly beside" (*para*, "beside," *hedra*, "a

seat"), is used in the best texts in 1 Cor. 9:13, RV, "wait upon (KJV, "at") (the altar)."¶ In the Sept., Prov. 1:21; 8:3.¶

Notes: (1) In 2 Thess. 3:5, KJV, *hupomonē*, "patience" (so RV), is rendered "patient waiting" (marg., "patience"). See PATIENCE. (2) For "lie in wait" in Eph. 4:14, KJV, see WILES. (3) For "lying in wait," Acts 20:19, KJV, and "laid wait," 20:3; 23:30, see PLOT.

WAKE

grēgoreō (γρηγορέω, 1127), translated "wake" in 1 Thess. 5:10, is rendered "watch" in the RV marg., as in the text in v. 6, and the RV in the twenty-one other places in which it occurs in the NT (save 1 Pet. 5:8, "be watchful"). It is not used in the metaphorical sense of "to be alive"; here it is set in contrast with *katheudō*, "to sleep," which is never used by the apostle with the meaning "to be dead" (it has this meaning only in the case of Jairus' daughter). Accordingly the meaning here is that of vigilance and expectancy as contrasted with laxity and indifference. All believers will live together with Christ from the time of the Rapture described in ch. 4; for all have spiritual life now, though their spiritual condition and attainment vary considerably. Those who are lax and fail to be watchful will suffer loss (1 Cor. 3:15; 9:27; 2 Cor. 5:10, e.g.), but the apostle is not here dealing with that aspect of the subject. What he does make clear is that the Rapture of believers at the second coming of Christ will depend solely on the death of Christ for them, and not upon their spiritual condition. The Rapture is not a matter of reward, but of salvation. See WATCH.

WALK

1. *peripateō* (περιπατέω, 4043) is used (*a*) physically, in the Synoptic Gospels (except Mark 7:5); always in the Acts except in 21:21; never in the Pauline Epistles, nor in those of John; (*b*) figuratively, "signifying the whole round of the activities of the individual life, whether of the unregenerate, Eph. 4:17, or of the believer, 1 Cor. 7:17; Col. 2:6. It is applied to the observance of religious ordinances, Acts 21:21; Heb. 13:9, marg., as well as to moral conduct. The Christian is to walk in newness of life, Rom. 6:4, after the spirit, 8:4, in honesty, 13:13, by faith, 2 Cor. 5:7, in good works, Eph. 2:10, in love, 5:2, in wisdom, Col. 4:5, in truth, 2 John 4, after the commandments of the Lord, v. 6. And, negatively, not after the flesh, Rom. 8:4; not after the manner of men, 1 Cor. 3:3; not in craftiness, 2 Cor. 4:2; not by sight, 5:7;

not in the vanity of the mind, Eph. 4:17; not disorderly, 2 Thess. 3:6."* See GO, *Note* (2) (*r*).

2. *poreuō* (πορεύω, 4198), for which see DEPART, No. 8, and GO, No. 1, is used in the middle voice and rendered "to walk" in Luke 1:6, of the general activities of life; so in Luke 13:33, KJV, "walk" (RV, "go on My way"); Acts 9:31; 14:16; 1 Pet. 4:3; 2 Pet. 2:10; Jude, 16, 18.

3. *emperipateō* (ἐμπεριπατέω, 1704), "to walk about in, or among" (*en*, "in," and No. 1), is used in 2 Cor. 6:16, of the activities of God in the lives of believers.¶

4. *stoicheō* (στοιχέω, 4748), from *stoichos*, "a row," signifies "to walk in line," and is used metaphorically of "walking" in relation to others (No. 1 is used more especially of the individual walk); in Acts 21:24, it is translated "walkest orderly"; in Rom. 4:12, "walk (in . . . steps)"; in Gal. 5:25 it is used of walking "by the Spirit," RV, in an exhortation to keep step with one another in submission of heart to the Holy Spirit, and therefore of keeping step with Christ, the great means of unity and harmony in a church (contrast No. 1 in v. 16; v. 25 begins a new section which extends to 6:10); in 6:16 it is used of walking by the rule expressed in vv. 14, 15; in Phil. 3:16 the reference is to the course pursued by the believer who makes "the prize of the high calling" the object of his ambition.¶ In the Sept., Eccl. 11:6.¶

5. *dierchomai* (διέρχομαι, 1330), "to go through" (*dia*), is rendered "to walk through" in the KJV of Matt. 12:43 and Luke 11:24 (RV, "passeth through"). See COME, No. 5, PASS, No. 2.

6. *orthopodeō* (ὀρθοποδέω, 3716), "to walk in a straight path" (*orthos*, "straight," *pous*, "a foot"), is used metaphorically in Gal. 2:14, signifying a "course of conduct" by which one leaves a straight track for others to follow ("walked . . . uprightly").¶

Note: In Mark 1:16, KJV, *paragō*, "to pass along" (RV, "passing along"), is translated "walked."

WALL

1. *teichos* (τεῖχος, 5038), "a wall," especially one around a town, is used (*a*) literally, Acts 9:25; 2 Cor. 11:33; Heb. 11:30; (*b*) figuratively, of the "wall" of the heavenly city, Rev. 21:12, 14, 15, 17, 18, 19.¶

2. *toichos* (τοῖχος, 5109), "a wall," especially of a house, is used figuratively in Acts 23:3, "(thou whited) wall."¶

---

* From *Notes on Thessalonians,* by Hogg and Vine, p. 67.

3. *mesotoichon* (μεσότοιχον, 3320), "a partition wall" (*mesos*, "middle," and No. 2), occurs in Eph. 2:14, figuratively of the separation of Gentile from Jew in their unregenerate state, a partition demolished by the Cross for both on acceptance of the gospel. Cf. PARTITION.¶

WALLET

pēra (πήρα, 4082), "a traveler's leather bag or pouch for holding provisions," is translated "wallet" in the RV (KJV, "scrip"), Matt. 10:10; Mark 6:8; Luke 9:3; 10:4; 22:35, 36.¶ Deissmann (*Light from the Ancient East*) regards it as an alms-bag.

WALLOW (Verb and Noun)

A. Verb.

kuliō (κυλίω, 2947) in the active voice denotes "to roll, roll along"; in the middle voice in Mark 9:20, rendered "wallowed."¶

B. Noun.

kulismos (κυλισμός, 2946**), "a rolling, wallowing," akin to A (some texts have *kulisma*), is used in 2 Pet. 2:22, of the proverbial sow that had been washed.¶

WANDER

A. Verb.

planaō (πλανάω, 4105), for which see DECEIT, C, No. 6, is translated "to wander" in Heb. 11:38, passive voice, lit., "were made to wander."

Note: In the KJV of 1 Tim. 5:13 and Heb. 11:37, *perierchomai*, "to go about or around," is translated "to wander about." See GO, No. 29.

B. Noun.

planētēs (πλανήτης, 4107), "a wanderer" (Eng., "planet"), is used metaphorically in Jude 13, of the evil teachers there mentioned as "wandering (stars)."¶ In the Sept., Hos. 9:17.¶

WANT (Noun and Verb)

A. Nouns.

1. *husterēsis* (ὑστέρησις, 5304), akin to B, No. 1 (below), occurs in Mark 12:14 and Phil. 4:11.¶

2. *husterēma* (ὑστέρημα, 5305) denotes (more concretely than No. 1) (α) "that which is lacking" (see LACK); (*b*) "need, poverty, want," rendered "want" in Luke 21:4 (KJV, "penury"); 2 Cor. 8:14 (twice); 9:12; 11:9 (2nd occurrence), RV, "want" (KJV, "that which was lacking").

3. *chreia* (χρεία, 5532) is rendered "want" in Phil. 2:25, KJV (RV, "need"). See BUSINESS.

B. Verbs.

1. *hustereō* (ὑστερέω, 5302) signifies "to be in want," Luke 15:14; 2 Cor. 11:9 (1st occurrence); Phil. 4:12, RV (KJV "to suffer need"); in John 2:3, KJV, "wanted" (RV, "failed"). See BEHIND, B, No. 1.

2. *leipō* (λείπω, 3007), "to leave," is rendered "to be wanting" in Titus 1:5 and 3:13, and in the KJV in Jas. 1:4. See LACK, C, No. 3.

WANTONNESS, WANTON, WANTONLY

A. Nouns.

1. *aselgeia* (ἀσέλγεια, 766), "lasciviousness, licentiousness," is rendered "wantonness" in 2 Pet. 2:18, KJV; see LASCIVIOUSNESS.

2. *strēnos* (στρῆνος, 4764), "insolent luxury," is rendered "wantonness" in Rev. 18:3, RV (marg., "luxury"; KJV, "delicacies," not a sufficiently strong rendering).¶

B. Verbs.

1. *strēniaō* (στρηνιάω, 4763), akin to A, No. 2, "to run riot," is rendered "waxed wanton" in Rev. 18:7, RV, and "lived wantonly" in v. 8. See DELICATELY, *Note* (1). The root of the verb is seen in the Latin *strenuus*. ¶

2. *katastrēniaō* (καταστρηνιάω, 2691), an intensive form of No. 1, "to wax wanton against," occurs in 1 Tim. 5:11.¶

WAR (Verb and Noun)

A. Verbs.

1. *polemeō* (πολεμέω, 4170) (Eng., "polemics"), "to fight, to make war," is used (*a*) literally, Rev. 12:7 (twice), RV; 13:4; 17:14; 19:11; (*b*) metaphorically, Rev. 2:16, RV; (*c*) hyperbolically, Jas. 4:2. See FIGHT, B, *Note* (1).¶

2. *strateuō* (στρατεύω, 4754), used in the middle voice, "to make war" (from *stratos*, "an encamped army"), is translated "to war" in 2 Cor. 10:3; metaphorically, of spiritual "conflict," 1 Tim. 1:18; 2 Tim. 2:3, KJV; Jas. 4:1; 1 Pet. 2:11. See SOLDIER, B.

3. *antistrateuomai* (ἀντιστρατεύομαι, 497), not found in the active voice *antistrateuō*, "to make war against" (*anti*), occurs in Rom. 7:23.¶

Note: For "men of war," Luke 23:11, KJV, see SOLDIER, No. 2.

B. Noun.

polemos (πόλεμος, 4171), "war" (akin to A, No. 1), is so translated in the RV, for KJV, "battle," 1 Cor. 14:8; Rev. 9:7, 9; 16:14; 20:8; for KJV, "fight," Heb. 11:34; KJV and RV in Jas. 4:1, hyperbolically of private "quarrels"; elsewhere, literally, e.g., Matt. 24:6; Rev. 11:7. See BATTLE.

WARD

1. *phulakē* (φυλακή, 5438), "a guard," is used of the place where persons are kept under guard (akin to *phulax*, "a keeper"), and translated "ward" in Acts 12:10. See CAGE, HOLD (Noun), IMPRISONMENT, PRISON, WATCH.

2. *tērēsis* (τήρησις, 5084) primarily denotes "a watching" (*tēreō*, "to watch"); hence "imprisonment, ward," Acts 4:3 (KJV, "hold"); 5:18, RV, "(public) ward" [KJV, "(common) prison"]. See HOLD (Noun), KEEPING, B, PRISON.

Note: For "were kept in ward," Gal. 3:23, see GUARD, B, No. 3, KEEP, No. 6.

WARE OF

phulassō (φυλάσσω, 5442) denotes "to guard, watch"; in 2 Tim. 4:15, "of (whom) be thou ware" (middle voice): see BEWARE, No. 3.

Note: For *sunoida*, translated "were ware" in Acts 14:6, KJV (RV, "became aware of it"), see KNOW, A, No. 6.

WARFARE

strateia, or -*tia* (στρατεία, 4756), primarily "a host or army," came to denote "a warfare," and is used of spiritual "conflict" in 2 Cor. 10:4; 1 Tim. 1:18.¶

Note: For the verb "to go a warfare," 1 Cor. 9:7, KJV, see SOLDIER, B, No. 1.

WARM (Verb)

thermainō (θερμαίνω, 2328), "to warm, heat" (Eng. "thermal," etc.), when used in the middle voice, signifies "to warm oneself," Mark 14:54, 67; John 18:18 (twice), 25; Jas. 2:16.¶

WARN

1. *noutheteō* (νουθετέω, 3560), "to put in mind, warn," is translated "to warn" in the KJV, in the passages mentioned under ADMONISH, B, No. 1 (which see); the RV always translates this word by the verb "to admonish."

2. *hupodeiknumi* (ὑποδείκνυμι, 5263), primarily, "to show secretly" (*hupo*, "under," *deiknumi*, "to show"), hence, generally, "to teach, make known," is translated "to warn" in Matt. 3:7; Luke 3:7; 12:5, RV (KJV, "forewarn"). See FOREWARN, *Note,* SHEW.

3. *chrēmatizō* (χρηματίζω, 5537), for which see ADMONISH, B, No. 3, is translated "to warn" in Matt. 2:12, 22; Acts 10:22; Heb. 8:5, RV (KJV, "admonished"); 11:7; 12:25, RV (KJV, "spake").

WAS, WAST, WERE, WERT

Note: When not part of another verb, or phrase, these translate *eimi*, "to be," e.g., Matt. 1:18, or the following: (*a*) *ginomai*, "to be-

come," e.g., Matt. 8:26; (*b*) *huparchō*, "to exist," especially when referring to an already existing condition, e.g., Luke 8:41; Acts 5:4 (2nd part); 16:3; 27:12; Rom. 4:19, KJV, "when he was" (RV, "he being"); (*c*) *echō*, "to have," e.g., Acts 12:15; (*d*) *apechō*, "to be away, to be distant," e.g., Luke 7:6; 24:13; (*e*) *mellō*, "to be about to," e.g., Luke 19:4; Acts 21:27, 37, KJV (RV, "was about to"); (*f*) *sumbainō*, "to come to pass, happen," e.g., Acts 21:35; (*g*) in Gal. 4:28, the preposition *kata*, "according to," is rendered "was," in the phrase "as Isaac was," lit., "like Isaac"; as Isaac's birth came by divine interposition, so does the spiritual birth of every believer.

WASH

1. *niptō* (νίπτω, 3538) is chiefly used of "washing part of the body," John 13:5 6, 8 (twice, figuratively in 2nd clause), 12, 14 (twice); in 1 Tim. 5:10, including the figurative sense; in the middle voice, to wash oneself, Matt. 6:17; 15:2; Mark 7:3; John 9:7, 11, 15; 13:10.¶ For the corresponding noun see BASON.

2. *aponiptō* (ἀπονίπτω, 633), "to wash off," is used in the middle voice, in Matt. 27:24.¶

3. *louō* (λούω, 3068) signifies "to bathe, to wash the body," (*a*) active voice, Acts 9:37; 16:33; (*b*) passive voice, John 13:10, RV, "bathed" (KJV, "washed"); Heb. 10:22, lit., "having been washed as to the body," metaphorical of the effect of the Word of God upon the activities of the believer; (*c*) middle voice, 2 Pet. 2:22. Some inferior mss. have it instead of *luō*, "to loose," in Rev. 1:5 (see RV).¶

4. *apolouō* (ἀπολούω, 628), "to wash off or away," is used in the middle voice, metaphorically, "to wash oneself," in Acts 22:16, where the command to Saul of Tarsus to "wash away" his sins indicates that by his public confession, he would testify to the removal of his sins, and to the complete change from his past life; this "washing away" was not in itself the actual remission of his sins, which had taken place at his conversion; the middle voice implies his own particular interest in the act (as with the preceding verb "baptize," lit., "baptize thyself," i.e., "get thyself baptized"); the aorist tenses mark the decisiveness of the acts; in 1 Cor. 6:11, lit., "ye washed yourselves clean"; here the middle voice (rendered in the Passive in KJV and RV, which do not distinguish between this and the next two passives; see RV marg.) again indicates that the converts at Corinth, by their obedience to the faith, voluntarily gave testimony to the complete spiritual change divinely wrought in them.¶ In the Sept., Job 9:30.¶

5. *plunō* (πλύνω, 4150) is used of "washing inanimate objects," e.g., "nets," Luke 5:2 (some texts have *apoplunō*); of "garments," figuratively, Rev. 7:14; 22:14 (in the best texts; the KJV translates those which have the verb *poieō*, "to do," followed by *tas entolas autou*, "His commandments").¶

6. *rhantizō* (ῥαντίζω, 4472), "to sprinkle," is used in the middle voice in Mark 7:4, in some ancient texts, of the acts of the Pharisees in their assiduous attention to the cleansing of themselves after coming from the market place (some texts have *baptizō* here). See SPRINKLE.

7. *brechō* (βρέχω, 1026), "to wet," is translated "to wash" in Luke 7:38, 44, KJV; the RV, "to wet" and "hath wetted," gives the correct rendering. See RAIN, B.

8. *baptizō* (βαπτίζω, 907) is rendered "washed" in Luke 11:38. See BAPTIZE.

Note: With regard to Nos. 1, 3, 5, the Sept. of Lev. 15:11 contains all three with their distinguishing characteristics, No. 1 being used of the hands, No. 3 of the whole body, No. 5 of the garments.

WASHING

1. *baptismos* (βαπτισμός, 909) denotes "the act of washing, ablution," with special reference to purification, Mark 7:4 (in some texts, v. 8); Heb. 6:2, "baptisms"; 9:10, "washings. See BAPTISM.¶

2. *loutron* (λουτρόν, 3067), "a bath, a laver" (akin to *louō*, see above), is used metaphorically of the Word of God, as the instrument of spiritual cleansing, Eph. 5:26; in Titus 3:5, of "the washing of regeneration" (see REGENERATION).¶ In the Sept., Song of Sol. 4:2; 6:6.¶

WASTE (Noun and Verb)

A. Noun.

apōleia (ἀπώλεια, 684), "destruction," is translated "waste" in Matt. 26:8; Mark 14:4. See DESTRUCTION, B, II, No. 1.

B. Verbs.

1. *diaskorpizō* (διασκορπίζω, 1287), "to scatter abroad," is used metaphorically of "squandering property," Luke 15:13; 16:1. See DISPERSE, SCATTER.

2. *portheō* (πορθέω, 4199), "to ravage," is rendered "wasted" in Gal. 1:13, KJV; see DESTROY, *Note,* HAVOC.

3. *lumainō* (λυμαίνω, 3075), "to outrage, maltreat," is used in the middle voice in Acts 8:3, of Saul's treatment of the church, RV, "laid waste" (KJV, "made havoc of").¶

WATCH (Noun and Verb), WATCHERS, WATCHFUL, WATCHINGS

A. Nouns.

1. *phulakē* (φυλακή, 5438) is used (*a*) with the meaning "a watch," actively, "a guarding," Luke 2:8, lit., "(keeping, *phulassō*) watches"; (*b*) of "the time during which guard was kept by night, a watch of the night," Matt. 14:25; 24:43; Mark 6:48; Luke 12:38. See CAGE, HOLD, IMPRISONMENT, PRISON.

Note: Among the Jews the night was divided into three "watches" (see, e.g., Exod. 14:24; Judg. 7:19), and this continued on through Roman times. The Romans divided the night into four "watches"; this was recognized among the Jews (see Mark 13:35).

2. *koustōdia* (κουστωδία, 2892), from Lat., *custodia* (cf. Eng., "custody"), is rendered "watch" in Matt. 27:65, 66 and 28:11, KJV: see GUARD.¶

3. *agrupnia* (ἀγρυπνία, 70), "sleeplessness" (akin to B, No. 4), is rendered "watchings" in 2 Cor. 6:5; 11:27.¶

B. Verbs.

1. *grēgoreō* (γρηγορέω, 1127), "to watch," is used (*a*) of "keeping awake," e.g., Matt. 24:43; 26:38, 40, 41; (*b*) of "spiritual alertness," e.g., Acts 20:31; 1 Cor. 16:13; Col. 4:2; 1 Thess. 5:6, 10 (for which see WAKE); 1 Pet. 5:8, RV, "be watchful" (KJV, "be vigilant"); Rev. 3:2, 3; 16:15.

2. *tēreō* (τηρέω, 5083), "to keep," is rendered "to watch," of those who kept guard at the cross, Matt. 27:36, 54; 28:4, RV, "watchers" (KJV, "keepers"), lit., "the watching ones." See HOLD, No. 8, KEEP, OBSERVE, PRESERVE, RESERVE.

3. *paratēreō* (παρατηρέω, 3906), "to observe," especially with sinister intent (*para*, "near," and No. 2), is rendered "to watch" in Mark 3:2; Luke 6:7; 14:1; 20:20; Acts 9:24. See OBSERVE.

4. *agrupneō* (ἀγρυπνέω, 69), "to be sleepless" (from *agreuō*, "to chase," and *hupnos*, "sleep"), is used metaphorically, "to be watchful," in Mark 13:33; Luke 21:36; Eph. 6:18; Heb. 13:17. The word expresses not mere wakefulness, but the "watchfulness" of those who are intent upon a thing.¶

5. *nēphō* (νήφω, 3525), "to abstain from wine," is used metaphorically of moral "alertness," and translated "to watch," in the KJV of 2 Tim. 4:5. See SOBER.

WATER (Noun and Verb), WATERING, WATERLESS

A. Noun.

hudōr (ὕδωρ, 5204), whence Eng. prefix, "hydro-," is used (*a*) of the natural element, frequently in the Gospels; in the plural especially in the Apocalypse; elsewhere, e.g., Heb. 9:19; Jas. 3:12; in 1 John 5:6, that Christ "came by water and blood," may refer either (1) to the elements that flowed from His side on the cross after His death, or, in view of the order of the words and the prepositions here used, (2) to His baptism in Jordan and His death on the cross. As to (1), the "water" would symbolize the moral and practical cleansing effected by the removal of defilement by our taking heed to the Word of God in heart, life and habit; cf. Lev. 14, as to the cleansing of the leper. As to (2), Jesus the Son of God came on His mission by, or through, "water" and blood, namely, at His baptism, when He publicly entered upon His mission and was declared to be the Son of God by the witness of the Father, and at the cross, when He publicly closed His witness; the apostle's statement thus counteracts the doctrine of the Gnostics that the divine *Logos* united Himself with the Man Jesus at His baptism, and left him at Gethsemane. On the contrary, He who was baptized and He who was crucified was the Son of God throughout in His combined deity and humanity.

The word "water" is used symbolically in John 3:5, either (1) of the Word of God, as in 1 Pet. 1:23 (cf. the symbolic use in Eph. 5:26), or, in view of the preposition *ek*, "out of," (2) of the truth conveyed by baptism, this being the expression, not the medium, the symbol, not the cause, of the believer's identification with Christ in His death, burial and resurrection. So the New Birth is, in one sense, the setting aside of all that the believer was according to the flesh, for it is evident that there must be an entirely new beginning. Some regard the *kai*, "and," in John 3:5, as epexegetic, = "even," in which case the "water" would be emblematic of the Spirit, as in John 7:38 (cf. 4:10, 14), but not in 1 John 5:8, where the Spirit and the "water" are distinguished. "The water of life," Rev. 21:6 and 22:1, 17, is emblematic of the maintenance of spiritual life in perpetuity. In Rev. 17:1 the "waters" are symbolic of nations, peoples, etc.

Note: For *potamos*, rendered "waters" in 2 Cor. 11:26, see RIVER.

B. Verb.

potizō (ποτίζω, 4222), "to give to drink," is used (*a*) naturally in Luke 13:15, "watering," with reference to animals; (*b*) figuratively, with reference to spiritual ministry to converts, 1 Cor. 3:6–8. See DRINK, B, No. 3.

Notes: (1) For *hudropoteō*, "to drink water," 1 Tim. 5:23, see DRINK, B, No. 5. (2) For the adjective *anudros*, "waterless" (RV), "without water," see DRY, No. 2.

WATERPOT

hudria (ὑδρία, 5201) occurs in John 2:6, 7; 4:28.¶

WAVE

1. *kuma* (κῦμα, 2949), from *kuō*, "to be pregnant, to swell," is used (*a*) literally in the plural, Matt. 8:24; 14:24; Mark 4:37 (Acts 27:41, in some mss.); (*b*) figuratively, Jude 13.¶

2. *salos* (σάλος, 4535) denotes "a tossing," especially the rolling swell of the sea, Luke 21:25, KJV, "waves" (RV, "billows").¶

3. *kludōn* (κλύδων, 2830), "a billow," is translated "wave" in Jas. 1:6, KJV (RV, "surge"); in Luke 8:24 it is translated "raging (of the water)." See RAGE, B.¶

WAVER, WAVERING

A. Adjective.

aklinēs (ἀκλινής, 186), "without bending" (*a*, negative, *klinō*, "to bend"), occurs in Heb. 10:23, KJV, "without wavering," RV, "that it waver not."¶

B. Verb.

diakrinō (διακρίνω, 1252) is rendered "to waver" in Rom. 4:20, RV (KJV, "staggered"); in Jas. 1:6 (twice). See DOUBT, No. 3.

WAX

1. *prokoptō* (προκόπτω, 4298), for which see ADVANCE, is rendered "to wax" in 2 Tim. 3:13.

2. *ginomai* (γίνομαι, 1096), "to become," is translated "waxed" in Luke 13:19, KJV (RV, "became"); in Heb. 11:34, KJV and RV, "waxed": see COME, No. 12, etc.

Note: This verb forms part of the translation of certain tenses of other verbs; see, e.g., BOLD, A, No. 2, COLD, C, CONFIDENT, B, No. 1, CORRUPT, A, No. 2, GROSS, OLD, D, No. 2, STRONG, B, No. 2, WANTON, B, Nos. 1 and 2, WEARY, No. 2, WROTH, No. 1.

WAY

1. *hodos* (ὁδός, 3598) denotes (*a*) "a natural path, road, way," frequent in the Synoptic Gospels; elsewhere, e.g., Acts 8:26; 1 Thess. 3:11; Jas. 2:25; Rev. 16:12; (*b*) "a traveler's way" (see JOURNEY); (*c*) metaphorically, of "a course of conduct," or "way of thinking," e.g., of righteousness, Matt. 21:32; 2 Pet. 2:21; of God,

Matt. 22:16, and parallels, i.e., the "way" instructed and approved by God; so Acts 18:26 and Heb. 3:10, "My ways" (cf. Rev. 15:3); of the Lord, Acts 18:25; "that leadeth to destruction," Matt. 7:13; " ... unto life," 7:14; of peace, Luke 1:79; Rom. 3:17; of Paul's "ways" in Christ, 1 Cor. 4:17 (plural); "more excellent" (of love), 1 Cor. 12:31; of truth, 2 Pet. 2:2; of the right "way," 2:15; of Balaam (id.); of Cain, Jude 11; of a "way" consisting in what is from God, e.g., of life, Acts 2:28 (plural); of salvation, Acts 16:17; personified, of Christ as the means of access to the Father, John 14:6; of the course followed and characterized by the followers of Christ, Acts 9:2; 19:9, 23; 24:22. See HIGHWAY.

Note: In Luke 5:19 and 19:4 the noun is not expressed in the original, but is understood.

2. *parodos* (πάροδος, 3938), "a passing or passage," is used with *en*, "in," 1 Cor. 16:7, "by the way" (lit, "in passing").¶

3. *tropos* (τρόπος, 5158), "a turning, a manner," is translated "way" in Rom. 3:2, "(every) way"; Phil. 1:18, "(in every) way." See CONVERSATION, MANNER, MEANS.

Notes: (1) In Jas. 1:11, KJV, *poreia*, "a journey, a going," is rendered "ways" (RV, "goings"). (2) In Heb. 12:17, *topos*, "a place," is rendered in KJV marg., "way (to change his mind)." (3) For the KJV rendering of *makran* "a good (or great) way off," Matt. 8:30; Luke 15:20, see FAR, B, No. 1. (4) In Luke 14:32, *porrō* is rendered "a great way off." (5) In Heb. 5:2, KJV, *planaō*, middle voice, "to wander," is rendered "(them) that are out of the way," RV, "(the) erring." (6) In Col. 2:14 and 2 Thess. 2:7, *ek mesou*, is translated "out of the way"; see MIDST, *Note* (1) (*e*). (7) For "two ways" in Mark 11:4, KJV, see STREET. (8) In John 10:1, the adverb *allachothen*, "from some other place" (from *allos*, "another"), is translated "some other way." (9) In 2 Pet. 3:1, the KJV translates *en* "by way of" ("by," RV). (10) In Gal. 2:5, the renderings "by," KJV, "in the way of," RV, serve to express the dative case of *hupotagē*, subjection. (11) For *propempō*, "to bring on one's way," Acts 15:3; 21:5, and the KJV of 2 Cor. 1:16 (RV, "to be set forward on my journey"), see BRING, No. 25. (12) *Aperchomai*, "to go away," is rendered "to go one's way," e.g., Matt. 13:25; 20:4; Mark 11:4; 12:12; Luke 19:32; John 11:46; Acts 9:17; Jas. 1:24: see GO, No. 14. (13) In Luke 8:14, KJV, *poreuomai*, "to go on one's way" (RV), is rendered "go forth"; in 13:33, KJV, "walk" (RV, "go on my way"); in Matt. 24:1, KJV, it is rendered "departed" (RV, "was going on his way"): see DEPART, No. 8. (14) In Acts 24:3, *pantē* is rendered "in all ways" (KJV, "always").¶ (15) In Rom. 3:12,

KJV, *ekklinō*, "to turn aside" (RV), is rendered "are gone out of the way." (16) See also ESCAPE, B, LASCIVIOUS.

WE

Note: When this is not part of the translation of a verb or phrase, it stands for some case of *hēmeis*, the plural of *egō*, "I"; this separate use of the pronoun is always emphatic. For "we ourselves," see OURSELVES.

WEAK, WEAKENED, WEAKER, WEAKNESS

A. Adjectives.

1. *asthenēs* (ἀσθενής, 772), lit., "strengthless" (see IMPOTENT), is translated "weak," (*a*) of physical "weakness," Matt. 26:41; Mark 14:38; 1 Cor. 1:27; 4:10; 11:30 (a judgment upon spiritual laxity in a church); 2 Cor. 10:10; 1 Pet. 3:7 (comparative degree); (*b*) in the spiritual sense, said of the rudiments of Jewish religion, in their inability to justify anyone, Gal. 4:9; of the Law, Heb. 7:18; in Rom. 5:6, RV, "weak" (KJV, "without strength"), of the inability of man to accomplish his salvation; (*c*) morally or ethically, 1 Cor. 8:7, 10; 9:22; (*d*) rhetorically, of God's actions according to the human estimate, 1 Cor. 1:25, "weakness," lit., "the weak things of God." See FEEBLE, SICK.

2. *adunatos* (ἀδύνατος, 102), lit., "not powerful," is translated "weak" in Rom. 15:1, of the infirmities of those whose scruples arise through lack of faith (see 14:22, 23), in the same sense as No. 1 (*c*); the change in the adjective (cf. 14:1) is due to the contrast with *dunatoi*, the "strong," who have not been specifically mentioned as such in ch. 14. See IMPOSSIBLE.

B. Verb.

astheneō (ἀσθενέω, 770), "to lack strength," is used in much the same way as A, No. 1, and translated "being ... weak" in Rom. 4:19, KJV (RV, "being weakened"); 8:3; 14:1, 2 (in some texts, 1 Cor. 8:9); 2 Cor. 11:21, 29 (twice); 12:10; 13:3, 4, 9. See DISEASED, IMPOTENT, SICK.

C. Noun.

astheneia (ἀσθένεια, 769), for which see INFIRMITY, is rendered "weakness," of the body, 1 Cor. 2:3; 15:43; 2 Cor. 11:30, RV; 12:5 (plural, RV), 9, 10, RV; Heb. 11:34; in 2 Cor. 13:4, "He was crucified through weakness" is said in respect of the physical sufferings to which Christ voluntarily submitted in giving Himself up to the death of the cross.

WEALTH

euporia (εὐπορία, 2142), primarily "facility" (*eu*, "well," *poros*, "a passage"), hence "plenty, wealth," occurs in Acts 19:25.¶ Cf. *euporeō*, "to be well provided for, to prosper," Acts 11:29.¶

Note: In 1 Cor. 10:24, the KJV, "*wealth*," RV, "*good*," is, lit., "the (thing) of the other."

WEAPONS

hoplon (ὅπλον, 3696), always in the plur., is translated "weapons" in John 18:3 and 2 Cor. 10:4, the latter metaphorically of those used in spiritual warfare. See ARMOR, INSTRUMENTS.

WEAR, WEARING

A. Verbs.

1. *phoreō* (φορέω, 5409), a frequentative form of *pherō*, "to bear," and denoting "repeated or habitual action," is chiefly used of clothing, weapons, etc., of soft raiment, Matt. 11:8; fine clothing, Jas. 2:3; the crown of thorns, John 19:5. See BEAR, No. 7.

2. *endidusko* (ἐνδιδύσκω, 1737), "to put on," is used in the active voice in Mark 15:17 (in good mss.; some have No. 3); in Luke 8:27 (middle voice), in some texts; the best have No. 3. For Luke 16:19, see CLOTHE, No. 3.¶

3. *enduō* (ἐνδύω, 1746) is rendered "to wear" in Luke 8:27 (middle voice; see No. 2). See CLOTHE, No. 2, PUT, No. 26.

4. *klinō* (κλίνω, 2827), "to bend, decline," is used of a day, "wearing" away, Luke 9:12 (in 24:29, "is far spent"). See BOW, No. 4, FLIGHT, B, LAY, No. 6, SPEND.

5. *hupōpiazō* (ὑπωπιάζω, 5299) is translated "wear (me) out" in Luke 18:5, RV (KJV, "weary"). For this and the somewhat different application in 1 Cor. 9:27, see BUFFET, No. 2.¶

B. Noun.

perithesis (περίθεσις, 4025), "a putting around or on" (*peri*, "around," *tithēmi*, "to put"), is used in 1 Pet. 3:3 of "wearing" jewels of gold (RV).¶

For WEARINESS, 2 Cor. 11:27, RV, see LABOR, No. 1

WEARY

1. *kopiaō* (κοπιάω, 2872), "to grow weary, be beaten out" (*kopos*, "a beating, toil"), is used of the Lord in John 4:6 (used in His own word "labor" in Matt. 11:28), in Rev. 2:3, RV. See LABOR, TOIL.

2. *kamnō* (κάμνω, 2577), "to be weary," is rendered "to wax weary" in Heb. 12:3, RV. See FAINT, No. 3, SICK.

3. *ekkakeō* or *enkakeō* (ἐκκακέω, 1573), for

which see FAINT, No. 2, is rendered "to be weary" in Gal. 6:9; 2 Thess. 3:13.

Note: For *hupōpiazō*, rendered "to weary" in Luke 18:5, KJV, see WEAR, A, No. 5.

WEATHER

1. *eudia* (εὐδία, 2105), akin to *eudios*, "calm," denotes "fair weather," Matt. 16:2.¶

2. *cheimōn* (χειμών, 5494), "winter," also "a winter storm," is translated "foul weather" in Matt. 16:3. See TEMPEST, WINTER.

For WEDDING see MARRIAGE

WEEK

sabbaton (σάββατον, 4521) is used (*a*) in the plural in the phrase "the first day of the week," Matt. 28:1; Mark 16:2, 9; Luke 24:1; John 20:1, 19; Acts 20:7; 1 Cor. 16:2. For this idiomatic use of the word see ONE, A, (5); (*b*) in the singular, Luke 18:12, "twice in the week," lit., "twice of the sabbath," i.e., twice in the days after the sabbath. See SABBATH.

WEEP, WEEPING

A. Verbs.

1. *klaiō* (κλαίω, 2799) is used of "any loud expression of grief," especially in mourning for the dead, Matt. 2:18; Mark 5:38, 39; 16:10; Luke 7:13; 8:52 (twice); John 11:31, 33 (twice); 20:11 (twice), 13, 15; Acts 9:39; otherwise, e.g., in exhortations, Luke 23:28; Rom. 12:15; Jas. 4:9; 5:1; negatively, "weep not," Luke 7:13; 8:52; 23:28; Rev. 5:5 (cf. Acts 21:13); in 18:9, RV, "shall weep" (KJV, "bewail"). See BEWAIL.

2. *dakruō* (δακρύω, 1145), "to shed tears" (*dakruon*, "a tear"), is used only of the Lord Jesus, John 11:35.¶

Note: Other synonymous verbs are *thrēneō*, "to mourn," of formal lamentation: see BEWAIL, Note (1); *alalazō*, "to wail"; *stenazō*, "to groan" (*oduromai*, "to lament audibly," is not used in NT; see the noun *odurmos*, "mourning").

B. Noun.

klauthmos (κλαυθμός, 2805), akin to A, No. 1, denotes "weeping, crying," Matt. 2:18; 8:12; 13:42, 50, RV (KJV, "wailing"); 22:13; 24:51; 25:30; Luke 13:28; Acts 20:37.¶

WEIGH, WEIGHT, WEIGHTY, WEIGHTIER

A. Verbs.

1. *bareō* (βαρέω, 916), "to weigh down," is so rendered in 2 Cor. 1:8, RV; see BURDEN, B, No. 1.

2. *histēmi* (ἵστημι, 2476), "to cause to stand," is used in Matt. 26:15, RV, "they

weighed (unto)" (of pieces of silver), KJV, metaphorically, "covenanted (with)."

B. Nouns.

1. *baros* (βάρος, 922), akin to A, is rendered "weight" in 2 Cor. 4:17. See BURDEN, A, No. 1.

2. *onkos* (ὄγκος, 3591) denotes "a bulk or mass"; hence, metaphorically, "an encumbrance, weight," Heb. 12:1.¶

C. Adjective.

barus (βαρύς, 926), "heavy" (akin to A and B, No. 1), is rendered "weighty" in 2 Cor. 10:10, of Paul's letters. The comparative degree is used in the neuter plural in Matt. 23:23, "(the) weightier matters (of the Law)." See GRIEVOUS, HEAVY.

WELCOME

1. *apodechomai* (ἀποδέχομαι, 588), "to receive gladly," is rendered "to welcome" in the RV of Luke 8:40; 9:11. See RECEIVE.

2. *hupolambanō* (ὑπολαμβάνω, 5274), "to take up, to entertain," is rendered "to welcome" in 3 John 8, RV, of a hearty "welcome" to servants of God. See RECEIVE.

WELL (Noun)

phrear (φρέαρ, 5421), "a pit," is translated a "well" in John 4:11, 12. See PIT.

Note: For *pēgē*, translated "well" in John 4:6 (twice), 14; 2 Pet. 2:17, see FOUNTAIN.

WELL (Adverb)

1. *kalōs* (καλῶς, 2573), "finely" (akin to *kalos*, "good, fair"), is usually translated "well," indicating what is done rightly; in the Epistles it is most frequent in 1 Tim. (3:4, 12, 13; 5:17); twice it is used as an exclamation of approval, Mark 12:32; Rom. 11:20; the comparative degree *kallion*, "very well," occurs in Acts 25:10. See GOOD, C, No. 1.

Note: The neuter form of the adjective *kalos*, with the article and the present participle of *poieō*, "to do," is translated "well-doing" in Gal. 6:9.

2. *eu* (εὖ, 2095), primarily the neuter of an old word, *eus*, "noble, good," is used (*a*) with verbs, e.g., Mark 14:7, "do (*poieō*) . . . good"; Acts 15:29 (*prassō*); Eph. 6:3 (*ginomai*, "to be"); (*b*) in replies, "good," "well done," Matt. 25:21, 23; in Luke 19:17, *eu ge* (in the best texts). The word is the opposite of *kakōs*, "evilly." See GOOD, C, No. 2.¶

Notes: (1) In 2 Tim. 1:18, *beltion*, the neuter form of what is used as the comparative degree of *agathos*, "good," is used adverbially and translated "very well."¶ (2) For John 2:10, "have well drunk" (RV, "freely"), see DRINK, B, No. 2. (3) *Hōs*, "as," with *kai*, "also (and)," is

rendered "as well as" in Acts 10:47 (*kathōs* in some mss.) and 1 Cor. 9:5. (4) In Heb 4:2 *kathaper*, "even as," with *kai*, is translated "as well as": see EVEN, No. 8.

WELL (do), WELL-DOING

A. Verbs.

1. *agathopoieō* (ἀγαθοποιέω, 15), "to do good" (*agathos*, "good," *poieō*, "to do"), is used (*a*) of such activity in general, 1 Pet. 2:15, "well-doing"; v. 20, "do well"; 3:6, 17; 3 John 11, "doeth good"; (*b*) of "acting for another's benefit," Mark 3:4; Luke 6:9, 33, 35.¶

2. *kalopoieō* (καλοποιέω, 2569), "to do well, excellently, act honorably" (*kalos*, "good," *poieō*, "to do"), occurs in 2 Thess. 3:13.¶ The two parts of the word occur separately in Rom. 7:21; 2 Cor. 13:7; Gal. 6:9; Jas. 4:17.

Notes: (1) The distinction between Nos. 1 and 2 follows that between *agathos* and *kalos* (see GOOD). (2) In John 11:12, KJV, *sōzō* (passive voice, "to be saved"), is rendered "he shall do well" (RV, "he will recover").

B. Noun.

agathopoiia (ἀγαθοποιία, 16), "well-doing" (akin to A, No. 1), occurs in 1 Pet. 4:19.¶

C. Adjective.

agathopoios (ἀγαθοποιός, 17), "doing good, beneficent," is translated "them that do well" in 1 Pet. 2:14, lit., "well-doing (ones)."¶

For WELL-BELOVED see BELOVED

WELL-NIGH

Note: This forms part of the translation of *sumplēroō*, "to fulfill," in Luke 9:51, "were well-nigh" come (see COME, No. 36), and *plēroō*, "to fulfill," in Acts 7:23, "was well-nigh . . .," lit., "a time (of forty years) was fulfilled (to him)" (see FULFILL, A, No. 1).

WELL PLEASED

A. Noun.

eudokia (εὐδοκία, 2107), "good pleasure," occurs in the genitive case in Luke 2:14, lit., "(men) of good pleasure" (SO RV marg.), RV, "(men) in whom He is well pleased" (the genitive is objective); the KJV, "good will (toward men)," follows the inferior texts which have the nominative. See DESIRE, PLEASURE, SEEM, WELL-PLEASING, WILL.

B. Verb.

eudokeō (εὐδοκέω, 2106), "to be well pleased": see PLEASE, A, No. 3, WILLING, B, No. 3.

WELL–PLEASING

A. Adjective.

euarestos (εὐάρεστος, 2101) is used in Rom. 12:1, 2, translated "acceptable (RV marg., "well-pleasing"); in the following the RV has "well-pleasing," Rom. 14:18; 2 Cor. 5:9; Eph. 5:10; in Phil. 4:18 and Col. 3:20 (RV and KJV); in Titus 2:9, RV, "well-pleasing" (KJV, "please . . . well"); in Heb. 13:21, RV and KJV. See ACCEPTABLE.¶

B. Verb.

euaresteō (εὐαρεστέω, 2100), akin to A, is rendered "to be well-pleasing" in Heb. 11:5, 6, RV (KJV, "please"); in Heb. 13:16, "is well pleased."¶

C. Noun.

eudokia (εὐδοκία, 2107), lit., "good pleasure," is rendered "well-pleasing" in Matt. 11:26 and Luke 10:21. See DESIRE, PLEASURE, SEEM, WELL PLEASED, WILL.

For WENT see GO

WEST

dusmē (δυσμή, 1424), "the quarter of the sun-setting" (*dusis*, "a sinking, setting"; *dunō*, "to sink"), hence, "the west," occurs in Matt. 8:11; 24:27; Luke 12:54 (some regard this as the sunset); 13:29; Rev. 21:13.¶

For WET, Luke 7:38, 44, RV, see WASH, No. 7

WHALE

kētos (κῆτος, 2785) denotes "a huge fish, a sea monster," Matt. 12:40.¶ In the Sept., Gen. 1:21; Job 3:8; 9:13; 26:12; Jonah 1:17 (twice); 2:1, 10.¶

WHAT

Notes: (1) Most frequently this is a translation of some form of the relative pronoun *hos* or the interrogative *tis*. (2) Other words are (*a*) *hoios*, "of what kind," e.g., 2 Cor. 10:11, RV (KJV, "such as"); 1 Thess. 1:5, "what manner of men"; 2 Tim. 3:11 (twice), lit., "what sorts of things," "what sorts of persecutions"; (*b*) *poios*, "what sort of," e.g., Matt. 21:23, 24, 27; 24:42, 43; Luke 5:19; 6:32–34; 20:2, 8; 24:19; John 12:33, "what manner of"; so in 18:32; 21:19; Rom. 3:27; 1 Cor. 15:35; in Jas. 4:14, "what"; 1 Pet. 2:20 and Rev. 3:3 (ditto); 1 Pet. 1:11, "what manner of"; (*c*) *hopoios*, "what sort of," 1 Cor. 3:13; "what manner of," 1 Thess. 1:9; (*d*) *hosos*, "how great," Mark 6:30 (twice), RV, "whatsoever"; Acts 15:12; Rom. 3:19, "what things soever"; Jude 10 (1st part), "what soever

things," RV; (2nd part) "what"; (*e*) *posos*, "how great, how much," 2 Cor. 7:11, "what (earnest care)," RV (*posos* here stands for the repeated words in the Eng. versions, the adjective not being repeated in the original); (*f*) *hostis*, "what (things)," Phil. 3:7; (*g*) in Matt. 26:40, *houtōs*, "thus, so," is used as an exclamatory expression, translated "What" (in a word immediately addressed by the Lord to Peter), lit., "So"; (*h*) for *potapos*, rendered "what" in Mark 13:1 (2nd part), KJV, see MANNER; (*i*) in 1 Cor. 6:16, 19, KJV, the particle *ē*, "or" (RV), is rendered "What?"; in 1 Cor. 14:36, KJV and RV, "what?" (*j*) in 1 Cor. 11:22, *gar*, "in truth, indeed," has its exclamatory use "What?" (3) In John 5:19 "but what" translates a phrase, lit., "if not anything." (4) In Matt. 8:33 "what" is, lit., "the things" (neuter plural of the article).

WHATSOEVER

Note: For this see *Notes* on words under WHAT. Frequently by the addition of the particle *an*, or the conjunction *ean*, "if," the phrase has the more general idea of "whatsoever," e.g., with *hos*, Matt. 10:11; with *hosos*, Matt. 17:12; with *hostis*, neuter form, Luke 10:35.

For WHEAT see CORN

For WHEEL, Jas. 3:6, RV, see COURSE, A, No. 4

For WHEN, WHENCE, WHENSOEVER, WHERE, etc., see †, p. 1

WHEREFORE

Note: This represents (1) some phrases introduced by the preposition *dia*, "on account of," *dia touto*, "on account of this," e.g., Matt. 12:31; Rom. 5:12; Eph. 1:15; 3 John 10; *dia hēn* (the accusative feminine of *hos*, "who"), "on account of which" (*aitia*, "a cause," being understood), e.g., Acts 10:21 (with *aitia*, expressed, Titus 1:13; Heb. 2:11); *dia ti* "on account of what?" (sometimes as one word, *diati*), e.g., Luke 19:23; Rom. 9:32; 2 Cor. 11:11; Rev. 17:7; (2) *dio* = *dia ho* (the neuter of the relative pronoun *hos*), "on account of which (thing)," e.g., Matt. 27:8; Acts 15:19; 20:31; 24:26; 25:26; 27:25, 34; Rom. 1:24; 15:7; 1 Cor. 12:3; 2 Cor. 2:8; 5:9; 6:17; Eph. 2:11; 3:13; 4:8, 25; 5:14; Phil. 2:9; 1 Thess. 5:11; Philem. 8; Heb. 3:7, 10; 10:5; 11:16; 12:12, 28; 13:12; Jas. 1:21; 4:6; 1 Pet. 1:13; 2 Pet. 1:10, 12; 3:14; (3) *dioper*, "for which very reason" (a strengthened form of the preceding), 1 Cor. 8:13; 10:14 (14:13 in some mss.);¶ (4) *hothen* (which denotes "whence," when used of direction or source, e.g., Matt. 12:44), used of cause and denoting "wherefore" in Heb. 2:17; 3:1; 7:25; 8:3; (5) *ti*, "what, why," John 9:27; Acts 22:30; Gal. 3:19, KJV (RV, "what"); (6) *heneka* with *tinos* (the genitive case of *ti*), "because of what," Acts 19:32; (7) *charin* with *hou*, the genitive case, neuter of *hos*, "for the sake of what," Luke 7:47; (8) *eis*, "unto," with *ti*, "what," Matt. 14:31; with *ho*, "which" (the accusative neuter of *hos*), 2 Thess. 1:11, KJV (RV, "to which end"); (9) *ara*, "so," 2 Cor. 7:12, KJV (RV, "so"); with *ge*, "at least," Matt. 7:20, KJV (RV, "therefore"); (10) *hina*, "in order that," with *ti*, "what," Matt. 9:4; (11) *toigaroun*, "therefore," rendered "wherefore" in Heb. 12:1, KJV; (12) in Matt. 26:50, *epi*, "unto," with *ho*, as in No. (8) above, KJV, "wherefore (art thou come)?" RV, "(*do* that) for which (thou art come)"; (13) *oun*, a particle expressing sequence or consequence, e.g., Matt. 24:26; Acts 6:3; (14) *hōste*, "so that," "wherefore," e.g., Rom. 7:12, 13; 1 Cor. 10:12; 11:27, 33; 14:22, 39; 2 Cor. 5:16; Gal. 3:24; 4:7; Phil. 4:1; 1 Thess. 4:18; 1 Pet. 4:19.

For **WHETHER** see †, p. 1

WHICH

Notes: (1) This is the translation of (*a*) the article with nouns, adjectives, numerals, participles, etc., e.g., "that which," etc.; (*b*) the relative pronoun *hos*, "who," in one of its forms (a frequent use); (*c*) *hostis*, "whoever," differing from *hos* by referring to a subject in general, as one of a class, e.g., Rom. 2:15; Gal. 4:24 (twice); 5:19; Rev. 2:24; 20:4; (*d*) the interrogative pronoun *tis*, "who? which?," e.g., Matt. 6:27; John 8:46; (*e*) *hoios*, "of what kind," e.g., Phil. 1:30; (*f*) *poios*, the interrogative of (*e*), e.g., John 10:32; (*g*) *hosos*, "whatsoever," etc.; plural, how many, translated "which" in Acts 9:39. (2) In Acts 8:26, KJV, *hautē* (the feminine of *houtos*, "this"), "the same" (RV), is translated "which." (3) In the triple title of God in Rev. 1:4, 8; 4:8, "which" is the translation, firstly, of the article with the present participle of *eimi*, to be, lit., "the (One) being," secondly, of the article with the imperfect tense of *eimi* (impossible of lit. translation, the title not being subject to grammatical change), thirdly, of the article with the present participle of *erchomai*, to come, lit., "the coming (One)"; in 11:17 and 16:5 the wording of the KJV and RV differs; in 11:17 the KJV follows the inferior mss. by adding "and art to come" (RV omits); in 16:5, the KJV, "and shalt be," represents *kai* ("and") followed by the article and the future participle of *eimi*, "to

be," lit., "and the (One) about to be"; the RV substitues the superior reading "Thou Holy One," lit., "the holy (One)": see HOLY, B, No. 2. (4) In Phil. 2:21, KJV, "the things of Jesus Christ" (RV, is rendered "the things which are Jesus Christ's."

WHILE, WHILES, WHILST

Notes: (1) See LITTLE, B, No. 1. (2) In Matt. 13:21, *proskairos estin*, lit., "is for a season," is rendered "dureth (RV, endureth) for a while." (3) *Chronos*, "time," is rendered "while" in Luke 18:4; John 7:33; 12:35 (1st part); 1 Cor. 16:7; *kairos*, "a season," "a while," Luke 8:13; in Acts 19:22, RV, "while" (KJV, "season"); for the different meanings of these words see SEASON. (4) In Acts 18:18, KJV, "a good while," is, lit., "sufficient days," RV, "many days." (5) In Acts 28:6, KJV, *epi polu*, lit., "upon much," is rendered "a great while" (RV, "long"). (6) For Mark 1:35 see DAY, B. (7) In Mark 15:44 *palai*, "long ago," is rendered "any while." (8) In Acts 27:33 and Heb. 3:13 *achri* (or *achris*) followed by *hou*, the genitive case of the relative pronoun *hos*, lit., "until which," is rendered "while"; cf. *en hō̧*, in Mark 2:19; Luke 5:34; John 5:7; *en tō̧*, in Luke 1:21, RV, "while"; in Heb. 3:15, "while it is said," is, lit., "in the being said" (*en*, with the article and the pres. infin., passive of *legō*); so, e.g., in Matt. 13:25 (9) In Heb. 10:33, AV., "whilst ye were made," partly translating the present participle of *theatrizomai*, "to become a gazing-stock," RV, "being made"; in the 2nd part, *ginomai*, "to become," is translated "whilst ye became," KJV (RV, "becoming").¶ (10) The conjunction *heōs*, "until," etc., has the meaning "while" in Matt. 14:22; Mark 6:45; 14:32; in some texts, John 9:4; 12:35, 36; with *hotou*, "whatever" (an oblique case, neuter, of *hostis*, "whoever"), "whiles," Matt. 5:25. (11) In Acts 20:11 *hikanos*, "sufficient," is rendered "a long while." (12) *Hōs*, as, "while" in Luke 24:32 (twice); John 12:35, 36; Acts 1:10; 10:17. (13) *Hotan*, "when," is rendered "while" in 1 Cor. 3:4, KJV (RV, "when"). (14) *Hote*, "when," is rendered "while" in John 17:12; Heb. 9:17. (15) In John 4:31 *metaxu*, "between," used with *en tō̧*, "in the," is rendered "meanwhile"; in Rom. 2:15 *metaxu* is itself rendered "the mean while" (RV, "between"). (16) In Acts 18:18, RV, *hikanos* is rendered "many" (KJV, "good"). (17) In 1 Pet. 1:6, RV, *oligon*, "a little," is rendered "for a little while" (KJV, "for a season").

WHISPERER, WHISPERING

1. *psithuristēs* (ψιθυριστής, 5588), "a whisperer," occurs in an evil sense in Rom. 1:29.¶

2. *psithurismos* (ψιθυρισμός, 5587), "a whispering," is used of "secret slander" in 2 Cor. 12:20.¶ In the Sept., Eccl. 10:11, of "a murmured enchantment."¶

Note: Synonymous with No. 1 is *katalalos*, "a backbiter" (Rom. 1:30¶), the distinction being that this denotes one guilty of open calumny, *psithuristēs*, one who does it clandestinely.

For WHIT see EVERY WHIT and NOTHING, No. 2

WHITE (Adjective and Verb)

A. Adjective.

leukos (λευκός, 3022) is used of (*a*) clothing (sometimes in the sense of "bright"), Matt. 17:2; 28:3; Mark 9:3; 16:5; Luke 9:29; John 20:12; Acts 1:10; symbolically, Rev. 3:4, 5, 18; 4:4; 6:11; 7:9, 13; 19:14 (2nd part); (*b*) hair, Matt. 5:36; Christ's head and hair (in a vision; cf. Dan. 7:9), Rev. 1:14 (twice); ripened grain, John 4:35; a stone, Rev. 2:17, an expression of the Lord's special delight in the overcomer, the new name on it being indicative of a secret communication of love and joy; a horse (in a vision), 6:2; 19:11 14 (1st part); a cloud, 14:14; the throne of God, 20:11.¶

Note: Lampros, "bright, clear," is rendered "white" in Rev. 15:6, KJV, of "white (linen)" (RV, "bright," following those mss. which have *lithon* "stone"); in 19:8 (RV, "bright"). See BRIGHT, CLEAR, GOODLY, *Note,* GORGEOUS.

B. Verbs.

1. *leukainō* (λευκαίνω, 3021), "to whiten, make white" (akin to A), is used in Mark 9:3; figuratively in Rev. 7:14.¶

2. *koniaō* (κονιάω, 2867), from *konia,* "dust, lime," denotes "to whiten, whitewash," of tombs, Matt. 23:27; figuratively of a hypocrite, Acts 23:3.¶ In the Sept., Deut. 27:2, 4; Prov. 21:9.¶

For WHITHER, WHITHERSOEVER, see †, p. 1.

WHO, WHOM, WHOSE

Notes: These are usually the translations of forms of the relative pronoun *hos,* or of the interrogative pronoun *tis;* otherwise of *hostis,* "whoever," usually of a more general subject than *hos,* e.g., Mark 15:7; Luke 23:19; Gal. 2:4; *hosos,* "as many as," Heb. 2:15; in Acts 13:7, KJV, *houtos,* "this (man)," is translated "who," RV, "the same."

WHOLE (made), WHOLLY, WHOLESOME

A. Adjectives.

1. *holos* (ὅλος, 3650), for which see ALL, A, No. 3, and ALTOGETHER, signifies "whole," (*a*) with a noun, e.g., Matt. 5:29, 30; Mark 8:36; 15:1, 16, 33; Luke 11:36 (1st part), though *holon* may here be used adverbially with *phōteinon,* "wholly light" [as in the 2nd part, RV, "wholly (full of light)"]; John 11:50; 1 Cor. 12:17 (1st part); 1 John 2:2; 5:19; (*b*) absolutely, as a noun, e.g., Matt. 13:33; 1 Cor. 12:17 (2nd part).

2. *pas* (πᾶς, 3956), for which see ALL, A, No. 1, is sometimes translated "the whole" when used with the article, e.g., Matt. 8:32, 34; Rom. 8:22.

3. *hapas* (ἅπας, 537), for which see ALL, A, No. 2, is rendered "the whole," e.g., in Luke 19:37; 23:1.

4. *holoklēros* (ὁλόκληρος, 3648), from No. 1 and *klēros,* "a lot," is rendered "whole" in 1 Thess. 5:23: see ENTIRE.

5. *hugiēs* (ὑγιής, 5199) (cf. Eng., "hygiene") is used especially in the Gospels of making sick folk "whole," Matt. 12:13; 15:31; Mark 3:5; 5:34; Luke 6:10; John 5:4, 6, 9, 11, 14, 15; 7:23; also Acts 4:10; of "sound (speech)," Titus 2:8. See SOUND.¶

6. *holotelēs* (ὁλοτελής, 3651), "wholly," 1 Thess. 5:23, is lit., "whole-complete" (A, No. 1, and *telos,* "an end"), i.e., "through and through"; the apostle's desire is that the sanctification of the believer may extend to every part of his being. The word is similar in meaning to No. 4; *holoklēros* draws attention to the person as a "whole," *holotelēs,* to the several parts which constitute him.¶

Note: In 1 Tim. 4:15, the sentence freely rendered "give thyself wholly to them" is, lit., "be in these (things)."

B. Verbs.

1. *hugiainō* (ὑγιαίνω, 5198), "to be in good health," akin to A, No. 5, is rendered "they that are whole" in Luke 5:31; "whole" in 7:10 (present participle); "wholesome" in 1 Tim. 6:3, KJV (RV, "sound"; marg., "healthful"). See HEALTH, SOUND.

2. *sōzō* (σώζω, 4982), "to save," is sometimes rendered "to make whole," and, in the passive voice, "to be made whole," or "to be whole," e.g., Matt. 9:21, 22 (twice), and parallel passages; Acts 4:9. See HEAL, SAVE.

3. *iaomai* (ἰάομαι, 2390), "to heal," is rendered "to make whole," Matt. 15:28; Acts 9:34, KJV (RV, "healeth"). See HEAL.

4. *ischuō* (ἰσχύω, 2480), "to be strong," is

rendered "they that are whole" in Matt. 9:12 and Mark 2:17. See ABLE, B, No. 4.

5. *diasōzō* (διασώζω, 1295), "to save thoroughly" (*dia*), is used in the passive voice and rendered "were made whole" in Matt. 14:36, RV (KJV, "were made perfectly whole"). See ESCAPE, HEAL, SAVE.

For WHORE, WHOREMONGER see FORNICATION, HARLOT

WHOSO, WHOSOEVER

Note: The same pronouns as those under WHO are used for the above, often with the addition of the particle *an* and a change of construction when a generalization is expressed. Some texts in Mark 15:6 have *hosper*, a strengthened form of *hos*, KJV, "whomsoever." For sentences introduced by the conjunction *ei* or *ean*, "if," see †, p. 1.

For WHY see †, p. 1

WICKED

1. *ponēros* (πονηρός, 4190), for which see BAD, No. 2, EVIL, A and B, No. 2, is translated "wicked" in the KJV and RV in Matt. 13:49; 18:32; 25:26; Luke 19:22; Acts 18:14; 1 Cor. 5:13; in the following the RV substitutes "evil" for KJV, "wicked": Matt. 12:45 (twice); 13:19; 16:4; Luke 11:26; Col. 1:21; 2 Thess. 3:2; and in the following, where Satan is mentioned as "the (or that) evil one": Matt. 13:38; Eph. 6:16; 1 John 2:13, 14; 3:12 (1st part); 5:18; in v. 19 for KJV, "wickedness"; he is so called also in KJV and RV in John 17:15; 2 Thess. 3:3; KJV only in Luke 11:4; in 3 John 10, KJV, the word is translated "malicious," RV, "wicked."

2. *athesmos* (ἄθεσμος, 113), "lawless" (*a*, negative, *thesmos*, "law, custom"), "wicked," occurs in 2 Pet. 2:7; 3:17.¶ An instance of the use of the word is found in the papyri, where a father breaks off his daughter's engagement because he learnt that her fiancé was giving himself over to lawless deeds (Moulton and Milligan, *Vocab.*).

Notes: (1) In Matt. 21:41, KJV, *kakos* (for which see BAD, No. 1, EVIL, A, No. 1), is translated "wicked" (RV, "miserable"). (2) In Acts 2:23 and 2 Thess 2:8, KJV, *anomos*, "lawless" (RV), is translated "wicked."

WICKEDNESS

1. *ponēria* (πονηρία, 4189), akin to *ponēros* (see above, No. 1), is always rendered "wickedness" save in Acts 3:26: see INIQUITY, No. 4.

2. *kakia* (κακία, 2549), "evil," is rendered "wickedness" in Acts 8:22; RV in Jas. 1:21, KJV, "naughtiness." See EVIL, B, No. 1, MALICE.

Notes: (1) For the KJV of 1 John 5:19 see WICKED, No. 1. (2) In Acts 25:5, KJV, the word *atopos* (RV, "amiss") is incorrectly rendered "wickedness."

For WIDE see BROAD

WIDOW

chēra (χήρα, 5503), Matt. 28:13 (in some texts); Mark 12:40, 42, 43; Luke 2:37; 4:25, 26, lit., "a woman a widow"; 7:12; 18:3, 5; 20:47; 21:2, 3; Acts 6:1; 9:39, 41; 1 Tim. 5:3 (twice), 4, 5, 11, 16 (twice); Jas. 1:27; 1 Tim. 5:9 refers to elderly "widows" (not an ecclesiastical "order"), recognized, for relief or maintenance by the church (cf. vv. 3, 16), as those who had fulfilled the conditions mentioned; where relief could be ministered by those who had relatives that were "widows" (a likely circumstance in large families), the church was not to be responsible; there is an intimation of the tendency to shelve individual responsibility at the expense of church funds. In Rev. 18:7, it is used figuratively of a city forsaken.¶

WIFE, WIVES

1. *gunē* (γυνή, 1135) denotes (1) "a woman, married or unmarried" (see WOMAN); (2) "a wife," e.g., Matt. 1:20; 1 Cor. 7:3, 4; in 1 Tim. 3:11, RV, "women," the reference may be to the "wives" of deacons, as the KJV takes it.

2. *gunaikeios* (γυναικεῖος, 1134), an adjective denoting "womanly, female," is used as a noun in 1 Pet. 3:7, KJV, "wife," RV, "woman."¶

Note: In John 19:25 the article stands idiomatically for "the *wife* (of)"; in Matt. 1:6, the article is rendered "her *that had been the wife* (of)."

WIFE'S MOTHER

penthera (πενθερά, 3994) denotes "a mother-in-law," Matt. 8:14; 10:35; Mark 1:30; Luke 4:38; 12:53 (twice).¶

WILD

agrios (ἄγριος, 66) denotes (*a*) "of or in fields" (*agros*, "a field"), hence, "not domestic," said of honey, Matt. 3:4; Mark 1:6; (*b*) "savage, fierce," Jude 13, RV, metaphorically, "wild (waves)," KJV, "raging."¶ It is used in the papyri of a malignant wound.

Note: In Rev. 6:8 the RV renders *thērion* (plural) "wild beasts" (KJV, "beasts").

WILDERNESS

1. *erēmia* (ἐρημία, 2047), "an uninhabited place," is translated "wilderness"in the KJV of Matt. 15:33 and Mark 8:4 (RV, "a desert place"); RV and KJV, "wilderness" in 2 Cor. 11:26. See DESERT, A. (In the Sept., Isa. 60:20; Ezek. 35:4, 9.¶)

2. *erēmos* (ἔρημος, 2048), an adjective signifying "desolate, deserted, lonely," is used as a noun, and rendered "wilderness" 32 times in the KJV; in Matt. 24:26 and John 6:31, RV, "wilderness" (KJV, "desert"). For the RV, "deserts" in Luke 5:16 and 8:29 see DESERT, B.

WILES

methodia, or —*eia* (μεθοδία, 3180) denotes "craft, deceit" (*meta*, "after," *hodos*, "a way"), "a cunning device, a wile," and is translated "wiles (of error)" in Eph. 4:14, RV [KJV paraphrases it, "they lie in wait (to deceive)"], lit., "(with a view to) the craft (singular) of deceit"; in 6:11, "the wiles (plural) (of the Devil.)"¶

WILFULLY, WILLFULLY

A. Adverb.

hekousiōs (ἐκουσείως, 1596) denotes "voluntarily, willingly," Heb. 10:26, (of sinning) "willfully"; in 1 Pet. 5:2, "willingly" (of exercising oversight over the flock of God).¶

B. Verb.

thelō (θέλω, 2309), "to will," used in the present participle in 2 Pet. 3:5, is rendered "willfully (forget)" in the RV, KJV, "willingly (are ignorant of)," lit., "this escapes them (i.e., their notice) willing (i.e. of their own will)." See WILL, C, No. 1, WILLING, B, No. 1.

WILL, WOULD

A. Nouns.

1. *thelēma* (θέλημα, 2307) signifies (*a*) objectively, "that which is willed, of the will of God," e.g., Matt. 18:14; Mark 3:35, the fulfilling being a sign of spiritual relationship to the Lord; John 4:34; 5:30; 6:39, 40; Acts 13:22, plural, "my desires"; Rom. 2:18; 12:2, lit., "the will of God, the good and perfect and acceptable"; here the repeated article is probably resumptive, the adjectives describing the will, as in the Eng. versions; Gal. 1:4; Eph. 1:9; 5:17, "of the Lord"; Col. 1:9; 4:12; 1 Thess. 4:3; 5:18, where it means "the gracious design," rather than "the determined resolve"; 2 Tim. 2:26, which should read "which have been taken captive by him" [(*autou*), i.e., by the Devil; the RV, "by the Lord's servant" is an interpretation; it does not correspond to the Greek] unto His (*ekeinou*) will" (i.e., "God's will"; the different

pronoun refers back to the subject of the sentence, viz., God); Heb. 10:10; Rev. 4:11, RV, "because of Thy will"; of human will, e.g., 1 Cor. 7:37; (*b*) subjectively, the "will" being spoken of as the emotion of being desirous, rather than as the thing "willed"; of the "will" of God, e.g., Rom. 1:10; 1 Cor. 1:1; 2 Cor. 1:1; 8:5; Eph. 1:1, 5, 11; Col. 1:1; 2 Tim. 1:1; Heb. 10:7, 9, 36; 1 John 2:17; 5:14; of human "will," e.g., John 1:13; Eph. 2:3, "the desires of the flesh"; 1 Pet. 4:3 (in some texts); 2 Pet. 1:21. See DESIRE, A, No. 5, PLEASURE, *Note* (1).

2. *thelēsis* (θέλησις, 2308) denotes "a willing, a wishing" [similar to No. 1 (*b*)], Heb. 2:4.¶

3. *boulēma* (βούλημα, 1013), "a deliberate design, that which is purposed," Rom. 9:19; 1 Pet. 4:3 (in the best texts). See PURPOSE, A, No. 1.

4. *eudokia* (εὐδοκία, 2107) (*eu*, "well," *dokeō*, "to think") is rendered "good will" in Luke 2:14, KJV (see WELL PLEASED); Phil. 1:15; see DESIRE, PLEASURE, SEEM, WELL-PLEASING.

5. *eunoia* (εὔνοια, 2133), "good will" (*eu*, "well," *nous*, "the mind"), occurs in Eph. 6:7 (in some texts, 1 Cor. 7:3).¶

Notes: (1) In Acts 13:36, KJV, *boulē*, "counsel" (RV), is translated "will." (2) In Rev. 17:17, KJV, *gnōmē*, "an opinion," RV, "mind," is translated "will." (3) For "will-worship," Col. 2:23, see WORSHIP, B, No. 2.

B. Adjectives.

1. *hekōn* (ἑκών, 1635), "of free will, willingly," occurs in Rom. 8:20, RV, "of its own will" (KJV, "willingly"); 1 Cor. 9:17, RV, "of my own will" (KJV, "willingly").¶ In the Sept., Exod. 21:13; Job 36:19.¶

2. *akōn* (ἄκων, 210), *a*, negative, and No. 1, "unwillingly," occurs in 1 Cor. 9:17, RV, "not of mine own will" (KJV, "against my will").¶ In the Sept., Job 14:17.¶

C. Verbs.

When "will" is not part of the translation of the future tense of verbs, it represents one of the following:

1. *thelō* (θέλω, 2309), for the force of which see DESIRE, B, No. 6, usually expresses "desire" or "design"; it is most frequently translated by "will" or "would"; see especially Rom. 7:15, 16, 18–21. In 1 Tim. 2:4, RV, "willeth" signifies the gracious "desire" of God for all men to be saved; not all are "willing" to accept His condition, depriving themselves either by the self-established criterion of their perverted reason, or because of their self-indulgent preference for sin. In John 6:21, the KJV renders the verb "willingly" (RV, "they were willing"); in 2 Pet. 3:5, KJV, the present participle is translated "willingly" (RV, "wilfully").

The following are RV renderings for the KJV, "will": Matt. 16:24, 25, "would"; "wouldest," 19:21 and 20:21; "would," 20:26, 27; Mark 8:34, 35; 10:43, 44; "would fain," Luke 13:31; "would," John 6:67; "willeth," 7:17; in 8:44, "it is your will (to do)"; "wouldest," Rom. 13:3; "would," 1 Cor. 14:35 and 1 Pet. 3:10.

2. *boulomai* (βούλομαι, 1014), for the force of which see DESIRE, B, No. 7, usually expresses the deliberate exercise of volition more strongly than No. 1, and is rendered as follows in the RV, where the KJV has "will": Matt. 11:27 and Luke 10:22, "willeth"; Jas. 4:4, "would"; in Jas. 3:4, RV, "willeth" (KJV, "listeth"). In Jas. 1:18 the perfect participle is translated "of His own will," lit. "having willed."

3. *mellō* (μέλλω, 3195), "to be about to," is translated "will" in Matt. 2:13 and John 7:35 (twice); "wilt," John 14:22; "will," Acts 17:31; "wouldest," 23:20; "will," 27:10 and Rev. 3:16. See ABOUT, B.

WILLING (Adjective and Verb)

A. Adjectives.

1. *prothumos* (πρόθυμος, 4289) is rendered "willing" in Matt. 26:41; Mark 14:38, RV. See READY, No. 2.

2. *hekousios* (ἑκούσιος, 1595**), "willing," is used with *kata* in Philem. 14, lit., "according to willing," RV, "of free will" (KJV, "willingly").¶

B. Verbs.

1. *thelō* (θέλω, 2309) is rendered "ye were willing" in John 5:35. See WILL, C, No. 1.

2. *boulomai* (βούλομαι, 1014) is rendered "(if) Thou be willing" in Luke 22:42; in 2 Pet. 3:9, KJV (RV, "wishing"). See WILL, C, No. 2.

3. *eudokeō* (εὐδοκέω, 2106), "to be well pleased, to think it good," is rendered "we are willing" in 2 Cor. 5:8; in 1 Thess. 2:8, KJV, "we were willing" (RV, "we were well pleased"). See PLEASE, PLEASURE.

Notes: (1) In 2 Cor. 8:3, KJV, *authairetos*, "of one's own accord" (RV), is rendered "willing of themselves"; in v. 17, "of his own accord." See ACCORD.¶ (2) For "willing to communicate," 1 Tim. 6:18, see COMMUNICATE, C.

For WILLING MIND see READINESS

WILLINGLY

Notes: (1) For *hekōn* see WILL, B, No. 1. (2) For *hekousiōs*, see WILLFULLY. (3) For Philem. 14 see WILLING, A, No. 2. (4) For 2 Pet. 3:5 see WILL, C, No. 1.

For WIN see POSSESS, A, No. 2

WIND (Noun)

1. *anemos* (ἄνεμος, 417), besides its literal meaning, is used metaphorically in Eph. 4:14, of variable teaching. In Matt. 24:31 and Mark 13:27 the four "winds" stand for the four cardinal points of the compass; so in Rev. 7:1, "the four winds of the earth" (cf. Jer. 49:36; Dan. 7:2); the contexts indicate that these are connected with the execution of divine judgments. Deissmann (*Bible Studies*) and Moulton and Milligan (*Vocab.*) illustrate the phrase from the papyri.

2. *pnoē* (πνοή, 4157), "a blowing, blast" (akin to *pneō*, "to blow"), is used of the rushing "wind" at Pentecost, Acts 2:2. See BREATH.

3. *pneuma* (πνεῦμα, 4151) is translated "wind" in John 3:8 (RV, marg., "the Spirit breatheth," the probable meaning); in Heb. 1:7 the RV has "winds" for KJV, "spirits." See SPIRIT.

Notes: (1) For *pneō*, "to blow" ("wind" in Acts 27:40), see BLOW, No. 1. (2) For *anemizō*, Jas. 1:6, "driven by the wind," see DRIVE, No. 8.¶

WIND (Verb)

1. *deō* (δέω, 1210), "to bind," is translated "wound (it in linen clothes)," John 19:40, KJV, of the body of Christ (RV, "bound"). See BIND, No. 1, TIE.

2. *sustellō* (συστέλλω, 4958) is translated "wound ... up" in Acts 5:6 (RV, "wrapped ... round"). See SHORTEN, No. 2, WRAP.

3. *eneileō* (ἐνειλέω, 1750), "to roll in, wind in," is used in Mark 15:46, of "winding" the cloth around the Lord's body, RV, "wound" (KJV, "wrapped").¶

WINDOW

thuris (θυρίς, 2376), a diminutive of *thura*, "a door," occurs in Acts 20:9; 2 Cor. 11:33.¶

WINE

1. *oinos* (οἶνος, 3631) is the general word for "wine." The mention of the bursting of the wineskins, Matt. 9:17; Mark 2:22; Luke 5:37, implies fermentation. See also Eph. 5:18 (cf. John 2:10; 1 Tim. 3:8; Titus 2:3). In Matt. 27:34, the RV has "wine" (KJV, "vinegar," translating the inferior reading *oxos*).

The drinking of "wine" could be a stumbling block and the apostle enjoins abstinence in this respect, as in others, so as to avoid giving an occasion of stumbling to a brother, Rom. 14:21. Contrast 1 Tim. 5:23, which has an entirely different connection. The word is used metaphorically (*a*) of the evils ministered to the nations by religious Babylon, 14:8; 17:2; 18:3;

(b) of the contents of the cup of divine wrath upon the nations and Babylon, Rev. 14:10; 16:19; 19:15.

2. *gleukos* (γλεῦκος, 1098) denotes sweet "new wine," or must, Acts 2:13, where the accusation shows that it was intoxicant and must have been undergoing fermentation some time.¶ In the Sept., Job 32:19.¶

Note: In instituting the Lord's Supper He speaks of the contents of the cup as the "fruit of the vine." So Mark 14:25.

For GIVEN TO WINE see BRAWLER, No. 1

WINEBIBBER

oinopotēs (οἰνοπότης, 3630), "a wine drinker" (*oinos*, and *potēs*, "a drinker"), is used in Matt. 11:19; Luke 7:34.¶ In the Sept., Prov. 23:20.¶

For WINEBIBBINGS see EXCESS, *Note* (2)

WINEPRESS, WINE-VAT

1. *lēnos* (ληνός, 3025) denotes "a trough or vat," used especially for the treading of grapes, Matt. 21:33. Not infrequently they were dug out in the soil or excavated in a rock, as in the rock vats in Palestine today. In Rev. 14:19, 20 (twice) and 19:15 (where *oinos* is added, lit., "the winepress of the wine") the word is used metaphorically with reference to the execution of divine judgment upon the gathered foes of the Jews at the close of this age preliminary to the establishment of the millennial kingdom.¶

2. *hupolēnion* (ὑπολήνιον, 5276) was "a vessel" or "trough" beneath the press itself (*hupo*, "beneath," and No. 1), for receiving the juice, Mark 12:1, RV, "a pit for the winepress."¶ In the Sept., Isa. 16:10; Joel 3:13; Hag. 2:16; Zech. 14:10.¶

For WINESKINS see SKIN

WING

pterux (πτέρυξ, 4420) is used of birds, Matt. 23:37; Luke 13:34; symbolically in Rev. 12:14, RV, "the two wings of the great eagle" (KJV, "two wings of a great eagle"), suggesting the definiteness of the action, the "wings" indicating rapidity and protection, an allusion, perhaps, to Exod. 19:4 and Deut. 32:11, 12; of the "living creatures" in a vision, Rev. 4:8; 9:9.¶ Cf. *pterugion*, "a pinnacle."

For WINK AT see OVERLOOK

WINTER (Noun and Verb)

A. Noun.

cheimōn (χειμών, 5494) denotes "winter," in Matt. 24:20; Mark 13:18; John 10:22; 2 Tim. 4:21. See TEMPEST.

B. Verb.

paracheimazō (παραχειμάζω, 3914) denotes "to winter at a place" (*para*, at, and A), Acts 27:12 (2nd part); 28:11; 1 Cor. 16:6; Titus 3:12.¶

Note: In Acts 27:12 (1st part) *paracheimasia*, "a wintering," is rendered "(to) winter in."¶

WIPE

1. *apomassō* (ἀπομάσσω, 631), "to wipe off, wipe clean" (*apo*, "from," *massō*, "to touch, handle"), is used in the middle voice, of "wiping" dust from the feet, Luke 10:11.¶

2. *ekmassō* (ἐκμάσσω, 1591), "to wipe out" (*ek*), "wipe dry," is used of "wiping" tears from Christ's feet, Luke 7:38, 44; John 11:2; 12:3; of Christ's "wiping" the disciples' feet, John 13:5.¶

3. *exaleiphō* (ἐξαλείφω, 1813), "to wipe out or away" (*ek*, or *ex*, "out," *aleiphō*, "to anoint"), is used metaphorically of "wiping" away tears from the eyes, Rev. 7:17; 21:4. See BLOT OUT.

WISDOM

1. *sophia* (σοφία, 4678) is used with reference to (a) God, Rom. 11:33; 1 Cor. 1:21, 24; 2:7; Eph. 3:10; Rev. 7:12; (b) Christ, Matt. 13:54; Mark 6:2; Luke 2:40, 52; 1 Cor. 1:30; Col. 2:3; Rev. 5:12; (c) "wisdom" personified, Matt. 11:19; Luke 7:35; 11:49; (d) human "wisdom" (1) in spiritual things, Luke 21:15; Acts 6:3, 10; 7:10; 1 Cor. 2:6 (1st part); 12:8; Eph. 1:8, 17; Col. 1:9, RV, "(spiritual) wisdom," 28; 3:16; 4:5; Jas. 1:5; 3:13, 17; 2 Pet. 3:15; Rev. 13:18; 17:9; (2) in the natural sphere, Matt. 12:42; Luke 11:31; Acts 7:22; 1 Cor. 1:17, 19, 20, 21 (twice), 22; 2:1, 4, 5, 6 (2nd part), 13; 3:19; 2 Cor. 1:12; Col. 2:23; (3) in its most debased form, Jas. 3:15, "earthly, sensual, devilish" (marg., "demoniacal").¶

2. *phronēsis* (φρόνησις, 5428), "understanding, prudence," i.e., a right use of *phrēn*, "the mind," is translated "wisdom" in Luke 1:17. See PRUDENCE.

Note: "While *sophia* is the insight into the true nature of things, *phronēsis* is the ability to discern modes of action with a view to their results; while *sophia* is theoretical, *phronēsis* is practical" (Lightfoot). *Sunesis*, "understanding, intelligence," is the critical faculty; this and *phronēsis* are particular applications of *sophia*.

WISE, WISER, WISELY

A. Adjectives.

1. *sophos* (σοφός, 4680) is used of (*a*) God, Rom. 16:27; in 1 Tim. 1:17 and Jude 25 *sophos* is absent, in the best mss. (see the RV), the comparative degree, *sophōteros*, occurs in 1 Cor. 1:25, where "foolishness" is simply in the human estimate; (*b*) spiritual teachers in Israel, Matt. 23:34; (*c*) believers endowed with spiritual and practical wisdom, Rom. 16:19; 1 Cor. 3:10; 6:5; Eph. 5:15; Jas. 3:13; (*d*) Jewish teachers in the time of Christ, Matt. 11:25; Luke 10:21; (*e*) the naturally learned, Rom. 1:14, 22; 1 Cor. 1:19, 20, 26, 27; 3:18–20.¶

2. *phronimos* (φρόνιμος, 5429), "prudent, sensible, practically wise," Matt. 7:24; 10:16; 24:45; 25:2, 4, 8, 9; Luke 12:42; 16:8 (comparative degree, *phronimōteros*); 1 Cor. 10:15; in an evil sense, "wise (in your own conceits)," lit., "wise (in yourselves)," i.e., "judged by the standard of your self-complacency," Rom. 11:25; 12:16; ironically, 1 Cor. 4:10; 2 Cor. 11:19.¶

B. Noun.

magos (μάγος, 3097) denotes "a Magian," one of a sacred caste, originally Median, who apparently conformed to the Persian religion while retaining their old beliefs; it is used in the plural, Matt. 2:1, 7, 16 (twice), "wise men." See also SORCERER.

C. Verbs.

1. *sophizō* (σοφίζω, 4679) is rendered "to make wise" in 2 Tim. 3:15: see DEVISED.

2. *suniēmi* or *suniō* (συνίημι, 4920), "to perceive, understand," is used negatively in 2 Cor. 10:12, KJV, "are not wise" (RV, "are without understanding"). See UNDERSTAND.

D. Adverb.

phronimōs (φρονίμως, 5430), "wisely" (akin to A, No. 2), occurs in Luke 16:8.¶

WISE (IN NO)

1. *ou mē* (οὐ μή), a double negative, expressing an emphatic negation, "by no means," is rendered "in no wise" in Matt. 10:42; Luke 18:17; John 6:37; Acts 13:41; Rev. 21:27.

2. *pantōs* (πάντως, 3843), "altogether, by all means," is used with the negative *ou* ("not") in Rom. 3:9, stating a complete denial, rendered "No, in no wise." See ALL, B, 3, ALTOGETHER, B, 1.

3. *panteles* (παντελές, 3838), the neuter of *pantelēs*, is used with the negative *mē*, and with *eis to*, "unto the," in Luke 13:11, and translated "in no wise," lit., "not to the uttermost": see UTTERMOST, No. 1.

For **WISE (ON THIS)** see **THUS**

WISH

1. *euchomai* (εὔχομαι, 2172) is rendered "to wish" in Acts 27:29 (RV marg., "prayed"); so Rom. 9:3; in 2 Cor. 13:9 and 3 John 2, RV, "pray": see PRAY.

2. *boulomai* (βούλομαι, 1014), in Mark 15:15, RV, is translated "wishing" (KJV, "willing"); so 2 Pet. 3:9; in Acts 25:22, RV, could wish" (KJV, "would"). See WILL, C, No. 2.

3. *thelō* (θέλω, 2309), in 1 Cor. 16:7, RV, is translated "wish" (KJV, "will"); Gal. 4:20, "I could wish" (KJV, "I desire"). See WILL, C, No. 1.

WIST

oida (οἶδα, Perf. of 1492), "to know," in the pluperfect tense (with imperfect meaning) is rendered "wist" (the past tense of the verb "to wit": cf. WOT) in Mark 9:6; 14:40; Luke 2:49; John 5:13; Acts 12:9; 23:5. See KNOW, No. 2.

WIT (TO)

A. Adverb.

hōs (ὡς, 5613), a relative adverb signifying "as," or "how," is used in 2 Cor. 5:19 to introduce the statement "that God was . . .," and rendered "to wit," lit., "how."

B. Verb.

gnōrizō (γνωρίζω, 1107), "to know, to make known," is rendered "we do (you) to wit" in 2 Cor. 8:1, KJV, RV, "we make known (to you)." See KNOW, No. 8.

Note: In Rom. 8:23 the italicized words "*to wit*" are added to specify the particular meaning of "adoption" there mentioned.

For **WITCHCRAFT** see **SORCERY**

For **WITH** see †, p. 1

WITHAL

hama (ἅμα, 260), at the same time, is rendered "withal" in Acts 24:26, RV (KJV, "also"); 1 Tim. 5:13 (with *kai*, "also"); Philem. 22.

Notes: (1) In Eph. 6:16, RV, the phrase *en pasin* (*en*, "in," and the dative plural of *pas*, "all") is rightly rendered "withal" (KJV, "above all"); the shield of faith is to accompany the use of all the other parts of the spiritual equipment. (2) In 1 Cor. 12:7 *sumpherō* is rendered "profit withal." See EXPEDIENT, PROFIT, B, No. 1. (3) In Acts 25:27, *kai*, "also," is rendered "withal."

WITHDRAW

1. *hupostellō* (ὑποστέλλω, 5288) is translated "withdraw" in Gal. 2:12: see DRAW, B, No. 4.

2. *apospaō* (ἀποσπάω, 645), in the passive voice, is translated "was withdrawn" in Luke 22:41, KJV: see PART (Verb), No. 3.

3. *anachōreō* (ἀναχωρέω, 402) is translated "to withdraw" in the RV of Matt. 2:22 and John 6:15; RV and KJV in Matt. 12:15 and Mark 3:7. See DEPART, No. 10.

4. *hupochōreō* (ὑποχωρέω, 5298), "to retire," is translated "withdrew Himself" in Luke 5:16; elsewhere in 9:10, RV, "withdrew apart" (KJV, "went aside"). See GO, No. 16.¶

5. *stellō* (στέλλω, 4724), "to bring together, gather up" (used of furling sails), hence, in the middle voice, signifies "to shrink from a person or thing," 2 Thess. 3:6, "withdraw"; elsewhere, 2 Cor. 8:20, "avoiding." See AVOID.¶ Cf. No. 1.

Note: In 1 Tim. 6:5, some texts have *aphistēmi*, rendered "withdraw thyself," KJV.

WITHER (away)

xērainō (ξηραίνω, 3583), "to dry up, parch, wither," is translated "to wither," (*a*) of plants, Matt. 13:6; 21:19, 20; Mark 4:6; 11:20, RV (KJV, "dried up"), 21; Luke 8:6; John 15:6; Jas. 1:11; 1 Pet. 1:24; (*b*) of members of the body, Mark 3:1, and, in some texts, 3. See DRY, B, OVERRIPE, PINE AWAY, RIPE.

Notes: (1) For the adjective *xēros*, "dry, withered," see DRY, A, No. 1. (2) For "whose fruit withereth," Jude 12, KJV, see AUTUMN.

WITHHOLD

kōluō (κωλύω, 2967), "to hinder, restrain," is translated "withhold (not)" in Luke 6:29, RV, KJV, "forbid (not) to take." See FORBID, HINDER, KEEP, *Note* (7), SUFFER, WITHSTAND.

Note: For "withholdeth" in 2 Thess. 2:6 see RESTRAIN.

WITHIN

Note: This is a translation of (*a*) *entos:* see INSIDE, No. 1; in Luke 17:21 the RV marg., "in the midst of," is to be preferred; the kingdom of God was not in the hearts of the Pharisees; (*b*) *en,* "of thinking or saying within oneself," e.g., Luke 7:39, 49 (marg., "among"); locally, e.g., Luke 19:44; (*c*) *esōthen,* 2 Cor. 7:5; Rev. 4:8; 5:1; "from within," Mark 7:21, 23; Luke 11:7; "within," Matt. 23:25; Luke 11:40, RV, "inside"; in Matt. 23:27, 28, RV, "inwardly"; (*d*) *esō,* John 20:26; Acts 5:23; 1 Cor. 5:12 (i.e., "within" the church); (*e*) *pros,* to, or with, in Mark 14:4, KJV, "within" (RV, "among"); (*f*) *dia,* "through," rendered "within (three days)" in Mark 14:58, KJV (RV, "in," looking through the time to the event, and in keeping with the metaphor of building); (*g*) *esōteros,* Heb. 6:19, the comparative degree of *esō,* used with the article translated "that within," lit., "the inner (part of the veil)," i.e., "inside": see INNER, No. 2; (*h*) in Luke 11:41, RV, *eneimi,* "to be in," is rendered "are within" (KJV, "ye have").

WITHOUT

Notes: (1) This is a translation of (*a*) *exō,* "outside," e.g., Matt. 12:46, 47; "(them that are) without," 1 Cor. 5:12, 13; Col. 4:5; 1 Thess. 4:12 (the unregenerate); Heb. 13:11–13; (*b*) *exōthen,* "from without," or "without," e.g., Mark 7:15, 18; Luke 11:40; 2 Cor. 7:5; 1 Tim. 3:7; as a preposition, Rev. 11:2; (*c*) *chōris,* "apart from," frequently used as a preposition, especially in Hebrews [4:15; 7:7, 20, 21; 9:7, 18, 22, 28; 11:6; in 11:40, RV, "apart from" (KJV, "without"); 12:8, 14]; (*d*) *aneu,* like *chōris,* but rarer, Matt. 10:29; Mark 13:2; 1 Pet. 3:1; 4:9;¶ (*e*) *ater,* Luke 22:6, marg., "without (tumult)"; v. 35;¶ (*f*) *ektos,* "out of, outside," 1 Cor. 6:18: see OTHER, OUT, OUTSIDE; (*g*) *parektos,* "besides, in addition," 2 Cor. 11:28, "(those things that are) without," RV, marg., "(the things which) I omit," or "(the things that come) out of course." (2) In Acts 5:26, *ou,* "not," *meta,* "with," is rendered "without (violence)." (3) In Acts 25:17, KJV, "without (any delay)" represents *poieō,* "to make," and *mēdemian,* "no," RV, "I made no (delay)." (4) For "without ceasing, Acts 12:5, KJV, see EARNESTLY, C, No. 1. (5) In many nouns the negative prefix *a* forms part of the word and is translated "without."

WITHSTAND

1. *kōluō* (κωλύω, 2967), "to hinder," is rendered "withstand" in Acts 11:17. See FORBID, HINDER.

2. *anthistēmi* (ἀνθίστημι, 436), "to set against," is translated "to withstand" in Acts 13:8 (middle voice); in the intransitive 2nd aorist, active voice, Eph. 6:13; 2 Tim. 3:8 (1st part; middle voice in 2nd part); 4:15. See RESIST.

WITNESS (Noun and Verb)

A. Nouns.

1. *martus* or *martur* (μάρτυς, 3144) (whence Eng., "martyr," one who bears "witness" by his death) denotes "one who can or does aver what he has seen or heard or knows"; it is used (*a*) of God, Rom. 1:9; 2 Cor. 1:23; Phil. 1:8; 1 Thess. 2:5, 10 (2nd part); (*b*) of Christ, Rev. 1:5; 3:14; (*c*) of those who "witness" for Christ by their death, Acts 22:20; Rev. 2:13; Rev. 17:6; (*d*) of the interpreters of God's counsels, yet to "witness" in Jerusalem in the times of the Antichrist, Rev. 11:3; (*e*) in a forensic sense, Matt. 18:16; 26:65; Mark 14:63; Acts 6:13; 7:58; 2 Cor. 13:1; 1 Tim. 5:19; Heb. 10:28; (*f*) in a historical

sense, Luke 11:48; 24:48; Acts 1:8, 22; 2:32; 3:15; 5:32; 10:39, 41; 13:31; 22:15; 26:16; 1 Thess. 2:10 (1st part); 1 Tim. 6:12; 2 Tim. 2:2; Heb. 12:1, "(a cloud) of witnesses," here of those mentioned in ch. 11, those whose lives and actions testified to the worth and effect of faith, and whose faith received "witness" in Scripture; 1 Pet. 5:1.¶

2. *marturia* (μαρτυρία, 3141), "testimony, a bearing witness," is translated "witness" in Mark 14:55, 56, 59; Luke 22:71; John 1:7, 19 (RV); 3:11, 32 and 33 (RV); 5:31, 32, 34 (RV), 36; RV in 8:13, 14, 17; 19:35; 21:24; KJV in Titus 1:13; KJV and RV in 1 John 5:9 (thrice), 10a; RV in 10b, 11; 3 John 12: see TESTIMONY, No. 2.

3. *marturion* (μαρτύριον, 3142), "testimony or witness as borne, a declaration of facts," is translated "witness" in Matt. 24:14, KJV; Acts 4:33; 7:44 (KJV); Jas. 5:3 (KJV): see TESTIMONY, No. 1.

4. *pseudomartus* or *-tur* (ψευδομάρτυς, 5571 and 3144) denotes "a false witness," Matt. 26:60; 1 Cor. 15:15.¶

5. *pseudomarturia* (ψευδομαρτυρία, 5577), "false witness," occurs in Matt. 15:19; 26:59.¶

B. Verbs.

1. *martureō* (μαρτυρέω, 3140) denotes (I) "to be a *martus*" (see A, No. 1), or "to bear witness to," sometimes rendered "to testify" (see TESTIFY, No. 1); it is used of the "witness" (*a*) of God the Father to Christ, John 5:32, 37; 8:18 (2nd part); 1 John 5:9, 10; to others, Acts 13:22; 15:8; Heb. 11:2, 4 (twice), 5, 39; (*b*) of Christ, John 3:11, 32; 4:44; 5:31; 7:7; 8:13, 14, 18 (1st part); 13:21; 18:37; Acts 14:3; 1 Tim. 6:13; Rev. 22:18, 20; of the Holy Spirit, to Christ, John 15:26; Heb. 10:15; 1 John 5:7, 8, RV, which rightly omits the latter part of v. 7 (it was a marginal gloss which crept into the original text: see THREE); it finds no support in Scripture; (*c*) of the Scriptures, to Christ, John 5:39; Heb. 7:8, 17; (*d*) of the works of Christ, to Himself, and of the circumstances connected with His death, John 5:36; 10:25; 1 John 5:8; (*e*) of prophets and apostles, to the righteousness of God, Rom. 3:21; to Christ, John 1:7, 8, 15, 32, 34; 3:26; 5:33, RV; 15:27; 19:35; 21:24; Acts 10:43; 23:11; 1 Cor. 15:15; 1 John 1:2; 4:14; Rev. 1:2; to doctrine, Acts 26:22 (in some texts, so KJV; see No. 2); to the Word of God, Rev. 1:2; (*f*) of others, concerning Christ, Luke 4:22; John 4:39; 12:17; (*g*) of believers to one another, John 3:28; 2 Cor. 8:3; Gal. 4:15; Col. 4:13; 1 Thess. 2:11 (in some texts: see No. 2); 3 John 3, 6, 12 (2nd part); (*h*) of the apostle Paul concerning Israel, Rom. 10:2; (*i*) of an angel, to the churches, Rev. 22:16; (*j*) of unbe-

lievers, concerning themselves, Matt. 23:31; concerning Christ, John 18:23; concerning others, John 2:25; Acts 22:5; 26:5; (II) "to give a good report, to approve of," Acts 6:3; 10:22; 16:2; 22:12; 1 Tim. 5:10; 3 John 12 (1st part); some would put Luke 4:22 here.¶

2. *marturomai* (μαρτύρομαι, 3143), strictly meaning "to summon as a witness," signifies "to affirm solemnly, adjure," and is used in the middle voice only, rendered "to testify" in Acts 20:26, RV (KJV, "I take . . . to record"); 26:22, RV, in the best texts [see No. 1 (*e*)]; Gal. 5:3; Eph. 4:17; 1 Thess. 2:11, in the best texts [see No. 1 (*g*)].¶

3. *summartureō* (συμμαρτυρέω, 4828) denotes "to bear witness with" (*sun*), Rom. 2:15; 8:16; 9:1.¶

4. *sunepimartureō* (συνεπιμαρτυρέω, 4901) denotes "to join in bearing witness with others," Heb. 2:4.¶

5. *katamartureō* (καταμαρτυρέω, 2649) denotes "to witness against" (*kata*), Matt. 26:62; 27:13; Mark 14:60 (in some mss., 15:4, for *katēgoreō*, "to accuse," RV).¶

6. *pseudomartureō* (ψευδομαρτυρέω, 5576), "to bear false witness" (*pseudēs*, "false"), occurs in Matt. 19:18; Mark 10:19; 14:56, 57; Luke 18:20; in some texts, Rom. 13:9.¶

C. Adjective.

amarturos (ἀμάρτυρος, 267) denotes "without witness" (*a*, negative, and *martus*), Acts 14:17.¶

WOE

ouai (οὐαί, 3759), an interjection, is used (*a*) in denunciation, Matt. 11:21; 18:7 (twice); eight times in ch. 23; 24:19; 26:24; Mark 13:17; 14:21; Luke 6:24, 25 (twice), 26; 10:13; six times in ch. 11; 17:1; 21:23; 22:22; 1 Cor. 9:16; Jude 11; Rev. 8:13 (thrice); 12:12; as a noun, Rev. 9:12 (twice); 11:14 (twice); (*b*) in grief, "alas," Rev. 18:10, 16, 19 (twice in each).¶

WOLF

lukos (λύκος, 3074) occurs in Matt. 10:16; Luke 10:3; John 10:12 (twice); metaphorically, Matt. 7:15; Acts 20:29.¶

WOMAN

1. *gunē* (γυνή, 1135), for which see also WIFE, is used of a "woman" unmarried or married, e.g., Matt. 11:11; 14:21; Luke 4:26, of a "widow"; Rom. 7:2; in the vocative case, used in addressing a "woman," it is a term not of reproof or severity, but of endearment or respect, Matt. 15:28; John 2:4, where the Lord's words to His mother at the wedding in Cana, are neither rebuff nor rebuke. The question is,

lit., "What to Me and to thee?" and the word "woman," the term of endearment, follows this. The meaning is "There is no obligation on Me or you, but love will supply the need." She confides in Him, He responds to her faith. There was lovingkindness in both hearts. His next words about "His hour" suit this; they were not unfamiliar to her. Cana is in the path to Calvary; Calvary was not yet, but it made the beginning of signs possible. See also 4:21; 19:26.

In Gal. 4:4 the phrase "born of a woman" is in accordance with the subject there, viz., the real humanity of the Lord Jesus; this the words attest. They declare the method of His incarnation and "suggest the means whereby that humanity was made free from the taint of sin consequent upon the Fall, viz., that He was not born through the natural process of ordinary generation, but was conceived by the power of the Holy Spirit... To have written 'born of a virgin' would have carried the argument in a wrong direction... Since that man is born of woman is a universal fact, the statement would be superfluous if the Lord Jesus were no more than man" (*Notes on Galatians*, by Hogg and Vine, pp. 184f.).

2. *gunaikarion* (γυναικάριον, 1133), a diminutive of No. 1, a "little woman," is used contemptuously in 2 Tim. 3:6, "a silly woman."¶

3. *presbuteros* (πρεσβύτερος, 4245), "elder, older," in the feminine plural, denotes "elder women" in 1 Tim. 5:2. See ELDER, A, No. 1.

4. *presbutis* (πρεσβῦτις, 4247), the feminine of *presbutēs*, "aged," is used in the plural and translated "aged women" in Titus 2:3.¶

5. *thēleia* (θήλεια, 2338**), the feminine of the adjective *thēlus*, denotes "female," and is used as a noun, Rom. 1:26, 27. See FEMALE.

WOMB

1. *koilia* (κοιλία, 2836) denotes "the womb," Matt. 19:12; Luke 1:15, 41, 42, 44; 2:21; 11:27; 23:29; John 3:4; Acts 3:2; 14:8; Gal. 1:15. See BELLY, No. 1.

2. *gastēr* (γαστήρ, 1064), is rendered "womb" in Luke 1:31. See BELLY, No. 2.

3. *mētra* (μήτρα, 3388), the matrix (akin to *mētēr*, "a mother"), occurs in Luke 2:23; Rom. 4:19.¶

WONDER (Noun and Verb)

A. Nouns.

1. *teras* (τέρας, 5059), "something strange," causing the beholder to marvel, is always used in the plural, always rendered "wonders," and generally follows *sēmeia*, "signs"; the opposite

order occurs in Acts 2:22, 43; 6:8, RV; 7:36; in Acts 2:19 "wonders" occurs alone. A sign is intended to appeal to the understanding, a "wonder" appeals to the imagination, a power (*dunamis*) indicates its source as supernatural. "Wonders" are manifested as divine operations in thirteen occurrences (9 times in Acts); three times they are ascribed to the work of Satan through human agents, Matt. 24:24; Mark 13:22 and 2 Thess. 2:9.

2. *thambos* (θάμβος, 2285), "amazement," is rendered "wonder" in Acts 3:10. See AMAZE, A, No. 2.

Notes: (1) For *thauma*, "a wonder" (rendered "admiration" in Rev. 17:6, KJV), see MARVEL. (2) In Rev. 12:1, 3 and 13:13 *sēmeion*, "a sign," is translated in the KJV, "wonder(s)," RV, "sign(s)." (3) In Acts 3:11 *ekthambos (ek*, intensive, and No. 2) is translated "greatly wondering."¶ (4) For *pseudos*, 2 Thess. 2:9, "lying wonders," see FALSE, B. Cf. AMAZE, B, Nos. 3 and 4.

B. Verb.

Note: For *thaumazō*, see MARVEL; for *existēmi*, Acts 8:13, KJV, see AMAZE, B, No. 1.

WONDERFUL (THING, WORK)

Notes: (1) In Matt. 7:22, KJV, *dunamis* (in the plural) is rendered "wonderful works" (RV, "mighty works," marg., "powers"). See POWER. (2) In Acts 2:11, KJV, the adjective *megaleios*, "magnificent," in the neuter plural with the article, is rendered "the wonderful works" (RV, "the mighty works").¶ (3) In Matt. 21:15, the neuter plural of the adjective *thaumasios*, "wonderful," is used as a noun, "wonderful things," lit., "wonders."

WONT

ethō (ἔθω, 1486), "to be accustomed," is used in the pluperfect tense (with imperfect meaning), *eiōtha*, rendered "was wont" in Matt. 27:15; Mark 10:1. See CUSTOM, B, No. 2, MANNER, A, *Note* (1).

Notes: (1) In Mark 15:8, "he was wont to do," RV, represents the imperfect tense of *poieō*, "to do" (KJV, "he had ever done"). (2) In Luke 22:39, KJV, *ethos*, "a custom," preceded by *kata* and the article, lit., "according to the (i.e., His) custom," is translated "as He was wont" (RV, "as His custom was"): see CUSTOM, A, No. 1. (3) In Acts 16:13 the KJV, "was wont," translates the texts which have the passive voice of *nomizō* with its meaning "to hold by custom"; the RV, "we supposed," translates the texts which have the imperfect tense, active, with the meaning "to consider, suppose."

WOOD

1. *xulon* (ξύλον, 3586) denotes "timber, wood for any use" 1 Cor. 3:12; Rev. 18:12 (twice). See STAFF, STOCKS, TREE.

2. *hule* (ὕλη, 5208) denotes "a wood, a forest," Jas. 3:5 (KJV, "matter," marg., "wood").¶ See MATTER, *Note* (3).

WOOL

erion (ἔριον, 2053) occurs in Heb. 9:19; Rev. 1:14.¶

WORD

1. *logos* (λόγος, 3056) denotes (I) "the expression of thought"—not the mere name of an object—(*a*) as embodying a conception or idea, e.g., Luke 7:7; 1 Cor. 14:9, 19; (*b*) a saying or statement, (1) by God, e.g., John 15:25; Rom. 9:9; 9:28, RV, "word" (KJV, "work"); Gal. 5:14; Heb. 4:12; (2) by Christ, e.g., Matt. 24:35 (plur.); John 2:22; 4:41; 14:23 (plur.); 15:20. In connection with (1) and (2) the phrase "the word of the Lord," i.e., the revealed will of God (very frequent in the OT), is used of a direct revelation given by Christ, 1 Thess. 4:15; of the gospel, Acts 8:25; 13:49; 15:35, 36; 16:32; 19:10; 1 Thess. 1:8; 2 Thess. 3:1; in this respect it is the message from the Lord, delivered with His authority and made effective by His power (cf. Acts 10:36); for other instances relating to the gospel see Acts 13:26; 14:3; 15:7; 1 Cor. 1:18, RV; 2 Cor. 2:17; 4:2; 5:19; 6:7; Gal. 6:6; Eph. 1:13; Phil. 2:16; Col. 1:5; Heb. 5:13; sometimes it is used as the sum of God's utterances, e.g., Mark 7:13; John 10:35; Rev. 1:2, 9; (*c*) discourse, speech, of instruction, etc., e.g., Acts 2:40; 1 Cor. 2:13; 12:8; 2 Cor. 1:18; 1 Thess. 1:5; 2 Thess. 2:15; Heb. 6:1, RV, marg.; doctrine, e.g., Matt. 13:20; Col. 3:16; 1 Tim. 4:6; 2 Tim. 1:13; Titus 1:9; 1 John 2:7;

(II) "The Personal Word," a title of the Son of God; this identification is substantiated by the statements of doctrine in John 1:1–18, declaring in verses 1 and 2 (1) His distinct and superfinite Personality, (2) His relation in the Godhead (*pros*, "with," not mere company, but the most intimate communion), (3) His deity; in v. 3 His creative power; in v. 14 His incarnation ("became flesh," expressing His voluntary act; not as KJV, "was made"), the reality and totality of His human nature, and His glory "as of the only begotten from the Father," RV (marg., "an only begotten from a father"), the absence of the article in each place lending stress to the nature and character of the relationship; His was the *shekinah* glory in open manifestation; v. 18 consummates the identification:

"the only-begotten Son (RV marg., many ancient authorities read "God only begotten,"), which is in the bosom of the Father, He hath declared Him," thus fulfilling the significance of the title "*Logos*," the "Word," the personal manifestation, not of a part of the divine nature, but of the whole deity (see IMAGE).

The title is used also in 1 John 1, "the Word of life" combining the two declarations in John 1:1 and 4 and Rev. 19:13 (for 1 John 5:7 see THREE).

2. *rhema* (ῥῆμα, 4487) denotes "that which is spoken, what is uttered in speech or writing"; in the singular, "a word," e.g., Matt. 12:36; 27:14; 2 Cor. 12:4; 13:1; Heb. 12:19; in the plural, speech, discourse, e.g., John 3:34; 8:20; Acts 2:14; 6:11, 13; 11:14; 13:42; 26:25; Rom. 10:18; 2 Pet. 3:2; Jude 17; it is used of the gospel in Rom. 10:8 (twice), 17, RV, "the word of Christ" (i.e., the "word" which preaches Christ); 10:18; 1 Pet. 1:25 (twice); of a statement, command, instruction, e.g., Matt. 26:75; Luke 1:37, RV, "(no) word (from God shall be void of power)"; v. 38; Acts 11:16; Heb. 11:3.

The significance of *rhema* (as distinct from *logos*) is exemplified in the injunction to take "the sword of the Spirit, which is the word of God," Eph. 6:17; here the reference is not to the whole Bible as such, but to the individual scripture which the Spirit brings to our remembrance for use in time of need, a prerequisite being the regular storing of the mind with Scripture.

Notes: (1) *Epos*, "a word," is used in a phrase in Heb. 7:9, lit., "(as to say) a word," RV, "(so to) say," KJV, "(as I may so) say"; *logos* is reasoned speech, *rhema*, an utterance, *epos*, "the articulated expression of a thought" (Abbott-Smith). (2) In Rom. 16:18, KJV, *chrestologia*, "useful discourse" (*chrestos*, "beneficial"), is rendered "good words" [RV, "smooth . . . (speech)"].¶ (3) For *logikos*, 1 Pet. 2:2 (RV, "spiritual"), rendered "of the word," KJV, see MILK. (4) For the verb *apangello*, rendered "to bring word," see BRING, No. 36. (5) In Matt. 2:13, KJV, *eipon*, "to tell" (RV), is rendered "bring . . . word." (6) For "enticing words," Col. 2:4, see ENTICE and PERSUASIVENESS. (7) For "strifes of words," 1 Tim. 6:4, KJV, and "strive . . . about words," 2 Tim. 2:14, see STRIFE, STRIVE. (8) For *suntomos*, Acts 24:4, "a few words," see FEW, B.¶ For the same phrase see FEW, A, Nos. 1 and 2.

WORK (Noun and Verb), WROUGHT

A. Nouns.

1. *ergon* (ἔργον, 2041) denotes (I) "work, employment, task," e.g., Mark 13:34; John

4:34; 17:4; Acts 13:2; Phil. 2:30; 1 Thess. 5:13; in Acts 5:38 with the idea of enterprise; (II) "a deed, act," (*a*) of God, e.g., John 6:28, 29; 9:3; 10:37; 14:10; Acts 13:41; Rom. 14:20; Heb. 1:10; 2:7; 3:9; 4:3, 4, 10; Rev. 15:3; (*b*) of Christ, e.g., Matt. 11:2; especially in John, 5:36; 7:3, 21; 10:25, 32, 33, 38; 14:11, 12; 15:24; Rev. 2:26; (*c*) of believers, e.g., Matt. 5:16; Mark 14:6; Acts 9:36; Rom. 13:3; Col. 1:10; 1 Thess. 1:3, "work of faith," here the initial act of faith at conversion (turning to God, v. 9); in 2 Thess. 1:11, "*every* work of faith," RV, denotes every activity undertaken for Christ's sake; 2:17; 1 Tim. 2:10; 5:10; 6:18; 2 Tim. 2:21; 3:17; Titus 2:7, 14; 3:1, 8, 14; Heb. 10:24; 13:21; frequent in James, as the effect of faith [in 1:25, KJV, "(a doer) of the work," RV, "(a doer) that work-eth"]; 1 Pet. 2:12; Rev. 2:2 and in several other places in chs. 2 and 3; 14:13; (*d*) of unbelievers, e.g., Matt. 23:3, 5; John 7:7; Acts 7:41 (for idols); Rom. 13:12; Eph. 5:11; Col. 1:21; Titus 1:16 (1st part); 1 John 3:12; Jude 15, RV; Rev. 2:6, RV; of those who seek justification by works, e.g., Rom. 9:32; Gal. 3:10; Eph. 2:9; described as the works of the law, e.g., Gal. 2:16; 3:2, 5; dead works, Heb. 6:1; 9:14; (*e*) of Babylon, Rev. 18:6; (*f*) of the Devil, John 8:41; 1 John 3:8. See DEED.

2. *ergasia* (ἐργασία, 2039) denotes "a work" or "business," also "a working, perform-ance," Eph. 4:19, where preceded by *eis*, "to," it is rendered "to work" (marg., "to make a trade of"). See DILIGENCE, GAIN.

Notes: (1) In Rom. 9:28, KJV, *logos*, "a word" (RV), is rendered "work." (2) For *pragma*, Jas. 3:16, rendered "work" in KJV, the RV has "deed." (3) For *praxis*, "a doing," Matt. 16:27, RV marg., KJV, "works," see DEED. (4) For the KJV, "much work," Acts 27:16, see DIFFICULTY. (5) For "workfellow," Rom. 16:21, KJV, see WORKER, No. 2. (6) In Matt. 14:2 and Mark 6:14, KJV, *dunameis*, "powers," RV, is translated "mighty works"; in Acts 2:22, RV, "mighty works," KJV, "miracles." (7) For "wonderful works" see WONDERFUL, *Note* (2).

B. Verbs.

1. *ergazomai* (ἐργάζομαι, 2038) is used (I) intransitively, e.g., Matt. 21:28; John 5:17; 9:4 (2nd part); Rom. 4:4, 5; 1 Cor. 4:12; 9:6; 1 Thess. 2:9; 4:11; 2 Thess. 3:8, 10–12 (for the play upon words in v. 11 see BUSYBODY, A); (II) transitively, (*a*) "to work something, produce, perform," e.g., Matt. 26:10, "she hath wrought"; John 6:28, 30; 9:4 (1st part); Acts 10:35; 13:41; Rom. 2:10; 13:10; 1 Cor. 16:10; 2 Cor. 7:10a, in the best texts, some have No. 2; Gal. 6:10, RV, "let us work"; Eph. 4:28; Heb. 11:33; 2 John 8; (*b*) "to earn by working, work for,"

John 6:27, RV, "work" (KJV, "labor"). See COM-MIT, DO, LABOR, MINISTER, TRADE.

2. *katergazomai* (κατεργάζομαι, 2716), an emphatic form of No. 1, signifies "to work out, achieve, effect by toil," rendered "to work" (past tense, "wrought") in Rom. 1:27; 2:9, RV; 4:15 (the Law brings men under condemnation and so renders them subject to divine wrath); 5:3; 7:8, 13; 15:18; 2 Cor. 4:17; 5:5; 7:10 (see No. 1), 11; 12:12; Phil. 2:12, where "your own salvation" refers especially to freedom from strife and vainglory; Jas. 1:3, 20; 1 Pet. 4:3. See DO, No. 5.

3. *energeō* (ἐνεργέω, 1754), lit., "to work in" (*en*, and A, No. 1), "to be active, operative," is used of "(*a*) God, 1 Cor. 12:6; Gal. 2:8; 3:5; Eph. 1:11, 20; 3:20; Phil. 2:13a; Col. 1:29; (*b*) the Holy Spirit, 1 Cor, 12:11; (*c*) the Word of God, 1 Thess. 2:13 (middle voice; KJV, 'effec-tually worketh'); (*d*) supernatural power, unde-fined, Matt. 14:2; Mark 6:14; (*e*) faith, as the energizer of love, Gal. 5:6; (*f*) the example of patience in suffering, 2 Cor. 1:6; (*g*) death (physical) and life (spiritual), 2 Cor. 4:12; (*h*) sinful passions, Rom. 7:5; (*i*) the spirit of the Evil One, Eph. 2:2; (*j*) the mystery of iniquity, 2 Thess. 2:7."*

To these may be added (*k*) the active re-sponse of believers to the inworking of God, Phil. 2:13b, RV, "to work (for)," KJV, "to do (of)"; (*l*) the supplication of the righteous, Jas. 5:16, RV, "in its working" (KJV, "effectual fer-vent").

4. *poieō* (ποιέω, 4160), "to do," is rendered "to work" in Matt. 20:12, KJV (RV, "spent"); Acts 15:12, "had wrought"; 19:11; 21:19; Heb. 13:21; Rev. 16:14; 19:20; 21:27, KJV (RV, "mak-eth"; marg., "doeth"). See DO.

5. *sunergeō* (συνεργέω, 4903), "to work with or together" (*sun*), occurs in Mark 16:20; Rom. 8:28, "work together"; 1 Cor. 16:16, "helpeth with"; 2 Cor. 6:1, "workers together," present participle, "working together"; the "*with Him*" represents nothing in the Greek; Jas. 2:22, "wrought with." See HELP.¶

6. *ginomai* (γίνομαι, 1096), "to become, take place," is rendered "wrought" in Mark 6:2; Acts 5:12, "were … wrought."

WORKER, WORKFELLOW, FELLOW WORKERS, WORKMAN

1. *ergatēs* (ἐργάτης, 2040) is translated "workers" in Luke 13:27 ("of iniquity"); 2 Cor. 11:13 ("deceitful"); Phil. 3:2 ("evil"); "work-

---

* From *Notes on Galatians*, by Hogg and Vine, pp. 114, 115.

man," Matt. 10:10, KJV (RV, "laborer"); "work-man," 2 Tim. 2:15; "workmen," Acts 19:25. See LABORER.

2. *sunergos* (συνεργός, 4904) denotes "a worker with," and is rendered "workfellow" in Rom. 16:21, KJV, RV, "fellow worker"; in Col. 4:11, "fellow workers" (see RV). See the RV, "God's fellow workers," in 1 Cor. 3:9. See COM-PANION, HELPER, LABORER, *Note*.

Note: For "workers at home," Titus 2:5, see HOME, B.

WORKING

1. *energeia* (ἐνέργεια, 1753) (Eng., "en-ergy") is used (1) of the "power" of God, (*a*) in the resurrection of Christ, Eph. 1:19; Col. 2:12, RV, "working" (KJV, "operation"); (*b*) in the call and enduement of Paul, Eph. 3:7; Col. 1:29; (*c*) in His retributive dealings in sending "a work-ing of error" (KJV, "strong delusion") upon those under the rule of the Man of Sin who receive not the love of the truth, but have pleas-ure in unrighteousness, 2 Thess. 2:11; (2) of the "power" of Christ (*a*) generally, Phil. 3:21; (*b*) in the church, individually, Eph. 4:16; (3) of the power of Satan in energizing the Man of Sin in his "parousia," 2 Thess. 2:9, "coming."¶

2. *energēma* (ἐνέργημα, 1755), "what is wrought," the effect produced by No. 1, occurs in 1 Cor. 12:6, RV, "workings" (KJV, "opera-tions"); v. 10.¶

For WORKMANSHIP see MADE, B

WORLD

1. *kosmos* (κόσμος, 2889), primarily "order, arrangement, ornament, adornment" (1 Pet. 3:3, see ADORN, B), is used to denote (*a*) the "earth," e.g., Matt. 13:35; John 21:25; Acts 17:24; Rom. 1:20 (probably here the universe: it had this meaning among the Greeks, owing to the order observable in it); 1 Tim. 6:7; Heb. 4:3; 9:26; (*b*) the "earth" in contrast with Heaven, 1 John 3:17 (perhaps also Rom. 4:13); (*c*) by metonymy, the "human race, mankind," e.g., Matt. 5:14; John 1:9 [here "that cometh (RV, 'coming') into the world" is said of Christ, not of "every man"; by His coming into the world He was the light for all men]; v. 10; 3:16, 17 (thrice), 19; 4:42, and frequently in Rom., 1 Cor. and 1 John; (*d*) "Gentiles" as distin-guished from Jews, e.g., Rom. 11:12, 15, where the meaning is that all who will may be recon-ciled (cf. 2 Cor. 5:19); (*e*) the "present condition of human affairs," in alienation from and op-position to God, e.g., John 7:7; 8:23; 14:30; 1 Cor. 2:12; Gal. 4:3; 6:14; Col. 2:8; Jas. 1:27; 1 John 4:5 (thrice); 5:19; (*f*) the "sum of tem-poral possessions," Matt. 16:26; 1 Cor. 7:31 (1st part); (*g*) metaphorically, of the "tongue" as "a world (of iniquity)," Jas. 3:6, expressive of mag-nitude and variety.

2. *aiōn* (αἰών, 165), "an age, a period of time," marked in the NT usage by spiritual or moral characteristics, is sometimes translated "world"; the RV marg. always has "age." The following are details concerning the world in this respect; its cares, Matt. 13:22; its sons, Luke 16:8; 20:34; its rulers, 1 Cor. 2:6, 8; its wisdom, 1 Cor. 1:20; 2:6; 3:18; its fashion, Rom. 12:2; its character, Gal. 1:4; its god, 2 Cor. 4:4. The phrase "the end of the world" should be ren-dered "the end of the age," in most places (see END, A, No. 2); in 1 Cor. 10:11, KJV, "the ends (*telē*) of the world," RV, "the ends of the ages," probably signifies the fulfillment of the divine purposes concerning the ages in regard to the church [this would come under END, A, No. 1, (*c*)]. In Heb 11:3 [lit., "the ages (have been prepared)"] the word indicates all that the suc-cessive periods contain; cf. 1:2.

Aiōn is always to be distinguished from *kos-mos*, even where the two seem to express the same idea, e.g., 1 Cor. 3:18, *aiōn*, v. 19, *kosmos*; the two are used together in Eph. 2:2, lit., "the age of this world." For a list of phrases contain-ing *aiōn*, with their respective meanings, see EVER, B.

3. *oikoumenē* (οἰκουμένη, 3625), "the in-habited earth" (see EARTH, No. 2), is used (*a*) of the whole inhabited world, Matt. 24:14; Luke 4:5; 21:26; Rom. 10:18; Heb. 1:6; Rev. 3:10; 16:14; by metonymy, of its inhabitants, Acts 17:31; Rev. 12:9; (*b*) of the Roman Em-pire, the world as viewed by the writer or speaker, Luke 2:1; Acts 11:28; 24:5; by meto-nymy, of its inhabitants, Acts 17:6; 19:27; (*c*) the inhabited world in a coming age, Heb. 2:5.¶

Notes: (1) In Rev. 13:3, KJV, *gē*, "the earth" (RV), is translated "world." (2) For phrases con-taining *aiōnios*, e.g., Rom. 16:25; 2 Tim. 1:9; Titus 1:2, see ETERNAL, No. 2.

WORLDLY

kosmikos (κοσμικός, 2886), "pertaining to this world," is used (*a*) in Heb. 9:1, of the tabernacle, KJV, "worldly," RV, "of this world" (i.e., made of mundane materials, adapted to this visible world, local and transitory); (*b*) in Titus 2:12, ethically, of "worldly lusts," or de-sires.¶

For WORLD RULERS, Eph. 6:12, RV, see RULER, No. 3

WORM

1. *skōlēx* (σκώληξ, 4663), "a worm which preys upon dead bodies," is used metaphorically by the Lord in Mark 9:48; in some mss. vv. 44, 46, cf. Isa. 66:24. The statement signifies the exclusion of the hope of restoration, the punishment being eternal.¶

2. *skōlēkobrōtos* (σκωληκόβρωτος, 4662) denotes "devored by worms" (*skōlēx*, and *bibrōskō*, "to eat"), Acts 12:23.¶

WORMWOOD

apsinthos (ἄψινθος, 894) (Eng., "absinthe"), a plant both bitter and deleterious, and growing in desolate places, figuratively suggestive of "calamity" (Lam. 3:15) and injustice (Amos 5:7), is used in Rev. 8:11 (twice; in the 1st part as a proper name).¶

WORSE

A. Adjectives.

1. *cheirōn* (χείρων, 5501), used as the comparative degree of *kakos*, "evil," describes (*a*) the condition of certain men, Matt. 12:45; Luke 11:26; 2 Pet. 2:20; (*b*) evil men themselves and seducers, 2 Tim. 3:13; (*c*) indolent men who refuse to provide for their own households, and are worse than unbelievers, 1 Tim. 5:8, RV; (*d*) a rent in a garment, Matt. 9:16; Mark 2:21; (*e*) an error, Matt. 27:64; (*f*) a person suffering from a malady, Mark 5:26; (*g*) a possible physical affliction, John 5:14; (*h*) a punishment, Heb. 10:29, "sorer." See SORE. ¶

2. *elassōn* or *elattōn* (ἐλάσσων, 1640) is said of wine in John 2:10. See LESS.

3. *hēssōn* or *hēttōn* (ἥσσων, 2276), "less, inferior," used in the neuter, after *epi*, "for," is translated "worse" in 1 Cor. 11:17; in 2 Cor. 12:15 the neuter, used adverbially, is translated "the less."¶

B. Verbs.

1. *hustereō* (ὑστερέω, 5302) is rendered "are we the worse" in 1 Cor. 8:8. See BEHIND, B, No. 1, COME, No. 39, DESTITUTE, FAIL, *Note* (2), LACK, WANT.

2. *proechō* (προέχω, 4281), "to hold before, promote," is rendered "are we better" in Rom. 3:9, KJV (passive voice); RV, "are we in worse case." See BETTER (be), *Note* (1).¶

WORSHIP (Verb and Noun), WORSHIPING

A. Verbs.

1. *proskuneō* (προσκυνέω, 4352), "to make obeisance, do reverence to" (from *pros*, "towards," and *kuneō*, "to kiss"), is the most frequent word rendered "to worship." It is used of an act of homage or reverence (*a*) to God, e.g., Matt. 4:10; John 4:21–24; 1 Cor. 14:25; Rev. 4:10; 5:14; 7:11; 11:16; 19:10 (2nd part) and 22:9; (*b*) to Christ, e.g., Matt. 2:2, 8, 11; 8:2; 9:18; 14:33; 15:25; 20:20; 28:9, 17; John 9:38; Heb. 1:6, in a quotation from the Sept. of Deut. 32:43, referring to Christ's second advent; (*c*) to a man, Matt. 18:26; (*d*) to the Dragon, by men, Rev. 13:4; (*e*) to the Beast, his human instrument, Rev. 13:4, 8, 12; 14:9, 11; (*f*) the image of the Beast, 13:15; 14:11; 16:2; (*g*) to demons, Rev. 9:20; (*h*) to idols, Acts 7:43.

Note: As to Matt. 18:26, this is mentioned as follows, in the "List of readings and renderings preferred by the American Committee" (see RV *Classes of Passages*, IV): "At the word 'worship' in Matt. 2:2, etc., add the marginal note 'The Greek word denotes an act of reverence, whether paid to man (see chap. 18:26) or to God (see chap. 4:10).'" The Note to John 9:38 in the American Standard Version in this connection is most unsound; it implies that Christ was a creature. J. N. Darby renders the verb "do homage" [see the Revised Preface to the Second Edition (1871) of his *New Translation*].

2. *sebomai* (σέβομαι, 4576), "to revere," stressing the feeling of awe or devotion, is used of "worship" (*a*) to God, Matt. 15:9; Mark 7:7; Acts 16:14; 18:7, 13; (*b*) to a goddess, Acts 19:27. See DEVOUT, No. 3.

3. *sebazomai* (σεβάζομαι, 4573), akin to No. 2, "to honor religiously," is used in Rom. 1:25.¶

4. *latreuō* (λατρεύω, 3000), "to serve, render religious service or homage," is translated "to worship" in Phil. 3:3, "(who) worship (by the Spirit of God)," RV, KJV, "(which) worship (God in the spirit)"; the RV renders it "to serve" (for KJV, "to worship") in Acts 7:42; 24:14; KJV and RV, "(the) worshipers" in Heb. 10:2, present participle, lit., "(the ones) worshiping." See SERVE.

5. *eusebeō* (εὐσεβέω, 2151), "to act piously towards," is translated "ye worship" in Acts 17:23. See PIETY (to show).

Notes: (1) The worship of God is nowhere defined in Scripture. A consideration of the above verbs shows that it is not confined to praise; broadly it may be regarded as the direct acknowledgement to God, of His nature, attributes, ways and claims, whether by the outgoing of the heart in praise and thanksgiving or by deed done in such acknowledgment. (2) In Acts 17:25 *therapeuō*, "to serve, do service to" (so RV), is rendered "is worshiped." See CURE, HEAL.

B. Nouns.

1. *sebasma* (σέβασμα, 4574) denotes "an object of worship" (akin to A, No. 3); Acts

17:23 (see DEVOTION); in 2 Thess. 2:4, "that is worshiped"; every object of "worship," whether the true God or pagan idols, will come under the ban of the Man of Sin.¶

2. *ethelothrēskeia* (or -*ia*) (ἐθελοθρησκεία, 1479), "will-worship" (*ethelō*, "to will," *thrēskeia*, "worship"), occurs in Col. 2:23, voluntarily adopted "worship," whether unbidden or forbidden, not that which is imposed by others, but which one affects.¶

3. *thrēskeia* (θρησκεία, 2356), for which see RELIGION, is translated "worshiping" in Col. 2:18.

Note: In Luke 14:10, KJV, *doxa*, "glory" (RV), is translated "worship."

WORSHIPER

1. *proskunētēs* (προσκυνητής, 4353), akin to *proskuneō* (see WORSHIP, A, No. 1), occurs in John 4:23.¶

2. *neōkoros* (νεωκόρος, 3511) is translated "worshiper" in Acts 19:35 KJV: see TEMPLE KEEPER.¶

3. *theosebēs* (θεοσεβής, 2318) denotes "reverencing God" (*theos*, "God," *sebomai*, see WORSHIP, A, No. 2), and is rendered "a worshiper of God" in John 9:31.¶ Cf. *theosebeia*, "godliness," 1 Tim. 2:10.¶

Note: For Heb. 10:2, see WORSHIP, A, No. 4.

WORTHY, WORTHILY

A. Adjectives.

1. *axios* (ἄξιος, 514), "of weight, worth, worthy," is said of persons and their deeds: (*a*) in a good sense, e.g., Matt. 10:10, 11, 13 (twice), 37 (twice), 38; 22:8; Luke 7:4; 10:7; 15:19, 21; John 1:27; Acts 13:25; 1 Tim. 5:18; 6:1; Heb. 11:38; Rev. 3:4; 4:11; 5:2, 4, 9, 12; (*b*) in a bad sense, Luke 12:48; 23:15; Acts 23:29; 25:11, 25; 26:31; Rom. 1:32; Rev. 16:6. See MEET, REWARD.

2. *hikanos* (ἱκανός, 2425), "sufficient," is translated "worthy" in this sense in Matt. 3:11 (marg., "sufficient"); so 8:8; Mark 1:7; Luke 3:16; 7:6. See ABILITY, C, No. 2, etc.

3. *enochos* (ἔνοχος, 1777), "held in, bound by," is translated "worthy (of death)" in Matt. 26:66 and Mark 14:64, RV (marg., "liable to"; KJV, "guilty"). See DANGER.

Notes: (1) In Jas. 2:7, KJV, *kalos*, "good, fair," is translated "worthy" (RV, "honorable"). (2) For the KJV of Eph. 4:1; Col. 1:10; 1 Thess. 2:12, see C, below.

B. Verbs.

1. *axioō* (ἀξιόω, 515), "to think or count worthy," is used (1) of the estimation formed by God (*a*) favorably, 2 Thess. 1:11, "may count (you) worthy (of your calling)," sugges-

tive of grace (it does not say "may make you worthy"); Heb. 3:3, "of more glory," of Christ in comparison with Moses; (*b*) unfavorably, 10:29, "of how much sorer punishment"; (2) by a centurion (negatively) concerning himself, Luke 7:7; (3) by a church, regarding its elders, 1 Tim. 5:17, where "honor" stands probably for "honorarium," i.e., "material support." See also DESIRE, B, No. 1 (Acts 28:22), THINK (Acts 15:38).¶

2. *kataxioō* (καταξιόω, 2661), a strengthened form of No. 1, occurs in Luke 20:35; 21:36, in some texts; Acts 5:41; 2 Thess. 1:5.¶ See ACCOUNT, A, No. 5.

C. Adverb.

axiōs (ἀξίως, 516), "worthily," so translated in the RV [with one exception, see (*c*)], for KJV, "worthy" and other renderings, (*a*) "worthily of God," 1 Thess. 2:12, of the Christian walk as it should be; 3 John 6, RV, of assisting servants of God in a way which reflects God's character and thoughts; (*b*) "worthily of the Lord," Col. 1:10; of the calling of believers, Eph. 4:1, in regard to their "walk" or manner of life; (*c*) "worthy of the gospel of Christ," Phil. 1:27, of a manner of life in accordance with what the gospel declares; (*d*) "worthily of the saints," RV, of receiving a fellow believer, Rom. 16:2, in such a manner as befits those who bear the name of "saints."¶ Deissmann (*Bible Studies*, pp. 248ff.) shows from various inscriptions that the phrase "worthily of the god" was very popular at Pergamum.

For WORTHY DEEDS, Acts 24:2, KJV, see CORRECTION

WOT

Note: This form, the 1st person singular and the plural of the present tense of an Anglo-Saxon verb *witan*, "to see" or "to know" (for the past tense cf. WIST), is a rendering of (1) *oida*, "to know," in Acts 3:17; 7:40; Rom. 11:2 (see KNOW, No. 2); (2) *gnōrizō*, "to come to know," in Phil. 1:22 (see KNOW, No. 8).

WOULD

Notes: (1) This is often a translation of various inflections of a Greek verb. When it represents a separate word, it is always emphatic, and is a translation of one or other of the verbs mentioned under WILL. (2) *Ophelon* (the 2nd aorist tense of *opheilō*, "to owe") expresses a wish, "I would that," either impracticable, 1 Cor. 4:8, RV (KJV, "would to God"); or possible, 2 Cor. 11:1; Gal. 5:12; Rev. 3:15. (3) *Euchomai*, "to pray," with the particle *an*, expressing a strong desire with a remote possibility of fulfillment, is used in Acts 26:29, "I would (to God, that)."

WOUND (Noun and Verb)

A. Noun.

trauma (τραῦμα, 5134), "a wound," occurs in Luke 10:34.¶

Note: Plēgē, "a blow, a stroke," is used in Luke 10:30 with *epitithēmi*, "to lay on," lit., "laid on blows," RV, "beat" (KJV, "wounded"). In Rev. 13:3, 12, *plēgē* is used with the genitive case of *thanatos*, "death," lit., "stroke of death," RV, "death stroke" (KJV, "deadly wound"); the rendering "wound" does not accurately give the meaning; in v. 14, with the genitive of *machaira*, "a sword," KJV, "wound" (RV, "stroke").

B. Verb.

traumatizō (τραυματίζω, 5135), "to wound" (from A), occurs in Luke 20:12 and Acts 19:16.¶

Note: In Rev. 13:3, KJV, *sphazō*, "to slay," is translated "wounded," RV, "smitten" (KJV and RV marg., "slain").

For **WOUND** (wrapped) see **WIND** (Verb)

WOVEN

huphantos (ὑφαντός, 5307), from *huphainō*, "to weave" (found in good mss. in Luke 12:27), is used of Christ's garment, John 19:23.¶

WRANGLINGS

diaparatribē (διαπαρατριβή, 3859v), found in 1 Tim. 6:5, denotes "constant strife," "obstinate contests" (Ellicott), "mutual irritations" (Field), KJV, "perverse disputings" (marg., "gallings one of another"), RV "wranglings." Some texts have *paradiatribē*. The preposition *dia-* is used intensively, indicating thoroughness, completeness.¶ The simple word *paratribē* (not found in the NT), denotes "hostility, enmity." See DISPUTE, No. 3.

WRAP

1. *eneileō* (ἐνειλέω, 1750), "to roll in, wind in," occurs in Mark 15:46; see WIND (Verb), No. 3.¶

2. *entulissō* (ἐντυλίσσω, 1794), "to roll in," occurs in Matt. 27:59; Luke 23:53; John 20:7: see ROLL, No. 5.¶

3. *sustellō* (συστέλλω, 4958), "to wrap" or "wind up," Acts 5:6; see WIND, No. 2; 1 Cor. 7:29, see SHORTEN, No. 2.¶

WRATH

1. *orgē* (ὀργή, 3709): see ANGER and *Notes* (1) and (2).

2. *thumos* (θυμός, 2372), "hot anger, passion," for which see ANGER, *Notes* (1) and (2), is translated "wrath" in Luke 4:28; Acts 19:28; Rom. 2:8, RV; Gal. 5:20; Eph. 4:31; Col. 3:8; Heb. 11:27; Rev. 12:12; 14:8, 10, 19; 15:1, 7; 16:1; 18:3; "wraths" in 2 Cor. 12:20; "fierceness" in Rev. 16:19; 19:15 (followed by No. 1).¶

3. *parorgismos* (παροργισμός, 3950) occurs in Eph. 4:26: see ANGER, A, *Note* (2).¶

Note: For the verb *parorgizō*, "to provoke to wrath," Eph. 6:4, KJV, see ANGER, B, No. 2.

WREST

strebloō (στρεβλόω, 4761), "to twist, to torture" (from *streblē*, "a winch" or "instrument of torture," and akin to *strephō*, "to turn"), is used metaphorically in 2 Pet. 3:16, of "wresting" the Scriptures on the part of the ignorant and unsteadfast.¶ In the Sept., 2 Sam. 22:27.¶

WRESTLE, WRESTLING

palē (πάλη, 3823), "a wrestling" (akin to *pallō*, "to sway, vibrate"), is used figuratively in Eph. 6:12, of the spiritual conflict engaged in by believers, RV, "(our) wrestling," KJV, "(we) wrestle."¶

WRETCHED

talaipōros (ταλαίπωρος, 5005), "distressed, miserable, wretched," is used in Rom. 7:24 and Rev. 3:17.¶ Cf. *talaipōria*, "misery," and *talaipōreō* (see AFFLICT).

WRINKLE

rhutis (ῥυτίς, 4512), from an obsolete verb *rhuō*, signifying "to draw together," occurs in Eph. 5:27, describing the flawlessness of the complete church, as the result of the love of Christ in giving Himself up for it, with the purpose of presenting it to Himself hereafter.¶

WRITE, WROTE, WRITTEN

A. Verbs.

1. *graphō* (γράφω, 1125) is used (*a*) of "forming letters" on a surface or writing material, John 8:6; Gal. 6:11, where the apostle speaks of his having "written" with large letters in his own hand, which not improbably means that at this point he took the pen from his amanuensis and finished the epistle himself; this is not negatived by the fact that the verb is in the aorist or past definite tense, lit., "I wrote," for in Greek idiom the writer of a letter put

himself beside the reader and spoke of it as having been "written" in the past; in Eng. we should say "I am writing," taking our point of view from the time at which we are doing it; cf. Philem. 19 (this Ep. is undoubtedly a holograph), where again the equivalent English translation is in the present tense (see also Acts 15:23; Rom. 15:15); possibly the apostle, in Galatians, was referring to his having "written" the body of the epistle but the former alternative seems the more likely; in 2 Thess. 3:17 he says that the closing salutation is written by his own hand and speaks of it as "the token in every epistle" which some understand as a purpose for the future rather than a custom; see, however, 1 Cor. 16:21 and Col. 4:18. The absence of the token from the other epistles of Paul can be explained differently, their authenticity not being dependent upon this; (b) "to commit to writing, to record," e.g., Luke 1:63; John 19:21, 22; it is used of Scripture as a standing authority, "it is written," e.g., Mark 1:2; Rom. 1:17 (cf. 2 Cor. 4:13); (c) of "writing directions or giving information," e.g., Rom. 10:5, "(Moses) writeth," RV (KJV, "describeth"); 15:15; 2 Cor. 7:12; (d) of "that which contained a record or message," e.g., Mark 10:4, 5; John 19:19; 21:25; Acts 23:25.

2. epistellō (ἐπιστέλλω, 1989) denotes "to send a message by letter, to write word" (stellō, "to send"; Eng., "epistle"), Acts 15:20; 21:25 (some mss. have apostellō, "to send"); Heb. 13:22.¶

3. prographō (προγράφω, 4270) denotes "to write before," Rom. 15:4 (in the best texts; some have graphō); Eph. 3:3. See SET (forth).

4. engraphō (ἐγγράφω, 1449) denotes "to write in," Luke 10:20; 2 Cor. 3:2, 3.¶

5. epigraphō (ἐπιγράφω, 1924) is rendered "to write over or upon" (epi) in Mark 15:26; figuratively, on the heart, Heb. 8:10; 10:16; on the gates of the heavenly Jerusalem, Rev. 21:12. See INSCRIPTION.

Notes: (1) For apographō, Heb. 12:23, KJV, "written," see ENROLL. (2) In 2 Cor. 3:7 "written" is a translation of en, "in," with the dative plural of gramma, a letter, lit., "in letters."

B. Adjective.

graptos (γραπτός, 1123), from A, No. 1, "written," occurs in Rom. 2:15.¶

WRITING

gramma (γράμμα, 1121), from graphō, "to write," is rendered "writings" in John 5:47. See LETTER, No. 1.

Notes: (1) For biblion, "writing," KJV in Matt. 19:7, see BILL, No. 1. (2) In John 19:19, KJV, "the writing (was)" is a translation of the perfect

participle, passive voice, of graphō, RV, "(there was) written."

WRITING TABLET (KJV, WRITING TABLE)

pinakidion (πινακίδιον, 4093) occurs in Luke 1:63, a diminutive of pinakis, "a tablet," which is a variant reading here.¶

WRONG (Noun and Verb), WRONGDOER, WRONGDOING

A. Nouns.

1. adikia (ἀδικία, 93), a, negative, dikē, "right," is translated "wrong" in 2 Pet. 2:13 (2nd part), 15, RV, "wrongdoing" (KJV, unrighteousness); in 2 Cor. 12:13, it is used ironically. See INIQUITY, UNJUST, UNRIGHTEOUSNESS.

2. adikēma (ἀδίκημα, 92) denotes "a misdeed, injury," in the concrete sense (in contrast to No. 1), Acts 18:14, "a matter of wrong"; 24:20, RV, "wrongdoing" (KJV, "evil doing"). See INIQUITY.

B. Verb.

adikeō (ἀδικέω, 91), "to do wrong," is used (a) intransitively, to act unrighteously, Acts 25:11, RV, "I am a wrongdoer" (KJV, "... an offender"); 1 Cor. 6:8; 2 Cor. 7:12 (1st part); Col. 3:25 (1st part); cf. Rev. 22:11 (see UNRIGHTEOUSNESS, B); (b) transitively, "to wrong," Matt. 20:13; Acts 7:24 (passive voice), 26, 27; 25:10; 2 Cor. 7:2, v. 12 (2nd part; passive voice); Gal. 4:12, "ye did (me no) wrong," anticipating a possible suggestion that his vigorous language was due to some personal grievance; the occasion referred to was that of his first visit; Col. 3:25 (2nd part), lit., "what he did wrong," which brings consequences both in this life and at the judgment seat of Christ; Philem. 18; 2 Pet. 2:13 (1st part); in the middle or passive voice, "to take or suffer wrong, to suffer (oneself) to be wronged," 1 Cor. 6:7. See HURT, OFFENDER, UNJUST.

WRONGFULLY

adikōs (ἀδίκως, 95), akin to the above, occurs in 1 Pet. 2:19.¶

Note: For "exact wrongfully," Luke 3:14, RV, see ACCUSE, B, No. 5.

WROTH (be)

1. orgizō (ὀργίζω, 3710), always in the middle or passive voice in the NT, is rendered "was (were) wroth" in Matt. 18:34; 22:7; Rev. 11:18, RV, (KJV, "were angry"); 12:17, RV, "waxed wroth." See ANGER, B, No. 1.

2. thumoō (θυμόω, 2373) signifies "to be very angry" (from thumos, "wrath, hot anger"),

"to be stirred into passion," Matt. 2:16, of Herod (passive voice).¶

3. *cholaō* (χολάω, 5520), primarily, "to be melancholy" (*cholē*, "gall"), signifies "to be

Y

YE, YOU, YOURSELVES, YOUR OWN SELVES

Notes: (1) These are most frequently the translations of various inflections of a verb; sometimes of the article before a nominative used as a vocative, e.g., Rev. 18:20, "ye saints, and ye apostles, and ye prophets" (lit., "the saints, etc."). When the 2nd person plural pronouns are used separately from a verb, they are usually one or other of the forms of *humeis*, the plural of *su*, "thou," and are frequently emphatic, especially when they are subjects of the verb, an emphasis always to be noticed, e.g., Matt. 5:13, 14, 48; 6:9, 19, 20; Mark 6:31, 37; John 15:27a; Rom. 1:6; 1 Cor. 3:17, 23; Gal. 3:28, 29a; Eph. 1:13a; 2:8; 2:11, 13; Phil. 2:18; Col. 3:4, 7a; 4:1; 1 Thess. 1:6; 2:10, 19, 20; 3:8; 2 Thess. 3:13; Jas. 5:8; 1 Pet. 2:9a; 1 John 2:20, 24 (1st and 3rd occurrences), 27a; 4:4; Jude 17, 20. (2) The addition of *autoi*, "yourselves," to the pronoun marks especial emphasis, e.g., Mark 6:31; John 3:28; 1 Cor. 11:13; 1 Thess. 4:9. Sometimes *autoi* is used without the pronoun, e.g., Luke 11:46, 52; Acts 2:22; 20:34; 1 Thess. 2:1; 3:3; 5:2; 2 Thess. 3:7; Heb. 13:3. (3) The reflexive pronoun "yourselves" represents the various plural forms of the reflexive pronoun *heautou* (frequently governed by some preposition), e.g., Matt. 3:9; 16:8; 23:31; 25:9; Mark 9:50; Luke 3:8; 12:33, 57; 16:9; 21:30, "of your own selves"; 21:34; Acts 5:35; in Rom. 11:25, "in your own (conceits)," lit., "in (*en;* some texts have *para,* 'among') yourselves"; so 12:16 (with *para*); 1 Pet. 4:8; Jude 20, 21; in Eph. 5:19, RV, "one to another" (KJV, and RV marg., "to yourselves").

Note: In 1 Thess. 5:11, KJV, *allēlous,* "one another" (RV), is rendered "yourselves together."

YEA, YES

1. *nai* (ναί, 3483), a particle of affirmation, is used (*a*) in answer to a question, Matt. 9:28; 11:9; 13:51; 17:25; 21:16; Luke 7:26; John 11:27; 21:15, 16; Acts 5:8; 22:27; Rom. 3:29; (*b*) in assent to an assertion, Matt. 15:27, RV (KJV, "truth"); Mark 7:28; Rev. 14:13; 16:7, RV (KJV, "even so"); (*c*) in confirmation of an assertion, Matt. 11:26 and Luke 10:21, RV (KJV, "even so"); Luke 11:51, RV (KJV, "verily"); 12:5; Phil. 4:3 (in the best texts); Philem. 20; (*d*) in solemn asseveration, Rev. 1:7 (KJV and RV, "even so"); 22:20, RV (KJV, "surely"); (*e*) in repetition for emphasis, Matt. 5:37; 2 Cor. 1:17; Jas. 5:12; (*f*) singly in contrast to *ou,* "nay," 2 Cor. 1:18, 19 (twice), 20, "(the) yea," RV.¶

2. *alla* (ἀλλά, 235), "but," is translated "yea" in John 16:2; Rom. 3:31, KJV (RV, "nay"); 1 Cor. 4:3; 2 Cor. 7:11 (six times); Gal. 4:17, KJV (RV, "nay"); Phil. 1:18; 2:17; 3:8; Jas. 2:18.

3. *kai* (καί, 2532), "and, even," is rendered "yea," e.g., Luke 2:35; John 16:32; 1 Cor. 2:10; 2 Cor. 8:3; in Acts 7:43, KJV (RV, "and").

4. *men oun* (μέν οὖν, 3304), i.e., *men-oun-ge,* "yea rather," occurs, e.g., in Luke 11:28; in Rom. 10:18, "yea (KJV, yes) verily"; in Phil. 3:8, RV, "yea verily" (KJV, "yea doubtless").

Notes: (1) In 1 Cor. 15:15 the RV translates *kai* by "and" (KJV, "yea"). (2) In Luke 24:22 the RV translates *alla kai* "moreover" (KJV, "yea . . . and"). (3) In 1 Cor. 16:6, KJV, *ē kai,* "or even" (RV), is translated "yea, and." (4) In 2 Cor. 5:16, KJV, the phrase *ei kai* (some texts have *ei de kai*) is translated "yea, though" (RV, "even though"). (5) In Phil. 2:8, RV, the particle *de,* "but," is translated "yea" (KJV, "even").

YEAR

A. Nouns.

1. *etos* (ἔτος, 2094) is used (*a*) to mark a point of time at or from which events take place, e.g., Luke 3:1 (dates were frequently reckoned from the time when a monarch began to reign); in Gal. 3:17 the time of the giving of the Law is stated as 430 "years" after the covenant of promise given to Abraham; there is no real discrepancy between this and Ex. 12:40; the apostle is not concerned with the exact

angry," John 7:23, RV, "are ye wroth" (KJV, " . . . angry").¶

For WROUGHT see WORK

duration of the interval; it certainly was not less than 430 "years"; the point of the argument is that the period was very considerable; Gal. 1:18 and 2:1 mark events in Paul's life; as to the former the point is that three "years" elapsed before he saw any of the apostles; in 2:1 the 14 "years" may date either from his conversion or from his visit to Peter mentioned in 1:18; the latter seems the more natural (for a full discussion of the subject see *Notes on Galatians* by Hogg and Vine, pp. 55ff.); (*b*) to mark a space of time, e.g., Matt. 9:20; Luke 12:19; 13:11; John 2:20; Acts 7:6, where the 400 "years" mark not merely the time that Israel was in bondage in Egypt, but the time that they sojourned or were strangers there (the RV puts a comma after the word "evil"); the Genevan Version renders Gen. 15:13 "thy posterity shall inhabit a strange land for 400 years"; Heb. 3:17; Rev. 20:2–7; (*c*) to date an event from one's birth, e.g., Mark 5:42; Luke 2:42; 3:23; John 8:57; Acts 4:22; 1 Tim. 5:9; (*d*) to mark recurring events, Luke 2:41 (with *kata*, used distributively); 13:7; (*e*) of an unlimited number, Heb. 1:12.

2. *eniautos* (ἐνιαυτός, 1763), originally "a cycle of time," is used (*a*) of a particular time marked by an event, e.g., Luke 4:19; John 11:49, 51; 18:13; Gal. 4:10; Rev. 9:15; (*b*) to mark a space of time, Acts 11:26; 18:11; Jas. 4:13; 5:17; (*c*) of that which takes place every year, Heb. 9:7; with *kata* [cf. (*d*) above], Heb. 9:25; 10:1, 3.¶

3. *dietia* (διετία, 1333) denotes "a space of two years" (*dis*, "twice," and No. 1), Acts 24:27; 28:30.¶

4. *trietia* (τριετία, 5148) denotes "a space of three years" (*treis*, "three," and No. 1), Acts 20:31.¶

Note: In Luke 1:7, 18, *hēmera*, "a day," is rendered "years."

B. Adjectives.

1. *dietēs* (διετής, 1332), akin to A, No. 3, denotes "lasting two years, two years old," Matt. 2:16.¶

2. *hekatontaetēs* (ἑκατονταετής, 1541) denotes "a hundred years old," Rom. 4:19.¶

C. Adverb.

perusi (πέρυσι, 4070), "last year, a year ago" (from *pera*, "beyond"), is used with *apo*, "from" 2 Cor. 8:10; 9:2.¶

Note: In Heb. 11:24, KJV, *ginomai*, "to become," with *megas*, "great," is rendered "when he was come to years" (RV, "when he was grown up").

For YES, see YEA

YESTERDAY

echthes or *chthes* (ἐχθές, 5504v) occurs in John 4:52; Acts 7:28; Heb. 13:8.¶

YET

Notes: This represents (1) the adverb *eti*, implying addition or duration, e.g., Matt. 12:40; Rom. 3:7; 5:6, 8; 9:19; in Heb. 12:26, 27, "yet ... more"; (2) *alla*, but, marking antithesis or transition, e.g., Mark 14:29; 1 Cor. 4:4, 15; 9:2; (3) *mentoi*, "nevertheless," John 4:27; 20:5; (4) *akmēn*, "even to this point of time" (the accusative case of *akmē*, "a point"), Matt. 15:16; ¶ (5) *ouketi*, "no longer," Mark 15:5, KJV, "yet ... nothing" (RV, "no more ... anything"); 2 Cor. 1:23, KJV, "not as yet"; "yet not," e.g. Gal. 2:20, KJV; (6) *oupō*, "not yet," John 7:39 and 1 Cor. 8:2 (*oudepō*, in some mss., KJV, "nothing yet"); *oudepō*, John 19:41, "never yet"; 20:9, "as yet ... not"; (7) *mēpō*, "not yet," Rom. 9:11; Heb. 9:8;¶ (8) *kai*, "and, even, also," "yet" in Luke 3:20; in Gal. 3:4, *ei ge kai*, KJV, "if ... yet" (RV, "if ... indeed"); (9) *ge*, a particle meaning "indeed," "yet," Luke 11:8; (10) *oudeis pōpote*, 19:30, RV, "no man ever yet," KJV, "yet never man," lit., "no one at any time (yet)"; (11) the following, in which the RV gives the correct meaning for the KJV, "yet": *ēdē*, "now," Mark 13:28; *pote*, "ever," Eph. 5:29 (KJV, "ever yet"); *kai ... de*, John 8:16, "yea and" (KJV, "and yet"); *ou pleious*, Acts 24:11, "not more"; (12) *mellō*, "to be about to," "are yet," Rev. 8:13; (13) other combinations with AND, AS, NOR, NOT.

YIELD

1. *didōmi* (δίδωμι, 1325), "to give," is translated "to yield," i.e., "to produce," in Matt. 13:8, RV (KJV, "brought forth"); Mark 4:7, 8. See GIVE.

2. *apodidōmi* (ἀποδίδωμι, 591), "to give up or back," is translated "to yield" in Heb. 12:11; Rev. 22:2 (in each case, of bearing fruit). See DELIVER, A, No. 3, etc.

3. *paristēmi* or *paristanō* (παρίστημι, 3936), "to present," is translated "to yield" in Rom. 6:13 (twice), 16, 19 (twice), RV, "to present," in each place. See COMMEND, etc.

4. *poieō* (ποιέω, 4160), "to make, to do," is translated "yield" in Jas. 3:12. See DO.

5. *aphiēmi* (ἀφίημι, 863), "to send away," is translated "yielded up (His spirit)" in Matt. 27:50 (cf. *paratithēmi*, "I commend," Luke 23:46, and *paradidōmi*, "He gave up," John 19:30). See FORGIVE, etc.

6. *peithō* (πείθω, 3982), "to persuade," in the passive voice, "to be persuaded," is translated

"do (not) thou yield," Acts 23:21. See PER-SUADE.

Note: In Acts 5:10, KJV, *ekpsuchō*, "to breathe one's last, expire" (*ek*, "out," *psuchē*, "the life"), is translated "yielded up" (RV, "gave up") the ghost." See GHOST (give up the), No. 2.

YOKE, YOKED

A. Nouns.

1. *zugos* (ζυγός, 2218), "a yoke," serving to couple two things together, is used (1) meta-phorically, (*a*) of submission to authority, Matt. 11:29, 30, of Christ's "yoke," not simply im-parted by Him but shared with Him; (*b*) of bondage, Acts 15:10 and Gal. 5:1, of bondage to the Law as a supposed means of salvation; (*c*) of bondservice to masters, 1 Tim. 6:1; (2) to denote "a balance," Rev. 6:5. See BALANCE.¶

2. *zeugos* (ζεῦγος, 2201), "a pair of ani-mals," Luke 14:19. See PAIR.

B. Verb.

heterozugeō (ἑτεροζυγέω, 2086), "to be un-equally yoked" (*heteros*, "another of a different sort," and A, No. 1), is used metaphorically in 2 Cor. 6:14.¶

YOKEFELLOW

sunzugos or *suzugos* (σύνζυγος, 4805), an adjective denoting "yoked together," is used as a noun in Phil. 4:3, "a yokefellow, fellow la-borer"; probably here it is a proper name, Syn-zygus, addressed as "true," or "genuine" (*gnēsios*), i.e., "properly so-called."¶

YONDER

ekei (ἐκεῖ, 1563), "there," is rendered "yon-der" in Matt. 26:36; "to yonder place," 17:20. See THERE, THITHER.

For YOU see YE

YOUNG, YOUNG (children, daughter, man, men, woman, women)

1. *neōteros* (νεώτερος, 3501), the compara-tive degree of *neos*, "new, youthful," is trans-lated "young" in John 21:18; in the plural, Acts 5:6, "young men" (marg., "younger"); Titus 2:6, KJV, RV, "younger men." See YOUNGER.

2. *neos* (νέος, 3501), in the feminine plural, denotes "young women," Titus 2:4. See NEW, No. 2.

3. *neanias* (νεανίας, 3494), "a young man," occurs in Acts 7:58; 20:9; 23:17, 18 (in some texts).¶

4. *neaniskos* (νεανίσκος, 3495), a diminu-tive of No. 3, "a youth, a young man," occurs in Matt. 19:20, 22; Mark 14:51 (1st part; RV

omits in 2nd part); 16:5; Luke 7:14; Acts 2:17; 5:10 (i.e., attendants); 23:18 (in the best texts), 22; 1 John 2:13, 14, of the second branch of the spiritual family.¶

5. *nossos* or *neossos* (νοσσός, 3502), "a young bird" (akin to No. 2), is translated "young" in Luke 2:24.¶ Cf. *nossia*, "a brood," Luke 13:34, and the noun *nossion*, used in the neuter plural, *nossia*, in Matt. 23:37, "chick-ens"; *nossion* is the diminutive of *nossos.*¶

Notes: (1) In Acts 20:12, KJV, *pais*, a "lad" (RV), is translated "young man." (2) In Mark 7:25, KJV, *thugatrion*, a diminutive of *thugatēr*, "a daughter," is rendered "young (RV, 'little') daughter." (3) In Mark 10:13, KJV, *paidion*, in the neuter plural, is rendered "young (RV, 'little') children." (4) In Acts 7:19, KJV, *brephos*, in the neuter plural, is rendered "young children," RV, "babes." See BABE, No. 1.

YOUNGER

1. *neōteros* (νεώτερος, 3501), for which see No. 1, above, occurs in Luke 15:12, 13; 22:26; 1 Tim. 5:1 ("younger men"); 5:2, feminine; v. 11, "younger (widows)"; v. 14, "younger (*wid-ows*)," RV, marg. and KJV, "younger (women)" (see WIDOW); 1 Pet. 5:5. For Titus 2:6 see YOUNG, No. 1.¶

2. *elassōn* (ἐλάσσων, 1640) is rendered "younger" in Rom. 9:12: see LESS.

YOUR, YOURS

Notes: (1) "Your" is most frequently the translation of *humōn*, lit., "of you," the genitive plural of *su*, "thou, you"; it is translated "yours" in 1 Cor. 3:21, 22; in 8:9, "of yours"; 16:18; 2 Cor. 12:14. In the following the dative plural, *humin*, lit., "to you," is translated "your"; Luke 16:11, lit., "(who will entrust) to you"; in 21:15 "your adversaries" is, lit., "(those opposed) to you"; in 1 Cor. 6:5 and 15:34, KJV, "(I speak to) your (shame)," RV, "(I say *this* to move) you (to shame)," is, lit., "(I speak unto a shame) to you." The accusative plural, *humas*, preceded by *kata*, "according to," is rendered in Acts 18:15 "your own (law)," RV, KJV, "your (law)," lit., "(of the law) according to you," with em-phasis and scorn; in Eph. 1:15 the same con-struction is used of faith, but *kata* here means "among," as in the RV, "(the faith . . . which is) among you," KJV, "your (faith)"; in John 14:26 "He shall . . . bring to your remembrance" is, lit., "He shall . . . put you in mind of." (2) The possessive pronoun, *humeteros*, "your," is used in Luke 6:20; John 7:6; 8:17; 15:20; Acts 27:34; Rom. 11:31; 1 Cor. 15:31; 16:17; 2 Cor. 8:8; Gal. 6:13; in Luke 16:12, "your own."¶ (3) In Rom. 16:19, KJV, the phrase *to epi humin*, lit., "the (matter) over you," is rendered "on your behalf" (RV, "over you," following the mss. which omit the neuter article *to*).

YOUTH

neotēs (νεότης, 3503), from *neos*, "new," occurs in Mark 10:20; Luke 18:21; Acts 26:4; 1 Tim. 4:12 (in some mss., Matt. 19:20).¶

YOUTHFUL

neōterikos (νεωτερικός, 3512), from *neōteros*, the comparative degree of *neos*, "new," is used especially of qualities, of lusts, 2 Tim. 2:22.¶

Z

ZEAL

zēlos (ζῆλος, 2205) denotes "zeal" in the following passages: John 2:17, with objective genitive, i.e., "zeal for Thine house"; so in Rom. 10:2, "a zeal for God"; in 2 Cor. 7:7, RV, "(your) zeal (for me)," KJV, "(your) fervent mind (toward me)"; used absolutely in 7:11; 9:2; Phil. 3:6 (in Col. 4:13 in some texts; the best have *ponos*, "labor," RV). See ENVY, *Note*, FERVENT, C, *Note* (2), INDIGNATION, A, *Note* (3), JEALOUSY.

ZEALOUS

A. Noun.

zēlōtēs (ζηλωτής, 2207) is used adjectivally, of "being zealous" (*a*) "of the Law," Acts 21:20; (*b*) "toward God," lit., "of God," 22:3, RV, "for God"; (*c*) "of spiritual gifts," 1 Cor. 14:12, i.e., for exercise of spiritual gifts (lit., "of spirits," but not to be interpreted literally); (*d*) "for (KJV, 'of') the traditions of my fathers," Gal. 1:14, of Paul's loyalty to Judaism before his conversion; (*e*) "of good works," Titus 2:14.

The word is, lit., "a zealot," i.e., "an uncompromising partisan." The "Zealots" was a name applied to an extreme section of the Pharisees, bitterly antagonistic to the Romans. Josephus (*Antiq.* xviii. 1. 1, 6; *B.J.* ii. 8. 1) refers to them

as the "fourth sect of Jewish philosophy" (i.e., in addition to the Pharisees, Sadducees, and Essenes), founded by Judas of Galilee (cf. Acts 5:37). After his rebellion in A.D. 6, the Zealots nursed the fires of revolt, which, bursting out afresh in A.D. 66, led to the destruction of Jerusalem in 70. To this sect Simon, one of the apostles, had belonged, Luke 6:15; Acts 1:13. The equivalent Hebrew and Aramaic term was "Cananaean" (Matt. 10:4); this is not connected with Canaan, as the KJV "Canaanite" would suggest, but is derived from Heb. *qannâ*, "jealous."¶

B. Verbs.

1. *zēloō* (ζηλόω, 2206), "to be jealous," also signifies "to seek or desire eagerly"; in Gal. 4:17, RV, "they zealously seek (you)," in the sense of taking a very warm interest in; so in v. 18, passive voice, "to be zealously sought" (KJV, "to be zealously affected"), i.e., to be the object of warm interest on the part of others; some texts have this verb in Rev. 3:19 (see No. 2). See AFFECT, *Note*, COVET, DESIRE, ENVY, JEALOUS.

2. *zēleuō* (ζηλεύω), a late and rare form of No. 1, is found in the best texts in Rev. 3:19, "be zealous."¶

Note: For *spoudazō*, Gal. 2:10, RV, see DILIGENT, B, No. 1.

ADDITIONAL NOTES

ON THE PARTICLE KAI (καί, 2532)

(*a*) The particle *kai*, "and," chiefly used for connecting words, clauses and sentences (the

copulative or connective use), not infrequently signifies "also." This is the *adjunctive*, or *amplificatory*, use, and it is to be distinguished from the purely copulative significance "and." A good illustration is provided in Matt. 8:9, in the words of the centurion, "I also am a man under authority." Other instances are Matt. 5:39, 40; 8:9; 10:18; 18:33; 20:4; Luke 11:49; 12:41, 54, 57; 20:3; John 5:26, "the Son also," RV; 7:3; 12:10; 14:1, 3, 7, 19; 15:9, 27; 17:24; Acts 11:17; Rom. 1:13; 6:11; 1 Cor. 7:3; 11:25; 15:30; Gal. 6:1; Phil. 4:12, "I know also," RV; 1 Thess. 3:12. In 1 Cor. 2:13 the *kai* phrase signifies "which are the very things we speak, with the like power of the Holy Spirit."

This use includes the meanings "so," or "just so," by way of comparison, as in Matt. 6:10, and "so also," e.g., John 13:33; cf. Rom. 11:16. In Heb. 7:26 the most authentic mss. have *kai* in the first sentence, which may be rendered "for such a High Priest also became us." Here it virtually has the meaning "precisely."

(*b*) Occasionally *kai* tends towards an *adversative* meaning, expressing a contrast, "yet," almost the equivalent of *alla*, "but"; see, e.g., Mark 12:12, "yet they feared"; Luke 20:19; John 18:28, "yet they themselves entered not." Some take it in this sense in Rom. 1:13, where, however, it may be simply parenthetic. Sometimes in the English versions the "yet" has been added in italics, as in 2 Cor. 6:8, 9, 10.

(*c*) In some passages *kai* has the meaning "and yet," e.g., Matt. 3:14, "and yet comest Thou to me?"; 6:26, "and yet (RV 'and,' KJV, 'yet') your Heavenly Father feedeth them"; Luke 18:7, "and yet He is longsuffering"; John 3:19, "and yet men loved the darkness"; 4:20, "and yet we say"; 6:49, "and yet they died"; 1 Cor. 5:2, "and yet ye are puffed up"; 1 John 2:9, "and yet hateth his brother." The same is probably the case in John 7:30, "and yet no man laid hands on Him"; some rule this and similar cases out because of the negative in the sentence following the *kai*, but that seems hardly tenable.

(*d*) In some passages it has a *temporal* significance, "then." In Luke 7:12 the *kai*, which is untranslated in the English versions, provides the meaning "then, behold, there was carried out"; so Acts 1:10, "then, behold, two men stood." This use is perhaps due to the influence of the Septuagint, reflecting the Hebrew idiom, especially when *idou* "behold" follows the *kai.*

(*e*) There is also the *inferential* use before a question, e.g., Mark 10:26, "then who can be saved?" RV. This is commonly expressed by the English "and," as in Luke 10:29; John 9:36.

(*f*) Occasionally it has almost the sense of *hoti,* "that," e.g., Matt. 26:15 (first part); Mark 14:40 (last part); Luke 5:12, 17, where, if the *kai* had been translated, the clause might be rendered "that, behold, a man ...," lit., " and

behold ... "; so v. 17; see also 9:51, where *kai,* "that," comes before "He steadfastly set"; in 12:15, "take heed that ye keep." What is said under (*d*), regarding the influence of the Septuagint, is applicable also to this significance.

(*g*) Sometimes it has the consecutive meaning of "and so": e.g., Matt. 5:15, "and so it shineth"; Phil. 4:7, "and so the peace ... "; Heb. 3:19, "and so we see."

(*h*) The *epexegetic* or *explanatory* use. This may be represented by the expressions "namely," "again," "and indeed," "that is to say"; it is usually translated by "and." In such cases not merely an addition is in view. In Matt. 21:5, "and upon a colt" means "that is to say, upon a colt." In John 1:16 the clause "and grace for grace" is explanatory of the "fullness." In John 12:48, "and receiveth not My sayings," is not simply an addition to "that rejecteth Me," it explains what the rejection involves, as the preceding verse shows. In Mark 14:1, "and the unleavened bread" is perhaps an instance, since the Passover feast is so defined in Luke 22:1. In Acts 23:6 the meaning is "the hope, namely, the resurrection of the dead." In Rom. 1:5 "grace and apostleship" may signify "grace expressed in apostleship." In Eph. 1:1 "and the faithful" does not mark a distinct class of believers, it defines "the saints"; but in this case it goes a little further than what is merely epexegetical, it adds a more distinctive epithet than the preceding and may be taken as meaning "yes indeed."

For the suggestion as to the epexegetic use of *kai* in John 3:5, "water, even the Spirit," see WATER.

In regard to Titus 3:5, "the renewing of the Holy Ghost" is coordinate with "the washing of regeneration," and some would regard it as precisely explanatory of that phrase, taking the *kai* as signifying "namely." Certainly the "renewing" is not an additional and separate impartation of the Holy Spirit; but the scope of the renewal is surely not limited to regeneration; the second clause goes further than what is merely epexegetic of the first. Just so in Rom. 12:2, "the renewing of your mind" is not a single act, accomplished once and for all, as in regeneration. See under RENEW, B. The Holy Ghost, as having been "shed on us," continues to act in renewing us, in order to maintain by His power the enjoyment of the relationship into which He has brought us. "The man is cleansed in connection with the new order of things; but the Holy Ghost is a source of an entirely new life, entirely new thoughts; not only of a new moral being, but of the communication of all that in which this new being develops itself ... He ever communicates more and more of the things of this new world into which He has brought us ... 'the renewing of the Holy Ghost' embraces all this ... so that it is not only that we are born of Him, but that He works in us, communicating to us all that is ours in Christ" (J. N. Darby). Both the washing and the renewing are His work.

(i) The *ascensive* use. This is somewhat similar to the epexegetic significance. It represents, however, an advance in thought upon what precedes and has the meaning "even." The context alone can determine the occurrences of this use. The following are some instances. In Matt. 5:46, 47, the phrases "even the publicans" and "even the Gentiles" represent an extension of thought in regard to the manner of reciprocity exhibited by those referred to, in comparison with those who, like the Pharisees, were considered superior to them. In Mark 1:27, "even the unclean spirits" represents an advance in the minds of the people concerning Christ's miraculous power, in comparison with the authority exercised by the Lord in less remarkable ways. So in Luke 10:17. In Acts 10:45, the *kai*, rendered "also," in the phrase "on the Gentiles also," seems necessary to be regarded in the same way, in view of the amazement manifested by those of the circumcision, and thus the rendering will be "even on the Gentiles was poured out the gift"; cf. 11:1.

In Rom. 13:5, the clause "but also for conscience sake" should probably be taken in this sense. In Gal. 2:13, the phrase "even Barnabas" represents an advance of thought in comparison with the waywardness of others; as much as to say, "the Apostle's closest associate, from whom something different might be expected, was surprisingly carried away." In Phil. 4:16 there are three occurrences of *kai*, the first ascensive, "even"; the second (untranslated) meaning "both," before the word "once"; the third meaning "and." In 1 Thess. 1:5, in the cause "and in the Holy Ghost," the *kai* rendered "and," is ascensive, conveying an extension of thought beyond "power"; that is to say, "power indeed, but the power of the Holy Spirit." In 1 Pet. 4:14 "the Spirit of God" is "the Spirit of glory." Here there is an advance in idea from the abstract to the personal. The phrase "the Spirit of God" does more than define "the Spirit of glory"; it is explanatory but ascensive also.

When preceded or followed by the conjunction *ei*, "if," the phrase signifies "even if," or "if even," e.g., Mark 14:29; Phil. 2:17; 1 Pet. 3:1.

ON THE PARTICLE DE (δέ, 1161)

The particle *de* has two chief uses, (a) *continuative* or *copulative*, signifying "and," or "in the next place," (b) *adversative*, signifying "but," or "on the other hand." The first of these, (a), is well illustrated in the genealogy in Matt. 1:2–16, the line being simply reckoned from Abraham to Christ. So in 2 Cor. 6:15, 16, where the *de* anticipates a negative more precisely than would be the case if *kai* had been used. In 1 Cor. 15:35; Heb. 12:6, e.g., the *de* "and (scourgeth)" is purely copulative.

(b) The adversative use distinguishes a word or clause from that which precedes. This is exemplified, for instance, in Matt. 5:22, 28, 32, 34, 39, 44, in each of which the *egō*, "I," stands out with pronounced stress by way of contrast. This use is very common. In Matt. 23:4 the first *de* is copulative, "Yea, they bind heavy burdens" (RV), the second is adversative, "but they themselves will not ... "

In John 3:1, RV, it may not at first sight seem clear whether the *de*, "Now," is copulative, introducing an illustration of Christ's absolute knowledge, or adversative, signifying "But." In the former case the significance would be that, however fair the exterior might be, as exemplified in Nicodemus, he needs to be born again. In the latter case it introduces a contrast, in regard to Nicodemus, to what has just been stated, that "Jesus did not trust Himself" (2:24) to those mentioned in v. 23. And, inasmuch as He certainly did afford to Nicodemus the opportunity of learning the truths of the New Birth and the kingdom of God, as a result of which he became a disciple ("secret" though he was), he may be introduced in the apostle's narrative as an exception to those who believed simply through seeing the signs accomplished by the Lord (2:23).

In Rom. 3:22, in the clause "even the righteousness," the *de* serves to annex not only an explanation, defining "a righteousness of God" (v. 21, RV), but an extension of the thought; so in 9:30, "even the righteousness which is of faith."

In 1 Cor. 2:6, in the clause "yet a wisdom," an exception (not an addition) is made to what precedes; some would regard this as belonging to (a) it seems, however, clearly adversative. In 4:7 the first *de* is copulative, "and what hast thou ... ?"; the second is adversative, "but if thou didst receive ... "

In 1 Thess. 5:21 "many ancient authorities insert 'but'" (see RV marg.), so translating *de*, between the two injunctions "despise not prophesyings" and "prove all things," and this is almost certainly the correct reading. In any case the injunctions are probably thus contrastingly to be connected.

In 2 Pet. 1:5–7, after the first *de*, which has

the meaning "yea," the six which follow, in the phrases giving virtues to be supplied, suggest the thought "but there is something further to be done." These are not merely connective, as expressed by the English "and," but adversative, as indicating a contrast to the possible idea that to add virtue to our faith is sufficient for the moral purpose in view.

De, in combination with the negatives *ou* and *mē* (*oude* and *mēde*, usually "but not," "and not," "neither," "nor,"), sometimes has the force of "even," e.g., *oude* in Matt. 6:29, "even Solomon ... was not arrayed ... "; Mark 6:31, lit., "(they had) not even leisure to eat"; Luke 7:9, lit., "not even in Israel have I found such faith"; John 7:5, "For even His brethren did not believe on Him"; Acts 4:32, lit., "not even one of them"; 1 Cor. 5:1, "not even among the Gentiles"; *mēde*, in Mark 2:2, "not even about the door"; 1 Cor 5:11, lit., "with such a one not even to eat."

ON THE PREPOSITIONS ANTI
(ἀντί, 473) AND **HUPER** (ὑπέρ, 5228)

The basic idea of *anti* is "facing." This may be a matter of opposition, unfriendliness or antagonism, or of agreement. These meanings are exemplified in compounds of the preposition with verbs, and in nouns. The following are instances: *antiparerchomai* in Luke 10:31, 32, where the verb is rendered "passed by on the other side," i.e., of the road, but facing the wounded man; *antiballō* in Luke 24:17, where the *anti* suggests that the two disciples, in exchanging words (see RV marg.), turned to face one another, indicating the earnest nature of their conversation. The idea of antagonism is seen in *antidikos*, "an adversary," Matt. 5:25, *antichristos*, "antichrist," 1 John 4:3, etc.

There is no instance of the uncompounded preposition signifying "against." Arising from the basic significance, however, there are several other meanings attaching to the separate use of the preposition. In the majority of the occurrences in the NT, the idea is that of "in the place of," "instead of," or of exchange; e.g., Matt. 5:38, "an eye for (*anti*) an eye"; Rom. 12:17, "evil for evil"; so 1 Thess, 5:15; 1 Pet. 3:9, and, in the same verse, "reviling for reviling." The ideas of substitution and exchange are combined, e.g., in Luke 11:11, "for a fish ... a serpent"; Heb. 12:16, "for one mess of meat ... his own birthright." So in Matt. 17:27, "a shekel (*statēr*) ... for thee and Me," where the phrase is condensed; that is to say, the exchange is that of the coin for the tax demanded from Christ

and Peter, rather than for the persons themselves. So in 1 Cor. 11:15, where the hair is a substitute for the covering.

Of special doctrinal importance are Matt. 20:28; Mark 10:45, "to give His life a ransom (*lutron*) for (*anti*) many." Here the substitutionary significance, "instead of," is clear, as also with the compound *antilutron* in 1 Tim. 2:6, "who gave Himself a ransom (*antitutron*) for (*huper*) all"; here the use of *huper*, "on behalf of," is noticeable. Christ gave Himself as a ransom (of a substitutionary character), not instead of all men, but on behalf of *all.* The actual substitution, as in the passages in Matthew and Mark, is expressed by the *anti*, instead of, "*many.*" The unrepentant man should not be told that Christ was his substitute, for in that case the exchange would hold good for him and though unregenerate he would not be in the place of death, a condition in which, however, he exists while unconverted. Accordingly the "many" are those who, through faith, are delivered from that condition. The substitutionary meaning is exemplified in Jas. 4:15, where the KJV and RV render the *anti* "for that" (RV, marg., "instead of").

In Heb. 12:2, "for (*anti*) the joy that was set before Him endured the cross," neither the thought of exchange nor that of substitution is conveyed; here the basic idea of facing is present. The cross and the joy faced each other in the mind of Christ and He chose the one with the other in view.

In John 1:16 the phrase "grace for grace" is used. The idea of "following upon" has been suggested, as wave follows wave. Is not the meaning that the grace we receive corresponds to the grace inherent in Christ, out of whose fullness we receive it?

The primary meaning of *huper* is "over," "above." Hence, metaphorically, with the accusative case, it is used of superiority, e.g., Matt. 10:24, "above his master" (or teacher); or of measure in excess, in the sense of beyond, e.g., 1 Cor. 4:6, "beyond the things that are written"; or "than," after a comparative, e.g., Luke 16:8; Heb. 4:12; or "more than," after a verb, e.g., Matt. 10:37. With the genitive it means "on behalf of, in the interests of," e.g., of prayer, Matt. 5:44; of giving up one's life, and especially of Christ's so doing for man's redemption, e.g., John 10:15; 1 Tim. 2:6, "on behalf of all" (see under *Anti*); 2 Thess. 2:1, "in the interest of (i.e., 'with a view to correcting your thoughts about') the Coming." The difficult passage, 1 Cor. 15:29, possibly comes here. With an alteration of the punctuation (feasible from the ms. point of view), the reference may be to baptism as taught elsewhere in the NT, and the verse may read thus: "Else what shall they do which are being baptized? (i.e., what purpose can they serve?); (it is) in the interest of the dead, if the dead are not raised at all. Why then are they baptized in the interest of them?" That is to say, they fulfill the ordinance in the interest of a Christ who is dead and in joint witness with (and therefore, in the interest of) believers who never will be raised, whereas an essential element in baptism is its testimony to the resurrection of Christ and of the believer.

In some passages *huper* may be used in the substitutionary sense, e.g., John 10:11, 15; Rom. 8:32; but it cannot be so taken in the majority of instances. Cf. 2 Cor. 5:15, in regard to which, while it might be said that Christ died in place of us, it cannot be said that Christ rose again in the place of us.

ON THE PREPOSITIONS APO (ἀπό, 575) AND EK (ἐκ, 1537).

The primary meaning of *apo* is "off"; this is illustrated in such compounds as *apokaluptō*, "to take the veil off, to reveal"; *apokoptō*, "to cut off"; hence there are different shades of meaning, the chief of which is "from" or "away from," e.g., Matt. 5:29, 30; 9:22; Luke 24:31, lit., "He became invisible from them"; Rom. 9:3.

The primary meaning of *ek* is "out of," e.g., Matt. 3:17, "a voice out of the heavens" (RV); 2 Cor. 9:7, lit., "out of necessity." Omitting such significances of *ek* as "origin, source, cause, occasion," etc., our consideration will here be confined to a certain similarity between *apo* and *ek*. Since *apo* and *ek* are both frequently to be translated by "from" they often approximate closely in meaning. The distinction is largely seen in this, that *apo* suggests a starting point from without, *ek* from within; this meaning is often involved in *apo*, but *apo* does not give prominence to the "within-ness," as *ek* usually does. For instance, *apo* is used in Matt. 3:16, where the RV rightly reads "Jesus ... went up straightway from the water"; in Mark 1:10 *ek* is used, "coming up out of the water"; *ek* (which stands in contrast to *eis* in v. 9) stresses more emphatically than *apo* the fact of His having been baptized in the water. In all instances where these prepositions appear to be used alternately this distinction is to be observed.

The literal meaning "out of" cannot be attached to *ek* in a considerable number of passages. In several instances *ek* obviously has the significance of "away from"; and where either meaning seems possible, the context, or some other passage, affords guidance. The following are examples in which *ek* does not mean "out of the midst of" or "out from within," but has much the same significance as *apo*: John 17:15, "that Thou shouldest keep them from the evil one"; 1 Cor. 9:19, "though I was free from all men"; 2 Cor. 1:10, "who delivered us from so great a death" (KJV); 2 Pet. 2:21, "to turn back from the holy commandment"; Rev. 15:2, "them that had come victorious from the beast, and from his image, and from the number of his name" (*ek* in each case).

Concerning the use of *ek*, in 1 Thess. 1:10, "Jesus, which delivereth (the present tense, as in the RV, is important) us from the wrath to come" [or, more closely to the original, "our Deliverer (cf. the same phrase in Rom. 11:26) from the coming wrath"], the passage makes clear that the wrath signifies the calamities to be visited by God upon men when the present period of grace is closed. As to whether the *ek* here denotes "out of the midst of" or "preservation from," this is determined by the statement in 5:9, that "God appointed us not unto wrath, but unto the obtaining of salvation"; the context there shows that the salvation is from the wrath just referred to. Accordingly the *ek* signifies "preservation from" in the same sense as *apo*, and not "out from the midst of."

ON THE PREPOSITION EN (ἐν, 1772)

En, "in," is the most common preposition. It has several meanings, e.g., "of place" (e.g., Heb. 1:3, lit., "on the right hand," i.e., in that position), and time, e.g., in 1 Thess. 2:19; 3:13; 1 John 2:28, in each of which the phrase "at His coming" (inadequately so rendered, and lit., "in His Parousia") combines place and time; the noun, while denoting a period, also signifies a presence involving accompanying circumstances, e.g., 1 Thess. 4:15.

Further consideration must here be confined to the instrumental use, often rendered "with" (though *en* in itself does not mean "with"), e.g., Matt. 5:13, "wherewith" (lit., 'in what,' i.e., by what means) shall it be salted"; 7:2, "with what measure ye mete." Sometimes the instrumental is associated with the locative significance (which indeed attaches to most of its uses), e.g., Luke 22:49, "shall we smite with the sword?" the smiting being viewed as located in the sword; so in Matt. 26:52, "shall perish with the sword"; cf. Rev. 2:16; 6:8; 13:10. In Matt. 12:24, "by (marg., 'in') Beelzebub," indicates that the casting out is located in Beelzebub. Cf.

Luke 1:51, "with His arm." In Heb. 11:37, the statement "they were slain with the sword" is, lit., "they died by (*en*) slaughter of the sword." There is a noticeable change in Rom. 12:21, from *hupo*, "by," to *en*, "with," in this instrumental and locative sense; the lit. rendering is "be not overcome by (*hupo*) evil, but overcome evil with (*en*) good," *en* expressing both means and circumstances. A very important instance of the instrumental *en* is in Rom. 3:25, where the RV, "faith, by His blood," corrects the KJV, "faith in His blood," and the commas which the RV inserts are necessary. Thus the statement reads "whom God set forth to be a propitiation, through faith, by His blood." Christ is a propitiation, by means of His blood, i.e., His expiatory death. Faith is exercised in the living God, not in the blood, which provides the basis of faith.

GREEK WORD INDEX

Note: The English words in the Index are not necessarily the meanings of the Greek words which are found under the English headings. The first number following each entry word refers to Strong's Greek Lexicon, the second to the page number in A Greek-English Lexicon of the New Testament and other Early Christian Literature *by Bauer, Arndt, and Gingrich, Second Edition (Chicago: 1979).*

A

abarēs [4; 1]
  burdensome
abba [5; 1]
  abba
abussos [12; 2]
  abyss, bottom, deep, pit
acharistos [884; 128]
  unthankful
acheiropoiētos [886; 128]
  hands (not made with)
achlus [887; 128]
  mist
achre(i)oō [889; 128]
  unprofitable
achreios [888; 128]
  unprofitable
achrēstos [890; 128]
  unprofitable
achri(s) [891; 128]
  until
achuron [892; 129]
  chaff
adapanos [77; 15]
  charge
adēlos [82; 16]
  appear (not), uncertain
adēlōs [84; 16]
  uncertainly
adēlotēs [83; 16]
  uncertain, uncertainly
adelphē [79; 15]
  believer, sister
adelphos [80; 15]
  brother
adelphotēs [81; 16]
  brotherhood
adēmoneō [85; 16]
  heaviness, heavy, trouble
adiakritos [87; 17]
  partiality, variance
adialeiptos [88; 17]
  cease, continual, unceasing
adialeiptōs [89; 17]
  cease, unceasingly
adiaphthoria [90; 17]
  uncorruptness
adikēma [92; 17]
  evil, iniquity, wrong
adikeō [91; 17]
  hurt, injure, offender, suffer,
  unjust, unrighteousness,
  wrong, wrong-doer

adikia [93; 17]
  iniquity, unjust,
  unrighteousness, wrong
adikos [94; 18]
  unjust, unrighteous
adikōs [95; 18]
  wrongfully
adō [103; 19]
  sing
adokimos [96; 18]
  cast, reject, reprobate
adolos [97; 18]
  guileless, sincere
adunateō [101; 19]
  impossible
adunatos [102; 19]
  impossible, impotent, weak
aei [104; 19]
  always, ever
aēr [109; 20]
  air
aetos [105; 19]
  eagle
agalliaō [21; 3]
  glad, joy, rejoice
agalliasis [20; 3] -
  gladness, joy
agamos [22; 4]
  unmarried
aganakteō [23; 4]
  displeased, indignation
aganaktēsis [24; 4]
  indignation
agapaō [25; 4]
  beloved, love
agapē [26; 5]
  charity, dear, feast, love
agapētos [27; 6]
  beloved, dear
agathopoieō [15; 2]
  good (to do), well, well-
  doing
agathopoiia [16; 2]
  well-doing
agathopoios [17; 2]
  well (do)
agathos [18; 2]
  benefit, good, goods, kind
agathōsunē [19; 3]
  goodness
agathourgeō [14; 3]
  good (to do)
agelē [34; 8]
  herd

agenealogētos [35; 8]
  genealogy
agenēs [36; 8]
  base
agnaphos [46; 10]
  new, undressed
agnoēma [51; 11]
  error, ignorance
agnoeō [50; 11]
  ignorant, ignorantly, know,
  understand
agnoia [52; 11]
  ignorance
agnōsia [56; 12]
  ignorance
agnōstos [57; 12]
  known, unknown
agō [71; 14]
  bring, carry, go, keep, lead,
  open
agōgē [72; 14]
  conduct, life, manner
agōn [73; 15]
  conflict, contention, fight,
  race
agōnia [74; 15]
  agony
agōnizomai [75; 15]
  fervently, fight, labor, strive
agora [58; 12]
  market, market-place, street
agoraios [60; 13]
  baser, court
agorazō [59; 12]
  buy, purchase, redeem
agra [61; 13]
  draught
agrammatos [62; 13]
  unlearned
agrauleō [63; 13]
  abide
agreuō [64; 13]
  catch
agrielaios [65; 13]
  olive, tree (*wild*)
agrios [66; 13]
  raging, wild
agros [68; 13]
  country, farm, field, ground,
  land, piece
agrupneō [69; 14]
  watch
agrupnia [70; 14]
  watching

aichmalōsia [161; 26]
  captivity
aichmalōteuō [162; 26]
  captive
aichmalōtizō [163; 27]
  captive, captivity
aichmalōtos [164; 27]
  captive
aïdios [126; 22]
  eternal, everlasting
aidōs [127; 22]
  ashamed, reverence,
  shamefastness
aigeios [122; 21]
  goat (skin)
aigialos [123; 21]
  beach, shore
aineō [134; 23]
  praise
ainesis [133; 23]
  praise
ainigma [135; 23]
  darkly
ainos [136; 23]
  praise
aiōn [165; 27]
  age, course, eternal, ever,
  evermore, world
aiōnios [166; 28]
  eternal, everlasting
aiphnidios [160; 26]
  sudden, unawares
airō [142; 24]
  away, bear, carry, doubt
  (make to), hoise up, hoist up,
  lift, loose, put, remove,
  suspense, take
aischrokerdēs [146; 25]
  filthy, lucre
aischrokerdōs [147; 25]
  filthy, lucre
aischrologia [148; 25]
  communication, filthy
aischros [150; 25]
  filthy, shame
aischrotēs [151; 25]
  filthiness
aischunē [152; 25]
  dishonesty, shame
*aischunō (-omai) [153; 25]
  ashamed
aisthanomai [143; 24]
  perceive
aisthēsis [144; 25]
  judgment
aisthētērion [145; 25]
  sense
aitēma [155; 26]
  ask, petition, request, require
aiteō [154; 25]
  ask, beg, call, crave, desire,
  request, require

aitia [156; 26]
  accusation, case, cause,
  charge, crime, fault
aitiōma [157v**; 26]
  charge, complaint
aition [158; 26]
  cause, fault
aitios [159; 26]
  author
akaireomai [170; 29]
  opportunity (lack)
akairōs [171; 29]
  season
akakos [172; 29]
  guileless, harmless, innocent,
  simple
akantha [173; 29]
  thorn(s) (of)
akanthinos [174; 29]
  thorns (of)
akarpos [175; 29]
  fruit, unfruitful
akatagnōstos [176; 29]
  condemn
akatakaluptos [177; 29]
  uncovered, unveiled
akatakritos [178; 29]
  uncondemned
akatalutos [179; 30]
  endless
akatapaustos [180; 30]
  cease
akataschetos [183; 30]
  unruly
akatastasia [181; 30]
  commotion, confusion,
  tumult
akatastatos [182; 30]
  restless, unstable
akatharsia [167; 28]
  uncleanness
akathartēs [168; 29]
  foul, unclean
akathartos [169; 29]
  filthy, foul, unclean
akeraios [185; 30]
  harmless, simple
aklinēs [186; 30]
  waver
akmazō [187; 30]
  ripe (to be fully)
akmēn [188; 30]
  yet
akoē [189; 30]
  ear, fame, hear, hearing,
  message, report, rumor
akoloutheō [190; 31]
  follow, reach
akōlutōs [209; 34]
  forbid
akōn [210; 34]
  will
akouō [191; 31]
  audience, ear, hear, hearer,

hearing, hearken, noise,
report
akrasia [192; 33]
  excess, incontinency
akratēs [193; 33]
  incontinent, self-control
  (without)
akratos [194; 33]
  mixture, unmixed
akribeia [195; 33]
  manner, strict
akribēs [196*; 33]
  straitest
akribesteron [197; 33*]
  carefully, exact, exactly,
  perfectly
akribestatos [196; 33*]
  straitest
akriboō [198; 33]
  inquire, learn
akribōs [199; 33]
  accurately, carefully,
  circumspectly, diligently,
  perfectly
akris [200; 33]
  locust
akroatērion [201; 33]
  hearing, place
akroatēs [202; 33]
  hearer
akrobustia [203; 33]
  uncircumcision
akrogōniaios [204; 33]
  chief, corner
akron [206; 34]
  end, tip, top, uttermost part
akrothinion [205; 33]
  spoil
akuroō [208; 34]
  disannul, effect, void
alabastron [211; 34]
  box, cruse
alalazō [214; 34]
  clanging, tinkle, wail
alalētos [215; 34]
  utter
alalos [216; 34]
  dumb
alazōn [213; 34]
  boast, boastful
alazon(e)ia [212; 34]
  boast, pride, vainglory, vaunt
aleiphō [218; 35]
  anoint
alektōr [220; 35]
  cock
alektorophōnia [219; 35]
  cock-crowing
alētheia [225; 35]
  true, truth, verity
alēthēs [227; 36]
  indeed, true, truly, truth
alētheuō [226; 36]
  truth

alēthinos [228; 37]
　true
alēthō [229; 37]
　grind
alēthōs [230; 37]
　indeed, surely, truth, true,
　truly, verily
aleuron [224; 35]
　meal
alisgēma [234; 37]
　pollution
alla [235; 38]
　nay, notwithstanding, rather,
　yea, yet
allachothen [237; 39]
　way
allachou [237v; 39]
　elsewhere
allassō [236; 39]
　change
allēgoreō [238; 39]
　allegory, contain
allēlōn [240; 39]
　each other, mutual, one
　another, other, themselves,
　together, yourselves
allogenēs [241; 39]
　stranger
allophulos [246; 41]
　nation
allos [243; 39]
　another, more, one,
　other (-s), otherwise, some
allōs [247; 41]
　otherwise
allotrioepiskopos [244; 40]
　busybody, meddler
allotrios [245; 40]
　alien, man's (another), other,
　strange, stranger
aloaō [248; 41]
　corn, thresh, tread
aloē [250; 41]
　aloes
alogos [249; 41]
　brute, unreasonable
alōpēx [258; 41]
　fox
alupos (-oteros) [253; 41]
　sorrowful (less)
alusitelēs [255; 41]
　unprofitable
amachos [269; 44]
　brawler
amaō [270; 44]
　mow, reap down
amarantinos [262; 42]
　fade
amarantos [263; 42]
　fade
amarturos [267; 44]
　witness
amathēs [261; 42]
　unlearned

ameleō [272; 44]
　light of (make), neglect,
　negligent, regard
amemptos [273; 45]
　blameless, faultless,
　unblameable
amemptōs [274; 45]
　blame (without), blameless,
　unblameably
amēn [281; 45]
　amen, verily
amerimnos [275; 45]
　care, carefulness, rid, secure
ametakinētos [277; 45]
　move, unmoveable
ametamelētos [278; 45]
　regret, repent, repentance
ametanoētos [279; 45]
　impenitent
ametathetos [276; 45]
　immutable, immutability
amethustos [271; 44]
　amethyst
amētōr [282; 46]
　mother
ametros [280; 45]
　measure
amiantos [283; 46]
　undefiled
ammos [285; 46]
　sand
amnos [286; 46]
　lamb
amoibē [287; 46]
　requite
amōmētos [298; 47]
　blameless, rebuke
amōmon [298a; 47]
　odor, spice
amōmos [299; 47]
　blame (without), blemish,
　faultless, unblameable
ampelōn [290; 47]
　vineyard
ampelos [288; 46]
　vine
ampelourgos [289; 47]
　vinedresser
amphiballō [297 and 906; 47]
　cast
amphiblēstron [293; 47]
　net
amphiennumi [294; 47]
　clothe
amphodon [296; 47]
　place, street
amphoteroi [297**; 47]
　master
amunō [292; 47]
　defend
ana [303; 49]
　apiece, each, every
anabainō [305; 50]
　arise, ascend, climb up,

　come, enter, go, grow, rise,
　spring
*anaballō (-omai) [306; 50]
　defer
anabathmos [304; 50]
　stair
anabibazō [307; 50]
　draw
anablepō [308; 50]
　look, receive, see, sight
anablepsis [309; 51]
　sight
anaboaō [310; 51]
　cry
anabolē [311; 51]
　delay
anachōreō [402; 63]
　depart, go, place, turn,
　withdraw
anachusis [401; 63]
　excess
anadechomai [324; 53]
　receive
anadeiknumi [322; 53]
　appoint, shew
anadeixis [323; 53]
　shewing
anadidōmi [325; 53]
　deliver
anagaion [508; 51]
　(see anōgeon)
anagennaō [313; 51]
　beget, born
anaginōskō [314; 51]
　read
*anagnōrizō (-omai) [319; 52]
　known
anagnōsis [320; 52]
　reading
anagō [321; 53]
　bring, depart, launch, lead,
　loose, offer, put, sail, set, take
anaid(e)ia [335; 54]
　importunity
anaireō [337; 54]
　death, kill, slay, take
anairesis [336; 54]
　death
anaitios [338; 55]
　blameless, guiltless
anakainizō [340; 55]
　renew
anakainoō [341; 55]
　renew
anakainōsis [342; 55]
　renewing
anakaluptō [343; 55]
　open, unlifted, untaken,
　unveiled
anakamptō [344; 55]
　return, turn
anakathizō [339; 55]
　sit

anakeimai [345; 55]
    guest, lean, lie, recline, set,
    sit, table (at the)

*anakephalaioō (-omai) [346; 55]
    comprehend, gather, sum up

anaklinō [347; 56]
    lay, sit

anakoptō [348; 56]
    hinder

anakrazō [349; 56]
    cry

anakrinō [350; 56]
    ask, discern, examine, judge,
    search

anakrisis [351; 56]
    examination

anakuliō [303 and 2947; 56]
    roll

anakuptō [352; 56]
    lift, look

analambanō [353; 56]
    receive, take

analēpsis [354; 57]
    receive

analiskō [355; 57]
    consume

analogia [356; 57]
    proportion

analogizomai [357; 57]
    consider

analos [358; 57]
    saltness

analuō [360; 57]
    depart, return

analusis [359; 57]
    departure

anamartētos [361; 57]
    sin

anamenō [362; 57]
    wait

anamimnēskō [363; 57]
    mind, remember,
    remembrance

anamnēsis [364; 58]
    remembrance

ananeoō [365; 58]
    renew

ananēphō [366; 58]
    awake, recover, sober

anangellō [312; 51]
    announce, declare, rehearse,
    report, shew, speak, tell,
    tidings

anankaios [316; 52]
    near, necessary

anankaioteros [316*; 52]
    needful

anankastōs [317; 52]
    constraint

anankazō [315; 52]
    compel, constrain

anankē [318; 52]
    distress, necessary, necessity,
    needs

anantirrhētos [368; 58]
    gainsay, speak

anantirrhētōs [369; 58]
    gainsay

anapauō [373; 58]
    ease, refresh, rest

anapausis [372; 58]
    rest

anapeithō [374; 59]
    persuade

anapempō [375; 59]
    send

anapē(i)ros [376; 59]
    maimed

anaphainō [398; 63]
    appear, discover

anapherō [399; 63]
    bear, bring, carry, lead, offer

anaphōneō [400; 63]
    voice

anapiptō [377; 59]
    lean, set, sit

anaplēroō [378; 59]
    fill, fulfill, supply

anapologētos [379; 60]
    excuse, inexcusable

anapsuchō [404; 63]
    refresh

anapsuxis [403; 63]
    refreshing

anaptō [381; 60]
    kindle

anaptussō [380; 60]
    open

anarithmētos [382; 60]
    innumerable

anaseiō [383; 60]
    move, stir

anaskeuazō [384; 60]
    subvert

anaspaō [385; 60]
    draw, pull

anastasis [386; 60]
    raise, resurrection, rising

anastatoō [387; 61]
    sedition, stir, trouble, turn,
    uproar

anastauroō [388; 61]
    crucify

anastenazō [389; 61]
    sigh

anastrephō [390; 61]
    abide, behave, conversation,
    live, overthrow, pass, return,
    use

anastrophē [391; 61]
    behavior, conversation, life,
    living, manner

anatassomai [392; 61]
    draw, order, set (forth)

anatellō [393; 62]
    arise, rise, rising, spring, up

anathallō [330; 54]
    flourish, revive

anathema [331; 54]
    curse, anathema

anathēma [334; 54]
    gift, offering

anathematizō [332; 54]
    curse, oath

anatheōreō [333; 54]
    behold, consider, observe

anatithēmi [394; 62]
    communicate, declare, lay

anatolē [395; 62]
    dayspring, east

anatrephō [397; 62]
    bring, nourish

anatrepō [396; 62]
    overthrow, subvert

anaxios [371; 58]
    unworthy

anaxiōs [371; 58]
    unworthily

anazaō [326; 53]
    alive, live, revive

anazēteō [327; 53]
    seek

anazōnnumi [328; 53]
    gird

anazōpureō [329; 54]
    stir

andrapodistēs [405; 63]
    men-stealers

andrizō [407; 64]
    men, quit

androphonos [409; 64]
    manslayer

anechomai (or *-chō*) [430; 65]
    bear, endure, forbear, suffer

anekdiēgētos [411; 64]
    unspeakable

aneklalētos [412; 64]
    unspeakable

anekleiptos [413; 64]
    fail

anēkō [433; 66]
    befit, convenient, fit

anektoteros [414; 64]
    tolerable

aneleēmōn [415; 64]
    unmerciful

aneleos [488; 64] (or *anil-*)
    [488; 69]
    mercy

anēmeros [434; 66]
    fierce

anemizō [416; 64]
    drive, wind

anemos [417; 64]
    wind

anendektos [418; 65]
    impossible

anenklētos [410; 64]
    blameless, unreprovable

anepaischuntos [422; 65]
    ashamed

anepilēptos [423; 65]
blameless, reproach,
unrebukeable
anepsios [431; 66]
cousin, sister
anēr [435; 66]
fellow, husband, man, sir
anerchomai [424; 65]
go
anesis [425; 65]
eased, indulgence, liberty,
relief, rest
anetazō [426; 65]
examine
anēthon [432; 66]
anise
aneu [427; 65]
without
aneuriskō [429; 65]
find
aneuthetos [428; 65]
commodious
anexeraunētos (or, -reu-) [419; 65]
unsearchable
anexichniastos [421; 65]
find, trace, unsearchable
anexikakos [420; 65]
forbearing, patient
angareuō [29; 6]
compel
angeion [30; 6]
vessel
angelia [31; 7]
message
angelos [32; 7]
angel, messenger
angos [30d; 8]
vessel
aniēmi [447; 69]
forbear, leave, loose
aniptos [449; 69]
unwashen
anistēmi [450; 70]
arise, lift, raise (up), rise,
stand
ankalē [43; 10]
arm
ankistron [44; 10]
hook
ankura [45; 10]
anchor
anō [507; 76]
above, brim, high, up
anochē [463; 72]
forbearance
anoētos [453; 70]
fool, foolish, unwise
anōgeon [508; 77]
room
anoia [454; 70]
folly, madness
anoigō [455; 70]
open

anoikodomeō [456; 71]
build
anoixis [457; 71]
open, opening
anomia [458; 71]
iniquity, lawlessness,
transgression,
unrighteousness
anomos [459; 72]
law, lawless, transgressor,
unlawful, wicked
anomōs [460; 72]
law
anōphelēs [512; 77]
unprofitable
anorthoō [461; 72]
lift, set, straight
anosios [462; 72]
unholy
anōterikos [510; 77]
upper
anōteron [511**; 77]
above, higher
anōthen [509; 77]
above, again, anew, first, top
antagōnizomai [464; 72]
strive
antallagma [465; 72]
exchange
antanaplēroō [466; 72]
fill
antapodidōmi [467; 73]
recompense, render, repay
antapodoma [468; 73]
recompense
antapodosis [469; 73]
recompense, reward
antapokrinomai [470; 73]
answer, reply
antechō (-omai) [472; 73]
hold, support
anteipon [473,
and aor. of 3004; 73]
gainsay, say
anthistēmi [436; 67]
resist, withstand
anthomologeomai [437; 67]
thanks
anthos [438; 67]
flower
anthrakia [439; 67]
coals
anthrax [449; 67]
coal
anthrōpareskos [441; 67]
men-pleasers
anthrōpinos [442; 67]
man's, men
anthrōpoktonos [443; 68]
murderer
anthrōpos [444; 68]
man, people, person
anthupateuō [445; 69]
proconsul

anthupatos [446; 69]
deputy, proconsul
anti [473; 73]
room
antiballō [474; 74]
have
antichristos [500; 76]
Antichrist
antidiatithēmi [475; 74]
oppose
antidikos [476; 74]
adversary
antikaleō [479; 74]
bid
antikathistēmi [478; 74]
resist
antikeimai [480; 74]
adversary, contrary, oppose
antilambanō (-omai) [482; 74]
help, partake, partaker,
support
antilegō [483; 74]
answer, contradict, deny,
gainsay, gainsayer, speak
antilē(m)psis [484; 75]
help
antilogia [485; 75]
contradiction, dispute,
gainsaying, strife
antiloidoreō [486; 75]
revile
antilutron [487; 75]
ransom
antimetreō [488; 75]
measure
antimisthia [489; 75]
recompense
antiparerchomai [492; 75]
pass
antipiptō [496; 75]
resist
antistrateuomai [497; 75]
war
*antitassō (-omai) [498; 76]
oppose, resist
antithesis [477; 74]
opposition
antitupos (-on) [499; 76]
figure, likeness, pattern
antlēma [502; 76]
draw
antleō [501; 76]
draw
antophthalmeō [503; 76]
bear, face
anudros [504; 76]
dry, water
anupokritos [505; 76]
dissimulation, hypocrisy,
unfeigned
anupotaktos [506; 76]
disobedient, put, subject,
unruly

aoratos [517; 79]
   invisible
apagō [520; 79]
   bring, carry, death, lead, take
apaideutos [521; 79]
   unlearned
apairō [522; 79]
   take
apaiteō [523; 80]
   require
apalgeō [524; 80]
   feel
apallassō [525; 80]
   deliver, depart, quit
apallotriō [526; 80]
   alien, alienated
*apanchō (-omai) [519; 79]
   hang
apangellō [518; 79]
   bring, declare, go, report,
   shew, tell, word
apantaō [528; 80]
   meet
apantēsis [529; 80]
   meet
aparabatos [531; 80]
   unchangeable
aparaskeuastos [532; 80]
   unprepared
aparchē [536; 81]
   firstfruit(s)
aparneomai [533; 81]
   deny
aparti [534; 81]
   henceforth, now (from)
apartismos [535; 81]
   complete, finish
apaspazomai [575 and 782; 81]
   bid farewell, leave, take
apataō [538; 81]
   beguile, deceive
apatē [539; 82]
   deceit, deceitful,
   deceitfulness, deceivableness
apatōr [540; 82]
   father
apaugasma [541; 82]
   brightness, effulgence
apechō [568; 84]
   abstain, enough, have,
   receive, was, etc.
apeidon [872; 82]
   (see *aphoraō*), (127)
apeilē [547; 83]
   straitly, threaten, threatening
apeileō [546; 82]
   threaten
apeimi [548; 83]
   absent
apeimi [549; 83]
   go
*apeipon (-omēn) [550; 83]
   renounce

apeirastos [551; 83]
   tempt
apeiros [552; 83]
   experience (without),
   unskilful
apeitheia [543; 82]
   disobedience, unbelief
apeitheō [544; 82]
   believe, disobedient, obey,
   unbelieving
apeithēs [545; 82]
   disobedient
apekdechomai [553; 83]
   look, wait
*apekdu (-omai) [554; 83]
   put, spoil
apekdusis [555; 83]
   putting
apelaunō [556; 83]
   drive
apelegmos [557; 83]
   disrepute, nought
apeleutheros [558; 83]
   freedman
apelpizō [560; 83]
   despair, hope
apenanti [561; 84]
   before, contrary, presence
aperantos [562; 84]
   endless
aperchomai [565; 84]
   come, depart, go, pass, way
aperispastōs [563; 84]
   distraction
aperitmētos [564; 84]
   uncircumcised
aphaireō [851; 124]
   cut, smite, take
aphanēs [852; 124]
   manifest
aphanismos [854; 124]
   vanishing
aphanizō [853; 124]
   consume, corrupt, disfigure,
   perish, vanish
aphantos [855; 124]
   vanish
aphedrōn [856; 124]
   draught
apheidia [857; 124]
   neglecting, severity
aphelotēs [858; 124]
   singleness
apheō [863; 125]
   (see *aphiēmi*)
aphesis [859; 125]
   deliverance, forgiveness,
   liberty, release, remission
aphiēmi [863; 125]
   alone, cease, cry, forgive,
   forsake, lay, leave, let, put,
   remit, send, suffer, utter, yield
aphikneomai [864; 126]
   come

aphilagathos [865; 126]
   despiser, lover
aphilarguros [866; 126]
   covetous, covetousness, free,
   lover
aphistēmi [868; 126]
   depart, draw, fall, refrain,
   withdraw
aphixis [867; 126]
   departing
aphnō [869; 127]
   suddenly
aphobōs [880; 127]
   fear
aphomoioō [871; 127]
   like
aphōnos [880; 127]
   dumb, signification
aphoraō (apheidon) [872; 127]
   look, see
aphorizō [873; 127]
   divide, separate, sever
aphormē [874; 127]
   occasion
aphrizō [875; 127]
   foam
aphrōn [878; 127]
   foolish, unwise
aphros [876; 127]
   foam
aphrosunē [877; 127]
   folly, foolishness, foolishly
aphtharsia [861; 125]
   immortality, incorruption,
   sincerity
aphthartos [862; 125]
   immortal, incorruptible
aphthoria [5356d; 125]
   uncorruptness
aphupnoō [879; 127]
   asleep
aphustereō [575 and 5302; 128]
   fraud
apisteō [569; 85]
   believe, disbelieve, faith
apistia [570; 85]
   belief, faith, unbelief
apistos [571; 85]
   believe, faithless, incredible,
   infidel, unbeliever,
   unbelieving, unfaithful
apo [575; 86]
   far, space
apobainō [576; 88]
   come, get, go, turn
apoballō [577; 88]
   cast
apoblepō [578; 89]
   look, respect
apoblētos [579; 89]
   refuse, reject
apobolē [580; 89]
   cast, loss

apochōreō [672; 102]
  depart
apochōrizō [673; 102]
  depart, part, remove
apochrēsis [671; 102]
  using
apodechomai [588; 90]
  accept, receive, welcome
apodeiknumi [584; 89]
  approve, prove, set, shew
apodeixis [585; 89]
  demonstration
apodekateuō [586v; 89]
  tithe
apodekatoō [586; 89]
  pay, tithe
apodektos [587; 90]
  acceptable
apodēmeō [589; 90]
  country, far, go, journey,
  travel
apodēmos [590; 90]
  far, journey, sojourn
apodidōmi [591; 90]
  deliver, give, pay, perform,
  recompense, render, repay,
  restore, reward, sell, yield
apodiorizō [592; 90]
  separate
apodochē [594; 91]
  acceptation
apodokimazō [593; 90]
  disallow, reject
apoginomai [581**; 89]
  die
apographē [582; 89]
  enrollment, taxing
apographō [583; 89]
  enroll, tax, write
apokalupsis [602; 92]
  appearing, coming, lighten,
  manifestation, revelation
apokaluptō [601; 92]
  reveal
apokaradokia [603; 92]
  expectation
apokatallassō [604; 92]
  reconcile
apokatastasis [605; 92]
  restitution, restoration
apokathistēmi [600; 91]
  (or *apokathistanō*), restore
apokeimai [606; 92]
  appoint, lay
apokephalizō [607; 93]
  behead
apokleiō [608; 93]
  shut
apokopto [609; 93]
  cut
apokrima [610; 93]
  answer, sentence
apokrinomai [611; 93]
  answer

apokrisis [612; 93]
  answer
apokruphos [614; 93]
  hid, hidden, secret
apokruptō [613; 93]
  hide
apokteinō [615; 93]
  death, kill, put, slay
apokueō [616; 94]
  beget, bring
apokuliō (or *-izō*) [617; 94]
  roll
apolambanō [618; 94]
  receive, take
apolausis [619; 94]
  enjoy, pleasure
apōleia [684; 103]
  destruction, perdition, perish,
  pernicious, waste
apoleichō [621; 95]
  lick
apoleipō [620; 94]
  leave, remain
apollumi [622; 95]
  destroy, destroyer, die, fall,
  lose, marred, perish
apologeomai [626; 95]
  answer, defense, excuse,
  speak
apologia [627; 96]
  answer, clearing, defense
apolouō [628; 96]
  wash
apoluō [630; 96]
  depart, dismiss, divorce,
  forgive, go, let, liberty, loose,
  put, release, send
apolutrōsis [629; 96]
  deliverance, redemption
apomassō (*-omai*) [631; 96]
  wipe
aponemō [632; 97]
  give
aponiptō [633; 97]
  wash
apopherō [667; 101]
  bring, carry
apopheugō [668; 101]
  escape
apophortizō [670; 102]
  unlade
apophthengomai [669; 102]
  say, speak, utterance
apopiptō [634; 97]
  fall
apoplanaō [635; 97]
  err, lead, seduce
apopleō [636; 97]
  sail
apoplunō [637; 97]
  wash
apopnigō [638; 97]
  choke

apopsuchō [674; 102]
  fail
aporeō [639; 97]
  doubt, perplex
aporia [640; 97]
  perplexity
aporphanizomai [642; 98]
  bereave
aporiptō [641; 97]
  cast
aposkeuazō [643; 98]
  baggage, carriage
aposkiasma [644; 98]
  cast, shadow
apospaō [645; 98]
  draw, get, part, withdraw
apostasia [646; 98]
  falling, forsake
apostasion [647; 98]
  divorcement
apostegazō [648; 98]
  uncover
apostellō [649; 98]
  liberty, put, send, set
apostereō [650; 94]
  bereft, defraud, destitute,
  fraud, suffer
apostolē [651; 99]
  apostleship
apostolos [652; 99]
  apostle, messenger, send
apostomatizō [653; 100]
  provoke
apostrephō [654; 100]
  bring, pervert, put, turn
apostugeō [655; 100]
  abhor
aposunagōgos [656; 100]
  synagogue (put out of the)
apotassō (*-omai*) [657; 100]
  bid farewell, farewell,
  forsake, leave, renounce,
  send, take
apoteleō [658; 100]
  do, finish, perform
apothēkē [596; 91]
  barn, garner
apotheō (*-omai*) [683; 103]
  cast, put, thrust
apothēsaurizō [597; 91]
  store
apothesis [595; 91]
  putting
apothlibō [598; 91]
  crush, press
apothnēskō [599; 91]
  die, perish
apotinassō [660; 101]
  shake
apotinō (or *-tio*) [661; 101]
  repay
apotithēmi [659; 101]
  cast, lay, put

apotolmaō [662; 101]
  bold
apotomia [663; 101]
  severity
apotomōs [664; 101]
  sharply, sharpness
apotrepō [665; 101]
  turn
apousia [666; 101]
  absence
aprositos [676; 102]
  approach
aproskopos [677; 102]
  offense, stumbling
aprosōpolēmptōs [678; 102]
  persons (respect of)
apseudēs [893; 129]
  lie
apsinthos [894; 129]
  wormwood
apsuchos [895; 129]
  life
aptaistos [699; 102]
  falling, stumbling
ara [685; 103]
  curse
ara [686; 103]
  doubt (no), haply, manner,
  perhaps, then, truly
arage [686 and 1065; 104]
  haply
archangelos [743; 111]
  archangel
archaios [744; 111]
  old
archē [746; 111]
  beginning, corner, estate,
  first, magistrate, power,
  principality, principles, rule,
  ruler
archēgos [747; 112]
  author, captain, prince
archieratikos [748; 112]
  priest
archiereus [749; 112]
  chief, priest
archipoimēn [750; 113]
  chief, shepherd
archisunagōgos [752; 113]
  chief, synagogue (ruler of
  the)
architektōn [753; 113]
  masterbuilder
architelōnēs [754; 113]
  chief, publican
architriklinos [755; 113]
  governor, ruler
archō (-omai) [756; 113]
  begin, beginning, rehearse,
  reign, rule
archōn [758; 113]
  chief, magistrate, prince,
  ruler

arēn [704; 106]
  lamb
areskeia [699; 105]
  pleasing
areskō [700; 105]
  please
arestos [701; 105]
  fit, please, reason
aretē [703; 105]
  excellence, praise, virtue
argeō [691; 104]
  linger
argos [692; 104]
  barren, idle, slow
argurion [694; 104]
  money, piece, silver
argurokopos [695; 105]
  silversmith
argureos [693; 104]
  silver
arguros [696; 105]
  silver
aristaō [709; 106]
  dine
aristeros [710; 106]
  left
ariston [712; 106]
  dinner
arithmeō [705; 106]
  number
arithmos [706; 106]
  number
arkeō [714; 107]
  content, enough, suffice,
  sufficient
arketos [713; 107]
  enough, suffice, sufficient
ark(t)os [715; 107]
  bear
arneomai [720; 107]
  deny, refuse
arnion [721; 108]
  lamb
arōma [759; 114]
  spice(s)
arotriaō [722; 108]
  plough (plow)
arotron [723; 108]
  plough (plow)
arrabōn [728; 109]
  earnest
ar(rh)aphos [729; 104]
  seam (without)
arrēn (or *arsēn*) [730; 109]
  male, man
arrhētos [731; 109]
  unspeakable
arrhōstos [732; 109]
  sick
arsenokoitēs [733; 109]
  abuser
artemōn [736; 110]
  foresail, mainsail

arti [737; 110]
  henceforth, hitherto, now,
  present
artigennētos [738; 110]
  newborn
artios [739; 110]
  complete, perfect
artos [740; 110]
  bread, loaf, shewbread
artuō [741; 111]
  season
asaleutos [761; 114]
  move, unmoveable
asbestos [762; 114]
  quench, unquenchable
aschēmōn [809; 119]
  uncomely
aschēmoneō [807; 119]
  behave, uncomely
aschēmosunē [808; 119]
  shame, unseemliness,
  unseemly
asebeia [763; 114]
  ungodliness, ungodly
asebeō [764; 114]
  ungodly
asebēs [765; 114]
  ungodly
aselgeia [766; 114]
  filthy, lasciviousness,
  wantonness
asēmos [767; 115]
  mean
asiarchēs [775; 116]
  chief
asitia [776; 116]
  abstinence, food
asitos [777; 116]
  fasting
askeō [778; 116]
  exercise
askos [779; 116]
  bottle, skin
asmenōs [780; 116]
  gladly
asophos [781; 116]
  unwise
asōtia [810; 119]
  excess, riot
asōtōs [811; 119]
  riotous
aspasmos [783; 117]
  greeting, salutation
aspazomai [782; 116]
  embrace, farewell, greet,
  leave, salute
asphaleia [803; 118]
  certainty, safety
asphalēs [804; 119]
  certain, certainty, safe, sure
asphalizō [805; 119]
  fast (to make), sure
asphalōs [806; 119]
  assuredly, safely

aspilos [784; 117]
    spot, unspotted
aspis [785; 117]
    asp
aspondos [786; 117]
    implacable, truce-breaker
assarion [787; 117]
    farthing
asson [788; 117]
    close
astateō [790; 117]
    certain, dwelling (place)
asteios [791; 117]
    beautiful, fair, goodly, proper
astēr [792; 117]
    star
astēriktos [793; 118]
    unstable
astheneia [769; 115]
    disease, infirmity, sickness,
    weakness
asthenēma [771; 115]
    infirmity
astheneō [770; 115]
    diseased, impotent, sick,
    weak
asthenēs [772; 115]
    feeble, impotent, sick, weak
astocheō [795; 118]
    err, swerve
astorgos [794; 118]
    affection
astrapē [796; 118]
    lightning, shining
astraptō [797; 118]
    dazzling, lighten, shine
astron [798; 118]
    star
asumphōnos [800; 118]
    agree
asunetos [801; 118]
    foolish, senseless,
    understanding
asunthetos [802; 118]
    covenant-breakers
atakteō [812; 119]
    behave, disorderly
ataktos [813; 119]
    disorderly, unruly
ataktōs [814; 119]
    disorderly
ateknos [815; 119]
    childless
atenizō [816; 119]
    behold, earnestly, fasten,
    look, set
ater [817; 120]
    absence, without
athanasia [110; 20]
    immortality
athemitos [111; 20]
    abominable, unlawful
atheos [112; 20]
    God (without)

athesmos [113; 21]
    wicked
atheteō [114; 21]
    bring, cast, despise, disannul,
    frustrate, nothing, nought,
    reject, void
athetēsis [115; 21]
    disannuling, put
athleō [118; 21]
    contend, strive
athlēsis [119; 21]
    conflict, fight
athōos [121; 21]
    innocent
athroizō [119a; 21]
    gather
athumeō [120; 21]
    discourage
atimaō [821; 120]
    handle
atimazō [818; 120]
    despise, dishonor, entreat,
    handle, shame, shamefully
atimia [819; 120]
    dishonor, disparagement,
    reproach, shame, vile
atimos [820; 120]
    despised, dishonor, honor
    (without)
atimoteros [820*; 120]
    honorable
atmis [822; 120]
    vapor
atomos [823; 120]
    moment
atopos [824; 120]
    amiss, harm, unreasonable,
    wickedness
auchmēros [850; 124]
    dark
augazō [826; 120]
    dawn, shine
augē [827; 120]
    day
aulē [833; 121]
    court, fold, hall, palace,
    praetorium
auleō [832; 121]
    pipe
aulētēs [834; 121]
    flute-players, piper
aulizomai [835; 121]
    abide, lodge
aulos [836; 121]
    pipe
aurion [839; 122]
    morrow, next day,
    tomorrow
austēros [840; 122]
    austere
autarkeia [841; 122]
    contentment, sufficiency
autarkēs [842; 122]
    content

authadēs [829; 120]
    self-willed
authairetos [830; 121]
    accord, willing
authenteō [831; 121]
    authority, dominion
autocheir [849; 124]
    hand (with one's own)
autokatakritos [843; 122]
    condemn
automatos [844; 122]
    accord, self
autoptēs [845; 122]
    eye-witness
autos [846; 122]
    company, halt, he, here,
    myself, ourselves, same, say,
    self, their, them, themselves,
    there, they, this, thou, thyself,
    very
autou [847; 124]
    here, there
auxanō [837; 121]
    grow, increase
auxēsis [838; 122]
    increase
axinē [513; 77]
    axe
axioō [515; 78]
    desire, think, worthy,
    worthily
axios [514; 78]
    due, meet, reward, worthy
axiōs [516; 78]
    become, godly, worthy
azumos [106; 19]
    bread

B

baion [902; 130]
    branch
ballantion [905; 130]
    bag
ballō [906; 130]
    arise, beat, cast, dung, lay,
    lie, pour, put, send, throw,
    thrust
baptisma [908; 132]
    baptism
baptismos [909; 132]
    baptism, washing
baptistēs [910; 132]
    Baptist
baptizō [907; 131]
    baptize
baptō [911; 132]
    dip
barbaros [915; 133]
    barbarian, barbarous
bareō [916; 133]
    charge, burden, heavy,
    overcharge, press, weigh

bareōs [917; 133]
dull
baros [920; 133]
burden, weight
barunō [925; 134]
overcharge
barus [926; 134]
grievous, heavy, weighty
barutimos [927; 134]
precious
basanismos [929; 134]
torment
basanistēs [930; 134]
tormentor
basanizō [928; 134]
distress, pain, toil, torment,
vex
basanos [931; 134]
torment
basileia [932; 134]
kingdom
basileion [933; 136]
court
basileios [934; 136]
king, royal
basileuō [936; 136]
king, reign
basileus [935; 136]
king
basilikos [937; 136]
king, nobleman, royal
basilissa [938; 137]
queen
basis [939; 137]
foot
baskainō [940; 137]
bewitch
bastazō [941; 137]
bear, carry, take
batheōs [901*; 130]
deeply, early
bathmos [898; 130]
degree
bathos [899; 130]
deep, deepness, depth
bathunō [900; 130]
deep
bathus [901; 130]
deep
batos [942; 137]
bramble, bush
batos [943; 137]
measure
batrachos [944; 137]
frog
battologeō [945; 137]
repetitions
bdelugma [946; 137]
abomination
bdeluktos [947; 138]
abominable
bdelussō [948; 138]
abhor, abominable

bebaioō [950; 138]
confirm, establish, stablish
bebaios [949; 138]
firm, force, stedfast, sure
bebaiōsis [951; 138]
confirmation
bebēloō [953; 138]
profane
bebēlos [952; 138]
profane
belial, -ar [955; 139]
Belial
belonē [956d; 139]
needle
belos [956; 139]
dart
beltion [957; 139]
well (adverb)
bēma [968; 140]
judgment-seat, throne
bērullos [969; 140]
beryl
bia [970; 140]
violence
biaios [972; 141]
mighty
biastēs [973; 141]
violence, violent
biazō [971; 140]
enter, force, press, suffer,
violence
biblaridion [974; 141]
book
biblion [975; 141]
bill, book, scroll, writing
biblos [976; 141]
book
bibrōskō [977; 141]
eat
bioō [980; 142]
live
bios [979; 141]
good(s), life, living
biōsis [981; 142]
life
biōtikos [982; 142]
life
blaberos [983; 142]
hurtful
blaptō [984; 142]
hurt
blasphēmeō [987; 142]
blaspheme, defame, rail,
report, revile
blasphēmia [988; 143]
blasphemy, evil speaking,
railing, speak
blasphēmos [989; 143]
blasphemous, railing (-ers)
blastanō [985; 142]
bring, bud, spring
blemma [990; 143]
seeing

blepō [991; 143]
behold, beware, heed (take),
lie, look, perceive, regard,
see, sight
blēteos [992; 144]
put
boaō [994; 144]
cry
boē [995; 144]
cry
boētheia [996; 144]
help
boētheō [997; 144]
help, succor
boēthos [998; 144]
helper
bolē [1000; 144]
cast, dart
bolis [1002; 144]
dart
bolizō [1001; 144]
dart, sound
bōmos [1041; 148]
altar
borboros [1004; 145]
mire
borras [1005; 145]
north
boskō [1006; 145]
feed, keep
botanē [1008; 145]
herb
bothunos [999; 144]
ditch, pit
botrus [1009; 145]
cluster
boulē [1012; 145]
advise, counsel, will
boulēma [1013; 145]
desire, purpose, will
bouleutēs [1010; 145]
counsellor
bouleuō [1011; 145]
consult, counsel, minded,
purpose
boulomai [1014; 146]
desire, determine, disposed,
fain, intend, list, minded,
will, willing, wish
bounos [1015; 146]
hill
bous [1016; 146]
ox
brabeion [1017; 146]
prize
brabeuō [1018; 146]
rule
brachiōn [1023; 147]
arm
brachus [1024; 147]
few, further, little, space,
while, words
bradunō [1019; 147]
slack, tarry

braduploeō [1020; 147]
   sail
bradus [1021; 147]
   slow
bradutēs [1022; 147]
   slackness
brechō [1026; 147]
   rain, wash
brephos [1025; 147]
   babe, child, infant, young
brochē [1028; 147]
   rain
brochos [1029; 147]
   snare
brōma [1033; 148]
   food, meat, victuals
brontē [1027; 147]
   thunder
brōsimos [1034; 148]
   eat, meat
brōsis [1035; 148]
   eating, food, meat, rust
bruchō [1031; 148]
   gnash
brugmos [1030; 147]
   gnashing
bruō [1032; 148]
   send
burseus [1038; 148]
   tanner
bussinos [1039; 148]
   linen (fine)
bussos [1040; 148]
   linen (fine)
buthizō [1036; 148]
   drown, sink
buthos [1037; 148]
   deep

C

chairō [5463; 873]
   farewell, glad, God-speed,
   greeting, hail, joy, rejoice
chalaō [5465; 874]
   let down, lower, strake, strike
chalaza [5464; 874]
   hail
chalepos [5467; 874]
   fierce, grievous, perilous
chalinagōgeō [5468; 874]
   bridle
chalinos [5469; 874]
   bit, bridle
chalkēdōn [5472; 874]
   chalcedony
chalkeos [5470; 875]
   brass
chalkeus [5471; 874]
   coppersmith
chalkion [5473; 874]
   brazen

chalkolibanon [5474; 875]
   brass
chalkos [5475; 875]
   brass, money
chamai [5476; 875]
   ground
chara [5479; 875]
   gladness, greatly, joy,
   joyfulness
charagma [5480; 876]
   graven, mark
charaktēr [5481; 876]
   image
charax [5482; 876]
   trench
charin [5484; 877]
   cause
charis [5485; 877]
   acceptable, benefit, bounty,
   favor, gift, grace, gracious,
   liberality, pleasure, thank(s),
   thankworthy
charisma [5486; 878]
   free, gift
charitoō [5487; 879]
   accepted, favor
charizomai [5483; 876]
   bestow, deliver, forgive,
   frankly, freely, give, grant
chartēs [5489, 879]
   paper
chasma [5490; 879]
   gulf
cheilos [5491; 879]
   lip, shore
cheimarrhos [5493; 879]
   brook
cheimazō [5492; 879]
   labor
cheimōn [5494; 879]
   tempest, weather, winter
cheir [5495; 879]
   hand
cheiragōgeō [5496; 880]
   hand (lead by the)
cheiragōgos [5497; 880]
   hand (lead by the)
cheirographon [5498; 880]
   bond, handwriting
cheirōn [5501; 881]
   sorer, worse
cheiropoiētos [5499; 880]
   hands (made by)
cheirotoneō [5500; 881]
   appoint, choose, ordain
cheroubim [5502; 881]
   cherubim
chēra [5503; 881]
   widow
chiliarchos [5506; 881]
   captain
chilias [5505; 882]
   thousand

chilioi [5507; 882]
   thousands
chiōn [5510; 882]
   snow
chitōn [5509; 882]
   clothes, coat, garment
chlamus [5511; 882]
   robe
chleuazō [5512; 882]
   mock
chliaros [5513; 882]
   lukewarm
chlōros [5515; 882]
   green, pale
choïkos [5517; 883]
   earthy
choinix [5518; 883]
   measure
choiros [5519; 883]
   swine
cholaō [5520; 883]
   angry, wroth (be)
cholē [5521; 883]
   gall
chōlos [5560; 889]
   cripple, halt, lame
choos (chous) [5522; 884]
   dust
chōra [5561; 889]
   coast, country, field, ground,
   land, region
chorēgeō [5524; 883]
   give, minister, supply
chōreō [5562; 889]
   come, contain, go, heart,
   pass, place, receive, room
chōrion [5564; 890]
   field, ground, land, parcel,
   pass, place, possession
chōris [5565; 890]
   apart, beside, separate,
   without
chōrizō [5563; 890]
   depart, put, separate
choros [5525; 883]
   dancing
chōros [5564; 891]
   north-west
chortasma [5527; 884]
   sustenance
chortazō [5526; 883]
   feed, fill, satisfy
chortos [5528; 884]
   blade, grass, hay
chraō (-aomai) [5531; 884]
   deal with, entreat, lend, treat,
   use
chrē [5534; 885]
   ought
chreia [5535; 884]
   business, lack, necessary,
   necessity, need, needful, use,
   want

chrēma [5536; 885]
money, riches

chrēmatismos [5538; 885]
answer

chrēmatizō [5537; 885]
admonish, call, reveal, speak,
warn

chreopheiletēs [5533; 885]
debtor

chrēsimos [5539; 885]
profit

chrēsis [5540; 885]
use

chrēsteuomai [5541; 886]
kind (be)

chrēstologia [5542; 886]
word

chrēstos [5543; 886]
better, easy, good, goodness,
gracious, kind

chrēstotēs [5544; 886]
gentleness, good, goodness,
kindness

chrēzō [5535; 885]
need

chriō [5548; 887]
anoint

chrisma [5545; 886]
anointing, unction

christos [5547; 886]
Christ

christianos [5546; 886]
Christian

chronizō [5549; 887]
delay, tarry

chronos [5550; 887]
delay, season, space, time,
while

chronotribeō [5557; 888]
spend, time

chrōs [5559; 889]
body

chruseos [5552; 888]
gold, golden

chrusion [5553; 888]
gold, jewels

chrusodaktulios [5554; 888]
gold ring, ring

chrusolithos [5555; 888]
chrysolite

chrusoō [5558; 889]
deck

chrusoprasos [5556; 888]
chrysoprasus

chrusos [5557; 888]
gold

chthes (or ech-) [5504; 881]
yesterday

D

daimōn [1142; 169]
demon, devil

daimoniōdēs [1141; 169]
devilish

daimonion [1140; 169]
demon

daimonizomai [1139; 169]
demon, possess

daknō [1143; 169]
bite

dakru (or -uon) [1144; 170]
tear

dakruō [1145; 170]
weep

daktulios [1146; 170]
ring

daktulos [1147; 170]
finger

damalis [1151; 170]
heifer

damazō [1150; 170]
tame

daneion [1156; 170]
debt

dan(e)istēs [1157; 170]
creditor, lender

daneizō [1155; 170]
borrow, lend

dapanaō [1159; 171]
charges, consume, spend

dapanē [1160; 171]
cost

de [1161; 171]
even, moreover, now, truly

dē [1211; 178]
now

dechomai [1209; 177]
accept, receive, take

deēsis [1162; 171]
prayer, request, supplication

dei [1163; 172]
behove, due, meet, must,
needful, needs, ought, should

deigma [1164; 172]
example

deigmatizō [1165; 172]
example, show (make a)

deiknumia (or -nuō) [1166; 172]
shew

deilia [1167; 173]
fear, fearfulness

deiliaō [1168; 173]
afraid, fearful

deilos [1169; 173]
fearful

deina [1170; 173]
such as

deinōs [1171; 173]
grievously, vehemently

deipneō [1172; 173]
sup

deipnon [1173; 173]
feast, supper

deisidaimōn [1174*; 173]
superstitious

deisidaimonia [1175; 173]
religion, superstition

deka [1176; 173]
ten

dekaduo [1177; 174]
twelve

dekapente [1178; 174]
fifteen

dekatē [1181; 174]
tenth, tithe

dekatessares [1180; 174]
fourteen

dekatoō [1183; 174]
pay, tithe

dekatos [1182; 174]
tenth

dektos [1184; 174]
acceptable

dēlaugōs [1212d; 178]
clearly

deleazō [1185; 174]
beguile, entice

dēloō [1213; 178]
declare, point, shew, signify

dēlos [1212; 178]
bewray, certain, evident,
manifest

dēmēgoreō [1215; 178]
oration

dēmiourgos [1217; 178]
maker

dēmos [1218; 179]
people

dēmosios [1219; 179]
common, openly, public,
publicly

dēnarion [1220; 179]
pence, penny, pennyworth

dendron [1186; 174]
tree

deō [1210; 177]
bind, knit, tie, wind

deomai [1189; 175]
beseech, pray, request

deos [5399d; 175]
awe

deon [1163; 175]
need

dēpou [1222; 179]
verily

derma [1192; 175]
goatskin

dermatinos [1193; 175]
leathern

derō [1194; 175]
beat, smite

desmē [1197; 176]
bundle

desmeō (or -euō), [1195; 175]
bind

desmios [1198; 176]
bond, prisoner

desmophulax [1200; 176]
jailor, prison-keeper

desmos [1199; 176]
band, bond, chain, string
desmōtērion [1201; 176]
prison, prison-house
desmōtēs [1202; 176]
prisoner
despotēs [1203; 176]
lord, master
deuro [1204; 176]
come, hither, hitherto
deute [1205; 176]
come
deuteraios [1206; 177]
next day, second
deuteroprōtos [1207; 177]
second
deuteros [1208; 177]
again, second, secondarily
dexiolabos [1187; 174]
spearman
dexios [1188; 174]
right, right hand, right side
dia [1223; 179]
means (by), occasion, space,
within
diabainō [1224; 181]
come, pass
diaballō [1225; 181]
accuse
diabebaioomai [1226; 181]
affirm
diablepō [1227; 181]
clearly, see
diabolos [1228; 182]
accuser, devil, slanderer
*diacheirizō (-omai) [1315; 191]
kill, slay
*diachōrizō (-omai) [1316; 191]
depart
diachleuazo [1223 and 5512; 191]
mock
diadechomai [1237; 182]
come, turn
diadēma [1238; 182]
crown
diadidōmi [1239; 182]
distribute, divide, give
diadochos [1240; 182]
room
diaginomai [1230; 182]
past, spent
diaginōskō [1231; 182]
determine, inquire, know
diagnōrizō [1232; 182]
known
diagnōsis [1233; 182]
decision, hearing
diagō [1236; 182]
lead, live
diagonguzō [1234; 182]
murmur
diagrēgoreō [1235; 182]
awake

diaireō [1244; 183]
divide
diairesis [1243; 183]
difference, diversity
diakatelenchomai [1246; 184]
confute, convince
diakathairō [1223 and 2508; 183]
purge
diakatharizō [1245; 183]
cleanse, purge
diakōluō [1254; 185]
forbid, hinder
diakoneō [1247; 184]
administer, minister, office,
serve
diakonia [1248; 184]
administration, minister,
ministration, ministering,
ministry, office, relief, service,
serving
diakonos [1249; 184]
deacon, minister, servant
diakosioi [1250; 185]
two hundred
*diakouō (-omai) [1251; 185]
hear
diakrinō [1252; 185]
contend, decide, difference,
discern, doubt, judge, partial,
put, stagger, waver
diakrisis [1253; 185]
decision, discern
dialaleō [1255; 185]
commune, noise
dialegomai [1256; 185]
discourse, dispute, preach,
reason, speak
dialeipō [1257; 185]
cease
dialektos [1258; 185]
language, tongue
diallassō [1259; 186]
reconcile
dialogismos [1261; 186]
disputation, disputing,
doubting, imagination,
reasoning, thought
dialogizomai [1260; 186]
cast, consider, dispute,
musing, reason, think
dialuō [1262; 186]
disperse, scatter
diamachomai [1264; 186]
strive
diamarturomai [1263; 186]
charge, testify, witness
diamenō [1265; 186]
continue, remain
diamerismos [1267; 186]
division
diamerizō [1266; 186]
cloven, divide, part

diangellō [1229; 182]
declare, preach, publish,
signify
dianemō [1268; 186]
spread
dianeuō [1269; 187]
beckon, signs (to make)
dianoēma [1270; 187]
thought
dianoia [1271; 187]
imagination, mind,
understanding
dianoigō [1272; 187]
open
dianuktereuō [1273; 187]
continue
dianuō [1274; 187]
finish
dia pantos [1275; 187]
always, continually
diaparatribē [3859v; 187]
disputing, wrangling
diaperaō [1276; 187]
cross, go, pass, sail
diaphanēs [1307; 190]
transparent
diaphēmizō [1310; 190]
blaze abroad, commonly,
fame, report
diapherō [1308; 190]
better, carry, differ, drive,
excellent, matter, publish,
spread, value
diapheugō [1309; 190]
escape
diaphoros [1313; 190]
differing, divers, excellent
diaphorōteros [1313*; 190*]
excellent
diaphtheirō [1311; 190]
corrupt, decay, destroy,
perish
diaphthora [1312; 190]
corruption
diaphulássō [1314; 191]
guard, keep
diapleō [1277; 187]
sail
diaponeō [1278; 187]
grieve, trouble
diaporeō [1280; 187]
doubt, perplex
diaporeuō (-omai) [1279; 187]
go, journey, pass
diapragmateuomai [1281; 187]
gain, trade
diapriō [1282; 187]
cut
diarpazō [1283; 188]
spoil
diarrhēgnumi (or *diarrhēsso*)
[1284; 188]
break, rend

diasapheō [1285; 188]
  explain, tell
diaseiō [1286; 188]
  fear, violence
diaskorpizō [1287; 188]
  disperse, scatter, strawed,
  waste
diasōzō [1295; 189]
  escape, heal, safe, save,
  whole
diaspaō [1288; 188]
  pluck, pull, rend, tear
diaspeirō [1289; 188]
  scatter
diaspora [1290; 188]
  disperse, scatter
diastellō (-omai) [1291; 188]
  charge, command
diastēma [1292; 188]
  space
diastolē [1293; 188]
  difference, distinction
diastrephō [1294; 189]
  perverse, pervert, turn
diatagē [1296; 189]
  disposition, ordinance
diatagma [1297; 189]
  commandment
diatarassō [1298; 189]
  trouble
diatassō [1299; 189]
  appoint, command, ordain,
  order
diateleō [1300; 189]
  continue
diatēreō [1301; 189]
  keep
diathēkē [1242; 183]
  covenant, testament
diati [1302; 189]
  wherefore
diatithēmi [1303; 189]
  appoint, make, testator
diatribō [1304; 190]
  abide, continue, tarry
diatrophē [1305; 190]
  food
diaugazō [1306; 190]
  dawn
diazōnnumi [1241; 182]
  gird
dichazō [1369; 200]
  variance
dichostasia [1370; 200]
  division, sedition
dichotomeō [1371; 200]
  cut
didachē [1322; 192]
  doctrine, teaching
didaktikos [1317; 191]
  teach
didaktos [1318; 191]
  taught, teach

didaskalia [1319; 191]
  doctrine, learning, teaching
didaskalos [1320; 191]
  doctor, master, teacher
didaskō [1321; 192]
  teach
didōmi [1325; 192]
  add, adventure, bestow,
  cause, commit, deliver, give,
  grant, make, minister, offer,
  power, put, receive, render,
  set, shew, smite, suffer, take,
  utter, yield
didrachmon [1323; 192]
  half-shekel, tribute
diegeirō [1326; 193]
  arise, awake, raise, stir up
diēgeomai [1334; 195]
  declare, shew, tell
diēgēsis [1335; 195]
  declaration, narrative
dienekēs [1336; 195]
  continually, ever
dienthumeomai [1223 and 1760;
  194] think
dierchomai [1330; 194]
  come, depart, go, pass,
  pierce, travel, walk
diermēneuō [1329; 194]
  expound, interpret,
  interpretation
diermēneutēs [1328; 194]
  interpreter
dierōtaō [1331; 194]
  inquiry
dietēs [1332; 194]
  year
dietia [1333; 194]
  year
diexodos [1327; 194]
  highway
diikneomai [1338; 195]
  pierce
diischurizomai [1340; 195]
  affirm
diistēmi [1339; 195]
  go, part, space
dikaiokrisia [1341; 195]
  judgment, righteous
dikaiōma [1345; 198]
  act, judgment, justification,
  ordinance, righteousness
dikaioō [1344; 197]
  free, justify, justifier,
  righteous
dikaios [1342; 195]
  just, meet, right, righteous
dikaiōs [1346; 198]
  justly, righteously,
  righteousness
dikaiōsis [1347; 198]
  justification
dikaiosunē [1343; 196]
  righteousness

dikastēs [1348; 198]
  judge
dikē [1349; 198]
  judgment, justice,
  punishment, vengeance
diktuon [1350; 198]
  net
dilogos [1351; 198]
  double-tongued
dio [1352; 198]
  wherefore
diodeuō [1353; 198]
  go, pass
diōgmos [1375; 201]
  persecution
diōkō [1377; 201]
  ensue, follow, give, persecute,
  persecution, press, pursue
diōktēs [1376; 201]
  persecutor
dioper [1355; 199]
  wherefore
diopetēs [1356; 199]
  fall
diorthōma [1357v; 199]
  correction, deed
diorthōsis [1357; 199]
  reformation
diorussō [1358; 199]
  break
diploō [1363; 199]
  double
diplous [1362; 199]
  double, twofold
dipsaō [1372; 200]
  thirst
dipsos [1373; 200]
  thirst
dipsuchos [1374; 201]
  double-minded
dis [1364; 199]
  again, twice
dischilioi [1367; 200]
  thousand
dismuriades [1364 and 3463; 199]
  thousand
distazō [1365; 200]
  doubt
distomos [1366; 200]
  edge, two-edged
dithalassos [1337; 195]
  sea
diülizō [1368; 200]
  strain out
dochē [1403; 206]
  feast
dōdeka [1427; 210]
  twelve
dōdekaphulon [1429; 210]
  tribes
dōdekatos [1428; 210]
  twelfth
dogma [1378; 201]
  decree, ordinance

dogmatizō [1379; 201]
  ordinance
dokeō [1380; 201]
  account, please, pleasure,
  reputation, repute, seem,
  suppose, think, trow
dokimazō [1381; 202]
  allow, approve, discern,
  examine, prove, refuse, try
dokimē [1382; 202]
  experience, experiment,
  probation, proof, trial
dokimion [1383; 203]
  proof, trial, try
dokimos [1384; 203]
  approved, tried
dokos [1385; 203]
  beam
doliŏo [1387; 203]
  deceit
dolios [1386; 203]
  deceitful
doloō [1389; 203]
  deceitfully, handle
dolos [1388; 203]
  craft, deceit, guile, subtilty
doma [1390; 203]
  gift
dōma [1430; 210]
  housetop
dōrea [1431; 210]
  gift
dōrean [1432; 210]
  cause, freely, nought, vain
dōrēma [1434; 210]
  boon, gift
dōreŏmai [1433; 210]
  give
dōron [1435; 210]
  gift, offering
dosis [1394; 204]
  gift
dotēs [1395; 205]
  giver
doulagōgeō [1396; 205]
  bondage, subjection
doulē [1399; 205]
  handmaid
douleia [1397; 205]
  bondage
douleuō [1398; 205]
  bondage, serve
douloō [1402; 206]
  bondage, enslaved, give,
  servant
doulos [1401; 205]
  bondman, bondservant,
  servant
doxa [1391; 203]
  dignity, glory, honor, praise,
  worship
doxazō [1392; 204]
  glorify, honor, magnify

drachmē [1406; 206]
  piece
drakōn [1404; 206]
  dragon
drassomai [1405; 206]
  take
drepanon [1407; 206]
  sickle
dromos [1408; 206]
  course
dunamai [1410; 207]
  able, can, may, possible,
  power
dunamis [1411; 207]
  ability, abundance, deed,
  meaning, might, miracle,
  power, strength, violence,
  virtue, wonderful (work),
  work
dunamoō [1412; 208]
  strengthen
dunastēs [1413; 208]
  authority, mighty, potentate
dunateō [1414; 208]
  able, mighty
dunatos (-on) [1415; 208]
  able, mighty, possible, power,
  strong
dunō [1416; 209]
  set
duo [1417; 209]
  twain, two
dusbastaktos [1419; 209]
  grievous
dusenterion [1420**; 209]
  dysentery
dusermēneutos [1421; 209]
  utter
duskolos [1422; 209]
  hard
duskolōs [1423; 209]
  hardly
dusmē [1424; 209]
  west
dusnoētos [1425; 209]
  understood
dusphēmeō [1418 and 5346;
  209] defame
dusphēmia [1426; 209]
  report

E

ē [2228; 342]
  either
ē [2229; 342]
  what, yea
ea [1436; 211]
  ah!, alone
eaō [1439; 212]
  commit, leave, let, suffer
ēcheō [2278; 349]
  roar, sound

echidna [2191; 331]
  viper
echō [2192; 331]
  ability, able, accompany, can,
  case, count, do, fare, follow,
  have, hold, keep, lie, next,
  old, possess, retain, take, use
ēchos [2279; 349]
  fame, roar, rumor, sound
echthes [5504v; 331]
  yesterday
echthra [2189; 331]
  enmity, hatred
echthros [2190; 331]
  enemy, foe
edaphizō [1474; 217]
  dash, ground
edaphos [1475; 217]
  ground
ēdē [2235; 344]
  already, now, time, yet
egeirō [1453; 214]
  arise, awake, lift, raise (up),
  rear, stand, take
egersis [1454; 215]
  resurrection
egō [1473; 217]
  I
eidea (or *idea*) [2397; 220]
  countenance
eidōlion [1493; 221]
  idol's temple
eidōlolatreia [1495; 221]
  idolatry
eidōlolatrēs [1496; 221]
  idolater
eidōlon [1497; 221]
  idol
eidōlothuton [1494; 221]
  idols (offered to), meat, offer,
  sacrifice
eidon [aor. of 3708; 220]
  (see *horaō*)
eidos [1491; 221]
  appearance, fashion, form,
  shape, sight
eikē [1500; 221]
  cause, vain (in), vainly
eikō [1502; 222]
  place
eikōn [1504; 222]
  image
eikosi [1501; 222]
  twenty
eilikrin(e)ia [1505; 222]
  sincerity
eilikrinēs [1506; 222]
  pure, sincere
eimi (to be) [1510; 222]
  come, have, hold, make,
  mean, might, pass, possible,
  was, etc.

eipon [3004; 226]
bid, call, command, say,
speak, tell, word
eirēnē [1515; 227]
peace, quietness, rest
eirēneuō [1514; 227]
peace, peaceably
eirēnikos [1516; 228]
peaceable
eirēnopoieō [1517; 228]
peace
eirēnopoios [1518; 228]
peacemaker
eirō (erō) [3004; 311]
make, say, speak, tell
eis [1519; 228]
regard (in...to)
eisagō [1521; 232]
bring, lead
eisakouō [1522; 232]
hear
eisdechomai [1523; 232]
receive
eiseimi [1524; 232]
enter, go
eiserchomai [1525; 232]
arise, come, enter, go
*eiskaleō (-omai) [1528; 233]
call
eisodos [1529; 233]
coming, enter, entering,
entrance
eispēdaō [1530; 233]
run, spring
eispherō [1533; 233]
bring, lead
eisporeuomai [1531; 233]
come, enter, go
eistrechō [1532; 233]
run
eita [1534; 233]
afterward, furthermore, then
ek [1537; 234]
means (by), of, out, out of
ekbainō [1543a; 237]
come, go
ekballō [1544; 237]
bring, cast, drive, expel,
leave, pluck (out), pull, put,
send, take, thrust
ekbasis [1545; 237]
end, escape, issue
ekbolē [1546; 238]
freight
ekcheō [1632; 247]
pour, run, shed, spill
ekchōreō [1633; 247]
depart
ekchun(n)ō [1632; 247]
gush out, pour, riotously,
run, shed, spill
ekdapanaomai [1550; 238]
spend

ekdechomai [1551; 238]
expect, look, tarry, wait
ekdēlos [1552; 238]
manifest
ekdēmeō [1553; 238]
absent
ekdidōmi [1554; 238]
let out
ekdiēgeomai [1555; 238]
declare
ekdikeō [1556; 238]
avenge, revenge
ekdikēsis [1557; 238]
avenge, punishment, revenge,
vengeance
ekdikos [1558; 238]
avenger, revenger
ekdiōkō [1559; 239]
drive, persecute
ekdochē [1561; 239]
expectation, looking
ekdotos [1560; 239]
deliver
ekduō [1562; 239]
strip, take, unclothed
ekei [1563; 239]
there, thither, yonder
ekeinos [1565; 239]
he, it, other, she, that, their,
them, they, this
ekeise [1566; 240]
there
ekeithen [1564; 239]
afterward, place, thence
(from), there
ekgamiskō [1548]
marriage (give in)
ekgamizō [1547; 238]
marriage (give in)
ekgonos [1549**; 238]
grandchildren, nephews
ekkaiō [1572; 240]
burn
ekkakeō [1573; 240]
(see *enkakeō*)
ekkathairō [1571; 240]
purge
ekkenteō [1574; 240]
pierce
ekklaō [1575; 240]
break
ekkleiō [1576; 240]
exclude
ekklēsia [1577; 240]
assembly, church
ekklinō [1578; 241]
avoid, eschew, go, turn, way
ekkolumbaō [1579; 241]
swim
ekkomizō [1580; 241]
carry (out)
ekkoptō [1581; 241]
cut, hew, hinder

ekkremannumi [1582; 242]
attentive, hang
eklaleō [1583; 242]
tell
eklampō [1584; 242]
shine
eklanthanomai [1585; 242]
forget
eklegō [1586; 242]
choice, choose
ekleipō [1587; 242]
fail
eklektos [1588; 242]
chosen, elect
eklogē [1589; 243]
chosen, election
ekluō [1590; 243]
faint
ekmassō [1591; 243]
wipe
ekmuktērizō [1592; 243]
deride, scoff
eknēphō [1594; 243]
awake
ekneuō [1593; 243]
convey
ekpalai [1597; 243]
long, old
ekpēdaō [1600a; 243]
run, spring
ekpeirazō [1598; 243]
tempt
ekpempō [1599; 243]
send
ekperissōs [1537 and 4057; 243]
vehemently
ekpetannumi [1600; 243]
spread, stretch
ekpherō [1627; 246]
bear, bring, carry
ekpheugō [1628; 246]
escape, flee
ekphobeō [1629; 247]
terrify
ekphobos [1630; 247]
fear
ekphuō [1631; 247]
put
ekpiptō [1601; 243]
cast, effect, fail, fall, nought
ekpleō [1602; 244]
sail
ekplēroō [1603; 244]
fulfill
ekplērōsis [1604; 244]
accomplishment
ekplēssō [1605; 244]
amaze, astonish
ekpneō [1606; 244]
ghost (give up the)
ekporeuō [1607; 244]
come, depart, go, issue,
proceed

ekporneuō [1608; 244]
  fornication
ekpsuchō [1634; 247]
  ghost (give up the), yield
ekptuō [1609; 244]
  reject
ekrizoō [1610; 244]
  pluck, root
ekstasis [1611; 245]
  amazement, astonishment,
  trance
ekstrephō [1612; 245]
  pervert, subvert
ektarassō [1613; 245]
  trouble
ekteinō [1614; 245]
  cast, lay, put, stretch
ekteleō [1615; 245]
  finish
ekteneia [1616; 245]
  earnestly, instantly
ektenēs [1618; 245]
  cease, fervent
ektenesteron [1617; 245*]
  earnestly
ektenōs [1619; 245]
  earnestly, fervently
ekthambeō [1568; 240]
  affright, amaze
ekthambos [1569; 240]
  wonder
ekthaumazō [1537 and 2296; 240]
  wonder
ekthetos [1570; 240]
  cast
ektinassō [1621; 245]
  shake
ektithēmi [1620; 245]
  cast, expound
ektos [1622; 246]
  except, other, out of, outside,
  unless, without
ektrephō [1625; 246]
  bring, nourish
ektrepō [1624; 246]
  avoid, turn
ektrōma [1626; 246]
  beget
ektromos [1740v; 246]
  fear
ekzēteō [1567; 240]
  inquire, require, seek
ekzētēsis [1537 and 2214; 240]
  questioning
elachistos [1646; 248]
  least, little, small
elachistoteros [1647; 248*]
  least
elaia [1636; 247]
  olive (berry), olive tree
elaion [1637; 247]
  oil
elaiōn [1638; 248]
  Olives, Olivet

elaphria [1644; 248]
  fickleness, lightness
elaphros [1645; 248]
  light
elassōn [1640; 248]
  less, under, worse, younger
elattoneō [1641; 248]
  lack
elattoō [1642; 248]
  decrease, lower
elaunō [1643; 248]
  carry, drive, row
eleeinos [1652; 249]
  miserable
eleeinoteros [1652*; 249*]
  miserable, pitiable (most)
eleēmōn [1655; 250]
  merciful
eleēmosunē [1654; 249]
  alms, almsdeeds
eleeō [1653; 249]
  compassion, mercy, obtain,
  receive
elegmos [1650v; 249]
  reproof
elenchō [1651; 249]
  convict, fault, rebuke,
  reprove
elenchos [1650; 249]
  reproof
elenxis [1649; 249]
  rebuke
eleos [1656; 250]
  mercy
elephantinos [1661; 251]
  ivory
eleusis [1660; 251]
  coming
eleutheria [1657; 250]
  freedom, liberty
eleutheroō [1659; 250]
  deliver, free
eleutheros [1658; 250]
  free, freeman, freewoman,
  liberty
ellogeō (or *-aō*) [1677; 252]
  account, impute
elpis [1680; 252]
  faith, hope
elpizō [1679; 252]
  hope, trust
emautou [1683; 253]
  me, myself
embainō [1684; 254]
  come, enter, get, go, step,
  take
emballō [1685; 254]
  cast
embaptō [1686; 254]
  dip
embateuō [1687; 254]
  dwell
embibazō [1688; 254]
  put

emblepō [1689; 254]
  behold, gaze, look, see
embrimaomai [1690; 254]
  charge, groan, murmur,
  straitly
eme, emoi [1691; 255]
  me
emeō [1692; 254]
  spue
emmainomai [1693; 255]
  mad
emmenō [1696; 255]
  continue
emos [1699; 255]
  me, my (mine), very
empaigmonē [1702d; 255]
  mockery
empaigmos [1701; 255]
  mocking
empaiktēs [1703; 255]
  mocker, scoffer
empaizō [1702; 255]
  mock
emperipateō [1704; 256]
  walk
emphanēs [1717; 257]
  manifest, openly, shew
emphanizō [1718; 257]
  appear, declare, inform,
  manifest, shew, signify
emphobos [1719; 257]
  affrighted, terrify, tremble
emphusaō [1720; 258]
  breathe
emphutos [1721; 258]
  engrafted, implanted
empiplaō [1705v; 256]
  fill
empiplēmi [1705; 256]
  fill, satisfy
empiprēmi (or *emprēthō*) [1714;
  256] burn
empiptō [1706; 256]
  fall
emplekō [1707; 256]
  entangle
emplokē [1708; 256]
  plaiting
empneō [1709; 256]
  breathe
emporeuomai [1710; 256]
  buy, merchandise, sell, trade
emporia [1711; 256]
  merchandise
emporion [1712; 257]
  merchandise
emporos [1713; 257]
  merchant
emprosthen [1715; 257]
  before, presence, sight of (in
  the)
emptuō [1716; 257]
  spit

en [1722; 258]
under, way (by...of), within

enalios [1724; 261]
sea

enankalizomai [1723; 261]
arm (physical)

enanti [1725; 261]
before, sight of (in the)

enantion [1726; 261]
before, contrariwise, sight of (in the)

enantios [1727; 262]
contrary

enarchomai [1728; 262]
begin

enchriō [1472; 217]
anoint

endechomai [1735; 262]
can

endeēs [1729; 262]
lack

endeigma [1730; 262]
token

endeiknumi [1731; 262]
shew

endeixis [1732; 262]
declare, proof, shew, token

endēmeō [1736; 263]
home, present

endiduskō [1737; 263]
clothe, wear

endikos [1738; 263]
just

endomēsis [1739; 263]
building

endoxazō [1740; 263]
glorify

endoxos [1741; 263]
glorious, glory, gorgeously, honorable

enduma [1742; 263]
clothing, garment, raiment

endunamoō [1743; 263]
enable, strength, strengthen, strong

endunō [1744; 263]
creep

enduō [1746; 264]
clothe, endue, have, put

endusis [1745; 263]
putting

enechō [1758; 265]
entangle, press, quarrel, set, urge

enedra (or *-dron*) [1747; 264]
lie in wait

enedreuō [1748; 264]
lie in wait

eneileō [1750; 264]
wrap

eneimi [1751; 264]
have, within

enenēkonta [1767d; 265]
ninety

eneos [1769; 265]
(see *enneos*)

energeia [1753; 265]
effectual, operation, strong, working

energēma [1755; 265]
operation, working

energeō [1754; 265]
do, effectual, mighty, shew, work

energēs [1756; 265]
active, effectual, powerful

eneulogeomai [1757; 265]
bless

engizō [1448; 213]
approach, come, draw, hand (at), near, nigh

engraphō [1449; 213]
write in

enguos [1450; 214]
surety

engus [1451; 214]
hand (at), near, nigh, ready

enguteron [1452; 214*]
nearer

eniautos [1763; 266]
year

enischuō [1765; 266]
strengthen

enistēmi [1764; 266]
come, hand (at), now, present

enkainia [1456; 215]
dedication

enkainizō [1457; 215]
consecrate, dedicate

enkakeō [1573v; 215]
faint, weary

enkaleō [1458; 215]
accuse, call, charge, implead, question

enkataleipō [1459; 215]
forsake, leave

enkathetos [1455; 215]
spy

enkatoikeō [1460; 216]
dwell

enkauchaomai [1722 and 2744; 216] glory

enkentrizō [1461; 216]
graff, graft

enklēma [1462; 216]
charge, crime, matter

enkomboomai [1463; 216]
clothe

enkopē [1464; 216]
hinder, hindrance

enkoptō [1465; 216]
hinder, tedious (to be)

enkrateia [1466; 216]
temperance

enkratēs [1468; 216]
temperate

enkrateuomai [1467; 216]
contain, continency, temperate

enkrinō [1469; 216]
number

enkruptō [1469; 216]
hide

enkuos [1471; 216]
child

ennatos [1766; 262]
ninth

ennea [1767; 267]
nine

enneos [1769; 267]
speechless

enneuō [1770; 267]
signs (to make)

ennoia [1771; 267]
intent, mind

ennomos [1772; 267]
law, lawful, regular

ennucha [1773*; 267]
day

enochleō [1776; 267]
trouble

enochos [1777; 267]
danger, guilty, subject, worthy

enoikeō [1774; 267]
dwell

enōpion [1799; 270]
before, presence, sight of (in the)

enorkizō [1722 and 3726; 267]
adjure, charge

enōtizomai [1801; 271]
hearken

entalma [1778; 268]
commandment, precept

entaphiasmos [1780; 268]
burying

entaphiazō [1779; 268]
bury, burial

entellō (-omai) [1781; 268]
charge, command, enjoined

enteuthen [1782; 268]
either, hence

enteuxis [1783; 268]
intercessions, prayer

enthade [1759; 266]
here, hither, there

enthen [1782v; 266]
hence

enthumeomai [1760; 266]
think

enthumēsis [1761; 266]
device, thought

entimos [1784; 268]
dear, honor, precious, reputation

entimoteros [1784*; 268*]
honorable

entolē [1785; 269]
commandment, precept

entopios [1786; 269]
  place
entos [1787; 269]
  inside, within
entrephō [1789; 269]
  nourish
entrepō [1788; 269]
  ashamed, regard, reverence,
  shame
entromos [1790; 269]
  fear, quake, trembling
entropē [1791; 269]
  shame
entruphaō [1792; 270]
  revel, sport
entulissō [1794; 270]
  roll, wrap
entunchano [1793; 270]
  deal with, intercessions,
  plead, suit
entupoō [1795; 270]
  engrave
enubrizō [1796; 270]
  despite
enupniazō [1797; 270]
  dream, dreamer
enupnion [1798; 270]
  dream
eoika [1503v; 280]
  like
epagō [1863; 281]
  bring
epagōnizomai [1864; 281]
  contend, earnestly
epaineō [1867; 281]
  commend, praise
epainos [1868; 281]
  praise
epairō [1869; 281]
  exalt, hoist up, lift, take
epaischunomai [1870; 282]
  ashamed
epaiteō [1871; 282]
  beg
epakoloutheō [1872; 282]
  follow
epakouō [1873; 282]
  hear
epakroaomai [1874; 282]
  hear
epanagō [1877; 282]
  launch, put, return, thrust
epanamimnēskō [1878; 282]
  mind, remembrance
epanankes [1876; 282]
  necessary
epanapau (-omai) [1879; 282]
  rest
epanerchomai [1880; 283]
  come, return
epangelia [1860; 280]
  message, promise
epangellō (-omai) [1861; 280]
  profess, promise

epangelma [1862; 281]
  promise
epanistēmi [1881; 283]
  rise
epanō [1883; 283]
  above, more
epanorthōsis [1882; 283]
  correction
epaphrizō [1890; 283]
  foam
eparatos [1883a; 283]
  accursed
eparch(e)ia [1885; 283]
  province
eparkeō [1884; 283]
  relieve
epathroizō [1865; 281]
  gather
epaulis [1886; 283]
  habitation
epaurion [1887; 283]
  follow, morrow, next day
epautophōrō [1888]
  act
epechō [1907; 285]
  heed, hold, mark, stay
epegeirō [1892; 284]
  raise, stir
epei [1893; 284]
  else, otherwise
epeidon [1896; 284]
  look
epeimi [1909 and 1510; 284]
  follow, next, next day
epeisagōgē [1898; 284]
  bringing
epeita [1899; 284]
  afterward(s), then
epekeina [1900; 284]
  beyond
epekteinō [1901; 284]
  reach, stretch
ependu (-omai) [1902; 284]
  clothe
ependutēs [1903; 285]
  clothing
eperchomai [1904; 285]
  come
epēreazō [1908; 285]
  accuse, despitefully, revile
eperōtaō [1905; 285]
  ask, demand, desire, question
eperōtēma [1906; 285]
  answer, interrogation
ephallomai [2177; 330]
  leap
ephapax [2178; 330]
  once
ephēmeria [2183; 330]
  course
ephēmeros [2184; 330]
  daily
epheuretēs [2182; 330]
  inventor

ephikneomai [2185; 330]
  reach
ephistēmi [2186; 330]
  assault, come, hand (at),
  instant, present, stand
ephphatha [2188; 331]
  ephphatha, open
epi [1909; 285]
  of, respect, space, time, under
epibainō [1910; 289]
  aboard, come, embark, enter,
  foot, go, ride, ship, sit, take
epiballō [1911; 289]
  beat, cast, fall, lay, put,
  stretch, think
epibareō [1912; 290]
  burden, chargeable,
  overcharge, press
epibibazō [1913; 290]
  set
epiblēma [1915; 290]
  piece
epiblepō [1914; 290]
  look, regard, respect
epiboaō [1916; 290]
  cry
epiboulē [1917; 290]
  plot
epicheireō [2021; 304]
  go, hand (take in), take
epicheō [2022; 305]
  pour
epichorēgeō [2023; 305]
  add, minister, supply
epichorēgia [2024; 305]
  supply
epichriō [2025; 305]
  anoint
epide [1896**; 291]
  behold
epidechomai [1926; 292]
  receive
epideiknumi [1925; 291]
  shew
epidēmeō [1927; 292]
  stranger, there
epidiatassō [1928; 292]
  add
epididōmi [1929; 292]
  deliver, give, offer
epidiorthoō [1930; 292]
  order
epiduō [1931; 292]
  go
epieikeia [1932; 292]
  clemency, gentleness
epieikēs [1933; 292]
  forbearance, gentle,
  moderation, patient
epigambreuō [1918; 290]
  marry
epigeios [1919; 290]
  earth, earthly, terrestrial

epiginomai [1920; 290]
   blow
epiginōskō [1921; 291]
   acknowledge, know,
   knowledge, perceive
epignōsis [1922; 291]
   acknowledgement, know,
   knowledge
epigraphē [1923; 291]
   superscription
epigraphō [1924; 291]
   inscription, write
*epikaleō (-omai) [1941; 294]
   appeal, call, surname
epikalumma [1942; 294]
   cloke
epikaluptō [1943; 294]
   cover
epikataratos [1944; 294]
   cursed
epikathizō [1940; 293]
   set
epikeimai [1945; 294]
   imposed, instant, lay, lie
epikellō (or epok-) [2207; 294]
   run
epikouria [1947; 294]
   help
epikrinō [1948; 295]
   give, sentence
epilambanō [1949; 295]
   catch, hold, lay, take
epilanthanomai [1950; 295]
   forget, forgetful
*epilegō (-omai) [1951; 295]
   call, choose
epileichō [1952a; 295]
   lick
epileipō [1952; 295]
   fail
epilēsmonē [1953; 295]
   forget, forgetful
epiloipos [1954; 295]
   rest (the)
epiluō [1956; 295]
   determine, expound, settle
epilusis [1955; 295]
   interpretation
epimartureō [1957; 296]
   testify
epimeleia [1958; 296]
   refresh
epimeleomai [1959; 296]
   care
epimelōs [1960; 296]
   diligently
epimenō [1961; 296]
   abide, continue, tarry
epineuō [1962; 296]
   consent
epinoia [1963; 296]
   thought
epiorkeō [1964; 296]
   forswear

epiorkos [1965; 296]
   perjured person
ēpios [2261; 348]
   gentle
epiousios [1967; 296]
   daily
epiphainō [2014; 304]
   appear, light
epiphaneia [2015; 304]
   appearing, brightness
epiphanēs [2016; 304]
   notable
epiphauō (or -auskō) [2017; 304]
   light, shine
epipherō [2018; 304]
   bring, take, visit
epiphōneō [2019; 304]
   cry, shout
epiphōskō [2020; 304]
   dawn, draw
epipiptō [1968; 297]
   fall, lie, press
epiplēssō [1969; 297]
   rebuke
epiporeuomai [1975; 298]
   come, resort
epipotheō [1971; 297]
   desire, long, lust
epipothēsis [1972; 298]
   desire, longing
epipothētos [1973; 298]
   long (verb)
epipothia [1974; 298]
   desire, longing
epirrhaptō [1976; 298]
   sew
epiriptō [1977; 298]
   cast
epischuō [2001; 302]
   fierce
episēmos [1978; 298]
   notable, note
episitismos [1979; 298]
   victuals
episkēnoō [1981; 298]
   rest
episkeptomai [1980; 298]
   look, visit
episkeuazō [643v; 298]
   baggage, carriage
episkiazō [1982; 298]
   overshadow
episkopē [1984; 299]
   bishop, bishoprick, office,
   visitation
episkopeō [1983; 298]
   carefully, exercise, look,
   oversight
episkopos [1985; 299]
   bishop, overseer
episōreuō [2002; 302]
   heap
epispaomai [1986; 299]
   uncircumcised

episphalēs [2000; 302]
   dangerous
epistamai [1987; 300]
   know, understand
epistasis [1999v; 300]
   come, press, raise, stir
epistatēs [1988; 300]
   master
epistellō [1989; 300]
   write
epistēmōn [1990; 300]
   endue, knowledge,
   understanding
epistērizō [1991; 300]
   confirm, strengthen
epistolē [1992; 300]
   epistle, letter
epistomizō [1993; 301]
   mouth, stop
epistrephō [1994; 301]
   come, convert, go, return,
   turn
epistrophē [1995; 301]
   conversion
episunagō [1996; 301]
   gather
episunagōgē [1997; 301]
   assembling, gathering
episuntrechō [1998; 301]
   come, run
episustasis [1999; 301]
   come, press, raise
epitagē [2003; 302]
   authority, commandment
epitassō [2004; 302]
   charge, command, enjoin
epitēdeios [2006; 302]
   needful
epiteleō [2005; 302]
   accomplish, complete, do,
   finish, make, perfect, perform
epithanatios [1935; 292]
   appointed, death, doomed
epithesis [1936; 293]
   laying on, putting
epithumeō [1937; 293]
   covert, desire, fain, lust
epithumētēs [1938; 293]
   lust
epithumia [1939; 293]
   concupiscence, coveting,
   desire, lust
epitimaō [2008; 303]
   charge, rebuke
epitimia [2009; 303]
   punishment
epitithēmi [2007; 302]
   add, lade, lay, put, set,
   surname
epitrepō [2010; 303]
   leave, let, liberty, license,
   permit, suffer
epitropē [2011; 303]
   commission

epitropos [2012; 303]
  guardian, steward, tutor
epitunchanō [2013; 303]
  obtain
epizēteō [1934; 292]
  desire, inquire, seek
epoikodomeō [2026; 305]
  build
eponomazō [2028; 305]
  call, name
epoptēs [2030; 305]
  eye-witness
epopteuō [2029; 305]
  behold
epos [2031; 305]
  so, word
epouranios [2032; 305]
  celestial, heavenly
erchomai [2064; 310]
  bring, come, enter, fall, go,
  grow, light (to...upon), next,
  pass, resort
eraunaō (or *ereu-*) [2045; 306]
  search
ereidō [2043; 308]
  stick fast, strike
erēmia [2047; 308]
  desert, place, wilderness
erēmoō [2049; 309]
  desolation, desolate, nought
erēmos [2048; 309]
  desert, desolate, solitary,
  wilderness
ēremos [2263; 348]
  quiet, tranquil
erēmōsis [2050; 309]
  desolation
erethizō [2042; 308]
  anger, provoke, stir
ereugomai [2044; 308]
  utter
ergasia [2039; 307]
  business, craft, diligence,
  gain, work
ergatēs [2040; 307]
  laborer, worker, workman
ergazomai [2038; 306]
  commit, do, gain, labor,
  minister, trade, work,
  working
ergon [2041; 307]
  deed, labor, work
erion [2053; 309]
  wool
eriphion [2055; 309]
  goat
eriphos [2056; 309]
  goat, kid
eris [2054; 309]
  contention, debate, strife,
  variance
erith(e)ia [2052; 309]
  contention, contentious,
  faction, strife

erizō [2051; 309]
  strive
erō (see *eirō*)
erōtaō [2065; 311]
  ask, beseech, desire, intreat,
  pray, request
eruthros [2063; 310]
  red
eschatos [2078; 313]
  end, last, lowest, part,
  uttermost
eschatōs [2079; 314]
  death
esō [2080; 314]
  inner, inward, within
esoptron [2072; 313]
  glass, mirror
esōteros [2082; 314]
  inner, within
esōthen [2081; 314]
  inside, inward, inwardly,
  within
esthēs [2066; 312]
  apparel, clothing, raiment,
  robe
esthēsis [2067; 312]
  apparel, garment
esthiō [2068; 312]
  devour, eat, live
ethelothrēsk(e)ia [1479; 218]
  worship
ethizō [1480; 218]
  custom
ethnarchēs [1481; 218]
  governor
ethnikos [1482; 218]
  Gentile(s), heathen
ethnikōs [1483; 218]
  Gentiles, manner
ethnos [1484; 218]
  Gentiles, heathen, nation,
  people
ethō [1486; 219]
  custom, manner, wont
ethos [1485; 218]
  custom, manner, wont
ēthos [2239; 344]
  manner
eti [2089; 315]
  also, even, further, longer,
  more, moreover, still,
  thenceforth, yet
etos [2094; 316]
  year
eu [2095; 317]
  good, well
euangelion [2098; 317]
  gospel
euangelistēs [2099; 318]
  evangelist
euangelizō [2097; 317]
  gospel, preach, shew, tidings
euaresteō [2100; 318]
  please, well-pleasing

euarestos [2101; 318]
  acceptable, well-pleasing
euarestōs [2102; 318]
  acceptably
eucharisteō [2168; 328]
  thank, thankful
eucharistia [2169; 328]
  thanks, thankfulness,
  thanksgiving
eucharistos [2170; 329]
  thankful
euchē [2171; 329]
  prayer, vow
euchomai [2172; 329]
  pray, wish, would
euchrēstos [2173; 329]
  profitable, use
eudia [2105; 319]
  fair, weather
eudokeō [2106; 319]
  please, pleasure, think,
  willing
eudokia [2107; 319]
  desire, pleasure, seem, well-
  pleasing, will, willing
euergesia [2108; 319]
  benefit, deed
euergeteō [2109; 320]
  good (to do)
euergetēs [2110; 320]
  benefactor
eugenēs [2104; 319]
  noble, nobleman
eugenesteros [2104*; 319*]
  noble
eukaireō [2119; 321]
  leisure, opportunity, spend,
  time
eukairia [2120; 321]
  opportunity
eukairos [2121; 321]
  convenient, need
eukairōs [2122; 321]
  conveniently, season
eukopōteros [2123; 321*]
  easier
eulabeia [2124; 321]
  fear, godly, reverence
eulabeomai [2125; 321]
  fear, godly, moved
eulabēs [2126; 322]
  devout
eulogeō [2127; 322]
  bless, praise
eulogētos [2128; 322]
  blessed
eulogia [2129; 322]
  blessing, bounty, fair, speech
eumetadotos [2130; 323]
  distribute
eunoeō [2132; 323]
  agree
eunoia [2133; 323]
  benevolence, will

eunouchizō [2134; 323]
eunuch
eunouchos [2135; 323]
eunuch
euōdia [2175; 329]
savor, smell
euodoō [2137; 323]
journey, prosper
euōnumos [2176; 329]
left
euparedros [2145v; 324]
attend
eupeithēs [2138; 324]
intreat
euperistatos [2139; 324]
beset, easily
euphēmia [2162; 327]
report
euphēmos [2163; 327]
report
euphoreō [2164; 327]
bring, plentifully
euphrainō [2165; 327]
fare, glad, merry, rejoice
euphrosunē [2167; 328]
gladness, joy
eupoieō
good (to do)
eupoiïa [2140; 324]
good
euporeō [2141; 324]
ability
euporia [2142; 324]
wealth
euprepeia [2143; 324]
grace
euprosdektos [2144; 324]
acceptable, accepted
euprosedros [2145; 324]
attend
euprosōpeō [2146; 324]
fair, show (make a)
eupsucheō [2174; 329]
comfort
euruchōros [2149; 326]
broad
euschēmōn [2158; 327]
comely, estate, honorable
euschēmonōs [2156; 327]
decently, honestly
euschēmosunē [2157; 327]
comeliness
eusebeia [2150; 326]
godliness, holiness
eusebeō [2151; 326]
piety (to shew), worship
eusebēs [2152; 326]
devout, godly
eusebōs [2153; 326]
godly
eusēmos [2154; 326]
understood
eusplanchnos [2155; 326]
pitiful, tenderhearted

eutheōs [2112; 320]
forthwith, immediately,
shortly, straightway
euthetos [2111; 320]
fit, meet
euthudromeō [2113; 320]
course
euthumeō [2114; 320]
cheer, cheerful, merry
euthumos [2115; 320]
cheer
euthumōs [2115*; 320]
cheerfully
euthumoteron [2115*; 320*]
cheerfully
euthunō [2116; 320]
governor, straight, steersman
euthus (adj.) [2117; 321]
right, straight
euthus (adv.) [2117; 321]
anon, forthwith,
immediately, straightway
euthutēs [2118; 321]
righteousness, uprightness
eutonōs [2159; 327]
mightily, powerfully,
vehemently
eutrapelia [2160; 327]
jesting
exagō [1806; 271]
bring, fetch, lead
exagorazō [1805; 271]
redeem
exaiphnēs [1810; 272]
suddenly
exaireō [1807; 271]
deliver, pluck, rescue
exairō [1808; 272]
put, take
*exaiteō (-omai) [1809; 272]
ask, desire
exakoloutheō [1811; 272]
follow
exaleiphō [1813; 272]
blot, wipe
exallomai [1814; 272]
leap
exanastasis [1815; 272]
resurrection
exanatellō [1816; 272]
spring
exangellō [1804; 271]
shew
exanistēmi [1817; 272]
raise (up), rise (see *arise*)
exapataō [1818; 273]
beguile, deceive
exapina [1819; 273]
suddenly
*exaporeō (-omai) [1820; 273]
despair
exapostellō [1821; 273]
send

exartizō [1822; 273]
accomplish, furnish
exastraptō [1823; 273]
dazzling, glister
exautēs [1824; 273]
forthwith, immediately,
presently, straightway
*exēcheō (-omai) [1837; 276]
sound
exegeirō [1825; 273]
raise (up)
exēgeomai [1834; 275]
declare, rehearse, tell
exeimi [1826; 273]
depart, get, go
exelenchō [1827; 274]
convict
exelkō [1828; 274]
draw
exerama [1829; 274]
vomit
exeraunaō [1830; 274]
search
exerchomai [1831; 274]
come, depart, escape, get, go,
proceed, spread
exesti [1832; 275]
lawful, let, may
exetazō [1833; 275]
ask, inquire, search
exischuō [1840; 276]
able
existēmi [1839; 276]
amaze, beside oneself,
bewitch, wonder
exō [1854; 279]
foreign, forth, outward,
strange, without
exochē [1851; 279]
principal
exodos [1841; 276]
decease, departure
exolothreuō [1842; 276]
destroy
exomologeō [1843; 277]
confess, consent, praise,
promise, thank
exorkistēs [1845; 277]
exorcist
exorkizō [1844; 277]
adjure
exorussō [1846; 277]
break, pluck
exōteros [1857; 280]
outer
exōthen [1855; 279]
outside, outward, outwardly,
without
exōtheō [1856; 280]
drive, thrust
exoudenoō [1847; 277]
nought

exousia [1849; 277]
   authority, jurisdiction, liberty,
   power, right, strength
exousiazō [1850; 279]
   authority, exercise, power
exoutheneō [1848; 277]
   account, contemptible,
   despise, esteem, least, nought
exupnizō [1852; 279]
   awake, sleep
exupnos [1853; 279]
   rouse, sleep

G

gala [1051; 149]
   milk
galēnē [1055; 150]
   calm
gameō [1060; 150]
   marry
gamiskō [1061; 151]
   marriage (give in)
gamizō [1061v; 151]
   marriage (give in)
gamos [1062; 151]
   feast, marriage, marriage
   feast, wedding
gangraina [1044; 149]
   canker, gangrene
gar [1063; 151]
   doubt (no), indeed,
   moreover, verily, what, why,
   yea, yet
gastēr [1064; 152]
   belly, glutton, womb
gaza [1047; 149]
   treasure
gazophulakion [1049; 149]
   treasury
ge [1065; 152]
   yet
gē [1093; 157]
   country, earth, ground, land,
   world
geenna [1067; 153]
   hell
geitōn [1069; 153]
   neighbor
gelaō [1070; 153]
   laugh
gelōs [1071; 153]
   laughter
gemizō [1072; 153]
   fill, full
gemō [1073; 153]
   full, laden
genea [1074; 153]
   age, generation, nation, time
genealogeō [1075; 154]
   descent, genealogy
genealogia [1076; 154]
   genealogy

genēma [1096d; 155]
   fruit
genesia [1077; 154]
   birthday
genesis [1078; 154]
   generation, nature, natural
genetē [1079; 155]
   birth
gennaō [1080; 155]
   bear, beget, bring forth,
   conceive, deliver, gender,
   made (be), spring
gennēma [1081; 155]
   fruit, generation, offspring
gennēsis [1083; 156]
   birth
gennētos [1084; 156]
   beget
genos [1085; 156]
   beget, country, countrymen,
   diversity, generation, kind,
   kindred, nation, offspring,
   stock
geōrgeō [1090; 157]
   dress, till
geōrgion [1091; 157]
   husbandry
geōrgos [1092; 157]
   husbandman
gēras [1094; 157]
   aged, old
gēraskō [1095; 158]
   aged, old
gerōn [1088; 157]
   old
gerousia [1087; 156]
   senate
geuō [1089; 157]
   eat, taste
ginomai [1096; 158]
   arise, assemble, become,
   befall, behave, bring, come,
   continue, divide, do, end,
   fall, far, finish, follow, forbid,
   grow, have, keep, marry,
   means (by...of), ordain, pass,
   past, perform, place (take),
   prefer, prove, publish, shew,
   sound, spent, spring, take,
   turn, use, was, etc., wax,
   work
ginōskō [1097; 160]
   allow, can, feel, know,
   knowledge, perceive, resolve,
   speak, sure, understand
gleukos [1098; 162]
   wine
glōssa [1100; 162]
   tongue
glōssokomon [1101; 162]
   bag
glukus [1099; 162]
   fresh, sweet

gnapheus [1102; 162]
   fuller
gnēsios [1103; 162]
   own, sincerity, true
gnēsiōs [1104; 163]
   naturally, truly
gnōmē [1106; 163]
   advice, agree, judgment,
   mind, purpose, will
gnophos [1105; 163]
   blackness
gnōrizō [1107; 163]
   certify, declare, know,
   understand, wit, wot
gnōsis [1108; 163]
   knowledge, science
gnōstēs [1109; 164]
   expert
gnōstos [1110; 164]
   acquaintance, known,
   notable
goēs [1114; 164]
   impostor, seducer
gomos [1117; 164]
   burden, merchandise
goneus [1118; 165]
   parents
gongusmos [1112; 164]
   grudging, murmuring
gongustēs [1113; 164]
   murmurer
gonguzō [1111; 164]
   murmur
gōnia [1137; 168]
   corner, quarter
gonu [1119; 165]
   knee, kneel
gonupeteō [1120; 165]
   bow, kneel
gramma [1121; 165]
   bill, learning, letter, scripture,
   writing
grammateus [1122; 165]
   scribe, townclerk
graōdēs [1126; 167]
   old wives
graphē [1124; 166]
   scripture
graphō [1125; 166]
   describe, write, writing
graptos [1123; 166]
   written
grēgoreō [1127; 167]
   vigilant, wake, watch,
   watchful
gumnasia [1129; 167]
   exercise
gumnazō [1128; 167]
   exercise
gumniteuō [1130; 167]
   naked
gumnos [1131; 167]
   bare, naked

gumnotēs [1132; 168]
    nakedness
gunaikarion [1133; 168]
    woman
gunaikeios [1134; 168]
    wife
gunē [1135; 168]
    wife, woman

H

hadēs [86; 16]
    Hades, hell
hadrotēs [100; 18]
    abundance, bounty
hagiasmos [38; 9]
    holiness, sanctification
hagiazo [37; 8]
    beloved, hallow, holy,
        sanctify
hagion [39; 9]
    sanctuary
hagios [40; 9]
    holy, saint, sanctuary
hagiōsunē [42; 10]
    holiness
hagiotēs [41; 10]
    holiness
hagneia [47; 10]
    purity
hagnismos [49; 11]
    purification
hagnizō [48; 11]
    purify
hagnos [53; 11]
    chaste, clear, pure
hagnōs [55; 12]
    sincerely
hagnotēs [54; 12]
    pureness, purity
haima [129; 22]
    blood
haimatekchusia [130; 23]
    blood
haimorrhoeō [131; 23]
    blood
haireō (-omai) [138; 24]
    choose
hairesis [139; 23]
    heresy, sect
hairetikos [141; 24]
    heretical
hairetizō [140; 24]
    choose
halieuō [232; 37]
    fish
halieus [231; 37]
    fisher, fisherman
halizō [233; 37]
    salt
hallēlouia [239; 39]
    Hallelujah

hallomai [242; 39]
    leap, spring
halōn [257; 41]
    threshing-floor
halōsis [259; 42]
    take
hal(a)s [251; 35]
    salt
halukos [250; 41]
    salt
halusis [254; 41]
    bond, chain
hama [260; 42]
    early, together, withal
hamartanō [264; 42]
    fault, offend, sin, trespass
hamartēma [265; 42]
    sin
hamartia [266; 43]
    offense, sin, sinful
hamartōlos [268; 44]
    sinful, sinner
hapalos [527; 80]
    tender
hapas [537; 81]
    all, every, whole
hapax [530; 80]
    once
haphē [860; 125]
    joint
haplous [573; 86]
    single
haplōs [574; 86]
    liberally
haplotēs [572; 85]
    bountifulness, liberal,
        liberality, simplicity,
        singleness
haptō [681; 102]
    handle, kindle, light, touch
harma [716; 107]
    chariot
harmos [719; 107]
    joint
harmozō [718; 107]
    espouse
harpagē [724; 108]
    extortion, ravening, spoiling
harpagmos [725; 108]
    prize, robbery
harpax [727; 109]
    extortioner, ravening
harpazō [726; 109]
    catch, force, pluck, pull,
        snatch, spoil, take
heautou (etc.) [1438; 211]
    herself, himself, his, his own,
        itself, one ... another, our
        own, ourselves, own, their,
        them, themselves, thyself,
        yourselves (see conceits)
hebdomēkonta [1440; 212]
    seventy, ten

hebdomēkontakis [1441; 213]
    seventy times
hebdomos [1442; 213]
    seventh
hebraïsti (or ebr-) [1447; 213]
    tongue (in Hebrew), (in the
        Hebrew)
hēdeōs [2234; 343]
    gladly
hēdista [2236; 344]
    gladly
hēdonē [2237; 344]
    lust, pleasure
hedraiōma [1477; 218]
    ground
hedraios [1476; 217]
    settled, stedfast
hēduosmon [2238; 344]
    mint
hēgemōn [2232; 343]
    governor, prince, ruler
hēgemoneuō [2230; 343]
    governor
hēgemonia [2231; 343]
    reign
hēgeomai [2233; 343]
    account, chief, count, esteem,
        governor, judge, rule,
        suppose, think
heilissō (or hel-) [1507; 222]
    fold, roll
heis [1520; 230]
    first, one, only, other
hekastos [1538; 236]
    each, every
hekastote [1539; 236]
    always, time
hekaton [1540; 236]
    hundred, hundredfold
hekatontaetēs [1541; 236]
    year
hekatontaplasiōn [1542; 237]
    hundredfold
hekatontarchēs [1543; 237]
    centurion
hekatontarchos [1543; 237]
    centurion
hēkō [2240; 344]
    come
hekōn [1635; 247]
    will, willingly
hekousios [1595**; 243]
    will, willingly
hekousiōs [1596; 243]
    wilfully, willingly
hektos [1623; 246]
    sixth
hēlikia [2244; 345]
    age, stature
hēlikos [2245; 345]
    great
hēlios [2246; 345]
    sun
helkō [1670; 251]
    drag, draw

helkoō [1669; 251]
    sore
helkos [1668; 251]
    sore
helkuō [1670; 251]
    drag, draw
hellēn [1672; 251]
    Gentiles
hēlos [2247; 345]
    nail
hēmeis (etc.) [2249; 345]
    company, our, ourselves, us,
    we
hēmera [2250; 345]
    age, daily, day, ever,
    judgment, time, year
hēmeteros [2251; 347]
    our, ours
hēmiōron [2256; 348]
    hour
hēmisus [2255; 348]
    half
hēmithanēs [2253; 348]
    (half) dead
hendeka [1733; 262]
    eleven
hendekatos [1734; 262]
    eleventh
heneka [1752; 264]
    cause
henotēs [1775; 267]
    unity
heortazō [1858; 280]
    feast
heortē [1859; 280]
    feast, holy day
heōs [2193; 334]
    far, much (as)
hepta [2033; 306]
    seven, seventh
heptakis [2034; 306]
    seven times
heptakischilioi [2035; 306]
    seven thousand
hermēneia [2058; 310]
    interpretation
hermēneuō [2059; 310]
    interpret, interpretation
herpeton [2062; 310]
    creeping, serpent
hespera [2073; 313]
    evening, eventide
hesperinos [2073*; 313]
    evening
hēssōn (see *hēttōn*)
hēsuchazō [2270; 349]
    cease, peace (hold one's),
    quiet, rest
hēsuchia [2271; 349]
    quietness, silence
hēsuchios [2272; 349]
    peaceable, quiet
hetairos [2083; 314]
    fellow, friend

heterodidaskaleō [2085; 314]
    teach
heteroglōssos [2084; 314]
    strange, tongue
heteros [2087; 315]
    another, neighbor, next day,
    other, strange, stranger
heterōs [2088; 315]
    otherwise
heterozugeō [2086; 314]
    another, yoke
hetoimasia [2091; 316]
    preparation
hetoimazō [2090; 316]
    hold, prepare, provide, ready
hetoimos [2092; 316]
    prepared, readiness, ready
hetoimōs [2093; 316]
    ready
hēttaomai [2274; 349]
    inferior, overcome
hēttēma [2275; 349]
    defect, dimishing, fault, loss
hēttōn [2276; 349]
    less, worse
heuriskō [2147; 324]
    find, get, obtain, perceive
hex [1803; 271]
    six
hexakosioi [1812; 272]
    six hundred
hexēkonta [1835; 276]
    sixty, sixtyfold
hexēs [1836; 276]
    afterwards, follow, morrow,
    next
hexis [1838; 276]
    use
hidrōs [2402; 371]
    sweat
hierateia [2405; 371]
    office, priesthood, priest's
    office
hierateuma [2406; 371]
    priesthood
hierateuō [2407; 371]
    execute, office, priest's office
hieratikos
    priest
hiereus [2409; 372]
    priest
hieron [2411; 372]
    temple
hieroprepēs [2412; 372]
    become, holiness, reverent
hieros [2413; 372]
    holy, sacred
hierosuleō [2416; 373]
    commit, sacrilege
hierosulos [2417; 373]
    robber
hierōsunē [2420; 373]
    priesthood

hierourgeō [2418; 373]
    minister
hikanoō [2427; 374]
    able, meet, sufficient
hikanos [2425; 374]
    able, content, enough, good,
    great, large, long, many,
    meet, much, security, sore,
    sufficient, worthy
hikanotēs [2426; 374]
    sufficiency
hiketēria [2428; 375]
    supplication
hilaros [2431; 375]
    cheerful
hilarotēs [2432; 375]
    cheerfulness
hilaskomai [2433; 375]
    merciful, propitiation,
    reconciliation
hilasmos [2434; 375]
    propitiation
hilastērion [2435; 375]
    mercy-seat, propitiation
hileōs [2436; 376]
    far, merciful
himas [2438; 376]
    latchet, thong
himation [2440; 376]
    apparel, clothes, garment,
    raiment, robe, vesture
himatismos [2441; 376]
    apparel, array, clothing,
    raiment, vesture
himatizō [2439; 376]
    clothe
himeiromai [2442; 376]
    affection, desire
hina [2443; 376]
    albeit, end, intent, lest, must,
    wherefore
hippeus [2460; 380]
    horsemen
hippikos [2461**; 380]
    horsemen
hippos [2462; 380]
    horse
histēmi [2476; 381]
    abide, appoint, bring, charge,
    continue, covenant, establish,
    holden, present, set, stand,
    stanch, weigh
historeō [2477; 383]
    see, visit
ho (1) [3588; 549]
    one (the), this
ho (2) [3739; 549]
    which
hode (*tode*) [3592; 553]
    manner, these, thus
hōde [5602; 895]
    here, hither, place, there
hodēgeō [3594; 553]
    guide, lead

hodēgos [3595; 553]
guide, leader
hodeuō [3593; 553]
journey
hodoiporeō [3596; 553]
go, journey
hodoiporia [3597; 553]
journey, journeyings
hodos [3598; 553]
highway, highwayside,
journey, way
hoios [3634; 562]
manner, such as, what,
which
holokautōma [3646; 564]
burnt (offering), offering
holoklēria [3647; 564]
soundness
holoklēros [3648; 564]
entire, whole
holos [3650; 564]
all, altogether, every whit,
whole
holōs [3654; 565]
actually, all, altogether,
commonly, utterly
holotelēs [3651; 565]
wholly
homeiromai (see himeiromai)
homichlē [3658a; 565]
mist
homileō [3656; 565]
commune, talk
homilia [3657; 565]
communication, company
homilos [3658; 565]
company
homoiazō [3662; 566]
agree
homoiōma [3667; 567]
like (made), likeness, shape,
similitude
homoioō [3666; 567]
like (make), liken, resemble
homoiopathēs [3663; 566]
passions
homoios [3664; 566]
like
homoiōs [3668; 567]
likewise, manner, so
homoiōsis [3669; 568]
likeness, similitude
homoiotēs [3665; 567]
like as, similitude
homologeō [3670; 568]
acknowledge, confess,
profess, promise, thanks,
vouchsafe
homologia [3671; 568]
confession, profession,
professed
homologoumenōs [3672; 569]
controversy (without)

homophrōn [3675; 569]
likeminded, mind, one
homōs [3676; 569]
even, yet
homotechnos [3673; 569]
craft, trade
homothumadon [3661; 566]
accord, mind
homou [3674; 569]
accord, together
hoplizō [3695; 575]
arm
hoplon [3696; 575]
armor, instruments, weapons
hopoios [3697; 575]
manner, sort, such as, what
hōra [5610; 896]
day, hour, instant, season,
short, time
hōraios [5611; 896]
beautiful
horama [3705; 577]
sight, vision
horaō (with eidon and optomai)
[3708; 577] appear, behold,
consider, heed (take), look,
look (to), perceive, see, shew
horasis [3706; 577]
look, sight, vision
horatos [3707; 577]
visible
horion [3725; 581]
border, coast
horizō [3724; 580]
declare, define, determine,
determinate, limit, ordain
horkizō [3726; 581]
adjure, charge
horkōmosia [3728; 581]
oath
horkos [3727; 581]
oath
hormaō [3729; 581]
run, rush, violently
hormē [3730; 581]
assault, impulse
hormēma [3731; 581]
violence
horothesia [3734; 582]
bound
hos [3739; 583]
he that, one...another, what,
whatsoever, which, who,
whosoever
hōs [5613; 897]
about, even as, like, wit (to),
while
hosakis [3740; 585]
oft, often
hōsanna [5614; 899]
Hosanna
hōsautōs [5615; 899]
even so, likewise, manner, so

hōsei [5616; 899]
about, like
hosge [585]
he that
hosios [3741; 585]
blessing, holy, mercy
hosiōs [3743; 585]
holily
hosiotēs [3742; 585]
holiness
hosos [3745; 586]
all, great, long, many, more,
much (as), what, whatsoever,
which, who, whosoever
hosper [3746; 586]
whosoever
hōsper [5618; 899]
even as, like as
hōste [5620; 899]
insomuch that, as, wherefore
hostis [3748; 586]
he that, such as, they, what,
which, who, whosoever
hotan [3752; 587]
while
hothen [3606; 555]
thence (from), wherefore
houtos [3778; 596]
fellow, he, one, same, she, so,
that, their, them, they, this,
which, who
houtō(-s) [3779; 597]
even so, fashion, like,
likewise, manner, so, thus,
what
huakinthinos [5191; 831]
jacinth
huakinthos [5192; 831]
jacinth
hualinos [5193; 831]
glass
hualos [5194; 831]
glass
hubris [5196; 832]
harm, hurt, reproach
hubristēs [5197; 832]
despiteful, injurious, insolent
hubrizō [5195; 831]
despitefully, entreat,
reproach, shamefully,
spitefully
hudōr [5204; 832]
water
hudria [5201; 832]
waterpot
hudrōpikos [5203; 832]
dropsy
hudropoteō [5202; 832]
drink, water
huetos [5205; 833]
rain

hugiainō [5198; 832]
 health, safe, sound (be),
 sound, whole, wholesome
hugiēs [5199; 832]
 sound, whole
hugros [5200; 832]
 green
huios [5207; 833]
 child, foal, son
huiothesia [5206; 833]
 adoption
hulē [5208; 836]
 matter, wood
humeis [5210; 836]
 ye, you, your
humeteros [5212; 836]
 your, yours
humneō [5214; 836]
 hymn, praise, sing
humnos [5215; 836]
 hymn
hupagō [5217; 836]
 depart, get, go
hupakoē [5218; 837]
 obedience, obedient, obey
hupakouō [5219; 837]
 answer, hearken, obedient,
 obey
hupandros [5220; 837]
 husband
hupantaō [5221; 837]
 meet
hupantēsis [5222; 837]
 meet
huparchō [5225; 838]
 exist, goods, have, live,
 possess, was (etc.)
huparchonta [5224; 837]
 substance
huparxis [5223; 837]
 goods, possession, substance
hupechō [5254; 842]
 suffer
hupeikō [5226; 838]
 submit
hupēkoos [5255; 842]
 obedient
hupenantios [5227; 838]
 adversary, contrary
huper [5228; 838]
 behalf, more, of, part
*huperairō (-omai) [5229; 839]
 exalt, overmuch
huperakmos [5230; 839]
 age, flower, pass
huperauxanō [5232; 840]
 grow
huperbainō [5233; 840]
 go, transgress
huperballō [5235; 840]
 exceed, excel, pass, surpass
huperballontōs [5234; 840]
 measure

huperbolē [5236; 840]
 abundance, exceeding, excel,
 excellency, excellent,
 greatness, measure
huperechō [5242; 840]
 better, excellency, higher,
 pass, supreme
hupereidon [5237; 840]
 overlook, wink
huperekchu(n)nō [5240; 840]
 run
huperekeina [5238; 840]
 beyond
huperekperissou [5528 and 1537
 and 4053; 840]
 abundantly, exceeding,
 exceedingly
huperekteinō [5239; 840]
 measure, overmuch, stretch
huperentunchanō [5241; 840]
 intercession
huperēphania [5243; 841]
 pride
huperēphanos [5244; 841]
 haughty, proud
hupēreteō [5256; 842]
 minister, serve
hupēretēs [5257; 842]
 attendant, minister, officer,
 servant
huperlian [6228 and 3029; 841]
 chiefest
hupernikaō [5245; 841]
 conquer
huperochē [5247; 841]
 authority, excellency, place
huperonkos [5246; 841]
 swelling
huperōon [5253; 842]
 chamber, room
huperperisseuō [5248; 841]
 abound, joyful, overflow
huperperissōs [5249; 842]
 measure
huperphroneō [5252; 842]
 think
huperpleonazō [5250; 842]
 abundant
huperupsoō [5251; 842]
 exalt
huphantos [5307; 849]
 woven
hupnos [5258; 843]
 sleep
hupo [5259; 843]
 under
hupoballō [5260; 843]
 suborn
hupochōreō [5298; 848]
 go, withdraw
hupodechomai [5264; 844]
 receive

hupodeigma [5262; 844]
 copy, ensample, example,
 pattern
hupodeiknumi [5263; 844]
 example, forewarn, shew,
 warn
hupodēma [5266; 844]
 shoe
hupodeō [5265; 844]
 bind, shod
hupodikos [5267; 844]
 guilty, judgment
hupogrammos [5261; 843]
 copy, example
hupokatō [5270; 844]
 under, underneath
hupokrinomai [5271; 845]
 feign
hupokrisis [5272; 845]
 dissimulation, hypocrisy
hupokritēs [5273; 845]
 hypocrite
hupolambanō [5274; 845]
 answer, receive, suppose,
 welcome
hupoleimma [5259 and 3005; 845]
 remnant
hupoleipō [5275; 845]
 leave
hupolēnion [5276; 845]
 wine-vat, pit
hupolimpanō [5277; 845]
 leave
hupomenō [5278; 845]
 abide, behind, endure,
 patient, patiently, suffer, take,
 tarry
hupomimnēskō [5279; 846]
 mind, remember,
 remembrance
hupomnēsis [5280; 846]
 remembrance
hupomonē [5281; 846]
 continuance, enduring,
 patience, patient, wait
huponoeō [5282; 846]
 deem, suppose, surmise,
 think
huponoia [5283; 846]
 surmising
hupopherō [5297; 848]
 bear, endure
hupōpiazō [5299; 848]
 buffet, wear, weary
hupopleō [5284; 846]
 lee, sail
hupopneō [5285; 846]
 blow
hupopodion [5286; 846]
 footstool
hupostasis [5287; 847]
 assurance, confidence,
 person, substance

hupostellō [5288; 847]
    draw (back), keep, shrink,
    shun, withdraw
hupostolē [5289; 847]
    draw (back)
hupostrephō [5290; 847]
    come, return, turn
hupostrōnnuō [5291; 847]
    spread
hupotagē [5292; 847]
    obedience, subjection
hupotassō [5293; 847]
    obedience, obedient, put,
    subdue, subject, subjection
hupotithēmi [5294; 848]
    lay, remembrance
hupotrechō [5295; 848]
    lee, run
hupotupōsis [5296; 848]
    ensample, form, pattern
hupozōnnumi [5269; 844]
    undergird
hupozugion [5268; 844]
    ass
hupsēlophroneō [5309; 850]
    high-minded
hupsēlos [5308; 849]
    high, highly
hupsistos [5310; 850]
    high, highest
hupsōma [5313; 851]
    height, high
hupsoō [5312; 850]
    exalt, lift
hupsos [5311; 850]
    estate, height, high
hus [5300; 848]
    sow
hussōpos [5301; 849]
    hyssop
husterēma [5303; 849]
    behind, lacking, penury,
    want
hustereō [5302; 849]
    behind, come, destitute, fail,
    fall, lack, need, short (come),
    want, worse
husterēsis [5304; 849]
    want
husteron [5305; 849]
    afterward(-s), last
husteros [5306; 849]
    later, latter

I

iama [2386; 368]
    healing
iaomai [2390; 368]
    heal, whole
iasis [2392; 368]
    cure, heal, healing

iaspis [2393; 368]
    jasper
iatros [2395; 368]
    physician
ichnos [2487; 384]
    step
ichthudion [2485; 384]
    fish
ichthus [2486; 384]
    fish
ide [2396; 369]; *idou* [2400; 370]
    behold, lo, see
idea (see *eidea*) [2397; 369]
idios [2398; 369]
    acquaintance, alone,
    business, company, due, his,
    his own, home, our own,
    own, private(-ly), proper,
    several, severally, their
idiōtēs [2399; 370]
    ignorant, rude, unlearned
iēsous [2424; 373]
    Jesus
ikmas [2429; 375]
    moisture
ios [2447; 378]
    poison, rust
iōta [2503; 386]
    jot
ioudaïkos [2451; 379]
    Jewish
ioudaïkōs [2452; 379]
    Jew (as do the)
ioudaios [2453; 379]
    Jew(s), Jewess, Jewish,
    Jewry
ioudaïsmos [2454; 379]
    Jews' religion
ioudaïzō [2450; 379]
    Jews (live as do the)
iris [2463; 380]
    rainbow
isangelos [2465; 380]
    angel
ischuō [2480; 383]
    able, avail, can, do, good,
    may, might, prevail, strength,
    whole, work
ischuros [2478; 383]
    boisterous, mighty, powerful,
    strong, valiant
ischuroteros [2478*; 383*]
    mightier, stronger
ischus [2479; 383]
    ability, might, power,
    strength
isopsuchos [2473; 381]
    likeminded
isos [2470; 381]
    agree, equal, like, much (as)
isōs [2481; 384]
    may
isotēs [2471; 381]
    equal, equality

isotimos [2472; 381]
    precious

K

kai [2532; 391]
    also, even, indeed, likewise,
    manner, moreover, very, yea,
    yet
kaige [2534; 394]
    (at) least
kainos [2537; 394]
    new
kainotēs [2538; 394]
    newness
kaiō [2545; 396]
    burn, light
kaiper [2539; 394]
    yet
kairos [2540; 394]
    always, opportunity, season,
    time, while
kakia [2549; 397]
    evil, malice, maliciousness,
    naughtiness, wickedness
kakoētheia [2550; 397]
    malignity
kakologeō [2551; 397]
    curse, evil, speak
kakoō [2559; 398]
    affect, afflict, entreat, evil,
    harm, hurt, vex
kakopatheia [2552; 397]
    affliction, suffering
kakopatheō [2553; 397]
    afflict, endure, hardship,
    suffer
kakopoieō [2554; 397]
    evil, harm
kakopoios [2555; 397]
    evil-doer, malefactor
kakos [2556; 397]
    bad, evil, harm, ill,
    miserable, noisome, wicked
kakōs [2560; 398]
    amiss, diseased, evil,
    grievously, miserably, sick,
    sore
kakōsis [2561; 398]
    affliction
kakoucheō [2558; 398]
    afflict, entreat, evil, suffer,
    torment
kakourgos [2557; 398]
    evil-doer, malefactor
kalamē [2562; 398]
    stubble
kalamos [2563; 398]
    pen, reed
kaleō [2564; 398]
    bid, call, name, surname
kallielaios [2565; 400]
    olive tree

kallion [2566; 400]
   well
kalodidaskalos [2567; 400]
   teacher
kalopoieō [2569; 400]
   well-doing
kalos [2570; 400]
   better, fair, good, goodly,
   honest, honorable, meet,
   seemly, worthy
kalōs [2573; 401]
   good, honestly, place, well
kalumma [2571; 400]
   veil
kaluptō [2572; 401]
   cover, hide
kamēlos [2574; 401]
   camel
kaminos [2575; 401]
   furnace
kammuō [2576; 402]
   close
kamnō [2577; 402]
   faint, sick, weary
kamptō [2578; 402]
   bow
kanōn [2583; 403]
   line, province, rule
kapēleuō [2585; 403]
   corrupt
kapnos [2586; 403]
   smoke
kardia [2588; 403]
   heart
kardiognōstēs [2589; 404]
   heart (knowing the),
   knowing
karphos [2595; 405]
   mote
karpophoros [2593; 405]
   fruitful
karpophoreō [2592; 405]
   bear, fruit, fruitful
karpos [2590; 404]
   fruit
kartereō [2594; 405]
   endure
kata [2596; 405]
   every, happen, manner, out
   of, pertain to, points, respect,
   was
katabainō [2597; 408]
   come, descend, fall, get, go,
   step
kataballō [2598; 408]
   cast, lay, smite
katabareō [2599; 408]
   burden
katabasis [2600; 409]
   descent
katabibazō [2601; 409]
   bring, thrust
katabolē [2602; 409]
   conceive, foundation

katabrabeuō [2603; 409]
   beguile, prize, reward, rob
katacheō [2708; 420]
   pour
katachraomai [2710; 420]
   abuse
katachthonios [2709; 420]
   earth
katadēlos [2612; 410]
   evident
katadeō [2611; 410]
   bind
katadikazō [2613; 410]
   condemn
katadikē [2613d; 410]
   judgment, sentence
katadiōkō [2614; 410]
   follow
katadouloō [2615; 410]
   bondage
katadunasteuō [2616; 410]
   oppress
katagelaō [2606; 409]
   laugh to scorn
kataginōskō [2607; 409]
   blame, condemn
katagnumi [2608; 409]
   break
katagō [2609; 410]
   bring, land, touch
katagōnizomai [2610; 410]
   subdue
kataischunō [2617; 410]
   ashamed, confound,
   dishonor, shame
katakaiō [2618; 411]
   burn
katakaluptō [2619; 411]
   cover
katakauchaomai [2620; 411]
   boast, glory, rejoice
katakeimai [2621; 411]
   keep, lie, sit
kataklaō [2622; 411]
   break
katakleiō [2623; 411]
   shut
kataklērodoteō [2624; 411]
   divide
kataklinō [2625; 411]
   meat, sit
kataklusmos [2627; 411]
   flood
katakluzō [2626; 411]
   overflow
katakoloutheō [2628; 412]
   follow
katakoptō [2629; 412]
   cut
katakrēmnizō [2630; 412]
   cast, headlong, throw
katakrima [2631; 412]
   condemnation

katakrinō [2632; 412]
   condemn
katakrisis [2633; 412]
   condemn, condemnation
katakurieuō [2634; 412]
   dominion, exercise, lord,
   master, overcome
katalaleō [2635; 412]
   speak
katalalia [2636; 412]
   backbiting, evil speaking
katalalos [2637; 412]
   backbiter
katalambanō [2638; 412]
   apprehend, attain, come,
   find, obtain, overtake,
   perceive, take
katalegō [2639; 413]
   enroll, number
kataleimma [2640; 413]
   remnant
kataleipō [2641; 413]
   behind, forsake, leave,
   reserve
katalithazō [2642; 413]
   stone
katallagē [2643; 414]
   atonement, reconciliation
katallassō [2644; 414]
   reconcile
kataloipos [2645; 414]
   residue
kataluma [2646; 414]
   guest-chamber, inn
kataluō [2647; 414]
   come, destroy, dissolve,
   guest, lodge, nought,
   overthrow, throw
katamanthanō [2648; 414]
   consider
katamartureō [2649; 414]
   witness
katamenō [2650; 414]
   abide
kata monas [2651; 414]
   alone
katanaliskō [2654; 414]
   consume
katanarkaō [2655; 414]
   burdensome, chargeable
kat(an)athema (414) [2652; 410]
   curse
katanathematizō [2653; 414]
   curse
kataneuō [2656; 415]
   beckon
katangeleus [2604; 409]
   setter forth
katangellō [2605; 409]
   declare, preach, proclaim,
   set, shew, teach
katanoeō [2657; 415]
   behold, consider, discover,
   perceive

katantaō [2658; 415]
arrive, attain, come, reach

*katanuss (-omai) [2660; 415]
prick

katanuxis [2659; 415]
stupor

katapateo [2662; 415]
foot, trample, tread

katapauō [2664; 416]
cease, rest, restrain

katapausis [2663; 415]
rest

katapetasma [2665; 416]
veil

kataphagō [aor. of 2719; 419]
devour, eat

katapherō [2702; 419]
bear down, fall, give, sink

katapheugō [2703; 420]
flee

kataphileō [2705; 420]
kiss

kataphroneō [2706; 420]
despise

kataphronētēs [2707; 420]
despiser

kataphtheirō [2704; 420]
corrupt

katapinō [2666; 416]
devour, drown, swallow

katapiptō [2667; 416]
fall

katapleō [2668; 416]
arrive

kataponeō [2669; 416]
distress, oppress, vex

katapontizō [2670; 417]
drown, sink

katapsuchō [2711; 421]
cool

katara [2671; 417]
curse, cursing

kataraomai [2672; 417]
curse

katargeō [2673; 417]
abolish, cease, cumber,
destroy, do, effect, fail, loose,
nought, pass, put, sever,
vanish, void

katarithmeō [2674; 417]
number

katartisis [2676; 418]
perfection

katartismos [2677; 418]
perfecting

katartizō [2675; 417]
fit, frame, join, mend,
perfect, prepare, restore

kataschesis [2697; 419]
possession

kataseiō [2678; 418]
beckon

kataskaptō [2679; 418]
dig, overthrow, ruin

kataskēnoō [2681; 418]
dwell, lodge, rest

kataskēnōsis [2682; 418]
nest

kataskeuazō [2680; 418]
build, make, ordain, prepare

kataskiazō [2683; 418]
overshadow

kataskopeō [2684; 418]
spy

kataskopos [2685; 418]
spy

katasophizomai [2686; 418]
deal with, subtilly

katasphazō [2695v; 419]
slay

katasphragizō [2696; 419]
seal

katastellō [2687; 419]
appease, quiet

katastēma [2688; 419]
behavior, demeanor

katastolē [2689; 419]
apparel, clothing

katastrephō [2690; 419]
dig, overthrow, ruin

katastrēniaō [2691; 419]
wanton

katastrōnnumi [2693; 419]
overthrow

katastrophē [2692; 419]
overthrow, subverting

katasurō [2694; 419]
hale

katatithēmi [2698; 419]
do, gain, lay, shew

katatomē [2699; 419]
concision

katatoxeuō [2700; 419]
thrust

katatrechō [2701; 419]
run

kataxioō [2661; 415]
account, count, worthy

katēcheō [2727; 423]
inform, instruct, teach

katechō [2722; 422]
have, hold, keep, make,
possess, restrain, retain, seize,
stay, take, withhold

katēgoreō [2723; 423]
accuse, witness

katēgoria [2724; 423]
accusation

katēgoros [2725; 423]
accuser

kateidōlos [2712; 421]
idols (full of)

katenanti [2713; 421]
before, sight of (in the)

katenōpion [2714; 421]
before, presence, sight of (in
the)

katēpheia [2726; 423]
heaviness

katephistemi [2721; 422]
insurrection, rise

katerchomai [2718; 422]
come, depart, descend, go,
land

katergazomai [2716; 421]
cause, do, perform, work

katesthiō [2719; 422]
devour, eat

katestrammena [2690**; 419]
ruin

kateuthunō [2720; 422]
direct, guide

katexousiazō [2715; 421]
authority, exercise

kathaireō [2507; 386]
cast, depose, destroy, pull
(down), put, take

kathairesis [2506; 386]
cast, destruction, pull

kathairō [2508; 386]
clean, purge

kathaper [2509; 387]
even as

kathaptō [2510; 387]
fasten

katharismos [2512; 387]
cleansing, purge, purification,
purifying

katharizō [2511; 387]
clean, cleanse, purge, purify

katharos [2513; 388]
clean, clear, pure

katharotēs [2514; 388]
cleanness, purifying

kathedra [2515; 388]
seat

kathēgētēs [2519; 388]
master

kathēkō [2520; 389]
convenient, fit, fitting

kathēmai [2521; 389]
dwell, seat, set, sit

kathēmerinos [2522; 389]
daily

katheudō [2518; 388]
asleep

kathexēs [2517; 388]
afterward, follow, order

kathezomai [2516; 388]
sit

kathiēmi [2524; 390]
let down

kathistēmi [2525; 390]
appoint, conduct, make,
ordain, ruler, set

kathizō [2523; 389]
continue, dwell, set, sit, tarry

katho [2526; 390]
according as, inasmuch as,
insomuch as

katholou [2527; 391]
  all
kathoplizō [2528; 391]
  arm
kathoraō [2529; 391]
  see
kathōs [2531; 391]
  according as, even as
kathoti [2530; 391]
  according as, inasmuch as
katioō [2728; 424]
  rust
katischuō [2729; 424]
  prevail
katō [2736; 425]
  beneath, bottom
katoikeō [2730; 424]
  dwell, dweller
katoikēsis [2731; 424]
  dwelling
katoikētērion [2732; 424]
  habitation
katoikia [2733; 424]
  habitation
katoikizō [2730d; 424]
  dwell
*katoptrizō (-omai) [2734; 424]
  behold, mirror
katorthōma [2735; 424]
  correction, deed
katōterō [2736; 425]
  under
katōteros [2737; 425]
  lower
kauchaomai [2744; 425]
  boast, glory, joy, rejoice
kauchēma [2745; 426]
  boasting, glory, glorying,
  rejoice
kauchēsis [2746; 426]
  boasting, glory, glorying,
  rejoice
kauma [2738; 425]
  heat
kaumatizō [2739; 425]
  scorch
kausis [2740; 425]
  burning
kausōn [2742; 425]
  burning, heat, scorching
kausoō [2741; 425]
  heat
kaustēriazō (or kautēr-) [2743;
  425] branded
keimai [2749; 426]
  appoint, lay, lie, made (be),
  set, there
keiria [2750; 427]
  grave-clothes
keirō [2751; 427]
  shear, shearer
keleuō [2753; 427]
  bid, command

keleusma [2752; 427]
  shout
kenodoxia [2754; 427]
  vainglory
kenodoxos [2755; 427]
  vainglory
kenoō [2758; 428]
  effect (of none), empty,
  reputation, vain, void
kenophōnia [2757; 428]
  babblings
kenos [2756; 427]
  empty, vain
kenōs [2761; 428]
  vain (in)
kēnsos [2778; 430]
  tribute
kentron [2759; 428]
  goad
kenturiōn [2760; 428]
  centurion
kephalaion [2774; 429]
  chief, point, sum
kephal(a)ioō [2775; 430]
  head (to wound in the)
kephalē [2776; 430]
  head
kephalis [2777; 430]
  roll
kēpos [2779; 430]
  garden
kēpouros [2780; 430]
  gardener
keraia (kerea) [2762; 428]
  tittle
kerameus [2763; 428]
  potter
keramikos [2764; 428]
  potter
keramion [2765; 428]
  pitcher
keramos [2766; 429]
  tiling
kerannumi [2767; 429]
  fill, mingle
keras [2768; 429]
  horn
keration [2769; 429]
  husks
kerdainō [2770; 429]
  gain, get
kerdos [2771; 429]
  gain, lucre
kērion [2781; 430]
  honey-comb
kerma [2772; 429]
  money
kermatistēs [2773; 429]
  changer
kērugma [2782; 430]
  message, preaching
kērussō [2784; 431]
  preach, preacher, preaching,
  proclaim, publish

kērux [2783; 431]
  preacher
kētos [2785; 431]
  whale
kibōtos [2787; 431]
  ark
kichrēmi [5531v; 433]
  lend
kinduneuō [2793; 432]
  danger
kindunos [2794; 432]
  peril
kineō [2795; 432]
  move, mover, remove, wag
kinēsis [2796; 432]
  moving
kinnamōmon [2792; 432]
  cinnamon
kithara [2788; 432]
  harp
kitharizō [2789; 432]
  harp
kitharōdos [2790; 432]
  harper
klados [2798; 433]
  branch
klaiō [2799; 433]
  bewail, weep
klaō [2806; 433]
  break
klasis [2800; 433]
  breaking
klasma [2801; 433]
  break, meat, piece
klauthmos [2805; 433]
  wailing, weeping
kleiō [2808; 434]
  shut
kleis [2807; 433]
  key
klēma [2814; 434]
  branch
klemma [2809; 434]
  theft
kleos [2811; 434]
  glory
kleptēs [2812; 434]
  thief
kleptō [2813; 434]
  steal
klēronomeō [2816; 434]
  heir, inherit
klēronomia [2817; 435]
  inheritance
klēronomos [2818; 435]
  heir
klēroō [2820; 435]
  heritage, inheritance
klēros [2819; 435]
  charge, inheritance, lot, part,
  portion
klēsis [2821; 435]
  call, calling

klētos [2822; 436]
  called
klibanos [2823; 436]
  oven
klima [2824; 436]
  part, region
klinarion [2825*; 436]
  bed
klinē [2825; 436]
  bed, table
klinidion [2826; 436]
  couch
klinō [2827; 436]
  bow, flight, lay, spent, wear
klisia [2828; 436]
  company
klopē [2829; 436]
  theft
kludōn [2830; 436]
  raging, wave
kludōnizomai [2831; 436]
  toss
knēthō [2833; 437]
  itching
kodrantēs [2835; 437]
  farthing
koilia [2836; 437]
  belly, womb
koimaō (-omai) [2837; 437]
  asleep, dead (to be: see *die*),
  fall
koimēsis [2838; 437]
  rest
koinōneō [2841; 438]
  communicate, distribute,
  fellowship, partake, partaker
koinōnia [2842; 438]
  communication,
  communion, contribution,
  distribution, fellowship
koinōnikos [2843; 439]
  communicate
koinōnos [2844; 439]
  companion, fellowship,
  partaker, partner
koinoō [2840; 438]
  call, common, defile, unclean
koinos [2839; 438]
  common, defiled, unclean,
  unholy
koitē [2845; 440]
  bed, chambering
koitōn [2846; 440]
  chamberlain
kokkinos [2847; 440]
  scarlet
kokkos [2848; 440]
  corn, grain
kolak(e)ia [2850; 440]
  flattery, flattering
kolaphizō [2852; 441]
  buffet
kolasis [2851; 440]
  punishment, torment

kolazō [2849; 440]
  punish
kollaō [2853; 441]
  cleave, company, join
kollourion [2854; 441]
  eye-salve
kollubistēs [2855; 442]
  changer
koloboō [2856; 442]
  shorten
kōlon [2966; 461]
  carcase
kolōnia [2862; 442]
  colony
kolpos [2859; 442]
  bay, bosom
kolumbaō [2860; 442]
  swim
kolumbēthra [2861; 442]
  pool
kōluō [2967; 461]
  forbid, hinder, keep, stay,
  suffer, withhold, withstand
komaō [2863; 442]
  hair
komē [2864; 442]
  hair
kōmē [2968; 461]
  town, village
komizō [2865; 442]
  bring, receive
kōmopolis [2969; 461]
  town
kōmos [2970; 461]
  revelling, rioting
kompsoteron [2866; 443]
  amend
koniaō [2867; 443]
  white
koniortos [2868; 443]
  dust
kopazō [2869; 443]
  cease
kōnōps [2971; 462]
  gnat
kopē [2871; 443]
  slaughter
kopetos [2870; 443]
  bewail
kophinos [2894; 447]
  basket, basketful
kōphos [2974; 462]
  deaf, dumb, speechless
kopiaō [2872; 443]
  bestow, labor, toil, weary
kopos [2873; 443]
  labor, toil, trouble, weariness
kopria [2874; 443]
  dung, dunghill
koprion [2874d; 443]
  dung
koptō [2875; 444]
  bewail, cut, mourn, wail

korasion [2877; 444]
  damsel, maid
korax [2876; 444]
  raven
korban [2878; 444]
  Corban
korbanas [2878; 444]
  treasury
korennumi [2880; 444]
  eat, enough, fill
koros [2884; 444]
  measure
kosmeō [2885; 445]
  adorn, garnish, trim
kosmikos [2886; 445]
  worldly
kosmios [2887; 445]
  behavior, modest, orderly
kosmokratōr [2888; 445]
  ruler
kosmos [2889; 445]
  adorning, world
koum(i) [2891; 447]
  talitha
kouphizō [2893; 447]
  lighten
koustōdia [2892; 447]
  guard, watch
krabbatos [2895; 447]
  bed, couch
kraipalē [2897; 448]
  surfeiting
kranion [2898; 448]
  Calvary, skull
kraspedon [2899; 448]
  border
krataioō [2901; 448]
  strengthen, strong
krataios [2900; 448]
  mighty
krateō [2902; 448]
  hands on (lay), hold, holden,
  keep, obtain, retain, take
kratistos [2903; 449]
  excellent, noble
kratos [2904; 449]
  dominion, power, strength
kraugazō [2905; 449]
  cry
krauge [2906; 449]
  clamor, cry, crying
krazō [2896; 447]
  cry
kreas [2907; 449]
  flesh
kreissōn (or -tt-) [2909; 449]
  better
kremannumi [2910; 450]
  hang, steep
krēmnos [2911; 450]
  steep
krima [2917; 450]
  condemnation, judgment,
  sentence

krinō [2919; 451]
call, conclude, condemn,
decree, determine, esteem,
judge, judgment, law, ordain,
sentence, think

krinon [2918; 451]
lily

krisis [2920; 452]
accusation, condemnation,
judgment

kritērion [2922; 453]
judge, judgment, judgment-
seat

kritēs [2923; 453]
judge

krithē [2915; 450]
barley

krithinos [2916; 450]
barley

kritikos [2924; 453]
discerner

krouō [2925; 453]
knock

kruphaios [2928d; 454]
secret

kruphē [2931; 454]
secret

kruptē [2926; 454]
cellar

kruptō [2928; 454]
hide, secretly

kruptos [2927; 454]
hid, hidden, inwardly, secret

krustallizō [2929; 454]
clear, crystal

krustallos [2930; 454]
crystal

ktaomai [2932; 455]
get, obtain, possess, provide,
purchase, win

ktēma [2933; 455]
possession

ktēnos [2934; 455]
beast, cattle

ktētōr [2935; 455]
possessor

ktisis [2937; 455]
building, creation, creature,
ordinance

ktisma [2938; 456]
creature

ktistēs [2939; 456]
Creator

ktizō [2936; 455]
create, Creator, make

kubeia (or *-bia*) [2940; 456]
sleight

kubernēsis [2941; 456]
government

kubernētēs [2942; 456]
master

kukleuō [2944v; 456]
compass

kukloō [2944; 456]
come, compass, stand

kuklō [2945; 456]
about, round about

kuklothen [2943; 456]
about, round about

kuliō [2947; 457]
wallow

kulismos [2946**; 457]
wallowing

kullos [2948; 457]
maimed

kuma [2949; 457]
wave

kumbalon [2950; 457]
cymbal

kuminon [2951; 457]
cummin

kunarion [2952; 457]
dog

kuōn [2965; 461]
dog

kuptō [2855; 458]
stoop

kuria [2959; 458]
lady

kuriakos [2960; 458]
Lord

kurieuō [2961; 458]
dominion, exercise, lord,
lordship

kurios [2962; 458]
lord, master, owner, sir

kuriotēs [2963; 460]
dominion, government

kuroō [2964; 461]
confirm

L

lachanon [3001; 467]
herb

lailaps [2978; 462]
storm, tempest

lakeō or lakaō [2997; 463]
burst

laktizō [2979; 463]
kick

laleō [2980; 463]
preach, say, speak, talk, tell,
utter

lalia [2981; 464]
saying, speech

lama [2982; 464]
lama

lambanō [2983; 464]
accept, attain, bring, call,
catch, find, have, hold,
obtain, receive, take

lampas [2985; 465]
lamp, light, torch

lampō [2989; 466]
light, shine

lampros [2986; 465]
bright, clear, fine, gay,
goodly, gorgeous, sumptuous,
white

lamprōs [2988; 466]
sumptuously

lamprotēs [2987; 466]
brightness

lanchanō [2975; 462]
lot, obtain, receive

lanthanō [2990; 466]
forget, hide, ignorant,
unawares

laos [2992; 466]
people

larunx [2995; 467]
throat

lathra [2977; 462]
privily, secretly

latomeō [2998; 467]
hew

latreia [2999; 467]
divine, service

latreuō [3000; 467]
serve, service, worship

laxeutos [2991; 466]
hewn

legeōn or *legiōn* [3003; 467]
legion

legō [3004; 468]
ask, bid, boast, call, describe,
give, mean, name,
pronounce, put, reckon, say,
speak, tell, utter

leimma [3005; 470]
remnant

leios [3006; 470]
smooth

leipō [3007; 470]
destitute, lack, want

leitourgeō [3008; 470]
minister

leitourgia [3009; 471]
ministration, ministry, service

leitourgikos [3010; 471]
ministering

leitourgos [3011; 471]
minister

lē(m)psis [3028; 473]
receiving

lēnos [3025; 473]
wine-press

lention [3012; 471]
towel

leōn [3023; 472]
lion

lepis [3013; 471]
scale

lepra [3014; 471]
leprosy

lepros [3015; 472]
leper

lepton [3016; 472]
mite

lēros [3026; 473]
    talk
lēstēs [3027; 473]
    robber, thief
lēthē [3024; 472]
    forget
leukaino [3021; 472]
    white
leukos [3022; 472]
    white
lian [3029; 473]
    exceeding, greatly, sore,
    while
libanos [3030; 473]
    frankincense
libanōtos [3031; 473]
    censer
likmaō [3039; 474]
    dust, grind, scatter
limēn [3040; 475]
    haven
limnē [3041; 475]
    lake
limos [3042; 475]
    famine, hunger
linon [3043; 475]
    flax, linen
liparos [3045; 475]
    dainty
lips [3047; 475]
    north-east, south-west
lithazō [3034; 473]
    stone
lithinos [3035; 474]
    stone
lithoboleō [3036; 474]
    stone
lithos [3037; 474]
    stone
lithostrōtos [3038; 474]
    pavement
litra [3046; 475]
    pound
logia [3048; 475]
    collection, gathering
logikos [3050; 476]
    milk, reasonable, spiritual,
    word
logion [3051; 476]
    oracle
logios [3052; 476]
    eloquent
logismos [3053; 476]
    imagination, thought
logizomai [3049; 475]
    account, charge, conclude,
    count, esteem, impute,
    number, reason, reckon,
    suppose, think
logomacheō [3054; 477]
    strive
logomachia [3055; 477]
    dispute, strife

logos [3056; 477]
    account, cause,
    communication, do, doctrine,
    fame, intent, matter, mouth,
    preaching, question, reason,
    reckon, report, rumor, saying,
    show, speech, talk, thing,
    tidings, treatise, utterance,
    word, work
loidoreō [3058; 479]
    revile
loidoria [3059; 479]
    railing, reproachfully, reviling
loidoros [3060; 479]
    railer, reviler
loimos [3061; 479]
    fellow, pestilence, pestilent
    fellow
loipon [3063; 479]
    besides, finally, furthermore,
    henceforth, moreover, now,
    then
loipos [3062**; 479]
    other, remain, remnant,
    residue, rest (the)
lonchē [3057; 479]
    spear
louō [3068; 480]
    bathed, wash
loutron [3067; 480]
    washing
luchnia [3087; 483]
    lampstand
luchnos [3088; 483]
    lamp, light
lukos [3074; 481]
    wolf
lumainō (*-omai*) [3075; 481]
    havoc, lay waste, waste
luō [3089; 483]
    break, destroy, dissolve,
    loose, melt, put, unloose
lupē [3077; 482]
    grief, grievous, grudingly,
    heaviness, sorrow
lupeō [3076; 481]
    grief, grieve, heaviness,
    sorrow, sorrowful, sorry
lusis [3080; 482]
    loose
lusiteleō [3081; 482]
    better (be)
lutron [3083; 482]
    ransom
lutroō [3084; 482]
    redeem
lutrōsis [3085; 483]
    redeem, redemption
lutrōtēs [3086; 483]
    deliverer

M

machaira [3162; 496]
    sword
machē [3163; 496]
    fighting, strife
machomai [3164; 496]
    fight, strive
mag(e)ia [3095; 484]
    sorcery
mageuō [3096; 484]
    sorcery
magos [3097; 484]
    sorcerer, wise
mainomai [3105; 486]
    beside oneself, mad
makarios [3107; 486]
    blessed, happy
makarismos [3108; 487]
    blessedness, blessing,
    gratulation
makarizō [3106; 486]
    bless, happy
makellon [3111; 487]
    shambles
makran [3112; 487]
    afar, far, hence, way
makrochronios [3118; 488]
    live, long
makros [3117; 488]
    far, long
makrothen [3113; 487]
    afar, far
makrothumeō [3114; 488]
    bear, endure, longsuffering,
    patient, patience, suffer
makrothumia [3115; 488]
    longsuffering, patience
makrothumōs [3116; 488]
    patiently
malakia [3119; 488]
    disease
malakos [3120; 488]
    effeminate
malista [3122; 488]
    chiefly, especially, most
mallon [3123; 489]
    more, rather
mammē [3125; 490]
    grandmother
mamōnas (or *mammon-*) [3126;
    490] mammon
mania [3130; 490]
    mad, madness
manna [3131; 490]
    manna
manteuomai [3132; 491]
    soothsaying
manthanō [3129; 490]
    learn, learned (be),
    understand
marainō [3133; 491]
    fade

maran-atha [3134; 491]
  Maran-atha
margaritēs [3135; 491]
  pearl
marmaros [3139; 492]
  marble
martureō [3140; 492]
  charge, give, obtain, report,
  testify, testimony, witness
marturia [3141; 493]
  report, testimony, witness
marturion [3142; 493]
  testimony, witness
marturomai [3143; 494]
  testify
martus (or *martur*) [3144; 494]
  witness
mas(s)aomai [3145; 495]
  gnaw
mastigoō [3146; 495]
  scourge
mastix [3148; 495]
  plague, scourging
mastizō [3147; 495]
  scourge
mastos [3149; 495]
  breast
mataiologia [3150; 495]
  talking (vain)
mataiologos [3151; 495]
  talkers (vain)
mataioō [3154; 495]
  vain
mataios [3152; 495]
  vain, vanity
mataiotēs [3153; 495]
  vanity
matēn [3155; 495]
  vain
mathētēs [3101; 485]
  disciple
mathēteuō [3100; 485]
  disciple, instruct, teach
mathētria [3102; 485]
  disciple
mē [3361; 515]
  lest, never, no one, nothing
mēde [3366; 517]
  much (as)
mēdeis (*-den*) [3367; 518]
  no man, no one, nothing
mēdepote [3368; 518]
  never
megalaucheō [3166; 496]
  boast
megaleios [3167; 496]
  great, mighty, wonderful
  (work)
megaleiotēs [3168; 496]
  magnificence, majesty,
  mighty
megaloprepēs [3169; 497]
  excellent

megalōs [3171; 497]
  greatly
megalōsunē [3172; 497]
  majesty
megalunō [3170; 497]
  enlarge, great, magnify, shew
megas [3173; 497]
  great, greatest, high, large,
  loud, matter, mighty, strong,
  years
megethos [3174; 498]
  greatness
megistan [3175**; 498]
  great, lord, prince
megistos [3176; 498]
  great
meizōn [3187; 499]
  best, elder, greater, greatest,
  more
meizoteros [3186; 499]
  greater
mēketi [3371; 518]
  henceforth, henceforward,
  no longer, no more
mēkos [3372; 518]
  length
mēkunō [3373; 518]
  grow
melan [3188; 499]
  ink
melas [3189; 499]
  black
melei [3199**; 500]
  care
meletaō [3191; 500]
  diligent, imagine, meditate,
  premeditate
meli [3192; 500]
  honey
melissios [3193; 500]
  honey-comb
mellō [3195; 500]
  about, almost, begin, come,
  hereafter, intend, mean,
  mind, point, ready, shall,
  should, tarry, was (etc.), will,
  yet
melō [3199; 500]
  care
melos [3196; 501]
  member
mēlōtē [3374; 518]
  sheepskin
membrana [3200; 502]
  parchment
memphomai [3201; 502]
  blame, fault
mempsimoiros [3202; 501]
  complainer
men [3303; 502]
  even, indeed, truly, verily
mēn [3375; 518]
  indeed

mēn [3376; 518]
  month
menō [3306; 503]
  abide, continue, dwell,
  endure, own, present,
  remain, stand, tarry
menoun, or *menounge* [3304; 503]
  nay, yea
mentoi [3305; 503]
  yet
mēnuō [3377; 519]
  shew, tell
mēpō [3380; 519]
  yet
mēpōs [3381; 519]
  haply, lest
mēpote [3379; 519]
  haply, lest, peradventure
mēpou [3361 and 4225; 519]
  haply, lest
merimna [3308; 504]
  care
merimnaō [3309; 505]
  care, careful, thought (to
  take)
meris [3310; 505]
  district, part, portion
merismos [3311; 505]
  dividing, gift
meristēs [3312; 505]
  divider
merizō [3307; 504]
  deal, difference, distribute,
  divide, give, part
mēros [3382; 519]
  thigh
meros [3313; 505]
  behalf, coast, country, course,
  craft, measure, part, piece,
  portion, respect, somewhat,
  sort, trade
mesēmbria [3314; 506]
  noon, south
mesitēs [3316; 506]
  mediator
mesiteuō [3315; 506]
  confirm, interposed
mesonuktion [3317; 507]
  midnight
mesoō [3322; 508]
  midst
mesos [3319; 507]
  between, midday, midnight,
  midst, way
mesotoichon [3320; 508]
  wall
mesouranēma [3321; 508]
  heaven
mestoō [3325; 508]
  fill
mestos [3324; 508]
  full
meta [3326; 508]
  hence

metabainō [3327; 510]
  depart, go, pass, remove
metaballō [3328; 510]
  change
metadidōmi [3330; 510]
  give, impart
metagō [3329; 510]
  turn
metairō [3332; 511]
  depart
metakaleō [3333; 511]
  call
metakineō [3334; 511]
  move
metalambanō [3335; 511]
  eat, have, partake, receive,
  take
metalēpsis [3336; 511]
  receive
metallassō [3337; 511]
  change, exchange
metamelomai [3338; 511]
  regret, repent
metamorphoō [3339; 511]
  change, transfigure,
  transform
metanoeō [3340; 511]
  repent
metanoia [3341; 512]
  repentance
metapempō [3343; 513]
  call, fetch, send
metaschēmatizō [3345; 513]
  change, fashion, figure,
  transform
metastrephō [3344; 513]
  pervert, turn
metathesis [3331; 511]
  change, removing, translation
metatithēmi [3346; 513]
  carry, change, remove,
  translate, turn
metaxu [3342; 512]
  between, next, while
mēte [3383; 519]
  much as
metechō [3348; 514]
  belong, part, partake,
  partaker, pertain
*meteōrizō (-omai) [3349; 514]
  doubtful
metepeita [3347; 514]
  afterward
mētēr [3384; 520]
  mother
methē [3178; 498]
  drunkenness
methermēneuō [3177; 498]
  interpret, interpretation
methistēmi (or *methistanō*) [3179;
  498] put, remove, translate,
  turn
method(e)ia [3180; 499]
  wiles

methorion [3181**; 499]
  border
methuō [3184; 499]
  drunk, drunken
methuskō [3182; 499]
  drunk, drunken
methusos [3183; 499]
  drunkard
metochē [3352; 514]
  fellowship
metochos [3353; 514]
  fellow, partaker, partner
metoikesia [3350; 514]
  bring, carrying away
metoikizō [3351; 514]
  carry away, remove
metōpon [3359; 515]
  forehead
mētra [3388; 520]
  womb
mētralōas (or *metrol-*) [3389; 520]
  mother
metreō [3354; 514]
  measure, mete
metrētēs [3355; 514]
  firkin
metriopatheō [3356; 514]
  bear, compassion, gently,
  little
metriōs [3357; 515]
metron [3358; 515]
  measure
mia [3391; 230]
  first, one
miainō [3392; 520]
  defile
miasma [3393; 521]
  defilement, pollution
miasmos [3394; 521]
  defilement, uncleanness
migma [3395; 521]
  mixture
mignumi [3396; 521]
  mingle
mikros (-on) (3397) [3398; 521]
  least, less, little, small, while
mikroteros [3398; 521*]
  least, less, little
milion [3400; 521]
  mile
mimeomai [3401; 521]
  follow, imitate
mimētēs [3402; 522]
  follower, imitator
*mimnēskō (-omai) [3403; 522]
  mindful, remember,
  remembrance
miseō [3404; 522]
  hate
misthapodosia [3405; 523]
  recompense
misthapodotēs [3406; 523]
  rewarder

misthios [3407; 523]
  hired, servant
misthōma [3410; 523]
  dwelling, hired house
misthoō [3409; 523]
  hire
misthos [3408; 523]
  hire, reward, wages
misthōtos [3411; 523]
  hired servant, hireling
mna [3414; 524]
  pound
mneia [3417; 524]
  mention, remembrance
mnēma [3418; 524]
  grave, sepulchre, tomb
mnēmē [3420; 524]
  remembrance
mnēmeion [3419; 524]
  grave, sepulchre, tomb
mnēmoneuō [3421; 525]
  mention, mindful, remember
mnēmosunon [3422; 525]
  memorial
mnēsteuō [3423; 525]
  betroth, espoused
mochthos [3449; 528]
  travail
modios [3426; 525]
  bushel
mogilalos [3424; 525]
  impediment
mogis [3425; 525]
  hardly
moichalis [3428; 526]
  adulteress, adulterous
moichaō [3429; 526]
  adultery
moicheia [3430; 526]
  adultery
moicheuō [3431; 526]
  adultery
moichos [3432; 526]
  adulterer
molis [3433; 526]
  difficulty, hardly
mōlōps [3468; 531]
  stripe
molunō [3435; 526]
  defile
molusmos [3436; 527]
  defilement, filthiness
mōmaomai [3469; 531]
  blame
mōmos [3470; 531]
  blemish
momphē [3437; 527]
  complaint
monē [3438; 527]
  abode, mansion
monogenēs [3439; 527]
  child, only, only begotten
monoō [3443; 528]
  desolate

monophthalmos [3442; 528]
    eye (with one)
monos (-on) [3441; 527]
    alone, only
mōrainō [3471; 531]
    foolish, savor
mōria [3472; 531]
    foolishness
mōrologia [3473; 531]
    foolish, talking (foolish)
mōros [3474; 531]
    fool, foolish, foolishness
morphē [3444; 528]
    form
morphoō [3445; 528]
    formed
morphōsis [3446; 528]
    form
moschopoieō [3447; 528]
    calf
moschos [3448; 528]
    calf
mousikos [3451; 528]
    minstrel
muelos [3452; 528]
    marrow
mueō [3453; 529]
    instruct, learn
mukaomai [3455; 529]
    roar
muktērizō [3456; 529]
    mock
mulikos [3457; 529]
    millstone
mulinos [3458v; 529]
    millstone
mulōn [3459; 529]
    mill
mulos [3458; 529]
    millstone
muōpazō [3467; 531]
    afar, see
murias [3461; 529]
    company, innumerable,
    thousand(s)
murioi [3463; 529]
    ten thousand
murizō [3462; 529]
    anoint
muron [3464; 529]
    ointment
mustērion [3466; 530]
    mystery
muthos [3454; 529]
    fable

N

nai [3483; 532]
    even so, surely, truth, verily,
    yea
naos [3485; 533]
    sanctuary, shrine, temple

nardos [3487; 534]
    spikenard
nauageō [3489; 534]
    shipwreck
nauklēros [3490; 534]
    owner
naus [3491; 534]
    ship
nautēs [3492; 534]
    mariners
nē [3513; 537]
    protest
neanias [3494; 534]
    young (man)
neaniskos [3495; 534]
    young (man)
nekroō [3499; 535]
    dead, mortify
nekros [3498; 534]
    dead
nekrōsis [3500; 535]
    deadness
neōkoros [3511; 537]
    temple-keeper, worshipper
neomēnia (or *noum-*) [3561; 535]
    moon
neophutos [3504; 536]
    novice
neos [3501; 535]
    fresh, new, young
n(e)ossos [3502; 536]
    young
neōterikos [3512; 537]
    youthful
neōteros [3501; 537]
    young, young (man),
    younger
neotēs [3503; 536]
    youth
nēphalios [3524; 538]
    sober, temperate
nephelē [3507; 536]
    cloud
nēphō [3525; 538]
    sober, watch
nephos [3509; 537]
    cloud
nephros [3510; 537]
    reins
nēpiazō [3515; 537]
    babe, child
nēpios [3516; 537]
    babe, child
nēsion [3519; 538]
    island
nēsos [3520; 538]
    island, isle
nēsteia [3521; 538]
    fast, fasting
nēsteuō [3522; 538]
    fast
nēstis [3523; 538]
    fasting

nēthō [3514; 537]
    spin
neuō [3506; 536]
    beckon
nikaō [3528; 539]
    conquer, overcome, prevail,
    victorious, victory
nikē [3529; 539]
    victory
nikos [3534; 539]
    victory
niptēr [3537; 540]
    bason
niptō [3538; 540]
    wash
noēma [3540; 540]
    device, mind, thought
noeō [3539; 540]
    consider, perceive, think,
    understand
nomē [3542; 541]
    eat, pasture
nomikos [3544; 541]
    law, lawyer
nomimōs [3545; 541]
    lawfully
nomisma [3546; 541]
    money
nomizō [3543; 541]
    suppose, think, wont
nomodidaskalos [3547; 541]
    doctor, teacher
nomos [3551; 542]
    law
nomothesia [3548; 541]
    law
nomotheteō [3549; 541]
    enact, establish, law
nomothetēs [3550; 542]
    lawgiver
nosēma [3553; 543]
    disease
noseō [3552; 543]
    dote, sick
nosos [3554; 543]
    disease, infirmity, sickness
*nosphizō (-omai) [3557; 543]
    keep, purloin
nossia [3555; 543]
    brood
nossion [3556; 543]
    brood
nothos [3541; 540]
    bastard
nōthros [3576; 547]
    dull, slothful, sluggish
notos [3558; 544]
    south, south wind
nōtos [3577; 547]
    back
nounechōs [3562; 544]
    discreetly
nous [3563; 544]
    mind, understanding

nouthesia [3559; 544]
　admonition
noutheteō [3560; 544]
　admonish, warn
nuchthēmeron [3574; 547]
　night and a day (a)
numphē [3565; 545]
　bride, daughter-in-law
numphios [3566; 545]
　bridegroom
numphōn [3567; 545]
　bride-chamber, wedding
nun [3568; 545]
　henceforth, late, now,
　present, time
nuni [3570; 546]
　now
nussō [3572; 547]
　pierce
nustazō [3573; 547]
　slumber
nux [3571; 546]
　night

O

ochleō [3791; 600]
　vex
ochlopoieō [3792; 600]
　company, crowd
ochlos [3793; 600]
　common, company, crowd,
　multitude, number, people
ochurōma [3794; 601]
　strongholds
ōdē [5603; 895]
　song
ōdin [5604; 895]
　pain, sorrow, travail
ōdinō [5605; 895]
　birth, travail
odous [3599; 555]
　tooth
odunaō [3600; 555]
　anguish, sorrow, torment
odunē [3601; 555]
　sorrow
odurmos [3602; 555]
　mourning
ogdoēkonta [3589; 552]
　fourscore
ogdoos [3590; 552]
　eighth
oida [perf. of 1492; 555]
　can, know, sure, tell, wist
oikeios [3609; 556]
　house, household
oikēma [3612; 557]
　cell, prison
oikeō [3611; 557]
　dwell
oiketeia [3610d; 556]
　household

oikētērion [3613; 557]
　habitation, house
oiketēs [3610; 557]
　household-servant, servant
oikia [3614; 557]
　home, house, household
oikiakos [3615; 557]
　household
oikodespoteō [3616; 558]
　guide, householder, rule
oikodespotēs [3617; 558]
　goodman, householder,
　master
oikodomē [3619; 558]
　building, edification, edify
oikodomeō [3618; 558]
　build, builder, edify,
　embolden
(*oikodomia*) [3620; 559]
　dispensation
oikonomeō [3621; 559]
　steward
oikonomia [3622; 559]
　dispensation, stewardship
oikonomos [3623; 560]
　chamberlain, governor,
　steward
oikos [3624; 560]
　family, home, house,
　household, temple
oikoumenē [3625; 561]
　earth, world
oikour(g)os [3626; 561]
　home
oikteirō [3627; 561]
　compassion, mercy
oiktirmōn [3629; 561]
　merciful, mercy
oiktirmos [3628; 561]
　compassion, mercy
oinophlugia [3632; 562]
　excess, wine, winebibbings
oinopotēs [3630; 562]
　wine-bibber
oinos [3631; 562]
　wine
oiomai (oimai) [3633; 562]
　suppose, think
okneō [3635; 563]
　delay
oknēros [3636; 563]
　grievous, irksome, slothful
oktaēmeros [3637; 563]
　eighth
oktō [3638; 563]
　eight
olethros [3639; 563]
　destruction
oligopistos [3640; 563]
　faith (of little)
oligopsuchos [3642; 564]
　fainthearted
oligōreō [3643; 564]
　despise, regard

oligos (-*on*) [3641; 563]
　few, little, season, small,
　space, while
ololuzō [3649; 564]
　howl
olothreuō [3645; 564]
　destroy
olothreutēs [3644; 564]
　destroyer
olunthos [3653; 565]
　fig
ombros [3655; 565]
　shower
omma [3659; 565]
　eye
omnumi (or *omnuō*) [3660; 565]
　swear
ōmos [5606; 895]
　shoulder
onar [3677; 569]
　dream
onarion [3678; 570]
　ass
oneidismos [3680; 570]
　reproach
oneidizō [3679; 570]
　cast, reproach, revile
oneidos [3681; 570]
　reproach
ōneomai [5608; 895]
　buy
onikos [3684; 570]
　millstone
oninēmi [3685; 570]
　joy
onkos [3591; 553]
　weight
onoma [3686; 570]
　call, name
onomazō [3687; 573]
　call, name
onos [3688; 574]
　ass
ontōs [3689; 574]
　certainly, clean, indeed, truth,
　verily
ōon [5609; 896]
　egg
opē [3692; 574]
　cave, hole, opening, place
opheilē [3782; 598]
　debt, due
opheilēma [3783; 598]
　debt
opheiletēs [3781; 598]
　debtor, offender, owe, sinner
opheilō [3784; 598]
　behove, bound (to be), debt,
　debtor, due, duty, guilty,
　indebted, must, needs, ought,
　owe, require, should
ōpheleia [5622; 900]
　advantage, profit

ōpheleō [5623; 900]
    advantage, bettered, prevail,
    profit
ōphelimos [5624; 900]
    profit, profitable
ophelon [3785; 599]
    would
ophelos [3786; 599]
    advantage, profit
ophis [3789; 600]
    serpent
ophrus [3790; 600]
    brow
ophthalmodoulia [3787; 599]
    eye-service
ophthalmos [3788; 599]
    eye, sight
opisō [3694; 575]
    back, backward, behind
opisthen [3693; 574]
    backside, behind
opōra [3703; 576]
    fruits
opsarion [3795; 601]
    fish
opse [3796; 601]
    even, end, late
opsia [3798**; 601]
    even, evening
opsimos [3797; 601]
    latter
opsis [3799; 601]
    appearance, countenance,
    face
opsōnion [3800; 602]
    charges, wages
optanō [3700; 576]
    appearing, see
optasia [3701; 576]
    vision
optomai (see *horaō*)
optos [3702; 576]
    broiled
orcheō [3738; 583]
    dance
oregō (*-omai*) [3713; 579]
    covet, desire, reach, seek
oreinos [3714; 580]
    country, hill
orexis [3715; 580]
    lust
orgē [3709; 578]
    anger, indignation,
    vengeance, wrath
orgilos [3711; 579]
    angry
orgizō [3710; 579]
    angry, wroth (be)
orguia [3712; 579]
    fathom
orneon [3732; 581]
    bird
ornis [3733; 582]
    hen

oros [3735; 582]
    hill, mount, mountain
orphanos [3737; 583]
    comfortless, desolate,
    fatherless
orthopodeō [3716; 580]
    walk
orthos [3717; 580]
    even, straight
orthōs [3723; 580]
    plain, right, rightly
orthotomeō [3718; 580]
    divide, handle
orthrinos [3720; 580]
    dawn, early, morning
orthrios [3721; 580]
    early
orthrizō [3719; 580]
    morning
orthros [3722; 580]
    dawn, early, morning
ōruomai [5612; 897]
    roar
orussō [3736; 582]
    dig
osmē [3744; 586]
    odor, savor
osphrēsis [3750; 587]
    smelling
osphus [3751; 587]
    loins
osteon [3747; 586]
    bone
ostrakinos [3749; 587]
    earthen
ōtarion [5621*; 900]
    ear
othonē [3607; 555]
    sheet
othonion [3608; 555]
    linen
ōtion [5621; 900]
    ear
ou (*ouk*) [3756; 590]
    nay, never, no man, nothing
oua [3758; 591]
    ah
ouai [3759; 591]
    woe
ouchi [3780; 598]
    nay
oudamōs [3760; 591]
    no wise (in)
oude [3761; 591]
    much (as)
oudeis (*-den*) [3762; 591]
    never, no man, no one,
    nothing, nought
oudepō [3764; 592]
    never, yet
oudepote [3763; 592]
    never, nothing

ouketi [3765; 592]
    henceforth, hereafter, no
    longer, no more, now, yet
oukoun [3766; 592]
    then
oun [3767; 592]
    now, so, then, verily
oupō [3768; 593]
    hitherto, yet
oura [3769; 593]
    tail
ouranios [3770; 593]
    heavenly
ouranos [3772; 593]
    air, heaven(s)
ouranothen [3771; 593]
    heaven
ous [3775; 595]
    ear
ousia [3776; 596]
    substance
outhen [3762; 591]
    nothing
oxos [3690; 574]
    vinegar
oxus [3691; 574]
    sharp, swift
ozō [3605; 555]
    stink

P

pachunō [3975; 638]
    gross (to wax)
pagideuō [3802; 602]
    ensnare, entangle
pagis [3803; 602]
    snare
pagos
    hill
paidagōgos [3807; 603]
    instructor, tutor
paidarion [3808; 603]
    child
paideia [3809; 603]
    chastening, chastisement,
    instruction
paideuō [3811; 603]
    chasten, chastise, correcting,
    instruct, learn, learned, teach
paideutēs [3810; 603]
    correct, instructor
paidion [3813; 604]
    child, damsel, young
paidiothen [3812; 604]
    child
paidiskē [3814; 604]
    bondmaid, damsel, maid,
    maiden
paiō [3817; 605]
    smite, strike
pais [3816; 604]
    boy, child, maid, maiden,

manservant, servant, son,
young man
paizō [3815; 604]
play
palai [3819; 605]
great, long, old, time, while
palaioō [3822; 606]
decay, old
palaios [3820; 605]
old
palaiotēs [3821; 606]
oldness
palē [3823; 606]
wrestle, wrestling
palin [3825; 606]
again
palingenesia [3824; 606]
regeneration
pamplēthei [3826; 607]
once, together
pampolus [3827; 607]
very
pandocheion [3829; 607]
inn
pandocheus [3830; 607]
host
panēguris [3831; 607]
assembly
panoikei [3832; 607]
house
panoplia [3833; 607]
armor
panourgia [3834; 608]
craftiness, subtilty
panourgos [3835; 608]
crafty
pantachē [3837v; 608]
everywhere
pantachothen [3836; 608]
every quarter
pantachou [3837; 608]
everywhere, place
pantē [3839; 608]
always, way
panteles [3838; 608]
uttermost
pantokratōr [3841; 608]
almighty
pantōs [3843; 609]
all, altogether, certainly,
doubt (no), means (by all),
surely, wise (in no)
pantote [3842; 609]
always, ever, evermore
pantothen [3840; 608]
every side, quarter, round
about
para [3844; 609]
contrary, more, nigh, of,
rather, side
parabainō [3845; 611]
fall, transgress, transgression
paraballō [3846; 611]
arrive, compare, touch

parabasis [3847; 611]
breaking, transgression
parabatēs [3848; 612]
breaker, transgressor
parabiazomai [3849; 612]
constrain
parabolē [3850; 612]
comparison, figure, parable
parabo(u)leuomai [3851; 612]
hazard
paracheimasia [3915; 623]
winter
paracheimazō [3914; 623]
winter
parachrēma [3916; 623]
forthwith, immediately
paradechomai [3858; 614]
receive
paradeigmatizō [3856; 614]
example, put, shame
paradeisos [3857; 614]
paradise
paradiatribē [3859; 614]
disputing, wrangling
paradidōmi [3860; 614]
betray, bring, cast, commend,
commit, deliver, give, hazard,
prison, put, ripe
paradosis [3862; 615]
ordinance, tradition
paradoxos [3861; 615]
strange
paraginomai [3854; 613]
arrive, come, go, part,
present, stand
paragō [3855; 613]
depart, pass, walk
paraineō [3867; 616]
admonish, exhort
paraiteomai [3868; 616]
avoid, excuse, intreat, refuse,
reject
parakaleō [3870; 617]
beseech, call, comfort, desire,
exhort, intreat, pray
parakaluptō [3871; 617]
conceal, hide
parakatathēkē [3872; 617]
commit
parakathezomai [3869v; 616]
sit
parakathizō [3869; 616]
sit
parakeimai [3873; 617]
present (to be)
paraklēsis [3874; 618]
comfort, consolation,
encouragement, exhortation,
intreaty
paraklētos [3875; 618]
Comforter
parakoē [3876; 618]
disobedience

parakoloutheō [3877; 618]
attain, follow, know, trace,
understand
parakouō [3878; 619]
hear
parakuptō [3879; 619]
look, stoop
paralambanō [3880; 619]
receive, take
paralegō [3881; 619]
coasting, sail
paralios [3882; 620]
coast, sea
parallagē [3883; 620]
variableness
paralogizomai [3884; 620]
beguile, deceive, delude
paraluo [3886; 620]
feeble, palsy (sick of)
paralutikos [3885; 620]
palsy (sick of)
paramenō [3887; 620]
abide, continue
paramutheomai [3888; 620]
comfort, console, encourage
paramuthia [3889; 620]
comfort
paramuthion [3890; 620]
comfort, consolation
parangelia [3852; 613]
charge, commandment,
straitly
parangellō [3853; 613]
charge, command, declare
paranomeō [3891; 621]
law
paranomia [3892; 621]
iniquity, transgression
parapherō [3911; 623]
remove, take
paraphroneō [3912; 623]
fool, beside oneself (to be)
paraphronia [3913; 623]
madness
parapikrainō [3893; 621]
provoke
parapikrasmos [3894; 621]
provocation
parapiptō [3895; 621]
fall
parapleō [3896; 621]
sail
paraplēsion [3897; 621]
nigh
paraplēsiōs [3898; 621]
likewise, manner
paraporeuomai [3899; 621]
go, pass
paraptōma [3900; 621]
fall, fault, offense, sin,
trespass
pararrhueō [3901; 621]
drift

parasēmos [3902; 622]
    sign
paraskeuazō [3903; 622]
    prepare, ready
paraskeuē [3904; 622]
    preparation
parateinō [3905; 622]
    continue, prolong
paratēreō [3906; 622]
    observe, watch
paratērēsis [3907; 622]
    observation, show
parathalassios [3864; 616]
    coast, sea
parathēkē [3866; 616]
    commit
paratheōreō [3865; 616]
    neglect
paratithēmi [3908; 622]
    allege, commend, commit,
    keeping, put, set
paratunchanō [3909; 623]
    meet (verb)
parautika [3910; 623]
    moment
parazēloō [3863; 616]
    jealousy, provoke
pardalis [3917; 623]
    leopard
parechō [3930; 626]
    bring, do, give, keep,
    minister, offer, render, shew,
    trouble
paredreuō [3917a; 624]
    wait
parēgoria [3931; 626]
    comfort
pareimi [3918; 624]
    come, have, here (to be),
    lack, present (to be)
pareisagō [3919; 624]
    bring
pareisaktos [3920; 624]
    privily, unawares
pareisdu(n)ō [3921; 624]
    creep, privily
pareiserchomai [3922; 624]
    come, enter, privily
pareispherō [3923; 625]
    add, give
parektos [3924; 625]
    except, saving, without
parembolē [3925; 625]
    army
parenochleō [3926; 625]
    trouble
parepidēmos [3927; 625]
    pilgrim, sojourner, stranger
parerchomai [3928; 625]
    come, go, pass, transgress
paresis [3929; 626]
    passing over, remission
pariēmi [3935; 627]
    hang

paristanō [3936; 627]
    present (verb), yield
paristēmi [3936; 627]
    bring, come, commend, give,
    present (verb), prove,
    provide, send, shew, stand,
    yield
parodos [3938; 628]
    way
paroichomai [3944; 629]
    pass
paroikeō [3939; 628]
    sojourn, stranger
paroikia [3940; 629]
    dwell, strangers, sojourning
paroikos [3941; 629]
    foreigner, sojourner, stranger
paroimia [3942; 629]
    parable
paroinos [3943; 629]
    brawler, wine
paromoiazō [3945; 629]
    like
paromoios [3946; 629]
    like
paropsis [3953; 630]
    platter
parorgismos [3950; 629]
    wrath
parorgizō [3949; 629]
    anger, provoke, wrath
parotrunō [3951; 629]
    stir, urge
parousia [3952; 629]
    coming, presence
paroxunō [3947; 629]
    provoke, stir
paroxusmos [3948; 629]
    contention, provoke
parrhēsia [3954; 630]
    boldness, confidence, freely,
    openly, plainly, plainness
parrhēsiazomai [3955; 631]
    bold, freely, preach
parthenia [3932; 626]
    virginity
parthenos [3933; 627]
    virgin
pas [3956; 631]
    all, every, everything,
    manner, many, one,
    whatsoever, whole,
    whosoever
pascha [3957; 633]
    Easter, passover
paschō [3958; 633]
    feel, passion, suffer
patassō [3960; 634]
    smite, strike
pateō [3961; 634]
    tread
patēr [3962; 635]
    father, parent

pathēma [3804; 602]
    affection, affliction, passion,
    suffering
pathētos [3805; 602]
    suffer
pathos [3806; 602]
    affection, lust, passion
patrolōas (or patral-) [3964; 637]
    murderer
patria [3965; 636]
    family, kindred
patriarchēs [3966; 636]
    patriarch
patrikos [3967; 637]
    father
patris [3968; 636]
    country
patrōos [3971; 637]
    father
patroparadotos [3970; 637]
    father, handed down, receive
pauō [3973; 638]
    cease, leave, refrain
pēchus [4083; 656]
    cubit
pēdalion [4079; 656]
    rudder
pedē [3976; 638]
    fetter
pedinos [3977; 638]
    place
pēganon [4076; 655]
    rue
pēgē [4077; 655]
    fountain, spring, well
pēgnumi [4078; 656]
    pitch
peinaō [3983; 640]
    hunger, hungry
peira [3984; 640]
    trial
peiraō [3987; 641]
    go, try
peirasmos [3986; 640]
    temptation, trial, try
peirazō [3985; 640]
    examine, go, prove, tempt,
    tempter, try
peismonē [3988; 641]
    persuasion
peitharcheō [3980; 638]
    hearken, obey
peithō [3982; 639]
    agree, assure, believe,
    confident, friend, obey,
    persuade, trust, urge, yield
peithos [3981; 639]
    enticing, persuasive
pelagos [3989; 641]
    depth, sea
pelekizō [3990; 641]
    behead
pēlikos [4080; 656]
    great, large

pēlos [4081; 656]
clay
pempō [3992; 641]
send, thrust
pemptos [3991; 641]
fifth
penēs [3993; 642]
poor
penichros [3998; 642]
poor
pentakis [3999; 643]
five times
pentakischilioi [4000; 643]
five, thousand
pentakosioi [4001; 643]
five (hundred)
pente [4002; 643]
five
pentekaidekatos [4003; 643]
fifteenth
pentēkonta [4004; 643]
fifty
pentēkostos [4005; 643]
Pentecost
pentheō [3996; 642]
bewail, mourn, wail
penthera [3994; 642]
mother-in-law, wife's mother
pentheros [3995; 642]
father-in-law
penthos [3997; 642]
mourning, sorrow
pepoithēsis [4006; 643]
confidence, trust
pēra [4082; 656]
wallet
peran [4008; 643]
beyond, side
peras [4009; 644]
end, final, part
peri [4012; 644]
of, pertain to, respect
periagō [4013; 645]
compass, go, lead
periaireō [4014; 645]
cast, take
periaptō [4012 and 681; 645]
kindle
periastraptō [4015; 645]
shine
periballō [4016; 646]
cast, clothe, put
periblepō [4017; 646]
look
peribolaion [4018; 646]
covering, mantle, veil, vesture
perichōros [4066; 653]
country, region
perideō [4019; 646]
bind
periechō [4023; 647]
contain

perierchomai [4022; 646]
circuit, compass, go, strolling, wander
periergazomai [4020; 646]
busybody
periergos [4021; 646]
arts, busybody, curious
periïstēmi [4026; 647]
avoid, stand
perikaluptō [4028; 647]
blindfold, cover, overlay
perikatharma [4027; 647]
filth
perikeimai [4029; 647]
bound (to be), compass, hang
perikephalaia [4030; 648]
helmet
perikratēs [4031; 648]
secure
perikruptō [4032; 648]
hide
perikukloō [4033; 648]
compass
perilampō [4034; 648]
shine
perileipō (-omai) [4035; 648]
leave, remain
perilupos [4036; 648]
sorrowful, sorry
perimenō [4037; 648]
wait
periochē [4042; 648]
place
perioikeō [4039; 648]
dwell
perioikos [4040; 648]
neighbor
periousios [4041; 648]
possession
peripateō [4043; 649]
go, occupy, walk
peripeirō [4044; 649]
pierce
peripherō [4064; 653]
bear, carry
periphroneō [4065; 653]
despise
peripipto [4045; 649]
fall
peripoieō (-omai) [4046; 650]
gain, purchase
peripoiēsis [4047; 650]
obtaining, possession, purchase, saving
peripsēma [4067; 653]
offscouring
perirrhēgnumi [4048; 650]
rend
perispaō [4049; 650]
cumber
perisseia [4050; 650]
abundance, overflowing

perisseuma [4051; 650]
abudance, leave, remain
perisseuō [4052; 650]
abound, abundance, better (be), enough, exceed, excel, increase, leave, remain, spare
perissos [4053; 651]
abundant, advantage, measure, more, superfluous
perissōs [4057; 651]
abundantly, exceedingly, measure, more
perissoteros (-on) (4054) [4055; 651] abundant, far, greater, more, overmuch
perissoterōs [4056; 651]
abundantly, earnest, exceedingly, more, rather
peristera [4058; 651]
dove
peritemnō [4059; 652]
circumcise
perithesis [4025; 647]
wearing
peritithēmi [4060; 652]
bestow, put, set
peritomē [4061; 652]
circumcision
peritrechō [4063; 653]
run
peritrepō [4062; 653]
turn
perix [4038; 648]
round about
perizōnnumi [4024; 647]
gird
perpereuomai [4068; 653]
vaunt
perusi [4070; 653]
year
petaomai [4072; 654]
fly
peteinon [4071; 654]
bird
petomai [4072; 654]
fly
petra [4073; 654]
rock
petrōdēs [4075; 655]
ground, rocky
petros [4074; 654]
stone
pezeuō [3978; 638]
foot, land
pezos [3979; 638]
foot
phagō [5315; 851]
eat, meat
phagos [5314; 851]
gluttonous
phailonēs [5341v; 851]
clothing

phainō [5316; 851]
appear, see, seem, shine, think

phaneroō [5319; 852]
appear, declare, manifest, shew

phaneros [5318; 852]
appear, known, manifest, openly, outwardly

phanerōs [5320; 853]
evidently, openly, publicly

phanerōsis [5321; 853]
manifestation

phanos [5322; 853]
lantern

phantasia [5325; 853]
pomp

phantasma [5326; 853]
apparition, spirit

phantazō [5324; 853]
appearance, sight

pharanx [5327; 853]
valley

pharisaios [5330; 853]
Pharisees

pharmak(e)ia [5331; 854]
sorcery, witchcraft

pharmakos (or *-keus*) (5332)
[5333; 854] sorcerer

phasis [5334; 854]
tidings

phaskō [5335; 854]
affirm, profess, say

phatnē [5336; 854]
manger

phaulos [5337; 854]
evil, ill, vessel

pheidomai [5339; 854]
forbear, spare

pheidomenōs [5340; 854]
sparingly

phelonēs [5341; 854]
clothing

phēmē [5345; 856]
fame

phēmi [5346; 856]
affirm, say

phengos [5338; 854]
light

pherō [5342; 854]
bear, bring, carry, come, drive, endure, go, lay, lead, move, press, reach, rushing, uphold

pheugō [5343; 855]
escape, flee

phialē [5357; 858]
bowl

philadelphia [5360; 858]
brother

philadelphos [5361; 858]
brethren

philagathos [5358; 858]
lover

philandros [5362; 858]
husband

philanthrōpia [5363; 858]
kindness, love

philanthrōpōs [5364; 858]
courteously, kindly

philarguria [5365; 859]
money (love of)

philarguros [5366; 859]
covetous, lover

philautos [5367; 859]
lover

philēdonos [5369; 859]
lover, pleasure

philēma [5370; 859]
kiss

phileō [5368; 859]
kiss, love

philia [5373; 859]
friendship

philoneikia [5379; 860]
contention, strife

philoneikos [5380; 860]
contentious

philophrōn [5391; 861]
courteous

philophronōs [5390; 861]
courteously

philoprōteuō [5383; 860]
pre-eminence

philos (philē) [5384; 861]
friend

philosophia [5385; 861]
philosophy

philosophos [5386; 861]
philosopher

philostorgos [5387; 861]
affection

philoteknos [5388; 861]
children

philotheos [5377; 860]
lover

philotimeomai [5389; 861]
aim, labor, strive, study

philoxenia [5381; 860]
entertain, hospitality, stranger

philoxenos [5382; 860]
hospitality, lover

phimoō [5392; 861]
muzzle, peace (hold one's), put, silence, speechless, still

phlogizō [5394; 862]
fire

phlox [5395; 862]
flame, flaming

phluareō [5396; 862]
prate

phluaros [5397; 862]
tattler

phobeō [5399; 862]
fear, marvel, reverence

phoberos [5398; 862]
fearful

phobētron [5400; 863]
fearful, sight, terror

phobos [5401; 863]
fear, terror

phoinix [5404; 864]
palm (tree)

phōleos [5454; 870]
hole

phōnē [5456; 870]
noise, sound, voice

phōneō [5455; 870]
call, cry

phoneuō [5407; 864]
kill, murder, slay

phoneus [5406; 864]
murderer

phonos [5408; 864]
murder, slaughter

phoreō [5409; 864]
bear, wear

phoros [5411; 865]
tribute

phortion [5413; 865]
burden, lading

phortizō [5412; 865]
lade

phortos [5414; 865]
lading

phōs [5457; 871]
light

phōsphoros [5459; 872]
day-star

phōstēr [5458; 872]
light

phōteinos [5460; 872]
bright, light

phōtismos [5462; 873]
light

phōtizō [5461; 872]
enlighten, light, lighten

phragellion [5416; 865]
scourge

phragelloō [5417; 865]
scourge

phragmos [5418; 865]
hedge, partition

phrassō [5420; 865]
stop

phrazō [5419; 865]
declare, explain

phrear [5421; 865]
pit, well

phrēn [5424; 865]
understanding

phrenapataō [5422; 865]
deceive

phrenapatēs [5423; 865]
deceiver

phrissō [5425; 866]
shudder, tremble

phronēma [5427; 866]
mind, minded

phroneō [5426; 866]
affection, careful, feel, mind,

minded, observe, regard,
savor, think, thought (to
take), understand
phronēsis [5428; 866]
prudence, wisdom
phronimos [5429; 866]
wise
phronimōs [5430; 866]
wisely
phrontizō [5431; 866]
careful
phroureō [5432; 867]
guard, keep
phruassō [5433; 867]
rage
phruganon [5434; 867]
stick
phthanō [5348; 856]
arrive, attain, come, precede
phthartos [5349; 857]
corruptible
phthengomai [5350; 857]
speak, utter
phtheirō [5351; 857]
corrupt, defile, destroy
phthinopōrinos [5352; 857]
autumn, fruit
phthoneō [5354; 857]
envy
phthongos [5353; 857]
sound
phthonos [5355; 857]
envy, envying
phthora [5356; 858]
corruption, destroy, perish
phugē [5437; 867]
flight
phulakē [5438; 867]
cage, hold (noun),
imprisonment, prison, ward,
watch
phulakizō [5439; 868]
imprison
phulaktērion [5440; 868]
phylactery
phulassō [5442; 868]
beware, guard, keep, observe,
preserve, save, ware of
phulax [5441; 868]
guard, keeper
phulē [5443; 868]
kindred, tribe
phullon [5444; 869]
leaf
phuō [5453; 870]
grow, spring
phurama [5445; 869]
lump
phusikos [5446; 869]
natural
phusikōs [5447; 869]
naturally
phusioō [5448; 869]
puff (up)

phusiōsis [5450; 870]
swelling
phusis [5449; 869]
kind (noun), nature, natural
phuteia [5451; 870]
plant
phuteuō [5452; 870]
plant
piazō [4084; 657]
apprehend, catch, hands
(lay...on), take
piezō [4085; 657]
press
pikrainō [4087; 657]
bitter
pikria [4088; 657]
bitterness
pikros [4089; 657]
bitter
pikrōs [4090; 657]
bitterly
pimplēmi (plēthō) [4130; 658]
accomplish, fill, furnish
pimprēmi [4092; 658]
swell
pinakidion [4093; 658]
writing-tablet
pinax [4094; 658]
charger, platter
pinō [4095; 658]
drink
piotēs [4096; 659]
fatness
pipraskō [4097; 659]
sell
piptō [4098; 659]
fail, fall, light (to...upon),
strike
pisteuō [4100; 660]
believe, believer, commit,
intrust, trust
pistikos [4101; 662]
spikenard
pistis [4102; 662]
assurance, belief, faith,
faithfulness, fidelity
pistoō [4104; 665]
assured
pistos [4103; 664]
believer, believing, faithful,
faithfully, sure, true
pithanologia [4086; 657]
enticing, persuasiveness
planaō [4105; 665]
deceive, err, lead, seduce,
wander, way
planē [4106; 665]
deceit, delusion, error
planētēs [4107; 666]
wandering
planos [4108; 666]
deceiver, seducing
plasma [4110; 666]
formed

plassō [4111; 666]
formed
plastos [4112; 666]
feigned
plateia [4113; 666]
street
platos [4114; 666]
broad
platunō [4115; 667]
broad, enlarge
platus [4116; 667]
wide
plax [4109; 666]
table
plēgē [4127; 668]
plague, stripe, wound
plegma [4117; 667]
braided
pleiōn (-on) [4119; 667]
above, excellent, greater,
long, longer, many, more,
most, number, yet
pleistos [4118; 667]
great, most
plekō [4120; 667]
plait
plēktēs [4131; 669]
striker
plēmmura [4132; 669]
flood
plēn [4133; 669]
except, notwithstanding,
rather
pleō [4126; 668]
sail
pleonazō [4121; 667]
abundant, increase, multiply,
over
pleonekteō [4122; 667]
advantage, defraud, gain,
wrong
pleonektēs [4123; 667]
covetous
pleonexia [4124; 667]
covetousness, extortion
plērēs [4134; 669]
full
plērōma [4138; 672]
fill up, fulfilling, fulness, put
plēroō [4137; 670]
accomplish, complete, end,
expire, fill, fulfill, preach,
supply, well-nigh
plērophoreō [4135; 670]
assure, believe, fulfill, know,
persuade, proclaim, proof
plērophoria [4136; 670]
assurance
plēsion [4139; 672]
near, neighbor
plēsmonē [4140; 673]
indulgence
plēssō [4141; 673]
smite

plēthō [4130]
(see *pimplēmi*)
plēthos [4128; 668]
assembly, bundle, company,
multitude
plēthunō [4129; 669]
abound, multiply
pleura [4125; 668]
side
ploiarion [4142; 673]
boat, ship
ploion [4143; 673]
boat, ship, shipping
ploos [4144; 673]
course, voyage
plousios [4145; 673]
rich, rich man
plousiōs [4146; 673]
abundantly, richly
plouteō [4147; 673]
get, goods, rich
ploutizō [4148; 674]
enrich, rich
ploutos [4149; 674]
riches
plunō [4150; 674]
wash
pneō [4154; 679]
blow, wind
pneuma [4151; 674]
breath, life, spirit, Spirit,
spiritual, wind
pneumatikos [4152; 678]
spiritual
pneumatikōs [4153; 679]
spiritually
pnigō [4155; 679]
choke, throat (take by the)
pniktos [4156; 679]
strangled
pnoē [4157; 680]
breath, wind
podērēs [4158; 680]
clothing, foot
poiēma [4161; 683]
made (be), workmanship
poieō [4160; 680]
abide, appoint, bear, bring,
cause, commit, continue,
deal with, do, execute,
exercise, fulfill, gain, give,
hold, keep, make, mean,
observe, ordain, perform,
provide, purpose, put, shew,
shoot forth, spend, take,
tarry, work, yield
poiēsis [4162; 683]
deed
poiētēs [4163; 683]
doer, poet
poikilos [4164; 683]
divers, manifold
poimainō [4165; 683]
cattle, feed, rule

poimēn [4166; 684]
pastor, shepherd
poimnē [4167; 684]
flock, fold
poimnion [4168; 684]
flock
poios [4169; 684]
manner, what, which
polemeō [4170; 685]
fight, war
polemos [4171; 685]
battle, fight, war
pōleō [4453; 731]
sell
polis [4172; 685]
city
politarchēs [4173; 686]
ruler
politeia [4174; 686]
citizenship, commonwealth,
freedom
politēs [4177; 686]
citizen
politeuma [4175; 686]
citizenship, commonwealth,
coversation
politeuō [4176; 686]
citizen, conversation, live
pollakis [4178; 686]
oft, often, oftentimes, oft-
times
pollaplasiōn [4179; 686]
manifold
pōlos [4454; 731]
colt
polulogia [4180; 687]
speaking (much)
polumerōs [4181; 687]
portion, time
polupoikilos [4182; 687]
manifold
polus [4183; 687]
abundant, common, great,
greatly, long, many, much,
oft, plenteous, sore, straitly
polusplanchnos [4184; 689]
pitiful
polutelēs [4185; 690]
costly, precious, price
polutimos [4186; 690]
costly, precious, price
polutropōs [4187; 690]
divers, manners
poma [4188; 690]
drink
ponēria [4189; 690]
iniquity, wickedness
ponēros [4190; 691]
bad, evil, grievous, harm,
malicious, person, vile,
wicked
ponos [4192; 691]
labor, pain

pōpote [4455; 732]
never, time
poreia [4197; 692]
journey, way
poreuō (-omai)) [4198; 692]
depart, go, journey, walk,
way
porismos [4200; 693]
gain
pornē [4204; 693]
harlot, whore
porneia [4202; 693]
fornication
porneuō [4203; 693]
fornication
pornos [4205; 693]
fornicator, whoremonger
pōroō [4456; 732]
blind, harden
pōrōsis [4457; 732]
blindness, hardening,
hardness
porphura [4209; 694]
purple
porphurous [4210; 694]
purple
porphuropōlis [4211; 694]
purple (seller of)
porrō [4206; 693]
far, way
porrōteron [4208; 694]
further
porrōthen [4207; 693]
afar
portheō [4199; 693]
destroy, havoc, waste
pōs (1) [4458; 732]
haply, means (by any, etc),
perhaps
pōs (2) [4459; 732]
manner, means
posakis [4212; 694]
oft, often
posis [4213; 694]
drink
posos [4214; 694]
great, long, many, what
potamophorētos [4216; 694]
flood, river
potamos [4215; 694]
flood, river, water
potapos [4217; 694]
manner, what
pote (1) [4218; 695]
aforetime, haply, last, length
(at), never, old, once, past,
sometimes, time, time
(some), (ever) yet
pote (2) [4219; 695]
long
potērion [4221; 695]
cup
potizō [4222; 695]
drink, feed, water

potos [4224; 696]
carousings
pou [4225; 696]
about, haply, place, room,
somewhere
pous [4228; 696]
foot
pragma [4229; 697]
business, matter, thing, work
pragmateia [4230; 697]
affair
pragmateuomai [4231; 697]
trade
praitōrion [4232; 697]
guard, hall, palace
praktōr [4233; 697]
officer
prasia [4237; 698]
ranks
prassō [4238; 698]
commit, deeds, do, exact,
extort, keep, practice,
require, use
praüpathia [4239 and 3958; 698]
meekness
praüs (or -os) [4239; 698]
meek
praütes (or -otēs) [4240; 699]
meekness
praxis [4234; 697]
deed, office, work
prēnēs [4248; 700]
fall, headlong, swell
prepō [4241; 699]
become, befit, comely
presbeia [4242; 699]
ambassage, message
presbeuō [4243; 699]
ambassador
presbuterion [4244; 699]
elder, estate
presbuteros [4245; 699]
elder, eldest, old
presbutēs [4246; 700]
aged, old
presbutis [4247; 700]
aged
prin [4250; 701]
before
prizō (or priō) [4249; 701]
saw asunder
proagō [4254; 702]
bring, foregoing, go
*proaireō (-omai) [4255; 702]
purpose
proaitiaomai [4256; 702]
charge, prove
proakouō [4257; 702]
hear
proamartanō [4258; 702]
sin
proaulion [4259; 702]
porch

probainō [4260; 702]
go, stricken (in years)
proballō [4261; 702]
put, shoot forth
probatikos [4262; 703]
sheep *gate,* sheep *market*
probation [4263*; 703]
sheep
probaton [4263; 703]
sheep
probibazō [4264; 703]
draw, instruct, put
problepō [4265; 703]
foresee, provide
procheirizō [4440; 724]
appoint, choose, make
procheirotoneō [4401; 724]
choose
prodēlos [4271; 704]
evident, manifest
prodidōmi [4272; 704]
give
prodotēs [4273; 704]
betrayer, traitor
prodromos [4274; 704]
forerunner
*proechō (-omai) [4281; 705]
better (be), case, worse
proēgeomai [4285; 706]
prefer
proeidon [4275; 704]
foresee, see
proeipon (prolegō) [(4302), 704]
foretell, forewarn, say, speak
proeirō [4280v]
tell
proelpizō [4276; 705]
hope, trust
proenarchomai [4278; 705]
begin
proepangellō (-omai) [4279; 705]
aforepromised, promise
proerchomai [4281; 705]
go, outgo, pass
proetoimazō [4282; 705]
ordain, prepare
proeuangelizomai [4283; 705]
preach
proginomai [4266; 703]
past
proginōskō [4267; 703]
foreknow, foreordain, know
prognōsis [4268; 703]
foreknowledge
progonos [4269; 704]
forefather, parents
prographō [4270; 704]
openly, ordain, set, write
proï [4404; 724]
early, morning
proïmos [4406; 725]
early
proïnos [4407; 725]
morning

proïos [4405; 724]
day, early, morning
proïstēmi [4291; 724]
maintain, over (to be), rule
*prokaleōmai [4292; 707]
provoke
prokatangellō [4293; 707]
foreshew, foretell, shew
prokatartizō [4294; 707]
make
prokeimai [4295; 707]
first, set
prokērussō [4296; 707]
preach
prokopē [4297; 707]
furtherance, profiting,
progress
prokoptō [4298; 707]
advance, increase, proceed,
profit, spent, wax
prokrima [4299; 708]
prefer, prejudice
prokuroō [4300; 708]
confirm
prolambanō [4301; 708]
come, overtake, take
prolegō [4302; 708]
(see *proeipon*)
promarturomai [4303; 708]
testify
promeletaō [4304; 708]
meditate
promerimnaō [4305; 708]
thought (to, take)
pronoeō [4306; 708]
provide, thought (to take)
pronoia [4307; 708]
providence, provision
prooraō [4308; 709]
foresee, see
proorizō [4309; 709]
determine, ordain,
predestinate
prosormizō [4358; 717]
draw
propaschō [4310; 709]
suffer
propatōr [4253 and 3962; 709]
forefather
propempō [4311; 709]
accompany, bring, conduct,
journey, set, way
propetēs [4312; 709]
heady, headstrong
prophasis [4392; 722]
cloke (pretense), excuse,
pretense, show (noun)
propherō [4393; 722]
bring
prophēteia [4394; 722]
prophecy, prophesying
prophētēs [4396; 723]
prophet

prophēteuō [4395; 723]
prophesy
prophētikos [4397; 724]
prophecy
prophētis [4398; 724]
prophetess
prophthanō [4399; 724]
speak
proporeuomai [4313; 709]
go
prōra [4408; 725]
foreship
pros [4314; 709]
belong, compare, nigh,
pertain to
prosabbaton [4315; 711]
sabbath
prosagō [4317; 711]
bring, draw
prosagōgē [4318; 711]
access
prosagoreuō [4316; 711]
call, name
prosaiteō [4319; 711]
beg
prosanabainō [4320; 711]
go
prosanaliskō [4321; 711]
spend
prosanaplēroō [4322; 711]
measure, supply
prosanatithēmi [4323; 711]
add, confer, impart
prosapeileō [4324; 711]
threaten
proschusis [4378; 720]
sprinkling
prosdapanaō [4325; 712]
spend
prosdechomai [4327; 712]
accept, allow, look (for),
receive, take, wait
prosdeomai [4326; 712]
need
prosdokaō [4328; 712]
expect, expectation, look
(for), tarry, wait
prosdokia [4329; 712]
expectation, looking (after)
proseaō [4330; 712]
suffer
prosechō [4337; 714]
attend, attendance, beware,
give, heed, regard
prosedreuō [4332; 712]
wait
prosengizō [4331; 712]
come
proselaō [4338; 714]
nail
prosēlutos [4339; 715]
proselyte
proserchomai [4334; 713]
come, consent, draw, go

prosergazomai [4333; 713]
gain
proseuchē [4335; 713]
earnestly, fervently, prayer
proseuchomai [4336; 713]
pray, prayer
proskairos [4340; 715]
season, temporal, time, while
proskaleō (-omai) [4341; 715]
call
proskartereō [4342; 715]
attend, continue, give,
instant, wait
proskarterēsis [4343; 715]
perseverance
proskephalaion [4344; 715]
pillow
prosklēroō [4345; 716]
consort
prosklisis [4346; 716]
partiality
proskollaō [4347; 716]
cleave, join
proskomma [4348; 716]
offense
proskopē [4349; 716]
offense
proskoptō [4350; 716]
beat, dash, smite, stumble
proskuliō [4351; 716]
roll
proskuneō [4352; 716]
beseech, worship
proskunētēs [4353; 717]
worshipper
proslaleō [4354; 717]
speak
proslambanō [4355; 717]
receive, take
proslē(m)psis [4356; 717]
receiving
prosmenō [4357; 717]
abide, cleave, continue, tarry
prosochthizō [4360; 717]
displease, grieve
prosōpolē(m)psia [4382; 720]
persons (respect of), receive
prosōpolē(m)pteō [4380; 720]
persons (respect of), receive
prosōpolē(m)ptēs [4381; 720]
persons (respect of), receive
prosōpon [4383; 720]
appearance, countenance,
face, fashion, person,
presence
prosormizō [4358; 717]
draw, moor
prosopheilō [4359; 717]
owe
prospēgnumi [4362; 718]
crucify
prospeinos [4361; 718]
hungry

prosphagion [4371; 719]
eat, meat
prosphatos [4372; 719]
new
prosphatōs [4373; 719]
lately
prospherō [4374; 719]
bring, deal with, do, offer,
present (verb), put
prosphilēs [4375; 720]
lovely
prosphōneō [4377; 720]
call, speak
prosphora [4376; 720]
offering
prospiptō [4363; 718]
beat, fall
prospoieō (-omai) [4364; 718]
make
prosporeuomai [4365; 718]
come
prospsauō [4379; 720]
touch
prosrēgnumi [4366; 718]
beat, break
prostassō [4367; 718]
bid, command
prostatis [4368; 718]
succorer
prostithēmi [4369; 718]
add, give, increase, lay,
proceed, speak
prostrechō [4370; 719]
run
protassō [4384; 721]
appoint
proteinō [4385; 721]
bind, tie
proteros (-on) (4386) [4387; 721]
aforetime, before, first,
former
prōteuō [4409; 725]
pre-eminence
prothesis [4286; 706]
purpose, shewbread
prothesmios [4287; 706]
appoint, term, time
prothumia [4288; 706]
forwardness, readiness,
willing
prothumos [4289; 706]
ready, willing
prothumōs [4290; 706]
ready
protithēmi [4388; 722]
purpose, set
prōtokathedria [4410; 725]
chief, seat, uppermost
prōtoklisia [4411; 725]
chief, place, room,
uppermost
prōton [4412; 725]
before, beginning, chiefly,
first

prōtos [4413; 725]
  best, chief, chiefest, estate,
  first, former, principal
prōtos [4413*; 727]
  first
prōtostatēs [4414; 726]
  ringleader
prōtotokia [4415; 726]
  birthright
prōtotokos [4416; 726]
  first-begotten, firstborn
protrechō [4390; 722]
  outrun, run
protrepō (-omai) [4389; 722]
  encourage, exhort
proüparchō [4391; 722]
  before, beforetime
prumna [4403; 724]
  stern
psallō [5567; 891]
  melody, praise, psalm, sing
psalmos [5568; 891]
  psalm
psēlaphaō [5584; 892]
  feel, handle, touch
psēphizō [5585; 892]
  count
psēphos [5586; 892]
  stone
pseudadelphos [5569; 891]
  brethren
pseudapostolos [5570; 891]
  apostle
pseudēs [5571; 891]
  false, liar
pseudochristos [5580; 892]
  false Christs (see *Christ*)
pseudodidaskalos [5572; 892]
  teacher, false teachers
pseudologos [5573; 891]
  lie
pseud (-omai) [5574; 891]
  falsely, lie
pseudomartureō [5576; 891]
  witness
pseudomarturia [5577; 892]
  witness
pseudomartus [5571 and 3144;
  892] witness
pseudōnumos [5581; 892]
  falsely
pseudoprophētēs [5578; 892]
  prophet
pseudos [5579; 892]
  falsehood, lie, lying
pseusma [5582; 892]
  lie
pseustēs [5583; 892]
  liar
psichion [5589; 893]
  crumb
psithurismos [5587; 892]
  whispering

psithuristēs [5588; 893]
  whisperer
psōchō [5597; 894]
  rub
psōmion [5596; 894]
  sop
psōmizō [5595; 894]
  bestow, feed
psuchē [5590; 893]
  heart, heartily, life, mind,
  soul
psuchikos [5591; 894]
  natural
psuchō [5594; 894]
  cold
psuchos [5592; 894]
  cold
psuchros [5593; 894]
  cold
ptaiō [4417; 727]
  fall, offend, stumble
ptēnon [4421; 727]
  bird
pterna [4418; 727]
  heel
pterugion [4419; 727]
  pinnacle
pterux [4420; 727]
  wing
ptōcheia [4432; 728]
  poverty
ptōcheuō [4433; 728]
  poor
ptōchos [4434; 728]
  beggar, beggarly, poor
ptoeō [4422; 727]
  terrify
ptoēsis [4423; 727]
  amazement, terror
ptōma [4430; 727]
  body, carcase, corpse
ptōsis [4431; 728]
  fall
ptuō [4429; 727]
  spit
ptuon [4425; 727]
  fan
pturō [4426; 727]
  affrighted, terrify
ptusma [4427; 727]
  spittle
ptussō [4428; 727]
  close (verb)
pugmē [4435; 728]
  diligently
puknos (-na) [4437; 729]
  often
puknoteron [4437*; 729*]
  oftener
pukteuō [4438; 729]
  fight
pulē [4439; 729]
  city, gate

pulōn [4440; 729]
  gate, porch
punthanomai [4441; 729]
  ask, inquire, understand
pur [4442; 729]
  fire
pura [4443; 730]
  fire
puressō [4445; 730]
  fever (be sick of)
puretos [4446; 730]
  fever
purgos [4444; 730]
  tower
purinos [4447; 731]
  fire
puroomai (-oō) [4448; 731]
  burn, fiery, fire, refined, try
purōsis [4451; 731]
  burning, fiery, trial
purrhazō [4449; 731]
  red
purrhos [4450; 731]
  red
puthōn [4436; 728]
  divination

R

rabbi (-ei) [4461; 733]
  master, Rabbi
rabbōni (or -ounei) [4462; 733]
  lord, Rabboni
rhabdizō [4463; 733]
  beat, rod
rhabdos [4464; 733]
  rod, staff
rhabdouchos [4465; 733]
  sergeant
rhadiourgēma [4467; 733]
  villany
rhadiourgia [4468; 733]
  villany
rhaka [4469; 733]
  raca
rhakos [4470; 734]
  cloth
rhantismos [4473; 734]
  sprinkling
rhantizō [4472; 734]
  sprinkle, wash
rhaphis [4476; 734]
  needle
rhapisma [4475; 734]
  blow (noun), smite, strike
rhapizō [4474; 734]
  palm, smite, strike
rhedē [4480; 734]
  chariot
rhēgma [4485; 735]
  ruin
rhēgnumi [4486; 735]
  break, burst, dash, rend, tear

rhēma [4487; 735]
saying, thing, word
rheō [4482; 735]
flow
rheō (see *eirō*) [4483]
command
rhētōr [4489; 735]
orator
rhētōs [4490; 736]
expressly
rhipē [4493; 736]
twinkling
rhipizō [4494; 736]
toss
rhiptō [4496; 736]
(or *rhipteō*), (4495), cast,
scatter, throw
rhiza [4491; 736]
root
rhizoō [4492; 736]
root
rhoizēdon [4500; 737]
noise
rhōmaios [4514; 738]
Roman
rhōmaïsti [4515; 738]
Latin
rhōmaïkos [4513; 738]
Latin
rhomphaia [4501; 737]
sword
rhōnnumi [4517; 738]
farewell
rhumē [4505; 737]
lane, street
rhuomai [4506; 737]
deliver, deliverer
rhupainō [4510v; 737]
filthy (to make)
rhuparia [4507; 738]
filthiness
rhuparos [4508; 738]
filthy, vile
rhupareuomai [4510; 738]
filthy
rhupos [4509; 738]
filth
rhusis [4511; 738]
issue
rhutis [4512; 738]
wrinkle

S

sabachthani [4518; 738]
sabachthani
sabaōth [4519; 738]
sabaoth
sabbatismos [4520; 739]
rest, sabbath
sabbaton [4521; 739]
sabbath, week

sagēnē [4522; 739]
net
sainō [4525; 740]
move
sakkos [4526; 740]
sackcloth
saleuō [4531; 740]
move, shake, stir
salos [4535; 741]
wave
salpinx [4536; 741]
trump, trumpet
salpistēs [4538; 741]
trumpeter
salpizō [4537; 741]
sound, trumpet
sandalion [4547; 742]
sandal
sanis [4548; 742]
board
sapphiros [4552; 742]
sapphire
sapros
bad, corrupt
sardinos [4555; 742]
sardine
sardios (-on) [4556; 742]
sardius
sardonux [4557; 742]
sardonyx
sarganē [4553; 742]
basket
sarkikos [4559; 742]
carnal, flesh, fleshly
sarkinos [4560; 743]
carnal, flesh, fleshy
saroō [4563; 744]
sweep
sarx [4561; 743]
flesh
satanas [4567; 744]
Satan
saton [4568; 745]
measure
sbennumi [4570; 745]
go, quench
schedon [4975; 797]
almost
schēma [4976; 797]
fashion
schisma [4978; 797]
division, rent, schism
schizō [4977; 797]
break, divide, open, rend,
rent
schoinion [4979; 797]
cord, rope
scholazō [4980; 797]
empty, give
scholē [4981; 798]
school
seautou [4572; 745]
thee, thyself

sebasma [4574; 745]
devotion, worship
sebastos [4575; 745]
emperor
sebazomai [4573; 745]
worship
sebō (-omai) [4576; 746]
devout, worship
seiō [4579; 746]
move, quake, shake, stir,
tremble
seira [4577; 746]
chain
seiros [4617a; 746]
pits
seismos [4578; 746]
earthquake, tempest
selēnē [4582; 746]
moon
selēniazō [4583; 746]
epileptic
sēmainō [4591; 747]
signify
sēmeion [4592; 747]
miracle, sign, token, wonder
sēmeioō [4593; 748]
note (verb)
sēmeron [4594; 749]
to-day, this day
semidalis [4585; 746]
flour
semnos [4586; 746]
grave (adjective), honest
semnotēs [4587; 747]
gravity, honesty, honorable
sēpō [4595; 749]
corrupt
sērikos (or *sir-*) [4596; 749]
silk
sēs [4597; 749]
moth
sētobrōtos [4598; 749]
moth-eaten
siagōn [4600; 749]
cheek
sidēreos [4603; 750]
iron
sidēros [4604; 750]
iron
sigaō [4601; 749]
close (verb), peace (hold
one's), secret, silence
sigē [4602; 749]
silence
sikarios [4607; 750]
assassin, murderer
sikera [4608; 750]
drink
simikinthion [4612; 751]
apron
sinapi [4615; 751]
mustard
sindōn [4616; 751]
linen

siniazō [4617; 751]
sift
siōpaō [4623; 752]
dumb, peace (hold one's)
siteutos [4618; 752]
fatted
sition [4621*; 752]
corn
sitistos [4619; 752]
fatling
sitometrion [4620; 752]
food, meat
sitos [4621; 752]
corn, wheat
skandalizō [4624; 752]
offend
skandalon [4625; 753]
fall, falling, offense
skaphē [4627; 753]
boat
skaptō [4626; 753]
dig
skelos [4628; 753]
leg
skēnē [4633; 754]
habitation, tabernacle
skēnōma [4638; 755]
habitation, tabernacle
skēnoō [4637; 755]
dwell, tabernacle
skēnopēgia [4634; 754]
tabernacle
skēnopoios [4635; 755]
tent-maker
skēnos [4636; 755]
tabernacle
skepasma [4629; 753]
covering, raiment
skeuē [4631; 754]
tackling
skeuos [4632; 754]
gear, goods, vessel
skia [4639; 755]
shadow
skirtaō [4640; 755]
leap
sklērokardia [4641; 756]
heart (hardness of)
sklēros [4642; 756]
fierce, hard, rough
sklērotēs [4643; 756]
hardness
sklērotrachēlos [4644; 756]
stiffnecked
sklērunō [4645; 756]
harden
skōlēkobrōtos [4662; 758]
worm
skōlēx [4663; 758]
worm
skolios [4646; 756]
crooked
skolops [4647; 756]
thorn

skopeō [4648; 756]
consider, heed (to take),
look, mark
skopos [4649; 756]
goal, mark
skorpios [4651; 757]
scorpion
skorpizō [4650; 757]
disperse, scatter
skoteinos [4652; 757]
dark, darkness
skotia [4653; 757]
dark, darkness
skotizō [4654; 757]
darken
skotoō [4656; 758]
darken, darkness
skotos [4655; 757]
darkness
skubalon [4657; 758]
dung
skullō [4660; 758]
distress, trouble
skulon [4661; 758]
spoil
skuthrōpos [4659; 758]
countenance
smaragdinos [4664; 758]
emerald
smaragdos [4665; 758]
emerald
smurna [4666; 758]
myrrh
smurnizō [4669; 759]
mingle, myrrh
sōma [4983; 799]
body, slave
sōmatikos [4984; 800]
bodily
sōmatikōs [4985; 800]
bodily
sophia [4678; 759]
wisdom
sophizo [4679; 760]
devised (cunningly), wise
sophos [4680; 760]
wise
sōphrōn [4998; 802]
discreet, sober, soberminded,
temperate
sōphroneō [4993; 802]
mind, sober, soberminded,
think, watch
sōphronismos [4995; 802]
discipline, mind
sōphronizō [4994; 802]
soberminded
sōphronōs [4996; 802]
soberly
sōphrosunē [4997; 802]
soberness, sobriety
sōreuō [4987; 800]
heap, lade

soros [4673; 759]
bier
sos [4674; 759]
thine, thy
sōtēr [4990; 800]
savior
sōtēria [4991; 801]
health, safety, salvation,
saving
sōtērion [4992; 801]
salvation
sōtērios [4992**; 801]
salvation
soudarion [4676; 759]
handkerchief, napkin
sōzō [4982; 798]
heal, recover, save, whole
spaō [4685; 761]
draw
sparassō [4682; 760]
rend, tear
sparganoō [4683; 760]
swaddling-clothes
spatalaō [4684; 761]
delicately, live, pleasure,
wanton
speira [4686; 761]
band
speirō [4687; 761]
receive, sow, sower
spekoulatōr [4688; 761]
guard, soldier
spēlaion [4693; 762]
cave, den
spendō [4689; 761]
offer
sperma [4690; 761]
issue, seed
spermologos [4691; 762]
babbler
speudō [4692; 762]
desire, earnestly, haste
sphagē [4967; 795]
slaughter
sphagion [4968; 796]
beast
sphazō (or *-ttō*) [4969; 796]
kill, slay, smite, wound
sphodra [4970; 796]
exceeding, exceedingly,
greatly, sore, very
sphodrōs [4971; 796]
exceedingly
sphragis [4973; 796]
seal
sphragizō [4972; 796]
seal
sphuron [4974; 797]
ankle-bones
spilas [4694; 762]
rock, spot
spiloō [4695; 762]
defile, spot

spilos [4696; 762]
  spot
splanchnon (-na) [4698; 763]
  affection, bowels,
  compassion, mercy
splanchnizomai [4697; 762]
  compassion
spodos [4700; 763]
  ashes
spongos [4699; 763]
  sponge
spora [4701; 763]
  seed
sporimos [4702; 763]
  corn, cornfield, field
sporos [4703; 763]
  seed
spoudaios [4705; 763]
  careful, diligent, earnest,
  forward
spoudaiōs [4709; 763]
  diligently, earnestly, instantly
spoudaioteros [4707; 763*]
  diligent, earnest
spoudaioterōs [4708; 763*]
  carefully, diligently
spoudazō [4704; 763]
  diligence, diligent, endeavor,
  forward, labor, study, zealous
spoudē [4710; 763]
  business, care, carefulness,
  diligence, earnestness,
  forwardness, haste
spuris [4711; 764]
  basket
stachus [4719; 765]
  corn, ear (of corn)
stadion [4712; 764]
  furlong, race
stamnos [4713; 764]
  pot
staphulē [4718; 765]
  grape
stasiastēs [7955v; 764]
  insurrection
stasis [4714; 764]
  dissension, insurrection, riot,
  sedition, standing, uproar
statēr [4715; 764]
  money, piece, shekel
stauroō [4717; 765]
  crucify
stauros [4716; 764]
  cross
stegē [4721; 765]
  roof
stegō [4722; 765]
  bear, forbear, suffer
steiros [4723; 766]
  barren
stēkō [4739; 767]
  stand
stellō [4724; 767]
  avoid, withdraw

stemma [4725; 766]
  garland
stenagmos [4726; 766]
  groaning
stenazō [4727; 766]
  grief, groan, murmur, sigh
stenochōreo [4729; 766]
  anguish, distress, straitened
stenochōria [4730; 766]
  anguish, distress
stenos [4728; 766]
  narrow
stephanoō [4737; 767]
  crown
stephanos [4735; 767]
  crown
stereōma [4733; 766]
  steadfastness
stereoō [4732; 766]
  establish, strength,
  strengthen, strong
stereos [4731; 766]
  firm, solid, steadfast, strong,
  sure
stērigmos [4740; 768]
  steadfastness
stērizō [4741; 768]
  establish, fix, set, strengthen
stēthos [4738; 767]
  breast
sthenoō [4599; 749]
  strengthen
stigma [4742; 768]
  mark
stigmē [4743; 768]
  moment
stilbō [4744; 768]
  shine
stoa [4745; 768]
  porch
stoibas [4746; 768]
  branch
stoicheion [4747; 768]
  elements, principles,
  rudiments
stoicheō [4748; 769]
  walk
stolē [4749; 769]
  clothing, robe
stoma [4750; 769]
  edge, face, mouth
stomachos [4751; 770]
  stomach
stratēgos [4755; 770]
  captain, magistrate
strateia [4752; 770]
  warfare
strateuma [4753; 770]
  army, soldier
*strateuō (-omai) [4754; 770]
  go, soldier, war, warfare
stratia (or -eia) [4756; 770]
  host (of angels, etc.), warfare

stratiōtēs [4757; 770]
  soldier
stratologeō [4758; 770]
  choose, enroll, soldier
stratopedarchēs [4759; 771]
  captain, guard
stratopedon [4760; 771]
  army
strebloō [4761; 771]
  wrest
strēniaō [4763; 771]
  deliciously, wanton
strēnos [4764; 771]
  delicacies, wantonness
strephō [4762; 771]
  convert, turn
strōnnumi [4766; 771] or *strōnnuō*
  furnish, spread
strouthion [4765; 771]
  sparrow
stugētos [4767; 771]
  hateful
stugnazō [4768; 771]
  countenance, lowring (to be)
stulos [4769; 772]
  pillar
su [4771; 772]
  thee, thine, thou, thy
sukaminos [4807; 776]
  sycamine
sukē (or sukea) [4808; 776]
  fig tree
sukomōrea [4809; 776]
  sycamore
sukon [4810; 776]
  fig
sukophanteō [4811; 776]
  accuse, exact (verb)
sulagōgeō [4812; 776]
  spoil
sulaō [4813; 776]
  rob
sullaleō [4814; 776]
  commune, confer, speak, talk
sullambanō [4815; 776]
  catch, conceive, help, seize,
  take
sullegō [4816; 777]
  gather
sullogizomai [4817; 777]
  reason
sullupeō [4818; 777]
  (see *sunl-*)
sumbainō [4819; 777]
  befall, happen, so, was, etc.
sumballō [4820; 777]
  confer, encounter, help,
  make, meet, ponder
sumbasileuō [4821; 777]
  reign
sumbibazō [4822; 777]
  assuredly, bring, compacted,
  conclude, instruct, knit
  together, prove

sumbouleuō [4823; 777]
consult, counsel
sumboulion [4824; 778]
consultation, council
sumboulos [4825; 778]
counsellor
summartureō [4828; 778]
testify, witness
summathētēs [4827; 778]
disciple
summerizō (-omai) [4829; 778]
partaker, portion
summetochos [4830; 778]
partaker
summimētēs [4831; 778]
follower, imitator
summorphizō [4833v; 778]
conformed
summorphoō [4833; 778]
conformable
summorphos [4832; 778]
conformed, fashion
sumparaginomai [4836; 779]
come, stand
sumparakaleō [4837; 779]
comfort
sumparalambanō [4838; 779]
take
sumparamenō [4839; 779]
continue
sumpareimi [4840; 779]
present (to be)
sumpaschō [4841; 779]
suffer
sumpatheō [4834; 778]
compassion, feeling, touch
sumpathēs [4835; 779]
compassion, compassionate
sumpempō [4842; 779]
send
sumperilambanō [4843; 779]
embrace
sumphēmi [4852; 780]
consent
sumpherō [4851; 780]
better (be), bring, expedient,
good (to be), profitable
sumpheron [4851d; 780]
profit
sumphōneō [4856; 780]
agree
sumphōnēsis [4857; 781]
concord
sumphōnia [4858; 781]
music
sumphōnos [4859; 781]
consent
sumphoros [4851d; 780]
profitable
sumphuletēs [4853; 780]
countryman
sumphuō [4855; 780]
grow, spring

sumphutos [4854; 780]
plant
sumpinō [4844; 779]
drink
sumplēroō [4845; 779]
come, fill, well-nigh
sumpnigō [4846; 779]
choke, throng
sumpolitēs [4847; 780]
citizen
sumporeuomai [4848; 780]
go, resort
sumposion [4849; 780]
company
sumpresbuteros [4850; 780]
elder
sumpsēphizō [4860; 781]
count
sumpsuchos [4861; 781]
accord
sunagō [4863; 782]
assemble, bestow, come,
gather, lead, resort, take
sunagōgē [4864; 782]
assembly, congregation,
synagogue
sunagōnizomai [4865; 783]
strive
sunaichmalōtos [4869; 783]
prisoner
sunairō [4868; 783]
reckon, take
sunakoloutheō [4870; 783]
follow
sunalizō [4871; 783]
assemble
sunallassō [4862 and 236; 784]
set
sunanabainō [4872; 784]
come
sunanakeimai [4873; 784]
meat, sit, table (at the)
sunanamignumi [4874; 784]
company
sunanpauomai [4875; 784]
find, refresh
sunantaō [4876; 784]
befall, meet
sunantēsis [4877; 784]
meet
sunantilambanō [4878; 784]
help
sunapagō [4879; 784]
carry, condescend, lead
sunapollumi [4881; 785]
perish
sunapostellō [4882; 785]
send
sunapothnēskō [4880; 784]
die
sunarmologeō [4883; 785]
fitly, frame, join
sunarpazō [4884; 785]
catch, seize

sunathleō [4866; 783]
labor, strive
sunathroizō [4867; 783]
call, gather
sunauxanō [4885; 785]
grow
sunchairō [4796; 775]
rejoice
suncheō [4797; 775]
or *sunchun(n)ō*
confound, confuse, stir,
uproar
sunchraomai [4798; 775]
dealings with
sunchusis [4799; 775]
confusion
sundeō [4887; 785]
bind
sundesmos [4886; 785]
band, bond
sundoulos [4889; 785]
servant
sundoxazō [4888; 785]
glorify
sundromē [4890; 785]
run
sunechō [4912; 789]
anguish, constrain, hold,
keep, press, sick, stop, strait,
straiten, take, throng
sunēdomai [4913; 789]
delight in
sunedrion [4892; 786]
council
sunegeirō [4891; 785]
raise, rise
suneidēsis [4893; 786]
conscience
suneidon [4894; 787]
(or *sunoida*), consider, know,
privy, ware
suneimi [4895; 787]
gather
suneiserchomai [4897; 787]
enter, go
sunekdēmos [4898; 787]
companion
suneklektos [4899; 787]
elect
sunelaunō [4900; 787]
set
sunēlikiōtēs [4915; 789]
equal, own
sunephistēmi [4911; 789]
rise (see *arise*)
sunepimartureō [4901; 787]
witness
sunepomai [4902; 787]
accompany
sunerchomai [4905; 788]
accompany, appear,
assemble, come, company,
go, resort

sunergeō [4903; 787]
    help, work, worker
sunergos [4904; 787]
    companion, helper, laborer,
    worker, work-fellow
sunesis [4907; 788]
    knowledge, prudence,
    understanding
sunesthiō [4906; 788]
    eat
sunētheia [4914; 789]
    custom
sunetos [4908; 788]
    prudent, understanding
suneudokeō [4909; 788]
    allow, consent, content,
    please
suneuōcheō (-omai) [4910; 789]
    feast
sungeneia [4772; 772]
    kindred
sungenēs [4773; 772]
    cousins, kin, kinsfolk,
    kinsman
sungeneus [4773;**, 772]
    kin, kinsfolk
sungenis [4773v; 772]
    cousin, kinswoman
sungnōmē [4774; 773]
    permission
suniēmi (or suniō) [4920; 790]
    consider, understand, wise
sunistēmi [4921; 790]
    approve, commend,
    compacted, consist, make,
    prove, stand
sunkakopatheō [4777; 773]
    hardship
sunkakoucheomai [4778; 773]
    affliction, entreat, suffer
sunkaleō [4779; 773]
    call
sunkaluptō [4780; 773]
    cover
sunkamptō [4781; 773]
    bow
sunkatabainō [4782; 773]
    go
sunkatapsēphizō (-omai) [4785;
    773] number
sunkatathesis [4783; 773]
    agreement
sunkatatithēmi [4784; 773]
    agree, consent
sunkathēmai [4775; 773]
    sit
sunkathizō [4776; 773]
    set, sit
sunkerannumi [4786; 773]
    mixed (with), temper
    together
sunkineō [4787; 773]
    stir

sunkleiō [4788; 774]
    conclude, inclose, shut
sunklēronomos [4789; 774]
    heir
sunkoinōneō [4790; 774]
    communicate, fellowship,
    partake(r)
sunkoinōnos [4791; 774]
    companion, partake, partaker
sunkomizō [4792; 774]
    carry
sunkrinō [4793; 774]
    compare
sunkuptō [4794; 775]
    bow
sunkuria [4795; 775]
    chance
sunlupeo (or sull) [0]
    grieve
sunochē [4928; 791]
    anguish, distress
sunodeuō [4922; 791]
    journey
sunodia [4023; 791]
    company
sunōdinō [4944; 793]
    travail
sunoida [4862, and perf.
    of 1492; 791]
    consider, know, privy, ware
sunoikeō [4924; 791]
    dwell
sunoikodomeō [4925; 791]
    build
sunomileō [4926; 791]
    talk
sunomoreō [4927; 791]
    join
sunōmosia [4945; 793]
    conspiracy
suntassō [4929; 791]
    appoint
sunteleia [4930; 792]
    end
sunteleō [4931; 792]
    complete, end, finish, fulfill,
    make
suntemnō [4932; 792]
    cut, short
suntēreō [4933; 792]
    keep, observe, preserve
sunthaptō [4916; 789]
    bury
sunthlaō [4917; 790]
    break
sunthlibō [4918; 790]
    throng
sunthruptō [4919; 790]
    break
suntithēmi [4934; 792]
    agree, covenant
suntomōs [4935; 793]
    few

suntrechō [4936; 793]
    run
suntribō [4937; 793]
    break, bruise
suntrimma [4938; 793]
    destruction
suntrophos [4939; 793]
    bring, foster-brother
suntunchanō [4940; 793]
    come
sunupokrinomai [4942; 793]
    dissemble
sunupourgeō [4943; 793]
    help
surō [4951; 794]
    drag, draw, hale
surophoinikissa [(4949); 794]
    (or *surophunissa*),
    Syrophoenician
surtis [4950; 794]
    quicksands
suschēmatizō [4964; 795]
    conform, fashion
susparassō [4952; 794]
    grievously, tear
sussēmon [4953; 794]
    token
sussōmos [4954; 794]
    body
sustasiastēs [4955; 794]
    insurrection
sustatikos [4956; 795]
    commendation
sustauroō [4957; 795]
    crucify
sustellō [4958; 795]
    short, wind, wrap
sustenazō [4959; 795]
    groan
sustoicheō [4960; 795]
    answer
sustratiōtēs [4961; 795]
    soldier
sustrephō [4962; 795]
    gather
sustrophē [4963; 795]
    banded, concourse
su(n)zaō [4800; 775]
    live
su(n)zēteō [4802; 775]
    dispute, inquire, question,
    reason
suzētēsis [4803; 775]
    disputation, reasoning
suzētētēs [4804; 775]
    disputer
su(n)zeugnumi [4801; 775]
    join
su(n)zōopoieō [4806; 776]
    quicken
su(n)zugos [4805; 775]
    yoke-fellow

T

tacha [5029; 806]
  peradventure, perhaps
tachei (en) [5034*; 807]
  quickly, shortly, speedily
tacheion [5032; 806]
  quickly, shortly
tacheōs [5030; 806]
  hastily, quickly, shortly,
  suddenly
tachinos [5031; 807]
  shortly, swift, swiftly
tachista [5033; 807]
  speed
tachu [5035; 807]
  lightly, quickly
tachus [5036; 807]
  swift
tagma [5001; 802]
  order
taktos [5002; 803]
  set
talaipōreō [5003; 803]
  afflict
talaipōria [5004; 803]
  misery
talaipōros [5005; 803]
  wretched
talantiaios [5006; 803]
  talent
talanton [5007; 803]
  talent
talitha [5008; 803]
  talitha
tameion [5009; 803]
  chamber
tapeinoō [5013; 804]
  abase, humble, low
tapeinophrōn [5011 and 5424;
  804] courteous, humble-
  minded
tapeinophrosunē [5012; 804]
  humbleness, humility,
  lowliness
tapeinos [5011; 804]
  base, cast, degree, estate,
  humble, low, lowly
tapeinōsis [5014; 805]
  estate, humiliation, low
  (estate)
taphē [5027; 806]
  burial
taphos [5028; 806]
  sepulchre, tomb
tarachē [5016; 805]
  trouble
tarachos [5017; 805]
  stir
tarassō [5015; 805]
  trouble
tartaroō [5020; 805]
  hell

tassō [5021; 805]
  appoint, determine, ordain,
  set
tauros [5022; 806]
  ox
taxis [5010; 803]
  order
technē [5078; 814]
  art, craft, trade
technitēs [5079; 814]
  builder, craftsman
teichos [5038; 808]
  wall
tekmērion [5039; 808]
  proof
teknion [5040; 808]
  child
teknogoneō [5041; 808]
  children
teknogonia [5042; 808]
  child-bearing
teknon [5043; 808]
  child, daughter, son
teknotropheō [5044; 808]
  children
tēkō [5080; 814]
  melt
tektōn [5045; 809]
  carpenter
tēlaugōs [5081; 814]
  clearly
teleioō [5048; 809]
  accomplish, consecrate, do,
  finish, fulfill, perfect
teleios [5046; 809]
  age, man, perfect
teleiōs [5049; 810]
  end, perfectly
teleiōsis [5050; 810]
  fulfillment, perfection
teleioteros [5046*; 809*]
  perfect
teleiotēs [5047; 809]
  perfection, perfectness
teleiōtēs [5051; 810]
  finisher
teleō [5055; 810]
  accomplish, end, expire, fill,
  finish, fulfill, go, pay,
  perform
telesphoreō [5052; 810]
  perfection
teleutaō [5053; 810]
  decease, die
teleutē [5054; 810]
  death
tēlikoutos [5082; 814]
  great, mighty
telōnēs [5057; 812]
  publican
telōnion [5058; 812]
  custom (toll)

telos [5056; 811]
  continual, custom (toll), end,
  ending, finally, uttermost
tephroō [5077; 814]
  ashes
teras [5059; 812]
  wonder
tēreō [5083; 814]
  charge, hold, keep, keeper,
  observe, preserve, reserve,
  watch
tērēsis [5084; 815]
  hold, keeping, prison, ward
tessarakonta [5062; 813]
  forty
tessarako ntaetēs [5063; 813]
  forty (years)
tessares [5064; 813]
  four
tessareskaidekatos [5065; 813]
  fourteenth
tetartaios [5066; 813]
  four
tetartos [5067; 813]
  four, fourth
tetra(a)rcheō [5075; 814]
  tetrarch
tetra(a)rchēs [5076; 814]
  tetrarch
tetradion [5069; 813]
  quaternion
tetragōnos [5068; 813]
  foursquare
tetrakischilioi [5070; 813]
  thousand
tetrakosia [5071; 813]
  four hundred
tetramēnos [5072; 813]
  months
tetraplous [5073; 813]
  fourfold
tetrapous [5074; 814]
  beast, fourfooted
thalassa [2281; 350]
  sea
thalpō [2282; 350]
  cherish
thambeō [2284; 350]
  amaze
thambos [2285; 350]
  amazement, wonder
thanasimos [2286; 350]
  deadly
thanatēphoros [2287; 350]
  deadly
thanatoō [2289; 351]
  dead, death, kill, mortify
thanatos [2288; 350]
  death
thaptō [2290; 351]
  bury
tharreō [2292; 352]
  bold, boldly, confident,
  confidence, courage

tharseō [2293; 352]
  cheer, comfort
tharsos [2294; 352]
  courage
thauma [2295; 352]
  marvel, wonder
thaumasios [2297; 352]
  wonderful (thing)
thaumastos [2298; 352]
  marvel, marvelous
thaumazō [2296; 352]
  marvel, wonder
thea [2299; 353]
  goddess
theaomai [2300; 353]
  behold, look, see
theatrizō [2301; 353]
  gazingstock
theatron [2302; 353]
  spectacle, theatre
theiōdēs [2306; 354]
  brimstone
theion [2303; 353]
  brimstone
theios [2304; 353]
  divine
theiotēs [2305; 354]
  Divinity
thēkē [2336; 360]
  sheath
thēlazō [2337; 360]
  suck, suckling
thēleia [2338**; 360]
  woman
thelēma [2307; 354]
  desire, pleasure, will
thelēsis [2308; 354]
  will
thelō [2309; 354]
  desire, disposed, fain,
  forward (be), intend, list,
  love, pleased, rather,
  unwilling, voluntary, will,
  willing, wish, would
thēlus [2338; 360]
  female, woman
themelioō [2311; 356]
  found, grounded, settle
themelios [2310; 355]
  foundation
theodidaktos [2312; 356]
  taught
theomacheō [2313; 356]
  fight
theomachos [2314; 356]
  fighting
theopneustos [2315; 356]
  inspiration
theōreō [2334; 360]
  behold, consider, look,
  perceive, see
theōria [2335; 360]
  sight

theos [2316; 356]
  God, godly
theosebeia [2317; 358]
  godliness
theosebēs [2318; 358]
  worshipper
theostugēs [2319; 358]
  hateful, hater
theotēs [2320; 358]
  Divinity
thēra [2339; 360]
  trap
therapeia [2322; 358]
  healing, household
therapeuō [2323; 359]
  cure, heal, worship
therapōn [2324; 359]
  servant
thēreuō [2340; 360]
  catch
thēriomacheō [2341; 360]
  fight
thērion [2342; 361]
  beast
therismos [2326; 359]
  harvest
theristēs [2327; 359]
  reaper
therizō [2325; 359]
  reap
thermainō [2328; 359]
  warm
thermē [2329; 359]
  heat
therso [2330; 359]
  summer
thēsaurizō [2343; 361]
  lay, store, treasure
thēsauros [2344; 361]
  treasure
thinganō [2345; 361]
  handle, touch
thlibō [2346; 362]
  afflict, narrow, press,
  straitened, throng,
  tribulation, trouble
thlipsis [2347; 362]
  afflict, affliction, anguish,
  burdened, distress,
  persecution, tribulation,
  trouble
thnēskō [2348; 362]
  die
thnētos [2349; 362]
  mortal, mortality
thōrax [2382; 367]
  breastplate
thorubazō [2351d; 362]
  trouble
thorubeō [2350; 362]
  ado, noise, trouble, tumult,
  uproar
thorubos [2351; 363]
  tumult, uproar

thrauō [2352; 363]
  bruise
thremma [2353; 363]
  cattle
thrēneō [2354; 363]
  bewail, mourn, wail
thrēnos [2355; 363]
  lamentation
thrēskeia [2356; 363]
  religion, worship
thrēskos [2357; 363]
  religious
thriambeuō [2358; 363]
  cause, lead, triumph
thrix [2359; 363]
  hair
throeō [2360; 364]
  trouble
thrombos [2361; 364]
  drop
thronos [2362; 364]
  seat, throne
thuella [2366; 365]
  tempest
thugatēr [2364; 364]
  daughter
thugatrion [2365; 365]
  daughter
thuïnos [2367; 365]
  thyine (wood)
thumiama [2368; 365]
  incense, odor
thumiaō [2370; 365]
  incense
thumiatērion [2369; 365]
  censer
thumomacheō [2371; 365]
  displease
thumoō [2373; 365]
  wroth (be)
thumos [2372; 365]
  anger, fierceness, indignation,
  wrath
thuō [2380; 367]
  kill, sacrifice, slay
thura [2374; 365]
  door, gate
thureos [2375; 366]
  shield
thuris [2376; 366]
  window
thurōros [2377; 366]
  door, porter
thusia [2378; 366]
  sacrifice
thusiastērion [2379; 366]
  altar
tiktō [5088; 816]
  beget, bear, bring, deliver,
  travail, usury
tillō [5089; 817]
  pluck
timaō [5091; 817]
  esteem, honor, price, value

timē [5092; 817]
    honor, precious, price, sum,
    value
timios [5093; 818]
    costly, dear, honorable,
    precious, reputation
timiotēs [5094; 818]
    costliness
timōreō [5097; 818]
    punish
timōria [5098; 818]
    punishment
tinō [5099; 818]
    punish
tis, ti (1) [5100; 819]
    certain, every, he, kind, man,
    manner, one, some,
    somebody, someone,
    something, somewhat
tis, ti (2) [5101; 818]
    what, whatever, which, who,
    whom
tithēmi [5087; 815]
    appoint, bow (verb),
    commit, conceive, give, lay,
    make, ordain, purpose, put,
    set, settle, sink
titlos [5102; 820]
    superscription, title
toichos [5109; 821]
    wall
toigaroun [5105; 821]
    wherefore
toinun [5106; 821]
    then
toioutos [5108; 821]
    fellow, such as
tokos [5110; 821]
    interest, usury
tolmaō [5111; 821]
    bold, dare
tolmēroterōs (-on) [5112; 822]
    boldly
tolmētēs [5113; 822]
    daring
tomos [5114*; 822]
    sharp
tomōteros [5114; 822*]
    sharper
topazion [5116; 822]
    topaz
topos [5117; 822]
    everywhere, opportunity,
    place, quarter, rocky, room,
    way
tosoutos [5118; 823]
    great, long, many, much
tote [5119; 823]
    then, time
tounantion [5121; 824]
    contrariwise
toxon [5115; 822]
    bow (noun)

trachēlizō [5136; 824]
    lay
trachēlos [5137; 825]
    neck
trachus [5138; 825]
    rocky, rough
tragos [5131; 824]
    goat
trapeza [5132; 824]
    bank, meat, table
trapezitēs [5133; 824]
    banker
trauma [5134; 824]
    wound
traumatizō [5135; 824]
    wound
trechō [5143; 825]
    course, run, rush
treis [5140; 825]
    three
tremō [5141; 825]
    tremble
trephō [5142; 825]
    bring, feed, nourish
triakonta [5144; 826]
    thirty, thirtyfold
triakosioi [5145; 826]
    three hundred
tribolos [5146; 826]
    thistle
tribos [5147; 826]
    path
trichinos [5155; 827]
    hair
trietia [5148; 826]
    year
trimēnos [5150**; 826]
    months
tris [5151; 826]
    thrice
trischilioi [5153; 826]
    thousand
tristegos [5152; 826]
    story
tritos [5154; 826]
    third, thirdly
trizō [5149; 826]
    gnash, grind
trochia [5163; 828]
    path
trochos [5164; 828]
    course, wheel
trōgō [5176; 829]
    eat
tromos [5156; 827]
    trembling
tropē [5157; 827]
    turning
trophē [5160; 827]
    food, meat
trophos [5162; 827]
    nurse
tropophoreō [5159; 827]
    bear, manner, suffer

tropos [5158; 827]
    conversation, even as,
    manner, means, way
trublion [5165; 828]
    dish
trugaō [5166; 828]
    gather
trugōn [5167; 828]
    dove
trumalia [5168; 828]
    eye
trupēma [5169; 828]
    eye
truphaō [5171; 828]
    delicately (live), pleasure
truphē [5172; 828]
    delicately, revel, riot
tuchōn [5177*; 829]
    special
tumpanizō [5178; 829]
    torture
tunchanō [5177; 829]
    attain, chance, common,
    enjoy, may, obtain
tuphloō [5186; 831]
    blind
tuphlos [5185; 830]
    blind
tuphō [5188; 831]
    smoke
tuphōnikos [5189; 831]
    tempestuous
tuphoō [5187; 831]
    high minded, pride, proud,
    puff (up), smoke
tupos [5179; 829]
    ensample, example, fashion,
    figure, form, manner, pattern,
    print
tuptō [5180; 830]
    beat, smite, strike, wound
turbazō [5182; 830]
    trouble

X

xenia [3578; 547]
    lodging
xenizō [3579; 547]
    entertain, lodge, strange
xenodocheō [3580; 548]
    stranger
xenos [3581; 548]
    host (of guests), strange,
    stranger
xērainō [3583; 548]
    dry, over-ripe, pine away,
    ripe, wither
xēros [3584; 548]
    dry, land, withered
xestēs [3582; 548]
    pot

xulinos [3585; 549]
    wood
xulon [3586; 549]
    staff, stocks, tree, wood
xuraō [3587; 549]
    shave

Z

zaō [2198; 336]
    lifetime, live, lively, living
zēloō [2206; 338]
    affect, covet, desire, earnestly,
    envy, jealous, seek, zealously
zēlos [2205; 337]
    envy, fervent, fierceness,
    indignation, jealousy, zeal
zēlōtēs [2207; 338]
    zealous

zēmia [2209; 338]
    loss
zēmioō [2210; 338]
    cast, forfeit, lose, loss, receive
zeō [2204; 337]
    fervent
zestos [2200; 337]
    hot
zētēma [223; 339]
    question
zēteō [2212; 338]
    about, desire, endeavor, go,
    inquire, require, seek
zētēsis [2214; 339]
    disputation, inquire, question
zeugos [2201; 337]
    pair, yoke
zeuktēria [2202; 337]
    band
zizanion [2215; 339]
    tares

zōē [2222; 340]
    life
zōgreō [2221; 340]
    captive, catch
zōnē [2223; 341]
    bag, girdle
zōnnumi [2224; 341]
    gird
zōogoneō [2225; 341]
    live, preserve, quicken
zōon [2226; 341]
    beast, creature
zōopoieō [2227; 341]
    life, quicken
zophos [2217; 339]
    blackness, darkness, mist
zugos [2218; 339]
    balance, pair, yoke
zumē [2219; 340]
    leaven
zumoō [2220; 340]
    leaven

TOPICAL INDEX

Introduction

The Topical Index to *Vine's Complete Expository Dictionary of Old and New Testament Words* enables you to find, in a single location, a comprehensive list of the Hebrew and Greek words that *Vine's* treats that are pertinent to the specific topic listed. This unique Index thus saves you time and will identify many more entries pertinent to the topics many users are studying than they would identify without the benefit of this exclusive tool. Because the Topical Index is thorough and generously cross-referenced, you can now mine the riches of *Vine's* careful definitions and insightful comments more thoroughly and completely than ever before.

Entries are arranged under twelve subject headings (see below) and numerous subdivisions. At the beginning of most of the subdivisions stands a summary of the words included (see, for example, the summary at the subdivision **General Revelation,** p. 2). The summary is followed by an *alphabetical* listing of the pertinent English entries from *Vine's,* beneath which are listed the Strong's numbers (where available), the transliterations of the Hebrew and Greek into English characters, and the *Vine's* page numbers. **Note that Strong's numbers in** regular type **refer to the Old Testament portion of** *Vine's* (for example, 1396). **But Strong's numbers in** *italic type* **refer to the New Testament portion of** *Vine's* (for example, *1396*).

The twelve subject headings (with beginning page numbers) follow:

REVELATION, p. 2   HUMAN BEINGS, p. 21
GOD, p. 3   SIN, p. 31
JESUS CHRIST, p. 6   SALVATION, p. 37
THE HOLY SPIRIT, p. 13   THE LIFE OF THE BELIEVER, p. 41
CREATION, p. 14   THE PEOPLE OF GOD, p. 50
SUPERNATURAL BEINGS, p. 20   THE FUTURE, p. 60

Following these and concluding the Index is a listing of General and Function words, such as pronouns and number words that, apart from specific uses with other words, convey little theological or expository content.

Suggestions for Use

1. First look up the word or concept in the main portions of *Vine's*. For example, we could look up "atonement" in both the Old Testament portion (p. 10) and in the New Testament portion (pp. 43–44).

2. If we did not know already, the comments in these entries would help us identify SIN and SALVATION as likely places to consult within the Topical Index.

3. We examine both of those for direct references to "atonement." By reading the comments at the beginning of the SIN subject heading (see p. 31), we discover that "atonement" is not listed here, although we may wish to examine the entries for the many terms directly related to "sin," which is the reason people need atonement.

4. By reading the comments at the beginning of the SALVATION subject heading (see p. 37), we discover many entries worth investigating: First we find a whole subdivision treating "atonement" in the Old Testament that lists pertinent entries such as "ALTAR," "TO ATONE, ATONEMENT," "BLOOD," "CONTINUAL, CONTINUALLY," "TO KILL," "OFFERING," and so forth. *Each entry will refer us to a discussion of one or more biblical words that relates directly to "atonement."* Here we discover the great benefit of this Topical Index: It pulls together a whole host of important words and entries from *Vine's* that we might not know how to compile on our own or, if we could compile it, it would take far more time than it takes to locate the list we want in a single place in the Topical Index.

Beyond this initial subdivision on atonement in the Old Testament, we find another subdivision concerning the atoning death of Jesus Christ (see p. 38). There is yet another host of important terms we may wish to explore. Note that in both subdivisions important *cross-references* are also displayed, encouraging us to continue our targeted research in even other areas.

5. Once we have identified subdivisions where the word or concept we wish to study is located, we look up as many discussions of specific words in *Vine's* as we wish to. We keep in mind that words listed with a Strong's number in regular type (for example, 1396) are discussed in the Old Testament portion, while words listed with a Strong's number in *italic type* (for example, *1396*) are found in the New Testament portion.

We discover that, with the Topical Index, *Vine's* yields up more of its treasured careful definitions and insightful comments concerning our word or concept than we likely would have found without the Topical Index. *Vine's* has become a Bible study tool more valuable than ever before!

REVELATION

General Revelation

The *creation reveals (revelation)* the wisdom and power of its Creator, so that all humanity has a natural awareness *(know)* of God.

See also CREATION, THE NATURAL ORDER

CREATE, CREATION, CREATOR, CREATURE

A. Verbs
1254 bārā', p. 51
7069 qānāh, p. 52
6213 'āśāh, p. 52
ktizō, p. 137

B. Nouns
2937 ktisis, p. 137
2938 ktisma, p. 137
2939 ktistēs, p. 137
2226 zōon, p. 137

KNOW, KNOWN, KNOWLEDGE

A. Verbs
1097 ginōskō, p. 346
1921 epiginōskō, p. 347

B. Adjective
1110 gnōstes, p. 348

REVEAL
601 apokaluptō, p. 531

REVELATION
602 apokalupsis, p. 532

Special Revelation

The Word of God

Scripture is the written *(to write)* and *inspired (sacred) word* of God. God *speaks* through the *books (to number, count)* of Scripture, both literally and figuratively *(allegory)*. His word is *active (pierce)* and *effectual*, *discerning* the thoughts and intentions of the heart.

All Scripture is *profitable* for teaching sound *doctrine*, for bringing *reproof, correction*, and for *instruction* in salvation through faith in Jesus Christ, who is himself the incarnate Word of God.

Believers are to be *doers*, rather than just *hearers* of the word, and are to feed *(eat; meditate; taste)* on God's word, allowing it to be *implanted* in their hearts.

See also JESUS CHRIST, NAMES AND TITLES OF

ACTIVE
1756 energēs, p. 12

ALLEGORY
238 allēgoreō, p. 22

BOOK
5612 sēper, p. 21
976 biblos, p. 74
975 biblion, p. 74
974 biblaridion, p. 74

CORRECTION
1882 epanorthōsis, p. 130

DISCERNING

C. Adjective
2924 kritikos, p. 171

DOCTRINE
1322 didachē, p. 180
1319 didaskalia, p. 180

DOER
4163 poiētēs, p. 180

TO EAT

A. Verb
398 'ākal, p. 67

EFFECTUAL

A. Adjective
1756 energēs, p. 194

HEARER
202 akroatēs, p. 296

IMPLANTED
1721 emphutos, p. 321

INSPIRATION OF GOD, INSPIRED BY GOD
2315 theopneustos, p. 328

INSTRUCTION

B. Noun
3809 paideia, p. 329

TO MEDITATE
1897 hāgāh, p. 150

TO NUMBER, COUNT

B. Noun
5612 sēper, p. 163

PIERCE
1338 diikneomai, p. 471

PROFITABLE

C. Adjective
5624 ōphelimos, p. 491

REPROOF, REPROVE

A. Noun
1650v elegmos, p. 527

B. Verb
1651 elenchō, p. 527

SACRED
2413 hieros, p. 543

SCRIPTURE
1124 graphē, p. 552
1121 gramma, p. 552

TO SPEAK

B. Noun
1697 dābār, p. 239

TASTE
1089 geuō, p. 619

WORD
3056 logos, p. 683
4487 rhema, p. 683

TO WRITE, WRITING

A. Verb
3789 kātab, p. 296

B. Noun
3791 kᵉtāb, p. 297

Prophecies, Miracles, and Visions

God *reveals (revelation)* himself in many ways, since it is impossible for people to discover him on their own *(mystery)*. He is revealed to a limited extent in the creation, but his person and nature are chiefly revealed through his Son, Jesus Christ, and through Scripture.

Revelation can *come* through *dreams, visions (to see, perceive; trance), oracles (load), signs, wonders,* and *miracles.* Or God may *appear* in theophanies in natural phenomena *(cloud; fire; bush),* in human form, or he may *speak* through *prophecy (foretell; to hear; to say, utter, affirm; prophesy).*

APPEAR, APPEARING

A. Verbs
5316 phainō, p. 31
2014 epiphainō, p. 31
398 anaphainō, p. 31
5319 phaneroō, p. 31
1718 emphanizō, p. 32
3700 optomai, p. 32
3700 optanō, p. 32

B. Nouns
602 apokalupsis, p. 32
2015 epiphaneia, p. 32

BUSH
942 batos, p. 84

CLOUD
6051 'ānān, p. 38
3509 nephos, p. 107
3507 nephelē, p. 107

TO COME
935 bô', p. 39

DREAM, DREAMER

A. Nouns
2472 ḥalôm, p. 62
3677 onar, p. 184
1798 enupnion, p. 184

B. Verbs
2492 ḥālam, p. 62
1797 enupniazō, p. 184

FIRE
784 'ēš, p. 82

FORETELL
4302 prolegō, p. 249

TO HEAR

B. Noun
8052 šᵉmû'āh, p. 108

LOAD
4853 maśśā', p. 139

MIRACLE
1411 dunamis, p. 412
4592 sēmeion, p. 412

MYSTERY
3466 mustērion, p. 424

ORACLE
3051 logion, p. 449

PROPHECY, PROPHESY, PROPHESYING

A. Nouns
5030 nābî', p. 190
4394 prophēteia, p. 492

B. Adjective
4397 prophētikos, p. 492

C. Verbs
5012 nābā', p. 190
4395 prophēteuo, p. 492

REVEAL
601 apokaluptō, p. 531
5537 chrēmatizo, p. 532

REVELATION
602   apokalupsis, p. 532

TO SAY, UTTER, AFFIRM

A. Verb
5002   neʾum, p. 216

B. Noun
5002   neʾum, p. 217

TO SEE, PERCEIVE

B. Noun
7203   rōʾeh, p. 219

SIGN
226   ʾôt, p. 229
4592   sēmeion, p. 575

TO SPEAK

A. Verb
1696   dābar, p. 239

B. Noun
1697   dābār, p. 239

TRANCE
1611   ekstasis, p. 639

VISION

A. Nouns
2377   ḥāzôu, p. 277
2384   ḥizzāyôn, p. 277
3705   horama, p. 662
3706   horasis, p. 662
3701   optasia, p. 662

B. Verb
2372   ḥāzāh, p. 277

WONDER

A. Nouns
4159   môpēt, p. 293
5059   teras, p. 682
2285   thambos, p. 682

Numbers

Some numbers that appear in Scripture have a special theological significance. God is *one*, and this denotes unity. *Three* is associated primarily with the doctrine of the Trinity, but also with periods of significant divine activity (*third* day, etc.). *Seven* (*seventh; seven times; seventy*) expresses completeness and perfection, while *six* (*sixth; sixty*) on the other hand, suggests incompleteness. The number *twelve* (*twelfth*) is suggestive of divine administration, and *forty* is used in Scripture in circumstances suggesting probation, separation, or judgment. (As with other entries, these are arranged an alphabetical, not numerical, sequence.)

FORTY
5062   tessarakonta, p. 253

ONE

A. Numeral
1520   heis, p. 446

SEVEN
2033   hepta, p. 565

SEVENTH
1442   hebdomos, p. 565

SEVEN TIMES
2034   heptakis, p. 565

SEVENTY
1440   hebdomēkonta, p. 565

SEVENTY TIMES
1441   hebdomēkontakis, p. 566

SIX
1803   hex, p. 579

SIXTH
1623   hektos, p. 579

SIXTY, SIXTYFOLD
1835   hexēkonta, p. 580

THREE
5143   treis, p. 631

TWELFTH
1428   dōdekatos, p. 648

TWELVE
1427   dōdeka, p. 648

GOD

Names and Titles Of

The *names* and titles of *God* reflect the greatness of his being and nature. In titles denoting his greatness, he is the *Almighty;* the first *(former);* the Most *High* *(to come up, ascend; highest);* the *Lord;* the Lord of Hosts *(Sabaoth);* the *Holy* One; the living God *(live);* the *Lawgiver.* In terms of his relationship with his people, he is *Father* and *Abba;* and in titles which reflect his activity, he is the *Redeemer;* the *Husbandman;* the *Maker* and *Author* of life. His character is shown in titles such as the *Amen* and the *stone (rock)* of Israel.

See also CREATION, THE NATURAL ORDER

ABBA
5   abba, p. 1

ALMIGHTY
3841   pantokratōr, p. 22

AMEN
281   amēn, p. 25

AUTHOR
159   aitios, p. 45
747   archēgos, p. 45

TO COME UP, ASCEND

B. Noun
5945   ʾelyôn, p. 41

FATHER

A. Nouns
1   ʾāb, p. 78
3962   patēr, p. 228

FORMER
7223   rišôn, p. 87

GOD
410   ʾēl, p. 96
426   ʾĕlāh, p. 96
433   ʾĕlôah, p. 97
410,
7706   ʾēl šadday, p. 97
410,
5769   ʾēl ʿōlām, p. 98
2316   theos, p. 271

HIGH, HIGHLY

A. Adjectives
1364   gābōah, p. 111
5308   hupsēlos, p. 304
5310   hupsistos, p. 304

B. Nouns
5311   hupsos, p. 304
5313   hupsōma, p. 304

HIGHEST
5310   hupsistos, p. 304

HOLY

A. Adjective
6918   qādôš, p. 113

HUSBANDMAN
1092   geōrgos, p. 315

LAWGIVER
3550   nomothetēs, p. 357

TO LIVE

C. Adjective
2416   ḥay, p. 138

LORD
113   ʾādôn *or* ʾădōnāy, p. 140
3068   yᵉhwāh, p. 140

MAKER
1217   dēmiourgos, p. 387

NAME

A. Nouns
8034   šēm, p. 158
3686   onoma, p. 425

B. Verbs
3687   onomazō, p. 425
2028   eponomazō, p. 426
4316   prosagoreuō, p. 426

REDEEM

A. Verb
1350   gāʾal, p. 194

ROCK
6697   ṣûr, p. 208

SABAOTH
4519   sabaōth, p. 542

STONE
68   ʾeben, p. 246

Character and Attributes Of

The *everlasting, invisible (spiritual), immutable (shadow; stand),* and one *true* God dwells in unapproachable *(approach) light* and *splendor. Honor, glory, majesty (magnificence; to be marvelous; noble),* and *power (ability; great; greatness; might; strong)* are due to his name. He is magnified *(magnify)* and highly *exalted (pride),* and his *manifold wisdom (wise)* is *unsearchable (deep).* He is *life* and bestows life.

His character and *will* are *perfect, complete,* and *divine.* He is *gracious (grace), kind, merciful (rich), compassionate,* and completely trustworthy *(to believe).* He shows his *love (loving-kindness)* and *faithfulness* to all. He is not *forgetful* or *slack,* and *knows* all things *(heart; foreknow, foreknowledge).* His *rule (reign; throne)* is *righteous (righteousness)* and *just.* His *burning anger (to be wroth; wrath)* is provoked because he is zealous *(to be jealous)* for his *holiness (fire; holy).*

ABILITY, ABLE
A. Nouns
1411   dunamis, p. 2
2479   ischus, p. 2

ANGER, BURNING
B. Noun
2740   ḥārôn, p. 5

APPROACH
B. Adjective
676   aprositos, p. 35

TO BELIEVE
A. Verb
539   'āman, p. 15

B. Nouns
530   'ĕmûnāh, p. 16
571   'ĕmet, p. 16

TO HAVE COMPASSION, BE MERCIFUL
A. Verbs
7355   rāḥam, p. 43
3627   oikteirō, p. 116

B. Nouns
7358   reḥem, p. 43
7356   raḥămîm, p. 43

C. Adjective
7349   raḥûm, p. 44

TO COMPLETE
A. Verb
7999   šālam, p. 44

B. Adjective
8003   šālēm, p. 44

DEEP, DEEPNESS, DEPTH
A. Noun
899   bathos, p. 154

DIVINE
A. Adjective
2304   theios, p. 178

EVER, EVERLASTING
5769   'ôlām, p. 72

TO BE EXALTED
A. Verb
7311   rûm, p. 73

B. Noun
4791   mārôm, p. 74

FAITHFULNESS
A. Noun
530   'ĕmûnāh, p. 75

FIRE
A. Noun
4442   pur, p. 239

FOREKNOW, FOREKNOWLEDGE
A. Verb
4267   proginōskō, p. 249

B. Noun
4268   prognōsis, p. 249

FORGET
A. Verb
1950   epilanthanomai, p. 250

GLORY
A. Nouns
8597   tip'eret, p. 92
1391   doxa, p. 267

B. Verb
6286   pā'ar, p. 93

GOOD, GOODNESS
A. Adjectives
2896   ṭôb, p. 99
18   agathos, p. 273
5543   chrēstos, p. 274

B. Noun
5544   chrēstotēs, p. 274

D. Verb
14   agathourgeo, p. 275

GRACE
5485   charis, p. 277

TO BE GRACIOUS, SHOW FAVOR
A. Verb
2603   ḥānan, p. 100

B. Noun
2580   ḥēn, p. 101

C. Adjective
2587   ḥannûn, p. 101

GREAT
3173   megas, p. 279

GREATNESS
3174   megethos, p. 280

HEART
2589   kardiognōstēs, p. 297

HOLINESS, HOLY
A. Noun
41   hagiotēs, p. 307

B. Adjectives
6918   qādôš, p. 113
40   hagios, p. 307
3741   hosios, p. 308

TO HONOR
B. Noun
3519   kābôd, p. 114

IMMUTABLE, IMMUTABILITY
276   ametathetos, p. 320

INVISIBLE
517   aoratos, p. 331

TO BE JEALOUS, ZEALOUS
A. Verb
7065   qānā', p. 124

B. Noun
7068   qin'āh, p. 125

C. Adjective
7067   qannā', p. 125

JUST, JUSTLY
A. Adjectives
1342   dikaios, p. 338
1738   endikos, p. 338

B. Adverb
1346   dikaiōs, p. 338

KIND, KINDNESS
A. Adjective
5543   chrēstos, p. 343

B. Verb
5541   chrēsteuomai, p. 343

C. Nouns
5544   chrēstotēs, p. 343
5363   philanthrōpia, p. 343

KNOW, KNOWN, KNOWLEDGE
A. Verbs
1097   ginōskō, p. 346
1492   oida, p. 346
4267   proginōskō, p. 347

C. Nouns
1108   gnōsis, p. 348
1922   epignōsis, p. 348

LIFE
A. Noun
2222   zōē, p. 367

LIVE
2198   zaō, p. 374

LIGHT
A. Noun
5457   phōs, p. 369

LOVE
A. Verbs
25   agapaō, p. 381
5368   phileō, p. 382

B. Nouns
26   agapē, p. 382
5363   philanthrōpia, p. 382

LOVING-KINDNESS
A. Noun
2617   ḥesed, p. 142

B. Adjective
2623   ḥāsîd, p. 143

MAGNIFICENCE
3168   megaleiotēs, p. 386

TO MAGNIFY
A. Verb
1431   gādal, p. 143

B. Nouns
1420   geḏûllāh, p. 144
1433   gōdel, p. 144

C. Adjective
1419   gādôl, p. 144

MAJESTY
3172   megalōsunē, p. 386

MANIFOLD
4182   polupoikilos, p. 390

TO BE MARVELOUS
A. Verb
6381   pālā', p. 149

B. Noun
6382   pele', p. 149

MERCIFUL, MERCY
A. Nouns
1656   eleos, p. 403
3628   oiktirmos, p. 404

B. Verbs
1653   eleeō, p. 404
3627   oikteirō, p. 404
2433   hilaskomai, p. 404

C. Adjectives

1655 eleēmōn, p. 404

3629 oiktirmōn, p. 404

2436 hileōs, p. 405

MIGHT

1369 gᵉbûrāh, p. 151

NOBLE

A. Noun

117 'addîr, p. 161

B. Adjective

117 'addîr, p. 161

C. Verb

639 'ap, p. 161

PERFECT

A. Adjectives

5049 teleios, p. 466

5046* teleioteros, p. 466

POWER

3581 kōaḥ, p. 183

1411 dunamis, p. 478

1849 exousia, p. 479

PRIDE

A. Verb

1342 gā'āh, p. 187

B. Noun

1347 gā'ôn, p. 187

REIGN

936 basileuō, p. 518

RICH

A. Adjective

4145 plousios, p. 533

RIGHTEOUS, RIGHTEOUSLY

A. Adjective

1342 dikaios, p. 534

B. Adverb

1346 dikaiōs, p. 535

RIGHTEOUSNESS

1343 dikaiosunē, p. 535

TO RULE

4910 māšal, p. 208

SHADOW

644 aposkiasma, p. 566

SLACK, SLACKNESS

A. Verb

1019 bradunō, p. 580

B. Noun

1022 bradutēs, p. 580

SPIRITUAL

A. Adjective

4152 pneumatikos, p. 594

B. Adverb

4153 pneumatikōs, p. 595

SPLENDOR

1935 hôd, p. 242

STAND

A. Verb

5975 'āmad, p. 243

STRONG

A. Adjective

2478 ischuros, p. 605

THRONE

3678 kissē', p. 262

TRUE, TRUTH

A. Adjective

228 alēthinos, p. 645

C. Noun

225 alētheia, p. 645

UNSEARCHABLE

419 anexeraunētos, p. 653

421 anexichniastos, p. 653

WILL, WOULD

A. Noun

2307 thelēma, p. 676

C. Verb

2309 thelō, p. 676

WISDOM

4678 sophia, p. 678

WISE

4680 sophos, p. 679

WRATH

A. Noun

2534 ḥēmāh, p. 296

TO BE WROTH, ANGRY

A. Verb

7107 qāṣap, p. 297

B. Noun

7110 qeṣep, p. 298

Works of God

God's mighty works can be seen throughout history: in the nation of Israel, in the ministry of Jesus Christ, and in the church. He *prospers (wealth)* his people, giving them *peace, security,* and *blessing (blessed; to be gracious, show favor; liberally)*. He *shepherds* them with care *(wing)* and *heals* the sick. His work is like that of a *potter* shaping the *clay.*

When his people are unfaithful, they come under his judgment *(to judge)*, but he does not *forget* them; and when they cry out to him, he *forgives* their sin and *redeems* them, *helping* them *(to go out, go forth; hero; to stretch out)* against their enemies *(avenge)*.

His saving *(to save)* and delivering *(to deliver)* work is seen supremely in his sending Jesus Christ to die for the sins of the world.

See also **CREATION**, THE NATURAL ORDER, GOD'S PROVIDENCE; **HUMAN BEINGS, THEIR CREATION AND FALL; THE PEOPLE OF GOD**, LIFE OF THE PEOPLE OF GOD; **THE FUTURE**, JUDGMENT.

AVENGE, AVENGER

A. Verbs

5358 nāqam, p. 10

1556 ekdikeō, p. 46

B. Nouns

5359 nāqām, p. 11

1558 ekdiktos, p. 46

1557 ekdikēsis, p. 46

BLESSED

835 'ašrê, p. 19

BLESSING

1293 bᵉrākāh, p. 18

CLAY

4081 pēlos, p. 103

TO DELIVER

A. Verb

3467 yāšaʻ, p. 57

B. Nouns

3444 yᵉšûʻāh, p. 57

3468 yēšaʻ, p. 58

8668 tᵉšûʻāh, p. 58

FAVOR

A. Noun

7522 rāṣôn, p. 79

B. Verb

7521 rāṣāh, p. 79

TO FORGET

7911 šākaḥ, p. 86

TO FORGIVE

5545 sālaḥ, p. 86

TO GO OUT, GO FORTH

A. Verb

3318 yāṣa', p. 95

TO BE GRACIOUS, SHOW FAVOR

A. Verb

2603 ḥānan, p. 100

B. Noun

2580 ḥēn, p. 101

C. Adjective

2587 ḥannûn, p. 101

TO HEAL

7495 rāpā', p. 107

TO HELP

5826 'āzar, p. 110

HERO

A. Noun

1368 gibbôr, p. 110

TO JUDGE

A. Verb

8199 šāpaṭ, p. 125

B. Noun

4941 mišpāṭ, p. 126

LIBERALLY

574 haplōs, p. 366

PEACE

A. Noun

7965 šālôm, p. 173

B. Verb

7999 šālēm, p. 174

C. Adjective

8003 šālēm, p. 174

POTTER

A. Noun

2763 kerameus, p. 478

TO PROSPER

6743 ṣālēaḥ, p. 191

2137 euodoō, p. 495

TO REDEEM

A. Verbs

1350 gā'al, p. 194

6299 pādāh, p. 195

3722 kāpar, p. 195

JESUS CHRIST

TO SAVE
A. Verb
3467 yāša', p. 214
B. Noun
3444 yᵉšû'āh, p. 215
SECURITY
A. Noun
4009 mibṭāḥ, p. 218
B. Verb
982 bāṭaḥ, p. 218
C. Adjective
982 beṭaḥ, p. 218
D. Adverb
983 beṭaḥ, p. 218
SEND
649 apostellō, p. 560
3992 pempō, p. 560
1821 exapostellō, p. 560
TO SHEPHERD
A. Verb
7462 rā'āh, p. 227
B. Noun
7462 rō'ēh, p. 228
TO BE SICK
B. Noun
2483 ḥŏlî, p. 229
TO STRETCH OUT
A. Verb
5186 nāṭāh, p. 248
WEALTH
1952 hôn, p. 286
WING
3671 kānāp, p. 289

Anthropomorphisms
(words describing God using terms
applying to humans)

Although God is Spirit, he is described in Scripture in human terms as having bodily parts (*arm; ear; eye; face; finger; foot; hand; head; heart; nose; right hand*).

Human actions are also attributed to him: he has a *voice* and *speaks* and *answers*, and he *walks, rides, takes*

away, and *goes out*. He looks (*to overlay, spy*) to *see* things and *hides* his face.

He also experiences *pleasure (desire)* and *savors* the smell of acceptable sacrifices.

TO ANSWER
6030 'ānāh, p. 6
ARM
2220 zᵉrôa', p. 8
1023 brachiōn, p. 37
DESIRE
A. Noun
2107 eudokia, p. 161
EAR
A. Noun
241 'ōzen, p. 65
EYE
5869 'ayin, p. 74
FACE
6440 pānîm, p. 75
FINGER
1147 daktulos, p. 239
FOOT
7272 regel, p. 85
TO GO OUT, GO FORTH
A. Verb
3318 yāṣa', p. 95
HAND
3027 yād, p. 104
5495 cheir, p. 288
HEAD
A. Noun
7218 rō'š, p. 105
HEART
A. Noun
3820 lēb, p. 108
TO HIDE
5641 sātar, p. 111
NOSE
639 'ap, p. 161
TO OVERLAY, SPY
A. Verb
6822 ṣāpāh, p. 170

PLEASURE
A. Noun
2656 ḥēpeṣ, p. 179
B. Verb
2654 ḥāpēṣ, p. 179
C. Adjective
2655 ḥāpēṣ, p. 179
TO RIDE
7392 rākab, p. 204
RIGHT HAND
3225 yāmîn, p. 204
SAVOR
A. Noun
7381 rêaḥ, p. 215
B. Verb
7306 rûaḥ, p. 216
TO SAY, SPEAK, ANSWER
A. Verb
559 'āmar, p. 216
B. Noun
561 'ēmer, p. 216
TO SEE, PERCEIVE
A. Verb
7200 rā'āh, p. 219
TO TAKE AWAY
A. Verb
3947 lāqaḥ, p. 255
VOICE
6963 qôl, p. 277
5456 phōnē, p. 662
TO WALK
1980 hālak, p. 279
1704 emperipateō, p. 664

The Trinity

Christian doctrine declares that there is only one true God, whose one being subsists in *three* persons (*appearance*): God the Father, God the Son, and God the Holy Spirit.

APPEARANCE
A. Noun
1491 eidos, p. 32
THREE
5143 treis, p. 631

JESUS CHRIST

Names and Titles Of

A number of titles applied to Jesus Christ are related to his person and ministry. In his Messianic titles, he is the *Aforepromised;* the *Anointed One;* the *Messiah (Christ);* the *Son (Only Begotten; seed)* of God; *King* of the Jews; the *Lion* of Judah; the *Comforter;* the *Counsellor;* the *Prophet (prophesy);* the Suffering *Servant;* the *Lamb* of God; the High *Priest (great);* the *Dayspring (east)* and *Day-star.*

In terms of his preeminence and authority, he is *Lord; Head; Prince; Chief* Shepherd; Chief *Cornerstone;*

the *Word* of God; the *firstborn;* the *firstfruits;* the *forerunner.*

In his act of salvation, he is *Jesus; Savior;* the *surety* and *Mediator* of the new covenant; the *rock* and the *Author* of life.

In the "I am" sayings of John's Gospel, he is the *bread* of *life;* the *door;* the light (*clear*); the true *vine;* the *way* and the *truth (Amen),* and his disciples frequently called him their *Master (Rabbi; Rabboni)* and *Teacher,* and after his resurrection, *Maran-atha.*

AFOREPROMISED
4279 proepangellomai, p. 18

TO ANOINT
B. Noun
4899 māšîaḥ, p. 5
AMEN
281 amēn, p. 25
AUTHOR
159 aitios, p. 45
747 archēgos, p. 45
BREAD
740 artos, p. 77
CHIEF
B. Nouns
749 archiereus, p. 98
750 archipoimēn, p. 99
204 akrogōniaios, p. 99

7

Character and Attributes Of

CHRIST
5547 christos, p. 101

CLEAR
A. Verb
2929 krustallizō, p. 104

COMFORTER
A. Noun
3875 paraklētos, p. 111

CORNER, CORNERSTONE
1137 gōnia, p. 129

COUNSELLOR
3289 yō'ēs, p. 49

DAYSPRING
395 anatolē, p. 147

DAY-STAR
5459 phōsphoros, p. 147

DOOR
2374 thura, p. 181

EAST
395 anatole, p. 192

FIRST-BEGOTTEN, FIRSTBORN
4416 prōtotokos, p. 240

FIRSTFRUITS
536 aparchē, p. 241

FORERUNNER
4274 prodromos, p. 249

GREAT
3173 megas, p. 279

HEAD
2776 kephalē, p. 294

JESUS
2424 iēsous, p. 333

KING
A. Noun
935 basileus, p. 343

LAMB
721 arnion, p. 351
286 amnos, p. 351

LIFE, LIVING, LIFE-GIVING
A. Noun
2222 zōē, p. 367

C. Verb
2227 zōopoieo, p. 368

LION
3023 leōn, p. 373

LIVE
2198 zaō, p. 374

LORD, LORDSHIP
A. Nouns
2962 kurios, p. 379
1203 despotēs, p. 380

C. Adjective
2960 kuriakos, p. 380

MARAN-ATHA
3134 maran-atha, p. 393

MASTER
A. Nouns
1320 didaskalos, p. 395
2962 kurios, p. 395
1203 despotēs, p. 395
4461 rabbei, p. 396
1988 epistatēs, p. 396
2519 kathēgētēs, p. 396

MEDIATOR
3316 mesitēs, p. 400

MESSIAH
A. Nouns
4899 māšîaḥ, p. 150
4888 mišḥāh, p. 151

B. Verb
4886 māšaḥ, p. 151

ONLY BEGOTTEN
3439 monogenēs, p. 447

PRIEST
2409 hiereus, p. 486
749 archiereus, p. 486

PRINCE
747 archēgos, p. 487
758 archōn, p. 487

PROPHET
5030 nābî', p. 190
4396 prophētēs, p. 493

RABBI
4461 rabbei or rabbi, p. 504

RABBONI
4462 rabbounei or rabbōni, p. 504

ROCK
4073 petra, p. 537

SAVIOR
4990 sōtēr, p. 548

SEED
4690 sperma, p. 557

TO SERVE
B. Noun
5650 'ebed, p. 224

SON
5207 huios, p. 584

SURETY
1450 enguos, p. 612

TEACHER
1320 didaskalos, p. 619

TRUE, TRUTH
A. Adjective
228 alēthinos, p. 645

C. Noun
225 alētheia, p. 645

VINE
288 ampelos, p. 660

WAY
3598 hodos, p. 668

WORD
3056 logos, p. 683

Character and Attributes Of

In the *unspeakable* gift of his Son, God's *glory, righteousness,* and *holiness* are reflected. Jesus is the *image (effulgence)* of God, bearing his *divinity (prize; substance)* in human likeness *(fashion; form),* but *undefiled* by *sin.* His words and deeds *(ability)* show God's *love, gentleness, clemency,* and *patience,* and God's *merciful, compassionate (grieve; groan),* and *gracious* nature in action. Jesus also exhibited the *joy* and *gladness (glad),* as well as the *anger* of God in his ministry. Jesus accepted limited *knowledge* as a consequence

of his humanity, but his *mind* and *wisdom* showed his intimate relationship with his Father. He was completely *obedient* and *faithful (behove)* to his Father's will and *humbled* himself to death on the cross.

Christ's existence *(exist)* is from the *beginning.* His authority *(rule)* belongs to him by *right,* and he has *preeminence* over all things.

ABILITY
A. Noun
1411 dunamis, p. 2

ANGER
A. Noun
3709 orgē, p. 26

BEGINNING
B. Noun
746 archē, p. 58

BEHOVE
3784 opheilō, p. 60
1163 dei, p. 60

CLEMENCY
1932 epieikeia, p. 104

COMPASSION, COMPASSIONATE
A. Verbs
4697 splanchnizomai, p. 116
4834 sumpatheō, p. 116
1653 eleeō, p. 117
3356 metriopatheō, p. 117

DIVINITY
2305 theiotēs, p. 178

EFFULGENCE
541 apaugasma, p. 195

EXIST
5225 huparchō, p. 217

FAITHFUL
4103 pistos, p. 223

FASHION
A. Noun
4976 schēma, p. 227

FORM
3444 morphē, p. 251
1491 eidos, p. 252

GENTLENESS
B. Noun
1932 epieikeia, p. 263

GLAD
A. Verb
21 agalliaō, p. 266

GLADNESS
20 agalliasis, p. 267

GLORY, GLORIOUS
A. Noun
1391 doxa, p. 267

B. Adjective
1741 endoxos, p. 268

GRACIOUS
5543 chrēstos, p. 277

GRIEVE
B. Verb
4818 sunlupeō, p. 281

GROAN
A. Verb
1690 embrimaomai, p. 282

HOLINESS
A. Noun
42   hagiōsunē, p. 307

HUMBLE
A. Adjective
5011   tapeinos, p. 314

IMAGE
5481   charaktēr, p. 319

JOY
A. Noun
5479   chara, p. 335

KNOW, KNOWLEDGE
A. Verbs
1097   ginōskō, p. 346
1492   oida, p. 346

C. Nouns
1108   gnōsis, p. 348
1922   epignōsis, p. 348

LIKENESS
3667   homoiōma, p. 372

LOVE
A. Verbs
25   agapaō, p. 381
5368   phileō, p. 382

MERCIFUL
B. Verb
1653   eleeō, p. 404

C. Adjective
1655   eleēmōn, p. 404

MIND
A. Noun
3563   nous, p. 408

OBEDIENCE
A. Noun
5218   hupakoē, p. 438

PATIENCE
A. Noun
5281   hupomonē, p. 462

PREEMINENCE
4409   prōteuō, p. 482

PRIZE
725   harpagmos, p. 489

RIGHT
A. Noun
1849   exousia, p. 534

B. Adjectives
1342   dikaios, p. 534
2117   euthus, p. 534

RIGHTEOUSNESS
1343   dikaiosunē, p. 535

RULE
B. Verb
4165   poimaino, p. 540

SIN
A. Noun
266   hamartia, p. 576

SUBSTANCE
5287   hupostasis, p. 607

UNDEFILED
283   amiantos, p. 650

UNSPEAKABLE
411   anekdiēgētos, p. 654

WISDOM
4678   sophia, p. 678

His Work and Ministry

His Incarnation, Birth, and Childhood

God sent (send) his Son into the world. Jesus was conceived of the Holy Spirit and born of the virgin Mary. He arose from the line of Judah. At his birth, because there was no room at the inn (guest-chamber), Mary wrapped the baby in swaddling clothes and laid him in a manger. Jesus' appearing as a babe was accompanied by supernatural signs. Wise men following a star brought gifts of gold, frankincense, and myrrh.

As a boy growing up, Jesus was obedient to his parents and was apprenticed to the trade of Joseph, his father by law, as a carpenter.

APPEAR, APPEARING
A. Verb
5316   phainō, p. 31

B. Noun
2015   epiphaneia, p. 32

ARISE, AROSE
393   anatellō, p. 37

BABE
1025   brephos, p. 48

BORN
1080   gennaō, p. 57

BIRTH
1083   gennēsis, p. 67

BOY
3816   pais, p. 76

CARPENTER
5405   tektōn, p. 90

FRANKINCENSE
2030   libanos, p. 255

GOLD
A. Noun
5557   chrusos, p. 273

GUEST-CHAMBER
2646   kataluma, p. 285

MANGER
5336   phatnē, p. 389

MYRRH
A. Noun
4666   smurna, p. 423

PARENTS
1118   goneus, p. 458

SEND
649   apostellō, p. 560
3992   pempō, p. 560
1821   exapostellō, p. 560

STAR
792   astēr, p. 598

SWADDLING CLOTHES
4683   sparganoō, p. 612

VIRGIN
3933   parthenos, p. 661

VIRGINITY
3932   parthenia, p. 661

WISE
B. Noun
3097   magos, p. 679

His Baptism and Temptation

Jesus was baptized by John in the River Jordan (water) at the start of his public ministry. At his baptism, a voice from heaven affirmed Jesus as God's Son in whom the Father was well-pleased, and the Holy Spirit descended on him bodily in the appearance (form) of a dove.

After his baptism, Jesus was led by the Spirit into the wilderness, where he was tempted (tempt) by the Devil for forty days.

See also REVELATION, SPECIFIC REVELATION: NUMBERS

APPEARANCE
A. Noun
1491   eidos, p. 32

BAPTISM, BAPTIST, BAPTIZE
A. Nouns
908   baptisma, p. 50
910   baptistēs, p. 50

B. Verb
907   baptizō, p. 50

BODILY
B. Adjective
4984   sōmatikos, p. 72

DOVE
4058   peristera, p. 182

FORM
1491   eidos, p. 252

LEAD, LED
321   anagō, p. 359

PLEASING, WELL-PLEASING
A. Verb
2106   eudokeō, p. 474

TEMPT
A. Verbs
3985   peirazō, p. 621
1598   ekpeirazō, p. 622

TEMPTER
Note, p. 622

WATER
A. Noun
5204   hudōr, p. 668

His Teaching

The teaching of Jesus Christ centered on the kingdom of God. He taught the multitude of people who followed him in parables (allege) and sayings. The parables of the mustard seed, the talents, and the tares are examples of his teaching.

Privately with his disciples he explained the meaning of these parables because the keys of the kingdom had been given to them.

ALLEGE
3908   paratithēmi, p. 22

DISCIPLE
A. Nouns
3101   mathētēs, p. 171
3102   mathētria, p. 172
4827   summathētēs, p. 172

B. Verb
3100 mathēteuō, p. 172

KEY
2807 kleis, p. 341

KINGDOM
932 basileia, p. 344

MULTITUDE
3793 ochlos, p. 421
4128 plēthos, p. 421

MUSTARD
4615 sinapi, p. 423

PARABLE
3850 parabolē, p. 457
3942 paroimia, p. 457

PRIVATELY
B. Adverbial Phrase
2596, kat' idian, p. 488
2398

SAYING
3056 logos, p. 549
4487 rhēma, p. 549

TALENT
A. Noun
5007 talanton, p. 617

B. Adjective
5006 talantiaios, p. 617

TARES
2215 zizanion, p. 618

His Miracles

Jesus Christ demonstrated the coming of the kingdom of God in his *healing* ministry, showing by his miracles that he was a man *approved* of God. He performed many *miracles, curing* those who had *dropsy, leprosy (leper)* and *palsy,* giving *sight* to the *blind (spittle),* and setting *loose* those who were *bound* and *possessed* by *demons.* He *lay* hands on those with *fever, disease,* and *infirmity* and healed all those who were *sick* and *maimed (halt).* A *deaf* and *dumb (speechless)* man was set free with a single command *(ephphatha)* from his infirmity, and a woman with an *issue* of blood was healed simply by touching the *border* of his garment. Jesus also healed an *epileptic* and a blind beggar *(beg)* and *raised* the dead, among whom was the daughter of Jairus *(talitha),* and Lazarus *(grave-clothes).* He also demonstrated his authority over nature by walking on water, so that his disciples thought he was a ghost *(apparition),* and in a storm he *rebuked* the wind and the *waves* became *calm.*

APPARITION
5326 phantasma, p. 31

APPROVE, APPROVED
A. Verb
584 apodeiknumi, p. 36

BEG, BEGGARLY
A. Verbs
1871 epaiteō, p. 56
4319 prosaiteō, p. 56

B. Adjective
4434 ptōchos, p. 56

BLIND
B. Adjective
5185 tuphlos, p. 70

BORDER
2899 kraspedon, p. 74

BOUND
4029 perikeimai, p. 75

CALM
1055 galēnē, p. 87

CURE
A. Nouns
2392 iasis, p. 141
2323 therapeuō, p. 141

DEAF
2974 kōphos, p. 148

DEMON, DEMONIAC
1139 daimonizomai, p. 158

DISEASE, DISEASED
A. Nouns
769 astheneia, p. 172
3119 malakia, p. 172
3554 nosos, p. 172

B. Verbs
770 astheneō, p. 172
2190, echō kakōs, p. 172
2556

DROPSY
5203 hudrōpikos, p. 185

DUMB
A. Adjective
216 alalos, p. 187

EPHPHATHA
Note, p. 204

EPILEPTIC
4583 selēniazō, p. 204

FEVER
A. Noun
4446 puretos, p. 233

B. Verb
4445 puressō, p. 234

GRAVE-CLOTHES
2750 keiria, p. 279

HALT
5560 chōlos, p. 288

HEAL, HEALING
A. Verbs
2323 therapeuō, p. 295
2390 iaomai, p. 295
4982 sōzō, p. 295
1295 diasōzō, p. 295

B. Nouns
2322 therapeia, p. 295
2386 iama, p. 295
2392 iasis, p. 295

IMPEDIMENT
3424 mogilalos, p. 320

INFIRMITY
769 astheneia, p. 324

ISSUE
4511 rhusis, p. 332

LAY
2007 epitithēmi, p. 358

LEPER
3015 lepros, p. 364

LEPROSY
3014 lepra, p. 364

LOOSE
A. Verb
630 apoluō, p. 379

MAIMED
376 anapēros *or* anapeiros, p. 386
2948 kullos, p. 386

MIRACLE
1411 dunamis, p. 412
4592 sēmeion, p. 412

PALSY
A. Adjective
3885 paralutikos, p. 457

B. Verb
3886 paraluō, p. 457

POSSESS
1139 daimonizomai, p. 477

RAISE
1453 egeirō, p. 505

REBUKE
A. Verb
2008 epitimaō, p. 510

SICK, SICKLY, SICKNESS
A. Verbs
770 astheneō, p. 573
2577 kamnō, p. 573
4912 sunechō, p. 574

B. Adjectives
772 asthenēs, p. 574
732 arrhōstos, p. 574

C. Nouns
769 astheneia, p. 574
3554 nosos, p. 574

SIGHT
A. Noun
309 anablepsis, p. 574

B. Verb
308 anablepō, p. 575

SPEECHLESS
2974 kōphos, p. 592

SPITTLE
4427 ptusma, p. 595

TALITHA
5008 taleitha *or* talitha, p. 618

WAVE
2949 kuma, p. 668
2830 kludōn, p. 668

His Transfiguration

On the *mount* of Transfiguration, Peter, James, and John were *eyewitnesses* of the *glory* of Jesus Christ. He was *transfigured* before them *(fashion)* and his *clothing* was *shining* and *dazzling.* Moses and Elijah appeared talking with Jesus and then a *cloud* enveloped them and God's voice was heard. When the voice had *past* they were alone.

CLOTHING
2441 himatismos, p. 106

CLOUD
3507 nephelē, p. 107

DAZZLING
1823 exastraptō, p. 147

EYEWITNESS
845 autoptēs, p. 220
2030 epoptēs, p. 220

FASHION

A. Noun

1491   eidos, p. 227

GLORY

A. Noun

1391   doxa, p. 267

MOUNT, MOUNTAIN

3735   oros, p. 418

PAST

A. Verb

1096   ginomai, p. 462

SHINE, SHINING

4744   stilbō, p. 571

TRANSFIGURE

3339   metamorphoō, p. 639

His Triumphal Entry

Jesus Christ entered Jerusalem in triumph riding (ride) on a colt, the foal of an ass. The crowd strewed palm branches along the way and shouted "hosanna."

He went into the temple area and with a scourge made of rope, he drove out the money changers who were buying and selling there.

ASS

3688   onos, p. 41

5268   hupozugion, p. 41

BRANCH

2798   klados, p. 76

4746   stoibas or stibas, p. 76

902   baion, p. 77

CHANGER

2855   kollubistēs, p. 96

2773   kermatistēs, p. 96

COLT

4454   pōlos, p. 108

FOAL

5207   huios, p. 244

HOSANNA

5614   hōsanna, p. 312

PALM

5404   phoinix, p. 456

RIDE

1910   epibainō, p. 534

ROPE

4979   schoinion, p. 539

SCOURGE

A. Noun

5416   phragellion, p. 551

His Suffering

Jesus Christ suffered many attempts by the Jews to seize him (cast him headlong) in order to put him to death, and they were constantly looking for an opportunity to ensnare and entangle him in his teaching.

In the garden of Gethsemane, at a stone's throw (cast) from the disciples, Jesus sweat drops of blood in his agony, as he wrestled with the cup of suffering that it was his Father's will for him to drink. Judas the traitor, who had been waiting for an opportunity, betrayed Jesus with a kiss.

The soldiers who arrested him took him first to the high priest and then to Pilate, the governor at the judgment hall in his palace, where they stripped and blindfolded him, put a scarlet (gorgeous) robe and a crown of thorns on him. They mocked him and spit on him, raining down blows upon his head as they beat him, but when threatened, he remained silent. Pilate declared himself innocent of the blood of Jesus as he sat on the judgment seat at the Stone Pavement, and Jesus was taken to be flogged with a scourge, suffering terrible stripes before being led away to be crucified.

AGONY

74   agōnia, p. 20

BEAT

1194   derō, p. 53

5180   tuptō, p. 54

BLINDFOLD

4028   perikaluptō, p. 70

BLOW

4475   rhapisma, p. 71

CAST

B. Noun

1000   bole, p. 92

CUP

4221   potērion, p. 141

DROP

2361   thrombos, p. 185

ENSNARE

3802   pagideuō, p. 202

ENTANGLE

1758   enechō, p. 203

GORGEOUS

2986   lampros, p. 275

GOVERNOR

A. Noun

2232   hēgemōn, p. 276

HALL

4232   praitōrion, p. 287

HEADLONG

2630   katakrēmnizō, p. 295

INNOCENT

121   athōos, p. 327

KISS

B. Verbs

5368   phileō, p. 345

2705   kataphileō, p. 345

LEAD, LED

520   apagō, p. 359

MOCK

A. Verb

1702   empaizō, p. 413

OPPORTUNITY

2120   eukairia, p. 449

PALACE

4232   praitōrion, p. 456

PAVEMENT

3038   lithostrōtos, p. 463

PRIEST

749   archiereus, p. 486

SCARLET

2847   kokkinos, p. 550

SCOURGE

B. Verb

5417   phragelloō, p. 551

SPIT

1716   emptuō, p. 595

STRIP

1562   ekduō, p. 604

STRIPE

4127   plēgē, p. 604

SUFFER

A. Verb

3958   paschō, p. 608

B. Adjective

3805   pathētos, p. 609

SWEAT

2402   hidrōs, p. 613

THORN

A. Noun

173   akantha, p. 629

B. Adjective

174   akanthinos, p. 630

THREATEN

546   apeileō, p. 631

TRAITOR

4273   prodotēs, p. 639

His Crucifixion and Death

The climax of Jesus Christ's suffering (his passion) was his death (weakness) on the cross (tree) at Calvary, the place of the skull. He refused the wine mixed with gall or myrrh that was offered to him to deaden his pain. The soldiers divided his clothing (seam; woven) amongst themselves by casting lots. Those passing by scoffed and wagged their heads at him (ah!). Pilate had a title fastened to the cross, a superscription that read "Jesus of Nazareth, the King of the Jews." Jesus' final words were "Eli, Eli, lama sabachthani." A sponge soaked with vinegar was put on a spear of hyssop and offered to Jesus to drink, but with a loud cry he bowed his head and gave up the ghost. At that moment, the veil of the temple was torn (break) in two from top to bottom. Because Jesus was already dead, the soldier did not break his legs as was customary, but instead pierced his side with a spear, before taking his body down from the cross.

AH!

3758   oua, p. 20

BOW, BOWED

2827   klinō, p. 75

BREAK

A. Verb

4977   schizō, p. 78

CALVARY

2898   kranion, p. 87

CLOTHING

5509   chitōn, p. 105

CROSS, CRUCIFY

A. Noun

4716   stauros, p. 138

B. Verbs

4717   stauroō, p. 138

4957 sustauroō, p. 138
4362 prospēgnumi, p. 138

CRY
B. Verbs
310 anaboaō, p. 140
2896 krazō, p. 140
5455 phōneō, p. 140

DEATH, DEATH-STROKE
C. Verbs
2289 thanatoō, p. 149
337 anaireō, p. 149
615 apokteinō, p. 150

DIVIDE
1266 diamerizō, p. 178

GALL
5521 cholē, p. 260

GHOST
1606 ekpneō, p. 264

HYSSOP
5301 hussōpos, p. 316

LAMA
2982 lama, p. 351

LEG
4628 skelos, p. 363

LOT, LOTS
A. Noun
2819 klēros, p. 381

MYRRH
B. Verb
4669 smurnizō, p. 424

PASSION
B. Verb
3958 paschō, p. 462

PIERCE
3572 nussō, p. 471

SABACHTHANI
4518 sabachthanei, p. 542

SCOFF
1592 ekmuktērizō, p. 550

SEAM
729 araphos *or* arrhaphos, p. 554

SIDE
A. Noun
4125 pleura, p. 574

SKULL
2898 kranion, p. 580

SPEAR
3057 lonchē, p. 591

SPONGE
4699 spongos, p. 596

SUFFER
3958 paschō, p. 608

SUPERSCRIPTION
1923 epigraphē, p. 610

TITLE
5102 titlos, p. 634

TOP
B. Phrases
Note, p. 637

TREE
3586 xulon, p. 642

VEIL
2665 katapetasma, p. 658

VINEGAR
3690 oxos, p. 661

WAG
2795 kineō, p. 663

WEAKNESS
C. Noun
769 astheneia, p. 669

WOVEN
5307 huphantos, p. 688

His Burial

Jesus was *anointed* for burial *(bury)* at Bethany before his crucifixion. A woman broke a *cruse (box)* of *spikenard ointment* over him in a symbolic act.

After Jesus' death, Joseph of Arimathea took Jesus' body *(depose)* and wrapped it with *spices* and *aloes* in strips of *linen* and laid it in a *garden tomb*. It was *Preparation* Day.

ALOES
250 aloē, p. 23

ANOINT, ANOINTING
3462 murizō, p. 28

BOX
211 alabastron, p. 76

BURY, BURYING
B. Verbs
1779 entaphiazō, p. 84
2290 thaptō, p. 84

CRUSE
211 alabastron, p. 139

DEPOSE
2507 kathaireō, p. 160

GARDEN
2779 kēpos, p. 261

LINEN, LINEN CLOTH, FINE LINEN
4616 sindōn, p. 372
3608 othonion, p. 373

OINTMENT
3464 muron, p. 444

PREPARATION
3904 paraskeuē, p. 483

SPICE(S)
759 arōma, p. 592

SPIKENARD
3487 nardos, p. 593

TOMB
3419 mnēmeion, p. 636

His Resurrection and Resurrection Appearances

On the *third* day Jesus Christ was *raised* from the dead. The disciples were initially filled with *doubt (incredible),* until they saw the empty grave-clothes *(apart; roll).* When Mary first saw him, she supposed him to be the *gardener.* But the disciples' doubt turned to joy at Jesus' *appearing (manifest)* to them after the *resurrection,* demonstrating that he was flesh and *bone* and not a ghost, and showing Thomas the *nail prints* in his hands. The resurrection declares *(determine)* Jesus Christ to be the Son of God.

APART
5565 chōris, p. 30

APPEARING
3700 optanō, p. 32

BONE
3747 osteon, p. 74

DETERMINE, DETERMINATE
3724 horizō, p. 165

DOUBT
A. Verb
639 aporeō, p. 182

GARDENER
2780 kēpouros, p. 261

INCREDIBLE
571 apistos, p. 323

MANIFEST
A. Adjective
1717 emphanēs, p. 390

NAIL
A. Noun
2247 hēlos, p. 425

PRINT
5179 tupos, p. 488

RAISE
1453 egeirō, p. 505
450 anistēmi, p. 506

RESURRECTION
386 anastasis, p. 531
1815 exanastasis, p. 531
1454 egersis, p. 531

ROLL
A. Verb
1794 entulissō, p. 538

THIRD
5154 tritos, p. 628

His Ascension and Exaltation

Forty days after his resurrection, Jesus Christ ascended *(arise; bear; lift)* into heaven *(bosom),* where he is *exalted* at God's *right* hand *crowned* with *glory* and *honor.* His appearance *(appear; countenance)* in glory, shining *(bright; shine)* like the *sun* in all its *strength,* was revealed to John in the vision in the Book of Revelation. His *hair* was white as *wool* and *snow,* his *eyes* were like *flames* of fire, and his feet like *burnished (burning)* brass.

See also REVELATION, SPECIFIC REVELATION: NUMBERS

APPEAR
A. Verb
5316 phainō, p. 31

ARISE
305 anabainō, p. 37

BEAR
399 anapherō, p. 52

BOSOM
2859 kolpos, p. 74

BRASS, BRAZEN
5474 chalkolibanon, p. 77

BRIGHT, BRIGHTNESS
A. Adjective
2986 lampros, p. 79

B. Nouns
2987 lamprotēs, p. 79
541 apaugasma, p. 79

BURNING
4448 puroomai, p. 84

BURNISHED
5474 chalkolibanon, p. 84

COUNTENANCE
3799 opsis, p. 133

CROWN
B. Verb
4737 stephanoō, p. 139

EXALT
A. Verbs
5312 hupsoō, p. 213
5251 huperupsoō, p. 213

EYE
3788 ophthalmos, p. 219

FLAME, FLAMING
5395 phlox, p. 242

GLORY
A. Noun
1391 doxa, p. 267

HAIR
A. Noun
2359 thrix, p. 287

HONOR
A. Noun
5092 timē, p. 310

LIFT
1869 epairō, p. 369

RIGHT, RIGHT HAND, RIGHT SIDE
1188 dexios, p. 534

SHINE
A. Verb
5316 phainō, p. 571

SNOW
5510 chiōn, p. 583

STRENGTH
A. Noun
1411 dunamis, p. 603

SUN
2246 hēlios, p. 610

WOOL
2053 erion, p. 683

His Victory

In his death on the cross, Jesus Christ *triumphed* over *(captive; show; spoil)* all the powers of evil arrayed against him and conquered death, which is now *swallowed* up in *victory.*

CAPTIVE, CAPTIVITY
A. Noun
161 aichmalōsia, p. 88

B. Verb
162 aichmalōteuō, p. 88

SHOW
1165 deigmatizō, p. 573

SPOIL, SPOILING
B. Verbs
4812 sulagōgeō, p. 595
554 apekduō, p. 595

SWALLOW
2666 katapinō, p. 612

TRIUMPH
2358 thriambeuō, p. 644

VICTORY
A. Nouns
3529 nikē, p. 660
3534 nikos, p. 660

Responses to Jesus

Jesus Christ elicited a variety of responses from those he encountered in his work and ministry. The *crowds (choke; crush)* and those he healed responded gladly and with faith *(believe),* as well as with *amazement (affrighted; beside oneself),* so that his *fame (blaze abroad)* spread. Some, however, *laughed* at him.

The obstinacy *(catch; close; hard; question; stumble)* of the Jews and the *indignation* of the religious leaders led them to *oppose* and *reject (deny; faithless; tread)* Jesus as their Messiah, attributing his power to demonic forces *(blaspheme),* while the response of the demons to Jesus was to *shudder (Ah!).*

See also HIS SUFFERING; **THE PEOPLE OF GOD,** JEWS AND GENTILES, WORSHIP OF GOD

AFFRIGHTED
A. Adjective
1719 emphobos, p. 18

B. Verb
1568 ekthambeō, p. 18

AH!
1436 ea, p. 20

AMAZE, AMAZEMENT
A. Nouns
1611 ekstasis, p. 24
2285 thambos, p. 24

B. Verbs
1839 existēmi, p. 25
1605 ekplēssō, p. 25
2284 thambeō, p. 25
1568 ekthambeō, p. 25

C. Adjective
1569 ekthambos, p. 25

BELIEVE, BELIEF, BELIEVERS
A. Verbs
4100 pisteuō, p. 61
3982 peithō, p. 61

B. Noun
4102 pistis, p. 61

C. Adjective
4103 pistos, p. 61

BESIDE ONESELF
1839 existēmi, p. 63

BLASPHEME, BLASPHEMY, BLASPHEMER, BLASPHEMOUS
A. Noun
988 blasphēmia, p. 69

B. Verb
987 blasphēmeō, p. 69

C. Adjective
989 blasphēmos, p. 69

BLAZE ABROAD
1310 diaphēmizō, p. 69

CATCH
4 agreuō, p. 92
2340 thēreuō, p. 92

CHOKE
4846 sumpnigō, p. 100

CLOSE
2576 kammuō, p. 105

CROWD
A. Noun
3793 ochlos, p. 139

B. Verb
3792 ochlopoieō, p. 139

CRUSH
598 apothlibō, p. 139

DENY
720 arneomai, p. 158
533 aparneomai, p. 158
483 antilegō, p. 158

FAITHLESS
571 apistos, p. 223

FAME
A. Noun
5345 phēmē, p. 225

B. Verb
1310 diaphēmizō, p. 225

GLAD, GLADLY
A. Verbs
5463 chairō, p. 266
21 agalliaō, p. 266

B. Adverb
2234 hēdeōs, p. 266

HARD, HARDEN, HARDENING, HARDNESS
B. Noun
4457 pōrōsis, p. 290

C. Verb
4456 pōroō, p. 290

INDIGNATION
B. Verb
23 aganakteō, p. 323

LAUGH, LAUGH TO SCORN
2606 katagelaō, p. 354

OPPOSE
498 antitassō, p. 449
475 antidiatithēmi, p. 449

QUESTION, QUESTIONING
A. Nouns
2214 zētēsis, p. 502
3056 logos, p. 503

B. Verbs
4802 suzēteō, p. 503
1905 eperōtaō, p. 503

REJECT
A. Verb
593 apodokimazō, p. 519

SHUDDER
5425 phrissō, p. 573

STUMBLE
4350 proskoptō, p. 606

TREAD
2662 katapateō, p. 641

Titles and Descriptions Of

The Holy *Spirit* is the *promised gift* of God. He is described metaphorically in terms which reflect his activity, such as a *wind* or *breath* and a *river* or *fountain.*

He is the *guide,* the *comforter,* and the *seal* of God's ownership on those who believe, as well as the guarantee *(earnest)* of the believer's future inheritance.

See also JESUS CHRIST, HIS WORK AND MINISTRY: HIS BAPTISM AND TEMPTATION

BREATH, BREATHE

A. Nouns
4157   pnoē, p. 79
4151   pneuma, p. 79

B. Verb
1720   emphusaō, p. 79

COMFORTER
3875   paraklētos, p. 111

EARNEST
728   arrabōn, p. 190

FOUNTAIN
4077   pēgē, p. 254

GIFT
1431   dōrea, p. 264

GUIDE

A. Noun
3595   hodēgos, p. 285

B. Verb
3594   hodēgeō, p. 285

PROMISE

A. Noun
1860   epangelia, p. 491

RIVER
4215   potamos, p. 536

SEAL

B. Verb
4972   sphragizō, p. 553

SPIRIT, BREATH
7307   rûaḥ, p. 240
4151   pneuma, p. 593

WIND
4157   pnoē, p. 677
4151   pneuma, p. 677

Work and Ministry of the Holy Spirit

In the Old Testament, the Holy Spirit only came on *(clothe)* particular people at specific times to impart wisdom and knowledge *(to think, devise),* to *speak (tongue)* to communicate God's will, or to change *(turn)* hearts and minds. But a time was foretold when the Holy Spirit would be poured out *(pour; shed)* on all flesh.

On the day of Pentecost when all the believers were gathered *(wait)* together, the Holy Spirit fell *(cloven; fall)* upon them, empowering *(power)* and *anointing* them for service and *witness* to Christ. *Full* of the Holy Spirit, they began speaking in other *languages.* Later, other believers were *baptized* in the Holy Spirit at the *laying on* of the apostles' hands.

The Holy Spirit is a person who can *grieve* when *quenched.* He is at work in the world to *convict (judge; judgment)* of sin. He *dwells* in the church and is at work in believers *(flow; live; spring; search)* to teach *(compare; taught)* them, to *renew* their *minds,* and to produce *(appear)* in them the likeness of Jesus *(transfigure)* through *sanctification.* He is the *adversary* of the flesh and *binds* believers together in unity. He *helps* believers in their *intercessions (groan)* and gives supernatural *gifts* of *grace:* the words of *wisdom (wise)* and *knowledge;* gifts of *faith, healing,* the working of *miracles, prophecy,* and *discernment (decision); tongues* and their *interpretation.* Those who are *led* by the Spirit will *reap* their reward, not only in the life to come, but in producing the *fruit* of the Spirit in their lives now: *love, joy, peace, longsuffering (patience), gentleness (kindness), goodness, faith, meekness,* and *temperance (continency).*

ADVERSARY
480   antikeimai, p. 15

ANOINTING

B. Noun
5545   chrisma, p. 28

APPEAR
1718   emphanizō, p. 32

BAPTIZE

B. Verb
907   baptizō, p. 50

BIND, BINDING
1210   deō, p. 66

TO CLOTHE
3847   lābaš, p. 38

CLOVEN
1266   diamerizō, p. 107

COMPARE, COMPARISON
4793   sunkrinō, p. 116

CONTINENCY
1467   enkrateuomai, p. 126

CONVICT
1651   elenchō, p. 128

DECISION

B. Noun
1253   diakrisis, p. 152

DISCERN, DISCERNER, DISCERNMENT

A. Verb
1252   diakrinō, p. 171

B. Noun
1253   diakrisis, p. 171

DWELL

A. Verbs
7931   šākan, p. 65
3611   oikeō, p. 187
2730d   katoikizō, p. 188
1774   enoikeō, p. 188

FAITH
4102   pistis, p. 222

FALL

B. Verb
1968   epipiptō, p. 224

FLOW
4482   rheō, p. 243

FRUIT, FRUITFUL

A. Nouns
2590   karpos, p. 256
1096d   genēma, p. 257

B. Adjective
2593   karpophoros, p. 257

FULL

A. Adjective
4134   plērēs, p. 258

GENTLE, GENTLENESS

A. Adjectives
1933   epieikēs, p. 263
2261   ēpios, p. 263

B. Noun
1932   epieikeia, p. 263

GIFT, GIVING
5486   charisma, p. 264
3311   merismos, p. 264

GOOD, GOODNESS

A. Adjective
5543   chrēstos, p. 274

B. Noun
5544   chrēstotēs, p. 274

GRACE
5485   charis, p. 277

GRIEVE

B. Verb
3076   lupeō, p. 281

GROAN, GROANING

B. Noun
4726   stenagmos, p. 282

HEALING
2386   iama, p. 295

HELP, HOLPEN

B. Verb
4878   sunantilambanō, p. 301

INTERCESSIONS

B. Verb
5241   huperentunchanō, p. 330

INTERPRET

A. Verbs
2059   hermēneuō, p. 330
1329   diermēneuō, p. 330

JOY, JOYFULNESS

A. Nouns
5479   chara, p. 335
20   agalliasis, p. 335
2167   euphrosunē, p. 335

B. Verbs
5463   chairō, p. 336
2744   kauchaomai, p. 336
21   agalliaō, p. 336
3685   oninēmi, p. 336

JUDGE

B. Verb
350   anakrinō, p. 336

JUDGMENT
2920   krisis, p. 337

KIND, KINDLY, KINDNESS
A. Adjective
5543   chrēstos, p. 343

B. Verb
5541   chrēsteuomai, p. 343

C. Nouns
5544   chrēstotes, p. 343
5363   philanthrōpia, p. 343

D. Adverb
5364   philanthrōpōs, p. 343

KNOW, KNOWN, KNOWLEDGE
A. Verbs
1097   ginōskō, p. 346
1492   oida, p. 346

C. Noun
1108   gnōsis, p. 348

LANGUAGE
1258   dialektos, p. 352

LAYING ON
1936   epithesis, p. 359

LEAD, LED
71   agō, p. 359

LIVE
2198   zaō, p. 374

LONGSUFFERING
A. Noun
3115   makrothumia, p. 377

B. Verb
3114   makrothumeō, p. 377

LOVE
A. Verbs
25   agapaō, p. 381
5368   phileō, p. 382

B. Nouns
26   agapē, p. 382
5363   philanthrōpia, p. 382

MEEK, MEEKNESS
A. Adjective
4239   praüs or praos, p. 401

B. Nouns
4240   praütēs or praotes, p. 401
4239,
3806   praüpathia, p. 401

MIND
A. Nouns
1271   dianoia, p. 408
5427   phronēma, p. 409

MIRACLES
1411   dunamis, p. 412

PATIENCE, PATIENT, PATIENTLY
A. Nouns
5281   hupomonē, p. 462
3115   makrothumia, p. 463

B. Verbs
5278   hupomenō, p. 463
3114   makrothumeō, p. 463

C. Adjectives
Notes, p. 463

D. Adverb
3116   makrothumōs, p. 463

PEACE, PEACEABLE, PEACEABLY
A. Noun
1515   eirēnē, p. 464

B. Verbs
1514   eirēneuō, p. 464
1517   eirēnopoieō, p. 464

C. Adjective
1516   eirēnikos, p. 464

TO POUR, FLOW
8210   šāpak, p. 183

POWER
B. Verb
1850   exousiazō, p. 479

PROPHECY
A. Noun
4394   prophēteia, p. 492

QUENCH
A. Verb
4570   sbennumi, p. 502

REAP
2325   therizō, p. 508

RENEW, RENEWING
A. Verb
365   ananeoō, p. 524

B. Noun
342   anakainōsis, p. 524

SANCTIFICATION, SANCTIFY
A. Noun
38   hagiasmos, p. 545

B. Verb
37   hagiazō, p. 546

SEARCH
2045   eraunaō or ereunaō, p. 554

SHED
1632   ekchunō or ekchunnō, p. 568

TO SPEAK
A. Verb
1696   dābar, p. 239

SPRING
A. Verb
242   hallomai, p. 597

TAUGHT
1318   didaktos, p. 619
2312   theodidaktos, p. 619

TEMPERANCE, TEMPERATE
A. Noun
1466   enkrateia, p. 620

B. Adjective
1468   enkratēs, p. 620

TO THINK, DEVISE
B. Adjective
2803   ḥāšab, p. 262

TONGUE(-S)
A. Nouns
3956   lāšôn, p. 264
1100   glōssa, p. 636
1258   dialektos, p. 636

B. Adjective
2084   heteroglōssos, p. 636

TRANSFIGURE
3339   metamorphoō, p. 639

TO TURN
A. Verb
2015   hāpak, p. 269

WAIT
4037   perimenō, p. 663

WISDOM
4678   sophia, p. 678
5428   phronēsis, p. 678

WISE
A. Adjective
4680   sophos, p. 679

WITNESS
B. Verb
3140   martureō, p. 681

CREATION

The Natural Order

God *created (to buy, acquire; craft; to consume; foundation)* the *heavens* and the *earth* and divinely arranged the order *(adorning)* in the *world.* He created *light,* divided it from the darkness, *called* the light *day,* the darkness *night,* and he *measured* out the *water* and *sea (deep; depth)* and separated it *(compacted)* from the dry *land.* He created the *grass,* the *flowers (lily; spin),* and the *trees (leaf; shoot forth; thyine; wood)* yielding *fruit,* and then the

sun, moon, and stars *(host),* setting them in motion *(turning).*

He also made the *birds (eagle; raven; sparrow)* and *winged* creatures *(moths; gnat)* to fly in the *air,* and every *fourfooted* creature *(bear; beast; fox; horse; ivory; leopard; lion; swine),* creeping thing *(viper; frog),* and sea creature *(whale),* that they might *multiply* and *fill* the earth. He also set precious metals *(copper; gold; silver), jewels (pearl),* and *stone (marble)* in the earth.

See also THE FUTURE, THE NEW ORDER

ADORNING
B. Noun
2889   kosmos, p. 14

AIR
109   aēr, p. 21
3772   ouranos, p. 21

BEAR
715   ark(t)os, p. 53

BEAST
929   beḥēmāh, p. 14

BIRD
4071   peteinon, p. 67

TO BUY, ACQUIRE
7069   qānāh, p. 28

TO CALL
A. Verb
7121 qārā', p. 29

COMPACTED
4921 sunistēmi, p. 115

TO CONSUME
A. Verb
3615 kālāh, p. 46

COPPER
5178 nᵉḥōšet, p. 48

CRAFT, CRAFTSMAN
5079 technitēs, p. 136

CREATE, CREATION, CREATOR, CREATURE
A. Verbs
1254 bārā', p. 51
7069 qānāh, p. 52
6213 'āśāh, p. 52
2936 ktizō, p. 137

B. Nouns
2937 ktisis, p. 137
2938 ktisma, p. 137
2939 ktistēs, p. 137

CREEPING
B. Noun
2062 herpeton, p. 138

DAY
3117 yôm, p. 54

DEEP
A. Noun
1037 buthos, p. 154

DEPTH
899 bathos, p. 160
3989 pelagos, p. 160

EAGLE
105 aetos, p. 189

EARTH
776 'ereṣ, p. 66

TO FILL
A. Verb
4390 mālē', p. 81

FLOWER
A. Noun
438 anthos, p. 243

FOUNDATION
A. Noun
2602 katabolē, p. 254

FOURFOOTED
5074 tetrapous, p. 254

FOX
258 alōpēx, p. 254

FROG
944 batrachos, p. 256

FRUIT
A. Noun
6529 pᵉrî, p. 88

B. Verb
6504 pārāh, p. 89

GNAT
2971 kōnōps, p. 269

GOLD
A. Nouns
2091 zāhāb, p. 98
5557 chrusos, p. 273

GRASS
5528 chortos, p. 278

HEAVENS
8064 šāmayim, p. 109

HORSE
5483 sûs, p. 116
2462 hippos, p. 312

HOST
A. Noun
6633 ṣābā', p. 116

IVORY
1661 elephantinos, p. 332

JEWELS
5553 chrusion, p. 334

LAND
127 'ădāmāh, p. 132
776 'ereṣ, p. 132
1093 gē, p. 352

LEAF
5444 phullon, p. 360

LEOPARD
3917 pardalis, p. 364

TO LIGHT, LIGHT
A. Verb
216 'ôr, p. 136

B. Noun
216 'ôr, p. 136

LILY
2918 krinon, p. 372

LION
738 'ărî, p. 137

MARBLE
3139 marmaros, p. 393

TO MEASURE
A. Verb
4058 mādad, p. 150

MOTH
4597 sēs, p. 418

TO MULTIPLY, INCREASE
A. Verb
7235 rābāh, p. 156

NIGHT
3915 laylāh, p. 160

PEARL
3135 margaritēs, p. 464

RAVEN
2876 korax, p. 507

SEA
3220 yām, p. 217

SHOOT FORTH
4261 proballō, p. 572

SILVER
A. Nouns
3701 kesep, p. 229
694 argurion, p. 576
696 arguros, p. 576

B. Adjective
693 argureos, p. 576

SPARROW
4765 strouthion, p. 590

SPIN
3514 nēthō, p. 593

STONE
A. Noun
3037 lithos, p. 600

SUN
8121 šemeš, p. 252
2246 hēlios, p. 610

SWINE
5519 choiros, p. 613

THYINE
2367 thuïnos, p. 633

TREE
6086 'ēṣ, p. 267
1186 dendron, p. 642

TURNING
5157 tropē, p. 647

VIPER
2191 echidna, p. 661

WATER
4325 mayim, p. 283
8415 tᵉhôm, p. 283

WHALE
2785 kētos, p. 672

WING
3671 kānāp, p. 289

WOOD
3586 xulon, p. 683
5208 hulē, p. 683

WORLD
2889 kosmos, p. 685

God's Providence

God *provides (to be satisfied)* for the needs of his creation, sustaining *(sustenance)* the natural order through Jesus Christ, in whom all things *consist.*
   See also WEATHER; **GOD, CHARACTER AND ATTRIBUTES OF, WORKS OF GOD**

CONSIST
1510 eimi, p. 124
4921 sunistēmi, p. 124

PROVIDE
A. Verb
4265 problepō, p. 495

TO BE SATISFIED
7646 śāba', p. 214

SUSTENANCE
5527 chortasma, p. 612

Creation's Future Redemption

God's perfect creation has been spoiled by sin, but will one day be completely renewed. Until then, however, the creation *groans* in *travail (vanity).*
   See also **THE FUTURE,** THE •
NEW ORDER

GROAN, GROANING
A. Verb
4959 sustenazō, p. 282

TRAVAIL
B. Verb
4944 sunōdinō, p. 641

VANITY
3153 mataiotēs, p. 658

Places

The *earth* comprises a great variety of places from *mountain ranges, hills,* and *rocky* places to *deserts* and *quicksands;* from *islands* and *seas (red; bay; beach; coast)* to *rivers (brook)* and *fountains (spring).*

BAY
2859 kolpos, p. 51

BEACH
123 aigialos, p. 52

BROOK
5493 cheimarrhos, p. 82

COAST, COASTING
A. Noun
3725 horion, p. 107
B. Adjective
3882 paralios, p. 107
C. Verb
3881 paralegō, p. 107

DESERT
A. Noun
2047 eremia, p. 161
B. Adjective
2048 erēmos, p. 161

EARTH
1093 gē, p. 191
3625 oikoumenē, p. 191

FOUNTAIN
4077 pēgē, p. 254

HILL
3735 oros, p. 304
3714 oreinos, p. 304
1015 bounos, p. 304

ISLAND, ISLE
3520 nēsos, p. 332
3519 nēsion, p. 332

MOUNTAIN RANGE
2022 har, p. 154

QUICKSANDS
Note, p. 503

RED
2063 eruthros, p. 515

RIVER, WADI
A. Nouns
5158 naḥal, p. 207
5104 nāhār, p. 207

ROCKY
4075 petrōdēs, p. 537

SEA
A. Nouns
3220 yām, p. 217
2281 thalassa, p. 552
3989 pelagos, p. 553
B. Adjectives
1724 enalios, p. 553
3882 paralios, p. 553
3864 parathalissios, p. 553
1337 dithalassos, p. 553

SPRING
B. Noun
4077 pēgē, p. 597

Time

Time is a creation of God marking the duration of life, which is measured by *days (daily; cock; dawn; early; to rise up early; even; evening; hour; midday; midnight; morning; morrow; next day; noon; night; today; tomorrow; yesterday), weeks, months (new moon),* and *years,* through changes in the *seasons (autumn; summer; temporal; winter).*

God also appoints particular times *(abolish; age; begin; former; complete; cease; end; ever; final; finish; fulfill; fullness; last; late; latter; term; swift; space; short; shortly)* for the unfolding of his purposes in history.

Because of the brevity of human life, it is imperative to make the most of *opportunities (chance; immediately; moment)* in the *present,* and not to *delay (tarry),* as time *continues* to *pass (past).*

ABOLISH
2673 katargeō, p. 3

AUTUMN
5352 phthinopōrinos, p. 46

AGE
A. Nouns
165 aiōn, p. 19
1074 genea, p. 19
2244 hēlikia, p. 19
2250 hēmera, p. 19
B. Adjectives
5230 huperakmos, p. 19
5046 teleios, p. 19

BEGIN, BEGINNING, BEGINNER
A. Verbs
756 archomai, p. 57
1728 enarchomai, p. 57
4278 proenarchomai, p. 57
3195 mellō, p. 57
B. Noun
746 archē, p. 58
C. Adverb
4412 prōton, p. 58

CEASE
A. Verbs
3973 pauō, p. 93
1257 dialeipō, p. 93
2270 hēsuchazō, p. 93
2869 kopazō, p. 93
863 aphiēmi, p. 93
2664 katapauō, p. 93

CHANCE
4795 sunkuria, p. 95
5177 ei tuchoi, p. 95

COCK, COCK-CROWING
220 alektōr, p. 107
219 alektorophōnia, p. 107

COMPLETE
A. Verbs
2005 epiteleō, p. 117
1822 exartizō, p. 117
4931 sunteleō, p. 117

4137 plēroō, p. 117
4135 plerophoreō, p. 117

CONTINUE, CONTINUANCE
1096 ginomai, p. 126
1300 diateleō, p. 126
1265 diamenō, p. 126
1696 emmenō, p. 127
1961 epimenō, p. 127
3887 paramenō, p. 127
4357 prosmenō, p. 127
4342 proskartereō, p. 127
1273 dianuktereuō, p. 127

DAILY
1967 epiousios, p. 143
2184 ephēmeros, p. 143
2522 kathēmerinos, p. 143

DAWN
A. Verbs
826 augazō, p. 146
1306 diaugazō, p. 146
2020 epiphōskō, p. 146
B. Noun
3722 orthros, p. 146

DAY
A. Nouns
3117 yôm, p. 54
2250 hēmera, p. 146
B. Adverb
1773**ennucha, p. 147

DELAY
A. Verbs
3635 okneō, p. 155
5549 chronizō, p. 156
B. Noun
311 anabolē, p. 156

EARLY
A. Noun
3722 orthros, p. 190
B. Adjective
3720 orthrinos, p. 190
C. Adverb
4404 prōi, p. 190

END, ENDING
A. Nouns
657 'epes, p. 68
7093 qēṣ, p. 69
7097 qāṣeh, p. 69
7098 qāṣāh, p. 69
319 'aḥărît, p. 70
5056 telos, p. 198
4930 sunteleia, p. 199
4009 peras, p. 199
B. Verbs
5055 teleō, p. 199
4931 sunteleō, p. 199
4137 plēroō, p. 199
C. Adjective
2078 eschatos, p. 199

EVEN, EVENING, EVENTIDE
A. Nouns
6153 'ereb, p. 71
2073 hespera, p. 208
3798**opsia, p. 208
B. Adverb
3796 opse, p. 208

WEEK
7620 šābûa', p. 286
4521 sabbaton, p. 670

WINTER
A. Noun
5494 cheimōn, p. 678
B. Verb
3914 paracheimazō, p. 678

YEAR
A. Nouns
8141 šānāh, p. 298
2094 etos, p. 690
1763 eniautos, p. 690
1333 dietia, p. 691
5148 trietia, p. 691
B. Adjectives
1332 dietēs, p. 691
1541 hekatontaetēs, p. 691
C. Adverb
4070 perusi, p. 691

YESTERDAY
5504v echthes or chthes, p. 691

Weather

The *weather* is under the control of God. Different climatic conditions are associated with different *seasons (summer; dry; heat; hot; warm; wither; winter; cool; cold; snow)* and reflect both the judgment of God *(hail; storm; tempest; tempestuous; thunder; lightning)*, his providence *(mist; rain; latter; moisture; shower; sun; east; west)*, and sometimes his presence *(cloud)*. The *wind (blow; north; northeast, northwest; south, south wind; southwest)* is also associated with God's presence in the world.

See also JESUS CHRIST, HIS WORK AND MINISTRY: HIS MIRACLES; CREATION, THE NATURAL ORDER; THE FUTURE, JUDGMENT

BLOW
4154 pneō, p. 71
5285 hupopneō, p. 71

CLOUD
6051 'ānān, p. 38

COLD
A. Noun
5592 psuchos, p. 108
B. Adjective
5593 psuchros, p. 108

COOL
2711 katapsuchō, p. 129

DRY
A. Adjectives
3584 xēros, p. 186
504 anudros, p. 186
B. Verb
3583 xērainō, p. 186

EAST
395 anatole, p. 192

HAIL
5464 chalaza, p. 286

HEAT
A. Nouns
2742 kausōn, p. 297
2738 kauma, p. 297
2329 thermē, p. 298

HOT
2200 zestos, p. 312

LATTER
3797 opsimos, p. 354

LIGHTNING
796 astrapē, p. 371

MIST
887 achlus, p. 413
3658a homichlē, p. 413
2217 zophos, p. 413

MOISTURE
2429 ikmas, p. 414

NORTH
1005 borras, p. 434

NORTHEAST, NORTHWEST
5566 chōros, p. 434

RAIN
A. Nouns
5205 huetos, p. 505
1028 brochē, p. 505
B. Verb
1026 brechō, p. 505

SEASON
A. Noun
2540 kairos, p. 554

SHOWER
3655 ombros, p. 573

SNOW
5510 chiōn, p. 583

SOUTH, SOUTH WIND
3558 notos, p. 589

SOUTHWEST
3047 lips, p. 590

STORM
2978 lailaps, p. 601

SUMMER
2330 theros, p. 609

SUN
2246 hēlios, p. 610

TEMPEST
2366 thuella, p. 621
4578 seismos, p. 621
5494 cheimōn, p. 621
2978 lailaps, p. 621

TEMPESTUOUS
5189 tuphōnikos, p. 621

THUNDER, THUNDERING
1027 brontē, p. 632

WARM
2328 thermainō, p. 666

WEATHER
2105 eudia, p. 670
5494 cheimōn, p. 670

WEST
1424 dusmē, p. 672

WIND
417 anemos, p. 677

WINTER
A. Noun
5494 cheimōn, p. 678

TO WITHER
3001 yābēš, p. 291

Plants, Food, and Agriculture

The economy of Israel was chiefly agricultural. The ground *(dust)* was cleared of *thorns* and *thistles*, irrigated *(pit; to give drink; water)*, and then plowed *(plough; till)* for the *sowing* of grain *(barley; corn; ear; husks; chaff)*, which, when harvested *(barn; basket; garner; sickle)* and threshed *(threshing-floor)*, was ground *(grind; mill; millstone)* into *flour* for making *bread (crumb; leaven)*, the staple diet in biblical times.

Animals *(cattle; herd; ox; fatling)* were *farmed (field; grass; mow)* for their *meat (dine; eat; sop; mess; meal; victuals)*, their *milk*, and their *skins*, as well as for sacrifice.

Plants were also a major source of *food* and materials *(flax; reeds)*. Fruit trees *(fig; fig tree; olives* [from which *olive oil* was made]; *sycamore; sycamine)* and especially *grapes (cluster; drink; vineyard; vinedresser; wine; winepress)* were widely cultivated.

The diet was supplemented with fish *(broiled; net)*, eggs *(hen)*, and honey *(honeycomb; sweet)*.

Herbs and spices *(anise, cinnamon; cummin; hyssop; mint; mustard; myrrh; rue)* had a variety of uses.

See also THE PEOPLE OF GOD, WORSHIP OF GOD

ANISE
432 anēthon, p. 28

BARLEY
A. Noun
2915 krithē, p. 51
B. Adjective
2916 krithinos, p. 51

BARN
596 apothēkē, p. 51

BASKET, BASKETFUL
2894 kophinos, p. 51
4711 spuris, p. 51
4553 sarganē, p. 51

BREAD
3899 leḥem, p. 23
4682 maṣṣāh, p. 24

BROILED
3702 optos, p. 81

CATTLE
504 'eleph, p. 32
2353 thremma, p. 92
934 ktēnos, p. 92

CHAFF
892 achuron, p. 95

CINNAMON
2792 kinnamōmon, p. 102

CLUSTER
1009 botrus, p. 107

CORN, CORNFIELD
4621 sitos, p. 129
4621* sition, p. 129
4702 sporimos, p. 129
4719 stachus, p. 129

CRUMB
5589 psichion, p. 139

CUMMIN
2951 kuminon, p. 140

DINE, DINNER
A. Verb
709 aristaō, p. 170
B. Noun
712 ariston, p. 170

DRINK, DRANK
A. Nouns
4188 poma, p. 184
4213 posis, p. 184
4608 sikera, p. 184
B. Verbs
8354 šātāh, p. 62
4095 pinō, p. 184
3184 methuō, p. 184
4222 potizō, p. 185
4844 sumpinō, p. 185
5202 hudropoteō, p. 185

DUST
A. Nouns
5522 chous or choos, p. 187
2868 koniortos, p. 187
B. Verb
3039 likmaō, p. 187

EAR (of corn)
4719 stachus, p. 190

EAT, EAT WITH, EATING
A. Verbs
2068 esthiō, p. 192
5315 phagō, p. 192
1089 geuō, p. 193
977 bibrōskō, p. 193
2719 kataphagō, p. 193
2880 korennumi, p. 193
4906 sunesthiō, p. 193
3542,
2192 nomēn echō, p. 193
B. Nouns
1035 brōsis, p. 193
4371 prosphagion, p. 193
C. Adjective
1034 brōsimos, p. 193

EGG
5609 ōon, p. 195

FARM
68 agros, p. 227

FATLING, FATTED
4619 sitistos, p. 229
4618 siteutos, p. 229

FIELD, CORNFIELD
7704 śādeh, p. 80
68 agros, p. 234
5561 chōra, p. 234
5564 chōrion, p. 234
4702 sporimos, p. 234

FIG
4810 sukon, p. 235
3653 olunthos, p. 235

FIG TREE
4808 sukē or sukea, p. 235

FISH, FISHER, FISHERMAN
A. Nouns
2486 ichthus, p. 241
2485 ichthudion, p. 241
3795 opsarion, p. 241
231 halieus, p. 241
B. Verb
232 halieuō, p. 241

FLAX
3043 linon, p. 242

FLOUR
4585 semidalis, p. 243

FOOD
5160 trophē, p. 245
1305 diatrophē, p. 245
1035 brōsis, p. 245
4620 sitometrion, p. 245
1033 brōma, p. 245

FRUIT, FRUITFUL
A. Nouns
6529 pᵉrî, p. 88
2590 karpos, p. 256
1096d genēma, p. 257
3703 opōra, p. 257
C. Verb
2592 karpophoreō, p. 257

GARNER
596 apothēkē, p. 261

TO GIVE DRINK
8248 šāqāh, p. 92

GRAIN
2848 kokkos, p. 278

GRAPE
4718 staphulē, p. 278

GRASS
5528 chortos, p. 278

GRIND
229 alēthō, p. 282
5149 trizō, p. 282

HEN
3733 ornis, p. 301

HERB
3001 lachanon, p. 302
1008 botanē, p. 302

HERD
1241 bāqār, p. 110
34 agelē, p. 302

HONEY, HONEYCOMB
3192 meli, p. 309
3193 melissios, p. 309

HUSKS
2769 keration, p. 316

HYSSOP
5301 hussōpos, p. 316

LEAVEN
A. Noun
2219 zumē, p. 362
B. Verb
2220 zumoō, p. 363

MEAL
224 aleuron, p. 398

MEAT
1033 brōma, p. 400
1035 brōsis, p. 400
1034 brōsimos, p. 400
5160 trophē, p. 400
5315 phagō, p. 400
5132 trapeza, p. 400

MESS
1035 brōsis, p. 405

MILK
1051 gala, p. 408

MILL
3459 mulōn, p. 408

MILLSTONE
A. Noun
3458 mulos, p. 408
B. Adjectives
3457 mulikos, p. 408
3458(v)mulinos, p. 408

MINT
2238 hēduosmon, p. 412

MOW
270 amaō, p. 420

MUSTARD
4615 sinapi, p. 423

MYRRH
4666 smurna, p. 423

NET
293 amphiblēstron, p. 430
1350 diktuon, p. 430
4522 sagēnē, p. 430

(OLIVE) OIL
A. Noun
8081 šemen, p. 170

OLIVES, OLIVE TREE
1636 elaia, p. 445
1638 elaiōn, p. 445
2565 kallielaios, p. 445
65 agrielaios, p. 445

OX
1016 bous, p. 455
5022 tauros, p. 455

PIT
875 bᵉ'ēr, p. 178

PLOUGH, PLOW
A. Noun
723 arotron, p. 475
B. Verbs
2790 ḥāraš, p. 179
722 arotriaō, p. 475

REED
2563 kalamos, p. 516

RUE
4076 pēganon, p. 539

SICKLE
1407 drepanon, p. 574

SKIN
779 askos, p. 580

SOP
5596 psōmion, p. 587

SOW, SOWER
A. Verb
2232 zāra', p. 238
4687 speirō, p. 590

B. Nouns
2233 zera', p. 238
5300 hus, p. 590

SWEET
1099 glukus, p. 613

SYCAMINE
4807 sukaminos, p. 614

SYCAMORE
4809 sukomorea, p. 614

THISTLE
5146 tribolos, p. 629

THORN
A. Nouns
173 akantha, p. 629
4647 skolops, p. 629

B. Adjective
174 akanthinos, p. 630

THRESH
248 aloaō, p. 631

THRESHING FLOOR
257 halōn, p. 631

TILL
1090 geōrgeō, p. 633

VICTUALS
1979 episitismos, p. 660

VINEDRESSER
289 ampelourgos, p. 661

VINEYARD
290 ampelōn, p. 661

WATER
4325 mayim, p. 283

WINE
3196 yayin, p. 288
3631 oinos, p. 677
1098 gleukos, p. 678

WINEPRESS, WINE-VAT
3025 lēnos, p. 678
5276 hupolēnion, p. 678

SUPERNATURAL BEINGS

Angelic Beings

Angels are supernatural, created beings, who minister to God and to believers, acting as messengers *(announce; send; tell)*, as agents of judgment *(destroy; smite; reaper)*, and as worshipers in heaven *(host; innumerable)*. They are *strong (ability)* and sometimes *contend* with other powers.

There are different orders of angels *(dignity; dominion)*, which include *archangels* and seraphim *(to burn)*.

Other supernatural beings depicted in Scripture are *winged* creatures *(beast; cherubim)*.

ABILITY
A. Noun
2479 ischus, p. 2

ANGEL
4397 mal'āk, p. 4
32 angelos, p. 26

ANNOUNCE
312 anangellō, p. 28

ARCHANGEL
743 archangelos, p. 36

BEAST
2226 zōon, p. 53

TO BURN
B. Noun
8314 šᵉrapîm, p. 27

CHERUBIM
5502 cheroubim, p. 98

CONTEND
1252 diakrinō, p. 125

DESTROY, DESTROYER, DESTRUCTION
A. Verb
3645 olothreuō, p. 164

B. Noun
3644 olothreutēs, p. 164

DIGNITY, DIGNITIES
1391 doxa, p. 169

DOMINION
A. Noun
2963 kuriotēs, p. 181

HOST
A. Nouns
6633 ṣābā', p. 116
4756 stratia, p. 312

INNUMERABLE
3461 murias, p. 327

REAPER
2327 theristēs, p. 509

TO SEND
A. Verbs
7971 šālaḥ, p. 221
649 apostellō, p. 560
3992 pempō, p. 560

SMITE
3960 patassō, p. 581

STRONG
A. Adjective
2478 ischuros, p. 605

TELL
3004 legō, p. 620

WING
3671 kānāp, p. 289
4420 pterux, p. 678

Satan, Names and Descriptions Of

As the *adversary (enemy)* of the person and purposes of God, *Satan (Belial; devil; dragon (red); evil, evil-doer)* often appears *(fashion)* as an angel of light in order to *deceive (device; serpent)* and *destroy (devour)* human beings, holding them *captive* to sin. He is the *accuser (slanderer)* and *tempter* of believers, and is likened to a *roaring* lion.

See also THE LIFE OF THE BELIEVER, THE LIFE OF FAITH: SPIRITUAL WARFARE

ACCUSER
1228 diabolos, p. 11
2725 katēgoros, p. 11

ADVERSARY
A. Noun
476 antidikos, p. 15

B. Verb
480 antikeimai, p. 15

C. Adjective
5227 hupenantios, p. 15

BELIAL
955 belial, p. 60

CAPTIVE
B. Verb
2221 zōgreō, p. 88

DECEIVE
C. Verb
4105 planaō, p. 151

DESTROY
A. Verb
3089 luō, p. 164

DEVICE
3540 noēma, p. 166

DEVIL, DEVILISH
1228 diabolos, p. 166

DEVOUR
2719 katesthiō *and* kataphagō, p. 166
2666 katapinō, p. 167

DRAGON
1404 drakōn, p. 183

ENEMY
2190 echthros, p. 200

EVIL, EVIL-DOER
B. Noun
4190 ponēros, p. 212

FASHION
C. Verb
3345 metaschēmatizō, p. 227

RED
A. Adjective
4450 purrhos, p. 515

ROAR
A. Verb
5612 ōruomai, p. 536

SATAN
7854 śāṭān, p. 213
4569 satanas, p. 547

SERPENT
3789 ophis, p. 562

SLANDERER
1228 diabolos, p. 580

TEMPTER
Note, p. 622

Agents of Satan

Satan works in the world through spiritual beings *(demon; principality; ruler)* under his control to *deceive, vex, dash,* and exert *dominion* over human beings.

See also **JESUS CHRIST,** HIS WORK AND MINISTRY: HIS MIRACLES

DASH
4486 rhēgnumi, p. 145

DECEIVER
4108 planos, p. 151

DEMON, DEMONIAC
A. Nouns
1142 daimōn, p. 157
1140 daimonion, p. 158

B. Verb
1139 daimonizomai, p. 158

C. Adjective
1141 daimoniōdēs, p. 158

DOMINION
B. Verb
2634 katakurieuō, p. 181

PRINCIPALITY
746 archē, p. 488

RULER
2888 kosmokrator, p. 540

VEX
3791 ochleō, p. 660

HUMAN BEINGS

Their Creation and Fall

God *formed* Adam from the *dust* of the ground. Because it was not good for Adam to be alone *(part)*, God formed Eve *(to tell)*, and the two became one flesh *(to cleave; join)*. *Man (male)* and *woman* were both made in the *image (likeness)* of God, *crowned* with glory and honor. God *set* them in the Garden of Eden and gave them *life* and dominion over everything that *lives* and instructed them to be *fruitful* and *multiply* upon the earth. But at the *fall*, Eve was *deceived* by the serpent and God banished *(send)* them from Eden.

See also **SIN,** THE NATURE OF SIN

CROWN
B. Verb
4737 stephanoō, p. 139

TO CLEAVE, CLING
1692 dābaq, p. 37

DECEIVE
C. Verbs
538 apataō, p. 151
1818 exapataō, p. 151

DUST
6083 ‘āpār, p. 63

FALL, FALLEN, FALLING, FELL
A. Nouns
4431 ptōsis, p. 223
3900 paraptōma, p. 223
646 apostasia, p. 223

B. Verbs
4098 piptō, p. 223
1706 empiptō, p. 224
3895 parapiptō, p. 224
5302 hustereō, p. 224
868 aphistēmi, p. 224
3845 parabainō, p. 224

TO FORM
3335 yāṣar, p. 86

FRUITFUL
B. Verb
6504 pārāh, p. 89

IMAGE
1504 eikōn, p. 318

JOIN
2853 kollaō, p. 334

4347 proskollaō, p. 334
4801 su(n)zeugnumi, p. 334

LIFE, LIFE-GIVING
A. Noun
2222 zōē, p. 367

C. Verb
2227 zōopoieō, p. 368

LIKENESS
B. Noun
1823 dᵉmût, p. 136

TO LIVE
A. Verb
2421 ḥāyāh, p. 137

B. Noun
2416 ḥay, p. 138

C. Adjective
2416 ḥay, p. 138

MALE
A. Noun
2145 zākār, p. 146

MAN
A. Nouns
120 ’ādām, p. 146
1397 geber, p. 147
376 ’îš, p. 148
582 ’ĕnôš, p. 149
970 bāḥûr, p. 149
444 anthrōpos, p. 388

TO MULTIPLY, INCREASE
A. Verb
7235 rābāh, p. 156

PART
A. Particle
905 bad, p. 172

B. Verb
909 bādad, p. 172

TO SEND
A. Verb
7971 šālaḥ, p. 221

TO SET ON, SET UP
A. Verb
7760 śîm, p. 226

TO TELL
C. Preposition
5048 neged, p. 258

WOMAN
802 ’iššāh, p. 292

The Nature of the Human Race

Human *nature* has three components:

- The *flesh* represents the physical aspect of human *(man's)* nature, which is *mortal* because of sin. The *body (blood; bone; slave)* is frail, human life is a mere *vapor (breath; vanish)*, and human nature is *carnal (fleshly)*.
- The *spirit (breath)* is that *inward (belly; joint)* part of people which gives them their identity and by which they think *(mind; conscience; imagination)*, feel *(heart; reins)*, and have *life*.
- The *soul* refers chiefly to that which is *natural* as opposed to that which is spiritual, and is the seat of the sentient element in human beings.

(These key terms express a wide range of meanings in the Old and New Testaments that cannot be adequately expressed in this compressed description of them. Each pertinent *Vine* entry should be examined closely to discover the nuances of meaning terms such as *flesh, spirit,* and *soul* expressed throughout the Bible.)

BELLY
2836 koilia, p. 61

BLOOD
A. Noun
129 haima, p. 70

BODY
A. Noun
4983 sōma, p. 72

BONE
6106 ‘eṣem, p. 20

BREATH
A. Nouns
1892 hebel, p. 25
4157 pnoē, p. 79
4151 pneuma, p. 79

CARNAL, CARNALLY
4559 sarkikos, p. 89
4560 sarkinos, p. 89

CONSCIENCE
4893 suneidēsis, p. 122

FLESH
1320 bāśār, p. 83
4561 sarx, p. 242

FLESHLY, FLESHY
4559 sarkikos, p. 243
4560 sarkinos, p. 243

HEART, HEARTILY
3820 lēb, p. 108
2588 kardia, p. 297
5590 psuchē, p. 297

IMAGINATION
3053 logismos, p. 319
1261 dialogismos, p. 319
1271 dianoia, p. 319

INWARD, INWARDLY
2080 esō, p. 331
2081 esōthen, p. 331

JOINT
719 harmos, p. 334

LIFE
A. Noun
5590 psuchē, p. 368

MAN'S, OF MAN, MANKIND
442 anthrōpinos, p. 389

MIND
A. Nouns
3563 nous, p. 408
1271 dianoia, p. 408
1771 ennoia, p. 408
3540 noēma, p. 408
1106 gnōmē, p. 408
5427 phronēma, p. 409

MORTAL, MORTALITY
2349 thnētos, p. 417

NATURAL, NATURALLY
A. Adjectives
5446 phusikos, p. 426
5591 psuchikos, p. 426
C. Adverb
5447 phusikōs, p. 427

NATURE
5449 phusis, p. 427
1078 genesis, p. 427

REINS
3510 nephros, p. 519

SLAVE
4983 sōma, p. 580

SOUL, SELF, LIFE
5315 nepeš, p. 237
5590 psuchē, p. 588

SPIRIT, BREATH
7307 rûaḥ, p. 240
4151 pneuma, p. 593

VANISH, VANISHING
A. Verb
853 aphanizō, p. 658

VAPOR
822 atmis, p. 658

Human Relationships

The *family* unit was ordained by God for the benefit (*benevolence*) of its members. In biblical times it referred to a much broader group of relatives than it generally does today in the west. As a group of relatives (*kin; kind; kindred; generation; tribe*), family could include *parents* (*father; mother*), sons (*brother*), daughters (*sister*), children (*small; offspring; weaker one; suck; young; youth*), cousins, grandmother, grandchildren, foster-brother, father-in-law, mother-in-law (*wife's mother*), as well as household servants (*to build; household; householder; bondman; goodman; hired servant; manservant; menservants; nurse*). Guests were accorded great honor, and good relations with *neighbors* (*countrymen; neighborhood*) were vital for the well-being of the community.

The *firstborn* (*birthday*) male (although not *bastards*) in a family had unique privileges (*heir; birthright; surname; forefather; handed down*) and *marriage* (*betroth; espoused; husband; wife; bride; virgin; unmarried*) was a solemn undertaking, although *divorce* was permissible under certain circumstances.

Friendship (*friend; acquaintance; companion; commune; company; to encounter; to discern*) could be a great blessing or a bad influence in the case of both *men* (*male; fellow*) and women (*damsel; female; maid; maiden; woman*).

ACQUAINTANCE
1110 gnōstos, p. 11
2398 idios, p. 11

BASTARD
3541 nothos, p. 51

BENEVOLENCE
2133 eunoia, p. 62

BETROTH
3423 mnēsteuō, p. 64

BIRTHDAY
1077 genesia, p. 67

BIRTHRIGHT
4415 prōtotokia, p. 67

BONDMAN, BONDMAID
1401 doulos, p. 73
3814 paidiskē, p. 73

BRIDE, BRIDEGROOM
3565 numphē, p. 79
3566 numphios, p. 79

BROTHER
251 'āḥ, p. 25

TO BUILD
A. Verb
1129 bānāh, p. 25
B. Nouns
1121 bēn, p. 26
1323 bat, p. 26

CHILD, CHILDREN, CHILD-BEARING, CHILDISH, CHILDLESS
A. Nouns
5043 teknon, p. 99
5207 huios, p. 99

3816 pais, p. 100
3813 paidion, p. 100
3808 paidarion, p. 100
3516 nēpios, p. 100
3439 monogenēs, p. 100
5042 teknogonia, p. 100
B. Verbs
5044 teknotropheō, p. 100
5041 teknogoneō, p. 100
C. Adjectives
1471 enkuos, p. 100
5388 philoteknos, p. 100
815 ateknos, p. 100

COMMUNE
1255 dialaleō, p. 114
3656 homileō, p. 114
4814 sullaleō, p. 114

COMPANION
A. Noun
7453 rēa', p. 42
B. Verb
7462 rā'āh, p. 43

COMPANY
A. Nouns and Phrases
3793 ochlos, p. 115
4923 sunodia, p. 115
4849 sumposion, p. 115
2828 klisia, p. 115
4128 plēthos, p. 115
3657 homilia, p. 115
3658 homilos, p. 115
2398 idios, p. 116
B. Verbs
4874 sunanamignumi, p. 116
4905 sunerchomai, p. 116

COUNTRYMEN
1085 genos, p. 133
4853 sumphuletēs, p. 133

COUSIN
431 anepsios, p. 135
4773v sungenis, p. 135

DAMSEL
2877 korasion, p. 143
3813 paidion, p. 143
3814 paidiskē, p. 144

DAUGHTER, DAUGHTER-IN-LAW
2364 thugatēr, p. 145
2365 thugatrion, p. 145
3933 parthenos, p. 145
3565 numphē, p. 146

TO DISCERN
5234 nākar, p. 60

DIVORCE, DIVORCEMENT
A. Verb
630 apoluō, p. 179
B. Noun
647 apostasion, p. 179

TO ENCOUNTER, BEFALL
7122 qārā', p. 68

ESPOUSED
718 harmozō, p. 206
3423 mnēsteuō, p. 206

FAMILY
4940 mišpāḥāh, p. 77
3624 oikos, p. 225
3965 patria, p. 225

FATHER
A. Noun
3962   patēr, p. 228
B. Adjectives
3971   patrōos, p. 229
3967   patrikos, p. 229
540   apatōr, p. 229
3970   patroparadotos, p. 229

FATHER-IN-LAW
3995   pentheros, p. 229

FELLOW
435   anēr, p. 232
2083   hetairos, p. 232
3353   metochos, p. 232

FEMALE
2338   thēlus, p. 233

FIRSTBORN
1060   bᵉkôr, p. 83

FOREFATHER
4269   progonos, p. 248
4253,
3962   propatōr, p. 248

FOSTER-BROTHER
4939   suntrophos, p. 253

FRIEND
A. Nouns
7453   rēaʻ, p. 88
5384   philos, p. 256
2083   hetairos, p. 256
B. Verb
3982   peithō, p. 256

FRIENDSHIP
5373   philia, p. 256

GENERATION
1074   genea, p. 262
1078   genesis, p. 262

GOODMAN
3617   oikodespotēs, p. 275

GRANDCHILDREN
1549**ekgonos, p. 278

GRANDMOTHER
3125   mammē, p. 278

GUEST
345   anakeimai, p. 284

HANDED DOWN
3970   patroparadotos, p. 288

HEIR
A. Nouns
2818   klēronomos, p. 300
4789   sunklēronomos, p. 300
B. Verb
2816   klēronomeō, p. 300

HIRED SERVANT, HIRELING
3411   misthōtos, p. 305
3407   misthios, p. 305

HOUSEHOLD
A. Nouns
3624   oikos, p. 313
3614   oikia, p. 313
3610d   oiketeia, p. 313
2322   therapeia, p. 313
B. Adjectives
3609   oikeios, p. 313
3615   oikiakos, p. 313

HOUSEHOLDER
A. Noun
3617   oikodespotēs, p. 314
B. Verb
3616   oikodespoteō, p. 314

HOUSEHOLD-SERVANT
3610   oiketēs, p. 314

HUSBAND
A. Noun
435   anēr, p. 315
B. Adjectives
5362   philandros, p. 315
5220   hupandros, p. 315

KIN, KINSFOLK, KINSMAN, KINSWOMAN
A. Adjective
4773   sungenēs, p. 342
B. Nouns
4773v   sungenis, p. 342
4773**sungeneus, p. 342

KIND
1085   genos, p. 342
5449   phusis, p. 343

KINDRED
4772   sungeneia, p. 343
1085   genos, p. 343

MAID, MAIDEN, MAIDSERVANT
3816   pais, p. 386
3814   paidiskē, p. 386
2877   korasion, p. 386

MAIDEN, VIRGIN
1330   bᵉtûlāh, p. 145
5959   ʻalmāh, p. 276
3933   parthenos, p. 661
3932   parthenia, p. 661

MALE
730   arsēn *or* arrēn, p. 387

MANSERVANT
3816   pais, p. 392

MARRIAGE, MARRY
A. Noun
1062   gamos, p. 394
B. Verbs
1060   gameō, p. 394
1061v   gamizō, p. 394
1061   gamiskō, p. 395
1548   ekgamiskō, p. 395
1547   ekgamizō, p. 395
1918   epigambreuō, p. 395

MEN
Notes, p. 403

MENSERVANTS
3816   pais, p. 403

MOTHER
517   ʼēm, p. 153
3384   mētēr, p. 418

MOTHER-IN-LAW
3994   penthera, p. 418

NEIGHBOR
1069   geitōn, p. 429
4040   perioikos, p. 429
4139   plēsion, p. 429

NEIGHBORHOOD
Note, p. 430

NURSE
5162   trophos, p. 437

OFFSPRING
1081   gennēma, p. 443
1085   genos, p. 443

PARENTS
1118   goneus, p. 458
4269   progonos, p. 458
3962   patēr, p. 458

SISTER
269   ʼāḥôt, p. 235
79   adelphē, p. 578

SMALL
A. Adjective
6996   qāṭān, p. 236
B. Verb
6994   qāṭōn, p. 236

SON
5207   huios, p. 584

SUCK, SUCKLING
2337   thēlazō, p. 608

SURNAME
1941   epikaleō, p. 612

TRIBE
5443   phulē, p. 643
1429   dōdekaphulos, p. 643

UNMARRIED
22   agamos, p. 652

VIRGIN *see* **MAIDEN**

WEAKER ONE, LITTLE ONE
2945   ṭap, p. 285

WIFE, WIVES
1135   gunē, p. 675
1134   gunaikeios, p. 675

WIFE'S MOTHER
3994   penthera, p. 675

WOMAN
1135   gunē, p. 681
1133   gunaikarion, p. 682
4245   presbuteros, p. 682
4247   presbutis, p. 682
2338**thēleia, p. 682

YOUNG
3501   neōteros, p. 692
3501   neos, p. 692
3494   neanias, p. 692
3495   neaniskos, p. 692
3502   nossos *or* neossos, p. 692

YOUTH
5288   naʻar, p. 299

Parts of the Body and Clothing

The *face (cheek; ear; eye; forehead; head; lip; mouth; nose)* is the main visual characteristic of a person. Along with other parts of the body *(arm; back; hand; right hand; palm; neck; knee; foot; heel)*, it is often associated in Scripture with certain gestures expressing mood and attitudes. Other parts of the body are simply functional *(ankle-bones; leg)* and/or they may be representative. *Bosom (breast)* is representative of motherhood, while *shoulder* denotes strength, and the *stomach* is associated with appetite.

Clothing (apparel; vesture) also carries symbolic meaning *(mantle; girdle; sandal; shoe; latchet). Garments (cover)* were originally provided by God for Adam and Eve, but soon became indicators of poverty *(bare; undressed; leather; sheepskin)* or wealth *(robe; purple; silk).*

Cloth was also used to make *aprons, handkerchiefs, napkins, towels,* and *sheets,* and women skilled with a *needle (sew)* were greatly admired and respected.

See also GOD, ANTHROPOMORPHISMS; THE LIFE OF THE BELIEVER, THE LIFE OF FAITH: SPIRITUAL WARFARE

ANKLE-BONES
4974 sphuron, p. 28

APPAREL, APPARELLED
2066 esthēs, p. 31
2067 esthēsis, p. 31
2440 himation, p. 31
2441 himatismos, p. 31
2689 katastolē, p. 31

APRON
4612 simikinthion, p. 36

ARM
2220 zᵉrôaʻ, p. 8
43 ankalē, p. 37

BACK
3577 nōtos, p. 48

BARE
1131 gumnos, p. 50

BOSOM
2436 ḥêq, p. 22

BREAST
4738 stēthos, p. 78
3149 mastos, p. 78

CHEEK
4600 siagōn, p. 97

CLOTH
4470 rhakos, p. 105

CLOTHING, CLOTHS, CLOTHES, CLOKE, COAT
534 phelonēs *or* phailonēs, p. 105
2440 himation, p. 105
5509 chitōn, p. 105
2441 himatismos, p. 106
1742 enduma, p. 106
1903 ependutēs, p. 106
2066 esthēs, p. 106
4749 stolē, p. 106

COVER, COVERING
A. Verbs
2572 kaluptō, p. 135
1943 epikaluptō, p. 135
4028 perikaluptō, p. 135
4780 sunkaluptō, p. 135
2619 katakaluptō, p. 135

B. Nouns
4018 peribolaion, p. 136
4629 skepasma, p. 136

EAR
A. Nouns
241 ʼōzen, p. 65
3775 ous, p. 189
5621 ōtion, p. 189
189 akoē, p. 189

EYE
5869 ʻayin, p. 74

FACE
6440 pānîm, p. 75
4383 prosōpon, p. 220

FOOT, FEET
A. Nouns
4228 pous, p. 246
939 basis, p. 246

FOREHEAD
3359 metōpon, p. 248

GARMENT
899 beged, p. 89
Note, p. 261

GIRDLE
2223 zōnē, p. 265

HAND
A. Adjective
5497 cheiragōgos, p. 288

B. Verbs
5496 cheiragōgeō, p. 288
2021 epicheireō, p. 288

C. Nouns
3027 yād, p. 104
849 autocheir, p. 288

HANDKERCHIEF
4676 soudarion, p. 289

HEAD
A. Noun
7218 rōʼš, p. 105

HEEL
4418 pterna, p. 299

KNEE
1119 gonu, p. 346

LATCHET
2438 himas, p. 353

LEATHER, LEATHERN
1193 dermatinos, p. 361

LEG
4628 skelos, p. 363

LIP
8193 śāpāh, p. 137
5491 cheilos, p. 373

MANTLE
4018 peribolaion, p. 392

MOUTH
A. Nouns
6310 peh, p. 155
4750 stoma, p. 419

NAPKIN
4676 soudarion, p. 426

NECK
5137 trachēlos, p. 428

NEEDLE
4476 rhaphis, p. 429
956d belonē, p. 429

NOSE
A. Noun
639 ʼap, p. 161

PALM
A. Noun
3709 kap, p. 171
Note, p. 456

PURPLE
4211 porphuropōlis, p. 499

RIGHT HAND
3225 yāmîn, p. 204

ROBE
4749 stolē, p. 537
5511 chlamus, p. 537
2440 himation, p. 537
2066 esthēs, p. 537

SANDAL
4547 sandalion, p. 546

SEW
1976 epiraptō *or* epirrhaptō, p. 566

SHEEPSKIN
3374 mēlōtē, p. 569

SHEET
3607 othonē, p. 569

SHOE
5266 hupodēma, p. 572

SHOULDER
5606 ōmos, p. 572

SILK
4596 sērikos *or* sirikos, p. 576

STOMACH
4751 stomachos, p. 600

TOWEL
3012 lention, p. 638

UNDRESSED
46 agnaphos, p. 651

VESTURE
2440 himation, p. 660
2441 himatismos, p. 660
4018 peribolaion, p. 660

Human Civilization

Human civilization comprises that network of social relationships, institutions, and values that make up the corporate aspect of human life. Society is organized in communities (for example, *city; town; village*) within *countries (border; boundary; colony; district; region),* with their associated governing institutions *(ruler; emperor; queen),* judicial systems *(court; senate; magistrate),* methods of criminal punishment *(cell; behead; jailer),* and means of defense *(army; gate; chariotry).*

Scripture amply illustrates the daily round of human activity *(to arise; kindle; sweep; swim; bathed; flee)* in biblical times, with its reference to everyday items *(bed; pillow; oven; pitcher; dish; couch)* to be found in *houses (roof; room; property),* and human *customs,* for example, regarding dead bodies *(bier; cave; sepulchre).* Education *(school),* arts and *crafts (entertain; dance; theater; poet), music (harp; cymbal; minstrel),* and the variety of occupations *(silversmith; soldier; tanner;*

tentmakers; physician; to work) carried on illustrate the rich variety of life in biblical times. *Business* and *trade (market; merchants; to sell)* and the associated coinage *(money; farthing; pence; shekel)* and weights and *measures (cubit; furlong; fathom)* were an integral part of daily life, as was *travel (street; compass; seafaring; boat; mariners)*.

Communication, both oral *(language; Latin)* and written *(narrative; letter; writing)*, was highly developed.

ABOARD
1910   epibainō, p. 3

ABSENCE, ABSENT
A. Noun
666   apousia, p. 5

B. Verbs
548   apeimi, p. 5
1553   ekdēmeō, p. 5

C. Preposition
817   ater, p. 5

ACCOUNT
B. Noun
3056   logos, p. 10

ADD
2007   epitithēmi, p. 12
4323   prosanatithēmi, p. 12
3923   pareispherō, p. 12

ADO
2350   thorubeō, p. 13

ADVENTURE
1325   didōmi, p. 15

AFFAIR
4230   pragmatia *or* pragmateia, p. 16

AGREE, AGREEMENT
A. Verbs
4856   sumphōneō, p. 20
4934   suntithēmi, p. 20
2132   eunoeō, p. 20
3982   peithō, p. 20

B. Noun
1106   gnōmē, p. 20

C. Adjectives
800   asumphōnos, p. 20
2470   isos, p. 20

ANCHOR
45   ankura, p. 26

ANSWER
A. Nouns
612   apokrisis, p. 29
627   apologia, p. 29

B. Verbs
611   apokrinomai, p. 29
470   antapokrinomai, p. 30
5274   hupolambanō, p. 30
626   apologeomai, p. 30
483   antilegō, p. 30
4960   sustoicheō, p. 30

APPEAL
1941   epikaleō, p. 31

APPEASE
2687   katastellō, p. 33

TO ARISE
A. Verb
6965   qûm, p. 6

B. Noun
4725   māqôm, p. 7

ARMY
4753   strateuma, p. 38
4760   stratopedon, p. 38
3925   parembolē, p. 38

ART, ARTS
5078   technē, p. 38

ASSASSIN
4607   sikarios, p. 42

ASSAULT
A. Verb
2186   ephistēmi, p. 42

B. Noun
3730   hormē, p. 42

AUSTERE
840   austēros, p. 45

AXE
513   axinē, p. 47

BAG
1101   glōssokomon, p. 47
905   ballantion, p. 49

BAGGAGE
643v   episkeuazō, p. 49

BALANCE
2218   zugos, p. 49

BAND, ARMY
1416   gᵉdûd, p. 12
4686   speira, p. 49
2202   zeuktēria, p. 49

BANK, BANKERS
5132   trapeza, p. 49
5133   trapezitēs, p. 50

BASON
3537   niptēr, p. 51

BATHED
3068   louō, p. 51

BATTLE
4171   polemos, p. 51

BEAM
1385   dokos, p. 52

BED
2825   klinē, p. 55
2825*   klinarion, p. 55
2845   koitē, p. 55
2895   krabbatos, p. 55

BEHEAD
607   apokephalizō, p. 59
3990   pelekizō, p. 59

BEWAIL
2799   klaiō, p. 65
2875   koptō, p. 65
3996   pentheō, p. 65

BID, BIDDEN, BADE, BID AGAIN
2564   kaleō, p. 66
2753   keleuō, p. 66
3004   eipon, p. 66
479   antikaleō, p. 66

BID FAREWELL
657   apotassō, p. 66
575,
782   apaspazomai, p. 66

BIER
4673   soros, p. 66

BILL
975   biblion, p. 66
1121   gramma, p. 66

BIND, BINDING
1210   deō, p. 66
4019   perideō, p. 66
5265   hupodeō, p. 66
2611   katadeō, p. 66
4887   sundeō, p. 66
1195   desmeuō *or* desmeō, p. 67

BOARD
4548   sanis, p. 71

BOAT
4142   ploiarion, p. 71
4143   ploion, p. 71
4627   skaphē, p. 71

BOOTY
7998   šālāl, p. 22

BORDER
3725   horion, p. 74

BORROW
1155   daneizō, p. 74

BOUND
3734   horothesia, p. 75

BOUNDARY
1366   gᵉbûl, p. 22

BOW
5115   toxon, p. 76

BRAIDED
4117   plegma, p. 76

BRASS, BRAZEN
5475   chalkos, p. 77
5470   chalkeos, p. 77
5473   chalkion, p. 77
5471   chalkeus, p. 77

TO BREAK
7665   šābar, p. 24

BRIDLE
A. Noun
5469   chalinos, p. 79

BRIM
507   anō, p. 80

BRING, BRINGING, BROUGHT
A. Verbs
5342   pherō, p. 80
399   anapherō, p. 80
667   apopherō, p. 80
1533   eispherō, p. 80
1627   ekphero, p. 80
2018   epipherō, p. 80
4393   propherō, p. 80
4374   prospherō, p. 80
4851   sumpherō, p. 80
71   ago, p. 80
321   anagō, p. 80
520   apagō, p. 80
1521   eisagō, p. 80
1806   exagō, p. 80
1863   epagō, p. 80
2609   katagō, p. 80
3919   pareisagō, p. 80
4254   proagō, p. 80
2865   komizō, p. 80
3930   parechō, p. 80
654   apostrephō, p. 80

2601 katabibazō, p. 80
4822 sumbibazō, p. 80
4311 propempō, p. 80
985 blastanō, p. 81
4160 poieō, p. 81
1544 ekballō, p. 81
5088 tiktō, p. 81
616 apokueō, p. 81
1080 gennaō, p. 81
2164 euphoreō, p. 81
5142 trephō, p. 81
397 anatrephō, p. 81
1625 ektrephō, p. 81
518 apangellō, p. 81

B. Noun
1898 epeisagōgē, p. 81

BROOD
3555 nossia, p. 81

BROW
3790 ophras, p. 82

BUNDLE
1197 desmē, p. 83
4128 plēthos, p. 83

TO BURN
A. Verb
8313 śārap, p. 27

BURST
4486 rhēgnumi, p. 84
2997 lakeō *or* laskō, p. 84

BUSHEL
3426 modios, p. 85

BUSINESS
A. Nouns
5532 chreia, p. 85
2039 ergasia, p. 85

B. Adjective
2398 idios, p. 85

CAGE
5438 phulakē, p. 86

CAPTAIN
5506 chiliarchos, p. 88
4755 stratēgos, p. 88

CARCASE
2966 kōlon, p. 89

CARRY
4792 sunkomizō, p. 90
1580 ekkomizō, p. 90
5342 pherō, p. 90
1308 diapherō, p. 90
3346 metatithēmi, p. 90
520 apagō, p. 90
4879 sunapagō, p. 90

CASE
2192 echō, p. 90
4281 proechō, p. 90

CAST
A. Verbs
906 ballō, p. 91
4496 rhiptō, p. 91
1601 ekpiptō, p. 91
577 apoballō, p. 91
1544 ekballō, p. 91
1685 emballō, p. 91
1911 epiballō, p. 91
2598 kataballō, p. 91
97,
906 amphiballō, p. 91

4016 periballō, p. 91
641 aporiptō, p. 91
1977 epiriptō, p. 91
683 apōtheō, p. 91
2507 kathaireō, p. 91
1260 dialogizomai, p. 91
659 apotithēmi, p. 91
1260 ektithēmi, p. 91
4014 periaireō, p. 91

B. Noun
1000 bole, p. 92

C. Adjective
96 adokimos, p. 92

TO CAST DOWN
7993 šālak, p. 32

CAVE
3692 opē, p. 93
4693 spēlaion, p. 93

CELL
3612 oikēma, p. 94

CENTURION
1543 hekatontarchos, p. 94
1543 hekatontarchēs, p. 94
2760 kenturiōn, p. 94

CHAMBERING
2845 koitē, p. 95

CHAMBERLAIN
2846 ho epi tou koitōnos, p. 95

CHARGER
4094 pinax, p. 97

CHARIOT
716 harma, p. 97
4480 rhedē, p. 97

CHARIOTRY
A. Nouns
7393 rekeb, p. 34
4818 merkābāh, p. 34

B. Verb
7392 rākab, p. 34

CIRCUIT
4022 perierchomai, p. 102

CITIZEN, CITIZENSHIP
4177 politēs, p. 103
4847 sumpolitēs, p. 103
4174 politeia, p. 103

CITY
5892 'îr, p. 35

CLAMOR
2906 kraugē, p. 103

CLANGING
214 alalazō, p. 103

TO CLEAVE, SPLIT
1234 bāqa', p. 38

COALS
440 anthrax, p. 107
439 anthrakia, p. 107

COLONY
2862 kolōnia, p. 108

COMMODIOUS
428 aneuthetos, p. 113

COMPASS
2944v kukleuō, p. 116
2944 kukloō, p. 116
4033 perikukloō, p. 116
4013 periagō, p. 116

4029 perikeimai, p. 116
4022 perierchomai, p. 116

COMPEL
315 anankazō, p. 117
29 angareuō, p. 117

CONCEAL
3871 parakaluptō, p. 118

CONCLUDE
4822 sumbibazō, p. 118

CONCOURSE
4963 suntrophē, p. 118

CONFER, CONFERENCE
4323 prosanatithēmi, p. 120
4814 sullaleō, p. 120
4820 sumballō, p. 120

CONFOUND, CONFUSE, CONFUSION
A. Nouns
181 akatastasia, p. 122
4799 sunchusis, p. 122

B. Verbs
4797 suncheō, p. 122
2617 kataischunō, p. 122

TO CONFRONT
6923 qādam, p. 45

CONSENT
A. Verbs
1843 exomologeō, p. 123
1962 epineuō, p. 123
4334 proserchomai, p. 123
4784 sunkatatithēmi, p. 123
4852 sumphēmi, p. 123
4909 suneudokeō, p. 123

B. Phrases

CONSPIRACY
4945 sunōmosia, p. 124

CONSULT, CONSULTATION
A. Verbs
1011 bouleuō, p. 124
4823 sumbouleuō, p. 124

B. Noun
4824 sumboulion, p. 124

CONTAIN
5562 chōreō, p. 125
4023 periechō, p. 125

COPY
5262 hupodeigma, p. 129

CORD
2256 ḥebel, p. 48
4979 schoinion, p. 129

COUCH
2826 klinidion, p. 132
2895 krabbatos, p. 132

COUNCIL, COUNCILLOR
4824 sumboulion, p. 132
4892 sunedrion, p. 132
1010 bouleutēs, p. 132

COUNSEL
A. Nouns
1012 boulē, p. 132
4825 sumboulos, p. 132

B. Verbs
1011 bouleuō, p. 132
4823 sumbouleuō, p. 132

COUNT
2192 echō, p. 132
2233 hēgeomai, p. 132
3049 logizomai, p. 132
5585 psēphizō, p. 133
4860 sumpsēphizō, p. 133

COUNTRY
A. Nouns
68 agros, p. 133
3968 patris, p. 133
5561 chōra, p. 133
4066 perichōros, p. 133
3313 meros, p. 133

B. Adjectives
510 anōterikos, p. 133
3714 oreinos, p. 133

C. Verb
589 apodēmeō, p. 133

COURT
2691 ḥāṣēr, p. 49
60 agoraios, p. 134
833 aulē, p. 134
933 basileion, p. 134

CRAFT, CRAFTSMAN
5078 technē, p. 136
5079 technitēs, p. 136
2039 ergasia, p. 137
3313 meros, p. 137

CROSS
1276 diaperaō, p. 138

CRY, CRYING
A. Nouns
2906 kraugē, p. 139
995 boē, p. 139

B. Verb
993 boaō, p. 139

CUBIT
520 'ammāh, p. 53
4083 pēchus, p. 140

CUSTOM (Toll)
5056 telos, p. 142

CUSTOM (Usage), ACCUSTOM
A. Nouns
1485 ethos, p. 142
4914 sunētheia, p. 142

B. Verbs
1480 ethizō, p. 142
1486 ethō, p. 142

CUT
2875 koptō, p. 142
609 apokoptō, p. 142
1581 ekkoptō, p. 142
2629 katakoptō, p. 142
1282 diapriō, p. 142
1371 dichotomeō, p. 142
4932 suntemnō, p. 143
851 aphaireō, p. 143

CYMBAL
2950 kumbalon, p. 143

DANCE
3738 orcheō, p. 144

DANCING
5525 choros, p. 144

DEAL WITH, HAVE DEALINGS WITH
1580 gāmal, p. 55

4160 poieō, p. 148
4374 prospherō, p. 148
4798 sunchraomai, p. 148

DECEASE
A. Noun
1841 exodos, p. 150

B. Verb
5053 teleutaō, p. 150

DECK
5558 chrusoō, p. 152

DEPARTING, DEPARTURE
359 analusis, p. 160
867 aphixis, p. 160

DISH
5165 trublion, p. 173

DISTRICT
3310 meris, p. 177

DITCH
999 bothunos, p. 177

DOORWAY
A. Noun
6607 petaḥ, p. 61

B. Verb
6605 pātaḥ, p. 62

DRAUGHT
61 agra, p. 183
856 aphedrōn, p. 183

DUNG
4657 skubalon, p. 187
2874d koprion, p. 187

DUNGHILL
2874 kopria, p. 187

DYSENTERY
1420**dusenterion, p. 188

EMPEROR
4575 sebastos, p. 197

ENEMY
341 'ōyēb, p. 70
6862 ṣar, p. 71

ENTERTAIN
3579 xenizō, p. 203

EPISTLE
1992 epistolē, p. 204

TO ESCAPE
4422 mālaṭ, p. 71

EUNUCH
A. Noun
2135 eunouchos, p. 208

B. Verb
2134 eunouchizō, p. 208

EXPERT
1109 gnōstēs, p. 218

FAN
4425 ptuon, p. 226

FARTHING
787 assarion, p. 227
2835 kodrantēs, p. 227

FAST
805 asphalizō, p. 228

FATHOM
3712 orguia, p. 229

FETCH
3343 metapempō, p. 233

FETTER
3976 pedē, p. 233

TO FIGHT
A. Verb
3898 lāḥam, p. 81

B. Noun
4421 milḥāmāh, p. 81

TO FIND
4672 māṣā', p. 82

FIRKIN
3355 metrētēs, p. 240

TO FLEE
1272 bāraḥ, p. 83
5127 nûs, p. 83

FLUTE-PLAYERS
834 aulētēs, p. 244

FOLD
833 aulē, p. 244

FORESAIL
736 artemōn, p. 249

FORESHIP
4408 prōra, p. 249

FREIGHT
1546 ekbolē, p. 256

FULLER
1102 gnapheus, p. 259

FURLONG
4712 stadion, p. 259

FURNACE
2575 kaminos, p. 259

GARNISH
2885 kosmeō, p. 261

GATE
8179 ša'ar, p. 89
4439 pulē, p. 261
4440 pulōn, p. 261

GEAR
4632 skeuos, p. 262

GOLD RING
5554 chrusodaktulios, p. 273

GOODS
5223 huparxis, p. 275
979 bios, p. 275
4632 skeuos, p. 275

GRAVE
3419 mnēmeion, p. 278
3418 mnēma, p. 278

GRAVEN
5480 charagma, p. 279

TO BE GREAT, HEAVY
A. Verb
7231 rābab, p. 101

B. Nouns
7230 rōb, p. 102
7227 rab, p. 102

C. Adjective
7227 rab, p. 102

GUARDIAN
2012 epitropos, p. 284

HALL
833 aulē, p. 287

HARP
A. Noun
2788 kithara, p. 291

B. Verb
2789   kitharizō, p. 291

HARPER
2790   kitharōdos, p. 291

TO HASTEN, MAKE HASTE
4116   māhar, p. 105

HAVEN
3040   limēn, p. 293

HEADLONG
4248   prēnēs, p. 295

HEW, HEW DOWN, HEWN
A. Verbs
1581   ekkoptō, p. 303
2998   latomeō, p. 303

B. Adjective
2991   laxeutos, p. 303

HIGHWAY, HIGHWAYSIDE
3598   hodos, p. 304

HIRE
A. Nouns
3408   misthos, p. 305
3409   misthoō, p. 305

HIRED HOUSE
3410   misthōma, p. 305

HOLE
5454   phōleos, p. 307
3692   opē, p. 307

HOOK
44   ankistron, p. 311

HOST
A. Noun
6633   ṣābā', p. 116

HOUSE
A. Nouns
3624   oikos, p. 313
3614   oikia, p. 313

B. Adverb
3832   panoikei, p. 313

HOUSETOP
1430   dōma, p. 314

IMPULSE
3730   hormē, p. 321

TO INHERIT
A. Verb
5157   nāḥal, p. 120

B. Noun
5159   naḥălāh, p. 121

INK
3188   melan, p. 326

INN
2646   kataluma, p. 326
3829   pandocheion, p. 326

INSCRIPTION
1924   epigraphō, p. 327

INSURRECTION
A. Nouns
4714   stasis, p. 329
4955v   stasiastēs, p. 329

B. Verb
2721   katephistēmi, p. 329

IRON
A. Noun
4604   sidēros, p. 331

B. Adjective
4603   sidēreos, p. 331

JAILER
1200   desmophulax, p. 332

JOURNEY, JOURNEYINGS
A. Nouns
3598   hodos, p. 334
3597   hodoiporia, p. 335

B. Verbs
4198   poreuomai, p. 335
1279   diaporeuō, p. 335
3596   hodoiporeō, p. 335
3593   hodeuō, p. 335
4922   sunodeuō, p. 335
2137   euodoō, p. 335
4311   propempō, p. 335
589   apodēmeō, p. 335

JURISDICTION
1849   exousia, p. 338

JUSTICE
1349   dikē, p. 338

KEEPER
5441   phulax, p. 341

KICK
2979   laktizō, p. 342

KINDLE
681   haptō, p. 343
4012,
681   periaptō, p. 343
381   anaptō, p. 343

LABOR
A. Nouns
2873   kopos, p. 349
4192   ponos, p. 349

B. Verbs
2872   kopiaō, p. 349
5492   cheimazō, p. 349

LADING
5413   phortion, p. 350

LANE
4505   rhumē, p. 352

LANGUAGE
1258   dialektos, p. 352

LANTERN
5322   phanos, p. 352

LATIN
4515   rhōmaisti, p. 354

LAUNCH
321   anagō, p. 354
1877   epanago, p. 354

LEAN
345   anakeimai, p. 360
377   anapiptō, p. 360

LEAP
242   hallomai, p. 360
4640   skirtaō, p. 360
1814   exallomai, p. 360
2177   ephallomai, p. 360

LEARNING
1121   gramma, p. 361
1319   didaskalia, p. 361

LEE
Note, p. 363

LETTER
1121   gramma, p. 365
1992   epistolē, p. 365

LEGION
3003   legiōn, p. 363

LEISURE
2119   eukaireō, p. 363

LEND, LENDER
A. Verbs
1155v   daneizō, p. 364
5531v   kichrēmi, p. 364

B. Noun
1157   danistēs *or* daneistēs, p. 364

LICK
1952a   epileichō, p. 366

TO LIE
A. Verb
7901   šākab, p. 135

B. Noun
4904   miškāb, p. 135

LIE IN WAIT
A. Verb
1748   enedreuō, p. 367

B. Noun
1747,
1749   enedra *or* enedron, p. 367

LOAD
4853   maśśā', p. 139

LODGE, LODGING
A. Verbs
835   aulizomai, p. 375
3681   kataskēnoō, p. 375
2647   kataluō, p. 375
3579   xenizō, p. 375

B. Noun
3578   xenia, p. 376

TO LOOK
5027   nābaṭ, p. 139

LOUD
3173   megas, p. 381

LUMP
5445   phurama, p. 384

MAGISTRATE
4755   stratēgos, p. 385
758   archōn, p. 385

TO MAKE HASTE, HASTEN
4116   māhar, p. 146

MARINERS
3492   nautēs, p. 393

MARKET, MARKETPLACE
58   agora, p. 394

TO MEASURE
A. Verb
4058   mādad, p. 150

B. Noun
4060   middāh, p. 150

MERCHANDISE
A. Nouns
1711   emporia, p. 403
1712   emporion, p. 403
1117   gomos, p. 403

B. Verb
1710   emporeuomai, p. 403

SEAT
A. Nouns
2515 kathedra, p. 555
4410 prōtokathedria, p. 555
B. Verb
2521 kathēmai, p. 555

SECRET
5475 sôd, p. 218

SEDITION
A. Nouns
4714 stasis, p. 556
1370 dichostasia, p. 556
B. Verb
387 anastatoō, p. 556

TO SELL
4376 mākar, p. 221
4453 pōleō, p. 559
4097 pipraskō, p. 559
591 apodidōmi, p. 559

SENATE
1087 gerousia, p. 559

SEPULCHRE
5028 taphos, p. 562

SERGEANT
4465 rhabdouchos, p. 562

TO SET IN ORDER
6186 'ārak, p. 225

TO SET, PLACE
7896 šît, p. 225

TO SET ON, SET UP
A. Verb
7760 sîm, p. 226

SHAMBLES
3111 makellon, p. 567

SHEATH
2336 thēkē, p. 568

SHEAR, SHEARER, SHORN
2751 keirō, p. 568

SHEKEL, HALF SHEKEL
4715 statēr, p. 569
1323 didrachmon, p. 569

SHIP, SHIPPING
4143 ploion, p. 571
4142 ploiarion, p. 571
3491 naus, p. 571

SHIPWRECK
3489 nauageō, p. 571

SILVERSMITH
695 argurokopos, p. 576

SINK
1036 buthizō, p. 578
2670 katapontizo, p. 578
5087 tithēmi, p. 578

SMELLING
3750 osphrēsis, p. 581

SOLDIER
A. Nouns
4757 stratiōtēs, p. 584
4753 strateuma, p. 584
4961 sustratiōtēs, p. 584
B. Verb
4754 strateuō, p. 584

SOUND
A. Nouns
5456 phōnē, p. 589

2279 ēchos, p. 589
5353 phthongos, p. 589
B. Verbs
2278 ēcheō, p. 589
1837 exēcheō, p. 589
4537 salpizō, p. 589
1001 bolizō, p. 589

SPEARMAN
1187 dexiolabos, p. 591

SPEECH
3056 logos, p. 591
5981 lalia, p. 592
2129 eulogia, p. 592
5542 chrēstologia, p. 592

SPY
A. Nouns
1455 enkathetos, p. 597
2685 kataskopos, p. 597

STAFF, STAVES
4464 rhabdos, p. 597
3586 xulon, p. 597

STAIR
304 anabathmos, p. 597

STEEP
2911 krēmnos, p. 599

STEP
A. Noun
6471 pa'am, p. 246

STERN
4403 prumna, p. 599

STICK
5434 phruganon, p. 600

STICK FAST
2043 ereidō, p. 600

STINK
3605 ozō, p. 600

STORY
5152 tristegos, p. 601

STREET
A. Noun
2351 ḫûṣ, p. 247
4113 plateia, p. 603
296 amphodon, p. 603

SUBURBS
A. Noun
4054 migrāš, p. 251

SUFFICIENCY
1767 day, p. 252

SWEEP
4563 saroō, p. 613

SWIM
2860 kolumbaō, p. 613
1579 ekkolumbaō, p. 613

SWORD
A. Noun
2719 ḥereb, p. 253
B. Verb
2719 ḥārab, p. 254

TABLE
5132 trapeza, p. 615
4109 plax, p. 615
345 anakeimai, p. 615

TO TAKE, HANDLE
8610 tāpaś, p. 255
270 'āḥaz, p. 255

TANNER
1038 burseus, p. 618

TO TELL
A. Verb
5046 nāgad, p. 257

TENTMAKERS
4635 skēnopoios, p. 623

TETRARCH
A. Noun
5076 tetraarchēs or tetrarchēs, p. 624
B. Verb
5075 tetraarcheō or tetrarcheō, p. 624

THEATER
2302 theatron, p. 625

THING(S)
3056 logos, p. 627
4229 pragma, p. 627

TILES, TILING
2766 keramos, p. 633

TIP
206 akron, p. 634

TORCH
2985 lampas, p. 637

TOWER
4026 migdāl, p. 266
4444 purgos, p. 638

TOWN
2969 kōmopolis, p. 638
2968 kōmē, p. 638

TOWN CLERK
1122 grammateus, p. 638

TRADE
A. Verbs
2038 ergazomai, p. 638
4231 pragmateuomai, p. 639
1281 diapragmateuomai, p. 639
1710 emporeuomai, p. 639
B. Nouns
5078 technē, p. 639
3313 meros, p. 639

TRAP
2339 thera, p. 640

TRAVEL
1330 dierchomai, p. 641

TREASURE
A. Noun
2344 thēsauros, p. 641

TREATISE
3056 logos, p. 642

TRENCH
5482 charax, p. 642

TRIBUTE
5411 phoros, p. 643
2778 kēnsos, p. 643
1323 didrachmon, p. 643

TRIM
2885 kosmeō, p. 644

TRUMPETER
4538 salpistēs, p. 646

TO TURN, TO TURN TOWARDS, TURN BACK
A. Verbs
2015 hāpak, p. 269

5437	sābab, p. 270
6437	pānāh, p. 271

B. Nouns

5439	sābîb, p. 271
6438	pinnāh, p. 272

UNDERGIRD

5269   hupozōnnumi, p. 650

UNLADE

670   apophortizo, p. 652

USING

671   apochrēsis, p. 656

VESSEL

3627   kᵉlî, p. 274

VILLAGE

2968   kōmē, p. 660

VOYAGE

4144   ploos *or* plous, p. 663

WALL

2346	hômāh, p. 280
5038	teichos, p. 664
5109	toichos, p. 664

WALLET

4082   pēra, p. 665

WAR

A. Verb

4170   polemeō, p. 665

B. Noun

4171   polemos, p. 665

WATERPOT

5201   hudria, p. 668

WAY

A. Nouns

1870	derek, p. 284
734	'ōraḥ, p. 285

TO WILL, BE WILLING

14   'ābāh, p. 288

TO WORK

A. Verbs

6466	pā'al, p. 293
6213	'āśāh, p. 293

B. Noun

4639   ma'áśeh, p. 294

WOUND

A. Noun

5134   trauma, p. 688

B. Verb

5135   traumatizō, p. 688

WRITING

1121   gramma, p. 689

WRITING TABLET

4093   pinakidion, p. 689

SIN

Scripture describes *sin* in many different terms, such as *iniquity (evil; wickedness), disobedience (lawless; unlawful; rebel), trespass (transgress), corruption (black; blemish; defile; filthiness; spot), ungodliness (unholy; unjust; unrighteousness),* and guilt *(guilty).* All attitudes and actions which result from a wrong relationship with God are *sinful.*

The Nature of Sin

BLACK, BLACKNESS

A. Adjective

3189   melas, p. 68

BLEMISH

A. Noun

3470   mōmos, p. 69

CORRUPT, CORRUPTION, CORRUPTIBLE

A. Verbs

2585	kapēleuō, p. 130
5351	phtheirō, p. 130
1311	diaphtheirō, p. 130
2704	kataphtheirō, p. 130
4595	sēpō, p. 130

B. Nouns

5356	phthora, p. 131
1312	diaphthora, p. 131

C. Adjectives

5349	phthartos, p. 131
4550	sapros, p. 131

DEFILE, DEFILEMENT

A. Verbs

2840	koinoō, p. 154
3392	miainō, p. 155
3435	molunō, p. 155
4695	spiloō, p. 155

B. Nouns

3393	miasma, p. 155
3394	miasmos, p. 155
3436	molusmos, p. 155

C. Adjective

2839   koinos, p. 155

DISOBEDIENCE, DISOBEDIENT

A. Nouns

543	apeitheia, p. 173
3876	parakoē, p. 173

B. Adjective

545   apeithēs, p. 173

C. Verb

544   apeitheō, p. 173

EVIL, EVIL-DOER

A. Adjectives

2556	kakos, p. 211
4190	ponēros, p. 211
5337	phaulos, p. 212

B. Nouns

2549	kakia, p. 212
4190	ponēros, p. 212
2556	kakon, p. 212
5337	phaulon, p. 212
2555	kakopoios, p. 212

C. Verbs

2559	kakoō, p. 212
2554	kakopoieō, p. 212

D. Adverb

2560   kakōs, p. 212

FILTHINESS, FILTHY

A. Nouns

151	aischrotēs, p. 237
4507	rhuparia, p. 237
3436	molusmos, p. 237
766	aselgeia, p. 237

B. Adjectives

150	aischros, p. 238
146	aischrokerdēs, p. 238
4508	rhuparos, p. 238

C. Adverb

147   aischrokerdōs, p. 238

D. Verb

4510v   rhupainō, p. 238

GUILTY

1777   enochos, p. 285

INIQUITY

A. Verb

5753   'āwāh, p. 121

B. Nouns

5771	'āwōn, p. 121
205	'āwen, p. 122
458	anomia, p. 326
93	adikia, p. 326
92	adikēma, p. 326
4189	ponēria, p. 326
3892	paranomia, p. 326

LAWLESS, LAWLESSNESS

A. Adjective

459   anomos, p. 357

B. Noun

458   anomia, p. 357

TO REBEL

A. Verb

4784   mārāh, p. 193

B. Noun

4805   mᵉrî, p. 193

C. Adjective

4805   mᵉrî, p. 194

SIN

A. Nouns

205	'āwen, p. 230
817	'āšām, p. 230
5999	'āmāl, p. 230
5771	'āwōn, p. 231
7563	rāšā', p. 231
2403	ḥaṭṭā't, p. 232
266	hamartia, p. 576
265	hamartēma, p. 577

B. Adjectives

7563	rāšā', p. 232
7451	ra', p. 232
361	anamartētos, p. 577

C. Verbs

5674	'ābar, p. 233
2398	ḥāṭā', p. 233
264	hamartanō, p. 577
4258	proamartanō, p. 577

SINFUL

268   hamartōlos, p. 578

SPOT

A. Nouns

4696	spilos, p. 596
4694	spilas, p. 596

SIN

B. Verb
4695 spiloō, p. 596

TRANSGRESS, TRANSGRESSION
A. Verbs
6586 pāša‘, p. 266
3845 parabainō, p. 639
5233 huperbainō, p. 640
3928 parerchomai, p. 640

B. Nouns
6588 peša‘, p. 266
3847 parabasis, p. 640
3892 paranomia, p. 640

TO TRESPASS
A. Verbs
4603 māʻal, p. 267
264 hamartanō, p. 643

B. Nouns
4604 maʻal, p. 268
3900 paraptōma, p. 642

UNGODLINESS
B. Adjective
765 asebēs, p. 651

C. Verb
764 asebeō, p. 651

UNHOLY
462 anosios, p. 651
2839 koinon, p. 651

UNJUST
94 adikos, p. 652

UNLAWFUL
111 athemitos, p. 652

UNRIGHTEOUSNESS
A. Noun
93 adikia, p. 653

B. Verb
91 adikeō, p. 653

WICKEDNESS
1100 beîîyaʻal, p. 288
4189 ponēria, p. 675
2549 kakia, p. 675

Sinners Described

A wide variety of terms are used in Scripture to describe all these who do *wrong (wrongfully; offender; malefactor; reprobate; transgressor)*. *Sinners* are *ungodly (unrighteous)*, without *God, wicked, abusers, men-pleasers*, and God-fighters *(fighting)*. *Unbelievers* are often *impenitent* and held in bondage *(bondman)* to sin.

ABUSE, ABUSERS
2710 katachraomai, p. 7

BONDMAN, BONDMAID
1401 doulos, p. 73

FIGHTING
B. Adjective
2314 theomachos, p. 235

GOD (without)
112 atheos, p. 272

IMPENITENT
279 ametanoētos, p. 320

MALEFACTOR
2557 kakourgos, p. 388
2555 kakopoios, p. 388

MEN-PLEASERS
441 anthrōpareskos, p. 403

OFFENDER
3781 opheiletēs, p. 442

REPROBATE
96 adokimos, p. 526

SINNER
268 hamartōlos, p. 578

TRANSGRESSOR
3848 parabatēs, p. 640
459 anomos, p. 640

UNBELIEVER
571 apistos, p. 649

UNGODLY
A. Noun
763 asebeia, p. 651

UNRIGHTEOUS
94 adikos, p. 653

WICKED
A. Noun
7563 rāšā‘, p. 287

B. Adjectives
7563 rāšā‘, p. 287
4190 ponēros, p. 675
113 athesmos, p. 675

C. Verb
7561 rāša‘, p. 288

WRONG, WRONGDOER, WRONGDOING
A. Nouns
93 adikia, p. 689
92 adikēma, p. 689

B. Verb
91 adikeō, p. 689

WRONGFULLY
95 adikōs, p. 689

Aspects of Sin

Sin is an *abomination (abominable; amiss; hate; miserable; noisome; perverse; vile)* in the sight of God that *alienates* humanity from him, leading to divine *condemnation (inclose)* and the *punishment (drown; punish)* of *death (dead; debt; decay; lose; recompence; wages)*.

Because of the *fall*, all human beings are held *captive (beset; branded; bondage; enslaved; sell)* to this *curse* of sin, and the human heart *(delusion; desire; devise; gross; thought)* has an inherent bias towards evil *(bad; base; carnal; crooked; dark; malignity; revive)*. Human weaknesses and failings *(fault)* are also sinful in themselves and may lead to further sin.

Ignorance (blindness; brute; dull; rude) and *folly (fool; foolishness; idle; barren; irksome; raca; stupid fellow; unwise)* are aspects of sin, as is *unbelief (disbelieve; unbelieving)* and hardness of *heart (hard; stiffnecked; to shut)*.

Sin produces *strife (blame)*, *shame (ashamed; reproach)*, dis-

honor and *toil*, and causes *harm (hurt; injure)* to both the sinner and to the one sinned against.

ABOMINABLE, ABOMINATION
A. Adjectives
111 athemitos, p. 4
947 bdeluktos, p. 4

B. Verbs
8581 tāʻab, p. 1
948 bdelussō, p. 4

C. Nouns
8441 tôʻēbāh, p. 1
946 bdelugma, p. 4

ALIENATE
526 apallotrioō, p. 21

AMISS
A. Adjective
824 atopos, p. 26

B. Adverb
2560 kakōs, p. 26

ASHAMED, SHAME
A. Verbs
153 aischunō, p. 39
1870 epaischunomai, p. 39
2617 kataischunō, p. 39
1788 entrepō, p. 39

B. Nouns
152 aischunē, p. 39
1791 entropē, p. 39

C. Adjectives
150 aischunos, p. 39
422 anepaischuntos, p. 39

BAD
2556 kakos, p. 48
4190 ponēros, p. 49
4550 sapros, p. 49

BARREN
692 argos, p. 51

BASE, BASER
60 agoraios, p. 51

BESET
2139 euperistatos, p. 63

BLAME
A. Verb
3469 mōmaomai, p. 68

B. Adjective
299 amōmos, p. 68

BLIND, BLINDNESS
A. Verbs
5186 tuphloō, p. 70
4456 pōroō, p. 70

B. Adjective
5185 tuphlos, p. 70

C. Noun
4457 pōrōsis, p. 70

BONDAGE
A. Noun
1397 douleia, p. 73

B. Verbs
1398 douleuō, p. 73
1402 douloō, p. 73
1396 doulagōgeō, p. 73
2615 katadouloō, p. 73

BRANDED
2743 kaustēriazo, p. 77

BRUTE
249   alogos, p. 82

CAPTIVE
B. Verb
163   aichmalōtizō, p. 88

CARNAL, CARNALLY
4559   sarkikos, p. 89
4560   sarkinos, p. 89

CONDEMN, CONDEMNATION
A. Verbs
2607   kataginōskō, p. 118
2613   katadikazō, p. 119
2919   krinō, p. 119
2632   katakrinō, p. 119

B. Nouns
2917   krima, p. 119
2631   katakrima, p. 119
2920   krisis, p. 119
2633   katakrisis, p. 119

C. Adjective
843   autokatakritos, p. 119

CROOKED
4646   skolios, p. 138

CURSE, CURSING, CURSED, ACCURSED
A. Nouns
685   ara, p. 141
2671   katara, p. 141
33   anathema, p. 141
2652   katathema, p. 141

B. Verbs
7043   qālal, p. 53
332   anathematizō, p. 141
2653   katanathematizō, p. 141
2672   kataraomai, p. 141
2551   kakologeō, p. 142

C. Adjectives
1944   epikataratos, p. 142
1883a   eparatos, p. 142

DARK, DARKEN, DARKLY, DARKNESS
A. Adjective
4652   skoteinos, p. 144

B. Nouns
4653   skotia, p. 144
4655   skotos, p. 145

C. Verbs
4654   skotizō, p. 145
4656   skotoō, p. 145

DEAD
3498   nekros, p. 148

DEATH
2288   thanatos, p. 149

DEBT
3783   opheilēma, p. 150

DECAY
3822   palaioō, p. 150
1311   diaphtheirō, p. 150

DELUSION
4106   planē, p. 157

DESIRE, DESIROUS
A. Noun
1939   epithumia, p. 161

B. Verb
2206   zēloō, p. 162

DEVICE
1761   enthumēsis, p. 166
3540   noēma, p. 166

DISBELIEVE
569   apisteō, p. 170

DISHONOR
A. Noun
819   atimia, p. 173

B. Adjective
820   atimos, p. 173

C. Verbs
818   atimazō, p. 173
2617   kataischunō, p. 173

DROWN
1036   buthizō, p. 185

DULL
A. Adjective
3576   nōthros, p. 186

B. Adverb
917   bareōs, p. 187

ENSLAVED
1402   douloō, p. 202

FALL, FALLEN, FALLING, FELL
A. Nouns
4431   ptōsis, p. 223
3900   paraptōma, p. 223
646   apostasia, p. 223

B. Verbs
4098   piptō, p. 223
1706   empiptō, p. 224
3895   parapiptō, p. 224
5302   hustereō, p. 224
868   aphistēmi, p. 224
3845   parabainō, p. 224

FAULT
A. Noun
158   aition, p. 229

C. Verbs
3201   memphomai, p. 229
1651   elenchō, p. 229

FOLLY
454   anoia, p. 245

FOOL, FOOLISH, FOOLISHLY, FOOLISHNESS
A. Adjectives
878   aphrōn, p. 246
453   anoētos, p. 246
3474   mōros, p. 246
801   asunetos, p. 246

B. Verbs
3471   mōrainō, p. 246
3912   paraphroneō, p. 246

C. Nouns
191   'ĕwîl, p. 85
200   'iwwelet, p. 85
5039   neᵇālāh, p. 85
3472   mōria, p. 246
877   aphrosunē, p. 246

GROSS
3975   pachunō, p. 283

HARD, HARDEN, HARDENING, HARDNESS
B. Nouns
4643   sklērotēs, p. 290
4457   pōrōsis, p. 290

C. Verbs
4456   pōroō, p. 290
4645   sklērunō, p. 290

HARM
A. Nouns
2556   kakos, p. 291
4190   ponēros, p. 291
5196   hubris, p. 291

B. Verbs
2559   kakoō, p. 291
2554   kakopoieō, p. 291

HATE, HATEFUL, HATER, HATRED
A. Verb
3404   miseō, p. 292

B. Adjective
4767   stugētos, p. 292

C. Nouns
2189   echthra, p. 292
2319   theostugēs, p. 292

HEART
4641   sklērokardia, p. 297

HURT, HURTFUL
A. Noun
5196   hubris, p. 315

B. Verbs
91   adikeō, p. 315
984   blaptō, p. 315
2559   kakoō, p. 315

C. Adjective
983   blaberos, p. 315

IDLE
692   argos, p. 316

IGNORANCE, IGNORANT, IGNORANTLY
A. Nouns
52   agnoia, p. 317
56   agnōsia, p. 317
51   agnoēma, p. 318

B. Verb
50   agnoeō, p. 318

INCLOSE
4788   sunkleiō, p. 322

INJURE, INJURIOUS, INJURY
A. Verb
91   adikeō, p. 326

B. Adjective
5197   hubristēs, p. 326

C. Noun
5196   hubris, p. 326

IRKSOME
3636   oknēros, p. 331

LOSE, LOSS, LOST
622   apollumi, p. 380
2210   zēmioō, p. 380

MALIGNITY
2550   kakoētheia, p. 388

MISERABLE, MISERABLY
A. Adjective
2556   kakos, p. 412

B. Adverb
2560   kakōs, p. 413

NOISOME
2556   kakos, p. 434

PERVERSE, PERVERT
654 apostrephō, p. 469
1294 diastrephō, p. 469
3344 metastrephō, p. 469
1612 ekstrephō, p. 469

PUNISH
2849 kolazō, p. 497
5097 timōreō, p. 497

PUNISHMENT
1557 ekdikēsis, p. 498
2009 epitimia, p. 498
2851 kolasis, p. 498
1349 dikē, p. 498
5098 timōria, p. 498

RACA
4469 raka, p. 504

RECOMPENCE, RECOMPENSE
A. Nouns
468 antapodoma, p. 513
469 antapodosis, p. 513
489 antimisthia, p. 513
3405 misthapodosia, p. 513
B. Verbs
467 antapodidōmi, p. 513
591 apodidōmi, p. 513

REPROACH
A. Nouns
3680 oneidismos, p. 526
3681 oneidos, p. 526
819 atimia, p. 526
B. Verbs
3679 oneidizō, p. 526
5195 hubrizō, p. 526

REVIVE
326 anazaō, p. 533

RUDE
2399 idiōtēs, p. 539

SELL
4097 pipraskō, p. 559

SHAME
A. Nouns
819 atimia, p. 567
152 aischunē, p. 567
1791 entropē, p. 567
808 aschēmosunē, p. 567
B. Adjective
150 aischros, p. 567
C. Verbs
818 atimazō, p. 567
1788 entrepō, p. 567
2617 kataischunō, p. 568
3856 paradeigmatizō, p. 568

TO SHUT
5462 sāgar, p. 228

STIFFNECKED
4644 sklērotrachēlos, p. 600

STRIFE
A. Verb
7378 rîb, p. 249
B. Noun
7379 rîb, p. 249
2054 eris, p. 604
2052 erithia (*or* -eia), p. 604
485 antilogia, p. 604
3163 machē, p. 604

5379 philoneikia, p. 604
3055 logomachia, p. 604

STUPID FELLOW
3684 kᵉsîl, p. 251

THOUGHT
1963 epinoia, p. 630
3540 noēma, p. 630
1270 dianoēma, p. 630
1761 enthumēsis, p. 630
3053 logismos, p. 630
1261 dialogismos, p. 630

TOIL
A. Verb
2872 kopiaō, p. 635
B. Noun
2873 kopos, p. 635

UNBELIEF
570 apistia, p. 649
543 apeitheta, p. 649

UNBELIEVING
A. Adjective
571 apistos, p. 649
B. Verb
544 apeitheō, p. 649

UNWISE
453 anoētos, p. 654
878 aphrōn, p. 654
781 asophos, p. 654

VILE
A. Noun
819 atimia, p. 660
B. Adjectives
4508 rhuparos, p. 660
4190 ponēros, p. 660

WAGES
3800 opsōnion, p. 663

Sinful Behavior

Sin affects every level of human existence and sinful behavior portrayed in Scripture includes sexual sins *(adultery; fornication; lasciviousness; loose conduct; lust; nakedness; wantonness)*, any kind of *excess (belly; carousings; dainty; delicately; drunk; effeminate; glutton; gluttonous; revel; surfeiting; winebibber)*, deceit *(cloke; conceits; conceive; dishonesty; dissimulation; defraud; feign; fraud; guile; hypocrisy; hypocrite; sleight; suborn; to think, devise; white; wiles)*, pride *(haughty; high-minded; proud; puff; self-willed; swelling; vainglory; vaunt)*, and all behavior which is *riotous (insolent; unruly; unseemly; violence)* and foolish *(dote)* or lazy *(slothful; sluggish)*.

Wrong attitudes towards *money (lucre; mammon)* are sinful and can lead to *oppressing (exact; extort; unmerciful)* others.

Stealing (rob; robber; theft), *murder (manslayers; murderer)*, *prejudice, envy, coveting, anger (bitterness)*, and all kinds of *malice (craftiness; despitefully; entice; villainy)* are condemned in Scripture,

---

and lack of *self-control (incontinency)*, evil *passions (affections)*, and *fickleness* are deplored.
See also IDOLATRY

ADULTERER, ADULTERY
A. Nouns
3432 moichos, p. 14
3428 moichalis, p. 14
3430 moicheia, p. 14
B. Verbs
3429 moichaō, p. 14
3431 moicheuō, p. 14

AFFECTION, AFFECTED
A. Nouns
3806 pathos, p. 16
3804 pathēma, p. 16
B. Adjective
794 astorgos, p. 16

ANGER, ANGRY
A. Noun
3709 orgē, p. 26
B. Verbs
3710 orgizō, p. 27
3949 parorgizō, p. 27
5520 cholaō, p. 27
C. Adjective
3711 orgilos, p. 27

BELLY
1064 gastēr, p. 61

BITTERNESS
4088 pikrainō, p. 68

CAROUSINGS
4224 potos, p. 90

CLOKE
1942 epikalumma, p. 104
4392 prophasis, p. 105

CONCEITS
1722,
1438 en heautois, p. 118

CONCEIVE
4815 sullambanō, p. 118
5087 tithēmi, p. 118

COVET, COVETOUS, COVETOUSNESS
A. Verbs
1937 epithumeō, p. 136
3713 oregō, p. 136
B. Nouns
1938 epithumētēs, p. 136
1939 epithumia, p. 136
4124 pleonexia, p. 136
C. Adjectives
4123 pleonektēs, p. 136
5366 philarguros, p. 136

CRAFTINESS, CRAFTY
A. Noun
3834 panourgia, p. 137
B. Adjective
3835 panourgos, p. 137
C. Noun
1388 dolos, p. 137

DAINTY
3045 liparos, p. 143

SELF-CONTROL (without)
193 akratēs, p. 559

SELF-WILLED
829 authadēs, p. 559

SLEIGHT
2940 kubia (*or* -eia), p. 581

SLOTHFUL
3576 nōthros, p. 581
3636 oknēros, p. 581

SLUGGISH
3576 nōthros, p. 581

STEAL
2813 kleptō, p. 599

SUBORN
5260 hupoballō, p. 607

SURFEITING
2897 kraipalē, p. 612

SWELLING
5450 phusiōsis, p. 613
5246 huperonkos, p. 613

THEFT
2829 klopē, p. 625
2809 klemma, p. 625

TO THINK, DEVISE
A. Verb
2803 ḥāšab, p. 261

UNMERCIFUL
415 aneleēmōn, p. 652

UNRULY
506 anupotaktos, p. 653
814 ataktos, p. 653

UNSEEMLINESS, UNSEEMLY
808 aschēmosunē, p. 654

VAINGLORY, VAINGLORIOUS
A. Nouns
2754 kenodoxia, p. 657
212 alazoneia *or* -ia, p. 657

B. Adjective
2755 kenodoxos, p. 657

VAUNT
4068 perpereuomai, p. 658

VILLAINY
4468 rhạdiourgia, p. 660
4467 rhạdiourgēma, p. 660

VIOLENCE
A. Noun
2555 ḥāmās, p. 276

WANTONNESS, WANTON, WANTONLY
A. Nouns
766 aselgeia, p. 665
4764 strēnos, p. 665

B. Verbs
4763 strēniaō, p. 665
2691 katastrēniaō, p. 665

WHITE
B. Verb
2867 koniaō, p. 674

WILES
3180 methodia *or* -eia, p. 676

WINEBIBBER
3630 oinopotēs, p. 678

Sinful Speech

The capacity of the *tongue (lip)* for *evil speaking (asp; poison)* requires it to be kept under control *(bridle; tame)*. The tongue *(double-tongued)* can be a source of all kinds of evil talk *(art; babbler; brawler; busybody; complainer; jesting; murmur; murmurer; prate; talkers; talking; tattler; whisperer)*, and can be used to *profane (blaspheme)*, lie *(false; falsehood; forswear; liar)*, defame *(accusation; slanderer)*, revile *(bite; backbiter; rail; spitefully)*, boast *(glory)*, and *flatter*.

ACCUSATION
B. Verbs
1908 epēreazō, p. 10
4811 sukophanteō, p. 11

ART, ARTS
4021 periergos, p. 38

ASP
785 aspis, p. 41

BABBLER, BABBLINGS
4691 spermologos, p. 48
2757 kenophōnia, p. 48

BACKBITER, BACKBITING
2637 katalalos, p. 48

BITE
1143 daknō, p. 68

BLASPHEME, BLASPHEMY, BLASPHEMER, BLASPHEMOUS
A. Noun
988 blasphēmia, p. 69

B. Verb
987 blasphēmeō, p. 69

C. Adjective
989 blasphēmos, p. 69

BOAST, BOASTER
A. Verbs
2744 kauchaomai, p. 71
3166 megalaucheō, p. 71

B. Nouns
213 alazōn, p. 71
212 alazoneia, p. 71

BRAWLER
3943 paroinos, p. 77

NOT A BRAWLER
269 amachos, p. 77

BRIDLE
B. Verb
5468 chalinagōgeō, p. 79

BUSYBODY
A. Verb
4020 periergazomai, p. 85

B. Adjective
4021 periergos, p. 85

C. Noun
244 allotrioepiskopos, p. 85

COMPLAINER, COMPLAINT
3202 mempsimoiros, p. 117
3437 momphē, p. 117

DEFAME
1418,
5346 dusphēmeō, p. 154

DOUBLE-TONGUED
1351 dilogos, p. 182

EVIL SPEAKING
988 blasphēmia, p. 212
2636 katalalia, p. 212

FALSE, FALSEHOOD
A. Adjectives
5571 pseudēs, p. 225
5581 pseudōnumos, p. 225

B. Nouns
8267 šeqer, p. 76
5579 pseudos, p. 225

C. Verb
5574 pseudō, p. 225

FLATTERY
2850 kolakia (*or* -eia), p. 242

FORSWEAR
1964 epiorkeō, p. 253

GLORY, GLORYING
A. Verbs
2744 kauchaomai, p. 268
2620 katakauchaomai, p. 268
1722,
2744 enkauchaomai, p. 268

B. Nouns
2745 kauchēma, p. 268
2746 kauchēsis, p. 268

JESTING
2160 eutrapelia, p. 333

LIAR
A. Noun
5583 pseustēs, p. 366

B. Adjective
5571 pseudēs, p. 366

LIE
A. Nouns
5579 pseudos, p. 366
5582 pseusma, p. 366

B. Adjective
5573 pseudologos, p. 367

C. Verb
5574 pseudō, p. 367

LIP
8193 śāpāh, p. 137

MURMUR, MURMURING
A. Verbs
1111 gonguzō, p. 422
1234 diagonguzō, p. 422
1690 embrimaomai, p. 422

B. Noun
1112 gongusmos, p. 422

MURMURER
1113 gongustēs, p. 422

POISON
2447 ios, p. 476

PRATE
5396 phluareō, p. 480

PROFANE
A. Adjective
952 bebēlos, p. 490

B. Verb
953 bebēloō, p. 490

RAIL, RAILER, RAILING
A. Verb
987   blasphēmeō, p. 505
B. Nouns
988   blasphēmia, p. 505
3059   loidoria, p. 505
C. Adjectives
989   blasphēmos, p. 505
3060   loidoros, p. 505

REVILE, REVILING, REVILER
A. Verbs
3058   loidoreō, p. 532
3679   oneidizō, p. 532
987   blasphēmeō, p. 532
486   antiloidoreō, p. 532
B. Adjective
3060   loidoros, p. 533
C. Noun
3059   loidoria, p. 533

SLANDERER
1228   diabolos, p. 580

SPEAKING
4180   pololugia, p. 591

SPITEFULLY
5195   hubrizō, p. 595

TALK
3026   lēros, p. 618

TALKERS
3151   mataiologos, p. 618

TALKING
3150   mataiologia, p. 618
3473   mōrologia, p. 618

TAME
1150   damazō, p. 618

TATTLER
5397   phluaros, p. 619

TONGUE
3956   lāšôn, p. 264

WHISPERER, WHISPERING
5588   psithuristēs, p. 673
5587   psithurismos, p. 674

Idolatry

Time and again in the promised land the Israelites were unfaithful to God, *provoking* him to anger by *turning towards (going a-whoring after)* the gods of *Canaan* and doing shameful (*burn; shame*) things. They set up pagan *altars* and *shrines* in *high places* for the worship of *idols* and *statues (Asherah, Baal; calf; goat-demons; goddess)*, even worshiping

the creation itself *(star; sun; tree)*. They also *practiced divination (soothsaying)* even though the Lord had warned them against such detestable practices, and they consulted the *spirits (of the dead)*, *necromancers*, and *enchanters*.

The use of magic arts *(curious)* and *sorcery (sorcerer)* was also widespread in New Testament times with food *sacrificed to idols (pollution)* by the *temple keepers* in *idol temples*, and the practice of worshiping men as gods *(garland)*.

ALTAR
1041   bōmos, p. 24

ASHERAH
842   'ašērāh, p. 8

BAAL, MASTER
1167   ba'al, p. 12

TO BURN
A. Verb
8313   śārap, p. 27

CALF
3448   moschos, p. 86
3447   moschopoieō, p. 86

CANAAN, CANAANITE
3667   kᵉna'an, p. 31
3669   kᵉna'ănî, p. 31

CURIOUS
Note, p. 141

DIVINATION
4436   puthōn, p. 178

TO DIVINE, PRACTICE DIVINATION
7080   qāsam, p. 61

ENCHANTER
825   'aššāp, p. 68

GARLAND
4725   stemma, p. 261

GOAT-DEMONS
8163   śā'îr, p. 96

GODDESS
2299   thea, p. 272

HIGH PLACE
1116   bāmāh, p. 112

IDOL
8655   tᵉrāpîm, p. 120
457   'ĕlîl, p. 120
1544   gillûlîm, p. 120
1497   eidōlon, p. 317

IDOLATER
1496   eidōlatrēs, p. 317

IDOLATRY
1495   eidōlolatria (*or* -eia), p. 317

IDOLS
2712   kateidōlos, p. 317
1494   eidōlothutos, p. 317
2413,
2378   hierothutos, p. 317

IDOL'S TEMPLE
1493   eidōlion (*or* eidōleion), p. 317

POLLUTION
234   alisgēma, p. 476

TO PROVOKE
3707   kā'as, p. 191

SHAME
A. Verb
954   bôš, p. 227
B. Noun
1322   bōšet, p. 227

SHRINE
3485   naos, p. 573

SOOTHSAYING
3132   manteuomai, p. 587

SORCERER
3097   magos, p. 587
5333   pharmakos, p. 587

SORCERY
A. Nouns
5331   pharmakia, p. 587
3095   magia, p. 587
B. Verb
3096   mageuō, p. 587

TO GO A-WHORING, BE A HARLOT
2181   zānāh, p. 286

SPIRIT (OF THE DEAD), NECROMANCER
178   'ôb, p. 241

STAR
798   astron, p. 598

STATUE
6754   ṣelem, p. 244

SUN
8121   šemeš, p. 252

TEMPLE KEEPER
3511   neōkoros, p. 621

TREE
352   'ayil, p. 267
436   'ēlôn, p. 267

TO TURN TOWARDS, TURN BACK
A. Verb
6437   pānāh, p. 271

SALVATION

Atonement

The Old Testament Sacrificial System

Under the Old Testament system of atonement, the *blood* of *beasts (heifers; bullocks; lambs; rams)* was *offered* as *sacrifice* at the *tabernacle* for sins. The animal had to be *perfect* if the Lord was to *accept (to think, devise)* the *burnt offering*. As *all* the

sacrifice was consumed on the altar, an offering made in this way was a pleasant *savor* to the Lord. The priests had specific instructions from the Lord on the *slaughter* of animals, how *to kill (strangled)* the *offering*, *sprinkle* the blood on the *altar*, and *burn incense (censer)* in order to *atone* for the sins of the people. Sacrifices had to be made *continually*

(continuity), although such regulations were only a *shadow* of things to come.

ACCEPT
7521   rāṣāh, p. 1

ALL
3632   kālîl, p. 2

ALTAR
4196   mizbēaḥ, p. 3
2379   thusiastērion, p. 23

TO ATONE, ATONEMENT

A. Verb
3722 kāpar, p. 10

B. Noun
3727 kappōret, p. 10
2643 katallagē, p. 43

BEAST
4968 sphagion, p. 53

BLOOD
1818 dām, p. 19
129 haima, p. 70
130 haimatekchusia, p. 71

BULLOCK
6499 pār, p. 26

TO BURN INCENSE

A. Verbs
6999 qāṭar, p. 27
7004 qᵉṭōret, p. 28

BURNT
3646 holokautōma, p. 84

CENSER
2369 thumiatērion, p. 94
3031 libanōtos, p. 94

CONTINUAL, CONTINUALLY

A. Adverbs
8548 tāmîd, p. 47
1223,
3956 dia pantos, p. 126
1519,
1336 eis to diēnekes, p. 126

B. Adjective
8548 tāmîd, p. 47

CONTINUITY

A. Noun
8548 tāmîd, p. 47

B. Adverb
8548 tāmîd, p. 48

HEIFER
1151 damalis, p. 299

INCENSE

A. Noun
2368 thumiama, p. 322

B. Verb
2370 thumiaō, p. 322

TO KILL
7819 šāḥaṭ, p. 127
615 apokteinō, p. 342
337 anaireō, p. 342
2380 thuō, p. 342
4969 sphazō or sphattō, p. 342

LAMB
3532 kebeś, p. 131
286 amnos, p. 351

TO OFFER
7133 qorbān, p. 165
4374 prospherō, p. 442
399 anapherō, p. 442

OFFERING
4503 minḥāh, p. 166
8641 tᵉrûmāh, p. 167
7133 qorbān, p. 168
7133 qurbān, p. 168
5930 'ōlāh, p. 168
801 'iššeh, p. 169
817 'āšām, p. 169
4376 prosphora, p. 442

3646 holokautōma, p. 442
334 anathēma, p. 442

PERFECT

A. Adjective
8549 tāmîm, p. 176

PRIESTHOOD, PRIEST'S OFFICE

A. Nouns
2420 hierōsunē, p. 487
2405 hierateia, p. 487

B. Verb
2407 hierateuō, p. 487

PROPITIATION

A. Verb
2433 hilaskomai, p. 493

B. Nouns
2435 hilastērion, p. 494
2434 hilasmos, p. 494

RAM
352 'ayil, p. 192

SACRIFICE

A. Nouns
2077 zebaḥ, p. 210
2378 thusia, p. 543

B. Verb
2380 thuō, p. 543

SAVOR

A. Nouns
7381 rêaḥ, p. 215
7306 rûaḥ, p. 216

SHADOW
4639 skia, p. 566

TO SLAUGHTER

A. Verb
2076 zābaḥ, p. 235

B. Nouns
2077 zebaḥ, p. 235
4196 mizbēaḥ, p. 236

SPRINKLE, SPRINKLING

A. Verb
2236 zāraq, p. 242

B. Nouns
4473 rhantismos, p. 597
4378 proschusis, p. 597

STRANGLED
4156 pniktos, p. 603

TABERNACLE
4633 skēnē, p. 614

TO THINK, DEVISE

A. Verb
2803 ḥāšab, p. 261

The Death of Jesus Christ

In his death on the cross, Jesus Christ fulfilled and replaced the Old Testament sacrificial system (*priesthood; unchangeable*). He offered up himself as the supreme, once-for-all *sacrifice (slay)* of *atonement* through the shedding (*sprinkling*) of his *blood*. By his one *act* of righteousness, *salvation (save)* as a free *gift* is for all who *believe*. In being *delivered* up to death (*interposed; taste*), Jesus accomplished several things:

- He paid the penalty of sin. In his body Jesus Christ bore

(*bear; nail; stripe*) the sins of the world so that humanity might receive *forgiveness (remission)* and that their sin would be *imputed* to Christ's *account,* in order that Christ's *righteousness* might be *reckoned* to their account. He was the *propitiation* of God's wrath against sin (*mercy seat*).
- He broke (*kill*) the power of sin by paying the *ransom* price (*buy, bought; deliver, deliverance, deliverer; exchange; redemption*), so that believers could be *free (discharged; liberty; release*) from slavery to sin.
- He removed the pollution of sin by making men *clean (blot out; washing)* through his blood.
- He destroyed (*abolish*) the *partition (hedge)* of sin to *reconcile* human beings to God and put them back into a right relationship (*justification*) with him, so that they may never again be separated (*die*) from God.

See also **JESUS CHRIST,** HIS WORK AND MINISTRY: HIS CRUCIFIXION AND DEATH

ABOLISH
2673 katargeō, p. 3

ACCOUNT

A. Verbs
1677 ellogeō, p. 9
3049 logizomai, p. 9

ACT
1345 dikaiōma, p. 11

TO ATONE

A. Verb
3722 kāpar, p. 10

B. Noun
3727 kappōret, p. 10

ATONEMENT
2643 katallagē, p. 43

BEAR
399 anapherō, p. 52
142 airō, p. 52

BELIEF, BELIEVE, BELIEVERS

A. Verbs
4100 pisteuō, p. 61
3982 peithō, p. 61

B. Noun
4102 pistis, p. 61

C. Adjective
4103 pistos, p. 61

BLOOD

A. Nouns
129 haima, p. 70
130 haimatekchusia, p. 71

BLOT OUT
1813 exaleiphō, p. 71

BUY, BOUGHT
59 agorazō, p. 85

CLEAN, CLEANNESS, CLEANSE, CLEANSING
A. Adjective
2513 katharos, p. 103
B. Verbs
2511 katharizō, p. 104
1245 diakatharizō, p. 104
C. Nouns
2512 katharismos, p. 104
2514 katharotēs, p. 104

DELIVER, DELIVERANCE, DELIVERER
A. Verbs
3860 paradidōmi, p. 156
1659 eleutheroō, p. 157
1807 exaireō, p. 157
4506 rhuomai, p. 157
B. Nouns
629 apolutrōsis, p. 157
859 aphesis, p. 157
3086 lutrōtēs, p. 157
C. Verbal Adjective
1560 ekdotos, p. 157

DIE, DEAD, DYING
599 apothnēskō, p. 167
4880 sunapothnēskō, p. 167

DISCHARGED
2673 katargeō, p. 171

EXCHANGE
465 antallagma, p. 215

FREE, FREEDOM, FREELY, FREEMAN, FREEMAN, FREEWOMAN
A. Adjective
1658 eleutheros, p. 255
B. Verb
1659 eleutheroō, p. 255
C. Nouns
1657 eleutheria, p. 255
558 apeleutheros, p. 255

FORGIVE, FORGAVE, FORGIVENESS
A. Verbs
863 aphiēmi, p. 250
5483 charizomai, p. 251
B. Noun
859 aphesis, p. 251

GIFT, GIVING
1435 dōron, p. 264

HEDGE
5418 phragmos, p. 299

IMPUTE
3049 logizomai, p. 322
1677 ellogaō or -eō, p. 322

INTERPOSED
3315 mesiteuō, p. 330

JUSTIFICATION, JUSTIFIER, JUSTIFY
A. Nouns
1347 dikaiōsis, p. 338
1345 dikaiōma, p. 339
B. Verb
1344 dikaioō, p. 339

KILL
615 apokteinō, p. 342
337 anaireō, p. 342

2380 thuō, p. 342
5407 phoneuō, p. 342
2289 thanatoō, p. 342
1315 diacheirizō, p. 342
4969 sphazō or sphattō, p. 342

LIBERTY
A. Nouns
425 anesis, p. 366
859 aphesis, p. 366
1657 eleutheria, p. 366
B. Adjective
1658 eleutheros, p. 366

MERCY SEAT
2435 hilastērion, p. 405

NAIL
B. Verb
4338 proseloō, p. 425

OFFER, OFFERING
A. Verbs
4374 prospherō, p. 442
399 anapherō, p. 442
B. Noun
4376 prosphora, p. 442

PARTITION
5418 phragmos, p. 460

PRIESTHOOD
A. Noun
2420 hierōsunē, p. 487

PROPITIATION
A. Verb
2433 hilaskomai, p. 493
B. Nouns
2435 hilastērion, p. 494
2434 hilasmos, p. 494

RANSOM
3083 lutron, p. 506

RECKON, RECKONING
3049 logizomai, p. 512

RECONCILE, RECONCILIATION
A. Verbs
2644 katallassō, p. 513
604 apokatallassō, p. 514
1259 diallassō, p. 514
B. Noun
2643 katallagē, p. 514

REDEEM, REDEMPTION
A. Verbs
1805 exagorazō, p. 515
3084 lutroō, p. 515
B. Nouns
3085 lutrōsis, p. 516
629 apolutrōsis, p. 516

RELEASE
630 apoluō, p. 520

REMISSION, REMIT
A. Nouns
859 aphesis, p. 522
3929 paresis, p. 522
B. Verb
863 aphiēmi, p. 522

RIGHTEOUSNESS
1345 dikaiōma, p. 535

SACRIFICE
A. Noun
2378 thusia, p. 543

B. Verb
2380 thuō, p. 543

SALVATION
A. Nouns
4991 sōtēria, p. 545
4992 sōtērion, p. 545
B. Adjective
4992**sōtērios, p. 545

SAVE, SAVING
A. Verbs
4982 sōzō, p. 547
1295 diasōzō, p. 548
B. Noun
4047 peripoiēsis, p. 548

SLAY, SLAIN, SLEW
4969 sphazō or sphattō, p. 581

SPRINKLE, SPRINKLING
A. Verb
4472 rhantizō, p. 597
B. Nouns
4473 rhantismos, p. 597
4378 proschusis, p. 597

STRIPE
3468 mōlōps, p. 604

TASTE
1089 geuō, p. 619

UNCHANGEABLE
531 aparabatos, p. 649

WASHING
3067 loutron, p. 667

Regeneration

Regeneration is the work of the Holy Spirit that brings *new life (anew; begin; new; newness; renewing)* to the inner being of believers and adopts *(adoption)* them into the *family* of God, making them become God's children *(beget)*. The Holy Spirit also gives *assurance* that believers are *accepted* as children of God and have *access* into God's presence.

Regeneration is accompanied by *conversion,* a turning to God in *repentance* and faith.

God *chooses* from the *beginning (appoint; choice; determine; predestinate)* to bring individuals to salvation through faith in Jesus Christ on account of his love and mercy.

See also THE HOLY SPIRIT, HIS WORK AND MINISTRY

ACCEPT, ACCEPTED, ACCEPTABLE
A. Verbs
1209 dechomai, p. 7
588 apodechomai, p. 7
4327 prosdechomai, p. 7
2983 lambanō, p. 7
B. Adjectives
1184 dektos, p. 7
587 apodektos, p. 7
2144 euprosdektos, p. 7
2101 euarestos, p. 7
C. Adverb
2102 euarestōs, p. 7

D. Nouns
594 apodochē, p. 7
5485 charis, p. 7

ACCESS
4318 prosagōgē, p. 7

ADOPTION
5206 huiothesia, p. 13

ANEW
509 anōthen, p. 26

APPOINT, APPOINTED
2476 histēmi, p. 33
2525 kathistēmi, p. 33
5087 tithēmi, p. 33
1303 diatithēmi, p. 33

ASSURANCE, ASSURE
A. Nouns
4102 pistis, p. 43
4136 plērophoria, p. 43
5287 hupostasis, p. 43

B. Verbs
4104 pistoō, p. 43
4135 plērophoreō, p. 43
3782 peithō, p. 43

BEGET
A. Verbs
1080 gennaō, p. 57
313 anagennaō, p. 57
616 apokueō, p. 57

BEGIN
1728 enarchomai, p. 57

BEGINNING
B. Noun
746 archē, p. 58

CHOICE, CHOOSE, CHOSEN
A. Verbs
977 bāḥar, p. 34
1586 eklegō, p. 100
1951 epilegō, p. 100
138 haireō, p. 100
140 hairetizo, p. 101
5500 cheirotoneō, p. 101
4401 procheirotoneō, p. 101

B. Adjective
1588 eklektos, p. 101

C. Noun
972 bāḥîr, p. 35

CONVERT, CONVERSION
A. Verbs
4762 strephō, p. 128
1994 epistrephō, p. 128

B. Noun
1995 epistrophē, p. 128

DETERMINE, DETERMINATE
4309 proorizō, p. 165

FAMILY
3965 patria, p. 225

JUSTIFICATION, JUSTIFIER, JUSTIFY
A. Nouns
1347 dikaiōsis, p. 338
1345 dikaiōma, p. 339

B. Verb
1344 dikaioō, p. 339

LIFE, LIFE-GIVING
A. Nouns
2222 zōē, p. 367
5590 psuchē, p. 367

C. Verb
2227 zōopoieō, p. 368

LIVE
2198 zaō, p. 374

NEW
C. Adjectives
2319 ḥādāš, p. 160
2537 kainos, p. 430
3501 neos, p. 431
4732 prosphatos, p. 431

NEWNESS
2538 kainotēs, p. 431

PREDESTINATE
4309 proorizō, p. 482

REGENERATION
3824 palingenesia, p. 517

RENEW, RENEWING
A. Verbs
341 anakainoō, p. 524
340 anakainizō, p. 524

REPENT, REPENTANCE
A. Verbs
3340 metanoeō, p. 525
3338 metamelomai, p. 525

B. Adjective
278 ametamelētos, p. 525

C. Noun
3341 metanoia, p. 525

Other Old Testament Aspects of Salvation

Salvation (to save) in the Old Testament was not understood exclusively as salvation from sin, but embraced the idea of being saved from anything from which deliverance (to deliver) was sought, such as enemies and troubles.

God's loving-kindness, power, and help are offered to his people in need of peace and deliverance from such situations.

God's choosing (to choose) to bring people into an intimate relationship with him, whereby they receive life and are made holy (to be righteous; to sanctify), goes as far back as Abram, and arises from God's covenant relationship with Abram and his descendants, by which God promises to remember the remnant of his people.

See also THE PEOPLE OF GOD, THE LIFE OF THE PEOPLE OF GOD: GOD'S SAVING ACTS

TO CHOOSE
A. Verb
977 bāḥar, p. 34

B. Noun
972 bāḥîr, p. 35

COVENANT
1285 bᵉrît, p. 50

TO DELIVER
A. Verb
3467 yāša', p. 57

B. Nouns
3444 yᵉšû'āh, p. 57
3468 yēša', p. 58
8668 tᵉšû'āh, p. 58

TO HELP
5826 'āzar, p. 110

HOLY
A. Adjective
6918 qādôš, p. 113

B. Verb
6942 qādēš or qādaš, p. 114

C. Noun
6944 qōdeš, p. 114

TO LIVE
B. Noun
2416 ḥay, p. 138

LOVING-KINDNESS
A. Noun
2617 ḥesed, p. 142

PEACE
A. Noun
7965 šālôm, p. 173

POWER
3581 kōaḥ, p. 183

TO REMEMBER
A. Verb
2142 zākar, p. 198

B. Noun
2143 zēker, p. 199

REMNANT
A. Nouns
7611 šᵉ'ērît, p. 199
7605 šᵉ'ār, p. 200

TO BE RIGHTEOUS
A. Verb
6663 ṣādaq, p. 205

B. Nouns
6664 ṣedeq, p. 205
6666 ṣᵉdāqāh, p. 205

C. Adjective
6662 ṣaddîq, p. 206

TO SANCTIFY
A. Verb
6942 qādaš, p. 210

B. Noun
6944 qōdeš, p. 212

C. Adjective
6918 qādôš, p. 213

TO SAVE
A. Verb
3467 yāša', p. 214

B. Noun
3444 yᵉšû'āh, p. 215

Other New Testament Aspects of Salvation

Many blessings accompany salvation (safe) for believers, as they are accorded the status and privileges of adoption (graft).

God calls people to belong (friendship) to him and to serve him *(laborer)* in the world. He sets believers apart *(holy; holiness; sanctify; sanctification),* granting them *access* into his presence, bestowing upon them *forgiveness, freedom, grace,* and *favor.*

Believers have *obtained* and *partake* of the inheritance *(inherit)* of *eternal* life, being at *peace* with God, and serving him in the *abundance* of new *life.*

ABUNDANCE, ABUNDANT, ABUNDANTLY, ABOUND

A. Nouns
100   hadrotēs, p. 5
4050 perisseia, p. 5
4051 perisseuma, p. 5

B. Verbs
4052 perisseuō, p. 6
5248 huperperisseuō, p. 6
4121 pleonazō, p. 6
5250 huperpleonazō, p. 6
4129 plēthunō, p. 6

C. Adjectives
4053 perissos, p. 6
4055 perissoteros, p. 6

D. Adverbs
4057 perissōs, p. 6
4056 perissoteros, p. 6
5249 huperperissōs, p. 6
5228 huperekperissou, p. 6
4146 plousiōs, p. 6

ACCESS
4318 prosagōgē, p. 7

ACCOMPANY
2192 echō, p. 8

ADOPTION
5206 huiothesia, p. 13

CALL, CALLED, CALLING
A. Verbs
2564 kaleō, p. 86
1528 eiskaleō, p. 86
1941 epikaleō, p. 86
4341 proskaleō, p. 86

B. Noun
2821 klēsis, p. 87

C. Adjective
2822 klētos, p. 87

ETERNAL
166   aiōnios, p. 207

FAVOR, FAVORED
A. Noun
5485 charis, p. 229

B. Verb
5487 charitoō, p. 229

FORGIVE, FORGAVE, FORGIVENESS
A. Verbs
863   aphiēmi, p. 250
5483 charizomai, p. 251

B. Noun
859   aphesis, p. 251

FREE, FREEDOM, FREELY, FREEMAN, FREEDMAN, FREEWOMAN
A. Adjective
1658 eleutheros, p. 255

B. Verb
1659 eleutheroō, p. 255

C. Nouns
1657 eleutheria, p. 255
558   apeleutheros, p. 255

D. Adverb
1432 dōrean, p. 256

FRIENDSHIP
5373 philia, p. 256

GRACE
5485 charis, p. 277

GRAFF, GRAFT
1461 enkentrizō, p. 277

HOLINESS, HOLY, HOLILY
A. Nouns
38   hagiasmos, p. 307
42   hagiōsunē, p. 307
41   hagiotēs, p. 307

B. Adjectives
40   hagios, p. 307
3741 hosios, p. 307

C. Adverb
3743 hosiōs, p. 308

D. Verb
37   hagiazō, p. 308

INHERIT, INHERITANCE
A. Verbs
2816 klēronomeō, p. 325
2820 klēroō, p. 325

B. Nouns
2817 klēronomia, p. 325
2819 klēros, p. 325

LABORER, FELLOW LABORER
2040 ergatēs, p. 349

LIFE, LIVING, LIFE-GIVING
A. Noun
2222 zōē, p. 367

C. Verb
2227 zōopoieō, p. 368

OBTAIN, OBTAINED
A. Verbs
5177 tunchanō, p. 439
2013 epitunchanō, p. 439
2975 lanchanō, p. 439
2983 lambanō, p. 439
2147 heuriskō, p. 439

B. Noun
4047 peripoiēsis, p. 440

PARTAKE, PARTAKER
A. Nouns
2844 koinōnos, p. 459
4791 sunkoinōnos, p. 459
4830 summetochos, p. 459

B. Verbs
2841 koinōneō, p. 459
4790 sunkoinōneō, p. 459

PEACE, PEACEABLE, PEACEABLY
A. Noun
1515 eirēnē, p. 464

B. Verbs
1514 eirēneuō, p. 464
1517 eirēnopoieō, p. 464

C. Adjective
1516 eirēnikos, p. 464

SAFE, SAFELY, SAFETY
B. Noun
4991 sōtēria, p. 543

SALVATION
A. Nouns
4991 sōtēria, p. 545
4992 sōtērion, p. 545

B. Adjective
*4992**sōtērios, p. 545

SANCTIFICATION, SANCTIFY
A. Noun
38   hagiasmos, p. 545

B. Verb
37   hagiazō, p. 546

THE LIFE OF THE BELIEVER

Character and Attitudes Of

The attitude of believers is characterized by their single-minded *(highly; light; single; eye) aim (goal)* to please God, always *zealous (diligence; endeavor; fervent; zeal)* for his *honor,* and presenting their bodies *(instruments; reasonable; vessel)* in *readiness (loins)* for *divine service.*

Christian character *perfects holiness (chaste; blame, blameless; devout; godliness; guiltless; pious; unblemished; upright; uprightness)* and *love* out of reverence for God. Believers are to be *honest (decently), gentle, compassionate (affection; bowels), modest (discreet; orderly),* diligent *(care; imagine),* so-*berminded (soberness), sincere,* and *guileless (harmless), conduct (behave)* which *befits (become)* the people of God. They are to be *faithful (faith; faithfulness; fidelity; to keep, watch, guard)* and vigilant *(wake; wait; watch),* responding to God in humility *(abase; courteous; to humble; humbleness of mind), trust,* and *obedience (to hear).* They are not to be anxious *(thought)* about anything, but are to be *content* in whatever situation they find themselves, *slow* to speak *(utterance)* and keeping the *unity* of the Spirit in the bond of peace. They are to earnestly *desire (delight in; thirst)* good things and to *covet (stir)* spiritual gifts, always maintaining a teachable *(instruction)* spirit.

In addition to these *virtues* the character of the believer exhibits joy *(rejoice; unspeakable), courage* (*bold; confidence; dare*), and blessing.

See also **HOLY SPIRIT**, HIS WORK AND MINISTRY

ABASE
5013   tapeinoō, p. 1

AFFECTION, AFFECTED
A. Noun
4698   splanchna, p. 16
B. Adjectives
794   astorgos, p. 16
5387   philostorgos, p. 16

AIM
5389   philotimeomai, p. 21

BECOME
A. Verb
4241   prepō, p. 55
B. Adjective
2412   hieroprepēs, p. 55

BEFIT, BEFITTING
4241   prēpo, p. 55
433   anēkō, p. 55

BEHAVE, BEHAVIOR
A. Verbs
390   anastrephō, p. 58
1096   ginomai, p. 58
812   atakteō, p. 59
807   aschēmoneō, p. 59
B. Nouns
391   anastrophē, p. 59
2688   katastēma, p. 59
C. Adjective
2887   kosmios, p. 59

BLAME, BLAMELESS
B. Adjectives
299   amōmos, p. 68
298   amōmētos, p. 68
273   amemptos, p. 68
338   anaitios, p. 68
423   anepilēptos, p. 68
410   anenklētos, p. 68
C. Adverb
274   amemptōs, p. 69

BLESS, BLESSED, BLESSEDNESS, BLESSING
A. Verb
3106   makarizō, p. 70
B. Adjective
3107   makarios, p. 70
C. Noun
3109   makarismos, p. 70

BOLD, BOLDNESS, BOLDLY
A. Verbs
2292   tharreō, p. 72
3955   parrhēsiazomai, p. 72
5111   tolmaō, p. 72
662   apotolmaō, p. 72
B. Noun
3954   parrhēsia, p. 72
C. Adverb
5112   tolmēroterōs, p. 73

BOWELS
4698   splanchnon, p. 76

CARE, CAREFULLY, CAREFULNESS
A. Nouns
3308   merimna, p. 89
4710   spoudē, p. 89
B. Verbs
3309   merimnaō, p. 89
3199**melei, p. 89
1959   epimeleomai, p. 89
5431   phrontizō, p. 89
5426   phroneō, p. 89
C. Adverbs
199   akribos, p. 89
4708   spoudaioterōs, p. 89

CHASTE
53   hagnos, p. 97

COMPASSION, COMPASSIONATE
B. Nouns
3628   oiktirmos, p. 117
4698   splanchnon, p. 117
C. Adjective
4835   sumpathēs, p. 117

CONDUCT
A. Noun
72   agōgē, p. 119

CONFIDENCE
A. Nouns
4006   pepoithēsis, p. 120
5287   hupostasis, p. 120
3954   parrhēsia, p. 121
B. Verbs
3982   peithō, p. 121
2292   tharreō, p. 121

CONTENT, CONTENTMENT
A. Verbs
174   arkeō, p. 125
4909   suneudokeō, p. 125
B. Adjectives
842   autarkēs, p. 125
2425   hikanos, p. 125
C. Noun
841   autarkeia, p. 126

COURAGE
A. Noun
2294   tharsos, p. 134
B. Verb
2292   tharreō, p. 134

COURTEOUS, COURTEOUSLY
A. Adjective
5012   tapeinophrōn, p. 134
B. Adverbs
5390   philophronōs, p. 134
5364   philanthrōpōs, p. 135

COVET
2206   zēloō, p. 136

DARE, DARING, DURST
A. Verb
5111   tolmaō, p. 144

DECENTLY
2156   euschēmonōs, p. 151

DELIGHT IN
4913   sunēdomai, p. 156

DESIRE, DESIROUS
A. Nouns
1972   epipothēsis, p. 161

2107   eudokia, p. 161
1972   epipothēsis, p. 161
1974   epipothia, p. 161
2307   thelēma, p. 161
B. Verbs
1937   epithumeō, p. 162
2065   erōtaō, p. 162
3713   oregō, p. 162
2309   thelō, p. 162
1014   boulomai, p. 162
2206   zēloō, p. 162

DEVOUT
2126   eulabēs, p. 167
2152   eusebēs, p. 167
4576   sebomai, p. 167

DILIGENCE, DILIGENT, DILIGENTLY
A. Nouns
2039   ergasia, p. 169
4710   spoudē, p. 169
B. Verbs
4704   spoudazō, p. 169
3191   meletaō, p. 169
C. Adjectives
4705   spoudaios, p. 169
4707   spoudaioteros, p. 169
D. Adverbs
1960   epimelōs, p. 169
4435   pugmē, p. 169
4709   spoudaiōs, p. 169
4708   spoudaioterōs, p. 169

DISCREET, DISCREETLY
A. Adjective
4998   sōphrōn, p. 172
B. Adverb
3562   nounechōs, p. 172

DIVINE
B. Noun
2999   latreia, p. 178

ENDEAVOR
4704   spoudazō, p. 199
2212   zēteō, p. 199

EYE
3788   ophthalmos, p. 219

FAITH
4102   pistis, p. 222

FAITH (of little)
3640   oligopistos, p. 223

FAITHFUL, FAITHFULLY
4103   pistos, p. 223

FAITHFULNESS
A. Noun
530   'ĕmûnāh, p. 75
Note, p. 223
B. Verb
539   'āman, p. 76

FERVENT, FERVENTLY
A. Adjective
1618   ektenēs, p. 233
B. Adverb
1619   ektenōs, p. 233
C. Verb
2204   zeō, p. 233

FIDELITY
4102   pistis, p. 234

553 apekdechomai, p. 663
4327 prosdechomai, p. 663
362 anamenō, p. 663

WAKE
1127 grēgoreō, p. 664

WATCH, WATCHERS, WATCHINGS
A. Nouns
5438 phulakē, p. 667
2892 koustōdia, p. 667
70 agrupnia, p. 667

B. Verbs
1127 grēgoreō, p. 667
5083 tēreō, p. 667
3906 paratēreō, p. 667
69 agrupneō, p. 667
3525 nēphō, p. 667

ZEAL
2205 zēlos, p. 693

ZEALOUS
A. Noun
2207 zēlōtēs, p. 693

B. Verbs
2206 zēloō, p. 693
2206 zēleuō, p. 693

Responsibilities to God

Prayer

Prayer (supplication) is the means by which believers communicate with God and receive guidance *(answer; direct)* for their lives. Effective *(avail)* prayer depends on faith and a right relationship with God.

Asking (importunity; knock; petition; plead; request) for oneself and for others *(intercessions; mention)* is an important aspect of prayer.

Scripture also gives guidance on the practicalities of prayer, like praying in secret *(chamber)*, postures for prayer *(kneeling; to spread out)*, and praying without *ceasing*, but not using vain *repetitions*.

See also **THE HOLY SPIRIT**, HIS WORK AND MINISTRY

ANSWER
A. Nouns
610 apokrima, p. 29
5538 chrēmatismos, p. 29

ASK
A. Verbs
7592 šā'al, p. 9
154 aiteō, p. 40
2065 erōtaō, p. 40
1905 eperōtaō, p. 40

B. Noun
155 aitēma, p. 40

AVAIL
2480 ischuō, p. 46

CEASE
B. Adjective
88 adialeiptos, p. 94

C. Adverb
89 adialeiptōs, p. 94

CHAMBER
5009 tameion, p. 95
5253 huperǭon, p. 95

DIRECT
2720 kateuthunō, p. 170

IMPORTUNITY
335 anaidia, p. 321

INTERCESSIONS
A. Noun
1783 enteuxis, p. 330

B. Verbs
1793 entunchanō, p. 330
5241 huperentunchanō, p. 330

KNEEL
1120 gonupeteō, p. 346

KNOCK
2925 krouō, p. 346

MENTION
A. Noun
3417 mneia, p. 403

B. Verb
3421 mnēmoneuō, p. 403

PETITION
155 aitēma, p. 470

PLEAD
1793 entunchanō, p. 474

PRAY, PRAYER
A. Verbs
6419 pālal, p. 185
2172 euchomai, p. 480
4336 proseuchomai, p. 480
2065 erōtaō, p. 480
1189 deomai, p. 480

B. Nouns
8605 tᵉpillāh, p. 186
2171 euchē, p. 480
4335 proseuchē, p. 480
1162 deēsis, p. 481
1783 enteuxis, p. 481

REPETITIONS
945 battalogeō *or* battologeō, p. 525

REQUEST
A. Nouns
155 aitēma, p. 527
1162 deēsis, p. 527

B. Verbs
1189 deomai, p. 527
154 aiteō, p. 527
2065 erōtaō, p. 527

TO SPREAD OUT
6566 pāraś, p. 242

SUPPLICATION
1162 deēsis, p. 610
2428 hiketēria, p. 610

Giving

The giving of possessions *(alms; boon; bounty; collection; contribution; supply; tithe)* and of *hospitality (host)* is a vital part of Christian worship and witness. Sacrificial giving is pleasing *(odor; savor)* to God.

Givers are to be *cheerful*, giving freely *(liberality)* of their own *accord* and not *grudgingly*, in recognition of the fact that human beings are *stewards* of what belongs to God and will one day give account of that stewardship.

ACCORD
B. Adjectives
830 authairetos, p. 9
844 automatos, p. 9

ALMS, ALMSDEEDS
1654 eleēmosunē, p. 23

BOON
1434 dōrēma, p. 74

BOUNTY, BOUNTIFULLY
2129 eulogia, p. 75
572 haplotēs, p. 75
5485 charis, p. 75
100 hadrotēs, p. 75

CHEER, CHEERFUL, CHEERFULLY, CHEERFULNESS
A. Verbs
2114 euthumeō, p. 97
2293 tharseō, p. 97

B. Adjectives
2115 euthumos, p. 98
2431 hilaros, p. 98

C. Adverb
2115* euthumōs, p. 98

D. Noun
2432 hilarotēs, p. 98

COLLECTION
3048 logia, p. 108

CONTRIBUTION
2842 koinōnia, p. 128

GIVER
1395 dotēs, p. 266

GRUDGINGLY
Note, p. 284

HOSPITALITY
A. Noun
5381 philoxenia, p. 312

B. Adjective
5382 philoxenos, p. 312

HOST
3581 xenos, p. 312
3830 pandocheus, p. 312

LIBERALITY
A. Noun
572 haplotēs, p. 366

ODOR
3744 osmē, p. 440

SAVOR
A. Nouns
2175 euōdia, p. 548
3744 osmē, p. 548

STEWARD, STEWARDSHIP
A. Nouns
3623 oikonomos, p. 599
2012 epitropos, p. 599
3622 oikonomia, p. 599

B. Verb
3621 oikonomeō, p. 600

SUPPLY
A. Verb
5524 chorēgeō, p. 610

TITHE
1183 dekatoō, p. 634
586 apodekatoō, p. 634
586v apodekateuō, p. 634

Remembering

Remembering (mindful of) God's past work in history and his dealings with his people is both an occasion for praise and thanksgiving, and an encouragement to believers. Sacred *stones, altars,* and *pillars (to stand)* are examples of commemorative *memorials.*

See also THE PEOPLE OF GOD, WORSHIP OF GOD: FEASTS AND FESTIVALS

ALTAR
2379 thusiastērion, p. 23

MEMORIAL
3422 mnēmosunon, p. 402

MINDFUL OF
5403 mimnēskō, p. 409
3421 mnēmoneuō, p. 410

PILLAR
4676 maṣṣēbāh, p. 178

REMEMBER, REMEMBRANCE, REMINDED

A. Verbs
2142 zākar, p. 198
3403 mimnēskō, p. 521
3421 mnēmoneuō, p. 521
363 anamimnēskō, p. 521
5279 hupomimnēskō, p. 522
1878 epanamimnēskō, p. 522

B. Nouns
2143 zēker *or* zeker, p. 199
364 anamnēsis, p. 522
5280 hupomnēsis, p. 522
3417 mneia, p. 522
3420 mnēmē, p. 522

TO STAND

A. Verb
5324 nāṣab, p. 243

B. Noun
5982 'ammûd, p. 244

STONE
68 'eben, p. 246

Responsibilities to Other Believers

Believers are to *prefer* one another, bearing *(bear)* with one another, particularly with those who are weak *(feeble; infirmity)* in their faith, and to *consider* how they may *provoke* one another to love and good deeds *(communicate; household).*

They are to *greet* one another with a holy *kiss* and to be of one mind *(accord; likeminded),* not going to litigation to *decide* their disputes *(account; life),* but living *(live)* and conducting themselves in accordance with the characteristics of the heavenly community.

ACCORD

A. Adverb
3661 homothumadon, p. 9

B. Adjective
4861 sumpsuchos, p. 9

ACCOUNT

A. Verb
1848 exoutheneō, p. 9

BEAR
3356 metriopatheō, p. 53
3114 makrothumeō, p. 53

COMMUNICATE, COMMUNICATION

A. Verbs
2841 koinōneō, p. 114
4790 sunkoinōneō, p. 114

B. Noun
2842 koinōnia, p. 114

C. Adjective
2843 koinōnikos, p. 114

CONSIDER
2657 katanoeō, p. 123

DECIDE

A. Verb
1252 diakrinō, p. 152

FEEBLE
772 asthenēs, p. 231

GREET, GREETING

A. Verbs
782 aspazomai, p. 281
5463 chairō, p. 281

B. Noun
783 aspasmos, p. 281

HOUSEHOLD

A. Noun
3624 oikos, p. 313

B. Adjective
3609 oikeios, p. 313

INFIRMITY
771 asthenēma, p. 324

KISS

A. Noun
5370 philēma, p. 345

LIFE, LIFETIME

A. Nouns
979 bios, p. 368
981 biōsis, p. 368
72 agōgē, p. 368
391 anastrophe, p. 368

B. Adjective
982 biōtikos, p. 368

LIKEMINDED
3675 homophrōn, p. 371

LIVE
390 anastrephō, p. 374
4176 politeuō, p. 375

PREFER, PREFERRING
4285 proēgeomai, p. 483

PROVOCATION, PROVOKE

A. Noun
3948 paroxusmos, p. 496

B. Verb
2042 erethizō, p. 496

Responsibilities to the World

To do good (maintain; well-doing) for the *benefit* of others is a characteristic of God which is reflected in the life of the believer. Scripture makes it clear that while salvation does not depend on good *deeds,* it does lead to them as believers are *constrained* by the love of God. Believers are to minister to the *poor (poverty)* and *needy (destitute)* and are not to *oppress (interest)* the *widow,* the *fatherless (bereaved; desolate),* and the *stranger (alien; foreign; forget; to sojourn).* They are to bring *comfort (consolation)* to the brokenhearted *(break; bruise; fainthearted), visit* the sick, and to be *peacemakers* and *ambassadors* for Christ, acting like *salt* and *light (lamp; lampstand; cellar)* in the world.

See also RESPONSIBILITIES TO GOD: GIVING; THE PEOPLE OF GOD, LIFE OF THE PEOPLE OF GOD: MINISTRY AND MISSION OF THE CHURCH

ALIEN
245 allotrios, p. 21

AMBASSADOR, AMBASSAGE

A. Verb
4243 presbeuō, p. 25

BENEFIT
2108 euergesia, p. 62
2110 euergetēs, p. 62
5485 charis, p. 62
18 agathon, p. 62

BEREAVED
642 aporphanizomai, p. 62

BREAK

A. Verb
4937 suntribō, p. 78

BRUISE
4937 suntribō, p. 82
2352 thrauō, p. 82

CELLAR
2926 kruptē, p. 94

COMFORT, COMFORTER, COMFORTLESS

A. Nouns
3874 paraklēsis, p. 110
3889 paramuthia, p. 111
3890 paramuthion, p. 111
3931 parēgoria, p. 111

B. Verbs
3870 parakaleō, p. 111
4837 sumparakaleō, p. 111
3888 paramutheomai, p. 111
2174 eupsucheō, p. 111

CONSOLATION, CONSOLE

A. Nouns
3874 paraklēsis, p. 124
3889 paramuthia, p. 124
3890 paramuthion, p. 124

B. Verb
3888 paramutheomai, p. 124

CONSTRAIN, CONSTRAINT
4912 sunechō, p. 124

DEED, DEEDS
2041 ergon, p. 153
4234 praxis, p. 153
4162 poiēsis, p. 153
2108 euergesia, p. 153

DESOLATE

B. Adjective

3739 orphanos, p. 162

DESTITUTE

650 apostereō, p. 164
5302 hustereō, p. 164
3007 leipō, p. 164

TO DO GOOD

A. Verb

3190 yāṭab, p. 61

B. Adjective

2896 ṭôb, p. 61

FAINTHEARTED

3642 oligopsuchos, p. 222

FATHERLESS

3737 orphanos, p. 229

FOREIGN, FOREIGNER

1854 exō, p. 248

FORGET, FORGETFUL

A. Verb

1950 epilanthanomai, p. 250

INTEREST

5110 tokos, p. 330

LAMP

2985 lampas, p. 351
3088 luchnos, p. 351

LAMPSTAND

3087 luchnia, p. 352

LIGHT, LIGHTEN

A. Nouns

5457 phōs, p. 369
5458 phōstēr, p. 370
5462 phōtismos, p. 370

B. Verbs

5461 phōtizō, p. 370
2017 epiphauskō, p. 370
2989 lampō, p. 370

MAINTAIN

4291 proistēmi, p. 386

NEEDY (PERSON)

A. Noun

34 'ebyôn, p. 159

OPPRESS

2616 katadunasteuō, p. 449
2669 kataponeō, p. 449

PEACEMAKER

1518 eirēnopoios, p. 464

POOR (PERSON), WEAK (PERSON)

A. Nouns

6041 'ānî, p. 180
1800 dal, p. 181
3993 penēs, p. 476

B. Verbs

1809 dālal, p. 182
6031 'ānāh, p. 182
4433 ptōcheuō, p. 476

C. Adjectives

6035 'ānāw, p. 182
4434 ptōchos, p. 476
3998 penichros, p. 476

POVERTY

4432 ptōcheia, p. 478

SALT, SALTNESS

A. Noun

251 halas, p. 544

B. Verb

233 halizō, p. 544

C. Adjective

358 analos, p. 545

SOJOURN, SOJOURNER, SOJOURNING

A. Verbs

1481 gûr, p. 236
3939 paroikeō, p. 583
1927 epidēmeō, p. 583

B. Adjectives

3941 paroikos, p. 583
590 apodēmos, p. 584
3927 parepidēmos, p. 584

C. Nouns

1616 gēr, p. 237
3940 paroikia, p. 584

STRANGER

A. Adjectives

3581 xenos, p. 603
245 allotrios, p. 603
241 allogenēs, p. 603

B. Verb

3580 xenodocheō, p. 603

C. Noun

5381 philoxenia, p. 603

VISIT

1980 episkeptomai, p. 662

WELL, WELL-DOING

A. Verbs

15 agathopoieō, p. 671
2569 kalopoieō, p. 671

B. Noun

16 agathopoiia, p. 671

C. Adjective

17 agathopoios, p. 671

WIDOW

490 'almānāh, p. 288
5503 chēra, p. 675

The Life of Faith

The Walk of Faith

The *walk (accurately; narrow; path; straight; way)* of faith is grounded in the need for believers to *abide (firm; cleave; root; stedfast)* in Christ, *abhorring (eschew; renounce; resist)* evil, *mortifying* the deeds of the body, and keeping themselves unspotted *(spot)* from the *world (worldly; conformed; fashion).* Scripture likens the life of faith to a *fight (buffet; contend)* or running *(run)* a race *(course)* to *gain* a prize *(crown; reward).* As believers *follow after (disciple; imitate; learn)* God in this way, he gives them the physical and moral *ability (conquer; strength; to be strong)* they need.

The walk of faith is one of *knowing (acknowledge; key)* God as a *friend* and *understanding (eye; apprehend; to see; perceive; senses; to take away)* him, although human understanding of God will always be limited. God is a *rewarder* of those who *seek (feel)* him and he gives *wis-*

dom (wise) for right living, as believers *meditate (eat)* on whatever things are *lovely.*

ABHOR

655 apostugeō, p. 1
948 bdelussō, p. 1

ABIDE, ABODE

3306 menō, p. 1
1961 epimenō, p. 1

ABILITY, ABLE

A. Nouns

1411 dunamis, p. 2
2479 ischus, p. 2

B. Verbs

1410 dunamai, p. 3
1412 dunamoō, p. 3
1414 dunateō, p. 3
2480 ischuō, p. 3
2192 echō, p. 3
2141 euporeō, p. 3

C. Adjectives

1415 dunatos, p. 3
2425 hikanos, p. 3

ACCURATELY

199 akribōs, p. 10

ACKNOWLEDGE(-MENT)

A. Verb

1921 epiginōskō, p. 11

B. Noun

1922 epignōsis, p. 11

APPREHEND

2638 katalambanō, p. 34

BUFFET

5299 hupōpiazō, p. 82

CLEAVE, CLAVE

2853 kollaō, p. 104
4347 proskollaō, p. 104
4357 prosmenō, p. 104

CONFORMED, CONFORMABLE

A. Verb

4833v summorphizō, p. 121

B. Adjectives

4832 summorphos, p. 122
4964 suschēmatizō, p. 122

CONQUER, CONQUEROR

3528 nikaō, p. 122
5245 hupernikaō, p. 122

CONTEND

118 athleō, p. 125
1252 diakrinō, p. 125
1864 epagōnizomai, p. 125

COURSE

A. Noun

1408 dromos, p. 134

CROWN

A. Noun

4735 stephanos, p. 139

B. Verb

4737 stephanoō, p. 139

DISCIPLE

A. Nouns

3101 mathētēs, p. 171
3102 mathētria, p. 172
4827 summathētēs, p. 172

B. Verb
3100 mathēteuō, p. 172

EAT, EAT WITH, EATING
A. Verb
5176 trōgō, p. 192

ESCHEW
1578 ekklinō, p. 206

EYE
5869 'ayin, p. 74

FASHION
C. Verb
4964 suschēmatizō, p. 227

FEEL, FEELING, FELT
5584 psēlaphaō, p. 232

FIGHT
A. Nouns
73 agōn, p. 235
119 athlēsis, p. 235

B. Verbs
75 agōnizomai, p. 235
4438 pukteuō, p. 235
3164 machomai, p. 235
2341 thēriomacheō, p. 235

FIRM
949 bebaios, p. 240

FOLLOW, FOLLOW AFTER
190 akoloutheō, p. 244
1872 epakoloutheō, p. 244
2628 katakoloutheō, p. 244
3877 parakoloutheō, p. 244
4870 sunakoloutheō, p. 244
1377 diōkō, p. 245
2614 katadiōkō, p. 245

FRIEND
A. Noun
5384 philos, p. 256

GAIN
B. Verb
2770 kerdainō, p. 260

IMITATE, IMITATOR
A. Verb
3401 mimeomai, p. 319

B. Nouns
3402 mimētēs, p. 319
4831 summimētēs, p. 320

KEY
2807 kleis, p. 341

KNOW, KNOWN, KNOWLEDGE, UNKNOWN
A. Verbs
5234 nākar, p. 130
1097 ginōskō, p. 346
1492 oida, p. 346
1921 epiginōskō, p. 347
4267 proginōskō, p. 347
1987 epistamai, p. 347
4923 sunoida, p. 347
50 agnoeō, p. 347
1107 gnōrizō, p. 347

B. Adjectives
1110 gnōstos, p. 348
5318 phaneros, p. 348
1990 epistēmōn, p. 348
57 agnōstos, p. 348

C. Nouns
1108 gnōsis, p. 348

1922 epignōsis, p. 348
56 agnōsia, p. 348

LEARN, LEARNED
3129 manthanō, p. 360
1097 ginōskō, p. 361

LOVELY
4375 prosphilēs, p. 383

MEDITATE
3191 meletaō, p. 400

MORTIFY
2289 thanatoō, p. 417
3499 nekroō, p. 417

NARROW
A. Adjective
4728 stenos, p. 426

B. Verb
2346 thlibō, p. 426

PATH
5147 tribos, p. 462
5163 trochia, p. 462

PERCEIVE
1097 ginōskō, p. 465
1921 epiginōskō, p. 465
3708 eidon, p. 465
2334 theōreō, p. 466
143 aisthanomai, p. 466
3539 noeō, p. 466
2657 katanoeō, p. 466
2638 katalambanō, p. 466

PRIZE
1017 brabeion, p. 489

RACE
73 agōn, p. 504
4712 stadion, p. 504

RENOUNCE
550 apeipon, p. 524
657 apotassō, p. 524

RESIST
436 anthistēmi, p. 528
478 antikathistēmi, p. 528

REWARD
A. Noun
3408 misthos, p. 533

REWARDER
3406 misthapodotēs, p. 533

ROOT
B. Verb
4492 rhizoō, p. 539

RUN, RAN
5143 trechō, p. 541

TO SEE, PERCEIVE
A. Verb
7200 rā'āh, p. 219

TO SEEK
A. Verbs
1245 bāqāš, p. 220
1875 dāraš, p. 220
2212 zēteō, p. 558
327 anazēteō, p. 558
1567 ekzēteō, p. 558
1934 epizēteō, p. 558
3713 oregō, p. 558

SENSES
145 aisthētērion, p. 561

SPOT
C. Adjective
784 aspilos, p. 596

STEDFAST, STEDFASTNESS
A. Adjectives
949 bebaios, p. 599
1476 hedraios, p. 599
4731 stereos, p. 599

B. Nouns
4733 stereōma, p. 599
4740 stērigmos, p. 599

STRAIGHT
A. Adjective
2117 euthus, p. 601

STRENGTH
2458 ḥayil, p. 247

TO BE STRONG
A. Verb
2388 ḥāzaq, p. 250

B. Adjective
2389 ḥāzāq, p. 250

TO TAKE AWAY
B. Noun
3948 leqaḥ, p. 256

UNDERSTAND, UNDERSTOOD
A. Verbs
7919 śākal, p. 273
995 bîn, p. 273
4920 suniēmi, p. 650
3539 noeō, p. 650
1097 ginōskō, p. 650
1987 epistamai, p. 650
4441 punthanomai, p. 651
1107 gnōrizō, p. 651
50 agnoeō, p. 651

B. Adjectives
2154 eusēmos, p. 651
1425 dusnoētos, p. 651

C. Nouns
998 bînah, p. 273
8394 teḇûnāh, p. 273
4905 maśkîl, p. 273

UNDERSTANDING
A. Nouns
3563 nous, p. 651
4907 sunesis, p. 651
1271 dianoia, p. 651

B. Adjective
801 asunetos, p. 651

WALK
4043 peripateō, p. 664

WAY
3598 hodos, p. 668

WISDOM
4678 sophia, p. 678
5428 phronēsis, p. 678

WISE, WISER, WISELY
A. Adjectives
2450 ḥākām, p. 290
4680 sophos, p. 679
5429 phronimos, p. 679

B. Noun
2451 ḥokmāh, p. 290

C. Verbs
2449 ḥākam, p. 291

4679 sophizō, p. 679
4920 suniēmi *or* suniō, p. 679

D. Adverb
5430 phronimōs, p. 679

WORLD
2889 kosmos, p. 685

WORLDLY
2886 kosmikos, p. 685

Spiritual Warfare

Spiritual *warfare (conflict; great; wrestle)* is a constant feature of the life of faith, but God has equipped believers with the spiritual *armor (bind, binding; breastplate; helmet; gird; loins; shield; withal)* and *weapons (left; sword)* necessary to *quench* the *fiery darts* of the enemy.

ARMS, ARMOR, TO ARM
A. Nouns
3696 hoplon, p. 37
3833 panoplia, p. 38
B. Verbs
3695 hoplizō, p. 38
2528 kathoplizō, p. 38

BIND, BINDING
5265 hupodeō, p. 66

BREASTPLATE
2382 thōrax, p. 78

CONFLICT
73 agōn, p. 121

DART
956 belos, p. 145

FIERY
4448 puroō, p. 234

GIRD, GIRDED, GIRT
4024 perizōnnumi, p. 264

GREAT
2245 hēlikos, p. 279

HELMET
4030 perikephalaia, p. 300

LEFT
710 aristeros, p. 363

LOINS
3751 osphus, p. 376

QUENCH
A. Verb
4570 sbennumi, p. 502

SHIELD
2375 thureos, p. 571

SWORD
3162 machaira, p. 613

WAR
A. Verb
4754 strateuō, p. 665

WARFARE
4756 strateia *or* -tia, p. 666

WEAPONS
3696 hoplon, p. 670

WITHAL
260 hama, p. 679

WRESTLE, WRESTLING
3823 palē, p. 688

Fasting

To *abstain (to eat; fast)* from food for a period of time is a discipline practiced by believers, not as an end in itself *(severity),* but as a sign of repentance or of seeking God.

ABSTAIN, ABSTINENCE
568 apechō, p. 5

TO EAT
A. Verb
398 'ākal, p. 67

FAST, FASTING
A. Nouns
3521 nēsteia, p. 227
3523 nēstis, p. 228
B. Verb
3522 nēsteuō, p. 228
C. Adjective
777 asitos, p. 228

SEVERITY
857 apheidia, p. 566

Growing in Faith

Believers are to *grow* in their faith and move on *(progress)* from rudimentary spiritual teaching *(novice; principles; drink; milk)* to maturity *(solid; meat).* Immaturity leads to an unstable *(toss)* Christian life.

Spiritual growth takes place through testing *(approve; proof; prove)* and *chastening (discipline; reprove; severity)* which proves the genuineness of faith and develops Christian character.

APPROVE, APPROVED
A. Verbs
1381 dokimazō, p. 35
4921 sunistēmi, p. 35

CHASTEN, CHASTENING, CHASTISE, CHASTISEMENT
A. Verb
3811 paideuō, p. 97
B. Noun
3809 paideia, p. 97

DISCIPLINE
4995 sōphronismos, p. 172

DRINK, DRANK
B. Verb
4222 potizō, p. 185

GROW
837 auxanō, p. 283
5232 huperauxanō, p. 283

MEAT
1035 brōsis, p. 400

MILK
1051 gala, p. 408

NOVICE
3504 neophutos, p. 436

PRINCIPLES
746 archē, p. 488

PROGRESS
4297 prokopē, p. 491

PROOF
1383 dokimion, p. 492

PROVE
A. Verbs
1381 dokimazō, p. 495
584 apodeiknumi, p. 495
3936 paristēmi, p. 495
3985 peirazō, p. 495
B. Noun
3986 peirasmos, p. 495

TO REPROVE
3198 yākaḥ, p. 203

SEVERITY
663 apotomia, p. 566

SOLID
4731 stereos, p. 584

TOSS
2831 kludōnizomai, p. 637

Threats to the Life of Faith

There are many *dangers (enemy; hinder)* to the life of faith, both physical and spiritual, which believers are to *beware* of *(abstain; attend; child; flee; heed; ware of).*

Wealth, while not condemned in Scripture, does have its dangers *(choke; rich; root),* and there are many *temptations (beguile; cumber; seduce)* to *wander* from the truth *(err; error)* and to become *discouraged (burden; faint; weary).*

Believers are *warned (forewarn)* not to go beyond their faith *(deal; proportion),* or to *waver (doubt; double-minded),* or to be afraid *(fear),* and to keep themselves from being unequally yoked *(separate; concord)* with unbelievers.

They are also *exhorted* in Scripture to *avoid disputes* and *jealousy (bitter),* and all things which lead to an *unfruitful (empty)* or *faithless* existence.

See also SIN, SINFUL BEHAVIOR; SINFUL SPEECH; IDOLATRY; THE PEOPLE OF GOD, LIFE OF THE PEOPLE OF GOD: PROBLEMS IN THE LIFE OF THE CHURCH

ABSTAIN, ABSTINENCE
568 apechō, p. 5

ATTEND
A. Verbs
4337 prosechō, p. 44
4342 proskartereō, p. 44
B. Adjective
2145v euparedros, p. 44

AVOID
1578 ekklinō, p. 47
1624 ektrepō, p. 47
3868 paraiteomai, p. 47
4026 periistēmi, p. 47
4724 stellō, p. 47

BEGUILE
538 apataō, p. 58
1818 exapataō, p. 58
3884 paralogizomai, p. 58
1185 deleazō, p. 58

BEWARE
991 blepō, p. 65
4337 prosechō, p. 65
5442 phulassō, p. 65

BITTER
A. Adjective
4089 pikros, p. 68

BURDEN, BURDENED
A. Noun
922 baros, p. 83
B. Verbs
916 bareō, p. 83
1912 epibareō, p. 83

CHILD
5040 teknion, p. 99

CHOKE
638 apopnigō, p. 100

CONCORD
4857 sumphōnēsis, p. 118

CUMBER
2673 katargeō, p. 140
4049 perispaō, p. 140

DANGER, DANGEROUS
A. Verb
2793 kinduneuō, p. 144
B. Adjectives
1777 enochos, p. 144
2000 episphalēs, p. 144

DEAL
3307 merizō, p. 148

DISCOURAGE
120 athumeō, p. 172

DISPUTE, DISPUTER, DISPUTING
A. Nouns
1261 dialogismos, p. 175
3055 logomachia, p. 175
3859v diaparatribē, p. 175
485 antilogia, p. 175
4804 suzētētēs, p. 175
B. Verb
1256 dialegomai, p. 175

DOUBLE-MINDED
1374 dipsuchos, p. 181

DOUBT, DOUBTING
A. Verbs
639 aporeō, p. 182
1280 diaporeō, p. 182
1252 diakrinō, p. 182
1365 distazō, p. 182
3349 meteōrizō, p. 182
5590,
142 psuchēn airō, p. 182
B. Noun
1261 dialogismos, p. 182

EMPTY
B. Adjective
2756 kenos, p. 198

ENEMY
2190 echthros, p. 200

ERR
4105 planaō, p. 205
635 apoplanaō, p. 205
795 astocheō, p. 205

ERROR
4106 planē, p. 205
51 agnoēma, p. 205

EXHORT, EXHORTATION
A. Verbs
3870 parakaleō, p. 217
3867 paraineō, p. 217
4389 protrepō, p. 217
B. Noun
3874 paraklēsis, p. 217

FAINT
1590 ekluō, p. 221
1573 enkakeō or ekkakeō, p. 222
2577 kamnō, p. 222

FAITHLESS
571 apistos, p. 223

FEAR, FEARFUL, FEARFULNESS
A. Nouns
5401 phobos, p. 229
1167 deilia, p. 230
B. Adjectives
5398 phoberos, p. 230
1169 deilos, p. 230
1630 ekphobos, p. 230
1790 entromos, p. 230
C. Adverb
880 aphobos, p. 230
D. Verb
5399 phobeō, p. 230

FLEE, FLED
5343 pheugō, p. 242
1628 ekpheugō, p. 242
2703 katapheugō, p. 242

FOREWARN
4302 prolegō, p. 250

HEED
991 blepō, p. 299
3708 horaō, p. 299
4337 prosechō, p. 299
1907 epechō, p. 299

HINDER, HINDRANCE
A. Verbs
1465 enkoptō, p. 305
2967 kōluō, p. 305
1254 diakōluō, p. 305
B. Noun
1464 enkopē, p. 305

JEALOUS, JEALOUSY
A. Noun
2205 zēlos, p. 332
B. Verbs
2206 zēloō, p. 332
3863 parazēloō, p. 333

PROPORTION
356 analogia, p. 494

RICH, RICHES, RICHLY, RICH MAN
A. Adjective
4145 plousios, p. 533
C. Noun
4149 ploutos, p. 533

ROOT
A. Noun
4491 rhiza, p. 539

SEDUCE, SEDUCING
A. Verbs
4105 planaō, p. 556
635 apoplanaō, p. 556
B. Adjective
4108 planos, p. 556

SEPARATE
A. Verb
873 aphorizō, p. 561

TEMPTATION
3986 peirasmos, p. 622

UNFRUITFUL
B. Adjective
175 akarpos, p. 257

WANDER
B. Noun
4107 planētēs, p. 665

WARE OF
5442 phulassō, p. 666

WARN
3560 noutheteō, p. 666
5263 hupodeiknumi, p. 666
5537 chrēmatizō, p. 666

WAVER, WAVERING
A. Adjective
186 aklinēs, p. 668
B. Verb
1252 diakrinō, p. 668

WEARY
2872 kopiaō, p. 670
2577 kamnō, p. 670
1573 ekkakeō or enkakeō, p. 670

The Suffering of Believers

That they will face *suffering (affliction; anguish; hardship; sorrow; tribulation), trials,* and *persecution (contradict; persecutor; waste)* should not come as a surprise to believers.

Scripture records the *torture (beat; saw asunder; scourge; scourgings; stocks; tormentors), imprisonment (bind; bond; chain; prison; prisoner; ward), hunger,* and other *hazards (thorn; banded; spectacle)* which confronted Paul and others as they preached the gospel of Jesus Christ.

Nevertheless, believers are encouraged to *endure (abide; bear)* suffering as good *soldiers,* without being *affrighted* or *ashamed,* knowing that if they share in the fellowship of Christ's sufferings *(baptism; behind, come behind; deadness; fill; fill up),* they will also share in his victory.

ABIDE
A. Verb
5278 hupomenō, p. 2

AFFLICT, AFFLICTION
A. Verbs
2558 kakoucheō, p. 17
2553 kakopatheō, p. 17
2346 thlibō, p. 17
5003 talaipōreō, p. 17

B. Nouns
2552   kakopatheia, p. 17
2561   kakōsis, p. 17
3804   pathēma, p. 17
2347   thlipsis, p. 17

AFFRIGHTED
4426   pturō, p. 18

ANGUISH
A. Nouns
4730   stenochōria, p. 27
4928   sunochē, p. 27

B. Verbs
4729   stenochōreō, p. 27
4912   sunechō, p. 28
3600   odunaō, p. 28

ASHAMED
A. Verbs
153   aischunō, p. 39
1870   epaischunomai, p. 39

C. Adjective
422   anepaischuntos, p. 39

BANDED
4160   poieō sustrophēn, p. 49

BAPTISM
A. Noun
908   baptisma, p. 50

BEAR
941   bastazō, p. 52
4064   peripherō, p. 52
5297   hupopherō, p. 52

BEAT
1194   derō, p. 53
5180   tuptō, p. 53
4463   rhabdizō, p. 53

BEHIND, COME BEHIND
C. Noun
5303   husterēma, p. 59

BIND, BINDING
4385   proteinō, p. 67

BOND
1199   desmos, p. 73
1198   desmios, p. 73

CHAIN
254   halusis, p. 95

CONTRADICT, CONTRADICTION
A. Verb
483   antilegō, p. 127

B. Noun
485   antilogia, p. 127

DEADNESS
3500   nekrōsis, p. 148

ENDURE, ENDURING
A. Verbs
3306   menō, p. 200
5278   hupomenō, p. 200
5342   pherō, p. 200
5297   hupopherō, p. 200
430   anechō, p. 200
2594   kartereō, p. 200
3114   makrothumeō, p. 200

B. Noun
5281   hupomonē, p. 200

FILL, FILL UP
466   antanaplēroō, p. 236

HARDSHIP
2553   kakopatheō, p. 290
4777   sunkakopatheō, p. 291

HAZARD
3860   paradidōmi, p. 294
3851   paraboleuomai, p. 294

HUNGER, HUNGERED, HUNGRY
A. Noun
3042   limos, p. 315

B. Verb
3983   peinaō, p. 315

C. Adjective
4361   prospeinos, p. 315

IMPRISON, IMPRISONMENT
A. Verb
5439   phulakizō, p. 321

B. Noun
5438   phulakē, p. 321

PERSECUTE, PERSECUTION
A. Verbs
1377   diōkō, p. 468
1559   ekdiōkō, p. 468

B. Noun
1375   diōgmos, p. 468

PERSECUTOR
1376   diōktēs, p. 468

PRISON, PRISON-HOUSE
1201   desmōtērion, p. 488
5438   phulakē, p. 488
5084   tērēsis, p. 488

PRISONER
1198   desmios, p. 488
1202   desmōtēs, p. 488
4869   sunaichmalōtos, p. 488

SAW ASUNDER
4249   prizō or priō, p. 548

SCOURGE
B. Verbs
3146   mastigoō, p. 551
3147   mastizō, p. 551

SCOURGING
3148   mastix, p. 551

SOLDIER
A. Nouns
4757   stratiōtēs, p. 584
4961   sustratiōtēs, p. 584

B. Verb
4754   strateuō, p. 584

SORROW
A. Nouns
3077   lupē, p. 588
3601   odunē, p. 588

B. Verbs
3076   lupeō, p. 588
3600   odunaō, p. 588

C. Adjective
4036   perilupos, p. 588

SPECTACLE
2302   theatron, p. 591

STOCKS
3586   xulon, p. 600

SUFFER
A. Verbs
430   anechō, p. 608
3958   paschō, p. 608
4310   propaschō, p. 608
4841   sumpaschō, p. 608
2558   kakoucheō, p. 608
4778   sunkakoucheomai, p. 609
3114   makrothumeō, p. 609
91   adikeō, p. 609

SUFFERING
3804   pathēma, p. 609

THORN
4647   skolops, p. 629

TORMENTOR
930   basanistēs, p. 637

TORTURE
5178   tumpanizō, p. 637

TRIAL
1382   dokimē, p. 643
3986   peirasmos, p. 643
4451   purōsis, p. 643

TRIBULATION
2347   thlipsis, p. 643

WARD
5438   phulakē, p. 666
5084   tērēsis, p. 666

WASTE
B. Verb
3075   lumainō, p. 667

THE PEOPLE OF GOD ——————

Old Testament Names for the People of God

God chose Israel to be his *heritage* and treasured *possession;* a *people* who were to be *separate* from those around them. The names for the Old Testament people of God reflect the nature of their relationship with God. He is the parent who has given them

birth *(bear; build)*, they are his *flock* and his *vineyard* which he has chosen to *plant.* The twelve *tribes* of Israel repeatedly suffered major catastrophes that brought them to the brink of extinction, but in his mercy, God always preserved a *remnant (to consume; to be left, remain; residue; remainder).*

TO BEAR
A. Verb
3205   yālad, p. 14

TO BUILD
1121   bēn, p. 26
1323   bat, p. 26

TO CONSUME
B. Noun
3617   kālāh, p. 47

FLOCK
6629 ṣō'n, p. 84

HERITAGE
2820 klēroō, p. 303

TO BE LEFT, REMAIN
A. Verb
3498 yātar, p. 134

B. Noun
3499 yeter, p. 134

PEOPLE
5971 'am, p. 174

TO PLANT
5193 nāṭa', p. 178

POSSESSION
5459 segullāh, p. 182

REMAINDER, REMNANT
A. Nouns
3499 yeter, p. 198
7611 še'ērît, p. 199
7605 še'ār, p. 200

B. Verb
7604 šā'ar, p. 200

RESIDUE
2645 kataloipos, p. 528

TO SEPARATE
A. Verb
5144 nāzar, p. 222

TRIBE
A. Nouns
4294 maṭṭeh, p. 268
7626 šēbeṭ, p. 269

VINEYARD
3754 kerem, p. 275

New Testament Names for the People of God

A number of names for the people of God in the New Testament emphasize different aspects of the relationship that believers have with God and with the world.

Christian (call) was first applied in New Testament times, but the *believers* were more commonly referred to as *saints* because of the righteousness that was theirs by faith, or as the *brethren (brothers)* as a sign of their belonging to the family of God. They are God's *children* by *adoption*, the *elect* or *chosen* ones. They are the *beloved* of God, a *royal* priesthood and *servants* of God.

As God's *flock* they are under the care of Christ, the Chief Shepherd of the *sheep;* while *remnant* contrasts the relatively small number saved by the gospel from the midst of unbelieving Israel. *Pilgrim* highlights the fact that believers are sojourners in the world, but they are not of it.

ADOPTION
5206 huiothesia, p. 13

BELIEF, BELIEVE, BELIEVERS
A. Verbs
4100 pisteuō, p. 61
3982 peithō, p. 61

B. Noun
4102 pistis, p. 61

C. Adjective
4103 pistos, p. 61

BELOVED
A. Adjective
27 agapētos, p. 62

B. Verb
25 agapaō, p. 62

BROTHER, BRETHREN, BROTHERHOOD, BROTHERLY
80 adelphos, p. 82

CALL, CALLED
A. Verb
5337 chrēmatizō, p. 87

CHILD, CHILDREN
5043 teknon, p. 99
5040 teknion, p. 99
5207 huios, p. 99
3816 pais, p. 100
3813 paidion, p. 100

CHOSEN
C. Noun
1589 eklogē, p. 101

ELECT, ELECTED, ELECTION
A. Adjective
1588 eklektos, p. 196

B. Noun
1589 eklogē, p. 196

CHRISTIAN
5546 christianos, p. 101

FAMILY
3624 oikos, p. 225
3965 patria, p. 225

FLOCK
4167 poimnē, p. 243
4168 poimnion, p. 243

PILGRIM
3927 parepidēmos, p. 471

REMNANT
3062**loipos, p. 522
3005 leimma, p. 522
5259,
3005 hupoleimma, p. 522

ROYAL
934 basileios, p. 539

SAINT(S)
40 hagios, p. 544

SERVANT
A. Nouns
1401 doulos, p. 562
1249 diakonos, p. 562
3816 pais, p. 562
5257 hupēretēs, p. 562
4889 sundoulos, p. 563

B. Verb
1402 douloō, p. 563

SHEEP
4263 probaton, p. 569
4263* probation, p. 569

Jews and Gentiles

The Jews were the descendants of the Old Testament Hebrew *people (to pass over)* and included the *Pharisees* and *scribes.*

The *Gentiles* are often referred to as the *nations* in the Old Testament, and in derogatory terms such as *barbarians, dogs,* and *publicans* in the New Testament. They and the *Syrophoenician* woman who came to Jesus were excluded from all the privileges associated with being a *Jew,* except for those *proselytes* who had converted to Judaism. In Christ, however, the distinction between Jew and Gentile is abolished.

See also JESUS CHRIST, RESPONSES TO JESUS

BARBARIAN, BARBAROUS
915 barbaros, p. 50

DOG
2965 kuōn, p. 181

GENTILES
A. Nouns
1484 ethnos, p. 262
1672 hellēn, p. 262

B. Adjective
1482 ethnikos, p. 263

C. Adverb
1483 ethnikōs, p. 263

JEW, JEWESS, JEWISH, JEWRY, JEWS' RELIGION
A. Adjectives
2453 ioudaios, p. 333
2451 ioudaikos, p. 334

B. Noun
2454 ioudaismos, p. 334

C. Verb
2450 ioudaizō, p. 334

D. Adverb
2452 ioudaikōs, p. 334

NATION
1471 gôy, p. 159
1484 ethnos, p. 426
1085 genos, p. 426
246 allophulos, p. 426

TO PASS OVER
B. Noun
5680 'ibrî, p. 173

PEOPLE
2992 laos, p. 465
1218 dēmos, p. 465
1484 ethnos, p. 465

PHARISEES
5330 pharisaios, p. 470

PROSELYTE
4339 prosēlutos, p. 495

PUBLICAN
5057 telōnēs, p. 497

SCRIBE
1122 grammateus, p. 551

SYROPHOENICIAN
4949 surophoinikissa *or* surophunissa, p. 614

The Life of the People of God

The Covenants

The covenant expressed God's committed relationship to, and his requirements of, his people. It was a solemn agreement often *confirmed* with an oath *(vouchsafe)* and with the use of *salt,* and accompanied by a sacrifice *(testator).*

God covenanted with Noah not to destroy the earth again by a *flood,* and gave the *rainbow* as a sign of the covenant.

God's covenant with Abraham was a *promise to bless (fatness)* the whole world in every *generation* through his descendants and to give him the *land* of Canaan. *Circumcision* was the outward sign of the *making* (or cutting) of this *covenant.*

The covenant at Sinai was accompanied by the giving of the Law *(to command; commandment).* Israel found it *impossible* to keep the Law, and *covenant-breakers (break; implacable)* led to the promise of a *new (dedicate)* covenant mediated through the death of Jesus Christ and sealed in his blood, where circumcision was spiritual *(concision)* rather than physical, as under the *old* covenant.

See also THE LAW; WORSHIP OF GOD IN ANCIENT ISRAEL: OATHS AND VOWS

TO BLESS
A. Verb
1288 bārak, p. 18
B. Noun
1293 berākāh, p. 18

BREAK, BREAKER, BREAKING, BRAKE
A. Verb
3089 luō, p. 78
B. Nouns
3847 parabasis, p. 78
3848 parabatēs, p. 78

CIRCUMCISION, UNCIRCUMCISION, CIRCUMCISE
A. Nouns
4061 peritomē, p. 102
203 akrobustia, p. 102
B. Adjective
564 aperitmētos, p. 102
C. Verbs
4135 mûl, p. 35
4059 peritemnō, p. 102
1986 epispaomai, p. 102

TO COMMAND
6680 ṣāwāh, p. 41
1299 diatassō, p. 111
2036 epō, p. 112
1781 entellō, p. 112
2004 epitassō, p. 112
2753 keleuō, p. 112
3853 parangellō, p. 112
4367 prostassō, p. 112

COMMANDMENT
4687 miṣwāh, p. 42
1297 diatagma, p. 112
1785 entolē, p. 112
1778 entalma, p. 112
2003 epitagē, p. 112

CONCISION
2699 katatomē, p. 118

CONFIRM, CONFIRMATION
A. Verbs
2964 kuroō, p. 121
4300 prokuroō, p. 121

COVENANT
A. Nouns
1285 berît, p. 50
1242 diathēkē, p. 135
B. Verb
4934 suntithēmi, p. 135

COVENANT-BREAKERS
802 asunthetos, p. 135

DEDICATE, DEDICATION
A. Verb
1457 enkainizō, p. 153

FATNESS
4096 piotēs, p. 229

FLOOD
A. Noun
2627 kataklusmos, p. 243

GENERATION
1755 dôr, p. 91

IMPLACABLE
786 aspondos, p. 320

IMPOSSIBLE
A. Adjective
102 adunatos, p. 321
B. Verb
101 adunateō, p. 321

LAND
127 'ădāmāh, p. 132
776 'ereṣ, p. 132

TO MAKE (CUT) A COVENANT
3772 kārat, p. 145

NEW
3501 neos, p. 431

OLD
A. Adjective
3820 palaios, p. 444

PROMISE
A. Noun
1860 epangelia, p. 491
B. Verb
1861 epangellō, p. 491

RAINBOW
2463 iris, p. 505

SALT
251 halas, p. 544

TESTATOR
1303 diatithēmi, p. 623

VOUCHSAFE
3670 homologeō, p. 663

God's Saving Acts
God's *saving* acts *(to number, visit, punish; to work)* reveal his nature and character. He delivered his people from Egypt and kept them *(to depart; to turn)* in their desert *wanderings,* providing them with food *(manna)* and water from the *rock.*

Horn is a symbol of God's strength and is frequently used in Scripture to emphasize his ability *to save.*

See also GOD, WORKS OF GOD

TO BURN
B. Noun
8314 śārap, p. 27

TO DEPART
5265 nāsa', p. 58

HORN
2768 keras, p. 312

MANNA
3131 manna, p. 390

TO NUMBER, VISIT, PUNISH
A. Verb
6485 pāqad, p. 164
B. Noun
6496 pāqîd, p. 164

ROCK
6697 ṣûr, p. 208

SAVE, SAVING
A. Verbs
3467 yāša', p. 214
4982 sōzō, p. 547
1295 diasōzō, p. 548
B. Nouns
3444 yešû'āh, p. 215
4047 peripoiēsis, p. 548

TO TURN
A. Verb
5437 sābab, p. 270

WANDER
A. Verb
4105 planaō, p. 665

TO WORK
A. Verbs
6466 pā'al, p. 293
6213 'āśah, p. 293
B. Noun
4639 ma'ăśeh, p. 294

The Nature and Foundation of the Church
The church is the *congregation (assemble; assembly)* of believers, both locally and universally. Scripture uses a number of metaphors to describe the church and Christ's relationship with the church.

- It is the *body (band; bond; compacted; joint; knit together; supply),* of which Jesus Christ is the *head.*
- It is a spiritual building *(build; frame)* in which Christ is both the *foundation* and chief *cornerstone,* built also on the foundation of the apostles and prophets *(masterbuilder).*
- It is the *bride (cherish; wrinkle)* of Christ and he is the bridegroom.

See also JESUS CHRIST, NAMES AND TITLES OF

ASSEMBLE
4863 sunagō, p. 42
4871 sunalizō, p. 42
4905 sunerchomai, p. 42

ASSEMBLY
1577 ekklesia, p. 42
3831 panēguris, p. 43

BAND
4886 sundesmos, p. 49

BODY
A. Noun
4983 sōma, p. 72

B. Adjective
4954 sussōmos, p. 72

BOND
4886 sundesmos, p. 73

BRIDE, BRIDEGROOM
3565 numphē, p. 79
3566 numphios, p. 79

BUILD
A. Verbs
3618 oikodomeō, p. 82
2026 epoikodomeō, p. 83
4925 sunoikodomeō, p. 83

B. Noun
3619 oikodomē, p. 83

CHERISH
2282 thalpō, p. 98

COMPACTED
4822 sumbibazō, p. 115

CONGREGATION
1577 ekklēsia, p. 122
4864 sunagōgē, p. 122

CORNER, CORNERSTONE
1137 gōnia, p. 129
746 archē, p. 129

FOUNDATION, FOUNDED
A. Nouns
2310 themelios *or* themelion, p. 254
2602 katabolē, p. 254

B. Verb
2311 themelioō, p. 254

FRAME
4883 sunarmologeō, p. 254

HEAD
2776 kephalē, p. 294

JOINT
860 haphē, p. 334

KNIT TOGETHER
4822 sumbibazō, p. 346

MASTERBUILDER
753 architektōn, p. 396

SUPPLY
A. Verb
2023 epichorēgeō, p. 611

B. Noun
2024 epichorēgia, p. 611

WRINKLE
4512 rhutis, p. 688

Activity and Government of God's People in the Old Testament

The Promised Land was *divided* up among the twelve *tribes* of Israel, according to descent (*genealogy; reckon*) from the *patriarchs*, and governed by Israel's leaders (*commander; elder; head; to judge; to keep, oversee; prince; to tell*) and their advisers (*to counsel*), until the *kingdom* of Israel was united under the *reign (throne)* of David.

Because of their persistent unfaithfulness, God sought to refine (*test*) the Israelites by suffering through *famine (wither)*, plague (*pestilence; to touch*), war, harsh *labor*, and ultimately through exiling them from the land (*carrying away; to be desolate; dispersion; to drive out; to forsake; to go away, leave; to perish; scatter*). Through such *calamity (reproach)*, they were *humbled (to repent; to mourn; to rend, tear; sackcloth; ashes)* and cried out (*to awake; to cry*) to God in their *distress*. When they returned (*to return*) to him, God always *restored (restoration)* them.

See also SIN, IDOLATRY

ASHES
A. Noun
4700 spodos, p. 39

TO AWAKE
5782 'ûr, p. 11

CALAMITY
343 'êd, p. 29

CARRYING AWAY
A. Noun
3350 metoikesia, p. 90

B. Verb
3351 metoikizō, p. 90

COMMANDER
8269 śar, p. 41

TO COUNSEL
A. Verb
3289 yā'aṣ, p. 49

B. Noun
3289 yā'aṣ, p. 49

TO CRY
6817 ṣā'aq, p. 52
2199 zā'aq, p. 52

TO BE DESOLATE
8074 šāmēm, p. 58

DISPERSION
B. Noun
1290 diaspora, p. 174

DISTRESS
A. Nouns
6869 ṣārāh, p. 60
6862 ṣar, p. 60

B. Verb
6887 ṣārar, p. 60

TO DIVIDE
A. Verb
2505 ḥālaq, p. 60

B. Noun
2506 ḥēleq, p. 61

TO DRIVE OUT
5080 nādaḥ, p. 63

ELDER, AGED
2204,
2205 zāqēn, p. 67

FAMINE
A. Noun
7458 rā'āb, p. 77
3042 limos, p. 225

B. Verb
7456 rā'ēb, p. 78

TO FORSAKE
5800 'azab, p. 87

GENEALOGY
A. Noun
1076 genealogia, p. 262

B. Verb
1075 genealogeō, p. 262

TO GO AWAY, LEAVE
A. Verb
1540 gālāh, p. 93

B. Noun
1473 gôlāh, p. 94

HEAD
7218 rō'š, p. 105

TO BE HUMBLED, AFFLICTED
A. Verb
6031 'ānāh, p. 119

B. Noun
6041 'ānî, p. 119

TO JUDGE
A. Verb
8199 šāpaṭ, p. 125

TO KEEP, OVERSEE
A. Verb
5329 nāṣaḥ, p. 126

B. Participle
5329 nāṣṣēaḥ, p. 126

KINGDOM
4438 malkût, p. 129
4467 mamlākāh, p. 129
4428 melek, p. 130

LABOR
A. Noun
5999 'āmāl, p. 131

B. Verb
5998 'amal, p. 131

TO MOURN
56 'ābal, p. 154

PATRIARCH
3966 patriarchēs, p. 463

TO PERISH
A. Verb
6 'ābad, p. 177

PESTILENCE
1698 deber, p. 178

PRINCE
A. Noun
5387 nāśî, p. 189

TO RECKON
A. Verb
3187 yāḥaś, p. 194

B. Noun
3188 yaḥaś, p. 194

TO REIGN
4427 mālak, p. 196

TO REND, TEAR
7167 qāra', p. 201

TO REPENT
5162 nāḥam, p. 201

REPROACH
A. Noun
2781 ḥerpāh, p. 202
B. Verb
2778 ḥārap, p. 203

RESTORATION
605 apokatastasis, p. 530

RESTORE
600 apokathistēmi or apokathistanō, p. 530

TO RETURN
A. Verb
7725 šûb, p. 203
B. Noun
4878 mᵉšûbāh, p. 204

SACKCLOTH
4526 sakkos, p. 543

TO SCATTER
6327 pûs, p. 217
B. Noun

TO TELL
5057 nāgrîd, p. 258

TO TEST
A. Verb
6884 ṣārap, p. 259
B. Noun

THRONE
3678 kissē', p. 262

TO TOUCH
B. Noun
5061 nega', p. 265

TRIBE
A. Nouns
4294 maṭṭeh, p. 268
7626 šēbeṭ, p. 269

WAR
A. Noun
4421 milḥāmāh, p. 281
B. Verb
3898 lāḥam, p. 281

TO WITHER
3001 yābēš, p. 291

The Priesthood

Priests were set apart *(anoint; to fill)* to *serve* the Lord and to *minister (attend; to come near; call)* to him in worship. Their priestly duties *(course; execute)* included the care of the priestly *clothing* such as the *ephod* with its precious *stones,* the casting of *lots (inheritance)* to discover the will of God, and the confining *(to shut)* of infectious diseases.

TO ANOINT
A. Verb
4886 māšaḥ, p. 5

ATTEND
A. Verb
4337 prosechō, p. 44

TO CALL
B. Noun
4744 miqrā', p. 30

CLOTHING
4749 stolē, p. 106

TO COME NEAR, APPROACH
5066 nāgaš, p. 40

COURSE
A. Noun
2183 ephēmeria, p. 134

ENDLESS
179 akatalutos, p. 200

EPHOD
646 'ēpôd, p. 71

EXECUTE
2407 hierateuō, p. 216

TO FILL
A. Verb
4390 mālē', p. 81

INHERITANCE
2819 klēros, p. 325

LOT
1486 gôrāl, p. 141

TO MINISTER, SERVE
A. Verb
8334 šārat, p. 152
B. Noun
8334 šārat, p. 152

PRIEST, PRIESTHOOD, PRIEST'S OFFICE
A. Nouns
3548 kōhēn, p. 188
2406 hierateuma, p. 487
B. Verb
3547 kāhan, p. 189

TO SERVE
A. Verbs
8334 šārat, p. 223
5647 'ābad, p. 224
B. Noun
5656 'ăbôdāh, p. 224
C. Participle
8334 šārat, p. 225

TO SHUT
5462 sāgar, p. 228

STONE
68 'eben, p. 246

The Law

The *Law* of Moses laid down the *statutes* and *ordinances (decree; disposition; imposed)* for God's people to follow. The *stone (engrave)* tablets of the *testimony* were a reminder *(phylactery)* of Israel's relationship and responsibility to God. The scribes *(to number, count)* and experts in the Mosaic *Law (doctor; lawyer; to take, handle)* were responsible *to teach* the people what was *lawful* for them to do. In the criminal law the testimony of *witnesses* was important for crimes carrying the death penalty *(stone).*

Not a single item *(jot)* of the Law will pass away or remain unfulfilled, but in his death on the cross Jesus Christ fulfilled the requirements of the Law.

See also **JESUS CHRIST, RESPONSES TO JESUS; SALVATION, ATONEMENT: THE DEATH OF JESUS CHRIST**

DECREE
1378 dogma, p. 153

DISPOSITION
1296 diatagē, p. 175

DOCTOR
1320 didaskalos, p. 180
3547 nomodidaskalos, p. 180

ENGRAVE
1795 entupoō, p. 201

IMPOSED
1945 epikeimai, p. 321

JOT
2503 iōta, p. 334

LAW
A. Nouns
8451 tôrāh, p. 133
3551 nomos, p. 354
3548 nomothesia, p. 356
B. Verbs
3549 nomotheteō, p. 356
2919 krinō, p. 356
3891 paranomeō, p. 356
C. Adjectives
3544 nomikos, p. 356
1772 ennomos, p. 356
459 anomos, p. 356
D. Adverb
460 anomōs, p. 356

LAWFUL, LAWFULLY
A. Verb
1832 exesti, p. 356
B. Adverb
3545 nomimōs, p. 356

LAWYER
3544 nomikos, p. 357

TO NUMBER, COUNT
B. Noun
5608 sōpēr, p. 164

PHYLACTERY
5440 phulaktērion, p. 470

STATUTE, ORDINANCE
A. Nouns
2706 ḥōq, p. 244
2708 ḥuqqāh, p. 245
1296 diatagē, p. 450
1378 dogma, p. 450
B. Verbs
2710 ḥāqaq, p. 245
1379 dogmatizō, p. 451

STONE
68 'eben, p. 246

TO TAKE, HANDLE
8610 tāpaś, p. 255

TO TEACH
A. Verb
3925 lāmad, p. 256
B. Noun
8451 tôrāh, p. 257
C. Adjective

TESTIMONY
5715 'ēdût, p. 260

WITNESS

A. Noun

5707 'ēd, p. 292

B. Verb

5749 'ûd, p. 292

The Ritual (Worship) Law

The ritual law gave the people ceremonial guidelines on which animals and activities were *unclean (common; foul)* for them and what they could and could not *eat* and *touch*. Provision was made for them *to be clean* from the things that *pollute* through *washing* with *water*.

TO BE CLEAN

A. Verb

2891 ṭāhēr, p. 36

B. Adjective

2889 ṭāhôr, p. 36

COMMON, COMMONLY

A. Adjective

2834 koinos, p. 113

B. Verb

2840 koinoō, p. 113

TO EAT

A. Verb

398 'ākal, p. 67

FOUL

169 akathartos, p. 253

TO POLLUTE

2490 ḥālal, p. 180

TO TOUCH

A. Verb

5060 nāga', p. 265

UNCLEAN

A. Adjectives

2931 ṭāmē', p. 272

169 akathartos, p. 649

2839 koinos, p. 649

B. Verbs

2930 ṭāmē', p. 272

2840 koinoō, p. 649

C. Nouns

2932 ṭum'āh, p. 272

167 akatharsia, p. 649

TO WASH

7364 rāḥas, p. 281

3526 kābas, p. 282

WATER

4325 mayim, p. 283

Activity and Government of God's People in the New Testament

Order in the church is maintained through a system of church *government (dispensation)* in which the *authority* of Jesus Christ is delegated to those who hold *office (appoint; ordain)* as *bishop, elder (ambassador; aged)*, and *deacon (degree)*. These are responsible for the *oversight (over)* of the church, and for the *laying on* of hands to *appoint (confirm)* others for particular work. These leaders must meet certain criteria

(gravity; wilfully) in order to *serve (service)*, and the church is to *submit* to them.

AGED

A. Nouns

4246 presbutēs, p. 20

4247 presbutis, p. 20

AMBASSADOR, AMBASSAGE

A. Verb

4243 presbeuō, p. 25

B. Noun

4242 presbeia, p. 25

APPOINT, APPOINTED

2476 histēmi, p. 33

2525 kathistēmi, p. 33

5087 tithēmi, p. 33

1303 diatithēmi, p. 33

5021 tassō, p. 33

1299 diatassō, p. 34

5500 cheirotoneō, p. 34

AUTHORITY

A. Nouns

1849 exousia, p. 45

2003 epitagē, p. 46

5247 huperochē, p. 46

1413 dunastēs, p. 46

B. Verbs

1850 exousiazō, p. 46

2175 katexousiazō, p. 46

831 authenteō, p. 46

BISHOP

1985 episkopos, p. 67

1984 episkopē, p. 67

CONFIRM, CONFIRMATION

A. Verbs

950 bebaioō, p. 121

1991 epistērizō, p. 121

DEACON

1249 diakonos, p. 147

DEGREE

898 bathmos, p. 155

DISPENSATION

3622 oikonomia, p. 174

ELDER, ELDEST

A. Adjectives

4245 presbuteros, p. 195

4850 sumpresbuteros, p. 196

3187 meizōn, p. 196

B. Noun

4244 presbuterion, p. 196

GOVERNMENT

2941 kubernēsis, p. 276

GRAVITY

4587 semnotēs, p. 279

LAYING ON

1936 epithesis, p. 359

OFFICE

A. Nouns

4234 praxis, p. 443

2405 hierateia, p. 443

B. Verb

2407 hierateuō, p. 443

ORDAIN

5087 tithēmi, p. 450

2525 kathistēmi, p. 450

5021 tassō, p. 450

1299 diatassō, p. 450

2919 krinō, p. 450

ORDER

A. Nouns

5010 taxis, p. 450

OVER

4291 proistēmi, p. 453

OVERSIGHT

1983 episkopeō, p. 454

SERVE

1247 diakoneō, p. 563

1398 douleuō, p. 563

3000 latreuō, p. 563

5256 hupereteō, p. 563

SERVICE, SERVING

1248 diakonia, p. 563

3009 leitourgia, p. 563

2999 latreia, p. 563

SUBMIT

5226 hupeikō, p. 607

WILFULLY

A. Adverb

1596 hekousiōs, p. 676

The Ministry and Mission of the Church

The mission *(commit; send)* of the church is to *preach (discourse; proclaim; tell; testify; testimony; witness)* and *teach (correct; instruct)* the message of the *gospel* of Jesus Christ to the world, handing on the *tradition* of the faith.

Preachers and *teachers* are to teach sound *doctrine* and be able to *expound* the word of God and give a *defense* of the faith, and to *admonish* when necessary. In addition to the *ministry* of preaching and teaching, other ministries given to the church are those of *apostle, prophet (prophetess), evangelist, pastor (feed; shepherd)*, and *helps (helper)*. In the *fellowship* of believers, however, all are called to *minister (add)* and to make *intercessions*.

ADD

2023 epichorēgeō, p. 12

ADMONITION, ADMONISH

A. Noun

3559 nouthesia, p. 13

B. Verbs

3560 noutheteō, p. 13

3867 paraineō, p. 13

5537 chrēmatizō, p. 13

APOSTLE, APOSTLESHIP

652 apostolos, p. 30

651 apostolē, p. 31

COMMIT, COMMISSION

A. Verbs

4100 pisteuō, p. 113

5087 tithēmi, p. 113

3908 paratithēmi, p. 113

B. Noun

3866 parathēkē, p. 113

Problems in the Life of the Church

Many forces threaten the church both from within and without.

Internal *wranglings (contention; defect), factions*, and *schisms* all cause *division,* while the immorality of the *love feasts (unworthily)* in the early church needed correction. Paul also had to address *disorderly behavior* in the church, issues concerning women in the church *(shamefastness; speak; unveiled),* and to bring correction to those striving for *preeminence.*

Impostors (rock; spy), false prophets, and *false teachers (bereaved; thief; pasture)* also seek to infiltrate the church to *bewitch (devour; subvert; itching)* believers by introducing *error (fable; gangrene; old wives')* and *heresy,* and by their *heretical* teaching *(stubble)* to divert others from the truth and into *sects. Religion, science,* and *superstitious* attitudes were additional threats to the church.

3948 paroxusmos, p. 126
5379 philoneikia, p. 126

B. Adjectives
269 amachos, p. 126
5380 philoneikos, p. 126

DEFECT
2275 hēttēma, p. 154

DEVOUR
2719 katesthiō *and* kataphagō,
     p. 166

DISORDERLY
A. Adjective
813 ataktos, p. 174
B. Adverb
814 ataktōs, p. 174
C. Verb
812 atakteō, p. 174

DIVISION
1307 dichostasia, p. 179
4978 schisma, p. 179

ERROR
4106 planē, p. 205
51 agnoēma, p. 205

FABLE
3454 muthos, p. 220

FACTION, FACTIOUS
2052 erithia (*or* -eia), p. 220

GANGRENE
1044 gangraina, p. 261

HERESY
139 hairesis, p. 303

HERETICAL
141 hairetikos, p. 303

ITCHING
2833 knēthō, p. 332

IMPOSTORS
1114 goēs, p. 321

LOVE FEASTS
26 agapē, p. 382

OLD WIVES'
1126 graōdēs, p. 445

PASTURE
3542 nomē, p. 462

PREEMINENCE
5383 philoprōteuō, p. 482

PROPHET, FALSE
5578 pseudoprophētēs, p. 493

RELIGION
2356 thrēskeia, p. 520
1175 deisidaimonia, p. 521

RELIGIOUS
2357 thrēskos, p. 521

ROCK
4694 spilas, p. 537

SCIENCE
1108 gnōsis, p. 550

SCHISM
4978 schisma, p. 550

SECT
139 hairesis, p. 555

SHAMEFASTNESS
127 aidōs, p. 568

SPEAK
2980 laleō, p. 590

SPY
B. Verb
2684 kataskopeō, p. 597

STUBBLE
2562 kalamē, p. 606

SUBVERT, SUBVERTING
A. Verb
384 anaskeuazō, p. 607
B. Noun
2692 katastrophē, p. 607

SUPERSTITIOUS
1175 deisidaimōn, p. 610

TEACHER, FALSE
5572 pseudodidaskalos, p. 620

THIEF, THIEVES
2812 kleptēs, p. 627

UNVEILED
177 akatakaluptos, p. 654

UNWORTHILY
A. Adverb
371 anaxiōs, p. 654

WRANGLINGS
3859 diaparatribē, p. 688

The Local Church
     The local church refers to those believers who *assemble* together in any locality. Metaphors which describe the universal church are also applied to the local church (*espoused; husbandry; pillar; temper together).*
     The letters of the New Testament are invariably addressed to local churches or particular individuals (*lady*) connected with the local church and address local issues (*government; rule),* as well as give warnings (*harlot; lukewarm; nakedness; spew).*

ASSEMBLE
4905 sunerchomai, p. 42

ESPOUSED
718 harmozō, p. 206

GOVERNMENT
2941 kubernēsis, p. 276

HARLOT
4204 pornē, p. 291

HUSBANDRY
1091 geōrgion, p. 315

LADY
2959 kuria, p. 350

LUKEWARM
5513 chliaros, p. 384

NAKEDNESS
C. Noun
1132 gumnotēs, p. 425

PILLAR
4769 stulos, p. 471

RULE
B. Verb
4291 proistēmi, p. 540

SPEW
1692 emeō, p. 592

TEMPER TOGETHER
4786 sunkerannumi, p. 620

Worship of God

     Human beings were created to be *worshipers (worship; to be great; glorify; magnify)* of God.
     Praise (bless; commend; hallelujah) and *thanksgiving, bowing* before God, and *confessing* his goodness in an attitude of *reverence* and *awe (fear)* are important elements of acceptable worship. *Rejoicing* in *song* and *singing psalms, hymns,* and *melodies* are major parts of worship, as is the *reading* of Scripture.
     See also SUPERNATURAL BEINGS, ANGELIC BEINGS; THE FUTURE, ETERNAL LIFE AND HEAVEN; REVELATION, WORD OF GOD

AWE
5399d deos, p. 47

BLESS, BLESSED, BLESSEDNESS, BLESSING
A. Verb
2127 eulogeō, p. 69
B. Adjective
2128 eulogētos, p. 70
C. Noun
2129 eulogia, p. 70

TO BOW, BEND
3766 kāra', p. 23
2578 kamptō, p. 75

COMMEND, COMMENDATION
A. Verb
1867 epaineō, p. 112

CONFESS, CONFESSION
A. Verbs
3034 yādāh, p. 44
3670 homologeō, p. 120
1843 exomologeō, p. 120
B. Noun
3671 homologia, p. 120

FEAR, FEARFUL, FEARFULNESS
A. Nouns
4172 môrā', p. 80
3374 yir'āh, p. 80
5401 phobos, p. 229
2124 eulabeia, p. 230
D. Verbs
3372 yārē', p. 79
5399 phobeō, p. 230
2125 eulabeomai, p. 230

GLORIFY
1392 doxazō, p. 267
1740 endoxazō, p. 267
4888 sundoxazō, p. 267

TO BE GREAT, HEAVY
A. Verb
3515 kābēd, p. 101

HALLELUJAH
239 hallēlouia, p. 287

HYMN
A. Noun
5215 humnos, p. 316
B. Verb
5214 humneō, p. 316

MAGNIFY
3170 megalunō, p. 386

MELODY
5567 psallō, p. 402

PRAISE

A. Nouns
8416 tᵉhillāh, p. 185
8426 tôdāh, p. 185
136 ainos, p. 479
1868 epainos, p. 479
133 ainesis, p. 480

B. Verbs
1984 hālal, p. 184
3034 yādāh, p. 184
134 aineō, p. 480
1867 epaineō, p. 480
5214 humneō, p. 480
5567 psallō, p. 480
1843 exomologeō, p. 480

PSALM
5568 psalmos, p. 497

READ, READING

A. Verb
314 anaginōskō, p. 507

B. Noun
320 anagnōsis, p. 507

TO REJOICE

A. Verb
8055 śāmaḥ, p. 196

B. Noun
8057 śimḥāh, p. 197

C. Adjective
8056 śāmēaḥ, p. 197

REVERENCE

A. Verbs
1788 entrepo, p. 532

B. Noun
2124 eulabeia, p. 532

REVERENT
2412 hieroprepēs, p. 532

TO SING

A. Verbs
7442 rānan, p. 234
7891 šîr, p. 234
103 ᾳdō, p. 578

B. Participle
7891 šîr, p. 234

C. Noun
7892 šîr, p. 234

SONG
5603 ōdē, p. 586

**THANK, THANKS, THANKFUL,
THANKFULNESS,
THANKSGIVING, THANKWORTHY**

A. Nouns
5485 charis, p. 624
2169 eucharistia, p. 624

B. Verbs
2168 eucharisteō, p. 625
1843 exomologeō, p. 625
437 anthomologeomai, p. 625

C. Adjective
2170 eucharistos, p. 625

WORSHIP, WORSHIPING

A. Verbs
7812 šāḥāh, p. 295
4352 proskuneō, p. 686
4576 sebomai, p. 686
4573 sebazomai, p. 686
3000 latreuō, p. 686
2151 eusebeō, p. 686

B. Nouns
4574 sebasma, p. 686
1479 ethelothrēskeia or -ia, p. 687
2356 thrēskeia, p. 687

WORSHIPER
4353 proskunētēs, p. 687
3511 neōkoros, p. 687
2318 theosebēs, p. 687

Worship of God
in Ancient Israel

The Place of Worship

   Until the completion (to be consumed) of the temple (part; pinnacle; porch; sea; sheep gate; treasury; to turn towards; watch) in Jerusalem, which became a place of pilgrimage (to come up, ascend), the worship of God centered on the tabernacle (sanctuary) housing the ark of the covenant containing the tablets of the Law, Aaron's rod (bud; to stretch out), and the jar of manna. During the wilderness years the tent of meeting outside the camp symbolized (fashion) God's presence (to dwell; house; shewbread) with his people.

   Moses, and later the high priest, would gather the congregation (assembly; stand) of Israel together to communicate God's will to the people, as it had been revealed to them.

   Synagogues as places of worship for the Jewish community were established later.

ARK
727 'ārōn, p. 7
2787 kibōtos, p. 37

ASSEMBLY

A. Noun
6951 qāhāl, p. 9

B. Verb
6950 qāhal, p. 10

BUD
985 blastanō, p. 82

CAMP
4264 maḥăneh, p. 30

TO COME UP, ASCEND

A. Verb
5927 'ālāh, p. 40

B. Noun
4699 ma'ălāh, p. 41

CONGREGATION
5712 'ēdāh, p. 45
4150 mô'ēd, p. 45

TO BE CONSUMED

A. Verb
8552 tāmam, p. 47

TO DWELL

A. Verbs
3427 yāšab, p. 64
7931 šākan, p. 65

B. Noun
4908 miškān, p. 65

FASHION

A. Noun
5179 tupos, p. 227

TO GATHER
6908 qābaṣ, p. 90

HOUSE
1004 bayit, p. 117
3624 oikos, p. 313

MANNA
3131 manna, p. 390

PART

A. Particle
905 bad, p. 172

PINNACLE
4419 pterugion, p. 472

PORCH
4745 stoa, p. 476

ROD

A. Noun
4464 rhabdos, p. 537

SANCTUARY
39 hagion, p. 546
3485 naos, p. 546

SEA
3220 yām, p. 217

SHEEP GATE, SHEEP MARKET
4262 probatikos, p. 569

SHEWBREAD
Note, p. 570

TO STAND

A. Verb
5975 'āmad, p. 243

TO STRETCH OUT

B. Noun
4294 maṭṭeh, p. 249

SYNAGOGUE
4864 sunagōgē, p. 614

TABERNACLE

A. Noun
4908 miškān, p. 254
4634 skēnopēgia, p. 615

B. Verb
7934 šākan, p. 255

TENT
168 'ōhel, p. 259

TEMPLE
1964 hêkāl, p. 258
2411 hieron, p. 621
3485 naos, p. 621

TREASURY
1049 gazophulakion, p. 641
2878 korbanas, p. 641

TO TURN TOWARDS, TURN BACK

B. Noun
6438 pinnāh, p. 272

C. Adjective
6442 pᵉnîmî, p. 272

WATCH
A. Nouns
4931 mišmeret, p. 282
4929 mišmār, p. 282

Sacrifices

The *blood* of *bullocks, lambs,* and *rams* were *offered* as *sacrifice.* The animal had to be *perfect (to be sick)* if the Lord was to *accept* the *burnt offering.* As *all* the sacrifice was consumed on the altar, an offering made in this way was a pleasant *savor* to the Lord. The priests had specific instructions from the Lord on the *slaughter* of animals, how *to kill* the *offering, sprinkle* the blood on the *altar* and *burn incense,* as well as the specific *feast* days on which certain offerings were to be made, such as that of the *sabbath* and the *new moon.*

See also SALVATION, ATONEMENT: THE OLD TESTAMENT SACRIFICIAL SYSTEM

ACCEPT
7521 rāṣāh, p. 1

ALL
3632 kālîl, p. 2

ALTAR
4196 mizbēaḥ, p. 3
2379 thusiastērion, p. 23

BEAST
4968 sphagion, p. 53

BLOOD
1818 dām, p. 19

BULLOCK
6499 pār, p. 26

TO BURN INCENSE
A. Verbs
6999 qāṭar, p. 27
7004 qᵉṭōret, p. 28

BURNT
3646 holokautōma, p. 84

CENSER
2369 thumiatērion, p. 94
3031 libanōtos, p. 94

CONTINUALLY
A. Adverb
8548 tāmîd, p. 47
B. Adjective
8548 tāmîd, p. 47

CONTINUITY
A. Noun
8548 tāmîd, p. 47
B. Adverb
8548 tāmîd, p. 48

HEIFER
1151 damalis, p. 299

INCENSE
A. Noun
2368 thumiama, p. 322
B. Verb
2370 thumiaō, p. 322

TO KILL
7819 šāḥaṭ, p. 127

LAMB
3532 kebeś, p. 131

TO OFFER
7133 qorbān, p. 165

OFFERING
4503 minḥāh, p. 166
8641 tᵉrûmāh, p. 167
7133 qorbān, p. 168
7133 qurbān, p. 168
5930 'ōlāh, p. 168
801 'iššeh, p. 169
817 'āšām, p. 169

PERFECT
A. Adjective
8549 tāmîm, p. 176

RAM
352 'ayil, p. 192

SACRIFICE
2077 zebaḥ, p. 210

SAVOR
A. Nouns
7381 rêaḥ, p. 215
7306 rûaḥ, p. 216

SHADOW
4639 skia, p. 566

TO BE SICK
A. Verb
2470 ḥālāh, p. 228

TO SLAUGHTER
A. Verb
2076 zābaḥ, p. 235
B. Nouns
2077 zebaḥ, p. 235
4196 mizbēaḥ, p. 236

TO SPRINKLE
2236 zāraq, p. 242

STRANGLED
4156 pniktos, p. 603

TO THINK, DEVISE
A. Verb
2803 ḥāšab, p. 261

Feasts and Festivals

The *feasts (holy day)* and festivals mentioned in the Old Testament commemorate either an event in Israel's history *(Dedication; Passover;* Unleavened *Bread),* or serve to mark the seasons *(year)* of the agricultural *(Firstfruits; Firstborn; Weeks)* and religious calendar *(to atone; New Moon; to cease; work; Sabbath).*

In the New Testament, some of these festivals are given new meaning, such as *Pentecost,* which was originally a *harvest* festival but came to celebrate the birth of the church, and also the festival of *Easter* was inaugurated.

TO ATONE
A. Verb
3722 kāpar, p. 10
B. Noun
3727 kappōret, p. 10

BREAD
4682 maṣṣāh, p. 24

TO CEASE
A. Verb
7673 šābat, p. 33
B. Noun
7676 šabbāt, p. 33

DEDICATION
B. Noun
1456 enkainia, p. 153

EASTER
3957 pascha, p. 192

FEAST
A. Nouns
2282 ḥag, p. 80
1859 heortē, p. 231
B. Verb
1858 heortazō, p. 231

FIRSTBORN
1061 bikkûrîm, p. 83

FIRSTFRUIT(S)
536 aparchē, p. 241

HOLY DAY
1859 heortē, p. 308

HARVEST
2326 therismos, p. 291

NEW MOON
B. Noun
2320 ḥōdeš, p. 160

PASSOVER
3957 pascha, p. 462

PENTECOST
4005 pentēkostos, p. 465

SABBATH
4521 sabbaton, p. 542
4315 prosabbaton, p. 543

WEEK
7620 šābûa', p. 286

TO WORK
6213 'āšāh, p. 293

YEAR
8141 šānāh, p. 298

Oaths and Vows

Oaths were *binding (to believe)* and could take the form of a *curse* or a pledge *(to blow).* They employed certain statements *(to add; to live)* and were used in covenantal formulas.

To *adjure* or *swear* an *oath* and take a *vow* signified allegiance to God. A Nazirite vow *(shave)* was a special period of being consecrated or made *separate* for the service of God, while *corban* was a gift offered to God as a vow.

See also THE LIFE OF THE PEOPLE OF GOD: COVENANTS

TO ADD
3254 yāsap, p. 2

ADJURE
3726 horkizo, p. 13
1844 exorkizō, p. 13
1722,
3726 enorkizō, p. 13

TO BELIEVE
C. Adverb
543 'āmēn, p. 17

TO BIND
631 'āsar, p. 17

TO BLOW
8628 tāqa', p. 20

CORBAN
2878 korban, p. 129

TO CURSE
A. Verbs
7043 qālal, p. 53
779 'ārar, p. 53
B. Noun
423 'ālāh, p. 54

TO LIVE
B. Noun
2416 ḥay, p. 138

OATH
3727 horkos, p. 438
3728 horkōmosia, p. 438

TO SEPARATE
B. Noun
5139 nāzîr, p. 223

SHAVE
3587 xuraō, p. 568

SWEAR, SWORN
7650 šāba', p. 253
3660 omnumi or omnuō, p. 613

VOW
A. Verb
5087 nādar, p. 278
B. Nouns
5088 neder, p. 278
2171 euchē, p. 663

Worship of God in the Church
The Ordinances of the Church
Baptism and the Lord's *Supper* were both instituted by Jesus Christ as symbols of faith in him.

Baptism signifies the *washing* away of sin and the *burying* of the old life and marks a person's entry into the church.

The *breaking* of *bread (eat)* and the wine *(drink)* celebrated at the *feast* of *Communion* are symbols of the sacrifice of the body and blood of Jesus given for sinful humanity. In this ceremony believers participate in the effects of both the death and resurrection of Jesus Christ and anticipate *(proclaim)* his return.

BAPTISM, BAPTIZE
A. Nouns
908 baptisma, p. 50
909 baptismos, p. 50
B. Verb
907 baptizō, p. 50

BREAD
740 artos, p. 77

BREAK
A. Verb
2806 klaō or klazō, p. 77
B. Noun
2800 klasis, p. 78

BURY
4916 sunthaptō, p. 84

COMMUNION
A. Noun
2842 koinōnia, p. 115
B. Adjective
2844 koinōnos, p. 115

DRINK, DRANK
B. Verb
4095 pinō, p. 184

EAT, EAT WITH, EATING
A. Verb
1089 geuō, p. 193

FEAST
A. Noun
1173 deipnon, p. 231

PROCLAIM
2605 katangellō, p. 490

SUPPER
1173 deipnon, p. 610

WASH
628 apolouō, p. 666

WASHING
909 baptismos, p. 667

THE FUTURE

End Times
The *end (approach)* times will be marked by *earthquakes (brimstone), pestilence (locust), bitterness (wormwood),* and *torment (gnaw; sorrow; travail);* the love of many will grow *cold,* and *false Christs* and *traitors (betray)* will abound. This is the beginning of God's final judgments *(flame)* on the earth and its inhabitants *(accomplish; complete; perfection).* The successive opening of the seven *seals* and the pouring out of the seven *bowls,* culminating in *silence* in heaven, discloses these events.

The *antichrist* and the *beast (diadem;* false *prophet),* rising from the *sand* of the sea, are the two figures who dominate the *latter* days, but God has promised to *cut short* those *last (later)* days because of the great *terror* and *tribulation* they will bring.

See also CREATION, TIME

ACCOMPLISH, ACCOMPLISHMENT
A. Verbs
4137 plēroō, p. 8
5055 teleō, p. 8
2055 epiteleō, p. 8
5048 teleioō, p. 8
4130 plēthō, p. 8

B. Noun
1604 ekplērōsis, p. 9

ANTICHRIST
500 antichristos, p. 30

APPROACH
A. Verb
1448 engizō, p. 35

BEAST
2342 thērion, p. 53

BETRAY, BETRAYER
A. Verb
3860 paradidōmi, p. 64
B. Noun
4273 prodotēs, p. 64

BITTER
B. Verb
4087 pikrainō, p. 68

BOWL
5357 phialē, p. 76

BRIMSTONE
2303 theion, p. 80
2306 theiōdēs, p. 80

CHRISTS (FALSE)
5580 pseudochristos, p. 101

COLD
C. Verb
5594 psuchō, p. 108

COMPLETE, COMPLETION
4931 sunteleō, p. 117

DIADEM
1238 diadēma, p. 167

EARTHQUAKE
4578 seismos, p. 191

END, ENDING
A. Nouns
7093 qēṣ, p. 69
5056 telos, p. 198
4930 sunteleia, p. 199
B. Verb
4931 sunteleō, p. 199
C. Adjective
2078 eschatos, p. 199

FLAME, FLAMING
5395 phlox, p. 242

GNAW
3145 masaomai or massaomai, p. 269

LAST
A. Adjective
2078 eschatos, p. 353
B. Adverb
5305 husteron, p. 353

LATER
5306 husteros, p. 354

LATTER
3797 opsimos, p. 354

LOCUST
200 akris, p. 375

PERFECTION, PERFECTING, PERFECTNESS

A. Nouns
5050   teleiōsis, p. 467
5047   teleiotēs, p. 467

B. Verb
5052   telesphoreō, p. 467

PESTILENCE
3061   loimos, p. 470

POUR
1632   ekcheō, p. 478

PROPHET
5578   pseudoprophētēs, p. 493

SAND
285   ammos, p. 546

SEAL

B. Verb
2696   katasphragizō, p. 553

SHAKE
4531   saleuō, p. 567

SHORT, SHORTEN
2856   koloboō, p. 572
4958   sustellō, p. 572

SILENCE

A. Noun
4602   sigē, p. 575

SORROW, SORROWFUL

A. Nouns
5604   ōdin, p. 588
3997   penthos, p. 588

TERROR
5401   phobos, p. 623
5400   phobētron, p. 623

TORMENT

A. Nouns
929   basanismos, p. 637
931   basanos, p. 637

B. Verb
928   basanizō, p. 637

TRAITOR
4273   prodotēs, p. 639

TRAVAIL

A. Noun
5604   ōdin, p. 640

TRIBULATION
2347   thlipsis, p. 643

WORMWOOD
894   apsinthos, p. 686

The Second Coming

The return (*appearing; coming*) of Jesus Christ is imminent (*door*) and will take place unexpectedly (*apprehend*).

When the *trump* of God sounds, Jesus, his name upon his *thigh* and his garment *dipped* in blood, will ride out from heaven. This *day* of the Lord (*star*) will be a day to *marvel* at and, like *lightning*, will be visible to all. Believers who are alive will be caught up (*catch; redemption*) to meet Jesus in the air and their bodies will *change* in the *twinkling* of an eye.

APPEARING

B. Noun
2015   epiphaneia, p. 32

APPREHEND
2638   katalambanō, p. 34

CATCH
726   harpazō, p. 92

CHANGE

B. Verb
236   allassō, p. 95

COMING
3952   parousia, p. 111

DAY
2250   hēmera, p. 146

DIP, DIPPED, DIPPETH
911   baptō, p. 170

DOOR
2374   thura, p. 181

LIGHTNING
796   astrapē, p. 371

MARVEL

B. Verb
2296   thaumazō, p. 395

REDEMPTION

B. Noun
629   apolutrōsis, p. 516

STAR
792   astēr, p. 598

THIGH
3382   mēros, p. 627

TRUMP, TRUMPET

A. Noun
4536   salpinx, p. 646

B. Verb
4537   salpizō, p. 646

TWINKLING
4493   rhipē, p. 648

Judgment

God's final *judgment* of the world will take place when Jesus Christ returns, and he will *pour out* his *wrath* to *execute vengeance* (*punishment; sentence*) upon, and to *destroy*, his enemies (*foe; footstool*).

God has *appointed* Jesus Christ as *judge*. The dead will be *raised* and the *books* opened, and each person will appear before God's *throne* (*judgment seat*) to give an account of their lives and to receive their due *reward*.

Scripture describes the consequences of God's judgment (*to be dismayed; to stumble, be weak; woe*) and uses a variety of symbols (*fire; sword; tongue; winepress; tread*) to illustrate its severity.

APPOINT, APPOINTED
2476   histēmi, p. 33
606   apokeimai, p. 34
3724   horizō, p. 34

BOOK
976   biblos, p. 74
975   biblion, p. 74
974   biblaridion, p. 74

DESTROY, DESTROYER, DESTRUCTION, DESTRUCTIVE

A. Verbs
8045   šāmad, p. 59
7843   šāḥat, p. 59

B. Noun
3639   olethros, p. 165

TO BE DISMAYED
2865   ḥātat, p. 60

EXECUTE
4160   poieō, p. 216

FIRE

A. Noun
4442   pur, p. 239

FOE
2190   echthros, p. 244

FOOTSTOOL
5286   hupopodion, p. 247

JUDGE

A. Noun
2923   kritēs, p. 336

B. Verb
2919   krinō, p. 336

JUDGMENT

A. Nouns
2920   krisis, p. 337
2917   krima, p. 337
2250   hēmera, p. 337
1106   gnōmē, p. 337

B. Adjective
5267   hupodikos, p. 337

JUDGMENT SEAT
968   bēma, p. 337
2922   kritērion, p. 338

TO POUR, FLOW
8210   šāpak, p. 183

PUNISHMENT
1557   ekdikēsis, p. 498
1349   dikē, p. 498
5098   timōria, p. 498

RAISE
1453   egeirō, p. 505
450   anistēmi, p. 506
1825   exegeirō, p. 506
4891   sunegeirō, p. 506

REWARD

A. Noun
3408   misthos, p. 533

B. Verb
591   apodidōmi, p. 533

SENTENCE

A. Noun
2917   krima, p. 561

TO STUMBLE, BE WEAK
3782   kāšal, p. 251

SWORD

A. Nouns
2719   ḥereb, p. 253
4501   rhomphaia, p. 613

THRONE
2362   thronos, p. 631

TONGUE
3956   lāšôn, p. 264

TREAD, TRODE, TRODDEN
3961   pateō, p. 641

VENGEANCE
1557 ekdikēsis, p. 659

WINEPRESS, WINE-VAT
3025 lēnos, p. 678

WOE
3759 ouai, p. 681

Eternal Life and Heaven

Heaven (Abraham's bosom; air; paradise), the *abode* of God, is the future *hope (sure)* of all believers, who will be *raised (up)* to *glory (burden; life-giving; live)* with Jesus Christ into an *inheritance* which is *eternal* and will not *fade (undefiled).*

The future spiritual body will be *clothed (clothing; white)* with *immortality* and *incorruption,* and believers will be *citizens* of the new Jerusalem.

The marriage supper *(feast)* of the Lamb will take place at the inauguration of God's kingdom.

See also SUPERNATURAL BEINGS, ANGELIC BEINGS

ABODE
B. Noun
3438 monē, p. 2

AIR
3772 ouranos, p. 21

BOSOM
2859 kolpos, p. 74

BURDEN
A. Nouns
922 baros, p. 83
5413 phortion, p. 83

CITIZEN, CITIZENSHIP
4175 politeuma, p. 103

CLOTHE
1746 enduō, p. 105
1902 enepduō, p. 105

CLOTHING
4749 stolē, p. 106

ETERNAL
166 aiōnios, p. 207

FADE
B. Adjectives (negative)
263 amarantos, p. 221
262 amarantinos, p. 221

FEAST
A. Nouns
1173 deipnon, p. 231
1062 gamos, p. 231

GLORY
A. Noun
1391 doxa, p. 267

HEAVEN
A. Nouns
3772 ouranos, p. 298
3321 mesouranēma, p. 298

HOPE
A. Noun
1680 elpis, p. 311

B. Verbs
1679 elpizō, p. 311

4276 proelpizō, p. 312
560 apelpizō, p. 312

IMMORTAL, IMMORTALITY
110 athanasia, p. 320

INCORRUPTION, INCORRUPTIBLE
B. Noun
861 aphtharsia, p. 131

C. Adjective
862 aphthartos, p. 131

INHERIT, INHERITANCE
A. Verbs
2816 klēronomeō, p. 325
2820 klēroō, p. 325

B. Nouns
2817 klēronomia, p. 325
2819 klēros, p. 325

LIFE-GIVING
C. Verb
2227 zōopoieō, p. 368

LIVE
2198 zaō, p. 374

PARADISE
3857 paradeisos, p. 457

RAISE
1825 exegeirō, p. 506

SURE
A. Adjectives
804 asphalēs, p. 611
949 bebaios, p. 611

UNDEFILED
283 amiantos, p. 650

WHITE
A. Adjective
3022 leukos, p. 674

B. Verb
3021 leukainō, p. 674

The New Order

The present heavens and the earth have been *stored* up for fire. At the conclusion of the age, God will roll up the heavens like a *scroll,* the *elements* will *melt (dissolve; heat),* and a *new* heaven and a new earth will come into being. The heavenly *city,* the new Jerusalem, will be built of pure *gold* like clear *glass.* It will be adorned with *costly* stones like *jasper, sapphire, chalcedony, emerald, sardonyx, sardius, chrysolite, beryl, topaz, chrysoprasus, jacinth,* and *amethyst,* and Jesus Christ will be its *light.*

AMETHYST
271 amethustos, p. 26

BERYL
969 bērullos, p. 62

CHALCEDONY
5472 chalkēdōn, p. 95

CHRYSOLITE
5555 chrusolithos, p. 101

CHRYSOPRASUS
5556 chrusoprasos, p. 102

CITY
4172 polis, p. 103

COST(LY)
A. Noun
5094 timiotēs, p. 131

B. Adjective
5093 timios, p. 131

CRYSTAL
A. Noun
2930 krustallos, p. 140

B. Verb
2929 krustallizō, p. 140

DISSOLVE
3089 luō, p. 176

ELEMENTS
4747 stoicheion, p. 196

EMERALD
A. Noun
4665 smaragdos, p. 197

B. Adjective
4664 smaragdinos, p. 197

GLASS, GLASSY
A. Noun
5194 hualos, p. 267

B. Adjective
5193 hualinos, p. 267

GOLD
2091 zāhāb, p. 98
5557 chrusos, p. 273

HEAT
B. Verb
2741 kausoō, p. 298

JACINTH
A. Noun
5192 huakinthos, p. 332

B. Adjective
5191 huakinthinos, p. 332

JASPER
2393 iaspis, p. 332

LIGHT
5458 phōstēr, p. 370

MELT
5080 tēkō, p. 402

NEW
2537 kainos, p. 430

SAPPHIRE
4552 sappheiros, p. 546

SARDIUS, SARDINE
4555 sardion *or* sardinos, p. 547

SARDONYX
4557 sardonux, p. 547

SCROLL
975 biblion, p. 552

STORE
2343 thēsaurizō, p. 601

TOPAZ
5116 topazion, p. 637

Death and Everlasting Punishment

Sleep *(asleep)* is often used as a metaphor for *death (die)* in Scripture, and *Sheol (to ask; bury; to go down; grave; Hades; house; land; pit; sepulchre; tomb)* is the destiny of all.

Hell, the place of *everlasting punishment (destroy)* in *darkness (outer;*

black) and *burning* in a *lake* of *unquenchable* fire, is the final outcome for all those who *forfeit* life (*perish*) by their rejection of God. It is a place of torment (*gnash; tooth; worm*) and separation (*fix; gulf*).

The Abyss (*bottomless*) is the abode of demons.

TO ASK
B. Noun
7585   šeʾôl, p. 9

ASLEEP, SLEEP
A. Verbs
2518   katheudō, p. 41
2837   koimaomai, p. 41

BLACK, BLACKNESS
B. Nouns
1105   gnophos, p. 68
2217   zophos, p. 68
3189   melas, p. 68

BOTTOMLESS
B. Adjective
12   abussos, p. 75

BURN, BURNING
2618   katakaiō, p. 84

TO BURY
A. Verb
6912   qābar, p. 28

B. Noun
6913   qeber, p. 28

DARKNESS
2217   zophos, p. 145

DEATH
4194   māwet, p. 55
2288   thanatos, p. 149

DESTROY, DESTROYER, DESTRUCTION
A. Verbs
622   apollumi, p. 164
2647   kataluō, p. 164
1842   exolothreuō, p. 164

B. Nouns
684   apōleia, p. 164
3639   olethros, p. 165
5356   phthora, p. 165

DIE, DEAD, DYING
4191   mût, p. 59
2348   thnēskō, p. 167
599   apothnēskō, p. 167
5053   teleutaō, p. 168
2837   koimaō, p. 168

EVERLASTING
166   aiōnios, p. 210
126   aidios, p. 210

FIX
4741   stērizō, p. 242

FORFEIT
2210   zēmioō, p. 250

GNASH, GNASHING
A. Verbs
1031   bruchō, p. 269
5149   trizō, p. 269

B. Noun
1030   brugmos, p. 269

TO GO DOWN
3381   yārad, p. 94

GRAVE
3419   mnēmeion, p. 278
3418   mnēma, p. 278

GULF
5490   chasma, p. 286

HADES
86   hadēs, p. 286

HELL
1067   geenna, p. 300

HOUSE
1004   bayit, p. 117

LAKE
3041   limnē, p. 350

LAND
776   ʾereṣ, p. 132

OUTER
1857   exōteros, p. 452

TO PERISH
A. Verbs
6   ʾābad, p. 177
622   apollumai, p. 467

PIT
5421   phrear, p. 472
12   abussos, p. 472

PUNISHMENT
1557   ekdikēsis, p. 498
2851   kolasis, p. 498

QUENCH, UNQUENCHABLE
B. Adjective
762   asbestos, p. 502

SEPULCHRE
5028   taphos, p. 562

SHEOL
7585   šeʾôl, p. 227

TOMB
3419   mnēmeion, p. 636
3418   mnēma, p. 636
5028   taphos, p. 636

TOOTH, TEETH
3599   odous, p. 637

WORM
4663   skōlēx, p. 686
4662   skōlēkobrōtos, p. 686

FUNCTION AND GENERAL WORDS

ABOUT
A. Adverbs
2943   kuklothen, p. 4

2945   kuklō, p. 4
4225   pou, p. 4
5613   hōs, p. 4
5616   hosei, p. 4
B. Verb
3195   mellō, p. 4

ABOVE
507   anō, p. 4
511   anōteron, p. 5
509   anōthen, p. 5

ACTUALLY
3654   holōs, p. 12

AFAR
3112   makran, p. 16
3113   makrothen, p. 16
4207   porrōthen, p. 16

AFORETIME
4218   pote, p. 18
4386   proteron, p. 18

AFTER, AFTERWARD
1564   ekeithen, p. 18
1836   hexēs, p. 18

2517   kathexēs, p. 18
3347   metepeita, p. 18
5305   husteron, p. 18

AGAIN
1364   dis, p. 18
3825   palin, p. 18

ALBEIT
2443   hina, p. 21

ALL
A. Noun
3605   kōl, p. 2

B. Adjectives
3606   kōl, p. 2
3632   kālîl, p. 2
3956   pas, p. 21
537   hapas, p. 21
3650   holos, p. 21

C. Adverbs
3654   holōs, p. 22
3843   pantōs, p. 22

D. Pronoun
3745   hosa, p. 22

ALMOST
A. Adverb
4975   schedon, p. 23

B. Verb
3195   mellō, p. 23

ALONE (LET ALONE)
A. Adjective
3441   monos, p. 23

B. Adverbs
3441   monon, p. 23
2651   kata monas, p. 23

C. Verb
863   aphiēmi, p. 23

ALREADY
2235   ēdē, p. 23

ALSO
2532   kai, p. 23
2089   eti, p. 23

ALTOGETHER
A. Adjective
3650   holos, p. 24

B. Adverbs
3843   pantōs, p. 24
3654   holōs, p. 24

ALWAY, ALWAYS
104   aei, p. 24
1539   hekastote, p. 24

1275 diapantos, p. 24
3839 pantē, p. 24

AMONG
A. Preposition
7130 qereb, p. 3
B. Noun
7130 qereb, p. 4

ANOTHER
243 allos, p. 29

ANYTHING
Note, p. 30

APART
5565 chōris, p. 30
      kat' idian, p. 30
2651 kata monas, p. 30

APIECE
303 ana, p. 30

AWAY
Note, p. 47

BACK, BACKSIDE, BACKWARD
3694 opisō, p. 48
3693 opisthen, p. 48

BEAUTIFUL
5611 hōraios, p. 54
791 asteios, p. 54

BEFORE, BEFORETIME
A. Adverbs
4412 prōton, p. 56
4386 proteron, p. 56
4250 prin, p. 56
1715 emprosthen, p. 56
1726 enantion, p. 56
1725 enanti, p. 56
561 apenanti, p. 56
2713 katenanti, p. 56
1799 enōpion, p. 56
2714 katenōpion, p. 56
B. Verb
4391 prouparchō, p. 56

BEHALF
3313 meros, p. 58
5228 huper, p. 58

BEHIND, COME BEHIND
A. Adverbs
310 'aḥar, p. 15
3693 opisthen, p. 59
B. Verbs
5302 hustereō, p. 59
5278 hupomenō, p. 59
C. Preposition
310 'aḥar, p. 15
D. Conjunction
310 'aḥar, p. 15

BEING
p. 60

BELONG
Note, p. 61

BENEATH
2736 katō, p. 62

BESIDE, BESIDES
5565 chōris, p. 63
3063 loipon, p. 63

BEST
4413 prōtos, p. 63
3187 meizōn, p. 63

BETTER
2909 kreissōn, p. 64
      kalon . . . mallon, p. 64

BETTER (be)
1308 diapherō, p. 64
4052 perisseuō, p. 64
3081 lusiteleō, p. 64
5242 huperechō, p. 64

BETTERED (to be)
5623 ōpheleō, p. 64

BETWEEN
996 bēn, p. 17
303,
3349 ana meson, p. 64
3342 metaxu, p. 65

BEWRAY
Note, p. 65

BEYOND
1900 epekeina, p. 65
4008 peran, p. 65

BRIEFLY
      di' oligōn, p. 79

BROAD, BREADTH
A. Adjective
2149 euruchōros, p. 81
B. Verb
4115 platunō, p. 81
C. Nouns
7341 rōḥab, p. 24
4114 platos, p. 81

BY
Note, p. 85

CAN (CANST, COULD, CANNOT)
3201 yākōl, p. 31
1410 dunamai, p. 87
2480 ischuō, p. 87, p. 132
2192 echō, p. 87, p. 132
1097 ginōskō, p. 88
1492 oida, p. 88
1510 esti, p. 88
1735 endechomai, p. 88

CAUSE
A. Nouns
156 aitia, p. 92
158 aition, p. 92
3056 logos, p. 92
1432 dōrean, p. 93
B. Verbs
4160 poieō, p. 93
1325 didōmi, p. 93

CLOSE
788 asson, p. 105

CONTRARIWISE
5121 t'ounantion, p. 127

DO, DONE
4160 poieō, p. 179
4238 prasso, p. 179
1096 ginomai, p. 179
2038 ergazomai, p. 179
2716 katergazomai, p. 180
2480 ischuō, p. 180
3930 parechō, p. 180

DOUBT, DOUBTLESS
3843 pantōs, p. 182
Notes, p. 182

EACH, EACH MAN, EACH ONE
1538 hekastos, p. 189

EACH OTHER
240 allēlōn, p. 189

EITHER
2228 ē, p. 195

ELSE
1893 epei, p. 197

ELSEWHERE
237v allachou, p. 197

ENOUGH
A. Adjectives
713 arketos, p. 201
2425 hikanos, p. 201
B. Verbs
714 arkeō, p. 201
568 apechō, p. 201

ESPECIALLY
3122 malista, p. 206

EVEN, EVEN AS, EVEN SO
2532 kai, p. 208
1161 de, p. 209
2089 eti, p. 209
5613 hōs, p. 209
3778 houtōs, p. 209
2531 kathōs, p. 209
5618 hōsper, p. 209
2509 kathaper, p. 209
3483 nai, p. 209
3676 homōs, p. 209

EVERY, EVERYONE, EVERYTHING
3956 pas, p. 210
537 hapas, p. 210
1538 hekastos, p. 210

EVERY WHIT
3650 holos, p. 211

EVERYWHERE, EVERY QUARTER, EVERY SIDE
3837v pantachē, p. 211
3837 pantachou, p. 211
3840 pantothen, p. 211

EXCEEDINGLY
A. Adverb
3966 meʼōd, p. 74

EXCEPT, EXCEPTED
1622 ektos, p. 215
3924 parektos, p. 215
4133 plēn, p. 215

EXPRESSLY
4490 rhētōs, p. 219

FAR
A. Adjective
3117 makros, p. 226
B. Adverbs
7368 rāḥaq, p. 78
3112 makran, p. 226
3113 makrothen, p. 226
4206 porrō, p. 226

FEW
A. Adjectives
3641 oligos, p. 234
1024 brachus, p. 234
B. Adverb
4935 suntomōs, p. 234

FOLLOWING
312 'aḥēr, p. 85

FOR NOTHING
2600 ḥinnām, p. 162
FORTH
1854 exō, p. 253
FORTHWITH
1824 exautēs, p. 253
2112 eutheōs, p. 253
2117 euthus, p. 253
FURTHER
2089 eti, p. 259
4208 porrōteron, p. 259
FURTHERMORE
1534 eita, p. 259
GET, GOT, GOTTEN
2147 heuriskō, p. 263
2932 ktaomai, p. 263
2770 kerdainō, p. 263
1826 exeimi, p. 263
5217 hupagō, p. 263
1831 exerchomai, p. 263
2597 katabainō, p. 263
1684 embainō, p. 263
576 apobainō, p. 263
GO, GO ONWARD
4198 poreuomai, p. 269
3899 paraporeuomai, p. 269
4313 proporeuomai, p. 269
1279 diaporeuomai, p. 269
1531 eisporeuomai, p. 269
4848 sumporeuomai, p. 269
71 agō, p. 269
5217 hupagō, p. 269
4013 periagō, p. 269
4254 proagō, p. 269
549 apeimi, p. 270
1524 eiseimi, p. 270
3327 metabainō, p. 270
565 aperchomai, p. 270
402 anachōreō, p. 270
5298 hupochōreō, p. 270
4281 proerchomai, p. 270
1931 epiduō, p. 270
4782 sunkatabainō, p. 270
4260 probainō, p. 270
576 apobainō, p. 270
4320 prosanabainō, p. 270
1826 exeimi, p. 270
4570 sbennumi, p. 270
5055 teleō, p. 270
1353 diodeuō, p. 270
589 apodēmeō, p. 270
424 anerchomai, p. 270
4022 perierchomai, p. 270
2021 epicheireō, p. 270
HAVE
2192 echō, p. 292
568 apechō, p. 293
1096 ginomai, p. 293
3335 metalambanō, p. 293
5225 huparchō, p. 293
474 antiballō, p. 293
1510 eimi, p. 293
1746 enduō, p. 293
HEAD
B. Adjective
7223 ri'šôn, p. 107

HENCE
1782v enthen, p. 301
1782 enteuthen, p. 301
HENCEFORTH, HENCEFORWARD
Notes, p. 302
HERE
5602 hōde, p. 302
1759 enthade, p. 302
847 autou, p. 302
3918 pareimi, p. 302
HEREAFTER
Notes, p. 302
HEREBY
Notes, p. 302
HEREIN
Note, p. 302
HEREOF
Notes, p. 302
HIGHER
A. Adverb
511** anōteron, p. 304
HITHER
5602 hōde, p. 305
1759 enthade, p. 306
HITHERTO
Notes, p. 306
INASMUCH AS
2526 katho, p. 322
          eph'hoson, p. 322
2530 kathoti, p. 322
          kath'hoson, p. 322
INDEED
3303 men, p. 323
227 alēthēs, p. 323
230 alēthōs, p. 323
3689 ontōs, p. 323
          kai gar, p. 323
          oude gar, p. 323
          alla kai, p. 323
2532 kai, p. 323
          ei mēti, p. 323
INNER
2080 esō, p. 326
2082 esōteros, p. 326
INSIDE
1787 entos, p. 327
2081 esōthen, p. 327
INSOMUCH THAT, or AS
5620 hōste, p. 328
2526 eis to, p. 328
          katho, p. 328
LARGE
3173 megas, p. 353
2425 hikanos, p. 353
4080 pēlikos, p. 353
LATELY
4373 prosphatōs, p. 354
LEAST
1646 elachistos, p. 361
1647 elachistoteros, p. 361
3398 mikros, p. 361
3398 mikroteros, p. 361
LEFT
2176 euōnumos, p. 363
LENGTH
3372 mēkos, p. 364

LENGTH (at)
4218 pote, p. 364
LESS
1640 elassōn, p. 364
3398 mikroteros, p. 364
2276 hēssōn, p. 364
LEST
3361 mē, p. 364
          hina mē, p. 364
3379 mēpote or mē pote, p. 364
3381 mēpōs or mē pōs, p. 364
3361,
4225 mēpou or mē pou, p. 365
LET
863 aphiēmi, p. 365
2010 epitrepō, p. 365
630 apoluō, p. 365
1439 eaō, p. 365
LIKE, LIKEN
A. Adjectives
3664 homoios, p. 371
2470 isos, p. 371
3946 paromoios, p. 371
B. Verbs
3666 homoioō, p. 371
1503v eoika, p. 371
3945 paromoiazō, p. 371
871 aphomoioō, p. 371
C. Adverbs
5613 hōs, p. 371
5618 hōsper, p. 371
LITTLE
A. Adjectives
3398 mikros, p. 373
3641 oligos, p. 373
1024 brachus, p. 373
1646 elachistos, p. 374
B. Adverbs
3397 mikron, p. 374
3641** oligon, p. 374
3357 metriōs, p. 374
MANY
4183 polus, p. 392
4119 pleiōn, p. 392
2425 hikanos, p. 392
3745 hosos, p. 392
4214 posos, p. 392
5118 tosoutos, p. 393
MAY, MAYEST, MIGHT
1410 dunamai, p. 397
1832 exesti, p. 397
2481 isōs, p. 397
5177 tunchanō, p. 397
MIDST
A. Adjective and Adverb
8432 tāwek, p. 151
3319 mesis, p. 406
B. Verb
3322 mesoō, p. 406
MORE
A. Adverbs
3123 mallon, p. 415
2089 eti, p. 415
3765 ouketi, p. 415
4054 perissoteron, p. 415
3187 meizon, p. 416

5228 huper, p. 416
    hoson, p. 416

B. Adjectives
4119 pleiōn, p. 416
4053 perissos, p. 416
4055 perissoteros, p. 416

MOREOVER
2089 eti, p. 416
2532 kai, p. 416
1161 de, p. 416
    alla kai, p. 416
    de kai, p. 416
    kai . . . de, p. 416
3063 loipon, p. 416

MOST
4119 pleion, p. 417
4118 pleistos, p. 417
3122 malista, p. 417

MUCH (AS)
Notes, p. 420

MUST
1163 dei, p. 422
3784 opheilō, p. 422

NAMELY
Notes, p. 426

NAY
3756 ou, p. 427
3780 ouchi, p. 427
235 alla, p. 427
3304 menounge, p. 427

NEAR, NEARER
A. Adverbs
1451 engus, p. 427
1452 enguteron, p. 427
4139 plēsion, p. 427

B. Adjective
316 anankaios, p. 427

C. Verb
1448 engizō, p. 427

NEVER
3763 oudepote, p. 430
3368 mēdepote, p. 430
3764 oudepō, p. 430

NEXT
1836 hexēs, p. 431
3342 metaxu, p. 431
2192 echō, p. 431
2064 erchomai, p. 432

NIGH
A. Adverbs
1451 engus, p. 432
3897 paraplēsion, p. 432

B. Verb
1448 engizō, p. 432

C. Preposition
3844 para, p. 432

NO
369 'ayin, p. 161

NO LONGER, NO MORE
3765 ouketi, p. 432
3371 mēketi, p. 432

NO MAN, NO ONE, NEITHER ANY MAN
Note, p. 433

NO WISE, ANYWISE
    ou mē, p. 433

3760 oudamōs, p. 433
    ou pantōs, p. 433

NOTHING
3762 ouden, p. 434
3367 mēden, p. 434
3756 ou, p. 435
3361 mē, p. 435
    ou . . . ti, p. 435
    mē . . . ti, p. 435
    mē ti, p. 435
    oude ti, p. 435

NOTWITHSTANDING
Note, p. 435

NOUGHT
A. Pronoun
3762 ouden, p. 435

B. Adverb
1432 dōrean, p. 435

C. Verbs
2673 katargeō, p. 435
1848 exoutheneō, p. 435
1847 exoudeneō *or* exoudenoō,
    p. 435
1601 ekpiptō, p. 435
114 atheteō, p. 435

NOW
A. Adverbs
3568 nun, p. 436
3570 nuni, p. 436
2235 ēdē, p. 436
737 arti, p. 436
534 aparti, p. 436
3063 loipon, p. 436

B. Conjunctions and Particles
3767 oun, p. 436
1161 de, p. 437
1211 dē, p. 437

OF
Note, p. 440

OFT, OFTEN, OFTENER, OFTENTIMES, OFT-TIMES
A. Adverbs
4178 pollakis, p. 443
*4183***polla, p. 443
4212 posakis, p. 443
3740 hosakis, p. 443
4437 pukna, p. 443
*4437** puknoteron, p. 443

B. Adjective
4437 puknos, p. 443

ONCE
530 hapax, p. 445
2178 ephapax, p. 445
4218 pote, p. 445

ONE ANOTHER or ONE . . . ANOTHER, ONE . . . THE OTHER
Notes, p. 446

ONLY
A. Adjective
3441 monos, p. 447

B. Adverbs
3441 monon, p. 447
4133 plēn, p. 447

OTHER
243 allos, p. 451
2087 heteros, p. 451
*3062***loipos, p. 451

245 allotrios, p. 451
240 allēlōn, p. 451
1520 heis, p. 451
1565 ekeinos, p. 451

OTHERWISE
243 allos, p. 451
247 allōs, p. 451
2088 heterōs, p. 451
1893 epei, p. 451

OUGHT
1163 dei, p. 451
3784 opheilō, p. 451
5534 chrē, p. 451

OUT, OUT OF
Notes, p. 452

OUTSIDE
1855 exōthen, p. 453
1622 ektos, p. 453

OUTWARD, OUTWARDLY
1854 exō, p. 453
1855 exōthen, p. 453

PARTLY
Notes, p. 460

PERADVENTURE
A. Adverbs
194 'ûlay, p. 176
5029 tacha, p. 465

B. Conjunction
3379 mēpote, p. 465

PERHAPS
5029 tacha, p. 467
686 ara, p. 467

PERTAIN TO
3348 metechō, p. 469

QUICKLY
5035 tachu, p. 503
5032 tacheion, p. 503
5030 tacheōs, p. 503
    en tachei, p. 503

RATHER
A. Adverb
3123 mallon, p. 507

B. Verb
2309 thelō, p. 507

C. Preposition
3844 para, p. 507

D. Conjunction
235 alla, p. 507

ROUND, ROUND ABOUT
2943 kuklothen, p. 539
3840 pantothen, 539
4038 perix, p. 539
2945 kuklō, p. 539

SAME
846 autos, p. 545
3778 houtos, p. 545

SELFSAME
Notes, p. 559

SHALL
3195 mellō, p. 567

SHOULD
3195 mellō, p. 572
1163 dei, p. 572

SMALL

A. Adjectives
6996   qāṭān, p. 236
      qāṭōn, p. 236
3398   mikros, p. 581
3641   oligos, p. 581

SO
Notes, p. 583

SOME, SOMEONE, SOMETHING, SOMEWHAT
Notes, p. 584

SOMEWHERE
4225   pou, p. 584

SORT

A. Adjective
3697   hopoios, p. 588

B. Noun
3313   meros, p. 588

STILL
2089   eti, p. 600

STREET

B. Adverb
2351   hûs, p. 247

SUCH AS
Notes, p. 607

SUDDENLY

A. Adjective
160   aiphnidios, p. 608

B. Adverbs
869   aphnō, p. 608
1810   exaiphnēs, p. 608
1819   exapina, p. 608

THEN
5119   tote, p. 626
1534   eita, p. 626
1899   epeita, p. 626
3063   loipon, p. 626
3767   oun, p. 626
3766   oukoun, p. 626

THENCE
1564   ekeithen, p. 626

THENCEFORTH
2089   eti, p. 626

THERE, THITHER
1563   ekei, p. 626
1566   ekeise, p. 626
1564   ekeithen, p. 626
1759   enthade, p. 626
847   autou, p. 626

THERE IS
3426   yēš, p. 260

THEREABOUT
Note, p. 626

THEREAT
Note, p. 626

THEREBY
Notes, p. 626

THEREIN, THEREINTO, THEREOF, THEREON, THEREOUT, THERETO, THEREUNTO, THEREUPON, THEREWITH
Note, p. 627

THIS, THESE
Note, p. 629

THOROUGHLY
Note, p. 630

THUS
3779   houtōs *or* houtō, p. 632

TO BE
1961   hāyāh, p. 13

TOGETHER

A. Adverbs
3162   yaḥad, p. 263
3162   yaḥdāw, p. 263
3674   homou, p. 635
260   hama, p. 635

C. Noun
3173   yāḥîd, p. 264

UNDER, UNDERNEATH
5270   hupokatō, p. 650
2736   katōterō, p. 650
1640   elasson, p. 650

UP
Notes, p. 655

VERY
Notes, p. 659

WAS, WAST, WERE, WERT
Note, p. 666

WELL-NIGH
Note, p. 671

WHAT
Notes, p. 672

WHATSOEVER
Note, p. 672

WHEREFORE
Note, p. 672

WHICH
Notes, p. 673

WHILE, WHILES, WHILST
Notes, p. 673

WHO, WHOM, WHOSE
Notes, p. 674

WILL, WOULD

C. Verbs
2309   thelō, p. 676
1014   boulomai, p. 676
3195   mellō, p. 676

WISE (IN NO)
      ou mē, p. 679
3843   pantōs, p. 679
3838   panteles, p. 679

WITHIN
Note, p. 680

WITHOUT
Notes, p. 680

WONT
1486   ethō, p. 682

WOT
Note, p. 687

WOULD
Notes, p. 687

YEA, YES
3483   nai, p. 690
235   alla, p. 690
2532   kai, p. 690
3304   men oun, p. 690

YET
Notes, p. 691

YONDER
1563   ekei, p. 692

Pronouns

HE
846   autos, p. 294
3778   houtos, p. 294
1565   ekeinos, p. 294

HE HIMSELF
846   autos, p. 294
1438   heauton, p. 294

HE THAT
3739   hos, p. 294
      hosge, p. 294

HIS, HIS OWN
Note, p. 305

I
1473   egō, p. 316

IT
Note, p. 332

ITSELF
Note, p. 332

ME
Notes, p. 397

MY (MINE)
1699   emos, p. 423

MYSELF
1683   emautou, p. 424
846   autos, p. 424

ONE

B. Pronouns
5100   tis, p. 446
3739   hos, p. 446

OUR, OURS
Notes, p. 452

OUR OWN
1438   heautōn, p. 452
2398   idios, p. 452

OURSELVES
Notes, p. 452

OWN
Notes, p. 455

SELF, SELVES
844   automatos, p. 559
846   autos, p. 559

SHE
Note, p. 568

THEE
Note, p. 625

THEIR, THEIRS
Note, p. 625

THEM, THEMSELVES
Note, p. 625

THEY, THEY THEMSELVES
Note, p. 627

THOU
Note, p. 630

THY, THINE, THINE OWN, THYSELF
Note, p. 633

US
p. 655

WE
Note, p. 669

YE, YOU, YOURSELVES, YOUR OWN SELVES
Notes, p. 690

YOUR, YOURS
Notes, p. 692

Numbers
See also REVELATION,
SPECIFIC REVELATION: NUMBERS

DOUBLE
A. Adjective
1362 diplous, p. 181
B. Verb
1363 diploō, p. 181

EIGHT, EIGHTEEN, EIGHTH
3688 oktō, p. 195
3590 ogdoos, p. 195
3637 oktaēmeros, p. 195

ELEVEN, ELEVENTH
1733 hendeka, p. 197
1734 hendekatos, p. 197

FIFTEEN, FIFTEENTH
1178 dekapente, p. 234

FIFTH
3991 pemptos, p. 235

FIFTY
4004 pentēkonta, p. 235

FIVE, FIVE TIMES
4002 pente, p. 242

FOURFOLD
5073 tetraploos, p. 254

FOUR, FOURTEEN, FOUR HUNDRED
5064 tessares, p. 254

FOURSCORE
3589 ogdoēkonta, p. 254

FOURSQUARE
5068 tetragōnos, p. 254

HALF
A. Nouns
2677 ḥăṣî, p. 103
2255 hēmisus, p. 287
B. Verb
2673 ḥāṣāh, p. 104

HUNDRED, HUNDREDFOLD
1540 hekaton, p. 315
1542 hekatontaplasiōn, p. 315

NINE
1767 ennea, p. 432

NINETY
1767d enenēkonta *or* ennēn-, p. 432

NINTH
1766 enatos *or* enn-, p. 432

PAIR
2201 zeugos, p. 456

QUARTER
3840 pantothen, p. 502

SEVERAL
2398 idios, p. 566

SEVERALLY
*2398***idią, p. 566

TEN
1176 deka, p. 622

TENTH
1181 dekatē, p. 623

THIRD, THIRDLY
5154 tritos, p. 628

THIRTY, THIRTYFOLD
5144 triakonta, p. 629

THOUSAND
5507 chilioi, p. 630
5505 chilias, p. 630

THREE HUNDRED
5145 triakosioi, p. 631

THRICE
5151 tris, p. 631

TWAIN, TWO
1417 duo, p. 648

TWENTY
1501 eikosi, p. 648

TWICE
1364 dis, p. 648

TWO HUNDRED
1250 diakosioi, p. 648